April 14–17, 2015
Singapore

Association for
Computing Machinery

Advancing Computing as a Science & Profession

ASIACCS'15

Proceedings of the 10th ACM Symposium on
Information, Computer and Communications Security

Sponsored by:

ACM SIGSAC

Supported by:

National Research Foundation (NRF), Baidu, and Huawei

Organized by:

Institute for Infocomm Research

Association for
Computing Machinery

Advancing Computing as a Science & Profession

The Association for Computing Machinery
2 Penn Plaza, Suite 701
New York, New York 10121-0701

ISBN: 978-1-4503-3245-3 (Digital)

ISBN: 978-1-4503-3894-3 (Print)

Additional copies may be ordered prepaid from:

ACM Order Department
PO Box 30777
New York, NY 10087-0777, USA

Phone: 1-800-342-6626 (USA and Canada)
+1-212-626-0500 (Global)
Fax: +1-212-944-1318
E-mail: acmhelp@acm.org
Hours of Operation: 8:30 am – 4:30 pm ET

Printed in the USA

ASIACCS 2015 Program Chairs' Welcome

As the Program Chairs, we are pleased to present herein the proceedings of the *10th ACM Symposium on Information, Computer and Communications Security* (*ASIACCS 2015*) held in Singapore, April 14-17, 2015.

ASIACCS 2015 is organized by the Institute for Infocomm Research (I^2R), supported by the National Research Foundation (NRF), Baidu, and Huawei. We received 269 submissions (not including some initial withdrawals) from 39 countries, which is the new record in the history of ASIACCS. This year's Program Committee comprising 79 security researchers from 18 countries, helped by 195 external reviewers, evaluated these submissions through thoughtful discussion and rigorous review procedure. The review process resulted in 48 full papers being accepted to the program, representing an acceptance rate of about 18%. In addition, 14 short papers and 7 posters are also included in the program.

Once again we have a very strong technical program along with 3 specialized pre-conference workshops: CPSS'15, IoTPTS'15 and SCC'15. We are also fortunate to have distinguished invited speakers, Shiuhpyng Shieh (founder of ASIACCS), Ahmad-Reza Sadeghi and Ravi Sandhu, who will provide various insights into security research opportunity in Internet of Things, legacy software protection, and attribute-based access control, respectively. These valuable and insightful talks can and will guide us to a better understanding on both fundamental and emerging topic areas in the field of information, computer and communications security.

Putting together *ASIACCS 2015* was a team effort. We first thank the authors of all submitted papers, and all attendees for their participation in the technical discussion during the conference. We are grateful to the Program Committee who worked very hard in reviewing papers and providing feedback for authors. On average, each individual reviewed 12 papers, and some members generously volunteered to help shepherd accepted papers toward improved presentations. Most members engaged in lively discussions and updated their reviews to reflect valuable insights derived from those discussions. We are also indebted to the external reviewers whose focused expertise significantly helped authors improve their submissions and provided substantial value to the feedback for authors.

We appreciate the effort and guidance of the Steering Committee Chair, Robert Deng and the chair of our sponsor ACM SIGSAC, Trent Jaeger. Also, we thank the *ASIACCS 2015* conference committee: the Honorary Chair, Lee Shiang Long, the General Chairs, Feng Bao and Steven Miller, the Organizing Chair, Shen-Tat Goh, the Publicity Chair, Shangyi Chen and Huaqun Guo, and the Publication Chair, Ying Qiu, for numerous discussions on how to produce an exceptional program and ensure a smooth logistic arrangement. Moreover, we want to thank the staff of the ACM for assisting us throughout the organization and publication process, and the Institute for Infocomm Research for its generous support.

We hope that you find this program interesting and thought-provoking and that the *ASIACCS 2015* will provide you with a valuable opportunity to share ideas with other researchers and practitioners in advancing the field of information, computer and communications security.

Jianying Zhou
ASIACCS'15 Program Co-Chair
Institute for Infocomm Research, Singapore

Gail-Joon Ahn
ASIACCS'15 Program Co-Chair
Arizona State University, USA

Table of Contents

Session 3: Malware Analysis

Session Chair: Ahmad-Reza Sadeghi *(Technische Universitaet Darmstadt)*

Keynote Address 3

Session Chair: Gail-Joon Ahn *(Arizona State University)*

Session 4A: Cyber-Physical Security

Session Chair: Jianying Zhou *(Institute for Infocomm Research)*

Session 4B: Cryptography

Session Chair: Guilin Wang *(Huawei International Pte Ltd)*

Session 5A: Network Security

Session Chair: Xuhua Ding *(Singapore Management University)*

Session 8B: Attack Analysis II

Session Chair: Debin Gao *(Singapore Management University)*

Short Paper 1A: Attacks & Vulnerabilities

Session Chair: S. P. T. Krishnan *(Institute for Infocomm Research)*

Short Paper 1B: Cryptographic Schemes

Session Chair: Matt Henricksen *(Institute for Infocomm Research)*

Short Paper 2A: Network Security

Session Chair: Xiaofeng Wang *(Indiana University)*

ASIACCS 2015 Organization

10th ACM Symposium on Information, Computer and Communications Security

Honorary Chair: Lee Shiang Long (*Institute for Infocomm Research, Singapore*)

General Chairs: Feng Bao (*Huawei Technologies Pte Ltd, Singapore*)
Steven Miller (*Singapore Management University, Singapore*)

Program Chairs: Jianying Zhou (*Institute for Infocomm Research, Singapore*)
Gail-Joon Ahn (*Arizona State University, USA*)

Steering Committee Chair: Robert Deng (*Singapore Management University, Singapore*)

Organizing Chair: Shen-Tat Goh (*Institute for Infocomm Research, Singapore*)

Publicity Chairs: Shangyi Chen (*Baidu, China*)
Huaqun Guo (*Institute for Infocomm Research, Singapore*)

Publication Chair: Ying Qiu (*Institute for Infocomm Research, Singapore*)

Program Committee: N. Asokan (University of Helsinki, Finland)
Elisa Bertino (Purdue University, USA)
Rainer Boehme (University of Munster, Germany)
Kevin Butler (University of Florida, USA)
Aldar C-F. Chan (ASTRI, HK)
Binbin Chen (Advanced Digital Sciences Center, Singapore)
Chen-Mou Cheng (National Taiwan University, Taiwan)
Sherman S. M. Chow (Chinese University of Hong Kong, HK)
Xuhua Ding (Singapore Management University, Singapore)
Xinshu Dong (Advanced Digital Sciences Center, Singapore)
Orr Dunkelman (University of Haifa, Israel)
Sara Foresti (The University of Milan, Italy)
Debin Gao (Singapore Management University, Singapore)
Dieter Gollmann (Hamburg University of Technology, Germany)
Guofei Gu (Texas A&M University, USA)
Yong Guan (Iowa State University, USA)
Jin Han (Twitter, USA)
Jinguang Han (Nanjing Univ. of Finance & Economics, China)
Feng Hao (Newcastle University, UK)
Matt Henricksen (Institute for Infocomm Research, Singapore)
Xinyi Huang (Fujian Normal University, China)

Program Committee (continued):

Murat Kantarcioglu (University of Texas at Dallas, USA)
Steve Kremer (INRIA, France)
S. P. T. Krishnan (Institute for Infocomm Research, Singapore)
Miroslaw Kutylowski (Wroclaw University of Technology, Poland)
Xuejia Lai (Shanghai Jiaotong University, China)
Adam J. Lee (University of Pittsburgh, USA)
Ming Li (Utah State University, USA)
Ninghui Li (Purdue University, USA)
Yingjiu Li (Singapore Management University, Singapore)
Zhenkai Liang (National University of Singapore, Singapore)
Zhiqiang Lin (University of Texas at Dallas, USA)
Dongdai Lin (Chinese Academy of Sciences, China)
Peng Liu (Pennsylvania State University, USA)
Javier Lopez (University of Malaga, Spain)
Di Ma (University of Michigan-Dearborn, USA)
Harsha Madhyastha (University of Michigan, USA)
Mark Manulis (University of Surrey, UK)
Aziz Mohaisen (Verisign Labs, USA)
Shiho Moriai (NICT, Japan)
Yi Mu (University of Wollongong, Australia)
Jianwei Niu (University of Texas at San Antonio, USA)
Guevara Noubir (Northeastern University, USA)
Daniela Oliveira (University of Florida, USA)
Xinming Ou (Kansas State University, USA)
Philippe Owezarski (LAAS-CNRS, France)
Mathias Payer (UC Berkeley, USA)
Zachary Peterson (Cal Poly, San Luis Obispo, USA)
Michalis Polychronakis (Columbia University, USA)
Georgios Portokalidis (Stevens Inst. of Tech., USA)
Kui Ren (State University of New York at Buffalo, USA)
Giovanni Russello (University of Auckland, NZ)
Mark Ryan (University of Birmingham, UK)
Ahmad-Reza Sadeghi (Technical University Darmstadt, Germany)
Rei Safavi-Naini (University of Calgary, Canada)
Pierangela Samarati (The University of Milan, Italy)
Joshua Schiffman (AMD, USA)
Dongwan Shin (New Mexico Tech, USA)
Christian Skalka (University of Vermont, USA)
Miguel Soriano (Universitat Politcnica de Catalunya, Spain)
Anna Squicciarini (Pennsylvania State University, USA)
Scott Stoller (Stony Brook University, USA)
Willy Susilo (University of Wollongong, Austrilia)
Patrick Tague (Carnegie Mellon University, USA)
Tsuyoshi Takagi (Kyushu University, Japan)

Program Committee (continued):

Gang Tan (Lehigh University, USA)
Vrizlynn Thing (Institute for Infocomm Research, Singapore)
Eugene Vasserman (Kansas State University, USA)
Hayawardh Vijayakumar (Pennsylvania State University, USA)
Tao Wan (Huawei, Canada)
Cong Wang (City University of Hong Kong, HK)
Guoliang Xue (Arizona State University, USA)
Danfeng Yao (Virginia Tech, USA)
David Yau (Singapore Univ. of Technology and Design, Singapore)
Ting Yu (Qatar Computing Research Institute, Qatar)
Jie Zhang (Nanyang Technological University, Singapore)
Rui Zhang (University of Hawaii, USA)
Yanchao Zhang (Arizona State University, USA)
Xiaoyong Zhou (Samsung Research, USA)

Additional reviewers:

A. Irissappane, Athirai
Agudo, Isaac
Alcaraz, Cristina
Ali, Syed Taha
Alrawi, Omar
Alvim, Mario S.
Amir-Mohammadian, Sepehr
Asghar, Muhammad Rizwan
Ashur, Tomer
Baldor, Kevin
Bardas, Alexandru G
Bates, Adam
Baykov, Robert
Bernstein, Daniel
Blaskiewicz, Przemyslaw
Blass, Erik-Oliver
Budianto, Enrico
Caballero-Gil, Cándido
Cai, Shaoying
Chang, Sang-Yoon
Chang, Yun-An
Chen, Haining
Chen, Jing
Chen, Ling
Chen, Rongmao
Chen, Xiaofeng
Chen, Yimin
Cheng, Long
Cheng, Yuan
Cheval, Vincent
Choo, Euijin
Chow, Yang-Wai
Chowdhury, Omar
Chua, Zheng Leong
Clarke, Dylan
Dai, Ting
Damopoulos, Dimitrios
Davi, Lucas
De Capitani Di Vimercati, Sabrina
Denzel, Michael
Dubovitskaya, Maria
Liao, Cong
Lim, Wee Yong
Liu, Hong
Liu, Jia
Liu, Jian
Liu, Joseph
Liu, Meicheng
Liu, Zhenhua
Livraga, Giovanni
Lu, Yao
Luhn, Sebastian
Ma, Yu Tak
Majcher, Krzysztof
Mao, Jieshen
Mayberry, Travis
Meng, Guozhu
Midi, Daniele
Ming, Jiang
Moataz, Tarik
Mood, Benjamin
Morozov, Kirill
Mutti, Simone
Nakanishi, Toru
Nieto, Ana
Niu, Ben
Nojima, Ryo
Nuñez, David
Ohkubo, Miyako
Ohtake, Go
Ordean, Mihai
Patel, Kunal
Pattuk, Erman
Phong, Le Trieu
Polakis, Iasonas
Pomonis, Marios
Qiao, Yechen
Quiring, Erwin
Rebollo-Monedero, David
Ren, Chuangang
Reyhanitabar, Reza
Rios, Ruben

Additional Reviewers (continued):

Elashry, Ibrahim
Emura, Keita
Fernandez, Carmen
Fernandez, Gerardo
Fu, Tom Z. J.
Fu, Yangchun
Garrison Iii, William C.
Gazeau, Ivan
Gerdes, Ryan
Golebiewski, Zbigniew
Grewal, Gurchetan
Gunasinghe, Hasini
Guo, Fuchun
Hakuta, Keisuke
Hanzlik, Lucjan
Hayashi, Takuya
He, Shibo
Hils, Maximilian
Hong, Kevin
Hu, Hong
Hu, Wenhui
Huang, Geshi
Hussain, Syed
Jhawar, Mahavir
Jia, Yaoqi
Jin, Xiaocong
Jorgensen, Zach
Kaplan, David
Kardas, Marcin
Khan, Muhammad Taimoor
Kiyomoto, Shinsaku
Klonowski, Marek
Ko, Li Ling
Kontaxis, Georgios
Kordy, Piotr
Krzywiecki, Lukasz
Kubiak, Przemysław
Kupcu, Alptekin
Kywe, Su Mon
Künnemann, Robert
Roy, Harichandan
Roy, Sankardas
Różański, Michał
Schoettle, Pascal
Seo, Anes Seung-Hyun
Shahandashti, Siamak
Shaon, Fahad
Su, Dong
Sulkowska, Malgorzata
Sun, Jingchao
Sun, Ruimin
Tamrakar, Sandeep
Tan, Darell
Tan, Rui
Thoma, Cory
Tian, Donghai
Tian, Jing
Ulusoy, Huseyin
Wachsmann, Christian
Wajjala, Phani
Wang, Boyang
Wang, Daniel
Wang, Ding
Wang, Hui
Wang, Lihua
Wang, Tun-Ju
Wang, Xiaofen
Wang, Xiaoyin
Wei, Fengguo
Won, Jongho
Xu, Chang
Xu, Hong
Xu, Jun
Xu, Ke
Xu, Lei
Xue, Weijia
Yang, Guomin
Yang, Weining
Yarom, Yuval
Yu, Jiangshan

Additional Reviewers (continued):

Lai, Russell W. F.
Lancrenon, Jean
Laube, Stefan
Lauks-Dutka, Anna
Le, Hoi
Lee, Peter Hyun-Jeen
Lemiesz, Jakub
Li, Jiguo
Li, Jin
Li, Lingjun
Li, Muyuan
Li, Nan
Li, Xiaolei
Li, Yan
Li, Yuping
Li, Zhen
Liang, Kaitai
Yu, Shucheng
Zhang, Jialong
Zhang, Jinxue
Zhang, Mingwu
Zhang, Rui
Zhang, Su
Zhang, Tao
Zhang, Ye
Zhang, Yuexin
Zhang, Zhongwen
Zhao, Bin
Zhao, Yongjun
Zheng, Xifan
Zhong, Hao
Zhou, Peng
Zhou, Yaqin

ASIACCS 2015 Sponsor & Supporters

10th ACM Symposium on Information, Computer and Communications Security

Organized by: A*STAR Institute for Infocomm Research

Sponsored by: acm SIGSAC

Supported by: National Research Foundation; Baidu 百度; HUAWEI

Emerging Security Threats and Countermeasures in IoT

Zhi-Kai Zhang, Michael Cheng Yi Cho, Shiuhpyng Shieh, *IEEE Fellow*
Department of Computer Science
National Chiao Tung University
Hsinchu, Taiwan
{skyzhang.cs99g, michcho.cs98g}@g2.nctu.edu.tw, ssp@cs.nctu.edu.tw

ABSTRACT
IoT (Internet of Things) diversifies the future Internet, and has drawn much attention. As more and more gadgets (i.e. Things) connected to the Internet, the huge amount of data exchanged has reached an unprecedented level. As sensitive and private information exchanged between things, privacy becomes a major concern. Among many important issues, scalability, transparency, and reliability are considered as new challenges that differentiate IoT from the conventional Internet. In this paper, we enumerate the IoT communication scenarios and investigate the threats to the large-scale, unreliable, pervasive computing environment. To cope with these new challenges, the conventional security architecture will be revisited. In particular, various authentication schemes will be evaluated to ensure the confidentiality and integrity of the exchanged data.

Categories and Subject Descriptors
K.6.5 [**Management of Computing and Information Systems**]: Security and Protection – *Authentication.*

General Terms
Security

Keywords
IoT; Security; Privacy; Communication; Authentication

1. INTRODUCTION
Internet of Thing (IoT) is a self-configuring and adaptive complex network that interconnects uniquely identifiable "Things" to the Internet through the use of interoperable communication protocols. The "Things", sometimes referred to as devices or objects interchangeably, have sensing/actuation and potential programmability capability. Information about the "Thing" can be collected from anywhere, at anytime, by anything. IoT attracts much attention as the economic prosperity generated by the technology [1]. One of the economic opportunities is based on the data that the "Things" on the Internet shared. The shared data is processed into information as the input for other "Things" or as reports for human to read [2]. Given the data that has been shared over a network medium, namely the Internet, it is important to protect the shared data as it may contain sensitive and private information [3]. With the growth of the technology on Big Data, the threat is severer since the attacker may obtain private information through the raw data leaked by the compromised objects. Thus, privacy preservation becomes a critical issue to address.

Privacy preservation has been a critical issue for information security. Significant amount of work has been done in the research area. Authentication methods and cryptographic mechanisms were used to protect user privacy. A well-designed authentication method ensures authenticity so that only the authorized personal or object has the access to the private information. On the other hand, cryptographic mechanisms ensure that sensitive and private information is protected during transmission, storage and processing. Due to the heterogeneity, battery capacity, and resource constraints of the "Things" in IoT, not all the "Things" in IoT has the capability to engage the available authentication methods and/or cryptographic mechanisms. For this reason, privacy preservation in IoT security needs to be revisited. The recent research on IoT privacy preservation is either at high level or based on physical layer communication security [4][5]. In this paper, we will focus on IoT privacy preservation in the application layer. We will construct various application scenarios to identify privacy preservation challenges. This information can be useful for the development of IoT applications that falls into these scenarios.

IEEE IoT Initiative recently launched new standards project [6], which will define an architectural framework for the IoT, including descriptions of various IoT domains, definitions of IoT domain abstractions, and identification of commonalities between different IoT domains. Furthermore, IEEE IoT Initiative launched IoT ecosystem study to determine the connective areas and potential gaps in the concept of IoT that could be addressed through pre-standards and standards activities.

The main concern that differentiates IoT from the conventional Internet is scalability. In IoT, billions of objects are connected to the network. The conventional naming policy may not be able handle the devices on this massive scale. The naming policy may need to be improved or redesigned to provide unique naming convention. In response to the evolution of naming, identification and authentication methods also need to be redesigned accordingly. Transparency and reliability are two other key challenges that make the design of identification and authentication methods even more difficult.

Transparency is an important issue for IoT security. Most users cannot patiently finish complex configuration steps to activate their smart devices. All the configuration settings should be nearly transparent to the users. Authentication operations should be designed as simple as possible. Although X.509 PKI may be powerful enough, it is not practical to assume that a naive user has

ASIA CCS'15, April 14–17, 2015, Singapore.

http://dx.doi.org/10.1145/2714576.2737091

the ability to successfully obtain and import valid certificates to a large number of IoT devices. One of the reasonable assumptions, for example, can be that users can find a passcode printed on the label of the device or the home gateway. Then the naming, identification, and authentication settings can be automatically executed after the passcode is entered. To achieve this goal, new standards need to be established. The desired standards may not need to be totally novel. It can be a combination of existent standards in related domains, such as UPnP, DLNA, and DNSSEC.

Reliability is another important issue for the IoT ecosystem. Due to limited resources and battery capacity, IoT objects and communication between them are error-prone. The heterogeneity of objects makes the ecosystem more complex. The implementation and evaluation of the devices and services become more difficult. Additionally, when errors occur, debugging and repairing are also more difficult in the IoT ecosystem. Therefore, not only robustness, but also easy debugging and one-step resumption should be taken into consideration during the development of identification and authentication schemes. Moreover, under a reasonable assumption, automatic self-monitoring and healing mechanisms are also desirable for the reason that debugging and repairing are difficult for naive users.

Security threats to IoT can be generally divided into two categories. In the first category, the threats, similar to the conventional network ecosystem, are against confidentiality, integrity, and availability (CIA). However, due to the large scale and heterogeneity of the objects, the complexity and severity of the security threats is much more serious. The other category of treats arises from the new property of IoT ecosystem. With IoT objects everywhere taking sensitive readings from heartbeats to room temperature at home, it can be expected that the data in the IoT ecosystem is more personal and dynamic. Because the huge number of IoT devices gather massive sensitive information about users, the data readings about its owner and the personal spaces are treated as personal assets where a leakage may reveal owner's geological location, health status, and living habits. Attackers may extract desired information and disclose personal privacy.

In response to the security threats, security requirements for privacy protection and preservation need to be defined properly in IoT. For the first aforementioned category of threats, security requirements should cover the additional concerns dealing with the large scale and heterogeneity of objects. For example, object-to-object (O2O) communication is inevitable given that IoT objects collaborate to achieve goals without human intervention. Therefore, the security requirements aiming at authentication models for IoT users/objects are important. For the second category of threats, the security requirements should cover a set of new protection models. The models should be able to handle the information gathering and leakage for the IoT objects, especially for resource-constrained devices, which only provide limited security protection. Without the protection models, private data can be misused by rouge users/objects, malicious data can cause object to misbehave, or alternation of exchanged data to deceive users/objects by a rouge party.

Software and system vulnerabilities of an IoT device are also a critical issue which can lead to backdoor problems. With software vulnerabilities, attackers exercise malicious intents, and plant a backdoor in a vulnerable IoT device to control the device. Due to the resource constraints and battery capacity of IoT devices, security mechanisms such as intrusion detection systems and antivirus which consume a fair amount of computation power are not suitable. With primitive protection mechanism, injecting backdoors into an IoT device is relatively easy. Both static and dynamic analysis techniques have been used to verify a program. Static analysis has the limitation to uncover the vulnerabilities in the real execution environment, while dynamic analysis is inadaptable to IoT for the lack of the computing power and battery capacity. More detail discussion about IoT software security can be found in articles [3]. In this paper, we will focus on object identity management and authentication in the IoT ecosystem.

This paper is organized as follows. Section 2 introduces the challenges to object identification and authentication for IoT communication, while section 3 introduces personal IoT communication scenarios, and identify authentication requirements. Section 4 lists authentication models for the personal IoT communication scenarios. Lastly, a conclusion is given in section 5.

2. Naming, Identification and Authentication

Wearable gadgets and smart home/office appliances are the main themes of Consumer Electronic Show (CES) 2015 [7]. Wearable gadgets take measurement and report it to mobile APPs. These collected data are then passed on to smart furniture and/or appliance in smart home/office to make adjustment accordingly. This is a common IoT application demonstrated in CES 2015. The communication scenario of information exchange can be broken into two categories according to the distance range, that is, domestic and foreign. Typical domestic communication is done locally without access to the public network (a.k.a. the Internet). Foreign communication, on the other hand, relies on the public network to distribute data to distant objects.

Heterogeneity of objects is expected in IoT where objects have limited resources, computing power and communication capability. With the nature of lightweight and portability, the communication capability of wearable devices is mostly in a short distance. Short-range wireless communication (i.e. domestic communication), such as Bluetooth and Zigbee [8], relies on pairing objects prior to data exchange. For wearable devices to extend the communication range (i.e. foreign communication), a delegator is required to relay the data traffic. Delegator is normally referred to as the gateway of communication [9]. For wearable devices made for mobility, the handheld device such as mobile phone is a suitable gateway to relay data. On the other hand, for home/office appliances, a hotspot such as wireless AP (Access Point) is a suitable candidate to relay data. Figure 1 illustrates the typical topology configuration for both long distance and short distance communication.

For domestic communication authentication, e.g. Bluetooth and Zigbee, basic security is provided in the link layer during object pairing where password is required. Once the object is paired, encryption is applied when data has been exchanged wirelessly [8]. On the other hand, foreign communication authentication, section 4 will enumerate a number of applicable authentication models.

Since IoT comes at a massive scale of objects, naming of the objects becomes more complex. Due to the heterogeneity of the objects and the network, conventional Internet naming and identification will not be applicable [3]. Uniquely naming the objects is one of the main challenges in IoT to be resolved before addressing object authentication. GS1 [10] suggested that the DNS naming scheme can be the naming basis of IoT given that

IoT is to be deployed on the Internet. Object Naming Service (ONS) [10] is part of GS1 EPCglobal [11] architecture framework that leverages DNS to locate authoritative metadata and services with given Electronic Product Code (EPC). The EPC is designed for the purpose of providing universal unique identity. ONS can also be integrated into DNS as a sub-domain of DNS. Therefore, the Internet becomes the communication medium for the device-naming domains.

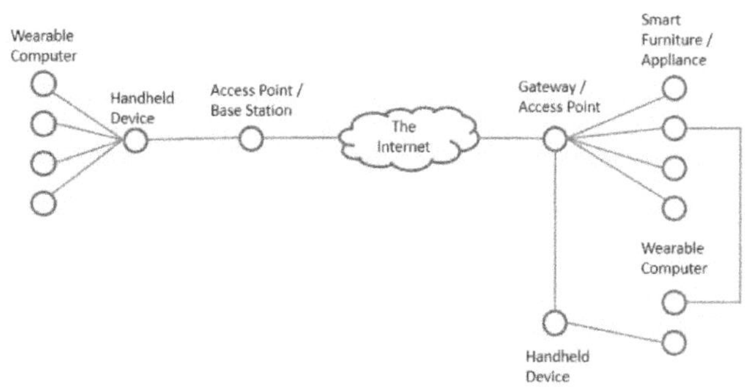

Figure 1. A typical IoT topology.

As an illustrator of the future Internet architecture, US NSF launched Future Internet Architecture Project (FIA Project) [12]. As a core sub-project of FIA Project, L. Zhang et al. proposed novel "Named Data Networking (NDN)" [13] which moves the network architecture from host-centric to data-centric. According to NDN, the identification and network routing are based on the name of the object instead of using conventional IP address. Naming in NDN is in a hierarchical structure, and is applicable to hierarchical nature of the current computer network structures. NDN has great impact, but is still in its infancy. There are still many new challenges, such as efficiency, name validation, signing key management, object authentication, and other security issues. These challenges remain unsolved and raise concerns.

3. IOT COMMUNICATION SCENARIOS

In this section, we will discuss various communication scenarios for IoT applications to exchange data. To model IoT communication scenarios, the administration domains of objects can be divided into *domestic* and *foreign domains*, based on the ownership of objects. An object of the *domestic domain* is administrated and owned by the home members while the object of a *foreign domain* is administrated and owned by outsiders. Each object is represented as a *peer*. A *domestic peer* represents an object that is registered to the domestic domain, while a *foreign peer* represents an object that is registered to a foreign domain. The communication of "things" can be formalized into three scenarios, namely, *basic scenario, extended scenario*, and *cloud scenario*. Details are given below.

3.1 Basic Communication Scenario

This basic communication scenario is regarded as domestic communication where wearable devices, smart furniture, and smart appliance exchange data within a closed network environment, such as home or organization (shown in Figure 2). For wearable devices that are incapable of making direct connection to an access point beyond the communication range, a delegator such as handheld device can play the role to relay data traffic to the access point so that the data can be transmitted to the destination. This communication scenario takes place in a closed network often referred as local area network (LAN), and the main challenges to data retrieval are as follows:

- Authentication and authorization to use the LAN
- Countermeasure for eavesdrop over wireless networks

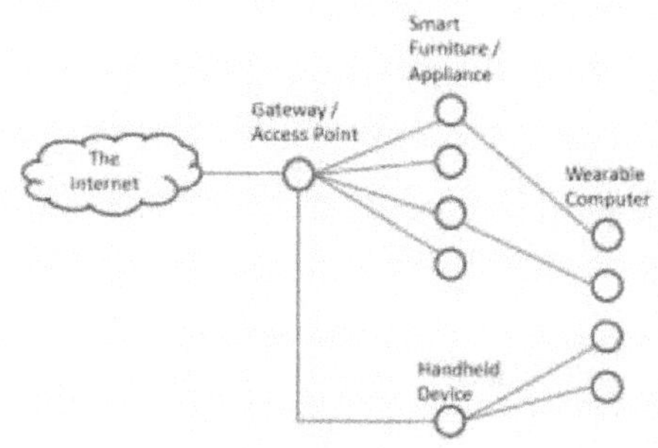

Figure 2, IoT communication in home/organization domain.

3.2 Extended Communication Scenario

Mobility is one of the features of wearable devices. Data must be exchangeable whilst a wearable device is on the move. Thus, public network (i.e. the Internet) is used to relay the exchanged data. Depending on the methods that data is exchanged and stored, network configurations can be divided into two types. Figure 3 depicts a simple network configuration for external resource access where resource and data distribution are decentralized. In this type of configuration, two gateways are employed to support communicate between the wearable devices and smart furniture/appliances. A gateway supports the local area network, while the mobile handheld device supports data relay for mobile wearable devices. As data exchanged, the two gateways handle data forwarding.

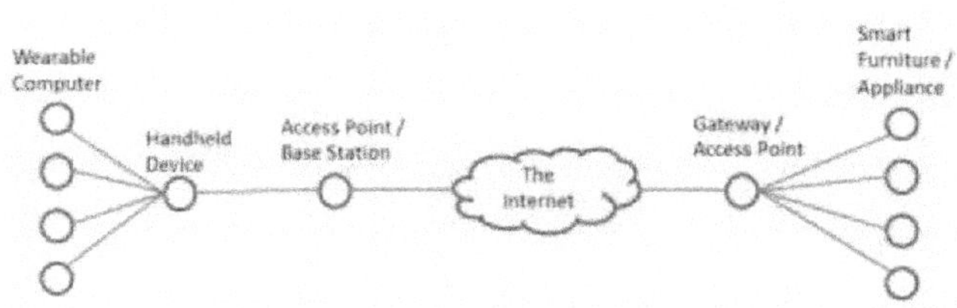

Figure 3, IoT communication over public network.

Figure 4 illustrates the network configuration where resource and data are centralized. Although the two network configurations are alike, the actual communication takes place using different approaches. In this approach, the data resource is centralized so that the objects do not communicate directly. All exchanged data is pushed and pulled from a central storage (i.e. the data pod). Regardless of centralized or decentralized network configurations, challenges to data retrieval are listed below:

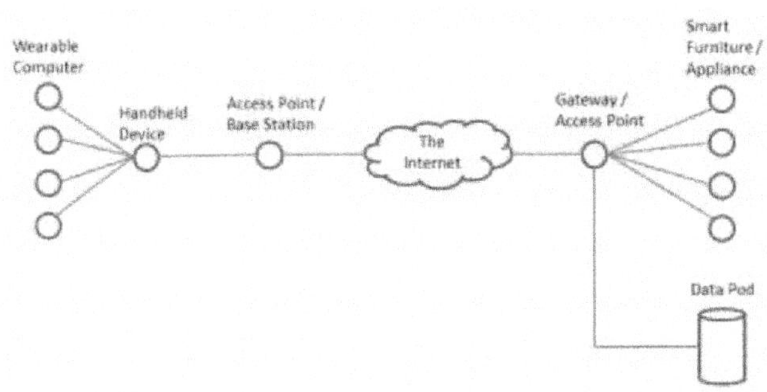

Figure 4, Centralized IoT communication over public network.

- Authentication and authorization to use the LAN
- Eavesdrop resistance over wireless networks
- Integrity assurance when using the public network
- Confidentiality assurance when using the public network

3.3 Cloud Communication Scenario

Cloud computing has been a hot topic in the recent years. Cloud computing will continue to thrive as IoT grows. The scenario involves vendors providing data storage service where data can be accessed from anywhere (shown in Figure 5). At the same time, data is replicated to prevent single point failure and ensure efficiency. The pushed data in the cloud service can also be computed for analytical purpose or for personal service recommendations. Unlike the aforementioned scenarios, the gateways of wearable devices, smart furniture, and smart appliances are only used to collect data for the cloud storage. In this context, data authentication is still needed to avoid pollution while transmitting collected data over the Internet to the cloud. The challenges to data collection is as follows:

- Authentication and authorization to use the LAN
- Eavesdrop resistance over wireless networks
- Confidentiality and integrity assurance over the Internet
- Authentication and authorization for the cloud service
- Confidentiality and integrity for the cloud storage

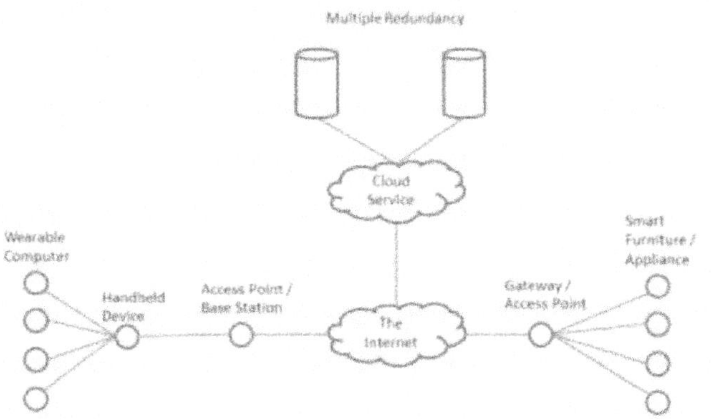

Figure 5, IoT with cloud computing.

4. AUTHENTICATION MODEL

In this section, authentication models are introduced to cope with the challenges incurred in various communication scenarios. Each authentication model is designed in an attempt to address the challenges in a communication scenario. These challenges are further elaborated as follows. For domestic communication, O2O (Object-to-Object) communication is applied to wearable devices and handheld devices. Due to resource constraints, wearable devices rely on more powerful computational objects, such as handheld device, to relay data. To authenticate, pairing mechanism is adopted when two objects are making connection. At the pairing stage, a simple password or pre-shared key is supplied before initializing the communication. When the data exchange begins, symmetric cryptosystems are suitable for preventing eavesdropping over wireless communication. For LAN communication, the conventional Wi-Fi protecting schemes are sufficient where a passphrase is used to authenticate the object to the network and prevent eavesdropping over wireless communication. These authentication schemes cover domestic communication while the following authentication schemes cover foreign communication where exchanged data is forwarded through the Internet.

4.1 Authentication by Gateway

In the authentication-by-gateway model, the authentication process relies on the gateway between the communication parties. To communicate with a domestic peer, a foreign peer first needs to be authenticated by the domestic gateway. Being authenticated, the subsequent exchanged data from the foreign peer is directed to the destination until the session is terminated. This authentication process is repeated for each communication session whenever the communication parties exchange data via the Internet. The authentication method can be as simple as ID-password scheme or any other scheme as long as it provides the proof of authorized identity. Similar to authentication-by-gateway model, research [14] has discussed a practical IoT communication example based on CoAP (Constrained Application Protocol) [15] that the resource-constrained objects cooperate with the gateway in UCN (Unconstrained Network) to achieve data authentication. The pros and cons of authentication-by-gateway scheme are listed below:

- Pros
  - The authentication method for foreign peers is independent of the authentication method for domestic peers.
  - Peer protection is centralized in the gateway. Since the gateway should be relatively powerful in terms of computation, the protection can be designed to be more complex to strengthen the security functionalities. On the other hand, the protection for the domestic peers can be designed to be lightweight. In this way, it is more applicable to the domestic peers that may have less computation power and requires less security functionalities.
- Cons
  - Single point failure, such as compromised gateway, exposes all the peers to threats.
  - The gateway can be a bottleneck since it is in charge of authenticating network traffic from communicating peers. At the same time, the gateway is also the only ingress and egress point of public network traffic. Thus, network traffic congestion problem is inevitable.

Applying this authentication model to the IoT communication model over public network, the gateway (i.e. the access points and the handheld devices) must be capable of authenticating foreign peers. An example of IoT applications is the IoT data collection and integration for e-health. In a health caring scenario, an elder may wear a smart bracelet continuously collecting his heartbeat and GPS location information. As the mobile gateway, a smart phone may be needed to collect raw data from the bracelet and upload them to a health care cloud. In this scenario, the smart phone may communicate with the bracelet through secure Bluetooth pairing and authenticate each other with the cloud through a DTLS [16] connection. This authentication model reduces data authentication workload on the communicating objects. Therefore, it is more suitable for resource-constrained objects such as the aforementioned bracelet. It is also applicable to centralized communication over public network. However, the downside of this authentication model is that the gateway is busy with processing authenticated sessions while forwarding network traffic to the public network. For standard home gateway such as home routers and access points, the high computing workload may be minor. However, it can be problematic to a gateway powered by battery.

4.2 Authentication by Security Token

In this authentication model, the gateway is responsible for initiating the authentication session when a foreign peer begins to exchange data with a domestic peer. At initiation, the gateway will establish a security token with the communicating parties. This security token may have a time-to-live or valid-period attribute to indicate security token validity by defining the time frame or the use count. For all sessions in the valid time period, the communicating peers exchange data using the security token for authentication purpose. Before the expiration of time-to-live or valid-period attribute, the gateway is free from succeeding authentication workload. Based on the concept of this category, the research [17] constructs a delegation-based authentication and authorization scheme for DTLS. The pros and cons of the authentication methods in this category are described as follows.

- Pros
  - The load for succeeding authentication after initialization is removed from the gateway.
  - It is suitable for resource-constrained peers where token-based authentication is considered to be lightweight in computation.
- Cons
  - Single point failure, such as compromised gateway, may expose peers to threats since the initial authentication session is performed by the gateway.
  - The design of a scheme using security tokens can be difficult because both security requirements and resource restriction of the peers must be taken into consideration simultaneously.

The authentication-by-security-token model relies on the domestic gateway to distribute a security token to the communicating peers. Upon receipt of the security token, the communicating peers use it to authenticate each other. This shifted the authentication workload to the communicating peers to alleviate the workload on the gateways. The valid period of a security token can be rather short if the communicating peers are resource-constrained objects which cannot afford strong security protection. Thus, this authentication model is still resource-constrained friendly. As a comparison to the previous authentication model, this model is also applicable to centralized communication over public network. The overhead for a gateway is to set up and manage the security tokens.

4.3 Authentication by Trust Chain

In this model, the trust relationship "peer A trusts peer B" is defined as follows. Peer A is convinced that the incoming data D is indeed from peer C, if peer B certifies that data D is from peer C. Therefore, a trust graph is constructed as a connected and directed graph in which the successor of a directed edge trusts the predecessor. The gateway is the predecessor of all the peers that are assigned to the domestic registration domain, and a public authority certifies the gateway. If two communication peers belonging to different trust graphs need to authenticate each other, one or multiple edges should be added to concatenate the two trust graphs in a proper manner. In this configuration, both peers can find particular predecessor which is trusted by itself and certifies the other peer. There are existent standards using a trust graph structure, such as X.509 PKI (IETF RFC 5280) and DNSSEC [18].

As an example, an authentication method based on X.509 PKI uses digital certificates for authentication. In the setup phase, the gateway must act as the concatenating point which requests a digital certificate from a public CA (Certificate Authority) and issues its own private, proprietary certificates to the domestic objects. For simplicity, the proprietary certificate does not need to follow the X.509 standard format; however, the communication peers must all agree on using the proprietary authentication method. After the setup phase, domestic peers can achieve mutual authentication with all the peers that trust the same proprietary CA. The pros and cons of the authentication-by-trust-chain model are listed below:

- Pros
  - After the setup phase, there will be no further authentication workload on the gateway. Thus, this authentication model reduces the workload for authentication.
  - This model is based on trust chain. In practice, authentication standards of this model are designed to provide better security functionalities compared to the basic authentication methods.
  - Instead of applying for a certificate for each domestic object, proprietary certificate authority is employed to reduce the cost of obtaining public certificates.
- Cons
  - This kind of authentication scheme is more complex, and may not be suitable for resource-constrained objects. A fair amount of computation power is required.
  - The authentication model uses similar methods for both domestic peers and foreign peers, which make it inflexible.
  - Single point of failure, such as a compromised gateway, may break the trust chain.

A prerequisite for this model is that a home/organization owner must have a certificate authority for all the objects, and this certificate authority must also obtained a digital certificate from an upper-tier to chain up the trust (i.e. trust graph concatenation). For traveling objects to phone home, no trust graph concatenation is required given that the digital certificate is issued by the domestic gateway. However, trust graph concatenation is required if an object is owned by an outsider. This will require communicating parties to acquire all the intermediate digital certificates to construct the chain of trust (i.e. trust graph concatenation). This authentication model shifts the authentication workload to the communicating objects. Therefore, it may not particularly suitable for certain resource-constrained objects.

4.4 Authentication by Global Trust Tree

Unlike the authentication-by-trust-chain model, a global trust tree is used instead. All the peers are registered in the global trust tree. As a result, all the peers can be authenticated globally. To our best knowledge, currently no global trust trees are available. DNSSEC can be a potential candidate to construct one [19]. However, some practical issues [20][21] will need to be resolved before moving forward. The pros and cons of this authentication model are as follows:

- Pros
  - Global trust graph is more reliable (in terms of management) comparing to the trust architecture using a private gateway.
  - The gateway does not intervene in authentication process, and thus can concentrate on network traffic forwarding tasks.
  - The underlying scheme is in general an international standard, which is more robust in achieving mutual authentication.
- Cons

- Global trust graph is not available in the current Internet framework.
- Constructing a global trust graph that includes all the objects in IoT is expensive and may be infeasible.
- Even if a global trust graph is available, the registration fee will be high as a whole for all the domestic objects.

In comparison with authentication-by-trust-chain, authentication-by-global-trust-tree can enforce strict rules to manage digital certificates. In this authentication model, the gateways of the communicating peers do not take part in authentication. Routing network traffic is their primary task. However, the communicating objects must be capable of performing data authentication, which may be problematic for some resource-constrained objects. Therefore, it is more appropriate in this authentication model to centralize data retrieval over the public network or cloud computing communication environment to reduce the amount of data exchanged.

5. CONCLUSION

In this paper, emerging security threats and countermeasures in IoT are investigated. In particular, challenges to sensitive and private information exchanged between travelling objects and objects at home/organization are evaluated. Naming, identity management, and authentication of IoT objects are the key issues for secure communication and data retrieval. Based on various communication scenarios in IoT, we enumerated a few potential authentication schemes that are applicable. Hopefully this attempt can motivate more future work to cope with security concerns in the deployment of IoT.

6. ACKNOWLEDGMENTS

This work is supported in part by Ministry of Science and Technology (MOST), Ministry of Education of Taiwan, Taiwan Information Security Center (TWISC), ITRI, III, iCAST, HTC, D-Link, Trend Micro Inc., Promise Inc., Chungshan Institute of Science and Technology, Bureau of Investigation, and Chunghwa Telecom, and Telecom Technology Center.

7. REFERENCES

[1] M. Ravindranath, (8 Jan 2014), *Cisco CEO at CES 2014: Internet of Things is a $19 trillion opportunity* [Online]. Available: http://www.washingtonpost.com/business/on-it/cisco-ceo-at-ces-2014-internet-of-things-is-a-19-trillion-opportunity/2014/01/08/8d456fba-789b-11e3-8963-b4b654bcc9b2_story.html.

[2] K. Aston, (22 Jun 2009), *That 'Internet of Things' Thing* [Online]. Available: http://www.rfidjournal.com/articles/view?4986.

[3] Z. K. Zhang, et al., "IoT Security: Ongoing Challenges and Research Opportunities," in *IEEE 7th International Conference on Service-Oriented Computing and Applications (SOCA 2014)*, Nov 2014, pp. 230-234.

[4] R. H. Weber, "Internet of Things – New Security and Privacy Challenges," in *Computer Law & Security Review*, vol. 26, issue 1, Jan 2010, pp. 23-30.

[5] C. M. Medaglia, and A. Serbanati, "An Overview of Privacy and Security Issues in the Internet of Things," in *the Internet of Things*, Jan 2010, pp. 389-395.

[6] R. Minerva, and A. Biru, "Towards a Definition of the Internet of Things," in *IEEE IoT Initiative White Paper*.

[7] R. Metz, (6 Jan 2015), *CES 2015: The Internet of Just About Everything* [Online]. Available: http://www.technologyreview.com/news/533941/ces-2015-the-internet-of-just-about-everything.

[8] J. S. Lee, Y. W. Su, and C. C. Shen, "A Comparative Study of Wireless Protocols: Bluetooth, UWB, ZigBee, and Wi-Fi," in *33rd Annual Conference of the IEEE Industrial Electronics Society (IECON 2007)*, Nov 2007, pp. 46-51.

[9] H. Chen, X. Jiao, and H. Li, "A Brief Introduction to IoT Gateway," in *IET International Conference on Communication Technology and Application (ICCTA 2011)*, Oct 2011, pp. 610-613.

[10] GS1, "GS1 Object Name Service (ONS) Version 2.0.1," in *Ratified Standard 2*, 2013.

[11] GS1, (5 Aug 2014), *EPCglobal Standards* [Online]. Available: http://www.gs1.org/gsmp/kc/epcglobal.

[12] National Science Foundation, (21 Sep 2014), *NSF Future Internet Architectures Project* [Online]. Available: http://www.nets-fia.net.

[13] L. Zhang, et al., "Named Data Networking," in *ACM SIGCOMM Computer Communication Review*, July 2014.

[14] R. Bonetto , et al., "Secure Communication for Smart IoT Objects: Protocol Stacks, Use Cases and Practical Examples," in *IEEE Int. Symp. on World of Wireless, Mobile, and Multimedia Networks (WoWMoM 2012)*, Jun 2012, pp. 1-7.

[15] E. Rescorla, and N. Modadugu, "Datagram Transport Layer Security Version 1.2" in *IETF RFC6347*, Jan 2012.

[16] Z. Shelby, K. Hartke, and C. Bormann, "The Constrained Application Protocol," in *IETF RFC7252*, Jun 2014.

[17] R. Hummen, et al., "Delegation-based authentication and authorization for the IP-based Internet of Things," in *11th Annual IEEE International Conference on Sensing, Communication, and Networking (SECON 2014)*, Jun 2014, pp.284-292.

[18] R. Arends, et al., "DNS Security Introduction and Requirements," in *IETF RFC4033*, Mar 2005.

[19] M. C. Y. Cho, P. Chen, and S. Shieh, "Dmail: a Globally Authenticated Email Service," in *IEEE Computer*, vol. 47, issue 5, May 2014, pp. 88-91.

[20] R. H. Weber, and R. Weber, "Security and Privacy" in *Internet of Things Legal Perspectives*. Springer, 2010, pp. 41-67.

[21] S. Evdokimov, B. Fabian, and O. Günther, "Multipolarity for the Object Naming Service," in *The Internet of Things Lecture Notes in Computer Science*, Vol. 4952, 2008, pp. 1-18.

Towards Discovering and Understanding Unexpected Hazards in Tailoring Antivirus Software for Android

Heqing Huang[†], Kai Chen[‡†], Chuangang Ren[†], Peng Liu[†], Sencun Zhu[†], Dinghao Wu[†]
[†]The Pennsylvania State University, University Park, PA, USA
[‡]Institute of Information Engineering, Chinese Academy of Sciences, China
{hhuang, szhu, cyr5126}@cse.psu.edu, {chenkai}@iie.ac.cn, {pliu, dwu}@ist.psu.edu

ABSTRACT

In its latest comparison of Android Virus Detectors (AVDs), the independent lab AV-TEST reports that they have around 95% malware detection rate. This only indicates that current AVDs on Android have good malware signature databases. When the AVDs are deployed on the fast-evolving mobile system, their effectiveness should also be measured on their runtime behavior. Therefore, we perform a comprehensive analysis on the design of top 30 AVDs tailored for Android. Our new understanding of the AVDs' design leads us to discover the hazards in adopting AVD solutions for Android, including hazards in malware scan (*malScan*) mechanisms and engine update (*engineUpdate*). First, the *malScan* mechanisms of all the analyzed AVDs lack *comprehensive* and *continuous* scan coverage. To measure the seriousness of the identified hazards, we implement targeted evasions at certain time (e.g., end of the scan) and locations (certain folders) and find that the evasions can work even under the assumption that the AVDs are equipped with "complete" virus definition files. Second, we discover that, during the *engineUpdate*, the Android system surprisingly nullifies all types of protection of the AVDs and exposes the system to high risks. We confirmed the presence of this vulnerable program logic in all versions of Google Android source code and other vendor customized system images.

Since AVDs have about 650–1070 million downloads on the Google store, we immediately reported these hazards to AVD vendors across 16 countries. Google also confirmed our discovered hazard in the *engineUpdate* procedure, so feature enhancements might be included in later versions. Our research sheds the light on the importance of taking the secure and preventive design strategies for AVD or other mission critical apps for fast-evolving mobile-systems.

Categories and Subject Descriptors

D.4.6 [Operating Systems]: Security and Protection–*Invasive software; Access controls*

Keywords

Mobile; Malware; Anti-malware; Vulnerability measurement

ASIA CCS'15, April 14–17, 2015, Singapore.

ACM 978-1-4503-3245-3/15/04 ...$15.00.
http://dx.doi.org/10.1145/2714576.2714589

1. INTRODUCTION

The increasing popularity of mobile computing devices (e.g., smartphones and tablets) attracts both normal users and malware writers. Among the popular mobile platforms, Android has not only conquered a lion's share of the market, but also gained 98.1% share of mobile malware detected in 2013 [13]. Many companies, including those reputable ones focusing on PC security as well as some new startups, have turned their attention to mobile platform security and tailored their antivirus detectors particularly for Android [2]. Every three months, the independent antivirus test lab, AV-TEST, generates a report [6], comparing the detection rates of Android Virus Detectors (AVDs). The latest report indicated that the malware signature databases (MSD) of popular AVDs under test have achieved on average about 95% high malware detection rate. However, since Android allows executing both ARM binaries and Dalvik bytecode file (e.g., *.so* and *.dex* files) from dynamically loaded payload files to better serve application (app) developers at runtime [43], it has been shown that more malware [53, 52] based on the dynamic code loading are created and spread through the widely used Android app repackaging techniques [26, 34, 32, 48, 49]. Therefore, besides evaluation based on the quality of the MSDs, the success of the AVD's design on the fast-evolving Android platform must also be measured based on its efficacy in identifying malware's dynamic behavior (e.g., dynamic malicious payloads dropping/executing).

In this work, we conduct the first comprehensive analysis of top 30 AVDs (listed in Table 1), which currently has a total of 650-1070 million user downloads for the Google-Play store alone. Previous works [44, 40] have only focused on evaluating the quality of Virus Definition File (VDF) for virus detectors based on the well-known AVD weaknesses (e.g., vulnerable to transformation attacks). We take it a step further and our analysis concentrates on the scanning mechanism of Android AVDs.

Protection Assumption I: We assume Android AVD vendors have developed a *complete* MSD, which has been updated with all the reported malicious payloads and all the possible obfuscated versions of the payloads. Note that under this assumption, the Android AVDs are immune to common transformation attacks [44, 40]. Bearing this assumption in mind, we would like to understand if there are still deficiencies in the malware scan (*malScan*) mechanism itself that can cause potential hazards.

Hazards in malScan. The *malScan* operation here means the general malware recognition mechanism, which fingerprints the malware based on the VDF updated from the MSD. Generally, there are two types of *malScan* operations for Android: *light monitoring malScan* and *heavy sweeping malScan.* Four out of the top 30 AVDs have implemented the *light monitoring malScan*, which leverages the APIs from the Android *FileObserver* class. This en-

Table 1: **Popular Android virus detectors (AVDs) in our study**

ID	Vendor	AVD package name & version #	Downloads #	ID	Vendor	AVD package name & version #	Downloads #
1	Avast	com.avast.android;.........3.0.6915	50M-100M	2	AntiyAVL	com.antiy.avlpro;................2.3.02	50K-100K
3	AVG	com.antivirus;.........................3.6	100M-150M	4	AegisLab	com.aegislab.sd3prj.av;.........2.1.5	100K-500K
5	Avira	com.avira.android;..................3.1	1M-5M	6	Qihoo360	com.qihoo360.mobilesafe;....4.0.1	150M-200M
7	Bitdefender	com.bitdefender.security;2.8.217	1M-5M	8	Bornaria	com.bornaria.antivirus;.......1.3.60	50K-100K
9	Kaspersky	com.kms (premium);.........11.2.3	5M-10M	10	F-Secure	com.fsecure.ms.dc;........9.0.14504	100K-500K
11	ESET	com.eset.ems2.gp;...........2.0.843	1M-5M	12	CleanMaster	com.cleanmaster.security;......5.1.0	100M-150M
13	Dr. Web	com.drweb.pro;................7.00.11	10M-50M	14	Ikarus	com.ikarus.mobile.security 1.7.20	100K-500K
15	Lookout	com.lookout;..........8.28-879ce69	50M-100M	16	Comodo	com.comodo.pimsecure;.......2.4.5	100K-500K
17	McAfee	com.wsandroid.suite;...4.0.0.143	5M-10M	18	CMCInfoSec	com.cmcinfosec.mbsec;3.11.18/u5	100K-500K
19	Norton	com.symantec.mbsec;....3.8.0.12	10M-50M	20	NetQin	com.nqmobile.antivirus20;..7.0.10	150M-200M
21	TrendMicro	com.trendmicro.tmmspsnl;....5.0	1M-5M	22	Sophos	com.sophos.smsec;..........3.0.1244	100K-500K
23	Tencent	com.tencent.qqpimsecure;.....4.6	1M-5M	24	Panda	com.pandasecurity.pandaav;.....1.1	100K-500K
25	Webroot	com.webroot.security;3.6.0.6579	500K-1M	26	AnGuanJia	com.anguanjia.safe;...............4.5.2	100K-500K
27	G Data	de.gdata.mobilesecurity;...24.5.4	500K-1M	28	Virusfighter	com.virusfighter.android;.......2.1.3	500K-1M
29	TrustGo	com.trustgo.mb.sec;..........1.3.13	5M-10M	30	Zoner	com.zoner.android.av;............1.8.3	1M-5M

ables the AVD developers to come up with an ad-hoc design to perform *continuous* monitoring. However, our further detailed measurement study shows that these four AVDs only monitor several selected folders (e.g., the file *Downloads* folder) and only focus on limited file types (e.g., Android Application Package (APK) file). Therefore, by dropping the malicious payload onto any non-monitored folders or simply using an archived version of a malicious payload, *light monitoring malScan* can be evaded. This analysis indicates that the *FileObserver* based *light monitoring malScan* lacks *comprehensiveness*.

On the other hand, all 30 tested AVDs have designed the *heavy sweeping malScan* operation, which is a *comprehensive* malware scan. However, it is just due to the comprehensiveness of this type of scan that distinguishable system resource (e.g., CPU and memory) usage patterns are emitted when scanning. Also, we find that Android records the per process/per thread resource usage statistics in $/proc/[PID]/stat$ and $/proc/[PID]/task/[TID]/stat$ respectively, thus the resource usage patterns of each AVD's process/threads are readily available for all unprivileged third party apps. As a result, the scanning status of *heavy sweeping malScan* can be revealed by fingerprinting the high peaks of the AVD's resource usages, which makes the scanning vulnerable to targeted evasions. Thus, adversaries can evade this scan by identifying its scanning period and perform malicious action subsequently. So to clearly differentiate their scanning and idle periods and provide proof-of-concept evasions, we leverage *Fast Fourier Transformation* (FFT) to preprocess the per process/thread usage signals. We design and implement a *signal steganography* technique to identify the scanning locations (folders). We demonstrate that the adversary can plan targeted evasions by recognizing the (sub)folders that have just been scanned. Our analysis shed the light on the importance of developing a malware scanning mechanism that has both the *comprehensive* and *continuous* scanning properties.

Protection Assumption II: We then further assume AVD keeps monitor the whole file system completely and efficiently, and it can even perform behavior-based detections efficiently. By adding such a strong protection, we aim to find if there are still security holes in deploying AVDs on Android system.

Hazards in engineUpdate. Our study and various sources [23, 10] also show that AVDs on the fast-evolving Android system tend to perform engine updates (*engineUpdate*) fairly frequently, since AVD *engineUpdates* serve for various important tasks, including *malScan* mechanism enhancement, vulnerabilities [8, 20, 21, 19] patching and other functionality improvement [7]. However, we discover that the critical *AVD engineUpdate* procedure itself can cause devastating hazards to AVD even under both *Protection Assumption I and II*. In Android, Package Manager Service (PMS) updates the engine by removing the whole APK file and killing the AVD processes. Various components in the system have to perform complicated tasks (e.g., Dalvik bytecode optimization, configuration file parsing and etc.) for the newly downloaded APK file before setting up the AVD engine and reactivating it. As any strong defense mechanism relies on continuous running processes of the AVDs, this seemingly safe but complicated design of Android app-updating mechanism surprisingly kills the AVD process and nullifies any *perfect* protections for a period of high risk, which is called *null-protection window*. What's worse, our analysis shows that some AVD developers leave the engines inactivated after finishing its update. The lack of consideration in the AVDs' design indicates that AVD developers have not realized the potential hazard in *engineUpdate* yet. Without the automatic relaunch functionality, users can be exposed under high risk for a longer period.

The main contributions of this paper are summarized as follows:

- *New Understanding and New Hazards.* We reverse-engineer 30 widely-deployed Android AVDs and build a framework to conduct the first empirical study towards a comprehensive understanding of their design logic. Our study discover new hazards in *malScan*, *engineUpdate* and other mission critical operations of Android AVDs.

- *Measurements and Implementation.* We fully measured various types of *malScan* mechanism on Android and then design and develop targeted evasions against antivirus based on FFT and *signal steganography* techniques. For the hazards in *engineUpdate*, besides measuring the length of the *null protection window* on various hardware devices, we identify and analyze the Android AOSP source code for the program logic that creates the vulnerable period. We then built a *model checker* to automatically verify the existence of the discovered hazard in all Google Android versions from v1.5–v4.4.4, as well as vendor customized OS images.

- *Industrial Impact.* Because of the seriousness of these hazards and the great impact of current Android AVDs (around one *billion* user downloads), we immediately reported our findings to the antivirus vendors across 16 countries, and proposed mitigations designs to them. Also, not only can this *engineUpdate* hazard hurt the AVD apps, but it will impact other Android apps that require continuous running/monitoring (e.g. Mobile Device Management apps (MDMs) or Intrusion Prevention Systems (IPSs)) as well. Hence, we reported the hazard and proposed feature enhancements to the security team at Google, and they responded immediately and confirmed our findings.

2. BACKGROUND

2.1 AVD Background

Android is an operating system built upon the Linux Kernel. On top of the Linux kernel, Android is loaded with four software layers, namely *System Libraries, Android Runtime, Application Framework* and *Application*. In addition to the native Linux basic access control mechanism, Android provides a fine-grained permission mechanism for all the apps running on the Application layer, including all the AVDs from third party vendors.

Generally, Android uses a standard template process, the Zygote, for all the Dalvik Virtual Machine (DVM) processes warm-up phase. Zygote is the parent process for all the Android DVM processes, including all the AVDs' main processes. Each AVD is assigned its own unique user ID (UID) at install time, and the access control bits for the relevant files and folders in the file system are then set accordingly by the system. The dedicated group ID (GID) numbers are assigned based on the requested permissions for system resources. For instance, if an AVD wants to perform scanning operations on the files in the *sdcard*, it must first request the *READ_EXTERNAL_STORAGE* permission. Then, the system adds a relevant GID number (1028) for it and the process is put into the *AID_SDCARD_R* group to enable its access to the *sdcard*.

In the current Android system, a Binder interprocess communication (IPC) mechanism is used for more efficient *Intents* based message passing. Intents can be used in different purposes. For the app relevant usages, it can be sent to start an activity, start a service, deliver/receive a broadcast and so on. The system delivers various broadcast intents for system events to the apps/services that have registered to it. An AVD app/system daemon usually listens to specific broadcast intents by registering a broadcast receiver in the file AndroidManifest.xml or programmatically registering the relevant receiver in the code. For example, if an AVD app wants to relaunch automatically after the system boots up, it has to register for the system-broadcasted intent *BOOT_COMPLETED*, which is issued by the system once the boot process is completed. Some AVDs perform scanning for newly installed apps through registering the *PACKAGE_ADDED* events generated from the Package Manager Service (PMS) component. Listening system-broadcasted intents enables the AVD to keep track of system events of interest that are happening and then take appropriate actions.

2.2 AVD Behavior Analyses

Table 1 lists 30 popular AVDs that we selected from Google Play in Feb. 2014, which enjoy a total user downloads of about one billion. We pick the top 30 AVDs based on their overall protection rankings, according to AV Test Reports [6] for the period of Jan. 2014–April. 2014. To better understand the internal design of virus detectors on the Android platform, we further build a framework to perform comprehensive analyses of the selected AVDs.

2.2.1 AVD Behavior Analysis Framework

Our framework, illustrated in Figure 1, includes *Dynamic Tester, Static Code Analyzer* and *Environment Information Collector* to collect relevant virus detectors deployment information from both Android framework and Linux layer of the system.

The *Dynamic Tester* is built to interact with the AVDs, so that we can repetitively test some interesting properties of AVDs' runtime behavior. We wrote python and shell scripts to glue together the ADB tool, the Monkey-Runner tool [4], and the DDMS tool [3] from Android Studio. Monkey-Runner is a testing program that can send user and system events for our testing purpose. We leverage DDMS, a common debugger for Android developers, to collect relevant execution traces for particular operations for further analysis.

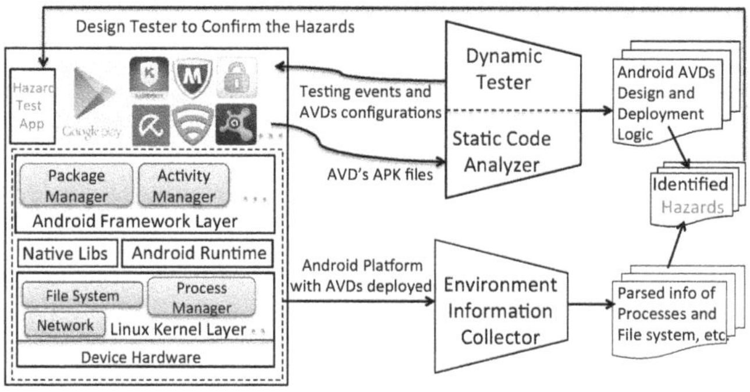

Figure 1: The AVD testing framework for Android platform

In the *Static Code Analyzer*, we first decompile the APKs of AVDs and then conduct analyses on the required *permissions* and registered *intent actions* in the corresponding broadcast receiver components. To further understand the design logic of AVDs, we build the control flow graph (CFG) upon the Android Dalvik bytecode disassembled from *baksmali* tool [16]. We adapt some of the analysis modules from Androguard [1] to construct the CFGs. We notice that most of the AVDs are not highly obfuscated, so the reverse engineering process is comparatively straightforward.

We also build an *Environment Information Collector* to analyze both the Android framework layer and the underneath Linux layer with all the AVDs installed, configured and running on the system. The purpose is to discover some effective public *information leakage channels*, which can help any third party app infer the AVDs' running status. For the Linux layer, we parse the information about the files and folders (e.g., access control bits) in the file system and the information about the running processes (e.g., the UID and GID numbers and their forking orders). Then we focus particularly on analyzing the information that is relevant to the installed AVDs. For the Android framework layer, we analyze relevant Android APIs to collect information about AVDs running status. After several rounds of automated testing and manual result verification, we discover several interesting *information leakage channels*, shown in Table 2, which will be especially valuable in determining the vulnerable periods of the running AVDs. Note that none of the discovered channels are protected by any Android permission yet.

2.2.2 Intents Registered and Permissions Claimed

In Table 3, we list the types and frequencies of the registered *intent actions* and claimed *permissions* of the 30 AVDs collected based on our reverse engineering result. Our analysis result indicates that current AVDs register lots of interesting permissions for privileged operations; for instance, the *KILL_PROCESSES* permission is used to kill suspicious background processes and the *ALERT_WINDOW* permission is claimed to help pop up urgent alert window from the system when suspicious status is identified. We also see that the current AVDs emphasize a *continuous* running status on the Android system. For instance, all these AVDs listen to the *BOOT_COMPLETED* system event to provide complete protection after the system boots up. They also obtain the *WAKE_LOCK* permission to periodically wake up the CPU to keep monitoring the system status. Events like *PACKAGE_ADDED* and *PACKAGE_REMOVED* are mostly registered to help monitor the newly installed/updated Android application package (APK) files. However, we still identify a loophole in its *engineUpdate* operation that unexpectedly nullifies the AVDs' protection.

Table 2: Information leakage channels used to infer AVDs' running status

ID	Probing Channels	Explanation
1	ActivityManager.getRunningAppProcesses()	Leaks DVM processes meta info (e.g., UID, PID, process name and etc.)
3	ActivityManager.getProcessMemoryInfo()	Leaks DVM process memory info (e.g., nativePSS, dalvikPrivateDirty and etc.)
4	PackageManager.getInstalledApplications()	Return a List of all the packages of installed applications
5	PackageManager.getPackagesForUid()	Leaks the names of all packages that are associated with a particular UID
6	PackageManager.sendBroadcast(Pkg_add)	Leaks the AVD or other apps' installation status
7	PackageManager.sendBroadcast(Pkg_rm)	Leaks the AVD or other apps' removal status
8	PackageManager.sendBroadcast(Pkg_updt)	Leaks the AVD or other apps' update status
9	Build.MODEL (HARDWARE)	Leaks device type and hardware specifications information
10	/proc/[AVD_pid]/stat	Leaks the relevant CPU usage info (e.g. utime, stime and etc.
11	/proc/[AVD_pid]/task/[AVD_tid]/stat	Leaks tasks CPU usage info of AVD process, used to purify the fingerprinting result
12	/proc/[AVD_pid]/statm	Leaks the memory usage info (e.g. the RSS, virtual memory size, etc.)
13	/proc/[AVD_pid]/status	Leaks the memory usage info (e.g., the RSS counts in pages)
14	JNI call stat() /data/data/[AVD_package]/*	Leaks all the files' meta info (e.g., size, creation date and etc.) in the subfolders
15	/system/bin/ps	Leaks all the running processes info including the DVM and non-DVM processes.
16	/proc/uid_stat/[AVD_uid]/snd(rcv)	Leaks the network usage info (e.g., send and received package sizes, etc.)

Table 3: Intents registered and permissions asked by AVDs

Intents Registered	#	Permissions Requested	#
MEDIA_REMOVED	4	SUPERUSER	1
MEDIA_CHECKING	5	BATTERY_STATS	12
PWR_DISCONNECTED	5	google.c2dm.RECEIVE	17
WIFI_STATE_CHANGED	6	KILL_PROCESSES	21
DATE_CHANGED	6	COARSE_LOCATION	21
SERVICE_STATE	7	ALERT_WINDOW	22
DIAL	7	WRITE_BOOKMARKS	22
MEDIA_UNMOUNTED	8	GET_ACCOUNTS	22
POWER_CONNECTED	8	READ_SMS	23
net.wifi.STATE_CHANGE	10	READ_BOOKMARKS	23
MEDIA_EJECT	10	READ_CONTACTS	25
USER_PRESENT	10	RECEIVE_SMS	25
ACTION_SHUTDOWN	12	SEND_SMS	25
NEW_OUTGOING-CALL	15	READ_LOGS	26
PHONE_STATE	17	GET_TASKS	26
PACKAGE_REPLACED	23	WAKE_LOCK	29
PACKAGE_REMOVED	30	EXTERNAL_STORAGE	30
PACKAGE_ADDED	30	READ_PHONE_STATE	30
BOOT_COMPLETED	30	BOOT_COMPLETED	30

Road map: The remainder of the paper continues as follows: Section 3 elaborates hazards relevant to the *malScan* mechanism, followed by the algorithm designed and implemented to confirm the hazards. Section 4 explains the exploring process of the hazard in AVD *engineUpdate* procedure and a model checker is developed to confirm the relevant vulnerable program logic. Other hazards are discussed in Section 5, followed by proposed mitigations. Section 6 reviews related works and Section 7 concludes this paper.

3. HAZARDS IN MALWARE SCAN

In this section, we report our study on the two malware scan (*malScan*) operations, namely the *light monitoring malScan* and the *heavy sweeping malScan*, and then followed by the discovered hazards for each type of *malScan* operations and their corresponding measurement results.

3.1 Malware Scan Behavior

Different from previous works on antivirus security measurement [44, 40] that targeting the weakness of the incomplete signature database, we assume that AVDs are all equipped with a *complete* VDF, which includes all known malicious payloads and their obfuscated counterparts. Hence, we use the easily recognizable malicious payloads from the well-known Malware Gnome Project [53] in our testing. This will force us to concentrate on analyzing the *malScan* mechanism itself when deployed on the Android platform. Similar to PC AVDs, the *malScan* operations are one of the core functionalities of AVDs for malware recognition based on up-to-date VDF.

Our analysis result shows that only four of the tested 30 AVDs have developed *light monitoring malScan*, which performs short-term scans for particular file system status changes. It leverages the *FileObserver* APIs provided by the Android framework, which is based on the *inotify()* system call to monitor the file system changes (e.g., create, modify, delete files/folders and etc.). For example, when a new file is downloaded into the $/sdcard/Downloads$, the AVD will perform a very quick scan for that particular file system status change on the folders, given that the particular folder is specified to be monitored in one of the registered FileObserver instances. However, our further analysis indicates that it can only focus on a few pre-selected folders (e.g., $/sdcard$) and the scan is lightweight, which means it cannot handle archive format.

On the other hand, all the 30 tested AVDs have implemented the *heavy sweeping malScan*, a comprehensive scan on the file system, which can be pre-scheduled or triggered directly by a user. It is usually performed by one or more Android service(s) or dedicated native process(es) (AVD # 9). This scan will consider most files, including archive files (e.g., *.apk*, *.tar* and *.zip*), in the target folder and its (sub)directories. It then fingerprints them against the VDF diligently. For instance, when targeting the $/data/app$ folder, it will check all the compressed app packages, the Android Application Package (APK) files of all installed apps, and iteratively scan through subdirectories and files in each APK file package. If an APK file happens to contain an archive file format, it will be uncompressed and scanned through all files contained in the archive file. Therefore, all of the tested AVDs rely on *heavy sweeping malScan* to perform comprehensive malware detection.

3.2 Light Monitoring malScan Hazard

To discover the potential hazards in *light monitoring malScans*, which leverage the *FileObserver* APIs, we use the *Dynamic Tester* to fully measure the effectiveness of the four AVDs. Our *Dynamic Tester* drops well-known malicious payloads on the $/sdcard$, which are recognized directly by all the four AVDs that have implemented this type of *malScan*. Then we configure the *Dynamic Tester* to test different dropping folders and using various archiving formats

Table 4: Light monitoring malware scan ineffectiveness

Tested Malicious Dropping Actions	Reacted AVD #
APK files (zipped) dropped on /sdcard	14
APK files (zipped) dropped on /sdcard/*/	None !!!
Native files (zipped) dropped on /sdcard	14, 15
Native files (zipped) dropped on /sdcard/*/	None !!!
APK files dropped on /sdcard/	13, 14, 15, 22(17.2s)
APK files dropped on /sdcard/*/	13, 15, 22
Native files dropped on /sdcard/	13, 14, 15
Native files dropped on /sdcard/*/	13

(e.g., zipped files). Table 4 contains the reacted AVDs for each specific measurement case. The result demonstrates that this type of scan is not effective, especially for zipped payloads dropped in a deeper-level folder of the targeted folder (e.g., $/sdcard/*/$). One reason that current AVDs cannot implement recursively file system monitoring due to the fact that this *FileObserver* APIs are not designed for comprehensive file system hooking.

From the result, we can also tell that AVD #15 from Lookout Inc., which is one of the top mobile security company targeting Android security for years, provides the best design for the *light monitoring malScan* among the tested AVDs. However, a design vulnerability in the AVD #15 has been discovered from our detailed analysis. The *light monitoring malScan* functionality is accidentally blocked when performing the *heavy sweeping malScan*. This buggy case indicates the problematic design of *light monitoring malScan* based on *FileObserver* APIs. Besides this problem, although our measurement shows that the AVD #22 Sophos can recognize malicious payloads in the $/sdcard$ directory, on average it takes 22.7s to react to the observed payload dropping events reported by the *FileObserver*. This vulnerability is due to an inappropriate way to handle the triggered events from the FileObserver object. During such a long reaction period, the adversary can easily finish his malicious actions based on the dropped payload and remove it before the *malScan* (its actual malware recognition action). We have reported the vulnerabilities to Lookout and Sophos respectively, and they have planned to fix them in the next versions.

Since *FileObserver* APIs provided by Google is not meant for AVD scanning purposes, these APIs cannot cover the whole file system comprehensively and efficiently. Thus, the ad-hoc design of the *light monitoring malScans* based on FileObserver is proven to be ineffective and problematic. Therefore, we are calling the need for specific hooking APIs for AVDs *light monitoring malScan* from platform designers, for instance, Samsung, Google and so on.

3.3 Heavy Sweeping malScan Hazard

Different from the *light monitoring malScan*, the *heavy sweeping malScan* is comprehensive, so it is usually hard to bypass. Especially, when the AVDs are equipped with the *complete* VDF. The *heavy sweeping malScan* is a series of expensive operations performed in a period, we call the period *high protection window*. Since it can be only triggered implicitly by a pre-defined schedule or explicitly by a user, this type of *malScan* can be very *comprehensive*, but lack of *continuous* protection. Therefore, if the adversary can identify the *high protection window*, it can potentially evade the detection by performing malicious actions after the scan.

To identify the *high protection window*, we want to analyze if the malScan reveals any side-effects, which is different from other non-scan operations. Based on the observations of *malScan* of the 30 AVDs, we notice that it is exactly this *comprehensive* scanning strategy that produces very distinguishable CPU and memory usage patterns. These patterns are distinct from other AVD operations (e.g., VDF updates or other managing tasks of AVDs). The result

Table 5: Heavy-sweeping malware scan configurations

Type	AVD #
Full Scan Only	5, 6, 7, 11, 15, 17, 21, 22, 25, 26, 29
Only Quick/Full	8, 9, 13, 14, 20, 24, 23, 27
App Only	1, 2, 4, 7, 12, 16, 17, 19, 20, 21, 27-30
Folder Only	1, 2, 3, 4, 9, 12, 13, 17, 18, 28, 30
Pre-scheduled	1, 2, 3, 4, 7, 9, 12, 16, 17, 19, 20, 21, 27, 29, 30

Table 6: Hardware specifications of four Android devices

Devices Name	OS versions	RAM	CPU cores,speed
Google Nexus 4	4.3 JB	2G	Quad,1.5kMHz
Asus Nexus 7 Tablet	4.1 JB	1G	Quad,1.3kMHz
Samsung Note 2	4.0 ICS	2G	Quad,1.6kMHz
Samsung Nexus S	2.2 Froyo	.5G	Single,1kMHz

from the *Environment Information Collector* in Table 2 shows that one can directly access the resource usage pattern (e.g., the utime and stime[1]) of AVDs from the file $/proc/[AVD\_pid]/stat$, which is accessible by the public. Here the *AVD_pid* is the process id of the AVD and the mapping between the AVD package name and its *pid* can be obtained through the probing channel #1 and #15.

Our further investigation shows that this Linux statistics file (*stat*), is created for the whole AVD process. Due to the multi-threaded programming of Android apps, the *stat* file for AVD process includes noise from other types of AVD operations, for example, a user interacting with the AVD app or other process management tasks (e.g. garbage collection) that are performed simultaneously on the background. To precisely identify the scanning operations and fingerprint the scanning period and locations, we discover that one can directly leverage the task information in the subdirectory of each $/proc/[AVD\_pid]/$ folder, namely the $/proc/[AVD\_pid]/task/[AVD\_tid]/stat$, #10 and #11 side channels. They reveal the utime and stime of a particular scanning task of an AVD process (e.g., start and end of the *heavy sweeping malScan*). Several dedicated tasks (main user interface or garbage collection threads) are assigned with fixed *tid* based on the *pid* offset. Thus, the noise introduced from these tasks or operations can be filtered out.

Another interesting observation is that some AVDs (e.g. # 9) use dedicated native process(es) for more efficient scanning, but this special improvement in *malScan* surprisingly hurts itself, as it simplifies the relevant *high protection window* fingerprinting procedure. One only has to identify the *pid* of the "/kav/libscan" native process of #9 through the *information leakage channels* #1 and #15. And then the relevant resource usage patterns for the comprehensive scanning tasks can be further collected through *channels* #10 and #11 of the "/kav/libscan" process.

Testing malScans and Collecting Scanning Traces.

To further explore the feasibility of fingerprinting the *heavy sweeping malScan* in real time and build proof-of-concept evasions from the collected system resource (e.g., CPU and memory) usages of the targeted AVD, we first run dynamic testing over all the AVDs' *heavy sweeping malScan*. The result of our dynamic testing, in Table 5, shows that current AVDs have three types of configurations for this *malScans*: 1) only one full scan; 2) quick/full scan, where a quick scan usually scans a subset of full scan's content (e.g., only the APK files); 3) flexible scan by selecting different targets (folders). In addition to the above, some AVDs also have user-scheduled scans at a particular time of a day or in a weekly/monthly basis. To perform one *malScan*, it usually takes 1-10 minutes, depending on the number and type of files/apps to be scanned. To build a bet-

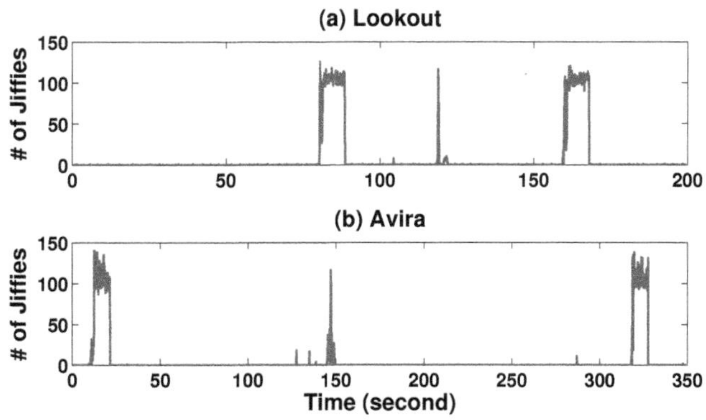

Figure 2: 6 minutes CPU usage (utime) temporal statistics of (a) AVD Lookout and (b) AVD Avira

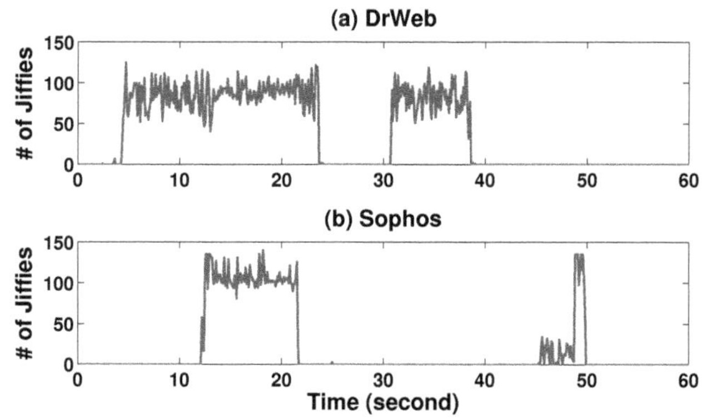

Figure 3: Comparison of full/quick scans' stime signal of (a) AVD Dr.Web and (b) AVD Sophos

ter fingerprinting algorithm, we collect the resource usage statistics for various *heavy sweeping malScan* configurations of all the 30 tested AVDs on four devices with different hardware specifications, as shown in Table 6. For each AVD on each device, we perform ten 30-minute tests to collect its corresponding resource usage statistics. We name the resource (e.g., CPU and memory) usage statistics for a particular job of an AVD as a *trace*. A *trace* generally contains all the relevant CPU and memory information (e.g., the utime, stime[1] of CPU and the VmSize, VmRSS[2] of the memory). For a particular AVD scan trace, we name each specific resource usage dynamics as a *signal*. For instance, the process's *utime signal* is a series of incremental values calculated based on the collected user mode CPU usage time (in Jiffies), which reflects the AVD's real-time CPU usage. Various signals can be sampled at adjustable rates (e.g., 1 sample/second or 5 sample/Minute).

Identify Heavy Sweeping malScans Traces.

Our first goal is to differentiate the traces of *heavy sweeping malScan* with traces from all other operations (e.g., VDF file updates, cloud Scan and etc.). Figure 2 contains 30-minute time series of two representative AVDs (AVD Lookout and Avira) during which the user triggers two *malScans* and various other random AVD operations. We remove part of the blank sub-period that contains no system resource statistics and present a 6-minute version in the paper. We observe that the utime pattern (stime has similar pattern) has an extremely aggressive CPU usage pattern in a continuous time period, which is the *high-protection window*, compared to all other small traces introduced by non-scan operations. Therefore, we use the average *utime, stime signals* in a sliding time window (around 30 seconds) to decide if the AVD's scan enters the *high-protection window*.

Differentiate Full and Quick Scans.

Besides identifying the *high-protection window*, we want to further differentiate the *high-protection window* of full and quick scans of one particular AVD, so that the adversary can start malicious actions (e.g., dropping/executing malicious payloads) right after the more comprehensive full scan, which is safer to evade detection. Figure 3 contains the *stime signal* of representative full and quick scans of two AVDs, from which we can tell that the quick scan is generally shorter (quicker) than full scan, and the stime signals' (utime is the same) peak and average values are pretty close to full scan. Based on this general heuristic, we can differentiate full and quick scan by collecting two *malScans* with very different signal lengths as benchmarks. Therefore, when the next *malScan* is identified, its signal length can be compared with the previously stored benchmarks. We also keep updating the corresponding benchmarks with the newly classified scan traces for different categories.

Signal Steganography based Scan Location Inference.

Our study also shows that some AVDs provide multiple ways of configuring the *heavy sweeping malScans* that target on various scanning locations. On rooted devices, some AVDs [12, 14] even enables the ability to scan most the important folders (e.g., $/sdcard$, $/data/app$, $/data/data$, $/system/app$ and etc.). Therefore, we seek to identify the precise location that the scanning has just happened. Because it is less likely for the AVD to re-scan the same location within a short period of time, one can design an evasion attack based on this assumption.

The scanning location inference idea is very intuitive. The goal is to infer if the scan is just sweeping through a particular folder of interest. To achieve this, we leave a special file, namely a *marker*, in that folder. The *marker* file is intentionally designed to exhibit special patterns in terms of CPU or other resource usages during AVD *heavy sweeping malScan*. Since only the *marker* file designer knows the embedded signal and later extracts it. We call this method, *signal steganography*.

Delay-of-Scan Hazard. The design of a unique marker file is based on our observations of the normal AVD scanning process. First, most of the AVDs have aggressive CPU usage, mainly caused by checking the files in the target folder. The pattern of CPU utilization during scanning varies depending on the type, size and structure of the (archive) files. Second, once encountering an archive file, most AVDs would have to first unzip the file before fingerprints it. The unzipping operations lead to less CPU utilization but more memory use, which exhibits certain patterns (the shape and frequency of CPU or memory utilization profiles). If one could make this special pattern continue for a significant long time (e.g., several seconds, which is actually unnoticeable compared to the minute-level scanning time), we can identify and extract it directly from the whole trace and finish the discovery of the embedded *sig-*

[1]utime is the user mode jiffies and stime is the kernel mode jiffies, which are the 14th and 15th field of the /proc/AVD_pid/stat file, respectively. Jiffies is a time measure based on a clock maintained by the kernel. CPU time, which is limited by the resolution of the software clock and measured by clock ticks (divided by sysconf(_SC_CLK_TCK). _SC_CLK_TCK is set to 100 in bionic/libc/unistd/sysconf.c for all Android OS versions.

[2]For an AVD process, the VmSize is the virtual memory size and VmRSS is the portion of a process' memory that is held in RAM, which are the 1st and 2nd fields of the s/proc/[AVD_pid]/statm, respectively.

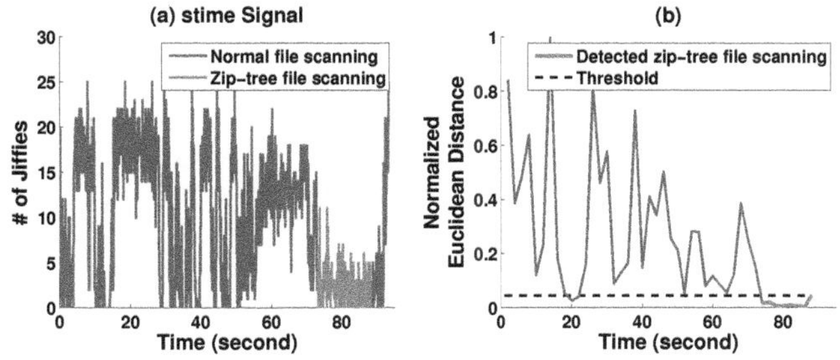

Figure 4: Stime signal (red line indicates zipTree scanning segment) of Panda Security

nal. To leverage these observations, we create a special archive file as the *marker*, which is a three-layer zip file called *zipTree*. Each parent node in this *zipTree* entry contains 10 zip files, and each one of the 10 zip files contains another 10 child-zip files. The inmost *leaf* zip file is an empty *.txt* file. The crafted *zipTree* is about 0.7KB in size, which can hold the *malScan* process for 9 seconds. We name this *Delay-of-Scan* hazard, which can potentially cause denial of service attack given a big enough *zipTree*. However, in our *signal steganography* based pattern recognition approach, we only need to delay the scan for a couple of seconds. In this way, we can precisely identify the scanning locations based on the marker that was dropped on the particular folder.

Figure 4(a) displays the stime signal of the scanning by Panda Security. It is noteworthy that the stime signal during *zipTree* scanning (as shown in a red line in the figure) exhibits patterns with three special *properties* compared to other parts of the signal: (1) the signal has a much lower mean value than other parts of the stime signal; (2) the signal shows stable patterns; that is, the signal is periodic and has relatively deterministic frequencies; (3) the stable pattern of the signal of *zipTree* file scanning lasts for considerably longer time compared with the other part in the signal. Based on these observations, we devise an efficient online algorithm, Algorithm 1, to recognize/extract the stime signal segments of *zipTree*. The algorithm is based on *Fast Fourier Transformation* (FFT) for the classic spectrum analysis that is widely used in signal processing. FFT transforms the sample signal from the time domain to the frequency domain, so our analysis is stable against potential time variations in the signal. More importantly, the frequency domain can still capture most part of the three properties of the signal. The idea is to determine *zipTree* scanning period by identifying a period of time that exhibits similar CPU utilization patterns (e.g., similar means and magnitude in different frequencies), or in one word, similar frequency spectrum characteristics that appeared repetitively. Once we identify a period with lower mean value signals (based on property (1)), we first perform FFT (line 9 in the Algorithm 1) to multiple sliding windows of the CPU utilization signal and generate a time series of frequency spectrum, a presentation of a time-series signal in the frequency domain. As is well known in signal processing, similar two frequency spectrum imply that the corresponding two time series sharing similar signal components at all frequencies. We then compute the *Euclidean Distance* of the neighboring spectrum (line 10). We determine two neighbor frequency spectrum as "similar" by checking if the euclidean distance between these spectrum is smaller than a self-adapted threshold (line 11). Since the archive files produce property (2) (3), the distance can be kept very small for an amount of time (several seconds, controlled by causing the *Delay-of-Scan* hazard), which is demonstrated in the red part of Figure 4(b). Although the stime signal length caused by the *Delay-of-Scan* hazard varies on different hardware devices, the repeated stable structure in the *zipTree* file ensures the periodicity of the low signal pattern regardless of hardware specifications. Note that for all the *malScan* inference measurements, we reach the desired results by using only the stime signals from the CPU patterns.

Algorithm 1 Pseudo-code for the algorithm to extract zipTree scanning pattern

```
1: zipfilescaning ← False
2: window[window_size] ← empty
3: spectrogram[window_size][ ] ← empty
4: k ← 0, mag_thresh ← α
5: dist_thresh ← β, len_thresh ← γ
6: while obtain new value V do
7:     update_Window(window, V)
8:     if mean(window) < mag_thresh then
9:         spectrogram[k][] ← FFT(window)
10:        distance ← Euclidea_Distance(spectrogram[k],
           spectrogram[k-1])
11:        if distance < dist_thresh and k > len_thresh then
12:            zipfilescaning ← True
13:        else
14:            zipfilescaning ← False
15:            erase(spectrogram)
16:            k ← 0
17:        end if
18:    else
19:        zipfilescaning ← False
20:        erase(spectrogram)
21:        k ← 0
22:    end if
23: end while
```

3.4 Targeted Evasions

Based on the discovered hazards, various targeted attacks can be designed. One potential attack scenario is based on repackaging [49, 32, 26, 48, 34] a benign carrier (RBC app) app, which does not contain any malicious payload for root exploiting, or privacy stealing. Therefore, the RBC app itself will not be judged as malicious during the install-time scan. After the RBC app is deployed on the system, it can leverage the *information leakage channel* #1 in Table 2 to check the name of the installed AVD and use the discovered hazard to infer its scanning status. Once it identifies a moment to its advantage (e.g., end of a *malScan*), malicious actions can be performed under the radar of the AVD's scans. For example, based on the similar analysis result from Table 4, one can drop malicious payloads to the folder that is not covered by the *light monitoring malScan*, load and execute them and then remove the evidence. Other remote evasions can also be designed. For instance, one can leverage remote vulnerability exploiting (e.g., code injection vulnerability in HTML5-based apps [37]) to hijack a running process's control flow, and then conduct the similar evasions to prevent the injected payloads from being identified.

4. HAZARDS IN ENGINE UPDATE

For an AVD equipped with complete VDF and perfect hooking mechanism, we consider the best moments to evade it is when its process(es) has not been activated yet. Our study result in Table 3 shows that all the tested AVD are listening on the *BOOT_COMPLETE* intent to automatically launch itself when the system boots up. This close a potential opportunity for evasions and indicates that AVD developers are aware of some similar hazards. However, after further analysis on the interaction between the AVD and the Android system, we identify a hazard in AVD's engine update (*engineUpdate*) procedure, that unexpectedly nullifies any strong protections an AVD provides for the system. Here we elaborate the AVD's *engineUpdate* operation in Android and analyze the hazard.

4.1 Engine Update Behavior and Hazard

The AVD *engineUpdate* operation provides essential updates for AVD *malScan* operation improvement, bug and vulnerability patching [7, 8, 20, 21, 19], and update-to-date protection [23]. Since the technical details of AVD's *engineUpdate* mechanism on Android have not been scrutinized before, to come up with a detailed full picture, we leverage our analysis framework and manual analysis based on runtime logs and related decompile Dalvik bytecode (the *smali* format). The *engineUpdate* operation is performed whenever an AVD developer posts an updated version of APK on Google Play. It can be either triggered by the user, or by the old AVD process automatically. The whole procedure is executed by the Android system, namely the Package Manager Service (PMS), the Activity Manager Service (AMS), *installd* daemon and etc. Lots of evidence [23, 10] show that AVDs update fairly frequently. Indeed, during a two-week period in March of 2014, we initially tested the process of *engineUpdate* operations using our analysis framework and noticed a high update ratio, 25 out of 30 tested AVD products have version updates from Google Play.

On the traditional PC platform, during the engine update procedure, an AVD will not shut down the whole AVD program, but only replace part of the necessary modules (e.g., DLL files or kernel drivers). However, we identify that on the Android platform, the updating procedure is different. One potential problem of this specific procedure is that the Android system will kill the AVD process(es) before the *engineUpdate*. This design is considered as valid and effective for most third party apps and help prevent unintended app update [15], but this specific design lacks detail analysis on potential security implications. Especially when considering from the perspective of AVD realtime protection and detection, this APK update mechanism introduces a serious flaw, as its complicated procedure renders the system lacking of AVD's protection for a period of high risk, which is called *null-protection window*.

In order to confirm the hazard, we further verify the existence of the *null-protection window* by checking the implementation logic in the Android AOSP code base. The relevant high-level program logic flow is generalized and presented in Figure 5 as a Finite State Automaton (FSA). In the device, the PMS from the Android framework layer listens on update requests and performs the actual work along with several other services. For instance, the *installd* daemon and the AMS have to collaborate with the PMS component to finish different tasks in the *engineUpdate* procedure. Based on the complicated design of app updates on Android, the system handles AVD version updates in several steps. After the new APK is downloaded and update is confirmed, the current AVD process is killed, and the old code directory ($/data/app$) and some relevant data files in the $/data/data/[AVD\_package]/*$ subdirectories are removed. Before relaunching the new process, the newly downloaded Android Package file (APK) of AVD is verified for the developer's signature, and followed by Dalvik bytecode optimization (e.g., *dex* to *odex*), configuration file parsing (e.g., permission registration based on the AndroidManifest.xml file) and etc. Note that the system never helps relaunch the previously killed process, which will expand the *null-protection window*. Due to this unavoidable *null-protection window* caused by the specific design for package updates of Android, the AVDs become vulnerable even under the strong *protection assumptions I and II*.

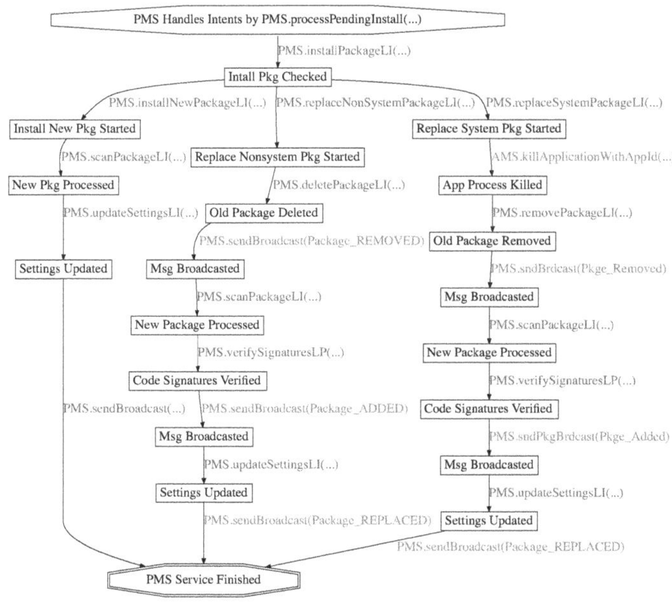

Figure 5: The constructed FSA of PMS for Android v4.4.4_r1

To leverage the exposed *null-protection window*, the adversary must infer if the AVD is performing the *engineUpdate* operation. During our runtime testing and code analysis, we find that PMS will broadcast a series of intents with different action fields, including *PACKAGE_REMOVED*, *PACKAGE_ADDED* and *PACKAGE_REPLACED* (red in Figure 5), so as to notify the other components to perform the corresponding tasks and keep them updated with the current app updating status. However, these broadcasted intents unexpectedly reveal the updating status of AVD to any unprivileged apps. So the malicious app can simply register these broadcast intents to get notified, and then start malicious operations during the exposed *null-protection window*. Our analysis framework also helps us identify several other leakage channels (e.g., channel #1, #4 and #14 in Table 2) that can infer this vulnerable status of AVD. This indicates simply restricting the receivers of the broadcasted intents cannot fully eliminate the hazard.

4.2 Null-protection Window Length

Next, we quantitatively measure the length of this *null-protection window* for various AVDs and devices. We conduct four groups of experiments based on four types of real devices, whose configurations are provided in Table 6 in Section 3. For each group, we try to test all the 30 AVDs' engine update operations and record their *null-protection window* lengths. For every AVD on each device, we test 10 times to obtain the mean value and relevant confidence interval. Our result indicates that the window lengths are quite stable; for example, the representative Symantec AVD has an average window length of 11.2 seconds, with a confidence interval [-0.13, 0.13] at the confidence level 95%. This is because of the routinely PMS updating logic and the atomic nature for most of the PMS method invocations during the execution. Due to space limits, we only show the mean values in Figure 4.2. Here, the x-axis is the average length of *null-protection window* in seconds, and the y-axis represents each AVD. For each AVD, to clearly compare the window lengths for four devices, we draw four horizontal bars in different colors. Longer bars are partly covered by shorter bars. We can see that for all AVDs, the *null-protection window* lengths in Samsung Note II and Google Nexus IV (LG) are the smallest, whereas Nexus S (Samsung) has the largest window, from about 9.2-16.8 seconds. Note that all the collected results are the theoretical lower bounds for the *null-protection window*, because in this test, our *Dynamic Testor* keeps sending launching events from *adb* tool during each tested AVD updating session. This guarantees the automatic AVD relaunch right after the AVD is updated.

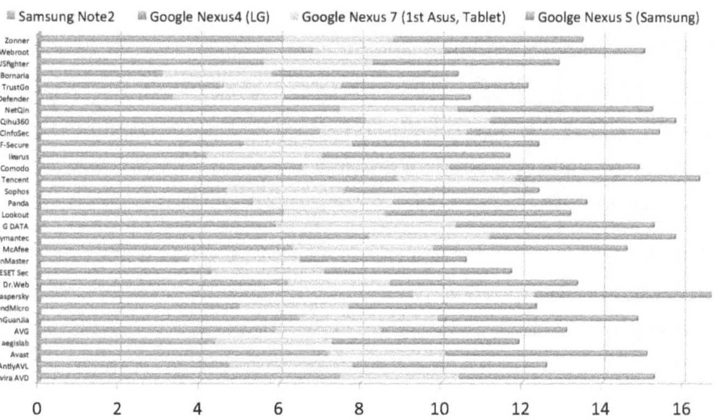

Figure 6: The *Null-protection Window* lengths (in seconds) for all 30 tested AVDs on four Android devices

Since we can automate the process of AVDs' relaunching, we think one might provide a preventive design to relaunch the AVD by the updated new AVD code itself immediately after the *engineUpdate* finishes. One interesting mitigation that we come up with is to add a *receiver* component in AVD to listen to the broadcasted *action.PACKAGE_REPLACED* intent, which indicates the finishing of the *engineUpdate*. Then this receiver of the updated new AVD engine is always triggered by this broadcasted intent right after the *engineUpdate* finishes. Within the registered receiver component, we then relaunch the main monitoring process automatically through Android APIs, *startActivity()*. Note that this mitigation does not solve the fundamental problem that the old AVD process is killed and the vulnerable period is created, but it can only reduce the *null-protection window* length to the theoretical lower bound (caused by the complicated updating operations carried out by the system). None of the 23 of the tested AVDs that registered the *action.PACKAGE_REPLACED* (in Table 3), are actually performing the preventive design for their own updates, but only use the registered receiver to start a service to scan other apps' updating for malware detection purpose. We report our findings to all the AVD vendors and propose this short-term mitigation to them. They responded to us immediately and confirmed the hazard. Similar patches will be provided in their next release based on our suggested mitigation. However, to completely eliminate the hazard, the PMS design should be enhanced. Since this hazard can be applicable to other apps that require continuous monitoring properties (e.g., Mobile Device Manager (MDM) [18], IPS [12, 14] and etc.), we reported this hazard to Google and they confirmed our findings and we are now working with them on possible feature enhancements for the relevant components and services.

4.3 Model Checking the Vulnerable Logic

To automate the process of verifying the pervasiveness of the vulnerable temporal logic in AVDs' engine update procedure, we leverage the model checking techniques, which have been applied widely [25, 29, 27] to perform system bugs and vulnerabilities examination and temporal property checking for both mobile and PC platforms. Our model checker for the Android platform is similar to Chen et al. [27], in the sense that we both check the reachability of certain temporal logic in the code. However, our model checker, particularly targets the Dalvik bytecode of the PMS in Android for the *engineUpdate*'s vulnerable temporal program logic.

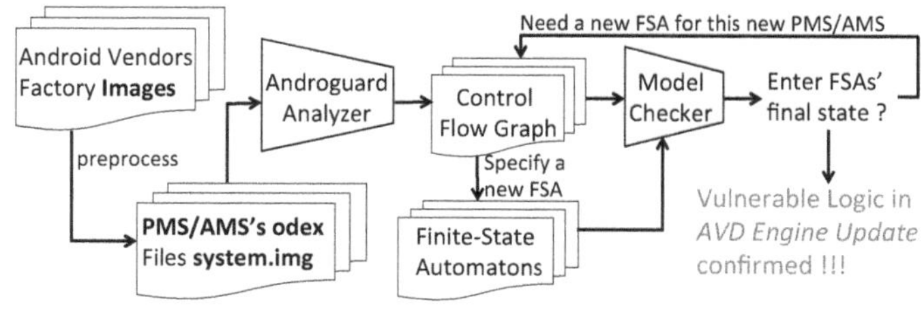

Figure 7: The model checking framework

Figure 7 shows the design of our model checking framework. The inputs are the Android factory images collected from multiple vendors. After the preprocessing phase, we extract the relevant *.odex* file of the PMS components in the system.img. The odex code, namely the optimized Dalvik bytecode, can be run directly on the targeted Dalvik VM. We decompile the odex file into Dalvik bytecode and produce the CFGs for these components. From the constructed CFGs, we first identify the relevant execution traces that correspond to the *engineUpdate*'s temporal logic. Then we construct FSAs to describe the relevant vulnerable program logic in PMS. Each edge in the FSA corresponds to a critical method invocation that brings the system state to the next state. For instance, Figure 5 is a simplified representation of one of the FSAs for the relevant vulnerable code in the PMS of Android version 4.4.4_r1. The completion of the *PMS.deletePackageLI()* invocation brings the state from STATE{"Replace Non-system Package Started"} to the STATE{"Old Package Deleted"}. Therefore, when we perform a model checking against the constructed CFG, whenever the system state STATE{"Replace Non-system Package Started"} encounters the *deletePackageLI()* method invocation in the PMS class file, our model checker will bring the current system state to the STATE{"Old Package Deleted"}. It then expects the next critical method invocation, namely *PMS.sndPkgBroadcast()*. Our model checker works in a depth-first-search manner to check the system states along the constructed CFGs. Whenever a sequence of method invocations is matched to a sequence of edges in the FSA that lead to the final STATE{"PMS Service Finished"}, a trace will be printed out for further verification. These traces help confirm the existence of the vulnerable logic for the AVD *engineUpdate* operation of the PMS component. We actually use the "liveness property" of model checking for vulnerability verification. Note that here we are to verify if something "good" will eventually happen, and here "good" means the identification of the exact vulnerable temporal logic in the PMS. Whenever the newly constructed CFGs of the PMS does not match the specified FSAs, we will check into the relevant CFGs to manually construct a new FSA for the unmatched PMS version. Most of the time, it is because the names of the methods are changed slightly, or a new wrapper is provided for an old method. It turns out that we only need to construct four FSAs to check the temporal logic of all PMS versions of Android OSes. The relevant mapping from FSAs to Android versions are given in Table 7. Due to the space limitation, we skipped some versions if our model checker reports no critical implementation variances.

Confirm the Goolge Android official factory Images.

To systematically check all Goolge Android factory images, we have downloaded all the factory images [9], which contain im-

Table 7: Android OS versions and relevant Models for PMS

OS versions	Release dates	Constructed FSAs
Android v4.4.4	19 June 2014	FSA of v4.4.4_r1
Android v4.4_r1	31 October 2013	FSA of v4.4.4_r1
Android v4.3_r2.1	14 July 2013	FSA ofv4.4.4_r1
Android v4.2_r1	13 November 2012	FSA of v4.4.4_r1
Android v4.1.2_r1	22 August 2012	FSA of v4.1.2_r1
Android v4.0.3_r1	16 December 2011	FSA of v4.1.2_r1
Android v2.3.7_r1	11 September 2011	FSA of v2.3.7_r1
Android v2.2_r1.1	29 June 2010	FSA of v2.3.7_r1
Android v2.1_r2	27 January 2010	FSA of v2.1_r2
Android v2.0_r1	14 October 2009	FSA of v2.1_r2
Android v1.6_r2	15 September 2009	FSA of v2.1_r2
Android v1.5_r4	30 April 2009	FSA of v2.1_r2

ages ranging from Android version v1.5_r4–v4.4.4_r1, totally 34 versions. Our model checker has verified that the same vulnerable logic in PMS appears from all the Android OS versions from v1.5_r4 (April 2009) to very recent v4.4.4_r1 (June 2014) for all Google official Android factory images.

Confirm the Vendor customized stock Images.

Due to the Android vendors' fragmentation problem [22, 5], we also download images from HTC and Samsung [17, 11] and conduct analysis on recently released stock images from multiple vendors, including Samsung (S4, S3 and S2 with Android v4.4.2, v4.0.4 and v2.3.4), HTC (One Mini, M7 with Android v4.4.2, v4.3), Sony (Xperia Z2 and Xperia M2 with Android v4.4 and v4.3) and LG (LGD958 Android v4.2.2). Our analysis also confirms that the same vulnerable PMS logic appears in all of them. It is because most of the customized stock images directly reuse most of the core design logic in mission critical components (e.g., PMS) from Google AOSP codebase.

Our finding demonstrates that some seemingly benign, but complicated updates in the system can cause surprising hazards to a stable system, which is similar to the takeaway message presented by Xing et al. [46]. But the newly discovered flaw resides in the PackageManager Service for AVDs' *engineUpdate* procedure, which can unexpectedly nullify any security protection from AVDs.

5. DISCUSSIONS

5.1 Mitigations

One proposed prevention for the discovered information leakage channels in Table 2 is based on more fine-grained mandatory access control. The Android system can leverage the existing SEAndroid [45] mechanism to restrict the public from accessing the channels under certain usage scenario with high security requirements. One specific policy refinement is to assign a new *subject domain* and relevant *allow* rules in the SEAndroid [45] policy database and then label a while-listed/authorized apps/services with the new subject domain. Consequently, only controlled/authorized accesses to different files under the $/proc/*$ (sub)folders are granted. However, this requires a solid understanding on different usage scenarios of various programs and the underlying Android system design specifics, so that the proposed mitigation will not block normal legitimate usability. One can model the relevant attacks in the mobile system into attack graph surface [33] and then enforce policy to block different leakage channels accordingly.

We propose another specific mitigation for the hazards in *heavy sweeping malScan*. For example, the underlying system may provide only the general usage statistics of AVDs (or other mission critical apps) by normalizing or delaying the reporting of system resource usage statistics (e.g., the CPU, memory and network) in relevant public channels in Table 2. Consequently, it is harder for an adversary to fingerprint an app's exact running status on the fly. The other way to reduce the risk is to introduce randomness into pre-scheduled scans. Instead of setting up an exact time, the user may specify a time window, in which an AVD can choose a random time to start scanning each day. A long-term mitigation is to improve the *malScan* operation and make scan operations *continuous* and *comprehensive* at the same time. According to our discussion with AVD vendors, this seems to be a future research topic, since *malScan* with both properties requires lots of testing and optimizations to be finally deployed on the resource limited mobile devices.

In addition to the designed short-term mitigations to AVD vendors in Section 4.2 for the *engineUpdate* hazard, we discuss with the Google security team that the system designers will have to re-architect the PMS component to close or reduce the *null-protection window* in the app-updating procedure. One suggestion to Google is to delete the old APK only after the new process has been reactivated, but this might cause conflicts on app's package names or other app management tasks (e.g., the install verification process). Since lots of apps have continuous monitoring requirements (e.g., MDMs, IPSs, and etc.), Google has to find a way to resolve those conflicts for this feature enhancement in PMS.

5.2 Other Hazards

In our study, we find the other two potential hazards, which indicate that the discovered hazards are just a tip of the iceberg. So we discuss the other two types of hazards which can enable the evasions of current Android AVDs.

Cloud based malScan Hazard.

During the analysis, we sense a trend of adding the cloud-based scanning strategy for mobile platforms, including AVD # 1, 2, 3, 23 and 26. Cloud-based scanning fits resource limited mobile devices, as it can offload the heavy computation to a remote server by sending out the collected information. However, since the per UID network usage statistics can be directly accessed through the discovered channel # 16 in Table 2 as well, an adversary can plan evasions and attacks against AVDs using the similar fingerprinting strategy described in the *heavy sweeping malScan* hazard.

Virus definition file (VDF) update Hazard.

All the AVDs store their VDF and other files/data in the subdirectories, $/data/data/[AVD\_package]/*$, which are strictly set to be *world-unreadable* and enforced by the Linux kernel in Android. Our further analysis based on *Environment Information Collector* shows that this solid design of app data privacy protection is not enough for VDFs' deployment, as an adversary only needs to know the file size or other meta-data information of relevant files (e.g., created/updated time) in the subdirectory to infer the updating status of the VDF or other sensitive files (e.g., scan result caching file). We design a zero-permission app to call the *stat()* system call thorugh JNI to directly probe the meta-data information of all these files in an AVD's data folder. The whole path parameter that leads to different files (e.g., VDF) can be first collected via offline analysis. Knowing this status information, lots of potential targeted evasions can be designed. For instance, we find that some AVDs (e.g., # 21) perform a fresh *heavy sweeping malScan* right after the VDF is updated, so the adversary can drop or decrypt the newly obfuscated known malicious payloads a few minutes after the VDF has been updated, so as to make its fresh scan useless.

6. RELATED WORK

Malware analysis and threat prevention techniques [47, 38] have been designed and applied for offline analysis. Also, various interesting anti-analysis techniques have been discussed [42, 28] for both mobile and PC malware. Our proof-of-concept evasion techniques are conceptually similar to anti-analysis techniques, but we focus on a new angle to emphasize more on the evasion of AVD's online protection mechanism. Zhou et al. [53] provided a study of Android malware, and similarly, the discovered hazards in this paper are also based on a systematic study of 30 popular AVDs.

Android app and system hazards have been discovered in [41, 30, 46, 51, 50]. Accidental data disclosure between apps in mobile and PC systems have been discussed in [39]. The discovered information leakage channels for various hazards in AVD are relevant to the unexpected data exposure from the system side. Jana et al. [36] also take the per process memory usage and CPU scheduling statistics as probing channels to leak program's secrets. We identify that we can even leverage per thread usages to conduct fine-grained inference. Pileup attacks [46] are also based on a flaw in PMS that targets system update. Our *engineUpdate* hazard is based on one newly discovered flaw in PMS (related to the app-update mechanism). Empirical studies [30] have been performed on several hazards in security critical components or modules in Android apps. Our study is performed on current AVD apps, and several hazards have been discovered and reported to AVD vendors.

Antivirus evasion techniques [40, 24, 35] have been studied previously. Android Dalvik bytecode polymorphic transformation attacks have been presented by Rastogi et al. [44] to target incomplete signature database. However, our study concentrates on the the malware recognition mechanism itself, and the result shows that the quality of AVD's *malScan* mechanism should be further improved when deployed on the Android platform. Fedler et al. [31] discuss the lack of on-demand file system hooking problem of Android antivirus. Our study shows that some of the AVDs have already leveraged *FileObserver* APIs for that purpose. However, we find that it is the lack of combination of scan comprehensiveness and continuity that causes the ineffectiveness of the current design. What's more, the discovered hazards in the AVD *engineUpdate* are completely orthogonal to the file system hooking problem. Because any strong protections have to rely on an activated AVD process, which is missing in the *null-protection window*.

7. CONCLUSION

Based on an analysis framework, we conduct an empirical study of top 30 AVDs on the current Android platform. We discovered several serious hazards related to AVD malware scan mechanism, engine update procedure and etc. We then develop techniques to measure the feasibility of exploiting the hazards in *malScan* and confirmed the vulnerable *engineUpdate* program logic in the Android system through static analysis and model checking techniques. We reported the discovered vulnerabilities and hazards to AVD vendors, all of them have confirmed our findings and will take some of the mitigations suggestions in their latest versions. We also discuss the vulnerable design in the PMS that causing the *null-protection window* to the Google security team. They also admit the problem and will consider feature enhancement on the PMS component.

As the malware and the Android system keep evolving, more secure and preventive design strategies for mission critical apps (e.g., AVDs, IPS [12, 14], MDM [18] and etc.) should be adopted to reduce the chance of getting unexpected failures and loopholes.

8. ACKNOWLEDGMENTS

The authors would like to thank the anonymous reviewers for their insightful comments that helped improve the presentation of this paper. This work was partially supported by ARO W911NF-09-1-0525 (MURI), NSF CCF-1320605, NSFC 61100226 and NSF CNS-1223710. Any opinions, findings and conclusions or recommendations expressed in this material are those of the authors and do not necessarily reflect the views of the National Science Foundation and Army Research Office.

9. REFERENCES

[1] AndroGuard: Android Dalvik Bytecode Analysis Framework. http://www.blackhat.com/html/bh-ad-11/bh-ad-11-briefings.html.

[2] Android antivirus companies. Technical report. http://www.zdnet.com/android-antivirus-comparison-review-malware-symantec-mcafee-kaspersky-sophos-norton-7000019189/.

[3] Android Dalvik Debug Monitor Server. http://developer.android.com/sdk/installing/studio-tips.html.

[4] Android Monkeyrunner. http://developer.android.com/guide/developing/tools/monkeyrunner_concepts.html.

[5] Android OS Version Relative Chart ending on April 1, 2014 . http://developer.android.com/about/dashboards/index.html.

[6] AV TEST report, Jan 2014. http://www.av-test.org/en/tests/mobile-devices/android/jan-2014/.

[7] Avast! Mobile Security protects against USSD attacks. http://blog.avast.com/2012/10/04/avast-mobile-security-protects-against-ussd-attacks/ .

[8] DoS attack on Lookout mobile security application. http://web.nvd.nist.gov/view/vuln/detail?vulnId=CVE-2013-3579.

[9] Factory Images for Nexus Devices. https://developers.google.com/android/nexus/images.

[10] Frequently updates of Antivirus Detection Engine, 2013. http://www.androiddrawer.com/15401/download-lookout-security-antivirus-8-30-1-app-apk/ .

[11] HTC Android Images from HTCdev. http://www.htcdev.com/devcenter/downloads/P00.

[12] Jinshan mobile duba. http://m.duba.net/.

[13] Kaspersky Lab Reports Mobile Malware in 2013. http://usa.kaspersky.com/about-us/press-center/press-releases/kaspersky-lab-reports-mobile-malware-2013-more-doubles-previous .

[14] LBE secrity guard. http://www.lbesec.com/.

[15] Prevent Unintended APP Update. http://www.symantec.com/connect/blogs/case-unintended-android-application-upgrade.

[16] Samli/Baksmali. http://code.google.com/p/smali/.

[17] Samsung Images from Samsung-updates. http://samsung-updates.com/.

[18] Samsung Mobile Device Management solution. http://www.samsung.com/global/business/mobile/solution/security/mobile-device-management/.

[19] The avast! AVD v2.0.4400 for Android allows attackers to cause a denial of service . http://cve.scap.org.cn/CVE-2013-0122.html.

[20] The Lookout AVD v8.17-8a39d3f for Android allows attackers to cause a denial of service . http://cve.scap.org.cn/CVE-2013-3579.html.

[21] The TrustGo AVD v1.3.6 for Android allows attackers to cause a DoS. http://cve.scap.org.cn/CVE-2013-3580.html.

[22] Android Platform Fragmentation. http://opensignal.com/reports/fragmentation-2013/, 2012.

[23] Frequently updates of Antivirus Detection Engine. http://m.aptoide.com/list/versions/com.lookout/83510, 2013.

[24] M. I. Al-Saleh and J. R. Crandall. Application-level reconnaissance: Timing channel attacks against antivirus software. In *4th USENIX Workshop on LEET 11'*.

[25] H. Chen, D. Dean, and D. Wagner. Model Checking One Million Lines of C Code. In *NDSS*, 2004.

[26] K. Chen, P. Liu, and Y. Zhang. Achieving accuracy and scalability simultaneously in detecting application clones on android markets. In *ICSE*, pages 175–186, 2014.

[27] K. Z. Chen, N. M. Johnson, V. D'Silva, S. Dai, K. MacNamara, T. R. Magrino, E. X. Wu, M. Rinard, and D. X. Song. Contextual policy enforcement in android applications with permission event graphs. In *NDSS*, 2013.

[28] X. Chen, J. Andersen, Z. M. Mao, M. Bailey, and J. Nazario. Towards an understanding of anti-virtualization and anti-debugging behavior in modern malware. In *DSN' 08*.

[29] M. Christodorescu, S. Jha, S. A. Seshia, D. Song, and R. E. Bryant. Semantics-aware malware detection. In *S&P '05*.

[30] M. Egele, D. Brumley, Y. Fratantonio, and C. Kruegel. An empirical study of cryptographic misuse in android applications. In *CCS '13*.

[31] R. Fedler, M. Kulicke, and J. Schutte. An antivirus API for Android malware recognition. In *Malicious and Unwanted Software:" The Americas"(MALWARE), 2013*.

[32] C. Gibler, R. Stevens, J. Crussell, H. Chen, H. Zang, and H. Choi. Adrob: Examining the landscape and impact of android application plagiarism. In *MobiSys '13*.

[33] H. Huang, S. Zhang, X. Ou, A. Prakash, and K. Sakallah. Distilling critical attack graph surface iteratively through minimum-cost sat solving. In *Proceedings of the 27th ACSAC*, pages 31–40. ACM, 2011.

[34] H. Huang, S. Zhu, P. Liu, and D. Wu. A framework for evaluating mobile app repackaging detection algorithms. In *Trust and Trustworthy Computing*. Springer, 2013.

[35] S. Jana and V. Shmatikov. Abusing file processing in malware detectors for fun and profit. In *SP' 12*.

[36] S. Jana and V. Shmatikov. Memento: Learning secrets from process footprints. In *S&P '12*.

[37] X. Jin, X. Hu, K. Ying, W. Du, H. Yin, and G. N. Peri. Code injection attacks on HTML5-based mobile apps: Characterization, detection and mitigation. In *CCS '14*.

[38] M. G. Kang, H. Yin, S. Hanna, S. McCamant, and D. Song. Emulating emulation-resistant malware. In *Proceedings of the 1st ACM Workshop on Virtual Machine Security*, 2009.

[39] A. Nadkarni and W. Enck. Preventing accidental data disclosure in modern operating systems. In *CCS '13*.

[40] J. Oberheide, M. Bailey, and F. Jahanian. PolyPack: an automated online packing service for optimal antivirus evasion. In *3rd USENIX on Offensive technologies*.

[41] J. Oberheide and F. Jahanian. Remote fingerprinting and exploitation of mail server antivirus engines, 2009.

[42] G. Pék, B. Bencsáth, and L. Buttyán. nEther: In-guest Detection of Out-of-the-guest Malware Analyzers. In *Proceedings of the Fourth European Workshop on System Security*, EUROSEC '11.

[43] S. Poeplau, Y. Fratantonio, A. Bianchi, C. Kruegel, and G. Vigna. Execute this! analyzing unsafe and malicious dynamic code loading in android applications. In *NDSS '14*.

[44] V. Rastogi, Y. Chen, and X. Jiang. Droidchameleon: evaluating android anti-malware against transformation attacks. In *asiaCCS*. ACM, 2013.

[45] S. Smalley and R. Craig. Security enhanced (se) android: Bringing flexible mac to android. In *NDSS*, 2013.

[46] L. Xing, X. Pan, R. Wang, K. Yuan, and X. Wang. Upgrading your android, elevating my malware: Privilege escalation through mobile os updating. In *IEEE Symposium on S&P 14*.

[47] L. K. Yan and H. Yin. Droidscope: seamlessly reconstructing the os and dalvik semantic views for dynamic android malware analysis. In *USENIX Sec '12*.

[48] F. Zhang, H. Huang, S. Zhu, D. Wu, and P. Liu. ViewDroid: Towards obfuscation-resilient mobile application repackaging detection. In *Proceedings of ACM WiSec '14*.

[49] W. Zhou, Y. Zhou, X. Jiang, and P. Ning. Detecting repackaged smartphone applications in third-party android marketplaces. In *Proceedings of CODASPY '12*. ACM.

[50] X. Zhou, S. Demetriou, D. He, M. Naveed, X. Pan, X. Wang, C. A. Gunter, and K. Nahrstedt. Identity, location, disease and more: inferring your secrets from android public resources. In *In ACM CCS*. ACM, 2013.

[51] X. Zhou, Y. Lee, N. Zhang, M. Naveed, and X. Wang. The peril of fragmentation: Security hazards in android device driver customizations. In *IEEE Symposium on S&P*, 2014.

[52] Y. Zhou and X. Jiang. An analysis of the anserverbot trojan. http://www.csc.ncsu.edu/faculty/jiang/pubs/AnserverBotAnalysis.pdf.

[53] Y. Zhou and X. Jiang. Dissecting android malware: Characterization and evolution. In *SP '12*. IEEE.

Hybrid User-level Sandboxing of Third-party Android Apps

Yajin Zhou†*, Kunal Patel†, Lei Wu†, Zhi Wang‡, and Xuxian Jiang†⋆
†North Carolina State University ‡Florida State University ⋆Qihoo 360
{yajin_zhou,kmpatel4, lwu4}@ncsu.edu, zwang@cs.fsu.edu, xjiang4@ncsu.edu

ABSTRACT

Users of Android phones increasingly entrust personal information to third-party apps. However, recent studies reveal that many apps, even benign ones, could leak sensitive information without user awareness or consent. Previous solutions either require to modify the Android framework thus significantly impairing their practical deployment, or could be easily defeated by malicious apps using a native library.

In this paper, we propose AppCage, a system that thoroughly confines the run-time behavior of third-party Android apps without requiring framework modifications or root privilege. AppCage leverages two complimentary user-level sandboxes to interpose and regulate an app's access to sensitive APIs. Specifically, *dex sandbox* hooks into the app's Dalvik virtual machine instance and redirects each sensitive framework API to a proxy which strictly enforces the user-defined policies, and *native sandbox* leverages software fault isolation to prevent the app's native libraries from directly accessing the protected APIs or subverting the dex sandbox. We have implemented a prototype of AppCage. Our evaluation shows that AppCage can successfully detect and block attempts to leak private information by third-party apps, and the performance overhead caused by AppCage is negligible for apps without native libraries and minor for apps with them.

Categories and Subject Descriptors

D.4.6 [**Security and Protection**]: Access control, Information flow controls

Keywords

Android; Software Fault Isolation; Dalvik Hooking

1. INTRODUCTION

Android has become the leading mobile platform with nearly 85% market share in the second quarter of 2014 [10]. This trend is accompanied by the vigorous increase of third-party Android apps that are available for users to download and install. However, recent studies reveal that third-party apps, including popular ones, could leak private information without user consent or awareness [12,19]. In light of these serious threats, there is a pressing need to strictly confine these apps, especially their access to sensitive data and dangerous operations. However, Android's existing permission system lacks flexibility for this purpose. An user has to grant *all* the permissions requested by an app in order to install it, and cannot make any adjustment to those permissions after installation.

To address this limitation, researchers have proposed a number of systems to enable fine-grained control of Android apps. They roughly fall into two categories: the first category consists of solutions that extend the Android framework (and even the kernel) to allow fine-tuning of the apps' permissions [5,14–16,27,33,37,45,55]. For example, AppFence [27] and TISSA [55] can be configured to return a mock location, instead of the real one, to the apps. Framework enhancement appears to be a natural solution. However, the requirement to update key Android components could strongly impair their practical deployment due to the deep fragmentation of the Android platform [46]. The second category includes the "in-app" mechanisms that control the app's access to sensitive APIs through (Dalvik) bytecode rewriting [13, 17, 18, 28] or native code interposing [47]. These systems do not require changes to the Android framework and thus can be readily deployed. Specifically, bytecode rewriting-based approaches insert inline reference monitors to regulate apps' behaviors. However, dynamically loaded classes (e.g., classes loaded by `DexClassLoader`) could pose serious challenges to these systems since the dynamically loaded bytecode is not available when statically rewriting the app. On the other hand, Aurasium [47] interposes the inter-process communication [2] between the app and remote Android services. Therefore, it can accommodate dynamic classes, but has to bridge the "semantic gap" by reconstructing high-level semantics from the exchanged raw messages, overall a tedious and error-prone task. More importantly, all those systems can be bypassed or subverted by a malicious app using a native library. For example, the app can leverage native code to tamper with the instrumented bytecode [1] or bypass security checks by "restoring the global offset table entries" [47].

In this paper, we present AppCage, a secure in-app mechanism to regulate the app's access to sensitive APIs and dangerous operations (e.g., making phone calls). Like other in-app mechanisms, AppCage does not need to change the Android framework; nor requires the root privilege, and thus can be readily deployed. Specifically, AppCage synthesizes a wrapper app for each target app (i.e., a third-party app to be confined). The wrapper sets up the dex sandbox for the app by hooking into its instance of Dalvik virtual machine and redirecting sensitive framework APIs to their respective

*Part of the work was done when the first author was an intern at Qihoo 360.

ASIA CCS'15, April 14–17, 2015, Singapore.

ACM 978-1-4503-3245-3/15/04 ...$15.00.
http://dx.doi.org/10.1145/2714576.2714598.

stubs. The stubs interpose the access to those APIs and enforce the user-defined policies. With API hooking, AppCage naturally supports dynamically loaded classes because the app eventually needs to call those APIs to retrieve sensitive data. However, API hooking alone could be subverted by the app using native code. To address this challenge, AppCage relies on a second sandbox, native sandbox, to confine the app's native code. The native sandbox leverages software fault isolation (SFI) [42] to ensure that the app's native libraries (including the system libraries they depend on) cannot escape from the sandbox or directly modify the code or data outside the sandbox. The app thus cannot tamper with the dex sandbox using native code. In addition, native sandbox prevents the app's native code from directly requesting sensitive data or performing dangerous operations via binder, the Android's ubiquitous interprocess communication mechanism. Combining those two sandboxes, AppCage can comprehensively interpose the app's access to key Android APIs and enforce user-defined policies to fine-tune the app's permissions.

We have implemented a prototype of AppCage and evaluated its effectiveness, compatibility, and performance. Our experiments show that AppCage can successfully detect and block attempts to leak the user's private data by both malicious and benign-but-invasive Android apps, and the security analysis demonstrates that native sandbox can protect our system from being bypassed or subverted. Moreover, the prototype is shown to be compatible with the popular Android apps we downloaded from the Google Play store, and it incurs negligible overhead for apps without native code and a mild 10.7% overhead for ones with native code. Given the protection offered by AppCage, we consider the performance of AppCage is acceptable for most daily uses.

In summary, this paper makes the following contributions:

- We propose hybrid user-level sandboxes to confine two components of an Android app – the bytecode and the native code. Particularly, dex sandbox relies on API hooking to reliably interpose the bytecode's access to key framework APIs, while native sandbox applies the proven technology of software fault isolation to confine the native code.
- Our native sandbox leverages both dynamic binary rewriting and static compiler-based binary instrumentation to reduce performance overhead. They enforce the same set of rules and can be seamlessly integrated.
- We have implemented and evaluated a prototype of AppCage. The experiment results show that AppCage is effective and compatible with popular apps, and it incurs acceptable overhead for daily use.

2. BACKGROUND AND THREAT MODEL

In this section, we briefly introduce some key concepts in Android to provide necessary background information of the proposed system, and then present the threat model.

2.1 Dalvik Virtual Machine

Most Android apps are written in the Java programming language and compiled into the bytecode for Dalvik VM. Dalvik VM is a shared library loaded into each running app and is responsible for executing the app's bytecode. To support later-binding of Java, Dalvik VM maintains a data structure for each Java class in the app (`ClassObject`) and one for each of its methods (`Method`). The `Method` structure in turn contains a pointer to the method's bytecode. Figure 1 shows a simple class and its representation in Dalvik VM. When `Sample.M` is called, the VM searches for `ClassObject`

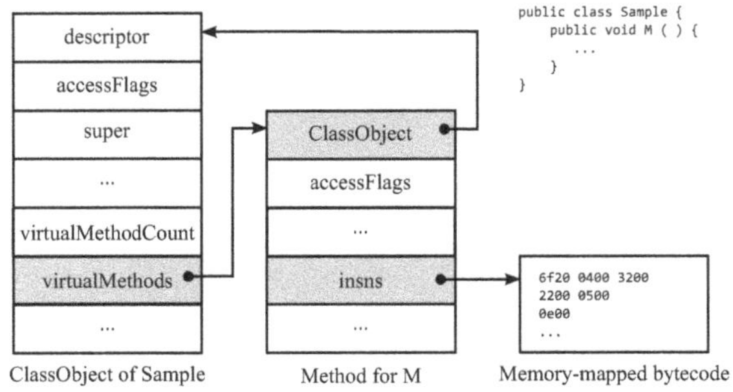

Figure 1: `ClassObject` and `Method` in Dalvik

of the class and further `Method` of the target method [11]. It then retrieves the bytecode of the method to decode and execute it.

Dalvik VM allows an app to dynamically load extra classes using `DexClassLoader`. The app can leverage this convenient capability to change its behavior at run-time. Dynamic class loading poses serious challenges to systems based on the bytecode rewriting because those classes are not available when the app is statically rewritten [17, 18, 28]. AppCage can naturally support this feature because it is based on the API hooking.

2.2 Java Native Interface

Java Native Interface (JNI) defines a framework for bytecode and native code to call each other. Android developers can use NDK to implement part of their apps in native languages such as C/C++. NDK compiles the source files into shared native libraries that can be dynamically loaded into the app by Dalvik VM under the request of the app's bytecode. Specifically, the VM uses the `dlopen` function to load the library into the app, and resolves the address of each imported library function using `dlsym`. These addresses are cached by the VM to avoid duplicated address resolution later. When a native function is invoked by the bytecode, it passes a special data structure of type `JNIEnv`, which allows the native code to interact with the bytecode [6, 39]. For example, the native function can use `JNIEnv->FindClass("Sample")` to locate the Java class `Sample` and subsequently call its functions. AppCage needs to interpose those key JNI related functions to (1) intercept the loading of native libraries and prepare the native sandbox for them, (2) and switch the run-time environment when entering and leaving the native sandbox.

2.3 Dynamic Loading and Linking

Android implements its own dynamic loader and linker for native libraries (`/system/bin/linker`). Unlike its counterpart in the desktop, Android's loader resolves all the external functions eagerly. For example, if the app's native code depends on the `__android_log_print` function in `liblog.so`, the loader will promptly load the library and recursively resolve the function address. Even though Android does not support lazy address resolution, the PLT/GOT [9] structure is still used for dynamic linking. More specifically, the compiler generates a stub in the PLT section for each external function. All calls to that function in the library are redirect to the stub, which simply contains an indirect branch to the address in the associated GOT entry. When a native library is loaded, the loader resolves the address of the external function and fills it in the GOT entry.

2.4 Threat Model

Similar to existing solutions [27, 55], we assume an adversary model where third-party apps are not trustworthy (e.g., they could leak personal information) but some of their features are desired by the user. Nevertheless, this privacy-aware user wishes to regulate

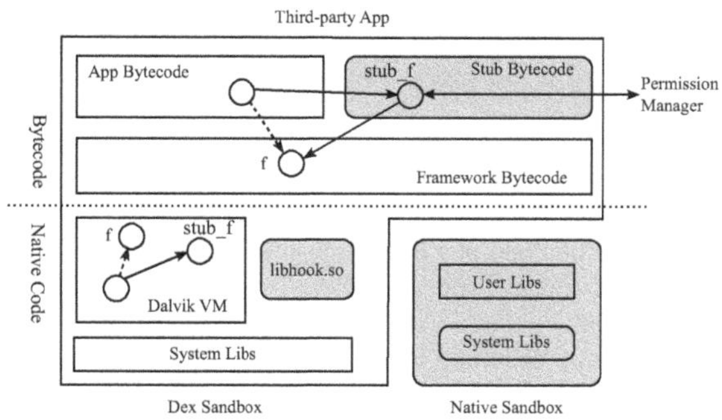

Figure 2: System architecture of AppCage

the apps' access to the private data and dangerous operations. Our system leverages a utility app that runs on the user's phone to instrument the target app, and this utility app is trusted. Moreover, we assume that the underlying Linux kernel and the Android middleware are trusted and attackers do *not* have the root privilege.

3. SYSTEM DESIGN

In this section, we describe the design of AppCage, particularly its hybrid user-level sandboxes: dex sandbox and native sandbox.

3.1 Overview

The goal of AppCage is to interpose key Android APIs to control the third-party app's access to private data and dangerous operations. Android apps consist of Dalvik bytecode and the optional native libraries. It is necessary to control both components of an app. AppCage provides dex sandbox and native sandbox for this purpose, respectively (Figure 2). To confine bytecode, AppCage hooks into Dalvik VM (`libhook.so`), and then manipulates its internal data structures to redirect each important Android API to its stub provided by AppCage. At run-time, the stub queries the permission manager whether the operation should be allowed, denied, or prompted to the user for confirmation. If the operation is allowed, the stub will then call the actual API on behalf of the original caller. Figure 2 shows how the framework method `f` is interposed by `stub_f`. Native sandbox applies software fault isolation to confine the app's native code. It prevents the app from using native code to subvert dex sandbox or directly request system services through binder, Android's lightweight remote procedure call mechanism [2]. Note that user libraries may depend on some system libraries such as `libc.so` or `libm.so`. AppCage provides a set of confined system libraries to the native sandbox. (Dalvik VM is still linked to the original system libraries.) With both sandboxes, AppCage has complete control over the app's access to sensitive APIs.

Use case: Figure 2 illustrates the run-time state of a confined app. In the following, we describe the use case of AppCage and how the sandboxes are initialized. AppCage provides a utility app that runs on the user's phone. For each third-party app to be installed, it generates a wrapper app that carries the whole original app, the bytecode of the stubs, and `libhook.so` (Figure 2). If the app has the native code, it also contains an instrumented copy of the native code. The wrapper requests the same permissions as the original app, and its entry point is assigned to a function in AppCage that is tasked to set up the sandboxes before executing the app [47]. The utility app also monitors the installation of new apps from the official and alternative app stores. For the former, it monitors the directory where the apps normally reside (`/data/app`) and prompts the user to uninstall the original app and replace it with the generated app. The process is mostly automated and the user only needs to click a few buttons when prompted. We cannot intercept the apps from the official app store because that requires the system privilege. For the latter, it can intercept the installation of the app by listening to the `INSTALL_PACKAGE` intent, and generate and install the wrapper app on-the-fly. The original app is not installed.

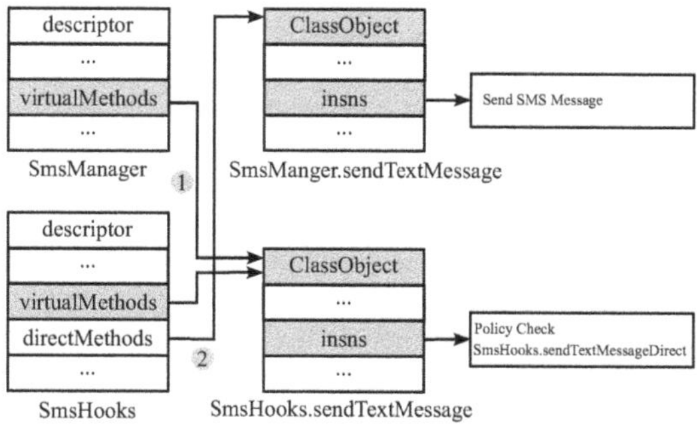

Figure 3: Dalvik hooking of `SmsManager.sendTextMessage`

3.2 Dex Sandbox

AppCage interposes the app's access to key framework APIs by essentially hooking those APIs. In contrast to previous systems that rewrite the app's bytecode for the same purpose [17, 18, 28], AppCage does not require extra efforts to support dynamically loaded classes and can tolerate obfuscation of the app's bytecode because the app eventually needs to call those interposed APIs to be effective.

AppCage's API hooking is implemented through direct manipulation of Dalvik VM's internal data structures. (We will discuss the compatibility issue raised in Section 5.3.) As mentioned in Section 2.1, Dalvik VM maintains a `ClassObject` data structure for each Java class in the app including those of the framework, through which we can find all the methods of the class. For each framework class that has sensitive methods, we manually create a stub class that contains the same set of stub methods [1]. The stub methods query the permission manager whether the operation should be allowed, and call the original methods if so.

Figure 3 shows an example of the `SmsManager` class, which allows an app to send text messages in the background via the predefined `sendTextMessage` method, possibly to premium numbers. To interpose this method, AppCage loads `SmsHooks`, the stub class for `SmsManager`, into the app, and manipulates the pointers in their corresponding `ClassObjects` so that `SmsManager.sendTextMessage` points to `SmsHooks.sendTextMessage` and the pointer to the original method `SmsManager.sendTextMessage` is stored in `SmsHooks`'s array of direct methods (arrow 1 and 2 in Figure 3, respectively). As such, the app will be redirected to `SmsHooks.sendTextMessage` when it tries to send a text message and subject to policy check. If the operation is allowed, `SmsHooks.sendTextMessage` calls the original method, which can be found in `SmsHooks`'s array of direct methods. Unlike virtual methods, direct methods are called directly without dynamic method resolution [11]. Hence, it is guaranteed that the original method will be called. By only manipulating method pointers, our system is compatible with the just-in-time compiling by Dalvik VM, a key technology to improve the system performa

3.3 Native Sandbox

Android allows its apps to use native code via the JNI interface (Section 2.2). Native code is often used to speed up performance-critical tasks such as rendering of 3D games. However, native code

[1] Most of this process can be automated. Doing it manually is acceptable since it is only a one-time effort.

could be exploited to subvert security schemes based on bytecode. For example, it can revert the changes to Dalvik VM's data structures made by AppCage. To address that, we adopt the software fault isolation (SFI) [42] technology to confine the app's native code. AppCage's native sandbox provides the following security guarantees: native code cannot write to memory out of the sandbox so that it cannot tamper with dex sandbox (memory read does not pose a threat to AppCage because sensitive data are maintained by Android's system service app); native code cannot escape from the sandbox; the access to dangerous instructions such as system call is regulated. Since source code of the app's native binary is not available, we use binary rewriting to implement software fault isolation.

Binary rewriting of the native code can take place at both installation time and run-time: AppCage instruments any native libraries discovered when generating the wrapper app (Section 3.1). It also hooks into the related JNI API to translate native libraries that are unknown during the installation, such as the encrypted libraries [3] or the downloaded ones. Our binary rewriter enforces the same set of rules as Native Client (NaCl) [38, 48]. Particularly, instructions are grouped into equal-sized bundles (16 bytes), and indirect branch instructions such as indirect call and return must target the boundary of a bundle. Moreover, the instructions inserted by AppCage (`bic` and `orr`) to confine an instruction must be put in the same bundle as that instruction so that they cannot be bypassed by indirect branches jumping over them. The rules of NaCl provide our native sandbox a solid theoretical and practical foundation in security. However, our binary rewriter needs to handle the app's native code in the binary format, while NaCl is a compiler plugin and thus requires the access to source code. Code generated by NaCl normally has less overhead than that by our binary rewriter. As such, AppCage also utilizes a modified NaCl compiler to confine system libraries that the app's native code rely on since their source code is readily available.

Even though ARM is a RISC architecture, rewriting ARM binaries is not straightforward: *1.)* an ARM binary can mix the ARM instructions (32 bits) and the THUMB-2 instructions (16 or 32 bits). *2.)* Constants are often embedded among instructions. We need to identify them and prevent them from being executed. *3.)* ARM instructions can directly refer the program counter (`pc`), often to read the embedded constants in code. Binary rewriting shifts the instructions around and may cause the wrong `pc` to be used. To address challenge 2 and 3, AppCage retains the original code section of the app's native code but makes it read-only and non-executable. The translated code section only contains instructions but not constants, which must be loaded from the original code section instead. AppCage also keeps a mapping between the original `pc` and the translated `pc` and converts them when necessary. To rewrite a binary, AppCage first disassembles it, breaks it into basic blocks, and instruments it as required by the native sandbox.

Disassembling Native Code: AppCage recursively disassembles the app's native code [50] using the exported functions as the initial starting points (the binary may be stripped and may not contain the complete symbol table.) Specifically, it keeps disassembling instructions from a starting point until a return instruction or other terminating instructions. Any targets of direct jumps or call instructions are added to a work list as the new starting points. After exhausting the work list, we start disassembling the leftover gaps with a trial-and-error strategy.

Our disassembler faces two challenges. First, constants are often embedded in-between instructions because they do not fit in the instruction (32 bits at most). To address that, we observe that constants are often collected at the end of functions and referred to with the `pc`-relative addressing mode, for example,

```
ldr r1, [pc, #284]
```

We accordingly treat the targets of `pc`-relative load instructions as constants. However, the heuristic may treat the real code as constants. This is handled at run-time by rewriting those missed instructions on demand. The second challenge is that a binary can consist of functions in the ARM and THUMB/THUMB-2 states. These states have different instruction length and encoding. AppCage needs to identify the instruction state to correctly disassemble them. This is solved as follows: first, branch instructions such as `B`, `BL` with an immediate offset, `BX`, and `BLX` specify the state of the target instruction in the encoding. AppCage decodes the targets accordingly using the target instruction encoding. Second, we use the context of a gap to infer its state. For example, if the instructions before and after a gap are in the THUMB state, the gap likely is also in that state. Third, if the previous heuristics fail to decide the instruction state, we assume the instructions are in the ARM state and start to disassemble them. We will restart the process in the THUMB state if errors are encountered, for example, if there are invalid instructions or the data flow in a peephole is inconsistent [44].

Note that the instruction mode which is determined by the heuristic, e.g., the branch target of an indirect branch instruction, may be wrong during statically disassembling. AppCage records the instruction mode for such instructions and compare it with the actual instruction mode at run-time. If there is a mismatch, then these instructions will be re-disassembled and instrumented at run-time.

Native Code Instrumentation: To rewrite the app's native code, AppCage breaks the disassembled instructions into basic blocks and then instruments each of them according to the instruction types. Figure 4 shows a concrete example for each such case.

a.) Memory write instructions: AppCage requires that memory write instructions can only target addresses within the sandbox. To this end, we position the native sandbox at an address that is 2^n-byte aligned with a length of 2^n. Consequently, we can confine memory writes by fixing the top $32-n$ bits of the target address to that of the sandbox. For example, if the sandbox is located at the range of `[0x40,000,000, 0x5F,FFF,FFF]`, we can use the following two instructions to confine memory writes (assuming `r0` is the base register):

```
bic r0, r0, #0xa0000000  /* clear bits 31,29 */
orr r0, r0, #0x40000000  /* set bits 30 */
```

Moreover, we put two guard pages around the sandbox, one at each end, to accommodate addressing modes with an immediate offset, which is always less than 4,096 in the ARM architecture (see case 1 in Figure 4 for an example). If the target address is calculated from several registers, we first save the address to a scratch register (spill one if necessary) and apply the same instructions as above to confine it. The memory write instruction is then patched to use the scratch register as the target (case 2 in Figure 4).

AppCage normally instruments every memory write instruction. One exception is those instructions with `sp` as the base register and an immediate offset. They are frequently used to update local variables. To reduce overhead, we do not instrument this type of instruction (case 3 in Figure 4), but instead instrument all instructions that update the `sp` register to guarantee that `sp` is within the sandbox (case 4 in Figure 4.)

b.) Branch instructions: the second category of instructions to rewrite consists of branch instructions, used for jumps and calls. Branch instructions can address the target with an immediate offset (direct branch) or with registers (indirect branch). Both types

(1) memory write: immediate offset

```
before:
 e2b8: e5840008  str r0, [r4, #8]

after:
 f8b0: e3c4420e  bic r4, r4, #0xe0000000
 f8b4: e5840008  str r0, [r4, #8]
```

Before writing data into memory,we mask off some bits of the target address. Since the immediate offset is within the 4K range, we can confine it by adding a guard page before and after the native sandbox.

(2) memory write: register offset

```
before:
 f054: e784e10c  str lr, [r4, ip, lsl#2]

after:
 1004: e084310c  add r3, r4, ip, lsl#2
 1008: e3c3320e  bic r3, r3, #0xe0000000
 100c: e583e000  str lr, [r3]
```

For instructions using the register offset,we allocate a scratch register (r3 in this case) first to store the target address of memory write, and then we mask off the related address bits. The original instruction is replaced by one using the scratch register.

(3) memory write: SP as the base register with immediate offset

```
before:
 114a0: e58d11d0  str r1, [sp, #464]

after:
 12f5c: e58d11d0  str r1, [sp, #464]
```

For instructions using the SP register as the base with immediate offset, we do not instrument them but instead ensure that SP is always within the sandbox by rewriting the instructions that update SP.

(4) computation : update SP

```
before:
 1c284: e084d005  add sp, r4, r5

after:
 10200: e084d005  add sp, r4, r5
 10204: e3cdd20e  bic sp, sp, #0xe0000000
```

We instrument instructions that update SP to make sure SP is always within the native sandbox.

(5) direct branch

```
before:
 dca4: 1affffbf  bne 0xdba8

after:
 f068: 1affffb3  bne 0xef3c
```

We need to patch the target of the direct branch instructions to its corresponding translated target.

(6) indirect branch: branch address on the stack

```
before:
 164f8: e8bd8002  pop {r1, pc}

after:
 18e10: e8bd0002  pop {r1}
 18e14: e59ff718  ldr pc, [pc, #1816] ;0x19534
 ...
 19534: 0001aae4
```

The registers other than PC will be popped first, and then it jumps to the indirect branch trampoline at offset 0x1aae4 (this address is patched by AppCage according to whether the PC is on the stack or in the reigster.) The trampoline fecthes the branch address from the stack and check whether it is valid. If so, it will jump to the address for execution.

(7) indirect branch: branch address in a register

```
before:
 164bc: e12fff1e  bx lr

after:
 18dcc: e59ff75c  ldr pc, [pc, #1884] ;0x19530
 ...
 19530: 0001aa88
```

Similar to case 6, it jumps to the indirect branch trampoline. This trampoline validates the branch target in the register and jumps to it for execution, if valid.

(8) using PC as the source register in non-branch instructions

```
before:
 14e80: e08f1001  add r1, pc, r1

after:
 1748c: e52d3004  push {r3}
 17490: e59f331c  ldr r3, [pc, #796] ;0x177b4
 17494: e0831001  add r1, r3, r1
 17498: e49d3004  pop {r3}
 ...
 177b4: 00014e88
```

We allocate a scratch register (r3 in this case), spill it when necessary, and load the original PC stored at address 0x177b4 into it. The original instruction is transformed to use this scratch register.

Figure 4: Instrumentation of native code by AppCage
(for simplicity, we assume the native sandbox is at the [0x0, 0x1FFFFFFF] address space range.)

of branch instructions need to be instrumented to ensure that the app's native code cannot escape from the sandbox. Direct branches can be handled completely during binary rewriting because their targets are known statically. We only need to verify that they target legitimate instructions in the sandbox and patch the immediate offsets accordingly (case 5 in Figure 4). Indirect branches require validation of the branch targets at run-time because they are unknown during translation. The address of the target may be on the stack (case 6 in Figure 4) or in a register (case 7 in Figure 4). AppCage uses a trampoline to handle the indirect branch instruction. The original instruction is replaced with a direct branch to its associated trampoline. The trampoline retrieves the original branch address and verifies that it lies within the sandbox. If so, the trampoline further converts the address to the translated target, with the help of the mapping between the original `pc` and the translated `pc`, and branches to it.

c.) Instructions using `pc` *as a general register:* in ARM, `pc` (program counter) can be directly accessed as a general register. Instructions using `pc` as the destination operand are in fact indirect branch instructions. This case has been discussed in b). If `pc` is used as the source operand, its value is decided by the address of the currently executing instruction, and thus is different from the original and intended value. For example, the following instruction at address `0x14e80` is relocated to `0x1748c` by the binary rewriter. When the app runs, the `pc` register has a value of `0x17494`, instead of the expected value of `0x14e88` (for historic reasons, `pc` in ARM is the address of the current instruction plus 8.)

```
14e80: add r1, pc, r1    -->    1748c: add r1, pc, r1
   PC: 0x14e88                     PC: 0x17494
```

To address this, we allocate a scratch register, load the original `pc` into it, and patch the instruction to use the scratch register instead of the current `pc` (case 8 in Figure 4).

d.) System call instruction: uncontrolled system calls can be exploited to subvert our system, for example, by tampering with the memory protection or calling system services through binder. As such, AppCage disallows direct system calls in the app's native libraries. The app instead has to access the kernel services through the APIs of the system libraries (e.g., `libc`). This is barely restrictive because very few apps, if any, rely on direct system calls. To prevent those libraries from being misused, AppCage provides a confined copy of the necessary system libraries to the native sandbox. During rewriting, *direct* system call instructions in the app's native code are replaced by branches to a function that terminates the current app.

System Libraries Instrumentation: the app's native code often relies on system libraries for service (e.g., `libc.so`). For performance reasons, AppCage uses the NaCl compiler for ARM [38] to sandbox the system libraries. Those libraries are loaded into the native sandbox by a custom loader and linked with the app's native code (Dalvik VM uses an unconfined version of the system libraries). Those libraries are subjected to the same constraints as the app's native code: memory writes and branch instructions must target locations within the native sandbox. However, NaCl compiler assumes that the lower 1GB memory is reserved for the sandbox. This cannot be guaranteed by AppCage because the location of native sandbox is unknown until it is initialized at run-time. Hence, we need to customize the NaCl compiler for our purpose.

NaCl uses the `bic` instruction to clear the most significant two bits of a branch target to ensure it is within the first 1GB of the address space. The last four bits of the target are also cleared to prevent the instrumented code from branching to the middle of an instruction bundle (16 bytes):

```
bic r0, r0, 0xc000000f   /*clear top 2 and the last 4 bits*/
```

For memory store instructions, NaCl uses the `tst` and `streq` instructions to conditionally execute the memory write if the address is inside the sandbox.

```
tst r0, #0xc0000000      /* within the first 1GB? */
streq r1, [r0, #12]      /* store to memory if so*/
```

Because native sandbox is not guaranteed to start at address 0, we modify the NaCl compiler to emit `bic` and `orr` instructions to confine sensitive instructions, similar to the binary rewriter. However, we have to keep the immediate values of those instructions undefined during translation because the location of native sandbox is unknown until it's initialized at run-time. AppCage's custom loader patches those instructions with the actual location of the sandbox.

JNI Interface: the app's bytecode and native code can call each other through the JNI interface. However, Dalvik VM and native sandbox have different contexts under AppCage such as stack, heap, and the code section. AppCage needs to intercept the JNI calls and switches the context accordingly. This has to be performed in both directions, from bytecode to native code and vice versa.

Bytecode can load and resolve native functions via Android's dynamic linker (`/system/bin/linker`) and call it through the JNI interface. To intercept those calls, we hook the `dlopen` and `dlsym` functions in Dalvik VM. The `dlopen` hook allows us to rewrite native libraries unseen during the installation (e.g., a newly downloaded library). Moreover, when `dlsym` is called to resolve a native function, we return its associated gate function in place of the target function. The gate prepares the execution context for the sandbox by copying over the parameters and switching the stack and registers. It then enters the sandbox to execute the target function. When the function returns, the gate switches the context back to Dalvik VM. Meanwhile, native code can also call exported bytecode functions through the `JNIEnv` structure. To intercept those calls, we replace the functions in `JNIEnv` with their stubs in the sandbox. The stub switches the execution environment to that of Dalvik VM and then calls the actual `JNIEnv` functions [39]. The direct reference to Java heap is processed through the copy-in and copy-out mechanism [39].

Table 1: Confined operations by the current prototype

Operation	Permissions
Send SMS	SEND_SMS
Read SMS	READ_SMS
Delete SMS	WRITE_SMS
Phone call	CALL_PHONE
Read contacts	READ_CONTACTS
Write contacts	WRITE_CONTACTS
Read call logs	READ_CALL_LOG
Get location	ACCESS_FINE_LOCATION ACCESS_COARSE_LOCATION
Network	INTERNET
Read IMEI	READ_PHONE_STATE

4. IMPLEMENTATION

We have implemented a prototype of AppCage. In particular, dex sandbox is implemented in the Java and C++ programming language, while native sandbox is implemented in C and the ARM assembly. In this section, we discuss the concrete implementation of this prototype.

4.1 Dex Sandbox

AppCage generates a wrapper app for a third-party app. The wrapper app consists of the original app and the additional components for the sandboxes. AppCage features both a dex sandbox for the bytecode and a native sandbox for native code. Dex sandbox hooks into the sensitive framework APIs to enforce the user-define policies. These policies are managed by a separate app (permission manager in Figure 2). Only permission manager can update the user policy database; other apps can read the database through an exported content provider interface. Table 1 lists the operations that our prototype can interpose. It is relatively easy to extend this list by adding more stubs. Permission manager can respond to a request with three verdicts: allow, deny, and prompt-to-user. It can be enhanced to return mock results (e.g., fake location) to improve its compatibility with third-party apps [27, 55].

Original App Loading: AppCage loads the embedded app into dex sandbox for execution. It leverages the `DexClassLoader` class for this purpose. However, this class loader is different from the class loader used by Dalvik VM to load the wrapper app and the stubs (`PathClassLoader`), and only classes loaded by the same class loader can refer to each other (this is also true for apps without AppCage). Therefore, classes in the original app cannot communicate with the stubs. To address this, we change the value of `pathList` of `PathClassLoader` to that of `DexClassLoader`. After that, the classes of the original app will behave like that they are loaded by the same loader as the stubs.

4.2 Native Sandbox

Native sandbox confines the app's native code into a continuous block of memory space. Figure 5 shows the layout of the app's address space at run-time. The memory for native sandbox is `256MB` aligned so that we can use the simple `bic` and `orr` instructions to control memory access. AppCage has a custom loader for the native code. It intercepts the app's requests to load the native code to sandbox it. Specifically, the loader will load both the original code section and the translated code section. The former is marked

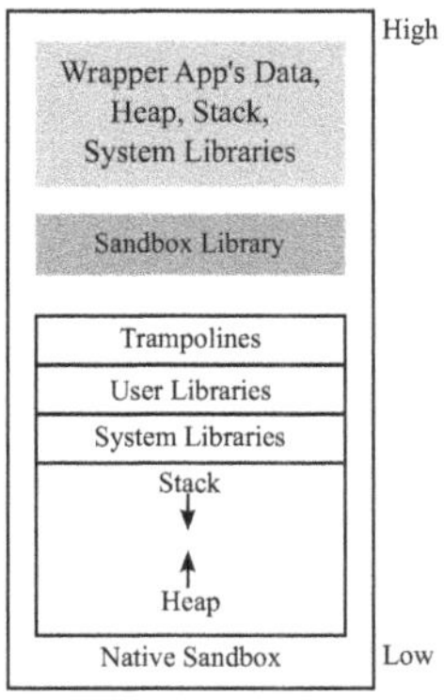

Figure 5: Memory layout of the native sandbox

as read-only and *non-executable*. We keep this section so that pc-relative instructions can access the correct memory. The loader also needs to fix various addresses in the translated code, such as those of the indirect jump trampolines.

Link to System Libraries: the app's native code is linked to NaCl-compiled system libraries. NaCl requires that branch targets aligned at the boundary of a bundle (16 bytes). This alignment ensures that the sandboxed code cannot jump into the middle of a bundle and bypass security checks. As such, we need to align return addresses of the native code at the boundary of a bundle. For example, the instruction at offset $0x4ae8$ calls `__android_log_print@plt`, which eventually jumps to the `__android_log_print` function in the system library. When this function in the system library returns, the last 4 bits of the `lr` register are masked out by NaCl [38]. When translating this instruction, we need to add padding instructions (`nop`) to ensure that the return address is 16 bytes aligned (`0x22b0` in the example).

```
4ae8:   ebfff8de    bl  2e68 <__android_log_print@plt>
-->
22a4:   e320f000    nop {0}
22a8:   e320f000    nop {0}
22ac:   ebfff772    bl  0x7c <__android_log_print@plt>
        /*lr = 0x22b0 */
```

Changes of System Libraries: AppCage provides the NaCl-compiled system libraries to the native sandbox. It makes the following additional changes for them to safely run in the sandbox:

First, the heap management functions in `libc` such as `malloc` are changed to allocate memory from the heap of the native sandbox, instead of the default heap. *Second*, we add security checks in some library functions. For example, the app should not be able to use `mprotect` to make the code section writable. Another example is the `ioctl` function in `libc`, which may be misused to send commands to the key Android services through the binder interface (`/dev/binder`), bypassing AppCage's policy check. *Third*, we relocate the thread local storage (TLS) to the native sandbox. Particularly, we allocate a special region inside the sandbox for TLS and change the `__get_tls` function accordingly. *Last*, callback functions may pose a problem for AppCage. For example, the app can register a callback function to the `qsort` function in `libc`. When `qsort` calls this function, a segmentation fault will be raised because the function is a part of the original code section, which is non-executable (Section 3.3). To address this, we register a signal handler to capture segmentation faults caused by those functions. In the signal handler, we lookup the translated callback function and dispatch to it.

Indirect Branch Trampolines: the indirect branch trampoline is fairly involved. It first saves the scratch registers and the status register, and retrieves the branch target from the stack or the register. The branch target (in the original code section) is then converted

```
   1a544: e24dd004 sub   sp, sp, #4 ; 0x4
   1a548: e92d400f push  {r0, r1, r2, r3, lr}
┌─ 1a54c: ea000000 b     0x1a554
│  1a550: e1200070 bkpt  0x0000
└→ 1a554: e10f2000 mrs   r2, CPSR //move status to r2
   1a558: e92d0004 push  {r2} //save status register on stack
┌─ 1a55c: ea000000 b     0x1a564
│  1a560: e1200070 bkpt  0x0000
└→ 1a564: e1a03000 mov   r3, r0 //move jump target (r0) to r3
   1a568: e59f25a8 ldr   r2, [pc, #1448] ; 0x1ab18
┌─ 1a56c: ea000000 b     0x1a574
│  1a570: e1200070 bkpt  0x0000
└→ 1a574: e12fff32 blx   r2 // retrieve the pc
   1a578: e8bd0004 pop   {r2} //pop status register to r2
┌─ 1a57c: ea000000 b     0x1a584
│  1a580: e1200070 bkpt  0x0000
└→ 1a584: e129f002 msr   CPSR_fc, r2 //restore status register
   1a588: e58d0014 str   r0, [sp, #20] //put new PC on stack
┌─ 1a58c: ea000000 b     0x1a594
│  1a590: e1200070 bkpt  0x0000
└→ 1a594: e8bd400f pop   {r0, r1, r2, r3, lr}
   1a598: e49df004 pop   {pc} //jump to new PC
   ..
   /* patch it to the function to get pc from stack or register*/
   1ab18: 00000000
```

Figure 6: An example of indirect branch trampoline

to the translated pc. At last, the trampoline restores the registers and branches to the target pc. Figure 6 shows a concrete example of the indirect branch trampoline. The trampoline has a non-trivial design because we cannot simply spill the scratch registers to the stack. For example, if the indirect branch instruction calls a function, some parameters may be saved on the stack. Changing the stack passes wrong values to those parameters. If the indirect branch instruction returns from a function, it could return to a wrong location, even out of the sandbox. The trampoline in Figure 6 guarantees the stack is not changed before branching.

Since the indirect branch trampoline is in the native sandbox, we need to prevent it from being misused by the native code. Binary rewriting guarantees that the app's native code cannot jump to the middle of a trampoline. This is because branches in the translated code can only target addresses in the mapping table of the original and translated `pcs`, and only the beginning of the trampoline is in this table. However, the native code may achieve the same goal by leveraging the indirect branches in the system libraries since they can target any bundles. To this end, we put the `bkpt` instruction at the code boundaries of the trampoline, and use `b` instruction to skip `bkpt` inside the trampoline [48]. Any attempts to jump into the trampoline from the NaCl-compiled system libraries will be captured because they can only target those boundaries (the `bkpt` instructions in the trampoline), a security rule enforced by the NaCl compiler.

4.3 Native Sandbox Optimizations

To reduce performance overhead, we apply several optimization techniques to the native sandbox.

Redundant Check Removal: when translating memory write instructions, we can analyze the register usage in an instruction bundle and remove redundant safety checks. For example, we only need to apply the confinement instructions to the first memory write instruction in the following case:

```
3324: str r3, [r4, #8]
3328: str r3, [r4, #20]
-->
/* native sandbox: [0x40000000, 0x5FFFFFFF] */
4400: bic r4, r4, #0xa0000000
4404: orr r4, r4, #0x40000000
4408: str r3, [r4, #8]
440c: str r3, [r4, #20]
```

Calls of System Library Functions: compilers use the PLT/GOT structure to support dynamic linking. Specifically, calls to an exter-

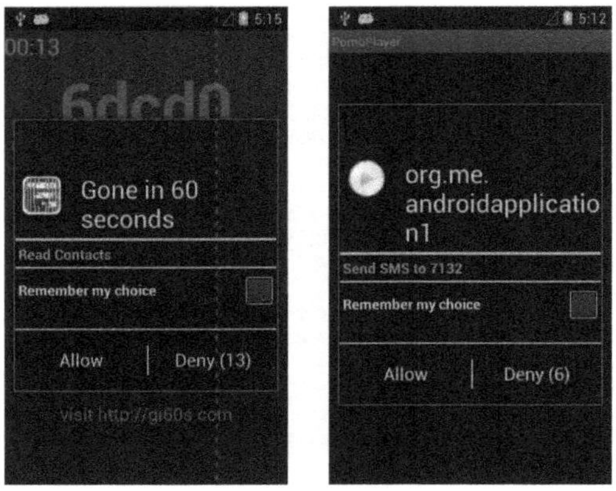

(a) Gone60 malware: reading contacts (b) FakePlayer: sending SMS to a premium number

Figure 7: AppCage detects malicious behaviors

nal function are patched to the function's stub in the PLT section, which indirectly branches to the function address in the associated GOT entry. The GOT entry is normally filled in by the dynamic linker after it resolves the address of the external function. In AppCage, the GOT entries are patched by our own custom loader and are guaranteed to be in the sandbox. Therefore, we do not need to rewrite the indirect branch instructions inside the PLT section (the GOT section is set to read-only after initialization.)

Function Return Optimization: ARM binaries often use the `pop` instruction to return from a function. Our binary rewriter treats the `pop` instruction using `pc` as the target operand as an indirect branch, which has a relatively heavy instrumentation (Section 4.2). Considering function return is highly frequent, we need to avoid the time-consuming indirect branch trampoline. To this end, we fetch the branch target into the `lr` register and add instructions to confine the value of `lr` before jumping to it. In particular, we mask off the last four bits of the return address to align it with the NaCl instruction bundle. The following instructions illustrate this optimization:

```
pop {r3, r4, pc}
-->
pop {r3, r4]
pop {lr}
/* native sandbox: [0x40000000, 0x5FFFFFFF] */
bic lr, lr, #0xa000000f
orr lr, lr, #0x40000000
bx  lr
```

Address Cache in Indirect Branch Trampolines: indirect branch trampolines need to look up the mapping between old `pc` and translated `pc`. Before looking up the table, we first search a small cache of the previously converted `pcs` (8 entries). This simple optimization has a high hit rate (90% for the `nbench` [7] benchmark.)

5. EVALUATION

In this section, we evaluate the effectiveness, compatibility, and performance of our prototype. The experiments are based on a Google Nexus S phone running Android 4.1.2 (build number JZ054K).

5.1 Effectiveness of AppCage

We used samples from 15 malware families obtained from the Android Malware Genome Project [52] and online malware [8] repository to evaluate the effectiveness of AppCage. Specifically, we try to trigger their malicious behaviors and check whether our prototype can capture all of them. However, some samples can only be triggered by commands from the defunct remote command and control (C&C) servers. For example, GoldDream waits for the commands to send SMS or make phone calls to premium numbers in the background. To address this, we redirect the traffic to the C&C servers to our local machines at the network level and send commands to these malware samples. Similarly, some malware samples need to be triggered by particular SMS messages. Table 2 lists these samples and the attempted malicious operations by them. AppCage successfully captures all the attempts by them to leak private information and perform dangerous operations. In the following, we present the details of the experiment with the Gone60 malware.

Gone60 was first discovered from the official Android Market in September 2011. When executed, it immediately reads the call logs, contacts and SMS messages in the phone and sends them to the remote server. We sideload this app on our test phone, AppCage intercepts the installation and installs a confined version of it. When the app is started, AppCage detects its attempts to read the sensitive information. Since we have not specified any policy for this app yet, AppCage prompts us to choose whether to allow or deny the access. Figure 7(a) shows the prompt generated by AppCage regarding `Gone60`'s access to the contacts. Figure 7(b) shows a similar prompt when `FakePlayer` tries to send SMS to a premium-rated number.

In addition to malware, we also experimented with some benign but invasive apps. These apps are not malicious, but may aggressively access the private information, say, for targeted ads. In our evaluation, AppCage can detect all the accesses and provide users an option to block them. For example, the `BestBuy` app requests the permissions to access location, send SMS, and make phone calls. The user can leverage AppCage to disallow this app to send SMS, but allow it to access location (e.g., to find the local BestBuy stores.)

5.2 Security Analysis

In this paper, we assume a threat model in which third-party apps are untrusted or even malicious. In this section, we explore possible attacks to bypass or subvert AppCage and the countermeasures built into our system.

Java Obfuscation: the bytecode of Android apps are often obfuscated. Java-based obfuscation does not affect the effectiveness of our system because dex sandbox is implemented in Dalvik VM unreachable to the bytecode (tamper-resistance), and the app still needs to call the interposed APIs to get private information. For example, Java reflection is often used to hide the actual framework APIs called by the app. AppCage can interpose this behavior because the function call will eventually be dispatched through the `Method` structure in Dalvik VM, where AppCage places its hook.

Dynamic Bytecode: Android apps can dynamically load external bytecode for execution. For example, they can download the bytecode from a remote server and use `DexClassLoader` or other loaders to execute it. This poses a threat to bytecode-rewriting systems because the new bytecode is not available during rewrite. This attack is not effective against our system for the same reason as Java obfuscation. AppCage is positioned to interpose the dynamically loaded bytecode.

Direct Calls to System Services: In Android, sensitive data are maintained by separate system service daemons and exported to third-party apps through the `binder` interface. An app can directly access those services through the `IBinder` interface (in Java) [26] or the raw IPC (in native code). For example, the app can obtain the `IBinder` interface of the location service to get the current location without using the high-level `LocationManager` class. AppCage can defeat such attacks by preventing the app from obtaining the `IBinder` instance of known system services (most legitimate apps

Table 2: AppCage successfully blocks malicious behaviors of samples in 15 malware families

Malware	Send SMS	Read/Delete SMS	Phone Calls	Location	Call Logs	Contacts	Internet	IMEI
FakePlayer	√							
YZHC	√	√						
GoldDream	√		√					
TapSnake				√				
NickiBot		√		√	√	√	√	√
DroidKungFu							√	√
BeanBot	√		√				√	√
Gone60		√			√	√	√	
SndApps							√	
HippoSMS	√	√					√	√
Zitmo		√					√	√
Zsone	√	√						
Spitmo		√					√	
DroidLive	√		√				√	√
Geinimi	√		√	√		√	√	√

Table 3: Some apps used in compatibility test (†: in seconds)

App	Size	Package Name	Time†
Job Search	474K	com.indeed.android.jobsearch	5.7
Comics	3.7M	com.iconology.comics	13.5
chase	1.8M	com.chase.sig.android	10.6
Domino's Pizza	7.2M	com.dominospizza	18.6
Early Detection Plan	4.6M	com.nbcf.edp	13.7
Super-Bright LED Flashlight	1.5M	com.surpax.ledflashlight.panel	4.8
Ebay	9.6M	com.ebay.mobile	37.9
The Weather Channel	7.2M	com.weather.Weather	27.9
Bug Rush Free	13M	com.fourpixels.td	22.2
Solitaire	8.7M	com.mobilityware.solitaire	18.6
Average	5.7 M	-	17.3

Table 4: Code size increase (†: sizes in kilobytes before and after instrumentation ‡: percentage of code size increased. ∗: percentage of padding. ♯: time in seconds.)

App	Native Library	Size†	Size†	%Inc.‡	%Pad∗	Time♯
Ebay	libredlaser.so	529.2	709.7	34.1	15.9	12.2
AngryBirds	libangrybirds.so	1,283.4	1,639.8	27.8	16.6	27.7
MiBench	libjpeg6a.so	213.7	283.5	32.3	12.5	5.4
	liblame.so	260.1	347.7	33.7	15.8	5.7
	libmad.so	115.7	147.5	27.5	7.9	2.6
	libtiff.so	195.4	257.0	31.5	10.1	5.2
Nbench	libnbench.so	82.2	103.3	29.2	13.1	2.2
Average	-	-	-	30.9	13.1	8.7

do not do this anyway). Moreover, the app can use native code to open the `binder` device and send commands to the system services using the `ioctl` system call. AppCage adds security checks in the `ioctl` function of `libc` to prevent it, and it disallows the native code to issue system calls directly (Section 3.3). Note that we only block the `ioctl` system call directly issued from user native libraries or the (confined) system libraries linked with user native libraries. The original communication channels to remote system services through the binder interface remain unchanged since they are going through original system libraries.

Tampering with Dalvik VM: the app may tamper with Dalvik VM using native code since they share the same address space [1]. For example, it can remove all the hooks of AppCage in Dalvik VM to disable the policy check. This attack can be foiled by our system because the app's native code is sandboxed and cannot write memory out of the sandbox. In addition, it cannot escape from the sandbox to execute untranslated code.

Attacking Native Sandbox: the app may also try to attack the native sandbox. For example, it may try to load unsandboxed native code or break out of the sandbox. Our system design is secure against those attacks. First, AppCage hooks into the Android's dynamic loader. It intercepts any attempt to load a native binary and ensures that all the loaded user binaries are instrumented and sandboxed. Second, even though AppCage uses both a binary rewriter and the customized NaCl compiler to instrument native code, they enforce the same set of rules as the Native Client, which has been proved to be reliable and secure [38,48], despite a few fixed implementation issues.

Synthetic Attack: to further evaluate the security of the native sandbox, we create several synthetic attacks that violate the native sandbox rules. The first one is to change the loaded app bytecode at run-time, i.e., by writing to the memory mapped bytecode. Our system can capture such an attempt since this attack invokes the mmap system calls (Section 3.3) to remap the memory space containing the bytecode as readable and writeable. The second one is to manipulate the Dalvik internal data structure to change the control flow of the app code using the native library at run-time. For instance, it manipulate the method pointer inside the Dalvik VM to invoke the sensitive APIs. Our system blocks this attack since it writes to the memory space outside the native sandbox.

5.3 Compatibility of AppCage

AppCage may cause compatibility issues for two reasons: first, some apps may not be accommodating to constraints imposed by AppCage's sandboxes, particularly the native sandbox. For example, AppCage disallows the app's native code to directly issue a system call. Meanwhile, dex sandbox should pose few problems because it is, in essential, a set of hooks. Overall, we expect this category of compatibility issues not to be serious because currently not many apps contain native code that has legitimate reasons to directly issue system calls [2]. These system calls usually go through the linked system library (libc for example). In fact, we do not find a case during our evaluation that legitimate user native libraries issue system calls directly. Second, our prototype permission manager only supports three coarse responses: allow, deny, and prompt-to-user. It is known that many apps will not fail gracefully when permissions are removed [25,27]. Issues in this category can generally be remedied by returning mock results, such as a mock location, instead of an error [27, 55]. However, resources such as network are hard to reconcile this way.

To test the compatibility of our current prototype, we downloaded 50 popular apps from the Google Play store. Some of the apps we tested are shown in Table 3. We first evaluate the compatibility issues caused by the sandboxes by configuring permission manager to always return `allow`. All the apps can run under AppCage and we have not met any glitches even with exhaus-

[2]Nevertheless, we still need to sandbox native code. Otherwise, malicious apps can easily subvert our system using a native library.

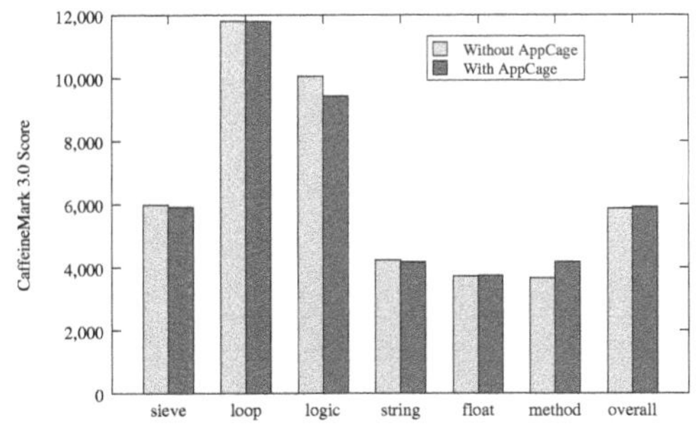

Figure 8: CaffeineMark with and without AppCage

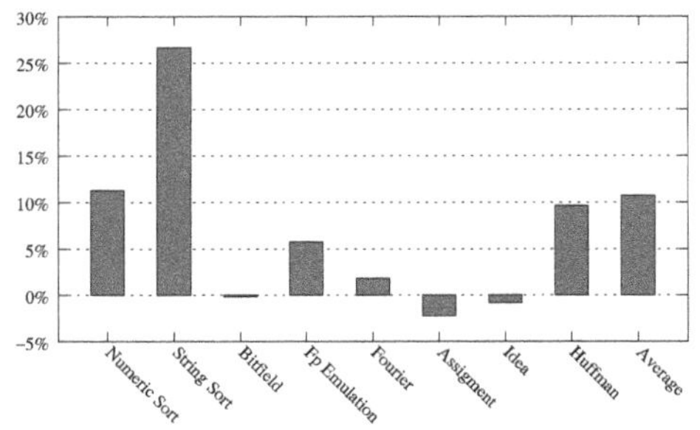

Figure 9: Normalized overhead of the native sandbox

tive interactions with the app (the result may not be definitive because we may have missed some code paths). We then evaluate the worst case of compatibility by configuring permission manager to always return `deny`. Under this stringent setting, some apps can only function partially but can still run. Only two apps crashed during our evaluation: `Bug Rush Free` and `Super-Bright LED Flashlight`. They immediately crashed when the access to the network and IMEI was denied, respectively. As aforementioned, the compatibility in this case can be improved by returning mock results if and when applicable.

We also evaluate the compatibility of the dex sandbox on different Android versions. We use five different Android versions, i.e., `2.3.6`, `4.0.4`, `4.1.2`, `4.2.2`, `4.3` in our test. Our experiments show that the dex sanbox can tolerant the changes of the Dalvik VM in different versions. We only need to slightly change the offset of the Dalvik VM data structure that needs to be hooked. This is implemented by maintaining a mapping table between the version numbers and the offsets of the Dalvik VM data structure that the dex sandbox are interested. Fortunately, this is a one time effort and the number of interested data structures is small (less than 10).

5.4 Performance Evaluation

We also evaluated the overhead introduced by AppCage including its impact to the code size, the installation time and the performance overhead.

Code Size: for each target app, AppCage generates a wrapper app that consists of the original app and other components to set up the sandboxes. This adds about 50KB of size to the original app (33KB for the stubs and 18KB for the library). Considering the average size of apps we tested is 5.7MB, the code size increase is less than 1%. There is additional code size increase due to the binary instrumentation for apps with native libraries. Table 4 shows the effect of binary instrumentation on the native code of two Android apps (`Ebay` and `Angry Birds`) and two benchmarks (`MiBench` and `Nbench`). The average increase is around 30%, and 13.1% of it can be contributed to the padding instructions to align code (Section 4).

Installation Time: AppCage will also increase installation time. For example, it needs to generate a wrapper app and *sign* it. Table 3 shows that the increase to the installation time is about 17 seconds for apps without native code. Moreover, binary rewriting could be time-consuming for large libraries. For example, AppCage spends about 27 seconds to rewrite the 1.2MB native code of `Angry Birds` (Table 4). Considering that native libraries are normally small and the binary rewriting is performed only once during installation, this increased installation time is acceptable, but maybe frustrating, in the practical deployment.

Performance Overhead: We also evaluated the run-time performance overhead introduced by AppCage. For bytecode, AppCage interposes its calls to some framework APIs. We used CaffeineMark, the standard Java benchmark to measure this overhead. The results in Figure 8 show that AppCage's dex sandbox only introduces negligible performance overhead to the bytecode. We obtained the similar results with an evaluation app that intensively invokes the confined framework APIs. Moreover, AppCage needs to communicate with permission manager (see Figure 2) to retrieve the policies. To measure the overhead introduced by this operation, we develop an app which continuously retrieves the policy for 10,000 times. It costs about 3.9 seconds in total for this app to complete. That is, the average time for each policy retrieval is about 0.39 millisecond. We believe this time introduced by AppCage is negligible that users cannot actually perceive it.

For native code, AppCage adds instructions to confine memory write and branches. To measure the overhead of native sandbox, we used Nbench [7], a computation-intensive benchmark of the CPU, FPU, and memory system performance. The average overhead of native sandbox is about 10.7% (Figure 9). The string sort benchmark has higher performance overhead because it heavily uses the `memmove` function in `libc` to move large blocks of data. `Libc` is built by a modified NaCl compiler and is the main source of the overhead for this benchmark. This is confirmed by the fact that the overhead will reduce dramatically if the benchmark is linked to a plain `libc`. This overhead can be reduced (to that of the original NaCl for ARM) if we position the sandbox in the same way as NaCl. This is not feasible unless we can change the default Android loader, a design we avoid for easy deployment. Similar to NaCl, there are three tests in Nbench perform better than the native execution. This is probably due to the caching effects of the code bundles [48].

6. DISCUSSION

First, compared to the systems that target the same problem [5, 14–16, 27, 33, 45, 55], AppCage is a more comprehensive and securer solution with its hybrid sandboxes. The ideal solution is for Google to *officially* support adjustment of permissions *after installation* [5]. However, there are two major issues that encumber this solution. First, Android is heavily fragmented with many versions and incompatible customization by major vendors [46]. It is not clear whether and when such update will be deployed to most of the users. In contrast, solutions such as AppCage can be immediately deployed. More importantly, as an official solution, the user would expect it to be compatible with *all* the apps in Google Play. It is a daunting task to update those millions of apps. It is questionable whether Google will ever deploy such a system (the experimental official permission manager has since been removed in a recent update to Android KitKat 4.4.2 [4].) Users likely have higher tolerance to the (inevitable) incompatibility of third-party solutions.

Second, AppCage prompts the user to choose to allow or deny the app's access to sensitive resources if no policy has been set (Figure 7). Compared to the prompt during installation, this *in-context* prompt is more effective and users are less likely to ignore it. Particularly, the research by Felt et al. shows that only 12% of the participants pay attention to the permission request at installation time [20], while 85% of them denied the location request for at least one app [21]. The system can also be extended to support community-based policy definition [35]. Moreover, the signature of the installed wrapper app is different from the original app, which may break the automatic update feature provided by the Google Play. Our system can monitor the version history of the apps on the Google Play and generate the wrapper app if a newer version is available.

Third, our current prototype only supports ARM, the dominate architecture for smartphones and tablets. Intel's x86 is an emerging architecture for mobile platforms. Our native sandbox can be extended to support x86 using similar techniques. In addition, our prototype does not support self-modify code. We leave it as a future work. Moreover, the indirect branch trampoline temporarily stores the target `pc` on the stack and branches to it using a `pop` instruction (Figure 6). This introduces a race condition where the target `pc` could be manipulated by another thread. The race condition can be avoided with an extra scratch register, and instructions to spill and restore the register. It would further complicate the design of the trampoline. However, the window of vulnerability is only four instructions, and the chance of successfully attacking it in practice is low. In fact, this race condition also affects other similar systems [32,49].

At last, since Android version 5.0, it uses a new runtime (ART) which leverages the ahead of time optimization to convert dex bytecode to a native binary. AppCage could be extended to support the ART runtime since this runtime still has the corresponding data structures to represent the Java classes and methods as the Dalvik VM (Figure 1). Accordingly, our system could take similar methods to hook these data structures in the ART runtime (libart.so). We take the ART support as one of the future work.

7. RELATED WORK

Android App Security: the first category of related work includes systems that expose privacy risks of third-party apps and systems to confine those apps. For example, researchers discover that private information could be leaked by benign apps [19], ad libraries [23], vulnerable apps [43], and malicious apps [52]. To mitigate this threat, researchers have proposed solutions to detect malicious or privacy-leaking apps. DroidRanger [54] and RiskRanker [24] are two systems to detect malicious apps on the official and alternative Android markets. Those systems can detect malicious app behaviors before they are installed on the user devices. However, they usually suffer from false negatives and false positives. On contrast, the interposition of AppCage cannot be bypassed by third-party apps.

There are also systems that extend the Android framework to provide fine-grained control of third-party apps at run-time [14–16, 27,33,55]. For example, AppFence [27] and TISSA [55] can return mock results of the sensitive resources such as the location. User-driven access control is a promising solution to provide in-context and non-disruptive permission granting [36]. While these systems may solve the problem in theory, the requirement to modify the Android framework significantly limits their practical deployment. In contrast, our system does not have such requirement and can be readily deployed. From another perspective, researchers have proposed to monitor and confine third-party apps in the user space with bytecode rewriting [17, 18, 28] or native library interposing [47] (Similar system also exists on other platforms [31].) For instance, AppGuard [13] is a closely-related system that instruments the target app and detours security-relevant methods to their guards functions through virtual machine internal data structure manipulation, a similar design as our dex sandbox (Section 3.2). Unfortunately, like other systems, it could be subverted by leveraging the native code. The native sandbox in AppCage is specifically designed to prevent this attack.

Software Fault Isolation AppCage leverages the software fault isolation (SFI) technology to sandbox native code. SFI has been widely researched and deployed [22, 29, 32, 34, 38, 42, 48, 50, 51]. Most of these systems target the x86 architecture [22, 29, 32, 34, 48, 50]. AppCage is designed for the ARM architecture, which has a different set of challenges (Section 3.3). ARMor [51] is a system providing SFI for the ARM architecture. However it does not support dynamic linking, and has a high performance overhead unsuitable to our system. Native Client for ARM [38] provides a customized compiler to generate confined ARM binaries. It thus requires source code access which is not available for the app's native code. ARMlock [53] implements an efficient fault isolation solution. However it requires the support from kernel space and thus cannot be used without the change to the phone's firmware. AppCage's native sandbox uses static binary translation to enforce the same proven rules of NaCl.

Robusta [39] and Arabica [40] are two closely related systems. They leverage Native Client and the JVMTI (JVM Tool Interface) to sandbox the native libraries of JVM, respectively. They have different assumptions than AppCage: Robusta requires to recompile the source code of the native libraries, and Arabica needs the support of JVMTI that is unavailable in Dalvik VM. Klinkoff *et al.* propose a SFI mechanism to protect managed code and the .NET run-time from the unmanaged code (or native code) [30]. They isolate unmanaged code in a separate process. Similarly, the NativeGuard [41] leverages the process boundary to isolate untrusted native libraries. AppCage takes a different design by isolating native code in the same process. While process-based isolation could be used in our system, one disadvantage is that every JNI call is transformed to a RPC call cross the process boundary, which is expensive and thus infeasible for our use cases.

8. CONCLUSION

We have presented the design, implementation, and evaluation of AppCage, a system to interpose and regulate third-party Android apps with hybrid user-level sandboxes, dex sandbox and native sandbox. Together, they enable AppCage to securely interpose the app's access to key APIs and services. We have implemented a prototype of AppCage. Our evaluation shows that AppCage can successfully detect and block the attempts to leak private data or perform dangerous operations by malware and invasive apps, and it also has an acceptable overhead, especially for apps without native code.

Acknowledgements The authors would like to thank the anonymous reviewers for their insightful comments that helped improve the presentation of this paper. This work was supported in part by the US National Science Foundation (NSF) under Grants 0855036 and 0952640. Any opinions, findings, and conclusions or recommendations expressed in this material are those of the authors and do not necessarily reflect the views of the NSF.

9. REFERENCES

[1] Android Security Analysis Challenge: Tampering Dalvik Bytecode During Runtime. `https://bluebox.com/technical/android-security-analysis-challenge-tampering-dalvik-bytecode-during-runtime/`.

[2] Binder. `http://developer.android.com/reference/android/os/Binder.html`.

[3] DroidKungFu Malware. `http://www.csc.ncsu.edu/faculty/jiang/DroidKungFu.html`.

[4] Googler: App Ops Was Never Meant For End Users, Used For Internal Testing And Debugging Only. http://www.androidpolice.com/2013/12/11/googler-app-ops-was-never-meant-for-end-users-used-for-internal-testing-and-debugging-only/.

[5] Hidden Permissions Manager Found in Android 4.3, Lets You Set the Rules. http://www.engadget.com/2013/07/26/hidden-permissions-manager-android-4-3/.

[6] JNI Tips. http://developer.android.com/training/articles/perf-jni.html.

[7] Linux/Unix nbench. http://www.tux.org/~mayer/linux/bmark.html.

[8] Mobile Malware Minidump. http://contagiominidump.blogspot.com/.

[9] PLT and GOT - the Key to Code Sharing and Dynamic Libraries. https://www.technovelty.org/linux/plt-and-got-the-key-to-code-sharing-and-dynamic-libraries.html.

[10] Smartphone OS Market Share, Q2 2014. http://www.idc.com/prodserv/smartphone-os-market-share.jsp.

[11] The Java Virtual Machine Specification. http://docs.oracle.com/javase/specs/jvms/se7/html/.

[12] Your Apps Are Watching You. http://online.wsj.com/news/articles/SB10001424052748704368004576027751867039730.

[13] M. Backes, S. Gerling, C. Hammer, M. Maffei, and P. von Styp-Rekowsky. AppGuard - Enforcing User Requirements on Android Apps. In *Proceedings of 19th International Conference on Tools and Algorithms for the Construction and Analysis of Systems*, 2012.

[14] A. R. Beresford, A. Rice, N. Skehin, and R. Sohan. MockDroid: Trading Privacy for Application Functionality on Smartphones. In *Proceedings of the 12th International Workshop on Mobile Computing System and Applications*, 2011.

[15] S. Bugiel, S. Heuser, and A.-R. Sadeghi. mytunes: Semantically linked and user-centric fine-grained privacy control on android. Technical Report TUD-CS-2012-0226, Center for Advanced Security Research Darmstadt, November 2012.

[16] S. Bugiel, S. Heuser, and A.-R. Sadeghi. Flexible and Fine-Grained Mandatory Access Control on Android for Diverse Security and Privacy Policies. In *Proceedings of the 22nd USENIX Security Symposium*, 2013.

[17] B. Davis and H. Chen. RetroSkeleton: RetroïňĄtting Android Apps. In *Proceedings of the 11th International Conference on Mobile Systems, Applications and Services*, 2013.

[18] B. Davis, B. Sanders, A. Khodaverdian, and H. Chen. I-ARM-Droid: A Rewriting Framework for In-App Reference Monitors for Android Applications. In *Proceedings of the IEEE Mobile Security Technology*, 2012.

[19] W. Enck, P. Gilbert, B. gon Chun, L. P. Cox, J. Jung, P. McDaniel, and A. N. Sheth. TaintDroid: An Information-Flow Tracking System for Realtime Privacy Monitoring on Smartphones. In *Proceedings of the 9th USENIX Symposium on Operating Systems Design and Implementation*, 2010.

[20] A. P. Felt, E. Hay, S. Egelman, A. Haneyy, E. Chin, and D. Wagner. Android Permissions: User Attention, Comprehension, and Behavior. In *Symposium on Usable Privacy and Security*, 2012.

[21] D. Fisher, L. Dorner, and D. Wagner. Short Paper: Location Privacy: User Behavior in the Field. In *Proceedings of the 2nd Annual ACM CCS Workshop on Security and Privacy in Smartphones and Mobile Devices*, 2012.

[22] B. Ford and R. Cox. Vx32: Lightweight User-level Sandboxing on the x86. In *Proceedings of the USENIX 2008 Annual Technical Conference*, 2008.

[23] M. Grace, W. Zhou, X. Jiang, and A.-R. Sadeghi. Unsafe Exposure Analysis of Mobile In-App Advertisements. In *Proceedings of the 5th ACM Conference on Security and Privacy in Wireless and Mobile Networks*, 2012.

[24] M. Grace, Y. Zhou, Q. Zhang, S. Zou, and X. Jiang. RiskRanker: Scalable and Accurate Zero-day Android Malware Detection. In *Proceedings of the 10th ACM International Conference on Mobile Systems, Applications and Services*, 2012.

[25] E. Gustafson, K. Kennedy, and H. Chen. Quantifying the Effects of Removing Permissions from Android Applications. In *IEEE Mobile Security Technologies*, 2013.

[26] H. Hao, V. Singh, and W. Du. On the Effectiveness of API-Level Access Control Using Bytecode Rewriting in Android. In *Proceedings of the 8th ACM Symposium on Information, Computer and Communications Security*, 2013.

[27] P. Hornyack, S. Han, J. Jung, S. Schechter, and D. Wetherall. These Aren't the Droids You're Looking For": Retroffiting Android to Protect Data from Imperious Applications. In *Proceedings of the 18th ACM Conference on Computer and Communications Security*, 2011.

[28] J. Jeon, K. K. Micinski, J. A. Vaughan, A. Fogel, N. Reddy, J. S. Foster, and T. Millstein. Dr. Android and Mr. Hide: Fine-grained Permissions in Android Applications . In *Proceedings of 2nd ACM CCS Workshop on Security and Privacy in Smartphones and Mobile Devices*, 2012.

[29] V. Kiriansky, D. Bruening, and S. Amarasinghe. Secure Execution via Program Shepherding. In *Proceedings of the 11th USENIX Security Symposium*, 2001.

[30] P. Klinkoff, E. Kirda, C. Kruegel, and G. Vigna. Extending .NET Security to Unmanaged Code. In *International Journal of Information Security*, 2007.

[31] B. Livshits and J. Jung. Automatic Mediation of Privacy-Sensitive Resource Access in Smartphone Applications. In *Proceedings of the 22nd USENIX Security Symposium*, 2013.

[32] S. McCamant and G. Morrisett. Evaluating SFI for a CISC Architecture. In *Proceedings of the 15th USENIX Security Symposium*, 2006.

[33] M. Nauman, S. Khan, M. Alam, and X. Zhang. Extending Android permission model and enforcement with user-deïňĄned runtime constraints. In *Proceedings of the 5th ACM Symposium on Information, Computer and Communications Security*, 2010.

[34] M. Payer and T. R. Gross. Fine-Grained User-Space Security Through Virtualization. In *Proceedings of the 7th International Conference of Virtual Execution Environments*, 2011.

[35] B. Rashidi, C. Fung, and T. Vu. RecDroid: A Resource Access Permission Control Portal and Recommendation Service for Smartphone Users. In *Proceedings of the ACM MobiCom workshop on Security and privacy in mobile environments*, 2014.

[36] F. Roesner, T. Kohno, A. Moshchuk, B. Parno, and H. J. Wang. User-Driven Access Control: Rethinking Permission Granting in Modern Operating Systems. In *Proceedings of the 33rd IEEE Symposium on Security and Privacy*, 2012.

[37] G. Russello, A. B. Jimenez, H. Naderi, and W. van der Mark. FireDroid: Hardening Security in Almost-Stock Android. In *Proceedings of the 29th Annual Computer Security Applications Conference*, 2013.

[38] D. Sehr, R. Muth, C. L. Biffle, V. Khimenko, E. Pasko, B. S. Yee, K. Schimpf, and B. Chen. Adapting Software Fault Isolation to Contemporary CPU Architectures. In *Proceedings of the 19th USENIX Security Symposium*, 2010.

[39] J. Siefers, G. Tan, and G. Morrisett. Robusta: Taming the Native Beast of the JVM. In *Proceedings of the 17th ACM Conference on Computer and Communications Security*, 2010.

[40] M. Sun and G. Tan. JVM-Portable Sandboxing of Java's Native Libraries. In *Proceedings of the 17th European Symposium on Research in Computer Security*, 2012.

[41] M. Sun and G. Tan. NativeGuard: Protecting Android Applications from Third-Party Native Libraries. In *Proceedings of the 7th ACM Conference on Security and Privacy in Wireless and Mobile Networks*, 2014.

[42] R. Wahbe, S. Lucco, T. E. Anderson, and S. L. Graham. Efficient Software-based Fault Isolation. In *Proceedings of the 14th ACM symposium on Operating systems principles*, 1993.

[43] R. Wang, L. Xing, X. Wang, and S. Chen. Unauthorized Origin Crossing on Mobile Platforms: Threats and Mitigation. In *Proceedings of the 20th ACM Conference on Computer and Communications Security*, 2013.

[44] X. Wang, C.-C. Pan, P. Liu, and S. Zhu. SigFree: A Signature-free Buffer Overflow Attack Blocker. In *Proceedings of the 15th IEEE Symposium on Security and Privacy*, 2006.

[45] C. Wu, Y. Zhou, K. Patel, Z. Liang, and X. Jiang. AirBag: Boosting Smartphone Resistance to Malware Infection. In *Proceedings of the 21st Network and Distributed System Security Symposium*, 2014.

[46] L. Wu, M. Grace, Y. Zhou, C. Wu, and X. Jiang. The Impact of Vendor Customizations on Android Security. In *Proceedings of the 20th ACM Conference on Computer and Communications Security*, 2013.

[47] R. Xu, H. Saidi, and R. Anderson. Aurasium: Practical Policy Enforcement for Android Applications. In *Proceedings of the 21th USENIX Security Symposium*, 2012.

[48] B. Yee, D. Sehr, G. Dardyk, B. Chen, R. Muth, T. Ormandy, S. Okasaka, N. Narula, and N. Fullagar. Native Client: A Sandbox for Portable, Untrusted x86 Native Code. In *Proceedings of the 30th IEEE Symposium on Security and Privacy*, 2009.

[49] C. Zhang, T. Wei, Z. Chen, L. Duan, L. Szekeres, S. McCamant, D. Song, and W. Zou. Practical control flow integrity & randomization for binary executables. In *Proceedings of the 34th IEEE Symposium on Security and Privacy*, 2013.

[50] M. Zhang and R. Sekar. Control-Flow Integrity For COTS Binaries. In *Proceedings of the 22rd USENIX Security Symposium*, 2013.

[51] L. Zhao, G. Li, B. D. Sutter, and J. Regehr. ARMor: Fully Verified Software Fault Isolation. In *Proceedings of the 11th International Conference on Embedded Software*, 2011.

[52] Y. Zhou and X. Jiang. Dissecting Android Malware: Characterization and Evolution. In *Proceedings of the 33rd IEEE Symposium on Security and Privacy*, 2012.

[53] Y. Zhou, X. Wang, Y. Chen, and Z. Wang. ARMlock: Hardware-based Fault Isolation for ARM . In *Proceedings of the 21st ACM Conference on Computer and Communications Security*, 2014.

[54] Y. Zhou, Z. Wang, W. Zhou, and X. Jiang. Hey, You, Get off of My Market: Detecting Malicious Apps in Official and Alternative Android Markets. In *Proceedings of the 19th Network and Distributed System Security Symposium*, 2012.

[55] Y. Zhou, X. Zhang, X. Jiang, and V. W. Freeh. Taming Information-Stealing Smartphone Applications (on Android). In *Proceedings of the 4th International Conference on Trust and Trustworthy Computing*, 2011.

On Designing an Efficient Distributed Black-Box Fuzzing System for Mobile Devices

Wang Hao Lee
Institute for Infocomm Research
Singapore
whlee@i2r.a-star.edu.sg

Murali Srirangam Ramanujam
Institute for Infocomm Research
Singapore
muralism@i2r.a-star.edu.sg

S. P. T. Krishnan
Institute for Infocomm Research
Singapore
krishnan@i2r.a-star.edu.sg

ABSTRACT

Security researchers who jailbreak iOS devices had crowd-sourced for system level vulnerabilities [1] for iOS. However, their success depended on whether a particular device owner encountered a crash in system-level code. To conduct voluntary security testing, Black-box fuzzing is one of the ideal low-cost and simple technique to find system level vulnerabilities for the less technical crowd. However, it is usually not the most effective method due to the large fuzzing space. At the same time, when fuzzing mobile devices such as today's smartphones, it is extremely time consuming to instrument mobile devices of varying versions of system software across the world. In this paper, we describe Mobile Vulnerability Discovery Pipeline (MVDP), a semi-automated, vulnerability discovery pipeline for mobile devices. MVDP is a carefully crafted process targeted to produce malicious output that is more likely to crash the target leading to vulnerability discovery. MVDP employs a few novel black-box fuzzing techniques such as distributed fuzzing, parameter selection, mutation position optimisation and selection of good seed files. To date, MVDP has discovered around 1900 crashing inputs and helped to identify 7 unique vulnerabilities across various Android and iOS phone models.

Categories and Subject Descriptors

D.4.6 [**Security and Protection**]: Invasive software—*Mobile Vulnerability*; D.2.5 [**Software Engineering**]: Testing and Debugging—*Distributed Debugging*

Keywords

Black-Box Fuzzing, Zero-Day Vulnerability, Crash Analysis, Smart-phones

ACM 978-1-4503-3245-3/15/04 ...$15.00.
http://dx.doi.org/10.1145/2714576.2714607.

1. INTRODUCTION

The increased sophistication of mobile devices brings with it many unknown vulnerabilities. It is critical to identify the vulnerabilities before attackers use them for 0-day exploits. The simplicity of black-box fuzzers allows non-security professionals to run security experiments and gather security related defects for the manufacturer or security researchers. On the other hand, the space for blind fuzzing is intractable and many duplicated fuzzed files or files with less meaningful mutations are produced. Hence, it is vital to devise techniques for discovering unknown vulnerabilities from a black-box perspective that yield higher detection-rates with fewer input tests. At a high level, three approaches to discovering software vulnerabilities exist: white-box, black-box and grey-box testing. The most suitable approach depends on the availability of the source codes, design specifications, size of source base and time and resources available. White box testing makes use of a program's source code to test the internal mechanism of the system or component. The openess of today's mobile Operating Systems today are mixed. Apple's iOS is generally closed source with some open-sourced components like XNU, `WebKit`, Objective-C runtime, `dyld` and so on. Debugging system level binaries are difficult without a Jailbreak which in itself is an exploit. Most of Google's Android OS is fully open-source with the exception of device drivers and UI customization [2]. The less popular Blackberry 10 and Windows Phone operating systems on the other hand are completely closed source. The complexity and size of the code-base would require significant time and resources for investigation. These code bases would also get updated before a researcher can sufficiently understand the system. In the context of voluntary security testing, it would be too intrusive to instrument a volunteer's device. Direct instrumentation of libraries that are common on mobile and desktop platforms on more robust desktop environments may accurately simulate the target environment, but target devices available around the world are actual live device targets providing the most accurate exploitation context. Furthermore, not every mobile device platform have common libraries with their desktop counterparts; for example, Webkit on iOS vs Mac OS X.

On the other hand, grey and black-box testing approaches require little or no knowledge of the architecture, respectively. As such, a large volume of test cases are needed to probe an unknown target. Black-box fuzzing at the extreme end of the spectrum, requires numerous unexpected or malformed inputs to test the response of the target. Although the basic idea may seem to lack elegance, it is highly effective in practice and simple in discovering critical bugs [3] even for users not coming from a security background. An average user has nearly 3 mobile devices according to a Sophos survey [4]. Shops also have unsold display-set devices switched on during the day. To harness the availability of idle devices and allow mainstream users to help researchers find security defects, we describe in this paper techniques such as distributed fuzzing, parameter selection, mutation position optimisation and selection of good seed files.

Audio, video and images are the most consumed media types on smartphones and drive-by-download exploits have been developed for these media in the past [5, 6, 7]. Hence, for this paper, we targeted the multimedia libraries (audio, video and images) on Android and iOS. Although only audio, video and images are tested in this paper, the technique is general and can be extended to include other data-formats that can be sent over the internet.

1.1 Fuzzing Challenges and Motivations

Black-box fuzzing is a popular, cheap and effective for finding bugs in applications for the masses. However, a good scalable black-box fuzzing architecture can always present challenges that need to be addressed before it can effectively enable vulnerability discovery. Overall, we summarize several challenges as below:

a) **Selecting good starting (seed) files**: The quality of the fuzzing output depends on the quality of seed files. This means the seed files from which the malformed inputs are generated must be of good quality [8]. The GIF file format, for example has several well-defined sections defined in its specification [9]. A good seed file should have all sections and sub-types of a particular data-format. More information about this is provided in Subsection 2.1.

b) **Virtually unlimited fuzzing space**: The fuzzing space for any file format can be exponentially large and exploring every single possibility can be next to impossible. For example, fuzz testing executed using binary files has is that it requires a large number of fault-inserted files to cover every test case [10]. As such, without much knowledge of the input format, we still need a method of generating and selecting fuzzing configurations that output fuzzed files containing a uniformly distributed set of mutation positions covering a diverse set of fields of the seed file.

c) **Fuzzing scalability**: If we were to generate test cases on the device itself, it is likely that the same malformed file is generated across multiple devices. This contributes to wasted computing power and less coverage of fuzzing space. There is also no means to compare test results across devices as each device might have performed the same or a different test. Hence, the fuzzed files should be generated only once and have copies distributed to different devices for testing. We need a server setup to coordinate the fuzz distribution across a great number of devices and collect and quantify the results.

When multiple devices of the same model and OS version are being fuzzed, there is a need to devise a method of balancing the inputs. With load balancing, more tests can be processed on a device/OS platform, duplicate tests can be eliminated and vulnerabilities can be discovered faster. This means that if we have multiple devices running the same OS version, the server must be able to identify them as of the same model and and allocate different inputs to each one of them.

When fuzzing many devices across the world, it is essential to have a new set of test input ready for the next arriving device of the same model and OS version. Storing fuzzed input thus require large amounts of storage space and the growth of space utilisation increases with the amount of devices connected to the test server. In addition, conducting tests across the internet requires massive network transfer of these test data much to the volunteer's deficit. Hence, we will need a means of optimizing the content being stored without comprimising on performance considerably.

With these challenges, it is noted that more efficient black-box fuzzing framework should be developed for discovering unknown vulnerabilities and bugs in mobile platforms, especially on smartphones.

1.2 Contributions

In this paper, we address the challenges described above and designed *Mobile Vulnerability Discovery Pipeline (MVDP)*, a scalable distributed fuzzing infrastructure for discovering unknown vulnerabilities for smartphones.

MVDP comprises of techniques to enable internet-scale voluntary security testing. The paper emphasizes the following key contributions for improvising black-box testing:

- **Ensuring universal uniqueness of fuzzes.** Sending the same file to the same device is a wastage of time, computing and network resources. Our paper presents FEET (Fuzzing Engine Evaluation Tool), a novel mechanism that ensures unique fuzzed files with well-distributed modification positions are prioritised.

- **Ensuring uniformity of fuzz campaigns (jobs).** Fuzzing is phased as jobs. Jobs are groups of `N` files analagous to a campaign in [11]. The basic idea of an optimized job in our case is that a job will contain a high diversity of modification positions as possible. Without considering too many intricacies of the file-format or system code from a black-box perspective, this technique attempts to ensure that a job tests out as many "fields" of a data-format as possible. This uniformity is measured using a chi-square test on all files in a job/fuzz epoch.

- **Improving Scalability and Fuzz Reuse.** It is mentioned in Section 1.1 that fuzz files are generated once and the copy is used to fuzz many devices, the side effect of it is the staggering growth of storage use when devices run out of test cases or arrival of more test devices. Diff-patches rather than use of actual file has a huge impact especially when it comes to MP4 and other storage-heavy files. Before fuzzing, the device creates the actual fuzz file by patching out the seed file. Refer to subsection 3.1.1 for more information on this approach.

By sending just the patches of the seed file rather than sending fuzzed files, we have been able to achieve up to 90% lesser network traffic. Each fuzzed file is a only BSDdiff patch file of approximately 500bytes. This makes it suitable for large scale fuzzing across the internet and future voluntary experiments by the general public on a large scale analagous to SETI@home [13] or BOINC [12].

Overall, MVDP comprises of various stages to generate good fuzzing output, hasten the process of vulnerability discovery and maximize the coverage of the test space. MVDP at its present stage discovers vulnerabilities of media file-formats but can be applied to target any data-format acessible over the internet.

The layout of the paper is organised as follows. Section 2 introduces the architecture of MVDP and its four operational stages. In Section 3 we share the implementation and experiments done. Section 3 sheds light on the results obtained and its implications. Section 4 lists related work, Section 5 talks about future work and Section 6 concludes the paper.

2. THE PROCESS

The Mobile Vulnerability Discovery Pipeline consists of several processes that can be programmed into server-end and device-end. Figure 1 provides an overview of the pipeline with the numbers representing the order of operations. The entire MVDP process can be described as *three* operating stages: the Quality Input Generation, Device and Task Management, and Crash Analysis.

2.1 Quality Input Generation

This is a semi-automated stage consisting of automatic downloading and initial good seed file selection. Additional manual augmentation of good seed files is advisable but optional. It aims to construct the best fuzzing configuration to be used such that the fuzzed files have good coverage and uniform distribution. The following sub-sections describe them in more detail.

2.1.1 Seed File Downloader (SFD)

To fuzz a data-format effectively, the clean input data (also known as seed files or initial files [14]) must cover as high field coverage as possible as defined in the respective file format RFC. To achieve this, data-format samples are downloaded and further manually augmented.

For the purpose of this paper, the main data inputs for fuzzing are file-based inputs. Rather than constructing such a file from scratch, files are downloaded from the internet. The search and download process is automated using web APIs They scans the Internet for seed files using the Google custom search Engine [15] and Microsoft Azure Search [16]. These raw inputs are given to SFAT.

2.1.2 Seed File Analysis Tool (SFAT)

SFAT compares, sorts and clusters the raw input files according to their protocol coverage. File format parsers like

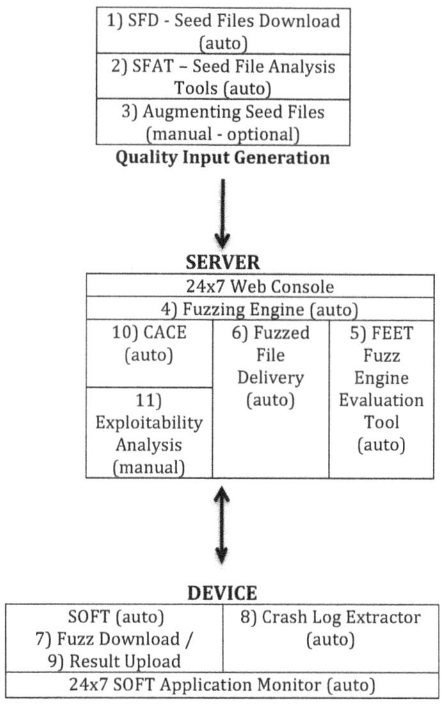

Figure 1: Architectural Flow Diagram of MVDP showing automatic and manual processes.

Hachoir [17] provides file information for the seed file selection algorithm (more in section 2.1.3) to calculate file format specification (RFC) coverage for a particular file. The files containing high data-format coverage are known as good seed files. In some protocols, there are mutually exclusive fields; each forming a sub-type of a file format. For example, in the case of PNG files, there are RGB and ICCP PNG file sub-types [18]. A PNG file can contain only either one of the ICCP or the sRGB chunk. In this case, SFAT automatically ignores files with field-coverage being total subsets of another downloaded file so sub-types are covered.

2.1.3 Seed File Selection Algorithm

SFAT is the tool to be run when a new binary file format is to be fuzzed using mutation fuzzing. It examines all seed files by using the following heuristics in the following order:

1. Top-Level Domain Score (TLD)
2. Field Score (F)
3. Field Occurrence Score (D)
4. Occurrence Distribution Score
5. File Size Score

The scoring is done for each file format separately and heuristics are used hierarchically. For the file formats we tested, there are (usually) many seed files with equally high TLD score; for example, internet downloaded PNG seed files with highest TLD scores have all 3-4 critical chunks [18] and 6 more ancillary chunks. These files with highest TLD scores are further ranked using Field Score. The best from Field Score is ranked by Field Occurrence Score and so on. If more than one seed file reaches the 5th level heuristic, the file with the smallest file size is selected.

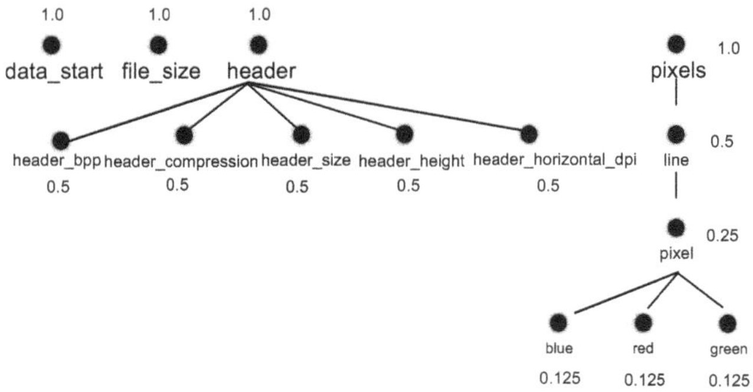

Figure 2: Field Score

(i) **Top-Level-Domain Score**

File-formats typically use markers/chunks to determine a major field. For example, PNG has 21 types of chunks out of which only 3 to 4 are mandatory [18]. Typically, the higher the number of top-level markers/chunks are, the better the seed file candidate.

(ii) **Field Score**

Given an instance of a file type F where there are n top-level domain fields we define the fields of file F as $< f_i.....f_n >$.

A weight is assigned to a field/sub-field to denote the significance of a field in a file-type instance. This weight value assignment scheme is experimental and can be changed accordingly. Within f_i where $i < n$, the set of weights for each subfields of a field f_i is denoted by $S_i =< s_{ij}...s_{im} >$, where m is the number of subfields of the field f_i.

The weight for each subfield is defined as s_{ij}. It is defined as: $s_{ij} = \frac{1}{(2^{l-1})}$ where l is the level of the field in the subfield tree.

By definition, top-level domain fields always have a weight of 1. The weight value decreases with tree height. For example, in BMP file format, the weight of a field called used_colors, (header/used_colors) is a second level sub-field and 'header' is the top-level-domain field. $\frac{1}{2^1} = 0.5$

Consider another example, if its a 4 level field e.g. (/pixels/line/pixel/red) $\frac{1}{2^3} = 0.125$

The total weight of a field f_i, denoted w_i is defined as:

$$w_i = \sum_{j=0}^{m} s_{ij} \tag{1}$$

Given the definitions above, we define the Field Score of file F as:

$$\prod_{i=0}^{N} w_i \tag{2}$$

where w_i = a weighted sum of the sub-fields and root field defined in Equation 1.

Consider the example of a Field score of a hypothetical file in Figure 2.

$$F = dataStart * FileSize * Header * Pixels$$
$$= 1.0 * 1.0 * 3.5 * 2.125 = \mathbf{7.4375}$$

In general, a higher field score represents a better seed file.

(iii) **Field Occurrence Score**

The field occurrence shows the number of times a field/subfield appears in the file. Let the field occurrence of a sub-field s_{ij} be o_j. The subfield weighted occurrence score B is given by:

$$B_{i,j} = o_{i,j} * s_{i,j} \tag{3}$$

From Equation 3 the field weighted occurrence score C is calculated as:

$$C_i = \sum_{j=0}^{m} B_j \tag{4}$$

Where m is the number of fields in the ith field. Given B_j and C_i, we can calculate the $fieldOccurrenceScore$ D as follows:

$$D = \sum_{i=0}^{n} C_i \tag{5}$$

A higher field occurrence score corresponds to a generally better seed file as it generally denotes a better overall spec coverage given the lack of time to read RFCs.

An example of a field occurrence score calculation is shown in Figure 3.

(iv) **Occurrence Distribution Score**

In occurrence distribution score, all fields or subfields are flattened and not weighted. We define the occurrence of a field/subfield as o_k. Let T be the total number of all subfields and fields of the input file and the set of all subfields and fields be k. We define the mean field/subfield occurrence as

$$\mu = \sum_{k=0}^{T} \frac{o_k}{(T)} \tag{6}$$

The file-wide standard deviation of the occurrences is given by:

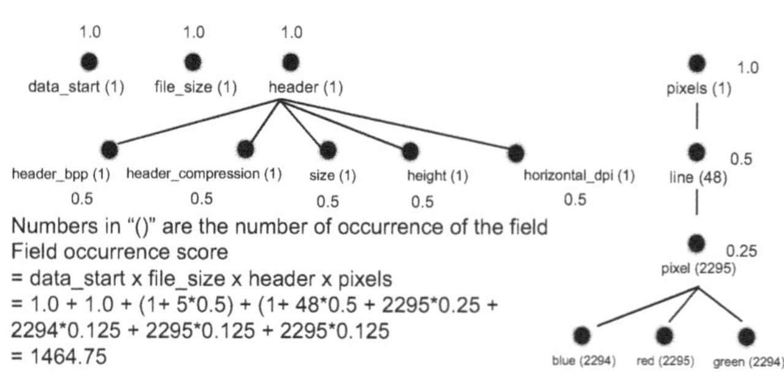

Figure 3: Field Occurrence Score

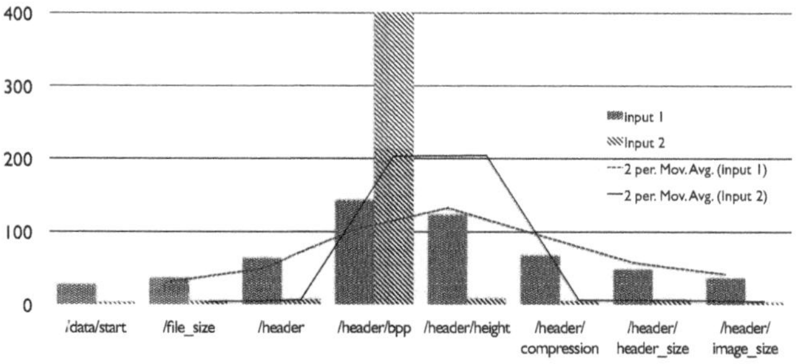

Figure 4: Occurrence Distribution Score

$$\sigma = \sqrt{(\frac{1}{n})} * (\sum_{k=0}^{T} (o_k - \mu)^2) \quad (7)$$

From Equation 6 and 7, the occurrence distribution score is calculated as:

$$occurrenceDistributionScore = \frac{\mu}{\sigma} \quad (8)$$

A higher field-wide occurence distribution score is less desirable. This is because mutation fuzzing will tend to fuzz only data in one field type. So the mean occurrence is taken into consideration. A higher occurrence distribution score is a better seed file. Figure 4 shows an example of a more desirable seed file (input 1) in terms of occurrence distribution score.

(v) **File Size Score**
Finally, after applying the above heuristics, if more than one seed file reaches this level, the best seed file the file with the smallest file. This is because the mutations by a fuzzer will be more likely to hit a wider range of fields. FEET also works more efficiently with a seed file of a smaller size. Patching a smaller seed file (see section 2.2.1) to produce a fuzzed file will also be faster.

The selected seed files are still downloaded from the internet and may not contain rare fields that are less commonly used. The combination of SFD and SFAT seeks to reduce the amount of rarer fields to be introduced by automatically selecting a high coverage seed file as a starting point. One can then instrument execution of a open source library supporting the data format (for example `libSkia` [19] is to PNG) to get maximum coverage. However, this technique is platform and application library dependant. Good code coverage in Skia on Android might not directly imply good code coverage on `ImageIO` [20] for iOS.

2.1.4 *Fuzzing Engine*

Seed files selected by SFAT are fed into a fuzzing engine and the results are evaluated to determine the best fuzzing configuration to use with test devices. Since the fuzzing is done on server end. Another fuzzing engine can be swapped out without affecting the SUT (system under test) in a remote corner of the internet. The fuzzer we created for this set of experiments is called Fe2 that mutates files with operators that mutate meta-data targeted at parsing logic.

Fe2 makes use of FEET described in Section 2.1.5 to automatically ensure that seed files have their mutations spread out throughout the protocol. Spreading the mutations throughout the protocol ensures that the fuzzer tests the handling of the file in all its protocol regions which may improve vulnerability detection due to the potential increase in code coverage.

Several different file fuzzing operators were implemented in Fe2. The operators are file-format agnostic so they can be used on several file formats.

(a) **Remove random string** - Removes a random section of random size and location in the input file. The objective is to stress the file parser by removing essential and nonessential parts of the input.

(b) **Add random string** - Adds a random string of random size to a random location. The objective is to add unexpected sections to the input file.

(c) **Change random string** - Changes multiple random sections. Randomizes the number and size of the sections, and the contents to be substituted. The objective is to determine if the file parser could recover from multiple errors in the input file.

(d) **Change random characters** - Replaces characters in the input file with random characters. Randomizes the number of locations selected for replacement and the replacement characters. The objective is to introduce unexpected characters.

(e) **Change cases** - These 2 operators seeks out and invert either the lowercase or uppercase ascii characters in the input file. It replaces single characters at one or more locations. Replaces one or more number of characters.

(f) **Replace null characters** - Finds null characters and replaces them with character A. This is similar to mutation operation (g) with the difference being single null characters instead of double. This operation probes libraries written in traditional C-style dynamic memory allocations with null-terminated strings. It aims to trigger buffer overflow errors in the parser.

(g) **Replace null string** - Finds instances of double null characters and replaces them with AA. The objective is to test file parsers dependent on double-null delimiters in C++ coded programs.

2.1.5 *Fuzzing Engine Evaluation Tool*

In order to determine the superiority of the fuzzed output, we have devised a Fuzzing Engine Evaluation Tool (FEET). FEET considers fuzzing parameters, uniqueness of the job and uniformity of the fuzzing space covered to evaluate the quality of the fuzzed output. Here we define a job to be a set of fuzzed files which were fuzzed with a particular fuzzing configuration. This notion is similar to a 'campaign' in [21] except larger numbers of up to 10000 files can be used in 1 job.

We define three levels of uniqueness for grouping of fuzzed input. They are local, global and universal uniqueness. The best fuzzing configuration has most files with universal uniqueness. All files for one file-type in MVDP have been selected to be globally unique.

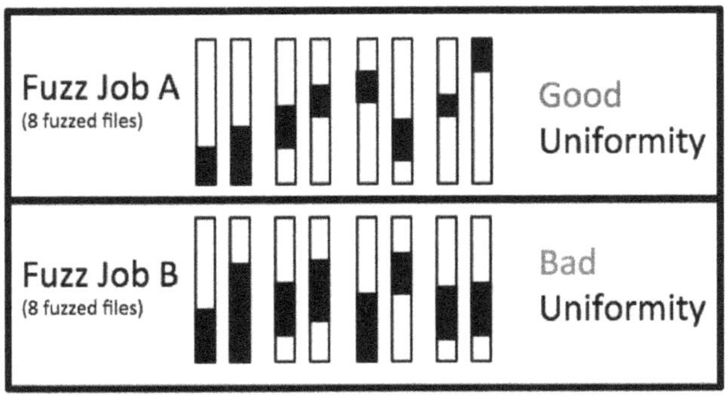

Figure 5: Different modification position distributions between 2 fuzz jobs (Black areas in a file are mutations)

a) **Local Uniqueness**
Local uniqueness is the percentage of unique fuzzed files in a job. Uniqueness of a file is determined by comparing the hash of the file against the hashes of all the remaining files within a job.

b) **Global Uniqueness**
There are usually millions of fuzzed files generated and packaged in several hundred jobs. Let D and G be 2 jobs with all locally unique files. Let d_i be a file in a job D and g_j be a file in job G, where $i, j > 0$. It is possible that $d_i \equiv g_j$ or even $D \equiv G$. Hence, for a fuzzed file to be globally unique, it must be unique across all jobs produced from a given fuzzer regardless of fuzzing parameters.

c) **Universal Uniqueness**
As MVDP is able to utilize several different fuzzers to produce fuzzed output, it is then possible for two fuzzers to produce 2 identical files. A fuzzed file is considered universally unique if it is both locally and globally unique and an identical copy of the fuzzed file is also not produced by another fuzzer within MVDP.

d) **Uniformity**
Fuzzing needs to concentrate on a specific location of the targeted data-type within a job. If the fuzzing is wildly distributed throughout the file, critical sections of files might be missed. Hence, we deduced that in each job, the fuzzing needs to be concentrated yet uniformly spread out in one particular section. As such, the definition of uniformity here refers to having a 'goodness-to-fit' between distributions of modified positions in a fuzz job against that of an even distribution of positions. An example of an evenly distributed fuzzed job and a non-evenly distributed fuzzed job is as shown in Figure 5.

The uniformity for seed file modification locations is measured using the chi-square test. We used the chi-square statistic χ^2 for a fuzzed job with k modifications as the uniformity distance:

$$\chi^2 = \sum_{1 \leq i \leq k} \frac{(Y_i - E)^2}{E} \tag{9}$$

where $Y_1, Y_2, \ldots, Y_k$ are the modifications positions in the fuzzed file and the expected position of each modification is E (where $1 < i < k$). The expected value E is given as:

$$E = \frac{\sum_{i=1}^{k} Y_i}{K} \tag{10}$$

After obtaining the chi-square distance for each job, we calculated the chi-squared probability using the uniformity distance with the degree of freedom being $K-1$. We ensured that all fuzzing jobs have a chi-squared probability > 0.05 to be considered uniform.

For each file format, we let FEET generate and analyse multiple jobs with various fuzzing configurations and select fuzzed jobs ranked by their chi-squared probability and uniqueness.

2.2 Device and Task Management

To test the Mobile OS's resistance to the malformed files, we would need to open/render each file individually and log the results. With the vast quantity of fuzzed files to be tested, we needed an automated system to deliver jobs to the devices, collect and consolidate results. Hence, we built the Security Testing Arsenal for Mobile Platforms (STAMP).

2.2.1 STAMP

STAMP is a server based system that automatically coordinates the flow of generating fuzzing jobs, distribute them to the devices, load balance the work among devices of the same type and collate the results for *centralised* graphical analysis and evaluation.

The problem of duplicate test cases is solved by generating the jobs within STAMP and distributing them to every new device to be tested. This also removes the waiting time for fuzzed files to be generated when a new device registers with STAMP. When a device registers with STAMP, there are already a large number of fuzzed inputs downloadable so the device can be tested without delay.

STAMP server holds history of all fuzzed files for newly registered unseen devices and generates new fuzzed file for seen devices. On a large scale of mobile clients, requests for fuzz files arrive faster than fuzz generation. The server then has to churn fuzz output at full-capacity creating exponential storage space growth. In addition, mobile network transfers are slow and less reliable especially for bigger file formats. To delay the rate of increase of storage use and reduce the amount of network data usage, we made use of the binary diff/patch utility. We generated patches between the fuzzed files and the Super Seed Files and stored the patches instead. This reduced the used space by more than 90%. This also greatly reduced the amount of network traffic (when sending the file from server to devices) and traded the download time for mobile device CPU's patching time. Today's mobile devices have sufficiently capable processors for patching files. Hence, this trade-off should be worthwhile.

2.2.2 STAMP clients

In the MVDP architecture in Figure 1, we mentioned about SOFT clients. These are small applications called SOFT (STAMP on-device Fuzzing Tool). SOFT clients are developed for each mobile platform. The client is easily portable to other mobile platforms if needed. The SOFT clients automatically interacts with the STAMP server to download jobs and patch them (since the fuzzed files in the server are stored as diff patches). Once a job is downloaded and patched, the SOFT client renders the fuzzed input using the native libraries/APIs provided by the OS. Upon completion of a job the clients reply to the server with the job results.

2.3 Crash Analysis

STAMP has a web interface which the security researcher can visit to obtain information about the fuzzing progress. The researcher can tell exactly which file caused a crash in a particular device at a particular time. All the STAMP reported crashes can be reproduced manually using the default application provided by the respective mobile OS. When doing so, logs on the mobile device (for example - Android) are monitored for any crashes. For example, image files are opened using the default Gallery application in Android. The Android system logs kernel errors during a crash into a Tombstone report; which are automatically extracted by using a shell script for further analysis. Similarly with iOS, the logs registering the stack trace, register values and fault locations during a crash are captured.

Inspection of crash dumps - Manual binning of all crash dumps is not scalable and is time consuming. With the Crash Automatic Classification Engine (CACE), this process has been automated. CACE processes the reports from Android's kernel crash logs (also known as tombstone) and iOS's crash logs to generate bins of unique vulnerabilities based on the type of crash. The bins are - Exploitable, Non-exploitable, Potentially Exploitable, Potentially non-exploitable or DOS. After CACE bins the crashes, researchers can focus on exploitable or potentially exploitable cases.

The key features of the engine are as follows:

- CACE is a rule based system to identify unique vulnerabilities that could have been exposed by multiple malformed files. The crash dumps are examined for terminated signal, fault address, terminated code (if exists) and the call stack along with the program counters. Hash value of all these entities combined form a unique ID for the vulnerability.

- CACE identifies the source of crash in binary (for iOS and Android) and in source locations (for Android). For example, if a crash occurs when opening an mp4 file on Android, CACE is able to point to the location in the source code/binary that led to the crash from the stack trace.

The unique vulnerabilities are then manually inspected for security issues. With the help of a scriptable disassembler. We inspect the libraries at the fault location to determine the nature of crash and severity level.

Depending on the type of access, crashes may or may not be exploitable. Various exception types and exploitability levels exist and we explored the approaches of CrashWrangler and Microsoft's !exploitable [22] to derive the common set of conditions for our own implementation; especially for Android where no crash triaging tool is available for security related purposes. In general, the SIGSEGV (11), SIGBUS (10) and SIGILL (4) on Unix flavoured Operating Systems such as Android and iOS are considered interesting to our experiments as they mean invalid memory access at the user space or kernel space and are possibly an indication of execution of data segments. Thus CACE automatically first filters out crashes containing these signals for exploration.

Next, based on the crashing address we found at the point of crash, we determine the instruction type last executed before the crash. Several types of ARM instruction classes correspond to read, write or execute instructions. Some examples are given below:

```
ldr r0, r1, r2;   - read
bl r1;            - execute
mov r1, [r4];     - write
```

When the last executed instruction before crashing is an unprivileged write or execute instruction, it is considered as potentially exploitable. Comparatively, crashes where the last instruction is an unprivileged read are not-likely exploitable.

2.4 Vulnerability Analysis

The degree of control the fuzz input has on exploitability is examined manually after a crash is binned by CACE. For every fuzzed input that corresponds to a potentially exploitable crash, we search for another existing crash with the same stack trace. For these two crashes with the same stack trace, we manually compare the crashing address value and its address contents/register value to be written or executed. If these address values or contents are relatively similar (ASLR slides library start addresses), then fuzz input does not influence the crash to a sufficently large extent and is henceforth considered as less interesting. On the other hand if the address/values for the similar crashes are all different, it means the crash is at least partially dependent on the given fuzzed input.

From time to time, it might not be possible to identify at least 2 potentially exploitable crashes with the same stack trace. When this happens, a diff operation is performed on the crashing input against the original seed file. The differences are recorded as we slowly move from the crashing input to the original seed file removing irrelevant file modifications. We stop removing modifications when we reach an input with a minimal set of modifications that produces the same crashing stack trace. When moving from the original crashing file to the minimal modification crashing file, the crashing address value and address contents/register values are examined for each crash. If the crash addresses or values are different during the minimisation process, this crash can be controlled from a given fuzzed input and is considered to be a crash where an exploit can be made.

3. IMPLEMENTATION AND EVALUATION

In this section we describe the experiment setup and discuss some of the important results obtained from MVDP.

3.1 Experimental Setup

All of our experiments were run on STAMP which is implemented as a server running Ubuntu 12.04 on an Intel Xeon E5-2697 v2 @ 2.70GHz 64 GB RAM. SFD, SFAT, Fe2 and FEET are implemented as Python scripts with the Python NumPy library. We modified hachoir-urwid [17] to provide SFAT with the structure of a recogonised file format in a hierarchical form. STAMP has been developed using Python's Django Framework with an interactive web-based

	Without BSDiff	With BSDiff
Storage Space	9.8mb	60kb
Fuzzing Time (if no crash)	1018s	1105s
Creation Time	63s	1864s
Network transmission	8.38s	0.46s

Table 1: Performance hit when using BSDiff to reduce storage requirement

dashboard, connecting to a MySQL database backend. The console allows for fuzz job monitoring, addition of jobs with user-preferred configuration, assignment of jobs to the devices, test device management, device progress monitoring, user administration and statistical visualization of crashes. HiCharts library was used to give a graphical representation of the number of crashes discovered and rate of discovery. This aids the security researcher in modifying the fuzzing configurations to better target vulnerable formats and regions.

The SOFT clients are developed using the Android and iOS SDKs. They are running on real devices or emulators. 5 x Intel Xeon E5-2650 v2 workstations with @2.60GHz 32GB RAM run the Android Emulator clients where each workstation runs 10 instances of Android emulators. We set up a fuzz farm a dozen iOS and Android devices in addition to running the Android emulators. The clients also verify any crashes discovered by the system and restart themselves upon a crash. On Android, for example, there is a service that constantly monitors the SOFT application to detect crashes. When the application is found to have crashed, the service takes the necessary steps to clean up and relaunch the application. The application then proceeds to retest the same file which caused the crash before moving onto the next test file. Information about whether the crash was reproducible is sent to the server. This has largely helped in reducing the waiting time between a crash and human intervention to restart the SOFT application. It has thus made it possible for SOFT to be running continuously for months with little/no supervision.

We conducted the fuzzing experiments on multiple Android Emulators running Android 2.3.7, 4.0.4, 4.1.2 and 4.2.1, popular devices from Samsung, LG, Motorola, Huawei and Google and all iOS devices. A total of approximately **5 million test cases** were evaluated in the system for formats PNG, GIF, JPEG, TIF, MP3 and MP4. Note that not all the devices finished processing all the jobs at the point of this paper as devices run at different speeds due to their hardware and software capabilities.

3.1.1 Storage Space Management

To mitigate the exponential disk space explosion from generating a few million fuzzed inputs, we developed a new way of producing and delivering the fuzzed input. Rather than directly generating the fuzzed input, BSDiff [23] patches are generated for each fuzzed input "diffed" against the seed file. These diff patches are stored on the server disk. Prior to fuzzing, the mobile device clients download a copy of the seed file and the BSDiff patches. The client then reconstructs the fuzzed files by applying the patch to the seed file. Finally the clients begins fuzzing by opening the files

With FEET	Without FEET
95.24	86.49
95.66	81.18
99.13	83.23
98.89	87.93
97.83	79.66
96.09	79.49
95.40	84.09
96.97	85.72
96.13	84.61
95.29	98.68

Table 2: Percentage uniqueness of first 10 jobs distributed to clients

reconstructed from the patches.

3.1.2 Crash Classification

To identify the module and function that caused the crash, the stack trace - obtained by the method described above - is parsed to get the filename of the shared library and its offset to the function. IDA pro is then invoked via a IDAPython script to read the shared library and identify the function and instruction causesing the crash. For Android devices, ADB's `logcat` output is parsed to look for crashes and CACE examines basic exploitability information. For iOS devices, CrashWrangler [24] is modified with access to ARM shared libraries and an ARM version of GDB/LLDB to triage iOS crashes.

3.1.3 Crash Similarity

For all reproducible identified crashes, a core-dump is generated and symbolicated. With the presence of ASLR, stack trace similarity is idenfitied based on function-names call sequence in the stack backtrace along with the ARM CPSR value before crash.

3.2 Experimental Parameters

We set up a fuzz farm consisting of a dozen iOS and Android devices in addition to running more than 100 Android emulators in Ubuntu desktops. The file formats tested are GIF, JPEG, PNG, MP3 and MP4 video. The fuzzing experiments were run for 2 weeks and the crashes are analysed by CACE. As we are still investigating several crashes to discover the vulnerabilities and to prevent attackers from exploiting them, we have anonymised the device identities.

For every stage of the vulnerability discovery pipeline, we define groups of metrics for our experimental findings categorised below:

3.2.1 SFAT Metrics

We evaluated all fuzzed results across all devices based on fuzzes created from 2 different mpeg-4 seed files across all devices. One mp4 file has lower field_scores, field_occurance_scores and occurancedistributionscores compared to the second mp4 file. The number of unique crashes and total number of crashes identified for each seed file to evaluate the effectiveness of SFAT.

3.2.2 FEET Metrics

We ran some GIF fuzzing experiments without FEET on several devices running Android 4.0.4 and compared the re-

FEET	Job ID	#Crashes	#Unique Bugs
Without FEET	1	1	1
	2	0	0
	3	0	0
	4	0	0
	5	0	0
	6	0	0
	7	0	0
	8	0	0
	9	0	0
With FEET	1	0	0
	2	0	0
	3	3	1
	4	3	1
	5	6	1
	6	0	0
	7	0	0
	8	0	0
	9	2	1

Table 3: Fuzzing on Android 4.0.4 Device 1 with and without FEET

sults with FEET to ascertain its effectiveness. A total of 9 jobs with 10000 files each were tested. The job IDs are fuzzed in order - i.e., ID 1 is fuzzed first and 9 last. We derived the following metrics to measure the effectiveness:

(a) **Uniqueness**

FEET tests the uniqueness of fuzz files produced by each fuzz configuration.A job in this experiment consisted of 10,000 fuzzed files. The more uniqueness a job has, the more diverse the individual test files in it. We of course prefer to maximise the uniqueness percentage as this means we are fuzzing more variety of files which in turn promises more chances of striking a crash.

(b) **Crash Arrival Rate**

We first compare the *crash arrival rate*, i.e. how fast can a crash be obtained using FEET selected fuzzing configurations against randomly selected fuzzing configurations.

(c) **Number of Crashes**

We also compare the *number of crashes* obtained using FEET selected fuzzing configurations against randomly selected fuzzing configurations.

(d) **Variety of bugs**

How many unique bugs are discovered using FEET selected fuzzing configurations against randomly selected fuzzing configurations.

3.2.3 STAMP Metrics

We analyse the speedup using distributed fuzzing 10,000 files against a fixed number of fuzzes.

3.3 Experimental Results

Please note that we have anonymised the device identities because we are still investigating several crashes to discover vulnerabilities.

3.3.1 FEET Results

(a) **Uniqueness**

Table 2 shows the percentage uniqueness of jobs distributed to clients. From the Table 2, we see that out of the 100,000 files in this experiment (10 jobs * 10,000 files per job), using FEET provides an average uniqueness factor of 96.67% compared to an average uniqueness factor of 85.11% without FEET.

For illustration purposes, let us consider that testing one JPG image on an iPhone takes 1 second (in reality, the time taken is much lesser). Let us have two iPhones side by side - one fuzzing inputs processed by FEET, and the other fuzzing inputs without FEET. Given 100,000 seconds, the first iPhone would have processed 96,670 unique images whereas the second iPhone would have processed 85,100 unique images. We can say the first iPhone "wasted" 3330 seconds out of 100,000 (a ratio of 0.033) whereas the second iPhone "wasted" 14,900 seconds (a ratio of 0.149) or around 4.5 times as much wastage. This gap only widens when we fuzz for longer durations.

(b) **Crash Arrival Rate Comparison** In Table 3, it can be seen that without using FEET, the device encountered the first crash in its first fuzzing job. However, that is the only crash found; hence this crash could be a one-off incident. Remaining jobs do not yield any crashes. This is in contrast with the utilisation of FEET to first determine uniformity and uniqueness of resulting configurations before generating patches. Crashes come only from the 3rd job onwards.

(c) **Number of Crashes**

There are 14 crashes discovered on the Android 4.0.4 device using FEET selected fuzzing configurations.

(d) **Variety of Bugs**

For the GIF file format, there is only one bug discovered by both FEET selected and randomly selected configurations.

Device	**Version**	**File Format**	**Crash Count**	**#Unique bugs**
Device 1	Android 2.3.x	GIF	825	1
Device 1	Android 2.3.x	MP4	9	2
Device 2	Android 4.0.x	GIF	253	1
Device 3	Android 4.0.x	GIF	708	1
Device 4	Android 4.1.x	PNG	19	1
Device 5	Android 4.2.x	MP3	27	2
Device 6	Android 4.3.x	MP3	13	2
Device 7	iOS 6.x	JPEG	25	1
Device 8	iOS 6.x	MP3	1	0
Device 9	iOS 6.x	JPEG	12	1
Device 10	iOS 6.1.x	JPEG	9	1

Table 5: Table of top 10 devices with maximum crashes found using STAMP.

Seed File	I	Field Occurance Score	Mean/StdDeviation	Size (KB)	#Unique Bugs	#Total Crashes
1.mp4	367.4	77.64	0.2	162	2	8
2.mp4	234.8	33.2	0.66	296	1	1

Table 4: Field score and occurance score for 2 mp4 files. Lesser score is better (See Section 2.1.2)

3.3.2 SFAT results

As the result shows in Table 4, the 1st file with higher field and occurance scores generally yield an overall better number of unique crashes and total crashes. We can conclude that SFAT's scoring mechanism is effective for finding a good seed file. The additional crashes are due to a location of the flag change corresponding to the size value of an TBPM (beats per minute) which is not present in 2.mp4.

3.3.3 STAMP results

Within the span of 2 weeks, STAMP conducted close to 5 million test cases and uncovered close to 1900 unique crashing inputs in both Android and iOS devices affecting GIF, JPEG, PNG, MP3 and MP4 video files. The speedup obtained (as shown in Table 6) from distributed parallel fuzzing of 4 devices of the same model achieves a better than expected 5.27. This is likely due to less (or no) crashes happening on some devices in parallel. Network latency may also play a part.

Overall, fuzzing speed depends on the file-type fuzzed. Video and audio files are significantly slower as they have to be played back even though the duration of all seed files are 1 second.

#GIF files fuzzed	#Devices	Time Taken
10000	4	55 min
	1	290 min

Table 6: Speedup obtained with distributed fuzzing Times include downloading, patching and fuzzing.

3.3.4 CACE - Variety of bugs

CACE triaged all discovered crashes discovered into 7 different bugs. They are detailed in Table 5. CACE traced the 1786 GIF crashes to a single bug in the LZW compression algorithm located in the Android 2D graphics library. That crash is an invalid read access and is not likely to be exploitable. On the other hand CACE deduced that the 19 PNG crashes are due to a potentially exploitable write to an invalid memory location also in the same Android 2D graphics library. The MP3 crash indicates an invalid address or address of corrupt block passed to `dlfree` to release memory. Further up the stack,it is actually discovered that the real error happened in the utilities library, where Android was actually trying to free a shared `StringBuffer`. This appears to be a use-after-free vulnerability. However, when `libc` is examined with IDA Pro, `r3` points to the address `0xdeadbaad` [25] intentionally to cause a segment violation and forcibly abort the playback. This is a countermeasure to address a possible heap corruption while rendering the file. The crash for MP3 is due to the TBPM flag set, a tag that is not always used in MP3 files; indicating the importance of fuzzing with a high coverage seed file. The single discovered JPEG crash for iOS is a memory leak bug where an extraordinarily large image dimensions are provided in a much smaller JPEG file. All bugs are reported to their respective manufacturers thus the anonymisation of the vulnerability information. We do not yet know if the bugs have been fixed by all affected vendors: Apple Google, OEM and telecom operators. This approach is in synonymous with responsible disclosure best practices.

3.3.5 Storage Utilisation

Table 1 shows the times taken for conducting a 1000 file PNG fuzz job with and without BSDiff.

The process trades storage space for only a minor loss in fuzzing speed as files have to be patched before every fuzzing experiment. A small and good seed file selected by SFAT helps too. On an iOS device, patching a 1000 job packet takes less than a minute. The main disadvantage of using BSDiff patching comes from a lot of CPU time and memory consumed while the patch for a file is produced [23]. This can be easily mitigated when running parallel threads of fuzzing on a high-performance server and running the tests on more instances of mobile devices of the same model.

3.4 Results Discussion

From our experiments, we found that preprocessing fuzzed inputs can be a worthwhile trade-off to make. In Subsection 3.2.2, **spending a few seconds on preprocessing prior to testing reduced the incidence of repeated tests by upto 4 times**. This of course is only a concern when dealing with a large number of test cases as was our case.

Usage of SFAT to maximise RFC coverage has benefits. As explained in Subsection 3.2.1, a file that would not have caused a crash was modified within the constraints of the file format. The resulting file then causes a crash in the target device due to the modified bit. This is just one example among many others and shows that **instead of blind fuzzing, intelligently crafting the inputs beforehand really pays dividends**. On the other hand, automatically downloaded and analysed seed files may not cover 100% of the code coverage as is evident from [14]. Manual insertion of less common fields are still necessary.

FEET is successful in creating fuzz jobs that yield a good number of crashes. It can be augmented by using the Blackbox fuzz scheduling techniques identified in [11] to select jobs based on a smaller epochs and assign weights to determine probability of selection of subsequent jobs after measuring crash ratio obtained from fuzzing one epoch. In this way we could get a crash arrival even faster than by the sole utilization of FEET.

To improve the bug variety discovered, fuzzing operators with a higher entropy such as bit-level operations could provide better results such as with zzuf[26].

The similarity of the number of crashes for multiple devices running Android 4.0.4 devices suggests that the bug is at the Android AOSP level that is independent of device manufacturer.

Usage of SOFT clients for browser renderable formats are still not very scalable to new platforms. For files renderable in the web browser, the mobile client can be made much simpler.

Exponential storage space growth is also mitigated at some expense of fuzzing speed. However, the payoff can be increased with more users joining the fuzzing experiments.

4. RELATED WORK

The concept of fuzzing was originally introduced in 1990 by Miller et al. [27]. The fuzzer's targets were Unix utilities. Since then a lot of research work has been conducted to improve the methodology of fuzzing. However, mobile Operating systems though Unix based do not expose command line utilities to the average user. With the changing IT landscape new data formats will be defined and existing formats will evolve - all of which require an investment of time and energy to adapt generational fuzzing methodology. Therefore, techniques that use probabilistic heuristics such as mutation ratio, belief metrics and mutation distribution such as our approach are some of the first attempts to provide intelligence to blind fuzzing.

Google [28] has the necessary space and resources to build a fuzzing farm where they have full-control of instrumentation. However, independant researchers and smaller labs have no such luxury. Crowdsourced vulnerability discovery on the other hand has limited control over the remote device.

BFF [29] by CERT is an automated system for finding defects in applications that run on the Linux and Mac OS X platforms. It is also integrated with a tool called CERT Triage Tools that classifies crashes by severity. BFF fuzzes applications which run on the same system as the BFF itself. It is one of the mutational fuzzers that fuzzes a single program with a collection of seeds and a set of mutation ratios. It uses a Multi-Armed-Bandit [32] algorithm to select the best seed-ratio pairs during a fuzz campaign. Due to the shared space, it is easier to coordinate fuzzing, amend fuzzing configuration by feedback and make use of system tools like GDB and Crashwrangler to capture back traces. Also, each fuzzed input is not retained. For testing every new application, the fuzzer is generated and testing cycle repeated. This introduces unnecessary fuzz generation time and duplication of malicious files. There is also no co-relation of fuzz inputs tested across applications or devices that distributed fuzzing provides. Although BFF as a framework is efficient, it is not applicable when the target is a mobile device and runs independently outside the vicinities of the fuzzer without volunteer's administrative access.

Automatic Exploit Generation [30] sought to automatically find vulnerabilities in an application and immediately write exploits for them. They have tested the tool on 14 open source projects and discovered 16 exploits. They make use of preconditioned symbolic execution of source and binary code analysis to come up with formula for exploits [30]. This means that they need to have access to the source code. In the mobile domain we know that that is not possible. Source code of Android version in devices is not released as they contain proprietary code, added on by the OEMs. This is even more true on iOS. Even if the source code does become accessible, the large program size poses a limitation to the extent of manual analysis possible. Additionally, with Mobile OS's implementing Address Space Randomizations (ASLR), symbolic execution methodologies are not effective.

The approach described in this paper for selection of good fuzzing configuration is analogous to the work by both Woo et. al. [11] and Householder et. al. [21]. The former studied how to find the greatest number of unique bugs in a fuzz campaign. They particularly developed an analytic framework using a mathematical model of black-box mutational fuzzing, which modeled black-box mutational fuzzing as a WCCP process with unknown weights and used the condition in the No Free Lunch theorem to decide a better online algorithm. The latter described a workflow for black-box fuzz testing and an algorithm for selecting fuzz parameters to maximize the number of unique application errors. They presented an implementation of the algorithm, which was used to find several previously unknown security vulnerabilities.

Robert et. al [11] have devised a general fuzz confguration scheduling problem-model for selection of seed files for fuzzing independent of the fuzzing scheduling algorithm. In our work on fuzzing, fuzz scheduling is mainly based on the knowledge of position modification. The authors Woo et. al [8] identified and tested several belief metrics based on past fuzzing results to select the next best seed/program pairs for fuzzing the following campaign. Like our approach, it uses no information of the target and the file format.

We can augment FEET by adopting CERT, Robert's[11] and Woo's[8] approach so a crash can be expected sooner.

To summarize, fuzz configuration scheduling algorithms and belief metrics can be used in conjunction with the selection of modification positioning to improve the number of unique bugs discovered. In particular, the modified positions can be a parameter to select different seed files or fuzz jobs consisting of a disparate set of modification positions based on previously performed experiments.

None of these related work however, address problems associated with fuzzing in a distributed client-server fashion such as pre-generation of fuzz input and reduction of storage overhead.

5. FUTURE WORK

This fuzzing paradigm works against downloadable content which includes documents and multimedia formats. All of which are vulnerable to today's drive-by attacks. However, system level components also involve network protocols and USB I/O protocols which speak directly to the operating system. Voluntary fuzzing should also expand to these targets as a future work.

MVDP uses byte or block level mutation operators. These operators can be offering overly coarse grained modifications that may be specialised to certain control elements of data formats. Future work can involve the exploration of more mutation operators that operate at the bit level, synonymous to the zzuf [26] fuzzer used by BFF.

We are also working on a specially crafted gateway appliance that can periodically fetch new crash information from STAMP. This information can include modification positions of files that successfully cause an exploitable crash in a particular target device. The modification information can be mapped to the initial/seed file to infer violations of data-format specification predicates. Subsequent incoming data-streams that match the set of failed predicates will be rejected by the gateway appliance before it reaches the end-host. This application is similar to anti-virus apps on devices, but it checks incoming files rather than applications. The application could also be made extensible by providing hooks into which other sources of information feed known attack signatures.

6. CONCLUSIONS

MVDP was designed to overcome the constraints internet-scale voluntary fuzzing. We used FEET to ensure the fuzzed files are highly unique and uniformly distributed. We designed a method to ensure that the seed files used for fuzzing are of high quality and RFC coverage. We also developed FEET to inform us of the best fuzzing configurations. STAMP and SOFT applications are designed to enable fuzz distribution and testing of the mobile device respectively. The CACE tool enabled automatic binning of unique vulnerabilities from crashes obtained from fuzz testing. Analysis of these crashes and visualizing them according to uniqueness, crash occurrence and severity give us a better chance at exploit generation for the sake of mobile security.

7. REFERENCES

[1] A. Imran, Chronic Dev Team Announces "Tool of Mass Exploitation", Install It Now To Help Community Find Exploits For Untethered Jailbreak *redmonpie.com*, November 27, 2011.

[2] J. Drake, Reversing and Auditing Android's Propietary Bits *RECon*, June, 2013.

[3] Michael Sutton, Adam Greene, and Pedram Amini. 2007. Fuzzing: Brute Force Vulnerability Discovery. Addison-Wesley Professional.

[4] Sophos Press Release: Users Weighed Down by Multiple Gadgets and Mobile Devices, New Sophos Survey Reveals March 18 2013, Sophos Ltd.

[5] National Cyber Awareness System - Vulnerability Summary for CVE-2012-0003 `http://web.nvd.nist.gov/view/vuln/detail?vulnId=CVE-2012-0003`

[6] National Cyber Awareness System - Vulnerability Summary for CVE-2013-0976: `http://web.nvd.nist.gov/view/vuln/detail?vulnId=CVE-2013-0976`

[7] National Cyber Awareness System - Vulnerability Summary for CVE-2013-1750 `http://web.nvd.nist.gov/view/vuln/detail?vulnId=CVE-2013-1750`

[8] A.Rebert, S.K.Cha, T.Avgerinos, J.Foote, D.Warren, G.Grieco, D.Brumley. Optimising Seed Selection for fuzzing In Proc. 23rd USENIX Security Symposium, 2014.

[9] Graphics Interchange Format, Version 89a, W3C; 31 July 1990.

[10] H.C.Kim, Y.H.Choi, D.H.Lee. Efficient file fuzz testing using automated analysis of binary file format. *Journal of Systems Architecture-Embedded Systems Design*, vol. 57, no. 3, pages 259-268, 2011.

[11] Maverick Woo, Sang Kil Cha, Samantha Gottlieb, and David Brumley. 2013. Scheduling black-box mutational fuzzing. In Proceedings of the 2013 ACM SIGSAC conference on Computer & communications security (CCS '13). ACM, New York, NY, USA, 511-522.

[12] Open-source software for volunteer computing and grid computing. https://boinc.berkeley.edu/

[13] SETI@home http://setiathome.ssl.berkeley.edu/

[14] C. Miller. How smart is intelligent fuzzing or - How stupid is dumb fuzzing? Independent Security Evaluators, August 3, 2007.

[15] Google Custom Search Engine. https://www.google.com/cse/

[16] Bing Search API. http://datamarket.azure.com/dataset/bing/search

[17] Hachoir Project. https://pypi.python.org/pypi/hachoir-core

[18] Information technology – Computer graphics and image processing – Portable Network Graphics (PNG): Functional specification. ISO/IEC 15948:2003 (E) W3C Recommendation 10 November 2003.

[19] Skia 2D graphics library - https://code.google.com/p/skia/

[20] Apple iOS `ImageIO` - `https://developer.apple.com/library/ios/documentation/GraphicsImaging/Conceptual/ImageIOGuide`

[21] A. D. Householder and J. M. Foote. Probability-Based Parameter Selection for Black-Box Fuzz Testing. Technical Report August, CERT, 2012

[22] !exploitable http://msecdbg.codeplex.com/

[23] Binary Diff Utility FreeBSD Man Pages

[24] Mac Developer Library: Apple Technical Note TN233, Accessing CrashWrangler to analyze crashes for security implications, March 2014

[25] (SIGSEGV), fault addr deadbaad https://groups.google.com/forum/#!topic/android-ndk/jQg6DM6-D6o

[26] C. Labs. zzuf: multi-purpose fuzzer. http://caca.zoy.org/wiki/zzuf.

[27] B. P. Miller, L. Fredriksen, and B. So. An Empirical Study of the Reliability of UNIX Utilities. *Communications of the ACM*, 33(12):32(44), 1990.

[28] Chris Evans, Matt Moore and Tavis Ormandy, Google Security Team: Fuzzing at scale http://googleonlinesecurity.blogspot.sg/2011/08/fuzzing-at-scale.html Friday, August 12, 2011

[29] Basic Fuzzing Framework. http://www.cert.org/vulnerability-analysis/tools/bff.cfm

[30] Thanassis Avgerinos, Sang Kil Cha, Alexandre Rebert, Edward J. Schwartz, Maverick Woo, and David Brumley. 2014. Automatic exploit generation. Commun. ACM 57, 2 (February 2014), 74-84.

[31] Hex-Rays IDA. https://www.hex-rays.com/products/ida/

[32] D. A. Berry and B. Fristedt. Bandit Problems:Sequential Allocation of Experiments. *Chapman and Hall*, 1985.

XiOS: Extended Application Sandboxing on iOS

Mihai Bucicoiu[1], Lucas Davi[2], Razvan Deaconescu[1], Ahmad-Reza Sadeghi[2]

[1]University "POLITEHNICA" of Bucharest, Romania
{mihai.bucicoiu,razvan.deaconescu}@cs.pub.ro

[2]Technische Universität Darmstadt
Intel Collaborative Research Institute for Secure Computing, Darmstadt, Germany
{lucas.davi,ahmad.sadeghi}@trust.cased.de

ABSTRACT

Until very recently it was widely believed that iOS malware is effectively blocked by Apple's vetting process and application sandboxing. However, the newly presented severe malicious app attacks (e.g., Jekyll) succeeded to undermine these protection measures and steal private data, post Twitter messages, send SMS, and make phone calls. Currently, no effective defenses against these attacks are known for iOS.

The main goal of this paper is to systematically analyze the recent attacks against iOS sandboxing and provide a practical security framework for iOS app hardening which is fully independent of the Apple's vetting process and particularly benefits enterprises to protect employees' iOS devices. The contribution of this paper is twofold: First, we show a new and generalized attack that significantly reduces the complexity of the recent attacks against iOS sandboxing. Second, we present the design and implementation of a novel and efficient iOS app hardening service, *XiOS*, that enables fine-grained application sandboxing, and mitigates the existing as well as our new attacks. In contrast to previous work in this domain (on iOS security), our approach does *not* require to *jailbreak* the device. We demonstrate the efficiency and effectiveness of *XiOS* by conducting several benchmarks as well as fine-grained policy enforcement on real-world iOS applications.

Categories and Subject Descriptors

D.4.6 [**Software**]: Operating Systems—*Security and Protection*

Keywords

binary instrumentation; sandboxing; mobile security; iOS

1. INTRODUCTION

iOS is after Android the most popular mobile operating system worldwide. It is deployed on well-known Apple devices such as iPhone, iPad, or iPod Touch, used by millions of users everyday. Apple maintains an app store, first introduced in July 2008, that hosts in Sep. 2014 more than 1,300,000 applications (apps) [28].

On the other hand, the popularity, the high number of features and apps, as well as the large amount of sensitive and private information that are available on iOS devices make them attractive targets for attackers. To address the security and privacy concerns, iOS enforces two main security principles: code signing and application sandboxing. The former ensures that only Apple-approved software can be executed on an iOS device while the latter technique guarantees that an app only performs operations within the boundaries of a pre-defined sandbox, and can neither disrupt nor access other applications. In particular, iOS distinguishes between *public* and *private* frameworks in its sandboxing model. Public frameworks comprise shared system libraries and APIs that can be accessed by *every* third-party app. For instance the AddressBook framework is a well-known available public framework that a developer is allowed to use in an iOS application [6]. In contrast, private frameworks and APIs should only be accessed by system applications. Prominent examples for private APIs are sending SMS messages or setting up a call.

As another line of defense, Apple also conducts application review/vetting for all apps that are to be published on the App Store, and rejects any application that attempts to invoke a private API. The folklore belief is that the vetting process is sufficient to effectively block malware from entering the App Store [17, 32].

However, recent research results shed new light on the security of iOS by demonstrating how to bypass the vetting process and iOS application sandboxing [19, 35]. The main idea of these attacks is to dynamically load private frameworks and invoke private APIs to induce malicious behavior without the user's consent. The attacks range from sending SMSs or emails to attacker specified addresses, posting Twitter tweets, abusing camera and audio, setting up phone calls, and stealing the device ID.

Some of these attacks use return-oriented programming [30] to hide and obfuscate the malicious functionality [35]. Such techniques impede the detection of malicious code and manifest the limits of any *off-line* application vetting approach.

Preventing these attacks is highly challenging due to the current system design of iOS. Prohibiting applications to load private frameworks is not a solution since public frameworks are not self-contained and need to interact with private frameworks to complete their tasks. Moreover, some public frameworks also contain private (hidden) API func-

ASIA CCS '15, April 14 - 17, 2015, Singapore, Singapore

http://dx.doi.org/10.1145/2714576.2714629.

tions, e.g., sending a Twitter message in background is a private API call inside a public framework [19].

Moreover, the recently proposed security enhancements for iOS (see Section 7) suffer from various deficiencies: these are either static and cannot detect attacks that trigger malicious behavior (only) at runtime [16], or require a jailbreak and induce performance overhead [15, 37].

Our goal in this paper is to provide a framework for app hardening that enables fine-grained app sandboxing on iOS and tackles the shortcomings of existing solutions, i.e., defeating the recent attacks against iOS sandboxing [19, 35]. In particular, we make the following contributions:

New malicious app attacks. We investigate previous attacks against iOS application sandboxing and significantly reduce their complexity. We show a new attack that requires no specific use of a public framework to access a private API, but rather exploits the *default* memory layout used in *all* iOS applications to invoke any private API of the adversary's choice. This allows us to construct general attack vectors on iOS application sandboxing.

Defense tool. We present the design and implementation of a novel mitigation service and tool, termed *XiOS*, for fine-grained application sandboxing on iOS tackling these attacks at API and function-level. In contrast to previous work in this domain [15, 37], our solution performs efficiently without requiring a *jailbreak* of the underlying device. We developed a new static binary rewriter for iOS that implants a reference monitor into the application's code, and protects, under reasonable assumptions, the reference monitor from the (potentially malicious) application without requiring the *source code* of the application. Our defense mechanism instruments all API calls and provides the following features: (i) API address hiding, and (ii) optional policy checks based on user, developer or administrators (e.g., enterprises) defined policies for public API calls.

Evaluation. We show the effectiveness and efficiency of our approach by applying it to several existing real-world iOS applications including Gensystek, WhatsApp, System Monitor, Music Notes and Frotz. Our evaluation shows that no overhead is added in terms of user-experience when *XiOS* is used to protect the application. We also show fine-grained policy enforcement for WhatsApp, allowing filtering of contacts information (see Section 6.4).

Advantages of our solution. Our defense technique does neither require a *jailbreak* nor the application's *source code*. Since our defense is implemented as a static binary rewriter, it can be applied just before an application is submitted to the App Store. On the one hand, it provides a useful tool for benign developers to harden their app from being compromised by a remote exploit that invokes private APIs. On the other hand, it can also be used by Apple to improve the vetting process by hardening potentially malicious apps with *XiOS*. In other words, *XiOS* (1) constrains malicious apps in their actions, and (2) hardens benign apps.

Compliance and independency. Our solution adheres to the existing design of private and public frameworks in iOS. It allows for flexible policy enforcement giving developers the possibility to define fine-grained access control policies for each app according to their own requirements. Finally, our solution is not dependent on application vetting, and can be deployed by enterprises to protect employees' devices, and still allowing the employees to use popular apps such as WhatsApp (see Section 4.5, and 6.3).

2. BACKGROUND

In this section, we recall the iOS security architecture and elaborate on related attacks against app sandboxing.

2.1 iOS Security

The main security mechanisms used on iOS are (1) code signing, (2) application vetting, (3) file system and data encryption, (4) memory randomization (ASLR) along with non-executable memory, and (5) application sandboxing.

Code signing ensures that only Apple-signed software can be executed on an iOS device. To bypass this restriction, users can jailbreak (root) their devices which allow them to arbitrarily install non-approved Apple software. Apple approves signed applications after a vetting process. Although the implementation details of application vetting are not public, Apple states that it *reviews all apps to ensure they are reliable, perform as expected, and are free of offensive material* [4]. Apple also deploys an AES-256 hardware crypto engine to encrypt the file system of an iOS device.

Address space layout randomization (ASLR) randomizes the start addresses of data and code segments. This makes runtime attacks like return-oriented programming that rely on fixed code addresses more cumbersome. Typically, ASLR is combined with the non-executable memory security model, which enforces that a memory page cannot be writable and executable at the same time [25]. This technique prevents runtime attacks that attempt to inject malicious code into an application's address space and execute it. iOS goes even one step further, and enforces code signing on memory pages at runtime: it prohibits any third-party app from dynamically generating code or changing existing (mapped) code.

An abstract view of the security architecture to realize *application sandboxing* on iOS is shown in Figure 1. iOS deploys sandboxing to isolate applications from each other, and to control access of applications to the operating system. In particular, we distinguish components on three software layers: (1) the kernel layer which provides basic system services (file system and network) and a kernel module to realize application sandboxing, (2) the Objective-C framework layer and a privacy setting service, and (3) the application layer where third-party and built-in apps are executing.

The main component to enforce application sandboxing resides in the iOS kernel, namely a TrustedBSD mandatory access control (MAC) module. This kernel module enforces sandboxing at the level of system calls and directory paths. Further, sandboxing is driven by sandboxing profiles which are pre-defined by Apple. The profiles consist of access control lists (ACLs) that either deny or grant access to certain system calls and file paths.

Apple defines a single sandboxing profile for third-party apps. Hence, all apps execute with the same privilege level. In particular, this profile prohibits App A to access code or data from other applications like App B (see Figure 1).

Apart from the TrustedBSD kernel module, there are several restrictions imposed by Apple indirectly related to application sandboxing. As mentioned before Apple distinguishes between public and private frameworks[1]. Private frameworks are reserved for iOS built-in and system applications. Although third-party applications are only allowed to access public APIs of a public framework, there is no fun-

[1]The list of all available frameworks can be downloaded from `http://theiphonewiki.com/wiki/System/Library/Frameworks`

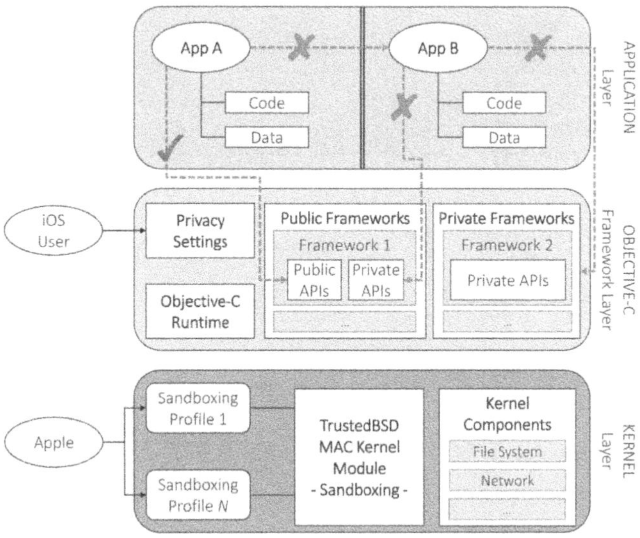

Figure 1: Basic iOS architecture to enforce application sandboxing

damental operating system mechanism that prevents the use of private APIs. Instead, Apple relies on the application vetting process to discover such unauthorized access requests.

Finally, since iOS version 6, iOS allows users to specify privacy settings on a per-app basis. Typically, iOS apps have by default access to private information such as contacts, device IDs, keyboard cache, or location. In order to restrict the access to this information, iOS users can arbitrarily configure privacy settings. In fact, this allows users to specify restrictions on some selected privacy-related *public* APIs. However, there is no general for all non-privacy related public APIs as well as private APIs.

2.2 Related Attacks on iOS Sandboxing

Recent attacks deploy a malicious third-party application that dynamically loads private frameworks and invokes private APIs without being detected by Apple's vetting process [35, 19]. In order to understand these attacks, we need to take a deeper look at how legitimate calls to private APIs in system apps are handled.

Typically, a call to a private API is internally handled as an external function call to a shared library. For this, a program requires that the library encapsulating that function is loaded into the application's address space. In addition, the runtime address of the desired function needs to be populated. In practice, this is achieved by dynamic loading [24]. In iOS, dynamic loading is provided by a dedicated library called `libdl.dylib`. We refer to this library as the dynamic loader. Specifically, the dynamic loader provides two fundamental methods: (1) *load-library* via the function `dlopen`, and (2) *load-address* using the `dlsym` function that determines the runtime address of a function residing in a library that has been already loaded. If an executable module (i.e., an application or a shared library) attempts to invoke a private API, then the linker will add the corresponding placeholders into the data section of the executable module. These placeholders will be automatically initialized with the correct addresses of *load-library* and *load-address* at load-time. Once the executable module starts executing, it can

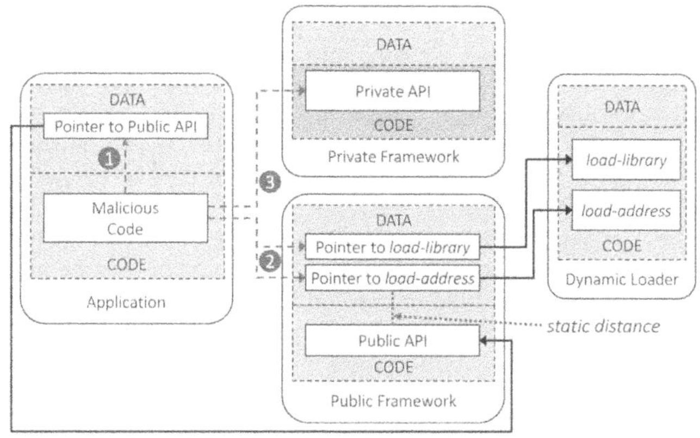

Figure 2: Dynamically invoking private APIs

invoke *load-library* to dynamically open a private framework, and subsequently issue *load-address* to retrieve the address of a private API and call it.

However, Apple prohibits any third-party application from using *load-library* and *load-address*, thereby preventing attempts to invoke private APIs. In the vetting process, one can simply check whether the application contains placeholders for these functions in the data section. On the other hand, public frameworks (developed by Apple) are allowed to use these functions. This leads to a confused deputy problem [20]: since third-party applications are allowed to load public frameworks, they can potentially misuse them to call a private API.

Figure 2 shows the general workflow of these attacks in detail. The malicious application legitimately links to a public framework (that uses *load-library* and *load-address*) and invokes a public API for benign reasons. Hence, the dynamic iOS loading process will populate the address of the public API into the data section of the malicious application. This allows the adversary to read out the address of the public API at runtime by de-referencing the designated placeholder in the data section (step 1). Effectively, this reveals the runtime location of the public API in memory. Based on this runtime address the adversary can determine the location of the two placeholders where the runtime addresses of *load-library* and *load-address* are stored (step 2). This is possible, because the relative offset (i.e., distance) between the start of the public API function and the two placeholders is constant, and can be pre-computed prior to execution. Once the adversary knows the address of *load-library* and *load-address*, he can call these functions to dynamically load a private framework of his choice and execute a private API (step 3).

In summary, existing attacks against iOS application sandboxing require (i) the availability of a public framework that necessarily uses dynamic loader functions *load-library* and *load-address*, and (ii) two address de-reference operations: one for the public API and another one for the address of either *load-library* or *load-address*.

3. DEVELOPING IMPROVED ATTACKS

Recent attacks require a public framework that either invokes *load- library* or *load-address* (as described in Section 2.2). Our investigation showed that out of 319 available public frameworks only 25 use *load-library* and 36 *load-*

address. Hence, one theoretical approach to defend against this attack is to rewrite some of the public frameworks and disable dynamic loading for them. However, by systematically analyzing and reverse-engineering the lazy binding mechanism used in iOS, we were able to launch the same attacks without requiring the application to link to *any* of the public frameworks. This not only significantly reduces the complexity of the attacks but also allows more general attacks, because the mechanisms we exploit in our attacks are by default enabled in *every* iOS application.

Specifically, we developed a simple iOS application using the standard settings in Xcode (which is the main IDE for iOS app development). By default, our application deploys lazy binding mechanisms. We traced back at assembler and binary-level[2] how lazy binding is performed in iOS, and were able to recognize that the lazy binding implementation is vulnerable to even simpler attacks.

In general, lazy binding dynamically (and transparently to the application) resolves the runtime address of a symbol (e.g., an external function or variable) the first time it is used [2]. In contrast, non-lazy binding resolves all the addresses of symbols once at application load-time. To support lazy binding, iOS maintains two data sections in iOS applications, one for non-lazy symbols and one for lazy symbols. One important symbol that is *always* defined in the section for non-lazy symbols is the external function **`dyld_stub_binder`**. This particular function realizes lazy binding: it resolves the runtime address of an external function that is defined in the lazy symbol section when it is accessed for the first time. Remarkably, this function is part of the dynamic loader library, the same library that contains *load-library* and *load-address*. Hence, an adversary can directly infer the address of the dynamic loader functions by de-referencing the address of **`dyld_stub_binder`** from the data section of the malicious application. Our improved attack completely removes the operations and attack requirements for Step 2 in Figure 2.

Note that the de-referencing of **`dyld_stub_binder`** makes no use of the string **`"dyld_stub_binder"`**, making the attack vector stealthy to static analysis methods. Its location offset inside the executable is statically precomputed using binary analysis. A potential attack would use the computed offset to retrieve the address of **`dyld_stub_binder`** from its location and then compute the address of *load-library* or *load-address*. This can be achieved offline due to the fact that all three functions are stored within the same library.

In contrast to previous work on bypassing iOS sandboxing [19, 35], our new attack does not require any specific public frameworks to be loaded. We also reduce the necessary attack steps: we only require a single address read from the data section of the application. Our attack has important implications: it can be applied to any iOS application since lazy binding is currently used for all iOS applications. Hence, given a benign application that contains a vulnerability, we can arbitrarily invoke private APIs using return-oriented programming.

In order to show the effectiveness of our new attack, we have developed an application for iOS 7 that dynamically invokes private APIs at runtime. We added to the application malicious code that can be used at runtime to derive the address of the private *createScreenIOSurface* API from the *UIWindow* class. Similar to previous attacks, our attack is triggered remotely, and continuously takes snapshots and sends them to a remote server controlled by us. We obfuscated and submitted our application to the App Store, and successfully passed the vetting process. Hence, our malicious app can still invoke private APIs in a stealthy manner without being detected by the vetting process using less dereferencing actions than existing attacks. The application was installed only on our testing device and then removed from the App Store. Moreover, we also stopped the server which remotely triggered the attack.

[2] using the Xcode debugger and IDAPro as disassembler

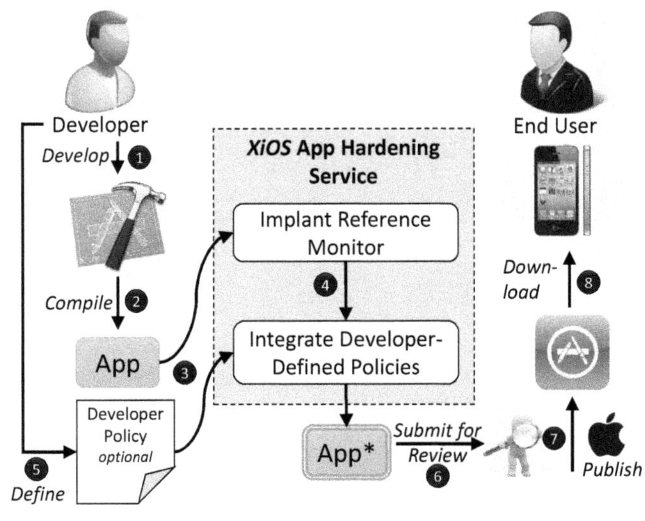

Figure 3: General approach and workflow of *XiOS*

4. OUR DEFENSE SERVICE *XiOS*

Mitigation of attacks against iOS sandboxing and, in particular our new attacks, is a challenging task due to several reasons: First, the attacks are based on exploiting lazy binding which is enabled by default on iOS due to performance reasons and cannot be simply disabled. Second, public frameworks are tightly coupled to private frameworks. Removing this interdependency would induce heavy design changes. Third, iOS is closed-source preventing direct extensions of the operating system with a reference monitor for private APIs.

In this section, we introduce the requirements on *XiOS* describe its workflow and system model, its components, and the corresponding security aspects. Finally, we discuss real-world deployment scenarios for *XiOS*.

4.1 Requirements and Assumptions

Given the above mentioned challenges, a defense tool needs to meet the following functional and security requirements:

R1: Preserve the benefits and efficiency features. In particular, mechanisms such as lazy binding should further be in place.

R2: Require no changes to the operating system and current software stack architecture of iOS. In particular, we need to ensure that private APIs are still accessible from public frameworks.

R3: Require no application's source code. Typically, the source code of iOS applications is not available, even

Apple's App Store only retrieves an application as a binary bundle.

R4: Integrate seamlessly into the existing application development and distribution process of iOS. In particular no jailbreak of the user's device is needed.

S1: Prevent (previous) attacks on iOS sandboxing [19, 35], and our novel attack (Section 3).

S2: The malicious application cannot bypass or disable our reference monitor (see Section 4.4).

We build our defense on the following assumptions:

A1: We assume that the target system enforces the principle of non-executable memory. Otherwise, an adversary could revert our security checks and circumvent our defense. As mentioned in Section 2.1, iOS deploys a very strict version of non-executable memory.

A2: Since our defense operates at application-level (due to R2), we obviously assume the underlying operating system kernel to be benign and not compromised.

A3: An adversary is not able to statically pre-compute the address of a private API or a critical function such as *load-library* and *load-address*. This is ensured by iOS since it applies ASLR to shared libraries.

4.2 System Model

As mentioned above (S1), the main goal of our solution is to prohibit the invocation of any private API from a third-party app to prevent attacks against app sandboxing. At the same time, we need to ensure that public frameworks can still access private APIs. Moreover, we generalize our design to enable fine-grained access control rules on public APIs. Our new hardening service *XiOS* achieves both (i) preventing invocations of private APIs, and (ii) enforcing developer-defined fine-grained access control rules on public APIs.

The workflow of *XiOS* is depicted in Figure 3. Our hardening service seamlessly integrates into Apple's application development process: after the developer has finished programming the app and compiling it (Step 1 and 2), the application is submitted to our hardening service via a web browser (Step 3). Next, the hardening process implants the *XiOS* reference monitor and some additional startup code into the application. The reference monitor and the startup code will hide traces of external API addresses including the address of `dyld_stub_binder`. Moreover, if the developer appended a policy for public APIs, we also embed these policies into the application (Step 4). To accomplish these tasks, *XiOS* makes use of binary instrumentation techniques (R3). Finally, the app is submitted to the App Store and can be later installed on users' devices (Step 6 to 8).

Our service always implants the reference monitor to prevent invocation of private APIs through the dynamic loader. In addition, it allows the developer to *optionally* append a custom policy for public APIs (Step 5). For instance, one could define a policy that restricts a messenger app (e.g., WhatsApp) to only upload a subset of the address book to the app server (due to privacy reasons). For this, we support different policy enforcement options: `allow`, `deny`, `log` or `modify`. In particular, the `modify` option allows the

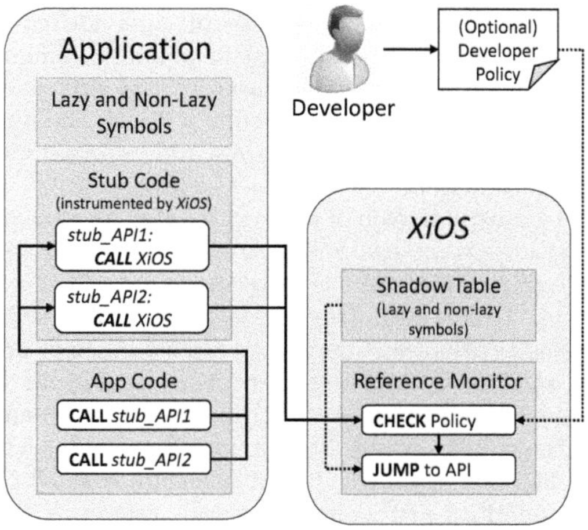

Figure 4: Instrumented *XiOS* App

replacement of the arguments passed to an external function and public API return values. Defining such policies is tightly coupled to the application purpose and its target users. Enterprises can integrate *XiOS* within their mobile device management (MDM) systems and harden all applications before they are deployed on employees' (personal) devices. Hence, enforcement of privacy-related policies can protect a company from being legally held responsible for information leakage [33].

It is also possible that an end-user submits an existing app to our service along with policies she desires to be enforced on that app. However, post-changes on existing apps would change the hash value of the application. This would imply re-submission to Apple's App Store to retrieve an updated Apple certification. Hence, the main purpose of *XiOS* is app hardening for both vulnerable benign and potentially malicious apps before Apple signs and uploads the app on the App Store.

4.3 Architecture

The high-level idea of *XiOS* app instrumentation is depicted in Figure 4. *XiOS* is directly implanted into the original iOS application (R2 and R4) and mainly contains a reference monitor that mediates all access requests of an application to an external library. The idea is here to completely hide public API calls and the `dyld_stub_binder` address from the app and redirect these requests to the reference monitor which is the only component that knows and can retrieve the runtime addresses of external functions.

There are three binary sections which are of particular interest: (1) the main app code section, (2) the so-called symbol stub code section, and (3) a data section where the lazy and non-lazy symbol pointers are stored. These sections correspond to the following iOS Mach-O binary sections: `__text` for the main app code, `__symbol_stub` for the symbol code section, `__la_symbol_table` and `__nl_symbol_table` for the lazy and non-lazy symbol data section.

Typically, when an iOS application attempts to invoke an external library function (i.e., a public API), the compiler will insert a dedicated stub for the desired function in the code stub section. Hence, the originating call to that external function effectively redirects the control-flow to the stub code section, e.g., a call to *stub_API1* or *stub_API2* in Figure 4. The stub code reads out the runtime address of the external function in either the lazy or non-lazy symbol data section. When the runtime address of the external function is not yet known, the stub code will ask the dynamic loader to resolve the runtime address and eventually invoke the external function.

To prevent exploitation of the lazy binding process and the leakage of important runtime addresses, we instrument the stub code section and remove its connection to the lazy symbol section. To this end, *XiOS* creates a duplicate of the lazy and non-lazy symbol section in a dedicated memory area denoted as *shadow table*. It also overwrites the original section with zeroes. In addition, we instrument each stub entry so that it always invokes our *XiOS* reference monitor when an external function is called. Thus, we ensure that all calls to external functions are redirected to our reference monitor, and simultaneously guarantee that a malicious application cannot read runtime addresses from the lazy and non-lazy symbol sections to launch attacks against app sandboxing.

Upon invocation, the reference monitor of *XiOS* performs as follows: first, it determines which external function the application attempts to execute. This is achieved by looking up the corresponding entry in the duplicate of the lazy and non-lazy symbol section. Next, it performs a policy check. For the invocation of public APIs, the (optional) developer-defined policies are consulted. The invocation of private APIs is prevented by the design of our reference monitor as it hides the crucial runtime addresses of public APIs and dynamic loader functions. However, the challenge is to still preserve the performance benefits of lazy binding. We tackle this as follows: when an external function is called for the first time, our reference monitor asks the dynamic loader to resolve the runtime address, and stores its value for later invocations in the shadow table.

4.4 Security Considerations

As mentioned in Section 4.1, we need to ensure the integrity of *XiOS* and prevent the untrusted application from reading the shadow table (S1 and S2). This is challenging as *XiOS* resides in the application's address space.

As explained above, the shadow table contains runtime addresses of public APIs and the dynamic loader functions. If an adversary can access these addresses then the attacks described in Section 2.2 and 3 can be launched. Ideally, the *XiOS* reference monitor should be executed in a separate process. However, due to the closed iOS, we can only implant it into the application itself to avoid a jailbreak (R4).

To only allow the reference monitor to access the shadow table, we need to enforce software fault isolation (SFI) [34], i.e., basically dividing an application in trusted and untrusted code parts. Since realizing SFI is cumbersome [40], we opted for a pragmatic SFI solution for our proof-of-concept implementation: Whenever the (untrusted) main application code is executing, *XiOS* marks all memory pages allocated for the shadow table as non-readable. In contrast, when the control is transferred to the reference monitor, *XiOS* changes the access rights of the pages back to readable. We demonstrate in Section 6 that modifying the access rights of the memory pages performs efficiently in *XiOS*. Although we fully support multithreading, an adversary can potentially trigger a policy validation, and force the iOS scheduler to switch to another thread while the shadow table is readable. We have not addressed this issue in our current proof-of-concept implementation, but currently we are working on ensuring that no other program thread is allowed to execute while the shadow table is set to readable.

As *XiOS* invokes memory management functions to prevent the main application from accessing the shadow table, we need to prevent the main application to exploit system calls to get access to the shadow table. Although it might seem that applications become limited by not allowing them to directly invoke system calls, this is not the case for iOS. Note that applications can still indirectly use system calls through external API functions that wrap their functionality and are mediated by our reference monitor. We prohibit all applications to directly invoke system calls using an in-house developed script that identifies invocations of system calls. Moreover, we have analyzed a large number of popular iOS applications (e.g., Facebook, Google Maps, YouTube, Angry Birds, Skype) and noticed that none uses directly system calls, hence, *XiOS* can be applied to them.

We also need to ensure that at application-start *XiOS* takes over the control first. Otherwise, an application could access the non-lazy symbol section to retrieve critical runtime addresses. Hence, we dispatch the entry point of an application such that *XiOS* is always executed first to setup the shadow table and zeroing out the original lazy and non-lazy symbol sections.

XiOS prevents attacks that attempt to jump over policy validation code. Since we instrument all stubs (see Figure 4), we ensure that policy validation always starts from its original entry point. Note that stub code cannot be modified by an adversary as the code is mapped as non-writable. A last chance for the adversary is to exploit an indirect jump, call or return to redirect the control-flow to the place after the policy check. These attacks can be prevented by control-flow integrity (CFI) for iOS [15], or by computing a secret value at the beginning of the policy check and checking the secret value at return of *XiOS* (see for instance checkpoint handling in [27]). We leave this as future work to further extend and improve *XiOS*.

4.5 XiOS Deployment

XiOS can be mainly deployed as an off-line remote hardening service in two scenarios. Primarily, it can be deployed by Apple or an enterprise before a new app is uploaded to the application store. This provides protection against malicious apps such as the one described in [19, 35])3. Alternatively, it can be deployed by (benign) developers that aim at hardening their apps from being remotely exploited and enforcing access control rules on public APIs.

For the former scenario, an enterprise can integrate *XiOS* into its Mobile Device Management infrastructure. Apple actively supports enterprise-specific app stores where employees can run applications that only need to be signed by the developer and the enterprise [5]. In this case, the applications are instrumented by *XiOS*, signed by the enterprise's administration, and the employee can download and install the hardened application over a custom enterprise application store.

The latter scenario allows benign developers to deploy *XiOS* to enforce fine-grained access control rules on public APIs. This provides better security than directly integrating access control rules into an app's source code, because an adversary could bypass these checks by jumping over the policy validation instructions. We prevent such attacks by enforcing every external function call to be dispatched over our instrumented code stubs. We are also currently working on an *XiOS* extension where such policies can be downloaded from and defined on a remote server.

5. IMPLEMENTATION

In this section we detail on our current implementation of *XiOS*. Considering that our hardening process works directly on the application's binary executable, and that the Mach-O file format is used by *all* iOS applications regardless of the operating system version, our implementation is applicable to any existing iOS app.

The first step of the hardening process is to search for direct invocations of system calls. To do so, we use binary disassembly tools (specifically IDAPro) to identify the assembler instruction used for system calls. On ARM, one can directly invoke a system call by using the `svc` (supervisor call) instruction[3]. In contrast to the x86 architecture, ARM instructions are aligned and any unaligned memory access generates a fault exception. Hence, an adversary must explicitly insert the `svc` instruction. We search for these instructions and raise an alarm if an app is using such an instruction.

In the remainder of this section we describe how calls to external functions are dispatched by *XiOS* and present the implementation of our reference monitor.

5.1 Dispatching External Function Calls

As already mentioned in Section 4.3, we instrument the stub code of an application to redirect execution to our reference monitor. Originally, each entry i in the stub code section consists of a load instruction that loads the address placed at entry i in the lazy symbol section into the program counter `pc`. Effectively, this instruction realizes an indirect jump where the target address is taken from memory (i.e., from the lazy symbol section). Recall that this requires the dynamic loader to relocate the runtime addresses of external functions in the lazy symbol section section either at load-time or on-demand at runtime, c.f. Section 2.

In our implementation, we replace the `pc`-load instruction in the stub code with a branch instruction that targets our reference monitor. Since both instructions have the same size no realignment of the binary is required. Specifically, we overwrite the original `ldr` (load register) instruction with a `b` (branch) as follows:

```
ldr pc,[lazy_sym_i] -> b reference_monitor
```

5.2 Reference Monitor

The reference monitor achieves two important goals: (1) replaces the iOS dynamic loader and offers a mechanism for dynamically searching the addresses of external functions while protecting them from being leaked to the main application, and (2) enforce developer-based policies.

The pseudo code of the reference monitor is shown in Algorithm 1. First, we determine the name and parameters of the hooked functions (lines 1-2). Second, based on the enforcement rules defined in the hardening process, we determine if the call to the external function is allowed or blocked (line 3). If the access to the external function is not granted, the program exits and, thus, blocks any information leakage. Third, if invocation is allowed and after marking the shadow table as readable and writable (line 5), the reference monitor verifies if a previous call to the same function has been made (line 6). If so, the address of the function can be retrieved from the shadow table (line 7) and the control-flow can be transferred to the external function (line 12). In case the function is called for the first time, we make use of the standard iOS dynamic loader to resolve the runtime address of the external function (line 9) and store it into the shadow table for future invocations (line 10). Finally, the reference monitor marks the shadow table as non-readable and non-writable (line 13).

Algorithm 1 Reference monitor - pseudo-code

```
1: params[] = read_params_from_registers();
2: fnct_name = decode_function_name();
3: execution = apply_pre_policies(fnct_name, params[]);
4: if (execution is granted) then
5:   unprotect(shadow_symbol_table);
6:   if shadow_symbol_table[fnct_name] not 0 then
7:     address = shadow_symbol_table[fnct_name];
8:   else
9:     address = bind(fnct_name);
10:    shadow_symbol_table[fnct_name] = address
11:  end if
12:  protect(shadow_symbol_table)
13:  execute_function_at(address);
14:  apply_post_policies(fnct_name, params[]);
15: end if
```

One technical challenge that our reference monitor needs to tackle concerns the resolving of a function's name at runtime. This is required to accurately enforce policies at function-level. To address this challenge, we exploit the fact how functions are called in ARM-compiled binaries. In general, a function can be called by means of a `bl` (branch with link) or a `blx` (branch with link and exchange) instruction. Both instructions have in common that they store the return address (which is simply the address following the `bl` or `blx` instruction) into ARM's dedicated link register `lr`. Hence, when an application attempts to invoke an external function, it actually uses a `blx` instruction targeting the corresponding entry i in the code stub section:

```
1. blx code_stub_i
```

Since we instrumented the code stub section (i.e., by replacing `pc`-loads with branch instructions to our reference monitor), the reference monitor will be invoked next:

```
2. b reference_monitor
```

Next, we let our reference monitor read the value of `lr` as it contains the return address. This allows us to dynamically calculate the address from where our reference monitor has been invoked. As we now know from where inside the main application the reference monitor has been called, we can dynamically compute the target address of `blx code_stub_i`. Specifically, we decode the `blx` instruction on-the-fly to determine the targeted entry i in the code stub section. Once we know i, we are able to resolve the function name from a pre-computed table stored within the reference monitor:

```
3. decode_function_name(i)
```

This table is generated during static analysis of the binary and contains a list with the names of all external functions used by the iOS application. In addition, the equivalent dynamic loader code to resolve a function's name is integrated

[3]Previously denoted as `swi` (software interrupt) instruction.

into our reference monitor. We have implemented the reference monitor using ARM assembly instructions.

5.3 Shadow Table

Recall that within a normal executable the addresses of lazy-resolved functions are stored in the lazy symbol section. Our approach for protecting lazy-resolved functions' addresses is based on the following three steps: (1) the entries from the lazy symbol section are stored into the shadow table, (2) we zeroise the entries in the lazy symbol section, and (3) we protect the shadow table from being accessed outside the reference monitor. Note that we need to maintain a separate table due to limitations of existing memory management capabilities, i.e., memory operations such as changing access rights can only be done at page level. Hence, we cannot apply such actions directly to sections from the data segment of an iOS application without affecting adjacent data.

The entries in the non-lazy symbol section are populated by the dynamic loader before the program starts executing. In order to prevent attackers from reading these values at the beginning of program execution, we add a small startup code that we refer to as *pre-main* which setups the reference monitor and the shadow table, and zeroise the original lazy and non-lazy symbol section. To this end, we overwrite the `LC_MAIN` command in the iOS Mach-O header with the start address of *pre-main*. Hence, *pre-main* is the code which is executed first when an application is launched. For protecting the memory region of our shadow table, we invoke the well-known *mprotect()* system call, which allows us to mark the shadow table as readable when the reference monitor is executed, and as non-readable when program control is passed back to the application.

An adversary could try bypassing the *mprotect*-based shadow table protection mechanism through accessible memory management functions. However, *XiOS* checks the arguments (if they target the shadow table) and disallows these call to prevent leakage of the shadow table.

Note that our binary rewriting does not impact the main code section of the application. Thus our mechanism has no impact on the internal flow and performance of the application, and avoids error-prone binary rewriting.

5.4 Developer-Defined Policies

XiOS allows the creation and integration of developer-defined policies. While the first one is highly dependent on the application that the policies are made for, for the second one we have implemented an easy way to add policies. Specifically, the developer provides *XiOS* with two predefined functions, i.e., *pre_external_call* and *post_external_call*, that are executed before and after each external function call. These functions need to be implemented in C and self-contained, i.e., cannot use other external functions such as *memcpy* as this would end up intercepted by *XiOS* and create a loop. In order to facilitate the job of the developer we can provide her with a set of pre-defined functions, e.g., she can use *xios_memcpy* instead of *memcpy*.

Within the *pre_external_call* and *post_external_call* functions, the developer has access to the function name, arguments and return value. Note that the return of a function can be a value or a pointer referring to internal buffers. *XiOS* can handle both cases. However, each external function takes a different number of arguments and returns a different type; thus, the developer must be aware of the signature for the functions she aims to handle. Moreover, with *XiOS*, the return values and the arguments can be changed. The following code snippet shows an example where an external call to the *NSLog* function will not be allowed:

```
int pre_external_call(const char *function_name,
    const unsigned long regs[]) {
  char nslog[6] = "NSLog";
  if (xios_strcmp(function_name, nslog) == 0)
    return FAIL;
}
```

Note that the reference monitor does not differentiate between invocations of C functions or Objective-C methods, as the Objective-C mechanism dispatches all objects' methods through a generic C function called *objc_msgSend*. With *XiOS* both can be analyzed in the same manner within the two pre-defined functions.

Developing self-contained policies in C maybe cumbersome. Hence, we are currently working on a service where the developer submits the app, and uses a simple interface to define rules and triggers *XiOS*'s hardening mechanism. This will enable convenient definition of custom policies.

6. EVALUATION

In this section we present a detailed evaluation of *XiOS* with respect to its effectiveness and efficiency. First, we analyze the effectiveness of our hardening process against previous and our own new attacks (see Section 2.2 and 3). Then, we evaluate the performance impact of our changes on the application, and measure the overhead they impose on a randomly selected set of both C and Objective-C functions. Moreover, we evaluate our hardening mechanism on several real-world applications.

6.1 Effectiveness

In order to test the effectiveness of *XiOS* we use our malicious sample application that we introduced in Section 3. In particular, we modified our sample application so that it includes both attack types: (1) exploiting a runtime address of a public API ([19, 35] and Section 2.2), and (2) exploiting the runtime address of the dynamic loader function to resolve lazy symbols (Section 3). To this end, we first apply *XiOS* to our sample malicious application. Afterwards, we deploy the hardened application on our test iOS device (iPhone 4 running iOS 7.0).

Previous Attacks: To test *XiOS* against previous attacks, we let our malicious application de-reference the runtime address of a public API. Specifically, we invoke the `CGImageSourceCreateWithURL` public API residing in the public `ImageIO` framework as `ImageIO` contains references to *load-library* and *load-address*. Since the runtime address of the public API is lazily resolved on-demand, its runtime address will be stored in the lazy symbol section after we have called the public API during normal program execution. However, since *XiOS* completely overwrites the original lazy and non-lazy symbol section with zeroes, the de-referenced value will be always zero rather than the runtime address of `CGImageSourceCreateWithURL`. In *XiOS*, the runtime address of the public API is on the shadow table which is only accessible from the *XiOS* reference monitor. This effectively prevents the first attack step of previous attacks [19, 35].

Our New Attack: Recall that our improved attack does not require the knowledge of a public API runtime address.

	printf	mmap	strerror	NSString alloc	NSUserName	NSTemporaryDirectory
1 Policy Check	0.029459	-0.018641	0.016662	0.041377	-0.013764	0.096091
10 Policy Checks	0.037107	-0.002330	0.023010	0.063399	0.105262	0.058099
100 Policy Checks	0.140015	0.088113	0.091601	0.260605	0.334400	0.228264

Table 1: Overhead for 10,000 calls (in seconds)

Instead, our attack attempts to access the runtime address of the dynamic loader function **`dyld_stub_binder`** which is present in every iOS application in the non-lazy symbol section. *XiOS* successfully prevents this attack similar to the previous attack as it hides runtime addresses of external functions contained in the non-lazy symbol section by overwriting this section with zero and maintaining the runtime addresses in the protected shadow table.

To summarize, in both attack instances (previous and our new one), *XiOS* prevents the malicious application from determining critical runtime addresses of function pointers that could be exploited to invoke a private API.

Since the pointers in the lazy and non-lazy symbol section are no longer available to the adversary, he may try to leak function addresses by inspecting return buffers, return values and return register values in public APIs that can be called. We prevent this by the use of policies that inspect the return information of a public API and zeroise or replace any sensitive pointer data.

On the other hand, the adversary could perform a complete memory scan to identify private APIs and dynamic loader functions based on signature or instruction matching. However, this requires the adversary to know exactly the location of all mapped memory pages. Otherwise, the application will crash upon read access on non-mapped memory. Moreover, many consecutive read operations from main application code to shared library code resembles a program anomaly which one can certainly monitor at runtime.

A current limitation of *XiOS* are attacks through an address of a global external variable stored in the non-lazy symbol section. This allows an adversary to use offset-based computation to retrieve the address of dynamic loader functions. We successfully tested this attack and it is indeed currently feasible in iOS, since the shared library code and its data section are always located at the same offset, irrespective of ASLR. Such attacks are only possible as the ASLR scheme implemented in iOS does not randomize the offset between the data and code section. Since our focus in *XiOS* resides on attacks based on function pointers and more fine-grained ASLR solves the issue, we did not implement a mechanism to hide data pointers which is an orthogonal problem and we leave as future work.

6.2 Efficiency

Our hardening mechanism is deployed by the reference monitor for each function call. The overhead is constant irrespective of the type of function called and depends on the number of policies. As described in Section 4.3, we intercept only calls to external functions. Thus, the main application code and instructions from shared libraries execute with native performance.

In order to determine the overhead of our approach per external call, we have selected a variety of functions and evaluated their execution time. Specifically, we have implemented an application that calls only the tested function and implanted a set of 1, 10, 100 policies using *XiOS*. We measure the execution time when running the application with and without policy enforcement. Each of the selected functions runs for 10,000 times. Note that the selected policies only perform a sanity check (i.e., verify the function's name and print its arguments) and do not prohibit execution of functions as this would end the testing procedure.

We present the results in Table 1. The overhead for running Objective-C functions 10,000 times is, at most, only of 0.33s, while the overhead for native-C functions is only 0.14s in the case of 100 policies. The negative numbers displayed for *mmap* and *NSUserName* show that the hardened application was actually faster than the vanilla version. This is due to the fact that we do not control how the operating system scheduler (i.e., closed-source OS) affects our tests.

During our tests, we analyzed the average number of function calls per second inside an app. For normal use (clicks, accessing resources) there are no more than 1,000 function calls per second. This means, that if an app were to use only the functions listed in Table 1 the overhead would at most be 0.033s; less than 5%.

We applied our enforcements on a popular iOS benchmark tool called Gensystek [1]. Figure 5 shows results for eight different benchmarks with different number of threads (1, 2 and 4) and with different number of policy checks (1, 10 and 100). The computation of an MD5 hash displays the most noticeable slowdown of 3.9x. However, similar heavy-CPU computation such as Floating point calculation/Arithmetic logical unit (FPU/ALU) show an overhead of only 1.5% when tested against 100 policy checks. The overhead for taking and saving a screenshot to disk is 4.3%. Moreover, *XiOS* induces less overhead than previous work, e.g., MoCFI adds up to 500% overhead for the PI calculation [15]. Note that every external function called is applied the 100 policy checks, irrespective of what the function does, as these checks were part of the reference monitor implementation. Within a more realistic scenario, there would only be a handful of functions that do these many policy checks, reducing the overall incurred overhead.

In terms of required memory, our experiments with *XiOS* on real applications show that no additional space is required for storing the reference monitor inside the executable. This is due to the fact that the reference monitor requires only 1KB and can be stored in unused space of the binary, such as the **`__TEXT`** segment. The shadow table requires 4K and is allocated dynamically when the application is executed. In our evaluation, less than 1KB was required for one policy. However, if complex policies (hence, more space required for storing the policies) are to be inserted, new code sections and memory pages can be added at the end of the application.

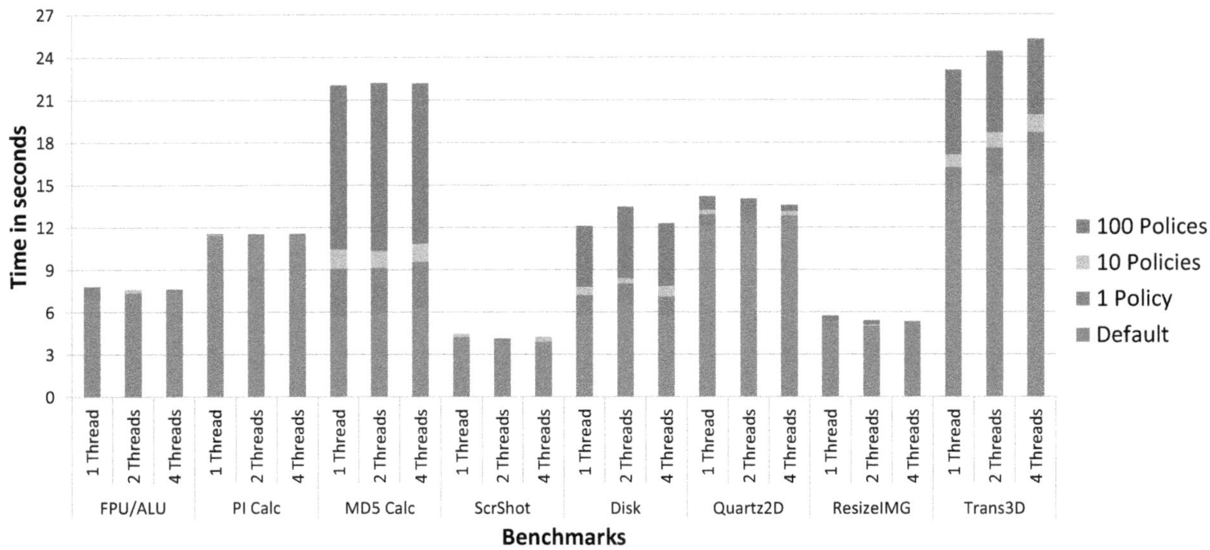

Figure 5: Gensystek Benchmark

No. of policies	SysMonitor	Frotz	MusicNotes
1	-8.78%	-9.05%	1.74%
10	3.68%	2.25%	-9.69%
100	21.39%	10.35%	-2.49%

Table 2: Loss in number of external functions calls

6.3 Study of Real World Apps

To demonstrate the effectiveness of our approach, we tested *XiOS* on several real-world applications such as Facebook, Twitter, Gmail, Youtube. In our experiences with the hardened applications we encountered no overhead. Moreover, we used our hardening service to apply policies to several applications such as System Monitor, Frotz, WhatsApp, MusicNotes and Gensystek. For testing the application behavior we sequentially used a number of 1, 10, and 100 policies and measured the number of external function calls with and without *XiOS* in a time frame of 30s. As before, policies are configured to allow all external calls. In order to access the application's binary (as iOS stores them encrypted), we made use of a well established tool, namely Clutch [14].

We compared "vanilla" application runs against hardened application runs. The results are shown in Table 2 as the percentage of loss in the number of external calls. Remarkably, *XiOS* does not reduce the number of external calls that are made within a given time frame. A noticeable overhead of 21% is noticed only when *XiOS* is configured with 100 policies for each external function call which is far from realistic but represents worst-case scenarios. The MusicNotes application allows users to play different sounds at a touch of a screen-keyboard. We did not encounter any noticeable delay when performing different tests.

6.4 Access Control on Public Applications

XiOS allows enterprises to create and apply their own policies on any application available on the App Store. In order to demonstrate how such policies can be created we have chosen one of the most used application today, namely the instant messenger WhatsApp [3]. One particular feature of WhatsApp is that it uses the phone number for identifying different users in the network. Moreover, the full address book is copied to the developer servers when the application is installed. *XiOS* allows filtering of the contacts to avoid that WhatsApp retrieves all the user's contacts.

Before creating the filtering policies we need to identify which functions are relevant and need to be instrumented. To do so, *XiOS* provides a script that can be used to identify all external functions invoked by the application along with the framework that they belong to. Specifically, WhatsApp uses *ABAddressBookGetPersonWithRecordID* within the *AddressBook* framework to extract the contacts from the address book.

Next, the developer can check the function's signature and specify policies according to the format shown in Section 5.4. In our particular use-case we prevent WhatsApp from accessing all contact phone numbers that belong to the domain `corporate`. Note that the domain name is maintained in the *kABPersonOrganizationProperty* field belonging to the class *ABRecordRef*. Hence, when WhatsApp retrieves the contacts, we simply validate for each record whether *kABPersonOrganizationProperty* is set to `corporate`. If so, we simply replace the entire record with `NULL`. Appendix A presents the specific implementation of the policy.

7. RELATED WORK

The work related to *XiOS* can be roughly classified into protection schemes for iOS and runtime protection mechanisms that aim at hiding function pointers and instrumenting function calls.

iOS Security: There are a few proposals that aim at enhancing the security of iOS-based systems. PiOS is a static privacy analysis tool that performs off-line path validation on an application's control-flow graph [16]. Although PiOS revealed that many apps leak the device ID to application developers, it cannot detect Jekyll-like attacks [35] where the malicious behavior is only triggered at runtime. On the other hand, MoCFI [15] and PSiOS [37] could potentially prevent the mentioned attacks by enforcing control-flow integrity (CFI) and fine-grained sandboxing policies. However, both solutions require a *jailbreak* and suffer from performance problems, which limit their deployment in practice. In contrast, *XiOS* avoids jailbreaking devices and only incurs modest performance overhead.

Runtime Protection Mechanisms: For Android-based systems, several Inline Reference Monitors (IRM) have been proposed recently. Most of them insert a policy hook or check before a critical function is called at Dalvik Bytecode level [7, 22]. Most closely to our approach is Aurasium [39], as it deploys a similar redirection technique: it overwrites entries of the global offset table (GOT) – that holds runtime addresses of lazy and non-lazy symbols – with the start address of policy check functions. However, in contrast to *XiOS*, it does not provide any mechanism to hide the actual runtime addresses in a shadow table. Hence, an adversary can deploy memory disclosure attacks to infer the runtime address of a critical function and directly redirecting execution to it (via an indirect branch instruction). Moreover, Aurasium can be bypassed through native code that directly invokes system calls [13].

Since the GOT is critical in many Linux-based systems to intiate runtime attacks, Xu et al. proposed a solution that randomizes the GOT section at load-time, but allow its address to be discovered through the procedure linkage table (PLT) section [38]. Roglia et al. improve this solution by randomizing the GOT section and rewriting the PLT region [29]. The mechanisms behind those two solutions can be migrated to the iOS operating system. However, in contrast to our solution, both proposals need to be integrated into the operating system as they require higher privileges to rewrite a binary at load-time.

Another approach to instrument function calls aims at adding a wrapper and verifying the parameters passed to the function [9, 8]. A common mechanism to load such interceptors is the Linux `LD_PRELOAD` linker facility which forces the application to use a wrapper function rather than the actual external function. However, since it is unrealistic that every external function is replaced by a wrapper (due to space and complexity reasons), an adversary can exploit the knowledge of the runtime address of one single (not instrumented) function to directly call a private API.

In the domain of runtime attack mitigation the security model of address space layout randomization (ASLR) is used against memory (i.e., function pointer) disclosure attacks. The basic idea is to randomize the start address of code and data segments. Recently, several schemes have been proposed to even enforce fine-grained code randomization [10, 18, 21, 26, 23, 36, 12, 11]. However, sophisticated memory disclosure attacks [31] can bypass ASLR-based schemes. Moreover, in order to mitigate the attacks presented in this paper (Section 2.2 and 3), one would need operating system support and a jailbreak, because ALSR needs to be applied to the dynamic loader and public/private frameworks.

8. SUMMARY AND FUTURE WORK

Recent attacks have demonstrated that the current design of iOS is vulnerable to a variety of attacks that undermine the iOS sandboxing model leading to the invocation of private APIs (e.g., sending text messages in background). While previous attacks rely on specific assumptions such as the availability of a public framework, we showed that the default iOS application structure by itself can be easily exploited to invoke dangerous private APIs.

Since existing solutions suffer from performance overhead or require a jailbreak, we introduce a new hardening service, *XiOS*, that implants an inline reference monitor into an iOS application to tackle these attacks without requiring a jailbreak or source code of the application. This reference monitor efficiently prevents an application from inferring addresses of private APIs, and at the same time enforces (optional) developer-defined policies on public APIs. We demonstrate the benefits of the latter by enabling a contacts filtering mechanism for the popular WhatsApp messenger.

In the future, we plan to extend *XiOS* with a web frontend, where end-users can conveniently upload their custom policies that are automatically translated into C code and deployed at runtime when the application is launched on the device. In addition, we also aim at validating entire call chains rather than only enforcing access control on a per function-level.

9. REFERENCES

[1] Gensystek benchmark. `http://www.ooparts-universe.com/apps/app\_gensystek.html`.

[2] Lazy binding. `http://developer.blackberry.com/native/documentation/core/com.qnx.doc.neutrino.prog/topic/devel_lazy_binding.html`.

[3] Whatsapp. `http://www.whatsapp.com/`.

[4] Apple Inc. App review. `https://developer.apple.com/appstore/guidelines.html`.

[5] Apple Inc. iOS developer enterprise program. `https://developer.apple.com/programs/ios/enterprise/`.

[6] Apple Inc. iOS frameworks. `https://developer.apple.com/library/ios/documentation/Miscellaneous/Conceptual/iPhoneOSTechOverview/iPhoneOSFrameworks/iPhoneOSFrameworks.html`.

[7] M. Backes, S. Gerling, C. Hammer, M. Maffei, and P. von Styp-Rekowsky. AppGuard: Enforcing user requirements on Android apps. In *International Conference on Tools and Algorithms for the Construction and Analysis of Systems (TACAS)*, 2013.

[8] A. Baratloo, N. Singh, and T. Tsai. Transparent run-time defense against stack smashing attacks. In *USENIX Annual Technical Conference (ATC)*, 2000.

[9] A. Barenghi, G. Pelosi, and F. Pozzi. Drop-in control flow hijacking prevention through dynamic library interception. In *Tenth International Conference on Information Technology: New Generations (ITNG)*, 2013.

[10] E. G. Barrantes, D. H. Ackley, T. S. Palmer, D. Stefanovic, and D. D. Zovi. Randomized instruction set emulation to disrupt binary code injection attacks. In *ACM Conference on Computer and Communications Security (CCS)*, 2003.

[11] S. Bhatkar, D. C. DuVarney, and R. Sekar. Address obfuscation: An efficient approach to combat a board range of memory error exploits. In *USENIX Security Symposium*, 2003.

[12] S. Bhatkar, R. Sekar, and D. C. DuVarney. Efficient techniques for comprehensive protection from memory error exploits. In *USENIX Security Symposium*, 2005.

[13] S. Bugiel, S. Heuser, and A.-R. Sadeghi. Flexible and fine-grained mandatory access control on android for

diverse security and privacy policies. In *USENIX Security Symposium*, 2013.

[14] Clutch. Clutch. https://github.com/KJCracks/Clutch.

[15] L. Davi, A. Dmitrienko, M. Egele, T. Fischer, T. Holz, R. Hund, S. Nürnberger, and A.-R. Sadeghi. MoCFI: A framework to mitigate control-flow attacks on smartphones. In *Network and Distributed System Security (NDSS)*, 2012.

[16] M. Egele, C. Kruegel, E. Kirda, and G. Vigna. PiOS: Detecting privacy leaks in iOS applications. In *Network and Distributed System Security (NDSS)*, 2011.

[17] A. P. Felt, M. Finifter, E. Chin, S. Hanna, and D. Wagner. A survey of mobile malware in the wild. In *ACM Workshop on Security and Privacy in Smartphones and Mobile Devices (SPSM)*, 2011.

[18] C. Giuffrida, A. Kuijsten, and A. S. Tanenbaum. Enhanced operating system security through efficient and fine-grained address space randomization. In *USENIX Security Symposium*, 2012.

[19] J. Han, S. M. Kywe, Q. Yan, F. Bao, R. Deng, D. Gao, Y. Li, and J. Zhou. Launching generic attacks on iOS with approved third-party applications. In *Applied Cryptography and Network Security (ACNS)*, 2013.

[20] N. Hardy. The confused deputy: (or why capabilities might have been invented). *SIGOPS'98 Oper. Syst. Rev.*, 1998.

[21] J. Hiser, A. Nguyen-Tuong, M. Co, M. Hall, and J. Davidson. Ilr: Where'd my gadgets go? In *IEEE Security and Privacy (Oakland)*, 2012.

[22] J. Jeon, K. K. Micinski, J. A. Vaughan, A. Fogel, N. Reddy, J. S. Foster, and T. Millstein. Dr. Android and Mr. Hide: Fine-grained permissions in Android applications. In *Workshop on Security and Privacy in Smartphones and Mobile Devices (SPSM)*, 2012.

[23] C. Kil, J. Jun, C. Bookholt, J. Xu, and P. Ning. Address space layout permutation (ASLP): Towards fine-grained randomization of commodity software. In *Annual Computer Security Applications Conference (ACSAC)*, 2006.

[24] H. Lu. ELF: From the programmer's perspective. http://linux4u.jinr.ru/usoft/WWW/www_debian.org/Documentation/elf/node7.html.

[25] Microsoft. Data Execution Prevention (DEP). http://support.microsoft.com/kb/875352/EN-US/, 2006.

[26] V. Pappas, M. Polychronakis, and A. D. Keromytis. Smashing the gadgets: Hindering return-oriented programming using in-place code randomization. In *IEEE Security and Privacy (Oakland)*, 2012.

[27] V. Pappas, M. Polychronakis, and A. D. Keromytis. Transparent ROP exploit mitigation using indirect branch tracing. In *USENIX Security Symposium*, 2013.

[28] PGbiz. Count of active applications in the App Store. http://www.pocketgamer.biz/metrics/app-store/app-count/, 2014.

[29] G. F. Roglia, L. Martignoni, R. Paleari, and D. Bruschi. Surgically returning to randomized lib(c). In *Annual Computer Security Applications Conference (ACSAC)*, 2009.

[30] H. Shacham. The geometry of innocent flesh on the bone: Return-into-libc without function calls (on the x86). In *ACM Conference on Computer and Communications Security (CCS)*, 2007.

[31] K. Z. Snow, F. Monrose, L. Davi, A. Dmitrienko, C. Liebchen, and A.-R. Sadeghi. Just-in-time code reuse: On the effectiveness of fine-grained address space layout randomization. In *IEEE Security and Privacy (Oakland)*, 2013.

[32] Symantec Corporation. 2013 internet security threat report, volume 18. http://www.symantec.com/security_response/publications/threatreport.jsp.

[33] T. Backdoor in top iPhone games stole user data, suit claims. http://www.theregister.co.uk/2009/11/06/iphone_games_storm8_lawsuit/, 2014.

[34] R. Wahbe, S. Lucco, T. E. Anderson, and S. L. Graham. Efficient software-based fault isolation. In *ACM Symposium on Operating Systems Principles (SOSP)*, 1993.

[35] T. Wang, K. Lu, L. Lu, S. Chung, and W. Lee. Jekyll on iOS: when benign apps become evil. In *USENIX Security Symposium*, 2013.

[36] R. Wartell, V. Mohan, K. W. Hamlen, and Z. Lin. Binary stirring: Self-randomizing instruction addresses of legacy x86 binary code. In *ACM Conference on Computer and Communications Security (CCS)*, 2012.

[37] T. Werthmann, R. Hund, L. Davi, A.-R. Sadeghi, and T. Holz. PSiOS: bring your own privacy & security to iOS devices. In *ACM SIGSAC Symposium on Information, Computer and Communications security (ASIACCS)*, 2013.

[38] J. Xu, Z. Kalbarczyk, and R. Iyer. Transparent runtime randomization for security. In *International Symposium on Reliable Distributed Systems*, 2003.

[39] R. Xu, H. Saïdi, and R. Anderson. Aurasium: Practical policy enforcement for Android applications. In *USENIX Security Symposium*, 2012.

[40] B. Yee, D. Sehr, G. Dardyk, J. B. Chen, R. Muth, T. Orm, S. Okasaka, N. Narula, N. Fullagar, and G. Inc. Native client: A sandbox for portable, untrusted x86 native code. In *IEEE Security and Privacy (Oakland)*, 2009.

APPENDIX

A. WHATSAPP POLICY DEFINITION

```
unsigned long post_external_call(const char
    *function_name, const unsigned long
    returned_value)
{
  if (xios_strcmp(function_name, addressGetID) ==
      0) {
    char * companyName =
        ABRecordCopyValue(person,
        kABPersonOrganizationProperty);
    if (xios_strcmp("corporate", companyName) ==
        0){
      return 0;
    }
  }
  return returned_value;
}
```

Securing Legacy Software against Real-World Code-Reuse Exploits: Utopia, Alchemy, or Possible Future?

Ahmad-Reza Sadeghi, Lucas Davi
Technische Universität Darmstadt, Germany and
Intel Collaborative Research Institute
for Secure Computing

Per Larsen
University of California, Irvine

ABSTRACT

Exploitation of memory-corruption vulnerabilities in widely-used software has been a threat for over two decades and no end seems to be in sight. Since performance and backwards compatibility trump security concerns, popular programs such as web browsers, servers, and office suites still contain large amounts of untrusted legacy code written in error-prone languages such as C and C++. At the same time, modern exploits are evolving quickly and routinely incorporate sophisticated techniques such as code reuse and memory disclosure. As a result, they bypass all widely deployed countermeasures including data execution prevention (DEP) and code randomization such as address space layout randomization (ASLR).

The good news is that the security community has recently introduced several promising prototype defenses that offer a more principled response to modern exploits. Even though these solutions have improved substantially over time, they are not perfect and weaknesses that allow bypasses are continually being discovered. Moreover, it remains to be seen whether these prototype defenses can be matured and integrated into operating systems, compilers, and other systems software.

This paper provides a brief overview of current state-of-the-art exploitation and defense techniques against run-time exploits and elaborates on innovative research prototypes that may one day stem the tide of sophisticated exploits. We also provide a brief analysis and categorization of existing defensive techniques and ongoing work in the areas of code randomization and control-flow integrity, and cover both hardware and software-based solutions.

Categories and Subject Descriptors

D.4.6 [**Software**]: Operating Systems—*Security and Protection*

Keywords

software exploitation; fine-grained randomization; control-flow integrity

1. INTRODUCTION

When the C language was designed four decades ago, computers were much less powerful, less networked, and thus much less exposed to malicious activities. In the pursuit of efficiency and flexibility, security features such as automatic memory management, strong typing, and overflow checks were omitted from C. As a result, programming errors can lead to memory corruption that causes unexpected program behavior and can be exploited for malicious purposes.

Modern systems incorporate a large amount of C/C++/Objective-C code and hand-written assembly code for performance and legacy reasons. This includes operating system kernels, web browsers, document viewers and language implementations for JavaScript, Flash, Java, PHP, etc. Despite the existence of many type-safe languages, members of the C family consistently inhabit the top ten in rankings of programming language popularity [54, 44]. This leaves the security research community with the challenge of mitigating exploits without abandoning the unsafe language features or introducing high overheads while at the same time remaining fully compatible with all existing code.

The goal of this paper is to give an overview of recent offensive and defensive systems security research in the context of runtime exploits. We start by giving a general overview of code reuse attacks (Section 1.1) and defenses (Section 1.2) and then describe offensive techniques that threaten to undermine the security of several improved defenses (Section 2). Finally, Section 3 highlights advanced defenses that aim to resist offensive techniques while at the same time offering practicality and efficiency.

1.1 From Code Injection to Code Reuse

The classic buffer overflow vulnerability allows an adversary to inject malicious code on the stack and overwrite a function's return address in order to direct execution to the exploit payload [3]. Stack smashing attacks became rare after deployment of techniques such as stack canaries [14]. However, attackers quickly adapted and moved to exploitation on the heap [42]. Modern operating systems defend against code injection attacks through Data Execution Prevention (DEP) [41]. DEP prohibits memory pages from being both writable and executable thereby preventing an adversary from injecting and directly executing code.

While standard defenses have all but obsoleted some types of attacks, new attacks have appeared in their place. In particular, code reuse emerged in response to the widespread deployment of DEP as it turns out that injecting malicious data is just as effective as malicious code injection [38]. The most popular variant of code reuse, return-oriented programming (ROP), reuses short code sequences, called gadgets, terminated by a return instruction (or another indirect branch) [48, 12]. ROP has been applied to many processor architectures: SPARC [9], Atmel AVR [22], PowerPC [35], and ARM [33]. In addition, ROP has been shown to be Turing-complete meaning that an adversary can generate arbitrary malicious execution.

1.2 Mitigating Code Reuse

We briefly introduce the most prominent techniques to prevent code reuse: code randomization and control-flow integrity.

Code randomization such as Address Space Layout Randomization (ASLR) can in principle prevent ROP attacks by making the location of gadgets unpredictable. Today, ASLR is enabled on nearly all modern operating systems including Windows, Linux, iOS, or Android. For the most part, current ASLR implementations randomize the base (start) address of segments such as the stack, heap, libraries, and the executable itself between consecutive runs of the application. The goal is to force adversaries to guess the location of the functions and instruction sequences needed to successfully launch a code reuse attack.

Unfortunately, ASLR suffers from two main problems: first, the entropy on 32-bit systems is too low, and thus ASLR is vulnerable to brute-force attacks [49]. Second, ASLR is highly vulnerable to *memory disclosure* attacks [47] where the adversary gains knowledge of a single runtime address and uses that information to infer the memory layout of the application.

To thwart these attacks, a number of fine-grained ASLR and code randomization schemes have been recently proposed [7, 32, 39, 28, 55, 30, 29]. The underlying idea in these works is to randomize the data and code structure, for instance, by shuffling functions or basic blocks (ideally for each program run [55]). The assumption underlying all these works is that the disclosure of a single address no longer allows an adversary to launch a code reuse attack. However, as will be explained in Section 2.1, more involved types of memory disclosure vulnerabilities can be exploited to bypass fine-grained code randomization.

Control-flow integrity (CFI) is another promising exploit mitigation mechanism [1, 2]. The main idea of CFI is to compute an application's control-flow graph (CFG) prior to execution, and then monitor its runtime behavior to ensure that the control-flow follows a legitimate path in the CFG. Any deviation from the CFG leads to a CFI exception and subsequent termination of the application.

Validating all indirect control-flow transfers can have a substantial performance impact that prevents widespread deployment. For instance, when validating function returns using a shadow stack, the average overhead of CFI can be as high as 21% [1] on average. Consequently, several CFI frameworks have been proposed that tackle the practical shortcomings of the original CFI approach. ROPecker [13] and kBouncer [40], for example, leverage the branch history table of modern x86 processors to perform a CFI check on a short history of executed branches. Zhang and Sekar [58] and Zhang et al. [57] applied coarse-grained CFI policies using binary rewriting to protect COTS binaries. In section 2.2, we will discuss the security implications of CFI policies that trade off security for efficiency.

2. ADVANCED ATTACKS

In this section we present two recent attack techniques that undermine modern exploit mitigation techniques. First, we present JIT-ROP, a just-in-time code-reuse attack that bypasses defenses that are based on randomizing the code layout of an application (Section 2.1). Second, we present an attack technique that bypasses several control-flow integrity approaches (Section 2.2). These attacks demonstrate weaknesses of two prominent exploit mitigation techniques, namely code randomization and control-flow integrity. They also motivate several improved mitigation techniques that we discuss in Section 3.

2.1 Just-In-Time Code Reuse

Just-in-time return-oriented programming (JIT-ROP) circumvents fine-grained ASLR by finding gadgets and generating the ROP payload at runtime using the scripting environment of the target application (e.g., a browser or document viewer). As with many real-world ROP attacks, the disclosure of a *single* runtime memory address is sufficient. However, in contrast to standard ROP attacks, JIT-ROP does not require the precise knowledge of the code part or function the memory address points to. It can use any code pointer such as a return address on the stack to instantiate the attack. Based on that leaked address, JIT-ROP discloses the contents of other memory pages by recursively searching for pointers to other code pages and generates the ROP payload at runtime.

The workflow of a JIT-ROP attack is shown in Figure 1. Here, we assume that fine-grained ASLR has been applied to each executable module in the address space of the (vulnerable) application. First, the adversary exploits a memory disclosure vulnerability to retrieve the runtime address of a code pointer ❶. One of the main observations of Snow et al. [51] is that the disclosed address will reside on a 4KB-aligned memory page ($Page_0$ in Figure 1). Hence, at runtime, one can identify the start and end of $Page_0$ ❷. Using a disassembler at runtime, $Page_0$ is then disassembled on-the-fly ❸. The disassembled page provides 4KB of gadget space ❹, and more importantly, it is likely that it contains direct branch instructions to other pages, e.g., a call to Func_B ❺. Since Func_B resides on another memory page (namely $Page_1$), JIT-ROP can again determine the page start and end, and disassemble $Page_1$ ❻. This procedure is repeated as long as new direct branches pointing to yet undiscovered memory pages can be identified ❼. Using the disassembled pages, a runtime gadget finder is then used to identify useful ROP gadgets (e.g., LOAD, STORE, or ADD ❽). Finally, the ROP payload is composed based on the discovered ROP gadgets and a high-level description of the desired functionality provided by the adversary ❾.

The threat of memory disclosure is not limited to JIT-ROP. For example, Shacham et al. [49], Bittau et al. [8] and Siebert et al. [50] all demonstrated how attackers can re-

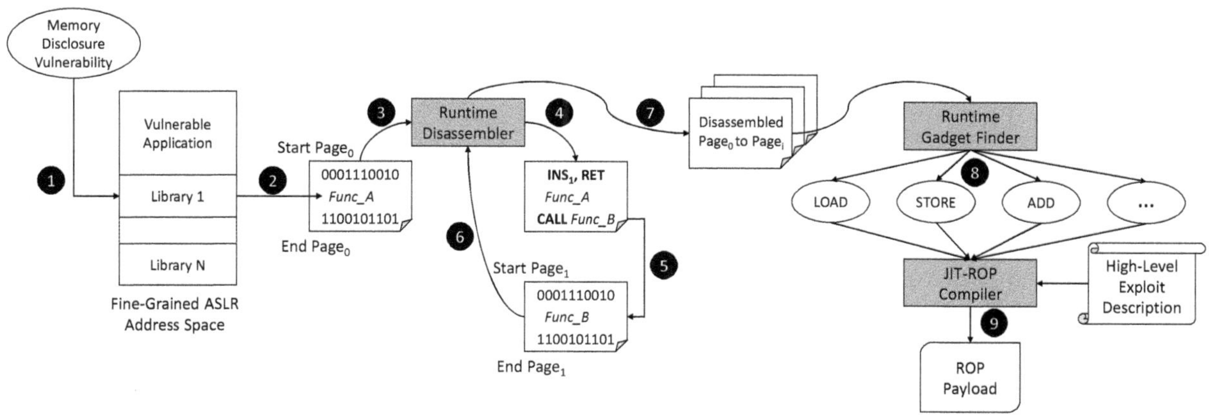

Figure 1: High-level overview of a JIT-ROP attack [51].

peatedly probe servers and analyze response characteristics to remotely bypass both coarse and fine-grained ASLR.

2.2 Bypassing Coarse-Grained CFI

The benefits of the so-called coarse-grained solutions come at the price of relaxing the original CFI policy. Abstractly speaking, coarse-grained CFI allows for CFG relaxations that allow many additional execution paths beyond those intended by the programmer. The most notable difference is that the coarse-grained CFI policy for return instructions only validates if the return address points to an instruction that follows directly after a call instruction [40, 58]. In contrast, the original policy for fine-grained CFI ensures that the return address points to the original caller of a function (based on a shadow stack). That is, a function return is only allowed to return to its original caller. On the other hand, several solutions use heuristics to compensate for the coarse-grained protection of returns, e.g., by monitoring the number of instructions executed between a pre-defined number of consecutive indirect branches [40, 13]. The goal is to detect the execution of a number of short instruction sequences which is a typical pattern of return-oriented programming attacks.

Davi et al. [18] conduct a systematic security analysis of the recently proposed CFI solutions including kBouncer [40], ROPecker [13], CFI for COTS binaries [58], ROPGuard [23], and Microsofts' EMET tool [36]. In particular, they derive a combined CFI policy that, for each type of indirect indirect branch and behavioral heuristic (e.g., the number of instruction executed between two indirect branches), uses the most restrictive setting among the aforementioned policies. Their security analysis demonstrates that based on the access to only a *single* — and commonly used system library in Windows — an adversary can still construct a Turing-complete gadget set. In particular, a new gadget type has been developed called *long-NOP*. This gadget bypasses heuristics that check for chains of short instruction sequences by invoking a long sequence that performs well-controlled memory writes without disrupting the actual payload, i.e., it also compensates for side-effects by saving registers before it is executed and loading them after the memory writes have been issued.

Other researchers have demonstrated weaknesses of coarse-grained CFI by constructing attacks that target specific CFI implementations. Göktas et al. [26] demonstrate attacks against the Compact Control-Flow Integrity and Randomization (CCFIR) [57] approach using call-preceded gadgets to invoke sensitive functions via direct calls. Carlini and Wagner [11] as well as Schuster et al. [46] demonstrate flushing attacks that eliminate return-oriented programming traces before a critical function is invoked.

3. ADVANCED DEFENSES

We now turn our attention to approaches that aim to withstand even the advanced exploitation techniques outlined in the previous section.

3.1 Fine-Grained Code Randomization

The introduction of JIT-ROP and other offensive techniques relying on memory disclosure, made it apparent that increasing the granularity of code randomization is not enough to thwart runtime exploits. There are two ways that defenders can address the threat of memory disclosure: 1) taking steps to prevent memory disclosure or 2) tolerating memory disclosure. We discuss each strategy in turn.

Hiding the code layout is one way to prevent adversaries from launching JIT-ROP attacks against diversified code. Backes and Nürnberger [6] proposed to prevent code discovery (Step ❼) in the original JIT-ROP approach by hiding pointers between code pages. Davi et al. [19] show that this approach is insecure because the adversary can harvest code pointers from C++ virtual tables instead of following pointers between code pages. Backes et al. [5] and Gionta et al. [25] later proposed two execute-only memory solutions: XnR and HideM respectively. However, these two approaches do not consider the threat of pointer harvesting.

Readactor by Crane et al. [16] aims at addressing some of the shortcomings of previous approaches. Specifically, it combines hardware-enforced execute-only memory and code pointer hiding to prevent both *direct* memory disclosure (code reads) and *indirect* disclosure through code pointer harvesting. In addition, Readactor scales beyond benchmarks to complex, real-world software such as browsers and JIT engines. One remaining challenge is that Readactor only runs on processors that support hardware accelerated paging[1] (HAP) and requires an operating system or kernel extension to exposes these features to application programs.

[1]Intel calls this feature Extended Page Tables while AMD markets this features as Nested Page Tables.

Control-flow randomization is an alternative way to tolerate code layout disclosure. Whereas Readactor, XnR, and HideM aim to *prevent* memory disclosure the Isomeron approach by Davi et al. [19] instead *tolerates* memory disclosure. A successful ROP attack requires an attacker to, among other things, 1) discover gadget addresses and 2) reliably transfer the control flow from one gadget to another. Most probabilistic defenses target the first requirement. Isomeron targets the second and therefore operates on the conservative assumption that adversaries know the code layout and instead randomizes control-flow transfers. In particular, Isomeron keeps two isomers (clones) of all functions in memory; one isomer retains the original program layout while the other is diversified. On each function call, Isomeron randomly determines whether the return instruction should switch execution to the other isomer or keep executing functions in the current isomer. Upon each function return, the result of the random trial is retrieved, and if a decision to switch was made, an offset (the distance between the calling function f and its isomer f') is added to the return address. Since the attacker does not know which return addresses will have an offset added and which will not, return addresses injected during a ROP attack will no longer be used "as is" and instead, the ROP attack becomes unreliable due to the possible addition of offsets to the injected gadget addresses. Since Isomeron is implemented as dynamic binary instrumentation framework it suffers from performance penalties and requires extra memory to hold the two program instances. In order to bring the performance overhead in line with efficient code layout randomization techniques [29, 20, 55], Isomeron could be integrated into a compiler.

Isomeron may be able to simultaneously protect against side-channel attacks in addition to code-reuse attacks. We observe that Crane et al. uses a similar control-flow randomization mechanism to rapidly alternate between two diversified program clones to thwart cache-based side-channel attacks [15]. We believe the two approaches can be readily combined.

3.2 Control-Flow Integrity

The literature on control-flow integrity is substantial. Consequently, we limit our discussion to recent and unconventional approaches.

CFI policy randomization prevents attacks against coarse-grained CFI. Opaque Control-Flow Integrity (O-CFI) is a hybrid approach that recasts CFI as a bounds checking problem [37]. Instead of checking the target address of each indirect branch against a list of valid targets, O-CFI checks that the target address is within the bounds defined by the maximal and minimal addresses in the list of valid targets. To avoid attacks wherein attackers construct a ROP chain that adheres to all bounds checks, O-CFI randomizes the code layout at load-time. Code layout randomization has the desirable side-effect of also randomizing the bounds that each ROP chain must adhere to. By protecting the bounds table against memory leakage vulnerabilities, O-CFI aims to resist JIT-ROP [51], Blind ROP [8], and gadget-stitching attacks [18, 26, 11, 27]. With an average overhead of 4.7%, O-CFI offers efficient protection on current processors. However, forthcoming Intel processors will include Memory Protection eXtensions (MPX) with support for hardware-accelerated bounds checking. Note that like Isomeron, O-CFI randomizes the code layout but *tolerates* code layout disclosure. Where Isomeron randomizes the control-flow, O-CFI constrains the control-flow using a random and thus unknown control-flow policy—in both cases, the adversary is unable to reliably chain ROP gadgets together. The current implementation of O-CFI is based on binary rewriting which makes it hard to recover a precise control-flow graph. A source-based implementation of O-CFI would be able to impose tighter bounds on indirect control-flow transfers (particularly for programs written in C++) and thus increase resilience to attacks.

Forward-edge CFI: In general, one can distinguish between backward and forward edges in the control-flow graph (CFG) of an application. The former are representative for function return instructions. In contrast, the latter edges are due to function call and jump instructions. Recently, a number of approaches have focused on applying CFI to forward-edges. In particular, compilers for C++ applications emit indirect call instructions to support virtual method calling via virtual tables. SAFEDISPATCH [31] and Google's CFI compiler [53] both ensure that an adversary cannot manipulate a virtual table (vtable) pointer so that it points to an adversary-controlled (malicious) vtable. However, these approaches require the source code of the application which might not be always readily available. In order to protect binary code, a number of CFI approaches have been presented recently [24, 56, 43]. Although these approaches require no access to source code, they are not as fine-grained as their compiler-based counterparts. A novel attack technique denoted as COOP (counterfeit object-oriented programming) undermines the CFI protection of these binary instrumentation-based defenses by invoking a chain of virtual methods through legitimate call sites to induce malicious program behavior [45].

Hardware-assisted CFI: The majority of research on CFI has focused on software-based solutions. However, hardware-based CFI approaches have several advantages over software-based counterparts: first, it is significantly more efficient. Second, CFI support in hardware easily allows compilers to harden software programs as only single CFI instructions need to be emitted rather than complex and large CFI checking code. Third, dedicated CFI hardware instructions and separate CFI memory provide an efficient and strong protection of critical CFI control-flow data.

The first hardware-based CFI approach has been presented by Budiu et al. [10]. They realized the original CFI proposal [1, 2] as a CFI state machine in a simulation environment of the Alpha processor. HAFIX is a recent hardware-based control-flow integrity protection that has been implemented on real hardware targeting Intel Siskiyou Peak and SPARC [17, 4]. It generates 2% performance overhead across different embedded benchmarks and focuses on thwart return-oriented programming attacks exploiting function returns.

As previously mentioned, the original software-based CFI implementation validates function returns using a shadow stack [2]: all return addresses that are pushed on the program's stack through call instructions are copied to a protected shadow stack. However shadow stack significantly decrease performance and lead to false positives for certain programming constructs (e.g., C++ exceptions with stack unwinding, setjmp/longjmp).

To reduce the cost of maintaining a shadow stack, HAFIX simply confines function returns to active call sites [17]. In other words, it forces a return to target a call-preceded instruction inside a function that is currently executing. This CFI policy can be efficiently implemented in hardware and requires only minimal changes to the compiler.

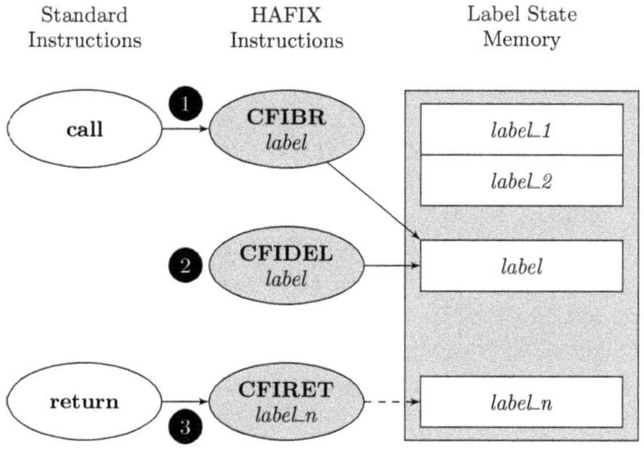

Figure 2: Abstract design of HAFIX

Figure 2 shows the underlying design to enforce the HAFIX CFI policy. To monitor functions that are currently executing, HAFIX requires the compiler to assign unique labels to each function. Further, it forces each subroutine upon call to issue a `CFIBR` instruction. This instruction loads the label of the function into a dedicated memory area, called the *label state memory*, to indicate that the function is active (Step ❶). Internally, direct and indirect call instructions lead to a processor state switch in which the processor only accepts `CFIBR`. To deactivate a function, HAFIX uses the `CFIDEL` instruction which effectively removes the label from the label state memory (Step ❷).

In HAFIX, return instructions need to target an active call site. This is enforced by switching the processor state where only the so-called `CFIRET` instruction is allowed. In this state, only a `CFIRET` that uses a currently active label in the label state memory is allowed (Step ❸). Otherwise, a CFI exception is raised.

On the compiler side, HAFIX only requires the compiler to emit the new CFI instructions at their corresponding places: `CFIBR` at function start, `CFIRET` at all call sites, and `CFIDEL` at function return.

HAFIX reduces the number of available call sites by 80% for static benchmark binaries. In other words, only every fifth call site is a valid target of a return. Obviously, the gadget space is further reduced for applications that link to shared libraries since only the instruction following the call of a library function is a valid target for the return.

Currently, HAFIX targets bare-metal code for static applications running on embedded processors. It remains to show how HAFIX can be applied to complex applications that also link to shared libraries and run on top of a operating system.

3.3 Code-Pointer Integrity

Based on a careful and detailed analysis of memory corruption [52], Szekeres et al. identified code-pointer integrity (CPI) as a defensive alternative to both code randomization and control-flow integrity. Whereas CFI seeks to detect invalid targets of control-flow transfers, CPI places sensitive control-flow data (e.g., function pointers and return addresses) in a "safe region" separated from all non-control-flow data. Kuznetsov et al. [34] presented the first implementation of code-pointer integrity. Although the worst-case overheads of CPI are high, the overall cost of protection is competitive with CFI and code randomization. CPI is no silver bullet, however, and bypasses have started to appear [21].

4. CONCLUSION

While we have barely skimmed the surface of modern offensive and defensive research, we hope to have brought some clarity to the exciting field of runtime exploits. We do not anticipate that any of the advanced defenses we have discussed will put an end to exploitation overnight. Instead, we expect slow but steady progress towards mature software-based defenses, slower progress towards support for hardware security mechanisms, and glacially slow progress towards safer languages. It is evident that building secure systems that contain large amounts of unsafe legacy code is a non-trivial if not impossible undertaking.

5. REFERENCES

[1] M. Abadi, M. Budiu, Ú. Erlingsson, and J. Ligatti. Control-flow integrity. In *ACM Conference on Computer and Communications Security*, CCS '05, pages 340–353, 2005.

[2] M. Abadi, M. Budiu, Ú. Erlingsson, and J. Ligatti. Control-flow integrity principles, implementations, and applications. *ACM Transactions on Information System Security*, 13:4:1–4:40, 2009.

[3] Aleph One. Smashing the stack for fun and profit. *Phrack Magazine*, 7(49), 1996. `http://www.phrack.org/issues.html?id=14&issue=49`.

[4] O. Arias, L. Davi, M. Hanreich, Y. Jin, P. Koeberl, D. Paul, A.-R. Sadeghi, and D. Sullivan. HAFIX: Hardware-assisted flow integrity extension. In *Design Automation Conference*, DAC '15, 2015.

[5] M. Backes, T. Holz, B. Kollenda, P. Koppe, S. Nürnberger, and J. Pewny. You can run but you can't read: Preventing disclosure exploits in executable code. In *ACM Conference on Computer and Communications Security*, CCS '14, 2014.

[6] M. Backes and S. Nürnberger. Oxymoron - making fine-grained memory randomization practical by allowing code sharing. In *USENIX Security Symposium*, 2014.

[7] S. Bhatkar, R. Sekar, and D. DuVarney. Efficient techniques for comprehensive protection from memory error exploits. In *USENIX Security Symposium*, 2005.

[8] A. Bittau, A. Belay, A. Mashtizadeh, D. Mazières, and D. Boneh. Hacking blind. In *IEEE Symposium on Security and Privacy*, S&P '14, 2014.

[9] E. Buchanan, R. Roemer, H. Shacham, and S. Savage. When good instructions go bad: generalizing return-oriented programming to RISC. In *ACM Conference on Computer and Communications Security*, CCS '08, 2008.

[10] M. Budiu, U. Erlingsson, and M. Abadi. Architectural support for software-based protection. In *Workshop on Architectural and System Support for Improving Software Dependability*, ASID '06, 2006.

[11] N. Carlini and D. Wagner. ROP is still dangerous: Breaking modern defenses. In *USENIX Security Symposium*, 2014.

[12] S. Checkoway, L. V. Davi, A. Dmitrienko, A.-R. Sadeghi, H. Shacham, and M. Winandy. Return-oriented programming without returns. In *ACM Conference on Computer and Communications Security*, CCS '10, 2010.

[13] Y. Cheng, Z. Zhou, Y. Miao, X. Ding, and R. H. Deng. ROPecker: A generic and practical approach for defending against ROP attacks. In *Network And Distributed System Security Symposium*, NDSS '14, 2014.

[14] C. Cowan, C. Pu, D. Maier, J. Walpole, P. Bakke, D. Beattie, A. Grier, P. Wagle, Q. Zhang, and H. Hinton. StackGuard: Automatic adaptive detection and prevention of buffer-overflow attacks. In *USENIX Security Symposium*, 1998.

[15] S. Crane, A. Homescu, S. Brunthaler, P. Larsen, and M. Franz. Thwarting cache side-channel attacks through dynamic software diversity. In *Network And Distributed System Security Symposium*, NDSS '15, 2015.

[16] S. Crane, C. Liebchen, A. Homescu, L. Davi, P. Larsen, A.-R. Sadeghi, S. Brunthaler, and M. Franz. Readactor: Practical code randomization resilient to memory disclosure. In *IEEE Symposium on Security and Privacy*, S&P '15, 2015.

[17] L. Davi, P. Koeberl, and A.-R. Sadeghi. Hardware-assisted fine-grained control-flow integrity: Towards efficient protection of embedded systems against software exploitation. In *Design Automation Conference - Special Session: Trusted Mobile Embedded Computing*, DAC '14, 2014.

[18] L. Davi, D. Lehmann, A.-R. Sadeghi, and F. Monrose. Stitching the gadgets: On the ineffectiveness of coarse-grained control-flow integrity protection. In *USENIX Security Symposium*, 2014.

[19] L. Davi, C. Liebchen, A.-R. Sadeghi, K. Z. Snow, and F. Monrose. Isomeron: Code randomization resilient to (just-in-time) return-oriented programming. In *Network And Distributed System Security Symposium*, NDSS '15, 2015.

[20] L. V. Davi, A. Dmitrienko, S. Nürnberger, and A.-R. Sadeghi. Gadge me if you can: secure and efficient ad-hoc instruction-level randomization for x86 and ARM. In *ACM Symposium on Information, Computer and Communications Security*, ASIACCS '13, 2013.

[21] I. Evans, S. Fingeret, J. Gonzalez, U. Otgonbaatar, T. Tang, H. Shrobe, S. Sidiroglou-Douskos, M. Rinard, and H. Okhravi. Missing the point: On the effectiveness of code pointer integrity. In *IEEE Symposium on Security and Privacy*, S&P '15, 2015.

[22] A. Francillon and C. Castelluccia. Code injection attacks on Harvard-architecture devices. In *ACM Conference on Computer and Communications Security*, CCS '08, 2008.

[23] I. Fratric. ROPGuard: Runtime prevention of return-oriented programming attacks. `http://www.ieee.hr/_download/repository/Ivan_Fratric.pdf`, 2012.

[24] R. Gawlik and T. Holz. Towards automated integrity protection of C++ virtual function tables in binary programs. In *Annual Computer Security Applications Conference*, ACSAC '14, 2014.

[25] J. Gionta, W. Enck, and P. Ning. Hidem: Protecting the contents of userspace memory in the face of disclosure vulnerabilities. In *ACM Conference on Data and Application Security and Privacy*, CODASPY '15, 2015.

[26] E. Göktas, E. Athanasopoulos, H. Bos, and G. Portokalidis. Out of control: Overcoming control-flow integrity. In *IEEE Symposium on Security and Privacy*, S&P '14, 2014.

[27] E. Göktas, E. Athanasopoulos, M. Polychronakis, H. Bos, and G. Portokalidis. Size does matter: Why using gadget-chain length to prevent code-reuse attacks is hard. In *USENIX Security Symposium*, 2014.

[28] J. Hiser, A. Nguyen-Tuong, M. Co, M. Hall, and J. W. Davidson. ILR: Where'd my gadgets go? In *IEEE Symposium on Security and Privacy*, S&P '12, 2012.

[29] A. Homescu, S. Neisius, P. Larsen, S. Brunthaler, and M. Franz. Profile-guided automatic software diversity. In *IEEE/ACM International Symposium on Code Generation and Optimization*, CGO '13, 2013.

[30] T. Jackson, A. Homescu, S. Crane, P. Larsen, S. Brunthaler, and M. Franz. Diversifying the software stack using randomized NOP insertion. In S. Jajodia, A. K. Ghosh, V. Subrahmanian, V. Swarup, C. Wang, and X. S. Wang, editors, *Moving Target Defense II*, volume 100 of *Advances in Information Security*. Springer New York, 2013.

[31] D. Jang, Z. Tatlock, and S. Lerner. SAFEDISPATCH: Securing C++ virtual calls from memory corruption attacks. In *Network And Distributed System Security Symposium*, NDSS '14, 2014.

[32] C. Kil, J. Jun, C. Bookholt, J. Xu, and P. Ning. Address space layout permutation (ASLP): Towards fine-grained randomization of commodity software. In *Annual Computer Security Applications Conference*, ACSAC '06, 2006.

[33] T. Kornau. Return-oriented programming for the ARM architecture. Master's thesis, Ruhr University Bochum, Germany, 2009.

[34] V. Kuznetsov, L. Szekeres, M. Payer, G. Candea, R. Sekar, and D. Song. Code-pointer integrity. In *USENIX Symposium on Operating Systems Design and Implementation*, OSDI '14, 2014.

[35] F. Lindner. Router exploitation. `http://www.blackhat.com/presentations/bh-usa-09/LINDNER/BHUSA09-Lindner-RouterExploit-SLIDES.pdf`, 2009.

[36] Microsoft. Enhanced Mitigation Experience Toolkit. `https://www.microsoft.com/emet`.

[37] V. Mohan, P. Larsen, S. Brunthaler, K. Hamlen, and M. Franz. Opaque control-flow integrity. In *Network And Distributed System Security Symposium*, NDSS '15, 2015.

[38] Nergal. The advanced return-into-lib(c) exploits: PaX case study. *Phrack Magazine*, 11(58), 2001. `http://www.phrack.org/issues.html?issue=58&id=4`.

[39] V. Pappas, M. Polychronakis, and A. D. Keromytis. Smashing the gadgets: Hindering return-oriented programming using in-place code randomization. In

IEEE Symposium on Security and Privacy, S&P '12, 2012.

[40] V. Pappas, M. Polychronakis, and A. D. Keromytis. Transparent ROP exploit mitigation using indirect branch tracing. In *USENIX Security Symposium*, 2013.

[41] PaX. *Homepage of The PaX Team*, 2001. `http://pax.grsecurity.net`.

[42] J. Pincus and B. Baker. Beyond stack smashing: Recent advances in exploiting buffer overruns. *IEEE Security & Privacy*, pages 20–27, 2004.

[43] A. Prakash, X. Hu, and H. Yin. vfGuard: Strict protection for virtual function calls in COTS C++ binaries. In *Network and Distributed System Security Symposium*, NDSS '15, 2015.

[44] The redmonk programming language rankings, 2015. `http://redmonk.com/sogrady/2015/01/14/language-rankings-1-15/`.

[45] F. Schuster, T. Tendyck, C. Liebchen, L. Davi, A.-R. Sadeghi, and T. Holz. Counterfeit object-oriented programming: On the difficulty of preventing code reuse attacks in C++ applications. In *IEEE Symposium on Security and Privacy*, S&P '15, 2015.

[46] F. Schuster, T. Tendyck, J. Pewny, A. Maaß, M. Steegmanns, M. Contag, and T. Holz. Evaluating the effectiveness of current anti-ROP defenses. In *International Symposium on Research in Attacks, Intrusions and Defenses*, RAID '14, 2014.

[47] F. J. Serna. The info leak era on software exploitation. In *Black Hat USA*, 2012.

[48] H. Shacham. The geometry of innocent flesh on the bone: Return-into-libc without function calls (on the x86). In *ACM Conference on Computer and Communications Security*, CCS '07, 2007.

[49] H. Shacham, M. Page, B. Pfaff, E. Goh, N. Modadugu, and D. Boneh. On the effectiveness of address-space randomization. In *ACM Conference on Computer and Communications Security*, CCS '04, 2004.

[50] J. Siebert, H. Okhravi, and E. Söderström. Information leaks without memory disclosures: Remote side channel attacks on diversified code. In *ACM Conference on Computer and Communications Security*, CCS '14, 2014.

[51] K. Z. Snow, F. Monrose, L. V. Davi, A. Dmitrienko, C. Liebchen, and A.-R. Sadeghi. Just-in-time code reuse: On the effectiveness of fine-grained address space layout randomization. In *IEEE Symposium on Security and Privacy*, S&P '13, 2013.

[52] L. Szekeres, M. Payer, T. Wei, and D. Song. SoK: eternal war in memory. In *IEEE Symposium on Security and Privacy*, S&P '13, 2013.

[53] C. Tice, T. Roeder, P. Collingbourne, S. Checkoway, Ú. Erlingsson, L. Lozano, and G. Pike. Enforcing forward-edge control-flow integrity in GCC & LLVM. In *USENIX Security Symposium*, 2014.

[54] Tiobe programming community index, 2015. `http://www.tiobe.com/index.php/content/paperinfo/tpci/index.html`.

[55] R. Wartell, V. Mohan, K. W. Hamlen, and Z. Lin. Binary stirring: self-randomizing instruction addresses of legacy x86 binary code. In *ACM Conference on Computer and Communications Security*, CCS '12, pages 157–168, 2012.

[56] C. Zhang, C. Song, K. Z. Chen, Z. Chen, and D. Song. VTint: Defending virtual function tables' integrity. In *Network and Distributed System Security Symposium*, NDSS '15, 2015.

[57] C. Zhang, T. Wei, Z. Chen, L. Duan, L. Szekeres, S. McCamant, D. Song, and W. Zou. Practical control flow integrity & randomization for binary executables. In *IEEE Symposium on Security and Privacy*, S&P '13, 2013.

[58] M. Zhang and R. Sekar. Control flow integrity for COTS binaries. In *USENIX Security Symposium*, 2013.

Enabling Encrypted Cloud Media Center with Secure Deduplication

Yifeng Zheng[†]* Xingliang Yuan[†]* Xinyu Wang[†], Jinghua Jiang[†‡], Cong Wang[†], Xiaolin Gui[‡]
[†]Department of Computer Science, City University of Hong Kong, Hong Kong
[‡]Department of Computer Science and Technology, Xi'an Jiaotong University, Xi'an, China
{yifezheng2, xinywang, congwang}@cityu.edu.hk,{xinglyuan3-c, jjinghua2-c}@my.cityu.edu.hk
xlgui@mail.xjtu.edu.cn

ABSTRACT

Multimedia contents, especially videos, are being exponentially generated today. Due to the limited local storage, people are willing to store the videos at the remote cloud media center for its low cost and scalable storage. However, videos may have to be encrypted before outsourcing for privacy concerns. For practical purposes, the cloud media center should also provide the deduplication functionality to eliminate the storage and bandwidth redundancy, and adaptively disseminate videos to heterogeneous networks and different devices to ensure the quality of service. In light of the observations, we present a secure architecture enabling the encrypted cloud media center. It builds on top of latest advancements on secure deduplication and video coding techniques, with fully functional system implementations on encrypted video deduplication and adaptive video dissemination services. Specifically, to support efficient adaptive dissemination, we utilize the scalable video coding (SVC) techniques and propose a tailored layer-level secure deduplication strategy to be compatible with the internal structure of SVC. Accordingly, we adopt a structure-compatible encryption mechanism and optimize the way how encrypted SVC videos are stored for fast retrieval and efficient dissemination. We thoroughly analyze the security strength of our system design with strong video protection. Furthermore, we give a prototype implementation with encrypted end-to-end deployment on Amazon cloud platform. Extensive experiments demonstrate the practicality of our system.

Categories and Subject Descriptors

H.3.5 [**Information Systems**]: Information Storage and Retrieval—*Online Information Services*; H.5.1 [**Information Systems**]: Information Interfaces and Representation—*Multimedia Information Systems*; E.3 [**Data**]: Data Encryption

*The first two authors contributed equally to this work.

ASIA CCS'15, April 14–17, 2015, Singapore, Singapore.

http://dx.doi.org/10.1145/2714576.2714628.

Keywords

Cloud Media Center; Secure Deduplication; Scalable Video Coding; Layer-level Deduplication

1. INTRODUCTION

With the explosive growth of multimedia technology and mobile devices with high-definition cameras, multimedia contents, especially videos, have already dominated the network traffic and demanded a great amount of hardware storage [8]. To handle such a rapidly growing trend, many existing and emerging applications based on videos are deployed at public clouds for its well-known advantages, e.g., availability, scalability, and economy [26]. However, the user privacy could be violated if content-sensitive videos are not protected properly in such an outsourcing environment [23]. In fact, current cloud-based data hosting services are shown to be vulnerable to security breaches. Data disclosure occurs frequently in recent years [15]. Therefore, addressing the privacy concerns becomes significant for building a cloud media center.

A plausible approach is to require each user to encrypt the videos using her secret key before sending them to public clouds. As long as the user's secret key is protected, video confidentiality can be guaranteed. But this approach prevents the cloud media center from supporting deduplication, a crucial function that can greatly save the network bandwidth and eliminate the storage redundancy in cloud services [14]. Identical videos encrypted by different users' secret keys would lead to different ciphertexts, making deduplication infeasible.

To support secure deduplication over encrypted videos, one might consider utilizing convergent encryption (CE) [10], which encrypts data with a key deterministically derived from the data itself (e.g., the hash value), so as to ensure the identical data will map to identical ciphertexts. However, CE is vulnerable to off-line brute-force attacks when the target message space is small or the data is predictable [2]. Besides, CE is under a weak security model, which does not consider the bounded leakage setting, where a certain amount of deterministically and efficiently extractable information of the data could be leaked [25]. Although some recent designs have improved the security of CE [2,14,17,25], it remains to be fully explored whether they can directly enable an encrypted cloud media center, which should simultaneously ensure the strong video confidentiality, provide immediate compatibility with the video structure, and deliver practical video dissemination services.

In practice, an encrypted cloud media center should be able to adaptively disseminate videos to heterogeneous networks and devices such as PCs, Mobile phones, Tablets and SmartTVs [12]. However, such adaptive dissemination might be disabled after encryption. Alternatively, one can ask each user to first generate different versions of videos from the same source, and then send all encrypted versions to the cloud. Yet, this method will incur a great amount of bandwidth and storage overhead, and thus increase the capital of using cloud services. Therefore, how to enable efficient adaptive video dissemination while supporting secure deduplication over encrypted videos, is the challenge we aim to tackle in this paper, for which we bring together techniques from both cryptography and video processing.

We first investigate the applicability of secure deduplication in the encrypted cloud media center and propose a non-trivial design to strongly protect video confidentiality. It takes into consideration the defenses against the adversaries in the bounded leakage setting, and the adversaries launching brute-force attacks over predictable videos, respectively. To support efficient adaptive dissemination, we exploit the scalable video coding (SVC) techniques [19]. SVC utilizes the concept of layers and enables multiple versions of the same video content to be embedded in a single video file, which can significantly improve the storage efficiency and dissemination scalability [24]. To make secure deduplication compatible with the structure of SVC, we propose a layer-level deduplication strategy tailored for SVC videos, enabling suitable deduplication for encrypted SVC videos.

Besides, we investigate the encryption of SVC videos [20, 22], and adopt a structure-compatible encryption mechanism and optimize the way encrypted SVC videos are stored for fast retrieval and efficient dissemination. Our thorough security analysis shows that video confidentiality is strongly protected in the proposed system design. We give a full implementation of an encrypted end-to-end cloud media center. which is deployed at Amazon EC2 instances and leverages Amazon DynamoDB as the video storage backend. Extensive experiments are conducted to justify the practicality of our system design.

Contributions. Our main contributions are listed below:

- We formulate a secure system framework for the encrypted cloud media center. It supports secure deduplication while protecting data confidentiality against malicious users and untrusted cloud. Building on top of latest literature on secure deduplication [2, 25], our framework supports the secure video deduplication in the bounded leakage setting, and defends the off-line brute-force attacks over predictable videos, respectively.

- We leverage the inherent characteristics of SVC videos in our design. We utilize an encryption mechanism which is compatible with the underlying SVC structure, and optimize the way how encrypted SVC videos are stored for fast retrieval. Meanwhile, the security of our system is thoroughly analyzed.

- We implement an end-to-end cloud media center system with roughly 17,000 lines of codes, which is fully deployed at Amazon AWS. We evaluate our system via various performance metrics on SVC videos with sizes up to 500MB. The results demonstrate the practicality of our system.

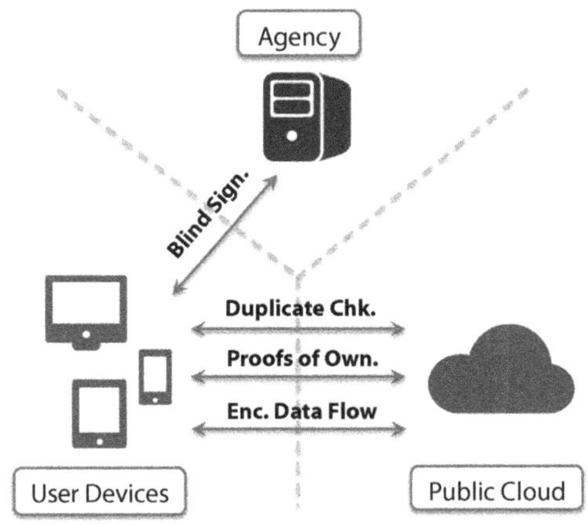

Figure 1: The proposed system framework.

The rest of this paper is organized as follows. Section 2 presents our problem formulation. Section 3 gives some preliminaries. Section 4 formulates the general secure deduplication framework. Section 5 gives the detailed construction for deduplication over encrypted SVC videos under the proposed framework. Section 6 presents the security analysis. Section 7 gives the implementation and performance evaluation. Section 8 describes the related works. Section 9 concludes the whole paper.

2. PROBLEM STATEMENT

2.1 System Model

Our system involves three entities: the cloud media center, the user, and the agency, as illustrated in Figure 1. Their roles are described below:

- The cloud media center (abbr. cloud) provides a video hosting platform, which stores users' encrypted videos and adaptively distributes them to cater for heterogeneous user devices and network bandwidth. It enforces secure client-side deduplication, i.e., duplicate check is performed before users upload videos.

- The user outsources her encrypted videos to the cloud, and possibly deletes the original ones at local. Later, the user may access her own videos. Video sharing is not the focus of this paper, although it can be achieved along with our design through techniques such as the attribute-based access control [23].

- The agency, hosted by a third party (e.g., a video service provider), facilitates our system to safeguard the confidentiality of user videos against off-line brute-force attacks. It assists users and cloud to perform the duplicate check in a controllable fashion, and enables users to perform the encryption that supports deduplication.

2.2 Threat Models

Our goal is to protect the confidentiality of users' videos. We will consider a strong security model for secure deduplication, i.e., the bounded leakage setting as in [25], where a certain amount of deterministically and efficiently extractable information about videos could be leaked. We will also be concerned with protection for both predictable and unpredictable videos.

Two types of adversaries are considered in our system: (1) *Malicious outside adversary.* The outside adversary may refer to a user who might obtain some knowledge (e.g., a hash value) of a video and try to earn the ownership of the target video from cloud. We assume that she will not upload a fake video to compromise the integrity of other users' videos. (2) *Honest-but-curious inside adversary.* The inside adversary may refer to cloud or the agency. On the one hand, cloud faithfully follows the designated deduplication scheme, yet intends to infer users' encrypted video contents. It might also manipulate one user or a number of users to harvest target video contents. On the other hand, the third-party agency dutifully executes the assigned functions, but also tries to extract useful information about users' videos. In this paper, we do not consider that cloud modifies or deletes users' videos. And we assume that there is no collusion between cloud and the agency.

3. PRELIMINARIES

3.1 Oblivious Pseudorandom Function

An oblivious pseudorandom function (OPRF) protocol enables two parties, say sender S and receiver R, to jointly and securely compute a pseudo-random function (PRF) $f_{sk}(x)$, where sk is the secret key of S and the input x is contributed by R. The OPRF protocol enforces that R only learns the output value $f_{sk}(x)$ and S learns nothing from the interactive process [11]. Verifiable OPRF schemes allow R to further verify whether the result $f_{sk}(\cdot)$ is correctly computed under S's secret key sk, via utilizing S's corresponding public key pk. Deterministic blind signatures can be used to build verifiable OPRF schemes [7]. In a blind signature scheme, a user is able to obtain and verify the digital signature of a message from a signer without revealing any data information. Meanwhile, the user cannot learn the signer's secret key. In this paper, we use the RSA-OPRF scheme built on RSA blind signatures [4] as a building block for our proposed system.

3.2 Scalable Video Coding

The SVC technique utilizes the concept of layers and enables multiple versions of the source video content to be embedded in a single file, i.e., a SVC video [19]. Intuitively, a SVC video is composed of a base layer, which represents the basic visual experience, and enhancement layers, which can improve the video by supplementing the base layer in different scalability dimensions (i.e., time, quality, resolution). In our system, we are particularly interested in the resolution scalability as the first instantiation. Through employing various inter-layer prediction methods, SVC removes the redundancy between different representations of the same video content [18]. It is noted that at the decoder side, a lower layer must be present if a higher layer exists but not the other way around. In other words, if the layers of a SVC video are discarded from the highest layer, the rest of layers are still decodable. Thus, a user can adaptively enjoy different versions of the same video content through a single SVC video.

Therefore, from the perspective of storage efficiency and dissemination scalability, it is advantageous to store SVC videos in the cloud media center to cater for heterogeneous network bandwidth and different devices. Without loss of generality, a SVC video SV with n layers can be denoted as $SV = (m_1, m_2, \ldots, m_n)$, where m_1 is the base layer and m_i is the $(i-1)th$ enhancement layer for $i \in [2, n]$ [23].

4. PROPOSED SECURE DEDUPLICATION FRAMEWORK

In this section, we present our secure deduplication framework that can protect users' videos in the bounded leakage setting, and defend off-line brute-force attacks over predictable videos, respectively. We start with describing our design intuition to address the threats mentioned in Section 2.2, and then elaborate on the detailed construction. We note that the framework is suitable for generic data, e.g., textual files and images.

4.1 Design Intuition

Our system targets secure client-side deduplication over encrypted videos. First, we consider secure client-side deduplication in a strong security model, i.e., the bounded leakage setting first proposed by Xu et al. in [25], where a certain amount of deterministically and efficiently extractable information of the plaintext data could be leaked. Under this setting, CE is not appropriate for use in our system since its data encryption key is not leakage resilient. Specifically, the private key in CE is derived from the data plaintext in a deterministic way and could be leaked *before* the encryption process. For similar reasons, using the plaintext hash as a proxy for the ownership of data can also be insecure under the leakage setting.

To address the threat posed by the bounded leakage setting, the following treatment inspired by [25] could be adopted. Firstly, deduplication is achieved by using the hash value $H(V)$ of the video V for duplicate check. Secondly, the video encryption key τ is selected randomly by the initial uploader, who also creates a one-time message-derived mask via a keyed hash function, i.e., $F_s(\cdot)$, to hide it, where s is a random string. Note that because τ is randomly generated, even the hash value of V is possibly leaked, the video is still protected as long as τ is hidden from cloud. Moreover, this type of masking can enable all the subsequent users who own the same video copies to obtain the random key τ and further prove to cloud that they indeed own the videos, by running a proofs-of-ownership (PoW) protocol with cloud.

Although the above treatment is resistant to the bounded leakage setting, it is not directly suitable for use in our system to provide strong protection for video confidentiality. In particular, the above treatment is vulnerable to off-line brute-force attacks over predictable videos. This vulnerability originates from the fact that the hash value is directly exposed to cloud for duplicate check and the random encryption key τ is only protected by V, which will be analyzed in detail shortly. In order to get rid of this vulnerability while still maintaining the security strength of the above treatment in the bounded leakage setting, we resort to an agency for assistance in our system, inspired by [2]. Specifically, we leverage the agency to securely produce message-derived tag α and label β via a RSA-OPRF protocol similar to [2]. The message-derived tag α is used for secure duplicate check and prevents cloud from directly accessing the video hash, while the message-derived label β is embedded in the mask during the initial upload and assists the recovery of the random key τ during the subsequent upload. We note that through this careful enhancement design, our system can also effectively prevent cloud from mounting off-line brute-force attacks over predictable videos and thus provide strong protection for video confidentiality, which will be analyzed in detail in Section 6.

4.2 Secure Deduplication Framework

We are now ready to present the detailed construction of the proposed secure deduplication framework. The work flow is illustrated in Figure 2. As shown, before uploading a video V, the user first needs to engage in the RSA-OPRF protocol with the agency to derive the message-derived tag α and label β of V, i.e., $\alpha = \mathsf{OPRF}_{k_1}^{RSA}(H(V))$ and $\beta = \mathsf{OPRF}_{k_2}^{RSA}(H(V))$, where k_1 and k_2 are two different secret keys of the agency for signing (we refer readers to Appendix for the details of the RSA-OPRF protocol). Then α is submitted to cloud for duplicate check. If it does not exist at the cloud side, the user is considered as the initial uploader of V; otherwise, the user is considered as the subsequent uploader.

Suppose user u is the initial one who uploads the video V after duplicate check. User u first encrypts V with a random key τ and produces the video ciphertext C_V. Then u generates a masked key r via using a keyed hash function $F(s, V \parallel \beta)$ to protect τ, where s is a random string, which will enable all subsequent users who indeed owns V to recover τ for correct decryption. Besides, τ is encrypted under u's private key sk to produce the ciphertext C_τ. Finally, u sends $\{C_V, s, r, C_\tau\}$ to cloud, and $H(C_V)$ is computed by cloud for the later use of PoW protocol. Suppose u' is a subsequent user who tries to upload V after the duplicate check. User u' has to run a PoW protocol with cloud to prove that she indeed owns V. Specifically, u' will request (r, s) from cloud, and utilizes V and β to recover the correct encryption key τ. Then u' encrypts V with τ to produce the ciphertext C_V and also computes $H(C_V)$. After that, $H(C_V)$ is sent to cloud for equality checking. After verification, u' is admitted as the owner of C_V. Finally, u' uses her private key sk' to encrypt the recovered τ and stores it at the cloud side. During the retrieval process, the user first downloads C_V and C_τ from cloud, and then uses its private key sk to decipher C_τ and further decrypt C_V with the recovered τ.

Differences compared with prior works. In the proposed deduplication framework, the message-derived tag α is used for duplicate check, and the random key τ is protected by a mask derived from the video V and the message-derived label β. Note that in [25], the hash value of data is directly exposed to cloud for duplicate check and the random key is only protected by the data. Therefore, if this approach is adopted for secure client-side deduplication, cloud can launch off-line brute-force attacks over predictable videos. Given the ciphertext C_V and knowing that its underlying video V is drawn from a dictionary $D_V = \{V_1, V_2, \ldots, V_n\}$, cloud can launch the following two types of off-line brute-force attacks to recover V. In the first attack, cloud can simply compare the received (stored) hash $H(V)$ with the computed hash of each V_i ($i \in [1, n]$) in D_V, and then recover the target video V when two hashes are found equal. In the second attack, cloud may first use each V_i in D_V to decrypt the masked random key and get a key candidate set $\mu_{set} = \{\mu_1, \mu_2, \ldots, \mu_n\}$. Then for each $i \in [1, n]$, cloud can

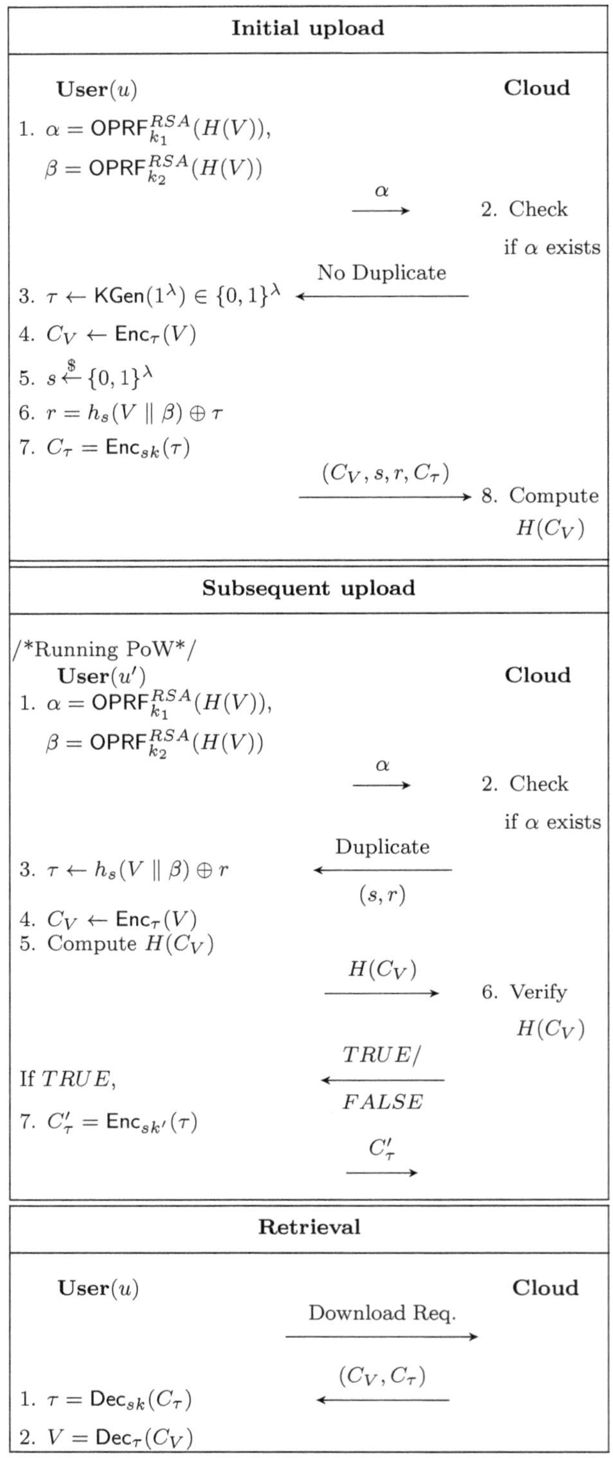

Figure 2: Overview of the system work flow. Here $\mathsf{E} = (\mathsf{KGen}, \mathsf{Enc}, \mathsf{Dec})$ is a deterministic symmetric encryption scheme with λ bits long key length and $h_K : \{0,1\}^* \rightarrow \{0,1\}^\lambda$ is a key-ed hash function. Note that it is omitted that a user runs KGen to derive the private key sk at the system setup.

use μ_i to decrypt the target video ciphertext C_V and compare the decryption result with V_i in the dictionary D_V to find the matched target video.

To securely use *server-side* deduplication and defend offline brute-force attacks over predictable data, Bellare et al. [2] propose an improved design based on CE. They resort to a semi-trusted party named key server for obliviously embedding a secret in the data hash used for encryption and do not consider any data leakage setting. Thus, if directly applied for secure deduplication in the bounded leakage setting, the data encryption key could be leaked as long as the hash is leaked [25]. Different from [2], our system targets client-side deduplication which saves both storage and bandwidth. Meanwhile, our design randomly selects keys for video encryption and protects them by masks derived from both users' videos and the blind signed hashes. Thus, the encryption key is well protected in the bounded leakage setting.

5. STRUCTURE-AWARE DEDUPLICATION OVER ENCRYPTED SVC VIDEOS

In this section, we exploit the internal structure of SVC videos to enforce layer-level deduplication under the proposed secure deduplication framework. We first motivate the importance of layer-level deduplication for SVC videos and then present the detailed construction.

5.1 Layer-Level Deduplication

The traditional file-level deduplication and block-level deduplication are not suitable for SVC videos. This misfit can be demonstrated by an intuitive and practical scenario. Suppose that a user, say u_a, owns the base layer and an enhancement layer for a source content, while another user, say u_b, only owns the base layer for the same source content. And u_a and u_b both used some cloud storage service with deduplication. Then, by file-level deduplication, the two different SVC videos of u_a and u_b can not be deduplicated since they have different contents at the file level. On the other hand, directly splitting a SVC video into blocks and performing block-level deduplication is not a desirable choice since the layers in a SVC video are formatted in a special structure [19,21] and applying block-level deduplication may destroy the structure of SVC video. To address the above challenges, we propose to exploit the layered nature of SVC videos to enforce layer-level deduplication, which treats each layer of a SVC video as a unit for deduplication.

5.2 Construction

Before presenting our construction of secure layer-level deduplication over encrypted SVC videos, we give two important observations that facilitate our design. First, we note that the base layer is the foundation of a SVC video and it also serves as the reference basis for higher enhancement layers [19]. This vital observation indicates that two SVC videos can hardly have duplicate layers if they do not have the same base layer, which inspires us to utilize the base layer for the duplicate check for a given SVC video. Second, users having the same base layer may possess different numbers of enhancement layers for the same source content under their heterogeneous devices and network environments.

Based on these important observations, the main idea for enforcing secure layer-level deduplication over encrypted SVC videos is introduced as follows: Before uploading a SVC video, the message-derived tag α_1 of the base layer and the number of layers are sent to cloud for duplicate check. If a match for α_1 is not found, it is considered that the SVC video does not contain any duplicate layers and thus all layers should be uploaded by the user. Otherwise, a SVC version with the same base layer has already been stored in cloud and thus the user's SVC video may contain a certain number of duplicate layers. In this case, if the user's SVC video has fewer layers than the SVC version in cloud, the PoW protocol needs to be run over all layers of the SVC video. Otherwise, the user only needs to run the PoW protocol over the duplicate layers contained in her SVC video and also uploads the additional layers. In our proposed secure deduplication framework, the construction with layer-level deduplication includes three phases which are described as follows:

Interaction with the agency. Before uploading a SVC video $SV = \{m_1, m_2, \ldots, m_n\}$ to cloud, the user first needs to engage in the RSA-OPRF protocol with the agency to derive the message-derived tag α_1 of the base layer and a message-derived label set $\{\beta_i\}_{1\leq i\leq n}$ for all layers, where $\alpha_1 = \mathsf{OPRF}^{RSA}_{k_1}(H(m_1))$ and $\beta_i = \mathsf{OPRF}^{RSA}_{k_2}(H(m_i))$.

Upload phase. After the interaction with the agency, the user sends α_1 and the number n of layers of SV to cloud for duplicate check. If a match for α_1 is not found, it is considered as the initial upload of SV. Suppose the initial uploader u has L layers (i.e., $n = L$). Then u performs the dedupable encryption as specified in the secure deduplication framework over each layer. For each layer m_i, u generates a layer ciphertext C_i, a masked layer key r_i along with a random string s_i, and a layer key ciphertext C_{τ_i}, where τ_i is the layer key. Then u sends $\{C_i, (s_i, r_i), C_{\tau_i}\}_{1\leq i\leq L}$ to cloud. Cloud will compute $H(C_i)$ over each layer ciphertext C_i for the later use of PoW protocol.

If a match for α_1 is found, it is indicated that a SVC version with the same base layer is already uploaded by some user. Thus, the upload request is considered as the subsequent upload. Suppose the subsequent uploader u' has L' layers (i.e., $n = L'$) and the already stored SVC version in cloud has L_c layers. The subsequent upload proceeds as follows. If $L' \leq L_c$, u' runs the PoW protocol over all her layers to earn the ownership from cloud. Recall that the layer keys $\{\tau_i\}_{1\leq i\leq L'}$ are recovered during the PoW process. Then u' encrypts each τ_i using the private key and stores them in cloud. If $L' > L_c$, for the L_c preceding layers (duplicates) $\{m_i\}_{1\leq i\leq L_c}$ of the SVC video, u' needs to run the PoW protocol over each of them to earn the ownership from cloud, and produces the ciphertexts $\{C'_{\tau_i}\}_{1\leq i\leq L_c}$ of the recovered layer keys $\{\tau_i\}_{1\leq i\leq L_c}$; for each additional layer m_i, where $L_c < i \leq L'$, u' produces a layer ciphertext C_i, a masked layer key r_i along with a random string s_i, and a layer key ciphertext C'_{τ_i}, where τ_i is the layer key. Then u' stores $\{C_i, (s_i, r_i)\}_{L_c<i\leq L'}$ along with $\{C'_{\tau_i}\}_{1\leq i\leq L'}$ in cloud. Note that for the case that $L' > L_c$, cloud updates L_c as L' when u' passes the PoW protocol enforced over all duplicate layers. Besides, if the number of layers actually owned by u' is less than the submitted one, cloud would not update L_c and only marks u' as the owner of the duplicate layers over which she passes the PoW protocol successfully. Therefore, regardless of the number of layers a user submits during a subsequent upload process, a user is marked as the owner of a duplicate layer only when she passes the PoW protocol over it.

Retrieval phase. During the retrieval process, the user u requests the number of layers she wants for a certain SVC video owned by her to cloud. Then the corresponding layer ciphertexts along with the layer key ciphertexts are returned to u. After that, u can use her secret key to recover each layer key and further recovers each layer.

6. SECURITY ANALYSIS

In this section, we give the security analysis of our system design in detail. We will demonstrate that our system addresses the threats from *Malicious outside adversary* and *Honest-but-curious inside adversary* respectively, as mentioned in Section 2.2, and meets the security goals.

Firstly, we consider the security against *Malicious outside adversary*. The outside adversary wants to use the hash $H(V)$ to gain the ownership of the video that does not belong to her from cloud. Note that the adversary with $H(V)$ can generate the message-derived tag α and label β through the agency. Recall that our PoW approach requires each subsequent user to compute the hash of encrypted video. Thus, the adversary should obtain the correct ciphertext, which means that she needs the plaintext V and the correct encryption key τ. Note that τ is protected via $F(s, V||\beta)$. Without V, the adversary cannot derive τ, not to mention the correct ciphertext. Hence, the PoW will fail and cloud will not be fooled to mark the outside adversary as a legitimate duplicate owner.

Secondly, we consider the security against *Honest-but-curious inside adversary*. As stated, the agency could be semi-trusted, which faithfully produces the message-derived tag and label via its private keys, but is interested in $H(V)$. Accordingly, our system adopts the blind signature (RSA-OPRF), so the input $H(V)$ is oblivious to the agency. On the other hand, we assume cloud is also curious but does not collude with the agency. Cloud stores the encrypted video C_V, the tag α for duplicate check, and the masked key $\tau \oplus F(s, V||\beta)$. We note that cloud is not able to obtain the plaintext V if the video is unpredictable. As mentioned, τ is well protected if cloud does not know V or β. Without τ, cloud cannot decrypt C_V.

Finally, our system can effectively prevent cloud from mounting the off-line brute-force attacks over predictable videos. As mentioned in Section 4.2, if cloud knows a relatively small message space (or a dictionary) underlying an encrypted video, it can compute all the message hashes in this dictionary. We note that leveraging the agency can defend off-line brute-force attacks. Firstly, our system resorts to an agency to assist the generation of message-derived tag α for duplicate check rather than directly exposing the hash $H(V)$ to cloud. Without the private key of the agency, cloud cannot produce the α for each candidate in the dictionary. In our system, it is required to interact with the agency to get α for each trial. Secondly, since cloud has the encrypted video C_V and the masked key $\tau \oplus F(s, V||\beta)$ (along with a random string s), it can try to recover the corresponding key and obtain the video plaintext. Likewise, cloud cannot produce the message-derived label β without requesting the agency. For each trial, cloud needs to interact with the agency to get β and unmask the key via xoring a mask derived from β and V. In a word, for predictable videos, our system can prevent the off-line brute-force attacks in a controllable fashion and turn it into online trials against cloud, which can be significantly slowed down by enforcing several proper rate limiting strategies [2].

Note that the proposed construction of secure deduplication over encrypted SVC videos is built under the secure deduplication framework. And the PoW scheme is enforced over each duplicate layer. Only the user who indeed owns the duplicate layers can earn the ownership.

7. EXPERIMENTS

7.1 Implementations

We implement our system prototype with roughly 7,000 lines of c++ code and 10,000 lines of java code. We use Thrift to create network services between entities with cross-language Remote Process Call (RPC)[1]. We use the GMP library [2] and the Openssl library [3] to perform our cryptography, i.e, blind signature, symmetric encryption (AES/CBC-256), and full-domain hash function (SHA-256). We collect videos from two benchmarks: VIRAT [16] and DASH [13]. We encode those videos into SVC videos (totally around 100GB) with the JSVM software[4], and decode them with the Open SVC decoder [6]. Meanwhile, we integrate the Open SVC decoder library to a open source video player MPlayer[5] and re-compile it to play the SVC videos. The implementations of each entity are described as follows:

- User client: it is developed in c++ and can process user's requests and call corresponding services. In the process of generating the message-derived tag α and label β, the client communicates with the agency. We also implement a basic access control mechanism including user login and register operations.

- Agency: it is also developed in c++. Once it receives the blinded input from client, the agency will compute the signature and response it to the client.

- Application server: it is implemented with java and has three functions. Firstly, it handles the user's request of duplicate check and replies with the result of querying on the storage server. Secondly, it verifies the ownership of videos by processing PoW. Lastly, after getting the download request, it verifies the access permission and replies the corresponding SVC videos.

- Storage server: it stores the encrypted SVC videos with tags for duplicate check and ciphertext hashes for PoW, and the user profiles with encrypted private keys and video ownerships. Here, we choose DynamoDB[6] as our storage backend. Note that our application server is running on Amazon EC2, which can efficiently communicate with DynamoDB.

SVC encryption. At a high level, each frame of a SVC video consists of a base layer and several enhancement layers [19]. To encrypt a SVC video, one straightforward method

[1]Apache Thrift: http://thrift.apache.org
[2]The CNU Multiple Precision Arithmetic Library: https://gmplib.org
[3]OpenSSL Project: http://www.openssl.org
[4]Joint Video Team: SVC reference software(jsvm software), 2011.
[5]MPlayer: http://www.mplayerhq.hu/design7/dload.html
[6]Amazon Web Service: http://aws.amazon.com/

(a) 144P (b) 240P (c) 1080P

Figure 3: Different qualities for a given SVC video.

is to perform symmetric encryption for each layer per frame. However, this method is not directly compatible with the underlying SVC structure [20,22]. From the perspective of the underlying structure, a SVC video bitstream is divided into network abstract layer units (NALUs). Each layer (both base layer and enhancement layers) has its own NALUs, and the NALUs can be identified to the corresponding layers from the attached header information [19]. If the whole layer is encrypted, a user client that requests a video cannot perform timely decryption until the whole ciphertext of one layer is downloaded, which in turn affects the timely decoding for playback, and degrades the user experience and service quality.

Instead of performing encryption at the layer level, we adopt NALU-level encryption inspired from [22], i.e., the payload of each NALU is encrypted individually and the related header information is left in cleartext. As a result, as long as one encrypted NALU is received, the client can perform decryption and then decoding. The processing of each layer can be performed in a pipelined fashion at the user client. For the implementation, the client extracts the layer's NALUs in the same layer for each frame, encrypts them one by one and uploads them to the storage backend.

Storage optimization. The NALUs within the same layer are grouped as a layer block by the storage server in our system. When the client wants to download the video, the storage server needs to fast locate the corresponding layer block and its NALUs. In the SVC standard [19], the NALUs are encoded together by adding the start code prefix, i.e., 0x00000001, between each NALU. Regarding our NALU-based encryption, using the start code to fetch NALUs may not meet the performance requirements for fast retrieval.

To optimize the storage, we use Key-Length-Value (KLV) encoding standard[7] to package the NALU. As a result, the storage server can efficiently distinguish each NALU. Explicitly, NALUs are encoded into Key-Length-Value triplets, where Key identifies the NALU (its frame ID), Length specifies the NALU's length, and Value is the NALU itself. Upon the retrieval of the SVC videos, the storage server can read the NALUs by the help of lengths, and combine them with the same frame ID.

7.2 Evaluation

7.2.1 Visual Experience

Figure 3 shows the different qualities (i.e., resolutions) for a given SVC video after the decryption and decoding at the user client. As shown, our security design does not affect the visual scalability of SVC. The more layers the video has, the higher quality the video is.

[7]BT.1563: Data encoding protocol using key-length-value: http://www.itu.int/rec/R-REC-BT.1563-1-201103-I/en

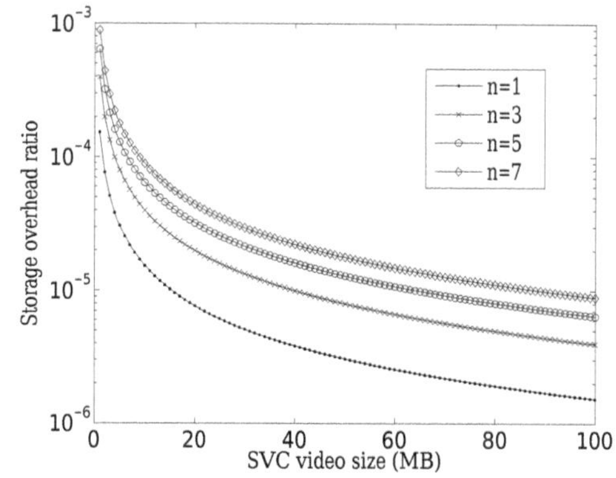

Figure 4: Ratio of the storage overhead to the SVC video size, under different numbers of layers, where n is the number of layers of a SVC video.

7.2.2 Performance

We report our system performance on the aspects of storage overhead, computation costs of different tasks for initial upload and time savings via deduplication. All measurement represents the mean of 10 trials.

Storage overhead. Our design incurs little storage overhead at cloud to support secure deduplication. As we adopt the layer-level deduplication, storing a SVC video with n layers, the storage overhead contains the tag α_1 (32 bytes) for duplicate check, n masked encryption key r with seed s (64 bytes per one) for the access of subsequent users, n owner key ciphertexts (32 bytes per one) and n hashes of the layer ciphertexts (32 bytes per one). Recall that we utilize only the message-derived tag of the base layer for duplicate check, since two SVC videos can hardly have duplicate layers if they do not have the same base layer [21].

In total, the storage overhead for a SVC video with n layers are equal to $32 + 64n + 32n + 32n = 32 + 128n$ bytes, which is roughly in linear to the number of layers and independent of the video size. The relation between the storage overhead and the sizes of SVC videos with different number of layers is displayed in Figure 4. As shown, the storage overhead is very low, compared with the video sizes under different number of layers. For example, given a SVC video with 1MB size and 7 layers, the storage overhead is only 928 bytes, just 0.09% of the video size. And for a fixed number of layers, the ratio quickly diminishes and becomes negligible as the video size gets larger.

Computation costs. We measure the time consumed by different computation tasks during the initial upload. Recall that the computation tasks consist of the following four components: 1. generation of message-derived tag α_1 via RSA-OPRF; 2. SVC video encryption; 3. generation of the masked key r (message-derived label β via RSA-OPRF included); 4. key τ encryption. We note that the time of key encryption is negligible compared to other tasks, so we focus on the first three ones, which are denoted as *vEnc*, *tGen*, and *rGen*, respectively. Besides, *vEnc* is regarded as the necessary operation to safeguard the data confidentiality. Thus, the computation overhead for secure deduplication lies in the other two components, i.e., *tGen* and *rGen*.

Figure 5 depicts the computation costs of the three components when different numbers of layers of a 95MB SVC

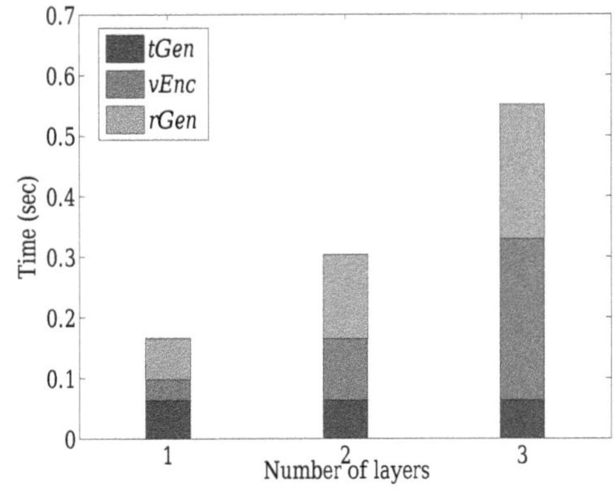

Figure 5: Time costs of different computation tasks for initially uploading different numbers of layers of a SVC video. There are totally three layers and the size is 95MB.

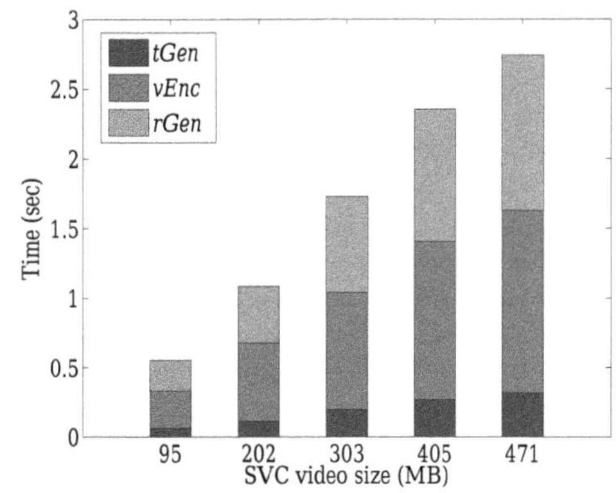

Figure 6: Time costs of different computation tasks for initially uploading SVC videos with the same number of layers but with different sizes. Here each SVC video has three layers.

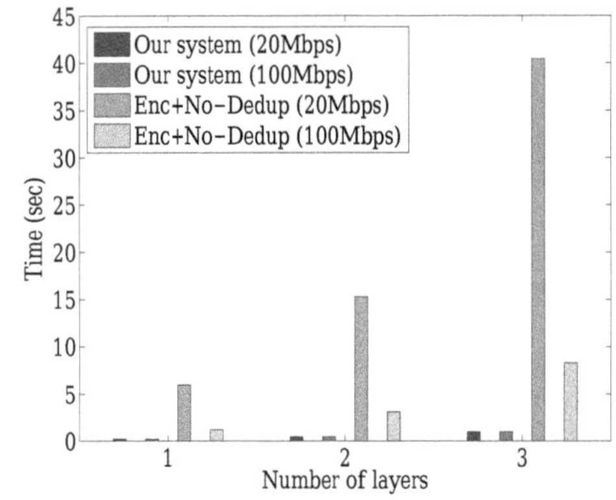

Figure 7: Running time comparisons between our system and Enc + No − Dedup setting, over different numbers of duplicate layers for a given 95MB SVC video, which totally has three layers.

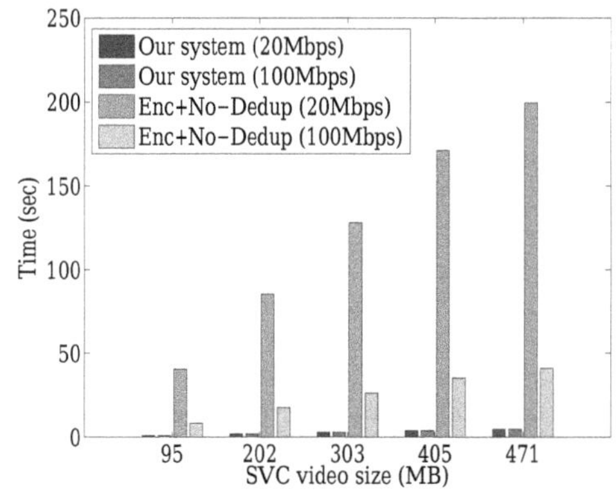

Figure 8: Running time comparisons between our system and Enc + No − Dedup setting, over SVC videos in different sizes but with the same number (three) of duplicate layers.

video is uploaded (totally three layers). The network delays in the RSA-OPRF protocol are not considered. It is observed that the time spent on *vEnc* and *rGen* increases linearly with the number of layers, since the related operations should be conducted for each layer. In contrast, *tGen* remains constant since it is only related to the base layer. Figure 6 shows the computation costs for SVC videos with different sizes but with the same number of layers. When the video sizes increase, the layer sizes increase as well, so each computation task will take more time to finish. Even though, our system is quite practical, e.g., the overall computation cost for a 471MB SVC video is less than 3 seconds.

Time savings. We measure the time savings for the user by using our secure deduplication system, compared with an Enc+No-Dedup policy that always sends the encrypted duplicate SVC videos (layers) to cloud. Two network settings are considered, including a fast network (20Mbps) and an extremely fast network (100Mbps) [1].

Figure 7 compares the running time between our deduplication design and the Ennc + No − Dedup policy, over different numbers of duplicate layers of a 95MB SVC video. Note that the running time in the compared policy includes the layer encryption time and the network transfer time of the layer ciphertexts, while our system includes all the operations specified above for a user to earn the ownership of duplicate layers from cloud. For both two network settings, our design always consumes much less time than the compared policy. The reason is that client-side deduplication is enforced in our system and duplicate layers would not be transferred through the network. Besides, it is noted that although some mechanisms such as the PoW protocol are involved in our system, the advantages in time savings rendered by deduplication remain unaffected. Figure 8 further compares the running time between our deduplication design and the policy over SVC videos in different sizes ranging from 95MB to 471MB with the same number of duplicate layers. As shown, for the 95MB SVC video in the 20 Mbps network setting, the compared policy takes 40.4484 seconds, while the time for our system is only 0.9681 seconds; in the 100 Mbps network setting, the compared policy takes 8.3025 seconds, while the time for our system is only 0.9676 seconds. On average, the time savings provided by our system can achieve about 97% in the 20Mbps network setting and about 88% in the 100Mbps network setting, respectively.

8. RELATED WORK

8.1 Secure Deduplication

Convergent encryption (CE) is first proposed by Douceur et al. [10] for secure deduplication, which enforces data confidentiality while enabling deduplciation. It encrypts/decrypts a file with a convergent key obtained through computing the hash value of the file content. Thus, the same file will always map to the same ciphertext, making deduplication feasible. Later, Bellare et al. [3] formalize CE under the name of message-locked encryption (MLE) and explore its application in secure space-efficient cloud storage, which can support both client-side and server-side deduplication. Recently, Li et al. [14] present a key management scheme based on secret sharing to protect the convergent keys in secure deduplication. The scheme constructs and distributes secret shares of keys across multiple independent servers. However, CE is inherently vulnerable to off-line brute-force attacks over predictable files [2]. The security of CE only holds for unpredictable files.

To securely use server-side deduplication and resist off-line brute-force attacks over predictable files in CE, Bellare et al. [2] resort to a key server (KS) to first provide message-based keys (i.e., hash values protected under the KS's secret key) without disclosing any information on the users' data. Then they adopt rate-limiting strategies on KS to mitigate the online brute-force attacks in practice. Another work proposed by Puzio et al. [17] employ a server to perform additional encryption over the convergent-encrypted data collected from all users. Without knowing the server's secret key, cloud cannot launch off-line brute-force attacks over predictable files. However, their design is only suited for server-side deduplication and the server has to suffer from heavy communication overhead.

Apart from the above inherent vulnerability, CE is insecure in the bounded leakage setting, where the data hash (i.e., the convergent key) may be disclosed [25]. Accordingly, Xu et al. [25] propose a client-side deduplication scheme for encrypted files in the bounded leakage setting. However, for predictable data, the proposed scheme does not consider the defense on the off-line brute-force attacks against the honest-but-curious cloud. Our system design enhances the security via the help of the agency.

8.2 Security Protection for SVC Videos

In [22], Wei et al. present a scalable and format-compliant encryption scheme to protect SVC bitstreams when being disseminated through an open network. The scheme constructs new NALUs to replace the original ones to preserving the SVC scalability. And the resulting encrypted SVC bitstream has the original SVC structure without emulation markers or illegal codewords for the standard SVC decoder, and thus achieves format-compliance. Deng et al. [9] propose an efficient block-based encryption scheme for SVC bitstream encryption. They consider a scenario where a pay TV broadcaster intends to provide a base layer version of the broadcasted program for everyone, but only allows authorized users to further get access to the enhancement layers. Therefore, the base layer is left in the cleartext while the enhancmenet layers are encrypted. The encryption of enhancement layers is achieved by employing secure pseudorandom permutations on macroblocks and subblocks. In [23], Wu et al. study the problem of attribute-based access control on SVC videos in cloud-based content sharing networks. Specifically, they present a novel multiple-message ciphertext policy attribute-based encryption (MCP-ABE) scheme, which can deliver multiple messages within one ciphertext, compared with the traditional CP-ABE scheme [5]. For a SVC video, the scheme constructs a key graph, encrypts layers with the corresponding keys and employs the MCP-ABE to encrypt the key graph. Users with different privileges can first decrypt the encryption of the key (sub)graph, and then decrypt the corresponding encrypted layers. Different from the above works, we investigate secure deduplication over encrypted SVC videos.

9. CONCLUSIONS

In this paper, we have designed and implemented an encrypted cloud media center that hosts encrypted SVC videos and supports secure deduplication. We first formulate a secure deduplication framework with strong protection for videos, which can protect the confidentiality in the bounded leakage setting and defend the off-line brute-force attacks over predictable data, respectively. Under the proposed framework, we then leverage the layered nature of SVC and propose the layer-level deduplication over encrypted SVC videos. We thoroughly analyze the security guarantee of our system against both malicious outside adversaries and honest-but-curious inside adversaries. Our implementation adopts the encryption strategy compatible with the structure and the format of SVC, and optimizes the way encrypted SVC videos are stored to improve the dissemination efficiency. The extensive experiments on Amazon cloud platform further demonstrate the practicality of our system.

In future work, we plan to investigate the support for multiple scalabilities (e.g., time and resolution) of SVC in our layer-level deduplication construction and extend our design for more general cases.

Acknowledgments

This work was supported in part by Research Grants Council of Hong Kong (Project No. CityU 138513), NSFC under grants 61472316 and 61172090, Ph.D. Programs Foundation of Ministry of Education of China under grant 201202-01110013, and Shaanxi Science and Technology Innovation Project under grant 2013SZS16-Z01/P01/K01. The authors would like to thank Prof. Robert H. Deng and Dr. Zhuo Wei for sharing their code in [23] on SVC related software during the early stage of this work.

10. REFERENCES

[1] Akamai. The Akamai State of the Internet Report. `http://www.akamai.com/stateoftheinternet/`.

[2] M. Bellare, S. Keelveedhi, and T. Ristenpart. Dupless: Server-aided encryption for deduplicated storage. In *Proc. of USENIX Security*, 2013.

[3] M. Bellare, S. Keelveedhi, and T. Ristenpart. Message-locked encryption and secure deduplication. In *Proc. of EUROCRYPT*, 2013.

[4] M. Bellare, C. Namprempre, D. Pointcheval, and M. Semanko. The one-more-rsa-inversion problems and the security of chaum's blind signature scheme. *Journal of Cryptology*, 16(3):185–215, 2003.

[5] J. Bethencourt, A. Sahai, and B. Waters. Ciphertext-policy attribute-based encryption. In *Proc. of IEEE SP*, 2007.

[6] M. Blestel and M. Raulet. Open svc decoder: a flexible svc library. In *Proc. of ACM MM*, 2010.

[7] J. Camenisch, G. Neven, and A. Shelat. Simulatable adaptive oblivious transfer. In *Proc. of EUROCRYPT*, 2007.

[8] Cisco Visual Networking Index. Global mobile data traffic forecast update: 2012-2017.

[9] R. H. Deng, X. Ding, Y. Wu, and Z. Wei. Efficient block-based transparent encryption for h.264/svc bitstreams. *Multimedia Systems*, 20(2):165–178, 2014.

[10] J. R. Douceur, A. Adya, W. J. Bolosky, D. Simon, and M. Theimer. Reclaiming space from duplicate files in a serverless distributed file system. In *Proc. of IEEE ICDCS*, 2002.

[11] S. Jarecki and X. Liu. Efficient oblivious pseudorandom function with applications to adaptive ot and secure computation of set intersection. In *Theory of Cryptography, Lecture Notes in Computer Science*, pages 577–594. Springer, 2009.

[12] A. Kathpal, M. Kulkarni, and A. Bakre. Analyzing compute vs. storage tradeoff for video-aware storage efficiency. In *Proc. of USENIX HotStorage*, 2012.

[13] S. Lederer, C. Müller, and C. Timmerer. Dynamic adaptive streaming over http dataset. In *Proc. of ACM MMSys*, 2012.

[14] J. Li, X. Chen, M. Li, J. Li, P. P. Lee, and W. Lou. Secure deduplication with efficient and reliable convergent key management. *IEEE Trans. on Parallel and Distributed Systems*, 25(6):1615–1625, 2014.

[15] North Carolina Daily. Snapchat nude photos, videos reportedly leaked online. `http://www.northcarolinadaily.com/index.php/sid/226634683`, 2014.

[16] S. Oh, A. Hoogs, A. Perera, N. Cuntoor, C.-C. Chen, J. T. Lee, S. Mukherjee, J. Aggarwal, H. Lee, L. Davis, et al. A large-scale benchmark dataset for event recognition in surveillance video. In *Proc. of IEEE CVPR*, 2011.

[17] P. Puzio, R. Molva, M. Önen, and S. Loureiro. Cloudedup: secure deduplication with encrypted data for cloud storage. In *Proc. of IEEE CloudCom*, 2013.

[18] Y. Sanchez, T. Schierl, C. Hellge, T. Wiegand, D. Hong, D. D. Vleeschauwer, W. V. Leekwijck, and Y. L. Louédec. Efficient http-based streaming using scalable video coding. *Signal Processing: Image Communication*, 27(4):329–342, 2012.

[19] H. Schwarz, D. Marpe, and T. Wiegand. Overview of the scalable video coding extension of the h.264/avc standard. *IEEE Trans. on Circuits and System for Video Technology*, 17(9):1103–1120, 2007.

[20] T. Stutz and A. Uhl. A survey of h. 264 avc/svc encryption. *IEEE Trans. on Circuits and Systems for Video Technology*, 22(3):325–339, 2012.

[21] Z. Wei, Y. Wu, R. H. Deng, and X. Ding. A hybrid scheme for authenticating scalable video codestreams. *IEEE Trans. on Information Forensics and Security*, 9(4):543–553, 2014.

[22] Z. Wei, Y. Wu, X. Ding, and R. H. Deng. A scalable and format-compliant encryption scheme for h.264/svc bitstreams. *Signal Processing: Image Communication*, 27(9):1011–1024, 2012.

[23] Y. Wu, Z. Wei, and R. H. Deng. Attribute-based access to scalable media in cloud-assisted content sharing networks. *IEEE Trans. on Multimedia*, 15(4):778–788, 2013.

[24] S. Xiang. Scalable streaming. `https://sites.google.com/site/svchttpstreaming/storagesaving`.

[25] J. Xu, E. Chang, and J. Zhou. Weak leakage-resilient client-side deduplication of encrypted data in cloud storage. In *Proc. of ACM AISACCS*, 2013.

[26] W. Zhu, C. Luo, J. Wang, and S. Li. Multimedia cloud computing. *IEEE Signal Processing Magazine*, 28(3):59–69, 2011.

APPENDIX

A. THE RSA-OPRF PROTOCOL

Table 1: The RSA-OPRF protocol. (N, e) and (N, d) are the agency's public key and secret key, respectively, which are as in the RSA system. M denotes the message to be signed. $\mathsf{H}_1 : \{0,1\}^* \to \mathbb{Z}_N^*$ and $\mathsf{H}_2 : \mathbb{Z}_N^* \to \{0,1\}^\lambda$ are two hash functions.

User		Agency
1. $\gamma \xleftarrow{\$} \mathbb{Z}_N^*$		
2. $h \leftarrow \mathsf{H}_1(M)$		
3. $x \leftarrow h \cdot \gamma^e mod N$		
	$\xrightarrow{x}$	
		4. $y \leftarrow x^d mod N$
	$\xleftarrow{y}$	
5. $z \leftarrow y \cdot \gamma^{-1} mod N$		
6. If $z^e mod N \neq h$ then ret $\perp$; Else ret $\mathsf{H}_2(z)$		

Group-oriented Proofs of Storage

Yujue Wang
1. School of Computer
Wuhan University, China
2. City University of Hong
Kong, Hong Kong S.A.R.
yjwang@whu.edu.cn

Qianhong Wu
School of Electronic and
Information Engineering
Beihang University
Beijing, China
qianhong.wu@buaa.edu.cn

Bo Qin
School of Information
Renmin University of China
Beijing, China
bo.qin@ruc.edu.cn

Xiaofeng Chen
State Key Laboratory of
Integrated Service Networks
Xidian University
Xi'an, China
xfchen@xidian.edu.cn

Xinyi Huang
School of Mathematics and
Computer Science
Fujian Normal University
Fuzhou, China
xyhuang81@gmail.com

Yunya Zhou
School of Electronic and
Information Engineering
Beihang University
Beijing, China
maomaozyy@163.com

ABSTRACT

We introduces and formalizes the notion of *group-oriented proofs of storage* (GPoS). In GPoS, each file owner, after being authorized as a member by a group manager, can outsource files to a group storage account maintained by an untrusted party, for example, a cloud storage server, while anyone can efficiently verify the integrity of the remotely stored files without seeing the files. The file owner's identity privacy is preserved against the cloud server while the group manager can trace the one who outsourced any suspicious file for liability investigation. By novelly identifying and exploiting several useful properties, that is, homomorphic composability and homomorphic verifiability in some signatures, we propose a generic GPoS construction relying on the security of the underlying signature scheme and the hardness of the computational Diffie–Hellman (CDH) problem. Following the generic construction, we instantiate a concrete GPoS scheme with the well-known Boneh–Boyen short signature. By leveraging the polynomial commitment technique, the proposed GPoS proposal is optimized with constant-size bandwidth consumption in proof of storage by the cloud server. Theoretical analyses and comparisons show that our GPoS proposal is advantageous over existing PoS-like schemes in user privacy, public audibility and/or performance in a multi-user setting.

Categories and Subject Descriptors

E.5 [**Data**]: Files

ASIA CCS'15, April 14–17, 2015, Singapore, Singapore.

http://dx.doi.org/10.1145/2714576.2714630 .

Keywords

Cloud storage, Proofs of Storage, Provable Data Possession, Proof of Retrievability, Public auditability

1. INTRODUCTION

Cloud computing provides convenient storage services to the clients and is widely believed to be a promising technique to reduce the clients' local hardware and software maintenance burden of large-scale data storage [6]. However, this remote storage paradigm also brings security concerns about integrity and privacy over the outsourced files [25, 7]. To address the integrity concern, a number of cryptographic concepts have been introduced, for example, Proofs of Storage [3], Provable Data Possession (PDP) [1] and Proofs of Retrievability (PoR) [11].

Although PoS/PDP/PoR have received considerable attentions, most existing proposals, for example, [2, 9, 11, 13, 15, 20, 22, 27], cannot well fit in some real-world applications. Consider a company purchases remote storage services from some cloud storage provider (CSP) for storing files. The employees should be authorized (e.g., by the IT department of the company) in a way such that they can upload files to the company's account maintained by the cloud storage server. It is easy to see that some specific information (e.g., identity) of the file owner should be embedded into the outsourced version of the file so that the company manager can know who outsourced the file if necessary. Otherwise, some dishonest employee may misuse/abuse his/her file-outsourcing capability and even worse, unauthorized outsiders may also upload malicious data to the company's cloud storage account without being caught. Also, the file uploading information may be used to count up the employee's workload, which is usually taken as a critical factor for evaluating employees' performance. However, it is usually the case that the company or the employees would not like to let the cloud storage server know the identity of the file owner who outsources the file.

1.1 Our Work

Motivated by the above application, we introduce and formalize a system of *group-oriented proof of storage* equipped with a number of enjoyable functionalities: (1) A trusted group manager issues secret keys associated with the members' unique identities. Every member can validate his/her secret key from the group manager. The members do not need to share any secret parameters among them. (2) Each group member can locally process the files with the issued secret key, without any further help from the group manager. The produced meta-data in the processed file is aggregatable, which implies economic bandwidth consumption and storage occupation. (3) Any one can serve as an auditor to validate the integrity of the outsourced files for unbounded times by only interacting with the cloud storage server. The integrity can be successfully audited with overwhelming probability without retrieving the outsourced file or inspecting all the file blocks. (4) The file owner is anonymous to the cloud storage server. The server can only know the file is uploaded by a legal member of some group, but cannot trace the identity of the member. In the meanwhile, the group manager can reveal the identity of the file owner for liability investigation.

We provide a secure generic construction of GPoS schemes. We first formalize the security model for GPoS schemes with public auditability. A GPoS scheme should be secure against conspiracy attacks from group members for forging secret keys and meta-data. It should be also able to prevent the cloud storage server involved in auditing the outsourced files from forging an integrity proof and from extracting the file owner's identity from maintained files. The meta-data must be (1) generated with a secret key issued by the group manager, (2) aggregatable, (3) publicly auditable, and (4) ownership privacy-preserving. These requirements raise a great challenge in GPoS construction. We manage to address this challenge by identifying some useful properties, that is, homomorphic composability and homomorphic verifiability (defined in Section 3.1) in some signature schemes. By exploiting these properties, we propose a generic GPoS construction proven secure if the underlying signature is existentially unforgeable and the standard Computational Diffie–Hellman (CDH) assumption holds.

We implement efficient concrete GPoS schemes. Observe that the well-known Boneh–Boyen short signature scheme [4] satisfies the required properties. By following the generic construction, we instantiate a practical GPoS scheme under the CDH assumption in the standard model. Particularly, the Boneh–Boyen short signature scheme is employed to issue secret keys for group members. The resulting GPoS scheme takes linearly computation and communication complexities. The instantiation is further optimized in terms of communication overheads and computation costs at the auditor side for auditing the integrity of the outsourced files. This optimization leverages the polynomial commitment technique [12] to commit to the aggregated file block, which means that the created commitment instead of the aggregated block itself will be responded to the auditor. To this end, the security of the optimized instantiation is reduced to the s-SDH assumption. One may observe that GPoS/PoS/PDP/PoR schemes built over symmetric bilinear groups may be optimized in the same way, which indicates that the polynomial commitment based communication optimization approach is general and universally useful.

The performance of our GPoS instantiations is comprehensively analyzed and compared. The analysis shows that our schemes are advantageous over existing PoS/PDP/PoR schemes in the multi-user setting. Our optimized instantiation enjoys an efficient tradeoff for the basic one, that is, although some additional but affordable computation burden is brought to the resource-redundant cloud server, the communication overheads are significantly saved during audition of the outsourced files. Particularly, the transmitted proof comprises of only three elements, independent of the sector number in a block and the block number in a challenge.

1.2 Related Work

Considerable efforts have been made to remotely check the integrity of the outsourced files in a single-user setting. Ateniese *et al.* [1] and Juels and Kaliski [11] independently investigated secure storage in untrusted clouds and introduced the notions of PDP and PoR, respectively. With these techniques, the integrity of the outsourced files can be audited without retrieving them back. Specifically, Ateniese *et al.*'s scheme supports unbounded number of integrity auditing. Shacham and Waters [13] proposed privately and publicly auditable PoR schemes with strong security proofs. In privately auditable PDP/PoR, the integrity of the outsourced file can only be audited by the one who has the corresponding secret key, that is, the file owner, while anyone can play the role as an auditor in publicly auditable schemes. Ateniese, Kamara, and Katz [3] showed how to convert a homomorphic identification protocol into a public-key homomorphic linear authenticator (HLA) and further constructed PoS from HLA. Dodis, Vadhan, and Wichs [8] improved PoR using the tools based on the coding and complexity theory. Wang *et al.* [20] incorporated a third party auditor (TPA) into the scheme. Such a TPA is able to audit the outsourced files on behalf of owners, but learns nothing about file contents. Zheng and Xu [30] discussed how to avoid maintaining multiple copies of the same file in PoS setting. In [24], Xu and Chang presented a privately auditable PoR using polynomial commitment technique [12], which greatly saves communication overheads compared with the scheme in [13]. Yuan and Yu [27] showed a publicly auditable PoR with the same polynomial commitment technique. Noticed too many heavy computations should be taken at the client side, Wang *et al.* [23] investigated how to offload PDP schemes by securely outsourcing them to a computation server.

In practice, there is a need of dynamic PDP/PoR/PoS schemes in which the outsourced files can be further updated at a block level with insertion, deletion and modification operations. Some early works [1, 2] can partially support those operations. The recent works [22, 9, 29] are equipped with all those functionalities. Among them, Wang *et al.*' scheme [22] is constructed using Merkle Hash Tree, while Erway *et al.*'s [9] schemes are based on the authenticated skip lists and RSA trees. Zhang and Blanton [29] presented a dynamic PDP scheme by employing balanced update trees. Built on oblivious RAM, Cash, Küpçü, and Wichs [5] investigated how to ensure the latest version of the outsourced file maintained by the storage server. Shi, Stefanov, and Papamanthou [14] provided a more efficient dynamic PoR based on special authenticated structures.

Some proposals have been proposed to address the integrity concern of the remote files in a multi-user setting. Wang, Li, and Li [16] investigated how to share data by a group of members through clouds. Although their scheme achieves privacy of the group member's identity in auditing the integrity, it cannot support public auditability or

Table 1: Comparison with Related Works in Multi-user Setting

Scheme	Issuing member's key	Shared secret para.	ID-based	Auditability	Ownership privacy
Wang, Li, and Li [16]	Group manager	Yes	×	TPA (Private)	✓
Wang, Li, and Li [17]	Local	No	×	TPA	✓
Wang *et al.* [15]	–	No	×	Public	✓
Wang, Li, and Li [19]	Group manager	Yes	×	TPA	✓
Wang *et al.* [18]	Local	No	×	TPA	×
Yuan and Yu [28]	Local	No	×	Public	×
Wang *et al.* [21]	Group manager	No	✓	Public*	✓
Yu *et al.* [26]	Local	Yes	×	TPA	×
Our instantiations	Group manager	No	✓	Public	✓

*The public auditor should hold a secret parameter of the file owner when auditing outsourced files.

identity-based deployment. In [17], they revisited the same problem using ring signatures. Each group member should locally prepare his/her secret key, instead of issuing by a group manager. Wang *et al.* [15] considered a scenario such that the group members do not hold secret keys. For any file to be outsourced, the file owner should process it by interacting with a security-mediator in a blind manner, which ensures that the mediator cannot know the file content. Wang, Li, and Li [19] proposed a secure cloud storage scheme that supports dynamic group member changes (for example, join and revocation). However, the group secret key must be delivered to all group members, which is not desirable in practice. Wang *et al.* [18] presented a scheme that enables user revocation without requiring any secret information to be shared among group members. Yuan and Yu [28] presented a scheme that supports multiple users in a group to modify the outsourced file. To this end, the involved members should locally generate secret keys and cooperate in producing public parameters in key generating algorithm. The scheme proposed by Wang *et al.* [21] requires the auditor to hold a secret parameter of file owner when verifying the integrity of the outsourced files. Also, in their scheme [21], the secret key of each group member consists of two elements in $\mathbb{G}$ and $\mathbb{Z}_p$. Yu *et al.*'s proposal [26] achieves ownership privacy-preserving against TPA when auditing the outsourced files, although the group members should locally generate their keys and interact to negotiate a pair of group public/secret keys.

Table 1 summarizes the comparison among the above mentioned PoS-related schemes in multi-user setting. They are compared in terms of comparable properties, that is, the manner of generating secret keys for group members, whether some secret parameters should be shared among group members, whether the scheme is proposed in identity-based setting, auditability of the outsourced files, and whether the identity of file owner is privacy-preserving against the cloud storage server. From the table, it can be seen that our schemes are advantageous over related schemes in ownership privacy, public audibility, freeness of sharing secret parameters and/or freeness of certificates (due to our identity-based design).

2. MODELLING GPOS

In this section, we define the architecture of GPoS schemes and formalize the corresponding security model as well.

2.1 System Architecture

A GPoS system involves four types of entities (as illustrated in Figure 1). The cloud storage server which is a semi-trusted party and maintained by some cloud storage provider, offers the remote storage services to cloud users, for example, file owners. This server also has powerful computation capability to respond the clients' requests. The group manager trusted by its members initiates the system and issues the secret keys for all the members. A file owner, that is, a group member, holds files and would like to outsource them to the cloud storage server. The auditor is also a cloud user, but may be not a group member. The group public information as well as the file tags of the outsourced files are accessible to the auditor. In this way, the auditor can audit the integrity of these files on behalf of group manager and the file owners.

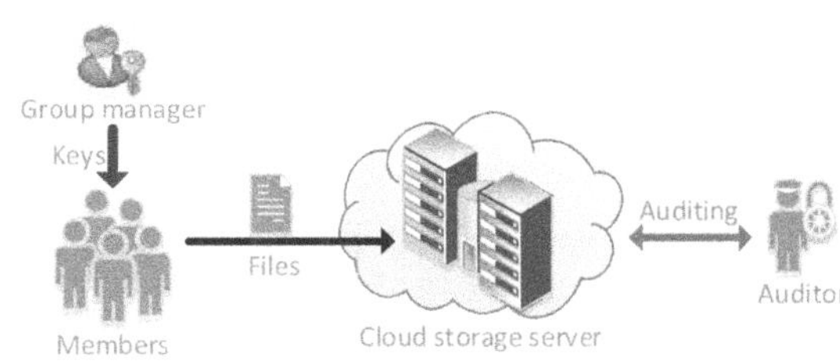

Figure 1: GPoS system model

2.2 Formal System Definition

A GPoS scheme with public auditability comprises six polynomial-time computable algorithms, that is, Setup, KeyExt, PrFile, Chall, PrfGen and Verify.

- $(\mathsf{gpk}, \mathsf{gsk}) \leftarrow \mathsf{Setup}(1^\lambda)$: On input a security parameter λ, the system setup algorithm, run by the group manager, outputs a pair of group public key and group secret key $(\mathsf{gpk}, \mathsf{gsk})$.

- $\mathsf{sk}_\ell \leftarrow \mathsf{KeyExt}(\mathsf{gpk}, \mathsf{gsk}, \mathsf{id}_\ell)$: On input a group public key gpk, a group secret key gsk and a member identity id_ℓ, the key extraction algorithm, run by the group manager, outputs a secret key sk_ℓ. This secret key is verifiable by its holder, that is, member id_ℓ, under group public key gpk.

- $(\tau, F^*) \leftarrow \mathsf{PrFile}(\mathsf{gpk}, \mathsf{sk}_\ell, F)$: On input a group public key gpk, a member's secret key sk_ℓ and a file $F \in \{0,1\}^*$, the processing file algorithm, run by the file owner id_ℓ (a group member), outputs a file tag τ and a processed file F^* that comprises of F and a number of meta-data $\vec{\sigma}$.

- $C \leftarrow \mathsf{Chall}(\mathsf{gpk}, \tau)$: On input a group public key gpk and a file tag τ, the challenge generation algorithm, run by the auditor, outputs a challenge C.
- $R \leftarrow \mathsf{PrfGen}(\mathsf{gpk}, F^*, C)$: On input a group public key gpk, a processed file F^* and a challenge C, the proof generation algorithm, run by the cloud storage server, outputs a proof R.
- $0/1 \leftarrow \mathsf{Verify}(\mathsf{gpk}, \tau, C, R)$: On input a group public key gpk, a file tag τ and a challenge/proof pair (C, R), the verification algorithm, run by the auditor, outputs "1" if R is a valid proof for C, or "0" otherwise.

Informally, the correctness property of a GPoS scheme requires that for any file that processed by any member in the group, if the cloud storage server performs honestly, then the proof R is valid for the challenge C in any round of integrity auditing protocol, that is, Chall-PrfGen-Verify. Formally, we have

DEFINITION 1 (CORRECTNESS). *A GPoS scheme* (Setup, KeyExt, PrFile, Chall, PrfGen, Verify) *is* correct *if for any group key pair* $(\mathsf{gpk}, \mathsf{gsk}) \leftarrow \mathsf{Setup}(1^\lambda)$*, any member* id_ℓ *with secret key* $\mathsf{sk}_\ell \leftarrow \mathsf{KeyExt}(\mathsf{gpk}, \mathsf{gsk}, \mathsf{id}_\ell)$*, and any file* $F \in \{0,1\}^*$*, let* $(\tau, F^*) \leftarrow \mathsf{PrFile}(\mathsf{gpk}, \mathsf{sk}_\ell, F)$*, the verification equation* $\mathsf{Verify}(\mathsf{gpk}, \tau, C, \mathsf{PrfGen}(\mathsf{gpk}, F^*, C)) = 1$ *holds for any challenge* $C \leftarrow \mathsf{Chall}(\mathsf{gpk}, \tau)$.

2.3 Adversary Model and Security Definitions

Note that we do not need to specially consider outsider attackers as they cannot be more powerful than insider attackers, that is, the colluding members or the server. Intuitively, a GPoS scheme may encounter the following conspiracy attacks from the group members and the cloud storage server.

- Secret key forgery. Several group members may collude to forge a secret key with respect to another group member.
- Meta-data forgery. The group members or the cloud storage server may forge meta-data for some file and group member.
- Proof forgery. The cloud storage server and group member may collude to forge a proof when auditing the integrity of some outsourced file with respect to some group member.

An insightful observation indicates the second type of attacks about meta-data forgery can be captured by the third case. Hence, in the following discussion, we only need to consider the secret key forgery and proof forgery. To capture them, we define a formal security model with the following game where a probabilistic polynomial-time (PPT) adversary $\mathcal{A}$ interacts with the challenger $\mathcal{C}$.

Setup: Suppose that the adversary controls a set S_c of corrupted members in the group and sends this set to $\mathcal{C}$. The challenger runs $\mathsf{Setup}(1^\lambda)$ to generate a pair of group public/secret keys $(\mathsf{gpk}, \mathsf{gsk})$ and gives gpk to $\mathcal{A}$.

Queries: The adversary adaptively queries the challenger. For each query, the challenger records the queried information as well as response in lists that are initiated as empty.

- *Key extraction:* The adversary adaptively queries the challenger to obtain the secret key of a member in the corrupted set S_c. The challenger returns the result of KeyExt for each queried member identity.
- *Processing file:* The adversary sends a file F and a member identity id_ℓ to the challenger. If the secret key of member id_ℓ has not been queried before, then the challenger should first run $\mathsf{KeyExt}(\mathsf{gpk}, \mathsf{gsk}, \mathsf{id}_\ell)$. The challenger computes $(\tau, F^*) \leftarrow \mathsf{PrFile}(\mathsf{gpk}, \mathsf{sk}_\ell, F)$ and sends (τ, F^*) to $\mathcal{A}$. Note that for each file, there is a unique file identifer in the file tag τ. For guaranteeing its uniqueness, we let it be randomly chosen by the challenger during the query.
- *Integrity auditing:* For any processed file in above processing file queries, the challenger (acting as the auditor) can audit its integrity by challenging the adversary (acting as the prover). That is, they jointly carry out the integrity auditing protocol. In detail, for any file F in the query list, the challenger can challenge $\mathcal{A}$ with $C \leftarrow \mathsf{Chall}(\mathsf{gpk}, \tau)$, and $\mathcal{A}$ responds with a proof R. Then, the challenger verifies R by invoking $\mathsf{Verify}(\mathsf{gpk}, \tau, C, R)$ and gives the results to $\mathcal{A}$.

End-Game: Finally, the adversary outputs a secret key sk'_ℓ for some member id'_ℓ, or a pair of challenge/proof (C', R') with regard to some file F' identified by file tag τ'.

DEFINITION 2 (SOUNDNESS). *A GPoS scheme is* sound *if for any PPT adversary* $\mathcal{A}$ *playing the above mentioned security game by interacting with the challenger, the outputs are neither of the following cases:*

- ***Case 1.*** *The secret key* sk'_ℓ *is valid under the group public key* gpk *for a member* id'_ℓ *but* $\mathsf{id}'_\ell \notin S_c$.
- ***Case 2.*** *The pair of challenge/proof* (C', R') *is valid but* R' *does not equal to that generated by the challenger from locally maintained information.*

A secure GPoS scheme also requires that, in the entire life span of an outsourced file, its owner identity should be hidden from the cloud storage server. Essentially, this *ownership privacy-preserving* property requires the files should be uploaded in the name of the group. As in the real application scenario, the files are uploaded by the employee under the company's account. Also, in any round of integrity auditing protocol with regard to any outsourced file, the cloud storage server should be able to respond with a valid integrity proof R without using the file owner's identity. More technically,

DEFINITION 3 (OWNERSHIP PRIVACY). *A GPoS scheme is* ownership privacy-preserving *against the cloud storage server if for any file* $F \in \{0,1\}^*$ *and any two distinct members* $\mathsf{id}_{\ell,1}$ *and* $\mathsf{id}_{\ell,2}$ *in the same group, the following two distributions are identical from the view of the cloud storage server:*

$$\left\{ \vec{\sigma}_1 : \begin{array}{r} (\mathsf{gpk}, \mathsf{gsk}) \leftarrow \mathsf{Setup}(1^\lambda), \\ \mathsf{sk}_{\ell,1} \leftarrow \mathsf{KeyExt}(\mathsf{gpk}, \mathsf{gsk}, \mathsf{id}_{\ell,1}), \\ (\tau_1, F_1^*) \leftarrow \mathsf{PrFile}(\mathsf{gpk}, \mathsf{sk}_{\ell,1}, F) \end{array} \right\},$$

and

$$\left\{ \vec{\sigma}_2 : \begin{array}{r} (\mathsf{gpk}, \mathsf{gsk}) \leftarrow \mathsf{Setup}(1^\lambda), \\ \mathsf{sk}_{\ell,2} \leftarrow \mathsf{KeyExt}(\mathsf{gpk}, \mathsf{gsk}, \mathsf{id}_{\ell,2}), \\ (\tau_2, F_2^*) \leftarrow \mathsf{PrFile}(\mathsf{gpk}, \mathsf{sk}_{\ell,2}, F) \end{array} \right\}.$$

3. GENERIC GPOS CONSTRUCTION

Suppose $\mathbb{G}_1 = \langle g_1 \rangle$ and $\mathbb{G}_2 = \langle g_2 \rangle$ be (multiplicative) cyclic groups of prime order p with efficient group actions. The groups $(\mathbb{G}_1, \mathbb{G}_2)$ are bilinear if there exists a (multiplicative) cyclic group $\mathbb{G}_T$ of the same order and an efficient bilinear map $\hat{e} : \mathbb{G}_1 \times \mathbb{G}_2 \rightarrow \mathbb{G}_T$ such that:

(1) Bilinearity: $\forall h \in \mathbb{G}_1, \hbar \in \mathbb{G}_2$, and $\forall \alpha, \beta \in \mathbb{Z}_p^*$, $\hat{e}(h^\alpha, \hbar^\beta) = \hat{e}(h, \hbar)^{\alpha\beta}$;

(2) Non-degeneracy: $\hat{e}(g_1, g_2) \neq 1$.

Our GPoS scheme and instantiations rely on the following well-known computational assumptions.

Computational Diffie–Hellman Assumption: Given a triple (g, g^α, g^β) for $\alpha, \beta \in_R \mathbb{Z}_p^*$, any PPT algorithm $\mathcal{A}$ has negligible probability, that is,

$$\Pr[\mathcal{A}(g, g^\alpha, g^\beta) = g^{\alpha\beta} : \alpha, \beta \in_R \mathbb{Z}_p^*]$$

to compute $g^{\alpha\beta}$.

s-Strong Diffie–Hellman (s-SDH) Assumption [4]: Given a $(s+1)$-tuple

$$(g, g^\alpha, \cdots, g^{\alpha^s})$$

for randomly chosen $\alpha \in_R \mathbb{Z}_p^*$, any PPT algorithm $\mathcal{A}$ has negligible probability

$$\Pr\left[\mathcal{A}(g, g^\alpha, \cdots, g^{\alpha^s}) = (z, g^{\frac{1}{\alpha+z}}) : \alpha \in_R \mathbb{Z}_p^*, z \in \mathbb{Z}_p^* \backslash \{-\alpha\}\right]$$

to compute a pair $(z, g^{\frac{1}{\alpha+z}})$.

3.1 Useful Properties in Signatures

To construct GPoS, we first need a secure way to generate secret keys for the group members. It is well-known that in group-oriented cryptographic primitives, the group members should not be allowed to (freely) generate secret keys by themselves. Instead, these keys are usually generated and distributed for all members by a (trusted) group manager. The secret key of a group member should be associated with his/her identity. To this end, the group manager usually signs the identity of the member and outputs the signature as the secret key of the member. An advantage of this approach is that it is naturally collusion-resistant in the sense that even colluding users cannot forge a valid secret key if the underlying signature is existentially unforgeable. However, this approach also brings a challenge in constructing group-oriented PoS schemes, not only because the files are processed by group members with their secret keys and each meta-data should incorporate at least a file identifier and a file block with many sectors, but also the produced meta-data should be aggregatable and publicly auditable. In fact, the situation will be even worse in constructing generic GPoS schemes equipped with user privacy.

We observe that some signature schemes enjoy several interesting properties useful to address the above challenge. We refer to these properties as homomorphic composability and homomorphic verifiability defined as follows. Let $\mathcal{S} = (\mathsf{KGen}, \mathsf{Sign}, \mathsf{Vrfy})$ be a signature scheme defined over some cyclic group $\mathbb{G} = \langle g \rangle$, and $\mathcal{M}$, $\mathcal{K}$ and Σ be the message space, secret key space and signature space of $\mathcal{S}$, respectively, where the signature space is assumed to be a finite multiplicative cyclic group.

Definition 4 (Homomorphic Composability). *A signature scheme $\mathcal{S}$ is $(\varphi, \digamma)$-homomorphic composable if*

(1) there exist two efficiently computable functions such as $\varphi : \mathcal{K} \times \mathcal{M} \rightarrow \mathcal{R}$ where $\mathcal{R}$ denotes some ring, and $\digamma : \mathbb{G} \times \mathcal{R} \rightarrow \Sigma$; and

(2) for each message $m \in_R \mathcal{M}$ and every key pair $(\mathsf{pk}, \mathsf{sk}) \leftarrow \mathcal{S}.\mathsf{KGen}(1^\lambda)$, the corresponding signature has the form $\sigma = \digamma(g, \varphi(\mathsf{sk}, m)) \leftarrow \mathcal{S}.\mathsf{Sign}(\mathsf{sk}, m)$. It holds that

$$\digamma(g, \varphi(\mathsf{sk}, m))^x = \digamma(g^x, \varphi(\mathsf{sk}, m))$$

for any value $x \in_R \mathcal{R}$, where $\digamma()^x$ is the exponentiation operation over Σ.

Definition 5 (Homomorphic Verifiability). *A signature scheme $\mathcal{S}$ is $(\varphi, \digamma)$-homomorphic verifiable if*

(1) there is an efficient test algorithm $\Xi(\mathsf{pk}; m, \sigma; \ddot{x}, \ddot{y})$ which takes a public key pk, a message/signature pair (m, σ), and a pair of elements $\ddot{x} \in \mathbb{G}$ and $\ddot{y} \in \Sigma$; and

(2) the algorithm Ξ outputs "1" if the given pair of message/signature is valid under pk, that is, $\mathcal{S}.\mathsf{Vrfy}(\mathsf{pk}, m, \sigma) = 1$, and $\varphi_1 = \varphi_2$ in $\mathcal{R}$, where $\varphi_1 = \digamma^{-1}(g, \sigma)$ and $\varphi_2 = \digamma^{-1}(\ddot{x}, \ddot{y})$. Otherwise, outputs "0".

We provide two exemplary signature schemes that satisfy these properties.

Boneh–Boyen scheme [4]. Let $\hat{e} : \mathbb{G}_1 \times \mathbb{G}_2 \rightarrow \mathbb{G}_T$ be an asymmetric bilinear map, where $\mathbb{G}_1 = \langle g_1 \rangle$, $\mathbb{G}_2 = \langle g_2 \rangle$ and $\mathbb{G}_T$ are (multiplicative) cyclic groups of prime order p.

- $\mathsf{KGen}(1^\lambda)$: Pick a random value $\gamma \in_R \mathbb{Z}_p^*$ to be the secret key sk, and compute $\varpi = g_2^\gamma$. The public key is
$$\mathsf{pk} = (\hat{e}, \mathbb{G}_1, \mathbb{G}_2, \mathbb{G}_T, g_1, g_2, p, \varpi)$$
- $\mathsf{Sign}(\mathsf{pk}, \mathsf{sk}, m)$: For any given message $m \in_R \mathbb{Z}_p$, compute the signature
$$\sigma = g_1^{\frac{1}{\gamma+m}}$$
If $m + \gamma = 0$, then set the signature as the identity element in $\mathbb{G}_1$.
- $\mathsf{Vrfy}(\mathsf{pk}, m, \sigma)$: If the equality
$$\hat{e}(\sigma, \varpi \cdot g_2^m) \stackrel{?}{=} \hat{e}(g_1, g_2)$$
holds, then the signature σ is valid for m and thus output "1"; otherwise, output "0".

We define

$$\varphi(\mathsf{sk}, m) = \frac{1}{\gamma + m} \mod p$$

and

$$\digamma(g_1, \varphi(\mathsf{sk}, m)) = g_1^{\varphi(\mathsf{sk}, m)}$$

For any $x \in_R \mathbb{Z}_p^*$, the function $\digamma$ satisfies homomorphic composability property, that is,

$$\digamma(g_1, \varphi(\mathsf{sk}, m))^x = g_1^{x \cdot \frac{1}{\gamma+m}} = \digamma(g_1^x, \varphi(\mathsf{sk}, m)).$$

Define the testing algorithm Ξ to output "1" if and only if both

$$\hat{e}(\sigma, \varpi \cdot g_2^m) = \hat{e}(g_1, g_2)$$

and

$$\hat{e}(\ddot{y}, \varpi \cdot g_2^m) = \hat{e}(\ddot{x}, g_2)$$

hold. Hence, it also satisfies homomorphic verifiability.

Gennaro–Halevi–Rabin scheme [10]. Let $H : \{0,1\}^* \rightarrow \{2n+1 : n \in \mathbb{Z}\}$ be a collision-resistant hash function.

- $\mathsf{KGen}(1^\lambda)$: Pick two random primes $p, q \in_R [2^\lambda, 2^{\lambda+1}]$ such that both $\frac{p-1}{2}$ and $\frac{q-1}{2}$ are also primes. Compute $N = pq$. Let $\mathbb{G}$ be a subgroup of squares in $\mathbb{Z}_N^*$. Pick a random element $g \in_R \mathbb{G}$. The secret key is $\mathsf{sk} = (p, q)$, and the public key is $\mathsf{pk} = (N, g)$.

- $\mathsf{Sign}(\mathsf{pk}, \mathsf{sk}, m)$: For any given message $m \in \{0,1\}^*$, compute the signature

$$\sigma = g^{\frac{1}{H(m)}}$$

- $\mathsf{Vrfy}(\mathsf{pk}, m, \sigma)$: If the equality

$$\sigma^{H(m)} \stackrel{?}{=} g$$

holds, then the signature σ is valid for m and thus output "1"; otherwise, output "0".

For GHR signature scheme, we have

$$\varphi(\mathsf{sk}, m) = \frac{1}{H(m)} \bmod \xi(N)$$

and

$$\digamma(g, \varphi(\mathsf{sk}, m)) = g^{\varphi(\mathsf{sk}, m)} \bmod N$$

where $\xi(N)$ is the Euler totient function of N. For any $x \in_R \mathbb{Z}^*$, the function $\digamma$ satisfies homomorphic composability property, that is,

$$\digamma(g, \varphi(\mathsf{sk}, m))^x = g^{x \cdot \frac{1}{H(m)}} = \digamma(g^x, \varphi(\mathsf{sk}, m)).$$

Define the testing algorithm Ξ to output "1" if and only if both

$$\sigma^{H(m)} = g$$

and

$$\ddot{y}^{H(m)} = \ddot{x}$$

hold. Hence, it also satisfies homomorphic verifiability.

3.2 Our GPoS Construction

Let $\mathcal{S}_k = (\mathsf{KGen}, \mathsf{Sign}, \mathsf{Vrfy})$ be a secure signature scheme which has the properties described in Section 3.1. Also let $\mathcal{S}_t = (\mathsf{KGen}, \mathsf{Sign}, \mathsf{Vrfy})$ be a secure standard signature scheme. Suppose the group consists of n members and $H_0 : \{0,1\}^* \to \mathcal{R}$ be a collision-resistant hash function.

For GPoS construction with the above defined properties, a group member id_ℓ only holds his/her secret key in the form of $\digamma(g, \varphi(\mathsf{gsk}, \mathsf{id}_\ell))$, where gsk denotes a group secret key. Thus, he/she cannot directly use gsk or $\varphi(\mathsf{gsk}, \mathsf{id}_\ell)$ for producing meta-data (signature for a file block). We explain how to employ trapdoor technique to circumvent this issue. In detail, the group member id_ℓ can randomly pick (secret) values $\alpha_i \in_R \mathcal{R}$ and compute the corresponding powers $u_i = g^{\alpha_i}$ as public parameters. When signing on a list of messages $\{m_i\}$, the member id_ℓ first evaluates a linear function

$$f_e = f(\{m_i, \alpha_i\}) = \sum \alpha_i m_i$$

over ring $\mathcal{R}$, and then computes

$$\sigma' = (\digamma(g, \varphi(\mathsf{gsk}, \mathsf{id}_\ell)))^{f_e} = \digamma(g^{f_e}, \varphi(\mathsf{gsk}, \mathsf{id}_\ell)).$$

In this way, it is easy to see that the component g^{f_e} can be recovered using public parameters $\{u_i\}$ and messages $\{m_i\}$.

Hence, under group public key gpk, the test algorithm Ξ can go through as follows

$$\Xi\left(\mathsf{gpk}; \mathsf{id}_\ell, \digamma(g, \varphi(\mathsf{gsk}, \mathsf{id}_\ell)); g^{f_e}, \sigma'\right) = 1.$$

Now we are ready to describe our generic construction.

$\mathsf{Setup}(1^\lambda)$**:** The group manager invokes $\mathcal{S}_k.\mathsf{KGen}(1^\lambda)$ to obtain a pair of public/secret keys, and sets them as the group public key and group secret key $(\mathsf{gpk}, \mathsf{gsk})$.

$\mathsf{KeyExt}(\mathsf{gpk}, \mathsf{gsk}, \mathsf{id}_\ell)$**:** For each member id_ℓ $(1 \le \ell \le n)$ in the group, the group manager computes a signature of his/her identity as follows

$$\mathsf{sk}_\ell \leftarrow \mathcal{S}_k.\mathsf{Sign}(\mathsf{gsk}, \mathsf{id}_\ell) \in \Sigma.$$

Such a signature serves as his/her secret key. When receiving sk_ℓ, the member id_ℓ is able to validate it by invoking $\mathcal{S}_k.\mathsf{Vrfy}$ with group public key gpk.

$\mathsf{PrFile}(\mathsf{gpk}, \mathsf{sk}_\ell, F)$**:** Given a file F, the member id_ℓ splits it into blocks such that each block has s sectors (as elements in $\mathcal{R}$) as follows

$$F = \{F_i = (f_{i,1}, \cdots, f_{i,s}) : 1 \le i \le r\}. \quad (1)$$

Then choose a random file identifier $fid \in_R \mathcal{R}$ and $(s+1)$ random values $\alpha_0, \alpha_1, \cdots, \alpha_s \in_R \mathcal{R}$. Compute

$$u_j = g^{\alpha_j} \in \mathbb{G}$$

for each $0 \le j \le s$. Let τ_0 be the concatenation string of

$$(\mathsf{gpk}, \mathsf{id}_\ell, u_0, u_1, \cdots, u_s, fid, r)$$

Generate the file tag by the following steps:

- Compute $(\mathsf{tpk}, \mathsf{tsk}) \leftarrow \mathcal{S}_t.\mathsf{KGen}(1^\lambda)$ to obtain a pair of public/secret keys;
- Compute $\vartheta \leftarrow \mathcal{S}_t.\mathsf{Sign}(\mathsf{tsk}, \tau_0)$ to obtain a signature of string τ_0.
- Send the file tag $\tau = (\tau_0, \mathsf{tpk}, \vartheta)$ to the group manager.

For each file block F_i $(1 \le i \le r)$, the member id_ℓ computes

$$\theta_i = \alpha_0 H_0(fid \parallel i) + \sum_{j=1}^{s} \alpha_j f_{i,j} \in \mathcal{R}$$

and generates meta-data as

$$\sigma_i \leftarrow \mathsf{sk}_\ell^{\theta_i} \in \Sigma$$

Send the processed file

$$F^* = \{(F_i, \sigma_i) : 1 \le i \le r\}$$

to the cloud storage server. Deletes the random values $\alpha_0, \alpha_1, \cdots, \alpha_s$, secret key tsk and the file locally.

$\mathsf{Chall}(\mathsf{gpk}, \tau)$**:** The auditor runs the algorithm as follows.

1. Invoke $\mathcal{S}_t.\mathsf{Vrfy}(\mathsf{tpk}, \tau_0, \vartheta)$ to validate the file tag τ. If it is invalid, outputs "0" and terminates.

2. Pick a random subset $Q \subseteq [1, r]$ and choose a random value $\beta_i \in_R \mathcal{R}$ for each $i \in Q$. Send the challenge

$$C = (fid, Q, \{\beta_i : i \in Q\})$$

to the cloud storage server.

$\mathsf{PrfGen}(\mathsf{gpk}, F^*, C)$: The cloud storage server computes the aggregated file block $\vec{\mu} = (\mu_1, \cdots, \mu_s)$ and meta-data σ as follows

$$\mu_j = \sum_{i \in Q} \beta_i f_{i,j} \in \mathcal{R} \text{ for each } j \in [1, s],$$

and

$$\sigma = \prod_{i \in Q} \sigma_i^{\beta_i} \in \Sigma. \quad (2)$$

Return the proof $R = (\vec{\mu}, \sigma)$ to the auditor.

$\mathsf{Verify}(\mathsf{gpk}, \tau, C, R)$: If R cannot be parsed, output "0" and terminates. Otherwise, check

$$\Xi\left(\mathsf{gpk}; \mathsf{id}_\ell, \mathsf{sk}_\ell; u_0^{\sum_{i \in Q} \beta_i H_0(fid \| i)} \cdot \prod_{j=1}^{s} u_j^{\mu_j}, \sigma\right) \stackrel{?}{=} 1. \quad (3)$$

If so, output "1"; otherwise, output "0".

3.3 The Security

THEOREM 1. *The proposed GPoS scheme is correct.*

PROOF. We only show Equation (3) holds as the other parts are straightforward. Observing that

$$\mathsf{sk}_\ell = F(g, \varphi(\mathsf{gsk}, \mathsf{id}_\ell))$$

we have

$$\begin{aligned}
\sigma &= \prod_{i \in Q} \sigma_i^{\beta_i} = \prod_{i \in Q} F\left(g, \varphi(\mathsf{gsk}, \mathsf{id}_\ell)\right)^{\theta_i \beta_i} \\
&= F\left(g, \varphi(\mathsf{gsk}, \mathsf{id}_\ell)\right)^{\sum_{i \in Q} \theta_i \beta_i} \\
&= F\left(g^{\sum_{i \in Q} \beta_i (\alpha_0 H_0(fid \| i) + \sum_{j=1}^{s} \alpha_j f_{i,j})}, \varphi(\mathsf{gsk}, \mathsf{id}_\ell)\right) \\
&= F\Big(\prod_{i \in Q} g^{\beta_i \alpha_0 H_0(fid \| i)} \cdot \prod_{i \in Q} \prod_{j=1}^{s} g^{\beta_i \alpha_j f_{i,j}}, \varphi(\mathsf{gsk}, \mathsf{id}_\ell)\Big) \\
&= F\Big(\prod_{i \in Q} g^{\beta_i \alpha_0 H_0(fid \| i)} \cdot \prod_{j=1}^{s} u_j^{\sum_{i \in Q} \beta_i f_{i,j}}, \varphi(\mathsf{gsk}, \mathsf{id}_\ell)\Big) \\
&= F\left(u_0^{\sum_{i \in Q} \beta_i H_0(fid \| i)} \cdot \prod_{j=1}^{s} u_j^{\mu_j}, \varphi(\mathsf{gsk}, \mathsf{id}_\ell)\right).
\end{aligned}$$

It can be seen that σ has the same component $\varphi(\mathsf{gsk}, \mathsf{id}_\ell)$ as the secret key sk_ℓ. According to the definition of algorithm Ξ, the correctness follows. □

THEOREM 2. *Suppose that the signature scheme $\mathcal{S}_t$ for file tags is existentially unforgeable. The proposed GPoS scheme is sound for any PPT adversary $\mathcal{A}$ if the CDH assumption holds.*

PROOF. Since the unforgeability of group members' secret keys is guaranteed by a secure signature scheme $\mathcal{S}_k$, it is omitted in the following discussion while only the soundness with regard to the integrity auditing of outsourced files is considered.

Suppose a PPT adversary $\mathcal{A}$ who controls a set S_c of group members and breaks the soundness of the proposed generic GPoS scheme. Let the adversary play the security game described in Definition 2 by interacting with the challenger $\mathcal{C}$. We show that if the adversary can output a (forged) valid pair of challenge/proof (C', R') with regard to a file F' and a tag τ', then we can construct an algorithm $\mathcal{B}$ by interacting with $\mathcal{A}$ to break the CDH assumption.

Setup: The adversary $\mathcal{A}$ sends the corrupted set S_c to $\mathcal{B}$. On input a security parameter λ, the challenger generates a pair of group public key and secret key $(\mathsf{gpk}, \mathsf{gsk})$. Send gpk to $\mathcal{B}$, who forwards it to the adversary $\mathcal{A}$.

Queries: The adversary can adaptively interact with the simulator $\mathcal{B}$ who maintains all the intermediate information, that is, all the queries and responses.

- *Processing file:* For each query from $\mathcal{A}$ with a file F and a member identity id_ℓ, the simulator $\mathcal{B}$ passes them to $\mathcal{C}$. If the identity has not been queried before, then the challenger first invokes KeyExt to extract a private key sk_ℓ for it. After running the algorithm PrFile, the challenger gives the private key sk_ℓ, a file tag τ and a list of meta-data $\{\sigma_i\}_{1 \le i \le r}$ to $\mathcal{B}$, where the file identifier fid (an element in τ) is randomly chosen by $\mathcal{C}$. The simulator $\mathcal{B}$ forwards the received information to $\mathcal{A}$. If $\mathsf{id}_\ell \notin S_c$, then sk_ℓ cannot be given to $\mathcal{A}$.

- *Integrity auditing:* For this type of queries, the simulator and the adversary play the roles as a verifier and a prover, respectively. For any file F that has been queried for processing, the simulator $\mathcal{B}$ runs $\mathsf{Chall}(\mathsf{gpk}, \tau)$ to generate a challenge

$$C = (fid, Q, \{\beta_i : i \in Q\})$$

and sends it to $\mathcal{A}$. The adversary responds with a proof $R = (\vec{\mu}, \sigma)$. The simulator verifies the proof P by running $\mathsf{Verify}(\mathsf{gpk}, \tau, C, R)$ and gives the verification results to $\mathcal{A}$.

End-Game: Finally, the adversary outputs a (forged) valid pair of challenge/proof (C', P') with regard to a file F' and a tag

$$\tau' = (\tau_0', \mathsf{tpk}, \vartheta')$$

that is, the pair of

$$C' = (fid, Q, \{\beta_i : i \in Q\})$$

and

$$R' = (\vec{\mu}', \sigma')$$

satisfy the testing algorithm Ξ. Note that file F' has been queried for processing. Assume it belongs to some member $\mathsf{id}_\ell \notin S_c$ and has identifier fid, both of which are specified in τ'. As we discussed, the forged and real proofs have the following representations, that is,

$$\begin{aligned}
\sigma' &= F\Big(u_0^{\sum_{i \in Q} \beta_i H_0(fid \| i)} \cdot \prod_{j=1}^{s} u_j^{\mu_j'}, \varphi(\mathsf{gsk}, \mathsf{id}_\ell)\Big) \\
&= F\left(g, \varphi(\mathsf{gsk}, \mathsf{id}_\ell)\right)^{\alpha_0 \sum_{i \in Q} \beta_i H_0(fid \| i) + \sum_{j=1}^{s} \alpha_j \mu_j'}
\end{aligned}$$

and

$$\sigma = \digamma\left(u_0^{\sum_{i\in Q}\beta_i H_0(fid\|i)} \cdot \prod_{j=1}^{s} u_j^{\mu_j}, \varphi(\mathsf{gsk}, \mathsf{id}_\ell)\right)$$
$$= \digamma\left(g, \varphi(\mathsf{gsk}, \mathsf{id}_\ell)\right)^{\alpha_0 \sum_{i\in Q}\beta_i H_0(fid\|i) + \sum_{j=1}^{s}\alpha_j\mu_j}.$$

Notice that, at least one pair of $\{(\mu'_j, \mu_j)\}_{1\le j\le s}$ should be different, since otherwise, $\sigma' = \sigma$ would also hold. Without loss of generality, assume $\mu'_1 \neq \mu_1$, while $\mu'_j = \mu_j$ for $2 \le j \le s$. In this case, the simulator, having the private key

$$\mathsf{sk}_\ell = \digamma(g, \varphi(\mathsf{gsk}, \mathsf{id}_\ell)) \in \mathbb{G}$$

and the public parameter $u_1 = g^{\alpha_1} \in \mathbb{G}$ with unknown exponents, can compute the CDH answer $\digamma(g, \varphi(\mathsf{gsk}, \mathsf{id}_\ell))^{\alpha_1}$ as follows

$$\left(\frac{\sigma'}{\sigma}\right)^{\frac{1}{\mu'_1-\mu_1}} = \left(\digamma(g, \varphi(\mathsf{gsk}, \mathsf{id}_\ell))^{\alpha_1(\mu'_1-\mu_1)}\right)^{\frac{1}{\mu'_1-\mu_1}}$$
$$= \digamma(g, \varphi(\mathsf{gsk}, \mathsf{id}_\ell))^{\alpha_1}.$$

Thus, the simulator breaks the CDH assumption. □

THEOREM 3. *The proposed GPoS scheme is ownership privacy-preserving against the cloud storage server.*

PROOF. On one hand, it is easy to see that, when auditing an outsourced file with respect to a group member id_ℓ, the cloud storage server does not know this specific membership. On the other hand, the produced meta-data in the processed file look random to the cloud server if the elements in both the ring $\mathcal{R}$ and the group $\mathbb{G}$ are uniformly distributed. Since all the values such as α_i-es are randomly chosen in $\mathcal{R}$, the meta-data $\sigma_i \in \mathbb{G}$ are random elements in $\mathbb{G}$ and independent of the file owner's identity in the view of the cloud storage server. □

4. INSTANTIATIONS

In this section, we first present an instantiation based on the Boneh–Boyen short signature [4]. We next show that a special type of GPoS instantiations can be further optimized with a polynomial commitment technique [12]. The signature scheme $\mathcal{S}_t$ is the same as in Section 3.2. Let $H_0 : \{0,1\}^* \to \mathbb{Z}_p^*$ be a collision-resistant hash function.

4.1 A CDH-based Instantiation

$\mathsf{Setup}(1^\lambda)$: The group manager picks a bilinear pairing $\hat{e} : \mathbb{G}\times\mathbb{G} \to \mathbb{G}_T$, where $\mathbb{G} = \langle g\rangle$ and $\mathbb{G}_T$ are cyclic groups of prime order p. Choose a random value $\gamma \in_R \mathbb{Z}_p^*$ and computes $\varpi = g^\gamma$. Let $H : \{0,1\}^* \to \mathbb{Z}_p^*$ be a collision-resistant hash function. The group public key is

$$\mathsf{gpk} = (\hat{e}, \mathbb{G}, \mathbb{G}_T, g, \varpi, H)$$

and the group secret key is $\mathsf{gsk} = \gamma$.

$\mathsf{KeyExt}(\mathsf{gpk}, \mathsf{gsk}, \mathsf{id}_\ell)$: For each member id_ℓ $(1 \le \ell \le n)$ in the group, the group manager computes a secret key

$$\mathsf{sk}_\ell = g^{\frac{1}{\gamma + H(\mathsf{id}_\ell)}}.$$

Once receiving sk_ℓ, the member id_ℓ can validate it by checking whether

$$\hat{e}\left(\mathsf{sk}_\ell, \varpi\cdot g^{H(\mathsf{id}_\ell)}\right) \stackrel{?}{=} \hat{e}(g, g)$$

holds.

$\mathsf{PrFile}(\mathsf{gpk}, \mathsf{sk}_\ell, F)$: The member id_ℓ splits the file F into blocks as shown in Equation (1). Choose a random file identifier $fid \in_R \mathbb{Z}_p^*$ and $(s+1)$ random values $\alpha_0, \alpha_1, \cdots, \alpha_s \in_R \mathbb{Z}_p^*$, and compute

$$u_j = g^{\alpha_j} \in \mathbb{G}$$

for each $0 \le j \le s$. Then, generate the file tag τ in the same way as in Section 3.2 and send it to the group manager.

For each file block F_i $(1 \le i \le r)$, do the follows:

- Compute

$$\theta_i = \alpha_0 H_0(fid \parallel i) + \sum_{j=1}^{s}\alpha_j f_{i,j} \in \mathbb{Z}_p$$

- Generate meta-data as

$$\sigma_i \leftarrow \mathsf{sk}_\ell^{\theta_i} \in \mathbb{G}$$

Then, send the processed file

$$F^* = \{(F_i, \sigma_i) : 1 \le i \le r\}$$

to the cloud storage server, and deletes the random values $\alpha_0, \alpha_1, \cdots, \alpha_s$, secret key tsk and the file locally.

$\mathsf{Chall}(\mathsf{gpk}, \tau)$: The auditor runs the algorithm in two steps.

1. The same to Section 3.2 for validating the file tag. If τ is invalid, output "0" and terminate.
2. Pick a random subset $Q \subseteq [1, r]$ and choose a random value $\beta_i \in_R \mathbb{Z}_p^*$ for each $i \in Q$. Send the challenge

$$C = (fid, Q, \{\beta_i : i \in Q\})$$

to the cloud storage server.

$\mathsf{PrfGen}(\mathsf{gpk}, F^*, C)$: Compute the aggregated file block $\vec{\mu} = (\mu_1, \cdots, \mu_s)$ as follows

$$\mu_j = \sum_{i\in Q}\beta_i f_{i,j} \mod p \text{ for each } j \in [1, s],$$

and calculate the aggregated meta-data σ as shown in Equation (2) but over $\mathbb{G}$. Return the proof $R = (\vec{\mu}, \sigma)$ to the auditor.

$\mathsf{Verify}(\mathsf{gpk}, \tau, C, R)$: If R cannot be parsed, output "0" and terminates. Otherwise, check whether the following equality holds

$$\hat{e}\left(\sigma, \varpi\cdot g^{H(\mathsf{id}_\ell)}\right) \stackrel{?}{=} \hat{e}\left(u_0^{\sum_{i\in Q}\beta_i H_0(fid\|i)} \cdot \prod_{j=1}^{s} u_j^{\mu_j}, g\right).$$

If so, output "1"; otherwise, output "0".

THEOREM 4. *The proposed GPoS instantiation is correct.*

PROOF. Observe the following equalities

$$
\begin{aligned}
&\hat{e}\left(\sigma, \varpi \cdot g^{H(\mathsf{id}_\ell)}\right) \\
&= \hat{e}\left(\prod_{i \in Q} \sigma_i^{\beta_i}, g^{\gamma} \cdot g^{H(\mathsf{id}_\ell)}\right) \\
&= \hat{e}\left(\prod_{i \in Q} \left(g^{\frac{1}{\gamma + H(\mathsf{id}_\ell)}}\right)^{\theta_i \beta_i}, g^{\gamma} \cdot g^{H(\mathsf{id}_\ell)}\right) \\
&= \hat{e}\left(\prod_{i \in Q} g^{\beta_i (\alpha_0 H_0(fid \| i) + \sum_{j=1}^{s} \alpha_j f_{i,j})}, g\right) \\
&= \hat{e}\left(\prod_{i \in Q} g^{\beta_i \alpha_0 H_0(fid \| i)} \cdot \prod_{i \in Q} \prod_{j=1}^{s} g^{\beta_i \alpha_j f_{i,j}}, g\right) \\
&= \hat{e}\left(\prod_{i \in Q} g^{\beta_i \alpha_0 H_0(fid \| i)} \cdot \prod_{j=1}^{s} u_j^{\sum_{i \in Q} \beta_i f_{i,j}}, g\right) \\
&= \hat{e}\left(u_0^{\sum_{i \in Q} \beta_i H_0(fid \| i)} \cdot \prod_{j=1}^{s} u_j^{\mu_j}, g\right).
\end{aligned}
$$

Hence, the correctness follows. □

According to Theorem 2 and Theorem 3, we have the following corollaries.

COROLLARY 1. *Suppose that the signature scheme $\mathcal{S}_t$ for file tags is existentially unforgeable. The proposed GPoS instantiation is sound for any PPT adversary $\mathcal{A}$ if the CDH assumption holds.*

COROLLARY 2. *The proposed GPoS instantiation is ownership privacy-preserving against the cloud storage server.*

For easiness to compare with the improved instantiation as shown in next section, the above instantiation is presented over symmetric bilinear groups. In fact, it can also be implemented over asymmetric bilinear groups, that is, by setting the group private key sk_ℓ, the public parameters u_i $(0 \le i \le s)$ and the meta-data $\{\sigma_i : 1 \le i \le r\}$ in $\mathbb{G}_1$, while defining ϖ in $\mathbb{G}_2$.

4.2 Optimized Instantiation

We proceed to optimize the above proposed GPoS instantiation by the leveraging polynomial commitment technique [12]. Our optimization approach is universal in the sense that the communication overheads for integrity auditing in a GPoS scheme may be further reduced if the PoS schemes are built over symmetric bilinear groups. At a high level, similarly to [24, 27], the public parameters u_j-es are generated using a single random element α, that is, they are associated with different powers of α. Furthermore, when an outsourced file is audited, a polynomial commitment with respect to the challenged blocks is produced by the cloud storage server and then validated by the auditor.

$\mathsf{Setup}(1^\lambda)$: The same to Section 4.1.

$\mathsf{KeyExt}(\mathsf{gpk}, \mathsf{gsk}, \mathsf{id}_\ell)$: The same to Section 4.1.

$\mathsf{PrFile}(\mathsf{gpk}, \mathsf{sk}_\ell, F)$: The member id_ℓ splits the file F into blocks as shown in Equation (1). Choose a random file identifier $fid \in_R \mathbb{Z}_p^*$ and two random values $\alpha_0, \alpha \in_R \mathbb{Z}_p^*$, and compute

$$v = g^{\alpha_0} \in \mathbb{G}$$

and

$$u_j = g^{\alpha^j} \in \mathbb{G}$$

for each $0 \le j \le s-1$. Generate the file tag τ and sends it to the group manager in the same way as Section 3.2 while τ_0 denotes a concatenation string of

$$(\mathsf{gpk}, \mathsf{id}_\ell, v, u_0, u_1, \cdots, u_{s-1}, fid, r)$$

For each file block F_i $(1 \le i \le r)$, do the follows:

- Compute

$$\theta_i = \alpha_0 H_0(fid \parallel i) + \phi_{\vec{\pi}_i}(\alpha) \mod p$$

where

$$\phi_{\vec{\pi}_i}(\alpha) = \sum_{j=0}^{s-1} f_{i,j} \alpha^j \mod p$$

- Generate the meta-data as $\sigma_i \leftarrow \mathsf{sk}_\ell^{\theta_i} \in \mathbb{G}$.

Then, send the processed file

$$F^* = \{(F_i, \sigma_i) : 1 \le i \le r\}$$

to the cloud storage server and locally discards the random values α_0, α, secret key tsk and the file information.

$\mathsf{Chall}(\mathsf{gpk}, \tau)$: The auditor runs the algorithm as follows.

1. The same to Section 3.2 for validating the file tag. If τ is invalid, outputs "0" and terminates.
2. Pick a random subset $Q \subseteq [1, r]$ and chooses two random values $z, \delta \in_R \mathbb{Z}_p^*$. Sends the challenge

$$C = (fid, Q, z, \delta)$$

to the cloud storage server.

$\mathsf{PrfGen}(\mathsf{gpk}, F^*, C)$: For each $i \in Q$, the cloud storage server calculates a value $\beta_i = \delta^i \mod p$. Generate the aggregated file block

$$\vec{\mu} = (\mu_0, \mu_1, \cdots, \mu_{s-1})$$

by computing

$$\mu_j = \sum_{i \in Q} \beta_i f_{i,j} \mod p \text{ for each } j \in [0, s-1],$$

and calculate the aggregated meta-data σ as shown in Equation (2) but over $\mathbb{G}$. Then, define a polynomial

$$\phi_{\vec{\mu}}(x) = \sum_{j=0}^{s-1} \mu_j x^j \mod p$$

and calculates $\kappa = \phi_{\vec{\mu}}(z) \mod p$. Compute the following polynomial

$$\psi_{\vec{\omega}}(x) = \frac{\phi_{\vec{\mu}}(x) - \phi_{\vec{\mu}}(z)}{x - z}$$

using polynomial long division. Let

$$\vec{\omega} = (\omega_0, \omega_1, \cdots, \omega_{s-2})$$

be the coefficient vector of $\psi_{\vec{\omega}}(x)$. Compute

$$\zeta = g^{\psi_{\vec{\omega}}(\alpha)} = \prod_{j=0}^{s-2} \left(g^{\alpha^j}\right)^{\omega_j}.$$

Return the proof $R = (\zeta, \kappa, \sigma)$ to the auditor.

$\mathsf{Verify}(\mathsf{gpk}, \tau, C, R)$: If R cannot be parsed, output "0" and terminate. Otherwise, check the following equality

$$\hat{e}\left(\sigma, \varpi \cdot g^{H(\mathsf{id}_\ell)}\right) \overset{?}{=} \hat{e}\left(\upsilon^{\sum_{i\in Q} \delta^i H_0(fid\|i)} \cdot g^{\kappa} \cdot \zeta^{-z}, g\right) \cdot \hat{e}(\zeta, u_1). \quad (4)$$

If so, output "1"; otherwise, output "0".

THEOREM 5. *The optimized GPoS instantiation is correct.*

PROOF. Since

$$\begin{aligned}
&\hat{e}\left(\sigma, \varpi \cdot g^{H(\mathsf{id}_\ell)}\right) \\
&= \hat{e}\left(\prod_{i\in Q} \sigma_i^{\beta_i}, g^{\gamma} \cdot g^{H(\mathsf{id}_\ell)}\right) \\
&= \hat{e}\left(\prod_{i\in Q} \left(g^{\frac{1}{\gamma + H(\mathsf{id}_\ell)}}\right)^{\theta_i \beta_i}, g^{\gamma} \cdot g^{H(\mathsf{id}_\ell)}\right) \\
&= \hat{e}\left(\prod_{i\in Q} g^{\beta_i(\alpha_0 H_0(fid\|i) + \phi_{\vec{\pi}_i}(\alpha))}, g\right) \\
&= \hat{e}\left(\prod_{i\in Q} \upsilon^{\beta_i H_0(fid\|i)} \cdot \prod_{i\in Q} g^{\beta_i \phi_{\vec{\pi}_i}(\alpha)}, g\right) \\
&= \hat{e}\left(\upsilon^{\sum_{i\in Q} \beta_i H_0(fid\|i)}, g\right) \hat{e}\left(g^{\sum_{i\in Q} \beta_i \phi_{\vec{\pi}_i}(\alpha)}, g\right) \\
&= \hat{e}\left(\upsilon^{\sum_{i\in Q} \delta^i H_0(fid\|i)}, g\right) \hat{e}\left(g^{\phi_{\vec{\mu}}(\alpha)}, g\right)
\end{aligned}$$

and

$$\begin{aligned}
&\hat{e}\left(g^{\kappa} \cdot \zeta^{-z}, g\right) \hat{e}(\zeta, u_1) \\
&= \hat{e}\left(g^{\phi_{\vec{\mu}}(z)} g^{-z\psi_{\vec{\omega}}(\alpha)}, g\right) \hat{e}\left(g^{\psi_{\vec{\omega}}(\alpha)}, g^{\alpha}\right) \\
&= \hat{e}\left(g^{(\alpha - z)\psi_{\vec{\omega}}(\alpha) + \phi_{\vec{\mu}}(z)}, g\right) \\
&= \hat{e}\left(g^{\phi_{\vec{\mu}}(\alpha) - \phi_{\vec{\mu}}(z) + \phi_{\vec{\mu}}(z)}, g\right) \\
&= \hat{e}\left(g^{\phi_{\vec{\mu}}(\alpha)}, g\right),
\end{aligned}$$

the verification equation (4) is satisfied. □

THEOREM 6. *Suppose that the signature scheme $\mathcal{S}_t$ for file tags is existentially unforgeable. The optimized GPoS instantiation is sound for any PPT adversary $\mathcal{A}$ if the s-SDH assumption holds.*

PROOF. Suppose that there is a PPT adversary $\mathcal{A}$ breaking the soundness of the improved GPoS instantiation. Similarly to Theorem 2, at the end of security game, the adversary outputs a (forged) valid pair of challenge/proof (C', R') with regard to a file F' with tag τ' and member id_ℓ, where file F' has been queried for processing. Suppose the challenge $C' = (fid, Q, z, \delta)$ and the proof $R' = (\zeta', \kappa', \sigma')$ Hence, the pair (C', R') satisfies Equation (4). However, since this pair is forged, R' must be unequal to that generated from the maintained information by the simulator. It further means that $(\zeta', \kappa') \neq (\zeta, \kappa)$, since otherwise, σ' would be equal to σ due to Equation (4). Then the simulator obtains two commitments (z, ζ', κ') and (z, ζ, κ) for the same polynomial and both for the evaluation at z. According to the security results [12] of polynomial commitment scheme due to Kate, Zaverucha and Goldberg, the simulator can find a solution $(-z, g^{\frac{1}{\alpha - z}})$ for the s-SDH instance $(\mathbb{G}, u_0, u_1, \cdots, u_{s-1})$ which contradicts the security assumption. □

According to Theorem 3, we have the following corollary.

COROLLARY 3. *The optimized GPoS instantiation is ownership privacy-preserving against the cloud storage server.*

5. PERFORMANCE EVALUATION

In this section, we evaluate and compare the performance of our GPoS instantiations.

5.1 Theoretical Analysis

For comparing the efficiency of both GPoS instantiations (see Section 4), we first analyse their computation costs in each stage. We only consider the most time-consuming computations, i.e., exponentiation and pairing in $\mathbb{G}$, $\mathbb{G}_T$ and $\mathbb{Z}_p$, etc., while the other light-weight operations such as additions and multiplications are omitted. In the table, $\mathtt{H}$ denotes one hash evaluation for both H and H_0, and $\mathtt{E}$ represents one exponentiation in $\mathbb{G}$ or $\mathbb{Z}_p$. That is, these evaluations are not discriminated in different groups or ring. The computation times for polynomial long division and a pairing evaluation are denoted by $\mathtt{D}$ and $\mathtt{P}$, respectively. The time to randomly sample an element from a group or a ring is also omitted in the analysis, since it is in fact much less than that taken by an exponentiation. We also treat the digital signature scheme $\mathcal{S}_t$ for file tag as a black-box. Specifically, we let $O(\mathcal{S}_{kgen})$, $O(\mathcal{S}_{sign})$ and $O(\mathcal{S}_{vrfy})$ denote the computation complexity of each algorithm in $\mathcal{S}_t$, that is, $\mathcal{S}_t.\mathsf{KGen}$, $\mathcal{S}_t.\mathsf{Sign}$ and $\mathcal{S}_t.\mathsf{Vrfy}$.

Table 2 summarizes the computational costs of every algorithm of both proposed instantiations. Both GPoS instantiations rely on the same key extracting algorithm to create secret keys for group members. Each key extraction takes one hash evaluation and one exponentiation in $\mathbb{G}$. Regarding the file processing algorithm, the secret values α^i $(2 \leq i \leq s-1)$ can be pre-computed by the group member in the optimized GPoS instantiation, then both instantiations take roughly the same computational complexity for processing a file. There are two ways for producing u_i in optimized GPoS instantiation. That is, either by computing $u_i = u_{i-1}^{\alpha}$ or by raising g to the power of a pre-computed value α^i. Both cases bring the identical complexity for preparing these values u_i. It can be seen from Table 2 that the algorithm PrFile in basic GPoS instantiation requires $(r+s+1)$ exponentiations in $\mathbb{G}$, which determines the overall efficiency for processing a file. In fact, r exponentiations are carried out for producing meta-data for r file blocks, while the other $(s+1)$ exponentiations are due to preparing public parameters $u_0, \cdots, u_s$. Consider a file F of L bytes. If it is split such that each sector has l bytes (as an element in $\mathbb{Z}_p$), then processing this file would take in total

$$T = \left\lceil \frac{L}{s \cdot l} \right\rceil + s + 1 \quad (5)$$

exponentiations. The case for the optimized GPoS instantiation is similar, that is, it would take $T' = T - 1$ exponentiations in $\mathbb{G}$. Furthermore, for processing file F with either GPoS instantiation, a preferable way is to set s as $\sqrt{L/l}$ since it would cost the minimum exponentiation operations.

For auditing an outsourced file in optimized instantiation, the cloud storage sever will carry out a bit more operations than the basic one. This is because that not only the coefficients β_i $(i \in Q)$ should be online calculated through exponentiations, but also an addition polynomial evaluation for κ, polynomial long division and multi-exponentiation for ζ need to be computed. This would not degrade practicality of the instantiations as the cloud servers are usually assumed to be powerful enough. At the auditor side for verification, the efficiency depends on the parameters $|Q|$ and s. If the auditor challenges a number of file blocks less than s, then the optimized GPoS instantiation is superior to the basic one. Note that most exponentiations taken by the auditor in optimized instantiation are due to computing the coefficients β_i ($i \in Q$). These computations can be carried out after sending out the challenge C and before receiving the response R from the cloud storage server. In this way, the auditor will take only $((|Q|+1)\mathtt{H}+4\mathtt{E}+3\mathtt{P})$ operations, which is much superior to that of basic instantiation.

We proceed to compare the communication overheads for both instantiations in auditing the integrity of the outsourced files. The details are summarized in Table 3 where S_G denotes the element size of $\mathbb{G}$. In optimized instantiation, the coefficients β_i ($i \in Q$) are not transmitted directly across the network as in basic instantiation, but generated by both the cloud storage server and the auditor. Thus, these additional computations greatly reduce the communications from the auditor to the cloud server. The similar communication reduction occurs for avoiding directly transmitting the aggregated file block from the cloud server to auditor. As shown in Section 4.2, this is realized by polynomial commitment to commit at a random point z. It can be seen from the Table that, the polynomial commitment trick brings great savings about the overall communication overheads.

Table 3: Communication overheads of auditing integrity in both instantiations

Instantiation	Communication overheads
Section 4.1	$(2\|Q\| + s)l + 1S_G$
Section 4.2	$(\|Q\| + 3)l + 2S_G$

6. CONCLUSION

In this paper, we introduced GPoS which guarantees the integrity of the outsourced group's files in clouds. We first formalized the system framework and the security model for GPoS schemes, and then proposed a generic GPoS construction. The construction is based on the newly identified properties of some digital signature schemes and a trapdoor trick. The effectiveness of this generic construction was showcased with two concrete instantiations over bilinear groups. The second instantiation illustrates extra advantageous features of lower communication overheads for auditing the outsourced files. We provided formal security proof and comprehensive performance evaluations. The analyses show that the proposed scheme and instantiations are secure and practical for real-world applications.

7. ACKNOWLEDGMENTS

We thank the anonymous reviewers for their valuable comments. This work was supported by the National Key Basic Research Program of China (973) (Grant No. 2012CB315905), National Natural Science Foundation of China (Grant Nos. 61370190, 61173154, 61272455, 61202450, 61472083, 61272501, 61402029, 61472429, and 61202465), and Beijing Natural Science Foundation (Grant Nos. 4132056 and 4122041), the Research Funds of Renmin University of China through project 14XNLF02 and the Open Research Fund of Beijing Key Laboratory of Trusted Computing.

8. REFERENCES

[1] G. Ateniese, R. Burns, R. Curtmola, J. Herring, L. Kissner, Z. Peterson, and D. Song. Provable Data Possession at Untrusted Stores. In *Proceedings of the 14th ACM Conference on Computer and Communications Security*, CCS'07, pages 598–609, New York, NY, USA, 2007. ACM.

[2] G. Ateniese, R. Di Pietro, L. V. Mancini, and G. Tsudik. Scalable and Efficient Provable Data Possession. In *Proceedings of the 4th International Conference on Security and Privacy in Communication Networks*, SecureComm'08. ACM, 2008.

[3] G. Ateniese, S. Kamara, and J. Katz. Proofs of Storage from Homomorphic Identification Protocols. In M. Matsui, editor, *Advances in Cryptology–ASIACRYPT 2009*, volume 5912 of *LNCS*, pages 319–333. Springer, Heidelberg, 2009.

[4] D. Boneh and X. Boyen. Short Signatures Without Random Oracles and the SDH Assumption in Bilinear Groups. *Journal of Cryptology*, 21(2):149–177, 2008.

[5] D. Cash, A. Küpçü, and D. Wichs. Dynamic Proofs of Retrievability via Oblivious RAM. In T. Johansson and P. Nguyen, editors, *Advances in Cryptology–EUROCRYPT 2013*, volume 7881 of *LNCS*, pages 279–295. Springer, Heidelberg, 2013.

[6] H. Deng, Q. Wu, B. Qin, S. S. M. Chow, J. Domingo-Ferrer, and W. Shi. Tracing and Revoking Leaked Credentials: Accountability in Leaking Sensitive Outsourced Data. In *Proceedings of the 9th ACM Symposium on Information, Computer and Communications Security*, ASIA CCS '14, pages 425–434, New York, NY, USA, 2014. ACM.

[7] H. Deng, Q. Wu, B. Qin, J. Mao, X. Liu, L. Zhang, and W. Shi. Who Is Touching My Cloud. In M. Kutyłowski and J. Vaidya, editors, *Computer Security–ESORICS 2014*, volume 8712 of *LNCS*, pages 362–379. Springer International Publishing, 2014.

[8] Y. Dodis, S. Vadhan, and D. Wichs. Proofs of Retrievability via Hardness Amplification. In O. Reingold, editor, *Theory of Cryptography*, volume 5444 of *LNCS*, pages 109–127. Springer, Heidelberg, 2009.

[9] C. Erway, A. Küpçü, C. Papamanthou, and R. Tamassia. Dynamic Provable Data Possession. In *Proceedings of the 16th ACM Conference on Computer and Communications Security*, CCS'09, pages 213–222, New York, NY, USA, 2009. ACM.

[10] R. Gennaro, S. Halevi, and T. Rabin. Secure Hash-and-Sign Signatures Without the Random Oracle. In J. Stern, editor, *Advances in Cryptology–EUROCRYPT'99*, volume 1592 of *LNCS*, pages 123–139. Springer, Heidelberg, 1999.

[11] A. Juels and B. S. Kaliski Jr. PoRs: Proofs of Retrievability for Large Files. In *Proceedings of the 14th ACM Conference on Computer and*

Table 2: Computation costs of each algorithm in both instantiations

Algorithm	Basic instantiation	Optimized instantiation
Setup	1E	1E
KeyExt	$n(1\mathtt{H}+1\mathtt{E})$	$n(1\mathtt{H}+1\mathtt{E})$
PrFile	$r\mathtt{H}+(r+s+1)\mathtt{E}+O(\mathcal{S}_{kgen})+O(\mathcal{S}_{sign})$	$r\mathtt{H}+(r+s)\mathtt{E}+O(\mathcal{S}_{kgen})+O(\mathcal{S}_{sign})$
Chall	$O(\mathcal{S}_{vrfy})$	$O(\mathcal{S}_{vrfy})$
PrfGen	$\lvert Q\rvert\mathtt{E}$	$(2\lvert Q\rvert+2s-3)\mathtt{E}+1\mathtt{D}$
Verify	$(\lvert Q\rvert+1)\mathtt{H}+(s+2)\mathtt{E}+2\mathtt{P}$	$(\lvert Q\rvert+1)\mathtt{H}+(\lvert Q\rvert+4)\mathtt{E}+3\mathtt{P}$

Communications Security, CCS'07, pages 584–597, New York, NY, USA, 2007. ACM.

[12] A. Kate, G. Zaverucha, and I. Goldberg. Constant-Size Commitments to Polynomials and Their Applications. In M. Abe, editor, *Advances in Cryptology–ASIACRYPT 2010*, volume 6477 of *LNCS*, pages 177–194. Springer, Heidelberg, 2010.

[13] H. Shacham and B. Waters. Compact Proofs of Retrievability. *Journal of Cryptology*, 26(3):442–483, 2013.

[14] E. Shi, E. Stefanov, and C. Papamanthou. Practical Dynamic Proofs of Retrievability. In *Proceedings of the 2013 ACM SIGSAC Conference on Computer and Communications Security*, CCS'13, pages 325–336, New York, NY, USA, 2013. ACM.

[15] B. Wang, S. S. M. Chow, M. Li, and H. Li. Storing Shared Data on the Cloud via Security-Mediator. In *Distributed Computing Systems (ICDCS), 2013 IEEE 33rd International Conference on*, pages 124–133, July 2013.

[16] B. Wang, B. Li, and H. Li. Knox: Privacy-Preserving Auditing for Shared Data with Large Groups in the Cloud. In F. Bao, P. Samarati, and J. Zhou, editors, *Applied Cryptography and Network Security*, volume 7341 of *LNCS*, pages 507–525. Springer, Heidelberg, 2012.

[17] B. Wang, B. Li, and H. Li. Oruta: Privacy-Preserving Public Auditing for Shared Data in the Cloud. In *Cloud Computing (CLOUD), 2012 IEEE 5th International Conference on*, pages 295–302, June 2012.

[18] B. Wang, B. Li, and H. Li. Public auditing for shared data with efficient user revocation in the cloud. In *INFOCOM, 2013 Proceedings IEEE*, pages 2904–2912, April 2013.

[19] B. Wang, H. Li, and M. Li. Privacy-preserving public auditing for shared cloud data supporting group dynamics. In *Communications (ICC), 2013 IEEE International Conference on*, pages 1946–1950, June 2013.

[20] C. Wang, S. S. M. Chow, Q. Wang, K. Ren, and W. Lou. Privacy-Preserving Public Auditing for Secure Cloud Storage. *Computers, IEEE Transactions on*, 62(2):362–375, Feb 2013.

[21] H. Wang, Q. Wu, B. Qin, and J. Domingo-Ferrer. Identity-based remote data possession checking in public clouds. *Information Security, IET*, 8(2):114–121, March 2014.

[22] Q. Wang, C. Wang, J. Li, K. Ren, and W. Lou. Enabling Public Verifiability and Data Dynamics for Storage Security in Cloud Computing. In M. Backes and P. Ning, editors, *Computer Security–ESORICS 2009*, volume 5789 of *LNCS*, pages 355–370. Springer, Heidelberg, 2009.

[23] Y. Wang, Q. Wu, D. S. Wong, B. Qin, S. S. M. Chow, Z. Liu, and X. Tan. Securely Outsourcing Exponentiations with Single Untrusted Program for Cloud Storage. In M. Kutyłowski and J. Vaidya, editors, *Computer Security–ESORICS 2014*, volume 8712 of *LNCS*, pages 326–343. Springer International Publishing, 2014.

[24] J. Xu and E.-C. Chang. Towards Efficient Proofs of Retrievability. In *Proceedings of the 7th ACM Symposium on Information, Computer and Communications Security*, ASIACCS '12, pages 79–80, New York, NY, USA, 2012. ACM.

[25] K. Yang and X. Jia. Data storage auditing service in cloud computing: challenges, methods and opportunities. *World Wide Web*, 15(4):409–428, 2012.

[26] Y. Yu, Y. Mu, J. Ni, J. Deng, and K. Huang. Identity Privacy-Preserving Public Auditing with Dynamic Group for Secure Mobile Cloud Storage. In M. H. Au, B. Carminati, and C. C. J. Kuo, editors, *Network and System Security*, volume 8792 of *LNCS*, pages 28–40. Springer International Publishing, 2014.

[27] J. Yuan and S. Yu. Proofs of Retrievability with Public Verifiability and Constant Communication Cost in Cloud. In *Proceedings of the 2013 International Workshop on Security in Cloud Computing*, Cloud Computing '13, pages 19–26, New York, NY, USA, 2013. ACM.

[28] J. Yuan and S. Yu. Efficient public integrity checking for cloud data sharing with multi-user modification. In *INFOCOM, 2014 Proceedings IEEE*, pages 2121–2129, April 2014.

[29] Y. Zhang and M. Blanton. Efficient Dynamic Provable Possession of Remote Data via Balanced Update Trees. In *Proceedings of the 8th ACM SIGSAC Symposium on Information, Computer and Communications Security*, ASIA CCS'13, pages 183–194, New York, NY, USA, 2013. ACM.

[30] Q. Zheng and S. Xu. Secure and Efficient Proof of Storage with Deduplication. In *Proceedings of the Second ACM Conference on Data and Application Security and Privacy*, CODASPY '12, pages 1–12, New York, NY, USA, 2012. ACM.

Lucky 13 Strikes Back

Gorka Irazoqui
Worcester Polytechnic Institute
girazoki@wpi.edu

Mehmet Sinan İnci
Worcester Polytechnic Institute
msinci@wpi.edu

Thomas Eisenbarth
Worcester Polytechnic Institute
teisenbarth@wpi.edu

Berk Sunar
Worcester Polytechnic Institute
sunar@wpi.edu

ABSTRACT

In this work we show how the Lucky 13 attack can be resurrected in the cloud by gaining access to a virtual machine co-located with the target. Our version of the attack exploits distinguishable cache access times enabled by VM deduplication to detect dummy function calls that only happen in case of an incorrectly CBC-padded TLS packet. Thereby, we gain back a new covert channel not considered in the original paper that enables the Lucky 13 attack. In fact, the new side channel is significantly more accurate, thus yielding a much more effective attack. We briefly survey prominent cryptographic libraries for this vulnerability. The attack currently succeeds to compromise PolarSSL, GnuTLS and CyaSSL on deduplication enabled platforms while the Lucky 13 patches in OpenSSL, Mozilla NSS and MatrixSSL are immune to this vulnerability. We conclude that, any program that follows secret data dependent execution flow is exploitable by side-channel attacks as shown in (but not limited to) our version of the Lucky 13 attack.

Keywords

Lucky 13 attack, Cross-VM attacks, virtualization, deduplication

1. MOTIVATION

The Transport Layer Security (TLS) family of protocols ensures the security of the entire communications infrastructure by providing confidentiality and integrity services across untrusted networks. Numerous web applications rely on TLS to secure client-server data traffic. Similarly distributed applications use TLS to establish a secure channel for transporting application-layer data with centralized cloud servers. At the higher level TLS uses X.509 certificates along with public key cryptography to authenticate the exchanged symmetric encryption keys and to authenticate the server. This session key is then used to ensure the integrity and confidentiality of the data exchanged over a secure session between the TLS client and server.

ASIA CCS'15, April 14–17, 2015, Singapore..

http://dx.doi.org/10.1145/2714576.2714625.

Starting as Secure Sockets Layer (SSL), after adoption by the IETF TLS has undergone many changes (SSL 1.0, 2.0, 3.0, TLS 1.0, 1.1, 1.2). Many releases were motivated by attacks targeting both the protocols and the underlying cryptographic schemes [38, 8, 7, 17, 29, 5, 16, 41]. In this work we focus on attacks targeting the padding procedure in TLS's MAC-Encode-Encrypt (MEE) primitive.

Implementation Attacks on TLS. Handling CBC IVs, and paddings in cryptographic algorithms has a long history of attacks and countermeasures, and is notoriously hard to get right in implementations. As early as in 1998 Bleichenbacher pointed to vulnerabilities in SSL 3.0 stemming from leaked error messages due to incorrectly padded plaintexts. Later Vaudenay [38] presented an attack in the symmetric key setting on SSL/TLS induced by CBC mode padding. The BEAST chosen plaintext attack (Browser Exploit Against SSL/TLS) [15] exploited a long-known cipher block chaining (CBC) mode IV vulnerability in TLS 1.0 [25] to achieve full plaintext recovery. The exploit is based on the earlier work in [32, 8, 7]. The padding oracle attack is most commonly applied to CBC encryption mode, where the server leaks whether the padding of an encrypted message was correctly formed or not. Depending on the specifics of the encryption scheme and the encapsulating protocol, this side-channel leakage may be escalated to a full message recovery attack. These are collectively referred to as *padding oracle attacks.* A more recent striking application of the aforementioned padding attacks was given by Bardou et al. [9] where many cryptographic hardware tokens were determined to be vulnerable. Specifically, Bardou et al. apply Vaudenay's CBC attack and improve Bleichenbacher's attack to significantly reduce the number of decryption oracle accesses, thereby making attacks feasible on slow tokens.

Even though in the last years the padding oracle attacks were considered a fixed vulnerability in the community, in 2013 a new kind of padding oracle attack was presented by AlFardan et al. [16]. The Lucky 13 attack was proposed to recover TLS/DTLS encrypted messages by exploiting a vulnerability in the implementation of HMAC. The attack works by carefully modifying network packets during transmission, and using network timing information to recover the plaintext byte-by-byte from TLS encrypted packets. The attack received significant attention from the media and industry. A great deal of work went into fixing the TLS vulnerability. A widely applied and immediate fix—using RC4 encryption instead of a block cipher in CBC mode—turned out to be ill-advised: The attack described in [5] exploits statistical biases in the RC4 key stream to recover parts of the plaintext using a large number of TLS encryptions. To fix the popular MEE mode that uses a block cipher in CBC mode, cryptographic library providers applied various techniques aimed to equalize packet processing times, e.g. by calling a dummy HMAC function. Since then modifications are being studied to solve attacks against MEE schemes and the Lucky 13 issue has been considered closed by the security community and the industry.

In this work, we revive the Lucky 13 attack on a number of prominent cryptographic libraries which have been *patched* to eliminate the network timing side-channel. We instead run our attacks in the cross-VM setting using cache access information to realize the Lucky 13 attack.

Cross-VM Attacks. Cross-VM attacks assume a co-located process running on the same physical hardware as a target process (e.g. same machine on different cores) can extract information from the target in spite of the VM sandboxing. Many side-channel attacks have been proposed that manage to recover sensitive data when a spy process is executed in the same OS as the victim. For instance, the early proposal by Bernstein [11] (and later in [12, 36, 18]) targets the time variation due to memory accesses to recover a AES encryption key. These techniques are now being moved to cloud servers to break sandboxing across virtual machines.

Cross-VM attacks assume the attacker to be able to co-locate with the victim. Co-location was considered a major obstacle until 2009 when Ristenpart et al. [31] demonstrated that it is possible to co-locate with a potential victim and extract sensitive data across VMs.This initial result fueled many other research targeting a co-located victim in a cloud system.

In 2011, Suzaki et al. [33, 34] exploited a memory saving OS-optimization called Kernel Samepage Merging (KSM) to recover data from another user and to identify a co-located user running in KVM hypervisors. Shortly later, Zhang et al. [42] used an access driven cache timing attack, namely *Prime and Probe* to recover an El Gamal decryption key from a victim process running in Xen VMs. In order to cope with multiple sources of microarchitectural noise, the authors used a hidden Markov model. In contrast to the work of Ristenpart et al. [31], the authors of [42] were able to extract fine grain information from a cryptographic implementation across VMs.

Recently the powerful *Flush+Reload* attack was used by Yarom et.al in cloud-like environments such as VMware ESXI and KVM to extract RSA [41, 10] and ECDSA keys, while Irazoqui et al. used the same detection method to recover AES keys from co-located VMware VMs [21].

1.1 Our Contribution

In this work we demonstrate that by mounting cache attacks it is possible to revive a modified Lucky 13 attack on many of the patched TLS libraries. Specifically, we show that it is possible to recover plaintexts from TLS encrypted sessions *across VM boundaries* by applying a *flush+reload* cache attack in VMware ESXi VMs. The vulnerability persists even if the VMs are running on different cores in the same machine. The attack works because some TLS libraries prevent the Lucky 13 attack by using *dummy functions* to ensure constant time executions. By monitoring the instruction cache, we detect accesses to these dummy functions and hence distinguish valid CBC-paddings, as done in the Lucky 13 attack. While requiring co-location, the cache side channel is less noisy than the network timing side channel originally exploited in [16], resulting in a more efficient attack. The effectiveness of the new attack is demonstrated on a number prominent cryptographic libraries: PolarSSL [30], GnuTLS [24], and CyaSSL [1]. Fortunately, our results also indicate that some libraries such as OpenSSL [35], Mozilla's NSS [26], and MatrixSSL [3] have been patched well and the new attack does not apply to them. These libraries feature carefully crafted constant run time execution while OpenSSL and Mozilla's NSS also ensure branch-free handling of MAC checking.

2. BACKGROUND

In this work we substitute the network timing channel with the cache timing channel as experienced in a Cross-VM setting. There is a very rich literature of cache attacks and here we only very briefly review cache timing attacks and focus on a more recent and effective cache attack variant, e.g **the *Flush+Reload* cache attack**.

Cache Architecture. The cache architecture is a set of components that reside between the CPU and the RAM. The principal function of the cache is to reduce the average access time to the main memory by exploiting spatial and temporal locality principles. When the CPU requests a memory line, the cache will be searched first to see if it is located there. If so, it is said that a cache *hit* has occurred and therefore, the access delay is much smaller. However when the data is not found in the cache, the CPU will try to find the memory line in the subsequent levels of cache or in the memory, which translates to greater delays. In this case it is said that a cache *miss* has occurred. When a cache miss occurs, the data is retrieved from the memory and a copy is stored in all levels of the cache hierarchy following both the spatial and temporal locality principles: recently accessed data and data in nearby locations are likely to be accessed soon.

Cache Side channel attacks. Cache based side channel attacks have been widely studied over the last two decades. It was in 1992 when the cache was first considered as a valid covert channel to extract sensitive information [20], and this approach was further studied theoretically later in [23, 28, 37]. In the last decade many implementations of cache based side channel attacks have been investigated. Bernstein in 2005 [11] recovered an AES keys due to microarchitectural time differences between different memory lines, whereas Osvik et al. studied the performance of different spy processes monitoring the data cache like *Prime and Probe* and *Evict+Time* on AES [27]. Only one year later, Bonneau et al. implemented a cache attack based on table look up collisions on AES [13].

Shortly later Aciiçmez showed that the instruction cache also leaks information by mounting an attack targeting RSA encryptions [4]. In a follow up work, Chen et al. improved the attack proposed in [4] and applied it in a more realistic scenario [14]. One year later, cache attacks were moved to the cloud by Zhang et al. where they managed to recover an El Gamal encryption key across XEN VMs [42].

Recently Gullasch et al. [19] demonstrated that deduplication features implemented in modern OSs can open a covert channel to recover sensitive information like AES keys with the *Flush+Reload* attack, but assuming to have control over the CFS. This approach was later followed by Yarom et al.

and Irazoqui et al. to recover RSA and AES keys respectively, even in cloud environments [41, 21]. Finally Benger et al. also showed that the security of ECDSA encryptions is compromised when the adversary is able to monitor cache accesses [10].

2.1 The Flush+Reload Technique

The *Flush+Reload* attack is a powerful cache-based side channel attack technique that checks if specific cache lines have been accessed or not by the code under attack. Gullasch et al. [18] first used this spy process on AES, although the authors did not brand their attack as *Flush+Reload* at the time. Later Yarom et al. [41, 10] used it to target specific functions instead of data. In their studies, they used the *Flush+Reload* technique to recover keys from RSA and ECDSA decryption processes. Here we briefly explain how *Flush+Reload* attack works. The attack is carried out in 3 stages:

- **Flush step:** In this stage, the attacker uses the `clflush` instruction to flush the desired memory lines from the cache and make sure that they go to the main memory. We have to remark here that the `clflush` command does not only flush the memory line from the cache hierarchy of the corresponding working core, but it flushes from all the caches of all the cores in the CPU. This is an important point: if it only flushed from the corresponding core's cache hierarchy, the attack would only work if the attacker and victim's processes were running on the same CPU core. This would have required a much stronger assumption than just being on the same physical machine.

- **Victim accessing step:** In this stage the attacker waits until the victim runs a fragment of the targeted code, which uses the memory lines that have been flushed in the first stage.

- **Reload step:** In this stage the attacker reloads the previously flushed memory lines and measures the time it takes to reload them. Depending on the reloading time, the attacker decides whether the victim accessed the memory line (in which case the memory line would be present in the cache) or if the victim did not access the corresponding memory line (in which case the memory line will not be present in the cache.) The timing difference between a cache hit and a cache miss makes this difference detectable by the attacker.

The fact that the attacker and the victim processes do not run on the same core is not a problem here. Even though there may be isolation at various levels of the cache, in most systems there is some level of cache that is shared between all the cores. Therefore, through this shared level of cache (typically the L3 cache), one can still distinguish between accesses to the main memory and accesses to the cache.

2.2 Memory Deduplication

Memory deduplication is an optimization technique that was originally introduced in Linux as KSM to improve the memory utilization by merging duplicate memory pages. KSM first appeared in Linux kernel version 2.6.32 [22, 2]. In this implementation, KSM kernel daemon **ksmd**, scans the user memory for potential pages to be shared among

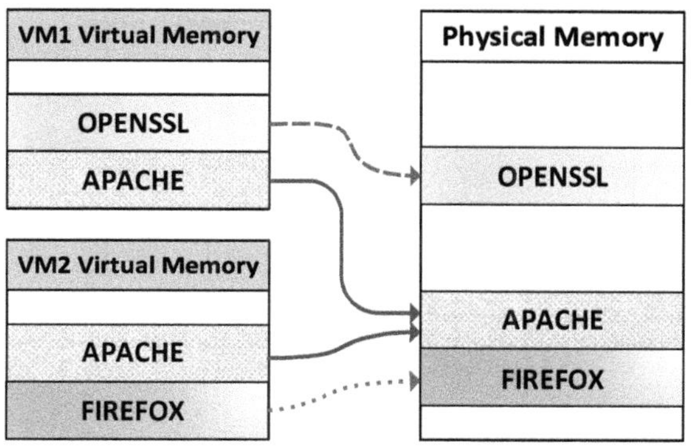

Figure 1: Memory Deduplication Scheme

users [6], creating signatures for these pages. The signatures are kept in the deduplication table for matching and merging. When two or more pages with the same signature are found, they are cross-checked completely to determine if they are identical in which case they are merged with the copy-on-write tag set.

Deduplication later became a standard technique for improving the memory utilization in VMMs. It is especially effective in virtual machine environments where multiple guest OSs co-reside on the same physical machine and share the physical memory. At the more abstract level, deduplication works by recognizing processes (or VMs) that place the same data in memory. This frequently happens when two processes use the same shared libraries. The deduplication scheme eliminates multiple copies from memory and allows the data to be shared between users and processes. Consequently, variations of memory deduplication techniques are now implemented in VMware ESXI [39, 40] and others such as KVM [2, 22] VMMs. Since KVM converts the Linux kernel into a hypervisor, it directly uses KSM as page sharing technique, whereas VMware uses Transparent Page Sharing (TPS).

Even though deduplication saves memory and thus allows more virtual machines to run on the host system, it also opens a door to side channel attacks. While the data in the cache cannot be modified or corrupted by an adversary, parallel access rights can be exploited to reveal secret information about processes executing in the target VM.

3. THE LUCKY 13 ATTACK

The Lucky 13 attack targets a vulnerability in the TLS (and DTLS) protocol design. The vulnerability is due to MAC-then-encrypt mode, in combination with the padding of the CBC encryption, also referred to as MEE-TLS-CBC. In the following, our description focuses on this popular mode. Vaudenay [38] showed how the CBC padding can be exploited for a message recovery attack. AlFardan et al. [16] showed—more than 10 years later—that the subsequent MAC verification introduces timing behavior that makes the message recovery attack feasible in practical settings. In fact, their work includes a comprehensive study of the vulnerability of several TLS libraries. In this section we give a brief description of the attack. For a more detailed description, please refer to the original paper [16].

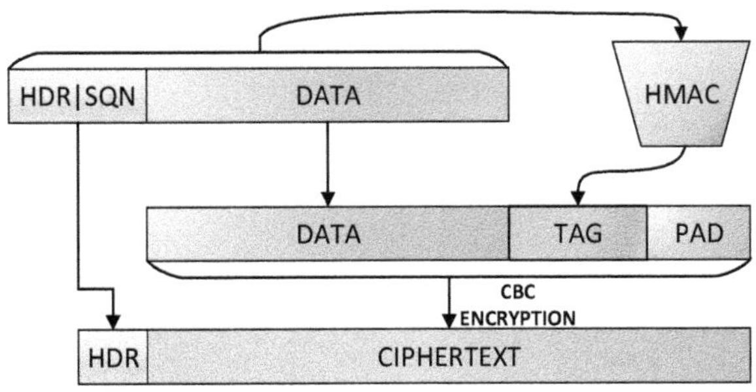

Figure 2: Encryption and authentication in the TLS record protocol when using HMAC and a block cipher in CBC mode.

3.1 The TLS Record Protocol

The TLS record protocol provides encryption and message authentication for bulk data transmitted in TLS. The basic operation of the protocol is depicted in Figure 2. When a payload is sent, a sequence number and a header are attached to it and a MAC tag is generated by any of the available HMAC choices. Once the MAC tag is generated, it is appended to the payload together with a padding. The payload, tag, and pad are then encrypted using a block cipher in CBC mode. The final message is formed by the encrypted ciphertext plus the header.

Upon receiving an encrypted packet, the receiver decrypts the ciphertext with the session key that was negotiated in the handshake process. Next, the padding and the MAC tag need to be removed. For this, first the receiver checks whether the size of the ciphertext is a multiple of the block size and makes sure that the ciphertext can accommodate minimally a zero-length record, a MAC tag, and at least one byte of padding. After decryption, the receiver checks if the recovered padding matches one of the allowed patterns. A standard way to implement this decoding step is to check the last byte of the plaintext, and to use it to determine how many of the trailing bytes belong to the padding. Once the padding is removed, and the plain payload is recovered, the receiver attaches the header and the sequence number and performs the HMAC operation. Finally, the computed tag is compared to the received tag. If they are equal, the contents of the message are concluded to be securely transmitted.

3.2 HMAC

The TLS record protocol uses the HMAC algorithm to compute the tag. The HMAC algorithm is based on a hash function H that performs the following operations:

$$\mathsf{HMAC}(K, m) = H((K \oplus opad)||H((K \oplus ipad)||M)$$

Common choices in TLS 1.2 for H are SHA-1, SHA-256 and the now defunct MD5. The message M is padded with a single 1 bit followed by zeros and an 8 byte length field. The pad aligns the data to a multiple of 64 bytes. $K \oplus opad$ already forms a 64 byte field, as well as $K \oplus ipad$. Therefore, the minimum number of compression function calls for a HMAC operation is 4. This means that depending on the number of bytes of the message, the HMAC operation is going to take more or less compression functions. To illustrate this, we are repeating the example given in [16] as follows. Assume that the plaintext size is 55 bytes. In this case an 8 byte length field is appended together with a padding of size 1, so that the total size is 64 bytes. Here in total the HMAC operation is going to take four compression function calls. However if the plaintext size is 58, an 8 byte length field is attached and 62 bytes of padding are appended to make the total size equal to 128 bytes. In this case, the total compression function calls are going to be equal to five. Distinguishing the number of performed compression function calls is the basic idea that enables the Lucky 13 attack.

3.3 CBC Encryption & Padding

Until the support of the Galois Counter Mode in TLS 1.2, block ciphers were always used in cipher block chaining (CBC) mode in TLS. Decryption of each block of a ciphertext C_i is performed as follows:

$$P_i = D_k(C_i) \oplus C_{i-1}$$

Here, P_i is the plaintext block and $D_k(\cdot)$ is the decryption under key k. For the prevalent AES, the block size is 16 bytes. The size of the message to be encrypted in CBC mode has to be indeed a multiple of the cipher block size. The TLS protocol specifies a padding as follows: the last padding byte indicates the length of the padding; the value of the remaining padding bytes is equal to the number of padding bytes needed. This means that if 3 bytes of padding is needed, the correct padding has to be 0x02|0x02|0x02. Possible TLS paddings are: 0x00, 0x01|0x01, 0x02|0x02|0x02, up to 0xff|0xff|...|0xff. Note that there are several valid paddings for each message length.

3.4 An Attack On CBC Encryption

We now discuss the basics of the Lucky 13 attack. For the purposes of this study the target cipher is going to be AES in CBC mode, as described above. Again, we are going to use the same example that AlFardan et al. gave in [16]. Assume that the sender is sending 4 non-IV blocks of 16 bytes each, one IV block, and the header number. Let's further assume that we are using SHA-1 to compute the MAC tag, in which case the digest size is 20 bytes. The header has a fixed length of 5 bytes and the sequence number would have a total size of 8 bytes. The payload would look like this:

$$\mathsf{HDR}|C_{IV}|C_1|C_2|C_3|C_4$$

Now assume that the attacker masks Δ in C_3. The decryption of C_4 is going to be as follows:

$$P_4^* = D_k(C_4) \oplus C_3 \oplus \Delta = P_4 \oplus \Delta$$

Focusing on the last two bytes $P_{4(14)}^*|P_{4(15)}^*$ three possible scenarios emerge:

Invalid padding This is the most probable case, where the plaintext ends with an invalid padding. Therefore, according to TLS protocol, this is treated as 0 padding. 20 bytes of MAC (SHA-1) are removed and the corresponding HMAC operation in the client side is performed on 44 bytes +13 bytes of header, in total 57 bytes. Therefore the HMAC evaluates 5 compression function calls.

Valid 0x00 padding If $P_{4(15)}^*$ is 0x00, this is considered as valid padding, and a single byte of padding is removed. Then the 20 bytes of digest are removed, and the HMAC operation in client side is done in 43+13 bytes, 56 in total, which takes 5 compression function calls.

Any other valid padding For instance, if we consider a valid padding of two bytes, the valid padding would be 0x01|0x01 and 2 bytes of padding are removed. Then 20 bytes of digest are removed, and the HMAC operation is performed over $42 + 13 = 55$ bytes, which means four compression function calls.

The Lucky 13 attack is based on detecting this difference between 4 and 5 compression function calls. Recall that if an attacker knows that a valid 0x01|0x01 padding was achieved, she can directly recover the last two bytes of P_4, since

$$0x01|0x01 = P_{4(14)}|P_{4(15)} \oplus \Delta_{(14)}|\Delta_{(15)}$$

Furthermore, she can keep on trying to recover the remaining bytes once she knows the first 2 bytes. The attacker needs to perform at most 2^{16} trials for detecting the last two bytes, and then up to 2^8 messages for each of the bytes that she wants to recover.

4. ANALYSIS OF LUCKY 13 PATCHES

The Lucky 13 attack triggered a series of patches for all major implementations of TLS [16]. In essence, all libraries were fixed to remove the timing side channel exploited by Lucky 13, i.e. implementations were updated to handle different CBC-paddings in constant time. However, different libraries used different approaches to achieve this:

- Some libraries implement *dummy functions* or processes,
- Others use *dummy data* to process the maximum allowed padding length in each MAC checking.

In the following, we discuss these different approaches for some of the most popular TLS libraries.

4.1 Patches Immune to Flush+Reload

In this section we will analyze those libraries that are secure against the flush and reload technique.

- **OpenSSL:** The Lucky 13 vulnerability was fixed in OpenSSL versions 1.0.1, 1.0.0k, and 0.9.8y by February 2013 without the use of a time consuming dummy function and by using dummy data. Basically, when a packet is received, the padding variation is considered and the maximum number of HMAC compression function evaluations needed to equalize the time is calculated. Then each compression function is computed directly, without calling any external function. For every message, the maximum number of compression functions are executed, so that no information is leaked through the time channel in case of the incorrect padding. Furthermore, the OpenSSL patch removed any data dependent branches ensuring a fixed data independent execution flow. This is a generic solution for microarchitectural leakage related attacks, i.e. cache timing or even branch prediction attacks.
- **Mozilla NSS:** This library is patched against the Lucky 13 attack in version 3.14.3 by using a constant time HMAC processing implementation. This implementation follows the approach of OpenSSL, calculating the number of maximum compression functions needed for a specific message and then computing the compression functions directly. This provides not only a countermeasure for both timing and cache access attacks, but also for branch prediction attacks.
- **MatrixSSL:** MatrixSSL is fixed against the Lucky 13 with the release of version 3.4.1 by adding timing countermeasures that reduce the effectiveness of the attack. In the fix, the library authors implemented a decoding scheme that does a sanity check on the largest possible block size. In this scheme, when the received message's padding length is incorrect, Matrix SSL runs a loop as if there was a full 256 bytes of padding. When there are no padding errors, the same operations are executed as in the case of an incorrect padding to sustain a constant time. Since there are no functions that are specifically called in the successful or unsuccessful padding cases, this library is not vulnerable to our *Flush+Reload* attack. In addition, Matrix SSL keeps track of all errors in the padding decoding and does the MAC checking regardless of valid or invalid padding rather than interrupting and finalizing the decoding process at the first error. However, since an if statement is used when the extra compression function is called, the library might be a suitable target for a branch prediction attack.

4.2 Patches Vulnerable to Flush+Reload

There are some patches that ensure constant time execution and therefore are immune to the original Lucky 13 attack [16] which are vulnerable to *Flush+Reload*. This implies a dummy function call or a different function call tree for valid and invalid paddings. Furthermore, if these calls are preceded by branch predictions, these patches might also be exploitable by branch prediction attacks. Some examples including code snippets are given below.

- **GnuTLS:** uses a `dummy_wait` function that performs an extra compression function whenever the padding is incorrect. This function makes the response time constant to fix the original Lucky 13 vulnerability. Since this function is only called in the case of incorrect padding, it can be detected by a co-located VM running a *Flush+Reload* attack.

```
if (memcmp (tag, &ciphertext->data[length],
tag_size) != 0 || pad_failed != 0)
  //HMAC was not the same.
{dummy_wait(params, compressed,pad_failed,
 pad,length+preamble_size);}
```

- **PolarSSL:** uses a dummy function called `md_process` to sustain constant time to fix the original Lucky 13 vulnerability. Basically the number of extra runs for a specific message is computed and added by `md_process`. Whenever this dummy function is called, a co-located adversary can learn that the last padding was incorrect and use this information to realize the Lucky 13 attack.

```
for( j = 0; j < extra_run; j++ )
  \\We need an extra run
md_process( &ssl->transform_in->
md_ctx_dec, ssl->in_msg );]*
```

- **CyaSSL:** was fixed against the Lucky 13 with the release of 2.5.0 on the same day the Lucky 13 vulnerability became public. In the fix, CyaSSL implements a timing resistant pad/verify check function called `TimingPadVerify` which uses the `Padcheck` function with dummy data for all padding length cases whether or not the padding length is correct. CyaSSL also does all the calculations such as the HMAC calculation for the *incorrect* padding cases which not only fixes the original Lucky 13 vulnerability but also prevents the detection of incorrect padding cases. This is due to the fact that the `Padcheck` function is called for both correctly and incorrectly padded messages which makes it impossible to detect with our *Flush+Reload* attack.

  However, for the correctly padded messages, CyaSSL calls the `CompressRounds` function which is detectable with *Flush+Reload* .Therefore, we monitor the correct padding instead of the incorrect padding cases.

  Correct padding case:

```
PadCheck(dummy, (byte)padLen,
MAX_PAD_SIZE - padLen - 1);
ret = ssl->hmac(ssl, verify, input,
pLen - padLen - 1 - t, content, 1);
CompressRounds(ssl, GetRounds(pLen,
padLen, t), dummy);
ConstantCompare(verify, input +
(pLen - padLen - 1 - t), t) != 0)
```

  Incorrect padding case:

```
CYASSL_MSG("PadCheck failed");
PadCheck(dummy, (byte)padLen,
MAX_PAD_SIZE - padLen - 1);
ssl->hmac(ssl, verify, input,
pLen - t, content, 1);
 //still compare
ConstantCompare(verify, input +
pLen - t, t);
```

5. REVIVING LUCKY 13 ON THE CLOUD

As the cross-network timing side channel has been closed (c.f. Section 4), the Lucky 13 attack as originally proposed no longer works on the recent releases of most cryptographic libraries. In this work we revive the Lucky 13 attack to target these (fixed) releases by gaining information through co-located VMs (a leakage channel not considered in the original paper) rather than the network timing exploited in the original attack.

5.1 Regaining the Timing Channel

Most cryptographic libraries and implementations have been largely fixed to yield an *almost* constant time when the MAC processing time is measured over the network. As discussed in Section 4, although there are some similarities in these patches, there are also subtle differences which—as we shall see—have significant implications on security. Some of the libraries not only closed the timing channel but also various cache access channels. In contrast, other libraries left an open door to implement access driven cache attacks on the protocol. In this section we analyze how an attacker can gain information about the number of compression functions performed during the HMAC operation by making use of leakages due to shared memory hierarchy in VMs located on the same machine. This is sufficient to re-implement the Lucky 13 attack.

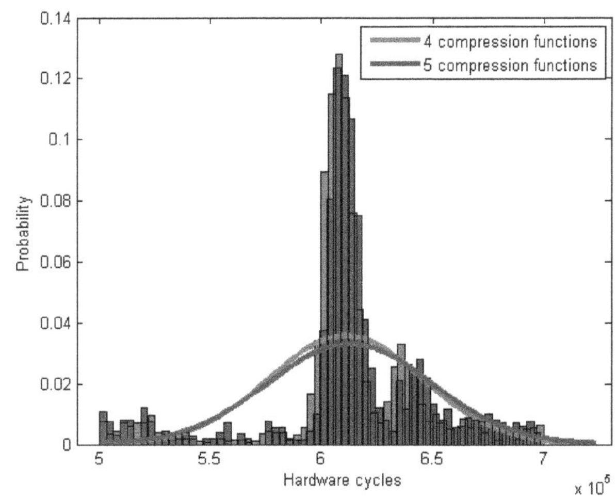

Figure 3: Histogram of network time measured for sent packages with valid (4 compression functions) and invalid (5 compression functions) paddings.

More precisely, during MAC processing depending on whether the actual MAC check terminates early or not, some libraries call a dummy function to equalize the processing time. Knowing if this dummy function is called or not reveals whether the received packet was processed as to either having a invalid padding, zero length padding or any other valid padding. In general, any difference in the execution flow between handling a well padded message, a zero padded message or an invalid padded message enables the Lucky 13 attack. This information is gained by the *Flush+Reload* technique if the cloud system enables deduplication features.

To validate this idea, we ran two experiments:

- In the first experiment we generated encrypted packets using PolarSSL client with valid and invalid paddings and measured the network time as shown in Figure 3. Note that, the network time in the two distributions obtained for valid and invalid paddings are essentially indistinguishable as intended by the patches.

- In the second experiment we see a completely different picture. Using PolarSSL we generated encrypted packets with valid and invalid paddings which were then sent to a PolarSSL server. Here instead, we measured the time it takes to load a specifically chosen PolarSSL library function running inside a co-located VM. Figure 4 shows the probability distributions for a function reloaded from L3 cache vs. a function reloaded from the main memory. The two distributions are clearly distinguishable and the misidentification rate (the area under the overlapping tails in the middle of the two distributions) is very small. Note that, this substitute timing channel provides much more precise timing that the network time. To see this more clearly, we refer the reader to Figure 2 in [16] where the network time

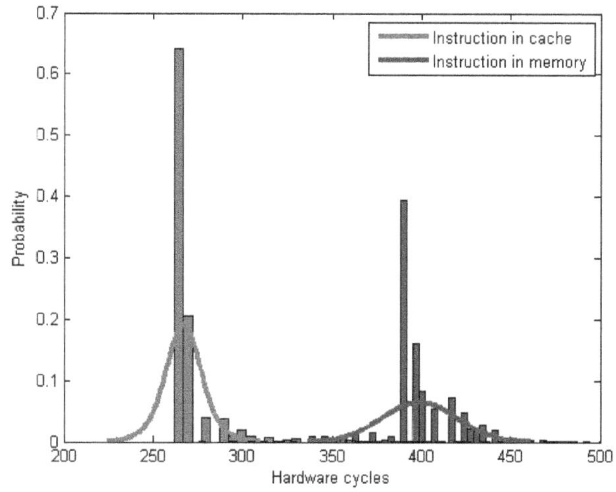

Figure 4: Histogram of access time measured for function calls from the L3 cache vs. a function called from the main memory.

is measured to obtain two overlapping Gaussians by measurements with OpenSSL encrypted traffic. This is not a surprise, since the network channel is significantly more noisy.

In conclusion, we regain a much more precise timing channel, by exploiting the discrepancy between L3 cache and memory accesses as measured by a co-located attacker. In what follows, we more concretely define the attack scenario, and then precisely define the steps of the new attack.

5.2 New Attack Scenario

In our attack scenario, the side channel information will be gained by monitoring the cache in a co-located VM. In the same way as in [16] we assume that the adversary captures, modifies, and replaces any message sent to the victim. However, TLS sessions work in such a way that when the protocol fails to decrypt a message, the session is closed. This is the reason why we focus in multi-session attacks where the same plaintext in the same place is being sent to the victim e.g. an encrypted password sent during user authentication.

The fact that we are working with a different method in a different scenario gives us some advantages and disadvantages over the previous Lucky 13 work:

Advantages:.

- Recent patches in cryptographic libraries mitigate the old Lucky 13 attack, but are still vulnerable in the new scenario.
- In the new scenario, no response from the server is needed. The old Lucky 13 attack needed a response to measure the time, which yielded a noisier environment in TLS than DTLS.
- The new attack does not suffer from the network channel noise. This source of noise was painful for the measurements as we can see in the original paper, where in case of TLS as many as 2^{14} trials were necessary to guess a single byte value.

Disadvantages:.

- Assumption of co-location: To target a specific victim, the attacker has to be co-located with that target. However the attacker could just reside in a physical machine and just wait for some potential random victim running a TLS operation.
- Other sources of noise: The attacker no longer has to deal with network channel noise, but still has to deal with other microarchitectural sources of noise, such as instruction prefetching. This new source of noise is translated in more traces needed, but as we will see, much less than in the original Lucky 13 attack. In Section 6 we explain how to deal with this new noise.

5.3 Attack Description

In this section we describe how an attacker uses *Flush+Reload* technique to gain access to information about the plaintext that is being sent to the victim.

- **Step 1 Function identification:** Identify different function calls in the TLS record decryption process to gain knowledge about suitable target functions for the spy process. The attacker can either calculate the offset of the function she is trying to monitor in the library, and then add the corresponding offset when the Address Space Layout Randomization (ASLR) moves her user address space. Another option is to disable the ASLR in the attackers VM, and use directly the virtual address corresponding to the function she is monitoring.
- **Step 2 Capture packet, mask and replace:** The attacker captures the packet that is being sent and masks it in those positions that are useful for the attack. Then she sends the modified packet to the victim.
- **Step 3 Flush targeted function from cache:** The flush and reload process starts after the attacker replaces the original version of the packet and sends it. The co-located VM flushes the function to ensure that no one but the victim ran the targeted function. Any subsequent execution of the targeted function will bear a faster reload time during the reload process.
- **Step 4 Reload target function & measure:** Reload the corresponding function memory line again and measure the reload time. According to a threshold that we set based on experimental measurements, we decide whether the dummy function was loaded from the cache (implying that the victim has executed the dummy function earlier) or was loaded from the main memory (implying the opposite).

Since the attacker has to deal with instruction prefetching, she will be constantly running *Flush+Reload* for a specified period of time. The attacker therefore distinguishes between functions preloaded and functions preloaded *and executed*, since the latter will stay for a longer period of time in the cache.

6. EXPERIMENT SETUP AND RESULTS

In this section we present our test environment together with our detection method in order to deal with different cache prefetch techniques that affect our measurements. Finally we present the results of our experiments for the PolarSSL, GnuTLS and CyaSSL libraries.

6.1 Experiment Setup

The experiments were run on an Intel i5-650 dual core at 3.2 GHz. Our physical server includes 256 KB per core L2 cache, and a 4 MB L3 cache shared between both cores. We used VMware ESXI 5.5.0 build number 162338 for virtualization. TPS is enabled with 4 KB pages. In this setting, our *Flush+Reload* technique can distinguish between L3 cache and main memory accesses.

For the TLS connection, we use an echo server which reads and re-sends the message that it receives, and a client communicating with it. Client and echo server are running in different virtual machines that use Ubuntu 12.04 guest OS. We modify the echo server functionality so that it adds a jitter in the encrypted reply message, modeling the Man in the Middle Attack. Once the message is sent, the echo server uses *Flush+Reload* to detect different function calls and concludes if the padding was correct or not. For the TLS connection, we use an echo server which reads and re-sends the message that it receives, and a client communicating with it. Client and echo server are running in different virtual machines that use Ubuntu 12.04 guest OS. We modify the echo server functionality so that it adds a jitter in the encrypted reply message, modeling the Man in the Middle Attack. Once the message is sent, the echo server uses *Flush+Reload* to detect different function calls and concludes if the padding was correct or not.

6.2 Dealing with Cache Prefetching

Modern CPUs implement cache prefetching in a number of ways. These techniques affect our experiments, since the monitored function can be prefetched to cache, even if it was not executed by the victim process. To avoid false positives, it is not sufficient to detect *if* the monitored functions were loaded to cache, but also for *how long* they have resided in the cache. This is achieved by counting the number of subsequent detections for the given function in one execution. Therefore, the attack process effectively distinguishes between *prefetched* functions and *prefetched and executed* functions.

We use experiments to determine a threshold (which differs across the libraries) to distinguish a prefetch and execute from a mere prefetch. For PolarSSL this threshold is based on observing three *Flush+Reload* accesses in a row. Assume that n is the number of subsequent accesses required to conclude that the function was executed. In the following we present the required hits for different libraries, i.e. the number of n-accesses required to decide whether the targeted function was executed or not.

6.3 Attack on PolarSSL1.3.6

Our first attack targets PolarSSL 1.3.6, with TLS 1.1. In the first scenario the attacker modifies the last two bytes of the encrypted message until she finds the Δ that leads to a 0x01|0x01 padding. Recall that 2^{16} different variations can be performed in the message. The first plot shows the success probability of guessing the right Δ versus L, where

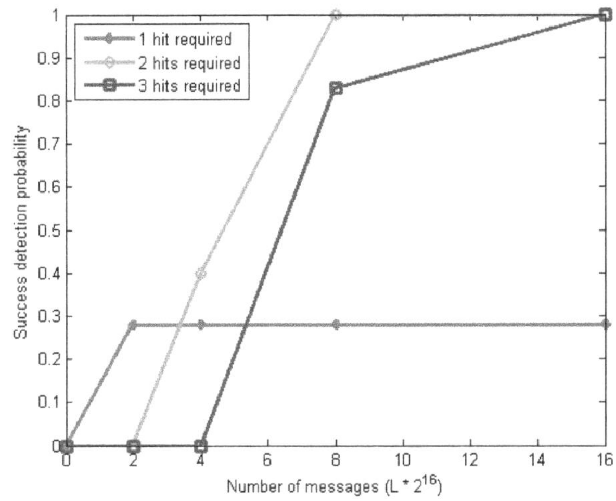

Figure 5: (PolarSSL 1.3.6) Success probability of recovering P_{14} and P_{15} vs. L, for different number of hits required. L refers to the number of 2^{16} traces needed, so the total number of messages is $2^{16} * L$.

L refers to the number of 2^{16} traces needed. For example $L = 4$ means that $2^{16} * 4$ messages are needed to detect the right Δ. Based on experimental results, we set the access threshold such that we consider a hit whenever the targeted function gets two accesses in a row.

The measurements were performed for different number of required hits. Figure 5 shows that requiring a single hit might not suffice since the attacker gets false positives, or for small number of messages she may miss the access at all. However when we require two hits, and if the attacker has a sufficient number of messages (in this case $L = 2^3$), the probability of guessing the right Δ is comfortably close to one. If the attacker increases the limit further to ensure an even lower number of false positives, she will need more messages to see the required number of hits. In the case of 3 hits, $L = 2^4$ is required to have a success probability close to one.

Figure 6 shows the success probability of correctly recovering P_{13}, once the attacker has recovered the last two bytes. Now the attacker is looking for the padding 0x02|0x02|0x02. We observed a similar behavior with respect to the previous case where with $L = 8$ and with a two hits requirement we will recover the correct byte with high probability. Again if the attacker increases the requirement to 3 hits, she will need more measurements; about $L = 16$ is sufficient in practice.

6.4 CyaSSL 3.0.0

Recall that the attack is much more effective if the attacker knows any of the preceding bytes of the plaintext, for example the last byte P_{15} of the plaintext. This would be the case in a javascript/web setting where adjusting the length of an initial HTTP request an attacker can ensure that there is only one unknown byte in the HTTP plaintext. In this case, the attacker would not need to try 2^{16} possible variations but only 2^8 variations for each byte that she wants to recover. This is the scenario that we analyzed in CyaSSL TLS 1.2, where we assumed that the attacker

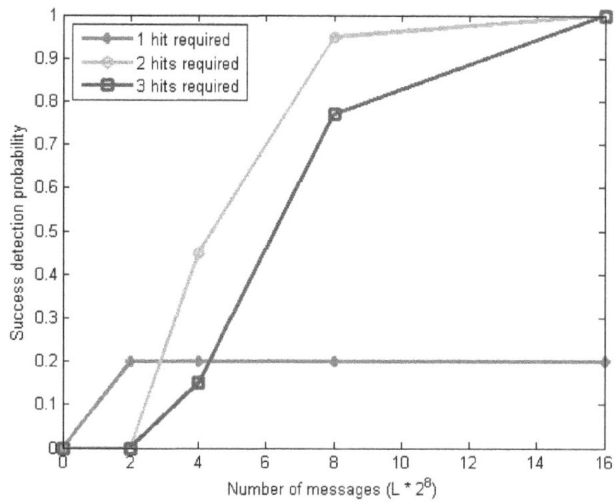

Figure 6: (PolarSSL 1.3.6) Success probability of recovering P_{13} assuming P_{14}, P_{15} known vs L, for different number of hits required. L refers to the number of 2^8 traces needed, so the total number of messages is $2^8 * L$.

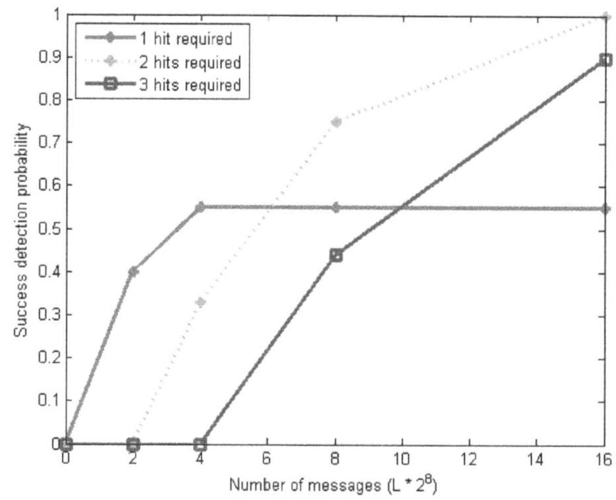

Figure 7: (CyaSSL3.0.0) Success Probability of recovering P_{14} assuming P_{15} known vs L, for different number of hits required. L refers to the number of 2^8 traces needed, so the total number of messages would be $2^8 * L$.

knows P_{15} and she wants to recover P_{14}. Now the attacker is again trying to obtain a 0x01|0x01 padding, but unlike in the previous case, she knows the Δ to make the last byte equal to 0x01. The implementation of CyaSSL behaves very similarly to the one of PolarSSL, where due to the access threshold, a one hit might lead to false positives. However, requiring two hits with a sufficient number of measurements is enough to obtain a success probability very close to one. The threshold is set as in the previous cases, where a hit is considered whenever we observe two *Flush+Reload* accesses in a row.

6.5 GnuTLS 3.2.0

Finally we present the results confirming that GnuTLS3.2.0 TLS 1.2 is also vulnerable to this kind of attack. Again, the measurements were taken assuming that the attacker knows the last byte P_{15} and she wants to recover P_{14}, i.e., she wants to observe the case where she injects a 0x01|0x01 padding. However GnuTLS's behavior shows some differences with respect to the previous cases. For the case of GnuTLS we find that if we set an access threshold of three accesses in a row (which would yield our desired hit), the probability of getting false positives is very low. Based on experimental measurements we observed that only when the dummy function is executed we observe such a behavior. However the attacker needs more messages to be able to detect one of these hits. Observing one hit indicates with high probability that the function was called, but we also consider the two hit case in case the attacker wants the probability of having false positives to be even lower. Based on the measurements we conclude that the attacker recovers the plaintext with very high probability, so we did not find it necessary to consider the three hit case.

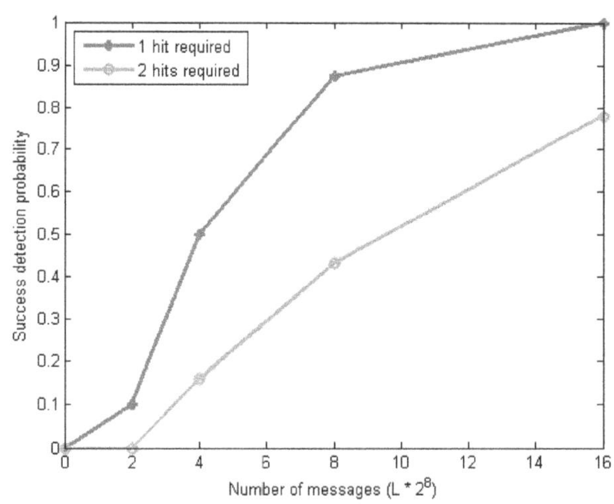

Figure 8: (GnuTLS3.2.0) Success Probability of recovering P_{14} assuming P_{15} known vs. L, for different number of hits required. L refers to the number of 2^8 traces needed, so the total number of messages would be $2^8 * L$.

7. COUNTERMEASURES

In this section we present various countermeasures that would prevent an attacker from implementing our modified Lucky 13 attack in a cloud environment. We first discuss software countermeasures, i.e, changes that can be made in the vulnerable cryptographic libraries to avoid the Lucky 13 attack. Then, we discuss more generic countermeasures to avoid the usage of *Flush+Reload* as a side channel technique to recover information. Note that library patches are less costly to implement than hardware based countermeasures.

On the downside, the software patches result in sub-optimal utilization of the memory hierarchy, thus, affecting the execution time performance.

Countermeasures in the cryptographic library: As our earlier survey of the library patches has revealed, there are two primary principles one needs to employ to securely patch cryptographic libraries against the cross-VM Lucky 13 attack:

- **Same function for valid/invalid padded cases:** The first pitfall that should be avoided takes place when a separate function call, e.g. a dummy function, is made to achieve a constant time implementation. This was part of the leakage exploited in this work where we monitor the dummy function calls made by another victim. In order to prevent it, a single function should be used during the entirety of the MAC operation of the message, as well as the additionally needed compression stages.
- **Same execution flow for valid/invalid padded cases:** This means that cryptographic library designers should avoid using message or key dependent branches that can leak information to an adversary monitoring the execution flow. Instead, logical operations like AND or XOR operations should be used to make the execution independent of vulnerable inputs. For instance, this solution has been adopted by OpenSSL, which calculates and always executes the maximum number of possible compression function calls.

An example algorithm that embodies these principles is presented in Algorithm 1. In the algorithm we are assuming that the maximum length of the processed message is 64 bytes, and that hash operations take 16 bytes of plaintext and that l is the length of the message once the padding is removed (for both correctly and incorrectly padded cases). The `md_process` function is used to perform the hash operations over all message blocks. This function puts the output in the hash variable. However, we use l to decide whether the output of the hash operation should be appended to the digest or not, depending on whether we are processing dummy data or the message. Note that the algorithm only uses a single function for both the valid message and the dummy data, thereby preventing execution flow distinguishing attacks. The code unifies the two separate execution flows.

Algorithm 1: Data independent execution flow for md_process

```
//M=Message,l=length Message without padding
Input  : M,l
//Digest of M
Output: digest(M)
//Assume hash operates on a 16 byte message,
  and we have a maximum length of 64
for i = 0 to 4 do
    valid=(16*i/l);
    md_process(M[16*i]*¬valid + dummy_data*valid,
    hash);
    Append(digest[i],hash*¬valid);
end
return digest;
```

(In the printed algorithm, ¬valid is shown as $\overline{\text{valid}}$.)

Preventing *Flush+Reload* : Since our version of the Lucky 13 attack uses the *Flush+Reload* technique to extract timing information, any *Flush+Reload* countermeasure will also disable our attack. Here we note a few common *Flush+Reload* countermeasures.

- **Disabling deduplication features:** Our detection method is based on shared memory features that are offered by VMMs. Although these features have the advantage of significantly saving memory, they can also be used as a side channel to snoop sensitive information from a co-located user. Therefore, disabling deduplication closes the covert channel necessary to perform the attack presented in this work.
- **Cache Partitioning:** This countermeasure should be performed at the hardware level, and consists in splitting the cache into pieces so that each user uses only a *private* portion of the cache. In this scenario even when memory deduplication is enabled, an attacker could not interfere with the victim's data in the cache, and would no longer be able to distinguish whether the monitored function was used or not.
- **Masking the cache loads:** This is a hardware-based countermeasure as well, where each user has a private masking value that is used when the data is loaded into cache and when the data being read from the cache. Since different users have different masking values, even when memory deduplication is enabled, attacker and victim would access the same data in memory through different cache addresses, preventing the attack in this work.

8. CONCLUSION

In this work we demonstrated that the Lucky 13 attack is still a threat in the cross-VM setting for a number of prominent cryptographic libraries already patched for the Lucky 13 attack. We discussed the different approaches taken by the major TLS libraries and showed that one class of timing side channel countermeasure, i.e, using dummy functions to achieve constant time execution, is vulnerable to cross-VM *Flush+Reload* attacks. With practical experiments we demonstrated that the side channel enabling Lucky 13 is still existent in PolarSSL, GnuTLS and CyaSSL if run in a deduplication enabled virtual machine. In fact, the new cache side channel is actually stronger, since it no longer suffers from network noise, making the attack succeed with significantly fewer observations than the original Lucky 13 attack in [16]. We also discussed how various crypto libraries fixed the Lucky 13 vulnerability in detail to better explain what makes a crypto library vulnerable to *Flush+Reload* based attacks.

In our test setting, we used the VMware ESXi with TPS enabled. This deduplication feature enabled us to detect dummy function calls that are implemented by the vulnerable libraries to equalize HMAC execution time in the case of incorrectly CBC-padded packets in TLS. Unlike in the case of vulnerable libraries, OpenSSL, Mozilla NSS, and MatrixSSL applied patches with a constant and padding-independent program flow to fix the Lucky 13 vulnerability. Libraries fixed this way are secure against the described attack.

With this study we showed that crypto library designers and authors should be careful about not implementing any data dependent execution paths and ensure true constant execution time. We conclude that, any function or process in a crypto library whose execution depends on the input data is exploitable by cache side-channel attacks and that libraries should be implemented accordingly.

9. ACKNOWLEDGMENTS

This work is supported by the National Science Foundation, under grant CNS-1318919 and CNS-1314770. We would like to thank the anonymous reviewers of AsiaCCS 2015 for their helpful comments. We would also like to thank Craig Shue for his help on understanding memory deduplication features.

10. REFERENCES

[1] CyaSSL: Embedded SSL library WolfSSL. `http://www.wolfssl.com/yaSSL/Home.html`, May 2014.

[2] Kernel samepage merging. `http://kernelnewbies.org/Linux_2_6_32\#head-d3f32e41df508090810388a57efce73f52660ccb/`, April 2014.

[3] MatrixSSL: Open source embedded SSL. May 2014.

[4] Acıİçmez, O. Yet another microarchitectural attack: Exploiting i-cache. In *Proceedings of the 2007 ACM Workshop on Computer Security Architecture* (New York, NY, USA, 2007), CSAW '07, ACM, pp. 11–18.

[5] AlFardan, N. J., Bernstein, D. J., Patterson, K. G., Poettering, B., and Schuldt, J. C. N. On the Security of RC4 in TLS. In *22nd USENIX Security Symposium* (2013).

[6] Arcangeli, A., Eidus, I., and Wright, C. Increasing memory density by using KSM. In *Proceedings of the Linux symposium* (2009), pp. 19–28.

[7] Bard, G. A challenging but feasible blockwise-adaptive chosen-plaintext attack on SSL. In *SECRYPT* (2006), pp. 99–109.

[8] Bard, G. V. The vulnerability of SSL to chosen plaintext attack. IACR Cryptology ePrint Archive 2004:111, 2004.

[9] Bardou, R., Focardi, R., Kawamoto, Y., Simionato, L., Steel, G., and Tsay, J.-K. Efficient padding oracle attacks on cryptographic hardware. In *CRYPTO* (2012), R. Safavi-Naini and R. Canetti, Eds., vol. 7417 of *Lecture Notes in Computer Science*, Springer, pp. 608–625.

[10] Benger, N., van de Pol, J., Smart, N. P., and Yarom, Y. "ooh aah... just a little bit": A small amount of side channel can go a long way. In *CHES* (2014), pp. 75–92.

[11] Bernstein, D. J. Cache-timing attacks on AES, 2004. URL: `http://cr.yp.to/papers.html#cachetiming`.

[12] Bonneau, J. Robust Final-Round Cache-Trace Attacks against AES.

[13] Bonneau, J., and Mironov, I. Cache-Collision Timing Attacks against AES. In *Cryptographic Hardware and Embedded Systems—CHES 2006* (2006), vol. 4249 of *Springer LNCS*, Springer, pp. 201–215.

[14] Chen Cai-Sen, Wang Tao, C. X.-C., and Ping, Z. An improved trace driven instruction cache timing attack on RSA. Cryptology ePrint Archive, Report 2011/557, 2011. `http://eprint.iacr.org/`.

[15] Duong, T., and Rizzo, J. Here come the XOR ninjas.

[16] Fardan, N. J. A., and Paterson, K. G. Lucky Thirteen: Breaking the TLS and DTLS Record Protocols. In *Security and Privacy (SP), 2013 IEEE Symposium on* (May 2013), pp. 526–540.

[17] Goodin, D. Hackers break SSL encryption used by millions of sites. `http://www.theregister.co.uk/2011/09/19/beast_exploits_paypal_ssl/`, 2011.

[18] Gullasch, D., Bangerter, E., and Krenn, S. Cache Games – Bringing Access-Based Cache Attacks on AES to Practice. *IEEE Symposium on Security and Privacy 0* (2011), 490–505.

[19] Gullasch, D., Bangerter, E., and Krenn, S. Cache Games – Bringing Access-Based Cache Attacks on AES to Practice. In *Proceedings of the 2011 IEEE Symposium on Security and Privacy* (Washington, DC, USA, 2011), SP '11, IEEE Computer Society, pp. 490–505.

[20] Hu, W.-M. Lattice scheduling and covert channels. In *Proceedings of the 1992 IEEE Symposium on Security and Privacy* (Washington, DC, USA, 1992), SP '92, IEEE Computer Society, pp. 52–.

[21] Irazoqui, G., İnci, M. S., Eisenbarth, T., and Sunar, B. Fine grain Cross-VM Attacks on Xen and VMware are possible. preprint available at `http://ecewp.ece.wpi.edu/wordpress/vernam/files/2014/04/main.pdf`.

[22] Jones, M. T. Anatomy of Linux kernel shared memory. `http://www.ibm.com/developerworks/linux/library/l-kernel-shared-memory/l-kernel-shared-memory-pdf.pdf/`, April 2010.

[23] Kelsey, J., Schneier, B., Wagner, D., and Hall, C. Side channel cryptanalysis of product ciphers. In *Computer SecurityÚESORICS 98*. Springer, 1998, pp. 97–110.

[24] Mavrogiannopoulos, N., and Josefsson, S. GnuTLS: The GnuTLS Transport Layer Security Library. May 2014.

[25] Moeller, B. Security of CBC ciphersuites in SSL/TLS: Problems and countermeasures. `http://www.openssl.org/?bodo/tls-cbc.txt`, April 2004.

[26] Mozilla. Mozilla NSS: Network security services. May 2014.

[27] Osvik, D. A., Shamir, A., and Tromer, E. Cache Attacks and Countermeasures: The Case of AES. In *Proceedings of the 2006 The Cryptographers' Track at the RSA Conference on Topics in Cryptology* (Berlin, Heidelberg, 2006), CT-RSA'06, Springer-Verlag, pp. 1–20.

[28] Page, D. Theoretical Use of Cache Memory as a Cryptanalytic Side-Channel, 2002.

[29] Paterson, K. G., Ristenpart, T., and Shrimpton, T. Tag size does matter: Attacks and proofs for the TLS record protocol. In *Advances in Cryptology–ASIACRYPT 2011*. Springer Berlin Heidelberg, 2011, pp. 372–389.

[30] PolarSSL. PolarSSL: Straightforward,secure communication. www.polarssl.org.

[31] Ristenpart, T., Tromer, E., Shacham, H., and Savage, S. Hey, you, get off of my cloud: Exploring information leakage in third-party compute clouds. In *Proceedings of the 16th ACM Conference on Computer and Communications Security* (New York, NY, USA, 2009), CCS '09, ACM, pp. 199–212.

[32] Rogaway, P. Problems with proposed IP cryptography. http://www.cs.ucdavis.edu/?rogaway/papers/draft-rogaway-ipsec-comments-00.txt, 1995.

[33] Suzaki, K., Iijima, K., Yagi, T., and Artho, C. Memory deduplication as a threat to the guest OS. In *Proceedings of the Fourth European Workshop on System Security* (2011), ACM, p. 1.

[34] Suzaki, K., Iijima, K., Yagi, T., and Artho, C. Software side channel attack on memory deduplication. *SOSP POSTER* (2011).

[35] The OpenSSL Project. OpenSSL: The open source toolkit for SSL/TLS. www.openssl.org, April 2003.

[36] Tromer, E., Osvik, D., and Shamir, A. Efficient Cache Attacks on AES, and Countermeasures. *Journal of Cryptology 23*, 1 (2010), 37–71.

[37] Tsunoo, Y., Saito, T., Suzaki, T., and Shigeri, M. Cryptanalysis of DES implemented on computers with cache. In *Proc. of CHES 2003, Springer LNCS* (2003), Springer-Verlag, pp. 62–76.

[38] Vaudenay, S. Security Flaws Induced by CBC Padding - Applications to SSL, IPSEC, WTLS. In *Proceedings of In Advances in Cryptology - EUROCRYPT'02* (2002), Springer-Verlag, pp. 534–546.

[39] VMWare. Understanding Memory Resource Management in VMware vSphere 5.0. http://www.vmware.com/files/pdf/mem_mgmt_perf_vsphere5.pdf.

[40] Waldspurger, C. A. Memory resource management in VMware ESX server. *ACM SIGOPS Operating Systems Review 36*, SI (2002), 181–194.

[41] Yarom, Y., and Falkner, K. Flush+reload: A high resolution, low noise, L3 cache side-channel attack. In *23rd USENIX Security Symposium (USENIX Security 14)* (San Diego, CA, Aug. 2014), USENIX Association, pp. 719–732.

[42] Zhang, Y., Juels, A., Reiter, M. K., and Ristenpart, T. Cross-VM side channels and their use to extract private keys. In *Proceedings of the 2012 ACM Conference on Computer and Communications Security* (New York, NY, USA, 2012), CCS '12, ACM, pp. 305–316.

An empirical analysis of ZeuS C&C lifetime

Carlos Gañán
Delft University of Technology
The Netherlands
c.h.g.hernandezganan@tudelft.nl

Orcun Cetin
Delft University of Technology
The Netherlands
F.O.Cetin@tudelft.nl

Michel van Eeten
Delft University of Technology
The Netherlands
M.J.G.vanEeten@tudelft.nl

ABSTRACT

Botnets continue to pose a significant threat to network-based applications and communications over the Internet. A key mitigation strategy has been to take down command and control infrastructure of the botnets. The efficiency of those mitigation methods has not been extensively studied. In this paper we investigate several observable characteristics of botnet command and controls (C&C) and estimate the variability in the survival rate of these C&Cs and the factors that are related to such variability. Furthermore, we show that different type of mitigation efforts have different impact. Kaplan-Meier analysis is performed to evaluate C&C survival ratios in the particular case of the ZeuS botnet. Using a lasso penalized Cox regression model, we identify the factors that influence the lifetime of a C&C. Location, malware family type, registrar, hosting type and popularity are the fundamental factors that explain this variability. Our results show that location and type of hosting are the two factors that affect more significantly the C&C lifetime. Thus, ZeuS C&Cs in certain regions of Asia are prone to stay online longer that those located in Europe.

Keywords

ZeuS malware, C2C lifetime, survival analysis

Categories and Subject Descriptors

K.6.5 [**Management of computing and information systems**]: Security and Protection; K.4.2 [**Computers and society**]: Social Issues

1. INTRODUCTION

A botnet comprises a set of malware-infected machines connected to the Internet that communicate to accomplish distributed criminal activities. Botnets support a wide array of criminal business models which represent a severe threat to the Internet economy, individuals' privacy, and national security.

ASIA CCS'15, April 14–17, 2015, Singapore..

http://dx.doi.org/10.1145/2714576.27145794.

One of the main strategies for combating botnets has been to disrupt the ability of the criminals to commandeer the botnet's resources. The criminals control the infected machines either directly via built-in commands, or indirectly via a command and control (C&C) infrastructure. Roughly speaking, C&C can rely on a centralized or a peer-to-peer architecture, enhanced by complementary techniques to ensure redundancy and resiliency against take-down attempts by defenders.

It is common to view C&C takedown as a primarily technical problem of reverse engineering the botnet's communication mechanisms and then disrupting it, by shutting down or manipulating key resources. What this view obscures, however, is that technological advances alone has proven insufficient to eradicate botnets [38]. Attempts to mitigate the proliferation of bots also have to take into account the incentives of the market actors that are needed to takedown criminal resources. Incentives are not just monetary, but also include reputation effects, legal constraints and the political environment in which these actors operate [37]. Understanding and aligning the incentives is as important as improving the technology in addressing cybersecurity threats.

Any attempt to improve these mitigation efforts will require identification of factors influencing the lifetime of botnet C&C. These factors help us to understand possible causes and identify pro-active and re-active countermeasures. To check the impact of both technological and socio-economic efforts towards mitigating botnets, we assess the lifetime duration of C&Cs depending on their characteristics. In this paper we use the ZeuS botnet [11] as case study to analyze these characteristics.

Zeus, Citadel and other variants of Zeus malware dominate the financial malware threat landscape and are responsible for huge business and costumer financial losses. According to a security report published in 2009, Zeus Crimeware along infected an estimated 3.6 million computers in the United States [11]. In order to mitigate the threat of the family of Zeus botnets, several takedown actions have been executed by both FBI and Microsoft. Some of them had an impact, but none of them brought down the botnets fully successfully.

Using three different data sources, we gather URLs related to C&Cs and analyze their characteristics, i.e., type of web server and web technologies. We investigate the relation between these characteristics and the C&C lifetime. Our results show that C&Cs running content management systems are less likely to host ZeuS than those are not running one, and that servers running *Tengine* are more likely to stay compromise longer than those running common servers like *Apache* or *nginx*.

Furthermore, we analyze the effectiveness of performed mitigating operations. We investigate the impact of four major mitigation efforts towards reducing the number of active C&Cs. Traditional time-series analysis shows significant differences among the take-down operations depending on the parties involved. Taking down a fraud friendly autonomous system is shown to be the most effective measure.

Survival analysis using Kaplan-Meier [22] estimates and Cox proportional hazards model [14] are used to determine potential differences in C&Cs lifetime, caused by different factors. A penalized likelihood algorithm is used to identify the importance of each factor and quantify their influence on the C&C's lifetime. Results show that the C&C's location and the hosting type are the main factors affecting the survival rate.

The rest of the paper is organized as follows. Section 2 describes the data collection methodology. Section 3 presents technological characteristics of ZeuS C&Cs. Section 4 analyzes the impact of different mitigation efforts. In Section 5 we evaluate C&C survival rate depending on several socio-demographic factors. Section 6 presents a lasso penalized Cox regression model to explain the importance of each factor. In section 7 we discus the related work and in section 8 we conclude.

2. DATA ON ZEUS COMMAND AND CONTROL SERVERS

2.1 Data Collection Methodology

The data set consists of 48,104 URLs associated with real C&C servers observed in the wild during approximately three years (the observation period varies depending on the data source). We use three independent data sources to collect ZeuS command and control URLs:

- *ZeuS Tracker* [5]: is a C&C panel tracker that provides the ability to track ZeuS command and control services and hosts of ZeuS files. It aims to provide system administrators with the possibility to block well-known ZeuS hosts and avoid ZeuS infections in their networks. The data-set consists of 18,889 URLs associated with C&Cs that were online at some point between 2009Q1 and 2014Q3. Let $\mathcal{Z}$ be the set of C&Cs from ZeuS tracker.

- *Cybercrime tracker* [1]: is a C&C panel tracker that lists the administration interfaces of certain in-the-wild botnets including ZeuS. Since 2013, this tracker is also integrated in Virus Total [3]. The data-set consists of 1,890 URLs associated with C&Cs that were online at some point between 2011Q4 and 2014Q3. Let $\mathcal{C}$ be the set of C&Cs from Cybercrime tracker.

- *Private honeypots*: consists of a list of botnet C&C servers captured by a company that specializes in threats intelligence using honeypots located all over the world. The data-set consists of 144,625 captured ZeuS configuration files. The configuration files were collected over a period of around two years (2011Q4-2013Q1) using two different methods: they are gathered by running live ZeuS samples or by emulating the malware to download configuration files. Let $\mathcal{P}$ be the set of C&Cs captured by these honeypots.

Table 1 shows the number of C&Cs per data source and the overlap among them. Most of the C&Cs in our data-set were captured by the private honeypots (56.80%) while Cybercrime tracker only captured a small amount (3.92%). It is also worth noting that there exists some overlap between the different data-sets. This overlap is insignificant between Cybercrime tracker and the private honeypots, while around 16.07% percent of the C&Cs present in the private data-set are also present in ZeuS tracker. On the other hand, 38,866 of the captured C&Cs are only present in one of the sources.

	Cardinality
$\mathcal{Z}$	18,889
$\mathcal{P}$	27,326
$\mathcal{C}$	1,890
$\mathcal{Z} \cap \mathcal{P}$	4,394
$\mathcal{Z} \cap \mathcal{C}$	119
$\mathcal{C} \cap \mathcal{P}$	8
$\mathcal{Z} \cap \mathcal{P} \cap \mathcal{C}$	6

Table 1: Number of C&Cs per source

From each C&C, we identify six different features: lifetime, ZeuS family type, location, hosting provider/AS number, registrar and popularity.

2.2 Summary statistics

We first discuss how the number of online C&Cs has evolved over time (see Fig. 1). The average number of online C&Cs (μ) varies highly depending on the data-set: Zeus tracker $\mu = 486.70$ ($\sigma = 164.15$), Cybercrime tracker $\mu = 84.77$ ($\sigma = 89.28$) and the private honeypots $\mu = 1,756.00$ ($\sigma = 328.01$). Though we observe that the different data sources captured different number of C&Cs, they all show a similar trend: the number of online C&Cs is converging to a common value independently of the data source. As can be seen in Fig. 1, a clear decreasing trend appeared in last quarter of 2014.

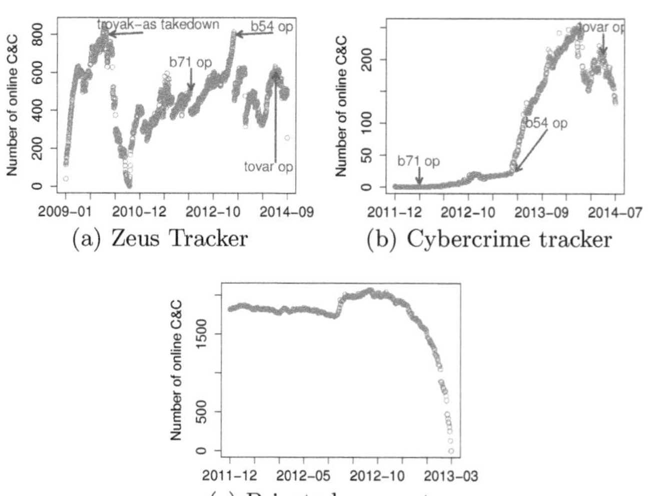

(a) Zeus Tracker

(b) Cybercrime tracker

(c) Private honeypots

Figure 1: Online C2C time series per source

We then study where these C&Cs are located (see Fig. 2). Our global data-set covers C&Cs located in 135 different countries. The top 10 countries in terms of hosting more C&Cs are United Stated (36.26%), Germany (14.05%), Russia (10.30%), Canada (4.25%), China (3.21%), Netherlands (3.11%), Ukraine (3.02%), United Kingdom (2.63%), India (2.35%) and France (1.45%). These 10 countries account for more than 80% of the total number of C&Cs, while the remaining 125 countries only account for less than 20%. This evidences that the number of C&Cs is related to the hosting industry market, i.e., a larger hosting industry increases the probability of hosting a C&C.

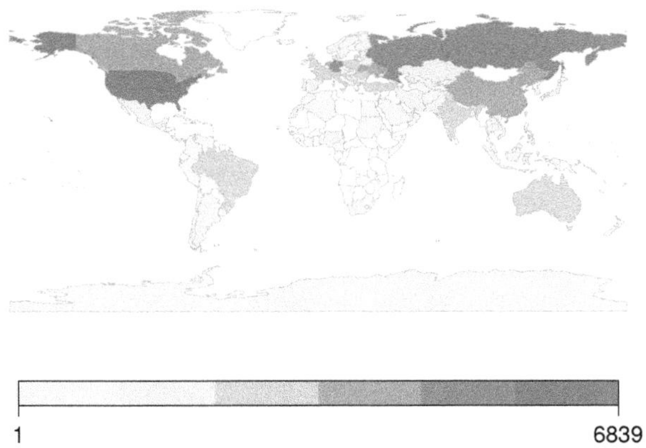

Figure 2: Number of C&C per country

Finally, we also analyze the distribution of the C&Cs among the different autonomous systems (AS). Table 2 shows the number of unique domains per data source. By comparing Table 1 and Table 2, we determine that several C&Cs are hosted in the same domain at some point in time. Moreover, it is also surprising that the number of unique IPs is smaller than the number of unique domains. That suggests that different domains share the same IP which evidences that shared hosting servers are being exploited as C&Cs. On the other hand, by comparing the number of ASes, we notice what part of the cyberspace is covered by each data source. ZeuS tracker is the most comprehensive in that sense, as it covers many more ASes than the other sources.

	# domains	Unique IPs	# ASes
Zeus Tracker	18,093	5,244	1181
Cybercrime tracker	1,647	1,135	449
Private honeypots	12,952	3,047	821

Table 2: Characteristics of the C&C domains per source

3. C&C CHARACTERISTICS

To further analyze why those particular servers were hosting C&C, we investigate their technical features. To that end, we scan all the C&Cs URLs using Netcraft toolbar [2].

First we analyze the uptime depending on the type of server. We define *uptime* as the amount of time since the C&C is detected until the C&C is taken down. Table 3 shows that there are appreciable differences in the uptime among different types of server. Though the frequency of the servers is related with their usage, the uptime is not. Tengine is the 9th top technology among web servers [4], but it hosts C&Cs for three times longer than traditional web servers such as Apache or Microsoft-IIS. We can also observe some significant differences among the different type of servers that host ZeuS C&Cs and the market share of these type of servers. That might indicate that these type of servers are more vulnerable or bot herders present some kind a preference towards infecting these type of web servers.

Server type	Avg. Uptime(h)	Observed	Expected)
Apache	1816.50	51.74%	59.4%
nginx	3276.78	27.92%	22.30%
Microsoft-IIS	2115.24	11.56%	13.5%
Tengine	6057.76	2.32%	0.17%
LiteSpeed	1142.90	1.66%	0.88%
cloudflare-nginx	2719.66	0.56%	0.58%
uServ	3191.97	0.25%	0.42%
lighttpd	2003.52	0.22%	0.75%
Microsoft-HTTPAPI	2993.71	0.17%	1.39%
YTS	1676.29	0.16%	0.04%
Squeegit	411.14	0.15%	0.02%
squid	1739.29	0.15%	0.20%
Apache-Coyote	1513.44	0.10%	0.29%
IdeaWebServer	1136.69	0.10%	0.40%
ghs	3913.35	0.08%	0.04%
IIS	3807.70	0.05%	1.07%
BladeStorm	2239.00	0.04%	0.04%
Zeus	666.00	0.04%	0.11%
PCX	950.20	0.03%	0.02%
Sun-ONE-Web-Server	34.40	0.03%	0.03%

Table 3: Uptime versus server type

Next we analyze the uptime depending on the type of content management system (CMS). Firstly, it is worth mentioning that only 36.77% of the C&Cs were hosted in a server running a CMS. The existence of sinkholes may have led to underestimate the number of C&Cs running on top of a CMS. However, the comparison among the different CMS types is representative of the ecosystem. Table 4 shows that there are important differences in the uptime among different types of CMS. Again we notice a similar trend that with the server type, i.e., some of the less popular CMSes host C&Cs for longer periods of time than the most popular ones. For instance, servers using Contao CMS lived ten times longer in average than those using WordPress.

CMS	Avg. Uptime(h)	Observed	Expected
WordPress	1164.96	54.65%	61.1%
Joomla	1293.88	31.42%	7.9%
Drupal	1421.91	2.16%	5.1%
Magento eCommerce	921.37	1.40%	2.7 %
Bitrix Site Manager	1077.08	1.08%	1.0%
osCommerce	690.87	1.02%	0.6%
zencart	4027.80	0.89%	0.4%
vBulletin	699.58	0.70%	1.1%
TYPO3	1015.38	0.57%	1.6%
Expression Engine	1256.30	0.51%	0.6%
OpenCart Shopping Cart	1214.93	0.51%	0.9%
phpBB	5564.10	0.38%	0.6%
Datalife Engine	4977.00	0.25%	0.9%
Google Sites	6964.00	0.25%	0.1%
DotNetNuke	2228.33	0.19%	0.9%
ECShop Shopping Cart	891.33	0.19%	0.2%
Simple Machines Forum	3070.00	0.19%	0.3%
concrete5	157.00	0.13%	0.2%
Contao CMS	11830.50	0.13%	0.2%

Table 4: Uptime versus content management system

Finally, we also analyze the different technologies searching for some pattern that would indicate that something is out of the ordinary. Table 5 describes the main statistics of the different technologies used by the C&Cs. Results show that 92.73% of the servers hosting C&C had some javascript code. This might indicate either that this technology represents a vulnerability or that certain ZeuS variants need javascript to run their C&C. In addition, sites that allow secure communication are less attractive to host a C&C and, in addition, they are cleaned faster.

	PHP	Javascript	Flash	SSL	Ajax	Perl
Observed Percentage	75.39%	92.73%	4.02%	19.08%	4.68%	14.04%
Expected Percentage	82.1%	88.1%	12.7%	48.9%	<0.1%	0.6%
Avg. Uptime(h) WITH	1993.36	2073.78	1259.27	1259.39	1381	1496.67
Avg. Uptime(h) WITHOUT	1898.04	1317.49	2050.66	2137.40	2031	2047.21

Table 5: Descriptive statistics C&C technologies

4. IMPACT OF MITIGATION MEASURES

In Section 2, we showed the evolution of the number of online C&Cs. In this section we analyze the impact of the different operations that took place to reduce that number.

During the period under observation, 4 interventions took place (see Fig. 1): troyak-AS takedown, b54 operation, b71 operation and tovar operation. As can be seen in Fig. 1a, on March 2010 the number of active ZeuS C&C servers dropped drastically. This drop was due to the takedown of Troyak-AS (AS50215), the upstream provider for the six worst ZeuS hosting ISPs. On March 2012, in operation b71, Microsoft obtained an ex parte temporary restraining order to seize domain names from botnet operators (in particular Zeus, SpyEye and Ice-IX variants). Again this operation caused a drop in the number of online C&Cs as shown in Fig. 1a. Note that the impact of this operation was not captured by cybercrime tracker (see Fig. 1b). This could be due to the fact that Microsoft took C&Cs that were operated mainly by researchers and security firms. Similarly, on June 2013, in operation b54, Microsoft in a collaborative action with the FBI took down several Citadel C&Cs that resulted in a significant disruption. The last operation -operation tovar- was performed on June 2014 by global law enforcement in conjunction with private partners to dismantle the Gameover Zeus. Note that these interventions only had a temporary impact on the botnet infrastructure but in any case it was possible to fully take down the botnet.

To assess the impact of the different interventions we model Zeus Tracker time series following the framework introduce by Box and Tiao [12]. This framework allows to measure how the interventions affected the number of online C&Cs by changing the mean function or the trend of the time series. To that end, we propose a basic univariate time series model is the Gaussian autoregressive moving average model:

$$\Phi(B)Z_t = \theta_0 + \theta(B)a_t, \tag{1}$$

where $\Phi(B) = 1 - \Phi_1 B - \ldots - \Phi_p B^p$ and $\theta(B) = 1 - \theta_1 B - \ldots - \theta_q B^q$ are polynomials in B of degrees p and q, respectively, θ_0 is a constant, B is the backshift operator such that $BZ_t = Z_{t-1}$, and a_t is a sequence of independent Gaussian variates with mean zero and variance σ_a^2.

More generally, we model the change in the mean function by an ARMAX-type specification so that it can handle intervention analysis and outliers. We consider two types of intervention: Level Shift and Transient Change. It is assumed that the intervention affects the mean function of the process, with the deviation from the unperturbed mean function modeled as the sum of the outputs of an ARMA filter of a number of covariates; the deviation is known as the transfer function. We consider two transient changes corresponding to the take-down Troyak-AS and operation tovar; and two level shifts corresponding to operations b51 and b54. The level shifts are included in the ARMA model from Eq. (1) by means of the indicator variable I_t that equals 1 in the intervention date and 0 otherwise. Transient changes are modeled as the sum of two ARMA filters of the corresponding indicator variable. Hence the transfer function equals:

$$\omega_0 I_t + \frac{\omega_1}{(1 - \omega_2 B)} I_t, \tag{2}$$

where I_t is a pulse function and ω_i is the deviation from the original time series caused by the intervention.

Table 6 shows the coefficients of the ARMAX model that best fit the time series series. To assess the goodness of the fit we compute the autocorrelation function of the residuals and the p-values. Fig. 3 shows that the standardized residuals do not show clusters of volatility. Similarly, the autocorrelation function shows no significant autocorrelation between the residuals and the p-values for the Ljung–Box statistics are all large, indicating that the residuals are patternless.

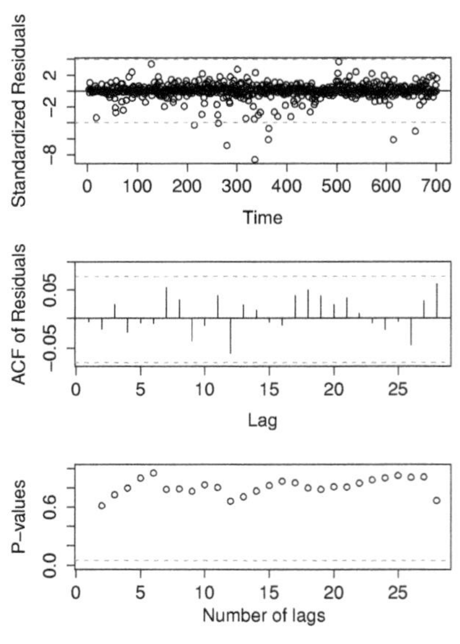

Figure 3: Diagnosis of the model fit

To compare the different interventions we analyze the value of the w_i coefficients. Comparing the ω_0 coefficients we can observe the change in the mean number of online C&Cs per intervention. The results corroborate the visual analysis, i.e., the take-down of Troyak-AS was the intervention that had a higher impact. The value of ω_2 determines how fast the effect of the intervention decays to zero. Again, the take-down of Troyak-AS had a longer persisting impact than the rest of the interventions.

5. FACTORS AFFECTING C&C UPTIME

In the previous sections, we have presented the technical characteristics of severs hosting C&Cs and showed how

		Troyak-AS			b71	b54	Tovar operation		
θ	Φ	ω_0	ω_1	ω_2	ω_0	ω_0	ω_0	ω_1	ω_2
-0.4031	0.5222	-181.3694	181.1214	0.0202	-17.0044	-19.8002	-61.7158	49.61	-0.2058
(0.1174)	(0.1073)	(44.5913)	(55.6024)	(0.0045)	(16.1217)	(17.3852)	(44.5918)	(23.1023)	(0.0125)

Table 6: Parameters (value and standard error) of the ARMAX model considering interventions

these affect the uptime. In this section, we analyze the impact of not only technical factors but also socio-demographic variables on the uptime of the C&Cs.

There exist several methods by which a botnet can be taken down [13]. Traditional methods include:

- Hosting provider de-peered
- Server hosting botnet cleans up/kicks off
- Public IRC servers takedown, expiration free web hosting
- Compromised host cleaned up/rebuilt
- DNS Revoked
- IP of C&C server blacklisted

These different take-down mechanisms involve different parties, e.g. registrars or hosting providers. In the following we evaluate and interpret the impact that have the different entities involved in these methods on the lifetime of the C&C. We perform a survival analysis using the time in hours to shut-down a C&C as the response variable. Our data consisted of overall C&C survival ($S(t)$), defined as the probability that a C&C is still online at a specific time during the study period. During that period, all C&Cs were initially online and may either have gone offline. Survival curves are estimated according to the Kaplan–Meier method [22], computed by updating the survival function after each event, without the assumption of an underlying probability distribution. Differences between survival curves were examined using a formal non-parametric statistical test called log-rank test [29]. It is worth noting that some C&Cs remain online at the end our study, making it impossible to observe when these are shut-down. C&Cs that remain online and in the search results at the end of our study are said to be right-censored.

We identify six different factors that might affect the lifetime of a C&Cs: location, malware variant, notification regime, hosting provider, registrar and popularity.

5.1 Location

First we analyze the impact of the location of the C&Cs on their lifetime. Fig. 4 shows the heat map of the average uptime of the C&C. Comparing the number of C&Cs hosted in each country to the average uptime of these C&C, we can observe a divergent pattern. While most of the C&Cs are hosted in the North America (41.29%), Europe (44.09%) and some populated countries in Asia (10.35%) (China and India), the worst countries in terms of average uptime are located in Africa, South America and China.

Fig. 5 shows the survival curves for the top 10 countries in terms of amount of C&Cs. We can appreciate that after the first 24 hours, the amount of C&Cs still online ranges from

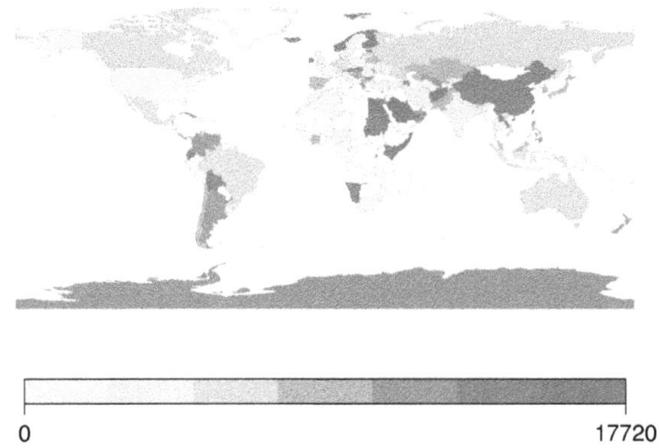

Figure 4: Country per C&C avg. uptime (hours)

78% to 85%. That indicates, that no matter the country, most of the C&Cs are alive for more than one day. Remarkably, the worst countries in terms of taking efficient measures against C&Cs are China, Canada and Russia. On the other hand, France and Netherlands are the countries that took C&Cs down faster.

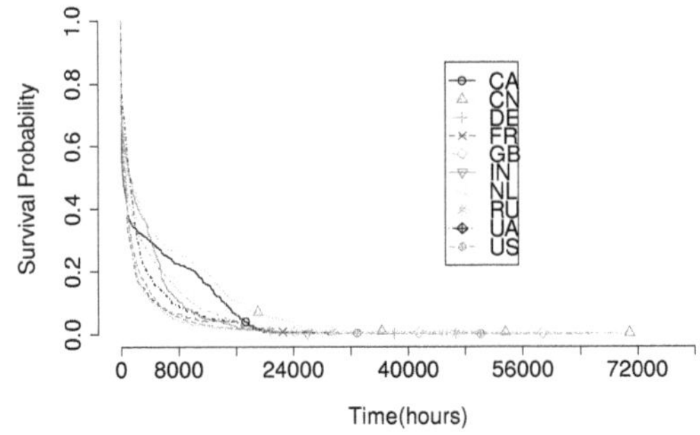

Figure 5: Kaplan-Meier estimates top 10 countries

To quantify the differences among different countries we perform a pairwise log-rank test[29]. Fig. 6 shows the results of the pairwise log-rank test for the top 20 countries in terms of amount of C&Cs. Blank tiles represent non-significant differences for a 5% confidence level. As expected, China and Russia survival curves are completely different to any other country. However, France survival rate is similar to the US, Romania, Netherlands, Macedonia, UK and Italy.

If we further analyzed the countries hosting ZeuS C&Cs with larger uptime, we notice that those countries have either lack of political stability, ineffective governance with high rates of terrorism or agents don't abide by the rules of society. Table 7 shows the top countries in terms of uptime the C&Cs along with different governance indicators

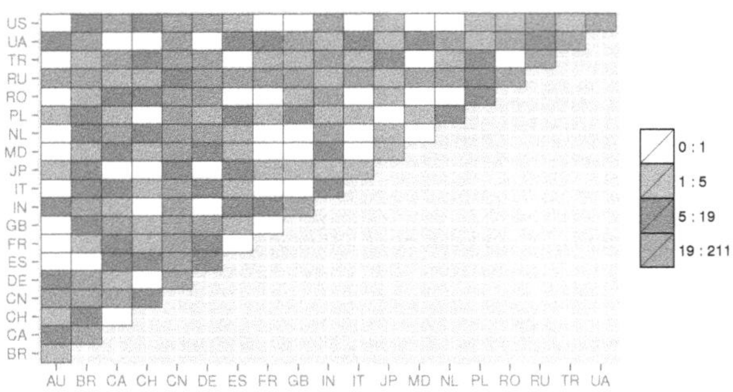

Figure 6: Differences between survival rates per country

[23]. Analyzing those indicators, we observe that the majority of these countries are below 1 which indicates political instability.

5.2 Malware variant

ZeuS malware has many variants among which the most prevalent ones are: Citadel, KINS, Ice-IX and the original ZeuS. All these variants have a similar purpose but the underneath communication protocol differs among them.

Fig. 7a shows the violin plot of the uptime for the 4 variants. We can appreciate differences both in terms of different moments as well as in the kernel density distribution of the uptime.

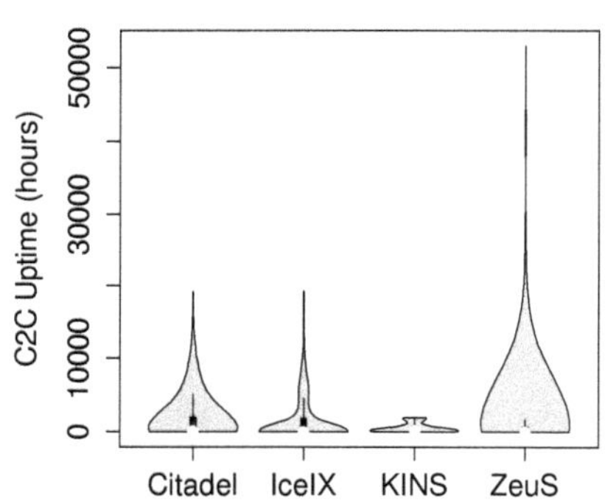

(a) Violin plot per ZeuS malware variant

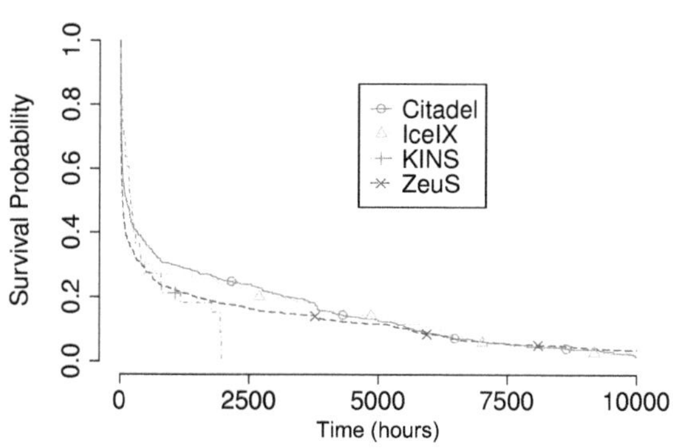

(b) Kaplan-Meier estimates per malware variant

Figure 7: C&C Uptime per ZeuS malware variant

ZeuS is the variant that lives longer, while KINS has the lowest average uptime. Then we analyzed the survival rate for each of the variants. Fig. 7b show the Kaplan-Meier estimates per variant. As can be seen, Citadel presents the highest survival rate while KINS presents the lowest. On the one hand, this might be due to the Citadel's anti-reverse engineering techniques which hinder the malware analysis process. On the other hand, KINS presents a vulnerability in the file upload process that makes it straightforward to take it over.

To measure the differences among the survival rate per ZeuS variant, we perform a pairwise log-rank test. Table 8 shows the results of these tests. As can be seen, all the curves are significantly different from each other. Citadel survival curve presents the biggest difference when compared to ZeuS survival curve, while is not that different from IceIX survival curve.

Malware	ZeuS		Citadel		IceIX		KINS	
	$\tilde{\chi}^2$	p-value	$\tilde{\chi}^2$	p-value	$\tilde{\chi}^2$	p-value	$\tilde{\chi}^2$	p-value
ZeuS			52.5	$4.27 \cdot 10^{-13}$	18.7	$1.5 \cdot 10^{-5}$	3.2	$7.3 \cdot 10^{-2}$
Citadel	52.5	$4.27 \cdot 10^{-13}$			3.5	$6.1 \cdot 10^{-2}$	19.1	$1.23 \cdot 10^{-5}$
IceIX	18.7	$1.5 \cdot 10^{-5}$	3.5	$6.1 \cdot 10^{-2}$			24.1	$9.34 \cdot 10^{-7}$
KINS	3.2	$7.3 \cdot 10^{-2}$	19.1	$1.23 \cdot 10^{-5}$	24.1	$9.34 \cdot 10^{-7}$		

Table 8: Log-rank test results per ZeuS variant

5.3 Notification regime

We further analyze the differences in terms of uptime for each of the data sources. Each data source has a different method to notify the URL of the detect C&Cs. ZeuS tracker presents a dynamic webpage that shows the online/offline C&Cs and also issues site summary and filter rules. Similarly, Cybercrime tracker also presents a dynamic webpage but they do not issue any type of periodic report/summary. Instead, Cybercrime tracker feeds one of the most prominent sources in terms of blacklisting checking as it is Virus Total [3]. On the other hand. the private company does not publicize any of the detected C&Cs. They only notify their customers about their existence so that they can take preventive measures.

We analyze how the different forms of notification affect the survival time of the C&Cs. Just comparing the average uptime we can already appreciate significant differences. C&Cs detected by ZeuS tracker stayed online an average of 1,328.64 hours, while the ones detected by Cybercrime tracker lived 22% less time. On the other hand, the C&Cs detected by the private company lived 2.8 times longer than the ones from ZeuS tracker.

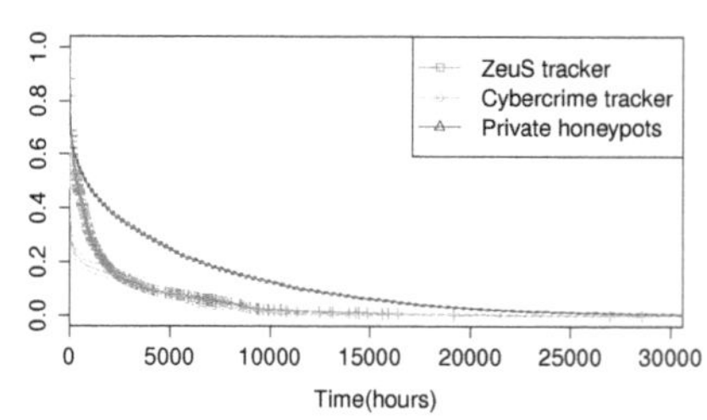

Figure 8: Uptime per source type

Then, we compare the different Kaplan-Meier estimates per data source. As expected, the C&Cs disclosed by Cybercrime tracker are the ones with lowest survival rates as they are included in the VirusTotal database that it is integrated by many companies. On the other hand, C&Cs detected by

Country	Political Stability	Gov. Effectiveness	Rule of Law	Uptime (hours)		
				Mean	Median	75th pctl
Virgin Islands (U.S.)	0.95	1.27	0.88	14143.00	14143.00	14143.00
St. Vincent&Grenadines	0.92	0.90	0.86	12557.00	12557.00	13198.50
Lao Pdr	0.06	-0.76	-0.77	10968.00	10968.00	12324.00
Somalia	-2.75	-2.21	-2.44	8841.00	8841.00	8841.00
Saudi Arabia	-0.41	0.06	0.26	8260.00	4138.00	12390.00
Tuvalu	1.32	-0.65	0.49	6472.82	757.50	9055.25
Rwanda	-0.08	0.00	-0.15	6470.00	3018.00	10521.00
Grenada	0.42	0.27	0.16	6262.00	6262.00	1710.00
Kenya	-1.15	-0.49	-0.74	5927.25	2465.00	7006.75
Palau	1.10	-0.59	0.90	5678.65	56785.65	3087.25
Afghanistan	-2.47	-1.43	-1.67	5574.00	5574.00	5574.00
Azerbaijan	-0.41	-0.46	-0.67	5505.33	84.00	8258.00
China	-0.55	-0.03	-0.46	5373.43	1318.00	8508.00
Samoa	1.01	0.14	0.72	4975.00	4318.00	12390.00
Cayman Islands	1.06	1.21	0.89	4767.33	2465.00	7691.00
Mexico	-0.74	0.31	-0.58	4664.13	1267.00	5378.75
Canada	1.03	1.77	1.74	4611.66	301.00	6273.50
Taiwan, China	0.86	1.19	1.04	4483.27	949.00	6726.00

Table 7: Governance indicators for top ZeuS hosting countries in terms of uptime (-2.5 to 2.5)

the private security company lived longer as they were not advertised publicly.

Table 9 shows the values of thee pairwise log-rank tests. The results show that all the survival curves are significantly different from each other. In particular, the survival curve from the private honeypots is well-differentiated from the other sources.

Source	ZeuS Tracker		Cybercrime		Priv. Honeypots	
	$\tilde{\chi}^2$	p-value	$\tilde{\chi}^2$	p-value	$\tilde{\chi}^2$	p-value
ZeuS Tracker			238	0	1,730	0
Cybercrime	238	0			664	0
Priv. Honeypots	1,730	0	664	0		

Table 9: Log-rank test results per data source

5.4 Hosting providers & Registrars

In this section we go a step further and we analyze the impact on the survival rate of the C&Cs of parties involved in the take-downs.

First we analyze the hosting providers. Identified C&Cs were hosted in 1,139 different hosting providers. Table 10 shows the top 10 hosting providers in terms of number of C&Cs. United Internet AG is the German Internet services company that hosted more ZeuS C&Cs during period of this study. In terms of average uptime, C&Cs located in Microsoft's hosting infrastructure lived longer[1].

To further understand these differences, the hosting provider are classified according to the hosting service they offer as in [5]:

- Bulletproof: is a service provided by some domain hosting or web hosting firms that allows their customer considerable leniency in the kinds of material they may upload and distribute,
- Hacked: these are sites owned by legitimate people/business but that were comprised at some point and hosted C&C,

[1]Note that Microsoft sinkholed ZeuS C&Cs in several occasions. Sinkholing might lead to inaccuracies in the uptime of the sinkholed domain names.

Hosting provider	# C&Cs	Avg. Uptime(h)
United Internet AG	5,006	3,975.54
Sprint	4,608	2,619.27
Microsoft Corporation	2,000	4,303.35
GoDaddy Inc	734	1,253.10
Hostinger Group	715	1,233.26
Endurance International	696	1,197.93
directi.com	658	2,818.34
FHE3 GmbH	560	3,100.40
Hurricane Electric	510	7,417.81
Hetzner Online AG	482	1,321.39

Table 10: Top hosting providers hosting ZeuS C&Cs

- Free hosting: is a hosting service that is free, usually advertisement-supported,
- Fast-Flux: is a hosting method used to hide servers or content behind an almost dynamic domain name.

According to this classification, 8.99% of the C&Cs are BulletProof, 0.01% are Fast-Flux, 2.43% Free hosting C&Cs, 24.19% Hacked and the rest didn't fit any of these categories. Then, we analyze the C&C uptime per category. As expected, Bulletproof and Fast-Flux providers are the ones that allow C&Cs to live longer. In this sense, C&Cs hosted by Fast-Flux providers stayed online for 2265.85 hours in average, while Hacked and Free-Hosted C&Cs only stayed online for less than 900 hours in average. Fig. 9 shows the survival curves for the four different types of hosting. As can be seen, "Fast-Flux" and "Bulletproof" hosting present the highest survival rates while "Free Hosting" and "Hacked websites" are cleaned up faster.

Finally, we compare the different survival curves by performing pairwise log-rank tests. Results show that not all the survival curves are significantly different from each other. At a 5% significant level, only "Bulletproof" is different from "Hacked" and "Free-hosting" from "Hacked". The rest of the survival curves are not significantly different among each other.

Next, we analyze how different registrars act in front of C&Cs that are registered by them. Different C&Cs were registered by more 400 different registrars. Table 12 shows

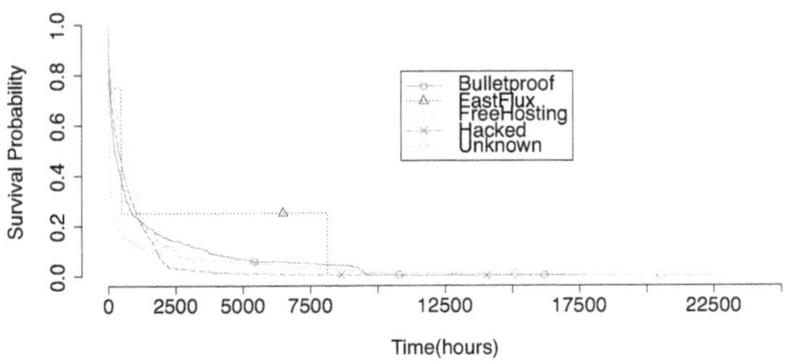

Figure 9: Kaplan-Meier estimates per hosting type

Hosting	Bulletproof		Hacked		Free-hosting		Fast-flux	
	$\tilde{\chi}^2$	p-value	$\tilde{\chi}^2$	p-value	$\tilde{\chi}^2$	p-value	$\tilde{\chi}^2$	p-value
Bulletproof			8.2	0.004	0.4	0.514	0.2	0.657
Hacked	8.2	0.004			3.7	0.054	1.4	0.237
Freehosting	0.4	0.514	3.7	0.054			1.0	0.319
Fast-flux	0.2	0.657	1.4	0.237	1.0	0.319		

Table 11: Log-rank test results per hosting type

top 10 registrars in terms of number of C&Cs. There is a clear relationship between rogue registrars and rogue hosting providers. For instance, 1&1 Internet AG is the main registrar in terms of number of C&Cs. This same registrar registered 84.85% of the domains hosted by United Internet AG. However, Sprint hosting provider has domains registered by more than 40 different registrars including 1&1 Internet AG (3.36%), GoDaddy.com (5.04%), ENOM inc. (11.34%), Public domain registry (3.89%), Bizcn.com (26.31%), Internetbs corp (8.06 %) and Markmonitor (10.86%).

Registrar	# C&Cs	Avg. Uptime(h)
1&1 Internet AG	1793	5184.15
GoDaddy.com LLC	1018	2242.02
ENOM inc	972	2415.95
Public domain registry	796	1485.88
Bizcn.com inc	648	3091.97
r01-reg-ripn	471	830.95
Dnbiz limited	426	8052.21
Internetbs corp	333	3612.56
Markmonitor inc	288	2789.80
ru-center-reg-ripn	268	2235.01

Table 12: Top 10 registrars

To check if different C&Cs present different survival rate depending on the registrar they used, we estimate the Kaplan-Meier curves. From Fig. 10 we can see that C&Cs under registrars in Europe present lower survival rates than those registered by Asiatic or American registrars.

Finally, we perform pairwise log-rank tests to compare the different survival curves. Fig. 11 shows the value of the χ^2 test. We can observe that different registrars perform quite different in terms of C&C survival rate.

5.5 Popularity

We use Google's PageRank [25] as a measure of the popularity of the URLs hosting C&Cs. We analyze Google's PageRank as one of the factors that influence the lifetime of the C&Cs. Google's PageRank is a variant of the eigenvector centrality measure used commonly in network analysis

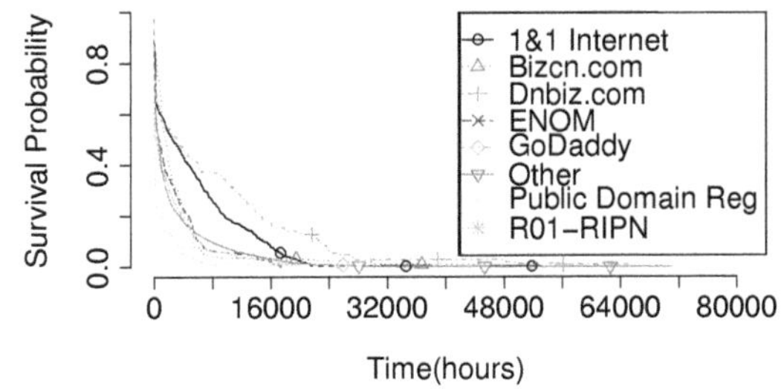

Figure 10: Kaplan-Meier estimates per registrar

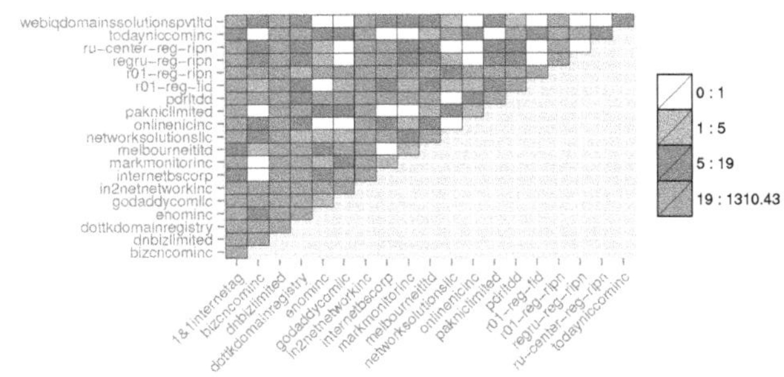

Figure 11: Pairwise log-rank test results per source

that basically counts link votes and determines which URLs are most important. Results show that 66.94% of the C&Cs were ranked as 'rank 0', 11.48% 'rank 1', 10.02% 'rank 2', 7.02% 'rank 3', 3.22% 'rank 4', 1.04 'rank 5', 0.17% 'rank 6', 0.03% 'rank 7' and 0.06% 'rank 8'. As expected, most of the URLs hosting C&Cs were not very popular.

Fig. 12 presents the average C&C uptime depending on the rank of the URL where the C&C was hosted. C&Cs with a rank ranging from 0 to 4 have similar average uptime. However, C&Cs with ranks between 5-10 present an evident decreasing trend, i.e., the higher is the rank the lower is the average uptime. Note that rank 7 C&Cs could be consider as an outlier as they only account for 0.03% of the number of C&Cs.

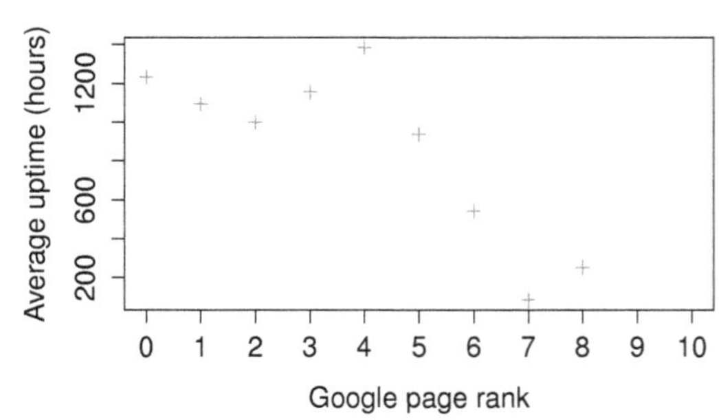

Figure 12: C&Cs avg. uptime depending on URL popularity

Finally, we compute the Kaplan-Meier estimates to compare the survival rates between C&Cs with different popularity. As can be seen in Fig. 13, there are significant differences among the difference curves. Rank 3 C&Cs live the longest while Rank 7/8 C&Cs are taken down in a matter of few hours.

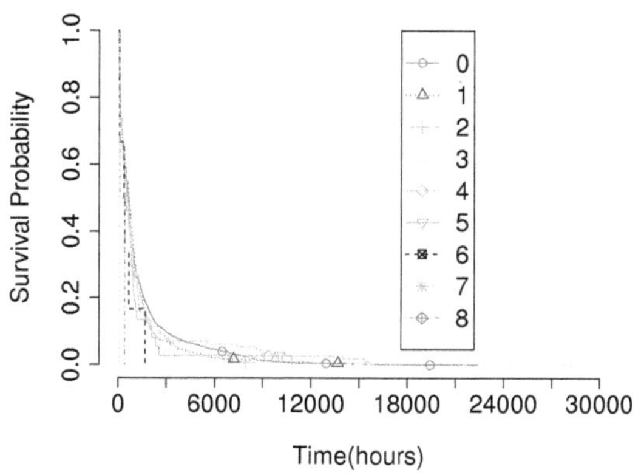

Figure 13: Kaplan-Meier estimates per domain popularity

6. STATISTICAL MODEL

To disentangle the effects of different demographic, technical, and social variables that could be associated with the life-cycle of ZeuS C&Cs, we use a Multivariate Cox proportional hazard model [14] of the form:

$$h(t) = h_0(t)e^{\beta_1 x_1 + \beta_2 x_2 + \cdots + \beta_m x_m} = h_0(t)e^{\beta^{\mathrm{T}}\mathbf{x}} = \quad (3)$$
$$= h_0(t)\exp(\beta_{1i}\mathrm{Country}_i + \beta_{2i}\mathrm{Family}_i +$$
$$+ \beta_{3i}\mathrm{AS}_i + \beta_{4i}\mathrm{Rank}_i + \beta_{4i}\mathrm{Hosting}_i),$$

where $h(t)$ is the hazard for C&C i at time t, $h_0(t)$ represents the baseline hazard and the factor $\exp(\beta_i x_i)$ describes the hazard for a particular covariate x_i. The covariates correspond to the variables described in the previous section.

Cox model establishes a mechanism which allows survival time varies with hazardous factors [14]. Thus we can find out which factors have significant impact on the lifetime of the C&Cs and forecast the survival probability according to the influence of factors. The dependent variable in Cox model is hazard probability at a given time t.

Traditional factor selection techniques are based on statistical test like Chi–Square or Information criteria to estimate the importance of each factor independently. However, in the previous section we have already shown that different factors are highly correlated, e.g. location and hosting providers. Thus, we need an algorithm that considers correlations between factors so that we detect and delete redundant factors effectively. To that end, we use Lasso (Least Absolute Shrinkage and Selection Operator) [36] to fit a regularized regression model to factors in such a way that the final model is a sparse solution in the factor space. Hence, the weight of redundant features in the final model would be zero. This means that we can remove these features from the model with no significant change in the C&C lifetime prediction. Lasso has a regularization penalty parameter, λ, that offers a trade-off between sparsity of the model and the accuracy of the prediction. Lower values for λ result in more relaxation of the regularization constraint which allows more features to have non–zero weights.

Fig. 14a shows the value of the coefficients as a function of λ. Each curve corresponds to a different factor. It shows the path of its coefficient against the ℓ1-norm of the whole coefficient vector at as λ varies. The axis above indicates the

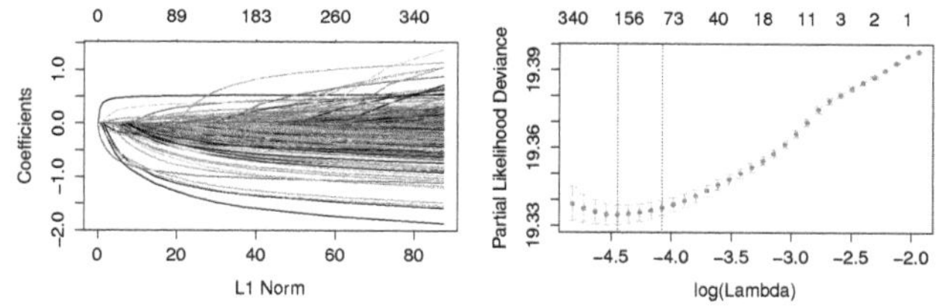

(a) Coefficients (b) cross-validation curve

Figure 14: Lasso model selection

number of nonzero coefficients at the current λ, which is the effective degrees of freedom for the Lasso. Fig. 14b shows the cross-validation curve (red dotted line), and upper and lower standard deviation curves along the λ sequence (error bars). The vertical dotted lines represent the values of λ that give minimum mean cross-validated error and the most regularized model such that error is within one standard error of the minimum respectively. As can be seen to obtain the minimum mean cross-validated error we have to include 180 factors.

λ	Selected Features
0.1442	Country={CA}
0.1314	Country={CA} Hosting={Hacked}
0.0825	Country={CA, RU} Hosting={Hacked}
0.0685	Country={CA, RU, AE} Hosting={Hacked} Family={ZeuS} ASN={33517, 50544}
...	...
0.0116	Country={AR, AZ, BY, BE, BR, BG, CA, KY, CN, CZ, EG, FR, HK, KZ, LV, LT, MT, MX, MD, PH, PT, RO, RU, RW, SK, TW, TH, UA, UK, VG} Hosting={Hacked} Family={ZeuS, Citadel, Ice, KINS} ASN={10029, 10474, 1101, 11340, 12140, 12322, 12406, 12481, 12573, 1267, 12849, 13147, 13193, 13237, 133165, 13335, 14037, 14080, 15497, 15830, 15967, 16125, 16257, 16509, 174, 18779, 19024, 19324, 19373, 19551, 19557, 196728, 199079, 19969, 20718, 20848, 20960, 21219, 24085, 24560, 24651, 25151, 25260, 25504, 25926, 26230, 26347, 26496, 278, 28824, 28917, 29290, 29761, 30083, 31103, 31133, 31147, 31252, 31727, 3249, 32592, 32613, 32780, 33317, 33517, 3352, 33922, 34011, 34187, 34702, 34788, 34977, 35088, 35908, 3598, 36351, 38370, 39020, 39647, 39756, 39779, 40244, 41175, 41310, 41786, 41794, 4250, 42668, 42831, 43060, 44018, 45324, 45887, 46062, 46816, 46844, 47242, 47544, 4765, 48031, 48172, 48185, 49126, 50274, 5033, 50544, 51248, 51743, 54301, 54456, 54718, 55470, 5588, 5617, 56309, 57043, 57910, 57972, 59491, 60708, 61214, 61255, 62416, 62567, 6429, 6903, 7381, 766, 790, 7922, 8001, 8075, 8426, 8447, 8560, 8828, 8926, 9070, 9121, 9198, 9269, 9891, 9916, 9918} Rank={0}

Table 13: Feature Selection using Lasso

Once fit, we can view the optimal λ value and a cross validated error plot to help evaluate our model. Table 13 shows a correlation between the selected factors and different values of λ. For $\lambda = 0.1442$, only one factor is selected. This means that, according to Lasso, if we want to forecast the lifetime of a C&C based on only one factor, checking where it is located would be our best choice. As we decrease the value of λ, more factors are selected according to their importance. The second most important factor is the type of hosting, specifically if the C&Cs is hosted in a hacked server. The last column in Table 13 shows the coefficients for λ that give the minimum mean cross-validated error. In this sparse factor set we have factors from all groups. For example,"ZeuS", "Citadel", "IceIX" and "KINS" are selected from the *Family* group. If we follow the Lasso path, factors get added and eliminated as λ decreases. We have a total of 180 factor selected from the 1,305 variables. In particular, we select 30 countries out of the 135 countries where C&Cs where located, we select 144 ASes out of the 1,153 ASes where C&Cs where located, we select all ZeuS family types, only "hacked" as hosting type and Google rank 0.

Then, we assess the goodness-of-fit of our model. Table 14 shows the values of various statistics. We calculate three different pseudo-R^2 parameters. All of them present low values which evidences that the impact of the factors is statistically significant but weak. Similarly, the concordance index has a value > 0.5 that implies that our model has good prediction capabilities.

AIC	pseudo-R^2			C-Index
	McFadden	Cox & Snell	Nagelkerke	
39231.74	0.022	0.254	0.254	0.661

Table 14: Goodness-of-fit of the model

Finally, we determine whether the fitted Cox regression model adequately describes the data. To that end, we consider the violation of the assumption of proportional hazards. To validate the proportional hazard assumption (PHA) we calculate the scaled Schoenfeld residuals [18]. These residuals can be calculated as:

$$\hat{\vec{r}}_i = \vec{x}_i - E[\vec{x}_i], \tag{4}$$

we compute the expected values at time t_i as:

$$\begin{aligned} E[\vec{x}_i] &= \sum_{k \in \mathcal{R}(t_i)} \vec{x}_k p(k \text{ dies at } t_i) \\ &= \frac{\sum_{k \in \mathcal{R}(t_i)} \vec{x}_k e^{\vec{\beta}\vec{x}_k}}{\sum_{j \in \mathcal{R}(t_i)} e^{\vec{\beta}\vec{x}_j}}, \end{aligned} \tag{5}$$

where the values of $\vec{\beta}$ are the fitted coefficients, and $\mathcal{R}(t)$ is the set of C&Cs that are still online at time t.

The scaled Schoenfeld residuals are:

$$\hat{\vec{r}}_i^* = [Var(\hat{\vec{r}}_i)]^{-1}\hat{\vec{r}}_i \approx m\, Var(\hat{\vec{\beta}})\hat{\vec{r}}_i, \tag{6}$$

where *Var* denotes a covariance matrix, and m is the number of uncensored survival times. $\hat{\vec{r}}_i$ is a length-n vector, and $Var(\hat{\vec{\beta}})$ is a $n \times n$ matrix, where m is the number of uncensored data points and n is the number of features. These residuals are centered on zero and should be independent of time if PHA is true. Deviations from this, i.e. residuals that exhibit some trend in time, indicate that the PHA is violated. The Schoenfeld residuals, at the time when a failure or death were to occur, are defined by the difference between the observed and expected covariate values at that time [18].

We compute the scaled Schoenfeld residuals for each factors and perform a chi-square test between the Kaplan-Meier transformed survival times and the Schoenfeld residuals. Fig. 15 represents the two-sided p-value for each χ^2 test run over the Schoenfeld residuals versus the survival function. Note that all the p-values are above 0.2 which proves that there is no evidence to reject the hypothesis that the residuals are uncorrelated with time.

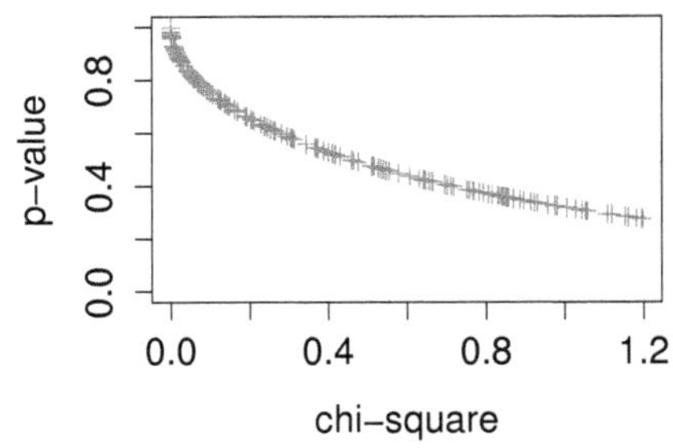

Figure 15: p-value of the χ^2 test over the scaled Schoenfeld residuals

7. RELATED WORK

While research has studied botnet identification and performance, no focus has been put into analyzing the factors that impact the lifetime of a command and control.

Rodríguez-Gómez et al. in [31] analyze the botnet life-cycle, understood as the sequence of stages that a botnet should successfully traverse in order to reach the success. They describe different defense mechanisms that affect the botnet during the different stages of its life-cycle. Apart from identifying these different stages, authors do not quantify the duration of each stage and do not identify the parties that are involved in the defense mechanism nor their role.

Researchers have also modeled the topology of different bot nets to gain insights into their life-cycle using deterministic [43, 42, 6, 20] and stochastic models [39, 26, 40, 41]. Recently, Khosroshahy et al. [24] developed a Markov-chain model that captures the dynamics of a botnet's life-cycle. However, the utility of the model is completely theoretical and it only allows to obtain expressions for the time dependent mean and variance of the population estimated size in each stage.

The rest of the literature is mainly focused on studying certain technical aspects like type of architecture, protocols or detection techniques [15, 27, 17, 19, 9, 8]. Different taxonomies have been proposed to classify botnets depending on their characteristics [16, 10, 33, 32].

Particularly, ZeuS botnet has also captured a lot of attention in the literature. The importance of ZeuS botnet is such that researchers have developed a tool for setting up and analyzing Zeus [21]. Stone-Gross [34] analyze the P2P variant of ZeuS in which disrupting the infrastructure (especially through legal action) becomes more difficult. Tajalizadehkhoob et al. [35] analyze the characteristics of the targets of ZeuS malware. Authors show that the critical bottleneck are the money mules, i.e., the accomplices to accept fraudulent ACH transfers who usually need to be within the same area or country as the victim to complete the transaction and reduce the risk of detection. Mohaisen et al. [28]

classify different version of ZeuS malware using several machine learning techniques using a behavior-based approach. They are able to identify 65 features that are unique and robust for identifying the different versions. Other research efforts have targeted at breaking ZeuS communication protocol. Ricardi et al. [30] propose a technique to break the encrypted malware communications, extracting the keystream used to encrypt such communications. Andriesse et al. [7] perform an in-depth analysis of the resilience Zeus botnet from the peer-to-peer perspective. Authors dissected the last version of the Zeus protocol describing the algorithm used and the resilient features applied. However, none of the previous research works have analyzed the factors that influence the lifetime of a ZeuS C&C.

8. CONCLUSIONS

This paper presents the first approach towards identifying the factors that affect the online time of the ZeuS C&Cs. Different technological characteristics are identified among the URLs where the C&Cs were hosted. Results showed some patterns that differ from the global market view. ZeuS C&Cs remained online for longer periods when hosted in some low usage web servers like Tengine or when using non-popular CMSes.

Furthermore, we proved from the Kaplan-Meier survival estimates there is a significant difference in survival by the location, notification regime, malware family, hosting provider, registrar and popularity of the C&Cs. On the other hand, the logrank test also showed that there was no significant difference in survival experience between the various categories of some covariates.

Multivariable Cox hazards regression model revealed that location, malware variant, AS number, hosting type and popularity were significant factors associated with the online time of the C&Cs. Via a penalized likelihood analysis we detected those categories with a major impact on the lifetime of ZeuS C&Cs. Our model presents good prediction capabilities (C-index 0.66).

Overall, our findings have important implications for information systems policy as well as for implementation of botnet defense techniques for ensuring the safety of network systems. Our prediction model can be use to estimate the lifetime of a given C&C and detect which factors represent the main hazard.

9. ACKNOWLEDGMENTS

The authors would like to thank Roman Huessy for sharing ZeuS C&C data. Also, thanks to TU Delft's ICT and Abuse staff (Lolke Boonstra, Adrian Cooke, and Paul Keekstra), SUFRNet (Wim Biemolt) for their support. This work was partly funded by the Netherlands Organisation for Scientific Research, grant number 628.001.022.

10. REFERENCES

[1] Cybercrime-Tracker. `http://cybercrime-tracker.net/`, Sept 2014.

[2] Netcraft Toolbar. `http://toolbar.netcraft.com/`, Oct 2014.

[3] Virus Total. `https://www.virustotal.com/`, Oct 2014.

[4] W3Techs- Web Technology Surveys. `http://w3techs.com/reports`, Oct 2014.

[5] ZeuS Tracker. `https://zeustracker.abuse.ch`, Sept 2014.

[6] M. Ajelli, R. Lo Cigno, and A. Montresor. Modeling botnets and epidemic malware. In *Communications (ICC), 2010 IEEE International Conference on*, pages 1–5, May 2010.

[7] D. Andriesse, C. Rossow, B. Stone-Gross, D. Plohmann, and H. Bos. Highly resilient peer-to-peer botnets are here: An analysis of Gameover Zeus. In *Malicious and Unwanted Software: "The Americas" (MALWARE), 2013 8th International Conference on*, pages 116–123, Oct 2013.

[8] M. Antonakakis, R. Perdisci, W. Lee, N. Vasiloglou, II, and D. Dagon. Detecting malware domains at the upper dns hierarchy. In *Proceedings of the 20th USENIX Conference on Security*, SEC'11, pages 27–27, 2011.

[9] M. Antonakakis, R. Perdisci, Y. Nadji, N. Vasiloglou, S. Abu-Nimeh, W. Lee, and D. Dagon. From throw-away traffic to bots: Detecting the rise of dga-based malware. In *Proceedings of the 21st USENIX Conference on Security Symposium*, Security'12, pages 24–24, 2012.

[10] M. Bailey, E. Cooke, F. Jahanian, Y. Xu, and M. Karir. A survey of botnet technology and defenses. In *Conference For Homeland Security, 2009. CATCH '09. Cybersecurity Applications Technology*, pages 299–304, March 2009.

[11] H. Binsalleeh, T. Ormerod, A. Boukhtouta, P. Sinha, A. Youssef, M. Debbabi, and L. Wang. On the analysis of the ZeuS botnet crimeware toolkit. In *Privacy Security and Trust (PST), 2010 Eighth Annual International Conference on*, pages 31–38, Aug 2010.

[12] G. Box and G. Tiao. Intervention analysis with applications to economic and environmental problems. *J. Am. Stat. Assoc.*, 70:70–79, 1975.

[13] D. Brown. Resilient botnet command and control with tor. In *DEF CON 18 - Hacking conference*, 2010.

[14] D. R. Cox. Regression models and life-tables. *Journal of the Royal Statistical Society. Series B (Methodological)*, 34(2):pp. 187–220, 1972.

[15] A. Dainotti, A. King, k. Claffy, F. Papale, and A. Pescapè. Analysis of a "/0" stealth scan from a botnet. In *Proceedings of the 2012 ACM Conference on Internet Measurement Conference*, IMC '12, pages 1–14, 2012.

[16] N. Daswani and M. Stoppelman. The Anatomy of Clickbot.A. In *Proceedings of the First Conference on First Workshop on Hot Topics in Understanding Botnets*, HotBots'07, pages 11–11, Berkeley, CA, USA, 2007. USENIX Association.

[17] S. García, M. Grill, J. Stiborek, and A. Zunino. An empirical comparison of botnet detection methods. *Comput. Secur.*, 45:100–123, Sept. 2014.

[18] P. M. Grambsch and T. M. Therneau. Proportional hazards tests and diagnostics based on weighted residuals. *Biometrika*, 81(3):515–526, 1994.

[19] F. Haddadi, D. Runkel, A. N. Zincir-Heywood, and M. I. Heywood. On Botnet Behaviour Analysis Using GP and C4.5. In *Proceedings of the 2014 Conference Companion on Genetic and Evolutionary Computation*

Companion, GECCO Comp '14, pages 1253–1260, 2014.

[20] Q. Han, W. Yu, Y. Zhang, and Z. Zhao. Modeling and evaluating of typical advanced peer-to-peer botnet. *Perform. Eval.*, 72:1–15, Feb. 2014.

[21] K. Hannah and S. Gianvecchio. Zeuslite: A Tool for Botnet Analysis in the Classroom. *J. Comput. Sci. Coll.*, 30(3):109–116, Jan. 2015.

[22] E. L. Kaplan and P. Meier. Nonparametric Estimation from Incomplete Observations. *Journal of the American Statistical Association*, 53(282):457–481, 1958.

[23] D. Kaufmann, A. Kraay, and M. Mastruzzi. The worldwide governance indicators. The World Bank, `http://info.worldbank.org/governance`, 2014.

[24] M. Khosroshahy, M. K. Mehmet Ali, and D. Qiu. The SIC Botnet Lifecycle Model: A Step Beyond Traditional Epidemiological Models. *Comput. Netw.*, 57(2):404–421, Feb. 2013.

[25] A. N. Langville and C. D. Meyer. *Google's PageRank and Beyond: The Science of Search Engine Rankings.* Princeton University Press, Princeton, NJ, USA, 2006.

[26] X. Li, H. Duan, W. Liu, and J. Wu. The growing model of botnets. In *Green Circuits and Systems (ICGCS), 2010 International Conference on*, pages 414–419, June 2010.

[27] M. M. Masud, J. Gao, L. Khan, J. Han, and B. Thuraisingham. Peer to peer botnet detection for cyber-security: A data mining approach. In *Proceedings of the 4th Annual Workshop on Cyber Security and Information Intelligence Research: Developing Strategies to Meet the Cyber Security and Information Intelligence Challenges Ahead*, CSIIRW '08, pages 39:1–39:2, 2008.

[28] A. Mohaisen and O. Alrawi. Unveiling Zeus: Automated Classification of Malware Samples. In *Proceedings of the 22Nd International Conference on World Wide Web Companion*, WWW '13 Companion, pages 829–832, 2013.

[29] R. Peto and J. Peto. Asymptotically efficient rank invariant test procedures. *Journal of the Royal Statistical Society. Series A (General)*, 135(2):pp. 185–207, 1972.

[30] M. Riccardi, R. Di Pietro, M. Palanques, and J. A. Vila. Titans' Revenge: Detecting Zeus via Its Own Flaws. *Comput. Netw.*, 57(2):422–435, Feb. 2013.

[31] R. A. Rodríguez-Gómez, G. Maciá-Fernández, and P. García-Teodoro. Survey and taxonomy of botnet research through life-cycle. *ACM Comput. Surv.*, 45(4):45:1–45:33, Aug. 2013.

[32] C. Rossow, D. Andriesse, T. Werner, B. Stone-Gross, D. Plohmann, C. Dietrich, and H. Bos. SoK: P2PWNED - Modeling and Evaluating the Resilience of Peer-to-Peer Botnets. In *Security and Privacy (SP), 2013 IEEE Symposium on*, pages 97–111, May 2013.

[33] S. S. C. Silva, R. M. P. Silva, R. C. G. Pinto, and R. M. Salles. Botnets: A survey. *Comput. Netw.*, 57(2):378–403, Feb. 2013.

[34] B. Stone-Gross. The Lifecycle of Peer-to-Peer (Gameover) ZeuS. Dell SecureWorks Counter Threat Unit(TM) Threat Intelligence, 2012.

[35] S. Tajalizadehkhoob, H. Asghari, C. Gañán, and M. van Eeten. Why Them? Extracting Intelligence about Target Selection from ZeuS Financial Malware. In *13th Annual Workshop on Economics of Information Security (WEIS 2014)*, pages 1–26, 2014.

[36] R. Tibshirani. Regression shrinkage and selection via the lasso. *Journal of the Royal Statistical Society, Series B*, 58:267–288, 1994.

[37] H. Tiirmaa-Klaar, J. Gassen, E. Gerhards-Padilla, and P. Martini. *Botnets.* SpringerBriefs in Cybersecurity. Springer, 2013.

[38] M. van Eeten, J. M. Bauer, H. Asghari, S. Tabatabaie, and D. Rand. The Role of Internet Service Providers in Botnet Mitigation: An Empirical Analysis Based on Spam Data. In *9th Annual Workshop on the Economics of Information Security*, WEIS 2010, 2010.

[39] E. Van Ruitenbeek and W. Sanders. Modeling peer-to-peer botnets. In *Quantitative Evaluation of Systems, 2008. QEST '08. Fifth International Conference on*, pages 307–316, Sept 2008.

[40] Q. Wang, Z. Chen, C. Chen, and N. Pissinou. On the robustness of the botnet topology formed by worm infection. In *Global Telecommunications Conference (GLOBECOM 2010), 2010 IEEE*, pages 1–6, Dec 2010.

[41] R. Weaver. A Probabilistic Population Study of the Conficker-C Botnet. In *Proceedings of the 11th International Conference on Passive and Active Measurement*, PAM'10, pages 181–190, 2010.

[42] W. Xin-liang, C. Lu-Ying, L. Fang, and L. Zhen-Ming. Analysis and modeling of the botnet propagation characteristics. In *Wireless Communications Networking and Mobile Computing (WiCOM), 2010 6th International Conference on*, pages 1–4, Sept 2010.

[43] C. C. Zou and R. Cunningham. Honeypot-aware advanced botnet construction and maintenance. In *Proceedings of the International Conference on Dependable Systems and Networks*, DSN '06, pages 199–208, 2006.

JSDC: A Hybrid Approach for JavaScript Malware Detection and Classification

Junjie Wang[†] Yinxing Xue[†] Yang Liu[†] Tian Huat Tan[‡]
[†]Nanyang Technological University
[‡]Singapore University of Technology and Design

ABSTRACT

Malicious JavaScript is one of the biggest threats in cyber security. Existing research and anti-virus products mainly focus on detection of JavaScript malware rather than classification. Usually, the detection will simply report the malware family name without elaborating details about attacks conducted by the malware. Worse yet, the reported family name may differ from one tool to another due to the different naming conventions. In this paper, we propose a hybrid approach to perform JavaScript malware detection and classification in an accurate and efficient way, which could not only explain the attack model but also potentially discover new malware variants and new vulnerabilities. Our approach starts with machine learning techniques to detect JavaScript malware using predicative features of textual information, program structures and risky function calls. For the detected malware, we classify them into eight known attack types according to their attack feature vector or dynamic execution traces by using machine learning and dynamic program analysis respectively. We implement our approach in a tool named JSDC, and conduct large-scale evaluations to show its effectiveness. The controlled experiments (with 942 malware) show that JSDC gives low false positive rate (0.2123%) and low false negative rate (0.8492%), compared with other tools. We further apply JSDC on 1,400,000 real-world JavaScript with over 1,500 malware reported, for which many anti-virus tools failed. Lastly, JSDC can effectively and accurately classify these detected malwares into either attack types.

1. INTRODUCTION

JavaScript is a widely-used client-side scripting language that provides active and dynamic content on the Internet. According to Microsoft's recent security report (Figure 81 in [12]), the prevalence of JavaScript leads to the largest number of malware detected by Microsoft in the first half year of 2013. Most of users typically rely on signature-based anti-virus products to detect malware. However, signature-based detection is not accurate, as it is neither resistant to obfuscation nor applicable to evolving variants of the same malware.

ASIA CCS'15, April 14–17, 2015, Singapore..

http://dx.doi.org/10.1145/2714576.2714620.

Detection of malicious JavaScript code can be classified into two lines: dynamic approaches and static approaches. Dynamic approaches are mostly based on low-interaction honey clients [25] and high-interaction honey clients [37, 34]. The problem of using honey client lies in the difficulty of setting up a virtual environment that captures the exploitations of all possible plug-ins. Most importantly, honey clients are extremely resource intensive, and it is not affordable to scan millions of scripts. Static approaches mainly adopt machine learning techniques to capture characteristics of malicious scripts. Most of them use obfuscated text information ([16, 27]), syntax information (e.g., AST [18, 26]) or (partial) dynamic information (e.g., API call [17, 33]) as the predicative features for classifying malicious and benign code.

Static and dynamic approaches both have merits and drawbacks. Dynamic approaches are effective, but not scalable. They are usually designed for specific attack types, not for general malware detection. Static approaches based on machine learning techniques or program similarity analysis are efficient, but with high false negative ratio. Besides, machine learning based detection can neither be used to model attack behaviors nor identify new attacks from emerging malware.

To our best knowledge, none of the aforementioned tools go beyond the mere detection of JavaScript malware. Towards an insightful summary and analysis of malware evolution trend, it is desirable to detect malware and further classify them according to the exploited *attack vector* and the corresponding *attack behaviors*. Considering the emergence of numerous new malware or their variants, knowing the attack type and the attack vector will greatly help domain experts for further analysis. Such an automated classification can significantly speed up the overall response to the malware and even shorten the time to discover the zero-day attacks or unknown vulnerabilities.

In this paper, we propose an automatic approach to perform JavaScript malware detection and classification by combining static analysis (via machine learning) and dynamic analysis to achieve both scalability and accuracy. To efficiently detect and classify malware, we propose a two-phase classification. The first phase is to classify malicious JavaScript samples from benign ones, while the second phase is to discover the attack type that a malicious script belongs to. In the first phase, we extract and analyze features that are generally predictive for malicious scripts. To address the obfuscation and dynamic code generation problems, we extend HtmlUnit [1] to obtain the final unpacked code. We extract features from document elements, source code and sensitive function call patterns. In the second phase, we focus on the features that are representative and unique for each attack type. To identify unique features relevant to a certain attack type, the inter-script analysis is adopted to find API usage patterns, which can serve as features of different attack types. For the suspicious candidates that fall into grey zone (uncertain in classification), we adopt the dynamic analysis to unveil the practical behaviors of the attack and match it to existing attack behavior models. For dynamic analysis, we instrument Firefox to capture the attack behaviors of malicious code. Holistically, static analysis assures the scalability while dynamic analysis on uncertain scripts improves the accuracy.

To sum up, this paper makes the following contributions:

- We propose an effective machine learning approach for JavaScript malware detection with predictive features like commenting style based on textual analysis and the feature of function calls with security risks based program analysis.
- We propose a combined approach for JavaScript malware classification by firstly using the machine learning approach with predictive features like function call patterns and the times of external references, and then further improving the accuracy using dynamic program analysis. Our approach achieves the scalability and accuracy.
- We develop the semantic models of the eight known JavaScript attacks in the form of Deterministic Finite Automata, which can not only help to explain the attack behavior, but also discover new malware variants and new vulnerabilities if the attack does not fall into any of the eight attack models.
- We implement out approach in a complete toolset and evaluate it using 20,000 web sites with 1,400,000 scripts. The result shows that our approach beats most mainstream anti-virus tools, with high accuracy and promising performance.

2. JAVASCRIPT MALWARE CATEGORIZATION

Computer Antivirus Research Organization gives each new discovered JavaScript malware a unique family name for identification, e.g., *TrojWare.JS.Agent.G*. Some organizations adopt it while others may have their own naming conventions. Thus, classification information provided by different organizations are neither congruent nor accurate to describe the attacks that the malware can launch. Besides, family-based classification provides no hints on the vulnerability exploited by the malware. A meaningful classification according to the vulnerability and the corresponding exploits is critical, especially for identifying new attacks. Such classification should be based on attack behaviors of the malware that exploit the vulnerability.

In accordance with Kaspersky Security Bulletin Overall Statistics 2013 [8], attacks targeting JRE, Adobe Acrobat Reader, browser, Adobe Flash and so on account up more than 95% of attacks launched by JavaScript code. Attack vector could be a good standard to classification, since it indicates location of vulnerability and the same type shares similar behavior pattern. We list the eight most common JavaScript attack types according to attack vectors as follows.

- *Type I: Attack targeting browser vulnerabilities.* This type of attack targets potential vulnerabilities (like CVE-2014-1567) of a browser of certain version or with certain plug-ins, and then exploits such vulnerabilities to trigger memory corruption. Consequently, it will lead to the malicious control of instruction registers.
- *Type II: Browser hijacking attack.* Browser hijacking is the modification of a web browser's settings performed without the user's permission. A browser hijacker may replace the existing home page, error page, or search page with its own. For instance, CVE-2007-2378 in the Google Web Toolkit (GWT) framework is a JavaScript hijacking attack, which illegally tracks personal data.
- *Type III: Attack targeting Adobe Flash.* ActionScript used in Adobe Flash and Adobe Air has a flaw of allowing chunks allocation in the heap. An exploit page uses vulnerabilities like CVE-2012-1535 to manipulate the heap layout, which induces heap spray attacks. Finally, the memory corruption results in running a ROP (Return Oriented Programming) chain.
- *Type IV: Attack targeting JRE.* Attacks take advantage of vulnerabilities in Oracle's J2SE JDK and JRE. The JVM security depends on the byte code verifier, the class loader, and the security manager. For instance, the vulnerability in Java 7 Update 11 (CVE-2013-1489) allows attackers to bypass all security mechanisms in the Java browser plug-in.
- *Type V: Attack based on multimedia.* Attacks are carried by multimedia files or files in other format supported by browsers, e.g., CSS based attacks. Generally, malicious downloadable resources (e.g., image and font files) can be deliberately designed to exploit vulnerabilities like CVE-2008-5506 to consume the network capacity of visitors, launch CSRF attacks, spy on visitors or run distributed denial-of-service (DDoS).
- *Type VI: Attack targeting Adobe PDF reader.* Vulnerability in Adobe Reader is being used by active attacks targeting individuals with malicious PDF files. For example, vulnerabilities like CVE-2011-2462 could cause a crash and potentially allow an attacker to take control of the affected system.
- *Type VII: Malicious redirecting attack.* Cybercriminals are constantly thinking up new ways to redirect unsuspecting visitors to their drive-by landing page. It includes "Meta Refresh redirecting", "JavaScript Redirect", "CSS redirecting", "OnError redirecting" and so on. This attack type is generally based on CWE-601.
- *Type VIII: Attack based on Web attack toolkits, e.g. Blacole.* Attack toolkits are increasingly available to an unskilled black market that is eager to participate in the speedy spread of malware. According to a recent report [2], Symantec reported that 61% of observed web-based threat activity could be directly attributed to attack kits.

Each attack type aims at representing a unique attack behavior that exploits a certain attack vector or share some certain event routine, e.g., attack type III, IV , V and VI scan the vulnerabilities in different origins. The above classification is at a more general concept level than family-based classification. For example, the popular malware family *Trojan.JS.Blacole* belongs to the attack type VIII, while the family *Trojan.JS.Iframe* is a malware of type VII. However, compared with the general term of attack type like *heap spray attack* [32], our classification is more specific as we consider attack vector of a heap spray. A heap spray attack can be an attack of type III, IV or V.

3. SYSTEM OVERVIEW OF JSDC

In this section, we sketch the overall workflow of our two-phase approach: JSDC, as depicted in Figure 1. The first phase is to identify the malicious (including highly suspicious) JavaScript snippets. Given malicious JavaScript snippets, the second phase is to further classify them according to their attack type. Thus, the classification process is applied twice, based on the features for malware detection and attack type classification. For the second classification, if there still exist any suspicious fragments that fall into the grey zone (the probability of a script being a certain attack type is non-dominant), dynamic confirmation is applied to execute this script and to capture its execution trace for further analysis.

We use the crawler Heritrix [29], to download web pages for detection. After Heritrix downloads a complete web page with HTML and JavaScript, we extract both internal and external JavaScript snippets. For the ease of feature extraction based on program information, we use HtmlUnit [1], a GUI-Less emulator of a full browser environment, which has fairly good JavaScript support, to obtain the unpacked code (e.g., the code dynamically generated during execution). Once we address the problem of obfuscation and dynamic code generation, we extract features from the source code and AST of the final unpacked code. Note that HtmlUnit is just used to parse and interpret the JavaScript code, without doing the actual rendering job. Thus, this step is regarded as mostly-static analysis [18].

With the training set of representative malicious and benign samples, we propose features that are predictive of malicious or benign intent (see Section 4). Firstly, textual features of the code are extracted based on textual analysis—word size, n-gram model, frequency of characters, commenting style, and entropy are extracted. After textual features are extracted, we use HtmlUnit to obtain the unpacked code, from which features about the program information can be extracted. The program information includes HTML properties and Document Object Model (DOM) operations, and the API usage patterns (i.e., patterns of function calls) in the JavaScript snippet. In addition, we also extract AST-based features, e.g., the tree depth, the pair of type and text from some AST nodes [18]. All these non-textual features are extracted to characterize the malicious behaviors.

To further distinguish eight different types of attacks, we reuse part of features about the program information for detection. Besides, we propose new features based on the vulnerability exploits or attack behaviors of different attack types. We identify the frequently used functions in different attack types. By considering parameters of these functions, we derive the features based on the pair of function and its parameters type. Additionally, features on the API usage patterns and inter-script references are also used.

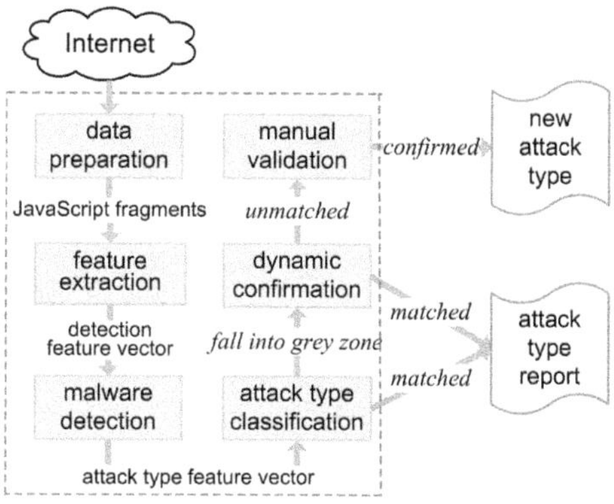

Figure 1: The work-flow of JSDC

Before the actual application of our approach in detection, we need to train the classifiers for predication. We have trained and evaluated each of the used classifiers using k-fold cross validation (CV). The usage of CV is mainly in settings where our goal is prediction, and we aim to estimate the accuracy of a predictive model for malware detection and classification. For the first classifier for malware detection, the training set includes both benign and malicious JavaScript snippets, and each snippet is labelled as malicious or benign. For the second classifier for malware classification according to attack type, the training set only includes malicious snippets and each of them is labelled with a known attack type.

During the process of classifying malicious scripts into different attack types, there are some uncertain results that fall into the grey zone (the classification results show that the probability of a script being a certain attack type is not significantly different from that of being others). This indicates that such scripts are not really similar to any existing malicious samples. For those uncertain ones, a further dynamic analysis is required to execute them and to capture their execution traces at runtime. We have some predefined or learned behaviour models from execution traces of the existing types of attack. More details on inferring attack models in DFAs and checking malware candidate with these models can be found in Section 5.

4. DETAILS OF FEATURE EXTRACTION

JavaScript owns dynamic features that incur security risks and make static analysis fail, e.g., no type checking, DOM based cross-cite scripting, client side open-redirecting and the dynamic code of Ajax [22]. JavaScript's flexibility is reflected in modifying everything ranging from an object's fields and methods to its parent object. Besides, JavaScript's dynamics allow to access and modify shared objects, and to dynamically run the injected code via functions like `eval()`, `setTimeout()`.

Obfuscation is widely adopted to hide the semantics of the JavaScript code from the human efforts' check. Benign JavaScript applications make use of obfuscation to protect intellectual property, while malicious JavaScript uses obfuscation (even multiple levels of obfuscations) to hide its true intent. The flexibility, dynamic features and obfuscation have made the malicious JavaScript code unreadable for human experts. Meanwhile, these characteristics also fail the purely-static approaches to detect malware accurately.

To extract representative features that cover the above characteristics of JavaScript, we adopt three types of analy-

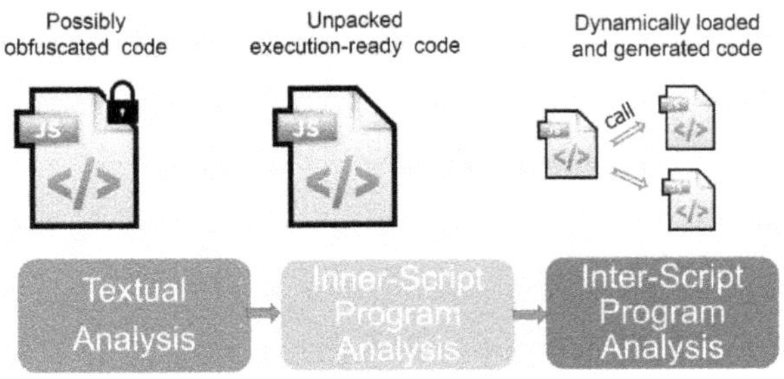

Figure 2: Feature extraction process

sis: textual, inner-script and inter-script analysis (see Figure 2). Textual analysis provides hints of the obfuscated attacks (see Section 4.1). Inner-script analysis (see Section 4.2) mainly provides program information on ASTs or function calls with security risks. Function call patterns and inter-script analysis (see Section 4.3) focus on the classification of attack types. The malicious sample s_1 in Figure 3, which is an obfuscated type I attack that loads external scripts, is used as an illustrative example.

Note that we annotate features only for detection with †, features only for attack type classification with ‡, and features for both purposes with ∗.

4.1 Textual Analysis

Textual analysis is applied to indicate both obfuscation and maliciousness, as it can tell the difference between obfuscated malicious scripts and obfuscated benign ones [16].

Longest word size†. Obfuscated JavaScript code usually contains long words, which signals the existence of encoding or encryption that is used for parameters of the function like eval. A script with very long word size (e.g., larger than 350 words [16]) is likely to be obfuscated. For example, in the obfuscated code in Figure 3(a), the size of the longest word is 814. After tokenization, the longest token size is calculated.

Entropy†. Entropy is a measure of unpredictability of information content, and it is used to analyze the distribution of different characters. Entropy is calculated as follows:

$$H(X) = -\sum_{i=1}^{N}(\frac{x_i}{T})log_{10}(\frac{x_i}{T}) \begin{cases} X = \{x_i, i = 0, 1, ..., N\} \\ T = \sum_{i=1}^{N} x_i \end{cases} \quad (1)$$

where x_i is the count of each characters and T counts all characters. Note that we omit the calculation of the count for space character since it is not part of the JavaScript code contents. The obfuscated code typically has low entropy than normal code, since it often contains repeated characters. It has been experimented that the entropy for obfuscated code is usually lower than 1.2, while the standard code has entropy from 1.2–2.1 [16]. The obfuscated code of s_1 has entropy of 1.1.

Byte occurrence frequency of specific character†. As obfuscated malicious code usually uses customized encoding, and it tends to use excessively specific characters. We use 1-gram model among n-gram model, to examine the occurrence frequency of characters (excluding the space character), which is equivalent to byte occurrence frequency. The byte occurrence is then divided by total characters for normalization. For example, in the obfuscated code in Figure 3(a), the comma character represents the most frequently used character (total of 232 characters), which represents a quarter of the total characters.

```
<!--
eval(String.fromCharCode(118,97,114,32,120,101,119,61,52,53,51,
56,48,48,53,52,51,59,118,97,114,32,103,104,103,52,53,61,34,110,
117,111,116,34,59,118,97,114,32,119,61,34,111,34,59,118,97,114,
32,114,101,54,61,34,108,108,46,34,59,118,97,114,32,104,50,104,
61,34,99,111,109,34,59,118,97,114,32,97,61,34,105,102,114,34,59,
118,97,114,32,115,61,34,104,116,116,34,59,100,111,99,117,109,
101,110,116,46,119,114,105,116,101,40,39,60,39,43,97,43,39,97,
109,101,32,115,114,39,43,39,99,61,34,39,43,115,43,39,112,58,47,
47,39,43,103,104,103,52,53,43,39,39,43,119,43,39,39,43,114,101,
54,43,39,39,43,104,50,104,43,39,47,39,43,39,34,32,119,105,100,
39,43,39,116,104,61,34,49,34,32,104,39,43,39,101,105,103,104,
116,61,34,51,34,62,60,47,105,102,39,43,39,114,97,109,101,62,39,
41,59,32,118,97,114,32,106,104,114,52,61,52,51,50,52,50,50,52));
//-->
```

(a) The original obfuscated version

```
var xew = 453800543;
var ghg45 = "nuot";
var w = "o";
var re6 = "ll.";
var h2h = "com";
var a = "ifr";
var s = "htt";
document.write("<"+a+"ame sr"+"c=\""+s+"p://"+ghg45+""+w+""+re6
+""+h2h+"/"+"\"wid"+"th=\"1\"h"+"eight=\"3\"></if"+"rame>");
var jhr4 = 4324224;
```

(b) The HtmlUnit unpacked version

Figure 3: A malicious sample s_1 of attack Type I

Commenting style†. There are two kinds of comment annotations in JavaScript. "//" is for single-line comments and "<!--. . . -->" for multiple-line or block comments. A basic evasion technique involves the mixture of these two kinds of comments. For example, the code in Figure 3(a) uses a pair of tags <!-- and //-->, which is expected to be commented out for execution, nevertheless, it is executed due to the fault-tolerance of the browser. The value of this feature records the occurrence frequency of such commenting style, e.g., there is one occurrence for the code in Figure 3(a).

4.2 Inner-Script Program Analysis

A web-page contains multiple JavaScript snippets, some are embedded (internal scripts), while some others are links to other JavaScript fies (external scripts). Analysis of the internal scripts are inner-script analysis, which is considered heavy weight for analysis of all JavaScript snippets. We delay the analysis of external scripts for inter-script analysis (see Section 4.3).

For the unpacked code in Figure 3(b), features about the program information are extracted to characterize the malicious behaviors. The program information includes HTML properties and Document Object Model (DOM) operations, the API usage pattern (i.e., the pattern of function calls) and AST-based features.

Function calls with security risks∗. Malicious JavaScript are usually accomplished by means of code generation, redirecting and DOM operations at runtime. In Figure 4, we list the functions that are with security risks by allowing dynamic code generation, loading or redirecting. Nevertheless, the functions are not used alone but together with some other assistant string operation functions (e.g., concat(), charCodeAt()) that can hide the malicious intention by encoding or encryption. We record the number of occurrences of a function call as a numeric feature, e.g., feature String.fromCharCode() and feature eval() in Figure 3(b) both have a value 1, as they are called only once.

AST features∗. We also consider hierarchical features extracted from the ASTs of unpacked code, e.g. the depth of the AST, the difference between the deepest depth of its subtrees and the shortest depth of its subtrees, the maximum

Function Name	Function Type	Possible Threats
eval() window.setInterval() window.setTimeout()	Dynamic code execution	Dynamic code generation
location.replace() location.assign()	Change current URL	Redirect to malicious URL
getUserAgent() getAppName()	Check browser	Target specific browser
getCookie() setCookie()	Cookie access	Manipulate Cookie
document.addEventListener() element.addEventListener()	Intercepting Events	Block user's operation or emulating
document.write() element.changeAttribute() document.writeln() element.innerHTML() element.insertBefore() element.replaceChild() element.appendChild()	DOM operation	Embed malicious script, invisible java applets, invisible iframe, invisible silverlight, etc.
String.charAt() String.charCodeAt() String.fromCharCode() String.indexOf() String.split()	String operation	Hide intension, by encoding and encryption

Figure 4: Functions with security risks

breadth and the versions of the AST during the generation of the final unpacked code.

There exists many similar assignments and function calls in the ASTs of malicious scripts—this reason leads to a large value of AST depth and maximum breadth. Furthermore, malicious scripts also use multiple levels of dynamic code generation like eval(), i.e., the parameter of one eval function call contains some other function call(s) like eval or document.write. During the process of unpacking these functions that support dynamic code generation, each time one such function like eval is parsed and interpreted, a new version of AST is built. Thus, by analysing the versions of ASTs, we can calculate the times of doing unpacking for functions that support dynamic code generation and loading in a script. Finally, the code in Figure 3(b) has an AST with a depth of 21, a width of 20 and a version number of 5.

Function call patterns‡. Different malicious attacks take advantage of distinct vulnerability and have their own behavior models. As API usage (or functional call) pattern is usually adopted to model program behavior, function call patterns can serve as the features predicating a possible type of attack. For the different attack types of samples in the training set, we apply frequent itemset mining on the function calls extracted from ASTs. A mined frequent itemset is a set of function calls that appear together with a support probability greater than a certain threshold. Specifically, we separately apply frequent itemset mining for samples of each attack type, and record all the maximum frequent itemsets with support greater than 20% for each attack type. Finally, 10 mined patterns are manually confirmed as valid function call patterns for the eight attack types.

In Figure 5, we show an example of function call patterns found common in Figure 3(b) for type I attack. As the function newActiveXObject() and createXMLHTTPRequest() are widely used by malware targeting vulnerability in ActiveX components, this pattern captures behaviors of such attack.

4.3 Inter-Script Program Analysis

In inter-script analysis, we count external scripts from other domains. In JSDC, we report malicious JavaScript code at the unit of a code snippet inside <script/>. In our training set, we find some of malicious samples are self-contained in one code snippet of <script/> and do not refer to other scripts to realize malicious intention. However,

Function call pattern:	Intension:
unescape()	obfuscation to evade checking
eval()	dynamic generation
GetCookie()	check Cookie
dateObject.toGMTString()	generate time String used in cookie
SetCookie()	set cookie to mark
document.write()	generate dynamic document content
document.createElement()	create new document element
element.appendChild()	append new element to current one
newActiveXObject()	create new Active object
createXMLHTTPRequest()	download exploit file to local system

Figure 5: An exemplar function call pattern from mining frequent itemsets in function calls

```
<script src="http://xxx.xxx.xxx/a.js"></script>
<script>
 new_element=document.createElement("script");
 new_element.setAttribute("type","text/javascript");
 new_element.setAttribute("src","a.js");//
 document.body.appendChild(new_element);
 function b() {
   a(); //a() is a function in a.js that contains malicious code
 }
</script>
```

Figure 6: A malicious sample s_2 that involves multiple JavaScript snippets

some malicious ones do not contain the actual malicious code. Instead, they just exploit the vulnerability and call some other third party scripts to accomplish the attack. For this type of attack that relies on some other scripts, we propose to adopt the inter-script program analysis.

We extract the times of referring to external scripts as numeric features. Besides, times of external function calls or variable access are also recorded as different numeric features. Our extension of HtmlUnit enables to parse and interpret the external scripts referred by the current one. As shown in Figure 6, the malicious attack refers to an external script "a.js", and it adds the "a.js" into its DOM as an element. Meanwhile, the function b is actually calling the malicious function a in "a.js" to launch the attack.

Miscellaneous and derived features‡. Given a suspicious script, to characterize the dynamically generated code or external scripts from other domains, we propose some features for attack type classification: feature *changeSRC* counts the number of changing of the *src* attribute (e.g., for <iframe src="..."/> tag); feature *changeSRC* counts the number of invocation of navigator.userAgent; derived statistic feature *domAndDynamicUsageCnt* counts the number of invocation for APIs that change DOM structure or supporting dynamic execution of JavaScript code in Figure 4; feature *dynamicUsageContentLen* stores the length of contents that are passed as arguments to APIs that support dynamic execution of JavaScript; lastly, feature *referenceError* counts the number of failures in its reference of external scripts. The usefulness of these features are discussed in Section 8.

Note that the inter-script program analysis is more computationally costly, compared with inner-script program analysis, due to the increased size of scripts that need to be analyzed. As inter-script analysis is only applicable to feature extraction for classification of detected malware, the overheads in analysing the comparatively small size of detected malicious are still acceptable in our approach.

5. DYNAMIC CONFIRMATION

To capture the attack behaviors of JavaScript malware at runtime, we propose to model and analyze JavaScript program behaviors by focusing on browser-level system calls. As system calls or actions (high level abstraction of similar system calls) are the interactions of a program with its environment (i.e., the browser in our study), it is effective to model program behaviors (including attack behaviors) based on system calls or actions [19]. Further, we propose to use Deterministic Finite Automata (DFA) to model attack behaviors, which is motivated by the work on detecting anomalous program behaviors based on Finite State Automate (FSA) [35]. The transitions of the DFA are actions, i.e., the high-level abstraction of system calls.

In [35], the dynamic analysis approach has been presented to automatically infer an FSA from a set of execution traces of binary executables. In this study, we have the similar idea, but we are modelling the attack behaviors of JavaScript malware based on browser-level system calls. Specifically, we instrument Mozilla Firefox and capture the method calls to Cross Platform Component Object Model (XPCOM) [10] as browser-level system calls. So our implementation is Firefox specific. The work-flow of dynamic confirmation is shown in Figure 7. First, we execute malicious JavaScript samples to get the training set of (both benign and malicious) execution traces. One good thing to web-based malware detection is no need for triggering. Generally, web-based malware are triggered automatically once the web page is loaded. Second, we perform a preprocessing to simplify these traces by removing security irrelevant system calls (those are not related to security or permission issues). For a common system call that happens in all malicious traces of the same attack type, we wrap it as an action. Then, the simplified traces are converted into action sequences. Finally, given all the actions as the alphabetic in a DFA and the existing action sequences as the training set, we adopt an off-line learning algorithm, i.e., regular positive negative inference (RPNI) [30], to infer a DFA from these execution traces. During the off-line learning, human experts (the authors) are involved to give some positive or negative counterexamples to refine the DFA step by step.

To identify the attack type of a possibly malicious script, we collect its execution traces and check them against these learned attack behaviour models in the form of DFA. If any trace is accepted by a certain DFA, the related script is considered as an instance of this attack type. If the traces of a script are not matched with any predefined or inferred behaviour model, JSDC suggests that this script is probably

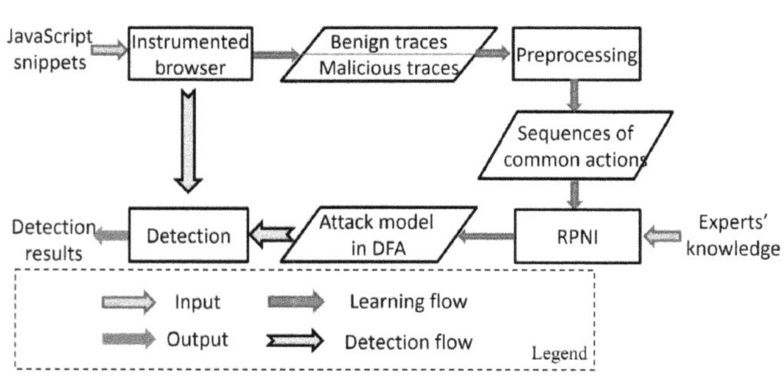

Figure 7: The work-flow of learning and detecting an attack type in dynamic confirmation

System calls	Actions
nsISupportsString.data	
nsICommandLine.resolveURI	$\Rightarrow a$
nsIObserverService.notifyObservers	
nsIWebNavigation.loadURI	$\Rightarrow b$
nsIScriptableUnicodeConverter.convertToByteArray	$\Rightarrow c$
nsICryptoHash.update	$\Rightarrow d$
nsILocalFile.append	$\Rightarrow e$
nsITimer.initWithCallback	$\Rightarrow f$
nsIIOService2.newURI	$\Rightarrow g$
nsIScriptableUnicodeConverter.convertToInputStream	
nsIBoxObject.setProperty	

Figure 8: An execution trace and the actions $\{a, b, c, d, e, f, g\}$ that appear in traces of type I attack

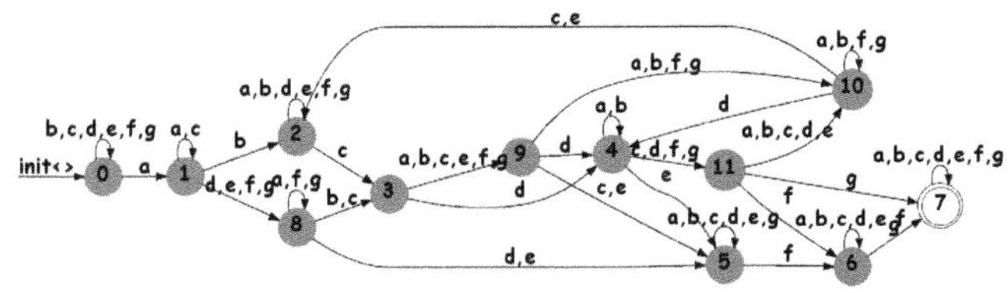

Figure 9: The illustrative DFA of the attack of s_1, which is a part of the actual DFA of type I attack

of a new attack type, or a benign script due to false positive cases introduced in detection.

Given a set of traces from samples of attack type I, we extract the common actions that appear in all malicious traces. Then all traces can be represented by action sequences. For example, the trace in Figure 8 can be represented as an action sequence $\langle a, b, c, d, e, f, g \rangle$. Then with all these action sequences, RPNI is applied to infer a DFA. Further with experts' knowledge, the refined DFA is attained and shown in Figure 9, which generate JavaScript code dynamically and exploit vulnerability of browser to download files into user's local file system. Given the sample s_1 in Figure 3, we can capture traces that are represented as sequences $\langle a, d, e, f, g \rangle$, $\langle a, b, c, d, e, f, g \rangle$ or $\langle a, b, c, b, c, d, e, f, g \rangle$. As these traces are accepted by the learned DFA, s_1 is of type I attack.

Note that for each attack type, we repeat the same workflow to learn an attack model in DFA. Totally, the eight learned models are available from the JSDC web-site [9]. To identify the possible attack type, the trace of a malicious script needs to be iteratively checked against each of these 8 DFAs, until one matched is found or all are not matched. The system call based behavior modelling is resistant to obfuscation owing to the dynamic analysis, and applicable to malware variants as it captures the essential behaviors of the same attack.

6. IMPLEMENTATION

In this section, we present our implementation details.

Crawler. We use the Heritrix public domain crawler [7] to crawl over 21,000 Internet web sites. Heritrix is a open-source, extensible, web-scale, archival-quality web crawler project. Heritrix is designed around the concepts of profiles and jobs [21]. A profile is a configuration of web crawler. A job is inherited from a profile and can override configuration options. Jobs are queued for processing and will be picked up by an idle crawler thread. Heritrix also supports custom workflows.

HtmlUnit Extension to Obtain Unpacked Code. Analyzing JavaScript with HtmlUnit, we are able to get the unpacked code (without obfuscation) prior to the actual time-consuming rendering. HtmlUnit is configured so that it does not try to resolve external dependencies (e.g., loading external JavaScript files or third party plugins) referred in the analysed JavaScript. Such a configuration is to make sure that our approach is scalable and light-weighted, since the time taken for the analysis could be quite long if we ensure all dependencies are fulfilled. Nevertheless, this is not a restrictive constraint, since with our experience, most JavaScript malware is designed to be standalone to maximize the chance for successful attack. In some rare events where the external dependencies affect the analysis of HtmlUnit, then our extension falls back to the plain syntactic analysis.

AST Generation and Functional Call Pattern Extraction. To build the AST of unpacked execution-ready code, We use Mozzila Rhino 1.7 [6]—an open source JavaScript engine. The reason to choose Rhino is due to its fault-tolerance and performance in parsing JavaScript code. Rhino is also integrated in HtmlUnit to build AST for the unpacked code that is ready for execution and rendering. We traverse the AST and extract all the function call nodes. We apply the frequent item-set mining implemented in WEKA, a Java-based open source machine learning toolkit [23], to mine function call patterns.

Classifiers. In [27], four types of classifiers, namely ADTree, Random Forest (RF), J48 and Näive Bayes (NB), have been used to solve the malware detection problem, which is a binary classification problem (malicious or benign). In the second phase of our approach, we are doing multi-class classification, to classify the malicious JavaScript code into eight attack types. Thus, we reuse the three classifiers that support multi-class classification, namely RF, J48 and NB. Besides, we also adopt Random Tree (RT).

All of these classifiers are available in the recent version of WEKA. We also use default parameters set-up for these classifiers. The detailed introduction of these classifiers is out of the scope of this paper. We provide a brief summary of each classifier as follows:

- RT: A classifier that build a decision tree with K randomly chosen attributes at each node. It supports estimation of class probabilities based on a hold-out set.
- RF: A non-probabilistic classifier that uses multiple decision trees for training, and predicting the classes by checking the most votes over all decision trees.
- J48: A non-probabilistic classifier that uses single decision tree for classification.
- NB: A probabilistic classifier based on Bayes' theorem with a strong (naive) independence assumptions between the features.

To address the noise due to the different ranges of feature values and treat features fairly, WEKA automatically normalizes values of all features via range and z-normalization. To achieve the best accuracy, WEKA also supports automatic feature selection algorithms.

7. EVALUATION

To test the effectiveness and efficiency of JSDC, we train 4 different classifiers mentioned in previous section with the training data set and perform predication for the testing data set. Particularly, controlled experiments on 20942 labelled scripts are conducted to evaluate the accuracy and run-time performance of JSDC. In addition to the controlled experiments, to exhibit the practical effectiveness, we also apply our approach on 1,400,000 unlabelled scripts to find wild malicious ones contained in public web sites.

Table 1: Data sets used in controlled experiments

Benign data set	#samples
Alexa-top500 websites	20000
Malicious data sets	**#samples**
Attack targeting browser vulnerabilities (type I)	150
Browser hijacking attack (type II)	28
Attack targeting Flash (type III)	81
Attack targeting JRE (type IV)	191
Attack based on multimedia (type V)	190
Attack targeting PDF reader (type VI)	101
Malicious redirecting attack (type VII)	92
Attack based on Web attack toolkits (type VIII)	109
Total	942

7.1 Data Set and Experiment Setup

The labelled data sets include 20000 benign samples and 942 malicious ones of 8 attack types, as shown in Table 1. Our malicious data sets originate from three sources. To include the existing common samples, we collect 200 samples of 8 attack types from well-known malware repositories VX-HEAVEN [4] and another 200 samples from OPENMALWARE [3]. To include the emerging and new attacks, we manually collect 542 samples from malicious websites reported by WEB INSPECTOR [5]. We test these total 942 malicious samples with the on-line service of 54 anti-virus tools provided on VIRUSTOTAL [11]. The results report that they are malicious. For the benign data set, we crawl 20,000 scripts from the Alexa-top500 websites[1], from each of which 40 scripts are randomly crawled. We scan them with two anti-virus tools AVAST! (version 2014.9.0.2021) and TRENDMICRO (version 10.4) to ensure that they are benign.

The unlabelled data sets include 1,400,000 scripts that are crawled by Heritrix with randomly selected seeds. Here, URLs in the list that a Web crawler starts with are called the seeds. Our seeds include general web sites of universities, governments, companies, discussion forums, etc. The training samples, testing samples and newly found malware in our study can be found from the JSDC web-site [9].

Our experimental environment is a Dell optiplex 990 PC (Intel Core i7-2600 3.40GHz, 8G memory), running Windows 7 64-bit Enterprise.

7.2 Evaluation of Malware Detection

7.2.1 Detection on the Labelled Data Sets

To test the accuracy of the classifiers for the labelled data sets, malicious and benign scripts are all mixed and then separated into multiple partitions. To avoid possible errors introduced in random partition of training set and testing set, we do not split all samples into a training partition (75%) and a predication partition (25%). Instead, we adopt 10-fold cross-validation (10-fold CV) strategy to train the 4 classifiers: RF, J48, NB and RT.

Accuracy of the trained classifiers. Table 2 shows the accuracies of trained classifiers on the labelled data sets. The accuracy is calculated by measuring the ratio of the number of successful classifications to the total number of samples. As there are more than 40 different features for classifica-

[1] http://www.alexa.com/topsites

Table 2: The accuracies of different classifiers

ML classifier	Accuracy	FP rate	FN rate
RandomForest (RF)	99.9522%	0.2123%	0.8492%
J48	99.8615%	0.7431%	2.335%
Näive Bayes (NB)	98.2237%	1.127%	4.5280%
RandomTree (RT)	99.8758%	0.3609%	1.4862%

```
<!--
if(navigator.userAgent.match(/(android|midp|j2me|symbian|
series 60|symbos|windowsmobile|windowsce|ppc|smartphone|
blackberry|mtk|bada|windows phone)/i)!==null){
window.location = "http://mirolend.h19.ru/away.php?sid=5";
} //-->
```

Figure 10: A code example of FN cases

tion of malicious and benign scripts, we use the function of automated searching and selection of predicate features in WEKA. Thus, as Table 2 shows, all the four classifiers have achieved an overall accuracy above 98%. Note that the overall accuracy is probably dominated by the large number of correct classification of benign sample. Thus, checking the specific false positive and false negative cases will provide more insightful observations.

In Table 2, the worst classifier is Näive Bayes, whose FN rate of malicious samples is 4.5280%. However, due to the overwhelming percentage of benign samples, a high FN rate (4.5%) of malicious samples does not affect the overall accuracy significantly. The other three classifiers have low FP rate. One of the FN cases for RF, J48 and RT is shown in Figure 10. This sample belongs to malicious redirects (type VII) and requires the client side to be a mobile device. Thus, HtmlUnit cannot parse and unpack the code properly so that the extracted feature vector is not accurate. Overall, the FN of malicious samples range from 0.3500% to 4.5280% for different classifiers. Thus, our tool achieves a detection ratio 99.65% (the RF classifer) on the whole labelled malicious samples. It is reasonable to get such high detection ratio, as in 10-fold CV the different folders (partitions) are mutually used for training and predication for each other.

Comparison with other tools. To compare the accuracy and performance of our approach with the state-of-the-art tools, we consider research prototype JSAND[2] [13] and other 11 popular anti-virus tools. The 11 anti-virus tools include the open-source anti-virus software CLAMAV[3] and the 2014 best reviewed ten anti-virus products[4]:—AVG, AVAST!, BITDEFENDER, F-SECURE, GDATA, KASPERSKY, MCAFEE, PANDA, SYMANTEC and TRENDMICRO. JSAND and CLAMAV are used in the previous study for comparison [33]. JSAND is available as on-line service from this link: https://wepawet.iseclab.org/index.php. CLAMAV and the best ten anti-virus tools are available as on-line service from VirusTotal [11]. To enable the latest JSAND 2.6 for detection, we upload 942 malicious samples and analyse them for five times to avoid the cached result provided by JSAND 1.3.

The results are summarized in Table 3. For each malicious sample we also count the number of tools, which succeed in detection, among the total 54 tools provided on VIRUSTOTAL. On average, each malicious sample is reported by 21 tools. Given any malicious sample in our labelled data sets, usually 6 to 7 among the best reviewed ten anti-virus tools can detect. These tools' detection ratio ranges from 5% to 93%. Note that we are not comparing these tools to find the best ones, but investigating the limitations of mainstream anti-virus tools. Our goal is to find the malicious scripts missed by JSAND and the best reviewed ten anti-virus tools. The best classifier RF in Table 2 can detect 939 out of 942 (99.68%) malicious samples. The failed cases are because of some implementation issues relating to our HtmlUnit-based infrastruction, which can not emulate all versions of mainstream browsers.

[2]JSAND supports three types of results, i.e., benign, suspicious and malicious. We consider it is detected if JSAND reports suspicious or malicious.

[3]CLAMAV: http://www.clamav.net/

[4]2014 Best Antivirus Software Review: http://anti-virus-software-review.toptenreviews.com/

Table 3: Detection Ratio of our approach and other tools on labelled malicious data sets

Tool	Detection %	Tool	Detection %
JSDC	99.68%	MCAFEE	59.87%
AVAST!	93.84%	SYMANTEC	27.28%
KASPERSKY	86.31%	JSAND	25.58%
GDATA	85.88%	TREND	22.08%
BITDEFENDER	83.23%	CLAMAV	9.24%
F-SECURE	82.38%	PANDA	5.31%
AVG	76.22%		

7.2.2 Detection on the Unlabelled Data Set

After we get the trained classifiers from the labelled data sets, we apply the learned model to unlabelled data sets for predication. Among these 1,400,000 wildly crawled scripts, the best trained classifier RF predicates 1,530 snippets as malicious.

To verify our prediction accuracy, we randomly select 100 from 1,530 reported unique samples. We manually inspect these 100 cases and find only 1 FP case in these 100 samples. For the rest 99 TP cases, we test them by other tools mentioned in Section 7.2.1. We find 11 out of 99 TP cases are missed by all the tools. For example, we found an exploit to CVE-2014-1580 is missed by all the tools. Mozilla Firefox before 33.0 does not properly initialize memory for GIF images, which allows remote attackers to obtain sensitive information from process memory via a crafted web page that triggers a sequence of rendering operations for truncated GIF data within a CANVAS element. The results in Table 4 show individual detection ratio for each tool. The best tool can achieve a detection ratio of 48.49%. We observe two facts: first, these tools perform much worse on the unlabelled samples than the labelled ones. Most of the labelled ones are from public repositories and may have been scanned by these tools, but unlabelled ones are new merging variants. Second, the ranking of detection ratio of these tools in Table 3 is generally consistent with the ranking in Table 4, although labelled and unlabelled samples are from different origins. The above observations imply that detection of wild and emerging malware is not easy. Note that our comparison mainly focuses on detection ratio (or FN ratio) rather than FP ratio, since existing studies [18, 33] have found that existing JavaScript malware detection tools have low FP but high FN.

7.2.3 Performance of Malware Detection

To know the potential of our approach being an off-line large-scale anti-virus tool or an on-line real-time scanner as a browser plugin, we investigate the performance of each step in malware detection.

Table 4: **Detection ratio of other tools on the 99 unique samples reported by our approach**

Tool	Detection%	Tool	Detection%
KASPERSKY	48.49%	MCAFEE	22.22%
AVAST!	46.47%	JSAND	10.10%
GDATA	34.34%	TREND	6.06%
BITDEFENDER	30.30%	SYMANTEC	3.03%
F-SECURE	30.30%	CLAMAV	2.02%
AVG	27.27%	PANDA	0.00%

Table 5: **The running time for different classifiers**

Operation	Num	Time(s)	Avg(ms)
Feature extraction	20942	1660.7	79.3
Training(RandomForest)	20942	0.785	0.037
Training(J48)	20942	0.364	0.017
Training(Näive Bayes)	20942	0.124	0.006
Training(RandomTree)	20942	0.275	0.013
Detection(RandomForest)	1,400,000	57.4	0.041
Detection(J48)	1,400,000	26.6	0.019
Detection(Näive Bayes)	1,400,000	8.4	0.006
Detection(RandomTree)	1,400,000	19.6	0.014

As shown in Table 5, we list the time used for different classifiers when the whole labelled data sets serve as the training set. The main overheads come from the feature extraction step. Although the total time of feature extraction for 20942 scripts in training sets is 1660.7 seconds, the average time for each script is just 79.3 ms. As mentioned in Section 4.3, feature extraction for effective inner and inter program analysis requires the execution ready code that is after several times of unpacking. Thus, unpacking code, generating ASTs and doing program analysis are the major time-consuming tasks at the step of feature extraction. However, feature extraction can be processed for only once, and the resulting feature vectors can be stored in database for future usage. Table 5 also lists the total training and detection time for different classifiers. For 20942 feature vectors, the training of classifiers only need less than 1 seconds. We can also observe that Näive Bayes classier, as the worst classifier in Table 2, exhibits the best performance—with only 0.006 ms needed for each script in detection stage. The sum of average feature extraction time and detection time approximately provides an estimate of the scanning time for a single script. Given the ignorable average detection time for each script, the average feature extraction time (79.3 ms) suggests that our approach can be used as a browser plug-in for real-time detection of malicious JavaScript.

To further evaluate the potential of our tool being an offline large-scale detector, we investigate the detection time needed for a large set of unlabelled scripts. Apart from feature extraction time, the detection only needs up to 1-2 minutes to classify 1.5 million scripts. In the real application of our approach for detection, we use Heritrix to crawl the pages and, meanwhile, HtmlUnit to unpack code and extract feature vectors. Thus, crawling and feature extraction are processed in parallel. The detection can be accomplished with different classifiers and different selected features.

7.3 Evaluation of Attack Type Classification

We measure the accuracy and performance of the attack type classification on the labelled and unlabelled samples. We further investigate when the dynamic confirmation is needed and how it can improve the overall accuracy.

7.3.1 Accuracy of the Trained Classifiers

Table 6: **The confusion matrix of using RandomForest on the 942 labelled malicious samples**

a	b	c	d	e	f	g	h	<–classified as
139	0	0	0	9	2	0	0	a = type I
0	23	4	0	0	0	0	1	b = type II
1	1	74	1	0	0	1	3	c = type III
0	0	2	179	9	0	1	0	d = type IV
1	0	0	0	179	10	0	0	e = type V
0	0	0	0	19	82	0	0	f = type VI
0	0	0	1	1	0	87	3	g = type VII
0	0	0	1	0	0	3	105	h = type VIII

Table 7: **Attack classification on the 1530 malicious ones detected from 1,400,000 unlabelled samples**

Type	type I	type II	type III	type IV
Num	113 (7.39%)	10 (0.65%)	75 (4.90%)	253 (16.54%)
Type	type V	type VI	type VII	type VIII
Num	202 (13.20%)	101 (6.60%)	350 (22.88%)	426 (27.84%)

We adopt 10-folder CV strategy to train the 4 classifiers (RF, J48, NB and RT) with the 942 labelled samples in Table 1. The accuracy of these 4 classifiers is 92.14% (RF), 90.22% (J48), 83.44% (NB) and 90.13% (RT), respectively. Table 6 shows how the 942 samples are classified into the 8 attack types according to RF. The sum of the entries on the matrix's main diagonal, namely 868 (92.1444%), are correctly classified samples. Among the 74 wrongly classified samples, 19 samples of type VI are wrongly classified as type V, while 10 of type V are wrongly classified as type VI. The direct reason is that some samples of type V and type VI are quite similar—their feature values show no significant differences. For the other 45 out of 74 wrongly classified cases, we find that most of them fall into the grey zone without a dominant certainty value for any attack type. The other three classifiers achieve slight worse accuracies. We also observe that they have similar problems in distinguishing type V and type VI, and classifying a number of uncertain cases. Thus, the trained classifiers can be ready for practical usage if we can address the above two problems via combining dynamic attack confirmation (see Section 7.4).

7.3.2 Predication on the Unlabelled Data Set

In Section 7.2.2, 1530 malicious samples are detected by our approach from 1.4 million unlabelled scripts. We apply the best trained classifiers, namely RF, to classify these samples into different attack types. The classification output is listed in Table 7. To measure the accuracy, we manually inspect 10% of samples of each type (for type II and type III that has few samples we randomly choose 10 samples). Totally, we check 164 samples and confirm that they are indeed malicious. On these 164 samples, the trained RF classifier achieves an accuracy of 87.8%, which means correctly classifying 144 out of 164 samples. Among the 20 mistakenly classified ones, 9 samples do not belong to any of the eight attack types and 11 samples are classified into the wrong types. We observe that 3 wrong cases are related to type V or VI confusion, and 9 cases fall into the grey zone. Thus, the sole supervised classification cannot accurately predicate the attack type of JavaScript malware, since feature values extracted by mostly-static analysis may not characterize the actual attack behaviors. Especially, for those cases that fall into grey zones, we need to apply dynamic confirmation to to analyse them by execution.

Table 8: The certainty value and the number of samples that fall into grey zone

certainty	certain#	total	uncertain#	uncertain %
1	764	1530	766	51.31%
⩾0.9	854	1530	676	50.07%
⩾0.8	994	1530	536	44.18%
⩾0.7	1296	1530	234	15.29%
⩾0.6	1311	1530	219	14.31%

7.4 Combining Dynamic Confirmation and Machine Learning Classification

The dynamic confirmation is applied on uncertain cases that fall into the grey zone during attack type classification.

To effectively select the uncertain cases, we investigate how the probabilities of the predicated class are distributed for the 1530 samples that are classified by RF in Section 7.3.2. In Table 8, we define the *certainty* as the dominant one among a sample's probabilities to be eight attack types. For example, *certainty* = 1 means there exists one dominant probability (100%) for a sample to be the related predicated attack type. *certain#* refers to the number of samples with this certainty value, i.e., 764 out of 1530 for *certainty* = 1. Thus, the number of uncertain cases without a dominant probability (*uncertain#*) is 766, which comprises 51.31% of the total 1530 samples.

Accuracy of Dynamic Attack Confirmation. From Table 8, we observe that 234 samples are without a dominant probability larger than 0.7 (234 samples are in the grey zone if *certainty* = 0.7). We apply the dynamic confirmation on these 234 samples. As described in Section 5, we learn a DFA for each attack type from the related ones in the training set of 942 samples. We separately execute the 234 samples and get 10 traces for each of them. Then these traces are used for acceptance check on the learned DFAs. If any trace is accepted, the corresponding sample is matched with the DFA of the compared attack type. Finally, we compare the matching results with manual verification results to measure the accuracy. Totally, the dynamic confirmation correctly classifies 220 samples out of 234, achieving an accuracy of 94.02%. Among eight attack types, type I shows the best accuracy (95%) for dynamic confirmation while type VI shows the worst (90.91%).

Thus, dynamic confirmation alone can achieve good accuracy for attack type classification. However, the problem is that it is not scalable. It takes about 1,544 seconds to analyse the 234 samples, i.e., averagely 6.6 seconds for each. Among 234 samples without a certainty value larger than 0.7, RF achieves an accuracy of 67.09%. Thus, among 234 grey zone samples, dynamic confirmation can rightly classify 63 more than RF.

Performance of Attack Type Classification.

As shown in Table 9, the training step of attack type classification takes about 0.01-0.12 seconds, which does not include the time of feature extraction. The predication step takes only about 0.001-0.05 seconds. Thus, the performance of these 4 classifiers is quite good, owing to the comparatively small number of samples to be handled in attack type classification. Besides, these classifiers also exhibit consistent performance — that is a classier fast in malware detection is also fast in attack type classification. Note that the time for feature extraction in this step is the same as that in malware detection step, as all feature values are extracted at once. Feature extraction averagely takes 0.1 second for each of 1530 detected malware.

Table 9: Running time of different classifiers in type classification

Operation	Num	Time(s)	Avg(ms)
Training(RandomForest)	942	0.1	0.11
Training(J48)	942	0.12	0.13
Training(Näive Bayes)	942	0.04	0.04
Training(RandomTree)	942	0.01	0.01
Detection(RandomForest)	1530	0.05	0.0033
Detection(J48)	1530	0.01	0.0006
Detection(Näive Bayes)	1530	0.001	0.00006
Detection(RandomTree)	1530	0.02	0.001

With regard to the time of dynamic confirmation on 234 samples, it takes 1,544 seconds. Including the 168 seconds used for classification (with feature extraction time for 1530 samples), it takes 1,712 seconds to finish identifying attack types for the 1530 malware, i.e., around 1 second per malware. Thus, combining this two techniques can improve the overall accuracy and meanwhile attain good performance.

8. DISCUSSION

Two- or one-phase machine learning classification? A concern is that how the accuracy will be if we make two phase classification into one—that is we do classification at once according to samples with benign labels and labels of eight attack types. On the 20942 training samples, the accuracy of the 4 trained classifiers is 90.99% (RF), 85.74% (J48), 77.15% (NB) and 88.27% (RT), respectively. We examine the results and find the difference for RF is not significant. Among 20000 benign samples, only one is wrongly classified for RF, while among 942 malicious samples, 84 are wrongly classified for RF. In contrast, 74 out of 942 are wrongly classified in our two phase classification of RF. But NB shows significant differences—it wrongly classifies 203 out of 942 malicious samples in one phase classification, in contrast, this number is 156 in our two phase classification. As the training time is almost ignorable if feature extraction is done, we consider two phase classification is worth.

Predicative features. We find that the malware detection has some decisive features: e.g., 98% of benign scripts use eval function only 0 or 1 times, while 87% malicious ones use more than 2 times, and as many as 1778 times. During attack type classification, we observe that there are no decisive features that can exclusively characterize a certain attack type. Instead, we indeed find some predicative features that can be effective in most cases. Specifically, among our 942 training malicious samples, we observe the following facts: 89% of Type I samples have feature $changeSRC < 1$; 52% of Type II have feature *element.appendChild* in Figure 4 with a value>20 ; 74% of Type III have feature *eval* in Figure 4 with a value>1000; 83% of Type IV have feature $GetUserAgent > 2.5$; 87% of Type V have feature $referenceError < 1$; 74% of Type VI have feature $invisibleIframe$=1, which means the frame is invisible; 79% of Type VII have feature $domAndDynamicUsageCnt$ <1; 67% of Type VIII have feature $dynamicUsaeContentLen$ >5000.

Thread to validity. First, the training sets are from three origins: VXHEAVEN, OPENMALWARE and WEB INSPECTOR. Thus, the collected samples directly affect the accuracy of trained classifiers. To address this problem, we need to further investigate the impact of sample size and representativeness on the results. Second, the parameters and set-up for machine learning classifiers are the default ones. Further investigation should be conducted to see the effects of parameters. Lastly, the dynamic attack confirmation relies on experts' knowledge to refine the learned DFA. The rationale of learned DFAs can affect the accuracy of attack confirmation—checking if a trace of a sample is accepted by the DFA of a certain attack type.

9. RELATED WORK

Since the past few years, JavaScript malware detection has intrigued the interest of security researchers and many approaches have been proposed. Existing approaches to JavaScript malware detection mostly rely on static analysis with machine learning techniques or dynamic analysis with behavioural abnormality checking. However, beyond the mere detection, there are few studies that focus on malware classification according to vulnerability or attack behaviors.

9.1 Machine Learning Approaches

In 2009, Likarish *et al.* [27] adopted 4 classifiers (i.e., NB, ADTree, SVM and RIPPER) to detect obfuscated JavaScript malware. The assumption of their approach is that malware utilizes obfuscation to hide the exploits and to evade the detection. They reported that features extracted from the strings of obfuscated scripts can distinguish obfuscated (malicious) scripts from non-obfuscated (benign) ones by machine learning classifiers. Likarish *et al.* acknowledged that the false positive rate is due to obfuscated but benign scripts, which poses threat to the assumption. However, in our study, we use not only features on obfuscation, but also other features on program information. By this, we can reduce false positive rate due to obfuscated but benign scripts.

In 2010, JSAND (JavaScript Anomaly-based aNalysis and Detection) [17] was presented to detect Drive-by Downloads (DbD) attacks. JSAND identifies 10 features characterizing intrinsic events of a drive-by download attack, and then uses these features for machine learning technique (NB) to detect malicious samples. These 10 features are extracted from 4 aspects (redirection, de-obfuscation, environmental context and exploitation) by dynamic anomaly detection with emulation in HtmlUnit [1]. Different from our work, JSAND adopts dynamic analysis and fails to investigate the impact of the different classifiers. Dynamic anomaly-based analysis can be effective but not efficient—JSAND needs 2:22 hours to scan the *Wepawet-bad dataset* which consists of 531 URLs.

Also in 2010, CUJO [33] uses hybrid analysis to on-the-fly capture program information (by static analysis) and execution traces (by dynamic analysis) of JavaScript program. The authors explored the distinct features for heap-spraying attacks and obfuscated attacks. But they failed to examine features for obfuscated but benign scripts, and overlooked classification according to vulnerabilities or attack behaviors as we do in this study. Note that CUJO requires executing every script to capture dynamic features, while our approach only executes scripts that fall into grey zone for dynamic confirmation. Finally, CUJO takes averagely 500ms to analyze a webpage. In contrast, JSDC takes about 80 ms in detection per script, including 70 ms for feature extraction and 10 ms for classification.

Later in 2011, Canali *et al.* [14] proposed a filter, called PROPHILER, to quickly filter out benign pages and forward to the costly analysis tools only the suspicious pages that are highly malicious. The filter's detection models are learned based on 70 features extracted from HTML contents of a page, from the associated JavaScript code, and from the corresponding URL. Then, multiple classifiers, Bayes Net(BN), J48, Logistic, RT and RF, are used to classify the malicious and benign web-pages. For JavaScript, the FP of these classifiers is good, ranging from 0.0% to 1.7%, but the FN ranges from 18.1% to 81%, which is worser than our approach.

In the same year, AST is used to extract characteristics for malicious JavaScript detection [18]. Curtsinger *et al.* [18] presented the tool ZOZZLE that predicates the benignity or maliciousness of JavaScript by leveraging features associated with AST contextual information. Around one to two thousand of features are extracted from the hierarchical structure and texts in ASTs, and then the classifier NB is applied. To remove the noise due to obfuscation, ZOZZLE uses Detours binary instrumentation to get the final, unpacked code for accurate AST generation. After tuning up with different set-up, the authors reported the FP ranges from 0.0003% to 4.5%, and the FN from 1.26% to 11.08%.

To sum up, none of the existing studies investigate the effective features for classifying JavaScript malware into various attack types as we do in this study. Additionally, we propose to apply dynamic confirmation to the cases that fall into grey zone in classification. By this, we can improve the overall accuracy and meanwhile achieve scalability.

9.2 Other Detection Techniques

Various approaches have been presented to detect specialized JavaScript malware in line with different attacks.

Attacks of obfuscated malware. In [16], the parameters for dangerous functions (`eval`, `document.write`, and so on) in web pages are processed to get 3 types of metrics data, i.e., N-gram, entropy and word size. The metrics data is compared with a certain threshold that is learned from empirical study to judge the maliciousness of the corresponding web page. Recently, JSTILL [38] detects obfuscated attacks based on the observation that—JavaScript has to be de-obfuscated before doing its malicious intention, but the deobfuscation process inevitably invokes certain functions.

Policy violation attacks. As early as in 2005, Hallaraker *et al.* [24] monitored the JavsScript execution and then checked the execution trace against the high-level security policies (e.g., the *same-origin* policy and the *signed-script* policy), to detect malicious attack behaviour.

Heap spread attacks. In 2009, Egele *et al.* [20] managed to detect heap spread attacks by checking instantiation of shell-code strings in the heap—specifically—checking if the string contains executable x86 code. The similar idea is adopted in NOZZLE [32], which individually examines all objects in the heap, interpreting object content as code and conducting a static analysis on the code to discover exploits.

JavaScript-bearing PDF documents. Tzermias *et al.* [36] presents MDSCAN, which instrumented Firefox SpiderMonkey. In such way, all the allocated string objects are scanned by the shellcode detector NEMU [31], and possible exploits are detected. MDSCAN failed to address this problem completely since it only searched for legitimate JavaScript inclusions (denoted by the /JS tag), while an attacker can easily circumvent this by encoding the script as text and evaluate it at runtime (e.g. via `eval`).

JavaScript worms. The tool SPECTATOR [28] detects a worm whenever a unusually long propagation chain is found. The idea is using a web proxy to monitor the cookie session and propagation chain for identification of worm replication.

In [15], PathCutter adopts the idea of running an individual script in different isolated and trusted components of web-pages. It prevents the propagation of worms by granting scripts the permission to do only legitimate operations.

10. CONCLUSION

A key to protecting user from exploitation is the rigorous eliminating of malware on Internet. To this end, we propose a method to accelerate the process of manual malware detection by suggesting potentially malware and their attack types to an analyst or an end-user. Our method not only learned features of maliciousness but also of attack type. Therefore, we can tell not only presence of malware, but malicious behaviors with attack approach information by virtue of dynamic attack confirmation. We also demonstrated our effectiveness and efficiency by empirical wild prediction. Among over 1,400,000 scripts, we find over 1,500 malware with 8 attack types. Our detection speed is scalable with below 80 ms per script. The attack type classification takes around 1 second for each malware, combining machine learning classifiers and dynamic attack confirmation.

11. ACKNOWLEDGEMENTS

This work is supported by "Formal Verification on Cloud" project under Grant No: M4081155.020 and "Vulnerability Detection in Binary Code" project under Grant No: M40 61366.680.

12. REFERENCES

[1] Htmlunit. http://htmlunit.sourceforge.net/.
[2] Internet security threat report. http://www.symantec.com/security_response/publications/threatreport.jsp.
[3] Openmalware. http://http://oc.gtisc.gatech.edu:8080/.
[4] Vxheaven. http://vxheavens.com/.
[5] Web inspector: Website security with malware scan and pci compliance. http://www.webinspector.com/.
[6] Rhino. https://developer.mozilla.org/en-US/docs/Mozilla/Projects/Rhino, 2005.
[7] The heritrix web crawler project. http://crawler.archive.org/, 2007.
[8] Kaspersky security bulletin 2013. http://media.kaspersky.com/pdf/KSB_2013_EN.pdf, 2013.
[9] JSDC. https://sites.google.com/site/jsmalwaredetection/models.html, 2014.
[10] MDN:XPCOM. https://developer.mozilla.org/en-US/docs/Mozilla/Tech/XPCOM, 2014.
[11] VirusTotal. https://www.virustotal.com/, 2014.
[12] Microsoft Security Intelligence Report,Volume 15. http://www.microsoft.com/security/sir/archive/default.aspx, Jan. 2013 to Jun. 2013.
[13] P. Agten, S. Van Acker, Y. Brondsema, P. H. Phung, L. Desmet, and F. Piessens. Jsand: Complete client-side sandboxing of third-party javascript without browser modifications. In *Proceedings of the 28th Annual Computer Security Applications Conference*, pages 1–10, New York, NY, USA, 2012. ACM.
[14] D. Canali, M. Cova, G. Vigna, and C. Kruegel. Prophiler: a fast filter for the large-scale detection of malicious web pages. In *WWW*, pages 197–206, 2011.
[15] Y. Cao, V. Yegneswaran, P. A. Porras, and Y. Chen. Pathcutter: Severing the self-propagation path of xss javascript worms in social web networks. In *NDSS*, 2012.
[16] Y. Choi, T. Kim, S. Choi, and C. Lee. Automatic detection for javascript obfuscation attacks in web pages through string pattern analysis. In *International Conference on Future Generation Information Technology*, pages 160–172, Berlin, Heidelberg, Germany, 2009.
[17] M. Cova, C. Krügel, and G. Vigna. Detection and analysis of drive-by-download attacks and malicious javascript code. In *WWW*, pages 281–290, 2010.
[18] C. Curtsinger, B. Livshits, B. Zorn, and C. Seifert. Zozzle: Fast and precise in-browser javascript malware detection. In *the 20th USENIX conference on Security*, Berkeley, CA, USA, 2011.
[19] M. Egele, T. Scholte, E. Kirda, and C. Kruegel. A survey on automated dynamic malware-analysis techniques and tools. *ACM Comput. Surv.*, 44(2):6, 2012.
[20] M. Egele, P. Wurzinger, C. Kruegel, and E. Kirda. Defending browsers against drive-by downloads: Mitigating heap-spraying code injection attacks. In *DIMVA*, pages 88–106, 2009.
[21] B. Feinstein and D. Peck. Caffeine monkey: Automated collection, detection and analysis of malicious javascript. In *DEFCON 15*, USA, 2007.
[22] J. J. Garrett et al. Ajax: A new approach to web applications. 2005.
[23] M. Hall, E. Frank, G. Holmes, B. Pfahringer, P. Reutemann, and I. H. Witten. The weka data mining software: an update. *ACM SIGKDD explorations newsletter*, 11(1):10–18, 2009.
[24] O. Hallaraker and G. Vigna. Detecting malicious javascript code in mozilla. In *ICECCS*, pages 85–94, 2005.
[25] A. Ikinci, T. Holz, and F. C. Freiling. Monkey-spider: Detecting malicious websites with low-interaction honeyclients. In *Sicherheit*, volume 8, pages 407–421, 2008.
[26] A. Kapravelos, Y. Shoshitaishvili, M. Cova, C. Kruegel, and G. Vigna. Revolver: An automated Approach to the Detection of Evasive Web-based Malware. In *USENIX Security*, pages 637–652, 2013.
[27] P. Likarish, E. Jung, and I. Jo. Obfuscated malicious javascript detection using classification techniques. In *MALWARE*, pages 47–54, Montreal, QC, Oct. 2009.
[28] V. B. Livshits and W. Cui. Spectator: Detection and containment of javascript worms. In *USENIX Annual Technical Conference*, pages 335–348, 2008.
[29] G. Mohr, M. Stack, I. Rnitovic, D. Avery, and M. Kimpton. Introduction to heritrix. In *4th International Web Archiving Workshop*, 2004.
[30] J. Oncina and P. Garcia. Inferring Regular Languages in Polynomial Update Time. *Pattern Recognition and Image Analysis*, pages 49–61, 1992.
[31] M. Polychronakis, K. G. Anagnostakis, and E. P. Markatos. An empirical study of real-world polymorphic code injection attacks. In *LEET*, 2009.
[32] P. Ratanaworabhan, V. B. Livshits, and B. G. Zorn. Nozzle: A defense against heap-spraying code injection attacks. In *USENIX Security Symposium*, pages 169–186, 2009.
[33] K. Rieck, T. Krueger, and A. Dewald. Cujo: efficient detection and prevention of drive-by-download attacks. In *ACSAC*, pages 31–39, 2010.
[34] M. Roesch et al. Snort: Lightweight intrusion detection for networks. In *LISA*, volume 99, pages 229–238, 1999.
[35] R. Sekar, M. Bendre, D. Dhurjati, and P. Bollineni. A fast automaton-based method for detecting anomalous program behaviors. In *IEEE Symposium on Security and Privacy*, pages 144–155, 2001.
[36] Z. Tzermias, G. Sykiotakis, M. Polychronakis, and E. P. Markatos. Combining static and dynamic analysis for the detection of malicious documents. In *EUROSEC*, page 4, 2011.
[37] Y.-M. Wang, D. Beck, X. Jiang, R. Roussev, C. Verbowski, S. Chen, and S. T. King. Automated web patrol with strider honeymonkeys: Finding web sites that exploit browser vulnerabilities. In *NDSS*, 2006.
[38] W. Xu, F. Zhang, and S. Zhu. Jstill: mostly static detection of obfuscated malicious javascript code. In *CODASPY*, pages 117–128, 2013.

Be Sensitive to Your Errors: Chaining Neyman-Pearson Criteria for Automated Malware Classification

Guanhua Yan
Department of Computer Science
Binghamton University, State University of New York
Binghamton, NY, U.S.A.
ghyan@binghamton.edu

ABSTRACT

Thwarting the severe threat posed by the voluminous malware variants demands effective, yet efficient, techniques for malware classification. Although machine learning offers a promising approach to automating malware classification, existing methods are oblivious of the costs associated with the different types of errors in malware classification, i.e., false positive errors and false negative errors. Such treatment adversely affects later applications of per-family malware analysis such as trend analysis. Against this backdrop, we propose a unified cost-sensitive framework for automated malware classification. This framework enforces the Neyman-Pearson criterion, which aims to maximize the detection rate under the constraint that the false positive rate should be no greater than a certain threshold. We develop a novel scheme to chain multiple Neyman-Pearson criteria on heterogeneous malware features, some of which may have missing values. Using a large malware dataset with labeled samples belonging to 12 families, we show that our method offers great flexibility in controlling different types of errors involved in malware classification and thus provides a valuable tool for malware defense.

Categories and Subject Descriptors

K.6.5 [**Management of Computing and Information Systems**]: Security and protection

Keywords

Malware, classification, Neyman-Pearson criterion

1. INTRODUCTION

The Internet is now inundated with numerous malware which are responsible for a wide range of malicious activities such as email spamming, botnets, and identity theft. As evidenced by the Symantec reports showing as many as 286 million malware variants were created in 2010 and 400 million in 2011 [35], we must equip ourselves with effective, yet scalable, solutions to mitigating the ever-growing malware threats. Traditional approaches based on malware signatures produced from AV (Anti-Virus) software companies have been shown fruitless in defending against current malware threats; some reports even go as far as claiming that the existing AV solutions are "dead" [11, 2].

In some previous efforts, machine learning has been offered as an alternative approach to classifying the vast volume of malware attacks [30, 14, 25, 27, 21, 32, 26, 1, 38]). Albeit promising, a few technical obstacles still remain as we apply machine learning to automated malware classification in practice. First, the numbers of malware variants belonging to different malware families are highly skewed [28]. Severe class imbalance across malware families poses significant challenges to controlling the accuracy of malware classification, as for a rare family with only a few instances, simply flagging every instance as negative would achieve high classification accuracy. Second, heterogeneous malware features can be extracted from malware programs [40]. Ideally, we would want to combine various types of features to achieve highly accurate malware classification. Existence of missing feature values hinders the deployment of standard machine learning techniques in a straightforward manner. Last but not least, malware samples that are accurately labeled are not easy to obtain, as it is difficult, if not impossible, to manually label a large number of malware variants, and it is hard to overcome the inconsistency among classification results by multiple AV software to find unbiased labeled samples by consensus [16, 18]. Hence, in many cases, we possess only a small number of malware samples that are confidently labeled along with a large number of unlabeled ones.

In this work we propose a unified malware classification framework that overcomes these challenges. This framework is built on an ensemble of cost-sensitive malware classifiers, each of which is trained individually on a type of features extracted from malware programs. Hence, even if we cannot collect one specific type of features from a malware program, the framework can still rely on other types of features to infer the family it should belong to. The cost-sensitive nature of individual classifiers offers us the flexibility of imposing different penalties on false positive and false negative errors. Taking advantage of how much penalties we assign to each type of classification errors, we enforce the Neyman-Pearson criterion [31, 4], which aims to maximize the detection rate of the ensemble classifier while ensuring that the false positive rate should be no greater than a certain threshold. When only a small number of malware samples are labeled, we leverage the structural information inherent

ASIA CCS'15, April 14–17, 2015, Singapore.

http://dx.doi.org/10.1145/2714576.2714578.

in a large amount of unlabeled data to train high-quality classifiers based on semi-supervised learning.

In a nutshell, our contributions made in this work can be summarized as follows. **(1)** We design and implement a unified cost-sensitive framework for automated malware classification, which overcomes various challenges we face in classifying large numbers of malware variants into their corresponding families in practice, such as missing feature values, class imbalance, and difficulty in obtaining accurately labeled samples. **(2)** To combine classification results from multiple cost-sensitive classifiers, we extend a well-established concept in hypothesis testing, Neyman-Pearson criterion [31, 4], and propose the *chain Neyman-Pearson criterion*, which can be used to ensure that the false positive rate of the ensemble classifier should be no greater than a certain threshold while maximizing its detection rate. **(3)** We apply the dynamic programming technique to search optimal configurations that satisfy the chain Neyman-Pearson criterion for individual classifiers, each trained on a specific type of malware features. **(4)** Using a malware dataset containing tens of thousands of malware instances belonging to 12 families, we demonstrate that our method offers great flexibility in controlling different types of errors involved in automated malware classification.

The rest of the paper is structured as follows. Section 2 presents the challenges in malware classification. Section 3 introduces a unified malware classification framework. Section 4 discusses how to train individual classifiers and Section 5 how to build an ensemble classifier. Section 6 shows the evaluation results. Section 7 discusses related work.

2. REALITY CHECK

Our study is based on a malware dataset from Offensive Computing [22] with 526,179 samples. While processing this dataset, we encounter the following three major challenges.

2.1 Labeled and unlabeled data

In order to know the family each malware variant belongs to, we upload its MD5 to the VirusTotal website [37] and obtain the detection results from 43 AV software. Among all these results, we consider only the detection results from the five major AV software, `McAfee`, `Kaspersky`, `Microsoft`, `ESET (NOD32)`, and `Symantec`. Next, we extract the malware family information from the detection result from each AV software. For instance, if Microsoft detects a malware program as `Trojan:Win32/Vundo.BY`, we then identify its family name as `Vundo`. Thereafter, we use the majority rule to label a malware instance: if four out of five AV software classify it as the same malware family, we assume it belong to that family. Using this method, we are able to label only 26,848 instances, which belong to 12 distinct malware families, `Bagle`, `Bifrose`, `Hupigon`, `Koobface`, `Ldpinch`, `Lmir`, `Rbot`, `Sdbot`, `Swizzor`, `Vundo`, `Zbot`, and `Zlob`. Conventional wisdom is that we train a classifier for each family based on only labeled data. The large amount of unlabeled data however contain rich structural information that can be further exploited to improve classification accuracy.

2.2 Class imbalance issue

Figure 1 shows the number of instances labeled in each family. The `Full` case includes both packed and unpacked instances, and the `Unpacked` case has only unpacked instances. The plot clearly shows high imbalance among different malware families. For instance, for the `Unpacked` case, the `Hupigon` family has 31.2 times as many instances as the `Bagle` family has. The class imbalance issue complicates the search for an optimal classifier [10]. For instance, consider a widely used measure, *classification accuracy*, which is defined to be the fraction of correctly classified instances. When we train an optimal classifier that maximizes classification accuracy from a dataset with only a few positive samples, a dummy classifier that simply classifies every instance as negative may stand out as the best one.

2.3 Missing feature values

We extract the following types of features from each malware program in our dataset. **(1) Hexdump 2-gram:** We use utility `hexdump` to produce byte sequences from each malware program, and a hexdump 2-gram feature is constructed by obtaining the frequencies of any two consecutive bytes in the program. **(2) Objdump 1-gram:** We use utility `objdump` to disassemble each malware program, and treat the concatenation of the prefix and the opcode in each instruction as a feature. The value of a feature is the frequency which which it appears in the program. **(3) PE header:** We extract information from the PE header of each malware program with utility `pefile`. We extract two types of features from PE headers. `PE-num`: numerical features extracted from PE headers, `PE-bool`: boolean features extracted from PE headers, such as bits in characteristic fields, whether a DLL is imported, and whether a system call in a DLL file is imported. **(4) PIN trace:** We execute each malware program in a controlled environment for five minutes and use Pin [12], a dynamic binary instrumentation tool, to dump the execution traces. We also extract two types of features from PIN traces. `PIN 2-gram`: the frequency of the ordered combination of opcodes in every two consecutive instructions, and `PIN SysCall`: the number of times that a system call has been invoked.

Figure 2 depicts the fraction of unpacked malware samples in each family that we are able to extract feature values successfully. Not surprisingly, we are able to extract `hexdump 2-gram` and `PE header` (including both `PE-num` and `PE-bool`) features successfully from every malware program. However, for those `objdump 1-gram` features, we cannot extract features from a significant portion of malware instances because objdump crashes during the disassembly process. This occurs similarly to Pin when we try to extract `PIN trace` (including both `PIN 2-gram` and `PIN SysCall`) features. Interestingly, there is no strong correlation between missing `objdump 1-gram` and `PIN trace` feature values: for some malware families (*e.g.*, Koobface, Zbot and Zlob), we are able to extract `objdump 1-gram` features from the majority of malware instances but can only extract `PIN trace` features from a small portion of malware instances.

3. A UNIFIED MALWARE CLASSIFICATION FRAMEWORK

A unified malware classification framework is illustrated in Figure 3. It works on a malware database that contains not only labeled malware programs but also a large number of unlabeled malware instances. Labeled malware samples can come from those identified manually by malware forensic analysts, or from consensus among multiple AV software. Due to the voluminous malware variants, many malware instances will remain as unlabeled in the malware database. Rather than ignoring these unlabeled samples, our frame-

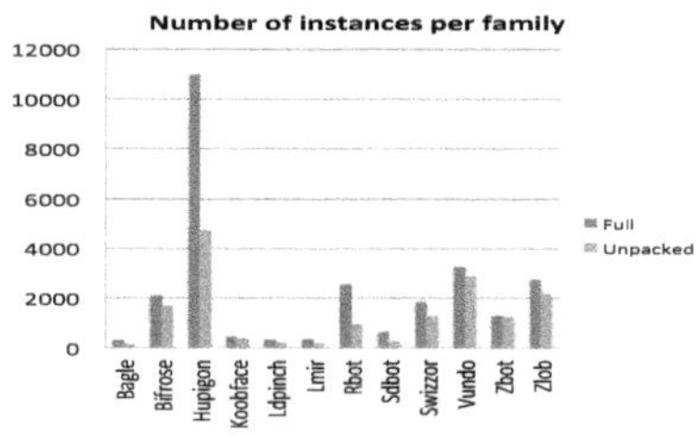

Figure 1: Imbalanced number of instances per family

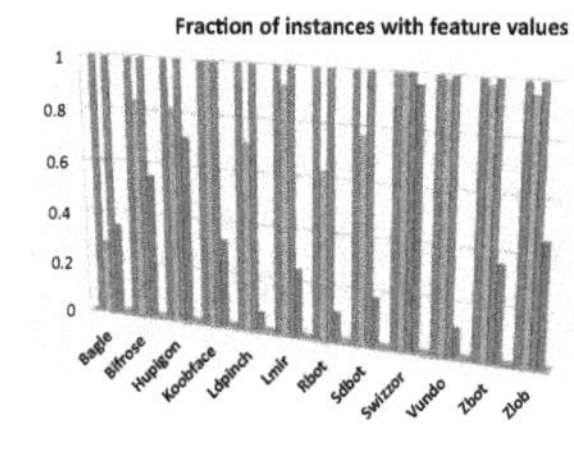

Figure 2: Fraction of instances with feature values per family

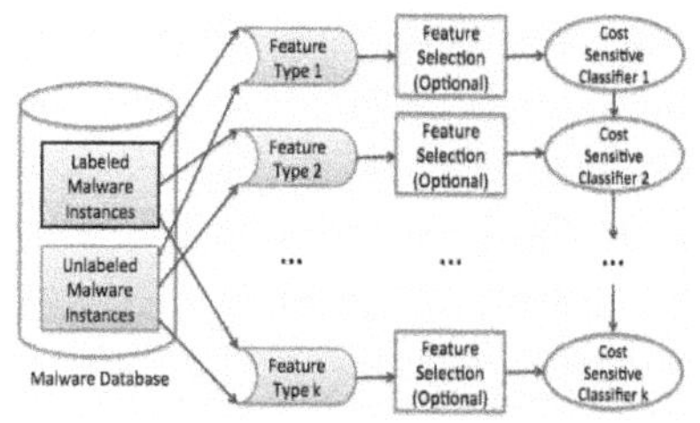

Figure 3: A unified malware classification framework

work exploits the structural information inherent among these unlabeled samples when training malware classifiers.

We extract various types of features from malware programs. There have been a large literature dedicated to discovering powerful features for malware detection or classification. In principle, our framework can integrate all these different types of features together, and provide a high-quality malware classifier based on their collective efforts. For each type of features extracted from malware programs, we may need to perform feature selection before training a classifier on them, because for some types of malware features, the number of features is so large that a classifier trained on all of them does not perform efficiently in practice, and for some classifiers, having more features does not necessarily mean that its performance is better than that when only a small number of features are used [40].

Once we have decided what features to use for each feature type, we use these features collected from both labeled and unlabeled malware instances to train a malware classifier. In parlance of machine learning, this process is semi-supervised learning. Semi-supervised learning contrasts with supervised learning, which relies on only labeled data when training a classifier. When labeled data are costly to obtain, the performance of supervised learning usually suffers because the distribution of labeled data used in the training dataset may not be representative of the true distribution of the new instances coming later. By contrast, semi-supervised learning exploits the structural information inherent in the large amount of unlabeled data to approximate better the true distribution of the instances which we will need to classify later. A fundamental assumption behind semi-supervised learning is that if two instances appear in the same cluster, they are likely to belong to the same class [6]. Based on this assumption, a semi-supervised classifier either propagates labeling information from labeled instances to those unlabeled ones belonging to the same cluster, or searches for classification boundaries through only sparse areas.

Another key component of our framework is the cost sensitiveness of the malware classifier we train on each type of features. When searching for an optimal classifier for a specific type of malware features, we apply the Neyman-Pearson criterion, which tries to maximize the detection rate under the constraint that the false positive rate must be no greater than a certain threshold [31, 4]. To enforce the Neyman-Pearson criterion, we use a cost-sensitive classifier with adjustable penalty weights on different types of classification errors. We search for an optimal setting from the parameter space of these weights, and use cross-validation techniques to ensure that the Neyman-Pearson criterion should be met.

With multiple individual classifiers, each of them may have its own opinion when we apply it on a new malware variant. As we may have missing features for a feature type, we assume that its corresponding classifier classifies it as negative. This naturally leads to a classifier ensemble based on the 'OR' rule: if any classifier decides that a new variant should belong to a specific malware family, the ensemble of classifiers believes it is a variant of that family; only all classifiers decide it is a negative sample does the ensemble classifier classifies it as negative. Such an 'OR' decision rule can be easily translated into a *sequence* of malware classifiers, each of which is trained on a specific type of malware features. If any of the classifiers decides a new sample is positive, the ensemble classifier terminates by flagging it as positive; only if the malware variant passes the tests of all individual classifiers can it be flagged as negative.

We further propose the chain Neyman-Pearson criterion, which is applicable to multiple classifiers that work in tandem. Under the chain Neyman-Pearson criterion, a dynamic programming method is used to spread the overall false positive rate allowed for the ensemble classifier over all the individual cost-sensitive classifiers as the constraints on their false positive rates.

We now theoretically analyze the ensemble classifier based on the 'OR' rule. Regarding the 'OR' rule that combines multiple classifiers, we have the following proposition about its Vapnik-Chervonenkis (VC) dimension, which measures the capacity of a classifier [36]:

Proposition 1. *Consider a hypothesis space H over domain $\mathbf{X} = \{0,1\}^n$, which is a set of $\{0,1\}$-valued functions. For each $h \in H$ and $\mathbf{x} = (x_1, x_2, ..., x_n) \in \mathbf{X}$, we have $h(\mathbf{x}) = \prod_{i=1}^{n} x_i$. The VC-dimension of H is then 2.*

PROOF. Consider two points in $\mathbf{X}$, $\mathbf{x}_0 = \mathbf{0}$ and $\mathbf{x}_1 \neq \mathbf{0}$. Clearly, any $h \in H$ can shatter the two points. However, for any three distinct points in $\mathbf{X}$, there must be at least two of them each containing at least one non-zero element. No hypothesis in H can shatter these two points.

We further have the following about the VC-dimension of the classifier ensemble combined with the 'OR' rule.

Proposition 2. *Consider a set of k binary classifiers, whose VC-dimensions are summed up to d. The VC-dimension of the classifier ensemble combined with the 'OR' rule is upper bounded by $(d+2)\log_2[3e(k+1)^2]$.*

PROOF. The k binary classifiers combined with the 'OR' rule can be deemed as a feed-forward architecture with $k+1$ computation nodes. The sum of all the computation nodes in this architecture is $d+2$ (note that the node corresponding to the 'OR' rule has a VC of 2, as seen from Proposition 1). According to Theorem 1 in [3], we have the number of realizable functions with m points, denoted by $\Delta(m)$, as follows:

$$\Delta(m) \leq ((k+1)em/(d+2))^{d+2}, \text{for } m \geq d+2. \quad (1)$$

We next show that if $m = (d+2)\log_2[3e(k+1)^2]$, it holds that $\Delta(m) < 2^m$. Note that:

$$\Delta((d+2)\log_2[3e(k+1)^2]) = [(k+1)e\log_2[3e(k+1)^2]]^{d+2}.$$

On the other hand, we have:

$$2^{(d+2)\log_2[3e(k+1)^2]} = [3e(k+1)^2]^{d+2}. \quad (2)$$

As we have both $\log_2(3e) < 3$ and $\log_2(k+1)^2 < 3k$ for $k \geq 1$. We thus have $\Delta(m) < 2^m$ when $m = (d+2)\log_2[3e(k+1)^2]$. Hence, the VC-dimension of the ensemble classifier is upper bounded by $(d+2)\log_2[3e(k+1)^2]$.

Therefore, the VC-dimension of the ensemble classifier is dominated by factor $d+2$, suggesting that the simple 'OR' rule does not improve significantly the capacity of the original set of classifiers, which agrees well with our intuition. Hence, our malware classification framework relies on individual classifiers that are sufficiently complicated in dividing malware families. To this end, we use the popular SVM classifier, whose VC dimension can be very high or even infinite when equipped with the radial basis kernel [5].

4. TRAINING INDIVIDUAL CLASSIFIERS

With the set of features chosen for each type of malware features, we prefer a classifier that is capable of not only performing semi-supervised learning but also having tunable parameters to impose different costs associated with different types of classification errors. Due to the extensibility of SVM for achieving both semi-supervised and cost-sensitive learning, it is used as the bedrock of individual malware classifiers in our framework. Consider two datasets, $\mathcal{D}_l = \{\langle \mathbf{x_i}, y_i \rangle\}_{i=1,...,n_l}$ where $y_i \in \{+1, -1\}$ and $\mathcal{D}_u = \{\mathbf{x_j^*}\}_{j=1,...,n_u}$, which contain labeled and unlabeled data, respectively. In order to train an SVM-type of classifier, we first project $\mathbf{x_i}$ or $\mathbf{x_j^*}$ into a Hilbert space with a mapping $\Phi : \mathbb{R}^d \to \mathcal{H}$, where d is the dimension of the feature space. In this Hilbert space, we search for a hyperplane with parameters $\mathbf{w}$ and b that minimizes the sum of margin errors, which are represented as ξ_i and ξ_j^*, respectively, for labeled and unlabeled training samples. Assuming that $I_+ = \{i : y_i = +1\}$, $I_- = \{i : y_i = -1\}$, $J_+ = \{j : y_j^* = +1\}$ and $J_- = \{j : y_j^* = -1\}$, the objective function is given by:

$$\begin{aligned} \min_{\mathbf{w}, b, \xi, \xi^*, \mathbf{y}^*} V(\mathbf{w}, b, \xi, \xi^*, \mathbf{y}^*) &= \frac{1}{2}||\mathbf{w}||^2 + \\ & C\rho \sum_{i \in I_+} \xi_i + C \sum_{i \in I_-} \xi_i + \\ & C^*\rho^* \sum_{j \in J_+} \xi_j^* + C^* \sum_{j \in J_-} \xi_j^* \quad (3) \end{aligned}$$

subject to:

$$\begin{aligned} y_i(\langle \mathbf{w}, \Phi(\mathbf{x_i}) \rangle_{\mathcal{H}} + b) \geq 1 - \xi_i, & \quad \forall \mathbf{x_i} \in \mathbf{X_l}, i = 1, ..., n_l \\ y_j^*(\langle \mathbf{w}, \Phi(\mathbf{x_j^*}) \rangle_{\mathcal{H}} + b) \geq 1 - \xi_j^*, & \quad \forall \mathbf{x_j^*} \in \mathbf{X_u}, j = 1, ..., n_u \\ \xi_i \geq 0, & \quad \forall i = 1, ..., n_l \\ \xi_j^* \geq 0, & \quad \forall j = 1, ..., n_u \\ y_j^* \in \{-1, +1\}, & \quad \forall j = 1, ..., n_u \end{aligned} \quad (4)$$

where C and C^* represent the cost parameters associated with margin errors induced by labeled and unlabeled training samples, respectively, and ρ and ρ^* are the cost ratios between margin errors on different sides induced by labeled and unlabeled training samples, respectively.

Our framework uses the *radial basis kernel* $k(\mathbf{x}, \mathbf{x}') = e^{-\frac{||\mathbf{x}-\mathbf{x}'||^2}{\sigma}}$. Moreover, we let C^* always be C and ρ^* be a constant. Hence, we have three tunable parameters C, ρ, and σ. Given fixed C, ρ, and σ, the current implementation of our framework uses `SVM-Light` [34] to solve Equation (3), although other alternative packages such as `libsvm` [17] can also be used here. In our experiments later, we always set ρ^* to the default value given by `SVM-Light`, although in principle this parameter can also be tuned.

Next, we consider how to search for the optimal configuration, where a *configuration* means a combination of tunable parameters C, ρ, and σ in Equation (3). For a given malware classifier, its performance can be evaluated based on both its false positive rate and its detection rate, which leads to a bi-criteria optimization problem. As it is a conflicting task to minimize the false positive rate while maximizing the detection rate, we apply the Neyman-Pearson criterion [31], which seeks for a classifier that maximizes the detection rate under the constraint that its false positive rate be no greater than a certain threshold. As we do not have a closed-form formula about the detection rate and the false positive rate of a classifier based on Equation (3), we resort to cross-validation to enforce the Neyman-Pearson criterion. More specifically, we divide the training data into m folds $\{F_i\}_{i=1,2,...,m}$. Each time, we use one of the folds F_i as the test data, and the remaining F_{-i} for the purpose of training. Given any configuration, we train a classifier on F_{-i} by solving Equation (3) and test its performance on F_i. For brevity, we use $\alpha_i(C, \rho, \sigma)$ and $\beta_i(C, \rho, \sigma)$ to denote the false positive rate and the detection rate of the classifier trained from F_{-i} on testing data F_i, respectively, under configuration (C, ρ, σ).

The Neyman-Pearson criterion can be written as follows:

$$\begin{aligned} & \text{argmax}_{C,\rho,\sigma} \tilde{\beta}(C, \rho, \sigma), & (5) \\ \text{subject to:} \quad & \tilde{\alpha}(C, \rho, \sigma) \leq \alpha^*, & (6) \\ \text{where } \tilde{\beta}(C, \rho, \sigma) &= \frac{1}{m}\sum_{i=1}^{m} \beta_i(C, \rho, \sigma) \\ \tilde{\alpha}(C, \rho, \sigma) &= \frac{1}{m}\sum_{i=1}^{m} \alpha_i(C, \rho, \sigma), \end{aligned}$$

and α^* is the threshold on the average false positive rate.

In order to compare two configurations $g_1 = (C_1, \rho_1, \sigma_1)$ and $g_2 = (C_2, \rho_2, \sigma_2)$, we say that $g_1 \prec g_2$ or g_1 *outperforms* g_2 if either of the following two cases hold:

$$\begin{aligned} \text{Case 1:} \quad & \tilde{\alpha}(C_1, \rho_1, \sigma_1) \leq \alpha^* \\ & \tilde{\alpha}(C_2, \rho_2, \sigma_2) \leq \alpha^*, \text{ and} \\ & \tilde{\beta}(C_1, \rho_1, \sigma_1) > \tilde{\beta}(C_2, \rho_2, \sigma_2) & (7) \\ \text{Case 2:} \quad & \tilde{\alpha}(C_2, \rho_2, \sigma_2) > \alpha^* \text{ and} \\ & \tilde{\alpha}(C_1, \rho_1, \sigma_1) < \tilde{\alpha}(C_2, \rho_2, \sigma_2). & (8) \end{aligned}$$

We also say that $g_1 \equiv g_2$ or g_1 *is equivalent to* g_2 if $\tilde{\alpha}(C_1, \rho_1, \sigma_1) = \tilde{\alpha}(C_2, \rho_2, \sigma_2)$ and $\tilde{\beta}(C_1, \rho_1, \sigma_1) = \tilde{\beta}(C_2, \rho_2, \sigma_2)$.

Accordingly, we say that g is *the best configuration* in a configuration set if it outperforms or is equivalent to any other configuration in the set. Originally, we planned to use the coordinate descent algorithm presented in [7] to search the best configuration. However, as we are not sure how many trials are needed for the algorithm to converge starting from any random point, the algorithm may spend a significant time on local search before exploring the entire configuration space. Hence, we decide to use the genetic algorithm, which performs local search and global search simultaneously, to find the best configuration for a given individual classifier. We treat parameters C, ρ, and σ as three types of chromosomes of the "population". In each generation, we select the k best configurations to breed the next generation. More specifically, given the current generation of the population, the next generation is reproduced as follows: **(1) Crossover:** For any two of the top k configurations, we average the values of each chromosome type. The intuition here is that the middle point between two good configurations is likely to be good. **(2) Partial mutation:** For each of the top k configurations, we replace any of its chromosomes with a randomly generated value of the corresponding type. Partial mutation explores points that differ from good configurations at only one chromosome. **(3) Full mutation:** We randomly generate values for all three types of chromosomes; full mutation prevents the search from converging to local optima. Among these three different reproduction schemes, crossover and partial mutation can be deemed as local search, as they search areas that are close to those configurations that are already found to be good; by contrast, the full mutation scheme regenerates a totally new configuration, which is used to explore good configurations in new regions at a global level.

The fitness function of a configuration $g = (C, \rho, \sigma)$ is defined as follows:

$$f(g) = \tilde{\beta}(C,\rho,\sigma) \cdot \delta(\tilde{\alpha}(C,\rho,\sigma) \leq \alpha^*) - \tilde{\alpha}(C,\rho,\sigma) \cdot \delta(\tilde{\alpha}(C,\rho,\sigma) > \alpha^*), \quad (9)$$

where $\delta(x)$ is 1 if x is true or 0 otherwise.

The algorithm is illustrated in Figure 4. The genetic algorithm has the following advantages. First, as mentioned earlier, it performs both local search and global search in each generation. This prevents the algorithm from getting stuck at local optima while improving the overall quality of the population from generation to generation. Second, both parameter k, which is used to control the number of good configurations from which to reproduce the next generation, and the number of generations that are eventually reproduced can be used to control the number of times that the search takes place. This thus provides a knob to decide how much time would be spent on searching the optimal configuration, given the computational resources available. Finally, the genetic algorithm can be easily parallelized by distributing the reproduction task over multiple processors.

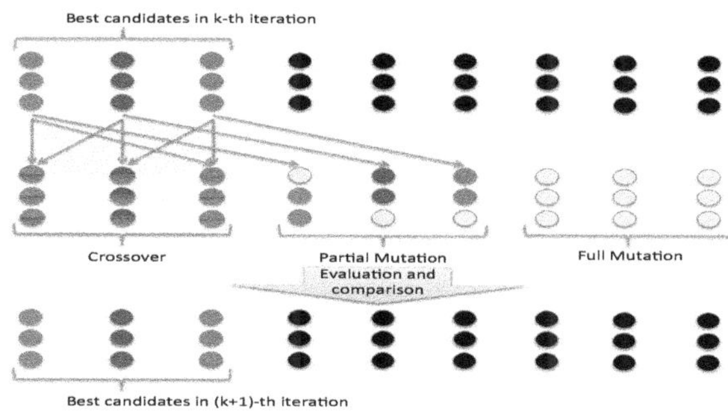

Figure 4: Illustration of genetic algorithm for searching optimal parameters

5. ENSEMBLE OF CLASSIFIERS

For each type of features, we can train a classifier as discussed in Section 4. The question that naturally follows is: given the classification results from multiple individual classifiers on a new malware instance, how should we decide whether it belongs to a specific family? One widely used rule is decision by majority, that is, the same decision made by the majority of the classifiers is chosen as the final verdict. The problem with the majority rule, however, is that we have to collect all types of features that are fed to these individual classifiers, which make independent decisions on classification. This can be time consuming, as for some types of features, it takes significant time and resources to collect their values from a new malware variant.

Due to this concern, our framework uses a simple 'OR' rule: as long as any classifier decides that a new malware instance belong to a specific family, the framework classifies it into that family. With such an 'OR' rule, our malware classification framework can draw classification results from individual classifiers in a sequential manner. As long as one classifier classifies the malware instance as positive, the framework does not need to consider the classification results by subsequent classifiers, and it is thus unnecessary to collect their corresponding types of features. In order to train the ensemble classifier as described, we enforce the *chain Neyman-Pearson criterion* on individual classifiers, which will be explained next.

5.1 Chain Neyman-Pearson Criterion

Suppose that the training data are divided into m folds $\{F_i\}_{i=1,2,...,m}$. Next, we train an individual classifier for the t-th type of features from each of $\{F_{-i}\}_{i=1,2,...m}$ and evaluate its performance on instances in F_i. Also suppose that from each malware sample we can extract T types of features. We now discuss how to modify the algorithm discussed in the previous section to train an individual classifier for the t-th type of features where $1 \leq t \leq T$.

Let $F_i^+ \subseteq F_i$ and $F_i^- \subseteq F_i$ be the set of positive and negative instances in fold F_i, respectively. Given any configuration $g = (C, \rho, \sigma)$ for the t-th type of features, let the set of positives that the candidate classifier trained from F_{-i} identifies from test data F_i be $\Theta_{t,i}(g)$. Define $\alpha^*_{1\to t}$ as:

$$\alpha^*_{1\to t} = \{\alpha^*_1, \alpha^*_2, ..., \alpha^*_t\}, \quad (12)$$

where $0 \leq \alpha^*_1 \leq \alpha^*_2 \leq ... \leq \alpha^*_t \leq 1$. Sequence $\alpha^*_{1\to t}$ contains false positive rate thresholds that are used to train the individual classifiers corresponding to the first t feature types.

We define $\Lambda(i,t)|_{\alpha^*_{1\to t}}$ and $\Delta(i,t)|_{\alpha^*_{1\to t}}$ recursively as in Figure 5. Hence, $\Lambda(i,t)|_{\alpha^*_{1\to t}}$ and $\Delta(i,t)|_{\alpha^*_{1\to t}}$ represent the *accumulative* set of true positives and false positives in the i-th fold, respectively, by the sequence of individual classifiers trained from the first t feature types under false positive thresholds $\alpha^*_{1\to t}$. The definitions of $\Lambda(i,t)|_{\alpha^*_{1\to t}}$ and $\Delta(i,t)|_{\alpha^*_{1\to t}}$ depend on $g^*_t|_{\alpha^*_{1\to t}}$, which, defined in Figure 6, is the best configuration found for the t-th feature type when the sequence of false positive rate thresholds used to train the individual classifiers for the first t feature types is $\alpha^*_{1\to t}$.

Hence, in contrast to the original Neyman-Pearson criterion given in Equation (5), we apply the chain Neyman-Pearson criterion: for the individual classifier trained for the t-th feature type, we search for the configuration with

$$\Lambda(i,t)|_{\alpha^*_{1\to t}} = \begin{cases} \Lambda(i,t-1)|_{\alpha^*_{1\to t-1}} \cup (\Theta_{t,i}(g^*_t|_{\alpha^*_{1\to t}}) \cap F^+_i) & t > 0 \\ \emptyset & t = 0 \end{cases} \tag{10}$$

$$\Delta(i,t)|_{\alpha^*_{1\to t}} = \begin{cases} \Delta(i,t-1)|_{\alpha^*_{1\to t-1}} \cup (\Theta_{t,i}(g^*_t|_{\alpha^*_{1\to t}}) \cap F^-_i) & t > 0 \\ \emptyset & t = 0 \end{cases} \tag{11}$$

Figure 5: Definition of $\Lambda(i,t)|_{\alpha^*_{1\to t}}$ and $\Delta(i,t)|_{\alpha^*_{1\to t}}$

$$\begin{aligned} g^*_t|_{\alpha^*_{1\to t}} &= \text{argmax}_{(C,\rho,\sigma)}\tilde{\beta}_t(C,\rho,\sigma)|_{\alpha^*_{1\to t}}, \\ \text{subject to:} & \quad \tilde{\alpha}_t(C,\rho,\sigma)|_{\alpha^*_{1\to t}} \le \alpha^*_t, \\ \text{with } \tilde{\beta}_t(C,\rho,\sigma)|_{\alpha^*_{1\to t}} &= \frac{1}{m}\sum_{i=1}^{m} \frac{|(\Theta_{t,i}(C,\rho,\sigma) \cap F^+_i) \cup \Lambda(i,t-1)|_{\alpha^*_{1\to t}}|}{|F^+_i|}, \\ \tilde{\alpha}_t(C,\rho,\sigma)|_{\alpha^*_{1\to t}} &= \frac{1}{m}\sum_{i=1}^{m} \frac{|(\Theta_{t,i}(C,\rho,\sigma) \cap F^-_i) \cup \Delta(i,t-1)|_{\alpha^*_{1\to t}}|}{|F^-_i|}, \end{aligned}$$

Figure 6: Definition of $g^*_t|_{\alpha^*_{1\to t}}$

the highest accumulative detection rate over the first t feature types under the constraint that the accumulative false positive rate over the first t feature types is no higher than α^*_t. With redefined $\tilde{\alpha}_t(C,\rho,\sigma)$ and $\tilde{\beta}_t(C,\rho,\sigma)$, we keep the same method of comparing two configurations as described in Section 4. Hence, given the current false positive rate threshold α^*_t, the algorithm presented in Section 4 can be used to train each individual classifier sequentially based on the chain Neyman-Pearson criterion.

5.2 Dynamic Programming

The application of the chain Neyman-Pearson criterion requires us to know the sequence of false positive thresholds, $\{\alpha^*_1, \alpha^*_2, ..., \alpha^*_T\}$, where T gives the total number of feature types in the classification framework. Given that the overall false positive rate threshold is α^*, we then should have $\alpha^*_T = \alpha^*$. Clearly, how to set these false positive rate thresholds affects the performance of the ensemble of classifiers trained based on the chain Neyman-Pearson criterion. In an extreme case, if we let α^*_1 be α^* and we can find a classifier based on the first feature type that has a false positive rate equal to α^*, then for the remaining feature types, the classifiers trained based on the chain Neyman-Pearson should not lead to any false positives in order for the ensemble of classifiers to have a false positive rate no greater than α^*.

Searching the continuous space of $\{\alpha^*_1, \alpha^*_2, ..., \alpha^*_T\}$ for an optimal configuration can be computationally prohibitive, as these parameters are dependent on each other. Moreover, during the search process, we want to tease out those features that contribute little to the accumulative classification performance, which is typically done in a separate feature selection process. To overcome these challenges, we propose a dynamic programming method, as illustrated in Figure 7, to search an optimal setting of $\alpha^*_{1\to T}$. Consider the following set of false positive rate thresholds that should be satisfied by individual classifiers,

$$\{0\alpha^*/D, 1\alpha^*/D, 2\alpha^*/D, ..., D\alpha^*/D\}, \tag{13}$$

where D is a predefined parameter, and we let the false positive rate thresholds in the sequence $\{\alpha^*_1, \alpha^*_2, ..., \alpha^*_T\}$ take values only from this set. For brevity, we define $\mathcal{D} = \{0, 1, ..., D\}$.

Threshold	Feature 1	...	Feature j-1	Feature j	...	Feature T
0α*/D	g*₁(0α*/D)		g*ⱼ₋₁(0α*/D)	g*ⱼ(0α*/D)		X
1α*/D	g*₁(1α*/D)		g*ⱼ₋₁(1α*/D)	g*ⱼ(1α*/D)		X
...	...		...	...		X
(i-1)α*/D	g*₁((i-1)α*/D)		g*ⱼ₋₁((i-1)α*/D)	g*ⱼ((i-1)α*/D)		X
iα*/D	g*₁(iα*/D)		g*ⱼ₋₁(iα*/D)	**g*ⱼ(iα*/D)**		X
...	...		...	...		X
α*	g*₁(α*)		g*ⱼ₋₁(α*)	g*ⱼ(α*)		g*_T(α*)

Figure 7: Dynamic programming for searching optimal configurations. $g^*_j(i\alpha^*/D)$, which is the best configuration when the false positive rate threshold over all the first j features is $i\alpha^*/D$, is obtained based on the best configurations in the previous column, $g^*_j(k\alpha^*/D)$ where $k = 0, 1, ..., i$. For the last feature (i.e., feature T), only the configuration under false positive rate threshold α^* needs to be computed.

Consider the t-th feature type, where $1 \le t \le T$, and any $d \in \mathcal{D}$. Given that the false positive rate threshold for the t-th feature type under the chain Neyman-Pearson criterion is $d\alpha^*/D$, we use the equations in Figure 8 to find recursively the optimal threshold for the false positive rate of the $(t-1)$-th feature type, which is $prev(t,d) \cdot \alpha^*/D$. The crux here is that when we search the optimal value for $prev(t,d)$, we check all possible false positive rate thresholds for the previous feature type (note that that previous threshold should be no greater than the current threshold), and use the one that leads to the best configuration for the current feature type under the chain Neyman-Pearson criterion. When we calculate the best configuration $g^*_t|_{d,d'}$ when the current and the last false positive rate thresholds are $d\alpha^*/D$ and $d'\alpha^*/D$, respectively, we keep track of both $\Lambda(i,t,d)$ and $\Delta(i,t,d)$, which represent the set of true positives and false positives, respectively, under the condition that the current false positive threshold is $d\alpha^*/D$ and the previous false positive thresholds are set to the values that recursively lead to the best configuration for the current feature type t.

The calculation can be done in an approach based on dynamic programming. For the first feature type (i.e., $t = 1$),

$$
\begin{aligned}
prev(t,d) &= \begin{cases} \text{argmax}_{d' \in \mathcal{D}} & g_t^*|_{d,d'} & t > 1 \\ & -1 & t = 1 \end{cases} \\
\text{where } \; g_t^*|_{d,d'} &= \text{argmax}_{(C,\rho,\sigma)} \tilde{\beta}_t(C,\rho,\sigma)|_{d'}, \\
\text{subject to:} & \quad \tilde{\alpha}_t(C,\rho,\sigma)|_{d'} \le d\alpha^*/D, \\
\text{with } \tilde{\beta}_t(C,\rho,\sigma)|_{d'} &= \frac{1}{m}\sum_{i=1}^{m} \frac{|(\Theta_{t,i}(C,\rho,\sigma) \cap F_i^+) \cup \Lambda(i,t-1,d')|}{|F_i^+|}, \\
\tilde{\alpha}_t(C,\rho,\sigma)|_{d'} &= \frac{1}{m}\sum_{i=1}^{m} \frac{|(\Theta_{t,i}(C,\rho,\sigma) \cap F_i^-) \cup \Delta(i,t-1,d')|}{|F_i^-|},
\end{aligned}
$$

Figure 8: Definition of $prev(t,d)$ and $g_t^*|_{d,d'}$

$$
\begin{aligned}
\Lambda(i,t,d) &= \begin{cases} \Lambda(i,t-1,prev(t,d)) \cup (\Theta_{t,i}(g_t^*|_{d,prev(t,d)}) \cap F_i^+) & t > 0 \\ \emptyset & t = 0 \end{cases} \\
\Delta(i,t,d) &= \begin{cases} \Delta(i,t-1,prev(t,d)) \cup (\Theta_{t,i}(g_t^*|_{d,prev(t,d)}) \cap F_i^-) & t > 0 \\ \emptyset & t = 0 \end{cases}
\end{aligned}
$$

Figure 9: Definition of $\Lambda(i,t,d)$ and $\Delta(i,t,d)$

we calculate the best configuration for each possible false positive rate threshold $d\alpha^*/D$, where $d \in \mathcal{D}$. Once the best configurations for the $(t-1)$-th feature type have been found, we search the best configuration for the t-th feature type for each possible false positive rate threshold $d\alpha^*/D$, where $d \in \mathcal{D}$. For any such d, we check the d possible false positive rate thresholds for the previous feature type (i.e., $0, 1\alpha^*/D, 2\alpha^*/D, ..., d\alpha^*/D$), and assuming that the previous classifier uses its best configuration for each of these false positive rate thresholds, we look for the best configuration for the current feature type.

It is noted that for the last feature type, i.e., the T-th feature type, we only need to consider the false positive rate threshold $D\alpha^*/D$. Define an *operation* to be an execution of the genetic algorithm, which is used to solve Equation (12). We have the following proposition:

Proposition 3. *If the dynamic programming algorithm performs as described, it takes* $2(D+1)+(T-2)\cdot\frac{(D+1)(D+2)}{2}$ *operations to calculate the best configurations.*

PROOF. For the first feature type, the algorithm performs $D+1$ operations that calculate the best configurations, each for a threshold $d\alpha^*/D$ with $d \in \mathcal{D}$. For the last feature type (i.e., the T-th feature type), the best configurations are only searched under the false positive rate threshold $D\alpha^*/D$; as the previous threshold for the $(T-1)$-th feature type can be any of $d\alpha^*/D$ with $0 \le d \le D$, $D+1$ operations that calculate the best configurations are performed. For the k-th feature type where $2 \le k \le T-1$, when the current false positive rate threshold is $d\alpha^*/D$, d operations that calculate the best configurations are performed (note that the previous threshold should be no greater than $d\alpha^*/D$). Hence, for each of these feature types, $\sum_{d=0}^{D} d = (D+1)(D+2)/2$ operations are performed. In total, there are thus $2(D+1)+(T-2)\cdot\frac{(D+1)(D+2)}{2}$ operations used to calculate the best configurations.

Implementation. If exhaustive search for optimal configurations were allowed, the detection rates with the configurations in the matrix in Figure 7 would be (weakly) monotonically improving from left top to right bottom. Due to a limited number of tries when searching for an optimal configuration with the genetic algorithm, it is however possible that no feasible configuration can be found or the configuration found has a false positive rate not falling into the current threshold range. In such circumstances, extra efforts are needed to ensure that classification performances of the entries in the matrix are indeed monotonically improving.

Let matrix M contain the configurations found; that is to say, $M(d,t)$ gives the configuration (α, β) found when the threshold on the false positive rate is $d\alpha^*/D$ for the t-th feature type; if no configuration is found, $M(d,t)$ is `null`. To optimize the process of finding the best configurations, we update the t-th column in two passes when the search for the t-th feature type is finished:

First pass: Consider the following example. The three thresholds on false positive rates are 0.01, 0.02, and 0.03. Suppose that the corresponding configurations found are (0.005, 0.8), (0.001, 0.99), and (0.025, 0.9). Hence, both the first two configurations have a false positive rate falling in the range [0, 0.01]. In this case, we use the second one to overrule the first one because it leads to a higher detection rate. Hence, in the first pass, for the configuration found for the d-th threshold, we proceed as follows:

(a.1) *Its false positive rate is higher than* $d\alpha^*/D$. As this violates the Neyman-Pearson criterion, we let $M(d,t)$ be `null`.

(a.2) *Its false positive rate is no greater than* $d\alpha^*/D$ *but higher than* $(d-1)\alpha^*/D$. In this case, we keep the current solution found for this threshold.

(a.3) *Its false positive rate is no greater than* $(d-1)\alpha^*/D$. Let the false positive rate of the solution found be r. We calculate $d' = \lceil rD/\alpha^* \rceil$ and compare the configuration previously found under the false positive rate threshold $d'\alpha^*/D$. If the current solution outperforms the previous configuration, we replace the previous configuration under the false positive rate threshold $d'\alpha^*/D$ with the current solution, and set the current solution under the false positive rate threshold $d\alpha^*/D$ to be `null`.

Second pass: Using the same example, after the first pass, the three configurations become (0.001, 0.99), `null`, and (0.025, 0.9). Note that albeit having a higher false positive rate, the third configuration has a lower detection rate, suggesting that it is dominated by the first configuration. Hence, in the second pass, we ensure that all configurations in the matrix M are ordered by the performances. Let $\max_\beta M_{i,j}$ be the maximum detection rate among the first i rows and j columns of matrix M. Without loss of generality, if $M_{i,j}$ is `null`, its detection rate is assumed to be 0.

For the d-th configuration where $1 \leq d \leq D$, let its detection rate be $\beta_{d,t}$. We have the following cases.

(b.1) $\max_\beta M_{d,t-1} \geq \max_\beta M_{d-1,t} \geq \beta_{d,t}$. This means that classification from the current feature type does not help improve the detection accuracy. Hence, we *inherit* the classification results from the previous feature type with the same false positive rate threshold without using the current feature type.

(b.2) $\max_\beta M_{d,t-1} \geq \max_\beta M_{d-1,t} \geq \beta_{d,t}$. This implies that the current feature type helps but increasing the false positive rate threshold does not help. We thus *deactivate* the configurations found from the current threshold for this feature type and will not consider any further results based on $M(d,t)$. We say that $M(d,t)$ is now *inactive*.

(b.3) $\beta_{d,t} > \max\{\max_\beta M_{d,t-1}, \max_\beta M_{d-1,t}\}$. This means that both the current threshold and the feature type help improving the detection accuracy, and we thus keep its classification results.

After the two passes, we ensure that performances of the configurations in matrix M, if they are active, must increase (weakly) monotonically as we increase the false positive rate threshold or add more feature types. These two passes are performed immediately for each feature type once the configurations are learned based on the chain Neyman-Pearson criterion under all the false positive rate thresholds. Due to the optimization applied in our implementation, the count stated in Proposition 3 provides only an upper bound on the real number of operations that have been executed.

It is noted that the overhead in feature extraction varies with the type of the features. When we train the ensemble classifier under the chain Neyman-Pearson criterion, feature groups are ordered based on their relative extraction overhead in an non-decreasing manner. Hence, costly features are used only if the cheap ones do not have sufficient discriminative power in classifying the malware family being considered.

6. EXPERIMENTS

We use those unpacked samples in the malware dataset described in Section 2 for performance evaluation, although in practice packed samples can be unpacked first before extracting features from them. Due to limited resources available, we extract features only for those samples that have been labeled. In total we have 15,494 labeled unpacked samples for experiments, and their family breakdown is as follows: `Bagle` (152), `Bifrose` (1677), `Hupigon` (4748), `Koobface` (371), `Ldpinch` (190), `Lmir` (181), `Rbot` (923), `Sdbot` (253), `Swizzor` (1276), `Vundo` (2852), `Zbot` (1231), and `Zlob` (2140). A classifier is built for each of these families, based on the one-against-all rule, which treats samples from the family under study as positive and all others as negative.

Among all the samples, we randomly choose 80% of them for training, and the remaining 20% for testing. In the training dataset, 75% of them are marked as unlabeled. When using the chain Neyman-Pearson criterion to train classifiers, we further divide the training dataset into five folds (i.e., $m = 5$ in Section 5.1), four of them used to search the best configurations and the remaining one used to evaluate the performance of a configuration. It is noted that during the training phase based on cross validation, the 20% of the test data are not available. Our task is to train a cost-sensitive classifier from the training dataset, and then label every instance in the test dataset. We set the false positive rate allowed for the ensemble classifier to be at most 5% (i.e., $\alpha^* = 0.05$). For the purpose of dynamic programming, we partition the overall false positive rate into 6 intervals, i.e., $D = 6$ in Equation (13).

Moreover, when using the genetic algorithm to search the optimal configuration, we generate candidate solutions for three generations, among which solutions in the first generation are randomly generated based on the full mutation scheme (see Figure 4). From the population of each generation, we choose the top three configurations for further reproduction. Hence, three new configurations are generated from crossover, and three others from partial mutation. In addition, three more are produced from full mutation. The size of the total population per generation is thus 9.

The six types of features mentioned in Section 2 are considered, `PE-num`, `PE-bool`, `Hexdump 2-gram`, `Objdump 1-gram`, `PIN 2-gram`, and `PIN SysCall`. We use the logistic regression method discussed in [40] to choose 100 features from each of the six feature types. When we search optimal configurations for each feature type, we order the six feature types based on the relative difficulty of obtaining their values. As both PE header features and `Hexdump 2-gram` features can be obtained in a deterministic manner, we consider them during the early phase of the classifier ensemble. `Objdump 1-gram` features require disassembly code of the executable programs, which can be obtained through static analysis. PIN features require dynamic execution of the programs, and are thus more difficult to obtain. Hence, we train individual classifiers sequentially according to the following order of the six feature types: `PE-num`, `PE-bool`, `Hexdump 2-gram`, `Objdump 1-gram`, `PIN 2-gram`, and `PIN SysCall`.

6.1 Classification Performance

Table 1 presents the average performances of the configurations found by our method over the five test folds in terms of false positive rates and detection rates. Clearly, for any of these malware families, it is not necessary to include all six feature types. For instance, for the `Swizzor`, `Zbot`, and `Zlob` families, only the features extracted from the PE headers are needed to classify their instances. This is desirable because for some feature types such as those from dynamic execution, it takes significant efforts to collect their feature values. Hence, our method based on the chain Neyman-Pearson criterion has the effect of selecting only those feature types that are useful for automated malware classification. Moreover, it is observed that classification of different malware families requires different types of features. For instance, `Hexdump 2-gram` features are only useful for the `Ldpinch` and the `Lmir` families but not the other ones. This is plausible

Table 1: **Performances trained under the chain Neyman-Pearson criterion. The numbers are the averages of 5-fold cross validation. '-' means that the feature type is not used. False positive rate threshold is 5%.**

Family	PE-num	PE-bool	Hexdump 2-gram	Objdump 1-gram	PIN 2-gram	PIN SysCall
Bagle	(0.34%, 91.3%)	(1.1%, 98.0%)	-	(1.6%, 100.0%)	-	-
Bifrose	(0.7%, 81.7%)	-	-	(2.0%, 91.2%)	(2.2%, 94.2%)	(2.5%, 95.8%)
Hupigon	(1.1%, 91.5%)	(1.9%, 98.4%)	-	-	-	(3.7%, 99.4%)
Koobface	(0.06%, 90.9%)	(0.09%, 94.6%)	-	(0.96%, 100%)	-	-
Ldpinch	(0.4%, 46.7%)	(1.9%, 83.1%)	(3.04%, 90.5%)	-	-	-
Lmir	(0.35%, 70.7%)	(0.4%, 92.8%)	(1.96%, 95%)	-	-	-
Rbot	(2.8%, 85.1%)	(3.2%, 91.5%)	-	-	-	(3.67%, 92.6%)
Sdbot	(1.2%, 58.3%)	(1.5%, 73.7%)	-	-	-	(1.6%, 76.5%)
Swizzor	(0.33%, 97.9%)	(0.5%, 99.7%)	-	-	-	-
Vundo	(0.33%, 95.6%)	(1.0%, 99.3%)	-	-	-	-
Zbot	(0.76%, 87.9%)	(1.6%, 92.2%)	-	-	(3.6%, 93.4%)	(4.0%, 96.0%)
Zlob	(1.5%, 98.6%)	(2.1%, 100.0%)	-	-	-	-

as the uniqueness of a malware family may manifest itself over only a specific subset of feature types. Our algorithm is able to find these distinguishing feature types.

Figure 10 shows the classification performance for each malware family. From Figure 10(1), we observe that the false positive rate for classifying the test samples in each malware family is no greater than the predefined threshold of 5% for each malware family, suggesting that the classifier ensemble trained is indeed able to enforce the Neyman-Pearson criterion. The detection rate per family is shown in Figure 10(2). For most of the families, we observe that the detection rate is above 90%, implying that the majority of the samples of these families can be identified by our method. For the `Sdbot` family, however, the detection rate is only around 70%. We note that for this family, during the training phase, our algorithm cannot find good configurations to achieve high classification accuracy anyway: the combination of PE header features and the `PIN-SysCall` features can only lead to an average detection rate of 76.5% based on 5-fold cross validation. Hence, the poor detection rate of `Sdbot` samples attributes to the six feature types used here which are unable to distinguish samples in the `Sdbot` family as effectively as those in the other ones. Comparing the detection rates in Figure 10(2) against those in Table 1, we find that the former are typically lower than the corresponding values by the classifier ensembles seen in Table 1. This is feasible as the detection rates in Figure 10(2) are obtained on the test data, which are invisible to the training phase; by contrast, during the training phase, we search configurations that lead to the highest detection rates under the false positive rate constraint using 5-fold cross validation, which are shown in Table 1.

For a classifier, let the number of true positives, false positives, true negatives, and false negatives be n_{tp}, n_{fp}, n_{tn} and n_{fn}, respectively. Its *precision* is $n_{tp}/(n_{tp}+n_{fp})$, and its *recall* $n_{tp}/(n_{tp}+n_{fn})$. The F-1 score, the harmonic mean of precision and recall, is $2n_{tp}/(2n_{tp}+n_{fp}+n_{fn})$. The precision, recall, and F-1 score of the classifier trained for each of the 12 malware families are shown in Figure 10(3). We note that the recall measures are high for most of the malware families (except the `Sdbot` family), because the recall measure is essentially the same as the detection rate. However, the precision measure can be low for some of the families, such as `Bagle`, `Ldpinch`, `Lmir`, and `Sdbot`. Common to these families is the fact that they are severely underrepresented, having a much smaller number of instances than the other families. Consider any malware family, whose samples comprise a fraction p of the entire dataset. Let the false positive rate and the detection rate of the classifier trained for this family be α and β, respectively. Then, we have:

$$\textit{precision} = \frac{p\beta}{(1-p)\alpha + p\beta} \leq \frac{1}{1+\alpha(1/p-1)}. \tag{14}$$

The inequality holds as $\beta \leq 1$, so if p is small, meaning that the malware family is significantly underrepresented, then $1/p - 1$ is large, and precision becomes small even though all positive samples can be detected successfully.

In some cases, however, it is important to have a classifier with high precision. For instance, if we need to study common characteristics shared by samples by a malware family, such as its unique string signatures, it is desirable to have a classifier that produces only a small fraction of false positives among the samples labeled as positive. For such cases, there are two solutions. First, we can use a smaller false positive rate in Equation (14), which can cancel the effect of $1/p-1$. For instance, we use a smaller false positive rate threshold 0.5%, and the classification performances for the `Ldpinch` and the `Lmir` families are shown as follows:

Measure	Ldpinch	Lmir
False positive rate	0.063%	0.16%
Detection rate	75.0%	88.6%
Precision	0.923	0.861
Recall	0.750	0.886
F1 Score	0.828	0.873

With a lower false positive rate threshold, the classifier trained by our framework reduces the false positive rate, and thus leads to a higher precision measure. Under this lower false positive rate threshold, the majority of the samples labeled as positive by the classifiers indeed belong to the malware families under study. For the `Lmir` family, although a false positive rate threshold of 0.5% is used, the detection rate is even higher than what we have observed when the false positive rate threshold is 5%. This results from the fluctuations due to randomness in searching for the optimal configurations by the genetic algorithm and the randomness in partitioning the dataset for training and testing.

An alternative way of training a classifier ensemble with a high precision measure is to slightly modify the chain Neyman-Pearson criterion: rather than ensuring that the accumulative false positive rate is no greater than a certain threshold, we search for configurations with the highest detection rates under the constraint that the precision measure should be no smaller than a predefined threshold. If such a threshold is set to be, say, 0.8, we expect the classifier to produce positive labels among which at least 80% of them are true positives.

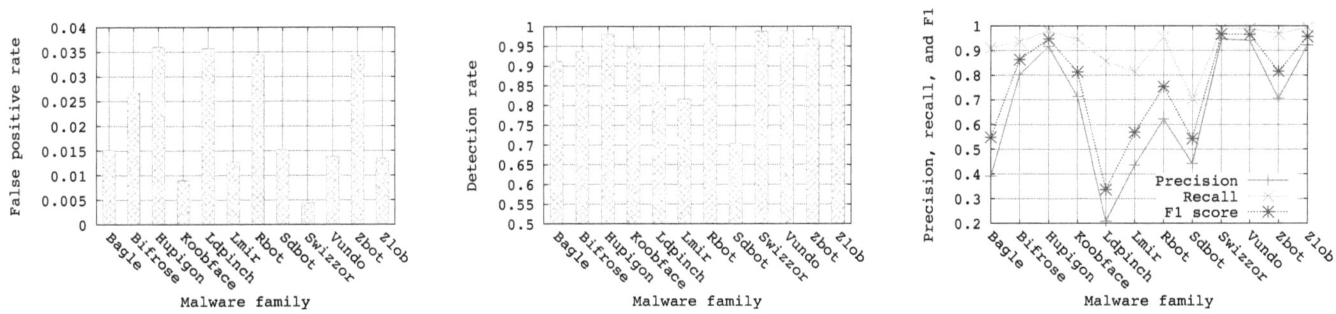

(1) False positive rate (2) Detection rate (3) F1 score

Figure 10: Performances of the classifiers trained under the chain Neyman-Pearson criterion

6.2 Performance Comparison

In the previous subsection, we have demonstrated the classification performance using the chain Neyman-Pearson criterion. Next we show how it compares against existing ensemble learning techniques. For the sake of performance comparison, we consider the following methods. (1) *Imputed*: We combine all the features used in the previous subsection together, and use the means of available values to impute those missing ones. We further use three standard classifiers, kNN, SVM, and decision trees (C4.5) to train classifiers from a subset of the imputed dataset. (2) *Boosting*: Using each of the three classifiers from (1) as the base learner, we further use the boosting method as the ensemble classifier. (3) *Bagging*: Using each of the three classifiers from (1) as the base learner, we further use the bagging method as the ensemble classifier. (4) *Stacking*: We stack all the three classifiers from (1) as the base learners together to create an ensemble classifier. Due to space limitation, we omit the details of these methods here and refer interested readers to the existing literature (e.g., [29, 8, 24]). For fair comparison, we use the implementations of these methods from a third-party machine learning software, `Orange` [23]. In order for other researchers to reproduce our results, we use the default settings in `Orange` in all the experiments, except that for the stacking scheme, we use kNN rather than Naive Bayes as the meta learner. Using the latter leads to very poor performance for malware classification (not shown here due to space limitation), and this has also been observed in our earlier work [40].

In a new set of experiments, 80% of samples are labeled and used to train the classifier and the remaining 20% are used for testing. Note that in the experiments, all the samples in the training dataset are labeled. The classification results are shown in Table 2. It is observed that none of the standard approaches is able to produce false positive rates below 5% for all the families: for each of these schemes, at least five families have false positive rates higher than 5%. Even with more labeled samples for training, the number of malware families with a detection rate below 80% varies from one to four among existing approaches, the best comparable to our proposed scheme. These results suggest that the ensemble classifier trained based upon the chain Neyman-Pearson criterion outperforms the existing methods.

The superior performance of our scheme is explained as follows. First, the implementation by Orange, the software we use for the standard methods, is not necessarily optimal. Second, our method aggressively searches the best parameter settings of the individual classifiers under the Neyman-Pearson criterion, but the standard solutions do not. Last but not least, our approach seeks to optimize the collective performance of the entire classifier ensemble in a sequential manner, which is not done by the existing methods.

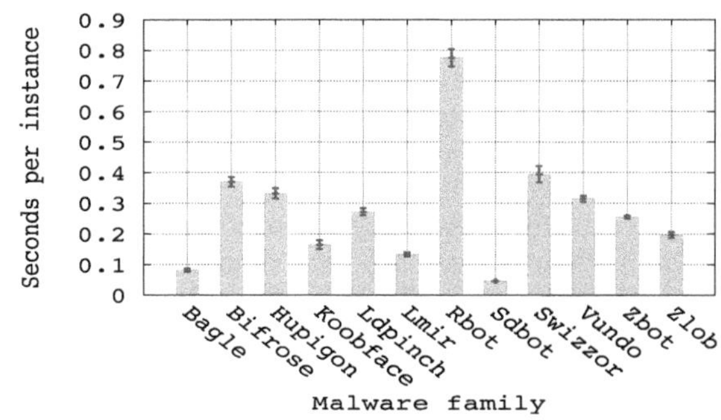

Figure 11: Execution time per instance

6.3 Execution Time for Online Classification

As our goal is to automate the process of malware classification, one may wonder whether our proposed malware classification framework is suitable for online malware classification. We thus perform another set of experiments to examine the average execution time spent on each malware instance in the test dataset. We run our method on a Linux workstation with 12 1.6Hz cores and 64G memory.

In our experiments, we only consider the execution time spent on malware classification. Hence, the time spent on collecting the features that are necessary for classification is *not* counted in the execution time we show here. The test dataset contains 3199 malware instances, which is fed to each of the 12 classifier ensembles we have trained in Table 1. For each classifier ensemble, we perform malware classification over the entire test dataset for 20 times. The mean execution time per family is shown in Figure 11, together with its standard deviation over these 20 runs.

Over all the 12 classifier ensembles, the mean execution time per malware instance is merely 0.2779 second, which suggests that when we apply our malware classification framework on a new malware variant to test whether it belongs to a specific family, the majority of the time would be spent on collecting necessary features that are used for classification, rather than the classification process itself. However, if we want to test whether a new malware variant belongs to any of existing families, we would have to test it against each of the classifier ensembles trained for these families. Still, even though we have to test the malware variant against the ensemble classifiers for 100 families, the total execution time

Table 2: Performance comparison. The experiments use 80% of labeled samples for training, and the other 20% for testing. All numbers are in percentage. False positive rates (FPR) higher than 5% and detection rates (DR) below 80% are shown in bold.

Family	Imputed						Boosting						Bagging						Stacking	
	KNN		Tree		SVM		KNN		Tree		SVM		KNN		Tree		SVM			
	FPR	DR	FPR	DR	FPR	DR	FPR	DR	FPR	DR	FPR	DR	FPR	DR	FPR	DR	FPR	DR	FPR	DR
Bagle	**13.2**	**60.6**	**10.8**	89.7	**6.7**	**9.0**	**9.1**	84.0	**10.8**	89.7	**6.7**	**9.0**	**12.0**	**61.3**	**8.0**	89.2	3.5	**22.1**	**8.1**	86.0
Bifrose	**6.5**	90.6	**5.3**	95.0	**8.0**	94.7	**6.4**	93.9	**5.3**	95.0	**8.0**	94.7	**6.7**	90.7	4.3	97.0	**8.5**	94.4	4.4	95.6
Hupigon	2.0	97.4	1.1	98.9	2.6	97.8	1.0	97.7	1.1	98.9	2.6	97.8	2.1	97.4	0.9	99.2	2.5	97.8	0.9	99.1
Koobface	**6.8**	98.6	3.7	97.9	1.2	98.1	**5.6**	94.1	3.7	97.9	1.2	98.1	**6.3**	98.1	3.0	97.8	1.4	98.2	2.6	97.3
Ldpinch	**17.9**	**65.9**	**15.4**	**79.6**	**19.3**	**74.2**	**12.5**	**69.2**	**15.4**	**79.6**	**19.3**	**74.2**	**14.9**	**65.1**	**5.6**	81.3	**15.3**	**72.2**	**9.9**	81.8
Lmir	**7.6**	**52.2**	**15.8**	82.8	**8.8**	80.7	**10.4**	80.1	**15.8**	82.8	**8.8**	80.7	**8.4**	**50.1**	**7.1**	87.2	**7.4**	80.1	**10.4**	84.7
Rbot	**31.8**	90.0	**7.4**	93.9	**23.3**	93.2	**25.8**	91.5	**7.4**	93.9	**23.3**	93.2	**32.5**	92.1	**7.3**	95.8	**21.8**	95.8	**6.6**	95.2
Sdbot	**18.3**	**36.7**	**23.9**	**73.2**	**22.4**	**45.8**	**33.6**	**50.3**	**23.9**	**73.2**	**22.4**	**45.8**	**9.5**	**36.2**	**18.2**	**75.2**	**8.0**	**46.0**	**20.0**	**74.9**
Swizzor	3.9	97.9	0.9	99.0	2.8	96.9	1.4	98.3	0.9	99.0	2.8	96.9	3.3	98.0	0.5	99.4	3.5	96.8	1.0	99.6
Vundo	3.1	97.6	1.7	98.4	1.4	98.9	1.3	98.1	1.7	98.4	1.4	98.9	3.1	97.7	1.2	99.2	1.4	98.9	1.0	99.2
Zbot	2.8	87.6	4.2	95.4	3.7	95.0	3.7	91.3	4.2	95.4	3.7	95.0	1.8	87.5	3.0	97.3	3.4	95.0	3.8	96.3
Zlob	**7.8**	98.3	1.4	98.5	3.0	98.2	4.1	98.5	1.4	98.5	3.0	98.2	**7.4**	98.3	0.7	99.0	2.9	98.3	1.9	99.0

is still expected to be less than half an minute. This time can be further reduced if multiple cores are used.

Interestingly, there are significant differences among the execution times by the classifier ensembles trained for the 12 malware families. On average, the classifier ensemble trained for the `Rbot` family takes the longest time, which is 0.776 second, and the one trained for the `Sdbot` family takes the least time, which is 0.0466 second. The differences can be attributed to a number of reasons, such as the set of features used for classification, fraction of positive samples, how likely positive samples can be detected at the early stage of the classifier ensemble, and the execution times of `SVM-Light` under various configurations.

6.4 Analysis of Genetic Algorithm

We next show how the genetic algorithm performs in finding the optimal configurations. We examine the executions of the genetic algorithm over all the 12 malware families, and find that about 50.8% of them do not return plausible solutions, which lead to unused feature types seen in Table 1 (i.e., those marked with '-'). Next we consider only the cases in which the genetic algorithm returns a plausible solution.

Generation	Fraction	Crossover	Partial Mutation	Full Mutation
1	49.2%	0	0	100%
2	24.6%	22.2%	35.6%	42.2%
3	26.2%	27.1%	39.6%	33.3%

The above table breaks down the fraction of solutions found from each generation. It is noted that almost half of the configurations found come from the first generation, which essentially uses full mutation to randomly generate solutions. Each of the second and third generations produces one fourth of the plausible solutions. One interesting observation is that among the solutions in the second and third generations, the full mutation scheme still contributes to a significant fraction of these solutions; however, when the reproduction process continues, the fraction of solutions randomly generated from full mutation decreases. This is because the evolutionary process gradually improves the quality of the population from both the crossover and the partial mutation schemes. Hence, if there are only a small number of searches used to find the optimal configuration, global search, which randomly explores the entire configuration space by full mutation, is more efficient in finding a good solution; however, with more searches allowed, local search, either crossover or partial mutation, is able to focus the searches in those regions with good solutions and can thus improve the current solutions more efficiently. This suggests that the genetic algorithm can combine the advantages of both local search and global search in finding optimal configurations.

7. RELATED WORK AND DISCUSSIONS

Due to scalability advantages over manual malware analysis, machine learning has been applied in a number of previous studies for distinguishing malware programs from benign ones (*e.g.*, [30, 14, 25, 27, 1, 32]). Malware detection is a different task from malware classification, which is the theme of this study, as the goal of the later is to classify malware variants into their corresponding families. In some recent works, machine learning has also been applied to automate the process of malware classification (*e.g.*, [21, 40, 15, 19, 38, 20, 39]). The main differences among these works lie in the types of features used for malware classification. Although the malware features used in this study are far from being exhaustive, they cover key malware features collected from both static analysis and dynamic analysis, and those features considered in the previous efforts can be easily incorporated in our malware classification framework based on the chain Neyman-Pearson criterion. More importantly, what really distinguishes our work from these previous efforts is that they *do not* consider different requirements on different types of errors induced by malware classification. For instance, if we want to study the trend of a malware family, we expect that the majority of the samples in this family should indeed belong to this family, which requires us to have a malware classifier with a low false positive rate even though we have to sacrifice its detection rate. Hence, it is of important to have the flexibility of balancing the false positive rate and the detection rate in malware classification, which cannot be achieved by any of existing methods.

The performance evaluation of of this work relies upon a malware dataset with labels derived from consensus from AV software detection results. It is known that the labels obtained in such a way may lead to a biased dataset [16, 18]. Even with such a flaw, it is noted that using the same dataset, the proposed solution outperforms standard ensemble learning techniques in classification performances. In the future, we plan to use other malware datasets with truthful labels to further evaluate our approach.

Like many other machine learning techniques, the proposed ensemble classifier is trained assuming that the test data would have the same or a similar distribution as the training data. However, the population of malware variants in a malware family can be nonstationary, which is called concept drift in parlance of machine learning [33]. In an adversarial environment, concept drift can bring significant challenges to malware classification [13]. Concept drift requires us to monitor changes of malware populations; if an abrupt change is observed, the classifiers need to be retrained. Adapting the proposed ensemble malware classifier to deal with concept drift remains as our future work.

In this work, we use the cost-sensitive SVM as the basic block to train individual classifiers. Davenport *et al.* considered how to tune the costs in cost-sensitive SVM based on the Neyman-Pearson criterion [7] with a coordinate descent method. The genetic algorithm used in this work can be easily parallelized, and has a single parameter (i.e., the number of generations) to control the number of search attempts.

The existing ensemble learning techniques, such as boosting, bagging, and stacking [9], can be orthogonal to our work: they can be used to improve the performance of an individual classifier when a specific feature type is considered in our malware classification framework. Moreover, the way in which our work combines multiple classifiers also differs from these existing techniques. First, the 'OR' rule used in our method enables us to take advantage of the correlation among multiple feature types: If adding a new feature type does not help improve the classification performance over previous feature types, our classification framework does not collect its values from a malware sample. Second, missing feature values render it difficult to apply existing methods directly. For example, given a malware sample, if we cannot collect values for a specific feature type, we cannot assign a weight to it in the boosting algorithm. Third, by applying the chain Neyman-Pearson criterion, we recursively train a set of classifiers that leads to the optimal performance collectively. Here, the performance of a classifier ensemble is evaluated according to the Neyman-Pearson criterion, rather than the classification errors used in some existing methods.

Acknowledgment We thank anonymous reviewers for their comments and our paper shepherd, Aziz Mohaisen, for his great help on improving the final version of this paper.

8. REFERENCES

[1] B. Anderson, D. Quist, J. Neil, C. Storlie, and T. Lane. Graph-based malware detection using dynamic analysis. *Journal of Computer Virology*, 7(4):247–258, 2011.

[2] `http://securitywatch.pcmag.com/security/323419-symantec-says-antivirus-is-dead-world-rolls-eyes`.

[3] E. B. Baum and D. Haussler. What size net gives valid generalization? *Neural computation*, 1(1):151–160, 1989.

[4] `http://cnx.org/content/m11548/1.2/`.

[5] C. J.C. Burges. A tutorial on support vector machines for pattern recognition. *Data mining and knowledge discovery*, 2(2):121–167, 1998.

[6] O. Chapelle, B. Schölkopf, and A. Zien. *Semi-supervised learning*, volume 2. MIT press Cambridge, 2006.

[7] M. A. Davenport, R. G. Baraniuk, and C. D. Scott. Tuning support vector machines for minimax and neyman-pearson classification. *IEEE Trans. Pattern Anal. Mach. Intell.*, 32(10):1888–1898, October 2010.

[8] T. G. Dietterich. Ensemble methods in machine learning. In *Multiple classifier systems*. Springer, 2000.

[9] T. Hastie, R. Tibshirani, and J. Friedman. *The elements of statistical learning: Data Mining, Inference, and Prediction*. Springer, 2009.

[10] H. He and E. A. Garcia. Learning from imbalanced data. *IEEE Trans. on Knowledge and Data Engineering*, 2009.

[11] `http://www.imperva.com/docs/HII_Assessing_the_Effectiveness_of_Antivirus_Solutions.pdf`.

[12] `http://www.pintool.org/`.

[13] A. Kantchelian, S. Afroz, L. Huang, A. C. Islam, B. Miller, M. C. Tschantz, R. Greenstadt, A. D. Joseph, and J. D. Tygar. Approaches to adversarial drift. In *ACM AISec'13*.

[14] J. Z. Kolter and M. A. Maloof. Learning to detect and classify malicious executables in the wild. *Journal of Maching Learning Research*, 7:2721–2744, December 2006.

[15] D. Kong and G. Yan. Discriminant malware distance learning on structural information for automated malware classification. In *Proceedings of ACM KDD'13*, 2013.

[16] P. Li, L. Liu, D. Gao, and M. K Reiter. On challenges in evaluating malware clustering. In *RAID'10*.

[17] `http://www.csie.ntu.edu.tw/~cjlin/libsvm/`.

[18] A. Mohaisen and O. Alrawi. AV-meter: An evaluation of antivirus scans and labels. In *Proceedings of DIMVA'14*.

[19] A. Mohaisen and O. Alrawi. Unveiling zeus: automated classification of malware samples. In *Proceedings of the 22nd international conference on WWW companion*, 2013.

[20] A. Mohaisen, A. G. West, A. Mankin, and O. Alrawi. Chatter: Exploring classification of malware based on the order of events. In *IEEE Conference on Communications and Network Security (CNS'14)*.

[21] L. Nataraj, V. Yegneswaran, P. Porras, and J. Zhang. A comparative assessment of malware classification using binary texture analysis and dynamic analysis. In *Proceedings of ACM AISec'11*.

[22] `http://www.offensivecomputing.net/`.

[23] `http://orange.biolab.si/`.

[24] N. C. Oza and K. Tumer. Classifier ensembles: Select real-world applications. *Information Fusion*, 9(1), 2008.

[25] R. Perdisci, A. Lanzi, and W. Lee. Mcboost: Boosting scalability in malware collection and analysis using statistical classification of executables. In *ACSAC'08*.

[26] K. Raman. Selecting features to classify malware. In *Proceedings of InfoSec Southwest*, 2012.

[27] K. Rieck, P. Trinius, C. Willems, and T. Holz. Automatic analysis of malware behavior using machine learning. *J. Comput. Secur.*, 19(4):639–668, December 2011.

[28] C. Rossow, C. J. Dietrich, C. Grier, C. Kreibich, V. Paxson, N. Pohlmann, H. Bos, and M. Van Steen. Prudent practices for designing malware experiments: Status quo and outlook. In *IEEE Symposium on Security and Privacy*, pages 65–79. IEEE, 2012.

[29] M. Saar-Tsechansky and F. Provost. Handling missing values when applying classification models. *Journal of Machine Learning Research*, 8:1623–1657, December 2007.

[30] M. G. Schultz, E. Eskin, E. Zadok, and S. J. Stolfo. Data mining methods for detection of new malicious executables. In *IEEE Symposium on Security and Privacy*, 2001.

[31] C. Scott and R. Nowak. A neyman-pearson approach to statistical learning. *IEEE Transactions on Information Theory*, 51(11), 2005.

[32] M. Z. Shafiq, S. M. Tabish, F. Mirza, and M. Farooq. Pe-miner: Mining structural information to detect malicious executables in realtime. In *RAID'09*.

[33] A. Singh, A. Walenstein, and A. Lakhotia. Tracking concept drift in malware families. In *Proceedings of ACM AISec'12*.

[34] `http://svmlight.joachims.org/`.

[35] Symantec Internet security threat report. Symantec Corporation, 2011.

[36] V. N. Vapnik and A. Y. Chervonenkis. On the uniform convergence of relative frequencies of events to their probabilities. *Theory of Probability & Its Applications*, 16(2):264–280, 1971.

[37] `https://www.virustotal.com/`.

[38] A. G. West and A. Mohaisen. Metadata-driven threat classification of network endpoints appearing in malware. In *Proceedings of DIMVA'14*.

[39] Z. Xu, J. Zhang, G. Gu, and Z. Lin. Autovac: Towards automatically extracting system resource constraints and generating vaccines for malware immunization.

[40] G. Yan, N. Brown, and D. Kong. Exploring discriminatory features for automated malware classification. In *Detection of Intrusions and Malware, and Vulnerability Assessment (DIMVA'13)*. 2013.

The Process Matters: Ensuring Data Veracity in Cyber-Physical Systems

Marina Krotofil
European Network for Cyber Security
The Hague, Netherlands

Jason Larsen
IOActive, Inc.
Seattle, WA 98104, USA

Dieter Gollmann
Hamburg University of Technology
Hamburg, Germany

ABSTRACT

Cyber-physical systems are characterized by an IT infrastructure controlling effects in the physical world. Attacks are intentional actions trying to cause undesired physical effects. When process data originating in the physical world is manipulated before being handed to the IT infrastructure, the data security property called "veracity" or trustworthiness will be violated. There is no canonical IT security solution guaranteeing that the inputs from a sensor faithfully represent reality. However, the laws of physics may help the defender to detect impossible or implausible sensor readings.

This paper proposes a process-aware approach to detect when a sensor signal is being maliciously manipulated. We present a set of lightweight real-time algorithms for spoofing sensor signals directly at the microcontroller of the field device. The detection of spoofed measurements takes the form of plausibility and consistency checks with the help of the correlation entropy in a cluster of related sensors. We use the Tennessee Eastman challenge process to demonstrate the performance of our approach and to highlight aspects relevant to the detection effectiveness.

Keywords

Cyber-physical systems, signal spoofing, veracity, cluster entropy, plausibility checks

1. INTRODUCTION

Miniaturization has led to the development of processors that have replaced analog components in many electronic products. Further integration of microprocessors with input and output components has evolved into microcontrollers, which became a part of purpose built computational systems embedded in applications in the physical world. Such systems consisting of computational and communication elements controlling physical entities with the help of sensors and actuators are called cyber-physical systems (CPS). On one hand embedded computers enable governing of physical applications to achieve desired outcomes. On the other hand, embedded computers can instruct physical systems to perform actions that are not intended.

A first generation of research on securing cyber-physical systems focused on the IT infrastructure deployed around industrial processes; it observed that in many cases appropriate network security measures were lacking putting the processes at risk. The dominant suggestion was to adapt state-of-the-art network security solutions such as cryptographic protocols, intrusion detection systems, and firewalls to the industrial application domain. These defenses primarily deal with attacks on the IT infrastructure. However an attacker might manipulate data at its source (where they are generated) before they are transmitted and become a part of IT infrastructure. Cryptographic protocols, for example, would then securely transmit "insecure" data, i.e. data potentially damaging the process. The challenge at hand therefore does not refer to *data integrity* but to the data trustworthiness or *veracity* (see Section 2).

A distinction has been drawn between *embedded systems* that use electronic and physical components developed separately by experts in their respective domains, and true *cyber-physical systems* where expertise in both domains must combined to advance the state of the art. The IT security approaches referred to above would then belong to the world of embedded systems. Defenses that can cope with manipulations of data at its source require a proper understanding of the physics of the processes controlled. With that we are taking a step towards cyber-physical security proper.

In this paper we assume an attacker that can manipulate actuators to cause tangible impact on the process and hides real process measurements from the process operator. We investigate methods for identifying those readings that have been manipulated. Specifically, we consider attacks generating believable artificial values and presenting those data to the operator to deceive her about the true state of a process. We explore such attacks in simulations of the well-known Tennessee-Eastman process (Section 3). Section 4 discusses methods for generating plausible fake data. Section 6 compares the performance of the statistical approaches described in Section 5 for detecting the sensor providing fake readings.

ASIA CCS '15, April 14 - 17, 2015, Singapore, Singapore

http://dx.doi.org/10.1145/2714576.2714599 ...$15.00.

2. VERACITY

Security is moving to the application plane. This can be observed in computer security where the reference monitor is moving from the operating system into the browser and into web pages. This trend can be also observed in communications security. An example is the HTTP protocol and the web services layer about it. The closer we get to securing the applications running on top of the IT infrastructure, the more urgently we need to ask whether the data provided by the infrastructure is actually fit for the intended purpose. This is then the question addressed in our work. Do the data received truthfully capture the aspects of the physical world relevant for the application at hand?

We refer to statements about aspects relevant in a given application domain as *assertions*. Assertions may be attributed to a source; authentication and non-repudiation verify whether this attribution is correct. Assertions may be true or false.

Veracity: *The property that an assertion truthfully reflects the aspect it makes a statement about.*

Cryptography provides data protection in the cyber space. "Trusting" sensor data just because they have been digitally signed does not help when the sensor readings have been manipulated before reading. Therefore veracity is not a property provided by familiar IT infrastructures. Veracity refers to aspects outside the IT infrastructure: the adversary is not an entity launching an attack in the infrastructure but an entity making false assertions. The data are already false when passed to the infrastructure.

Veracity is not an entirely new notion. It corresponds to external consistency in the field of databases and a similar definition has been given for mobile agent systems [3]:

Veracity: *The concept that an agent will not knowingly communicate false information.*

Our definition does not differentiate between assertions that are false on purpose and assertions that are false by accident. This distinction does not matter for the application; the application would react to a false assertion in the same way in both cases. The distinction matters in the design of countermeasures. Borselius, e.g., comments that veracity cannot be effectively enforced in mobile agent systems as the required redundancy for such a protection system is likely to make the mobile agent system useless [3].

2.1 Manipulation at the Process Level

The lowest level of manipulation possible is the actual physics of the process itself. Even if two sensors are segregated electronically, the process may connect them to each other. When the logic of a field device operates on a particular datum, that datum may actually be an aggregate of other data even if that process value was directly measured from the process. Take for example a pressure measurement. Depending on the process, changes in pressure may be the result of temperature, flow, volume, or reaction speed. A simultaneous change in temperature and volume may be incorrectly interpreted as a change in reaction speed. Incorrect interpretation of unmeasured quantities (here reaction speed) has led to a number of industrial accidents in the past.

This has given rise to a number of theoretical attacks such as pulsing a pump in sync with the sensor sampling rate to make the sensor show an alias instead of the true average value. In many cases the operator can only observe the process through the sensors and must have faith that the sensors describe the true underlying physics. This faith can be used by an attacker even where an estimator is used to mathematically solve for the error in the system. An example from electric power is where complementary disturbances are caused in adjacent nodes to cancel out the residual error in a state estimator.

Consider another example in which the process itself can be modeled as *"hidden impact data"*. Boyle's law describes a physical relationship between pressure, volume, and temperature just like data flows are combined in a controller to describe various relationships. If one control loop manipulates a process, it will cause a change in the value of a sensor which could be interpreted as a data flow.

Consider as an example a process unit that produces ammonia where pressure in a vessel is maintained with a pump. Maintaining the right ammonia pressure is critical to the financial health of the plant, therefore its control loop is closely monitored. Another pump is responsible for the out flow of the ammonia from the vessel but is not considered critical to the economy of the plant. It may be possible to set up a standing wave between the two pumps that has a direct impact on the ability of the first pump to perform its function. In that case the state of the non-critical pump can be considered having "hidden impact" on another control loop that contains the critical pump. The unseen state of the second pump is critical to the functionality of the first pump even though there are no electronic data flows between the two control loops.

2.2 Manipulation at the Sensor Level

In cyber-physical systems process-related data are generated in the physical world. A common design in sensors is to vary voltage or amperage in response to a physical phenomenon. To provide useful units of measurements, the analog signal must be *calibrated* and *scaled* first. Improperly calibrated measuring instrument can be a source of safety accidents. An example is an explosion at BP Texas City Refinery (15 people killed, 180 injured) [20]. The root cause of that tragedy was critical alarms and control instrumentation providing false indications. Due to calibration errors the splitter tower level indicator showed that the tower level was declining when it was actually overfilling with flammable liquid hydrocarbons. As a result the operator kept filling the tower. Further chain of events eventually led to an explosion. Hence, manipulating instrument calibration is a potentially dangerous attack vector.

The analog signal is converted into a digital signal by the controller. While a sensor can be purely analog, it is now more common for a microcontroller to be embedded into the sensor itself [15]. In the case of most 4-20 mA sensors, a microcontroller produces the analog signal that is sent to the controller replacing the amplified version of the original signal. A sensor is considered to be a monolithic unit that is validated via calibration, but the presence of a digital stage in the sensor allows malicious logic where a sensor behaves maliciously but always passes calibration tests.

In process automation field devices are considered fully trusted [16] and the data originated by the devices are correspondingly considered trustworthy. If the attacker manages to tamper with the data (e.g. spoof) directly on the sensor, before it is sent to the communication infrastructure, the veracity of the data will be violated.

2.3 Ensuring Veracity

At the level where physical measurements are turned into data, veracity can be achieved in two ways. First, if the environment warrants a sufficient degree of physical protection tamper-resistant "trustworthy" sensors can be deployed, i.e. we rely on physical security. Second, if the environment cannot be easily controlled, countermeasures can take the

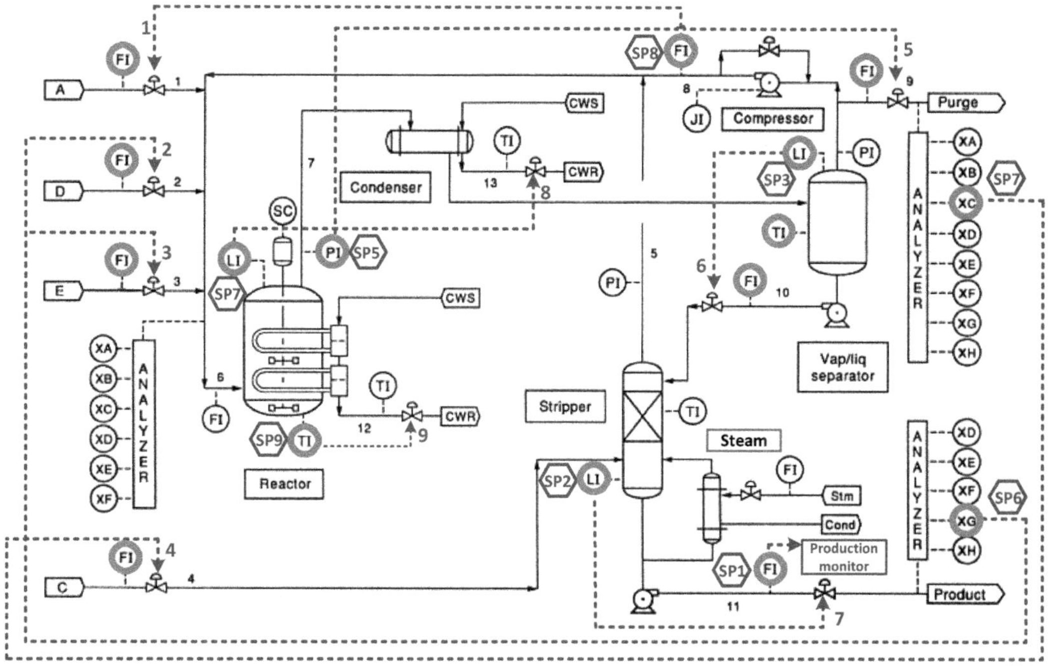

Figure 1: Plantwide chemical process under control–based on [12]

form of consistency or plausibility checks on the received sensor inputs. Sensor readings can be false on purpose (due to attack) or by accident (sensor failure). Although this distinction does not matter for the application, it matters for the design of the countermeasures.

Redundancy and consistency checks such as majority voting have been used for detecting accidental sensor failures. With intentional attacks defenses cannot be built on the basis of statistical independence and may take the form of plausibility and/or consistency checks. In this case models of the physical space under observation are used to judge to which extent individual sensor readings are consistent with the overall state of the system derived from all the readings. It is possible to further model the relationship between different aspects of the physical process (e.g. temperature and pressure) in order to detect impossible sensor readings or flag implausible readings as suspicious. Changes in the plant configuration are not required to implement such countermeasures that make them practical.

3. TENNESSEE EASTMAN CHALLENGE PROCESS

The Tennessee Eastman (TE) process is a modified model of a real plant-wide industrial process [6]. The authors intentionally omitted certain details of the process to protect its proprietary nature. This makes TE an excellent case study because the *a priori* information about the process is limited and thus allows emulation of the "grey-box" exploitation use cases. For our empirical analysis we use the TE Matlab model developed by Ricker [18].

The plant produces two liquid (*liq*) products from four fresh gaseous (*g*) reactants during two irreversible exothermic reactions involving chemicals A, C, D, E, G and H:

$$A(g) + C(g) + D(g) \rightarrow G(liq), \qquad \text{Product 1,}$$
$$A(g) + C(g) + E(g) \rightarrow H(liq), \qquad \text{Product 2.}$$

The process has five major operation units: the reactor, the product condenser, a vapor-liquid separator, a recycle compressor and a product stripper as shown in Fig. 1. The gaseous reactants and products are not specifically identified. Feed C is not pure and consists of 48.5% A and 51% C. The byproducts and inert gases are purged from the system in the vapor phase using a vapor-liquid separator; products G and H exit the stripper base and are separated in a downstream refining section.

The plant has 12 valves for manipulation. In total 41 measurements are involved in process monitoring; the first 22 are continuous, the rest are sampled composition analyses from chromatographs with a delay of 0.1 or 0.25 hours, depending on the process variable. The simulation model control scheme consists of 18 proportional-integral (PI) controllers, 16 process measurements XMEAS{1;2;3;4;5;7;8;9;10;11;12;14;15;17;31;40} and 9 set points which form 8 multivariable control loops and one single feedback control loop [12]. The full notation and units of process and manipulated variables can be found in [6].

The process description includes a flowsheet, steady-state material and energy balance as well as operational constraints of both the optimal steady-state operations and the process shutdown limits. Depending on her goal (economic or physical disruption), the attacker would have to violate these specified constraints. By default the process operates in a steady state (without disturbances). However, the original problem statement includes typical set points and load changes, which along with other listed disturbances illustrate different aspects of process operations. In total there are 20 disturbance modes IDV{1-20} and four set point changes. This information is valuable to an attacker as any change in operations causes variations in the process behavior which in turn is visible in the process measurements (sensor signals).

The default simulation time of a single experiment is 72 hours. Real-time process simulation is conducted with signals sampled at a rate of f_s=2000 s/h (samples per hour). After a simulation is completed, the process data is down-sampled to 100 s/h before being stored in the Matlab workspace. We conduct our analysis on the data sampled with f_s=100s/h. The original Matlab model does not allow any randomness in the simulations to guarantee the repeatability of the plant operation disturbances, so each simulation run produces identical results. In order to obtain statistically significant results we modified the original model to generate a new seed for the random number generator for each simulation run while preserving underlying dynamics of process behavior.

3.1 Simulation of Attacks

We assume an attacker aiming to cause tangible impact on the process and to hide real process measurements from the process operator. In the context of cyber-physical systems the attacker can either tamper with the sensor signals or modify the manipulated variables (MV) issued by the controller. To simulate attacks on the process, we use the attacker model proposed in [5]. In particular, we extended the Simulink model of the TE process to simulate integrity attacks and DoS attacks on the manipulated variables (actuators).

Let $Y_i(t)$ be a manipulated variable i at time t, $0 \leq t \leq T$, and T be the duration of the simulation; time is discrete. The attack interval T_a is arbitrary and is bounded by the simulation run time. In our setting, we simulate a manipulated MV Y_i' as follows:

$$Y_i'(t) = \begin{cases} Y_i(t), & \text{for } t \notin T_a \\ Y_i^a(t), & \text{for } t \in T_a, \end{cases}$$

where $Y_i^a(t)$ is the modified manipulated variable (attack value).

During a *DoS attack*, new controller commands do not reach the actuator. If the attack starts at time t_a, we have:

$$Y_i^a(t) = Y_i(t_a - 1).$$

where Y_t^a is the stale MV (the last MV received by the actuator before the DoS attack).

4. SENSOR SIGNAL SPOOFING

If the process upset desired by the attacker is not instantaneous, plant operators may notice process changes and take corrective measures to bring the process back into its steady state. Moreover, if the operator attributes the process behavior to unnatural causes, she can initiate an immediate incident investigation. Out of these considerations an attacker might prefer to hide the real process measurements from the operator.

Falsifying a sensor signal is a matter of art as much as science. In theory, it is possible to falsify sensor signal that would be undetectable given enough time and CPU power. In real world scenarios the attacker is constrained by engineering, time, effort, and other factors. The core computers of an industrial control system are capable of significant computation, but the individual measuring instruments are almost universally based on small microcontrollers that have limited computing and storage resources.

The techniques used to spoof a signal are a tradeoff between storage and computation. At one end of the spectrum, an attacker can use a "record-and-playback" approach. The sensor signals are recorded at a convenient time and then played back during the attack. Depending on the type of the process (continuous or batch), data from a previous day or a previous batch is recorded and played back during the attack. This type of spoofing approach was used in Stuxnet [11]. However, this method can require large amounts of storage depending on the number of sensors signals that need to be spoofed. At the other end of the spectrum, the attacker can build a model of the process and then run that model in real time to produce spoofed process measurements. Building and running a usable model of the process is an onerous task and requires significant computational and storage resources [21]. Also it requires a large body of detailed knowledge about the process that the attacker has to gain directly from the process she is trying to spoof.

As alternative, in this paper we consider a spoofing technique that can be run on the small microcontrollers used by sensors. It is based on a set of lightweight real-time algorithms which builds a small model of a single sensor signal and allows accurate reconstruction of process measurement dynamics and sensor signal noise.

4.1 Runs Analysis

The technique described is this section is used to replicate the noise floor of a sensor signal. The design goal is to produce sensor noise that is believable to a human observer in the smallest footprint possible. It means accurately reproducing noise amplitude and a number of visible spikes and gaps from the original data.

The technique is based on Bradley's Runs Test for comparing random sequences from his collection of the Distribution-Free Statistical Tests [4]. The algorithm counts the number of runs in two pseudo-random sequences and then compares the distribution of those runs as a measure of the similarity of the underlying randomness. Our algorithm counts the runs in the sensor noise treating it like a pseudo-random sequence to build a distribution. It then uses that distribution to generate sensor noise that mimics the original. The approach works across a wide variety of sensor signals and does not require the attacker to have *a-priori* knowledge of the noise parameters.

The technique is best described by example. Consider the following sequence as if it was a set of consecutive samples from a sensor:

[33.47, 34.73, 37.77, 36.56, 35.31, 30.15, 39.64, 35.08, 37.22, 34.18, 30.84, 38.47, 35.9, 31.12, 32.19, 30.39, 35.39, 31.08, 37.15, 34.24, 36.63, 37.4, 31.49, 37.11, 38.27, 39.97, 34.16, 38.85, 32.6, 32.69, 32.64, 35.41...]

The technique first counts the number of increasing or decreasing values in a row called "runs up" or "runs down". The subsequence [33.47, 34.73, 37.77] increases over three consecutive numbers and can be described as a "run up of 3" or simply "+3". The next subsequence [36.56, 35.31, 30.15] decreases over three consecutive numbers and can be described as a "run down of 3" or simply "-3". The run can be further described by the total distance traveled. The subsequence [34.73, 37.77] travels 37.77-33.47=4.30 units and can be described with the shorthand (+3;4.3). The original sequence can be converted into the runs notation as following:

[(3;1.21), (-3;9.49), (1;4.56), (-1;2.14), (1;3.04), (-2;7.63), (1;2.57), (-2;1.07), (1;1.8), (-1;5.0), (1;4.31), (-1;6.07), (1;2.91), (-1;2.39), (2;5.91), (-1;5.62), (3;5.81), (-1;4.69), (1;6.25), (-1;0.09), (1;0.05), (-1;2.77), (1;0.38), (-1;4.3)...]

The average distance moved by each length of run can be described with a single distribution (Fig. 2a). This distribution describes the dynamic nature of the input sensor noise and can be used to generate sensor noise that looks similar to a human eye. The algorithm constructs the noise as a series of line connected segments from the distribution where the X value of the line segment is the length of the run (Fig. 2b) and the Y value of the line segment is the average distance traveled. Each line segment is not equally represented in the input data and should not be equally represented in the spoofed data. Thus, a run of +2 is far more common than a run of +5 in most data sets. The ratio of +2 to +5 can be determined by simply counting their occurrences in the input data set.

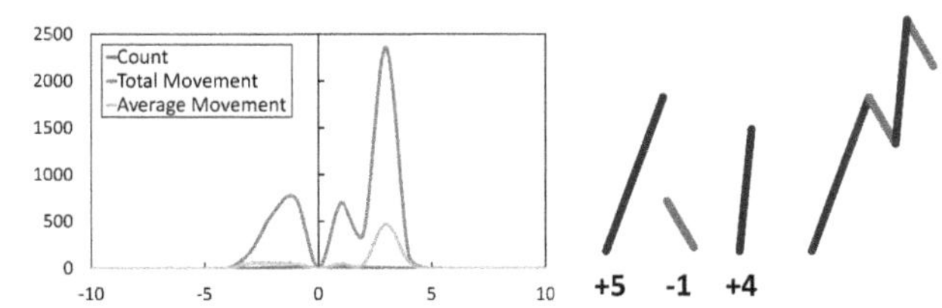

(a) Runs distribution (b) Noise synthesis

Figure 2: Attributes of Runs Analysis

The noise generation algorithm is simple. A line segment is chosen from either the positive half or the negative half of the distribution at random. The random choice is weighted so that the ratio of +2 to +5 is maintained. The random noise should not be allowed to drift too far from the sensor reading shown to the operator. This is accomplished by choosing from the positive runs when the value is lower than desired and the negative runs when the value is higher than desired.

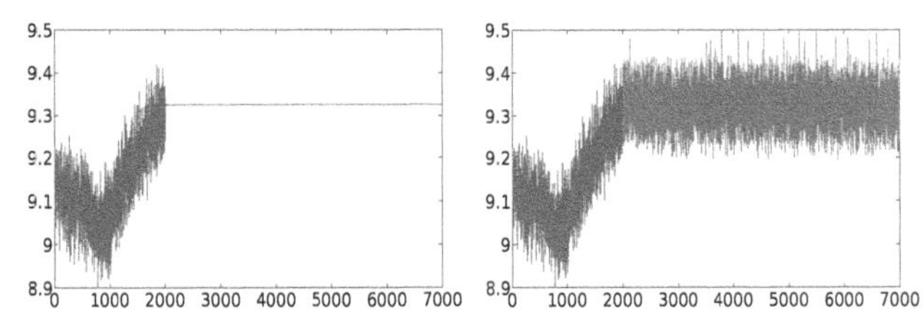

(a) "Frozen" sensor signal (b) Synthesized noise profile

Figure 3: Synthesized sensor signal noise with Runs Algorithm over the "frozen" sensor signal

Fig. 3 visualizes the results of the Runs Test algorithm. The original noise shown in Fig. 3a is used as the training set. As can be observed in Fig. 3b the human important features of the noise such as noise floor width, distribution of spikes and gaps are generated in a believable way.

For the experiment shown in Fig. 3, the runs code (in assembly) was hand optimized for the target microcontroller (ARM) and required approximately 400 bytes of combined code and data for the entire algorithm.

4.2 Triangle Approximation

While sensor noise accounts for the background oscillations of the sensing hardware, the feedback mechanisms enforce a dynamic process behavior that is also visible to the operator. Many sensor signals in a steady state do not deviate much from a set point and look more like a flat line with a sensor noise (Fig. 4a). If the sensor signal is dynamic, a disturbance kicks in or the operator changes operational settings, the attacker will need to construct a believable dynamic behavior of a signal.

As noted above, the microcontrollers used to measure process state in field equipment have limited processing power. Even when it would be possible to build a complex model of the dynamic nature of the signal, such models are usually too complex to implement on the limited resources available.

The raw units coming from the sensory package may be in an arbitrary scale. Also, process data can be measured in various units. Thus the attacker needs a scale-independent technique. In our approach we describe the dynamic nature of the process by fitting line segments to the process data. Fig. 4b shows an arbitrary sensory data with a series of line segments fitted over the top. The line segments give a sufficient estimation of the dynamic nature of the data. The algorithm that fits the line segment is dynamic, it will generate more line segments when the data is changing rapidly and fewer line segments when the data is level.

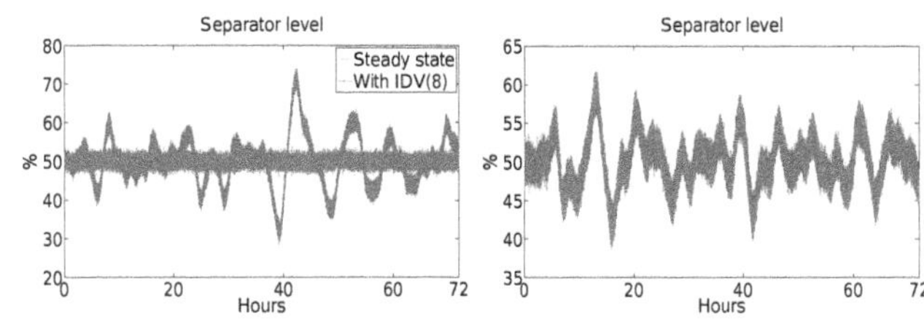

(a) Sensor signal in steady state and with a disturbance (b) Line segment signal approximation

Figure 4: Extraction of the dynamic sensor signal trend with line segment approximation

Conceptually approximation is based on a triangle starting at the last vertex and growing to the right. Two rays are sent out from the vertex until too many points fall outside the triangle described by the two rays. In that case a vertex is declared, the angle is adjusted and the process starts over. The details of the algorithm are given in Appendix A. Depending on the number of line segments needed to be stored in memory, the triangle algorithms requires approximately 700 bytes of combined code and data.

4.3 Sensor Signal Spoofing

Depending on the noise level and shape of the signal, the real-time sensor signals in the TE process can be roughly divided into four distinct groups (Fig. 5). Type 1 is characterized by a few distinct peaks and a low noise level. Type 2 is distinguished by the multiple noisy signal peaks. Type 3 can be described as a very noisy variation of a Type 1 signal. The type 4 signal distinguishes itself by an overall slow signal amplitude change with high amplitude noise. Depending on the state of the process, sensor signals can change their properties substantially. For example, A feed flow F_A is of Type 4 in a steady state, of Type 2 under disturbance IDV(11) and of Type 1 under IDV(8).

Fig. 6 demonstrates the steps of the proposed signal spoofing approach in the example of a signal of Type 3. The spoofing process starts with a learning phase when the attacker determines sensor noise characteristics, extracts the dynamic behavior of the sensor signal in the form of line segments and determines the signal mean. During the actual spoofing phase, the attacker combines line segments in a

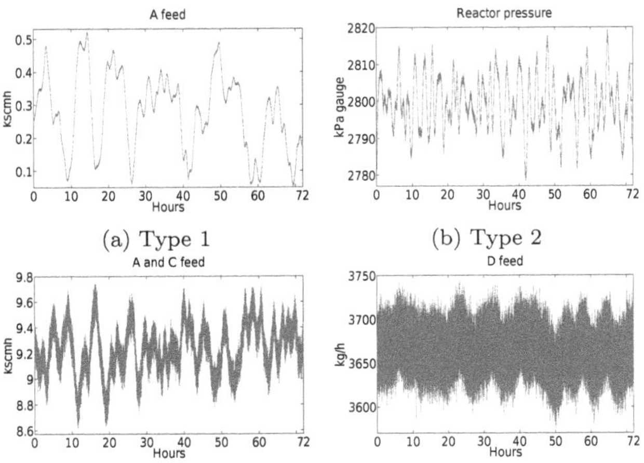

(a) Type 1 (b) Type 2

(c) Type 3 (d) Type 4

Figure 5: Different types of sensor signals in TE process

random fashion placing them around the learned mean value in such a way that the synthesized signal evenly fluctuates around the mean (Fig. 6a). Sensor noise is then added on top of the line segment-approximated signal (Fig. 6b).

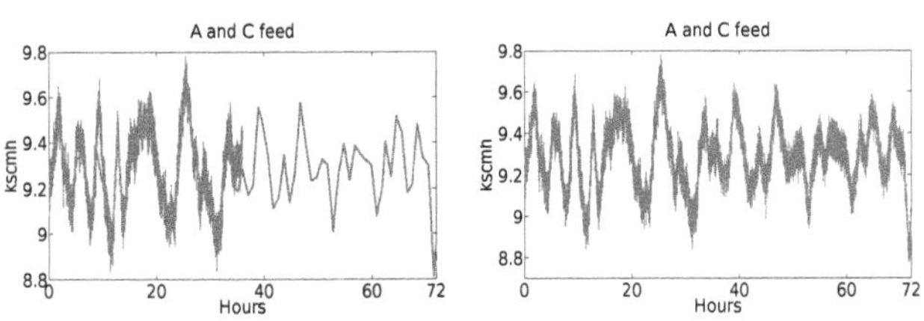

(a) Signal spoof with triangle approximation (b) Spoofed signal with added noise

Figure 6: Steps of signal spoofing

5. INFORMATION-THEORETIC DETECTION APPROACH

Entropy is a metric from communication theory, originally intended for analyzing signals [19]. It is an abstract measure for the coincidence or information contained in a data set (continuous or discrete). The more randomness the data contains, the higher its entropy actually is. The essential advantage of the entropy metric is that it can be calculated for various data sets which have different semantic meanings, even without proper knowledge or understanding of these meanings. In this work we investigate the applicability of the entropy metric to detecting inconsistent and/or implausible sensor signal(s) in a cluster of correlated signals.

Definition: The entropy of a discrete data set X with the finite alphabet $C_X = \{x_1, x_2, \ldots, x_m\}$, where each data item belongs to a character set $x \in C_X$ is defined as:

$$H(X) = \sum_{x \in C_X} P(x) log_a \frac{1}{P(x)}, \quad (1)$$

where $P(x)$ is the probability of x in X.

The base a of the logarithm specifies the unit of the information measure. We set $a = 2$ to measure entropy in bits.

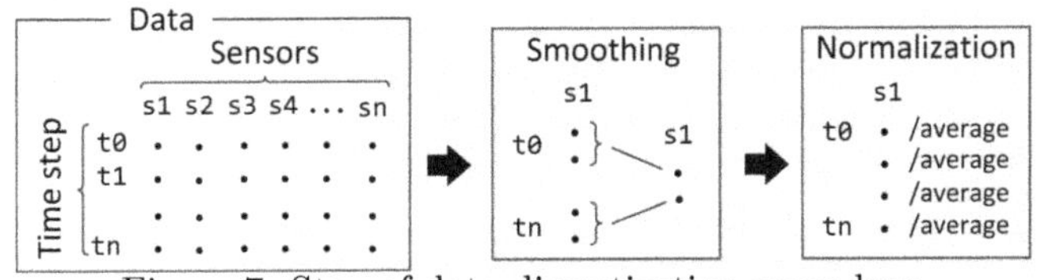

Figure 7: Step of data discretization procedure

5.1 Data Preparation

Process measurements from the TE model are given in double-precision format. With this level of precision it is unlikely that there are two or more identical occurrences of data items matching in all fifteen decimal places. Consequently, each data item of the set is unique, yielding a characteristic probability distribution: In a set N, which contains n items, each $x \in N$ has the probability of occurrence equal to $1/n$. As a result, the data sets from two different simulations without discretization will have identical entropy because of identical probability distributions functions. Therefore, in order for entropy to yield meaningful and comparative results, we first further discretize the simulated data. The data preparation process is partially based on [1] and is visualized in Fig. 7.

In the approach from [1], the normalized data are mapped into one of 64 uniformly sized bins. This quantization method was not suitable for the sensor data from the TE process in the presence of attacks as the limited amount of bins resulted in a large number of mapping collisions. Therefore we derived our own discretization function f without limiting the number of bins. For all $z \in \mathbb{R}$ with $\lfloor |z| \rfloor = x \in \mathbb{N}_0$, and $\lfloor 10 * (|z| - x) \rfloor = y \in \mathbb{N}_0$, $f(z) \in \mathbb{Z}$ is derived as:

$$f(z) = \begin{cases} -(10 \cdot x + y), & \text{for } z < 0 \\ 0, & \text{for } z = 0 \\ 10 \cdot x + y, & \text{for } z > 0 \end{cases}$$

where $\lfloor a \rfloor$ is the floor function $\lfloor a \rfloor = max\{b \in \mathbb{Z} | b \leq a\}$.

Table 1 gives an example of the discretization mapping. All values from a certain range are mapped into a corresponding bin. For instance, all values in the range [0–0,1] are mapped into bin $f(z) = +1$.

z	x	y	f(z)
..1,3	1	3	+13
..1,2	1	2	+12
...			
..0,1	0	1	+1
..0	0	0	0
..-0,1	0	1	-1

Table 1: Illustration of the discretization process

5.2 Plant-Wide and Sensor Entropy

Once the simulation data are preprocessed, the entropy can be computed according to Eq. 1 either (i) for all sensors at each time step yielding a plant-wide entropy (pwe) measurement or (ii) for a particular sensor over a period of time yielding a sensor entropy value (se) as visualized in Fig. 8.

The system-wide entropy is particularly effective in detecting single or multiple anomalies, which have a large-scale impact on the whole system and affect multiple sensor measurements. Fig. 9a depicts two sensor signals from the TE process, XMEAS{7;10}, in a steady state which were temporarily effected by the plant-wide disturbance IDV(8). As

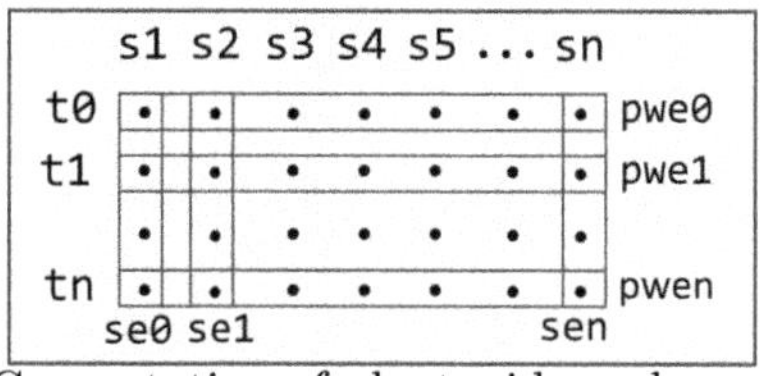

Figure 8: Computation of plant-wide and sensor entropy

can be seen in Fig. 9b, the plant-wide entropy has changed substantially during the disturbance period causing an overall rise of the mean entropy value (red line) in comparison to the steady state plant-wide entropy (green line). Although plant-wide entropy can indicate that there is a system-wide change in a measurement set, it does not provide any information on the source of the disturbance: the affected sensors remain unknown.

In contrast, sensor-specific entropy is not only useful in detecting changes in the process state but also allows for locating the affected sensors. Fig. 9c suggests that the most affected sensors are XMEAS{1;10} which can with certainty be attributed to the disturbance in the reactor unit. However, sensor-specific entropy is rendered useless if an attacker manages to spoof attack-indicating sensor signals in a way that their entropy will not deviate from normal.

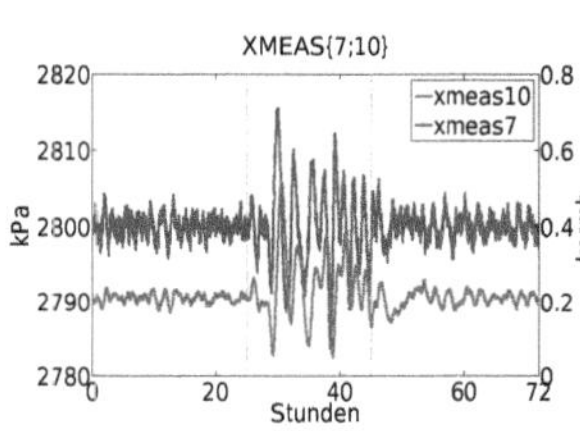

(a) Sensor signals with temporary disturbance

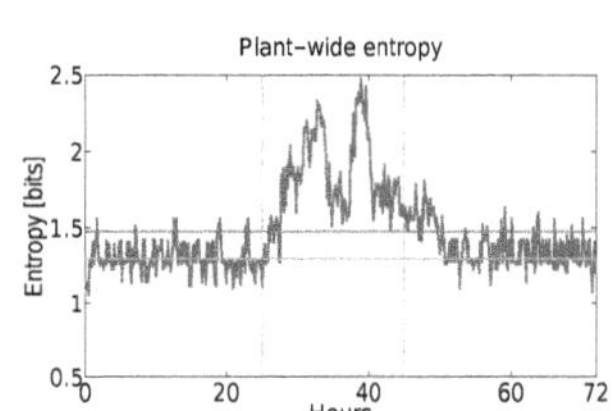

(b) Plant-wide entropy

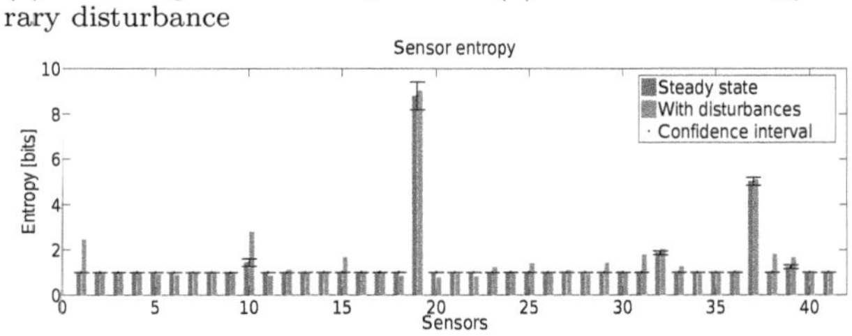

(c) Sensor entropy; 95% confidence interval is calculated using Student's t-distribution based on 100 simulation runs

Figure 9: Plant-wide and sensor entropy

5.3 Cluster Entropy

Disturbances (of both natural and malicious causes) in real complex systems rarely influence the measurements of a single sensor. Instead they have a correlated influence on multiple parts of the process (multiple sensors). Discovering these correlations allows for identifying clusters of related sensors, namely groups of measurements whose dynamic behavior is tightly correlated over time.

> The hypothesis we investigate is that spoofed signals while appearing genuine at first glance, will not be correlated with the rest of the signals in the cluster. We call this type of detection *plausibility check.*

The viability of such a hypothesis is based on the several limitations of the attacker. The attacker must not know which sensors form a cluster. As a result she does not know which sensor signals to match to remain correlated to other signals in the cluster. In addition, the attacker cannot observe and reproduce signals simultaneously in real-time because this would require her to look into the future.

The approach to computing cluster entropy is based on [1] and is illustrated in Fig. 10. To begin, the correlation matrix is computed between each pair of sensors. Then the sensors are clustered by partitioning the correspondent adjacency graph. Within each cluster the correlation coefficient is computed for each sensor within a specific non-overlapping window of time. The entropy of the correlation indexes can be used to determine time series when one or few sensors in the cluster become uncorrelated.

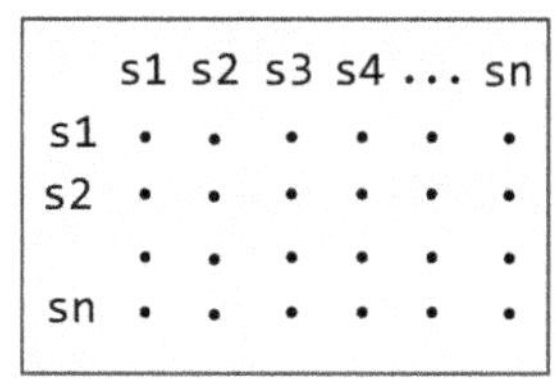

(a) Sensors correlation matrix

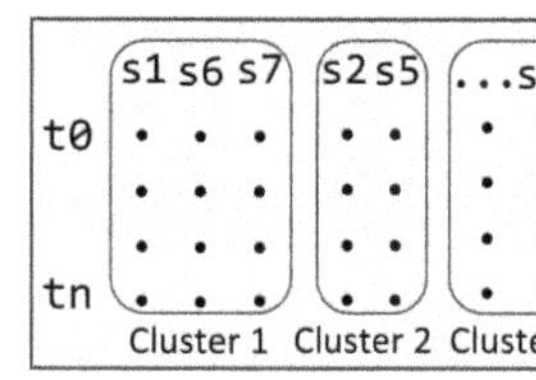

(b) Sensor clusters

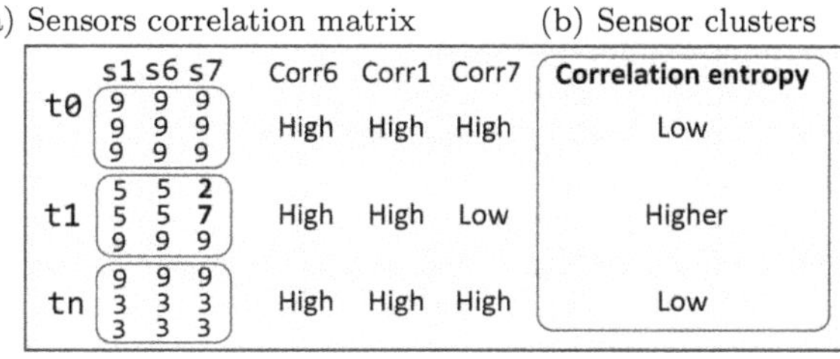

(c) Correlation entropy

Figure 10: Computation of cluster entropy

6. EXPERIMENTAL RESULTS

To evaluate our detection approach we conduct an experimental analysis for two operational modes: (i) in steady state and (ii) with disturbances. For our analysis we have selected disturbance IDV(8) which stands for the variation in the reactor feed. This disturbance is successfully absorbed by the process and does not impact operations but causes noticeable unpredictable deviations in sensor signals.

6.1 Sensors Clustering

As stated in Section 5.3, sensors from the same cluster are more correlated with each other (by some metric) than with sensors from the other clusters. To identify signals that form a cluster, it is necessary to compute pairwise correlation coefficients between all the sensor signals first. We identify the distance between two sensors with the help of the Pearson correlation coefficient r [17] that takes values between $+1$ and -1, where $+1$ is total positive correlation, 0 is no correlation, and -1 is total negative correlation. The result of this operation is a $n \times n$ distance matrix, where $n = 41$, the number of process measurements in the TE process.

The pairwise linear dependencies between the sensors can be visualized with a help of a scatter plot (Fig. 11). Correlations equal to $+1$ or -1 correspond to data points lying exactly on a line (like in the highlighted red squares). The direction of the slope (ascending or descending) determines the sign of the correlation (positive or negative). The further data points scatter from the line, the smaller the correlation coefficient is. Horizontal lines usually stand for undefined correlation. There are no guidelines for the interpretation of a correlation coefficient – it depends on the context and purposes. A correlation of 0.8 may be very low when verifying a physical law using high-quality instruments, but may be regarded as very high in social sciences where there may be a greater contribution from complicating factors.

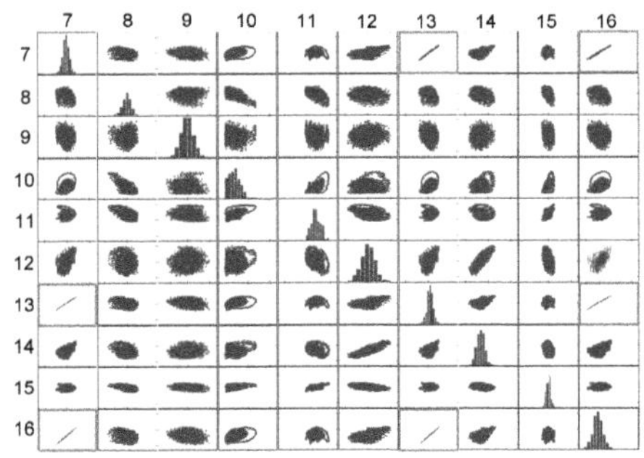

Figure 11: Pairwise sensor correlation coefficients

6.1.1 *Graph partitioning*

The correlation matrix represents an adjacency graph, where sensors that are closer together are linked by edges of greater weight. In this case, identification of sensor clusters takes the form of graph partitioning. Since edge weights represent the correlation between sensors, the objective of the partitioning would be to produce a clustering that has strongly weighted edges between nodes in the same cluster and weakly weighted edges between nodes belonging to different clusters.

We have used METIS [7], an open-source tool-kit for graph partitioning, which includes several multilevel graph partitioning algorithms [8]. METIS allows partitioning an unstructured graph into a user-specified number k of parts using either the multilevel recursive bisection [9] or the multilevel k-way partitioning [10] paradigms. We opted for the latter because it partitions the graph evenly and provides additional partitioning optimization capabilities. In particular, the algorithm tries to minimize the aggregate weight between the partitions. This objective is commonly referred to as the edge-cut. To work with METIS we developed a routine to call the partitioning algorithms from the Matlab environment.

One of the challenges was to identify the optimal number of partitions or clusters, k. In the context of the TE process, partitioning into smaller clusters delivered better detection results. We identified the optimal number of partitions as $k \approx 10-13$. To ensure accurate clustering we verified partitioning results by checking against the correlation matrix (or scatter plot) and by inspecting sensor signals visually. Thus, METIS had identified sensors XMEAS{7;13;16} as belonging to the same cluster. The correctness of this result can be confirmed with the scatter plot on Fig. 11 (red squares) and with the plots of the corresponding process measurements. As can be seen in Fig. 12, the signals are indeed strongly correlated (correlation coefficient ≈ 0.95).

6.2 Detection of Spoofed Signals

To simulate an attack on the reactor unit, we conduct a data integrity attack on the purge valve XMV(10). In

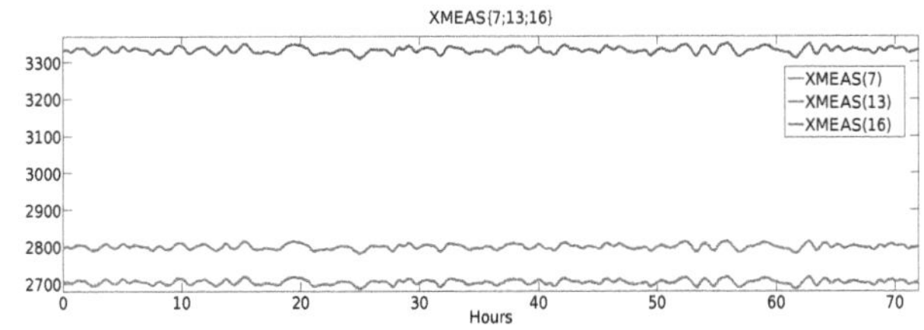

Figure 12: Correlated sensor signals forming a cluster

particular, we forge manipulated variables sent to the valve forcing it to open. Such an attack causes reactor pressure to decrease resulting in significantly higher operational costs. The attacker hides the real reactor pressure state from the operator by forging (spoofing) the correspondent process measurements to look normal (red signal) as depicted in Fig. 13a. Whereas the increase in the plant-wide entropy (red line in Fig. 13b) indicates a significant change in the plant state, sensor entropy cannot provide much information about the source of the problem as the entropy of the correspondent sensor XMEAS(7) does not exceed the normal value (Fig. 13c).

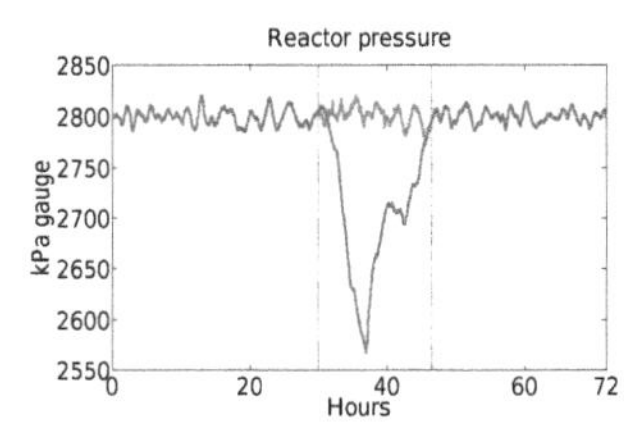

(a) Spoofed state of the reactor

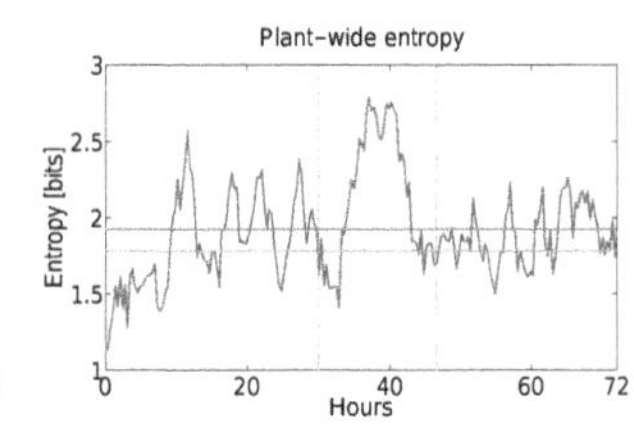

(b) Change of the plant-wide entropy

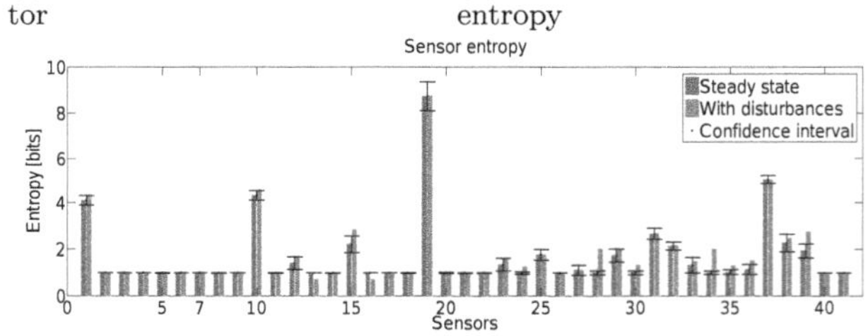

(c) Failed detection with sensor entropy

Figure 13: Detection of integrity attack on XMV(10)

In contrast, cluster entropy (Fig. 14a) demonstrates an increase in the correlation entropy indicating a (more) non-correlated behavior of the signals within the cluster in the "attack"-window (indicated by vertical lines). The time-window for computing entropy was set to $tw = 45$ min or 75 samples. In addition, we had to perform a slight smoothing of sensor signals with a moving average to reduce high-frequency noise in data. This step is necessary as heavy noise conditions complicate the extraction of the correlation coefficients.

Note that even outside of the attack window the correlation entropy moves between 0 and 1; this is an uncharacteristic behavior suggesting strong correlation between the signals. This flaw is the result of the entropy being computed over non-overlapping time windows. Thus, even few non-correlated signal samples cause an increase in correlation entropy in that time window.

The situation is even worse in case of weakly correlated sensors. Fig. 14b demonstrates the detection of a spoofed signal in a cluster formed by XMEAS{5;6;23} with $r \approx 0.85$.

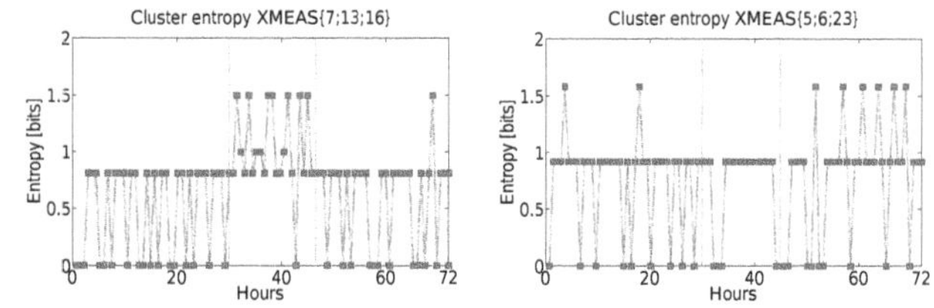

(a) Detection in cluster of strongly correlated sensors (b) Detection in cluster of weaker correlated sensors

Figure 14: Cluster entropy

As can be seen, not only does a higher entropy level dominate outside of the attack window, but we also did not clearly detect the attack. Non-correlated samples of the spoofed signals became distributed over several time windows without causing clear increases of the entropy values in the attack window. To mitigate the weakness of detection with non-overlapping time-window cluster entropy, we apply a sliding window-entropy detection.

6.2.1 *Detection with Sliding Time-Window Entropy*

The principle of computing sliding time-window entropy (twe) is illustrated in Fig. 15; t stands for the time stamps of the sensor readings. As before, the entropy is computed for a predefined time window. However, at each step the time-window slides only one sample further, i.e. one sample is discarded and one sample is added to the window (as opposed sliding by a fixed time-window). The advantage of this approach is that it allows computing entropy over larger time windows. In this case even if a single sample is erroneously uncorrelated it has little impact on the overall entropy in the entire window. What is more important, at some point in time the "entropy" window will largely overlap with the attack window (in red) enabling unambiguous detection of the presence of an uncorrelated signal in a cluster.

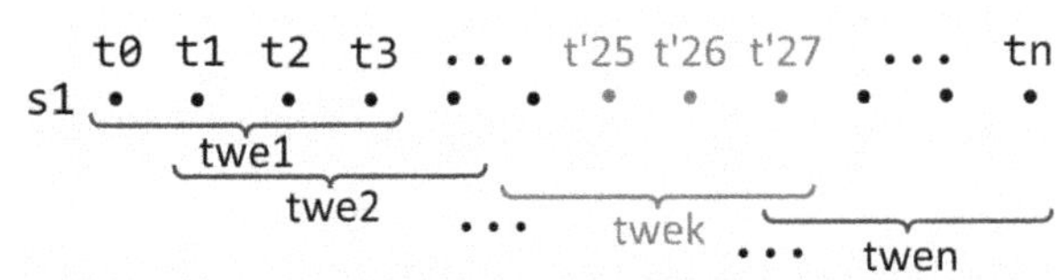

Figure 15: Computation of sliding time-window entropy

Fig. 16 demonstrates detection of spoofed signals with sliding time-window entropy in cluster XMEAS{5;6;23}, with disturbance IDV(8) active (Fig. 16a, 16c) and in a steady state (Fig. 16b, 16d). The time-window is set to $tw = 12$ hours. Spoofed signals are shown in red. It should be noted, that this method is characterized by a slight detection delay. This is because for the correlation entropy to increase it is required to have a certain dominant number of uncorrelated samples in a cluster. For the same reason cluster entropy remains higher for some time after the spoofing attack ends.

6.2.2 *Use Case: Powerful Attacker*

We now assume a worst case scenario when the attacker (i) knows which sensor signals form a cluster, (ii) spoofs all the signals making them looking authentic as shown in Fig. 17a. In this scenario, while all signals in a cluster are *plausible*, they will not be *consistent* because they lack correlation. This assertion is based on the assumption of the attacker's inability to reconcile signal spoofing processes in

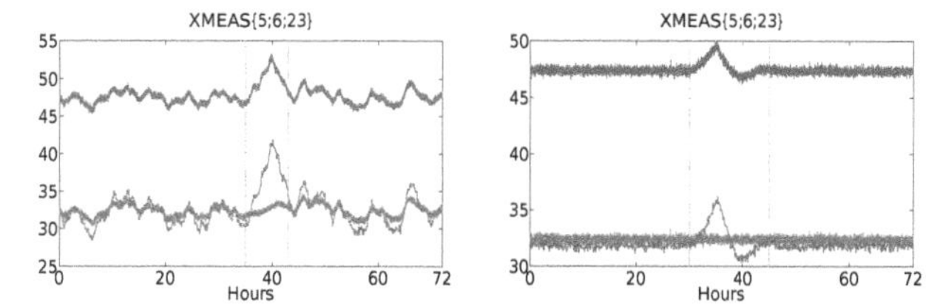

(a) Spoofed signal (red) in the cluster, with disturbance (b) Spoofed signal (red) in the cluster, steady state

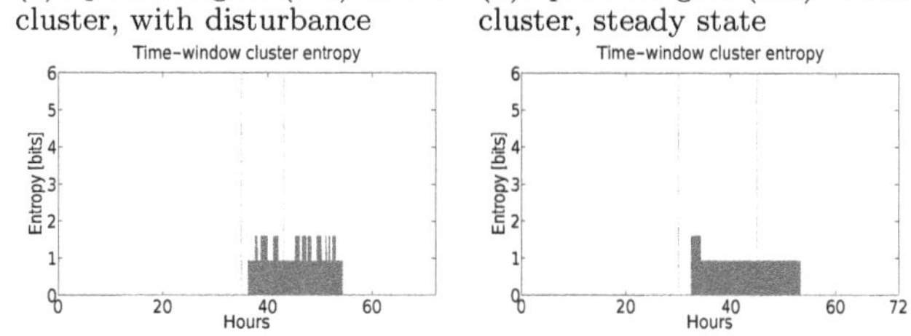

(c) Cluster entropy, with disturbance (d) Cluster entropy, steady state

Figure 16: Detection of spoofed signals, with a plant disturbance and in a steady state

real time. Thus, the attacker synthesizes spoofed signals by assembling together line segments "learned" for those particular type and scale of signals. To synthesize correlated signals, the attacker must be able to pick "correlated" line segments out of a bin of segments for each signal. This turns the attacker's task into a sequential object inspection problem, which is not solvable in real time. Lack of correlation between the spoofed signals can be detected by computing the time-window entropy of the corresponding cluster (Fig. 17b). We call this type of spoofed signals detection *consistency check.*

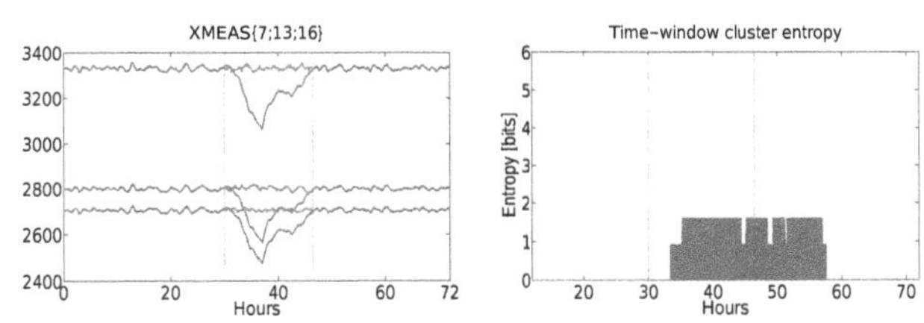

(a) Spoofed and real signals in cluster (b) Cluster entropy

Figure 17: Detection when all signals in cluster are spoofed

Further, we investigate the detection of (all) spoofed signals in a cluster when the process is in a steady state. As stated before, most sensor signals in the TE process in steady state do not deviate far from their set points and look more like a flat line with added noise. Computing the correlation entropy of such signals requires significant signal smoothing to uncover underlying (long-term) signal dynamics.

Real and spoofed (in red) signals of XMEAS(20) from cluster XMEAS{11;18;20;22} are depicted in Fig. 18a. The rest of the signals are also accurately spoofed but are not shown in the figure due to visual layout considerations. As can be seen in Fig. 18b, without smoothing it is not possible to determine correlation coefficients of steady noisy signals. In contrast, prior signal smoothing allows detection of inconsistency even in seemingly flat signals (Fig. 18c). The selection of the appropriate smoothing width m depends on the noise profile and sampling frequency of the signal. In

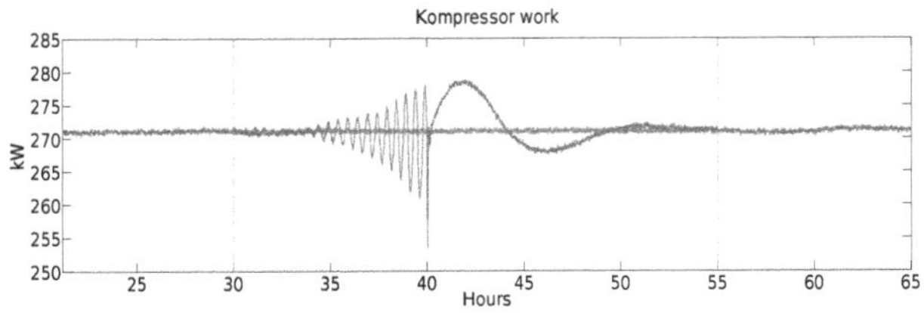

(a) Signal spoof, steady state

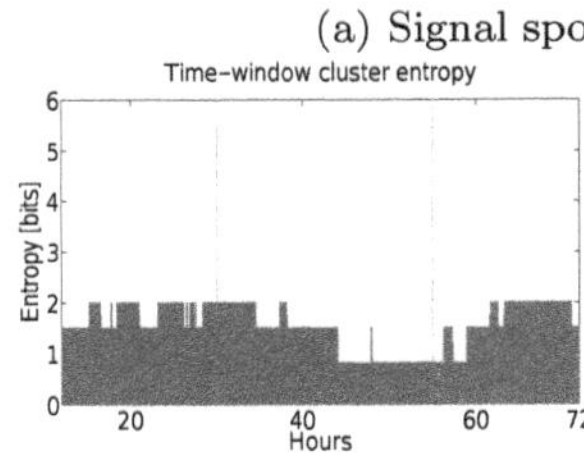

(b) Cluster entropy without smoothing

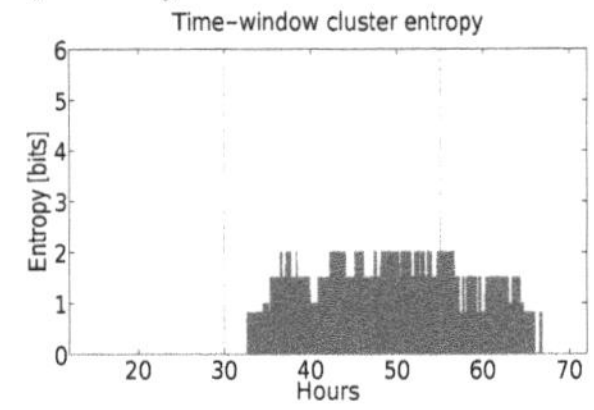

(c) Cluster entropy with smoothing

Figure 18: Detection of spoofed sensor signals in steady state

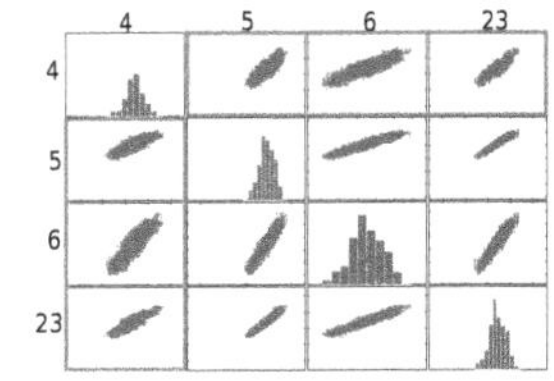

(a) XMEAS{4;5;6;23}, with IDV (8)

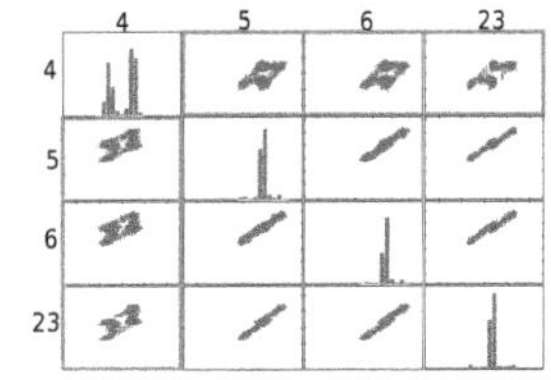

(b) XMEAS{4;5;6;23}, with IDV (1)

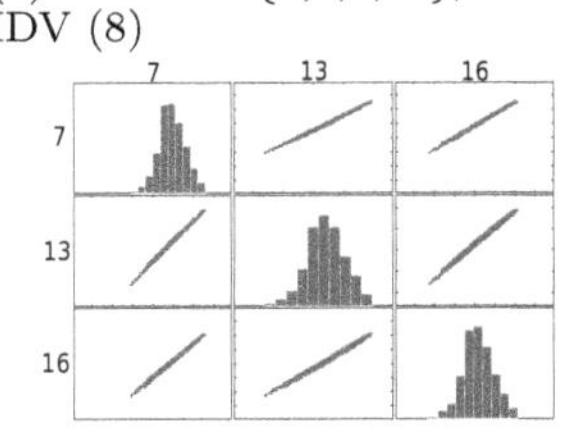

(c) XMEAS{7;13;16}, with IDV (8)

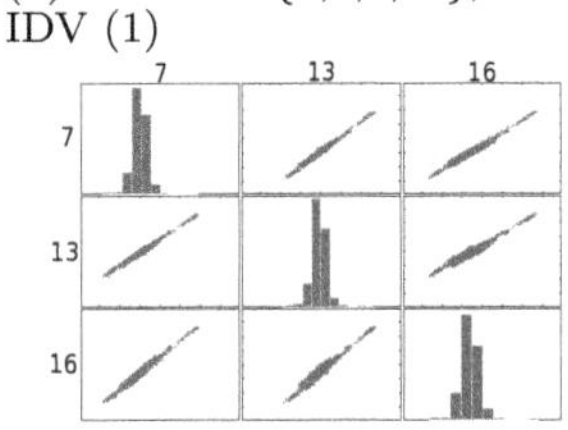

(d) XMEAS{7;13;16}, with IDV (1)

Figure 19: Correlation inconsistency

our experiment we set $m = 850$.

6.2.3 *Detection Complexities*

We verified the effectiveness of our approach by testing the detection of spoofed signals (i) during different operational conditions and (ii) under several attack scenarios. Although the approach delivers robust performance, inaccurately identified clusters may hamper its effectiveness.

During our analysis we discovered that pairwise correlation coefficients within a cluster may change depending upon the state of the process. As can be seen in Fig. 19a all sensors in the cluster formed by XMEAS{4;5;6;23} demonstrate homogeneous correlational relationships under disturbance IDV(8). However, signal XMEAS(4) becomes uncorrelated to the rest of the signals under disturbance IDV(1) which stands for a change in reactants A/C feed ratio (Fig. 19b, in red squares). Exhaustive analysis of this cluster shows that XMEAS(4) does not belong to the group in the majority of scenarios. Therefore we have excluded it from the cluster.

In contrast, the cluster formed by XMEAS{7;13;16} has consistently demonstrated strong dependencies between the sensors (Fig. 19c, 19d). Finding such clusters of sensors with stable correlations is essential for avoiding/reducing falls positive alarms.

6.2.4 *Increasing Detection Robustness*

While signals in cluster XMEAS{7;13;16} always remain correlated, the cluster can be rendered insecure by a powerful attacker. This cluster is formed by three identical signals in terms of signal type (Type 3) and signal scale. As a result, the attacker only needs to spoof one signal which she can re-use (re-play) to spoof other signals as well. In this case all three signals in the cluster will be *plausible* and *correlated.* Logically, our approach cannot detect such an attack.

To increase detection robustness it is therefore reasonable to form clusters consisting of different types of signals and/or of different scales. Fig. 20a depicts two signals XMEAS{20;22} of the same type (Type 1) but having different scales. These signals belong to the same cluster and we assume an attacker using XMEAS(22) to extract signal characteristics for a later simultaneous spoofing attack. As can be seen in Fig. 20a, the attacker is not successful due to the differences in signal scaling. The line segments extracted from signal XMEAS(22) are too short to believably reproduce XMEAS(20). The additional advantage of these signals is that they are hard to spoof accurately with the techniques proposed in this paper.

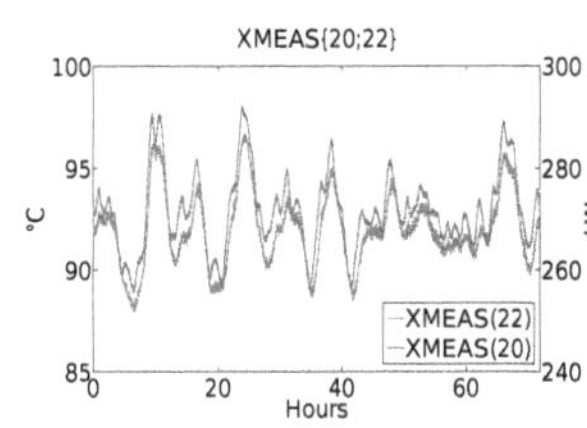

(a) Similar signals of different scaling

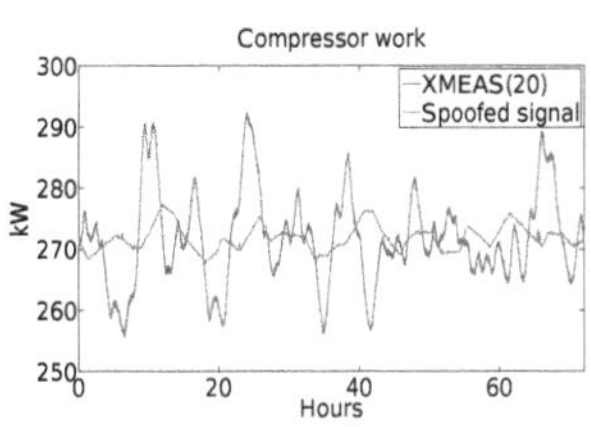

(b) Spoofing failure

Figure 20: Spoofing of a signal by learning a signal of different scaling

Although accounting for scaling and adding additional algorithms for spoofing different types of signals are solvable problems, they force the attacker to account for more issues and to write larger code (which eventually may not fit into a small microcontroller), and in general to exert more effort to perform an attack.

6.3 Discussion

In the course of our experiments, selection of the right approach to clustering sensor signals turned to be most crucial and time-consuming. We found that it is most accurate with human assistance and thorough testing of correlations under different operational conditions. With hundreds or thousands of sensors in a facility it could be an onerous task which would benefit from a reliable automated solution. However, the clustering process is sustainable in that once it is done, it need not be revisited or changed often.

In the context of the TE process, most signals do not show clear dependencies in the steady state due flat dynamics. In order to identify the distances between the signals the system needs to be given a stimulus to observe which signals respond to the input in a correlated manner (Fig. 21a). Verification of the cluster can be automated with "negative" detection. Thus, we verified clusters by applying temporary disturbance (both natural and malicious) and measured cor-

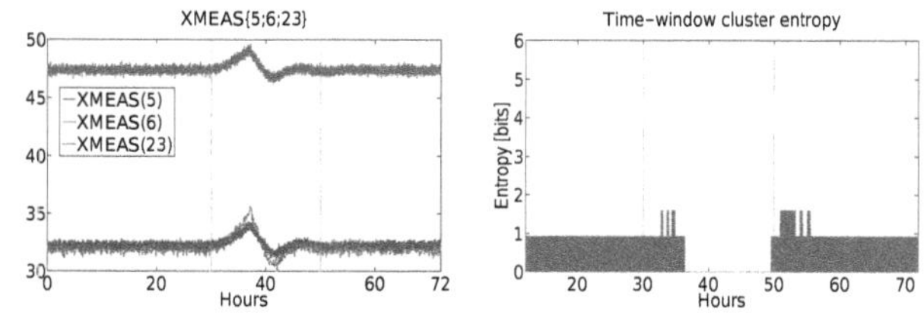

(a) Response to a stimuli in a cluster

(b) Correlation entropy

Figure 21: Identification of signal dependencies

relation entropy. If signals react to the stimuli identically, the correlation entropy will be zero (Fig. 21b). Note that we do not smooth signals for this type of detection.

To increase detection robustness it is not only advisable to include signals of different types and scales but also signals from distant locations. Attackers generally uses malicious code in places where there is a single point of data manipulation. A group of sensors located on a single bus can be manipulated at this common interface. Therefore forming clusters of sensors on different buses provides more protection by reducing the chance of having all sensors in the cluster spoofed.

In (petro)chemical facilities detection robustness can be further improved by including measurements of product variables or quality indices. These are offline data obtained by the analyzer by performing a chemical analysis of the final product. Component analyzers are placed at the critical process locations to control the chemical composition of the process flows. Each analyzer is characterized by its sampling frequency (how often does it take a probe from the stream) and by the dead time (time between tasking a sample and when analysis is complete). Because of the dead time such signals have a step-like form (Fig. 22). In case it is possible to ensure the security of the analyzing process, signals of quality indices can be used as "known good" signals in clusters.

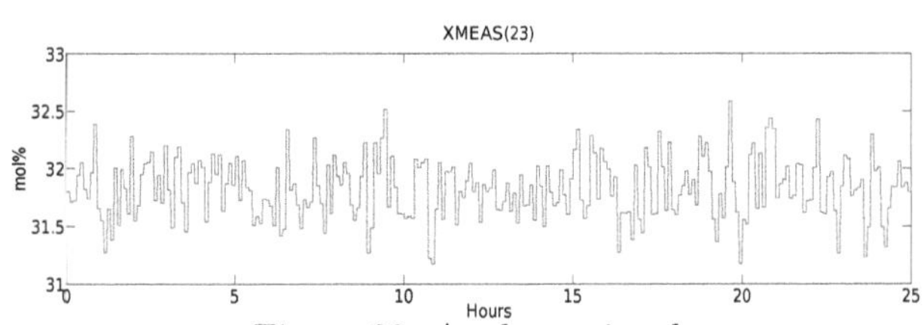

Figure 22: Analyzer signal

There are three analyzers in the TE process generating 19 signals XMEAS{23-41} with lag times from 10 to 25 minutes. The majority of them are strongly correlated with the other real-time process measurements. Particularly, we tested our approach on the cluster XMEAS{5;6;23} which includes signal XMEAS(23) from the analyzer that measures *mol%* of component *A* in the reactor feed.

7. RELATED WORK

In the work closest to ours Agogino and Tumer [1] investigate the applicability of entropy-based anomaly detection techniques to detect and locate anomalies in the space shuttle main engines. We have extended the proposed approach by introducing sliding time-window anomaly detection which allowed us to significantly increase the accuracy of the detection. Wang et.al. [22] developed an intrusion detection approach for false data injection attacks which relies on the correlation graphs (for system variables) and state relation graphs (for system states) to describe the valid behavior patterns of the target system. The proposed approach is heavily dependent on knowledge of the possible and invalid system states. The complexity of modeling continuous processes and in particular of a plant-wide process dynamic [2] limits the application of such an approach. In contrast, our approach does not require knowledge of the plant states. McAvoy and Wolthusen [14] describe an anomaly detection approach based on proxy measurements to detect attacks disguised in the noise of sensor signals. Utilizing control laws, they compare the estimated system output using real-time numerical simulation along with the actual output to detect attacker manipulations. Similarly to the work [22], the necessity of having a plant or operational unit model can be an insurmountable obstacle in implementing such detection solutions. In [13] the authors propose an approach for detecting falsified control systems states with the help of encrypted and thus secure ("known") sensor measurements. By relying on a randomly selected limited set of sensors, the algorithm imposes little additional computational and bandwidth costs. Whilst this approach is feasible for application in a plant-wide control scheme, the advantage of the entropy-based approach is the lack of required changes to existing IT operational practices.

8. CONCLUSION

The attacker's goal in the Process Control Domain is to cause an impact on some physical process. Correspondingly, in the context of the cyber-physical systems, a "security-in-depth" approach would mean extending security protections to the level of the physical process itself. In this paper we investigated the question of data veracity specifically for cyber-physical systems. In particular, we proposed a process-aware approach for detecting when a sensor signal is being intentionally manipulated before it is submitted to the IT infrastructure.

In the control domain sensory data generally are considered trustworthy. We have proposed a set of techniques to synthesize believable but fake sensor signal which can fit into a microcontroller embedded in a measuring instrument. There is no canonical IT security solution that can guarantee that the inputs from a sensor faithfully represent the reality. To overcome the limitations of securing process data with information security approaches we propose a process-aware detection technique based on the correlation entropy in a cluster of the related sensors. The detection technique takes a form of plausibility and consistency checks.

We have verified the effectiveness of our approach by testing the detection of spoofed signals during different operational conditions. The cluster entropy method has demonstrated robust performance for different scenarios of spoofed signals. Care must be taken while forming the clusters as improperly formed clusters may result in fault positives.

Acknowledgments

The authors are thankful to the students Alexander Winnicki and Alexander Isakov for the helpful assistance and dedicated attitude to the testing, tuning and verifying of the proposed approaches.

9. REFERENCES

[1] A. Agogino and K. Tumer. Entropy based anomaly detection applied to space shuttle main engines. In *Aerospace Conference, 2006 IEEE*, pages 1–7, 2006.

[2] T. Backx, O. Bosgra, and W. Marquardt. Integration of Model Predictive Control and Optimization of Processes. Technical report, The Chair of Process Systems Engineering, University of Aachen, 2000.

[3] N. Borselius. Mobile agent security. *Electronics & Communication Engineering Journal*, 14(5):211–118, 2002.

[4] J. V. Bradley. *Distribution-Free Statistical Tests.* Prentice Hall, 1968.

[5] A. A. Cárdenas, S. Amin, Z.-S. Lin, Y.-L. Huang, C.-Y. Huang, and S. Sastry. Attacks against process control systems: risk assessment, detection, and response. In *ASIACCS'11*, pages 355–366, 2011.

[6] J. J. Downs and E. F. Vogel. A plant-wide industrial process control problem. *Computers & Chemical Engineering*, 17(3):245–255, 1993.

[7] Karupis Lab. METIS - Serial Graph Partitioning and Fill-Reducing Matrix Ordering. `http://glaros.dtc.umn.edu/gkhome/views/metis`. retrieved: July, 2014.

[8] G. Karypis and V. Kumar. Multilevel graph partitioning schemes. In *The 24th International Conference on Parallel Processing*, pages 113–122, 1995.

[9] G. Karypis and V. Kumar. A fast and high quality multilevel scheme for partitioning irregular graphs. *SIAM Journal on Scientific Computing*, 20(1):359–392, 1998.

[10] G. Karypis and V. Kumar. Multilevel k-way partitioning scheme for irregular graphs. *Journal of Parallel and Distributed Computing*, 48:96–129, 1998.

[11] R. Langner. To kill a centrifuge. Technical report, Langner Communications, 2013.

[12] T. Larsson, K. Hestetun, E. Hovland, and S. Skogestad. Self-optimizing control of a large-scale plant: The Tennessee Eastmann process. *Ind. Eng. Chem. Res.*, 40(22):4488–4901, 2001.

[13] O. Linda, M. Manic, and M. McQueen. Improving Control System Cyber-State Awareness Using Known Secure Sensor Measurements. In *Critical Information Infrastructures Security*, volume 7722 of *LNCS*, pages 46–58. 2013.

[14] T. R. McEvoy and S. D. Wolthusen. Detecting Sensor Signal Manipulations in Non-Linear Chemical Processes. In *Critical Infrastructure Protection IV*, pages 81–94, 2010.

[15] C. McIntyre. Using Smart Instrumentation. *Plant Engineering: online magazine*, 2011. `http://www.controleng.com/single-article/using-smart-instrumentation/a0ec350155bb86c8f65377ba66e59df8.html`.

[16] L. Neitzel and B. Huba. Top ten differences between ICS and IT cybersecurity. *InTech*, 61(3):12–18, 2014.

[17] W. H. Press, B. P. Flannery, S. A. Teukolsky, and W. T. Vetterling. *Numerical Recipes in FORTRAN: The Art of Scientific Computing,*. Cambridge University Press, 1992.

[18] N. L. Ricker. Tennessee Eastman Challenge Archive. `http://depts.washington.edu/control/LARRY/TE/download.html`. retrieved: May, 2013.

[19] C. E. Shannon and W. Weaver. *The Mathematical Theory of Communications.* University of Illinois Press, 1949.

[20] U.S. Chemical Safety and Hazard Investigation Board. BP America Refinery Explosion: Final Investigation Report. 2007.

[21] A. Vodencarevic, H. Kleine Buning, O. Niggemann, and A. Maier. Identifying behavior models for process plants. In *Emerging Technologies Factory Automation, 2011 IEEE 16th Conference on*, pages 1–8, 2011.

[22] Y. Wang, Z. Xu, J. Zhang, L. Xu, H. Wang, and G. Gu. SRID: State Relation Based Intrusion Detection for False Data Injection Attacks in SCADA. In *Computer Security – ESORICS 2014*, volume 8713 of *LNCS*, pages 401–418. 2014.

APPENDIX

A. TRIANGLE APPROXIMATION ALGORITHM

1. Declare a vertex at the first value;
2. Choose an arbitrary starting window of the size n. Calculate or estimate a sensor signal smoothing factor $s = log(n)$;
3. Note the minimum and the maximum values in the window;
4. Draw a triangle from the origin through the minimum and maximum values and ending in a vertical line at n;
5. Declare a vertex at the midpoint of the vertical line at n;
6. Start drawing a second triangle from the vertex using the slopes of the previous triangle;
7. Count (y, z) samples that are (above,below) the triangle;
8. When y or $z > s$ declare a vertex at the midpoint of the vertical line through the current sample;
9. If $y < z$ increase the slope of the top line and decrease the slope of the bottom line, otherwise do the opposite;
10. If the number of samples between the current sample and the last vertex $< 4n$ then increase n
11. If at any time there has been no vertex in $4n$ samples, declare a vertex at the midpoint of the line through the current sample and decrease n.
12. Go to step 6.

Efficient Implementation of ECDH Key Exchange for MSP430-Based Wireless Sensor Networks

Zhe Liu
University of Luxembourg
Luxembourg
zhe.liu@uni.lu

Hwajeong Seo
Pusan National University
Republic of Korea
hwajeong84@gmail.com

Zhi Hu
Central South University
P.R. China
huzhi@math.pku.edu.cn

Xinyi Huang
Fujian Normal University
P.R. China
xyhuang81@gmail.com

Johann Großschädl
University of Luxembourg
Luxembourg
johann.groszschaedl@uni.lu

ABSTRACT

Public-Key Cryptography (PKC) is an indispensable building block of modern security protocols, and, thus, essential for secure communication over insecure networks. Despite a significant body of research devoted to making PKC more "lightweight," it is still commonly perceived that software implementations of PKC are computationally too expensive for practical use in ultra-low power devices such as wireless sensor nodes. In the present paper we aim to challenge this perception and present a highly-optimized implementation of Elliptic Curve Cryptography (ECC) for the TI MSP430 series of 16-bit microcontrollers. Our software is inspired by MoTE-ECC and supports scalar multiplication on two families of elliptic curves, namely Montgomery and twisted Edwards curves. However, in contrast to MoTE-ECC, we use pseudo-Mersenne prime fields as underlying algebraic structure to facilitate inter-operability with existing ECC implementations. We introduce a novel "zig-zag" technique for multiple-precision squaring on the MSP430 and assess its execution time. Similar to MoTE-ECC, we employ the Montgomery model for variable-base scalar multiplications and the twisted Edwards model if the base point is fixed (e.g. to generate an ephemeral key pair). Our experiments show that the two scalar multiplications needed to perform an ephemeral ECDH key exchange can be accomplished in 4.88 million clock cycles altogether (using a 159-bit prime field), which sets a new speed record for ephemeral ECDH on a 16-bit processor. We also describe the curve generation process and analyze the execution time of various field and point arithmetic operations on curves over a 159-bit and a 191-bit pseudo-Mersenne prime field.

ASIA CCS'15, April 14–17, 2015, Singapore, Singapore.

http://dx.doi.org/10.1145/2714576.2714608.

Categories and Subject Descriptors

E.3 [**Data**]: Data Encryption—*Public Key Cryptosystems*; K.6.5 [**Management of Computing and Information Systems**]: Security and Protection

General Terms

Algorithms, Experimentation, Performance, Security

Keywords

Wireless sensor networks, Ephemeral ECDH key exchange, Multi-precision arithmetic, Pseudo-Mersenne prime

1. INTRODUCTION

In recent years, the security of Wireless Sensor Networks (WSNs) has been an active area of research, mainly due to the widespread deployment of WSN technology in critical application domains like medical monitoring, traffic control or disaster detection [1]. The wireless nature of communication among sensor nodes implies that WSNs face the same security threats as other wireless networks; for example, an attacker may eavesdrop on the communication, inject false messages, or replay old messages [17]. In addition, WSNs can be subject to many other, very specific attacks that are difficult to defend against [17]. Deploying sensor nodes in an unattended environment exposes them to attackers who could tamper with individual nodes or even capture a node with the goal of extracting sensitive information stored on it. Strong cryptography is essential to protect stored data against unauthorized access or to thwart eavesdropping on the communication between nodes. However, sophisticated cryptographic algorithms introduce significant overheads in terms of execution time and energy consumption, which is undesirable for resource-restricted devices such as wireless sensor nodes. A state-of-the-art sensor node features an 8 or 16-bit microcontroller clocked at a frequency of less than 10 MHz and is equipped with a few kB of RAM and up to 256 kB of flash memory for storing program code. Despite these computational constraints, the (by far) most precious resource of a wireless sensor node is energy. Once deployed in the field, the sensor nodes are expected to work several months, or even years, with the energy of two AA batteries that can not be easily recharged or replaced.

A prerequisite for secure (i.e. encrypted) communication between two sensor nodes is the establishment of a shared secret key. Standardized security protocols like SSL or TLS utilize Public-Key Cryptography (PKC) to set up a shared key between a client and a server, either through key transport based on RSA or by means of key agreement based on the Diffie-Hellman scheme. However, due to the restricted resources of wireless sensor nodes, it was generally believed that PKC is not feasible for WSNs [1]. Therefore, a large body of research has been devoted to find more lightweight approaches for establishing shared keys between nodes, see e.g. [17] and [12, Section 1.1] for a brief overview. A simple idea is *random key pre-distribution*, where, prior to deployment, each sensor node is loaded with a set of keys chosen randomly from a large key pool so that any two nodes will share (at least) one key with a certain probability. While this approach is fairly easy to implement and preserves the scarce resources of the nodes (since no costly cryptographic operations are involved), it has limitations with respect to scalability and resilience to node capture. Another method to obtain pairwise secret keys in a WSN is to use a trusted third party (e.g. the base station) as a *key distribution center* that generates, upon request, a unique "link key" for a pair of nodes. This approach requires each node to share a long-term key with the trusted third party, which is used to transfer the link key securely (i.e. encrypted) to the two nodes. However, key establishment techniques relying on a key distribution center require communication among three parties, possibly over large distances, which is expensive in terms of energy.

In 2004, Gura et al [7] published a now-classical paper in which they demonstrated that, in contrast to conventional wisdom, strong PKC is feasible for small battery-powered sensor nodes. In particular, they showed that Elliptic Curve Cryptography (ECC) [8], when carefully implemented and optimized, is computationally less costly than was believed at that time. For example, a scalar multiplication (which is the major operation of an ECC cryptosystem) in a 160-bit elliptic curve group (providing a similar level of security as 1024-bit RSA) can be executed in only 0.81 seconds on an 8-bit ATmega128 microcontroller clocked at 8.0 MHz. The feasibility of ECC on such resource-restricted sensor nodes paved the way to another option for key establishment in a WSN, namely the well-known Elliptic Curve Diffie-Hellman (ECDH) key exchange protocol. ECDH is quite similar to the traditional Diffie-Hellman protocol, but operates in an elliptic curve group $E(\mathbb{F}_q)$ instead of $\mathbb{Z}_p^*$ [8]. As mentioned before, the computationally expensive part of virtually all ECC schemes, including ECDH, is scalar multiplication, an operation of the form $k \cdot P$ whereby P is a point of prime order n on an elliptic curve, and k is simply an integer in the range $[1, n-1]$. There exist two major variants of the ECDH protocol, namely static and ephemeral ECDH. The latter yields a unique secret key in each run of the protocol and, hence, can provide forward secrecy, but this comes at the cost of an additional scalar multiplication. Ephemeral ECDH requires each node to execute two scalar multiplications; one by a fixed base point (to generate an ephemeral key pair) and the other by a variable base point (to obtain the shared secret key).

The feasibility of performing ECC on resource-restricted sensor nodes does not necessarily imply that ECDH is an attractive option for key establishment in a WSN [23]. Even though ECDH has clear advantages over other techniques for key establishment with respect to communication energy cost, it is still widely believed that scalar multiplication is too computation-intensive and, therefore, consuming too much energy for "real-word" WSN applications. To address this critique, a large body of research has been devoted to improve the performance of scalar multiplication on 8 and 16-bit microcontrollers with the goal of making ECC more attractive for resource-restricted environments. Besides the 8-bit ATmega128, also Texas Instruments' MSP430 series of low-power microcontrollers [24] has been frequently used as experimental platform since it can be found in a range of sensor nodes (e.g. the Tmote Sky). One of the first ECC software implementations for the TI MSP430 was reported by Wang et al [25], who achieved an execution time of 25.0 and 28.1 million cycles for a fixed-base and a variable-base scalar multiplication, respectively, using a Weierstraß curve over a 160-bit prime field. The by far most important ECC software for MSP430-based WSNs is TinyECC [14], whose source code is openly available and has been incorporated into numerous WSN research projects. TinyECC supports elliptic curves over 128, 160, and 192-bit primes fields and is highly scalable and configurable. In the past 5 years, the majority of research focussed on improving the execution time of the arithmetic operations in the underlying prime field, in particular the multiplication; examples for this line of research are [5, 9, 18, 20, 23, 27]. Only very recently, a second approach to speed up ECC on the MSP430 platform has been investigated, namely the use of "special" families of curves (e.g. Montgomery curves [19] or twisted Edwards curves [3]) to improve the point arithmetic; representative papers in this context are [10, 13]. A scalar multiplication on Curve25519 (a Montgomery curve over a 255-bit prime field [2]) can be executed in only 9,14 million clock cycles on an MSP430 with a (16×16)-bit multiplier [10].

In this paper, we describe an efficient ECC implementation that achieves record-setting execution times for fixed-base and variable-base scalar multiplication on an MSP430 processor. We managed to push the performance envelope through the right selection of curve models (and associated domain parameters) combined with a careful optimization of the point/field arithmetic. All previous implementations of ECC for MSP430 processors used either a conventional Weierstraß curve (e.g. [20, 23, 27]) or a Montgomery curve of unreasonably large order (e.g. [10]), both of which wastes execution time and, thus, energy. In contrast, our software supports Montgomery and Edwards curves over a 159 and a 191-bit prime field, which represents a good compromise between performance and security. Our implementation is inspired by MoTE-ECC [16], but we use pseudo-Mersenne prime fields instead of the so-called Optimal Prime Fields (OPFs) [15] to facilitate inter-operability with other ECC implementations. We implemented and optimized all field operations from scratch in Assembly language, whereby we paid particular attention to the squaring since it was often ignored in related work. Thanks to our special combination of curve parameters and efficient point/field arithmetic, we managed to significantly improve the state-of-the-art.

2. ELLIPTIC CURVES

Ephemeral ECDH requires each of the two sensor nodes involved in the key exchange to carry out two scalar multiplications; one to generate an ephemeral key pair and the other to get the shared key. The first scalar multiplication uses a fixed and a-priori-known point as input, namely the generator G of the elliptic-curve group, whereas the second scalar multiplication has to be carried out with a random point not known in advance. Consequently, each of the two nodes has to perform both a fixed-base and a variable-base scalar multiplication [8]. Recently, Liu et al [16] introduced MoTE-ECC, an optimized software library for ECC on the 8-bit AVR platform that allows for very efficient execution of ephemeral ECDH key exchange in a WSN. MoTE-ECC uses both the Montgomery model and the twisted Edwards model, whereby solely the x-coordinates of the public keys are transferred, as in [2], which reduces the communication energy cost and makes point compression [8] obsolete. The fixed-base scalar multiplication is performed on a twisted Edwards curve, and the variable-base scalar multiplication on the birationally-equivalent Montgomery curve. In this way, MoTE-ECC is able to combine the individual computational advantages of the twisted Edwards model and the Montgomery model. Our implementation for the MSP430 follows this approach and, thus, we also support both curve models. In the rest of this section, we first recap the basics of Montgomery and twisted Edwards curves, and then we elaborate on the curve generation process.

2.1 Montgomery & Twisted Edwards Curves

In 1987, Peter Montgomery [19] presented a special class of elliptic curves with unique implementation properties. In formal terms, a so-called Montgomery curve E_M over $\mathbb{F}_p$ is defined through an equation of the form

$$E_M: \; By^2 = x^3 + Ax^2 + x, \tag{1}$$

where $A \in \mathbb{F}_p \setminus \{-2, 2\}$ and $B \in \mathbb{F}_p \setminus \{0\}$. A characteristic feature of such curves is that a scalar multiplication can be executed using only the x-coordinate of the base point and all intermediate points. The so-called Montgomery ladder is a special technique for computing $Q = k \cdot P$ that performs a differential point addition (i.e. an addition of two points P_1, P_2 whose difference $P_1 - P_2$ is known) and a doubling in each step. Since the y-coordinate is not involved in the computation, a differential point addition can be executed very efficiently with three multiplications (i.e. 3M) and two squarings (i.e. 2S) in the underlying finite field. Doubling a point requires two multiplications (i.e. 2M), two squarings (i.e. 2S), as well as a multiplication by $(A-4)/2$, which is normally a cheap operation when the curve parameter A is chosen properly [2]. For each bit of the scalar k, the Montgomery ladder has to execute a "ladder step" consisting of a point addition and a point doubling; both costs 5M and 4S altogether. Besides efficiency, the Montgomery ladder also features a highly regular execution pattern, which helps to thwart certain implementation attacks.

Twisted Edwards curves were introduced by Bernstein et al in 2008 [3] and are currently considered to be one of the fastest means to implement ECC. A twisted Edwards curve E_T over prime field $\mathbb{F}_p$ can be defined as

$$E_T: \; ax^2 + y^2 = 1 + dx^2y^2, \tag{2}$$

where $a, d \in \mathbb{F}_p$ and $ad(a-d) \neq 0$. These curves possess a remarkable addition law that can be complete when a is a square in $\mathbb{F}_p$ and d a non-square. Completeness means the addition produces the correct result for any two points on the curve E_T, without exception, even if one of the points is the neutral element $\mathcal{O} = (0, 1)$ [3]. Similar to most of the previous implementations, we adopt the so-called extended twisted Edwards coordinates introduced in [11], which are particularly efficient when parameter $a = -1$. After some straightforward optimizations of the original formulae from [11], a mixed point addition can be carried out using seven multiplications (7M), while three multiplications (3M) and four squarings (4S) are necessary to double a point. Mixed here means that one of the points to be added is given in extended projective coordinates, and the other in extended affine coordinates. We represent a projective point via the quintuple $(X : Y : E : H : Z)$, whereby $EH = T = XY/Z$ is the fourth coordinate from [11]. An extended affine point is a triple $(u : v : w)$ where $u = (x + y)/2$, $v = (y - x)/2$, and $w = dxy$. Besides efficiency, twisted Edwards curves have a second major advantage, namely that scalar multiplication can be easily made resistant against Simple Power Analysis (SPA) thanks to the completeness of the addition law.

Bernstein et al formally proved in [3] that every twisted Edwards curve E_T over a non-binary field $\mathbb{F}_q$ is birationally equivalent over $\mathbb{F}_q$ to a Montgomery curve E_M and vice versa. They also gave a set of formulae for the conversion of points on E_T to points on E_M and back.

2.2 Generation of MoTE Curves

A MoTE curve can be described as a Montgomery curve that is birationally equivalent to a twisted Edwards curve with a fast and complete addition law [16]. "Fast" in this context means that we can apply the 7M mixed-addition formula mentioned above, which is only possible when the curve parameter a is -1. On the other hand, completeness of the twisted Edwards addition requires a to be a square in $\mathbb{F}_p$ and d a non-square. Consequently, it is only possible to have a fast and complete addition law when $a = -1$ is a square in the underlying prime field $\mathbb{F}_p$, which is the case if and only if $p \equiv 1 \bmod 4$. In other words, a MoTE curve can only be generated over a prime field $\mathbb{F}_p$ whose order is congruent to 1 modulo 4 [6, 16]. The authors of the original MoTE-ECC paper [16] used so-called Optimal Prime Fields (OPFs) as underlying algebraic structure, which are defined by primes of the form $p = u \cdot 2^k + 1$ where u has a length of up to 16 bits [15]. While such primes are always congruent to 1 mod 4, they have the disadvantage that the computation of square roots mod p is costly, which poses a problem for application scenarios where point compression is desirable[1]. A further drawback of OPFs is that, despite their excellent arithmetic properties (see e.g. [15]), they are not (yet) widely supported by other ECC implementations for WSNs. Therefore, and since we want our software to be suitable for applications that require point compression, we eventually decided to not use OPFs.

Our ECC software for 16-bit TI MSP430 microcontrollers employs pseudo-Mersenne prime fields in order to facilitate inter-operability with other implementations and support a variety of ECC protocols and applications, including ones that require point compression. Although we focus only on ECDH key exchange in this paper, the two MoTE curves we present in this section are not limited to ECDH but can

[1]It should be noted that point compression is obsolete in an "x-coordinate-only" ECDH key exchange as described in the MoTE-ECC paper [16] and earlier in [2]. The ability to efficiently de-compress a point is mainly useful for schemes that need both the x and y coordinate (e.g. signatures).

be used with any other scheme. A pseudo-Mersenne prime has the form $p = 2^k - c$ where c is small enough to fit into a single register on the target platform, which means c can be (at most) 16 bits long in our case. In order to achieve both a complete addition law and fast square-root computations, we use primes that are congruent to 5 mod 8. Since $p \equiv 5 \bmod 8$ implies $p \equiv 1 \bmod 4$, the parameter $a = -1$ is clearly a square modulo p. On the other hand, if a prime p satisfies $p \equiv 5 \bmod 8$, it is possible to compute the square root of an element of $\mathbb{F}_p$ in a fairly efficient way using the method of Atkin [6], which, in essence, costs an exponentiation modulo p. Following the approach of Bernstein from [2], we adopt primes with a bitlength slightly less than the "nominal" length, e.g. 159 instead of 160 bits. To be more concrete, the exponent k of our pseudo-Mersenne primes is a multiple of 32 minus 1. Using primes that leave one bit of "headroom" simplifies the implementation of arithmetic operations modulo p if one aims for both high performance and some basic resistance against SPA attacks [13]. Once the exponent k is fixed, a suitable value for c needs to be determined, which we simply did by choosing the minimal c so that $p = 2^k - c$ is a prime congruent to 5 modulo 8. In this way, we found the 159-bit prime $p = 2^{159} - 91$ and the 191-bit prime $p = 2^{191} - 19$.

When generating elliptic curves for cryptographic applications, one needs to take into account both security and efficiency requirements. The SafeCurves website [4] defines a number of criteria a curve has to satisfy to be considered secure, whereby it distinguishes between ECC security and ECDLP security. On top of the list of requirements for the latter is that the group of rational points on a given curve contains a large subgroup of prime order ℓ [4]. SafeCurves requires ℓ to be at least 2^{200}, in which case computing the ECDLP is infeasible with today's technology. However, the requirement to use groups of such large order contradicts with the common practice of using groups of order between 2^{160} and 2^{192} for WSN applications, see e.g. [14]. This is, in general, due to the fact that sensor nodes are a low-value target for cryptanalytic attacks, and, consequently, orders of about 2^{160} still provide ample protection for applications in such areas like home automation. Furthermore, it has to be taken into account that the ECDLP is almost never the weakest link in the security of WSNs [17]. In practice, the most serious vulnerability of sensor nodes is their physical exposure to attackers along with the lack of tamper resistance. A serious attacker would never attempt to break the ECDLP in a 160-bit group as he can get the secret key in a much cheaper way via reverse engineering. Therefore, we decided to use elliptic curves with orders of about 2^{160} and 2^{192}; both orders are well established and supported in the WSN research community.

As specified in [6], the "Montgomery shape" of a MoTE curve is given by an equation of the form

$$E_M: \ -(A+2)y^2 = x^3 + Ax^2 + x, \qquad (3)$$

which means the parameter $B = -(A+2)$. This contrasts with the "conventional" approach of using $B = 1$ as in the case of e.g. Curve25519 [2]. Choosing a Montgomery curve with $B = -(A+2)$ has the the advantage that such a curve is "directly" birationally equivalent to a twisted Edwards curve possessing a fast addition law [11], i.e. to a twisted Edwards curve with $a = -1$. Given a Montgomery curve with parameters A, B as in Equation (1), the parameters of the birationally-equivalent twisted Edwards curve can be computed as follows (see [3] for details).

$$a = (A+2)/B \quad \text{and} \quad d = (A-2)/B \qquad (4)$$

Therefore, when $B = -(A+2)$, the curve parameter a we obtain is $a = (A+2)/(-(A+2)) = -1$, which simplifies the conversion of points between the Montgomery and the twisted Edwards shape (see [6] for additional details). On the other hand, when $B = 1$, the conversion of a point on the Montgomery curve to a point on the birationally-equivalent twisted Edwards curve with $a = (A+2)/B$ and then from there to an isomorphic twisted Edwards curve of the form $-x^2 + y^2 = 1 + (-d/a)x^2y^2$ (which allows one to use the fast 7M addition formula) is more complex and requires the pre-computation of $1/\sqrt{-a}$ as explained in [11, Section 3.1]. The parameter A of the Montgomery form of a MoTE curve is chosen such that $A - 2$ is a square and $A + 2$ is a non-square in $\mathbb{F}_p$, in which case $d = (A-2)/(-(A+2))$ is also a non-square (at least if $p \equiv 1 \bmod 4$) and the twisted Edwards addition law is complete. Last, but not least, the parameter A is congruent to 2 mod 4 to ensure $(A+2)/4$ is small and a multiplication by $(A+2)/4$ can be performed efficiently. Taking all this and some further considerations (e.g. twist security) into account, we generated the MoTE curves P159 and P191, which we specify below. The "P" in the name of these curves stands for pseudo-Mersenne prime and the subsequent 3-digit number denotes the bitlength.

MoTE Curve P159

P159 is a MoTE curve over the 159-bit prime field $\mathbb{F}_p$ given by $p = 2^{159} - 91$. The Montgomery shape of curve P159 is defined through the equation

$$E_{M159}: \ -3191568y^2 = x^3 + 3191566x^2 + x \qquad (5)$$

(i.e. $A = 3191566$ and $B = -(A+2) = -3191568$). This Montgomery curve is birationally equivalent to the twisted Edwards curve of the form

$$E_{T159}: \ -x^2 + y^2 = 1 + dx^2y^2, \qquad (6)$$

where $d = 837225916393474870456088348941705219765626$ 63492. Curve P159 has an order of $q = 4\ell < p$ where ℓ is a prime slightly smaller than 2^{157}. On the other hand, the quadratic twist of P159 has an order of $q' = 8\ell' > p$ where ℓ' is a prime slightly larger than 2^{156}. In other words, curve P159 has a co-factor of 4, whereas its quadratic twist has a co-factor of 8. Both the curve and its twist have a large embedding degree of above 2^{100}. Moreover, curve P159 has a large CM field discriminant that fully complies with the SafeCurves requirements (see [6] for further details).

MoTE Curve P191

P191 is a MoTE curve over the 191-bit prime field $\mathbb{F}_p$ given by $p = 2^{191} - 19$. The Montgomery shape of curve P159 is defined through the equation

$$E_{M191}: \ -2678312y^2 = x^3 + 2678310x^2 + x \qquad (7)$$

(i.e. $A = 2678310$ and $B = -(A+2) = -2678312$). This Montgomery curve is birationally equivalent to the twisted Edwards curve of the form

$$E_{T191}: \ -x^2 + y^2 = 1 + dx^2y^2, \qquad (8)$$

where $d = 1039515076553220231993780426167499664788 13$ 474077612237402. Curve P191 has very similar features as curve P159 with respect to order (resp. co-factor) of curve and twist, embedding degree of curve and twist, as well as CM field discriminant. A more detailed description of this curve can be found in [6].

3. FIELD ARITHMETIC

Most practical implementations of ECC adopt some kind of "special" prime fields to speed up the modular reduction operation; well-known examples are fields whose order is a Mersenne-like prime, e.g. a generalized or pseudo-Mersenne prime. In this section, we will focus only on the latter class of primes. A so-called pseudo-Mersenne prime has the form $p = 2^k - c$ where c is small in relation to 2^k; typically, c is chosen to fit into a register of the target processor. This is clearly met by the primes $p = 2^{159} - 91$ and $p = 2^{191} - 19$ from the previous section. The major idea of fast reduction modulo a pseudo-Mersenne prime $p = 2^k - c$ is to utilize the congruence relation $2^k \equiv c \bmod p$ repetitively until the obtained residue has the same bitlength as p. Suppose z is an integer of a length of $l > k$ bits. At first, z needs to be split up into a lower part z_L comprising the k least significant bits of z and an upper part z_H that comprises all the other bits, i.e. we can write $z = z_H 2^k + z_L$. Now, we have to substitute 2^k by c and get

$$z = z_H 2^k + z_L \equiv z_H c + z_L \tag{9}$$

This new value for z is, of course, in the same residue class as the original z, but at least $k - 1$ bits shorter. To obtain a further reduced result, we simply apply this substitution repeatedly until z has the same bitlength as p.

The elements of a prime field $\mathbb{F}_p$ with $p = 2^k - c$ are the integers from 0 to $p - 1$, which are at most k bits long. As usual, we represent the field elements in the form of arrays of w-bit words, where w corresponds to the word-size of the target processor, i.e. $w = 16$ in our case. A k-bit operand consists of exactly $m = \lceil k/w \rceil$ words, which means $m = 10$ for 159-bit operands and $m = 12$ for $k = 191$. We will use indexed lowercase letters to denote the individual words in an array, e.g. $a \in \mathbb{F}_p$ is stored in an m-word array of the form $a = (a_{m-1}, \ldots, a_1, a_0)$ with $0 \le a_i < 2^w$ where a_0 and a_{m-1} represent the least and most significant w-bit word of a, respectively. Similar to numerous other ECC software implementations, e.g. [15], we adopt the idea of incomplete modular reduction, which means all arithmetic operations modulo p accept operands that are not fully reduced (and hence not less than p), as long as they fit into m words. In our case, the operands can be up to $n = mw = k + 1$ bits long because the exponent k of the primes we use is not a multiple of w but one bit shorter. To give a more concrete example, the operands of the arithmetic operations modulo our 159-bit prime can be up to $n = 160$ bits long and also the results can have a length of up to 160 bits.

3.1 Addition and Subtraction

An addition of two elements of $\mathbb{F}_p$ is, basically, a normal integer addition, yielding a sum that can be (at most) one bit longer than the operands, followed by a reduction mod p. Algorithm 1 shows our implementation of the addition modulo a k-bit pseudo-Mersenne prime p, whereby we use a similar notation as in Section 2.2.1 of [8]. The word-wise additions in line 3 and line 9 are add-with-carry operations with ε representing the carry bit. As explained above, the operands a, b do not necessarily need to be smaller than p, but they must fit into m words, i.e. they can be up to $n = k + 1$ bits long. The first part of Algorithm 1 performs a conventional multiple-precision addition, yielding a sum of up to $n + 1$ bits, of which n bits are stored in the words of s and the final carry bit in ε. In line 5 we combine the "excess bits" (i.e. ε and the most significant bit of s_{m-1}) in t, which corresponds to z_H in Equation (9). Since the sum s before reduction is (at most) $n + 1$ bits long, t can have a length of two bits, i.e. $0 \le t \le 3$. The next step (line 6) is to clear the most significant bit of s_{m-1}, after which the sum s is at most k bits long. Now we multiply t by c, add the product to s_0, and finally propagate the carry up to s_{m-1}. The result is at most $k + 1$ bits long because it had a length of k bits before the addition of $t \cdot c$. Thus, it can be used as operand in another field operation. Note that the modular addition in Algorithm 1 has a constant execution time as it does not contain any conditional statements.

Algorithm 1. Addition modulo a pseudo-Mersenne prime

Input: Two m-word operands $a = (a_{m-1}, \ldots, a_0)$ and $b = (b_{m-1}, \ldots, b_0)$, and a prime of the form $p = 2^k - c$.
Output: Modular sum $s = a + b \bmod p = (s_{m-1}, \ldots, s_0)$.
1: $(\varepsilon, s_0) \leftarrow a_0 + b_0$
2: **for** $i = 1$ to $m - 1$ **do**
3: $\quad (\varepsilon, s_i) \leftarrow a_i + b_i + \varepsilon$
4: **end for**
5: $t \leftarrow (\varepsilon \ll 1) + (s_{m-1} \gg 15)$ $\quad \{0 \le t \le 3\}$
6: $s_{m-1} \leftarrow s_{m-1}$ & 0x7fff $\quad$ {clear the MSB of s_{m-1}}
7: $(\varepsilon, s_0) \leftarrow t \cdot c + s_0$ $\quad$ {main step of reduction}
8: **for** $i = 1$ to $m - 1$ **do**
9: $\quad (\varepsilon, s_i) \leftarrow s_i + \varepsilon$
10: **end for**
11: **return** s

A subtraction in $\mathbb{F}_p$ can be performed in a similar way as the modular addition described above. To prevent negative results, we execute the subtraction $s = a - b \bmod p$ via an operation of the form $s = 3p + a - b \bmod p$. Since we use pseudo-Mersenne primes, the addition of $3p$ does not cause much overhead due to the fact that most words of $3p$ have the same value, namely $2^w - 1$, and so they do not need to be loaded from memory. The reduction step can be done in exactly the same way as described above.

3.2 Multiplication and Squaring

Multiplication and squaring in $\mathbb{F}_p$ are in general the two most performance-critical field operations performed in the course of a scalar multiplication [8]. When using a pseudo-Mersenne prime, it is common practice to do the reduction mod p after the multiplication instead of executing them in an interleaved fashion as in [15]. Also our implementation for the MSP430 follows this basic approach. Some MSP430 models feature a memory-mapped hardware multiplier able to execute (16×16)-bit multiply and multiply-accumulate operations on both signed and unsigned integers [24]. Since the multiplier is a memory-mapped peripheral, it has to be accessed by writing the two operands to specific locations in memory. Concretely, the first operand of a multiply or a MAC operation has to be written to one of four addresses (`MPY`, `MPYS`, `MAC`, or `MACS`) and this address determines the actual operation to be issued. The second operand must be written to another specific address (`OP2`), and once this has happened, the selected operation is immediately executed

[24]. After a few clock cycles, the 32-bit result is available at the addresses RESLO (lower 16 bits) and RESHI (upper 16 bits). In the case of a MAC operation, the product of the two operands is added to the content of RESHI|RESLO and the obtained cumulative sum is written back to RESHI and RESLO [24]. The carry bit produced by the accumulation is written to another address, namely SUMEXT. When several multiplications with one and the same operand need to be carried out, it is possible to "re-use" this operand, provided that it is the first operand. Namely, the first operand can be used in consecutive multiplications or consecutive MAC operations without having to write it again to one of the four addresses that select the type of operation.

Multiple-Precision Multiplication

Most ECC implementations for the MSP430 platform use the so-called product-scanning technique (or an optimized variant of it) to perform multi-precision multiplication, see e.g. [5, 21, 22]. The product-scanning method computes the product of two multiple-precision integers in a column-wise fashion and performs MAC operations in its loops, i.e. two w-bit words are multiplied and the $2w$-bit product is added to a cumulative sum. Hence, the product-scanning method performs well on MSP430 processors. Our implementation is also based on product scanning, but we incorporated a number of low-level optimizations. For example, we use all free registers to "cache" 16-bit words of the operands so as to minimize the number of memory accesses. Moreover, we adapt the order in which the partial products are processed with the goal of increasing the number of subsequent MAC operations that can use one and the same operand. In this way, we can save a few clock cycles as the re-used operand has to be written to MAC only once. Listing 1 shows a code snippet that illustrates the computation of the first two partial products of a column. The MOV instructions in line 1 and 2 write two operand words (which are accessed via the pointers APTR and BPTR) to MAC and OP2. As explained above, the 32-bit result of a MAC operation is placed in RESHI and RESLO, while the carry from the accumulation is written to SUMEXT. In line 3 and 7, the carry bit is added into a register named CARRY. More precisely, the carry from the first MAC operation of a column can be directly moved to CARRY, while subsequent carries need to be added.

```
1:    MOV @APTR+, &MAC
2:    MOV @BPTR, &OP2
3:    MOV &SUMEXT, CARRY
4:    SUB #2, BPTR
5:    MOV @APTR+, &MAC
6:    MOV @BPTR, &OP2
7:    ADD &SUMEXT, CARRY
8:    SUB #2, BPTR
```

Listing 1: Product-scanning technique using MAC operations

Multiple-Precision Squaring

Since squaring received rather modest attention in previous work (and was completely ignored in e.g. [18]), it bears the potential for noticeable speed-ups through optimization. In essence, squaring is a special case of multiplication since all partial products of the form $a_i \cdot a_j$ with $i \neq j$ appear twice in the result due to the fact that $a_i \cdot a_j = a_j \cdot a_i$. Dedicated squaring techniques compute these partial products once and then double them, which reduces the number of word-level multiplication or MAC operations by nearly 50%. The squaring routine we implemented involves two steps; in the first step, all partial products to be doubled are generated and summed up. Then, in the second step, the intermediate result obtained so far is doubled and the partial products from the "'main diagonal" (i.e. the partial products that are themselves squares of the form $a_i \cdot a_i$) are added to yield the full result. The first step can be optimized in the same way as the multi-precision multiplication, which means we should use free registers to "cache" operand words and we should re-order the processing of partial products with the goal of executing a number of consecutive MAC operations with the same first operand. For example, once a_0 has been written to address MAC, we can process the partial products $a_0 \cdot a_2$ and $a_0 \cdot a_3$ by only writing a_2 and a_3 to OP2.

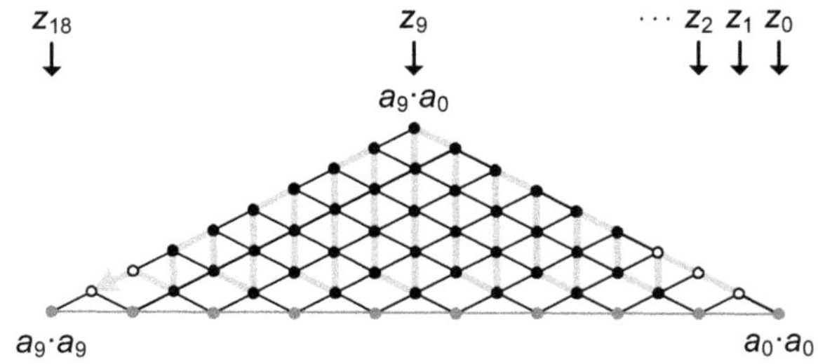

Figure 1: Zig-zag squaring of a 160-bit integer

```
CLR R15
MOV R15, &RESLO
MOV R15, &RESHI
// A[0]*A[1]
MOV @APTR, &MAC
MOV @APTR2+, &OP2
MOV &RESLO, 2(R14)
MOV &RESHI, &RESLO
MOV R15, &RESHI
// A[0]*A[2]
MOV @APTR2+, &OP2
MOV &RESLO, 4(R14)
MOV &RESHI, &RESLO
MOV R15, &RESHI
// A[0]*A[3]
MOV @APTR2+, &OP2
```

Listing 2: Zig-zag squaring using MAC operations

Taking all these optimization strategies into account, we found that the most efficient way to perform the first step is to process the partial products in a "zig-zag" fashion as illustrated by the thick yellow line in Figure 1. We call this approach "zig-zag squaring" because it is somewhat related to the zig-zag multiplication described in [27]. Each dot in Figure 1 represents one partial product. The computation starts at the right corner and proceeds to the left. Both the first column on the yellow line (i.e. the column yielding the word z_1 of $z = a^2$) and the second column (z_2) consist of a single partial product each, namely $a_0 \cdot a_1$ and $a_0 \cdot a_2$, while the third column (producing the word z_3) contains the two partial products $a_0 \cdot a_3$ and $a_1 \cdot a_2$. Listing 2 demonstrates the computation of the first three partial products on the yellow line, whereby this code snippet shows that a_0 needs to be written to the address MAC only once and can then be used as operand in three MAC operations. The first three partial products (i.e. $a_0 \cdot a_1$, $a_0 \cdot a_2$, and $a_0 \cdot a_3$) allow some special optimizations as their accumulation into `RESLO` and `RESHI` can not cause an overflow, i.e. `SUMEXT` is 0 and does not need to be added to register `CARRY`. This also simplifies the w-bit right-shift of the cumulative sum, which has to be performed at the end of each column in order to ensure a proper alignment of the partial products. The white dots in Figure 1 indicate all partial products that do not require a carry propagation. When the first step of the squaring is completed, the intermediate result has to be doubled and the partial products located on the red line at the bottom of Figure 1 (i.e. $a_0 \cdot a_0$ to $a_9 \cdot a_9$) must be added, which can be done together with the doubling in one pass.

Modular Reduction

Since the operands of a multiplication or squaring may be incompletely reduced, the resulting product or square has a length of (up to) $2n = 2k + 2$ bits, and, therefore, always fits into $2m$ words. Our implementation of the reduction is fully optimized for pseudo-Mersenne primes $p = 2^k - c$ and consists of two steps. Let z be a $2m$-word product. In the first step, z is split into an upper part z_H that comprises the m most significant words and a lower part z_L with all the other words. At the beginning of this section we defined the exponent k of our primes to be a multiple of 32 minus 1, which implies that k is a multiple of w minus 1. Thus, we have $2p = 2(2^k - c) = 2^n - d$ where $n = k + 1 = mw$ and $d = 2c$. Given $z = z_H \cdot 2^{mw} + z_L$, the first reduction step is to compute $z' \equiv z \bmod p$ as follows

$$z' = z_H \cdot d + z_L \qquad (10)$$

Taking our 159-bit prime $p = 2^{159} - 91$ as an example, we have $d = 2c = 182$. Since the two operands to be multiplied must be less than 2^{160} each, it can be shown that z' has a maximum length of 168 bits and fits into 11 words. Using $2p$ instead of p in the first reduction step allows us to avoid shift operations, which would otherwise be necessary since k is not a multiple of the word size. The second step of the reduction operation is the same as in the modular addition (i.e. line 5 to 10 in Algorithm 1), except that the variable t has to be composed of z'_m (shifted one bit to the left) and the MSB of z'_{m-1}. More formally, $t = z'/2^k$, which means t has a length of 9 bits in our 159-bit example. The product $t \cdot c$ has a length of 16 bits, and, consequently, the result we get after the second reduction step is at most 160 bits as in the modular addition.

3.3 Fermat-Based Inversion

Using projective coordinates for the point arithmetic has the advantage that only a single inversion in $\mathbb{F}_p$ needs to be executed, namely at the very end of a scalar multiplication to convert the result from projective to affine coordinates [8]. There exist two principal approaches for performing an inversion in $\mathbb{F}_p$, namely the Extended Euclidean Algorithm (EEA) and inversion via exponentiation based on Fermat's little theorem. The EAA is, in general, more efficient than Fermat's technique, but has an irregular execution pattern and an operand-dependent execution time, both of which is problematic if one aims for resistance against side-channel attacks. Therefore, we implemented the inversion by means of an exponentiation of the form $a = z^{-1} \equiv z^{p-2} \bmod p$. In order to minimize the number of modular multiplications needed for this exponentiation, we use an addition-chain as shown in Algorithm 2 for our 159-bit prime. The comments in each line specify the computational cost of the operation carried out in that line, i.e. the number of multiplications (M) and squarings (S). Also given is the intermediate value of the exponent based on all operations executed until that line. In total, an inversion modulo our 159-bit prime costs 158 squarings and 11 multiplications.

Algorithm 2. Fermat-based inversion mod $p = 2^{159} - 91$

Input: Integer a satisfying $1 \le a \le p - 1$.
Output: Inverse $z = a^{p-2} \bmod p = a^{-1} \bmod p$.

1: $a_2 \leftarrow a^2$ {exp: 2, cost: 0M+1S}
2: $a_3 \leftarrow a_2 \cdot a$ {exp: 3, cost: 1M+0S}
3: $a_{15} \leftarrow (a_3)^{2^2} \cdot a_3$ {exp: 15, cost: 2S+1M}
4: $t_1 \leftarrow (a_{15})^{2^4} \cdot a_{15}$ {exp: $2^8 - 1$, cost: 4S+1M}
5: $t_2 \leftarrow (t_1)^{2^8} \cdot t_1$ {exp: $2^{16} - 1$, cost: 8S+1M}
6: $t_3 \leftarrow (t_2)^{2^{16}} \cdot t_2$ {exp: $2^{32} - 1$, cost: 16S+1M}
7: $t_4 \leftarrow (t_3)^{2^{32}} \cdot t_3$ {exp: $2^{64} - 1$, cost: 32S+1M}
8: $t_5 \leftarrow (t_4)^{2^{64}} \cdot t_4$ {exp: $2^{128} - 1$, cost: 64S+1M}
9: $t_6 \leftarrow ((t_5)^{2^{16}} \cdot t_2)^{2^8} \cdot t_1$ {exp: $2^{152} - 1$, cost: 24S+2M}
10: $z \leftarrow ((t_6)^{2^2} \cdot a)^{2^5} \cdot a_3$ {exp: $2^{159} - 93$, cost: 7S+2M}
11: **return** z

A Fermat-based inversion modulo $p = 2^{191} - 19$ can be performed in a similar fashion using an optimized addition chain, whereby the overall computational cost amounts to 190 modular squarings and 12 modular multiplications.

4. EXPERIMENTAL RESULTS

Ephemeral ECDH key exchange requires each of the two involved nodes to perform a fixed-base and a variable-base scalar multiplication. Since our implementation is based on MoTE curves, we can execute the former with a fixed-base comb method (using the twisted Edwards model), whereas the second scalar multiplication can take advantage of the existence of a birationally-equivalent Montgomery model and its high efficiency in variable-base scenarios. Similar to Curve25519 [2], we exchange only the x-coordinates of the ephemeral public keys. Thus, it is necessary to convert the point obtained as result of the first scalar multiplication to a point on the equivalent Montgomery curve. This can be done in combination with the projective-affine conversion so that only one inversion is necessary for both conversions (see [16] for the conversion formulae).

Operation	159 bit	191 bit
Addition	108	133
Subtraction	124	156
Multiplication	1,828	2,555
Squaring	1,505	1,983
Inversion	268,547	419,823

Table 1: Execution time (in clock cycles) of field arithmetic operations.

We determined the execution time of various arithmetic operations with help of the cycle-accurate simulator that is part of IAR Embedded Workbench 6.10 using the F1611 as target device. Table 1 summarizes the results of the field

Implementation	Field Mul	Fixed SM	Variab SM	Full ECDH	Regular	Device
Implementations using curves over a 159 or 160-bit prime field						
Liu and Ning [14]	n/a	12,645,000	12,645,000	25,290,000	No	MSP430F1611
Marin et al [18]	6,293	10,020,000	10,020,000	20,040,000	No	n/a
Wenger and Werner [27]	3,112	8,779,931	8,779,931	17,559,862	n/a	MSP430F1611
Hinterwälder et al [9]	2,266	6,312,785	6,312,785	12,625,570	No	MSP430F2618
Szczechowiak et al [23]	2,736	5,760,000	5,760,000	11,520,000	No	MSP430F1611
Wenger [26]	1,905	5,721,420	5,721,420	11,442,840	Yes	MSP430C11x1
Gouvêa and López [5]	1,952	1,831,063	4,417,661	6,248,724	No	n/a
This work (curve P159)	1,828	1,635,056	3,248,819	4,883,875	Yes	MSP430F1611
Implementations using curves over a 191 or 192-bit prime field						
Wenger and Werner [27]	n/a	11,949,000	11,949,000	23,898,000	n/a	MSP430F1611
Wenger [26]	2,559	9,100,128	9,100,128	18,200,256	Yes	MSP430C11x1
This work (curve P191)	2,555	2,604,338	5,121,517	7,725,855	Yes	MSP430F1611

Table 3: Execution times (in clock cycles) of our ECC software and some previous implementations.

arithmetic for both of our prime fields. For example, a full multiplication (including reduction) in our 159-bit field has an execution time of just 1828 clock cycles, which improves the 160-bit multiplication times in [5] and [26] by 124 and 77 cycles, respectively. An execution time of 1828 cycles is, to our knowledge, the best result for multiplication in a prime field of about 160 bits ever reported in the literature and, therefore, represents a new speed record. Squaring in our 159-bit prime field is approximately 18% faster than a multiplication, whereas a the Fermat-based inversion has an execution time of roughly 147 multiplications. Note that all field operations listed in Table 1 have a regular execution profile and a constant execution time, independent of the actual value of the operands, which helps to thwart certain implementation attacks.

Operation	159 bit	191 bit
TE Point Add.	14,685	19,852
TE Point Dbl.	13,263	17,514
Mon Point Add.	10,276	13,586
Mon Point Dbl.	8,183	10,733

Table 2: Execution time (in clock cycles) of point addition and point doubling.

We implemented the point arithmetic (i.e. point addition and doubling) in C, whereby we used Assembly functions for the field operations as subroutines. The execution times for the Montgomery shape and the twisted Edwards shape on both curve P159 and P191 are specified in Table 2. As expected, the point arithmetic on the Montgomery curve is faster than that on the twisted Edwards curve, mainly due to the fact that the differential point addition/doubling on a Montgomery curve does not involve the y coordinate. In summary, the simulation results in Table 2 agree with the number of field multiplications and squarings as analyzed in Subsection 2.1. A fixed-base scalar multiplication using the twisted Edwards model of MoTE curve P159 requires approximately $1.635 \cdot 10^6$ cycles on the MSP430F1611. We perform a fixed-base scalar multiplication via a fixed-base comb method with and pre-computed multiples of the base point so that four bits the the scalar can be processed at a time. A detailed description of this comb method, which is highly regular and has constant (i.e. operand-independent) execution time, can be found in [16]. As mentioned at the outset of this section, the fixed-base scalar multiplication also includes the conversion of the obtained point from the twisted Edwards curve to the birationally-equivalent Montgomery curve, on which the second scalar multiplication is performed. However, since this second scalar multiplication is variable-base, we use the Montgomery ladder to execute it in an efficient fashion. Taking curve P159 as example, the second (i.e. variable-base) scalar multiplication executes in $3.249 \cdot 10^6$ cycles, which means the total computation time of ephemeral ECDH amounts to $4.884 \cdot 10^6$ cycles.

Table 3 compares our work with previous ECC software implementations for MSP430 devices in terms of execution time of a field multiplication (second column), a fixed-base scalar multiplication (third column), a variable-base scalar multiplication (fourth column), and an ECDH key exchange (fifth column). Also specified is whether an implementation features a regular execution profile (sixth column) and the specific device (seventh column). Our implementations on both curve P159 and curve P191 significantly improve the state-of-the-art; for example, ECDH on curve P159 outperforms the best previous implementation (i.e. [5]) by more than 21.84%. However, it should be taken into account in this comparison that most of the previous implementations only considered variable-base scalar multiplication.

5. CONCLUSIONS

We presented a high-speed implementation of ephemeral ECDH key exchange based on MoTE elliptic curves for the MSP430 family of microcontrollers. Our software exploits the birational equivalence between the Montgomery model and the twisted Edwards model of a MoTE curve with the goal of maximizing the performance of both fixed-base and arbitrary-base scalar multiplication. When using a MoTE curve over a 159-bit pseudo-Mersenne prime, a fixed-base scalar multiplication (using the twisted Edwards form and eight pre-computed points) takes $1.635 \cdot 10^6$ cycles on an MSP430F1611, while a variable-base scalar multiplication on the birationally-equivalent Montgomery curve requires $3.249 \cdot 10^6$ clock cycles. Consequently, both scalar multiplications can be executed in only $4.884 \cdot 10^6$ cycles, which sets a new speed record for the computation of an ephemeral ECDH key exchange on the MSP430 platform and improves the previously best result in the literature by 21,84%. We achieved this performance gain through a careful selection of curve models and domain parameters, aiming for a good balance between security and efficiency, combined with a highly-optimized implementation of the low-level field and group arithmetic.

6. ACKNOWLEDGEMENTS

Zhe Liu is supported by the Fonds National de la Recherche (FNR) Luxembourg under AFR grant no. 1359142.

Hwajeong Seo is supported by the MSIP (Ministry of Science, ICT and Future Planning), Korea, under the ITRC (Information Technology Research Center) support program (NIPA-2014-H0301-14-1048) supervised by the NIPA (National IT Industry Promotion Agency.

Xinyi Huang is supported by National Natural Science Foundation of China (61472083, U1405255, 61202450), Fok Ying Tung Education Foundation (141065), Ph.D. Programs Foundation of the Ministry of Education of China (2012350 3120001), Program for New Century Excellent Talents in Fujian University (JA14067), Distinguished Young Scholars Fund of Department of Education, Fujian Province, China (JA13062).

7. REFERENCES

[1] I. F. Akyildiz and M. C. Vuran. *Wireless Sensor Networks.* John Wiley and Sons, 2010.

[2] D. J. Bernstein. Curve25519: New Diffie-Hellman speed records. In *Public Key Cryptography — PKC 2006*, vol. 3958 of *Lecture Notes in Computer Science*, pp. 207–228. Springer Verlag, 2006.

[3] D. J. Bernstein, P. Birkner, M. Joye, T. Lange, and C. Peters. Twisted Edwards curves. In *Progress in Cryptology — AFRICACRYPT 2008*, vol. 5023 of *Lecture Notes in Computer Science*, pp. 389–405. Springer Verlag, 2008.

[4] D. J. Bernstein and T. Lange. SafeCurves: Choosing safe curves for elliptic-curve cryptography. Avialable online at `http://safecurves.cr.yp.to`, 2013.

[5] C. P. Gouvêa and J. López. Software implementation of pairing-based cryptography on sensor networks using the MSP430 microcontroller. In *Progress in Cryptology — INDOCRYPT 2009*, vol. 5922 of *Lecture Notes in Computer Science*, pp. 248–262. Springer Verlag, 2009.

[6] J. Großschädl. A family of implementation-friendly MoTE elliptic curves. Technical report TR-LACS-2013-01, Laboratory of Algorithmics, Cryptology and Security (LACS), University of Luxembourg, Luxembourg, 2013.

[7] N. Gura, A. Patel, A. S. Wander, H. Eberle, and S. Chang Shantz. Comparing elliptic curve cryptography and RSA on 8-bit CPUs. In *Cryptographic Hardware and Embedded Systems — CHES 2004*, vol. 3156 of *Lecture Notes in Computer Science*, pp. 119–132. Springer Verlag, 2004.

[8] D. R. Hankerson, A. J. Menezes, and S. A. Vanstone. *Guide to Elliptic Curve Cryptography.* Springer Verlag, 2004.

[9] G. Hinterwälder, C. Paar, and W. P. Burleson. Privacy preserving payments on computational RFID devices with application in intelligent transportation systems. In *Radio Frequency Identification Security and Privacy Issues — RFIDSec 2012*, vol. 7739 of *Lecture Notes in Computer Science*, pp. 109–122. Springer Verlag, 2012.

[10] G. Hinterwälder, A. Moradi, M. Hutter, P. Schwabe, and C. Paar. Full-size high-security ECC implementation on MSP430 microcontrollers. In *Progress in Cryptology — LATINCRYPT 2014*, vol. 8895 of *Lecture Notes in Computer Science*, pp. 22–38. Springer Verlag, 2015.

[11] H. Hişil, K. K.-H. Wong, G. Carter, and E. Dawson. Twisted Edwards curves revisited. In *Advances in Cryptology — ASIACRYPT 2008*, vol. 5350 of *Lecture Notes in Computer Science*, pp. 326–343. Springer Verlag, 2008.

[12] C. Lederer, R. Mader, M. Koschuch, J. Großschädl, A. Szekely, and S. Tillich. Energy-efficient implementation of ECDH key exchange for wireless sensor networks. In *Information Security Theory and Practice — WISTP 2009*, vol. 5746 of *Lecture Notes in Computer Science*, pp. 112–127. Springer Verlag, 2009.

[13] L. Li, J. Großschädl, Z. Liu, and Q. Xu. Energy-efficient elliptic curve cryptography for MSP430-based wireless sensor nodes. Preprint, submitted for publication, 2015.

[14] A. Liu and P. Ning. TinyECC: A configurable library for elliptic curve cryptography in wireless sensor networks. In *Proceedings of the 7th International Conference on Information Processing in Sensor Networks (IPSN 2008)*, pp. 245–256. IEEE Computer Society, 2008.

[15] Z. Liu, J. Großschädl, and D. S. Wong. Low-weight primes for lightweight elliptic curve cryptography on 8-bit AVR processors. In *Information Security and Cryptology — INSCRYPT 2013*, vol. 8567 of *Lecture Notes in Computer Science*, pp. 217–235. Springer Verlag, 2014.

[16] Z. Liu, E. Wenger, and J. Großschädl. MoTE-ECC: Energy-scalable elliptic curve cryptography for wireless sensor networks. In *Applied Cryptography and Network Security — ACNS 2014*, vol. 8479 of *Lecture Notes in Computer Science*, pp. 361–379. Springer Verlag, 2014.

[17] J. Lopez and J. Zhou. *Wireless Sensor Network Security*, vol. 1 of *Cryptology and Information Security Series.* IOS Press, 2008.

[18] L. Marin, A. J. Jara, and A. F. Gómez-Skarmeta. Shifting primes: Extension of pseudo-Mersenne primes to optimize ECC for MSP430-based future Internet of things devices. In *Availability, Reliability and Security for Business, Enterprise and Health Information Systems*, vol. 6908 of *Lecture Notes in Computer Science*, pp. 205–219. Springer Verlag, 2011.

[19] P. L. Montgomery. Speeding the Pollard and elliptic curve methods of factorization. *Mathematics of Computation*, 48(177):243–264, Jan. 1987.

[20] C. Pendl, M. Pelnar, and M. Hutter. Elliptic curve cryptography on the WISP UHF RFID tag. In *RFID Security and Privacy — RFIDSec 2011*, vol. 7055 of *Lecture Notes in Computer Science*, pp. 32–47. Springer Verlag, 2012.

[21] H. Seo, Y. Lee, H. Kim, T. Park, and H. Kim. Binary and prime field multiplication for public key cryptography on embedded microprocessors. *Security and Communication Networks*, 7(4):774–787, Apr. 2014.

[22] H. Seo, K.-A. Shim, and H. Kim. Performance enhancement of TinyECC based on multiplication optimizations. *Security and Communication Networks*, 6(2):151–160, Feb. 2013.

[23] P. Szczechowiak, L. B. Oliveira, M. Scott, M. Collier, and R. Dahab. NanoECC: Testing the limits of elliptic curve cryptography in sensor networks. In *Wireless Sensor Networks — EWSN 2008*, vol. 4913 of *Lecture Notes in Computer Science*, pp. 305–320. Springer Verlag, 2008.

[24] Texas Instruments, Inc. MSP430x1xx Family User's Guide (Rev. F). Manual, vailable for download at `http://www.ti.com/lit/ug/slau049f/slau049f.pdf`, 2006.

[25] H. Wang, B. Sheng, and Q. Li. Elliptic curve cryptography-based access control in sensor networks. *International Journal of Security and Networks*, 1(3–4):127–137, Dec. 2006.

[26] E. Wenger. Hardware architectures for MSP430-based wireless sensor nodes performing elliptic curve cryptography. In *Applied Cryptography and Network Security — ACNS 2013*, vol. 7954 of *Lecture Notes in Computer Science*, pp. 290–306. Springer Verlag, 2013.

[27] E. Wenger and M. Werner. Evaluating 16-bit processors for elliptic curve cryptography. In *Smart Card Research and Advanced Applications — CARDIS 2011*, vol. 7079 of *Lecture Notes in Computer Science*, pp. 166–181. Springer Verlag, 2011.

Systematic Low Leakage Coding for Physical Unclonable Functions

Matthias Hiller
Institute for Security in Information Technology, Technische Universität München
matthias.hiller@tum.de

Meng-Day (Mandel) Yu
Verayo, Inc.
COSIC, KU Leuven and CSAIL, MIT
myu@verayo.com

Michael Pehl
Institute for Security in Information Technology, Technische Universität München
m.pehl@tum.de

ABSTRACT

Physical Unclonable Functions (PUFs) derive unique secrets from internal manufacturing variations in integrated circuits. This work shows that key generation with PUFs is a practical application of the generic information theoretic problem of secret key agreement with a compound source.

We present an improved secure sketch construction with our new optimal syndrome coding scheme for PUFs, Systematic Low Leakage Coding (SLLC). Our scheme provides inherent information theoretic security without the need of a hash function or strong extractor, and optimal asymptotic performance concerning maximum key size and minimum helper data size. The secrecy leakage is bounded by a small epsilon that goes to zero for sufficiently good PUFs.

The reference implementation for an ASIC application scenario shows that our scheme does not require the 47% hardware overhead for the hash function that is mandatory for the state-of-the-art approaches.

Categories and Subject Descriptors

K.6.5 [**Management of Computing and Information Systems**]: Security and Protection
; E.4 [**Coding and Information Theory**]: Error Control Codes

Keywords

Physical Unclonable Functions; Information Theory; Fuzzy Extractor; Secure Sketch; Syndrome Coding; Secret Key Generation; Compound Source; ASIC.

1. INTRODUCTION

Secure and reliable cryptographic keys are a prerequisite to apply cryptography in embedded systems, operating in unprotected environments. Physical Unclonable Functions (PUFs) [1, 2, 3, 4, 5, 6, 7] are circuits that measure manufacturing variations to derive a unique secret inside a device to use it as a cryptographic key or to authenticate a device. One main advantage of PUFs is that they provide secure keys for circuits manufactured in standard CMOS technology that do not have access to state-of-the art secure storage solutions such as secure flash memory [8]. This makes PUFs especially promising for lightweight cryptographic scenarios with resource constrained devices [9].

ASIA CCS'15, April 14–17, 2015, Singapore.

http://dx.doi.org/10.1145/2714576.2714588

Similar to measuring biometric patterns in nature, silicon PUFs generate unique patterns inside chips during runtime. PUF circuits are designed to amplify the effects of manufacturing variations in the circuit and extract a unique response pattern for each device. These PUF circuits can be modeled mathematically as random variables with unique properties for each chip that return PUF responses as outcomes. PUF responses are sensitive to measurement noise, environmental changes and aging. So, the PUF responses vary slightly between different measurements, and also over time. Almost all existing PUF types need additional algorithmic support to generate keys that fulfill cryptographic requirements and have a sufficiently low error probability over their entire lifetime.

To derive a secure key from a PUF, we have to ensure that the PUF response has a reasonable amount of entropy. The generation procedure creates helper data that is used later to reconstruct the key in the reproduction phase. The helper data is public so that it can be observed by the adversary. Algorithms for secret key generation with PUFs are a vivid research topic in the hardware security community [3, 10, 11, 12, 13, 14, 15, 16, 17, 18].

Improvements on algorithmic level and new implementations pushed the limits in efficiency and reliability. Some key generation algorithms for PUFs can be seen as *secure sketches* [19]. In general, the current approaches typically require at least two algorithmic components for the post-processing of the raw PUF data:

- *Syndrome coding* schemes address the issue to create public helper data that enables error correction, and for some approaches also the first error correction steps are carried out in the syndrome decoder [12, 14, 15]. During *generation*, public helper data is created. Later during *reproduction*, the cryptographic key is computed from a noisy PUF response and the helper data. The challenge in creating helper data lies in the contradicting interests of revealing information about the PUF that permits error correction, while keeping the parts used for the cryptographic key secret.

- An *error-correcting code* [20] corrects the remaining errors in the output of the syndrome decoder. Here, it is important that the code is designed to reach the target bit error probability of the key for a given application scenario and PUF. Strict hardware constraints on the size of the decoder pose new challenges on algorithmic and implementation level to design specific low area decoders for this purpose.

We focus on syndrome coding in this work and assume that optimal error-correcting codes with specific properties are given. The construction and efficient implementation of error-correcting codes is out of the scope of this paper.

In [12, 14, 15], it has been proven that the discussed pointer based syndrome coding solutions are information theoretically secure for sufficiently good PUFs. Therefore, the outcome of the error-correcting code can be output directly as a cryptographic key. In contrast, the secure sketches in [19] have to be extended to fuzzy extractors with an additional hash function to derive a cryptographically secure key.

Note that all current approaches have a downside that they either discard PUF response bits so that they do not extract all available secret information or that they are only cryptographically and not information theoretically secure. In this work, we will present a method that overcomes these shortcomings and shows optimal performance and information theoretic security at the same time.

Research in the information theory community led to a better understanding of different key agreement scenarios and adversary models on an abstract level [21, 22, 23, 24, 25, 26]. As one typical problem in information theory, a source returns two correlated output sequences. Two legitimate parties observe one sequence each and derive a common secret by exchanging messages over a public communication channel. Analyzing the asymptotic behavior of this abstract problem gave new insights to understand its fundamental properties, especially the limits of how much key information can be extracted and how much public communication is necessary. Our work shows that secret key generation with PUFs can be seen as a practical use case of the abstract scenario of secret key agreement from correlated sequences drawn from a very recent source model, called *compound source* [26].

In the same work ([26]), Boche and Schäfer introduced an optimal key agreement protocol for a compound source using random code constructions. Random codes show optimal theoretical properties, but are in general hardly suitable for implementation in embedded devices since large random codebooks have to be stored. Whereas previous theoretical work such as [23] only considers aspects of the key, [26] also took the size of the transmitted data into account. Based on this work, we will present a deterministic coding scheme with similar properties that can be implemented in practice.

To introduce our new approach on a solid theoretical basis, we will go from the abstract to a more concrete level, and finally into a practical setting, over the sections of this work.

Our contributions

- This work provides the first information theoretic model that fully represents the problem of secure key generation with PUFs. We translate the practical problem of key generation with PUFs directly into information theoretic models and highlight the corresponding parts as well as possible simplifications.
- Our new syndrome coding scheme *Systematic Low Leakage Coding* (SLLC) is the first optimal syndrome coding scheme that fulfills common requirements in information theoretic security. Using error-correcting codes with systematic encoding separates the codeword into an information and a redundancy part. Storing only helper data for the redundancy part minimizes the helper data size and brings the leakage of the key through the helper data close to zero for sufficiently good PUFs. Returning only the information part as key ensures information theoretic security. In addition, reference secure sketch constructions are compared to SLLC on an information theoretic level.
- The implementation part sketching a lightweight ASIC implementation with a small BCH decoder shows that the low secrecy leakage of SLLC has significant benefits in practice. It enables information theoretic security, removes the area-intensive hash function that is necessary for other approaches and minimizes the helper data size.

Outline

The first contribution of the paper is to reveal the correspondence between the practical problem of secret key generation with PUFs and the theoretical compound source model in Section 2. Section 3 introduces the mathematical notation used in the paper. The information theoretic preliminaries and definitions are presented in Section 4. We discuss the existing optimal random coding scheme in Section 5 and present our new deterministic scheme SLLC in Section 6. The evaluation in Section 7 compares our new scheme to popular secure sketch constructions and Section 8 discusses SLLC in relation to the state of the art in a practical setting. Section 9 draws our conclusions over this work.

2. EQUIVALENCE OF SECURE KEY GENERATION WITH PUFS AND KEY AGREEMENT FROM COMPOUND SOURCES

In this section, we show that secure key generation with PUFs is equivalent to key agreement from correlated sources as shown in Figure 1 from a high-level point of view. In contrast to previous work [27, 23], the compound source provides a more detailed model because the effects of various physical parameters can be represented as states of the source.

For secure key generation with PUFs, a PUF behaves like a random variable that is evaluated in the generation procedure to compute the helper data. Later on, the PUF acts like a correlated random variable, depending on the random variable and the environmental conditions. It is evaluated multiple times in the field to generate the cryptographic key whenever it is needed.

In the information theoretic setting, two parties, Alice and Bob, both have access to one output sequence of a joint source of randomness. The sequences are drawn from a joint probability distribution such that they are correlated, but in general not identical. Therefore, error correction is necessary. Alice corresponds to the PUF during the generation

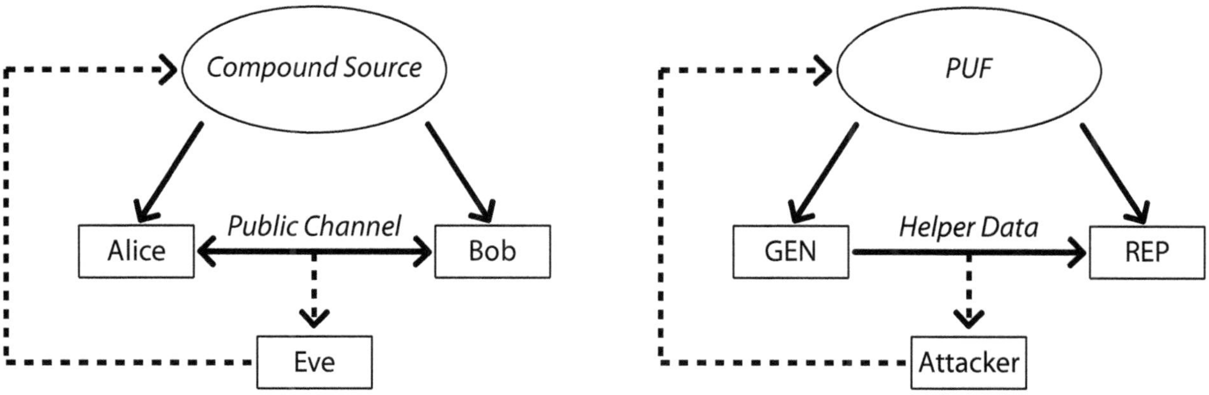

Figure 1: Analogies between the key agreement from a compound source and secret key generation from a PUF

	Information Theoretic Model	Key Generation with PUFs
Source of randomness	Compound Source	PUF
Communication between parties	Public Communication Channel	External Helper Data
Influence of attacker	State of the Compound Source	Operating Conditions of PUF
Distance between parties	Space	Time

Table 1: Comparison of key generation with a PUF and secret key agreement with a compound source

procedure in the manufacturing environment and Bob to the PUF during the reproduction procedure in the field.

The following four criteria show the most prominent equivalents between the two problems:

Source of randomness.

Generating and reproducing one PUF key can be seen as one key agreement between Alice and Bob in the information theoretic scenario, with the difference that Bob can also transmit data to Alice whereas the PUF key reproduction takes place later and we cannot go back in time.

Reading out a PUF twice under different environmental conditions can be interpreted as Alice and Bob evaluating correlated sequences. However, we assume that the helper data of a PUF is generated in a fixed and protected manufacturing environment that is not accessible to the attacker. Therefore, we can remove the state dependency in the sequence of Alice.

The state depends on the environmental conditions and age of the PUF and defines the distribution of the random variable observed by Bob. The random process that determines which actual outcome is drawn from this distribution corresponds to thermal and measurement noise.

Communication between parties.

Storing external helper data permits a communication from helper data generation to key reproduction. In an information theoretic sense, this is equivalent to a noiseless one-way channel from Alice to Bob. Mostly, a bidirectional communication between Alice and Bob is permitted in the theoretical setup. However, the optimal protocol in [26] only requires one-way communication.

Influence of attacker.

We assume that the attacker can determine the operating conditions of the PUF by setting the external voltage, operating the PUF in an environment with a specific temperature, or aging the device. The operating conditions correspond to the state of the compound source. Further, the attacker can read out the helper data, which corresponds to an adversary eavesdropping the public communication.

Distance between parties.

Typically, communication is carried out between two parties that are separated in space using for example a wireless or cable connection. In the PUF scenario, two PUF responses are separated in time. For an adversary with unlimited computational power in the theoretical setting, both scenarios have the same properties.

In practice, a wireless transmission over space can have stricter timing constraints for the computation for the adversary. However, this is more important for other scenarios where an active wiretapper manipulates the public communication between Alice and Bob, which is not considered in this work.

Note that the discussed work does not check, whether the reproduced key is correct or not. See e.g. [28] if the authenticity of the key also has to be ensured.

In a use case, the information theoretic protocol is run several times to establish new session keys between Alice and Bob. Therefore, both parties agree on a new key each time the protocol is carried out. This corresponds to the manufacturing process of PUFs, where multiple different PUFs are manufactured. The source statistics of the PUFs are identical, but the actual sequences and the derived keys vary.

For a single PUF, one set of helper data is generated and then the same key is reproduced multiple times. Alice's part is only executed once so that Alice's sequence from the source, the derived key, and the public helper data remain constant over the lifetime of the PUF. Only Bob's source sequence and his reproduced key can vary from key generation to key generation.

Taking the previous points into consideration, the PUF scenario can be seen as a typically more resource restricted special case of the generic information theoretic model of secure key agreement from a compound source. See Table 1 for a compact representation of the results.

3. NOTATION

Random variables are denoted in capital italic letters, e.g. X. Scalars, such as outcomes of random variables, are written in small italic letters, e.g. x. Calligraphic letters indicate sets and $|\mathcal{X}|$ is the cardinality of the set $\mathcal{X}$.

Further, a superscript over a letter, e.g. X^n, denotes a vector of n instances of X. X_i^j selects elements i to j of X^n. $P_X(x)$ denotes the probability distribution or, more formally, the probability mass function, of X for $x \in \mathcal{X}$. Matrices are written in bold capital letters. Let $\mathbf{A}^T$ be $\mathbf{A}$ transposed. Concatenations are indicated with two vertical lines ($||$).

For random variables X and Y, $X|Y$ means X under condition Y. Let $H(X)$ stand for the Shannon entropy of X and $H(XY)$ for the joint entropy of X and Y, and let $I(X;Y)$ be the mutual information between X and Y [29].

For a better readability, we will switch between integer representations of numbers and their binary representations in $GF(2^n)$ without marking the binary representation explicitly. In cases that require special emphasis, the binary representation of i in $GF(2^n)$, $n \in \mathbb{Z}^+$, is denoted with $b_n(i)$.

4. INFORMATION THEORETIC PRELIMINARIES AND DEFINITIONS

In this work, we apply the compound source model for the first time to PUFs. Therefore, we present the required models and definitions in this section. Figure 2 shows two parties, Alice and Bob, that want to agree on a mutual secret key while keeping the adversary Eve ignorant. A compound source is a source with multiple correlated outputs and an internal state s selected from set $\mathcal{S}$. Alice and Bob observe different outputs of the same discrete memoryless multiple compound source [26] and use the outputs of the source to generate a common secret. Memoryless means that the n output pairs (x, y) of the source are drawn independently. Empirical entropy evaluations of PUFs, e.g. [30], show that this assumption also holds in practice for popular PUF types like the SRAM PUF so that we can apply this theory.

In the following, we will consider the compound source shown in Figure 2. It has two generic outputs X_s and Y_s with joint probability distribution $P_{XY,s}(x, y)$ depending on the state $s \in \mathcal{S}$. The state s can be set by the adversary Eve. X_s and Y_s with marginal distributions $P_{X,s}(x)$, $P_{Y,s}(y)$ are not accessible to the adversary.

Alice and Bob cannot observe both random variables at once. To establish a joint secret, Bob can observe his marginal distribution $P_{Y,s}(y)$ to make an estimate of s. He can further make a rough estimate of X_s by observing Y_s.

This behavior is represented mathematically as probabilistic memoryless channel $\mathcal{T}_s$ between Alice and Bob with input $x \in \mathcal{X}$ and output $y \in \mathcal{Y}$. The effect of the channel is characterized by the conditioned probability distribution $P_{Y|X,s}$, since the output of the channel Y_s depends on the input X_s. For a specific $s \in \mathcal{S}$, the channel $\mathcal{T}_s$ is given by the set of the conditional probabilities for all (x, y) pairs.

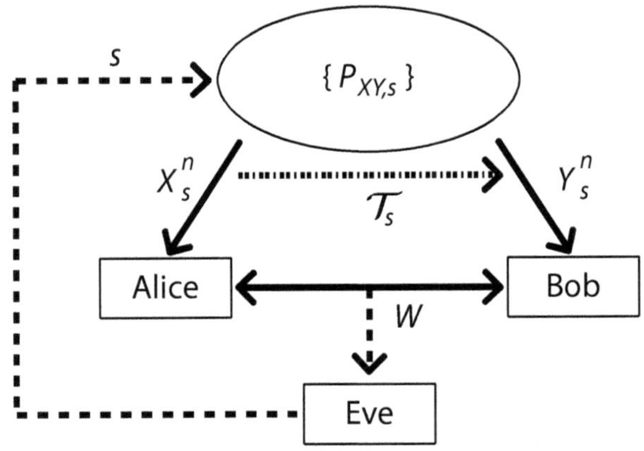

Figure 2: Secret key generation with a compound source

$$\mathcal{T}_s = \left\{ P_{Y|X,s}(x, y) = \frac{P_{XY,s}(x, y)}{P_{X,s}(x)} : x \in \mathcal{X}, y \in \mathcal{Y} \right\} \quad (1)$$

Public communication, or helper data, between Alice and Bob supports this estimation. Alice establishes secret key K and Bob secret key L from the same key space $\mathcal{K}$, with $K, L \in \mathcal{K}$, after observing the two sequences ${X_s}^n$ and ${Y_s}^n$ of length n drawn from the joint probability distribution $P_{XY,s}(x, y)$ and exchanging data over the public channel.

In Section 2, we have shown that this information theoretic model corresponds to the practical behavior of a PUF with an initial response ${X_s}^n$. In contrast to previous models, the compound source can represent that subsequent responses ${Y_s}^n$ depend on environmental factors such as temperature, voltage or aging that can be potentially controlled by the attacker.

The public communication, that is typically carried out over space in a communication scenario, corresponds to storing the helper data W in external non-volatile memory that is accessed again later in time to reproduce a key. A secret key K is established during manufacturing and later on, key L is reproduced in the field. We aim for a reliable key generation protocol, so $k = l$, with $K \mapsto k$ and $L \mapsto l$, should hold with a high probability.

Definition of an achievable rate

A *key rate* R_{key} specifies the amount of secret information that can be derived reliably from each (x, y) pair. This can be interpreted as the ratio between key length and PUF size. Referring to Ahlswede and Csiszar [21], Boche and Schäfer defined in [26] that a key rate R_{key} is an *achievable key rate*, if for any $\epsilon > 0$ and n_ϵ there exists a key generation protocol with source output length $n > n_\epsilon$ where K and L satisfy the following four conditions for every $s \in \mathcal{S}$:

$$\Pr[k \neq l] < \epsilon \tag{2a}$$
$$I(W;K) < \epsilon \tag{2b}$$
$$\frac{1}{n}H(K) > R_{key} - \epsilon \tag{2c}$$
$$\frac{1}{n}\log_2|\mathcal{K}| < \frac{1}{n}H(K) + \epsilon \tag{2d}$$

Condition 2a ensures the reliability of the generated key K, or more formally that the probability that an incorrect key L is reproduced, is smaller than ϵ. From a security point of view, it is important that no significant amount of key information K leaks through the helper data W, so according to Condition 2b the helper data leaks less than ϵ about the key. The rate R_{key} quantifies the performance of the scheme. The rate is the central criterion that quantifies this performance. For a meaningful measure, the amount of actual key information $H(K)$ has to be close to the specified rate R_{key}, as stated in Condition 2c. Bounded by ϵ, Condition 2d states that the key space $\mathcal{K}$ is only slightly larger than the entropy of the key $H(K)$, such that the generated key has good cryptographic quality.

Capacity definitions

In information theory, a capacity is defined as the best achievable rate. Depending if a capacity C is defined as upper or lower bound of a measure, it is the supremum or infimum over all achievable rates R.

The key capacity C_{key} of a compound source is defined as the supremum over all achievable key rates R_{key}. The authors in [26] show that the key capacity of the compound source is given by the minimum mutual information between both outcomes of the source over all possible states such that

$$C_{key} = \sup_{R_{key} \text{ is achievable rate}} R_{key} \tag{3}$$
$$= \min_{s \in S} I(X_s, Y_s) \tag{4}$$

Reconstructing X_s from Y_s with joint distribution $P_{XY,s}$ requires in average $H(X_s|Y_s)$ bits. The helper data capacity C_{hd} is the minimum helper data size that has to be assigned to be able to restore X_s from Y_s for any state of the source. Therefore, the minimum helper data size is given by

$$C_{hd} = \max_{s \in S} H(X_s|Y_s) \tag{5}$$

See [26] for the proofs.

These theoretical bounds permit to evaluate schemes not only in comparison to previous work. They also give designers quantitative information on how far a scheme can still be improved until the absolute limits are reached.

Code definition

Typically, error-correcting codes are defined by the code length n, the code size (or number of information bits) k and the minimum distance between any two codewords d [20]. Sometimes, also the minimum number of correctable errors $t = \lfloor \frac{d-1}{2} \rfloor$ is used. Code $\mathcal{C}$ is defined as set containing all codewords C_i, $i = 1, ..., 2^k$.

The Channel Coding Theorem [29] shows that there exist codes for a channel $\mathcal{T}_s$ with capacity $C_\mathcal{T}$ where the probability of a decoding error is smaller than a small $\epsilon > 0$ if the code length n is larger than an n_ϵ for every ϵ and rate $R_{Code} = \frac{k}{n} < C_\mathcal{T}$.

Similar to [26], we define codes with code length n, code size k and maximum probability of a decoding error for a given channel as (n, k, ϵ) codes for the theoretical part. For the practical part, we will use (n, k, d) codes.

5. AN OPTIMAL SYNDROME CODING SCHEME WITH RANDOM CODES

Boche and Schäfer introduced an optimal combined syndrome coding and error correction construction for a compound source in [26]. In this work, we are the first who apply this approach to PUFs. The scheme creates a large number of random codes such that any ${X_s}^n$ is a codeword of one of the codes with probability close to one. Alice transmits the number of the code as helper data to indicate Bob which code to use for decoding ${Y_s}^n$. The adversary Eve only knows that ${X_s}^n$ is one of the 2^k codewords of the code with the number that is transmitted. However, she received no information which codeword is equal to ${X_s}^n$. Therefore, this information can be used as secret key.

For the sake of simplicity, we will only discuss the use case for PUFs where X^n is evaluated in a controlled manufacturing environment in which the state of the source is fixed. To achieve error probabilities $< \epsilon$ for all possible states and a small $\epsilon > 0$, we use (n, k, ε) error-correcting codes with rate

$$R_{Code} = \frac{k}{n} = \max_{s \in S} H(X|Y_s) \tag{6}$$

Before running the actual key agreement process, m random (n, k, ϵ) codes $\mathcal{C}_i$ $(i = 0, ..., m-1)$ with disjoint codewords are created. The codes $\mathcal{C}_i$ are created in sequential order, starting with code $\mathcal{C}_0$. As code generation procedure of codeword C_j $(j \in 0, ..., 2^k - 1)$ of code $\mathcal{C}_i$, we draw an output sequence of length n and with distribution P_X from the source (PUF). If C_j is not already a codeword of the code $\mathcal{C}_i$ $(C_j \notin \mathcal{C}_i = \{C_0, ..., C_{j-1}\})$ or any other previously generated code $\mathcal{C}_0$,...,$\mathcal{C}_{i-1}$ $(C_j \notin \bigcup_{l=0}^{i-1} \mathcal{C}_l)$, the new codeword C_j is added to $\mathcal{C}_i$. Otherwise, the sequence is discarded and a new sequence is drawn. This process is continued until all m codes contain 2^k codewords.

The union over all codes covers the most likely output sequences X^n, so if the number of codes m is sufficiently large

$$\Pr[X^n \in \bigcup_{i=0}^{m-1} \mathcal{C}_i] > 1 - \eta \tag{7}$$

for a small $\eta > 0$. Note that the codebooks are public, so also accessible to the adversary Eve.

Starting with the actual key agreement, Alice draws the sequence X^n from the source. She transmits (or the PUF saves) the index i of the selected code $\mathcal{C}_i$ as helper data W such that

$$W(X^n) = \begin{cases} i, & \text{if } X^n \in \mathcal{C}_i, \text{and } i \in \{0, ..., m-1\} \\ 0, & otherwise \end{cases} \tag{8}$$

According to Eqn 7, the probability of the "'otherwise"' case in Eqn. 8 is bounded by η so that this helper data generation process is sufficiently reliable.

All codes are (n, k, ϵ) codes for the given channel, so Bob (or the PUF in the field) can reconstruct the correct key L from W and $Y_s{}^n$ with a small error probability such that

$$\Pr[k \neq l | X^n \in \mathcal{C}_i] < \epsilon \tag{9}$$

Considering both error events given in Eqns. 7 and 9 leads to an overall error probability of

$$\Pr[k \neq l] < \epsilon + \eta \tag{10}$$

The proofs in [26] show that this approach is capacity achieving and that the security condition, Condition 2b in the definition, is satisfied with $I(W; K) = 0$ for i.i.d. PUF response bits.

Random codes show properties of (n, k, ϵ) codes, so the error correction problem is solved in theory. However, Alice and Bob have to store all random codebooks, which makes this approach infeasible in practice, especially for PUFs when they are used in resource constrained lightweight embedded systems.

6. SYSTEMATIC LOW LEAKAGE CODING FOR PUFS

In this section, we introduce a capacity achieving syndrome coding construction for PUFs, inspired by the random coding construction discussed in the previous section. As main advantage over the approach discussed in the previous section, our new syndrome coding scheme does not have to store any random codebooks. This facilitates implementations in practice.

We replace the random codebook generation with a deterministic procedure where all codes are derived from one parent code. In the following, we also assume that (n, k, ϵ) code $\mathcal{C}$ achieves a rate of R_{Code} for the channel such that decoding errors occur with a probability $< \epsilon$. We assume that there exists a systematic encoding scheme for code $\mathcal{C}$ such that for all codewords $C \in \mathcal{C}$, the first k codeword bits are equal to the information bits $c_1^k = x_1^k$.

This assumption holds for many popular code classes, such as BCH, Reed-Solomon, convolutional, LDPC codes and many other code classes, see e.g. [20].

SLLC code construction

In the following, we use one (n, k, ϵ) block code with systematic encoding and create all other codes as cosets of the basic code. For the i-th coset of the code $\mathcal{C}$, the binary representation of i is XORed on the last $n-k$ bits of each codeword to create code $\mathcal{C}_i$. Iterating over i from 1 to $2^{n-k}-1$, we are able to assign exactly one code $\mathcal{C}_i$ to each element in $GF(2^n)$.

Let $\mathbf{I}_{n-k}$ be the $((n-k) \times (n-k))$ identity matrix and $\mathbf{A}$ a $((n-k) \times k)$ matrix. For systematic encoding, the code $\mathcal{C}$ has a parity check matrix $\mathbf{H}$ in the form [20]

$$\mathbf{H} = (\mathbf{A} || \mathbf{I}_{n-k}) \tag{11}$$

This leads to a generator matrix $\mathbf{G}$ with

$$\mathbf{G} = (\mathbf{I}_k || \mathbf{A}^T) \tag{12}$$

Let φ_n: $GF(2^k) \mapsto GF(2^n)$ be the encoder of the code $\mathcal{C}$ and $b_k(l)$ the binary representation of l in $GF(2^k)$. For our new approach, we define the code $\mathcal{C}_0$ as

$$\mathcal{C}_0 = \left\{ \varphi_n(b_k(l)) \oplus (0^k || b_{n-k}(0)) \ : \ l = 0, ..., 2^k - 1 \right\} \tag{13}$$

We derive all other codes $\mathcal{C}_i$, $i = 1, ..., 2^k - 1$ as follows:

$$\mathcal{C}_i = \left\{ \varphi_n(b_k(l)) \oplus (0^k || b_{n-k}(i)) \ : \ l = 0, ..., 2^k - 1 \right\} \tag{14}$$

Given the n-bit PUF response X^n, the helper data W^{n-k} is generated by storing code index i.

$$W^{n-k} = b_{n-k}(i) = \left[\varphi_n(X^k) \oplus X^n \right]_{k+1}^n \tag{15}$$

Since for all systematic codes,

$$[\varphi_n(X^k)]_1^k = X_1^k \tag{16}$$

the $n-k$ least significant bits return the binary representation of i. This representation separates the secret key part X_1^k from the redundancy part X_{k+1}^n. The operation $\varphi_n(X^k) \oplus X^n$ can be interpreted as masking the redundancy $[\varphi_n(X^k)]_{k+1}^n$, that leaks key information, with unused PUF bits X_{k+1}^n.

Using indices from 0 to $2^{n-k}-1$, we are able to cover the entire output space X^n such that there exists a code $\mathcal{C}_i$ for all $X^n \in GF(2^n)$ with $X^n \in \mathcal{C}_i$. We can guarantee that $X^n \in \bigcup_{i=0}^{m-1} \mathcal{C}_i$ because $\bigcup_{i=0}^{m-1} \mathcal{C}_i = GF(2^n)$. Therefore, Eqn. 7 holds with $\eta = 0$.

In contrast to the state-of-the-art secure sketches, where a hash function is mandatory, the first k bits of the corrected PUF response can be used directly as secret key without hashing if $H(X^k) > k - \epsilon$ and $I(X^k; X_{k+1}^n) < \epsilon$. If the entropy of X^k is lower, a standard data compression function g_l, see e.g. [29], can be used to compress the corrected PUF response to a key $K = g_l(X^k)$ such that $H(K) > l - \epsilon$ for a small $\epsilon > 0$.

During reproduction, $\hat{Y}^k$ is reconstructed from Y_s^n and $W^{n-k} = b_{n-k}(i)$. Let $\gamma_k = \varphi_n{}^{-1}$: $GF(2^n) \mapsto GF(2^k)$ be the decoder of the code $\mathcal{C}$.

$$\hat{Y}_s^k = \gamma_k(Y_s^n \oplus (0^k || b_{n-k}(i))) \tag{17}$$

Remark

In a typical communications scenario, cosets are used to characterize errors. All vectors in the jth coset have the same error pattern $b_n(j) \in GF(2^n)$, $j \in \{1, ..., 2^{n-1}\}$, that is added to each codeword. For bounded minimum distance decoding [20], the decoder can correct errors by finding j if the Hamming weight of $b_n(j)$ is bounded by

$$wt(b_n(j)) \leq \lfloor \frac{d-1}{2} \rfloor \tag{18}$$

In contrast, we use $b_{n-k}(i)$, $i \in \{1, ..., 2^{n-k}-1\}$, to modify the last $n-k$ bits of codewords to generate the ith subcode. Then, $b_{n-k}(i)$ is transmitted as side information to the decoder. We can represent $Y_s{}^n$ as

$$Y_s{}^n = X^n \oplus b_n(j) \quad (19)$$

Using $X^n = \varphi_n(X^k) \oplus (0^k || b_{n-k}(i))$ gives

$$Y_s{}^n = \varphi_n(X^k) \oplus (0^k || b_{n-k}(i)) \oplus b_n(j) \quad (20)$$

Since $b_{n-k}(i)$ is known through the helper data, the decoder can correct any error as long as Eqn. 18 holds. The systematic encoding enables to generate the subcode without changing the first k bits. Therefore, we can obtain the corrected key $\hat{Y}_s^k$ by

$$\hat{Y}_s^k = \gamma_k \left(\varphi_n(X^k) \oplus b_n(j) \right) \quad (21)$$

Note that Eqn. 17 is equivalent to Eqn. 21. Eqn. 21 leads back to the default decoding problem in the standard communications case where the decoder γ_k can be used.

Example

In this toy example, we use our new scheme SLLC together with a $(n = 7, k = 4, d = 3)$ Hamming code with systematic encoding to demonstrate underlying mechanism[1]. 3 bits of helper data are stored. The code has the following generator matrix **G**

$$\mathbf{G} = \left(\begin{array}{cccc||ccc} 1 & 0 & 0 & 0 & 0 & 1 & 1 \\ 0 & 1 & 0 & 0 & 1 & 0 & 1 \\ 0 & 0 & 1 & 0 & 1 & 1 & 0 \\ 0 & 0 & 0 & 1 & 1 & 1 & 1 \end{array} \right), \quad (22)$$

and parity check matrix **H** [20]

$$\mathbf{H} = \left(\begin{array}{cccc||ccc} 0 & 1 & 1 & 1 & 1 & 0 & 0 \\ 1 & 0 & 1 & 1 & 0 & 1 & 0 \\ 1 & 1 & 0 & 1 & 0 & 0 & 1 \end{array} \right) \quad (23)$$

Let the PUF outputs return random sequence $x_1^7 = 1001010$. The encoder of the Hamming code encodes x_1^4 to codeword c_1^7

$$c_1^7 = x_1^4 \cdot \mathbf{G} = 1001100 \quad (24)$$

Storing the 3 least significant bits directly would leak information about the key and thus violate Condition 2b in Section 4. In the new scheme, we mask the redundancy part with fresh PUF bits to bring the leakage close to zero or eliminate it completely. The XOR between PUF response and codeword gives the code index as follows (cf. 15)

$$\begin{aligned} w_1^3 &= b_3(i) && (25) \\ &= x_5^7 \oplus c_5^7 && (26) \\ &= 010 \oplus 100 && (27) \\ &= 110 && (28) \end{aligned}$$

Therefore, index 6 is stored as helper data value. The Hamming code can correct one error, which will be labeled in bold notation in the following. Assuming $y_1^7 = 10\mathbf{1}1010$ as PUF response in the field, the syndrome decoder reconstructs

[1]We recommend using more complex and powerful codes for a good error correction capability in practice.

$$\begin{aligned} \tilde{c}_1^7 &= y_1^4 || (y_5^7 \oplus w_1^3) && (29) \\ &= 10\mathbf{1}1 || (010 \oplus 110) && (30) \\ &= 10\mathbf{1}1100 && (31) \end{aligned}$$

The Hamming decoder corrects $\tilde{c}_1^7$ to $\hat{c}_1^7 = 10\mathbf{0}1100$ which gives us $\hat{y}_1^7 = 10\mathbf{0}1010$. This example shows how we can combine SLLC and an error-correcting code to correct errors such that

$$\hat{y}_1^4 = x_1^4, \text{ or in general } k = l \quad (32)$$

Although it is only a toy example, we have shown that SLLC permits error-tolerant secure key generation by using error-correcting codes with systematic encoding.

7. EVALUATION

This section addresses the theoretical properties of SLLC, first to show that it has optimal asymptotic behavior for large block sizes such that the capacities can be achieved. Afterwards, the secrecy leakage of SLLC is compared to two popular secure sketch constructions, namely the code-offset and the syndrome construction. For the convenience of the reader, the reference constructions are briefly discussed in Appendix A.

The overview at the end of this section shows that SLLC is currently the only deterministic scheme that achieves the secret key and the helper data capacity, and also inherently ensures information theoretic security.

In general, good PUFs have a sufficiently high entropy but do not necessarily show perfectly i.i.d. behavior. For the security proof, we therefore loosen the i.i.d. assumption to a wider assumption $H(X^n) = n - \epsilon_A$ and $H(X^k) = k - \epsilon_B$ that can also represent correlations. Further, let $H(W) = n - k - \epsilon_W$ with $\epsilon_A > \epsilon_B + \epsilon_W$.

Achievable rate of SLLC

Lemma 1:

Rate k/n is an achievable rate for SLLC and an (n, k, ϵ_1) code with systematic encoding where Conditions 2a to 2d are bounded by a finite ϵ.

Proof:

This section proves that Conditions 2a to 2d in Section 4 are fulfilled such that rate k/n is an achievable key rate for a compound source with channel $\mathcal{T}_s$ using SLLC and an (n, k, ϵ_1) code $\mathcal{C}$. We will bound ϵ_i for each condition, maximizing finally over all four ϵ_i by one ϵ.

Condition 2a.

ϵ_1 follows immediately from the block error rate of the reproduced key p_B that depends on the code $\mathcal{C}$ and the channel $\mathcal{T}_s$.

In practice, it can be computed by bounding techniques [20] or simulation.

$$\Pr[k \neq l] = p_B < \epsilon_1 \quad (33)$$

Condition 2b.

$$I(K;W) = H(W) + H(K) - H(WK) \quad (34)$$
$$= H(\varphi_n(X_1^k)_{k+1}^n \oplus X_{k+1}^n) + H(X_1^k) - H(X_1^n) \quad (35)$$
$$= (n - k - \epsilon_W) + (k - \epsilon_B) - (n - \epsilon_A) \quad (36)$$
$$(37)$$

Therefore,

$$I(K;W) < \epsilon_2 \quad (38)$$

with $\epsilon_2 > \epsilon_A - \epsilon_B - \epsilon_W$.

Condition 2c.

$$\frac{1}{n}H(K) > R_{key} - \epsilon_3 \quad (39)$$

with Rate $R_{key} = k/n$

$$\frac{1}{n}H(X_1^k) > \frac{k}{n} - \epsilon_3 \quad (40)$$
$$\frac{1}{n}(k - H(X_1^k)) < \epsilon_3 \quad (41)$$

Condition 2d.

$$\frac{1}{n}\log_2|\mathcal{K}| < \frac{1}{n}H(K) + \epsilon_4 \quad (42)$$
$$\frac{k}{n} < \frac{1}{n}H(X_1^k) + \epsilon_4 \quad (43)$$
$$\frac{1}{n}(k - H(X_1^k)) < \epsilon_4 \quad (44)$$

Therefore, $R_{key} = k/n$ is an achievable key rate for $n_\epsilon = n$ and

$$\epsilon = \max(\epsilon_1, \epsilon_2, \epsilon_3, \epsilon_4) \quad (45)$$

■

Corollary:

For an ideal PUF with $\Pr[x = 0] = \Pr[x = 1] = 0.5$ and i.i.d outputs, Rate R_{key} is achievable with $\epsilon = \epsilon_1$.

Proof:

Due to i.i.d. PUF outputs, $H(X_{k+1}^n) = n - k$. Further, $H(X_1^k) = k$. Therefore, $\epsilon_2 \to 0, \epsilon_3 \to 0, \epsilon_4 \to 0$ which gives $\epsilon = \epsilon_1$. So, secret key rate k/n is achievable with an (n, k, ϵ_1) code.

■

Lemma 2:

The secret key rate R_{key} and the helper data rate R_{hd} of SLLC achieve the capacities of the source.

Proof:

We have shown that SLLC can achieve a rate $R_{key} = \frac{k}{n}$. In this proof we denote the code size with k_n to highlight that k depends on n for a given ϵ. A capacity achieving (n, k_n, ϵ) code $\mathcal{C}$ for a channel $\mathcal{T}$ has rate R_{key} such that

$$\lim_{n\to\infty} R_{key} = \lim_{n\to\infty} \frac{k_n}{n} = C_{\mathcal{T}} = C_{key} \quad (46)$$

By definition, the capacity achieving code $\mathcal{C}$ has redundancy $n - k_n$ with

$$\lim_{n\to\infty} R_{hd} = \lim_{n\to\infty} \frac{n - k_n}{n} = C_{hd} \quad (47)$$

■

Therefore, we have shown that our systematic coding scheme SLLC fulfills typical information theoretic requirements because the error probability and the security parameters are bounded by ϵ. In addition, our scheme is optimal in a sense that it is capacity achieving such that a maximum key size can be extracted and the required helper data size is brought down to the theoretical limit in an asymptotic setting.

Secrecy leakage in comparison to state-of-the-art secure sketches

The leakage through the helper data is a central security measure since the helper data is accessible to the attacker. Secure sketches using the code-offset construction, the syndrome construction and SLLC all return the corrected PUF response or parts of it as preliminary key. We compare the achievable key rates as well as the key leakage of the three approaches in this section.

The security analysis does not make any assumptions on the PUF. However, it is difficult to compute $H(W)$ in the generic case. To show the ideal case, we add the analysis with a nearly perfect PUF.

Systematic low leakage coding:

For SLLC, the secrecy leakage is given in Equation 38. For nearly optimal i.i.d. PUFs with entropy $H(X^n) = n - \epsilon_A$ and $\epsilon_A \ll 1$, the leakage goes to zero.

Code-offset construction:

The code-offset construction is briefly sketched in A.1. Ignatenko and Willems discussed the leakage in detail in [23] from an information theoretic point of view. A cryptographic upper bound for the leakage is presented in [31] and applied in [32].

In this scenario, the attacker knows that the PUF response X^n was XORed with a random codeword C^n. Therefore, the helper data leaks $H(C^n)$ bits of the restored secret.

$$I(X^n; W^n) = H(W^n) - H(C^n) \quad (48)$$
$$= H(X^n \oplus C^n) - H(C^n) \quad (49)$$

The code has 2^k codewords. Therefore, $H(C^n) \leq k$. For a nearly optimal PUF with entropy $H(X^n) = n - \epsilon$ and $H(C^n) = k$

$$I(X^n; W^n) = H(X^n) - H(C^n) \quad (50)$$
$$= n - k - \epsilon \quad (51)$$

Key generation from internal PUF Response	max R_{key}	min R_{HD}	$I(X;W)$	$I(X;W)$ (perfect PUF)
SLLC	C_{key}	C_{hd}	$H(W^{n-k}) - H(X^n) + H(X^k)$	$< \epsilon$
Random Coding [26]	C_{key}	C_{hd}	0 [26]	0
Code-Offset [19]	C_{key}	1	$H(W^n) - H(C^n)$ [23]	$< n - k + \epsilon$
Syndrome Construction [19]	C_{key}	C_{hd}	$H(W^{n-k})$ [13]	$n - k$

Table 2: Theoretical comparison to related work

Key generation from internal PUF Response	Helper data size	Leakage	Hash function required	Estimated area
SLLC	36 bit	0 bit	no	$\approx 4500\ GE$
Code-Offset [19]	155 bit	36 bit	yes	$\approx 6600\ GE$
Syndrome Construction [19]	36 bit	36 bit	yes	$\approx 6600\ GE$

Table 3: Practical comparison to related work for non-optimized implementations

As a consequence, even for a PUF with nearly optimal properties $n - k + \epsilon$ PUF bits leak, which is significantly higher as for SLLC.

Syndrome construction:

For the syndrome construction presented in [19] and discussed in A.2, two factors affect the leakage through the syndrome $W^{n-k} = X^n \cdot \mathbf{H}^T$. The overall leakage is bounded by the entropy of the PUF $H(X^n)$.

$$H(W^{n-k}) = H(X^n \cdot \mathbf{H}^T) \leq H(X^n) \tag{52}$$

Further, $|W^{n-k}| = n - k$ such that at most $n - k$ bits can be exposed by the helper data. Therefore,

$$I(X^n; W^{n-k}) = \min\{H(X^n), n - k\} \tag{53}$$

Again, for a nearly optimal PUF with $H(X^n) = n - \epsilon$, $n - k$ bits are exposed, whereas SLLC only leaks ϵ.

Remarks:

To design a system with a code-offset or syndrome secure sketch, a hash function is required to provide a cryptographically secure key. For hardware implementations such as [11, 13], lightweight hashes such as Toeplitz hashing [33] or SPONGENT [34] were used.

Maes *et al.* proposed in [13] to use strong extractors [35] to achieve information theoretic security. However, to the best of our knowledge the proposal using a strong extractor was not implemented yet.

In contrast, our new approach SLLC provides a leakage going to zero, according to Eqn. 38, for sufficiently good PUFs as soon as

$$H(X^n) - H(X^k) > n - k - \epsilon \tag{54}$$

holds with a small ϵ. In the random coding approach in [26], a constant leakage of zero can be achieved since the codewords have the same distribution as the PUF response even for low entropy PUFs.

For future research, the secrecy leakage ϵ in SLLC can be reduced with careful code design where $C^n_{k+1}(X^k_1)$ is chosen such that it can be fully masked by X^n_{k+1}. This approach enables nearly zero leakage also for PUFs with lower entropy.

Therefore, we are able to provide a stronger security with a simpler architecture that does not require a cryptographic hash function or even a strong extractor. In the case that $H(X^k_1) < k - \epsilon$, a simple data compression algorithm without cryptographic properties can be used to create a fuzzy extractor since no leakage has to be mitigated.

Theoretical comparison to related work

The performance evaluation in Table 2 shows the achievable rates and the leakage for different secure sketch constructions. All discussed approaches can achieve the key capacity C_{key} and also all except the code-offset construction achieve the minimum helper data size C_{hd}. However, SLLC and the random coding approach are the only ones that inherently provide information theoretic security. This makes, to the best of our knowledge, SLLC to the first capacity achieving and inherently information theoretically secure construction that can be implemented in practice.

8. IMPLEMENTATION

One of the main use cases of PUFs is providing a low or medium security level for standard CMOS circuits that do not have access to sophisticated security technologies that are used in chip cards and other high-security products. In the context of commercial products that are not intended for governmental or otherwise standardized use, reducing the key entropy from 128 bit to 126 or even less than 120 does not affect the security level significantly. If the implementation complexity is reduced therefore, this is a trade-off designers (or their managers) might be willing to take.

From a practical point of view, 100 bits still offer a decent security level, as stated by government agencies e.g. [36, 37]. Entropy estimations of PUF responses such as [30] show that several PUFs already show this desired security level without further privacy amplification.

With the trend towards more reliable and secure PUFs at the circuit level, e.g. [38], PUFs with bit error probabilities during provisioning of 10^{-5} and lower can be manufactured. Therefore, less powerful error correction is necessary to generate reliable keys. The structure has only negligible bias and correlation so that it offers close to optimum security so that the last column in Table 2 holds in a good approximation.

Calculating the bit error probability according to e.g. [20] shows that in this case, a compact high-rate $(55, 43, 5)$ code already leads to a key regeneration failure rate of $7.87 \cdot 10^{-11}$. This is below the Failure in Time (FIT) specification of most, if not all, popular silicon processes (typical FIT failure rate ranges from $1 \cdot 10^{-9}$ to $2 \cdot 10^{-8}$ [39]).

In our example, we chose a BCH $(55, 43, 5)$ code in a systematic construction, which is a shortened version of a BCH $(63, 51, 5)$ code [20]. Running this three times results in $55 \cdot 3 = 165$ PUF bits consumed to derive $43 \cdot 3 = 129$ data bits for the key, and using $(55 - 43) \cdot 3 = 36$ helper data bits.

The proof-of-concept BCH decoding core is a modified version of the one used in [40] and requires 4441 NAND2 equivalent gates in an ASIC implementation, synthesized using Synopsys Design Compiler, comprising of 194 flip-flops and the rest conventional standard-cell combinatorial logic. It uses a serialized input and output interface. The latency is 372 clock cycles per block, and three blocks (1116 cycles) are required to generate a 128-bit key. The decoder operates in $GF(2^6)$ with field elements constructed using the primitive polynomial $p(x) = 1 + X + X^6$. The generator polynomial used to generate the codewords for the (55,43,5) BCH code is $g(x) = \left((1 + X + X^6) \cdot (1 + X + X^2 + X^4 + X^6)\right)$. Since the code is shortened, the first 6 data bits of each 63 bit block are regarded as fixed to 0.

Note that the SLLC decoder only has a negligible impact on the overall implementation size. It can be implemented as a 6 bit counter and a comparator that decides if an input bit is within the information part of the codeword and fed directly into the BCH decoder, or if it is XORed with a helper data bit.

In addition to the BCH decoder, the code-offset and syndrome methods require a hash function. Compact implementations of popular lightweight hash functions like SPONGENT (256/256/16) [34] or PHOTON (256/32/32) [41] require around 2300 GE and 2150 GE, respectively.

Table 3 compares the helper data size, the secret key leakage and an estimated gate count for SLLC, the code-offset and the syndrome method. It can be seen that SLLC is the only approach that combines minimal helper data size and zero leakage through the helper data. For both other approaches $n - k = 36$ bit of the PUF response are revealed.

Due to SLLC, we can use 128 of the 129 data bits directly as keying bits, without processing them through a hash function. The overhead for helper data is only 36 bits.

The area is estimated by adding the size of the BCH decoder and the hash function, if necessary. In a modular implementation where the BCH module and the hash module are distinct, SLLC method requires only the BCH module of an estimated 4400 GE. With code-offset or syndrome construction, an additional an estimated 2150 GE is required for the hash, for a total of an estimated 6500 GE. This is an extra 47% overhead that SLLC avoids. This result is shown in Table 3.

There is the option to decrease the size of the implementation by designing a more advanced joint BCH decoder and SPONGENT module to share resources, e.g. registers. The savings are limited by the fact that the state registers of the hash function cannot be shared with the BCH decoder after the first codeword is hashed into the state. However, there are still possibilities to share other registers or logic that do not always contain valid data.

With an overhead of less than 4,500 gates, 36 extra helper data bits, and the use of SLLC which eliminates the use of a key hashing function, a 47% overhead in GE is avoided compared to the code-offset and syndrome method. In addition, the required helper data is cut to 24% of the code-offset method. We also achieve information theoretic security, and do not have to make additional assumptions on the security of the hash function. From a practical standpoint, there is an additional module less to secure, e.g. against the side-channel attack in [42].

We drive the reliability of high reliability PUF circuits such as [38] into a realm where the PUF key generation reliability is below the failure rate of the underlying silicon device, and also help to account for aging and other environmental effects not yet characterized in [38] and related publications.

9. CONCLUSIONS

Secure key generation with PUFs lies at the intersection of cryptology and information theoretic security on the theoretical side and secure hardware implementations as application. This work transfers recent results from information theory to design a new scheme that is suitable for implementation. As first step, we show the correspondence between the practical problem and a recent theoretical model of using a compound source.

Moreover, this work presents Systematic Low Leakage Coding (SLLC), the first capacity achieving syndrome coding scheme for PUFs that achieves maximum key size and minimum helper data size under the constraint that the leakage of the key through the helper data can be brought close to zero for sufficiently good PUFs. We discuss information theoretic preliminaries and the immediate theoretical predecessor to motivate our work and to set in a larger context.

Our approach uses error-correcting codes with systematic encoding to split the codeword in an information part and a redundancy part. Storing masked helper data only for the redundancy part is the lowest possible amount and reduces the leakage close to zero. A theoretical comparison to related work shows that our scheme is currently the only capacity achieving scheme with information theoretic security while other secure sketch constructions only achieve cryptographic security and require an additional security assumption on the hash function.

The case study demonstrated the advantages of SLLC in a practical setting, namely minimal helper data and that no hash function is mandatory to generate secure keys.

Acknowledgements

The authors would like to thank the anonymous reviewers for their helpful comments. This work was partly funded by the German Federal Ministry of Education and Research (BMBF) in the project SIBASE through grant number 01IS13020A and the Bavaria California Technology Center (BaCaTeC) through grant number 2014-1/9.

APPENDIX

A. REVIEW OF STATE-OF-THE-ART SECURE SKETCHES

The code-offset and syndrome construction are two popular secure sketches introduced by Dodis *et al.* in [19].

A.1 Code-Offset

The code-offset construction is based on the fuzzy commitment scheme by Juels and Wattenberg [43]. For helper data generation, a random number Z^k is selected. The encoder φ_n of the code creates a random codeword $C^n = \varphi_n(Z^k)$ that is XORed with X^n.

$$W^n = X^n \oplus \varphi_n(Z^k) \quad (55)$$
$$= X^n \oplus C^n \quad (56)$$

During reproduction, the decoder γ_k computes the corrected PUF response $\hat{Y}^n$ from Y^n and W^n. First, $\hat{Z}^k$ is computed by

$$\hat{Z}^k = \gamma_k (Y^n \oplus W^n) \quad (57)$$

Then, $\hat{Y}^n$ is given by the corrected codeword $\hat{C}^n = \varphi_n(\hat{Z}^k)$ and W^n such that,

$$\hat{Y}^n = \hat{C}^n \oplus W^n \quad (58)$$

A.2 Syndrome Construction

The presented method uses the parity-check matrix $\mathbf{H}$ of the code to generate the helper data. Using the steps described [13], the helper data is generated according to

$$W^{n-k} = X^n \cdot \mathbf{H}^T \quad (59)$$

During reproduction Y^n is interpreted as $Y^n = X^n + E^n$ with an error vector E^n. The syndrome S^{n-k} is computed by

$$S^{n-k} = Y^n \cdot \mathbf{H}^T \oplus W^{n-k} \quad (60)$$
$$= (X^n \cdot \mathbf{H}^T) \oplus (E^n \cdot \mathbf{H}^T) \oplus W^{n-k} \quad (61)$$
$$= E^n \cdot \mathbf{H}^T \quad (62)$$

For an (n, k, d) code and $HW(E^n) \leq \lfloor \frac{d-1}{2} \rfloor$, Y^n can be decoded to $\hat{Y}^n$.

For algebraic codes, there exists an analogous definition for a syndrome polynomial such that the discussed method can also be applied BCH codes.

Both approaches were already implemented in hardware, e.g. [11] and [13]. A comprehensive theoretical analysis can be found in [23, 24].

B. REFERENCES

[1] D. Lim, J. W. Lee, B. Gassend, G. E. Suh, M. van Dijk, and S. Devadas, "Extracting secret keys from integrated circuits," *IEEE Transactions on Very Large Scale Integration (VLSI) Systems*, vol. 13, no. 10, pp. 1200–1205, 2005.

[2] G. E. Suh and S. Devadas, "Physical unclonable functions for device authentication and secret key generation," in *ACM/IEEE Design Automation Conference (DAC)*, 2007, pp. 9–14.

[3] J. Guajardo, S. S. Kumar, G. J. Schrijen, and P. Tuyls, "FPGA intrinsic PUFs and their use for IP protection," in *Workshop on Cryptographic Hardware and Embedded Systems (CHES)*, ser. LNCS, P. Paillier and I. Verbauwhede, Eds., vol. 4727. Springer Berlin / Heidelberg, 2007, pp. 63–80.

[4] M. Majzoobi, F. Koushanfar, and M. Potkonjak, "Lightweight secure PUFs," in *IEEE/ACM International Conference on Computer-Aided Design (ICCAD)*, 2008, pp. 670–673.

[5] F. Armknecht, R. Maes, A.-R. Sadeghi, F.-X. Standaert, and C. Wachsmann, "A formal foundation for the security features of physical functions," in *IEEE Symposium on Security and Privacy (S&P)*, 2011, pp. 397–412.

[6] A. Maiti and P. Schaumont, "Improved ring oscillator PUF: An FPGA-friendly secure primitive," *Journal of Cryptology*, vol. 24, no. 2, pp. 375–397, 2011.

[7] R. Maes, "Physically unclonable functions: Constructions, properties and applications," Dissertation, Katholieke Universiteit Leuven, 2012.

[8] H. Handschuh and E. Trichina, "Securing flash technology," in *Workshop on Fault Diagnosis and Tolerance in Cryptography (FDTC)*. IEEE, 2007, pp. 3–20.

[9] A. Poschmann, "Lightweight cryptography - cryptographic engineering for a pervasive world," Dissertation, Ruhr-University Bochum, 2009.

[10] C. Bösch, J. Guajardo, A.-R. Sadeghi, J. Shokrollahi, and P. Tuyls, "Efficient helper data key extractor on FPGAs," in *Workshop on Cryptographic Hardware and Embedded Systems (CHES)*, ser. LNCS, E. Oswald and P. Rohatgi, Eds., vol. 5154. Springer Berlin / Heidelberg, 2008, pp. 181–197.

[11] R. Maes, P. Tuyls, and I. Verbauwhede, "Low-overhead implementation of a soft decision helper data algorithm for SRAM PUFs," in *Workshop on Cryptographic Hardware and Embedded Systems (CHES)*, C. Clavier and K. Gaj, Eds. Springer Berlin / Heidelberg, 2009, pp. 332–347.

[12] M. Yu and S. Devadas, "Secure and robust error correction for physical unclonable functions," *IEEE Design & Test of Computers*, vol. 27, no. 1, pp. 48–65, 2010.

[13] R. Maes, A. Van Herrewege, and I. Verbauwhede, "PUFKY: A fully functional PUF-based cryptographic key generator," in *Workshop on Cryptographic Hardware and Embedded Systems (CHES)*, ser. LNCS, E. Prouff and P. Schaumont, Eds., vol. 7428. Springer Berlin / Heidelberg, 2012, pp. 302–319.

[14] M. Hiller, D. Merli, F. Stumpf, and G. Sigl, "Complementary IBS: Application specific error correction for PUFs," in *IEEE International Symposium on Hardware-Oriented Security and Trust (HOST)*, 2012, pp. 1–6.

[15] M. Hiller, M. Weiner, L. Rodrigues Lima, M. Birkner, and G. Sigl, "Breaking through fixed PUF block limitations with differential sequence coding and

convolutional codes," in *International Workshop on Trustworthy Embedded Devices (TrustED)*. ACM, 2013, pp. 43–54.

[16] M. Hiller and G. Sigl, "Increasing the efficiency of syndrome coding for PUFs with helper data compression," in *Design, Automation & Test in Europe (DATE)*. ACM/IEEE, 2014.

[17] X. Kan, M. T. Rahman, D. Forte, H. Yu, S. Mei, and M. Tehranipoor, "Bit selection algorithm suitable for high-volume production of SRAM-PUF," in *IEEE International Symposium on Hardware-Oriented Security and Trust (HOST)*, 2014, pp. 101–106.

[18] S. Müelich, S. Puchinger, M. Bossert, M. Hiller, and G. Sigl, "Error correction for physical unclonable functions using generalized concatenated codes," in *International Workshop on Algebraic and Combinatorial Coding Theory (ACCT)*, 2014.

[19] Y. Dodis, L. Reyzin, and A. Smith, "Fuzzy extractors: How to generate strong keys from biometrics and other noisy data," in *Advances in Cryptology (EUROCRYPT)*, ser. LNCS, C. Cachin and J. L. Camenisch, Eds., vol. 3027. Springer Berlin / Heidelberg, 2004, pp. 523–540.

[20] M. Bossert, *Channel Coding for Telecommunications*. New York: John Wiley & Sons, 1999.

[21] R. Ahlswede and I. Csiszar, "Common randomness in information theory and cryptography - Part I: Secret sharing," *IEEE Transactions on Information Theory*, vol. 39, no. 4, pp. 1121–1132, 1993.

[22] U. Maurer, "Secret key agreement by public discussion from common information," *IEEE Transactions on Information Theory*, vol. 39, pp. 733–742, 1993.

[23] T. Ignatenko and F. M. J. Willems, "Information leakage in fuzzy commitment schemes," *IEEE Transactions on Information Forensics and Security*, vol. 5, no. 2, pp. 337–348, 2010.

[24] ——, "Biometric security from an information-theoretical perspective," *Foundations and Trends in Communications and Information Theory*, vol. 7, no. 2-3, pp. 135–316, 2012.

[25] A. Khisti, S. N. Diggavi, and G. W. Wornell, "Secret-key generation using correlated sources and channels," *IEEE Transactions on Information Theory*, vol. 58, no. 2, pp. 652–670, 2012.

[26] H. Boche and R. F. Wyrembelski, "Secret key generation using compound sources - optimal key-rates and communication costs," in *International ITG Conference on Systems, Communications and Coding (SCC)*. IEEE, 2013.

[27] P. Tuyls and J. Goseling, "Capacity and examples of template-protecting biometric authentication systems," in *Biometric Authentication International Workshop (BioAW)*, ser. LNCS, D. Maltoni and A. Jain, Eds., vol. 3087. Springer Berlin / Heidelberg, 2004, pp. 158–170.

[28] Y. Dodis, B. Kanukurthi, J. Katz, L. Reyzin, and A. Smith, "Robust fuzzy extractors and authenticated key agreement from close secrets," *IEEE Transactions on Information Theory*, vol. 58, no. 9, pp. 6207–6222, 2012.

[29] T. M. Cover and J. A. Thomas, *Elements of Information Theory*, 2nd ed. New York: Wiley, 2006.

[30] S. Katzenbeisser, U. Kocabas, V. Rozic, A.-R. Sadeghi, I. Verbauwhede, and C. Wachsmann, "PUFs: Myth, fact or busted? a security evaluation of physically unclonable functions (PUFs) cast in silicon," in *Workshop on Cryptographic Hardware and Embedded Systems (CHES)*, ser. LNCS, E. Prouff and P. Schaumont, Eds., vol. 7428. Springer Berlin / Heidelberg, 2012, pp. 283–301.

[31] Y. Dodis, R. Ostrovsky, L. Reyzin, and A. Smith, "Fuzzy extractors: How to generate strong keys from biometrics and other noisy data," *SIAM Journal on Computing*, vol. 38, no. 1, pp. 97–139, 2008.

[32] P. Koeberl, L. Jiangtao, A. Rajan, and W. Wei, "Entropy loss in PUF-based key generation schemes: The repetition code pitfall," in *IEEE International Symposium on Hardware-Oriented Security and Trust (HOST)*. IEEE, 2014, pp. 44–49.

[33] H. Krawczyk, "LFSR-based hashing and authentication," in *Advances in Cryptology (CRYPTO)*, ser. LNCS, Y. Desmedt, Ed., vol. 839. Springer Berlin / Heidelberg, 1994, pp. 129–139.

[34] A. Bogdanov, M. Knezevic, G. Leander, D. Toz, K. Varici, and I. Verbauwhede, "SPONGENT: The design space of lightweight cryptographic hashing," *IEEE Transactions on Computers*, vol. 62, no. 10, pp. 2041–2053, 2013.

[35] N. Nisan and D. Zuckerman, "Randomness is linear in space," *Journal of Computer and System Sciences*, vol. 52, no. 1, pp. 43–52, 1996.

[36] European Union Agency for Network and Information Security, "Algorithms, key sizes and parameters report - 2013 recommendations," Tech. Rep., 2013.

[37] Bundesamt für Sicherheit in der Informationstechnik, "Kryptographische Verfahren: Empfehlungen und Schlüssellängen (BSI TR-02102-1)," Tech. Rep., 2014.

[38] C. Böhm and M. Hofer, *Physical Unclonable Functions in Theory and Practice*. Springer, 2013.

[39] Xilinx, Inc., "Device reliability report UG116 (v10.1)," Tech. Rep., 2014.

[40] M. Yu, R. Sowell, A. Singh, D. M'Raihi, and S. Devadas, "Performance metrics and empirical results of a PUF cryptographic key generation ASIC," in *IEEE International Symposium on Hardware-Oriented Security and Trust (HOST)*, 2012, pp. 108–115.

[41] J. Guo, T. Peyrin, and A. Poschmann, "The PHOTON family of lightweight hash functions," in *Advances in Cryptology (CRYPTO)*, ser. LNCS, P. Rogaway, Ed., vol. 6841. Springer Berlin / Heidelberg, 2011, pp. 222–239.

[42] D. Merli, D. Schuster, F. Stumpf, and G. Sigl, "Side-channel analysis of PUFs and fuzzy extractors," in *International Conference on Trust and Trustworthy Computing (TRUST)*, ser. LNCS, J. M. McCune, B. Balacheff, A. Perrig, A.-R. Sadeghi, A. Sasse, and Y. Beres, Eds., vol. 6740. Springer Berlin / Heidelberg, 2011, pp. 33–47.

[43] A. Juels and M. Wattenberg, "A fuzzy commitment scheme," in *ACM Conference on Computer and Communications Security (CCS)*. ACM, 1999, pp. 28–36.

Vehicular Platooning in an Adversarial Environment

Soodeh Dadras, Ryan M. Gerdes, and Rajnikant Sharma
Dept. of Electrical and Computer Engineering
Utah State University
Logan, UT, USA
soodeh.dadras@aggiemail.usu.edu, {ryan.gerdes, rajnikant.sharma}@usu.edu

ABSTRACT

In this paper, we show that a single, maliciously controlled vehicle can destabilize a vehicular platoon, to catastrophic effect, through local modifications to the prevailing control law. Specifically, by combining changes to the gains of the associated law with the appropriate vehicle movements, the attacker can cause the platoon to oscillate at a resonant frequency, causing accidents that could result in serious injury or death. We determine the range of gains, and their corresponding frequencies, that allow an attacker to violate the string stability and stability criteria at different positions in the platoon. Furthermore, we prove that the attack can be successful at any position in the platoon and at frequencies that can be realized by the other vehicles in the platoon. Our work implies that neither the string stability nor stability conditions, when used singly, ensure proper platoon operation, and that neither can be used to ensure the other. Finally, we show that an attacker is theoretically capable of gaining control over the individual position and velocity (states) of other vehicles in the platoon; two attacks are demonstrated for this vulnerability.

Categories and Subject Descriptors

C.4 [**Performance of Systems**]: Reliability, availability, and serviceability; I.2.8 [**Artificial Intelligence**]: Problem Solving, Control Methods, and Search—*control theory*; I.2.9 [**Artificial Intelligence**]: Robotics—*autonomous vehicles*; K.4.1 [**Computers and Society**]: Public Policy Issues—*abuse and crime involving computers*

General Terms

Security, Reliability, Performance

Keywords

autonomous and automated vehicles; vehicle platoon; adaptive cruise control; cooperative adaptive cruise control; attack

ASIA CCS'15, April 14–17, 2015, Singapore.

ACM 978-1-4503-3245-3/15/04 ...$15.00.
http://dx.doi.org/10.1145/2714576.2714619.

1. INTRODUCTION

The vehicular platooning concept, wherein a group of vehicles act as a single unit through coordination of movements, dates back to at least the 1970s [18], and rose to prominence in U.S. during the 1990s with the California Partners for Advanced Transit and Highways (PATH) program [30]. It continues to be of interest to academics, governments, and industry [3, 17, 24], and has seen several recent demonstrations [7, 31], in no small part because of its potential benefits, which include increases in safety, roadway capacity, and efficiency [4, 11, 13].

While many aspects of platooning are active areas of research, e.g. transportation impacts, mechanical and control concerns [2, 20, 21], comparatively little work has examined platooning in an adversarial environment. In fact, we are only aware of two such works: [16] examined platooning under the effects of jamming, while [15] showed that neighbor influences in platoons could lead to increased energy usage. In this work we consider an attacker seeking to destabilize or take control of a platoon through purely local modifications to the control system of the vehicle under their control. Our analysis shows that the primary design criterion of platooned systems (stability) can be violated by such means, and that catastrophic accidents, more severe than simply ignoring the control laws, can be effected.

A critical characteristic of vehicle platoons is that they be *string stable*. In the case of a homogeneous platoon of vehicles (i.e. all vehicles have the same performance characteristics), string stability guarantees system stability [8] and, in the absence of particular inflows/outflows, the prevention of traffic flow instability [10, 32]. As we show, it is possible for a malicious actor to induce both instability and string instability and, if perpetrated on a large enough scale, we conjecture, create traffic flow instability.

An important distinction is also made as to the roles of vehicles in a platoon. Generally, a platoon will have a leader that is responsible for setting the trajectory and speed of the vehicles behind it. The following vehicles (followers) share a common control algorithm that prescribes how they are to react to perturbations in steady-state operation (e.g. the leader speeding up or slowing down). In this work we also examine the extent to which a malicious actor in control of a following vehicle could subvert the role of the leader and, even more disconcertingly, control the movements (state) of other followers, to an arbitrary degree.

Finally, while the majority of this work focuses on analyzing our attack against a single controller (proportional-derivative) employed with particular platooning algorithm

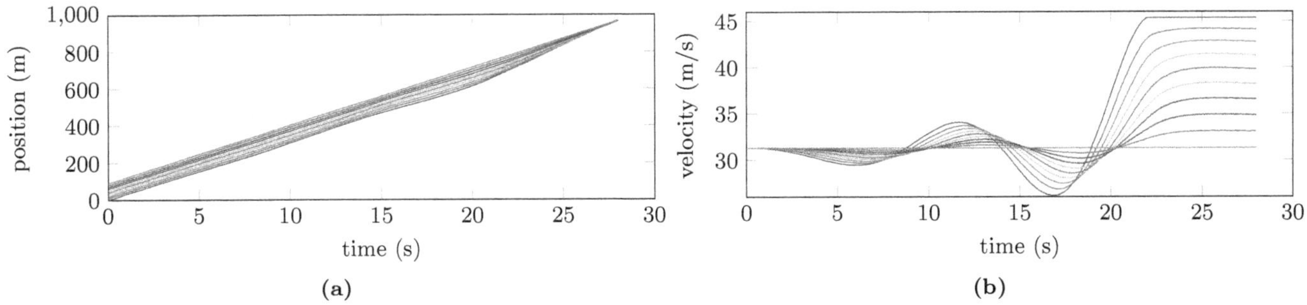

Figure 1: Position and velocity of a platoon under attack. An attacker in the last position leverages instability to cause the platoon to crash into the leader at heightened velocities (time of impact ≈ 27 s).

(bidirectional), we believe that our attack is general enough to be applicable to a wide variety of controllers/algorithms. To justify this supposition we show how a non-linear controller, based on sliding mode control, when used with a unidirectional platooning algorithm, can be manipulated to produce similar unstable behavior that can be utilized by an attacker. What we hope our attack conveys is that control system designers must consider the possibility that vehicles may attempt to actively undermine the operation of a platoon by targeting the control strategy.

1.1 Motivating example

While system instabilities are generally catastrophic, an attacker could also leverage instabilities to target vehicles, in a controlled manner, for crashes with effects far greater than if the instability were not employed. For example, an attacker at the rear of a platoon who wishes to target the leader could simply ignore the control law governing the platoon and accelerate, which would indeed cause preceding vehicles to crash into the leader. The severity of the accident will depend on the relative velocities of the vehicles, with respect to the leader, at the time of impact. However, to maximize relative velocity, the attacker could instead introduce an instability and then cause the vehicles to oscillate at the resulting resonant frequency. Each subsequent period of the oscillation will cause the followers to brake more and accelerate more (increasing/decreasing their maximum/minimum velocity). Before the vehicles have crashed into the leader, and while they are at their maximum velocity, the attacker need only stop accelerating to have the other followers maintain their heightened velocities as they crash into the leader (Figure 1). We have found that the mean relative velocities when the attacker leverages instability can be 60% greater than when the attacker simply accelerates, while the kinetic energy at time of impact can be 160% higher.

1.2 Related work

Within the platooning literature, the work that comes closest to examining platooning in an adversarial environment concerns the stability/string stability of heterogenous platoons [29]. In [12,28], controllers were proposed to maintain the string stability/stability of heterogeneous platoons; however, these controllers were designed without considering the actions of malicious actors. In particular, they assume that vehicles will adhere to the strictures of the control law and that the information provided by vehicles is genuine. Thus, they are unlikely to be able to maintain the integrity of a platoon in the presence of an attacker. The aforementioned work also showed that, in the heterogeneous case, stability does not necessarily imply string stability. We go further and show that in the adversarial case neither is implied by the other; i.e. it is possible to have a platoon that is string stable but not stable or one that is stable but not string stable.

Within the broader work on the security of cyber-physical systems (CPS), the authors of [5] mention that CPSs are uniquely vulnerable to an attack that causes the system to resonate (become unstable), which is one of the goals of our attacker (the other being to wrest control of the platoon from the leader). They do not, however, describe an exact mechanism for carrying out the attack (other than sensor or controller compromise), as such an attack is specific the particular CPS under consideration. We show how such an attack could be effected against a platoon by an attacker in control of only a single vehicle. Barreto et al. [1] analyzed how an attacker could affect a system, in terms of controllability and stability, when given control over actuators and sensors. Our attack differs in that an attacker alters the state matrix directly and can only know/modify their own control input (though they needn't necessarily use it to carry out the attack).

Our attack vector bears some resemblance to an insider version of the replay attack of [27], in that the attacker is part of the CPS and is therefore able inject control inputs legitimately, though the attacker does not need to gain control of sensors to carry out the attack. A single autonomous vehicle was destabilized using a variant of the replay attack that used false-data injection (FDI) in [25]. Our attack is effected through malicious vehicle movement/response and FDI is unnecessary.

Finally, to the best of our knowledge, the formalism we use to model our attacker was first proposed in [26] to define misbehaving agents in consensus networks. We note that the attack is also unidentifiable in the sense of [26].

1.3 Paper structure

The remainder of the paper is organized as follows. In Section 2 we describe the platoon control algorithm selected for analysis and lay out our threat model. The stability and string stability of a platoon under adversarial conditions is examined in Section 3. Section 4 covers the extent to which an attacker can usurp control of the platoon from the leader and affect the states of other vehicles. The security implications of our findings are discussed in Section 5. Finally, we conclude and offer avenues of future work in Section 6.

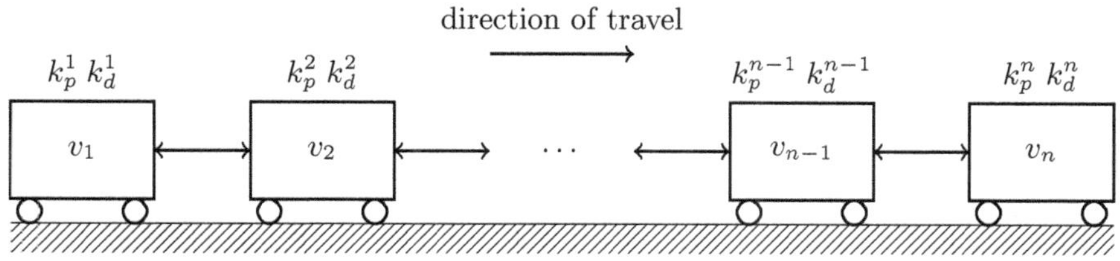

(a)

platoon size	3	4	5	6
$k_d \geq$	2.1	2.7	3.3	4.2
platoon size	7	8	9	10
$k_d \geq$	5.1	6	7	7.7

(b)

Figure 2: (a) An n-vehicle platoon employing a bi-directional control law. Arrows represent the flow of information. (b) The minimum derivate gains necessary to guarantee string stability ($k_p = 1$).

2. PLATOON AND THREAT MODELS

We formally describe the platooning law of our system, the rationale for selecting it, and the capabilities and goals of the attacker.

2.1 Platoon model

Our analysis focuses on exploiting longitudinal control laws for platooning, which are intended to maintain the separation/velocity of vehicles in a platoon as they follow a straight line. While it may be possible to exploit lateral control laws, too, longitudinal control represents an inherently coupled system (a CPS), where the movements of one vehicle have the potential to influence others.[1] In addition, vehicles with longitudinal control (in the form of adaptive cruise control) are available from all major auto manufacturers. Thus, we consider a straight, dedicated platooning lane with a platoon traveling at a constant velocity. All of the vehicles in the platoon are assumed to share the same performance characteristics (i.e. the platoon is homogenous); nonlinearities in vehicle performance can be linearized through feedback linearization techniques [19].

Following the reasoning set forth at the end of the Introduction, of the dozen of control laws available [20, 21], we selected a platooning law that is simple enough for straightforward analysis and presentation, but also has several characteristics deemed desirable by the platooning community. Specifically, we use the bi-directional (predecessor-follower) proportional-derivative (PD) controller of [33] to demonstrate the catastrophic effect a malicious actor can have on platooning operations. This control law is capable of maintaining a constant separation, d, between vehicles, based solely on local sensing. This is important because it allows us to show that an attacker can affect the platoon solely through malicious movement and needn't rely on interfering with communication between vehicles, as in [16].

Formally, the dynamics of a platoon with n vehicles (Figure 2a) employing this control law are described by the following system of equations

$$
\begin{aligned}
\dot{x}_1 &= v_1 \\
\dot{v}_1 &= -k_p^1 x_1 + k_p^1 x_2 - k_p^1 d - k_d^1 v_1 + k_d^1 v_2 \\
\dot{x}_2 &= v_2 \\
\dot{v}_2 &= k_p^2 x_1 - k_p^2 x_2 + k_p^2 d + k_p^2 x_3 - k_p^2 x_2 - k_p^2 d \\
&\quad + k_d^2 v_1 - 2k_d^2 v_2 + k_d^2 v_3 \\
&\vdots \\
\dot{x}_{n-1} &= v_{n-1} \\
\dot{v}_{n-1} &= k_p^{n-1} x_{n-2} - k_p^{n-1} x_{n-1} + k_p^{n-1} d + k_p^{n-1} x_n - k_p^{n-1} x_{n-1} \\
&\quad - k_p^{n-1} d + k_d^{n-1} v_{n-2} - 2k_d^{n-1} v_{n-1} + k_d^{n-1} v_n \\
\dot{x}_n &= v_n \\
\dot{v}_n &= k_p^n x_{n-1} - k_p^n x_n + k_p^n d + k_d^n v_{n-1} - k_d^n v_n + u
\end{aligned}
\tag{1}
$$

where x_i and v_i represent the position and velocity, respectively, of the ith vehicle ($\dot{a}$ denotes the first derivative with respect to time of the variable a) and k_p^i and k_d^i represent their proportional and derivate gains. For normal platooning operations k_p^i and k_d^i are the same for each vehicles (we thus dispense with the superscript unless referring to the gains for a vehicle in a particular position). k_p is traditionally fixed at one, while k_d varies according to the size of the platoon (Figure 2b). Here, u represents the control input for the leader (the nth vehicle). In the steady-state u is generally taken to equal zero; however, we note that $k_p^n \neq 0$ and $k_d^n \neq 0$ implies that the followers would be able to influence the leader's movements, unless u is set to cancel out the follower movements, which would effectively set $k_p^n = k_d^n = 0$. In any case, from the security perspective it seems inadvisable for followers to be able to influence the leader. This ambiguity is of consequence for our controllability analysis (Section 4).

2.2 Threat models

We examine the case of a single actor in control of a vehicle within an already established platoon, traveling at a constant speed, who attempts to destabilize (Section 3) or take control (Section 4) of the platoon. In the context of the present work, the attacker may accomplish this by causing the vehicle under their control to subvert or ignore the control law established for maintaining follower separation. This implies that the controller gains of the attacker's vehicle could be modified and should movement in one direction be prescribed by the control law, the vehicle is free to ignore it. The attacker's vehicle is taken to have exactly the same capabilities as the other vehicles in the platoon.

Because we desire to demonstrate that an attacker is capable of disrupting/controlling platooning operations without being assigned nominal control of the platoon, we assume that the attacker does not act as the leader of the platoon. We note, however, that because of the symmetry of the control law (Equation 1), any influence that the first vehicle in the platoon is able to effect could be carried out by the leader.

The equivalent state-space representation of the linear time-invariant (LTI) system defined by (1) in the presence

[1]Even in the case of strictly autonomous vehicles, a control law is needed to maintain separation between vehicles. Thus, a string of such vehicles, employing the same control law, could become coupled in a platoon-like manner.

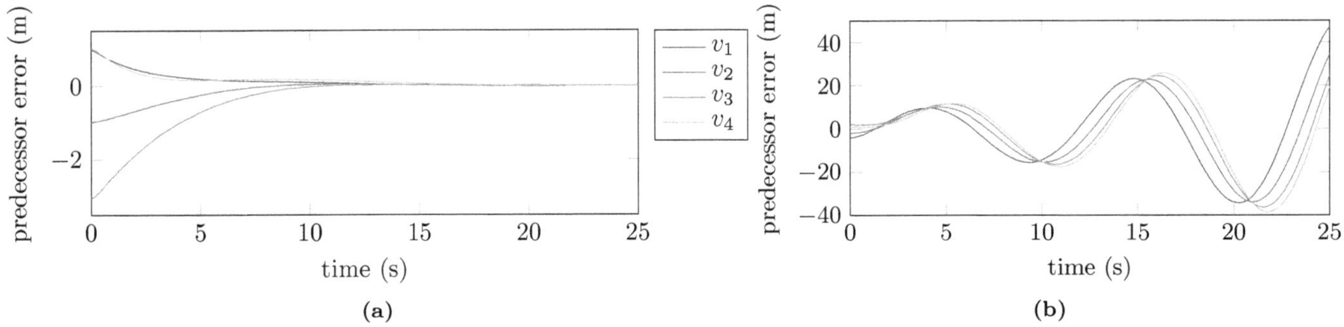

Figure 3: The position error between a vehicle and its predecessor due to initial differences in spacing and velocity for a five vehicle platoon. When the platoon is (a) stable the error reduces to zero, but when (b) unstable the error growth is unbounded.

of an attacker is

$$\begin{aligned} \dot{\mathbf{x}} &= A\mathbf{x} + B\mathbf{u} \\ \mathbf{y} &= C\mathbf{x} \end{aligned} \tag{2}$$

where $\mathbf{x} = [x_1,\ v_1,\ x_2,\ v_2,\ \cdots,\ x_n,\ v_n]^\top \in \mathbb{R}^{2n}$ are the states of all the vehicles in the platoon, $A \in \mathbb{R}^{2n\times 2n}$, $B \in \mathbb{R}^{2n\times 2}$, $C \in \mathbb{R}^{2n\times 2n}$, and $\mathbf{u} = [u_l\, u_a]^\intercal$. C is the identity matrix (because we assume that all the vehicle states are measurable), B has non-zero entries corresponding to the leader and the attacker control, u_l and $u_a = a \sin \omega t$, respectively, where a is the amplitude of the attacker's input and ω is the frequency at which the input oscillates.

The goals and methods of the attacker may be stated formally as: 1) to introduce instability/string instability by modifying the entries in A controlled by the attacker so as to produce an instability and then realize a $u_a = a \sin \omega t$ to effect the instability, and 2) to control the platoon by selecting the entires in A and B under their influence to make the system controllable and then derive a controller for u_a that allows them to move the system to a desired state.

3. PLATOON STABILITY

The stability of an LTI system (2) is given by [6]:

DEFINITION 1 (MARGINAL AND ASYMPTOTIC STABILITY). *The homogeneous LTI system $\dot{\mathbf{x}} = A\mathbf{x}$ is said to be marginally asymptotically stable if, for every initial condition $\mathbf{x}(t_0) = \mathbf{x}_0$, the homogeneous state-space response $\mathbf{x}(t) = \Phi(t, t_0)\mathbf{x}_0$, $\forall t \geq 0$, where $\Phi(t, t_0)$ is the state transition matrix, is uniformly bounded. The system is asymptotically stable if $\mathbf{x}(t) \Rightarrow 0$ as $t \Rightarrow \infty$.*

The homogeneous LTI system is both marginally and asymptotically stable if all the eigenvalues of A have negative real part [6].

DEFINITION 2 (BIBO STABILITY). *The homogeneous LTI system (2) is said to be bounded input bounded output (BIBO) stable if every bounded input $\mathbf{u}$ has a bounded forced response y.*

If a system is asymptotically stable (i.e., if all the eigenvalues of A have a negative real part) then the system is (BIBO) stable [6]. Figure 3 shows the response of a five vehicle platoon to initial errors in spacing and velocity when the platoon is asymptotically stable (Figure 3a) and unstable (Figure 3b).

In what follows, we prove that by modifying the derivative gain of a single vehicle under their control and applying an sinusoidal acceleration, an attacker can produce both instability and string instability in a platoon. The range of gains and the frequencies corresponding to the resultant unstable modes are discussed.

As per [33], we assume that non-attacker (victim) vehicles select the same set of gains, k_p and k_d, chosen based on platoon size, to ensure stability. We denote the attacker derivate gain as $\tilde{k}_d$; the attacker uses the same proportional gain as the rest of the vehicles in the platoon.

3.1 String instability

The stability/string stability condition in the homogeneous case states that spacing errors between vehicles should attenuate as they move upstream. Allowing $z_i = x_i - x_{i+1}$ to represent the spacing error between the ith and i^{th}+1 vehicles, the string stability criterion may be stated as [33]

$$|G_i(s)| = \left|\frac{z_i}{z_{i+1}}\right| < 1 \text{ for } i = 1, \ldots, n-2 \tag{3}$$

where $s = \jmath\omega$ and ω is the angular frequency. $|G_i(s)|$ represents the magnitude of the (error) transfer function between the ith and i^{th}+1 vehicles. The transfer function varies according to the relative position of the vehicles and their gains; thus the effects of an attacker changing their gain, in an attempt to violate (3), will depend upon the relative position of the attacker. To understand the attacker's impact requires that we derive the form of the transfer function for an attacker at each possible position. We perform the requisite derivation for an attacker at the first position here and then simply provide the expressions for the remainder of the positions.

3.1.1 Transfer function derivation

To aid in this task, we first transform the system dynamics given in (1) to error coordinates

$$\begin{aligned} z_1 &= x_1 - x_2 \\ y_1 &= \dot{z}_1 = v_1 - v_2 \\ z_2 &= x_2 - x_3 \\ y_2 &= \dot{z}_2 = v_2 - v_3 \\ &\vdots \end{aligned} \tag{4}$$

$$z_{n-2} = x_{n-2} - x_{n-1}$$
$$y_{n-2} = \dot{z}_{n-2} = v_{n-2} - v_{n-1}$$
$$z_{n-1} = x_{n-1} - x_n$$
$$y_{n-1} = \dot{z}_{n-1} = v_{n-1} - v_n$$

The resulting equations in error coordinates for an attacker at the first position are then

$$
\begin{aligned}
\dot{z}_1 &= y_1 \\
\dot{y}_1 &= -2k_p z_1 + k_p z_2 - (k_d + \tilde{k}_d) y_1 + k_d y_2 \\
\dot{z}_2 &= y_2 \\
\dot{y}_2 &= k_p z_1 - 2k_p z_2 + k_p z_3 + k_d y_1 - 2k_d y_2 + k_d y_3 \\
&\vdots \\
\dot{z}_{n-2} &= y_{n-2} \\
\dot{y}_{n-2} &= k_p z_{n-3} - 2k_p z_{n-2} + k_p z_{n-1} \\
&\quad + k_d y_{n-3} - 2k_d y_{n-2} + k_d y_{n-1} \\
\dot{z}_{n-1} &= y_{n-1} \\
\dot{y}_{n-1} &= k_p z_{n-2} - 2k_p z_{n-1} + k_d y_{n-2} - 2k_d y_{n-1} + u
\end{aligned}
\tag{5}
$$

To find $|G_1(s)| = \left|\frac{z_1}{z_2}\right|$ we have that

$$
\begin{aligned}
\dot{y}_1 &= z_2 - 2z_1 + k_d y_2 - (\tilde{k}_d + k_d) y_1 \\
&\Rightarrow \ddot{z}_1 = z_2 - 2z_{n-1} + k_d \dot{z}_2 - (\tilde{k}_d + k_d)\dot{z}_1 \\
&\Rightarrow s^2 z_1 + s(\tilde{k}_d + k_d) z_1 + 2z_1 = z_2 + k_d s z_2 \\
&\Rightarrow (s^2 + s(\tilde{k}_d + k_d) + 2) z_1 = (1 + k_d s) z_2
\end{aligned}
$$

which results in

$$|G_1(s)| = \left|\frac{z_1}{z_2}\right| = \left|\frac{1 + k_d s}{s^2 + s(\tilde{k}_d + k_d) + 2}\right| \tag{6}$$

Similarly, for $|G_2(s)| = \left|\frac{z_2}{z_3}\right|$

$$
\begin{aligned}
\dot{y}_2 &= z_3 - 2z_2 + z_1 + k_d y_3 - 2k_d y_2 + k_d y_1 \\
&\Rightarrow \ddot{z}_2 = z_3 - 2z_2 + z_1 + k_d \dot{z}_3 - 2k_d \dot{z}_2 + k_d \dot{z}_1 \\
&\Rightarrow s^2 z_2 + 2k_d s z_2 + 2z_2 = z_3 + k_d s z_3 + z_1 + k_d s z_1 \\
&\Rightarrow (s^2 + 2k_d s + 2) z_2 = (1 + k_d s) z_3 + (1 + k_d s) z_1 \\
&\Rightarrow (s^2 + 2k_d s + 2) z_2 = (1 + k_d s) z_3 \\
&\quad + (1 + k_d s)\frac{1 + k_d s}{s^2 + s(\tilde{k}_d + k_d) + 2} z_2 \\
&\Rightarrow (s^2 + 2k_d s + 2 - (1 + k_d s)\frac{1 + k_d s}{s^2 + s(\tilde{k}_d + k_d) + 2}) z_2 \\
&\quad = (1 + k_d s) z_3
\end{aligned}
$$

yields

$$|G_2(s)| = \left|\frac{z_2}{z_3}\right| = \left|\frac{\frac{1+k_d s}{s^2+2k_d s+2}}{1 - \frac{1+k_d s}{s^2+2k_d s+2} G_1}\right| \tag{7}$$

to simplify the transfer functions we define

$$g_1 = \frac{1 + \tilde{k}_d s}{s^2 + s(\tilde{k}_d + k_d) + 2} \qquad g_2 = \frac{1 + k_d s}{s^2 + s(\tilde{k}_d + k_d) + 2}$$
$$g_3 = \frac{1 + k_d s}{s^2 + 2k_d s + 2}$$

$|G_3(s)|$ to $|G_{n-2}(s)|$ follow a similar pattern as $|G_2(s)|$; thus, the transfer functions for the platoon when an attacker is in the first position may be stated as

$$
\begin{aligned}
&|G_1(s)| = |g_2|, |G_2(s)| = \left|\frac{g_3}{1 - G_1 g_3}\right|, \cdots, \\
&|G_i(s)| = \left|\frac{g_3}{1 - G_{i-1} g_3}\right|, \cdots, |G_{n-2}(s)| = \left|\frac{g_3}{1 - G_{n-3} g_3}\right|
\end{aligned}
\tag{8}
$$

We refer the reader to [9] for the definitions of the transfer functions for the remaining attacker positions.

3.1.2 String instability analysis

To violate the string stability condition an attacker must select a gain, $\tilde{k}_d$, such that the inequality of (3) is reversed. Even though the attacker gain may appear in more than one transfer function, the attacker need only cause a single $|G_i(s)| = \left|\frac{z_i}{z_{i+1}}\right| > 1$ to breach the stability criterion. In what follows we demonstrate how an attacker in the first position should select their gain to achieve this; we then offer an algorithm that generalizes the procedure for the remaining positions.

Beginning from the analysis given above, we have that

$$|G_1(s)| = \sqrt{\Re(G_1)^2 + \Im(G_1)^2} \tag{9}$$

where $\Re(\cdot)$ and $\Im(\cdot)$ denote the real and imaginary parts, respectively, of $G_1(s)$. Considering each separately, we have

$$
\begin{aligned}
\Re &= \frac{(-1 + k_d \tilde{k}_d + (k_d)^2) w^2 + 2}{w^4 + w^2((k_d)^2 + (\tilde{k}_d)^2 + 2k_d \tilde{k}_d - 4) + 4} \\
\Im &= \frac{(-k_d w^3 + w(k_d - \tilde{k}_d))}{w^4 + w^2((k_d)^2 + (\tilde{k}_d)^2 + 2k_d \tilde{k}_d - 4) + 4}
\end{aligned}
\tag{10}
$$

The attacker wishes to satisfy $\sqrt{\Re(G_1)^2 + \Im(G_1)^2} > 1$. Using (10) we can rewrite this condition as

$$\alpha(\tilde{k}_d)^2 + \beta(\tilde{k}_d) + \gamma > 0 \tag{11}$$

where $\alpha = 1$, $\beta = 2k_d$ and $\gamma = \dfrac{w^4 - 4w^2 + 3}{w^2}$. To make (11) greater than zero for some value of $\tilde{k}_d$ requires that $\Delta = \beta^2 - 4\alpha\gamma > 0$, which results in

$$(k_d)^2 > \frac{w^4 - 4w^2 + 3}{w^2} \tag{12}$$

Thus, to make the system string unstable an attacker should choose a $\tilde{k}_d$ that lies between the roots of (12); i.e. $k_d - \sqrt{(k_d)^2 - \frac{w^4-4w^2+3}{w^2}} < \tilde{k}_d < k_d + \sqrt{(k_d)^2 - \frac{w^4-4w^2+3}{w^2}}$. We note that if k_d is selected such that $(k_d)^2 < \frac{w^4-4w^2+3}{w^2}$ the system is string stable and cannot be made string unstable. However, a k_d smaller than the minimum values given in Figure 2b would compromise string stability for other vehicles, and furthermore, as we show in Section 3.2, small values of k_d make it easier for an attacker to destabilize the platoon.

Beyond an attacker in the first position, symbolic analysis becomes tedious. We therefore propose an algorithm for numerically determining $\tilde{k}_d$ for a platoon of size n that uses a derivate gain of k_d, at a given ω (Algorithm 1). The general procedure for an attacker at the ith position is to evaluate the real and imaginary parts of the first transfer function, G_i, where $\tilde{k}_d$ appears and arrange the results into the form of (11). Table 1 provides the range of gains, as a function of attacker position, that make a ten vehicle platoon unstable for $\omega = \{\pi/4,\ \pi/2,\ \pi,\ 2\pi\}$ rad s^{-1}. We note that, in general, the lower the frequency of string instability, the higher the attacker gain can be to effect it.

Algorithm 1: Finding the attacker gain to make the platoon string unstable.

Input : k_d, n and ω (a normal vehicle gain, platoon size, and frequency)
Output: $\tilde{k}_d$ (gain for the attacker which makes the platoon string unstable)
$i \leftarrow$ first transfer function affected by attacker;
$\alpha(\tilde{k}_d)^2 + \beta(\tilde{k}_d) + \gamma > 0 \leftarrow \Im(G_i)^2 + \Re(G_i)^2 > 1$;
$\Delta \leftarrow \beta^2 - 4\alpha\gamma$;
if $\alpha > 0$ *and* $\Delta > 0$ **then**
  $\tilde{k}_d$ should be chosen between $\dfrac{-\beta \pm \sqrt{\Delta}}{2\alpha}$;
else if $\alpha < 0$ *and* $\Delta > 0$ **then**
  $\tilde{k}_d$ should be chosen out of $\dfrac{-\beta \pm \sqrt{\Delta}}{2\alpha}$;
else if $\alpha < 0$ *and* $\Delta < 0$ **then**
  an attacker can not make the platoon string unstable;
else if $\alpha = 0$ **then**
  $\tilde{k}_d < \dfrac{-\gamma}{\beta}$;
else
  platoon is always string unstable;
end

3.2 Instability

An attacker can make the platoon asymptotically and BIBO unstable only by changing the eigenvalues of A (by making real part of at least one eigenvalue positive). We first prove that an attacker can introduce an instability into a platoon, and then show that this instability can be effected through malicious movements on the part of the attacker.

3.2.1 *Attacker gain derivation*

To prove that an attacker can cause a platoon to become unstable by changing its derivative gain (i.e. $\tilde{k}_d \neq k_d$), we use the error coordinates formulation given by (4). For an n vehicle platoon, the state matrix, $A \in \mathbb{R}^{2(n-1)\times 2(n-1)}$, for the error coordinates will, however, depend on the position of the attacker.

The general form of A, in the absence of an attacker, is given by

$$A = \begin{bmatrix} 0 & 1 & 0 & 0 & 0 & 0 & 0 & \cdots & 0 \\ -2k_p & -2k_d & k_p & k_d & 0 & 0 & 0 & \cdots & 0 \\ 0 & 0 & 0 & 1 & 0 & 0 & 0 & \cdots & 0 \\ k_p & k_d & -2k_p & -2k_d & k_p & k_d & 0 & \cdots & 0 \\ & & & & \ddots & & & & \\ 0 & \cdots & 0 & 0 & 0 & 0 & 0 & 0 & 1 \\ 0 & \cdots & 0 & 0 & 0 & k_p & k_d & -2k_p & -2k_d \end{bmatrix} \tag{13}$$

Allow $A(i,j)$ to represent access to the element at the ith row and j^{th} column of A. When an attacker is present at the first position, only $A(2,2) = -k_d - \tilde{k}_d$ of (13) needs to be changed. An attacker in the ith position, $1 < i < n-1$, will change the following elements of (13)

$$\begin{aligned} &A(2(i-1),2(i-1)) = -k_d - \tilde{k}_d,\ A(2(i-1),2i) = \tilde{k}_d \\ &A(2i,2(i-1)) = \tilde{k}_d,\ A(2i,2i) = -k_d - \tilde{k}_d \end{aligned} \tag{14}$$

When the attacker position is $i = n-1$, only $A(2(i-1),2(i-1)) = -k_d - \tilde{k}_d$ of (13) is changed.

LEMMA 1. *A platoon cannot be stable if the real part of a single eigenvalue of A is greater than zero. An attacker who selects a derivative gain $\tilde{k}_d < -k_d$ will cause A to have at least one eigenvalue with a positive, real part and therefore make the platoon unstable.*

PROOF. The non-symmetric matrix A will necessarily have an eigenvalue with a positive, real component if an $x \in \mathbb{R}^{2(n-1)}$ can be found such that $x^\intercal Ax > 0$. The gains in the absence of an attacker are selected to ensure that the state matrix of (13) will produce $x^\intercal Ax < 0$ for every x and that the eigenvalues of (13) will have only negative, real components. Thus, for an attacker to create instability, the vector x must contain at least one element such that the product $x^\intercal Ax$ includes $\tilde{k}_d$.

For an attacker in the first position we select $x = [0\ 1\ 0\ \cdots\ 0]^\intercal$ with $A(2,2) = -k_d - \tilde{k}_d$

$$x^\intercal Ax = A(2,2) = -k_d - \tilde{k}_d > 0 \Rightarrow \tilde{k}_d < -k_d \tag{15}$$

Similarly, for an attacker in the ith position, $1 < i < n$, we select $x(2(i-1)) = 1$ with the remaining elements of x set to zero and the modifications to A given by (14) (we note that that for $i = n-1$ only $A(2(i-1),2(i-1))$ is changed)

$$x^\intercal Ax = A(2(i-1),2(i-1)) = -k_d - \tilde{k}_d > 0 \Rightarrow \tilde{k}_d < -k_d \tag{16}$$

$\therefore \forall \tilde{k}_d < -k_d$ will make a platoon unstable, independent of the position of the attacker. □

We note that the above analysis does not necessarily determine the maximum attacker gain that will result in instability. In fact, it gives a necessary rather than sufficient value for the attacker gain; i.e. $\tilde{k}_d > -k_d$ may still produce instability. To find the maximum attacker gain, we calculated the gain margin of the characteristic equation for platoons of size $n = [3, 10]$, using attacker positions of $i = 1, \cdots, n-1$. Figure 4a gives the maximum attacker gains to produce instability, as a function of platoon size and attacker position.

3.2.2 *Frequency response of the platoon*

We have demonstrated that it is possible for an attacker, through judicious selection of their derivative gain, to cause a platoon to violate the stability criterion. It is not, however, sufficient for the system to contain a potential unstable mode: the attacker must be able to effect the instability through the movement of their vehicle (i.e. accelerate/brake in an oscillatory fashion). This requires that an attacker, in reference to (2), either realize a control input at the frequency of the instability ω or introduce a position/velocity error. In either case, the vehicles in the platoon must be capable of oscillating at ω. For the attack to be feasible we thus stipulate that the frequency of the instability be less

Table 1: Attacker gains to guarantee string instability for a ten vehicle platoon, with respect to attacker position and frequency. $\tilde{k}_d$ must be within the given intervals; $k_d = 7.7$.

ω \ position	1	2	3	4	5	6	7	8	9
2π	$> -12.59, < -2.81$	< -6.16	< -8.41	< -10.24	< -10.22	< -10.06	< -10.03	< -10.04	< -10.04
π	$> -15.03, < -0.37$	< -4.25	< -3.45	< -4.42	< -5.15	< -5.28	< -5.21	< -5.15	< -5.13
$\pi/2$	$> -15.58, < 0.18$	< -3.83	< -2.02	< -1.75	< -1.98	< -2.30	< -2.5	< -2.55	< -2.54
$\pi/4$	$> -15.92, < 0.52$	< -3.95	< -1.83	< -1.04	< -0.62	< -0.42	< -0.38	< -0.44	< -0.52

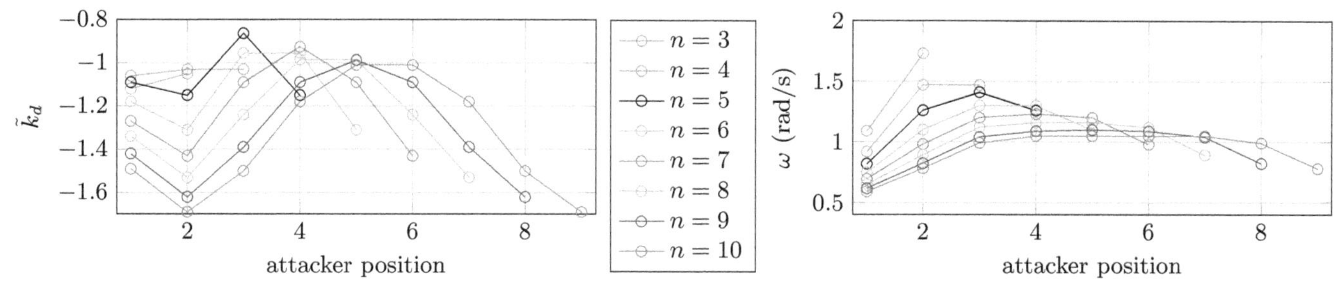

(a) (b)

Figure 4: (a) Maximum attacker gains that produce instability, as function of attacker position and platoon size, n. (b) The frequencies of instability corresponding to maximum attacker gains.

than or equal to one hertz ($\omega \leq 2\pi$); we also applied this condition for string instability (Table 1). Figure 4b gives the unstable frequency for the maximum attacker gain that causes instability, with respect to attacker position and platoon size, found in Section 3.2; at every position the attack is feasible. Figure 5 further demonstrates that an attacker can meet our feasibility constraint for a wide range gains, at every position in ten vehicle platoon (when an attacker gain resulted in multiple instabilities, we selected the one with the highest frequency).

The exact response of the system to the instability introduced by the attacker may be calculated as follows. The solution of the LTI state-space system (2) with $u = a \sin \omega_t$ can be written as $\mathbf{x}(t) = \mathbf{x}_h(t) + \mathbf{x}_f(t)$, where $\mathbf{x}_h(t) = e^{At}\mathbf{x}_0$ is the zero-input or homogeneous solution and $\mathbf{x}_f(t) = a\alpha \sin(\omega_t + \phi)$ is the zero-state or forced response [6]. In the forced response α is the magnitude of the transfer function $\hat{g}(s) = C(sI - A)^{-1}B$, computed at $s = j\omega$, and ϕ is the phase angle of the transfer function, computed at $s = j\omega$. Referring to the stability conditions discussed earlier, we can say that if all the eigenvalues of A have negative real parts, the homogeneous part $\mathbf{x}_h(t) \to 0$ and $\mathbf{x}(t)$ is then equal to the forced response $\mathbf{x}_f(t)$. In other words, the the LTI system response oscillates with the attacker's frequency ω. The oscillations in this case are bounded, not fulfilling attacker's objectives.

In order to create growing (unbounded) oscillations, the attacker has to change the eigenvalues of A (i.e. make the real part of at least one eigenvalue positive) by changing $\tilde{k}_d$, as shown in the previous section. Changing $\tilde{k}_d$ can result in two types of behavior, depending on the k_d used by the platoon.

1) *If the attacker selects $\tilde{k}_d < -k_d$ and k_d is near the minimum value given in Figure 2b* then in addition to making the real parts of up to two eigenvalues positive, imaginary parts to some of the remaining eigenvalues of A may also be introduced. This will result in oscillating $\mathbf{x}_h(t)$ with growing amplitude (caused by the negative damping introduced by the attacker) and with frequency $\omega_d = \omega_n\sqrt{1-\zeta^2}$ with growing amplitude, where ω_n is the natural frequency of the platoon, and ζ is the damping coefficient. The natural frequency ω_n is the magnitude of the poles with an imaginary part. This implies that the time response of the platoon states, $\mathbf{x}(t) = \mathbf{x}_h(t) + \mathbf{x}_f(t)$, is sum of two signals oscillating at two different frequencies ω_d and ω and that the amplitude of the oscillations grow with time.

2) *If the attacker selects $\tilde{k}_d < -k_d$ and k_d is much greater than the minimum value given in Figure 2b* then, unlike the above scenario, the attacker is only able to make the real parts of up to two eigenvalues positive, but not introduce imaginary parts to any eigenvalues of A. This will result in exponentially growing $\mathbf{x}_h(t)$ (caused by the negative damping introduced by the attacker) without any oscillations. This implies that the time response of platoon states, $\mathbf{x}(t) = \mathbf{x}_h(t) + \mathbf{x}_f(t)$, grows with time and oscillates at the attacker's frequency ω.

3.3 Comparing string stability and stability

In the case of a homogeneous platoon, string stability (SS) will ensure stability (S); however, in the adversarial case neither implies the other. To prove that $SS \nRightarrow S$ and $S \nRightarrow SS$, it is sufficient to find one example in which the system is stable but not string stable and another example in which it is string stable but not stable. For the former case, we select $n = 20$, $k_d = 14$, and an attacker at position one with $\tilde{k}_d = -0.2$, which results in stability/string instability at $\omega = 2.1\,\mathrm{rad\,s^{-1}}$, while for the latter we use $n = 3$, $k_d = 2.5$, and an attacker at position one with $\tilde{k}_d = -5$ to produce instability/string stability at $\omega = 0.474\,\mathrm{rad\,s^{-1}}$ (Figure 6 depicts the string stable/string unstable regions vs. $\tilde{k}_d$ for these cases).

4. PLATOON CONTROLLABILITY

In this section we investigate the controllability of the platoon from an attacker's perspective; i.e. whether an attacker can cause other vehicles in the platoon to take on arbitrary

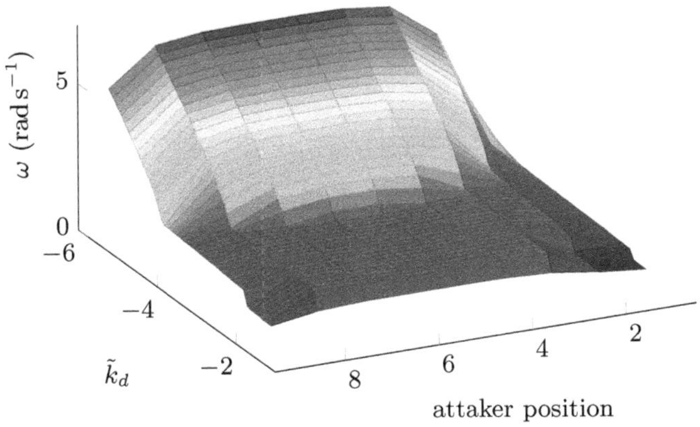

Figure 5: Frequencies at which a ten vehicle platoon can be made unstable, with respect to attacker position and gain.

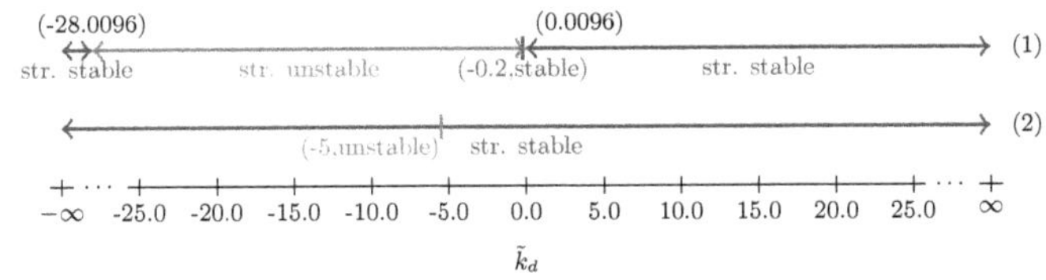

Figure 6: Attacker at position one. (1) system stable but not string stable. (2) system string stable but not stable.

states and by doing so fully control their movements (separation between neighboring vehicles and velocity).

DEFINITION 3 (CONTROLLABILITY). *A system is said to be controllable if and only if it is possible, by means of the input, to transfer the system from one state to another state in finite time.*

A LTI system represented by

$$\dot{x} = Ax + Bu \tag{17}$$

where $x \in \mathbb{R}^n$, $A \in \mathbb{R}^{n \times n}$, $u \in \mathbb{R}^m$, and $B \in \mathbb{R}^{n \times m}$. is controllable if the controllability matrix

$$\mathcal{C} = \left[\begin{array}{ccccc} B & AB & A^2B & \cdots & A^{n-1}B \end{array}\right] \tag{18}$$

is full rank (i.e $rank(\mathcal{C}) = n$) [6].

In what follows, we perform a controllability analysis to determine an attacker's ability to control the states (position and velocity) of other vehicles in the platoon. A general controllability framework for dynamic systems was investigated from a security perspective in [1]. We are specifically interested in whether an attacker can control the states of all the other vehicles or only some vehicle states in a platoon. To comment on the controllability of the vehicle platoon with an attacker planning malicious control, we consider a five vehicle platoon using error coordinates. Due to the regularity of the state matrix, only three attacker positions need to be examined. Because of the ambiguity in how the control law is to be applied (end of Section 2.1), we investigate controllability for two different leader behaviors: 1) the leader is not affected by followers and 2) the leader responds to the perturbations of followers as any other vehicle in the platoon would.

4.1 Lead vehicle unaffected by followers

In this scenario the lead vehicle is not applying the vehicle platooning control law and moves at a constant speed ($k_p^n = k_d^n = 0, u_l = 0$). Equations of motion for the lead vehicle (5th vehicle) can be written as

$$\dot{x}_5 = v_5$$
$$\dot{v}_5 = 0.$$

We use relative equations of motion for controllability analysis. Under this scenario we investigate controllability of three cases for attacker at first, second, and third position.

Attacker at 1st position. A and B matrices for the LTI system in (17) for a five vehicle platoon with attacker in the first position can be written as

$$A = \begin{bmatrix} 0 & 1 & 0 & 0 & 0 & 0 & 0 & 0 \\ -2k_p & -2k_d & k_p & k_d & 0 & 0 & 0 & 0 \\ 0 & 0 & 0 & 1 & 0 & 0 & 0 & 0 \\ k_p & k_d & -2k_p & -2k_d & k_p & k_d & 0 & 0 \\ 0 & 0 & 0 & 0 & 0 & 1 & 0 & 0 \\ 0 & 0 & k_p & k_d & -2k_p & -2k_d & k_p & k_d \\ 0 & 0 & 0 & 0 & 0 & 0 & 0 & 1 \\ 0 & 0 & 0 & 0 & k_p & k_d & -k_p & k_d \end{bmatrix}$$

$$B = \left[\begin{array}{cccccccc} 0 & 1 & 0 & 0 & 0 & 0 & 0 & 0 \end{array}\right]^\top.$$

We can compute the controllability matrix $\mathcal{C}$ for the above system using (18). It can be verified that

$$\det(\mathcal{C}) = k_p^{12} \neq 0$$

Therefore we can say that $rank(\mathcal{C}) = 8$ meaning that system is controllable and the attacker can control relative position and velocity between all the vehicles.

Attacker at 2nd position. A and B matrices for the LTI system in (17) for a five vehicle platoon with attacker in the second position can be written as

$$A = \begin{bmatrix} 0 & 1 & 0 & 0 & 0 & 0 & 0 & 0 \\ -2k_p & -2k_d & k_p & k_d & 0 & 0 & 0 & 0 \\ 0 & 0 & 0 & 1 & 0 & 0 & 0 & 0 \\ k_p & k_d & -2k_p & -2k_d & k_p & k_d & 0 & 0 \\ 0 & 0 & 0 & 0 & 0 & 1 & 0 & 0 \\ 0 & 0 & k_p & k_d & -2k_p & -2k_d & k_p & k_d \\ 0 & 0 & 0 & 0 & 0 & 0 & 0 & 1 \\ 0 & 0 & 0 & 0 & k_p & k_d & -k_p & -k_d \end{bmatrix}$$

$$B = \left[\begin{array}{cccccccc} 0 & -1 & 0 & 1 & 0 & 0 & 0 & 0 \end{array}\right]^\top.$$

We can compute the controllability matrix $\mathcal{C}$ for the above system using (18). It can be verified that

$$\det(\mathcal{C}) = 0$$

It can be verified that $rank(\mathcal{C}) = 6 < 8$ meaning that system is not fully controllable when the attacker is at second position.

To find out uncontrollable states we perform similarity transformation to bring the controllability matrix into Row Reduced Echelon Form (RREF) which is given by

$$RREF(\mathcal{C}) = \begin{bmatrix} 1 & 0 & 0 & 0 & 0 & 0 & 0 & 0 \\ 0 & 1 & 0 & 0 & 0 & 0 & 0 & 0 \\ 0 & 0 & 1 & 0 & 0 & 0 & a_1 & a_2 \\ 0 & 0 & 0 & 1 & 0 & 0 & a_3 & a_4 \\ 0 & 0 & 0 & 0 & 1 & 0 & a_5 & a_6 \\ 0 & 0 & 0 & 0 & 0 & 1 & a_7 & a_8 \end{bmatrix} \tag{19}$$

Table 2: Five vehicle controllability results

Case	Position#1	Position#2	Position#3
1 ($\dot{v}_5 = 0$)	Cont	Uncont	Cont
2 ($\dot{v}_5 \neq 0$)	Cont	Cont	Uncont

where $a_1 = -3k_p^2$, $a_2 = 12k_dk_p^2$, $a_3 = -6k_dk_p$, $a_4 = 24k_d^2k_p - 3k_p^2$, $a_5 = -3k_d^2 - 4k_p$, $a_6 = 12k_d^3 + 10k_pk_d$, $a_7 = -4k_d$, $a_8 = 13k_d^2 - 4k_p$. The six controllable states can then be written as

$$X_{cont} = \begin{bmatrix} z_1 \\ y_1 \\ z_2 + a_1z_4 + a_2y_4 \\ y_2 + a_3z_4 + a_4y_4 \\ z_3 + a_5z_4 + a_6y_4 \\ y_3 + a_7z_4 + a_8y_4 \end{bmatrix}$$

where $z_1 = x_1 - x_2$, $y_1 = v_1 - v_2$, $z_2 = x_2 - x_3$, $y_2 = v_2 - v_3$, $z_3 = x_3 - x_4$, $y_3 = v_3 - v_4$, $z_4 = x_4 - x_5$, and $y_4 = v_4 - v_5$ are relative position and velocity coordinates.

Attacker at 3rd position. A and B matrices for the LTI system in (17) for a five vehicle platoon with attacker in the third position can be written as

$$A = \begin{bmatrix} 0 & 1 & 0 & 0 & 0 & 0 & 0 & 0 \\ -2k_p & -2k_d & k_p & k_d & 0 & 0 & 0 & 0 \\ 0 & 0 & 0 & 1 & 0 & 0 & 0 & 0 \\ k_p & k_d & -2k_p & -2k_d & k_p & k_d & 0 & 0 \\ 0 & 0 & 0 & 0 & 0 & 1 & 0 & 0 \\ 0 & 0 & k_p & k_d & -2k_p & -2k_d & k_p & k_d \\ 0 & 0 & 0 & 0 & 0 & 0 & 0 & 1 \\ 0 & 0 & 0 & 0 & k_p & k_d & -k_p & -k_d \end{bmatrix}$$

$B = \begin{bmatrix} 0 & 0 & 0 & -1 & 0 & 1 & 0 & 0 \end{bmatrix}^\top$.

We can compute the controllability matrix $\mathcal{C}$ for the above system using (18). It can be verified that

$$\det(\mathcal{C}) = k_p^{12} \neq 0$$

Therefore we can say that $rank(\mathcal{C}) = 8$ meaning that system is controllable and the attacker at the third position can control relative position and velocity between all the vehicles.

4.2 Lead vehicle affected by followers

In this scenario the lead vehicle is also applying the vehicle platooning control law meaning the attacker can also affect the leader's motion in this case ($k_p^n = k_p, k_d^n = k_d, u_l = 0$). Equations of motion for the lead vehicle (5th vehicle) can be written as

$$\dot{x}_5 = v_5$$
$$\dot{v}_5 = k_p(x_4 - x_5) + k_d(v_4 - v_5).$$

Under this scenario we investigated the controllability for the three cases of an attacker at first, second, and third position, as above. Table 2 summarizes the controllability analysis results for the two types of leader behavior. Note: an attacker in the third position for the second case is able to control four states, which are a combination of several individual vehicle states, as in the case of an attacker in the second position in the first case.

Based on our analysis we conclude that the symmetry of an attacker's position makes the system uncontrollable, from the attacker's perspective. For an attacker to completely control the platoon, the attacker must be situated at certain positions, which are determined by how the leader implements the platooning control law; partial control (which may or may not allow an attacker to control other vehicle states individually) is possible from every position in the platoon.

Having determined which states an attacker can control, the next step is to create a controller for u_a that allows an attacker to control its own motion in such a way as to regulate distance and velocity between two adjacent vehicles. We consider the feasibility of designing such controllers in Section 5.2. This type of attack is distinct from, and more powerful than, an attack in which the attacker's gains are changed to destabilize the platoon, as it provides more flexibility (individual states, or a subset of vehicle states, may be controlled, to a perhaps arbitrary) and safety to the attacker (the attacker needn't be affected by the attack).

5. DISCUSSION

The security/safety implications of the findings presented in Sections 3 and 4 are discussed.

5.1 Stability

An attacker able to violate string stability on a large enough scale (i.e. an attacker in control of several compromised vehicles) and in the right conditions (i.e. high traffic densities) could effect traffic flow instability; e.g. the creation of phantom traffic jams. Within a single platoon, violations of string stability would lead to greater than anticipated vehicle separations, which would possibly negate the fuel savings of the platoon, or allow an attacker to carry out the attack of [15] more effectively.

The example given in Section 1.1 illustrates how a single attacker can leverage instability to target the leader of a platoon. By changing our threat model slightly, in order accommodate an attacker in control of two vehicles or two colluding attackers, we can also illustrate how a single, non-leader vehicle can be targeted. In this case the two attackers are positioned at the first and ninth position of a ten vehicle platoon. They begin to accelerate and brake contrariwise (one breaks while the other accelerates) at an unstable frequency. Vehicles following the fifth vehicle will brake at the same time vehicles preceding the fifth accelerate (and vice versa); the fifth vehicle will not be disturbed. Eventually the oscillation produced grows so great that the vehicles collide at the center point of the platoon; i.e. the platoon collapses in on the fifth vehicle (Figure 7). By employing different amplitudes for their respective oscillations, the attackers could target vehicles at other positions for the same attack.

We note that countering such attacker-induced instabilities is not a simple matter of damping out the normal modes of the system. Figure 8 shows the position/velocity gain for the ninth vehicle in a platoon due to a perturbation from an attacker situated at the first position of the platoon. The wide bandwidth of the gain shows that even if the attacker doesn't oscillate at the natural frequency of the system, they can still cause significant deviations in velocity/position for the victim (essentially each subsequent period of oscillation by the attacker will cause position/velocity deviations at least twice as great as the last for the victim). Additionally, while constraining allowable vehicle behavior (e.g. maximum velocity) decreases the effect of attack, lim-

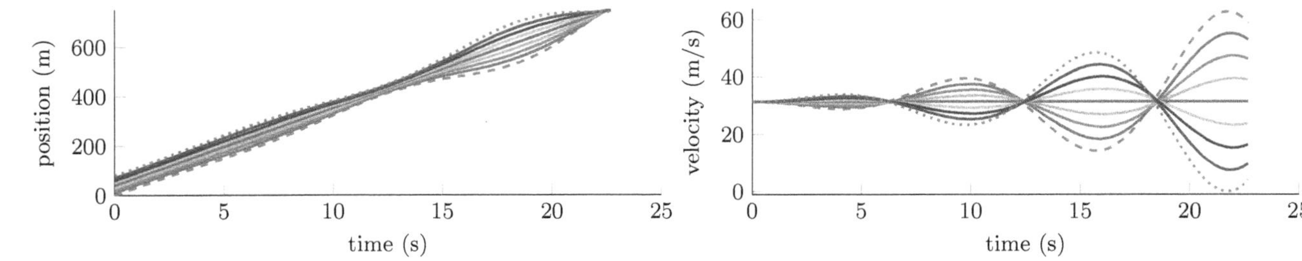

(a) (b)

Figure 7: Position and velocity of a platoon under attack. (a)/(b) Two attackers cause the platoon to collapse in on itself by oscillating at the resonant frequency, but 180° out of phase.

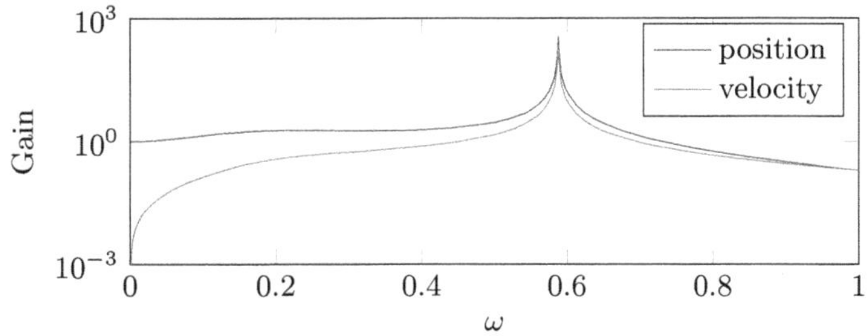

Figure 8: Position/velocity gains of ninth vehicle in ten vehicle platoon for attacker in first position. The attacker can cause significant changes to the vehicle even when not oscillating at the resonant frequency.

its per se cannot prevent it from being deployed to increase the severity of accidents. For example, if the vehicles in the above two-attacker example are limited to a maximum velocity of $35\,\mathrm{m\,s^{-1}}$ and accelerations in the range of $\pm 5\,\mathrm{m\,s^{-2}}$, a collision resulting from an instability would still see relative velocities 35% greater, and kinetic energy 81% greater, at time of impact than if the attackers had simply decelerated/accelerated at $\pm 5\,\mathrm{m\,s^{-2}}$.

Generality of attack

To demonstrate the widespread applicability of our attack, we consider a platoon following a unidirectional algorithm [33] employing a second order sliding mode controller [14]. The control objective in this instance is to make the velocities of the following vehicles converge to that of the leader's; only information about the preceding vehicle is used. Again, assuming an ideal vehicle model, the dynamics of the ith vehicle are given by:

$$\begin{aligned} \dot{x}_i &= v_i \\ \dot{v}_i &= a_i \\ \dot{a}_i &= \frac{1}{h}(-W_M sign[s_i(t) - \frac{1}{2}s_{max,i}]) \end{aligned} \tag{20}$$

where x_i, v_i, and a_i denote the position, velocity, and acceleration of the vehicle, W_M is a gain taken to be greater than four times the maximum vehicle acceleration, a_{max}, and $s_{max,i}$ is the extermal value of the signal of $s_i = x_i - x_{i+1} + s_{d0} + hv_i$, with s_{d0} being a desired minimum vehicle spacing at rest and h a "headway time".

As in the case of PD control, the attacker must first be able to make the system unstable through a change of gain(s). The resulting resonant frequency must then be achievable by the other vehicles in order to effect the attack. We first prove that an attacker can make the platoon unstable, and then show that the resulting frequencies for some gain changes satisfy our feasibility condition ($\omega \leq 2\pi$).

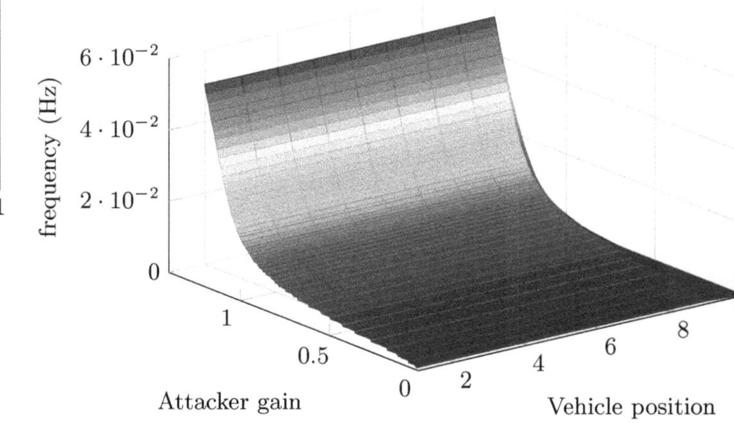

Figure 9: Frequencies at which each vehicle in a ten vehicle platoon will resonate; non-linear controller used for each vehicle, with unidirectional platoon algorithm. Attacker at position nine.

LEMMA 2. *The states of the system will not converge to the desired value of $s_i = 0$ (i.e. an attacker can make the system unstable) if the attacker selects for its gain, W_M, in $(0, 4a_{max})$.*

PROOF. In [14], convergence is proved via the contraction property. Should an attacker choose their gain such that it violates the contraction property, the state trajectory will not converge to the origin of state plane. The contraction property holds for the system if $\frac{2a_{max}}{W_M - 2a_{max}} < 1$. If W_M is chosen from $(0, 4a_{max})$ the strict inequality is violated. This holds for all initial conditions. □

By varying the attacker's gain and simulating the system response ($W_M = 5a_{max}$ was used for victim vehicles), we have found that the platoon will resonate at feasible frequencies for attacker gains over the range $(0, 1.2a_{max})$ (Figure 9). The location of the attacker in the platoon does not affect the resonant frequency, but, because of the unidirectional nature of the platooning algorithm, the attacker is only able to force following vehicles to oscillate. All vehicles oscillate at the same frequency.

5.2 Controllability

As we showed in Section 4, it is theoretically possible for an attacker to control the states of individual vehicles in the platoon, assuming they are at the proper position. However, controlling states of other vehicles just by controlling an attacker's motion falls under single input multiple output (SIMO) control, which has not been addressed in the controls literature very extensively. The SIMO control problem has been solved for slow dynamic systems, such as control of a dam river system, where the action variable is the upstream discharge and the controlled variable the downstream discharge [22, 23]. In an extension of this work we intend to solve the SIMO control problem in order to design a controller that allows an attacker to control their motion to regulate other vehicles' position and velocity. The results of the controllability analysis presented above should thus been seen as the uncovering of a new vulnerability in vehicle platooning. For an attacker to exploit this vulnerability will require advances in the area of SIMO control.

Another problem in designing SIMO attacker control is the conditionality of the control matrix. Even when the system is fully controllable (full rank), the controllability matrix is badly conditioned (very high condition number). This means even though the attacker can theoretically control all the other vehicle states, to practically design a controller we may have to change the structure of the A and B matrices to improve the condition number of the controllability matrix. In future work, we will explore the use of false data injection to accomplish this.

While we are not able to offer a general-purpose controller that would allow an attacker to control arbitrary vehicle states, we can provide a controller that gives an attacker arbitrary control over preceding vehicles' separation, without changing the attacker's gain(s).

LEMMA 3. *Vehicles preceding an attacker will be separated by an amount equal to the attacker's desired spacing.*

PROOF. Allow d_{atk} to be the attacker's desired spacing for the platoon and d the desired platoon spacing in the absence of an attacker. Using these values with (1) for an attacker in the first position (rear of the platoon), we have that at steady state (i.e. $\dot{v}_1 = \dot{v}_2 = \cdots = \dot{v}_n = 0$ and $v_1 = v_2 = \cdots = v_n$):

$$\begin{aligned}
\dot{x}_1 &= v_1 \\
\dot{v}_1 &= -k_p x_1 + k_p x_2 - k_p d_{atk} = 0 \\
\dot{x}_2 &= v_2 \\
\dot{v}_2 &= k_p x_1 - k_p x_2 + k_p d \\
&\quad + k_p x_3 - k_p x_2 - k_p d = 0 \\
&\vdots \\
\dot{x}_{n-1} &= v_{n-1} \\
\dot{v}_{n-1} &= k_p x_{n-2} - k_p x_{n-1} + k_p d \\
&\quad + k_p x_n - k_p x_{n-1} - k_p d = 0 \\
\dot{x}_n &= v_n \\
\dot{v}_n &= 0
\end{aligned} \tag{21}$$

Rearranging and canceling terms for $\dot{v}_1$, we find that $x_2 - x_1 = d_{atk}$. Substituting this value recursively into the subsequent $\dot{v}_i$ equations yields $x_i - x_{i-1} = d_{atk}$ for $1 < i < n-1$. Following the same procedure for an attacker in the jth position, we have that $x_{i+1} - x_i = d$ for $1 < i < j$ and $x_{i+1} - x_i = d_{atk}$ for $j < i < n-1$.

$\therefore$ For all vehicles preceding them, the attacker is able to specify the spacing policy. □

The utility of this attack lies in an attacker being able to set $d_{atk} \leq 0$, which results in the platoon collapsing in on itself (more negative values of d_{atk} will cause this to happen at greater relative velocities). By setting $d_{atk} \sim \sin \omega t$ an attacker would cause vehicles in the platoon to oscillate back and forth in a controlled manner that would not invite collisions. Such movements would force vehicles to brake and accelerate, continuously, which would cause excess energy expenditure (i.e. wasting of fuel), as in [15].

6. CONCLUSION AND FUTURE WORK

We have shown that a vehicle with a modified control system, operated by a maliciously minded actor, can destabilize a platoon employing a PD controller that uses predecessor and follower distances and velocities to maintain a constant separation. Our work demonstrates the need for creators of future platooning control laws to consider the presence of an adversary in the design process. Additionally, we proved that an attacker can theoretically control the relative position and velocity of surrounding vehicles.

Future work will focus on the designing of countermeasures, including the possible use of dynamic gain scheduling for vehicles in a platoon. It is hoped that by obfuscating the exact gains of other vehicles, an attacker would be prevented from calculating their own gain to achieve resonance. We will also examine the susceptibility of platooning/platooning-like laws that rely only on predecessor information and/or employ communication to relay information (e.g. adaptive and cooperative adaptive cruise control systems), which are already present in, or are under development for, commercial systems. Finally, we will endeavor to advance SIMO control to the point where we can create a controller to exploit an attacker's ability to control other vehicle states.

7. ACKNOWLEDGEMENTS

This material is based in part upon work supported by the National Science Foundation under Grant No. 1410000.

8. REFERENCES

[1] C. Barreto, A. A. CÃąrdenas, and N. Quijano. Controllability of dynamical systems: Threat models and reactive security. In S. Das, C. Nita-Rotaru, and M. Kantarcioglu, editors, *Decision and Game Theory for Security*, volume 8252 of *Lecture Notes in Computer Science*, pages 45–64. Springer International Publishing, 2013.

[2] L. D. Baskar, B. De Schutter, J. Hellendoorn, and Z. Papp. Traffic control and intelligent vehicle highway systems: a survey. *IET Intelligent Transport Systems*, 5(1):38–52, 2011.

[3] C. Bergenhem, S. Shladover, E. Coelingh, C. Englund, and S. Tsugawa. Overview of platooning systems. In *Proceedings of the 19th ITS World Congress, Oct 22-26, Vienna, Austria (2012)*, 2012.

[4] J. Carbaugh, D. N. Godbole, and R. Sengupta. Safety and capacity analysis of automated and manual

highway systems. *Transportation Research Part C: Emerging Technologies*, 6(1):69–99, 1998.

[5] A. Cardenas, S. Amin, B. Sinopoli, A. Giani, A. Perrig, and S. Sastry. Challenges for securing cyber physical systems. In *Workshop on future directions in cyber-physical systems security*, 2009.

[6] C.-T. Chen. *Linear system theory and design*. Oxford University Press, Inc., 1995.

[7] E. Coelingh and S. Solyom. All aboard the robotic road train. *IEEE Spectrum*, November 2012. [Online; accessed 30-Sept-2013].

[8] P. Cook. Conditions for string stability. *Systems & Control Letters*, 54(10):991–998, 2005.

[9] S. Dadras, R. M. Gerdes, and R. Sharma. Transfer functions for string instability. Technical report, `http://www.eng.usu.edu/ece/faculty/rgerdes/papers/tech/transferSI.pdf`, 2015.

[10] S. Darbha and K. Rajagopal. Intelligent cruise control systems and traffic flow stability. *Transportation Research Part C: Emerging Technologies*, 7(6):329–352, 1999.

[11] A. Davila, E. del Pozo, E. Aramburu, and A. Freixas. Environmental benefits of vehicle platooning. *Human Factors*, 2012:05–17, 2012.

[12] W. Dunbar and D. Caveney. Distributed receding horizon control of vehicle platoons: Stability and string stability. *Automatic Control, IEEE Transactions on*, 57(3):620–633, March 2012.

[13] C. Featherstone and M. Lowson. Viability and benefits of platooning in automated transport systems. `http://www.cybercars.org/docs/CTF%20Lowson%20Report.pdf`, 2004. [Technical report; online; accessed 04-June-2014].

[14] A. Ferrara and C. Vecchio. Sliding mode control for automatic driving of a platoon of vehicles. In *Variable Structure Systems, 2006. VSS'06. International Workshop on*, pages 262–267, June 2006.

[15] R. M. Gerdes, C. Winstead, and K. Heaslip. Cps: An efficiency-motivated attack against autonomous vehicular transportation. In *Proceedings of the 29th Annual Computer Security Applications Conference*, ACSAC '13, pages 99–108, New York, NY, USA, 2013. ACM.

[16] J. J. Haas. The effects of wireless jamming on vehicle platooning. `https://wiki.engr.illinois.edu/download/attachments/19826169/jjhaas2_platoon_jamming.pdf`, 2009. [Tech report; online; accessed 04-June-2014].

[17] HDT Truckinginfo. Project to test 'platooning' trucks. `http://www.truckinginfo.com/channel/fuel-smarts/news/story/2013/10/project-to-test-platooning-trucks.aspx`, 2013. [Online; accessed 04-June-2014].

[18] P. Ioannou. *Automated Highway Systems*. Springer, 1997.

[19] A. Isidori. *Nonlinear Control Systems*. Number v.1 in Communications and Control Engineering. Springer, 1995.

[20] P. Kavathekar and Y. Chen. Draft: Vehicle platooning: A brief survey and categorization. In *Proceedings of The ASME 2011 International Design Engineering Technical Conferences and Computers and Information in Engineering Conference*, volume 2011, pages 829–845. ASME, 2011.

[21] A. Khodayari, A. Ghaffari, S. Ameli, and J. Flahatgar. A historical review on lateral and longitudinal control of autonomous vehicle motions. In *Mechanical and Electrical Technology (ICMET), 2010 2nd International Conference on*, pages 421–429, Sept 2010.

[22] X. Litrico. Robust imc flow control of simo dam-river open-channel systems. *Control Systems Technology, IEEE Transactions on*, 10(3):432–437, 2002.

[23] X. Litrico and J. Pomet. Nonlinear modelling and control of a long river stretch. In *European Control Conference, Cambridge, UK*, 2003.

[24] X.-Y. Lu, S. E. Shladover, and C. Nowakowski. Partial automation for truck platooning. `http://www.automatedvehiclessymposium.org/callforposters/partial-automation`, 2014. [Poster presented at TRB Automated Vehicle Symposium 2014; accessed 04-June-2014].

[25] Y. Mo and B. Sinopoli. Integrity attacks on cyber-physical systems. In *Proceedings of the 1st International Conference on High Confidence Networked Systems*, HiCoNS '12, pages 47–54, New York, NY, USA, 2012. ACM.

[26] F. Pasqualetti, A. Bicchi, and F. Bullo. Consensus computation in unreliable networks: A system theoretic approach. *Automatic Control, IEEE Transactions on*, 57(1):90–104, Jan 2012.

[27] F. Pasqualetti, F. Dorfler, and F. Bullo. Attack detection and identification in cyber-physical systems. *Automatic Control, IEEE Transactions on*, 58(11):2715–2729, Nov 2013.

[28] E. Shaw and J. Hedrick. Controller design for string stable heterogeneous vehicle strings. In *Decision and Control, 2007 46th IEEE Conference on*, pages 2868–2875, Dec 2007.

[29] E. Shaw and J. Hedrick. String stability analysis for heterogeneous vehicle strings. In *American Control Conference, 2007. ACC '07*, pages 3118–3125, July 2007.

[30] S. Shladover. Path at 20—history and major milestones. *Intelligent Transportation Systems, IEEE Transactions on*, 8(4):584–592, Dec 2007.

[31] S. Shladover. Recent international activity in cooperative vehicle-highway automation systems. `http://www.fhwa.dot.gov/advancedresearch/pubs/12033/index.cfm`, 2012. [U.S. Department of Transportation Federal Highway Administration Report FHWA-HRT-12-033;Online; accessed 04-June-2014].

[32] J. Wang and R. Rajamani. Should adaptive cruise-control systems be designed to maintain a constant time gap between vehicles? *Vehicular Technology, IEEE Transactions on*, 53(5):1480–1490, Sept 2004.

[33] D. Yanakiev and I. Kanellakopoulos. A simplified framework for string stability analysis in ahs. In *In the Proceedings of the 13th IFAC World Congress*, pages 177–182, 1996.

NTRUReEncrypt: An Efficient Proxy Re-Encryption Scheme Based on NTRU

David Nuñez
Universidad de Málaga
Network, Information and Computer Security Laboratory (NICS Lab)
Málaga, Spain
dnunez@lcc.uma.es

Isaac Agudo
Universidad de Málaga
Network, Information and Computer Security Laboratory (NICS Lab)
Málaga, Spain
isaac@lcc.uma.es

Javier Lopez
Universidad de Málaga
Network, Information and Computer Security Laboratory (NICS Lab)
Málaga, Spain
jlm@lcc.uma.es

ABSTRACT

The use of alternative foundations for constructing more secure and efficient cryptographic schemes is a topic worth exploring. In the case of proxy re-encryption, the vast majority of schemes are based on number theoretic problems such as the discrete logarithm. In this paper we present NTRUReEncrypt, a new bidirectional and multihop proxy re-encryption scheme based on NTRU, a widely known lattice-based cryptosystem. We provide two versions of our scheme: the first one is based on the conventional NTRU encryption scheme and, although it lacks a security proof, remains as efficient as its predecessor; the second one is based on a variant of NTRU proposed by Stehlé and Steinfeld, which is proven CPA-secure under the hardness of the Ring-LWE problem. To the best of our knowledge, our proposals are the first proxy re-encryption schemes to be based on the NTRU primitive. In addition, we provide experimental results to show the efficiency of our proposal, as well as a comparison with previous proxy re-encryption schemes, which confirms that our first scheme outperforms the rest by an order of magnitude.

Categories and Subject Descriptors

E.3 [**Data Encryption**]: Public Key Cryptosystems

1. INTRODUCTION

Proxy re-encryption is a type of public-key cryptographic scheme that enables a user to delegate her decryption rights to other users. From a high-level viewpoint, a proxy re-encryption scheme is an asymmetric encryption scheme that permits a proxy to transform ciphertexts under Alice's public key pk_A into ciphertexts decryptable by Bob's secret key sk_B. In order to do this, the proxy is given a re-encryption key $rk_{A\to B}$, which makes this process possible. So, besides defining traditional encryption and decryption functions, a proxy re-encryption scheme also defines a re-encryption function for executing the transformation.

Since the introduction of proxy re-encryption by Blaze et al. in 1998 [11], many proxy re-encryption schemes have been proposed. The vast majority of these schemes are based on bilinear pairings, which have several drawbacks. For instance, pairings are known to be computationally intensive operations. With respect to security, pairing-based proxy re-encryption schemes ultimately rely on the hardness of the discrete logarithm problem. This poses a problem in the case that efficient cryptanalytic attacks against the discrete logarithm problem are developed or quantum computation becomes practical. This problem is also applicable to other schemes not based on pairings but that also depend on the discrete logarithm or on integer factorization assumptions.

Apart from bilinear pairings, the use of other foundations for constructing proxy re-encryption schemes has received little attention. Recently, some lattice-based proxy re-encryption schemes have been proposed [29, 4]. Lattice-based cryptography is a promising field, chiefly because of its role in post-quantum cryptography, but in some particular cases, also for its efficiency. As a prime example of widely-accepted and efficient lattice-based cryptosystem we find NTRU, which was introduced in 1996 by Hoffstein, Pipher and Silverman [20]. Since then, it has remained as the most practical lattice-based public-key cryptosystem, at the point of being standardized by IEEE Std 1363.1-2008 [28] and ANSI X9.98-2010 [2]. One of the main reasons of NTRU's popularity is its overwhelming performance with respect to traditional public-key cryptosystems. For instance, optimized versions of NTRU executed on a GPU proved to be up to 1000 times faster than RSA and 100 times faster than ECC [19]. The results behind the efficiency of NTRU are explained by the simplicity of its basic underlying operation, which is the convolution, i.e., the polynomial multiplication. NTRU uses polynomials with relatively small coefficients, so multiplications can be efficiently performed, even in constrained devices [8]. Another implication of this is that the size of the keys is relatively compact, when compared to other lattice-based schemes. In addition, the convolution operation can even be parallelized, which is very convenient as multicore and GPU processors are becoming more relevant nowadays.

One of the main drawbacks of NTRU is that it lacks a formal security proof, so its security stems from the practicality of best known attacks. This has meant that, over the

ASIA CCS'15, April 14–17, 2015, Singapore, Singapore

http://dx.doi.org/10.1145/2714576.2714585 .

years, NTRU has followed a somewhat "break-and-repair" approach, where advances in attacks have stimulated changes in the scheme and its set of parameters, although it has remained essentially the same. In order to advance towards solving this gap, Stehlé and Steinfeld proposed in 2011 a provable-secure variant of NTRU [25, 26], whose security is based on the assumed hardness of lattice problems.

Our contribution. In this paper, we propose new bidirectional proxy re-encryption schemes based on NTRU. Our first result, NTRUReEncrypt, is a slight modification of the conventional NTRU encryption scheme; this proposal extends the original scheme in order to support re-encryption, thus it remains just as efficient. However, it lacks of a formal security proof, as does NTRU. For this reason, we also present PS-NTRUReEncrypt, a provably-secure version based on the variant of the NTRU primitive proposed by Stehlé and Steinfeld in [25, 26]. To the best of our knowledge these are the first proxy re-encryption schemes based on NTRU, and one of the first to be based on lattices. In addition, we complement our proposal with an experimental comparison of the performance of several proxy re-encryption schemes, which confirms that our first scheme outperforms the rest by an order of magnitude.

Related work. The notion of proxy re-encryption was introduced in 1998 by Blaze et al. [11]; their proposal, which is usually referred to as the BBS scheme, is bidirectional (it is trivial to obtain $rk_{B\to A}$ from $rk_{A\to B}$) and multihop (the re-encryption process can be repeated multiple times), but not resistant to collusions between the proxy and one of the users. Ateniese, Fu, Green and Hohenberger proposed in [6] new proxy re-encryption schemes based on bilinear pairings. Their schemes are unidirectional, unihop and resistant to collusions. Green and Ateniese propose an identity-based proxy re-encryption scheme in [18]; however, this scheme is not resistant to collusions. An improved proposal that is secure against chosen-ciphertext attacks (CCA) is presented in [13], but again, it is not collusion-resistant. In [12], Canetti and Hohenberger present a CCA-secure bidirectional scheme; based on this security model, Libert and Vergnaud propose in [21] a unidirectional scheme with chosen-ciphertext security in the standard model. Another interesting proposal is presented in [5], where the authors define the notion of *key privacy* in the context of proxy re-encryption, which prevents the proxy to derive the identities of both sender and receiver from a re-encryption key.

As mentioned, the security in these schemes is based on number theoretic assumptions, such as the hardness of the discrete logarithm problem, but the use of other foundations for constructing proxy re-encryption schemes has been much less explored. In [29], Xagawa and Tanaka present the first lattice-based proxy re-encryption sheme, which relies on the Learning With Errors (LWE) problem; this scheme is bidirectional, multihop and CPA-secure. After this seminal work, Aono et al [4] proposed a unidirectional and multihop scheme, also based on the LWE problem.

With regard to the NTRU primitive, it has already been used as the basis for constructing other cryptographic schemes, such as multikey fully homomorphic encryption [22], private information retrieval [3], and public key traitor tracing scheme [23].

Organization. The rest of this paper is organized as follows: In Section 2, we provide some basic definitions for bidirectional proxy re-encryption schemes. In Section 3, we describe the NTRU encryption scheme and, based on it, we present our bidirectional proxy re-encryption scheme NTRUReEncrypt. In Section 4, we describe the provably-secure version of NTRU from Stehlé and Steinfeld and present our second scheme, PS-NTRUReEncrypt. In Section 5, we describe the experimental results from a prototype implementation of our proposals, as well as a comparison with previous proxy re-encryption schemes. Finally, Section 6 concludes the paper and future work is outlined.

2. DEFINITIONS

In this section, we provide some basic definitions relevant to bidirectional proxy re-encryption schemes. We first define the specification of a bidirectional CPA-secure proxy re-encryption scheme, based on the one given by Canetti and Hohenberger [12].

Definition 1. Bidirectional PRE. A bidirectional proxy re-encryption scheme is a tuple of algorithms (Setup, KeyGen, ReKeyGen, Enc, ReEnc, Dec):

- Setup(1^k) $\to$ *params*. On input the security parameter 1^k, the setup algorithm Setup outputs the parameters *params*[1].
- KeyGen() $\to$ (pk_A, sk_A). The key generation algorithm KeyGen outputs a pair of public and secret keys (pk_A, sk_A) for user A.
- ReKeyGen(sk_A, sk_B) $\to$ $rk_{A\to B}$. On input the secret keys sk_A and sk_B, the re-encryption key generation algorithm ReKeyGen outputs a re-encryption key $rk_{A\to B}$.
- Enc(pk_A, M) $\to$ C_A. On input the public key pk_A and a message $M \in \mathcal{M}$, the encryption algorithm Enc outputs a ciphertext $C_A \in \mathcal{C}$.
- ReEnc($rk_{A\to B}, C_A$) $\to$ C_B. On input a re-encryption key $rk_{A\to B}$ and a ciphertext $C_A \in \mathcal{C}$, the re-encryption algorithm ReEnc outputs a second ciphertext $C_B \in \mathcal{C}$.
- Dec(sk_A, C_A) $\to$ M. On input the secret key sk_A and a ciphertext $C_A \in \mathcal{C}$, the decryption algorithm Dec outputs a message $M \in \mathcal{M}$.

Once we have defined which are the inputs and outputs of a bidirectional proxy re-encryption scheme, we formulate the concept of correctness, also based on the one given by [12]. In this case, as these kinds of schemes are usually multihop, we refer to multihop correctness (i.e., ciphertexts that can be re-encrypted multiple times).

Definition 2. Multihop Correctness. A bidirectional PRE scheme (Setup, KeyGen, ReKeyGen, Enc, ReEnc, Dec) is multihop correct with respect to plaintext space $\mathcal{M}$ if:

- For all (pk_A, sk_A) output by KeyGen and all messages $M \in \mathcal{M}$, it holds that Dec(sk_A, Enc(pk_A, M)) $= M$.
- For any sequence of pairs (pk_i, sk_i) output by KeyGen, with $0 \le i \le N$, all re-encryption keys $rk_{j\to j+1}$ output by ReKeyGen(sk_j, sk_{j+1}), with $j < N$, all messages

[1] In the following, we will assume *params* is globally known, so we will omit it in the functions.

$M \in \mathcal{M}$, and all ciphertexts C_1 output by $\mathsf{Enc}(pk_1, M)$, it holds that:

$$\mathsf{Dec}(sk_N, \mathsf{ReEnc}(rk_{N-1\to N}, ...\mathsf{ReEnc}(rk_{1\to 2}, C_1))) = M$$

If for any $M \in \mathcal{M}$ correctness holds only with probability 1 minus a negligible quantity, we say that the scheme is correct with respect to $\mathcal{M}$.

Finally, we define the security game we use for bidirectional CPA-secure proxy re-encryption schemes. This definition is adapted from [12], [29] and [5].

Definition 3. Bidirectional PRE CPA-security game Let k be the security parameter. Let $\mathcal{A}$ be the adversary, and $\mathcal{H}, \mathcal{C}$ the sets of indices of honest and corrupt users, respectively. The game consists of an execution of $\mathcal{A}$ with the following oracles, which can be invoked multiple times in any order, subject to the constraints below:

Phase 0: The challenger takes a security parameter 1^k, obtains global parameters $params \leftarrow \mathsf{Setup}(1^k)$ and initializes sets $\mathcal{H}, \mathcal{C}$ to $\emptyset$. The challenger generates the public key pk^* of target user i^*, adds i^* to $\mathcal{H}$, and sends pk^* to the adversary.

Phase 1:

- Uncorrupted key generation $\mathcal{O}_{honest}$: On input an index i, where $i \notin \mathcal{H} \cup \mathcal{C}$, the oracle obtains a new keypair $(pk_i, sk_i) \leftarrow \mathsf{KeyGen}()$ and adds index i to $\mathcal{H}$. The adversary receives pk_i.
- Corrupted key generation $\mathcal{O}_{corrupt}$: On input an index i, where $i \notin \mathcal{H} \cup \mathcal{C}$, the oracle obtains a new keypair $(pk_i, sk_i) \leftarrow \mathsf{KeyGen}()$ and adds index i to $\mathcal{C}$. The adversary receives (pk_i, sk_i).

Phase 2:

- Re-encryption key generation $\mathcal{O}_{rkgen}$: On input (i, j), where $i \neq j$, and either $i, j \in \mathcal{H}$ or $i, j \in \mathcal{C}$, the oracle returns $rk_{i\to j} \leftarrow \mathsf{ReKeyGen}(sk_i, sk_j)$.
- Challenge oracle $\mathcal{O}_{challenge}$: This oracle can be queried only once. On input (M_0, M_1), the oracle chooses a bit $b \leftarrow \{0, 1\}$ and returns the challenge ciphertext $C^* \leftarrow \mathsf{Enc}(pk^*, M_b)$, where pk^* corresponds to the public key of target user i^*.

Phase 3:

- Decision: Eventually, $\mathcal{A}$ outputs guess $b' \in \{0, 1\}$. $\mathcal{A}$ wins the game if and only if $b' = b$.

As already noted in [5], we only allow queries to $\mathcal{O}_{rkgen}$ where users are either both corrupt or both honest. Otherwise, in a bidirectional setting these queries would corrupt honest users and could be used to simulate a decryption oracle, which is not considered in CPA security. That is, we are adopting a static corruption model. Note that we have not included a re-encryption oracle. On the one hand, in the case of CPA security and multihop schemes, the addition of a re-encryption oracle that allows to re-encrypt ciphertexts from honest to corrupt users could be used to simulate a decryption oracle, which is by definition out of the scope of CPA. On the other hand, restricting the re-encryption oracle only to the honest-to-honest and corrupt-to-corrupt cases would result in a superfluous oracle, since the same capabilities are acheived by means of $\mathcal{O}_{rkgen}$. For these reasons, a re-encryption oracle is not provided.

3. A PROXY RE-ENCRYPTION SCHEME BASED ON NTRU

In this section we firstly introduce the conventional NTRU encryption scheme and describe its operation. Then, we extend it in order to construct a bidirectional multihop proxy re-encryption scheme.

3.1 The NTRU Encryption Scheme

The NTRU encryption scheme, originally proposed by Hoffstein, Pipher and Silverman in [20], is one of the first public key encryption schemes based on lattices. The main reason behind the interest in NTRU is its efficiency, which is much better than other public-key cryptosystems and is even comparable to symmetric ciphers. In addition, its security is conjectured to be based on hard problems over lattices, although it lacks a formal proof.

We now briefly describe the operation of NTRU. The original NTRU cryptosystem is defined over the quotient ring $\mathcal{R}_{NTRU} = \mathbb{Z}[x]/(x^n - 1)$, where n is a prime parameter. Thus, elements of the ring $\mathcal{R}_{NTRU}$ are integer polynomials of degree less than n; the operators $+$ and $\cdot$ denote addition and multiplication in $\mathcal{R}_{NTRU}$, respectively. Other parameters of NTRU are the integer q, which is a small power of 2 of the same order of magnitude than n, and the small polynomial $p \in \mathcal{R}_{NTRU}$, which usually takes values $p = 3$ or $p = x + 2$. In general, operations over polynomials will be performed in $\mathcal{R}_{NTRU}$ modulo q or p, which will be denoted respectively as $\mathcal{R}_{NTRU}/q$ and $\mathcal{R}_{NTRU}/p$.

In NTRU, the private key sk consists of a polynomial $f \in \mathcal{R}_{NTRU}$ chosen at random, with a determined number of coefficients equal to 0, -1, and 1. The polynomial f must have an inverse in $\mathcal{R}_{NTRU}/q$ and $\mathcal{R}_{NTRU}/p$, respectively, f_q^{-1} and f_p^{-1}. For efficiency, f can be chosen to be congruent to 1 modulo p. The public key pk consists of the polynomial $h = p \cdot g \cdot f_q^{-1} \mod q$, where $g \in \mathcal{R}_{NTRU}$ is chosen at random.

The encryption process is very simple: a plaintext M from message space $\mathcal{R}_{NTRU}/p$ is encrypted to ciphertext $C = h \cdot s + M \mod q$, where s is a small random polynomial in $\mathcal{R}_{NTRU}$. For decrypting a ciphertext C, one must first compute $C' = f \cdot C$ and reduce it modulo q. If the original polynomial C' is sufficiently small then the result of the reduction is $pgs + fM \in \mathcal{R}_{NTRU}/q$. Next, C' is reducted modulo p, obtaining fM. Finally, this result is multiplied by f_p^{-1} to extract the original message M; note that the last step is redundant if f was selected congruent to 1 modulo p.

3.2 NTRUReEncrypt

Based on the NTRU encryption scheme, we define the proxy re-encryption scheme NTRUReEncrypt. Our proposal is essentialy an extension of the scheme that includes the definition of the re-encryption and re-encryption key generation algorithms. One of the fundamental differences of our scheme with respect to the original NTRU is that the secret polynomial f has to be congruent to $1 \mod p$, not for efficiency reasons, but because it is necessary to correctly decrypt re-encrypted ciphertexts.

3.2.1 *The scheme*

Now we present our scheme NTRUReEncrypt. In the following, the delegator is represented by user A, whereas the delegatee is user B. Our scheme is specified by the following algorithms:

- KeyGen(): The output of the key generation algorithm for user A is a pair of public and secret keys (pk_A, sk_A). If first chooses a pair of polynomials $(f_A, g_A) \in \mathcal{R}^2_{NTRU}$ at random, with a determined number of coefficients equal to 0, -1, and 1, as in the conventional NTRU scheme. The only added requirement is that f_A has to be congruent to 1 modulo p. As in the original case, f_A must have an inverse in $\mathcal{R}_{NTRU}/q$, denoted by f_A^{-1}. Note that now it is not necessary the inverse of f_A modulo p. The private key sk_A is the polynomial f_A, whereas the public key pk_A consists of the polynomial $h_A = p \cdot g_A \cdot f_A^{-1} \mod q$.
- ReKeyGen(sk_A, sk_B): On input the secret keys $sk_A = f_A$ and $sk_B = f_B$, the re-encryption key generation algorithm ReKeyGen computes the re-encryption key between users A and B as $rk_{A\to B} = sk_A \cdot sk_B^{-1} = f_A \cdot f_B^{-1}$. The re-encryption key can be computed by means of a simple three-party protocol, so neither A, B nor the proxy learns any secret key. The protocol, originally proposed in [12], is as follows: A selects a random $r \in \mathcal{R}_{NTRU}/q$ and sends $r \cdot f_A \mod q$ to B and r to the proxy; next, B sends $r \cdot f_A \cdot f_B^{-1} \mod q$ to the proxy, who computes $rk_{A\to B} = f_A \cdot f_B^{-1} \mod q$.
- Enc(pk_A, M): On input the public key pk_A and a message $M \in \mathcal{R}_{NTRU}/p$, the encryption algorithm Enc generates a small random polynomial $s \in \mathcal{R}_{NTRU}$, and outputs the ciphertext $C_A = h_A s + M$.
- ReEnc($rk_{A\to B}, C_A$): On input a re-encryption key $rk_{A\to B}$ and a ciphertext C_A, the re-encryption algorithm ReEnc samples a random polynomial $e \in \mathcal{R}_{NTRU}$ and outputs ciphertext $C_B = C_A \cdot rk_{A\to B} + pe$.
- Dec(sk_A, C_A): On input the secret key $sk_A = f_A$ and a ciphertext C_A, the decryption algorithm Dec computes $C'_A = (C_A \cdot f_A) \mod q$ and outputs the original message $M = (C'_A \mod p)$.

Note that if ciphertexts are not re-encrypted, NTRUReEncrypt behaves in exactly the same way as the original NTRU encryption scheme.

3.2.2 Correctness

Now, we informally explain the reason why the re-encryption process works. Re-encrypted ciphertexts are of the form:

$$\begin{aligned} C_B &= C_A \cdot rk_{A\to B} + pe \\ &= (pg_A f_A^{-1} s + M) \cdot f_A f_B^{-1} + pe \\ &= pg_A f_B^{-1} s + pe + f_A f_B^{-1} M \end{aligned}$$

When decrypting a re-encrypted ciphertext, the delegatee multiplies the ciphertext with the secret key f_B:

$$\begin{aligned} C_B \cdot f_B &= (pg_A f_B^{-1} s + pe + f_A f_B^{-1} M) \cdot f_B \\ &= pg_A s + pe f_B + f_A M \end{aligned}$$

Now, taking modulo p, we get rid of the additional terms. Recall that we require secret key polynomial f_A to fulfill $f_A = 1 \mod p$, so $(C_B \cdot f_B) \mod p = (pg_A s + pe f_B + f_A M) \mod p = M$, which is the original message.

The inclusion of the random term e during the re-encryption phase is necessary in order to prevent a simple ciphertext-only attack from the delegatee. Imagine that a re-encrypted ciphertext is of the form $C_B = C_A \cdot rk_{A\to B} = C_A \cdot f_A \cdot f_B^{-1}$; that is, without the random term e. Then, the delegatee could extract the secret key of the delegator based on the observation that $C_B \cdot f_B = C_A \cdot f_A$ holds, since $C_B = C_A \cdot rk_{A\to B}$. Next, assuming that C_A is invertible modulo q, the attacker can extract the secret key by computing $f_A = C_A^{-1} \cdot C_B \cdot f_B$.

The scheme is also multihop, that is, it supports multiple re-encryptions. However, this property is limited, since the addition of the error term during the re-encryption produces an increasing error that grows on each hop, until eventually, decryption fails. Our experiments show that this depends heavily on the choice of parameters. This issue is discussed in more detail in Section 5.1.

3.2.3 Analysis

The resulting proxy re-encryption scheme preserves the performance level of the original NTRU; a detailed experimentation on this matter is presented in Sections 5.1 and 5.2. These experimental results show that NTRUReEncrypt outperforms other proxy re-encryption schemes by an order of magnitude.

A theoretical analysis of the computational costs associated with NTRUReEncrypt shows that the main algorithms, namely encryption, decryption and re-encryption, only need a single multiplication (actually, re-encryption takes an additional multiplication for computing the term pe, but this can be computed beforehand and, in addition, the polynomial p is small and known in advance). As already stated in the introduction, the core operation in NTRU is the multiplication of polynomials, which can be done in $O(n \log n)$ time using the Fast Fourier Transform (FFT) [19].

Table 1: Space costs of NTRUReEncrypt

Element	Size
Keys	$O(n \cdot \log_2 q)$
Message	$O(n)$
Ciphertext	$O(n \cdot \log_2 q)$
Ciphertext expansion	$O(\log_2 q)$

As for the space costs associated to NTRUReEncrypt, Table 1 presents a theoretical analysis of the size of the messages, keys, and ciphertexts, as well as a measure of the ciphertext expansion it produces. It can be seen that the expansion is logarithmic in the parameter q, and that the size of keys is within $O(n \log_2 q)$. This can be put in contrast with other lattice-based cryptosystems, such as the proxy re-encryption scheme from Aono et al [4], where keys and messages are tipically matrices whose dimensions grow linearly with the parameter n. This implies that the size of these matrices is at least quadratic with respect to n.

Table 2 illustrates this fact by showing a comparison between Aono's scheme and ours. The space costs from Aono's scheme are determined by the parameters shown in [4] for the case of 143 bits of security and 128-bit plaintexts, whereas our figures are calculated using a parameter set that achieves 256 bits of security and supports up to 186-bits plaintexts. More details about the parameters used are given in Section 5.1. It can be seen that our space costs are lower in

Table 2: Comparison of space costs (in KB)

Size	Aono et al. [4]	NTRUReEncrypt
Public keys	60.00	1.57
Secret key	60.00	1.57
Re-Encryption key	2520.00	1.57
Ciphertext	0.66	1.57

comparison, even considering the difference in bits of security. In the case of re-encryption keys, the difference in size is remarkable as it grows up to 3 orders of magnitude. On the other hand, our ciphertexts are slightly bigger. Another interesting fact is that we use the same kind of polynomials for conveying all the types of keys and ciphertexts, so the space costs are the same in all cases (1.57 KB).

It is easy to check that our scheme is bidirectional. Given $rk_{A \to B} = f_A f_B^{-1}$, the proxy can easily compute $rk_{B \to A} = (rk_{A \to B})^{-1} = f_B f_A^{-1}$. This property is a consequence of how re-encryption keys are constructed ($rk_{A \to B} = sk_A \cdot sk_B^{-1}$), in the same way as in other bidirectional schemes [11, 12, 27].

With respect to the security of the scheme, we cannot overcome the problem of NTRU lacking a formal security proof. However, we can study it from a practical way, as NTRU does. For instance, the time required for a lattice-based attack to the public key is conjectured to be exponential in n [20]. This is also relevant to the re-encryption scheme since extracting private keys from the re-encryption key is at least as hard as attacking NTRU public key, as they are constructed in the same way: for instance, the public key of user B is of the form $pg_B f_B^{-1}$, whereas re-encryption key $rk_{A \to B}$ is of the form $f_A f_B^{-1}$. In NTRU, the polynomials f are larger than the polynomials g, i.e., they have more non-zero terms, so the term f_A of a re-encryption key would be larger than the term pg_B of a public key. However, as it happens to the majority of bidirectional proxy re-encryption schemes [11, 12, 27], our scheme is not collusion-safe. That is, it is vulnerable to a collusion of the proxy and the users, since extracting the delegator's secret key f_A is as simple as computing $rk_{A \to B} \cdot f_B$. The same problem applies to the delegatee's secret key.

As a way to provide a formal security proof of our scheme, we explored how this problem has been addressed in the literature. An interesting approach is made by Stehlé and Steinfeld in [25, 26], where they present a variant of NTRU which is proven CPA-secure under lattice-based assumptions. Based on this solution, we build a second version of our NTRU-based proxy re-encryption scheme, called PS-NTRUReEncrypt, which is provably-secure.

4. PROVABLY SECURE NTRUREENCRYPT

In this section we provide a second proxy re-encryption scheme, called PS-NTRUReEncrypt, that is provable secure under a hard problem for lattices, namely the Ring-LWE assumption. Before explaining our provably-secure scheme, we must first establish some background concepts; after that, we describe the NTRU variant proposed in [25, 26] by Stehlé and Steinfeld, which serves as a basis for our second scheme.

4.1 Background

Before continuing, we provide some basic definitions and present the notation that is used throughout this section. Most of this definitions and notation is taken from [25, 26].

Let $\Phi(x) = x^n + 1$, with n a power of 2; that is, $\Phi(x)$ is the $2n$-th cyclotomic polynomial. Let q be a prime integer such that $q = 1 \mod 2n$. Let $\mathcal{R}$ be the ring $\mathbb{Z}[x]/\Phi(x)$, and $\mathcal{R}_q = \mathcal{R}/q = \mathbb{Z}_q[x]/\Phi(x)$. We will denote the set of invertible elements of $\mathcal{R}_q$ as $\mathcal{R}_q^\times$. Although elements of $\mathcal{R}$ are polynomials, we often treat them as vectors. We denote by $\|\cdot\|$ and $\|\cdot\|_\infty$ the Euclidean norm and infinite norm, respectively. During the proofs in Section 4.3.1 and 4.3.2, we use the asymptotic notations $O(\cdot), \omega(\cdot), \Omega(\cdot)$. A function $f(n)$ is negligible if $f(n) = n^{-\omega(1)}$.

The Ring Learning With Errors (Ring-LWE) problem is a hard decisional problem based on lattices introduced by Lyubaskevsky et al in [24]. In this paper, we use an adapted version of this problem found in [25, 26].

Definition 4. The Ring-LWE problem. Let $s \in \mathcal{R}_q$ and ψ a distribution over $\mathcal{R}_q^\times$, then we define $A_{s,\psi}^\times$ as the distribution that samples pairs of the form (a, b), where a is chosen uniformly from $\mathcal{R}_q^\times$ and $b = a \cdot s + e$, for some e sampled from ψ. The distribution $A_{s,\psi}^\times$ is also called the Ring-LWE distribution. The Ring-LWE problem is to distinguish distribution $A_{s,\psi}^\times$ from a uniform distribution over $\mathcal{R}_q^\times \times \mathcal{R}_q$. The Ring-LWE assumption is that this problem is computationally infeasible.

This variant of the Ring Learning With Errors problem is denoted in [25, 26] as the R-LWE$_{\text{HNF}}^\times$ problem; however, we will not use that notation for simplicity. As in [25, 26], the error distributions ψ are sampled from a family of distributions Ψ_α, with parameter α; for more details of the definition of these distributions, see [25, 26].

4.2 Provably Secure NTRU

Stehlé and Steinfeld proposed in [25, 26] a variant of the NTRU primitive which is proven CPA-secure under the hardness assumption of the Ring-LWE problem. This scheme is defined over the rings $\mathcal{R}$ and $\mathcal{R}_q$, determined by parameters n and q, as defined in previous section. The plaintext space $\mathcal{M}$ corresponds to the ring $\mathcal{R}/p$, where $p \in \mathcal{R}_q^\times$ is also a parameter of the scheme; as conventional NTRU, typical values for this parameter are $p = 3$ and $p = x + 2$, but in this scheme one may choose $p = 2$, since q is prime. The parameter α characterizes the family of distributions Ψ_α, and the parameter σ is the standard deviation of the Gaussian distribution used during the key generation algorithm. Thus, gobal parameters are a tuple $(n, q, p, \alpha, \sigma)$. The algorithms of this encryption scheme are the following:

- KeyGen(): The output of the key generation algorithm for user A is the pair of public and secret keys $(pk_A, sk_A) \in \mathcal{R}_q^\times \times \mathcal{R}_q^\times$. Let $D_{\mathbb{Z}^n,\sigma}$ be the Gaussian distribution over $\mathbb{Z}^n$ with standard deviation σ. The keys are computed as follows:
    1. Sample f' from $D_{\mathbb{Z}^n,\sigma}$; let $f_A = 1 + p \cdot f'$; if ($f_A \mod q) \notin \mathcal{R}_q^\times$, resample.
    2. Sample g_A from $D_{\mathbb{Z}^n,\sigma}$; if $(g_A \mod q) \notin \mathcal{R}_q^\times$, resample.
    3. Compute $h_A = p \cdot g_A \cdot f_A^{-1}$.
    4. Return secret key $sk_A = f_A$ and $pk_A = h_A$.
- Enc(pk_A, M): On input the public key pk_A and a message $M \in \mathcal{M}$, sample noise polynomials s, e from a

distribution from Ψ_α, and output ciphertext $C_A = h_A s + pe + M \in \mathcal{R}_q$.

- $\mathsf{Dec}(sk_A, C_A)$. On input the secret key $sk_A = f_A$ and a ciphertext C_A, the decryption algorithm Dec computes $C'_A = C_A \cdot f_A$ and outputs the message $M = (C'_A \mod p) \in \mathcal{M}$.

It can be seen that the operation of this scheme is very similar to the original NTRU, except for the generation of the keys and the inclusion of a noise term during encryptions. The authors prove that this NTRU variant is CPA-secure, over the hardness of the Ring-LWE problem. They also prove the correctness of their proposal, by establishing the conditions for avoiding decryption failures. Both proofs will serve as a basis for ours.

4.3 Provably-Secure NTRUReEncrypt

In this section we present the scheme PS-NTRUReEncrypt, which is based on the provably-secure variant of NTRU described in the previous section. This scheme uses the same global parameters as before, a tuple $(n, q, p, \alpha, \sigma)$. This scheme is defined by the following algorithms:

- $\mathsf{KeyGen}()$: The output of the key generation algorithm for user A is the pair of public and secret keys $(pk_A, sk_A) \in \mathcal{R}_q^\times \times \mathcal{R}_q^\times$. The keys are computed as follows:

  1. Sample f' from $D_{\mathbb{Z}^n,\sigma}$; let $f_A = 1 + p \cdot f'$; if $(f_A \mod q) \notin \mathcal{R}_q^\times$, resample.
  2. Sample g_A from $D_{\mathbb{Z}^n,\sigma}$; if $(g_A \mod q) \notin \mathcal{R}_q^\times$, resample.
  3. Compute $h_A = p \cdot g_A \cdot f_A^{-1}$.
  4. Return secret key $sk_A = f_A$ and $pk_A = h_A$.

- $\mathsf{ReKeyGen}(sk_A, sk_B)$: On input the secret keys $sk_A = f_A$ and $sk_B = f_B$, the re-encryption key generation algorithm ReKeyGen computes the re-encryption key between users A and B as $rk_{A\to B} = sk_A \cdot sk_B^{-1} = f_A \cdot f_B^{-1}$.

- $\mathsf{Enc}(pk_A, M)$: On input the public key pk_A and a message $M \in \mathcal{M}$, the encryption algorithm Enc samples noise polynomials s, e from a distribution from Ψ_α, and outputs ciphertext $C_A = h_A s + pe + M \in \mathcal{R}_q$.

- $\mathsf{ReEnc}(rk_{A\to B}, C_A)$: On input a re-encryption key $rk_{A\to B}$ and a ciphertext C_A, the re-encryption algorithm ReEnc samples noise polynomial e' from a distribution from Ψ_α and outputs ciphertext $C_B = C_A \cdot rk_{A\to B} + pe' \in \mathcal{R}_q$.

- $\mathsf{Dec}(sk_A, C_A)$. On input the secret key $sk_A = f_A$ and a ciphertext C_A, the decryption algorithm Dec computes $C'_A = C_A \cdot f_A$ and outputs the message $M = (C'_A \mod p) \in \mathcal{M}$.

It can be seen that this scheme is an extension of the one from Stehlé and Steinfeld, by including the definition of the re-encryption and re-encryption key generation algorithms. Note also that the same three-party protocol for computing the re-encryption key described in Section 3.2 for NTRUReEncrypt can be applied here.

4.3.1 *Correctness*

Following the description of the encryption, decryption and re-encryption algorithms, it is easy to informally check that the correctness conditions defined in Def. 2 are fulfilled:

- For all (pk_A, sk_A) output by KeyGen and all messages $M \in \mathcal{M}$, it holds that $\mathsf{Dec}(sk_A, \mathsf{Enc}(pk_A, M)) = M$.

  The evaluation of the encryption of an arbitraty message $M \in \mathcal{M}$ gives $\mathsf{Dec}(psg_A f_A^{-1} + pe + M, sk_A)$ as a result. Next, as described in the decryption algorithm, we take $C' = f_A \cdot (psg_A f_A^{-1} + pe + M) = psg_A + pef_A + Mf_A$. Finally, since $f_A = 1 \mod p$ and $psg_A = pef_A = 0 \mod p$, we have that $C' \mod p = M$.

- For any sequence of pairs (pk_i, sk_i) output by KeyGen, with $0 \le i \le N$, all re-encryption keys $rk_{j\to j+1}$ output by $\mathsf{ReKeyGen}(sk_j, sk_{j+1})$, with $j < N$, all messages $M \in \mathcal{M}$, and all ciphertexts C_1 output by $\mathsf{Enc}(pk_1, M)$, it holds that:

  $\mathsf{Dec}(sk_N, \mathsf{ReEnc}(rk_{N-1\to N}, ...\mathsf{ReEnc}(rk_{1\to 2}, C_1))) = M$

  If for any $M \in \mathcal{M}$ correctness holds only with probability 1 minus a negligible quantity, we say that the scheme is correct with respect to $\mathcal{M}$.

  Let us assume the sequence of secret keys $f_0, f_1, ..., f_N$. Since our scheme is multi-hop, a ciphertext re-encrypted N times will be of the form:

$$
\begin{aligned}
C_N &= pg_0 f_N^{-1} s + pe_0 f_0 f_N^{-1} + pe_1 f_1 f_N^{-1} + ... \\
&\quad + pe_{N-1} f_{N-1} f_N^{-1} + pe_N + M f_0 f_N^{-1} \\
&= pg_0 f_N^{-1} s + \left[\sum_{i=0}^{N-1} pe_i f_i f_N^{-1}\right] + pe_N + M f_0 f_N^{-1} \quad (1)
\end{aligned}
$$

  where e_i denotes the additional error terms added during the re-encryptions, and e_0 is the error term from the first (and unique) encryption. When decrypting C_N, and assuming there are no decryption failures, one obtains:

$$
C'_N = C_N \cdot f_N = pg_0 s + \left[\sum_{i=0}^{N} pe_i f_i\right] + M f_0 \quad (2)
$$

  Since, $f_0 = 1 \mod p$ and $pg_0 s = pe_i f_i = 0 \mod p$, for $0 \ge i \ge N$, then we have that $C'_N \mod p = M$.

In the informal proof above, we have not considered the possibility of decryption failures. This is a recurrent issue from the first definition of the NTRU cryptosystem. It can be seen that the re-encryption process produces an increase in the error terms of the ciphertexts, which can potentially lead to decryption failures. We will now describe the correctness conditions of NTRUReEncrypt and prove that the decryption algorithm is capable of handling with this increase. This proof is basically a slight extension of the one given in [26, Lemma 3.7] and generalizes single encryption as well as multiple re-encryptions; in this case, single encryption is a handled as a particular case of multihop re-encryption (taking the number of re-encryptions $N = 0$).

THEOREM 1. *If $deg(p) \leq 1$, $\omega(n^{0.25}\log n)\alpha N\|p\|^2\sigma \leq 1$, and $n^{0.75} \leq \alpha q$, then the decryption algorithm of PS-NTRUReEncrypt succeeds in recovering M with probability $1 - n^{-\omega(1)}$ over the choice of s, e_i, f_i, g_i, for $0 \leq i \leq N$.*

PROOF. As stated, a ciphertext C_N re-encrypted N times has the form described in Equation 1. When decrypting C_N, the decryption algorithm computes C'_N, as described in Equation 2. This computation is implicitly performed modulo q, so $C'_N \in \mathcal{R}_q$. However, let us define $C''_N \in \mathcal{R}$, that is, not modulo q:

$$C''_N = pg_0s + \left[\sum_{i=0}^{N} pe_if_i\right] + Mf_0 \in \mathcal{R}$$

In order for the decryption algorithm to succeed $\|C''_N\|_\infty \leq q/2$, so $C'_N = C''_N$ in $\mathcal{R}$. Since $f_0 = 1 \mod p$ and $pg_0s = pe_if_i = 0 \mod p$, for $0 \leq i \leq N$, then we have that $C''_N \mod p = C'_N \mod p = M$ and the decryption algorithm succeeds. Then, it is sufficient to give an upper bound on the probability that $\|C''_N\|_\infty \geq q/2$.

From Lemma 1 (see Appendix A), polynomials g_0 and f_i, for $0 \geq i \geq N$, have Euclidean norms $\leq 4\sqrt{n}\|p\|\sigma$, with probability $\geq 1 - 2^{-n+3}$. From the properties of the ring $\mathcal{R}$ [17], we know that for all $u, v \in \mathcal{R}$, $\|u \cdot v\| \leq \sqrt{n} \cdot \|u\| \cdot \|v\|$. As a particular case, since $deg(p) \leq 1$, then $\|p \cdot u\| \leq 2\|p\| \cdot \|u\|$. Hence, it follows that $\|pf_i\|, \|pg_0\| \leq 8\sqrt{n}\|p\|^2\sigma$, with probability $\geq 1-2^{-n+3}$. Now, from Lemma 2 (see Appendix A), if $n^{0.25} \leq \alpha q$ we have that with probability $\geq 1-n^{-\omega(1)}$:

$$\|pf_ie_i\|_\infty, \|pg_0s\|_\infty \leq 8\alpha q n^{0.25}\omega(\log n)\|p\|^2\sigma$$

Apart from this, since $\|M\| \leq \|p\|$ [26], we know that:

$$\|f_0M\|_\infty \leq \|f_0M\| \leq 4n\|p\|^2\sigma$$

Hence $\|C''_N\|_\infty \leq \left[8(N+2)\alpha q n^{0.25}\omega(\log n) + 4n\right]\|p\|^2\sigma$, and taking $n^{0.75} \leq \alpha q$, then:

$$\|C''_N\|_\infty \leq (8N+20)\alpha q n^{0.25}\omega(\log n)\|p\|^2\sigma$$

As we assumed initially that $\omega(n^{0.25}\log n)\alpha N\|p\|^2\sigma \leq 1$, then we have that $\|C''_N\|_\infty \leq q/2$, with probability $\geq 1 - n^{-\omega(1)}$. □

It can be seen that for the case of single encryption ($N = 0$), the determined bounds are the same than in [26, Lemma 3.7].

4.3.2 Security proof

In this section, we proceed to prove that the scheme PS-NTRUReEncrypt is CPA-secure. This proof is also based on the one given in [26, Lemma 3.8].

THEOREM 2. *Suppose that n is a power of 2, and q a prime number such that $q = 1 \mod 2n$. Let $\epsilon \in (0, \frac{1}{3}), \delta > 0, p \in \mathcal{R}_q^\times$ and $\sigma \geq n\sqrt{ln(8nq)} \cdot q^{\frac{1}{2}+\epsilon}$. If there exists and IND-CPA attack against PS-NTRUReEncrypt with probability $\frac{1}{2}+\delta$, then there exists an algorithm that solves the Ring-LWE problem with probability $\frac{\delta}{2} - q^{-\Omega(n)}$.*

PROOF. Let us assume, by contradiction, that we have an adversary $\mathcal{A}$ that breaks PS-NTRUReEncrypt with probability $\frac{1}{2} + \delta$. We construct an algorithm $\mathcal{B}$ against the Ring-LWE problem as follows:

Let $\mathcal{O}_{sample}$ be an oracle that samples tuples (h', C') from either the uniform distribution over $\mathcal{R}_q^\times \times \mathcal{R}_q$ or $A_{s,\psi}^\times$. Algorithm $\mathcal{B}$ first gets a sample (h', C') from $\mathcal{O}_{sample}$. Next, $\mathcal{B}$ generates target public key $pk^* = h^* = p \cdot h'$ and gives pk^* to $\mathcal{A}$. Note that, regardless of the input distribution, h' will be sampled uniformly from $\mathcal{R}_q^\times$, and since $p \in \mathcal{R}_q^\times$, then $h^* = p \cdot h'$ is uniformly random in $\mathcal{R}_q^\times$; however, by [26, Theorem 3], h^* is within negligible statistical distance $q^{-\Omega(n)}$ to public keys generated by KeyGen. $\mathcal{B}$ will also generate an invalid, but correctly distributed, secret key polynomial f^* as described in the first step of the key generation process, so target secret key is $sk^* = f^*$.

Both honest and corrupted key generation are done as in the PS-NTRUReEncrypt scheme. Re-encryption key generation queries are done using the secret keys derived on the key generation queries. Once $\mathcal{A}$ queries the challenge oracle with inputs M_0 and M_1, $\mathcal{B}$ randomly picks $b \leftarrow \{0, 1\}$, and constructs the challenge ciphertext as $C^* = p \cdot C' + M_b$. Adversary $\mathcal{A}$ receives C^* and, eventually, outputs its guess b'; if $b' = b$, then algorithm $\mathcal{B}$ outputs 1.

On the one hand, when the input to $\mathcal{B}$ is a sample from $A_{s,\psi}^\times$, then it will be of the form $(h', C' = h's + e)$, for some $s, e \leftarrow \psi$. In this case, the challenge ciphertext C^* is a correct encryption of M_b under h^*, since $C^* = p \cdot C' + M_b = p(h's+e)+M_b = h^*s+pe+M_b$, and $\mathcal{A}$ will succeed in distinguishing M_b with probability $\frac{1}{2} + \delta - q^{-\Omega(n)}$. Hence, $\mathcal{B}$ will determine that the sample was from the $A_{s,\psi}^\times$ distribution with the same probability.

On the other hand, when the sample is from the uniform distribution over $\mathcal{R}_q^\times \times \mathcal{R}_q$ then C' is uniformily random in $\mathcal{R}_q$, and since $p \in \mathcal{R}_q^\times$, so is $p \cdot C'$. The challenge ciphertext $C^* = p \cdot C' + M_b$ will be then uniformily random in $\mathcal{R}_q$, as in the original distribution of ciphertexts, and independent of b. In this case, algorithm $\mathcal{B}$ does not have any advantage in distinguishing the distribution and outputs 1 with probability $\frac{1}{2}$. Overall, algorithm $\mathcal{B}$ succeeds with probability $(\frac{1}{2})(\frac{1}{2}+\delta-q^{-\Omega(n)})+(\frac{1}{2})(\frac{1}{2}) = \frac{1}{2}+\frac{\delta}{2}-q^{-\Omega(n)}$. This contradicts the Ring-LWE assumption when δ is non-negligible.

□

Remark: In this simulation, each re-encryption key that involves the target public key is invalid, as generating a re-encryption key implies knowledge of the secret keys of the users involved. In this case, the target public key is constructed from $\mathcal{O}_{sample}$, so the simulator does not know the corresponding secret key. However, since the secret key of the target used generated at the beginning of the simulation is correctly distributed, any re-encryption key computed from this secret key is indistinguishable from a valid one. A similar argument is made in [18].

4.3.3 Analysis

The properties of PS-NTRUReEncrypt are the same as our first scheme. These properties are:

- Bidirectional: Given $rk_{A\to B} = f_Af_B^{-1}$, one can easily compute $rk_{B\to A} = (rk_{A\to B})^{-1} = f_Bf_A^{-1}$.
- Multihop: It supports multiple re-encryptions, as shown in Section 4.3.1. Note that an error term is included during the re-encryption process, so the noise grows on each hop. Nevertheless, the correctness conditions presented before guarantee that the decryption

succeeds with overwhelming probability for proper parameters (which include the devised maximum number of hops, N). See also the results presented on Section 5.3.

- Not collusion-safe: This scheme suffers from the same vulnerability as NTRUReEncrypt, so secret keys can be extracted from the re-encryption key if the proxy colludes with a user involved. This problem is common in bidirectional proxy re-encryption schemes.

Table 3 shows the computational costs associated to PS-NTRUReEncrypt. As for our first scheme NTRUReEncrypt, the main operation here is the multiplication of polynomials, which is denoted by t_m. In addition, another potentially costly operation is sampling from the noise distribution, denoted by t_s. We distinguish here between on-line and off-line operations, as the latter can be performed beforehand (e.g., sampling noise terms).

Table 3: Time costs of PS-NTRUReEncrypt

Operation	On-line	Off-line
Encryption	t_m	$t_m + 2t_s$
Re-Encryption	t_m	$t_m + t_s$
Decryption	t_m	–

With regard to the theoretical space costs, this scheme shares the same results as NTRUReEncrypt, presented in Table 1. However, when considering an experimental instantiation, the parameters used would not be the same, which implies that the experimental costs vary. In addition, given that we lack of a formal analysis for quantifying the level of security that is provided by the scheme, it is not possible to make a direct comparison. An experimental analysis of the costs of PS-NTRUReEncrypt is presented in Section 5.3.

5. SOME EXPERIMENTAL RESULTS

In order to validate the viability of the proposed proxy re-encryption schemes, we have developed and tested an implementation of our proposals. Since we propose two schemes, we have two different implementations. NTRUReEncrypt is implemented on top of an available open-source Java implementation of NTRU [1]. For PS-NTRUReEncrypt, due to its non-standard nature, we had to code it from scratch; however, we made use of the functionalities provided by the Java Lattice-Based Cryptography (jLBC) library [14]. Our execution enviroment consists on an Intel Core 2 Duo @ 2.66 GHz. Although this processor has two cores, our implementation only uses one of them, as it is not parallel.

5.1 Performance of NTRUReEncrypt

The first experiment consisted of measuring the performance of the first proposed scheme using different set of parameters. We have used the parameter sets proposed in [28], although other parameters could be studied. Besides the basic implementation, we have made also some optimizations, such as the possibility of using product-form polynomials [28], which has a great effect on performance.

In Table 4, we give the execution times for the encryption, decryption and re-encryption for each parameter set. Parameters are represented by a tuple (*n, prod, k*), where *prod* is a boolean parameter that indicates the use of product-form polynomials, and k is the claimed security level (in bits). Additional parameters are fixed, such as $q = 2048$ and $p = 3$.

For each set of parameters, the experiment consisted of a looped execution, where a random message from the plaintext space is sequentially encrypted, re-encrypted and decrypted, and new keys are used on each iteration. The time for each operation is computed as the average of 100 iterations. Since sampling random elements is an operation that can be performed off-line, we decided to exclude it from the time measurements; thus, times reflected in this experiment only reflect the operations that must be performed on-line. This approach was also followed by [19].

Table 4: Computation time (in ms) and number of hops of NTRUReEncrypt for different parameters

Parameters	Enc.	Dec.	Re-Enc.	# Hops
(439, no, 128)	0.64	0.30	0.24	5
(439, yes, 128)	0.16	0.30	0.23	5
(1087, no, 256)	1.39	1.25	1.05	21
(1087, yes, 256)	0.48	1.26	1.07	15
(1171, no, 256)	0.80	1.12	1.14	21
(1171, yes, 256)	0.43	1.22	1.15	14
(1499, no, 256)	0.74	1.78	1.73	50
(1499, yes, 256)	0.32	1.67	1.66	42

For example, the sixth set of parameters was already used for a previous NTRU benchmark [19], and we can see that our results are consistent with their study, where they obtained a measure of approximately 0.31 ms for encryption (3220 encryptions per second).

In addition, Table 4 also shows the average number of re-encryptions supported by each parameter set. As stated in Section 3.2.2, the inclusion of the error term *pe* during the re-encryption process produces an increasing error that grows on each hop, causing a decryption failure at some point. It can be seen that this depends on the choice of parameters, so increasing the parameters actually decreases the probability of decryption failure.

5.2 Comparison of NTRUReEncrypt with other proxy re-encryption schemes

In order to benchmark our proposal with respect to other proxy re-encryption schemes, we have implemented three schemes. Two of them share similar properties than ours (i.e., bidirectional and multihop). One of them is the BBS scheme [11], which is CPA-secure as ours, while the other is the one proposed by Weng et al [27], which is proven CCA-secure; note, however, that the latter scheme achieves a better notion of security than ours, and hence, the comparison is unbalanced in this case. Both of them are implemented in Java using elliptic curve cryptography over a prime field. Specifically, we used the NIST P-256 curve, which provides 128 bits of security [10]. In addition, and for the sake of comparison, we have also implemented a third scheme from Aono et al [4]; note that in this case, this scheme is not bidirectional. For our scheme, we have used the *ees1171ep1* parameter set from [28], which achieves 256 bits of security. This parameter set corresponds to the sixth row of Table 4. We chose this parameter set because it was already used for a previous NTRU benchmark [19]. With regard to the experimental setting, we have used the same environment as before.

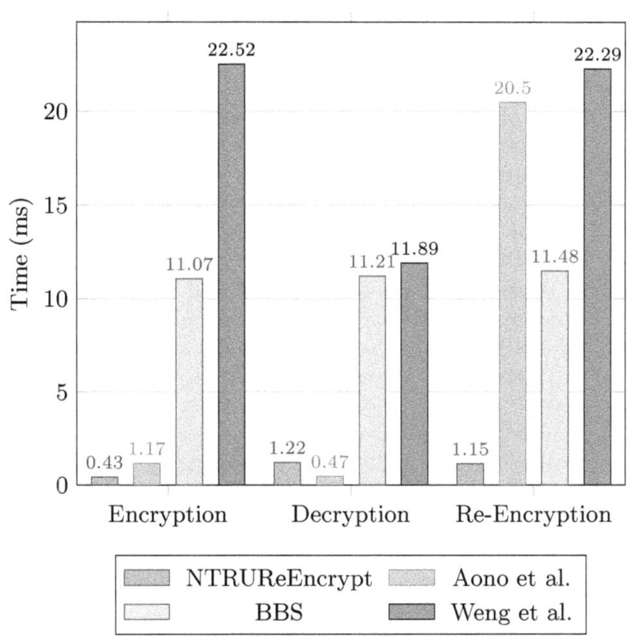

Figure 1: Comparison with other proxy re-encryption schemes

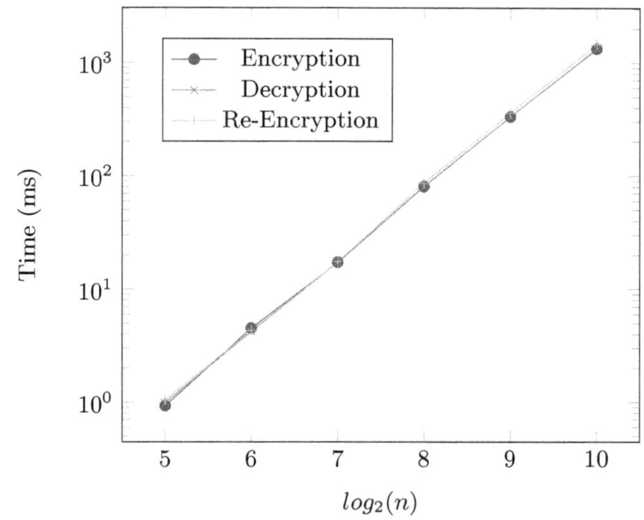

Figure 2: Performance of PS-NTRUReEncrypt

Figure 1 shows the results of our experiment. It can be seen that our scheme outperforms the others, as it is between 10 and 20 times faster. The scheme from Aono et al shows a similar performance in encryption and decryption, but is 20 times slower for re-encryption. The results obtained for our scheme are consistent with previous benchmarks for NTRU [19], as we used the same parameters.

For our experiment, we also implemented other unidirectional schemes, specifically, the ones from Ateniese et al [7] and Libert and Vergnaud [21]. However, we exclude them from this comparison since they are much slower due to the use of bilinear pairings; Appendix B presents these omitted results.

5.3 Performance of PS-NTRUReEncrypt

Table 5 shows the computation time of the main operations of PS-NTRUReEncrypt. It can be seen that the computation time for the main operations is approximately the same for each parameter set. This is also shown in Figure 2. Note that this figure is in logarithm scale, so the growth in computation time is exponential as n increases. This is a consequence of requiring that n is a power of 2, which restricts the choice of parameters.

Table 5: Computation time (in ms) of PS-NTRUReEncrypt for different parameters

Parameters	Enc.	Dec.	Re-Enc.
$n = 32, \log_2 q = 23$	0.93	0.99	1.05
$n = 64, \log_2 q = 28$	4.53	4.23	4.32
$n = 128, \log_2 q = 32$	17.28	17.32	17.45
$n = 256, \log_2 q = 37$	80.64	81.045	86.56
$n = 512, \log_2 q = 41$	333.75	334.07	359.54
$n = 1024, \log_2 q = 46$	1333.03	1344.10	1461.46

Unlike the first scheme, we do not provide a comparison of PS-NTRUReEncrypt to other proxy re-encryption schemes. We cannot directly compare it to other schemes without properly analizing the security level it achieves, which is done indirectly through evaluating the security against the best known lattice attacks [26].

With regard to the number of hops of this scheme, the results now are much better than in NTRUReEncrypt, where we had just up to 50 re-encryptions, with the parameter sets used. In this case, we were unable to find a maximum number of hops, having executed more than 10000 re-encryptions for each parameter set, without finding any decryption failure. This lead us to think that the parameters used in PS-NTRUReEncrypt are actually very conservative, which explains also that its performance is lower than NTRUReEncrypt. These parameters are, however, derived from the theoretic assumptions; it is an open problem to find ways to decrease them.

Other factor that could impact the results is that the implementation is not as optimized as NTRUReEncrypt, since we had to code it from scratch. In order to improve our implementation, we can make use of optimizations such as faster algorithms for polynomial multiplication, based on the Fast Fourier Transform (FFT).

Table 6: Space costs (in KB) of PS-NTRUReEncrypt for different parameters

Parameters	Size of polynomials
$n = 32, \log_2 q = 23$	0.09
$n = 64, \log_2 q = 28$	0.22
$n = 128, \log_2 q = 32$	0.50
$n = 256, \log_2 q = 37$	1.16
$n = 512, \log_2 q = 41$	2.56
$n = 1024, \log_2 q = 46$	5.75

As for the space costs, Table 6 shows the size in KB of the polynomials produced by different parameters. Recall that in our schemes, all the elements of the cryptosystem (i.e., public and secret keys, re-encryption keys, and ciphertexts) are represented by the same kind of polynomials.

6. CONCLUSIONS

In this paper we describe NTRUReEncrypt, a highly-efficient proxy re-encryption scheme based on the NTRU cryptosystem. This scheme is bidirectional and multihop, but not collusion-resistant. The key strength of this scheme is its performance. Experimental results show that this scheme outperforms previous proposals by an order of magnitude, and there is room for even more improvement, for instance using parallelization techniques, as shown in [19]. We believe that the level of efficiency shown by NTRUReEncrypt opens up new practical applications of proxy re-encryption in constrained environments. In addition to this scheme, we propose PS-NTRUReEncrypt, a provably-secure variant that is CPA-secure under the hardness of lattice problems, namely the Ring-LWE problem.

With regard to future work, there are several areas with potential for improvement. The most pressing are achieving CCA-security and the definition of a unidirectional and collision-resistant scheme. Another subject is improving the parameters of NTRUReEncrypt, since this could decrease the probability of decryption failures after multiple re-encryptions. Additionaly, it would be interesting to come up with better bounds for the provably-secure version and an analysis of the selection of parameters based on the best known attacks. Finally, we want also to extend the experimental analysis to other lattice-based proxy re-encryption schemes.

7. ACKNOWLEDGMENTS

This work was partly supported by the Junta de Andalucía through the project FISICCO (P11-TIC-07223) and by the Spanish Ministry of Economy and Competitiveness through the PERSIST project (TIN2013-41739-R). The first author has been funded by a FPI fellowship from the Junta de Andalucía through the project PISCIS (P10-TIC-06334).

8. REFERENCES

[1] Java implementation of NTRUEncrypt and NTRUSign. http://tbuktu.github.io/ntru/.

[2] ANSI X9.98: Lattice-based polynomial public key establishment algorithm for the financial services industry. Technical report, ANSI, 2010.

[3] C. Aguilar-Melchor and P. Gaborit. A lattice-based computationally-efficient private information retrieval protocol. *Cryptol. ePrint Arch., Report*, 446, 2007.

[4] Y. Aono, X. Boyen, L. T. Phong, and L. Wang. Key-private proxy re-encryption under LWE. In *Progress in Cryptology–INDOCRYPT 2013*, pages 1–18. Springer, 2013.

[5] G. Ateniese, K. Benson, and S. Hohenberger. Key-private proxy re-encryption. *Topics in Cryptology–CT-RSA 2009*, pages 279–294, 2009.

[6] G. Ateniese, K. Fu, M. Green, and S. Hohenberger. Improved proxy re-encryption schemes with applications to secure distributed storage. In *Proceedings of the 12th Annual Network and Distributed System Security Symposium*, pages 29–44, 2005.

[7] G. Ateniese, K. Fu, M. Green, and S. Hohenberger. Improved proxy re-encryption schemes with applications to secure distributed storage. *ACM Transactions on Information and System Security (TISSEC)*, 9(1):1–30, 2006.

[8] D. V. Bailey, D. Coffin, A. Elbirt, J. H. Silverman, and A. D. Woodbury. NTRU in constrained devices. In *Cryptographic Hardware and Embedded Systems—CHES 2001*, pages 262–272. Springer, 2001.

[9] E. Barker, W. Barker, W. Burr, W. Polk, and M. Smid. Recommendation for key management — part 1: General. Technical report, 2005.

[10] E. Barker, L. Chen, A. Roginsky, and M. Smid. Recommendation for Pair-Wise Key Establishment Schemes Using Discrete Logarithm Cryptography. NIST special publication 800-56A (Revision 2), NIST, May 2013.

[11] M. Blaze, G. Bleumer, and M. Strauss. Divertible protocols and atomic proxy cryptography. *Advances in Cryptology—EUROCRYPT'98*, pages 127–144, 1998.

[12] R. Canetti and S. Hohenberger. Chosen-ciphertext secure proxy re-encryption. In *Proceedings of the 14th ACM conference on Computer and communications security*, pages 185–194. ACM, 2007.

[13] C. Chu and W. Tzeng. Identity-based proxy re-encryption without random oracles. *Information Security*, pages 189–202, 2007.

[14] A. De Caro. Java Lattice Based Cryptography Library (jLBC). http://gas.dia.unisa.it/projects/jlbc/.

[15] A. De Caro and V. Iovino. jPBC: Java pairing based cryptography. In *Proceedings of the 16th IEEE Symposium on Computers and Communications, ISCC 2011*, pages 850–855. IEEE, 2011.

[16] S. D. Galbraith, K. G. Paterson, and N. P. Smart. Pairings for cryptographers. *Discrete Applied Mathematics*, 156(16):3113–3121, 2008.

[17] C. Gentry. Fully homomorphic encryption using ideal lattices. In *Proceedings of the Forty-first Annual ACM Symposium on Theory of Computing*, STOC '09, pages 169–178, New York, NY, USA, 2009. ACM.

[18] M. Green and G. Ateniese. Identity-based proxy re-encryption. In *Applied Cryptography and Network Security*, pages 288–306. Springer, 2007.

[19] J. Hermans, F. Vercauteren, and B. Preneel. Speed records for ntru. In *Topics in Cryptology-CT-RSA 2010*, pages 73–88. Springer, 2010.

[20] J. Hoffstein, J. Pipher, and J. H. Silverman. Ntru: A ring-based public key cryptosystem. In *Algorithmic number theory*, pages 267–288. Springer, 1998.

[21] B. Libert and D. Vergnaud. Unidirectional chosen-ciphertext secure proxy re-encryption. *Information Theory, IEEE Transactions on*, 57(3):1786–1802, 2011.

[22] A. López-Alt, E. Tromer, and V. Vaikuntanathan. On-the-fly multiparty computation on the cloud via multikey fully homomorphic encryption. In *Proceedings of the 44th symposium on Theory of Computing*, pages 1219–1234. ACM, 2012.

[23] X. Lv, B. Yang, and C. Pei. Efficient traitor tracing scheme based on ntru. In *Parallel and Distributed Computing, Applications and Technologies, 2005. PDCAT 2005. Sixth International Conference on*, pages 120–124. IEEE, 2005.

[24] V. Lyubashevsky, C. Peikert, and O. Regev. On ideal lattices and learning with errors over rings. *Journal of the ACM (JACM)*, 60(6):43, 2013.
[25] D. Stehlé and R. Steinfeld. Making NTRU as secure as worst-case problems over ideal lattices. In *Advances in Cryptology–EUROCRYPT 2011*, pages 27–47. Springer, 2011.
[26] D. Stehlé and R. Steinfeld. Making NTRUEncrypt and NTRUSign as secure as standard worst-case problems over ideal lattices. *IACR Cryptology ePrint Archive*, 2013:4, 2013.
[27] J. Weng, R. H. Deng, S. Liu, and K. Chen. Chosen-ciphertext secure bidirectional proxy re-encryption schemes without pairings. *Information Sciences*, 180(24):5077–5089, 2010.
[28] W. Whyte, N. Howgrave-Graham, J. Hoffstein, J. Pipher, J. Silverman, and P. Hirschhorn. IEEE P1363.1: Draft standard for public-key cryptographic techniques based on hard problems over lattices. Technical report, IEEE, 2008.
[29] K. Xagawa and K. Tanaka. Proxy re-encryption based on learning with errors. In *Proceedings of the 2010 Symposium on Cryptography and Information Security (SCIS 2010)*, 2010.

APPENDIX

A. SECONDARY LEMMAS

In this section we present two secondary lemmas, both presented in [26]. The first lemma provides bounds for the secret keys generated using the key generation algorithm:

LEMMA 1. *[26, Lemma 3.6] Let n be a power of 2, q a prime so that $q = 1 \mod 2n$, and $deg(p) \leq 1$. Let $\sigma \geq \sqrt{n \log n} \cdot q^{1/n}$. The secret key polynomials f and g returned by the KeyGen algorithm satisfy $\|f\| \leq 4\sqrt{n}\|p\|\sigma$ and $\|g\| \leq \sqrt{n}\sigma$, with probability $\geq 1 - 2^{-n+3}$.*

The second lemma provides bounds to the product of arbitrary polynomials of $\mathcal{R}$ with samples from a distribution from Ψ_α:

LEMMA 2. *[26, Lemma 2.10] Let $y, r \in \mathcal{R}$, with r fixed and y sampled from a distribution from Ψ_α, with $\alpha q \geq n^{0.25}$. Then: $Pr\left[\|yr\|_\infty \geq \alpha q n^{-0.25} \omega(\log n) \cdot \|r\|\right] \leq n^{-\omega(1)}$*

B. PERFORMANCE EVALUATION OF PROXY RE-ENCRYPTION SCHEMES

In addition to the schemes shown in the experimental comparison, we also implemented two more schemes from Ateniese et al [7] and Libert and Vergnaud [21], both of them unidirectional and the latter secure against chosen ciphertext attacks. However, being based on pairings, these schemes have proven to be much slower, so we drop them from our main analysis. Since we are unaware of any previous work that benchmarks actual implementations of proxy re-encryption schemes, we decided to include this evaluation as an appendix.

We implemented these additional schemes using the jPBC library [15], a pairing-based cryptography library for Java. As for the cryptographic details, we used a supersingular curve of the form $y^2 = x^3 + x$, with a 256-bit group order and 3072 bits for the field size, which achieves 128 bits of security [16][9]. Additionally, we have made extensive use of exponentiation and pairing preprocessing of frequently-used elements for efficiency reasons. This is a very useful functionality of jPBC that allows the preprocessing of exponentiation operations for efficiency reasons, since there are several elements that are frequently exponentiated, such as the generators of the groups and the public keys.

Table 7: Computation time of several proxy re-encryption schemes (in ms)

Scheme	Enc.	Dec.	Re-Enc.
NTRUReEncrypt	0.43	1.22	1.15
Aono et al [4]	1.17	0.47	20.5
BBS [11]	11.07	11.21	11.48
Weng et al [27]	22.52	11.89	22.29
Ateniese et al [7]	22.76	13.76	83.52
Libert and Vergnaud [21]	155.27	443.87	386.93

Table 7 shows the results obtained from our experiments, including the schemes from Ateniese et al. and from Libert and Vergnaud. For the particular case of re-encryption, which is the most common operation for most applications of proxy re-encryption, it can be seen that NTRUReEncrypt outperforms the others. Note also that the security level for the proxy re-encryption schemes is 128 bits, while the provided by NTRUReEncrypt with the used parameters is 256 bits; if we increase the parameters in the rest of the schemes in order to achieve 256 bits of security, then these times would be much higher.

Identity-Set-based Broadcast Encryption supporting "Cut-or-Select" with Short Ciphertext

Yan Zhu, Xin Wang
School of Computer and Communication Engineering,
University of Science and Technology Beijing,
Beijing 100083, China
zhuyan@ustb.edu.cn

Di Ma
Computer and Information Science,
University of Michigan-Dearborn,
Dearborn, MI 48128
dmadma@umich.edu

RuiQi Guo
School of Computer and Communication Engineering,
University of Science and Technology Beijing,
Beijing 100083, China
guoruiqi7@163.com

ABSTRACT

In this paper we present an identity-set-based broadcast encryption scheme with three working modes: *positive membership* (Select-mode), *all member* (All-mode), and *negative membership* (Cut-mode) over the user identity set, simultaneously. The core of our scheme is the implementation of cryptographic representation of subset by using two aggregation functions: Zeros-based aggregation and Poles-based aggregation. These two aggregation functions are capable of compressing any subset into one element in a bilinear map group for determining the membership between an element and a subset. Our scheme achieves the optimal bound of $O(1)$-size for either ciphertext (consisting of just two elements) or decryption key (one element) for an identity set of large size. We prove that our scheme is secure under the General Diffie-Hellman Exponent (GDHE) assumption.

Categories and Subject Descriptors

E.3 [**Data Encryption**]: Public key cryptosystems; C.2.0 [**Computer-Communication Networks**]: General—*Security and protection*; D.4.6 [**Operating Systems**]: Security and Protection—*Cryptographic controls*

General Terms

Security, Design, Algorithms, Performance

Keywords

Group-oriented Encryption, Cryptographic Representation of Subset, Negative Membership, Set Membership, Identity-Set-based Encryption

1. INTRODUCTION

Broadcast encryption (BE) is a group-oriented cryptosystem in which a broadcaster encrypts messages and transmits them to a group of users $\mathcal{U}$ who are listening to a broadcast channel and use their private keys to decrypt received messages. [1, 2, 3] One remarkable feature of broadcast encryption is that each user has a unique private key. In the public key setting for $n = |\mathcal{U}|$ users, this feature means that broadcast encryption has a one-to-many (or $1 : n$) public/private key structure. In other words, many different private keys correspond to one public key. This kind of key structure is completely different from traditional $1 : 1$ public/private key structure. The benefits gained from this $1 : n$ key structure include additional functionalities such as traitor tracing [4], dynamic revocation, and so on.

Broadcast encryption can be widely used in many application scenarios ranging from TV subscription services, DVD copyright protection, and encrypted file systems, to secure communication of social networks, e.g., Email, Blog, Web communities. Existing broadcast encryption schemes can be roughly categorized into two groups (related work is discussed in Section 7):

- Category I: Broadcast for multiple designated receivers where a broadcast message is sent securely to a small subset of users $\mathcal{S}$ and $|\mathcal{S}| \ll n$ [2, 5];
- Category II: Broadcast without multiple revoked receivers where a broadcast message is sent to all BUT a small set of revoked users $\mathcal{R}$ and $|\mathcal{R}| \ll n$ [6].

Usually, these two categories of broadcast encryption do not replace each other when n is large, so they can be thought as two complementary approaches. There is little systematic work for integrating these two categories of broadcast encryption into a secure BE system [2, 7, 8] from literature.

The two mechanisms, one-time *designation or inclusion* (of Category I) and *revocation or exclusion* (of Category II) for a subset of users, are extremely important for large-scale IT systems with large-size users. For example, in email system or Blog sites, we often communicate with several specified friends, but also sometimes broadcast to almost users in community. To sum up, we list some desirable features for developing a practical and flexible BE scheme:

1. The scheme should be able to support large-size users and new user's joining at an arbitrary time;
2. Two broadcast mechanisms, designation and revocation, should be supported simultaneously, and the ciphertext size should be independent on the number of designated or revoked users;

ASIA CCS'15, April 14–17, 2015, Singapore.
Copyright © 2015 ACM 978-1-4503-3245-3/15/04 ...$15.00.
http://dx.doi.org/10.1145/2714576.2714602 .

3. For easy-to-use, the user's identity (similar as identity-based encryption) should be employed to memory and distinguish the different users;

Our Motivation and Roadmap. In this paper our goal is to develop a new group-oriented encryption which supports two broadcast mechanisms, designation and revocation, simultaneously. We believe that the foundation of constructing such an encryption system is to achieve *cryptographic decisional problem of set membership*, that is, given a subset $\mathcal{S}$ and an element e in $\mathcal{U}$, determine whether or not e belongs to $\mathcal{S}$ (i.e., $e \in \mathcal{S}$ or $e \notin \mathcal{S}$) in a secure (or non-deceptive) way. Obviously, our desired cryptosystem could be constructed by solving the above problem.

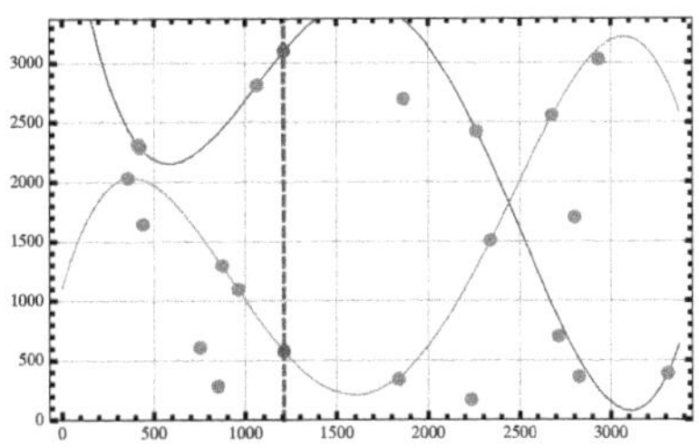

Figure 1: Example of cryptographic representation of subset and aggregation function.

Our approach of solving the above problem is to realize the cryptographic representation of any given subset, and then design a secure aggregation function to compress the subset into a constant-size random element, which would be used to construct our desired encryption system. Further, we show an example of our approach in Figure 1, in which such an approach can be realized by four following steps:

1. Given a set $\mathcal{U} = \{e_1, \cdots, e_n\}$, we map each element e_i into a random point v_i in cryptographic space, where the partial information of these points is published as the public key mpk (see the red points in Figure 1);
2. Given a subset $\mathcal{S} \subseteq \mathcal{U}$, we construct a curve $c(x)$ through all random points $\{v_i\}$ included in $\mathcal{S}$ (see two curves in Figure 1, each of which was interpolated from points);
3. We introduce a random secret γ and then the aggregation function is defined as the corresponding point $c(\gamma)$ in this curve, that is, $Aggregate(mpk,\mathcal{S}) \rightarrow c(\gamma)$, where mpk is the public cryptographic parameters (see the dashed blue line and the intersections of this line and two curves);
4. We define the security feature of function that intend to ensure the security of aggregation under the malicious attacks (see Definition 3 and 4 in Section 3.1).

Finally, we expect to use this kind of aggregation for developing our encryption scheme. The privacy and randomness of aggregation point $c(\gamma)$ will provide guarantee for the security of our scheme. Moreover, the compression property of aggregation function can ensure the $O(1)$-size ciphertext.

Our Contributions. In this paper we first present a new identity-Set-based Broadcast Encryption (SBE) based on cryptographic decisional problem of set membership. By supporting both designation and revocation simultaneously, our scheme allows a nice property of "**Cut-or-Select**". That is, a broadcaster is able to send a message to some selected users or to all but some revoked ones. In detail, our work is listed as follows:

- We propose a new approach to solve cryptographic decisional problem of set membership by designing two aggregation functions: Zeros-based aggregation and Poles-based aggregation. Two corresponding fast algorithms are developed to compress any subset quickly into a constant-size element for designation and revocation mechanisms.
- We present the construction of a SBE scheme with three operation modes over the set of user identities: *positive membership, all member, negative membership* for any subset of users, simultaneously. Moreover, our scheme achieve the optimal bound of $O(1)$-size for either ciphertexts or decryption keys.
- We prove the security of two aggregation functions and provide a complete security proof of our SBE scheme based on general Diffie-Hellman exponent (GDHE) assumption. Our scheme is secure for arbitrarily large collusion of corrupted users. Moreover, our experiments show that our SBE scheme is simple, easy-to-implement and high performance, as well as short (128-byte) and constant-size ciphertext for any size subset.

Organization. The preliminaries and definition of SBE are provided in Section 2. We propose an effective solution for cryptographic set membership in 3.1. Our SBE scheme in Section 3. We present the security and performance analysis in Section 4, 5, and 6. Related work is presented in Section 7 and Section 8 concludes the Lab.

2. OUR DEFINITION OF SBE

We now give a formal definition of identity-Set-based Broadcast Encryption (SBE) with key encapsulation mechanism [2], which is made up of four algorithms, shown as follows:

Setup($\mathbb{S}$): takes as input a bilinear map group system $\mathbb{S}$. It outputs a public key mpk and a master secret key msk, where mpk contains a list of user's profiles pp.

KeyGen(msk, ID_k): takes as input msk and a user's identity ID_k. It outputs the user's secret key sk_k and adds a user's profile pp_k to pp, i.e., $\mathrm{pp} = \mathrm{pp} \cup \{pp_k\}$.

Encrypt($mpk, \mathcal{S}, mode$): takes as input mpk, a set of user's identities $\mathcal{S}$, and a mode of operation $mode$, where $mode$ belongs to one of three modes in $\{u \in \mathcal{S}, u \in \mathrm{All}, u \notin \mathcal{S}\}$. It outputs a ciphertext C and a random session key ek, where $(\mathcal{S}, mode)$ is included in C.

Decrypt(mpk, sk_k, C): takes as input mpk, a ciphertext C, and a user's secret key sk_k. If this user satisfies the access mode $mode$ then the algorithm will decrypt the ciphertext C and return a session key ek.

In SBE scheme, the *user's profile* includes the identity of this user and a public parameter generated in registry. Our scheme makes use of these profiles to realize encryption and decryption for a subset of users. As a group-oriented cryptosystem, we employ a list of profiles to realize the management of memberships. According to the different of operations, the set of users $\mathcal{S}$ will be used in three cases:

Select-mode ($\mathbf{u} \in \mathcal{S}$): used to specify multiple receivers, where $\mathcal{S}$ denotes a set of specified users, such that the user $u \in \mathcal{S}$ will be authorized to decrypt the message.

All-mode ($\mathbf{u} \in$ All): used to specify all receivers, and all users is specified to decrypt the message.

Cut-mode ($u \notin \mathcal{S}$): used to revoke multiple receivers, where $\mathcal{S}$ denotes a set of revoked users, such that the user $u \notin \mathcal{S}$ will be authorized to decrypt the message.

Consider all possible mpk from $Setup(\mathbb{S}) \rightarrow (mpk, msk)$, a valid ciphertext C from $Encrypt(mpk, \mathcal{S}, mode) \rightarrow (\mathrm{C}, ek)$ and $KeyGen(msk, \mathrm{ID}_k) \rightarrow sk_k$. If the user's identity ID_k satisfies the operation mode $(\mathcal{S}, mode)$ in C, then the decryption algorithm will retrieve the session key ek, i.e.,

$$\Pr\left[\begin{array}{c} Decrypt(mpk, sk_k, \mathrm{C}) = ek : \\ mode(\mathrm{ID}_k, \mathcal{S}) = 1 \end{array}\right] = 1,$$

where $mode(\mathrm{ID}_k, \mathcal{S}) = 1$ denotes the boolean judgment over $mode := \{u \in \mathcal{S}, u \in \mathrm{All}, u \notin \mathcal{S}\}$ for a certain ID_k and a set of user's identities $\mathcal{S}$.

We now describe a game-based security definition of our SBE scheme. We define a selective-set model for proving the security of SBE under chosen plaintext attack (CPA). Given a challenge ciphertext C^* with $(\mathcal{S}^*, mode)$, the attacker can repeatedly ask for secret keys $\mathcal{R} = \{(\mathrm{ID}_i, sk_i)\}$ corresponding to a given $mode$ used in C^*, but we have $mode(\mathrm{ID}_i, \mathcal{S}) = 0$ for all possible ID_i in the corrupted keys $\mathcal{R}$, where i is a user counter. The security game follows.

- **Setup.** Given a $mode$ and a set $\mathcal{S}^*$, the challenger runs the Setup algorithm and gives mpk to the adversary.
- **Learning.** The adversary makes n times repeated private keys queries for a user's identity ID_i. The challenger returns $\mathrm{KeyGen}(\mathrm{MK}, \phi) \rightarrow (sk_i, pp_i)$ if $mode(\mathrm{ID}_i, \mathcal{S}^*) = 0$. Otherwise, it merely returns a public profile pp_i, where t is the number of all corrupted secret keys and $|\mathcal{S}^*| = n - t$.
- **Challenge.** The challenger completes $\mathrm{Encrypt}(mpk, \mathcal{S}^*, mode) = (\mathrm{C}, ek)$, and then flips a random coin $b = \{0, 1\}$ and sets $ek_b = ek$ and ek_{1-b} to a random element of $\mathbb{G}_T$. The ciphertext (C, ek_0, ek_1) is given to the adversary.
- **Guess.** The adversary outputs a guess b' of b.

The advantage of an adversary $\mathcal{A}$ in this game is defined as $Adv^{\mathrm{IND}, mode}_{\mathrm{SBE}, \mathcal{A}}(n, t) = |\Pr[b' = b] - 1/2|$ for three modes. A SBE scheme is (n, t)-secure against colluders [3, 9] if all polynomial time adversaries have at most a negligible advantage in the above game.

3. OUR CONSTRUCTION

3.1 Aggregation Functions of Subsets

In this section, we illustrate our basic idea to design cryptographic construction for set membership. In our idea, the core notion is cryptographic representation of subset based on aggregation functions. Given a set $\mathcal{U}$, an **aggregation function** is a cryptographic function to compress the information of any subset $\mathcal{S} \subseteq \mathcal{U}$ into a constant-size value. The output of aggregation function is called the *cryptographic representation of subset.* The definition of this function is stated as follows:

Definition 1 (Aggregate function). *Let $\mathcal{PK}$ denote the public key space over a group $\mathbb{G}$ and $\mathcal{U} = \{e_1, \cdots, e_n\}$ be a set of elements, the function Aggregate : $\mathcal{PK} \times 2^U \rightarrow \mathbb{G}$ is a deterministic polynomial time algorithm satisfying:*

$$Aggregate(mpk, \mathcal{S}) = R_{\mathcal{S}}, \quad (1)$$

where mpk is the public key in $\mathcal{PK}$, a subset $\mathcal{S} \subseteq \mathcal{U}$, and $R_{\mathcal{S}}$ is a random enough element in $\mathbb{G}$ to avoid guessing.

This kind of aggregation function is our core in our SBE scheme and foundation of cryptographic decisional problem of set membership (see Section 1). In this paper, we use this kind of function to build membership and negative membership. More importantly, the constant size ciphertext can be implemented in our SBE scheme only if the compression property can be efficiently realized. Based on the presented approach in Section 1, we present two aggregate functions, ZerosAggr and PolesAggr, that realize the decision over positive membership and negative membership, respectively.

Before our aggregation functions are introduced, we first give the definition of zeros and poles in a function as follows:

Definition 2 (Zeros and Poles). *A rational polynomial function has the form $H(x) = \frac{P(x)}{Q(x)}$ that is the quotient of two polynomial $P(x)$ and $Q(x)$. We say the value z is a zero of $H(x)$ if $P(z) = 0$, and z is a pole of $H(x)$ if $Q(z) = 0$.*

Next, we propose two aggregation functions, ZerosAggr and PolesAggr, for $u \in \{v_i\}$ and $u \notin \{v_i\}$ as below. Given a subset $\mathcal{S} = \{e'_1, \cdots, e'_m\} \subseteq \mathcal{U}$, we define a polynomial $f_{\mathcal{S}}(x)$ of degree $m+1$ over $\mathcal{S}$,

$$f_{\mathcal{S}}(x) = x(x + x'_1) \cdots (x + x'_m) = x \prod_{e'_i \in \mathcal{S}} (x + x'_i) \pmod p,$$

in which the hash value of elements in $\mathcal{S}$ is considered as the negative root of this polynomial and let $x'_i = hash(e'_i)$. [1] Next, given a secret γ, we propose the definition of aggregation function that can aggregate the information of $\mathcal{S}$ into the constant-size value $g^{f_{\mathcal{S}}(\gamma)}$ based on the polynomial $f_{\mathcal{S}}(x)$. We call it the Zeros-based Aggregation (in short, **ZerosAggr**) function which is defined as follows:

Definition 3 (Zeros-based Aggregation). *Given a subset $\mathcal{S} = \{e_1, \cdots, e_m\} \in \mathcal{U}$ and a cyclic group $\mathbb{G}$, an algorithm is called Zeros-based Aggregation function if there exists a polynomial-time algorithm ZerosAggr that outputs*

$$G_{\mathcal{S}} = \mathrm{ZerosAggr}(mpk, \mathcal{S}) = g^{\gamma \cdot \prod_{e_i \in \mathcal{S}} (\gamma + x_i)}, \quad (2)$$

where, $mpk = \{g_i = g^{\gamma^i}\}_{i \in [1, |\mathcal{U}|]}$ is the public parameter, g is a generator in $\mathbb{G}$, $x_i = hash(e_i)$ and γ is a secret.

Similarly, we here introduce a new construction, called poles-based aggregation (in short, **PolesAggr**). Given a subset $\mathcal{R} = \{e'_1, \cdots, e'_m\} \subseteq \mathcal{U}$, we also make use of the hash values of elements in $\mathcal{R}$ as the negative poles of polynomial, that is, we define a polynomial $g_{\mathcal{R}}(x)$ of degree $|\mathcal{R}| = m$ as

$$g_{\mathcal{R}}(x) = \frac{1}{(x + x'_1) \cdots (x + x'_m)} = \frac{1}{\prod_{e'_i \in \mathcal{R}} (x + x'_i)} \pmod p,$$

where $x'_i = hash(e'_i)$. It is obvious that $g_{\mathcal{R}}(x)$ is unique for the different subset $\mathcal{R}$. Next, we propose the formal definition of poles-based aggregation based on $g_{\mathcal{R}}(x)$ over a cyclic group $\mathbb{G}$ and a generator h in it, as follows:

Definition 4 (Poles-based Aggregation). *Given a subset $\mathcal{R} = \{e_1, \cdots, e_m\} \in \mathcal{U}$ and a cyclic group $\mathbb{G}$, an algorithm is called Poles-based Aggregation function if there exists a polynomial-time algorithm PolesAggr that outputs*

$$H_{\mathcal{R}} = \mathrm{PolesAggr}(mpk, \mathcal{R}) = h^{\frac{1}{\prod_{e_i \in \mathcal{R}} (\gamma + x_i)}}, \quad (3)$$

where, $mpk = \{h_i = h^{\frac{1}{\gamma + x_i}}\}_{e_i \in \mathcal{U}}$ is the public parameter, h is a generator in $\mathbb{G}$, $x_i = hash(e_i)$ and γ is a secret.

[1] $f_{\mathcal{S}}(x) = x \prod_{e'_i \in \mathcal{S}} (x - (-x'_i)) = x \prod_{e'_i \in \mathcal{S}} (x + x'_i) \pmod p$.

Setup($\mathbb{S}$): chooses two elements $G \xleftarrow{R} \mathbb{G}_1$, $H \xleftarrow{R} \mathbb{G}_2$, and two exponents $\gamma, \epsilon \xleftarrow{R} \mathbb{Z}_p^*$. And then set $R = e(G,H)^\epsilon$ and sets $G_k = G^{\gamma^k}$ for $k \in [1,m]$. The master key is outputted as $msk = (\gamma, \epsilon, G, G^\epsilon)$ and the public key is $mpk = \{\mathbb{S}, H, R, \{G_k\}_{k\in[1,m]}, pp = \phi\}$.

KeyGen(msk, ID_k): Given an user's identity ID_k, defines $x_k = hash(\mathrm{ID}_k)$ and computers the k-th user's secret key

$$sk_k = G^{\frac{x_k \epsilon}{\gamma + x_k}}, \quad and \quad H_k = H^{\frac{\epsilon}{\gamma+x_k}},$$

where, $pp_k = (\mathrm{ID}_k, H_k)$ is appended to pp, i.e., pp = pp $\cup \{pp_k\}$.

Encrypt($mpk, \mathcal{S}, mode$): picks a random $s \xleftarrow{R} \mathbb{Z}_p^*$ and executes the following process:

- Case $mode := (u \in \mathcal{S})$: invokes **PolesAggr**$(mpk, \mathcal{S}) \to H_\mathcal{S} = H^{\epsilon \prod_{e_i \in \mathcal{S}} \frac{1}{\gamma + x_i}}$, then computes

$$C_1 = H^s, \quad \text{and} \quad C_2 = (H_\mathcal{S})^s.$$

- Case $mode := (u \notin \mathcal{S})$: invokes **ZerosAggr**$(mpk, \mathcal{S}) \to G_\mathcal{S} = G^{\gamma \cdot \prod_{e_i \in \mathcal{S}}(\gamma + x_i)}$, then computes

$$C_1 = H^s, \quad \text{and} \quad C_2 = (G_\mathcal{S})^s$$

Finally, the ciphertext is published as $C = (\mathcal{S}, mode, C_1, C_2)$. The corresponded session key is $ek = R^s$.

Decrypt(mpk, sk_k, C): chooses one action from two following cases according to the $mode$ in C:

- Case $mode := (u \in \mathcal{S})$: checks whether ID_k is a member of $\mathcal{S}$, that is, $\mathrm{ID}_k \in \mathcal{S}$. If true, it sets $\mathcal{S}_- = \mathcal{S} \setminus \{\mathrm{ID}_k\}$ and invokes **ZerosAggr**$(mpk, \mathcal{S}_-) \to G_{\mathcal{S}_-} = G^{\gamma \cdot \prod_{e_i \in \mathcal{S}_-}(\gamma + x_i)}$. Next it retrieves the session key

$$ek' = e(sk_k, C_1) \cdot e(G_{\mathcal{S}_-}, C_2). \tag{4}$$

- Case $mode := (u \notin \mathcal{S})$: checks whether ID_k satisfies the relation $\mathrm{ID}_k \notin \mathcal{S}$. If true, it sets $\mathcal{S}_+ = \mathcal{S} \cup \{\mathrm{ID}_k\}$ and invokes **PolesAggr**$(mpk, \mathcal{S}_+) \to H_{\mathcal{S}_+} = H^{\epsilon \prod_{e_i \in \mathcal{S}_+} \frac{1}{(\gamma + x_i)}}$. Next, it also retrieves the session key

$$ek' = e(sk_k, C_1) \cdot e(C_2, H_{\mathcal{S}_+}). \tag{5}$$

Figure 2: The full construction of set-based broadcast encryption (SBE).

3.2 Our Construction

We now present our SBE scheme with three modes, such as Select, All, and Cut. In this scheme, we assume that each user has a unique identity ID (e.g., email address) and all users in cryptosystem make up a full set $\mathcal{U} = \{\mathrm{ID}_1, \cdots, \mathrm{ID}_n\}$, where the size of $\mathcal{U}$ is not restricted. Given a subset of users $\mathcal{S}$ in $\mathcal{U}$, we now present the SBE construction providing two basic access control mechanisms: positive membership decision over $u \in \mathcal{S}$ and negative membership decision over $u \notin \mathcal{S}$, simultaneously.

Our SBE scheme is illustrated in Figure 4. In this scheme, we choose the bilinear map system $\mathbb{S} = (p, \mathbb{G}_1, \mathbb{G}_2, \mathbb{G}_T, e(\cdot,\cdot))$ of prime order p and two generators g and h in $\mathbb{G}_1$ and $\mathbb{G}_2$, respectively [10, 11], where p is the order of groups. Additionally, the algorithm will employ a hash function $hash : \{0,1\}^* \to \mathbb{Z}_p^*$, mapping any identity ID described as a binary string to a random element $x_i \in \mathbb{Z}_p^*$, that is, $x_i = hash(\mathrm{ID}_i)$. This scheme is described as follows:

- Setup: we redefine two random elements G and H as the generators in $\mathbb{G}_1$ and $\mathbb{G}_2$, respectively. We require $G \neq g$ and G is a secret. Let m be the maximum number of aggregated users in the *ZerosAggr* algorithm. Usually, we set $m \leq n/2$ because the sender can use Select-mode when the size of $\mathcal{S}$ is greater than $n/2$. In addition, the public profile pp is used to list all users in system and their public tags, i.e., $\{(\mathrm{ID}_i, H_i)\}$. The initial status is defined as $\varnothing$. As a group-oriented cryptosystem, the parameter pp is usually shared through public media, e.g., web, facebook, where each user can search his friends profiles in a convenient way. Note that, we must keep two values, G and G^ϵ, secret because of the following reasons:
  - When the adversary knows the value G^ϵ, the decryption is executed by using

  $$e(G^\epsilon, C_1) = e(G^\epsilon, H^s) = e(G,H)^{s\epsilon} = ek.$$

  - When the adversary knows G and a sub-ciphertext $C_2 = H^{\frac{s\epsilon}{\gamma + x_i}}$, the decryption is implemented by

  $$e(G_1 \cdot G^{x_i}, C_2) = e(G^{\gamma + x_i}, H^{\frac{s\epsilon}{\gamma+x_i}}) = e(G,H)^{s\epsilon} = ek.$$

- KeyGen: given a unique identity ID_k, the user's secret key sk_k is only an element in $\mathbb{G}_1$. In addition, the new user's profile pp_k is also appended into pp. The scheme allows adding new members into the system anytime, and the total number of users is unlimited in the system.
- Encrypt: the sender may select one of Select and Cut mechanisms to implement secure broadcast, where there is no limit for the number of "cut-or-section" users. These two mechanisms employ two *Aggregate* functions, ZerosAggr for Cut-mode and PolesAggr for Select-mode, which can aggregate all information of user's identities in $\mathcal{S}$ into two group elements $G_\mathcal{S}$ and $H_\mathcal{S}$, respectively. We will introduce this algorithm in detail in Section 3.4. And then, the pair $(H, G_\mathcal{S})$ or $(H, H_\mathcal{S})$ is used to generate the ciphertext

$$(C_1, C_2) = \begin{cases} (H^s, (H_\mathcal{S})^s) & \text{for } (u \in \mathcal{S}) \\ (H^s, (G_\mathcal{S})^s) & \text{for } (u \notin \mathcal{S}) \end{cases}$$

Note that, a significant feature of our scheme is short and constant-size ciphertext.

- Decrypt: this process only needs two steps for a successful decryption: firstly, the receiver invokes two *Aggregate* functions, ZerosAggr for Select-mode and PolesAggr for Cut-mode, taken as input $\mathcal{S}_-$ or $\mathcal{S}_+$, respectively. Secondly, the above result will be used to decrypt the ciphertext by using two bilinear maps.

We verify that the decryption works correctly as follows:

Case $mode := (u \in \mathcal{S})$**:** when $\mathrm{ID}_k \in \mathcal{S}$, we have $\mathcal{S}_- = \mathcal{S} \setminus \{e_k\}$ and $G_{\mathcal{S}_-} = G^{\prod_{e_i\in\mathcal{S}, e_i\neq e_k}(\gamma+x_i)}$ can be computed from the *ZerosAggr* algorithm. Based on this value, we check whether the triple (C_1, C_2) in ciphertext matches the private key sk_k by using

$$\begin{aligned} & e(sk_k, C_1)\cdot e(G_{\mathcal{S}_-}, C_2) \\ = \; & e\left(G^{\frac{x_k\epsilon}{\gamma+x_k}}, H^s\right)\cdot e\left(G^{\frac{\gamma}{\gamma+x_k}\prod_{e_i\in\mathcal{S}}(\gamma+x_i)}, H^{s\cdot\epsilon\prod_{e_i\in\mathcal{S}}\frac{1}{\gamma+x_i}}\right) \\ = \; & e(G,H)^{\frac{x_k s\epsilon}{\gamma+x_k}}\cdot e(G,H)^{\frac{\gamma s\epsilon}{\gamma+x_k}} = e(G,H)^{s\epsilon} = R^s = ek. \end{aligned}$$

Case $mode := (u \notin \mathcal{S})$**:** when $\mathrm{ID}_k \notin \mathcal{S}$, we have $\mathcal{S}_+ = \mathcal{S} \cup \{e_k\}$ and $H_{\mathcal{S}_+} = H^{\frac{1}{\gamma+x_k}\prod_{e_i\in\mathcal{S}}\frac{1}{(\gamma+x_i)}}$ can be computed from the *PolesAggr* algorithm. Based on this value, we check whether the triple (C_1, C_2) in ciphertext matches the private key sk_k by using

$$\begin{aligned} & e(sk_k, C_1)\cdot e(C_2, H_{\mathcal{S}_+}) \\ = \; & e\left(G^{\frac{x_k\epsilon}{\gamma+x_k}}, H^s\right)\cdot e\left(G^{s\gamma\prod_{e_i\in\mathcal{S}}(\gamma+x_i)}, H^{\frac{\epsilon}{\gamma+x_k}\prod_{e_k\in\mathcal{S}}\frac{1}{\gamma+x_i}}\right) \\ = \; & e(G,H)^{\frac{x_k s\epsilon}{\gamma+x_k}}\cdot e(G,H)^{\frac{\gamma s\epsilon}{\gamma+x_k}} = e(G,H)^{s\epsilon} = R^s = ek. \end{aligned}$$

In summary, our scheme is easy-to-understand and the ciphertexts and decryption keys are constant size.

3.3 Construction for All-mode

We provide a solution for mode $u \in$ All, that means that all users can be authorized only if everyone of them holds a valid key. This mode is usually realized based on Select-mode with $\mathcal{S} = \mathcal{U}$, but it need to provide a complete list of all users. A more effective method is to consider All-mode as a special case of Cut-mode with $\mathcal{S} = \varnothing$, where $\varnothing$ denotes the empty set. The reason is that $u \in$ All is logically equivalent to $u \notin \varnothing$. In this case, the work mode is defined as $u \notin \varnothing$. We provide this process as follows:

- Encrypt$(mpk, \varnothing, u \in \mathrm{All})$: picks a random integer $s \in \mathbb{Z}_p$ and computes the following cipertext $C = (\varnothing, u \in \mathrm{All}, C_1, C_2)$, where

  $$C_1 = H^s, \qquad C_2 = G_1^s.$$

  The corresponded session key is $ek = R^s$.

- Decrypt(mpk, sk_k, C): When the mode $u \in$ All in C is found, it makes use of sk_k and the corresponding public profile H_k to recover ek

  $$\begin{aligned} ek &= e(sk_k, C_2)\cdot e(C_1, H_k) \\ &= e\left(G^{\frac{x_k\epsilon}{\gamma+x_k}}, H^s\right)\cdot e\left(G^{s\gamma}, H^{\frac{1}{\gamma+x_k}}\right) \\ &= e(G,H)^{\frac{x_k s\epsilon}{\gamma+x_k}}\cdot e(G,H)^{\frac{\gamma s\epsilon}{\gamma+x_k}} = e(G,H)^{s\epsilon} = R^s. \end{aligned}$$

In contrast with Select-mode with $\mathcal{S} = \mathcal{U}$, our construction does not require to invoke the aggregation function. Moreover, the broadcaster does not need to provide (or know) a list of all users' identities, such that the total number of receivers is unlimited in one time broadcast.

3.4 Construction of Aggregation Functions

Given a subset $\mathcal{S}$, the aggregate functions defined in Equation (2) and (3) are used repeatedly in our constructions, such that it is crucial to compute the output values $(G_\mathcal{S}, H_\mathcal{S})$ from the public key mpk in an efficient way. We provide a fast recursive method to realize them as follows:

3.4.1 Implement of ZerosAggr function

To implement fast ZerosAggr, we first extract the related information $\{G_i = G^{\gamma^i}\}_{i\in[1,m]}$ from mpk, where γ is an unknown secret. Let $|\mathcal{S}| = t$ and we require $t < m$. We provide a fast recursive way to realize the ZerosAggr function: given all $\{x_i = hash(e_i)\}_{e_i\in\mathcal{S}}$, we define the polynomial of x as

$$f_\mathcal{S}(x) = x\prod_{e_i\in\mathcal{S}}(x + x_i) = \sum_{k=0}^{t} a_k x^{k+1} \pmod p$$

and compute the coefficient $a_k \in \mathbb{Z}_p$ for all $k \in [0, t]$. We can use the recursive process to obtain these coefficients. Let $a_i^{(j)}$ denote the value of a_i at the j-th cycle for $j = 1, \cdots, t$ and $i = 0, \cdots, j$. For each cycle, a new x_k is appended into the polynomial. After an inital coefficient is set as $a_0^{(0)} = 1$, the coefficients can be computed repeatedly in each cycle as

$$\begin{cases} a_k^{(k)} &= a_{k-1}^{(k-1)} & (k \geq 1) \\ a_{k-1}^{(k)} &= a_{k-2}^{(k-1)} + a_{k-1}^{(k-1)}\cdot x_k & (k \geq 2) \\ \cdots & \cdots & \\ a_1^{(k)} &= a_0^{(k-1)} + a_1^{(k-1)}\cdot x_k & (k \geq 2) \\ a_0^{(k)} &= a_0^{(k-1)}\cdot x_k & (k \geq 1) \end{cases}.$$

After t cycles running, the value $a_0^{(t)}, \cdots, a_t^{(t)}$ are outputted as $a_0, \cdots, a_t$. It is obvious that the output of ZerosAppr is $G_\mathcal{S} = G^{f_\mathcal{S}(\gamma)}$. In face, although γ is unknown, we make use of $(G_1, \cdots, G_m)$ and $t < m$ to compute $G_\mathcal{S}$ as following

$$\begin{aligned} G_\mathcal{S} &= G^{f_\mathcal{S}(\gamma)} = G^{\gamma\cdot\prod_{e_i\in\mathcal{S}}(\gamma+x_i)} \\ &= G^{\sum_{k=1}^{t+1} a_{k-1}\cdot\gamma^k} = \prod_{k=1}^{t+1} G_k^{a_{k-1}}. \end{aligned} \tag{6}$$

Note that, when $\mathcal{S} = \emptyset$ and $t = 0$, the output of this algorithm is $ZerosAggr(mpk, \mathcal{S}) = G_1$. This value is used to realize the broadcast for all users.

```
Algorithm ZerosAggr(mpk, S)
  B[1] = 1;
  for i = 1 to t do
    B[i + 1] = B[i];
    for j = i downto 2 do
      B[j] = B[j − 1] + B[j] * x_i;
    end for
    B[1] = B[1] * x_i;
  end for
  sum = 1;
  for k = 1 to t + 1 do
    sum = sum * pow(G_k, B[k]);
  end for
  Return sum;
```

Figure 3: The zeros-based aggregation function.

Based on this recursive process, we present a fast algorithm, call ZoresAggr, shown in Algorithm 3. In this algorithm, we design a double-loop structure for computing the coefficients $(a_0, \cdots, a_t)$ of the polynomial $f_{\mathcal{S}}(x)$, where $B[1] = a_0, \cdots, B[t+1] = a_t$. And then, the final result is computed by accumulating all items $G_k^{a_{k-1}} = pow(G_k, B[k])$ for $k = 1, \cdots, t+1$. In this process, the function $pow(\cdot)$ is invoked to obtain the power of element in $\mathbb{G}_1$, that is, $pow(G_k, B[k]) = G_k^{B[k]} = G_k^{a_{k-1}}$.

3.4.2 Implement of PolesAggr function

To implement fast pole-based aggregation, we first extract the information $\{(x_i, H_i = H^{\frac{\epsilon}{\gamma+x_i}})\}_{e_i \in \mathcal{S}}$ from mpk. Given H_i and H_j, it is easy to obtain the aggregation equation

$$(H_j/H_i)^{\frac{1}{x_i - x_j}} = (H^{\frac{\epsilon}{\gamma+x_j}}/H^{\frac{\epsilon}{\gamma+x_i}})^{\frac{1}{x_i-x_j}} = H^{\frac{\epsilon}{(\gamma+x_i)(\gamma+x_j)}},$$

where $x_i \neq x_j$ is a prerequisite for this equation. The value $\frac{1}{x_i - x_j}$ modulo p can be computed by using extended Euclidean algorithm (called xGCD) in $\mathbb{Z}_p^*$.

Next, we expand this equation to multi-value cases. We define a new notation $B_{i,j}$ that denotes the aggregation of all values $(H_i, \cdots, H_j)$, where $1 \leq i < j \leq t$ and $B_{i,j} = H^{\frac{\epsilon}{\prod_{k=i}^{j}(\gamma+x_k)}}$. In terms of Equation (7), we can compute

$$\begin{aligned} B_{i,j+1} &= (B_{i,j}/B_{i+1,j+1})^{\frac{1}{x_{j+1}-x_i}} \\ &= (H^{\frac{\epsilon}{\prod_{k=i}^{j}(\gamma+x_k)}}/H^{\frac{\epsilon}{\prod_{k=i+1}^{j+1}(\gamma+x_k)}})^{\frac{1}{x_{j+1}-x_i}} \\ &= (H^{\frac{\epsilon}{\gamma+x_i}}/H^{\frac{\epsilon}{\gamma+x_{j+1}}})^{\frac{1}{x_{j+1}-x_i}\cdot\frac{1}{\prod_{k=i+1}^{j}(\gamma+x_k)}} \\ &= H^{\frac{\epsilon}{(\gamma+x_i)(\gamma+x_{j+1})}\cdot\frac{1}{\prod_{k=i+1}^{j}(\gamma+x_k)}} = H^{\frac{\epsilon}{\prod_{k=i}^{j+1}(\gamma+x_k)}}. \end{aligned}$$

Finally, the output value $H_{\mathcal{S}} = B_{1,t}$ can be completed by sequentially computing $B_{i,j}$ for $j \in [1, t-i]$ (where i varies from 1 to $t-1$) according to the following recursive process

$$\begin{cases} B_{i,i} = H_i \quad \forall i \in [1,t], \\ B_{i,j+1} = (B_{i,j}/B_{i+1,j+1})^{\frac{1}{x_{j+1}-x_i}}, \\ \qquad i \in [1, t-1],\ j \in [1, t-i], \end{cases} \tag{7}$$

where $B_{i,i}$ is the initial input H_i for $i = [1, t]$.

```
Algorithm PolesAggr(mpk, S)
  for k = 1 to t do
    B[k] = H_k
  end for
  for i = 1 to t − 1 do
    for j = 1 to t − i do
      if x_{j+i} = x_j then
        Return 0.
      end if
      tmp_1 = x_j − x_{j+i};
      tmp_2 = invert(tmp_1, p);
      tmp_3 = B[j + 1]/B[j];
      B[j] = pow(tmp_3, tmp_2);
    end for
  end for
  Return B[1];
```

Figure 4: The poles-based aggregation function.

We provide the above recursive algorithm, called PolesAggr, in Algorithm 4. This fast algorithm is derived from Equation (7). During the aggregation process, the double loops are used to compute the value of $B[j] = B_{j,j+i}$ for $i = 1, \cdots, t-1$ and $j = 1, \cdots, t-i$, repeatedly. In each loop, the output value 0 denotes the error if there exist two equivalent values x_{j+i} and x_j. This means that two identities are identical (or a hash collision occurred, but this is unlikely to happen because two identities ID_{j+i} and ID_j are equivalent with negligible probability according to the property of cryptographic hash function). Next, two functions, $invert(\cdot)$ and $pow(\cdot)$, are used to compute the inverse element and the power of element, that is, $tmp_2 = 1/tmp_1 \pmod p$ and $B[j] = tmp_3^{tmp_2} \in \mathbb{G}_2$.

4. SECURE ANALYSIS

4.1 Security Analysis for Our SBE Scheme

We prove the semantic security of our system by relying on the General Diffie-Hellman Exponent (GDHE) framework in [3, 5]. We overview the GDHE framework in Appendix A. *We will not analyze All-mode because this mode can be realized as a special case of Cut-mode*, that is, $\mathcal{S} = \varnothing$. We start by defining the following computational problem.

According to construction of two aggregation functions, we assume $f(x)$ and $g(x)$ be two known random polynomials of respective degree t and $n-t$ with pairwise distinct roots,

$$\begin{cases} f(X) = \prod_{i=1}^{t}(X + x_i) = \sum_{i=0}^{t} a_i \cdot X^i, \\ g(X) = \prod_{i=1}^{n-t}(X + x_i') = \sum_{i=0}^{n-t} b_i \cdot X^i. \end{cases}$$

Moreover, $h(x, y, z) = f(x)g(x)yz$ be a three-variable polynomial in a bilinear group system $\mathbb{S} = (p, \mathbb{G}_1, \mathbb{G}_2, \mathbb{G}_T, e(\cdot,\cdot))$.

Based on these two polynomials, we provide a new computational problem, called GDHE_1 problem, which is used to prove the semantic security of our SBE scheme for Select-mode ($u \in \mathcal{S}$). This problem is defined as follows:

THEOREM 1 ((n,t)-GDHE_1 PROBLEM). *Let $\gamma, \varsigma, \epsilon \in \mathbb{Z}_p^*$ be three secret random variables, $f(X)$ and $g(X)$ are two polynomials described above, and $\hat{G}, \hat{H}$ be generators of $\mathbb{S}$. Given the values in (F_1, F_2, F_3)-$GDHE_1$ problem with*

$$\begin{cases} F_1(\gamma,\varsigma,\epsilon) = \left\langle \hat{G}^{\epsilon}, \hat{G}^{\gamma\epsilon}, \cdots, \hat{G}^{\gamma^{t-1}\epsilon}, \hat{G}^{\gamma f(\gamma)}, \cdots, \hat{G}^{\gamma^m f(\gamma)} \right\rangle, \\ F_2(\gamma,\varsigma,\epsilon) = \left\langle \begin{matrix} \hat{H}^{\epsilon}, \hat{H}^{\gamma\epsilon}, \cdots, \hat{H}^{\gamma^n \epsilon}, \\ \hat{H}^{f(\gamma)g(\gamma)}, \hat{H}^{\varsigma f(\gamma)g(\gamma)}, \hat{H}^{\varsigma\epsilon f(\gamma)} \end{matrix} \right\rangle, \\ F_3(\gamma,\varsigma,\epsilon) = e(\hat{G},\hat{H})^{\epsilon f^2(\gamma)g(\gamma)}, \end{cases}$$

and $T \xleftarrow{R} \mathbb{G}_T$, decide whether $e(\hat{G},\hat{H})^{\varsigma\cdot\epsilon\cdot f^2(\gamma)\cdot g(\gamma)} = T$. For any algorithm $\mathcal{A}$ that makes a total of at most q queries to the oracles computing the group operation and the bilinear pairing, the advantage of $\mathcal{A}$ is $Adv^{\mathrm{IND}}_{\mathrm{GDHE}_1,\mathcal{A}}(n,t) \leq \frac{(q+2s+2)^2 \cdot d}{2p}$, where $s = n+t+m+4$ and $d = 2n$.

We provide the proof of this theorem in Appendix B. In this proof, we reduce this problem to the weakest case $\mathbb{G}_1 = \mathbb{G}_2 = \mathbb{G}$, so that the polynomials (F_1, F_2, F_3, T) in bilinear map group are converted to three polynomials (P, Q, h) in bilinear map group. Then we prove that h is independent of (P, Q) and complete the final proof based on Theorem 4 in Appendix. In fact, we also show the security of this assumption based on the following analysis: Considering that ς only appears in $\hat{H}^{\varsigma\epsilon f(\gamma)}$ and $\hat{H}^{\varsigma f(\gamma)g(\gamma)}$, we only pick them out for three following cases:

Case $\hat{H}^{\varsigma\epsilon f(\gamma)}$: we need to find $\hat{G}^{f(\gamma)g(\gamma)}$ to meet $e(\hat{G}^{f(\gamma)g(\gamma)}, \hat{H}^{\varsigma\epsilon f(\gamma)}) = T$. Let $g(x) = \prod_{i=1}^{n-t}(x + x_i') = \sum_{i=0}^{n-t} b_i \cdot x^i$, where $b_0 = x_1' x_2' \cdots x_{n-t}' \neq 0$ because all $x_i' \neq 0$. So that, this polynomial $f(x)g(x)$ is represented as

$$f(x)g(x) = \sum_{i=0}^{n-t} a_i(x^i f(x)) = b_0 f(x) + \sum_{i=1}^{n-t} b_i(x^i f(x)).$$

But it is infeasible for computing $\hat{G}^{f(\gamma)g(\gamma)} = (\hat{G}^{f(\gamma)})^{b_0} \cdot (\hat{G}^{\gamma^i f(\gamma)})^{b_i}$ because there dose not exist the item $\hat{G}^{f(x)}$ from all known items $\hat{G}^{\gamma f(\gamma)}, \cdots, \hat{G}^{\gamma^m f(\gamma)}$.

Case $\hat{H}^{\varsigma f(\gamma)g(\gamma)}$: we need to find $\hat{G}^{\epsilon f(\gamma)}$ to meet $e(\hat{G}^{\epsilon f(\gamma)}, \hat{H}^{\varsigma f(\gamma)g(\gamma)}) = T$ and it is also infeasible because $f(x) = \prod_{i=1}^{t}(x + x_i) = \sum_{i=0}^{t} a_i \cdot x^i = \sum_{i=0}^{t-1} a_i \cdot x^i + x^t$ is a polynomial of degree t and $a_t = 1$, such that $\hat{G}^{\epsilon f(\gamma)} = \prod_{i=0}^{t-1}(\hat{G}^{\epsilon\gamma^i})^{a_i} \cdot \hat{G}^{\gamma^t}$ cannot be built from all known $\hat{G}^{\epsilon}, \hat{G}^{\gamma\epsilon}, \cdots, \hat{G}^{\gamma^{t-1}\epsilon}$.

Linear combination between $\hat{H}^{\varsigma\epsilon f(\gamma)}$ **and** $\hat{H}^{\varsigma f(\gamma)g(\gamma)}$: assume that there exist two coefficients a, b to satisfy

$$e(\hat{G}^{f(\gamma)\frac{a\gamma g(\gamma)}{\gamma + x_i'}}, \hat{H}^{\varsigma\epsilon f(\gamma)}) \cdot e(\hat{G}^{\epsilon\frac{bf(\gamma)}{\gamma + x_i}}, \hat{H}^{\varsigma f(\gamma)g(\gamma)}) = T$$

So that, we have $\frac{a\gamma}{\gamma + x_i'} + \frac{b}{\gamma + x_i} = 1$. To solve this equation, we have $(a-1)\gamma^2 + (ax_i + b - x_i - x_i')\gamma + (bx_i' - x_i x_i') = 0$. It is easy find that our solution is $a = 1$ and $b = x_i = x_i'$, but it contradicts with the assumption of $x_i \neq x_i'$ for all x_i and x_i' in $f(\gamma)$ and $g(\gamma)$.

Next, we provide another problem, called GDHE_2 problem, which is used to prove the security of our SBE scheme for negative membership (Cut-mode on $u \notin \mathcal{S}$):

THEOREM 2 ((n,t)-GDHE_2 PROBLEM). *Let $\gamma, \varsigma, \epsilon \in \mathbb{Z}_p^*$ be three secret random variables, $f(X)$ and $g(X)$ are two polynomials described above, and $\hat{G}, \hat{H}$ be generators of $\mathbb{S}$. Given the values in (F_1, F_2, F_3)-$GDHE_2$ problem with*

$$\begin{cases} F_1(\gamma,\varsigma,\epsilon) &= \left\langle \begin{array}{c} \hat{G}^{\epsilon}, \hat{G}^{\gamma\epsilon}, \cdots, \hat{G}^{\gamma^{t-1}\epsilon}, \\ \hat{G}^{\gamma f(\gamma)}, \cdots, \hat{G}^{\gamma^m f(\gamma)}, \hat{G}^{\varsigma\gamma f^2(\gamma)} \end{array} \right\rangle, \\ F_2(\gamma,\varsigma,\epsilon) &= \left\langle \begin{array}{c} \hat{H}^{\epsilon}, \hat{H}^{\gamma\epsilon}, \cdots, \hat{H}^{\gamma^n\epsilon}, \\ \hat{H}^{f(\gamma)g(\gamma)}, \hat{H}^{\varsigma f(\gamma)g(\gamma)} \end{array} \right\rangle, \\ F_3(\gamma,\varsigma,\epsilon) &= e(\hat{G},\hat{H})^{\epsilon f^2(\gamma)g(\gamma)}, \end{cases}$$

and $T \xleftarrow{R} \mathbb{G}_T$, decide whether $e(\hat{G},\hat{H})^{\varsigma \cdot f^2(\gamma)\cdot g(\gamma)} = T$. For any algorithm $\mathcal{A}$ that makes a total of at most q queries to the oracles computing the group operation and the bilinear pairing, the advantage of $\mathcal{A}$ is $Adv^{\text{IND}}_{\text{GDHE}_2,\mathcal{A}}(n,t) \leq \frac{(q+2s+2)^2 \cdot d}{2p}$, where $s = n + t + m + 4$ and $d = 2n$.

We provide the proof of this theorem in Appendix C. We here give a simple comparison with GDHE_1 and GDHE_2 in Table 1. As seen from this table, most of items are shared between two problems except a slight different: GDHE_1 has a unique item $\hat{G}^{\varsigma\gamma f^2(\gamma)}$ and GDHE_2 is $\hat{H}^{\varsigma\epsilon f(\gamma)}$. This means that there is a strong correlation between two problems.

Table 1: Comparison with GDHE_1 and GDHE_2

	Common Elements	GDHE_1	GDHE_2
F_1	$\hat{G}^{\epsilon}, \hat{G}^{\gamma\epsilon}, \cdots, \hat{G}^{\gamma^{t-1}\epsilon}$, $\hat{G}^{\gamma f(\gamma)}, \cdots, \hat{G}^{\gamma^m f(\gamma)}$		$\hat{G}^{\varsigma\gamma f^2(\gamma)}$
F_2	$\hat{H}^{\epsilon}, \hat{H}^{\gamma\epsilon}, \cdots, \hat{H}^{\gamma^n\epsilon}$, $\hat{H}^{f(\gamma)g(\gamma)}, \hat{H}^{\varsigma f(\gamma)g(\gamma)}$	$\hat{H}^{\varsigma\epsilon f(\gamma)}$	
F_3	$e(\hat{G},\hat{H})^{\epsilon f^2(\gamma)g(\gamma)}$		

We now prove the semantic security of our SBE scheme based on the security model in Section 2, which has the semantic security against chosen plaintext attacks (IND-CPA) with colluders. Usually, we need two separate proofs that prove the security of SBE scheme under two different modes, Select-mode and Cut-mode, respectively. However, we found that these two proofs has too many similarities according to the comparison result in Table 1. Therefore, we combine two proofs into a full proof of our SBE scheme. Based on (n,t)-GTDHE_1 and (n,t)-GTDHE_2, the security of our SBE scheme satisfies the following theorem:

THEOREM 3 (SECURITY OF SBE SCHEME). *Our SBE scheme for both Select-mode and Cut-mode is semantically secure against chosen plaintext attacks with colluders assuming the (n,t)-$GDHE_1$ and (n,t)-$GDHE_2$ problem is hard in $\mathbb{S}$ for $0 \leq t \leq n$.*

The proof of this theorem is presented in Appendix D. Note that, our scheme is secure for arbitrary large collusion of corrupted users because the number of corrupted users t is not restricted in the above theorem.

5. PERFORMANCE EVALUATION

5.1 Parameter Gneration

Our scheme is constructed on the general bilinear map group system $\mathbb{S} = (p, \mathbb{G}_1, \mathbb{G}_2, \mathbb{G}_T, e(\cdot,\cdot))$ with prime order p, where decisional Diffie-Hellman is hard. We set up our systems using bilinear pairings introduced by Boneh and Franklin [10]. We define the bilinear pairing takes the form $e : E(\mathbb{F}_q) \times E(\mathbb{F}_q) \to \mathbb{F}^*_{q^2}$ (The definition given here is from [11, 12]), where p is a prime and $k = 2$ is the embedding degree (or security multiplier). It turns out the total number of elements is $\sharp E(\mathbb{F}_q) = q + 1$ and $\sharp E(\mathbb{F}_{q^2}) = (q+1)^2$. The order p is some prime factor of $q+1$. We invoke this kind of pairing directly based on the Stanford's PBC library [2]. In order to ensure the security of our scheme, we uses 256-bit base field, which is equivalent to 128-bit security (κ=128-bit) for symmetric encryption [13].

5.2 Performance Analysis

We first provide the performance analysis from two aspects: computation costs and communication overheads. Here, we assume that t denotes the size of included or excluded subset and m denotes the manixium number of aggregated users. We present the computation cost of our SBE scheme in Table 2. We use $[E]$ to denote the computation cost of an exponent operation in $\mathbb{G}$, namely, g^x, where x is a positive integer in $\mathbb{Z}_p$ and $g \in \mathbb{G}$ or $\mathbb{G}_T$. We neglect the computation cost of algebraic operations and simple modular arithmetic operations because they run fast enough [14]. The most complex operation is the computation of a bilinear map $e(\cdot,\cdot)$ between two elliptic points (denoted as $[B]$). The symbols $ZAgg(t)$ and $PAgg(t)$ denote two aggregation algorithms where t denotes the size of subset. It is easy to find that the encryption and decryption costs are related to the performance of aggregation algorithms, but if the aggregation algorithms are excluded, all algorithms have the constant number of operations after m, t are set.

Then, we analyze the storage and communication costs of our scheme. This means that the length of integer is $l_0 = |q|$ in $\mathbb{Z}_p$. Similarly, we have $l_1 = l_2 = 2|q|$ in $\mathbb{G}_1$ and $\mathbb{G}_2$, and $l_T = 2|q|$ in $\mathbb{G}_T$ for the embedding degree $k = 2$. The storage and communication costs of our scheme is shown in Table 3. We neglect the storage/communication cost of the

[2]http://crypto.standord.edu/pbc/times.html

Table 2: Computation overhead of our scheme.

	SBE		
	All	Select	Cut
Setup	$(1+m)[E]+1[B]$		
KeyGen	$2[E]$		
Encrypt	$3[E]$	PAgg(t)+$3[E]$	ZAgg(t)+$3[E]$
Decrypt	$2[B]$	ZAgg(t)+$2[B]$	PAgg(t)+$2[B]$

subset of user's identities because the size of each identity cannot too large as a easy-to-remember string. It is also easy to find that the private key, the ciphertext, and the session key has the constant and short size (e.g., only 64-byte for a ciphertext with point compression) regardless of the size of subset in ciphertext.

Table 3: The storage/communication overhead.

Algorithm		SBE	Our system
Setup	PK	$l_2 + l_T + ml_1 + nl_2$	(m+n+2)*64-Byte
	mk	$l_0 + l_T$	192Byte
KeyGen	$SK^{(k)}$	l_1	64-Byte
Encrypt	C	$l_1 + l_2$	128-Byte
Decrypt	ek	l_T	64-Byte

In short, our scheme has the advantages as follows:

- The computation cost is low if there exist fast algorithms to realize the aggregation of subset.
- The size of private key and ciphertext is constant and short regardless of the size of subset in ciphertext.

The size of public key is related to the size of community (or the total number of users). This is not a large problem in applications because the users have access to a large shared storage medium in which the profiles can be stored [2]. For example, we usually provide a on-line search service for identity query from the profile list in public key. In other applications, each user only needs to store part of profiles, such as his friends' identities, because encryption and decryption just need to input a subset of specified users rather than to know all users.

6. EXPERIMENTAL RESULTS

Using GMP and JPBC libraries, we have developed a Java-language cryptographic library upon which our SBE cryptosystem can be constructed. This Java library contains Pairing-based algorithms on elliptic curves and has been tested on both Windows and Mac OSX platforms. Our SBE cryptosystem is a lightweight software about 600 lines of code built on Eclipse. To evaluate the performance of our SBE cryptosystem, our experiments are run in a Mac laptop with 2.0GHz processor and 4G RAM.

6.0.1 Performance of Aggregation Functions

At first, we evaluate the performance of two aggregation functions. It is easy to analyze the computational costs of two functions from Section 3.4: the ZeorsAggr function needs $O(t^2)$ times multiplication operations in $\mathbb{Z}_p^*$ and $O(t)$ times exponent operations in $\mathbb{G}_1$; and the PolesAggr function needs $O(t^2)$ times exponent operations in $\mathbb{G}_2$ and $O(t^2)$ times xGCD operations in $\mathbb{Z}_p^*$. Hence, the computational costs of PolesAggr is far greater than (roughly t times as) that of ZerosAggr due to the cost of operations in $\mathbb{G}_1$ and $\mathbb{G}_2$ is much larger than that in $\mathbb{Z}_p^*$.

We give the result of experiments for two aggregation functions in Figure 5, in which time consumptions of two

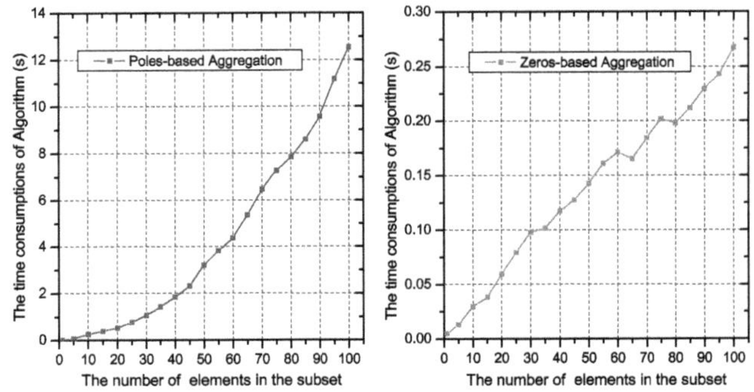

Figure 5: Time overheads of aggregation functions.

functions are showed under the different size of subsets (from 10 to 100). From this figure, it is easy to find that the computational costs of ZerosAggr is proportional to the size of subset, and the costs of PolesAggr grows rapidly for the sustained growth of subset sizes. The memory overheads of two algorithms are proportional to the size of subset. These results are completely consistent with our previous theoretical analysis. However, the time consumption is still high for a large-size subset, so that we can improve the performance by using parallel algorithm or fast elliptic curve algorithm.

6.0.2 Performance under Different Modes

We next analyze the performance of encryption and decryption processes according to three modes, including All, Select, and Cut in Figure 6. The left sugfigure shows the time consumption of encryption for these three modes in which the encryption overhead in Select-mode is greatest of all. The similar result of decryption is showed in the right subfigure but the decryption overhead in Cut-mode is greatest of all instead of Select-mode. When the system is not large, the users can choose Select-mode or Cut-mode according to application requirements, e.g., the Select-mode is used to reduce the overhead of decryption for mobile terminals with limited power (smart phone or sensor node) while leaving heavy encryption for high-power servers. In addition, the aggregation functions could be preprocessed in some applications with the fixed receivers, such that encryption and decryption can be achieved rapidly.

The same results are listed in Table 4. As seen from this table, the overhead of encryption or decryption is constant in All-mode no matter how large the total number of users is in system. In Select-mode, the encryption overhead is more higher than that of decryption due to the time consumption of PolesAggr is much larger than that of ZerosAggr. The similar situation also appears in Cut-mode where the decryption overhead is more higher than that of encryption based on the same reason. However, no matter what mode we pick, the ciphertext is only two points on an elliptic curve and the size of ciphertexts is constant for any mode.

Table 4: Time consumption of encryption and decryption under the different modes.

Size	Encryption			Decryption		
	All	Select	Cut	All	Select	Cut
1	0.00959	0.01106	0.01585	0.01059	0.01267	0.0137
20	0.01239	0.55603	0.11251	0.01056	0.10591	0.63935
40	0.01164	2.21912	0.22061	0.01046	0.21214	2.39276
60	0.0109	5.02113	0.3162	0.00815	0.31277	5.30531
80	0.01055	8.99909	0.418	0.0081	0.41469	9.40407
100	0.01066	14.19017	0.5107	0.00775	0.50979	14.6477

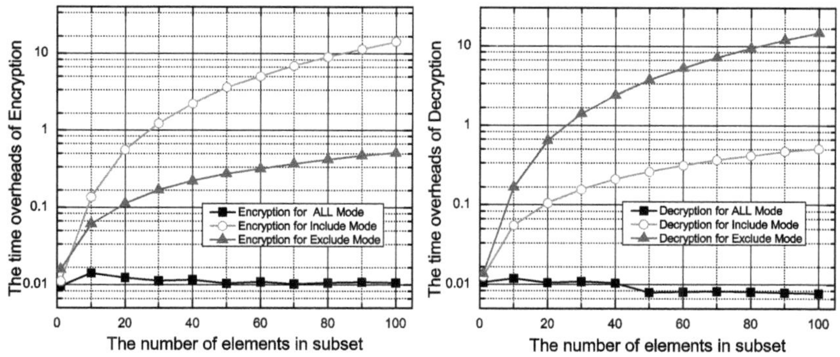

Figure 6: Time overheads of different modes in SBE.

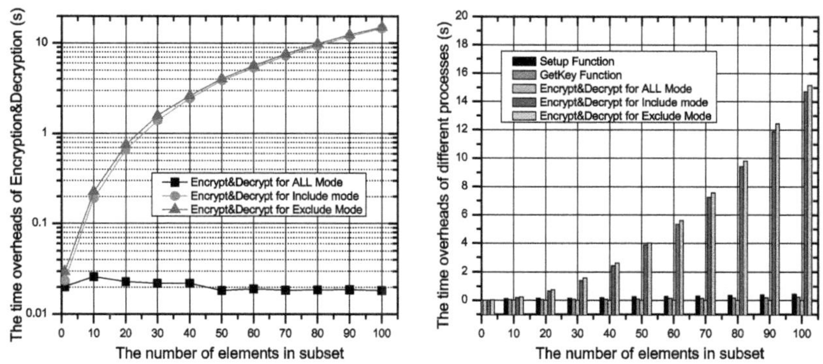

Figure 7: Time overhead of different algorithms in SBE.

6.0.3 *Performance of SBE Cryptosystem*

Finally, we provide the result of experiments to illustrate the performance of our SBE cryptosystem. Our experiments were implemented by a test (and demo) routine about 1000 lines of code. At first, we tested the total overheads of encryption and decryption under the different modes. As seen from left of Figure 7, encryption and decryption in Select-mode has the same overhead as Cut-mode. This result is the same with our theoretical analysis.

Next, we show time consumption of four functions, Setup, KeyGen, Encrypt and Decrypt, under different size of subsets (from 10 to 100) in right of Figure 7. In this experiment, we require two functions, Setup and GenKey, deal with all elements in a given subsets. Their overheads are proportional to the subset size but are still small. From this figure, the overhead of Setup or KeyGen is far less than that of encryption and decryption. In summary, our experiments show that our SBE scheme is simple, easy-to-implement, and high performance.

7. RELATED WORK

Fiat and Naor [1] were the first to formally explore broadcast encryption. They presented a private-key solution which was secure against a collusion of t users and has ciphertext size of $O(t \log^2 t \log n)$. Naor et al. [6] presented a fully collusion secure BE system that is efficient for broadcasting to all, but a small set of revoked users. However that these systems do not support public-key encryption, the first public-key BE scheme was proposed by Dois et al. [9]. Boneh and Silverberg also show that n-linear maps give the ultimate *fully collusion secure* scheme with constant public key, private key, and ciphertext size. Soon after this, the bilinear maps became the basis for many subsequent proposals, including Delerablée et al. [5] proposed identity-based broadcast encryption and gave a selective CPA secure scheme. Existing broadcast encryption can be divided into two category:

One category is broadcast with multiple revoked receivers, meaning that we broadcast to all but a small set of revoked users $\mathcal{R}$ and $|\mathcal{R}| \ll n$. The best known systems are the scheme of Delerablée et al.[5] which achieves the optimal bound of $O(1)$-size either for ciphertexts or decryption keys for any subset of revoked users. More importantly, several dynamic behaviors, e.g., dynamic user joining, key updating, were supported by their BE systems.

Another category is broadcast for multiple designated receivers, where message is sent to a small subset of users $\mathcal{S}$, and $|\mathcal{S}| \ll n$. Untill now, the best known systems are the scheme of Boneh, Gentry and Waters [2] which achieves $O(\sqrt{n})$-size ciphertexts and public keys for any subset of receivers, where each user's private keys are of constant size. Their trivial scheme where both ciphertexts and private keys are of constant size and public key size is linear in total number of users is more efficient when $|\mathcal{S}| < O(\sqrt{n})$. However, their upper bound on the number of possible users n must be chosen at initialization time, so that new users cannot join dynamically the system. In summary, these work gave us many important inspirations for our research.

8. CONCLUSION

In this paper we present a new group-oriented cryptosystem, called set-based broadcast encryption. Our main contribution is to give the first cryptographic constructions for the decision problem of positive membership and negative membership. for future work, we will improve the performance and apply our scheme into some practical applications, e.g., broadcasting, keyword searching, and voting.

Acknowledgment

The authors would like to express their thanks to Dijiang Huang at Arizona State University and Kui Ren at State Univesity of New York at Buffalo for helpful suggestions and encouragement. This work is supported by the National 973 Program (Grant No. 2013CB329605) and the National Natural Science Foundation of China (Grant Nos. 61170264 and 61472032).

9. REFERENCES

[1] Amos Fiat and Moni Naor. Broadcast encryption. In *Advances in Cryptology - CRYPTO '93, 13th Annual International Cryptology Conference, Santa Barbara, California, USA, August 22-26, 1993, Proceedings*, pages 480–491, 1993.

[2] Dan Boneh, Craig Gentry, and Brent Waters. Collusion resistant broadcast encryption with short ciphertexts and private keys. In *Advances in Cryptology - CRYPTO 2005: 25th Annual International Cryptology Conference, Santa Barbara, California, USA, August 14-18, 2005, Proceedings*, pages 258–275, 2005.

[3] Dan Boneh, Xavier Boyen, and Eu-Jin Goh. Hierarchical identity based encryption with constant size ciphertext. In *Advances in Cryptology - EUROCRYPT 2005, 24th Annual International Conference on the Theory and Applications of Cryptographic Techniques, Aarhus, Denmark, May 22-26, 2005, Proceedings*, pages 440–456, 2005.

[4] Dan Boneh and Matthew K. Franklin. An efficient public key traitor tracing scheme. In *Advances in Cryptology - CRYPTO '99, 19th Annual International Cryptology Conference, Santa Barbara, California, USA, August 15-19, 1999, Proceedings*, pages 338–353, 1999.

[5] Cécile Delerablée. Identity-based broadcast encryption with constant size ciphertexts and private keys. In *Advances in Cryptology - ASIACRYPT 2007, 13th International Conference on the Theory and Application of Cryptology and Information Security, Kuching, Malaysia, December 2-6, 2007, Proceedings*, pages 200–215. 2007.

[6] Dalit Naor, Moni Naor, and Jeffery Lotspiech. Revocation and tracing schemes for stateless receivers. In *Advances in Cryptology - CRYPTO 2001, 21st Annual International Cryptology Conference, Santa Barbara, California, USA, August 19-23, 2001, Proceedings*, pages 41–62, 2001.

[7] Duong Hieu Phan, David Pointcheval, Siamak Fayyaz Shahandashti, and Mario Strefler. Adaptive CCA broadcast encryption with constant-size secret keys and ciphertexts. volume 12, pages 251–265, 2013.

[8] Dan Boneh, Brent Waters, and Mark Zhandry. Low overhead broadcast encryption from multilinear maps. In *Advances in Cryptology - CRYPTO 2014 - 34th Annual Cryptology Conference, Santa Barbara, CA, USA, August 17-21, 2014, Proceedings, Part I*, pages 206–223. 2014.

[9] Yevgeniy Dodis and Nelly Fazio. Public key broadcast encryption for stateless receivers. In *Security and Privacy in Digital Rights Management, ACM CCS-9 Workshop, DRM 2002, Washington, DC, USA, November 18, 2002, Revised Papers*, pages 61–80, 2002.

[10] Dan Boneh and Matthew K. Franklin. Identity-based encryption from the weil pairing. In *Advances in Cryptology - CRYPTO 2001, 21st Annual International Cryptology Conference, Santa Barbara, California, USA, August 19-23, 2001, Proceedings*, pages 213–229, 2001.

[11] Jean-Luc Beuchat, Nicolas Brisebarre, Jérémie Detrey, and Eiji Okamoto. Arithmetic operators for pairing-based cryptography. In *Cryptographic Hardware and Embedded Systems - CHES 2007, 9th International Workshop, Vienna, Austria, September 10-13, 2007, Proceedings*, pages 239–255, 2007.

[12] Honggang Hu, Lei Hu, and Dengguo Feng. On a class of pseudorandom sequences from elliptic curves over finite fields. *IEEE Transactions on Information Theory*, 53(7):2598–2605, 2007.

[13] Bogdan Warinschi Gaven Watson Nigel P. Smart, Vincent Rijmen. Algorithms, key sizes and parameters report. european union agency for network and information security (enisa), 2013.

[14] Paulo S. L. M. Barreto, Steven D. Galbraith, Colm O'Eigeartaigh, and Michael Scott. Efficient pairing computation on supersingular abelian varieties. *Des. Codes Cryptography*, 42(3):239–271, 2007.

APPENDIX

A. GDHE ASSUMPTION

We give a rough overview of the General Diffie-Hellman Exponent (GDHE) assumption introduced by Boneh, Boyen and Goh [3] that will be used to analyze the security of our scheme. We only consider the GDHE assumption under the weakest case $\mathbb{G}_1 = \mathbb{G}_2 = \mathbb{G}$ in the general bilinear map group system $\mathbb{S} = (p, \mathbb{G}_1, \mathbb{G}_2, \mathbb{G}_T, e(\cdot,\cdot))$ with prime order p. Let $\mathbb{G}$ and $\mathbb{G}_T$ be groups of order p and $e : \mathbb{G} \times \mathbb{G} \to \mathbb{G}_T$ be a non-degenerate bilinear map.

Definition 5 (GDHE Problem, [3]). *Let $P, Q \in \mathbb{F}_p[X_1, \cdots, X_m]^s$ be two s-tuples of m-variate polynomials over $\mathbb{F}_p$ and generators $\hat{G}, \hat{H} \in \mathbb{G}$, where $s, m \in \mathbb{Z}^+$. We write $P = (p_1, \cdots, p_s)$ and $Q = (q_1, \cdots, q_s)$. Given a vector*

$$S = \left(\hat{G}^{P(x_1,\cdots,x_m)}, e(\hat{G}, \hat{H})^{Q(x_1,\cdots,x_m)} \right) \in \mathbb{G}^s \times \mathbb{G}_T^s$$

and $T \xleftarrow{R} \mathbb{G}_T$, decide whether $T = e(\hat{G}, \hat{H})^{h(x_1,\cdots,x_m)}$, where the polynomial $h \in \mathbb{F}_p[X_1, \cdots, X_m]$.

It is easy to find that almost previous decisional Diffie-Hellman assumptions can be reduced into GDHE assumption. We say that an algorithm $\mathcal{A}$ that outputs $b \in \{0, 1\}$ has advantage ϵ in solving the GDHE problem if

$$Adv_{\mathrm{GDHE}}^{\mathrm{IND}}(\mathcal{A}) = \left| \begin{array}{c} \Pr[\mathcal{A}(S, e(\hat{G}, \hat{H})^{h(x_1,\cdots,x_m)}) = 0] \\ -\Pr[\mathcal{A}(S, T) = 0] \end{array} \right| > \epsilon.$$

The following theorem gives a lower bound on the advantage of a generic algorithm in solving the decision (P, Q, h)-Diffie-Hellman problem.

Theorem 4 ([3], Theorem A.2). *Let $P, Q \in \mathbb{F}_p[X_1, \cdots, X_m]^s$ be two s-tuples of m-variate polynomials over $\mathbb{F}_p$ and $h \in \mathbb{F}_p[X_1, \cdots, X_m]$. Let $d = max(2d_P, d_Q, d_h)$, where d_P (resp. d_Q, d_h) denote the maximal degree of elements of P (resp. of Q, h). If h is* ***independent*** *of (P, Q) then for any $\mathcal{A}$ that makes a total of at most q queries to the oracles (computing the group operation in $\mathbb{G}, \mathbb{G}_T$ and the bilinear pairing $e : \mathbb{G} \times \mathbb{G} \to \mathbb{G}_T$), one has $Adv_{\mathrm{GDHE}}^{\mathrm{IND}}(\mathcal{A}) \leq \frac{(q+2s+2)^3 \cdot d}{2p}$.*

In this theorem, we define that a polynomial h is independent on the sets (P, Q) if there does not exist $s^2 + s$ constant $\{a_{ij}\}_{i,j=1}^s, \{b_k\}_{k=1}^s$, such that $h = \sum_{i,j=1}^s a_{ij} p_i p_j + \sum_{k=1}^s b_k q_k$. The security analysis of our schemes relies directly on these two theorems.

B. PROOF OF THEOREM 1

Proof. We consider the weakest case $\mathbb{G}_1 = \mathbb{G}_2 = \mathbb{G}$ and thus pose $\hat{H} = \hat{G}^u$, where u is a random variate. In the (F_1, F_2, F_3, T)-GDHE$_1$ problem, if one replace γ by x, ϵ by v, and ς by y, we see that our problem is reformulated as

(P,Q,h)-GDHE, where F_1, F_2 are integrated into P, F_3 and T correspond to Q and h, respectively. Such that, we have

$$\begin{cases} P(x,y,u,v) &= \begin{pmatrix} 1, v, xv, x^2v, \cdots, x^{t-1}v, \\ xf(x), \cdots, x^m f(x), \\ uv, uvx, \cdots, uvx^n, uf(x)g(x), \\ uvyf(x), uyf(x)g(x) \end{pmatrix} \\ Q(x,y,u,v) &= (1, uvf^2(x)g(x)) \\ h(x,y,u,v) &= uvyf^2(x)g(x) \end{cases}$$

where $d = 2n$, $m = 4$ and $s = t + m + n + 4$. According to the analysis method in [3], we next show that the polynomial h is independent of (P,Q), that is, no coefficients $\{a_{ij}\}_{i,j=1}^s, \{b_k\}_{k=1}^s$ exist such that $h = \sum_{i,j=1}^s a_{ij}p_ip_j + \sum_{l=1}^s b_l q_l$, where the polynomials p_i and q_i are the one listed in P and Q above. Considering that y only appears in $(uvyf(x), uyf(x)g(x))$, we must pick them out for all cases. A simple analysis method is to find the multiples of uvy from all possible products of two polynomials $(uvyf(x), uyf(x)g(x))$ in P. The polynomials $(uv, uvx, \cdots, uvx^n)$ can be excluded because $(uvyf(x), uyf(x)g(x))$ have contained u. Further, the polynomials $(v, xv, x^2v, \cdots, x^{t-1}v)$ also conflict with $uvyf(x)$ because they all contain v. So, we consider three cases:

- For the former $uvyf(x)$, we need to find the polynomial $h(x,y,u,v)/uvyf(x) = f(x)g(x)$. Let $g(x) = \prod_{i=1}^{n-t}(x + x'_i) = \sum_{i=0}^{n-t} b_i \cdot x^i$, where $b_0 = x'_1 x'_2 \cdots x'_{n-t} \neq 0$ because all $x'_i \neq 0$. So, $f(x)g(x)$ is represented as
$$f(x)g(x) = \sum_{i=0}^{n-t} a_i(x^i f(x)) = b_0 f(x) + \sum_{i=1}^{n-t} b_i(x^i f(x)).$$
but it is infeasible for computing it because there dose not exist the polynomial $f(x)$ in $P(x,y,u,v)$ even though we can get $(xf(x), \cdots, x^l f(x))$ from $P(x,y,u,v)$.
- For the latter $uyf(x)g(x)$, we need to find the polynomial $h(x,y,u,v)/uyf(x)g(x) = vf(x)$ and it is also infeasible because the polynomial $f(x) = \prod_{i=1}^t (x + x_i) = \sum_{i=0}^t a_i \cdot x^i = \sum_{i=0}^{t-1} a_i \cdot x^i + x^t$, which is a polynomial of t degree and $a_t = 1$, cannot be built from $(v, xv, \cdots, x^{t-1}v)$.
- For linear combination between $uvyf(x)$ and $uyf(x)g(x)$, assume that there exist two coefficients a, b to satisfy
$$h(x,y,u,v) = a \cdot uvyf(x) \cdot p_1 + b \cdot uyf(x)g(x) \cdot p_2.$$
So that, we have $vf(x)g(x) = avp_1 + bg(x)p_2$. To satisfy it, p_1 is merely derived from $(xf(x), \cdots, x^l f(x))$ and p_2 is from $(v, xv, \cdots, x^{t-1}v)$. This means $xf(x)|p_1$. Next we have $avp_1 = g(x)(vf(x) - bp_2)$, so we have $g(x)|p_1$. These two results show $xf(x)g(x)|p_1$. Since $p_1|g(x)(vf(x) - bp_2)$, we have $xf(x)|(vf(x) - bp_2)$. However, we know p_2 is a polynomial of x with at most degree $t-1$, so $(vf(x) - bp_2)$ is a polynomial of x with degree t. This is a contradiction with the fact that $xf(x)$ has degree $t+1$.

Hence, no linear combination among the polynomials from the known P, Q loads to h. This means that h is independent of (P,Q). Hence, the advantage of adversary is $Adv_{\text{GDHE}_1,\mathcal{A}}^{\text{IND}}(n,t) \leq \frac{(q+2s+2)^3 \cdot d}{2p}$ according to Theorem (4). □

C. PROOF OF THEOREM 2

PROOF. This proof is similar to the previous proof. We also consider the weakest case $\mathbb{G}_1 = \mathbb{G}_2 = \mathbb{G}$. We see that our problem (F_1, F_2, F_3, T)-GDHE is reformulated as (P,Q,h)-GDHE, where the result after conversion is

$$\begin{cases} P(x,y,u,v) &= \begin{pmatrix} 1, v, xv, x^2v, \cdots, x^{t-1}v, \\ xf(x), \cdots, x^m f(x), \\ uv, uvx, \cdots, uvx^n, uf(x)g(x), \\ yxf^2(x), uyf(x)g(x) \end{pmatrix} \\ Q(x,y,u,v) &= (1, uvf^2(x)g(x)) \\ h(x,y,u,v) &= uvyf^2(x)g(x) \end{cases}$$

where $d = 2n$, $m = 4$ and $s = n + t + m + 4$. We show that the polynomial h is independent of (P,Q). Considering that y only appears in $(yxf^2(x), uyf(x)g(x))$, we must pick them out for all cases. Next, there only exist the polynomials, $(uv, uvx, \cdots, uvx^n)$, which contain uv, so we have the candidate combination between $yxf^2(x)$ and these polynomials, but the combination between $uyf(x)g(x))$ and them will be excluded. Such that, we only need to consider three cases:

- For the former $(yxf^2(x)$, we need to find the polynomial $h(x,y,u,v)/yxf^2(x) = uvg(x)/x$, but it is infeasible for all $(uv, uvx, \cdots, uvx^n)$ because $g(x) = \prod_{i=1}^{n-t}(x + x'_i)$ is not divisible by x when all $x'_i \neq 0$ for $i = 1, \cdots, n-t$.
- For the latter $uyf(x)g(x))$, we need to find the polynomial $h(x,y,u,v)/uyf(x)g(x) = vf(x)$ and it is also infeasible because $f(x) = \prod_{i=1}^t (x + x_i) = \sum_{i=0}^t a_i x^i = x^t + \sum_{i=0}^{t-1} a_i x^i$, which is a polynomial of t degree, cannot be built from $(v, xv, \cdots, x^{t-1}v)$.
- For linear combination between $yxf^2(x)$ and $uyf(x)g(x)$, assume that there exist two coefficients a, b to satisfy
$$h(x,y,u,v) = a(yxf^2(x))(uv\tfrac{g(x)}{x+x'_i}) + b(uyf(x)g(x))(\tfrac{vf(x)}{x+x_i}).$$
So that, we have $\frac{ax}{x+x'_i} + \frac{b}{x+x_i} = 1$. To solve this equation, we have $(a-1)x^2 + (ax_i + b - x_i - x'_i)x + (bx'_i - x_i x'_i) = 0$. It is easy find that our solution is $a = 1$ and $b = x_i = x'_i$, but it contradicts with the assumption of $x_i \neq x'_i$ for all x_i and x'_i in $f(x)$ and $g(x)$.

Hence, no linear combination among the polynomials from P, Q loads to h. This also means that h is independent of (P,Q). Therefore, we obtain the advantage of adversary $Adv_{\text{GDHE}_2,\mathcal{A}}^{\text{IND}}(n,t) \leq \frac{(q+2s+2)^3 \cdot d}{2p}$ according to Theorem (4). □

D. PROOF OF THEOREM 3

PROOF. Suppose there exists an adversary $\mathcal{A}$ can break our SBE scheme with the advantage $Adv_{\text{SBE},\mathcal{A}}^{\text{IND},mode}(n,t)$ for either Select-mode or Cut-mode. Our objective is to build a PPT algorithm $\mathcal{B}$ to solve the above (n,t)-GDHE$_1$ or (n,t)-GDHE$_2$ problem by using the advantage of $\mathcal{A}$. Since there merely exists a slight different between GDHE$_1$ and GDHE$_2$: $\hat{H}^{\varsigma\epsilon f(\gamma)}$ lies in GDHE$_1$ but $\hat{G}^{\varsigma\gamma f^2(\gamma)}$ in GDHE$_2$ (see Table 1), such that we merge them into one proof, as follows:

Initial. According to the assumption that $\mathcal{B}$ is given as input an (n,t)-GDHE$_1$ or (n,t)-GDHE$_2$ instance. From this instance, $\mathcal{B}$ does not know $\gamma, \varsigma, \epsilon$ but knows $2n$ random integers $x_i, x'_i, a_i, b_i \in \mathbb{Z}_p^*$ in $f(x)$ and $g(x)$, where any pairwise (x_i, x'_i) are not equal to each other. Firstly, $\mathcal{B}$ defines a set of identities $\mathcal{U}$, and then require $\mathcal{A}$ to choose randomly a challenge subset $\mathcal{S}$ from $\mathcal{U}$ such that $\mathcal{R} = \mathcal{U} \setminus \mathcal{S}$, where $|\mathcal{U}| = n$ and $\mathcal{R} = t$. Secondly, $\mathcal{B}$ formally sets $G = \hat{G}^{f(\gamma)}$ (but he can by no means compute the value of G) and $H = \hat{H}^{f(\gamma)g(\gamma)}$. In order to compute H, we first need to compute the polynomial coefficients c_i of $f(X) \cdot g(X) = \prod_{i=1}^{t}(X + x_i) \cdot \prod_{i=1}^{n-t}(X + x'_i) = \sum_{i=0}^{n} c_i \cdot X^i$, where all x_i and x'_i are known, and then $H = \prod_{i=0}^{n}(\hat{H}^{\epsilon\gamma^i})^{c_i}$ is computed from $\hat{H}^{\epsilon}, \hat{H}^{\gamma\epsilon}, \cdots, \hat{H}^{\gamma^n\epsilon}$. Based on them, it computes easily the public parameter:

$$mpk = \begin{cases} H &= \hat{H}^{f(\gamma)g(\gamma)} &= \prod_{i=0}^{n}(\hat{H}^{\epsilon\gamma^i})^{c_i}, \\ R &= e(G,H)^{\epsilon} &= e(\hat{G},\hat{H})^{\epsilon f^2(\gamma)g(\gamma)}, \\ G_k &= G^{\gamma^k} &= \hat{G}^{\gamma^k f(\gamma)} \quad \text{for } k = [1,m]. \end{cases}$$

Learning. In this phase, the adversary $\mathcal{A}$ can issue up to n times secret-key queries $\{\text{ID}_i\}$ to gain the information of this cryptosystem. For each query ID_i, we consider two following cases: $\text{ID} \in \mathcal{S}$ and $\text{ID}_i \in \mathcal{R}$:

Case $\text{ID}_i \in \mathcal{R}$: $\mathcal{B}$ chooses randomly an element x_i and let $x_i = hash(\text{ID}_i)$. Then $\mathcal{B}$ defines the polynomial

$$f_i(X) = \frac{f(X)}{X + x_i} = \prod_{k=1,k\neq i}^{t}(X+x_i) = \sum_{k=0}^{t-1} a'_k X^k$$

of degree $t-1$ for $i \in [1,t]$. Based on the known values $(\hat{G}^{\epsilon}, \hat{G}^{\epsilon\gamma}, \cdots, \hat{G}^{\epsilon\gamma^{t-1}})$, $\mathcal{B}$ generates the secret key of the corrupted users

$$\begin{aligned} sk^{(i)} &= G^{\frac{x_i\epsilon}{\gamma+x_i}} = \hat{G}^{\epsilon\frac{x_i f(\gamma)}{\gamma+x_i}} = \hat{G}^{\epsilon x_i f_i(\gamma)} \\ &= \left(\hat{G}^{\epsilon\sum_{j=0}^{t-1} a'_j\gamma^j}\right)^{x_i} = \left(\prod_{j=0}^{t-1}\left(\hat{G}^{\epsilon\gamma^j}\right)^{a'_j}\right)^{x_i}. \end{aligned}$$

Similarly, $\mathcal{B}$ computes the coefficients b'_k of the polynomial $f_i(X)g(X) = \sum_{k=1}^{n-1} b'_k X^k$ and then uses $(\hat{H}^{\epsilon}, \hat{H}^{\epsilon\gamma}, \cdots, \hat{H}^{\epsilon\gamma^n})$ to compute

$$H_i = H^{\frac{\epsilon}{\gamma+x_i}} = \hat{H}^{\epsilon f_i(\gamma)g(\gamma)} = \prod_{k=0}^{n-1}(\hat{H}^{\gamma^k\epsilon})^{b'_k},$$

where b'_k is a known integer for all $k = [0, n-1]$. Finally, $\mathcal{B}$ sends $sk^{(i)}$ and $pp_i = (\text{ID}_i, H_i)$ to $\mathcal{A}$. Note that, all these keys $\{sk^{(i)}\}_{\text{ID}_i\in\mathcal{R}}$ are available for the ciphertext which is encrypted by the public encryption key.

Case $\text{ID}_i \in \mathcal{S}$: $\mathcal{B}$ chooses randomly an element x'_i and let $x'_i = hash(\text{ID}_i)$. $\mathcal{B}$ is merely required to use the above-mentioned approach to generate (ID_i, H_i), that is, $\mathcal{B}$ define $g_i(X) = \frac{g(X)}{X+x'_i}$ for $i \in [1, n-t]$ and computes $H_i = \hat{H}^{f(\gamma)g_i(\gamma)}$ in terms of $(\hat{H}^{\epsilon}, \hat{H}^{\epsilon\gamma}, \cdots, \hat{H}^{\epsilon\gamma^n})$. Finally, $\mathcal{B}$ sends $pp_i = (\text{ID}_i, H_i)$ to $\mathcal{A}$.

Note that the total number of attribute values is n. H_i can be computed easily because the polynomials $f_i g$ and fg_i are of degree $n-1$. In addition, $\mathcal{A}$ can query the hash value $x_i = h(\text{ID}_i)$ at any time if $\text{ID}_i \in \mathcal{R}$. Otherwise, $\mathcal{B}$ returns the hash value $x'_i = h(\text{ID}_i)$.

Challenge. $\mathcal{B}$ defines $\varsigma = s$, but ς is unknown for $\mathcal{B}$. Next, according to the given challenge $mode^*$, $\mathcal{B}$ chooses one of two modes, $u \in \mathcal{S}$ and $u \notin \mathcal{S}$ to compute the challenge ciphertext from two given instances, GDHE_1 or GDHE_2, respectively. The ciphertext is generated as follows:

- $u \in \mathcal{S}$: $\mathcal{B}$ constructs a ciphertext as follows:

$$\begin{cases} C_1 &= H^s &= \hat{H}^{\varsigma f(\gamma)g(\gamma)}, \\ C_2 &= H^{\frac{s\epsilon}{g(\gamma)}} &= \hat{H}^{\varsigma\epsilon f(\gamma)}, \end{cases}$$

where $\mathcal{B}$ get these two values from GDHE_1 instance.

- $u \notin \mathcal{S}$: $\mathcal{B}$ constructs a ciphertext as follows:

$$\begin{cases} C_1 &= H^s &= \hat{H}^{\varsigma f(\gamma)g(\gamma)}, \\ C_2 &= G^{s\gamma f(\gamma)} &= \hat{G}^{\varsigma\gamma f^2(\gamma)}, \end{cases}$$

where $\mathcal{B}$ get these two values from GDHE_2 instance.

For both cases, $\mathcal{B}$ defines the session key ek as T. $\mathcal{B}$ now selects a random bit $b \leftarrow \{0,1\}$, sets $ek_b = T$ and sets ek_{1-b} to a random element of $\mathbb{G}_T$. Finally, $\mathcal{B}$ sends the challenge $\mathcal{C} = (C^*, ek_0, ek_1)$ to $\mathcal{A}$, where $C^* = (\mathcal{S}, mode^*, C_1, C_2)$.

Note that, as seen from Section 4.1, there exists a slight different between GDHE_1 and GDHE_2: $\hat{H}^{\varsigma\epsilon f(\gamma)}$ lies in GDHE_1 but $\hat{G}^{\varsigma\gamma f^2(\gamma)}$ in GDHE_2, which is responsible for the different of the above ciphertexts.

Guess. $\mathcal{A}$ returns a guess $b' \in \{0,1\}$ to $\mathcal{B}$. If $b = b'$, $\mathcal{B}$ outputs 1, otherwise 0.

We now analyze the validate of $\mathcal{B}$ as follows: if the given value T is valid, i.e., $T = e(\hat{G},\hat{H})^{\varsigma\epsilon f^2(\gamma)g(\gamma)}$, the challenge C^* and ek will be valid because

$$\begin{aligned} ek &= e(G,H)^{s\epsilon} = e(\hat{G}^{f(\gamma)}, \hat{H}^{f(\gamma)g(\gamma)})^{\varsigma\epsilon} \\ &= e(\hat{G},\hat{H})^{\varsigma\epsilon f^2(\gamma)g(\gamma)} = T. \end{aligned}$$

In this case, we have the success probability of $\mathcal{B}$ is

$$\begin{aligned} \Pr[b = \mathcal{A}(\mathcal{C})|T = ek] &= Pr[b = b'|T = ek] \\ &= \Pr[b' = 1|b = 1 \wedge T = ek]\cdot\Pr[b = 1] + \\ &\quad \Pr[b' = 0|b = 0 \wedge T = ek]\cdot\Pr[b = 0] \\ &= \Pr[b' = 1|b = 1 \wedge T = ek]\cdot\tfrac{1}{2} + \\ &\quad \Pr[b' = 0|b = 0 \wedge T = ek]\cdot\tfrac{1}{2} \end{aligned}$$

Otherwise, the adversary $\mathcal{A}$ randomly guesses and picks an answer b' with 1/2 possibility, such that $\Pr[b = b'|T \xleftarrow{R} \mathbb{G}_T] = \Pr[b \neq b'|T \xleftarrow{R} \mathbb{G}_T] = 1/2$,. Based on them, we have

$$\begin{aligned} &Adv^{\text{IND}}_{\text{GDHE}_{1,2},\mathcal{B}}(n,t) \\ &= |\Pr[b = b'|T = ek] - \Pr[b = b'|T \xleftarrow{R} \mathbb{G}_T]| \\ &= |\Pr[b' = 1|b = 1 \wedge T = ek]\cdot\tfrac{1}{2} + \\ &\quad \Pr[b' = 0|b = 0 \wedge T = ek]\cdot\tfrac{1}{2} - \tfrac{1}{2}| \\ &= \frac{1}{2}\left| \begin{array}{l} \Pr[b' = 1|b = 1 \wedge T = ek] - \\ \Pr[b' = 1|b = 0 \wedge T = ek] \end{array} \right| \end{aligned}$$

Based on $Adv^{\text{IND}}_{\text{SBE},\mathcal{A}}(n,t)$ in Section 2, we have the following equation under the precondition of $T = ek$:

$$\begin{aligned} Adv^{\text{IND},mode}_{\text{SBE},\mathcal{A}}(n,t) &= |\Pr[b' = b] - 1/2| \\ &= \tfrac{1}{2}|\Pr[b' = b] - \Pr[b' \neq b]| \\ &= \tfrac{1}{2}|\Pr[b' = 1|b = 1] - \Pr[b' = 1|b = 0]|. \end{aligned}$$

Summing up, we get that the equation $Adv^{\text{IND}}_{\text{GDHE}_{1,2},\mathcal{B}}(n,t) = Adv^{\text{IND},mode}_{\text{SBE},\mathcal{A}}(n,t)$ for two modes. According to Theorem 1 and 2, we have proved that $Adv^{\text{IND}}_{\text{GDHE}_{1,2},\mathcal{B}}(n,t) \leq \frac{(q+2s+2)^2\cdot d}{2p}$, where $s = n+t+m+4$ and $d = 2n$. Thus, $Adv^{\text{IND},mode}_{\text{SBE},\mathcal{A}}(n,t)$ also satisfies the same negligible success probability. $\square$

Automated Identification of Cryptographic Primitives in Binary Code with Data Flow Graph Isomorphism

Pierre Lestringant* Frédéric Guihéry* Pierre-Alain Fouque†

*AMOSSYS
R&D Security Lab
Rennes, France
first.last@amossys.fr

†Université de Rennes 1 and
Institut Universitaire de France
Rennes, France
first.last@univ-rennes1.fr

ABSTRACT

Softwares use cryptographic algorithms to secure their communications and to protect their internal data. However the algorithm choice, its implementation design and the generation methods of its input parameters may have dramatic consequences on the security of the data it was initially supposed to protect. Therefore to assess the security of a binary program involving cryptography, analysts need to check that none of these points will cause a system vulnerability. It implies, as a first step, to precisely identify and locate the cryptographic code in the binary program. Since binary analysis is a difficult and cumbersome task, it is interesting to devise a method to automatically retrieve cryptographic primitives and their parameters.

In this paper, we present a novel approach to automatically identify symmetric cryptographic algorithms and their parameters inside binary code. Our approach is static and based on Data Flow Graph (DFG) isomorphism. To cope with binary codes produced from different source codes and by different compilers and options, the DFGs is normalized using code rewrite mechanisms. Our approach differs from previous works, that either use statistical criteria leading to imprecise results, or rely on heavy dynamic instrumentation. To validate our approach, we present experimental results on a set of synthetic samples including several cryptographic algorithms, binary code of well-known cryptographic libraries and reference source implementation compiled using different compilers and options.

Categories and Subject Descriptors

D.2.7 [**Distribution, Maintenance, and Enhancement**]: Restructuring—*reverse engineering, and reengineering*; D.4.6 [**Information Systems Applications**]: Cryptographic controls; I.2.8 [**Problem Solving, Control Methods, and Search**]: Graph and tree search strategies

Keywords

Static Binary Analysis, Reverse Engineering, Cryptography

ASIA CCS'15, April 14–17, 2015, Singapore.

ACM 978-1-4503-3245-3/15/04 ...$15.00.
http://dx.doi.org/10.1145/2714576.2714639.

1. INTRODUCTION

When assessing software security, analysts pay special attention to cryptographic algorithms for several reasons. First the algorithm choice may be problematic. Algorithms that have not been thoroughly analyzed or for which practical attacks have been published are insecure and should not be used. For instance, practical collision can be found for the MD5 hash function [33], however it is still not uncommon to find it in applications. Second, the algorithm's implementation may not be compliant with the specifications. It was the case for GnuPG that used a faster implementation of the signature scheme DSA by relying on smaller nonces [23]. This was instrumental in an attack that enabled to recover the signer's private key in less than a second. Because such liberties taken from the specifications may reduce the algorithm security, they should be detected so that they can be carefully analyzed. Third, the algorithm's implementation may leak information about secret data. Today, it is well-known that the most efficient attacks use side-channel information. Thus it is essential to check if these attacks exist on the implementation being evaluated. The cache timing attack against the table implementation of AES [26] and the recent attack based on acoustic leakage against RSA [12] are good examples of practical side-channel attacks. Finally, despite a secure implementation, poorly generated input parameters can still affect the system security. Therefore the analyst will be particularly interested in how the key, the IV or the padding are generated. For instance, attacks known as padding oracle [21, 28] target insecure padding scheme.

The ability to conduct these analyses at the binary level is important because source code is not always available. And even when it is, the compiler may introduce security breaches [5, 30] that can only be revealed by looking at the binary code. It is clear that a first prerequisite will be to find and identify cryptographic primitives in binary code. Therefore, designing automated mechanisms to address this specific problem should be highly profitable for security experts who have a limited amount of time to assess the security of software.

The solution we proposed, based on static analysis and more particularly on data flow graph isomorphism is able to identify and accurately locate cryptographic algorithms and their parameters inside binary executables. Our solution targets symmetric cryptographic algorithms. We choose not to address the problem of code obfuscation because the objective of our method is to deal with the kind of general software that is typically reviewed during product certification and not to specifically target applications such as malwares that would have involved heavy obfuscation. In summary, this paper makes the following contributions:

- We present a sound and efficient approach to automatically identify and locate symmetric cryptographic algorithms and their parameters in binary code.
- We propose a normalization process and a signature matching scheme that is resistant against compiler optimizations and source code variations.
- We present the results of an experimental study that demonstrates the efficiency of our approach on well-known cryptographic libraries.

The remainder of the paper is structured as follows. In Section 2 we present more formally the previous works on the field of cryptographic identification. Then, we present at a high-level our solution in Section 3: the DFG is described in Section 4, the normalization process in Section 5, the signature design in Section 6 and the subgraph isomorphism algorithm due to Ullman is recalled in Section 7. Finally, in Section 8 we give experimental results.

2. RELATED WORK

The topic of cryptographic primitives identification in binary programs has been previously addressed. In this Section we will first present and discuss the limitations of two characteristics used to identify cryptographic code: data constant and input/output relationship. Finally we will briefly list other lines of work that are closely related.

2.1 Data Constant

Symmetric cryptographic algorithms often contain specific constants. These constants range from a single value of a few bits to large lookup tables of several kilobytes. Because it is unlikely to find them in different algorithms, they can be used to identify cryptographic code. This is a widely used technique and it has been implemented in several publicly available tools, such as Findcrypt2 (IDA plugin) [14], KANAL (PEiD plugin), or H&C Detector, to name but a few. As far as we know all tools based on constant identification solely rely on static analysis. However we should bear in mind that constant identification can also be performed using dynamic analysis. This is particularly useful in the case of packed programs, or for constants that are dynamically computed.

Despite its simplicity and its efficiency the constant identification technique does not meet our precision and reliability requirements. We exhibit some of the limitations of constant identification with the following example, that uses an AES table implementation as a target. A reminder on possible AES implementations is given in Appendix A. Given a binary program, let us assume the AES S-Box has been detected by one of the previously listed tools. The precise location of the AES encryption/decryption routines still needs to be investigated. In fact multiple parts of the program can access the S-Box, such as: the AES key schedule (either for encryption or decryption) or a 4 kilobytes lookup tables generation routine. Moreover the parameters (including the key size) have not been identified. Finally, the detected algorithm could be another cryptographic primitive that uses the AES S-Box, such as the Fugue hash function [15] or the LEX stream cipher [6].

To conclude, constant identification may be a very effective first step, but it should not be used as a standalone technique to precisely and completely uncover cryptographic primitives.

2.2 Input/Output Relationship

The I/O relationship identification technique relies on the following hypothesis: given a cryptographic primitive $f : I \rightarrow O$, the relationship between an input value and the corresponding output value identifies f with an overwhelming probability. In other words, if during an execution a program fragment reads a value $i \in I$ and writes a value $o \in O$ such that $f(i) = o$, we can conclude that this fragment implements the primitive f.

From a practical perspective, the targeted program is first executed in a Dynamic Binary Instrumentation (DBI) environment. The exact values manipulated by the program are recorded in an execution trace. The execution trace is then split into fragments using the loop abstraction according to the hypothesis that cryptographic code manipulates their arguments within loops. This observation is used to narrow the search space by only considering what happens inside loops' body. For each fragment F a set of input and output arguments (called respectively I_F and O_F) are reconstructed from its instructions' operands. Finally, given a database of cryptographic reference implementations P, we search $f \in P$ such that: $i \in I_F$ and $f(i) \in O_F$.

Gröbert *et al.* [13] were the first to use the I/O relationship to recognize cryptographic primitives. Zhao *et al.* [34] also used the I/O relationship, but instead of using the loop abstraction to extract candidates, they split the trace in terms of functions. More recently, Calvet *et al.* [7] proposed a complete and detailed tool named Aligot based on the I/O relationship. Aligot includes a new loop definition and the analysis of the data flow between loops to produce the best candidate for I/O testing.

However in our opinion two problems remain unaddressed by this approach. The first problem is fragment extraction in the case of unrolled loops. Loop unrolling is a common technique used by software engineers or compilers to reduce branch penalties and increase instruction level parallelism. It is not uncommon to encounter unrolled loops in cryptographic code as performance is a major concern. However according to our observations even Calvet loop's definition is unable to cope with unrolled loop: since loop unrolling is not the ultimate step of an optimization process, unrolled loops are not the exact repetition of a sequence of dynamic instructions.

The second problem concerns the parameters reconstruction. Instruction's operands have to be aggregated to form input and output parameters for reference implementations. Previous works [13, 34, 7] have provided rules to concatenate memory operands (based on spatial proximity either in code or in memory). However nothing has been proposed to concatenate register operands. Without external information, we must resort to a brute force approach. Given n operands, the number of parameters resulting from every combination and permutation of k operands, is: $\frac{n!}{(n-k)!}$. This is not tractable in practice if we consider that the same parameter may be distributed in the memory and in registers, as it is for instance often the case for the states of the

AES or MD5. In that case n is the sum of the number of registers operands an the number of memory operands.

To conclude, the I/O relationship identification method has several qualities: parameters identification, no false positive and resilient against implementation variations. However we have identified two blind spots: unrolled loops and parameters reconstruction.

2.3 Miscellaneous

In this section we list works that do not directly address the problem of cryptographic identification, but are closely related. A first line of work is automatic decryption of encrypted communication received by a binary executable. Given a known or an unknown decryption algorithm, the objective is to automatically retrieve decrypted data from the process memory. This problem deserves to be mentioned here, since it requires to detect where and when the cryptographic code is and implies at least to identify the output parameter (or conversely the input parameter for encryption). Lutz [20] was the first to address this problem in the context of malware analysis. He devised a dynamic technique based on data tainting and several heuristics including loops, integer arithmetic operations and entropy (an entropy drop may indicate a decryption). ReFormat [31] is a tool designed to automate the protocol reverse engineering of encrypted messages. It also uses data tainting to track the encrypted data in memory, but solely relies on arithmetic and bitwise instructions to discern the decryption phase. Finally Wang *et al.* [29] proposed a novel approach for automated Digital Rights Management (DRM) removal from streaming media. Their approach is driven by real-time constraints. The decryption algorithm is revealed by a randomness decrease in memory buffers manipulated by loops. According to this study randomness should be preferred over entropy to dissociate encrypted data from compressed data.

A second closely related area is binary clone detection. It is a more general problem but some of the techniques used might be of some interest for cryptographic primitive identification. Sæbjørnsen *et al.* [25] based their binary clone detection on the comparison of features vectors, which characterize a code fragment in terms of instruction mnemonics and operands. Finally, Rendezvous [19] identifies binary code fragment using statistical model relying on instruction mnemonics, Control Flow Graph (CFG) subgraph and data constants. Experiments carried out by the authors show resilience to the use of different compilers and compiler's options.

3. SOLUTION OVERVIEW

DFGs are a natural way to represent the dependencies between operations. They are also convenient to rewrite program code, i.e. to modify the code without breaking its semantics, as illustrated by their many uses in the compiler field for code optimizations [4]. For those two reasons the DFG representation appears well suited to address the problem of cryptographic algorithm identification. First it will be easy to extract specific subsets of related operations to form accurate signatures. Second, it will be possible to remove some of the variations that exist between different instances of the same algorithm, by rewriting the DFG. These variations have either been introduced in the source code or during the compilation. Ideally there should be a unique signature that matches every instance. Thus these variations should be removed leading to a canonical form that contains the signature.

In a nutshell, our identification method is a three-step process. First given as input a piece of assembly code we build the corresponding DFG. Second we normalize this DFG using rewrite rules. Third we search for subgraphs in the DFG that are isomorphic to the graph signature of a given cryptographic algorithm. If such a subgraph is found, we conclude that the assembly code implements the corresponding algorithm. Figure 1 shows the flowchart of our identification method.

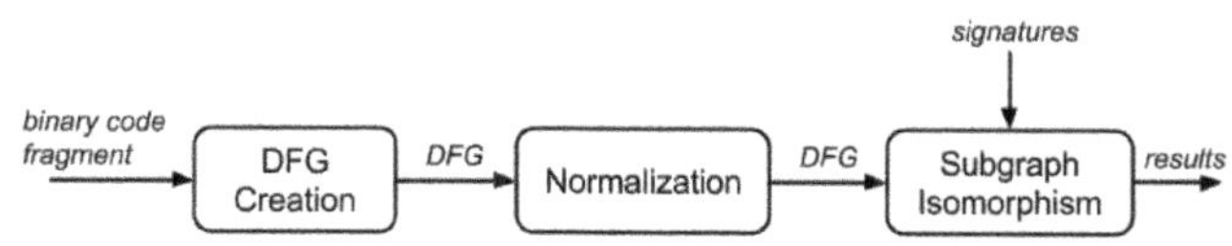

Figure 1: Simple flowchart of the DFG signature based identification technique

It is natural to wonder if CFGs could be used in a similar process. However, due to performance and security considerations (typically to resist timing attacks), the implementation of symmetric cryptographic algorithms tends to avoid conditional instructions. For example there is no conditional instruction in a standard MD5 implementation (Appendix B). Furthermore CFG may vary from one algorithm instance to another due to loop unrolling. For those reasons, control flow information does not seem relevant for symmetric cryptographic identification and we choose to solely rely on the DFG. To take full advantage of this simplification, we make the assumption of straight-line programs where every loop has been unrolled and every function call has been inlined.

To achieve acceptable performances, our method should not be applied directly to the code of a whole program. In fact the second and third steps are computationally intensive and the smaller the DFG is, the faster they will be executed. Therefore, only preselected program fragments should be submitted to the identification process. However unlike the I/O identification method (described in Section 2.2), there is no hard constraint on the fragment extraction mechanism in our case. Obviously the cryptographic code should be included in one fragment, but using large fragments does not affect the method reliability. In fact, the subgraph isomorphism algorithm is able to detect signatures even though they are surrounded by additional elements. Some of the criteria that may be used to extract suitable code fragments are discussed in Section 8.

4. DATA FLOW GRAPH CONSTRUCTION

4.1 Model of DFG

A DFG is a Directed Acyclic Graph (DAG) that represents the data dependency between a set of operations. A vertex represents either an arithmetic/logic operation or an input variable. An edge from vertex v_1 to vertex v_2 means that v_1 (or the value produced by v_1, if v_1 is an operation) is an input operand for operation v_2. Each operation produces one result and takes a non-empty unordered set of operands as input. For non commutative operations, edges may be tagged using special labels to clearly identify the role of each operand. We also distinguish constant from non-constant input variables. Constant variables have a fixed known value derived from immediate operands of the x86 assembly code; non-constant variables have an unknown value defined either by a register or by a memory location. Memory accesses are potentially considered as both input/output variables and operations, and as such they are handled separately.

4.2 From Assembly to DFG

From the assembly code of a program fragment F, we build the corresponding DFG: $G_F = (V, E)$ (V is a set of vertices and E is a set of edges) by iterating over the instructions of F. Each instruction $i \in F$ is translated into a set of operations O_i which can be empty (if i has no effect on G_F, for instance because it is a branch instruction) or contain one to several vertices (multiple operations may be required to reproduce the behavior of complex instructions). Depending on the type of the instruction's input operands, we take the following actions:

Immediate. We add a constant input variable to G_F. This vertex holds the value of the immediate operand and is linked by an edge to O_i.

Register. We add an edge between the last definition of the register and O_i. In practice, we maintain an array that associates each register with the vertex holding the reference to its current value. This reference can be null if the register has not yet been used in F (In that case a new input vertex is added to the graph), or it can point to either an input variable (the register was read but not set in F) or an operation (the last to have written in the register).

Memory. Memory operands are accessed through special operations: `load` for memory read and `store` for memory write. These two operations take as input operand an address which computation is explicitly transcribed in G_F. We also keep track of the order in which memory accesses are made in the program fragment.

4.3 Example

We illustrate our DFG model and the translation process with an example. This example is based on a custom Even-Mansour cipher [11] with a 32-bit substitution box as the public permutation. If we note p the plaintext, k the key and S the substitution box, the ciphertext is equal to the following expression: $S(p \oplus k) \oplus k$. An x86 assembly implementation of this encryption algorithm is given in Figure 2 and the corresponding DFG is given in Figure 3. Input variables are represented inside rectangles and operations inside circles. The relative order of memory accesses is specified by an index. This example will be pursued through Section 5 and Section 6.

```
mov     ebx,DWORD PTR [esp+0x8]      ; load key
pop     ecx                          ; load plaintext
xor     ebx,ecx                      ; = p ^ k
mov     ecx,DWORD PTR [SBOX+ebx*4]   ; = S(p ^ k)
mov     ebx,DWORD PTR [esp+0x4]      ; load key
xor     ecx,ebx                      ; = S(p ^ k) ^ k
```

Figure 2: A possible x86 assembly code for the custom encryption algorithm. Given a plaintext p, an encryption key k, the custom algorithm computes $S(p \oplus k) \oplus k$ where S is a substitution box.

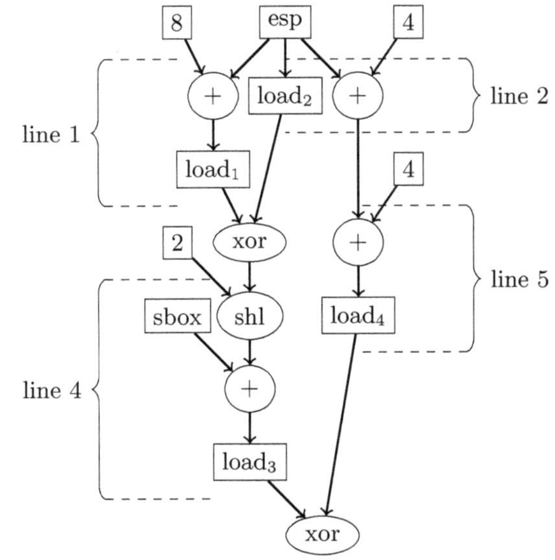

Figure 3: DFG derived from the assembly code of the custom encryption algorithm given in Figure 2. Input variables are represented inside rectangles and operations inside circles.

5. NORMALIZATION

The goal of normalization is to modify the DFG without breaking its semantics in order to maximize the chance of finding an algorithm's signatures. In other words we try to remove the variations that may have been introduced by either the developer, the optimizations of the compiler or the translation into machine code.

Once the DFG of a code fragment has been constructed, we normalize it using a set of rewrite rules. Since it is hard to understand how a particular rule can affect the others, we simply iterate the application of the rewrite rules until we reach a fixed-point, which we consider to be the canonical form of the DFG. We assume that the set of rewrite rules does not contain conflicting rules that will cause an endless loop. In practice the canonical form is reached in less than ten iterations for most cases.

We use three types of rewrite rules: normalization rules, memory simplification rules and general simplification rules.

5.1 Normalization Rules

Normalization rules are used when several instructions can be used to perform the same operation. We arbitrarily choose one as the normalized version and we create rules to convert from the others. Examples of normalization rules that we use, are given in the table below:

Original	Normalized	
$\mathtt{a} \oplus \mathtt{0xff..f}$	$\sim \mathtt{a}$	
$\mathtt{rol(a, cst_1)}$	$\mathtt{ror(a, cst_2)}$	with $\mathtt{cst_2} = \mathtt{size(a)} - \mathtt{cst_1}$
$\mathtt{a} - \mathtt{cst_1}$	$\mathtt{a} + \mathtt{cst_2}$	with $\mathtt{cst_2} = -\mathtt{cst_1}$
$\mathtt{a} \oplus \mathtt{a}$	$\mathtt{0}$	
$\mathtt{a} \times 2^{\mathtt{n}}$	$\mathtt{a} << \mathtt{n}$	

5.2 Memory Access Simplification Rules

During the generation of the DFG, every memory access has been replaced by a `load` or a `store` operation. However, many of them are caused by registers filling and spilling and are irrelevant to the algorithm identification. Most of all, it is necessary for normalized graphs to be independent from where local variables are stored (either in registers or memory). A consequence is that normalized graphs should be free of any memory operation except for the ones corresponding to input or output variables. We devise three rules to simplify memory accesses. For each memory address, i.e. each vertex of the DFG that is used as an address operand by at least one memory operation, we compute the corresponding sequence of memory operations. Then, we traverse the sequences and perform simplifications for the following patterns:

- `store` after `store`: the first `store` has no effect, it can be removed.
- `load` after `store`: the output of the `load` is equal to the input of the `store`, the `load` can be removed.
- `load` after `load`: the two operations output the same value, they can be merged.

However, the problem of aliasing is yet to be solved. Aliasing happens when two different vertices are equal to the same address value. In such cases, the address sequence computed for both vertices will be incomplete. As a first consequence, we may miss additional simplification cases. This is not a concern however, since we can assume that these will eventually be dealt with by other simplification rules (such as common subexpression elimination). The second consequence is more problematic: simplifications performed with incomplete sequences may break semantics of the code irreversibly. This happens in the following cases:

- if an aliased `load` happens between two memory `store`.
- if an aliased `store` happens between a memory `store` and a memory `load`.
- if an aliased `store` happens between two memory `load`.

To address this problem, we can use a may-alias analysis. When a possible aliasing issue is detected we split the sequences of memory operations. The result is a set of sequences that are free of any aliasing conflict and that can be safely simplified. However, if the may-alias analysis is too inclusive, several legitimate simplification cases will be discarded. This is the main drawback of that method.

An example of memory access simplification is given in the right hand side of Figure 4. Two `load` operations are performed for the same address ($esp + 8$), there is no memory write in-between (that is to say no possible aliasing issue), thus according to the simplification rules they can be merged.

5.3 General Simplification Rules

We wish to achieve two goals with the general simplifications rules. The first goal is to find which memory accesses are made at a same address in order to enable the memory simplifications described previously. The second goal is to optimize the DFG of non optimized code. In fact compiler optimizations are not necessarily reversible. Hence if we have to reach the same normalized representation from two versions: one well optimized and the other not, the only possibility left is to optimize code that is not well optimized. For example let us assume the following sequence of instructions and its optimized counterpart:

$$\begin{array}{lcl} \mathtt{b} = \mathtt{a} >> \mathtt{16} & & \mathtt{e} = \mathtt{a} >> \mathtt{14} \\ \mathtt{c} = \mathtt{b} \wedge \mathtt{0xff} & \longrightarrow & \mathtt{d} = \mathtt{e} \wedge \mathtt{0x2fc} \\ \mathtt{d} = \mathtt{c} << \mathtt{2} & & \end{array}$$

Let us assume that a certain compiler happens to perform this optimization. It is obvious that it will be hard to be undone: how do we guess there was a right shift operation at the end of the sequence? Its normalized representation should definitely be the optimized one. As a result, every time the original sequence is encountered it will have to be optimized.

At this point one might think that the amount of work required to match modern compilers data flow optimizations is going to be tremendous. However due to the straight line hypothesis we made, it is simpler than it might look. In fact the program fragment F can be seen as a single basic block with one entry point and one exit point. Thus the simplification rules required to catch up with maximal optimization levels only have to be applied locally to a single basic block. These rules can be divided in two main mechanisms: common subexpression elimination and constant simplification.

Common Subexpression Elimination

Common subexpression elimination is a classical compiler technique to remove redundant operations. If two operations share the same set of input operands, then they obviously produce the same output. Consequently one of them can safely be removed from the graph.

Common subexpression elimination is especially important for memory addresses. In fact in x86 code, the effective address computation is generally performed every time a memory access is made. As a consequence it is hard to detect if two memory accesses are made at the same location, since their address operand systematically belongs to different vertices. Common subexpression elimination will merge effective address computations resulting from the same set of operands (base, index, scale and displacement). As a result some memory accesses will explicitly share address vertex in the graph and thence it will be possible to perform the memory simplification rules described previously.

An example of subexpression elimination is given on the center of Figure 4. Two additions take as input *ESP* and 8. One of them was removed, leaving the graph with two memory `load` sharing the same address vertex.

Constant Simplification Rules

We can perform constant simplification in the following case:

1. If every input operands of an arithmetic/logic operation is a constant variable. The operation can be replaced by the result.
2. If an arithmetic/logic operation has an operand which is equal to either the identity element or the absorbing element of that operation (if they exist).

However it is sometimes required to rearrange sequences of associative operations to perform constant simplification. This requirement is illustrated on the left hand side of Figure 4 where two consecutive additions involving constant variables can be simplified if they are rearranged. Another kind of rearranging strategy that enables further constant simplification is distribution. It is especially important for memory address simplification due to the scale parameter of the x86 addressing mode.

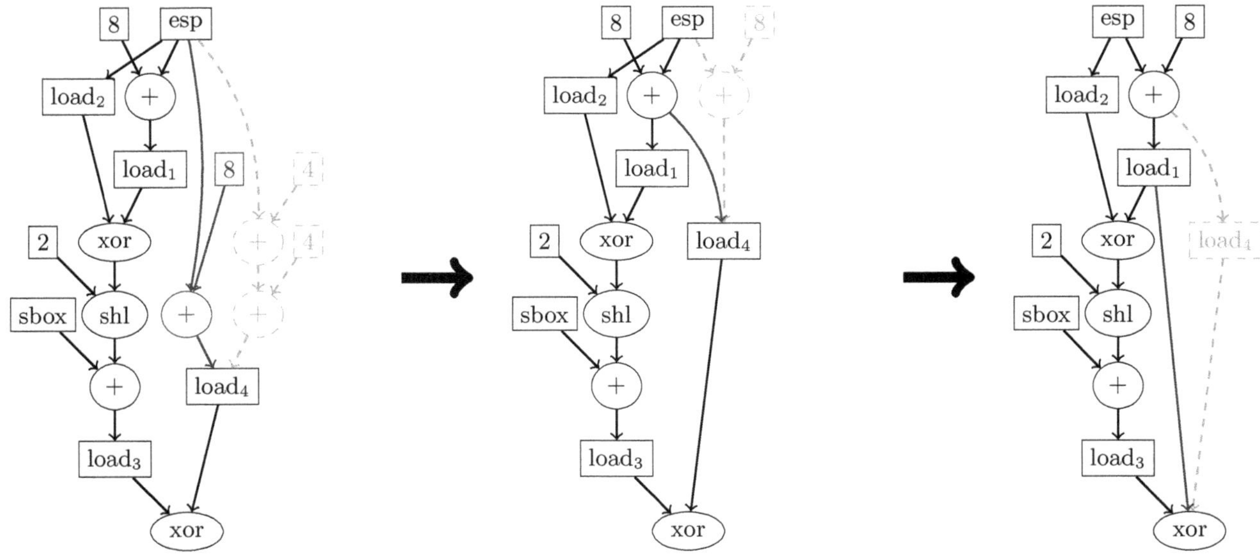

Figure 4: During the normalization process three transformation rules can be applied to the DFG of Figure 3. For each, the initial state is recalled in dashed red and the result is given in dark green. From the left to the right we successively perform: a constant simplification, a common subexpression elimination and a memory simplification.

For that purpose we design two additional rewrite rules. The first rule merges consecutive associative operations involving constant variables. The second rule distributes distributive couple of operations involving constant variables.

6. SIGNATURE

A signature is a distinctive subgraph shared between the normalized DFG of every instance of an algorithm. Signatures should be as complete and precise as possible in order to reduce the number of false positives and to reveal every feature of the algorithm that we might be interested in. Since our objective is to precisely locate the algorithm and its parameters, the signatures must cover the full length of the algorithm and must not be limited to some specific fragments. But conversely, signatures should not be too restrictive so as to match the largest range of possible implementations. Ideally the normalization process should be able to transform any instance of an algorithm into a unique representation. However, the level of analysis and understanding required is sometimes far beyond the reach of our rewrite rules. When it happens, one may favor a more generic signature that leaves the part subject to variations unspecified rather than to multiply the number of required signatures.

6.1 Signature Creation

We currently do not implement an automatic mechanism to create new signatures, and they have to be generated manually. Obviously, this requires some knowledge of the assembly language and a good understanding of the algorithm implementation. However, there is no prerequisite regarding the normalization process in theory. In fact, to be compliant with the rewrite rules, a signature can always be normalized after its creation, like any other DFG.

6.2 Macro Signature

Despite the normalization step and careful signature designs, multiple signatures are sometimes required to cover a wide range of implementations. In such cases, to reduce their number, we introduce macro signatures to model context-free graph grammar. The key idea is to append to the DFG a special vertex every time a signature is detected. It makes possible to issue higher level queries through macro signatures containing reference to signatures that have already been encountered. More formally a macro signature is a graph containing usual DFG vertices (terminal symbols) and also vertices representing other signatures (non terminal symbols). We use a bottom-up parsing algorithm relying on a subgraph isomorphism solver (discussed in Section 7). Starting from the signatures containing only terminal symbols, a special vertex is appended to the DFG every time an instance of a signature is found. These vertices are labeled according to their corresponding signature. Notice that different signatures can result in vertices of equal labels. A macro signature s_1 can be searched when every signature s_2 such that $s_1 \Rightarrow s_2$ was searched.

Macro signature are of high interest to reduce the number of signatures that need to be tested. In fact, variations that affect disjoint parts of a DFG can be searched independently. Let us assume an algorithm divided into n disjoint parts, each of them with $a_i, 1 \leq i \leq n$ different ways of being implemented. Without macro signatures, the number of signatures that have to be tested to cover the full algorithm is $\prod_{i=1}^{n} a_i$. However, using macro signatures, each part can be searched independently, covering every case with only $\sum_{i=1}^{n} a_i$ signatures. A practical example is given in Section 8.1.

Additionally, macro signatures may be used to break down large graphs into smaller ones, leading to better performances. This strategy is illustrated in Section 8.2.

6.3 Example

We continue the running example and create a signature for our toy cipher. Assuming we want to locate the parameters of our algorithm, the signature should at least contain one vertex for each of them: the plaintext, the key and the ciphertext and at least a path linking them together. Although macro signatures were far from being mandatory in that case, we intentionally choose to use one for illustrating purpose. We first create a signature that covers the access to the substitution box (address computation plus memory read). This signature is then reused in another signature where the two `xor` operations and the parameters' vertices have been appended. This second signature is complete and should be able to accurately identify our algorithm. These signatures and the way they match the normalized DFG of Figure 4 are shown in Figure 5. A specific label $*$ is used for input variables. This label can be matched with any other label (it is mandatory for input variables since they may have produced by any operation). The two steps of the parsing process are illustrated in Figure 5. First, on the left hand side the substitution box signature is being searched. Second, on the right hand side after appending a new vertex (drawn in a rounded rectangle with the label sig_1) corresponding to the successfull match of the first signature, the complete signature is being searched.

7. SUBGRAPH ISOMORPHISM

This is the final step of our solution. Given a normalized DFG and a set of signatures, we want to know which signatures are contained in the DFG. To this end we use the subgraph isomorphism algorithm proposed by Ullmann [27]. A short description of this algorithm is given as follows.

As a reminder, a graph $G_A = \{V_A, E_A\}$ is a subgraph of $G_B = \{V_B, E_B\}$ if $V_A \subset V_B$ and $E_A \subset E_B$. A graph $G_A = \{V_A, E_A\}$ is said to be isomorphic to $G_B = \{V_B, E_B\}$ if there is a function $f : V_A \mapsto V_B$ such that: $(v, w) \in E_A \Leftrightarrow (f(v), f(w)) \in E_B$. Given a signature $S = \{V_S, E_S\}$ and a normalized DFG $D = \{V_D, E_D\}$, we want to find all subgraphs of D that are isomorphic to S. With respect to the above definitions, our problem can be reformulated as follows: we want to enumerate every function $f : V_S \to V_D$ such that:

$$(v, w) \in E_S \Rightarrow (f(v), f(w)) \in E_D \quad (1)$$

Subgraph isomorphism can be achieved using a rather simple depth-first tree-search procedure. For each vertices of the signature: $v \in V_S$, we maintain a set of possible assignment called A_v. A_v is initialized with vertices of D that have the same label than v. The algorithm works by recursively picking one element in each possible assignment sets such that condition 1 hold true. The f function is defined by: $f(v) = u$ where u is the vertex that has been picked in A_v.

Ullmann introduced an additional refinement procedure that takes advantage of the vertices that have already been picked to reduce the possibilities for future picks. Let v and w be vertices of S such that $(v, w) \in E_S$. Given $x \in A_u$, if there is no vertex $y \in A_w$ such that $(x, y) \in E_D$, then x can be removed from A_v. In fact, picking x from A_v will necessarily break condition 1. Every time an element is removed or picked from one of the possible assignment sets, we apply this new criteria trying to remove as many elements as possible from the other possible assignment sets. A pseudo code for Ullmann subgraph isomorphism algorithm is given in Algorithm 1.

Despite a high theoretical complexity (the subgraph isomorphism problem is NP complete) we were able to achieve acceptable performance using Ullmann algorithm in our context. Experimental data regarding the execution time are presented and discussed in Section 8.2.

Algorithm 1 Ullmann Subgraph Isomorphism

```
function SUBGRAPH ISOMORPHISM(S, D)
    ∀v ∈ V_S initialize A_v. Δ ← {A_v, v ∈ V_S}
    f is undefined for every vertex of V_S
    RECURSIVE SEARCH(S, D, f, Δ)
end function

function RECURSIVE SEARCH(S, D, f, Δ)
    if ∀v ∈ V_S, f(v) is defined then
        f defines a valid subgraph isomorphism ⌑
    else
        UPDATE(Δ)
        pick v ∈ V_S such that f(v) is undefined
        while A_v ≠ ∅ do
            pick u ∈ A_v. f(v) ← u
            RECURSIVE SEARCH(S, D, f, copy(Δ))
            remove u from A_v and set f(v) undefined
        end while
    end if
end function

function UPDATE(Δ)
    for all (v, w) ∈ E_S | f(v) is undefined do
        for all x ∈ A_v do
            if f is defined for w then
                A_w ← {f(w)}
            end if
            if {y ∈ V_D, (x, y) ∈ E_D} ∩ A_w = ∅ then
                remove x from A_v
                UPDATE(Δ) return
            end if
        end for
    end for
end function
```

8. EXPERIMENTAL EVALUATION

The goal of the experimental evaluation is to demonstrate the validity of our approach. It involves two claims in particular: first that the normalization process is able to effectively remove implementation variations, and second that it is possible to create graph signatures that match every instance of an algorithm once normalized. For that purpose, we have implemented a prototype and run it on multiple test programs. As a first evaluation of our method, we thought it was more relevant to analyze the performance on synthetic samples rather than to directly confront our prototype with real life programs. Synthetic samples are convenient to thoroughly evaluate the solution in well controlled environments. Furthermore as mentioned in Section 3 our method takes preselected fragments of binary code as input. It is clear that the prototype performances depend more on the fragment's code rather than on the fragment's origin. Thus synthetic samples sound perfectly relevant for our testing purpose.

Although we do not address the problem of fragment extraction in our work, we list here few heuristics that can be used as front end filters to extract candidates. These heuristics are taken from the related works discussed in Section 2.

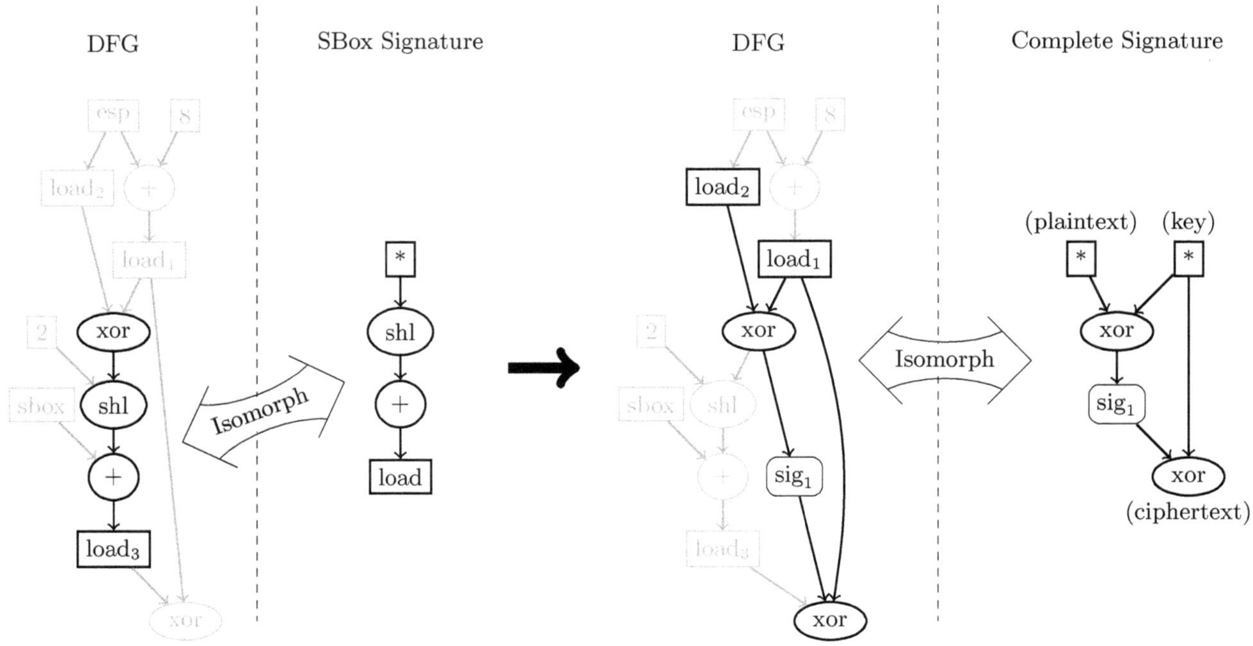

Figure 5: Signature detection: for the two steps of the parsing process we recall the DFG and the signature that is being searched. The signature match is drawn in black and the rest of the DFG in light gray.

Function. Symmetric cryptographic algorithms are usually implemented in a single function that does not call any sub function. Based on this observation we can extract every function which maps to a vertex with no direct successor in the call graph.

Constant. As previously stated constants can be used to identify cryptographic code. Code regions surrounding identified constants are good candidates for implementing cryptographic primitives.

Mnemonic. The DFG normalization may modify some instruction's mnemonic. Nevertheless most of them will remain unmodified (or at least will be changed in an easily predictable way). A first and effective step would be to filter code regions based on the mnemonics of their instructions.

From an implementation perspective the straight line code requirement is obtained using DBI. During a program execution, every executed instruction is recorded and then analyzed statically by our prototype.

In this section we present the results we obtained for three cryptographic primitives: the XTEA block cipher, the MD5 hash function and the AES block cipher. For each of them two groups of tests were performed. The first group is designed to extensively evaluate the influence of the compiler and its options on the primitive detection. Given a publicly available reference source code, we compiled it using several compilers and multiple optimization levels. The second group of tests is aimed at assessing the efficiency of our method on *real* cryptographic binary code and to show its resilience to source code variations. To do so we created synthetic samples that use well known cryptographic libraries that were used as distributed in their respective Debian package.

Finally we discuss the performance of our approach.

8.1 Results on Samples Testing

We will try to justify here why our method does not produce any false positive. First, the normalization process preserves the semantics. This is mandatory since semantics discrepancies amplified by the whole set of rewriting rules could have dramatic effects on both the false positive and the false negative ratio. Second, Ullmann algorithm for the subgraph isomorphism problem returns exact solutions and not approximations. Thence when a signature is detected, the code fragment does implement the mechanism described by the signature. Of course we do not deny that if the signature is not distinctive enough, it will appear in the DFG of other algorithms.

XTEA

The first algorithm we have tested is XTEA (a reminder on XTEA and its implementation is given in Appendix C). We used one signature for the encryption algorithm and one signature for the decryption algorithm. They are composed of approximately 500 vertices each and cover the 32 cycles of a classical implementation. We evaluated the resilience to variations in the compilation process by using the C source code given on the Wikipedia page of XTEA [1]. The results are presented in Table 1.

We use three different compilers with four optimization levels ranging from `-o0` (not optimized) to `-o3` (fully optimized). Only two levels have been used for MSVC (Microsoft Visual Studio Compiler), they correspond to the standard settings of the debug and release mode. Our prototype was able to correctly identify the algorithm in every case for both encryption and decryption.

The second testing phase involved three cryptographic libraries: Crypto++ [2], LibTomCrypt [10] and Botan [1].

[1]`http://en.wikipedia.org/w/index.php?title=XTEA&oldid=618892433`

Table 1: XTEA signature detection for different conditions of compilation.

	GCC 4.9.1 (Linux 32-bit)	Clang 3.5.0 (Linux 32-bit)	MSVC 17.00 (Windows 32-bit)
−o0	ok	ok	ok
−o1	ok	ok	-
−o2	ok	ok	ok
−o3	ok	ok	-

The identification was successful for these three libraries. The only difficulty we faced was about the key scheduling. The XTEA key scheduling is fairly simple, thus it can either be performed in an early initialization phase resulting in a round key buffer (as in LibTomCrypt) or it can be directly computed within the main encryption/decryption loop (as in Crypto++ or Botan). This difference cannot be removed by the normalization step, hence it should be dealt with at the signature level. The option we chose was to remove the key scheduling from the signature to keep a unique signature for both versions. Even though the key remains unidentified it is acceptable since at least, the round key buffer (first version) or the key scheduling final operations (second version) are identified as part of the signature input variables.

MD5

The second algorithm we have tested is MD5 (a reminder on MD5 and its implementation is given in Appendix B). For reasons that will soon become apparent we used macro signatures. Let us assume for the moment the following layout for the signatures: one signature for each different round functions and a macro signature that congregates the round signatures to form the 64 rounds of the Feistel network. For the first series of tests we took the C implementation given in the appendices of the RFC [24] and we recompiled it using different compilers and optimization levels. The results are presented in the Table 2.

Table 2: MD5 signature detection for different conditions of compilation.

	GCC 4.9.1 (Linux 32-bit)	Clang 3.5.0 (Linux 32-bit)	MSVC 17.00 (Windows 32-bit)
−o0	ok	ok	Partial
−o1	ok	ok	-
−o2	ok	ok	Partial
−o3	ok	ok	-

The identification of the final macro signature representing the Feistel network was successful except for MSVC. In the case of MSVC not all of the 64 round signatures were correctly detected for the second message chunk. Consequently the final signature, that depends on the correct identification of every round, was not detected for the second message chunk. This problem can be explained in two points that are detailed as follows.

Rotation. Every round function includes a rotation. Because there is no rotation operator in the C language, it has to be implemented using two `shift` and an `or` operator. Some compilers recognize this specific pattern and translate it to the rotation instruction of the x86 instructions set. However MSVC does not always perform this translation and sometimes keeps the expanded form. Due to the optimizations performed later by MSVC and to our own rewrite rules (particularly distributing left shifts over additions for constant operand, refer to Section 5.3) it would have been challenging to design a rewrite rule to detect and replace the expanded form by a single rotation vertex. We choose to tackle this problem at the signature level. It is a perfect example to illustrate the interest of macro signatures. Each round, after the normalization process, can still be implemented in two different ways: either with the rotation operation or with the expanded form. The overall number of combinations for the 64 rounds is 2^{64}. It is obviously impossible to test 2^{64} signatures. Instead, with macro signatures we only have to double the number of round signatures (from 4 to 8).

Constant state. For the first message chunk the state is initialized with constant values. Because of the rewrite rules designed to promote numeric simplification (Section 5.3) operations involving the initial state are merged with surrounding operations. It happens in the case of MSVC for the expanded form of the rotation at the beginning of the second chunk, scrambling the expected signature pattern. This issue is still being investigated and we believe that a more complete common subexpression elimination algorithm (capable of removing common subexpression distributed over several vertices and not only two) might be able to solve this issue.

We based our second testing phase on the following libraries: Crypto++, LibTomCrypt and OpenSSL [3]. The result were successful and we faced none of the previously described difficulties since rotations were always implemented by the x86 instruction and the initial state was never perceived as constant due to the API design which is such that the initialization is performed in another function outside the code fragment.

AES

The last algorithm we tested is the table implementation of AES (a reminder on AES and its implementation is given in Appendix A). We built three signatures, one for each key size. The signatures are the same for encryption and decryption, only the look up tables change. We choose the source code provided by Gladman on his website for the first series of test. The results are presented in the Table 3.

Table 3: AES signature detection for different conditions of compilation.

	GCC 4.9.1 (Linux 32-bit)	Clang 3.5.0 (Linux 32-bit)	MSVC 17.00 (Windows 32-bit)
−o0	ok	ok	ok
−o1	ok	ok	-
−o2	ok	ok	ok
−o3	ok	ok	-

Our prototype was able to successfully detect the signature in every case. For the second testing phase involving well known cryptographic libraries we used Crypto++, LibTomCrypt and Botan. We were only able to test the decryption for the Crypto++ library, since the encryption uses MMX and SSE2 instructions which were not supported by our DFG creation routine at the time when the tests were done. Aside from Crypto++'s encryption algorithm the identification was successful in every cases.

8.2 Performance

The subgraph isomorphism problem is a well known NP-complete problem, but it can be solved efficiently in the majority of the cases encountered in our context. Table 4 presents some of the execution times we obtained with our prototype for the subgraph isomorphism step on a common laptop computer. Each column corresponds to a code fragment (taken from the LibTomCrypt library) and each row corresponds to a signature.

Table 4: Execution times for the signature matching step, on a common laptop computer.

	TEA 753 vertices	MD5 904 vertices	AES_{256} 1687 vertices
TEA 1 cycle (16 vertices)	5ms	< 1ms	< 1ms
TEA 32 cycles (450 vertices)	102ms	< 1ms	< 1ms
MD5 1 round (10 vertices)	< 1ms	9ms	< 1ms
MD5 64 rounds (372 vertices)	< 1ms	26ms	< 1ms
AES 1 round (76 vertices)	< 1ms	< 1ms	442ms
AES 14 rounds (1012 vertices)	< 1ms	< 1ms	2.22s

When the signature was not detected, the cell is colored in gray. We first notice that our prototype quickly (< 1ms) eludes cases where the code fragment does not match the signature. It is a reassuring result, since it will be the most common scenario while testing large databases of signatures with weak fragment selection heuristics. Second, we observe that large signatures (the ones covering several rounds) take significantly more time than smaller ones (covering just one round). Based on that observation, it may be tempting to use macro signatures to reduce the signature's size and thus to achieve better performances. For instance if we split the AES 14-round signature into two signatures: the first one covering one round (approximatively 70 vertices) and the second one linking the 14 rounds together (approximatively 130 vertices), the execution time is reduced: 1.3s instead of 2.3s. However the number of vertices is not the only parameter to influence the execution time. Sometimes larger signatures imply stronger structural constrains between their vertices and the subgraph isomorphism algorithm will be able converge more rapidly towards the solution.

Regarding the normalization step, every rewrite rule is linear with the number of vertices, except for the common subexpression rule which is quadratic (at least for its naive implementation). However as previously stated, the rewrite rules are iteratively applied until a fixed-point is reached. Thus, the execution time also depends on the distance between the original DFG and its normalized version. In practice the execution time of the normalization does not exceed the execution time of the signature matching.

To conclude, despite the theoretical complexity of the underlying algorithm, the execution times we observed on synthetic samples seem acceptable.

9. CONCLUSION

In this paper we presented a new method for symmetric cryptographic algorithms identification in binary programs. To this end we introduced a DFG representation. This representation was first used in a normalization step designed to increase the detection capability, by erasing the peculiarities of each instance of an algorithm. Then, the normalized DFG was compared to the signatures of database using a subgraph isomorphism algorithm. Signatures cover the full length of the algorithm and not only an isolated group of distinctive instructions. Thus our approach does not produce any false positive and the input and output parameters of the cryptographic primitive are automatically identified as part of the signature boundary. We built a prototype and tested it against several synthetic samples covering three cryptographic algorithms: XTEA, MD5 and AES. We showed detailed results proving that our approach was resistant to a large range of compilation conditions. We also provided results on well known cryptographic libraries.

As future work, we plan to cover block cipher modes of operation by leveraging the concept of macro-signature we have presented in this paper and we envisage to extend our approach to automatically identify public key cryptographic algorithms. In order to make our contribution more practical for security auditors to support more algorithms, we aim at automatically generating signatures from reference implementation. Finally we left for future researches the delicate problem of dealing with obfuscated code.

10. ACKNOWLEDGMENTS

The authors are grateful to Pierre Karpman for his help and his useful feedbacks.

11. REFERENCES

[1] Botan. `http://botan.randombit.net/`.
[2] Crypto++. `http://www.cryptopp.com/`.
[3] Openssl. `https://www.openssl.org/`.
[4] A. V. Aho, R. Sethi, and J. D. Ullman. *Compilers: Princiles, Techniques, and Tools.* Addison-Wesley, 1986.
[5] G. Balakrishnan and T. W. Reps. WYSINWYX: what you see is not what you execute. *ACM Trans. Program. Lang. Syst.*, 32(6), 2010.
[6] A. Biryukov. The design of a stream cipher lex. In E. Biham and A. M. Youssef, editors, *Selected Areas in Cryptography*, volume 4356 of *Lecture Notes in Computer Science*, pages 67–75. Springer, 2006.
[7] J. Calvet, J. M. Fernandez, and J.-Y. Marion. Aligot: cryptographic function identification in obfuscated binary programs. In T. Yu, G. Danezis, and V. D. Gligor, editors, *ACM Conference on Computer and Communications Security*, pages 169–182. ACM, 2012.
[8] C. Clavier and K. Gaj, editors. *Cryptographic Hardware and Embedded Systems - CHES 2009, 11th International Workshop, Lausanne, Switzerland, September 6-9, 2009, Proceedings*, volume 5747 of *Lecture Notes in Computer Science.* Springer, 2009.
[9] J. Daemen and V. Rijmen. *The Design of Rijndael: AES - The Advanced Encryption Standard.* Information Security and Cryptography. Springer, 2002.

[10] T. S. Denis. Libtomcrypt. `http://libtom.org/`.

[11] S. Even and Y. Mansour. A construction of a cipher from a single pseudorandom permutation. *J. Cryptology*, 10(3):151–162, 1997.

[12] D. Genkin, A. Shamir, and E. Tromer. RSA key extraction via low-bandwidth acoustic cryptanalysis. In J. A. Garay and R. Gennaro, editors, *Advances in Cryptology - CRYPTO 2014 - 34th Annual Cryptology Conference, Santa Barbara, CA, USA, August 17-21, 2014, Proceedings, Part I*, volume 8616 of *Lecture Notes in Computer Science*, pages 444–461. Springer, 2014.

[13] F. Gröbert, C. Willems, and T. Holz. Automated identification of cryptographic primitives in binary programs. In R. Sommer, D. Balzarotti, and G. Maier, editors, *RAID*, volume 6961 of *Lecture Notes in Computer Science*, pages 41–60. Springer, 2011.

[14] I. Guilfanov. Findcrypt2. `http://www.hexblog.com/?p=28`, February 2006.

[15] S. Halevi, W. E. Hall, and C. S. Jutla. The hash function "fugue". *IACR Cryptology ePrint Archive*, 2014:423, 2014.

[16] M. Hamburg. Accelerating aes with vector permute instructions. In Clavier and Gaj [8], pages 18–32.

[17] E. Käsper and P. Schwabe. Faster and timing-attack resistant aes-gcm. In Clavier and Gaj [8], pages 1–17.

[18] J. Kelsey, B. Schneier, and D. Wagner. Related-key cryptanalysis of 3-way, biham-des, cast, des-x, newdes, rc2, and TEA. In Y. Han, T. Okamoto, and S. Qing, editors, *Information and Communication Security, First International Conference, ICICS'97, Beijing, China, November 11-14, 1997, Proceedings*, volume 1334 of *Lecture Notes in Computer Science*, pages 233–246. Springer, 1997.

[19] W. M. Khoo, A. Mycroft, and R. Anderson. Rendezvous: a search engine for binary code. In T. Zimmermann, M. D. Penta, and S. Kim, editors, *Proceedings of the 10th Working Conference on Mining Software Repositories, MSR '13, San Francisco, CA, USA, May 18-19, 2013*, pages 329–338. IEEE / ACM, 2013.

[20] N. Lutz. Towards revealing attacker's intent by automatically decrypting network traffic. Master's thesis, ETH Zurich, July 2008.

[21] J. Manger. A chosen ciphertext attack on RSA optimal asymmetric encryption padding (OAEP) as standardized in PKCS #1 v2.0. In J. Kilian, editor, *Advances in Cryptology - CRYPTO 2001, 21st Annual International Cryptology Conference, Santa Barbara, California, USA, August 19-23, 2001, Proceedings*, volume 2139 of *Lecture Notes in Computer Science*, pages 230–238. Springer, 2001.

[22] M. Matsui and J. Nakajima. On the power of bitslice implementation on intel core2 processor. In P. Paillier and I. Verbauwhede, editors, *CHES*, volume 4727 of *Lecture Notes in Computer Science*, pages 121–134. Springer, 2007.

[23] P. Q. Nguyen. Can we trust cryptographic software? cryptographic flaws in GNU privacy guard v1.2.3. In C. Cachin and J. Camenisch, editors, *Advances in Cryptology - EUROCRYPT 2004, International Conference on the Theory and Applications of Cryptographic Techniques, Interlaken, Switzerland, May 2-6, 2004, Proceedings*, volume 3027 of *Lecture Notes in Computer Science*, pages 555–570. Springer, 2004.

[24] R. Rivest. The MD5 Message-Digest Algorithm. RFC 1321, April 1992.

[25] A. Sæbjørnsen, J. Willcock, T. Panas, D. J. Quinlan, and Z. Su. Detecting code clones in binary executables. In G. Rothermel and L. K. Dillon, editors, *Proceedings of the Eighteenth International Symposium on Software Testing and Analysis, ISSTA 2009, Chicago, IL, USA, July 19-23, 2009*, pages 117–128. ACM, 2009.

[26] E. Tromer, D. A. Osvik, and A. Shamir. Efficient cache attacks on aes, and countermeasures. *J. Cryptology*, 23(1):37–71, 2010.

[27] J. R. Ullmann. An algorithm for subgraph isomorphism. *J. ACM*, 23(1):31–42, 1976.

[28] S. Vaudenay. Security flaws induced by CBC padding - applications to ssl, ipsec, WTLS ... In L. R. Knudsen, editor, *Advances in Cryptology - EUROCRYPT 2002, International Conference on the Theory and Applications of Cryptographic Techniques, Amsterdam, The Netherlands, April 28 - May 2, 2002, Proceedings*, volume 2332 of *Lecture Notes in Computer Science*, pages 534–546. Springer, 2002.

[29] R. Wang, Y. Shoshitaishvili, C. Kruegel, and G. Vigna. Steal this movie: Automatically bypassing DRM protection in streaming media services. In S. T. King, editor, *USENIX Security*, pages 687–702. USENIX Association, 2013.

[30] X. Wang, N. Zeldovich, M. F. Kaashoek, and A. Solar-Lezama. Towards optimization-safe systems: analyzing the impact of undefined behavior. In M. Kaminsky and M. Dahlin, editors, *ACM SIGOPS 24th Symposium on Operating Systems Principles, SOSP '13, Farmington, PA, USA, November 3-6, 2013*, pages 260–275. ACM, 2013.

[31] Z. Wang, X. Jiang, W. Cui, X. Wang, and M. Grace. Reformat: Automatic reverse engineering of encrypted messages. In M. Backes and P. Ning, editors, *ESORICS*, volume 5789 of *Lecture Notes in Computer Science*, pages 200–215. Springer, 2009.

[32] D. J. Wheeler and R. M. Needham. Tea, a tiny encryption algorithm. In B. Preneel, editor, *Fast Software Encryption: Second International Workshop. Leuven, Belgium, 14-16 December 1994, Proceedings*, volume 1008 of *Lecture Notes in Computer Science*, pages 363–366. Springer, 1994.

[33] T. Xie, F. Liu, and D. Feng. Fast collision attack on MD5. *IACR Cryptology ePrint Archive*, 2013:170, 2013.

[34] R. Zhao, D. Gu, J. Li, and R. Yu. Detection and analysis of cryptographic data inside software. In X. Lai, J. Zhou, and H. Li, editors, *Information Security, 14th International Conference, ISC 2011, Xi'an, China, October 26-29, 2011. Proceedings*, volume 7001 of *Lecture Notes in Computer Science*, pages 182–196. Springer, 2011.

APPENDIX

A. AES IMPLEMENTATION REMINDER

The Advanced Encryption Standard (AES) [9] is a Substitution Permutation Network (SPN) that can be instantiated using three different key bit-lengths: 128, 192, and 256. The 128-bit plaintext initializes the internal state viewed as a 4×4 matrix of bytes seen as elements of the finite field $GF(2^8)$, which is defined via the irreducible polynomial $x^8 + x^4 + x^3 + x + 1$ over $GF(2)$. Depending on the version of the AES, N_r rounds are applied to that state: $N_r = 10$ for AES-128, $N_r = 12$ for AES-192 and $N_r = 14$ for AES-256. Each of the N_r AES round applies four operations to the state matrix (except the last one where the *MixColumns* is omitted):

- *AddRoundKey*: adds a 128-bit subkey to the state.
- *SubBytes*: applies the same 8-bit to 8-bit invertible S-Box S 16 times in parallel on each byte of the state.
- *ShiftRows*: shifts the i-th row left by i positions.
- *MixColumns*: replaces each of the four column C of the state by $M \times C$ where M is a constant 4×4 maximum distance separable matrix over $GF(2^8)$.

After the N_r-th round has been applied, a final subkey is added to the internal state to produce the ciphertext. A key expansion algorithm is used to produce the $N_r + 1$ sub keys required for all AES variants.

From an implementation perspective, the *ShiftRows* and the *MixColumns* can be combined with the *SubBytes* resulting in 4 lookup tables of 1 kilobyte each. We introduce the following notations: A_i is the state at round i, divided in four 32-bits word and T_i $(0 \leq i \leq 3)$ is a function that given a 32-bit word, extracts the ith most significant byte and returns the associated 32-bit word in the ith lookup table. For each full round $(1 \leq i \leq N_r - 1)$, the combination of the *ShiftRows*, *MixColumns* and *SubBytes* can be implemented using the following pseudo code (we have omitted the *AddRoundKey* for brevity):

$$
\begin{aligned}
A_{i+1}[0] &= T_0(A_i[0]) \oplus T_1(A_i[1]) \oplus T_2(A_i[2]) \oplus T_3(A_i[3]) \\
A_{i+1}[1] &= T_0(A_i[1]) \oplus T_1(A_i[2]) \oplus T_2(A_i[3]) \oplus T_3(A_i[0]) \\
A_{i+1}[2] &= T_0(A_i[2]) \oplus T_1(A_i[3]) \oplus T_2(A_i[0]) \oplus T_3(A_i[1]) \\
A_{i+1}[3] &= T_0(A_i[3]) \oplus T_1(A_i[0]) \oplus T_2(A_i[1]) \oplus T_3(A_i[2])
\end{aligned}
$$

This implementation is the most widespread and it is usually referred to as the tables implementation. However, it is not the only way to efficiently implement the AES. Matsui *et al.* [22] and Käsper *et al.* [17] proposed two bitsliced implementations. In bitsliced modes, several blocks are processed in parallel taking advantage of the SMID architecture. Nevertheless bitsliced can only be used in parallel modes of operation (such as the counter mode for instance). Hamburg [16] demonstrated that it is feasible to implement a single block AES encryption with vector permute instructions. Finally recent CPUs have dedicated AES instructions to reach the best performances and the highest security levels. These alternative implementations have been mentioned here for completeness. This work only covers the tables implementation.

B. MD5 IMPLEMENTATION REMINDER

MD5 [24] is a cryptographic hash function that given a message of any size produces a 128-bit hash. The message is divided into 512-bit chunks with a padding being applied to the last chunk. The MD5 algorithm is based on a four-branch Feistel network that operates on a 128-bit state. It is composed of 64 rounds. We use the following notations: f_i is the round function of round i, $\{k_i, 1 \leq i \leq 64\}$ is a set of specific constants, M is an input message chunk and $(A_{1,i}, A_{2,i}, A_{3,i}, A_{4,i})$ is the 128-bit state at the beginning of round i, divided into four words of 32 bits. At each round $(1 \leq i \leq 64)$ the state is updated according to the following equations:

$$
\begin{aligned}
A_{1,i+1} &= A_{4,i} \\
A_{2,i+1} &= f_i(A_{1,i}, A_{2,i}, A_{3,i}, A_{4,i}, M, k_i) \\
A_{3,i+1} &= A_{2,i} \\
A_{4,i+1} &= A_{3,i}
\end{aligned}
$$

The round function f_i contains a boolean function that changes every 16 rounds (4 distinct boolean functions are used for the 64 rounds). Apart from this boolean function, the round function remains the same for every round. Usually the 64 rounds are directly unrolled in the source code. This is for instance the case of the C source code given in the appendix of the RFC).

For the first two series of rounds (round 1 to 16 and round 17 to 32) two different formulas might be used to compute the boolean functions. A different formula that the one provided in the RFC might be used for improved efficiency (it can be implemented using fewer bitwise instructions).

C. TEA & XTEA IMPLEMENTATION REMINDER

Tiny Encryption Algorithm (TEA) [32] is a 64-bit block cipher with a 128-bit key. It is based on a two-branch Feistel network that operates on a 64-bit state. Rounds are usually regrouped in pairs forming cycles. The recommended number of cycles is 32. However TEA suffers from related-key attacks [18]. To solve this weakness Needham and Wheeler proposed an extended version of TEA named XTEA. XTEA has a different key scheduling and a different round function.

Both TEA and XTEA have been designed as small C programs performing simple operations on 32-bit words. The only implementation variation we are aware of concerns the key scheduling. Since the key scheduling is extremely simple some implementations do not compute the round keys separately but they do it directly in each round.

Related Randomness Attacks for Public Key Cryptosystems

Tsz Hon Yuen
Huawei, Singapore
Yuen.Tsz.Hon@huawei.com

Cong Zhang
Rutgers University, NJ, USA
cz200@cs.rutgers.edu

Sherman S. M. Chow
The Chinese University of Hong Kong, Hong Kong
sherman@ie.cuhk.edu.hk

Siu Ming Yiu
The University of Hong Kong
Hong Kong
smyiu@cs.hku.hk

ABSTRACT

We initiate the study of *related randomness attack* in the face of a number of practical attacks in public key cryptography, ranges from active attacks like fault-injection, to passive attacks like software (mis)implementation on choosing random numbers. Our new definitions cover the well-known related-key attacks (RKA) where secret keys are related, and a number of new attacks, namely, related encryption randomness attacks, related signing randomness attacks, and related public key attacks. We provide generic constructions for security against these attacks, which are efficiently built upon normal encryption and signature schemes, leveraging RKA-secure pseudorandom function and generator.

Categories and Subject Descriptors

E.3 [**Data Encryption**]: Public key cryptosystems

Keywords

related-key attack; related-randomness attack; public key encryption; identity-based encryption; signatures

1. INTRODUCTION

Generating randomness is crucial to the security of modern cryptosystems, from generating password salts and producing nonce for authentication, to picking randomness for public key cryptosystems, including generations of public key pairs, encryptions, and signatures.

There exist cryptographically secure pseudorandom number generators (PRNG), but researches show that many programmers fail to understand its importance. Recently, Lenstra *et al.* [16] tested the validity of the assumption that different random coins are used to generate each key. They collected a large number of openly accessible public keys and discovered common primes in 0.2% of RSA public-keys.

ASIA CCS'15, April 14–17, 2015, Singapore, Singapore.

http://dx.doi.org/10.1145/2714576.2714622.

Heninger *et al.* [13] performed a large survey and found that 0.75% of TLS certificates share keys due to insufficient entropy during key generation. They obtained RSA private keys for 0.50% of TLS hosts and 0.03% of SSH hosts, because their public keys shared non-trivial common factors, and DSA private keys for 1.03% of SSH hosts, due to insufficient signature randomness. They also discovered boot-time entropy hole in the Linux PRNG.

For PRNGs themselves, Argyros and Kiayias [1] exploits randomness vulnerabilities in PHP applications, which lacks a built-in cryptographically secure PRNG. Michaelis *et al.* [18] uncovered significant weaknesses of PRNG SecureRandom of several Java runtime libraries including Apache Harmony used in Android, GNU classpath, and Bouncy Castle.

One may argue that security is guaranteed if cryptographically secure PRNG is correctly applied and implemented. However, fault injection [11, 8] can induce modifications in a hardware-stored key, including the key of a pseudorandom function (PRF). The key of the PRF itself may be vulnerable to related-key attack [5]. It is important to consider the security of cryptosystems under such weak randomness.

In this paper, we propose the formal model of *related randomness attack.* Firstly, we consider the randomness used to generate secret keys. This type of attacks is termed as the related-key attack (RKA), and it is well-known for blockciphers, PRF [5], and public key cryptosystems [4]. Secondly, we consider the randomness used to encrypt or sign a message. To the best of the authors' knowledge, related randomness attacks in these two contexts are not previously formalized (except a recent and independent work on public-key encryption [19]). Finally, we consider the related randomness in public key. They appear to be the same as the RKA since the public key is usually a deterministic function of the secret key. However, we show examples that related public keys may induce security problems, without accessing the (related) secret keys. This paper proposes new models to capture and constructions for security against these attacks.

1.1 Related-Key Attacks

Related-key attacks (RKA) are practical against real blockciphers such as AES [9]. Under RKA, an adversary can obtain input-output examples of the blockcipher, not only under the target key K, but also under some related keys. Security against RKA is a popular blockcipher design goal. Bellare *et al.* [4] leverage the RKA security for a suite of high-level primitives in public key cryptosystems. They showed how to construct Φ-RKA secure signatures and Φ-RKA secure public key encryption (PKE) against chosen ciphertext attack from Φ-RKA secure identity-based encryption (IBE).

Recently, Bellare *et al.* [6] proposed a framework to convert normal IBE schemes into Φ-RKA secure IBE schemes, which covers schemes with security in the random oracle model and in the standard model. We make a technical observation that Φ-RKA secure IBE is easy to construct in the random oracle model, where $\Phi = \{\phi^*_\Delta : \Delta \in \mathcal{K}\}$ where $(\mathcal{K}, *)$ is a group under the operation $*$, and $\phi^*_\Delta(K) = K * \Delta$ for all $K \in \mathcal{K}$. This allows a larger class of RKA when compared with affine space, the class of RKA supported by the existing RKA-secure IBE instantiated from Boneh-Franklin IBE [6].

1.2 Related Encryption Randomness Attack

Related key attack is widely studied for different primitives. Also, the problem of fresh randomness is considered in leakage-resilient cryptography. However, there is little concern for the use of related randomness in encryption and signatures. To be more explicit, consider the following example in C++. In most programming textbook, it is suggested to generate a random number by the function *rand()*. The seed of the random number is usually set by the function *srand(time(null))*. So, the seed of two different function calls to *srand* is actually related to the time difference of the function calls. If such randomness is used by the encryptor, then security problems may arise. Even the more complicated seeding algorithm of a number of Java runtime libraries are shown to be error prone [18].

Model. In order to model the related encryption randomness attack on the challenge ciphertext, we have to provide an extra *encryption oracle* which takes a message M, an identity ID and a function ϕ as inputs and outputs $\mathtt{Enc}(\mathsf{mpk}, \mathsf{ID}, M; \phi(R^*))$, where R^* is the randomness used in the challenge ciphertext. Obviously, to rule out simple attack, we do not allow M to be one of the challenge message when ID is the challenge identity and ϕ is the identity function.

We can show that all concrete constructions of RKA-secure IBE proposed by Bellare *et al.* [6] are not secure when this new attack is considered. Take the example of the Boneh-Franklin IBE (with g^α as the master public key), the encryption process using the randomness r is as follows:

$$C_0^* = M^* \cdot \hat{e}(g^\alpha, H(\mathsf{ID}^*))^r, \quad C_1^* = g^r.$$

If the attacker can ask for the encryption of arbitrary message M' for the same ID^* with ϕ being an identity function, he can obtain the same $\hat{e}(g^\alpha, H(\mathsf{ID}^*))^r$ easily and learn M^* encrypted by the challenge ciphertext C^*.

Construction. A simple idea is to use the correlated-input secure hash function (CI-hash) [12] H to generate the randomness used in the original encryption $\mathtt{Enc}$. For example, a new encryption algorithm $\bar{\mathtt{Enc}}$ can be:

$$\bar{\mathtt{Enc}}(\mathsf{mpk}, \mathsf{ID}, M; r) = \mathtt{Enc}(\mathsf{mpk}, \mathsf{ID}, M; H(r||\mathsf{ID}||M)).$$

CI-hash [12] provides *one-wayness*, *unpredictability*, and *pseudorandomness* even if related randomness are used as the hash inputs. Goyal *et al.* showed that fully secure CI-hash can be constructed from RKA-secure PRF [3]. However, the CI-hash is a keyed hash function. The key itself may still suffer from "related public key" attack, since the hash key used in different cryptosystems may be related. CI-hash only considers security of correlated inputs, but not related hash keys. We may need to treat the hash key as some common reference strings and assume that it is honestly generated.

In this paper, instead of using the CI-hash, we use RKA-secure PRF [3] directly. We treat the randomness r as the key of the RKA-secure PRF F and $\mathsf{ID}||M$ as its input[1]. We thus reduce the problem of related encryption randomness ed to the related-key attack of PRF.

1.3 Related Signing Randomness Attack

A signing algorithm can suffer from practical attacks if the signing randomness is chosen from a low entropy source. If a DSA key is used to sign two different messages using the same ephemeral key, then the long-term secret key is immediately computable from the public key and the signatures. Heninger *et al.* [13] recovered DSA private keys for 1.6% of SSH hosts, because of insufficient signature randomness.

Model. The original Φ-RKA security model for signatures allows the adversary to obtain the (related) signature $\mathsf{Sign}(\phi(\mathsf{sk}), M)$ for any $\phi \in \Phi$ and any message M, such that M is not equal to the forgery message or ϕ is not the identity function. Our new model allows an extra level of Φ_r-related signing randomness attack, such that the signing oracle outputs $\mathsf{Sign}(\phi(\mathsf{sk}), M; \phi_r(R))$ for any $\phi_r \in \Phi_r$, where R is a fixed string. It allows the attacker to obtain signatures of related signing randomness.

Construction. Our solution is similar to the Φ-RKA-secure signature scheme by Bellare *et al.* [4]. They used Φ-RKA secure pseudorandom number generator (PRG) to generate the randomness of the key generation algorithm, in order to achieve Φ-RKA security for signatures. We also use the same Φ-RKA secure PRG to generate the signing randomness to achieve related signing randomness security at the same time. The advantage of our scheme is that our scheme has minimal modification to the existing signature schemes, and it is easy to update the existing implementation to cope with the related signing randomness attack.

1.4 Related Public Key Attack

One of the motivations of modeling RKA in public key cryptosystems is to protect against fault injection attack. It can be viewed as an *active* attack when the relation injected into the system is chosen by the attacker. On the other hand, it is possible that one may misuse different cryptographic primitives with related secret and public key pairs. For example, Alice uses the key pairs (x, g^x) for her online banking transaction, uses the key pairs $(x+\Delta, g^{x+\Delta})$ for her email communication, uses the key pairs $(x + 2\Delta, g^{x+2\Delta})$, $(x+3\Delta, g^{x+3\Delta})$ for other applications. Alice may do so voluntarily due to ignorance, or she may not be aware of such relation introduced by the software implementation of choosing key pairs (recall C++ example of the related encryption attack). It can be viewed as a *passive* attack since the attack can be performed by simply observing the relationship between public keys.

Compared to our definition of related public key attack (RPA), Bellare *et al.* [4] also proposed a similar notion of "strong Φ-RKA security", which additionally outputs a related public key during the oracle query of the RKA security

[1]By [12, Theorem 6], it is equivalent to a CI-hash of key $\mathsf{ID}||M$ and input r.

game. However, they claimed that they "*are not aware of this having any application-relevance but wish to highlight it because the constructions possess it*". In this paper, we propose a separation of RPA from RKA by showing a concrete attack on a multiple-recipient encryption scheme [15] with related public keys. This attack does not even require the use of the RKA oracle query.

Model. Modeling the related public key is not trivial. If the relationship between public keys are publicly computable, no oracle is needed and RPA is not properly captured. As a result, the relationship must be computed using the secret key (such that the adversary cannot compute it himself), and yet the computation must be related to the generation of the public key.

We find that the Φ_p-related public key attack model can be applied to *separable* scheme [4], which means that the public key pk is a deterministic function $\mathcal{T}$ of the secret key sk and some public parameters π. In the security model, we additionally allow the adversary to query a key generation oracle with input $\phi_p \in \Phi_p$, to obtain $\mathcal{T}(\pi, \phi_p(\mathsf{sk}))$. This model is applicable to both signatures and encryption schemes.

Construction. Bellare *et al.* proved that a signature scheme can be strengthened to be strong Φ_K-RKA secure by using Φ_K-RKA secure pseudorandom generator (PRG), by assuming either Φ_K is *claw-free*, or the PRG is also secure in the Φ_K*-identity-collision-resistant* model. We want to investigate if one can build a signature scheme from a weaker assumption, if only RPA security is considered. It is useful when the user is confident in defending against active attacks, but still want to avoid the passive RPA attack.

We propose a framework to convert many RPA-insecure signature schemes into one secure in the RPA model. It is simple, efficient, and avoids the claw-free assumption on the leakage function.

ORGANIZATION. We first review some background knowledge in the next section. Section §3 shows that RKA-secure IBE is easy to construct in the random oracle model. In §4, we define the new security model for IBE for this paper, give a generic construction and its security proof. In §5, we extend the related randomness attack to signatures. In §6, we show the related public key attack and give a solution. Finally, we conclude our paper in §7.

2. BACKGROUND

2.1 Pseudorandom Functions

A pseudorandom function (PRF) family is specified by an efficient probabilistic parameter generation algorithm $\mathsf{Gen}_{\mathsf{prf}}$ which takes as input a security parameter 1^λ and outputs the description of a function π including a description of the function's keyspace $\mathcal{K}$, domain $\mathcal{D}$, and range $\mathcal{R}$, i.e., a PRF function family $F : \mathcal{K} \times \mathcal{D} \to \mathcal{R}$ takes a key $k \in \mathcal{K}$ and input $x \in \mathcal{D}$ and returns an output $F(k, x) \in \mathcal{R}$.

The Φ-RKA-security of pseudorandom function [4] is defined by the security game with an adversary $\mathcal{A}$. Firstly, the challenger runs $\pi \leftarrow \mathsf{Gen}_{\mathsf{prf}}$, picks a random key $k \in \mathcal{K}$ and a random bit $b \in \{0, 1\}$. The challenger gives π to the adversary. The adversary $\mathcal{A}$ asks the oracle $RKFn(\phi, x)$ for $\phi \in \Phi$ and $x \in \mathcal{D}$. If $b = 1$, the oracle returns $F(\phi(k), x)$. If $b = 0$, the oracle picks T uniformly at random from $\mathcal{R}$ and returns T. Note that if $(\phi(k), x)$ is the same as a certain oracle query in the past, the oracle always returns the same T. Finally, $\mathcal{A}$ returns a guess bit b' and wins if $b = b'$. The advantage of $\mathcal{A}$ is the probability of $\mathcal{A}$ wins minus 1/2.

2.2 Pseudorandom Generators

Pseudorandom Generators (PRG) is specified by a parameter generation algorithm $\mathtt{Setup}(1^\lambda)$ which outputs param; a key generation algorithm $\mathcal{K}(\mathsf{param})$ which outputs a key K; an evaluation algorithm $\mathcal{G}(K)$ which outputs T, with $t = |T|$ is publicly known.

The Φ-RKA security of PRG [4] is defined by the following security game with an adversary $\mathcal{A}$. Firstly, the challenger runs $\mathsf{param} \leftarrow \mathtt{Setup}(1^\lambda)$, picks a random key $K \in \mathcal{K}(\mathsf{param})$ and a random bit $b \in \{0, 1\}$. The challenger gives param to the adversary. The adversary $\mathcal{A}$ ask the oracle $RKGen(\phi)$ where $\phi \in \Phi$. If $b = 1$, the oracle returns $\mathcal{G}(\phi(K))$. If $b = 0$, the oracle picks T uniformly random from $\{0, 1\}^t$ and returns T. Note that if the value of $\phi(K)$ is the same as some past oracle queries, the oracle always return the same T. Finally, $\mathcal{A}$ returns a guess bit b' and wins if $b = b'$. The advantage of $\mathcal{A}$ is the probability of $\mathcal{A}$ wins minus 1/2.

The Φ-identity-collision-resistance (ICR) security of PRG defined by the following security game with an adversary $\mathcal{A}$. Firstly, the challenger runs $\mathsf{param} \leftarrow \mathtt{Setup}(1^\lambda)$, picks a random key $K \in \mathcal{K}(\mathsf{param})$ and calculates $T_0 = \mathcal{G}(K)$. The challenger gives param to the adversary. The adversary $\mathcal{A}$ ask the oracle $RKGen(\phi)$ where $\phi \in \Phi$. The oracle returns $S = \mathcal{G}(\phi(K))$. Finally, $\mathcal{A}$ wins if there exists an oracle query with input ϕ such that $K' = \phi(K) \neq K$ and $S = T_0$. The advantage of $\mathcal{A}$ is the probability of $\mathcal{A}$ wins.

3. RKA-SECURE IBE IN THE ROM

We make the technical observation that Φ-RKA secure identity-based encryption (IBE) is easy to construct in the random oracle model. We observe that Lucks [17] showed that it is easy to strengthen a given PRF to be a Φ-RKA one by hashing the key with a random oracle before use, where $\Phi = \{\phi^*_\Delta : \Delta \in \mathcal{K}\}$, $(\mathcal{K}, *)$ is a group under the operation $*$, and $\phi^*_\Delta(K) = K * \Delta$ for all $K \in \mathcal{K}$. Since Bellare *et al.* [4] showed Φ-RKA secure IBE, CCA-secure PKE and signatures can be constructed from a Φ-RKA secure PRF and an instance of IBE with traditional security, CCA-secure PKE, and signatures respectively. Therefore, we observe that Φ-RKA secure IBE can also be constructed by hashing the master secret key with a random oracle before use.

There are two advantages of the our approach. Firstly, applying the existing transformation [6] on Boneh-Franklin IBE is slightly less efficient since the hash function takes a longer input (hashing the identity and the master public key). Secondly, our method allows Φ to be a large group-induced class when compared with linear relation [6].

4. RELATED ENCRYPTION RANDOMNESS

We showed a related encryption randomness attack on RKA-secure IBE [6] in Section 1 for the same identity. Even if the related randomness is used to encrypt other messages to another identity, it may still help the attacker. Here we show a stronger attack against the Boneh-Boyen IBE [10], with (α, β) as the master secret key. The encryption of a challenge message M^* to the challenge identity ID^*

$$C^*_0 = M^* \cdot \hat{e}(g, g)^r, \quad C^*_1 = g^{r(\alpha + \mathsf{ID}^*)}, \quad C^*_2 = g^{\beta r}.$$

If the attacker can ask for the encryption of arbitrary message M' and identity $\mathsf{ID} \neq \mathsf{ID}^*$, with $\phi(r) = Ar+B$ (an affine space related randomness), he can obtain $\hat{e}(g,g)^r$ easily and win the security game.

4.1 Related Key & Randomness Attack for IBE

An IBE scheme consists of four probabilistic polynomial-time (PPT) algorithms:

1. $\mathtt{Setup}$: On input a security parameter 1^λ, it generates a master public key mpk and a master secret key msk.
2. $\mathtt{Ext}$: On input msk and an identity ID from an identity space $\mathcal{I}$, it outputs an identity-based secret key $\mathsf{sk}_{\mathsf{ID}}$.
3. $\mathtt{Enc}$: On input $\mathsf{mpk}, \mathsf{ID}$ and a message M from a message space $\mathcal{M}$, it outputs a ciphertext $\mathfrak{C}$.
4. $\mathtt{Dec}$: On input $\mathsf{sk}_{\mathsf{ID}}$, and $\mathfrak{C}$, it outputs a message M or $\perp$ symbolizing the failure of decryption.

Correctness. $\forall M \in \mathcal{M}$ and $\forall \mathsf{ID} \in \mathcal{I}$, $M \leftarrow \mathtt{Dec}(\mathsf{sk}_{\mathsf{ID}}, \mathtt{Enc}(\mathsf{mpk}, \mathsf{ID}, M))$, where $(\mathsf{mpk}, \mathsf{msk}) \leftarrow \mathtt{Setup}(1^\lambda)$, $\mathsf{sk}_{\mathsf{ID}} \leftarrow \mathtt{Ext}(\mathsf{msk}, \mathsf{ID})$.

We consider the following indistinguishability game against adaptive chosen identity and chosen plaintext attacks (IND-ID-CPA) for semantic security with related key and randomness attack. The game (Φ_k, Φ_r)-RKRA-IBE is defined as follows.

1. Setup. The challenger runs $(\mathsf{mpk}, \mathsf{msk}) \leftarrow \mathtt{Setup}(1^\lambda)$ and gives mpk to the adversary $\mathcal{A}$.
2. Query 1. The following oracles can be queried by $\mathcal{A}$:
   - Extraction Oracle $\mathcal{KEO}(\mathsf{ID}, \phi)$: On input $\mathsf{ID} \in \mathcal{I}, \phi \in \Phi_k$, it outputs $\mathtt{Ext}(\phi(\mathsf{msk}), \mathsf{ID})$.
3. Challenge. $\mathcal{A}$ sends two messages $M_0, M_1 \in \mathcal{M}$ and an identity $\mathsf{ID}^* \in \mathcal{I}$ to the challenger. The challenger picks a random bit b' and computes $\mathfrak{C}^* \leftarrow \mathtt{Enc}(\mathsf{mpk}, \mathsf{ID}^*, M_{b'}; R^*)$ using a randomness R^*. The challenger sends $\mathfrak{C}^*$ to $\mathcal{A}$.
4. Query 2. The following oracles can be queried by $\mathcal{A}$:
   - Extraction Oracle $\mathcal{KEO}(\mathsf{ID}, \phi)$: On input $\mathsf{ID} \in \mathcal{I}, \phi \in \Phi_k$, it outputs $\mathtt{Ext}(\phi(\mathsf{msk}), \mathsf{ID})$.
   - Encryption Oracle $\mathcal{EO}(M, \phi, \mathsf{ID})$: On input a message $M, \phi \in \Phi_r$ and an identity ID, it returns $\mathtt{Enc}(\mathsf{mpk}, \mathsf{ID}, M; \phi(R^*))$.
5. Output. $\mathcal{A}$ returns a guess b^* of b'.

$\mathcal{A}$ wins the game if $b' = b^*$, there was no query to $\mathcal{KEO}$ with input $\mathsf{ID} = \mathsf{ID}^*$ and ϕ is an identity map, and no query to $\mathcal{EO}$ with input $M = M_0^*$ or M_1^*, $\mathsf{ID} = \mathsf{ID}^*$ and ϕ is an identity map. The advantage of $\mathcal{A}$ is $\left|\Pr[\mathcal{A} \text{ wins}] - \frac{1}{2}\right|$.

An IBE scheme is (t, ϵ)-(Φ_k, Φ_r)-RKRA IND-ID-CPA secure if there is no t-time attacker $\mathcal{A}$ with advantage ϵ in the (Φ_k, Φ_r)-RKRA-IBE game above.

If there is no related randomness attack, then the attacker cannot query the encryption oracle. In this case, we say that an IBE scheme is (t, ϵ)-Φ_k-RKA (related key attack) IND-ID-CPA secure if there is no t-time attacker $\mathcal{A}$ with advantage ϵ in the $(\Phi_k, \emptyset)$-RKRA-IBE game above.

If there is no related-key attack, then the attacker cannot query the extraction oracle. In this case, we say that an IBE scheme is (t, ϵ)-Φ_r-RRA (related encryption randomness attack) IND-ID-CPA secure if there is no t-time attacker $\mathcal{A}$ with advantage ϵ in the $(\emptyset, \Phi_r)$-RKRA-IBE game above.

A similar definition for public key encryption (PKE) is given in Appendix A for completeness.

4.2 Generic Construction

We propose the use RKA-secure pseudorandom function (PRF) [3] to handle the encryption randomness. We treat the randomness r as the key of the RKA-secure PRF F and $\mathsf{ID}||M$ as its input. The identity and the message are treated as the input of the PRF, to prevent the attack we have shown against Boneh-Boyen IBE. The problem of related encryption randomness is reduced to the related-key attack of PRF.

Suppose $\Pi = (\mathtt{Setup}, \mathtt{Ext}, \mathtt{Enc}, \mathtt{Dec})$ is a IND-ID-CPA secure IBE scheme with security parameter 1^λ, the identity space $\mathcal{I}$, the message space $\mathcal{M}$ and the randomness space used in encryption $\mathcal{R}$. Suppose $F : \mathcal{K} \times (\mathcal{I}||\mathcal{M}) \rightarrow \mathcal{R}$ is a Φ-RKA secure PRF with generator $\mathsf{Gen}_{\mathsf{prf}}$. Define

- $\hat{\mathtt{Setup}}(1^\lambda)$: It runs $(\mathsf{mpk}, \mathsf{msk}) \leftarrow \mathtt{Setup}(1^\lambda)$ and runs $\mathsf{Gen}_{\mathsf{prf}}(1^\lambda)$ to get $F : \mathcal{K} \times \mathcal{D} \rightarrow \mathcal{R}$, where $\mathcal{D}$ is the identity space $\mathcal{I}$ concatenates with the message space $\mathcal{M}$. It outputs $\hat{\mathsf{mpk}} = (\mathsf{mpk}, F)$ and msk.
- $\hat{\mathtt{Enc}}(\mathsf{mpk}, \mathsf{ID}, M)$: It picks a random key $r \in \mathcal{K}$ and returns $\mathtt{Enc}(\mathsf{mpk}, \mathsf{ID}, M; F(r, \mathsf{ID}||M))$.

Then we obtain an RRA-secure IBE scheme $\hat{\Pi} = (\hat{\mathtt{Setup}}, \mathtt{Ext}, \hat{\mathtt{Enc}}, \mathtt{Dec})$.

THEOREM 1. *The IBE scheme $\hat{\Pi}$ is Φ-RRA IND-ID-CPA secure if Π is IND-ID-CPA secure and $\mathcal{F}$ is a Φ-RKA secure PRF.*

PROOF. We can prove the theorem by hybrid security games. The main part of the proof is to show statistical indistinguishability between these games. The output of each games consists of the view of the adversary $\mathcal{A}$ as well as a bit b chosen by the challenger $\mathcal{C}$ representing its choice of which message M_0^*, M_1^* to encrypt. Denote Game 0 to be the original Φ-RRA security game. Denote Game 1 to be the same as the Game 0, except that for the encryption oracle query and the challenge phase, it outputs $\hat{\mathtt{Enc}}(\mathsf{mpk}, \mathsf{ID}, M; r')$ where r' is randomly chosen from $\mathcal{R}$.

LEMMA 1. *No PPT adversary can distinguish* Game *1 and* Game *0 if $\mathcal{F}$ is a Φ-RKA secure PRF.*

PROOF. Suppose the simulator $\mathcal{B}$ is given a Φ-RKA PRF family F from its challenger $\mathcal{C}$. For the encryption oracle query with input (ID, M, ϕ):

- It asks its challenger $\mathcal{C}$ for the oracle $RKFn(\phi, \mathsf{ID}||M)$ and obtains $\bar{r}$. It outputs $\hat{\mathtt{Enc}}(\mathsf{mpk}, \mathsf{ID}, M; \bar{r})$.

For the challenge phase, $\mathcal{B}$ picks a random bit b, sets ϕ as an identity map and asks its challenger $\mathcal{C}$ for the oracle $RKFn(\phi, \mathsf{ID}^*||M_b^*)$. $\mathcal{B}$ obtains r^* and outputs $C^* \leftarrow \hat{\mathtt{Enc}}(\mathsf{mpk}, \mathsf{ID}^*, M_b^*; r^*)$.

It is easy to see that if the challenger $\mathcal{C}$'s choice of $b = 1$, then $\mathcal{B}$ simulates Game 0; if the challenger $\mathcal{C}$'s choice of $b = 0$, then $\mathcal{B}$ simulates Game 1. Therefore Game 1 is indistinguishable from Game 0 if F is a Φ-RKA secure PRF. $\square$

LEMMA 2. *The advantage of $\mathcal{A}$ in* Game 1 *is negligible if* Π *is IND-ID-CPA secure.*

PROOF. Observe that in Game 1, all oracle outputs are not related to r^*. Therefore, the encryption oracle does not help the attacker to win the game. The rest of the simulation is the same as the underlying IBE scheme. Thus, the advantage of $\mathcal{A}$ in Game 1 is negligible if Π is IND-ID-CPA secure. □

Combining the above lemmas, the IBE scheme $\hat{\Pi}$ is Φ-RRA IND-ID-CPA secure. □

Extension. Our result can be applied to different areas. Similarly, we can prove the following lemma for RKRA-secure IBE.

LEMMA 3. *The IBE scheme* $\hat{\Pi}$ *is* (Φ_k, Φ_r)*-RKRA IND-ID-CPA secure if* Π *is* Φ_k*-RKA IND-ID-CPA secure and* $\mathcal{F}$ *is a* Φ_r*-RKA secure PRF.*

It can also been easily shown that the theorem still holds for CCA security.

5. RELATED SIGNING RANDOMNESS

For the case of signatures, both the secret key and the singing randomness are chosen by the signer. The adversary only needs to obtain leakage from a single party. For some signature schemes, anyone can re-randomize a signature σ for a message M into another signature σ' for M, and hence it is legitimate to generate a signature with related randomness for the same message. On the other hand, it is not possible for many signature schemes, such as signatures from the Fiat-Shamir transformation.

For the related signing randomness attack, we should avoid the attacker to generate a new signature for *different* messages, even if we know certain ways to obtain related randomness. We first consider the existential unforgeability against related key and related (signing) randomness attack, such that the attacker cannot re-randomize a signature for a different message.

5.1 Related Randomness Attack for Signatures

A signature scheme consists of four PPT algorithms:

1. $\mathtt{Setup}$: On input a security parameter 1^λ, it generates a system parameter param.

2. $\mathtt{Gen}$: On input param, it generates a public key pk and a secret key sk.

3. $\mathtt{Sign}$: On input $\mathsf{param}, \mathsf{sk}$ and a message M from a message space $\mathcal{M}$, it outputs a signature σ.

4. $\mathtt{Verify}$: On input $\mathsf{param}, \mathsf{pk}$, M and σ, it outputs 1 for valid signature or 0 otherwise.

Correctness. $\forall M \in \mathcal{M}$, $1 \leftarrow \mathtt{Verify}(\mathsf{param}, \mathsf{pk}, M, \mathtt{Sign}(\mathsf{param}, \mathsf{sk}, M))$, where $(\mathsf{pk}, \mathsf{sk}) \leftarrow \mathtt{Gen}(\mathsf{param})$, $\mathsf{param} \leftarrow \mathtt{Setup}(1^\lambda)$.

We consider the following unforgeability game against chosen message attacks (EUF-CMA) for security with related-key, related signing randomness attack. The game (Φ_k, Φ_r)-RKRA-Sig is defined as follows.

1. Setup. The challenger runs $\mathsf{param} \leftarrow \mathtt{Setup}(1^\lambda)$, $(\mathsf{pk}, \mathsf{sk}) \leftarrow \mathtt{Gen}(\mathsf{param})$ and gives $\mathsf{param}, \mathsf{pk}$ to the adversary $\mathcal{A}$. The challenger samples the signing randomness r.

2. Query 1. The following oracles can be queried by $\mathcal{A}$:

   - Signing Oracle $\mathcal{SO}(M, \phi_k, \phi_r)$: On input a message M, a key leakage $\phi_k \in \Phi_k$ and a randomness leakage $\phi_r \in \Phi_r$, it returns a signature $\sigma \leftarrow \mathtt{Sign}(\mathsf{param}, \phi_k(\mathsf{sk}), M; \phi_r(r))$.

3. Output. $\mathcal{A}$ returns a signature σ^* on a message M^*.

$\mathcal{A}$ wins the game if $1 \leftarrow \mathtt{Verify}(\mathsf{param}, \mathsf{pk}, M^*, \sigma^*)$, there was no query to $\mathcal{SO}$ with input message M^* and $\phi_k(\mathsf{sk}) = \mathsf{sk}$. The advantage of $\mathcal{A}$ is $\Pr[\mathcal{A} \text{ wins}]$.

A signature scheme is (t, ϵ)-(Φ_k, Φ_r)-RKRA EUF-CMA secure if there is no t-time attacker $\mathcal{A}$ with advantage ϵ in the (Φ_k, Φ_r)-RKRA-Sig game above.

5.2 Generic Construction

We give a generic construction of RKRA EUF-CMA secure signature scheme from RKA-secure pseudorandom generator (PRG). The construction is similar to the RKA EUF-CMA secure signature scheme by Bellare *et al.* [4]. Suppose $(\mathtt{Setup}, \mathtt{Gen}, \mathtt{Sign}, \mathtt{Verify})$ be a EUF-CMA secure signature scheme, and $(\mathtt{Setup}', \mathcal{K}, \mathcal{G})$ be an RKA-secure PRG. We give our new construction as follows.

- $\hat{\mathtt{Setup}}(1^\lambda)$: It runs $\mathsf{param} \leftarrow \mathtt{Setup}(1^\lambda)$ and $\mathsf{param}' \leftarrow \mathtt{Setup}'(1^\lambda)$, and outputs $\hat{\mathsf{param}} = \mathsf{param}||\mathsf{param}'$.

- $\hat{\mathtt{Gen}}(\hat{\mathsf{param}})$: It samples a random $K \leftarrow \mathcal{K}(\mathsf{param}')$ and runs $(\mathsf{pk}, \mathsf{sk}) \leftarrow \mathtt{Gen}(\mathsf{param}; \mathcal{G}(K))$. It outputs $\hat{\mathsf{pk}} = \mathsf{pk}$ and $\hat{\mathsf{sk}} = K$.

- $\hat{\mathtt{Sign}}(\hat{\mathsf{param}}, K, M)$: It runs $(\mathsf{pk}, \mathsf{sk}) \leftarrow \mathtt{Gen}(\mathsf{param}; \mathcal{G}(K))$ and samples a random $R \leftarrow \mathcal{K}(\mathsf{param}')$. It outputs $\sigma = \hat{\mathtt{Sign}}(\mathsf{param}, \mathsf{sk}, M; \mathcal{G}(R))$.

- $\hat{\mathtt{Verify}}(\hat{\mathsf{param}}, \mathsf{pk}, M, \sigma)$: It outputs the result of $\mathtt{Verify}$ $(\mathsf{param}, \mathsf{pk}, M, \sigma)$.

THEOREM 2. *The above signature scheme is* $(\Phi_k \cup \Phi_c, \Phi_r)$*-RKRA EUF-CMA secure, if the underlying signature is EUF-CMA secure, the underlying PRG is* $(\Phi_r \cup \Phi_k)$*-RKA secure and* Φ_k*-ICR secure; and* Φ_c *is the class of constant related-key deriving functions associated to* Φ_k.

PROOF. We prove the security of our scheme by a sequence of security games:

- Game_0 is the original $(\Phi_k \cup \Phi_c, \Phi_r)$-RKRA EUF-CMA security game.

- Game_1 is the same as Game_0, except that for each signing oracle query, the simulator runs $(\mathsf{pk}, \mathsf{sk}) \leftarrow \mathtt{Gen}(\mathsf{param}; \mathcal{G}(K))$ and picks R' uniformly random from the range of $\mathcal{G}$. It returns $\sigma = \hat{\mathtt{Sign}}(\mathsf{param}, \mathsf{sk}, M; R')$.

We have to show that the advantage of $\mathcal{A}$ in Game_1 and Game_0 differs by ϵ, where ϵ is the probability of breaking the Φ_r-RKA security of the underlying PRG. Suppose the simulator $\mathcal{B}$ is given param' from the challenger of the Φ_r-RKA security game. It runs $\mathsf{param} \leftarrow \mathtt{Setup}(1^\lambda)$, samples a random $K \leftarrow \mathcal{K}(\mathsf{param}')$ and runs $(\mathsf{pk}, \mathsf{sk}) \leftarrow \mathtt{Gen}(\mathsf{param}; \mathcal{G}(K))$. It sets $\hat{\mathsf{sk}} = K$, and outputs ($\hat{\mathsf{param}} = \mathsf{param}||\mathsf{param}'$, $\hat{\mathsf{pk}} = \mathsf{pk}$) to the adversary $\mathcal{A}$.

For the signing oracle queries with input (M, ϕ_k, ϕ_r), $\mathcal{B}$ runs $(\mathsf{pk}', \mathsf{sk}') \leftarrow \mathtt{Gen}(\mathsf{param}; \mathcal{G}(\phi_k(K)))$ and queries the $\mathsf{GenOracle}(\phi_r)$ to its challenger. The challenger returns a value T which is either equal to $\mathcal{G}(\phi_r(R))$ or a uniformly random number from the range of $\mathcal{G}$. Then $\mathcal{B}$ outputs $\sigma = \hat{\mathtt{Sign}}(\mathsf{param}, \mathsf{sk}', M; T)$ and sends to $\mathcal{A}$.

Therefore if the adversary can distinguish between Game_0 and Game_1, then $\mathcal{B}$ can answer $T = \phi_r(R)$ or T is a random number, which breaks the Φ_r-RKA security of the underlying PRG.

Finally, observe that Game_1 is the same as the $(\Phi_k \cup \Phi_c)$-RKA EUF-CMA security game. The adversary cannot win with a non-negligible probability if the underlying signature is EUF-CMA secure, the underlying PRG is Φ_k-RKA secure and Φ_k-ICR secure, where Φ_c is the class of constant related-key deriving functions associated to Φ_k. □

6. RELATED PUBLIC KEY ATTACK

The related public key attack (RPA) seems to be a natural extension of RKA. In this section, we will propose a security model to capture the RPA. Bellare *et al.* [4] considered a similar model with combined RPA with RKA, but they did not show any relevant attack. We will demonstrate two concrete attacks on encryption and signature schemes with related public keys. In fact, our attacks do not require the oracles provided by the RKA, and hence it shows the separation between the RKA and the RPA models.

6.1 Examples of Related Public Key Attack

We demonstrate two practical related public key attacks, one for encryption and one for signatures.

Multi-Recipient Encryption. Bellare *et al.* [2] showed that randomness re-use is secure for *multi-recipient encryption* schemes. It can also be viewed as a special case of *related encryption randomness* security, where the relation is an identity map. Their security model rules out the *rouge-key* attack, where an adversary registers public keys created as a function of other public keys. They assume that the adversary cannot register a public key without knowing the corresponding secret key. However, if the public keys of two or more recipients are related (e.g. Bob encrypts an email to multiple email accounts of Alice using different public keys, but the public keys are actually related), the rouge-key attack also succeeds. It is because such relation is generated by an legitimate user knowing the secret key. One example of rouge-key attack on ElGamal-based scheme [15] was presented [2, Section 4]. We demonstrate it in the context of related public key attack as follows.

Scheme. Suppose a sender wants to send message M_i to receiver i encrypted under the latter's ElGamal public key g^{x_i}, for $i \in [1, n]$. Kurosawa [15] considered picking just one r at random, setting $C_i = (g^r, g^{x_i r} \cdot M_i)$ and send C_i to receiver i for all $i \in [1, n]$. This scheme is known as the ElGamal-based multi-recipient encryption.

Attack. Now suppose the public keys of some receivers are related, e.g. g^x, g^{2x}, g^{3x}. Thus the adversary sees the three corresponding ciphertexts $(g^r, g^{xr} \cdot M_1), (g^r, g^{2xr} \cdot M_2), (g^r, g^{3xr} \cdot M_3)$. From them it can compute $[g^{rx} \cdot M_1] \cdot [g^{2rx} \cdot M_2] \cdot [g^{3rx} \cdot M_3]^{-1} = M_1 M_2 / M_3$. If two plaintexts are known, the third one can be calculated easily without using any related secret key during the calculation. This scheme is not secure in this sense if there is related public key.

Ring Signatures. Related public key attack also applies to the *ring signatures*. We can show that if the attacker obtains a ring signature with respect to $(pk_1, pk_2, \ldots, pk_n)$, the attacker can convert it into a signature with respect to $(\phi(pk_1), pk_2, \ldots, pk_n)$, where $\phi(pk_1)$ is a related public key.

Scheme. Consider the ring signature scheme [14] using the classic Schnorr signatures. For simplicity, we consider the two users case. Denote g to be a generator of a multiplicative subgroup of $\mathbb{Z}_p^*$ with order q and $H : \{0,1\}^* \to \mathbb{Z}_q$ is a collision resistant hash function. Suppose Alice and Bob have key pairs $(x_1, y_1 = g^{x_1})$ and $(x_2, y_2 = g^{x_2})$ respectively. To sign a message M, Alice randomly picks $r, r_1 \in \mathbb{Z}_q^*$ and computes

$$R_2 = g^{r_2}, \quad R_1 = g^r y_2^{-H(M,R_2)}, \quad \sigma = r + r_2 + x_1 H(M, R_1).$$

The ring signature is $(R_1, R_2, h_1, h_2, \sigma)$, where $h_i = H(M, R_i)$ for $i = 1, 2$. The verification algorithm is to check if h_1, h_2 are correct hash outputs, and if

$$R_1 R_2 y_1^{h_1} y_2^{h_2} = g^{\sigma}.$$

Attack. Suppose the attacker issues a typical query for the signing oracle of x_1 to sign M with public keys (y_1, y_2) and receives $(R_1, R_2, h_1, h_2, \sigma)$. The attacker then picks Δ and asks the KeyGen Oracle to obtain y_3, which is a public key related to y_2 via the relation $y_3 = g^{x_2+\Delta}$. Then the attacker can calculate

$$\sigma' = \sigma - \Delta h_2.$$

$(R_1, R_2, h_1, h_2, \sigma')$ is a valid signature for the message M and public keys (y_1, y_3) since

$$R_1 R_2 y_1^{h_1} y_3^{h_2} = R_1 R_2 y_1^{h_1} (y_2 g^{\Delta})^{h_2} = g^{\sigma + h_2 \Delta} = g^{\sigma'}.$$

A similar attack has been shown to illustrate the difference between fixed-ring attack and chosen-subring attack in ring signatures [7]. Our related public key is a special kind of *adversarially-chosen key* in the chosen-subring attack, yet the adversary does not know the corresponding secret key in our model.

6.2 Modeling Related Public Key Attack

We propose the security model of related public key attack (RPA). In the usual syntax of public key cryptosystems, the public and secret keys are generated together by the algorithm $\mathsf{KeyGen}(1^\lambda)$. In most practical schemes, the secret key is usually chosen first and the public key is a deterministic function of the secret key and some public parameters. A scheme is called *separable* [4] if there exists algorithms:

- $\mathsf{Setup}(1^\lambda)$: It is a probabilistic algorithm which outputs the public parameters π.
- $\mathsf{KeyGen}(\pi)$: It is a probabilistic algorithm which outputs a key pair $(\mathsf{pk}, \mathsf{sk})$, where $\mathsf{pk} = \mathcal{T}(\pi, \mathsf{sk})$ and $\mathcal{T}$ is a deterministic algorithm.

We only consider separable schemes in the rest of this section.

In the security game with Φ_P-RPA security for separable schemes, we additionally allow the adversary to query a KeyGen Oracle:

- KeyGen Oracle(ϕ): On input a function $\phi \in \Phi_P$, it returns $\hat{\mathsf{pk}} = \mathcal{T}(\pi, \phi(\mathsf{sk}))$.

The adversary can win the game not only by attacking on the (challenge) public key pk, but also on any $\hat{\mathsf{pk}}$ returned by the KeyGen Oracle.

Comparison between RPA and Strong Φ_K-RKA. Bellare *et al.* [4] proposed a similar notion of strong Φ_K-RKA security for signatures and PKE. In their security model, there is only a signing oracle with input a message M and $\phi \in \Phi_K$. The oracle outputs $\sigma \leftarrow \mathsf{Sign}(\phi(\mathsf{sk}), M)$ and $\hat{\mathsf{pk}} = \mathcal{T}(\pi, \phi(\mathsf{sk}))$. The adversary wins the game if the forgery signature is valid for any $(M, \hat{\mathsf{pk}})$ used by the oracle. Conceptually, they embed our KeyGen Oracle into the signing oracle for RKA security.

Bellare *et al.* [4] also proposed analogous security definitions for CCA-secure PKE. The decryption oracle outputs a related public key $\hat{\mathsf{pk}}$ and the decryption under the related secret key $\phi(\mathsf{sk})$. In the challenge phase, the adversary can ask for the challenge ciphertext encrypted for some $\hat{\mathsf{pk}}$.

We note that our model is more general than the strong Φ_K-RKA security [4]. It is because the attacker may obtain related public keys (which is a passive attack by just observing available public keys) but cannot launch related (secret) key attack (which is an active attack, such as fault injection). It is not necessary to consider both attacks together. Therefore, our model provides a separation for different attacks and provides better classification.

Consider the attack on multi-recipient encryption schemes in §6.1. The successful attacker only requires the formation of related public keys and the knowledge of some plaintexts. The former is captured by our KeyGen Oracle, while the latter is the challenge message chosen by the attacker. Therefore the attack in §6.1 is captured in our model, but not by the strong Φ_K-RKA security [4].

6.3 Generic Construction

Let $\Pi' = (\mathsf{Setup}', \mathsf{KeyGen}', \mathsf{Sign}', \mathsf{Verify}')$ be a signature scheme which is not RPA secure in the sense that, given a signature σ on a message m for parameter π and public key pk, and a group induced operation $\phi \in \Phi$, there exists a polynomial time algorithm to find $\bar{\sigma}$ such that

$$\mathsf{Verify}'(\pi, \mathsf{pk}, \sigma, M) = \mathsf{Verify}'(\pi, \mathcal{T}(\pi, \phi(\mathsf{sk})), \bar{\sigma}, M).$$

We call such scheme Φ-*RPA fix-message insecure.*

We find that we can achieve RPA security for Φ-RPA fix-message insecure signatures if the underlying scheme has a property called Φ-*public key malleability.* It means that for a separable scheme with parameter π, public key pk, secret key sk, and $\phi \in \Phi$, there exists a polynomial time algorithm to find $\bar{\mathsf{pk}}$ such that

$$\bar{\mathsf{pk}} = \mathcal{T}(\pi, \phi(\mathsf{sk})).$$

Many existing key systems have the public key malleability property. For example, consider the discrete logarithm based system with $\mathsf{sk} = x$ and $\mathsf{pk} = g^x$, public key malleability holds for affine space transformation for Φ. Let $\phi(x) = Ax + B$ for some $A, B \in \mathbb{Z}$. Then it is easy to compute g^{Ax+B}.

We start with the Φ-RPA fix-message insecure secure signature scheme $\Pi' = (\mathsf{Setup}', \mathsf{KeyGen}', \mathsf{Sign}', \mathsf{Verify}')$ with Φ-public key malleability. We now build another signature scheme Π as follows:

- Setup: On input the security parameter 1^λ, it outputs $\pi \leftarrow \mathsf{Setup}'(1^\lambda)$.
- KeyGen: On input param, it outputs $(\mathsf{pk}, \mathsf{sk}) \leftarrow \mathsf{KeyGen}'(\pi)$.
- Sign: On input a message M, sk and π, returns $\sigma \leftarrow \mathsf{Sign}'(\pi, \mathsf{sk}, M||\mathsf{pk})$.
- Verify: On input a signature σ, a message M, π and pk, it outputs $\mathsf{Verify}(\pi, \mathsf{pk}, \sigma, M||\mathsf{pk})$.

THEOREM 3. *If Π' is a EUF-CMA secure separable signature scheme with Φ_A-public key malleability but Φ_B-RPA fix-message insecure, then Π is a Φ_P-RPA, EUF-CMA secure signature scheme, where $\Phi_P = \Phi_A \cap \Phi_B$ is some class of group induced operations.*

PROOF. Suppose the simulator $\mathcal{B}$ is given π, pk from the challenger $\mathcal{C}$ of Π'. $\mathcal{B}$ forwards π, pk to the adversary $\mathcal{A}$.

For the Signing Oracle query with input M, $\mathcal{B}$ asks $\mathcal{C}$ to answer the signature on the message $M||\mathsf{pk}$. For the KeyGen Oracle query with input $\phi \in \Phi_P$, $\mathcal{B}$ answers $\bar{\mathsf{pk}} = \mathcal{T}(\pi, \phi(\mathsf{sk}))$ by the Φ_A-public key malleability property.

Finally, $\mathcal{A}$ returns a forgery σ^* on a message M^* with respect to the public key $\bar{\mathsf{pk}}$ such that $\mathsf{Verify}(\pi, \bar{\mathsf{pk}}, \sigma^*, M^*||\bar{\mathsf{pk}}) = 1$. If $\bar{\mathsf{pk}} = \mathsf{pk}$, then M^* must not be asked in the signing oracle. Then $\mathcal{B}$ returns σ^* to $\mathcal{C}$ as the signature to the message $M^*||\mathsf{pk}$. Else, $\bar{\mathsf{pk}}$ is the output of the KeyGen Oracle for some input ϕ. Then $\mathcal{B}$ transforms σ^* to $\hat{\sigma}$ such that $\mathsf{Verify}(\pi, \mathsf{pk}, \hat{\sigma}, M^*||\bar{\mathsf{pk}})$ by the Φ_B-RPA fix-message insecurity. This transformation is possible since ϕ^{-1} exists for group induced operations in Φ_P. $\mathcal{B}$ returns $\hat{\sigma}$ to $\mathcal{C}$ as the signature to the message $M^*||\bar{\mathsf{pk}}$, since such message was never asked to the signing oracle of $\mathcal{C}$. If $\mathcal{A}$ wins, then $\mathcal{B}$ breaks the EUF-CMA security of Π'. □

We can obtain a similar conversion for strongly unforgeable (SUF-CMA) signatures. Suppose the signature scheme Π' is not RPA secure in a way that given a signature σ on a message m for a public key pk, and some $\phi \in \Phi$, there exists a polynomial time algorithm to find $(\bar{\sigma}, \bar{M}) \neq (\sigma, M)$ such that

$$\mathsf{Verify}'(\pi, \mathsf{pk}, \sigma, M) = \mathsf{Verify}'(\pi, \mathcal{T}(\pi, \phi(\mathsf{sk})), \bar{\sigma}, \bar{M}).$$

We call such scheme Φ-*RPA insecure.* Using such signature scheme Π', we can build another signature scheme Π same as above.

THEOREM 4. *If Π' is a SUF-CMA secure separable signature scheme with Φ_A-public key malleability but Φ_B-RPA insecure, then Π is a Φ_P-RPA, SUF-CMA secure signature scheme, where $\Phi_P = \Phi_A \cap \Phi_B$ is some class of group induced operations.*

PROOF. Suppose the simulator $\mathcal{B}$ is given π, pk from the challenger $\mathcal{C}$ of Π'. $\mathcal{B}$ forwards π, pk to the adversary $\mathcal{A}$.

For the Signing Oracle query with input M, $\mathcal{B}$ asks $\mathcal{C}$ to answer the signature on the message $M||\mathsf{pk}$. For the KeyGen Oracle query with input ϕ, $\mathcal{B}$ answers $\bar{\mathsf{pk}} = \mathcal{T}(\pi, \phi(\mathsf{sk}))$ by the Φ_A-public key malleability property.

Finally, $\mathcal{A}$ returns a forgery σ^* on a message M^* with respect to the public key $\bar{\mathsf{pk}}$ such that $\mathsf{Verify}(\pi, \bar{\mathsf{pk}}, \sigma^*, M^*||\bar{\mathsf{pk}}) = 1$. If $\bar{\mathsf{pk}} = \mathsf{pk}$, then M^* must not be asked in the signing oracle. Then $\mathcal{B}$ returns σ^* to $\mathcal{C}$ as the signature to the message $M^*||\mathsf{pk}$. Else, $\bar{\mathsf{pk}}$ is the output of the KeyGen Oracle for some input ϕ. Then $\mathcal{B}$ transforms $(\sigma^*, M^*||\bar{\mathsf{pk}})$ to $(\hat{\sigma}, \hat{M})$ such that $\mathsf{Verify}(\pi, \mathsf{pk}, \hat{\sigma}, \hat{M}) = 1$ by the Φ_B-RPA fix-message insecurity. This transformation is possible since ϕ^{-1} exists for group induced operations in Φ_P. $\mathcal{B}$ returns $\hat{\sigma}$ to $\mathcal{C}$ as the signature to the message $\hat{M}$, since such pair of $(\hat{\sigma}, \hat{M})$ was never asked to the signing oracle of $\mathcal{C}$. If $\mathcal{A}$ wins, then $\mathcal{B}$ breaks the SUF-CMA security of Π'. □

7. CONCLUSION

We propose a framework which includes the existing related (secret) key attack, and the new models of related encryption randomness attack, related signing randomness attack, and related public key attack. Corresponding, we propose generic constructions to achieve security under these related randomness attacks. We hope our work to be useful in building cryptosystems in the face of practical attacks resulted from fault injection or poor implementation of pseudorandom number generators.

8. ACKNOWLEDGMENTS

Sherman S.M. Chow would like to acknowledge the support from Early Career Scheme and Early Career Award of the Research Grants Council, Hong Kong (CUHK 439713). S.M. Yiu would like to acknowledge the support from the Seed Funding Programme for Basic Research (201311159040), HKU and NSFC/RGC Joint Research Scheme, Hong Kong (N_HKU 729/13).

9. REFERENCES

[1] G. Argyros and A. Kiayias. I forgot your password: randomness attacks against PHP applications. In *USENIX*, Security'12, page 6. USENIX Association, 2012.

[2] M. Bellare, A. Boldyreva, and J. Staddon. Randomness Re-use in Multi-recipient Encryption Schemes. In Y. Desmedt, editor, *PKC 2003*, volume 2567 of *LNCS*, pages 85–99. Springer, 2003.

[3] M. Bellare and D. Cash. Pseudorandom Functions and Permutations Provably Secure against Related-Key Attacks. In T. Rabin, editor, *CRYPTO 2010*, volume 6223 of *LNCS*, pages 666–684. Springer, 2010.

[4] M. Bellare, D. Cash, and R. Miller. Cryptography Secure against Related-Key Attacks and Tampering. In D. H. Lee and X. Wang, editors, *ASIACRYPT 2011*, volume 7073 of *LNCS*, pages 486–503. Springer, 2011.

[5] M. Bellare and T. Kohno. A Theoretical Treatment of Related-Key Attacks: RKA-PRPs, RKA-PRFs, and Applications. In E. Biham, editor, *EUROCRYPT 2003*, volume 2656 of *LNCS*, pages 491–506. Springer, 2003.

[6] M. Bellare, K. G. Paterson, and S. Thomson. RKA Security beyond the Linear Barrier: IBE, Encryption and Signatures. In X. Wang and K. Sako, editors, *ASIACRYPT 2012*, volume 7658 of *LNCS*, pages 331–348. Springer, 2012.

[7] A. Bender, J. Katz, and R. Morselli. Ring Signatures: Stronger Definitions, and Constructions without Random Oracles. In S. Halevi and T. Rabin, editors, *TCC 2006*, volume 3816 of *LNCS*, pages 60–79. Springer, 2006.

[8] E. Biham and A. Shamir. Differential Fault Analysis of Secret Key Cryptosystems. In B. S. K. Jr., editor, *CRYPTO '97*, volume 1294 of *LNCS*, pages 513–525. Springer, 1997.

[9] A. Biryukov, D. Khovratovich, and I. Nikolic. Distinguisher and Related-Key Attack on the Full AES-256. In S. Halevi, editor, *CRYPTO 2009*, volume 5677 of *LNCS*, pages 231–249. Springer, 2009.

[10] D. Boneh and X. Boyen. Efficient Selective-ID Secure Identity-Based Encryption Without Random Oracles. In C. Cachin and J. Camenisch, editors, *EUROCRYPT 2004*, volume 3027 of *LNCS*, pages 223–238. Springer, 2004.

[11] D. Boneh, R. A. DeMillo, and R. J. Lipton. On the Importance of Checking Cryptographic Protocols for Faults (Extended Abstract). In W. Fumy, editor, *EUROCRYPT '97*, volume 1233 of *LNCS*, pages 37–51. Springer, 1997.

[12] V. Goyal, A. O'Neill, and V. Rao. Correlated-Input Secure Hash Functions. In Y. Ishai, editor, *TCC 2011*, volume 6597 of *LNCS*, pages 182–200. Springer, 2011.

[13] N. Heninger, Z. Durumeric, E. Wustrow, and J. A. Halderman. Mining your Ps and Qs: detection of widespread weak keys in network devices. In *USENIX*, Security'12, page 35. USENIX Association, 2012.

[14] J. Herranz and G. Sáez. Forking Lemmas for Ring Signature Schemes. In T. Johansson and S. Maitra, editors, *INDOCRYPT 2003*, volume 2904 of *LNCS*, pages 266–279. Springer, 2003.

[15] K. Kurosawa. Multi-recipient Public-Key Encryption with Shortened Ciphertext. In D. Naccache and P. Paillier, editors, *PKC 2002*, volume 2274 of *LNCS*, pages 48–63. Springer, 2002.

[16] A. K. Lenstra, J. P. Hughes, M. Augier, J. W. Bos, T. Kleinjung, and C. Wachter. Public Keys. In R. Safavi-Naini and R. Canetti, editors, *CRYPTO 2012*, volume 7417 of *LNCS*, pages 626–642. Springer, 2012.

[17] S. Lucks. Ciphers Secure against Related-Key Attacks. In B. K. Roy and W. Meier, editors, *FSE 2004*, volume 3017 of *LNCS*, pages 359–370. Springer, 2004.

[18] K. Michaelis, C. Meyer, and J. Schwenk. Randomly Failed! The State of Randomness in Current Java Implementations. In E. Dawson, editor, *CT-RSA 2013*, volume 7779 of *LNCS*, pages 129–144. Springer, 2013.

[19] K. G. Paterson, J. C. N. Schuldt, and D. L. Sibborn. Related Randomness Attacks for Public Key Encryption. In *PKC 2014*, volume 8383 of *LNCS*, pages 465–482. Springer, 2014.

APPENDIX

A. RELATED KEY AND RANDOMNESS ATTACK MODEL FOR PKE

An encryption scheme consists of three PPT algorithms:

1. `Setup`: On input a security parameter 1^λ, it generates a public key pk and a secret key sk.
2. `Enc`: On input pk and a message M from a message space $\mathcal{M}$, it outputs a ciphertext $\mathfrak{C}$.
3. `Dec`: On input sk, and $\mathfrak{C}$, it outputs a message M or $\perp$ symbolizing the failure of decryption.

Correctness. $\forall M \in \mathcal{M}$, $M \leftarrow \texttt{Dec}(\mathsf{sk}, \texttt{Enc}(\mathsf{pk}, M))$, where $(\mathsf{pk}, \mathsf{sk}) \leftarrow \texttt{Setup}(1^\lambda)$.

We consider the following indistinguishability based game against chosen ciphertext attacks (IND-CCA) for semantic security with related-key, related encryption randomness attack. The game (Φ_k, Φ_r)-RKRA-PKE is defined as follows.

1. Setup. The challenger runs $(\mathsf{pk}, \mathsf{sk}) \leftarrow \texttt{Setup}(1^\lambda)$ and gives pk to the adversary $\mathcal{A}$.
2. Query 1. The following oracles can be queried by $\mathcal{A}$:
   - Decryption Oracle $\mathcal{DO}(C, \phi)$: On input a ciphertext C and a key leakage $\phi \in \Phi_k$, it returns a message $m/\perp \leftarrow \texttt{Dec}(\phi(\mathsf{sk}), C)$.
3. Challenge. $\mathcal{A}$ sends two messages $M_0, M_1 \in \mathcal{M}$ to the challenger. The challenger picks a random bit b' and computes $\mathfrak{C}^* \leftarrow \texttt{Enc}(\mathsf{pk}, M_{b'}; R^*)$ using the randomness R^*. The challenger sends $\mathfrak{C}^*$ to $\mathcal{A}$.
4. Query 2. The following oracles can be queried by $\mathcal{A}$:
   - Decryption Oracle $\mathcal{DO}(C, \phi)$: On input a ciphertext C and a key leakage $\phi \in \Phi_k$, it returns a message $m/\perp \leftarrow \texttt{Dec}(\phi(\mathsf{sk}), C)$.
   - Encryption Oracle $\mathcal{EO}(M, \phi)$: On input a message M and a randomness leakage $\phi \in \Phi_r$, it returns $\texttt{Enc}(\mathsf{pk}, M; \phi(R^*))$.
5. Output. $\mathcal{A}$ returns a guess b^* of b'.

$\mathcal{A}$ wins the game if $b' = b^*$, there was no query to $\mathcal{DO}$ with input $C = C^*$ and ϕ is an identity map, and no query to $\mathcal{EO}$ with input $M = M_0^*$ or M_1^*, and ϕ is an identity map. The advantage of $\mathcal{A}$ is $\left|\Pr[\mathcal{A} \text{ wins}] - \frac{1}{2}\right|$.

An encryption scheme is (t, ϵ)-(Φ_k, Φ_r)-RKRA IND-CCA secure if there is no t-time attacker $\mathcal{A}$ with advantage ϵ in the (Φ_k, Φ_r)-RKRA-PKE game above.

If there is no related randomness attack, then the attacker cannot query the encryption oracle. In this case, we say that an encryption scheme is (t, ϵ)-Φ_k-RKA IND-CCA secure if there is no t-time attacker $\mathcal{A}$ with advantage ϵ in the game above.

If there is no related key attack, then the attacker cannot query the decryption oracle with input $\phi \in \Phi_K$. In this case, we say that an encryption scheme is (t, ϵ)-Φ_r-RRA IND-CCA secure if there is no t-time attacker $\mathcal{A}$ with advantage ϵ in the game above.

TLS Record Protocol: Security Analysis and Defense-in-depth Countermeasures for HTTPS

Olivier Levillain
ANSSI
olivier.levillain@ssi.gouv.fr

Baptiste Gourdin
Sekoia
baptiste.gourdin@sekoia.fr

Hervé Debar
Télécom SudParis
herve.debar@telecom-sudparis.eu

ABSTRACT

TLS and its main application HTTPS are an essential part of internet security. Since 2011, several attacks against the TLS Record protocol have been presented. To remediate these flaws, countermeasures have been proposed. They were usually specific to a particular attack, and were sometimes in contradiction with one another. All the proofs of concept targeted HTTPS and relied on the repetition of some secret element inside the TLS tunnel. In the HTTPS context, such secrets are pervasive, be they authentication cookies or anti-CSRF tokens. We present a comprehensive state of the art of attacks on the Record protocol and the associated proposed countermeasures. In parallel to the community efforts to find reliable long term solutions, we propose masking mechanisms to avoid the repetition of sensitive elements, at the transport or application level. We also assess the feasibility and efficiency of such defense-in-depth mechanisms. The recent POODLE vulnerability confirmed that our proposals could thwart unknown attacks, since they would have blocked it.

1. INTRODUCTION

SSL (Secure Sockets Layer) is a cryptographic protocol designed by Netscape in 1995 to protect the confidentiality and integrity of HTTP connections. Since 2001, the protocol has been maintained by the IETF (Internet Engineering Task Force) and renamed TLS (Transport Layer Security). Designed in 2008, the current version of the protocol is TLS 1.2 [9]. The original objective of SSL/TLS was to secure online-shopping and banking web sites. With the deployment of web services using the so-called Web 2.0, its use has broadened drastically.

TLS typical use consists of two consecutive phases: the *Handshake protocol* negotiates the cryptographic algorithms and keys, and authenticates the server to the client using certificates; the second phase, the *Record protocol*, protects the confidentiality and integrity of subsequent messages, called records, carrying the application data. In this article, we only consider attacks on TLS Record layer, letting aside handshake-related subtleties such as session resumption, renegotiation or client authentication.

ASIA CCS'15, April 14–17, 2015, Singapore..

ACM 978-1-4503-3245-3/15/04 ...$15.00.
http://dx.doi.org/10.1145/2714576.2714592.

Depending on the handshake outcome, the records can be protected using one of the three following cryptographic schemes: *MAC-then-encrypt with a streamcipher*, available since SSL inception (as of today, only RC4 is standardized); *MAC-then-encrypt with a blockcipher using CBC mode*, available since SSL inception; *AEAD* (Authenticated Encryption with Additional Data), available from TLS 1.2 only (e.g. AES using GCM mode). Optionally, the plaintext can be compressed before cryptographic transformations occurs. Fig. 1 describes the three possible workflows.

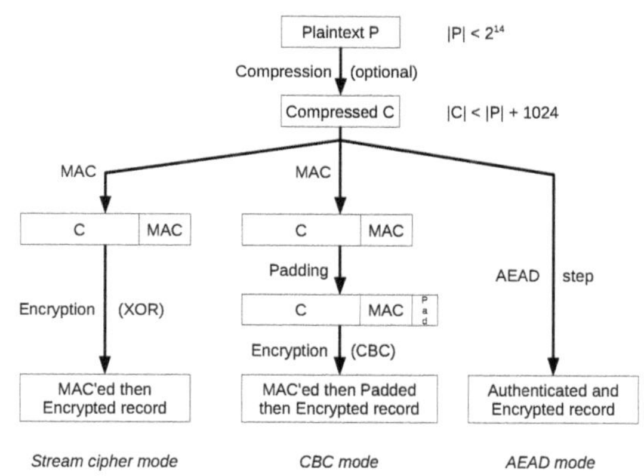

Figure 1: TLS Record protocol (streamcipher mode, CBC mode and AEAD mode).

Since 2011, several researchers have presented attacks affecting the Record protocol confidentiality. Each time, to prove the applicability of their findings, they implemented attacks against HTTPS. Typical HTTP secrets are cookies and anti-CSRF tokens. If stolen, they enable attacks like message replay, session highjacking or web site compromising. Fundamental to state maintenance in web applications, they are usually transmitted several times both within sessions and across different sessions. As a matter of fact, each proof of concept relied on one of these secret elements repeatedly transmitted inside TLS connections. Thus, a way to thwart attacks exploiting this kind of repetitions, existing or still unknown, is to mask the secrets so the attacks become inefficient in practice. In this article, we focus on cookie protection. HTTP Basic/Digest Authentication, and server-side attacks are discussed in the appendices.

Sec. 2 describes several recent attacks, and the proposed countermeasures. Sec. 3 presents our attacker model and the masking principle. Two proofs of concept have been implemented to assess the applicability and efficiency of our proposals. Sec. 4 describes those implementations, whereas Sec. 5 analyses the effectiveness of the proposed mechanisms, as well as their impact on performance.

Our contribution is threefold: first, we propose a comprehensive analysis of recent attacks on TLS Record layer with their countermeasures; then we present a new defense-in-depth approach to the problem, orthogonal to the current efforts towards long-term solutions, and illustrate them with two proofs of concepts; finally, we analyse those implementations, security- and performance-wise.

2. ATTACKS ON THE RECORD PROTOCOL

This section describes five recent attacks published between 2011 and 2014, targeting a session cookie sent by the client.

2.1 BEAST: implicit IV in CBC mode

In 1995, Rogaway described an adaptive chosen plaintext attack against the CBC mode with a predictable IV [30]. In 2002 [21], it was noticed that TLS used predictable IVs, since the last encrypted block of a record is used as the next record IV. However, this attack was deemed impractical at the time, or at least challenging citeBard04–tls-cpa,Bard06–tls-cpa, since it was an adaptive chosen plaintext attack. The situation changed in 2011 when Duong and Rizzo presented BEAST (Browser Exploit Against SSL/TLS) [10], a proof of concept of the vulnerability. Fig. 2 (left-side) details the "Encryption (CBC)" step presented in Fig. 1, when implicit IV is used.

Using the notations of Fig. 2, the attacker can "guess" that the value of P_1 is equal to some $P^\star$ and check the validity of her guess. Indeed, after the two records have been sent, she knows C_5 will be the next record IV. Thus she sends $P_6 = P^\star \oplus C_5 \oplus C_0$ as the next plaintext block, and observes $C_6 = E(P_6 \oplus C_5) = E(P^\star \oplus C_0)$. If the guess was correct (i.e. P_1 is $P^\star$), $C_6 = C_1$, which is observable. The corresponding encryption step is given on the right side of the figure.

Furthermore, to avoid having to guess a whole block, the proof of concept cleverly aligns the blocks so that the block to guess only contains one unknown byte. For instance, if the attacker knows P_1 is `":SESSION_TOKEN=?"` where ? is unknown, she only needs at most 256 attempts (128 on average) to recover the byte (or even less, if the targeted byte belongs to a constrained charset).

Finally, to send the chosen plaintext data in the same TLS session as the target web application, the Same Origin Policy (SOP[1]) [4] must be bypassed. Due to the complexity of the web ecosystem, vulnerabilities allowing SOP violations are regularly found on standard browsers and web applications[2].

[1]SOP is a fundamental security property implemented in web browsers, intended to prevent scripts loaded from a given site from communicating freely with another site

[2]Early BEAST implementations used WebSockets. Authors had to use a Java bug when WebSockets were randomised.

Hypotheses and prerequisites

- The connexion uses CBC mode with an implicit IV;
- The ciphertext is observable;
- The plaintext is partially controlled, adaptively;
- Multiple connections containing the same secret can be triggered.

Proposed countermeasures

Switch to TLS 1.1. This is the long term solution, since TLS 1.1 introduces an explicit (and unpredictable) IV for each record. Yet, TLS 1.1 is still not widely deployed, as shown by different studies [28, 19]. What is worse, to accommodate broken implementations, up-to-date browsers use a fallback strategy when a TLS connection fails, and retry using older versions (TLS 1.0 or SSLv3).

Use TLS 1.2 AEAD suites. AES-GCM or AES-CCM are not vulnerable to this attack, but they are only available with TLS 1.2. As for TLS 1.1, this protocol version is not widely deployed, and may be subject to a downgrade attack.

Use RC4 to avoid CBC mode. With TLS 1.0 and earlier versions, this is an efficient way to counter *this* attack, and it can be deployed easily and reliably (but Sec. 2.4 shows this is not an overall acceptable solution).

Randomize the IV by splitting the record. By splitting the records to send in two records, the first one containing the first byte of the original record, and the second one the remaining data, the attack still works, but only on the first byte. This so-called "$1/n-1$ split" is efficient and implemented in major browsers[3].

Fix SOP violations and XSS bugs. To mount the attack, forged requests must be sent to the target, either by bypassing the SOP or by exploiting a Cross Site Scripting (XSS) vulnerability. It is obviously desirable to fix all these bugs, but the ever-evolving web ecosystem makes this goal difficult to reach.

2.2 CRIME & TIME: client-side compression

In 2012, Duong and Rizzo published another attack against TLS named CRIME (Compression Ratio Info-leak Made Easy) [29]. Again, their objective was to recover a secret cookie. The attack is based on the compression step in the Record protocol and assumes the attacker is able to choose part of the cleartext, e.g. the URL path. The following year, another research team presented the TIME (Timing Info-leak Made Easy) attack [32], a variant of the CRIME attack, relying on a different feedback method.

Let's assume the secret cookie, `SESSION_ID`, is an hexadecimal string, and that the attacker can trigger successive HTTPS connections while controlling part of the cleartext (typically the URL path). This does not violate the Same Origin Policy, and the resulting HTTP requests will contain both the forged URL (`www.target.com/SESSION_ID=X` in our example, `X` being an hexadecimal character) and the cookies corresponding to the target. When these requests are compressed, the redundancy will be maximum when the attacker has guessed the secret correctly, which should re-

[3]Initially, a "$0/n$ split" had been implemented in OpenSSL, but it proved to break some implementations, despite empty ApplicationData records being licit.

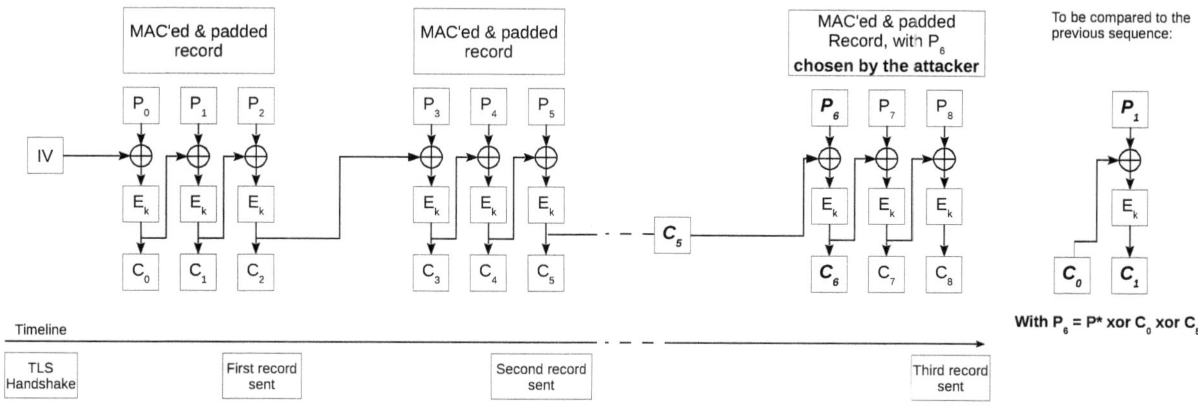

Figure 2: [Left] CBC with implicit IV in SSL/TLS before TLS 1.1: IV is generated during the handshake, then all records are encrypted as a continuous CBC flow. [Right] To check whether $P_1 = P^\star$, the attacker encrypts a record starting with plaintext block P_6, and compares the output C_6 to C_1, previously observed.

sult in a better compression. To make this phenomenon observable, the attacker needs the record to get smaller[4].

CRIME and TIME propose two different methods to observe the impact of compression on the plaintext. CRIME simply relies on the encrypted packet sizes, assuming the attacker is able to capture the victim's traffic. TIME uses a different feedback method: the variation of transmission time between a correct guess (where compression is more efficient) and an incorrect one[5]. To amplify the effect of a compressed plaintext being one byte shorter, the idea behind TIME is to forge a plaintext such that the encrypted packet just crosses the TCP window size and requires a TCP ACK from the server before sending the remaining byte. This way, when the attacker guesses the correct character, the compression kicks in and the encrypted data contains one byte less, which does not require to wait a Round Trip Time for the ACK. This difference in timing is observable from the client-side script launching the requests.

Hypotheses and prerequisites

- TLS compression is activated;
- The ciphertext length is observable, e.g. via packet sizes or timing leaks;
- Plaintext can be loosely controlled by the attacker;
- Multiple connections containing the same secret can be triggered.

Proposed countermeasures

Disable TLS compression. This blocks the attack completely, and has no significant impact on performance.

Randomize the packet length. Several proposals were made to add random-length padding to application messages (adding random bytes or slicing the HTTP content in chunks). Unless the added data is significant enough (which is equivalent in practice to disabling compression), these proposals essentially force the attacker to collect more data, but do not fundamentally invalidate the attack.

Restrictions on cross-site requests. If cross-site requests were forbidden (or at least excluded sensitive information like authentication cookies), the attacker would first need to exploit an XSS to mount this attack, but many web applications would also break.

[4]To this aim, some parameters need to be tuned, like the block alignment (with CBC encryption) and a way to reset the compression dictionary (the main compression algorithm in TLS, Defalte, is stateful).

[5]TIME authors also described an attack to recover server-sent anti-CSRF tokens. Appendix B presents details on server-side compression attacks and countermeasures.

2.3 Lucky 13: CBC padding oracle

In TLS, when a blockcipher is used with CBC, the plaintext is MAC'ed then padded and encrypted, which allows for attacks exploiting padding oracles, first introduced by Vaudenay in 2002 [33]. As soon as an attacker can distinguish between a MAC error and a CBC padding error, be it through an out-of-band message or a timing difference, she can gain information about the plaintext.

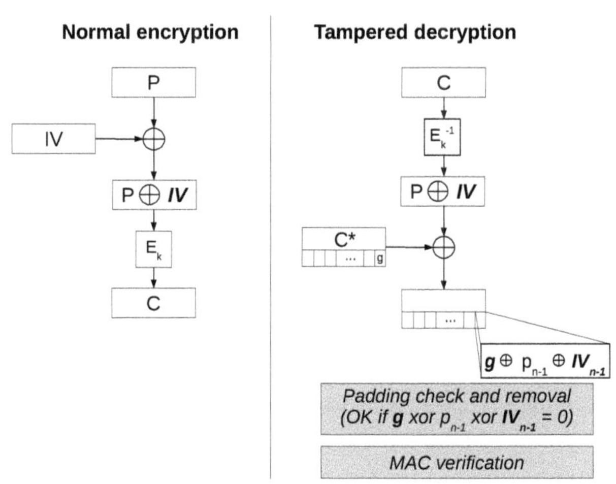

Figure 3: CBC encryption and decryption, in the light of a padding oracle exploitation. Blocks C, $C^\star$ (in particular its last byte g) and IV are known.

When decrypting a CBC-encrypted record, the recovered plaintext should end with a valid padding: p bytes all valued $p-1$ (for example, blocks ending with 00, 0101, 020202, etc. are correctly padded). Let $P = p_0 p_1 \cdots p_{n-1}$ be a plaintext block, and $C = c_0 c_1 \cdots c_{n-1}$ be the corresponding ciphertext (see Fig. 3, on the left side). To guess the value of p_{n-1}, the attacker can send a fake ciphertext containing two blocks: $C^\star C$, with C being the ciphertext block to recover and $C^\star$ a random block, ending with $c^\star_{n-1} = g$ (the decryption of the second block is described in Fig. 3, on the right side). If the guessed byte g is indeed equal to $p_{n-1} \oplus IV_{n-1}$, the output of E_k^{-1} will end with a null byte, the padding will be correct, and this will lead to a MAC error (since the attacker can not create a valid MAC). Otherwise, if the guess is incorrect, the padding will be incorrect, with overwhelming probability[6].

If the attacker can distinguish between MAC errors and CBC padding errors, she can use the resulting padding oracle to guess the content of a block, one byte at a time. Indeed, once the attacker has identified the last byte p_{n-1}, she can try and find whether $p_{n-2} = g$ with $C^\star$ ending this time with $(g \oplus 01)|(p_{n-1} \oplus 01)$, and so on.

The initial specifications of SSL/TLS stated that both error cases (invalid MAC and padding error) should lead to different alert messages. However, this was not directly useful from the attacker point of view, since the alert was encrypted. Another way to differentiate the two error cases is to measure the time needed to reject the invalid packet. When no MAC is performed, the answer is returned faster. That is why TLS 1.1 [8] contains a note stating that *implementations MUST ensure that record processing time is essentially the same whether or not the padding is correct.*

Moreover, such attacks were initially considered impractical against TLS since modified records would eventually trigger a MAC error, be rejected, and cause the whole session to close. In 2012, Paterson et al. studied the applicability of this attack to DTLS [23]. Datagram TLS (DTLS) [27] is a cryptographic protocol similar to TLS relying on UDP instead of TCP; since UDP is not a reliable transport layer, datagrams may be lost or corrupted. Furthermore, DTLS does not close a session when a MAC error is encountered (nor does it emit a warning). The authors identified a timing attack that made it possible to distinguish a padding error from a MAC error (to amplify the timing info-leak, several identical consecutive packets are sent on the wire).

In case of a padding error, the standard implementation of TLS CBC decryption assumes a fixed-length pad, which, according to the implementation note quoted earlier, *leaves a small timing channel, since MAC performance depends to some extent on the size of the data fragment, but it is not believed to be large enough to be exploitable.* It was established in 2013 that this small info-leak was in fact exploitable in TLS to obtain a padding oracle [2]. Moreover, when the target is a constant secret string repeatedly sent in the encrypted channel, it does not matter that the TLS session is closed and that the keying material changes accross sessions. The proof of concept was named Lucky 13, after the size of the pseudo-header MAC'ed with the message.

[6]To be precise, there is a 2^{-16} probability to get a plaintext ending with 01 01, a 2^{-24} to get 02 02 02, and so on. To eliminate those false positives, the attacker can simply repeat the operation with a different random string in $C^\star$.

Hypotheses and prerequisites

- The connexion uses CBC with a timing info-leak;
- The attacker is able to intercept and modify packets;
- Multiple connections containing the same secret can be triggered.

Proposed countermeasures

Add random delays to CBC-mode decryption step. This would only increase the complexity of the attack (requiring more samples to compute the mean value).

Implement constant-time MAC-then-Encrypt. Such implementations counter the attack, but the code needed to obtain efficient record processing in effectively constant time is complex (the OpenSSL patch is almost 300 lines long).

Use RC4 to avoid CBC mode. As for BEAST, it thwarts *this* attack but is inconsistent with other measures.

Use TLS 1.2 AEAD suites. As for BEAST, this works but is hard to deploy reliably.

Switch to Encrypt-then-MAC. This would solve the problem, but the specification [16] is still young. Moreover, it relies on an extension, which would lead to the same deployment and reliability issues as TLS 1.2.

2.4 RC4 biases

RC4 is a stream cipher designed by Rivest in 1987. It is very simple to implement and has very good performance in software. It has thus been widely adopted in protocols (WiFi encryption protocols WEP and WPA, or TLS for example). Since 1995, several statistical biases have been identified in the first bytes of an RC4 keystream. These flaws eventually led to very efficient attacks against WEP [31].

As these attacks rely on initial biases of the keystream, it was proposed to drop the first n bytes of the keystream, but later findings show the existence of additional statistical biases, even after the initial bytes [12]. In 2013, two research teams presented practical attacks against the encryption of the same fixed sequence of plaintext using large numbers of different keys [18, 1], which apply to HTTPS cookies.

Here is a short description of the most efficient attacks on RC4, presented in the article by AlFardan et al. Their single-byte bias attack relies on the fact that the first 256 bytes of the keystream are strongly biased. The researchers generated a lot of RC4 keystreams to observe the actual distribution of each of the 256 first bytes. Using an empirical reference of 2^{45} keystreams, it is possible to recover the first 256 bytes of a plaintext, as soon as it is encrypted a sufficient number of times; this number varies from 2^{24} to 2^{32} as a function of the byte position in the 256 bytes keystream. Using the reference distribution and the encrypted distribution, the idea is to find the most probable byte value, by measuring the distance between the reference distribution and each of the candidate keystreams.

However, the attack is hard to implement, since it requires a lot of different TLS connections, and only works for data sent in the first few bytes. To overcome these limitations, the researchers also used long-term biases described by Fluhrer and McGrew [12] on consecutive bytes to perform a practical attack requiring more keystream, but which could work in a pipelined HTTPS stream (i.e. using different messages within the same TLS connection). This double-byte bias attack is more practical than the single-byte bias one, and a proof of concept was developed to recover an HTTP cookie.

Hypotheses and prerequisites

- TLS uses RC4 to encrypt data;
- The attacker is able to observe encrypted packets;
- Multiple connections containing the same secret can be triggered.

Proposed countermeasures

Use CBC mode to avoid RC4. This is an efficient way to counter *this* attack, and it can be deployed easily and reliably. Obviously, this recommendation is in contradiction with the *Use RC4* recommendation (from Sec. 2.1 and 2.3).

Use TLS 1.2 AEAD suites. This works but leads to deployment and reliability issues.

Use another streamcipher. ChaCha20 [5] is currently under examination by the IETF as an alternative stream cipher. Such a change could be easier to deploy than a protocol version switch, as the ciphersuite negotiation is usually better supported, but it will still require some time[7].

Throw away the first bytes of the keystream. This behavior could be specified in TLS (with a new ciphersuite or extension) or HTTP (by padding the beginning of messages), but we know exploitable long-term RC4 biases exist.

Randomize the packet length. As for compression attacks, random padding would only increase the complexity.

2.5 POODLE: another padding oracle

In October 2014, Möller, Duong and Kotowicz presented POODLE (Padding Oracle on Downgraded Legacy Encryption) [22], another padding oracle targeting SSLv3 CBC mode. The old SSL version indeed handles CBC padding in a specific way: when n bytes are needed to pad a plaintext, the last byte is set to $n-1$ (as in TLS, described in Sec. 2.3), but the other bytes can take any arbitrary value. An attacker can use this liberty to get a padding oracle.

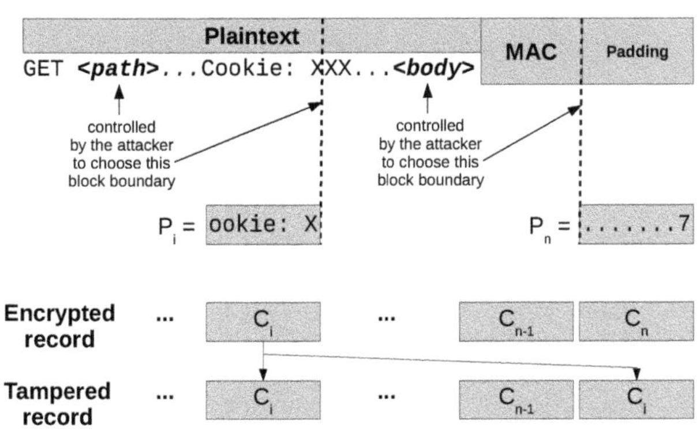

Figure 4: POODLE attack exploiting SSLv3 CBC Padding, assuming an 8-byte blockcipher.

Let's assume an attacker can trigger requests to the vulnerable site using SSLv3 and CBC mode. Since she may alter the path fragment in the URL, she may prepare the request in such a way that the cookie ends on a block frontier. Moreover, she may include a request body of arbitrary length after the headers, which allows her to get a plaintext message (once the MAC is appended) whose length is a multiple of the block size (see Fig 4). This way, a whole block would be added in the padding phase. Such a block has only one constraint: the last byte must be $n-1$ where n is the block length.

Once the request is sent by the browser, the attacker needs to modify the record on the wire. She must replace the all-padding block by the block where the last byte is to be guessed, as shown in Fig. 4. If the decryption of the last blocks leads to the correct value $(n-1)$, the rest of the block is ignored and the record is accepted by the server. It means the last byte of $E_k^{-1}(C_i) \oplus C_{n-1}$ is $n-1$, and that the last byte of P_i is $C_{n-1} \oplus C_{i-1} \oplus (n-1)$. If the padding does not end with $n-1$, the decryption will need to a MAC error and to the end of the connection. If the attacker retries, another key will be used and C_{n-1} will be randomized. Thus, each byte can be guessed with a 2^{-8} probability, which results in 256 requests needed to recover each byte of the secret value.

It is interesting to note that this attack relies on the browser using a fallback strategy, and on the server to accept the obsolete SSLv3 version of the protocol.

Hypotheses and prerequisites

- The connection uses SSLv3 with CBC mode;
- Plaintext can be loosely controlled by the attacker;
- The attacker is able to intercept and modify packets;
- Multiple connections containing the same secret can be triggered.

Proposed countermeasures

Use TLS 1.0. Since this powerful padding oracle is only present in SSLv3, forbidding this deprecated version is an efficient countermeasure. Moreover, only a small portion of the internet still relies on this version of the protocol, which makes this measure also practical.

Use RC4 to avoid CBC mode.

Use TLS 1.2 AEAD suites.

Switch to Encrypt-then-MAC. These three countermeasures work, with the same reservations as before.

Anti poodle record splitting. Opera and Google's developper Adam Langley proposed to split SSLv3 CBC records to counter the POODLE attack. The proposed splitting method is supposed to avoid whole blocks of padding. Yet, POODLE paved the way for new SSLv3 padding oracle attacks, which may not be blocked this way.

TLS_FALLBACK_SCSV. Möller and Langley proposed a mechanism to avoid browser fallbacks when a higher version is supported by both the client and the server, using a fake signaling ciphersuite. This would indeed block downgrade attacks and POODLE in particular, between up-to-date parties. Yet, legacy SSLv3 stacks would still be at risk.

2.6 Comparative analysis of these attacks

To mitigate these threats, many countermeasures have been proposed. Our analysis shows that some of them have no real effect on the attacks: throwing the first bytes of RC4 keystream, randomizing the packet length or adding random

[7]Moreover, the current draft actually specifies an AEAD suite, not a streamcipher one, which would require TLS 1.2.

Countermeasures	Dep.	Rel.	HTTP	Beast	L 13	RC4	*IME	POODLE
Structural changes to TLS								
Use TLS 1.0	+	+	+					+
Use TLS 1.1	−	−	+	+				+
Encrypt-then-MAC	− −	−	+		+			
Changes related to TLS ciphersuites or compression methods								
Use CBC mode	+	+	+			+		
Use RC4	+	+	+	+	+			+
Use a new stream cipher	−	+	+	+	+	+		+
Use AEAD (TLS 1.2)	− −	−	+	+	+	+		+
No TLS compression	+	+	+				+	
Changes related to TLS implementations								
$1/n-1$ split	−	+	+	+				
Constant-time CBC	−	+	+		+			
Anti poodle splitting	−	+	+					+
Other countermeasures in related work								
Single-use cookie	− −	+	−	+		+	+	+
One-Time Cookies [7]	− −	−	+	p	p	p	p	p
Countermeasures presented in this article								
TLS scrambling	− −	+	+	+	+	+	+	+
MCookies (server)	−	+	+	+		+	+	+
MCookies (client/server)	− −	+	+	+	+	+	+	+

Table 1: Summary of the proposed countermeasures.

delays to CBC-mode decryption. Others require significant changes to the architecture of web applications and would be hard to enforce: restricting cross-site requests or fixing all SOP/XSS bugs. The remaining countermeasures are listed in Table 1, and compared using different criteria:

- **Dep.** relates to the ease of **deployment** of the proposed solution. In particular, studies [24, 19] shed light on the problem of existing intolerance, e.g. new TLS versions raising important compatibility issues;
- **Reliability (Rel.)** corresponds to the assurance we have the countermeasure will not be easily bypassed between a client and a server both implementing the solution. The idea is to capture the possible down-negotiation and fall-back strategies (for example issues related to TLS version negotiation);
- **HTTP** assesses the compatibility of the measure with HTTP use-case. Current web applications have to e.g. accommodate with multi-tab browsing. Countermeasures should not break or limit such features;
- A set of columns state whether the countermeasure is efficient against each attack (**BEAST**, **L13**, **RC4**, ***IME** for compression attacks, and **POODLE**), "p" meaning the measure only partially blocks the attack.

The last lines of the table describe countermeasures proposed in related work (Sec. 6) and our proposals (Sec. 4).

3. ATTACKER MODEL AND THE MASKING PRINCIPLE

The legitimate actors we consider are: the user agent (e.g. Firefox), the HTTP(S) server (e.g. Apache) and the web application (a program written in PHP or Python for example). The web application may rely on a framework designed to abstract the inherent complexity of web development (e.g. Django or Zend). The attacker we consider is an active network attacker, able to read, modify or delete packets between the client and the server. We also assume, as for each of the attacks presented in Sec. 2, that a secret cookie is repeated across different TLS messages.

Given a TLS session, we assume the attacker is able to retrieve some information about κ consecutive bytes of the corresponding plaintext. Typically, $\kappa = 1$, and the attacker is able to check whether a cleartext byte is equal to a guessed value. Thus, by repeating the attack on constant plaintext bytes, she can recover this part of the plaintext.

To draw a parallel with side-channel attacks [6, 15, 26], such attacks may be called first order attacks. To deal with them, a typical countermeasure is to mask the secret value: each time a secret s of κ bytes must be transmitted, a random value m (the mask) of the same length would be chosen and the pair $(m, m \oplus s)$ would be sent instead of s. This way, the value can trivially be recomputed by the other party, but the representation on the wire is different for every message. If the secret s to mask is longer than κ, s can be split in κ-byte words, masked by the same mask. Alternatively, it is possible to choose a longer mask to cover the secret entirely.

Masking all secrets using a fresh mask would force the attacker to mount a second order attack, that is find a way to simultaneously retrieve information about the mask and the masked value, to learn something about the secret.

Most of the attacks described in Sec. 2 are designed to recover the plaintext one byte at a time, which makes them first order attacks with $\kappa = 1$. Some attacks against RC4 also exploit statistical biases on two consecutive bytes, which also corresponds to our model (for $\kappa = 2$).

In practice, the BEAST, CRIME, TIME and Lucky 13 attacks could easily be extended to guess κ consecutive bytes at once (for example, for BEAST, this would mean aligning the boundary of the block to guess differently). However, the complexity to recover κ bytes at once would be proportional to $2^{8\kappa}$ (instead of $\kappa \cdot 2^8$), which limits κ to small values in practice. To be conservative, we consider the maximum number of recoverable successive bytes κ to be 8.

Overall, the recent attacks against TLS Record layer can all be considered as first order attacks (with $\kappa \leq 8$). So, masking secret values using unique 8-byte random strings will mitigate these attacks. In the following sections we present two implementations of this concept applied to the transport and the application level.

Concerning RC4, it can be noted that other known biases exist and are related to distinct distant groups of keystream bytes. Thus, second order attacks against RC4 might be possible by exploiting such biases. We briefly discuss this case in the conclusion.

4. PROPOSED MECHANISMS

This section presents generic mechanisms to mitigate the impact of TLS security flaws, by leveraging the masking principle. The first one acts at the transport (TLS) layer, while the second one works at the application (HTTP) level.

4.1 TLS Scramble: Masking at the TLS level

The idea of masking application data at the transport level is not new in TLS. During the specification of WebSockets [11], a recent HTML5 feature, a randomization step was added to avoid confusion between WebSocket traffic and other protocols, that could be leveraged by an attacker. WebSocket randomizes client-to-server traffic using 4-byte long masks. An interesting side effect of this change was to block the early version of the BEAST attack, forcing Duong and Rizzo to rewrite their exploit using Java instead of WebSockets.

4.1.1 *A fake compression method: Scramble*

As shown in Fig. 1, record processing may optionally compress the plaintext before the cryptographic transformations. This step takes a plaintext record of at most 2^{14} bytes, and produces a compressed record that can be at most 1024 bytes longer than the plaintext.

To generalize the idea behind WebSockets masking, we define a *fake* compression algorithm, Scramble. Given a κ parameter (the mask length) and a plaintext P, the way Scramble *compresses* P is as follows:

- the `scramble_record` method generates a κ-byte random string m;
- m is repeated, and possibly truncated, to be as long as P. The result is a masking string M;
- the *compressed* record is $m|P \oplus M$, which is exactly κ-byte longer than P.

The `unscramble_record` operation is straightforward:

- on receiving a *compressed* string c, which should contain at least κ bytes, extract the first κ bytes of c as the mask m, and call X the remaining string;
- expand m to be as long as X to obtain M;
- the *uncompressed* value is $M \oplus X$.

4.1.2 *Implementation in OpenSSL*

To check the feasibility of this idea, we implemented the Scramble compression method in OpenSSL (v1.0.1) with 8-byte masks. The patch affects the `crypto/comp` directory. It adds `c_scramble.c`, a 75-line file describing the method, as well as trivial changes to `comp.h` and to the corresponding `Makefile`. The `scramble_record` function is given in Appendix C. To test the method with real connections, we also patched `apps/s_client.c` and `apps/s_server.c` to exchange data over the scrambled channel.

4.2 MCookies: Masking at the application level

Another way to tackle the problem is to mask secret values at the application level, which requires less bandwidth (only relevant elements would need to be masked) and avoids modifying TLS stacks. In this section, we propose a method to mask cookies at the HTTP level.

4.2.1 *MCookies principle*

Usually, HTTP cookies work as specified in Fig. 5: a server can define cookies to be stored by its client, then each time this client sends a request to the server, the cookies are added to the headers [3]. In some cases, they may also be read and modified by client-side scripts.

If we only consider cookies that are never read nor modified by client-side scripts, there is a simple way to break this repetition while modifying only the HTTP server, which is described in Fig. 6:

- **Cookie definition:** when the web application sets such a cookie (e.g. calling `set-cookie(SESSID,` V`)`), the HTTP layer rewrites the `Set-cookie` header to send `SESSID=`$M : M \oplus V$ instead of `SESSID=`V[8].
- **Cookie restitution (and redefinition):** for each request containing a `SESSID=`$X : Y$ cookie, the HTTP server transmits `SESSID=`$X \oplus Y$ (the unmasked cookie) to the web application. Then, three cases may arise:
  - the web application updates the cookie, which is covered by the Cookie definition step;
  - it can erase the cookie by setting an outdated expiration time, in which case the HTTP layer simply transmits the header as is;
  - otherwise (the cookie is left unchanged by the application), the HTTP server sets a new version of the cookie, M':$M' \oplus V$, that is the same initial value masked using a fresh random mask.

4.2.2 *Discussion of MCookies feasibility*

To select the senstive cookies to protect, a simple way would be to define a static list of cookie names, but a natural heuristic is to protect every cookie flagged both `httpOnly` and `secure`. Only considering `httpOnly` cookies guarantees that client-side script have no access to the cookie value, leaving the HTTP server free to change the cookie representation at will. However, from the web application point of view, the cookie value sent and received remains the same. Moreover, protecting a non-`secure` cookie is pointless as this one can be easily stolen with our attacker model in general[9].

[8]Since M and $M \oplus V$ are binary strings, Base64 is used.

[9]Even when cookies are sent without the `secure` attribute, security mechanisms like HSTS (HTTP Strict Transport Security [17]) can forbid cleartext communications.

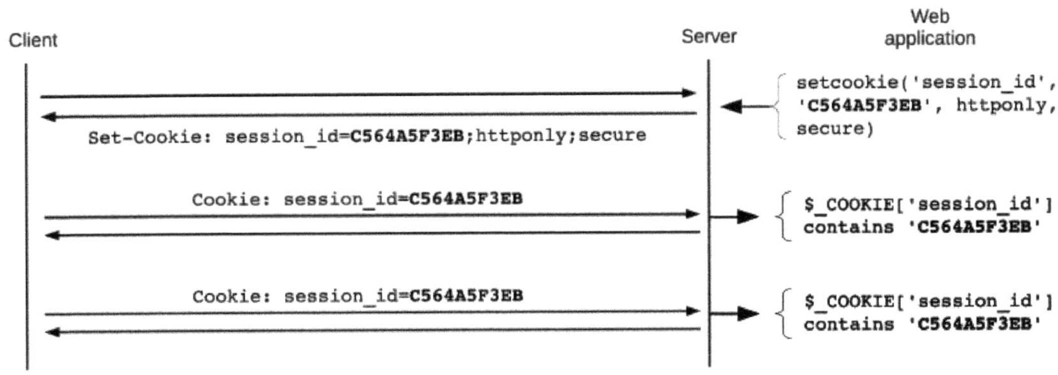

Figure 5: HTTP cookies: definition and restitution.

Figure 6: Definition and restitution of MCookies

Yet, rewriting the cookies on every request has negative consequences. First, it adds extra-bandwidth in server messages. Second, the original cookie attributes (`Expires`, `Max-Age`, `Domain`, `Path`) are lost in the process. These attributes would need to be specified at each redefinition to keep application cookies constistency. To fix this problem, the attributes from the original `Set-cookie` header are encoded inside the masked cookie: a sensitive cookie V with attributes A would be transmitted to the client as $M\!:\!M \oplus V\!:\!A$. It would thus be possible to remember the correct attributes for each request.

By fixing the attribute problem, we amplified the bandwidth overhead. However, we can use smaller representations for several attributes, since each request carries information that can help rebuild the `Domain` and `Path` attributes. For domains, we can keep only the number of subdomains in the domain and the presence of a starting dot. For example, the `.example.com` domain would become `.2`, whereas `sub.example.com` would become `3`. Indeed, the exact domain can be rebuilt using the `Host` header in the request. Therefore, we only need a single byte to encode domains, using the sign bit to store the presence of the starting dot, leaving 7 bits for the node count. A similar transformation can be applied to path attributes. Finally, the expiration attribute can be converted into a 8-byte timestamp.

Another drawback of MCookies is that they cannot prevent active network attacks (such as Lucky 13). Indeed, when the record packets are modified by the attacker, they are seen as corrupted records by the server TLS stack, and discarded. Since the HTTP server never receives the corresponding request, it cannot answer with a freshly masked cookie. To counter active attacks, the browser could monitor failed successive HTTPS connections for each origin and, after a given number of broken connections, erase the cookies associated to this domain. Drawbacks of this countermeasure are twofold:

- the client has to be modified to maintain this counter;
- setting a correct threshold is hard: the trigger should be effective against real attacks, but a low threshold would easily break HTTPS sessions on poor quality network connections.

To overcome MCookies limitations, we extend MCookies with a new HTTP header: `Masked-Cookie`. This extension requires a change in the browser that is now put in charge of masking cookies.

4.2.3 *Masked-Cookie headers*

In addition to the MCookies mechanism, we introduce a new `Set-Cookie` attribute, `masked` to signal to the client the presence of masking. Then, a compliant client would, for each request, send this cookie in a new header, `Masked-Cookie`, with the value here masked by the client : `Masked-`

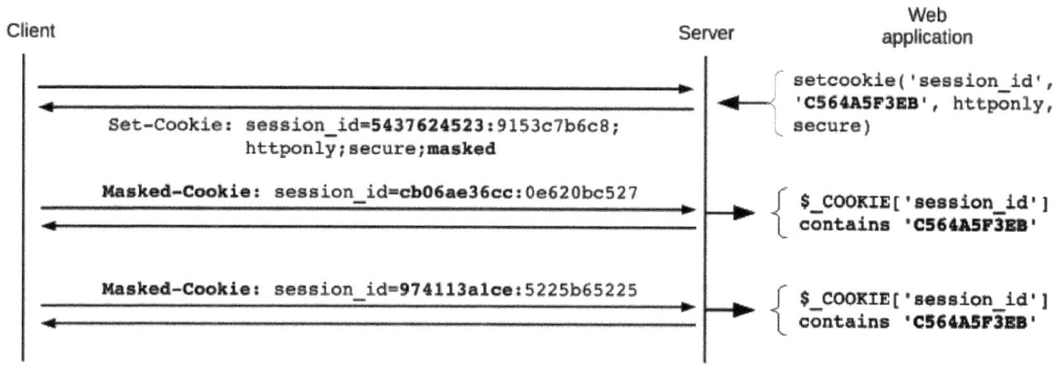

Figure 7: Use of `Masked-Cookie` headers: masking is done by the client.

`Cookie: SESSID=`M':$M' \oplus V$. Fig. 7 describes the protocol use of this new header.

By moving the cookie masking process to the client side, active attacks are no more effective. Faced with a compliant client, a server only needs to define MCookies once, so the extra bandwidth cost is essentially removed. On the other hand, a standard client will ignore the `masked` attribute, and the server will fall back on the previous behavior.

4.2.4 Apache Implementation

Implementing MCookies can easily be done as a filter module for HTTP servers. We chose Apache for our proof of concept, since it is open-source, and currently the most deployed HTTP server (its market share is estimated at 45 % by Netcraft[10] and at 65 % by W3Techs[11]).

Apache exposes a powerful module system with hooks allowing to interact with the request and response processing. In order to mask the cookies sent by the server during the emission of the `Set-Cookie` header, we hook the response process using an `output_filter`, defined by `mod_filter`. To this aim, we call the `ap_register_output_filter` and `ap_add_output_filter_handle` functions. Then, to unmask the cookies received via `Cookies` headers from the client, we hook the request handling. The `input_filter` hook happening too late in the process, we use an earlier control point, when headers are parsed, using `ap_hook_header_parser`. The last step is to send a new representation of the cookie parsed in the request, along with the response; this step is easy to implement since request cookies are available from the `output_filter` hooks.

The overall code to implement the MCookies (including the Base64 code to encode the masked value safely) is around 500 lines of C. It handles both the MCookie rewriting, without compression, and the `Masked-Cookie` extension.

4.2.5 Masked-Cookies for Chromium

Chromium is currently the most popular web browser. As it is open-source and modular, we decided to patch this web browser to prove the feasibility of `Masked-Cookies` headers in a real world context. The overall C++ patch for Chromium (version 31) only counts 241 lines. It adds the `masked` attribute to the internal cookie representation, the `CanonicalCookie` class, as a new attribute. Masking and unmasking are implemented in the `CanonicalCookie::Create` and `CookieMonster::BuildCookieLine` methods.

[10] `http://www.netcraft.com`
[11] `http://w3techs.com`

5. ANALYSIS OF MASKING MECHANISMS

5.1 Security analysis

5.1.1 TLS Scramble method

Specified as a new TLS compression method, TLS Scramble would require deployment efforts. However, once deployed, TLS compression negotiation would be reliable, since it is similar to ciphersuite negotiation, which is known to work between all TLS stacks.

TLS Scramble disables real TLS compression, trivialy defeating CRIME and TIME attacks. This technique is also efficient against BEAST, Lucky 13, RC4-biases and POODLE attacks, since they only recover the secret one byte at a time, and that Scramble makes this byte a moving target.

It is however important to notice that TLS Scrambling masks the entire messages, and not only the secret values, which means this method does not meet the principle described in section 3 *per se*. In particular, some attacks relying on mixing secret values and attacker's guess might still work, e.g. compression attacks in the application layer.

5.1.2 MCookies

MCookies randomize only the cookie values sent by the client, which fits exactly our masking principle. As long as secrets are masked, first-order attacks will be defeated by MCookies: this is the case for passive network attacks like BEAST, client-side compression attacks and RC4-biases.

To be effective, MCookies need HTTP requests to reach the server and the corresponding answers (containing a freshly masked cookie) to get back to the client. Active network attackers may be able to block such answers. Even if they do not, Lucky 13 can not be blocked by MCookies, since each tampered request will lead to a server-side TLS error, thus breaking the connection. For POODLE, a lucky guess will lead to a valid record, and the server will be able to send a new cookie representation, which may still be blocked by the attacker. So MCookies are inefficient against active attacks.

Apart from thwarting most of the attacks, MCookies have the advantage of requiring only a small modification of the HTTP server, leaving the browser and the web application untouched, which makes it a reliable solution to deploy.

5.1.3 *MCookies with* `Masked-Cookies` *headers*

As MCookies, this extended mechanism fits the masking principle. Moreover, since sensitive cookies are masked by the browser, every request will be masked differently, even in the presence of an active attacker: all the studied attacks are covered by the countermeasure.

Moreover, this mechanism is backward compatible: it is possible with the same HTTPS server to handle old and new clients, taking advantage of the new `Masked-Cookies` headers when available, but still defeating passive network attacks with older clients.

5.2 Performance analysis

5.2.1 *TLS Scrambling overhead analysis*

Masking plaintext data at the TLS level is easy to implement, and is completely transparent from the application layer point of view. Yet, it presents two major drawbacks:

- each and every record has to be κ-byte longer, even for short messages;
- deploying a new compression method in TLS would be hard, since deploying new ciphersuites (an easier operation) can take years.

Performance-wise, the CPU overhead is negligible, and the network bandwidth overhead is less than 1 % in bytes.

5.2.2 *MCookies network overhead analysis*

At application level, the masking of cookie values increases the HTTP requests and responses size by adding the mask and the attributes to the initial cookie value and by sending new headers. In order to quantify this overhead, we built a script that simulates MCookies on a real internet navigation traffic. It computes the overheads according to whether the web browser used supports `Masked-Cookies` headers or not.

Traffic type	**Raw traffic volume**	**Extra bandwidth**		
		w/o UA support		with UA
		naive	compr.	support
Sensitive	24 MB	+20.1 %	+14.9 %	+10.8 %
Overall	122 MB	+4.1 %	+3.0 %	+2.2 %

Table 2: Network overhead evalulation

We instrumented a web browser (Chromium) to analyse HTTP requests and responses from HTTPS secured traffic obtained during the following one day scenario. The user logs in Google, Facebook, Twitter, Dropbox, an RSS aggregator, and some other web sites; he keeps tabs opened on multiple pages for each services, uses them during the day and browses other websites as well. 8,185 HTTP requests (122 MB) were retrieved. Among these, 4,823 requests (24 MB) actually set or sent sensitives cookies.

With this HTTP trace, the script processes sequentially each request and simulates the overheads induced by installing the MCookie module on every reached host. We identify every sensitive cookie by looking at the `httpOnly` and `secure` flags. Table 2 describes the extra bandwidth in different situations: without User-Agent support (that is using MCookies), either with naïve or compressed encoding, and with User-Agent support (the `Masked-Cookies` headers). The results show a significant overhead on requests containing sensitive cookies. However, when looking at the big picture, the overall HTTPS traffic, this overhead turns out to be rather small. Finally, compared to the entire web communications, both HTTP and HTTPS, the cost induced by cookie masking proves to be negligible.

5.2.3 *Apache module system overhead analysis*

To evaluate the efficiency of MCookies and assess their scalability, we performed a web server benchmark with and without the MCookies module enabled. In order to evaluate the module overhead, we ran the benchmarking tool on a single HTML page. Furthermore, we also benchmarked the module on a Wordpress website for a more realistic scenario. Each request sent embedded three different sentitive cookies.

The host used for this evaluation was an Intel Xeon X5650 with 6Go of RAM running a Debian system with an Apache (v2.4.7) web server, a Mysql (v5.5) database server and hosting a Wordpress (v3.8.1) web site.

	Vanilla server	**MCookies enabled**	
		w/o UA support	with UA support
Static page	384	318 (-17 %)	382
Wordpress page	221	212 (-4 %)	220

Table 3: Performance results (transactions/second)

We used Siege[12] in benchmark mode to assess the number of transactions the web server is capable to process per second with the three scenarios. The results, as described in Table 3, show a small decrease of 4 % of the Wordpress web server capacity when dealing with User-Agents without the support of this mechanism, whereas the overhead is negligible otherwise. However, for a static page served to a User-Agent with no `Masked-Cookie` header support, performance are much more degraded, but this is a worst-case scenario, since static web sites rarely produce sensitive cookies.

6. RELATED WORK

To avoid repeating the same cookie across different TLS messages, a natural idea would be to change its value for every new connection, or at least to limit the cookie lifetime. In fact, PHP proposes a way to handle session identifiers this way with the `session_regenerate_id` function, usually called after a user logged in, to decorrelate the old and the new sessions and avoid session fixation attacks[13]. Short-lived cookies (which could even be pushed to single-use cookies) should thwart all passive attacks, but choosing the right lifetime is not easy. In fact, mitigating attacks would require a very short lifetime, which could easily lead to out-of-sync cookies when dealing with parallel HTTP connections. Modern web sites heavily use JavaScript asynchronous requests, and session regenerations are known to provoke requests concurrency errors[14]. This is why MCookies are designed to always have the same *intended* value.

One-Time Cookies [7] are another solution to protect plaintext HTTP cookies against replay, by having the client bind

[12]`http://www.joedog.org/siege-home/`

[13]`http://www.acros.si/papers/session_fixation.pdf`

[14]Our 1-day HTTPS capture actually contains such concurrent requests, that would be problematic.

the cookie with the request sent. This mechanism uses cryptographic mechanisms (symmetric encryption and HMAC) and borrows the idea of Kerberos tickets and proposes an elegant solution requiring no server-side state. Applied to HTTPS and our attacker model, One-Time Cookies (OTC) do not counter attacks, since repeating the same exact request would lead to the same OTC; however, the value retrieved could only be replayed for the request in question, which would limit the scope of the attacks. Moreover, as OTC rely on specific HTTP headers, their implementation requires browser and server/web application modifications. With regard to the Record protocol attacks exposed here, `Masked-Cookie` headers are much simpler to implement (no cryptographic primitives are needed).

Both solutions (single-use cookies and One-Time Cookies) are described in Table 1. Other alternative cookie protocols have been proposed, such as [14, 20], but they share OTC advantage (unique cookies bound to the request data) and drawbacks (heavy changes needed on both end points).

7. CONCLUSION

We have studied recent attacks on TLS Record protocol, and thoroughly analyzed the proposed countermeasures. In practice, the countermeasures implemented in most of the software are specific to each attack: $1/n-1$ split for BEAST, constant-time CBC decryption for Lucky 13, deprecation of RC4, disabling TLS compression for CRIME and TIME, and deprecation of SSLv3 for POODLE.

In parallel, we showed that all the attacks relied on the common assumption that a secret would be repeatedly sent in different TLS sessions. We suggested a common model to describe these attacks. We also proposed to reuse the concept of masking, borrowed from the side-channel community, to mitigate the attacks. Such a technique can be implemented as a complementary measure, a defense-in-depth strategy. We described different ways this countermeasure could be implemented, and wrote two proofs of concept to check its feasibility to protect cookies.

At the TLS level, our Scramble compression method builds on the idea of WebSockets masking, which actually blocked the BEAST attack. At the HTTP level, our MCookies extend the idea of single-use cookies, without requiring complex changes in web protocols and applications. Masking allows for a defense-in-depth strategy, giving developers and integrators more time to solve the crisis. It would have been effective against the presented attacks, and might be against yet unknown ones. The recent POODLE attack did in fact meet all the criteria, and was published after we implemented our proposals. The fact it would have been blocked by our proofs of concept actually validates our work.

We would however make it clear that masking is designed to be a defense-in-depth measure *in addition* to specific countermeasures, not instead of them. When a cryptographic algorithm or scheme shows significant weaknesses, they should be phased out and correctly patched. In the particular case of RC4, we now know a lot of statistical biases, some of which can lead to efficient first order attacks, but realistic second order attacks could be the next attack against TLS Record layer. All the masking proposals could be easily extended to use two (or three) masks instead of one. Yet we consider RC4 is a good example of a streamcipher that should have been phased out a long time ago, since many RC4 practical and theoretical flaws have been known for a decade.

8. REFERENCES

[1] N. J. AlFardan, D. Bernstein, K. G. Paterson, B. Poettering, and J. C. N. Schuldt. On the security of RC4 in TLS and WPA. In *USENIX Security*, 2013.

[2] N. J. AlFardan and K. G. Paterson. Lucky Thirteen: Breaking the TLS and DTLS Record Protocols. In *IEEE SSP*, 2013.

[3] A. Barth. HTTP State Management Mechanism. RFC 6265, 2011.

[4] A. Barth. The Web Origin Concept. RFC 6454, 2011.

[5] D. Bernstein. ChaCha, a variant of Salsa20. cr.yp.to/papers.html#chacha, 2008.

[6] S. Chari, C. S. Jutla, J. R. Rao, and P. Rohatgi. Towards sound approaches to counteract power-analysis attacks. In *CRYPTO*, 1999.

[7] I. Dacosta, S. Chakradeo, M. Ahamad, and P. Traynor. One-time cookies: Preventing session hijacking attacks with stateless authentication tokens. *ACM Trans. Internet Techn.*, 2012.

[8] T. Dierks and E. Rescorla. TLS Protocol Version 1.1. RFC 4346, 2006.

[9] T. Dierks and E. Rescorla. TLS Protocol Version 1.2. RFC 5246, 2008.

[10] T. Duong and J. Rizzo. BEAST: Surprising crypto attack against HTTPS. Ekoparty, 2011.

[11] I. Fette and A. Melnikov. The WebSocket Protocol. RFC 6455, 2011.

[12] S. Fluhrer and D. McGrew. Statistical Analysis of the Alleged RC4 Keystream Generator. In *FSE*, 2000.

[13] J. Franks, P. Hallam-Baker, J. Hostetler, S. Lawrence, P. Leach, A. Luotonen, and L. Stewart. HTTP Authentication: Basic and Digest Access Authentication. RFC 2617, 1999.

[14] K. Fu, E. Sit, K. Smith, and N. Feamster. The Dos and Don'ts of Client Authentication on the Web. In *USENIX Security*, 2001.

[15] L. Goubin and J. Patarin. DES and Differential Power Analysis The "Duplication" Method. In *CHES*, 1999.

[16] P. Gutmann. Encrypt-then-MAC for Transport Layer Security (TLS) and Datagram Transport Layer Security (DTLS). RFC 7366, 2014.

[17] J. Hodges, C. Jackson, and A. Barth. HTTP Strict Transport Security (HSTS). RFC 6797, 2012.

[18] T. Isobe, T. Ohigashi, Y. Waatanabe, and M. Morii. Full Plaintext Recovery Attack on Broadcast RC4. In *FSE*, 2013.

[19] O. Levillain, A. Ebalard, H. Debar, and B Morin. One Year of SSL Measurement. In *ACSAC*, 2012.

[20] A. X. Liu, J. M. Kovacs, C. Huang, and M. G. Gouda. A Secure Cookie Protocol. In *IEEE ICCCN*, 2005.

[21] B. Möller. Security of CBC Ciphersuites in SSL/TLS: Problems and Countermeasures, 2002-2004.

[22] B. Möller, T. Duong, and K. Kotowicz. Google Security Advisory: This POODLE Bites: Exploiting The SSL 3.0 Fallback, 2014.

[23] K. G. Paterson and N. J. AlFardan. Plaintext Recovery Attacks Against DTLS. In *NDSS*, 2012.

[24] Y. N. Pettersen. Renego patched servers: A long-term interoperability time bomb brewing. My Opera blog: Implementer's notes, 2010.

[25] A. Prado, N. Harris, and Y. Gluck. SSL, Gone in 30 seconds - A BREACH beyond CRIME. Black Hat USA, 2013.
[26] E. Prouff and M. Rivain. Masking against side-channel attacks: a formal security proof. In *Eurocrypt*, 2013.
[27] E. Rescorla and N. Modadugu. DTLS Version 1.2. RFC 6347, 2012.
[28] I. Ristic. Internet SSL Survey, Talk at BlackHat 2010. Black Hat USA, 2010.
[29] J. Rizzo and T. Duong. The CRIME attack. Ekoparty, 2012.
[30] P. Rogaway. IETF Draft: Problems with proposed IP Cryptography, 1995.
[31] A. Stubblefield, J. Ioannidis, and A. Rubin. Using the Fluhrer, Mantin, and Shamir Attack to Break WEP. In *NDSS*, 2002.
[32] A. Shulman T. Be'ery. A Perfect CRIME? TIME Will Tell. Black Hat EU, 2013.
[33] S. Vaudenay. Security Flaws Induced by CBC Padding Applications to SSL, IPsec, WTLS. In *Eurocrypt*, 2002.

APPENDIX

A. HTTP BASIC/DIGEST AUTH

In this paper, we discussed cookie protection. Other methods exist to authenticate the client at the HTTP layer: Basic and Digest Authentication [13]. In practice, they are rarely used, as the user interfaces do not allow for a clean integration with modern web applications (e.g. no logout feature).

Both headers are as vulnerable as cookies w.r.t. the described attacks. For Basic Authentication, it is not clear how they could be randomized: there can be no equivalent to MCookies, unless the mechanism is deeply changed. For Digest Authentication however, the standard already allows for possible randomizations resembling MCookies, producing a new server nonce value for each new request. Such policy would defeat all passive network attacks, since the client would produce a different header for each request.

B. SERVER-SIDE COMPRESSION

B.1 TIME and BREACH

In the TIME attack, in addition to targeting client-side compression, the researchers proposed to target server-side secret information repeatedly sent on the wire. For example, Cross-Site Request Forgeries (CSRF) are usually blocked by having the server insert a token in forms, which is later checked on form submission. Such anti-CSRF tokens are usually reused for a given user and a certain amount of time.

Server-side messages can be compressed using two different mechanisms. In addition to the aforementioned TLS compression, the server can also use HTTP compression. This HTTP compression is also a target of the attack, as the attacker can inject attacker-controlled data in the server answer (preferably close to the targeted token in the payload). This is the principle of the BREACH attack [25], an attack aiming at retrieving the anti-CSRF token sent by the server.

Hypotheses and prerequisites

- TLS or HTTP compression is activated;
- The ciphertext length is observable;
- The answer containing the target token is partially controlled by the attacker, e.g. using a reflected field;
- Multiple connections containing the secret can be triggered by the attacker.

Proposed countermeasures

Disable TLS and HTTP compression. As for client-side compression, this measure blocks the attack. In fact, TLS compression can be (and has been) disabled, but HTTP compression is essential to reduce bandwidth and disabling it would drastically increase the size of HTTP responses.

Randomize the packet length. See Sec. 2.2.

Structurally modify web applications to separate secrets from attacker-controlled content. If sensitive information and attacker-controlled content come from different servers, compression contexts are distinct and the attack does not hold. Yet, this requires significant changes.

Change the token value for each request (single-use token). It would block the attack but it also requires an important change in the way anti-CSRF tokens usually work.

B.2 MTokens: Making anti-CSRF tokens

To mitigate server-side attacks, the CSRF tokens (and similar objects) could easily be protected using a technique close to MCookies, i.e. by masking the token with a different value for each message. The *intended* value of the token would remain the same, avoiding out-of-sync problems, while randomizing the data that is sent over the network. Implementing this would require very very small changes to web applications (or even no change at all if web frameworks are modified): it would simply amount to replacing every call to the function producing the token (which we will call `write_csrftoken()`) with `mask(write_csrftoken())`, and each call to the function getting the token from the client form (`read_csrftoken()`) with `unmask(read_csrftoken())`.

Security analysis

MTokens require small modifications in web applications (or in frameworks), so they are easy to deploy, reliable and compatible with web applications, especially if the changes are made in the framework. They are effective against server-side first order attacks against anti-CSRF tokens in general.

C. TLS SCRAMBLING FUNCTION

The core of the Scramble compression method is the `scramble_record` function (and `unscramble_record`, its counterpart), which is implemented as follows

```
static int scramble_record(COMP_CTX *ctx,
  uchar *out, uint olen, uchar *in, uint ilen)
{
  uchar mask[MSIZE];

  if (olen < (ilen + MSIZE)) return -1;
  if (RAND()->bytes(mask, MSIZE) < 0) return -1;
  memcpy (out, &mask, MSIZE);

  out = out + MSIZE;
  for (int i = 0; i < ilen; i++)
    *(out++) = *(in++) ^ mask.bytes[i % MSIZE];
  return (ilen + MSIZE);
}
```

Enabling IP Protection for Outsourced Integrated Circuit Design

Xingliang Yuan
Department of CS
City University of Hong Kong
Hong Kong
xl.y@my.cityu.edu.hk

Cong Wang
Department of CS
City University of Hong Kong
Hong Kong
congwang@cityu.edu.hk

Kui Ren
Department of CSE
University at Buffalo
United States
kuiren@buffalo.edu

ABSTRACT

As today's integrated circuit (IC) has easily involved millions and even billions of gates, known as very large-scale integration (VLSI), one natural trend is to move such prohibitive in-house design procedure to the low-cost public cloud. However, such a migration is also raising a challenging request on practical and privacy-preserving techniques to safeguard the sensitive IC design data, i.e., the Intellectual Property (IP). In this paper, we initiate the first study along the direction, and present a practical system for privacy-preserving IC timing analysis, which refers to an essential and expensive procedure via repeated evaluations of timing delays on a gate-level circuit. For privacy protection, our system leverages a key observation that many IP blocks are universally reused and shared across different IC designs, and thus only a small portion of critical IP blocks need to be protected. By carefully extracting such critical design data from the whole circuit, our system only outsources the non-critical data to the public cloud. As such "data splitting" does not readily facilitate correct timing analysis, we then develop specialized algorithms to enable the public cloud to take only the non-critical data and return intermediate results. Such results can later be integrated with critical design data by the local server for fast timing analysis. We also propose a heuristic algorithm to considerably reduce the bandwidth cost in the system. Through rigorous security analysis, we show our system is resilient to IC reverse engineering and protects both the critical IP gate-level design and functionality. We evaluate our system over large IC benchmarks with up to a million of gates to show the efficiency and effectiveness.

Categories and Subject Descriptors

B.7 [**Integrated Circuits**]: Miscellaneous; K.6.5 [**Management of Computing and Information Systems**]: Security and Protection

ASIA CCS'15, April 14–17, 2015, Singapore, Singapore

http://dx.doi.org/10.1145/2714576.2714601 .

Keywords

Secure outsourcing; Integrated circuits; IP protection; Timing analysis

1. INTRODUCTION

The steady scaling down of transistor size and remarkable innovations in electronic design automation (EDA) have made it possible today to fit millions and even billions of gates into a single integrated circuit (IC), known as very large-scale integration (VLSI). To deliver the circuit final physical layout from the design specification [25], engineers have to comply with the rigorous and expensive IC design procedures over such large-scaled data, including functional verification, circuit equivalence checking, timing and power analysis, etc. For design optimization, such procedure needs to be further conducted in an iterative and incremental manner, exacerbating the relentlessly growing design complexity and the inexorable demand of computing resources. To economically keep up with the intensive design processing on VLSI circuits, one natural trend is to move the in-house procedures to the public cloud, taking advantages of its low-cost and scalable computing resources, and parallel batch processing capabilities [2]. While cloud provides opportunities and means to deliver greater value with cheaper cost, such a migration is also demanding practical and privacy-preserving techniques to safeguard the sensitive IC design data, i.e., the Intellectual Property (IP)[1] [2, 18, 26].

Previous study has shown hardware infringement could result in dramatic capital loss at least over $5 billion USD per year [26]. Hence, IP protection is indispensable in IC design. To defend against IP infringement, various hardware watermarking [1] and fingerprinting techniques [23] have been proposed, with the goal of tagging and tracking possible illegal IP usages after physical hardware manufacturing. Meanwhile, some proactive protection approaches, like IC obfuscation via camouflage gates [21] and splitting manufacturing [15], have also been proposed recently, with the goal of concealing IP at the stage of manufacturing. Although effective, we argue that all those designs are focusing on the IP protection after the IC design procedure has been completely finalized. None of them have considered the potential security challenges, when the overall IC design procedures are migrated off premises, i.e., on the public cloud.

[1]IP block is a reusable unit of hardware description language (HDL), logic, cell, or layout design that is the intellectual property of one party.

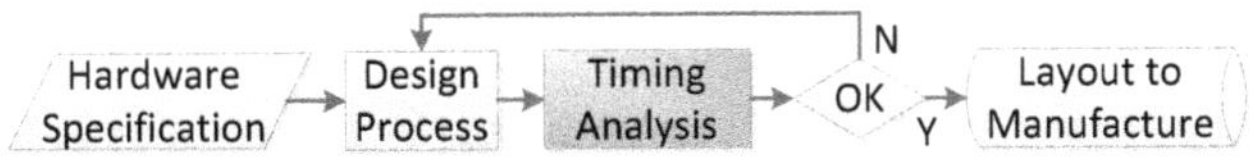

Figure 1: IC design flow

In this paper, we initiate the study of this challenging problem, how to enable secure IC design outsourcing with privacy-assured IP protection, and present our first result in this effort, a practical system for outsourced privacy-preserving timing analysis on integrated circuits. As an essential procedure of IC design shown in Figure 1, timing analysis evaluates the circuit timing performance and verifies the timing constraints to guarantee the circuit design specification and runtime reliability before IC fabrication [25]. To tolerate process variations in fabrication, one widely adopted approach is statistical timing analysis, which requires repeated evaluations of the longest path delay on a gate-level circuit timing graph via Monte Carlo simulations [11]. To predict IC's timing performance with a measurable confidence, such statistical simulations usually need to be evaluated more than tens of thousands of times. And the cost of each simulation is in proportional to the size of circuits, i.e., the number of gates and interconnects [25]. In particular, on a modern PC with an Intel 3.6GHz CPU, it takes nearly an hour on a circuit with about 25,000 logic gates to perform 64,000 Monte Carlo simulations [7]. Since today's IC design can easily involve millions and even billions of gates, the resulting computation cost is prohibitive even for well-financed IC design companies.

Design intuitions. In order to enable practical and privacy-preserving timing analysis on integrated circuits, our system leverages a key observation on IP reuse design philosophy [19,25]. Namely, many IP blocks are universally reused and shared across different IC designs for the saving of redundant development effort, and thus only a small portion of critical IP blocks need to be protected, especially those newly designed ones. The reasons are the following: Firstly, many IP blocks in IC are standard design units, such as memory, bus I/O, arithmetic units, etc [25]. They are by nature non-sensitive design data and do not need to be protected. Secondly, as indicated by recent surveys [5,14], the percentage of the newly designed blocks on a full IC today is just less than 10% as of 2014. And this percentage will be continuously decreasing, due to the increasing reuse of standard or aging IP blocks across different IC designs.

Based on above observations, our design intuition is to carefully extract the small portion of critical design data from the whole circuit on the local private server, and only outsource the large portion of non-critical design data to the public cloud, so as to achieve the IP protection. We argue that such a design choice, i.e., placing all non-critical IP blocks on the public cloud, is also beneficial to the IP reuse philosophy. Many computations over the non-critical design data can be carried out only once and shared/reused on a globally available cloud infrastructure.

Design challenges. However, simply splitting the critical design data from the non-critical one does not readily facilitate correct timing analysis. This is because most state-of-the-art algorithms for finding the longest path delay on a circuit timing graph require the sequential processing of each graph vertex[2] Directly applying them will inevitably bring in huge interactions between the public cloud and the private server due to our "data splitting". Thus, we have to develop a new algorithm, which should break the computation dependency between the critical and non-critical data, such that cloud can finish the intensive workloads only based on the non-critical data and return intermediate results. For that purpose, we have carefully crafted a splitting algorithm on the circuit timing graph, by leveraging that the subpaths of longest paths are also longest paths. The resulting algorithm allows only one-round interaction, where the intermediate results can be returned in one batch and integrated by the local private server for finalizing timing analysis. The protection of IP lies in the fact that all critical IPs never leave the on-premises server.

Besides the new algorithm design, another practical challenge faced in our system is how to reduce the size of intermediate results returned by the public cloud. Because the Monte Carlo simulations on VLSI circuits normally need to be conducted for tens of thousands of times to achieve sufficient confident timing analysis results, the size of intermediate results can be large. To reduce the bandwidth cost, we propose a heuristic algorithm that is able to transform the intermediate results, represented as timing graphs, into equivalent graphs with much fewer edges.

Contributions. Our contributions are summarized below:

- We propose the first practical and privacy-preserving system to outsource timing analysis, one of the most expensive and critical IC design procedures, on integrated circuits. The system delicately extracts and reserves the critical IP blocks and only outsources the non-critical design data to the public cloud.
- Our design enables cloud to conduct intensive workloads on the non-critical data only and return intermediate results, which can later be integrated by the local server with critical design data for finalizing timing analysis. We also design a heuristic algorithm to considerably reduce the size of the intermediate results for better communication efficiency.
- Our security analysis demonstrates our system is resilient to the state-of-the-art IC reverse engineering [24] on the critical IP gate-level design and functionality. Especially for the IP functionality protection, we prove that our system is secure such that the reverse engineering, i.e., *I/O pattern analysis* reveals the critical IP functionality with negligible probability.
- We implement our system prototype and evaluate the system performance on a large scale IC benchmark IWLS2005 [3], which contains circuits with nearly one million gates. Our evaluation shows the local computational saving is up to 91% when the critical IP blocks are around 10% of the whole IC, as indicated in recent surveys [5,14].

Our system makes one-step closer towards secure IC design migration to the public cloud [2]. It can be considered as a building-block for other EDA applications to further encourage IP-protected IC design outsourcing via IP reuse.

[2]One well-known algorithm is the Program Evaluation and Review Technique (PERT) [25] which traverses the graph vertices in the topologically sorted order. Details can be seen in Section 2 and Appendix.

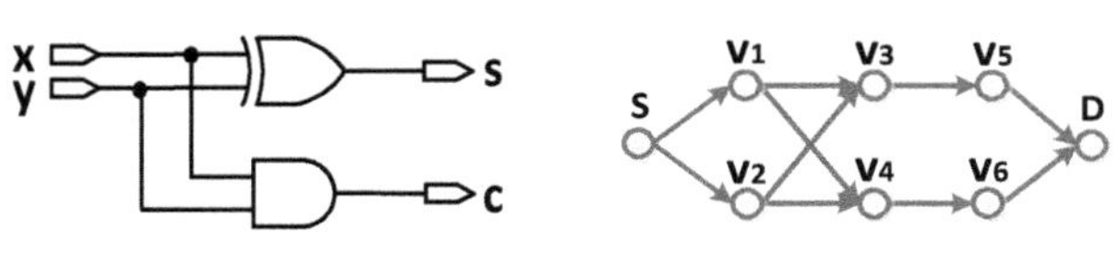

(a) Gate-level Design (b) Timing Graph

Figure 2: Gate-level design and timing graph of half-adder

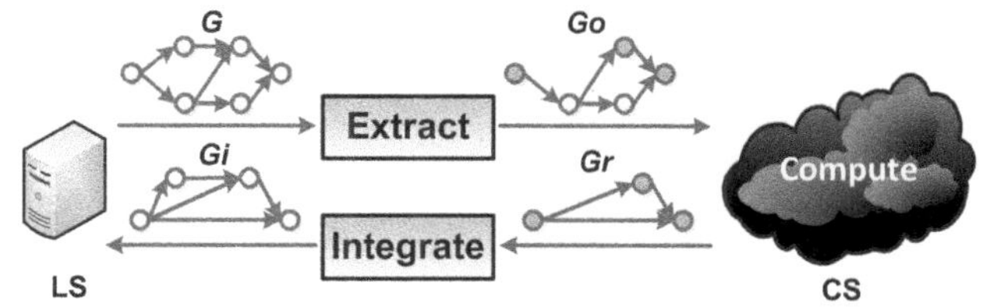

Figure 3: System design overview

Organization. Section 2 introduces the preliminaries and notations. Section 3 presents the system model, attack assumptions, and design goals. Afterwards, Section 4 elaborates on our system design. Security analysis is discussed in Section 5. Prototype evaluations are reported in Section 6. Section 7 gives a comprehensive overview on related works, with Section 8 concluding the whole paper.

2. PRELIMINARIES AND NOTATIONS

IC design flow. An overview of IC design flow is shown in Figure 1: design engineers first describe IC's functionality and behaviour by hardware description language (HDL) according to design specifications. The logic-synthesis then transforms HDL codes to the logic gate-level design. By selecting the logic gates from the standard cell library[3], IC's gate-level design, also known as netlist [25] is generated with collections of standard cells and electronic connections. After that, timing analysis estimates the expected time for how long the signal propagates from IC's inputs to outputs over its gate-level design. Only if there is no violation on timing constraints and the timing performance meets the design specification, the circuit layout will be generated and delivered for fabrication. Timing analysis is supposed to ensure the circuit performance and runtime reliability.

Timing analysis. Precisely, timing analysis is to evaluate IC's longest path delay. The problem is formulated as the longest path problem on a weighted directed-acyclic graph (DAG) [7, 11]. The timing graph $G(V, E)$ is derived from the gate-level netlist, where vertex set $V = \{v_i\}$ represents gates, inputs, and outputs, directed edge set $E = \{e_{i,j}\}$ represents interconnects (electronic wires). Adjacent lists are used to represent $G(V, E)$, where $v_i.adj_{out}, v_i.adj_{in}$ denote v_i's outgoing and incoming neighbors respectively. Edge $e_{i,j}$ is assigned with a non-negative weight d_i, which corresponds to the gate delay[4]. Figure 2 illustrates the gate-level design of 1 bit half-adder and its modeled timing graph, where v_1 and v_2 represent input x and y; v_5 and v_6 represent output s and c; v_3 is 2-input *xor* gate and v_4 is 2-input *and* gate; source S connects to all inputs and sink D is connected from all outputs. Given the timing graph, one common approach, the Program Evaluation and Review Technique (PERT), can be used to obtain the longest path delay through sequential computations following a vertex-based linear order, i.e., topological-order (see Appendix).

To tolerate the effects of process variations in fabrication, which lead to random delays at logic gates and interconnects, statistical timing analysis (STA) via Monte Carlo simulations are widely adopted. In STA, statistical models of device parameters and delay are first built. Then the probability distribution of IC's longest path delay is estimated via Monte Carlo simulations, which delivers the accurate timing measurements and encompasses the complicated statistical models [11]. Within simulations, process or device parameters are sampled from their statistical models to generate the deterministic delays based on the delay model. Then PERT runs repeatedly through the full-circuit timing graph to obtain the longest path distribution which is defined as χ and derived from $\{D_1, \ldots, D_n\}$, where D_i is the longest path delay for the ith simulation. Because our system carefully extracts the critical timing graph from the non-critical one and aims to intentionally separate the computation on the two part, PERT is no longer directly applicable, because of its requirement on the sequential processing of vertices.

[3]The standard cell library usually contains the logic gate schematic, layout, abstract and timing information, etc.

[4]Following the standard practice [7, 11], we ignore the interconnect delay as it is usually negligible compared to the gate delay. We note that it does not affect the design correctness.

3. PROBLEM STATEMENT

3.1 System Model

Our system includes two entities, as shown in Figure 3: the *local private server* (LS), who may represent IC design companies; the *public cloud servers* (CS), who provide computing as services. LS attempts to leverage CS to perform timing analysis on integrated circuits for cost saving and productivity improvement, while protecting the critical IPs from CS.

Our design leverages the IC reuse philosophy and achieves privacy-preserving by extracting the critical IP design data, such as those newly designed blocks, from the whole circuit. LS first formulates a full-circuit timing graph G, and then extracts the critical subgraphs G_c from G to reserve it locally. Here G_c covers all the critical IP blocks. After that, the remaining timing graph, denoted as G_o, is sent to CS, who will conduct intensive Monte Carlo simulation workloads over G_o and return intermediate results, denoted as G_r. G_r is a reduced size timing graph with multiple weights per edge derived from multiple Monte Carlo simulations. Upon receiving G_r, LS integrates G_r with G_c to form a new graph G_i, and finalizes timing analysis to derive the longest path distribution χ.

3.2 Threat Models and Attack Assumptions

In this paper, we assume LS is trustworthy, and mainly consider an "honest-but-curious" public cloud, which performs the specified computations faithfully but is interested in the critical IC design data theft. Typically, two types of design data protection are considered for critical IP blocks: 1) **critical gate-level design;** 2) **critical IP functionality**. In our design, cloud only sees the outsourced non-critical IP blocks, while the critical IP blocks, especially their gate-level designs and related computations, never leave the local private server. Hence, we mainly focus on the IP functionality protection against IC reverse engineering.

As widely recognized by the state-of-the-art [21, 24], the most effective reverse engineering on IP functionality can be summarized as *I/O pattern analysis*. Explicitly, given a sufficient number of random input bit sequences and the corresponding bit outputs (I/O patterns), the IP functionality might be inferred or even resolved by finding the input sequence and the output sequence matching between the unknown IP blocks and existing IP blocks with known functionalities. We assume "honest-but-curious" cloud tries to infer the possible I/O vertices of critical IPs from the non-critical IPs, which it can see, for *I/O pattern analysis*. We want to achieve that such reverse engineering will hardly succeed with negligible probability.

3.3 Design Goals

With above attack models and assumptions, our system should achieve the following design goals: 1) Critical data protection: no critical design data including gate-level design and functionalities can be leaked or reverse engineered from the input or the output of the outsourced computing workloads at public cloud. 2) Correctness: the timing analysis results from our framework should be exactly the same as the ones computed from the original timing analysis approach. 3) Efficiency: the local computation should be substantially less than performing timing analysis over the full IC. The communication cost should be minimized.

4. OUR PROPOSED DESIGN

This section presents our practical privacy-preserving timing analysis system. We start from the system functions, and then elaborate on them including the extraction methodology for the critical timing graph, the pairwise longest path computation for conducting Monte Carlo simulations over non-critical timing graph, a heuristic reduction algorithm on cloud's intermediate results, and the integration on intermediate results with the reserved critical timing graph.

4.1 System Framework

The processes at LS comprise two functions Extract and Integrate. The process on CS is represented by one function Compute. Each function is summarized below:

- Extract(G) $\rightarrow \{G_c, G_o\}$: The function protects critical IP design data and functionalities. It takes the full circuit timing graph G as input, and outputs the critical timing graph G_c and the outsourced timing graph G_o.
- Compute(G_o, N) $\rightarrow \{G_r\}$: The function performs simulations at CS. It takes G_o and the number of Monte Carlo simulations N as inputs, and outputs the intermediate results G_r.
- Integrate(G_c, G_r, N) $\rightarrow \{\chi\}$: The function obtains the final timing analysis result. It takes G_c, G_r and N as inputs, and outputs the longest path distribution χ.

4.2 Critical Subgraph Extraction

One fundamental requirement of our timing analysis system is to protect the critical design data. We leverage the observation of IP reuse design methodology [19, 25]. Most of the reused IP blocks are standard, and the critical design

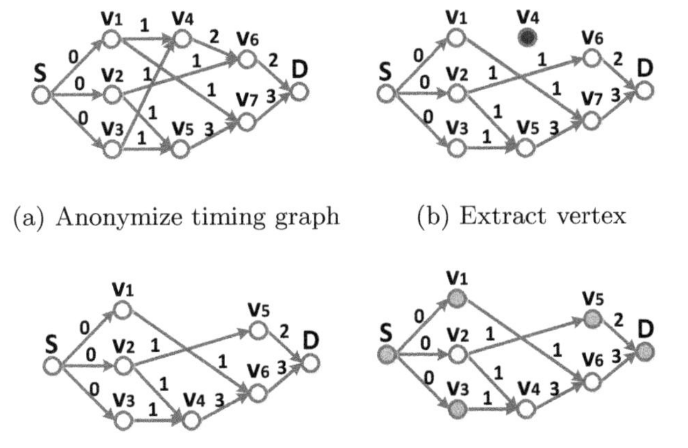

(a) Anonymize timing graph (b) Extract vertex

(c) Re-index vertices (d) Color boundary vertices

Figure 4: The procedure of Extract function

data such as newly designed IP blocks are only a small portion in the whole design. Therefore, we plan to extract the corresponding critical timing graph from the full-circuit timing graph, and simultaneously generate a non-critical outsourced timing graph. Our extraction does not place any critical design data to CS, and it further ensures the correct computation at CS on outsourced data and facilitates the subsequent integration at LS.

An illustrative example. To illustrate our idea, we consider a simple example of extracting discrete vertices in Figure 4. The circuit timing graph with topological-order indexed vertices is firstly anonymized as shown in Figure 4a. Assume that v_4 is critical, we then extract v_4 and its adjacent weighted edges in Figure 4b, to prevent reverse engineering from using such information to identify its representative gate and functionality. However, v_4 is possibly revealed from the vertex index information. Accordingly, we re-index the vertices by starting from 1 continuously to be compatible with the topological-order, shown in Figure 4c. Such index mapping information is reserved locally for the correctness of integration later. While doing so achieves privacy protection, it does not facilitate the correct computation at CS. Therefore, we have to further provide CS with some hints, i.e., v_4's adjacent vertices, source S and sink D should be gray colored as boundary vertices in Figure 4d. As shown in Section 5, revealing these hints does not compromise the security. To present Extract formally, we first give some auxiliary definitions:

Definition 1 (SUB CRITICAL TIMING GRAPH). *Sub critical timing graph is defined as* G_i^s*, where* $1 \leq i \leq n$*. They map to the total* n *critical IP blocks.* G^s *is the union set, where* $G^s = G_1^s(V_1^s, E_1^s) \bigcup G_2^s(V_2^s, E_2^s) \bigcup \ldots \bigcup G_n^s(V_n^s, E_n^s)$.

Definition 2 (BOUNDARY VERTEX). *The vertex adjacent to* G_i^s *is defined as boundary vertex* v_i^b*. And source* S *and sink* D *are also set to boundary vertices. The set of boundary vertices is defined as* V^b.

Definition 3 (BOUNDARY EDGE). *The edge with boundary vertex is defined as boundary edge* $e_{i,j}^b$*. The set of boundary edges is defined as* E^b.

Algorithm 1: Single-source prime path $SPP(v_i)$:

Data: v_i: $P_{i,j}$'s starting vertex v_i, where $v_i \in V^b$.
Result: $W_{i,j}$: the weights of $P_{i,j}$.
begin
  for *each* $v_j \in V_o$ **do**
    $t_j \leftarrow 0$; $l_j \leftarrow 0$;
  $l_i \leftarrow 1$;
  for $j \leftarrow i+1$ *to* $|V_o|$ **do**
    for *each* $v_k \in v_j.adj_{in}$ **do**
      if $l_k = 1$ **then**
        $t_j \leftarrow \max\{w_{k,j} + t_k, t_j\}$;
        $l_j \leftarrow 1$;
    if $v_j \in V^b$ **then**
      $W_{i,j}.insert(t_j)$;

Algorithm 2: Compute on the outsourced timing graph Compute(G_o, N)

Data: G_o: the outsourced timing graph;
N: the number of MC simulations.
Result: G_r: the reduced timing graph.
begin
  for $n \leftarrow 0$ *to* N **do**
    // Generate gate delays (See Appendix).
    $WeightGen(G_o)$;
    for *each* $v_i \in v^b$*, and* $v_i.adj_{out} \neq \emptyset$ **do**
      // Compute prime path weights;
      $SPP(v_i)$;
    // Reduce bandwidth;
    $G_r \leftarrow Transform(G_r)$; ;

Definition 4 (Critical timing graph). *Critical timing graph is defined as $G_c(V_c, E_c)$, where $V_c = V^s \bigcup V^b$ and $E_c = E^s \bigcup E^b$.*

Definition 5 (Outsourced timing graph). *Outsourced timing graph is defined as $G_o(V_o, E_o)$, where $V_o = (V - V_c) \bigcup V^b$ and $E_o = E - E_c$.*

Based on the definitions, Extract is conducted as follows:
1) *Extract critical timing graph*: Critical IP blocks' corresponding timing graphs G^s are all extracted from G, and V^b and E^b which are adjacent to G^s is extracted too. As a result, G_c including G^s, V^b and E^b is reserved at LS.
2) *Re-index vertices*: The inconsecutive indexes indicate the gate numbers in critical IP blocks, so we re-index V_o in consecutive order starting from value 1. It is compatible with the topological-order for computation correctness later.
3) *Color boundary vertices*: Boundary vertices V^b are gray colored in G_o to indicate the starting and ending vertices of truncated paths for the outsourced workloads at CS and the integration for final timing analysis at LS.

Purpose of boundary vertices. For correctness, the boundary vertices are colored in the outsourced timing graph. It not only enables cloud to generate the intermediate results, but also ensures the correct integration later at the local server. Although cloud wants to infer the input and output vertices from those boundary vertices for IC reverse engineering, we note that such limited capability of cloud is not able to compromise the confidentiality of critical IP design data. We show that the IP protection of our system still holds from the security analysis later in Section 5.

Guideline on defining critical IP blocks. In practice, IC companies also want to protect IP blocks with sensitive functionalities in addition to newly designed ones. For examples, some IP blocks are security-critical and safety-critical [18]. The former ones contribute to economic and national security as they could be fundamental building blocks for commercial, industrial, and national security electronic systems. The latter ones are used in automotive systems and healthcare applications which affect human safety and personal privacy. Those IP blocks revealing other sensitive information should be extracted too. We note that introducing more critical IP blocks will introduce more computation cost locally, but it is necessary for IP protection.

4.3 Compute on Outsourced Timing Graph

Originally, each simulation of timing analysis computes the longest path from source S to sink D, while G_o only contains the non-critical truncated subpaths. For the state-of-the-art longest path algorithms like PERT, they are usually based on the sequential processing of vertices, and directly applying them will result in tremendous interactions between CS and LS. To overcome such obstacle, we propose Compute to perform pairwise longest path computation based on boundary vertex information indicated in Extract. That design provides benefits in two-fold: it can shift most workloads to CS; it only requires one round interaction to return the intermediate results while ensuring the correctness of computations in Integrate later. For security, Compute only carries out computations over G_o without retrieving any data from LS.

Our new design still utilizes the topologically-sorted order of vertices for correctness and efficiency, but targets the pairwise longest paths that start and end only at boundary vertices. We leverage the fact that the subpaths of longest paths are also longest paths. Hence, we propose to find all the boundary-vertex pairwise subpaths, and each of those longest subpaths can be further treated as a directed edge with some weight equivalent to the path weight. Accordingly, Compute will obtain all boundary-vertex pairwise longest paths for each simulation, and load them to a reduced timing graph, as the intermediate results for Integrate.

Prime path computation . To solve the problem, we propose a single-source prime path (*SPP*) algorithm which will be called multiple times in each simulation. Here, we present several definitions for the algorithm flow in Algorithm 1:

Definition 6 (Boundary-vertex pairwise path). *Boundary-vertex pairwise path $p_{i,j}$ is defined as a set of ordered edges from v_i and v_j, where v_i and v_j are the only boundary vertices along the path.*

Definition 7 (Prime path). *Prime path $P_{i,j}$ is defined as the longest $p_{i,j}$ from v_i to v_j.*

Definition 8 (Prime path weights). *Prime path weights are defined as $W_{i,j}$, where $W_{i,j}$ is a set of $\{W^k_{i,j}\}$, and $W^k_{i,j}$ is derived from the k-th simulations.*

$SPP(v_i)$ starts from one of boundary vertices v_i and performs one round graph traversal to obtain all weights of

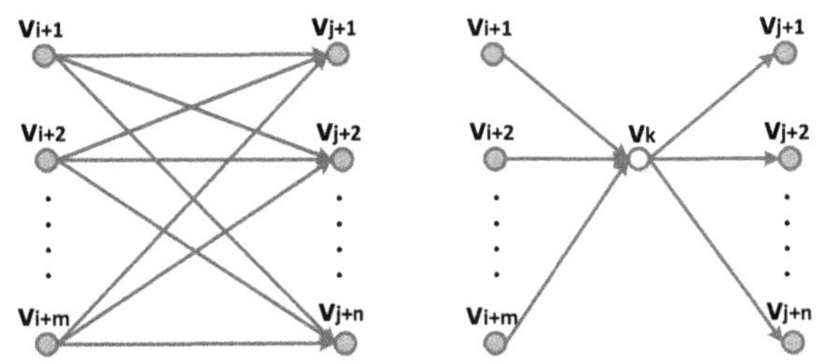

(a) Prime paths $\{P_{i,j}\}$ in G_r (b) $\{P_{i,j}\}$ that pass v_k

Figure 5: Observation on bandwidth reduction

prime paths which start from v_i. Initially, the longest path weight t_j from v_i to v_j is set to 0 for all vertices in V_o. Note that the vertex indexes still follow the topological-order after re-indexing in Extract. To leverage such benefit while guaranteeing the correctness, only vertices on prime paths $\{p_{i,j}\}$ should be processed. As vertices on $\{p_{i,j}\}$ are all reachable from v_i, we introduce a reachable label l_i to indicate the reachability. In line 6 of Algorithm 1, if v_k is reachable from v_i, where v_k is in v_j's incoming adjacent list $v_j.adj_{in}$, v_j is also reachable from v_i. Then v_j should be processed in line 7 and l_j should be updated too. When another boundary vertex v_j is processed, t_j is inserted to $W_{i,j}$. $SPP(v_i)$ terminates when the last vertices in V_o is processed.

As shown, $SPP(v_i)$ does not have to traverse the whole G_o as long as v_i is in the middle of V_o. The complexity is bounded by $O(|V_o| + |E_o|)$. After all boundary vertices are processed, G_o is simultaneously reduced as a relatively small graph called the reduced timing graph G_r, which contains the boundary vertices only, and its edge number $|E_r|$ is equal to the number of prime paths. When all N simulations are completed, each edge in G_r will obtain N weights. And G_r is the intermediate result for integration later at LS.

Acceleration via parallel computing. To further accelerate Compute, we can leverage the parallel computing with cloud. In Monte Carlo simulations, because each simulation is independent of any other ones, Compute can naturally be conducted in parallel through distributing Monte Carlo simulations on G_o over multiple cloud servers.

4.4 Bandwidth Reduction

After Compute at cloud, the reduced graph G_r has fewer edges than G_o. However, it still introduces potentially large bandwidth cost. Each edge in G_r has multiple weights due to Monte Carlo simulations, and the number of which can be over tens of thousands. Specifically, if a floating point number with 4-byte is used to denote the edge weight, each edge will cost 160KB for 40K simulations. For example, the G_r for benchmark circuit $b18$ shown later in Section 6.2 roughly contains 600 edges and the bandwidth cost is nearly 1Gb. For practical concerns, we design a bandwidth reduction algorithm by transforming G_r to an equivalent timing graph G'_r with even fewer edges.

Observations on intermediate result reduction. The key observation is that: many primes paths share the same sub longest paths and their starting or ending vertices can be used for graph transformation. Figure 5 illustrates our idea explicitly. There exists a number mn of prime paths $\{P_{i,j}\}_{mn}$ in G_r, where every boundary vertex from v_{i+1} to v_{i+m} has prime paths that end at every boundary one from v_{j+1} to v_{j+n}. If all those prime paths pass v_k, G_r can be transformed to another timing graph. During the transformation, v_k is defined as bridge vertex and set as new boundary vertex splitting those prime paths. Meantime, the sub longest path weights are assigned. As a result, mn edges are removed and $m+n$ edges are introduced. We define the saving as β_k for v_k, where $\beta_k = m_k n_k - (m_k + n_k)$. As long as β_k is positive, the bandwidth will be saved.

Algorithm 3: Transform the reduced timing graph $Transform(G_r)$

Data: $G_r(V_r, E_r)$: the reduced timing graph;
Result: $G'_r(V'_r, E'_r)$: the transformed timing graph.
begin
  for $\forall v_k$, *where* $v_k \in P_{i,j}$ **do**
    compute β_k;
    if $\beta_k > 0$ **then**
      $Q.push(\beta_k)$;
  $Sort(Q)$ in descending order;
  $Q_{src} \leftarrow \emptyset$, $Q_{sink} \leftarrow \emptyset$;
  while $Q \neq \emptyset$ **do**
    find v_k, where $\beta_k \leftarrow Q.pop$;
    if $Q_{src} \bigcap Q^k_{src} = \emptyset$ *and* $Q_{sink} \bigcap Q^k_{sink} = \emptyset$ **then**
      $V^b.insert(v_k)$;
      for *each* $e_{i,j}$ *passing* v_k, *where* $v_i \in Q^k_{src}$, $v_j \in Q^k_{sink}$ **do**
        $E_r.delete(e_{i,j})$;
      for *each* $e_{i,k}$ **do**
        $E_r.insert(e_{i,k})$, $w_{i,k} \leftarrow t^i_k$;
      for *each* $e_{k,j}$, *and* $e_{k,j} \notin E_r$ **do**
        $E_r.insert(e_{k,j})$, $w_{k,j} \leftarrow t^i_j - t^i_k$;
      $Q_{src}.push(Q^k_{src})$, $Q_{sink}.push(Q^k_{sink})$;

Based on the observation, our heuristic approach first requires algorithm *SPP* to trace and cache all vertices like v_k, and then selects new boundary vertices in the descending order of their related savings to invoke the above *Transform*. Since the tracing and caching is integrated in one-pass *SPP*, the introduced overhead is acceptable, which is also shown later from our evaluation in Section 6.

Heuristic implementation. Our implementation of bandwidth reduction is presented in Algorithm 3. It is embedded in each simulation of Compute as shown in Algorithm 2. In particular, all the $\{P_{i,j}\}$ are traced in each *SPP*, i.e., the vertex's ancestor on a prime path is updated and cached after the max operation in *SPP*. With the prime path information, subroutine *Transform* transforms the graph G_r to G'_r with fewer edges. We heuristically evaluate all the cached bridge vertices $\{v_k\}$ with positive saving $\{\beta_k\}$, where $\{\beta_k\}$ are stored in a descending order at a queue Q. The first element of Q is popped up because of its maximum saving. Then we find the corresponding bridge vertices v_k and color it as boundary vertex. After that, $e_{i,j}$ is removed, while $e_{i,k}$ and $e_{k,j}$ are introduced with updated weights.

Ordering by $\{\beta_k\}$, the corresponding vertices are set as bridge ones sequentially if they have no overlapping on their paths' source and sink boundary vertices respectively. Such heuristic strategy is to avoid repetitive transformations. If overlap is allowed, the intersection will be processed redundantly over different bridge vertices. For the implementation, Q^k_{src} and Q^k_{sink} are used to store the source and sink vertices for v_k. Q_{src} and Q_{sink} are used to store the source and sink vertices that the bridge vertices already have for the overlap checking. Our design is heuristic rather than optimized, but it still performs well in the practical experiment later. We also note that such saving is usually design dependent. The more prime paths with share vertices, the more saving will be gained.

4.5 Integration

Upon receiving the reduced timing graph G_r, LS integrates G_r with G_c to compute the longest path distribution. For the graph integration, the vertex indexes are firstly recovered by the reserved mapping information. Then the adjacent list for each boundary vertex in G_c and G_r are combined together. As CS computes the boundary-vertex pairwise longest paths for each simulation, G_i is equivalent to G except the outsourced paths are replaced by edges with pre-computed weights. Therefore, the state-of-the-art timing analysis algorithm can be used to obtain the longest path delay distribution as before, i.e., LS does not need to modify the algorithm design and implementation. As the computation related to critical timing graph is performed at LS, the path delays of critical IP blocks and the IC longest path delay distribution are privacy preserving.

Note that the computation cost is proportional to the size of critical IP blocks. The reason is that the sampling process dominates the total runtime of timing analysis and G_r will not introduce new vertices in G_i comparing G_c. Even G_i has more edges than G_c, the runtime of graph traversal is negligible to the sampling which will be demonstrated in Section 6. And the new boundary vertices after bandwidth reduction will not introduce too much overhead either, because those vertices are not the boundary ones at the beginning and their delay sampling process is already completed.

4.6 Discussions

Our proposed mechanism and system can be extended to other EDA applications such as design verifications and optimizations. Design data can be partitioned according to the criticality. However, we note that our design only works for applications involving public and sensitive data and the effectiveness depends on the portion of sensitive data. In timing analysis, the more critical IP blocks a circuit contains, the less saving will be gained from our system. If almost all the design data is sensitive, our design will become ineffective. Even so, our design can still be widely adopted, since many applications in most real-life scenarios comprise both public and private data [27].

More generally, our design can be applied to graph-based applications related on web graphs, social networks, transportation networks and so on, as long as they contains sensitive contents. For example, path recommendation in navigation or location-based services can split the computation. Paths that are close to user's private locations (e.g., home, school and hospital) are kept at user's local device. Computation related to the private information can be carried out at local after the computation over public data at the cloud side. For social graph-based services, the private relationship can be maintained at user's local side., e.g., friend discovery can generate the final recommendation list after filtering the intermediate results from public graphs.

5. SECURITY ANALYSIS

In this section, we demonstrate that our system protects the gate-level design and the functionalities of critical IP blocks as stated in Section 3. Recall that our system extracts and always keeps the critical IP gate-level design at the local private server, including the sensitive timing characteristics and related timing analysis results. Under such design, cloud has no access to the critical IP gate-level design. However, it wants to infer the critical IP functionality through the aforementioned *I/O pattern analysis*. *I/O pattern analysis* refers to the widely recognized reverse engineering technique [21, 24], which tries to build the truth table of IP functionality by observing deduced output bit sequences from a sufficient number of random input bit sequences. Recent works on IC camouflage and IC obfuscation [20, 21] evaluate their protection effectiveness against such *I/O pattern analysis*, and quantify the security strength via the Hamming distance between correct and corrupted outputs.

In our design, cloud wants to infer the possible I/O vertices of the critical IPs from the boundary vertices of non-critical IPs and then launch the *I/O pattern analysis*. To quantify the security strength of IP functionality protection, we follow the security framework from [20, 21]. Explicitly, we also use the Hamming distance to measure the hardness of reverse engineering. The larger the Hamming distance between the guessed and the correct outputs is, the less information on IP functionality is considered to be disclosed. And for each input sequence, such Hamming distance should be larger than some given threshold.

Formally, we consider that some certain IP block has y bit output, and λ is the security parameter, where $\lambda < y$. For a sufficient number of c random inputs, if the Hamming distance between the correct and guessed outputs is less or equal than λ for each input, the reverse engineering succeeds. If the Hamming distance is larger than threshold λ, we consider our IP functionality protection is secure. Note that since the gate-level design of critical IP blocks is kept locally and fully unknown to cloud, cloud can only guess the outputs randomly for each input sequence. For the given y, λ and c, such successful probability P is the following: $P = (\sum_{\lambda<k\leq y} \binom{y}{k}/2^y)^c$.

As the parameter settings suggested by the existing works [20, 21], a sufficient large c can range from a few hundred to a few thousand, and λ as $y/2$ for high obscureness. Thus, the security strength is considered acceptable when at least 50% guessed output bits are different from correct ones for each of c input sequences. In this setting, $P = (\sum_{y/2<k\leq y} \binom{y}{k}/2^y)^c = ((2^y - \binom{y}{y/2})/2^{y+1})^c$. The above derivation is because of $\sum_{0\leq k\leq y} \binom{y}{k} = 2^y$. Given the upper bound [16] that $\binom{y}{k} \geq (\frac{n}{k})^k$, for $1 \leq k \leq n$, we have $\binom{y}{y/2} \geq (\frac{y}{y/2})^{y/2} = 2^{\frac{y}{2}}$. Therefore, $P \leq (\frac{1}{2} - \frac{1}{2^{y/2+1}})^c$. Here, P is negligible when applying a sufficient large number of random input sequences, e.g., $c = 1000$. It demonstrates that IP functionality is hardly to be inferred from the number of I/O only.

Further, we can carefully design the critical IP blocks extraction algorithm, which could introduce a number of additional boundary vertices to further obfuscate the I/Os of

Table 1: Performance Evaluation of Privacy-preserving Timing Analysis System

Benchmark					Timing evaluation at LS				Per inst. at CS
Name	#V $\|V\|$	#E $\|E\|$	Critical $\frac{\|V_i\|}{\|V\|}$	Public 1- $\frac{\|V_i\|}{\|V\|}$	Extract t_e(s)	Integrate t_i(s)	Baseline t(s)	Saving $1-\frac{t_i}{t}$	Compute t_o(s)
b18	114K	217K	9%	91%	1.8	1.4K	14K	91%	0.6K
b19	232K	439K	10%	90%	3.6	3.3K	30K	89%	0.9K
leon3mp	546K	112K	11%	89%	10.1	8.8K	73K	88%	7K
netcard	725K	1316K	10%	90%	11.5	9.9K	95K	90%	9K
leon2	781K	1476K	9%	91%	12.4	10.6K	104K	90%	11K
leon3	900K	1865K	11%	89%	17.2	13.9K	120K	88%	13K

the critical IP blocks, e.g., by introducing more I/O vertices shared between multiple IP blocks or including non-critical I/O vertices in the critical IP blocks. Such methodology could further harden the security strength of our critical IP block protection.

6. EXPERIMENTAL EVALUATIONS

In this section, we evaluate our proposed privacy-preserving timing analysis system on large benchmark circuits. The results demonstrate that our system saves a considerable computation time at LS. Then, we quantify the overhead of our privacy-preserving design through the computation cost at both LS and CS, and the bandwidth cost between local and cloud. Finally, we estimate the capital on real-world cloud services to show that the benefit of shortening overall system response time overwhelms the investment on outsourcing computation to CS.

6.1 Experiment Setup

Benchmarks and critical IP simulation. We derive the experimental circuits from IC benchmark IWLS 2005 [3]. Benchmark circuits with over one hundred thousand gates are selected. The largest circuit contains nearly one million gates. We adopt the famous canonical first-order delay model [7] to generate the deterministic gate delay for each simulation (See Appendix). We assume the delay is Gaussian distributed and we sample Gaussian numbers independently for various device parameters. For simplicity, we assign the mean of each gate delay as its outgoing edge number, and ignore the interconnect delays. We note that such treatment will not affect our design correctness. Afterwards, the number of simulations is set to $40k$, i.e., the golden number of Monte Carlo simulation [11], which leads to a confident estimation error interval within 1%.

We use the circuit partition tool *hMETIS*[5] to create virtual critical and non-critical IP blocks. *hMETIS* is a widely adopted tool to package IP blocks, which can successfully partition the circuit while minimizing the number of interconnects between blocks. Since our objective is mainly on the performance evaluation, we omit the identification of critical IP blocks on benchmark circuits. Based on the recent surveys [5, 14], the total number of IP blocks in a full circuit is around 80 on average. Thus, we partition each benchmark circuit into 80 blocks, where the size of each block is slightly different. Those surveys also report that the newly designed IP blocks are around 10% in a full circuit. And in the experiment, we treat those newly designed IP blocks as critical ones. Regarding the estimated ratio, around 10% blocks are selected randomly as virtual critical ones. We note that such ratio could vary in practice. Later, we will analyze that the smaller ratio of critical IP blocks, the more computation saving will be gained.

Implementation. Our system is implemented in *c++* with *gcc O2* optimization. A commodity computer with Intel i7 CPU and $8GB$ RAM is used at LS. Compute are running on remote servers with 144 Intel Xeon E5 CPU threads and $128GB$ RAM to simulate the environment of cloud servers. The distributed high throughput computing framework HTCondor[6] is used to execute 100 Compute instances parallelly, where each runs 400 simulations, satisfying $40K$ rule of thumb Monte Carlo simulations [11]. In our experiment, 7 device parameters are set for the delay model [11], so the Gaussian random number generator will be invoked by 7 times to output a deterministic gate delay. Random number generation is more expensive than arithmetic operations and graph traversal, and dominates the cost of Monte Carlo based timing analysis. Basically, there are two typical approaches to generate random numbers in simulations. One is to generate random numbers on-the-fly within each simulation. The other is to pre-compute and cache the random numbers to reuse them. The latter approach demands a large amount of storage or memory for caching a large amount of random numbers. Thus, we adopt the former approach to generate random gate delays.

6.2 Performance Analysis

Computation cost evaluation. In Table 1, the columns under "Benchmark" summarize the benchmark circuit size, the critical IP block ratio (Critical) and the non-critical IP block ratio (Public) in a full circuit. The computation cost is reported for both LS and CS. t_e, t_i, and t_o are the time performance of Extract, Integrate and Compute on each computing instances respectively. We also run the state-of-the-art timing analysis (i.e., PERT) at LS to obtain the baseline t for comparison.

The time of Monte Carlo timing analysis is roughly proportional to the number of vertices according to baseline t. In Table 1, if LS runs PERT based timing analysis, it takes roughly 120,000 seconds, i.e., 34 hours, for the circuit with nearly 1 million of gates, which is quite expensive. Using our system, LS now only runs PERT over critical IP blocks for around 3.8 hours. The local saving is 88%, roughly equal to the ratio of outsourced public IP blocks 89%. We note

[5]hMETIS: the Hypergraph & Circuit Partitioning tool, online at `http://glaros.dtc.umn.edu/gkhome/metis/hmetis/overview`

[6]HTCondor: the open source distributed computing software, online at `http://research.cs.wisc.edu/htcondor/`

Table 2: System Overhead and Runtime Speedup Evaluation

Benchmark		System overhead		System response time	
Name	$\#V_b$ $\lvert V_b\rvert$	Baseline t(ks)	Total time $m * t_o + t_i$(ks)	Response time $t_o + t_i$(ks)	Speedup $\frac{t_o+t_i}{t}$
b18	0.6K	14	64.2	2.2	6.3 ×
b19	0.5K	30	96.6	4.2	7.1 ×
leon3mp	2.4K	73	708.8	15.8	4.6 ×
netcard	3.8K	95	909.9	18.9	5.0 ×
leon2	3.3K	104	1110.6	21.6	4.8 ×
leon3	1.5K	120	1313.9	26.9	4.5 ×

that the saving is slightly smaller than the public ratio due to the overhead of other operations in Integrate such as the vertex index recovering. As mentioned in Section 4.6, if the critical ratio increases, CS will process less non-critical data. Hence, the saving gained from CS will decrease and the local cost will increase linearly in the total size of critical IP blocks. As a result, our system effectiveness will be reduced if an IC contains a large portion of critical design data.

Compute introduces the computational overhead comparing to PERT due to the splitting of sequential computation for privacy concerns. In Table 2, we evaluate the overall time cost of our system, which is equal to the summation of Integrate time and the Compute time $t_i + m * t_o$, where m is 100, the number of Compute instances in our setting. From Algorithm 1, the complexity of pair-wised graph traversal in Compute is $O(N|V_b|(|V_o| + |E_o|))$. Therefore, when the size of outsourced timing graph and the number of boundary vertices go large, the overhead will increase. In this experiment, the total time is roughly 10 times than the baseline time, but such overhead can be amortized due to the parallel simulations across multiple instances.

As mentioned, each simulation in Compute is independent, executing it in a parallel and scalable manner leads to faster the response time of CS to generate G_r, and improves the system response time for overall timing analysis, where system response time is equal to the time interval of running timing analysis at both LS and CS $t_i + t_o$. Table 2 also presents our system response time speedup from the benefits of parallel Compute. The system response time under the setting of 100 Compute instances is average 5 times faster than the baseline. Such speedup can be further maximized on the scalable cloud by using more instances to perform Compute. Note that we ignore the transmission time of intermediate results because $1GB$ data can be downloaded for seconds by dedicated connections. Therefore, IC design companies can rent more instances to shorten the cycle of timing analysis and IC design, which will result in early market share and huge profile margin in IC industry. Given that, the additional overhead of our design is tolerable.

Bandwidth cost and reduction evaluation. Figure 6 depicts the bandwidth cost between LS and CS. We focus on analyzing the data transfer bandwidth from CS to LS. In our experiment, floating-point number (4 bytes) is used to represent an edge weight, so the bandwidth cost of intermediate results, i.e., the size of reduced timing graph G_r, are equal to $4N|E_r|$ for N simulations. The reduced bandwidth cost is also reported after applying our heuristic reduction algorithm, and the average saving ratio is 47%. Note that the saving varies and it is design dependent. The more prime paths that share vertices, the more saving will be obtained.

As mentioned, through high speed transmission, LS is expected to receive G_r in dozens of seconds or less. Hence, such overhead can be deemed acceptable considering that the large portion of workload is shifted to CS. Meantime, the upload cost from LS to CS is negligible to the intermediate results G_r, because only the outsourced graph and related coefficients of delay models will be uploaded to CS.

Price estimation on using real cloud infrastructure. To show the economy of our proposed system in real world, we estimate the price when using the services such as Amazon EC2 and Amazon Direct Connect[7]. For the computing instances, we select the Compute Optimized Instance with 32 cores, and the rent fee is \$0.36 per hour. Assume that 4 instances with total over 100 cores are rent for 100 parallel Compute running on HTCondor. The price paid for computation can be estimated. Amazon Direct Connect's $1G$ port speed is \$0.30 per hour and the data transfer price is \$0.03 per GB. In Figure 7, more computing resources are purchased when the circuit size increases, while the charges on bandwidth is within a certain range. The estimated charges on using Amazon web services are only few US dollars which is extremely economic. Thus, comparing the possible huge profit margin from shorting the design procedure, the investment on using cloud infrastructure is negligible.

7. RELATED WORKS

Integrated circuit IP protections. Many works on hardware watermarking [1] and fingerprint techniques [23] are proposed to tag and track used/reused components within several processes of IC design flow. Hence, IC design companies can claim the authorship and prevent the illegal copies by the manufactory. However, the above protection techniques don't provide proactive prevention of IP theft, such as threats on functionality and structural design. They only afford a very low-level form of security which does not meet our protection goal. To protect IC's functionality, hardware metering schemes [4] are designed to provide post-fabrication control for IP design companies. Power, timing measurements and analyses based techniques are proposed to detect the malicious manufacturing such as Trojan circuitries [13]. Other works on hardware obfuscation adds dummy gates as IC camouflaging to resist the reverse engineering [21], but those camouflaging gates will introduce overhead in IC design procedure on analysis and verification. Besides, such technique focuses on functionality protection, and a part of netlist is disclosed.

[7]AWS Direct Connect: Private Network Connection to AWS, online at `http://aws.amazon.com/directconnect/`

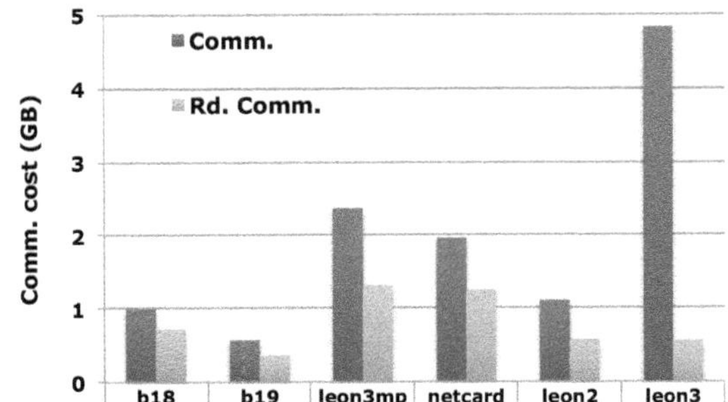

	b18	b19	leon3mp	netcard	leon2	leon3
Comm.	0.99	0.57	2.37	1.96	1.11	4.82
Rd. Comm.	0.72	0.36	1.31	1.25	0.57	0.56

Figure 6: Bandwidth cost with and without reduction

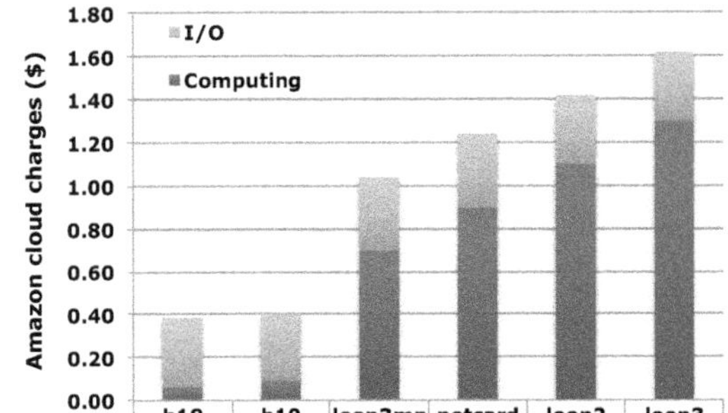

	b18	b19	leon3mp	netcard	leon2	leon3
I/O	0.32	0.31	0.34	0.34	0.32	0.32
Computing	0.06	0.09	0.70	0.90	1.10	1.30

Figure 7: Estimated Charges on Amazon

Meanwhile, several works also leverage the idea of "split" to ensure the confidentiality of IC's full knowledge. In [22], the layout of IC is split into different layers or multiple partitions to prevent an attacker from obtaining the gate-level netlist and improve the security strength against reverse engineering on I/O relationships. Such split manufacturing for obfuscation is further investigated in [15]. The precise notion of security is provided, and the computational ability of attackers and the complexity are thoroughly analyzed. However, the above protections focus on the security in the post-fabrication of IC design procedure at the IC foundry. We note that our system focuses on the different stage of IC design procedure to provide a security guarantee for the design automation outsourced at cloud.

Privacy-preserving computation outsourcing. There are several works that utilize hybrid cloud to perform privacy-preserving intensive computations. In [27], Sedic, a hybrid cloud framework, is proposed to perform MapReduce tasks involving sensitive data. It splits the data and computation workload by security labels. The private data are uploaded to private nodes and private tasks are assigned to private nodes, while public data and tasks are outsourced to public nodes. Our design shares the similar hybrid clouds alike approaches for privacy-preserving computation. However, Sedic is built on Hadoop - a MapReduce framework, which focuses on how to auto-place the MapReduce tasks according the data security label, while we focus on graph-based computations. In Sedic, the implicitly assumption is that the computation on public data by default can be separated from private data, which is no longer the case in our problem and requires specialized new algorithm design.

Another related work based via hybrid clouds studies the private human genomic sequence mappings in DNA analysis [9]. The proposed approach splits the genomic sequence mapping tasks into *Seeding* and *Extension*. Public cloud runs *Seeding* which compares the hashed seeds to the hashed reference previously computed and uploaded to cloud. *Extension* at private cloud checks the edit distance for every matched pair derived from *Seeding*. Their design does not split the input data. Instead, they prepossess the input for security consideration and split the computation process.

Privacy-preserving graph-based computation. Recall that a circuit gate-level timing graph is generated as the inputs for timing analysis and optimizations. Therefore, we study privacy-preserving graph publishing and graph-based computation. For privacy-preserving graph publishing, a graph partition scheme called k-isomorphism partitions the graph into k disjoint components [10]. And another graph encryption scheme is designed for encrypting graph data while allowing for neighbour and adjacency queries [8]. However, they don't support computations over the encrypted or partitioned graph traversal.

Several studies emphasize on privacy-preserving graph-based computation. In [12], the original graph is transformed into a linked graph and a set of outsourced graphs for the shortest path query. Their topologies are totally different with the original graph and the edge weights of outsourced graph should be computed before being transferred to cloud. In [17], private information retrieval (PIR) protocol is used as building blocks. Client poses a query through a multiple round protocol on the encrypted connection to compute the shortest path. In [6], privacy-preserving graph algorithms are realized by techniques like linear secret sharing, threshold homomorphic encryption, or Boolean garbled circuits. And their approach only support the matrix presentation of graph which is more expensive than adjacent list presentation for sparse graphs, while circuit graph is usually sparse. In a word, those works will introduce a great amount of overhead on graph transformation, encryption, bandwidth due to over ten thousands of simulations in timing analysis.

8. CONCLUSION

This paper proposes the first privacy-preserving system to outsource timing analysis on integrated circuits. Our design is built on the observation from IP reuse - the modern IC design methodology. Most of reused IP blocks are standard units and universally shared. Therefore, our system protects the critical design in a "data-splitting" way, which extracts the critical data from the whole design and outsources the non-critical data to cloud. To break the computation dependency over critical and non-critical data, we design a new algorithm to enable intensive computations over the outsourced data at cloud, so cloud can generate intermediate results, which the local private server can integrate with the critical design data for finalizing timing analysis results. The sufficient evaluation demonstrates our design achieves the security, efficiency, correctness, and economy.

In future, we will extend our system to other computations that involve both public and sensitive data and complete our system by adding the verification module to verify the computations from cloud.

Acknowledgment

This work was supported in part by Research Grants Council of Hong Kong (Project No. CityU 138513), and by US National Science Foundation under grant CNS-1262277.

9. REFERENCES

[1] A. B. Kahng et al. Constraint-based watermarking techniques for design IP protection. *IEEE TCAD*, 20(10):1236–1252, 2001.

[2] A. Kuehlmann et al. Does IC design have a future in the clouds. In *Proc. of DAC*, 2010.

[3] C. Albrecht. IWLS 2005 benchmarks. In *International Workshop for Logic Synthesis (IWLS): http://www.iwls.org*, 2005.

[4] Y. Alkabani and F. Koushanfar. Active hardware metering for intellectual property protection and security. In *Proc. of USENIX Security*, 2007.

[5] B. Bailey. How much of the chip does IP fill. Online at `http://www.eetimes.com/author.asp?section_id=36&doc_id=1287320`, 2013.

[6] M. Blanton, A. Steele, and M. Alisagari. Data-oblivious graph algorithms for secure computation and outsourcing. In *Proc. of AISACCS*, 2013.

[7] C. Visweswariah et al. First-order incremental block-based statistical timing analysis. *IEEE TCAD*, 25(10):2170–2180, 2006.

[8] M. Chase and S. Kamara. Structured encryption and controlled disclosure. In *Proc. of ASIACRYPT*. 2010.

[9] Y. Chen, B. Peng, X. Wang, and H. Tang. Large-scale privacy-preserving mapping of human genomic sequences on hybrid clouds. In *Proc. of NDSS*, 2012.

[10] J. Cheng, A. W. Fu, and J. Liu. K-isomorphism: privacy preserving network publication against structural attacks. In *Proc. of SIGMOD*, 2010.

[11] C. Forzan and D. Pandini. Statistical static timing analysis: A survey. *The VLSI Journal on INTEGRATION*, 42(3):409–435, 2009.

[12] J. Gao, Y. Xu, R. Jin, J. Zhou, T. Wang, and D. Yang. Neighborhood-privacy protected shortest distance computing in cloud. In *Proc. of SIGMOD*, 2011.

[13] Y. L. Gwon, H. Kung, and D. Vlah. DISTROY: Detecting integrated circuit Trojans with compressive measurements. In *Proc. of HotSec*, 2011.

[14] A. Hamid. Design reuse without verification reuse is useless. Online at `http://www.eetimes.com/document.asp?doc_id=1280157`, 2012.

[15] F. Imeson, A. Emtenan, S. Garg, and M. V. Tripunitara. Securing computer hardware using 3D Integrated Circuit (IC) technology and split manufacturing for obfuscation. In *Proc. of USENIX Security*, 2013.

[16] M. Mitzenmacher and E. Upfal. *Probability and computing: Randomized algorithms and probabilistic analysis*. Cambridge University Press, 2005.

[17] K. Mouratidis and M. L. Yiu. Shortest path computation with no information leakage. *Proc. of the VLDB Endowment*, 5(8):692–703, 2012.

[18] Office of Technology Evaluation at Bureau of Industry and Security in U.S. Department of Commerce. U.S. Integrated circuit design and fabrication capability. Online at `http://www.bis.doc.gov`, 2009.

[19] R. Saleh et al. System-on-chip: reuse and integration. *Proc. of the IEEE*, 94(6):1050–1069, 2006.

[20] J. Rajendran, Y. Pino, O. Sinanoglu, and R. Karri. Logic encryption: A fault analysis perspective. In *Proc. of DATE*, 2012.

[21] J. Rajendran, M. Sam, O. Sinanoglu, and R. Karri. Security analysis of integrated circuit camouflaging. In *Proc. of ACM CCS*, 2013.

[22] J. Rajendran, O. Sinanoglu, and R. Karri. Is split manufacturing secure? In *Proc. of DATE*, 2013.

[23] S. Maeda et al. An artificial fingerprint device (AFD): a study of identification number applications utilizing characteristics variation of polycrystalline silicon TFTs. *IEEE TED*, 50(6):1451–1458, 2003.

[24] R. Torrance and D. James. The state-of-the-art in IC reverse engineering. In *Proc. of Cryptographic Hardware and Embedded Systems*. Springer, 2009.

[25] N. Westte and D. Harris. *CMOS VLSI Design*. Pearson-Addison-Wesley, 2011.

[26] L. Yuan, G. Qu, L. Ghouti, and A. Bouridane. VLSI design IP protection: solutions, new challenges, and opportunities. In *Proc. of IEEE NASA/ESA on Adaptive Hardware and Systems*, 2006.

[27] K. Zhang, X. Zhou, Y. Chen, X. Wang, and Y. Ruan. Sedic: privacy-aware data intensive computing on hybrid clouds. In *Proc. of ACM CCS*, 2011.

APPENDIX

PERT Algorithm. The Program Evaluation and Review Technique (PERT) in Algorithm 4 is used to compute the longest path delay for a given circuit timing graph.

Algorithm 4: PERT Critical Path Delay

Data: $G(V, E)$: the circuit timing graph;
Result: D: the longest path delay.
begin
    Topologically sorting $G(V, E)$;
    for *each* $v_i \in V$ **do**
        $t_i \leftarrow 0$;
    for $i \leftarrow 2$ *to* $|V|$ **do**
        for *each* $v_j \in v_i.adj_{in}$ **do**
            $t_i \leftarrow \max\{w_{j,i} + t_j, t_i\}$
    $D \leftarrow t_{|V|}$

Delay model. The canonical first-order delay model [7] is defined as: $d = a_0 + \sum_{i=1}^{n} a_i \Delta x_i + a_{n+1} \Delta R_a$, where d is the gate delay, a_0 is the mean of delay, Δx_i represents the variation of X_i, i.e., a device parameter with correlations on other parameters, ΔR_a is the variation of an independent random variable R_a, i.e., a device parameter independent with others, a_i is the sensitivity of each variation. We assume that the random gate delay is Gaussian distributed. By scaling the sensitivity a_i, Δx_i and ΔR_a are unit Gaussian distributed $N(0, 1)$.

A Secure Communication Protocol for Drones and Smart Objects

Jongho Won
Department of Computer Science
Purdue University, IN, USA
won12@purdue.edu

Seung-Hyun Seo
Department of Computer Science
Purdue University, IN, USA
seosh77@gmail.com

Elisa Bertino
Cyber Center
Purdue University, IN, USA
bertino@purdue.edu

ABSTRACT

In many envisioned drone-based applications, drones will communicate with many different smart objects, such as sensors and embedded devices. Securing such communications requires an effective and efficient encryption key establishment protocol. However, the design of such a protocol must take into account constrained resources of smart objects and the mobility of drones. In this paper, a secure communication protocol between drones and smart objects is presented. To support the required security functions, such as authenticated key agreement, non-repudiation, and user revocation, we propose an efficient Certificateless Signcryption Tag Key Encapsulation Mechanism (eCLSC-TKEM). eCLSC-TKEM reduces the time required to establish a shared key between a drone and a smart object by minimizing the computational overhead at the smart object. Also, our protocol improves drone's efficiency by utilizing dual channels which allows many smart objects to concurrently execute eCLSC-TKEM. We evaluate our protocol on commercially available devices, namely AR.Drone2.0 and TelosB, by using a parking management testbed. Our experimental results show that our protocol is much more efficient than other protocols.

Categories and Subject Descriptors

C.2.2 [**Compute-Communication Networks**]: Network Protocols; E.3 [**Data Encryption**]: Public key cryptosystems

General Terms

Security, Design

Keywords

Certificateless Signcryption; Drone Communications

1. INTRODUCTION

Over recent years, drones are increasingly being used not only for military tasks, but also for civilian tasks, such as environment and traffic monitoring, delivery services, and aerial surveys. An Australian textbook rental startup company, Zookal, has already started using drones to deliver books. Amazon will soon start a new delivery method, Amazon Prime Air, which would offer 30-minute deliveries using drone-like octocopters. Also, some research projects [22, 29] have adopted drones as mobile collectors for monitoring applications based on wireless sensor networks (WSNs). For example, on-ground sensors can be deployed in farms to monitor the conditions of soil and drones can periodically collect information from these sensors and perform in-network processing of this information. In such context, drones can also be used for communicating with the on-ground sensors in order to send the sensors re-configuration instructions, such as instructing the sensors to change the sampling rates.

In many current and foreseen applications involving drones, including the Internet of Things (IoT), security is an important requirement. Drones, as many computing devices, are vulnerable to malicious attacks such as impersonation, manipulation and interception. Moreover, since drones may move around in unattended hostile areas with collected sensor data, they are vulnerable to physical capture. It is thus critical to address security requirements, such as authentication, non-repudiation, confidentiality and integrity, and securing communications between drones and other devices (referred to as smart objects in what follows), such as on-ground sensors. An important security building block is represented by cryptography which in turn requires a key management scheme. However, implementing a key management scheme suitable for WSNs that involve both smart objects and drones is quite challenging because of (1) the mobility and limited flight time of drones and (2) the constrained resources of smart objects.

Most encryption key management schemes proposed for WSNs adopt a symmetric-key-based approach instead of an asymmetric-key-based approach in order to address the limited energy and processing capability of sensors [6, 8]. However, the symmetric-key-based approach suffers from high communication overhead and requires large amounts of memory space to store the shared pairwise keys. Also such approach is not scalable, not resilient against compromises, and unable to support adequate node mobility. Public key cryptography (PKC) is relatively more expensive than symmetric key encryption in terms of computational costs, but recent improvements in the implementation of elliptic curve cryptography (ECC) [13] have demonstrated the practical applicability of PKC to WSNs. In order to enhance

ASIA CCS'15, April 14–17, 2015, Singapore..

http://dx.doi.org/10.1145/2714576.2714616.

scalability and flexibility, asymmetric key based approaches that use ECC and identity-based PKC have been proposed for WSNs [15, 27, 7]. However, ECC-based schemes with certificates [27] and pairing operation-based ID-PKC [15, 7] schemes, when directly applied to WSNs, suffer from certificate management overhead and computational overhead from pairing operations, respectively. Moreover, since drones, unlike sensors, are likely to record a wide range of information, they can become a target for physical capture. We thus need an approach to minimize information leakage in the event that a drone is captured by attackers.

To address security and efficiency requirements for communications between drones and smart objects, we present the efficient Certificate-less Signcryption Tag Key Encapsulation Mechanism (eCLSC-TKEM) which supports authenticated key agreement and non-repudiation. The key feature of eCLSC-TKEM is to combine one-way key agreement and digital signatures into one efficient algorithm. Since eCLSC-TKEM is based on certificateless PKC (CL-PKC), it inherits the advantages of CL-PKC such as the elimination of the overhead resulting from the certificate management and the key escrow problem. eCLSC-TKEM supports user revocation by adopting Boneh et al.'s revocation technique [5] which adds a valid time period to the partial private keys that are issued. After the time period expires, new private keys are generated. Therefore, if a drone is captured, information leakage is limited to the time period during which the private keys were valid. To improve efficiency, eCLSC-TKEM minimizes the computational overhead at the smart object. The entire system efficiency highly depends on the computation time required by the smart object rather than the drone since a smart object is equipped with a low speed processor, while the drone has a PC-like processor. The contributions of our paper are summarized as follows.

- An efficient Certificateless Signcryption Tag Key Encapsulation Mechanism (eCLSC-TKEM) is proposed. The formal security model and a security proof are provided. Based on eCLSC-TKEM, a secure communication protocol for drone applications is presented. Our protocol is the most energy-efficient protocol supporting sharing of symmetric encryption keys for secure communications and non-repudiation.
- The *dual channel strategy* is introduced to concurrently perform eCLSC-TKEM with many smart objects at the same time, and thus to save the drone's energy.
- A secure communication protocol for the real drone application, i.e., smart parking management, has been implemented. The performance of eCLSC-TKEM has been evaluated in a testbed consisting of the commercially available devices AR.Drone2.0 and TelosB.

The remainder of this paper is organized as follows: In Section 2, we briefly discuss related work and requirements for drone-related communication protocols. In Section 3, we introduce our eCLSC-TKEM and dual channel strategy. In Section 4, we describe the design of our protocol through an example application. Then, the performance of our protocol is evaluated in Section 5. In Section 6, the security model and proof of eCLSC-TKEM are presented. Then, we outline conclusions and future works in Section 7.

2. BACKGROUND

2.1 Mobile data collectors in WSN

Several approaches [22, 25, 4, 29, 23, 18] have been proposed for using mobile data collectors in WSNs because of their advantages over traditional static WSNs such as connectivity, cost, reliability and energy efficiency. However, the use of mobile collectors introduces new security risks because mobile collectors are privileged nodes storing collected data and are exposed to physical capture. Zhou et al. [29] analyzed the security impact of mobile collector compromises and proposed a key pre-distribution scheme for group-based sensor networks. Song et al. [23] proposed a privilege-dependent pairwise key establishment scheme. This scheme revokes the privileges of a compromised mobile collector immediately after its compromise is detected. Rasheed et al. [18] proposed a secure data collection mechanism based on hash chains under the assumption that a mobile collector moves along a predetermined path. In this protocol, once a mobile collector is authenticated, a cluster head transfers aggregated data to the mobile collector. Although these protocols deal with the compromise of mobile collectors, their scalability is limited since they are based on symmetric key pre-distribution. Our protocol addresses the scalability problem by taking advantage of an asymmetric-key approach, while minimizing the computational overhead at the sensors.

To save the energy of sensor nodes or to extend the contact time between sensor nodes and mobile collectors, previous approaches [19, 28] adopted multiple radios/channels. However, these approaches did not consider the impact of slow public key operations at resource-constraint sensor nodes on mobile collectors.

2.2 CLSC-TKEM and CL-AKA

The authenticated key agreement (AKA) scheme is one of the most fundamental cryptographic mechanisms. It supports user authentication and generates shared secret keys between two parties over an insecure network. Traditional PKC-based AKA has the overhead of certificate management, whereas ID-PKC based AKA has the key escrow problem. To solve those issues, Al-Riyami et al. introduced certificateless public key cryptography (CL-PKC) [3]. Then, several certificateless authenticated key agreement (CL-AKA) protocols were built based on bilinear pairings. However, since the computational costs required for pairing operations are much higher than those for standard operations, such as EC point multiplication, it is hard to implement pairing-based applications on resource-constrained devices. Several pairing-free CL-AKA protocols [10, 9, 26, 24] have thus been proposed. However, most of those protocols were proved to be insecure and only two of them still remain secure: Sun's CL-AKA [24] and Yang's CL-AKA [26]. Recently, Li et al. [12] proposed a certificateless signcryption tag KEM (CLSC-TKEM) protocol. CLSC-TKEM supports not only practical authenticated key agreement but also designated verifier signature. Later, Selvi et al. [20] showed a security weakness in Li et al.'s CLSC-TKEM and presented an improved CLSC-TKEM. Since both CLSC-TKEM protocols [12, 20] rely on bilinear pairing operations, they are not suitable for resource-constrained devices. Recently, Seo et al. [21] proposed a pairing-free CLSC-TKEM protocol that does not use bilinear pairing operations. However, none of the existing CL-AKA and CLSC-TKEM protocols addresses

Table 1: Comparison of protocols

Protocol	Computational overhead on a smart object (on-line)	Security functionality			
		Key agreement	User authentication	Non-repudiation	User revocation
Yang's CL-AKA [26]	9EM + 1V (8EM + 1V)	yes	yes	no	no
Sun's CL-AKA [24]	6EM (5EM)	yes	yes	no	no
CLSC-TKEM [21]	5EM (3EM)	yes	yes	yes	no
eCLSC-TKEM	4EM (2EM)	yes	yes	yes	yes

EM: EC point multiplication, V: signature verification. 'On-line' means the computational overhead except ephemeral public key generations such as U and V generation in our protocol. The 'On-line' overhead is more meaningful than the entire overhead since ephemeral public keys can be generated in advance before a key agreement protocol starts.

user revocation which means that if drones are captured, the attacker will have full access not only to the information already collected and recorded in the drone, but also to future information to be collected by the drone.

In order to minimize information leakage in case of physical capture of drones, eCLSC-KTEM utilizes Boneh et al.'s revocation technique [5]. The key generation center (KGC) in eCLSC-TKEM adds time constraint to its partial private keys. In other words, partial private keys issued in eCLSC-TKEM are only valid for specified time periods. After the time period ends, new private keys will be generated. By adding this time constraint, we limit information leakage. To revoke a compromised drone, the KGC stops issuing partial private/public keys, including a valid time component, to the drone. Our approach prevents unauthorized users from being able to generate full private/public keys for future time periods. Although eCLSC-TKEM does not completely eliminate the risk of information leakage in case of physical capture, it limits the amount of compromised information to the information acquired during the last time period right before the revocation took place. Table 1 summarizes the comparison between eCLSC-TKEM and existing pairing-free CL-AKA and CLSC-TKEM.

2.3 Requirements for secure drone communications

The requirements for a communication protocol between drones and smart objects are summarized in terms of security and efficiency as follows.

- **Security** First, authenticated key establishment should be supported for confidentiality and user authentication. Second, it should be possible to verify the integrity of data and support non-repudiation. Third, information leakage should be minimized in the event that a drone is captured and its secret key is exposed. Finally, different access rights to smart objects should be supported for drones. Only authenticated/authorized drones should have access to smart objects' internal data according to their rights.
- **Efficiency** Since drones and smart objects are battery-powered, energy efficiency as well as security is a critical issue. Therefore, protocol executions should be completed as soon as possible to save energy. A drone usually has PC-like processing speed while a smart object has sensor-like processing speed. It is thus critical that protocols impose minimal computational overhead on smart objects. In addition, a drone may communicate with many smart objects at the same time. Therefore, the protocol should support concurrent cryptographic operations.

3. BUILDING BLOCKS

In this section, eCLSC-TKEM and the dual channel strategy are presented as major building blocks for our secure drone communication protocol.

3.1 eCLSC-TKEM

Unlike existing protocols, eCLCS-TKEM satisfies all the security requirements such as authenticated key agreement, non-repudiation and user revocation with the minimum computational overhead at smart objects (see Table 1). Note that the CL-AKA protocols [26, 24] satisfy only the first requirement. To support non-repudiation, the CL-AKA protocols must be extended with a signature scheme. Although CLSC-TKEM satisfies the first and second requirements, it does not support user revocation or multiple access rights. eCLSC-TKEM is a 8-tuple: (SetUp, SetSecretValue, PartialPrivateKeyExtract, SetPrivateKey, SetPublicKey, SymmetricKeyGen, Encapsulation Decapsulation). The description of each probabilistic polynomial time algorithm is as follows.

1) SetUp: This algorithm is run by the KGC to generate the system parameters `params` and a master secret key `msk`, given a security parameter k as input. KGC takes a security parameter $k \in \mathbb{Z}^+$ as input, and returns two system parameters: Ω and the KGC's master private key msk. Given k, the KGC performs the following steps:

- Chooses a k-bit prime q and determine the tuple $\{F_q, E/F_q, G_q, P\}$, where the point P is the generator of G_q.
- Chooses the master key $x \in \mathbb{Z}_q^*$ uniformly at random and computes the system public key $P_{pub} = xP$.
- Chooses cryptographic hash functions $H_0 : \{0,1\}^* \times G_q^2 \times \{0,1\}^* \to \mathbb{Z}_q^*$, $H_1 : G_q^3 \times \{0,1\}^* \times G_q \to \{0,1\}^n$, $H_2 : G_q \times \{0,1\}^* \times G_q \times \{0,1\}^* \times G_q \times \{0,1\}^* \times G_q \to \mathbb{Z}_q^*$, and $H_3 : G_q \times \{0,1\}^* \times G_q \times \{0,1\}^* \times G_q \times \{0,1\}^* \times G_q \to \mathbb{Z}_q^*$. Here, n is the key length of a DEM.
- Publishes $\Omega = \{F_q, E/F_q, G_q, P, P_{pub}, H_0, H_1, H_2, H_3\}$ as the system's parameter and keeps the master key x secret.

2) SetSecretValue: This algorithm is run by each entity to generate a secret value and the corresponding public value for oneself. The entity A with an identity ID_A chooses $x_A \in \mathbb{Z}_q^*$ uniformly at random as its secret value and generates the corresponding public key as $P_A = x_A P$.

3) PartialPrivateKeyExtract: The KGC runs this algorithm to generate the partial private key of a user. It takes the KGC's master secret key, the id of the user ID_A, the permitted time period t_A and the system parameter as inputs. It returns the partial private key of the entity. In order to obtain the partial private key, the entity A sends (ID_A, P_A) to the KGC. The KGC then executes the following steps:

- Chooses $r_A \in \mathbb{Z}_q^*$ and computes $R_A = r_A P$.
- Computes $d_A = r_A + xH_0(ID_A, R_A, P_A, t_A) \bmod q$.

The partial private key of the entity A is d_A. The entity can validate its private key by checking whether $d_A P = R_A + H_0(ID_A, R_A, P_A, t_A) P_{pub}$ holds.

4) SetPrivateKey: This algorithm is run by each entity to generate the full private key. The entity A takes the pair $sk_A = (d_A, x_A)$ as its full private key.

5) SetPublicKey: This algorithm is run by each entity to generate the full public key. The entity A takes the pair $pk_A = (P_A, R_A)$ as its full public key.

6) SymmetricKeyGen: This algorithm is run by the sender A to obtain the symmetric key K and an internal state information ω, which is not known to the receiver B. Given the sender (entity A)'s identity ID_A, the full public key pk_A, the full private key sk_A, the receiver (entity B)'s identity ID_B, the time interval t_B and the full public key pk_B as inputs, the sender executes this symmetric key generation algorithm to obtain the symmetric key K as follows:

- Chooses $l_A, s_A \in \mathbb{Z}_q^*$ and computes $U = l_A P$, $V = s_A P$.
- Computes $Y = R_B + H_0(ID_B, R_B, P_B, t_B) \cdot P_{pub} + P_B$, $T = s_A \cdot Y (= s_A \cdot (H_0(ID_B, R_B, P_B, t_B) \cdot P_{pub} + R_B + P_B))$ and $K = H_1(Y, V, T, ID_B, P_B)$.
- Outputs K and the intermediate information $\omega = (l_A, s_A, U, V, T, ID_A, pk_A, sk_A, ID_B, pk_B, t_B)$.

7) Encapsulation: This algorithm is executed by the sender A to obtain the encapsulation φ. It takes ω corresponding to K and an arbitrary tag τ as inputs. Given a state information ω and an arbitrary tag τ, the sender A obtains the encapsulation φ by performing the following steps:

- Computes $H = H_2(U, \tau, T, ID_A, P_A, ID_B, P_B)$, $H' = H_3(U, \tau, T, ID_A, P_A, ID_B, P_B)$ and $W = d_A + l_A \cdot H + x_A \cdot H'$
- Outputs $\varphi = (U, V, W)$.

8) Decapsulation: This algorithm is executed by the receiver B to obtain the key K encapsulated in φ. Given the encapsulation φ, a tag τ, the sender's identity ID_A, full public key pk_A, the time interval t_A the receiver's identity ID_B, the full public key pk_B and the full private key sk_B, the key K is computed as follows:

- Computes $Y = (d_B + x_B) \cdot P\ (= (r_B + xH_0(ID_B, R_B, P_B, t_B) + x_B) \cdot P = R_B + H_0(ID_B, R_B, P_B, t_B) \cdot P_{pub} + P_B)$, $T = (d_B + x_B) \cdot V (= (d_B + x_B) \cdot s_A P = s_A \cdot Y)$.
- Computes $H = H_2(U, \tau, T, ID_A, P_A, ID_B, P_B)$ and $H' = H_3(U, \tau, T, ID_A, P_A, ID_B, P_B)$.
- If $W \cdot P = R_A + H_0(ID_A, R_A, P_A, t_A) \cdot P_{pub} + H \cdot U + H' \cdot P_A$, outputs $K = H_1(Y, V, T, ID_B, P_B)$.

  Otherwise, outputs an invalid encapsulation error. The correctness of the above equation is as follows:

$$\begin{aligned} W \cdot P &= (d_A + l_A \cdot H + x_A \cdot H') \cdot P \\ &= d_A \cdot P + l_A \cdot P \cdot H + x_A \cdot P \cdot H' \\ &= (r_A + xH_0(ID_A, R_A, P_A, t_A)) \cdot P + U \cdot H + H' \cdot P_A \\ &= R_A + H_0(ID_A, R_A, P_A, t_A) \cdot P_{pub} + H \cdot U + H' \cdot P_A \end{aligned}$$

3.2 Dual Channel Strategy for Concurrency using LPL

Since smart objects and drones are battery-powered, their energy should be efficiently used. Our protocol utilizes dual channels and low power listening (LPL) [1]. The asynchronous duty cycling technique, known as LPL, is one of most promising power-saving techniques for WSNs and results in higher performance than synchronous duty cycling techniques in terms of energy and throughput [17].

Each smart object has one radio and changes its channel according to its situations, while drones are equipped with two radios, i.e., the wake-up radio and the data radio. As depicted in Fig. 1, a smart object periodically turns a radio transceiver on (wake-up) and off (sleep) on the wake-up channel to save its energy. Through the wake-up radio, a mobile drone continuously broadcasts wake-up signals including its ID and public keys. When a smart object wakes up, it quickly checks whether the wake-up channel is busy. If the wake-up channel is idle, the smart object can save energy by sleeping again until the next wake-up time. If a mobile drone broadcasting the wake-up signals approaches some smart objects, the wake-up channel becomes busy. If the smart objects listen the wake-up signals, they stay awake and receive a whole wake-up signal. Then, each smart object concurrently initiates SymmetricKeyGen and Encapsulation and switches the channel from the wake-up channel to the data channel. The Encapsulation output is transmitted to the drones using the data channel. These concurrent executions of eCLSC-TKEM in smart objects can save drone's energy. If a drone has only one radio, it might require precise time synchronization with smart objects to make schedules or perform eCLSC-TKEM with each smart object one by one, which results in a waste of its limited flight time.

4. SECURE COMMUNICATION PROTOCOL FOR DRONES

In this section, we illustrate the design of our protocols in the context of a smart parking management application.

4.1 Smart parking management

Today's parking management is a manual, labor-intensive process. Parking enforcement officers must periodically patrol on-street parking areas and check cars one by one to identify cars that are parked over time . By utilizing drones and sensors, parking management can be more efficient and cost effective. Cars might attach an independent device equipped with a GPS and a radio transceiver. For example, an university can issue those independent devices to registered car owners as parking permits for parking management on its campus. Then, a drone would patrol time limited parking areas and collect information from every parked car. Information includes the identity and location of the car, the type of parking permit and the current time. By collecting this information at certain time intervals, drones can detect if a car is parked at an invalid zone or has been parked at the same spot for longer than the time limit.

In this scenario, since privacy-sensitive information is involved, only authorized drones should be allowed to collect this information. More importantly, since the information is used to fine drivers who parked their cars illegally, a protocol must support non-repudiation and integrity of the collected information.

4.2 Registration

We assume that every car is equipped with a smart object which includes a low-speed CPU, a small memory, a GPS sensor and a radio transceiver. The smart object (A) generates its own secret value (x_A) and corresponding public key (P_A) by executing the SetSecretValue algorithm. For each smart object, the KGC generates a partial private/public key pair (d_A, R_A) by executing the PartialPrivateKeyExtract algorithm and transfers it to the smart object through a se-

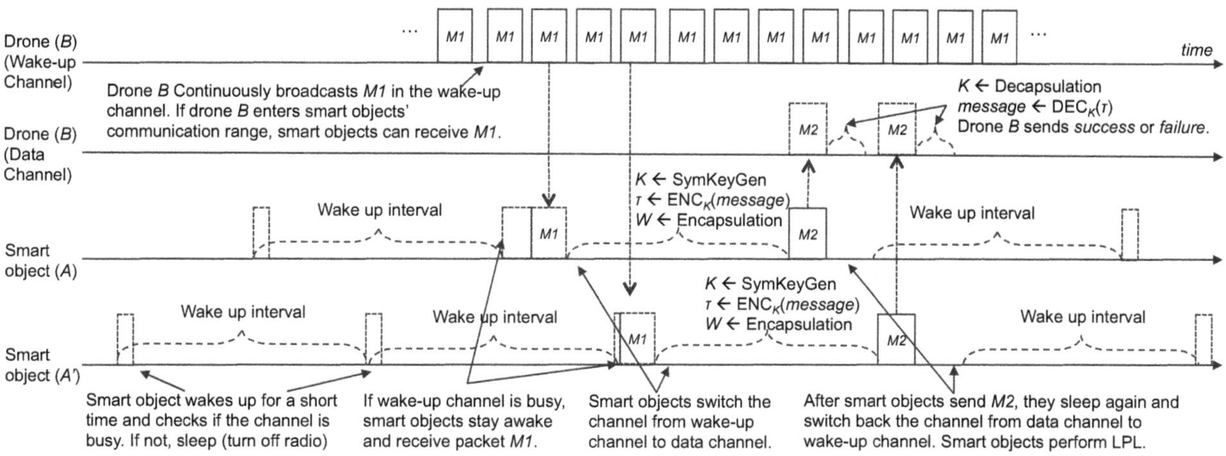

Figure 1: Solid-line square: packet transmission, dash-line square: listen or packet reception. $M1 = \{ID_B, P_B, R_B, t_B\}$, $M2 = \{ID_A, P_A, R_A, t_A, U, V, W, \tau\}$, Decapsulation result (success/failure) transmissions are omitted.

cure channel. Note that the partial private key is only valid for a certain period of time, for example one year, since a permitted time period is included in t_A of the PartialPrivateKeyExtract algorithm. Thus, a car owner should periodically renew the partial private/public key. We assume that a drone stays in a secure place when it is off duty. The drone (B) generates its secret value (x_B) and corresponding public key (P_B) by executing the SetSecretValue algorithm. Before the drone goes out to patrol, it requests a partial private/public key (d_B, R_B) from the KGC. The partial private key is only valid for the maximum flight time, for example 30 minutes; this time period is inserted into t_B of PartialPrivateKeyExtract algorithm. Therefore, in the event that the drone is compromised, the information leakage is limited to this time period. Similarly, access rights granted to the drone are also inserted in t_B.

4.3 Key establishment using dual channels

Fig. 1 illustrates the flow of our protocol. A smart object (A) runs LPL in the wake-up channel and tries to detect wake-up signals from a drone. The drone (B) continuously broadcasts wake-up signals ($M1$) in the wake-up channel while moving, so that smart objects can detect $M1$ when they awake. $M1$ contains the drone's ID (ID_B), the public keys (P_B, R_B) and the permitted time period/access right (t_B). If a smart object wakes up and receives $M1$, it stops LPL and generates a symmetric key (K) by performing SymmetricKeyGen. Then, using K, the smart object generates a ciphertext (τ) by encrypting messages, such as permit type, location information (loc) and current time (ct). After the smart object generates W by executing the Encapsulation algorithm, it switches the channel from the wake-up channel to the data channel and sends $M2$ to B. Since τ is signed by A as part of the Encapsulation, A cannot repudiate τ afterward. $M2$ contains the ID of the smart object (ID_A), the public keys (P_A, R_A), the permitted time period (t_A), ephemeral public keys (U, V), the result value of Encapsulation (W), and the ciphertext (τ).

If the drone receives $M2$, it executes Decapsulation. If the validation process is successful, the drone (B) generates K and decrypts τ using K. Right after obtaining loc and ct from τ, B compares loc and ct with its own current location (loc') and current time (ct'), respectively. Then, based on the comparison outcome, it may perform additional actions. For example, if $|loc - loc'| > 10m$ or $ct - ct' > 5$ mins, B might take actions such as taking a picture of the car or sending a message to a human manager. Finally, B sends the decapsulation result to A. If the result is successful, both the drone (B) and the smart object (A) can use K to exchange encrypted messages.

5. EXPERIMENTS

To evaluate our protocol, we implemented not only our protocol, but also the CL-AKA [26, 24] and CLSC-TKEM [21] protocols on the commercially available devices AR.Drone2.0 [2] and TelosB sensors.

5.1 Experiment Setup

5.1.1 Drone

AR.Drone2.0 [2] is a quad-copter equipped with front and ground cameras and a Wi-Fi (2.4GHz). It has a 1GHz 32-bit ARM cortex A8 CPU and a 1Gbit DDR2 RAM. The main board of the AR.Drone2.0 runs the BusyBox based GNU/Linux distribution with 2.6.32 kernel. After the drone is booted, it works as a Wi-Fi access point. The drone can be controlled from smartphones or laptops by sending UDP control commands through the Wi-Fi. As ECC library, we adopted the micro-ecc [14] optimized for the ARM processor. To compile our code, we used a 32-bit Linux machine since our code had to be cross-compiled for the 32-bit ARM architecture. Then, we transferred the compiled code to AR.Drone2.0 using FTP and executed it by Telnet.

For the wake-up radio and the data radio, two TelosBs were connected to the drone using USB-to-serial interfaces (see Fig. 2). The data radio is connected to an external USB-to-serial interface which is located nearby the battery connector. The wake-up radio is connected to a pin connector on the main board. TelosB is equipped with a CC2420 IEEE 802.15.4 radio transceiver which works at the 2.4GHz ISM band. To avoid interferences between the Wi-Fi and the IEEE 802.15.4 radios, the channel 6 was selected as the Wi-Fi channel and the channel 11 and 26 were selected as the wake-up channel and the data channel, respectively.

5.1.2 Smart object

We used a TelosB equipped with an extremely low speed CPU (TIMSP430 F1161) as a smart object in order to show that our protocol works well even with low speed devices.

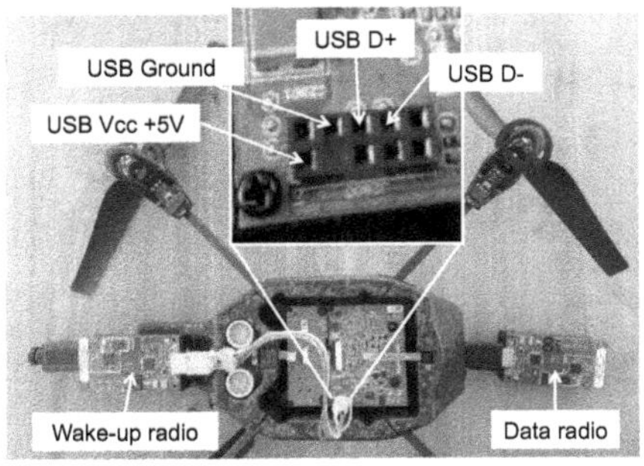

Figure 2: Dual radios attached on AR.Drone2.0

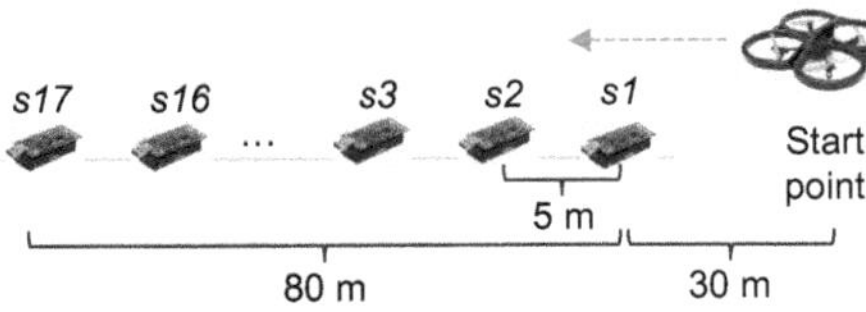

Figure 3: Network topology

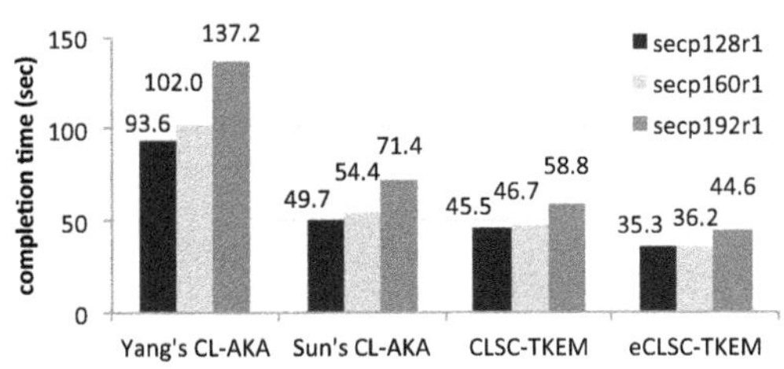

Figure 4: Impact of key bit size

Although the maximum communication range of CC2420 is approximately 100m when the RF power is set to 0dBm, we set the RF power to -7dBm to save power and its communication range became roughly 30m. TelosB is operated by TinyOS 2.0 which is an open-source operating system designed for low-power devices. We used the LPL functionalities in TinyOS 2.0. In addition, TinyECC [13] was used as the basic ECC operations of our protocol.

5.1.3 *Network topology*

Fig. 3 illustrates network topology which mimics the scenario of the smart parking management. 17 smart objects are deployed at 5m intervals in a line and a drone starts from the starting point which is 30m apart from $s1$ at an altitude of 10m. The mission of the drone is to collect messages from all smart objects. and the mission completion time of the drone was measured. The drone proceeds from the start point to $s17$. If the drone reaches a smart object (sx), but is unable to finish the data collection task with sx, the drone waits until the collection is completed.

5.2 Experimental results

5.2.1 *Impact of key bit size*

Fig. 4 shows the mission completion time of four protocols with different ECC key bit sizes when the system adopts 5sec wake-up interval and dual channels. When secp160r1 is used, the mission completion time of our protocol is 36.2sec which is 1.3, 1.5 and 2.8 times faster than Seo's CLSC-TKEM, Sun's CL-AKA and Yang's CL-AKA, respectively. The completion time of each protocol increases as the key bit size increases. However, the difference between a 128-bit key and a 160-bit key is much smaller than the difference between a 160-bit key and a 192-bit key, which implies that a 160-bit key may be a reasonable choice since it provides better security than a 128-bit key with a very small time increase. These results are confirmed by Table 2 which compares the computation time measurements of each protocol on a smart object with different ECC curves. The computation time at a smart object in our protocol is 1.4, 1.8 and 3.8 times faster than Seo's CLSC-TKEM, Sun's CL-AKA and Yang's CL-AKA, respectively, when secp160r1 is used. Note that in our protocol the smart object is required to compute only two EC point multiplications after it starts communicating with the drone (online), while the other protocols require more than two EC point multiplications (see Table 1). These results are similar to the completion time results since the overall performance highly depends on the computation time at the smart object.

Table 2: Comparison of the on-line computation time of a smart object (unit: second)

Protocol	secp128r1	secp160r1	secp192r1
Yang's CL-AKA [26]	32.84	36.22	50.43
Sun's CL-AKA [24]	15.10	16.98	23.84
CLSC-TKEM [21]	13.37	13.87	18.77
eCLSC-TKEM	9.25	9.61	13.03

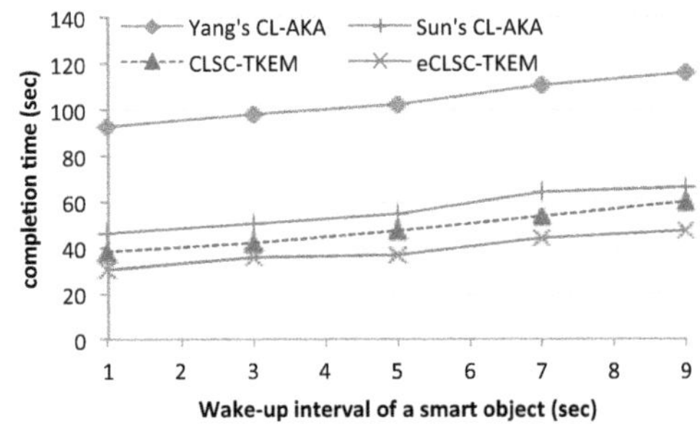

Figure 5: Impact of interval between wake-ups

5.2.2 *Impact of interval between wake-ups*

We analyzed the impact of the wake-up interval of smart objects when the system adopts secp160r1 and dual channels. As shown in Fig. 5, our protocol, compared to CLSC-TKEM and Sun's CL-AKA, has a similar completion time with longer intervals between wake-ups, thus saving energy in smart objects. Specifically, the mission completion time of our protocol is 46.8sec when the wake-up interval is 9sec. However, in CLSC-TKEM, the wake-up interval that achieves a similar mission completion time, i.e., 46.7sec, is 5sec. In Sun's protocol, the wake-up interval that achieves the similar mission completion time, i.e., 46.2sec, is 1sec. As a result, by using our protocol a smart object can save energy 1.8 and 9 times more than when using the CLSC-TKEM and Sun's CL-AKA, respectively, if the mission completion times of three protocols are equally set.

5.2.3 *Impact of drone's altitude*

Since our protocol is efficient, a drone using our protocol does not require a long contact time with smart objects and thus complete the mission faster than others even at a higher altitude. For example, based on experiments we have carried out, the time required by eCLSC-TKEM to complete a mission at an altitude of 20m was 47sec, whereas the time required by CLSC-TKEM at an altitude of 5m was 49sec. [1]

[1]secp160r1 and 5sec wake-up interval are used. These detailed results are not included in the paper for lack of space.

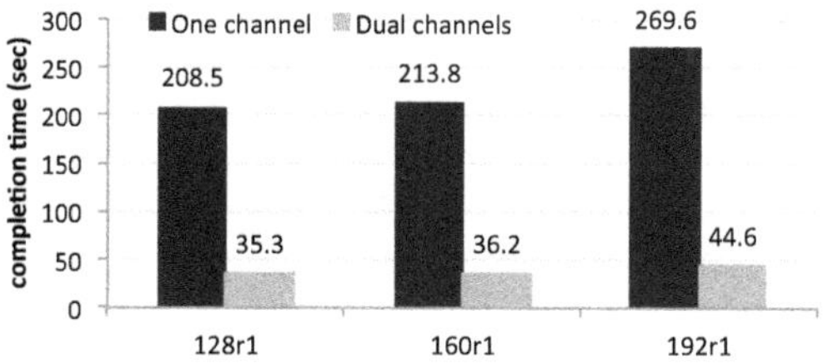

Figure 6: Impact of the dual channel strategy

5.2.4 *Impact of dual channel strategy*

Finally, Fig. 6 shows the impact of the dual channel strategy on the system when the wake-up interval is 5sec. For the key establishment scheme, eCLSC-TKEM is utilized. The drone completes the mission approximately 6 times faster than when only one channel is used. If the dual channel strategy is adopted, the drone can take advantage of independent dual channels. The drone can continuously broadcast the wake-up signals on the wake-up channel while, at the same time, it can exchange eCLSC-TKEM output with smart objects on the data channel. The experiment results shown in Fig. 6 refer to the case in which 3 or 4 smart objects are in the communication range of the drone (see also Fig.5). The results show that all the smart objects in the range are able to concurrently initiate the execution of the eCLSC-TKEM protocol once they receive the wakeup signal. However, if only one channel is used, the drone must perform eCLSC-TKEM with smart objects one by one. In the one-channel system, the drone broadcasts the wake-up signals. Once a smart object receives the wake-up signal, it sends an acknowledge to the drone. Then, the drone must stop broadcasting the wake-up signals to receive the eCLSC-TKEM output from the smart object. If the whole process of eCLSC-TKEM with the smart object is successfully finished, the drone starts broadcasting the wake-up signals again to wake up another smart object. Since each smart object takes much longer time for the execution of the eCLSC-TKEM protocol than the drone, the drone must wait wasting its limited flight time doing nothing. As a result, the dual channel strategy is essential for efficient and secure communication protocols that support many different security functions.

6. SECURITY ANALYSIS

6.1 Security Model of eCLSC-TKEM

An efficient certificateless signcryption tag KEM must consider three types of adversaries: $\mathcal{A}_{\mathcal{I}}$, $\mathcal{A}_{\mathcal{II}}$ and $\mathcal{A}_{\mathcal{III}}$. $\mathcal{A}_{\mathcal{I}}$ represents a dishonest user who can replace other user's public keys but has no knowledge about the master secret key of the KGC. $\mathcal{A}_{\mathcal{II}}$ represents a malicious KGC which has knowledge of the KGC's master secret key. However, $\mathcal{A}_{\mathcal{II}}$ is unable to replace the users' public keys. $\mathcal{A}_{\mathcal{III}}$ represents a previously functional user, whose partial private/public keys have been revoked by the KGC. $\mathcal{A}_{\mathcal{III}}$ cannot replace other users' public keys. Except for the consideration of $\mathcal{A}_{\mathcal{III}}$, the security model of eCLSC-TKEM is similar to that of CLSC-TKEM [20, 12]. eCLSC-TKEM must satisfy confidentiality, that is, indistinguishability against an adaptive chosen ciphertext and identity attacks (IND-CCA2), and unforgeability, that is, existential unforgeability against adaptive chosen messages and identity attacks (EUF-CMA). In order to describe the security model of eCLSC-TKEM, we consider the two formal games IND-eCLSC-TKEM-CCA2 game and EUF-eCLSC-TKEM-CMA game.

1) IND-eCLSC-TKEM-CCA2 Game: The adversary $\mathcal{A}$ can be either $\mathcal{A}_{\mathcal{I}}$, $\mathcal{A}_{\mathcal{II}}$ or $\mathcal{A}_{\mathcal{III}}$. The challenger $\mathcal{C}$ should keep a history of query-answers while interacting with adversaries. $\mathcal{C}$ runs the SetUp() algorithm to generate the public parameters `params` and the master private key `msk` respectively. If $\mathcal{A}$ is either $\mathcal{A}_{\mathcal{I}}$ or $\mathcal{A}_{\mathcal{III}}$, $\mathcal{C}$ gives `params` to $\mathcal{A}$ while keeping `msk` secret. If $\mathcal{A}$ is $\mathcal{A}_{\mathcal{II}}$, $\mathcal{C}$ gives both `params` and `msk` to $\mathcal{A}$.

Phase I: $\mathcal{A}$ may perform a polynomially bounded number of the following queries in an adaptive fashion.

- **Extract-Secret-Value queries**: $\mathcal{C}$ runs SetSecretValue to get x_U with identity ID_U, and then returns it to $\mathcal{A}_{\mathcal{I}}$. In the case of $\mathcal{A}_{\mathcal{III}}$, $\mathcal{C}$ runs SetSecretValue before the challenge time period and returns x_U to $\mathcal{A}_{\mathcal{III}}$. The adversary $\mathcal{A}_{\mathcal{I}}$ or $\mathcal{A}_{\mathcal{III}}$ cannot query any identity for which the corresponding public key has been replaced. $\mathcal{A}_{\mathcal{II}}$ is excluded in this query.
- **Extract-Partial-Private-Key queries**: In the case of $\mathcal{A} \in \{\mathcal{A}_{\mathcal{I}}, \mathcal{A}_{\mathcal{II}}\}$, these can be made for all identities except for the target identity. If $\mathcal{A}$ is $\mathcal{A}_{\mathcal{III}}$, these can be made for any identity before the challenge time period. $\mathcal{C}$ runs PartialPrivateKeyExtract to obtain the partial private key d_U and the permitted time period t_U. Then $\mathcal{C}$ sends d_U and t_U to $\mathcal{A}$.
- **Request-Public-Key queries**: In the case of $\mathcal{A} \in \{\mathcal{A}_{\mathcal{I}}, \mathcal{A}_{\mathcal{II}}\}$, $\mathcal{C}$ runs SetPublicKey to get the full public key pk_U and then returns it to $\mathcal{A}_{\mathcal{I}}$. If $\mathcal{A}$ is $\mathcal{A}_{\mathcal{III}}$, $\mathcal{C}$ runs SetPublicKey to get the full public key pk_U and returns it to $\mathcal{A}_{\mathcal{III}}$ before the challenge time period.
- **Public-Key-Replacement queries**: $\mathcal{A}_{\mathcal{I}}$ may replace the public key pk_U corresponding to the user identity ID_U with any value pk'_U of $\mathcal{A}_{\mathcal{I}}$'s choice. $\mathcal{A}_{\mathcal{II}}$ and $\mathcal{A}_{\mathcal{III}}$ are excluded in this query.
- **Symmetric Key Generation queries**: In the case of $\mathcal{A} \in \{\mathcal{A}_{\mathcal{I}}, \mathcal{A}_{\mathcal{II}}\}$, $\mathcal{A}$ chooses a sender's identity ID_A and a receiver's identity ID_B. $\mathcal{C}$ obtains the private key of the sender, sk_A and t_B from the corresponding "query-answer" list. Then, $\mathcal{C}$ runs SymmetricKeyGen to obtain the symmetric key K and an internal state information ω by using ID_A, ID_B, sk_A, pk_B and t_B. It stores ω while keeping the ω secret from the view of $\mathcal{A}$. Finally, $\mathcal{C}$ sends K to $\mathcal{A}$. $\mathcal{C}$ may not obtain the sender's secret value if the associated public value of the sender A is replaced. In this case, $\mathcal{A}$ is required to provide the secret value of A to $\mathcal{C}$. We do not allow queries where $ID_A = ID_B$. If $\mathcal{A}$ is $\mathcal{A}_{\mathcal{III}}$, $\mathcal{C}$ runs the above operations for any time instant before the challenge time period.
- **Key Encapsulation queries**: In the case of $\mathcal{A} \in \{\mathcal{A}_{\mathcal{I}}, \mathcal{A}_{\mathcal{II}}\}$, $\mathcal{A}$ produces an arbitrary tag τ for sender A. $\mathcal{C}$ checks whether there exists a corresponding ω value. If ω has been previously stored, then $\mathcal{C}$ computes $(\varphi) \leftarrow$ Encapsulation(ω, τ), deletes ω and returns φ to $\mathcal{A}$. Otherwise, $\mathcal{C}$ returns $\perp$ and terminates. In case that $\mathcal{A}$ is $\mathcal{A}_{\mathcal{III}}$, $\mathcal{C}$ runs the above operations for any time instant before the challenge time period.
- **Key Decapsulation queries**: In the case of $\mathcal{A} \in \{\mathcal{A}_{\mathcal{I}}, \mathcal{A}_{\mathcal{II}}\}$, $\mathcal{A}$ produces an encapsulation φ, a tag τ, the sender's identity ID_A, the public key pk_A, the receiver's identity ID_B and the public key pk_B. $\mathcal{C}$ obtains the receiver's private key sk_B and t_A from the corresponding "query-answer" list. $\mathcal{C}$ runs Decapsulation by using ID_A, ID_B, pk_A, sk_B, t_A, φ and τ. $\mathcal{C}$ may not be aware of the corresponding secret value if the associated public value of

ID_B is replaced. In this case $\mathcal{A}$ must provide the secret value of B to $\mathcal{C}$. We do not allow the queries where $ID_A = ID_B$. If $\mathcal{A}$ is $\mathcal{A}_{III}$, $\mathcal{C}$ runs the above operations for any time instant before the challenge time period.

Challenge: At the end of Phase I decided by $\mathcal{A} \in \{\mathcal{A}_I, \mathcal{A}_{II}\}$, $\mathcal{A}$ generates a sender identity ID_{A^*} and a receiver identity ID_{B^*} on which $\mathcal{A}$ wishes to be challenged. Here, ID_{B^*} must not be queried to extract a sk_{B^*} in Phase I. Also, in case that $\mathcal{A}$ is $\mathcal{A}_I$, ID_{B^*} may not be equal to an identity for which both the public key has been replaced and the partial private key has been extracted. At the end of Phase I which is decided by $\mathcal{A} \in \{\mathcal{A}_{III}\}$, $\mathcal{A}_{III}$ generates a sender identity ID_{A^*} and a receiver identity ID_{B^*} on which $\mathcal{A}_{III}$ wishes to be challenged for some instant t'_{A^*} such that $t'_{A^*} > t_{A^*}$ (after he has been revoked). In the revoked period, $\mathcal{A}_{III}$ has access to no new information. Now, $\mathcal{C}$ computes $(K_1, \omega^*) \leftarrow$ $\mathsf{SymmetricKeyGen}(\mathtt{params}, ID_{A^*}, pk_{A^*}, sk_{A^*}, ID_{B^*}, pk_{B^*}, t_{B^*})$ and chooses $K_0 \in_R \mathcal{K}$, where $\mathcal{K}$ is the key space of the eCLSC-TKEM. The $\mathcal{C}$ chooses a bit $\delta \in_R \{0,1\}$ and sends K_δ to $\mathcal{A}$. $\mathcal{A}$ generates an arbitrary tag τ^* and sends it to $\mathcal{C}$. $\mathcal{C}$ computes $(\varphi^*) \leftarrow \mathsf{Encapsulation}(\omega^*, \tau^*)$ and sends φ^* to $\mathcal{A}$ as a challenge encapsulation.

Phase II: In the case that $\mathcal{A}$ is $\mathcal{A}_I$ or $\mathcal{A}_{II}$, $\mathcal{A}$ can perform a polynomially bounded number of queries adaptively as in Phase I. However, when $\mathcal{A}$ is $\mathcal{A}_{III}$, the notable difference is that $\mathcal{A}$ can perform a polynomially bounded number of queries adaptively, before the beginning of the challenge period as in Phase I. $\mathcal{A}$ may not make Extract-full-Private-Key queries on ID_{B^*}. In $\mathcal{A}_I$, if the public key of ID_{B^*} has been replaced before the challenge phase, $\mathcal{A}_I$ may not extract the partial private key for ID_{B^*}. Moreover, $\mathcal{A}$ may not make a key decapsulation query on (K_δ, φ^*) under ID_{A^*} and ID_{B^*}, unless the public key $pk_{ID_{A^*}}$ or $pk_{ID_{B^*}}$ has been replaced after the challenge phase.
Guess: $\mathcal{A}$ outputs a bit δ' and wins the game if $\delta' = \delta$.

The advantage of $\mathcal{A}$ is defined as $Adv^{IND-CCA2}(\mathcal{A}) = |2Pr[\delta' = \delta] - 1|$, where $Pr[\delta' = \delta]$ denotes the probability that $\delta' = \delta$. A eCLSC-TKEM is IND-CCA2 secure if there is no probabilistic polynomial-time adversary in the above games with non-negligible advantage in the security parameter k. The security of eCLSC-TKEM is based on the assumed intractability of the one-sided gap Diffie-Hellman problem (OGDH) [11].

2) EUF-eCLSC-TKEM-CMA Game: The Forger $\mathcal{F}$ can be either $\mathcal{F}_I$, $\mathcal{F}_{II}$ or $\mathcal{F}_{III}$. The challenger $\mathcal{C}$ should keep a history of the query-answers while interacting with adversaries. $\mathcal{C}$ runs the $\mathsf{SetUp}()$ algorithm to generate the public parameters $\mathtt{params}$ and the master private key $\mathtt{msk}$ respectively. If $\mathcal{F}$ is either $\mathcal{F}_I$ or $\mathcal{F}_{III}$, $\mathcal{C}$ gives $\mathtt{params}$ to $\mathcal{F}$ while keeping $\mathtt{msk}$ secret. If $\mathcal{F}$ is $\mathcal{F}_{II}$, $\mathcal{C}$ gives both $\mathtt{params}$ and $\mathtt{msk}$ to $\mathcal{F}$.

Training Phase: $\mathcal{F}$ may make a polynomially bounded number of queries to random oracles $H_i(0 \leq i \leq 3)$ at any time and $\mathcal{C}$ responds as follows:
All the oracles and queries needed in the training phase are identical to the queries allowed in Phase I of the IND-eCLSC-TKEM-CCA2 game.

Forgery: At the end of the Training Phase which is decided by $\mathcal{F} \in \{\mathcal{F}_I, \mathcal{F}_{II}\}$, $\mathcal{F}$ produces an encapsulation $\langle \tau^*, \varphi^*, ID_{A^*}, ID_{B^*} \rangle$ on a arbitrary tag τ^*, where ID_{A^*} is the sender identity and ID_{B^*} is the receiver identity. At the end of the Training Phase decided by $\mathcal{F} = \mathcal{F}_{III}$, $\mathcal{F}_{III}$ generates a sender identity ID_{A^*} and a receiver identity ID_{B^*} on which $\mathcal{F}_{III}$ wishes to be challenged for some instant t'_{A^*} such that $t'_{A^*} > t_{A^*}$ (after $\mathcal{F}_{III}$ has been revoked). Then, $\mathcal{F}$ sends $\langle \tau^*, \varphi^*, ID_{A^*}, ID_{B^*} \rangle$ to $\mathcal{C}$. If $\mathcal{F}$ is $\mathcal{F}_I$, during the Training Phase, the partial private key for ID_{A^*} must not be queried and the public key for ID_{A^*} must not be replaced simultaneously. If $\mathcal{F}$ is $\mathcal{F}_{II}$, the secret value x_{A^*} for ID_{A^*} must not be queried and the public key for ID_{A^*} must not be replaced, simultaneously. Moreover φ^* must not be returned by the key encapsulation oracle on the input $(\tau^*, \omega^*, ID_{A^*}, ID_{B^*})$ during the Training Phase. If the output of $\mathsf{Decapsulation}(\mathtt{params}, ID_{A^*}, pk_{A^*}, t_{A^*}, ID_{B^*}, pk_{B^*}, sk_{B^*}, \varphi^*, \tau^*)$ is valid, $\mathcal{F} \in \{\mathcal{F}_I, \mathcal{F}_{II}\}$ wins the game. If the output of $\mathsf{Decapsulation}(\mathtt{params}, ID_{A^*}, pk_{A^*}, t'_{A^*}, ID_{B^*}, pk_{B^*}, sk_{B^*}, \varphi^*, \tau^*)$ is valid, $\mathcal{F} = \mathcal{F}_{III}$ wins the game.

The advantage of $\mathcal{F}$ is defined as the probability with which it wins the EUF-pCLSC-TKEM-CMA game. A eCLSC-TKEM satisfies existential unforgeability against an adaptively chosen message attack (EUF-eCLSC-TKEM-CMA), if no polynomially bounded forger $\mathcal{F}$ has non-negligible advantage in the above EUF-eCLSC-TKEM-CMA game between $\mathcal{C}$ and $\mathcal{F}$

6.2 Security Proof

In this section, we provide the formal security proof for the confidentiality and the existential unforgeability of our eCLSC-TKEM. The security of our eCLSC-TKEM relies on the hardness of the following problems.

Definition of OGDH For a group G_q with a generator P and a fixed point Q, the one-sided gap Diffie-Hellman problem (OGDH) [11] is defined as follows: for $x, y \in \mathsf{Z}_q^*$, given Q, R, compute xyP by accessing an one-sided decision Diffie-Hellman (ODDH) Oracle, where $Q = xP$ and $R = yP$.

Definition of ODDH For a group G_q with a generator P and a fixed point Q, the one-sided decision Diffie-Hellman oracle (ODDH) [11] is an oracle that for any $R', S' \in \mathsf{G}_q$ correctly answers the question: Is $z' \equiv xy' \pmod{p}$, where $x, y', z' \in \mathsf{Z}_q^*$ are integers such that $Q = xP, R' = y'P, S' = z'P$?

Definition of ECDLP The elliptic curve discrete log problem (ECDLP) is defined as follows: given a random instance P, Q, find a number $x \in \mathsf{Z}_q^*$ such that $Q = xP$.

Theorem 1. *In the random oracle model, the eCLSC-TKEM is IND-CCA2 secure under the assumption that the one-sided gap Diffie-Hellman (OGDH) problem is intractable.*
The Theorem 1 is proved based on Lemmas 1, 2 and 3. We adopt the security proof techniques from [21]. The proof of Lemma 3 is in the appendix, whereas the proofs of Lemmas 1 and 2 are omitted due to the space limitation.

Lemma 1. In the random oracle model, if there exists an adversary $\mathcal{A}_I$ against the IND-eCLSC-TKEM-CCA2-I security of the eCLSC-TKEM with advantage a non-negligible δ, then an algorithm $\mathcal{C}$ exists that solves the OGDH problem with the following advantage ε

$$\varepsilon \geq \delta \cdot (1 - \frac{q_{ppri}}{q_C \cdot q_{H_0}}) \cdot (1 - \frac{q_{sv}}{q_C \cdot q_{H_0}}) \cdot (\frac{1}{q_C \cdot q_{H_0} - q_{ppri} - q_{sv}}) \cdot (\frac{1}{q_{H_1}})$$

Here, q_{H_0}, q_{H_1}, q_C, q_{ppri} and q_{sv} are the maximum number of queries that the PPT adversary may ask random oracles H_0 and H_1, create (ID_i), extract-partial-private-key queries and extract-secret-value queries.

Lemma 2. In the random oracle model, if there exists an adversary $\mathcal{A}_{\mathcal{II}}$ against the IND-eCLSC-TKEM-CCA2-II security of the eCLSC-TKEM with advantage a non-negligible δ, then there exist an algorithm $\mathcal{C}$ that solves the OGDH problem with the following advantage ε

$$\varepsilon \geq \delta \cdot (1 - \frac{q_{sv}}{q_C \cdot q_{H_0}}) \cdot (1 - \frac{q_{pkR}}{q_C \cdot q_{H_0}}) \cdot (\frac{1}{q_C \cdot q_{H_0} - q_{sv} - q_{pkR}}) \cdot (\frac{1}{q_{H_1}})$$

Here, q_{H_0}, q_{H_1}, q_C, q_{pkR} and q_{sv} are the maximum number of queries that the PPT adversary may ask random oracles H_0 and H_1, create (ID_i), public-key-replacement queries and extract-secret-value queries.

Lemma 3. In the random oracle model, if there exists an adversary $\mathcal{A}_{\mathcal{III}}$ against the IND-eCLSC-TKEM-CCA2-III security of the eCLSC-TKEM with advantage a non-negligible δ, then an algorithm $\mathcal{C}$ exists that solves the OGDH problem with the following advantage ε

$$\varepsilon \geq \delta \cdot (1 - \frac{t^\star}{t}) \cdot (1 - \frac{1}{q}) \cdot (\frac{1}{q_C \cdot q_{H_0} - q_{ppri} - q_{sv}}) \cdot (\frac{1}{q_{H_1}})$$

Here, q_{H_0}, q_{H_1}, q_C, q_{ppri} and q_{sv} are the maximum number of queries that the PPT adversary may ask random oracles H_0 and H_1, create (ID_i), extract-partial-private-key queries and extract-secret-value queries. t denotes the total possible time assuming that the time begins at 0. $t^\star$ is a valid time period of the target identity.

Theorem 2. *In the random oracle model, the eCLSC-TKEM is EUF-CMA secure under the assumption that the elliptic curve discrete logarithm problem (ECDLP) is intractable.*
Theorem 2 is proved based on Lemmas 4, 5 and 6. We adopt the security proof techniques from [21]. The proof of Lemma 6 is in the appendix, whereas the proofs of Lemmas 4 and 5 are omitted due to the space limitation.

Lemma 4. In the random oracle model, if there exists a forger $\mathcal{F}_{\mathcal{I}}$ against the EUF-eCLSC-TKEM-CMA-I security of the eCLSC-TKEM with advantage a non-negligible δ, then there exists an algorithm $\mathcal{C}$ that solves the ECDLP with the following advantage ε

$$\varepsilon \geq \delta \cdot q_E \cdot (1 - \frac{q_{H_0} \cdot q_C}{q}) \cdot (1 - \frac{q_{H_2}^2}{q}) \cdot (1 - \frac{q_{H_3}^2}{q}) \cdot (1 + \frac{1}{q}) \cdot (\frac{1}{q_C}) \cdot (1 - \frac{q_{ppri}}{q_{H_0}}) \cdot (1 - \frac{q_{sv}}{q_{H_0}})$$

Here, q_C, q_E, q_{H_i}, q_{ppri} and q_{sv} are the maximum number of queries that the forger may make create (ID_i) queries, key encapsulation queries, random oracle queries to H_i $(0 \leq i \leq 3)$, extract-partial-private-key queries and extract-secret-value queries.

Lemma 5. In the random oracle model, if there exists a forger $\mathcal{F}_{\mathcal{II}}$ against the EUF-eCLSC-TKEM-CMA-II security of the eCLSC-TKEM with advantage a non-negligible δ, then there exists an algorithm $\mathcal{C}$ that solves the ECDLP with the following advantage ε

$$\varepsilon \geq \delta \cdot q_E \cdot (1 - \frac{q_{H_0} \cdot q_C}{q}) \cdot (1 - \frac{q_{H_2}^2}{q}) \cdot (1 - \frac{q_{H_3}^2}{q}) \cdot (1 + \frac{1}{q}) \cdot (\frac{1}{q_C}) \cdot (1 - \frac{q_{sv}}{q_{H_0}}) \cdot (1 - \frac{q_{pkR}}{q_{H_0}})$$

Here, q_C, q_E, q_{H_i}, q_{pkR} and q_{sv} are the maximum number of queries that the forger may make create (ID_i) queries, key encapsulation queries, random oracle queries to H_i $(0 \leq i \leq 3)$, public key replacement queries and extract-secret-value queries.

Lemma 6. In the random oracle model, if there exists a forger $\mathcal{F}_{\mathcal{III}}$ against the EUF-eCLSC-TKEM-CMA-III security of the eCLSC-TKEM with advantage a non-negligible δ, then there exists an algorithm $\mathcal{C}$ that solves the ECDLP with the following advantage ε

$$\varepsilon \geq \delta \cdot q_E \cdot (1 - \frac{q_{H_0} \cdot q_C}{q}) \cdot (1 - \frac{q_{H_2}^2}{q}) \cdot (1 - \frac{q_{H_3}^2}{q}) \cdot (1 + \frac{1}{q}) \cdot (\frac{1}{q_C}) \cdot (1 - \frac{t^\star}{t})$$

Here, q_C, q_E and q_{H_i} are the maximum number of queries that the forger may make create (ID_i) queries, key encapsulation queries, random oracle queries to H_i $(0 \leq i \leq 3)$. t denotes the total possible time and assuming that the time begins at 0. $t^\star$ is a valid time period of target identity

7. CONCLUSIONS AND FUTURE WORKS

In this paper, a secure communication protocol between drones and smart objects is presented. To satisfy security and efficiency requirements, we propose the eCLSC-TKEM with the dual channel strategy. Our protocol efficiently supports four security functions: key agreement, user authentication, non-repudiation, and user revocation. Our experimental analysis carried in a smart parking management testbed shows that our protocol is 1.3, 1.5 and 2.8 times faster than other protocols, i.e., Seo's CLSC-TKEM [21], Sun's CL-AKA [24] and Yang's CL-AKA [26], respectively.

As future work, we plan to investigate how to mitigate the $O(N)$ key update overhead at the KGC (N is the number of users). The overhead at the KGC can be dispersed by introducing intermediate entities between the KGC and drones. The KGC issues a valid partial private key not to directly drones but to the entity who is responsible for drones' operations. The entity can generate proxy partial private keys for drones using its valid partial private key. The key idea of the proxy partial private key might be similar to the proxy certificate or the proxy signature.

Acknowledgments

The work reported in this paper has been partially supported by the Purdue Cyber Center and by the National Science Foundation under grant CNS-1111512.

8. REFERENCES

[1] Low power listening, http://tinyos.stanford.edu/tinyos-wiki/index.php/writing_low-power_applications.

[2] Parrot, http://ardrone2.parrot.com.

[3] S. Al-Riyami and K. Paterson. Certificateless public key cryptography. In C.-S. Laih, editor, *ASIACRYPT*, volume 2894 of *LNCS*, pages 452–473. Springer, 2003.

[4] G. Anastasi, M. Conti, E. Monaldi, and A. Passarella. An adaptive data-transfer protocol for sensor networks with data mules. In *WoWMoM*, pages 1–8, 2007.

[5] D. Boneh and M. K. Franklin. Identity-based encryption from the weil pairing. In *Proceedings of CRYPTO '01*, pages 213–229. Springer, 2001.

[6] H. Chan, A. Perrig, and D. Song. Random key predistribution schemes for sensor networks. In *IEEE Symposium on Security and Privacy*, 2003.

[7] K. Chatterjee, A. De, and D. Gupta. An improved id-based key management scheme in wireless sensor network. In *Advances in Swarm Intelligence*, volume 7332 of *LNCS*, pages 351–359. Springer, 2012.

[8] W. Du, J. Deng, Y. S. Han, and P. K. Varshney. A pairwise key pre-distribution scheme for wireless sensor networks. In *CCS '03. Proceedings*, 2003.

[9] M. Geng and F. Zhang. Provably secure certificateless two-party authenticated key agreement protocol without pairing. In *CIS '09*, pages 208–212, 2009.

[10] D. He, J. Chen, and J. Hu. A pairing-free certificateless authenticated key agreement protocol. *Int. Journal of Comm. Sys.*, pages 221–230, 2012.

[11] N. Koblitz and A. Menezes. Intractable problems in cryptography. In *Proc. 9th International Conf. Finite Fields and Their Applications*, 2010.

[12] F. Li, M. Shirase, and T. Takagi. Certificateless hybrid signcryption. In *Information Security Practice and Experience*, volume 5451 of *LNCS*. Springer, 2009.

[13] A. Liu and P. Ning. Tinyecc: A configurable library for elliptic curve cryptography in wireless sensor networks. In *IPSN '08*, pages 245–256, April 2008.

[14] K. MacKay. https://github.com/kmackay/micro-ecc.

[15] S. M. Mizanur Rahman and K. El-Khatib. Private key agreement and secure communication for heterogeneous sensor networks. *J. Parallel Distrib. Comput.*, 70(8):858–870, Aug. 2010.

[16] D. Pointcheval and J. Stern. Security arguments for digital signatures and blind signatures. *JOURNAL OF CRYPTOLOGY*, 13:361–396, 2000.

[17] J. Polastre, J. Hill, and D. Culler. Versatile low power media access for wireless sensor networks. In *Proceedings of the ACM SenSys '04*, 2004.

[18] A. Rasheed and R. Mahapatra. Secure data collection scheme in wireless sensor network with mobile sink. In *IEEE NCA '08*, 2008.

[19] C. Schurgers, V. Tsiatsis, S. Ganeriwal, and M. Srivastava. Optimizing sensor networks in the energy-latency-density design space. *Mobile Computing, IEEE Trans. on*, 1(1):70–80, Jan 2002.

[20] S. Selvi, S. Vivek, and C. Rangan. Certificateless kem and hybrid signcryption schemes revisited. In *Information Security, Practice and Experience*, volume 6047 of *LNCS*, pages 294–307. Springer, 2010.

[21] S. Seo and E. Bertino. Elliptic curve cryptography based certificateless hybrid signcryption scheme without pairing, http://www.cerias.purdue.edu/apps /reports_and_papers/view/4698. *CERIAS report*, '13.

[22] R. Shah, S. Roy, S. Jain, and W. Brunette. Data mules: modeling a three-tier architecture for sparse sensor networks. In *SNPA '03, Proceedings*, 2003.

[23] H. Song, S. Zhu, W. Zhang, and G. Cao. Least privilege and privilege deprivation: Toward tolerating mobile sink compromises in wireless sensor networks. *ACM Trans. Sen. Netw.*, 4(4):23:1–23:34, Sept. 2008.

[24] H. Sun, Q. Wen, H. Zhang, and Z. Jin. A novel pairing-free certificateless authenticated key agreement protocol with provable security. *Frontiers of Computer Science*, 7(4):544–557, 2013.

[25] Y. Tirta, Z. Li, Y.-H. Lu, and S. Bagchi. Efficient collection of sensor data in remote fields using mobile collectors. In *ICCCN '04. Proceedings*, 2004.

[26] G. Yang and C.-H. Tan. Strongly secure certificateless key exchange without pairing. In *ASIACCS*, 2011.

[27] X. Zhang, J. He, and Q. Wei. Eddk: Energy-efficient distributed deterministic key management for wireless sensor networks. *EURASIP Journal on Wireless Communications and Networking*, 2011.

[28] W. Zhao, M. Ammar, and E. Zegura. A message ferrying approach for data delivery in sparse mobile ad hoc networks. In *ACM MobiHoc*, pages 187–198, 2004.

[29] L. Zhou, J. Ni, and C. Ravishankar. Supporting secure communication and data collection in mobile sensor networks. In *INFOCOM '06. Proceedings*, 2006.

APPENDIX

A. PROOF OF LEMMA 3

Suppose that there exists a Type III adversary $\mathcal{A}_{\mathcal{III}}$ who can break the IND-eCLSC-TKEM-CCA2-III security of the eCLSC-TKEM with a non-negligible probability in polynomial time. A challenger $\mathcal{C}$ is challenged with an instance of the OGDH (One-sided Gap Diffie-Hellman) problem. $\mathcal{C}$ can utilize $\mathcal{A}_{\mathcal{III}}$ to compute the solution of the OGDH instance by accessing a ODDH (One-sided Decision Diffie-Hellman)oracle. $\mathcal{C}$ sets the master private/public key pair as $(x, P_{pub} = xP)$, where P is the generator of the group G_q and the hash functions $H_i(0 \leq i \leq 3)$ are treated as random oracles. $\mathcal{C}$ sends the system parameters $\Omega = \{F_q, E/F_q, G_q, P, P_{pub}, H_0, H_1, H_2, H_3\}$ to $\mathcal{A}_{\mathcal{III}}$. To maintain the consistency, $\mathcal{C}$ maintains lists $L_i(0 \leq i \leq 3)$). It also maintains a list of issued private keys and public keys including valid time period in L_k. $\mathcal{C}$ can simulate the challenger's execution of each phase of the formal Game. Let $\mathcal{C}$ select a random index j, where $1 \leq j \leq q_C$ and fix ID_j as the target identity for the challenge phase. Let's that $\mathcal{A}_{\mathcal{III}}$ was revoked at the time interval beginning at $t^\star$.

Phase 1: $\mathcal{A}_{\mathcal{III}}$ may make use of all random oracles $H_i(0 \leq i \leq 3)$ at any time and $\mathcal{C}$ responds as follows:

Create(ID_i): When $\mathcal{A}_{\mathcal{III}}$ submits a Create(ID_i) query to $\mathcal{C}$, $\mathcal{C}$ responds as follows: (1) If case 1 ($ID_i \neq ID_j$) or case 2 ($ID_i = ID_j$ and $t_j < t^\star$), $\mathcal{C}$ picks $e_i, b_i, x_i \in_R Z_q^*$, then sets $H_0(ID_i, R_i, P_i, t_i) = -e_i$, $R_i = e_i P_{pub} + b_i P$ and computes the public key as $P_i = x_i P$. $d_i = b_i$ and it satisfies the equation $d_i P = R_i + H_0(ID_i, R_i, P_i, t_i)P_{pub}$. $\mathcal{C}$ inserts $\langle ID_i, R_i, P_i, t_i, -e_i\rangle$ into the list L_0 and $\langle ID_i, d_i, x_i, R_i, P_i, t_i\rangle$ into the list L_k. (2) If $ID_i = ID_j$ and $t_j > t^\star$, $\mathcal{C}$ chooses $e_j, x_j \in_R Z_q^*$ and sets $H_0(ID_j, R_j, P_j, t_j) = -e_j$, $P_j = x_j P$, and $R_j = e_j P_{pub} - P_j + aP$. Here, $\mathcal{C}$ does not know a. $\mathcal{C}$ uses the aP given in the instance of the OGDH problem. $\mathcal{C}$ inserts $\langle ID_j, R_j, P_j, t_j, -e_j\rangle$ into the list L_0 and

$\langle ID_j, \perp, x_j, R_j, P_j, t_j\rangle$ into the list L_k.

H_0 **queries**: When $\mathcal{A}_{III}$ submits a H_0 query with ID_i, $\mathcal{C}$ searches the list L_0. If there is a tuple $\langle ID_i, R_i, P_i, t_i, -e_i\rangle$, $\mathcal{C}$ responds with the previous value $-e_i$. Otherwise, $\mathcal{C}$ chooses $e_i \in_R Z_q^*$ and returns $-e_i$ as the answer. Then, $\mathcal{C}$ inserts $\langle ID_i, R_i, P_i, t_i, -e_i\rangle$ into the list L_0.

H_1 **queries**: When $\mathcal{A}_{III}$ submits a H_1 query with $(Y_i, V_i, T_i, ID_i, P_i)$, $\mathcal{C}$ checks whether the ODDH oracle returns 1 when queried with (aP, V_i, T_i). If the ODDH oracle returns 1, $\mathcal{C}$ outputs T_i and stop. Then $\mathcal{C}$ goes through the L_1 with entries $\langle Y_i, V_i, *, ID_i, P_i, l_i\rangle$, for different values of l_i, such that the ODDH oracle returns 1 when queried on the tuple (aP, V_i, T_i). Note that in this case $ID_i = ID_j$ and $t_j > t^\star$. If such a tuple exists, it returns l_i and replaces the symbol $*$ with T_i. Otherwise, $\mathcal{C}$ chooses $l \in_R \{0,1\}^n$ and updates the L_1, which is initially empty, with a tuple containing the input and return values. $\mathcal{C}$ then returns l to $\mathcal{A}_{III}$.

H_2 **queries**: $\mathcal{C}$ checks whether $\langle U, \tau, T, ID_A, P_A, ID_B, P_B, h_i\rangle$ exists in the L_2. If it exists, $\mathcal{C}$ returns $H = h_i$ to $\mathcal{A}_{III}$. Otherwise, $\mathcal{C}$ chooses $h_i \in_R Z_q^*$, adds $\langle U, \tau, T, ID_A, P_A, ID_B, P_B, h_i\rangle$ to the L_2 and returns $H = h_i$ to $\mathcal{A}_{III}$.

H_3 **queries**: $\mathcal{C}$ checks whether $\langle U, \tau, T, ID_A, P_A, ID_B, P_B, h'_i\rangle$ exists in the L_3. If it exists, $\mathcal{C}$ returns $H' = h'_i$ to $\mathcal{A}_{III}$. Otherwise, $\mathcal{C}$ chooses $h'_i \in_R Z_q^*$, adds $\langle U, \tau, T, ID_A, P_A, ID_B, P_B, h'_i\rangle$ to the L_3 and returns $H' = h'_i$ to $\mathcal{A}_{III}$.

Extract-Partial-Private-Key queries: In order to respond to the query for the partial private key of a user with ID_i, $\mathcal{C}$ performs the following steps: (1) If $ID_i = ID_j$ and $t_j > t^\star$, $\mathcal{C}$ aborts the execution. (2) If case 1 ($ID_i \neq ID_j$) or case 2 ($ID_i = ID_j$ and $t_j < t^\star$), $\mathcal{C}$ retrieves $\langle ID_i, d_i, x_i, R_i, P_i, t_i\rangle$ from L_k, returns (d_i, R_i) which satisfies the equation $d_i P = R_i + H_0(ID_i, R_i, P_i, t_i)P_{pub}$.

Extract-Secret-Value queries: $\mathcal{A}_{III}$ produces ID_i to $\mathcal{C}$ and requests a secret value of ID_i. If case 1 (the public key of ID_i has not been replaced and $ID_i \neq ID_j$) or case 2 (the public key of ID_i has not been replaced, $ID_i = ID_j$ and $t_j < t^\star$), then $\mathcal{C}$ responds with x_i by retrieving from L_k. If $\mathcal{A}_{III}$ has already replaced the public key of ID_i, $\mathcal{C}$ does not provide the corresponding secret value to $\mathcal{A}_{III}$. If $ID_i = ID_j$ and $t_j > t^\star$, $\mathcal{C}$ aborts.

Request-Public-Key queries: $\mathcal{A}_{III}$ produces ID_i to $\mathcal{C}$ and requests a public key of ID_i. $\mathcal{C}$ checks in the L_k for $\langle ID_i, d_i, x_i, R_i, P_i, t_i\rangle$. If it exists, $\mathcal{C}$ returns the corresponding public key (R_i, P_i, t_i). Otherwise, $\mathcal{C}$ recalls Create(ID_i) query to obtain (R_i, P_i, t_i) and returns (R_i, P_i, t_i).

Public-Key-Replacement queries: $\mathcal{A}_{III}$ chooses values (R'_i, P'_i, t'_i) to replace the public key (R_i, P_i, t_i) of ID_i. $\mathcal{C}$ updates the corresponding tuple in the L_k as $\langle ID_i, -, -, R'_i, P'_i, t'_i\rangle$. The current value of the user's public key is used by $\mathcal{C}$ for responses to any queries made by $\mathcal{A}_{III}$.

Symmetric Key Generation queries: $\mathcal{A}_{III}$ produces a sender's ID_A, public key (R_A, P_A, t_A), the receiver's ID_B and public key (R_B, P_B, t_B) to $\mathcal{C}$. For each query (ID_A, ID_B), $\mathcal{C}$ proceeds as follows: (1) If case 1 ($ID_A \neq ID_j$) or case 2 ($ID_A = ID_j$ and $t_j < t^\star$), $\mathcal{C}$ computes sk_A corresponding to ID_A by executing the Extract-Partial-Private-Key and Extract-Secret-Value algorithm. Then, $\mathcal{C}$ gets K and ω by running the actual SymmetricKeyGen algorithm. $\mathcal{C}$ stores ω and overwrite any previous value. $\mathcal{C}$ sends K to $\mathcal{A}_{III}$. (2) If $ID_A = ID_j$ and $t_j > t^\star$, $\mathcal{C}$ chooses $r_1, r_2, h_t, h'_t \in_R Z_q^*$ and computes $U = r_1 P - {h_t}^{-1} \cdot aP + {h_t}^{-1} \cdot P_t$, $V = r_2 P$, $Y = R_B + H_0(ID_B, R_B, P_B, t_B) \cdot P_{pub} + P_B$, $T = r_2 \cdot Y \bmod q {=} r_2 \cdot (H_0(ID_B, R_B, P_B, t_B)P_{pub} + R_B + P_B) \bmod q$ and $K = H_1(Y, V, T, ID_B, P_B)$, where R_B and P_B are obtained by calling the Request-Public-Key query oracle on ID_B. Note that ω is $\omega = (r_1, r_2, h_t, h'_t, U, V, T, ID_A, pk_A, ID_B, pk_B)$. (3) $\mathcal{C}$ goes through the L_1 looking for an entry (Y, V, T, ID_B, P_B, k) for some k such that ODDH(P_B, V, Y)=1. If such an entry exists, it computes $K \leftarrow l$. Otherwise it uses a random l and updates the L_1 with $(Y, V, *, ID_B, P_B, l)$. $\mathcal{C}$ stores ω and sends K to $\mathcal{A}_{III}$.

Key Encapsulation queries: $\mathcal{A}_{III}$ produces an arbitrary tag τ, the sender's ID_A, public key (R_A, P_A, t_A), the receiver's ID_B and public key (R_B, P_B, t_B) and sends them to $\mathcal{C}$. The full private key of the sender $sk_A = (d_A, x_A)$ is obtained from the L_k. $\mathcal{C}$ checks whether a corresponding ω value has been stored previously. (1) If ω does not exist, $\mathcal{C}$ returns an invalid reply. (2) If case 1 (a corresponding ω exists and $ID_A \neq ID_j$) or case 2 (a corresponding ω exists, $ID_A = ID_j$ and $t_j < t^\star$), then $\mathcal{C}$ computes φ with ω and τ by using the actual Encapsulation algorithm, and deletes ω. (3) If a corresponding ω exists, $ID_A = ID_j$ and $t_j > t^\star$, then $\mathcal{C}$ computes φ by performing the following steps. Note that ω is $(r_1, r_2, h_j, h'_j, U, V, T, ID_A, pk_A, ID_B, pk_B)$ and $\mathcal{C}$ does not know the private key corresponding to ID_t. So $\mathcal{C}$ should perform the encapsulation in a different way:

- $H = h_j$ and add $\langle U, \tau, T, ID_A, P_A, ID_B, P_B, h_j\rangle$ to L_2.
- $H' = h'_j$ and add $\langle U, \tau, T, ID_A, P_A, ID_B, P_B, h'_j\rangle$ to L_3.
- Compute $W = h_j \cdot r_1 + h'_j \cdot x_A$.
- Output $\varphi = (U, V, W)$ as the encapsulation.

We show that $\mathcal{A}_{III}$ can pass the verification of $\varphi = (U, V, W)$ to validate the encapsulation, because the equality $W \cdot P = R_A + H_0(ID_A, R_A, P_A, t_A) \cdot P_{pub} + H \cdot U + H' \cdot P_A$ holds as follows: $R_A + H_0(ID_A, R_A, P_A, t_A) \cdot P_{pub} + H \cdot U + H' \cdot P_A = aP + e_j P_{pub} - P_j + (-e_j) \cdot P_{pub} + H \cdot (r_1 P - {h_j}^{-1} \cdot aP + {h_j}^{-1} \cdot P_j) + H' \cdot P_A = h_j \cdot r_1 P + h'_j \cdot P_A {=} W \cdot P$

Key Decapsulation queries: $\mathcal{A}_{III}$ produces an encapsulation $\varphi = (U, V, W)$, a tag τ, the sender's ID_A, the public key (R_A, P_A, t_A), the receiver's ID_B and the public key (R_B, P_B, t_B) to $\mathcal{C}$. The full private key of the receiver $sk_B = (d_B, x_B)$ is obtained from the list L_k. (1) If case 1 ($ID_B \neq ID_j$) or case 2 ($ID_B = ID_j$ and $t_j < t^\star$), then $\mathcal{C}$ computes the decapsulation of φ by using the actual Decapsulation algorithm. (2) If $ID_B = ID_t$ and $t_j > t^\star$, then the point cannot be computed. In order to return a consistent answer, $\mathcal{C}$ computes K from φ as follows:

- Searches in the L_2 and L_3 for entries $\langle U, \tau, T, ID_A, P_A, ID_B, P_B, h_j\rangle$ and $\langle U, \tau, T, ID_A, P_A, ID_B, P_B, h'_j\rangle$, respectively.
- If $H = h_j$ and $H' = h'_j$ exist then $\mathcal{C}$ checks whether the equality $W \cdot P = R_A + H_0(ID_A, R_A, P_A, t_A) \cdot P_{pub} + H \cdot U + H' \cdot P_A$ holds.
- If the above equality holds, the T is retrieved from the L_2 and L_3. Both the T values should be equal.
- $\mathcal{C}$ goes through L_1 and looks for $\langle Y, V, T, ID_B, P_B, l\rangle$ such that the ODDH oracle returns 1 when queried on the (aP, V, T). If such entry exists, the corresponding $K \leftarrow l$ value is returned as the decapsulation of φ.
- If $\mathcal{C}$ reaches this point of execution, it puts the entry $\langle Y, V, *, ID_B, P_B, l\rangle$ for a random l on the L_1 and returns $K \leftarrow l$. The $*$ denotes an unknown value. The identity component with $*$ is a receiver ID_B.

Challenge: At the end of Phase I, $\mathcal{A}_{III}$ sends a sender's ID_{A*} and a receiver's ID_{B*} to $\mathcal{C}$. Here, the partial private key of the revoked receiver was not queried in Phase I. Let the time $t'^*_j \in (t^*_j, t^*_j + \alpha)$. $\mathcal{C}$ aborts the game if case 1 ($ID_{B*} \neq ID_j$) or case 2 ($ID_{B*} = ID_j$ and $t'^*_j < t^\star$). Otherwise, $\mathcal{C}$ performs the following steps to compute the challenge encapsulation φ^*: (1) Choose $r \in_R Z_q^*$ and compute $U^* = rP$. (2) Set $V^* = bP$ and choose $T^* \in_R G_q$. Here, $\mathcal{C}$ does not know b. $\mathcal{C}$ uses the bP given in the instance of the OGDH problem. (3) Choose $K_0 \in_R \mathcal{K}$, where $\mathcal{K}$ is the key space of the eCLSC-TKEM. (4) Choose a random hash value l^* and set $K_1 = l^*$. (5) $\mathcal{C}$ chooses a bit $\delta \in_R \{0,1\}$ and sends K_δ to $\mathcal{A}_{III}$. (6) $\mathcal{A}_{III}$ generates τ^* and sends it to $\mathcal{C}$. (7) Choose $h_i, h'_i \in_R \mathbb{Z}_q^*$, store $\langle U^*, \tau^*, T^*, ID_{A*}, P_{A*}, ID_{B*}, P_{B*}, h_i\rangle$ to the L_2 and $\langle U^*, \tau^*, T^*, ID_{A*}, P_{A*}, ID_{B*}, P_{B*}, h'_i\rangle$ to the L_3. (8) Since $\mathcal{C}$ knows the sender's private key, $\mathcal{C}$ computes $W^* = d_{A*} + r \cdot h_i + x_{A*} \cdot h'_i$. (9) $\mathcal{C}$ returns $\varphi^* = \langle U^*, V^*, W^*\rangle$.

Phase II: $\mathcal{A}_{III}$ adaptively queries the oracles as in Phase I. Besides it cannot query decapsulation on φ^*.

Guess: Since $\mathcal{A}_{III}$ can break the IND-eCLSC-TKEM-CCA2-III security (which is assumed at the beginning of the proof), $\mathcal{A}_{III}$ should have asked a H_1 query with $(Y^*, V^*, T^*, ID_{B^*}, P_{B^*})$ as inputs. It is to be noted that $T^* = b \cdot Y^* = b \cdot (-e_j \cdot P_{pub} + e_j \cdot P_{pub} - P_j + aP + P_{B^*}) = ab \cdot P$, where $P_j = P_{B*}$ because of $ID_j = ID_{B*}$. Therefore, if the L_1 has q_{H_1} queries corresponding to the sender ID_{A^*} and receiver ID_{B^*}, one of the T^*'s among q_{H_1} values stored in the list L_1 is the solution for the OGDH problem instance. $\mathcal{C}$ chooses one T value uniformly at random from the q_{H_1} values from the L_1 and outputs it as the solution for the OGDH instance.

Analysis: $\mathcal{C}$ lets E_1, E_2 and E_3 be the events in which $\mathcal{C}$ aborts the IND-eCLSC-TKEM-CCA2-III game.

(1) E_1: The $\mathcal{A}_{III}$ returns decapsulation for $t'^*_j < t^\star$). The probability is $Pr[E_1] = \frac{t^\star}{t}$. t denotes the total possible time and assuming that the time begins at 0.

(2) E_2: An invalid public key replacement by $\mathcal{A}_{III}$ was not detected. The probability is $Pr[E_2] = \frac{1}{q}$.

(3) E_3: $\mathcal{A}_{III}$ does not choose the target identity ID_j during the challenge. The probability is $Pr[E_3] = 1 - \frac{1}{q_C \cdot q_{H_0} - q_{ppri} - q_{sv}}$.

Thus, the probability that $\mathcal{C}$ does not abort the IND-eCLSC-TKEM-CCA2-III game is

$$Pr[\neg E_1 \wedge \neg E_2 \wedge \neg E_3] = (1 - \frac{t^\star}{t}) \cdot (1 - \frac{1}{q}) \cdot (\frac{1}{q_C \cdot q_{H_0} - q_{ppri} - q_{sv}})$$

The probability that $\mathcal{C}$ randomly chooses the T from L_1 and T is the solution of OGDH problem is $\frac{1}{q_{H_1}}$. So, the probability that $\mathcal{C}$ finds the OGDH instance is as follows:

$$Pr[\mathcal{C}] = \delta \cdot (1 - \frac{t^\star}{t}) \cdot (1 - \frac{1}{q}) \cdot (\frac{1}{q_C \cdot q_{H_0} - q_{ppri} - q_{sv}}) \cdot (\frac{1}{q_{H_1}})$$

Therefore, the $Pr[\mathcal{C}]$ is non-negligible, because δ is non-negligible. This contradicts the OGDH assumption.

B. PROOF OF LEMMA 6

A challenger $\mathcal{C}$ is challenged with an instance of the ECDLP. To solve the ECDLP, given $\langle P, bP\rangle \in G_q$, $\mathcal{C}$ must find b. Let $\mathcal{F}_{III}$ be a forger who is able to break the EUF-eCLSC-TKEM-CMA-III security of the eCLSC-TKEM. $\mathcal{C}$ can utilize $\mathcal{F}_{III}$ to compute the solution b of the ECDLP instance by playing the following interactive game with $\mathcal{F}_{III}$. To solve the ECDLP, $\mathcal{C}$ sets the master private/public key pair as $(x, P_{pub} = xP)$, where P is the generator of the group G_q and the hash functions $H_i (0 \leq i \leq 3)$ are treated as random oracles. The $\mathcal{C}$ sends the system parameter $\Omega = \{F_q, E/F_q, G_q, P, P_{pub}, H_0, H_1, H_2, H_3\}$ to $\mathcal{F}_{III}$. In order to avoid the inconsistency between the responses to the hash queries, $\mathcal{C}$ maintains lists $L_i (0 \leq i \leq 3)$). It also maintains a list L_k to maintain the list of issued private keys and public keys including the valid time period. $\mathcal{C}$ can simulate the Challenger's execution of each phase of the formal game.

Training Phase: $\mathcal{F}_{III}$ may make a series of polynomially bounded number of queries to random oracles $H_i (0 \leq i \leq 3)$ at any time and $\mathcal{C}$ responds as follows: All the oracles and queries needed in the training phase are identical to those of the Create(ID_i) queries, H_0 queries, H_1 queries, H_2 queries, H_3 queries, Extract-Partial-Private-Key queries, Extract-Secret-Value queries, Public-Key-Replacement queries, Symmetric Key Generation queries, Key Encapsulation queries and Key Decapsulation queries in IND-pCLSC-TKEM-CCA2-III game.

Forgery: Eventually, $\mathcal{F}_{III}$ returns a valid encapsulation $\langle \tau, \varphi = (U, V, W), ID_A, ID_B\rangle$ on a arbitrary tag τ, where ID_A is the sender identity and ID_B is the receiver identity, to $\mathcal{C}$. If $ID_A = ID_j$ and $t'^*_j > t^\star$, $\mathcal{C}$ aborts the execution of this game. Otherwise, $\mathcal{C}$ searches the list L_2 and outputs another valid encapsulation $\langle \tau, \varphi^* = (U, V, W^*), ID_A, ID_B\rangle$ with different h_i^* such that $h_i^* \neq h_i$ on the same τ as done in forking lemma [16]. Thus, we can get $W \cdot P = R_A - e_j \cdot P_{pub} + h_i \cdot U + h'_i \cdot P_A$ and $W^* \cdot P = R_A - e_j \cdot P_{pub} + h_i^* \cdot U + h'_i \cdot P_A$. Let $U = bP$. Then if we subtract these two equations, we get following value.

$W^* \cdot P - W \cdot P = h_i^* \cdot U - h_i \cdot U$

$\Rightarrow (W^* - W)P = (h_i^* - h_i) \cdot U$

$\Rightarrow (W^* - W)P = (h_i^* - h_i) \cdot bP$

$\Rightarrow (W^* - W) \cdot (h_i^* - h_i)^{-1} = b$

Therefore, $\mathcal{F}_{III}$ solves the ECDLP as $b = \frac{W^* - W}{h_i^* - h_i}$ using the algorithm $\mathcal{C}$ for given a random instance $\langle P, bP\rangle \in G_q$.

Analysis: In order to assess the probability of success of the challenger $\mathcal{C}$. We assume that $\mathcal{F}_{III}$ can ask q_C create (ID_i) queries, q_E key-encapsulation queries and q_{H_i} random oracle queries to H_i ($0 \leq i \leq 3$). We also assume that $\mathcal{F}_{III}/$ never repeats H_i ($0 \leq i \leq 3$) a query with the same input.

(1) The success probability of the Create(ID_i) query execution is $(1 - \frac{q_{H_0}}{q})^{q_C} \geq 1 - \frac{q_{H_0} \cdot q_C}{q}$.

(2) The success probability of the H_2 query execution is $(1 - \frac{q_{H_2}}{q})^{q_{H_2}} \geq 1 - \frac{q_{H_2}^2}{q}$.

(3) The success probability of the H_3 query execution/ is $(1 - \frac{q_{H_3}}{q})^{q_{H_3}} \geq 1 - \frac{q_{H_3}^2}{q}$.

(4) The success probability of the key encapsulation query execution is $\frac{q_E}{(1 - \frac{1}{q})} \geq q_E \cdot (1 + \frac{1}{q})$.

(5) The probability of both $ID_i = ID_j$ and $t'^*_j > t^\star$ is $\frac{1}{q_C} \cdot (1 - \frac{t^\star}{t})$. t denotes the total possible time and assuming that the time begins at 0.

Thus, the success probability that $\mathcal{C}$ can win the EUF-eCLSC-TKEM-CMA-III game is

$$\varepsilon \geq \delta \cdot q_E \cdot (1 - \frac{q_{H_0} \cdot q_C}{q}) \cdot (1 - \frac{q_{H_2}^2}{q}) \cdot (1 - \frac{q_{H_3}^2}{q}) \cdot (1 + \frac{1}{q}) \cdot (\frac{1}{q_C}) \cdot (1 - \frac{t^\star}{t})$$

Therefore, the probability that $\mathcal{C}$ computes the solution of ECDLP is non-negligible, because δ is non-negligible.

Message Integrity Protection over Wireless Channel by Countering Signal Cancellation: Theory and Practice

Yantian Hou*, Ming Li*, Ruchir Chauhan*, Ryan M. Gerdes*, Kai Zeng†
houyantian@gmail.com, ming.li@usu.edu, ryan.gerdes@usu.edu, kzeng2@gmu.edu
*Utah State University, Logan, UT 84322
†George Mason University, Fairfax, Virginia 22030

ABSTRACT

Physical layer message integrity protection and authentication by countering signal-cancellation has been shown as a promising alternative to traditional pure cryptographic message authentication protocols, due to the non-necessity of neither pre-shared secrets nor secure channels. However, the security of such an approach remained an open problem due to the lack of systematic security modeling and quantitative analysis. In this paper, we first establish a novel correlated jamming framework to study the optimal signal-cancellation attacker's behavior and utility using game-theory, which precisely captures the attacker's knowledge using its correlated channel estimates in various channel environments. Besides, we design a practical physical layer message integrity protection protocol based on ON/OFF keying and Manchester coding, which provides quantitative security guarantees in the real-world. Such a guarantee is achieved by bounding the attacker's knowledge about the future channel via proactively measuring channel statistics (mimic the attacker), so as to derive a lower-bound to the defender's signal-detection probability under optimal correlated jamming attacks. We conduct extensive experiments and simulations to show the security and performance of the proposed scheme. We believe our novel threat modeling and quantitative security analysis methodology can benefit a wide range of physical layer security problems.

1. INTRODUCTION

Message integrity protection and authentication are two fundamental security services in the Internet-of-Things, given the exponential growth of wireless sensors and mobile devices [1]. Traditionally, such services have assumed the existence of pre-shared secret keys or secure channels. However, in many scenarios these premises may not be satisfied, e.g. when initial security associations need to be established among two or more constrained wireless devices. Generally, secret keys need to be distributed either via an off-line secure channel or using a public key infrastructure (PKI). But key pre-distribution may not be always feasible due to the lack of hardware interfaces and the absence of a global PKI. Some existing research proposed using out-of-band (OOB) secure auxiliary channels to build message authentication protocols without pre-shared keys [23, 3, 8, 4, 16, 17]. However, an OOB channel would require special hardware and non-trivial human interaction, while its security has been revisited [18]. In addition, whenever keys are stolen or compromised, re-keying involves significant human effort as well.

Ideally, we want to provide message integrity protection and authentication without relying on pre-shared keys or secure channels. That is, to establish the veracity of a message and its source using only wireless in-band transmissions. Čapkun et. al. [5] showed that it is possible to construct such an in-band integrity protection primitive, by preventing signal-cancellation in the wireless channel and combine it with unidirectional error detection codes. Later a few works have followed up in this direction. However, an important question remained unanswered about its security. Since the security depends on the infeasibility of signal-cancellation, work should be done to evaluate to which extent this is true, i.e. there lacks quantitative analysis of its security. Recently, Pöpper et. al. [19] demonstrated a practical relaying attack that can fully cancel the source's signal in some cases. In fact, the probability of adversarial signal-cancellation heavily depends on the wireless channel conditions. But again, so far only qualitative results are available, while no quantitative security guarantee can been provided by any of the previous designs.

Unfortunately, in general such a security guarantee is quite challenging to establish for any wireless physical-layer security mechanism. This is primarily due to a lack of systematic modeling of attacker's behaviors in this area, unlike well-known methodologies for cryptography. To do so one needs to connect knowledge from information-theory, wireless communications and practical aspects of security. In addition, the fact that wireless is an open medium makes it easy for common attacks to be launched, thus threat modeling needs to be comprehensive. A smart and strategic attacker who is knowledgeable about the wireless channel environment must be assumed. In fact, we will show that the channel state information (CSI) can be viewed as a partial secret of the legitimate communicating pairs, and we can systematically bound attacker's knowledge about this information in reality. Moreover, the attacker can possess advanced hardware and processing capabilities such as multi-antennas and directional antennas. Many other existing

ASIA CCS'15, April 14–17, 2015, Singapore..

http://dx.doi.org/10.1145/2714576.2714617.

physical layer security schemes failed to provide any security [24, 20] when the attacker is powerful as such.

In this paper, we first present a systematic threat modeling for signal cancellation attacks. In our model, the attacker exploits the intrinsic channel correlation existing in various domain(s) (e.g. temporal, spatial and frequency domains) to estimate the CSI of the legitimate communication pair with help of advanced hardware (such as directional antenna or multi-antenna). We then develop a correlated jamming and defense framework based on previous pure theoretical study in correlated jamming [12]. Our framework captures the attacker's knowledge about the legitimate communication pair's CSI using a correlation coefficient. We consider both indoor and outdoor environments in our system model. The correlated jamming and defense process is modeled as a zero-sum game, in which the attacker aims at minimizing receiver's signal detection probability, while the defender seeks to maximize this probability. Under this framework, we theoretically analyze the optimal attack/defense strategies and detection probability under correlated jamming, given any correlation coefficient.

Based on the theoretical results, we propose a practical physical-layer message integrity protection scheme that can achieve provable security guarantees. The protocol builds upon and can be regarded as an add-on to previous works using ON/OFF keying and Manchester coding. Our idea is to let the legitimate pair proactively make a worst case estimation of the attacker's knowledge of their CSI (mimic the attacker), and use that to derive a lower-bound of the signal detection probability under optimal cancellation attacks. A key challenge is how to bound the attacker's knowledge given that it can measure correlated channels at an arbitrary location, time and frequency. In our protocol, we deal with one of the strongest CSI estimation attack in temporal, frequency and spatial domains. We assume the attacker can obtain accurate CSI measurements (full knowledge) of the legitimate pair in the past, based on which it predicts the CSI in the future for optimal correlated jamming. Interestingly, by extracting the intrinsic randomness and unpredictability of the wireless channel over time, we can achieve an arbitrary goal of minimum signal detection probability by tuning the number of symbols in each ON slot.

Finally, we validate our theoretical analysis results using simulation, which shows that signal cancellation is indeed most effective when the attacker adopts the optimal jamming strategy. We also show the impact of attacker's correlation coefficient and the detection threshold to the system security level and achievable link throughput. In addition, we carry out real-world experiments and implement our scheme on USRP GNU radio devices. We found that by actively randomizing the physical channel using external disturbances, we can turn an indoor static channel into a dynamic channel which can defend against signal cancellation attack more effectively.

This paper is organized as follows. Sec. 2 presents the background and motivation to our threat modeling, followed by the system and attack models in Sec. 3. In Sec. 4, we present the game-theoretical framework to analyze the attacker/defender's strategies and their optimal utilities. Sec. 5 gives our physical layer message integrity protection scheme. Sec. 6 contains the simulation evaluation results. In Sec. 7, we present the implementation and experimental study, and discussions. Sec. 8 gives an overview of related work. Sec. 9 concludes the paper.

2. BACKGROUND AND MOTIVATION

2.1 In-band Message Integrity Protection and Authentication

A few previous works proposed in-band message integrity protection and authentication schemes without relying on pre-shared secret keys [5, 7, 10]. The common underlying idea is to combine ON/OFF keying with unidirectional error detection code. By using this coding method, bit 1 is encoded into ON_OFF slots and bit 0 is encoded into OFF_ON slots. To provide message integrity protection, a data packet is sent first using normal modulation, followed by a cryptographic hash calculated over the message which is encoded using the ON/OFF keying approach (idea is also shown in Fig. 4). The security of this approach is based on the infeasibility of signal cancellation in the wireless channel, which ensures that only unidirectional bit modification is feasible, i.e. attacker could only change OFF slot into ON slot but not in the opposite direction. Therefore any tampering with the original message will be detected (w.h.p.), and the authentication property can be derived based on integrity protection and the presence of the participating devices (authentication through presence [5]). Anti-signal-cancellation is achieved by setting the signal to be random in each ON slot, and based on the assumption that attacker could not extract any knowledge of the source signal and the channel thus it cannot cancel the signal.

However, this assumption is too strong because practical signal cancellation attack has been demonstrated [19], which uses a pair of directional antennas to relay the source signal such that the phase differs by $k\pi$ from the direct signal at the receiver. It is also referred to as correlated jamming [14]. This type of attack aims at completely cancelling out the received signal, by assuming the attacker knows the transmitted source signal x (or a correlated version of it). This is achieved in [19] by using directional antennas, such that the attacker obtains x from A in real time, and it has almost complete knowledge of the direct channel from A to B (which is a stable indoor channel). Through correlated jamming, the attacker has the potential to modify/cancel any signal in wireless channel, and the message integrity will not be protected. Thus, it is essential to investigate the possibility of signal cancellation in the real-world, so as to provide quantitative security guarantees.

2.2 Quantifying Adversary's Knowledge in Correlated Jamming

Previous results on the signal cancellation attack are qualitative [19], which show that a static environment leads to higher chance of cancellation. While some theoretical results are known in correlated jamming, the legitimate pair's CSI h is assumed to be either perfectly known by the attacker, or not known but only statistics are available. However, in practice this is often not the case. Instead, the attacker's knowledge about the channel can lie between these two extremes. And how can we quantify the attacker's capability remained as an open problem. Intuitively, the more accurate the attacker could estimate the legitimate pair's channel h, the more effective it could launch the correlated jamming attack. Therefore, we can use the correlation coefficient $r_{h\bar{g}}$ to

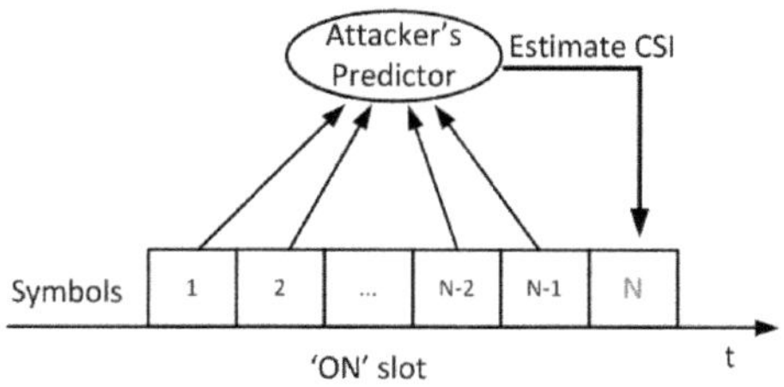

Figure 1: Example of CSI prediction attack.

quantize the correlated jammer's capability, where g denotes the attacker's estimation of h.

Generally, the attacker can exploit correlations in three domains to obtain knowledge of legitimate h: spatial domain, temporal domain, and frequency domain. In the spatial dimension, previous works [13, 11] demonstrated high correlations between channels where the receivers (or transmitters) are close to each other (typically within half wavelength). He et. al. [9] even showed that, the attacker can obtain a very accurate estimation of the legitimate pair's channel by placing multiple eavesdroppers around the legitimate receiver. The idea is to let all the eavesdroppers measure the channel simultaneously, and then combine them into a linear minimum mean square error (LMMSE) estimator. The estimation error can decrease to zero with increased number of eavesdroppers in some cases.

It has also been shown by previous works that channel is self-correlated in time domain. The correlated time scale is typically measured by the channel coherence time, which is usually several ms in dynamic environment and hundreds of ms in static environments.

Similarly, channel correlation exists in the frequency domain. The attacker can also exploit CSI measurements made in adjacent channels to derive a better estimate of the CSI in the frequency used by the legitimate pair.

In a word, the attacker could leverage channel correlation in any of the three domains and combine them. Such correlation should be considered in the threat model and design of any anti-signal-cancellation based integrity protection scheme.

In this paper, we first derive a theoretic result showing that the attacker's successful cancellation probability increases with its channel correlation with the legitimate one. However, in reality it is difficult (if not impossible) to know the attacker's capabilities in advance (e.g., location, device type, number), and it seems hopeless to upper-bound the attacker's knowledge about the legitimate channel. Fortunately, since correlated jamming is an active attack, it is only effective when the jamming signal is in the same frequency. Also, it must be timely – attacker's channel estimation needs to be done in real-time without any delay, otherwise the jamming opportunity will be missed. Therefore, even though the attacker can accurately measure the historical legitimate CSI via spatial and frequency domain correlation, it still needs to predict the CSI in the present (and future) in order to generate its correlated jamming signal (illustrated in Fig. 1). Any approach to obtain the current channel knowledge through measurements takes time, and after that the optimal jamming opportunity is already missed. That means, we can exploit the intrinsic time-domain unpredictability of the legitimate channel to prevent it from knowing the future CSI. To do so, in our scheme the legitimate TX/RX quantify the CSI's self-correlation in the time domain and use that to bound the knowledge of attacker.

3. MODEL AND ASSUMPTIONS

3.1 System Model

In our model, Alice communicates with Bob through a wireless channel. There are two types of transmission modes. In the first one (normal mode) a message is transmitted using standard modulation and data rates, such like 802.11 OFDM. The second one is called the ON/OFF keying mode, where information bits (like the hash of a normal message) are all encoded using ON/OFF keying combined with unidirectional error detection codes (e.g., Manchester coding). In each ON slot, a normal packet with random content is transmitted, while in OFF slots Alice remains silent. For this mode Bob uses energy detection to decode the received signal. Periodically (e.g., per symbol interval), Bob obtains a received signal strength (RSS) and compares it with a threshold (α). If the RSS is larger than α for N_s samples then an ON slot is detected. We assume each transmitted signal $x \in \mathbb{C}$ is arbitrary. The channel state $h \in \mathbb{C}$ between Alice and Bob is modeled under Rayleigh fading with additive white Gaussian noise n in outdoor environment, and Rician model in indoor environments.

3.2 Threat Model

The attacker's general goal is to break integrity protection, i.e., modify the message without being detected. For the normal mode, we assume the adversary can arbitrarily eavesdrop, inject, modify, replay, and block the message (standard Dolev-Yao model). For the ON/OFF keying mode, we assume a correlated jammer C who knows the exact transmitted signal x, and C's goal is to cancel out the signal received at Bob. To learn x in real-time, C can place a directional antenna closely to the legitimate transmitter A. To create and deliver a correlated jamming signal at B, C will utilize x and her "knowledge" about the CSI h from A to B. Essentially, C possesses a correlated version of h denoted as g (correlation coefficient denoted as $r \in [0, 1]$), which could be estimated from measurements (as shown in Fig. 2).

There are two types of attackers our model depending on their capabilities. We always assume the attacker cannot replace A or B, nor simply block the communication using a Faraday Cage. We do not restrict the number and type of devices the attacker may have. It can either generate its own signals or relay and process the signals from A to B.

Type I: This type of attacker relies on statistical or background information to estimate h, but makes no effort to obtain the accurate measurement of h. For example, channel propagation models can be used to derive the stable (Line-of-Sight/LoS) part of the CSI based on the distance, and large-scale fading/shadowing effects can also be predicted. However the attacker cannot derive a correlated version for the dynamic/small-scale part. This model is adopted by [19] under a stable indoor scenario, where A-B, A-C and C-B channels are all assumed constant.

Type II: This type of attacker can obtain up-to-date and correlated estimation about A to B's CSI using information from any of the three domains mentioned in previous section. For example, it could place multiple receivers close to B, and measure the channel for each transmitted symbol continuously. In the worst case, it obtains the exact A-B channel for every symbol in the past and uses them to predict the future CSI.

In a word, the Type I attacker could only get the knowledge about the stable part of CSI, while the Type II attacker could also get partial knowledge of the dynamic part. We note that, the type II attack model is stronger and more general than previous works [19, 7, 5, 10], as the attacker can do real-time signal processing to generate a correlated jamming signal based on source x and the correlated CSI.

4. OPTIMAL STRATEGIES FOR SIGNAL CANCELLATION ATTACK AND DEFENSE

4.1 Game Theoretic Framework

In this section, we theoretically analyze the signal cancellation attack for one symbol in an ON slot. We model the cancellation and anti-cancellation process as a game. The attacker's goal is to transmit a signal correlated with x such that the detection probability P_d of the combined received signal is minimized at B. Therefore we define the attacker's utility function as $U_a = -P_d$. The legitimate pair's strategy is to maximize the signal detection probability and their utility function is $U_l = P_d$. Obviously, this is a zero-sum game.

For the strategy space, let the correlated jammer generate a linear signal [12, 22, 21] that is $agx + v$, in which a is a variable controlled by jammer, g is attacker's knowledge about h (an estimated or correlated version), and v is additive white Gaussian noise with variance σ_v. Thus the overall received signal will be:

$$y = (h + ag)x + n + v \quad (1)$$

W.l.o.g., we use the Rician model for A-B channel (Rayleigh model is a special case). In this model, the channel h is composed of two parts: one is the deterministic LoS component h', the other is the random Gaussian distributed fading component h''. Thus the channel is denoted by $h = h' + h''$.

We assume the attacker could estimate the LoS part precisely. The estimation g is further divided into two parts $g = g' + g''$. The attacker's strategy consists of a tuple $\mathbf{a} = [a', a'', \sigma_v]$ corresponding to each component. Its transmit power can be easily derived based on $\mathbf{a}$, g, the power of x and v, and here we assume it is not bounded. To include the attacker's power in its strategy under power constraint will be our future work. On the other hand, the defender's strategy consists of A's transmit power.

Under this model, the received signal can be represented by:

$$y = (h' + a'g')x + (h'' + a''g'')x + n + v \quad (2)$$

4.2 Optimal Attack Strategy

Because the LoS and NLoS signal components are independent from each other, the attacker can cancel the two components separately.

4.2.1 LoS Component Strategy

As the LoS channel component h' is assumed to be precisely known, we have $g' = h'$. Therefore we can easily derive the optimal attack strategy for the LoS component:

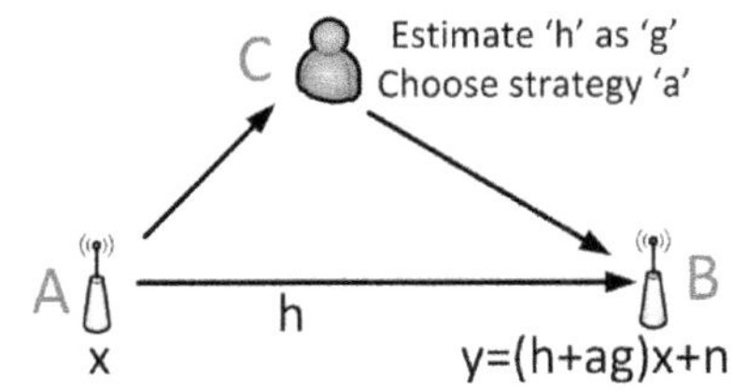

Figure 2: The system model

THEOREM 4.1. *The optimal LoS component cancellation strategy is:*

$$a' = -1 \quad (3)$$

The above indicates that, the attacker will reverse the LoS signal's phase to completely cancel it out at the receiver side.

4.2.2 NLoS Component Strategy

Given that the LoS component can be completely cancelled, we analyze the optimal attack strategy for NLoS part. We start from deriving the distribution of received power of this component under correlated jamming.

Type I attacker. For the type I attacker, the estimated channel g'' is independent from h''. Since the source signal x is randomly distributed, the power detected by receiver is $P_y = \sigma_x^2|h''|^2 + |a''g''|^2\sigma_x^2 + \sigma_n^2 + \sigma_v^2$, where $\sigma_x, \sigma_n, \sigma_v$ are the variance (power) of the source signal and noises, respectively. We can see that the variable $|h''|^2$ follows gamma distribution $\Gamma(1, 2\sigma^2)$ as $|h''|$ is Rayleigh distributed, where $\sigma^2 = \frac{1}{2}E[h''\overline{h''}]$.

THEOREM 4.2. *Given detection threshold α, the probability that a symbol within an ON slot be detected under type I attacker's correlated jamming is:*

$$P_d(\sigma^2) = e^{-\frac{\alpha - \sigma_n^2 - \sigma_v^2 - |a''g''|^2\sigma_x^2}{2\sigma_x^2\sigma^2}} \quad (4)$$

From the detection probability, we derive the optimal NLoS attack strategy:

THEOREM 4.3. *The NLoS part optimal strategy for type I attacker is:*

$$(a'' = 0, \sigma_v^2 = 0) \quad (5)$$

Due to space limit, the proof is omitted. As shown in Theorem 4.3, the best strategy for type I attacker is to not jam the NLoS part. This is because, the estimated channel g'' is not correlated with the real channel h''. Thus any non-zero signal will only add more noise at the receiver B, which increases the detection probability instead.

Type II attacker. According to the type II attacker model, the estimated channel g'' is correlated with h''. Thus in the power expression $P_y = \sigma_x^2(h'' + a''g'')^2 + \sigma_n^2 + \sigma_v^2$, the component $|h'' + a''g''|^2$ follows Gamma distribution $\Gamma(1, 2\sigma^2)$ since $(h'' + a''g'')$ is a CSCG random variable, where $\sigma^2 = \frac{1}{2}E[(h'' + a''g'')\overline{(h'' + a''g'')}]$. In addition, the part $\sigma_x^2|h''+a''g''|^2$ also follows Gamma distribution $\Gamma(1, 2\sigma_x^2\sigma^2)$, because $\sigma_x(h'' + a''g'')$ is a CSCG random variable.

THEOREM 4.4. *Given detection threshold α, the probability that a symbol within an ON slot be detected under type II attacker's correlated jamming is:*

$$P_d(\sigma^2) = e^{-\frac{\alpha - \sigma_n^2 - \sigma_v^2}{2\sigma_x^2\sigma^2}} \quad (6)$$

According to equation 6, the detection probability is related to the estimated channel g''. Thus we will first analyze the effect of parameter σ^2 on the detection probability.

THEOREM 4.5. *The detection probability $P_d(\sigma^2)$ is a non-decreasing function with respect to σ^2.*

The proof is in Appendix. According to Theorem 4.4, the minimum detection probability is achieved when σ^2 is infinitely close to 0:

$$\lim_{\sigma^2 \to 0} P_d(\sigma^2) = 0 \tag{7}$$

The above result shows, the perfect attack precisely estimates channel h'' such that the jamming signal is exactly the opposite of the received signal from A to B, thus the original signal will be completely attenuated. However, this is an extreme case in which perfect CSI is assumed known by attacker. Some previous works are based on this extreme case [12, 14], under which the link from A to B has zero capacity. In this paper we consider a more realistic general case in which the real CSI h'' and the attacker's estimated CSI g'' is correlated with arbitrary $r_{h''\overline{g''}}$.

THEOREM 4.6. *The NLoS part's optimal correlated jamming strategy is:*

$$(a'' = -\frac{E[h''\bar{g''}]}{\sigma_g^2}, \sigma_v^2 = 0) \tag{8}$$

The proof is in Appendix. Given the optimal strategy of attacker, we can use Eq. (14) in Appendix to derive the minimum variance $\sigma_{min}^2 = \frac{1}{2}\sigma_h^2(1 - |r_{h\bar{g}}|^2)$, where $|r_{h''\overline{g''}}|$ is the correlation coefficient. Substitute it into Eq. (6), we get the minimum detection probability:

$$P_d(\sigma_{min}^2) = e^{-\frac{\alpha - \sigma_n^2 - \sigma_v^2}{\sigma_x^2 \sigma_h^2 (1 - |r_{h''\overline{g''}}|^2)}} \tag{9}$$

From the analysis above, we can see that the minimum detection probability decreases with the increase of attacker's correlation coefficient $|r_{h''\overline{g''}}|$. Also, previous works that either assumed a 0 or 1 correlation coefficient are two extreme cases of our result.

4.3 Optimal Defender Strategy

Next we analyze the legitimate pair's optimal strategy. From the above, the type I attacker is only a special case of type II attacker when $r_{h''\overline{g''}} = 0$. In our model, the signal x is independent with h''. The only transmitter parameter that has influence on the final detection probability is the power σ_x^2. From Eq. (9), we can easily see that the detection probability increases when σ_x^2 increases. In reality, the transmitter's power is limited, thus it indicates that the transmitter should always choose its largest power level to defend against correlated jamming attacks.

5. INTEGRITY PROTECTION SCHEME

5.1 Design Overview

In this section, we present our integrity protection protocol. We first devise an approach to upper-bound the attacker's knowledge (correlation) under type II attack, specifically the CSI prediction attack. The idea is to extract the A-B CSI by the legitimate receiver B through channel probing, and mimic the attacker's strategy to quantify the intrinsic time-domain correlation (or unpredictability) in the channel itself, assuming perfect estimation of historical CSI by the attacker. Based on this correlation, we calculate the maximum signal cancellation probability (or minimum signal detection probability) for each symbol under correlated jamming attacks using our theoretic framework. Given a targeted security requirement (signal cancellation probability for each ON slot), we derive the transmission parameters (the number of symbols needed in each ON slot). Then the transmitter applies the parameter during its ON/OFF keying to protect message integrity, while the receiver uses energy detection to recover the source information bits. To enhance efficiency, the transmitter sends a normal message packet followed by ON/OFF keying encoding the hash of the message, which is sent in the same wireless channel such that no out-of-band communication is needed.

Input: $n_{default}$ to both A and B, P_s
Setup phase:
1. User starts receiver B and transmitter A
2. A sends an ON/OFF keying sync signal s to B using $n_{default}$
3. A sends a probing packet e to B (long known symbol sequence)
4. B measures the CSI for each received symbol
5. B mimics the attacker to calculate $r_{h_e''\overline{g_e''}}$ between g_e'' and h_e'' and channel variance $\sigma_{h_e''}$
6. B picks α, and calculates the minimal number of needed symbols n based on $r_{h_e''\overline{g_e''}}$ to satisfy P_s
7. B immediately notifies A the derived n via ON/OFF keying encoding
Online phase:
8. A and B update n, then A transmits each message followed by its hash using ON/OFF keying and Manchester coding

Figure 3: Overview of the Message Integrity Protection Protocol. n: amount of symbols in each ON slot; P_s: minimum guarantee of detection probability in each ON slot; α: energy detection threshold at B.

Our integrity protection protocol is divided into two phases: The first one is called setup phase, within which the channel is measured, and based on that we calculate the channel correlation coefficient and the necessary amount of symbols n in each ON slot. The second one is the online phase, during which we transmit the original message and the integrity-protected bits (hash in our case) using the parameter derived in the setup phase. Note that, to follow the optimal defender strategy, the transmitter always sends signals/packets using the highest available transmission power and antenna gain.

5.2 The Setup Phase

First the user initiates the protocol by starting both the transmitter and receiver. Initially, the transmitting parameter $n_{default}$ will be set to a large enough default value. The default parameter can be obtained from known channel statistics or hardcoded into the devices. When the protocol starts, the devices have no much knowledge about the channel itself, thus it is reasonable to assume a worst case scenario (almost static channel). Note that the default parameter is chosen based on conservative estimation, so as to guarantee the security for the transmission of the sync message, and parameter of n back to A from B. This may bring some time overhead due to the conservative default parameter. However it is a one-time overhead in the initialization phase, thus is not a big concern. The setup phase ends after the receiver sends back its calculated parameter n to A.

5.2.1 Synchronization

If node A wants to transmit to B, it first needs to determine the length of each slot based on the channel correlation measurement. A synchronization signal s is needed to notify the receiver to begin measurement of channel correlation. This can be done by sending a standard sync message s containing the node IDs and the initiation intent, followed by the ON/OFF keying mode encoding of its hash using $n_{default}$ as the number of symbols. By knowing there is only one legitimate transmitter within range, the receiver can detect any malicious modifications to the synchronization signal. If the attacker also tries to initiate the measurement with the receiver, two duplicate sync sequences will be detected and an alarm will be sounded at B.

5.2.2 Channel Measurement

After sending the sync sequence, the transmitter will immediately send a packet e (or several of them sent back to back) with many repeated known symbols to the receiver. The receiver will measure a CSI sequence from the received signal. The CSI h_{e_i} is computed by taking every received symbol e'_i after converting the signal to baseband (before channel equalization), and divide it by the sent symbol e_i (both complex numbers). Moreover, the receiver decodes each packet to check whether the result is the same as the known sent symbols (e.g., all '1' bits), to prevent an attacker interfering with the CSI measurement. Note the specific value of CSI measured in this step has nothing to do with the future ON/OFF keying transmission. It is only the channel statistics that we need to derive.

5.2.3 Channel Correlation Estimation

After the channel measurement, the receiver obtains $h_{e_i} = h'_{e_i} + h''_{e_i}$, $i \in [1, M]$ where M is the number of CSI samples. It then use this sample channel to mimic the attacker to obtain a upper-bound of spatial-temporal correlation. Based on our attack model, the slow-channing/LoS component h' can be cancelled by the correlated jammer. So we need to eliminate this slow-changing/LoS component from channel h. In practice, we can use a Savitzky-Golay filter to separate the slow-changing and fast-changing components in the CSI [2]. Therefore we will focus on the remaining fast-changing/NLoS part h''. We assume the attacker leverages the time domain correlation by using l historical CSI measurements $h''_{N-l}, ..., h''_{N-1}$ to predict the current channel h''_N. For example, it can use the auto-regression model which is a tool for predicting a time series of data [15]. When l=1, it reduces to the simple case when $h''_N = h''_{N-1}$. For each $i \in [l+1, M]$, the attacker can obtain a predicted CSI from the historical CSI, and we denote this predicted sequence as g''_e. Assuming the channel statistics doesn't change between the offline and online phases, we can calculate the correlation coefficient $r_{h''_e \overline{g''_e}}$ of the two sequences g''_e and h''_e (both for $i \in [l+1, M]$), and use it as an estimated upper-bound of attacker's channel correlation $r_{h''\overline{g''}}$. Besides, the receiver

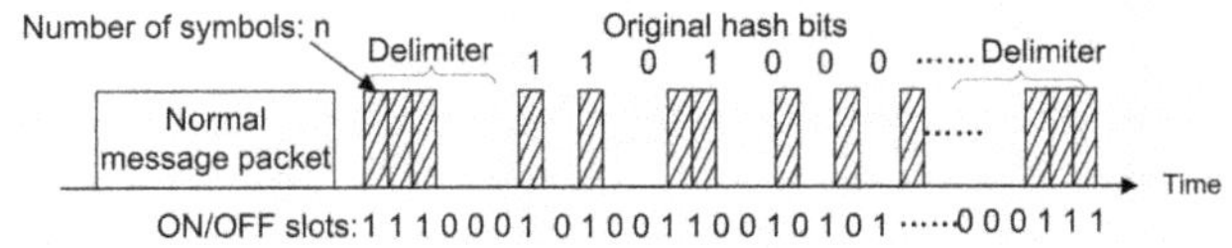

Figure 4: The messaging structure in the online phase.

also calculates the variance of the dynamic component $\sigma_{h''_e}$ and use that as an estimation of $\sigma_{h''}$ and $\sigma_{g''}$.

5.2.4 Deriving the Minimum Symbol Amount

Given the bound of attacker's correlation coefficient, we substitute it along with others parameters (including $\sigma_{h''}$, σ_x, α) into Eq. (9) in the theoretical analysis section. Then we can derive the detection probability P_d, and the minimum necessary amount of symbols n in each ON slot:

THEOREM 5.1. *Given the required minimum detection probability in each ON slot P_s, the minimal number of symbols is:*

$$n = \lfloor log_{1-P_d}^{1-P_s} \rfloor \tag{10}$$

The proof is in Appendix. Once n is determined, the receiver B immediately notifies the transmitter A to update this parameter, by using ON/OFF keying and Manchester coding to send n to A using the default parameter $n_{default}$.

5.3 The Online Phase: Data Transmission

In the online phase, the TX and RX devices start integrity-protected data transmission using parameter n. The message structure in this phase consists of two parts (shown in Fig. 4): a normal packet containing the message m followed by a L-bit cryptographic hash $H(m)$ encoded using ON/OFF keying and Manchester coding. To ensure the receiver knows the message boundary, node A transmits an I-code delimiter "111000" both in the beginning and the end of each ON/OFF keying sequence. This delimiter is guaranteed to be different from any message bits encoded using ON/OFF keying and Manchester coding. The receiver uses energy detection to detect each ON/OFF slot, and then decode the hash string $H'(m)$, it checks whether $H'(m) = H(m)$. If so, the integrity verification is passed for m.

The above basic online protocol can be extended to different application scenarios. For example, suppose in-band communication is needed (i.e., coexist with other traffic in the same band like normal WiFi or ZigBee). To avoid interfering with other links, similar to TEP [7], we can add a Clear-To-Send (CTS) signal in front of the whole message, which reserves the channel for the period until the ON/OFF sequence ends. The two devices can exchange an authenticated Diffie-Hellman key assuming knowledge of presence of each other. If we have a dedicated channel such as a satellite link where source information is broadcasted continuously, then source authentication can also be achieved [5].

5.4 Security Analysis

Integrity Protection. First, due to the collision resistance of cryptographic hash functions, it is infeasible for the attacker to find another $m' \neq m$ such that $H(m') = H(m)$. Second, if the attacker modifies any one or more bits in the original message, approximately half of the hash bits

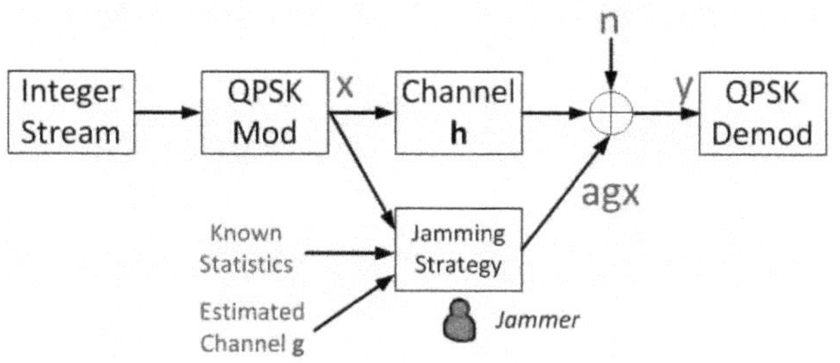

Figure 5: The simulation diagram of correlated jamming.

will flip. For each flipped bit, one ON slot needs to be converted into an OFF slot. So the probability that the attacker successfully passes verification is approximately $(1 - P_s)^{L/2}$ (negligible). Thus, message integrity can be guaranteed under our attack model since we choose n to satisfy a minimum per-ON slot detection probability P_s, such that any tampering with the message m will be detected w.h.p.

Security of CSI measurement. In the setup phase, the attacker can try to interfere with the CSI measurement packet(s). If she manages to lower the perceived correlation coefficient $r_{h''_e \overline{g''_e}}$ at the receiver, the calculated n will be smaller and also the security guarantee. But if she increases the perceived correlation, it will decrease the link's throughput but increase security. We can defend against such attack in several ways. (1) Observe that to lower $r_{h''_e \overline{g''_e}}$ the attacker should generate a random jamming signal (or noise) with little correlation. It will make the received message undecodable (or a very high symbol error rate), so that the receiver will sound an alarm; whereas in normal situations the symbol error rate will be small. The attacker can also try jamming with very high power to induce capturing effect, but since the transmitter is already sending with maximum power, this will create a high RSSI at the receiver which again raises suspicion. (2) In non-mobile situations, the channel correlation statistics in different locations can be pre-gathered securely and made publicly known (such as being kept in a database). Once the receiver measures the channel and calculated $r_{h\bar{g}}$, it will compare with the preloaded data, and abort if it finds a discrepancy.

5.5 Overhead Analysis

In our protocol, the overhead is mainly brought by the setup phase. The transmissions of synchronization signals and feedback of n require $(b_s + b_n)/R_{data} + 4n_{default} \cdot L \cdot \Delta_t$ time in total, in which b_s and b_n stand for the bit length of message s and n, respectively, R_{data} is the normal data rate,Δ_t is the symbol duration. The ON/OFF keying takes up the majority of transmission time. For example, assume in reality the maximum $|r_{h\bar{g}}| = 0.9$ (conservative estimate), then $n_{default} = 10$ would suffice. AssumeΔ_t is 1ms and let $L = 256$, then we can get the time overhead is around 10 seconds. The step of sending e and calculating $r_{h''_e \overline{g''_e}}$ and $\sigma_{h''_e}$ brings only a small overhead, since typically one probing packet (lasts less than 1 second) is enough to collect a representative CSI sequence. However, we should note that this overhead is one-time. Our scheme is most suitable to a static scenario where the channel statistic doesn't change overtime. If we want to apply it to mobile settings, we may need to re-do the setup phase and update the parameter n

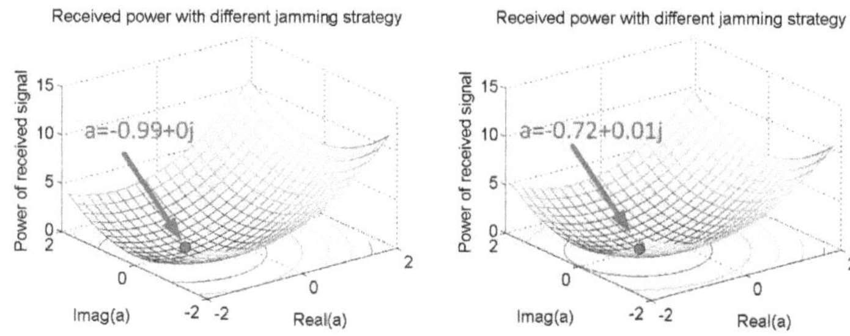

(a) (b)

Figure 6: The curved surface denotes average powers of received signal under different attacking strategies. The red dot is the optimal strategy derived by our theoretical analysis. The left figure shows the case when channel correlation coefficient $|r_{h\bar{g}}| = 1$. The right figure shows the case of $|r_{h\bar{g}}| = 0.7$.

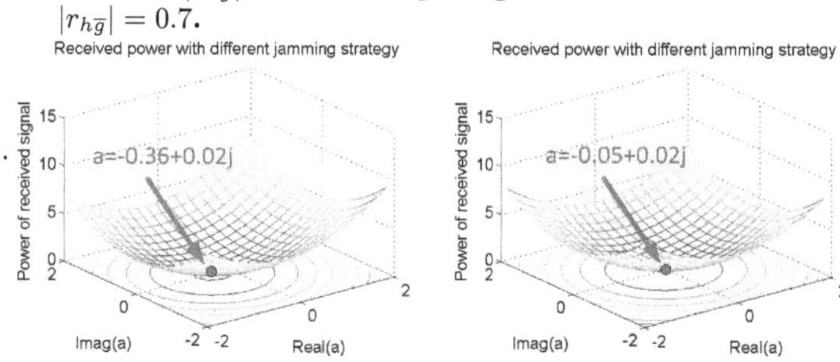

(a) (b)

Figure 7: The left figure shows the case when channel correlation coefficient $|r_{h\bar{g}}| = 0.3$. The right figure shows the case of $|r_{h\bar{g}}| = 0$.

periodically. However, for applications such as key establishment, only a few messages need to be exchanged, so we can still assume the channel does not change even in the mobile cases. Fully handling mobile settings will be part of our future work.

6. SIMULATION EVALUATION

In this section we use Matlab simulation to validate the correctness of our correlated jamming analysis. Then we evaluate the throughput of our scheme.

6.1 Effectiveness of Correlated Jamming

To analyze the effectiveness of correlated jamming attack, we study the received signal power in the presence of correlated jamming. We choose NLoS Rayleigh fading channel in this simulation. We generate two CSI sequences with a given correlation coefficient $r_{h\bar{g}}$ to simulate the legitimate channel and attacker's estimation. For convenience, we assume A's transmission power is $0dB$, and we normalize the channel gain to be 1. The SNR at the receiver side is assumed to be $25dB$. The signal is modulated using QPSK. We assume the attacker knows $r_{h\bar{g}}$ and the estimated channel's variance σ_g^2, thus can calculate its best jamming strategy a. The simulation result is shown in Fig. 5.

6.1.1 Optimal Jamming Strategy

We first validate the theoretical analysis of optimal jamming strategy. We test several cases, each with a different

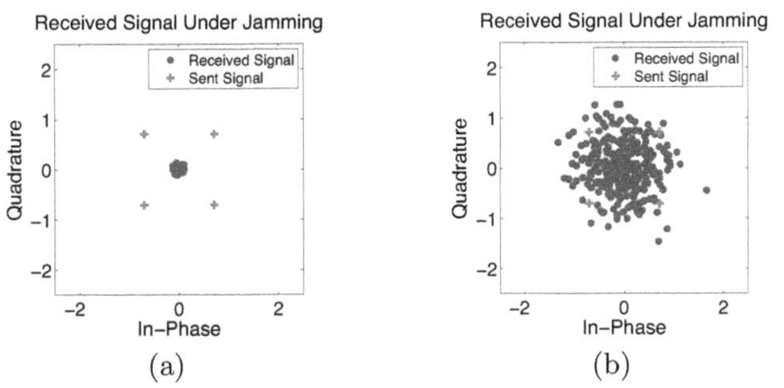

Figure 8: The received signal's constellation under optimal correlated jamming. Left: channel correlation coefficient $|r_{h\bar{g}}| = 1$. Right: $|r_{h\bar{g}}| = 0.7$.

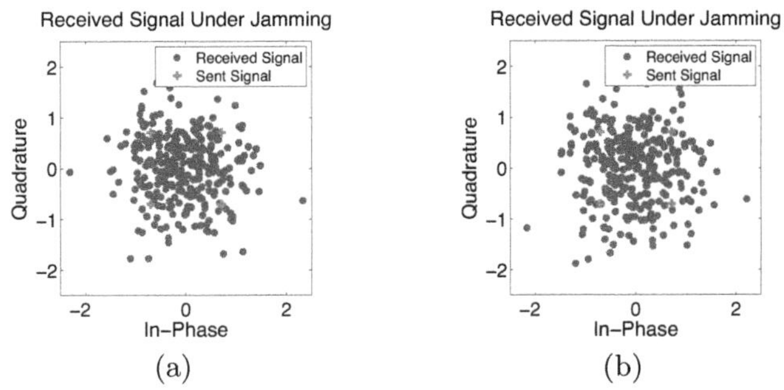

Figure 9: Left: channel correlation coefficient $|r_{h\bar{g}}| = 0.3$. Right: $|r_{h\bar{g}}| = 0$.

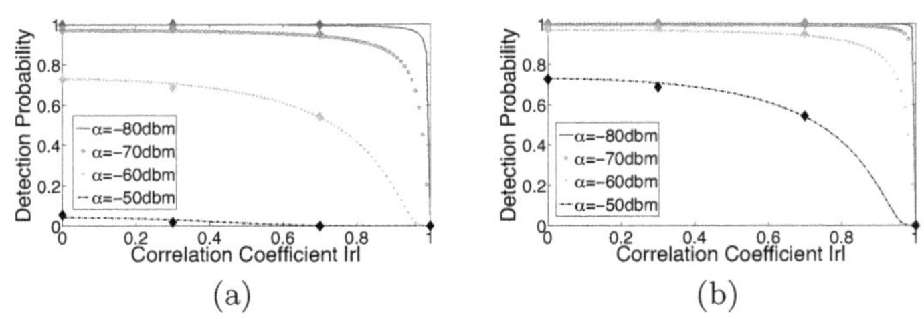

Figure 10: The energy detection probability in each ON slot under different detection thresholds α. Subfigure (a) and (b) uses $0dbm$ and $10dbm$ for transmission power respectively.

correlation coefficient $r_{h\bar{g}}$. The simulation results are shown in Figs. 6 and 7. The curved surface illustrates the average power of received signal under correlated jamming with different attacker strategies. The red dot in the center is the optimal jamming strategy derived from theoretical analysis in Section IV. We can see that the power of received signal always achieves the minimum when the jammer applies the optimal strategy, thus confirming the correctness of our theoretical analysis.

From Figs. 6 and 7, we have another insight. When $|r_{h\bar{g}}|$ decreases from 1 to 0, the amplitude of attacker's jamming coefficient a also decreases from $|a| \approx 1$ to $|a| \approx 0$. This phenomenon corresponds to our intuition: the higher the accuracy of jammer's estimation about h, the more confidence it has, then the more energy it uses to cancel out the signal. When the correlation coefficient $|r_{h\bar{g}}|$ is small, the jammer chooses to be quiet, because extra jamming signal is more likely to increase the received signal's power, instead of weakening it.

6.1.2 *Jamming Effectiveness*

Next we evaluate the impact of optimal jamming strategy to the received signal's power under various channel correlation coefficients. We assume random symbols are sent. The results are shown in Figs. 8 and 9. We can see that when the correlation coefficient is 1, all points concentrate around the original point, i.e. the received signal's average power is close to 0 (the transmitted signal x is almost completely cancelled out). The remaining power is caused by noise. When the channel correlation coefficient decreases, the amplitude (and power) of received signal increases. Specifically, when $|r_{h\bar{g}}| = 0.7$ and 0.3, average powers are 0.46 and 0.87. When $|r_{h\bar{g}}|$ drops to 0, the average power is nearly 1, which means the signal is not canceled at all.

6.2 Signal Detection Probability

Next we will quantize the effectiveness of the defense mechanism by studying its detection probability. The background noise is chosen to be $-95dBm$. We choose the frequency as $2.4Ghz$. The transmission power is set to be 0 or $10dBm$. The distance between legitimate sender and receiver is $5m$. The channels are generated following Rayleigh distribution, together with path-loss model with path-loss exponent as 3.

The detection probability results are shown in Fig. 10. We set the detection threshold α at different values. The continuous lines are generated from theoretical calculation, while the big diamond dots are derived from simulation. We can see that our simulation results are consistent with the theoretical results. We can also observe that: 1) A higher correlation coefficient will yield a lower detection probability. 2) The higher threshold we choose, the lower the detection probability is. 3) Higher transmitting power can increase the detection probability.

6.3 Throughput Analysis

Next we analyze the throughput of our scheme. If we only consider using the ON/OFF keying mode to carry data, given the parameter n and security requirement P_s, we can derive the maximum link throughput between A and B: $c = \frac{1}{2\lfloor log_{1-P_d}^{1-P_s} \rfloor \cdot \Delta t}$ (ignore decoding errors). If we consider both normal mode and the hash ON/OFF encoding, the maximum throughput will be $c' = \frac{L_{data}}{T_{data} + 2L \cdot \lfloor log_{1-P_d}^{1-P_s} \rfloor \cdot \Delta t}$, where L_{data} and T_{data} are the bit length and transmission time of a normal data packet, respectively, while L is hash length. We can see that the higher the per-symbol detection probability P_d, the higher the throughput.

For simplicity, we evaluate the ON/OFF keying mode only. Let the symbol duration be $0.35ms$. The security requirement for successfully detecting each ON slot is set to be $P_s = 0.999999$. All other parameters are the same as in the previous sub-section.

The minimal number of symbols under the given security requirement is shown in Fig.11, and the corresponding maximum link throughput is shown in Fig.12. We have several observations. 1) As the correlation coefficient $|r|$ increases, the energy detection probability in each ON slot decreases, which leads to an increasing number of needed symbols and a decreasing link throughput. This corresponds to our intuition that the more accurate the jammer's estimation about channel h, the more symbols we need in order to achieve

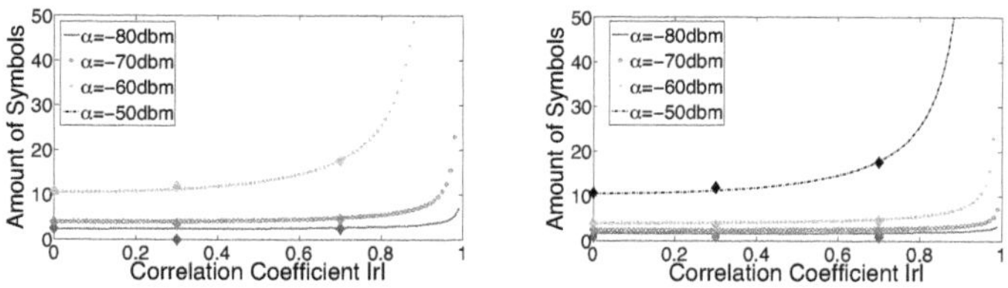

(a) (b)

Figure 11: The minimum necessary amount of symbols under different detection thresholds α, given $P_s = 0.999999$. Subfigure (a) and (b) use $0dbm$ and $10dbm$ transmission power respectively. The black curve in subfigure (a) is not shown as it is above 300.

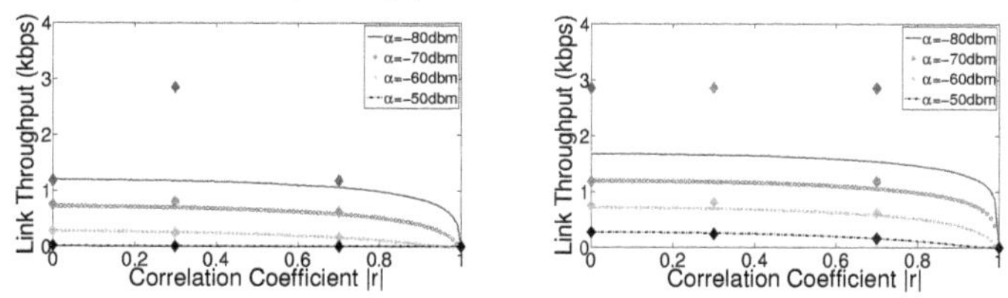

(a) (b)

Figure 12: The link throughput under different detection thresholds α, given $P_s = 0.999999$ detection probability. The length of each symbol is $0.35ms$. Subfigure (a) and (b) are with $0dbm$ and $10dbm$ transmitting power respectively.

the same security requirement. 2) With the increase of detection threshold α, the detection probability decreases, and the necessary amount of symbols increases. We note that, in reality the detection threshold is set based on the noise level. The higher the noise level, the higher the threshold should we use, which can decrease the false positive rate for OFF slots. The tradeoff is that, this will decrease the true positive probability (for ON slots) and also the link throughput eventually.

Note that, in Fig. 12, some of the result points for low detection thresholds seem far away from our theoretical calculation. This is because the high detection probability leads to enlarged error in the minimal number of symbols in our discrete simulation, which could be remedied by choosing longer symbol sequences in simulation.

7. EXPERIMENT AND IMPLEMENTATION

In this section, we first carry out experiments to measure the CSI of real indoor environments as a case study, and analyze the temporal domain channel correlation to show how it affects the security of our scheme. Then we implement our ON-OFF keying scheme on USRP devices to show the performance.

7.1 Experiment Setup

We setup two USRP GNU radio N210 devices with SBX daughter boards on a table in an indoor lab, the distance between them is about $0.5m$. The transmitting power is 20 dbm, and each symbol duration is $0.35ms$. We tested two scenarios: 1) static channel without external disturbance; 2) dynamic channel by using automatic random disturbance. In our case we attach several aluminum foil strips on the transmitting antenna, and use an electric fan to blow air

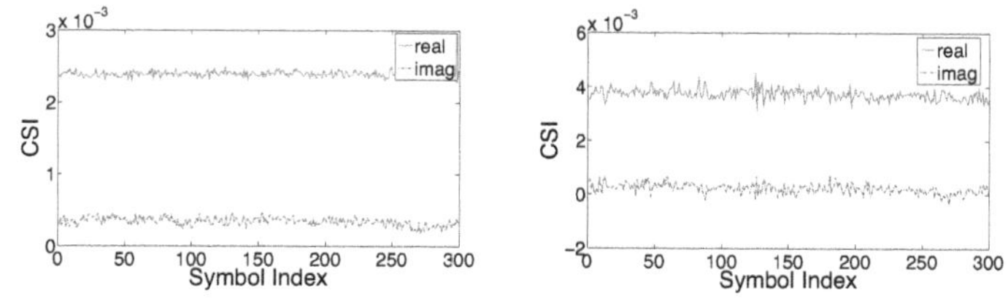

(a) (b)

Figure 13: Subfigure (a) shows the channel CSI measured between transmitter and receiver in static scenario. (b) shows the artificial dynamic channel scenario.

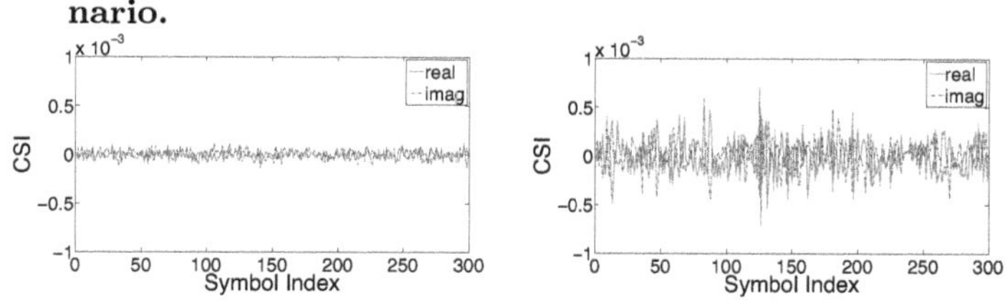

(a) (b)

Figure 14: Subfigure (a) shows the NLoS CSI component extracted between transmitter and receiver in static case. (b) shows artificial dynamic channel scenario.

towards it so the foil vibrates randomly. The second experiment's layout is shown in Fig. 17 (a).

We implement an OFDM transmitter and receiver on the USRP devices. The transmitter sends 5 packets in a row with known symbols in the 2.4GHz band with bandwidth set to 500kHz. In order to obtain the true physical channel state, we connect the two USRPs with a MIMO cable to synchronize their clocks to eliminate the impact of frequency and phase offset. In reality, if the devices are far apart and no cable is available, we can use accurate external clocks such as GPS clocks to synchronize TX/RX. The receiver extracts the frequency domain CSI for each symbol in one OFDM subcarrier from baseband before equalization, and we analyze the CSI sequence on the computer using Matlab. Because each OFDM subcarrier is narrow-band (7.8kHz), the frequency domain CSI is equivalent to time domain CSI. In the first scenario, since the devices are close to each other, the LoS part is strong and thus the channel is very stable. Therefore it is an ideal case for the attacker.

7.2 CSI Randomness and Correlation

To mimic the correlated jamming attacker, after obtaining the CSI h, we first eliminate its static component and obtain the remaining dynamic component. We use the Savitzky-Golay filter to separate the slow-changing (mainly caused by LoS) and fast-changing components. To generate the attacker's estimated CSI sequence g, we use autoregression with the exact previous two CSI samples to predict the next sample. Then we analyze the correlation between h and g and compute the minimum necessary number of symbols, which is used to derive the maximum secure link throughput.

The experiment result for scenario 1) is shown in Fig. 13 (a). We can see that the CSI between the transmitter and receiver is quite stable, due to the static channel condition. However, there is still a small fast-changing and random component (caused by noise and other factors). The fast-

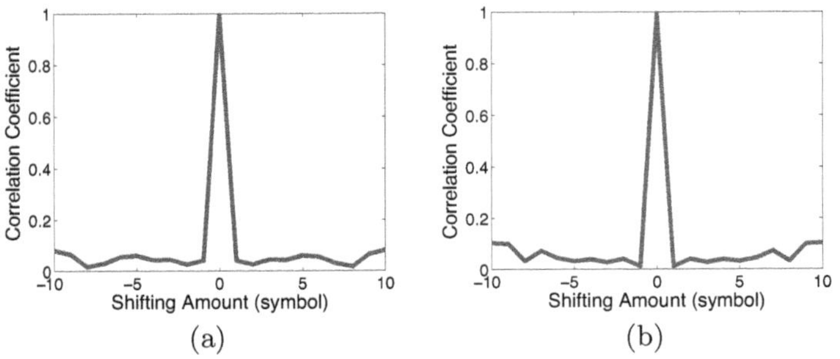

Figure 15: Subfigure (a) shows the auto-correlation coefficient of the NLoS CSI sequence in static scenario. (b) shows the artificial dynamic channel scenario.

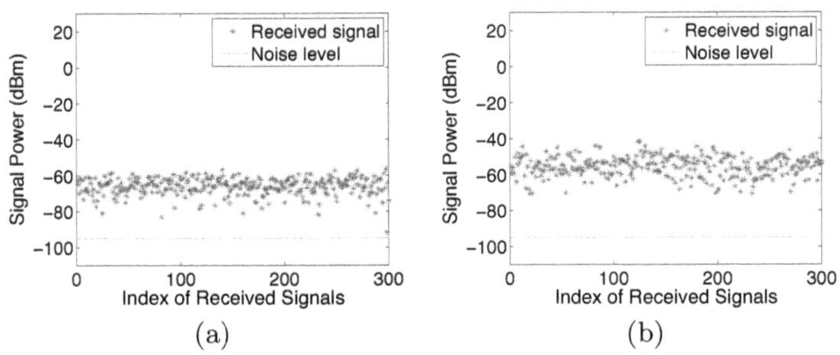

Figure 16: Subfigure (a) shows the received power level under optimal correlated jamming attack in static scenario. (b) shows the artificial dynamic channel scenario.

changing CSI component is shown in Fig. 14 (a). We can see that this part's randomness is high. To verify this we calculate this sequence's auto-correlation coefficient and show the result in Fig. 15. The correlation coefficient drops below 0.1 after one symbol's duration, which is about 0.35 ms.

On the other hand, in the artificial dynamic case shown in Fig. 14 (b) it has a higher variance than in the static case. The average gain of the NLoS component is $-84dB$ for static case and $-72dB$ for dynamic case, which means it is barely large enough compared with background noise level in static scenario. However, in the artificial dynamic scenario, the received power level is about $12dB$ higher, which will result in higher detection probability, thus higher secure link throughput. We then plot the received signals' power levels after removing the LoS component in Fig. 16. We can see that the received signals' power levels are both higher than the noise level; but if we use a higher detection threshold, the static case will need much more number of symbols to defend against signal cancellation. This shows by actively randomizing the channel, we can achieve better integrity protection under the same throughput, or achieve a higher secure link throughput under the same security guarantee.

We can calculate ON/OFF keying parameters for both scenarios. After the CSI statistics estimation, we derived $r_{h_e'' \overline{g_e''}} < 0.1$ for both scenarios. Along with $\sigma^2_{h''}$ and detection threshold $\alpha = -90dbm$, we derive the necessary amount for each slot as $n = 2.2$ and $n = 1.5$ for the static and dynamic scenarios respectively; In reality we choose $n = 3$ and $n = 2$, respectively. The theoretical maximum link throughput of the ON/OFF mode can be derived as $1.29kbps$ and $1.86kbps$, respectively. More comparison results of the two scenarios under different thresholds are shown in Table 1.

Threshold	-90dBm	-80dBm	-70dBm	-60dBm
Static n	2.2	3.8	9.7	217
Dynamic n	1.5	2.1	3.4	7.5
Static R(kbps)	1.3	0.7	0.3	0.01
Dynamic R(kbps)	1.8	1.3	0.8	0.4

Table 1: The comparison of symbol number in ON slots (n) and ON/OFF mode throughput under different detection thresholds and channel conditions.

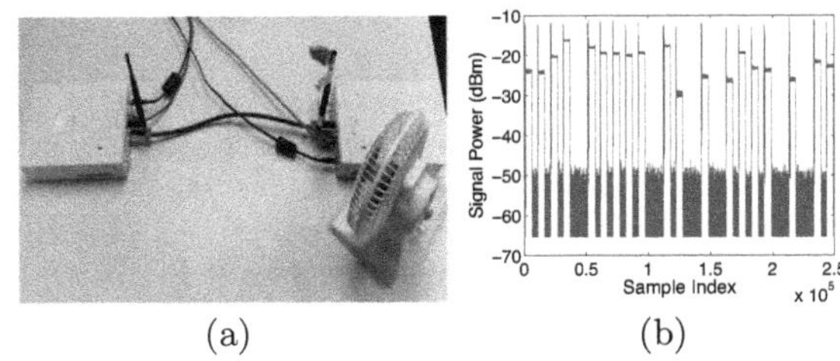

Figure 17: Subfigure (a) shows the experiment layout; (b) illustrates the receiving power of ON/OFF key energy detection method with 3 symbols in a ON slot. The sampling rate is $500ksps$.

7.3 Protocol Implementation

We have implemented a basic prototype of our integrity-protection scheme in USRPs. By now our prototype can achieve three main functions: synchronization, channel measurement, and ON/OFF keying encoded hash transmission. For synchronization and hash transmission, they are all based on ON/OFF keying encoding and energy detection decoding, which is the key part in the implementation.

The transmitting gain is $30dB$ and receiving gain is $15dB$. The noise floor is about $-50dBm$. We use the static scenario's parameter $n = 3$ as an example and the received power sequence is shown in Fig. 17 (b). The receiver counts the number of high power samples in each slot and compare it with the threshold. We note that there is an implementation issue: the ON and OFF slots are not exactly the same in length and there is a lag after each ON slot (in Fig. 17 (b)). This is because when the USRP switches from ON to OFF, there is always a time delay induced by hardware. This delay could be tolerated when the ON slot is long. However for the short slots, it will prevent the receiver from decoding an OFF slot between two ON slots. To remedy it we make the OFF slots longer, beyond the end of the lag. The throughput will be decreased, however as the original ON slot is short, so such a loss of throughput is tolerable. If we enlarge the OFF slot and make each ON/OFF to be 22 ms, the derived practical throughput is $45bps$ for ON/OFF keying mode. After adjusting the length of OFF slot, we achieve zero bit error with random sequences of 10^5 bits long. If the message transmitted in the normal mode is 4096 Bytes long at $500kbps$ and hash length is 256 bits, this yields an overall throughput of $5.75kbps$.

7.4 Discussion

Although indoor channel is typically stable, we use active channel disturbance to make it a more dynamic channel to better defend against signal cancellation attacks. In outdoor scenarios, the slow-changing/LoS component is typically weak and the channel is dynamic due to fading, so it will be harder for the attacker to cancel out the signal. Evaluating our scheme in outdoor scenarios will be part of the future work.

In our protocol, we only considered the type of attack which uses estimated future CSI (spatial and temporal domain) to carry out jamming. This type of attack includes the one proposed in [19] as a special case. In the future we will consider another type of attack, especially spatial correlated jamming where the jammer itself is located near to the TX or RX and one of its own channels is correlated with legitimate CSI h. The attacker in this case does not need to measure and estimate h, but needs to do additional processing of signal x and relay it. However, since it does not know h and thus the correlation coefficient, it is hard to achieve optimal cancellation. To defend it we can impose a restricted region around the TX/RX to prevent the attacker from being too close, to upper-bound its spatial correlation. With our channel changing approach, such correlation should decrease compared with static channel case.

8. RELATED WORK

Physical Layer Message Integrity Protection and Authentication: The integrity code (I-code) proposed by Čapkun et. al. in [5] protects the message integrity transmitted in an insecure wireless channel. It provides message tamper-evidence using unidirectional error detection code, based on the infeasibility of signal cancellation. Similarly, Tamper-Evident Pairing (TEP) proposed by Gollakota et. al [7] is an in-band device pairing protocol for 802.11 devices, which protects message integrity by embedding cryptographic authentication information (e.g., a hash) into the physical signals. Both of the above works assume that wireless signal cancellation is infeasible. However, Pöpper et. al. demonstrated a practical cancellation attack using a pair of directional antennas in [19], under quasi-static channel conditions. Recently, Hou et. al. proposed Chorus [10], which extends the idea of in-band message authentication to a group of devices, and adapts the uncoordinated frequency hopping (UFH) mechanism to defend against correlated signal cancellation. However, it assumes the attacker does not possess advanced real-time processing capabilities and is located at some distance away from the legitimate pair. In summary, a quantitative security guarantee is still lacking for anti-signal-cancellation based message integrity protection schemes. In this paper, our proposed defense approach can be applied to any protocol with the same core idea.

Correlated Jamming: Médard and Goldsmith [14] first studied the capacity of wireless channels under correlated jamming. This work considers two cases: first, the jammer has complete knowledge of the transmitted signal, and second, the jammer could only obtain partial knowledge of the transmitted signal through eavesdropping. The channel is always assumed to be constant and known by the jammer. It is shown that the channel capacity decreases to zero. Kashyap et. al. [12] also studied channel capacity under correlated jamming, and they expand to MIMO case and assume the CSI is totally random (attacker only knows the statistics). Shafiee and Ulukus [22, 21] continued the research of correlated jamming and expanded to the multi-user scenario. All these works try to maximize the link capacity in the information theory sense, while our work considers a more practical goal - the energy detection probability which is the key to integrity protection. In addition, in our work we consider a different model by assuming the attacker can obtain an arbitrarily correlated CSI, which is more practical. We study the relationship between link throughput and the correlation coefficient between the attacker's estimated channel and the real channel. Recently, Chang et. al. proposed a countermeasure for signal-cancellation based jamming [6], by introducing redundancy frequency offsets at the transmitter-side. However, it can only prevent a weak form of correlated jamming attack where the attacker generates its own signal but cannot prevent the relaying attacks.

9. CONCLUSION

In this work, we studied the security of physical layer message integrity protection scheme. We established a correlated jamming framework to model the attacker's behavior. We quantitatively analyzed the security guarantee for physical layer message integrity protection protocol under correlated jamming attack with arbitrary CSI-estimation correlation coefficient. Based on the analysis we proposed a physical layer message integrity protection protocol which achieves any given security requirement. Extensive experiments and simulations results are shown to verify the correctness of our optimal jamming strategy analysis and to evaluate the achievable throughput under different security requirements. In the future, we will extend our scheme to the case of MIMO.

10. ACKNOWLEDGMENTS

We would like to thank the anonymous reviewers for helpful comments. We thank Dan Shan for helpful discussions on USRP implementation. This work was supported in part by the US National Science Foundation under grants CNS-1410000, CNS-1350655 and CNS-1502584.

11. REFERENCES

[1] Top 50 internet of things applications - ranking. `http://www.libelium.com/top_50_iot_sensor_applications_ranking/`.

[2] S. Ali, V. Sivaraman, and D. Ostry. Secret key generation rate vs. reconciliation cost using wireless channel characteristics in body area networks. In *Embedded and Ubiquitous Computing (EUC), 2010 IEEE/IFIP 8th International Conference on*, pages 644–650, Dec 2010.

[3] D. Balfanz, D. K. Smetters, P. Stewart, and H. C. Wong. Talking to strangers: authentication in ad-hoc wireless networks. In *NDSS '02*, 2002.

[4] M. Cagalj, S. Capkun, and J.-P. Hubaux. Key agreement in peer-to-peer wireless networks. *Proceedings of the IEEE*, 94(2):467–478, Feb. 2006.

[5] S. Capkun, M. Cagalj, R. Rengaswamy, I. Tsigkogiannis, J.-P. Hubaux, and M. Srivastava. Integrity codes: Message integrity protection and authentication over insecure channels. *Dependable and Secure Computing, IEEE Transactions on*, 5(4):208–223, Oct 2008.

[6] S.-Y. Chang, Y.-C. Hu, J. Chiang, and S.-Y. Chang. Redundancy offset narrow spectrum: countermeasure for signal-cancellation based jamming. In *Proceedings of the 11th ACM international symposium on Mobility management and wireless access*, pages 51–58. ACM, 2013.

[7] S. Gollakota, N. Ahmed, N. Zeldovich, and D. Katabi. Secure in-band wireless pairing. In *USENIX security symposium*, 2011.

[8] M. T. Goodrich, M. Sirivianos, J. Solis, G. Tsudik, and E. Uzun. Loud and clear: Human-verifiable authentication based on audio. In *In IEEE ICDCS 2006*, page 10, 2006.

[9] X. He, H. Dai, W. Shen, and P. Ning. Is link signature dependable for wireless security? In *INFOCOM, 2013 Proceedings IEEE*, pages 200–204, April 2013.

[10] Y. Hou, M. Li, and J. D. Guttman. Chorus: Scalable in-band trust establishment for multiple constrained devices over the insecure wireless channel. In *Proceedings of the Sixth ACM Conference on Security and Privacy in Wireless and Mobile Networks*, WiSec '13, pages 167–178, New York, NY, USA, 2013. ACM.

[11] P. Kafle, A. Intarapanich, A. Sesay, J. McRory, and R. Davies. Spatial correlation and capacity measurements for wideband mimo channels in indoor office environment. *Wireless Communications, IEEE Transactions on*, 7(5):1560–1571, May 2008.

[12] A. Kashyap, T. Basar, and R. Srikant. Correlated jamming on mimo gaussian fading channels. *Information Theory, IEEE Transactions on*, 50(9):2119–2123, Sept 2004.

[13] P. Kyritsi, D. Cox, R. Valenzuela, and P. Wolniansky. Correlation analysis based on mimo channel measurements in an indoor environment. *Selected Areas in Communications, IEEE Journal on*, 21(5):713–720, June 2003.

[14] A. G. M. MÃľdard. Capacity of correlated jamming channels. In *Allerton Conference on Communications, Computing and Control*, 1997.

[15] H. Madsen. *Time Series Analysis: Forecasting and Control*, volume 77. CRC Press, 2008.

[16] J. M. McCune, A. Perrig, and M. K. Reiter. Seeing-is-believing: Using camera phones for human-verifiable authentication. In *IEEE S & P*, pages 110–124, 2005.

[17] L. Nguyen and A. Roscoe. Authentication protocols based on low-bandwidth unspoofable channels: a comparative survey. *Journal of Computer Security*, 19(1):139–201, 2011.

[18] T. Perkovic, M. Cagalj, T. Mastelic, N. Saxena, and D. Begusic. Secure initialization of multiple constrained wireless devices for an unaided user. *Mobile Computing, IEEE Transactions on*, 11(2):337–351, Feb 2012.

[19] C. Pöpper, N. O. Tippenhauer, B. Danev, and S. Capkun. Investigation of signal and message manipulations on the wireless channel. ESORICS'11, pages 40–59, 2011.

[20] M. Schulz, A. Loch, and M. Hollick. Practical known-plaintext attacks against physical layer security in wireless mimo systems. *Proceedings of the Network and Distributed System Security Symposium, NDSS 2014*, 2014.

[21] S. Shafiee and S. Ulukus. Capacity of multiple access channels with correlated jamming. In *Military Communications Conference, 2005. MILCOM 2005. IEEE*, pages 218–224 Vol. 1, Oct 2005.

[22] S. Shafiee and S. Ulukus. Mutual information games in multiuser channels with correlated jamming. *Information Theory, IEEE Transactions on*, 55(10):4598–4607, Oct 2009.

[23] F. Stajano and R. J. Anderson. The resurrecting duckling: Security issues for ad-hoc wireless networks. In *IWSP '00*, pages 172–194, 2000.

[24] N. Tippenhauer, L. Malisa, A. Ranganathan, and S. Capkun. On limitations of friendly jamming for confidentiality. In *Security and Privacy (SP), 2013 IEEE Symposium on*, pages 160–173, May 2013.

12. APPENDIX

12.1 Proof of Theorem 4.5

PROOF. We will show the monotonicity w.r.t $k = \sigma^2$. According to Leibniz integral rule we have:

$$P_d'(k) = \int_{\alpha-\sigma_n^2-\sigma_v^2}^{\infty} \frac{d}{dk}\frac{e^{-\frac{r}{2k\sigma_x^2}}}{2k\sigma_x^2}\,\mathrm{d}r \tag{11}$$

$$= \int_{\alpha-\sigma_n^2-\sigma_v^2}^{\infty} \frac{(r-2k\sigma_x^2)\cdot e^{-\frac{r}{2k\sigma_x^2}}}{4k^3\sigma_x^4}\,\mathrm{d}r \tag{12}$$

$$= \left.\frac{-r}{2k^2\sigma_x^2 e^{\frac{r}{2k\sigma_x^2}}}\right|_{r=\alpha-\sigma_n^2-\sigma_v^2}^{r=\infty} \tag{13}$$

It is easy to see from equation 13 that $P_d'(k) > 0, \forall k > 0$, which means the smaller $k = \sigma^2$ brings smaller detection probability. □

12.2 Proof of Theorem 4.6

PROOF. We start from expression of the variance of random variable $\beta = h + ag$. The variance σ^2 is denoted as:

$$\begin{aligned}
2\sigma^2 &= E|h+ag|^2,\\
&= E[(h+ag)\overline{(h+ag)}],\\
&= E[(h+ag)(\overline{h}+\overline{ga})],\\
&= \sigma_h^2 + E[h\overline{(ag)}] + E[(ag)\overline{h}] + |a|^2\sigma_g^2,\\
&= \sigma_h^2 + |a|^2\sigma_g^2 + \overline{a}E[h\overline{g}] + aE[\overline{(h\overline{g})}],\\
&= \sigma_h^2 + |a|^2\sigma_g^2 + 2Re\{a\}Re\{E[h\overline{g}]\} + 2Im\{a\}Im\{E[h\overline{g}]\},\\
&= \sigma_h^2 + (Re\{a\}^2 + Im\{a\}^2)\sigma_g^2 + 2Re\{a\}Re\{E[h\overline{g}]\}\\
&\quad + 2Im\{a\}Im\{E[h\overline{g}]\}
\end{aligned} \tag{14}$$

From above we can see that σ^2 is a convex function w.r.t $Re\{a\}$ and $Im\{a\}$. By setting partial derivatives to zero, We can get $Re\{a\}* = -\frac{Re\{E[h\overline{g}]\}}{\sigma_g^2}$, $Im\{a\}* = -\frac{Im\{E[h\overline{g}]\}}{\sigma_g^2}$.

The proof of $\sigma_v^2 = 0$ is similar to that of type I attacker, thus it is not presented here. □

12.3 Proof of Theorem 5.1

PROOF. The probability of signal $'ON'$ being not detected at one symbol is $(1-p_d)$, thus consider n continuous symbols, the probability of $'ON'$ being not detected within all n symbols is $(1-p_d)^n$. By making it lower than the non-secure probability $1-p_s$, we can derive the necessary amount of symbols:

$$n = \lfloor log_{1-p_d}^{1-p_s} \rfloor \tag{15}$$

□

Formal Analysis of Enhanced Authorization in the TPM 2.0

Jianxiong Shao, Yu Qin, Dengguo Feng and Weijin Wang
Trusted Computing and Information Assurance Laboratory,
Institute of Software, Chinese Academy of Sciences, Beijing, China
{shaojianxiong, qin_yu, feng, wangweijin}@tca.iscas.ac.cn

ABSTRACT

The Trusted Platform Module (TPM) is a system component that provides a hardware-based approach to establish trust in a platform by providing protected storage, robust platform integrity measurement, secure platform attestation and other secure functionalities. The access to TPM commands and TPM-resident key objects are protected via an authorization mechanism. Enhanced Authorization (EA) is a new mechanism introduced by the TPM 2.0 to provide a rich authorization model for specifying flexible access control policies for TPM-resident objects.

In our paper, we conduct a formal verification of the EA mechanism. Firstly, we propose a model of the TPM 2.0 EA mechanism in a variant of the applied pi calculus. Secondly, we identify and formalize the security properties of the EA mechanism (Prop.1 and 2) in its design. We also give out a misuse problem that is easily to be neglected (Lemma 7). Thirdly, using the SAPIC tool and the tamarin prover, we have verified both the two security properties. Meanwhile, we have found 3 misuse cases and one of them leads to an attack on the application in [12].

Categories and Subject Descriptors

D.2.4 [**Software/Program Verification**]: Formal methods

General Terms

Security

Keywords

TPM; Formal Verification; Enhanced Authorization; Trusted Computing

1. INTRODUCTION

The Trusted Platform Module (TPM) is an important system component separated from the system on which it reports (the host system). The only interaction is through the interface, i.e. application programming interface (API), predefined in the TPM specification. Through API commands, the TPM offers facilities to enable trustworthy computation and communication over open networks. The TPM specification [1] is an industry standard proposed by a computer industry consortium called the Trusted Computing Group (TCG). TPM 1.2 specification has become the ISO standard [2]. Hundreds of millions of TPMs are deployed in a wide range of devices ranging from servers and personal computers to mobile devices.

However, several papers have indicated the vulnerabilities in the TPM 1.2 API designs [3, 4, 5, 6, 7], particularly in relation to the secrecy and authentication properties. The attacks on the TPM include the replay attack on TPM authorization protocols [3], the impersonation attack on shared authdata [4], the offline dictionary attack on weak authdata [5], and the illegitimate acquirement of certificates on selected TPM keys [7]. These attacks highlight the importance of formal analysis and verification of the TPM API commands.

To enhance the security and functionalities of the TPM, TCG continues to revise the TPM specifications. In 2013, TCG has published the TPM 2.0 specifications [8]. New version fixes the known flaws in the TPM 1.2 and makes several changes and enhancements from the previous versions especially on the authorization mechanisms. The TPM 2.0 API defines 3 authorization types: password, HMAC, and policy. The last one is denoted by the enhanced authorization (EA), which allows object owners and administrators to require specific policy assertions to be satisfied before access to a protected object is allowed. The policy relies on the object's *authPolicy* setting. The EA mechanism extends the original platform configuration register (PCR) binding operation in TPM 1.2 with more authorization assertions. Moreover, the EA mechanism has a top priority since the other two kinds can be disabled by the specific settings of attributes.

We provide, to the best of our knowledge, the first formal analysis and verification of the TPM 2.0 EA model in our paper. Firstly, we propose a formal model for the API analysis of the simplified TPM 2.0 EA mechanism in the stateful applied pi calculus [9, 10]. Our model could cover almost all aspects of the EA functionalities except for the *CounterTimer* assertion. Secondly, we define and formalize the security properties (Prop.1 and 2) of the EA mechanism in its design. We have met two challenges in this part. The first is that there is more than one expression for a given policy. We solve it by transforming the policy into a dis-

ASIA CCS'15, April 14–17, 2015, Singapore, Singapore.

http://dx.doi.org/10.1145/2714576.2714610.

junctive normal form and providing a generic way to compute the authPolicy setting for it. The second challenge is that the universal quantifier over the policy setting makes it difficult to verify Prop.1. We solve it by dividing the whole proof into a chain of pieces (Lemma 1 and 2) which can be verified and composed by induction. We also identify a misuse problem (Lemma 7). At last, using the SAPIC tool [9] and the tamarin prover [11], we have verified both the two security properties of the EA model. In our analysis, three misuse cases are discovered. The first one is for the *NV* assertion. It leads to an attack on the application in [12], where an NV counter is used to restrict the number of PIN attempts. We find that a malicious user can double this number by using one more session. The other two focus on a theoretical analysis of the race conditions when the TPM APIs are implemented in a concurrency-based model.

Related Work. A few researches have been done for the formal analysis and verification of the TPM 2.0 specifications on direct anonymous attestation [13, 14], protected storage [15], and the traditional HMAC-based authorization [16]. However, there are no results about the formal verification of TPM 2.0 EA mechanism as far as we know. In [12], the first accessible description of the TPM 2.0 EA model is provided and being used to build an Electronic Identification (eID) architecture. They limit the scope of security analysis only to the eID requirements without considering the security properties of EA mechanism, although they acknowledge its formal verification is a worthy pursuit. However, we find that the NV assertion is misused in their application, which might lead to an attack. Some researches have been done for the formal verification of the PCR binding operations in the TPM 1.2 API commands. In [17], a logic for reasoning about the properties of secure systems based on the PCRs is proposed. However, their model assumes that the TPM functions well and does not provide an API analysis as in our model. Another technique presented in [18] extends the logic used in the tool ProVerif [19] with a binary predicate to introduce a non-monotonic global state. Their model focuses on the usage of the PCR to build a chain of trust. This method is generalized to a tool StatVerif [10] but it could only handle a finite number of memory cells. Thus it cannot be used to analyze the TPM API with unbounded number of objects, which has been done by our model.

The paper is organized as follows. In Section 2 we give a brief introduction to the stateful applied pi calculus and the TPM 2.0 EA mechanism. In Section 3 we model the EA mechanism in TPM API commands and its security properties. In Section 4 we present the results of the formal verification of EA and 3 misuse cases. We conclude in Section 5.

2. PRELIMINARIES

2.1 Stateful applied pi calculus

Stateful applied pi calculus is a variant of the applied pi calculus first proposed in [10]. In addition to the usual operators for concurrency, replication, name restriction, communication, and condition, it offers the constructs for manipulation of an explicit global state. In this subsection, we will give a brief introduction to the syntax and semantics of the stateful applied pi calculus, and the trace formulas for the formalization of security properties. The details can be found in [9, 10].

The syntax of terms assumes two disjoint, infinite sets $\mathcal{N}$ and $\mathcal{V}$ of *names* and *variables*. A *signature* Σ consists of a finite set of function symbols, each with an arity. A function symbol with arity 0 is a constant. *Terms*, ranged over by M, N, are built up from names and variables by function applications, which is described in **Table 1**. We denote by $\sigma = \{^{t_1}/_{x_1}, \cdots, ^{t_n}/_{x_n}\}$ the substitution which maps x_i to t_i. Terms are equipped with an equational theory $=_E$ to capture the cryptographic primitives used by protocols. We give an example of the digital signature scheme below.

Example 1. Digital signature scheme can be modeled by a signature $\Sigma = \{\text{Sig}/2, \text{PK}/1, \text{CkSig}/2\}$ equipped with an equational theory defined by $\text{CkSig}(\text{Sig}(m, k), \text{PK}(k)) =_E m$. It allows to check whether the message m is correctly signed by the key k.

The syntax of *processes* is described in **Table 1**. 0 denotes the terminal process. $P|Q$ is the parallel composition of processes P and Q and $!P$ the replication of P, allowing an unbounded number of sessions in protocol executions. The construct $\nu n; P$ binds the name n in P and models the generation of a fresh, random value. Processes out $([M,]N); P$ and in $([M,]N); P$ represent the output, respectively input, of message N on channel M. Note that if the channel M is unique and public, it can be omitted from the expressions. The process if $M = N$ then P [else Q] will execute P if $M =_E N$ and Q otherwise. The branch else Q can be trailed when Q is 0. The event construct F is merely used for annotating processes and will be used in the definition of trace formulas. The construct insert M, N binds the value N to a handle M. Successive inserts allow to change this binding. The delete M operation simply flushes the mapping for the handle M. The lookup M as x in P [else Q] allows to retrieve the value associated to M, binding it to the variable x in P. If the mapping is undefined for M, the process behaves as Q. The process lock $M; P$ locks the resource handle M for the subsequent process P. When the resource M is locked, another parallel process that intends to access M has to wait until a primitive unlock $M; P'$. This is essential for formalizing API where the parallel commands cannot read and update a common memory.

We give an informal description of the semantics of processes and the trace. The formal definition could be found in [9] (Section 3.2). The semantics is defined by a set of the labelled transition relations between process configuration to model the single-step execution (transition) of processes. The transitions are labelled by facts. $\mathcal{F}$, the set of facts, includes two subsets, one for the event construct F, the other for the attacker's deduction of new message M, denoted by $\text{K}(M)$. The trace of a process P, denoted by $tr^P = [F_1, \cdots, F_n]$ where $F_i \in \mathcal{F}$, is defined by a finite sequence of facts, which have been executed. It is the possible executions that the process P admits. Given a ground process P, the set of traces of P is $Tr(P) = \{[F_1, \cdots, F_n] | \exists tr^P = [F_1, \cdots, F_n]\}$. For a sequence tr, $idx(tr)$ is the set of positions in tr, and the i-th label is denoted by tr_i for $i \in idx(tr)$.

In the following, we give out the definitions of trace formula and its validity, which are the same to the definitions 8, 9, 10 in [9]. These definitions could help us formalize the security properties of the TPM 2.0 EA mechanism. Trace formula is described in a two-sorted first-order logic. The sort *temp* is used for timepoints. A valuation θ is a function from variables to ground terms and timepoints that respects sorts.

Table 1: Syntax of processes

$\langle M, N\rangle ::=$	terms
$a, b, c, m, n, h, ...$	names
$x, y, z, ...$	variable
$f(M_1, ..., M_n), f \in \Sigma$ of arity n	function
$\langle P, Q\rangle ::=$	processes
0	termination
$P\|Q$	concurrency
$!P$	replication
$\nu n; P$	restriction
$\text{out}([M,]N); P$	output
$\text{in}([M,]N); P$	input
if $M = N$ then P [else Q]	conditional
event $F; P$	event
insert $M, N; P$	state
delete $M, N; P$	delete
lookup M as x in P [else Q]	read
lock $M; P$	lock state
unlock $M; P$	unlock state

Definition 1(Trace formulas). A trace atom is either false $\perp$, a term equality $M_1 \approx M_2$, a timepoint ordering $i < j$, a timepoint equality $i = j$, or an action $F@i$ for a fact $F \in \mathcal{F}$ and a timepoint i. A trace formula is a first-order formula over trace atoms.

Definition 2(Satisfaction relation). The satisfaction relation $(tr, \theta) \models \phi$ between trace tr, valuation θ and trace formula ϕ is defined as follows:

$$
\begin{array}{lll}
(tr,\theta) \models \perp & \text{never} \\
(tr,\theta) \models F@i & \text{iff} & \theta(i) \in idx(tr) \text{ and } F\theta =_E tr_{\theta(i)} \\
(tr,\theta) \models i < j & \text{iff} & \theta(i) < \theta(j) \\
(tr,\theta) \models i = j & \text{iff} & \theta(i) = \theta(j) \\
(tr,\theta) \models M_1 \approx M_2 & \text{iff} & M_1\theta =_E M_2\theta \\
(tr,\theta) \models \neg\phi & \text{iff} & \text{not } (tr,\theta) \models \phi \\
(tr,\theta) \models \phi_1 \wedge \phi_2 & \text{iff} & (tr,\theta) \models \phi_1 \text{ and } (tr,\theta) \models \phi_2 \\
(tr,\theta) \models \exists x.\phi & \text{iff} & \text{there is } u \text{ such that} \\
& & (tr, \theta[x \mapsto u]) \models \phi
\end{array}
$$

Definition 3(Validity). Given a ground process P, a trace formula ϕ is said to be valid for the set of the process P's traces $Tr(P)$, written $Tr(P) \models^{\forall} \phi$, if for any trace $tr^P \in Tr(P)$ and any valuation θ we have that $(tr^P, \theta) \models \phi$.

Example 2. The following trace formula expresses the correspondence property. It holds if each occurrence of event Ev_2 is preceded by an event Ev_1.

$$
\begin{aligned}
\phi := \forall x_1, \cdots, x_m, t_2.\ & Ev_2(x_1, \cdots, x_m)@t_2 \Rightarrow \\
& \exists t_1.\ Ev_1(M_1, \cdots, M_n)@t_1 \wedge t_1 < t_2.
\end{aligned}
$$

2.2 The enhanced authorization in the TPM

In the TPM 2.0 specification, the TPM stores key objects in its shielded memory, and access to these internal objects require authorizations. By using the enhanced authorization mechanism, the creator of the object can require specific tests or actions to be performed before it is operated by some specific TPM commands. In this case, the authorization is a proof that the TPM has completed the required actions. It should be provided by the user of these commands.

The specific requirements, defined as policy, are encapsulated in a value called *authPolicy* within the data structure of the object. Once the creator of the object sets the authPolicy value, it cannot be modified. In order to use the object, the user should first start a policy session located in the TPM's shielded memory and then invoke a sequence of policy assertion commands to complete the tests required by the policy. These commands will check some conditions and modify the session's *policyDigest* and other context values. After executing all the assertion commands required by the policy, the TPM keeps a policy session. This session accumulates all policy information needed to make the authorization decision. Finally, the user references the object accompanied with the session in the command, which is to be authorized. If the session's policyDigest matches the object's authPolicy (and some other optional conditions are valid), then the command is authorized to operate the object.

In this subsection, we will give a brief overview of the EA mechanism in the TPM 2.0, including the classification of the policy assertion commands and the way they update the policy session's context. We also give an example of how the EA mechanism works. Details of EA could be found in the specification [8] (Section 19.7, Part I).

2.2.1 Policy assertions

In a policy for authorization, an assertion is a statement of something that must be true before the policy is satisfied. For example, an assertion may be that the selected platform configuration register (PCR) in the TPM should have the desired value to allow an object to be authorized for use in a command. The policy assertion commands are defined in [8] (Section 19.7.6, Part I). In part 3, the policy commands are with the names of the form `TPM2_PolicyXXX()` where `"XXX"` is a Label of the type of policy assertions. In this subsection, we will give a classification of the policy assertion commands. The assertion commands are listed in **Table 2**. The table also includes the actions that the TPM will take in each command, the description of each assertion, and the classification.

Two or more assertions can be combined by logical connectives AND and OR. First, we describe an AND way. There is no explicit AND command. An AND policy may be expressed in an equation as a sequence of assertions that must all be satisfied. To verify it, the user should sequentially invoke all the assertion commands in the equation with the same policy session. These commands will validate the assertions and update the session's policyDigest (optionally with other context values). The final digest value indicates the evaluated policy. In each assertion command, the policyDigest value is computed as

$$polD_{new} := \text{HASH}\,(polD_{old} || polLabel_{new} || Param_{new}) \quad (1)$$

where $polLabel_{new}$ identifies the new policy assertion and $Param_{new}$ is the parameters associated to the assertion. For example in `TPM2_PolicyPCR`, $polLabel_{new}$ equals 'PCR' and $Param_{new}$ is the desired PCR value. The way of computation is like a chain to record the sequential evaluation of the assertions in an AND policy.

The TPM 2.0 has classified the AND policy assertion commands into 3 different types: immediate, deferred and combined. For an immediate command, the TPM validates the assertion of the input values and then updates the ses-

Table 2: Policy assertion commands

Label	Actions	Description of assertion	classification
NV	validate selected NV (Non-Volatile) update polD (policyDigest)	NV Index has the desired relationship with the input value	Immediate
PCR	validate selected pcr update polD, pcrUpdateCounter	Selected pcr has the desired value	Combined
CounterTimer	validate internal clock update polD	Internal clock has the desired relationship with the input value	Immediate
CpHash	update polD, cpHash	Auth for commands with a specified cpHash	Deferred
NameHash	update polD, nameHash	Auth for commands with a specified nameHash	Deferred
CommandCode	update polD, commandCode	Auth for a specified command	Deferred
DuplicationSelect	update polD, cpHash, commandCode	Auth for `TPM2_Duplicate` with a specified cpHash	Deferred
AuthValue	update polD, isAuthValueNeeded	an HMAC keyed on the authValue required	Deferred
Password	update polD, isPasswordNeeded	a password required	Deferred
Locality	update polD, locality	Auth for commands executed at specified locality	Deferred
PhysicalPresence	update polD, isPPRequired	physical presence required	Deferred
NvWritten	update polD, checkNvWritten, NvWrittenState	NV Index has the desired attribute for written	Deferred
Signed	validate signature of param update polD, timeout	Auth bound with session (used once), specified polRef, expiration for auth	Combined
Secret	validate HMAC of param update polD, timeout	Auth bound with session (used once), specified polRef, expiration for auth	Combined
Ticket	validate tickets for specific authorization update polD, timeout	specified cpHash, expiration for auth	Combined
Authorize	validate and update polD	polD has been signed by a specified key	Authorize
OR	validate and update polD	polD is in the list of digest	OR

sion's policyDigest if and only if the assertion is valid. For a deferred command, the TPM conducts no validation but only updates the policyDigest based on the input values and records some parameters in the session's context. These parameters will be checked when the session is used for authorization. For a combined assertion, the TPM both validates some conditions of the input and records some parameters in the session's context.

Among the AND policy assertion commands, there is a special assertion, `TPM2_PolicyAuthorize`, which allows a dynamical permission of new policies. It is an immediate assertion, but we consider it independently. When this assertion is included in a policy, it allows a designated entity (with a signing key) to authorize a policyDigest to be included in the policy by signing it. During the evaluation of this assertion, a signature of the session's current policyDigest value should be provided and verified by the TPM. If the signature is verified, the session's current policyDigest value is updated by the public part of the signing key as

$$polD_{new} := \text{HASH}\left(0\cdots0 \| \text{'Authorize'} \| \left(pk, polR\right)\right) \quad (2)$$

For OR connection, it allows a certain list of branches for the OR policy. Each branch corresponds to one digest value. During the evaluation of the assertion command `TPM2_PolicyOR`, the TPM compares the session's current policyDigest value with a list of digest values provided by the caller. If the current one is in the list, the TPM will set the current policyDigest to zero, concatenate all the digests in the list, and update the new policyDigest as

$$polD_{new} := \text{HASH}\left(0\cdots0 \| \text{'OR'} \| digestLists\right) \quad (3)$$

2.2.2 *An example for the EA mechanism*

We will give a simple example for how the EA mechanism works in the TPM API commands. The administrator needs to create a signing key on the platform with a TPM. He may require that Alice can sign with this key, but only Bob can certify it, and further,

- Alice (with a signing key sk_A) can only sign with this key five times (as measured by the NV counter);
- Bob (with a signing key sk_B) can only certify the key when the platform is in a certain state (as measured by the PCR).

First, the administrator should set an authPolicy value for the policy. It is set by the following computation.

$$\begin{aligned}
aP &:= \text{HASH}(0\cdots0 \| \text{'OR'} \| Z_1 \| Z_2)\\
Z_1 &:= \text{HASH}(Z_N \| \text{'Signed'} \| PK(sk_A) \| \text{'Alice'})\\
Z_2 &:= \text{HASH}(Z_P \| \text{'Signed'} \| PK(sk_B) \| \text{'Bob'})\\
Z_N &:= \text{HASH}(Z_{C1} \| \text{'NV'} \| NVC1 \| LT \| 5)\\
Z_P &:= \text{HASH}(Z_{C2} \| \text{'PCR'} \| PCR1 \| v)\\
Z_{C1} &:= \text{HASH}(0\cdots0 \| \text{'CmdCode'} \| \text{CC_Sign})\\
Z_{C2} &:= \text{HASH}(0\cdots0 \| \text{'CmdCode'} \| \text{CC_Certify})
\end{aligned}$$

By calling the commands `TPM2_Create`$(aP) \to kB$ and `TPM2_Load`(kB) $\to hK$, the administrator creates a signing key in the TPM. He also sets the NV counter $NVC1$ to 0 and requires that each use of signing with this key will cause the counter value plus 1[1].

Suppose Alice wants to sign with this key. Before she uses it, Alice should do the following steps to get the authorization session. If any step fails, Alice cannot use the key.

1. By calling `TPM2_StartAuthSession`$() \to (hS, nt)$, Alice starts a new policy session with the policyDigest initialized to $0\cdots0$.

2. She calls the assertion command `TPM2_CommandCode`$(hS$, CC_Sign) to update the session's commandCode to CC_Sign. The policyDigest is extended to Z_{C1}.

[1]This can be done by a more complex setting of Z_1, which is described in [12](Section 4.2.2). For simplicity, we just suppose it can be achieved here.

3. She triggers the command TPM2_PolicyNV(hS, $NVC1$, LT, 5) to validate that the counter $NVC1$'s value is less than 5. If valid, the TPM updates the policyDigest to Z_N, which accumulates the name of the NV Index, the comparison operation LT, and the operand '5'.

4. By using Alice's signing key, she can obtain a signature $\sigma_A = \text{Sig}(\langle nt, \text{'Alice'}\rangle, sk_A)$ where nt is the session's nonce, the text 'Alice' is called the policy reference ($polR$), which is an opaque value determined by the authorizing entity (Alice). Then she calls the command **TPM2_PolicySigned**(hS, σ_A, 'Alice', $PK(sk_A)$) to validate the signature. If valid, the TPM updates the policyDigest to Z_1, which encapsulates her public key and the signed label.

5. She calls the command TPM2_PolicyOR(hS, $\langle Z_1, Z_2\rangle$) to check that the session's current policyDigest is on the list $\langle Z_1, Z_2\rangle$. If valid, the TPM updates the session's policyDigest to a value equals aP.

6. Alice triggers the command **TPM2_Sign**(hK, hS, msg). The TPM will check the authorization according to the input handles. Since the session's policyDigest matches the key's authPolicy value and the session's commandCode value equals the authorized command's code CC_Sign, the TPM executes the command to sign msg. The TPM also increments $NVC1$ by 1.

It is similar for Bob to get the authorization for the command **TPM2_Certify**(), except he should use the command code CC_Certify in **TPM2_CommandCode**() and the assertion command **TPM2_PolicyPCR**() instead of **TPM2_PolicyNV**().

3. MODEL OF EA IN TPM 2.0 API

3.1 An overview of the model

In this section, we will propose a model of security API analysis in a stateful process calculus introduced in Section 2.1. This model, as a framework, is applied to the API analysis of EA mechanism in TPM 2.0. The main process is as follows.

$$\begin{aligned} P_{main} &:= P_{Init}; !(P_1|P_2|\cdots) \\ P_{Init} &:= \nu \tilde{k}_I; \bar{P}_{Init} \\ P_i &:= \text{in}(\langle 'Label'_i, \tilde{x}_i\rangle); \nu\tilde{k}_i; [\text{lock } \tilde{h}_i;]\bar{P}_i; \\ &\quad\ \text{out}(\langle \tilde{M}_i\rangle)[; \text{unlock } \tilde{h}_i] \end{aligned}$$

This is a general model. The instantiation is in Section 3.2. P_{main} is the main process of the API, in which P_{Init} and P_i respectively model the program of initialization and the specific commands. Initialization of the TPM is executed before all the other commands. The process $\nu\tilde{k}_I$ models the generation of global values. $\bar{P}_{Init}$ is the concrete initialization process of the TPM internal states. All the commands P_i could be executed concurrently and repeatedly. Each command has one input and one output. The process $\nu\tilde{k}_i$ models the generation of fresh local values. The lock $\tilde{h}_i$ process locks all the resource handles $\tilde{h}_i$ operated by the following concrete execution processes in $\bar{P}_i$ and decides exclusive access to them until a process unlock $\tilde{h}_i$. The (un)lock processes in square brackets might be omitted according to the two execution modes of the TPM API. There are no communication and (un)lock processes in the concrete execution process $\bar{P}_i$. All the unbound variables in $\bar{P}_i$ should be bound in the input variables $\tilde{x}_i$. In fact, $\bar{P}_i$ deals with the handle maps, which are usually modeled as global states.

We will give an informal description for the threat model. We assume the administrator creates the object and sets its authPolicy value. The malicious user, as the adversary, needs to gain authorization for the uses of the object and tries to violate the policy assertions encapsulated in its authPolicy value. The adversary model is formalized in a classic Dolev-Yao style. The malicious user, as the adversary, could only receive and send messages on the public channel as well as deduce terms. He could call all the API commands with any parameters in his knowledge. However, the adversary cannot touch the internal states except through the API provided by the TPM.

By injecting the processes lock $\tilde{h}_i$ and unlock $\tilde{h}_i$ into the command processes P_i, we establish two modes for the execution model of TPM API commands.

Mode 1, with (un)lock processes, specifies that all the commands are called sequentially and cannot be executed in parallel. Each command gains exclusive access to its resources. This execution mode is suitable for the TPM API implemented by a dedicated chip.

Mode 2, without (un)lock processes, models a concurrency based TPM API. Although TPM is originally designed to be implemented as a dedicated chip and does not allow concurrent execution of commands, the TPM 2.0 specification [8] (Section 9.3, Part I) mentions another reasonable implementation. This version of a TPM is implemented as the code run on the host processor in a hardware-based Trusted Execution Environments (TEEs). They provide secure, integrity-protected processing environments, consisting of processing, memory and storage capabilities, that are isolated from the regular processing environment. This mode may allow concurrent execution of commands. There are several different schemes for achieving this mode including System Management Mode, Trust Zone^{TM}, and processor virtualization. In mode 2, the security API should be analyzed more carefully due to race conditions.

3.2 Modeling the TPM commands

In this section, we instantiate the above model to formalize the TPM API commands described in Section 2.2. We do not limit the number of sessions started by the adversary. However, there are 109 commands in part 3 of the TPM 2.0 specifications [8] in total. EA mechanism can be applied to Most of them. One of the most difficult problems we have faced is the high complexity of the analysis. Thus we need to do 3 simplifications in our model.

First, we need to simplify the object management commands. We find that the policy set by the internal object's authPolicy is not type-specific. Thus we use a generic type instead of any specific one. We also give out a fictional framework of commands for the management of this type, including 2 commands: TPM2_NewObj and TPM2_UseObj for the creation and use of such an object. In the first command, a new authPolicy value is set for the created object. In fact, it completes the sequential executions of the real TPM 2.0 API commands TPM2_Create and TPM2_Load. In the second command, a session should be provided for the authorization and an authorization check is done. It simulates the real TPM function CheckPolicyAuthSession() which is performed before any commands that need a policy based authorization. We also introduce the assumption that each session could be used for authorization only once. This assumption appears to be quite reasonable since the session is initialized after each use in the practical case.

Second, we cut off several branches for the authorization checking logic. In the practical case, all of the session's context values should be checked before the authorized command is executed. In our model, we just check the authPolicy value in the command **TPM2_UseObj**. Instead we set the events CmdXXX(*ap*, *ctv*) to denote the check of the context value *ctv* but with no block if failed. Actually, we do not care whether such a check is successful or failed in our model. We do care the fact that in the authorized command, the session's context values *ctv* should be consistent with the policy encapsulated in the authPolicy value *ap*. If it is verified, *ctv* could be used in a check in the practical case. More details about this security property is described in Section 3.3. In this way, we cut off 2 checking logic branches for each context value[2].

Third, we do not model an internal clock of the TPM. The internal clock mechanism could be modeled as a monotonic increasing counter which is incremented every time a command is called. However, adding such a counter to our model will increase the complexity of analyzing. Thus we omit the time-related policy in our model, which includes the CounterTimer assertion and the input parameter *timeout* in the combined assertions. It does no harm to the soundness of our model since the caller could disable time-related policy in the practical case. For the other internal states, we take only one NV Index and one PCR. All the results in our paper could be generalized to a model with a finite number of NV Indexes and PCRs without any extra efforts.

The signature used in our model is $\Sigma := \{H/1, zero/0, nvh/0, pcrh/0, PK/1, Sig/2, CkSig/2\}$ with the equation $CkSig(Sig(m, k), PK(k)) = m$. Besides the digital signature functions PK/1, Sig/2, CkSig/2 described in Example 1, the function H/1 specifies the digest function used in PCR extending and policy digest updating. zero/0 is the initial value for some session's context values. We use *nvh*/0 for the handle of the NV Index and *pcrh*/0 for the handle of the PCR.

Now we are able to model the main process of the EA mechanism in the TPM API according to our model in Section 3.1. For simplicity, we divide the commands into 3 groups of parallel processes: management of objects and sessions (P_O with 3 commands), management of the internal states (P_S with 2 commands), and policy assertion commands (P_A with 14 commands). Thus, the main process is $P_{TPM} = P_I; !(P_O|P_S|P_A)$. Note that our model includes 2 modes which respectively specify the TPM API implemented in hardware and software. For simplicity, we only give out Mode 1 with (un)lock processes. Mode 2 can be obtained by omitting them.

The process of initialization P_I is described in **Table 3**. P_I initializes the value of NV and PCR with zero/0. The context of the PCR includes a monotonic counter *pcrUpdateCounter* (denoted by label 'pcrUpdC') which is incremented by 'one' every time the PCR value is changed. We model this counter as a multiset only consisting of the symbols 'zero' and 'one'. The union operator is denoted with a plus sign (+).

P_O includes 3 commands: $P_O := P_{NewObj} | P_{UseObj} | P_{StartAS}$. The details are described in **Table 4**. P_{NewObj} for the command **TPM2_NewObj** takes as input the *authPolicy* value *ap*, binds it to a fresh handle, and outputs the handle. P_{UseObj} for the command **TPM2_UseObj** conducts an authorization check for the object *hObj* through the policy session with the input handle *hS*. Note that we omit several events CmdXXX(*ap*, *ctv*) here since they are similar to CmdCPH. $P_{StartAS}$ for the command **TPM2_StartAuthSession** is invoked to generate a new policy session and initialize the session's context values.

Table 3: The process of initialization

$P_I :=$ insert ⟨'NV', *nvh*⟩, zero;
insert ⟨'PCRV', *pcrh*⟩, zero;
insert ⟨'pcrUpdC', *pcrh*⟩, 'zero';

P_S includes 2 commands: $P_S := P_{NVWrite} | P_{PCRExtend}$. For the NV Index, the internal state is modified by $P_{NVWrite}$ and for PCR by $P_{PCRExtend}$. Note that when the 'PCRV' value is extended, the old counter 'pcrUpdC' plus 'one' makes the new counter value. The details are given in **Table 4**.

P_A contains 14 policy assertion commands, which includes the assertions in **Table 2** except for the CounterTimer assertion, Secret assertion, and Ticket assertion. As in **Table 2**, the policy assertion commands can be divided into 5 classifications: immediate, deferred, combined, assertion OR, and assertion Authorize. For the limited space, we only present 6 commands. We present the typical one for each classification except for the combined assertions, for which we present two assertions. The full model including the rest assertions are listed in the full version of this paper. Note that all the assertion commands take as input a policy session's handle *h* and update the session's policyDigest (labeled by 'polD') according to the equations (1) to (3) in Section 2.2.1. We denote it by a hash digest of a 3-tuple. The first element is for the old policyDigest, the second is for the label of the assertion command, and the third is a vector of some input parameters used in the assertion.

- The immediate assertion group includes two assertions: NV and CounterTimer. As we have clarified before, we omit the CounterTimer assertion. The command P_{NV}, for NV assertion, takes as input a comparison value *v* and validates that it matches the current NV's context value *nv*. If matched, TPM will update the 'polD' of the input session according to the equation (1). Note that the immediate assertion might be misused in a deferred manner, which is described in Section 4.
- The deferred assertion group includes 9 commands as in **Table 2**. These commands just need two operations: updating the policyDigest value and modifying some specific context values of the session. In convenience we present P_{cpHash} for the assertion CpHash as an example. This command takes as input a value *cph* that should be used to modify the session's context 'cpHash'. This modification will be checked in the authorized command P_{UseObj} by the event CmdCPH(*ap*, *cph*), which is described in Section 3.3. P_{cpHash} also updates the input session's context 'polD' according to the equation (1).
- The combined assertions are composed of 4 assertions: Signed, Secret, Ticket, and PCR. The Signed and Se-

[2]One is for default setting and one for failed validation

Table 4: The processes of API commands

```
P_NewObj :=
in(⟨'NewObj', ap⟩);
ν h;
lock h;
insert ⟨'AuthP', h⟩, ap;
out(h);
unlock h
```

```
P_StartAS :=
in(⟨'StartAS'⟩); ν h; ν nt;
lock h;
event SessionBind(nt, h)
insert ⟨'PolD', h⟩, zero;
insert ⟨'cpHash', h⟩, zero;
insert ⟨'nameHash', h⟩, zero;
insert ⟨'commandCode', h⟩, zero;
insert ⟨'commandLocality', h⟩, zero;
insert ⟨'isPPRequired', h⟩, 'CLEAR';
insert ⟨'isAuthValueNeeded', h⟩, 'CLEAR';
insert ⟨'isPasswordNeeded', h⟩, 'CLEAR';
insert ⟨'pcrUC', h⟩, 'zero';
insert ⟨'NonceTPM', h⟩, nt;
insert ⟨'checkNVWritten', h⟩, 'CLEAR';
insert ⟨'nvWrittenState', h⟩, zero;
out(⟨h, nt⟩);
unlock h
```

```
P_PCRExtend :=
in(⟨'PCRExtend', v⟩);
lock pcrh;
lookup ⟨'PCRV', pcrh⟩ as pcrv in
lookup ⟨'pcrUpdC', pcrh⟩ as pc in
event PCRExtend(pc);
insert ⟨'pcrUpdC', pcrh⟩, pc + 'one';
insert ⟨'PCRV', pcrh⟩, H(⟨pcrv, v⟩);
unlock pcrh
```

```
P_PCR :=
in(⟨'PolicyPCR', h, v⟩);
lock h; lock pcrh;
lookup ⟨'PCRV', pcrh⟩ as pcrv in
lookup ⟨'PolD', h⟩ as pd in
if v = pcrv then
  event Pol('PCR', h, pd, v);
  insert ⟨'PolD', h⟩, H(⟨pd, 'PCR', v⟩);
  lookup ⟨'pcrUpdC', pcrh⟩ as pc in
  insert ⟨'pcrUC', h⟩, pc;
  unlock pcrh; unlock h
else unlock pcrh; unlock h
```

```
P_cpHash :=
in(⟨'PolicyCpHash', h, cph⟩);
lock h;
lookup ⟨'PolD', h⟩ as pd in
event Pol('CpHash', h, pd, cph);
insert ⟨'PolD', h⟩, H(⟨pd, 'CpHash', cph⟩);
insert ⟨'cpHash', h⟩, cph
unlock h;
```

```
P_Authorize
in(⟨'PolicyAuthorize', h, sig, pk, polR⟩);
lock h;
lookup ⟨'PolD', h⟩ as pd in
if CkSig(sig, pk) = ⟨pd, polR⟩ then
  event Pol('Authorize', h, zero, ⟨pk, polR⟩);
  insert ⟨'PolD', h⟩, H(⟨zero, 'Authorize', ⟨pk, polR⟩⟩);
  unlock h
else unlock h
```

```
P_UseObj :=
in(⟨'UseObj', hObj, hS⟩);
lock hObj; lock hS; lock pcrh; lock nvh;
lookup ⟨'AuthP', hObj⟩ as ap in
lookup ⟨'cpHash', hS⟩ as cph in
lookup ⟨'nameHash', hS⟩ as nmh in
lookup ⟨'commandCode', hS⟩ as cc in
lookup ⟨'commandLocality', hS⟩ as Loc in
lookup ⟨'isPPRequired', hS⟩ as PP in
lookup ⟨'isAuthValueNeeded', hS⟩ as AV in
lookup ⟨'isPasswordNeeded', hS⟩ as PW in
lookup ⟨'checkNVWritten', hS⟩ as NW in
lookup ⟨'nvWrittenState', hS⟩ as WS in
lookup ⟨'NV', nvh⟩ as nv in
lookup ⟨'PCRV', pcrh⟩ as pcrv in
lookup ⟨'pcrUpdC', pcrh⟩ as pc in
lookup ⟨'pcrUC', hS⟩ as pcS in
lookup ⟨'PolD', hS⟩ as pd in
unlock nvh; unlock pcrh; unlock hS; unlock hObj;
if pd = ap then
  event UseObj(ap, hS);
  event CmdCPH(ap, cph);
  event CmdNV(ap, nv);
  event CmdPCRV(ap, pcrv, pc, pcS);
  out('Success')
```

```
P_NVWrite :=
in(⟨'NVWrite', v⟩);
lock nvh;
insert ⟨'NV', nvh⟩, v;
unlock nvh
```

```
P_NV :=
in(⟨'PolicyNV', h, v⟩);
lock nvh; lock h;
lookup ⟨'NV', nvh⟩ as nv in
lookup ⟨'PolD', h⟩ as pd in
if v = nv then
  event Pol('NV', h, pd, v);
  insert ⟨'PolD', h⟩, H(⟨pd, 'NV', v⟩);
  unlock h; unlock nvh
```

```
P_Signed :=
in(⟨'PolicySigned', h, sig, pk, polR⟩);
lock h;
lookup ⟨'PolD', h⟩ as pd in
lookup ⟨'NonceTPM', h⟩ as nt in
if CkSig(sig, pk) = ⟨nt, polR⟩ then
  event Pol('Signed', h, pd, ⟨pk, polR⟩);
  insert ⟨'PolD', h⟩, H(⟨pd, 'Signed', ⟨pk, polR⟩⟩);
  unlock h
else unlock h
```

```
P_OR :=
in(⟨'PolicyOR', h, ⟨ld, rd⟩⟩);
lock h;
lookup ⟨'PolD', h⟩ as pd in
if pd = ld then
  event Pol('OR', h, pd, ⟨ld, rd⟩);
  insert ⟨'PolD', h⟩, H(⟨zero, 'OR', ⟨ld, rd⟩⟩);
  unlock h
  else if pd = rd then
    event Pol('OR', h, pd, ⟨ld, rd⟩);
    insert ⟨'PolD', h⟩, H(⟨zero, 'OR', ⟨ld, rd⟩⟩);
    unlock h
    else unlock h
```

cret assertions convey an authorization by signing a set of parameters that indicate the nature of the authorization. In the former assertion command, the signature is signed by an asymmetric signing key and in the latter one, the signature is signed by an HMAC key. The signed parameters include nonceTPM (nt) for binding the authorization to the specified session, and policy reference ($polR$) for an opaque value relating to the authorizing entity (An example could be found in Section 2.2.2). These two commands both can output an HMAC (called a ticket) which can be used in the Ticket assertion, which functions in the same way. Since the 3 assertion commands have similar operations, we only present one typical command P_{Signed} for the Signed assertion. P_{Signed} takes as input a signature sig and its verification key pk (instead of a handle for pk, in the practical case). The TPM validates the signature and updates the session's context 'polD' according to the equation (1).

- We present the command P_{PCR} for combined assertion PCR. This command takes as input a digest value v and validates that it matches the current PCR's context 'PCRV' value $pcrv$. If matched, TPM will update the 'polD' of the input session according to the equation (1). Note that in P_{PCR}, the session's context 'pcrUC' is updated by the PCR's context 'pcrUpdC' for a future match in the authorized command P_{UseObj}. This mechanism is set to defend against time-of-check time-of-use (TOCTOU) attack.

- The assertion command `TPM2_PolicyAuthorize` is modeled as $P_{Authorize}$. By using the input public key pk, the TPM validates that the input value sig is a signature of the session's current policyDigest pd and the policy reference $polR$. If valid, the TPM updates the session's context 'polD' according to the equation (2). In the real TPM, the signature is verified by another command. Successful validation produces a TPM-specific ticket (HMAC). We merge the validation into the assertion command since the ticket is signed by a TPM hierarchy proof value and is unforgeable (Section 11.4.5.3 and 14.4, Part I, specification [8]).

- The OR assertion command `TPM2_PolicyOR` takes as input a digest list of at most 8 digests. In our model we cut this number to 2 in P_{OR}, since it can be expanded by using cascading OR assertions. The command P_{OR} takes as input a pair of digest values $\langle ld, rd\rangle$ and checks whether the session's policyDigest pd matches ld or rd, or neither. If matched, the TPM updates the session's context 'polD' according to the equation (3).

In our model, the main process of the EA mechanism in TPM API is as follows. We present the full model transcripts of the two modes in [20].

$$\begin{aligned}
P_{TPM} &:= P_I; !(P_O|P_S|P_A)\\
P_O &:= P_{NewObj}|P_{UseObj}|P_{StartAS}\\
P_S &:= P_{NVWrite}|P_{PCRExtend}\\
P_A &:= P_{PCR}|P_{NV}|P_{Signed}|P_{Authorize}|P_{OR}|P_{cpHash}|\\
&\quad P_{nameHash}|P_{commandCode}|P_{locality}|P_{PhysicalPresence}|\\
&\quad P_{AuthValue}|P_{Password}|P_{DuplicationSelect}|P_{NvWritten}.
\end{aligned}$$

3.3 Modeling the security properties

The security properties of EA mechanism are not explicitly explained in the TPM 2.0 specifications, although some hints are provided. The specification [8] (Section 19.7, Part I) states that "Enhanced authorization is a TPM capability that allows entity-creators or administrators to require **specific tests** or **actions** to be performed before an action can be completed. The specific policy is encapsulated in a value called an authPolicy that is associated with an entity". We give out an informal description of the security properties of EA mechanism.

1. (For required **specific actions**) If the TPM has executed the authorized command, it MUST have executed a sequence of policy assertion commands corresponding to the policy encapsulated in the object's *authPolicy*;

2. (For required **specific tests**) If the TPM has executed the authorized command, its execution environment MUST have been tested to be consistent with the policy encapsulated in the object's *authPolicy*.

3.3.1 Formalization of Property 1

The adversary model has been described in Section 3.1. In the formalization of the first property, we have met two challenges. The first is that there is more than one expression of the authPolicy setting for a given policy. We solve it by transforming a given policy into a disjunctive normal form and providing a generic way to compute the authPolicy setting for it.

As stated in Section 2.2.1, the policy can be expressed by the OR and AND combinations of policy assertions. We denote by $Assert(polLabel, Param)$ all the assertions listed in **Table 2** except for the OR assertion (which we call AND assertions). $polLabel$ is for the Label of the assertion and $Param$ for the parameters in equation (1). Although for the AND assertions the order of execution matters, we could list all the possible permutations and combine them by using the OR connective. Thus a policy can be expressed in a disjunctive normal form (DNF):

$$\text{policy} = \bigvee_{i=1}^{n} \bigwedge_{j=1}^{m_i} Assert(L_{i,j}, pm_{i,j}). \quad (4)$$

Given the policy, we provide a generic way to set the corresponding authPolicy value ap.

For $n = 1$, $(1 \le j \le m_1)$

$$\begin{aligned}
ap &:= \mathrm{H}(\langle ap_{1,1}, L_{1,1}, pm_{1,1}\rangle)\\
ap_{1,j} &:= \mathrm{H}(\langle ap_{1,j+1}, L_{1,j}, pm_{1,j}\rangle)\\
ap_{1,m_1+1} &:= \text{zero}
\end{aligned}$$

As we have stated in Section 2.2.1, ap encodes the unique branch for AND assertions by linking $ap_{1,j}$ to $ap_{1,j+1}$. Note that in each branch, the test order is from $j = m_1$ to 1.

For $n \ge 2$, $(0 \le k \le n-2,\ 1 \le i \le n,\ 1 \le j \le m_i)$

$$\begin{aligned}
ap &:= rd_0\\
rd_k &:= \mathrm{H}(\langle \text{zero}, \text{'OR'}, \langle ld_{k+1}, rd_{k+1}\rangle\rangle)\\
rd_{n-1} &:= ld_n\\
ld_i &:= \mathrm{H}(\langle ap_{i,1}, L_{i,1}, pm_{i,1}\rangle)\\
ap_{i,j} &:= \mathrm{H}(\langle ap_{i,j+1}, L_{i,j}, pm_{i,j}\rangle)\\
ap_{i,m_i+1} &:= \text{zero}
\end{aligned}$$

Each ld_i encodes the i-th branch by linking $ap_{i,j}$ to $ap_{i,j+1}$. Each rd_k encodes the remained disjunctive formula from $i = k+1$ to n. The OR assertion connects ld_i with rd_i.

With the expression of the specific authPolicy values for any given policies in (4), we can formalize Property 1. Each assertion in the policy should be preceded by one execution of the policy assertion command, which is denoted by the event Pol.

Property 1(*SpecAct*). For the authPolicy value ap corresponding to any given policies in a disjunctive normal form (4), it should have $Tr(P_{TPM}) \models^{\forall} \phi$, where $t_{i,0} = t_0$ for $1 \leq i \leq n$ and

$$\phi := \forall h_S, t_0.\text{UseObj}(ap, h_S)@t_0 \Rightarrow \bigvee_{i=1}^{n} \bigwedge_{j=1}^{m_i} (\exists t_{i,j}.\text{Pol}(L_{i,j}, h_S, ap_{i,j+1}, pm_{i,j})@t_{i,j} \wedge t_{i,j} < t_{i,j-1}).$$

Example 3. In Section 2.2.2, we give a simple example of the EA mechanism. Its policy in disjunctive normal form is as follows. Due to the simplification in our model, we omit some parameters in the 'NV' and 'PCR' assertions

$$\begin{pmatrix} Assert(\text{'Signed'}, \langle \text{PK}(sk_A), \text{'Alice'}\rangle)\wedge \\ Assert(\text{'NV'}, 5) \wedge Assert(\text{'CmdCode'}, \text{CC\_Sign}) \end{pmatrix} \vee \begin{pmatrix} Assert(\text{'Signed'}, \langle \text{PK}(sk_B), \text{'Bob'}\rangle)\wedge \\ Assert(\text{'PCR'}, v) \wedge Assert(\text{'CmdCode'}, \text{CC\_Certify}) \end{pmatrix}$$

The trace formula to be verified is as follows.

$$\phi := \forall h_S, t_0.\text{UseObj}(aP, h_S)@t_0 \Rightarrow \begin{pmatrix} \exists t_{11}, t_{12}, t_{13}.t_{13} < t_{12} \wedge t_{12} < t_{11} \wedge t_{11} < t_0 \wedge \\ \text{Pol}(\text{'Signed'}, h_S, Z_N, \langle \text{PK}(sk_A), \text{'Alice'}\rangle)@t_{11}\wedge \\ \text{Pol}(\text{'NV'}, h_S, Z_{C1}, 5)@t_{12}\wedge \\ \text{Pol}(\text{'CmdCode'}, h_S, \text{zero}, \text{CC\_Sign})@t_{13} \end{pmatrix} \vee \begin{pmatrix} \exists t_{21}, t_{22}, t_{23}.t_{23} < t_{22} \wedge t_{22} < t_{21} \wedge t_{21} < t_0 \wedge \\ \text{Pol}(\text{'Signed'}, h_S, Z_P, \langle \text{PK}(sk_B), \text{'Bob'}\rangle)@t_{21}\wedge \\ \text{Pol}(\text{'PCR'}, h_S, Z_{C2}, v)@t_{22}\wedge \\ \text{Pol}(\text{'CmdCode'}, h_S, \text{zero}, \text{CC\_Certify})@t_{23} \end{pmatrix}$$

The second challenge we have met is that the universal quantifier over the authPolicy value makes it difficult to verify Property 1. In fact, the number of branches n and the length of digest chain m_i is unbounded. We solve this problem by using the linking of digest chain in the event and divides the whole proof into a chain of pieces. If we can prove the fact that every piece of the chain is true and can be reused, then we could give out a whole proof for Property 1. We achieve this goal by providing 2 lemmas.

Lemma 1(*CorUsePol*). $Tr(P_{TPM}) \models^{\forall} \phi_1$, where

$$\begin{aligned} &\phi_1 := \forall h_S, pd, L, pm, t_0. \\ &\text{UseObj}(\text{H}(\langle pd, L, pm\rangle), h_S)@t_0 \Rightarrow \\ &(\exists t_1.L \neq \text{'OR'} \wedge \text{Pol}(L, h_S, pd, pm)@t_1 \wedge t_1 < t_0)\vee \\ &\begin{pmatrix} \exists ld, rd, t_2.L = \text{'OR'} \wedge pd = \text{zero} \wedge pm = \langle ld, rd\rangle\wedge \\ \text{Pol}(L, h_S, ld, pm)@t_2 \wedge t_2 < t_0 \end{pmatrix} \vee \\ &\begin{pmatrix} \exists ld, rd, t_3.L = \text{'OR'} \wedge pd = \text{zero} \wedge pm = \langle ld, rd\rangle\wedge \\ \text{Pol}(L, h_S, rd, pm)@t_3 \wedge t_3 < t_0 \end{pmatrix}. \end{aligned}$$

Lemma 1 states that any execution of the event UseObj with ap $= \text{H}(\langle pd, L, pm\rangle)$ and h_S should be preceded by the execution of the event Pol with the same payload L, h_S, pd, and pm. There are 3 branches. For the case that $L \neq$'OR', it is an AND assertion with the old policyDigest in the event Pol equals pd. For the other two cases that $L =$'OR', the policyDigest pd in the event UseObj should be zero but the old policyDigest in the event Pol should be either ld or rd in the digest list pm.

Lemma 2(*CorPol1Pol2*). $Tr(P_{TPM}) \models^{\forall} \phi_2$, where

$$\begin{aligned} &\phi_2 := \forall L_1, pm_1, L_2, pm_2, pd, h_S, t_0. \\ &\text{Pol}(L_1, h_S, \text{H}(\langle pd, L_2, pm_2\rangle), pm_1)@t_0 \Rightarrow \\ &(\exists t_1.L \neq \text{'OR'} \wedge \text{Pol}(L_2, h_S, pd, pm_2)@t_1 \wedge t_1 < t_0)\vee \\ &\begin{pmatrix} \exists ld, rd, t_2.L_2 = \text{'OR'} \wedge pd = \text{zero} \wedge pm_2 = \langle ld, rd\rangle\wedge \\ \text{Pol}(\text{'OR'}, h_S, ld, pm_2)@t_2 \wedge t_2 < t_0 \end{pmatrix} \vee \\ &\begin{pmatrix} \exists ld, rd, t_3.L_2 = \text{'OR'} \wedge pd = \text{zero} \wedge pm_2 = \langle ld, rd\rangle\wedge \\ \text{Pol}(\text{'OR'}, h_S, rd, pm_2)@t_3 \wedge t_3 < t_0 \end{pmatrix}. \end{aligned}$$

Lemma 2 states that any execution of the event Pol with the policyDigest $polD = \text{H}(\langle pd, L_2, pm_2\rangle)$ should be preceded by the execution of another event Pol with the payloads encapsulated in $polD$ and the same policy session handle h_S. As in the lemma *CorUsePol*, we should differentiate 3 branches of L_2.

(**Proof sketch of Property 1.**) If Lemma 1 and Lemma 2 are both verified, we can prove Property 1. In the following, we give a sketch. The formal proof could be found in the full version of this paper. Given an authPolicy value ap, by lemma 1, the event UseObj(ap, h_S) should be preceded by the execution of an event Pol according to the end part of the digest chain ap. There might be three cases. For case 1, the end part is an AND assertion. Then the number of branches n is one. By using the inductive method, it is trivial to give out the proof by lemma 2 (for only one branch). If the end part is an OR assertion, then we will go into the left part case, which is similar to case 1, and the right part case, which can be proved by lemma 2 through the induction method. The conclusion of ϕ in Property 1 can be achieved by omitting all the events Pol labeled with the OR assertion in the proof we have obtained.

3.3.2 Formalization of Property 2

The second property requires specific tests before the execution of the authorized command. The assertions are classified into 5 groups as in **Table 2**, which are managed separately. By TPM design, the tests for the immediate NV assertion and the OR assertion are performed in their respective policy assertion commands (in an immediate manner). We have stated that in Property 1, the use of object should be preceded by the execution of the corresponding policy assertion commands, which have performed the immediate assertion tests. Thus we do not need to consider these two assertions. For the deferred assertions, we use the CpHash assertion as a standard. The verification of the other deferred assertions such as NameHash and CommandCode are similar to that of the CpHash assertion. It is trivial to extend the analysis results. Thus we only focus on the CpHash assertion. In the following, we give out Lemma 3 to Lemma 6 respectively for the Authorize assertion, the combined Signed assertion, the deferred CpHash assertion, and the PCR assertion.

Lemma 3(*PolAuth*). $Tr(P_{TPM}) \models^{\forall} \phi_3$, where

$$\begin{aligned} &\phi_3 := \forall h_S, sk, polR, t_0. \\ &\text{Pol}(\text{'Authorize'}, h_S, \text{zero}, \langle \text{PK}(sk), polR\rangle)@t_0 \Rightarrow \\ &(\exists pd, t_1.\text{K}(\text{Sig}(\langle pd, polR\rangle, sk))@t_1 \wedge t_1 < t_0) \end{aligned}$$

Lemma 4(*PolSigned*). $Tr(P_{TPM}) \models^{\forall} \phi_4$, where

$$\begin{aligned} &\phi_4 := \forall h_S, sk, pd, polR, t_0. \\ &\text{Pol}(\text{'Signed'}, h_S, pd, \langle \text{PK}(sk), polR\rangle)@t_0 \Rightarrow \\ &\begin{pmatrix} \exists nt, t_1, t_2.\text{K}(\text{Sig}(\langle nt, polR\rangle, sk))@t_1 \wedge t_1 < t_0\wedge \\ \text{SessionBind}(nt, h_S)@t_2 \wedge t_2 < t_0 \end{pmatrix} \end{aligned}$$

Lemma 3 and Lemma 4 respectively states that in order to successfully execute the Authorize and Signed assertion commands, the attacker should know the signature of some specific payloads (pd and $polR$ for 'Authorize'; nt and $polR$ for 'Signed'). Note that for the Signed assertion, the signed nt should be bound with the policy session h_S.

Lemma 5(*PolCpHash*). $Tr(P_{TPM}) \models^{\forall} \phi_5$, where

$$\phi_5 := \forall pd, ch_1, ch_2, t. \\ \text{CmdCPH}(\text{H}(\langle pd, \text{'CpHash'}, ch_1\rangle), ch_2)@t \Rightarrow (ch_1 = ch_2)$$

Lemma 6(*PolPCR*). $Tr(P_{TPM}) \models^{\forall} \phi_6$, where

$$\phi_6 := \forall pd, pc, pcrv_1, pcrv_2, t. \\ \text{CmdPCRV}(\text{H}(\langle pd, \text{'PCR'}, pcrv_1\rangle), pcrv_2, pc, pc)@t \\ \Rightarrow (pcrv_1 = pcrv_2)$$

Lemma 5 states that in the authorized command, the session's context value should be consistent with the policy set in the object's authPolicy. This lemma is for the CpHash assertion. As stated in Section 3.2, we use the event CmdCPH(ap, ch) to denote the check of the context value ch with no block if failed. Thus the verification of Lemma 5 means that the session's context ch_2 equals ch_1 set in ap and can be used in a check in the practical case. Lemma 6 is similar. It means that when TPM executes the authorized command, the PCR should have the desired value specified in the object's authPolicy. In this lemma, the session's context 'pcrUC' equals the PCR's current counter 'pcrUpdC' to force a match of the PCR value. This is equivalent to the case that the command P_{UseObj} only executes the event CmdPCRV after checking that 'pcrUC' and 'pcrUpdC' match. Note that the repetition of the same assertion commands can replace the previous policy settings. Thus in Lemma 5 and Lemma 6, we assume that the end part of ap is respectively the CpHash and PCR assertion.

With lemma 3 to 6, we could give out Property 2 for the TPM 2.0 EA mechanism.

Property 2(*SpecTest*). $Tr(P_{TPM}) \models^{\forall} \phi_3 \wedge \phi_4 \wedge \phi_5 \wedge \phi_6$.

Property 1 and 2 are two security properties stated by the design of TPM 2.0 specifications. However, we find that the administrator is likely to misuse the immediate NV assertion in a deferred manner. Thus we propose Lemma 7 to analyze this case.

Lemma 7(*CmdNV*). $Tr(P_{TPM}) \models^{\forall} \phi_7$, where

$$\phi_7 := \forall pd, nv_1, nv_2, t. \\ \text{CmdNV}(\text{H}(\langle pd, \text{'NV'}, nv_1\rangle), nv_2)@t \Rightarrow (nv_1 = nv_2)$$

It is similar to lemma 6. nv_1 is the desired NV value set in authPolicy. nv_2 is the NV Index value at the authorization decision moment. If lemma 7 is falsified, which means $nv_1 \neq nv_2$, then there exists an attack on the misuse case.

4. ANALYSIS RESULTS OF EA

In this section, we conduct an experiment to analyze the security properties of the EA mechanism in the TPM 2.0. Using the tool SAPIC [9], our model of the EA mechanism in Section 3.2 could be translated into the script of rewriting systems, that can be automatically analyzed by the tamarin prover [11]. The script contains 267 multiset rewriting rules and axioms for Mode 1 and 213 rules for Mode 2. We choose the tamarin prover as the analyzer since it supports an interactive mode with a GUI which allows to manually guide the tool in its proof. The analyzing results are summarized in **Table 5**. The running times on PC with Intel Core(TM)2 Quad 2.66GHz and 4GB RAM are less than 2 minutes. All the formal proof transcripts presented in this section can be found in [20]. They can be automatically verified by the tamarin-prover.

4.1 Results for Mode 1

For mode 1, the lemmas 1 to 6 have been verified. Among them, the lemmas *PolCpHash* and *PolPCR* are verified manually by using the interactive mode of the tamarin prover. By proving Property 1 and 2, we have achieved a formal verification of the EA mechanism in TPM 2.0 design. However, as we have mentioned in Section 3.3, the administrator of the TPM may misuse the NV assertion in a deferred manner. In this case, we have proved that the lemma *CmdNV* is falsified. We have found a TOCTOU attack in this case.

We present a sketch for the interaction in the proof of the lemmas *PolPCR* and *PolCpHash*. In the verification of the lemma *PolPCR*, we introduce an auxiliary formula ψ and verify the lemma *Counter* that $Tr(P_{TPM}) \models^{\forall} \psi$ by using the inductive method. It states that the PCR counter 'pcrUpdC' is monotonically increasing, where

Lemma 8(*Counter*). $Tr(P_{TPM}) \models^{\forall} \psi$, where

$$\psi := \forall c_1, c_2, t_1, t_2. \text{PCRExtend}(c_1)@t_1 \wedge \text{PCRExtend}(c_2)@t_2 \\ \Rightarrow ((t_1 < t_2 \wedge \exists z. c_1 + z = c_2) \vee (t_2 < t_1) \vee (t_1 = t_2)).$$

With the lemma *Counter*, we can prove the lemma *PolPCR* step by step. The tamarin prover transfers the formula $p \Rightarrow c$ to a constraint system $p \wedge \text{not}(c)$, thus we get the condition $pcrv_1 \neq pcrv_2$ and try to find a contradiction. $ap = \text{H}(\langle pd, \text{'PCR'}, pcrv_1\rangle)$ means that the event CmdPCRV should be preceded by a PCR assertion command, in which the TPM checks the 'PCRV' of pcrh as $pcrv_1$ and inserts the session's 'pcrUC' (by lock) with the value pc. This context of pcrh should be inserted by a command $P_{PCRExtend}$ or by initialization P_I. Since the current 'pcrUpdC' of pcrh has the same value pc but the current 'PCRV' of pcrh has a different value pcrv$_2$, this context of pcrh should be inserted by another $P_{PCRExtend}$ command. We could find a contradiction with the lemma *Counter* by selecting these two $P_{PCRExtend}$ commands. For the lemma *CmdCPH*, it could be easily verified by selecting the two commands P_{cpHash} which respectively insert the session's 'polD' and 'cpHash' since $ch_1 \neq ch_2$.

TOCTOU attack. For the immediate NV assertion, the time of check is at the assertion command `TPM2_PolicyNV` but the time of authorization decision is at the authorized command `TPM2_UseObj`. It is possible for the adversary to cause the NV value to change between these two commands, which might lead to an attack if the administrator does not expect its happening.

We present an attack of the policy setting in [12] (Section 4.2.2). Their scheme binds the PIN value to multiple keys stored on personal device and uses the policy NV assertion to restrict the number of PIN attempts to 3. The policy for the key authorization is policy $= Assert(\text{'Secret'}, \text{PIN\_handle}) \wedge \bigvee_{n=0}^{2} \{Assert(\text{'NV'}, n{+}1) \wedge Assert(\text{'NV'}, n)\}$. It can be rewritten in DNF: policy $= \bigvee_{n=0}^{2} \{Assert(\text{'Secret'}, \text{PIN\_handle}) \wedge Assert(\text{'NV'}, n+1) \wedge Assert(\text{'NV'}, n)\}$. n is the current NV counter value and the initial value is 0. Since the order of verification of policy is reversed in each OR branch. To ver-

Table 5: Results of analyzing

Lemmas	Property	Mode 1		Mode 2	
		Results	Automated Run	Results	Automated Run
CorUsePol	Prop.1	verified	yes (257 steps)	verified	yes (257 steps)
CorPol1Pol2		verified	yes (615 steps)	verified	yes (549 steps)
PolAuth	Prop.2	verified	yes (4 steps)	verified	yes (4 steps)
PolSigned		verified	yes (6 steps)	verified	yes (6 steps)
PolCpHash		verified	no (200 selections)	falsified	no (36 selections)
PolPCR		verified	no (352 selections)	falsified	no (59 selections)
CmdNV	misuse	falsified	no (83 selections)	falsified	no (37 selections)

ify the policy setting, the user invokes the first NV assertion command to check its value matches n, increments the NV counter by one, and again invokes the second NV assertion command with $n+1$. Then the user attempts to enter and verify the PIN value by using the Secret assertion. In this assertion, the PIN_handle (associated with the PIN value as its authorization value) is extended into the session's policy digest only if an hmac keyed on the PIN value is inputted into the TPM by the user. At last, the user invokes the OR assertion command, which only accepts the successful verification of PIN value within 3 attempts. It is supposed to restrict the number of authorizations.

However, a malicious user can double this number by using one more policy session. Suppose that the personal device is stolen by a malicious user who does not know the PIN value. He attempts to guess the low-entropy PIN value by brute force. Suppose that the user starts 2 sessions S_1 and S_2, he can use S_1 to invoke the first NV assertion command with $n = 0$ and sequentially use S_2 still with $n = 0$. Then he increments the NV counter by one, and sequentially uses S_1 and S_2 to invoke the second NV assertion command with $n + 1 = 1$. Now he can use S_1 and S_2 to invoke the Secret assertion command to try 2 PIN candidates since the 2 sessions both have the same policy digest. Now the malicious user achieves 2 attempts but only increments the counter by 1. With $n = 1$ and $n = 2$, the user can double the number of attempts by the same way.

To avoid the misuse, the administrator should be cautious when using the immediate assertions. For the NV assertion, we suggest the current specifications change it to a deferred assertion just like the PCR assertion and add a *NVUpdateCounter* which acts a similar role as *pcrUpdateCounter*. For [12] based on current specification, we suggest the administrator uses the TPM 2.0 dictionary attack (DA) protection mechanism (Section 19.11, Part I, specification [8]) that provides protection against guessing or exhaustive searches of authorization values stored within the TPM.

4.2 Results for Mode 2

For mode 2, lemmas 1 to 4 are all verified. Lemma *CmdNV* is falsified due to the same attack in Mode 1. Lemmas *PolCpHash* and *PolPCR* are falsified due to the race conditions. The race conditions are only possible when the API commands can be executed in parallel. The two race conditions may lead to theoretical attacks in mode 2.

Race-condition-1. For the lemma *PolCpHash*, we find that the order of modifying session's context in the deferred assertion commands causes race conditions. Note that in all of these commands, the TPM modifies the session's *policyDigest* before it modifies the other context values. If the adversary can simultaneously invoke the deferred assertion command `TPM2_PolicyCpHash` and the authorized command `TPM2_UseObj` with the same session handle, then it is possible for the TPM to firstly update the session's policyDigest in the assertion command, and secondly conduct the authPolicy check in the authorized command before the assertion command modifies the session's context values. In this way, the adversary has a chance to bypass the deferred assertion checks since the context values are not modified.

Race-condition-2. For the lemma *PolPCR*, we find that the time difference in the command `TPM2_PolicyPCR` between the check of PCR value and the modification of the session's context pcrUC causes the race condition. Note that in this command, the TPM checks the PCR value before it copies the PCR's counter pcrUpdC into the session's context pcrUC for a future match. If the adversary can simultaneously invoke the commands `TPM2_PCRExtend` and `TPM_PolicyPCR`, then it is possible for the TPM to firstly check the PCR value, secondly change the PCR's value and counter in the extending command, and thirdly modify the session's context. In this way, the adversary has a chance to bypass the defence of the TOCTOU attack.

Although the probability of making a successful attack might be very small, we suggest to disable the execution mode 2. The TPM specification gives manufactures some leeway in its implementation. Our results of formal analysis show that the TPM resources should be locked when used to prevent the race conditions. It is easy to be achieved by using an I/O buffer and only allowing the execution of the next command when the last command returns a result.

5. CONCLUSION

In this paper, we have conducted a formal verification and analysis of the enhanced authorization (EA) mechanism in the TPM 2.0 API. We have proposed a model of security API analysis in process calculus with global states. We have identified and formalized the two security properties of EA mechanism in its design. Using SAPIC tool and tamarin prover, we have verified both the two security properties and discovered 3 misuse cases in the present EA mechanism.

As future work, we foresee extending our model with more TPM API commands such as those involved in attestation and platform integrity measurement. We also plan to improve and apply our formal verification results to the security analysis of more EA-based applications in Trusted Network Connection (TNC), digital rights management (DRM), Bring Your Own Device (BYOD), etc. We expect to do some improvements on our model when dealing with counters. Since at present it cannot be verified by the prover automatically.

Acknowledgments

We would like to thank all the anonymous reviewers who have reviewed our work and have provided us with valuable feedbacks. The research presented in this paper is supported by the National Basic Research Program of China (No. 2013CB338003) and National Natural Science Foundation of China (No. 91118006, No.61202414).

6. REFERENCES

[1] Trusted Computing Group. TPM Specification version 1.2. Parts 1–3, revision. http://www.trustedcomputinggroup.org/resources/tpm_main_specification.

[2] ISO/IEC PAS DIS 11889: Information technology –Security techniques – Trusted Platform Module.

[3] D. Bruschi, L. Cavallaro, A. Lanzi, and M. Monga. Replay attack in TCG specification and solution. In *Proceedings of ACSAC 2005*, volume 10, pages 127–137, Tucson, AZ (USA), December 2005. ACSAC, IEEE Computer Society.

[4] L. Chen and M. Ryan. Attack, solution and verification for shared authorisation data in TCG TPM. In P. Degano and J. Guttman, editors, *Formal Aspects in Security and Trust*, volume 5983 of *Lecture Notes in Computer Science*, pages 201–216. Springer Berlin Heidelberg, 2010.

[5] L. Chen and M. Ryan. Offline dictionary attack on tcg tpm weak authorisation data, and solution. In D. Gawrock, H. Reimer, A.-R. Sadeghi, and C. Vishik, editors, *Future of Trust in Computing*, pages 193–196. Vieweg Teubner, 2009.

[6] S. Delaune, S. Kremer, M. Ryan, and G. Steel. A formal analysis of authentication in the TPM. In P. Degano, S. Etalle, and J. Guttman, editors, *Formal Aspects of Security and Trust*, volume 6561 of *Lecture Notes in Computer Science*, pages 111–125. Springer Berlin Heidelberg, 2011.

[7] S. Gurgens, C. Rudolph, D. Scheuermann, M. Atts, and R. Plaga. Security evaluation of scenarios based on the TCG's TPM specification. In J. Biskup and J. Lĺőpez, editors, *Computer Security–ESORICS 2007*, volume 4734 of *Lecture Notes in Computer Science*, pages 438–453. Springer Berlin Heidelberg, 2007.

[8] Trusted Computing Group. TPM Specification version 2.0. Parts 1–4, revision. http://www.trustedcomputinggroup.org/resources/tpm_main_specification.

[9] S. Kremer and R. Künnemann. Automated analysis of security protocols with global state. IEEE Symposium on Security and Privacy, 2014. http://sapic.gforge.inria.fr/.

[10] M. Arapinis, E. Ritter, and M. Ryan. Statverif: Verification of stateful processes. In *Computer Security Foundations Symposium (CSF), 2011 IEEE 24th*, pages 33–47, June 2011.

[11] B. Schmidt, S. Meier, C. Cremers, and D. Basin. Automated analysis of diffie-hellman protocols and advanced security properties. In *Computer Security Foundations Symposium (CSF), 2012 IEEE 25th*, pages 78–94, June 2012.

[12] T. Nyman, J.E. Ekberg, N. Asokan. Citizen Electronic Identities using TPM 2.0. *Trustworthy Embedded Devices 2014*. http://arxiv.org/abs/1409.1023.

[13] L. Chen and J. Li. Flexible and scalable digital signatures in tpm 2.0. In *Proceedings of the 2013 ACM SIGSAC Conference on Computer and Communications Security*, CCS '13, pages 37–48, New York, NY, USA, 2013. ACM.

[14] L. Xi. DAA-related APIs in TPM 2.0 Revisited. Cryptology ePrint Archive, 2014. https://eprint.iacr.org/2014/052.

[15] J. Shao, D. Feng, and Y. Qin. Type-based analysis of protected storage in the tpm. In S. Qing, J. Zhou, and D. Liu, editors, *Information and Communications Security*, volume 8233 of *Lecture Notes in Computer Science*, pages 135–150. Springer International Publishing, 2013.

[16] W. Wang, Y. Qin, and D. Feng. Automated proof for authorization protocols of tpm 2.0 in computational model. In X. Huang and J. Zhou, editors, *Information Security Practice and Experience*, volume 8434 of *Lecture Notes in Computer Science*, pages 144–158. Springer International Publishing, 2014.

[17] A. Datta, J. Franklin, D. Garg, and D. Kaynar. A logic of secure systems and its application to trusted computing. In *Proceedings of the 2009 30th IEEE Symposium on Security and Privacy*, SP '09, pages 221–236, Washington, DC, USA, 2009. IEEE Computer Society.

[18] S. Delaune, S. Kremer, M. D. Ryan, and G. Steel. Formal analysis of protocols based on tpm state registers. In *Proceedings of the 2011 IEEE 24th Computer Security Foundations Symposium*, CSF '11, pages 66–80, Washington, DC, USA, 2011. IEEE Computer Society.

[19] B. Blanchet. An efficient cryptographic protocol verifier based on prolog rules. In *Proceedings of the 14th IEEE Workshop on Computer Security Foundations*, CSFW '01, pages 82–, Washington, DC, USA, 2001. IEEE Computer Society.

[20] TPM2-EA-formal-verification. https://github.com/sjxzmc/TPM2-EA-formal-verification/

GuardMR: Fine-grained Security Policy Enforcement for MapReduce Systems

Huseyin Ulusoy #1, Pietro Colombo *2, Elena Ferrari *3, Murat Kantarcioglu #4, Erman Pattuk #5
The University of Texas at Dallas
800 W. Campbell Rd, Richardson TX, 75080
[1] huseyin.ulusoy@utdallas.edu [4] muratk@utdallas.edu [5] erman.pattuk@utdallas.edu
* Università degli Studi dell'Insubria
Via Mazzini 5, 21100 Varese - Italy
[2] pietro.colombo@uninsubria.it [3] elena.ferrari@uninsubria.it

ABSTRACT

Executing data analytics tasks in MapReduce systems introduces new security and privacy concerns as the processed unstructured datasets may contain sensitive information (e.g., social security numbers, business sensitive information) at the level of individual records, and the existing file-level access control mechanisms provide all or nothing access to the entire dataset. To address these concerns, we propose GUARDMR which is a novel, modular framework that can enforce fine-grained security policies at the key-value level in MapReduce systems. The presented security policies can dynamically create authorized views of data resources based on the organizational roles of the MapReduce users. GUARDMR further simplifies the specification of authorized views via automatically generating the bytecode of the functions necessary for creating the views, from the high level specification language (i.e., OCL). It facilitates enforcement of a broad, flexible set of policies that can handle the complexity demanded by high volume, high variety, unstructured datasets and general MapReduce computation without any modification to the underlying MapReduce system and operating system. Our evaluation results indicate that GUARDMR provides fine-grained access control for Apache Hadoop system with easy maintainability and very low overhead.

Categories and Subject Descriptors

H.2 [**DATABASE MANAGEMENT**]; H.2.4 [**Systems**]: Distributed databases; H.2.7 [**Database Administration**]: Security, integrity, and protection

Keywords

Big Data; MapReduce sytems; fine-grained access control

1. INTRODUCTION

Increasing data accumulation and processing have been fundamentally changing the computation environments for several years. Our daily activities, ranging from updating status in social networks to sharing images via mobile devices, produce enormous heterogeneous datasets known as *Big Data*. These datasets are processed to extract information by many devoted organizations, including large-scale Internet companies and government agencies. However, processing Big Data goes beyond most traditional data management systems, where the higher velocity and greater variety of Big Data requires more flexible and adaptable systems. Over the past several years, many systems have been proposed to handle the complexity demanded by Big Data. Among them, MapReduce systems (e.g., Apache Hadoop) have become one of the most widely used Big Data systems, due in part to horizontal data partitioning and flexible computation model.

The popularity of MapReduce systems has raised significant concerns about security and privacy, though. The current access control mechanism integrated into MapReduce systems regulates the access at the level of file-system resources, but data processing is achieved on individual data records. Since the processed datasets are unstructured and the content of records are diverse, some of the records may contain sensitive and private information, ranging from *personally identifiable information* to *business sensitive information*. This sensitive information might be disclosed by the potentially malicious MapReduce jobs as file-based access permissions are valid for all records in a file, and file-based access control mechanisms do not allow selective processing of the data in a given file. To address this issue, the MapReduce model needs fine-grained access control (FGAC) enforcing the security policies at the level of key-value pairs while creating dynamic authorized views of data resources according to the security clearance of the MapReduce users.

For example, let us consider an online shopping company, which is interested in processing its *click logs* for ad-targeting algorithms (e.g., SalesForce.com Inc. as presented in [1]). To that end, the dominant approach is that the company loads the log files into Apache Hadoop; the employees of the company writes MapReduce jobs analyzing customer behaviors and preferences, where each employee has different job description and security clearance. For simplicity, let us assume each action of costumers is stored as records in Hadoop File system (HDFS). The MapReduce jobs, submitted by a user who has access rights to log file, can read all the information in the log file while performing data analytics tasks. However, some of the records in the log file may contain sensitive and private information, e.g., the identity of customers, sensitive product purchases, credit card numbers, contact of customers, etc. If access permission is given to the entire log file, a possibly malicious employee can disclose such sensitive information by running MapReduce jobs. These malicious actions may re-

ASIA CCS'15, April 14–17, 2015, Singapore..

ACM 978-1-4503-3245-3/15/04 ...$15.00.
http://dx.doi.org/10.1145/2714576.2714624

sult in privacy violation, reputation loss of company, etc. A typical *Extract, Transform and Load (ETL)* strategy—the data is preprocessed by a trusted entity sanitizing the sensitive records before the data analytics tasks are performed—does not address this problem as the employees have different roles, and therefore different security clearances. For each security clearance, a separate file needs to be created by sanitizing the records according to the employee's job description, where exponential number of data duplications (one duplication per employee) causes disastrous monetary and computative results for Big Data. On the other hand, granting access to the dynamically created authorized data views containing only authorized records of the file defined for the role of employee, will significantly reduce the risk of such privacy violations.

FGAC has been successfully integrated into some commercial relational database management systems (e.g., Oracle VPD [2]). Based on this previous experience, industry and academic experts have already observed that FGAC is a must-have addition to MapReduce systems as the model becomes more widely adopted [3, 4, 5]. Although FGAC promises significant improvement for the security of MapReduce systems, to our knowledge, there is no study in the literature about FGAC targeting the unstructured datasets in MapReduce systems except an initial work [6].

[6] proposes to apply *history independent functions*—the functions that are independently run on multiple input instances while only using the corresponding instance's data without sharing any information between the functions—on the individual records to restrict the access in MapReduce systems. In theory, the history independent functions can sanitize the sensitive entries in the records and filter out the unauthorized ones. However, each history independent function has to be defined in the domain of specific input data types (i.e., the data types of key-value pairs), while in MapReduce systems a job can implement its own data view of a resource by means of self-defined preprocessing functions and can come up with new data types (e.g., Custom RecordReader and key-value classes in Hadoop). [6] does not consider these ad-hoc data types, and define the functions for one specific data type. If another data type is used in the jobs, the jobs is conservatively rejected. This imposes the use of restricted data types on the job writers, and reduces the utility and flexibility of the MapReduce computation. For a more general FGAC system, the user-defined data types and preprocessing functions need to be supported, yet there are two main challenges for that: 1) the malicious preprocessing functions may try to obfuscate/encrypt the data so as to circumvent the history independent functions; 2) for each data resource in the system, there can be multiple (even infinite) data views as new jobs can always introduce new data types. To that end, GUARDMR proposes an access control model that includes the entities about the trusted data types and preprocessing functions used in the MapReduce. The model is equipped with the administrative functions that allow to add new data types and preprocessing functions after a proper security analysis. Since our authorized view specification technique is based on high-level OCL statements, the derivation of the existing policies for new data types is easy and more manageable.

With the aim to achieve all the aforementioned challenging goals, in this paper, we propose GUARDMR, an FGAC framework for MapReduce systems. GUARDMR supports the system administrators with three provided facilities: 1) the proposed access control model for policy specification in the MapReduce computation, while handling the user-defined preprocessing functions and adhoc data types; 2) a formal specification approach to the definition of authorized views of the target dataset at high level of abstraction through object constraint language (OCL) specifications; 3) a mechanisms to automatically generate and integrate the bytecode that implements the above-mentioned OCL specifications (i.e., authorized data views).

The main contributions of this paper are summarized as follows:

- We formalize the fine-grained access control problem for general MapReduce computation and propose an access control model, which regulates the access at the level of key-value pairs of data resources, and forms the dynamic view-based access control of relational databases in the MapReduce.
- We propose an innovative method to generate history independent functions from the high level OCL specifications, and to automatically generate the implementations of functions in Java bytecode.
- We show how the generated implementation of functions can be enforced upon MapReduce computation by ensuring the security and completeness of the imposed policy enforcement. Thus, GUARDMR is designed as a separate module that is completely independent of underlying MapReduce and operating systems by staying orthogonal to the changes in these systems.
- We implemented a prototype of GUARDMR demonstrating that the access control can be regulated at the level of key-values when unstructured datasets (e.g., tweets, crawled images, etc.) are processed, and even if the untrusted users can use their own preprocessing functions and data types. Our empirical results indicate that GUARDMR enforces FGAC in Hadoop while incurring very small overhead

The rest of the paper is organized as follows. Background knowledge is summarized in Sec. 2. The thread model is discusses in Sec. 3. The access control model is formally defined for the MapReduce in Sec. 4. The overview of system is explained in Sec. 5. The design of our implementation is detailed in Sec. 6. Our empirical results are evaluated in Sec. 7. Related studies are discussed in Sec. 8. Finally, the paper is concluded in Sec. 9.

2. BACKGROUND

This section provides the background information on MapReduce and object constraint language (OCL), which are two core technologies that GUARDMR is based on.

2.1 MapReduce Model

MapReduce is a programming model and associated implementations for processing and storing large data sets [7]. The model is based on processing different chunks of large input files in parallel using commodity hardwares. The MapReduce tasks—the processes separately handling the chunks of data—are defined by the users as *Map* and *Reduce* functions. These tasks compose a computation environment that can handle the datasets without predefined structures that are hard to process with the traditional databases. This flexibility makes it a popular system that more than half of the Fortune 50 uses Apache Hadoop [8].

The MapReduce model can be expressed as 5-step parallel computations: (1) *Pre-process:* The input data is pre-processed to form a valid format for the subsequent steps. For example in Hadoop, RecordReader classes read the input from HDFS and produce key-value pairs. (2) *Map:* The input key-value pairs are processed by producing intermediate key-value pairs. (3) *Shuffle:* The intermediate pairs are transfered to the reduce functions by assigning the pairs having the same key to the same reduce functions. (4) *Reduce:* The intermediate pairs are processed by forming smaller set of pairs. (5) *Post-process:* The outputs of reduce functions are combined and written to HDFS.

2.2 The Object Constraint Language (OCL)

The Object Constraint Language (OCL) [9] is a formal language supporting the specification of structural and behavioral properties of elements into target UML models. The language is commonly used for the specification of class invariants constraints, and pre and post conditions to the execution of operations. However, OCL also allows the specification of new class operations and attributes not natively provided by the classes of the target model, and derivation and initialization expressions related to class attributes.

Although the language natively targets UML models, advanced OCL frameworks such as Dresden OCL Toolkit [10], support the specification and evaluation of OCL specifications on Java models. Following this line, in this paper we use Dresden OCL Toolkit to automatically integrate into a Java application 1) enforcement mechanisms of OCL constraints, and 2) complementary structural and behavioral properties. OCL Toolkit allows considering a set of Java classes as the target model with respect to which OCL specifications are defined. It provides tools to automatically derive AspectJ code from the OCL specifications, which enforces the specified OCL constraints and implements the specified class operations, attributes, derivation and initialization expressions. The bytecode of the generated aspects is weaved into the bytecode of the classes composing the target Java model such that the complementary features are integrated as native properties of the target classes. A more exhaustive explanation of the approach is provided in Sec. 6.

3. THREAT MODEL

In this paper, we consider the following attack scenario for general MapReduce model: Many unstructured Big Data resources, possibly containing sensitive and private information, are stored in a MapReduce system. Multiple users with different roles process the data resources via the MapReduce jobs. The jobs contain ad-hoc Map and Reduce functions along with user-defined pre-processing functions and data types. The users are regarded as untrusted and have malicious intentions, e.g., they try to disclose the sensitive entries that their roles do not allow to access. A set of trusted agents, administrators, try to prevent sensitive information leakages. To that end, they dynamically create the authorized data views for each user's role and the data resource residing in the MapReduce system such that when the MapReduce jobs access the data resources via the legitimate MapReduce interface, the filters specified by the administrators dynamically creates authorized views on the datasets.

The MapReduce systems provide only one legitimate method to access the input data for submitted MapReduce jobs, which is through a preprocessing function that breaks the data into key-value pairs (e.g., RecordReader interface in Apache Hadoop). However, the jobs include arbitrary code and data, where a malicious user can easily place a malicious code to circumvent RecordReader. We have performed two attacks to show the feasibility of this vulnerability. In the first attack, we have placed a code inside a MapReduce job that accesses to raw input data (or any data stored in the corresponding data node) via Java I/O API. In the second attack, the malicious code opens a socket as a backdoor to communicate with our malicious server. Both attacks show that the MapReduce jobs must be confined to prevent these security breaches and policy violations. There are numerous studies [11, 12, 13] in the literature to circumscribe untrusted codes and programs. These studies can be employed to immunize MapReduce system against such attacks by potentially malicious MapReduce jobs.

Since the users are not trusted, the data preprocessing functions and data types submitted by the malicious users may try to obfuscate/encrypt the data to circumvent access control system and the authorized views. To prevent this possibility, the used data preprocessing functions and data types need to be analyzed in advance by the trusted security agents, the administrator. The safe data types are allowed to be used in the MapReduce jobs and stored by our access control model. Unless the users provide their new data types in advance for security analysis, those types are not accepted by our access control model and conservatively rejected by GUARDMR.

GUARDMR is defined in such a way that, if Map-Reduce jobs access data resources only through the RecordReader interface, and the jobs are executed in a secure sandbox, security and completeness requirements of data management systems are fulfilled. More precisely, GUARDMR is defined to fulfil the *security* requirement, based on which it has to forbid Map-Reduce jobs to access data which according to the specified access control policies cannot be accessed. In addition, GUARDMR is defined to satisfy the *completeness* requirement, based on which it has to ensure that Map-Reduce jobs access data if the specified access control policies authorize the access.

After introducing the access control model proposed for GUARDMR in Section 4, and describing how GUARDMR implements and allows one to integrate FGAC into Hadoop in Section 5 and 6, in Section 6.3 we will state *security* and *completeness* properties that prove that GUARDMR satisfies the above mentioned correctness requirements.

4. THE ACCESS CONTROL MODEL

The proposed fine-grained access control model includes both elements specifically designed for MapReduce scenarios and selected core features of the proposed NIST standard for role based access control [14]. Let us start focusing on the MapReduce related aspects. Data resources accessed by MapReduce jobs are modeled as a collection of data records characterized by the fields *key* and *value*, each representing a data type possibly composed of several fields. The adopted types depend on the characteristics of an application scenario (the users can define their own ad-hoc data types).

DEFINITION 1. *A data resource Dr is denoted as a pair ⟨Id, Lp⟩, where Id is the identifier of the data resource (e.g., a file name), and Lp is an ordered list of pairs ⟨k:K, v:V⟩, where k and v are instances of the data types K and V, respectively.*

The key-value pairs composing a given data resource are all modeled by the same data types and thus are characterized by the same type of properties. As such, assuming that *typeOf(o)* is a function that derives the type of a generic instance *o*, we get that $\forall\langle k, v\rangle, \langle k', v'\rangle \in Dr.Lp(k \neq k' \wedge v \neq v') \rightarrow$ *typeOf(k)=typeOf(k')* $\wedge$ *typeOf(v)=typeOf(v')*[1].

Example 1 Let Tw_{ds} be the identifier of a dataset Dr_{tw} of Twitter messages specified as a textual file. Each message *m* in Dr_{tw}

[1]Hereafter we refer to a component *cp* of an element *el* with the notation $el.cp$, therefore $Dr.Lp$ denotes the component *Lp* of Dr.

contains arbitrary text with no predefined format. The considered data resource is therefore represented by means of the tuple $\langle Tw_{ds}, \bigcup_{m \in Dr_{tw}} \langle k_m, v_m \rangle \rangle$, where k_m: *Integer* specifies the progressive number of the message within the dataset, whereas v_m:*String* models the message content.

Filter is the key element of our access control model and it is used to build authorized views on the protected data resources. The application of a filter results into a view on the resource *Dr*, which consists of a set of *key-value* pairs. The new generated pairs can be different with respect to cardinality and values, from the original pairs. Let *Lp* denote the set of key-value pairs characterizing *Dr* and *Lp'* be the collection of pairs derived through the application of filter *F* on *Dr*. *F* is defined in such a way that, for each pair $\langle k', v' \rangle$ in *Lp'*, there exists a pair $\langle k, v \rangle$ in *Dr.Lp* such that the data types characterizing *k'* and *v'* are the same as the ones of *k* and *v*, and the values of *k'* and *v'* are derived from those of *k* and *v*. The derivation is achieved by means of the *key-derivation* function *dk*: $K \rightarrow K$, and the *value derivation* function *dv*: $V \rightarrow V$, respectively defined for the data types *K* and *V* characterizing the pairs in *Dr.Lp*. More precisely, $\forall \langle k', v' \rangle \in Lp' \rightarrow \exists \langle k, v \rangle \in Lp \wedge$ *typeOf(k)=typeOf(k')* $\wedge$ *typeOf(v)=typeOf(v')*$\wedge k' = dk(k) \wedge v' = dv(v)$. Given a key-value pair $\langle k, v \rangle$ in *Dr.Lp*, due to the filter application, either $\langle k, v \rangle$ is mapped to a key value pair $\langle k', v' \rangle$ in *Lp'* through the derivation functions or it is not used to build the authorized view. The selection of key value pairs is achieved by the *pair selection* function *ps*: $\langle K \times V \rangle \rightarrow$ *boolean*.

DEFINITION 2. *A filter F is denoted as a tuple ⟨Id,ps,dk,dv⟩, where Id is the filter identifier, whereas ps, dk and dv respectively identify a pair selection, key derivation and value derivation functions. The rationale of filter application is the execution of a function ff: dom(ps) → dom(ps), which operates on the abstract representation Lp of a data resource Dr in such a way that* $ff = \bigcup_{\langle k,v \rangle \in \Gamma} \langle dk(k), dv(v) \rangle$, *where* $\Gamma = \{\langle k, v \rangle \in Dr.Lp | ps(k, v)\}$.

Example 2 Let F be a filter operating on the representations of data resources specified as a pairs of textual fields (i.e., *K=V=String*), and let us suppose that F builds a view within which phone numbers are obfuscated and pairs containing values that include email addresses are pruned out. Let dk and dv denote the *key derivation* and *value derivation* functions of F. dk is defined to return the current value of the analyzed key, i.e. $\forall k : Integer \rightarrow dk(k) = k$, whereas dv is defined in such a way to obfuscate phone numbers possibly specified within the analyzed value. More precisely, let *split* be a function that partitions a string into a list of textual tokens, and let *isPN* and *isEm* be boolean functions that check, by means of regular expressions, whether a textual token matches the format of a telephone number and an email address, respectively, and let Σ denote a string concatenation operation. Then, dv is defined as follows:

$$dv(v) = \sum_{t \in split(v)} \begin{cases} \text{“***”}, \text{if isPN(t)=true} \\ t \quad \text{, else} \end{cases}$$

Finally, let ps denote the *pair selection* function of F. ps is defined in such a way that it is only satisfied when *v* does not contain an email addresses. More precisely,

$$ps(k, v) = \bigwedge_{t \in split(v)} \neg isEm(t)$$

The above three functions are composed to form the filter tuple $\langle F, ps, dk, dv \rangle$. Filters are assigned to data resources and authorized to users that cover given roles.

DEFINITION 3. *A filter authorization is denoted as a triple ⟨Dr,F,R⟩, where Dr identifies a data resource, F is the identifier of a filter, and R the identifier of a role.*

Example 3 Let R be a role and let Fa be a filter authorization $\langle Tw_{ds}, F, R \rangle$. Suppose that Fa grants users covering role R the permit to access the data resource Dr_{tw} (referred to in Example 1) through the application of filter F illustrated in Example 2. Due to the filter application all phone numbers are obfuscated and messages containing an email addresses are pruned out.

Role and role related conceptual elements included in our model correspond to the elements presented in [14], as such, hereafter we only mention them. User represents the straightforward concept of a stakeholder who submits a MapReduce Job and it is modeled as a pair ⟨*Id, Ps*⟩, where *Id* is the identifier of the user within the system, whereas *Ps* models an optional set of properties (e.g., name). Role models a set of users that cover the same functionalities within an organization and therefore they should have the same authorized views on data resources. Roles are hierarchically organized as inverted trees. Senior roles implicitly inherit the filter authorizations specified for their ancestors (junior roles), and junior roles acquire the user membership of their descendant roles. A role R is modeled as a pair ⟨*Id, Ar*⟩, where *Id* is the role identifier and *Ar* is the identifier of the ancestor (more junior) role that precedes R in the inverted tree.

User sessions represent execution scenarios within which a user activates a set of roles among those he/she is authorized to play with the aim to execute specific jobs. A session is modeled as triple ⟨*Id, U, Rs*⟩, where *Id* is the session identifier, *U* the user identifier, and *Rs* the set of roles activated by U.

Static Separation of Duty (SSD) and Dynamic Separation of Duty (DSD) prevent users from covering multiple conflicting roles. Both are modeled as a pair $\langle Rs, n \rangle$, where *n* represents the maximum number of roles belonging to the roles set *Rs*, which can be covered by the same user. SSD constrains the roles assignable to a user in any scenario, whereas DSD regulates the role activation within specific user sessions.

The conceptual elements characterizing an application scenario are grouped into several sets: *Fs* collects the filters; *FAs*, the filter authorizations; *DRs*, the data resources; *DTs*, the considered data types for keys and values; *DFs*, the key and value derivation functions, *PSs*, the pair selection functions; *Us*, the involved users; *Rs*, the involved roles; *Ua*, the user assignments; *Ss*, the user sessions; *SSDs/DSDs*, the static/dynamic separation of duty constraints. A set of administrative and review functions allow one to access and possibly modify the elements collected into these sets.

In addition, our access control model supports most of the RBAC administrative functions presented in [14]. For instance, dedicated functions allow one to add or delete a user or a role, to add or delete the inheritance relationship between roles, assign or deassign a user to a role, create or delete a user session, add or drop an active role to/from a session, create or delete a SSD/DSD constraint, add or remove a role to/from a SSD/DSD constraint. The interested readers can refer to [14] for the thorough description of these functions.

5. SYSTEM OVERVIEW

GuardMR is composed of two main components: access control module and reference monitor. The access control model presented in Sec. 4 and its administrative functions are realized as a Java application in the access control module, where the conceptual entities (e.g., Roles, Filter) are implemented as Java classes. The management of the Java classes that model the access control entities characterizing an application scenario is handled by the methods that implement the administrative functions of the access control model (e.g., add/modify/delete role, filter). These methods generate and manipulate classes using the facilities of *Javassist* [15], a class library for Java bytecodes manipulation. An automatic code generation approach is used to integrate into the Access control module mechanisms that enforce the necessary conditions (e.g., add authorization $\langle Dr,F,R \rangle$ unless there is already one in the list of filter authorizations *FAs*) to the execution of administrative functions as OCL constraints. A similar approach is also used for the generation of code implementing pair selection, key and value derivation functions specified as OCL operations. Dresden OCL Toolkit is used to automatically generate AspectJ code from OCL statements, which is then automatically integrated.

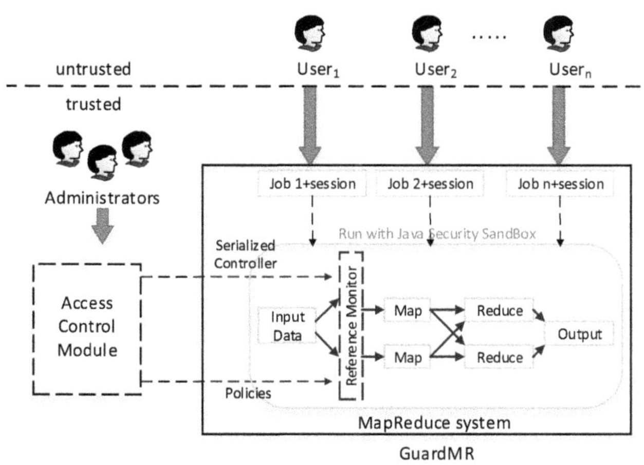

Figure 1: GuardMR Setup

The reference monitor enforces the specified security policies to the underlying MapReduce system. It needs to interact with access control module to derive information related to the policies to be enforced. To that end, all conceptual classes and complementing AspectJ code are gathered by access control module in an umbrella class, *Controller*, which is serialized into the HDFS to be reachable from all distributed nodes of MapReduce system. The reference monitor interposes the data flow of MapReduce just after pre-process of input data and before map functions (see Sec. 2.1). By using the controller class, it assigns the authorized filter to the job and creates an authorized view of data accordingly. This form of reference monitor achieves high modularity and independence employing AspectJ dynamic weaving facilities to intercept MapReduce core-function calls, which does not modify the source code of MapReduce and stays orthogonal to the changes in the MapReduce system (see Sec. 6.2).

Fig. 1 shows the overview of GuardMR setup, where thick and dashed arrows indicate the actions of administrators/users and GuardMR respectively, and dashed boxes indicate two modules of GuardMR. In this setup, GuardMR has to intercept all outside communication of MapReduce system so that the untrusted users cannot directly access to the MapReduce system other than designated interfaces. The administrators manage the access control module and specify the security policies through it. They are also responsible from the data and add/delete/modify the files in the MapReduce system.

GuardMR system is transparent to the users such that they write MapReduce jobs as usual and send it to GuardMR along with the required parameters, such as input/output identifiers and job specific variables. A submitted job is first inspected on whether it contains malicious code or not. The jobs containing calls to native libraries (e.g., Java's native code) or self-generating code (e.g., Java Reflection API) are subject to security analysis (self-modifying codes, e.g., reflection and unorthodox data transformations —encryption and obfuscation of plain data in employed data types—are always subject to investigation in computer security; often computer viruses follow these approaches). If the job is accepted, a session object containing the role(s) activated by the user is injected into the job. Injection is carried out by means of the private inter-type declaration facilities of AspectJ, which cannot be tampered by the job. Then, GuardMR runs the job on behalf of the user, and by doing so leverage the current file-level access control policy of MapReduce system. Thus, the outputs of jobs are protected by *Discretionary access control (DAC)* mechanism enforced by current MapReduce systems (e.g., Apache Hadoop after version 1.X). Note that the output of MapReduce jobs are not subject to the FGAC proposed in this paper as they are the property of users submitting the corresponding MapReduce job. Coarse-grained file-based DAC is more suitable for these outputs. Furthermore, the submitted job is run by GuardMR in a secure sandbox to prevent the illegitimate data accesses circumventing the enforcement mechanism. In the current implementation, GuardMR employs Java Security [11] to restrict the jobs (e.g., accesses to the data resources through Java I/O library are subject to Java security policies). We are planning to support native libraries in the future by integrating GuardMR with the Robusta system[13].

6. THE FRAMEWORK

In this section, we present the details of GuardMR framework, which consists of two main modules: a MapReduce independent access control module realizing the model described in Sec. 4, and a reference monitor designed to enforce the proposed access control model in Apache Hadoop.

6.1 The access control module

Within the access control module, the conceptual elements of the access control model (e.g., Roles, Filters, etc.) have been implemented as Java classes.

Filter is a generic abstract class parametrized over the types of key and value pairs of a data resource. *Filter* declares the abstract methods *dk*, *dv* and *ps*, which logically correspond to the derivation and pair selection functions of the access control model (see Def. 2) and are implemented by concrete extensions of this abstract class specified for a given scenario.

Other classes (e.g., Role, FilterAuthorization, Session, etc.) are defined in such a way to specify the components of the homonymous elements of the access control model (see Sec. 4) as class attributes. For instance, a filter authorization triple $\langle Dr,F,R \rangle$ in Def. 3 is represented as a FilterAuthorization class including the attributes of types *String*, *Class<? extends Filter>* and *Class<? extends Role>*, which keep track of the authorized data resource, filter and role, respectively.

As showed in Sec. 5, Class *Controller* represents the core of the entire module as it keeps track of all elements that characterize an access control scenario and implements all administrative and review functions mentioned in Sec. 5. *Controller* attributes group conceptual elements of access control model based on their types. For instance, *fS:Set<Class<? extends Filter> >* groups the scenario's filters, *faS: Set<Class<? extends FilterAuthorization> >* collects the filter authorizations, and *dmS: Set<Class<?> >* keeps track of the data manipulation classes. The implementation of review functions is straightforward since they only select elements from the collections of elements stored within *Controller*. Similarly, the implementation of administrative functions is also elementary as most of these functions simply add, update and remove elements from/to *Controller*.

The necessary conditions to the execution of administrative functions mentioned in Sec. 5 (e.g., add authorization $\langle Dr,F,R \rangle$ unless there is already one in the list of filter authorizations *FAs*) are realized by means of aspect-oriented programming. Firstly, the constraints are specified as OCL expressions, and corresponding AspectJ code is automatically derived from the expressions by using the facilities of the Dresden OCL Toolkit. Then, the derived AspectJ code is in-lined into the *Controller* class, where they complement the features of the Java classes in the application model including *pointcuts* that intercept the methods invocation and check if the conditions are satisfied, altering the execution flow in case the conditions are not met.

In addition to the classes implementing the conceptual elements of access control model, the access control module includes classes that are used to generate filters as extension of the previously mention abstract class *Filter*. These include *data type* classes, which model the types of keys and values that filters can handle (set by the users in the jobs), and *data manipulation* classes, that implement the functions able to process the data types referred to by keys and values, which are later used by filters to build authorized views on the target resources. For instance, in application scenarios concerning textual resources, a data manipulation class can include string handler methods. Data type and data manipulation classes can be either predefined Java classes of the MapReduce system or external class libraries, or ad-hoc defined Java classes. The access control module also allows the administrators to import external library code after a proper security analysis. The imported code is considered as trusted, and stored among the classes referred to by *Controller*. For instance, it is possible to import regular expression handlers defined within the external library Jakarta/Regexp [16].

Filter specification is performed by the administrators through concrete extensions of the abstract class *Filter* by providing the implementation of abstract methods *dk*, *dv*, and *ps* as OCL statements. Concrete filters are automatically defined by GUARDMR for a given pair of *data type* classes *K* and *V* and include a set of attributes *inF*, which refer to the instances of *data manipulation* classes used to handle the processing of data items of type *K* and *V*. To that end, the access control module provides editing functionalities supporting the definition of new data type, data manipulation, and filter classes. Administrators are not in charge of directly defining the source code of these classes. In contrast, they use editing tools in the access control module aimed to supervise and constrain the definition, raise the level of abstraction at which the implementation is defined, and ease the definition activity. New classes are generated at runtime with a two steps process. In the first phase, the skeleton of the classes is generated using Javassist facilities [15], which allows defining the bytecode of non existent classes starting from the abstract descriptions of the class structure specified via instances of the Javassist class *CtClass*. The second phase targets the automatic definition of the derivation and pair selection methods that are then integrated within the newly generated filter class skeletons, as well as the optional definition of data manipulation functions.The definition approach for derivation, pair selection, and data manipulation methods is based on the OCL specification of these functions and the automatic generation of AspectJ code implementing them. The bytecode of the generated aspects is then weaved with the one of the previously defined classes.

Example 4 Let us suppose that Bob, a system admin, aims at generating a filter that sanitizes phone numbers possibly specified within the unstructured text included in the *value* component of key-value pairs. As such, Bob starts generating the concrete filter class *PhoneFilter*. As none of the existing data manipulation classes defined within the considered access control scenario specifies proper string management functions, Bob introduces the skeleton of a data manipulation class denoted *TextHandler*. Let us suppose that a string manipulation library includes the class *RegExHandler* which provides regular expressions management functionalities. In particular, *RegExHandler* includes: *regex(s,rx)*, a method checking if *s* matches the regular expression *rx*, and *split(s,ss)*, a method tokenizing *s* using *ss* as separator. *TextHandler* is defined in such a way to include an attribute *rh* of type *RegExHandler*. Bob also defines the OCL specification of the *TextHandler* method *sanitize*, which is shown in Listing 1.

Listing 1: TextHandler methods

```
context TextHandler
def: sanitize(s: String, rx: String)
 : String = if self.rh.regex(s,rx)
              then '***' else s endif
```

The method receives a textual token *s* and a regular expression *rx* as input, and if *s* matches the regular expression *rx*, it returns the constant string "***" sanitizing the original string, otherwise it returns the original string *s*. In a similar way, Bob also specifies the method *tokenize(s,rx)*, which tokenizes the input string *s* using the regular expression *rx* as token separator. *PhoneFilter* is generated as including the attribute *th* of type *TextHandler*, the newly generated data manipulation class. The method *dv* of *PhoneFilter* is specified to tokenize the string received as input and to apply the sanitization to each composing token. The OCL code of *dv* is shown in List. 2.

Listing 2: PhoneFilter methods

```
context PhoneSanitizer::
dv(value: String):String
body: th.tokenize(value,'\\s')->
 iterate(el: String; ret:String='' |
  ret+ th.sanitize(el,'\\d{3}-\\d{3}-\\d{4}'))
```

Bob does not explicitly specify the method *dk* of *PhoneFilter*, since it does not alter the key component of the analyzed pair. In this case, the OCL specification of *dk*, which is automatically derived by the access control module, simply returns the original key which is specified as input parameter of *dk*. In a similar way, Bob does not provide the OCL specification of the pair selection method *ps*. In this case, the automatically derived OCL specification returns true for each key-value pair received as input. Since the OCL specifications of *dk* and *ps* are straightforward we do not report them here. Once the OCL specification has been completed, Bob invokes the code generation functionality of the access control module, which is based on the AspectJ code generation facilities of Dresden OCL toolkit. After generating the code, the new classes are registered within Controller and can be therefore referred to by *FilterAuthorizations*.

The application of a filter $\langle Id,ps,dk,dv \rangle$ on a data resource Dr results in creation of a data view. The number of authorized views which have to be specified via OCL is proportional to the number of roles and allowed data types. In other words, for each type of key-value pairs and role, a filter needs to be defined by the administrators. This requirement is similar to the FGAC policies of the relational database management systems, where for each relation and role a policy need to be defined by the administrators. Moreover, for new data types which are a variety of existing data type, the existing filters can be used with minor modification due to high level of abstraction of OCL. For example, *PhoneFilter* given in Listing 2 can easily be adapted to the data type *Text* as Text data type is based on the data type *String*.

6.2 Reference Monitor

A reference monitor regulates the execution of MapReduce jobs based on the access control policies specified using the access control module presented in Sec. 6.1, which are automatically serialized by GUARDMR as shared data resources in the HDFS. The monitor is implemented as a Java application by mean of Aspect-oriented Programming. It operates within the host Hadoop system interacting with the access control module to derive information related to the policies to be enforced.

The monitor constrains the submitted jobs to access data resources by means of authorized views built by filters. The monitor automatically integrates the filters into the submitted MapReduce jobs through the enhancement of the specified *RecordReader* classes. A MapReduce job specifies a *RecordReader RR* class, which defines the logic of how the mappers access the target data resources. *RR* is substituted by the monitor with an automatically generated enhanced RecordReader RR', which integrates into *RR* methods the execution of derivation and pair selection functions specified for an authorized filter. Filters are assigned based on the filter authorizations specified within the access control module, according to the roles activated by the users and the type of key-value pairs that are processed by the mappers.

RecordReader is a generic abstract class parametrized over the generic types K and V. For each *InputSplit* (a Hadoop class modeling a portion of data resource), a given instance of *RecordReader* builds a representation of the considered portion of resource as a list of specified key-value pairs. Mappers are allowed to access the pairs by means of *RecordReader* methods. *RecordReader* specifies, among others, the methods *getCurrentKey*, *getCurrentValue*, and *nextKeyValue*, which allow accessing the pairs characterizing the abstract representation of the considered InputSplit. The access to key-value pairs is regulated by means of an iterator operating over the pairs of the collection. *nextKeyValue* checks if there exists a pair that follows the one referred to by the iterator, and if this condition is satisfied, it moves the iterator pointer to the next pair, whereas *getCurrentKey* and *getCurrentValue* return the key and value component of the currently referred pair, respectively. Enhanced *RecordReaders* redefines these three methods by integrating the execution of pair selection and key/value derivation functions of authorized filters.

The monitor has been implemented as an AspectJ *aspect* responsible for generating the extended *RecordReader*. The aspect intercepts the invocation of method *createRecordReader* performed during the initialization phase of the MapReduce job, which targets the generation of an instance of the *RecordReader* class specified for the job. The interception is achieved by means of the AspectJ pointcut *formatIntercept* shown in Listing 3.

Listing 3: The monitor's Pointcut formatIntercept

```
pointcut formatIntercept(InputFormat i,
    InputSplit s, TaskAttemptContext t):
  call(* InputFormat.createRecordReader(...))
    && target(i) && args(s,t);
```

The enhanced *RecordReader* is defined by means of a simple generation process implemented by an *advice* specified for the pointcut *formatIntercept*. Listing 4 shows the pseudocode of a simplified extract of the advice.

Listing 4: The monitor's Advice

```
RecordReader around(InputFormat i,
 InputSplit s,TaskAttemptContext t):
formatIntercept(i,s,t){
 try{
  Controller ctrl= Controller.getModel(ctrlf);
  Class<? extends Filter> fC=
   ctrl.getAuthorizedFilter(s,t);
  RecordReader rr =  proceed(i,s,t);
  Class<? extends RecordReader> eRR=
   ClassFactory.generateERR(rr.getClass(),fC);
  return (RecordReader) eRR.newInstance();
 }...
}
```

The generation is carried out by means of a sequential process composed of 4 activities: 1) deserialization of the access control information specified by a serialized Controller object stored in the HDFS; 2) assignment of the authorized filter; 3) derivation of the enhanced *RecordReader* class that integrates the authorized filter; and, finally, 4) generation of an instance of the enhanced *RecordReader* which is returned to the caller. If during the execution of the advice any of the above mentioned activities throws an exception (e.g., no authorized filter has been found), the *RecordReader* creation is aborted and the execution of the job is conservatively blocked. Note that these exceptions cannot be caught by the jobs as the exceptions are thrown from Hadoop core-layer before the job code begins to execute. For example, if an unknown RecordReader class (i.e., a class which is not tested or analyzed by the administrators) is used by the job, the activity 3 throws an exception as an untrusted RR can try to obfuscate/encrypt the data to circumvent the filters.

Listing 5: Function *getAuthorizedFilter*

```
Filter getAuthorizedFilter
(InputSplit s, TaskAttemptContext t)
  throws NoFilter{
 Set(FilterAuthorization) faS=
  this.getFilterAuthorizations();
 String dr = ((FileSplit)s).getPath();
 Set(Class<? extends Role>) rS=
  t.getSession().getActiveRoles();
 Class K = t.getKeyClass();
 Class V = t.getValueClass();
 for(FilterAuthorization fa:faS){
  if(this.checkDr(fa.obj,dr) &&
    this.checkRole(fa.cr,rS) &&
    this.checkType(fa.getK(),K) &&
    this.checkType(fa.getV(),V)){
   return fa.FilterClass;
  }
 }throw new NoFilter();
}
```

The path of the file that contains the access control policies and related elements, which are stored within the serialized instance of *Controller*, is set as a configurable property of the monitor.[2] The deserialization is handled by the static method *getModel* of class *Controller*. The function is straightforward and exploits basic Java IO serialization APIs. The authorized filter is determined via the Controller method *getAuthorizedFilter*, whose pseudocode is shown in Listing 5, through the analysis of the filter authorizations collected within *Controller*.

The list of authorizations is derived through the execution of the review function *getAuthorizedFilter* of *Controller*. Each authorization *fa* belonging to the list *faS* is separately analyzed. The goal is to identify a *FilterAuthorization* whose components comply with the information derived from the job execution context.

In order to consider a *FilterAuthorization fa* as a possible applicable authorization, the data resource component *obj* and the role information *cr* of *fa* have to match the data resource and role(s) of the running job. Hadoop API allows determining the data resource accessed by the submitted job through the analysis of the *InputSplit* accessed by the *RecordReader* under definition (i.e., the one whose instantiation has been intercepted). However, role information is not directly accessible through Hadoop APIs, as Hadoop is only aware of the identifier of user who has submitted the job. To derive the role[3] that has been activated by the involved user, the monitor retrieves the session object which was injected into the job when it was accepted by GUARDMR (see Sec. 5). To this end, the reference monitor invokes the *getSession()* method of *TaskAttemptContext*, which is injected via AspectJ as private inter-type declared method (the job cannot access this method since it is declared as private).

In Hadoop, a data resource can be read by the distinct jobs parameterized over different and possibly custom data types (e.g., a textual dataset can be read as values having *Text* and *String* classes). Some of them may have malicious forms (e.g., obfuscated and encrypted) aimed at bypassing filters. For this reason, GuardMR exclusively allows the definition of concrete filter classes parametrized over data types preventively approved by system administrators. The set of allowed data types is managed by administrators on the basis of application scenarios requirements. The reference monitor extract information related to the data type handled by the submitted job by accessing the corresponding *TaskAttemptContext* object. If an unsupported data type is detected, the job is conservatively rejected.

Listing 6: ERR methods

```
public K getCurrentKey(){
 return f.dk(super.getCurrentKey());
}
public V getCurrentValue(){
 return f.dv(super.getCurrentValue());
}
public boolean nextKeyValue(){
 boolean nkv=false;
 while((nkv=super.nextKeyValue()) &&
  !f.ps(super.getCurrentKey(),
        super.getCurrentValue())
 ){;}
 return nkv;
}
```

If all above checks succeed, then the filter authorization *fa* is applicable to the job submission request, and its filter class is integrated into the enhanced *RecordReader*. More precisely, as shown in Listing 4, after identifying the target filter class *fC*, the advice generates an instance *rr* of the original *RecordReader* class referred to by the submitted job. Afterwords, the *ClassFactory*[4] method *generateERR* is invoked to generate an enhanced *RecordReader* class extending the class referred to by *rr*. More precisely, let *RR* be the *RecordReader* class specified as input of *generateERR* (i.e., *RR* corresponds to *rr.getClass()*), and let *K* and *V* be the types of the keys and values referred to by *RR*. The enhanced *RecordReader* generated by *generateERR* is a class *ERR* that extends *RR*, specified in such a way to include an attribute *f* of type *fC* and to define the methods *getCurrentKey*, *getCurrentValue* and *nextKeyValue* based on the corresponding methods of *RR* and the pair selection and derivation functions of *fC*. The pseudocode of these methods is shown in Listing 6.

Finally, the advice generates an instance of the derived enhanced *RecordReader* class *eRR* which is returned to the caller, and will be used by a Mapper to access the target data resource. Class polymorphism ensures that mappers invoke the enhanced methods on the returned object as it was an instance of the original *RecordReader* class.

6.3 Security Analysis

The correctness of GUARDMR is stated by Theorems 1 and 2 introduced in the remaining of this section, whose formal proofs are presented in Appendix A. Proofs rely on two main assumptions: (1) MapReduce jobs access data resources only through the RecordReader interface, for which GUARDMR runs the jobs in secure sandbox; (2) The code generation and byte-code manipulation activities are correctly performed by the Dresden OCL toolkit and the Javassist framework. In addition, correctness proof also relies on the correct implementation of administrative functions. To that end, the access control model specifies pre and post conditions to the execution of these functions, and the AspectJ code automatically derived from the OCL specification of these constraints have been integrated into the access control module to check the conditions at run-time.

The basic rationale behind Theorem 1 is that if access control policies forbid the access to a data item *D*, GUARDMR does not allow Map-Reduce jobs to access *D*. More precisely, let us consider an application scenario *S'* where a user *U* submits a job *J* to Hadoop system that integrates GuardMR. Let *R* be the role activated by *U* within a user session. Let us suppose *J* accesses a data *D* by means of a RecordReader *RR*, which builds a view on *D* composed of key-value of type *K* and *V*. Let us assume that within S' there exists a filter authorization *fa* that authorizes users covering the role *R* to access the data resource *D* through the application of filter *F*.

THEOREM 1 (SECURITY). *Within* S', *there does not exist any key-value pair* $\langle k', v' \rangle$ *accessed by a mapper of J which is not derived from a pair* $\langle k, v \rangle$ *generated by RR such that* $ps(k,v)=true \wedge dk(k)=k' \wedge dv(v)=v'$, *where filter* $F=\langle Id,ps,dk,dv \rangle$ *is assigned to J by* GUARDMR.

The rationale behind Theorem 2 is that GUARDMR does not prevent a Map-Reduce job *J* from accessing a data item *D* if the access control policies specified for *D* grants *J* the access to *D*. For the purposes of specifying the theorem statement, in addition to scenario *S'*, let us now consider a scenario *S* within which *U* submits *J* to an Hadoop system that does not integrate GUARDMR.

[2]For space limitations we do not describe here how customizable Monitor properties are handled.

[3]In this paper, we assume that a single role is activated during each session.

[4]ClassFactory is a complementary class of the monitor which collects methods that, relying on Javassist facilities, allow the automatic definition the enhanced RecordReader classes.

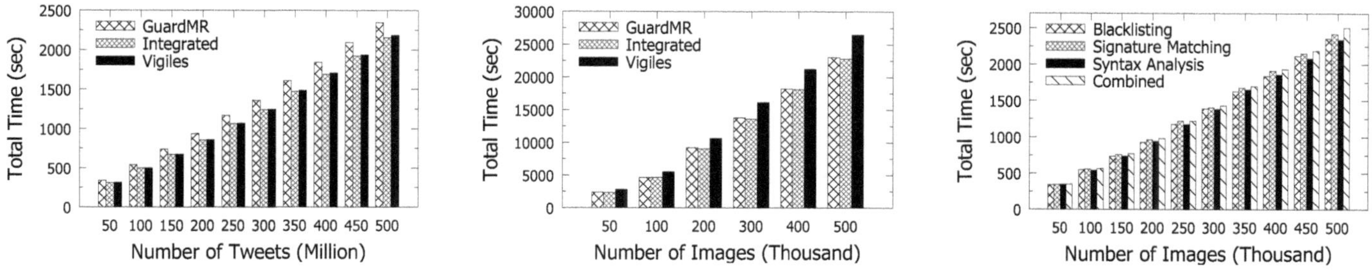

(a) Performance on Text Dataset (b) Performance on Image Dataset (c) Performance of Four Sample Filters

Figure 2: Performance of Three Systems for Single End-user Setup

THEOREM 2 (COMPLETENESS). *If a key-value pair* $\langle k, v\rangle$ *is accessed by a Mapper of J in S and* $\langle k, v\rangle$ *satisfies the pair selection function ps of F,* $\langle k, v\rangle$ *has to be in the view of D derived by the enhanced RecordReader RR′ of J in S′.*

7. EVALUATION

We evaluated the efficiency and scalability of GUARDMR via a series of experiments. We first explain the experiment setup, datasets, scenarios, then present the empirical results.

7.1 Setup

The experiments are conducted on a cluster containing a master and 6 slave nodes. The master node has an Intel Xeon 8 cores processor with 32 GB of main memory. Each slave node consists of an Intel Xeon 8 cores processor with 2TB disk space and 32GB of main memory. Hadoop 1.2.1 and AspectJ 1.7.4 are installed on each node in the cluster. To enable runtime weaving required for GUARDMR, Hadoop is configured to run the MapReduce tasks with the load-time weaving JAR of AspectJ (i.e., *aspectjweaver.jar*); the security policies in the form of aspects are stored in the HDFS. Note that GUARDMR is exceptionally modular such that any Hadoop distribution or version (e.g., Hadoop version 1.X and 2.X, Clouderan etc.) could be used in the experiments.

7.2 Datasets

We performed our experiments on two real-world Big Data corpora, which are sufficiently large enough to measure the overhead of GUARDMR. The first dataset used in the experiments is based on textual data. We used a Twitter corpus, which is crawled from January 13, 2013 to July 17, 2013. The dataset contains hundreds of million tweets posted from all over the world in many different languages. The tweets use a diverse set of character-encoding schemes, such as US-ASCII, GBK, EUC-JP. The content of tweets are varying from textual messages to URLs and different kinds of smilies. We randomly sampled the corpus and formed 10 input files stored as block-compressed text files in HDFS. The files contains 50M, 100M, ... , 500M tweets where the compressed version of files allocate approximately 5GB, 10GB, ... , 50GB space in HDFS, respectively.

The second dataset used in the experiments is based on image data. We used an image corpus containing images in various formats (e.g., JPEG, PNG and BMP) crawled via Google images. The contents of images are varying from human photos taken with phones to graphic-based iconic figures. We randomly sampled the corpus and formed 6 input files, where the images organized as *SequenceFiles* containing the pairs of an identifier and image binary in their original encoding as key-value pairs. The files are composed of 50K, 100K, 200K, 300K, 400K and 500K images, allocating 28 GB, 56 GB, 84 GB, 112 GB and 140 GB in HDFS, respectively. Note that since we observed a constant overhead percentage proportional to size of datasets in our experiments, we did not repeat the experiments on bigger datasets.

7.3 Scenarios

We created two scenarios for Twitter and image datasets. For Twitter datasets, the users submit a MapReduce job that counts how often the words occur in a given input file. To that end, the popular benchmark of Hadoop, *WordCount*, is employed. To show the feasibility of proposed access control model, we specified four filters employing three different state of the art detection techniques: *Blacklisting*, *Signature Matching*, *Syntax analysis*, and combination of all three. In blacklisting, a set of sensitive keywords containing 3000 human and company names is formed as a *Hashmap* for exact matching. The blacklisting filter uses this hashmap to detect whether the tweets include blacklisted words or not; If such a word is detected, it is sanitized. In signature matching, a set of signatures, including phone number, ssn and address information, in the form of regular expressions is used in the pattern matching. The signature filter sanitizes any word(s) in the tweets matching with the regular expression of the signatures. In syntax analysis, it is aimed to determine the meta-information about the data through syntactic analysis. For instance, the language and thus location information can be detected through encoding analysis. A possible scenario is to create a view of tweets only containing Chinese character-encoding schemes for a user whose role is related to market research in China. The syntax filter, therefore, only allows the tweets having Chinese character-encoding schemes.

For image datasets, the users submit a job that selects the images according to a given criteria and write in a separate file. The admins consider any human face existing in the images as sensitive information and prepare a security policy that sanitizes the images by placing a thin black strip to the eyes of humans. In the specification of image policy, the *Haar face recognition* algorithm of OpenCV library [17] is employed to detect a human face and the parts around eyes are darkened by modifying pixels.

7.4 Results

We compared the performance of GUARDMR with two other approaches. In the first approach called *integrated* version, we implemented the reference monitor detailed in Sec. 6.2 in the Hadoop source code to determine the overhead of our modular reference monitor caused by runtime weaving. To that end, we enhanced all the concrete RecordReader classes with our reference monitor such that when three methods of the RecordReaders (see. Sec. 6) are

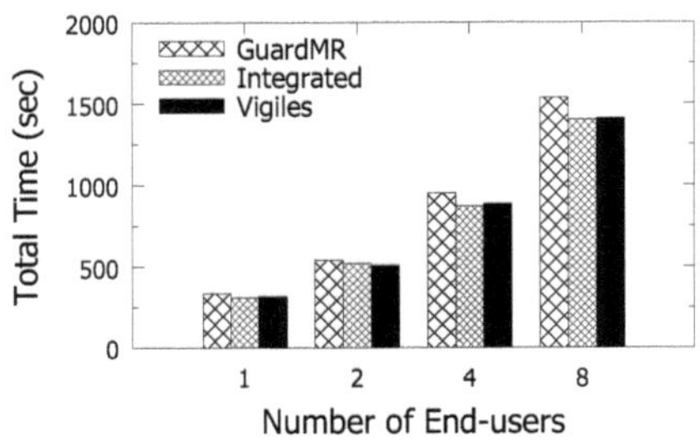

(a) Performance on Text Dataset

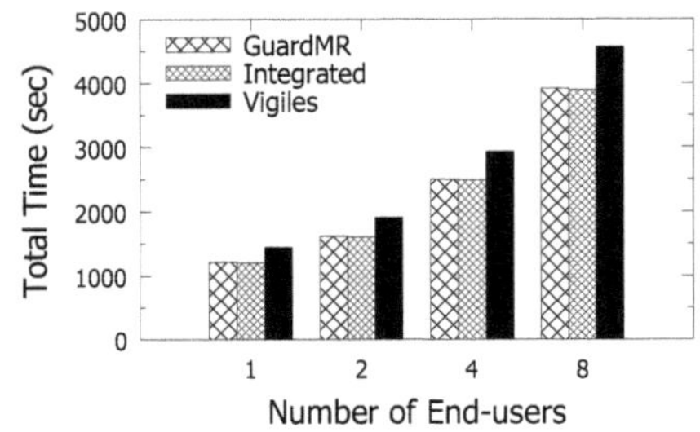

(b) Performance on Image Dataset

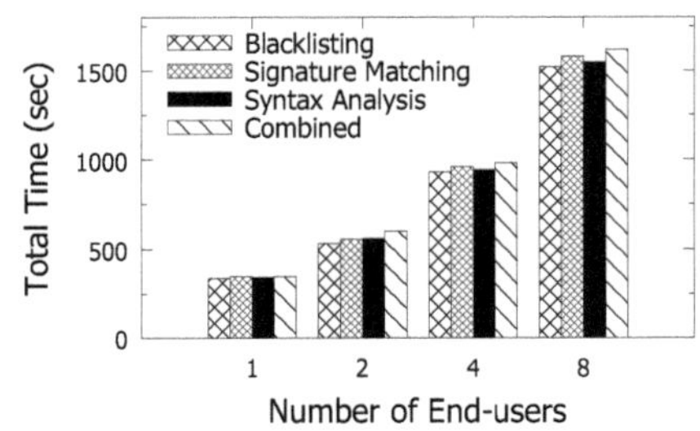

(c) Performance of Four Sample Filters

Figure 3: Performance of Three Systems for Multi End-users Setup

called, the same security policies are applied to the generated key-value pairs. The integrated version, however, is only for experiment purpose and does not form a proper reference monitor, because it can easily be circumvented by the MapReduce jobs with self-defined RecordReaders. The second approach is the *Vigiles* system [6]. In this system, the security policies are specified through Java programming language as *AspectJ aspects* and weaved into Hadoop bytecode via AspectJ bytecode weaving. We run the jobs 5 times for each Twitter dataset and 3 times for each image dataset, where the standard derivation is less than 1% in each experiment. The total running time of experiments exceeded 12 days. The average of results is used in the presented graphs.

First of all, we compared the performance of three systems when only a single job is running on the Hadoop. Fig. 2(a) shows the total running time of WordCount job when the blacklisting filter is employed in three systems. Integrated version outperforms the others followed by the Vigiles system. The average overhead of GUARDMR and Vigiles with respect to integrated version is 9% and 0.5%, respectively. The small performance difference of GUARDMR is caused by the reflection operations performed in the reference monitor (see Sec. 6.2). Fig. 2(b) shows the running time of image selection job when the human eyes are sanitized by the three systems. Integrated version again outperforms the others followed by GUARDMR. However, this time the average overhead of GUARDMR and Vigiles with respect to integrated version is 0.70% and 17.60%, respectively. For GUARDMR, the average overhead of image experiment is smaller than the average overhead of text experiment, because the running time of image experiment is longer while the cost of reflection is constant. On the other hand, Vigiles incur a huge overhead due the its bytecode weaving approach that is unable to use Just-in-time (JIT) compiler of JVM. As discussed in [6, 18], the external libraries which are excessively leveraging JIT optimizations (e.g., regular expressions, image processing operations) perform poorly in Vigiles setup. GUARDMR does not suffer from the same problem, because runtime weaving can leverage JIT compiler. Moreover, Fig. 2(c) shows the comparison of four defined policies for single job scenario.

Moreover, we compared the performance of three systems when multiple MapReduce jobs are simultaneously running on the Hadoop. Fig. 3(a) shows the total running time of WordCount MapReduce job when the blacklisting filter is employed in three systems. We observe similar results of single job experiment that integrated version outperforms the others. The average overhead of GUARDMR and Vigiles with respect to integrated version is 7.60% and 0.20%, respectively. Fig. 3(b) shows the running time of image selection MapReduce job when the human eyes are sanitized by the three systems via the same policy. The average overhead of GUARDMR and Vigiles with respect to integrated version is 0.50% and 18.20%, respectively. Fig. 3(c) shows the comparison of four defined policies for multiple jobs scenario.

These empirical results indicate that GUARDMR has many advantages over other two systems (e.g., practical policy specification, enforcement mechanism with proved security, built-in access control model, and high modularity and flexibility) while only incurring small overhead. On the other hand, integrated version cannot provide a secure environment as self-defined RecordReaders in the jobs would bypass it. Similarly in Vigiles, all operations in an access control model ,e.g., policy specification and function assignment to the jobs, have to be accomplished by hard-coding via Java programming language as AspectJ aspects.

8. RELATED WORK

We review two fields of studies related to GUARDMR: Security applications for MapReduce and FGAC in relational databases.

Security Applications For MapReduce: *Apache Accumulo* [19] is a sorted, distributed key-value store based on Google's *BigTable* [20] designed and built on top of *Apache Hadoop.* Accumulo improves the BigTable design in the form of cell-based access control and a server-side programming mechanism that can modify key-value pairs at various points in the data management process. Similarly, *BigSecret* [21] enables secure querying of cell-level encrypted data in HBase. *SecureMR* [22] is an integrity assurance framework built on top of MapReduce model. It provides a decentralized replication-based integrity verification scheme to protect the integrity of MapReduce in open systems. *Airavat* [23] is an application for MapReduce system where the security and privacy are guaranteed for distributed computations on sensitive data. It employs SElinux [24] for mandatory access control and information flow control. It also provides individual privacy guarantees via *differentially private* MapReduce computation results. *Sedic* [25] and *Tagged-MapReduce* [26] propose secure MapReduce processing for the labeled datasets on the hybrid cloud setup by considering public nodes as semi-trusted. *Silver Lining* [27] enforces mandatory information flow policies at the level of files on Apache Hadoop. Similar to our system, it achieves high modularity by implementing the security policies by means of *In-lined Reference Monitors*. However, none of the aforementioned systems address the FGAC challenges for all types of data (viz., structured, unstructured, semi-structured data) in the generic MapReduce model even though each of them addresses different security/privacy issues.

FGAC for MapReduce systems has recently attracted attention in both industry and academia. *Apache Sentry* [28] developed by Cloudera targets to deliver fine-grained authorization to datasets stored in Apache Hadoop. Although it provides fine-grained access management for the system built atop Apache Hadoop (i.e., Hive, Impala, and Search), it assumes that the data is organized as relational tables and cannot provide FGAC for the MapReduce programming model. *Vigiles* [6] is an FGAC system developed for MapReduce, which proposes to apply history independent functions on the individual records of datasets before MapReduce jobs access them. Vigiles lacks a method to formally specify the history independent functions, and instead proposes to implement the functions by means of Java programming language and in-line them into the MapReduce computation via aspect-oriented programming. This method suffers from inferior usability as policy specification requires a lot of programming effort such that the system administrator has to deal with the interior architecture of MapReduce system (e.g., system administrator needs to find suitable interior functions for the aspect-oriented hooks), and a small change within access control policies can correspond to huge re-implementation effort. Moreover, unlike GUARDMR, it does not consider the many aspects and challenges of FGAC in MapReduce, (e.g., ad-hoc data types used in the MapReduce jobs, difference views of same datasets, etc.) strictly limiting the applicability of the approach.

FGAC in Relational Databases: Virtual Private Database (VPD) [2] has been included as an FGAC component in Oracle DBMS since Oracle8i. VPD allows to specify predicates as strings appended to the WHERE clause of the queries. In 2004, Rizvi et al. [29] generalized the query modification approach as *Truman model*, where each user's view of database can be inconsistent with additional information derived from external sources. They addressed this issue by rewriting queries using only the authorized views. Alternatively, LeFevre et al. [30] introduced *table semantics* model, where the queries remain the same while the tables are effectively modified by injecting dynamically created views. Agrawal et al. [31] proposed to use grant commands of DBMS to provide cell level access control. In 2007, Chaudhuri et al. [32] proposed to use predicated grants by considering other features (e.g., aggregate authorization, user groups, authorization groups, etc.). Rosenthal and Sciore [33] extended this approach for management of predicated grants as well. However, these approaches are not applicable to MapReduce model due to the lack of structured query languages in MapReduce systems, where the above approaches leverages the features specific to relational databases (e.g., *grant* commands, SQL, etc.).

9. CONCLUSION

In this paper, we studied fine-grained access control for MapReduce computation. We focused on the automatic generation of dynamic authorized views of input data resources from the high level OCL specifications. The generated data views are expressive enough to handle the datasets without predefined structures in MapReduce systems. We further showed that how these authorized data views can be enforced on the MapReduce computation by means of a modular reference monitor. The proposed reference monitor does not need to customize the source code or API of underlying MapReduce system and operating system while guaranteeing the security and completeness of the policy enforcement. We demonstrated the feasibility of GUARDMR by implementing and evaluating it in Apache Hadoop. Our empirical results illustrate the efficiency and scalability of GUARDMR with low overhead.

10. ACKNOWLEDGMENTS

This work is partially supported by the following grants: Air Force Office of Scientific Research FA9550-12-1-0082, National Institutes of Health Grants 1R0-1LM009989 and 1R01HG006844, National Science Foundation (NSF) Grants Career-CNS-0845803, CNS-1111529, CNS-1228198 and Army Research Office Grant W911NF-12-1-0558.

11. REFERENCES

[1] D. Logothetis, C. Trezzo, K. C. Webb, and K. Yocum, "In-situ mapreduce for log processing," in *USENIX*, 2011, pp. 9–9.

[2] K. Browder and M. A. Davidson, "The virtual private database in oracle9ir2," *Oracle Technical White Paper*, vol. 500, 2002.

[3] C. Mohan, "History repeats itself: sensible and nonsensql aspects of the nosql hoopla," in *EDBT*. ACM, 2013, pp. 11–16.

[4] K. W. Hamlen, M. Kantarcioglu, L. Khan, and B. Thuraisingham, "Security issues for cloud computing," *International Journal of Information Security and Privacy (IJISP)*, vol. 4, no. 2, pp. 36–48, April–June 2010.

[5] "Top ten big data security and privacy challenges," http://www.isaca.org/Groups/Professional-English/big-data/GroupDocuments/Big_Data_Top_Ten_v1.pdf, accessed: 2014-10-29.

[6] H. Ulusoy, M. Kantarcioglu, K. Hamlen, and E. Pattuk, "Vigiles: Fine-grained access control for mapreduce systems," in *IEEE BigData*, 2014.

[7] J. Dean and S. Ghemawat, "Mapreduce: simplified data processing on large clusters," *Commun. ACM*, vol. 51, no. 1, pp. 107–113, Jan. 2008.

[8] "Apache hadoop version 4," http://www.seamicro.com/node/354, accessed: 2014-05-11.

[9] "Object constraint language (ocl)," http://www.omg.org/spec/OCL, accessed: 2014-05-11.

[10] "Dresden ocl toolkit," http://www.dresden-ocl.org, 2014-05-11.

[11] L. Gong, M. Mueller, and H. Prafullch, "Going beyond the sandbox: An overview of the new security architecture in the java development kit 1.2," in *USENIX*, 1997, pp. 103–112.

[12] I. Goldberg, D. Wagner, R. Thomas, and E. A. Brewer, "A secure environment for untrusted helper applications: Confining the wily hacker," in *Proceedings of the 1996 USENIX Security Symposium*, 1996.

[13] M. Sun, G. Tan, J. Siefers, B. Zeng, and G. Morrisett, "Bringing java's wild native world under control," *ACM Trans. Inf. Syst. Secur.*, 2013.

[14] D. F. Ferraiolo, R. Sandhu, S. Gavrila, D. R. Kuhn, and R. Chandramouli, "Proposed nist standard for role-based access control," vol. 4, no. 3. ACM, Aug. 2001.

[15] "Javassist project," http://www.javassist.org, accessed: 2014-05-11.

[16] "Apache jakarta project," http://jakarta.apache.org/regexp/, 2014-05-11.

[17] G. Bradski, "The opencv library," *Doctor Dobbs Journal*, vol. 25, no. 11, pp. 120–126, 2000.

[18] E. Hilsdale and J. Hugunin, "Advice weaving in aspectj," in *Aspect-oriented software development*. ACM, 2004, pp. 26–35.

[19] "Apache accumulo," http://accumulo.apache.org/, accessed: 2014-05-11.

[20] F. Chang, J. Dean, S. Ghemawat, W. C. Hsieh, D. A. Wallach, M. Burrows, T. Chandra, A. Fikes, and R. E. Gruber, "Bigtable: A distributed storage system for structured data," *in TOCS*, vol. 26, no. 2, p. 4, 2008.

[21] E. Pattuk, M. Kantarcioglu, V. Khadilkar, H. Ulusoy, and S. Mehrotra, "Bigsecret: A secure data management framework for key-value stores," in *IEEE CLOUD*, 2013.

[22] W. Wei, J. Du, T. Yu, and X. Gu, "Securemr: A service integrity assurance framework for mapreduce," in *ACSAC*, 2009, pp. 73–82.

[23] I. Roy, S. T. V. Setty, A. Kilzer, V. Shmatikov, and E. Witchel, "Airavat: Security and privacy for mapreduce," in *USENIX*, 2010, pp. 20–20.

[24] "Selinux," http://selinuxproject.org/, accessed: 2014-05-11.

[25] K. Zhang, X. Zhou, Y. Chen, X. Wang, and Y. Ruan, "Sedic: privacy-aware data intensive computing on hybrid clouds," in *CCS*, 2011, pp. 515–526.

[26] C. Zhang, E.-C. Chang, and R. H. Yap, "Tagged-mapreduce: A general framework for secure computing with mixed-sensitivity data on hybrid clouds."

[27] S. M. Khan, K. W. Hamlen, and M. Kantarcioglu, "Silver lining: Enforcing secure information flow at the cloud edge," in *IEEE Cloud Engineering (IC2E)*, 2014, pp. 37–46.

[28] "Apache sentry," http://www.cloudera.com/content/cloudera/en/products-and-services/cdh/sentry.html, accessed: 2014-05-08.

[29] S. Rizvi, A. Mendelzon, S. Sudarshan, and P. Roy, "Extending query rewriting techniques for fine-grained access control," in *SIGMOD*, 2004.

[30] K. LeFevre, R. Agrawal, V. Ercegovac, R. Ramakrishnan, Y. Xu, and D. DeWitt, "Limiting disclosure in hippocratic databases," in *VLDB*. VLDB Endowment, 2004, pp. 108–119.

[31] R. Agrawal, P. Bird, T. Grandison, J. Kiernan, S. Logan, and W. Rjaibi, "Extending relational database systems to automatically enforce privacy policies," in *ICDE*. IEEE, 2005, pp. 1013–1022.

[32] S. Chaudhuri, T. Dutta, and S. Sudarshan, "Fine grained authorization through predicated grants," in *ICDE*. IEEE, 2007, pp. 1174–1183.

[33] A. Rosenthal and E. Sciore, "Extending sqlŠs grant operation to limit privileges," in *Data and Application Security*. Springer, 2002.

APPENDIX

A. PROOFS

Rationale behind the proof of Theorem 1: Theorem 1 is proved by contradiction, showing that if we assume the existence of a key value pair accessed by a mapper of J which is not generated by RR we fall in contradiction.

Proof for Theorem 1: Suppose for the sake of contradiction that there exists a key-value pair $\langle k', v' \rangle$ such that $\langle k', v' \rangle$ is accessed by a mapper of *J*, and there does not exist a pair $\langle k, v \rangle$ generated by *RR* such that $ps(k,v)=true \wedge dk(k)=k' \wedge dv(v)=v'$. Once Hadoop receives *J*, it invokes an instantiation of *RR* for each *InputSplit* of *D*. The enforcement monitor intercepts this requests (see Listing 3) and activates the generation of the enhanced RecordReader (see Listing 4). The monitor invokes method *getAuthorizedFilter* on *Controller* (see Listing 5) to check if a valid filter authorization exists. It can be proved that if there was no valid filter authorization, the reference monitor would block the execution of J. However, based on the assumptions this is not the case. Indeed, after identifying the data *D* accessed by *J*, *R* activated by *U* and the types *K* and *V* handled by the Mappers of *J*, an authorization *fa* is also identified, which authorizes the execution of *J* subject to the application of *F* referred to by *fa*.

Therefore, the monitor generates an enhanced *RR* denoted RR' and returns it to the caller so that the Mappers of J interact with instances of RR' to access *D*. RR' is defined in such a way to filter the key-value pairs through the application of *F*. By construction of RR' (see Listing 6) and by definition of Filter (see Def. 2), a pair $\langle k', v' \rangle$ is included in the authorized view of *D* and it is accessible by a *Mapper* if there exists a pair $\langle k, v \rangle$ generated by *RR* from which $\langle k', v' \rangle$ is derived. More precisely, let Lp' be the view on *D* generated by RR' through the application of the filter *F* to the collection of key-value pairs generated by *RR*. For each pair $\langle k, v \rangle$ generated by *RR* such that *k=RR.getCurrentKey()* and *v=RR.getCurrentValue()*, if $ps(k,v)=true$, the pair $\langle dk(k), dv(v) \rangle$ is part of Lp'. By assumption $\langle k', v' \rangle$ is accessed by a *Mapper*, this implies that $\langle k', v' \rangle$ is included in Lp', which in turn implies there exists a pair $\langle k, v \rangle$ generated by *RR* (i.e., *k=RR.getCurrentKey()* and *v=RR.getCurrentValue()*), such that $ps(k,v)=true \wedge dk(k)=k' \wedge dv(v)=v'$, which contradicts the hypothesis.□

Rationale behind the proof of Theorem 2: Theorem 2 is also proved by contradiction, showing that according to GUARDMR specification, if we assume the existence of a key value pair $\langle k, v \rangle$ which 1) is accessed by a mapper of J within S, and 2) satisfies the selection function *ps* of *F* within *S'*, and we assume that $\langle k, v \rangle$ is not used in the view of *D* built by RR', we fall in contradiction.

Proof for Theorem 2: Let us suppose by contradiction that there exists a pair $\langle k, v \rangle$, where $k{:}K$, and $v{:}V$, such that $\langle k, v \rangle$ is accessed by a mapper of *J* in *S*, $\langle k, v \rangle$ satisfies the pair selection function *ps* of *F*, and $\langle k, v \rangle$ is not used in the view of *D* built by RR'.

By the definition of reference monitor (see Section 6.2), *RR* is the parent class of RR'. Since $\langle k, v \rangle$ is accessed by a mapper of *J* in *S* by assumptions, at a given point of the execution of J, the iterator of *RR* refers to a pair such that *RR.getCurrentKey()=k* and *RR.getCurrentValue()=v*. The method *nextKeyValue* of RR' is defined in such a way to prune out from the set of pairs generated by *RR* all those pairs that do not satisfy *ps* of *F* (see Listing 6). More precisely, as shown in Listing 6, the definition of the RR' method *nextKeyValue* is based on the methods *nextKeyValue*, *getCurrentKey* and *getCurrentValue* of the parent class *RR*. A key-value pair is selected to build the authorized view on *D* if it is also referred to by *RR* (i.e., *RR.nextKeyValue()=true*) and *ps* executed specifying as input parameters the key and value resulting from the execution of *getCurrentKey* and *getCurrentValue* of *RR* is satisfied. Based on previous reasoning there exists a pair $\langle k, v \rangle$ referred to by *RR* such that *RR.getCurrentKey()=k* and *RR.getCurrentValue()=v*, and based on the assumptions, the pair selection function *ps* of *F* evaluated with respect to such a pair is satisfied, i.e., $ps(k, v)=true$. We derive that $\langle k, v \rangle$ is also used by RR' to generate the authorized view on *D*, which contradicts the hypothesis.□

Automated Synthesis of Run-time Monitors to Enforce Authorization Policies in Business Processes*

Clara Bertolissi
Fondazione Bruno Kessler
University of Marseille
clara.bertolissi@lif.univ-mrs.fr

Daniel Ricardo dos Santos
Fondazione Bruno Kessler
SAP Labs France
University of Trento
dossantos@fbk.eu

Silvio Ranise
Fondazione Bruno Kessler
ranise@fbk.eu

ABSTRACT

Run-time monitors are crucial to the development of security-aware workflow management systems, which need to mediate access to their resources by enforcing authorization policies and constraints, such as Separation of Duty. In this paper, we introduce a precise technique to synthesize run-time monitors capable of ensuring the successful termination of workflows while enforcing authorization policies and constraints. An extensive experimental evaluation shows the scalability of our technique on the important class of hierarchically specified security-sensitive workflows with several hundreds of tasks.

Categories and Subject Descriptors

D.4.6 [**Operating Systems**]: Security and Protection; K.6.5 [**Management of Computing and Information Systems**]: Security and Protection

Keywords

Run-time Enforcement, Workflow Satisfiability

1. INTRODUCTION

It is common that workflow management systems support the execution of business processes. A workflow specifies a collection of tasks and the causal relationships between them. The execution of tasks is initiated by humans or software agents executing on their behalf. Security-related dependencies are specified as additional constraints on the execution of the various tasks. In an organization, a workflow task is executed by a user who should be entitled to do so; e.g., the teller of a bank may create a loan request whereas only a manager may accept it. Additional authorization constraints are usually imposed on task execution, such as Separation of Duty (SoD) or Bound of Duty (BoD) whereby two distinct users or the same user, respectively, must execute two tasks. Below, following [2], we call "security-sensitive" this kind of workflows.

The *Workflow Satisfiability Problem* (WSP) consists of checking if there exists an assignment of users to tasks such that a security-sensitive workflow successfully terminates while satisfying all authorization constraints. Such a problem has been studied in several papers; see, e.g., [27, 20]. The run-time version of the WSP consists of answering sequences of user requests at execution time and ensuring successful termination together with the satisfaction of authorization constraints. This problem has received less attention and only an approximate solution is available [3, 4].

The **main contribution** of this paper is an automated technique to synthesize run-time monitors capable of ensuring the successful termination of workflows while enforcing authorization policies and SoD/BoD constraints, thus solving the run-time version of the WSP. Changes in the authorization policies can be accommodated without re-running from scratch the approach. Section 2 illustrates the main steps underlying the technique on a simple example. Section 3 gives full details and states several theorems guaranteeing the correctness of the approach. **Another contribution** of the paper is an extensive experimental evaluation of the proposed technique on hierarchically structured workflows, i.e. complex workflows that can be decomposed in subflows. Section 4 describes a prototype implementation of the technique and how the structure of hierarchic specifications can be exploited to make our approach scale to large workflow systems containing hundreds of tasks. Section 4.1 discusses the performances of our technique on two workflow systems inspired by realistic use-cases while Section 4.2 studies its scalability on synthetic benchmarks inspired by those in [12] containing up to 500 tasks. Our findings clearly show the scalability of the proposed technique on hierarchic workflows. Section 5 discusses related work and Section 6 concludes the paper by giving hints to future work.

2. A TRIP REQUEST EXAMPLE

We describe our approach to synthesize run-time monitors for security-sensitive workflows on a trip request process. The workflow is composed of five tasks—each one indicated by a box labeled by Trip request ($t1$), Car rental

*This work was partly supported by the EU under grant FP7-PEOPLE-SECENTIS and the RESTATE Programme, co-funded by the European Union under the FP7 COFUND Marie Curie Action—Grant agreement no. 267224.

ASIA CCS'15, April 14–17, 2015, Singapore.

ACM 978-1-4503-3245-3/15/04 $15.00.
http://dx.doi.org/10.1145/2714576.2714633.

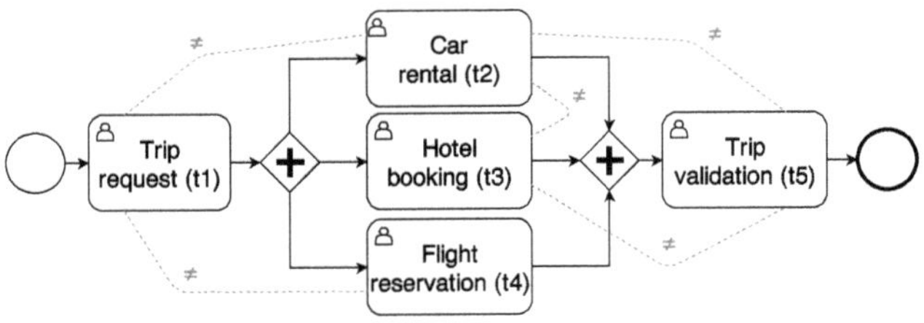

Figure 1: Workflow in extended BPM notation

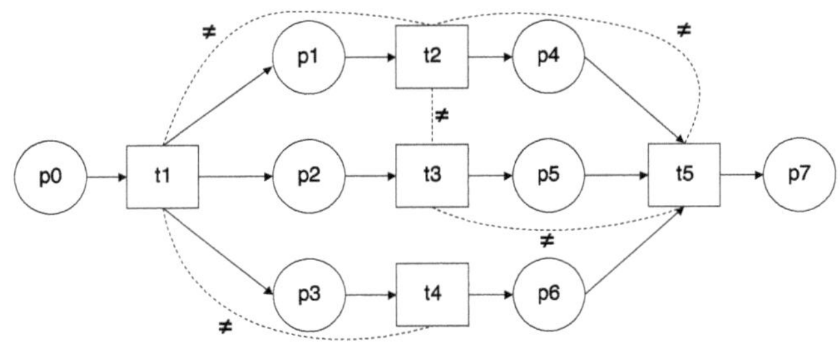

Figure 2: Workflow as an extended Petri net

($t2$), Hotel booking ($t3$), Flight reservation ($t4$), and Trip validation ($t5$)—whose execution is constrained as follows (cf. solid arrows and diamonds labeled with $+$): $t1$ must be executed first, then $t2$, $t3$ and $t4$ can be executed in any order, and when all have been performed, $t5$ can be executed, thereby terminating the workflow. Additionally, each task is executed under the responsibility of a user (indicated by the small icon inside the boxes corresponding to the various tasks) who has the right to execute it according to some access control policy—not shown in Figure 1—and the five authorization constraints depicted as dashed lines labeled by the symbol $\neq$ for Separation of Duty (SoD). So, for example, the authorization constraint connecting the boxes of $t1$ and $t2$ requires the user executing $t2$ to be distinct from the one that has executed $t1$, i.e. the user who requests the trip cannot also rent a car.

Our goal is to synthesize a run-time monitor, capable of ensuring that all execution and authorization constraints are satisfied. Our approach is organized in two phases: off-line and on-line.

Off-line. We first construct a symbolic transition system S whose executions correspond to those of the security-sensitive workflow. Then, we use a symbolic model checker to explore all possible terminating executions of the workflow which satisfy both the causality and the authorization constraints. We assume the model checker to be able to return a symbolic representation R of the set of all states, called reachable, encountered during the exploration of the terminating executions of S. We use particular classes of formulae in first-order logic to be the symbolic representations of S and R.

On-line. We derive a Datalog program M from the formulae R, representing the set of states reachable in the terminating executions of S and the policy P specifying which user can perform which task. The Datalog program M derived in this way is the monitor capable of guaranteeing that any request of a user to execute a task is permitted by P, satisfies the authorization constraints (such as SoD), and the workflow can terminate its execution.

We illustrate the two phases on the security-sensitive workflow in Figure 1.

2.1 Off-line phase

First of all, we build the symbolic transition system S in two steps: (i) we adopt the standard approach (see, e.g., [24]) of using (extensions of) Petri nets [19] to formalize the semantics of workflows and (ii) we adapt the well-known translation of Petri nets to symbolic transition systems (see, e.g., [21]) to the class of extended Petri nets used in this paper.

Figure 2 shows the extended Petri net that can be automatically derived from the BPM notation of Figure 1. Tasks are modeled as transitions or events (the boxes in the figure) whereas places (the circles in the figure) encode their enabling conditions. At the beginning, there will be just one token in place $p0$ which enables the execution of transition $t1$. This corresponds to the execution constraint that task $t1$ must be performed before all the others. The execution of $t1$ removes the token in $p0$ and puts a token in $p1$, another in $p2$, and yet another in $p3$; this enables the execution of $t2$, $t3$, and $t4$. Indeed, this corresponds to the causality constraint that $t2$, $t3$, and $t4$ can be executed in any order after $t1$ and before $t5$. In fact, the executions of $t2$, $t3$, and $t4$ remove the tokens in $p1$, $p2$, $p3$ and put a token in $p4$, $p5$, and $p6$ which, in turn, enables the execution of $t5$. This removes the token in $p4$, $p5$, $p6$ and put a token in $p7$ which enables no more transitions. This corresponds to the fact that $t5$ is the last task to be executed. The fact that there is at most one token per place is an invariant of the Petri net. This allows us to symbolically represent the net as follows: we introduce a Boolean variable per place (named as the places in Figure 2) together with a Boolean variable representing the fact that a task has already been executed (denoted by d_t and if assigned to true implies that task t has been executed). So, for instance, the enabling condition for the execution constraint on task $t1$ can be expressed as $p0 \wedge \neg d_{t1}$ meaning that the token is in place $p0$ and transition $t1$ has not yet been executed. The effect of executing transition $t1$ is to assign F(alse) to $p0$ and T(rue) to $p1$, $p2$, $p3$, and d_{t1}; in symbols, we write $p0, p1, p2, p3, d_{t1} := F, T, T, T, T$. The other transitions are modeled similarly.

Besides the constraints on the execution of tasks, Figure 2 shows also the same authorization constraints of Figure 1. These are obtained by taking into consideration both the access control policy P granting or denying users the right

Table 1: Workflow as symbolic transition system

event	enabled		action	
	CF	Auth	CF	Auth
$t1(u)$	$p0 \wedge \neg d_{t1}$	$a_{t1}(u)$	$p0, p1, p2, p3, d_{t1} := F, T, T, T, T$	$h_{t1}(u) := T$
$t2(u)$	$p1 \wedge \neg d_{t2}$	$a_{t2}(u) \wedge \neg h_{t3}(u) \wedge \neg h_{t1}(u)$	$p1, p4, d_{t2} := F, T, T$	$h_{t2}(u) := T$
$t3(u)$	$p2 \wedge \neg d_{t3}$	$a_{t3}(u) \wedge \neg h_{t2}(u)$	$p2, p5, d_{t3} := F, T, T$	$h_{t3}(u) := T$
$t4(u)$	$p3 \wedge \neg d_{t4}$	$a_{t4}(u) \wedge \neg h_{t1}(u)$	$p3, p6, d_{t4} := F, T, T$	$h_{t4}(u) := T$
$t5(u)$	$p4 \wedge p5 \wedge p6 \wedge \neg d_{t5}$	$a_{t5}(u) \wedge \neg h_{t3}(u) \wedge \neg h_{t2}(u)$	$p4, p5, p6, p7, d_{t5} := F, F, F, T, T$	$h_{t5}(u) := T$

to execute tasks and the SoD constraints between pairs of tasks. To formalize these, we introduce two functions a_t and h_t from users to Boolean, for each task t, which are such that $a_t(u)$ is true iff u has the right to execute t according to the policy P and $h_t(u)$ is true iff u has executed task t. Notice that a_t is a function that behaves as an abstract interface to the policy P whereas h_t is a function that evolves over time and keeps track of which users have executed which tasks. For instance, the enabling condition for the authorization constraint on task $t1$ is simply $a_{t1}(u)$, i.e. it is required that the user u has the right to execute $t1$, and the effect of its execution is to record that u has executed $t1$, i.e. $h_{t1}(u) := T$ (notice that this assignment leaves unchanged the value returned by h_{t1} for any user u' distinct from u). Notice that it is useless to take into account the SoD constraints between $t1$ and $t2$, $t4$ when executing $t1$ since $t2$ and $t4$ will always be executed afterwards. As another example, let us consider the enabling condition for the authorization constraint on $t2$: besides requiring that u has the right to execute $t2$ (i.e. $a_{t2}(u)$), we also need to require the SoD constraints with $t1$ and $t3$ (not that with $t5$ since this will be executed afterwards), i.e. that u has executed neither $t1$ (i.e. $\neg h_{t1}(u)$) nor $t3$ (i.e. $\neg h_{t3}(u)$). The authorization constraints on the other tasks are modeled in a similar way.

Table 1 shows the formalization of all transitions in the extended Petri net of Figure 2. The first column reports the name of the transition together with the fact that it is dependent on the user u taking the responsibility of its execution. The second column shows the enabling condition divided in two parts: CF, pertaining to the execution constraints, and Auth, to the authorization constraints. The third and last column list the effects of the execution of the transition again divided in two parts: CF, for the workflow, and Auth, for the authorization.

The initial state of the security-sensitive workflow is described by the *initial* formula

$$p0 \wedge \bigwedge_{i=1,\ldots,7} \neg pi \wedge \bigwedge_{i=1,\ldots,5} \neg d_{ti} \wedge \bigwedge_{i=1,\ldots,5} \forall u.\neg h_{ti}(u) \qquad (1)$$

saying that there is just one token in $p0$, no task has been executed, and indeed no user has yet executed any of the tasks, whereas a state of a terminating execution of the workflow by the *goal* or *final* formula

$$p7 \wedge \bigwedge_{i=0,\ldots,6} \neg pi \wedge \bigwedge_{i=1,\ldots,5} d_{ti} \qquad (2)$$

saying that there is just one token in $p7$ and all the tasks have been executed.

Formally, the way in which we specify the transition systems corresponding to security-sensitive workflows can be seen as an extended version of the assertional framework proposed in [22]. We emphasize that obtaining, from the extended BPM notation of Figure 1, the symbolic representation S of the initial and goal formulae with that of the transitions in Table 1 is a fully automated process.

Exploring the search space. After obtaining the symbolic representation of the initial and goal states together with the transitions of the security-sensitive workflow, we invoke a symbolic model checker in order to compute the symbolic representation R of the set of (reachable) states visited while executing all possible sequences of transitions leading from an initial to a goal state. A crucial assumption of our approach is that the model checker is able to compute

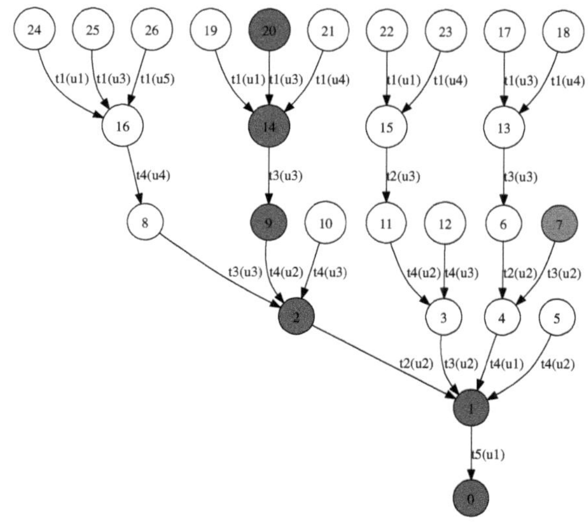

Figure 3: Graph-like representation of the set of reachable states for the workflow in Figure 1

R for any finite number of users. By doing this, the interface functions a_t's can be instantiated with any policy P, i.e. containing any number of users. As a consequence, changes in the authorization policy do not imply to re-run the off-line phase. In summary, our goal is to compute a parametric—in the number n of users—representation of the set of states visited while executing all possible terminating sequences of transitions. From now on, we write R_n to emphasize this fact.

Although the computation of R_n seems to be a daunting task, there exist techniques available in the literature about parameterized model checking (see the seminal paper [1]) that allow us to do this. Among those available, we have chosen the Model Checking Modulo Theories approach proposed in [16] for it uses first-order formulae as the symbolic representation of transition systems and the availability of tools, such as MCMT [17], which are capable of returning the set of reachable states as a first-order formula.

For instance, Figure 3 shows a graph-like representation of the formula R_n for the security-sensitive workflow described by the symbolic transition system derived from Figure 1. Each node is associated to a first-order formula: node 0 (bottom of the figure) is labeled by the goal formula (2), nodes 17–26 (top of the figure) are labeled by formulae describing sets of states that have non-empty intersection with the set of initial states characterized by the initial formula (1), all other nodes (namely, those from 1 to 16) are labeled with formulae describing sets of states that are visited by executing transitions (labeling the arcs of the graph) belonging to a terminating sequence of executions of the workflow. For instance, node 1 is labeled by the formula

$$\begin{aligned} \neg p0 \wedge \neg p1 \wedge \neg p2 \wedge \neg p3 \wedge p4 \wedge p5 \wedge p6 \quad \wedge \\ d_{t1} \wedge d_{t2} \wedge d_{t3} \wedge d_{t4} \wedge \neg d_{t5} \quad \wedge \\ (a_{t5}(u1) \wedge \neg h_{t2}(u1) \wedge \neg h_{t3}(u1)) \end{aligned}$$

describing the set of states from which it is possible to reach a goal state when some user $u1$ takes the responsibility to execute task $t5$. The first two lines in the formula above require that there is a token in places $p4$, $p5$, $p6$ (thereby enabling transition $t5$), tasks $t1$, $t2$, $t3$, $t4$ have been executed, and $t5$ has not yet been performed. The last line requires that user $u1$ has the right to execute $t5$ and that he/she has performed neither $t2$ nor $t3$ (because of the SoD constraints between $t5$ and $t2$ or $t3$). In general, let us consider an arc $\nu \xrightarrow{t(u)} \nu'$ in the graph of Figure 3: the formula labeling node ν describes the set of states from which it is possible to reach the set of states described by the formula labeling node ν' when user u executes task t. Thus, the paths starting from one of the nodes 17–26 (labeled by formulae representing states with non-empty intersection with the set of initial states) and ending in node 0 (labeled by the goal formula) describe all possible terminating executions of the workflow in Figure 1 (although nodes 5, 7, 10 and 12 seem to be exceptions, this is not the case: explaining their role requires a more precise description of how the graph is built and will be discussed in the next section). For instance, the sequence of blue nodes describes the terminating sequence $t1, t3, t4, t2, t5$ of task executions by the users $u3$, $u3$, $u2$, $u2$, and $u1$, respectively. It is easy to check that this sequence satisfies both the execution and the authorization constraints required by the workflow in BPM notation of Figure 1. In fact, $t1$ is executed first, $t5$ is executed last, and $t2, t3, t4$ are executed in between; there are three *distinct* users $u1, u2, u3$ that can execute the five tasks without violating any of the SoD constraints. By considering all possible paths in the graph of Figure 3, it is easy to see that there should be at least three distinct users to be able to terminate the security-sensitive workflow in Figure 1. From what we said above, the formula R_n representing the set of states visited during terminating sequences of task executions of the security-sensitive workflow in Figure 1 can be obtained by taking the disjunction of the formulae labeling the nodes in the graph of Figure 3 except for the one labeling node 0 since, by construction, no task is enabled in the set of states represented by that formula. Let r_ν be the formula labeling node ν, then

$$R_n := \bigvee_{\nu \in N} r_\nu \quad (3)$$

where N is the set of nodes in the graph (in the case of Figure 3, we have $N = \{1, ..., 26\}$).

2.2 On-line phase

Once MCMT has returned the first-order formula R_n describing the set of states visited during any terminating executions for a (finite but unknown) number n of users, we can derive a Datalog [10] program which constitutes the run-time monitor of the security-sensitive workflow formalized by the symbolic transition system used to compute R_n. Then, we can add the specification of the interface functions a_{t1}, ..., a_{t5} for a given value of n.

We have chosen Datalog as the programming paradigm in which to encode monitors for three main reasons. First, it is well-known [18] that a wide variety of access control policies can be easily expressed in Datalog. Second, Datalog permits efficient computations: the class of Datalog programs resulting from translating formulae R_n permits to answer queries in *LogSpace* (see below for more details). Third, it is possible to further translate the class of Datalog programs we produce to SQL statements so that run-time monitors can be easily implemented as database-backed applications. In the rest of this section, we describe how it is possible to derive Datalog programs from formulae describing the set of reachable states computed by the model checker and then how to add the definitions of the interface functions a_{t1}, ..., a_{t5}.

From R_n to Datalog. Recall the form (3) of R_n. It is not difficult to see that each r_ν can be seen as the conjunction of a formula r_ν^{CF} containing the Boolean functions $p0, ..., p7$ for places and $d_{t1}, ..., d_{t5}$ keeping track of task execution with a formula r_ν^{Auth} of the form

$$a_t(u0) \wedge \rho_\nu^{\text{Auth}}(u0, u1, ..., uk)$$

where $u0$ identifies the user taking the responsibility to execute task t, ρ_ν^{Auth} is a formula containing the variables $u0, u1, ..., uk$, the interface functions $a_{t1}, ..., a_{t5}$, the history functions $h_{t1}, ..., h_{t5}$, and all disequalities between pairwise distinct variables from $u0, u1, ..., uk$ (indeed, if there are no variables, there is no need to add such disequalities). For instance, formula r_1 labeling node 1 in Figure 3 is $r_1^{\text{CF}} \wedge r_1^{\text{Auth}}$ where

$$\begin{aligned} r_1^{\text{CF}} &:= \neg p0 \wedge \neg p1 \wedge \neg p2 \wedge \neg p3 \wedge p4 \wedge p5 \wedge p6 \wedge \\ &\quad\; d_{t1} \wedge d_{t2} \wedge d_{t3} \wedge d_{t4} \wedge \neg d_{t5} \\ r_1^{\text{Auth}} &:= \rho_1^{\text{Auth}}(u1) \\ \rho_\nu^{\text{Auth}}(u1) &:= a_{t5}(u1) \wedge \neg h_{t2}(u1) \wedge \neg h_{t3}(u1) \end{aligned}$$

with $u0$ renamed to $u1$.

In general, each r_ν in the expression (3) for the formula R_n can be written as

$$r_\nu^{\text{CF}} \wedge a_t(u0) \wedge \rho_\nu^{\text{Auth}}(u0, u1, ..., uk) \quad (4)$$

and describes a set of states in which user $u0$ executes task t while guaranteeing that the workflow will terminate since ν is one of the nodes in the graph computed by the model checker while generating all terminating sequences of tasks. In other words, (4) implies that $u0$ can execute task t or, equivalently written as a Datalog clause: $can\_do(u0, t) \leftarrow$ (4), where *can_do* is a Boolean function returning true iff a user (first argument) is entitled to execute a task (second argument) while all execution and authorization constraints are satisfied and the workflow can terminate. Notice that $can\_do(u0, t) \leftarrow$ (4) is a Datalog clause. So, we generate the following Datalog clauses

$$can\_do(u0, t) \leftarrow r_\nu^{\text{CF}} \wedge a_t(u0) \wedge \rho_\nu^{\text{Auth}}(u0, u1, ..., uk) \quad (5)$$

for each $\nu \in N$. In the following, let D_n be the Datalog program composed of all the clauses of the form (5). For instance, the Datalog clause corresponding to node 1 is

$$\begin{aligned} can\_do(u1, t5) \quad \leftarrow \quad & \neg p0 \wedge \neg p1 \wedge \neg p2 \wedge \neg p3 \wedge p4 \wedge p5 \wedge p6 \wedge \\ & d_{t1} \wedge d_{t2} \wedge d_{t3} \wedge d_{t4} \wedge \neg d_{t5} \wedge \\ & a_{t5}(u1) \wedge \neg h_{t2}(u1) \wedge \neg h_{t3}(u1) . \end{aligned}$$

It is not difficult to show that $can\_do(u, t)$ iff there exists a disjunct of the form (4) in R_n for a given number n of users. Finally, observe that clauses of the form (5) contain negations but are non-recursive.

Specifying the policy P. We are left with the problem of specifying the access control policy P for a given number n of users. As already observed above, there should be at least three distinct users in the system to be able to terminate the execution of the workflow in Figure 1. So, to illustrate, let $U = \{a, b, c\}$ be the set of users and use the RBAC model to express the policy. This means that we have a set $R = \{r_1, r_2, r_3\}$ of roles which are indirections between users and (permissions to execute) tasks. Let $UA = \{(a, r1), (a, r2), (a, r3), (b, r2), (b, r3), (c, r2)\}$ be the user-role assignments and $TA = \{(r_3, t1), (r_2, t2), (r_2, t3), (r_1, t4), (r_2, t5)\}$ be the role-task assignment. Then, a user u can execute task t iff there exists a role r such that $(u, r) \in UA$ and $(r, t) \in TA$. This can be formalized by the following Datalog clauses:

$ua(a, r1)$ $ua(a, r2)$ $ua(a, r3)$ $ua(b, r2)$ $ua(b, r3)$ $ua(c, r2)$
$pa(r_3, t1)$ $pa(r_2, t2)$ $pa(r_2, t3)$ $pa(r_1, t4)$ $pa(r_2, t5)$
$a_t(u) \leftarrow ua(u, r) \wedge pa(r, t)$ for each $t \in \{t1, ..., t5\}$

and denoted by D_P. By taking the union of the clauses of D_n and D_P, we build a Datalog program $M_{n=3}$ allowing us to monitor the security-sensitive workflow of Figure 1. I.e. $M_{n=3}$ is capable of answering queries of the form $can\_do(u, t)$ in such a way that all execution and authorization constraints are satisfied and the workflow execution terminates. An example of a run of the monitor is in Table 2, where each line represents a state of the system; columns CF and Auth describe the values of the variables in that state ("Token in" shows which places have a token and the various h_{ti} hold the name of the user who executed task t_i); $can\_do(u, t)$ represents user u requesting to execute task t and 'Resp' is the corresponding response returned by the monitor (grant or deny the request). The execution in the table shows two denied requests, one in line 0 and one in line 2. In line 0, user a requests to execute task $t1$ but this is not possible since a is the only user authorized to execute $t4$, and if a executes $t1$, he/she will not be allowed to execute $t4$ because of the SoD constraint between $t1$ and $t4$ (see Figure 1). In line 2, user b requests to execute task $t2$ but again this is not possible since b has already executed task $t1$ and this would violate the SoD constraint between $t1$ and $t2$. All the other requests are granted, as they do not violate neither execution nor authorization constraints.

So far, we have described the key ideas underlying our technique while neglecting efficiency considerations related to the enumeration of all possible terminating execution sequences of the security-sensitive workflow. If we want our approach to scale up and handle real-world workflows, we have to design suitable heuristics as discussed in Section 4.

Table 2: A run of the monitor program $M_{n=3}$ for the security-sensitive workflow in Figure 1

	CF	Auth					*can_do*	
#	Token in	h_{t1}	h_{t2}	h_{t3}	h_{t4}	h_{t5}	(u, t)	Resp.
0	$p0$	-	-	-	-	-	$(a, t1)$	deny
1	$p0$	-	-	-	-	-	$(b, t1)$	grant
2	$p1, p2, p3$	b	-	-	-	-	$(b, t2)$	deny
3	$p1, p2, p3$	b	-	-	-	-	$(a, t2)$	grant
4	$p4, p2, p3$	b	a	-	-	-	$(c, t3)$	grant
5	$p4, p5, p3$	b	a	c	-	-	$(a, t4)$	grant
6	$p4, p5, p6$	b	a	c	a	-	$(b, t5)$	grant
7	$p7$	b	a	c	a	b	-	-

3. AUTOMATED SYNTHESIS OF RUN-TIME MONITORS

Considering the specification of workflows as transition systems presented in Section 2, we now describe how a symbolic model checker can compute a reachability graph that represents all terminating executions of the workflow (off-line phase) and how this is then translated to a Datalog program that implements the run-time monitor for the WSP (on-line phase).

3.1 Off-line

As already observed in Section 2.1, it is standard to use (extensions of) Petri nets to give a formal semantics to workflows written in BPM notation [24]. In turn, it is well-known how to represent (extension of) Petri nets as state transition systems (see, e.g., [21]), that are composed of a set of *state variables* and a set of *events*, as proposed in [22]. A *state* of the system is defined by the values of the variables. A *predicate* (Boolean function) over the state variables implicitly defines a set of states, i.e. the one containing the values of the variables for which the predicate evaluates to true. A state *satisfies* a predicate iff it belongs to the set of states implicitly defined by the predicate. An event has an *enabling condition*, which is a predicate on the state variables, and an *action*, which updates the state variables. When the enabling condition of an event evaluates to true in a given state s, we say that the event is *enabled* at s. Executing an event enabled at state s results in a new state s' obtained by applying the update of the event to the values of the variables in s. A *behavior* is a sequence of the form $s_0 \xrightarrow{e_0} s_1 \xrightarrow{e_1} \cdots$ where s_i is a state, e_i is an event, and state s_{i+1} is obtained by executing event e_i in state s_i, for $i = 0, 1, ...$ We say that a state s_n is *reachable* from a state s_0 iff there exists a behavior $s_0 \xrightarrow{e_0} s_1 \xrightarrow{e_1} \cdots s_{n-1} \xrightarrow{e_{n-1}} s_n$.

For the class of security-sensitive workflows considered in this paper, the set V of state variables is the union of a set V_{CF} and a set V_{Auth} where the former contains a Boolean variable p_i for each place in the Petri net (for $i = 0, 1, ...$) and a Boolean variable d_t for each transition t in the Petri net, whereas the latter contains two function variables a_t and h_t mapping the set U of users to Booleans for each transition t in the net. Intuitively, p_i is true iff there is a token in the corresponding place, d_t is true iff task t has been executed, $a_t(u)$ is true iff user u has the right to execute task t, and $h_t(u)$ is true iff user u has executed task t. The enabling condition and the action of an event t are of the following forms: $enabled_{\mathrm{CF}} \wedge enabled_{\mathrm{Auth}}$ and $act_{CF}||act_{Auth}$, respectively, where $enabled_{\mathrm{CF}}$ is a predicate over V_{CF}, $enabled_{\mathrm{Auth}}$ is a predicate over V_{Auth}, act_{CF} (act_{Auth}, resp.) is the parallel ($||$) updates of (some of) the variables in V_{CF} (V_{Auth}, resp.), which are written as $x_1, ..., x_k := v_1, ..., v_k$ for x_i a state variable and v_i is the value to which x_i should be updated to. An update of a function variable f from users to Booleans is written as $f(u) := b$ where u is a user, b is a Boolean value, and after the update the function is identical to the previous one except at u for which the value b is returned. An event is a tuple $(t(u), enabled_{\mathrm{CF}} \wedge enabled_{\mathrm{Auth}}, act_{CF}||act_{Auth})$ written as

$$t(u) : enabled_{\mathrm{CF}} \wedge enabled_{\mathrm{Auth}} \rightarrow act_{CF}||act_{Auth} \quad (6)$$

where t is the name of the event (taken from a finite set) and u is a user. Notice that an event is parametric with respect to a user; thus, (6) specifies a collection of events, one for every u in the set U of users. A *security-sensitive (state) transition system over the finite set U of users* is a tuple $(V_{\text{CF}} \cup V_{\text{Auth}}, Tr)$ where U is a finite set of users, $V_{\text{CF}} \cup V_{\text{Auth}}$ is the set of state variables as described above, and Tr is the set of events obtained by considering all users in U.

Let $\mathcal{U}$ be an unbounded set of users and $S = (V_{\text{CF}} \cup V_{\text{Auth}}, Tr)$ be a security-sensitive workflow over a finite set $U \subseteq \mathcal{U}$, I and F be two predicates over $V_{\text{CF}} \cup V_{\text{Auth}}$ and V_{CF}, respectively, characterizing the set of *initial* and *final* states. (Intuitively, F describes the set of states in which the security-sensitive workflow terminates: to express this, the variables in V_{CF} are sufficient.) The goal of the off-line phase is to compute the set $B(S, I, F)$ of all behaviors $s_0 \xrightarrow{e_0} s_1 \xrightarrow{e_1} \cdots s_{n-1} \xrightarrow{e_{n-1}} s_n$ such that s_0 is an initial state (i.e. satisfies I) and s_n is a final state (i.e. satisfies F), for every finite sub-set U of users in $\mathcal{U}$.

Symbolic behaviors. We solve the problem of enumerating all possible behaviors of a security-sensitive workflow $S = (V_{\text{CF}} \cup V_{\text{Auth}}, Tr)$ for every sub-set U of users in $\mathcal{U}$ by using a symbolic representation for S and U. We use first-order logic formulae [15] to represent sets of states. A *state formula* is a first-order formula containing (at most) the state variables in $V_{\text{CF}} \cup V_{\text{Auth}} \cup V_{\text{User}}$ as free variables where V_{User} is a set of variables taking values over the set U of users. A state formula P evaluates to true (in symbols, $s, v \models P$) or false (in symbols, $s, v \not\models P$) in a state s of the system and for an assignment v of the user variables (i.e. a mapping from V_{User} to U): for each variable x in $V_{\text{CF}} \cup V_{\text{Auth}} \cup V_{\text{User}}$ that appears free in P, replace x by its value in s or v and then evaluate the resulting formula. In other words, state formulae define predicates or, equivalently, sets of states. Examples of state formulae are (1) and (2) describing the sets of initial and final states, respectively, of the security-sensitive workflow in Figure 2. A *symbolic event* is a tuple of the form (6) where, this time, u is a first-order variable in V_{User}, $enabled_{\text{CF}}$ is a state formula over V_{CF}, and $enabled_{\text{Auth}}$ is a state formula over $V_{\text{Auth}} \cup V_{\text{User}}$, act_{CF} is as before, and act_{Auth} is of the form $f(u) := b$ where b is a Boolean value and u is the same variable in the label $t(u)$. A *symbolic security-sensitive transition system* is a tuple $(V_{\text{CF}} \cup V_{\text{Auth}} \cup V_{\text{user}}, Ev)$ where $V_{\text{CF}} \cup V_{\text{Auth}}$ is the set of state variables, V_{User} is the set of user variables, and Ev is a finite set of symbolic events. The semantics of a symbolic security-sensitive transition system $(V_{\text{CF}} \cup V_{\text{Auth}} \cup V_{\text{User}}, Ev)$ is axiomatically defined by using the notion of weakest liberal precondition (wlp) [14]:

$$\mathsf{wlp}(Ev, P) \;:=\; \bigvee_{(t(u):en \rightarrow act) \in Ev} (en \wedge P[act]) \qquad (7)$$

where $P[act]$ denotes the formula obtained from P by substituting the state variable v with the value b when the assignment $v := b$ is in act_{CF} and substituting $v(x)$ with either $v(x) \vee x = u$ when $v(x) := true$ is in act_{Auth} or with $v(x) \wedge x \neq u$ when $v(x) := false$ is in act_{Auth} for x in V_{User} and $act := act_{\text{CF}} \wedge act_{\text{Auth}}$. When Ev is a singleton containing a single symbolic event ev, we write $\mathsf{wlp}(ev, P)$ instead of $\mathsf{wlp}(\{ev\}, P)$. Notice that $\mathsf{wlp}(Ev, P)$ is equivalent to $\bigvee_{ev \in Ev} \mathsf{wlp}(ev, P)$. To make expressions more compact, we also write $\mathsf{wlp}(t(u), P)$ instead of $\mathsf{wlp}(t(u) : en \rightarrow act, P)$.

To illustrate, we compute $\mathsf{wlp}(t5(u), (2))$ where the symbolic event $t5(u)$ is defined in Table 1 by using (7):

$$\left(\begin{array}{l} p4 \wedge p5 \wedge p6 \wedge \neg d_{t5} \wedge \\ a_{t5}(u) \wedge \neg h_{t3}(u) \wedge \neg h_{t2}(u) \end{array} \right) \wedge (\bigwedge_{i=0,\ldots,3} \neg pi \wedge \bigwedge_{i=0,\ldots,4} d_{ti})$$

which is equivalent to

$$\begin{array}{l} (\bigwedge_{i=0,\ldots,3} pi \wedge \neg p4 \wedge \neg p5 \wedge \neg p6 \wedge \bigwedge_{i=1,\ldots,4} d_{ti} \wedge \neg d_{t5}) \wedge \\ \qquad a_{t5}(u1) \wedge \neg h_{t3}(u1) \wedge \neg h_{t2}(u1)) \end{array}$$

and it identifies those states in which there is a token in places $p4$, $p5$, and $p6$, task $t5$ has not yet been executed whereas tasks $t1$, ..., $t4$ have been executed, user $u1$ has the right to execute $t5$ and has executed neither $t2$ nor $t3$. This is exactly the formula labeling node 1 in Figure 3.

A *symbolic behavior* is a sequence of the form $P_0 \xrightarrow{e_0} P_1 \xrightarrow{e_1} \cdots \xrightarrow{e_{n-1}} P_n$ where P_i is a state formula and e_i is a symbolic event such that (a) $P_0 \wedge I$ is satisfiable, (b) P_i is logically equivalent to $\mathsf{wlp}(e_i, P_{i+1})$ for $i = 0, ..., n-1$, and (c) P_n is F for I and F formulae characterizing the initial and final states, respectively. The crucial advantage of symbolic events is the use of variables to represent users instead of enumerating them. To illustrate, consider a simple security-sensitive workflow with just two tasks t_1, t_2 such that t_1 should be executed before t_2 and there is a SoD constraint between them. If the cardinality of the set U of users is n, then the cardinality of the set of all possible behaviors is $n^2 - n$. By using symbolic events, we can represent all such behaviors by a single symbolic behavior $P_0 \xrightarrow{t_1(u1)} P_1 \xrightarrow{t_2(u2)} P_2$ with the proviso that $u1 \neq u2$ where $u1, u2$ are variables. Before stating formally this result, we need to introduce the notion of security-sensitive transition system $T = (V_{\text{CF}} \cup V_{\text{Auth}}, Ev_T)$ *associated to a symbolic security-sensitive transition system* $S = (V_{CF} \cup V_{Auth} \cup V_{User}, Ev_S)$ *and a finite set* $U \subseteq \mathcal{U}$ *of users*: if the symbolic event $t(ui) : en_S \rightarrow act_S$ is in Ev_S, then Ev_T contains an event $t(u_i) : en \rightarrow act$ where u is a user in U, en is the predicate interpreting the formula obtained from en_S by substituting the variable ui with u_i and all other user variables with users in U (in all possible ways), and act is obtained from act_S by substituting ui with u_i.

THEOREM 3.1. *Let $S = (V_{CF} \cup V_{Auth} \cup V_{User}, Ev_S)$ be a symbolic security-sensitive transition system and $T = (V_{CF} \cup V_{Auth}, Ev_T)$ be the associated security-sensitive transition system for the set $U \subseteq \mathcal{U}$ of users. If $s_0 \xrightarrow{t_0(u_0)} s_1 \xrightarrow{t_1(u_1)} \cdots s_{n-1} \xrightarrow{t_{n-1}(u_{n-1})} s_n$ is a behavior of T for $u_0, ..., u_{n-1}$ in U, then there exists a symbolic behavior $P_0 \xrightarrow{t_0(u0)} P_1 \xrightarrow{t_1(u1)} \cdots \xrightarrow{t_{n-1}(un-1)} P_n$ such that $s_i, v_i \models P_i$ with $v_i(ui) = u_i$ for $i = 0, ..., n-1$ and $s_n, v_{n-1} \models P_n$.*

This result tells us that a symbolic behavior is an adequate (and hopefully compact) representation of a set of behaviors. The proof is by a standard induction on the length of the behaviors and exploits the fact that the enforcement of authorization constraints depends only on two aspects: the identity of users (via the state variables a_t's modeling the interface to the concrete authorization policy establishing if a user has the right to execute a task) and the history of the computation (via the state variables h_t's keeping track of who has executed which tasks so that SoD and BoD constraints can be guaranteed to hold).

Computation of symbolic behaviors. Algorithm 1 computes the set of all possible symbolic behaviors of a symbolic security-sensitive workflow. It takes as input the symbolic security-sensitive workflow S together with the state formula F defining the set of final states and returns a labeled graph RG, called *reachability graph*, whose set of labeled paths is the set of all symbolic behaviors of S ending with F. The procedure incrementally builds the reachability graph RG by updating the set N of nodes, the set E of edges, and the labeling function λ from N to state formulae. Initially (line 1), a new node i is created (by invoking the auxiliary function `new`, which returns a "fresh" node—i.e. distinct from any other node already in N—at each invocation), N is assigned to the singleton containing node i, which is also labeled (via λ) by the final formula F. The algorithm also maintains the set TBV of nodes to be visited, which is made equal to N. Then, the main loop (lines 2–14) is entered by checking if there are some nodes to be visited (line 2). At each iteration, it is first (line 3) checked whether the set of states identified by the wlp of the formula $\lambda[i]$ with respect to the set Ev_S of symbolic events is included in the union of the sets of states that have been already generated. This is done by invoking `subsumed`(i,N,N') which returns true iff, for each symbolic event $ev \in Ev_S$, there exists a sub-set N' of $N - \{i\}$ and $wlp(ev, \lambda[i])$ implies the formula $\bigvee_{j\in N'} \lambda[j]$ (notice that the third argument N' is passed by reference). If this is the case, we can avoid to add a new node ν to N labeled by $wlp(ev, \lambda[i])$ as the symbolic behaviors arriving in ν have already been generated when visiting the nodes in N'. Thus, we can delete node i from TBV, add a new node j labeled by $wlp(ev, \lambda[i])$ together with an edge from j to i labeled by $\overline{ev}$ and—by invoking the auxiliary function `connect`—duplicate the initial part of each path passing through a node n' in N' by replacing n' with j provided that the newly created path is a symbolic behavior of the symbolic transition system. To illustrate, consider node 7 in Figure 3 (colored in red): $wlp(ti(u), \lambda[7])$ is unsatisfiable for $i = 1, 3, 4, 5$ (and can thus be ignored) whereas $wlp(t2(u3), \lambda[7])$ is satisfiable and implies $\lambda[13]$; this is checked by invoking `subsumed` with $N' = \{13\}$. Thus, we create a new node (say) 29, with $\lambda[29]$ equal to $wlp(t2(u3), \lambda[7])$, draw an edge from 29 to 7 with label $t2(u3)$, duplicate the initial parts of the paths passing through node 13 (namely $\lambda[17] \stackrel{t1(u3)}{\longrightarrow} \lambda[13]$ and $\lambda[18] \stackrel{t1(u4)}{\longrightarrow} \lambda[13]$) while replacing 13 with 29 (thus obtaining $\lambda[17] \stackrel{t1(u3)}{\longrightarrow} \lambda[29]$ and $\lambda[18] \stackrel{t1(u4)}{\longrightarrow} \lambda[29]$), and then check that the newly created paths, namely

$$\lambda[17] \stackrel{t1(u3)}{\longrightarrow} \lambda[29] \stackrel{t2(u3)}{\longrightarrow} \lambda[7] \stackrel{t3(u2)}{\longrightarrow} \lambda[4] \stackrel{t4(u1)}{\longrightarrow} \lambda[4] \stackrel{t5(u1)}{\longrightarrow} \lambda[0] \text{ and}$$
$$\lambda[18] \stackrel{t1(u4)}{\longrightarrow} \lambda[29] \stackrel{t2(u3)}{\longrightarrow} \lambda[7] \stackrel{t3(u2)}{\longrightarrow} \lambda[4] \stackrel{t4(u1)}{\longrightarrow} \lambda[4] \stackrel{t5(u1)}{\longrightarrow} \lambda[0],$$

are symbolic behaviors. It turns out that only the latter is so, since the former violates the SoD constraint between $t1$ and $t2$. We thus add only the path $\lambda[18] \stackrel{t1(u4)}{\longrightarrow} \lambda[29] \stackrel{t2(u3)}{\longrightarrow} \lambda[7]$ to the graph in Figure 3. Nodes 5, 10, and 12 are handled similarly. These extensions to the graph in Figure 3 are omitted to keep it readable.

Algorithm 1 Building a symbolic reachability graph

Input: $S = (V_{\text{CF}} \cup V_{\text{Auth}} \cup V_{\text{User}}, Ev_S)$ and F
Output: $RG = (N, \lambda, E)$
1: $i \leftarrow$ new(); $N \leftarrow \{i\}$; $E \leftarrow \emptyset$; $\lambda[i] \leftarrow F$; $TBV \leftarrow \{i\}$;
2: **while** $TBV \neq \emptyset$ **do**
3:   **if** `subsumed`(i,N,N') **then**
4:     `connect`(N',i); $TBV \leftarrow TBV - \{i\}$;
5:   **end if**
6:   **for all** $ev \in Ev_S$ **do**
7:     $P \leftarrow$ wlp$(ev, \lambda[i])$;
8:     **if** P is satisfiable **then**
9:       $j \leftarrow$ new(); $N \leftarrow N \cup \{j\}$; $E \leftarrow E \cup \{(i, \overline{ev}, j)\}$;
10:       $\lambda[j] \leftarrow P$; $TBV \leftarrow TBV \cup \{j\}$;
11:     **end if**
12:   **end for**
13:   $i \leftarrow$ `pickOne`(TBV); $TBV \leftarrow TBV - \{i\}$;
14: **end while**
15: **return** (N, λ, E);

If node i is not subsumed by those in N (i.e. `subsumed`(i,N) returns false), we compute the wlp with respect to all symbolic events (inner loop 6–11). I.e., for each ev in Ev_S, we compute wlp$(ev, \lambda[i])$ labeling the node i being visited (line 6) and verify if it defines a set of states which is non-empty, by checking the satisfiability of the resulting formula (line 7). If this is the case, we add a fresh node j, labeled by the wlp just computed, to N, an edge from i to j labeled by the name $\overline{ev}$ of the symbolic event ev, and add the newly created node j to the set TBV (lines 8 and 9). For instance, when computing the wlp of the formula labeling node 0 in Figure 3, we found out that only the symbolic event named $t5(u1)$ generates a formula denoting a non-empty set of states and thus we added node 1 labeled by such a formula and an edge from 1 to 0 labeled by $t5(u1)$. After exiting the inner loop, if the set TBV of nodes to be visited is non-empty, we consider another node to be visited by invoking the auxiliary function `pickOne`(TBV) which non-deterministically selects an element from TBV (when this is empty, `pickOne` returns a distinguished element), which is then deleted, and we start the main loop again.

THEOREM 3.2. *Let I be the initial state formula. If Algorithm 1 returns the reachability graph RG when taking as input the symbolic security-sensitive transition system $S = (V_{CF} \cup V_{Auth} \cup V_{User}, Ev_S)$ and the final state formula F, then the set of all symbolic behaviors of S is the set of labeled paths in RG starting with a node labeled by a formula whose conjunction with I is satisfiable and ending with a node labeled by F.*

The proof of this theorem uses the definition of wlp and the properties discussed above about the auxiliary functions `subsumed` and `connect`. It is possible to show that Algorithm 1 always terminates by adapting the results in [8].

3.2 On-line

Theorem 3.2 implies that starting from an initial state (i.e. one satisfying the initial formula I) in the reachability graph computed by Algorithm 1, it is always possible to reach a final state (i.e. one satisfying the final formula F). If no event can be enabled infinitely often without being executed—called *strong fairness*—then a final state is eventually reached. (As observed in [25], the assumption of strong fairness is reasonable in the context of workflow management since decisions to execute tasks are under the responsibility of applications or humans.) This is the key to prove the following result, underlying the correctness of the automated technique—to be described below—for extracting (part of) the monitor from the reachability graph computed by Algorithm 1.

THEOREM 3.3. *Let* $S = (V_{CF} \cup V_{Auth} \cup V_{User}, Ev_S)$ *be a symbolic security-sensitive transition system and* $T = (V_{CF} \cup V_{Auth}, Ev_T)$ *be the associated security-sensitive transition system for the finite set* $U \subseteq \mathcal{U}$ *of users. Furthermore, let* $RG = (N, \lambda, E)$ *be the symbolic reachability graph computed by Algorithm 1 when taking as input* S *and a final state formula* F*. If the state* s *satisfies a formula* $\lambda[i]$ *for some* $i \in N$*, then there exists a behavior* $s_0 \overset{t_0(u_0)}{\to} s_1 \overset{t_1(u_1)}{\to} \cdots s_{n-1} \overset{t_{n-1}(u_{n-1})}{\longrightarrow} s_n$ *of* T *such that (i)* $s_0 = s$*, (ii)* s_n *satisfies* F*, and (iii)* $(i, t(x), j) \in E$ *with* $t_0 = t$ *and* $s_0(x) = u_0$*.*

Thus, if T is in state s and we want to know if a certain user u_0 can execute task t_0 while guaranteeing that the authorization constraints are satisfied and the workflow terminates, it is sufficient to find a node of the reachability graph that is satisfied by the s and one of the outgoing edges is labeled by t_0. Indeed, this is exactly the task a monitor is supposed to perform! To make this operational, we observe that we can associate the Datalog clause [10]

$$can\_do(u,t) \quad \leftarrow \quad \Gamma \wedge C_k[i]$$

for each node $i \in N$ and edge $(i, t(u), j) \in E$, where Γ is the conjunction of atoms of the form $is\_user(x)$ for each variable x in $C_k[i]$ with $RG = (N, \lambda, E)$ and $\bigvee_{k=1}^{n_i} C_k[i]$ is the disjunctive normal form of $\lambda[i]$. Let $D(RG)$ be the set of Datalog clauses built in this way from the reachability graph RG. (It is straightforward to check that $D(RG)$ is non-recursive; see [10] for a precise definition). Formally, the addition of Γ is needed to make $D(RG)$ a safe Datalog program (see again [10] for a precise definition) so that answering queries always terminates.

After building the Datalog program $D(RG)$, it is straightforward to build a run-time monitor. Let U be a finite set of users, $A \subseteq V_{\text{Auth}}$ be the sub-set of state variables a_t's modeling the interface to the concrete authorization policy establishing if a user has the right to execute a task, and P be a Datalog program formalizing an authorization policy (i.e. P contains a clause of the form $is\_user(u)$ for each $u \in U$ and clauses whose heads contain only the predicates in A). We call P a *Datalog authorization policy program over the interface variables in* V_{Auth}. (How to write authorization policies in Datalog is outside the scope of this paper, the interested reader is pointed to [18].) Any assignment over the states variables in $V_{\text{CF}} \cup (V_{\text{Auth}} - A)$ can be represented by a set Σ of Datalog facts of the forms p, $\neg p$, $h_t(u)$, or $\neg h_t(u)$ for $p \in V_{\text{CF}}$ and $h_t \in (V_{\text{Auth}} - A)$. We call Σ a *partial Datalog state over the state variables in* $V_{CF} \cup (V_{Auth} - A)$.

THEOREM 3.4. *Let* $S = (V_{CF} \cup V_{Auth} \cup V_{User}, Ev_S)$ *be a symbolic security-sensitive transition system,* $T = (V_{CF} \cup V_{Auth}, Ev_T)$ *be the associated security-sensitive transition system for the finite set* $U \subseteq \mathcal{U}$ *of users, and* $RG = (N, \lambda, E)$ *be the symbolic reachability graph computed by Algorithm 1 when taking as input* S *and a final state formula* F*. Additionally, let* P *be a Datalog authorization policy over the interface variables in* V_{Auth} *and* Σ *be a partial Datalog state. A user* $u \in U$ *can execute task* t *guaranteeing the satisfaction of all authorization constraints and the termination of the workflow iff the query* $can\_do(u, t)$ *is answered positively by the Datalog program* $D(RG) \cup P \cup \Sigma$*.*

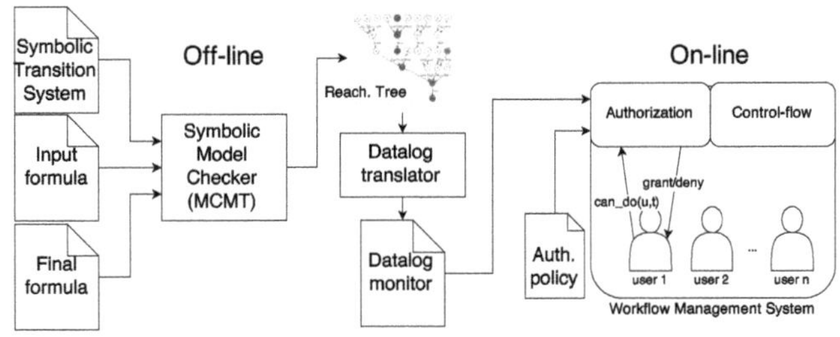

Figure 4: Architecture of the implementation

This is the main result of the paper and guarantees the correctness of our procedure to synthesize run-time monitors. It is a consequence of the definition of Datalog authorization policy program, partial Datalog state, and Theorem 3.3. Notice that when both $D(RG)$ and P are non-recursive (stratified) Datalog programs, queries can be answered very efficiently in *LogSpace* and can be translated to SQL without aggregate operators (such as AVG and COUNT).

4. EXPERIMENTS

We have implemented the technique for the automated synthesis of monitors in a tool whose architecture is depicted in Figure 4. On the left (Off-line), we have a symbolic model checker (MCMT [17]) that, given a symbolic transition system representing a workflow together with initial and final formulae, computes the reachability graph according to Algorithm 1. The graph is then passed to the Datalog translator—implemented in Python (v2.7.5)—which creates a Datalog program as explained in Section 3.2. On the right of Figure 4 (On-line), we use pyDatalog (v0.14.5) as our Datalog engine to answer authorization queries of the form *"can user u execute task t and guarantee the successful termination of the workflow?"*.

For a first evaluation of the scalability of our technique, we focus on an important class of workflows encountered in practice, namely those designed according to a hierarchical decomposition principle. The idea is to split a complex workflow into subflows which are again decomposed into smaller subflows up to a desired level of detail. Several workflows management systems support this style of workflow specification following an established line of works in both academy (see, e.g., [23]) and industry (see, e.g., the "SAP Modeling Handbook," available on-line at `http://wiki.scn.sap.com/wiki/display/ModHandbook/Process+Hierarchy`). Hierarchic workflows are structured according to the notion of *task refinement*, i.e. a task can be refined into a subflow. To illustrate, the workflow on the left of Figure 5 contains the task Bookings, which can be refined by the workflow on the right of the same picture. This means that by replacing task Bookings with the workflow on the right of the figure, we derive the workflow in Figure 1.

Besides fostering reuse and simplifying maintenance of complex workflows, hierarchic specifications allow for the development of a divide-and-conquer strategy when applying

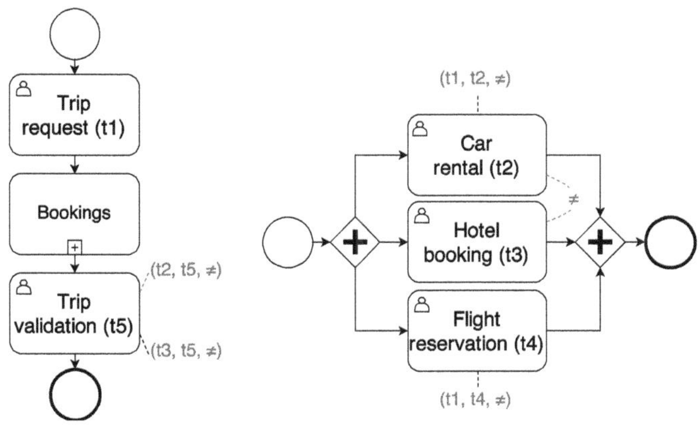

Figure 5: Hierarchic specification of the trip request example workflow (cf. Figure 1)

Algorithm 1. I.e., given a hierarchic workflow, it is possible to compute its monitor for the WSP by first computing the monitors for each of the subflows separately and then "gluing" them together. To understand what we mean by "gluing," let us consider the hierarchic workflow in Figure 5. We run the Algorithm 1 first on the workflow on the left, on that on the right, and we run the Datalog translator on the resulting reachability graphs to obtain the Datalog programs $D(RG_l)$ and $D(RG_r)$, respectively. Let p_i^l, p_f^l and p_i^r, p_f^r be the predicates corresponding to the initial and final places of the Petri nets representing the workflows on the left and on the right of Figure 5. The Datalog program for the hierarchic workflow (equivalent to the workflow in Figure 1) can be obtained by adding the clauses $p_i^r \leftarrow p_f^l$ (to transfer the control flow from the workflow on the left to that on the right) and $p_i^l \leftarrow p_f^r$ (to transfer back the control flow from the workflow on the right to that on the left) to $D(RG_l) \cup D(RG_r)$ and finally removing the clauses in which the identifier of the task Bookings occur. As can be seen in the example, it is possible to have authorization constraints that span different subflows. For each constraint in this case, a literal $\neg h_t(u)$ is added to the corresponding transition in the symbolic transition system. For instance, the SoD constraint $(t1, t2, \neq)$ adds the literal $\neg h_{t1}(u)$ to the enabling condition of $t2$. These literals are unconstrained when each subflow is taken separately, but after the "gluing" process, they act as any other constraint.

This modular approach to synthesizing monitors has been implemented in our tool and is key to scalability. In fact, without using hierarchic specifications, for a workflow with up to 5 tasks, running Algorithm 1 (the most expensive step of our technique) takes few seconds on a standard laptop; for 6 tasks, around a minute; and for 7 tasks, already two hours and a half! Since hierarchic specifications are so important for scalability, we have designed and implemented heuristics that, given monolithic workflows, are capable of deriving equivalent hierarchic specifications. For lack of space, we leave their description to future work and assume in the following that our tool is presented with hierarchic workflows. As observed above, hierarchic specifications of workflows are frequently available so that results from experiments on them already give significant indications about the efficiency of techniques for synthesizing run-time monitors for the WSP.

4.1 Real-world workflows

We have experimented with some real-world workflows taken from related works and present here two cases in details. These examples show the expressiveness of our approach and illustrate the use of all the basic control-flow patterns (such as sequence and exclusive choice) besides advanced patterns for arbitrary loops [26]. Figure 6 shows the two examples in extended BPM notation, where—following [3]—the circles marked by the depiction of a user leaving a door represent *release points* and the gray lines show the authorization constraints. A release point is a special event whereby the history of executions of the workflow is erased, so that authorization constraints can be handled in loops.

Drug dispensation process [4] (left of Figure 6). The execution of an instance of this workflow starts with a Patient requesting drugs to a Nurse ($t1$). The Nurse consults the Patient's record and sends it to a PrivacyAdvocate ($t2$), who decides if this data should be anonymized ($t3$ and $t4$). If the drug prescription has therapeutic notes, they must be reviewed by a Therapist ($t5$) and in parallel, a Researcher can add data related to experimental drugs ($t6$). In the end a Pharmacist either approves or denies the process ($t7$) and a Nurse carries out the related tasks: collect and dispense the drugs ($t9$ and $t10$) or notify the Patient ($t8$). A SoD constraint for this workflow, not shown in the Figure, is $(t1, t7, \neq)$: the same user cannot act as Patient and Pharmacist, so that a Pharmacist cannot dispense drugs to himself.

A workflow of this size (10 tasks) would be intractable for our tool. Thus, we come up with a hierarchic specification consisting of two subflows to be executed one after the other; the former is refined to the subflow containing tasks t_1, ..., t_4 and the latter the subflow with tasks t_5, ..., t_{10}. According to some control flow operators, not all tasks must be executed in the workflow for its successful termination. In fact, tasks $t4$, $t5$ and $t6$ may or may not be executed depending on certain conditions (e.g., "*anonymize?*") while tasks $t8$ and $t9$ are mutually exclusive. To represent the decisions that have to be taken to complete the workflow, we create transitions for the various branches whose enabling conditions depend on additional variables—called *environment variables*—modeling non-deterministic choices of the environment. For instance, the fact that task $t7$ is followed by the decision point *approved?* can be represented by the following two transitions:

$$\begin{aligned} t_7^{true}(u) &= p6 \wedge p7 \wedge \neg d_{t7} \wedge app \wedge a_{t7} \wedge \neg h_{t1}(u) \rightarrow \\ &\quad p6, p7, p10, d_{t7}, h_{t7}(u) := F, F, T, T, T \\ t_7^{false}(u) &= p6 \wedge p7 \wedge \neg d_{t7} \wedge \neg app \wedge a_{t7} \wedge \neg h_{t1}(u) \rightarrow \\ &\quad p6, p7, p8, d_{t7}, h_{t7}(u) := F, F, T, T, T\,. \end{aligned}$$

When the environment variable *app* is true (cf. t_7^{true}), tasks $t9$ and $t10$ must be executed; when it is false (t_7^{false}), only task $t8$ is executed. Besides permitting the precise representation of the control flow, environment variables allow for writing final formulae differentiating between the alternative execution. For example, assuming a Petri net representation of the drug dispensation process that has a place $p4$ after $t4$ and before $t5$, we run the model checker on the first subflow with the final formula

$$\begin{aligned} &(\neg p0 \wedge \neg p1 \wedge ... \wedge p4 \wedge d_{t1} \wedge d_{t2} \wedge d_{t3} \wedge d_{t4}) \quad \vee \\ &(\neg p0 \wedge \neg p1 \wedge ... \wedge \neg p4 \wedge d_{t1} \wedge d_{t2} \wedge d_{t3} \wedge \neg d_{t4}) \quad . \end{aligned}$$

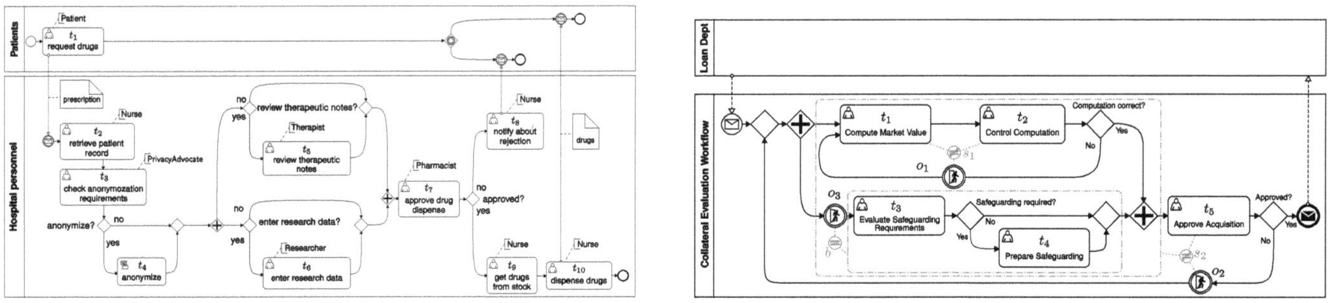

Figure 6: Left: Drug dispensation process from [4]. Right: Collateral evaluation workflow, from [3]

A similar final formula can be derived for the second subflow.

The reachability graph computed for the first subflow contains 200 nodes while that for second 231 nodes. Using a MacBook laptop (see below for a detailed description of its configuration), the time spent to compute the reachability graph and translate it to a Datalog program is around 15s (roughly, 3s for the first and 12s for the second). The time taken by the synthesized monitor to answer access requests is almost negligible.

Collateral evaluation workflow [3] (right of Figure 6). It is executed to evaluate a collateral pledge for a loan. The main difference with the previous workflow is the presence of loops, exemplified by the decision points *Computation correct?* and *Approved?*. This workflow has only 5 tasks, so we do not need to transform it to an equivalent hierarchic specification. Similarly to conditionals, we add environment variables to model decision points and suitable transitions for loops. For instance, task $t2$ is followed by the decision point—encoded by the environment variable $l1$—of the first loop which can be represented by transitions t_2^{true} when $l1$ is true and the loop is taken and t_2^{false} when $l1$ is false and the loop is not taken. The enabling condition of the transitions are analogous to what was shown above while the updates take into account the use of release points when updating the history variables h_t's in order to support the use of authorization constraints in loops as discussed in [3].

The reachability graph for the collateral evaluation process has 135 nodes and the time spent for computing it is around 4s. As before, answering authorization constraints in the on-line phase is immediate.

4.2 Synthetic benchmarks

To test the scalability of our approach, we have extended the generator of random workflows used in [12][1] to produce hierarchic workflows. Our generator has the following parameters: n_w, the number of subflows and n_{tw}, the number of tasks in each subflow ($n_t = n_w \cdot n_{tw}$ is the total number of tasks; n_u, the number of users; p_a, the authorization density which is the ratio, expressed as a percentage, between the cardinality of $\bigcup_t \{a_t(u) = true | u \text{ is a user}\}$ and $n_t \cdot n_u$ (where t ranges over the set of tasks); and p_c, the constraint density which is the ration between the number of SoD constraints in the set C and n_t.

The generator also produces random (finite) sequences $(r_0, r_1, ..., r_n)$ of authorization requests where $r_i = (t, u)$ for t a task and u a user, encoding the question "can u perform task t according to the authorization policy specified by the a_t's and the constraints in C while guaranteeing its termination?"

According to our experience with real-world workflows (cf. Section 4.1), we set n_{tw} to 5 and increase the number n_w of subflows so that the total number n_t of tasks in the generated workflows range from 10 to 500 (notice that [12] considers workflows with at most 150 tasks). More precisely, we let $n_t = 10, 20, ..., 150, 200, 250, ..., 500$ and, following [12], $n_u = n_t$, $p_a = 100\%, 50\%, 10\%$, $p_c = 5\%, 10\%, 20\%$.

Figure 7 shows the behavior of our prototype tool, for the off-line (left) and on-line (right) phases, on the hierarchic workflows produced by the random generator with the parameters described above. The x-axis shows the number n_t of task in the workflow, the y-axis the timings in seconds, each line corresponds to different values for the pair (p_a, p_c) of parameters (recall that $n_u = n_t$). The timings are obtained on a MacBook 2014 laptop with a 1.3GHz dual-core Intel Core i5 processor and 8GB of RAM, running MAC OS X 10.9.4.

It is clear that the computation time of our tool in both the on-line and off-line phases is linear in the number of tasks in the workflows for any value of the pair (p_a, p_c) of parameters. For the off-line phase, this is so because of the divide-and-conquer strategy described above and supported by hierarchic workflows. For the on-line phase, the linear growth is due to the fact that the synthesized Datalog programs belong to a class whose requests can be answered in linear-time. Notice also that that for workflows with $n_t \leq 200$, the (median) time to answer a request is under 1 second while for workflows with $200 < n_t \leq 500$, it is around 1.6 seconds. This clearly demonstrates that the monitors synthesized by our tool are suitable to be used on-line.

To give an idea of the distribution of the answers given by the synthesized monitors to the randomly generated sequences of authorization requests, Figure 8 shows the number of denied (in red) and granted (in green) requests (y-axis) for workflows with $n_t = 10, ..., 400$ (x-axis) and $(p_a, p_c) = (10, 20)$ (the number shown on the x-axis must be multiplied by 10 to obtain the number of tasks in the workflow). We believe that these results clearly show the scalability and practical applicability of our approach on the important class of hierarchically specified workflows.

5. RELATED WORK

Verification of array-based systems. Model Checking Modulo Theories [16] is an approach for the verification of array-based systems based on the computation of pre-

[1]We would like to thank the authors for sharing their source code with us.

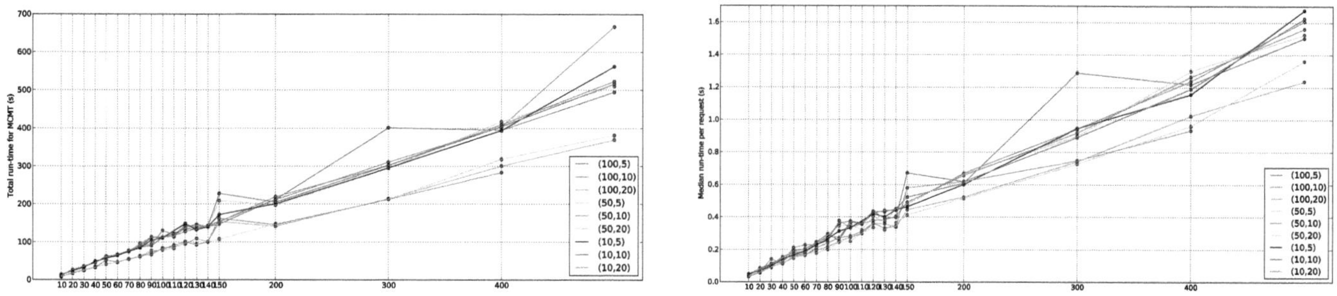

Figure 7: Total run-time of off-line (left) and online (right) phase by the number of tasks in all configurations

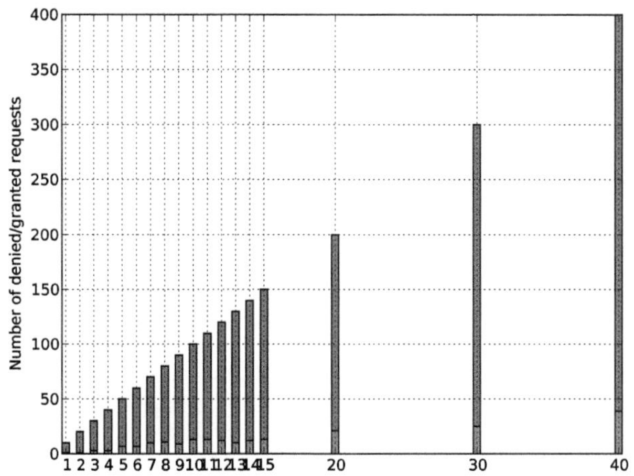

Figure 8: Number of granted (green) and denied (red) requests for increasing values of n_t with $(p_a, p_c) = (10, 20)$

images of a set of states using first-order formulae and on reducing fix-point checks to SMT solving. This approach is implemented by the model checker MCMT [17]. The link between array-based systems and security-sensitive workflows was given in [8], where composed array-based systems represent security-sensitive workflows, with a terminating procedure for the verification of reachability properties for this class of systems.

Workflow Satisfiability. Bertino et al. [6] described the specification and enforcement of authorization constraints in workflow management systems, presenting constraints as clauses in a logic program and an exponential algorithm for assigning users and roles to tasks without violating them, but considering only linear workflows. Crampton [11] showed another model for specifying constraints, considering workflows as DAGs, and an algorithm to determine whether there is an assignment of users to tasks that satisfies the constraints, showing that it can be incorporated into a reference monitor. [13] extended the previous work to consider the effects of delegation on satisfiability, showing algorithms to only allow delegations that can still satisfy a workflow. Crampton et al. [12] used model checking on an NP-complete fragment of linear temporal logic to decide the satisfiability of workflow instances. The authors presented three different encodings in LTL(F) that can compute a set of solutions, minimal user bases and a safe bound on resiliency. The synthesis of monitors was left as future work.

Wang and Li [27] proposed a role-and-relation based access control model that allows to describe the relationships between users and thus specify complex authorization constraints. The authors showed that the WSP is NP-complete in their model and that this intractability is inherent in authorization systems supporting simple constraints. They showed that with only equality and inequality relations, using the number of tasks as a parameter renders the WSP fixed-parameter tractable. They also reduced the problem to SAT. Yang et al. [20] studied the complexity of several formulations of the WSP, considering the possibility of different control-flow patterns, and showed that, in general, the problem is intractable.

Basin et al. [5] considered the problem of choosing authorization policies that allow a successful workflow execution and an optimal balance between system protection and user empowerment. They treat the problem as an optimization problem (finding the cost-minimizing authorization policy that allows a successful workflow execution) and show that, in the role-based case, it is NP-complete. They generalize the decision problem of whether a given authorization policy allows a successful workflow execution to the notion of an optimal authorization policy that satisfies this property. In a following work, Basin et al. [4] used the Separation of Duties Algebra (SoDA) to enforce SoD constraints in a dynamic, service-oriented enterprise environment. The authors generalized SoDA's semantics to workflow traces that satisfy a term and refined it for control-flow and role-based authorizations. Their formalization, based on CSP, is the base for provisioning SoD as a Service, with an implementation using a workflow engine and a SoD enforcement monitor. [4] is the closest to us in terms of monitor implementation, but their monitor only verifies if a trace of a workflow satisfies a SoDA term, being incapable of checking whether there is a future trace that can be concatenated in order to satisfy the workflow.

This work. This work extends the results in [7, 9] by describing a fully automated technique, arguing its correctness, providing an implementation, and a thorough experimental evaluation. The main advantages of our work with respect to the others discussed above is the specification of the security-sensitive workflows as array-based systems, the consideration of an off-line and an on-line phase and the composition of sub- workflows. These three characteristics allow us to efficiently compute all terminating executions of large instances of workflows for a finite but unbounded number of users and then translate it to a Datalog program that acts as an efficient run-time monitor.

6. CONCLUSIONS

We have introduced and implemented a precise technique to automatically synthesize run-time monitors capable of ensuring the successful termination of workflows while enforcing authorization policies and SoD constraints, thus solving the run-time version of the WSP. It consists of an off-line phase in which we compute a symbolic representation of all possible behaviors of a workflow and an on-line phase in which the monitor is derived from such a symbolic representation. An advantage of the technique is that changes in the policies can be taken into account without re-running the off-line phase since only an abstract interface to policies is required. The interface is refined to the concrete policy only in the on-line phase. We have also described the assumptions for the correctness of the technique (cf. Theorem 3.4). An extensive experimental evaluation with an implementation of the technique shows the scalability of our approach on the important class of hierarchic workflows.

As future work, we plan to present a detailed description of our heuristics to obtain equivalent hierarchic specification of monolithic workflows. This would allows us to enlarge the scope of applicability of our approach even further. We also intend to integrate our prototype in available workflow execution engines—e.g., the one available in the SAP HANA platform (`http://www.sap.com/hana`)—to collect data about the performances of our monitors on real workflows, and compare the results with those in this paper. This would be an important step towards the creation of a library of benchmarks to set a standard for the evaluation of workflow analysis techniques.

7. REFERENCES

[1] P. A. Abdulla, K. Cerans, B. Jonsson, and Y.-K. Tsay. General decidability theorems for infinite-state systems. In *Proc. of LICS*, pages 313–321, 1996.

[2] A. Armando and S. E. Ponta. Model Checking of Security-sensitive Business Processes. In *6th Int. Ws. on Formal Aspects in Security and Trust (FAST)*, 2009.

[3] D. Basin, S. J. Burri, and G. Karjoth. Obstruction-free authorization enforcement: Aligning security with business objectives. In *Proc. of CSF'11*, pages 99–113, Washington, DC., 2011. IEEE Computer Society.

[4] D. Basin, S. J. Burri, and G. Karjoth. Dynamic enforcement of abstract separation of duty constraints. *ACM TISSeC*, 15(3):13:1–13:30, Nov. 2012.

[5] D. Basin, S. J. Burri, and G. Karjoth. Optimal workflow-aware authorizations. In *Proc. of SACMAT '12*, pages 93–102, New York, NY, 2012. ACM.

[6] E. Bertino, E. Ferrari, and V. Atluri. The specification and enforcement of authorization constraints in workflow management systems. *TISSeC*, 2:65–104, 1999.

[7] C. Bertolissi and S. Ranise. A Methodology to build run-time Monitors for Security-Aware Workflows. In *Proc. of ICITST'13*. IEEE, 2013.

[8] C. Bertolissi and S. Ranise. Verification of Composed Array-based Systems with Applications to Security-Aware Workflows. In *Proc. of FROCOS'13*. Springer, 2013.

[9] C. Bertolissi and S. Ranise. A smt–based methodology for monitoring of security–aware workflows. *Int. J. of ITST*, 5(3):275–290, 01 2014.

[10] S. Ceri, G. Gottlob, and L. Tanca. What You Always Wanted to Know About Datalog (And Never Dared to Ask). *IEEE TKDE*, 1(1):146–166, 1989.

[11] J. Crampton. A reference monitor for workflow systems with constrained task execution. In *10th ACM SACMAT*, pages 38–47. ACM, 2005.

[12] J. Crampton, M. Huth, and J.-P. Kuo. Authorized workflow schemas: deciding realizability through ltl(f) model checking. *STTT*, 16(1):31–48, 2014.

[13] J. Crampton and H. Khambhammettu. Delegation and satisfiability in workflow systems. In *SACMAT*, pages 31–40, New York, NY, USA, 2008. ACM.

[14] E. W. Dijkstra. *A Discipline of Programming*. Prentice-Hall, 1976.

[15] H. B. Enderton. *A Mathematical Introduction to Logic*. Academic Press, New York-London, 1972.

[16] S. Ghilardi and S. Ranise. Backward reachability of array-based systems by SMT solving: Termination and invariant synthesis. *In LMCS, Vol. 6, Issue 4*, 2010.

[17] S. Ghilardi and S. Ranise. MCMT: A Model Checker Modulo Theories. In *IJCAR*, volume 6173 of *LNCS*, pages 22–29, 2010.

[18] N. Li and J. C. Mitchell. Datalog with constraints: a foundation for trust management languages. In *PADL'03*, pages 58–73, 2003.

[19] T. Murata. Petri nets: properties, analysis and applications. *Proc. of the IEEE*, 77(4):541–580, 1989.

[20] I. R. P. Yang, X. Xie and S. Lu. Satisfiability analysis of workflows with control-flow patterns and authorization constraints. *IEEE TSC*, 99, 2013.

[21] S. Sankaranarayanan, H. Sipma, and Z. Manna. Petri net analysis using invariant generation. In *In Verification: Theory and Practice, LNCS 2772*, pages 682–701. Springer Verlag, 2003.

[22] A. U. Shankar. An Introduction to Assertional Reasoning for Concurrent Systems. *ACM Comput. Surv.*, 25(3):225–262, Sept. 1993.

[23] W. van der Aalst. Workflow verification: Finding control-flow errors using petri-net-based techniques. In *Business Process Management*, volume 1806 of *LNCS*, pages 161–183. Springer, 2000.

[24] W. van der Aalst and A. H. M. T. Hofstede. Yawl: Yet another workflow language. *Inf. Systems*, 30:245–275, 2003.

[25] W. van der Aalst, K. van Hee, A. ter Hofstede, N. Sidorova, H. Verbeek, M. Voorhoeve, and M. Wynn. Soundness of workflow nets: classification, decidability, and analysis. *Formal Aspects of Comp.*, 23(3):333–363, 2011.

[26] W. M. P. Van Der Aalst, A. H. M. Ter Hofstede, B. Kiepuszewski, and A. P. Barros. Workflow patterns. *Distrib. Parallel Databases*, 14(1):5–51, July 2003.

[27] Q. Wang and N. Li. Satisfiability and resiliency in workflow authorization systems. *TISSeC*, 13:40:1–40:35, December 2010.

AppPolicyModules: Mandatory Access Control for Third-Party Apps

Enrico Bacis
enrico.bacis@unibg.it

Simone Mutti
simone.mutti@unibg.it

Stefano Paraboschi
parabosc@unibg.it

Università degli Studi di Bergamo, Italy
Department of Management, Information and Production Engineering

ABSTRACT

Android has recently introduced the support for Mandatory Access Control, which extends previous security services relying on the Android Permission Framework and on the kernel-level Discretionary Access Control. This extension has been obtained with the use of SELinux and its adaptation to Android (SEAndroid). Currently, the use of the MAC model is limited to the protection of system resources. All the apps that are installed by users fall in a single undifferentiated domain, *untrusted_app*. We propose an extension of the architecture that permits to associate with each app a dedicated MAC policy, contained in a dedicated *appPolicyModule*, in order to protect app resources even from malware with root privileges.

A crucial difference with respect to the support for policy modules already available in some SELinux implementations is the need to constrain the policies in order to guarantee that an app policy is not able to manipulate the system policy. We present the security requirements that have to be satisfied by the support for modules and show that our solution satisfies these requirements. The support for appPolicyModules can also be the basis for the automatic generation of policies, with a stricter enforcement of Android permissions. A prototype has been implemented and experimental results show a minimal performance overhead for app installation and runtime.

Categories and Subject Descriptors

D.4.6 [**Security and Protection**]: Access control

Keywords

Android, App Security, Policy Modularity, Administrative Policies, Mandatory Access Control, SELinux

1. INTRODUCTION

Mobile operating systems play a central role in the evolution of Information and Communication Technologies. One of the clearest trends of the past few years has been the adoption by users of mobile portable devices, replacing personal computers as the reference platform for the delivery of many ICT resources and services. The rapid success and wide deployment of mobile operating systems has also introduced a number of challenging security requirements, making explicit the need for an improvement of security technology.

The mobile scenario is indeed characterized by two mutually reinforcing aspects. On one hand, mobile devices are high-value targets, since they offer a direct financial incentive in the use of the credit that can be associated with the device or in the abuse of the available payment services (e.g., Google Wallet, telephone credit and mobile banking) [13,18]. In addition, mobile devices permit the recovery of large collections of personal information and are the target of choice if an adversary wants to monitor the location and behavior of an individual. On the other hand, the system presents a high exposure, with users of modern mobile devices continuously adding new *apps* to their devices, to support a large variety of functions (we follow the common convention and use the term *app* to denote applications for a mobile operating system).

The risks are then greater and different from those of classical operating systems [2]. The frequent installation of external code creates an important threat. The design of security solutions for mobile operating systems has to consider a careful balance between, on one side, the need for users to easily extend with unpredictable apps the set of functions of the system and, on the other side, the need for the system to be protected from potentially malicious apps.

It is to note that the greatest threats derive from apps that are offered through delivery channels that are alternative to the "official" *app markets* (e.g., [19]), whose number of app installations is increasing rapidly, pointing out the need of wider security layers. Apps in official markets, instead, are verified by the market owner and the ones detected as misbehaving are promptly removed from the market. The correct management of the app market is crucial, nevertheless it is not able by itself to fully mitigate the security concerns. The mobile operating systems have to provide a line of defense internal to the device against apps that, due to malicious intent or the presence of flaws in system components or other apps, may let an adversary abuse the system.

1.1 Rationale of the approach

The approach that we propose follows the principles of the Android security model, which aims at isolating from each other the apps that are executed by the system. Each app is confined within an assigned domain and interaction between

ASIA CCS'15, April 14–17, 2015, Singapore..

http://dx.doi.org/10.1145/2714576.2714626.

the elements of the system is managed by a privileged component, which enforces the restrictions specified by a policy. The approach presented in the paper aims at strengthening this barrier, introducing an additional mechanism to guarantee that apps are isolated and cannot manipulate the behavior of other apps. The additional mechanism is obtained with an adaptation of the services of a Mandatory Access Control (MAC) model, which enriches the Discretionary Access Control (DAC) services native to the Linux kernel.

MAC models are commonly perceived as offering a significant contribution to the security of systems. However, one drawback of MAC models is represented by *policy management* which is a especially critical in complex systems such as Android, where each OEM tries to customize the MAC policy for its own devices. Samsung KNOX is the most well-known example. Policy customization provides benefits in terms of security, but it inevitably leads to *policy fragmentation.* Our work tries to do a step ahead in the policy standardization defining a set of *entry points* which can be used by both OEMs and developers in order to extend, under specific constraints, the MAC policy to fulfill their own security requirements and subsequently try to mitigate the policy fragmentation problem.

Apps can only become known to the system when the owner asks for their installation. The MAC policy has then to be dynamic, with the ability to react to the installation and deletion of apps, which requires modularity and the capability to incrementally update the security policy, with a policy module associated with an app. We use the term appPolicyModule to characterize it (when space is limited, like in table headers, we may use the acronym APM). The support for appPolicyModules allows app developers to benefit from the presence of a MAC model, letting them define security policies that increase the protection the app can get against attacks coming from other apps, which may try to manipulate the app and exploit its vulnerabilities.

1.2 Outline

Section 2 provides an overview of the Android security architecture, describing the role of the MAC model introduced by SEAndroid. Section 3 describes the threat to third-party apps that the policy modules want to mitigate. Section 4 presents a model of SELinux policies, used in Section 5 to formalize the requirements that policy modules have to satisfy. Section 6 introduces the syntax used by appPolicyModules. Section 7 illustrates how the use of appPolicyModules can improve the support of Android permissions. In Section 8 we discuss the performance results. Section 9 provides a comparison with previous work in the area. Finally, Section 10 draws a few concluding remarks.

2. ANDROID SECURITY ARCHITECTURE

The Android security model shows a direct correspondence with the overall Android architecture, which is organized in three layers (from bottom to top): (a) an underlying Linux kernel, (b) a middleware framework, and (c) an upper application layer. The Linux kernel in the lowest layer provides low-level services and device drivers to other layers and it differs from a traditional Linux kernel, because it aims at running in an embedded environment and does not have all the features of a traditional Linux distribution. The second layer, the middleware framework, is composed of native Android libraries, runtime modules (e.g., the Dalvik Virtual Machine and the alternative Android Runtime ART) and an application support framework. The third layer is composed by apps. Apps are divided into two categories: (i) pre-installed apps (e.g., Web browser, phone dialer) and (ii) *third-party* apps installed by the user. In the paper we focus on the consideration of third-party apps, since the pre-installed ones are already covered by the system policy.

Android provides distinct security mechanisms at the distinct layers. The Linux security model based on user identifiers (*uid*) and group identifiers (*gid*) operates at the lowest layer, with each app receiving a dedicated *uid* and *gid*. The granularity of this access control model is at the level of files and processes, reusing all the features of the classical DAC model of Unix/Linux, with a compact *acl* that describes for each resource the operations permitted respectively to the owner, members of the resource group, and every user of the system.

At the application layer, Android uses fine-grained permissions to allow apps or components to interact with other apps/components or critical resources. The *Android Permission Framework* contains a rich and structured collection of privileges, in the 4.4.4 version more than 200, focused on the management of the large variety of resources that are offered by the operating system to apps. The access control model assumes that apps specify in their manifest the set of privileges that will be required for their execution. At installation time, users of Android devices have to explicitly accept the request for privileges by the app; in case the user does not accept the app request, the app is not installed.

2.1 SEAndroid

Recently, the SEAndroid initiative [15] has led to a significant extension of the security services, with the integration of Security Enhanced Linux (SELinux) [12] into the Android operating system. The goal of SEAndroid is to build a *mandatory access control* (MAC) model in Android using SELinux to enforce kernel-level MAC, introducing a set of middleware MAC extensions to the Android Permission Framework. SELinux originally started as the Flux Advanced Security Kernel (FLASK) [10] development by the Utah University Flux team and the US Department of Defense. The development was enhanced by the NSA and released as open source software. SELinux policies are expressed at the level of *security context* (also known as *security label* or just *label*). SELinux requires a security context to be associated with every process (or subject) and object, which is used to decide whether access is allowed or not as defined by the policy. Every request a process generates to access a resource will be accepted only if it is authorized by both the classical DAC access control service and by the SELinux policy. The advantage of SELinux compared to the DAC model are its flexibility (the design of Linux assumes a *root* user that has full access to DAC-protected resources) and the fact that process and resource labels can be assigned and updated in a way that is specified at system level by the SELinux policy (in the DAC model owners are able to fully control the resources).

The middleware MAC extension chosen to bridge the gap between SELinux and the Android permission framework is called *install-time MAC* [15] (several middleware MACs have been developed, but only the install-time MAC has been integrated into the AOSP). This mechanism allows to check an app against a MAC policy (i.e., *mac_permissions.xml*).

The integration of this middleware MAC ensures that the policy checks are unbypassable and always applied when apps are installed and when they are loaded during system startup.

The current design of SEAndroid aims at protecting core system resources from possible flaws in the implementation of security in the Android Permission Framework or at the DAC level. The exploitation of vulnerabilities becomes harder due to the constraints on privilege escalation that are introduced by SELinux. Unfortunately, the current use of SELinux in Android aims at protecting the system components and trusted apps from abuses by third-party apps. All the third-party apps fall within a single *untrusted_app* domain and an app interested in getting protection from other apps or from internal vulnerabilities can only rely on Android permissions and the Linux DAC support. This is a significant limitation, since apps can get a concrete benefit from the specification of their own policy.

3. THREAT MODEL

In Android each app receives a dedicated *uid* and *gid* at install-time. These identifiers are used to set the user and the group owner of the resources installed by the app in the default data directory, which is */data/data/"package_name"*. By default, the apps databases, settings, and all other data go there. Since user data for an application also resides in */data/data/"package_name"*, it is important that only that application has access to that particular folder. This confinement of the data folders permits to enforce a strict isolation from other applications. In Android this isolation is only enforced at DAC level, but this is not enough to protect the app and its own resources by other apps with *root* privileges. Android, by default, comes with a restricted set of permissions for its user and the installed applications (i.e., no root privileges). Despite this, apps can gain root privileges in two ways and use it to provide desirable additional features for users, but a malicious app may also abuse it to bypass Android's security measures.

On one hand many benign apps require root privileges to accomplish their job. For example, *Titanium Backup* [17] is one of Google Play's best-selling apps and it needs root privileges to backup system and user applications along with their data. In this scenario, the user typically flashes a recovery console on the device which has the permission to write on the system partition and from there she installs an app such as *SuperSU* or *Superuser* in order to gain and manage root privileges. After that, the user can give root privileges to other applications. According to Google, users install non-malicious rooting apps by a ratio of 671 per million in 2014 (increased by 38% compared to the 491 per million in 2013 [11]). Moreover, there are successful community-ROMs, such as CyanogenMod with over 10 million installations, that provide root access to the user by default. Here, the user is aware of the fact that some apps act as root in the system and have access to everything, however she does not know how these privileges are used and she has to trust the app.

On the other hand, a malware could exploit a bug in a system component and gain root privileges to freely access the whole system in order to steal personal information or perform fraudulent actions. In this scenario the user is unaware of the fact that an app acts as root. Over the years Android has been attacked by threatening malware apps such as *DroidDreamLight*, which affected 30,000-120,000 users in May 2011 [3]. Recently the app *towelroot* has been released which, exploiting the *CVE-2014-3153* bug of Linux kernel, permits to "root the device" without the need to flash a recovery console, and gives root privileges potentially to all apps. This bug affects all Android versions up to 4.4.4 and thus represents a significant threat in the current DAC-only protection of private app resources.

Our proposal provides a solution to both scenarios through the use of appPolicyModules defined by the app and attached to the SELinux system policy.

3.1 Example

Hereinafter, we define a running example that we use as a proof of concept of our solution. *Dolphin Browser* [7] is considered one of the most successful mobile browsers for Android[1] with over 100 million downloads. It uses the *Webkit* engine and provides several features such as *gesture browsing* and *browsing boost*. We use it to show how the threat model defined in the previous section affects the current DAC-only security isolation of a real app and its private data. In Section 5 we use this example to identify the requirements and then we will illustrate how the use of a dedicated appPolicyModule can provide better security for its private data. The Android permissions requested by the app are:

```
android.permission-group.NETWORK
android.permission-group.ACCOUNTS
android.permission-group.LOCATION
android.permission-group.MICROPHONE
android.permission-group.CAMERA
```

Many browsers include a password manager component that stores confidential information such as usernames and passwords. The common strategy used by almost all the mobile browsers we have analyzed is to keep the credentials in a SQLite database. Following Google's best practices for developing secure apps, the password database is saved in the app data folder, which should be accessible only to the app itself. Another best practice (not used by Dolphin browser) to provide additional protection for sensitive data, is to encrypt local files using a key that is not directly accessible to the application. For example, a key can be placed in a *KeyStore* and protected with a user password that is not stored on the device. While this does not protect data from a root compromise that can monitor the user inputting the password, it can provide protection for a lost device without file system encryption.

Some of the browsers we have analyzed (e.g., *Google Chrome*) store the passwords in plaintext in the database, while others use some form of encryption (e.g., *Dolphin Browser*, *Firefox*). The decision to keep the passwords in plaintext can appear as a weakness, but even when the information is stored in an encrypted form, if the data needs to be recovered automatically by the app without the need of addi-

[1]At the time of writing *Chrome* is the most used mobile browser for Android devices; however, due to the fact that *Chrome* is included in the *Gapps*, it does not belong to the *untrusted_app* domain but to the *isolated_app* domain, thus it is not considered as a third-party app. The same discussion and threat model presented for Dolphin Browser is also valid for *Google Chrome for Android*. Moreover, all the passwords that the user saved in the Desktop version of Google Chrome using the same login details are available in the Android database.

tional information not stored on the device (e.g., a master password known only by the user), a malware could use the same resources used by the legitimate application to retrieve the information.

There are a number of ways one can obtain the Java code back from the APK in order to study the app behavior, to replicate it and to extract the encrypted information. To encrypt the passwords, *Dolphin Browser* used to adopt a static key, which was obtainable by simply looking at the decompiled bytecode. Newer versions of the browser derive the key from the *android_id* of the device, generated during the first boot, whose use is encouraged by the Android Developers community to generate device-specific passwords.

We were able to obtain the decrypted passwords from the *password.db* decompiling the app and studying its behavior. In the same way, a malware that managed to obtain root privileges can access the database and decrypt all the user credentials.

4. SELINUX POLICY MODEL

SELinux uses a *closed* policy model, denying every access request that is not explicitly permitted. The SELinux policy is defined using rules, which produce a set of authorizations. The SELinux model is quite rich and offers a number of features that increase its expressive power and flexibility. For instance, SELinux is able to manage a Multi-Level Security model, with the representation of sensitivity labels and categories. These features are used in some systems that rely on SELinux (e.g., Samsung Knox), but they are not currently used in AOSP, which is our reference platform. We then propose a simpler model that allows us to better characterize our approach.

The model uses names with an "av" prefix, like avType instead of "type", to provide a more precise definition. In the remainder of the paper, we will sometimes used the simpler terms (i.e., type instead of avType) when we see no ambiguity in their use. The "av" prefix stands for "access vector" and is used in SELinux to characterize the rules defining the policy, called AV Rules. The basic elements of this model are:

avType: represents an identifier that can be used to describe both the subject and the target of an authorization; an avType denotes a security domain or the profile of a process or resource in the system; the avType is used to build labels for processes and resources.

avClass: represents the kind of resource (e.g., file, process) that will be the target of an authorization; an implementation of SELinux in a system will have to provide in its setup a set of avClasses consistent with the variety of resources that the system is able to manage.

avPermission: represents the possible actions a source can apply on a target of a specific avClass, specified in the setup of SELinux; every avClass *cl* has its own set of avPermissions, represented by *cl.permissions* (e.g., $file.permissions = \{read, write, execute, \ldots\}$).

In order to give a formal representation of the SELinux policy, we introduce the concept of avAuthorization.

DEFINITION 1. *Given a set T of avTypes, a set C of avClasses, and a set P of avPermissions, an* ***avAuthorization*** *a is a quadruple* ⟨ source, target, class, action ⟩, *where:*

source $\in T$ *represents the process (the security principal of the authorization);*

target $\in T$ *is associated with the object that is accessed by the* source*;*

class $\in C$ *denotes the type of resource that is accessed in the operation;*

action $\in \{P \cap \text{class.permissions}\}$ *is the specific avPermission, which has to be compatible with the avClass.*

Each avAuthorization describes a specific request that is permitted in the system.

EXAMPLE 1. *Consider an app whose process is associated with the avType myapp that wants to read a file both in the internal and external sdcard. The required avAuthorizations are as follows:* ⟨ myapp, sdcard_internal, file, read ⟩, ⟨ myapp, sdcard_external, file, read ⟩.

DEFINITION 2. *An* **avAuthzPolicy** *is a set of avAuthorizations.*

The avAuthzPolicy is derived from the specification of a collection of *avRules.* avRules can be positive or negative, support the use of patterns for the specification of sources and targets, and may use avAttributes.

DEFINITION 3. *An* **avAttribute** *is an identifier that can be used in the construction of avRules. It can be used to support the definition of collections of avAuthorizations. The collection of avAttribute identifiers in a system must be separate from the domain of avTypes.*

DEFINITION 4. *Given a set T of avTypes, a set C of avClasses, a set A of avAttributes, and a set P of avPermissions, an* **avRule** *is a quintuple* ⟨ ruleType, ruleSource, ruleTarget, ruleClass, ruleAction ⟩, *where:*

ruleType *is either* allow *or* neverallow*;*[2]

ruleSource *is a* pattern, *structured in two parts: (a) a set of positive elements $p_i \in T \cup A$, and (b) an optional set of negative elements $n_i \in T \cup A$;*

ruleTarget *is a* pattern, *with the same structure as the* ruleSource*;*

ruleClass *is a set of avClasses, i.e., each $c_i \in C$, denoting the types of resource that are considered by the avRule;*

ruleAction *is a set of avPermissions, where we assume that each $a_j \in \cap_i c_i$.permissions, i.e., all the elements have to be compatible with all the avClasses specified in the avRule.*

Each avRule can be represented in a textual form, listing the five components following the order above. The textual notation for patterns keeps all the elements within curly braces, preceding the set of negative elements with a "-" character; a colon separates the ruleTarget from the ruleClass.

EXAMPLE 2. *In order to group the common avAuthorizations granted to myapp it is possible to create the avAttribute sdcard and assign it to the sdcard_internal and sdcard_external (through the use of* typeattribute, *defined below). Then, the avAuthorizations defined in Example 1 can*

[2]SELinux also supports the *auditallow* and *dontaudit* rules, which describe the configuration of the auditing services. The model we describe can be easily extended to manage these services.

be derived by the following avRule: ⟨ allow, myapp, sdcard, file, read ⟩.

The avRules provide a higher-level representation of avAuthorizations. Every *allow* avRule is managed with an expansion of the sets associated with the source, target, class, and action. In general, a cartesian product is computed of all the elements in the positive part. The negative portion of each pattern is used to specify exceptions in the consideration of the positive portion of the pattern.

EXAMPLE 3. *In order to provide myapp the avAuthorizations needed to create and write files and directories labeled with an avType that has the avAttribute sdcard, defined in Example 2, with the exception of the avType sdcard_internal, the required avRule is as follows:* ⟨ myapp, { sdcard -sdcard_internal }, { file dir }, { create write } ⟩.

An element that has a strong impact on the derivation of the low-level avAuthzPolicy is the definition of the association between avTypes and avAttributes.

DEFINITION 5. *The* typeattribute *statement associates an avType with one or more avAttributes. The syntax of* typeattribute *appears in Table 1. The interpretation is that the avType will be associated with all the privileges that have been granted to the avAttribute.*

DEFINITION 6. *An* **avRulePolicy** *is a set of avRules and* typeattribute *statements.*

The avAuthzPolicy is obtained by a compilation of the avRulePolicy. The compilation is executed by the *checkpolicy* tool, with a sequence of three steps: (a) the typeattribute statements are processed, creating new avRules for every avRule where the avAttribute appears, replacing the avAttribute with the avTypes; (b) all the *allow* rules are expanded, producing a set of avAuthorizations; (c) all the *neverallow* rules are expanded and the policy is checked for the presence of conflicts: if even one avAuthorization produced by the expansion of *neverallow* rules matches an avAuthorization produced by *allow* rules, the compilation stops and an empty policy is produced.

5. REQUIREMENTS

Analyzing the introduction of appPolicyModules in the management of per-app security, we need to consider the different cases that emerge from the combination of the *system policy* and an appPolicyModule. From the model presented above, we note that every avAuthorization defined in an SELinux policy has a *source* avType and a *target* avType. These types may be defined in either the *system policy* or the appPolicyModule. We then have four types of avAuthorization, depending on the origin of the source and target domains. Each configuration is associated with a specific requirement that must be satisfied by appPolicyModules.

Each requirement will be described and formalized using a simple formalization that expresses each requirement as a constraint on the relationship between the system avAuthzPolicy AV, derived from the system avRulePolicy S, and the avAuthzPolicy AV', obtained after the integration of an appPolicyModule M with S. We will show in Section 6 that our proposed language and restrictions for the appPolicyModules satisfy all the requirements. We assume that

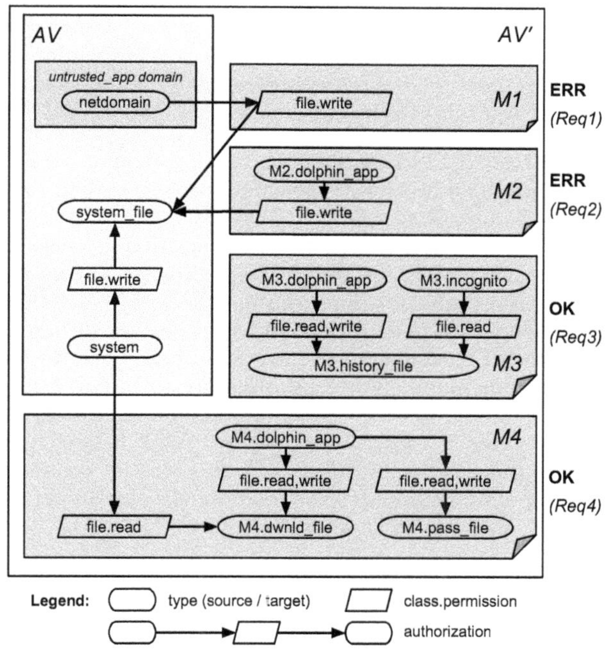

Figure 1: Examples of both compliant and non-compliant modules to illustrate requirements.

there is an avType that describes the domain of safe-to-use resources and actions, called *untrusted_app*, which protects system resources from the abuse of third-party apps (this is the name actually used in the current SEAndroid policy).

An example referring to the *Dolphin Browser* app will also be presented for every requirement, to clarify the impact in the design of the policy. To denote the type of avAuthorization, we use a compact notation where S and A represent respectively the system and appPolicyModule origin of the avType, with this structure: *source* → *target*.

Req1 ($S \rightarrow S$), No impact on the system policy: the app must not change the system policy and can only impact on processes and resources associated with the app itself.

An appPolicyModule is intended to extend the system policy and to be managed by the same software modules that manage the system policy. Since third-party apps can not be trusted a priori, it is imperative that the provided appPolicyModule must not be able to have an impact on privileges where source and target are system types.

More formally, AV must be contained into AV' and all the avAuthorizations appearing in $AV' - AV$ have to present as source or target avTypes defined in M (a set represented by notation $M.newAvTypes$).

I.e., $AV \subseteq AV' \;\wedge\; \forall a \in (AV' \setminus AV) \;\rightarrow$
$\quad a.source \in M.newAvTypes \vee a.target \in M.newAvTypes$

EXAMPLE 4 (FIGURE 1, M1). *The APM associated with* Dolphin Browser *can specify access privileges only on its own resources, such as its own password database, but must not be able to specify authorizations on system resources. Without this restriction the appPolicyModule could provide* unstrusted_app *write access to the type* platform_app_data_file *and corrupt the system resources, or enhance the privileges of system resources that the app can access, creating unpredictable vulnerabilities. Consider the appPolicyModule* M1 *in Figure 1. The module defines an authorization that modifies the behavior of the system policy because* netdomain *should not have write access to files labeled as* system_file. *Thus* M1 *will not be installed due to the violation of* Req1.

Req2 ($A \rightarrow S$), No escalation: the app cannot specify a policy that provides to its types more privileges than those available to *untrusted_app*.

New domains declared in an appPolicyModule must always operate within the boundaries defined by the system policy as acceptable for the execution of apps. When a new application is installed, its domain has to be created "under" the *untrusted_app* domain, so the system policy can flexibly define the maximum allowed privileges for third-party apps.

More formally, all the avAuthorizations introduced by the appPolicyModule M that have an avType t belonging to the avTypes defined by M as a source will be contained in the set of avAuthorizations that have the system-defined *untrusted_app* avType as source.

I.e., $\forall\ a' \in (AV' \setminus AV) \mid$
$a'.source \in M.newAvTypes \wedge a'.target \notin M.newAvTypes \rightarrow$
$\exists a \in AV \mid$
$(a.source = untrusted\_app \wedge a'.target = a.target \wedge$
$a'.class = a.class \wedge a'.action = a.action)$

The constraint forces the avAuthzPolicy to assign to all the types introduced by the appPolicyModule a set of authorizations that corresponds to privileges available to the *untrusted_app* avType. Then, each privilege must have the same class and action of a privilege already assigned to *untrusted_app*.

Example 5 (Figure 1, M2). *As highlighted by appPolicyModule* M2 *in Figure 1, appPolicyModules can only request a subset of the privileges granted to the* untrusted_app *domain. The APM* M2 *tries to give* M2.dolphin_app *the privilege of writing files labeled as* system_file, *that is not granted to the* untrusted_app *domain. Thus* M2 *will not be installed due to the violation of* Req2.

Req3 ($A \rightarrow A$), Flexible internal structure: apps may provide many functionalities and use different services (e.g., geolocalization, social networks). The appPolicyModule has to provide the flexibility of defining multiple domains with different privileges so that the app, according to the functionality in use, may switch to the one that represents the "least privilege" domain needed to accomplish the job, in order to limit potential vulnerabilities deriving from internal flaws.

Greater flexibility derives from the possibility to freely manage privileges for internal types over internal resources, building a MAC model that remains completely under the control of the app.

More formally, there can exist a pair of new avTypes t and t' introduced by M such that in $AV' \setminus AV$ t receives a privilege that t' does not have.

I.e., if $\exists t \in M.newAvTypes \wedge t' \in M.newAvTypes \wedge$
$a \in AV' \wedge a.source = t \not\rightarrow$
$\exists a' \in AV' \mid a'.source = t' \wedge a.target = a'.target \wedge$
$a.class = a'.class \wedge a.action = a'.action$

Example 6 (Figure 1, M3). Dolphin Browser *provides the* anonymous surfing *(*incognito*) mode, which allows the user to surf the web without storing permanently the history and the cookies, and in general aiming at leaving no trace in persistent memory of the navigation session. In order to enhance its security and protect the user even from possible app flaws, the appPolicyModule could specify a switch of context (i.e., it may change the SELinux domain associated with its process) when the user enters the incognito mode. In Figure 1 the APM* M3 *specifies that the domain* M3.dolphin_app *can read and write files labeled as* M3.history_file, *while the domain* M3.incognito, *used during anonymous surfing, drops the privilege of writing the files, preventing the leakage of resources that may leave a trace of the navigation session.*

Req4 ($S \rightarrow A$), Protection from external threats: users of mobile devices may unconsciously install malware apps from untrusted sources that, exploiting some security vulnerabilities, could compromise the entire system or other apps (e.g., steal user information). To mitigate the risk, an appPolicyModule should provide a common way to isolate the app's critical resources. The use of MAC support offers protection even against threats coming from the system itself, like a malicious app that abuses root privileges.

The app can protect its resources from other apps, specifying its own types and defining in a flexible way which system components may or may not access the domains introduced by the APM. This requirement depends on the ability of the MAC model to let app types be protected against system-level elements, an aspect that SELinux supports and not available in classical multi-level systems, which assume a rigid hierarchical structure. Indeed, in the SELinux policy model every privilege has to be explicitly authorized and new avTypes are not accessible by system avTypes unless a dedicated rule is introduced in the appPolicyModule.

More formally, the appPolicyModule M can introduce an avAuthorization that gives to an avType introduced by M a privilege that is not necessarily available to a type in the system policy.

I.e., if $\exists\ t \in M.newAvTypes \wedge a \in AV' \wedge\ a.source = t \not\rightarrow$
$\exists a' \in AV\ | a'.source \notin M.newAvTypes \wedge a.target = a'.target \wedge$
$a.class = a'.class \wedge a.action = a'.action.$

Example 7 (Figure 1, M4). *The* Dolphin browser *can grant to the* system *type the privilege to read the* dwnld_file *files, used to label the downloaded files, while it prevents the access to the* pass_file *files used to label the password file.*

There are other environments where SELinux is used, like the Redhat Fedora distribution of Linux, that already supports SELinux modules, but the requirements presented above do not apply to them. The reason is that the trust assumptions are different. The modules used in Redhat Fedora permit to structure the security policy, they are trusted and free to revise in arbitrary ways the system policy. Modules in Android are not trusted and it is mandatory that they cannot be used to introduce vulnerabilities in the system.

Additional requirements, not associated with a formal treatment, have also to be considered.

- Not all the developers have the knowledge or are interested to secure their apps with SELinux, so in order not to impede the development they have to experience the same development and installation process, with no impact on their activities. This requirement will be considered in Section 7.

- In order to facilitate the deployment, the solution has to be compatible with the implementation of SELinux offered by SEAndroid. This is considered in Section 8.

6. POLICY MODULE LANGUAGE

We now present the concrete structure of appPolicyModules. We introduce the subset of the SELinux statements used in their definition and describe the additional statements that will be automatically added to the appPolicyModule by a pre-processor. A critical design requirement is the compatibility with the SELinux implementation available today, which facilitates the adoption of the proposed approach.

Each module presents a head and a body (see right side Figure 2). The head describes all the identifiers that the appPolicyModule reuses from the system policy. This is represented by the *require* statement. In case a name appears that is not known to the system, the compilation fails.

The body of the appPolicyModule can make use of the following SELinux statements: *typebounds*, *type*, *attribute*, *typeattribute*, *allow*, *neverallow*, and *typetransition*. These statements are the only ones that can be used in the definition of the appPolicyModule. The syntax for these statements is succinctly presented in Table 1.

The *typebounds* statement permits to specify that the collection of privileges of the bounded avType has to fall within the boundaries of another avType. The *typebounds* statement will raise an exception when an *allow* rule introduces a privilege for a bounded type in the source that does not match an existing rule for the bounding type.

```
type dolphin_app;
type dolphin_app_incognito;
typebounds untrusted_app dolphin_app,
    dolphin_app_incognito;
allow dolphin_app app_data_file:file
    {read write};
allow dolphin_app_incognito
    app_data_file:file {read};
```

Listing 1: Example of use of *typebounds*. In the system policy there is a rule `allow untrusted_app app_data_file:file {read write};`

The evaluation of compatibility takes into account the presence of other *typebounds* statements in the target, considering as correct the use in the target of an avType that is bounded by the type appearing in the higher-level rule. In the example in Listing 1, the verification by typebounds is satisfied, because both the *allow* rules use in the target an avType that is considered compatible with the *untrusted_app* type. It is useful to emphasize that the *typebounds* statement does not assign the authorizations to the bounded domain, it only sets its upper bound. This is a core principle in our scenario, where policy writers are outside of the trust domain of the core system resources.

The *type* statement permits to introduce new avTypes. To avoid name conflicts between types defined in different modules, the pre-processing adds a prefix that derives from the app name to every identifier (we omit in the examples the representation of this step). If it does not already appear in the module, the pre-processing step will add a *typebounds* statement for every introduced type that will constrain the authorizations referring to types in the system policy to lie within the *untrusted_app* type. The *attribute* statement declares an identifier that can be used to define rules. SELinux policies make extensive use of avAttributes to provide a structure to policies. No constraint needs to be introduced on the definition of new attributes. Attributes produce an effect on the policy when they are used in the *typeattribute* statement, which has been presented above. The pre-processing checks that every *type_id* used in a *typeattribute* statement must be defined inside the appPolicyModule. Without this constraint, a module could violate *Req1* and *Req2*, compromising the system policy and possibly performing an escalation of privileges, by assigning attributes to the *untrusted_app* type. The *allow* and *neverallow* statements permit to create avRules. The pre-processing checks that all the avRules present as a source or target one of the avTypes and avAttributes introduced by the module.

Table 1: Simplified SELinux syntax used in APMs.

Statement	Syntax
attribute	attribute *attribute_id* ';'
type	type *type_id* (',' *attribute_id*)* ';'
typeattribute	typeattribute *type_id attribute_id* (',' *attribute_id*)* ';'
typebounds	typebounds *bounding bounded* (',' *bounded*)* ';'
typetransition	type_transition *type_id type_id*':' '{'*class_id*+'}' *type_id* ';'
allow	allow '{'*pattern*+ ('-'*pattern*)* '}' '{'*pattern*+ ('-'*pattern*)* '}' '{'*class_id*+'}' '{'*perm_id*+'}' ';'
neverallow	neverallow '{'*pattern*+ ('-'*pattern*)* '}' '{'*pattern*+ ('-'*pattern*)* '}' '{'*class_id*+'}' '{'*perm_id*+'}' ';'

The element *pattern=(type_id|attribute_id)* is not included in the SELinux statements; we use it here to provide a more readable description of the syntax.

Finally, the *typetransition* statement permits to describe the admissible transitions between avTypes at runtime. We introduce the constraint, checked by the pre-processor, that the avType defined as first parameter has to be an avType defined in the module. The *type_transition* statement is used to perform *object* and *domain* transitions.

- An *object transition* occurs when an object needs to be relabeled (i.e., a file label is changed).
- A *domain transition* occurs when a process with one avType (we call it *transition-startpoint*) switches to another avType (we call it *transition-endpoint*), enacting different avAuthorizations from the original ones. An app could define different domains with limited avAuthorizations and use them when performing specific actions. We note that for a domain transition to succeed, we must grant three different avAuthorizations to the transition-startpoint type.

With respect to object transitions, there is no need to further constrain them, because the process domain must have the corresponding avAuthorizations to be able to create objects with the new label. With respect to domain transitions, when a type transition is authorized and the transition-startpoint type is given the three additional authorizations, the transition-startpoint type is actually able to benefit from all the authorizations that have the transition-endpoint as the source. This is a potential risk in the definition of the policy, because the *typebounds* statement does not extend its evaluation to the consideration of the types that are reachable through type transitions. The current AOSP system policy does not give to *untrusted_app* any type transition privilege, and at the moment there is no danger, but to avoid any risk we enforce the constraint to accept in the appPolicyModule only type transitions that have a transition-endpoint bounded within *untrusted_app*.

6.1 Correctness

We want to show that the appPolicyModules will satisfy the four requirements described in Section 5.

With respect to *Req1 (S→S), No impact on the system policy*, we note that the appPolicyModule statements do not have an impact on the system policy, because all the *allow* and *neverallow* statements have to specify as source or target a new avType, guaranteed to be outside of the system policy.

The correctness with respect to *Req2 (A→S), No escalation* is guaranteed through the use of the *typebounds* statements associated with all the avTypes that appear as source in the *allow* statements. It is to note that the *neverallow* rules do not have to be considered here, because they may only cause the rejection of the appPolicyModule by the compiler, but they cannot lead to the escalation of privileges for the new avTypes. The consideration by the compiler of the *typebounds* statements indeed verifies that each *allow* rule r' in the appPolicyModule that refers to system types has a corresponding *allow* rule r associated with *untrusted_app*.

The respect of *Req3* and *Req4* can be demonstrated with a simple example of an appPolicyModule that shows the desired behavior. Requirement *Req3 (A→A), Flexible internal structure* is satisfied by the example in Listing 1, which shows two new avTypes *dolphin_app* and *dolphin_app_incognito*, associated with distinct privileges.

Requirement *Req4 (S→A), Protection from external threats* is supported by the same example: without an explicit rule giving permission, a process associated with *untrusted_app* is not authorized to access files associated with *dolphin_app*.

7. MAPPING ANDROID PERMISSIONS

The introduction of *appPolicyModules* improves the definition and enforcement of the security requirements associated with each app. However, in the approach presented in the previous section, we assumed that the extension to the MAC policy has to be defined by the developer, who knows the service provided by the app and its source code. Due to the size of the community, we can expect that many app developers will either be unfamiliar with the SELinux syntax and semantics, or know SELinux but not want to use it, avoiding the introduction of strict security boundaries to the app beyond those associated with *untrusted_app*. There is also the risk generated by the presence in devices of a variety of versions of the system policy and the need to guarantee that the appPolicyModule is compatible with it.

However, we observe that the app developers that can be expected to be most interested in using the services of the MAC model are expert developers responsible for the construction of critical apps (e.g., apps for secure encrypted communication, or for key management, or for the access to financial and banking services). This community is possibly small, but their role is extremely critical. They can be expected to overcome the obstacles to the use of appPolicyModules. In addition, the deployment of the policy modularity services opens the door to a number of other services. We consider here how it is possible to use them to enforce a stricter model on the management of Android permissions, relying on the automatic generation of appModulePolicies, solving all the issues identified above.

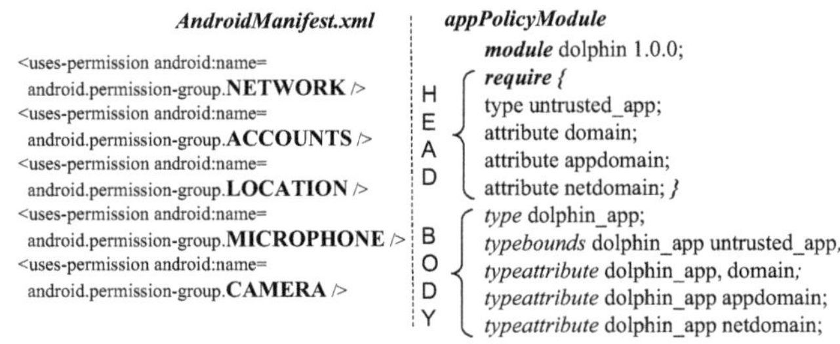

Figure 2: Generation of the Dolphin browser appPolicyModule starting from the permissions in the app manifest.

Looking at the workflow to build an app, developers are already familiar with the definition of security requirements in the *AndroidManifest.xml*, through the use of the tag *uses-permission*. In fact, in order to access system resources (e.g., access to the user's current location) the app has to explicitly request the associated Android permissions (e.g., *android.permission-group.LOCATION*), which correspond both to a set of concrete actions at the OS level and to a set of *avPermissions* granted at the SELinux level (e.g., *open*, *read* on files and directories). The system already offers both a high-level representation and a low-level representation of the privileges needed to access a resource, but they are not integrated and what happens, in the absence of policy modularity, is that the app is associated with the *untrusted_app* domain, which is allowed to use all the actions that correspond to the access to all the resources that are invokable by apps, essentially using for protection only Android permissions. The integration of security policies at the Android permission and MAC levels offers a more robust enforcement of the app policy.

This can be realized introducing a mechanism that bridges the gap between different levels, through the analysis of the high-level policy (i.e., the permissions asked by the app within the Android Permission Framework) and the automatic generation of an appPolicyModule that maps those Android permissions to a corresponding collection of SELinux statements. The generator starts from the representation of the app security requirements expressed in the *AndroidManifest.xml*, builds a logical model of the structure of the *appPolicyModule*, and it finally produces the concrete implementation of the *appPolicyModule* and verifies that all the security restrictions are satisfied.

A necessary step in the construction of the mechanism is the identification of a mapping between policies at the distinct levels. The Android Permission Framework contains more than 200 permissions and most of them present a mapping between the Android permission and a dedicated SELinux domain, already specified in the system policy. The current system policy does not cover all the permissions; e.g., the *downloads*, *calendar*, and *media content* resources are associated with the single *platform_app_data_file* type. We expect this aspect to be manageable with a revision of the policy. However, there is a number of Android permissions that can only be partially supported by this mechanism due to current limitations in the security mechanisms provided by internal components (e.g., SQLite).

To summarize, it is already possible to capture most Android permissions in a precise way and some of them with some leeway, leading in all cases to a significant reduction in the size of the MAC domain compared to what would otherwise be associated with an app. We provide in Figure 2 an example of the appPolicyModule that would be generated for the Dolphin browser described in Section 3.1. We note that every app will have to be associated with the *domain* and *appdomain* attributes, which provide all the basic privileges required to let an app execute in the system. The head of the module will then have to introduce the *require* declarations that specify this attribute, together with the *untrusted_app* type and the *netdomain* attribute. The body of the module introduces the *dolphin_app* type, the *typebounds* and all the MAC privileges required to access the network and other resources/services. Due to the current SELinux policy structure the access to the *ACCOUNTS*, *LOCATION MICROPHONE* and *CAMERA* services are mitigated by the *system_server*. The *system_server* is the core of the Android system which manages most of the framework services. The access to the requested services is granted by the *system_server* to the *appdomain* type and through the use of the rule *typeattribute dolphin_app appdomain* the *dolphin_app* type inherits these privileges.

In general, with the availability of appPolicyModules, the system could evolve from a scenario where each app is given at installation time access at the SELinux layer to the whole *untrusted_app* domain, to a scenario where each app is associated with the portion of *untrusted_app* domain that is really needed for its execution, with a better support of the classical "least-privilege" security principle.

8. IMPLEMENTATION

The work done by Smalley et al. in [15] represents the basis for our work. We have introduced a set of extensions in order to enrich the current implementation and manage appPolicyModules. We now provide a description of the challenges to enable the concrete use of appPolicyModules in Android. The system has been implemented with an open source license, extending the current version 4.4.4 of the AOSP (link omitted for the anonymity constraints); adaptation to Android L is planned as soon as it will be released.

The current SELinux implementation for Android spans different levels of the Android stack. At the *Application Framework* level, the *SELinux* class provides access to the centralized Java Native Interface (JNI) bindings for SELinux interaction. The *android_os_SELinux.cpp* file represents the JNI bridge. At the *Libraries* level, the SELinux implementation consists of the *libsepol* and *libselinux* libraries. The former provides an API for the manipulation of SELinux binary policies. The latter provides the APIs to get and set process and file security contexts and to obtain security policy decisions.

The first challenges to the integration of appPolicyModules in Android appeared in the adaptation of the current SELinux libraries and in the addition of the libraries needed to build, link and check the appPolicyModules. These libraries are part of the full SELinux environment and are included in the major Linux distributions, but the activation

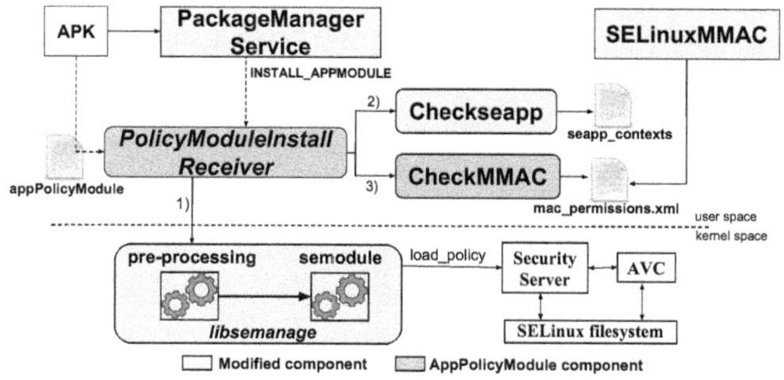

Figure 3: appPolicyModule Architecture.

of policy modules in SELinux for Android required more than a simple cross-compilation.

8.1 Changes to SELinux

The work we did at the SELinux level can be structured into four major activities.

First, the *libselinux* library was modified with the introduction of additional features needed by the *libsemanage* library, such as the *selinux-config.c* module. We modified the *checkpolicy* tool in order to build automatically the binary policy at version 26 (standard SELinux implementations support version 29 of the binary policy). In the current SEAndroid implementation the binary policy version range is between 15 and 26. This constraint is enforced by the *load_policy* method when a policy reload is triggered.

Second, the *libsemanage* library, which provides APIs for the manipulation of SELinux binary policies and binary policy modules, was adapted to fulfill the new requirements. Due to the differences in scenario, architecture and requirements, some functions, such as the *genhomedircon* service, were disabled. The *genhomedircon* service is used to generate file context configuration entries for user home directories based on their default roles and is run when building the policy. However, in Android, though there is the possibility to create several users for a single device, they do not have a *home* directory.

Third, the source code of the *semodule* executable was extended in order to correctly interact with the modified version of the *libsemanage* library. The *semodule* tool is used to manage SELinux policy modules, including installation, upgrade, listing and removal of modules. The *semodule* tool may also be used to force a rebuild of the policy from the module repository and/or to force a reload of the policy without performing any other transaction.

Figure 3 shows an abstract representation of the complete architecture introduced in order to manage the appPolicyModules. Fourth, in addition to the modifications on the set of SELinux libraries, to meet the requirements introduced in Section 2 a pre-processing phase was introduced. This phase supports the creation of constraints introduced in Section 4. Thanks to the modularity provided by SELinux, we were able to implement the pre-processing phase reusing several SELinux components.

8.2 Changes to Android

The second set of challenges concerns the app installation process, which starts from the APK file that contains the app. The *PackageManagerService* class provides the APIs that actually manage app installation, uninstallation, and update. The *PackageManagerService* component provides the functions to parse the *APK* file and to assign the SELinux label to the app. The label is retrieved by the *SELinuxMMAC* class from the *mac_permissions.xml* file. The file maps the app certificate to a SELinux label. In the current AOSP version, all third-party apps are assigned to the default stanza of the *mac_permissions.xml* file, regardless of their certificate. To address this limitation and assign to the app the right SELinux type, we introduced a new install service, named *PolicyModuleInstallReceiver*. This service is triggered by an Intent and manages the installation workflow of an appPolicyModule. The workflow is structured as follows:

1. trigger the installation of the policy module, update the SELinux policy and check its correctness;
2. update the *seapp_contexts* file used to label app processes and app package directories;
3. update the *mac_permissions.xml* file used by *SELinuxMMAC* to retrieve the type to assign to the app. This file is used in conjunction with *seapp_contexts*.

8.2.1 Update SELinux policy

The use of the *PolicyModuleInstallReceiver* service requires to broadcast an *intent.action.INSTALL_APPMODULE* intent. When the service receives the intent it performs a JNI call to the *libsemanage* library, which validates (i.e., preprocessing phase), links, expands the module (i.e., *semodule* tool) and triggers the reload of the binary policy.

8.2.2 Update seapp_contexts

In order to meet the requirements Req3 and Req4 described in Section 5 the app processes and the app package directories have to be labeled accordingly to the appPolicyModule. In the current AOSP implementation the security context assigned to app processes, respectively app package directories, is retrieved from the seapp_context file by the *selinux_android_setcontext*, respectively *selinux_android_setfilecon2*.

In order to manage the addition of new entries in the *seapp_contexts* file the *checkseapp* utility was extended. Currently, *checkseapp* is used during the AOSP build process to validate the *seapp_contexts* file against policy. The extension permits to dynamically manage the addition/removal of an entry in the *seapp_contexts* according to the domains defined in the appPolicyModule.

To allow AOSP components such as *Zygote* to spawn applications in the correct domain, an update of the *mac_permissions.xml* is needed.

8.2.3 Update mac_permissions.xml

This file is used to configure the install MMAC policy. More specifically this file is used in conjunction with the *seapp_contexts* file in order to determine the *seinfo* label to assign to the app. The *seinfo* value is subsequently used to determine the SELinux security context for the app process and its */data/data* directory based on the *seapp_contexts* configuration.

The information needed to build a stanza for the *mac_permissions.xml* file are (i) the app's X.509 certificate and (ii) the *seinfo* label. The stanza is built on the fly by the *checkMMAC* Java class retrieving the information directly from the parsed *apk* and the entry added to the *seapp_contexts*

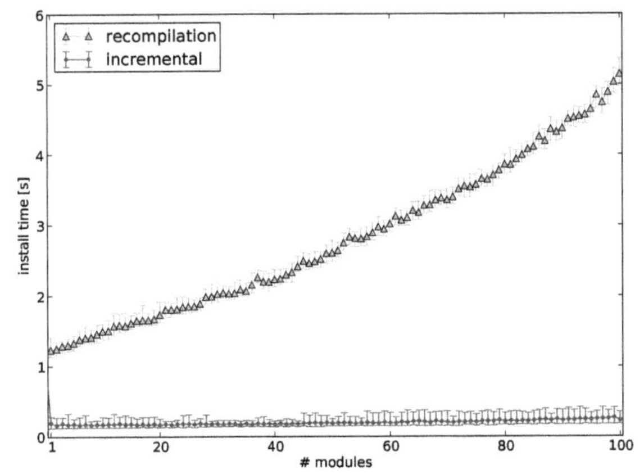

Figure 4: Installation time: comparison between the full recompilation and the incremental approach.

file. After stanza creation, an update is triggered to insert and refresh the whole *mac_permissions.xml* file. This is needed in order to let *SELinuxMMAC* retrieve the right *seinfo* label for the new app.

8.3 Performance

As it was clearly expressed in the design of SEAndroid [15], it is necessary to have a minimal overhead in terms of performance, both at app installation time and during regular system runtime. We executed a series of experiments for the evaluation of the performance impact of the techniques presented in this paper. Experiments have been run on a Nexus 7 2013 aosp_flo_userdebug 4.4.2_r2. The Android runtime used was ART.

8.3.1 Installation time

We evaluated the performance overhead of our approach at app installation time, due to the fact that the process to install an app was extended in order to manage appPolicyModules. Two different approaches were developed; the first one is consistent with the approach used for SELinux in Fedora. When a new module is ready to be installed, the *libsemanage* tool creates a new version of the policy and re-installs all the old modules plus the new one. If the new policy passes the checking step, then the new policy is stored into the system, otherwise a rollback occurs. This approach introduces a non negligible overhead, because it requires to reconsider the whole policy every time a new module is added to the system. This option is natural for SELinux in Fedora, because the modules are created by trusted entities and they are free to modify the system policy, with a number of types in the existing binary representation that may have to be updated. As we have already discussed, the requirements associated with the use of appPolicyModules in Android are different, because in our scenario an appPolicyModule cannot modify the system policy (*Req1* in Section 5). In addition to the security benefit, this requirement also leads to a simplification of the management of policy modules, because the re-installation of the system policy and all the other modules is not needed. This permits to provide an "incremental" solution, with a significant reduction in the appPolicyModule installation time.

The graph in Figure 4 describes the time observed in a scenario where the current system policy has been extended with 100 modules, adding the modules one by one. The tests were run 100 times. Each element in the graph describes the range of measured values and the average. The observations in the upper part of the graph show that as the number of modules increases, the re-compilation approach shows a significant increase in the compilation time, due to the fact that at each step the policy becomes larger and its full recompilation more expensive. The incremental approach instead shows a constant response time, with no observable impact deriving from the increase in the size of the overall policy. The average installation time for the incremental approach, which is the one to use, is near to 0.2 s, compatible with the requirements of real systems.

8.3.2 Runtime

We evaluated the performance overhead of our approach at runtime, considering two scenarios with different binary policy sizes.

Table 2: Binary policies used in the tests.

policy	#rules	size
sepolicy	1319	73KB
sepolicy +1000 APMs	35319	631KB

For runtime analysis we used two well known benchmark apps: (i) AnTuTu [1] by AnTuTu Labs and (ii) Benchmark by Softweg [16]. Under both benchmarks, we ensured that the same number of apps/services were loaded and running.

Table 3: AntuTu Benchmark (100 iterations), higher values are better

	sepolicy	sepolicy +1000 APMs
svm	1130.467	1132.867
smt	3334.533	3341.400
database	630.600	631.333
sram	1534.840	1538.533
float	1938.600	1939.200
snand	1159.320	1159.400
memory	1121.280	1120.800
integer	2285.933	2284.133

AnTuTu Benchmark is a popular Android utility for benchmarking devices. As it was explained in [15], the overhead introduced by SELinux is very limited and it only affects *sdwrite*, *sdread* and *database I/O* tests. The tests performed by Smalley et al. take into account a "static" policy. In our scenario the policy size is not static, but it changes at each installation and can potentially become quite large. However, experimental results highlight how the policy size does not affect the system performance. Table 3 shows the results of the benchmark. The impact of the larger policy is not detectable by the experiments.

Table 4 shows the results provided by *Benchmark* app developed by Softweg. Similarly to the results obtained by AnTuTu, SELinux does not affect CPU and graphics scores. For the filesystem and sdcard tests, the overhead introduced by the increased size of the policy is negligible. As highlighted by the *create and delete* tests, the time taken to create or delete 1000 empty files increased by less than 1 percent. As explained by Smalley et al. [15] the *create and delete* tests can be viewed as a worst case, since the overhead of managing the *security context* is not amortized over any real usage of the file.

Table 4: Softweg Benchmark (100 iterations): for the Total File System score, higher values are better

	sepolicy	sepolicy +1000 APMs
Create 250 empty files	1.222 s	1.230 s
Create 1000 empty files	0.302 s	0.303 s
Delete 250 empty files	0.351 s	0.351 s
Delete 1000 empty files	0.130 s	0.130 s
Total file system score	342.835	341.158

9. RELATED WORK

In the past few years a strong interest has been dedicated to the investigation of Android security. Several solutions have been proposed to increase the security of the system and to protect the apps and system components from a variety of threats. The central role of the proposal by Smalley et al. [15] has already been discussed. We summarize here other important contributions in the area.

TaintDroid, proposed in [8] by Enck et al., provides functions to detect the unauthorized leakage of sensitive data. *TaintDroid* uses dynamic taint analysis (i.e., taint tracking) to monitor the exchange of sensitive information among third-party apps. While this solution try to identify the information leakage, our proposal goes one step further impeding the leakage at the SELinux level.

Other solutions, such as *FlaskDroid* [6], *TrustDroid* [5] and *XManDroid* [4] show greater similarity to our work.

FlaskDroid [6] is a security architecture for the Android OS that instantiates different security solutions. It is inspired by the concepts of the *Flask* architecture and is based on SEAndroid. *FlaskDroid* provides mandatory access control on both Android's middleware and kernel layers. This represents an enhancement in terms of the isolation that is provided between separate components, but the two MAC levels are not coordinated and largely use *booleans* in the SELinux policy. In the current SEAndroid implementation, the use of booleans inside the policy is strongly discouraged, for two main reasons: (i) it could introduce compatibility problems, and (ii) it could undermine the default security goals being enforced via SELinux in AOSP itself. Compared to our proposal, the focus of *Flaskdroid* is the security of system modules and the security of third-party apps is not supported. *Flaskdroid* does not permit to dynamically add policy modules without a recompilation of the entire policy.

TrustDroid [5] and *XManDroid* [4] provide mandatory access control at both the middleware layer and at the kernel layer. At the kernel layer, they rely upon *TOMOYO* Linux [9], a path-based MAC framework. *TOMOYO* supports policy updates at runtime, but the security model of SELinux is more flexible and supports richer policies.

RootGuard [14] is an enhanced root-management system which monitors system calls, to detect the abnormal behavior of apps (i.e., malware) with root privileges. It is composed by three components (i) *SuperuserEx*, (ii) *Policy storage database*, and (iii) *Kernel module*, which span the different levels of the Android architecture. The *SuperuserEx* is built on top of the open source Superuser app, the *Policy storage database* is used to store the *RootGuard* policy and the *Kernel module* introduces a set of *hooks* in order to intercept system calls. This implementation is similar to the one used by SELinux, but all the SELinux code is already in the mainline Linux kernel and provides a more robust solution.

10. CONCLUSIONS

Security is correctly perceived, both by technical experts and customers, as a crucial property of mobile operating systems. The integration of SELinux into Android is a significant step toward the realization of more robust and more flexible security services. The attention that has been dedicated in the SEAndroid initiative toward the protection of system components is understandable and consistent with the high priority associated with the protection of core privileged resources. Our approach is the natural extension of that work, which demonstrated a successful deployment, toward a more detailed consideration of the presence of apps.

The paper shows that the potential for the application of policy modules associated with each app is quite extensive, supporting scenarios where developers define their own app policy, and scenarios where policies are automatically generated to improve the enforcement of privileges and the isolation of apps. The extensive level of reuse of SELinux constructs that characterizes the language for the appPolicyModules demonstrates the flexibility of SELinux and facilitates the deployment of the proposed solution. An analysis of the evolution of the official SEAndroid project confirms that appPolicyModules identify a concrete need and that Android is evolving in this direction.

11. ACKNOWLEDGEMENTS

This work was partially supported by a Google Research Award (winter 2014), by the Italian Ministry of Research within the PRIN project "GenData 2020" and by the EC within the 7FP and H2020, respectively, under grant agreements 257129 and 644579.

12. REFERENCES

[1] AnTuTu labs. AnTuTu Benchmark. `https://play.google.com/store/apps/details?id=com.antutu.ABenchMark`.

[2] M. Arrigoni Neri, M. Guarnieri, E. Magri, S. Mutti, and S. Paraboschi. Conflict Detection in Security Policies using Semantic Web Technology. In *Proc. of IEEE ESTEL - Security Track*, 2012.

[3] M. Balanza, K. Alintanahin, O. Abendan, J. Dizon, and B. Caraig. Droiddreamlight lurks behind legitimate android apps. In *Malicious and Unwanted Software (MALWARE), 2011 6th International Conference on*, pages 73–78. IEEE, 2011.

[4] S. Bugiel, L. Davi, A. Dmitrienko, T. Fischer, A.-R. Sadeghi, and B. Shastry. Towards taming privilege-escalation attacks on android. In *19th Annual Network & Distributed System Security Symposium (NDSS)*, volume 17, pages 18–25, 2012.

[5] S. Bugiel, L. Davi, A. Dmitrienko, S. Heuser, A.-R. Sadeghi, and B. Shastry. Practical and lightweight domain isolation on android. In *Proceedings of the 1st ACM workshop on Security and privacy in smartphones and mobile devices*. ACM, 2011.

[6] S. Bugiel, S. Heuser, and A.-R. Sadeghi. Flexible and fine-grained mandatory access control on android for diverse security and privacy policies. In *22nd USENIX Security Symposium*. USENIX, 2013.

[7] Dolphin Browser. Dolphin Browser for Android. `https://play.google.com/store/apps/details?id=mobi.mgeek.TunnyBrowser`.

[8] W. Enck, P. Gilbert, B.-G. Chun, L. P. Cox, J. Jung, P. McDaniel, and A. Sheth. Taintdroid: An information-flow tracking system for realtime privacy monitoring on smartphones. In *OSDI*, volume 10, 2010.

[9] T. Harada, T. Horie, and K. Tanaka. Task oriented management obviates your onus on linux. In *Linux Conference*, volume 3, 2004.

[10] J. Lepreau, R. Spencer, S. Smalley, P. Loscocco, M. Hibler, and D. Andersen. The flask security architecture: System support for diverse security policies, 2006.

[11] A. Ludwig. Android - practical security from the ground up, October 2013. `http://goo.gl/zORIwu`.

[12] F. Mayer, K. MacMillan, and D. Caplan. *SELinux by Example: Using Security Enhanced Linux (Prentice Hall Open Source Software Development Series)*. Prentice Hall PTR, NJ, USA, 2006.

[13] C. Mulliner, W. Robertson, and E. Kirda. Virtualswindle: An automated attack against in-app billing on android. In *Proceedings of the 9th ACM Symposium on Information, Computer and Communications Security*, ASIACCS '14, pages 459–470, New York, NY, USA, 2014. ACM.

[14] Y. Shao, X. Luo, and C. Qian. Rootguard: Protecting rooted android phones. *Computer*, 47(6):32–40, 2014.

[15] S. Smalley and R. Craig. Security enhanced (se) android: Bringing flexible mac to android. In *Network and Distributed System Security Symposium (NDSS 13)*, 2013.

[16] Softweg. Benchmark. `https://play.google.com/store/apps/details?id=softweg.hw.performance`.

[17] Titanium Track. Titanium Backup. `https://play.google.com/store/apps/details?id=com.keramidas.TitaniumBackup`.

[18] C. Yang, V. Yegneswaran, P. Porras, and G. Gu. Detecting money-stealing apps in alternative android markets. In *Proceedings of the 2012 ACM Conference on Computer and Communications Security*, CCS '12, pages 1034–1036, New York, NY, USA, 2012. ACM.

[19] Y. Zhou, Z. Wang, W. Zhou, and X. Jiang. Hey, you, get off of my market: Detecting malicious apps in official and alternative android markets. In *NDSS*, 2012.

Now You See Me: Hide and Seek in Physical Address Space

Ning Zhang
Virginia Polytechnic Institute and State University
Blacksburg, VA, USA
ningzhang@vt.edu

Kun Sun
College of William and Mary
Williamsburg, VA, USA
ksun@wm.edu

Wenjing Lou
Virginia Polytechnic Institute and State University
Blacksburg, VA, USA
wjlou@vt.edu

Y. Thomas Hou
Virginia Polytechnic Institute and State University
Blacksburg, VA, USA
thou@vt.edu

Sushil Jajodia
George Mason University
Fairfax, VA, USA
jajodia@gmu.edu

ABSTRACT

With the growing complexity of computing systems, memory based forensic techniques are becoming instrumental in digital investigations. Digital forensic examiners can unravel what happened on a system by acquiring and inspecting in-memory data. Meanwhile, attackers have developed numerous anti-forensic mechanisms to defeat existing memory forensic techniques by manipulation of system software such as OS kernel. To counter anti-forensic techniques, some recent researches suggest that memory acquisition process can be trusted if the acquisition module has not been tampered with and all the operations are performed without relying on any untrusted software including the operating system.

However, in this paper, we show that it is possible for malware to bypass the current state-of-art trusted memory acquisition module by manipulating the physical address space layout, which is shared between physical memory and I/O devices on x86 platforms. This fundamental design on x86 platform enables an attacker to build an OS agnostic anti-forensic system. Base on this finding, we propose Hidden in I/O Space (HIveS) which manipulates CPU registers to alter such physical address layout. The system uses a novel *I/O Shadowing* technique to lock a memory region named *HIveS memory* into I/O address space, so all operation requests to the HIveS memory will be redirected to the I/O bus instead of the memory controller. To access the HIveS memory, the attacker unlocks the memory by mapping it back into the memory address space. Two novel techniques, *Blackbox Write* and *TLB Camouflage*, are developed to further protect the unlocked HIveS memory against memory forensics while allowing attackers to access it. A HIveS prototype is built and tested against a set of memory acquisition tools for both Windows and Linux running on x86 platform. Lastly, we propose potential countermeasures to detect and mitigate HIveS.

ASIA CCS'15, April 14–17, 2015, Singapore..

http://dx.doi.org/10.1145/2714576.2714600.

Categories and Subject Descriptors

D.2.11 [**Software Engineering**]: [Software Architectures - Information hiding]; K.6.5 [**Management of Computing and Information Systems**]: [Security and Protection - Invasive software]

General Terms

Design, System

Keywords

Digital Forensics; Memory Acquisition; System Security; Rootkits

1. INTRODUCTION

Digital forensics is the science on collecting and presenting digital evidence. With the ever increasing use of computing systems in our daily life, computers and networks have become not only the personal portal to instant information, but also a platform that criminals exploit to commit crimes. Digital forensics is now one of the services sought at the very beginning of all types of investigation - criminal, civil, and corporate [7, 13].

Disk forensic methods and tools have matured in the past two decades, offering comprehensive capabilities to extract and visualize artifacts from nonvolatile storage images. With the prevalence of memory hiding techniques and the need to evade disk forensic, adversaries are starting to hide the presence of malicious code and data only in the memory [8, 16, 15]. To tackle this problem, forensic examiners are increasingly relying on live memory forensics to uncover the malicious contents in the memory [7].

There are two general memory acquisition approaches: *software based* approach and *hardware based* approach. Software based solutions rely on a trusted memory acquisition module in the operating system to acquire the memory through the processor [35, 21]. Hardware based solutions often utilize dedicated I/O devices, such as network interface card, to capture physical memory image via direct memory access (DMA) [10, 28, 39] with the processor totally bypassed. Some hardware based approaches use the remanence of physical memory to extract sensitive data from memory module in systems that are powered off for a short time [11, 18].

To counter live memory forensics, attackers have developed a number of anti-forensic techniques to sabotage the memory acquisition process [19]. Current anti-forensic techniques against software based memory acquisition rely on manipulating the software used in the memory acquisition process. Some examples include modifying the acquisition module or the OS kernel [20, 34, 15], hooking operating system APIs [32], or installing a thin hypervisor on the fly [29]. Based on this observation, Stüttgen et al. recently suggested that the memory acquisition process can be trusted with two conditions. The first one is that the acquisition module has not been tampered with, and the second one states all the operations are performed without relying on the operating system or any other untrusted software [35]. However, in this paper, we show that this assumption is not true by presenting Hidden in I/O Space (HIveS), an operating system (OS) agnostic anti-forensic mechanism, that is capable of evading the most updated software based memory forensics tools.

Physical address space on x86 platform is shared between physical memory and I/O devices. Memory access to a physical address gets directed to either the memory controller or the I/O bus based on where it is located in the address space layout. This physical address layout is also what memory forensics tools use to understand where the physical memory regions are located. Memory forensic tools obtain this layout information by interacting with operating system or BIOS, and they assume this layout is correct and updated. We show that this condition can be easily violated by presenting HIveS. HIveS alters the machine physical address layout while the system is in operational state by modifying registers in the processor. With this mispresented address layout, HIveS can conceal a memory region called *HIveS memory* from being observed and acquired by memory forensics tools.

The basic idea is to map (or lock) the HIveS memory into the I/O space, so that any operation on the physical memory address will be redirected to the I/O bus instead of the memory controller. When the HIveS memory is locked, its memory contents cannot be accessed by any processor, including the one(s) controlled by the attacker. When the attacker wants to access the HIveS memory, she would first unlock the memory region by mapping it back into the memory address space. To protect the unlocked HIveS memory against memory forensics, we propose two novel techniques, *Blackbox Write* and *TLB Camouflage*. Blackbox Write enables only write access to the HIveS memory by creating asymmetric read and write destinations between the memory space and the I/O space. TLB Camouflage exploits TLB cache incoherency among multi-core processors to ensure exclusive read and write access for a single processor core to the HIveS memory.

HIveS is operating system agnostic, since it only changes the system hardware configurations. We build a prototype of HIveS on an x86 desktop with an AMD FX processor running both Windows and Linux. Since HIveS conceals the presence of malware without changing any system software including BIOS, hypervisor or OS kernel, it can effectively defeat the most updated software based memory acquisition tools on both Windows and Linux. Furthermore, we extend HIveS with a number of existing anti-forensic techniques, such as *RAM-less encryption* and *Cache based I/O storage*, to defeat hardware based memory acquisition approaches.

We propose several countermeasures for detecting and mitigating HIveS. One seemingly simple solution is to directly inspect the CPU registers that may have been manipulated by HIveS. However, since legitimate peripheral device drivers may also change the same set of CPU registers, it remains a challenge to distinguish normal configurations from malicious usages, and maybe impossible without crashing the system on some hardware platforms.

To summarize, we make the following contributions.

- We present HIveS, a system that exploits hardware features in x86 platform to subvert the foundation of memory acquisition. HIveS is an OS agnostic anti-forensic mechanism that can defeat memory forensic techniques by concealing the HIveS memory in the I/O space.
- We develop two novel techniques to enable covert operations on the unlocked HIveS memory against memory forensics. Blackbox Write grants only the write privilege to the HIveS memory, and TLB Camouflage can grant malicious users exclusive read and write access to the HIveS memory.
- A prototype of HIveS is built on the x86 platform to demonstrate its capability on concealing the HIveS memory against a number of most updated memory forensics tools on both Windows and Linux.
- We propose potential countermeasures to detect and mitigate HIveS. As an arms race, we show that HIveS can be enhanced to further evade hardware based memory acquisition solutions.

The remainder of the paper is organized as follows. Section 2 describes some background knowledge on x86 memory address space. We present the HIveS framework in Section 3 and discuss its extensions in Section 4. A prototype implementation is detailed in Section 5. We propose potential countermeasures in Section 6. Section 8 discusses the related works. Finally, we conclude the paper in Section 9.

2. BACKGROUND

The entire range of memory addresses accessible by x86 processors is often referred to as *physical address space*. Contrary to popular believes, the length of such address space usually does not equal to the amount of actual physical memory installed on the platform. This is because some of the address is mapped to the bus for I/O devices, instead of dynamic random access memory (DRAM). A typical memory layout of systems with AMD processors is shown in Figure 1, where the shaded areas are backed by DRAM, and the areas without shade are backed by I/O devices. This memory layout is used by the Memory Map Unit (MMU) to route memory requests from the processor to either DRAM or memory-mapped I/O (MMIO).

The memory setting of an x86 system is initialized by the BIOS at hardware reset and parsed by the operating system during the system bootstrap [9]. The layout is configured via several configuration registers in the North Bridge (NB) and the processor. DRAM Base/Limit register pair is among the earliest ones configured by the BIOS. They define the ranges of physical address space

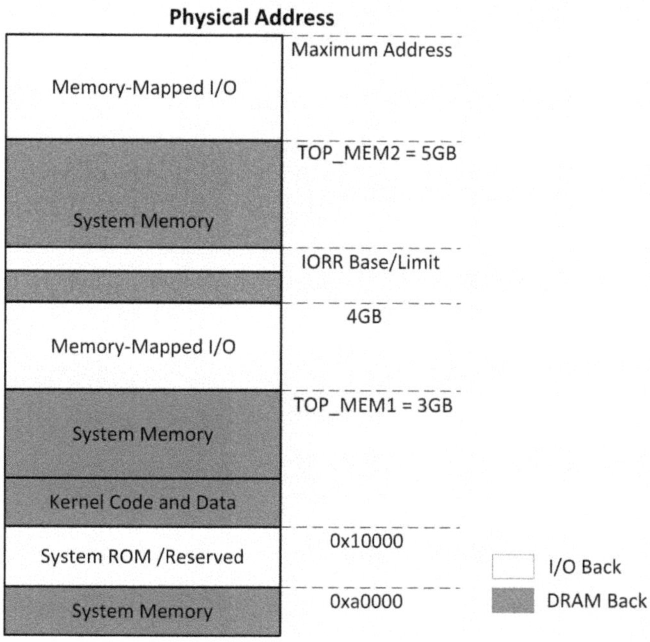

Figure 1: Physical Address Layout on AMD Architecture

mapped to DRAM in the north bridge. Any access to these areas will be forwarded to the DRAM Controller (DCT). These registers are configured by the BIOS with the result of system memory probing during hardware initialization. Therefore they are designed to be lock-once (i.e., write-once). The values cannot be changed until the next system reset.

The next set of registers that shapes the memory layout consists of two Mode Specific Registers (MSR) Top Of Memory (TOM) registers. AMD processors allow system software to use TOM registers to specify where memory accesses are directed for a given address range [2]. There are two TOM registers, *TOP_MEM1 (TOM1)* and *TOP_MEM2 (TOM2)*. Figure 1 shows that the address range from 0 to TOM1 as well as the address range from 4GB to TOM2 are set as system memory on this AMD system. Access requests within these two ranges are directed to the DRAM, while requests outside these two ranges are directed to the I/O space. The purpose of these two registers is to offer the operating system software the ability to carve out large memory space to organize DRAM and I/O devices. Even though they can be changed even when the system is operational, unlike the DRAM Base/Limit register, it is rare to change the memory address allocation after the system starts up. This is because the DRAM boundaries, governed by DRAM Base/Limit registers, have already been determined. Lastly, systems usually stop functioning if these registers are changed, since the OS kernel was not expecting the change of hardware configuration while the system is running.

The last set of registers that shapes the layout is also MSR in the processor. They are the Input Output Remap Registers (IORR). These set of registers can create a special mapping beyond the base setting to direct specific read/write access of any address space between the I/O space and the DRAM space. This set of registers are designed to enable system software to shadow ROM device in memory to improve the system performance.

3. HIVES FRAMEWORK

In the ongoing battle between attackers and digital forensics examiners, memory acquisition is becoming an important technique for evidence collection. From the perspective of an attacker, we design HIveS, an anti-forensic system. It is capable of evading acquisition by software based memory forensics tools on a designated range of physical memory chosen by the attacker. We call this range of memory *HIveS memory*. It can be used by attackers to store malicious code or sensitive data.

A high level block diagram of the HIveS system is shown in Figure 2. For simplicity, we show a generic x86 multi-core architecture with one processor consisting of two cores. Each processor core has its own cache and TLB.

When a processor core needs to access the DRAM memory, it sends a request to the north bridge. The MUX inside the north bridge is responsible of forwarding the memory request to either the DRAM controller or the south bridge based on the physical address layout. This layout was initialized by the BIOS, then further defined by the operating system using model-specific registers (MSRs) including the top of memory (TOM) registers and the I/O range registers (IORRs). When the physical address is mapped to the I/O space, the request is forwarded to the south bridge. When the physical address falls in the DRAM range, the memory request goes through the DRAM controller to the physical memory.

HIveS has two states, *locked* and *unlocked*. When it is in the locked state, the HIveS memory is completely inaccessible to any processor core. This is because all access attempts are forwarded to the I/O space once HIveS is locked. While the system remains in this state, even the malicious core (e.g., Core 1 in Figure 2) cannot access the HIveS memory. When the attacker needs to access the HIveS memory, she can set HIveS to unlocked state, where only the malicious core can access the HIveS memory, and memory requests from all other cores are redirected to another DRAM region. Lastly, since HIveS relies only on hardware configurations to conceal the HIveS memory, it is OS agnostic. Moreover, it leaves no trace in memory. Unlike some of the current rootkits that modifies kernel data structures or operating system APIs, HIveS cannot be detected by checking the integrity of the OS.

3.1 Inaccessibility in the Locked State

Considering the use case of a password stealing rootkit, whose goal is to steal passwords and store them quietly in some place before an opportunity to exfiltrate, there is no need for the rootkit to read from or write to the memory where the stolen passwords are stored until it is ready to transmit. HIveS is designed to an anti-forensic tool, so we develop a novel *I/O Shadowing* technique to block all processor cores from accessing the HIveS memory. The basic idea of I/O shadowing is to dynamically manipulate the configuration of a memory range so that even if it is backed by the DRAM in the physical address space, any read/write request will be redirected to the I/O space. The real contents in the DRAM memory are shadowed by the memory-mapped I/O (MMIO).

Among the various controls that shapes the memory layout, there are two MSRs that can be controlled by the system software when the system is operational. They are TOM and IORR.

Though TOM registers can be modified after the system boots up, any modification of the TOM registers can greatly affect the

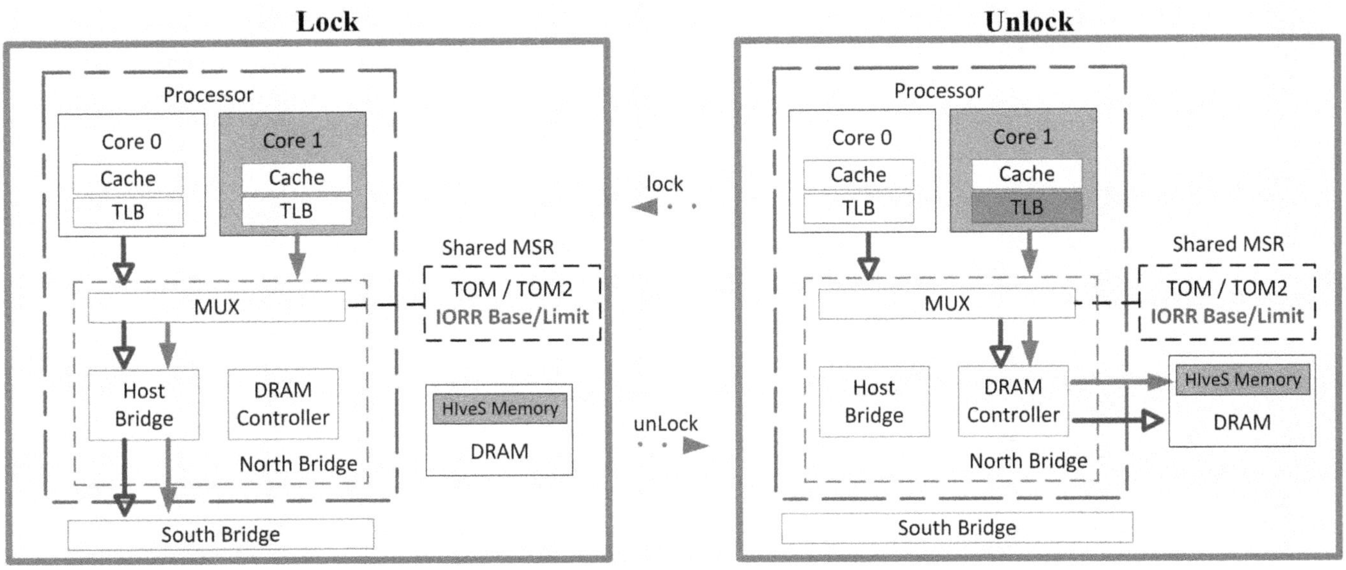

Figure 2: Architecture of HIveS

system stability, since the OS kernel uses the TOM registers in many default system settings. Furthermore, TOM modifications can only change the boundary between the default I/O area and the DRAM area. Even if system instability was not an issue, the manipulation would be very limited.

We instead use I/O range registers (IORRs) to adaptively prevent all processor cores from accessing the HIveS memory. IORRs are variable-range memory type range registers (MTRRs). They can be used to specify if reads and writes in any physical address range should map to system memory or memory-mapped I/O (MMIO). In AMD architecture [2], up to two address ranges of varying sizes can be controlled using IORRs. Figure 1 shows an example that maps an area of system RAM between 4GB and 5GB into MMIO using one IORR.

Each IORR has a pair of registers, *IORR base register* and *IORR mask register*. The IORR mask register contains the length of the region and a valid bit indicating whether the IORR configuration pair is active. IORR base register contains the starting address of the IORR region, as well as two important flag bits, *WrMem* and *RdMem* [2]. When these two bits are set to 1, the north bridge directs read/write requests for this physical address range to system memory. When these bits are cleared to 0, all reads/write requests are directed to memory-mapped I/O.

The RdMem and WrMem bits in IORR are originally designed for shadowing ROMs of I/O devices in DRAM memory to improve system performance. The system can create a shadow region by setting $WrMem = 1$ and $RdMem = 0$ for a dedicated memory range and then copy the ROM from I/O device into DRAM memory. Once the copy operation is completed, the system changes the bit value to $WrMem = 0$ and $RdMem = 1$. Now the memory reads are directed to the faster copy in the DRAM memory instead of ROM of the device; write requests are still being directed to the ROM, but the ROM simply ignores any write request.

The I/O shadowing provided by IORRs can be misused to redirect processor requests of a valid system memory area to the I/O space. When both RdMem and WrMem bits are set to 0 in the IORR, all read and write requests to the HIveS memory will be redirected to the I/O space. With this configuration, the HIveS memory becomes inaccessible for all processor cores. Since both Windows and Linux operating systems make no assumptions on the default configurations and usages of IORRs, the modification of unused IORR registers has no impact on the OS reliability. In addition, IORR registers offers great adaptability in both the location and size of the HIveS memory.

3.2 Exclusive Access in the Unlocked State

The HIveS memory in the unlocked state is designed to allow an exclusive access from the processor core controlled by the attacker, while preventing acquisition by the processor cores that perform memory forensics. IORRs are registers shared by all processor cores, so any modification on one IORR register affects all the processor cores in the system. When an attackers needs to access the HIveS memory in a single core system, she can simply unlock HIveS memory by disabling the I/O shadowing, read or modify contents in the HIveS memory, and then lock it by enabling the I/O shadowing. However, it becomes a challenge to ensure an exclusive access to HIveS memory with parallel execution in a multi-core system, since the forensic examiner can be collecting memory with the other running core. We develop two new techniques, *Blackbox Write* and *TLB Camouflage*, to solve this problem.

3.2.1 Blackbox Write

When an attacker with an active keylogger uses HIveS memory to store the collected sensitive data, it will be writing to the HIveS memory most of the time and does not need to frequently read it back. On the other hand, forensic examiners are interested only on reading the memory contents. In order to preserve the integrity of the evidence, memory forensic tools always read the memory contents and never write to the memory.

Based on the above asymmetric operations between the attackers and the examiners, we develop *Blackbox Write* to redirect all

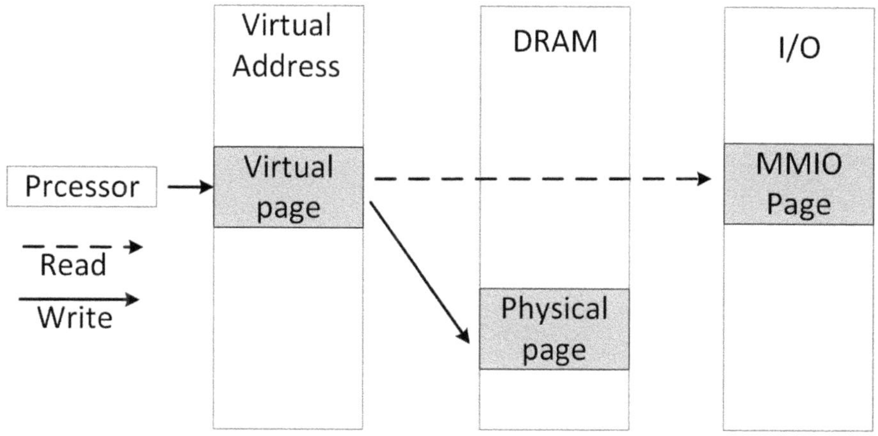

Figure 3: Blackbox Write

Algorithm 1: TLB Camouflage

begin
- allocate a new memory page;
- pause all other running cores;
- all cores flush TLBs;
- modify the new page PTE to point to the HIveS memory;
- malicious core read/write the virtual address;
- malicious core TLB entry loaded;
- modify the new page PTE back to regular address;
- resume all other cores;

memory read requests to the I/O space by setting $RdMem = 0$ in IORR and send all the memory write requests to the HIveS memory by setting $WrMem = 1$. With this setting, attackers can write new contents into the HIveS memory while preventing forensic examiners from reading and analyzing it. Because there is no real I/O device in the I/O hub to respond to the memory reads, a default value (e.g, $0xFF$ in AMD FX processor [4]) is returned instead. Note the examiner can also write into the HIveS memory, however actively modifying memory is a an act of compromising evidence, which is against the principle of digital forensics.

The attacker eventually needs to send the data in the HIveS memory to a remote machine. For instance, after a fix amount of user key strokes have been stealthily recorded, the keylogger can send the data to a remote server using network packets. Instead of unlocking processor's read access to the HIveS memory, the attacker can manage to read the HIveS memory by a peripheral device via DMA. To prevent random peripheral devices from reading the HIveS memory, HIveS can set the IOMMU to only allow a designated peripheral device to access the HIveS memory. Thus, a network interface adapter can read the key stoke logs from the HIveS memory via DMA and exfiltrate them.

3.2.2 TLB Camouflage

Blackbox write is an effective technique for malware that continuously stores sensitive data in a secret place with little need to read back, such as keyloggers. However, when the malware needs to unlock the HIveS memory for continuous read and write, it leaves a large time window for memory forensic tools to acquire the HIveS memory. We propose TLB Camouflage technique to mitigate this problem. Figure 4 shows the basic idea of TLB camouflage, where the unlocked HIveS memory can only be accessed by the malicious Core 1 that is controlled by the attacker, while the read and write requests from Core 2 for memory forensics are redirected to another memory space. TLB camouflage enables exclusive access to HIveS memory by creating an incoherent view of memory mapping between cores, allowing the HIveS memory contents be accessed only by the processor core that is running the malicious software.

Modern operating systems enable paging mechanism to translate virtual memory address into physical memory address before passing the memory access request to DRAM Controller (DCT) [9]. Translation-Lookaside Buffer (TLB), also known as page-translation caches, is designed to reduce the performance penalty during the time-consuming address translation process [2]. Only one memory access per virtual memory request is required when the translation for the demanding page is present in the TLB (a TLB hit). When there is no entry in the TLB for the demanding page, a TLB miss occurs. And the translation information for the page is copied from a page table entry (PTE) into the TLB (a TLB reload).

Each processor core has its own TLB [2, 3]. When the operating system changes a page mapping, the TLB won't be automatically updated to reflect the new virtual to physical address translation. TLB camouflage exploits this property to create a page translation incoherence among different processor cores.

A pseudo code of TLB Camouflage is shown in Algorithm 1. The idea is to create an incoherent cache entry in the TLB caches among the running processor cores. A new page is allocated in the kernel for the page translation manipulation, such that the rest of the system would not be affected. Then, all the other processor cores are paused. At this point, the malicious core can flush the TLB and to make sure that there is no preexisting translation stored for the our newly allocated page already. The PTE of the allocated page is then modified to point to HIveS memory, and several LDR instructions are then used to force a translation table walk and TLB reload. And the malicious core would have a TLB entry mapping to HIveS memory. Then the PTE is modified back to the original values, and the other cores are resumed. Technically, the TLB entry for the allocated page of malicious core is incoherent, and contains

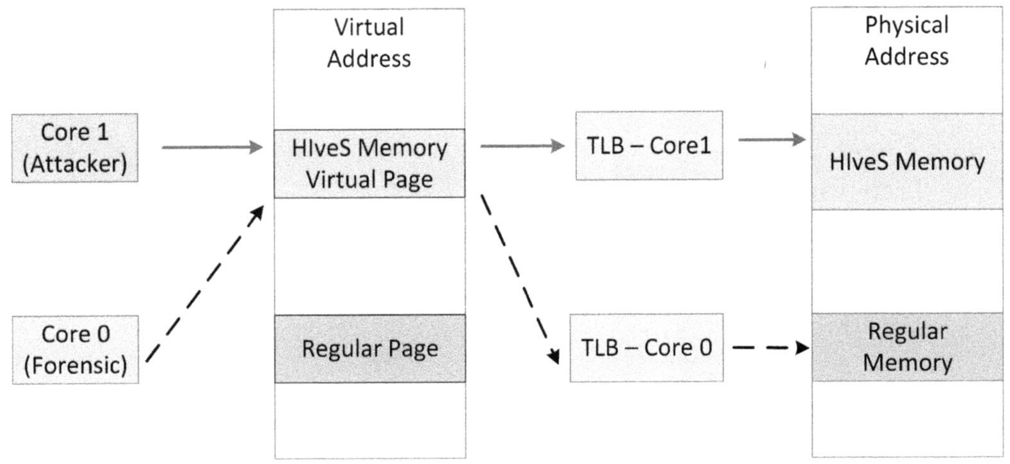

Figure 4: TLB Camouflage

a false mapping. And this is exactly what we need. In Figure 4, when Core 2 requests to access the virtual page of the HIveS memory, it will get the content in the regular memory. On the other hand, since the malicious Core 1 has an incoherrent TLB entry pointed to the HIveS memory address, it can access the HIveS memory if the TLB entry has not been flushed out.

TLB camouflage technique greatly increases the usability of HIveS memory, which can be used not only as a temporary storage with few interactions, but also as an interactive memory storage to support more malicious operations.

However, TLB Camouflage has some limitations. First, not all forensic tools rely on the existing kernel page tables to map virtual addresses to physical addresses [35]. In this case, TLB camouflage won't work since it depends on manipulating the kernel page tables. Second, the TLB entry should be sustained all the time; otherwise, the malicious core cannot access the HIveS memory either. Since TLB locking capability is not supported by the latest x86 architecture, malicious code has to freshen the TLB entry periodically in order to keep it active in TLB depending on the processor implementation.

3.3 HIveS Memory Access Property

When the HIveS memory is in the locked state by applying the I/O shadowing technique, none of processor cores can read or write the HIveS memory. Most of the time, the attacker does not need to access the HIveS memory at all, so it can lock the memory for a better protection. However, the attacker has to unlock the memory eventually to access it. When the attacker only needs to write to the HIveS memory, it can use the Blackbox Write technique. Moreover, if the attacker also needs to frequently read the memory contents, it can use the TLB Camouflage technique. Table 1 shows the different access privileges to the HIveS memory for both attackers and forensic examiners when applying different anti-forensic techniques.

HIveS is operating system agnostic, so the HIveS memory can be concealed on x86 platforms for both Windows and Linux. However, we need to develop a kernel module on Linux or a device driver on Windows with the root privilege to set the hardware registers. Contrary to current rootkits that modify kernel data structures or routines in the operating system, HIveS does not leave any trace in the memory or hard disk, so it cannot be detected by checking the integrity of the OS image in the memory and the hard disk.

4. HIVES EXTENSION

HIveS is mainly developed to defeat software based memory acquisition methods that rely on a trusted software module in the operating system to acquire the physical memory through the processor to memory interface. Both I/O Shadowing and Blackbox Write rely on modifying the IORR registers, and TLB Camouflage creates an incoherent page translation in TLB caches of multiple processor cores. All the modifications are made on the processor, and thus only affect processing of memory request originated from the processor. On the other hand, hardware based memory acquisition solutions can detect HIveS, since a dedicated I/O device can capture physical memory image via direct memory access, which totally bypasses the processor hardware configurations made by HIveS. Moreover, the Cold Boot technique [18] exploits the physical remanence property of memory chips to directly extract sensitive data from the chips. Cold boot technique resets the system and invalidates all configurations prior to system reset. To enhance the capability of HIveS against the hardware based forensics tools, we propose to retrofit a number of existing techniques in HIveS, including IOMMU, RAM-less encryption, and Cache based I/O storage.

4.1 Hiding from I/O Devices

We propose to use IOMMU to evade physical memory forensics by I/O devices via DMA. Similar to the translation from virtual memory address to physical memory address performed by MMU, IOMMU is a hardware device that translates device DMA addresses into proper physical memory addresses. Each I/O device is assigned a protected domain with a set of I/O page tables that define the corresponding memory addresses. During a DMA transfer, the IOMMU intercepts the access message from the I/O bus and checks its cache (IOTLB) for the I/O to memory address translation along with the access right. IOMMU is controlled with in-memory tables and memory-mapped registers. Once a DMA request passes IOMMU, it is then processed by the north bridge.

Table 1: Comparison of Access to HIveS Memory

	Attacker Read	Attacker Write	Regular Read	Regular Write
I/O Shadowing	no	no	no	no
Blackbox Write	no	yes	no	yes
TLB Camouflage	yes	yes	no	no

The north bridge then forwards the request either to the I/O hub or the DRAM controller base on the ranges defined by DRAM Base/Limit and MMIO Base/Limit registers. Therefore, HIveS can set the IOMMU to only allow a peripheral device to perform DMA into assigned regions, thus preventing a full system memory acquisition with DMA. When the IOMMU is not available on some old systems, the DMA can also be redirected by manipulating the north bridge using MMIO Base/Limit registers. The main idea is to modify the MMIO Base/Limit registers to bounce DMA reads back to the I/O hub. The details can be found in [30].

4.2 Hiding from Cold Boot

There are two solutions to evade Cold Boot based memory acquisition mechanisms: *RAM-less encryption* and *Cache based I/O storage*.

RAM-less encryption. The basic idea is that attacker encrypts all the memory contents in the HIveS memory with a secret key stored in CPU registers [24, 33]. Since operating systems do not use all the MTRR and IORR register pairs all the time, HIveS can encrypt the HIveS memory using AES and store the encryption key in unused MTRR or IORR registers. Thus, even if the physical memory is completely acquired through Cold Boot, the contents of HIveS are still being protected, because the encryption key in the CPU registers is lost forever due to the system reset.

Cache based I/O storage. The idea is to save a small HIveS memory only in the CPU cache [22, 26, 17] and then mask it with I/O Shadowing technique. When the memory address is set to cacheable in the page table entry and both RdMem and WrMem bits in the IORR base register are set to 1, any write to that location will trigger a cache line fill if the memory contents are not yet loaded in the cache. When the HIveS system is unlocked, the attacker can simply write data into memory as usual. When the HIveS system is locked, the HIveS memory is cached and masked by I/O shadowing. Therefore, neither I/O devices nor the processor can read out the HIveS memory in the cache via DMA. However, it remains a challenge to maintain the contents in the cache considering the limited cache control provided by the x86 architecture [2, 3].

5. IMPLEMENTATION AND EVALUATION

We build a prototype of HIveS on an x86 desktop with AMD FX processor. The motherboard is ASUS M4 A96 R2.0, running a AMD FX-8320 8-core processor with single bank DDR3 4GB memory. The 4GB memory is relatively small but it shortens the time for memory acquisition and it is large enough to demonstrate all the functionality of HIveS.

To illustrate the effectiveness of the HIveS memory, we implement a keylogger rootkit called *HIL* that uses HIveS memory to store the keystrokes so that the stolen information cannot be detected by memory forensics. We implement HIL prototypes on both Windows and Linux. On Ubuntu 13.04, we implement a Linux kernel module to support all the techniques in HIveS. On 64-bit Windows 7, we implement a kernel mode device driver as a keylogger and use WinDbg debugger to configure the IORR pair.

We implement I/O shadowing, Blackbox Write, and TLB Camouflage techniques and evaluate their effectiveness using a number of most updated software based memory forensic tools. We also implement RAM-less encryption and cache based I/O Storage techniques to demonstrate the capability of HIveS to evade Cold Boot based physical memory forensics.

5.1 I/O Shadowing

Since modification of MSR require privilege mode, we implemented most of the functionalities in a kernel module. User space programs can communicate with the kernel module through *procfs* export. For I/O shadowing, the kernel module is responsible for manipulating the IORR register to set the base and the size of the HIveS memory, as well as the WrMem and RdMem flag bits. With the physical address and HIveS running mode passed in through procfs, the module first masks off the lower 12 bit of the physical address, and inserts it into bits 12 to 47 in I/O Range Base register, *MSRC001_0016*, since the physical addressing in AMD x64 is 47 bit. The bits 3 and 4 of the register are RdMem bit and WrMem bit respectively. For I/O Shadowing, we clear both bit 3 and bit 4 to redirect both read and write requests into the I/O space.

The IORR base register should always be written first, since the IORR mask register, *MSRC001_0017*, contains a *valid* bit, which will immediately enable the IORR pair once this bit is set. Therefore, we cannot set the two IORR registers in reverse order; otherwise, the system will fail and hang itself. In the AMD FX system [2], the valid bit is bit 11 of the IORR mask register.

Although the detailed HIveS implementation is different on Linux and Windows, the workflow remains the same. We first load HIveS as a kernel module in the system. An 1MB area at physical address offset of *0x10c800000* is allocated to be the HIveS memory. With RdMem and WrMem both set, we fill the memory with repeating pattern of *0x12345678*. Once the pattern is written, we flush the cache to make sure that these patterns are written into the memory. Then we enable I/O shadowing to lock the HIveS memory by clearing both the WrMem and RdMem bits. At this point, all the contents in the HIveS memory should be protected against memory forensic tools.

We verify that none of the software based memory forensic tools that we tested is able to capture the HIveS memory protected by the I/O shadowing technique. Table 2 summarizes the tools that we use in our experiments. Tools such as the Linux base memory acquisition tool LiME [36] obtain the physical memory layout of the system by parsing kernel data structure. For each valid memory re-

Table 2: Verification against memory forensic tools

Tool	Tool Version	OS	Examine IORR	With HIveS	Without HIveS
UnitTest	1.0	Linux	No	No Detection	Identified
LiME	1.1	Linux	No	No Detection	Identified
MemDump	1.01	Linux	No	No Detection	Identified
DD	8.13	Linux	No	No Detection	Identified
WinPmem	2.3.1	Windows	No	No Detection	Identified
Mem Marshall	1.0	Windows	No	No Detection	Identified
Memoryze	3.0	Windows	No	No Detection	Identified
Dumpit	1.3.2	Windows	No	No Detection	Identified

gion, it calls *kmap* function to map virtual pages to physical pages to read the content.

Table 2 shows that none of these memory forensic tools can detect the HIveS memory through searching the special repeating pattern *0x12345678* when the I/O shadowing is enabled. However, when the memory dumps are taken again after the I/O shadowing is disabled, we can identify the repeating pattern in the memory dumps. None of the tools can detect HIveS, since all the processor memory accesses can be manipulated by the IORR registers and all the software based tools utilize processor to access memory.

5.2 Blackbox Write and TLB Camouflage

Blackbox Write only provides write access to the HIveS memory and prevents any read access. We implement it by clearing the RdMem bit and setting the WrMem bit. To disable Blackbox Write, we simply clear the valid bit of the IORR pair. To verify its effectiveness, we set up the keylogger to work in the Blackbox Write mode. Instead of filling the HIveS memory with repeating pattern *0x12345678*. We run the keylogger, and manually type in "this is a HIveS blackbox write test!". When Blackbox Write is enabled, we dump the memory using the memory acquisition tools, including LiME, MemDump, and WinPmem, to capture the entire physical memory images. And we verify that the sentence we typed was not found in the acquired memory image. Immediately after the first round of memory dump, we disable Blackbox Write to allow both read and write access to the HIveS memory and perform memory dumping again. This time, we were able to find the logs of what we just typed.

TLB camouflage protects the HIveS memory by only allowing read and write access to a single processor core. After pausing all other cores, we flush the TLBs of all cores. Next, we disable all interrupts on the malicious core and then read the contents of the HIveS memory into a temporary memory space. The kernel module then goes in a busy loop accessing the memory location continuously to sustain the TLB entry in the malicious core's TLB. We confirm that only a single processor core can access the HIveS memory by dumping the memory images using different processor cores and searching the coded repeating pattern.

5.3 RAM-less Encryption

For RAM-less encryption, we use a secret key to XOR the plaintext instead of using the AES function, since the feasibility of RAM-less encryption has already been verified [24, 33] and our focus is on testing the stability of the MSRs for storing the secret key. In particular, we use the unused MTRR registers and IORR registers, which can be identified by checking the valid bit. On our AMD platform, there are eight MTRR pairs per core plus two shared core IORR registers. When the valid bit is cleared, the register is not used by the system. The bits provided by these registers are large enough to store a short encryption key.

5.4 Cache based I/O Storage

We perform a simple experiment to verify that the cache based I/O storage is able to keep the sensitive data in the cache only. Similarly, a repeating pattern *0x12345678* is written into the HIveS memory. Now the pattern should be stored in the cache. Next, we execute an *INVD* instruction, which invalidates all cache content without writing them back to the physical memory. If the pattern is indeed in the cache, after the execution of *INVD* instruction, such written pattern should no longer be observable. In our experiment, since the memory read back after *INVD* is not *0x12345678*, and therefore the modifications to the memory we wrote was truly stored in the cache. However, when the processor is busy, such contents stored in the cache is flushed out to the physical DRAM in a very short time.

6. HIVES LIMITATIONS AND COUNTERMEASURES

6.1 HIveS Limitations

Though the prototype shows promising potential on using HIveS to conceal malicious code and sensitive data in HIveS memory, the system has some limitations.

First, since the basic idea behind HIveS is the manipulation of physical address layout, system architecture with a fixed or reliable way to retrieve the physical address layout is not vulnerable to this attack. Furthermore, our implementation of HIveS relies on manipulating hardware registers in the AMD processor [2], therefore porting of the malware to other platforms requires careful design changes and examinations. As with most other advanced anti-forensic rootkits, HIveS requires kernel privilege to manipulate the system registers, and thus it is not available to user space malwares.

Second, HIveS achieves stealthiness by redirecting memory access on the hardware level. This inherently implies all software based accesses to the memory are redirected. Therefore HIveS cannot be used to store the current executing code. As a result, malware code that utilizes this storage, as presented in our prototype, is left in the memory and could be captured and analyzed by forensic examiners.

Lastly, HIveS focuses on defeating the software based memory acquisition approaches, so it has to be augmented with other anti-forensic mechanisms to defeat the hardware based memory acquisition approaches. Those mechanisms increase the complexity of HIveS and possibly make the targeted system unstable.

6.2 Countermeasures

HIveS is a system to subvert the organization of physical address layout. In order to defeat HIveS, it is important to get a reliable representation of the true address layout. Unfortunately, there is currently no architecturally supported method to verify the truthfulness of the layout. For the rest of the discussion, we focus on how to defeat our HIveS implementation on AMD platforms.

First, we know that the manipulation of IORR is essential in HIveS, and since IORR registers are only available on AMD processors, HIveS as a system does not work well in Intel family processor from HIveS, though several techniques we presented in HIveS may still apply.

Second, the use of IORR can be a good hint of the presence of HIveS memory in the system. It can be identified by simply inspecting the valid bit in the IORR mask register. A forensic examiner can also detect the existence of HIveS by measuring the timing for memory operations. When I/O shadowing is enabled, all memory access goes through the I/O bus and takes much longer to complete.

Note that legitimate I/O devices may also use the IORR to map physical memory address to the I/O space. For instance, AGP video driver in Linux kernel uses the IORR register in some cases. Since AMD provides two pairs of IORR registers, a forensic examiner can also examine the difference of the two pairs. Yet, such analysis could be quite system dependent. It is difficult to determine if the use of IORR registers is benign or malicious. The forensic examiner may assume the use of IORR is malicious and directly modify the value of this IORR register to reveal the memory contents. However, if the use of IORR is benign and system originated, such direct manipulation may crash the system. A more conservative approach might be to read out the contents from the address range without modifying any of the registers. Even though this might cause system instability as well, the probability of a system catastrophic failure caused by memory read is much smaller. If all the bytes read back are all identical values $0xFF$ or $0x00$, then most likely there is no real I/O device behind these I/O addresses.

Finally, HIveS can be detected by Cold Boot if we don't apply the HIveS extensions such as RAM-less encryption. Forensic examiners can first dump the registers, including all the MSRs and debugging registers from all processor cores. All system cache can then be flushed back into memory. Then the system is reset to extract memory content exploiting the memory remanence characteristics. This however changes many system configurations in the system as well as some memory contents, which violates the forensic principle of not altering the crime scene.

7. EXTENSION AND FUTURE WORK

While some of the limitations discussed above are unavoidable, such as dependence on architecture and operating system, some others can be overcome. We discuss possible extensions of HIveS in this section.

7.1 Eliminating Memory Traces

One of the limitations discussed above is that the storage can only be used to store data collected by the malware instead of protecting the entire malware. The forensic examiner might be able to analyze the malware memory to discover the manipulation of address layout. One key insight is that, the physical address layout manipulation performed by HIveS is very infrequent if not one time. Furthermore, the amount of code required to alter this layout is very small, most likely a single instruction or two. Taking our prototype as an example, the kernel module initialization routine can use one instruction to change the IORR register then immediately erasing the previous instruction by zeroing it. This leaves a very small time window, three instruction execution time, for the forensic examiner to capture the image and discover the use of IORR in the malware. The practical chance of catching such moment is close to zero.

7.2 Extending HIveS to Intel Platforms

The IORR registers HIveS exploited to alter the physical address layout is AMD specific unfortunately. To the best of our knowledge, there is no such MSR in the Intel platform [3]. This does not imply HIveS is impossible on Intel. Malware authors will need to find another way to alter the physical address layout to launch the attack. For example, Intel Memory Controller Hub (MCH) chipsets also provide capability to recover addressable memory space lost to MMIO space [1]. One can modify the REMAPBASE and REMAPLIMIT register in the chipset to manipulate the physical address layout (also known as system address space in Intel manuals).

7.3 HIveS for Defense

Techniques in computer security are like weapons, it can be used either to defend the righteousness or cause damage to the society. For instance, virtual machine based rootkit (VMBR) introduced by Rutkowska et al. [29] has been used to capture host image in forensic memory analysis [23, 40]. Similarly, though we present HIveS as a powerful anti-forensic tool, it can certainly be developed and used as a defense tool to protect sensitive data against malicious memory scanning. For example, application passwords can be stored in HIveS memory without having to worry about malware reading the passwords from the physical memory.

8. RELATED WORKS

There is an ongoing arms race between the attackers and the forensic examiners in computer forensics [34, 20, 25, 37]. Memory forensic analysis is becoming an indispensable tool for forensic examiners nowadays, and they have two ways to acquire computer memory: software based methods that use a trusted software module to access memory through the CPU processor [11, 21, 39, 28, 35, 14, 31, 36, 12] and hardware based methods that rely on dedicated I/O devices to access physical memory image via Direct Memory Access [10, 35, 27, 6].

Software based memory acquisition techniques rely on the CPU processor to acquire physical memory through the operating system. Unfortunately, after recognizing this dependency, attackers have developed anti-forensic techniques to compromise the memory acquisition process, such as directly modifying the acquisition module or the OS kernel data structure [8, 20, 34, 15], using rootkits to hook operating system APIs [32], or installing a thin hypervisor on the fly [29].

To defeat those anti-forensic techniques, Stüttgen et al. [35] propose an anti-forensic resilient method to acquire physical memory by eliminating its dependence on the operating system routines and data structures. Schatze [31] proposes to bootstrap a trusted new execution environment from the normal one to make sure that the operating system is free of malware. System management mode (SMM) can also be used to create a trusted isolated execution environment [28, 39]. Some researchers propose to go deeper than the operating system level and use hardware virtualization to avoid the memory acquisition software being subverted by rootkits [23, 40].

Stüttgen et al. suggest that the memory acquisition process can be trusted if the acquisition module has not been tampered with and all the operations are performed without relying on the operating system or any other untrusted software [35]. However, in this paper, we show that this assumption is not true. The main reason is that the physical memory layout seen by the processor can be manipulated through the hardware configurations on the chipset. Attackers can misuse hardware configurations to modify this layout and conceal the presence of malware.

A number of hardware based memory acquisition methods have been developed recently [27, 38, 5, 10], using a trusted peripheral device to capture the physical memory image via DMA. Since it does not rely on the CPU processor to get the physical memory, the hardware based approaches can successfully prevent those anti-forensic techniques that are originally designed to defeat the software based approaches. However, Rutkowska [30] shows that it is possible to present a different view of the physical memory to the peripherals by reprogramming the north bridge. Therefore, in-memory data acquired by DMAs could be compromised as well [28, 35].

A special type of memory acquisition technique relies on the unique remanence property of physical DRAM [18, 11]. Despite the popular belief that volatile contents in DRAM are gone once the computer resets or powers off, Halderman et al. [18] demonstrate a Cold Boot attack that can reliably recover the contents in the memory modules even after the power has been cut off for a short period of time. Though the original Cold Boot is demonstrated as an attack to steal cryptographic keys and other sensitive data from the RAM, it is also an effective method that can be used for reliably acquiring physical memory.

9. CONCLUSIONS

In this paper, we propose a different approach to anti-memory forensic. Instead of looking at ways to conceal presence by operating system object manipulation, we can defeat current memory acquisition methods by manipulating the physical address layout, a design architectural feature on modern x86 platforms.

HIveS is an anti-forensic mechanism to conceal in-memory data shadowed behind the I/O address space. Besides I/O Shadowing technique to prevent forensic memory acquisition tools from reading the HIveS memory contents via processor, we also use Blackbox Write and TLB Camouflage to enable the attacker exclusive write access and provide a single malicious core exclusive read and write access, respectively. Furthermore, we propose several addons to the basic framework to further hide from physical memory forensics.

A prototype of HIveS is built on an AMD platform to show that none of the popular memory acquisition tools we tested can capture the memory data protected by HIveS. Several countermeasures are discussed in the end. In the future, we intend to further investigate possible mechanisms to retrieve trustworthy physical address layout.

Acknowledgment

This work was supported in part by US National Science Foundation under grants CNS-1217889 and CNS-1405747. Dr. Kun Sun's work is partially supported by U.S. Army Research Office under Grant W911NF-12-1-0060, W911NF-12-1-0448 and U.S. Office of Naval Research under Grant N00014-11-1-0471

10. REFERENCES

[1] Intel Chipset 4 GB System Memory Support . Feb 2005.

[2] Advanced Micro Devices. Amd64 Architecture Programmer's Manual. Vol. 2, may 2013.

[3] Intel 64 and IA-32 Architectures Software Developer's Manual. sep 2013.

[4] Advanced Micro Devices, Inc. BIOS and Kernel Developer's Guide (BKDG) For AMD Family 15h Processors, Rev 3.23.

[5] R. BBN. Fred: Forensic ram extraction device. `http://www.digitalintelligence.com/products/fred/`.

[6] M. Becher, M. Dornseif, and C. N. Klein. FireWire All Your Memory are Belong to us. *Proceedings of CanSecWest*, 2005.

[7] N. Beebe. Digital forensic research: The good, the bad and the unaddressed. In *Advances in digital forensics V*, pages 17–36. Springer, 2009.

[8] D. Bilby. Low down and dirty: Anti-forensic rootkits. *BlackHat Japan*, 2006.

[9] D. Bovet and M. Cesati. *Understanding the Linux kernel.* O'reilly, 2007.

[10] B. D. Carrier and J. Grand. A hardware-based memory acquisition procedure for digital investigations. *Digital Investigation*, 1(1):50 – 60, 2004.

[11] E. Chan, S. Venkataraman, F. David, A. Chaugule, and R. Campbell. Forenscope: A framework for live forensics. In *Proceedings of the 26th Annual Computer Security Applications Conference*, pages 307–316. ACM, 2010.

[12] M. Cohen, D. Bilby, and G. Caronni. Distributed forensics and incident response in the enterprise. *digital investigation*, 8:S101–S110, 2011.

[13] N. R. Council. Strengthening Forensic Science in the United States: A Path Forward. `https://www.ncjrs.gov/pdffiles1/nij/grants/228091.pdf`, 2009.

[14] D. Farmer and W. Venema. *Forensic discovery*, volume 18. Addison-Wesley Reading, 2005.

[15] E. Florio. When malware meets rootkits. *Virus Bulletin*, 2005.

[16] S. L. Garfinkel. Digital forensics research: The next 10 years. *Digital Investigation*, 7:S64–S73, 2010.

[17] L. Guan, J. L. amd Bo Luo, and J. Jing. Copker: Computing with Private Keys without RAM. In *In Network and Distributed System Security Symposium (NDSS)*, 2014.

[18] J. A. Halderman, S. D. Schoen, N. Heninger, W. Clarkson, W. Paul, J. A. Calandrino, A. J. Feldman, J. Appelbaum, and E. W. Felten. Lest we remember: cold-boot attacks on encryption keys. *Communications of the ACM*, 52(5):91–98, 2009.

[19] R. Harris. Arriving at an anti-forensics consensus: Examining how to define and control the anti-forensics problem. *digital investigation*, 3:44–49, 2006.

[20] T. Haruyama and H. Suzuki. One-byte modifications for breaking memory forensic analysis. *Black Hat Europe*, 2012.

[21] E. Libster and J. D. Kornblum. A proposal for an integrated memory acquisition mechanism. *SIGOPS Oper. Syst. Rev.*, 42(3):14–20, Apr. 2008.

[22] Y. Lu, L. Lo, G. Watson, and R. Minnich. CAR: Using Cache as RAM in LinuxBIOS. `http://rere.qmqm.pl/~mirq/cache_as_ram_lb_09142006.pdf`.

[23] L. Martignoni, A. Fattori, R. Paleari, and L. Cavallaro. Live and trustworthy forensic analysis of commodity production systems. In *Recent Advances in Intrusion Detection*, pages 297–316. Springer, 2010.

[24] T. Müller, F. C. Freiling, and A. Dewald. Tresor runs encryption securely outside ram. In *USENIX Security Symposium*, 2011.

[25] T. Newsham, C. Palmer, A. Stamos, and J. Burns. Breaking forensics software: Weaknesses in critical evidence collection. In *Proceedings of the 2007 Black Hat Conference*, 2007.

[26] J. Pabel. Frozencache: Mitigating cold-boot attacks for full-disk-encryption software. In *27th Chaos Communication Congress*, 2010.

[27] N. L. Petroni Jr, T. Fraser, J. Molina, and W. A. Arbaugh. Copilot-a coprocessor-based kernel runtime integrity monitor. In *USENIX Security Symposium*, pages 179–194, 2004.

[28] A. Reina, A. Fattori, F. Pagani, L. Cavallaro, and D. Bruschi. When hardware meets software: A bulletproof solution to forensic memory acquisition. In *Proceedings of the 28th Annual Computer Security Applications Conference*, ACSAC '12, pages 79–88, New York, NY, USA, 2012. ACM.

[29] J. Rutkowska. Subverting vistatm kernel for fun and profit. *Black Hat Briefings*, 2006.

[30] J. Rutkowska. Beyond the CPU: Defeating hardware based RAM acquisition. *Proceedings of BlackHat DC 2007*, 2007.

[31] B. Schatz. Bodysnatcher: Towards reliable volatile memory acquisition by software. *digital investigation*, 4:126–134, 2007.

[32] D. Sd. Linux on-the-fly kernel patching without lkm. *Volume 0x0b, Issue 0x3a, Phile# 0x07 of 0x0e-Phrack Magazine-http://www. phrack-dont-give-a-shit-about-dmca. org/show. php*, 2001.

[33] P. Simmons. Security through amnesia: a software-based solution to the cold boot attack on disk encryption. In *Proceedings of the 27th Annual Computer Security Applications Conference*, pages 73–82. ACM, 2011.

[34] S. Sparks and J. Butler. Shadow walker: Raising the bar for rootkit detection. *Black Hat Japan*, pages 504–533, 2005.

[35] J. Stüttgen and M. Cohen. Anti-forensic resilient memory acquisition. *Digital Investigation*, 10:S105–S115, 2013.

[36] J. Sylve. Lime-linux memory extractor. *ShmooConâĂŹ12*, 2012.

[37] S. Vömel and F. C. Freiling. A survey of main memory acquisition and analysis techniques for the windows operating system. *Digital Investigation*, 8(1):3–22, 2011.

[38] J. Wang, A. Stavrou, and A. K. Ghosh. Hypercheck: A hardware-assisted integrity monitor. In *RAID*, pages 158–177, 2010.

[39] J. Wang, F. Zhang, K. Sun, and A. Stavrou. Firmware-assisted memory acquisition and analysis tools for digital forensics. In *Systematic Approaches to Digital Forensic Engineering (SADFE), 2011 IEEE Sixth International Workshop on*, pages 1–5. IEEE, 2011.

[40] M. Yu, Q. Lin, B. Li, Z. Qi, and H. Guan. Vis: virtualization enhanced live acquisition for native system. In *Proceedings of the Second Asia-Pacific Workshop on Systems*, page 13. ACM, 2011.

TrustLogin: Securing Password-Login on Commodity Operating Systems

Fengwei Zhang
George Mason University
Fairfax, VA, USA
fzhang4@gmu.edu

Kevin Leach
University of Virginia
Charlottesville, VA, USA
kjl2y@virginia.edu

Haining Wang
University of Delaware
Newark, DE, USA
hnw@udel.edu

Angelos Stavrou
George Mason University
Fairfax, VA, USA
astavrou@gmu.edu

ABSTRACT

With the increasing prevalence of Web 2.0 and cloud computing, password-based logins play an increasingly important role on user-end systems. We use passwords to authenticate ourselves to countless applications and services. However, login credentials can be easily stolen by attackers. In this paper, we present a framework, TrustLogin, to secure password-based logins on commodity operating systems. TrustLogin leverages System Management Mode to protect the login credentials from malware even when OS is compromised. TrustLogin does not modify any system software in either client or server and is transparent to users, applications, and servers. We conduct two study cases of the framework on legacy and secure applications, and the experimental results demonstrate that TrustLogin is able to protect login credentials from real-world keyloggers on Windows and Linux platforms. TrustLogin is robust against spoofing attacks. Moreover, the experimental results also show TrustLogin introduces a low overhead with the tested applications.

Categories and Subject Descriptors

D.4.6 [**Operating Systems**]: Security and Protection—*Invasive software*; B.4.2 [**Hardware**]: Input/Output Devices—*Channels and controllers*

Keywords

Login Password; System Management Mode; Keyloggers

1. INTRODUCTION

Logging in is part of daily practice in the modern world. We use it to authenticate ourselves to applications for resource accesses. Consequently, login credentials are one of the top targets for attackers. For example, keylogger malware found on UC Irvine health center computers in May 2014, and it is estimated that 1,813 students and 23 non-students were impacted [7]. Additionally, it is reported that attackers have stolen credit card information for customers who shopped at 63 Barnes & Noble stores using keyloggers [3]. A case study has shown that 10,775 unique bank account credentials were stolen by keyloggers in a seven-month period [22]. Protecting login credentials is a critical part of daily life.

Nowadays, operating systems are complex and rely on millions of lines of code to operate (e.g., the Linux kernel has about 17 million lines of code [35]). The large Trusted Computing Base (TCB) of these OSes inevitably creates vulnerabilities that could be exploited by attackers. The Common Vulnerabilities and Exposures (CVE) list shows that 240 vulnerabilities have been found for the Linux kernel [2]. An attacker can easily leverage these vulnerabilities to create rootkits and keyloggers.

On top of an untrusted OS, no matter how secure the network applications are, the sensitive data used by secure applications is at risk of leakage. For example, an attacker can install a stealthy keylogger after compromising the OS, so the banking login information entered in a web browser can be obtained by the attacker without a user awareness. Therefore, the protection of the user's sensitive data during network operations is crucial; we need to prevent malicious behaviors of attackers on network applications.

In this paper, we present TrustLogin, a framework to securely perform login operations on commodity operating systems. Even if the operating system and applications are compromised, an attacker is not able to reveal the login password from the host. TrustLogin leverages System Management Mode (SMM), a CPU mode that exists in x86 architecture, to transparently protect the login credentials from keyloggers. Since we assume the attackers have ring 0 privilege, all of the software including the operating system cannot be trusted. SMM is a separate CPU mode with isolated execution memory, and it is inaccessible from the OS, which satisfies the needs of our system.

When users enter their passwords, TrustLogin automatically switches into SMM and records the keystroke. It provides a randomly generated string to the OS kernel and then the network driver prepares the login packets. When the login packets arrive at the network card, TrustLogin switches

ASIA CCS'15, April 14–17, 2015, Singapore..

http://dx.doi.org/10.1145/2714576.2714614 .

into SMM again and replaces the placeholder with the real password. Under the protection of TrustLogin , rootkits (e.g, keyloggers) cannot steal the sensitive data even with ring 0 privilege. To defend spoofing attacks, we implement two novel techniques that ensure the trust path when switching to SMM. They use the LED lights on keyboard and the PC speaker to interact with users. More importantly, TrustLogin does not modify application- and OS-code, and it is transparent from client and server sides.

To demonstrate the effectiveness of our approach, we conduct two study cases to use TrustLogin with legacy and secure applications. We test TrustLogin with real-world keyloggers on both Windows and Linux platforms, and the experiment results show that TrustLogin is able to protect the login password against them. We also measure the performance overhead introduced by executing code in SMM. Our results show SMM switching only takes about 8 microseconds. TrustLogin takes 33 milliseconds to store and replace a keystroke and most of the time is consumed by trusted path indication (i.e., playing a melody and showing a LED light sequence); it spends 30 microseconds on injecting the password back to a login packet for the tested application. The contributions of this paper are summarized as follows:

- We propose a framework, TrustLogin, to secure passwords when logging in on commodity operating systems. It leverages System Management Mode to protect the sensitive data from exposing to rootkits and thus guarantees the security on the local host.
- TrustLogin does not modify application- and OS- code, and it is transparent from both user-ends and servers. TrustLogin does not rely on hypervisor or OS code, and it introduces a minimal trusted code.
- We implement our framework on legacy and secure applications. We also demonstrate that TrustLogin can prevent real-world keyloggers from stealing passwords on Windows and Linux platforms.
- TrustLogin is robust against spoofing attacks by ensuring the trusted path of SMM switching. The performance experiments show that TrustLogin is lightweight and efficient to use.

The rest of the paper is organized as follows. Section 2 explains the background of the work. We discuss the threat model and assumptions in Section 3. Section 4 outlines the system architecture and implementation of TrustLogin. We propose the login case studies in Section 5. The discussion and limitation of TrustLogin is explained in Section 6. We present the related work in Section 7. Section 8 concludes the paper and discusses future work.

2. BACKGROUND

2.1 Advanced Programmable Interrupt Controller

The Advanced Programmable Interrupt Controller (APIC) is used to handle the communication between CPU and peripherals. There are two components in the Intel APIC system, the Local APIC (LAPIC) and the I/O APIC. The LAPIC performs two primary functions for the processor: 1) It receives interrupts from an external I/O APIC and sends these to the processor core for handling; 2) it sends and receives Interprocessor Interrupt (IPI) messages to and from other logical processors. The LAPIC is integrated in the CPU and each processor core has a LAPIC. The external I/O APIC is part of the system chipset. Its primary function is to receive the interrupts from I/O devices and forwards them to the LAPIC as interrupt messages. Normally each peripheral bus has an I/O APIC. In TrustLogin, we reconfigure APIC to generate SMIs.

2.2 System Management Mode

System Management Mode (SMM) is a CPU mode available in all x86 architecture. It is similar to Real and Protected Modes. Originally, it was designed for implementing system control functions such as power management. In recent years, it has been used for system introspection, debugging and so on. SMM is implemented by the Basic Input/Output System (BIOS). Before the system boots up, the BIOS loads SMM code into System Management RAM (SMRAM), a special memory region that is inaccessible from any other CPU mode. SMM is triggered by asserting the System Management Interrupt (SMI) pin on the motherboard. Both hardware and software are able to assert this pin, although the specific method depends on the chipset. After assertion, the system automatically saves its CPU states into SMRAM, and then executes the SMI handler code. A `RSM` instruction is executed at the end of the SMI hander to switch back to Protected Mode. In TrustLogin, we use SMM as a trusted execution environment to implement critical operations.

3. THREAT MODEL AND ASSUMPTIONS

3.1 Keylogger

Keyloggers can be classified into two types: hardware- and software-based. Hardware-based keyloggers are small electronic devices that are used to capture the keystrokes. They are often built in the keyboard itself and have separate non-volatile memory to store the keystrokes. Hardware keyloggers do not require installation of any software or power source for their operations. For instance, there are some commercial hardware keyloggers available [8]. In this paper, we do not consider this type of keylogger, and we assume the keyboard is not malicious.

Software-based keyloggers are installed within the operating system, and most of the keyloggers in the real world are this type. There are two kinds of software keyloggers: user- and kernel-level. For instance, a user-level keylogger can use the `GetKeyboardState` API function to capture keystrokes in Windows. This kind of keylogger is efficient but also easily detected. Kernel-level keyloggers are implemented at the kernel level and require administrator privilege to install. For example, a keyboard filter driver can be used to stealthily capture keystrokes [37]. TrustLogin considers software-based keyloggers as the threat model, and it guarantees that keystrokes cannot be stolen if such a keylogger is present.

3.2 Assumptions

TrustLogin assumes that the attackers have unlimited computing resources and can exploit zero-day vulnerabilities of the host OS and desktop applications. We only consider attacks against the host machine; network attacks are out of the scope of this paper. We do not consider phishing at-

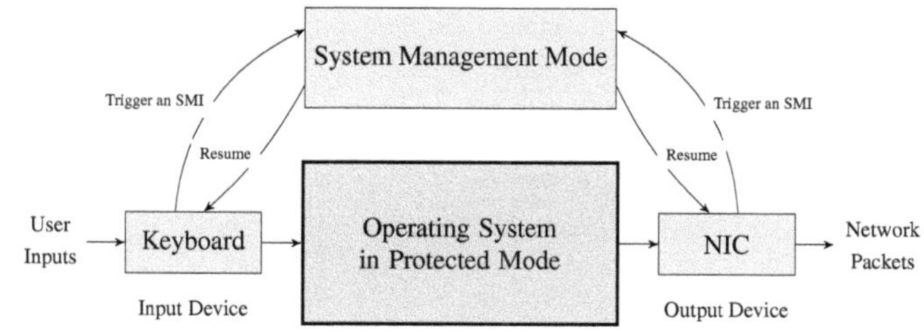

Figure 1: Architecture of TrustLogin

tacks, which trick users to send their credentials to a remote host. We assume the hardware and firmware of the host machine are trusted, and the attacker cannot flash the BIOS or modify the firmware. We assume SMRAM is locked and remains intact after boot, and the attacker cannot change the SMI handler. We assume that the attacker does not have physical access to the machine. We do not consider Denial-of-Service (DoS) attacks against our system. Ring 0 malware can easily disable SMI triggering and stop the login process.

4. SYSTEM FRAMEWORK

Figure 1 shows the architecture of TrustLogin. There are four rectangles in the figure; the green rectangles represent trusted components, including the keyboard, Network Interface Card (NIC), and System Management Mode (SMM). The red rectangle represents the operating system in Protected Mode, which may have been compromised by attackers. When a user inputs the sensitive information (e.g., password) from the keyboard, the keyboard automatically triggers an SMI for every key press. The SMI handler (which executes in SMM) records the keystrokes and inserts bogus place-holders in the keyboard buffer. After resuming Protected Mode, the OS only handles the place-holders. In other words, the attackers with ring 0 privilege can only retrieve the string of place-holders. When the login packet is about to transmit, TrustLogin triggers another SMI by using the network card. The SMI handler replaces the bogus place-holders with the original keystrokes in the network packet. We also make sure the packet leaves the network card within the SMI handler so that malware cannot read the packet. Next, we explain the system step by step.

4.1 Entering Secure Input Mode

In TrustLogin, we have two modes for the system. One is the secure input mode, and the other one is the normal input mode. In the secure input mode, TrustLogin intercepts all of the keystrokes and protect them from the keyloggers or rootkits. When the user is about to enter the sensitive information (e.g., password), he or she needs to switch to the secure input mode. Past systems have used a variety of ways to notify the system. For instance, Bumpy [34] uses "@@" as a Secure Attention Sequence (SAS) to signal the system that the user is about to enter sensitive inputs.

One requirement of switching into the Secure Input Mode is that the entering method should be rarely used by default. Ideally, it should be unique (e.g., a dedicated hardware switch [40]), but SAS-like "@@" sequence also works. The other requirement is usability. In TrustLogin, we simply use the key combination, `Ctr+Alt+1`, to signal our system and enter the secure input mode. When TrustLogin reads an Enter key in the secure input mode, it stops intercepting keystrokes and switches to the normal input mode. Since users often end password inputs by pressing Enter, this is reasonable.

4.2 Intercepting Keystrokes

TrustLogin intercepts every keystroke and records them in the SMRAM in the secure input mode. Before introducing how keystrokes are intercepted in TrustLogin, we will explain how keystrokes are handled normally.

The input/output devices (e.g., keyboard) connect to the Southbridge (a.k.a. I/O controller Hub). Whenever a key is pressed or released, the keyboard notifies the I/O Advanced Programmable Interrupt Controller (APIC) in the Southbridge. I/O APIC looks up the I/O redirection table based on the Interrupt Request (IRQ), and then creates the corresponding interrupt message. The IRQ for the keyboard is 1, and the interrupt message includes the Delivery Mode (DM), Fixed, and the interrupt vector, `0x93`. The interrupt message goes through the PCI and system buses, and arrives at the local APIC in the CPU. Based on the DM and interrupt vector, the local APIC looks up the Interrupt Descriptor Table (IDT), and then the CPU jumps to the base address of the OS keyboard interrupt handler. The OS keyboard interrupt handler starts to execute keyboard handling functions. Specifically, it reads the keyboard data registers by accessing port `0x60` and may display the key value on the display monitor. Figure 2 shows the keystroke handling process.

Note that there are two interrupts for each keystroke: key press and key release. When the key is pressed or released, the keyboard sends a message known as "scan code" to the keyboard controller output buffer that the OS handler read later. There are two different types of scan codes: "make codes" and "break codes." A make code is sent when a key is pressed, and a break code is sent when a key is released. Every key has a unique make code and break code. There are three different sets of scan codes. Our keyboard uses the scan code set 1 [6]. For example, the make code of the `A` key is `0x1E`, and its break code is `0x9E`. If a user keeps holding the key, the keyboard would continue to send interrupts with the make code. When the user releases the key, the break code would be written into the output buffer of the keyboard controller.

To record the keystrokes, TrustLogin raises an SMI during the key press or release handling process and saves the keystrokes in the SMRAM. Additionally, we also save the scan code set mapping in the SMI handler to figure out which key is pressed or released. Next, we explain two approaches that we implement to trigger an SMI during the keystroke handling.

4.2.1 *I/O Trap Approach*

TrustLogin can use hardware I/O traps to generate an SMI [12]. The I/O trap feature allows SMI trapping on access to any I/O port using `IN` or `OUT` instruction. As mentioned, the OS interrupt handler needs to read the keyboard data register by accessing port `0x60`. If we configure the SMI I/O trap, an SMI would be triggered when the OS handler reads the keyboard data registers. In this way, we are able to intercept all keystrokes and save them in the SMRAM. When the OS keyboard interrupt handler

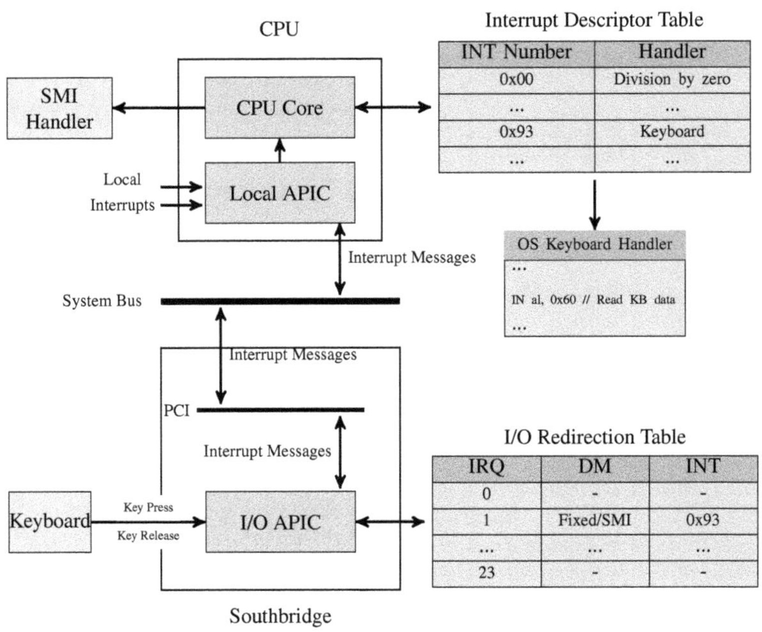

Figure 2: Keystroke Handling in TrustLogin

executes `IN al, 0x60` instruction, the system automatically generates an SMI. However, this `IN` instruction would not be executed again when resuming the OS in Protected Mode. To address this problem, the SMI handler needs to read the key value from the keyboard data register and store it in the `EAX` as if no trap has been created. Additionally, we need to disable the SMI I/O trap in the SMI handler. Otherwise, an SMI will be buffered when accessing the I/O port. In that case, the SMI will be immediately triggered after exiting SMM and the system will halt. Note that Wecherowski demonstrated similar triggering approach in [43].

4.2.2 *I/O APIC Rerouting Approach*

The other approach of triggering SMIs is to reroute keyboard interrupt by reconfiguring I/O APIC. As shown in Figure 2, The Delivery Mode (DM) of the I/O redirection table can be configured as "SMI" instead of "Fixed" normally. In other words, we are able to deliver an SMI to the CPU for every keyboard interrupt; that is, every key press causes our code to execute in SMM. Next, we store the keystroke to the SMRAM by reading the keyboard data register in the SMI handler.

We read the 1-byte scan code from the keyboard data register by reading I/O port `0x60`. After extracting the scan code, we map the scan code to the key value using the scan code set 1 table. Next, we store the key in the SMRAM. Since this approach reroutes the keyboard interrupt to an SMI, the original keyboard interrupt is not handled. To address this problem, we configure the keyboard control register (i.e., IO port `0x64`) to reissue the interrupt. We write the command code, 0xD2, to the control register. This special command means the next byte written to the keyboard data register (i.e., I/O port `0x60`) will be as if it came from the keyboard [42]. We write a replaced scan code back to the data register after writing the command code. After exiting SMM, another interrupt is generated due to the new data in the keyboard data register. Additionally, we need to disable SMI triggering in I/O APIC when reissuing the interrupt in the SMI handler. This makes sure that the reissued interrupt is a normal keyboard interrupt with "fixed" as the DM. Otherwise, an immediate SMI will be generated after exiting SMM, which causes an infinite loop (deadlock). The method for accessing the I/O APIC or keyboard controller is specified in the Southbridge datasheet [42].

Embleton et al. also used a similar approach to generate SMIs in [20]. However, we did not see that the I/O read operation of the keyboard data register was destructive in the SMI handler; we were able to read the data register multiple times until a new value was written. Additionally, it uses interprocessor interrupts (IPI) to reissue the interrupt by configuring the Interrupt Command Register (ICR), while we simultaneously write to the keyboard control register to reissue the normal interrupt.

4.2.3 *Universal Serial Bus Keyboard*

Universal Serial Bus (USB) is a popular external interface standard that enables communication between the computer and other peripherals. There are currently three versions of USB in use: USB 1.1, 2.0, and 3.0. A USB system has a host controller, and it sits between the USB device and the operating system. USB 1.1 uses Universal Host Controller Interface (UHCI) [26]; USB 2.0 uses Enhanced Host Controller Interface (EHCI) [23]; and the recent USB 3.0 uses eXtensible Host Controller Interface (XHCI) [24]. From the manuals of these standards, all of the them support triggering SMIs. For instance, XHCI uses a 32-bit register to enable SMIs for every xHCI/USB event it needs to track, and we are able to trigger an SMI for every key press required by TrustLogin. This register is located at xHCI Extended Capabilities Pointer (XECP) + `0x04`, and we can find XECP from the base address of the XHCI + `0x10`. Similar registers that enable SMIs can also be found at EHCI and UHCI. Moreover, Schiffman and Kaplana [38] demonstrated that USB keyboards can generate SMIs.

4.3 Generating Placeholders

To replace the original password, we generate a placeholder for each keystroke intercepted in the SMI handler. One of the simplest methods is to replace each keystroke with a constant character (e.g., character 'p'). However, this method cannot pass the security checks that ensure the strength of the password. For instance, most of the password policies require that passwords contain at least one digit, one lowercase character, one uppercase character, and one special character. Although these checks are usually performed on the server side, they could be done on the client application. To address this problem, TrustLogin replaces a keystroke based on its type. TrustLogin substitutes the original keystroke with a random one of the same type.

We use a linear-congruential algorithm to generate a pseudo-random number n in the SMI handler. The parameters of the linear-congruential algorithm we used are from Numerical Recipes [44]. Next, we use $n \bmod k$, where k is the cardinality of the corresponding type (e.g., 26 each for lower- or uppercase characters) to generate a random character. In terms of the special characters, different applications or servers may have a different set of valid special characters. For instance, the American Express website does not allow special characters like '.' in the password, while Bank of America and CitiBank do accept it. TrustLogin assumes the application allows six special characters as follows: dot, underscore, star, percent, question mark, and sharp. We can always update the set of special characters based on the application requirements. Next, we discuss how the network card intercepts packets and replaces the placeholders with the original password.

4.4 Intercepting Network Packets

TrustLogin starts to intercept the network packets when the Enter key is received in the secure input mode. This means the user has finished entering the password and the OS is about to transmit the login credentials. We use a popular commercial PCI-based network card, Intel e1000 [25], to demonstrate this in TrustLogin.

Message Signaled Interrupts (MSIs) are an optional feature incorporated into PCI devices. They essentially allow a PCI device to generate an interrupt without having to make use of a physical interrupt pin on the connector. Introduced in PCI version 2.2, MSIs allow the device to send a variety of different interrupts to the CPU via the chipset. One such interrupt is the SMI. We can configure the MSI configuration registers (offset 0xF0 to 0xFF) in the PCI configuration space to enable SMI triggering.

When MSIs are enabled, the network card generates a message when any of the unmasked bits in the Interrupt Cause Read register (ICR) are set to 1 [25]. The ICR contains all interrupt conditions for the network card. Each time an interrupt occurs, the corresponding interrupt bit is set in the register. The interrupts are enabled through Interrupt Mask Set/Read Register (IMS). For instance, the first bit of IMS sets a mask for Transmit Descriptor Written Back (TDWB). When the hardware finishes transmitting a packet, it sets a status bit back to the transmit descriptor; this action could be an interrupt condition. In TrustLogin, we reroute this interrupt to an SMI by using MSI. This means we can trigger an SMI for each packet when it is transmitted. In the SMI handler, we then inspect all of the transmit descriptors in the transmit queue and search for the login packet. It is possible that the first packet that generates the SMI is the login packet. To address this edge case, we create a transmit descriptor in the SMI handler beforehand and make sure the first SMI from NIC is triggered by this transmit descriptor. This transmit descriptor is created when TrustLogin enables the NIC's SMI triggering by rerouting TDWB interrupts to an SMI. Note that the transmit queue may become empty before finding the login packet, so we may miss the first transmit descriptor that arrives at the empty transmit queue. Thus, we insert a transmit descriptor whenever the transmit queue becomes empty until identifying the login packet.

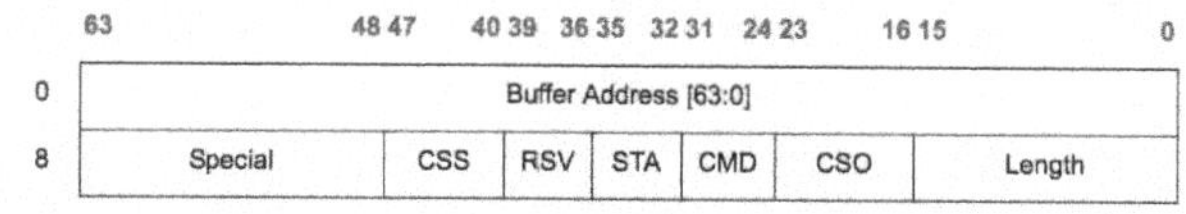

Figure 3: Transmit Descriptor Format [25]

Figure 3 shows the format of the transmit descriptor structure. Buffer Address points to the data in the host memory. The CMD (i.e., command) field specifies the RS (i.e., report status) bit. With this bit set, the hardware writes a status bit back to the STA (i.e., status) field in the descriptor when a packet is transmitted. For the inserted packet, we set the RS bit and NULL to the Buffer Address so that it transfers no data. We also makes sure all of the inspected packets have the RS bit set.

To replace the placeholders in the network packets, TrustLogin can simply search the sequence of the placeholders in the packets. We can use the Transmit Descriptor Base Address (TDBA) and Transmit Descriptor Tail (TDT) to find the addresses of the transmit descriptors. The transmit descriptor structure contains all of the information about the packet including the address of the payload. Note that the addresses here are physical addresses (i.e., no paging) because the Direct Memory Access (DMA) engine of the NIC only understands the physical addresses. One challenge of this method is that the network packets are encrypted (e.g., TLS) and Section **??** discusses this further. After the SMI handler finds and replaces the placeholders, it waits until the packet leaves the host to avoid further sensitive data leakage. Moreover, the attacker may use NIC's diagnostic registers to access transmitted packet connects. We empty the NIC's internal Packet Buffer Memory (PBM) by writing 16KB random data since the size of the internal buffer of our testing NIC is 16KB [25].

4.5 Ensuring Trusted Path

One challenge of TrustLogin is the reliability of triggering SMIs. As shown in Figure 2, The I/O redirection table in red is not trusted. An attacker with ring 0 privilege can modify the table to intercept an SMI, and then prepare a fake switching process so that the users think that he or she is in the SMM. In this case, the attacker can trick the user and get the password. This is a typical spoofing attack. There has been some research tackling this problem [41, 34, 40, 32]. Bumpy [34] uses an external smartphone as the trusted monitor to acknowledge the switching. SecureSwitch [40] and Lockdown [41] use a dedicated switch to ensure the trust path. Cloud Terminal [32] uses a UI with strawberries on the screen as a shared secret to prevent spoofing attack. In

TrustLogin, we implement two novel methods to prevent the spoofing attacks. One approach is to use the keyboard Light Emitting Diode (LED) lights, and the other is to use the PC speaker. Next, we explain the implementation details of these two approaches.

4.5.1 Keyboard LED Lights

We use the LED lights on the keyboard to ensure the trust path. Usually, there are three LED lights on the keyboard, indicating Num, Caps, and Scroll locks. The users can set a shared secret LED light sequence to indicate that the system is in SMM. For instance, we can refer to scroll lock as 0, number lock as 1, and caps lock as 2. {[0 on]→[0 off]→[1 on]→[1 off]→[2 on]→[2 off]} is a LED light sequence. When the system switches into SMM, the SMI handler performs the shared secret LED light sequence so that the user knows the system is in SMM–not tricked by attackers.

To program the keyboard LED lights, we write a command byte, `0xED`, into the keyboard data register, and then write a LED state byte to the same I/O port. Bit 0 is for scroll lock; bit 1 is for number lock; bit 2 is for caps lock. Value 1 means on and 0 indicates off. Since every keystroke generates two interrupts (i.e., key press and release), TrustLogin only shows the LED light sequence when the key is released. We can easily identify a key release by checking the value of the scan code (greater than `0x80` [6]).

To help the user to identify the LED light sequence, we set a time delay between two lights. For instance, there should be a time delay between [0 off] and [1 on] for distinction. In TrustLogin, each light is on for 1 `ms`, and we set the same time delay when switching lights. The authors can identify that sequence based on their observations in the experiments. The user can adjust the time delay based on their preference.

```
    mov $0x30D40, %ecx   ;1 CPU cycle
DELAY:
    nop                  ;1 CPU cycle
    nop                  ;1 CPU cycle
    nop                  ;1 CPU cycle
    loop DELAY           ;8 CPU cycles
```

Listing 1: Assembly Code that Introduces 1 `ms` Delay on Our Testbed

Listing 1 shows the assembly code that introduces a 1 `ms` delay on our testbed. This delay function loads a counter, `0x30D40` or 200,000 in decimal, into `EAX`, and spinlocks until the counter is 0. The value, 200,000, is calculated from the time it takes to execute the loop instructions on our testbed. The testbed has an AMD Sempron LE-1250 2.2 GHz processor with AMD K8 chipset. The `MOV` and `NOP` instructions take 1 CPU cycle and the `LOOP` instruction takes 8 CPU cycles [5]. We also assume it takes 7 CPU cycles for a `LOOP` instruction when the contents of `EAX` is zero. The equations explain the steps that calculates the counter for performing 1 `ms` time delay on our testbed.

$$TimeDelay = \frac{ClockCycles}{ClockSpeed}$$

$$1ms = \frac{1 + N * (1 + 1 + 1) + (N - 1) * 8 + 7}{2.2GHz} \Longrightarrow N = 200,000$$

4.5.2 PC Speaker

We also use the PC speaker to ensure the trusted path. TrustLogin plays simple music on the PC speaker when each key is pressed in the secure input mode. The users can choose their favorite melodies and embed them in the SMI handler. By recognizing their selected tone sequence, they can ensure that an SMI is triggered for their every key press. Thus, the selected music should be short but recognizable. TrustLogin plays a C major scale in the SMI handler to demonstrate this idea. Table 3 in Appendix shows the notes and corresponding frequencies for one complete octave starting from a middle C. We set the middle C as 523.25 Hz based on a musical reference guide [1].

To play a tone, we program the Intel 8253 Programmable Interval Timer (PIT) in the SMI handler to generate musical notes. The 8253 PIT performs timing and counting functions, and it exists in all x86 machines. In modern machines, it is included as part of the motherboard's southbridge. This timer has three counters (Counters 0, 1, and 2), and we use the third counter (Counter 2) to generate tones via the PC Speaker. We can generate different kinds of tones by adjusting the output frequency. The output frequency is calculated by loading a divisor into the 8253 PIT.

$$Divisor = IF/OF,$$

where IF is the input frequency of the 8253 PIT. IF used by the PIT chip is about 1.19 MHz, and OF is the output frequency. Column 3 of Table 3 shows the calculated divisors for the musical notes of an octave based on their output frequencies.

Playing a note on the PC speaker takes the following steps: 1) Configure mode/command register of the PIT chip through port `0x43` with value `0xB6`, which selects channel 2 to use and sets the mode to accept divisors; 2) load a divisor into channel 2 through port `0x42`; 3) turn on bit 0 and bit 1 of port `0x61` to enable the connection between PIT chip and the PC speaker; 4) set a time for the note to play; 5) turn off the PC speaker by configuring port `0x61`. Similar to the LED lights sequnce, we need to set a time delay so that the users can easily identify the music. In TrustLogin, each note is produced in 1 `ms`, and we set the same time of the delay between every two notes.

5. CASE STUDY

We study legacy and secure applications to demonstrate the effectiveness of TrustLogin. For the legacy applications that we referenced, they are normally built on a client-server architecture, and authentication occurs using a plaintext username/password pair. We consider Remote Shell (rsh), File Transfer Protocol (FTP), and Telent legacy applications. Note that TrustLogin is OS-agnostic for legacy applications because it does not need to reconstruct the semantics of OS kernels and rebuilds the packet in the NIC. For the secure applications that we noted, their network traffic securely encrypted. We consider Secure Shell (SSH), Secure File Transfer Protocol (SFTP), and Transport Layer Security (TLS) secure protocols.

5.1 Hardware and Software Specifications

We conduct the case study on a physical machine, which uses an ASUS M2V-MX_SE motherboard with an AMD K8 Northbridge and a VIA VT8237r Southbridge. It has a 2.2 GHz AMD LE- 1250 CPU and 2GB Kingston DDR2 RAM. We use a Dell PS/2 keyboard and PCI-based Intel 82541 Gigabit Ethernet Controller as the triggering devices. To program SMM, we use the open-source BIOS, Coreboot [19]. We also install Microsoft Windows 7 and CentOS 5.5 on this machine.

5.2 Case Study I: Legacy Applications

For legacy applications, we use FTP as the study example. Next, we demonstrate the effectiveness of our system on both Windows and Linux platforms. Figure 4 shows the screenshots of the FTP login with and without TrustLogin on Windows and Linux. We create an FTP account on a server. The username and password for the account is `hack3r` and `AsiaCCS.`, respectively. On Windows, we install the Free Keylogger Pro version 1.0 [4] and use the FTP client to connect to the server. We first start the keylogger to log keystrokes. Next, we login to the FTP server without TrustLogin enabled. As shown in subfigure 4(a), we can see that the keylogger records the timestamp, application name, username, and password in a file. The red rectangle shows the password is `AsiaCCS.` as recorded by the keylogger. Then, we enable TrustLogin and login to the FTP server again. However, the password recorded by the keylogger has been changed to a random string generated by TrustLogin. In other words, the keylogger cannot steal the real password when TrustLogin is enabled. We install Logkeys version 0.1.1a [9] on the CentOS 5.5, and subfigure 4(b) shows the results. Similar to the experiments on Windows, we login to the FTP server with and without TrustLogin enabled. We can see that the keylogger logs the random placeholders when TrustLogin enabled, and the keylogger cannot steal the login password. Note that attackers can easily steal the passwords from legacy applications by sniffing out the network. However, TrustLogin is used to address the general problem of securing keystrokes on the local host. Here studying the legacy applications emphasizes that TrustLogin is a framework that works with various applications to prevent keyloggers.

5.3 Case Study II: Secure Applications

TrustLogin replaces the password placeholders in a network packet when the packet is about to transmit. However, since most of the network packets are encrypted, we cannot simply search for the placeholder sequence though the encrypted data. For example, Transport Layer Security (TLS) encrypts the data of network connections in the application layer.

Secure Shell (SSH) is one of the most popular application protocols for access to shell accounts on Unix-based systems. There are several client authentication methods supported by SSH. For instance, we can use a public and private key pair to authenticate the client. However, we only consider the password-based authentication method in this paper. The password-based authentication method is the most commonly used authentication mechanisms in SSH. The SSH server simply uses a username and password to authenticate the client, and the password transmitted by the client to the server is encrypted by a session symmetric key. Unlike the legacy applications, we cannot simply search for the login packet and replace the original password. To address this problem, TrustLogin decrypts and re-encrypts the login packets using the session symmetric key. Next, we explain how we find the session states like the session key.

As mentioned, SSH protocol uses a session symmetric key to encrypt the traffic. To decrypt the login packet, we first need to find the session states in the memory. Fortunately, SMM is able to access all of the physical memory because it has the highest privilege. TrustLogin uses signature-based searching. Typically, software data structures inevitably create some signatures in memory. For example, researchers extract SSL private key in memory by validating RSA/DSA structures on multiple applications including Apache, SSH, and OpenVPN [18].

We use `session_state` structure as the signature for the searching. The `session_state` structure stores the session information for SSH communication. By analyzing the source code of OpenSSH [11], some fields of `session_state` structure in the `packet.c` file are static before users authenticate themselves. For instance, the `max_packet_size` field is set to constant, 0x8000. Listing 2 shows part of `session_state` structure, and these fields are static and continuous. Thus, TrustLogin uses this static signature as the search string and then finds the session states in memory. Since we assume malware has ring 0 privilege, an advanced malware can prepare a fake session key to TrustLogin. This attack breaks the login process but cannot steal the real password. Note that a DoS attack is out of the scope of this paper.

```
struct session_state {
  /* default maximum packet size, 0x8000 */
  u_int max_packet_size;
  /* Flag indicating whether this module has been
     initialized, 0x1 */
  int initialized;
  /* Set to true if connection is interactive, 0x0 */
  int interactive_mode;
  /* Set to true if we are the server side, 0x0 */
  int server_side;
  /* Set to true if we are authenticated, 0x0 */
  int after_authentication;
  /* Default before login, 0x0 */
  int keep_alive_timeouts;
  /* The maximum time that we will wait to send or
     receive a packet, -1, 0xffffffff */
  int packet_timeout_ms;
```

Listing 2: Static fields of Session Structure in SSH Source Code

One naive approach for implementation would be searching byte-by-byte through all of physical memory, but this is very slow. We instead search only the SSH instance in TrustLogin. Since only the physical memory is visible to SMM, we must reconstruct semantics of the raw data. In other words, we must understand the location of the SSH process and what its content means in memory. This is referred to as the "semantic gap problem." Recently, researchers proposed an array of approaches to address this problem [27], including hand-crafted data structure signatures [28, 47] and automated learning and bridging [30, 21]. Similar to the previous systems [28, 47], we manually reconstruct the semantics using kernel data structure signatures.

We first use the `ESP` value saved in the SMRAM to calculate the pointer to the current process's `task_struct`. Alternatively, we can obtain the address of the `init_task` from the `System.map` file. Next, we traverse the doubly linked list of `task_structs` or `run_lists` to locate the SSH process by comparing the `comm` field. Note that multiple instances of SSH could be running at the same time in the memory. We use the `prev` field for the transversal, which ensures that the first SSH process found is the last process launched. In this case, we assume the user interacts with the most recently launched SSH instance. Next, we obtain a pointer to the

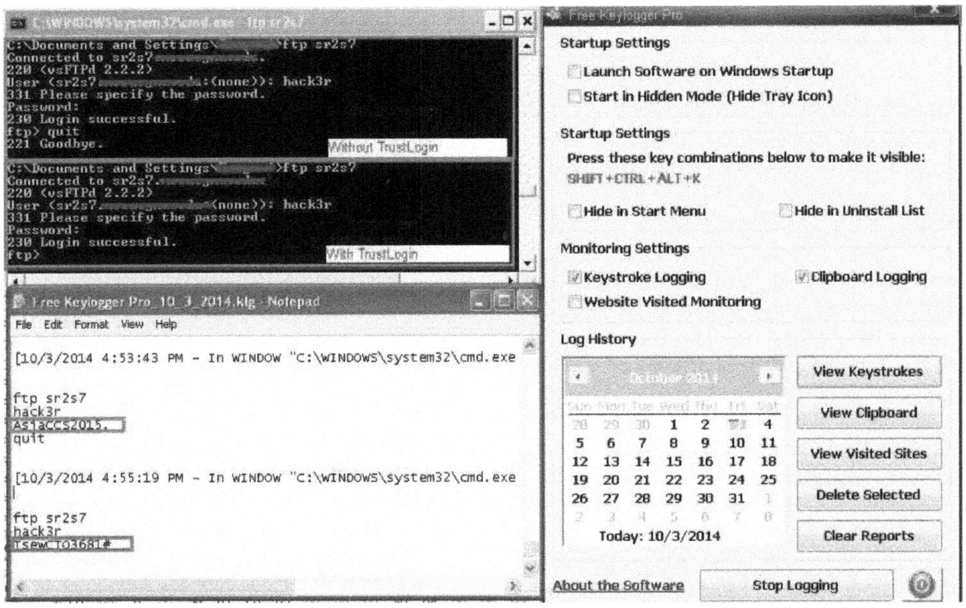

(a) FTP Login With and Without TrustLogin on Windows

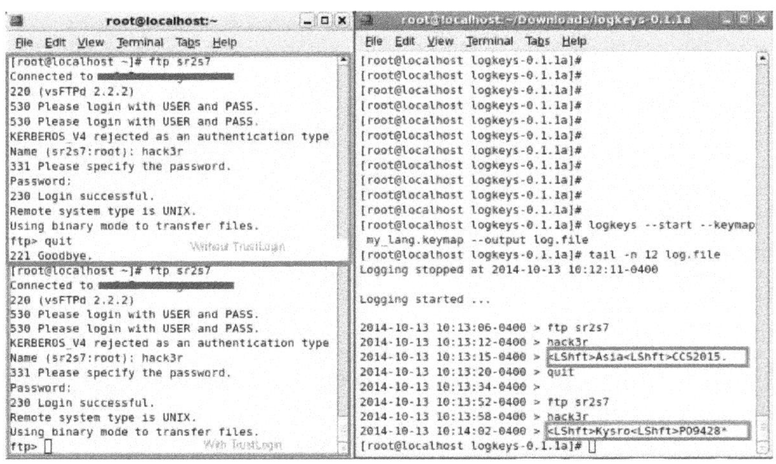

(b) FTP Login With and Without TrustLogin on Linux

Figure 4: FTP Login With and Without TrustLogin on Windows and Linux

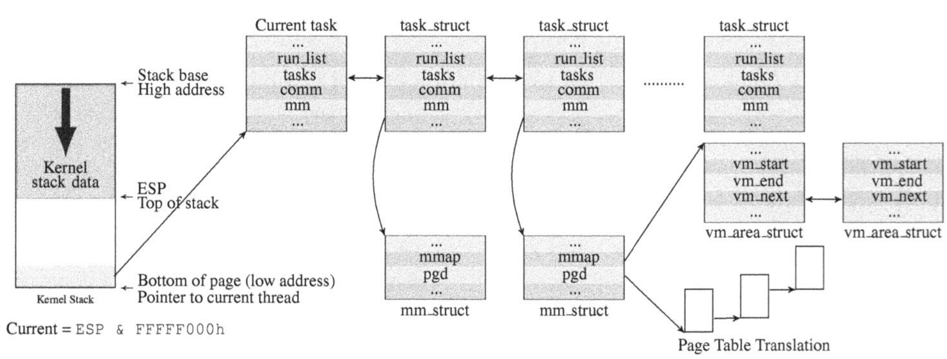

Figure 5: Filling the Semantic Gap by Using Kernel Data Structures in Linux

mm_struct from the mm field in task_struct. The mmap field in the mm_struct points to the head of the list of memory regions with the type vm_area_struct. The memory region object contains vm_start and vm_end fields, which define the start and end addresses of the memory region. Figure 5 shows the semantic reconstruction using kernel data structures in Linux. As pointed out in [27], all of the current solutions to the semantic gap assumes the kernel data structures are benign. Our semantic reconstruction approach also assumes this. We search the session_state signature in the memory regions of the SSH process, which achieves a better performance than the linear searching approach. Section 5.4 details the overheads of these two approaches.

All pointers in these structures are virtual. However, SMM does not use paging, meaning it addresses physical memory directly. Thus, we must translate addresses manually from virtual to physical space. For kernel-space structures (e.g., task_struct and mm_struct), there is a constant offset, 0xc0000000, to move from virtual to physical space. For userspace structures (e.g., vm_start and vm_end), we locate and employ the process's page tables. Fortunately, the pgd field in the mm_struct stores the cr3 value that tells us the location of the global page directory. After we retrieve all of the required information from memory, we decrypt the data and replace the placeholder sequence with the real password in the packet. Finally, we rebuild the network packet with the corresponding checksum by using the functions from OpenSSH source code.

5.4 Performance Evaluation

In order to understand the performance overhead of our system, we measure the runtime of each individual operation in the SMI handler. In TrustLogin, we have two parts of the handling code in the SMI handler; one is to handle the SMI triggered by the keyboard (i.e., KB SMI), and the other part is executed when the NIC triggers an SMI (i.e., NIC SMI). The KB SMI contains 7 steps.

1. Play a melody
2. Show an LED sequence
3. Disable keyboard SMIs (prevent reissuing)
4. Read the keystroke from the keyboard data register and save it in SMRAM
5. If Enter is pressed, break out and enable NIC SMIs
6. Generate random scan code and replace the keystroke
7. Enable keyboard SMIs for subsequent keystroke

Additionally, the NIC SMI consists of 3 operations.

1. Locate received packet in NIC memory
2. Search packets and inject original password
3. Disable NIC SMIs after password is injected

We measure the time delay for all of these operations in the SMI handler. As mentioned in Section 2, the hardware automatically saves and resumes the CPU context when switching to SMM. We also measure the overhead induced by switching to and resuming from SMM.

Table 1 shows the time breakdown of each operation. We use the Time Stamp Counter (TSC) to measure the time delay for each operation. We first record the TSC value at the beginning and end of each operation. Next, we use the CPU frequency to divide the difference in the TSC register to compute how much time this operation. We conduct the experiment based on the FTP login for 30 trials. We calculate the mean, standard deviation, and 95% confidence interval for each operation. From Table 1 we can see that the total time for KB SMIs is about 32 ms. Note that most of the time is consumed by playing the melody and showing the LED sequence. Each note in the melody and each part of the LED sequence takes 1 ms (See Section 4.5 for details). The total time of the NIC SMI code and SMM switching are only about 30 and 8 μs, respectively.

Table 1: Breakdown of the SMI Handler Runtime (Time: μs)

	Operations	Mean	STD	95% CI
KB SMI	Play music	26,244	3,675	[25,199,27,288]
	Show LED	6,317	251	[6,245,6,388]
	Disable KB SMI	1.47	0.21	[1.40,1.53]
	Read keystroke	2.38	0.33	[2.28,2.47]
	Enable NIC SMI	8.40	0.05	[8.39,8.419]
	Replace keystroke	8.94	1.27	[8.57,9.30]
	Enable KB SMI	1.14	0.17	[1.09,1.19]
	Total of KB SMI	32,583		
NIC SMI	Read NIC registers	3.96	0.10	[3.93,3.99]
	Search packets	18.27	1.18	[17.93,18.60]
	Disable NIC SMI	7.44	0.05	[7.42,7.45]
	Total of NIC SMI	29.67		
	Switch into SMM	3.29	0.08	[3.27,3.32]
	Resume from SMM	4.58	0.10	[4.55,4.61]
	Total of switching	7.87		

Table 2: Comparison between Linear Searching and Semantic Searching

Approaches	Search Space	Time
Linear Searching	2 GB	70.21 s
Semantic Searching	18 MB	(1.39+227.45) ms

As mentioned in Section ??, searching the SSH session states after reconstructing the memory semantic (called semantic searching) achieves a better performance than linear searching. To demonstrate this, we compare the linear searching with the semantic searching. We conduct the experiment on the Linux machine. We installed the latest OpenSSH client version 6.6p1 on the testbed, and the testing machine has 2GB physical memory. For linear searching, we compare the signature of the session states with the 2GB memory byte-by-byte. As for semantic searching, we first find the SSH process in memory using kernel data structures and then only search the memory regions pointed by mmap. After a user types ssh username@hostname in a terminal, the SSH server waits for the password from the client. At this time, we trigger an SMI and let the SMI handler perform both searching methods. We also use the TSC to measure the time it takes for each approach.

Table 2 shows the comparison between linear searching and semantic searching. The linear searching has 2 GB of searching space and takes about 70 seconds to find the session states. The semantic searching only has about 18 MB of searching space; it takes 1.39 ms to fill the semantic gap and 227 ms for searching.

6. LIMITATIONS AND DISCUSSION

TrustLogin provides a framework to secure password-based logins on commodity operating systems, and it can be applied to many network applications. We demonstrate the effectiveness by using legacy and secure applications. To port more secure applications working with TrustLogin, we need to decrypt and rebuild the relevant login packet, which requires application-specific efforts.

Additionally, an advanced keylogger may directly read the keyboard buffer to retrieve the keystrokes using DMA. For example, Ladakis et al. [29] proposed a GPU-based keylogger that directly reads the keyboard buffer from the GPU through DMA. In TrustLogin, the CPU has been switched to SMM, but DMA is able to read the keyboard buffer at the same time that SMM accesses it. In other words, there is a race between SMM and DMA. From the experimental results in Table 1 we can see that TrustLogin only takes a couple of microseconds (i.e., 3.29+2.38+8.94=14.61 μs) to switch into SMM and replace the scan code in the keyboard buffer. However, the GPU-based keylogger needs to periodically poll and monitor the keyboard buffer for new keystrokes, and the suggested polling interval is 90 milliseconds in the prototype of the GPU-based keylogger [29]. As stated in the paper, higher frequency of polling may affect the proper display of the graphics, and the user may notice the abnormal event. Thus, TrustLogin is able to defend a GPU-based keylogger as long as the polling interval does not pass below 15 microseconds.

There have been a number of attacks against SMM [16]. Wojtczuk and Rutkowska [46] have demonstrated a cache poisoning attack by configuring the Memory Type Range Registers (MTRR) to execute malicious code in the cache instead of SMRAM. However, this architectural bug has been fixed by the Intel in recent chipsets by adding System Management Range Register (SMRR). Additionally, the MITRE team discovered a buffer overflow vulnerability in SMM [17], but this bug is specific to the code implemented in the BIOS and is not an architectural bug. Recently, Wojtczuk and Kallenberg [45] presented an SMM attack by manipulating UEFI boot script. The UEFI boot script is a data structure interpreted by UEFI firmware during S3 resume. When the boot script executes, system registers like BIOS_CNTL (SPI flash write protection) or TSEG (SMM protection from DMA) are not set so that attackers can force an S3 sleep to take control of SMM. Fortunately, as stated in the paper [45], the BIOS update around the end of 2014 fixed this vulnerability.

7. RELATED WORK

Researchers have proposed several trustworthy computing environments to execute sensitive workloads. SICE [14] leverages SMM to provide an isolated execution environment to protect sensitive workloads in cloud servers. It does not rely on any software component in the host environment and supports up to 4GB of isolated memory. SecureSwitch [40] is another isolated computing environment for executing sensitive workloads. It relies on the S3 sleep mode (i.e., suspend to RAM) in the BIOS to switch between trusted and untrusted OSes. Flicker [33] uses Late Launch to enable execution of a Piece of Application Logic (PAL). Unlike these trustworthy computing environments, TrustLogin is lightweight and only protects the sensitive network inputs.

One of the closest works is Bumpy [34], a Flicker-based system for securing sensitive network input. It handles inputs in a special code module that is executed in an isolated environment using the Flicker. Bumpy can protect user's sensitive web inputs even with a compromised OS or web browser. However, Bumpy requires modification of the web application and web server, while TrustLogin does not and works transparently.

Cloud Terminal [32] is a micro-hypervisor and provides secure access to sensitive applications from an untrusted OS. It moves most application logic to a remote server called the Cloud Rendering Engine and only runs a light-weight Secure Thin Terminal on the end host, so end-users can securely execute sensitive applications. It also uses the Flicker to setup the micro-hypervisor. Cloud Terminal has the same threat model as TrustLogin, while TrustLogin uses existing hardware features without using a micro-hypervisor and has a smaller TCB.

Borders and Prakash proposed a Trusted Input Proxy (TIP) [15] to secure network inputs. The TIP runs as a module in a separate VM that proxies network connections of the primary VM. It also uses the placeholder approach to substitute the actual sensitive data. Neither TIP nor TrustLogin require modification of web browser and server, and they are transparent to users. As stated in the limitation section of this paper, TIP relies on a virtual machine monitor. It also introduces a large trusted code base and significant slowdown for I/O intensive applications. TrustLogin is a hardware-assisted method working on bare metal, which overcomes the shortcomings in TIP.

MP-Auth [31] uses a mobile device to encrypt the password under the public key of an intended server, and passes the encrypted password to the host for authentication. The host can only access a one-time password so that it can prevent keyloggers and phishing attacks. oPass [39] leverages a user's cellphone and short message service to thwart credential stealing and password reuse attacks. Recently, Google provided a 2-step verification for the Gmail login. The 2-step verification requires something you know (i.e., password) and something you have (i.e., cell phone). Even if an attacker compromises the password, she still needs the cell phone to get into the account, so the 2-step verification provides an extra layer of security. Compared to TrustLogin, MP-Auth, oPass, and 2-step verification propose a new protocol between the web browser and web server. That is, they modify the network application and server to fit their new protocols. TrustLogin is built on existing authentication protocols and is transparent to network applications and servers.

In recent years, an array of SMM-based systems have been implemented. On one hand, researchers use SMM to implement stealthy rookits [20, 38]. For instance, the National Security Agency (NSA) uses SMM to build an array of rootkits including DEITYBOUNCE for DELL and IRONCHEF for HP Proliant servers [10]. On the other hand, researchers leverage SMM to build security defense systems. For example, HyperCheck [49] and Hypersentry [13] are SMM-based systems used to check the integrity of the hypervisors. Spectre [47] and IOCheck [48] are introspection frameworks for detecting malicious malware in the live memory and firmware, respectively. SMMDumper [36] uses SMM to reliably acquire physical memory for forensics purposes.

8. CONCLUSIONS AND FUTURE WORKS

In this paper, we presented TrustLogin, a novel framework for securing password-login via System Management Mode. We do not trust underlying applications and OS on the target system, and TrustLogin is able to prevent rootkits and stealthy malware from stealing sensitive data from the local host. Since TrustLogin does not change any software on the client and server sides, it is transparent to users and applied applications. We implemented our framework on legacy and secure applications. The experiment results show that TrustLogin is robust against keyloggers on both Windows and Linux platforms. TrustLogin is able to defend spoofing attacks and guarantees the trust path of SMM switching. Our performance evaluation results show that TrustLogin is light-weight and only takes 8 microseconds for SMM switching.

As explained in the threat model, the current prototype of TrustLogin cannot defend against phishing attacks and only protects the login credentials on the local host, so we plan to mitigate this attack in our future work. For instance, we can ask users to type the destination hostame/IP address before entering the login credentials. Similar to intercepting the login credentials, we store the destination hostname/IP address in SMRAM. Note that this hostname/IP address cannot be modified by malware because we intercept the keystrokes before the OS receives them. When TrustLogin injects the login credentials back to the network packet, we also check the destination IP address of that packet and make sure it matches the one in SMRAM. If it matches, we can guarantee that the packet would be delivered to the user's desired destination. Note that the malware cannot change the IP address after the checking procedure because the SMI handler waits until the packet physically leaves NIC. Since humans are used to remembering hostnames instead of IP addresses, the SMI handler may need to implement an `nslookup` utility to translate the hostname to the IP address.

9. ACKNOWLEDGEMENTS

The authors would like to thank all of the reviewers for their valuable comments and suggestions. This work is supported by the National Science Foundation Grant No. CNS 1421747 and II-NEW 1205453, Defense Advanced Research Projects Agency Contract FA8650-11-C-7190, and ONR Grant N00014-13-1-0088. Opinions, findings, conclusions and recommendations expressed in this material are those of the authors and do not necessarily reflect the views of the US Government or the Navy.

10. REFERENCES

[1] C-Scale Frequency Reference Guide for Musicians. `http://www.ronelmm.com/tones/cscale.html`.

[2] Common Vulnerabilities and Exposures list. `http://www.cvedetails.com/vulnerability-list/vendor_id-33/product_id-47/cvssscoremin-7/cvssscoremax-7.99/Linux-Linux-Kernel.html`. Access time: 07/06/2014.

[3] Credit Card Data Breach at Barnes & Noble Stores. `http://www.nytimes.com/2012/10/24/business/hackers-get-credit-data-at-barnes-noble.html?_r=3&`.

[4] Free Keylogger Pro. `http://freekeyloggerpro.com/`.

[5] Intel 64 and IA-32 Architectures Optimization Reference Manual. `http://www.intel.com/content/www/us/en/architecture-and-technology/64-ia-32-architectures-optimization-manual.html`.

[6] Keyboard Scan Code Set 1. `http://www.computer-engineering.org/ps2keyboard/scancodes1.html`.

[7] Keylogger Malware Found on UC Irvine Health Center Computers. http://www.scmagazine.com/keylogger-malware-found-on-three-uc-irvine-health-center-computers/article/347204/.

[8] Keylogger Products. `http://www.keylogger.org`.

[9] Logkeys Linux keylogger. `https://code.google.com/p/logkeys/`.

[10] NSA's ANT Division Catalog of Exploits for Nearly Every Major Software/Hardware/Firmware. `http://Leaksource.wordpress.com`.

[11] OpenSSH. `http://www.openssh.com`. Access time: 09/01/2014.

[12] Advanced Micro Devices, Inc. BIOS and Kernel Developer's Guide for AMD Athlon 64 and AMD Opteron Processors. `http://support.amd.com/TechDocs/26094.PDF`.

[13] A. M. Azab, P. Ning, Z. Wang, X. Jiang, X. Zhang, and N. C. Skalsky. HyperSentry: Enabling Stealthy In-Context Measurement of Hypervisor Integrity. In *Proceedings of the 17th ACM Conference on Computer and Communications Security (CCS'10)*, 2010.

[14] A. M. Azab, P. Ning, and X. Zhang. SICE: A Hardware-level Strongly Isolated Computing Environment for x86 Multi-core Platforms. In *Proceedings of the 18th ACM Conference on Computer and Communications Security (CCS'11)*, 2011.

[15] K. Borders and A. Prakash. Securing network input via a trusted input proxy. In *Proceedings of the 2nd USENIX workshop on Hot topics in security*, 2007.

[16] Y. Bulygin, J. Loucaides, A. Furtak, O. Bazhaniuk, and A. Matrosov. Summary of Attacks Against BIOS and Secure Boot. In *Defcon-22*, 2014.

[17] J. Butterworth, C. Kallenberg, and X. Kovah. BIOS Chronomancy: Fixing the Core Root of Trust for Measurement. In *Proceedings of the 20th ACM Conference on Computer and Communications Security (CCS'13)*, 2013.

[18] N. Collignon. In-memory Extraction of SSL Private Keys. `http://c0decstuff.blogspot.com/2011/01/in-memory-extraction-of-ssl-private.html`, 2011.

[19] Coreboot. Open-Source BIOS. `http://www.coreboot.org/`.

[20] S. Embleton, S. Sparks, and C. Zou. SMM rootkits: A New Breed of OS Independent Malware. In *Proceedings of the 4th International Conference on Security and Privacy in Communication Networks (SecureComm'08)*, 2008.

[21] Y. Fu and Z. Lin. Space Traveling across VM: Automatically Bridging the Semantic Gap in Virtual Machine Introspection via Online Kernel Data Redirection. In *Proceedings of the 33rd IEEE Symposium on Security and Privacy (S&P'12)*, 2012.

[22] T. Holz, M. Engelberth, and F. Freiling. Learning More About the Underground Economy: A Case-Study of Keyloggers and Dropzones. In *Proceedings of The 14th European Symposium on Research in Computer Security (ESORICS'09)*, 2009.

[23] Intel. Enhanced Host Controller Interface Specification for Universal Serial Bus. `http://www.intel.com/content/dam/www/public/us/en/documents/technical-specifications/ehci-specification-for-usb.pdf`.

[24] Intel. eXtensible Host Controller Interface for Universal Serial Bus (xHCI). `http://www.intel.com/content/dam/www/public/us/en/documents/technical-specifications/extensible-host-controler-interface-usb-xhci.pdf`.

[25] Intel. PCI/PCI-X GbE Family of Controllers: Software Developer Manual. `http://www.intel.com/content/www/us/en/ethernet-controllers/pci-pci-x-family-gbe-controllers-software-dev-manual.html`.

[26] Intel. Universal Host Controller Interface (UHCI) Design Guide. `ftp.netbsd.org/pub/NetBSD/misc/blymn/uhci11d.pdf`.

[27] B. Jain, M. B. Baig, D. Zhang, D. E. Porter, and R. Sion. SoK: Introspections on Trust and the Semantic Gap. In *Proceedings of the 35th IEEE Symposium on Security and Privacy (S&P'14)*, 2014.

[28] X. Jiang, X. Wang, and D. Xu. Stealthy Malware Detection Through VMM-based Out-of-the-box Semantic View Reconstruction. In *Proceedings of the 14th ACM Conference on Computer and Communications Security (CCS'07)*, 2007.

[29] E. Ladakis, L. Koromilas, G. Vasiliadis, M. Polychronakis, and S. Ioannidis. You Can Type, but You Can't Hide: A Stealthy GPU-based Keylogger. In *Proceedings of the European Workshop on System Security (EuroSec'13).*, 2013.

[30] T. Leek, M. Zhivich, J. Giffin, and W. Lee. Virtuoso: Narrowing the Semantic Gap in Virtual Machine Introspection. In *Proceedings of the 32nd IEEE Symposium on Security and Privacy (S&P'11)*, 2011.

[31] M. Mannan and P. van Oorschot. Leveraging Personal Devices for Stronger Password Authentication from Untrusted Computers. *Journal of Computer Security*, 2011.

[32] L. Martignoni, P. Poosankam, M. Zaharia, J. Han, S. McCamant, D. Song, V. Paxson, A. Perrig, S. Shenker, and I. Stoica. Cloud Terminal: Secure Access to Sensitive Applications from Untrusted Systems. In *Proceedings of the 2012 USENIX Conference on Annual Technical Conference (USENIX ATC'12)*, 2012.

[33] J. McCune, B. Parno, A. Perrig, M. Reiter, and H. Isozaki. Flicker: An Execution Infrastructure for TCB Minimization. In *Proceedings of the 3rd ACM SIGOPS/EuroSys European Conference on Computer Systems*, 2008.

[34] J. M. McCune, A. Perrig, and M. K. Reiter. Safe passage for passwords and other sensitive data. In *NDSS*, 2009.

[35] Ohloh. Black Duck Software, Inc. `http://www.ohloh.net`. Access time: 7/16/2014.

[36] A. Reina, A. Fattori, F. Pagani, L. Cavallaro, and D. Bruschi. When Hardware Meets Software: A Bulletproof Solution to Forensic Memory Acquisition. In *Proceedings of the Annual Computer Security Applications Conference (ACSAC'12)*, 2012.

[37] S. Sagiroglu and G. Canbek. Keyloggers. *Technology and Society Magazine, IEEE*, 2009.

[38] J. Schiffman and D. Kaplan. The SMM Rootkit Revisited: Fun with USB. In *Proceedings of 9th International Conference on Availability, Reliability and Security (ARES'14)*, 2014.

[39] H.-M. Sun, Y.-H. Chen, and Y.-H. Lin. oPass: A User Authentication Protocol Resistant to Password Stealing and Password Reuse Attacks. *Information Forensics and Security, IEEE Transactions on*, 2012.

[40] K. Sun, J. Wang, F. Zhang, and A. Stavrou. SecureSwitch: BIOS-Assisted Isolation and Switch between Trusted and Untrusted Commodity OSes. In *Proceedings of the 19th Annual Network & Distributed System Security Symposium (NDSS'12)*, 2012.

[41] A. Vasudevan, B. Parno, N. Qu, V. Gligor, and A. Perrig. Lockdown: A Safe and Practical Environment for Security Applications (CMU-CyLab-09-011). Technical report, 2009.

[42] VIA. VT8237R Southbridge. `http://www.via.com.tw/`.

[43] F. Wecherowski. A Real SMM Rootkit: Reversing and Hooking BIOS SMI Handlers. *Phrack Magazine*, 2009.

[44] H. William, S. A. Teukolsky, W. T. Vetterling, and B. P. Flannery. *Numerical Recipes: The Art of Scientific Computing.* Cambridge University Press, New York, 2007.

[45] R. Wojtczuk and C. Kallenberg. Attacking UEFI Boot Script. `http://events.ccc.de/congress/2014/Fahrplan/system/attachments/2566/original/venamis_whitepaper.pdf`, 2014.

[46] R. Wojtczuk and J. Rutkowska. Attacking SMM Memory via Intel CPU Cache Poisoning, 2009.

[47] F. Zhang, K. Leach, K. Sun, and A. Stavrou. SPECTRE: A Dependable Introspection Framework via System Management Mode. In *Proceedings of the 43rd Annual IEEE/IFIP International Conference on Dependable Systems and Networks (DSN'13)*, 2013.

[48] F. Zhang, H. Wang, K. Leach, and A. Stavrou. A Framework to Secure Peripherals at Runtime. In *Proceedings of The 19th European Symposium on Research in Computer Security (ESORICS'14).*, 2014.

[49] F. Zhang, J. Wang, K. Sun, and A. Stavrou. HyperCheck: A Hardware-assisted Integrity Monitor. In *IEEE Transactions on Dependable and Secure Computing (TDSC'14)*, 2014.

APPENDIX

Table 3: Musical Notes of an Octave

Musical Note	Frequency (Hz)	Divisor
C	523.25	0x08E2
D	587.33	0x07EA
E	659.26	0x070D
F	783.99	0x06A8
G	783.99	0x05EE
A	880.00	0x0548
B	987.77	0x04B5
C	1046.50	0x0471

Efficient Virtualization-Based Application Protection Against Untrusted Operating System

Yueqiang Cheng*
CyLab, Carnegie Mellon University
4720 Forbes Ave
Pittsburgh, PA, USA
chengyue@andrew.cmu.edu

Xuhua Ding
Singapore Management University
80 Stamford Rd
Singapore, 178902
xhding@smu.edu.sg

Robert H. Deng
Singapore Management University
80 Stamford Rd
Singapore, 178902
robertdeng@smu.edu.sg

ABSTRACT

Commodity monolithic operating systems are abundant with vulnerabilities that lead to rootkit attacks. Once an operating system is subverted, the data and execution of user applications are fully exposed to the adversary, regardless whether they are designed and implemented with security considerations. Existing application protection schemes have various drawbacks, such as high performance overhead, large Trusted Computing Base (TCB), or hardware modification. In this paper, we present the design and implementation of AppShield, a hypervisor-based approach that reliably safeguards code, data and execution integrity of a critical application, in a more efficient way than existing systems. The protection overhead is localized to the protected application only, so that unprotected applications and the operating system run without any performance loss. In addition to the performance advantage, AppShield tackles several newly identified threats in this paper which are not systematically addressed previously. We build a prototype of AppShield with a tiny hypervisor, and experiment with AppShield by running several off-the-shelf applications on a Linux platform. The results testify to AppShield's low performance costs in terms of CPU computation, disk I/O and network I/O.

Categories and Subject Descriptors

D.4.6 [**Security and Protection**]: Isolated Execution Environment

General Terms

Security

Keywords

Address Space Isolation, Untrusted OS, Application Protection, Isolated Execution Environment

*The work was done at Singapore Management University.

ASIA CCS'15, April 14–17, 2015, Singapore, Singapore.

http://dx.doi.org/10.1145/2714576.2714618 .

1. INTRODUCTION

With a superior privilege than user applications, the commodity monolithic operating systems are often regarded as the security basis of systems. A conundrum facing the end users is that the commodity OSes are not always trustworthy as expected. Their enormous code size and broad attack surfaces make them vulnerable to attacks. Once an OS is subverted, all applications and sensitive data are at the mercy of the attacker. Moreover, some high-profile end users and organizations are even concerned about whether the commodity operating systems in their use are purposely implemented with trapdoors to invade their privacy or data secrecy.

To cope with OS level attacks, various mechanisms [23, 22, 28, 3, 6, 34, 31, 5, 29] have been proposed to protect critical applications without trusting the operating system. self-contained code Among them, the approaches like Flicker [23], TrustVisor [22] and Fides [28] are only applicable to self-contained code with predefined inputs and outputs (e.g., inputs are the initial parameters and outputs are the final returns). Those code cannot even make the basic system calls for dynamic memory allocation or deallocation. Although MiniBox [20] extends the functionality by supporting system calls of the self-contained code, it still has several limitations, such as lack of multi-thread support and limiting to sandbox-capable modules.

To protect a full-fledged application, several systems [29, 21, 2, 9, 6, 34, 31, 5, 14, 17] are proposed. Among them, AEGIS [29], XOM OS [21], Bastion [2] and SecureME [9] require hardware modifications, which is apparently impractical for current commodity platforms. Intel's upcoming Software Guard Extensions (SGX) [10] technology provides a suite of hardware extension for software protection which requires significant changes on the software level, and therefore is not compatible with legacy applications. Proxos [31] and Terra [14] introduce a dedicated trusted virtual machine for the protected applications, an approach with a dramatically expanded TCB size and therefore a weaker security assurance.

The systems like OverShadow [6], CHAOS [5], SP^3 [34], InkTag [17] aim to protect the whole process without requiring hardware modifications or a trusted VM. However, they all rely on the costly encryption/decryption operations and are subject to the newly identified attacks (as described in Section 3.2.1) whereby the kernel manipulates the address mapping, e.g., the malicious OS could swap two address translation mappings to break the data/code integrity without directly modifying the data/code of the protected application. Virtual Ghost [12] prevents the kernel from illicitly accessing application memory by instrumenting memory access instructions and enforcing a complete control flow integrity in the kernel, which are usually not applicable for commodity OSes (e.g., Windows) in practice.

In this paper, we propose AppShield, a novel system which *reliably*, *efficiently* and *transparently* protects data secrecy and integrity of a critical application, as well as its execution integrity, against OS-level malware attacks (Figure 1). AppShield leverages the virtualization techniques [19] to isolate the application's address space such that all accesses from the kernel are blocked except those explicitly authorized by the application through system calls. The protected application utilizes the main memory in the same fashion as in a normal setting, since it can request the kernel to (de)allocate memory buffers. Its memory accesses are in the native speed without computation-heavy encryption/decryption or being intercepted. Furthermore, AppShield also achieves *performance isolation* which isolates the performance loss only to the protected application, keeping those unprotected applications not affected. Our scheme is complementary to secure I/O (e.g., DriverGuard [8] and Trusted Path [35]) and encrypted I/O (e.g., SSL for network data) schemes such that they can jointly provide a holistic protection on the application and its I/O data.

We have implemented a prototype of AppShield which consists of a bare-metal hypervisor with roughly $29K$ SLOC and a tiny kernel module of around $2K$ SLOC. We have experimented the prototype with several applications (e.g., Apache) and run a suite of benchmark tests. The experiment results demonstrate that AppShield incurs insignificant performance costs in CPU computation, disk I/O and network I/O.

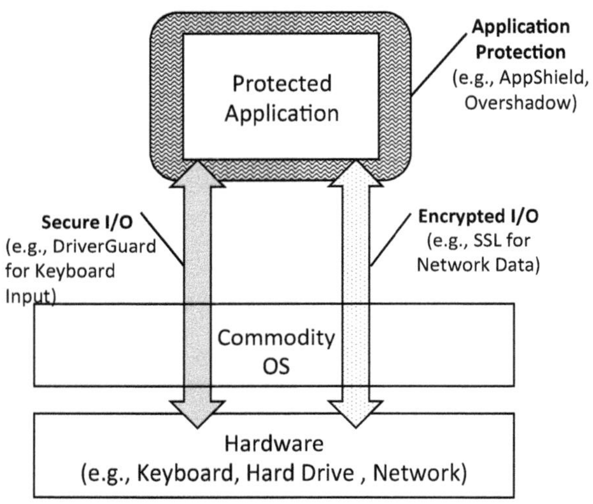

Figure 1: Protections for application and its data. Our scheme is complementary to secure I/O and encrypted I/O schemes.

To summarize, our contributions of this paper are listed below.

- We discover several address mapping attacks which are not addressed by existing application protection schemes. Through these attacks, the malicious kernel can tamper with the protected application's data secrecy and execution integrity.
- We design AppShield to protect execution integrity, data secrecy and integrity of an off-the-shelf application which is allowed to issue system calls.
- Compared with existing work in the literature, our AppShield design achieves better performance by avoiding computation-heavy cryptographic operations and enforcing performance isolation in the sense that the performance loss is incurred to the protected application *only*.
- We build a prototype of AppShield and evaluate it with several commonly used applications and benchmark tools. The experiments show that AppShield does not introduce high overhead to the system.

ORGANIZATION. In the next section, we define the problem by specifying the threat model, our objectives and an overview of AppShield. In Section 3, we describe the dynamic address space isolation together with newly identified threats. The secure address space switch and the support of data exchanges are presented in Section 4 and Section 5, respectively. The implementation and evaluation of AppShield are reported in Section 6. We discuss the related work in Section 7 and conclude this paper in Section 8.

2. SYNOPSIS

2.1 The Model

In this work, we defend against kernel-level malware attacks on a critical application by tampering with the latter's data and/or execution. The adversary can run arbitrary code and launch DMA operations in the victim platform. Nonetheless the adversary does not have physical control over the platform. All hardware and peripheral devices, together with their firmware, are considered as trusted. In other words, the platform's chipset and all peripheral devices operate as expected, namely, following their specifications and not containing Trojan-Horse circuits or microcode that respond to commands of the adversary. In our model, we trust the a bare-metal hypervisor in use, which has a tiny code size and limited number of interfaces. Moreover, we assume our hypervisor intercepts and emulates the System Management Mode (SMM) operations in order to tackle SMM-based attacks by leveraging SMM containerization. In fact, Intel has supported such mechanism [19].

Neither side channel attacks nor application availability is in the scope of our study. We also suppose that no ill-formed inputs can subvert the control flow of the critical application which can be achieved by input sanitation and proper code development. It is *orthogonal* to our work to enhance code security (e.g., fixing bugs) of the protected applications.

Our goal is to protect a critical application execution integrity and data security within the application memory space. The critical application may use cryptographic techniques to protect its derived data for disk and network I/O, and may leverage existing secure I/O path schemes like [8, 35] to protect the raw I/O data for peripheral devices such as a keyboard and a fingerprint reader.

2.2 Design Principles

In the design of AppShield, we follow the four principles described below. Firstly, it should support and protect the application's system calls. The critical application can safely issue system calls to request the services (e.g., memory allocation) from the operating systems even though the latter is not trusted.

Secondly, no significant performance impact should be inflicted by AppShield on the protected application and on the platform as a whole. Ideally, the protected application accesses the main memory in the native speed without being interposed on or going through an encryption/decryption procedure. Moreover, the mechanism should take a limited performance toll on the protection application, whereas other unprotected applications and the OS are not affected. We term this property as *performance localization* in this paper.

Thirdly, out of the practicality consideration, we intend to design AppShield to be compatible and even transparent to legacy off-the-shelf applications. The requirement of significant source code or binary code modifications hinders the adoption of AppShield in practice. Note that the compiling and installation of the kernel module do not rely on the source code of the operating system.

Lastly, as a widely accepted design principle, the TCB of the security mechanism should be kept small and simple, which ensures that the risk of subverting the TCB is minimal. Therefore, it excludes the approach of using a trusted virtual machine where an operating system is part of the TCB.

2.3 AppShield Overview

The high level idea of AppShield is to dynamically isolate the target application's context (registers) and address space from the rest of the platform (including the kernel) in an exclusive fashion, while its system calls are securely mediated by the hypervisor to fend off attacks. For the easiness of presentation, we use CAP in the rest of the paper to denote the critical application under AppShield's protection.

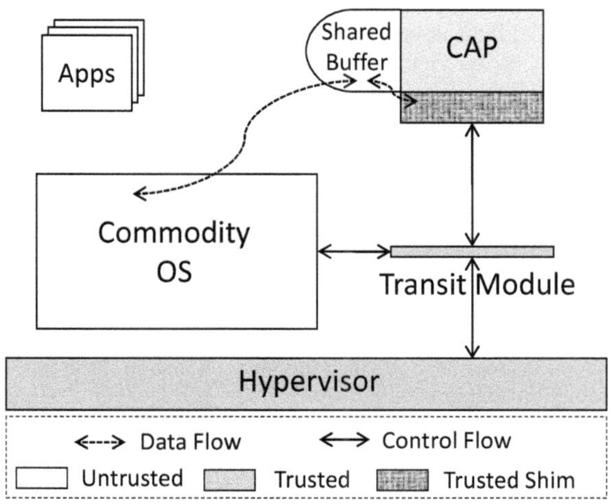

Figure 2: The architecture of AppShield. The data flows (dotted lines) between the protected Critical APplication (CAP) always go through the shared buffer and mediated by the *shim* code. The control flows (solid lines) between CAP and the OS are mediated by the Transit Module. The executions of transit module and the trust shim are protected by the hypervisor.

Figure 2 depicts the architecture of AppShield. It consists of a bare-metal hypervisor, a *transit module* in the guest kernel[1] space mediating *control flow* transitions between CAP and the kernel, and a *shim code* in the user space assisting inbound and outbound *data flows*. Both the transit module and the shim code are self-contained and safeguarded by the hypervisor to defend against attacks from the kernel and malicious DMA requests as in [8, 22]. The AppShield hypervisor as the root of trust in our system could boot up using SRTM [32] (Static Root of Trust for Measurements) and DRTM [18] (Dynamic Root of Trust for Measurements) techniques. Thus, we could install AppShield during runtime, even if the guest operating system is already infected before installing the hypervisor, because any integrity violation could be verified.

CAP runs in an address space isolated from the rest of the guest domain, while the guest OS and other unprotected applications on the platform run as usual without being affected. The page table of CAP is managed by the guest OS, but its updates are intercepted and verified by the hypervisor to defend against various attacks including the new ones introduced in Section 3.2.1. Data flows in system calls are mediated by the shim code which is essentially a wrapper of `libc` libraries. Thus, it does *not* require source code of libc and any modification on the protected application. The main task of the shim is to marshal the system call parameters by exporting the data needed by the system call routine into the shared buffer accessible to the kernel.

The transit module regulates the control flow transitions between CAP and the guest kernel. The transitions are triggered by the events including system calls, exceptions and interrupts. In order to respond to those events before the guest kernel, the new handlers within the transit module are invoked before the handlers in the kernel so as to prevent the context switch from being manipulated.

3. DYNAMIC ADDRESS SPACE ISOLATION AND VERIFICATION

Dynamic address space isolation is the bedrock of AppShield. In this section, we first elaborate how the hypervisor isolates a predefined address space of CAP. Then, we explain how the isolation is dynamically adapted to the changes of the memory boundary at run-time. While our description follows Intel virtualization technology, the approach is applicable with AMD's as well.

3.1 Dynamic Address Space Isolation

In a nutshell, the physical memory assigned to the guest is divided into two separated regions by the hypervisor. One (trusted) region is used for CAP while another (untrusted) region is for the guest OS and other applications. The hypervisor configures IOMMU to prevent malicious DMA requests to access the trusted region. To prevent illicit software access, the memory dichotomy as depicted in Figure 3 is realized by two suites of Extended Page Tables (EPTs) maintained by the hypervisor, respectively. The EPT enforced address space isolation ensures that the guest OS and other untrusted applications can never access the memory regions assigned to CAP; on the other hand, CAP cannot access memory regions belonging to the guest system either. For the sake of clarification, we use *AppShield EPT* to refer to the ones dedicated for CAP. In the following, we only focus on the EPT configuration. The details of applying the proper EPT are described in Section 4 which elaborates the context switches between CAP and the guest OS.

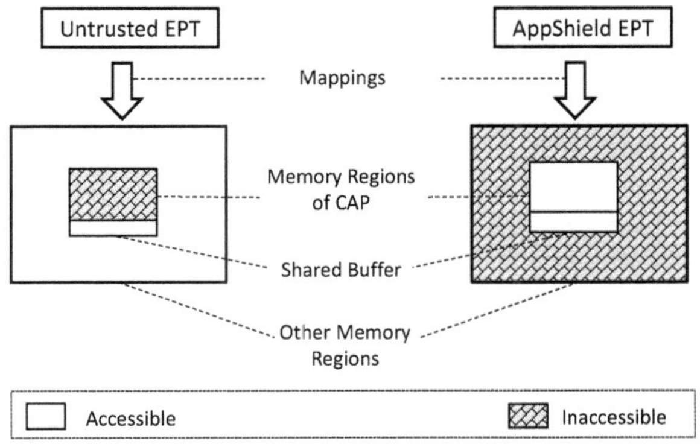

Figure 3: Address Space Isolation. With the AppShield EPT, only the memory regions of CAP and the shared buffer are accessible and other memory regions are inaccessible. In contrast, with the original EPT, CAP's regions except the shared buffer are inaccessible.

[1]Guest kernel refers to the kernel running in the guest VM.

3.1.1 Activation and Deactivation

The hypervisor exports two hypercalls for CAP to activate and deactivate the protection. The activation hypercall is issued before CAP's main function is entered. In response, the hypervisor obtains the page table base address from CR3 register and traverses the page table entries (PTEs) belonging to the application, so that it locates all pages within the address space, including the shared libraries. Note that the transit module copies the shared libraries into the isolated space region, and keeps all original shared libraries to be used by the untrusted applications. Both the traversed guest PTEs and the pages pointed by them constitute the physical memory region that needs to be separated from the guest. The hypervisor creates the AppShield EPT for this region and marks the corresponding entries in the original EPT as inaccessible, so that the guest cannot visit the isolated region. Once the application's code and data are isolated, the hypervisor can validate its launch-time integrity, supposing that the integrity of the protected application has been priorly authenticated by a signature or an HMAC tag. In addition, the hypervisor measures its integrity and ensures that its memory region does not overlap with existing ones.

With the deactivation hypercall, CAP notifies the hypervisor to disable the protection. In response, the hypervisor first ensures that it is issued by CAP, and then destroys the AppShield EPT and restores the entries in the original EPTs.

3.1.2 Tracking Address Space Updates

One of the main tasks of isolating a full-fledged application is that its memory region evolves over time, due to dynamic memory allocation and deallocation as a result of relevant system calls (e.g., *brk*) which are invoked by the corresponding memory usage functions in the libc library, such as *malloc* and *free*.

The details of how AppShield mediates system calls are described in the next section. Here we focus on explaining how the hypervisor dynamically maintains address space isolation, which demands the hypervisor to track memory space updates at runtime.

To track page table updates, one design option is to let the hypervisor directly manages a dedicated guest page table for the CAP. Obviously, it significantly increases the hypervisor complexity which weakens the security strength. The paraverfication technique approach used by InkTag [17] is another alternative. However it requires massive modifications of the OS. To follow the design principles we put forth in Section 2.2, our design utilizes paravirtualization as Xen [1] whereby the guest page tables, being set as read-only, are managed by the kernel and any updates are trapped into the hypervisor and conducted by the hypervisor.

3.2 Address Space Verification

Although the malicious kernel does not have a direct write access to CAP's guest page table, it may manipulate the virtual and/or physical address of the newly allocated memory regions to compromise CAP's security without accessing the latter's memory space. One such example is the Iago attack [4] which relies on a vulnerability in libc libraries. In the following, we first show several newly discovered attacks in the same vein, but in a more generalized setting, and then we show how the hypervisor in AppShield verifies an address space update (before isolating it) to counter these attacks.

3.2.1 Address Mapping Manipulation

In general, address mapping manipulation attacks can be launched by the kernel in response to any system calls that result in page table updates. Without loss of generality, we use buffer allocation as an example to illustrate the attacks.

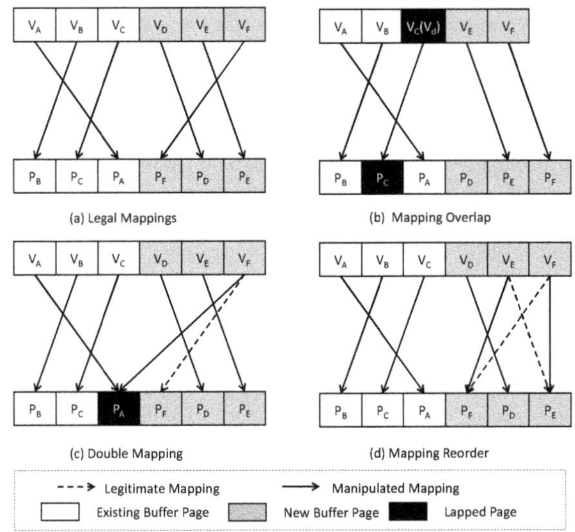

Figure 4: Address mapping manipulation attacks. $V_A, \cdots, V_F$ **are regions in the virtual addresses and** $P_A, \cdots, P_F$ **are their guest physical pages respectively.**

Suppose a CAP's buffer contains three consecutive pages at virtual address V_A, V_B and V_C respectively and CAP requests a new buffer. When there is no attack, the newly allocated buffer's virtual address and physical addresses do not overlap with any existing regions, as illustrated in Figure 4-(a), where they are at virtual address V_D, V_E and V_F. In the following, we show four types of manipulation attacks.

Mapping Overlap Attack. The malicious kernel may overlap two memory regions in both virtual and physical address space. As illustrated in Figure 4-(b), the new buffer is set to the pages located at V_D to V_E. The overlapping of V_C and V_D leads to undesired modifications of data in P_C when the application attempts to update the first page of the allocated buffer (through the mapping from V_D to P_C). Obviously this attack breaches data integrity. It can also subvert the control flow of CAP when the overlapping memory is in the application stack and the modifications change the stored return address(es).

Double Mapping Attack. This attack maps two or more virtual pages to one physical page in the user space. In double mapping attack, there are only overlaps in the physical address space but no overlap in the virtual address space, which is the main difference with the mapping overlap attack. As shown in Figure 4-(c), a write to V_A affects the result of a read operation at V_F. This attack is more stealthy than the mapping-overlap attack, as the physical addresses are transparent to the code running in the virtual space which is not tampered with at all.

Mapping Re-order Attack. The mapping re-order attack is to re-order the existing address mappings between the virtual addresses and the physical addresses. As shown in Figure 4-(d), CAP retrieves wrong data when it reads from V_F. As a result, CAP's data or control flow can be manipulated by the malicious kernel.

Mapping Release Attack. In this attack, the malicious kernel release one or more existing mappings without any system call requests from the protected application. The mapping-release could induce the hypervisor to give up the protection on those pages since they are not considered in CAP's addresses space. By doing so, the guest OS can freely access the data on those released pages.

Essentially, these attacks can be neutralized by the hypervisor via monitoring and verifying changes to the guest page tables. To the best of our knowledge, no existing work precisely describe the verification procedures and many of them [6, 34] suffer from one or more aforementioned attacks. Moreover, it is not easy to efficiently verify them due to frequent page table updates.

3.2.2 *Context Information Collection*

In order to determine whether an address space change is legitimate, the hypervisor needs to be aware of the present memory layout, the application's intent to memory updates and the resulting page table updates following the system calls.

The existing memory layout (the mapping relationship between guest virtual addresses to guest physical addresses) is collected by traversing CAP's guest page table. The collected information is trustworthy since it is collected by the hypervisor and the guest page table is set as read-only so that the kernel cannot directly update it.

To determine the intent of the application relevant to memory updates, one possible way is to allow the hypervisor to intercept all system calls that are potentially used by the CAP to allocate or deallocate memory. In order to correctly interpret the memory updates information (i.e., the based address and the size), the hypervisor has to know the exact semantic meaning of all parameters and return values. It inevitably increases the complexity of the hypervisor and thereby dampens its security. In our paper, the trusted shim running in the user space closely works with the CAP. Thus, it knows the system calls used by the CAP and their semantic meanings, e.g., the parameter of the *malloc* is the memory size and the return value is the based address of the new allocated buffer. Through several hypercalls, the trusted shim securely pass such information to the hypervisor.

3.2.3 *Verification Details*

In page table update verification, the hypervisor and the shim code jointly enforce the following policies for protecting the address space of a CAP.

1. The page table of CAP should be non-writable for the untrusted guest OS. Any update should be intercepted by the hypervisor.

2. The newly added memory region should not overlap with any existing memory region, in both the virtual address space and the guest physical address space.

3. Once the mappings between the virtual addresses and the guest physical addresses are fixed, they are not allowed to be re-mapped.

4. The memory regions can be only released upon CAP's requests, and the page data should be cleaned before allowing the guest OS to manage/access it.

The shim code checks the overlap in the virtual address space after system calls, because it wraps all libc functions related to system calls and therefore has the entire virtual address layout. Taking *mmap* as an example, the trusted shim stores the size of the memory-mapped region through the second parameter of *mmap* and the base address through the return value. Such information are securely deposited in an ordered list which is inaccessible from the kernel since the address space of the CAP is isolated by the hypervisor. For each new allocated memory region, the trusted shim verifies it with existing ones. If there is no overlap, it then updates the maintained list and passes the execution flow to the CAP; otherwise it will issue a hypercall to the hypervisor to inform the policy violation.

To defend against double mapping and mapping reorder attacks in the page table updates, the hypervisor interprets the present mapping (denoted as M) and the resulting mapping M', and analyzes the intent of this update. If the guest kernel is to build a new mapping (i.e., M is empty and M' points to a guest physical page), the hypervisor verifies if the new pointed physical page is occupied before. If it is already occupied, it is a double mapping attack and the request is denied; otherwise the update is approved. If the guest OS aims to remap/reorder the mappings (i.e., both M and M' point to the guest physical pages), the hypervisor directly rejects it.

If the guest kernel aims to free an existing mapping (i.e., M points to a guest physical page while M' is empty), the hypervisor verifies whether it has been priorly informed with CAP's such requests via the shim code's hypercall. The addresses and sizes of those memory pages to be freed are stored in a list in the hypervisor space. By searching the list, the hypervisor decides if the current page is the one that CAP aims to release. If it is not, the hypervisor rejects the update; otherwise it approves it and updates the list by deleting the corresponding record. Note that the data on the releases memory page is zeroed by the trusted shim once it gets the release requests from the CAP.

Note that all mapping updates should be driven by the requests from the application itself. Thus, the above verification algorithm does not prevent normal memory sharing within user space, e.g., a JIT compiler may request two virtual address for its code, one read/execute only, the other for writing.

4. SECURE ADDRESS SPACE SWITCH

Events like system calls, interrupts and exceptions lead to context switches between CAP and the kernel. Different from the conventional user-kernel context switch, the switch between CAP and the kernel involves address space switches, since they run in two exclusively separated address spaces.

When CAP is in execution, the transit module in AppShield handles all interrupts and prevents the kernel from exploiting the context switch to attack CAP. Its main tasks are to facilitate the context switch and to safeguard CAP's context information. It also notifies the hypervisor to perform address space switch. As shown in Figure 5, when an interrupt is raised, the control flow leaves from CAP to the kernel. Once the event is processed by the kernel, the flow goes back to CAP. We proceed to elaborate the details of context switch.

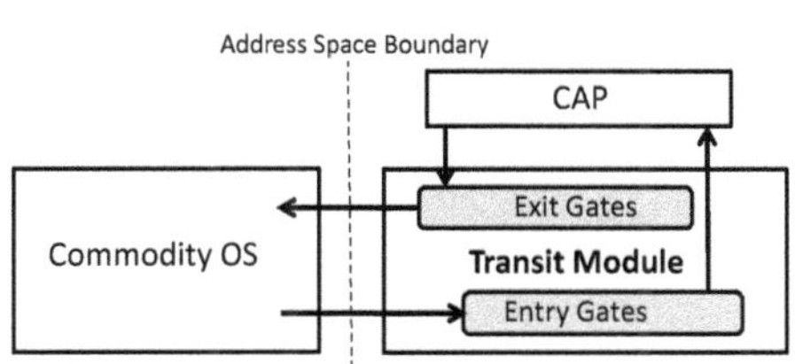

Figure 5: Control flow between the CAP and the guest kernel. Each control flow of CAP starts from an entry gate and ends with an exit gate.

4.1 Components of Transit Module

The transit module is a self-contained kernel module with its execution being protected by the hypervisor using the mechanism described in [27]. Specifically, the memory regions occupied by the transit module is isolated by the hypervisor, such that the untrusted commodity OS can not modify the data and the code. The control flows of the transit module execution *always* start from the predefined addresses called *entry/exit gates* as in Figure 5.

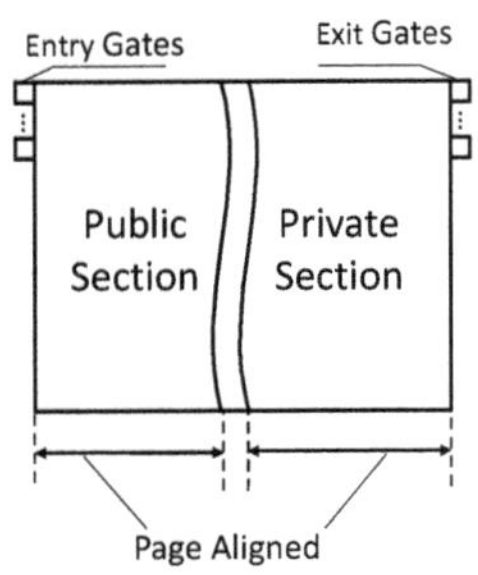

Figure 6: The format of transit module

The transit module has two sections (Figure 6), which are page aligned for facilitating memory protection. The first section is the *public section* which contains information that is read-only for the transit module and the commodity OS. The second section is the *private section* which contains private data. Accesses to the private section are only allowed if they are from the transit module; other accesses originated from outside of the transit module are blocked by the hypervisor. The transit module comprise an AppShield Interrupt Descriptor Table (IDT) which points to a set of its own interrupt handlers called *AppShield interrupt handlers*. Note that the interrupts are still handled by the guest kernel as in the normal setting, not by the transit module. As explained in subsequent sections, the transit module is for AppShield to capture events and protect the context switch without having performance effect on the kernel or other applications.

An AppShield interrupt handler is composed of two code stubs (Figure 7): the *entry gate* in the public section and the *exit gate* in the private section. The control flow of the transit module always starts from one of the entry/exit gates. The exit gate handles the context switch from CAP in protection to the guest kernel while the entry gate handles the switch back to CAP. More details of their working mechanisms are presented in Section 4.3.

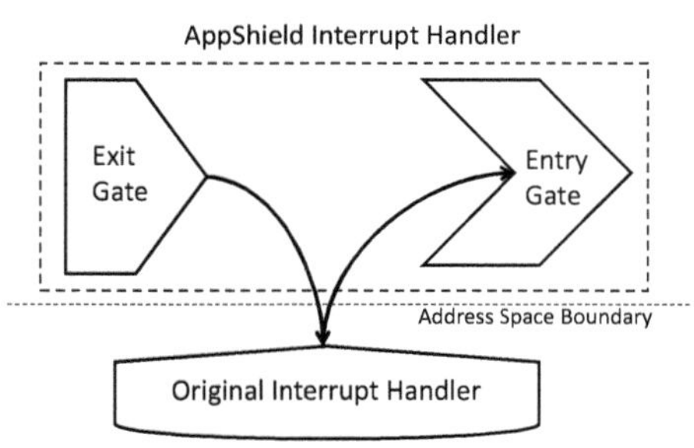

Figure 7: An AppShield interrupt handler consists of one pair of gates, which invokes the original interrupt handler to response the corresponding interrupt and mediates the return from the kernel to CAP.

4.2 Event Capture

The hypervisor in AppShield does not intercept interrupt events since it will significantly affect the platform performance. When AppShield is activated, the hypervisor loads and protects the transit module which captures events within CAP, so that unrelated applications are not involved.

The AppShield IDT contains the pointers pointing to the AppShield interrupt handlers. The hypervisor installs the AppShield IDT to the CPU occupied by CAP by setting its IDTR register in the VMCS structure. Consequently, the AppShield interrupt handlers become the first responders to interrupts on the CPU occupied by CAP. They use hypercalls to notify the hypervisor when necessary. When the guest OS is running, it still uses the original IDT and interrupt handlers. The switch of the two IDTs follows the switch of the address space. As illustrated in Figure 8, the original IDT is uninstalled and the secure IDT is installed for the CAP execution.

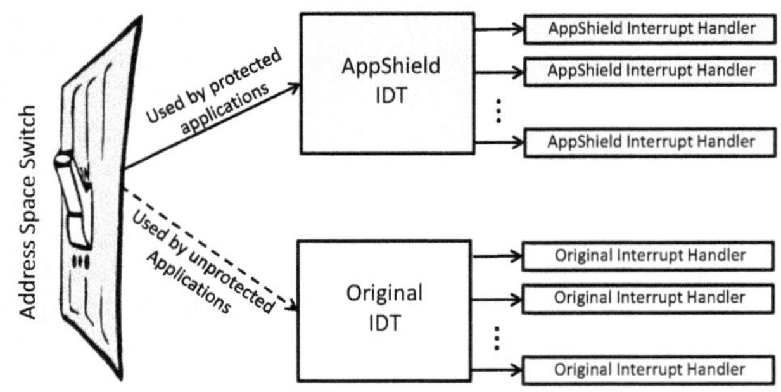

Figure 8: Performance Overhead Localization. When the context switches to CAP, the normal IDT is uninstalled and the secure IDT is installed.

By using two sets of interrupt handlers, our design achieves performance overhead localization, because the transit module is only invoked when CAP is interrupted. AppShield is not involved with the executions of other applications or the guest OS.

4.3 Context and Address Space Switch

Figure 9 depicts the control flow of event handling with two context switches at the exit gate and the entry gate. When an interrupt is raised during CAP's execution, the exit gate of the AppShield interrupt handler sets out to the context. Under the protection of the hypervisor, the exit gate first prepares a buffer and saves CAP's context in the transit module's private section. It then creates a dummy context for the kernel to execute within. Note that the dummy context should *not* be randomly generated since some context information is used by the kernel to serve for the application. For instance, the EIP should point to the corresponding interrupt handler so that the original handler can serve the interrupt. Specifically, we only need to hide the information in the general registers (i.e., EAX, EBX, ECX, EDX, ESI, EDI, EBP) since they may contain sensitive CAP data. In the case of system call context switch, we also need to keep the parameters in the corresponding registers.

To allow the execution flow to securely come back to the transit module, the return address of the dummy context is set to point to the corresponding entry gate. In the end, the exit gate then issues a hypercall to inform the hypervisor to restore the original page tables so that the interrupt handler in the guest kernel can properly execute.

Once the guest interrupt handler finishes its process, the control is returned to the entry gate. The entry gate issues a hypercall to request the hypervisor to restore the AppShield EPT and guest page tables. After ensuring that the request is indeed from the legitimate entry gate, the hypervisor restores the AppShield EPT and installs the AppShield IDT, so that the entry gate can properly restore the saved context and resume the interrupted CAP execution.

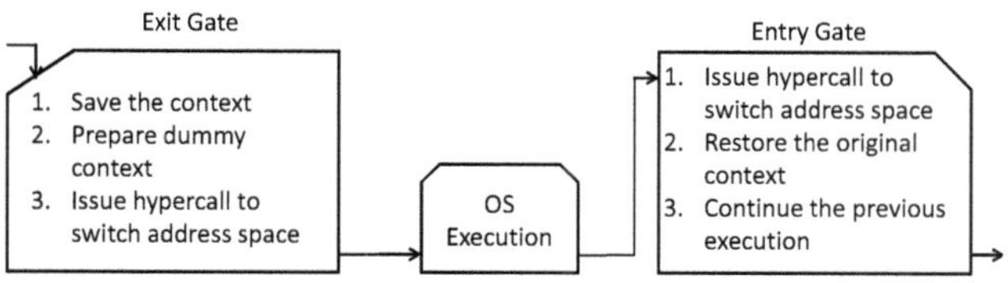

Figure 9: A typical address space switch always starts with an exit gate and ends with an entry gate. The commodity OS handles the events that trigger the address space switch.

4.4 Special Considerations

4.4.1 Fast-System-Call Cost Localization

Platforms with modern processor and chipset support fast system call mechanisms by introducing new instructions. The SYSENTRER(SYSCALL) instruction traps the CPU to the kernel mode while the SYSEXIT(SYSRET) instruction transfers the CPU back to the user mode. In this paper we use SYSENTER and SYSEXIT instruction pair to illustrate the localization mechanism.

The SYSENTER instruction sets the registers (i.e., CS, EIP, SS and ESP) according to values specified by the operating system in certain Model-Specific Registers (MSR), and triggers the CPU to trap into the kernel mode. To localize the performance overhead to CAP, the hypervisor uses an additional set of MSR dedicated for CAP, where EIP value in the corresponding MSR (i.e., SYSENTER_EIP_MSR) is set to point to the corresponding exit gate within the transit module. By doing so, all fast system calls will be intercepted the transit module. The guest kernel uses its own MSRs. The two sets of registers are switched following address space switches. Note that the context backup and restoration are still handled by the pairs of the exit and entry gates. ItâĂŹs a well known fact that when multiple processors are present in a system, every processor has its own set of MSRs. Thus, the modifications of MSRs for the protected application do not affect other applications running on other processors.

4.4.2 Multi-Thread Execution

AppShield supports multi-thread execution of CAP. The child threads could be user threads, which are completely maintained by CAP in user space, or light weight processes which share the same address space with their parent and are scheduled by the guest OS.

The user threads do not have their own contexts since they do not have the kernel structure for scheduling. Therefore, they are transparent to AppShield. In contrast, light weight process threads may have multiple user contexts for CAP, since each of them has its own corresponding structures (e.g., the kernel stack) for scheduling. These threads may run in parallel and trap into the guest OS simultaneously. Therefore, by using the base addresses of their kernel stacks as the identifiers, the transit module can distinguish each of them, and save/restore the respective contexts.

5. SYSTEM CALL MEDIATION

The system call from CAP to the guest kernel reveals some application data when they are passed to the kernel as parameters. AppShield provides a *spatial-temporal* protection [9] for the data involved in the system call. It ensures that the guest OS can only access the authorized data (spatial protection) during the execution of the system call (temporal protection). The previous sections have explained that temporal protection is achieved by address space isolation and secure context switch. In this section, we describe how AppShield enforces spatial protection through system call adaption. According to the security risks, we adapt those low risk system calls and emulate those high risk ones.

5.1 System Call Adaption

In the majority of system calls, the application information needed by the kernel, if any, is passed as parameters and there is no need for the kernel to access the application address space. These calls are not adapted in AppShield.

Nonetheless, system calls with parameters of the pointer type (e.g., a pointer pointing to the file name in *open*), requires the kernel to access the application's space to acquire needed information. In order to prevent the kernel misuse such accesses, it is desirable to adapt those system calls with parameter marshaling.

To ensure spatial protection, two approaches of parameter marshaling have been proposed in the literature. One approach as used in [6] is to interact with the hypervisor eight times to safely move the decrypted data into a newly allocated shared/public buffer. Obviously, the multiple round interaction with the hypervisor is detrimental to the system performance. The other approach as in [9] incurs less context switches as it decrypts the data and overwrites the cipher text using the same buffer. Nonetheless, both approaches use encryption algorithms which consume an order of magnitude more CPU cycles than conventional system calls. Therefore, the performance deteriorates significantly when CAP frequently issues system calls. We summarize the performance cost of the parameter marshaling in a system call in these two approaches (i.e., Overshadow and SecureME) together with our scheme in Table 1.

	Crypto. Operations	Data Movement	Context Switch (#)
OverShadow [6]	yes	yes	8
SecureME[9], InkTag[17]	yes	yes	2
AppShield	no	yes	2

Table 1: The time cost of the parameter marshaling in a system call. Our scheme is relatively efficient because we give up the costly cryptographic operations and reduce the switch times.

In our scheme, the trusted shim creates a shared region in its user space, and issues a hypercall to inform the hypervisor that the shared region is accessible for the guest OS. In this way, the guest OS can only access the data within the shared region, but cannot access any other regions within the user space of the CAP.

To adapt system calls, we develop the shim code with the semantics of each system call, i.e. the parameter semantics and the return values. In addition, the semantics also includes the data flow direction, i.e. whether the memory buffer referred to by the parameter is to receive data from the guest kernel, or store the data to be sent out to the kernel.

Specifically, for the data that the CAP attempts to send out, the shim simply copies the data into a buffer allocated in the shared region, and updates the corresponding parameter to refer to the new buffer. To receive data from the guest OS, the shim should reserve a buffer in the shared region. The shim then saves the base address of the original buffer, and updates the corresponding parameter to refer to the reserved one. When the system call returns, the shim copies the received data into the original buffer and continues the execution.

Configurations	Descriptions
CPU	Intel i7-2600 with 3.40GHZ
Memory	3GB DDR3 1333MHZ
Network Card	Intel Device 1502 with 1Gbps
Disk	ATA 7200RPM
OS	Ubuntu 10.04 with Kernel 2.6.32.59

Table 2: The configurations of the experiment machine.

5.2 System Call Emulation

There are several system calls whereby the system call adaption technique is not applicable to resolve the conflict between the system call service and the security requirement. Specifically, such system calls are not designed for exchanging data. Instead, they are used to introspect or manipulate the application by accessing or modifying its internal state. For such system calls, we have to emulate them in the transit module.

The fast user mutex system call (*futex*) allows an application to wait for a value at a given address, and to wake up other applications waiting on a particular address. The handler of *futex* not only directly accesses the process's space, but also binds some information (e.g., a hash bucket) with the address. Therefore, the system call adaption technique described previous leads to the failure of *futex* as the information is bound to an incorrect address.

Other system calls requiring emulation are for signal handling, where the guest kernel needs to prepare a temporary execution context for the application and transfers the execution control to a preregistered handler to handle the corresponding signal. The critical security issue here is that the guest kernel needs to be authorized to manipulate the application context. Such authorization may be exploited to reveal and tamper with the application data, e.g., involve a function to send plain text outside.

CAVEAT Note that the *ptrace* system call is not allowed in AppShield since its working mechanism requires the guest OS to directly read the content of the user space, or to modify the data or even code of the specific addresses, which cannot be reconciled with the security requirements. We do not emulate this system call.

6. IMPLEMENTATION AND EVALUATION

We have implemented a prototype of AppShield on a PC with Intel i7-2600 (3.4GHZ), 3GB memory and Ubuntu 10.04 with kernel 2.6.32.59 (Table 2). The prototype consists of a dedicated hypervisor [7] running on the bare-metal hardware, and a Linux loadable module as the transit module. The code base of the hypervisor is around $29K$ SLOC with $218KB$ binary size. The transit module consists of around $2K$ SLOC, and the trusted shim is around $1K$ SLOC.

Trusted Shim. We do not modify the source code of the application or the shared libraries. Instead, we create the shim as a wrapper of libc, and allow it to intercept the function calls that are supposed to call the libc functions. Specifically, on the Linux system, an application usually needs shared libraries at run-time, and the dynamic linker loads those shared libraries in whatever order it needs them. However, when LD_PRELOAD is set for a shared library, it will be loaded before any other libraries, including the libc library. Pre-loading a library means that its functions will be used before others of the same name. We use this feature in our implementation, saving the cost of the source code modification.

The trusted shim needs to do some initialization and preparation for the protection and the interception, such as allocating the shared buffer and informing the hypervisor to protected the application. However, those functions for intercepting system calls are passively invoked, meaning that they do not execute until the application explicitly calls them. To solve this problem, we resort to another feature - constructor function. A constructor function marked with *.init* will be called by the dynamic linker when the library is loaded. The trusted shim in our implementation supports 56 most commonly used system calls as listed in Table 3 below.

System Calls	
Files	open, close, read, write, chdir writev, access, fstat64, uname, poll, fcntl statfs64, fstatfs64, getdents64, getdents stat64, lseek, _llseek, getcwd, fchdir, ioctl
Network	bind, listen, accept, sendto, recvfrom, accept4, select connect, send, recv, getsockname, socketcall
Memory	mmap2, munmap, mremap, brk, mprotect
Process	getpid, gettid, getgroups32, set_thread_area getuid, geteuid, getgid, getegid exit_groud, tgkill, getrlimit, exit
Time	time, clock_gettime, gettimeofday
Others	futex, rt_sigaction, rt_sigprocmask, sigaltstack

Table 3: Supported system calls.

Implementation Challenges. The techniques used in the system call interception and parameter marshaling are not as trivial as they seem. The operations of each system call and the related data structures are rather complex. For example, *socketcall* supports many possible operations on the selected file. The operation is determined by a *command* parameter. There are up to 20 command options, and the commands could impact the meanings of other parameters and invoke different data structures. Handling all these variations requires both deep understanding and careful implementation. The challenges of implementing performance isolation are related to the installation of interrupt handlers which involve special steps (e.g., saving context) in the assembly code before invoking the corresponding native C-code handler. The assembly code needs to prepare the stack and registers (e.g., as parameters) for the native handler. Since this piece of code usually breaks the stack layout and alters the register values, those information have to be stored properly right before executing the code and are restored by the code right before invoking the C-code handler. All these operations are further complicated by the requirement that they should be finished in an atomic way. Any interrupt during the operations overwrites the saved context and/or breaks the stack layout.

6.1 Micro Benchmark

In the micro benchmark, we evaluate the cost of the address space switch (Table 4). An address space switch event can be divided into three parts: protection mode switch, context backup and restoration. The protection mode switch includes a hypercall, IDTR and EPT switching. The context backup consists of saving registers (including general, flag, control registers, and MMX/SSE/AVX registers) and creating a dummy context. The context restoration is to load all the saved registers. The cost of address space switch is relatively high, because it contains the costly memory access from hypervisor space to guest space, i.e., inserting the return address to the kernel stack. All three costs constitute the latency for the system to handle a particular interrupt or exception.

The cost for a system call is composed of the address-space switch cost and the parameter marshaling cost. The latter varies with different system calls. For instance, there is no such cost for *getpid*, while *write* involves a data copy. Thus, we do not provide individual evaluation. However, they are reflected in macro

Operation	Time (μs)
Out of Protected Address Space	1.72
Back to Protected Address Space	1.33
Context Backup	0.11
Context Restoration	0.08

Table 4: The micro-benchmark results for address space switch.

benchmarking which evaluate the whole application performance overhead.

6.2 Macro Benchmark

In macro benchmarking, we apply AppShield on several applications (including Apache, and *ls*, *vim* on Linux) as well as benchmark tools, and measure their performance effects on computation, disk and network I/O.

6.2.1 AppShield Impacts on Performance

SPEC CINT2006 [11] is an industry-standard benchmark intended for measuring the performance of the CPU and memory. We executed SPEC CINT2006 in two setups: with and without AppShield protection. Without AppShield protection, the performance overhead is due to the virtualization itself. The full evaluation has been reported in [7]. Generally, it only introduces 0.2% to 10.3% performance overhead. In addition to the virtualization cost, AppShield has 0.01% slowdown on average. The primary source of virtualization overhead is VM exits due to interrupts and privileged instructions [15]. Figure 10 shows the results.

6.2.2 Computation centric programs

We measure the AppShield's protection on computation-intensive programs. In our experiment, we measure three encryption algorithms (i.e., AES, RC4 and RSA) from *OpenSSL 0.9.8k* package. We run these algorithms to encrypt/decrypt messages with different lengths, from 32bytes to 2048 bytes. The measurement results in Figure 11 shows that the protection effects on the computation programs is quite small.

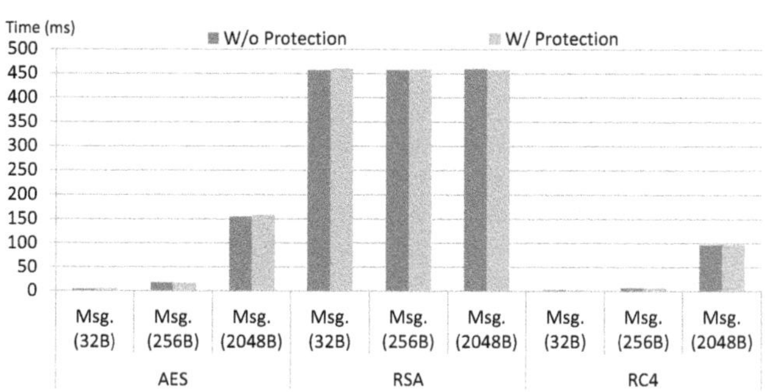

Figure 11: The effects of AppShield protection on computation

6.2.3 Disk I/O centric programs

The disk I/O benchmark includes three sub-benchmarks to evaluate the overhead in disk reading, writing and copying. Disk I/O benchmark reads/writes data from/to files with different sizes. In our experiments, the file size is 64MB, and the read/write granularity is from 512B to 4MB. Experiments with a larger file and a smaller buffer result in more system calls, and consequently introduce more context switches. However, with the increasing of the buffer size, the performance is better, which is also proved by the experiment results in Figure 12. For example, the performance overheads with 4KB-granularity are quite high, and have (81.91%, 71.84%, 74.57%) for (read, write, copy) respectively, while the performance overhead with 256KB-granularity are very small, only has (0.68%, 4.52%, 0.00%) for (read, write and copy) respectively. Note that the overhead is mainly introduced by data copy and context backup/restoration.

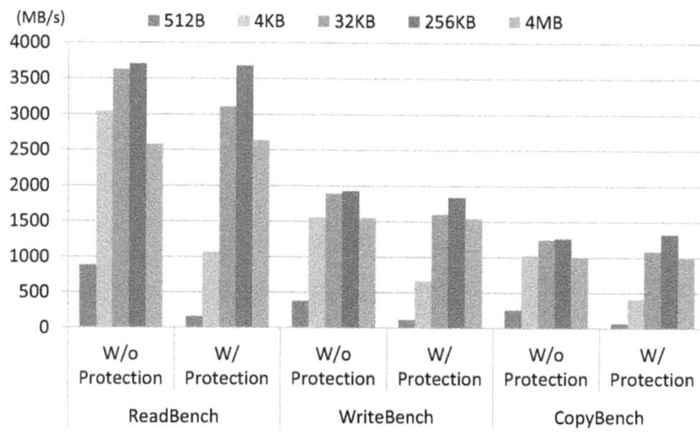

Figure 12: The disk I/O Benchmark

6.2.4 Network I/O Benchmark

We measured the network performance with the Apache web server. The server is configured in worker mode with one main process and 20 threads. We run the standard *ApacheBench* included in the Apache utility tools. We execute 10,000 web requests, at the concurrency level of 100 to fetch the default index page. The web client and the Apache server are in the same LAN. With AppShield, the Apache web server serves requests with 1.20% overhead in throughput, and about 3.05% overhead in waiting time and 1.86% overhead in processing time. We also compare AppShield against Overshadow[6] and InkTag [17] in Table 6. Note that Apache may cache the frequently requested pages, without issuing disk I/O for each request, which helps to reduce the overhead. We also compare the network performances under Overshadow, InkTag and AppShield protections, The results that are listed in Table 6 also indicate that our scheme have the lowest performance overhead and latency on network I/O.

	Linux	AppShield	Overhead
Throughput (req/s)	321	317	1%
Conn. Processing (ms)	160	163	2%
Conn. Waiting (ms)	131	135	3%

Table 5: The benchmark results of Apache performance

	Overhead		
	OverShadow	InkTag	AppShield
Req. Throughput	100%	2%	1%
Conn. Latency	–	13%	3%

Table 6: Network performance comparisons with Overshadow and InkTag.

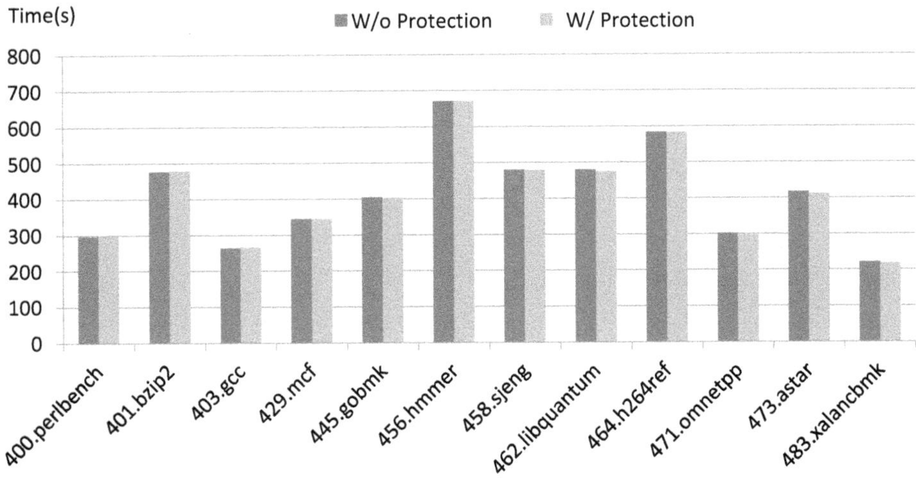

Figure 10: SPECint 2006 Result. AppShield introduces insignificant slowdown.

7. RELATED WORK

There are several approaches proposed to protect application code and data, and all of them attempted to remove the OS out of TCB to provide a higher-assurance execution environment.

7.1 Self-contained Code Protection

Flicker [23] system built on the TPM-based Dynamic Root Of Trust (DROT) technology can create an isolation environment to protect a piece of code and data. Due to the limitation of the TPM, the latency of the Flicker system is quite high. To minimize the latency, TrustVisor [22] scheme are proposed. By leveraging virtualization technology, TrustVisor virtualizes the physical TPM into Virtual TPMs (VTPMs) and migrate them into hypervisor space. Note that both schemes focus on the protection of a small piece of code and data. Both schemes only protect self-contained code with pre-defined inputs and outputs (e.g., inputs are the initial parameters and outputs are the final returns), and they do not support the protection with dynamic memory allocation and system calls. The increasing of the protection scope, such as protecting the whole application, may lead both schemes to failure. MiniBox [20] attempts to extend the functionality of the self-contained code by combining virtualization-based memory isolation and user-space sandbox (e.g., Google Native Client) techniques. But it still have several limitations to support a whole legacy application, such as lack of multi-thread support and limiting to sandbox-capable applications.

7.2 Whole Application Protection

Secure-Processor-Based Protection. AEGIS [29] and XOM OS [21] are secure-processor based approaches that provide compartments to isolate one application from others. Both of them incur poor computability since they require substantial modifications on the OSes and applications. AEGIS [29] also provide an alternative implementation, which requires to build security into the OS.

Bastion [2] and SecureME [9] aim to deal with untrusted OS and untrusted hardware attacks simultaneously with the assistance of a secure processor. Bastion focuses on the protection of a security module, while SecureME attempts to provide privacy and integrity for data and code of the application. SecureME requires modifications on both OSes and applications.

In addition, a Processor-Measured Application Protection Service P-MAPS [25] is announced by Intel, which is built upon Intel TXT [18] and Intel VT [19] hardware capabilities. P-MAPS provides runtime isolation to protect standard applications with small TCB. P-MAPS is quite similar to our scheme at a high level. However, the details of P-MAPS are unavailable for public to conduct an in-depth comparison.

Intel Software Guard Extensions (SGX) technology [10] is able to to protect an application by extending hardware processors. It introduces Enclave - isolated memory of code and data within an application's address space. It enforces that only code executing within the enclave can access data within the same enclave. Any accesses even they are from privileged software or SMM will be rejected. The exchanged data between processor cache and main memory are encrypted. Thus, bus sniffing attack does not work. Comparing with AppShield, Intel SGX could achieve stronger security (e.g., it is able to defend against the bus sniffing attack which would work in AppShield). However, its performance would be slower as it requires lots of encryptions and decryptions on data exchange between processor cache and main memory. Note that all memory accesses in AppShield setting is native speed, without any encryption or decryption.

Microkernel-Based Protection. EROS[26], Perseus[24], Microsoft's NGSCB [13] and Nizza [16] are microkernel(or small kernel) based solutions. They attempt to run commodity OS and untrusted applications in the low-assurance partitions, and run the applications with higher security requirements in the high-assurance partitions, which are isolated and protected by the microkernel itself. However, all of them incur compatibility issue since they may require splitting or even redesigning on the applications.

Virtualization-Based Protection. The approaches like TERRA [14] and Proxos [31] are hypervisor-based trust partitioning systems. They protect applications by isolating them into trusted domains with application-specific OSes. These systems incurs large TCB since they include all secure domains inside. In addition, they are still vulnerable once the application-specific OSes are compromised.

OverShadow [6], CHAOS [5] and SP^3 [34] aim to protect the whole application execution against malicious application and OSes. However, all of them need complex encryption and decryption operations on the application data. Obviously, these additional costly cryptographic operations may reduce the performance and increase the latency of the whole system, especially for the protected application. In addition, none of them claims that they protect applications from the mapping reorder attack. Thus, the data and code integrity may still be broken by potentially compromised OS. InkTag [17] is an approach that protects the whole application and verifies the OS behaviors through paraverfication technique. The paraverfication technique needs to modify the source code of the kernel, which is not always available. Thus, it may lead to the failure of the protection on the close-source OSes, e.g., Windows. Virtual Ghost [12] provides application security by providing *ghost memory*. However, it requires compiler instrumentation on kernel code that is not always available for commodity platforms. In addition, it requires *complete* control-flow integrity checking at runtime, which is extremely hard to achieve in reality.

BIOS-Based Protection. Lockdown [33] system relies on a BIOS-assisted lightweight hypervisor and an ACPI-based mechanism to provide two switchable worlds - green world for trusted applications and red world for untrusted applications. Lockdown uses a trusted path built upon LEDs to provide a verifiable protection. The main drawback of the Lockdown system is the switch latency is too high, roughly 40 seconds. SecureSwitch [30] system that is quite similar to Lockdown also leverages a BIOS-assisted mechanism for secure instantiation and management of trusted execution environments. The switch latency is relatively smaller, roughly 6 seconds. Essentially, both approaches needs to shut down one world to run another one, meaning that they can not simultaneously execute two worlds. However, our AppShield allows the coexistence, meaning the protected applications can simultaneously executed with the untrusted/unprotected applications in a system.

8. CONCLUSIONS

In this paper, we have presented the designed and implementation of AppShield, which reliably and flexibly protects critical applications with complete isolation, rich functionalities and high efficiency. The design of AppShield has taken into consideration several newly identified threats where the kernel manipulates the address mapping. We have implemented the prototype of AppShield with a small bare-metal hypervisor. We have evaluated the performance impacts on CPU computation, disk I/O and network I/O using micro and macro benchmarks. The experiments show that AppShield is lightweight and efficient.

9. ACKNOWLEDGMENTS

The authors would like to thank the anonymous reviewers for their insightful comments that greatly helped improve the paper. This research was funded in the Singapore Management University through a research grant *C220/MSS13C005* from the Ministry of Education Academic Research Tier 1.

10. REFERENCES

[1] Paul Barham, Boris Dragovic, Keir Fraser, Steven Hand, Tim Harris, Alex Ho, Rolf Neugebauer, Ian Pratt, and Andrew Warfield. Xen and the art of virtualization. In *SOSP '03: Proceedings of the nineteenth ACM symposium on Operating systems principles*, pages 164–177, New York, NY, USA, 2003. ACM.

[2] D. Champagne and R.B. Lee. Scalable architectural support for trusted software. In *High Performance Computer Architecture (HPCA), 2010 IEEE 16th International Symposium on*, pages 1–12. IEEE, 2010.

[3] David Champagne and Ruby B. Lee. Scalable architectural support for trusted software. pages 1–12. IEEE Computer Society, 2010.

[4] Stephen Checkoway and Hovav Shacham. Iago attacks: why the system call api is a bad untrusted rpc interface. In *Proceedings of the eighteenth international conference on Architectural support for programming languages and operating systems*, ASPLOS '13, pages 253–264, New York, NY, USA, 2013. ACM.

[5] H. Chen, F. Zhang, C. Chen, Z. Yang, R. Chen, B. Zang, P.C. Yew, and W. Mao. Tamper-resistant execution in an untrusted operating system using a virtual machine monitor. Technical Report FDUPPITR-2007-0801, Parallel Processing Institute, Fudan University, August 2007.

[6] Xiaoxin Chen, Tal Garfinkel, E. Christopher Lewis, Pratap Subrahmanyam, Carl A. Waldspurger, Dan Boneh, Jeffrey Dwoskin, and Dan R.K. Ports. Overshadow: a virtualization-based approach to retrofitting protection in commodity operating systems. In *Proceedings of the 13th international conference on Architectural support for programming languages and operating systems*, ASPLOS XIII, pages 2–13, New York, NY, USA, 2008. ACM.

[7] Yueqiang Cheng and Xuhua Ding. Guardian: Hypervisor as security foothold for personal computers. In *Trust and Trustworthy Computing*, pages 19–36. Springer Berlin Heidelberg, 2013.

[8] Yueqiang Cheng, Xuhua Ding, and Robert H. Deng. Driverguard: a fine-grained protection on I/O flows. In *Proceedings of the 16th European conference on Research in computer security*, ESORICS'11, pages 227–244, Berlin, Heidelberg, 2011. Springer-Verlag.

[9] Siddhartha Chhabra, Brian Rogers, Yan Solihin, and Milos Prvulovic. Secureme: a hardware-software approach to full system security. In *Proceedings of the international conference on Supercomputing*, ICS '11, pages 108–119, New York, NY, USA, 2011. ACM.

[10] Intel Corporation. Innovative instructions and software model for isolated execution. http://privatecore.com/wp-content/uploads/2013/06/HASP-instruction-presentation-release.pdf.

[11] Standard Performance Evaluation Corporation. Spec cint2006. http://www.spec.org/.

[12] John Criswell, Nathan Dautenhahn, and Vikram Adve. Virtual ghost: Protecting applications from hostile operating systems. ASPLOS '14, pages 81–96. ACM, 2014.

[13] Paul England, Butler Lampson, John Manferdelli, Marcus Peinado, and Bryan Willman. A trusted open platform. *Computer*, 36(7):55–62, July 2003.

[14] Tal Garfinkel, Ben Pfaff, Jim Chow, Mendel Rosenblum, and Dan Boneh. Terra: a virtual machine-based platform for trusted computing. In *Proceedings of the 9th ACM Symposium on Operating Systems Principles*, pages 193–206, New York, NY, USA, 2003. ACM.

[15] Abel Gordon, Nadav Amit, Nadav Har'El, Muli Ben-Yehuda, Alex Landau, Assaf Schuster, and Dan Tsafrir. Eli: bare-metal performance for i/o virtualization. In *Proceedings of the seventeenth international conference on Architectural Support for Programming Languages and Operating Systems*, ASPLOS XVII, pages 411–422, New York, NY, USA, 2012. ACM.

[16] H. Hartig, M. Hohmuth, N. Feske, C. Helmuth, A. Lackorzynski, F. Mehnert, and M. Peter. The nizza

secure-system architecture. In *Collaborative Computing: Networking, Applications and Worksharing, 2005 International Conference on*, pages 10–pp. IEEE, 2005.

[17] Owen S. Hofmann, Sangman Kim, Alan M. Dunn, Michael Z. Lee, and Emmett Witchel. Inktag: secure applications on an untrusted operating system. In *Proceedings of the eighteenth international conference on Architectural support for programming languages and operating systems*, ASPLOS '13, pages 265–278, New York, NY, USA, 2013. ACM.

[18] Intel. Intel Trusted Execution Technology (Intel TXT) software development guide. Dec 2009.

[19] Intel. Intel 64 and IA-32 architectures software developer's manual combined volumes: 1, 2a, 2b, 2c, 3a, 3b and 3c. October 2011.

[20] Yanlin Li, Adrian Perrig, Jonathan M McCune, James Newsome, Brandon Baker, and Will Drewry. Minibox: A two-way sandbox for x86 native code (cmu-cylab-14-001). 2014.

[21] David Lie, Chandramohan A. Thekkath, and Mark Horowitz. Implementing an untrusted operating system on trusted hardware. In *Proceedings of the nineteenth ACM symposium on Operating systems principles*, SOSP '03, pages 178–192, New York, NY, USA, 2003. ACM.

[22] Jonathan M. McCune, Yanlin Li, Ning Qu, Zongwei Zhou, Anupam Datta, Virgil Gligor, and Adrian Perrig. Trustvisor: Efficient tcb reduction and attestation. In *Proceedings of the 2010 IEEE Symposium on Security and Privacy*, SP '10, pages 143–158, Washington, DC, USA, 2010. IEEE Computer Society.

[23] Jonathan M. McCune, Bryan J. Parno, Adrian Perrig, Michael K. Reiter, and Hiroshi Isozaki. Flicker: an execution infrastructure for tcb minimization. In *Proceedings of the 3rd ACM SIGOPS/EuroSys European Conference on Computer Systems 2008*, Eurosys '08, pages 315–328, New York, NY, USA, 2008. ACM.

[24] B. Pfitzmann, J. Riordan, C. Stüble, M. Waidner, and A. Weber. The perseus system architecture. In *VIS*, pages 1–18, 2001.

[25] R. Sahita, U. Warrier, and P. Dewan. Dynamic software application protection. *Intel Corporation, Apr*, 2009.

[26] J.S. Shapiro. *EROS: A capability system*. PhD thesis, University of Pennsylvania, 1999.

[27] Monirul I. Sharif, Wenke Lee, Weidong Cui, and Andrea Lanzi. Secure in-vm monitoring using hardware virtualization. In *Proceedings of the 16th ACM conference on Computer and communications security*, CCS '09, pages 477–487, New York, NY, USA, 2009. ACM.

[28] Raoul Strackx and Frank Piessens. Fides: selectively hardening software application components against kernel-level or process-level malware. In *Proceedings of the 2012 ACM conference on Computer and communications security*, CCS '12, pages 2–13, New York, NY, USA, 2012. ACM.

[29] G. Edward Suh, Dwaine Clarke, Blaise Gassend, Marten van Dijk, and Srinivas Devadas. Aegis: architecture for tamper-evident and tamper-resistant processing. In *Proceedings of the 17th annual international conference on Supercomputing*, ICS '03, pages 160–171, New York, NY, USA, 2003. ACM.

[30] Kun Sun, Jiang Wang, Fengwei Zhang, and Angelos Stavrou. Secureswitch: Bios-assisted isolation and switch between trusted and untrusted commodity oses. In *Proceedings of the 19th Annual Network and Distributed System Security Symposium*, 2012.

[31] Richard Ta-Min, Lionel Litty, and David Lie. Splitting interfaces: making trust between applications and operating systems configurable. In *Proceedings of the 7th symposium on Operating systems design and implementation*, OSDI '06, pages 279–292, Berkeley, CA, USA, 2006. USENIX Association.

[32] Trusted Computing Group. TPM main specification. Main Specification Version 1.2 rev. 85, February 2005.

[33] Amit Vasudevan, Bryan Parno, Ning Qu, Virgil D. Gligor, and Adrian Perrig. Lockdown: towards a safe and practical architecture for security applications on commodity platforms. In *Proceedings of the 5th international conference on Trust and Trustworthy Computing*, TRUST'12, pages 34–54, Berlin, Heidelberg, 2012. Springer-Verlag.

[34] Jisoo Yang and Kang G. Shin. Using hypervisor to provide data secrecy for user applications on a per-page basis. In *Proceedings of the fourth ACM SIGPLAN/SIGOPS international conference on Virtual execution environments*, VEE '08, pages 71–80, New York, NY, USA, 2008. ACM.

[35] Zongwei Zhou, Virgil D. Gligor, James Newsome, and Jonathan M. McCune. Building verifiable trusted path on commodity x86 computers. In *Proceedings of the IEEE Symposium on Security and Privacy*, May 2012.

Fixing Races For Good: Portable and Reliable UNIX File-System Race Detection

Xiang Cai*
Twitter, Inc.
141 Portland St.
Cambidge, MA
xcai@twitter.com

Rucha Lale*
Credit Suisse
11 Madison Ave.
New York, NY 10010
rucha.lale@credit-suisse.com

Xincheng Zhang*
Google, Inc.
1600 Amphitheater Pkwy.
Mountain View, CA 94043
xinczhan@google.com

Rob Johnson
Computer Science Dept.
Stony Brook University
Stony Brook, NY 11777
rob@cs.stonybrook.edu

ABSTRACT

We present a system for performing arbitrary sequences of file-system operations and provably detecting any violation of serializable isolation semantics, i.e. any interleaving of attacker and defender actions is equivalent to a non-interleaved sequence of attacker and defender actions. Thus, our system provides a provably secure defense against all UNIX file-name race conditions, including the infamous `access/open` race. Our solution operates entirely in user-space and is portable to any POSIX.1-2008 system, making it usable today. Developers can adopt our solution selectively, using it for security-critical code and using the standard POSIX interface for non-security-critical parts of their programs. Furthermore, the proofs of correctness suggest several simple improvements to the POSIX standard.

Categories and Subject Descriptors

K.6.5 [**MANAGEMENT OF COMPUTING AND INFORMATION SYSTEMS**]: Security and Protection—*Unauthorized access*; D.4.6 [**OPERATING SYSTEMS**]: Security and Protection—*Access controls*

General Terms

Security

Keywords

File-system Races; Intrusion Detection; Operating-system Security

*This work was completed while the authors were at Stony Brook University.

ASIA CCS'15, April 14–17, 2015, Singapore..

ACM 978-1-4503-3245-3/15/04 ...$15.00.
http://dx.doi.org/10.1145/2714576.2714581.

1. INTRODUCTION

This paper presents a general, portable, provably correct solution to the UNIX race condition problem [2]. Our solution detects violations of "serializable" isolation semantics for file-name-based operations, i.e. it verifies that a sequence of interleaved attacker and defender actions is equivalent to a sequence of non-interleaved actions with the same result. This frees application developers from the difficult task of reasoning about the correctness of their code when the file system may be changing beneath them. Instead, they can simply prove their algorithms correct in isolation and use our theorem to prove their algorithm is safe in the presence of an attacker. We provide safe implementations of every basic file-system operation, e.g. `open`, `lstat`, etc., and application developers can combine these operations in any order. Applications using our system can declare pseudo-transactions (i.e. transactions guaranteeing only isolation) and can perform inter-process coordination by sharing internal transaction state. Our solution operates entirely in user-space and is portable to any POSIX.1-2008 compliant system.

Our library detects violations of serializable isolation by maintaining an internal model of the file-system state and checking that every access is consistent with the model. Our library performs path resolution, including resolving symbolic links, in user-space so that it can check that every step of the path is consistent with the file-system model.

We performed micro-benchmarks to compare our solution to several previously-proposed solutions to the `access/open` race. Our library out-performs atomic k-race but is slower than the original k-race algorithm and the original `access/open` paradigm. However, this is not an apples-to-apples comparison because none of the competing solutions is secure.

Previous file-system race defenses, discussed in Section 2, all had at least one deficiency: they weren't portable, they weren't secure, or they weren't general. Our implementation is portable to any POSIX.1-2008 system. We provide proofs of security for our algorithms. Programmers can use our library to perform arbitrary sequences of file-system operations with serializable semantics. Furthermore, our library is easy to use – in most cases programmers can simply replace calls to `open` with `trace_open`, etc. The library also provides programmers with direct access to its internal path resolution function which in many cases can enable programmers to further simplify their code.

In summary, we describe an easy-to-use, portable, efficient, and provably-secure library for accessing UNIX file systems without race conditions and that supports arbitrary sequences of operations within each pseudo-transaction.

2. RELATED WORK

UNIX file-system race conditions have been a continuous problem for over two decades [2] and, despite numerous proposals for solving them [2, 5, 6, 8, 11, 12, 13, 16, 18, 20, 21, 22, 23], there is still no general, portable, secure way for applications to access the file system in a race-free way [11]. File systems are such a fundamental component of any operating system, it is surprising that this problem has persisted for so long. File-system race conditions are an important class of security vulnerabilities. The Common Vulnerabilities and Exposures database lists 46 file-system race conditions discovered in the last 5 years [9], almost all of which enable an attacker to obtain root privileges. This list certainly under-estimates the prevalence of file race conditions, since these bugs are subtle and since almost every application must access the file system in some way. CWE includes general race conditions in their 2009 list of "Top 25 Most Dangerous Programming Errors" [7], and include file-system race conditions as an important subset of this class of bugs. Unlike buffer overflows, applications written in any language can contain file access race conditions, and there is currently no known, general way for application developers to avoid these vulnerabilities. Researchers have shown that, contrary to popular belief, these bugs are easy to exploit reliably [3, 4].

Previously proposed solutions are inadequate. Static analyses for detecting file-system races in application source code [2, 5, 17] have numerous false positives and negatives and, even when they do detect a bug, the developer may not have any easy way to fix it. Kernel-based run-time race detectors and preventers are OS-specific, may not catch all kinds of races [8], may be vulnerable to attack [4], and have not seen widespread use. The user-space path-walking solution proposed by Tsafrir, et al., is not general – it is designed specifically for "check/use" system call pairs and hence does not check consistency across multiple file-system operations. Our system fixes both these deficiencies. Several researchers have proposed improvements to the UNIX file-system interface [11]. Some of these extensions are simple, cleanly solve specific race conditions (e.g. the `O_RUID` flag to `open`), and hence have a reasonable chance of being standardized within the next decade. More general solutions, such as OS or file-system transactions [15, 23], are worthy long-term goals, but are unlikely to become standardized in commercial UNIX systems within the next decade, leaving developers and administrators unable to avoid these vulnerabilities. Researchers have also proposed probabilistic race defenses [11, 18], but these schemes have repeatedly been shown to be non-secure [3, 4]. As a result, in current practice, each program contains its own custom routines for accessing the file system in a race-free way. This results in duplication of functionality, forces many programmers to become experts in file-system semantics, limitations, and quirks, and causes numerous security vulnerabilities.

Our solution builds on the notion of user-space path walking [19] and ideas from kernel-based race condition detectors [4]. User-space path walking moves the task of resolving symbolic links and multi-component paths from the OS to applications, enabling programs to enforce application-specific filename resolution policies. Kernel-based detectors keep a table of file lookup results and verify that they are consistent. Kernel-based detectors are not portable and are imperfect because they do not have knowledge of the application's file-system transactions [4]. Our solution moves both path resolution and consistency checks to user-space, yielding a portable and complete solution to UNIX race conditions.

3. UNIX RACE CONDITIONS

Figure 1 shows several code snippets that are vulnerable to race-condition attacks. In Figure 1(a), a setuid-root program attempts to open a file accessible by its invoker but, by changing the file system between the `access` and `open` calls, an attacker can trick this program into reading any file on the system. The `deltree` function in Figure 1(b) is derived from a real bug in a `/tmp` cleaning program [20]. By moving `dir` while the program is inside, an attacker can trick the cleaner into deleting files of his choice. Figure 1(c) shows a program that checks for the existence of a file and creates it if it does not exist. An attacker that creates the file, or even just a link to an existing file, after the existence check can control the owner and permissions of the file and can insert arbitrary data into it. The `run` function in Figure 1(d) is a simplified version of a race condition in the suPHP program [10]. suPHP allows users to run PHP scripts with the user ID of the script file's owner, but if the script file is specified through a symbolic link, then the link must have the same owner as the link's target. An attacker could change the target of the link immediately before or after the last call to `lstat` in order to run arbitrary code with another user's privileges.

These examples demonstrate several important points that we must keep in mind when designing a solution to the UNIX file-system race problem:

- Race conditions can involve many different file operations, such as `chdir`, `open`, `access`, `chmod`, `creat`, `mkdir`, etc., so our solution must cover all these operations.
- The `deltree` example, demonstrates that two related calls may be separated by a large number of intervening file access operations, so a solution that handles only pairs of related calls is not adequate.
- A filename may consist of several path components, such as `/tmp/foo/bar`, and an attacker may attempt to change any one of these components during an attack.
- Race conditions can involve many different file properties – existence, non-existence, protection bits, their location within the file system, etc. – so we should provide isolation for all these properties.
- Races can involve system calls that fail, as in the `stat` in Figure 1(c), so our defense system should provide race detection for all calls, even failing ones.
- Programmers tend to write file-system code in the most straightforward way they can, so our safe access library should provide race-free access no matter how the programmer uses it.

Note that none of the vulnerable programs in Figure 1 involve file contents. This is not an accident. None of the 46 race condition bugs we surveyed involved races on file contents, so we exclude file contents from the scope of our solution. We believe this is justified for two reasons. First, as noted before, content races are extremely rare. Second, content races can occur only after a malicious program has gained access to a sensitive file. By preventing races on file meta-data operations, such as permission changes and file creation events, we can prevent most races on the content within those files. Our defense mechanism does detect changes to a file's size in certain cases, though. For example, many programmers assume that, after creating a file, it will have size 0. We detect violations of this natural assumption where appropriate. We leave extending our solution to file contents as future work.

```
void main(int argc, char **argv)
{
  int fd;
  if (access(argv[1], R_OK) != 0)
    exit(1);
  fd = open(argv[1], O_RDONLY);
  /* Use fd... */
}
```

(a)

```
void deltree(char *dir)
{
  chdir(dir);
  /* Recursively delete
     contents of dir ... */
  chdir("..");
}
```

(b)

```
int mktmpfile(char *fname)
{
  int fd = -1;
  struct stat buf;
  if (stat(fname,
           &buf) < 0)
    fd = open(fname,
              O_CREAT,
              S_IRWXU);
  return fd;
}
```

(c)

```
int run(char *exe)
{
  struct stat s[3];
  lstat(exe, &s[0]);
  stat(exe, &s[1]);
  if (s[0].st_uid != s[1].st_uid)
    exit(1);
  lstat(exe, &s[2]);
  setreuid(s[2].st_uid,
           s[2].st_uid);
  execl(exe, NULL);
}
```

(d)

Figure 1: Four example programs vulnerable to race attacks. (a) An attacker can change the mapping from filenames to files between the `access` and `open` calls, tricking the program into opening a secret file. (b) An attacker can move `dir` while the programming is traversing the sub-tree beneath `dir`, causing the program to delete files it did not intend to delete. (c) An attacker can create the file before the victim does, and hence can control the permissions and owner of the file, or even cause the program to open some other file that already exists on the system. (d) An attacker that modifies the symbolic link `exe` either immediately before or after the last call to `lstat` can execute arbitrary code as another user.

4. DESIGN OVERVIEW

Our goal is to provide isolation for a defender program. Any interleaving of actions by the defender and another process should either result in a "consistency error" or be equivalent to a non-interleaved ordering of the defender and other process' actions. To be specific, each time the defender tries to access an object in the file system, it will check that observed information about the object is consistent with previously-observed file-system state. Note that we focus only on the defender's view of the file system because we do not provide isolation for the attacker, and hence it is reasonable and sufficient to just look at the defender's file-system accesses.

In order to obtain enough information about the defender's access to the file system, we need to solve two problems:

- We should verify consistency for all the defender's file-system accesses, including intermediate directories accessed while resolving a longer path.
- The defender should access each file-system object atomically.

Figure 2 shows our design overview. We perform the path resolution in user-space so that we can observe all the file-system accesses performed by the defender. As shown in Figure 2, the user-space path walker will resolve each component, *atom*, of a given path, and get certain information about *atom* by calling the atomic accessor. It then compares the information with the file-system model's previous state to see whether there is any inconsistency. If the consistency check is satisfied, it will proceed to the next component in the path, repeating this process until it reaches the end of the path.

The atomic accessor interacts with the real file system and is guaranteed to access the object atomically. After accessing the *atom*, the atomic accessor will return all the information needed to perform consistency checks against the file-system model. The implementation of atomic accessor will be discussed later on.

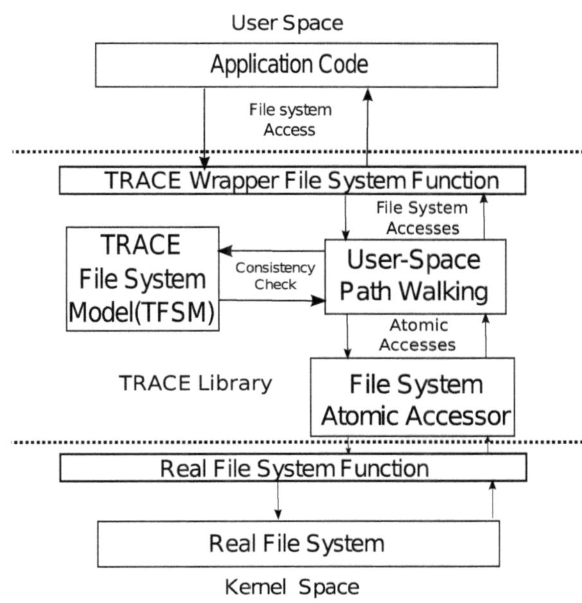

Figure 2: Design Overview.

5. FILE-SYSTEM MODEL

We must prove our algorithms correct with respect to some model of the UNIX file system and API. This model must specify the operations available to the attacker and defender and how those operations can be interleaved. This model will also make explicit which aspects of the file system are not covered by our solution. We first explain the UNIX file system as a graph with nodes and edges. We then describe the operations the attacker can perform on the file system. Our model gives the attacker a powerful low-level inter-

```
struct stat {
  dev_t      st_dev;      /* ID of device holding file */
  ino_t      st_ino;      /* inode number */
  mode_t     st_mode;     /* protection */
  nlink_t    st_nlink;    /* number of hard links */
  uid_t      st_uid;      /* user ID of owner */
  gid_t      st_gid;      /* group ID of owner */
  dev_t      st_rdev;     /* device ID if special file */
  off_t      st_size;     /* total size, in bytes */
  blksize_t st_blksize;  /* file system I/O blocksize */
  blkcnt_t   st_blocks;   /* num. alloced 512B blocks */
  time_t     st_atime;    /* time of last access */
  time_t     st_mtime;    /* time of last modification */
  time_t     st_ctime;    /* time of last status mod */
};
```

Figure 3: The inode information returned by `stat` [14].

face for manipulating the file system. The defender, however, must work with the standard POSIX API, so we finish by describing our assumptions about the POSIX calls used by our defense.

The file-system model. We model the file system as a directed graph with edges labeled by path components. We will treat links from one directory to another as two links: the link from parent to child and the ".." link from child to parent. Nodes in the graph correspond to allocated file-system inodes and edges correspond to file-system hard links. Each node has some associated meta-data, as represented by the POSIX-defined `stat` structure, shown in Figure 3.

We assume the reader is familiar with the POSIX file-system API, but make a few clarifying remarks. We assume that the type of an inode cannot be changed after the inode is allocated – we know of no operating system that allows such an operation. Similarly, we assume the `st_rdev` field cannot be changed once an inode is allocated. Most UNIX kernels allow at most one link to directory inodes – our defense will respect this limit, but we will consider attackers that can violate it. We will allow attackers to make multiple links to a single directory, but we will constrain each directory's ".." link to point back to one of its parents. We will assume the ".." entry is always available, so the attacker can only change it atomically from one parent to another. Although the target of symbolic links is not contained in the POSIX `stat` structure, we will model it as another inode attribute. For technical reasons explained later, we assume that the defender only tests whether a file's `st_nlink` field is non-zero.

We assume that inode numbers are never re-used. Many operating systems now support generation numbers in inodes, enabling us to detect when inode numbers are re-used. In those OSes, as long as the OS never re-uses an inode number-generation number ordered pair, our algorithm will be secure.

Attacker operations. Given this graph-based file-system model, an attacker can perform only a few basic operations: allocate a new inode, lookup the inode referenced by a directory entry, create a new link or destroy an existing link, and get or set an inode's meta-data attributes. We can further simplify this model by ignoring any attacker operations that do not modify the file system, i.e. link and attribute lookups. Writes to a file's contents will, in our model, simply be optional updates to the file's size attribute. Table 1 summarizes the file-system operations available to the attacker in our model. We assume that each of these operations is executed atomically within the kernel.

Access-control is governed by each object's owner (`st_uid`), group (`st_gid`), and permission bits encoded in `st_mode`. We assume that the attacker is not root and does not control any process with the same user-ID as the defender. An attacker with root privileges or with the same UID as the defender does not need to exploit file-system race conditions – she can directly modify the file system herself. The attacker and defender may share one or more group IDs. We assume the OS implements the POSIX access control rules, with the following clarification that we have observed in real systems: creating and removing links require both search and write permissions on the directory containing the link.

We assume the attacker can perform any of the basic operations – allocate, link, unlink, and setattr – at any point in time as long as the permissions checks pass at that moment and as long as the atomicity assumptions described below are preserved.

Defense assumptions. Our solution uses file-descriptor-based POSIX system calls, such as `fstat`, `close`, `fchdir`, etc., the POSIX-standardized "at" system calls, e.g. `openat`, `fstatat`, `readlinkat`, etc., and a few other special-purpose APIs, such as `chroot`, that have no file-descriptor-based or at-style counterpart. We assume that file-descriptor-based calls execute atomically. We assume that at-style APIs execute atomically when called with a pathname that consists of a single path component (i.e. one that does not contain "/" or is exactly equal to "/") and when passed any required flags to prevent them from following symbolic links. We will use the miscellaneous other functions in a restricted way that will make concurrency a non-issue, e.g. all call to `chroot` are of the form `chroot(".")`. We also assume that these system calls do not modify any objects in the filesystem other than those specified in the arguments to the call. Otherwise, our defense might incorrectly flag those changes as races.

We believe that the system calls described above will execute atomically. The key observation is that the results of these system calls only depend on a few pieces of filesystem state – the attributes of a directory inode, the state of a link in that directory, and the attributes of the target inode of the link – and that each piece of state only needs to be examined once during the execution of the system call. Thus any concurrent operations performed by the attacker must occur either before or after the defender's system examines the affected object, and hence can be viewed as happening either before or after the defender's entire system call. Furthermore, our recent experimental work on race attacks on Linux, FreeBSD, OpenBSD, and OpenSolaris found empirically that, on all the systems, these types of system calls executed atomically [4].

6. SERIALIZABLE FILE-SYSTEM ACCESS

Our goal is to provide file-system access that programmers can reason about extremely easily. The simplest scenario for developers to reason about is isolated access, i.e. their program is the only program running on the system, so we will strive to create the illusion of perfect isolation, i.e. serializable isolation [1]. The notion of serializable isolation comes from the database community, where a database is said to support serializable isolation if there exists an ordering of all the transactions executed on the database such that the result is the same as the (possibly interleaved) execution ordering that the database actually performs.

Our system deviates from a pure database-oriented approach in several ways. First, since we are not assuming OS support, we cannot assume that all operations on the file system will be using our file access protocol. For example, if our system maintains an internal set of locks, there is no reason to expect an attacker to respect our locking discipline. Our system does not handle roll-back in the event of an isolation failure. This would be desirable, but is difficult to accomplish without OS support. Instead, our solution merely in-

Operation	Notes
inode allocate(device, type, ...)	Allocate a new inode with the given type. For symlinks, the additional parameter specifies the target. For device files, the parameter specifies the target device.
link(inode src, inode dst, string name)	Creates the link "name" in the directory specified by inode src to the object (file or directory) dst.
unlink(inode src, string name)	Deletes the link "name" from the directory specified by inode src.
setattr(inode i, field f, int value)	Updates meta-data field f of inode i with the given value.

Table 1: Our model of file-system operations available to the attacker.

forms the defending application of the violation. In the database notion of isolation, the serialized schedule and interleaved schedule must consist of the same sets of operations – only the order is different. In our system, we require only a one-sided notion of isolation in which the defender's actions are unchanged. We guarantee only that an interleaving of defender and attacker actions is equivalent to a non-interleaved sequence of the same defender actions and *possibly different* attacker actions. Thus any attack that can be accomplished by an interleaved attacker can also be accomplished by a non-interleaved attacker.

Preliminaries. Our proofs will take a sequence of interleaved attacker and defender actions and modify them, without changing the state of the defender or the final state of the file system, so that all the attacker actions occur before or after all the defender actions. Note that we can assume the attacker performs all its calls to allocate() before the defender takes any actions. This assumption is safe since the defender cannot read or write the allocated objects until they have links created to them, which must occur after they are allocated. Thus, any sequence of attacker actions can be reduced to a triple (D, A, S), where D is a set of edges to be deleted from the graph, A is a set of edges to be created in the graph, and S is a set of setattr operations to be performed on nodes of the graph.

6.1 Serializable `open`/`fstat`

User-space path walking requires programs to `openat` each path component and obtain its `stat` information, so the walker can determine whether the component is a directory, symlink, or file. The generally accepted "race-free" method for doing this is to call `openat` on the component and use `fstat` to obtain the `stat` information. Although the file-descriptor returned by `openat` is an immutable reference to the file, this method cannot detect all serializability violations, and it also is not applicable when the call to `openat` fails. Fore example, when the `openat` fails, e.g. with `EEXIST`, we would still like to obtain stat information for the file so we can check consistency of future system calls involving that file. In this case, we must use the `fstatat` system call. We must further check that the results of the `fstatat` system call are consistent with the error code returned by `openat`. For example, `fstatat` should not fail with `ENOENT` after the `openat` fails with `EEXIST`.

Algorithm 1 shows our routine for opening and stating a file, and Table 2 summarizes the consistency checks performed by the OPENSTAT-CHECK routine. Intuitively, the OPENSTAT routine performs the `openat/fstat` algorithm and then checks that all the error codes and `stat` information are consistent. For example, if the `openat` call failed with `EACCES`, then OPENSTAT-CHECK verifies that the permissions in the stat information are consistent with this outcome.

Theorem 1. *Suppose that* OPENSTAT *is called with valid flags that contain `O_EXCL` if they contain `O_CREAT`, a valid file-descriptor that was created with the `O_SEARCH` and `O_DIRECTORY` flags, an atom argument that does not contain "/" or is equal to "/". For any interleaving of attacker actions, if* OPENSTAT *does not throw `ERACEDETECTED`, then there is a non-interleaved sequence of attacker actions that yields the same defender and file-system state.*

Algorithm 1 Routine for opening and stat-ing a file and detecting any violations of serializable semantics.

```
Require: If flags & O_CREAT, then flags & O_EXCL.
function OPENSTAT(parent, parent-fd, atom, flags, mode)
    child ←⊥
    child-fd ← openat (parent-fd, atom, flags, mode)
    openerrno ← errno

    if child-fd ≥ 0 then
        if fstat (child-fd, &child.stat-info) ≠ 0 then
            throw ERACEDETECTED
    else
        child-fd ← openerrno   ▷ Return open error in child-fd
        fstatat (parent-fd, atom, &child.stat-info,
                 AT_SYMLINK_NOFOLLOW)
        staterrno ← errno
        if IS-SYMBOLIC-LINK(child.stat-info) then
            if readlinkat (parent-fd, atom,
                           child.symlink-target,
                           PATH_MAX) ≠ 0 then
                throw ERACEDETECTED

    ▷ Throw ERACEDETECTED if there is an inconsistency.
    OPENSTAT-CHECK(parent, flags, mode, child, openerrno,
                   staterrno)
    return (child, child-fd)
```

Proof: Suppose the file system is in state F when the defender calls `openat`, that afterwards it is in state F', that the attacker then performs edge deletions D, edge additions A, and setattrs S, transitioning the file system to state F'', and then the defender executes its stat call, as shown below:

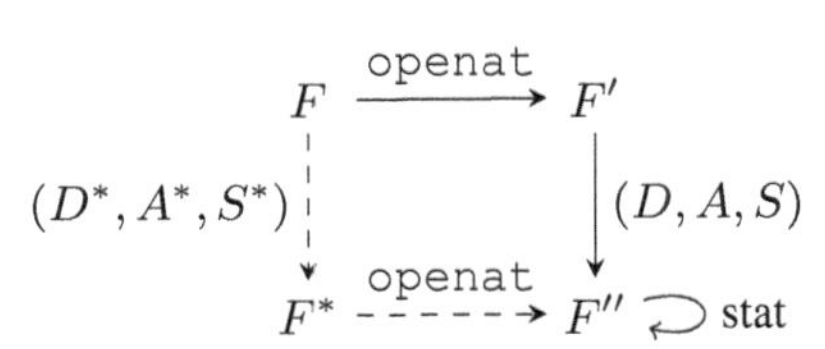

We will show that, if OPENSTAT does not throw `ERACEDETECTED`, then there exists a file system state F^* and sequence of attacker actions a (D^*, A^*, S^*) that complete the above diagram, i.e. they result in the same final file-system state and yield the same results to the defender's `openat` and stat calls.

Define F^* as follows. If $F = F'$, i.e. if the `openat` call did not create a new file, then set $F^* = F''$. Otherwise, set F^* equal to F'' with the node pointed to by the "atom" edge, and the "atom" edge

flags	openerrno	staterrno	Additional conditions
O_CREAT	Success	N/A	User can write to parent and child looks new, i.e. has the requested permission bits (minus umask bits), is of the correct file type (i.e. is not a symlink), has a link count of one, has correct owner, has a valid group, and has size zero.
!O_CREAT	Success	N/A	Child is not a symlink, has at least one hard link, is a directory if O_DIRECTORY was specified, has permissions consistent with requested access (i.e. read and/or write), and has size zero if O_TRUNC was specified.
O_CREAT	EACCES	ENOENT	Defender lacks write permission on parent.
*	EACCES	Success	Defender lacks requested access to file.
O_CREAT	EEXIST	Success	None
*	EISDIR	Success	Defender requested write access.
*	ELOOP	Success	Child is a symlink and has size equal to the string-length of the link's target path.
!O_CREAT	ENOENT	ENOENT	None
O_DIRECTORY	ENOTDIR	Success	Child is not a directory.

Table 2: Rules for checking consistency of results obtained during OPENSTAT. Any result not listed in this table indicates a potential race condition. Keep in mind that any call to OPENSTAT where O_CREAT is set must also set O_EXCL.

itself, removed. We know that, if $F \neq F'$, then F'' must contain an "atom" edge because otherwise OPENSTAT-CHECK would have throw ERACEDETECTED. We also know that the file pointed to by this edge must be equivalent to a newly created file, i.e. its size is 0, it has exactly one hard link, etc.

By examining Table 2, one can verify that executing openat on a file system in state F^* will transition the file system to state F'' and will yield the same results as executing openat on F. Thus the bottom edge in the above diagram exists.

We now just need to show there exists an a^* that transforms F into F^*.

If $F' = F$, then define $(D^*, A^*, S^*) = (D, A, S)$. In this case, executing (D^*, A^*, S^*) on state F is the same as executing (D, A, S) in state F', which will yield file system state $F'' = F^*$.

Now suppose that $F' \neq F$, i.e. the defender's openat call creates a new file, "atom". If the attacker doesn't modify this link or the attributes of the newly-created file, then we can execute the attackers actions on file system F, as above.

If the attacker deletes this newly created link, then, since the later call to OPENSTAT-CHECK succeeds, he must recreate it. The recreated link may point to a different file, but that file must be functionally indistinguishible from the new file created by the defender, i.e. it must have the same owner, must have size 0, must have exactly 1 link to it in state F'', etc.

So we have two cases. If the attacker leaves the newly-created link unchanged, then he also cannot perform any changes to the attributes of the newly created file, since otherwise OPENSTAT-CHECK would detect the changes. In this case, we can execute (D, A, S) on file system state F to transform it into state F^*.

If the attacker changes the "atom" link from pointing to the newly created file f' to a previously existing file f'', he may also then perform some setattr calls on f' and f''. The setattr calls on f'', however, must leave it in the state of a newly created file. Thus, in this case, the attacker can transform F into F^* by performing the same sequence of actions, except applying all changes to f' to f'', instead. In other words, the attacker does not change the "atom" link to point to f''; any edges it created to point to f' should be created to point to f'' instead; and any setattr calls the attacker performed on f' should be performed on f'' instead.

Finally, the defender may also modify the file system by specifying the O_TRUNC flag. In this case, F^* should be equal to F'', except that the size of the file pointed to by the "atom" link should be the same as it is in F. It is easy to verify that, in this case, the attacker's original sequence of operations, (S, A, D), will transform F into F^*. ■

We now point out several subtleties of the theorem and proof.

There are a few cases in the POSIX specification where implementers have some choice as to which error code to return. For example, if the flags to openat are O_RDONLY | O_DIRECTORY[1], and the path refers to a non-directory for which the calling process does not have read permission, then the kernel may return either EACCES or ENOTDIR. An attacker could use this ambiguity to modify the file system between the openat and fstatat calls without detection, as long as he modifies it to a new state that is consistent with the results of the openat.

Real kernels will presumably check these conditions in some order and therefore will always return one or the other. To be portable, our consistency-checking routine can verify only that a kernel is allowed by the POSIX standard to return the observed error code, it cannot verify that the actual kernel would behave as observed. Thus there may be some interleavings of attacker actions on real kernels which are not equivalent to non-interleaved sequences on the same kernel, yet which are accepted by OPENSTAT-CHECK.

POSIX-compliant applications should assume the kernel might return any valid error code in these situations, though, and therefore should be unaffected.

We also do not support O_CREAT without O_EXCL due to its inherent ambiguity. First, POSIX is not clear what happens when an openat call has flags O_RDONLY | O_CREAT and the given path refers to a readable directory. The POSIX standard states that, if the file exists, the O_CREAT flag should have no effect unless O_EXCL is also set, so the openat call should succeed. However, the presence of the O_CREAT flag strongly suggests the application intends to open a file, and implementations we have tested return an error in this case. Second, using the O_CREAT flag without O_EXCL can result in some non-serializable sequences of events. For example, if the openat call creates a new file and the attacker is able to write to it before the fstat call, then any equivalent non-interleaved sequence must have the attacker create the atom link to a non-empty file with the defender's user ID before the openat call. If, for example, the file system contains no files owned by the defender, then this is impossible. Applications that need the O_CREAT behavior can emulate it by using our routines to open the

[1]Indicating that the openat should succeed only if the path refers to a directory.

file without O_CREAT and, if that fails, try again with O_CREAT | O_EXCL.

A POSIX-aware operating system may define additional error codes that are not part of the POSIX standard or may re-use POSIX error codes for other error conditions. Alternatively, some systems may allow openat and other system calls to succeed even though the stat information examined by OPENSTAT-CHECK indicates the call should fail. For example, systems that implement the POSIX draft standard for ACLs can allow a call to succeed even when the standard permission bits indicate it should fail. In these cases, OPENSTAT-CHECK will return ERACEDETECTED even though no race may have occurred. Thus, our system will have false positives whenever the behavior of the underlying operating system deviates from strict POSIX compliance.

Some applications may not need the full protection provided by our scheme. For example, if an application never looks at the value of the st_nlink field, then it doesn't matter if the attacker causes any changes to this field. For such an application, the strict checking performed by OPENSTAT might cause false positives. These applications could use a relaxed version of OPENSTAT customized to their needs. However, this paper presents an OPENSTAT implementation that can detect serializability violations for all applications.

6.2 Serializable User-space Path Walking

Algorithm 2 Algorithm for checking the consistency of parent/child links between directories.

```
T ← empty table

function PATHRES-CHECK(parent, atom, openflags, new-child-info, child-fd)
    if ∃ entry of form (parent, atom, old-child-info) ∈ T then
        if old-child-info, new-child-info, openflags, and child-fd match any of the conditions in Table 3 then
            return OK
        else
            throw ERACEDETECTED
    else
        return OK

function RECORD-LINK(source-info, atom, dest-info)
    if (source-info, atom, dest-info) ∈ T then
        return
    if atom ≠".." ∧ IS-DIRECTORY(dest-info) then
        PATHRES-CHECK(dest-info, "..", 0, source-info, 0)
        RECORD-LINK(dest-info, ".." source-info)
    if ∃ an entry of form (source-info, atom, DNE) ∈ T then
        remove it                          ▷ OPENSTAT created a file.
    insert (source-info, atom, dest-info) into T
```

The OPENSTAT routine can handle only a single path component. The PATHRES routine presented in Algorithm 3 makes repeated calls to OPENSTAT and performs additional consistency checks in order to handle arbitrary paths while verifying serializable isolation semantics.

The PATHRES function walks the given path, using OPENSTAT (or recursive calls to itself) to obtain file-descriptors for each atom. As it walks the path, it keeps an open file handle for the previous path component, which is used by some of the consistency checks and some higher-level operations discussed in Section 6.3. As with OPENSTAT, PATHRES does not allow O_CREAT without O_EXCL in its flags argument. The PATHRES function also needs information about the current working directory so that it knows where to start resolutions. This is also used when resolving symbolic links, since links are resolved relative to the directory in which they reside.

Algorithm 3 The main user-space path resolution algorithm. Upon success, returns stat information and file-descriptors about the last two elements in path. Note that if the last element of the path does not exist, then it still returns information about the second-to-last element.

```
Require: The path is not the empty string, and if flags &
    O_CREAT, then flags & O_EXCL.
function PATHRES(cwd, cwd-fd, path, flags, mode)
    child ← cwd
    child-fd ← dup (cwd-fd)
    parent ← ⊥
    parent-fd ← −1

    for each atom in path do
            ▷ Close old file descriptors and shift child to parent.
        if child-fd < 0 then
            throw child-fd
        if parent-fd ≥ 0 then
            close (parent-fd)
        parent ← child
        parent-fd ← child-fd
        child ← ⊥
        child-fd ← −1

                        ▷ Decide whether atom must be a directory.
        if atom is not the last element of path then
            openflags ← O_SEARCH | O_DIRECTORY
        else if atom ends with "/" then
            openflags ← flags | O_DIRECTORY
        else
            openflags ← flags

        (child, child-fd) ← OPENSTAT(parent, parent-fd, atom,
                                     openflags, mode)
        PATHRES-CHECK(parent, atom, openflags, child,
                      child-fd)
        RECORD-LINK(parent, atom, child)

                                ▷ Recursively resolve symbolic links.
        if IS-SYMBOLIC-LINK(child.stat-info) then
            if atom is not last element of path then
                (parent, parent-fd, child, child-fd)
                ← PATHRES(parent, parent-fd,
                          child.symlink-target,
                          O_SEARCH | O_DIRECTORY,
                          mode)
            else if !(flags & O_NOFOLLOW) then
                (parent, parent-fd, child, child-fd)
                ← PATHRES(parent, parent-fd,
                          child.symlink-target,
                          flags, mode)

    return (parent, parent-fd, child, child-fd)
```

The consistency-checking routine keeps state about earlier name lookups and checks that the current lookup results are consistent with the stored results. We say that the total set of observed results is consistent if the defender could observe those results while exe-

Old child info	New child info	openflags	child-fd	Other conditions
No info	*	*	*	None
DNE	DNE	*	< 0	None
DNE	$\neq$DNE	O_CREAT	≥ 0	None
d	d'	!O_CREAT	*	$d = d'$
d	d'	O_CREAT	< 0	$d = d'$

Table 3: PATHRES-CHECK consistency rules. Any outcome not listed in this table causes PATHRES-CHECK to throw ERACEDETECTED. In this table, "DNE" means that the information indicates that the file does not exist.

cuting in isolation. From the file-system model in Section 5, there are four aspects to consistency:

- Two lookups of the same atom in the same directory should produce the same result, i.e. the atom should either not exist in both lookups or point to the same target in both lookups.
- The attributes associated with any inode should be the same every time the defender examines them.
- The link ".." in directory d points to a directory d' iff there exists a link in d' that points to d.
- The defender should never observe more links to an inode than are indicated in the inode's st_nlink field. Since we assume the defender does not examine the st_nlink field except to observe whether it is non-zero, we actually need to enforce only a weaker condition: the defender never observes a link to an inode with st_nlink equal to 0. This is enforced by OPENSTAT-CHECK, which verifies that all stat information it obtains has st_nlink greater than zero.

The only exception to these invariants is that, when the defender modifies the file system, e.g. by creating a new file, it should expect to see the effects of that change in future file-system accesses.

The PATHRES-CHECK and RECORD-LINK functions check these invariants. The PATHRES-CHECK function checks that each observation of the same file-system object gives the same results. RECORD-LINK checks that parent/child directory links are consistent.

Both functions use a table of results of past file-system operations. Entries in the table are of the form (d, n, c), where d is the stat information for some directory, n is a single path component, and c is the stat information (and symlink target, if applicable) obtained from a call to OPENSTAT with d as the parent directory and n as the atom. Note that c can therefore take on two basic forms – positive entries indicating that the given n existed last time it was looked up, or negative entries indicating that n did not exist.

PATHRES-CHECK uses its parent and atom arguments to lookup results from the last time it performed a lookup on atom in parent. It then verifies that the new information about the child is consistent with the old information. Table 3 shows the consistency-checking rules. PATHRES-CHECK verifies that, when old information about the child is available and the OPENSTAT did not create a new file, the old results are identical to the new results. Since the child info contains the device and inode numbers of the child, comparing this information implicitly confirms that the old and new results refer to the same file-system object. Thus, PATHRES-CHECK enforces the first two consistency rules mentioned above.

RECORD-LINK enforces the consistency of parent/child links and updates the table of observations. RECORD-LINK enforces consistency by treating every resolution of a forward link as if it were also a resolution of the implied ".." link. It then calls PATHRES-CHECK to verify that the implied ".." link is consistent with any actual resolutions of the ".." link in the dest-info directory. This ensures that the results obtained when resolving forward links are consistent with results from resolving ".." links.

Theorem 2. *Suppose* PATHRES *is called with cwd, cwd-fd, and flags s.t. cwd-fd was created with O_DIRECTORY | O_SEARCH, cwd is the corresponding* stat *information, and flags has O_EXCL if it has O_CREAT. If* PATHRES *does not throw ERACEDETECTED, then its execution is serializable.*

Proof: First, notice that PATHRES only interacts with the file system through OPENSTAT. The other two system calls that it makes – dup and close – only inspect and update the defender's open file table and hence cannot be affected by attacker actions.

Furthermore, a simple inductive argument shows that PATHRES always calls OPENSTAT with valid parent, parent-fd, atom, and flags arguments, as defined in Theorem 1. If PATHRES does not throw ERACEDETECTED, then none of its calls to OPENSTAT could have thrown ERACEDETECTED, either. Thus all the OPENSTAT calls are, individually, serializable.

As argued above, if all the results obtained via OPENSTAT pass all the consistency checks defined in PATHRES-CHECK and RECORD-LINK, then the defender could have observed those results while executing in isolation.

Each of the defender's OPENSTAT calls observes some parts of the file system, e.g. the attributes of the parent argument, the state of the atom link, and the attributes of the child, if it exists. Note that PATHRES may observe the same part of the file system multiple times, e.g. if it resolves a path of the form "$x/../x$". Thus the attacker's file-system modifications fall into three categories: (1) modifications to a file-system object o that occur before the first time that PATHRES observes any information about o, (2) modifications to a file-system object o that occur after the last time that PATHRES observes any information about o, and (3) modifications to a file-system object o that occur between the first and last times that PATHRES observes any information about o.

Attacker modifications to object o that occur before the defender's first observation can be scheduled to occur before PATHRES begins execution. Similarly, attacker modifications to object o that occur after the defender's last observation can be scheduled to occur after PATHRES completes execution. Attacker modifications the occur between two observations must have no net effect, since otherwise the consistency checks performed by PATHRES-CHECK and RECORD-LINK would not succeed.

Hence the execution of PATHRES is serializable. ■

The theorem also applies to multiple invocations of PATHRES, so long as the state collected by RECORD-LINK is maintained throughout the execution. Thus applications can string together multiple calls to PATHRES with serializable semantics.

The PATHRES function never removes entries from its state, so it may grow unboundedly. Our prototype includes transaction begin and end functions that initialize and free PATHRES' state. The transaction-begin function also creates a handle on the current working directory that can be used as the cwd argument to PATHRES.

The system as described does not support cooperating processes that manipulate the file system in concert, e.g. where one process creates a file and another process polls the file system waiting for it to be created. Cooperating processes can solve this problem by storing their state in shared memory, with suitable locking to prevent concurrent access.

6.3 Serializable POSIX API Wrappers

The PATHRES function has the desirable property that, during a single transaction, all calls to PATHRES will detect any violation of serialization semantics. However, the PATHRES function is not a complete system – it is just a basic building block for implementing other file-system access functions. We now describe how to write PATHRES wrappers that emulate other POSIX APIs. By implementing these other APIs on top of PATHRES, a developer can make arbitrary sequences of calls to the wrappers and be assured that any violation of serialization semantics will be detected. Some functions, such as `open`, `stat`, and `creat`, can be implemented very straightforwardly using PATHRES. Other file-system operations require additional work, as explained below.

`access`. The `access` system call is famously prone to races. Tsafrir, et al. proposed user-space path walking as a solution to the `access`/`open` race [19]. Our solution is conceptually the same: we re-implement the access-control logic in user-space and verify that the process's real user and group IDs enable the requested access. The advantage of our scheme is that calls to our `access` implementation can be combined with arbitrary other operations, whereas other proposed defenses support only the `access`/`open` paradigm [19]. In our implementation, PATHRES takes an additional argument specifying a function pointer that is called at each step of the resolution. This function pointer can enforce arbitrary path resolution policies, including the policy defined by `access`.

`mkdir` and `symlink`. Unlike `openat`, `mkdirat` creates a new file-system object without returning a file-descriptor for that object. This makes it difficult to access the newly-created directory in a race-free way. For example, an attacker may be able to replace the new directory with another directory of his choice. We can solve this problem by writing a MKDIROPENSTAT function analogous to the OPENSTAT function in Algorithm 1. This task could be greatly simplified if the POSIX definition for `openat` were extended so that specifying `O_CREAT | O_EXCL | O_DIRECTORY | O_SEARCH` would create and open the specified directory.

After successfully creating a new directory, the wrapper must record the new directory in the table of past file-system observations. In addition to recording the inode information for the new directory, it must also remember that the directory is empty, so that a serialization violation will be reported if the defender ever observes a link that it did not create in the directory. See the discussion of `readdir` below for more on the infrastructure for monitoring the contents of directories.

`symlink` can be handled similarly.

`link`, `unlink`, `rmdir`, and `rename`. To implement a version of `link` that can detect serialization violations when used inside a transaction, we can use PATHRES to resolve the `oldpath` and `newpath` arguments to `link`, call `linkat` with the resulting parent directory file-descriptors, verify that the results of the `link` operation are consistent with the results of the earlier PATHRES calls, and finally update PATHRES' internal state to reflect the change. Although this is serializable, it does not detect serialization violations as soon as possible. For example, an attacker might change the target of `oldpath` after the PATHRES calls, causing the application to create a link to a file other than the intended one. The defender would discover the substitution if it ever resolved the newly created link within the same transaction, but this might not happen until much later, and it might never happen if the application ends the transaction. This differs from the semantics of creating a file with PATHRES– any serialization violation that occurs while creating the file is reported immediately. Therefore, in order to provide the same early-detection semantics as when creating a file, a serializable implementation of `link` should use `fstatat` to verify that the new link points to the correct file. We can implement `unlink`, `rmdir`, and `rename` similarly, i.e. by checking that the link is gone and, in the case of `rename`, that the new link points to the correct file.

`chmod` and `chown`. It might appear to be trivial to implement a race-free version of `chmod` using PATHRES: obtain a file-descriptor using PATHRES and then use `fchmod` on that descriptor. The problem is that, although an object's owner always has permission to `chmod` the object, he may not have permission to `open` it for reading or writing. However, only a file's owner may successfully `chmod` it, so we can resolve this problem by using PATHRES to obtain a file-descriptor for the parent directory, using `fchmodat` to grant the file's owner read access to the file, and then using the PATHRES/`fchmod` technique. If an attacker manages to change the target of the path passed to the first `fchmodat` call, then the only damage would be to either cause the `fchmodat` call to fail or to grant the defender read access to one of his own files. A failing `fchmodat` call would indicate a race condition. If the `fchmod` succeeds, then subsequent PATHRES call would detect the change unless the attacker switches the link to point back to its original target after the `fchmodat`. In this case, the PATHRES call would fail to open the file, also indicating a race. Thus, no matter what the attacker does, he will be detected. `chown` can be handled similarly.

This complexity could be avoided by introducing a new `O_STAT` flag for `open` and `openat`. File descriptors obtained with this flag would not support reading or writing (and hence would not require those permissions), but would be valid arguments to the `fchmod` system call. Note that the caller would not need to be the owner of the file for the `open` call to succeed, but would need to be the owner for the `fchmod` to succeed.

`readdir` and related functions. After an application scans the entries in a directory, it expects that future scans of the directory will yield the same result, that deleting all the entries discovered during the scan will result in an empty directory, that creating a file with a name not seen during the scan will not fail with `EEXIST`, etc. Returning to our analogy with databases, directory scans correspond to range queries, and our goal of serializable file-system access corresponds to the requirement that we prevent "phantom reads" [1].

Unfortunately, the POSIX specification of `readdir` gives implementers a lot of freedom in order to enable optimizations. For example, if a new entry in a directory is created after an application calls `opendir`, then that entry may or may not be visited by subsequent calls to `readdir`. Likewise, entries deleted after the application calls `opendir` may still show up in `readdir` results. Given this flexibility, it is quite difficult to determine whether a `readdir` result constitutes a serializability violation.

Instead, our implementation sacrifices some performance for simplicity. When the application makes a call to our implementation of `opendir` (or `rewinddir`), our implementation scans the entire directory and uses PATHRES to resolve each entry found. It then checks these entries against prior knowledge about the directory, and then checks, for all future accesses to the directory, that no new files appear. It also ensures that all entries that are already known to exist in the directory are returned at some point during the scan. It then copies these entries into a buffer allocated for the current call to `opendir`. Future calls to `readdir` are satisfied by pulling entries from the buffer. The `opendir` scan also marks the PATHRES state information for that directory as "scanned". If PATHRES ever observes an entry in that directory that is not in its list of entries and is not created by the application, then it raises an `ERACEDETECTED` error. This strategy can be proved to detect serialization violations using the same techniques as in the proofs of Theorems 1 and 2.

7. USING OUR DEFENSE

Using our file access library is quite easy. In most cases, programmers need only identify the crucial sequences of system calls that form a transaction, add calls to our transaction-begin and end functions, and change calls to standard file-system access functions to their trace-ified versions.

This is sufficient to solve all TOCTTOU races in which an application checks a set of pre-conditions, such as file ownership or permissions, before performing a single action, such as creating a file or executing a script. A defender that uses the trace library to perform the checks and execute the action within a single transaction can be assured that the action will be performed only if the file system has not changed since the time of the checks. This would solve the TOCTTOU races in the examples in Figures 1(a), 1(c), and 1(d).

Figure 1(b) shows a program vulnerable to a race condition other than a TOCTTOU race, but it can still be fixed by using our library. The programmer can create a top-level wrapper that begins a transaction, calls `deltree`, and then ends the transaction. Within `deltree`, all file-system access calls are changed to their trace equivalents. Any change to the file system during the recursive traversal will result in an error, allowing the application to bail out before doing any damage to the file system.

Deciding where to place transactions is application-specific, but some applications have a structure that can make the task simpler. For example, some SMTP servers use a helper program to append mail to local users' mailboxes. In these cases, the helper program can simply start a transaction at the beginning of `main` and change all file-system calls to their trace versions. Programs with more complex behavior will require the developer to determine where to place transactions.

Our defense can detect isolation violations, but the application must handle recovery. In some cases, this may be easy. For example, in most TOCTTOU races, the application doesn't make any changes to the file system, except possibly during the last system call in a transaction. Thus, no recovery is necessary, since the last system call will succeed if and only if the whole transaction succeeds. If a serialization violation is detected after the application has made changes to the file system, then recovery may be impossible, since the file system has changed in potentially arbitrary ways. Consequently, developers should strive to write their file-system access code so that it can terminate in the middle of a transaction without leaving the system in a vulnerable state. Although this imposes some burden on programmers, it is still substantially easier to reason about prefixes of isolated executions than all possible executions that may be interleaved with an attacker.

Finally, developers may encounter false positives from using our library. For example, their OS may return a non-standard error code in some situations, or the developer may want multiple cooperating processes to modify the file system concurrently. The latter is easy to handle: the programmer can modify his suite of utilities to all share transaction state, so that one process will not raise an alarm based on changes made by another cooperating process. A false positive created by a non-standard OS behavior would be difficult to correct – the application developer could try to design around it, e.g. by using a different system call with the same functionality, if one is available, but in some cases the only option may be to change the OS to match POSIX behavior, or to change the trace library to accept the OS behavior.

If the programmer does not control the entire suite of software that may be accessing the file system, e.g. imagine many different mail processing utilities written by multiple authors that all process a user's mail directory, then he can combine trace transactions with other systems used to manage concurrent access to the file system. For example, if concurrent access to a directory is governed by a lock file, then the programmer can rewrite his code to start a transaction before attempting to acquire the lock. If the program fails to acquire the lock, it can end the transaction and start again. Note that the transaction may generate an `ERACEDETECTED` exception while attempting to acquire the lock, but this can be safely ignored. Once the process acquires the lock, it can then proceed as normal, using our trace library to access the file system. Any race condition detected after acquiring the lock will not be a false positive – it will indicate another program that is not following the locking protocol and therefore should be changed.

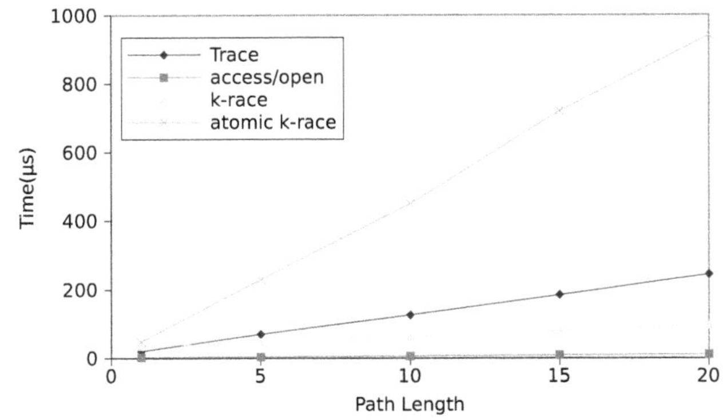

Figure 5: Performance of Trace, k-open, atomic k-open, and `access/open` on our low-end machine.

8. SECURITY EVALUATION

The proofs presented in this paper provide strong evidence of the security of our scheme, but we can also demonstrate its security empirically. Figure 4 shows two snippets of code for testing our scheme's security. These snippets are derived from the programs in Figure 1(b) and (c). In the present snippets, we have inserted an attacker action between the two relevant defender operations. Thus, these tests make the most optimistic assumption for an attacker – that he can reliably intervene between defender operations. Despite this generous assumption, we confirmed that our scheme detected the attack in both cases.

9. PERFORMANCE

We evaluate our system against other proposed defenses against the `access/open` race. We ran our tests on a machine with a Pentium 2.8GHz dual core CPU, 2GB of RAM, an 11krpm 160GB hard disk. The machine was running 32-bit Ubuntu Linux with a 2.6.31-21-generic kernel.

access/open. Figure 5 shows the performance, averaged over 500 trials, of four race defenses executing on our low-end test machine. The `access/open` scheme is the classic, insecure idiom, k-race was proposed at USENIX Security 2004 [11], and atomic k-race was proposed at USENIX FAST 2008 [18]. Note that none of these other schemes is secure. We significantly outperform atomic k-race, since it also performs user-space path walking, but has to perform 14 system calls per step, as opposed to only 2 calls per step for our scheme. The original k-race algorithm is faster, but it still performs 14 system calls and is not secure. Simply calling `access/open` is very fast, but also not secure.

```
if((fd = trace_chdir("/tmp/a/b")) < 0)
  return fd;
if((fd = trace_unlink("./foo")) < 0)
  return fd;

/* attacker's operation */
system("mv /tmp/a/b /tmp");

if((fd = trace_chdir("..")) < 0)
  return fd;
printf("cwd is %s\n", getcwd(cwd, 100));
```

(a)

```
if(trace_stat(argv[1], &buf) < 0){

  /* attacker's operation */
  open(argv[1], O_CREAT, S_IRWXU);

  fd = trace_open(argv[1], O_CREAT,
                  S_IRWXU);
}
printf("fd is %d\n\n", fd);
```

(b)

Figure 4: Trace-ified version of the programs in Figures 1(b) and 1(c).

10. CONCLUSION

The challenges discussed in this paper demonstrate that writing correct, race-free file-system manipulation code is extremely difficult. Many programs must access the file system securely, though, and the lack of a simple solution has led to many security bugs and much wasted developer effort.

This paper presents a general solution to the UNIX file-system race condition problem. Our solution works on any POSIX-compliant operating system and provides very strong security guarantees, making it easy for application developers to write secure code in whatever way seems most natural to them. Developers can employ our solution selectively – gaining high security during critical parts of their application and high performance elsewhere.

Our solution uses many ideas from previous kernel-level race condition detectors [20] and user-space path walking, as proposed by Tsafrir, et al. [19]. We improve upon these prior solutions in portability, generality, and security. As noted by Tsafrir, et al., user space path walking also enables trusted applications to enforce their own security policies. Defining useful application-specific user-space extensions to the basic POSIX file-system interface could be an interesting direction for future research.

We have also identified several small changes to the POSIX API that would make it easier to write race-free code. `openat` could be extended to create directories and to open files solely for access to their `stat` information. More ambitiously, one could consider extending the POSIX API to include an orthogonal and clean set of APIs similar to those outlined in Table 1.

The main limitation of our defense is that, when a race is discovered, it cannot roll back any file-system changes that have already been made by the application. Even worse, some file-system changes, such as `link`, can only detect races after the fact. The defense may also generate false positives in some circumstances. Addressing these limitations in a portable and provably-correct way may be fruitful ground for future research.

Availability

The code in this paper is available from `http://www.splat.cs.sunysb.edu/`.

11. REFERENCES

[1] H. Berenson, P. Bernstein, J. Gray, J. Melton, E. O'Neil, and P. O'Neil. A critique of ANSI SQL isolation levels. In *SIGMOD '95: Proceedings of the 1995 ACM SIGMOD international conference on Management of data*, pages 1–10, New York, NY, USA, 1995. ACM.

[2] M. Bishop and M. Dilger. Checking for race conditions in file accesses. *Computing Systems*, 9(2):131–152, Spring 1996.

[3] N. Borisov, R. Johnson, N. Sastry, and D. Wagner. Fixing races for fun and profit: how to abuse atime. In *SSYM'05: Proceedings of the 14th conference on USENIX Security Symposium*, pages 20–20, Berkeley, CA, USA, 2005. USENIX Association.

[4] X. Cai, Y. Gui, and R. Johnson. Exploiting UNIX file-system races via algorithmic complexity attacks. In *IEEE Symposium on Security and Privacy*, 2009.

[5] H. Chen and D. Wagner. MOPS: an infrastructure for examining security properties of software. In *Proceedings of the 9th ACM Conference on Computer and Communications Security (CCS)*, pages 235–244, Washington, DC, Nov. 18–22, 2002.

[6] B. Chess. Improving computer security using extended static checking. *Proceedings of the 23rd Annual IEEE Symposium on Security and Privacy*, 2002.

[7] S. Christey, B. Martin, M. Brown, and A. Paller. 2009 CWE/SANS top 25 most dangerous programming errors. Technical report, CWE/SANS, 2009.

[8] C. Cowan, S. Beattie, C. Wright, and G. Kroah-Hartman. Raceguard: Kernel protection from temporary file race vulnerabilities. In *In Proceedings of the 10th USENIX Security Symposium*. USENIX Association, 2001.

[9] Common vulnerabilities and exposures. `http://cve.mitre.org`.

[10] CVE Maintainers. CVE-2008-1614. Technical report, Common Vulnerabilities and Exposures Database, 2008.

[11] D. Dean and A. J. Hu. Fixing races for fun and profit: how to use access(2). In *Proceedings of the 13th USENIX Security Symposium*. USENIX Association, 2004.

[12] C. Ko, G. Fink, and K. Levitt. Automated detection of vulnerabilities in privileged programs by execution monitoring. In *In Proceedings of the 10th Annual Computer Security Applications Conference*, pages 134–144, 1994.

[13] K.-S. Lhee and S. J. Chapin. Detection of file-based race conditions. *International Journal of Information Security*, 4(1-2):105–119, 2005.

[14] Linux man-pages project. *STAT(2): Linux Programmer's Manual*, 3.23 edition, September 2009.

[15] D. E. Porter, O. S. Hofmann, C. J. Rossbach, A. Benn, and E. Witchel. Operating system transactions. In *Proceedings of the 22nd ACM Symposium on Operating Systems Principles*, 2009.

[16] C. Pu and J. Wei. A methodical defense against TOCTTOU attacks: The EDGI approach. In *Proceedings of the 2006 International Symposium on Secure Software Engineering*, March 2006.

[17] B. Schwarz, H. Chen, D. Wagner, G. Morrison, J. West, J. Lin, and W. Tu. Model checking an entire linux distribution for security violations. Technical Report UCB/CSD-05-1384, UC Berkeley, April 2005.

[18] D. Tsafrir, T. Hertz, D. Wagner, and D. Da Silva. Portably solving file TOCTTOU races with hardness amplification. In *Proceedings of the 6th USENIX Conference on File and Storage Technologies*, February 2008.

[19] D. Tsafrir, T. Hertz, D. Wagner, and D. D. Silva. Portably preventing file race attacks with user-mode path resolution. Technical Report RC24572, IBM T. J. Watson Research Center, Yorktown Heights, NY, June 2008.

[20] E. Tsyrklevich and B. Yee. Dynamic detection and prevention of race conditions in file accesses. In *Proceedings of the 12th USENIX Security Symposium*, pages 243–256, August 2003.

[21] P. Uppuluri, U. Joshi, and A. Ray. Preventing race condition attacks on file-systems. In *SAC '05: Proceedings of the 2005 ACM symposium on Applied computing*, pages 346–353, New York, NY, USA, 2005. ACM.

[22] J. Viega, J. T. Bloch, Y. Kohno, and G. Mcgraw. ITS4: a static vulnerability scanner for C and C++ code. In *Proceedings of the 16th Annual Conference on Computer Security Applications (ACSAC)*, pages 257–267, 2000.

[23] C. P. Wright, R. Spillane, G. Sivathanu, and E. Zadok. Extending ACID Semantics to the File System. *ACM Transactions on Storage (TOS)*, 3(2):1–42, June 2007.

Software Watermarking using Return-Oriented Programming

Haoyu Ma* ma-haoyu@163.com
Kangjie Lu† kjlu@gatech.edu
Xinjie Ma*,‡ xjma@smu.edu.sg
Haining Zhang* guage_110@sohu.com
Chunfu Jia*,§ cfjia@nankai.edu.cn
Debin Gao‡ dbgao@smu.edu.sg

*College of Computer and Control Engineering, Nankai University, China
†School of Computer Science, Georgia Institute of Technology, USA
‡School of Information Systems, Singapore Management University, Singapore
§Information Security Evaluation Center of Civil Aviation, Civil Aviation University of China, China

ABSTRACT

We propose a novel dynamic software watermarking design based on Return-Oriented Programming (ROP). Our design formats watermarking code into well-crafted data arrangements that look like normal data but could be triggered to execute. Once triggered, the pre-constructed ROP execution will recover the hidden watermark message. The proposed ROP-based watermarking technique is more stealthy and resilient over existing techniques since the watermarking code is allocated dynamically into data region and therefore out of reach of attacks based on code analysis. Evaluations show that our design not only achieves satisfying stealth and resilience, but also causes significantly lower overhead to the watermarked program.

Categories and Subject Descriptors

K.5.1 [**Legal Aspects of Computing**]: Hardware/Software Protection – Proprietary rights

General Terms

Security

Keywords

Software watermarking, return-oriented programming, reverse engineering, code obfuscation

1. INTRODUCTION

Software theft and pirating have always been important concerns in software industry. In fighting against such intellectual property violations, software watermarking is considered a valuable tool. Like media watermarking, software watermarking embeds a secret message into a subject program which can be extracted to identify the copyright owner or authentic user of the program.

Existing software watermarking designs can be divided into static and dynamic watermarking [10]. The former embeds the watermark message directly in program's text, while the later hides it in program's runtime states or dynamic data. Since dynamic watermarking retrieves the hidden message by running along a specific path of the watermarked program and examining its specific behavior, it is usually considered a more reliable and secure solution [9].

Nevertheless, despite the progress made on dynamic watermarking, there are well-documented limitations with existing techniques [9]. First, existing solutions of dynamic watermarking introduce special data structures and instruction patterns which could be targeted by attackers to locate the hidden watermark. Second, code inserted by dynamic watermarking is usually rather independent from the other parts of the program, and thus can be suspicious. Finally, because previous designs, e.g., [8,21,23], use an external extractor to recover the watermark from program's execution recordings, sometimes the watermarked program needs to leave some information for the extractor to find the hidden watermark, which might also be exploited by attackers in undoing it. Existing research suggests that these problems be solved by integrating other protection techniques [23]; yet doing so also significantly decreases the efficiency of the watermarking technique [9].

In general, dynamic watermarking is to give the program a new execution path (which presents the watermark). However, with regular programming techniques, it's nearly impossible to also conceal the existence of this new execution path. In this paper, we present a innovative solution to this difficulty – a novel dynamic watermarking design based on *Return-Oriented Programming* (henceforth ROP), a well-known software exploit technique [4,14,16,26,27]. We show that, although initially proposed for malicious purposes, ROP can be applied in benign uses like software watermarking and works surprisingly well.

Our approach "assembles" the watermarking code out of a group of small, special instruction pieces picked from existing code, resulting an unexpected execution path that can only be chained with ROP. We also modify the subject program so that it prepares all other resources needed to chain

ASIA CCS'15, April 14–17, 2015, Singapore, Singapore

http://dx.doi.org/10.1145/2714576.2714582.

this watermarking path on-the-fly in its heap region. Only when triggered by the secret input will the program transfer its control to the hidden ROP path, which then extracts the embedded watermark. Our method ensures that the watermarked program does not have an explicit code stream that belongs exclusively to watermarking, so that when our watermarking module lurks it functionally doesn't exist, preventing it from being spotted by software analyses.

To our best knowledge, our approach is the first dynamic watermarking technique that performs execution of watermarking using solely instructions from other existing code modules. This not only keeps the watermarking code out of the scope of analysis tools, but also helps it survive various distortive attacks. Moreover, since ROP is initially developed to defeat protections against code injection exploits, our approach also involves no suspicious behavior like violation of W⊕X, DEP, or code signing. We present evaluations of program stealth and resilience in Section 4. Results show that our approach is able to make watermarking semantics untraceable by powerful static analysis tools, thus succeeds in concealing watermarking behaviors.

Another benefit of arranging the watermarking module in the form of ROP is better integration with the original program without creating suspicious data structures as in most existing work [11,21]. We show that components of the watermark, which are inserted as ROP resources, can be spread out and blended with the program's other runtime data more easily and flexibly, minimizing suspicion from analyses that aim to locate them. Our evaluation demonstrates that our design achieves satisfying static stealth in merging the watermark into subject programs.

Last but not the least, instead of using an external extractor, our approach plants an ROP trigger inside the watermarked program to activate the ROP execution and to extract the watermark. This avoids leaking hints that could assist watermark recovering to third parties as in existing techniques [8, 11, 20, 21].

The rest of the paper is organized as follows. In Section 2 we introduce the background as well as existing research on aspects related to our design. The ideology and implementation of ROP-based watermarking is given in Section 3. Section 4 presents evaluations on the proposed solution along with comparisons with previous watermarking methods. We discuss applicability and compatibility issues of applying ROP in watermarking in Section 5. Section 6 concludes the paper.

2. RELATED WORK

2.1 Software watermarking

The goal of software watermarking is to embed an identifying message into a piece of software which could later be extracted to recognize the ownership or certain authentic information of the watermarked software.

Some schemes statically embed watermark into program's text by, e.g., relocating registers or modifying program's abstract semantics [12,18]. Others focus on dynamic approaches in which the watermark is embedded in program's runtime behavior [8, 11, 19–21, 23, 25, 31].

Previous work on dynamic watermarking falls into two categories. Graph-based watermarking, first introduced by Collberg et al. [10], is one of the most well-understood software watermarking method [11, 23, 31, 34]. These schemes encode watermark messages into heap-allocated graph structures. Watermark extraction is done by examining graph structures built by the program with external watermark extraction routines and recognizing the graph that represents the watermark message. Another category of dynamic watermarking attempts to encode the watermark in special states of the program's control flow and extract the watermark by analyzing specific execution traces of the program, such as multi-thread behavior [21], conditional branching [8, 20], or value of opaque predicates [19].

A common characteristic of the above methods is that they require special components added into the program that serve solely for watermarking (e.g., data structures representing graph nodes [11,34], special thread components [21]). Many of them leave distinguishable features on regular running since the watermark extraction relies on external observation/examination to the program. For example, watermarking schemes based on thread behavior or dynamic execution path require locating and monitoring special thread components or certain branch instructions externally [9].

2.2 Return-oriented programming

Initially proposed by Shacham [27], return-oriented programming has become a major step in the advance of malicious code. While protection mechanisms like W⊕X and DEP are used by more and more operation systems to fight against code injection attacks, ROP provides a new way of exploitiation for arbitrary computation and bypasses the above protections since it does not inject any new code.

ROP was started on x86 architecture [5, 26] and later extended to many other platforms, e.g., the SPARC [4], ARM [16], etc. ROP attack is now not only fully automated, but able to be initiated during the executing of target program [15, 29]. Furthermore, ROP is also proven to be useful in compromising iOS applications [32] where code injection is not allowed.

2.3 Program steganography with ROP

Though introduced as an attacking technique, recently the argument on whether ROP can be used in a benign way has been brought to researchers' attention. In particular, RopSteg [17] was proposed for code protection that attempts to hide selected code portion of a program by executing their "unintended matches" located elsewhere. In the sense of hiding certain code blocks of a piece of software, RopSteg and our ROP-based software watermarking share similar purposes. However, RopSteg's design assumes a scenario where tampering with program code is not of the best interest of the attackers, which is certainly not true in software watermarking since removing a specific part of the program (that for watermarking) is exactly the purpose of attacks. When used directly for software watermarking, RopSteg has the following drawbacks.

First, RopSteg replaces the protected code portion with *ROP generator* and *ROP board* for jumping into and returning from the unintended matches. In watermarking this means that RopSteg still introduces new code of special pattern that only executes in watermark extraction. This could make the embedded watermark even easier to be located.

Second, RopSteg does not withstand distortive attacks in the sense that any simple program transformation applied to the RopStegged program would most likely destroy the

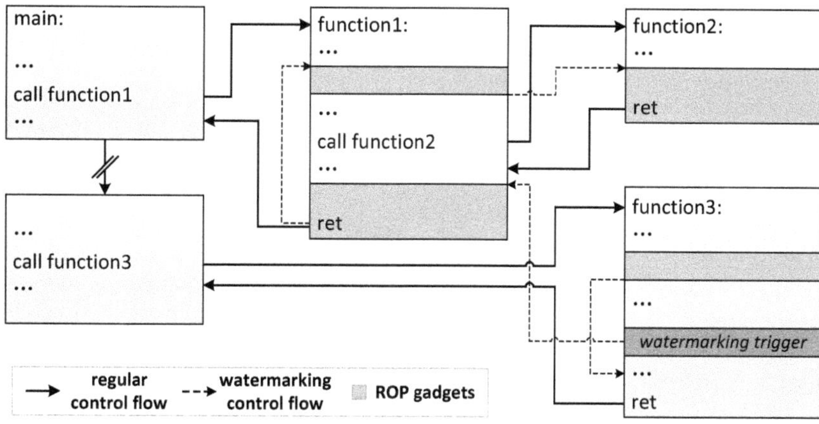

Figure 1: Overview of ROP-based watermarking

unintended matches of the hidden instructions. This makes it a fragile solution for watermark embedding.

3. ROP-BASED DYNAMIC SOFTWARE WATERMARKING

3.1 Threat model and assumptions

A dynamic watermarking design consists of a watermark *embedder* and a watermark *recognition protocol*. The watermark embedder, denoted as $E(\cdot,\cdot,\cdot)$, takes as input the subject program P, a watermark object ω, and an input setting $\delta \in \Delta$ (aka the "secret input"), and outputs the watermarked program $P' = E(P, \omega, \delta)$. The goal is to make $P'(\delta) = P(\delta) + \Omega$ at semantic level, where Ω is the executable form of ω, while preserving the semantics for other inputs, i.e., $P'(i) = P(i)\ \forall i \neq \delta$. The watermark recognition protocol $R(\cdot)$ extracts ω from P' when it runs with the secret input, i.e. $\omega = R(P'(\delta))$.

In general, an adversary may launch the following attacks on P':

Additive attack which turns P' into P'' in order to insert a bogus watermark υ, such that for an adversary-specified $\sigma \in \Delta^1$, $R(P''(\sigma)) = \upsilon$.

Subtractive/distortive attack which turns P' into P'' so that the authentic watermark ω is removed or compromised, i.e. $R(P''(\delta)) \neq \omega$.

The adversary is assumed to possess full control of P'. He could modify it using any semantic-preserving transformations, and observe and analyze its behavior both statically and dynamically. Nonetheless, the adversary is not al-mighty either. In practice, it is considered to be blind on a number of key information [10], namely:

1. Whether P' has been watermarked;
2. The original program P;
3. The secret input δ.

Our ROP-based watermarking inherits the above assumptions and considers the same general attack model. Furthermore, we extend the concept of the recognition protocol R to be more than just an algorithm or software analysis toolkit, but to also include the entire system environment setting in which the program is to be executed. The reason of such a definition will be explained in Section 5.

[1]Whether σ satisfies $\sigma \neq \delta$ is not important here.

3.2 Overview

The reason of ROP being so popular in malicious uses is that it formats its "code" in a form that is not to be run directly, but to help creating unexpected executions out of a program using its own instructions. Due to this special way of organizing executables, ROP also makes it very difficult for analysts to detect or understand the new "code" stream it creates. In other words, the execution path introduced by ROP is functionally "invisible". This could very well be a solution to building a dynamic software watermarking that, unlike existing ones, achieves minimum visibility while maintaining strong resilience.

It is important to first understand that an ROP "code" consists of 2 portions:

1. small pieces of instructions called "gadgets" that end with return or indirect call/jump, which are located somewhere in the existing executables; and
2. a carefully crafted bit string called the "payload" consisting of addresses of these gadgets as well as other variables they need in the execution.

ROP works by executing the gadgets with the payload strings, which means that for the new execution path it creates, nothing more than some extra data needs to be built. Therefore, the idea of ROP-based watermarking is to construct the actual watermarking code with ROP gadgets, while introducing extra code that builds a payload to control the gadgets. As briefly demonstrated in Figure 1, program modified in this way will transfer control to the selected gadgets when given the secret input[2] which takes over and presents the hidden watermark, and then return back to the program's normal routine. Since building ROP payload does not change the way in which the original program works, the extra code added by this method can always be executed during regular use of program instead of being kept idle and raising suspicions.

[2]These gadgets may be intended code pieces of the program or unintended instruction sequences in the middle of some code session (in case of CISC instruction set).

To give an example, suppose that we are to embed the watermark "007" into the target program by putting it into a 4-byte character string S (see Figure 2). In this example, payload construction involves preparing a sequence controlling the following gadgets and variables on the heap (shaded area in Figure 2):

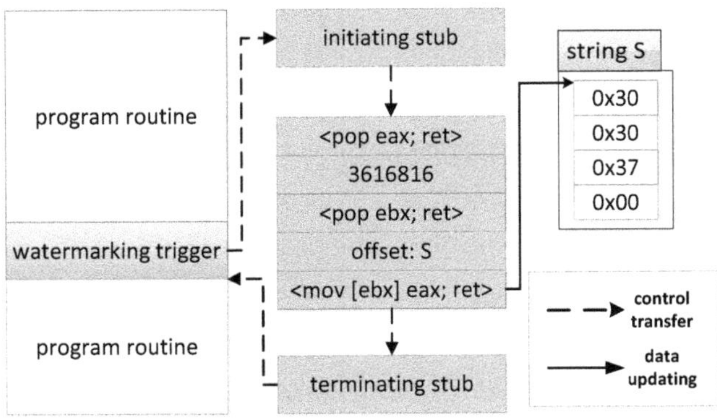

Figure 2: A simple example of ROP-based watermarking

- An initiating stub to store the current stack pointer and the address to return to, and to modify the stack pointer to point to the watermarking code;
- The watermarking code consisting of three gadgets `<pop eax; ret>`, `<pop ebx; ret>`, and `<mov [ebx], eax; ret>` which complete a memory writing chain;
- A constant 3616816 (corresponding to the ASCII code of string "007") and the address of string S which will be used by the memory writing gadgets;
- A terminating stub that recovers the original stack layout and goes back to regular program execution.

When the watermark extraction procedure is triggered, the embedded ROP first loads 3616816 and the address of S into register `eax` and `ebx`, respectively, then updates S to the watermark message "007"[3].

Typically, executing a well-designed ROP relies on injecting the payload on the stack in advance of turning to the gadgets, to ensure not only that the gadgets are given all operands they required but also that the indirect control instructions correctly find their successors so that gadgets are executed in the exact sequence as planned. Therefore, the way to construct and plant payload is a critical link of ROP. In malicious exploits, this is usually done by inputting external data to the program via some vulnerable routines, and the injected payload corrupts the original stack environment without concerning potential consequences (e.g., segmentation fault after the ROP execution). However, in case of software watermarking, the following issues have to be considered:

1. since the embedded ROP is for presenting a watermark, the payload has to be built all by the program itself;
2. code used in constructing the payload should not appear to be suspicious when compared to the original program;
3. after retrieving the watermark, ROP should return control to normal execution without sabotaging the program's normal execution.

[3]Note that it is only for simplicity that the watermark message is directly written in the ROP payload. In real implementation, this can be easily avoided with more complex gadget combinations.

Besides these, we also need to bypass protection mechanisms, e.g., Address Space Layout Randomization (ASLR). Clearly the old-fashioned way of launching an ROP for malicious attack is inappropriate in ROP-based watermarking. Instead, we need to propose a customized technique for our purposes. In the following subsections, we present each step of our scheme in more detail.

3.3 Locating watermarking gadgets

As mentioned in Section 3.2, ROP execution is constructed on the basis of instruction pieces called gadgets located from existing code regions, thus our first step is to find gadgets useful in watermark generation. However, using instructions inside the program itself is susceptible to simple program transformation attacks (as discussed in Section 2.3).

To provide resistance to the transformation attacks, we make use of the shared libraries (e.g. `libc.so` for UNIX and `kernel32.dll` for Windows). Such libraries are linked to almost any programs and cannot be easily modified. Therefore, we choose to search for watermarking gadgets from these system libraries, since semantic-preserving transformations on the watermarked program cannot prevent it from correctly targeting gadgets inside such legacy code.

Because we are using ROP only to hide watermarking behavior, gadgets to be executed needs to have no more than the following functions:

Register loading to load watermark messages and target memory addresses into registers. Note that this may not be as simple as a `<pop; ret>` sequence. Arithmetic/logical/shifting operations are also included.

Memory writing to write the value of source register to the memory area pointed to by the address in the target register, e.g., `<mov [eax], ecx; ret>`.

Stack shifting to control stack pointer, allowing watermarking ROP to be linked without being redirected with additional code. These are basically special register loading gadgets, since their only target is the stack pointer register.

Transferring to record the current position of instruction pointer when the program is directed to ROP, and to recover after the watermarking code is executed. Besides a specific combination of the former types of gadgets, we specifically exploit register exchange gadgets like `<xchg eax, esp; ret>` here since they can store the current stack pointer for later usage.

Since the introduction of ROP, many have proposed automatic searching of useful instruction sequences [15,26,29]. We make use of these existing techniques to locate the gadgets we need from system libraries. To be compatible with ASLR-enabled systems, we record gadgets by their offsets from entries of certain functions in the libraries, so that at runtime their absolute address can be computed easily with the assistant of function pointers.

Projects/libs	Size(KB)	Gadget types			
		Register loading	Memory writing	Stack shifting	Transferring
bzip2	63.488	22	2	2	1
hmmer	204.288	8	*NA*	*NA*	1
lbm	24.064	8	*NA*	*NA*	1
mcf	18.432	8	*NA*	*NA*	1
sjeng	105.984	12	1	1	1
soplex	306.688	24	*NA*	*NA*	1
libc.so.6	1335.56	9	5	2	4
kernel32.dll	857.6	13	2	8	3

Table 1: Number of available gadgets in projects and libraries

We search these four types of gadgets in a collection of SPECint-2006 benchmark projects as well as two system libraries `libc.so.6` and `kernel32.dll`. Only gadgets that complete a functional chain are recorded as available. Results shown in Table 1 confirm that both system libraries provide fully functional gadget sets for watermarking, while the same searching on small program modules are likely to fail. In addition, we found that typically gadgets of the equivalent function can be found at more than one locations, which could provide flexibility in formatting the payload.

3.4 Distributive and dynamic construction of watermarking payload

Constructing a reasonable watermark in ROP typically requires to execute dozens of gadgets, thus the payload used to chain the gadgets up would be of notable length. The code used to construct such payload would then be even longer, leaving potential targets for attackers. However, as briefly mentioned in Section 1, an important advantage of our ROP-based watermarking technique is to be able to spread out the watermarking components throughout the execution path to minimize suspicion from program analysis. Our design splits the watermarking payload into small segments to be constructed in different functions of the program which we called "carriers". With a number of carriers, we managed to embed just a small piece of code in each carrier that controls only a few gadgets, largely reducing the suspicion raised since the inserted code is almost negligible compared to the size of the original carriers. Refer to Section 4 for security evaluations on this.

We use TEMU, the dynamic analysis component of BitBlaze binary analysis platform [30], to trace the execution of the program with the secret input and to record all functions that are executed on the path along with their size, invoking frequency, and a call graph showing the control flow among them. Each function on this execution path is a carrier candidate for the watermarking payload. We sort the carriers by their size and embed longer segments of the payload in larger carriers since they provide better cover for the additional code.

Instead of storing the watermarking payload inside static data region, we construct the payload segments "on the fly". That is, only when a carrier is executed will the payload segment it carries be created in the program's heap area (we choose not to do this in carriers' stack frame in order to minimize the affect to program's normal execution caused by watermarking). We diversify the forms in which the payload segments are constructed to make it harder to recognize a pattern that indicates watermarking. Payload segments could be arranged as

- Integer arrays;
- Character strings;
- Selected variables of newly created instances of composite data structures (e.g., C structs and C++ classes).

Figure 3 shows examples on how the watermarking payload stored in a linear memory space can be built with different types of program objects. As we can see, the same piece of payload corresponding to the gadget <pop eax; ret> could stand in different ways: an integer array with two elements, two variables next to each other in an instance of a struct/class. We construct the payload based on the data structures that are already in the subject program and do not create new types of structures serving solely for watermarking which could be targets for attackers.

Furthermore, since the payload segments are formatted as heap-allocated data pieces, it's easy to use them in computing other variables owned by the program. Doing so creates active connections between the watermark components and the subject program, making them more difficult to be disabled even if they are somehow spotted by the adversary.

3.5 Payload chaining via stack pointer manipulation

Although splitting watermarking payload into short segments and distributing them among multiple carriers improve security, we still need a way to ensure that the discretely distributed payload pieces can be chained into a continuous stream during watermark extraction so that the ROP execution under their control works correctly.

As shown in Figure 4, when the watermarking payload is cut into segments, we attach stack-shifting gadgets at the end of them. In this way, each of the segments is responsible to relocate the stack frame correctly to the exact memory address of the next one, so that the watermarking payload works as if it were a continuous piece.

As discussed in the previous subsection, segments of the watermarking payload are constructed dynamically. During runtime whene one of them is constructed, the watermarked program checks if its previous and/or following segment had already been constructed. If either of them exists, the program chains the segments together by updating their stack

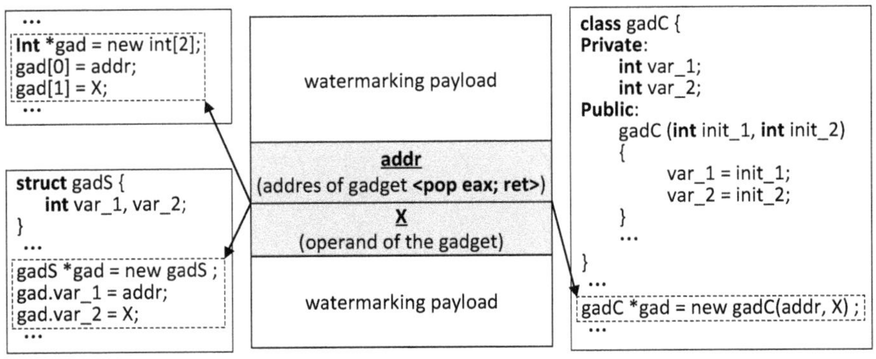

Figure 3: The diversity of payload formatting in ROP-based watermarking

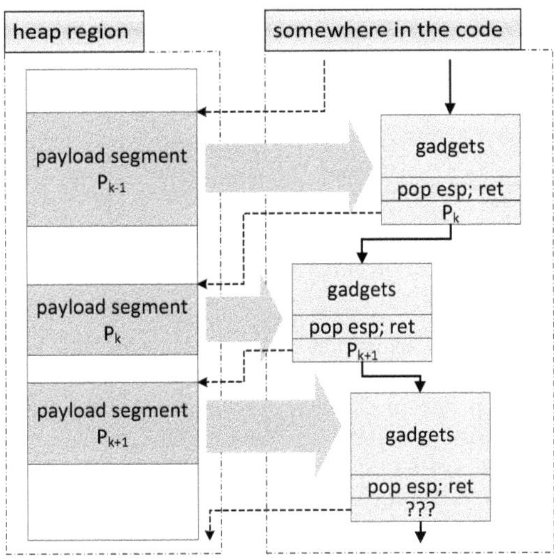

Figure 4: Chaining discrete payload segments via stack shifting gadgets (The dash arrows indicate stack pointer relocation while solid arrows indicate ROP execution flow)

shifting gadgets. Since the segments are generated one after another (although they may not be in the strict order as when they are used), each of them would either link itself to its neighbors or get linked by the neighbors.

3.6 Triggering ROP via function pointer overwriting

Now that the watermarking payload is chained up for execution. The last missing piece in the ROP-based watermarking is to instantiate the execution of the hidden watermarking path. This involves transitioning from normal execution of the program to ROP execution of the pre-selected gadgets, and we don't want instructions that perform such a transition to look suspicious.

We use a function pointer for triggering the ROP execution. The reason of this design choice is because a function pointer not only allows control transfer to the ROP gadgets via a simple overwriting of its value, but also provides a natural way of loading the initiating stub of the watermarking payload (given in the example in Section 3.2) directly onto the stack as function parameters. Usually this watermarking trigger points to a dummy function we added to the program so that in normal execution the trigger calls the dummy function and performs computations that do not affect the rest of the program. Upon inputting the secret input, the value of trigger is overwritten to point to the first gadget of the initiating stub (while the other parts of this stub will be pushed on the stack later by the trigger). Later when the trigger is invoked, gadgets of the initiating stub get executed, which save the current environment and transfer control to the first segment of watermarking payload.

The next question is how to encode the trigger condition (testing the secret input). A simple solution is to use a conditional block (e.g., an `if` statement) to compare current program input with the constant secret input. However, such conditional block introduces branching in the control flow graph and could attract attention of program analysis. Here we propose a novel idea to conceal such branching, see Figure 5. We exploit the right shifting operation so that only when *Input* equals to *Key* will the variable x be set to 0. As a result, the program is able to conditionally determine the function pointer's value without explicitly introducing control flow transfer instructions.

```
void RopTrigger_A (int Input, int Key)
{
    int a=Input-Key;
    int b=Key-Input;
    a>>31;
    b>>31:
    /* if Input==Key, then x=0, otherwise x
       =-1 */
    int x=a^b;
    /* overwriting */
    &funcPt=addressA*(0-x)+addressB*(1+x);
    funcPt(Initial_Gadgets);
}
```

Figure 5: Testing trigger condition without branching

Note that the above example is only a raw implementation of our watermark trigger. In practice there are many ways to build the same function in more complex form so that the embedded trigger is harder to locate or analyze. For example, we can use the hash value of *Key* to compute a and b as similarly suggested in [28]. Simple right shifting can be replaced with equivalent arithmetic combinations. Pointer aliasing may also be applied to the function pointer overwriting. Finally, code block of the trigger can be taken apart and merged with another functional module to decrease its visibility.

3.7 Implementation

Our ROP-based watermarking toolkit is implemented in a set of python scripts consisting of a *gadget scanner*, a *trace processor* and a *code re-writer*, as shown in Figure 6.

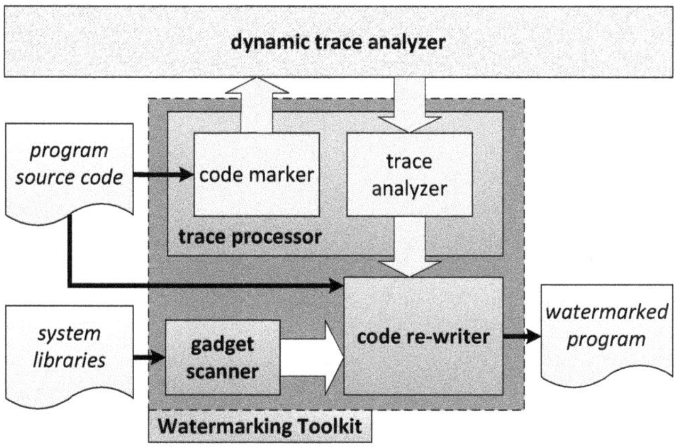

Figure 6: Implementation of ROP-based watermarking

Gadget scanner analyzes the system libraries, selects available gadgets of the four types given in Section 3.3 and creates a gadget database. It also generates the ROP payload that chains the candidate gadgets into the watermarking code.

Meanwhile, the trace processor analyzes the execution traces of the subject program under the secret input to find available carriers for watermarking payload. It not only finds the entry points of carriers but also records which parts of them are executed in the given trace.

After these preparations, code re-writer modifies the program's source code to embed the watermark. First, it divides the payload provided by the gadget scanner into segments and generates code for building and linking them. Following that, it distributes these code into the carriers, and also plants the dummy function as well as the ROP trigger. Finally, the modified source code is re-compiled, resulting the watermarked program.

Secret trace analysis is a tricky part of the watermarking since the analyzer only records execution on *binary* level while the watermark is embedded to the *source code*. To fill this gap, our trace processor consists of a *code marker* and a *trace analyzer*.

First, code marker makes a special copy of the program's source code by marking entry points and end points of functions as well as conditional code blocks in them with ineffective inline assembly sequences (which we called *tags*). We format these tags so that they are not only easy to be recognized, but also tell the exact locations in the corresponding source files they are assigned to. In particular, we let each tag to be started and ended with a `<mov edx, edx>` instruction, which never occurs in regular binaries. Additionally, a global junk variable is added in the program, with each tag carrying instructions that write the file ID and line number of the marked position in sequence to this junk variable. consequently, the resulting executable from the marked source is run with the secret trace recorded, and the trace analyzer can simply search for the inserted tags to figure out exactly which part of the source code is executed.

The trace processor is implemented as a total of 207 lines of scripts, in which the code marker takes 135 lines and the trace analyzer takes 72 lines. Code re-writer script consists of 191 lines due to the need of generating code for payload preparation in addition to scanning and re-writing source files. Gadget scanner is extended from GALILEO [27], an existing gadget searching algorithm.

4. EVALUATION

In this section, we subject our ROP-based watermarking to a number of security analyses and present the results. We also measure the static and dynamic overhead.

Security of software watermarking is usually evaluated in terms of the *stealth*, *credibility*, and *resilience*. Stealth typically refers to how well the watermark blends in the code or data around it; credibility describes how precisely the watermark can be retrieved; while resilience measures the resistance against determined attempts at discovery or removal. ROP-based watermarking extracts a watermark as a direct result of executing the embedded ROP gadgets; thus its credibility is quite self-evident. Therefore, in this section, we mainly focus on analyzing stealth and resilience of our approach. Meanwhile, the overhead caused by applying the ROP-based watermarking is also evaluated on three aspects – time it takes to generate the watermark, increment in code size, and the additional heap space required.

We apply our scheme on a number of subject programs from the SPECint-2006 test suite which are subject programs that previous research chose to work with [23]. The experimental watermarking is designed to simply output a watermark message on the screen. All tests were run on a PC with a 2.66GHz Intel Core 2 Quad CPU, 4GB memory, and Windows 7 operating system.

4.1 Static stealth

Static stealth of software watermarking measures how well a watermark fits into the program around it. As mentioned in Section 3, the ROP-based watermarking needs to insert a small amount of code into the program for constructing its payload. Therefore, static stealth plays an important role in evaluating our design. The good news is that code introduced by our ROP-based watermarking is only for creating and updating the payload segments which appear to be program data. It is broken down to instruction level and distributed over many carriers in the program (see Section 3.4). Considering the diversity of such code as also discussed in Section 3.4, we expect that ROP-based watermarking presents good static stealth in this measurement.

We adopt the static stealth measurement introduced by Collberg et al. [11], briefly described as follows:

- First, given a piece of watermarking code that generates an x-bit watermark, a *dictionary* is created as an instruction level profile. This is done by sweeping a peephole (of which the size is set to one to three instructions as suggested by Collberg et al.) over the instruction stream of the watermarking code, while distinct instruction combinations observed in the scanning are added as new *words* to the dictionary.
- Second, to measure whether the watermarking code is stealthy in a program, all words in the dictionary are then searched in the original and watermarked programs. The more words appearing in them, the better the watermarking code fits into the program.

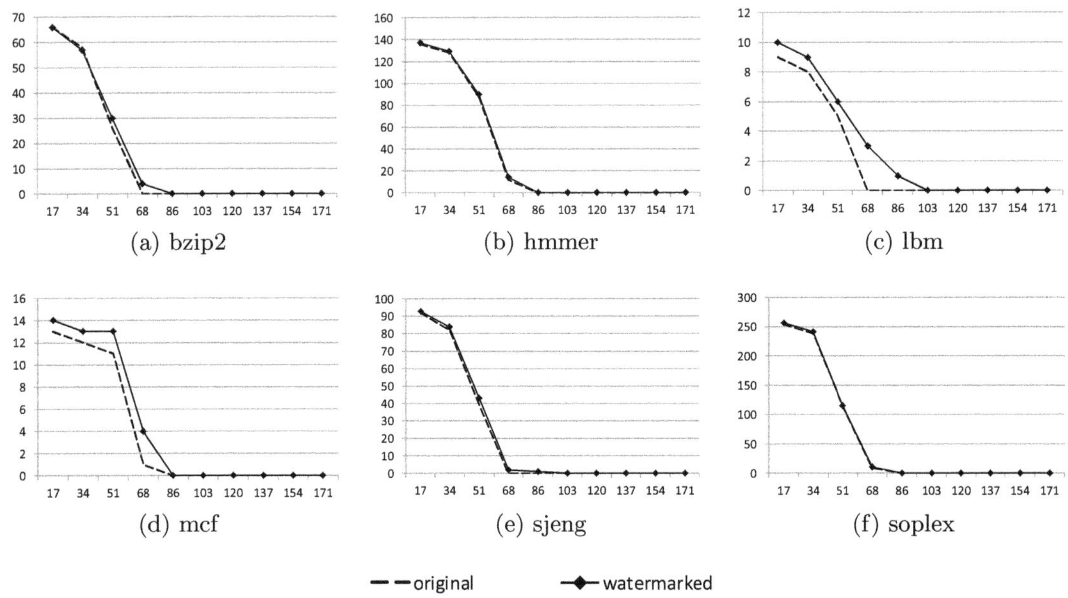

Figure 8: Locality evaluation on static stealth

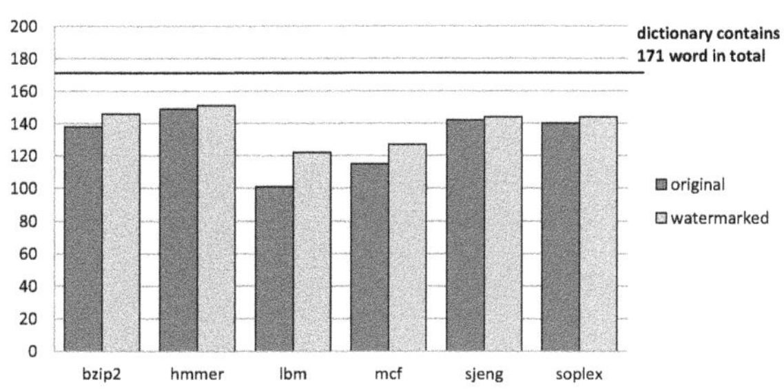

Figure 7: Static stealth of ROP-based watermarking

We apply our ROP-based watermarking on six benchmark programs `bzip2`, `hmmer`, `lbm`, `mcf`, `sjeng`, and `soplex` to embed a 192-bit watermark. By analyzing the watermarking code inserted into the six watermarked program, we identify a total of 171 words in the dictionary. Figure 7 shows the number of words in the dictionary that are found in the original and watermarked programs.

There are two important takeaways from these results. First, we observe that between 70 and 85 percent of the words in the dictionary of watermarking code already exists in the original programs. This shows that most of the code introduced by our ROP-based watermarking can be seen in the ordinary program, making it hard for attackers to look for special instruction sequences that could serve as signatures for detection. Second, we find that even in the watermarked programs, there are only 72 to 88 percent of the words in the dictionary being observed. Meanwhile, the differences between results on the original programs and the watermarked programs are pretty small – making the original and watermarked programs relatively indistinguishable in this analysis.

We further extend this experiment to perform a locality evaluation by running a considerably large sliding window (200 instructions in our experiment, since the watermarking code itself only has 271 instructions in total) over the programs' instruction stream. Again, we look for words from the dictionary when running the sliding window, one step to the right when the number of words found is below a threshold, or 200 steps to the right otherwise to avoid double counting. Locations where the number of words found exceeds the threshold are considered "hotspots" that have similar profile compared to the watermarking code, and will be marked as suspicious. Figure 8 shows the result where the horizontal axis shows different threshold settings and the vertical axis shows the number of "hotspots" found.

Results are consistent with those from the previous experiment, where few windows in which over 50% coverage of watermarking dictionary are reported. When comparing the results for the original and the watermarked programs, there is no significant increase on the number of hotspots.

4.2 Dependence analysis on watermarking components

In the second analysis on the stealth of the watermarking technique, we assume a more realistic scenario where the attacker manages to locate one distinguishable component used in the watermark, and tries to trace the other parts of it with dependency analysis to the exposed component. Existing watermarking schemes can be vulnerable on this aspect since certain features used by their external extractor to recognize watermark may also be exploited by adversaries, while the connections between their code and data are directly exposed to analyses.

As an example, we simulate such a dependency analysis on the CT watermarking technique [10], one representative watermarking techniques proposed in the literature. In the simulation, we set the root node of the heap-allocated watermark graph to be static, as if it is recognized already. IDA pro 6.4 is then used to launch a dependency analysis starting from the given root node in order to find anything that are semantically connected. Figure 9 shows the analysis result, where we find that based on the exposed root node, IDA pro is able to detect a dependency graph connecting all functions that participate in the watermark generation, making it relatively easy for attackers to narrow down to specific functions in searching for the watermarking code.

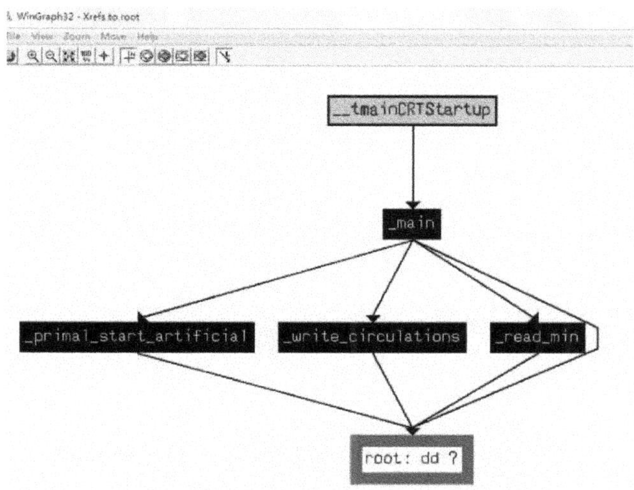

Figure 9: Dependency analysis result of CT watermarking

In contrast, our ROP-based watermarking payload stay in the data region of the program, thus from normal perspective it has no explicit connection to the corresponding gadgets, making the watermarking semantics "invisible" to code analyses (including dependence analysis), i.e. the code stream in charge of writing the watermark message into program's memory then printing it out literally does not exist when the embedded ROP is not triggered. For verification, we perform a similar simulation on our design, in which we intentionally let the watermarking code write the hidden message in a *static* character string that can be easily picked up by a static analyzer, and again look for semantically connected portions from the program. However, IDA pro encounters a failure to reach anything that have dependencies on the exposed string, i.e., it believes that semantically there is no instruction in the watermarked program that tries to read or modify the string at all.

To confirm this result, we dynamically execute the watermarked program and monitor the target string to find out instructions that operate upon it. Figure 10 shows screenshots of this dynamic analysis (before and after the exposed character string is overwritten). We can see that instructions operating on the target string are actually unintended instructions from the shared library that are beyond the scope of the analyzer. This confirms that there is zero dependency found in the watermarked program.

Note that the above simulation is only for demonstrating the difference on semantic visibility between our design and the previous work. In our ROP-based watermarking, we do not actually use such a static string to store the watermark message, and therefore the dependency analysis might even have no ground to begin with.

4.3 Resilience

In this subsection, we discuss the strength of our design against distortion attacks in which the adversary attempts to destroy the watermark by twisting the binary of watermarked program. Common binary obfuscations (including function and basic block reordering, function inlining and outlining, data restructuring, etc.) are the main approaches of distortion attack while program packing and optimizing are also included in the adversaries' arsenal.

Intuitively, semantic-preserving transformations do not affect our design because they do not change the way gadgets are constructed. One possibility, though, is to target parameters of the function pointer for triggering ROP execution. However, the trigger function pointer works via a indirect call, whose target is hard to be determined at binary level. Theoretically, a complete distortion on the trigger needs to locate all indirect calls and modify all their potential targets including those imported to the program (which are highly error-prone). This makes the adversary's task impractical.

We test the resilience of all our watermarked programs against transformation of a selection of well-known tools:

- *xenocode*, performs binary-level obfuscation including encrypting static strings, randomly inserting redundant ineffective instructions, and obfuscating program's control flow [3];
- *UPX*, provides high-quality packing and compression on softwares [2]; and
- *LLVM optimizer*, enables various source- and target-independent binary optimizations, some of which perform decompilation/recompilation on target code [1].

Results show that after transformations, the watermarked programs can still correctly generate and chain the watermarking payload, and the hidden watermarks can still be correctly extracted. This not only indicates the good resilience of our design, but also shows that our ROP-based watermarking has potentially high compatibility should we want to combine it with other protection mechanisms.

4.4 Overhead

In this subsection, we evaluate the performance overhead of our design in comparison with graph-based watermarking. Intuitively, ROP-based watermarking involves far less overhead in both execution time and heap space because it does not need to encode the watermark into complex data structures (e.g., a graph).

In our experiments, we apply the CT watermarking technique to encode the watermark into radix graphs because it is widely considered to be the most efficient solution in graph-based watermarking [11]. All programs involved in the test are compiled under the same setting, and programs watermarked with both methods do not have any additional protection mechanisms integrated. Table 2 shows the result for runtime overhead, while Figure 11 presents results for static program size increments.

We find that the runtime overhead of a ROP-based watermarked programs is significantly smaller than that in the graph-based one – in some cases more than two orders of magnitude smaller. Our method also experiences smaller increase in program size.

We also evaluate the size of heap-allocated data structures that are constructed for the watermark. Results are very much identical for all six programs, in which CT watermarking uses 1,536 bytes of heap space to encode a 192-bit

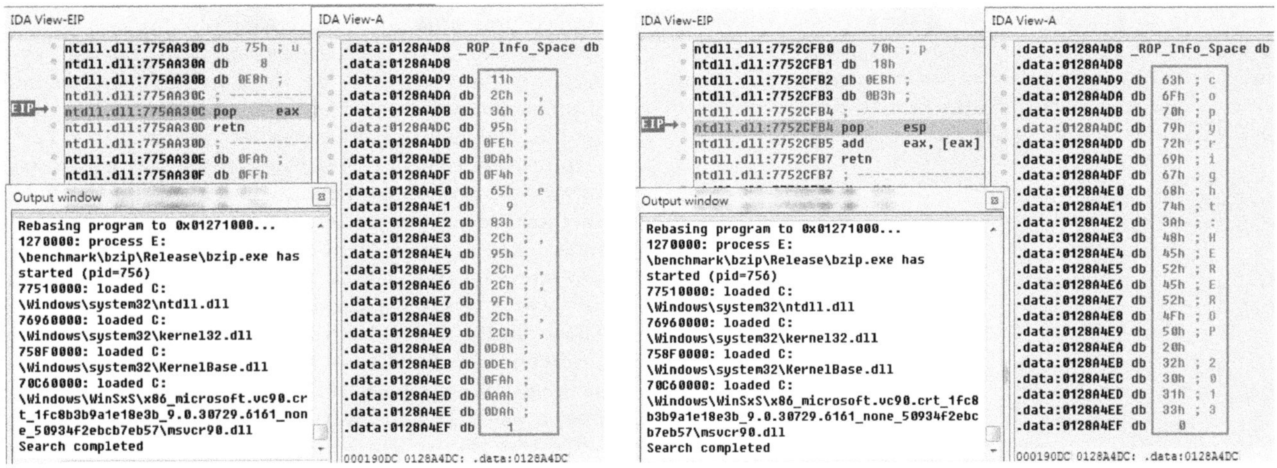

(a) Before string overwriting (b) After string overwriting

Figure 10: Unintended instructions that overwrite the watermark string in our design

benchmark	runtime overhead (ms)	
	ROP-based watermarking	graph-based watermarking
bzip2	1.33	154.94
hmmer	6.48	10897.63
lbm	536.61	41363.07
mcf	88.62	47177.45
sjeng	19.04	4262.94
soplex	2.03	4.61

Table 2: Runtime overhead

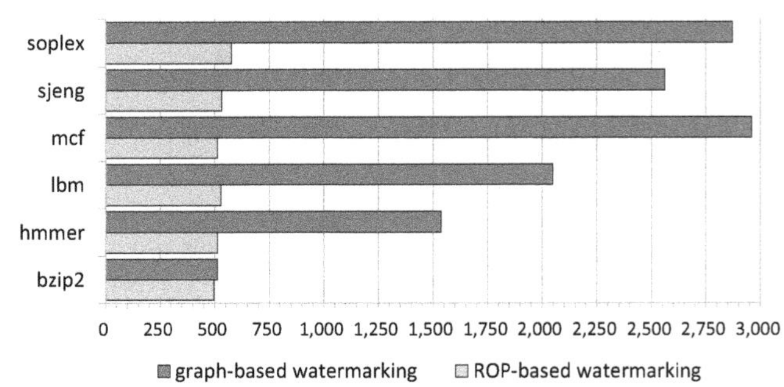

Figure 11: Increment in program size (bytes)

watermark into a radix graph, whereas our ROP-based watermarking uses 156 or 188 bytes when the gadgets are formatted in integer arrays or in structs/classes, respectively. Again, our ROP-based watermarking has a clear advantage.

4.5 Our method vs. RopSteg

In this subsection, we give a comparison between our method and RopSteg when applied to hide software watermark. As discussed in Section 2, RopSteg is a general tool for hiding code portions of a program with ROP. It has a different threat model compared to software watermarking and is susceptible to simple program transformation attacks. In this subsection, we, instead, focus on two evaluations. First, the amount of additional instructions inserted that participate dynamically in normal runs of the program (without watermark generation) and in watermark generation. This is an important security evaluation of software watermarking because instructions dedicated to watermark generation (those not participated in normal runs of the program at all) are suspicious and attract program analysis. Second, we also evaluate the program size increments. Table 3 shows the average result for the six benchmark programs we have tested, since the results are very much constant among them (shown in the previous subsection for our method and discussed in [17] for RopSteg).

Our ROP-based watermarking is designed based on an idea that instructions introduced by watermarking should be amphibious – they should be executed in regular runs of the program (without watermark generation). Our evaluation (second column of Table 3 confirms that our design meets this criteria, as 100% of the newly added instructions participate in normal runs of the programs. Meanwhile, only 61% of the instructions inserted by RopSteg participated in normal executions of the programs. In addition, the total size increment caused by RopSteg is larger than our method.

5. DISCUSSION

5.1 ROP defenses

A number of ROP defenses have been proposed to detect and stop ROP execution [6,7,13,22,24,33]. One can imagine that if triggered on a system with ROP defense deployed, the embedded ROP execution in the program transformed with our ROP-based watermarking would set off an alarm, and that specific execution where watermark extraction took place might be terminated.

However, watermark extraction is a special scenario that only happens when certain concerned party tries to either prove the software's ownership or to identify the authorized users. That's why a special input is used to trigger the watermark execution. In our ROP-based watermarking, nor-

Method	Newly inserted instructions executed		Program size increase
	Normal run (without watermark generation)	Watermark generation	
Our work	100%	0%	512
RopSteg	61.5%	38.5%	650

Table 3: Overhead comparison between our method and RopSteg

mal executions of the watermarked program will show no characteristics of ROP execution at all, and therefore do not conflict with ROP defenses. Although it is true that extracting watermark hidden with our design presents ROP behaviors, we believe that given that watermark extraction is such a special event, it is reasonable to simply run the watermarked program in a specialized environment or temporarily turn off the ROP defense.

5.2 Compatibility

Our design is implemented and evaluated under the x86 instruction architecture. Effectiveness and efficiency on other architectures, such as SPARC or ARM, might vary from our current results. That said, there have been reports of successful ROP on various platforms [4, 14, 16], which suggest that our proposal could work on these platforms, too.

Nevertheless, our design makes use of gadgets from shared libraries, suggesting that the watermark extraction depends on the execution environment, e.g. library versions, to correctly re-build the ROP execution path. One possible solution is to source for multiple sets of watermarking payload strings, each corresponding to a distinct version of the selected libraries, so that the watermarked program can detect the environment on which it is running and point the watermarking trigger to the corresponding watermarking payload. We leave this as future work.

5.3 Library Replacement Attack

At this moment, a potential weakness of our ROP-based watermarking is the so-called library replacement attack, i.e. the adversary replaces the original dynamic libraries that would link to the watermarked program, say L, with its custom library L' that may be bundled in the software package. So long as there are gadgets locate in L, such replacement could render errors during ROP and therefore compromise the watermark recovery process. In the extreme case, the adversary could replace all dynamic libraries just in case it does not know where the gadgets reside. We plan to improve our approach on this aspect in the near future. Possible ways might include exploiting gadgets inside libraries that cannot be circumvented (this is possible in some operation system, e.g. any program runs on windows system must load `Kernel32.dll` which provides system API), or introducing tamper-proofing approaches that at runtime check whether the loaded libraries are compromised.

6. CONCLUSION

We proposed a novel dynamic software watermarking design that embeds and exhibits watermark through a memory error exploiting technique named return-oriented programming. Our ROP-based watermarking is able to transform important watermarking code into ROP gadgets and build them in the data region. The watermark can be extracted by activating ROP execution along these gadgets constructed. Evaluations show that compared to previous works, our design achieves better stealth because of its fine-grained code distribution. Analysis and experiments also suggest that our design not only presents good resilience against attacks with code obfuscation and re-packing, but also causes notably lower overhead.

We take our ROP-based watermarking as a successful attempt of turning a malicious approach (return-oriented programming in this case) into a benign usage. We also believe that this work opens a rather different view for software watermarking – instead of hiding messages in special executions, we could make execution itself invisible.

7. ACKNOWLEDGMENTS

This project is partly supported by the National Key Basic Research Program of China (Grant No. 2013CB834204), the National Natural Science Foundation of China (Grant No. 61272423, 61303213), the Natural Science Foundation of Tianjin (Grant No. 14JCYBJC15300), and the Open Project Foundation of Information Security Evaluation Center of Civil Aviation, Civil Aviation University of China (Grant No. CAAC-ISECCA-201403).

8. REFERENCES

[1] The llvm compiler infrastructure. http://llvm.org/.

[2] Upx: the ultimate packer for executables. http://upx.sourceforge.net/.

[3] Xenocode. http://www.xenocode.com.

[4] E. Buchanan, H. Roemer, H. Shacham, and S. Savage. When good instructions go bad: Generalizing return-oriented programming to risc. In *Proceedings of the 15th ACM conference on Computer and communications security (CCS)*, pages 27–38, 2008.

[5] S. Checkoway, L. Davi, A. Dmitrienko, A.-R. Sadeghi, H. Shacham, and M. Winandy. Return-oriented programming without returns. In *Proceedings of the 17th ACM conference on Computer and communications security (CCS)*, pages 559–572, 2010.

[6] P. Chen, H. Xiao, X. Shen, X. Yin, B. Mao, and L. Xie. Drop: Detecting return-oriented programming malicious code. In *Proceedings of the 5th International Conference of Information Systems Security (ICISS)*, pages 163–177, 2009.

[7] Y. Cheng, Z. Zhou, M. Yu, X. Ding, and R. H. Deng. Ropecker: A generic and practical approach for defending against rop attacks. In *Symposium on Network and Distributed System Security (NDSS)*, 2014.

[8] C. Collberg, E. Carter, S. Debray, A. Huntwork, J. Kececioglu, C. Linn, and M. Stepp. Dynamic path-based software watermarking. In *Proceedings of*

the ACM SIGPLAN 2004 conference on Programming language design and implementation (PLDI), pages 107–118, 2004.

[9] C. Collberg and J. Nagra. *Surreptitious Software — Obfuscation, Watermarking, and Tamperproofing for Software Protection.* Software Security Series. Addison-Wesley, 2009.

[10] C. Collberg and C. Thomborson. Software watermarking: models and dynamic embeddings. In *Proceedings of the 26th ACM SIGPLAN-SIGACT Symposium on Principles of Programming Languages (POPL)*, pages 311–324, 1999.

[11] C. Collberg, C. Thomborson, and G. M. Townsend. Dynamic graph-based software watermarking. Technical Report TR04-08, Department of Computer Science, The University of Arizona, 2004.

[12] P. Cousot and R. Cousot. An abstract interpretation-based framework for software watermarking. In *Proceedings of the 31th ACM SIGPLAN-SIGACT Symposium on Principles of Programming Languages (POPL)*, pages 173–185, 2004.

[13] L. Davi, A. Sadeghiy, and M. Winandyz. Ropdefender: A detection tool to defend against return-oriented programming attacks. In *Proceedings of the 6th ACM Symposium on Information, Computer and Communications Security (ASIACCS)*, pages 40–51, 2011.

[14] A. Francillon and C. Castelluccia. Code injection attacks on harvard-architecture devices. In *Proceedings of the 15th ACM conference on Computer and communications security (CCS)*, pages 15–26, 2008.

[15] T. Holz and F. Freiling. Return-oriented rootkits: Bypassing kernel code integrity protection mechanisms. In *Proceedings of the 19nd USENIX conference on Security (USENIX Security)*, pages 383–398, 2009.

[16] T. Kornau. Return oriented programming for the arm architecture. Master's thesis, Ruhr-Universität, Bochum, 2010.

[17] K. Lu, S. Xiong, and D. Gao. Ropsteg: Program steganography with return oriented programming. In *Proceedings of the 4th ACM Conference on Data and Application Security and Privacy (CODASPY)*, pages 265–272, 2014.

[18] G. Myles and C. Collberg. Software watermarking through register allocation: Implementation, analysis, and attacks. In *Proceedings of the 6th International Conference of Information Security and Cryptology (ICISC)*, pages 274–293, 2003.

[19] G. Myles and C. Collberg. Software watermarking via opaque predicates: Implementation, analysis, and attacks. *Electronic Commerce Research*, 6(2):155–171, 2006.

[20] G. Myles and H. Jin. Self-validating branch-based software watermarking. In *Proceedings of the 7th International Workshop of Information Hiding (IH)*, pages 342–356, 2005.

[21] J. Nagra and C. Thomborson. Threading software watermarks. In *Proceedings of the 6th International Workshop of Information Hiding (IH)*, pages 208–223, 2004.

[22] K. Onarlioglu, L. Bilge, A. Lanzi, D. Balzarotti, and E. Kirda. G-free: defeating return-oriented programming through gadget-less binaries. In *Proceedings of the 26th Annual Computer Security Applications Conference (ACSAC)*, pages 49–58, 2010.

[23] J. Palsberg, S. Krishnaswamy, M. Kwon, D. Ma, Q. Shao, and Y. Zhang. Experience with software watermarking. In *Proceedings of the 16th Annual Conference of Computer Security Applications (ACSAC)*, pages 308–316, 2000.

[24] V. Pappas. kbouncer: Efficient and transparent rop mitigation. Technical report, Columbia University, 2012.

[25] C. Ren, K. Chen, and P. Liu. Droidmarking: Resilient software watermarking for impeding android application repackaging. In *Proceedings of the 29th ACM/IEEE international conference on Automated software engineering (ASE)*, pages 635–646, 2014.

[26] R. Roemer, E. Buchanan, H. Shacham, and S. Savage. Return-oriented programming: Systems, languages, and applications. *ACM Transactions on Information and System Security (TISSEC)*, 15(1):2, 2012.

[27] H. Shacham. The geometry of innocent flesh on the bone: Return-into-libc without function calls (on the x86). In *Proceedings of the 14th ACM conference on Computer and communications security (CCS)*, pages 552–561, 2007.

[28] M. Sharif, A. Lanzi, J. Giffin, and W. Lee. Impeding malware analysis using conditional code obfuscation. In *Proceedings of the 16th Annual Network & Distributed System Security Symposium (NDSS)*, 2008.

[29] K. Z. Snow, F. Monrose, L. Davi, A. Dmitrienko, C. Liebchen, and C. Sadeghi. Just-in-time code reuse: On the effectiveness of fine-grained address space layout randomization. In *Proceedings of the 34rd IEEE Symposium on Security and Privacy (S&P)*, pages 574–588, 2013.

[30] D. Song, D. Brumley, H. Yin, J. Caballero, I. Jager, M. G. Kang, Z. Liang, J. Newsome, P. Poosankam, and P. Saxena. Bitblaze: A new approach to computer security via binary analysis. In *Proceedings of the 4th International Conference on Information Systems Security (ICISS)*, pages 1–25, 2008.

[31] R. Venkatesan, V. Vazirani, and S.Sinha. A graph theoretic approach to software watermarking. In *Proceedings of the 4th International Workshop of Information Hiding (IH)*, pages 157–168, 2001.

[32] T. Wang, K. Lu, L. Lu, S. Chung, and W. Lee. Jekyll on ios: When benign apps become evil. In *Proceedings of the 22nd USENIX conference on Security (USENIX Security)*, pages 559–572, 2013.

[33] C. Zhang, T. Wei, Z. Chen, L. Duan, S. McCamant, L. Szekeres, D. Song, and W. Zou. Practical control flow integrity & randomization for binary executables. In *Proceedings of the 34rd IEEE Symposium on Security and Privacy (S&P)*, pages 559–573, 2013.

[34] W. Zhou, X. Zhang, and X. Jiang. Appink: Watermarking android apps for repackaging deterrence. In *Proceedings of the 8th ACM Symposium on InformAtion, Computer and Communications Security (ASIACCS)*, pages 1–12, 2013.

The Limits of Composable Crypto with Transferable Setup Devices

Ioana Boureanu
Akamai Technologies Limited
London
UK
icarlson@akamai.com

Miyako Ohkubo
NICT
Tokyo
Japan
m.ohkubo@nict.go.jp

Serge Vaudenay
EPFL
Lausanne
Switzerland
serge.vaudenay@epfl.ch

ABSTRACT

UC security realized with setup devices imposes that single instances of these setups are used. In most cases, UC-realization relies further on other properties of the setups devices, like tamper-resistance. But what happens in stronger versions of the UC framework, like EUC or JUC, where multiple instances of these setups are allowed? Can we formalise what it is about setups like these which makes them sometimes hinder UC, JUC, EUC realizability?

In this paper, we answer this question. As such, we formally introduce *transferable setups*, which can be viewed as setup devices that do not (publicly) disclose if they have been maliciously passed on. Further, we prove the *general result* that one cannot realize oblivious transfer (OT) or any "interesting" 2-party protocol using transferable setups in the EUC model.

As a by-product, we show that physically unclonable functions (PUFs) themselves are transferable devices, which means that one cannot use PUFs as a global setups; this is interesting because non-transferability is a weaker requirement than locality, which until now was the property informally blamed for UC-impossibility results regarding PUFs as global setups.

If setups are transferable (i.e., they can be passed on from one party to another without explicit disclosure of a malicious transfer), then they will not intrinsically leak if a relay attack takes place. Indeed, we further prove that if relay attacks are possible then oblivious transfer cannot be realized in the JUC model.

Linked to the prevention of relaying, authenticated channels have historically been an essential building stone of the UC model. Related to this, we show how to strengthen some existing protocols UC-realized with PUFs, and render them not only UC-secure but also JUC-secure.

Categories and Subject Descriptors

E.3 [**Data encryption**]: [Public key cryptosystems]

Keywords

universal comparability; relay attacks; physically unclonable functions

1. INTRODUCTION

UC-composable [5] cryptographic primitives give us the very sought-after secure guarantees when it comes to the design of cryptographic protocols. And, the skeptical can even go beyond and aim for stronger models, like the JUC (joint-state UC), EUC (externalized UC), GUC (generalized UC) [6], where realizability is even harder. However there is a fundamentally limiting impossibility result by Canetti *et al.* [7]: two-party secure computations are UC-impossible in the UC plain model. To bypass this, the UC models are augmented with helping building blocks, also called (UC) setups.

In this paper, we look at designing composable cryptographic primitives, especially in stronger UC frameworks (like JUC, EUC) and at how relaying comes in the way of that. We link relay attacks to whether they are apparent/visible at the level of the crypto setups used therein, via the notion of *transferable setups*. An instance of such setups is given by the much spoken-of PUFs (physical unclonable functions) [17, 24, 16, 10, 13, 25]. We then look at how the often-assumed authenticated channels have come to defeat relaying within the UC framework.

For completeness, we will first summarize the general settings of UC models with and without setups, underlining certain important details on the communication model and the legitimate use of setups.

A UC overview.

Plain UC. In the UC framework, we consider several participants and an environment. They all run their purported algorithms. Some participants may be corrupted, in which case they behave as the adversary instructs them to. Participants receive inputs from the environment and send their final outputs to the environment. It is assumed that all algorithms are probabilistic polynomial-time algorithms. The UC models comprises two symbolic worlds that should behave similarly, i.e., a real world where the protocol π is run, and an ideal world where the idealized version of the protocol is executed; this idealized version is usually denoted via an ideal (target) functionality $\mathcal{F}_{target}$. Let us detail slightly. In the real world, a set of honest participants is assumed to run their corresponding part of π. In the ideal world, honest participants are "dummies" who just forward inputs/outputs to the ideal functionality $\mathcal{F}_{target}$. We say that this functionality is UC-realized by the protocol π if for every real adversary, there exists an ideal adversary (also called simulator) such that for every environment $\mathcal{Z}$, the real and the ideal worlds are indistinguishable in terms of the output of $\mathcal{Z}$. This definition is accompanied by a composition theorem: every complex experiment using one instance of π as a subroutine emulates a corresponding experiment using (the dummy protocol based on) $\mathcal{F}_{target}$ instead. This substitution can of course be used recursively.

Communication Models in UC. In the original UC papers [5], it was assumed that the channels were secure; we will henceforth refer to that UC-model as the *secure-channel UC*. However, this assumption was consequently [6] dropped; we will henceforth refer to this later UC-model as the *insecure-channel UC*. The latter means that in the case of honest real-world executions, one can imagine man-in-the-middle adversaries mounting attacks. To bypass this issue, most UC-secure constructions assume or intrinsically require authenticated channels between the participants[1]. Participants can identify where an incoming message comes from and where an outgoing message goes to. Note that the UC models also assume that such authenticated channels are not visible to the adversary.

Hybrid UC. Unfortunately, virtually no interesting ideal functionalities can be realized by protocols in the plain UC setting [7]. So, one turns to the hybrid model, where participants can further access a setup functionality $\mathcal{F}_{\texttt{setup}}$, in both the real and the ideal worlds. This defines the $\mathcal{F}_{\texttt{setup}}$-UC-realization. Roughly speaking, a protocol π is said to be realized in the $\mathcal{F}_{\texttt{setup}}$-hybrid model if π is now built using calls to the ideal functionality $\mathcal{F}_{\texttt{setup}}$, in such a way that one instance of the corresponding "physical" setup will only be used in one protocol session of π. One clear disadvantage is that composition only works for *one single* session of π which is using a "physical" instance of the setup given via $\mathcal{F}_{\texttt{setup}}$ at one point in time. Namely, such a $\mathcal{F}_{\texttt{setup}}$ UC-functionality is always so that it models the following: "duplicates" of the (physical) UC setup-device that $\mathcal{F}_{\texttt{setup}}$ is modelling will be issued for every new session of π. Moreover, no other process should access $\mathcal{F}_{\texttt{setup}}$ when π is already using it (i.e., the environment $\mathcal{Z}$ cannot directly access $\mathcal{F}_{\texttt{setup}}$). In UC terms, for π to be UC-composable using $\mathcal{F}_{\texttt{setup}}$, π needs to be "subroutine respecting" [6].

EUC and GUC. From UC, one moves to the EUC formalization [6] by allowing the environment to access the $\mathcal{F}_{\texttt{setup}}$ as well. EUC-realization and EUC-composition are simply UC-realization and UC-composition respectively where the environment is empowered in this way. I.e., EUC still refers to *one* session of a protocol, but –in EUC– all parties have access to a *global* setup, even if it is still only *one (physical) instance of such a setup*. In the GUC framework [6], the environment is even more powerful as he has access to other protocols running simultaneously in the network. Also, in GUC, the target protocol has several simultaneously running sessions, which the GUC-environment can have adaptive (I/O) access to. GUC-realization is defined with respect to this all-powerful environment. A result of equivalence between some type of GUC-composition and some type of EUC-composition exists [6]. For this equivalence to hold, the communication is restricted again, in that it still only allows "subroutine-respecting" protocols. A protocol π is $\mathcal{F}_{\texttt{setup}}$-subroutine respecting if no subroutine of a party in π takes I/O from any non-subroutine of π (other than a single instance of $\mathcal{F}_{\texttt{setup}}$ and the environment). With such a restriction in place, a weaker EUC-realization/EUC-composition is defined, i.e., EUC-realization that applies to $\mathcal{F}_{\texttt{setup}}$-subroutine respecting protocols, which was proven equivalent to the GUC-realization.

JUC. There also exists a model in between the hybrid-UC and EUC, namely JUC [9]. In the definition of the $\mathcal{F}_{\texttt{setup}}$-JUC realization, we consider several groups of participants, each running their own instance of π in the real world, and "playing" with their own instance of $\mathcal{F}_{target}$ in the ideal world. The protocol participants can all jointly access $\mathcal{F}_{\texttt{setup}}$, but the environment cannot. The environment must also provide all inputs at once, i.e., the simultaneous sessions of π cannot be initialized adaptively. This notion makes feasible a complex composition in some limited way. Namely, for each set of sessions of π which can only be initialized with inputs in parallel, we can substitute each session with an instance of $\mathcal{F}_{target}$, and use the same instance of $\mathcal{F}_{\texttt{setup}}$ for this set (and this set only).

UC setups of interest. UC hybrid models, with setups of tamper-evident and tamper-resistant devices, have been employed to UC-realize bit-commitments (COM), oblivious transfers (OT), coin flipping, polling schemes [15, 18, 14, 19, 20, 22, 21, 2, 3], etc. More recently, a new type of tamper-resilient devices has been modelled as setups to create UC-secure OT and COM [4, 23], namely PUFs (physically unclonable functions). Different assumptions [4] have been taken to model these PUFs: e.g., super-polynomial sizes of the input domains, well-spread domains, freshness of usage, honest behavior, etc. In [23], malicious PUFs are also modelled.

Contributions.

I. In this paper, we first look at how UC setups can in fact lead to impossibility results in certain flavors of the UC model. To this end, we formalize *transferable setups*, which can be viewed as devices that do not (publicly) disclose if they have been maliciously passed on. For instance, transferable setups will not publicly output, e.g., the identifiers of the parties who are physically accessing them. We show that OT is not EUC-realizable if transferable setups are to be used. So, transferable setups cannot be global.

We will show that many of the well-known tamper-resilient devices, PUFs included, can be modelled as what we call *transferable setups*. More specifically, we show that those used in in [14, 19, 20, 22, 21, 2, 4, 23] can, while those used in [15, 18, 2] cannot.

II. We also formalize *relay attacks* in the context of using UC setups. Using this formalism, we then show that an OT protocol subject to a relay attack cannot be JUC-secure.

III. We then look at how relaying and PUFs were handled in the latest UC protocols using these setups. We observe that if PUFs are reusable amongst sessions, or that if we do not assume channel authentication within UC, then the OT protocol in [4] is not UC-secure in the $\mathcal{F}_{\texttt{PUF}}$-hybrid model.

We then show a manner to render the OT protocol in [4] even JUC-secure, by strengthening the protocol.

We discuss other related protocols and setups in the literature and obtain similar results with the protocols from [11, 12, 23].

Organization. We define and observe transferable setup in Section 2. The EUC-impossibilities with transferable setups, as well as other related JUC-imposibilities are discussed in Section 3. We give several examples of transferable setups in Section 4. Section 5 shows how to make JUC-secure OT protocol out of from UC-secure OT protocol that uses transferable setup. We conclude in Section 6.

2. UC SETUPS, TRANSFERABILITY AND RELAYING

Intuitive description of transferability.

This section will give a mathematical expression for the following scenario.

Scenario for transferability. Assume that parties A, B and C are engaged in a communication protocol involving some setup-device. Assume further that B and C are malicious, and A thinks

[1]In the UC literature, it is not always clear when authenticated channels are assumed, but most of the UC protocols do implicitly rely on this assumption of the model. There are a few feasibility results without it [1].

she is communicating with B when in fact she is communicating with C. Roughly speaking, the setup used therein is transferable if the fact that A is mis-lead w.r.t. its interlocutor is not prevented by/via the outputs of this setup.

By separating the notions of party/participant, algorithm, and setup being used, this section will formalise the idea behind transferable setups. This is needed in order to formulate and prove a formal (E)UC impossibility result.

Participants, algorithms and transferability.

We distinguish between a physical *participant* (e.g., a computer, a HSM) and the actual *algorithm* that is run by this physical participant (e.g., the client-side SSH installed on a computer). We will now formalise how these participants and algorithms interact together within a protocol execution. E.g., pieces of software can interact together on the same machine, and each piece can independently deliver several outputs: an SSL client algorithm can send some messages directly on port 443 and some other messages to the network configuration daemon of the same physical machine.

Participants can be viewed as identifiable entities/parties taking part in real/idealized execution: e.g., a physical machine with an identifiable IP address. Participants, functionalities, and the environment run *algorithms*. They are connected with each others by some bi-directional channels. For simplicity, we assume only two ends for every channel. We assume that algorithms have different input/output communication ports which can be "plugged" to the port of other algorithms, or to the communication channel of a participant. I.e., in a real-world setting, this would be akin to one algorithm being called by another algorithm and/or used by a device/party. Also, algorithms are not aware how their communication ports are plugged. At the same time, honest participants are correctly "plugged". I.e., the SSL algorithm does not "care" on which port messages are delivered, but a correctly/standardly configured SSL server will have port 443 open and it will be listening on it.

Participants, functionalities, and the environment have an identifier. Algorithms could use the identifier of participants as part of their communication. I.e., the SSL-handshake algorithm will verify a certificate against a given hostname that identifies the server. Indeed, algorithms could receive such identifiers as input, e.g., to instruct them which role they are supposed to "play" and with whom they are supposed to communicate. This is akin to instantiated an object of a generic class with specific parameters, or calling a function with specific arguments, e.g., instantiate the server-side (object) of a program with a server-identifier called "server1" to speak to a client instantiated as "client3". To denote that an algorithm $\mathtt{alg}$ runs with some given identifiers $id_1,\ldots,id_n$, we simply write $alg(id_1,\ldots,id_n)$. These identifiers can also be hard-coded in the algorithm. For instance, we can assume that the algorithm of a UC setup functionality $\mathcal{F}_{\mathtt{setup}}$ is correctly "plugged" and that all identifiers are hard-coded. In this way, $\mathcal{F}_{\mathtt{setup}}$ always knows from which participant a message comes in, and to which participant a message is to be sent to. However, for participants and their algorithms, there is no guarantee that the "plugging" and/or the input-manipulation runs correctly. This is so since inputs can be (maliciously) handled, e.g., if the algorithm is run by a corrupted participant.

Transferability.

In the context of communicating parties, using setups, we will also formalize how an unobservable relay can be achieved, i.e., a relay that no party/setup can be aware of. To do so, we will introduce a series of experiments (i.e., interactive games of machines/participants and algorithms) depicted in Fig. 1 and denoted $\mathbf{exp_1}$, $\mathbf{exp_2}$, $\mathbf{exp}'_1$ and $\mathbf{exp}'_2$.

The transferability/relay-defining experiments in Fig. 1. Assume an arbitrary 2-party protocol defined by two algorithms *sdr* (sender) and *rcv* (receiver). We assume that *sdr* is designed to be run by party P_1 and to communicate with party P_2, and that *rcv* is designed to be run by P_2 and to communicate with P_1 (I.e., this is as if the previously mentioned identifiers, here denoted P_1 and P_2, were hard-coded in *sdr* and *rcv*). The participant denoted with $\mathcal{Z}$ is executing an arbitrary algorithm with two communication ports, no input (port) and one output (port). Both algorithms *sdr* and *rcv* have an input/output port (connected to $\mathcal{Z}$), a setup port (connected to $\mathcal{F}_{\mathtt{setup}}$), and an extra communication port to communicate with their counterpart. This is depicted in the upper, leftmost part of Fig.1, denoted $\mathbf{exp_1}$. In this experiment denoted $\mathbf{exp_1}$, P_1 indeed executes *sdr* (sender), P_2 executes *rcv* (receiver) with correctly connected communication ports. A second experiment is shown on the upper right part of Fig. 1 and is denoted $\mathbf{exp_2}$. In this second experiment exp_2, P_3 is running two concurrent algorithms: the *rcv* (receiver) algorithm and $\mathtt{tr}^{P_1P_2}_{P_2P_3}$ (some "relay-accommodating" translator).

The aim of experiments $\mathbf{exp_1}$ and $\mathbf{exp_2}$ in Fig. 1. This is here is as follows: $\mathbf{exp_2}$ will appear (to the outside world) just like $\mathbf{exp_1}$., only that –in $\mathbf{exp_2}$– the outputs by the *sdr* algorithm are relayed from P_1 to the P_3 party, who is the one running the *rcv* algorithm in $\mathbf{exp_2}$; All of this is done transparently to Z and all other parties involved. For this transparency to be achieved, we introduced the $\mathtt{tr}^{P_1P_2}_{P_2P_3}$: a mechanisation facilitating whatever translation (of identifiers) needs to take place. Intuitively, via $\mathtt{tr}^{P_1P_2}_{P_2P_3}$'s "translation", the *rcv* (receiver) algorithm behaves as if it was run by P_2 communicating with P_1 in the upper part of $\mathbf{exp_2}$'s last block, while in its lower part, *rcv* behaves as if it is run by P_3 communicating with P_2.

We define similar experiments $\mathbf{exp}'_1$ and $\mathbf{exp}'_2$, in a symmetric way.

The first communication port of $\mathcal{Z}$ is connected to P_1 in both experiments. The second port of $\mathcal{Z}$ is connected to (the channel of) P_2 in the first experiment, and to P_3 in the second experiment. The algorithm $\mathtt{tr}^{P_1P_2}_{P_2P_3}$ uses two ports: the upper and the lower one. The input/output port of *rcv* is connected to $\mathcal{Z}$, its communication port is connected to P_2, and its setup port is connected to the upper port of $\mathtt{tr}^{P_1P_2}_{P_2P_3}$. The lower port of $\mathtt{tr}^{P_1P_2}_{P_2P_3}$ is connected (to the channel) to $\mathcal{F}_{\mathtt{setup}}$. In both experiments, we assume that P_1 executes *sdr* with correctly connected communication ports.

Let us now formalize the requirements of the setups, in order for the above (informal) transparent relaying to be the case.

Definition 1. (Transferable Setup) Assume some participants and identifiers P_1,P_2,P_3. Let $\mathcal{F}_{\mathtt{setup}}$ be a setup functionality and $\mathtt{relay}(P_1,P_2,P_3)$ be an algorithm. We say that $\mathcal{F}_{\mathtt{setup}}$ is a $\mathtt{relay}$-transferable setup if there exists some algorithms $\mathtt{tr}=\mathtt{tr}^{P_1P_2}_{P_2P_3}$ and $\mathtt{tr}'=\mathtt{tr}^{P_2P_3}_{P_1P_2}$ such that for any 2-party protocol $\pi=(\mathtt{alg}_1,\mathtt{alg}_2)$ as per the above and any $\mathcal{Z}$, the above experiments in $(\mathsf{exp}_1,\mathsf{exp}_2)$ and $(\mathsf{exp}'_1,\mathsf{exp}'_2)$ produce indistinguishable outcomes in each respective tuple.

In Section 4, we are going to show which "modern" UC setups are transferable and which are not; in anticipation, PUFs [4] are transferable, but tamper-resistant hardware [15] are not.

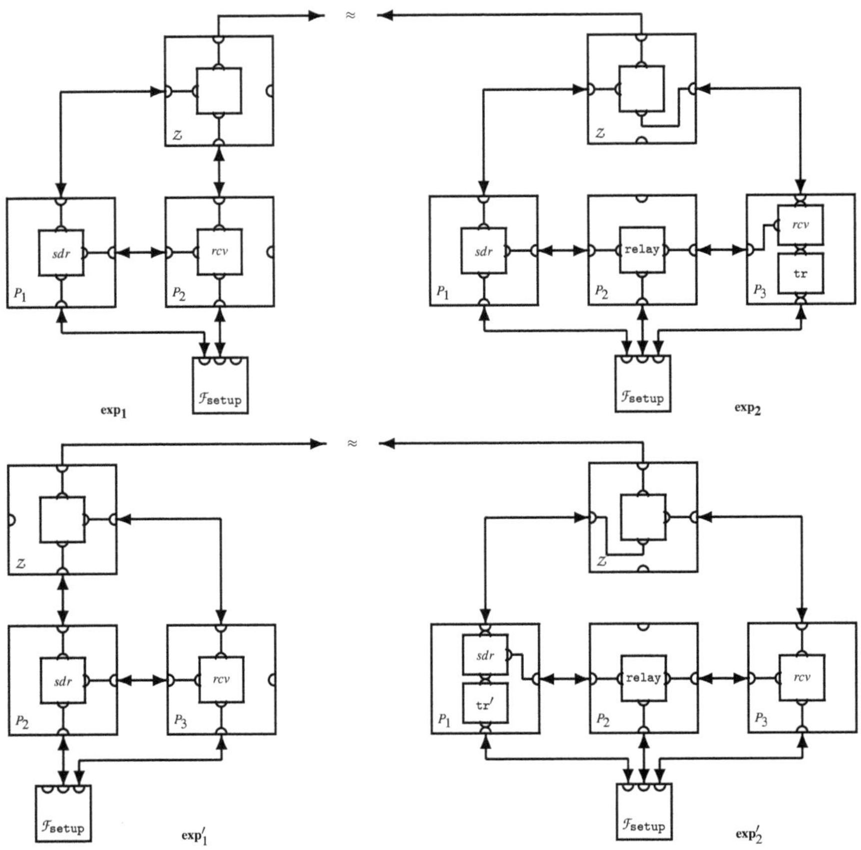

Figure 1: Transferable Setup.

We are now going to formalize the notion of relay attacks, in presence of transferable setups.

Definition 2. (Relay Attack (Fig. 2)) Let $\mathcal{F}_{\texttt{setup}}$ be a $\texttt{relay}$-transferable setup, for $\texttt{relay}(P_1,P_2,P_3)$, P_1, P_2, P_3 as before. We consider a 2-party protocol $\pi=(\texttt{alg}_1(P_1,P_2),\texttt{alg}_2(P_1,P_2))$ based on the functionality $\mathcal{F}_{\texttt{setup}}$ in which *sdr* and *rcv* receive two hard-coded identifiers. We say that π is subject to relay attacks if for any $\mathcal{Z}$, the two following experiments are indistinguishable to any environment: 1. participant P_1 runs $sdr(P_1,P_3)$ with the communication port connected (to the channel) to participant P_3, participant P_3 runs $rcv(P_1,P_3)$ with the communication port connected (to the channel) to participant P_1; 2. participant P_1 runs $sdr(P_1,P_2)$ with the communication port connected (to the channel) to participant P_2, participant P_3 runs $rcv(P_2,P_3)$ with the communication port connected (to the channel) to participant P_2, participant P_2 runs $\texttt{relay}(P_1,P_2,P_3)$, as per the definition of $\texttt{relay}$-transferable setups.

3. IMPOSSIBILITY RESULTS IN UC WITH TRANSFERABLE SETUPS & RELAYING

In this section, we will see how transferability affects EUC-realization.

3.1 Transferable Setups & EUC-Impossibility

THEOREM 1. *If $\mathcal{F}_{\texttt{setup}}$ is a $\texttt{relay}$-transferable setup for some symmetric $\texttt{relay}$ algorithm, then there is no protocol which $\mathcal{F}_{\texttt{setup}}$-EUC-realizes $\mathcal{F}_{OT}$.*

The intuition of the proof.

The idea of the proof is classical. Start from the premise that an arbitrary protocol $\pi=(\texttt{alg}_s,\texttt{alg}_r)$ would $\mathcal{F}_{\texttt{setup}}$-EUC-realize $\mathcal{F}_{OT}$. Then, create a series of runs of this protocol and of the $\mathcal{F}_{OT}$ functionality respectively, such that these runs are pair-wise and/or transitively indistinguishable, yet you arrive at some (distinguishability-based) contradiction. Thus, conclude that no such protocol $\pi=(\texttt{alg}_s,\texttt{alg}_r)$ could have in fact $\mathcal{F}_{\texttt{setup}}$-EUC realized $\mathcal{F}_{OT}$.

To get to this contradiction, we will basically use the existence of the ideal-world simulator $\mathcal{S}im$ (given the initial presumption that $\pi=(\texttt{alg}_s,\texttt{alg}_r)$ would $\mathcal{F}_{\texttt{setup}}$-EUC-realize $\mathcal{F}_{OT}$ say running with one of the inputs as a bit b). Then, this $\mathcal{S}im$ must be able to "extract" the correct bit b to send to $\mathcal{F}_{OT}$. We will then make $\mathcal{S}im$ internally available to a corrupt participant in a new (real-world) run of the protocol. The executions run via such a corrupt party (in the real world) will not be indistinguishably simulatable (in an ideal counterpart). To build the series of indistinguishable experiments we apply transformation steps provided either by the (supposed) $\mathcal{F}_{\texttt{setup}}$-EUC realization of $\mathcal{F}_{OT}$ or by the definition of transferable setups.

Note1.

It seems intuitive that if a setup is transferable, then it loses "globality", hence it cannot serve as an EUC-setup. However, the separation between "globality" and non-transferability is not known. I.e., if a setup is non-global, it does not mean it is transferable,

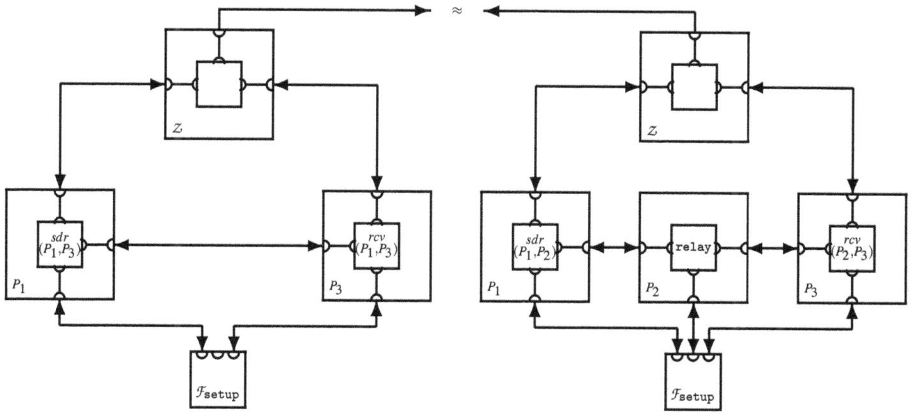

Figure 2: Relay Attack.

nor do we know how many other well-distinguishable properties may lie between transferable and non-global, or between global and non-transferable. Moreover, this is the first time a compact class of global setups, which lead to lack of realizability, has been formally characterised.

Note2.

This proof strategy to be seen below (but not the methodology of symmetric algorithms and relay-transferable setups) is akin to that of splitting adversaries in [8]. Thus, our result above seems to also be an extension from UC-impossibility results to EUC-impossibility results, when the class of relay-transferable setups are used. Along similar lines, the above OT-impossibility result should extend and, like in [8], apply to all same-output non-trivial 2-party protocols.

PROOF. We start with a protocol $\pi = (\texttt{alg}_s, \texttt{alg}_r)$ and assume contrary to our current theorem that π would $\mathcal{F}_{\texttt{setup}}$-EUC realize $\mathcal{F}_{OT}$. If this is the case then for every adversary that will corrupt π (in the real world), there exists a simulator running an algorithm $\mathcal{S}im$ that would mimic it (in the ideal world) in such a way that no (EUC) environment $\mathcal{Z}$ can tell the difference (between the two worlds).

In what follows we consider an environment and three participants P_1, P_2, P_3, together with $\mathcal{F}_{\texttt{setup}}$.

In the first three experiments, the environment is running and algorithm G generating two strings s_0 and s_1 and a bit b, sending s_0 and s_1 to a left participant and b to a right one, getting from the right participant some s, and giving as an outcome 1 if and only if $s = s_b$.

In the first experiment, denoted $\mathbf{exp_1}$ in Fig. 3, the left participant is connected to P_1 who is running $\texttt{alg}_s$ with P_2. The right one is connected to P_2 who is running $\texttt{alg}_r$ with P_1. So, this experiment always outputs 1.

At the higher level, we can simply view $\mathbf{exp_1}$ *as* P_1 *running an honest sender-side algorithm and* P_2 *running an honest receiver-side algorithm within an 1-out-of-2 two-party OT protocol* π.

Using the transferability assumption (marked with "(1)" in Fig. 3), a direct consequence of Def. 1 shows that this is equivalent to a second experiment in which the left participant is still connected to P_1, still running $\texttt{alg}_s$ with P_2, but the right one is connected to P_3, now running $\texttt{alg}_r$ and $\texttt{tr}^{P_1P_2}_{P_2P_3}$ with P_2. The participant P_2 is now running $\texttt{relay}(P_1,P_2,P_3)$. Please see the top two experiments of Fig. 3.

At a higher level, this second experiment $\mathbf{exp_2}$ *shows how mainly the receiver-side is getting corrupted (and, above all, impersonated). I.e., the receiver-side is now being run by some* P_3*, but* P_1 *thinks he is sending messages to some* P_2*; meanwhile, the receiver-side messages produced inside* P_3 *will be received by the man-in-the-middle* P_2 *and then fed by* P_2 *back to* P_1.

We can define a new environment putting the old one and P_3 together (see the doted line on the second diagram in Fig. 3, $\mathbf{exp_2}$ and $\mathbf{exp_3}$).

Thus, in $\mathbf{exp_2}$*, we simply have an EUC environment (within* $\mathbf{exp_2}$*'s dotted line) which runs the receiver-side inside himself, and we have an adversary in the person of* P_2 *who simply relays between this environment and an honest sender-side algorithm run inside* P_1*. This EUC real-world execution now becomes fundamental to the proof (because we presumed it would be simulatable).*

Let us apply the EUC-realizability assumption (marked with "(2)" in Fig. 3). Then, this second, real-life EUC experiment $\mathbf{exp_2}$ is equivalent to a third, ideal-life EUC experiment $\mathbf{exp_3}$. In $\mathbf{exp_3}$, P_1 is a dummy sender forwarding messages to $\mathcal{F}_{\texttt{OT}}$, P_2 is running a simulator exchanging messages with $\mathcal{F}_{OT}$, and the environment is as before, i.e., the (old, G-based) environment and P_3 are still being run as in $\mathbf{exp_2}$.

According to the assumption of EUC-realizability assumption, $\mathcal{S}im$ *is able to produce a bit* b' *to send to* $\mathcal{F}_{\texttt{OT}}$*,* $\mathcal{F}_{\texttt{OT}}$ *gives him back a state* $s_{b'}$ *such that, with a high probability,* $b' = b$ *and then* $s_{b'}$ *is equal to* s_b *(i.e., with* s*).*

In the next experiments, the environment is still generating s_0, s_1, b, sending b to a right participant (who is still connected to P_3 at this time), waiting for a bit b' from a left participant (that we connect to P_2 for the moment) and sending him back $s_{b'}$. The environment expects some s or s_b from the right participant and outputs 1 if and only if $s_{b'} = s_b$.

By redirecting the simulator's port to the environment (marked with "(3)" in Fig. 3), we obtain an experiment which is obviously equivalent to the previous one. We denote by G' the algorithm of the environment.

The simple step from $\mathbf{exp_3}$*to* $\mathbf{exp_4}$ *was first to include a simulated version of* $\mathcal{F}_{OT}$ *inside the run done by* $\mathcal{Z}$*. Then, (algorithm of) the dummy* P_1 *was also silently "pushed inside"* $\mathcal{Z}$*. This is why we renamed his internal algorithm from G to* G'*. This is possible without distinguishability repercussions since* $\mathcal{F}_{OT}$ *does not state who queries what, i.e., it makes no public announcements that would hinter its simulated "inclusion" within* $\mathcal{Z}$*, and* P_1 *did practically nothing.*

We now apply the transferability with (P_3, P_2, P_1) (marked with "(4)" in Fig. 4). We obtain that P_2 runs $\texttt{relay}(P_3,P_2,P_1)$ with the

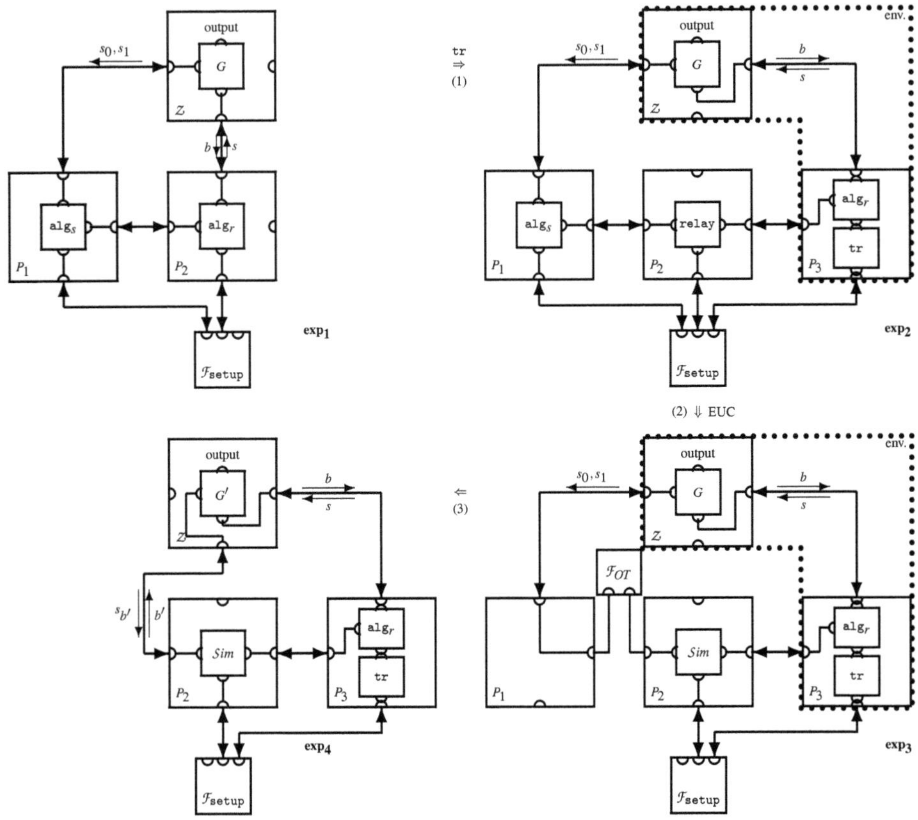

Figure 3: Reductions (1) to (3).

left port connected to P_3 and the right port connected to P_1. But, due to the symmetry, this is equivalent to $\mathtt{relay}(P_1, P_2, P_3)$ with the left port connected to P_1 and the right port connected to P_3. Now, P_1 is running the simulator connected to a translator.

We apply again (marked with "(5)" in Fig. 4) the transferability (backwards) to move back to the situation where P_2 is running $\mathtt{alg}_r$ correctly connected, and P_3 unused.

We have now arrived to some clearer, new real-world (UC) executions depicted in $\mathbf{exp_6}$*. We can see it in the following way.* $\mathcal{Z}$ *is running an OT session called* π_1 *(on* s_0, s_1, b*) with a receiver in the person of* P_2*. Out of this,* $\mathcal{Z}$ *gets* $s = s_b$ *from* P_2*. And,* P_1 *interacts as a sender with the honest receiver* P_2 *according to the OT protocol* π*, in a session called* π_3*. At the same time,* $\mathcal{Z}$ *is running another OT session called* π_2 *(on* b'*) with a (corrupt) party in the person of* P_1*.* P_1 *is acting as an OT-receiver for* $\mathcal{Z}$ *inside* π_2*. Out of this,* $\mathcal{Z}$ *should send* $s_{b'}$ *to* P_1*, where* b' *is provided by* P_1 *via* $\mathcal{S}im$*. Since* $\mathcal{S}im$ *should be able to extract* b *out of the run in* π_3*, then with an overwhelming probability,* b' *should be equal to* b *and then* $s_{b'}$ *should be equal to* s_b *with an overwhelming probability. So, in these real-world executions the environment with output* 1*, with an overwhelming probability.*

Finally, we apply (marked with "(6)" in Fig. 4) the EUC assumption again (actually, the UC assumption is enough in this case, since the environment is not using $\mathcal{F}_{\mathtt{setup}}$). Due to our reductions, in the ideal-world execution depicted in $\mathbf{exp_7}$, the output must also be 1 (except with negligible probability).

In $\mathbf{exp_7}$, in the session π_1, we obtain that P_2 is honestly receiving a bit b and giving it to $\mathcal{F}_{\mathtt{OT}}$, P_1 sends some s'_0, s'_1 to $\mathcal{F}_{\mathtt{OT}}$, $\mathcal{F}_{\mathtt{OT}}$ sends s'_b back to P_2, P_2 then sends this s'_b as s back to $\mathcal{Z}$. In the session π_2, P_1 is running a simulator $\mathcal{S}im'$ to send some b'' to the environment $\mathcal{Z}$, to get $s_{b''}$ in return from $\mathcal{Z}$.

The question is whether $s_{b''}$ is still equal to s (like $s_{b'}$ was in $\mathbf{exp_6}$). Clearly, if $b = b''$, then this holds with probability 1 (i.e., then $s_{b''} = s_b \equiv s$). But if $b \neq b''$ (which happens with probability $\frac{1}{2}$), this can only work if the simulator $\mathcal{S}im'$ can correctly guess $s'_{\bar{b}}$. Given that there is at least one bit of information in $s'_{\bar{b}}$, the outcome of the experiment is 1 with probability lower than $\frac{3}{4}$, which contradicts the initial assumption (i.e., $\mathbf{exp_7}$ cannot perfectly emulate $\mathbf{exp_6}$, which goes back to $\mathbf{exp_4}$ not perfectly emulating $\mathbf{exp_3}$, which refutes the EUC-realizability in the first place). □

Other EUC impossibilities with transferable setups.

We believe that this can be taken further, to some other types of protocols (like the impossibility in [8] was). For instance, we can easily show with a similar proof the same result for commitment.[2] A natural question, given our results, is whether we can EUC-realize key exchange $\mathcal{F}_{KE}$ (since practice likes to do key exchange with PUFs), based on transferable setups. The answer is that we cannot.

THEOREM 2. *If* $\mathcal{F}_{\mathtt{setup}}$ *is a* $\mathtt{relay}$*-transferable setup for some symmetric* $\mathtt{relay}$ *algorithm, then there is no protocol which* $\mathcal{F}_{\mathtt{setup}}$*-EUC-realizes* $\mathcal{F}_{COM}$ *or* $\mathcal{F}_{KE}$*.*

---

[2] Care is to be taken at the fact that commitment-transactions are done in two phases.

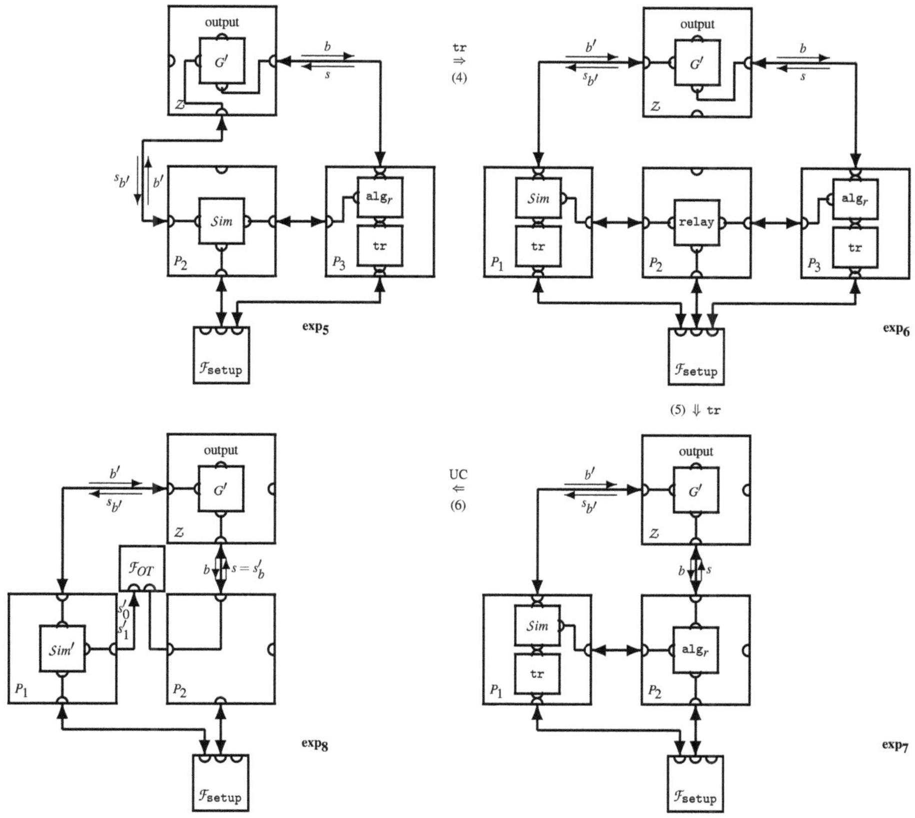

Figure 4: Reductions (4) to (6).

The intuition of the proof.

If we have a protocol EUC-realizing $\mathcal{F}_{KE}$, we can consider an experiment with Alice and Bob, where Alice is malicious and just forwards everything to the environment. Due to transferability, this is the same as Alice and Bob running the protocol honestly. Due to EUC-security, there must be an ideal adversary who as follows. First, this ideal adversary makes Alice and dummy Bob run $\mathcal{F}_{\text{KE}}$ and get the exchanged key K. Then, it can simulate Bob's protocol to the environment running Alice's protocol in such a way that the protocol terminate with the key K. Now, take the algorithm of this ideal adversary and consider another experiment where Bob is malicious and running this algorithm. This will make a honest Alice terminate the KE protocol on a key K chosen by the environment and given to Bob. But now, it is clear that the ideal world cannot force $\mathcal{F}_{\text{KE}}$ to make Alice receive some K chosen by the environment. So, there is a contradiction with EUC security.

3.2 Relaying & JUC-Impossibility

We now move to JUC-security and show that it is hindered by relay attacks, formalized in Def. 2.

THEOREM 3. *If* $\pi = (\texttt{alg}_s, \texttt{alg}_r)$ *is an OT protocol based on* $\mathcal{F}_{\texttt{setup}}$ *and* π *is subject to relay attacks, then* π *does not* $\mathcal{F}_{\texttt{setup}}$*-JUC-realizes* $\mathcal{F}_{OT}$.

PROOF. Consider a JUC (real-world) experiment of two sessions of the OT protocol in $\mathcal{F}_{\texttt{setup}}$ hybrid model, with a sender S_1 and a receiver R_1, and a sender S_2 and receiver R_2, in the two respective sessions. The environment $\mathcal{Z}$ chooses $s_0^{(i)}$ and $s_1^{(i)}$ and sends them to the honest participant S_i, where $i = 1,2$. $\mathcal{Z}$ also selects a bit $b^{(i)}$ and sends it to the honest participant R_i, where $i = 1,2$. The outcome s coming for R_2 will be given back to the environment. The environment outputs 1 if and only if $s = s_b^{(1)}$. We consider the following execution of this real-world experiment where R_1 and S_2 are corrupted. In first session π_1 of π, using a setup function $\mathcal{F}_{\texttt{setup}}$, S_1 runs with $(s_0^{(1)}, s_1^{(1)})$ with the adversary $\mathcal{A}$ who does the following: $\mathcal{A}$ relays the protocol sessions from S_1 to R_2 (as well as the physical setup instance, as per the transferability assumption). The above real-world execution is illustrated in Fig. 5.

Due to the transferability assumption, this is indistinguishable from S_1 and R_2 running the protocol together. So, in this real-world execution, the environment outputs 1 with probability 1 (as he would do if S_1 and R_2 running the protocol together).

Let us now describe the corresponding ideal-world execution. The ideal adversary $\mathcal{S}im$ (namely $\mathcal{S}im(R_1)$) learns $s_\beta^{(1)}$, but has no information about $s_{\bar\beta}$. Equally, $\mathcal{S}im$ (namely $\mathcal{S}im(S_2)$) knows nothing about $b^{(2)}$. So, with the output by the dummy R_2, in this ideal-world execution, the environment outputs 1 with a probability close to $\frac{1}{2}$.

Thus, we exemplified a JUC real-world execution of an arbitrary 1-out-of-2 2-party OT that is distinguishable from its ideal-world counterpart. Thus, OT is not JUC-secure in $\mathcal{F}_{\texttt{setup}}$-hybrid model, when $\mathcal{F}_{\texttt{setup}}$ is transferable and relaying is possible. □

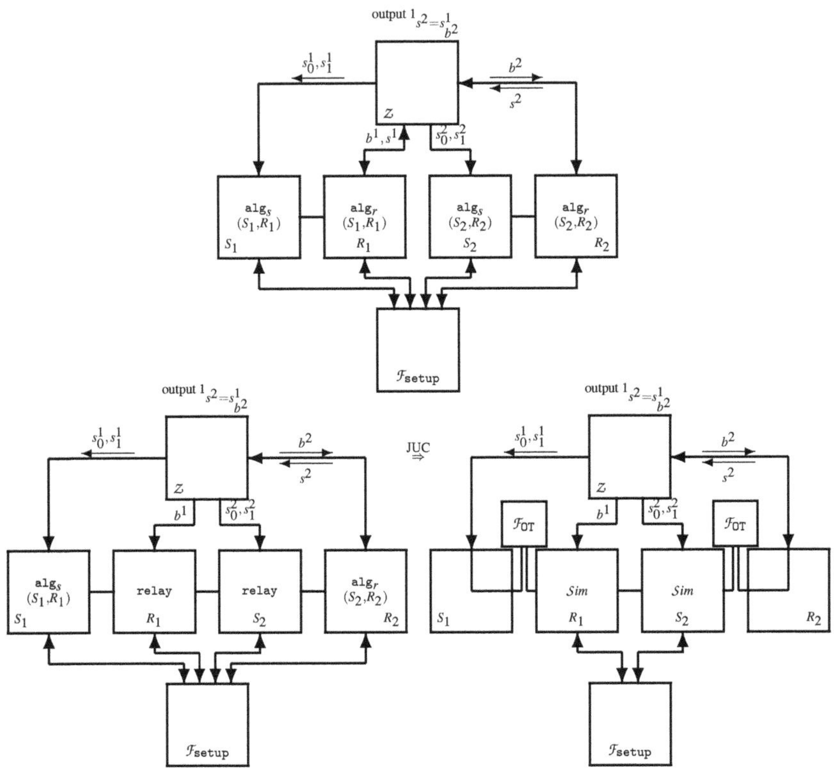

Figure 5: Relay Attack against JUC Security.

4. ACTUAL TRANSFERABLE SETUP DEVICES

Examples of transferable setups.

We will show prove/discuss the transferability of certain known UC setup devices. One of these is $\mathcal{F}_{\mathrm{PUF}}$, modelling PUFs, as they were formalised in [4].

THEOREM 4. *$\mathcal{F}_{\mathrm{PUF}}$ defined in [4] is* `relay`*-transferable setup.*

PROOF. Let us consider a 2-party protocol π run using PUFs (i.e., $\mathcal{F}_{\mathrm{PUF}}$). We presume some hard-coded identifiers P_1, P_2, and two algorithms *sdr*, *rcv* respectively used by parties with these identifiers. Let the run of this protocol by the parties above denote an experiment called $\mathbf{exp_1}$ (as in the left hand side of Fig. 1). Let P_3 be another hard-coded identifier, to be used by a third party. We will define two more algorithms, `relay` and `tr` and we will prove that — with $P_1, P_2, P_2, \mathtt{alg}_1, \mathtt{alg}_2, \mathcal{F}_{\mathrm{PUF}}$ and `relay` and `tr` — we can build an execution of π, in an experiment $\mathbf{exp_2}$, indistinguishable from $\mathbf{exp_1}$. The same holds for $\mathbf{exp}'_1$ and $\mathbf{exp}'_2$. Consequently, $\mathcal{F}_{\mathrm{PUF}}$ is `relay`-transferable setup as per Def. 1.

A `relay` *algorithm:* This is relaying messages in an intuitive way: whatever comes from the left port is forwarded to the right port and vice versa. Messages from $\mathcal{F}_{\mathrm{PUF}}$ are ignored except the notifications of a received handover: if `relay` receives $(\mathtt{handover}_{\mathrm{PUF}}, \mathtt{sid}, P_i)$ for $i = 1, 3$, it sends back $m = (\mathtt{handover}_{\mathrm{PUF}}, \mathtt{sid}, P_j)$ with j such that $\{i, j\} = \{1, 3\}$ to forward the PUF to the other participant. Since we consider 2-party protocols, whenever `relay` receives a message from $\mathcal{F}_{\mathrm{PUF}}$, it could only have originated from *sdr* or *rcv*. So, other handed over PUFs are just ignored by `relay`.

A $\mathtt{tr}^{P_1P_2}_{P'_1P'_2}$ *algorithm:* This translates identifiers in an intuitive way: if it receives $m = (\mathtt{init}_{\mathrm{PUF}}, \mathtt{sid}, P_j)$ from the top port, then $\mathtt{tr}^{P_1P_2}_{P'_1P'_2}$ sends $(\mathtt{init}_{\mathrm{PUF}}, \mathtt{sid}, P'_j)$ to the bottom one. The response of form $(\mathtt{initialized}_{\mathrm{PUF}}, \mathtt{sid})$ from the bottom port is forwarded to the top one. If $m = (\mathtt{eval}_{\mathrm{PUF}}, P_j, c)$ comes from the top, then $\mathtt{tr}^{P_1P_2}_{P'_1P'_2}$ sends $(\mathtt{init}_{\mathrm{PUF}}, P'_j, c)$ to the bottom. Then, the response of form $(\mathtt{eval'ed}_{\mathrm{PUF}}, \mathtt{sid}, c, r)$ from the bottom is forwarded to the top. Finally, after it receives the message $m = (\mathtt{handover}_{\mathrm{PUF}}, \mathtt{sid}, P_j, P_i)$ from the top, $(\mathtt{handover}_{\mathrm{PUF}}, \mathtt{sid}, P'_j, P'_i)$ is sent by $\mathtt{tr}^{P_1P_2}_{P'_1P'_2}$ to the bottom, and $m = (\mathtt{handover}_{\mathrm{PUF}}, \mathtt{sid}, P'_i)$ coming from the bottom makes $\mathtt{tr}^{P_1P_2}_{P'_1P'_2}$ send the message $(\mathtt{handover}_{\mathrm{PUF}}, \mathtt{sid}, P_i)$ to the top.

For $P'_1 = P_3$ and $P'_2 = P_3$, we show by induction that any step in $\mathbf{exp_1}$ matches one (or several) steps in $\mathbf{exp_2}$. So, the simulation is perfect. □

Let us now consider other setup assumptions. Tamper-proof hardware is used in [15] and is described using $\mathcal{F}_{wrap}$. According to the definition, $\mathcal{F}_{wrap}$ is not a transferable setup since it is assumed that the creator of the tamper-proof device intends to have this device be used only by one user, whose id is recorded in the device, and the thus-wise recorded id cannot be changed. Tamper-resistant devices $\mathcal{F}_{TA}$ are building blocks in a model called the trusted agent model [18]; like $\mathcal{F}_{wrap}$, $\mathcal{F}_{TA}$ is not a transferable setup. This is because there is no opportunity for handing it over as per the device's definition in [18]. Tamper-evident envelopes presented in [21] can be considered relay-transferable setups, because such an envelope includes only the sender's id (and a value), and the envelope sent to a user can be diverted to another user. However, purported tamper-evident envelopes $\mathcal{F}^{DE}_{Oneseal}$ (a variant of the above envelopes), proposed by [2], are not transferable. It is because such an envelope is aimed only for an intended recipient and cannot be diverted to another recipient.

5. COMPOSABILITY & TRANSFERABLE DEVICES – FURTHER ASPECTS

We will now report on further issues with the UC-security of recent protocols that were particularly based on PUFs, which we showed above to be transferable devices. (These discussions could extend to other transferable devices.)

Then we will propose some solutions to bypass the issues highlighted in the first part of the section.

To set the basis of the discussions, in Fig. 6, we first recall the *PUFOT* protocol from [4], an OT protocol based on PUFs.[3] We simplified the description of the protocols as follows: 1). we are assuming non-noisy PUFs (which allows to get rid of the fuzzy extraction); 2). we removed the multiple OT capabilities. It is fairly easy to check that our observations extend to the original PUFOT protocol. In this way, we treat PUFs as access-controlled random oracles. (Malicious PUFs could later be introduced as arbitrary oracles.) Basically, the receiver initializes a PUF, gets one random

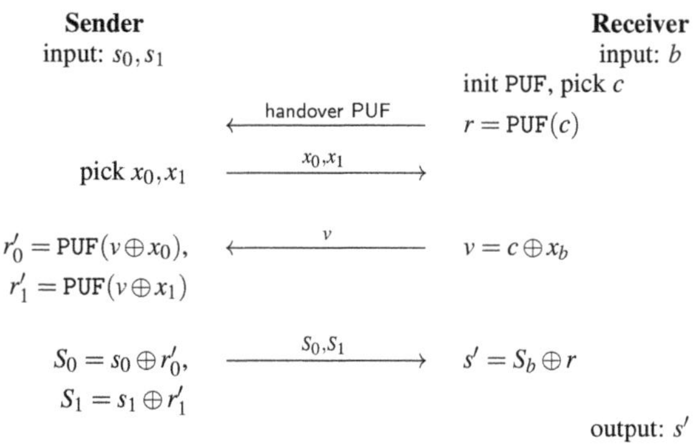

Figure 6: The (Simplified) PUFOT Protocol.

$(c, \mathrm{PUF}(c))$ pair, and hands over the PUF to the sender.[4] The sender selects two values x_0 and x_1 and sends them to the receiver. The receiver responds by $v = c \oplus x_b$ which perfectly hides b. The sender computes $r'_0 = \mathrm{PUF}(v \oplus x_0)$ and $r'_1 = \mathrm{PUF}(v \oplus x_1)$ as one of these must be the r known by the receiver. The receiver cannot know both since he cannot predict $x_0 \oplus x_1$. Finally, the sender used r'_0 and r'_1 to encrypt s_0 and s_1 respectively. The receiver is then able to decrypt s_b.

5.1 Two Issues in UC-security: Reusing PUFs and Authenticating Channels

Honest reuse of PUFs in PUFOT.

We now observe that the PUF instances/devices cannot be handed over again after one session of PUFOT. Indeed, if a PUF-instance is used in one session of PUFOT and then handed-over by the sender, then the first session is insecure. To see that, let us assume that a PUF instance can be reused after a session of the PUFOT with sender S and receiver R. As we know, when the session finishes, the sender S will hold the PUF. We assume that S hands over the PUF after the session. During this hand-over, the adversary that overheard the session is able to query the PUF on the value $c' = c \oplus x_0 \oplus x_1$ and learn r'_{1-b}. Then, he can decrypt s_{1-b} and break the OT requirements.

[3]Note that [26, 27] have shown a weakness of this protocol.

[4]On Fig. 6, "handover PUF" is a shorthand to mean that the receiver sends a hand-over command to $\mathcal{F}_{\mathrm{PUF}}$ and that the sender waits for being granted access to the PUF.

This observation states a version of the PAM-impossibility results in [28]. Our formulation/proof above is much simpler, and in fact natural.

Consequently, PUFs must be destroyed after a protocol is completed. Note that the PUFOT protocol allows multiple OTs with the same sender and receiver. But since the PUF is not be handed over, this imposes that the OT sessions are from the same sender to the same receiver. After all sessions completed, the PUF cannot be used anymore and must be destroyed. So, attacks based on honest reuse of PUFs can be avoided.

Malicious reuse of PUFs in PUFOT.

The PUFOT protocol is subject to relay attacks as per Def. 2, which could be seen as a malicious reuse of a PUF. So, due to Th. 3, it does not $\mathcal{F}_{\mathrm{PUF}}$-JUC realize $\mathcal{F}_{OT}$.

Actually, there is no practical way to prevent an adversary from reusing a PUF. This entails that the PUC model [4] does not compose in the classical sense, even to the weak level of JUC.

Malleability in PUFOT and its successors.

The PUFOT protocol has another shortcoming. Namely, it makes the oblivious transfer malleable: when messages are not authenticated, a man-in-the-middle in the OT between two honest participants can transform the $sdr(s_0, s_1)$ into $sdr(s_1, s_0)$ by exchanging S_0 and S_1 and by replacing v by $v \oplus x_0 \oplus x_1$: $rcv(b)$ will obtain s_{1-b} instead of s_b. This only requires the capability to corrupt the communication between the two participants. So, this property shall be a concern for the practicality of PUFOT.

When using PUFOT to implement a bit commitment [4], this translates into an man-in-the-middle attack to transform the commitment to b to a commitment to $1 - b$.

A similar problem occurs in the [23] protocol. (See Appendix A for details.) The same goes for the commitment protocol of [11, 12]. Although these protocols are UC-secure, this observation shows that it is not the case without the authenticated channel assumption. This is clearly stated in [4, 11, 12], but it is not mentioned in [23].

There could be another subtle form of malleability which could be a concern in practice: assume a man-in-the-middle adversary who could substitute the PUF which is handed over by R to S. Concretely, the adversary substitutes the PUF in a way that he runs independently a receiver protocol with S using a random $\bar{b}$, finishing by giving $s_{\bar{b}}$, and a sender protocol with R, using two strings $\bar{s}_0$ and $\bar{s}_1$ such that $\bar{s}_{\bar{b}} = f(s_{\bar{b}})$ and the other string $s_{1-\bar{b}}$ is random. Finally, R receives $f(s_b)$ if $b = \bar{b}$ and something random otherwise. This is still a malleability problem. It applies to all protocols using PUFs. Fortunately, the PUF formalisation does not allow substituting the PUF during the hand-over process. Indeed, when P_i hands over a PUF to P_j, upon reception, $\mathcal{F}_{\mathrm{PUF}}$ tells P_j that the PUF was sent by P_i, and $\mathcal{F}_{\mathrm{PUF}}$ also delivers a receipt to P_i saying that the PUF was well received by P_j. So, the PUF which is sent by R must be the one received by S, even in a protocol under attack. So, there is an *intrinsic authentication* of PUFs in the handover process of $\mathcal{F}_{\mathrm{PUF}}$ and this can be used to avoid the authenticated channel assumption. Even assuming a weaker PUF formalisation where the PUF delivery could be corrupted, the authors of [23] proposed a way to avoid this attack based on the unpredictability of PUFs.

5.2 Strengthening PUFOT (still using authenticated channels)

We will avoid relay attacks by strengthening the PUFOT protocol. Our *Strengthened PUF Oblivious Transfer* protocol (SPOT) is depicted in Fig. 7. Essentially, we bind the PUF query to the sender

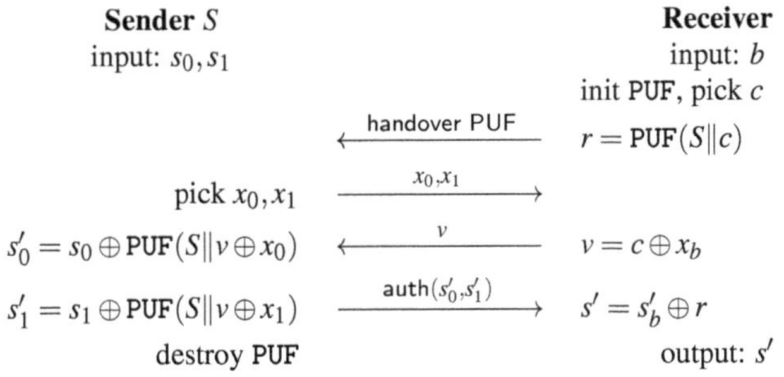

Figure 7: The (Simplified) SPOT Protocol.

S by adding S in the query. As one can see, this is a minor change, and it brings more security.

THEOREM 5. *Assuming authenticated channels, the SPOT protocol on Fig. 7 $\mathcal{F}_{\mathtt{PUF}}$-JUC-realizes $\mathcal{F}_{\mathtt{OT}}$.*

PROOF SKETCH. Following the JUC setting, we have several participants S_j (corrupted or not) receiving (s_0^j, s_1^j) from $\mathcal{Z}$ at the beginning and running the sender protocol with several participants R_i (corrupted or not) receiving b^i from $\mathcal{Z}$ at the beginning and running the receiver protocol, respectively. At the end, they send there output s^i to $\mathcal{Z}$ who produces the outcome of the experiment. Of course, $\mathcal{Z}$ may interact with corrupted participants in between sending the inputs and receiving the outputs.

We consider an environment $\mathcal{Z}$ and an adversary $\mathcal{A}$ in a JUC setting, and we want to construct an ideal-world adversary $\mathcal{S}im$. This $\mathcal{S}im$ runs a simulation $\bar{\mathcal{A}}$ of $\mathcal{A}$ to simulate the corrupted participants as in the real world. $\bar{\mathcal{A}}$ will also have to interact with $\mathcal{F}_{\mathtt{PUF}}$. Since neither any honest participant nor the environment is assumed to interact with $\mathcal{F}_{\mathtt{PUF}}$, $\mathcal{S}im$ needs not hand over any PUF. He just uses $\mathcal{F}_{\mathtt{PUF}}$ for simulating the interaction with real PUFs. The hand-over processing is simulated. $\mathcal{S}im$ also has to interact with $\mathcal{F}_{\mathtt{OT}}$ on behalf of corrupted participants and to feed $\bar{\mathcal{A}}$ with communications between honest participants (since we assume the authenticated channel UC framework).

To run $\bar{\mathcal{A}}$, $\mathcal{S}im$ needs to simulate some honest participants $\bar{S}_j$ and $\bar{R}_i$ while the ideal participants S_j and R_i (with inputs unknown to $\mathcal{S}im$) are interacting with $\mathcal{F}_{\mathtt{OT}}$. In what follows, we consider

$$Views_{real}(\mathcal{Z}, \mathcal{A}, S, R) =$$

$$\langle View_{real}(\mathcal{Z}), View_{real}(\mathcal{A}), (View_{real}(S_j))_j, (View_{real}(R_i))_i \rangle$$

the collection of the views of $\mathcal{Z}$, $\mathcal{A}$, all honest S_j and R_i in the real world, and

$$Views_{ideal}(\mathcal{Z}, \mathcal{S}im) = \langle View_{ideal}(\mathcal{Z}), View_{ideal}(\mathcal{S}im) \rangle$$

the collection of the views of $\mathcal{Z}$ and $\mathcal{S}im$ in the ideal world. (Since the ideal S_j and R_i are just forwarding inputs from $\mathcal{Z}$, we can ignore their views which are redundant with the one of $\mathcal{Z}$.) We denote by $V_{\mathcal{Z}}$ the first view in a collection V. So, $Views_{real}(\mathcal{Z}, \mathcal{A}, S, R)_{\mathcal{Z}} = View_{real}(\mathcal{Z})$. Below, we construct $Views_{sim}$ as a function $Views_{sim} = f(Views_{ideal}(\mathcal{Z}, \mathcal{S}im))$ such that $Views_{real}(\mathcal{Z}, \mathcal{A}, S, R)$ and $Views_{sim}$ are indistinguishable and that $View_{ideal}(\mathcal{Z}) = (Views_{sim})_{\mathcal{Z}}$. We deduce from this construction that $View_{ideal}(\mathcal{Z})$ is indistinguishable from $View_{real}(\mathcal{Z})$, which is what we had to prove.

To prove indistinguishability, we just have to say that the inputs and responses from $\mathcal{F}_{\mathtt{PUF}}$ have a correct distribution and that running the real world on the same input produces the same views.

To define $Views_{sim} = f(Views_{ideal}(\mathcal{Z}, \mathcal{S}im))$, we just concatenate $View_{ideal}(\mathcal{Z})$, $View_{ideal}(\bar{\mathcal{A}})$, and the (reconstructed) views of each honest $\bar{S}_j$ and $\bar{R}_i$. All is computed from $View_{ideal}(\mathcal{S}im)$ by running $\bar{\mathcal{A}}$ and the simulator for the honest $\bar{S}_j$ and $\bar{R}_i$, except for $View_{ideal}(\mathcal{Z})$ which is already part of $Views_{ideal}(\mathcal{Z}, \mathcal{S}im)$. As we will see, $\bar{S}_j$ and $\bar{R}_i$ are simulated but we can reconstruct a meaningful view for S_j and R_i afterwards.

To make the simulation work, $\mathcal{S}im$ has to simulate the honest participants $\bar{S}_j$ and $\bar{R}_i$ interacting with $\bar{\mathcal{A}}$. One problem is that $\mathcal{S}im$ is not always aware of which inputs S_j and R_i receive from $\mathcal{Z}$. Another issue for $\mathcal{S}im$ is to simulate the interaction with $\mathcal{F}_{\mathtt{OT}}$ on behalf of corrupted participants interacting with honest ones. The interaction between two malicious participants is fully taken care of by $\bar{\mathcal{A}}$.

Incidentally, we notice that $\mathcal{S}im$ is aware of all interaction (queries and answers) with all PUFs.

To define $\mathcal{S}im$ and f, we maintain two sets Q and Q' of $(\mathtt{sid}_{\mathtt{PUF}}, q)$ queries. The set Q includes actual queries to the PUF while the set Q' contains undecided queries, which could have been made by some honest receiver. These two sets are originally empty. Whenever $\bar{\mathcal{A}}$ is making a query to PUF, the corresponding pair is added in Q. During the simulation for a honest receiver $\bar{R}_i$, some undetermined queries will be added in Q' as detailed below.

To simulate a honest $\bar{R}_i$, $\mathcal{S}im$ simply takes a fresh PUF, waits for some x_0, x_1, and selects a random string v. Then, $\mathcal{S}im$ queries both $\mathtt{PUF}(S\|v \oplus x_0)$ and $\mathtt{PUF}(S\|v \oplus x_1)$ and inserts both queries in Q'. To reconstruct the view of R_i in $Views_{sim} = f(Views_{ideal}(\mathcal{Z}, \mathcal{S}im))$, we take $c = v \oplus x_b$ as the random coins of R_i (where b is computed from $View_{ideal}(\mathcal{Z})$) and the response from PUF to the query corresponding to b. Clearly, the coins have a correct distribution and the simulation is perfect. If S is corrupted, $\mathcal{S}im$ further has to submit some s_0, s_1 to $\mathcal{F}_{\mathtt{OT}}$ for R_i. After receiving s'_0, s'_1, $\mathcal{S}im$ can get both s_0 and s_1 and submit them to $\mathcal{F}_{\mathtt{OT}}$, and the ideal R_i will get s_b like in the real world.

To simulate a honest $\bar{S}_j$, we pick x_0 and x_1 normally and wait for v. The corresponding PUF is now handed by a honest sender and not supposed to be queried any more by $\bar{\mathcal{A}}$. We can check if the queries $\mathtt{PUF}(S\|v \oplus x_0)$ and $\mathtt{PUF}(S\|v \oplus x_1)$ exist in Q or Q'. Then, there are two cases to analyse.

In the first case, there is at most one of the two queries in $Q \cup Q'$ and we can set b to the value such that $\mathtt{PUF}(S\|v \oplus x_b)$ is the existing query. If there is none, we just set b to a random value. So, $\mathcal{S}im$ can make the corrupted R_i send b to $\mathcal{F}_{\mathtt{OT}}$ to deduce s_b. Then, we construct s'_b based on s_b and set s'_{1-b} to a random string. Whatever $\bar{A}$ is doing is equivalent to running the real world with a correct s_b and some random s_{1-b}. But $\bar{A}$ cannot have any access to the correct value of s_{1-b} due to the non-existent query to the PUF. So, the executions produce equivalent results. In the reconstructed view of S_j, the non-queried PUF value is set to $s'_{1-b} \oplus s_{1-b}$ where s_{1-b} is taken from $View_{ideal}(\mathcal{Z})$. Since the PUF output is random and the PUF is no longer used, this reconstructed view perfectly simulates S_j running with input s_0 and s_1.

In the second case, both possible queries are in $Q \cup Q'$. Note that the PUF handed by S cannot have been queried after $\bar{S}_j$ selected x_0 and x_1. Since the probability that $x_0 \oplus x_1$ matches the XOR between two existing queries is negligible, both queries cannot be in $Q \cup Q'$ at this time and none can later be added in Q: it can only be the case that some queries were added in Q' afterwards. If only one is added in Q' and the other is already existing, then it means that a simulation for a honest receiver managed to select some random vector hitting an existing query. This occurs with negligible probability. So, the two values must have been added in Q'. Clearly, this comes from the above simulation of a honest receiver $\bar{R}_i$ who is undecided about b and who received some $\bar{x}_0$ and $\bar{x}_1$. The queries have form $S\|v\oplus\bar{x}_b$. Due to this structure, it must be the case that these two participants are really interacting with each other and have seen some protocol messages $x_0, x_1, \bar{v}$ (for the sender) and $\bar{x}_0, \bar{x}_1, v$ (for the receiver) leading to the same pairs $\{\bar{v}\oplus x_0, \bar{v}\oplus x_1\}$ and $\{v\oplus\bar{x}_0 = v\oplus\bar{x}_1\}$. So, $x_0\oplus x_1 = \bar{x}_0\oplus\bar{x}_1$. Since $\mathtt{sid}_{\mathtt{PUF}}$ is the same, they also have seen the same PUF. By looking at the receiver protocol, we can see that the adversary cannot know any $v\oplus\bar{x}_i$ before he got v from the receiver. This occurs after giving $\bar{x}_0$ and $\bar{x}_1$. If either of the possible values of $\bar{v}\oplus x_i$ is known before $\bar{S}_j$ selects x_0 and x_1, then v must have been released by the receiver before. So, it is unlikely that $x_0\oplus x_1 = \bar{x}_0\oplus\bar{x}_1$. Therefore, the probability that the adversary queries the PUF with either of the possible values of $\bar{v}\oplus x_j$, before x_0 and x_1 have been released, is negligible. Similarly, he has no chance to query the PUF after learning these values. So, he knows nothing about the decryption keys for s'_0 and s'_1. The simulator $\bar{S}_j$ can thus use some random s'_0 and s'_1. The reconstructed view for $\bar{S}_j$ works as above, by changing the table value of the PUF. Since s'_0 and s'_1 cannot be corrupted, the receiver $\bar{R}_i$ must receive them unchanged. In this situation, we have to change slightly the simulator $\bar{R}_i$ which was described before: indeed, we cannot extract s_0 and s_1 from these random values. But fortunately, we do not need to submit s_0 and s_1 to $\mathcal{F}_{\mathrm{OT}}$. This was done by the ideal S_j already. □

Note that the above theorem (and proof) only holds in JUC, but does not hold in GUC. This is because, in JUC, all sessions and the PUF usages inter-sessions will have one single, all-encompassing interface with the environment, as if they were all part of one macro-session; in GUC, by contrast, the environment (and thus the combined adversarial body) has fine-tuned, inter-session access to the PUF and has separate access/control to and over each individual session. Thus, the simulation in the proof above would default in GUC.

6. CONCLUSIONS

It is important to know not only what we can realize with (UC-)setup devices, but also what shortfalls they bring to the crypto world. In that sense, in this paper, we looked at UC-setup devices that may hinder EUC/JUC realization. We singled these out and characterized them formally. We thuswise denote the class of transferable setups; informally, these are setup devices which do not (publicly) disclose if they have been maliciously passed on. A subset of these are the well-known physical unclonable functions (PUFs).

We proved that one cannot realize oblivious transfer (OT) or any other "interesting" 2-party protocol using transferable setups in the EUC model.

Furthermore, if relay attacks are possible then oblivious transfer cannot be realized in the JUC model either. As a by-product, we show that the protocols proposed built with PUFs by Brzuska *et al.* at CRYPTO 2011, by Ostrovsky *et al.* at EUROCRYPT 2013, by Damgård and Scafuro at ASIACRYPT 2013, are subject to relaying thus not being JUC secure. In addition to this, they all need authenticated channels. We also discuss this need, to some extend.

We showed how to strengthen one of these PUF-based protocols to make them JUC-secure.

7. REFERENCES

[1] Boaz Barak, Ran Canetti, Yehuda Lindell, Rafael Pass, and Tal Rabin. Secure computation without authentication. *Journal of Cryptology*, 24(4):720–760, October 2011.

[2] Ioana Boureanu and Serge Vaudenay. Several weak bit-commitments using seal-once tamper-evident devices. In *Proceedings of the 6th International Conference on Provable Security*, ProvSec'12, pages 70–87, Berlin, Heidelberg, 2012. Springer-Verlag.

[3] Ioana Boureanu and Serge Vaudenay. Compact and efficient uc commitments under atomic-exchanges. In *Proceedings of the 17th International Conference on Information Security and Cryptology*, ICISC 2014, Berlin, Heidelberg, 2015. Springer-Verlag. to appear.

[4] Christina Brzuska, Marc Fischlin, Heike Schröder, and Stefan Katzenbeisser. Physically uncloneable functions in the universal composition framework. In *CRYPTO*, pages 51–70, 2011.

[5] R. Canetti. A Unified Framework for Analyzing Security of Protocols. *Electronic Colloquium on Computational Complexity (ECCC)*, 8(16), 2001.

[6] R. Canetti, Y. Dodis, R. Pass, and S. Walfish. Universally Composable Security with Global Setup. Cryptology ePrint Archive, Report 2006/432, 2006. `http://eprint.iacr.org/`.

[7] Ran Canetti, Eyal Kushilevitz, and Yehuda Lindell. On the limitations of universally composable two-party computation without set-up assumptions. In Eli Biham, editor, *Advances in Cryptology, Proceedings of the 22nd Annual International Conference on the Theory and Applications of Cryptographic Techniques, EUROCRYPT*, volume 2656 of *Lecture Notes in Computer Science*, pages 68–86. Springer, 2003.

[8] Ran Canetti, Eyal Kushilevitz, and Yehuda Lindell. On the limitations of universally composable two-party computation without set-up assumptions. *J. Cryptology*, 19(2):135–167, 2006.

[9] Ran Canetti and Tal Rabin. Universal composition with joint state. Cryptology ePrint Archive, Report 2002/047, 2002. `http://eprint.iacr.org/`.

[10] Cheun Ngen Chong, Dan Jiang, Jiagang Zhang, and Long Guo. Anti-counterfeiting with a random pattern. In *Proceedings of the 2008 Second International Conference on Emerging Security Information, Systems and Technologies*, SECURWARE 2008, pages 146–153, Washington, DC, USA, 2008. IEEE Computer Society.

[11] Ivan Damgård and Alessandra Scafuro. Unconditionally secure and universally composable commitments from physical assumptions. Cryptology ePrint Archive, Report 2013/108, 2013. `http://eprint.iacr.org/`.

[12] Ivan Damgård and Alessandra Scafuro. Unconditionally secure and universally composable commitments from physical assumptions. In *In Proceedings of the International Conference on the Theory and Application of Cryptographic Techniques, ASIACRYPT '13*, pages 100–119, 2013.

[13] Sezer Goren, H. Fatih Ugurdag, Abdullah Yildiz, and Ozgur Ozkurt. FPGA design security with time division multiplexed PUFs. In *Proceedings of the International Conference on High Performance Computing and Simulation (HPCS)*, volume 28, pages 608–614, July 2010.

[14] V. Goyal, Y. Ishai, A. Sahai, R. Venkatesan, and A. Wadia. Founding Cryptography on Tamper-Proof Hardware Tokens. In *Theory of Cryptography*, pages 308–326, 2010.

[15] J. Katz. Universally Composable Multi-party Computation Using Tamper-Proof Hardware. In *Theory and Application of Cryptographic Techniques*, pages 115–128, 2007.

[16] Roel Maes, Pim Tuyls, and Ingrid Verbauwhede. Low-overhead implementation of a soft decision helper data algorithm for sram pufs. In *Proceedings of the 11th International Workshop on Cryptographic Hardware and Embedded Systems*, CHES 2009, pages 332–347, Berlin, Heidelberg, 2009. Springer-Verlag.

[17] Roel Maes and Ingrid Verbauwhede. Physically unclonable functions: A study on the state of the art and future research directions. In *Towards Hardware-Intrinsic Security*, pages 3–37. Springer, 2010.

[18] P. Mateus and S. Vaudenay. On Tamper-Resistance from a Theoretical Viewpoint. In *Proceedings of the 11th International Workshop on Cryptographic Hardware and Embedded Systems(CHES)*, volume 5747 of *Lecture Notes in Computer Science*, pages 411–428. Springer, 2009.

[19] T. Moran and M. Naor. Basing Cryptographic Protocols on Tamper-Evident Seals. In *Proceedings of the 32nd International Colloquium on Automata, Languages and Programming (ICALP)*, volume 3580 of *Lecture Notes in Computer Science*, pages 285–297. Springer-Verlag, Jul 2005.

[20] T. Moran and M. Naor. Polling with Physical Envelopes: A Rigorous Analysis of a Human-Centric Protocol. In *Advances in Cryptology, Proceedings of the 25th Annual International Conference on Theory and Application of Cryptographic Techniques – EUROCRYPT*, volume 4004 of *Lecture Notes in Computer Science*, pages 88–108. Springer Berlin / Heidelberg, May 2006.

[21] T. Moran and M. Naor. Basing Cryptographic Protocols on Tamper-Evident Seals. *Theoretical Computer Science*, 411:1283–1310, March 2010.

[22] T. Moran and G. Segev. David and Goliath Commitments: UC Computation for Asymmetric Parties Using Tamper-Proof Hardware. In *Theory and Application of Cryptographic Techniques*, pages 527–544, 2008.

[23] Rafail Ostrovsky, Alessandra Scafuro, Ivan Visconti, and Akshay Wadia. Universally composable secure computation with (malicious) physically uncloneable functions. In *Advances in Cryptology, Proceedings of the 32nd Annual International Conference on the Theory and Applications of Cryptographic Techniques, EUROCRYPT*, pages 702–718, 2013.

[24] Ravikanth S. Pappu. *Physical one-way functions*. PhD thesis, Massachusetts Institute of Technology, March 2001.

[25] Masoud Rostami, Mehrdad Majzoobi, Farinaz Koushanfar, Dan S. Wallach, and Srinivas Devadas. Robust and reverse-engineering resilient PUF authentication and key-exchange by substring matching. *IEEE Transactions on Emerging Topics in Computing*, 2014. to appear.

[26] Ulrich Rührmair and Marten van Dijk. On the practical use of physical unclonable functions in oblivious transfer and bit commitment protocols. *J. Cryptographic Engineering*, 3(1):17–28, 2013.

[27] Ulrich Rührmair and Marten van Dijk. PUFs in security protocols: Attack models and security evaluations. In *2013 IEEE Symposium on Security and Privacy, SP 2013, Berkeley, CA, USA, May 19-22, 2013*, pages 286–300. IEEE Computer Society, 2013.

[28] Marten van Dijk and Ulrich Rührmair. Physical unclonable functions in cryptographic protocols: Security proofs and impossibility results. Cryptology ePrint Archive, Report 2012/228, 2012. `http://eprint.iacr.org/`.

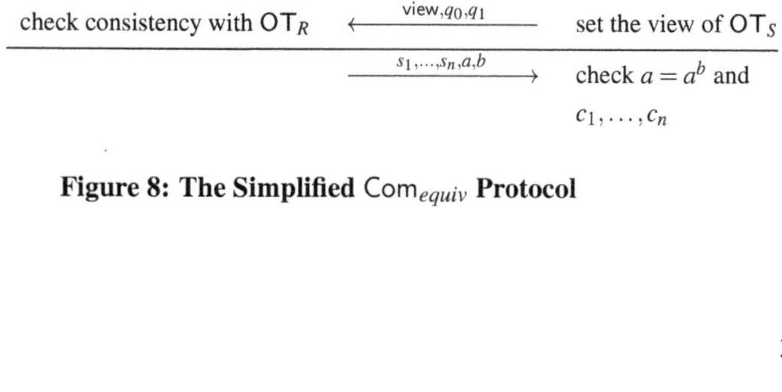

Figure 8: The Simplified Com_{equiv} Protocol

APPENDIX

A. AUTHENTICATED CHANNELS & UC-SECURITY WITH PUFS

In [23], there are two commitment protocols using PUFs. One is inherited from the protocol of Brzuska *et al.* and, like it, it requires authentication of communication as an extra assumption on top of the insecure-channel UC model; this assumption is stated clearly in [4]. The other, completely novel protocol in [23] also requires authenticated channels, even if this is not stated in the paper.

To see that this is the case, we sketch a man-in-the-middle attack against the Com_{equiv}, if the UC channels therein were not authenticated. The protocol is recalled on Fig. 8. Note that the input r is the result of a previous coin flipping protocol in the full commitment protocol by [23]. It is known by the adversary. The step where S sends some c_i's based on r to R is known as the Naor commitment of a_b. It is opened by giving $s_1, \ldots, s_n$ with a. The protocol uses a subprotocol OT where R plays the role of the sender. This protocol runs based on a view to be disclosed later on, so that S – playing the role of the receiver– can check for consistencies.

Thus, imagine a honest receiver R following the protocol, in –let us say– session 1 of Com_{equiv}. I.e., R chooses q_0 and q_1, queries PUF_R on one of them, obtains a_i, with $i \in \{0,1\}$, and then hands over the PUF to the honest sender S. He then runs the inner OT protocol on q_0, q_1. The man-in-the-middle (MiM) adversary $\mathcal{A}$ is playing two different protocols with S and R. To R in session 1, he runs the OT protocol with a random bit $\overline{b}$, As expected, this man-in-the-middle gets out of the OT protocol a state $q_{\overline{b}}$. In the OT session which is run with S, let us call it session 2, $\mathcal{A}$ selects q'_0 and q'_1 such that $q'_{1-\overline{b}} = q_{\overline{b}}$ and $q'_{\overline{b}}$ is random. Supposing that S inputted a bit b into the OT protocol, then this sender S gets q'_b as the OT output. So, $q'_b = q_{1-b}$ with probability $\frac{1}{2}$. Then, the Naor commitment c from S to R is left unchanged. The view (with the OT inputs) that $\mathcal{A}$ sends to S is set so that it is consistent with q'_0 and q'_1. In the opening, the Naor commitment is left unchanged but the bit b is replaced by $\overline{b}$.

In this MiM-infected real world execution, R receives $\overline{b} = 1 - b$ with probability $\frac{1}{2}$. Of course, this will never be the case in the ideal-world execution. This is due to S and R being honest and the commitment functionality making sure that only the bit b set by S can be opened to R. So, authentication is a requirement in order for the Com_{equiv} protocol in [23] to enjoy UC-security.

Asymmetric Cross-cryptosystem Re-encryption Applicable to Efficient and Secure Mobile Access to Outsourced Data

Hua Deng
School of Computer
Wuhan University
Wuhan, P. R. China
denghua@whu.edu.cn

Qianhong Wu
School of Electronic and Information Engineering
Beihang University, P.R. China
qianhong.wu@buaa.edu.cn

Bo Qin
School of Information
Renmin University of China
Beijing, P. R. China
bo.qin@ruc.edu.cn

Willy Susilo
School of Computer Science and Software Engineering
University of Wollongong
Wollongong, Australia
wsusilo@uow.edu.au

Joseph Liu
Institute for Infocomm Research (I2R)
Singapore
ksliu9@gmail.com

Wenchang Shi
School of Information
Renmin University of China
Beijing, P. R. China
wenchang@ruc.edu.cn

ABSTRACT

With the increasing development of pervasive computing and wireless bandwidth communication, more mobile devices are used to access sensitive data stored in remote servers. In such applications, a practical issue emerges such as how to exploit the sufficient resource of a server so that the file owners can enforce fine-grained access control over the remotely stored files, while enable resource-limited mobile devices to easily access the protected data, especially if the storage server maintained by a third party is untrusted. This challenge mainly arises from the asymmetric capacity among the participants, i.e., the capacity limited mobile devices and the resource abundant server (and file owners equipped with fixed computers). To meet the security requirements in mobile access to sensitive data, we propose a new encryption paradigm, referred to as asymmetric cross-cryptosystem re-encryption (ACCRE) by leveraging the asymmetric capacity of the participants. In ACCRE, relatively light-weight identity-based encryption (IBE) is deployed in mobile devices, while resource-consuming but versatile identity-based broadcast encryption (IBBE) is deployed in servers and fixed computers of the file owners. The core of ACCRE is a novel ciphertext conversion mechanism that allows an authorized proxy to convert a complicated IBBE ciphertext into a simple IBE ciphertext affordable to mobile devices, without leaking any sensitive information to the proxy. Following this paradigm, we propose an efficient ACCRE scheme with its security formally reduced to the security of the underlying IBE and IBBE schemes. Thorough theoretical analyses and extensive experiments confirm that the scheme takes very small cost for mobile devices to access encrypted data and is practical to secure mobile computing applications.

ASIA CCS'15, April 14–17, 2015, Singapore, Singapore

http://dx.doi.org/10.1145/2714576.2714632 .

Categories and Subject Descriptors

E.3 [**Data**]: Data Encryption

Keywords

Data Security; Identity-based broadcast encryption; Identity-based encryption; Proxy re-encryption

1. INTRODUCTION

With pervasive advances in information and wireless communication technologies, mobile devices such as smart phones and tablets have been widely used in data outsourced systems (e.g., cloud storage [8]) to access the outsourced data. In such applications, users can leverage their potable devices to access the data maintained by a third party through Internet or wireless communication. For instance, outdoor users can use mobile phones to access their private photos outsourced from their desktops; doctors can make timely diagnoses with mobile access to the patients' electronic health records [20] and in mobile office, employees may use their tablets to process sensitive company business assigned by their managers in offices via cloud computing services.

Data security is one of the main concerns in such applications. Outsourced data are usually encrypted [19] to prevent untrusted storage servers from knowing the sensitive contents. Identity-based broadcast encryption (IBBE) [10] is especially appealing to resource-abundant data owners as it allows the owners to enforce fine-grained and flexible precise access control over the outsourced data by specifying which users can access what digital contents. In contrast, identity-based encryption (IBE) [3] is especially interesting to mobile devices due to its almost light-weight feature and freeness of complicated public-key certificates.

Now we encounter a clear gap in such applications. The file owners having powerful computing devices such as desktop computers would like to employ resource-consuming but versatile IBBE [11] to enforce flexible access control over their outsourced data [16]. However, the mobile users with capacity-constraint computing devices would like to deploy resource-saving IBE to access the outsourced data. Then a natural question arises: *Can we design a security mechanism enabling devices equipped with IBE to access IBBE encrypted files directly?*

Consider a mobile office application in which the above problem may be realistic. The employees are associated with unique identities and their desktop computers in offices are equipped with an identity-based broadcast encryption (IBBE) system to protect data security. Under IBBE, the employee Alice can securely share her data with a group of employees so that all the employees can simultaneously access the same data. On the other hand, another employee Bob works outside his offices and processes data by using mobile devices such as iPads or Android tablets. At some point, Bob also requests to access the data encrypted by Alice. Unfortunately, the data has already been encrypted as an IBBE ciphertext and Alice (or any other employees able to access the encrypted data) may not want to decrypt the IBBE encrypted data and then encrypt it to Bob using the IBE encryption. A more elegant approach is required for precessing the previously encrypted data so that it is also decryptable by Bob.

A plausible solution to the above application might be proxy re-encryption (PRE) [1]. We note that identity-based PRE schemes [14, 9] allow a proxy to convert an IBE ciphertext for one user into a ciphertext for another user, but they do not support the required "broadcasting" mechanism for Alice. In view of limited resources of mobile devices, other solutions also try to convert a complicated ciphertext into a simple one so that mobile devices can easily access. The computation outsourcing techniques [36] enable mobile devices to outsource large computation tasks in decrypting complicated ciphertexts. However, these techniques require the mobile users to interact with a computing server for help to complete the computation tasks whenever the mobile users need to decrypt a ciphertext, which is inefficient due to the frequent interactions with the computing server. The ciphertext delegation approach [33] is also a kind of encrypted data conversion but only allows a ciphertext for an access policy to be "re-encrypted" to a more restrictive policy, which is not necessary to reduce the computation overheads of the target decryptor. Furthermore, it requires Alice to know the identity of Bob when encrypting, which is opposite to the above motivating scenario.

Indeed, what needed is an asymmetric cross-cryptosystem re-encryption that bridges an IBBE system to be employed for powerful computing devices and an IBE system to be employed for resource-limited mobile devices. The re-encryption mechanism allows a data owner to delegate the access rights of the IBBE encrypted data to a user having an IBE decryption key, without requiring the data owner to know the identity of the target user in advance nor leaking any sensitive information about the original digital contents to any unauthorized user.

1.1 Our Contributions

In this paper, we introduce and formalize a new concept of asymmetric cross-cryptosystem re-encryption (ACCRE) to convert encrypted data for resource-asymmetric computing devices. The ACCRE seems an amazing and useful cryptographic tool in practice. However, it involves two separate encryption systems (IBBE and IBE) with very different parameters, e.g., public keys, secret keys, and respective algorithms, which inevitably makes it challenging to formalize its security definition and realize practical ACCRE schemes.

We present a framework of the ACCRE and define its security. The ACCRE system involves an IBBE system and an IBE system that work independently in their standard ways. When a user wants to share his data with others, the user can encrypt the data with the set of identities of the receivers and then outsource the resulting IBBE encrypted file to a storage service provider. Later, the user may also want to authorize a mobile user to access his data. Instead of downloading and decrypting the encrypted file, the user just generates a conversion key without any help of the mobile user and then gives this key to a proxy. The proxy applies this key to convert the user's IBBE encrypted file into an IBE encrypted file so that the mobile user can access using his normal IBE decryption key. We define a semantic security notion for ACCRE. Due to the conversion feature, the adversary is allowed to additionally query the conversion keys. We require even such an adversary cannot distinguish the ciphertexts of the messages of the attacker's choice.

We propose a provably secure ACCRE scheme with short ciphertexts and secret keys. One challenge is the asymmetric structures of an IBBE ciphertext and an IBE one. An IBBE ciphertext is associated with multiple identities while that of IBE is associated with only one. It is hard to replace the identities involved in the original ciphertext with a single identity, without disclosing any information about the encrypted data. We address this challenge by proposing a *key blinding* technique and constructing the ACCRE scheme on a variant of the IBE scheme [3] and the IBBE scheme [10]. With the key blinding technique, one can safely entrust the proxy with the conversion task without leaking one's secret key or the digital contents of the original file, even if the proxy colludes with unauthorized users.

We conduct thorough analysis of the proposed ACCRE scheme. Its security is formally reduced to the security of the underling IBBE and IBE schemes. We also perform a comprehensive performance evaluation. Both the theoretical analysis and the experimental results confirm that a mobile user takes negligible cost to decrypt a converted ciphertext, compared to that to decrypt an IBBE one. The costs for conversion key generation and file conversion are also less for more powerful computing devices. The analysis shows our ACCRE is a promising solution to secure mobile access to outsourced data.

1.2 Organization

Section 2 reviews the related work in the literature. In Section 3, we describes our system framework and the system model. Section 4 presents the proposed scheme. In Section 5, we formally prove the security of the proposed scheme in a rigorous definition. We analyze the performance of the proposed scheme both theoretically and experimentally in Section 6. Section 7 concludes the paper.

2. RELATED WORK

Data security is a major concern in data outsourcing applications. Pavlović and Miklavčič [32] adopted the secure socket layer (SSL) protocol to secure sensitive digital medical records transmitted through Internet. Tan *et al.* [35] employed IBE in body sensor networks to protect the sensitive health information outsourced to doctors. Deng *et al.* [11] employed IBBE to protect data security and allows multiple users to access the same outsourced data while a trusted third party to trace corrupted users. Liu *et al.* [27] suggested hierarchical IBBE in which the key generation and distribution can be delegated to one's subordinates. Chu *et al.* [8] proposed a key-aggregate cryptosystem to secure data outsourced to cloud storage systems and Li *et al.* applied the flexible attribute-based encryption (ABE) to protect the privacy of outsourced personal health records. Liu *et al.* [28] enhanced chosen-plaintext secure ABE with adaptively chosen ciphertext security at a marginal cost. The leakage tracing mechanism was further realized in cloud storage with ABE for fine-grained access control [13].

Mobile access to encrypted data needs to take into consideration the low computing capability of mobile devices. Zhang *et al.* [38] leveraged network coding to reduce the energy consumed by data encryption in mobile ad hoc networks. Liu, Chu and Chow [26, 7, 6] used the concept of online/offline in IBE setting to offload the heavy computation into a third party. Hwu *et al.* [16] employed IBE on mobile devices to eliminate the overheads of the authenticity of public keys. Wang *et al.* [36] proposed an exponentiation outsourcing to reduce the computation complexity in decryption, although it requires the help of a third party. To reduce the complicated computations of mobile users in decrypting ABE ciphertexts, Green *et al.* [15] proposed an outsourcing technique that allows a mobile user to outsource a majority of decryption computation to a third party. Their scheme mainly focuses on the reduction of decryption computation and does not consider the access rights delegation from one to another. Recently, Sahai *et al.* [33] provides a ciphertext delegation that can convert an ABE ciphertext for an access policy into a ciphertext for a more restrictive one. Since IBBE and IBE can be roughly viewed as special cases of ABE, one may attempt to apply Sahai *et al.*'s solution to the motivating scenario to convert a ciphertext for an access set of multiple identities into a ciphertext for a single identity. However, due to the requirement that only more restrictive access policy can be delegated to, this solution requires the identity regarding the converted ciphertext to be appear in the access set in advance, which would be undesirable for the application. Deng *et al.* [12] recently propose hierarchical ABE so that the key generation can be delegated to lower level users and relieve the burden of the high-hierarchy users. But their scheme does not relieve the computation burden of the decryptors. Our scheme does not fall into such restrictions since it applies a different technique, proxy re-encryption. Further, our scheme directly employs the efficient IBE on mobile users, thus there is no need to reduce the decryption computation any more.

Proxy re-encryption (PRE), first formulated by Blaze *et al.* [2], is a useful cryptographic tool that can transform a ciphertext for a public key into a ciphertext for another public key. As remarked in [1], Blaze *et al.*'s scheme is inherent *bidirectional*, that is, the re-encryption key allows translating ciphertexts not only from Alice to Bob, but also from Bob to Alice. Ivan and Dodis [17] constructed a unidirectional proxy encryption by splitting a decryption key into two parts, one of which is for the proxy and the other is for Bob. This scheme protects delegatee's security, although requires the delegatee Bob to store additional secrets before being delegated to. Following Ivan and Dodis's work, Ateniese *et al.* [1] proposed a unidirectional PRE scheme that eliminates the storage need of extra secrets before re-encryption. Canetti and Hohenberger [5] improved Ateniese *et al.*'s schemes to be chosen-ciphertext secure, although this scheme is bidirectional. Subsequently, Libert and Vergnaud [25] presented the first replayable chosen-ciphertext secure unidirectional PRE scheme in the standard model. Matsuda *et al.* [30] introduced a new primitive referred to as re-applicable lossy trapdoor function and applied this function to achieve a chosen-ciphertext secure PRE scheme in the standard model. Weng *et al.* [37] made a careful observation on the Matsuda *et al.*'s scheme and indicated some dissatisfactions of the security.

There are some extensions of PRE to support identity-based cryptosystem. Green and Ateniese [14] extended the PRE to support identity-based encryption, resulting into an identity-based proxy re-encryption (IBPRE). In an IBPRE scheme, the identity of a user plays the role of a traditional public key and in re-encryption, a ciphertext under an identity is converted into a ciphertext under another identity. Chu and Tzeng [9] presented an IBPRE scheme proved chosen-ciphertext secure in the standard model. Matsuo [31] linked the traditional public-key systems and identity-based encryption systems by presenting a hybrid proxy re-encryption system. This PRE scheme allows a ciphertext in PKI-based systems to be converted into a ciphertext for an identity in IBE system, although it does not support the broadcasting mechanism in encryption. Liang [23] deployed the concept of PRE to achieve revocability in identity-based setting and further generalized the concept of PRE into any DFA-based functional setting [21]. Shao [34] extended the concept of IBPRE to that of anonymous IBPRE (AIBPRE) and proposed an AIBPRE scheme to achieve the anonymity of recipients. A fully-anonymous functional PRE scheme is presented by Kawai and Takashima [18] recently. To achieve more flexible encryption, some attribute-based proxy re-encryption (ABPRE) schemes [24, 29, 22] have been proposed. In ABPRE systems, a ciphertext for an access policy is able to be re-encrypted to a different access policy (this access policy is not constrained to be more restrictive than the original one). Given that the cryptographic computations in attribute-based encryption are often too complicated, these schemes seem not very suitable for the mobile devices that often possess limited computing capability.

The existing PRE schemes do not achieve re-encryption from a complicated cryptosystem to a simple cryptosystem. In contrast, the proposed ACCRE scheme directly employs IBE on mobile devices in view of their limited resources. The ACCRE allows a proxy to transform a ciphertext of an IBBE system into a ciphertext of an IBE system, without requiring any participation of a third party or the user specified to access the IBE ciphertext, nor extra secret storage for the specified user. Hence, a user can efficiently convert his IBBE secured file into a simple IBE secured one that can be accessed by a mobile user at a low cost.

3. PROBLEM STATEMENT AND SYSTEM MODEL

3.1 Problem Statement

We consider securing data between computing devices equipped with asymmetric capacities, i.e., mobile devices such as smart phones, and powerful computing devices such as desktops and servers. Mobile devices employ an identity-based encryption (IBE) scheme to meet their constraint resources while powerful desktops and servers employ an identity-based broadcast encryption (IBBE) scheme for the purpose of versatile access control over the data to be outsourced. The users equipped with the IBBE can encrypt data via the IBBE encryption so that a set of specified users can access the same data. The users equipped with the IBE are able to encrypt their data by calling the IBE encryption. Hence there are two kinds of ciphertexts, i.e, IBBE ciphertexts and IBE ciphertexts. When a user in IBBE system wishes to authorize a user in IBE system to access the data that is previously encrypted in an IBBE ciphertext, the problem is how to enable the IBBE user (authorizing a powerful proxy) to securely convert the IBBE ciphertext into the IBE ciphertext decryptable by the authorized IBE user with the following constraints.

1. The IBBE users are not required to install the IBE system.
2. The IBE users are not required to install the IBBE system.
3. The IBBE user who wants to transmit his/her data does not need to decrypt the IBBE ciphertext.

3.2 System Model

We address the above problem by introducing and formalizing a new proxy re-encryption paradigm referred to as asymmetric cross-cryptosystem re-encryption (ACCRE). The system architecture is illustrated in Figure 1. In the ACCRE framework, there are five parties described as follows.

- Administrator (Admin): a party which is responsible for publishing public parameters and issuing access credentials (i.e., decryption keys).
- Data storage provider (DSP): a party which provides storage services for data owners.
- Data owners: the users who encrypt their data using IBBE and then outsource the encrypted data to the DSP.
- Data consumers: the users who can access the data encrypted in IBE ciphertexts if they have the correct access credentials issued by Admin.
- Proxy: a party which converts the files encrypted in IBBE into the files encrypted in IBE if having the conversion keys given by the data owners.

In an ACCRE system, IBBE and IBE are employed for data owners and data consumers respectively. Although these two cryptosystems can also contain data consumers and data owners, we ignore these users in their own systems to concentrate on the file conversion functionality. The data owners in ACCRE can encrypt their data with a set of identities through the IBBE encryption and thus obtain IBBE ciphertexts. When a data owner wants to transform his/her IBBE secured file stored in DSP into an IBE encrypted file with the identity of the data consumer, the data owner does not need to decrypt the IBBE ciphertext. Instead, the data owner generates a conversion key (CK) using his/her secret key and the identity of the data consumer and then sends CK to the proxy. The proxy downloads the data owner's file from DSP and applies the conversion key to transform the IBBE encrypted file into the IBE encrypted one that can be decrypted by the intended data consumer. We note that during the whole file conversion, the data owner is online only when sending the conversion key; and neither the DSP nor the data consumer is required to participate.

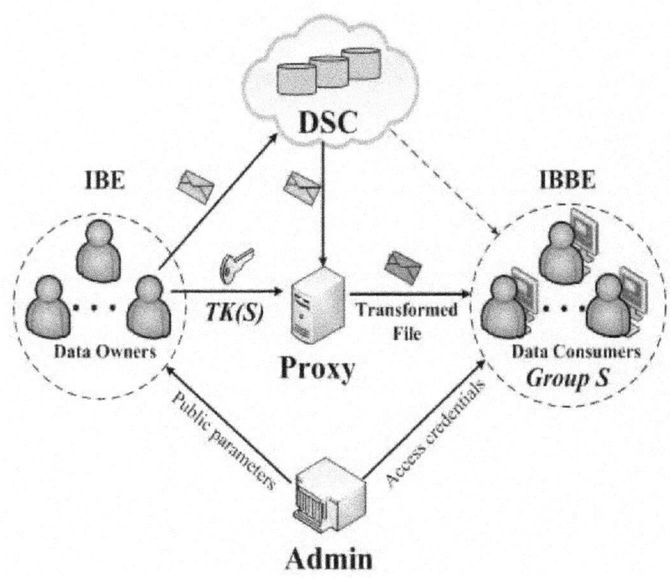

Figure 1: System Model

3.3 Security Model and Assumptions

As in previous work, we assume that the Admin is fully trusted. The DSP and the proxy are assumed to be honest-but-curious in that they may be curious about the the content of files and some secret information about the data owners, but they still honestly perform the tasks assigned to. The DSP and the proxy, as well as the data consumers may try to access the content of files stored in DSP without any authorization.

To capture realistic attacks, we define an adversary which is able to compromise all the parities, except the Admin, the owner of target data and the data consumer who has the correct access credentials (decryption key) to the target data. We require that even for such adversary, any useful information about the data will be not leaked. We note that this is a strong notion of security since it resists attacks from all unauthorized parities. The formal security model will be given in Section 5.

4. PROPOSED ACCRE SCHEME

Before presenting our ACCRE scheme, we first introduce some basic idea in driving the construction.

4.1 Basic Idea

In an ACCRE system, data owners encrypt their data and outsource the encrypted files to DSP for sharing. For instance, the employees of a company encrypt their data via the IBBE so that a number of authorized employees can download and then access the data. In meanwhile, another employee outside office works with a mobile device involving an IBE decryption key. When a data owner wants to authorize the employee working outside with the access rights to his/her IBBE encrypted file, the data owner can generate a conversion key and calls the proxy, e.g., the IT center of the company, to transform the IBBE encrypted file into an IBE encrypted one so that the specified employee can access with the IBE decryption key.

We construct the ACCRE scheme by using the the IBBE scheme [10] and a variant of the IBE scheme [3]. The biggest obstacle in the ACCRE construction is the asymmetric structure of the IBBE ciphertexts and the IBE ciphertexts. Specifically, the IBBE ciphertext is generated with a set of identities, whereas an IBE ciphertext is associated with a single identity. Then, in the conversion of the IBBE ciphertext into an IBE ciphertext, multiple identities should be replaced with the identity of intended IBE user without revealing the underlying message. Further, the underlying message is usually blinded by a random value to protect the security, it seems problematic to replace the multiple identities without knowledge about the random value.

We overcome the above challenge by using a *key blinding* technique. Coarsely, in the conversion key generation, the data owner blinds his/her IBBE secret key with a random value and then encrypts the random value with the identity of the specified data consumer via the IBE encryption. Given the conversion key, the proxy applies the blinded secret key of the data owner to "partially" decrypt the IBBE ciphertext, which results an IBE ciphertext additionally blinded by the random value. Then the data consumer with the identity specified in the conversion key can first recover the random value and finally obtain the data in plaintext.

4.2 The Construction

We now describe our ACCRE scheme which is built in a bilinear map groups system $(p, \mathbb{G}, \mathbb{G}_T, \hat{e}) \leftarrow \mathcal{G}(1^\lambda)$. This bilinear group system is defined as follows. Let $\mathcal{G}(1^\lambda)$ be a generator with input the security parameter λ. It generates two cyclic groups $\mathbb{G}$ and $\mathbb{G}_T$. We say that $\mathbb{G}$ is a bilinear group if there exists an efficient map $\hat{e} : \mathbb{G} \times \mathbb{G} \rightarrow \mathbb{G}_T$ satisfying: i) $\hat{e}(g^a, h^b) = \hat{e}(g,h)^{ab}$ for all $g, h \in \mathbb{G}$ and all $a, b \in \mathbb{Z}_p$; and ii) $\hat{e}(g,h) \neq 1$. The ACCRE system consists of the following procedures.

System Setup: The admin calls the **Setup** algorithm to create system public key PK and a master secret key MSK, where PK involves the public key of IBE and the public key of $IBBE$, denoted by PK_{IBE} and PK_{IBBE} respectively. The public key PK is public to other parties while MSK must be kept secret.

$(MPK, MSK) \leftarrow$ **Setup**(1^λ): Choose a bilinear group $\mathbb{G}$ of prime order p with generator g. Choose random elements $h \in \mathbb{G}$ and $\alpha \in \mathbb{Z}_p$. Select a hash function $H : \{0,1\}^* \rightarrow \mathbb{Z}_p^*$, as well as a coding function $F^1 : \mathbb{G}_T \rightarrow \mathbb{G}$. Set m as the maximal size of the broadcasting receiver set and compute

$$g_1 = g^\alpha, h^\alpha, h^{\alpha^2}, ..., h^{\alpha^m}$$

Define the public key

$$PK = \left(g_1, \hat{e}(g,h), h, h^\alpha, ..., h^{\alpha^m}, H(\cdot), F(\cdot)\right)$$

[1]This function could be defined as follows: given an element $e(g, g^x) \in \mathbb{G}_T$ for a value $x \in \mathbb{Z}_p$, output $g^x \in \mathbb{G}$.

and the master secret key $MSK = (g, \alpha)$. The IBBE public key PK_{IBBE} is defined the same as PK and the IBE public key PK_{IBE} is set as

$$PK_{IBE} = (g_1, \hat{e}(g,h), h, h^\alpha, H(\cdot), F(\cdot))$$

which is a part of PK.

User Registration: When a new user associated with an identity ID requires to join the system, the Admin first checks whether this user is valid or not. If yes, the Admin generates an access credentials for this user. In the ACCRE system, although there are two kinds of encryption systems, the Admin does not need to differentiate which encryption system (IBBE or IBE) the requiring user belongs to, but just calls the following algorithm to generate an access credential for the user.

$SK_{ID} \leftarrow$ **KeyGen**(PK, MSK, ID): This algorithm takes as inputs the public key PK, the master secret key MSK, and the identity ID of the new user. The algorithm hashes the identity ID to be $H(ID) \in \mathbb{Z}_p$ and outputs

$$SK_{ID} = g^{\frac{1}{\alpha + H(ID)}}.$$

We note that a user with an identity ID has the same access credential in IBBE and IBE. That is, assuming that $SK_{IBBE,ID}$ and $SK_{IBE,ID}$ is the access credentials of user ID in IBBE and IBE respectively, then we have $SK_{ID} = SK_{IBBE,ID} = SK_{IBE,ID}$. This would save the overheads of the Admin in issuing users' access credentials since it generates the same credential for an identity no matter involved in IBBE or IBE.

File Creation: When a data owner in IBBE wants to share his/her data with a set S of users, the data owner creates a file to be stored in DSP by the following steps. First, the owner encrypts the file with a random symmetric session key DEK of some symmetric cryptosystem such as AES. Second, the owner encrypts the symmetric session key DEK with the set S of identities of the users the data owner wants to share data with. The procedure runs as follows.

$CT_S \leftarrow$ **Encrypt**(PK, S, M): This algorithm takes as inputs the public key PK, a set of identities $S = \{ID_i\}_{i=1}^n$ with $n < m$ and a message $M \in \mathbb{G}_T$, where M is a representation of the symmetric key DEK to be encrypted. The algorithm chooses a random $s \in \mathbb{Z}_p^*$ and computes

$$C_0 = M \cdot \hat{e}(g,h)^s, \quad C_1 = g_1^{-s}, \quad C_2 = h^{s \prod_{i=1}^n (\alpha + H(ID_i))}.$$

Then output $CT_S = (C_0, C_1, C_2)$. This CT_S and the ciphertext of the data under the symmetric key form the encrypted file stored in DSP.

Conversion Key Generation: Suppose that a data has already been encrypted by the IBBE and outsourced to DSP. When a user ID_j having access to the data wants to authorize a mobile user ID (i.e., an IBE user) to access the data, the user ID_j needs to first generate a conversion key by calling the following algorithm and then gives this key to the proxy.

$CK_{S \rightarrow ID} \leftarrow$ **CKGen**(PK, SK_{ID_j}, S, ID): The algorithm takes as inputs the public key PK, the secret key SK_{ID_j}, the identity set $S = \{ID_i\}_{i=1}^n$ involving ID_j and the identity ID of the intended IBE data consumer. The algorithm generates a conversion key $CK_{S \rightarrow ID}$ that can transform an

IBBE ciphertext associated with the identity set S into an IBE ciphertext associated with ID. The algorithm proceeds as follows. Choose a random $k \in \mathbb{G}_T$ and compute

$$SK'_{ID_j} = SK_{ID_j} \cdot F(k)^{\prod_{i=1,i\neq j}^{n} H(ID_i)}.$$

Choose a random $r \in \mathbb{Z}_p$ and compute

$$E_0 = k\hat{e}(g,h)^r, E_1 = h^{r(\alpha+H(ID))}$$

to form an IBE ciphertext (E_0, E_1) for k and ID. Finally, output the conversion key as

$$CK_{S\to ID} = (SK'_{ID_j}, E_0, E_1).$$

We note that in this procedure the user ID_j is online only when sending the conversion key and neither the DSP nor the data consumer ID is required to participate in generating the conversion key.

File Conversion: Given a conversion key $CK_{S\to ID}$, the proxy can transform an IBBE ciphertext CT_S with set S into an IBE ciphertext CT_{ID} for an identity ID. The proxy first downloads the encrypted file from DSP and applies the conversion key to convert the file by calling the following algorithm.

$CT_{ID} \leftarrow$ **ReEnc**$(PK, CK_{S\to ID}, CT_S)$: The algorithm takes as inputs the public key PK, the IBBE ciphertext CT_S and the conversion key $CK_{S\to ID}$ that is given by the user $ID_j \in S$. It computes

$$\begin{aligned} K &= \left[\hat{e}\left(C_1, h^{\Delta_{S,j}}\right)\cdot \hat{e}\left(SK'_{ID_j}, C_2\right)\right]^{\frac{1}{\prod_{i=1,i\neq j}^{n} H(ID_i)}}, \\ &= \hat{e}(g,h)^s \cdot \hat{e}(F(k), C_2), \end{aligned}$$

where

$$\Delta_{S,j} = \frac{1}{\alpha}\left(\prod_{i=1,i\neq j}^{n}(\alpha + H(ID_i)) - \prod_{i=1,i\neq j}^{n} H(ID_i)\right).$$

Then compute

$$C'_0 = C_0/K = M/\hat{e}(F(k), C_2).$$

Finally, output

$$CT_{ID} = (C'_0, C_2, E_0, E_1).$$

File Access: When a user requires an IBBE secured file stored in DSP, the DSP returns the corresponding file. The users first decrypts the IBBE ciphertext to obtain the symmetric key and then uses the symmetric key to finally obtain the data. The decryption of IBBE ciphertext is identical to that in [10] and described as follows.

$M \leftarrow$ **Decrypt**$_{IBBE}(PK, CT_{ID}, SK_S)$: The algorithm takes as inputs the public key PK, the access credential SK_{ID_j} of user $ID_j \in S$ and the IBBE ciphertext $CT_S = (C_0, C_1, C_2)$. It computes

$$\begin{aligned} M' &= \left(\hat{e}\left(C_1, h^{\Delta_{S,j}}\right)\cdot \hat{e}\left(SK_{ID_j}, C_2\right)\right)^{\frac{1}{\prod_{i=1,i\neq j}^{n} H(ID_i)}} \\ &= \hat{e}(g,h)^s \end{aligned}$$

and outputs $M = C_0/M'$.

When a user ID requires a converted file, the proxy returns the corresponding file. Similarly, the user first decrypts the IBE ciphertext transformed from an IBBE ciphertext to get the symmetric key and then uses the symmetric key to recover the data. The decryption of the converted ciphertext is described by the following algorithm.

$M \leftarrow$ **Decrypt**$_{Conv}(PK_{IBE}, CT_{ID}, SK_{ID})$: The algorithm takes as inputs the public key PK_{IBE}, the access credential SK_{ID} of user ID and the converted ciphertext $CT_{ID} = (C'_0, C_2, E_0, E_1)$. It performs

$$k = E_0/\hat{e}(SK_{ID}, E_1)$$

and outputs

$$M = C'_0 \cdot \hat{e}(F(k), C_2).$$

The basic idea of this algorithm is first running the IBE decryption to recover the blinding value k and then re-blinding C'_0 to recover M by performing one bilinear pairing.

Correctness. For the decryption of an IBBE ciphertext, the correctness follows from that of IBBE decryption described in [10]: If CT_S is well formed for S, we have that

$$\begin{aligned} M' &= \left(\hat{e}\left(g^{-\alpha s}, h^{\Delta_{S,j}}\right)\cdot\right. \\ &\quad \left.\hat{e}\left(g^{\frac{1}{\alpha+H(ID_j)}}, h^{s\prod_{i=1}^{n}(\alpha+H(ID_i))}\right)\right)^{\frac{1}{\prod_{i=1,i\neq j}^{n} H(ID_i)}} \\ &= \left(\hat{e}(g,h)^{-s\prod_{i=1,i\neq j}^{n}(\alpha+H(ID_i))+s\prod_{i=1,i\neq j}^{n} H(ID_i)}\cdot\right. \\ &\quad \left.\hat{e}(g,h)^{s\prod_{i=1,i\neq j}^{n}(\alpha+H(ID_i))}\right)^{\frac{1}{\prod_{i=1,i\neq j}^{n} H(ID_i)}} \\ &= \left(\hat{e}(g,h)^{s\prod_{i=1,i\neq j}^{n} H(ID_i)}\right)^{\frac{1}{\prod_{i=1,i\neq j}^{n} H(ID_i)}} \\ &= \hat{e}(g,h)^s. \end{aligned}$$

Thus, $M = C_0/M' = M\hat{e}(g,h)^s/\hat{e}(g,h)^s$.

We now show the correctness of the decryption for a converted ciphertext. First, in the file conversion, we have that

$$\begin{aligned} K' &= \hat{e}\left(g^{-\alpha s}, h^{\Delta_{S,j}}\right)\cdot \\ &\quad \hat{e}\left(g^{\frac{1}{\alpha+H(ID_j)}}\cdot F(k)^{\prod_{i=1,i\neq j}^{n} H(ID_i)}, h^{s\left(\prod_{i=1}^{n}(\alpha+H(ID_i))\right)}\right), \\ &= \hat{e}\left(g^{-\alpha s}, h^{\Delta_{S,j}}\right)\cdot \hat{e}(g,h)^{s\prod_{i=1,i\neq j}^{n}(\alpha+H(ID_i))}\cdot \\ &\quad \hat{e}\left(F(k)^{\prod_{i=1,i\neq j}^{n} H(ID_i)}, C_2\right), \\ &= \hat{e}(g,h)^{-s\prod_{i=1,i\neq j}^{n}(\alpha+H(ID_i))+s\prod_{i=1,i\neq j}^{n} H(ID_i)}\cdot \\ &\quad \hat{e}(g,h)^{s\prod_{i=1,i\neq j}^{n}(\alpha+H(ID_i))}\cdot \hat{e}\left(F(k)^{\prod_{i=1,i\neq j}^{n} H(ID_i)}, C_2\right), \\ &= \left(\hat{e}(g,h)^s\cdot \hat{e}(F(k), C_2)\right)^{\prod_{i=1,i\neq j}^{n} H(ID_i)} \end{aligned}$$

and

$$K = (K')^{\frac{1}{\prod_{i=1,i\neq j}^{n} H(ID_i)}} = \hat{e}(g,h)^s\cdot \hat{e}(F(k), C_2).$$

It then follows that

$$\begin{aligned} C'_0 &= C_0/K = M\hat{e}(g,h)^s/\left(\hat{e}(g,h)^s\cdot \hat{e}(F(k), C_2)\right) \\ &= M/\hat{e}(F(k), C_2). \end{aligned}$$

Next, in the decryption, we have that

$$\begin{aligned} k &= k\hat{e}(g,h)^r/\hat{e}\left(g^{\frac{1}{\alpha+H(ID)}}, h^{r(\alpha+H(ID))}\right) \\ &= k\hat{e}(g,h)^r/\hat{e}(g,h)^r \end{aligned}$$

which allows to compute $F(k) \in \mathbb{G}$. It follows that

$$M = C'_0 \cdot \hat{e}(F(k), C_2).$$

5. SECURITY ANALYSIS

In this section, we evaluate the security of the ACCRE system. Since the ACCRE involves an IBBE and an IBE, the security involves the standard security definitions of these two primitives, which can be found in [10] and [4], respectively. In this analysis, we focus on the security due to the introduction of file conversion in the security definition. At a high level, a secure ACCRE system should guarantee that unauthorized users cannot get any useful information about the content of the IBBE secured file stored in DSP, even if they could access the system public key, compromise the access credentials of other unauthorized users, and collude with the DSP. Further, since the IBBE encrypted files can be transformed into IBE encrypted ones, the secure ACCRE system should additionally resist the attacks from the collusion of unauthorized users and the proxy.

To capture these attacks, we define an adversary that is able to access the public keys of IBBE and IBE, collude with users (no matter in IBBE or IBE) by querying their decryption keys, and compromise the proxy by having the conversion keys. The adversary declares two equal-length messages and a set S^* of identities. It is then challenged by an IBBE ciphertext for one of the messages under the set S^*. The security of ACCRE states that even for such adversary, it cannot distinguish which message is used to create the ciphertext. To avoid trivial solutions, we require that the adversary cannot query the decryption keys for the challenge ciphertext. Moreover, the adversary should be restricted in some way so that it cannot query the conversion keys that can transform the challenge ciphertext into the ciphertexts for which the adversary holds decryption keys. Formally, the security of ACCRE is defined by the following game played between a challenger and the adversary.

Init: The adversary $\mathcal{A}$ declares a set of identities, S^* to be attacked.

Setup: The challenger runs the **Setup** algorithm to obtain the system public keys PK and master secret keys MSK. It gives PK to the adversary $\mathcal{A}$.

Phase 1: The adversary $\mathcal{A}$ issues queries $Q_1, ..., Q_{q'}$ to the challenger, where Q_i for $1 \leq i \leq q'$ is one of the following queries:

> **Reveal**(ID). $\mathcal{A}$ queries the decryption key for identity $ID \notin S^*$ of either IBBE or IBE. In response, the challenger runs the algorithm **KeyGen**(PK, MSK, ID) to output key SK_{ID} and returns this key to $\mathcal{A}$.
>
> **CKReveal**$(S \to ID)$. $\mathcal{A}$ queries the conversion key from identity set S to an identity ID. In response, the challenger runs the algorithm **CKGen**$(PK, SK_{ID'}, S, ID)$ to output key $CK_{S\to ID}$ and gives this key to $\mathcal{A}$, where the decryption key $SK_{ID'} \leftarrow$ **KeyGen**(PK, MSK, ID') for $ID' \in S$.

Challenge: The adversary $\mathcal{A}$ outputs two equal-length messages M_0 and M_1. The restriction is that (1) the adversary cannot query **Reveal**(ID) for any $ID \in S^*$; and (2) the adversary $\mathcal{A}$ can query at most one of two queries **CKReveal**$(S^* \to ID)$ and **Reveal**(ID) for any ID. The challenger then flips a coin $b \in \{0,1\}$, encrypts M_b under S^* and returns the ciphertext CT_{S^*} to $\mathcal{A}$.

Phase 2: The adversary $\mathcal{A}$ issues queries $Q_{q'+1}, ..., Q_q$ to the challenger just as in Phase 1, with the constraints that (1) it cannot query **Reveal**(ID) for any $ID \in S^*$; and (2) it can query at most one of two queries **CKReveal**$(S^* \to ID)$ and **Reveal**(ID) for any ID.

Guess: The adversary $\mathcal{A}$ outputs a guess $b' \in \{0,1\}$.

The advantage of an attacker $\mathcal{A}$ in this game is defined as

$$Adv_{\mathcal{A}} = |\Pr[b = b'] - 1/2|.$$

DEFINITION 1. *An ACCRE system is secure if all polynomial time adversaries have at most a negligible advantage in the above game.*

In the ACCRE system, there are two kinds of ciphertexts, i.e., IBBE ciphertexts and converted IBE ciphertexts. However, we do not additionally challenge the adversary with the IBE ciphertext in the security definition above, which means that the adversary is not required to declare an identity to be attacked in Init phase. This is because that the adversary is able to query the conversion keys and convert the challenge IBBE ciphertext into an IBE one by using the queried conversion keys.

The following theorem shows the security of ACCRE in the above security definition, with the proofs given in Appendix A.

THEOREM 1. *Our ACCRE scheme is secure if the underlying IBBE and IBE are both secure. In particular, if there exist an adversary $\mathcal{A}$ which has an advantage $Adv_{\mathcal{A}}$ in breaking the security of the ACCRE system, then we can construct an algorithm $\mathcal{B}$ that breaks the security of the underlying IBBE and IBE schemes with advantage ϵ_1 and ϵ_2, respectively, satisfying $\epsilon_1 + \epsilon_2 \geq Adv_{\mathcal{A}}/e(1 + q_K)$, where e is the base of natural logarithm and q_K is the maximum number of $\mathcal{A}$'s key queries.*

From the above theorem, it can be seen that if the advantages of breaking the security of IBBE and the security of IBE are both negligible, then the advantage in breaking the security of ACCRE is also negligible, which means that the ACCRE system resists the attacks from any polynomial-time adversary defined in Definition 1.

6. PERFORMANCE EVALUATION

In this section, we evaluate the performance of the ACCRE system both theoretically and experimentally.

6.1 Theoretical Analysis

We analyze the computation complexity of each procedure of the ACCRE system. We do not take into account the computation overheads of the symmetric encryption and decryption, since they are only related to the data size and independent of the file conversion mechanism of ACCRE. We focus on the most expensive operations, i.e., exponentiations and bilinear maps, in the asymmetric cryptosystems. The time consumed by an exponentiation and a bilinear map is denoted by t_e and t_p, respectively.

Table 1 summarizes the computation cost of each procedure in the ACCRE. In this table, m denotes the maximum number of users authorized to access an IBBE secured file and $n(< m)$ denotes the number of users specified by the data owner in file creation. Table 1 clearly reveals the efficiency of the file conversion mechanism: the data owner just needs four exponentiations to produce a conversion key

Table 1: Computation

Operation	Computational Complexity
System Setup	$(m+1) \cdot t_e + t_p$
User Registration	$1 \cdot t_e$
File Creation	$(n+3) \cdot t_e$
CK **Generation**	$4 \cdot t_e$
File Conversion	$n \cdot t_e + 2 \cdot t_p$
Original File Access	$n \cdot t_e + 2 \cdot t_p$
Converted File Access	$2 \cdot t_p$

that can transform his/her IBBE encrypted file into an IBE encrypted one; and the data consumer with correct IBE decryption key takes only two bilinear pairing operations to recover the symmetric key. This allows a resource-limited mobile to take little energy to access an encrypted file. Besides, since the proxy in the file conversion actually decrypts the IBBE ciphertext to obtain a blinded symmetric key, the computation complexity of the file conversion is the same as that of the original file access (decryption for an IBBE ciphertext), which means that the proxy does not need to take extra costs to convert a file other than a normal IBBE decryption. These features show that our ACCRE scheme provides a promising method to securely transform encrypted data from the IBBE cryptosystem to the different IBE cryptosystem.

Table 2 compares our ACCRE scheme with some related work that also achieve transforming a ciphertext for a public key into a ciphertext for another public key, in terms of the performance, interaction (required or not) and the cross-cryptosystem (supported or not). In this table, the schemes proposed in [14] and [9] are constructed in identity-based settings. Although these schemes achieve the constant size of public key, secret key, original ciphertext, conversion key and converted ciphertext, they transform encrypted files in the same identity-based encryption system. Hence, the data owner cannot specify a group of users to access the data at first, but only one single user. This restricts the schemes from being employed for more complicated data sharing systems allowing multiple authorized visitors. The schemes [24] and [29] are constructed in attribute-based encryption and thus allow multiple matching visitors to access a file. However, in accessing a converted file, the number of the time-consuming bilinear pairings required in the decryption is linear with the number N of total attributes in the system. This would be unaffordable to mobile devices such as mobile phones and tablets that usually possess limited computing capability. The scheme [31] supports the cross-cryptosystem that allows to transform a file encrypted in one PKE cryptosystem into a file encrypted in another cryptosystem (IBE), whereas it requires the interaction between the data owner who delegates the access rights and the data consumer authorized to access converted file during the conversion process.

Table 2 reveals the superior practicality of our scheme. It can be seen that the users in IBE store very short public key and secret decryption keys and take only two bilinear pairings in accessing a converted file. Compared to [24] and [29], the original file, the conversion key, the converted file of our scheme are very short. Our scheme allows many authorized users to access the original file, in contrast to allowed single one in [14, 9, 31]. Our scheme does not require any participation of the Admin or the specified data consumer in the file conversion, hence the data owners can convert their files more conveniently. Moreover, our ACCRE supports the cross-cryptosystem re-encryption that allows to transforms an IBBE encrypted file into an IBE encrypted one. Therefore, a mobile user equipped with an IBE decryption can at a low cost access a data previously encrypted by a more complicated encryption system. These confirm the practical attractiveness of our ACCRE scheme.

Our ACCRE solution allows a mobile user with resource-limited devices to access encrypted files at a low cost. We note that there exist some other solutions that also result less consumptions for the mobile users to access encrypted files. Table 3 compares our ACCRE with these solutions. We are interested on the public key, decryption key, ciphertext to be stored on a mobile user and the number of bilinear pairings computed by a mobile user in decryption. Hence, we evaluate the size of the public key, decryption key and ciphertext needed to be stored and the bilinear pairings required to be computed by a mobile user in this comparison.

Table 3 reveals the advantageous features of ACCRE in its applications to mobile access. Compared to the standard IBE scheme [3] that does not support file conversion, our scheme achieves the similar size of both public key and decryption key and the same number of required bilinear pairings. The solution [15] provides an outsourcing mechanism to convert a long ABE ciphertext (linear in the number l of attributes associated with the ciphertext) into a short ElGamal-type one so that the mobile user can decrypt without performing any bilinear pairing. This solution reduces the computations of decryption performed by a mobile user, but it does not support the access rights delegation that the data owners are allowed to delegate the access rights to their data to other users. The solution [33] provides a delegation in ABE that allows a ciphertext to be re-encrypted to a more restrictive policy. In a trivial application of [33], one could transform a ciphertext into a ciphertext for the access policy that contains only the identity of the mobile user. Thus, the complicated ciphertext is converted into a short one that the mobile user only needs few bilinear pairing to decrypt. However, this use of [33] requires the identity of the mobile user to be *in advance* specified in the access policy of the original ciphertext, while in some applications the data owners may not know who will ask to access their data in the future. The IBBE scheme [10] that our scheme bases on also achieves less consumption on mobile users except more space to store the longer public key. Similar with [33], it also requires the identity of the mobile user to be *pre-specified* in encryption. Our ACCRE scheme achieves the less consumption of mobile users. Furthermore, it allows the data owner to delegate the access rights to his encrypted data to a mobile user who is not involved in the access policy beforehand. These comparisons show the charming features of our scheme to convert encrypted data for mobile access in data outsourced environments.

6.2 Experimental Results

We conducted a series of experiments to evaluate the performance of ACCRE system in isolation (i.e., without considering the network lag, file I/O, etc.). The experiments are performed on two hardware platforms: a PC desktop with

Table 2: Comparison with Related Work

	Public Key Size	Secret key Size	Original CT Size	Conversion Key Size	Converted CT Size	$\hat{e}(,)$ in Decryption	Non-interaction	Cross-cryptosystem
[14]	2	1	2	3	4	2	√	×
[9]	3	2	3	5	5	3	√	×
[31]	**PKE:** 3 **IBE:** 4	**PKE:** 3 **IBE:** 2	4	3	3	2	×	√
[24]	$3N+3$	$2N$	$N+3$	$3N+4$	$N+6$	$N+3$	√	×
[29]	$3N+5$	$2N+1$	$N+3$	$3N+4$	$N+6$	$2N+2$	√	×
Ours	**IBBE:** $m+3$ **IBE:** 4	**IBBE:** 1 **IBE:** 1	3	3	4	2	√	√

Table 3: Comparison with Related Work Resulting Less Consumptions on Mobile Users

	Public Key Size	Secret Key Size	Original CT Size	Converted CT Size	$\hat{e}(,)$ in Decryption	Ciphertext Conversion	Non-pre-Specification	Access rights Delegation
[3]	4	2	3	⊥	2	×	⊥	×
[10]	$m+3$	1	3	⊥	2	×	⊥	×
[15]	3	1	$2l+2$	2	0	√	×	×
[33]	3	3	$l+2$	3	3	√	×	√
Ours	4	1	3	4	2	√	√	√

a 4-core Intel Core i3-2130 CPU running 3.40GHz and a Samsung mobile phone I9100 with a dual-core Exynos 4210 CPU, running at 1.2GHz. The operations in bilinear groups are implemented by using the Standford PBC library 0.5.12 (available at http://crypto.stanford.edu/pbc). In the experiments, we evaluate the performance of each procedure of ACCRE.

In the ACCRE, the performance of file creation and conversion key generation both depend on the parameter n, i.e., the number of users allowed to access a data encrypted in an IBBE ciphertext. To reflect the affection of the parameter n on the system performance, we conducted experiments with different number of allowed users. In a practical example such as a company's data sharing system, it seems reasonable to assume that the maximum number of employees authorized to access a file would be no more than one hundred. Therefore, we evaluated the performance of ACCRE with parameter $n = 10, 20, 30, ..., 100$.

In the system setup procedure, the Admin outputs the public key of size linear in m. For a fixed $m = 100$, the time to generate the system public key is about 435 ms, which is a negligible consumption to an Admin that usually possesses more powerful computing capability than our PC desktop.

In the user admission procedure, the Admin generates a decryption key for a user no matter in IBBE or IBE. The time consumed by the Admin to generate a decryption key is just nearly 8.10 ms, which is also a negligible cost to the Admin.

Figure 2 shows the time consumed by a data owner to create an IBBE secured file to be stored in DSP. It can be seen that the time consumed in the IBBE encryption is linear with the number of users allowed to access the same data. Even for the largest number $n = 100$, the time consumed by the asymmetric encryption in this procedure is just about

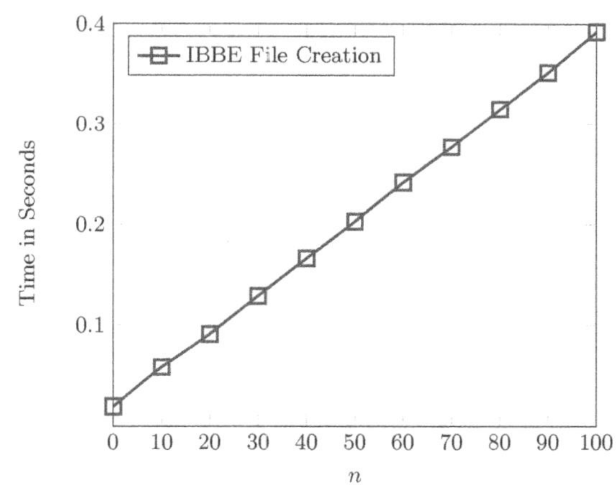

Figure 2: Time Consumed in File Creation

0.4 s, which is very low cost for the data owners to encrypt their data to be outsourced.

Figure 3 shows the time consumed in conversion key (CK) generation procedure and file conversion procedure respectively. In the CK generation, for an IBBE ciphertext, the data owner generating CK runs an IBE encryption for the identity of the intended data consumer. Although the data owner computes a product of the hash values of the identities involved in the IBBE ciphertext, the computations are performed in $\mathbb{Z}_p$ and the cost time are negligible compared to the time cost by the operations in $\mathbb{G}$. Therefore, the time consumed by the conversion key generation is almost independent of the number of authorized users. We simulated the file conversion procedure of the proxy also on the PC platform. Figure 3 shows that the time consumed by the proxy to convert an IBBE ciphertext into an IBE ciphertext is linear with the number of users authorized to decrypt the

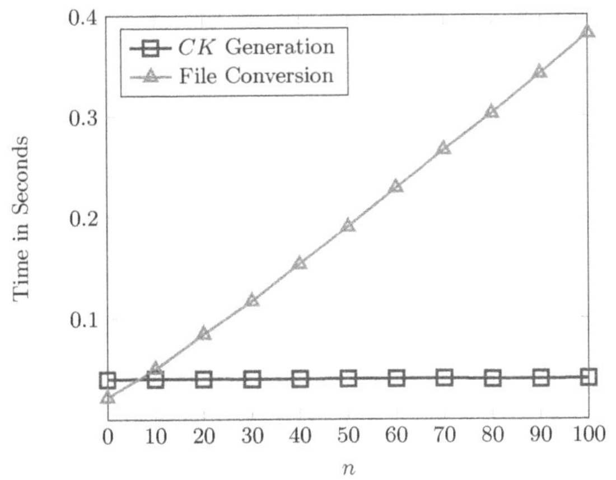

Figure 3: Time Consumed in Conversion Key Generation and File Conversion

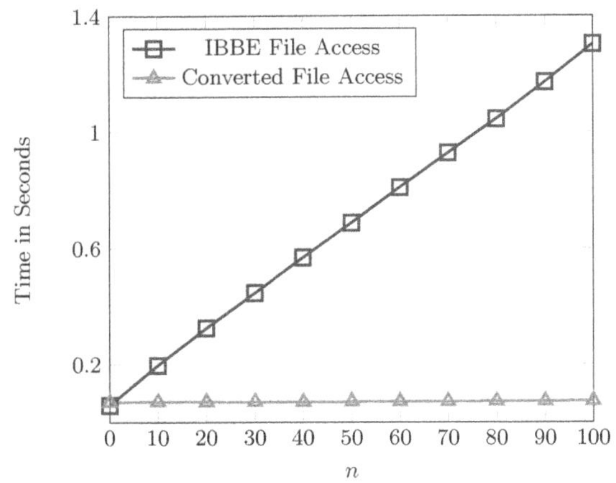

Figure 4: Time Consumed in IBBE File and Converted File Access on Mobile Phone

IBBE ciphertext. This confirms that the proxy performs one decryption of IBBE to convert an IBBE encrypted file.

Figure 4 shows the time consumed by the mobile phone to access a converted file is much less that that to access an IBBE encrypted file (original file). It can be seen that the time cost by the IBBE decryption grows linearly with the number of authorized users. Due to the less powerful computing capability than the PC desktop, the mobile phone takes much more time to decrypt an IBBE encrypted file. For the largest number $n = 100$, the time consumed by the IBBE decryption performed on the mobile phone is nearly 1.4 s. Figure 4 demonstrates that the time consumed by the mobile phone to access a converted file is independent of the number of authorized users. Since the decryption for a converted file only requires two bilinear pairings, the time consumed by the mobile phone in this procedure is millisecond-level. Hence, the data consumer can take a less cost to access the data that is previously encrypted in an IBBE ciphertext.

From the above experimental results, our ACCRE scheme provides an efficient way for data owners to protect their data. Before outsourcing the data to the DSP, the data owners can encrypt the data at a very low cost through the IBBE so that a group of authorized users can access. When deciding to transmit the outsourced data to a user equipped with IBE, the data owner takes an even less time to generate a conversion key. The file conversion mechanism transforms an IBBE encrypted file into an IBE encrypted one so that the IBE user can recover the data without altering his/her IBE decryption key nor spending much time. During the file conversion, the DSP, the Admin and the IBE user are not required to take part in the process. These features make our ACCRE practical to securely transform an encrypted file into another one easily accessible to a mobile device.

7. CONCLUSION

In this paper we proposed a new encryption paradigm, referred to as asymmetric cross-cryptosystem re-encryption (ACCRE) to convert encrypted data for resource-asymmetric computing devices. The novelty of the ACCRE is that it integrates a complicated yet versatile IBBE scheme and a simple yet efficient IBE scheme with a secure ciphertext conversion from the former to the latter. This feature renders the ACCRE especially suitable for the applications where an IBBE and an IBE are deployed for resource-asymmetric computing devices and a conversion mechanism is required to transform the complicated IBBE ciphertext into a simple IBE ciphertext affordable to resource-limited access devices. We constructed an ACCRE scheme with short ciphertexts and secret keys by proposing a key blinding technique and using an IBE scheme compatible with an existing IBBE scheme. We proved the security of the proposed ACCRE scheme in a rigorous definition. The theoretical and experimental analyses showed that mobile users take little costs to access encrypted data. We note none of existing re-encryption schemes between different cryptosystems, i.e., the Matsuo PKE-to-IBE scheme [31] and our IBBE-to-IBE scheme, are secure against collusions from the proxy and non-authorized users but cannot prevent collusion attacks from a malicious proxy and authorized re-encryption receivers. This may incurs practical vulnerabilities in some applications. Hence, it seems interesting to design re-encryption scheme secure against this kind of strong colluding attacks.

8. ACKNOWLEDGEMENTS

We thank the anonymous reviewers for the invaluable comments to improve the paper. This paper was supported by the National Key Basic Research Program (973 program) under project 2012CB315905, the Natural Science Foundation of China under projects 61370190, 61173154, 61272501, 61202465, 61472029, 61472429 and 61472083, by the Beijing Natural Science Foundation under projects 4132056 and 4122041, the Research Funds of Renmin University of China through project 14XNLF02 and the Open Research Fund of Beijing Key Laboratory of Trusted Computing.

9. REFERENCES

[1] G. Ateniese, K. Fu, M. Green, and S. Hohenberger. Improved proxy re-encryption schemes with applications to secure distributed storage. *Information and System Security (TISSEC), ACM Transactions on*, 9(1):1–30, 2006.

[2] M. Blaze, G. Bleumer, and M. Strauss. Divertible protocols and atomic proxy cryptography. In *EUROCRYPT 1998*, pages 127–144. Springer, 1998.

[3] D. Boneh and X. Boyen. Efficient selective-id secure identity-based encryption without random oracles. In *EUROCRYPT 2004*, pages 223–238. Springer, 2004.

[4] D. Boneh and M. Franklin. Identity-based encryption from the weil pairing. In *CRYPTO 2001*, pages 213–229. Springer, 2001.

[5] R. Canetti and S. Hohenberger. Chosen-ciphertext secure proxy re-encryption. In *ACM CCS 2007*, pages 185–194. ACM, 2007.

[6] S. S. M. Chow, J. K. Liu, and J. Zhou. Identity-based online/offline key encapsulation and encryption. In *ASIACCS 2011*, pages 52–60. ACM, 2011.

[7] C. Chu, J. K. Liu, J. Zhou, F. Bao, and R. H. Deng. Practical id-based encryption for wireless sensor network. In *ASIACCS 2010*, pages 337–340. ACM, 2010.

[8] C. K. Chu, S. S. M. Chow, W. G. Tzeng, J. Zhou, and R. H. Deng. Key-aggregate cryptosystem for scalable data sharing in cloud storage. *Parallel and Distributed Systems, IEEE Transactions on*, 25(2):468–477, 2014.

[9] C. K. Chu and W. G. Tzeng. Identity-based proxy re-encryption without random oracles. In *ISC 2007*, pages 189–202. Springer, 2007.

[10] C. Delerablée. Identity-based broadcast encryption with constant size ciphertexts and private keys. In *ASIACRYPT 2007*, pages 200–215. Springer, 2007.

[11] H. Deng, Q. Wu, B. Qin, S. S. M. Chow, J. Domingo-Ferrer, and W. Shi. Tracing and revoking leaked credentials: accountability in leaking sensitive outsourced data. In *ASIACCS*, pages 425–434. ACM, 2014.

[12] H. Deng, Q. Wu, B. Qin, J. Domingo-Ferrer, L. Zhang, J. Liu, and W. Shi. Ciphertext-policy hierarchical attribute-based encryption with short ciphertexts. *Information Sciences*, 275:370–384, 2014.

[13] H. Deng, Q. Wu, B. Qin, J. Mao, X. Liu, L. Zhang, and W. Shi. Who is touching my cloud. In *ESORICS 2014*, volume 8712 of *Lecture Notes in Computer Science*, pages 362–379. Springer, 2014.

[14] M. Green and G. Ateniese. Identity-based proxy re-encryption. In *ACNS 2007*, pages 288–306. Springer, 2007.

[15] M. Green, S. Hohenberger, and B. Waters. Outsourcing the decryption of abe ciphertexts. In *USENIX Security Symposium 2011*. 2011,3.

[16] J. S. Hwu, R. J. Chen, and Y. B. Lin. An efficient identity-based cryptosystem for end-to-end mobile security. *Wireless Communications, IEEE Transactions on*, 5(9):2586–2593, 2006.

[17] A. Ivan and Y. Dodis. Proxy cryptography revisited. In *NDSS 2003*. 2003.

[18] Y. Kawai and K. Takashima. Fully-anonymous functional proxy-re-encryption. Cryptology ePrint Archive, Report 2013/318, 2013.

[19] B. Lee. Unified public key infrastructure supporting both certificate-based and id-based cryptography. In *ARES 2010*, pages 54–61. IEEE, 2010.

[20] M. Li, S. Yu, Y. Zheng, K. Ren, and W. Lou. Scalable and secure sharing of personal health records in cloud computing using attribute-based encryption. *Parallel and Distributed Systems, IEEE Transactions on*, 24(1):131–143, 2013.

[21] K. Liang, M. H. Au, J. K. Liu, W. Susilo, D. S. Wong, G. Yang, T. V. X. Phuong, and Q. Xie. A DFA-Based Functional Proxy Re-Encryption Scheme for Secure Public Cloud Data Sharing. *IEEE Transactions on Information Forensics and Security*, 9(10):1667–1680, 2014.

[22] K. Liang, M. H. Au, J. K. Liu, W. Susilo, D. S. Wong, G. Yang, Y. Yu, and A. Yang. A secure and efficient ciphertext-policy attribute-based proxy re-encryption for cloud data sharing. *Future Generation Computer Systems*, 2015. To Appear.

[23] K. Liang, J. K. Liu, D. S. Wong, and W. Susilo. An efficient cloud-based revocable identity-based proxy re-encryption scheme for public clouds data sharing. In *ESORICS 2014*, volume 8712 of *Lecture Notes in Computer Science*, pages 257–272. Springer, 2014.

[24] X. Liang, Z. Cao, H. Lin, and J. Shao. Attribute based proxy re-encryption with delegating capabilities. In *ASIACCS 2009*, pages 276–286. ACM, 2009.

[25] B. Libert and D. Vergnaud. Unidirectional chosen-ciphertext secure proxy re-encryption. In *PKC 2008*, pages 360–379. Springer, 2008.

[26] J. K. Liu and J. Zhou. An efficient identity-based online/offline encryption scheme. In *ACNS 2009*, volume 5536 of *Lecture Notes in Computer Science*, pages 156–167, 2009.

[27] W. Liu, J. Liu, Q. Wu, and B. Qin. Hierarchical identity-based broadcast encryption. In *ACISP 2014*, volume 8544 of *Lecture Notes in Computer Science*, pages 242–257. Springer, 2014.

[28] W. Liu, J. Liu, Q. Wu, B. Qin, and Y. Zhou. Practical direct chosen ciphertext secure key-policy attribute-based encryption with public ciphertext test. In *ESORICS 2014*, volume 8713 of *Lecture Notes in Computer Science*, pages 91–108. Springer, 2014.

[29] S. Luo, J. Hu, and Z. Chen. Ciphertext policy attribute-based proxy re-encryption. In *ICICS 2010*, pages 401–415. Springer, 2010.

[30] T. Matsuda, R. Nishimaki, and K. Tanaka. Cca proxy re-encryption without bilinear maps in the standard model. In *PKC 2010*, pages 261–278. Springer, 2010.

[31] T. Matsuo. Proxy re-encryption systems for identity-based encryption. In *Pairing 2007*, pages 247–267. Springer, 2007.

[32] Pavlović and Miklavčič. Web-based electronic data collection system to support electrochemotherapy clinical trial. *Information Technology in Biomedicine, IEEE Transactions on*, 11(2):222–230, 2007.

[33] A. Sahai, H. Seyalioglu, and B. Waters. Dynamic credentials and ciphertext delegation for attribute-based encryption. In *CRYPTO 2012*, pages 199–217. Springer, 2012.

[34] J. Shao. Anonymous id-based proxy re-encryption. In *ACISP 2012*, pages 364–375. Springer, 2012.

[35] C. C. Tan, H. Wang, S. Zhong, and Q. Li. Ibe-lite: a lightweight identity-based cryptography for body sensor networks. *Information Technology in Biomedicine, IEEE Transactions on*, 13(6):926–932, 2009.

[36] Y. Wang, Q. Wu, D. S. Wong, B. Qin, S. S. M. Chow, Z. Liu, and X. Tan. Securely outsourcing

exponentiations with single untrusted program for cloud storage. In *ESORICS 2014*, pages 326–343. Springer, 2014.

[37] J. Weng, Y. Zhao, and G. Hanaoka. On the security of a bidirectional proxy re-encryption scheme from pkc 2010. In *PKC 2011*, pages 284–295. Springer, 2011.

[38] P. Zhang, C. Lin, Y. Jiang, Y. Fan, and X. Shen. A lightweight encryption scheme for network-coded mobile ad hoc networks. *Parallel and Distributed Systems, IEEE Transactions on*, 25(9):2211–2221, 2014.

APPENDIX

A. PROOF OF THEOREM 1

The IBBE scheme involved in ACCRE system has been proved to be secure in [10]. The underlying IBE scheme is a variant of the IBE scheme [3] in that the random value in the denominator of the secret key's exponent in the IBE scheme [3] is replaced by the hashed value $H(ID)$ in our scheme. Using H as a random oracle, we can still obtain a secure IBE scheme by manipulating the random values in queried secret keys.

We now prove the security of ACCRE after the introduction of file conversion. Given an adversary $\mathcal{A}$ breaking the ACCRE, we build an algorithm $\mathcal{B}$ which interacts with $\mathcal{A}$ to break the security of the IBBE scheme in [10] or the IBE scheme. As defined in Definition 1, we have to respond to $\mathcal{A}$' **CKReveal**$(S \to ID)$ queries. To do so, we need to call the key generation oracle of the IBBE scheme and then leverage the output keys to run the **CKGen** algorithm to obtain the requested conversion keys. If the adversary $\mathcal{A}$ queries a conversion key for the challenge identity set S^* (which is allowed by the security definition), the algorithm $\mathcal{B}$ cannot simulate such a key since the definition of the security of the IBBE forbids generating a decryption key for the challenge identity set. To overcome this problem, we make $\mathcal{B}$ output the correct keys with a determined probability, while outputs random keys with the complementary probability. Then, similar to [9], we create a table $(\beta \in \{0,1\}, S, ID, CK)$, where $\beta = 1$ means that $\mathcal{B}$ outputs a correct key and $\beta = 0$ means that $\mathcal{B}$ outputs a random key. We also need to prove the indistinguishability of the correct conversion keys and random ones in $\mathcal{A}$'s view.

The algorithm $\mathcal{B}$ first runs the setup algorithm of the IBBE scheme [10] to get public key PK. The algorithm $\mathcal{B}$ also maintains a table (β, S, ID, CK) initialized to be empty. Algorithm $\mathcal{B}$ interacts with adversary $\mathcal{A}$ as follows.

Init. The adversary $\mathcal{A}$ outputs an identity set S^*.

Setup. Algorithm $\mathcal{B}$ gives the public key PK to $\mathcal{A}$.

Phase 1. The adversary $\mathcal{A}$ makes the following queries:

Reveal$(ID \notin S^*)$. Algorithm $\mathcal{B}$ responds by generating a decryption key. It flips a random $\beta \in \{0,1\}$ so that $\Pr[\beta = 1]$ with a probability θ which we will determine later. When $\beta = 0$, or $(0, *, ID, *)$ exists on the table, where $*$ denotes the wildcard, $\mathcal{B}$ aborts. Otherwise, $\mathcal{B}$ calls the key generation oracle of the IBBE scheme by taking in ID to output a secret key for ID and returns this key to $\mathcal{A}$. Finally, algorithm $\mathcal{B}$ writes $(\beta, *, ID, \perp)$ in the table.

CKReveal$(S \to ID)$. Algorithm $\mathcal{B}$ flips a random $\beta \in \{0,1\}$ just as in the **Reveal** stage. If $\beta = 1$ and $S \neq S^*$, or $(1, S, *, \perp)$ exists on the table, algorithm $\mathcal{B}$ requests the key generation oracle of the IBBE scheme to create a secret key with identity in S and applies this key to the **CKGen** algorithm to generate a conversion key CK from S to ID, then $\mathcal{B}$ gives CK to $\mathcal{A}$. Otherwise, $\mathcal{B}$ returns a random conversion key $CK = (D, R_0, R_1)$, where D is a random element of $\mathbb{G}$ and (R_0, R_1) can be seen an IBE ciphertext for some message. Finally, $\mathcal{B}$ writes (β, S, ID, CK) in the table.

Challenge. The adversary $\mathcal{A}$ outputs two messages M_0 and M_1. If there is a record $(1, S^*, ID', CK')$ for any ID' and CK' in the table, algorithm $\mathcal{B}$ aborts. Otherwise, $\mathcal{B}$ gives the challenge (S^*, M_0, M_1) to the encryption oracle of the IBBE scheme and returns the challenge ciphertext to $\mathcal{A}$.

Phase 2. Phase 1 is repeated except the forbidden queries described in Definition 1.

Guess. The adversary $\mathcal{A}$ outputs its guess $b' \in \{0,1\}$ and $\mathcal{B}$ outputs the same bit.

We now determine the upper-bounded probability of $\mathcal{B}$ in breaking the security of the IBBE scheme [10] and the IBE scheme. We note that $\mathcal{B}$ perfectly simulates the real scheme if it does not abort and always outputs correct keys. We first describe the probability that $\mathcal{B}$ aborts. Let q_K denote the number of $\mathcal{A}$' secret key queries. Then the probability of $\mathcal{B}$ aborting in phase 1 and phase 2 is θ^{q_K}. Besides, the probability that $\mathcal{B}$ aborts in the challenge phase is $1-\theta$. Hence, the probability that $\mathcal{B}$ aborts in the whole game is $\theta^{q_K}(1-\theta)$, which has a maximum value $1-1/(q_K+1)$. Using this value, we can obtain the probability that $\mathcal{B}$ aborts is at least $1/e(1+q_K)$.

We next discuss the probability of $\mathcal{A}$ in distinguishing a correct key from a random one. The random conversion key is in the form of (D, R_0, R_1), where $D \xleftarrow{R} \mathbb{G}_T$, and the correct conversion key is in the form of $(SK_{ID_j}F(k), E_0, E_1)$, where (E_0, E_1) is an IBE ciphertext for k. We can see that SK_{ID_j} is randomized by $F(k)$. The only way to distinguish these two keys is to distinguish (R_0, R_1) from (E_0, E_1). However, this is equivalent to breaking the security of the IBE scheme. Then the probability of $\mathcal{A}$ in distinguishing correct keys from random keys is negligible.

The adversary's successful distinguishability of the message encrypted in the challenge ciphertext is identical to breaking the security of the IBBE scheme.

Therefore, given the advantage $Adv_{\mathcal{A}}$ of $\mathcal{A}$ breaking the security of our scheme, the algorithm $\mathcal{B}$ can break the security of the IBBE scheme with an advantage ϵ_1 and the security of the IBE scheme with an advantage ϵ_2, satisfying $\epsilon_1 + \epsilon_2 \geq Adv_{\mathcal{A}}/e(1+q_K)$.

Block Programs: Improving Efficiency of Verifiable Computation for Circuits with Repeated Substructures

Gang Xu
Department of Electrical and Computer Engineering
Iowa State University
Ames, Iowa 50011
gxu@iastate.edu

George Amariucai
Department of Electrical and Computer Engineering
Iowa State University
Ames, Iowa 50011
gamari@iastate.edu

Yong Guan
Department of Electrical and Computer Engineering
Iowa State University
Ames, Iowa 50011
guan@iastate.edu

ABSTRACT

In the cloud computing paradigm, clients outsource computation to professional service providers. However, service providers may be error-prone or otherwise not entirely trustworthy, and therefore oftentimes the returned results need to be thoroughly verified. As such, the problem of verifiable computation has been motivating a rapidly-growing body of research, yielding increasingly-efficient systems, which currently achieve nearly-practical verifiable computation. Most recent solutions firstly transform the computation task into an arithmetic circuit, and then based on this circuit they design a verification protocol using argument systems.

In this paper we focus on the verification protocol *after* the circuit generation. We notice the state of the art involve a considerable cost, including the verifier's *amortized cost*, (i.e., the cost that needs to be amortized over a large number of work instances), and the prover's *cost of proof generation*. The most efficient argument systems still incur an amortized cost that is linear in the size of the circuit. In this paper, we show that verifiable computation can be made more efficient by taking advantage of computations with corresponding circuits containing repeated substructures (e.g. loops). Since loops play a pivotal role in the real world of computing (not only compute-intensive computations but also data-intensive computations such as big data applications), we take loops as a typical example, propose a new verification protocol for repeated structures and show that the circuit generated from computation with loops can indeed lead to a lower amortized cost and a lower cost of proof generation. Using the theory of arithmetic circuit complexity we prove that for most programs our design results in very significant savings. Our verification design for loops is based on Block Programs (BPs), an innovative encoding scheme for circuits with repeated structures.

ASIA CCS'15, April 14–17, 2015, Singapore..

http://dx.doi.org/10.1145/2714576.2714631.

Categories and Subject Descriptors

F.2.0 [**Theory of Computation**]: Analysis of Algorithms and Problem Complexity—*General*; K.6.5 [**Management of Computing and Information Systems**]: Security and Protection

General Terms

Algorithms, Security, Theory

Keywords

Cloud computing, Big data, Verifiable computation, Argument systems, PCPs, QAPs, Block Programs, Amortized costs, Loops.

1. INTRODUCTION

The surging popularity of the cloud computing paradigm has rendered a new type of service: computation as a commodity. While using this service, companies and individual users must no longer maintain expensive computing assets. They just outsource any burdensome computational workload to the cloud and enjoy additional perks, like expert technical consulting. But while outsourcing computation provides appealing benefits, one must fully consider a critical security issue: there is no guarantee on the correctness of the results returned by the cloud server, which may be error-prone or otherwise not entirely trustworthy. Thus an immediate need for result assurance naturally arises.

This need motivates a growing body of research on *verifiable computation*, and in particular, works focused on verification protocols for general-purpose computation. Since verifying the result of general computation can be abstracted to classical problems in the theory of computation, such as interactive proof (IP) systems [18] and probabilistically checkable proof (PCP) systems [1, 2], the security community naturally turned to the model of these classical proof systems, attempting to refine theory toward implementation. In their designs, the server plays the role of a *prover* trying to convince the client, who plays the role of a *verifier*, that the result is correct. A recent line of work strives for verifying computation based on *argument systems* [10, 21, 22], a notable variant of the PCP model. They hold a more practical assumption that, in addition to the verifier being polynomial-time probabilistic, the prover is also computationally bounded. Breakthroughs [19, 25, 26, 24, 11, 29] in argument systems have made PCP-based approaches more practical. Another important line of work [16, 24,

23, 7] makes attempts to adopt the recent finding of a new characterization of the NP complexity class – the *Quadratic Span Programs (QSPs)* (and *Quadratic Arithmetic Programs (QAPs)*) [16]. Based on theoretical innovations of QAP [16], a nearly practical verifiable computation system called Pinocchio was introduced in [23].

In the context of verifiable computation, there are two stages: one in which the outsouced computation task, which is a piece of code written in the form of a high-level language (e.g. C), is transformed into an arithmetic circuit, and another in which the actual verification protocol is performed to check that the prover correctly evaluated the circuit generated in the first stage. The core of the first transformation stage is a specific compiler, as known as a circuit generator. State-of-the-art compilers includes vnTinyRAM [7, 8] and the compilers in Zaatar and Pinocchio. These compiler techniques are beyond the scope of this paper, and we review these compilers for completeness in Section 7. In this paper, we are interested in the second stage, namely, the actual verification protocol. In the rest of our paper, we assume that the underlying circuit representation has been generated using the aforementioned circuit generators.

Although encouraging results have been emerging, the high costs still stymie their practicality. In particular, the biggest performance concerns are around further reducing the *amortized cost* of verification, and reducing the *cost of proof generation.* Zaatar [24] and Pinocchio [23] are two representatives of the state of the art in verifiable computation. The verification protocols in both Zaatar and Pinocchio can be viewed as argument systems with *amortizing*, namely, proof systems that require a high cost for the verifier that needs to be amortized over a large number of work instances. In Pinocchio, the verifier needs to publish a public key and hold a matching verification key. Both the cost of constructing this verification key and the public key are amortized over all possible work instances of the same circuit. In Zaatar, the verifier must invest in the expensive construction of the commitment and all the PCP queries before he performs the actual verification operations for each instance. This amortized cost grows linearly with the circuit size in both Zaatar and Pinocchio, and it can be prohibitive, especially for large circuits, which are widely used in many practical scenarios. Meanwhile, the costs of proof generation in Zaatar and Pinocchio grow at least linearly with the circuit size. Assuming the circuit size of the computation task is $\mathcal{S}$, then the cost of proof generation in Zaatar is asymptotically $O(\mathcal{S} \cdot log^2(\mathcal{S}))$ and the cost of proof generation in Pinocchio is asymptotically $O(\mathcal{S})$.

From a theoretical perspective, one natural question is whether it is possible to have sub-linear time (in the size of the circuit) amortized cost and cost of proof generation. To the best of our knowledge, this remains an open question. From a practical perspective, the first requirement is to further reduce both amortized cost and cost of proof generation, which act as chief obstacles in verifiable computation.

To tackle these problems, instead of merely focusing on optimizing current verification algorithms regardless of the structure of the computation tasks, like in most recent works, in this paper we take into account the structure of the circuit based on which the computation tasks are verified.

We observe that *repeated structures* play a pivotal role in the arithmetic circuit based on which verification protocol is performed. The compilers of Zaatar and Pinocchio analyze any high-level program piece by piece and generate the corresponding circuit in a straightforward way: for instance, loops are unrolled in a naive way. We notice that almost every computation (e.g. Big Data!) employs loops. Moreover, these computations are the most likely tasks to be outsourced to the cloud server. Repeated structures show up frequently in the circuit generated by Zaatar's and Pinocchio's compilers. Meanwhile, vnTinyRAM universally transforms any C program with fixed number of execution steps into one single arithmetic circuit, which also contains lots of repeated subcircuits such as C_{mem}, C_{exe} and the multiplexers in the Waksman networks [8].

Repeated structures (e.g. looping structures) are not well addressed in the current research on verification protocols. As observed in [26, 29], looping can not be handled concisely. Hence, if we can take advantage of repeated structures in the circuits of these computations and handle the verification better, we could make verifiable computation more efficient.

Since we use terminology of loops intensively in this paper, we explain them here. In our paper, the *loop body* is the piece of code describing the executions inside the loop. One *loop iteration* refers to one execution of the loop body.

In this paper, we address the problems proposed above, argue that verifiable computation can be made cheaper by taking advantage of computations whose circuits contain repeated substructures (e.g. loops), and achieve cheaper verifiable computation through efficient loop-handling. Our contributions are:

- We give a first-step answer to the question of existence of sub-linear amortized cost (in the size of the circuit) in verifiable computation. We show that for circuits that have repeated structure (e.g. loops) we can reduce the amortized cost into the sum of two parts, one of which is verifying one loop iteration (which does not scale with the number of loop repetitions) and the other is linear in the *degree* of the sub-computation (one loop iteration) and the number of executions of the sub-computation. (From the theory of arithmetic circuit complexity, the latter is usually far less than the amortized cost of existing algorithms, which is linear in the *size* of the whole circuit.)
- We also reduce the prover's cost of proof generation from quasilinear in the *size* of the circuit corresponding to the loop body (like in Zaatar) to quasilinear in the *degree* of the circuit corresponding to the loop body.
- We propose Block Programs (BPs), an innovative encoding scheme for circuits with repeated structure, based on which we build our verification design for loops. As a theoretical generalization of QAPs [16], BPs imply a way to verify results computed by a circuit composed of identical substructures, and may also have potential in distributed and/or parallel computing scenarios.
- In terms of round complexity of interaction, our design fills the gap in verifiable computation. More specifically, our design runs only one more round than Zaatar, but much fewer than GKR [17]. Recall that Pinocchio-style systems are non-interactive and Zaatar needs two rounds of interaction. However, IP-base systems (e.g. GKR) require even more rounds.

The rest of this paper is structured as follows. We formally present the problem in Section 2. We start our demonstration with a brief exposition of QAP and Zaatar as the preliminaries in Section 3, since our protocols are related to the works of [24, 23]. In Section 4, we propose our theoretical result, a generalization of QAPs ([16]). Then, in Section 5, we apply our theoretical finding to the loop structures and describe the full solution to verifying the result computed by a loop. In Section 6, we analyze the complexity of our design and compare with existing work. Analysis shows the efficiency of our design. We review the related work in Section 7. Section 8 concludes our findings.

2. PROBLEM STATEMENT

In the context of cloud computing, we propose a computation architecture involving two parties: the client $\mathcal{V}$, who is computationally weak, has computation tasks to be delegated to the cloud; the cloud server $\mathcal{P}$, who is computationally powerful, provides computing services to the client. After receiving the computation task, $\mathcal{P}$ performs the computation and returns the results to $\mathcal{V}$. Later, $\mathcal{V}$ runs the verification protocol with $\mathcal{P}$ to ensure the correctness of the returned result. The computation task is a piece of code written in a high-level programming language. In the verification stage, this piece of code is transformed into an arithmetic circuit form. Existing compilers can turn high-level programs into (non-deterministic) circuits [26, 24, 23]. Since this phase is outside the scope of the current paper, we directly assume the computation task is formalized into an arithmetic circuit in the verification stage. We assume this piece of code is a loop program and in the verification stage, this program is formalized into a *loop circuit* (we will further illustrate loop circuits in Section 5).

3. PRELIMINARIES

3.1 Quadratic Programs

Recently Gennaro, Gentry, Parno and Raykova introduced a new characterization of the NP complexity class – the *Quadratic Span Programs (QSPs)* (and *Quadratic Arithmetic Programs (QAPs)*) [16, 23]. They showed that NP can be defined as the set of languages with proofs that can be efficiently verified by QSPs (or QAPs). Similarly to PCPs – another characterization of NP, which has already been widely used to obtain verifiable computation schemes – QSPs/QAPs are considered to be well-suited for verifiable computation and zero-knowledge schemes. One limitation of QSPs is that they inherently compute boolean circuits. But since arithmetic circuits are more natural and efficient in real-world computation tasks, we focus on QAPs, the counterpart of QSPs dealing with arithmetic circuit evaluation.

DEFINITION 1. (Quadratic Arithmetic Programs [16]) *A QAP Q over field $\mathbb{F}$ contains 3 sets of $W'+1$ polynomials: $\{A_w(t)\}$, $\{B_w(t)\}$, $\{C_w(t)\}$, for $w \in \{0, 1, \cdots, W'\}$, and a target polynomial $D(t)$. For function $\Psi : \mathbb{F}^N \mapsto \mathbb{F}^{N'}$, we say Q computes Ψ if the following holds: $(z_1, \cdots, z_{N+N'}) \in \mathbb{F}^{N+N'}$ is a valid assignment of Ψ's inputs and outputs, iff there exist coefficients $z_{N+N'+1}, \cdots, z_{W'}$ such that $D(t)$ divides $P(t)$, where $P(t) = \left(\sum_{w=1}^{W'} z_w \cdot A_w(t) + A_0(t)\right) \cdot \left(\sum_{w=1}^{W'} z_w \cdot B_w(t) + B_0(t)\right) - \left(\sum_{w=1}^{W'} z_w \cdot C_w(t) + C_0(t)\right)$. Namely, there exists a polynomial $H(t)$ such that $D(t) \cdot H(t) = P(t)$.*

Given an arithmetic circuit computing function Ψ, its corresponding QAP can be constructed by polynomial interpolation. Consider the set of circuit wires corresponding to the inputs and outputs of the circuit, and also the outputs of all multiplication gates. Each one of these wires is assigned three interpolation polynomials in Lagrange form, encoding whether the wire is a left input, right input, or output of each multiplication gate [16, 23]. The resulting set of polynomials is a complete description of the original circuit.

3.2 A Recent Efficient Argument System: Zaatar

The very recent work of [9] observes that QAPs can also be viewed as linear PCPs. By re-designing the PCP query generation and replacing the quadratic consistency checks and circuit correctness checks with the divisibility check of a QAP, Setty et al. successfully fit QAPs into the framework of Ginger [26]. The result is the novel protocol *Zaatar* [24], which significantly reduces the prover's workload. The key observation of Zaatar is that the evaluation of the polynomial $P(t)$ at the point $t = \tau$ can be simply written as: $P(\tau) = (\langle Z, q\rangle + A_0(\tau)) \cdot (\langle Z, q'\rangle + B_0(\tau)) - (\langle Z, q''\rangle + C_0(\tau))$, where $Z = (z_1, z_2, \cdots, z_{W'})$, $q = (A_1(\tau), A_2(\tau), \cdots, A_{W'}(\tau))$, $q' = (B_1(\tau), B_2(\tau), \cdots, B_{W'}(\tau))$, and $q'' = (C_1(\tau), \cdots, C_{W'}(\tau))$. Thus, $P(\tau)$ can be evaluated through three standard PCP queries to the dot product oracle $\pi_Z(\cdot) = \langle Z, \cdot\rangle$. If we represent the polynomials $H(t)$ explicitly: $H(t) = h_{|C_Z|} t^{|C_Z|} + \cdots + h_1 t + h_0$ (where C_Z is the set of constraints in Zaatar), similar observations on $H(\tau)$ can be made: $H(\tau) = \langle K_H, q_H\rangle$ where $K_H = (h_0, h_1, \cdots, h_{|C_Z|})$ and $q_H = (1, \tau, \tau^2, \cdots, \tau^{|C_Z|})$. Thus, $H(\tau)$ can also be evaluated through one PCP query to the oracle $\pi_H(\cdot) = \langle K_H, \cdot\rangle$. If Z consists of the input X with width $|X| = N$, output Y with width $|Y| = N'$ and intermediate results R with $|R| = W' - (N + N')$, then in order to guarantee that Y is the correct output when the input is X, the verifier needs to compute a part of $\langle Z, q\rangle$, and also a part of $\langle Z, q'\rangle$ and $\langle Z, q''\rangle$, by himself. Consequently, $\mathcal{V}$ only queries the linear function oracle $\pi_R(\cdot) = \langle R, \cdot\rangle$, instead of $\pi_Z(\cdot)$. Zaatar inherits the single-commit-multi-decommit protocol from Ginger [26].

4. OUR THEORETICAL RESULTS: BLOCK PROGRAMS (BPS)

Just as QSPs are a natural extension of span programs (SPs) [20], our new form of arithmetization which we call Block Programs (BPs), is a natural extension of Quadratic Arithmetic Programs (QAPs). We focus on a kind of general circuits, which may be an arithmetic circuit or a boolean circuit, that is composed of *identical* units. This elementary unit, which we call *block*, can be a simple NAND gate. But it is more common to be a more complex *sub-circuit*. This kind of sub-circuit can be multiple-input-multiple-output. The sub-circuits can be viewed as pseudo-gates, a generalized form of gates. Consider a scenario where the whole circuit is composed of this kind of sub-circuits just like in Figure 1, where all blocks are identical. We define BPs as follows.

DEFINITION 2. (Block Programs)(BPs, Generalization of Quadratic Arithmetic Programs (QAPs) [16])
We assume that a circuit computing a function $\Psi : \mathbb{F}^N \mapsto \mathbb{F}^{N'}$ is composed of identical substructures, all of which compute the same function: $\psi : \mathbb{F}^V \mapsto \mathbb{F}^M$. ($\psi$ implies M func-

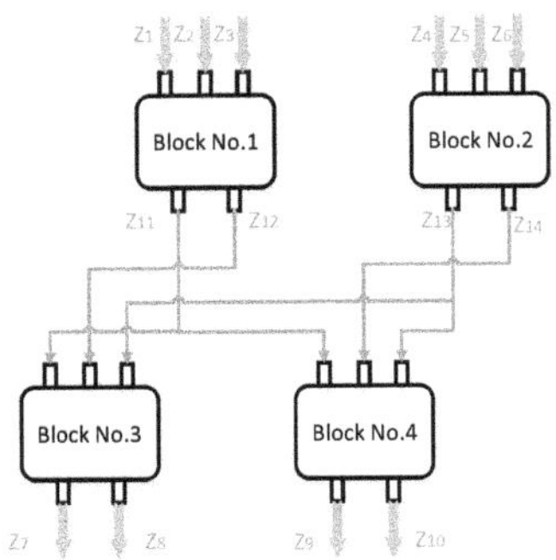

Figure 1: Computing through Blocks

	Meaning	Range
v	Index of Input of a Block	$1, \cdots, V$
j	Index of Output of a Block	$1, \cdots, M$
k	Index of Blocks	$1, \cdots, K$
w	Index of wires in the circuit	$1, \cdots, W$
w_1	w is represented as (w_1, w_2)	$1, \cdots, M+Q$
w_2	w is represented as (w_1, w_2)	$1, \cdots, K$
N	the number of inputs of the circuit	
N'	the number of outputs of the circuit	
i	Index of Direct Input of a Block	$1, \cdots, M$
u	Index of Extra Input of a Block	$1, \cdots, Q$

Figure 2: Notations

tions $\psi_j : \mathbb{F}^V \mapsto \mathbb{F}$ where $j = 1, 2, \cdots, M$. Each of these M functions is associated to one of the outputs of ψ.)

A BP $\mathcal{Q}$ over field $\mathbb{F}$ contains V sets of W polynomials: $\{A_{1w}(t)\}$, $\{A_{2w}(t)\}$, $\cdots$, $\{A_{Vw}(t)\}$, and M sets of W polynomials : $\{B_{1w}(t)\}$, $\{B_{2w}(t)\}$, $\cdots$, $\{B_{Mw}(t)\}$, for $w \in \{1, \cdots, W\}$, and a target polynomial $D(t)$. We say $\mathcal{Q}$ computes Ψ using block ψ if the following holds:

$(z_1, z_2, \cdots, z_{N+N'}) \in \mathbb{F}^{N+N'}$ is a valid assignment of Ψ's inputs and outputs, if and only if there exist coefficients $z_{N+N'+1}, \cdots, z_W$ such that $D(t)$ divides $P_j(t)$, $(j = 1, \cdots, M)$, where $P_j(t) =$

$$\psi_j\left(\sum_{w=1}^{W} z_w \cdot A_{1w}(t), \cdots, \sum_{w=1}^{W} z_w \cdot A_{Vw}(t)\right) - [\sum_{w=1}^{W} z_w \cdot B_{jw}(t)]. \tag{4.1}$$

In other words, for each j, there exists a polynomial $H_j(t)$ such that $D(t) \cdot H_j(t) = P_j(t)$, where $j = 1, 2, \cdots, M$.

After we define Block Programs, two natural questions are: (1) do Block Programs exist? (2) if yes, how to construct Block Programs? Here, we will show the existence of Block Programs by constructing corresponding BPs by polynomial interpolation. In particular, given a circuit that computes Ψ and is composed of identical blocks denoted by $\psi : \mathbb{F}^V \mapsto \mathbb{F}^M$ as above, we firstly construct a group of interpolation polynomials in Lagrange form. Then, we prove that the constructed polynomials form the BP that computes Ψ.

Suppose the circuit is composed of K blocks. We pick an arbitrary value σ_k for each block. When we pick these K values from $\mathbb{F}$, we make sure all these values are different from each other. We define the target polynomial as follows: $D(t) = \prod_{k=1}^{K}(t - \sigma_k)$. Now we consider the set of all the inputs of the circuit, and all the outputs of each block. Firstly, we label each input of the whole circuit and each output from a block with an index w, where $w \in \{1, 2, \cdots, W\}$ and W is the total number of all *wires*, namely, all the inputs of the whole circuit and all the outputs of each block. We can easily deduce that $W = N + K \cdot M$. (Recall that N is the number of inputs to the whole circuit, K is the number of blocks, and M is the number of outputs from a block) Then the values of each input of the whole circuit and each output from a block can be denoted by z_w. Secondly, we assign $V + M$ interpolation polynomials in Lagrange form to each wire, indicating whether the corresponding value z_w is the v-th input, or the j-th output of each block, where $v = 1, 2, \cdots, V$ and $j = 1, 2, \cdots, M$. These polynomials indeed determine how these blocks are interconnected. Thus, the resulting set of polynomials is a complete description of the original circuit. Specifically, we let the polynomials $\{A_{vw}(t)\}$ (for $w = 1, 2, \cdots, W$) encode the v-th input into each block, where $v = 1, 2, \cdots, V$ and let $\{B_{jw}(t)\}$ (for $w = 1, 2, \cdots, W$) encode the j-th output from each block, where $j = 1, 2, \cdots, M$. In particular, we let

$$A_{vw}(\sigma_k) = \begin{cases} 1 & \text{if } z_w \text{ is the } v\text{-th input to the } k\text{-th block;} \\ 0 & \text{otherwise.} \end{cases} \tag{4.2}$$

$$B_{jw}(\sigma_k) = \begin{cases} 1 & \text{if } z_w \text{ is the } j\text{-th output from the } k\text{-th block;} \\ 0 & \text{otherwise.} \end{cases} \tag{4.3}$$

Based on the evaluations at the K values $\sigma_1, \cdots, \sigma_K$, it is straightforward to construct $\{A_{vw}(t)\}$ and $\{B_{jw}(t)\}$, for $w = 1, \cdots, W$, $v = 1, \cdots, V$, and $j = 1, \cdots, M$ using interpolation polynomials in Lagrange form. Let $\mathcal{K}$ be the set of indices: $\mathcal{K} = \{1, 2, \cdots, K\}$. Then, $A_{vw}(t) = \sum_{k \in \mathcal{K}} A_{vw}(\sigma_k) \cdot \frac{\prod_{k^* \in \mathcal{K}, k^* \neq k}(t - \sigma_{k^*})}{\prod_{k^* \in \mathcal{K}, k^* \neq k}(\sigma_k - \sigma_{k^*})}$, and $B_{jw}(t) = \sum_{k \in \mathcal{K}} B_{jw}(\sigma_k) \cdot \frac{\prod_{k^* \in \mathcal{K}, k^* \neq k}(t - \sigma_{k^*})}{\prod_{k^* \in \mathcal{K}, k^* \neq k}(\sigma_k - \sigma_{k^*})}$.

We can show that $\{A_{vw}(t)\}$ and $\{B_{jw}(t)\}$, which we have constructed using interpolation polynomials in Lagrange form, constitute a BP that computes Ψ, where $w = 1, 2, \cdots, W$, $v = 1, 2, \cdots, V$, and $j = 1, 2, \cdots, M$.

THEOREM 1. *For a circuit which computes a function $\Psi : \mathbb{F}^N \mapsto \mathbb{F}^{N'}$, if the circuit is composed of identical blocks denoted by $\psi : \mathbb{F}^V \mapsto \mathbb{F}^M$, then $\{A_{vw}(t)\}$ and $\{B_{jw}(t)\}$ constructed above constitute a BP that compute Ψ, where $w = 1, 2, \cdots, W$, $v = 1, 2, \cdots, V$, and $j = 1, 2, \cdots, M$.*

PROOF. The rough idea of the proof is as follows. If we evaluate $\{A_{vw}(t)\}$ and $\{B_{jw}(t)\}$ in σ_k, for $w = 1, 2, \cdots, W$, $v = 1, 2, \cdots, V$, and $j = 1, 2, \cdots, M$, which we have constructed, we can observe that this makes the equation (4.1) become:

$$\begin{aligned} P_j(\sigma_k) =& \psi_j(\text{the kth block's inputs}) - \\ & (\text{the kth block's output}). \end{aligned} \tag{4.4}$$

This means that if the output is correct, then $P_j(\sigma_k) = 0$. Namely, σ_k is a root of $P_j(t)$, which in turn means that $(t - \sigma_k)$ divides $P_j(t)$. If all blocks are computed correctly, this results in $D(t)$ dividing $P_j(t)$. □

5. OUR SCHEME: INTERACTIVE VERIFICATION FOR LOOPS

In this section, we use the previously described Block Programs to develop the full solution to the verification of a "loop" computation. Since the theoretical results in Section 4 apply to all general circuits that have repeated substructures, which are not limited to those circuits that a piece of "loop" code is mapped to, we are not directly ready for designing the verification protocol for a "loop" computation. Thus, in Section 5.1, we further refine the theoretical results we have developed in Section 4, to loop-specific results which are more appropriate for the blocks to which a piece of "loop" code is mapped. Then, in Section 5.2, we demonstrate our verification protocol for "loop" computations using Block Programs.

5.1 Theoretical Results for Loop Circuits

As stated in Section 2, the computation task is a piece of "loop" code written in a high-level programming language. In the verification stage, this piece of code is transformed into an arithmetic circuit form using existing compilers such as [26, 24, 23]. This arithmetic circuit, to which we map a piece of code describing a loop, is called as a *loop circuit.*

It is straightforward to abstract the structure of this circuit as follows. As shown in Figure 3, a loop circuit is a series of identical blocks, the output of each of which serves as the input for the next. Each block, which is an arithmetic circuit or boolean circuit, is actually one loop iteration of the original "loop" code. Meanwhile, since each loop iteration may have extra inputs from the outside of the whole piece of code, (e.g. in the big data processing scenarios) each block may have corresponding extra inputs from the outside of the circuit. The block is demonstrated in Figure 4, where $\mathtt{EX}_1^{(2)}, \mathtt{EX}_2^{(2)}, \cdots, \mathtt{EX}_Q^{(2)}$ are the extra inputs.

In Section 4, we show that for a circuit that has repeated substructures there exists a BP that computes that circuit. We have introduced the theoretical results that show how to construct the corresponding BP, and how to determine whether a given (inputs, outputs) tuple is valid for that circuit using BPs. Since a loop circuit has repeated substructures, we can easily apply our previous results to loops.

Now, we consider a loop circuit as shown in Figure 3. The circuit's functionality is to compute a function $\Psi : \mathbb{F}^{M+K\cdot Q} \mapsto \mathbb{F}^M$. The circuit is composed of identical blocks as shown in Figure 4, denoted by $\psi : \mathbb{F}^{M+Q} \mapsto \mathbb{F}^M$. The block ψ can also be formulated as M functions: $\psi_j : \mathbb{F}^{M+Q} \mapsto \mathbb{F}$, for $j = 1, 2, \cdots, M$. By Theorem 1, we can construct a BP $\mathcal{Q}$ that computes Ψ, where $\mathcal{Q}$ consists of a target polynomial $D(t)$, $M+Q$ sets of $K\cdot(M+Q)+M$ polynomials (See Figure 2 for notations): $\{A_{1,w}(t)\}$, $\{A_{2,w}(t)\}$, $\cdots$, $\{A_{M,w}(t)\}$, and M sets of $K\cdot(M+Q)+M$ polynomials: $\{B_{1,w}(t)\}$, $\{B_{2,w}(t)\}$, $\cdots$, $\{B_{M,w}(t)\}$, where w is the index which represents the labels of wires and $K\cdot(M+Q)+M$ is the number of the wires.

Since a "loop" circuit has a regular structure, we label the wires with a pair of indices and get explicit expressions of the corresponding Block Programs. Then we can simplify these Block Programs into succinct expressions denoted by $A_k(t), k = 1, 2, \cdots K$. Namely, we let w be (w_1, w_2) and denote each wire by $\mathtt{Z}_{w_1,w_2}$ as shown in Figure 3. Correspondingly, each polynomial in $\mathcal{Q}$ is denoted by $\{A_{v,(w_1,w_2)}(t)\}$ or $\{B_{j,(w_1,w_2)}(t)\}$ where $v, w_1 \in \{1, 2, \cdots, M, M+1, \cdots, M+Q\}$, $j \in \{1, 2, \cdots, M\}$, and $w_2 \in \{1, 2, \cdots, K+1\}$. The explicit expressions of $\mathcal{Q}$ are as follows: Let $\mathcal{K}$ be the set of indices, $\mathcal{K} = \{1, 2, \cdots, K\}$. If $\sigma_1, \sigma_2, \cdots, \sigma_K$ are distinct values, each of which is picked from $\mathbb{F}$, then,

$A_{v,(w_1,w_2)}(t) = \sum_{k\in\mathcal{K}} A_{v,(w_1,w_2)}(\sigma_k) \cdot \frac{\prod_{k^*\in\mathcal{K},k^*\neq k}(t-\sigma_{k^*})}{\prod_{k^*\in\mathcal{K},k^*\neq k}(\sigma_k-\sigma_{k^*})}$, and

$B_{j,(w_1,w_2)}(t) = \sum_{k\in\mathcal{K}} B_{j,(w_1,w_2)}(\sigma_k) \cdot \frac{\prod_{k^*\in\mathcal{K},k^*\neq k}(t-\sigma_{k^*})}{\prod_{k^*\in\mathcal{K},k^*\neq k}(\sigma_k-\sigma_{k^*})}$, where

$A_{v,(w_1,w_2)}(\sigma_k)$ and $B_{j,(w_1,w_2)}(\sigma_k)$ are determined by the interconnection of the blocks in the circuit: $A_{v,(w_1,w_2)}(\sigma_k)$ is 1 if $\mathtt{Z}_{w_1,w_2}$ is the v-th input of the k-th block and 0 otherwise; $B_{j,(w_1,w_2)}(\sigma_k)$ is 1 if $\mathtt{Z}_{w_1,w_2}$ is the j-th output from the k-th block and 0 otherwise. From the circuit's structure, we can simplify the above as follows: $A_{v,(w_1,w_2)}(\sigma_k)$ is 1 if $w_1 = v, w_2 = k$ and 0 otherwise; $B_{j,(w_1,w_2)}(\sigma_k)$ is 1 if $w_1 = j, w_2 = k+1$ and 0 otherwise.

Thus, $A_{v,(w_1,w_2)}(t) = \begin{cases} \frac{\prod_{k\in\mathcal{K},k\neq w_2}(t-\sigma_k)}{\prod_{k\in\mathcal{K},k\neq w_2}(\sigma_{w_2}-\sigma_k)} & \text{if } {w_1=v,\text{and} \atop 1\leq w_2\leq K,} \\ 0 \text{ otherwise.} \end{cases}$

$B_{j,(w_1,w_2)}(t) = \begin{cases} \frac{\prod_{k\in\mathcal{K},k\neq w_2-1}(t-\sigma_k)}{\prod_{k\in\mathcal{K},k\neq w_2-1}(\sigma_{(w_2-1)}-\sigma_k)} & \text{if } {w_1=j,\text{ and} \atop 2\leq w_2\leq K+1,} \\ 0 \text{ otherwise} \end{cases}$. If

we define $A_k(t) = \frac{\prod_{k'\in\mathcal{K},k'\neq k}(t-\sigma_{k'})}{\prod_{k'\in\mathcal{K},k'\neq k}(\sigma_k-\sigma_{k'})}$, then, the block program can be expressed by $A_k(t)$ where $k = 1, 2, \cdots, K$:

$$A_{v,(w_1,w_2)}(t) = \begin{cases} A_{w_2}(t) & \text{if } w_1 = v, 1 \leq w_2 \leq K \\ 0 & \text{otherwise.} \end{cases} \tag{5.1}$$

$$B_{j,(w_1,w_2)}(t) = \begin{cases} A_{w_2-1}(t) & \text{if } w_1 = j, 2 \leq w_2 \leq K+1 \\ 0 & \text{otherwise.} \end{cases} \tag{5.2}$$

If we express the corresponding Block Programs by these $A_k(t)$, instantiate the wire values, and plug them into Definition 2, we directly have the following result for loop circuits.

COROLLARY 2. *We consider a loop circuit which computes a function $\Psi : \mathbb{F}^{M+K\cdot Q} \mapsto \mathbb{F}^M$. As in Figure 3, this loop circuit is composed of successive blocks which are identical and denoted by $\psi : \mathbb{F}^{M+Q} \mapsto \mathbb{F}^M$. Naturally, the block can be formulated as M functions: $\psi_j : \mathbb{F}^{M+Q} \mapsto \mathbb{F}$, $j = 1, 2, \cdots, M$. Let $\mathcal{Q}$ be the block program that computes Ψ using block ψ. Then, for inputs $(\mathtt{Z}_{1,1}, \mathtt{Z}_{2,1}, \cdots, \mathtt{Z}_{M,1}) \in \mathbb{F}^M$ and the extra inputs $\mathtt{Z}_{M+1,1}$, $\mathtt{Z}_{M+2,1}$, $\cdots$, $\mathtt{Z}_{M+Q,1}$, $\cdots$, $\mathtt{Z}_{M+1,K}$, $\mathtt{Z}_{M+2,K}$, $\cdots$, $\mathtt{Z}_{M+Q,K}$, all of which are in $\mathbb{F}$, the corresponding outputs of the circuit are $(\mathtt{Z}_{1,K+1}, \mathtt{Z}_{2,K+1}, \cdots, \mathtt{Z}_{M,K+1}) \in \mathbb{F}^M$, iff there exist coefficients (they are actually the inner wire values) $(\mathtt{Z}_{1,2}, \cdots, \mathtt{Z}_{M,2}) \in \mathbb{F}^M$, $(\mathtt{Z}_{1,3}, \cdots, \mathtt{Z}_{M,3}) \in \mathbb{F}^M$, $\cdots$, $(\mathtt{Z}_{1,K}, \cdots, \mathtt{Z}_{M,K}) \in \mathbb{F}^M$ such that $D(t)$ divides $P_j(t)$ $(j = 1, 2, \cdots, M)$ where $P_j(t) =$*

$$\psi_j\left(\sum_{k=1}^{K} \mathtt{Z}_{1,k}\cdot A_k(t), \cdots, \sum_{k=1}^{K} \mathtt{Z}_{M,k}\cdot A_k(t), \sum_{k=1}^{K} \mathtt{Z}_{M+1,k}\cdot A_k(t), \cdots, \sum_{k=1}^{K} \mathtt{Z}_{M+Q,k}\cdot A_k(t)\right) - \left(\sum_{k=1}^{K} \mathtt{Z}_{j,k+1}\cdot A_k(t)\right). \tag{5.3}$$

In other words, there exists a polynomial $H_j(t)$ for each $P_j(t)$ $(j = 1, 2, \cdots, M)$, such that $D(t)\cdot H_j(t) = P_j(t)$.

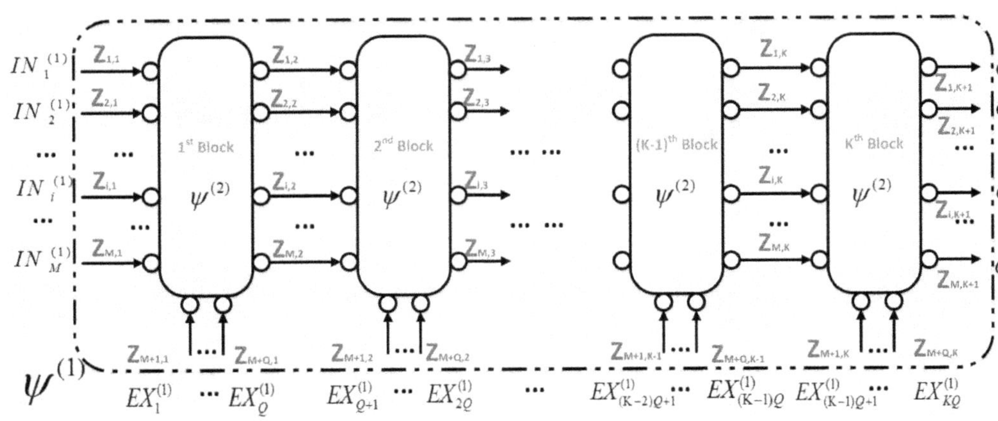

Figure 3: A Loop Circuit

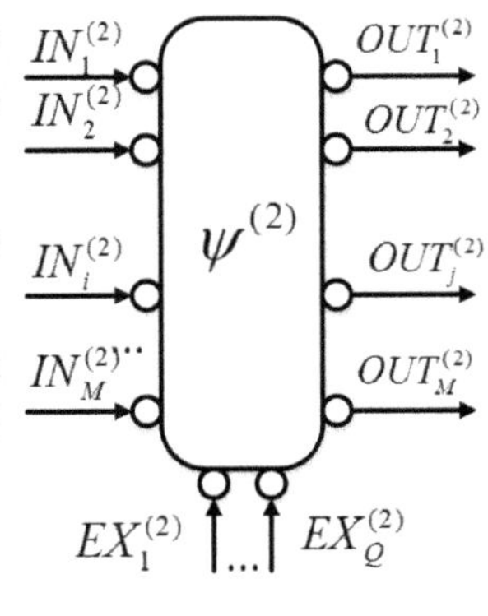

Figure 4: One Single Block

PROOF. Since the loop circuit is a circuit which is composed of identical blocks, by Definition 2, for the purported intermediate wire values $(\mathrm{z}_{1,2},\cdots,\mathrm{z}_{M,2})$, $(\mathrm{z}_{1,3},\cdots,\mathrm{z}_{M,3})$, $\cdots$, $(\mathrm{z}_{1,K},\cdots,\mathrm{z}_{M,K})$, it suffices to prove (5.3) is equivalent to (4.1) in the context of loop circuits. In the context of loop circuits, (4.1) is:

$$P_j(t) = \psi_j\Big(\sum_{w_1=1}^{M+Q}\sum_{w_2=1}^{K+1} \mathrm{z}_{w_1,w_2}\cdot A_{1,(w_1,w_2)}(t), \cdots, \sum_{w_1=1}^{M+Q}\sum_{w_2=1}^{K+1} \mathrm{z}_{w_1,w_2}\cdot A_{M+Q,(w_1,w_2)}(t)\Big) - \Big(\sum_{w_1=1}^{M+Q}\sum_{w_2=1}^{K+1} \mathrm{z}_{w_1,w_2}\cdot B_{j,(w_1,w_2)}(t)\Big). \quad (5.4)$$

If we instantiate $A_{v,(w_1,w_2)}(t)$, $B_{j,(w_1,w_2)}(t)$ using (5.1) and (5.2), we immediately get (5.3). The conclusion follows. □

5.2 Our Interactive Verification for Loops

Corollary 2 implies a way to verify a result computed by a "loop" circuit using BPs. To convince $\mathcal{V}$ that the result is correct, by the Corollary 2, it suffices to show the existence of those intermediate results and the polynomial $H_j(t)$ which satisfy the divisibility $D(t)\cdot H_j(t) = P_j(t)$.

The divisibility itself can be checked probabilistically: for polynomials $P_j(t)$, $H_j(t)$ and $D(t)$, $\mathcal{V}$ randomly picks $\tau \in \mathbb{F}$ and checks whether $D(\tau)\cdot H_j(\tau) = P_j(\tau)$. (We will show how to evaluate $D(\tau)$, $H_j(\tau)$ and $P_j(\tau)$ later.) If the result is correct, $\mathcal{P}$ must be able to find $H_j(t)$ such that $P_j(t) = H_j(t)\cdot D(t)$, then for any $\tau\in\mathbb{F}$, $D(\tau)\cdot H_j(\tau) = P_j(\tau)$. If the result is not correct, then for any $H_j(t)$, $D(\tau)\cdot H_j(\tau) \neq P_j(\tau)$ except with a small probability.

To check the existence of the intermediate results and the polynomial $H_j(t)$, one naive idea is to let $\mathcal{P}$ output the intermediate results and $H_j(t)$, and let $\mathcal{V}$ evaluate $H_j(\tau)$ and use the intermediate results to check the divisibility. Instead of this expensive approach, we use a "commit and query" method. Roughly speaking, we have $\mathcal{P}$ commit to the intermediate results and $H_j(t)$ first. Then, when $\mathcal{V}$ needs to use the intermediate results and $H_j(\tau)$, he will query $\mathcal{P}$ to get purported values and finally check the divisibility. (We will show the "commit and query" method in details later.)

Now we show how we evaluate $D(\tau)$, $H_j(\tau)$ and $P_j(\tau)$. For $D(\tau)$, $\mathcal{V}$ can construct $D(t)$ himself and evaluate $D(\tau)$ himself. In our protocol, neither $\mathcal{V}$ nor $\mathcal{P}$ will materialize $P_j(\tau)$. $P_j(t)$ involves three sets of polynomials: the polynomials that abstract the outputs of the blocks: $G_j(t) = \sum_{k=1}^{K}\mathrm{z}_{j,k+1}\cdot A_k(t), j = 1,2\cdots M$; the polynomials that abstract the inputs of the blocks: $f_{\mathrm{IN}_i}(t) = \sum_{k=1}^{K}\mathrm{z}_{i,k}\cdot A_k(t), i = 1,2\cdots M$; and the polynomials that abstract the extra inputs of the blocks: $f_{\mathrm{EX}_u}(t) = \sum_{k=1}^{K}\mathrm{EX}^{(1)}_{[(k-1)\cdot Q]+u}\cdot A_k(t), u = 1,2,\cdots,Q$, where $\mathrm{EX}^{(1)}_{(k-1)\cdot Q+u} = \mathrm{z}_{u+M,k}$. $\mathcal{V}$ can construct $f_{\mathrm{EX}_u}(t)$ and evaluate $f_{\mathrm{EX}_u}(\tau)$ himself. We observe that $G_j(t)$ and $f_{\mathrm{IN}_i}(t)$ are the only parts in the divisibility equation (5.3) that involve the intermediate results. When evaluating them, neither $\mathcal{V}$ nor $\mathcal{P}$ genuinely materializes the polynomial. We view $G_j(t)$, $f_{\mathrm{IN}_i}(t)$ and $H_j(t)$ to be linear functions, denoted by π_{G_j} $(j = 1,\cdots,M)$, π_{IN_i} $(i = 1,\cdots,M)$, π_{H_j} $(j = 1,\cdots,M)$, respectively. We have $\mathcal{P}$ commit to them first[1], then have $\mathcal{V}$ evaluate these polynomials through querying $\mathcal{P}$ on these committed functions, as in [25, 26, 24]. More specifically, as a PCP style protocol, in our protocol, $\mathcal{P}$ holds a proof l and $\mathcal{V}$ holds a query q. When queried with q, $\mathcal{P}$ responds with the evaluation of the linear function $\pi(q) = \langle l, q\rangle$ (where $\langle\cdot,\cdot\rangle$ is the inner product of two vectors), which should be the evaluation of $l(t)$ at the point $t=\tau$. For example, if l represents the coefficient vector of the polynomial $l(t)$ and $q = (1,\tau,\tau^2,\cdots,)$, then $\pi(q)$ is $l(\tau)$. To evaluate $G_j(\tau)$, $\mathcal{V}$ queries $\mathcal{P}$ with: $q_G = (A_1(\tau), A_2(\tau)\cdots, A_{K-1}(\tau))$. To evaluate $f_{\mathrm{IN}_i}(\tau)$, $\mathcal{V}$ queries $\mathcal{P}$ with: $q_{IN} = (A_2(\tau), A_3(\tau)\cdots, A_K(\tau))$. To evaluate $H_j(\tau)$, $\mathcal{V}$ queries $\mathcal{P}$ with: $q_H = (1,\tau,\tau^2,\cdots)$. The length of q_H is equal to the highest degree of all $H_j(t)$ $(j = 1,\cdots M)$.

So far we have demonstrated all the techniques we will use. Now we show our interactive verification protocol as in Figure 5. Note that before verification, $\mathcal{V}$ sends the loop program and $(\mathrm{z}_{1,1},\mathrm{z}_{2,1},\cdots,\mathrm{z}_{M,1})$ $(\mathrm{z}_{M+1,1},\mathrm{z}_{M+2,1},\cdots,\mathrm{z}_{M+Q,1})$ $\cdots$ $(\mathrm{z}_{M+1,K},\mathrm{z}_{M+2,K},\cdots,\mathrm{z}_{M+Q,K})$ to $\mathcal{P}$; on these inputs $\mathcal{P}$ computes and returns the results: $(\mathrm{z}_{1,K+1},\cdots,\mathrm{z}_{M,K+1})$. Our idea is to prove that the wire values between repeated substructures are calculated correctly, and then prove that the blocks themselves are computed correctly, rather than trying to verify the entire circuit in one round. The ad-

[1]Since the commit/decommit and corresponding linearity tests are mature techniques as in [25, 26, 24], we omit the details here

vantage of this approach is that, since all blocks have identical structure, the verification of all blocks can be done together as though all blocks are collapsed into a single block. Let the loop circuit contain K loop iterations. We view the whole circuit from a two-layer perspective. In the first layer's perspective, the circuit consists of one big block, which we call the first layer block and denote by a function $\psi^{(1)} : \mathbb{F}^{M+K\cdot Q} \mapsto \mathbb{F}^M$. In the second layer's perspective, the circuit consists of K smaller blocks, which we call the second layer block and denote by a function $\psi^{(2)} : \mathbb{F}^{M+K\cdot Q/K} \mapsto \mathbb{F}^M$. Each of the second layer blocks is one loop iteration. We reduce the task of verifying (for $j = 1, 2, \cdots, M$)

$$\mathtt{OUT}_j^{(1)} = \psi_j^{(1)}(\mathtt{IN}_1^{(1)}, \cdots, \mathtt{IN}_M^{(1)}, \mathtt{EX}_1^{(1)}, \cdots, \mathtt{EX}_{Q\cdot K}^{(1)}), \quad (5.5)$$

to the task of verifying (for $j = 1, 2, \cdots, M$)

$$\mathtt{OUT}_j^{(2)} = \psi_j^{(2)}(\mathtt{IN}_1^{(2)}, \cdots, \mathtt{IN}_M^{(2)}, \mathtt{EX}_1^{(2)}, \cdots, \mathtt{EX}_Q^{(2)}), \quad (5.6)$$

(Here we want to abstract each layer to a block. We denote inputs (directly from the previous iteration) to this block by IN, extra inputs (from the outside of the iterations) by EX, and outputs from the block by OUT. Because we have multiple layers, we identify inputs/outputs/extra inputs to each layer by an upper index. Therefore, in our special case layer 1 (the whole circuit) has inputs $\mathtt{IN}_1^{(1)}, \cdots, \mathtt{IN}_M^{(1)}$, outputs $\mathtt{OUT}_1^{(1)}, \cdots, \mathtt{OUT}_M^{(1)}$, and extra inputs $\mathtt{EX}_1^{(1)}, \cdots, \mathtt{EX}_{Q\cdot K}^{(1)}$, as in Figure 3, where the second layer (one loop iteration) has inputs $\mathtt{IN}_1^{(2)}, \cdots, \mathtt{IN}_M^{(2)}$, extra inputs $\mathtt{EX}_1^{(2)}, \cdots, \mathtt{EX}_Q^{(2)}$, and output $\mathtt{OUT}_1^{(2)}, \cdots, \mathtt{OUT}_M^{(2)}$, as in Figure 4. It is advantageous to use this notation because when verifying the iterations, we collapse all of them into a single iteration, such that $\mathtt{IN}_1^{(2)}, \cdots$, $\mathtt{OUT}_1^{(2)}, \cdots$, and $\mathtt{EX}_1^{(2)}, \cdots$ are aggregates of the individual iterations' inputs, outputs and extra inputs.)

To verify (5.6), $\mathcal{V}$ can compute itself, or let $\mathcal{P}$ perform some other verification protocols like Pinocchio [23], Zaatar [24], etc. We omit the details here.

5.3 Security Analysis

Now, we provide the completeness and soundness of our design.

THEOREM 3. *(Completeness) As in Figure 3, the inputs are* $(\mathtt{z}_{1,1}, \mathtt{z}_{2,1}, \cdots, \mathtt{z}_{M,1})$, $(\mathtt{z}_{M+1,1}, \mathtt{z}_{M+2,1}, \cdots, \mathtt{z}_{M+Q,1})$, $\cdots$, $(\mathtt{z}_{M+1,K}, \mathtt{z}_{M+2,K}, \cdots, \mathtt{z}_{M+Q,K})$, *and* $(\mathcal{P}, \mathcal{V})$ *run the protocol in Figure 5. If the results* $(\mathtt{z}_{1,K+1}, \mathtt{z}_{2,K+1}, \cdots, \mathtt{z}_{M,K+1})$ *are correct, then* $Pr\{\mathcal{V} \text{ accepts}\} = 1$.

To prove the completeness(Theorem 3), the idea is to show that an honest prover is able to provide the correct proof associated with the correct results. This correct proof will pass all the checks with probability 1. This is straightforward and we omit the details here.

THEOREM 4. *(Soundness) As in Figure 3, assume the inputs are* $(\mathtt{z}_{1,1}, \mathtt{z}_{2,1}, \cdots, \mathtt{z}_{M,1})$, $(\mathtt{z}_{M+1,1}, \mathtt{z}_{M+2,1}, \cdots, \mathtt{z}_{M+Q,1})$, $\cdots$, $(\mathtt{z}_{M+1,K}, \mathtt{z}_{M+2,K}, \cdots, \mathtt{z}_{M+Q,K})$, *and* $\mathcal{P}$ *and* $\mathcal{V}$ *proceed according to Figure 5. There exists a constant* $\kappa < 1$ *such that if results* $(\mathtt{z}_{1,K+1}, \mathtt{z}_{2,K+1}, \cdots, \mathtt{z}_{M,K+1})$ *are not correct, then* $Pr\{\mathcal{V} \text{ accepts}\} < \kappa$ *holds for any purported proofs. The probability is over the randomness of both* $\mathcal{V}$ *and* $\mathcal{P}$ *in both phases in our protocol. This is equivalent to: if* $Pr\{\mathcal{V} \text{ accepts}\} > \kappa$*, the purported results are correct.*

The proof of the soundness is in Appendix A.

5.4 Improving the Performance through Batching

One question left over is whether, if $\mathcal{V}$ queries different linear proofs, he should re-generate the queries for each proof. If so, the cost of issuing queries will be prohibitive. Our idea is to reuse τ and corresponding divisibility query for all linear proofs. We achieve this by making our protocol work in a batching style, which implies two levels: (1) same queries work over many computation instances, namely $\mathcal{V}$ verifies computation in batches; (2) for one computation instance, $\mathcal{V}$ uses the same τ and corresponding queries for all proofs in the same layer.

This batching technique was firstly proposed in [25], where $\mathcal{V}$ generates one single commitment query $\mathtt{Enc}(r)$(the query to get the commitment information) and one single set of PCP queries for β proofs. In the commitment phase, $\mathcal{P}$ replies to $\mathcal{V}$ with β pieces of commitment information $\mathtt{Enc}(s_1)$, $\mathtt{Enc}(s_2), \cdots, \mathtt{Enc}(s_\beta)$, one for each of the β proofs. In the decommitment phase, $\mathcal{V}$ issues the decommitment query based on the commitment query $\mathtt{Enc}(r)$ and the set of PCP queries and receives β answers, one for each of the β proofs. $\mathcal{V}$ will perform the decommitment check separately. It is proved that this batching technique will not impair the soundness of the verification protocol ([25], Appendix C, Theorem C.1). This immediately implies the correctness and soundness of our first level "batching", as that in [24].

For the second level of "batching", we are targeting to use one single commitment query and one single set of PCP queries for all these proofs. Firstly, we notice that the bottom line of batching is that $\mathcal{P}$ is not allowed to output the answer for one proof after he learns whether $\mathcal{V}$ accepts or rejects another proof (the so-called Verifier Rejection Problem [15]) Thus, we move all the decommitment tests to the last step in our protocol, which is performed after all verification is done. Secondly, since our protocol is an interactive protocol, the soundness holds only under the restriction that $\mathcal{V}$'s τ and his verdict in each layer does not help $\mathcal{P}$ deviate from the protocol and generate proofs in the next layer to cheat $\mathcal{V}$. Thus, if we use Zaatar [24] to verify one loop iteration, we need to guarantee that the randomly generated number for the divisibility test in Zaatar should be different from our τ.

6. PERFORMANCE EVALUATION

In this section, we analyze the performance of our design and compare it with existing work. We firstly compare the complexity of the algorithms. Then, we compare the "experimental results" of our design with all existing work. However, we model, rather than measure, their performance. For our design, we built a model of its performance based on the latest performance results for [24], while for the others, we used previously published models [24, 23]. Analysis shows the efficiency of our design.

6.1 Performance Analysis and Comparison

We are targeting at reducing the amortized part of cost (for the verifier) and the proof generation cost (for the prover). Now, in the context of loop circuits, we compare the cost of our protocol with Zaatar and Pinocchio as in Figure 6. We use the published performance models of Zaatar [24] and Pinocchio [23]. For Pinocchio, we only list the most burdensome part in Figure 6; for Zaatar, given that Zaatar's circuit

Setup

Step 1: $\mathcal{V}$ randomly generates $\tau \in \mathbb{F}$ and $q_H = (1, \tau, \tau^2, \cdots, \tau^V)$, $q_G = (A_1(\tau), A_2(\tau) \cdots, A_{K-1}(\tau))$, $q_{IN} = (A_2(\tau), A_3(\tau) \cdots, A_K(\tau))$
Step 2: $\mathcal{V}$ generates the commitment query according to the commitment protocol as in Pepper [25], and sends it to $\mathcal{P}$;
Step 3: $\mathcal{V}$ generates $\sigma_1, \cdots, \sigma_K$ and constructs the BP for the circuit.

Verification

Step 4: Both $\mathcal{P}$ and $\mathcal{V}$ computes $\mathtt{IN}_i^{(1)}$, $\mathtt{EX}_{(k-1)\cdot Q+u}^{(1)}$, and $\mathtt{OUT}_j^{(1)}$: $\mathtt{IN}_i^{(1)} \leftarrow \mathtt{Z}_{i,1}$, $(i = 1, 2, \cdots, M)$;
$\mathtt{EX}_{(k-1)\cdot Q+u}^{(1)} \leftarrow \mathtt{Z}_{u+M,k}$, where $u = 1, 2 \cdots Q$ and $k = 1, 2, \cdots, K$; $\mathtt{OUT}_j^{(1)} \leftarrow \mathtt{Z}_{j,K+1}$, $(j = 1, 2, \cdots, M)$
Step 5: $\mathcal{P}$ computes intermediate results $\mathtt{Z}_{w_1,w_2}$, linear functions π_{H_j}, π_{G_j}, $\pi_{\mathtt{IN}_i}$ for all i, j, replies the commitment information for all proofs.
Step 6: $\mathcal{V}$ sends $\mathcal{P}$ these queries: q_H, q_G, q_{IN},$\mathcal{P}$ replies: $\pi_{H_j}(q_H)$, $\pi_{G_j}(q_G)$, $\pi_{\mathtt{IN}_i}(q_{IN})$ $(i, j \in \{1, 2, \cdots, M\})$
Step 7: $\mathcal{V}$ checks the linearity of these proofs. If any fails, reject;
Step 8: $\mathcal{P}$ sends $\mathtt{OUT}_j^{(2)}$; $\mathcal{V}$ checks whether $\mathtt{OUT}_j^{(2)} = D(\tau) \cdot \pi_{H_j}(q_H) + \pi_{G_j}(q_G) + A_K(\tau) \cdot \mathtt{OUT}_j^{(1)}$, where $j = 1, \cdots, M$. If not, reject.
Step 9: $\mathcal{V}$ updates $\mathtt{IN}_i^{(2)}$, $i = 1, 2, \cdots, M$: $\mathtt{IN}_i^{(2)} = \pi_{\mathtt{IN}_i}(q_{IN}) + \mathtt{IN}_i^{(1)} \cdot A_1(\tau)$; and updates $\mathtt{EX}_u^{(2)}$ by computing: $\mathtt{EX}_u^{(2)} \leftarrow f_{\mathtt{EX}_u}(\tau)$ $(u = 1, 2, \cdots, Q)$.
Step 10: $\mathcal{P}$ convinces $\mathcal{V}$ that $\mathtt{OUT}_j^{(2)} = \psi_j^{(2)}(\mathtt{IN}_1^{(2)}, \cdots, \mathtt{IN}_M^{(2)}, \mathtt{EX}_1^{(2)}, \cdots, \mathtt{EX}_Q^{(2)})$
Step 11: $\mathcal{V}$ performs the decommitment check for every proofs. If any fails, $\mathcal{V}$ rejects.
Step 12: If the running of our protocol goes here, accept.

Figure 5: Our Verification Protocol

is formulated into constraints, we view the number of constraints in Zaatar as the number of multiplication gates (circuit size). Then, the number of variables in the constraints (excluding inputs and outputs) in Zaatar equals the circuit size minus the number of input/output wires.

Remember that our verification design has two layers, the first layer proves that the wire values between repeated substructures are calculated correctly, and then the second layer proves that the blocks themselves are computed correctly. At the second layer in our protocol, the result of a single loop iteration needs to be verified. We use existing methods as a building block to perform the verification. In Figure 6, the last terms in the column of our design's cost model (e.g., $C^Z_{na}(1)$, $\frac{1}{K}C^Z_a(K)$, etc.) represent the cost for the verification of one loop iteration in our protocol. In our protocol, if $\mathcal{V}$ adopts Zaatar or Pinocchio as the verification block for one loop iteration, this part of cost will usually be only $\frac{1}{K}$ of the total cost that $\mathcal{V}$ pays if $\mathcal{V}$ uses Zaatar or Pinocchio to verify the whole loop. In particular, the second layer verification(verification of one loop iteration) also contains amortized cost, which is linear in the size of the circuit associated with the loop body. For simplicity, We choose Zaatar to show our cost model.

Now we show why the amortized cost in our protocol is much less that its counterparts in all existing protocols: our design has the following properties: First, it has more flexibility in amortizing. Our protocol has a benefit that the first part of amortized cost, denoted by C^*_a, can be amortized over instances which have the same loop structure and the same degree of the polynomial that the circuit of the loop body computes. (Notice: these instances can have different circuits for the loop body, as long as the circuit the loop bodies compute have the same degree.) This property renders our protocol superior to existing works, in which costs can only be amortized to instances that share the same circuit. Namely, even if our amortized cost is the same as its counterparts, our protocol can be amortized to more instances than other protocols. Second, it has smaller costs. Even if the amortized part for verifying the one exection of the loop body, denoted by $C^\dagger_a$, counteracts a part of cost, the total amortized cost in our protocol is still far less than that of Zaatar in the loop circuit. Notice the total amortized cost in our protocol is $[C^*_a + C^\dagger_a] \sim [O(K \cdot D) + O(C)]$. Zaatar has amortized cost which is linear in the size of the whole circuit, denoted by $C^Z_a \sim O(K \cdot C)$. Recall that K is the number of loop iterations (executions of the loop body) and D is the degree of the polynomial that the circuit of the loop body computes. (The loop body is equivalent to an arithmetic circuit and the arithmetic circuit computes a polynomial.) C is the size of the circuit that the loop body is equivalent to. We can prove that the amortized cost in our protocol is usually far less than the amortized cost in existing work.

Although C^*_a and C^Z_a seems similar, in general, they are largely different. We know arithmetic circuits are the standard model for computing polynomials. In other words, an output of an arithmetic circuit is a polynomial in the input variables. The arithmetic complexity is characterized by the size of the arithmetic circuit. From the theory of arithmetic circuit complexity, we know *most* polynomials have high arithmetic complexity ([13], Section 4). More specifically, a detailed analysis using a counting argument shows that most polynomials in n variables and degree d require circuits of size at least $\Omega(\sqrt{\binom{n+d}{d}})$ ([27], Section 3.1). Here *most* means that the number of polynomials that have small circuits (i.e. smaller than the lower bound above) is much smaller than the total number of polynomials. In most cases, to compute an n-variate polynomial of degree d requires a circuit of size at least $\Omega(\sqrt{\binom{n+d}{d}})$. In our context, $n = M + Q$ and $d = D$. Then, by this lower bound, C is at least $\Omega(\sqrt{\binom{M+Q+D}{D}})$ which is much more than D, since $\Omega\left(\sqrt{\binom{M+Q+D}{D}}\right) \sim \Omega\left(\sqrt{\frac{(M+Q+D)^{M+Q+D+\frac{1}{2}}}{(M+Q)^{M+Q+\frac{1}{2}} \cdot D^{D+\frac{1}{2}}}}\right)$ by Stirling's approximation. For Given M and Q, this is an exponential function of D.

Similarly, we improve the prover's cost of proof generation from quasilinear in the size of the circuit of the loop body (like in Zaatar) to quasilinear in the degree of the circuit of the loop body, with an additional cost for generating the proof of one loop iteration. This is also a big improvement according to the analysis above.

6.2 An Example for Performance Comparison

To have a clear picture of these costs and how powerful our method is in verification of real-world iterative computation, we look at a real loop. We look at an example of successive matrix multiplication, which is widely used in communications, signal processing, and control systems. The code to compute: $xA_0 \cdots A_K$, where x is a $1 \times K$ vector and A_i, $(i = 0, \cdots K)$ are $M \times M$ matrices. It is easy to write this into a "for" loop. Let A be a 1000×1000 matrix and the

	Zaatar (Loop ver.)	Pinocchio (Loop ver.)	Our Algm
$\mathcal{V}$'s Total non-amortized cost	$C^Z_{na}(K) = 2\texttt{Dec} + \rho \cdot (6M + 3Q \cdot K + 6\rho_{lin} + 4) \cdot \texttt{Mult}$	$C^P_{na} = 11\texttt{Map}$	$C_{na}(K) = 3M \cdot \texttt{Dec} + \rho \cdot (6M + Q \cdot K + 9M\rho_{lin}) \cdot \texttt{Mult} + C^Z_{na}(1)$
$\mathcal{V}$'s Total amortized cost	$C^Z_a(K) = (2K \cdot C) \cdot \texttt{Enc} + \rho \cdot \rho_{lin} \cdot 2 \cdot (2K \cdot C) \cdot \texttt{Rand} + \rho \cdot [\texttt{Rand} + (\texttt{Div}) \cdot K \cdot C] + (\rho_{lin} \cdot 3 \cdot (2K \cdot C) + (3K \cdot C + 6K \cdot C + K_1 + 3K_2)) \cdot \rho \cdot \texttt{Mult}$	$C^P_a(K) = [10(K \cdot C)] \cdot \texttt{Exp}$	$C_a(K) = (K \cdot D) \cdot [\texttt{Enc} + 2\rho \cdot \rho_{lin} \cdot (\texttt{Rand} + \texttt{Mult}) + 2\rho \cdot \texttt{Mult}] + \rho \cdot (\texttt{Div} + 3 \cdot \texttt{Mult}) \cdot K + \frac{1}{K} C^Z_a(K)$
Task Computing	Comp	Comp	Comp
$\mathcal{P}$: Construct proof vector	$C^Z_p(K) = 3\texttt{Mult} \cdot (K \cdot C) \cdot log^2(K \cdot C)$	$C^P_p(K) = 8\texttt{Muex} \cdot (K \cdot C)$	$C_p(K) = 3\texttt{Mult} \cdot (K \cdot D - K) \cdot log^2(K \cdot D - K) + C^Z_p(1)$
$\mathcal{P}$: Issue PCP responses	$C^Z_i(K) = (\texttt{Oper} + (\rho \cdot (6\rho_{lin} + 4) + 1) \cdot \texttt{Mult}) \cdot (2K \cdot C)$	N/A	$C_i(K) = [\texttt{Oper} + (\rho \cdot (3\rho_{lin} + 2) \cdot M + 1) \cdot \texttt{Mult}] \cdot (K \cdot D) + C^Z_i(1)$

Map: cost of bilinear map in $\mathbb{G} \times \mathbb{G} \mapsto \mathbb{G}_T$
Div: cost of division over $\mathbb{F}$
Rand: cost of pseudorandomly generating an element in $\mathbb{F}$
Dec: cost of decryption over $\mathbb{F}$
Comp: cost of evaluating the whole circuit
Muex: cost of multiplication over exponent
D: degree of the polynomial that the circuit of the loop body computes
K_1: number of additive terms in the constraints of Ginger, Zaatar's underlying protocol
K: number of loop iterations
Exp: cost of exponential operation in $\mathbb{G}$
Mult: cost of multiplication over $\mathbb{F}$
Q: number of the extra input of one loop iteration
Enc: cost of encryption over $\mathbb{F}$
Oper: cost of ciphertext add plus multiply
ρ: number of iteration of verification for one instance
ρ_{lin}: number of iterations of linearity tests in one iteration of verification.
K_2: number of distinct additive degree-2 terms in the constraints of Ginger, Zaatar's underlying protocol
M: the number of input (or output) of one loop iteration
C: size of the circuit of the loop body

Figure 6: Comparison of Cost for Verifier in Each Instance

	Zaatar	Pinocchio	Our Algm[a]
$\mathcal{V}$'s Cost (Non-amortized)	$1.10h$	$9.9ms$	$1281s + 7.70s$
$\mathcal{V}$'s Cost (Amortized)	$96.76h$	$164.3h$	$0.29s + 696.67s$
Task Computing	$160s$	$160s$	$160s$
$\mathcal{P}$: Construct proof	$111.34h$	$445.56h$	$38.6ms + 381s$
$\mathcal{P}$: Issue responses	$124.38h$	N/A	$158.8s + 895.5s$

Map: $0.9ms$
Div: $3\mu s$, 220-bit
Rand: $260ns$, 220-bit
Oper: $130\mu s$, 220-bit
ρ: 8
Dec: $170\mu s$, 220 bits
Exp: $118.3\mu s$, fixed base, optimized for twist curve
Mult: $320ns$, 220-bit
Muex: $401.0\mu s$, 254-bit, optimized for twist curve
ρ_{lin}: 20
Enc: $88\mu s$, 220 bits

[a]Note: we list the cost for both the first layer and the second layer in our design, connected by "+".

Figure 7: An Loop Example and Its Cost

number of executions be $K = 500$. Let the width of the inputs/outputs be $M = 1000$, the width of the extra inputs for each execution $Q = M^2$, and the circuit size of the loop body $C = M^2$. It is easy to see the polynomial that the circuit of each loop body computes is quadratic, thus $D = 2$. We use published models ([24, 23]) and instantiate the costs as in Figure 7. All the costs of basic operations are borrowed from Zaatar [24] and Pinocchio [23]. We can see that, for the amortized cost and the prover's cost, our protocol is far superior to the other two. This also implies that in our protocol smaller breakeven batching size suffices to guarantee that the average cost for verification per instance is less than re-computing.

6.3 Further Discussion

If we examine our protocol carefully, a natural question will arise: why cannot the block be of size $K_0 \cdot C$ such that $K_0 \neq 1$? Moreover, if we group K_0 successive loop iterations into large blocks ($K_0 < K$), then we can further group several sequential big blocks into a bigger block. The whole circuit can be viewed as a multiple-layer structure. More specifically, we can view the whole circuit as one big block, which we call the first layer block and denote by a function $\psi^{(1)} : \mathbb{F}^{M+K \cdot Q} \mapsto \mathbb{F}^M$. In the second layer's perspective, the circuit consists of K_0 smaller blocks, which we call the second layer block and denote by a function $\psi^{(2)} : \mathbb{F}^{M+K \cdot Q/K_0} \mapsto \mathbb{F}^M$, and so forth. In each layer, several blocks constitute the circuit. The block in the l-th layer is denoted by a function $\psi^{(l)} : \mathbb{F}^{M+K \cdot Q/(K_0^{l-1})} \mapsto \mathbb{F}^M$. The l-th layer block is composed of K_0 lower layer blocks, i.e. the $l+1$ layer blocks. At the L-th layer, the last layer, each of the blocks is equivalent to one loop iteration. Note that the reduction of our verification can go further recursively in this multiple-layer view. According to our current protocol, the correctness of computing $\psi^{(1)}$ is reduced to the correctness of computing $\psi^{(2)}$. Similarly, the correctness of computing $\psi^{(2)}$ is reduced to the correctness of computing $\psi^{(3)}$. We can keep doing this until we meet the last layer.

At a first glance, this recursive protocol seems promising. However, it is the first layer that dominates the cost. This implies that this method introduces high cost due to the recursion. More specifically, if we have multiple-layer blocks, then from $\psi^{(1)}(\cdot) = \psi^{(2)}(\psi^{(2)}(\cdots(\psi^{(2)}(\cdot))\cdots))$, we see the degree of the polynomial a block computes increases exponentially. Simple analysis will show that the cost of the first layer dominates and therefore the cost for this recursive method is proportional to $O(D^K)$, which is much more than our current protocol. Recall in our current protocol, the block is one loop iteration. Thus, the degree of the polynomial this block computes is D. This is also the reason why sequential circuits – where the output of each gate is an input to the next gate – is the worst-case scenario for our protocol. Such circuits are better tackled with Zaatar, Pinocchio, etc.

7. RELATED WORK

Extensive research has been motivated by the problem of verifying computation, striving for verifying the result of general computation. Verifying the result of general computation can be viewed as originating from similar but more abstract problems in the theory of computation, such as interactive proof (IP) systems [18] and probabilistically checkable proof (PCP) systems [1, 2]. Until recently, the security community has been extending and refining classical proof systems, attempting to make theoretical cryptographic protocols practical.

Extending provides basic theoretical models and meaningful tools for applications. Existing verifiable computation schemes fall into three broad categories. The first line of verifiable computation systems [25, 26, 24, 31] is based on the IKO argument system which is first proposed by Ishai et al. [19]. In these systems, the proof for the result correctness is formulated into a linear PCP with a commitment which is constructed in the pre-processing phase. This line of work made PCP-based approaches more practical- very efficient if batching over a large number of computation instances, while requiring only standard cryptographic assumptions.

Parno et al. start another line of work [24, 23, 7] which is based on the recent finding of a new characterization of the NP complexity class -QSPs/QAPs [16], such as Pinocchio, which supports public verifiability and zero-knowledge. Similarly, by compiling programs to an innovative circuit representation [6], Ben-Sasson et al. provides another publicly verifiable and zero-knowledge scheme BCGTV [7, 8]. Our work inherits the property of the linear-PCP style designs and does not provide zero-knowledge, either. The only work built on linear-PCP (like Pepper/Ginger/Zaatar) that is known to support zero-knowledge proof is XAG [31].

Motivated by the delegation of computation (GKR [17]), IP systems provides the third line of work to assure the client that an untrusted prover has actually performed the correct computation (CRR [12], CMT [14]). In this line of work, Thaler also finds that circuits that satisfy a specific condition can have much lower cost on the pre-processing stage [28]. However, their circuits need to satisfy either a so-called "regular" wiring pattern condition or the "data-parallel" structure requirement (namely, a sub-computation is applied *independently* to different pieces of data). Besides, Thaler's work still has verifier's cost linear in the size of the circuit. All GKR-style systems typically require far more interaction, introducing much more bandwidth costs.

As an interesting hybrid-architecture protocol, Allspice [29] integrates both Zaatar and CMT in such a way that it automatically determines which one would be more efficient to verify the computation and runs the better of the two. Another study [5] has been pursuing argument systems that avoid a pre-processing phase for the verifier. Those argument systems are based on short PCPs, and existing work on this topic is still only theoretical.

Since state-of-the-art verification protocols are based on arithmetic circuit, the compiler which transforms the outsource task (typically a program written in high level languages such as C) into a circuit representation plays a very important role in this area. Zaatar's and Pinocchio's compilers map a large class of computations into corresponding arithmetic circuits, using special-purpose encodings. Another line of compilers, TinyRAM [7] and vnTinyRAM [8], use an innovative technique [6] and compiles universally programs in C with the same number of executions to one same circuit. This compiler has better performance for programs consisting of lots of memory accesss and control flow than Zaatar's and Pinocchio's, while the compilers of Zaatar and Pinocchio do better in programs which are close to "circuit" forms [8]. Walfish et al. evaluate these compilers in [30] and claim TinyRAM's circuit representation is orders of magnitude larger than the representation in Pinocchio and Zaatar.

8. CONCLUSIONS

This paper addresses two fundamental problems in the verifiable computation (we focus on the verification protocol part which is right after circuit generation): 1) whether and what computations can have lower amortized cost and proof generation cost; 2) how to handle loops concisely after circuit generation.

We give a first-step answer by showing that for computation with loops, we can use Block Programs, our new theoretical result, to reduce the verifier's amortized cost to the sum of two parts, one of which is merely verification of one loop iteration (which does not scale with the number of loop repetitions) and the other is linear in the *degree* of the circuit of the loop body and the number of loop iterations. From the theory of arithmetic circuit complexity, the degree of most circuits will be far less than their size. Hence the verifier's amortized costs in our design is far less than the counterpart of existing algorithms, which are linear in the *size* of the whole circuit. We also improve the prover's cost of proof generation from quasilinear in the size of the circuit of the loop body to quasilinear in the degree of the circuit of the loop body, attached with a cost of generating a proof for one loop iteration, achieving great savings similarly.

For applications that require a large number of loop executions (which is common in not only compute-intensive computations but also data-intensive computations such as big data applications), and have loop bodies the degree of which is far less than their size (from the theory of arithmetic circuit complexity, this is nature: the degree of *most* circuits will be far less than their size), our approach is expected to perform better than existing verifiable computation protocols. However, for "deep" loop bodies, in which the output of each gate is an input to the next gate, standard algorithms like Zaatar and Pinocchio would probably do better.

9. ACKNOWLEDGMENTS

We appreciate anonymous reviewers for valuable suggestions and comments. This material is based upon work supported in part by the National Science Foundation under Grant No. 1320351.

10. REFERENCES

[1] S. Arora and S. Safra. Probabilistic checking of proofs; a new characterization of np. In *Proceedings of the 33rd Annual Symposium on Foundations of Computer Science*, SFCS '92, pages 2–13, Washington, DC, USA, 1992.

[2] L. Babai, L. Fortnow, L. A. Levin, and M. Szegedy. Checking computations in polylogarithmic time. In *Proceedings of the twenty-third annual ACM symposium on Theory of computing*, STOC '91, pages 21–32, New York, NY, USA, 1991.

[3] M. Bellare, S. Goldwasser, C. Lund, and A. Russell. Efficient probabilistically checkable proofs and applications to approximations. In *Proceedings of the Twenty-fifth Annual ACM Symposium on Theory of Computing*, STOC '93, pages 294–304, New York, NY, USA, 1993. ACM.

[4] M. Bellare, M. Kiwi, and M. Sudan. Linearity testing in characteristic two. *IEEE Transactions on Information Theory*, 1996.

[5] E. Ben-Sasson, A. Chiesa, D. Genkin, and E. Tromer. On the concrete-efficiency threshold of probabilistically-checkable proofs. *Electronic Colloquium on Computational Complexity (ECCC)*, 19:45, 2012.

[6] E. Ben-Sasson, A. Chiesa, D. Genkin, and E. Tromer. Fast reductions from rams to delegatable succinct constraint satisfaction problems: extended abstract. In *ITCS*, pages 401–414, 2013.

[7] E. Ben-Sasson, A. Chiesa, D. Genkin, E. Tromer, and M. Virza. SNARKs for C: Verifying program executions succinctly and in zero knowledge. In *Proceedings of the 33rd Annual International Cryptology Conference*, CRYPTO '13, pages 90–108, 2013.

[8] E. Ben-Sasson, A. Chiesa, E. Tromer, and M. Virza. Succinct non-interactive zero knowledge for a von neumann architecture. In *Proceedings of the 23rd USENIX Security Symposium, San Diego, CA, USA, August 20-22, 2014.*, pages 781–796, 2014.

[9] N. Bitansky, A. Chiesa, Y. Ishai, O. Paneth, and R. Ostrovsky. Succinct non-interactive arguments via linear interactive proofs. In *Proceedings of the 10th Theory of Cryptography Conference on Theory of Cryptography*, TCC'13, pages 315–333, Berlin, Heidelberg, 2013. Springer-Verlag.

[10] G. Brassard, D. Chaum, and C. Crépeau. Minimum disclosure proofs of knowledge. *J. Comput. Syst. Sci.*, 37(2):156–189, 1988.

[11] B. Braun, A. J. Feldman, Z. A. Ren, S. Setty, A. J. Blumberg, and M. Walfish. Verifying computations with state. In *SOSP*, 2013.

[12] R. Canetti, B. Riva, and G. N. Rothblum. Two 1-round protocols for delegation of computation. Cryptology ePrint Archive, Report 2011/518, 2011. http://eprint.iacr.org/.

[13] X. Chen, N. Kayal, and A. Wigderson. *Partial Derivatives in Arithmetic Complexity and Beyond (Foundations and Trends(R) in Theoretical Computer Science)*. Now Publishers Inc., Hanover, MA, USA, 2011.

[14] G. Cormode, M. Mitzenmacher, and J. Thaler. Practical verified computation with streaming interactive proofs. In *Proceedings of the 3rd Innovations in Theoretical Computer Science Conference*, ITCS '12, pages 90–112, New York, NY, USA, 2012. ACM.

[15] R. Gennaro, C. Gentry, and B. Parno. Non-interactive verifiable computing: outsourcing computation to untrusted workers. In *Proceedings of the 30th annual conference on Advances in cryptology*, CRYPTO'10, pages 465–482, Berlin, Heidelberg, 2010. Springer-Verlag.

[16] R. Gennaro, C. Gentry, B. Parno, and M. Raykova. Quadratic span programs and succinct nizks without pcps. In *Proceedings of the IACR Eurocrypt Conference*, Eurocrypt 13, 2013.

[17] S. Goldwasser, Y. T. Kalai, and G. N. Rothblum. Delegating computation: interactive proofs for muggles. In *Proceedings of the 40th annual ACM symposium on Theory of computing*, STOC '08, pages 113–122, New York, NY, USA, 2008. ACM.

[18] S. Goldwasser, S. Micali, and C. Rackoff. The knowledge complexity of interactive proof systems. *SIAM J. Comput.*, 18(1):186–208, Feb. 1989.

[19] Y. Ishai, E. Kushilevitz, and R. Ostrovsky. Efficient arguments without short pcps. In *Proceedings of the Twenty-Second Annual IEEE Conference on Computational Complexity*, CCC '07, pages 278–291, Washington, DC, USA, 2007.

[20] M. Karchmer and A. Wigderson. On span programs. In *In Proc. of the 8th IEEE Structure in Complexity Theory*, pages 102–111. IEEE Computer Society Press, 1993.

[21] J. Kilian. A note on efficient zero-knowledge proofs and arguments (extended abstract). In *Proceedings of the twenty-fourth annual ACM symposium on Theory of computing*, STOC '92, pages 723–732, New York, NY, USA.

[22] J. Kilian. Improved efficient arguments (preliminary version). In *Proceedings of the 15th Annual International Cryptology Conference on Advances in Cryptology*, CRYPTO '95, pages 311–324, London, UK, UK, 1995. Springer-Verlag.

[23] B. Parno, C. Gentry, J. Howell, and M. Raykova. Pinocchio: nearly practical verifiable computation. In *the IEEE Symposium on Security and Privacy*, IEEE S&P 13, 2013.

[24] S. Setty, B. Braun, V. Vu, A. J. Blumberg, B. Parno, and M. Walfish. Resolving the conflict between generality and plausibility in verified computation. EuroSys '13, 2013.

[25] S. Setty, R. McPherson, A. J. Blumberg, and M. Walfish. Making argument systems for outsourced computation practical (sometimes). In *NDSS*, 2012.

[26] S. Setty, V. Vu, N. Panpalia, B. Braun, A. J. Blumberg, and M. Walfish. Taking proof-based verified computation a few steps closer to practicality. In *USENIX Security*, 2012.

[27] A. Shpilka and A. Yehudayoff. Arithmetic circuits: A survey of recent results and open questions. *Found. Trends Theor. Comput. Sci.*, 5:207–388, Mar. 2010.

[28] J. Thaler. Time-optimal interactive proofs for circuit evaluation. In *CRYPTO (2)*, pages 71–89, 2013.

[29] V. Vu, S. Setty, A. J. Blumberg, and M. Walfish. A hybrid architecture for interactive verifiable computation. In *the IEEE Symposium on Security and Privacy*, IEEE S&P 13, 2013.

[30] M. Walfish and A. J. Blumberg. Verifying computations without reexecuting them: from theoretical possibility to near-practicality. *Electronic Colloquium on Computational Complexity (ECCC)*, 20:165, 2013.

[31] G. Xu, G. Amariucai, and Y. Guan. Delegation of computation with verification outsourcing: Curious verifiers. In *Proceedings of the ACM Symposium on Principles of Distributed Computing*, PODC '13. ACM, 2013.

APPENDIX

A. PROOF OF SOUNDNESS

To better illustrate the logical flow of the soundness proof, we first provide the following simple experiment. Suppose $\mathcal{P}$ must choose between two boxes (the left and the right box), each containing a number of white balls and black balls. The right box stands for the correct proof, while the left box for the wrong proof. White balls represent tests that pass, black balls represent tests that fail. By the completeness argument, we know that all the balls in the right box are white. On the other hand, the left box contains both white and black balls. The prover $\mathcal{P}$ chooses one of the boxes, and places it in a dark room (the room stands for the prover's commitment). The verifier $\mathcal{V}$ has to test the box, to see whether the prover chose the wrong proof. To accomplish this, $\mathcal{V}$ enters the dark room and picks a ball from the box. Then $\mathcal{V}$ exits the room and looks at the ball. Our proof flows as follows. 1. We first show that if $\mathcal{V}$ were to randomly pick a ball from the left box, then $Pr\{\text{the ball is white}\} < \kappa_0^M$, where κ_0^M is some small positive constant (that is, the left box contains mostly black balls). 2. We then reason that, if for the box in the dark room we have $Pr\{\text{the ball is white}\} > \kappa_0^M$, then the box has to be the right box.

Our soundness proof is a bit less straightforward. To make it work, we have to first condition our probabilities on the event that all proofs provided by the prover are linear. In Lemma 6, we show that, if the verifier provides the wrong result (and consequently the wrong proof), then $Pr\{\mathcal{V} \text{ accepts } | \text{all purported proofs are linear }\} < \kappa_0^M$. Now looking back to Theorem 4, to prove the soundness it suffices to show the existence of κ. We start our proof by providing an explicit value κ^*. It now suffices to prove that, if the probability that the verifier accepts (not conditioned on anything) is greater than κ^*, then the purported results are correct. So we show that, if the probability that the verifier accepts is greater than κ^*, then we have $Pr\{\mathcal{V} \text{ accepts } | \text{all purported proofs are linear}\} > \kappa_0^M$, Finally, we bootstrap our argument as above, reasoning that unless the results of the computation are correct, a contradiction ensues with Lemma 6.

Let us proceed. For simplicity, we extract a part of purely mathematical transformation from our proof into Lemma 5.

LEMMA 5. *In the context of loop circuits (as in Figure 3),*

$$D(\tau)\cdot H_j(\tau)=\psi_j^{(2)}\Big(\sum_{k=2}^{K}\mathtt{Z}_{1,k}\cdot A_k(\tau)+\mathtt{IN}_1^{(1)}\cdot A_1(\tau),\cdots,$$
$$\sum_{k=2}^{K}\mathtt{Z}_{M,k}\cdot A_k(\tau)+\mathtt{IN}_M^{(1)}\cdot A_1(\tau),\sum_{k=1}^{K}\mathtt{EX}^{(1)}_{[(k-1)\cdot Q]+1}\cdot A_k(\tau),$$
$$\cdots,\sum_{k=1}^{K}\mathtt{EX}^{(1)}_{[(k-1)\cdot Q]+Q}\cdot A_k(\tau)\Big)-\Big(\sum_{k=1}^{K-1}\mathtt{Z}_{j,k+1}\cdot A_k(t)$$
$$+A_K(\tau)\cdot\mathtt{OUT}_j^{(1)}\Big) \quad (A.1)$$

is equivalent to $\mathtt{OUT}_j^{(2)}=\psi_j^{(2)}(\mathtt{IN}_1^{(2)},\cdots,\mathtt{IN}_M^{(2)},\mathtt{EX}_1^{(2)},\cdots,\mathtt{EX}_Q^{(2)})$, *for inputs* $\mathtt{IN}_1^{(1)},\cdots,\mathtt{IN}_M^{(1)}$, *extra inputs* $\mathtt{EX}_1^{(1)},\cdots,\mathtt{EX}_{Q\cdot K}^{(1)}$, *and outputs* $\mathtt{OUT}_1^{(1)},\cdots,\mathtt{OUT}_M^{(1)}$, *and* $\mathtt{IN}_1^{(2)},\cdots,\mathtt{IN}_M^{(2)}$, $\mathtt{EX}_1^{(2)},\cdots,\mathtt{EX}_Q^{(2)}$, $\mathtt{OUT}_1^{(2)},\cdots,\mathtt{OUT}_M^{(2)}$ *are defined in terms of* τ *as in Figure 5.*

A simple change of variable suffices to prove it.

LEMMA 6. *Let* $\mathcal{V}$ *and* $\mathcal{P}$ *run our protocol as in Figure 5. If the results of the computation task are not correct, for the cases that all purported proofs* π_{G_j} $(j=1,\cdots,M)$, $\pi_{\mathtt{IN}_i}$ $(i=1,\cdots,M)$, π_{H_j} $(j=1,\cdots,M)$ *are linear functions, we have* $Pr\{\mathcal{V}$ *accepts* $|$*all purported proofs are linear*$\}<\kappa_0^M$, *where* $\kappa_0=\frac{K\cdot D}{|\mathbb{F}|}$ *or* κ_{Zaatar}, D *is the degree of the polynomial that the circuit of the loop body computes and* K *is the number of loop iterations. The probability is over the randomness of both* $\mathcal{V}$ *and* $\mathcal{P}$ *in both phases our protocol.*

PROOF. Under the condition that all purported proofs π_{G_j} $(j=1,\cdots,M)$, $\pi_{\mathtt{IN}_i}$ $(i=1,\cdots,M)$, π_{H_j} $(j=1,\cdots,M)$ are linear functions, all the linearity tests pass. Then, $\mathcal{V}$ accepts if

$$\mathtt{OUT}_j^{(2)}=\psi_j^{(2)}(\mathtt{IN}_1^{(2)},\cdots,\mathtt{IN}_M^{(2)},\mathtt{EX}_1^{(2)},\cdots,\mathtt{EX}_Q^{(2)}). \quad (A.2)$$

This is checked by computing himself or using existing protocols, like Zaatar or Pinocchio. If he computes himself, by Lemma 5, the verifier accepts only when the following holds:

$$D(\tau)\cdot H_j(\tau)=\psi_j^{(2)}\Big(\sum_{k=2}^{K}\mathtt{Z}_{1,k}\cdot A_k(\tau)+\mathtt{IN}_1^{(1)}\cdot A_1(\tau),\cdots,$$
$$\sum_{k=2}^{K}\mathtt{Z}_{M,k}\cdot A_k(\tau)+\mathtt{IN}_M^{(1)}\cdot A_1(\tau),\sum_{k=1}^{K}\mathtt{EX}^{(1)}_{[(k-1)\cdot Q]+1}\cdot A_k(\tau),\cdots,$$
$$\sum_{k=1}^{K}\mathtt{EX}^{(1)}_{[(k-1)\cdot Q]+Q}\cdot A_k(\tau)\Big)-[\sum_{k=1}^{K-1}\mathtt{Z}_{j,k+1}\cdot A_k(\tau)+A_K(\tau)\cdot\mathtt{OUT}_j^{(1)}]. \quad (A.3)$$

This is a simple test of the following at the point $t=\tau$:

$$D(t)\cdot H_j(t)=\psi_j^{(2)}\Big(\sum_{k=2}^{K}\mathtt{Z}_{1,k}\cdot A_k(t)+\mathtt{IN}_1^{(1)}\cdot A_1(t),\cdots,$$
$$\sum_{k=2}^{K}\mathtt{Z}_{M,k}\cdot A_k(t)+\mathtt{IN}_M^{(1)}\cdot A_1(t),\sum_{k=1}^{K}\mathtt{EX}^{(1)}_{[(k-1)\cdot Q]+1}\cdot A_k(t),\cdots,$$
$$\sum_{k=1}^{K}\mathtt{EX}^{(1)}_{[(k-1)\cdot Q]+Q}\cdot A_k(t)\Big)-[\sum_{k=1}^{K-1}\mathtt{Z}_{j,k+1}\cdot A_k(t)+A_K(t)\cdot\mathtt{OUT}_j^{(1)}]. \quad (A.4)$$

However, since the results are not correct, by Corollary 2, for any $j=1,2,\cdots,M$, there is no $H_j(t)$ for which (A.4) holds. Thus, $\mathcal{V}$ wrongly accepts only if τ is a root of (A.4). By Schwartz-Zippel lemma, the probability that $\mathcal{V}$ wrongly accepts is bounded above by $\frac{K\cdot D}{|\mathbb{F}|}$, where D is the degree of the polynomial that the circuit of the loop body computes and K is the number of loop iterations. If $\mathcal{V}$ uses Zaatar to check (A.2), then the probability is bounded above by κ_{Zaatar} (refer to [24], Apdx. A.2). Notice the divisibility tests will run M times. Thus, if the results of the computation are not correct, then, $Pr\{\mathcal{V}$ accepts$|$ all purported proofs are linear $\}<\kappa_0^M$, where $\kappa_0=\frac{K\cdot D}{|F|}$ or κ_{Zaatar}. The probability is over the randomness of $\mathcal{V}$ and $\mathcal{P}$ in both phases our protocol. □

The proof of Theorem 4 is as follows (our articulation follows [24]):

PROOF. We address the general cases where maybe not all purported proofs π_{G_j} $(j=1,\cdots,M)$, $\pi_{\mathtt{IN}_i}$ $(i=1,\cdots,M)$, π_{H_j} $(j=1,\cdots,M)$ are linear functions. We define $\kappa^*=max\{(1-3\delta+6\delta^2)^{\rho_{lin}},6M\delta+\kappa_0^M\}$ (where ρ_{lin} is the number of linearity tests, and $0<\delta<\delta^*$, δ^* is the lesser root of $6\delta^2-3\delta+2/9=0$), and claim this κ^* is the κ we are looking for. Now, we prove our claim. It suffices to prove: if $Pr\{\mathcal{V}$ accepts$\}>\kappa^*$, then the purported results are correct. (This statement is equivalent to the requirement for κ.) The probability is over the randomness of both $\mathcal{V}$ and $\mathcal{P}$ in both phases our protocol.

$Pr\{\mathcal{V}$ accepts$\}>\kappa^*$ implies that both linearity tests and the divisibility tests pass with probability greater than κ^*. Then, we know the linearity tests pass with probability greater than $(1-3\delta+6\delta^2)^{\rho_{lin}}$. If the linearity tests pass with probability greater than $(1-3\delta+6\delta^2)^{\rho_{lin}}$, then the proof is δ-close to linear; this follows from results of Bellare et al. [4, 3]; see the analysis in the extended version of [25], Apdx. A.2. Suppose $Pr\{\mathcal{V}$ accepts$\}>\kappa^*$, then we also have $Pr\{\mathcal{V}$ accepts$\}>6M\delta+\kappa_0^M$. If we exclude the cases that any of the queries in the divisibility tests "hit" the non-linear part, the remaining cases are those that all the queries in the divisibility tests "hit" the linear part of the purported proofs. Let E_H be the event that all the queries in the divisibility tests "hit" the linear part of the purported proofs. Since one query in the divisibility tests "hit" the non-linear part is δ, by union bound, $Pr\{\overline{E_H}\}\le 6M\delta$. Thus, $Pr\{\mathcal{V}$ accepts, $\overline{E_H}\}<Pr\{\overline{E_H}\}<6M\delta$. Since

$$Pr\{\mathcal{V}\text{ accepts}\}=Pr\{\mathcal{V}\text{ accepts, }E_H\}+Pr\{\mathcal{V}\text{ accepts, }\overline{E_H}\}, \quad (A.5)$$

and $Pr\{\mathcal{V}$ accepts$\}>6M\delta+\kappa_0^M$, we have

$$Pr\{\mathcal{V}\text{ accepts, }E_H\}>\kappa_0^M. \quad (A.6)$$

Then, we have $Pr\{\mathcal{V}$ accepts$|E_H\}>Pr\{\mathcal{V}$ accepts, $E_H\}>\kappa_0^M$. Since the effect of testing the divisibility using all the queries that "hit" the linear part of the purported proofs is exactly the same as testing the divisibility under the condition that all purported proofs are linear, we will have :

$$Pr\{\mathcal{V}\text{ accepts}|\text{all purported proofs are linear}\}>\kappa_0^M \quad (A.7)$$

(A.7) implies the purported results are correct. Otherwise, if the purported results are not correct, by Lemma 6, we will have $Pr\{\mathcal{V}$ accepts$|$all purported proofs are linear$\}<\kappa_0^M$, which contradicts (A.7). □

Secure Bilinear Pairing Outsourcing Made More Efficient and Flexible

Haibo Tian*
[1]School of Information Science and Technology,Sun Yat-sen University
[2]Guangdong Provincial Key Laboratory of Information Security, Guangzhou 510006, China
tianhb@mail.sysu.edu.cn

Fangguo Zhang
[1]School of Information Science and Technology, Sun Yat-sen University
[2]Guangdong Provincial Key Laboratory of Information Security, Guangzhou 510006, China
[3]Department of Computer Science and Engineering University at Buffalo, State University of New York, NY 14260-2500, U.S.A.
isszhfg@mail.sysu.edu.cn

Kui Ren
Department of Computer Science and Engineering University at Buffalo, State University of New York, NY 14260-2500, U.S.A.
kuiren@buffalo.edu

ABSTRACT

The increasing availability of cloud computing allows more and more mobile devices to outsource expensive computations. Among these computations, bilinear pairing is very fundamental and frequently-used by many modern cryptographic protocols. Currently, the most efficient outsourcing algorithm of bilinear pairings requires about 5 point additions in $\mathbb{G}_1$ and $\mathbb{G}_2$ and 4 multiplications in $\mathbb{G}_T$ under the one-malicious version of a two-untrusted-program assumption. And the result of the algorithm is checkable with a probability about $1/2$. In this paper, we improve the state-of-the-art by proposing two new outsourcing algorithms for bilinear pairings. One is a more efficient outsourcing algorithm under the same assumption with the same checkability. The other is more flexible under a two-untrusted-program assumption with improved checkability. Both algorithms are better suited to various applications where on-line computations are strictly limited due to the lack of available computing resources.

Categories and Subject Descriptors

F.2.1 [**Numerical Algorithms and Problems**]: Computations in finite fields; E.3 [**DATA ENCRYPTION**]: Public key cryptosystems

General Terms

Privacy

*The Corresponding Author

ASIA CCS'15, April 14–17, 2015, Singapore.

http://dx.doi.org/10.1145/2714576.2714615.

Keywords

Secure Outsourcing; Bilinear Pairings; Efficiency; Checkability

1. INTRODUCTION

The development of cloud computing enables people to access almost unlimited computing resources in an on-demand fashion. People with mobile devices or other energy-limited devices may benefit from this pattern to fulfill some complex computations that are unaffordable in their devices alone, such as linear programming [27] and convex optimization [32]. In the setting of cryptographic applications, it is satisfactory if a device could outsource some energy-consuming operations to a cloud, and keep the security properties of the applications unchanged [22]. As a basic operation in pairing-based cryptographic applications, the bilinear pairing evaluation attracts researchers to study suitable security model and efficient implementations for outsourcing.

There are mainly three aspects about the security model.

- The first is about secrecy. Some sensitive information involved in an outsourced process should be kept secrete. The requirement comes from a semi-trusted cloud server assumption where a cloud server may be curious to peek client's data. In practice, cloud servers are usually owned by some corporations that may be not trusted by clients. So this assumption is sound.
- The second is about checkability. The result of an outsourced computation should be checkable at least with some probability. This requirement again comes from the semi-trusted cloud server assumption. A service program in a could server may have bugs or malicious functions. It is also attractive for a cloud server to finish a computing task as soon as possible, which may lead to incomplete computation or even zero computation where simply a wrong result is returned.
- The last aspect is about assumptions on the number and trustability of programs to implement an algorith-

m. A one-untrusted-program (OUP) assumption allows only one program to implement an algorithm, and the program could be malicious. A one-malicious version of a two-untrusted-program (OMTUP) assumption allows two programs to implement an algorithm, and only one of them could be malicious. A two-untrusted-program (TUP) assumption allows two programs to implement an algorithm and both of them could be malicious.

In practice, the OUP assumption needs a client to access only one program to outsource its computation task. An algorithm under the OUP assumption usually needs more computations than under other assumptions. Most outsourcing algorithms for bilinear pairings are under the OUP assumption. The OMTUP and TUP assumptions need a client to access two programs. Under the OMTUP assumption, the two programs are expected to be produced by different vendors. Under the TUP assumption, the two programs may be from the same vendor.

The efficiency of an algorithm with outsourced computation is a basic goal and is the reason of the existence of such an algorithm. Considering bilinear pairings, before the work of Chen et al. [12], all outsourcing algorithms [16, 13, 8] need scalar multiplications and exponentiations. The fast implementations of bilinear pairings on energy-limited devices [24, 25] almost make the effort of pairings outsourcing useless. Just for some parameter sets, there are some benefits to outsource bilinear pairings. The outsourcing algorithm in [12] only needs a few point additions in $\mathbb{G}_1$ and $\mathbb{G}_2$ and multiplications in $\mathbb{G}_T$, which makes their work valuable.

Since a bilinear pairing is a basic operation in pairing based applications, a pairing outsourcing algorithm has a wide usage. Chen et al. [12] gave two examples. One is the well-known Boneh-Franlin identity-based encryption scheme [4]. The other is the Cha-Cheon identity-based signature scheme [14]. Both schemes need on-line pairing evaluations. Their results show that the on-line computations are largely reduced.

We notice the similarity of on-line/off-line computation algorithms and the outsourcing algorithms in [17, 12, 28, 8]. They all need some off-line computations to support the on-line computations. The difference is whether the on-line computations are outsourced. From this standpoint, we may view the mentioned algorithms as extensions to on-line/off-line computation algorithms to save the on-line computing resources. So we claim the algorithms are suitable to applications where on-line computations have strict limitations on available computing resources. In practice, the off-line computations may be finished when a mobile device is charging or simply be finished by another device that puts the off-line computation results to the mobile device.

This paper mainly proposes two outsourcing algorithms. One is a more efficient bilinear pairing outsourcing algorithm in the framework of [12]. The other is an algorithm in a more flexible framework with a better checkability. We also give two pre-computation algorithms for the two outsourcing algorithms respectively that are based on a well-known EBPV algorithm.

1.1 Related Works

The outsourcing computation of cryptographic operations is a technique that has been studied for a long time [19, 9, 18]. There are also some generic constructions [33, 7] for secure outsourcing computation. For the special case of bilinear pairing outsourcing, the closely related works are as follows.

Girault and Lefranc [16] proposed some protocols for pairing-based schemes for the first time. They suggest a method to blind a point. Suppose two points $A \in \mathbb{G}_1$ and $B \in \mathbb{G}_2$. A client wants to compute $e(A, B)$ and to hide the point B from a server. The client could select a random value $u \in \mathbb{Z}_q$ where q is the order of $\mathbb{G}_1$ and $\mathbb{G}_2$. And the client sends A and uB to the server. After the server returns $e(A, uB)$, the client could recover $e(A, B)$.

Chevallier-Mames et al. [2, 13] proposed a protocol for secure delegation of the elliptic-curve pairing. The secure delegation in their proposal means that both points could be hidden from a server, and that the server's computation result is checkable. Basically, they make a server compute two comparable results to check the correctness of a pairing evaluation. Kang et al. [3] proposed a simpler protocol to improve the efficiency of the protocol in [2]. They feed a server with a set of new points and obtain two comparable results with a smaller cost.

Tsang et al. [21] proposed the concept of batch pairing delegation, and constructed several protocols for different types of bilinear pairings. They showed that the batch pairing delegation was more efficient than multiple runs of non-batch delegation protocols at that time.

Wu et al. [30, 31] focused on server-aided signature verification. They specially study the verification of Boneh-Lynn-Shacham (BLS) signature [5]. Their final construction shows a similar idea to exploit two comparable results returned by a server to check the correctness of server's computation. Wang et al. [29] proposed a new security model in the setting of server-aided verification. Chow et al. [15] proposed another new model in the same setting, and proposed a method to exploit pairing delegation protocols [21] for signature verification.

Canard et al. [8] proposed a new method to delegate a pairing evaluation. Their construction shows again the similar idea to use two comparable results returned by a server to check the correctness of server's computation. They contribute a new efficient construction to implement such an idea. Their construction for public points outsourcing needs two scalar multiplications in $\mathbb{G}_1$ and $\mathbb{G}_2$, one exponentiation in $\mathbb{G}_T$ and a membership test in $\mathbb{G}_T$. They noticed the work of Ana and Francisco [25] where an optimal-Ate pairing over Barreto-Naehrig curves [1] was implemented. They then argue that the benefit of pairings outsourcing may be the save of area to implement a pairing evaluation. In fact, Scott et al. [24] have showed an implementation of cryptographic pairings on smart cards, where the Section 7 shows that a pairing outsourcing algorithm is only meaningful for Ate pairings.

Surprisingly, Chen et al. [12] proposed an efficient algorithm for secure outsourcing of bilinear pairings. They only require a client to compute 5 point additions in $\mathbb{G}_1$ and $\mathbb{G}_2$ and 4 multiplications in $\mathbb{G}_T$. No scalar multiplications or exponentiations are needed.

1.2 Contributions

More Efficient Algorithm: We exploit a trick in [24, 8] to use an inverse of a random value in a pre-computation phase. Basically, suppose $e(A, B)$ is expected to be outsourced. We let a server compute $e(A+x_1P_1, B+x_1^{-1}x_2P_2)$ where P_1 and P_2 are generators of $\mathbb{G}_1$ and $\mathbb{G}_2$, respectively. Note $e(x_1P_1, x_1^{-1}x_2P_2) = e(P_1, P_2)^{x_2}$. Then some computations in [12] could be saved. We also observe that some computations in [12] could be further pre-computed. For example, the second query to the program U_1 in [12] is not related to the inputs (A, B). That computation could be pre-computed, and the queries to U_1 could be reduced.

Pre-computation Algorithms: The outsourcing algorithm in [12] needs precomputations of three six-tuples each of which includes three scalar multiplications and one pairing evaluation. We propose two algorithms based on a well-known EBPV algorithm [20] for precomputations. We further exploit an idea in [28] to build a dynamic table where each entry is used to outsource a pairing evaluation. Our efficient algorithm needs ten random elements for one pairing evaluation. The other algorithm needs twelve random elements for one pairing evaluation.

Two Untrusted Programs: We notice that an algorithm under the OUP assumption may need more computations than under the OMTUP and TUP assumptions. And the OMTUP assumption may be not well-suited to some practical deployment of cloud services. For example, many cloud services may be based on the same platform provided by a vendor. We then propose a flexible algorithm under the TUP assumption. We let two programs compute two closely related outputs whose relationship could be checked by a client with a small cost, similar to [2, 30, 8]. We emphasize that an algorithm secure under the OMTUP assumption may have different behaviors under the TUP assumption. For example, our efficient algorithm and an algorithm in [10, 11] exploit the OMTUP assumption to check a result by comparing two values returned by two programs while a client does not know a correct answer. This trick is invalid under the TUP assumption.

Improvement on Checkability: The outsourcing algorithm under the TUP assumption has a probability $(1-1/3s)^2$ to check the result for a security parameter s. Our method gives a client a choice to improve the checkability at the cost of several computations. Note that in some applications of outsourcing algorithms, the checkability may be crucial. For example, if a signature verification procedure employs a bilinear pairing outsourcing algorithm, the checkability of the outsourcing algorithm determines the correctness of the signature verification procedure. Chow et al. [15] discussed this problem in their security analysis section.

1.3 Organizations

The next section shows the pre-computation algorithms based on EBPV. Section 3 is a more efficient outsourcing algorithm for bilinear pairings with the descriptions of security model and proofs. The algorithm under the TUP assumption and its proofs are in Section 4. Section 5 includes a comparison. The last section concludes the paper.

2. PRE-COMPUTATION ALGORITHMS

2.1 EBPV

Boyko, Peinado and Venkatesan [6] proposed a method to speed up discrete log and factoring based schemes via precomputations. It is called as BPV algorithm. Nguyen, Shparlinski and Stern [20] showed an extension of the BPV algorithm called as EBPV algorithm. We here review the EBPV algorithm in [20] as follows.

Let g be a generator of a cyclic multiplicative group $\mathbb{Z}_p^*$ with order q where p and q are two large primes.

- *Preprocessing Step*: Generate n random integers α_1, ..., $\alpha_n \in \mathbb{Z}_q$. For $j = 1, \ldots, n$, compute $\beta_j = g^{\alpha_j} \bmod p$, and store the values of α_j and β_j in a table.
- *Pair Generation*: When a pair (x, g^x) is needed, randomly generate $S \in \{1, \ldots, n\}$ such that $|S| = k$. For each $j \in S$, randomly select $\chi_j \in \{1, \ldots, h-1\}$ where $h > 1$ is a small integer. Compute

$$x = \sum_{j \in S} \alpha_j \chi_j \bmod q \tag{1}$$

and

$$X = \prod_{j \in S} \beta_j^{\chi_j} \bmod p. \tag{2}$$

If $x = 0 \bmod q$, start again. Otherwise return the pair (x, X).

Note that Nguyen et al. [20] have studied the distribution of modular sums and have shown that by choosing a suitable parameter set, the statistical distance between the distribution of a modular sum and the uniform distribution could be arbitrarily small.

2.2 Bilinear Pairings

In the setting of bilinear pairings, we use the following symbols. Let $\mathbb{G}_1$ and $\mathbb{G}_2$ be two cyclic additive groups generated by P_1 and P_2 respectively. The order of $\mathbb{G}_1$ and $\mathbb{G}_2$ is a large prime and also denoted by the symbol q. Define $\mathbb{G}_T$ to be a cyclic multiplicative group of the same order q. A bilinear pairing is defined as a map $e : \mathbb{G}_1 \times \mathbb{G}_2 \rightarrow \mathbb{G}_T$ with the following properties:

- Bilinear: $e(aR, bQ) = e(R, Q)^{ab}$ for any $R \in \mathbb{G}_1$, $Q \in \mathbb{G}_2$ and $a, b \in \mathbb{Z}_q^*$.
- Non-degenerate: There are $R \in \mathbb{G}_1$ and $Q \in \mathbb{G}_2$ such that $e(R, Q) \neq 1$.
- Computable: There is an efficient algorithm to compute $e(R, Q)$ for any $R \in \mathbb{G}_1$ and $Q \in \mathbb{G}_2$.

Since the EBPV algorithm has no limitations on the cyclic groups, it could be trivially applied to the setting of bilinear pairings.

2.3 Dynamic Table

Wang et al. [28] proposed a BPV$^+$ algorithm employing two tables. One table is a static table to store precomputations. The other is a dynamic table that maintains some pairs of elements produced by a BPV algorithm [6]. On each invocation of their BPV$^+$ algorithm, an entry in the dynamic table is used and removed. The dynamic table is expected to be replenished with some fresh random pairs in an idle time of a device. Obviously, this method could be used together with the EBPV algorithm smoothly.

2.4 *RandA*

We next give the first pre-computation algorithm *RandA*. It prepares random vectors for our more efficient algorithm with outsourced computation. The subscripts of random values are kept the same as they in the corresponding outsourcing algorithm. It includes a static table ST and a dynamic table DT.

- *Preprocessing Step*: Generate n random integers $\alpha_1, \ldots, \alpha_n \in \mathbb{Z}_q$. For $j = 1, \ldots, n$ compute $\beta_{j1} = \alpha_j P_1$ and $\beta_{j2} = \alpha_j P_2$, and store the values of α_j, β_{j1} and β_{j2} in a static table ST. Compute $e(P_1, P_2)$ and store the value in ST.

- *Vector Generation*: When a table DT needs a new entry, it is produced as follows. Randomly generate $S \in \{1, \ldots, n\}$ such that $|S| = k$. For each $j \in S$, randomly select $\chi_j \in \{1, \ldots, h-1\}$ where $h > 1$ is a small integer. Compute

$$x_1 = \sum_{j \in S} \alpha_j \chi_j \bmod q \tag{3}$$

If $x_1 = 0 \bmod q$, start again. Else compute

$$x_1 P_1 = \sum_{j \in S} \chi_j \beta_{j1}. \tag{4}$$

Following the above procedure, compute similarly the vectors (x_3, x_3P_1), (x_4, x_4P_2), (x_7, x_7P_1) and (x_8, x_8P_2). Then randomly select $x_2, x_5, x_6 \in \mathbb{Z}_q^*$ and compute

$$\begin{array}{l} 1.\ x_1^{-1}x_2P_2, \\ 2.\ x_1x_2^{-1}x_5P_1, \\ 3.\ x_1^{-1}x_6P_2, \\ 4.\ e(P_1,P_2)^{x_7x_8}, \\ 5.\ e(P_1,P_2)^{x_5+x_6-x_2}. \end{array} \tag{5}$$

The entry

$$\begin{array}{l} (x_1P_1, x_3P_1, x_1x_2^{-1}x_5P_1, x_7P_1, \\ x_1^{-1}x_2P_2, x_4P_2, x_1^{-1}x_6P_2, x_8P_2, \\ e(P_1,P_2)^{x_7x_8}, e(P_1,P_2)^{x_5+x_6-x_2}). \end{array} \tag{6}$$

are stored in the DT table. On each invocation of *RandA*, an entry is returned and removed from DT. And the DT is replenished with fresh random values in an idle time of a device.

2.5 *RandB*

Our flexible algorithm under the TUP assumption needs the following *RandB* algorithm to prepare random vectors. The subscripts of random values are also kept the same as they in the corresponding outsourcing algorithm.

- *Preprocessing Step*: The table ST is filled in the same way as that in the *RandA* algorithm.

- *Vector Generation*: When a table DT needs a new entry, it is produced as follows. A pair (x_1, x_1P_1) is fast sampled in the same way as the *RandA* algorithm. Then randomly select $x_2, x_3, x_4 \in \mathbb{Z}_q^*$, and compute

$$\begin{array}{l} 1.\ x_1x_2^{-1}x_3P_1, \\ 2.\ x_1^{-1}x_2P_2, \\ 3.\ x_1^{-1}x_4P_2, \\ 4.\ (e(P_1,P_2)^{x_3+x_4-x_2}, \end{array} \tag{7}$$

The entry

$$\begin{array}{l} (x_1P_1, x_1x_2^{-1}x_3P_1, \\ x_1^{-1}x_2P_2, x_1^{-1}x_4P_2 \\ e(P_1,P_2)^{x_3+x_4-x_2}). \end{array} \tag{8}$$

Table 1: Comparison of Precomputations

	Scheme [12]	Algorithm A	Algorithm B
SM	9	3	6
ME	0	2	2
PE	3	0	0
PA	-	$5(k+h-3)$	$2(k+h-3)$

are stored in the DT table. On each invocation of *RandB*, an entry is returned and removed from DT. And the DT is replenished with fresh random values in an idle time of a device.

2.6 Comparisons

We show the precomputations needed for a pairing evaluation in our two algorithms and that in Chen et al.'s algorithm [12]. We name our efficient algorithm in Section 3 as "Algorithm A". The algorithm with outsourced computation in Section 4 is called as "Algorithm B". We then note that for a outsourced pairing evaluation, the *RandA* algorithm is called once in Algorithm A, and the *RandB* algorithm is called twice in Algorithm B, and Chen et al. need three times six-tuple in their algorithm. We use SM to denote a scalar multiplication, ME a modular exponentiation, PE a pairing evaluation and PA a point addition. The numbers of SM and PA include all operations in $\mathbb{G}_1$ and $\mathbb{G}_2$. The value k is the size of a set S in the algorithms *RandA* and *RandB*. According to the parameter sets in [20], the value k is about twenties and the value h is less than 10. It is also noted in [20] that the computation cost of the value X is about $k + h - 3$ group operations. The comparison result is in Table 1. It is obvious that *RandA* and *RandB* algorithms need less computations. Note that the computations in *Preprocessing Step* are not included since they are produced once and used many times.

3. AN EFFICIENT ALGORITHM

This section includes the construction of our "Algorithm A" and its related security model and proofs.

3.1 Construction of Algorithm A

We use $U_i(R,Q) \to e(R,Q)$, $i \in \{1,2\}$, to denote the party U_i taking (R,Q) as inputs and producing $e(R,Q)$ as an output. And we use T to denote a trusted device with limited computation resources. System parameters include $(\mathbb{G}_1, \mathbb{G}_2, \mathbb{G}_T, e, q, P_1, P_2)$ that are defined in Section 2.2. The inputs of algorithm A are points $A \in \mathbb{G}_1$ and $B \in \mathbb{G}_2$. The output of algorithm A is expected to be $e(A,B)$. The algorithm is executed as follows.

- *Init*: T calls *RandA* to fetch random values

$$\begin{array}{l} (x_1P_1, x_3P_1, x_1x_2^{-1}x_5P_1, x_7P_1, \\ x_1^{-1}x_2P_2, x_4P_2, x_1^{-1}x_6P_2, x_8P_2, \\ e(P_1,P_2)^{x_7x_8}, e(P_1,P_2)^{x_5+x_6-x_2}). \end{array} \tag{9}$$

- *Computation*: T queries U_1 in random orders

  1. $U_1(A + x_1P_1, B + x_1^{-1}x_2P_2) \to \alpha_1$;
  2. $U_1(x_3P_1, x_4P_2) \to \alpha_2$;

  Similarly, T queries U_2 in random orders

  1. $U_2(A + x_1x_2^{-1}x_5P_1, -x_1^{-1}x_2P_2) \to \alpha_1'$;

2. $U_2(-x_1P_1, B + x_1^{-1}x_6P_2) \rightarrow \alpha_2'$;
3. $U_2(x_3P_1, x_4P_2) \rightarrow \alpha_3'$;
4. $U_2(x_7P_1, x_8P_2) \rightarrow \alpha_4'$;

- *Recover*: T checks whether

$$\alpha_2 = \alpha_3'$$

and

$$e(P_1, P_2)^{x_7x_8} = \alpha_4'.$$

If the equations hold, it computes

$$o = \alpha_1\alpha_1'\alpha_2'e(P_1, P_2)^{x_5+x_6-x_2}$$

and produces o as an output. Otherwise, it rejects and produces "Error".

3.2 Security Model

Chen et al. [12] proved their algorithm in a security model proposed in [17]. We introduce the model as follows.

An outsourcing model includes three players, a trusted party T, an untrusted party U and an untrusted environment E. The party T has limited computation resource and tries to outsource its computation task to the party U. The party U may be a program written by E and installed on a computing device. The party E produces the program U and interacts indirectly with U through T. The goal of E and U is to learn something interesting about T. The goal of T is to implement an algorithm Alg by interacting with U. An outsourcing implementation of an algorithm is secure if U and E could learn nothing interesting about T's inputs and outputs.

Next is the formal definition of "an algorithm with outsource I/O" [17, 12].

Definition 1. An algorithm with outsource I/O takes five inputs and produces three outputs which are divided to secret, protected and unprotected categories according to the knowledge of U and E. An input or output is secret if neither E nor U knows it. If only E knows an input or output, it is called as protected. Otherwise, an input or output is unprotected. An honest party produces the first three inputs known as honest secret, honest protected, and honest unprotected inputs. The environment E produces the following adversarial protected, and adversarial unprotected inputs. The algorithm produces secret, protected and unprotected outputs.

The security definition of an algorithm with outsource I/O is mainly to ensure that the party E knows nothing about the secret input and output of an implementation T^U even if the party U is produced by the party E.

Definition 2. Let Alg be an algorithm with outsource I/O. An implementation T^U of Alg is secure if:

1. T^U is a correct implementation of Alg;
2. For all probabilistic polynomial time adversaries E and U, there are probabilistic expected polynomial time simulators (S_1, S_2) such that the following pairs of random variables are computationally indistinguishable.
   - Pair One: $EVIEW_{real} \sim EVIEW_{ideal}$ that are views of the party E participating two processes.
     - $EVIEW_{real} = EVIEW_{real}^i$ if $stop^i = TRUE$ where

       $EVIEW_{real}^i = (estate^i, y_p^i, y_u^i)$ and
       $(istate^i, x_{hs}^i, x_{hp}^i, x_{hu}^i) \leftarrow I(1^\kappa, istate^{i-1})$;
       $(estate^i, j^i, x_{ap}^i, x_{au}^i, stop^i) \leftarrow$
       $E(1^\kappa, EVIEW_{real}^{i-1}, x_{hp}^i, x_{hu}^i)$;
       $(tstate^i, ustate^i, y_s^i, y_p^i, y_u^i) \leftarrow$
       $T^{U(ustate^{i-1})}(tstate^{i-1}, x_{hs}^{j^i}, x_{hp}^{j^i}, x_{hu}^{j^i}, x_{ap}^i, x_{au}^i)$.

       The algorithm I is honest to take a security parameter κ and its $i-1$ round internal states $istate^{i-1}$ and to produce its i round honest state and honest inputs $(x_{hs}^i, x_{hp}^i, x_{hu}^i)$ for T^U. The adversary E takes κ, x_{hp}^i, x_{hu}^i and its $i-1$ round view $EVIEW_{real}^{i-1}$ as inputs to produce its i round internal state $estate^i$, the order of honest inputs j^i, the i round adversarial inputs x_{ap}^i and x_{au}^i, and a terminal signal $stop^i$. The adversary U takes its $i-1$ round internal state $ustate^{i-1}$ to interact with T in the round i interaction. The implementation T^U takes the five inputs and the $i-1$ round internal state $tstate^{i-1}$ of T to produce the round i internal states of T and U, and the three round i outputs. All states are initially empty.
     - $EVIEW_{ideal} = EVIEW_{ideal}^i$ if $stop^i = TRUE$ where

       $EVIEW_{ideal}^i = (estate^i, z_p^i, z_u^i)$ and
       $(istate^i, x_{hs}^i, x_{hp}^i, x_{hu}^i) \leftarrow I(1^\kappa, istate^{i-1})$;
       $(estate^i, j^i, x_{ap}^i, x_{au}^i, stop^i) \leftarrow$
       $E(1^\kappa, EVIEW_{ideal}^{i-1}, x_{hp}^i, x_{hu}^i)$;
       $(astate^i, y_s^i, y_p^i, y_u^i) \leftarrow$
       $Alg(astate^{i-1}, x_{hs}^{j^i}, x_{hp}^{j^i}, x_{hu}^{j^i}, x_{ap}^i, x_{au}^i)$;
       $(sstate^i, ustate^i, Y_p^i, Y_u^i, rep^i) \leftarrow$
       $S_1^{U(ustate^{i-1})}(sstate^{i-1}, x_{hp}^{j^i}, x_{hu}^{j^i}, x_{ap}^i, x_{au}^i, y_p^i, y_u^i)$;
       $(z_p^i, z_u^i) = rep^i(Y_p^i, Y_u^i) + (1 - rep^i)(y_p^i, y_u^i)$.

       The algorithms I, E and U are similar to those in the real process. The algorithm Alg takes the five inputs and the $i-1$ round internal state $astate^{i-1}$ of Alg to produce the three outputs and the round i state. The simulated implementation S_1^U takes its $i-1$ round internal state $sstate^{i-1}$ and all the protected and unprotected inputs and outputs to produce the round i internal states of S_1 and U, the simulated protected and unprotected output Y_p^i and Y_u^i and a response signal $rep^i \in \{0, 1\}$. The response signal is used to determine the round i outputs z_p^i and z_u^i for $EVIEW_{ideal}^i$.
   - Pair Two: $UVIEW_{real} \sim UVIEW_{ideal}$ that are views of the party U participating two processes.
     - $UVIEW_{real} = UVIEW_{real}^i$ if $stop^i = TRUE$ where $UVIEW_{real}^i = (ustate^i)$ and the $ustate^i$ is defined in the $EVIEW_{real}^i$ of the above "Pair One" definition.
     - $UVIEW_{ideal} = UVIEW_{ideal}^i$ if $stop^i = TRUE$

where

$UVIEW^i_{ideal} = ustate^i$ and
$(istate^i, x^i_{hs}, x^i_{hp}, x^i_{hu}) \leftarrow I(1^\kappa, istate^{i-1})$;
$(estate^i, j^i, x^i_{ap}, x^i_{au}, stop^i) \leftarrow$
$E(1^\kappa, estate^{i-1}, x^i_{hp}, x^i_{hu}, y^{i-1}_p, y^{i-1}_u)$;
$(astate^i, y^i_s, y^i_p, y^i_u) \leftarrow$
$Alg(astate^{i-1}, x^{j^i}_{hs}, x^{j^i}_{hp}, x^{j^i}_{hu}, x^i_{ap}, x^i_{au})$;
$(sstate^i, ustate^i) \leftarrow$
$S_2^{U(ustate^{i-1})}(sstate^{i-1}, x^{j^i}_{hu}, x^i_{au})$.

The algorithms I and E are the same as those in the $EVIEW^i_{real}$ of the above "Pair One" definition. The algorithm Alg is defined in the same way as that in the $EVIEW^i_{ideal}$ of the above "Pair One" definition. The simulated implementation S_2^U takes its round $i-1$ state and unprotected inputs to produce two round i states for the simulator S_2 and U.

An algorithm with outsource I/O should be more efficient than the algorithm runs in a single device. This is formally defined as "α-Efficient Secure Outsourcing".

Definition 3. A pair of algorithms (T, U) is α-efficient secure outsourcing if T^U is a secure implementation of the algorithm Alg, and if for any input x, the running time of T is no more than an α-multiplicative factor of the running time of Alg.

Since the computation is outsourced to an untrusted party U, it is crucial to check the correctness of the result. This requirement is formally defined as "β-Checkable Secure Outsourcing".

Definition 4. A pair of algorithms (T, U) is β-checkable secure outsourcing if T^U is a secure implementation of the algorithm Alg, and if for any input x, T could detect any deviations of U from U's advertised functionality during the execution of T^U with a probability no less than β.

In summary, an efficient, checkable and secure outsourcing is defined as "(α, β)-Outsource Security".

Definition 5. A pair of algorithms (T, U) has the (α, β)-outsource security property if it is α-efficient and β-checkable secure outsourcing.

According to the number and trustability of the party U, the OMTUP assumption is defined as follows:

Definition 6. If the party U denotes two noninteractive programs (U_1, U_2), and if only one of them U_i, $i \in_R \{1, 2\}$, is malicious, the algorithms (T, U) are implemented under an OMTUP assumption.

3.3 Proofs

THEOREM 1. *The algorithms $(T, (U_1, U_2))$ of "Algorithm A" are an outsource-secure implementation of a pairing evaluation under the OMTUP assumption where the input (A, B) may be honest, secret, honest, protected, or adversarial, protected.*

PROOF. The correctness is obvious from the following equation:

$$\begin{aligned} o &= \alpha_1 \alpha'_1 \alpha'_2 e(P_1, P_2)^{x_5 + x_6 - x_2} \\ &= e(A, B) e(P_1, P_2)^{x_2} e(P_1, P_2)^{-x_5} \\ &\quad e(P_1, P_2)^{-x_6} e(P_1, P_2)^{x_5 + x_6 - x_2} \\ &= e(A, B) \end{aligned} \tag{10}$$

Next, we focus on the security aspect.

- $EVIEW_{real} \sim EVIEW_{ideal}$:

  For a round i, if the input (A, B) is protected or unprotected, the simulator S_1 behaves in the same way as in a real round. Else if (A, B) is an honest, secret input, the simulator S_1 behaves as follows. S_1 randomly selects points $(t_1P_1, t_2P_2, t_3P_1, t_4P_2)$ for U_1 to form random queries. S_1 also randomly selects points $(t_5P_1, t_6P_2, t_7P_2, t_8P_2, t_9P_1, t_{10}P_2)$ for U_2 to form random queries together with t_3P_1, and t_4P_2. More clearly,

  - $U_1(t_1P_1, t_2P_2) \to \alpha_1$;
  - $U_1(t_3P_1, t_4P_2) \to \alpha_2$;
  - $U_2(t_5P_1, t_6P_2) \to \alpha'_1$;
  - $U_2(t_7P_1, t_8P_2) \to \alpha'_2$;
  - $U_2(t_3P_1, t_4P_2) \to \alpha'_3$;
  - $U_2(t_9P_1, t_{10}P_2) \to \alpha'_4$.

  Next, according to the responses of U_1 and U_2, S_1 behaves as follows.

  - If $\alpha_2 \neq \alpha'_3$ or $e(t_9P_1, t_{10}P_2) \neq \alpha'_4$, S_1 produces Y^i_p ="Error", $Y^i_u = \emptyset$ and $rep^i = 1$.
  - If all responses are correct, S_1 sets $Y^i_p = \emptyset$, $Y^i_u = \emptyset$ and $rep^i = 0$.
  - Otherwise, S_1 selects a random value $o_r \in \mathbb{G}_T$ and sets $Y^i_p = o_r$, $Y^i_u = \emptyset$ and $rep^i = 1$.

  For each case, S_1 saves the appropriate states.

  The distributions of inputs in the real and ideal experiments are computationally indistinguishable for U_1 and U_2. In the ideal experiment, the inputs to U_1 or U_2 are chosen uniformly at random. In a real experiment, the inputs to U_1 or U_2 are independently re-randomized. Note that for U_1 or U_2, each input has a new random value that is different to the random values of other inputs.

  If U_1 and U_2 behave honestly in the round i, S_1 uses the Alg to give the correct output that is the same as the output of T^{U_1, U_2}. If U_1 and U_2 are dishonest, with a probability $1/2$, S_1 and T produce "Error". With a probability $1 - 1/2$, S_1 and T are cheated to produce a random output. Note that U_1 and U_2's responses are multiplied by a random value that is known only by T or S_1, and the party E knows nothing about the honest, secret input. Then we conclude that $EVIEW^i_{real} \sim EVIEW^i_{ideal}$, and then $EVIEW_{real} \sim EVIEW_{ideal}$ by a hybrid argument.

- $UVIEW_{real} \sim UVIEW_{ideal}$:

  For a round i, the simulator S_2 uses the same strategy as S_1 to produce random queries for U_1 and U_2, and saves its states and the states of U_1 and U_2. Note that E could not communicate directly with U_1 and U_2 after they are installed on a computing device. So E could not tell U_1 and U_2 that the simulator produces nothing as an output. And U_1, U_2 could not collaborate to test the random inputs since they are noninteractive. Then U_1 and U_2 could not distinguish random queries from real queries for the same reason as they interact with S_1. Then we conclude that $UVIEW^i_{real} \sim UVIEW^i_{ideal}$, and then $UVIEW_{real} \sim UVIEW_{ideal}$ by a hybrid argument.

□

THEOREM 2. *The algorithms $(T,(U_1,U_2))$ of "Algorithm A" are a $(\mathcal{O}(\frac{1}{logq}), 1/2)$-outsource secure implementation of a pairing evaluation under the OMTUP assumption .*

PROOF. The computation of algorithm A includes a call to *RandA*, 4 point additions in $\mathbb{G}_1$ and $\mathbb{G}_2$, and 3 multiplications in $\mathbb{G}_T$. Since we use a dynamic table, the call to *RandA* is a table-lookup operation and the online cost could be omitted. As noted in [12], it takes roughly $\mathcal{O}(logq)$ multiplications to compute a bilinear pair. So the algorithms $(T,(U_1,U_2))$ are a $\mathcal{O}(1/logq)$-efficient secure outsourcing.

U_1 could not distinguish a test query from a real query. Note that we are under the OMTUP assumption, at least one response about the test query is assumed to be honest. So if U_1 is dishonest, it fails with a probability 1/2. U_2 could not distinguish the two test queries from the real queries. One test query is verified by the party T under the OMTUP assumption. The other is verified by the party T with a pre-computed value. So if U_2 is dishonest, it fails with a probability 1/2. □

4. A FLEXIBLE ALGORITHM

This section includes the construction of "Algorithm B" and its related security model and proofs.

4.1 Construction of Algorithm B

Algorithm B uses the same symbols as the algorithm A.

- *Init*: T calls *RandB* two times to produce values

$$(x_1P_1, x_1x_2^{-1}x_3P_1,\\ x_1^{-1}x_2P_2, x_1^{-1}x_4P_2\\ e(P_1,P_2)^{x_3+x_4-x_2})$$

and

$$(x'_1P_1, x'_1x_2'^{-1}x'_3P_1,\\ x_1'^{-1}x'_2P_2, x_1'^{-1}x'_4P_2\\ e(P_1,P_2)^{x'_3+x'_4-x'_2}).$$

It randomly selects a small integer $t \in \{1,\ldots,s\}$.

- *Computation*: T queries U_1 in a random order
  1. $U_1(A+x_1P_1, B+x_1^{-1}x_2P_2) \rightarrow \alpha_1$;
  2. $U_1(tA+x'_1x_2'^{-1}x'_3P_1, -x_1'^{-1}x'_2P_2) \rightarrow \alpha_2$;
  3. $U_1(-x'_1P_1, B+x_1'^{-1}x'_4P_2) \rightarrow \alpha_3$;

  Similarly, T queries U_2 in a random order
  1. $U_2(tA+x'_1P_1, B+x_1'^{-1}x'_2P_2) \rightarrow \alpha'_1$;
  2. $U_2(A+x_1x_2^{-1}x_3P_1, -x_1^{-1}x_2P_2) \rightarrow \alpha'_2$;
  3. $U_2(-x_1P_1, B+x_1^{-1}x_4P_2) \rightarrow \alpha'_3$;
- *Recover*: T computes

$$o = \alpha_1\alpha'_2\alpha'_3e(P_1,P_2)^{x_3+x_4-x_2}$$

and

$$o' = \alpha'_1\alpha_2\alpha_3e(P_1,P_2)^{x'_3+x'_4-x'_2}.$$

If $o^t = o'$ and $o \in \mathbb{G}_T$, T produces o as an output. Otherwise, it rejects and produces "Error".

REMARK 4.1. *According to a comment in [8], the membership test of an output is necessary. It is intended to ensure that a malicious program does not modify a response by multiplying an element of small orders. For some parameter sets [23, 1], the membership test does not need an exponentiation. A more general solution is to outsource the membership test operation. Since U_1 or U_2 knows the order q, we may use a secure public-exponent-secret-base outsourcing algorithm [34] to compute o^q and compare the result with $e(P_1,P_2)$ to determine whether $o \in \mathbb{G}_T$. Note that since q is the order of $\mathbb{G}_T$, the blind factors in [34] should not be selected from $\mathbb{G}_T$.*

We further propose the following wrapper protocol for membership test in the setting of elliptic curve pairings where $\mathbb{G}_T$ is a subgroup of $\mathbb{F}^*_{p^\lambda}$. Note p is a prime number and λ is the embedding degree that is the smallest integer such that $q|p^\lambda-1$. We use a public-exponent-public-base exponentiation outsourcing algorithm [26] as a subroutine.

- *Off-line Phase: T randomly selects $u \in \mathbb{F}^*_{p^\lambda}$ and computes u^q.*
- *On-line Phase:*
  1. *T computes $v = uo$ and calls a public-exponent-public-base outsourcing algorithm to compute v^q.*
  2. *T checks whether $v^q = u^q$. If the equation holds, T believe that $o \in \mathbb{G}_T$.*

The simple protocol adds two online multiplications in $\mathbb{F}^*_{p^\lambda}$. The checkability is the same as that of the subroutine.

4.2 Security Model

Note that all definitions in Section 3.2 except the Definition 6 do not consider the number and trustability of programs, and they could be reused here. To emphasize the TUP assumption, we give the following definition.

Definition 7. If the party U denotes two noninteractive programs (U_1,U_2), and if U_1, U_2 are malicious, the algorithms (T,U) are implemented under an TUP assumption.

4.3 Proofs

THEOREM 3. *The algorithms $(T,(U_1,U_2))$ of "Algorithm B" are an outsource-secure implementation of a pairing evaluation under the TUP assumption where the input (a,u) may be honest, secret, honest, protected, or adversarial, protected.*

PROOF. The correctness is obvious from the following two equations:

$$\begin{aligned} o &= \alpha_1\alpha'_2\alpha'_3e(P_1,P_2)^{x_3+x_4-x_2} \\ &= e(A,B)e(P_1,P_2)^{x_2}e(P_1,P_2)^{x_3+x_4-x_2} \\ &\quad e(P_1,P_2)^{-x_3}e(P_1,P_2)^{-x_4} \\ &= e(A,B) \end{aligned} \tag{11}$$

$$\begin{aligned} o' &= \alpha'_1\alpha_2\alpha_3e(P_1,P_2)^{x'_1+x'_2-1} \\ &= e(A,B)^te(P_1,P_2)^{x'_2}e(P_1,P_2)^{x'_3+x'_4-x'_2} \\ &\quad e(P_1,P_2)^{-x'_3}e(P_1,P_2)^{-x'_4} \\ &= e(A,B)^t \end{aligned} \tag{12}$$

Next, we focus on the security aspect.

- $EVIEW_{real} \sim EVIEW_{ideal}$:

  For a round i, if the input (A, B) is protected or unprotected, the simulator S_1 behaves in the same way as in a real round. Else if (A, B) is an honest, secret input, the simulator S_1 behaves as follows. S_1 randomly selects points $(t_1P_1, t_2P_2, t_3P_1, t_4P_2, t_5P_1, t_6P_2)$ and $t \in \{1, \ldots, s\}$ for U_1 and U_2 to form random queries. More clearly,

  - $U_1(t_1P_1, t_2P_2) \rightarrow \alpha_1$;
  - $U_1(tt_3P_1, t_4P_2) \rightarrow \alpha_2$;
  - $U_1(tt_5P_1, t_6P_2) \rightarrow \alpha_3$;
  - $U_2(tt_1P_1, t_2P_2) \rightarrow \alpha'_1$;
  - $U_2(t_3P_1, t_4P_2) \rightarrow \alpha'_2$;
  - $U_2(t_5P_1, t_6P_2) \rightarrow \alpha'_3$;

  Next, according to the responses of U_1 and U_2, S_1 behaves as follows.

  - If $(\alpha_1\alpha'_2\alpha'_3)^t \neq \alpha'_1\alpha_2\alpha_3$, S_1 produces Y_p^i ="Error", $Y_u^i = \emptyset$ and $rep^i = 1$.
  - If all responses are correct, S_1 sets $Y_p^i = \emptyset$, $Y_u^i = \emptyset$ and $rep^i = 0$.
  - Otherwise, S_1 selects a random value $o_r \in \mathbb{G}_T$ and sets $Y_p^i = o_r$, $Y_u^i = \emptyset$ and $rep^i = 1$.

  For each case, S_1 saves the appropriate states.

  The distributions of inputs in the real and ideal experiments are computationally indistinguishable for U_1 and U_2. In the ideal experiment, the inputs to U_1 or U_2 are chosen uniformly at random. In a real experiment, the inputs to U_1 or U_2 are independently rerandomized. Note that for U_1 or U_2, each input has a new random value that is different to the random values of other inputs.

  If U_1 and U_2 behave honestly in the round i, S_1 uses the Alg to give the correct output that is the same as the output of T^{U_1,U_2}. If U_1 and U_2 are dishonest, with a probability about $(1-1/3s)^2$, S_1 and T produce "Error". With a probability about $1/3s(2-1/3s)$, S_1 and T are cheated to produce a random output. Note that in a real experiment, U_1 and U_2's responses are multiplied by a random value that is known only by T, and the party E knows nothing about the honest, secret input (A, B). In an ideal experiment, U_1 and U_2's responses are checked by the simulator. If their responses pass the check equation and are not correct, a random output is then produced, which means that U_1 or(and) U_2 has(have) guessed the value t and the order of inputs, and returns wrong results. Then we conclude that $EVIEW^i_{real} \sim EVIEW^i_{ideal}$, and then $EVIEW_{real} \sim EVIEW_{ideal}$ by a hybrid argument.

- $UVIEW_{real} \sim UVIEW_{ideal}$:

  For a round i, the simulator S_2 uses the same strategy as S_1 to produce random queries for U_1 and U_2, and saves its states and the states of U_1 and U_2. Note that E could not communicate directly with U_1 and U_2 after they are installed on a computing device. So E could not tell U_1 and U_2 that the simulator produces nothing as an output. And U_1, U_2 could not collaborate to obtain extra information about the inputs since they are noninteractive. Then U_1 and U_2 could not distinguish random inputs from real inputs. Then we conclude that $UVIEW^i_{real} \sim UVIEW^i_{ideal}$, and then $UVIEW_{real} \sim UVIEW_{ideal}$ by a hybrid argument.

□

THEOREM 4. *The algorithms $(T, (U_1, U_2))$ of "Algorithm B" are a $(\mathcal{O}(\frac{logs}{logq}), (1-1/3s)^2)$-outsource secure implementation of a pairing evaluation.*

PROOF. Algorithm B includes two calls to the *RandB* algorithm, and $\mathcal{O}(logt)$ point additions and $\mathcal{O}(logt)$ modular multiplications. We use a dynamic table and the calls to *RandB* are table-lookup operations. We then claim that the online computation is about $\mathcal{O}(logs)$ since $t \in \{1, \ldots, s\}$. As we noted in Theorem 2, it takes roughly $\mathcal{O}(logq)$ multiplications to compute a bilinear pair. So the algorithms $(T, (U_1, U_2))$ are a $\mathcal{O}(logs/logq)$-efficient secure outsourcing.

We assume two malicious U_1 and U_2 without interactions. The checking equation $o^t = o'$ could be written as

$$\begin{aligned} & (e(P_1, P_2)^{x_3+x_4-x_2})^t \alpha_1^t \alpha_2^{-1} \alpha_3^{-1} \\ = \; & e(P_1, P_2)^{x'_3+x'_4-x'_2} \alpha'_1 \alpha'^{-t}_2 \alpha'^{-t}_3. \end{aligned} \quad (13)$$

In the right side of the equation (13), if U_2 wants to change α'_2 or α'_3 and to keep the equation holding, it should know the value t. In the left side, if U_1 wants to change the product of $\alpha_2\alpha_3$ and to keep the equation holding, it should know the value t. If U_2 changes only α'_1 and U_1 changes only the product of $\alpha_2\alpha_3$ and they keep the equation holding, then the product of $\alpha'_1\alpha_2\alpha_3$ keeps unchanged and the output is correct.

Now suppose U_i, $i \in_R \{1, 2\}$ guesses a correct value t. Considering U_1, it now has to identify the query to produce α_1 out of the three queries. Since the inputs to U_1 are in a random order, the probability is 1/3 for U_1 to identify the query. Similarly, U_2 has to identify α'_1 with a probability 1/3.

In summary, the chance for U_1 or U_2 to change their outputs and to keep the verification equation holding is to guess the value t and the inputting order correctly. The probability of successful checking is then $(1-1/3s)^2$. □

5. COMPARISON

We show two tables to compare the efficiency and security properties between our algorithms and two up-to-date algorithms [8, 12]. The "Alg. [8]" refers to their main protocol for public points outsourcing. They propose a general conversion for secure bilinear pairing delegation. That conversion adds 2 scalar multiplications and 1 modular exponentiation, which leads to a more inefficient implementation. For "Algorithm B", we set $s = 4$ to give a concrete example about computations and computations. Note again the value s is configurable. The symbols SM, ME and PA are defined in Section 2.6 denoting a scalar multiplication, a modular exponentiation and a point addition. The symbol MT denotes a membership test operation, and MM a modular multiplication. From Table 2, it is obvious that our "Algorithm A" has the best efficiency.

Table 3 shows the properties of different algorithms. It is obvious the algorithm in [8] is under a convenient OUP assumption and has the best checkability. However, the works

Table 2: Efficiency Comparison of Up-to-date Algorithms

	SM	ME	MT	PA	MM
Alg. [8]	2	1	1	2	1
Alg. [12]	0	0	0	5	4
Alg. A	0	0	0	4	3
Alg. B	0	0	1	$\mathcal{O}(logs)$	$\mathcal{O}(logs)$
Alg. B ($s = 4$)	0	0	1	10	8

Table 3: Properties Comparison of Up-to-date Algorithms

	Assumptions	Secrecy	Checkability
Alg. [8]	OUP	No	1
Alg. [12]	OMTUP	YES	1/2
Alg. A	OMTUP	YES	1/2
Alg. B	TUP	YES	$(1 - 1/3s)^2$
Alg. B ($s = 4$)	TUP	YES	0.84

in [25, 24] shows that their algorithm is meaningful for only some parameters. Comparatively, our "Algorithm B" shows an alternative approach to balance the security properties and efficiency. The algorithm needs no scalar multiplications or modular exponentiations as the algorithm in [12]. And the client needs not to check the vendor of a program to satisfy the OMTUP assumption. And a client could set s larger to get a better checkability at the cost of more computations. So we claim the algorithm B as a more flexible algorithm. If $s = 4$, the probability to check a result is about 0.84. Note that the "Algorithm B" is under the TUP assumption. If the algorithm [12] is under the same TUP assumption, their checkability is about 0.25.

6. CONCLUSION

This paper showed two algorithms for bilinear pairing outsourcing. One is more efficient than the state-of-the-art algorithms. The other is more flexible to be deployed in a really two-malicious-program environment, and enables an approach to balance the computation cost and the checkability. It also showed two pre-computation algorithms to compute off-line random vectors. Further, we are implementing our algorithms for low power devices to study the computation, memory and communication costs in practice with real world examples.

7. ACKNOWLEDGMENTS

This work was supported in part by the National Natural Science Foundation of China under No. 61379154 and U1135001, Huawei Grant YB2013120027, and US National Science Foundation under grant CNS-1262277.

8. REFERENCES

[1] Paulo S L. M. Barreto and Michael Naehrig. Pairing-friendly elliptic curves of prime order. In Bart Preneel and Stafford Tavares, editors, *Selected Areas in Cryptography*, pages 319–331, 2006.

[2] Chevallier-Mames Benoit, Coron Jean-Sebastien, McCullagh Noel, Naccache David, and Scott Michael. Secure delegation of elliptic-curve pairing. Cryptology ePrint Archive, Report 2005/150, 2005. http://eprint.iacr.org/.

[3] Kang Bo Gyeong, Lee Moon Sung, and Park Je Hong. Efficient delegation of pairing computation. Cryptology ePrint Archive, Report 2005/259, 2005. http://eprint.iacr.org/.

[4] Dan Boneh and Matt Franklin. Identity-based encryption from the weil pairing. In Joe Kilian, editor, *Advances in Cryptology - CRYPTO 2001*, volume 2139 of *Lecture Notes in Computer Science*, pages 213–229. Springer Berlin Heidelberg, 2001.

[5] Dan Boneh, Ben Lynn, and Hovav Shacham. Short signatures from the weil pairing. *Journal of Cryptology*, 17(4):297–319, 2004.

[6] Victor Boyko, Marcus Peinado, and Ramarathnam Venkatesan. Speeding up discrete log and factoring based schemes via precomputations. In Kaisa Nyberg, editor, *Advances in Cryptology - EUROCRYPT'98*, pages 221–235, 1998.

[7] Sĺębastien Canard, Iwen Coisel, Julien Devigne, Cĺęcilia Gallais, Thomas Peters, and Olivier Sanders. Toward generic method for server-aided cryptography. In Sihan Qing, Jianying Zhou, and Dongmei Liu, editors, *Information and Communications Security*, volume 8233 of *Lecture Notes in Computer Science*, pages 373–392. Springer International Publishing, 2013.

[8] Sĺębastien Canard, Julien Devigne, and Olivier Sanders. Delegating a pairing can be both secure and efficient. In Ioana Boureanu, Philippe Owesarski, and Serge Vaudenay, editors, *Applied Cryptography and Network Security*, pages 549–565, 2014.

[9] David Chaum and TorbenPryds Pedersen. Wallet databases with observers. In ErnestF Brickell, editor, *Advances in Cryptology - CRYPTO'92*, volume 740 of *Lecture Notes in Computer Science*, pages 89–105. Springer Berlin Heidelberg, 1993.

[10] Xiaofeng Chen, Jin Li, Jianfeng Ma, Qiang Tang, and Wenjing Lou. New algorithms for secure outsourcing of modular exponentiations. In Sara Foresti, Moti Yung, and Fabio Martinelli, editors, *Computer Security ĺC ESORICS 2012*, pages 541–556, 2012.

[11] Xiaofeng Chen, Jin Li, Jianfeng Ma, Qiang Tang, and Wenjing Lou. New algorithms for secure outsourcing of modular exponentiations. *Ieee Transactions on Parallel And Distributed Systems*, 25(9):2386–2396, 2014.

[12] Xiaofeng Chen, Willy Susilo, Jin Li, Duncan S. Wong, Jianfeng Ma, Shaohua Tang, and Qiang Tang. Efficient algorithms for secure outsourcing of bilinear pairings. *Theoretical Computer Science*, (In Press), 2014.

[13] Benoit Chevallier-Mames, Jean-Sĺębastien Coron, Noel McCullagh, David Naccache, and Michael Scott. Secure delegation of elliptic-curve pairing. In Dieter Gollmann, Jean-Louis Lanet, and Julien Iguchi-Cartigny, editors, *Smart Card Research and Advanced Application*, pages 24–35, 2010.

[14] JaeCha Choon and Jung Hee Cheon. An identity-based signature from gap diffie-hellman groups. In YvoG Desmedt, editor, *Public Key Cryptography - PKC 2003*, volume 2567 of *Lecture*

Notes in Computer Science, pages 18–30. Springer Berlin Heidelberg, 2002.

[15] Sherman S. M. Chow, Man Ho Au, and Willy Susilo. Server-aided signatures verification secure against collusion attack. *Information Security Technical Report*, 17(3):46–57, 2013.

[16] Marc Girault and David Lefranc. Server-aided verification: Theory and practice. In Bimal Roy, editor, *Advances in Cryptology - ASIACRYPT 2005*, pages 605–623, 2005.

[17] Susan Hohenberger and Anna Lysyanskaya. How to securely outsource cryptographic computations. In Joe Kilian, editor, *Theory of Cryptography*, pages 264–282, 2005.

[18] ChaeHoon Lim and PilJoong Lee. Server(prover/signer)-aided verification of identity proofs and signatures. In LouisC Guillou and Jean-Jacques Quisquater, editors, *Advances in Cryptology - EUROCRYPT'95*, volume 921 of *Lecture Notes in Computer Science*, pages 64–78. Springer Berlin Heidelberg, 1995.

[19] Tsutomu Matsumoto, Koki Kato, and Hideki Imai. Speeding up secret computations with insecure auxiliary devices. In Shafi Goldwasser, editor, *Advances in Cryptology - CRYPTOąŕ 88*, volume 403 of *Lecture Notes in Computer Science*, pages 497–506. Springer New York, 1990.

[20] PhongQ Nguyen, IgorE Shparlinski, and Jacques Stern. Distribution of modular sums and the security of the server aided exponentiation. In Kwok-Yan Lam, Igor Shparlinski, Huaxiong Wang, and Chaoping Xing, editors, *Cryptography and Computational Number Theory*, volume 20 of *Progress in Computer Science and Applied Logic*, pages 331–342. Birkhauser Basel, 2001.

[21] Tsang Patrick P., Chow Sherman S. M., and Smith Sean W. Batch pairing delegation. In *Proceedings of the Security 2nd international conference on Advances in information and computer security*, pages 74–90, Nara, Japan, 2007.

[22] Kui Ren, Cong Wang, and Qian Wang. Security challenges for the public cloud. *Internet Computing, IEEE*, 6(1):69–73, 2012.

[23] Michael Scott. Unbalancing pairing-based key exchange protocols. Cryptology ePrint Archive, Report 2013/688, 2013. http://eprint.iacr.org/.

[24] Michael Scott, Neil Costigan, and Wesam Abdulwahab. Implementing cryptographic pairings on smartcards. In Louis Goubin and Mitsuru Matsui, editors, *Cryptographic Hardware and Embedded Systems - CHES 2006*, pages 134–147, 2006.

[25] AnaHelena Slćnchez and Francisco RodrÍłguez-HenrÍłquez. Neon implementation of an attribute-based encryption scheme. In Michael Jacobson, Michael Locasto, Payman Mohassel, and Reihaneh Safavi-Naini, editors, *Applied Cryptography and Network Security*, pages 322–338, 2013.

[26] Marten Van Dijk, Dwaine Clarke, Blaise Gassend, G. Edward Suh, and Srinivas Devadas. Speeding up exponentiation using an untrusted computational resource. *Designs, Codes and Cryptography*, 39(2):253–273, 2006.

[27] Cong Wang, Kui Ren, and Jia Wang. Secure and practical outsourcing of linear programming in cloud computing. In *INFOCOM, 2011 Proceedings IEEE*, pages 820–828, 2011.

[28] Yujue Wang, Qianhong Wu, DuncanS Wong, Bo Qin, ShermanS M. Chow, Zhen Liu, and Xiao Tan. Securely outsourcing exponentiations with single untrusted program for cloud storage. In Miroslaw Kutylowski and Jaideep Vaidya, editors, *Computer Security - ESORICS 2014*, pages 326–343, 2014.

[29] Zhiwei Wang, Licheng Wang, Yixian Yang, and Zhengming Hu. Comment on wu et al.'s server-aided verification signature schemes. *International Journal of Network Security*, 10(3):238–240, 2010.

[30] Wei Wu, Yi Mu, Willy Susilo, and Xinyi Huang. Server-aided verification signatures: Definitions and new constructions. In Joonsang Baek, Feng Bao, Kefei Chen, and Xuejia Lai, editors, *Provable Security*, pages 141–155, 2008.

[31] Wei Wu, Yi Mu, Willy Susilo, and Xinyi Huang. Provably secure server-aided verification signatures. *Computers & Mathematics with Applications*, 61(7):1705–1723, 2011.

[32] Zhen Xu, Cong Wang, Qian Wang, Kui Ren, and Lingyu Wang. Proof-carrying cloud computation: The case of convex optimization. In *INFOCOM, 2013 Proceedings IEEE*, pages 610–614, 2013.

[33] Andrew C. Yao. Protocols for secure computations. In *Foundations of Computer Science, 1982. SFCS '08. 23rd Annual Symposium on*, pages 160–164, 1982.

[34] Fangguo Zhang, Xu Ma, and Shengli Liu. Efficient computation outsourcing for inverting a class of homomorphic functions. *Information Sciences*, 286(1):19–28, 2014.

On Information-theoretic Measures for Quantifying Privacy Protection of Time-series Data

Chris Y.T. Ma
Advanced Digital Sciences Center
Singapore
chris.ma@adsc.com.sg

David K.Y. Yau
Singapore University of Technology and Design
Advanced Digital Sciences Center
Singapore
david_yau@sutd.edu.sg

ABSTRACT

Privacy protection of time-series data, such as traces of household electricity usage reported by smart meters, is of much practical importance. Solutions are available to improve data privacy by perturbing clear traces to produce noisy versions visible to adversaries, e.g., in battery-based load hiding (BLH) against non-intrusive load monitoring (NILM). A foundational task for research progress in the area is the definition of privacy measures that can truly evaluate the effectiveness of proposed protection methods. It is a difficult problem since resilience against any attack algorithms known to the designer is inconclusive, given that adversaries could discover or indeed already know stronger algorithms for attacks. A more basic measure is information-theoretic in nature, which quantifies the inherent information available for exploitation by an adversary, independent of *how* the adversary exploits it or indeed any assumed computational limitations of the adversary. In this paper, we analyze information-theoretic measures for privacy protection and apply them to several existing protection methods against NILM. We argue that although these measures abstract away the details of attacks, the *kind* of information the adversary considers plays a key role in the evaluation, and that a new measure of *offline conditional entropy* is better suited for evaluating the privacy of perturbed real-world time-series data, compared with other existing measures.

Categories and Subject Descriptors

E.3 [**Data**]: Data Encryption

Keywords

Privacy Protection; Privacy Measure; Conditional Entropy; Correlated Time-series

1. INTRODUCTION

Privacy protection of time-series data is of much practical importance. Such data includes mobility traces in location-based services [40], or household electricity consumption measured by smart meters for demand response [7]. If users' privacy is not assured in these applications, they will not opt in as participants. Or if they do, then should the leak of sensitive information actually happen, damaging outcomes may ensue such as abuse of consumer rights or lawsuits [32, 47].

In view of the privacy problem, solutions are available that perturb a clear trace of time-series data to produce a noisy version, and make sure that any would-be adversaries will have access to the noisy version only [22]. The extent of perturbation may be constrained by the capability of the defense mechanism. This is the case, for example, in battery-based load hiding (BLH) [21, 23, 27, 46] of smart meter reports against non-intrusive load monitoring (NILM) [4, 11, 31, 43], whose privacy concerns are well documented [32, 47].

In other situations, the perturbation is constrained by the need to preserve enough accuracy of the data for various application needs. This is the case, for example, in inferring congestion index of roads as a location-based service (LBS) [8]. When the accuracy of positioning is low, congestion may be inferred at a wrong location.

While the design of specific privacy protection is interesting, a foundational task for advances in the area is the definition of proper measures that can truly assess the privacy of the protection. Some measures focus on protecting the identity of a participant without considering the information content of the corresponding data. One example is k-anonymity [41], which although widely employed, is unsatisfactory in various semantic aspects. For example, k-anonymity ignores the diversity of data [26], i.e., hiding a data point among k other identical data points is of dubious usefulness. Some patches, such as l-diversity [26] and m-invariance [45], have been applied to k-anonymity to address the problems.

An alternative information-theoretic viewpoint is to measure directly the amount of original information that is contained in the noisy data, i.e., the common information between them. The idea is that if the amount of private information available for learning in the noisy data is small, then the privacy loss will be bounded by that amount, independent of *how* the adversary operates. Hence, if a protection method satisfies privacy in this information-theoretic sense, the privacy is strong in that there is no danger that an attack will be discovered to breach the protection. This property is appealing compared with resilience proved against specific attacks [48], since we cannot rule out the possibility of stronger attacks. It is also appealing compared with resilience proved assuming computational limitations of the

ASIA CCS'15, April 14–17, 2015, Singapore.

http://dx.doi.org/10.1145/2714576.2714577.

adversary, such as the hardness of factoring the product of two large prime numbers in RSA cryptography [38].

If elements in a data trace are uncorrelated temporally, information-theoretic privacy can be given by the concept of *mutual information* [2], denoted by $I(X;Y)$, where X and Y are random variables corresponding to the clear and noisy data distributions, respectively. Real-world time-series exhibit obvious correlations in time, however. For example, a household's electricity consumption at time t is likely to be similar to the consumption at $t+\delta$, for small δ; a user's locations at t and $t+\delta$ are likely to be close as well. In general, adversaries will be able to exploit these correlations in privacy attacks.

Hence, even though information-theoretic measures abstract away the operational details of attacks, its use still raises questions about the *kinds* of information the adversary is assumed to use in the attacks. Prior work has taken initial steps in accounting for information present in the temporal correlations of data. Specifically, Yang *et al.* consider the mutual information between distributions of *pairs* of consecutive data points as symbols [46]. Their construct is Markov-like in that a data point is assumed to depend on the immediately preceding data point only.

Typically, real-world data exhibits much more persistent temporal correlation than Markov, i.e., the autocorrelation decreases slowly with the time shift [10, Chapter 5]. In this paper, we focus on the protection of smart meter readings from a household that support emerging demand-response smart grid applications. In this case, the readings collected by a smart meter, as shown in Fig. 1, have long temporal correlation. How this feature impacts privacy protection of time-series data has not been studied in a systematic manner. In this paper, we undertake such a study.

We investigate the following four sets of privacy measures that subsume state-of-the-art measures used in prior work to evaluate BLH or more general time-series data:

- A baseline definition of mutual information (MI) uses individual elements in a time-series as symbols [2]. This baseline has been widely employed in privacy research [33, 42, 44], but it does not account for the data's temporal correlation. A recent definition of MI considers two consecutive data points as symbols [46], which provides an initial limited attempt to incorporate the effects of correlated data. In this paper, our goal is to characterize the temporal correlation comprehensively. Hence, we evaluate a general notion of MI that uses length-k sequences of data points as symbols, for any integer $k > 0$.

- Koo *et al.* adapt the baseline MI to a normalized version (NMI) [23]. The intent is to measure the *fraction* of information that is available, rather than the absolute amount. We evaluate this variational view also for our parameterized MI measure above.

- *Conditional entropy* (CE) has been proposed for online prediction problems, e.g., optimal paging of a mobile phone based on its location history [6]. The length of the last k, $k > 0$, data points used as history to guide the prediction is a parameter whose choice should depend on the complexity (i.e., entropy) of the phone's movement patterns. We adapt this measure to privacy protection. In this case, since we are interested in how much the noisy trace tells us about the clear trace, our new definition of this measure conditions the entropy of the clear data on the *noisy* data, which is different from the original definition.

- Beyond CE, we propose a new *offline conditional entropy* (OCE) measure to account for the full information available to the adversary when he tries to compromise the privacy of some clear data points. Specifically, the adversary may exploit any range of revealed noisy data points as guiding information. Without loss of generality, we measure the entropy of a clear ("present") data point, conditional on the corresponding noisy data point, as well as the preceding ("historical") k and subsequent ("future") k noisy data points, where $k \geq 0$.

We compare the four privacy measures over different values of k, in order to expose the impact of the temporal correlation. We use a balance of synthetic and real data to ensure useful comparisons.

First, we postulate axiomatic properties of desirable privacy measures in their ability to bring out the true information content of time-series data. We test the four proposed privacy measures against the axiomatic properties, by subjecting them to synthetic test data generated by data models specifically designed to ensure the information content. Our major findings are:

- We use an automaton data model (Sec. 6.3) to show that, because of the original prediction intent of conditional entropy (CE), it fails to account for all available information in a privacy attack. In contrast, the MI, NMI, and OCE measures do not suffer from this limitation, meaning that for a large enough k, they can account for all information in the noisy trace that can be exploited by the adversary.

- Although the MI measure can encompass all the available information, its values across k are not comparable. This is because, as k grows, MI grows inherently due to the increased diversity of longer symbols, so that the quantification of information loss occurs over a moving basis. Moreover, using NMI as a relative information measure does not solve the problem. In either case, because of inherent increase of symbol diversity with k, MI or NMI does not satisfy the axiomatic property that it should stabilize at some k when applied to time-series data generated by an order-l Markov model (Sec. 6.4).

- Unlike the MI and NMI measures, OCE always measures the uncertainty of clear data points conditional on the noisy data. Its meaning is therefore not affected by k. Specifically, when it is applied to the protection of data where the relationship between the noisy data points and the clear data point can be described by an order-l Markov model (Sec. 6.3), it quantifies successfully marginal gains in the adversary's knowledge as k grows, and stabilizes at the smallest k sufficient to fully capture the order of information in the noisy traces.

- In summary, OCE appears to be superior in that it satisfies our axiomatic properties of desirable privacy measures.

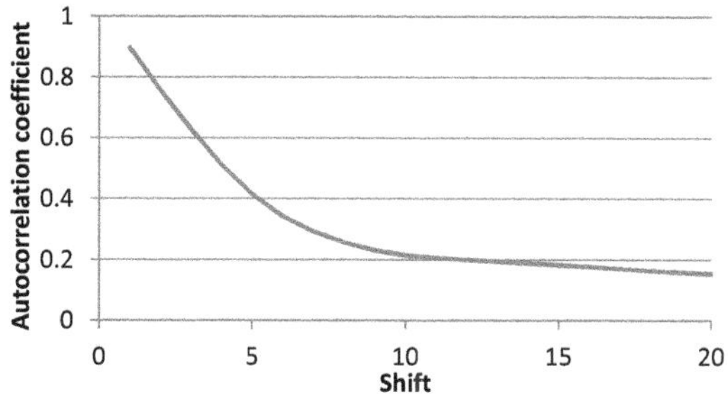

Figure 1: Auto-correlation coefficient as a function of shifting in time (minutes), which measures the correlation of data in the temporal dimension. Smart meter readings collected from a household in the U.K. [36] in one minute intervals for one year.

Second, we test the proposed privacy measures using data from the application domain of BLH protected smart meter readings against NILM. We focus on MI vs. OCE. In particular, MI has been widely used in the existing literature for privacy quantification [33, 42, 44, 46]. We study foremost BLH protection methods including best-effort (BE) [21], non-intrusive load leveling (NILL) [27], and lazy stepping (LS) [46]. We show that, for our focus domain of temporally correlated time-series data, it is crucial for the measures to expose the scope of information used in the attack. Specifically, a good privacy measure must be able to quantify how the privacy protection weakens as the adversary exploits progressively larger scopes of data correlation present in real-world smart meter data. This requires a measure whose meaning remains constant as k changes, which is not satisfied by conventional MI but by the proposed OCE measure. Our quantitative results show that although LS becomes weaker as k increases, it remains better than BE and NILL over the range of k that is relevant for smart meter data in the real world.

We also study a novel and realistic attack on BLH, in which the adversary compromises the control software running on a smoothing battery system, in order to expose private usage of household appliances through a covert channel of normal smart meter readings. Our attack mimics the control steps in the LS algorithm with a slight modification to leak important physical state information of the household electrical system at strategic moments. The success of the attack hinges on exploiting temporal correlations naturally occurring in real-world smart meter data, which again substantiates the importance of accounting for the correlation comprehensively by privacy measures, beyond prior state-of-the-art measures used to evaluate BLH. Specifically, our result shows that the attack appears ineffective at small k, and its damage only becomes evident when measured by our proposed OCE measure for a big enough k.

The remainder of the paper is organized as follows. We define the privacy protection problem in Sec. 2. We present related work in Sec. 3. In Sec. 4 we discuss the importance of collecting smart meter data readings, its privacy concerns, and state-of-the-art mitigation strategies for the concerns. In Sec. 5 we give details of the four privacy measures used in our study. We test these measures in Sec. 6 against various protection strategies for data traces generated by synthetic models designed to ensure specific information content of the data. In Sec. 7 we test the privacy measures against BLH-protected smart meter readings, either collected in the real world or generated by realistic, validated smart-meter data models. Our results quantify the importance of temporal correlations that are present in real or realistic data traces. Sec. 8 concludes.

2. PROBLEM DEFINITION

We consider the problem of quantifying the protection of time-series data by different privacy-preserving strategies. This is an important problem because of existing and growing practice to collect time-series data for supporting applications such as smart-meter enabled demand-response and location-based services for mobile nodes. To address clear privacy concerns, different perturbation strategies have been proposed to cloak the time-series data before making it available to the service provider. A proper privacy measure to quantify the true effectiveness of the protection is crucial, to avoid embarrassing scenarios of inadvertent data reidentification [41].

We let a trace of clear time-series data be a stochastic process $\mathcal{X} = \{X_i\}$, where i is the time index and the X_i's form a sequence of random variables, and let $\mathcal{X}^l$ be the stochastic process in which the symbols are the set of l consecutive data points in $\mathcal{X}$, $l > 0$. We let the corresponding noisy time-series data generated by a privacy-preserving strategy be a stochastic process $\mathcal{Y} = \{Y_i\}$, where i is the time index and the Y_i's form a sequence of random variables, and let $\mathcal{Y}^l$ be the stochastic process in which the symbols are the set of l consecutive data points in $\mathcal{Y}$, $l > 0$. We wish to design an information-theoretic measure to compare the similarity between $\mathcal{X}$ and $\mathcal{Y}$, in which the *dissimilarity* between the two processes represents the level of privacy protection provided by a privacy-preserving strategy. As discussed in Sec. 1, an information-theoretic approach avoids the need to assume specific attack strategies or computational power of the adversary. As temporal correlations naturally occur in time-series data, which can be exploited by an adversary to infer the private information, it is crucial for a privacy measure to expose the impact of such correlations.

Notice that we consider the information content between $\mathcal{X}$ and $\mathcal{Y}$, i.e., the clear time-series data and its corresponding perturbed version generated by a privacy-preserving strategy. In applications where a number of anonymous users participated in the data collection process, the comparison between clear data and its corresponding perturbed version may be seen as a worst case scenario where the adversary has already de-anonymized the traces, and the perturbation of data by the strategy is a last line of defense. This worst case scenario is realistic, however, because in certain applications, a few pieces of side information (such as a few time-location pairs of victims in trajectory tracing) can already de-anonymize the traces [13, 25].

3. RELATED WORK

Different privacy notions [24, 26, 41, 45] have been used to guide the publication of databases of private data. These results demonstrate resilience (i.e., small leaks of information) against specific known attacks. They are inconclusive, however, since we cannot rule out the existence of stronger attacks.

Furthermore, the kind of information used by a measure to quantify privacy greatly affects the effectiveness of the measure. It has been shown that k-anonymization [41], which is an information-theoretic measure of protecting the identity of a participant by ensuring the size of an anonymity set, does not capture the diversity of the anonymity set [26]. To address the issue, l-diversity [26] has been proposed. The attempt is not fully successful, however. Li and Li [24] show that l-diversity fails to ensure that the diversity in a generalized class is similar to that of the original data. This may allow the adversary to gain knowledge of a victim's attribute, though perhaps not its exact value. They then propose a t-closeness notion [24], which ensures that the distance of a sensitive attribute's distribution in one class is no more than a threshold t from that of the whole table. Xiao and Tao [45] further propose m-invariance to limit the risk of privacy disclosure in data re-publications, since potential correlations among snapshots of data in different publication instances may be used to derive sensitive information. The long sequence of attempts to improve the series of measures reflects the difficulties of getting these measures right.

The trajectory of mobile nodes in location-based services constitutes an important kind of private time-series data, and its protection has been widely studied [5, 14, 17, 18, 19, 20, 30]. One approach is to mix requests from different anonymized users together by a trusted anonymizing proxy [5]. Another approach is to reduce the spatial/temporal granularity of the location information made available to the service provider while achieving satisfactory service performance [14, 17, 18]. Henrici and Muller [19] propose the use of one-time identifiers for privacy protection. Hoh *et al.* [20] devise a protection strategy to release user data only when certain privacy constraints are met. Meyerowitz and Choudhury [30] propose to send fake requests alongside real requests, to reduce the service provider's ability to trace a mobile node over time. The authors of [17, 18] quantify the performance of their privacy protection by showing that k-anonymity is satisfied, while the authors of [5, 20, 30] quantify the performance by measuring the uncertainty of the adversary in tracking a victim.

Differential privacy [15] is considered a strong notion of privacy and is of much current interest in privacy research [16, 28]. It guides the design of a query mechanism for a dataset, so that the impact of any specific data point to an *aggregate* query result will be almost unnoticeable to a curious adversary. It also ensures that one cannot infer reliably whether specific individuals participate in the dataset. Since differential privacy is about hiding an individual in aggregates, it is mainly useful for statistical results. For example, it allows aggregators [29] in smart grid demand-response [7] to obtain the total electricity consumption of users in real time, to enable control decisions such as load curtailment [29], without revealing the individual consumption [1, 9, 34, 39]. However, differential privacy is not applicable to the protection of individual traces that is a required solution against NILM attacks.

Against NILM, a popular approach to protecting a consumption trace is battery-based load hiding (BLH) [21, 23, 27, 46]. In the approach, a household makes use of the charging/discharging of a local battery to smooth the demand seen by a smart meter, which reports its measurements to an independent system operator (ISO). The smoothing, whose extent is constrained by the battery capacity, hides discrete jumps in the data which might reveal when a household turns on/off individual appliances, for example. Existing measures that quantify the goodness of the protection by different similarity notions between the clear and protected traces include relative feature mass [27], entropy [21, 27], and mutual information [23, 46]. All these measures, however, do not consider temporal correlations of data in the traces. This omission could easily lead to wrong conclusions.

Rebollo-Monedero *et al.* [35] propose a general framework for measuring privacy as an adversary's estimation error. For estimating single data points, this framework encompasses notions such as k-anonymity, differential privacy, and mutual information. For estimating sequences of data points that are i.i.d., they show that the estimation error is related to the asymptotic equipartition property (AEP) [12] that there exists a typical subset of sequences almost certain to occur. AEP generalizes to entropy rates [3] for stationary ergodic sequences. They do not provide an explicit and systematic account of how temporal correlation in application data sequences may impact the privacy protection. Our work provides understanding of how correlated data in these sequences can be used to infer any specific single data points.

4. PROTECTING PRIVACY OF SMART METER READINGS

We now discuss the specific problem of protecting smart meter readings as temporally correlated time-series data. We first review major existing BLH algorithms. We then present a novel covert-channel attack on the BLH algorithm, which will expose the importance of privacy quantification under long temporal correlation.

4.1 Battery-based Load Hiding Algorithms

We briefly review three foremost BLH algorithms in the literature. In the discussion, we let $d(t)$ be the real load (measured in power) from a household at time t, $e(t)$ be the corresponding regulated load after being smoothed out by the battery (i.e., the load measured by the smart meter), $\beta_c > 0$ be the maximum battery charging rate (in power), and $\beta_d > 0$ be the maximum battery discharging rate.

Best Effort (BE) [21]
This algorithm tries to maintain $e(t)$ by charging the battery if the real load drops below the previously measured value, i.e., $d(t) < e(t-1)$, and the charging rate of the battery is $e(t-1)-d(t)$; or discharging the battery if the real load rises above the previously measured value, i.e., $d(t) > e(t-1)$, and the discharging rate of the battery is $d(t) - e(t-1)$.

However, there are four cases when the battery fails to meet the target. These four cases are as follows: (i) $d(t) < e(t-1)$ and the excess power is greater than the charging rate, β_c, of the battery. In this case, the battery regulates the load by maximally charging itself, i.e., $e(t) = d(t) + \beta_c$; (ii) The battery will be overcharged if we have $e(t) = e(t-1)$. In this case, the battery does not regulate the load, and we have $e(t) = d(t)$; (iii) $e(t-1) < d(t)$ and the power needed from the battery is greater than the discharging rate, β_d, of the battery. In this case, the battery regulates the load by maximally discharging itself, i.e., $e(t) = d(t) - \beta_d$; and (iv) The battery will be over-discharged (below empty) if we have $e(t) = e(t-1)$. In this case, the battery does not regulate the load, and we have $e(t) = d(t)$.

Non-Intrusive Load Leveling (NILL) [27]
This algorithm also tries to maintain $e(t)$. However, instead of using the previous measured load $e(t-1)$ as the tar-

get to maintain, the algorithm computes a *target load* to be preserved, which is related to the average amount of load computed from history. The authors claim that this helps reduce the changes in power acquired from the power grid. This is indeed the case when the battery capacity is large, so that the deviation from the target load can be mostly complemented by the battery [27].

The target load is also constantly adjusted when the battery fails to meet the target, which reflects persistent deviations in the demand of the household. The failure scenarios for NILL to maintain the target load are similar to the BE case: (i) $d(t) < e(t-1)$ and the excess power is greater than the charging rate, β_c, of the battery. In this case, the battery regulates the load by maximally charging itself, i.e., $e(t) = d(t) + \beta_c$; (ii) The battery will be overcharged if we have $e(t) = e(t-1)$. In this case, the target load is recomputed as a weighted average of the previous target and the average load d since the last recovery. However, the target load is not used immediately, since the system will be in a "high recovery state," in which $e(t)$ is set so that the battery is gradually discharged. The system only leaves the recovery state when the battery is half-emptied or the current demand $d(t)$ is higher than a certain value above $e(t-1)$; (iii) $e(t-1) < d(t)$ and the power needed from the battery is greater than the discharging rate, β_d, of the battery. In this case, the battery regulates the load by maximally discharging itself, i.e., $e(t) = d(t) - \beta_d$; and (iv) The battery will be over-discharged if we have $e(t) = e(t-1)$. In this case, the target load is recomputed as a weighted average of the previous target and the average load d since the last recovery. However, the target load is not used immediately, since the system will be in a "low recovery state," in which $e(t)$ is set so that the battery is gradually charged. The system only exits the recovery state when the battery is half-filled or the current demand $d(t)$ is lower than a certain fraction of $e(t-1)$.

Lazy Stepping (LS) [46]
Similar to the previous two algorithms, this algorithm tries to maintain $e(t)$. This algorithm protects privacy by restricting the measured load to some discrete levels. In particular, the measured load is quantized into levels. The separation between different levels, β, is related to the charging and discharging rates of the battery by the equation $\beta = \min(\beta_c, \beta_d)$, such that the measured load can always be regulated to one of those levels by charging or discharging the battery to make up for the difference from the real demand. As a result, the measured load is limited to these levels without revealing the real demand or its changes.

In Sec. 7, we implement the LS1 approach proposed in [46], which regulates the measured load as follows: (i) When keeping $e(t) = e(t-1)$ will result in overcharging the battery, then set the output to the level that is just *below* $d(t)$ to discharge the battery; (ii) When keeping $e(t) = e(t-1)$ will result in over-discharging the battery, then set the output to the level that is just *above* $d(t)$ to charge the battery; (iii) When $d(t)$ is too low or too high relative to $e(t-1)$, i.e., $e(t-1) - d(t) > \beta$ or $d(t) - e(t-1) > \beta$, respectively, then set the output to the level that is just *above* $d(t)$ to charge the battery if the battery is below half full. Otherwise, the output is set to the level that is just *below* $d(t)$ to discharge the battery.

4.2 Privacy Attack Using Smart Meter Readings as Covert Channel

Once BLH algorithms are deployed on smoothing battery systems, they will naturally become the targets of attacks by adversaries to defeat the privacy protection. As inexpensive consumer-grade devices, the battery systems are vulnerable to software attacks. Specifically, assume that an adversary can surreptitiously modify control software implementing the BLH, say through malware injection, but the battery system does not have an explicit communication channel for sending any learned private information directly to the adversary. Furthermore, assume that the adversary cannot compromise the smart metering infrastructure (i.e., the smart meters measure electricity consumption normally and report it normally). But the adversary can observe the reported smart meter readings, which is a standard assumption in NILM attacks.

We consider the case where LS1 is used as the privacy-preserving algorithm, and the adversary modifies it to a malicious version, which we call LS1a. It turns out that LS1a only needs a slight modification to LS1 to leak compromised private information to the adversary, using the normal smart meter readings as a covert channel. Specifically, in cases (i) and (iii) when the LS algorithm needs to reduce the regulated load (because the battery is almost full or the charge rate is too high), the malicious version forgets the reduced regulated load in the next time instance, and instead tries to use the regulated load before the reduction as the target load to be preserved. As an illustration, let t be the time instance at which the apparent load is reduced because of the mentioned reasons, i.e., $e(t) < e(t-1)$, the malicious control will try to set $e(t+1) = e(t-1)$ instead of $e(t+1) = e(t)$. Only in cases (ii) and (iii) when the LS algorithm needs to increase the regulated load, the malicious version will update the target load to be preserved afterwards.

This slight change is surprisingly significant, in that it will allow to leak the status of the battery, or the range of magnitudes of the real load that triggered the $e(t)$ update, through the normal smart meter readings. The inference by the adversary is as follows.

We assume that the real load that triggered the $e(t)$ update remains roughly the same at $t+1$ because the sampling frequency is high, i.e., $d(t+1) \approx d(t)$. Consider that in LS1a, if $e(t)$ is updated under condition (i) (i.e., the battery would be overcharged if $e(t) = e(t-1)$), then there are two possible outcomes at $t+1$ as follows, (a) the battery discharges enough to support charging, so that we have $e(t+1) = e(t-1)$; or (b) the battery discharges insufficiently to support charging, so that we have $e(t+1) = e(t)$. On the other hand, if $e(t)$ is updated under condition (iii) (i.e., the charging rate exceeds the maximum possible value, $d(t) - e(t-1) > \beta$), then there are four possible outcomes at $t+1$ as follows, (a) the battery was below 50% charged at t, was charged at t, and now is above 50% charged, so we have $e(t+1) = e(t) - \beta$; (b) the battery was below 50% charged at t, was charged at t, but now is still below 50% charged, so that we have $e(t+1) = e(t)$; (c) the battery was above 50% charged at t, was discharged at t, and now is below 50% charged, so we have $e(t+1) = e(t) + \beta$; or (d) the battery was above 50% charged at t, was discharged at t, but now is still above 50% charged, so we have $e(t+1) = e(t)$.

Based on the above analysis, if the adversary observes that $e(t+1) = e(t-1)$, he can then conclude that it is the scenario of (i)(a); if the adversary observes that $e(t+1) = e(t) - \beta$, he can then conclude that it is the scenario of (iii)(a); and if the adversary observes that $e(t+1) = e(t)+\beta$, he can then conclude that it is the scenario of (iii)(c). The knowledge so gained, together with inference of the battery charging/discharging rate β the adversary makes from past smart meter readings, will allow the adversary to estimate a possible range of the real reading at $e(t+1)$, hence $e(t)$ also under the assumption that the real load remains about the same over a short time period.

Notice that the adversary can apply the same inference for the later time instances to further refine his estimates of the real load, provided that the regulated load is not increased in cases (ii) and (iii), and the duration of time is relatively short so that the real load remains roughly the same during the period.

5. PRIVACY MEASURES

We now present the four privacy measures that we will evaluate in this paper. They are information-theoretic measures that quantify the common information between the original private data to be protected and its noisy version that is revealed to observers, including curious adversaries who aim to infer the private information. Importantly, in contrast to most similar measures in the literature, our measures are all parameterized to reveal explicitly the order of correlated information that can be used in a privacy attack. The first three measures do so by generalizing basic notions already proposed in related work. The fourth measure is a new one that we define, that admits comprehensively different scopes of information truly available for attack while retaining a constant meaning independent of the specific scope considered. In our discussion, we will use the notations of $\mathcal{X} = \{X_i\}$ and $\mathcal{Y} = \{Y_i\}$, whose definitions are given in Sec. 2.

5.1 Mutual Information (MI)

An arguably most natural notion to measure information content common to the clear and noisy data is that of mutual information (MI), which indeed has been widely used in privacy research [33, 42, 44, 46]. MI quantifies the mutual dependence between two random variables X and Y. It is defined as follows.

$$I(X;Y) = \sum_{x\in\mathcal{X}^1}\sum_{y\in\mathcal{Y}^1} p(x,y)\log\left(\frac{p(x,y)}{p(x)p(y)}\right).$$

The smaller the measure, the lower the mutual dependence between the clear data points and the perturbed ones, and the better the privacy protection.

MI can be defined for sequences of data points, rather than individual data points, as symbols. In BLH, privacy quantification has taken a modest step in this direction [46], where the definition of MI uses pairs of consecutive data points as symbols:

$$I(X;Y) = \sum_{\mathbf{x}\in\mathcal{X}^2}\sum_{\mathbf{y}\in\mathcal{Y}^2} p(\mathbf{x},\mathbf{y})\log\left(\frac{p(\mathbf{x},\mathbf{y})}{p(\mathbf{x})p(\mathbf{y})}\right). \quad (1)$$

It is clear that pairs of data points may not capture all relevant orders of information in real data. In this paper, we will therefore consider a general notion of MI applied to length-k data sequences for general $k > 0$: $\mathbf{x} \in \mathcal{X}^k$ and $\mathbf{y} \in \mathcal{Y}^k$ in Eq. 1. While this extension is conceptually simple, we must take care to ensure that the length of data used to test a privacy measure is long enough to produce steady-state results after convergence. This issue is of much practical importance because the required length increases with k due to increased symbol diversity. We will address this practical challenge in Sec. 7.

5.2 Normalized Mutual Information (NMI)

A variant privacy measure to MI is the mutual information normalized by the entropy of the clear data trace [23]. The definition of this NMI measure is as follows.

$$C_{YX} = \frac{I(X;Y)}{H(X)} = \frac{\sum_{x\in\mathcal{X}^1}\sum_{y\in\mathcal{Y}^1} p(x,y)\log\left(\frac{p(x,y)}{p(x)p(y)}\right)}{\sum_{x\in\mathcal{X}^1} p(x)\log(p(x))}.$$

The reason for the division is to normalize the computed MI to give the *fraction* of information of the clear data trace that is exposed by the perturbed data trace. We adapt this normalization similarly to our parameterized notion of MI by k, for $k > 0$.

5.3 Conditional Entropy (CE)

Conditional entropy has been used to capture the uncertainty of the position of a mobile user as a function of the length of historical data points used to infer the position [6]. The measure is defined as $H(X_{k+1}|X_k, X_{k-1}, ..., X_1)$ when length-k, $k > 0$, historical data points are used. We adapt this uncertainty notion of clear data to the case of privacy protection. To do so, we define our CE measure to quantify the uncertainty of a clear data point as a function of the length of previous noisy data points used in the inference. Specifically, we define the CE as

$$\begin{aligned}&H(X_{k+1}|Y_k, Y_{k-1}, ..., Y_1)\\ &= \sum_{\mathbf{y}\in\mathcal{Y}^k} p(\mathbf{y})H(X_{k+1}|Y_k = \mathbf{y}_k, Y_{k-1} = \mathbf{y}_{k-1}, ..., Y_1 = \mathbf{y}_1)\\ &= -\sum_{\mathbf{y}\in\mathcal{Y}^k} p(\mathbf{y})\sum_{x\in\mathcal{X}^1} p(X_{k+1} = x|\mathbf{y})\log p(X_{k+1} = x|\mathbf{y}),\end{aligned}$$

where k is the length of past data points used from the noisy trace, $k > 0$. The larger the CE, the higher the uncertainty of the clear data points, hence the better the privacy protection.

5.4 Offline Conditional Entropy (OCE)

We now propose a new privacy measure of *offline conditional entropy* (OCE). This measure accounts for the full information available to the adversary when he tries to infer some clear data points. Specifically, the adversary may exploit any range of noisy data points as guiding information. Without loss of generality, the OCE is defined with respect to a range of $2k+1$ data points in the neighborhood of the clear data point, for general $k \geq 0$:

$$\begin{aligned}&H(X_{k+1}|Y_1, Y_2, ..., Y_{2k+1})\\ &= \sum_{\mathbf{y}\in\mathcal{Y}^{2k+1}} p(\mathbf{y})H(X_{k+1}|Y_1 = \mathbf{y}_1, Y_2 = \mathbf{y}_2, ..., Y_{2k+1} = \mathbf{y}_{2k+1})\\ &= -\sum_{\mathbf{y}\in\mathcal{Y}^{2k+1}} p(\mathbf{y})\sum_{x\in\mathcal{X}^1} p(X_{k+1} = x|\mathbf{y})\log p(X_{k+1} = x|\mathbf{y}).\end{aligned}$$

Similar to CE, the larger the OCE, the higher the uncertainty of the clear data points, and the better the privacy protection.

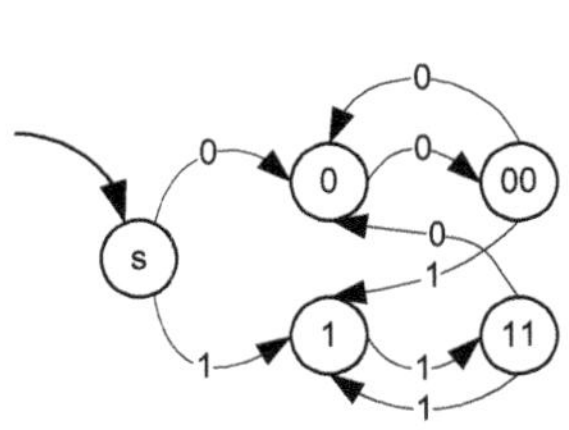

Figure 2: Automaton for trace generation.

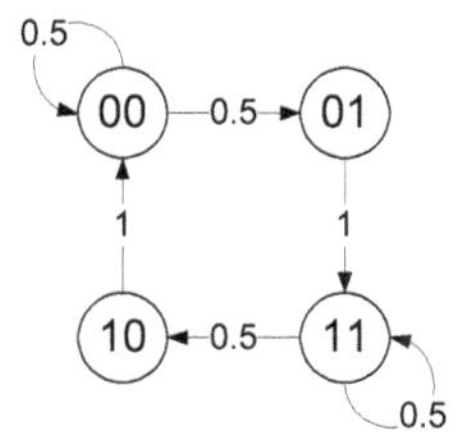

Figure 3: Order-2 Markov model for trace generation.

6. AXIOMATIC PROPERTIES OF PRIVACY MEASURES

In this section, we assess the proposed privacy measures by postulating desirable axiomatic properties that they should satisfy to be practically useful, in that these properties are evidence that a measure can bring out the true information content available in a privacy attack. In testing the privacy measures for these axiomatic properties, a main issue is to ensure that the test data has the intended information content by design. We use specifically designed synthetic data models to generate the required data. We report two such data models in the generation: (i) a data automaton, and (ii) an order-2 Markov chain. Application of the measures to real-world traces will be presented in Sec. 7.

Traces generated by data automaton. Data points in this trace set are limited to the range of integers $[0, 1]$. Specifically, the even index data points are equal to their corresponding previous odd index data points, and the odd index data points are drawn uniformly at random from $[0, 1]$. Fig. 2 shows the automaton used to generate the trace of integers. An example trace generated from the automaton is $\{1, 1, 0, 0, 0, 0, ...\}$.

Notice that we cannot represent the generation of this dataset by a Markov model of any order. It is because no matter how high the order of the Markov model, there will always exist patterns of all identical symbols (albeit occurring at small probabilities), so that we cannot tell if the leading symbol of such a pattern is at an odd or even index to determine the next data point following the pattern, i.e., whether it should be identical to the previous data point or it should be picked randomly from the range of $[0, 1]$.

Our use of this dataset with repeating symbols gives us a ready method to control the degree of correlation existing between the data points of the original trace and those of the perturbed trace.

Traces generated by Markov model. Data points in this trace set are also limited to the range of integers $[0, 1]$. They are generated by the order-2 Markov model shown in Fig. 3. Notice that each data value is repeated at least once in this trace. $\{1, 1, 1, 0, 0, 0, 0, 1, 1, ...\}$ is an example trace. This dataset allows us to control the order of data correlation in the original trace used to test a privacy measure.

6.1 Axiomatic properties

We postulate two axiomatic properties for a desirable privacy measure:

1. The measure accounts for all available information in a privacy attack.
2. The measure quantifies how the privacy protection weakens as the adversary exploits progressively larger scopes of data correlation present in the data. The strength of protection should stabilize at some scope k when applied to time-series data generated by an order-l Markov model.

6.2 Protection strategies

We now evaluate the four measures we proposed in Sec. 5 against the axiomatic properties we presented above. We consider four strategies for protecting the synthetic data:

- **No data point is perturbed.** This acts as a baseline when there is no protection at all.
- **Randomly perturbing 50% of data points.** This strategy perturbs 50% of the data points (chosen uniformly at random) by replacing them with integer values drawn uniformly at random from the range of $[0, 1]$.
- **Deterministically perturbing even indexed data points.** This strategy perturbs the same number of data points as the previous strategy on average, but the perturbation applies to all the even indexed (i.e., deterministic) data points only – they are replaced with integer values drawn uniformly at random from the range of $[0, 1]$.
- **Deterministically perturbing odd indexed data points.** This strategy works in the same way as the previous one, but it perturbs all the odd indexed data points and them only.

For traces generated by the data automaton, it is easy to see that the perturbation of a random 50% of the data points gives the best protection, whereas the two deterministic choices of the perturbed data points (i.e., either even or odd indexed) have the same protection, and this protection is in turn better than no perturbation at all.

6.3 Results – traces generated by data automaton

We test satisfaction of the first axiomatic property using traces generated by the data automaton, for each of the four protection strategies. Fig. 4 reports the privacy protection according to the four measures in Sec. 5. From the figure, notice that CE (Fig. 4(a)) fails to show that the two deterministic perturbation strategies offer equally poor privacy protection. This is because the online nature of CE causes it to determine the uncertainty of original data points based on their corresponding preceding data points only. Hence, it erroneously concludes that perturbing the odd entries will give much better protection than perturbing the even ones. In contrast, OCE (Fig. 4(b)), MI (Fig. 4(c)), and NMI (Fig. 4(d)) do not suffer from this limited view. They show that the two deterministic perturbation strategies achieve the same performance for the same k.

The perturbed version of the traces generated by the data automaton in Fig. 2 also allows us to test the privacy measures against the second axiomatic property. It is because in these traces, the entries with a separation greater than one time index are unrelated. Hence, the useful scope of information to the adversary is limited to $k = 1$ of CE and OCE, corresponding to the published data point either right before or after the data point that the adversary wishes to

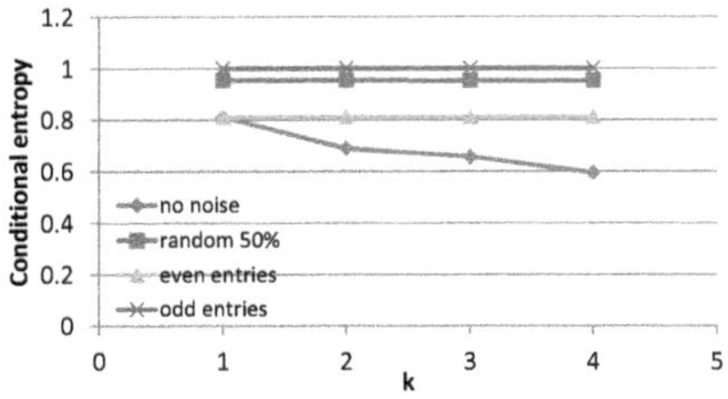

(a) Conditional entropy

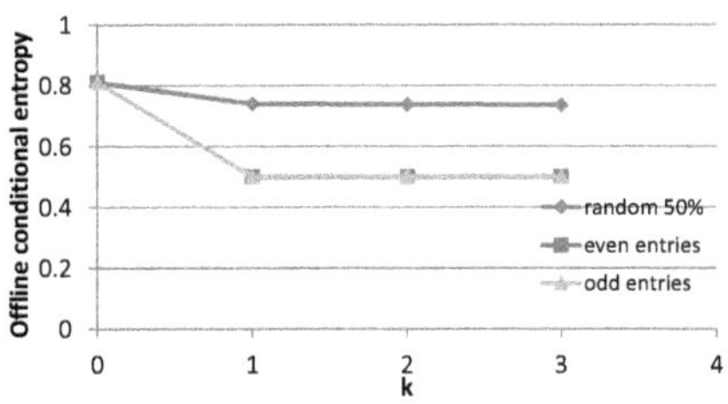

(b) Offline conditional entropy

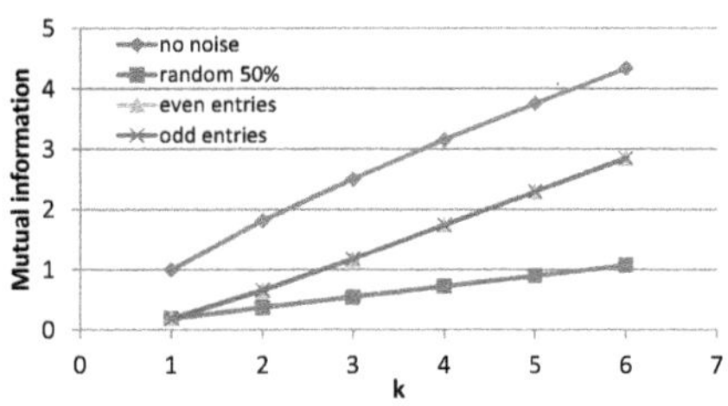

(c) Mutual information

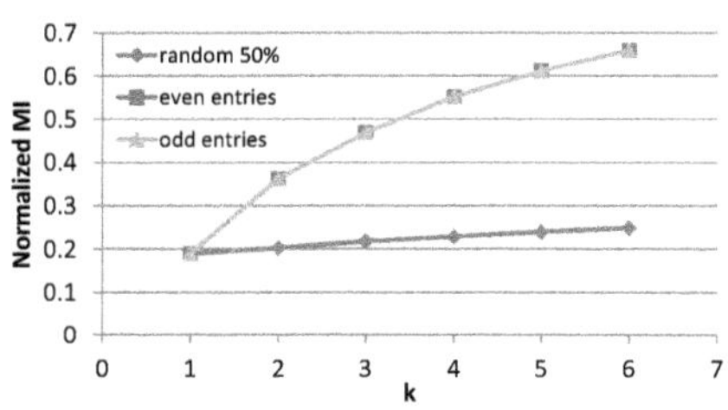

(d) Normalized mutual information

Figure 4: Measure of privacy protection by different measures. Traces are generated by data automaton.

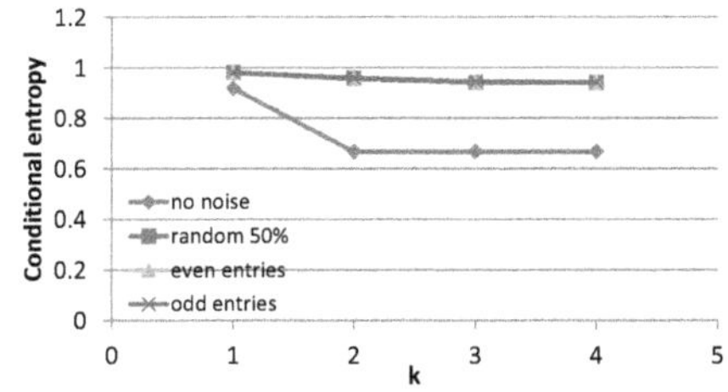

(a) Conditional entropy

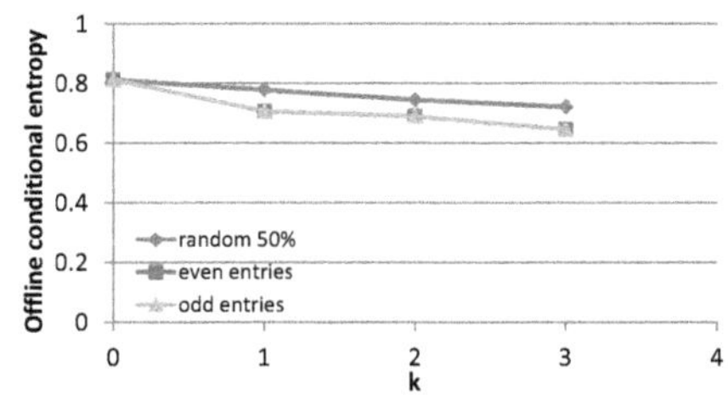

(b) Offline conditional entropy

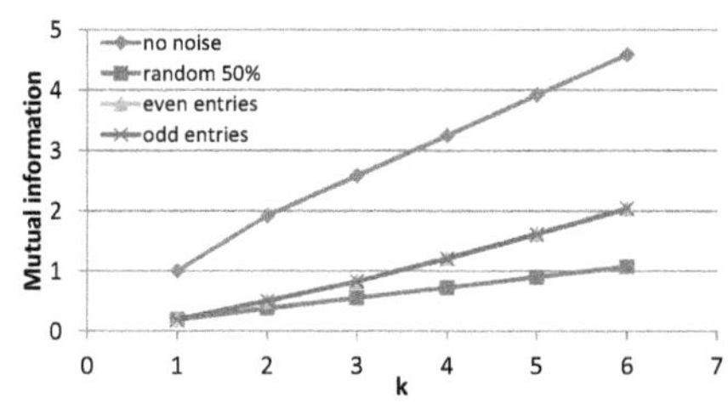

(c) Mutual information

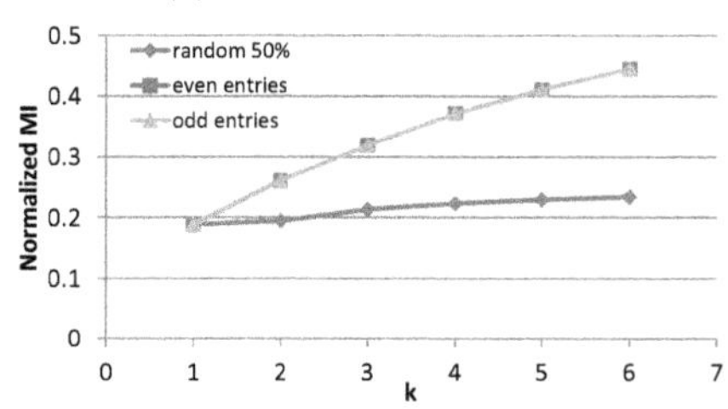

(d) Normalized mutual information

Figure 5: Measure of privacy protection by different measures. Traces are generated by order-2 Markov model.

reveal. Observe that for CE (Fig. 4(a)) or OCE (Fig. 4(b)), the privacy measure indeed stabilizes at $k = 1$ for all the perturbation methods, thus verifying the second axiomatic property. On the other hand, the MI (Fig. 4(c)) and NMI (Fig. 4(d)) measures do not stabilize at $k = 2$, i.e., considering two data points together.

6.4 Results – Traces generated by Markov model

We now test the privacy measures against the second axiomatic property using the four protection strategies (Sec. 6.2) and traces generated by the Markov model in Fig. 3, where the data points are integers within the range of $[0, 1]$.

Fig. 5 reports the measured privacy protection according to the different measures. Fig. 5(a) shows that for no perturbation, the protection according to CE weakens until $k = 2$, which agrees with the order of the Markov model used to generate the test data. It remains stable at this minimum protection afterwards, when k grows beyond the Markov order of the trace. The results also show that perturbations have the general effect of increasing the Markov order of the data traces. Hence, when perturbations are applied, the CE and OCE values may drop further, albeit by relatively small amounts, as k grows beyond two. To be maximally effective, the adversary may thus need to use longer data patterns in his attacks. On the other hand, Fig. 5(c) and Fig. 5(d) show that for the no perturbation case, MI and NMI keep increasing (i.e., do not stabilize) after the k considered grows beyond the Markov order of the trace, i.e., they do not satisfy the second axiomatic property. It is because when k increases, MI and NMI always have a tendency to grow due to the significantly increased diversity of symbols.

6.5 Discussions

In summary, CE does not satisfy the first axiomatic property, i.e., it fails to account for all available information in an attack. On the other hand, although MI and NMI satisfy the first property, they do not satisfy the second one. In particular, their measure of privacy (or its loss) over a moving basis makes their results hard to interpret across k, which is an important limitation. Of the measures evaluated, OCE is the only one that satisfies both the axiomatic properties.

Hence, it appears to be the best suited for measuring the privacy protection of temporally correlated data traces.

7. BLH EXPERIMENTS

In this section we use the proposed privacy measures to quantify the performance of the different privacy protection strategies we presented in Sec. 4 for BLH.

7.1 Dataset

We evaluate the performance of the different BLH algorithms presented in Sec. 4 using real smart meter readings collected from the U.K. [36], as well as synthetic ones generated using an energy demand model developed in [37].

U.K. dataset [36]. This dataset contains power meter readings collected from 22 households in the U.K. at a sampling interval of one minute in 2008 and 2009.

Synthetic dataset [37]. As we discussed in Sec. 5, the use of a large k for performance evaluation requires a long enough data trace to produce steady-state results after convergence. To ensure that the relative performance of different BLH algorithms remains valid as the adversary exploits progressively longer data patterns, we assess the performance of these BLH algorithms using five years long synthetic traces also, well beyond the available length of the U.K. real-world dataset. We now present how we generate the synthetic smart meter traces.

The generator model [37] is configured using the data collected from [36]. It generates the power usage of a household in different days from 33 possible appliances and some other light fixtures up to a sampling interval of one minute. The generator takes as input parameters the number of persons in the household, the month of the year, and the type of the day (e.g., weekday or weekend) to generate the occupancy of the house, the usage of the appliances, and hence the total power usage.

We utilize the generator to generate years long meter readings of a household with specific input parameters (e.g., the household has three persons). In particular, we modified the generator so that it can generate continual meter readings according to the month of the year and types of days according to the calendar. The generated traces of smart meter readings are for five years, from 2008 to 2012.

7.2 Privacy concern of data

According to [46], the changes between consecutive smart meter readings are more important than the clear data to an adversary because many of the NILM techniques [4, 31, 43] use the changes to infer the type of appliance being used. Hence, we apply the privacy measures on the changes between consecutive smart meter readings rather than on the raw data to quantify the performance of the BLH algorithms.

7.3 Comparison of different BLH algorithms

We evaluate and compare the privacy protection of the three protection strategies, i.e., BE, NILL, and LS1, as a function of the length of data patterns exploited by the adversary, under different capacities of the battery in the household's battery smoothing system. The charging and discharging rates of the battery are set to values such that the battery is fully charged from empty or fully discharged from full in an hour.

Since we have shown in Sec. 6 that conditional entropy (CE) is not a good privacy measure and normalized mutual information (NMI) gives no further information than mutual information (MI), in this section we only compare the evaluation results obtained by offline conditional entropy (OCE) and mutual information (MI).

U.K. data. We present the evaluation using real data in the U.K. dataset [36], particularly data from a smart meter collected in 2008.

Fig. 6 shows the OCE value computed for the different protection strategies as a function of k considered by the privacy measure, under different battery capacity in the BLH smoothing. Fig. 6 shows that when $k = 1$ (i.e., the uncertainty of a clear data point conditioned on the corresponding perturbed data point, a perturbed data point in the past, and another one in the future), the effectiveness of the three protection strategies is similar to that reported in [46], i.e., LS1 gives the best protection whereas NILL gives the worst. When k is increased to four (i.e., the adversary utilizes more information from the "past" and "future"), the comparison result is similar. Furthermore, we can observe from the figure that when the adversary uses longer patterns to exploit the temporal correlation in the time-series data, the protection provided by each strategy invariably decreases as measured by OCE.

Fig. 7 compares the privacy protection of different BLH methods according to MI. A similar conclusion can be drawn from this measure as from OCE on the relative performance of the different BLH algorithms – it remains the same as k varies. However, unlike OCE, it is not easy to tell from MI how increased exploitation of the data temporal correlation may help the adversary in the attack. This is because for MI, the quantification of information content occurs over a moving basis.

Synthetic data. We now compare the performance of different BLH algorithms using the five years long synthetic traces. Fig. 8 shows the comparison of the different algorithms as they are quantified by OCE, whereas Fig. 9 shows the comparison quantified using MI.

The results for the synthetic traces are similar to those from the real traces. The BLH algorithms achieve the same relative performance, and this relative performance remains unchanged as k increases. Moreover, it is straightforward to use OCE to quantify the privacy impact of a larger k for the adversary, but the same is not true of MI.

The malicious version of LS1. We now evaluate the impact of LS1a, the malicious version presented in Sec. 4.2 of the LS1 BLH algorithm. Recall that LS1a mimics the working of LS1 but with a slight modification to leak private information to the adversary through normally reported smart meter readings as a covert channel.

Fig. 10 presents the simulation results of LS1 and its malicious version LS1a. We can observe from the figure that the harm of the malicious version is not obvious when k is small, i.e., LS1a has similar performance as LS1 in that regime. However, it would be incorrect to dismiss the attack as ineffective. This is because when k increases, it becomes apparent that the protection of LS1a is in fact much weaker than that of LS1. If we further compare the performance of LS1a with that of BE, i.e., Fig. 10 versus Fig. 6 and Fig. 7, we can see that LS1a under-performs even BE when k is large. Hence, it is crucial to use a proper privacy measure

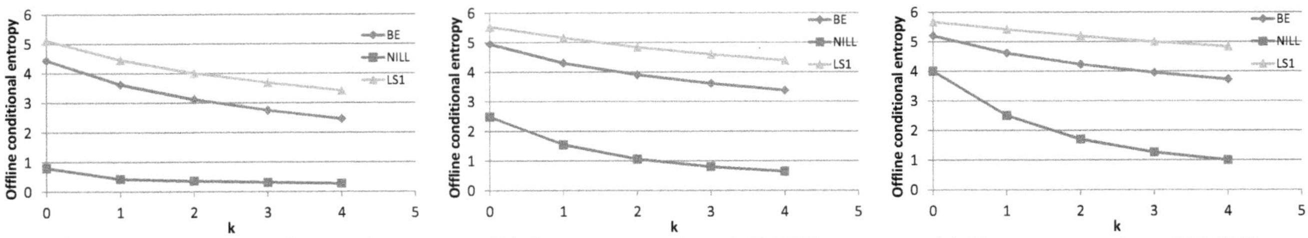

(a) Battery capacity of 100 Wh (b) Battery capacity of 400 Wh (c) Battery capacity of 800 Wh

Figure 6: Comparing the performance of the three BLH protection approaches using OCE. A larger value means better protection. Readings of one meter from the U.K. The relative performance of different BLH algorithm remains the same when k increases.

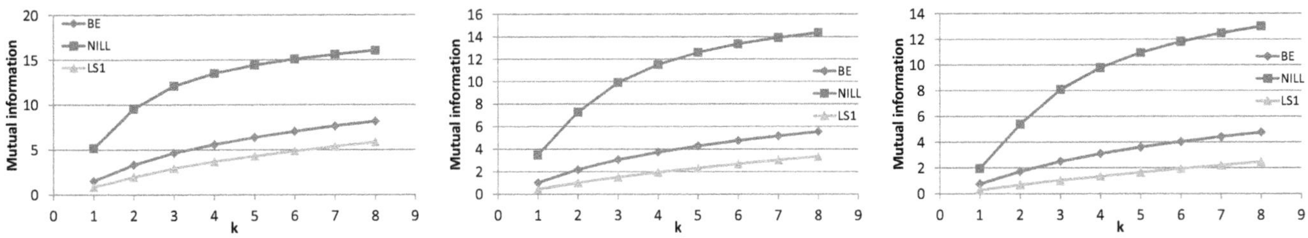

(a) Battery capacity of 100 Wh (b) Battery capacity of 400 Wh (c) Battery capacity of 800 Wh

Figure 7: Comparing the performance of the three BLH protection approaches using MI. A smaller value means better protection. Readings of one meter from the U.K. The relative performance of different BLH algorithm remains the same when k increases.

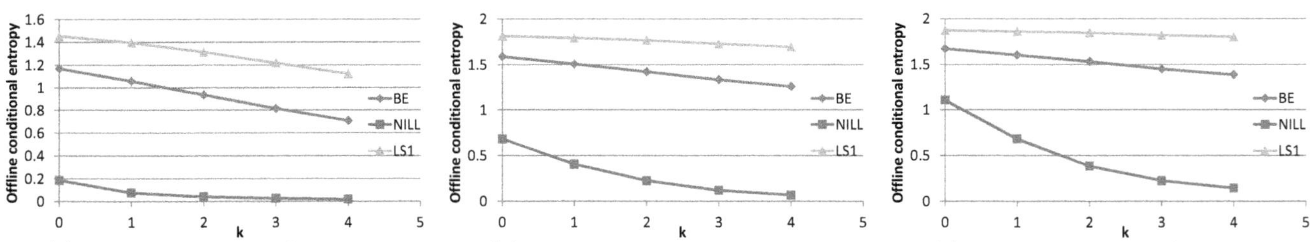

(a) Battery capacity of 100 Wh (b) Battery capacity of 400 Wh (c) Battery capacity of 800 Wh

Figure 8: Comparing the performance of the three BLH protection methods using OCE. A larger value means better protection. Synthetic meter readings of length 5 years. Similar to the case of real data, the relative performance of different BLH algorithms remains the same when k increases.

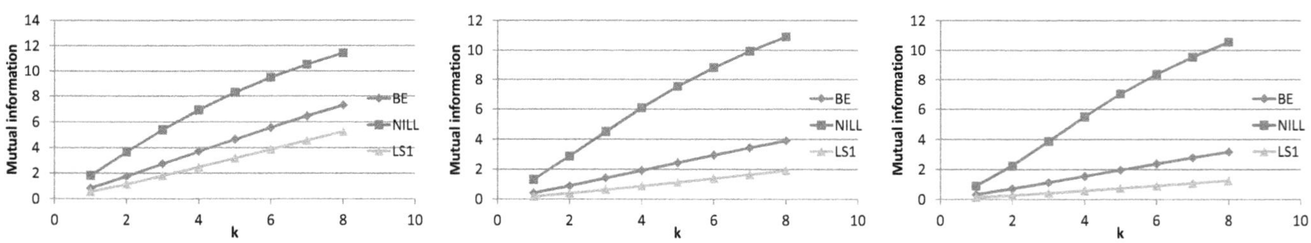

(a) Battery capacity of 100 Wh (b) Battery capacity of 400 Wh (c) Battery capacity of 800 Wh

Figure 9: Comparing the performance of the three BLH protection methods using MI. A smaller value means better protection. Synthetic meter readings of length 5 years. Similar to the case of real data, the relative performance of different BLH algorithms remains the same when k increases.

to expose LS1a's ability to infer significant private information from temporally correlated data.

7.4 Discussions

We provided a first systematic comparative study of the major existing BLH algorithms across a comprehensive range of k, the scope of data used in a privacy attack. While the ranking of the algorithms by our study agrees with prior results in the literature that either do not consider the correlation or only consider it minimally (e.g., $k = 2$ for MI), our new results on the hitherto unstudied range of k are important, given the clear presence of long temporal correlations in real world data (e.g., traces of household electricity consumption) and the undisputed ability of adversaries to actually exploit this correlation. Particularly, our analysis of a novel covert channel attack on BLH protection of smart

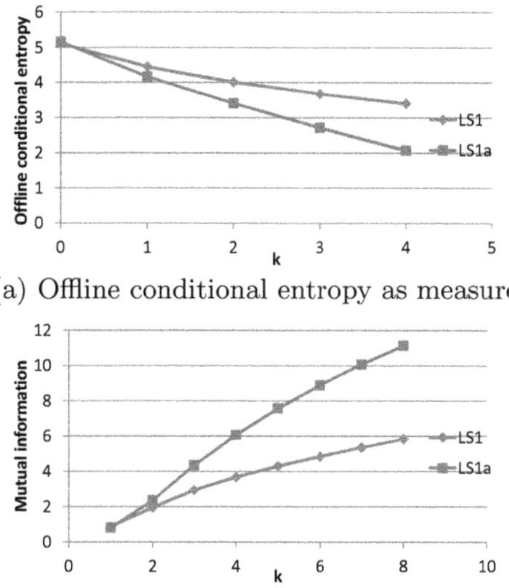

(a) Offline conditional entropy as measure

(b) Mutual information as measure

Figure 10: Comparing the performance of LS1 and LS1a using OCE and MI. Readings of one meter from the U.K. Battery capacity of 100 Wh.

meter data shows that whereas the attack may appear inconsequential when k is small, its true power is demonstrated only when it is evaluated at a large enough k.

8. CONCLUSION

In this paper we presented a systematic study of the impact of temporal correlation in time-series data on the quantification of the data's privacy protection. We evaluated four sets of information-theoretic privacy measures, including three that are adopted from existing measures in the literature and a new measure of offline conditional entropy (OCE) that we proposed. By an automaton- and a Markov-driven data model, we demonstrated that OCE satisfies both of our proposed axiomatic properties of desirable privacy measures, whereas the other measures do not.

We then used OCE to evaluate the performance of three foremost existing BLH algorithms for privacy protection of smart meter data traces, and demonstrated the advantages of this evaluation compared with mutual information. We used a balance of real world U.K. traces and long synthetic traces generated from realistic (and validated) power usage models to ensure the relevance and convergence of our results. Our results provided a first confirmation of the ranking of these algorithms when long data correlations (i.e., a large value of the k parameter used in the privacy measures) are considered, beyond the regime studied in earlier work. We also presented a novel covert channel attack on BLH protection, in which a slight malicious modification of the LS1 algorithm at strategic moments can leak significant private information about a household's usage of appliances. This attack is interesting in its own right in that it only requires an eminently feasible compromise of the BLH system's control software – similar attacks have been repeatedly observed for consumer grade devices – but otherwise it leverages a normally functioning smart meter infrastructure to report the private information. Importantly, the true power of the malicious control becomes clear only when it is evaluated at a large enough value of k.

9. ACKNOWLEDGEMENTS

This research was supported in part by Singapore's Agency for Science, Technology, and Research (A*STAR) under the Human Sixth Sense Programme, in part by S'pore Ministry of Education under grant numbers SUTD-ZJU-RES-01-2013 and SRG-ISTD-2013-060, in part by National Natural Science Foundation of China (NSFC) under grant number 61429301, and in part by U.S. National Science Foundation under grant number CNS-0963715.

10. REFERENCES

[1] G. Ács and C. Castelluccia. I have a DREAM!: differentially private smart metering. In *Proc. of IH*, May 2011.

[2] J. Aczel and Z. Daroczy. *On Measures of Information and Their Characterizations.* Academic Press, 1975.

[3] P. Algoet and T. Cover. A sandwich proof of the Shannon-McMillan-Breiman theorem. *The Annals of Probability*, 16(2), 1998.

[4] C. Beckel, W. Kleiminger, T. Staake, and S. Santini. Improving device-level electricity consumption breakdowns in private households using ON/OFF events. *ACM SIGBED Review - Special Issue on the 3rd International Workshop on Networks of Cooperating Objects (CONET 2012)*, 9(3), July 2012.

[5] A. Beresford and F. Stajano. Location privacy in pervasive computing. *Pervasive Computing, IEEE*, 2(1), Jan 2003.

[6] A. Bhattacharya and S. K. Das. LeZi-update: an information-theoretic framework for personal mobility tracking in PCS networks. *Wireless Networks*, 8(2–3), March 2002.

[7] S. Borenstein, M. Jaske, and A. Rosenfeld. Dynamic pricing, advanced metering, and demand response in electricity markets. Technical Report CSEMWP105, Center for the Study of Energy Markets, October 2002.

[8] R. Cayford and T. Johnson. Operational parameters affecting use of anonymous cell phone tracking for generating traffic information. *Institute of transportation studies for the 82th TRB Annual Meeting*, 1(3), January 2003.

[9] T.-H. Chan, E. Shi, and D. Song. Privacy-Preserving Stream Aggregation with Fault Tolerance. In *Proc. of FC*, February 2012.

[10] S. Chatterjee and J. S. Simonoff. *Handbook of Regression Analysis.* John Wiley & Sons, Inc., 2012.

[11] F. Chen, J. Dai, B. Wang, S. Sahu, M. Naphade, and C.-T. Lu. Activity analysis based on low sample rate smart meters. In *Proc. of ACM SIGKDD*, August 2011.

[12] T. Cover and J. Thomas. *Elements of Information Theory, 2nd Edn.* Wiley, New York, 2006.

[13] Y.-A. de Montjoye, C. Hidalgo, M. Verleysen, and V. Blondel. Unique in the Crowd: The privacy bounds of human mobility. *Nature Scientific Report*, March 2013.

[14] M. Duckham and L. Kulik. A Formal Model of Obfuscation and Negotiation for Location Privacy. In *Proc. of PERVASIVE*, May 2005.

[15] C. Dwork. Differential privacy. In *Proc. of ICALP*, July 2006.

[16] C. Dwork. Differential privacy: A survey of results. In *Proc. of TAMC*, April 2008.

[17] B. Gedik and L. Liu. Location Privacy in Mobile Systems: A Personalized Anonymization Model. In *Proc. of IEEE ICDCS*, June 2005.

[18] M. Gruteser and D. Grunwald. Anonymous Usage of Location-Based Services through Spatial and Temporal Cloaking. In *Proc. of ACM MobiSys*, May 2003.

[19] D. Henrici and P. Muller. Hash-based enhancement of location privacy for radio-frequency identification devices using varying identifiers. In *Proc. of IEEE PerCom*, March 2004.

[20] B. Hoh, M. Gruteser, H. Xiong, and A. Alrabady. Preserving Privacy in GPS Traces via Uncertainty-Aware Path Cloaking. In *Proc. of ACM CCS*, October 2007.

[21] G. Kalogridis, C. Efthymiou, S. Denic, T. Lewis, and R. Cepeda. Privacy for smart meters: Towards undetectable appliance load signatures. In *Proc. of IEEE SmartGridComm*, October 2010.

[22] H. Kargupta, S. Datta, Q. Wang, and K. Sivakumar. On the privacy preserving properties of random data perturbation techniques. In *Proc. of IEEE ICDM*, November 2003.

[23] J. Koo, X. Lin, and S. Bagchi. PRIVATUS: Wallet-Friendly Privacy Protection for Smart Meters. In *Proc. of ESORICS*, September 2012.

[24] N. Li and T. Li. t-closeness: Privacy beyond k-anonymity and l-diversity. In *Proc. of IEEE ICDE*, April 2007.

[25] C. Y. T. Ma, D. K. Y. Yau, N. K. Yip, and N. S. V. Rao. Privacy Vulnerabilities of Published Anonymous Mobility Traces. *IEEE/ACM Transactions on Networking*, 21(3), June 2013.

[26] A. Machanavajjhala, J. Gehrke, D. Kifer, and M. Venkitasubramaniam. l-diversity: Privacy beyond k-anonymity. In *Proc. of IEEE ICDE*, April 2006.

[27] S. McLaughlin, P. McDaniel, and W. Aiello. Protecting consumer privacy from electric load monitoring. In *Proc. of ACM CCS*, October 2011.

[28] F. McSherry and K. Talwar. Mechanism Design via Differential Privacy. In *Proc. of IEEE FOCS*, October 2007.

[29] J. Medina, N. Muller, and I. Roytelman. Demand response and distribution grid operations: Opportunities and challenges. *IEEE Trans. Smart Grid*, 1(2), 2010.

[30] J. Meyerowitz and R. R. Choudhury. Hiding Stars with Fireworks: Location Privacy through Camouflage. In *Proc. of ACM MobiCom*, September 2009.

[31] S. N. Patel, T. Robertson, J. A. Kientz, M. S. Reynolds, and G. D. Abowd. At the flick of a switch: detecting and classifying unique electrical events on the residential power line. In *Proc. of UbiComp*, September 2007.

[32] E. L. Quinn. Smart metering and privacy: Existing law and competing policies. *A report for the Colorado Public Utilities Commission*, 2009.

[33] S. R. Rajagopalan, L. Sankar, S. Mohajer, and H. V. Poor. Smart meter privacy: A utility-privacy framework. In *Proc. of IEEE SmartGridComm*, October 2011.

[34] V. Rastogi and S. Nath. Differentially private aggregation of distributed time-series with transformation and encryption. In *Proc. of ACM SIGMOD*, June 2010.

[35] D. Rebollo-Monedero, J. Parra-Arnau, C. Diaz, and J. Forné. On the measurement of privacy as an attacker's estimation error. *International Journal of Information Security*, 12(2), 2013.

[36] I. Richardson and M. Thomson. One-Minute Resolution Domestic Electricity Use Data, 2008-2009 [computer file]. Colchester, Essex: UK Data Archive [distributor], October 2010. SN: 6583, http://dx.doi.org/10.5255/UKDA-SN-6583-1. `http://discover.ukdataservice.ac.uk/catalogue?sn=6583`.

[37] I. Richardson, M. Thomson, D. Infield, and C. Clifford. Domestic electricity use: A high-resolution energy demand model. *Energy and Buildings*, 42(10), 2010.

[38] R. L. Rivest, A. Shamir, and L. Adleman. A method for obtaining digital signatures and public key cryptosystems. *Communications of ACM*, 21:120–126, 1978.

[39] E. Shi, R. Chow, T.-H. Chan, D. Song, and E. Rieffel. Privacy-preserving aggregation of time-series data. In *Proc. of NDSS*, February 2011.

[40] S. Steiniger, M. Neun, and A. Edwardes. Foundations of Location Based Services. *Lecture Notes on LBS, Department of Geography, University of Zurich*, 2006.

[41] L. Sweeney. k-anonymity: a model for protecting privacy. *International Journal on Uncertainty, Fuzziness and Knowledge-based Systems*, 10(5), 2002.

[42] D. Varodayan and A. Khisti. Smart meter privacy using a rechargeable battery: Minimizing the rate of information leakage. In *Proc. of IEEE ICASSP*, May 2011.

[43] M. Weiss, A. Helfenstein, F. Mattern, and T. Staake. Leveraging smart meter data to recognize home appliances. In *Proc. of IEEE PerCom*, March 2012.

[44] T. Wu, Y. Xue, and Y. Cui. Preserving traffic privacy in wireless mesh networks. In *Proc. of ACM WOWMOM*, June 2006.

[45] X. Xiao and Y. Tao. M-invariance: towards privacy preserving re-publication of dynamic datasets. In *Proc. of ACM SIGMOD*, June 2007.

[46] W. Yang, N. Li, Y. Qi, W. Qardaji, S. McLaughlin, and P. McDaniel. Minimizing Private Data Disclosures in the Smart Grid. In *Proc. of ACM CCS*, October 2012.

[47] G. P. Zachary. Saving Smart Meters From a Backlash. *IEEE Spectrum*, August 2011.

[48] B. Zhou and J. Pei. Preserving privacy in social networks against neighborhood attacks. In *Proc. of IEEE ICDE*, April 2008.

Privacy-Preserving Association Rule Mining in Cloud Computing

Xun Yi
School of Computer Science and Information Technology
RMIT University
Melbourne, VIC 3001, Australia
xun.yi@rmit.edu.au

Fang-Yu Rao
Department of Computer Science
Purdue University
West Lafayette, IN 47907, USA
raof@purdue.edu

Elisa Bertino
Department of Computer Science
Purdue University
West Lafayette, IN 47907, USA
bertino@purdue.edu

Athman Bouguettaya
School of Computer Science and Information Technology
RMIT University
Melbourne, VIC 3001, Australia
athman.bouguettaya@rmit.edu.au

ABSTRACT

Recently, the paradigm of data mining-as-a-service in cloud computing environment has been attracting interests. In this paradigm, a company (data owner), lacking data storage, computational resources and expertise, stores its data in the cloud and outsources its mining tasks to the cloud service provider (server). In order to protect the privacy of the outsourced database and the association rules mined, k-anonymity, k-support, and k-privacy techniques have been proposed to perturb the data before it is uploaded to the server. These techniques are computationally expensive. If the data owner has resources to use these techniques, then it is often able to execute association rule mining locally. In this paper, we consider a scenario where a user (data owner) encrypts its data and stores it in the cloud. To mine association rules from its data, the user outsources the task to n (≥ 2) "semi-honest" servers, which cooperate to perform association rule mining on the encrypted data in the cloud and return encrypted association rules to the user. In this setting, we provide three solutions to protecting data privacy during association rule mining. Our solutions are built on the distributed ElGamal cryptosystem and achieve item privacy, transaction privacy and database privacy, respectively, as long as at least one out of the n servers is honest. To reduce the possibility that all servers are compromised, the user can use servers from different cloud providers. Our implementation and experiments demonstrate that our solutions are practical.

1. INTRODUCTION

Cloud computing is the result of evolution and adoption of existing technologies and paradigms. The goal of cloud computing is to allow users to take benefits from all of these technologies, without the need for deep knowledge about or expertise in each one of them. The cloud aims to cut costs, and help the users focus on their core business instead of being impeded by IT obstacles.

The discovery of frequent patterns, association rules, and correlation relationships among huge amounts of data is useful to business intelligence. A typical example of frequent itemset mining is the market basket analysis. This process analyzes customer buying habits by finding associations between the different items that customers place in their "shopping baskets". The discovery of such associations can help retailers develop marketing strategies by gaining insight into which items are frequently purchased together by customers. For instance, if customers are buying milk, how likely are they to also buy bread (and what kind of bread) on the same trip to the supermarket? Such information can lead to increased sales by helping retailers do selective marketing and plan their shelf space [5].

For a decade, it has been seen a growing interest in the paradigm of data mining-as-a-service in cloud computing environment [9, 11, 4]. In this paradigm, a company (data owner), lacking data storage, computational resources and expertise, stores its data in cloud and outsources its mining tasks to the cloud service provider (server). Without doubt, the data mining-as-a-service benefits business intelligence. However, there exists a serious privacy issue in the paradigms, that is, the server has access to the data of the company and may learn business secrets from it.

On the other hand, in the paradigm of outsourcing data mining tasks to the cloud, the company (data owner) is assumed to lack data storage, computational resources and expertise. However, transforming a database to k-support anonymity or k-privacy is computationally expensive. If the data owner has resources to use these techniques, then it is often able to execute association rule mining, such as the Apriori algorithm [1], locally.

In this paper, we consider a cloud computing environment where the data owner does not have a large local data storage and chooses to store all its transaction data in the cloud. It may need to continuously add new transactions to its database in the cloud. In addition, the data owner does not have computation resources to run data

ASIA CCS'15, April 14–17, 2015, Singapore..

http://dx.doi.org/10.1145/2714576.2714603.

mining algorithms locally and even does not have knowledge of k-anonymity and data mining algorithms.

To protect data privacy, the data owner employs the ElGamal cryptosystem [2] to encrypt all items in a transaction, i.e., the data owner generates its public/private key pair and then encrypts all items with the public key, before uploading the transaction onto the cloud. Note that the ElGamal encryptions of the same item look completely different.

When outsourcing the data mining task, the data owner chooses n ($n \geq 2$) different servers in the cloud. It splits its private key into n pieces and distributes them to the n servers, respectively. The private key is secure as long as not all the n servers collude. To reduce the possibility that all servers are compromised, the user can use servers from different cloud service providers. We assume that at least one out of n servers is honest. In addition, the data owner sends an encryption of the minimum support threshold to the n servers. We assume that each server is "semi-honest", i.e., it honestly follows the data mining algorithm but may be curious about the privacy of the data, e.g., the supports of itemsets or association rules.

Under this model, we formally define three privacy requirements for association rule mining over the encrypted transaction database. According to the three privacy requirements, we give three solutions, mainly built on the distributed ElGamal cryptosystem, for the n servers to cooperate to mine association rules from the encrypted data in the cloud and return to the data owner encrypted association rules with encrypted supports.

Our first solution is built on the Plaintext Equality Test (PET) technique [7], by which the n servers can cooperate to determine the equality of two plaintexts on the basis of their encryptions without the need for decryption. The basic idea is using PET to identify the encryptions of the same item in the encrypted transactions and replace them with the same encryption. Then the Aprori algorithm is applied to the replacement of the transaction database. Our first solution does not hide the support of each itemset and therefore it may be vulnerable to the background knowledge-based attack.

To hide the support of each itemset, we provide the second solution in which each server adds fake transactions (encrypted by the public key of the data owner) into the encrypted database and the original and fake transactions are then mixed by the ElGamal re-encryptions and random permutations performed by all servers. Next, like our first solution, PET is used to identify and replace the encryptions of the same item. When applying the Aprori algorithm to the replacement of the transaction database, the effect of the fake transactions is removed by all the servers and the real support of the itemset is then compared with the encrypted minimum support threshold using the conditional gate [10]. Our second solution can hide the real support of each itemset, but it does not hide the original transactions completely.

To hide the original transactions completely, we provide the third solution in which each server counts the support of an itemset in a subset of the database and n servers then jointly derive the support of the itemset in the whole database. Each time before counting the support of an itemset, all transactions are shuffled so that the structure of transactions can be hidden. Next, like our second solution, the encrypted support of the itemset and the encrypted minimum support threshold are compared using the conditional gate.

Compared with the previous work on outsourcing of association rule mining, our work reduces the requirements of data storage, computation resources and expertise for the data owner. What the data owner is required to do is encrypting its data before uploading it to the cloud and decrypting the mined association rules received from the cloud.

The rest of the paper is organized as the following: Section 2 reviews the works that have already been done in the literature; Section 3 introduces some techniques for developing our solutions; Section 4 describes our model for privacy-preserving association rule mining in cloud computing environments; Sections 5 to 7 give our solutions on the basis of the model. Sections 8 and 9 provide the security and performance analysis; and Section 10 discusses the implementation and experiments. The last section concludes our work.

2. RELATED WORK

To protect the data privacy of the company and yet enable the server to perform association rule mining on the data in the cloud, a naive solution is for the data owner to hide the meanings of items in its transaction database by replacing items with integers (where the same item is replaced with the same integer while different items are replaced with different integers). This one-to-one substitution approach does not hide the frequencies of items. If the server has precise knowledge on frequencies of some items, it can re-identify some items, in particular, the top frequent items. For example, suppose that bread is the most frequent item in retail transaction databases and an integer a appears most frequently in the transformed database, the server can conclude that the integer a represents bread.

The background knowledge based attack was first addressed by Wong et al. [12] in 2007. To prevent it, they proposed a one-to-n item mapping that transform transactions non-deterministically. The basic idea is to add fake items into the transaction database. Assume that I is the set of items in the original database and m is a one-to-one mapping from items to integers. The data owner adds a set of fake items F to the dictionary J (i.e., $|J| = |I| + |F|$) and maps each item x onto $M(x) = \{m(x)\} \cup f$, where f is a random subset of F. For example, suppose that $I = \{a, b, c\}$, $m(a) = 1, m(b) = 2, m(c) = 3$ and $F = \{4, 5\}$, a possible one-to-n item mapping M can be defined as $M(a) = \{1, 4, 5\}$, $M(b) = \{2\}$, $M(c) = \{3, 5\}$, $M(a, b) = M(a) \cup M(b) = \{1, 2, 4, 5\}$ and so on. In this way, even if the server has some rough estimates of the frequencies of itemsets, it is not easy to find out the distribution of the true itemsets in the transformed database.

The approach of adding fake items has two weaknesses. The first weakness is that each fake item has the same probability of being added to each transaction, and thus appears with similar frequencies when the number of transactions is large. The second weakness is that fake items are added to transactions independently of the items already present. As a result, each fake item in f is independent of all other items x. This second observation holds even if the frequency of each fake item is different. Based on these observations, in 2009, Molloy et al. [8] presented a frequency analysis based attack to Wong et al.'s algorithm. By this attack, the independently added fake items can be removed by detecting the low correlations between items, and some top frequent items were re-identified successfully.

In 2010, Tai et al. [11] proposed a new approach, based on k-support anonymity, to protect each sensitive item with $k-1$ other items of similar support. For example, a retail transaction database contains 5 transactions, $t_1 = \{wine\}, t_2 = \{cigar, wine\}, t_3 = \{cigar, tea\}, t_4 = \{beer, cigar, wine\}$, and $t_5 = \{beer, tea, wine\}$. Suppose that $beer$, $cigar$, $wine$, tea are replaced with a, b, c, h, respectively. A transformed transaction database with 3-support anonymity is: $t_1 = \{c, d, g\}, t_2 = \{b, d, g\}, t_3 = \{b, h\}$, $t_4 = \{a, b, c\}$, and $t_5 = \{a, c, d, h\}$, where d, g are two fake items. We can see that each of three items a, g, h has 2 supports and each of three items b, c, d has 3 supports. Tai et al. transforms the frequent itemset mining to the generalized/multi-level frequent itemset mining, and limits the additional item occurrences with the help of a pseudo taxonomy tree. Their approach can protect the sensitive information with the k-support anonymity.

Recently, Giannotti et al. [4] extended the concept of k-support anonymity to k-privacy. While k-support anonymity requires that each transformed item cannot be distinguished from at least $k-1$ other items, k-privacy requires that each transformed itemset (i.e., a set of items) cannot be distinguished from at least $k-1$ other itemset with the same size (i.e., the same number of items). They proposed an approach to transform a database to achieve k-privacy. Their approach consists of three main steps: (1) using a 1-to-1 mapping to replace each plain item. Assume that the resulted database is D; (2) grouping items for k-privacy; (3) adding fake transactions to achieve k-privacy. The constructed fake transactions are added to D to form a database D^*, which is submitted with a minimum support threshold to the server. After the server returns the computed frequent patterns from D^*, the data owner removes the effect of the fake transactions. For example, if the support of an itemset E in D^* is x and the support of E in $D^* \backslash D$ is y, then the real support of E in D is $x-y$.

The difference between the privacy-preserving approaches proposed by Tai et al. [11] and Giannotti et al. [4] is that Tai et al. added fake items to the data to achieve k-support anonymity while Giannotti et al. added fake transactions to the data to achieve k-privacy.

3. PRELIMINARIES

3.1 ElGamal Cryptosystem

The ElGamal cryptosystem [2] consists of key generation, encryption, and decryption algorithms as follows.

- Key Generation: On input a security parameter k, it publishes a multiplicative cyclic group $\mathbb{G}$ of prime order q with a generator g, such that discrete logarithm problem over the group $\mathbb{G}$ is hard. Then it chooses a private key x randomly from $\mathbb{Z}_q^* = \{1, 2, \cdots, q-1\}$ and computes a public key $y = g^x$. The private key x is kept secret while the public key y can be known to everyone.

- Encryption: On inputs a message $m \in \mathbb{G}$ and the public key y, it chooses an integer r randomly from $\mathbb{Z}_q^*$ and outputs a ciphertext $C = \mathsf{E}(m) = (A, B)$, where $A = g^r$ and $B = m \cdot y^r$.

- Decryption: On inputs a ciphertext (A, B), and the private key x, it outputs the plaintext $m = \mathsf{D}(C) = B/A^x$.

The ElGamal decryption algorithm is correct because

$$B/A^x = m \cdot y^r/(g^r)^x = m \cdot (g^x)^r/g^{rx} = m.$$

The ElGamal cryptosystem has two important properties for privacy protection as follows.

Homomorphic Property - Given the encryptions of two messages m_1 and m_2, denoted as $\mathsf{E}(m_1) = (A_1, B_1) = (g^{r_1}, m_1 y^{r_1})$ and $\mathsf{E}(m_2) = (A_2, B_2) = (g^{r_2}, m_2 y^{r_2})$, one can compute the encryption of the multiplication $m_1 m_2$ of the two messages, that is, $\mathsf{E}(m_1 m_2) = (A_1 A_2, B_1 B_2)$. This property is correct because

$$B_1 B_2/(A_1 A_2)^x = m_1 y^{r_1} m_2 y^{r_2}/(g^{r_1} g^{r_2})^x = m_1 m_2.$$

Based on this property, we can see that $\mathsf{E}(m^n) = (A^n, B^n)$ for any positive integer n. We denote $\mathsf{E}(m_1)\mathsf{E}(m_2) = (A_1 A_2, B_1 B_2)$ and $\mathsf{E}(m)^n = (A^n, B^n)$.

Re-encryption Property - Given an encryption of a message m, denoted as $\mathsf{E}(m) = (A, B)$, one can compute another encryption of the message, denoted as $\mathsf{RE}(\mathsf{E}(m))$, that is, $(A', B') = (Ag^{r'}, By^{r'})$, where r' is randomly chosen from Z_q^*. This property is correct because

$$By^{r'}/(Ag^{r'})^x = Bg^{xr'}/(A^x g^{r'x}) = B/A^x = m.$$

3.2 Distributed ElGamal Cryptosystem

The ElGamal cryptosystem has been used in a distributed environment [3] in a threshold manner. A simplified distributed ElGamal cryptosystem for n servers $S_1, S_2, \cdots, S_n$ can be described as follows.

- Key Generation: On input a security parameter k, it publishes a multiplicative cyclic group $\mathbb{G}$ of prime order q with a generator g, such that discrete logarithm problem over the group $\mathbb{G}$ is hard. Then each server S_i chooses a private key x_i randomly from $\mathbb{Z}_q^*$ and computes a public key $y_i = g^{x_i}$. The private key x_i is known to S_i only while the public key y_i is known to everyone. Let $y = \prod_{i=1}^n y_i = g^{\sum_{i=1}^n x_i}$, which is the common public key for the n servers.

- Encryption: On inputs a message $m \in \mathbb{G}$ and the common public key y, it chooses an integer r randomly from $\mathbb{Z}_q^*$ and outputs a ciphertext $C = \mathsf{E}(m) = (A, B)$, where $A = g^r$ and $B = m \cdot y^r$.

- Decryption: On inputs a ciphertext (A, B), each server S_i outputs $A_i = A^{x_i}$. Then the algorithm outputs the plaintext $m = \mathsf{D}(C) = B/\prod_{i=1}^n A^{x_i}$.

The decryption algorithm of the distributed ElGamal scheme is correct because

$$B/\prod_{i=1}^{n} A^{x_i} = m \cdot y^r/g^{r\sum_{i=1}^n x_i} = m \cdot y^r/y^r = m.$$

3.3 Distributed Plaintext Equality Test

Distributed plaintext equality test (PET) was introduced by Jakobsson and Juels [7] to test if two plaintexts are equal, given their ElGamal encryptions, without disclosing the two plaintexts.

Assume the same setting as distributed ElGamal cryptosystem, a simplified PET can be described as follows:

- Blindness: Given two ElGamal encryptions $C_1 = (A_1, B_1)$ and $C_2 = (A_2, B_2)$, to test if they are encryptions of the same plaintext, each server S_i chooses an integer r_i randomly from $\mathbb{Z}_q^*$ and outputs $A_i' = (A_1/A_2)^{r_i}$ and $B_i' = (B_1/B_2)^{r_i}$.

- Test: Let $C = (A', B') = (\prod_{i=1}^n A_i', \prod_{i=1}^n B_i')$. The n servers decrypt C as described in the decryption algorithm in Section 3.2. If $\mathsf{D}(C) = 1$, then the two ciphertexts represent the encryption of the same plaintext. This is denoted by $\mathsf{PET}(C_1, C_2) = 1$. Otherwise, the plaintexts are not equal. This is denoted by $\mathsf{PET}(C_1, C_2) = 0$.

When (A_1, B_1) and (A_2, B_2) are encryptions of the same plaintext, (A_i', B_i') is an encryption of 1 and therefore (A', B') is an encryption of 1 as well. Otherwise, (A_i', B_i') is an encryption of a random number and therefore (A', B') is an encryption of a random number as well.

3.4 Conditional Gate

Conditional gate [10] allows n (≥ 2) parties to multiply two encrypted values a and b without disclosing a and b, as long as a is restricted to a two-valued domain. It can be realized by the distributed ElGamal cryptosystem.

Assume the same setting as distributed ElGamal cryptosystem. Let $\mathsf{E}(g^a), \mathsf{E}(g^b)$ denote ElGamal encryptions, with $a \in \{-1, 1\}$ and $b \in \mathbb{Z}_q$, the n server jointly compute $W = \mathsf{E}(g^{ab})$ using the conditional gate as follows.

- Let $U_0 = \mathsf{E}(g^a)$ and $V_0 = \mathsf{E}(g^b)$
- For $i = 1, 2 \cdots, n$, the server S_i takes U_{i-1} and V_{i-1} as input and outputs $U_i = \mathsf{RE}(U_{i-1}^{r_i})$ and $V_i = \mathsf{RE}(V_{i-1}^{r_i})$, where r_i is randomly chosen from $\{-1, 1\}$.
- The n servers jointly decrypt U_n to obtain $g^{a \prod_{i=1}^{n} r_i}$. Because $a, r_i \in \{-1, 1\}$, it is easy to know $a' = a \prod_{i=1}^{n} r_i \in \{-1, 1\}$.
- Let $W = V_n^{a'}$.

The conditional gate correctly computes $\mathsf{E}(g^{ab})$ because

$$V_n^{a'} = \mathsf{E}(g^{b \prod_{i=1}^{n} r_i})^{a'} = \mathsf{E}(g^{ab (\prod_{i=1}^{n} r_i)^2}) = \mathsf{E}(g^{ab}).$$

Based on the conditional gate, the n servers can jointly compute $\mathsf{E}(g^{ab})$ given $\mathsf{E}(g^a)$ and $\mathsf{E}(g^b)$ for $a, b \in \{0, 1\}$ as follows.

$$\mathsf{E}(g^{ab}) = \mathsf{E}(g^{((2a-1)b+b)2^{-1}}) = (\mathsf{E}(g^{(2a-1)b})\mathsf{E}(g^b))^{2^{-1}}.$$

Note that $2a - 1 \in \{-1, 1\}$ when $a \in \{0, 1\}$ and $\mathsf{E}(g^{(2a-1)b})$ can be computed with the conditional gate as above.

Furthermore, given encrypted bit representations $\mathsf{E}(x) = (\mathsf{E}(g^{x_{m-1}}), \cdots, \mathsf{E}(g^{x_1}), \mathsf{E}(g^{x_0}))$ and $\mathsf{E}(y) = (\mathsf{E}(g^{y_{m-1}}), \cdots, \mathsf{E}(g^{y_1}), \mathsf{E}(g^{y_0}))$ of two numbers x and y, the n servers can jointly compute the bits of $x+y$, given by $\mathsf{E}(z) = \mathsf{E}(x+y) = (\mathsf{E}(g^{c_{m-1}}), \mathsf{E}(g^{z_{m-1}}), \cdots, \mathsf{E}(g^{z_1}), \mathsf{E}(g^{z_0}))$ as follows:

$$\mathsf{E}(g^{c_i}) = \mathsf{E}(g^{x_i y_i})\mathsf{E}(g^{x_i c_{i-1}})\mathsf{E}(g^{y_i c_{i-1}})\mathsf{E}(g^{-2x_i y_i c_{i-1}}),$$

$$\mathsf{E}(g^{z_i}) = \mathsf{E}(g^{x_i})\mathsf{E}(g^{y_i})\mathsf{E}(g^{c_{i-1}})\mathsf{E}(g^{-2c_i}),$$

for $i = 0, 1, \cdots, m-1$, where $c_{-1} = 0$. We denote $\mathsf{E}(x+y) = \mathsf{E}(x) \boxplus \mathsf{E}(y)$.

3.5 Two's Complement

Two's complement system is the most common method of representing signed integers on computers ([6]). A positive integer in two's complement always has a 0 in the leftmost bit (sign bit) and is represented the same way as an unsigned binary integer. To negate a number, we invert all the bits and add one.

Comparison of two integers is often implemented with two's complement. Given the m-bit representations $(x_{m-1} \cdots x_1 x_0)$ and $(y_{m-1} \cdots y_1 y_0)$ of two numbers x and y, where the sign bits $x_{m-1} = 0$ and $y_{m-1} = 0$, the two's complement of $-y$, denoted as $\overline{-y}$, is $(\overline{y_{m-1}} \cdots \overline{y_1}\ \overline{y_0}) + 1$ where $\overline{y_i} = 1 - y_i$, let $z = (z_{m-1} \cdots z_1 z_0) = x + \overline{-y}$. If the sign bit $z_{m-1} = 0$, $x \geq y$ and otherwise $x < y$.

4. MODEL

Our model considers a cloud computing environment with clients and servers. The clients are assumed to lack data storage, computational resources and expertise, while the servers can provide the client with various services, including data storage and data mining services. Our model with one client, one database (DB) server and n data mining (DM) servers can be illustrated in Fig. 1.

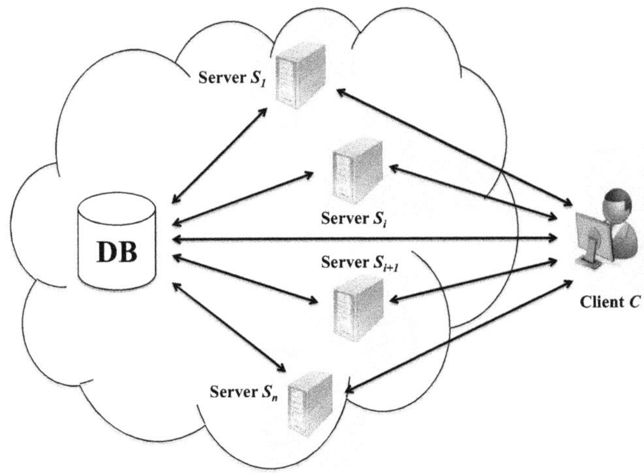

Figure 1: Our Model for Privacy-Preserving Data Mining in the Cloud

In Fig. 1, the client stores its data in the DB server in the cloud. To protect its data privacy, the ElGamal cryptosystem is used. At first, the client generates its ElGamal public/private key pair. Then it encrypts its data with its ElGamal public key before uploading it to the DB server. To mine association rules from the encrypted data, the client selects n DM servers in the cloud, where $n \geq 2$, and splits its private key into n pieces and distributed them to the n DM servers, respectively. The n DM servers can cooperate to decrypt encrypted data on behalf of the client and thus can be thought as decryption servers as well. To reduce the possibility that all servers are compromised, the user can use servers from different cloud providers.

All servers (either DB or DM servers) are assumed to be "semi-honest", i.e., they follows protocols or algorithms exactly, but may be curious about the data privacy of the client. In addition, **at least one out of n DM servers is assumed to be trusted not to collude with other DM servers**. In view of this, the n servers can cooperate to decrypt the encrypted data only if they are required by data mining algorithms.

Our model aims to protect the data privacy of the client which outsources its data mining task to the n DM servers and the DB server.

This paper focuses on association rule mining and thus we only consider a database composed of transactions. Each transaction contains a transaction identity (ID) and a set of items. Each item in the transaction is encrypted and stored in the DB server. The DB server does not know the private key of the client and therefore cannot decrypt any transaction.

When performing association rule mining on the encrypted transaction database, the basic privacy requirement is protecting the privacy of items. We formally define the item privacy of association rule mining over the encrypted transaction database with a game as follows.

Definition 1. An association rule mining algorithm over the encrypted transaction database has *item privacy* if any adversary does not have a non-negligible additional probability more than 1/2 to win the following game:

- The adversary is provided with the public key of the client, chooses two distinct items a_0 and a_1 and sends them to a challenger.
- The challenger randomly chooses a bit b, encrypts a_b with the public key of the client and returns an encryption of a_b to the adversary.
- The n DM servers and the DB server run the association rule mining algorithm over the encrypted transaction database.
- The adversary guesses the bit selected by the challenger, denoted as b'. If $b' = b$, the adversary wins the game.

An association rule mining algorithm with item privacy cannot guarantee the privacy of the support of itemsets. For example, in a transaction database, the same items are replaced with an encryption of the item and the replacement of the database is then forwarded to the DB server for association rule mining. On the basis of Definition 1, the association rule mining algorithm has item privacy. But the adversary can still learn the supports of the encrypted items and perform the background knowledge-based attack.

To prevent the background knowledge-based attack, one approach is letting each DM server add noisy transactions (encrypted by the public key of the client) into the encrypted transaction database, like [4], and mix the original and noisy transactions by re-encryption and random shuffling, and then remove the effect of the noisy transactions during association rule mining. The noisy transactions can hide the real supports of itemsets. In this case, any attacker, possibly an insider, such as a DM server or a coalition of DM servers, must not distinguish the original transactions and the noisy transactions. Otherwise, the noisy transactions can be easily removed.

We formally define the *transaction privacy* of association rule mining over the encrypted transaction database by a game as follows.

Definition 2. An association rule mining algorithm over the encrypted transaction database, composed of the original transactions (encrypted) and the noisy transactions (encrypted), has *transaction privacy* if any adversary does not have a non-negligible additional probability more than 1/2 to win the following game:

- The adversary is provided with the public key of the client, the set of transactions (encrypted) in the original transaction database, denoted as T, and a set of noisy transactions (encrypted), denoted as T'. The adversary chooses two distinct transactions t_0 and t_1 and sends them to a challenger, where t_0, t_1 are from T and T', respectively and contain the same number of items (encrypted). We assume that t_1 is not a noisy transaction generated by the adversary or its coalition in the case that the adversary is a DM server.
- The challenger randomly chooses a bit b.
- The n DM servers and the DB server run the association rule mining algorithm over the encrypted transaction database.
- The challenger keeps all status of t_b during the association rule mining and returns them to the adversary.
- The adversary guesses the bit selected by the challenger, denoted as b'. If $b' = b$, the adversary wins the game.

Despite of the existence of noisy transactions, an association rule mining algorithm with transaction privacy may still reveal certain information about the original transactions such as the probability of a transaction to be an original transaction.

An ideal association rule mining to ensure the privacy of the transaction database must not disclose any information about the original data except for the information about whether an encrypted itemset is frequent or not. We formally define the *database privacy* of association rule mining by a game as follows:

Definition 3. An association rule mining algorithm over the encrypted transaction database has *database privacy* if any adversary does not have a non-negligible additional probability more than 1/2 to win the following game:

- The adversary is provided with the public key of the client, chooses two different transaction databases D_0 and D_1 with the same frequent itemsets and the same size and sends D_0 and D_1 to the challenger.
- The challenger randomly chooses a bit b.
- The n DM server and the DB server run the association rule mining algorithm on the transaction database D_b and returns all the intermediate outcomes and final outcomes to the adversary.
- The adversary guesses the bit selected by the challenger, denoted as b'. If $b' = b$, the adversary wins the game.

In the above three privacy requirements for association rule mining, item privacy is the basic privacy requirement, transaction privacy is higher than item privacy, and database privacy is the highest of the three privacy requirements.

5. ASSOCIATION RULE MINING WITH ITEM PRIVACY

In this section, we give our solution for association rule mining with item privacy.

5.1 Setup

First of all, on input a security parameter k, the cloud publishes a multiplicative cyclic group $\mathbb{G}$ of prime order q with a generator g, such that the discrete logarithm over the group $\mathbb{G}$ is hard.

In addition, the cloud publishes a standard item table which maps any item to a group element in $\mathbb{G}$, such that an item a is mapped to a code $g^{h(a)}$, where h is a collision-resistant hash functions from $\{0,1\}^*$ to an element in $\mathbb{Z}_q^*$.

A client chooses a private key x randomly from $\mathbb{Z}_q^* = \{1, 2, \cdots, q-1\}$ and computes a public key $y = g^x$. For a transaction $t = (\mathsf{TID}, a_1, a_2, \cdots, a_\lambda)$, where TID is the transaction identity and a_i is an item, the client looks up the code of each item in the transaction from the standard item table and encrypts the code with its public key y as described in Section 3.1. Then the client uploads the encrypted transaction composed of encrypted items to the DB server.

To outsource the association rule mining task to the cloud, the client chooses n (≥ 2) DM servers from different cloud providers. Next, the client splits its private key into n pieces $x_1, x_2, \cdots, x_n$ such that $\sum_{i=1}^{n} x_i = x \pmod q$. Then, the client distributes $x_1, x_2, \cdots, x_n$ to the n DM servers, respectively, via secure channels as shown in Fig. 1. For instance, the client encrypts x_i with the public key of the ith DM server S_i and sends the encryption to the server.

For association rule mining, the client sends the minimum support and confidence to the DB server.

5.2 Same Item Identification

In the encrypted transaction database, the same item has different encryptions because the ElGamal encryption is probabilistic. To mine the frequent itemsets from the encrypted transaction database, denoted as $T = \{t_1, t_2, \cdots, t_\ell\}$, the n DM servers and the DB server cooperate to identify the encryptions of the same item and replace them with one encryption of the item by Algorithm 1.

Algorithm 1 Same Item Identification (DB server and n DM Servers)

Input: $T = \{t_1, t_2, \cdots, t_\ell\}, y$ (public), $x_1, x_2, \cdots, x_n$ (private)
Output: $T' = \{t'_1, t'_2, \cdots, t'_\ell\}$
1: $t'_1 \leftarrow t_1, T' \leftarrow \{t'_1\}, t'_2 = t'_3 = \cdots = t'_\ell \leftarrow \emptyset$.
2: for $i = 1$ to $\ell - 1$ {
3: if ($t_i \neq \emptyset$) {
4: for any $c \in t_i$ {
5: for $j = i + 1$ to ℓ {
6: if ($t_j \neq \emptyset$) {
7: for any $c' \in t_j$ {
8: n DM servers cooperate to run $\mathsf{PET}(c, c')$
9: if ($\mathsf{PET}(c, c') = 1$) $\{t'_j \leftarrow t'_j \cup \{c\}; t_j \leftarrow t_j - \{c'\};$ $j \leftarrow j + 1$; go to Step 5; }
10: } //end for at Step 7
11: } //end if at Step 6
12: } //end for at Step 5
13: } //end for at Step 4
14: } //end if at Step 3
15: $t'_{i+1} \leftarrow t'_{i+1} \cup t_{i+1}$.
16: } //end for at Step 2
17: **return** T'

In Algorithm 1, the DB server executes all lines except for the Plaintext Equality Test (PET) at Step 8, which requires those n DM servers to cooperate as described in Sections 3.2 and 3.3. For efficiency, we assume that each DM server in PET sends (A'_i, B'_i) to the DB server which computes and broadcasts (A', B') to all DM servers, and each DM server in the distributed ElGamal decryption sends A_i to the DB server which computes and broadcasts the decryption result.

Theorem 1 (Correctness) Algorithm 1 does not change the content of the transaction database, i.e., $\mathsf{D}(T') = \mathsf{D}(T)$, where D stands for the ElGamal decryption.

Proof We only need to prove $\mathsf{D}(t'_i) = \mathsf{D}(t_i)$ for any i. It is obvious that $\mathsf{D}(t'_1) = \mathsf{D}(t_1)$. Let us consider t_i and t'_i for $2 \leq i \leq \ell$. For the first $i - 1$ loops at Step 2, the transaction t'_i is filled with the items in the transaction t_i which are the same as some items in the transactions $t_1, t_2, \cdots, t_{i-1}$ at Step 9. In the end of $i - 1$ loops at Step 15, the transaction t'_i is added with the items in the transaction t_i which are not the same as any item in the transactions $t_1, t_2, \cdots, t_{i-1}$. Therefore, the two transactions t'_i and t_i have the same items, i.e., $\mathsf{D}(t'_i) = \mathsf{D}(t_i)$. □

5.3 Association Rule Mining on Encrypted Data

Because the different encryptions of the same item in the encrypted transaction database have been replaced by one encryption of the item, the DB server can now count the support of any encrypted itemset. Therefore, the DB server can run the Apriori algorithm [1] on the replacement of the encrypted database T' according to the minimum support provided by the client.

By the Apriori algorithm, the DB server can find all frequent encrypted itemsets according to the minimum support and then construct the association rules. Then the DB server returns the strong encrypted association rules satisfying the minimum support and confidence to the client.

In the end, the client decrypts the encrypted strong association rules and looks up the standard item table to determine the items in the association rules.

During the association rule mining, all items in the transaction database are encrypted all the time. Therefore, this solution achieves the item privacy. However, this solution cannot withstand the background knowledge-based attack because the supports of encrypted itemsets in the encrypted transaction database are known to the DB server in the cloud.

6. ASSOCIATION RULE MINING WITH TRANSACTION PRIVACY

In this section, we give our solution for association rule mining with transaction privacy. This solution can hide the real supports of the encrypted itemsets in the encrypted transaction database by adding noisy transactions.

6.1 Setup

The setting of this solution is the same as described in Section 5.1 except that the client sends an encryption of the minimum support δ to the DB server instead of the plain minimum support.

Assume that there are ℓ transactions in the database and $m = \lceil \log_2 \ell \rceil$ and the binary expression of δ is $(w_{m-1} \cdots w_1 w_0)$. The encryption of δ takes a form of

$$\mathsf{E}(\delta) = \{\mathsf{E}(g^{w_{m-1}}), \cdots, \mathsf{E}(g^{w_1}), \mathsf{E}(g^{w_0})\}$$

where $w_i \in \{0, 1\}$.

We do not consider the minimum confidence here. We assume that the DB server and the n DM servers cooperate to mine all frequent encrypted itemsets and return them with their encrypted supports to the client. After decryption, the client can easily construct strong association rules satisfying the minimum support and confidence locally.

6.2 Item Dictionary Anonymization

To construct a noisy transaction, the DM servers need to refer to a dictionary of possible items. We assume that all possible items in the original transaction database are $\{a_1, a_2, \cdots, a_\gamma\}$. The DM servers may directly select and encrypt some items from the dictionary and then put the encrypted items into a noisy transaction. This way makes it hard to remove the effect of the noisy transactions without decryption when mining frequent itemsets.

To facilitate the removal of the noisy transactions, the DB server and the n DM servers cooperate to anonymize the dictionary of all possible items to obtain a list of encrypted items $\{c_1, c_2, \cdots, c_\gamma\}$ with Algorithm 2 such that nobody knows the mapping between the dictionary $\{a_1, a_2, \cdots, a_\gamma\}$ and the anonymized dictionary $\{c_1, c_2, \cdots, c_\gamma\}$ as long as one of the n DM servers is honest.

In Algorithm 2, the DB server executes Steps 1 to 4 and forwards $c_1, c_2, \cdots, c_\gamma$ to the first DM server at Step 5. The n DM servers then anonymize the dictionary alternatively at Steps 6 and 7. In the end, the last DM servers returns the anonymized dictionary to the DB server, which publishes it in the cloud.

6.3 Transaction Anonymization

Based on the anonymized dictionary, the DM servers can select and re-encrypt some encrypted items in the dictionary and put them into noisy transactions, which are then sent to the DB server.

To produce noisy transactions appropriate for the original encrypted transaction database, the DB server groups the original

Algorithm 2 Item Dictionary Anonymization (DB server and n DM Server)

Input: $\{a_1, a_2, \cdots, a_\gamma\}, y$ (public)
Output: $\{c_1, c_2, \cdots, c_\gamma\}$

1: for $i = 1$ to γ {
2: DB server looks up the code a_i' of a_i from standard item table;
3: DB server encrypts a_i' to form $c_i = (g^r, a_i' y^r)$, where r is randomly chosen from $\mathbb{Z}_q^*$.
4: } //end for at Step 1
5: for $j = 1$ to n {
6: Server S_j mixes $c_1, c_2, \cdots, c_\gamma$ by re-encryption and randomly shuffling;
7: Server S_j forwards the results to Server S_{j+1} if $j < n$.
8: } // end for at Step 5
9: **return** $(c_1, c_2, \cdots, c_\gamma)$

transactions on the basis of the number of items a transaction contains. Assume that the original transaction database $T = \{t_1, t_2, \cdots, t_\ell\}$ is grouped into $\{T_1, T_2, \cdots, T_\lambda\}$, where T_i is the set of all transactions with i items and λ is the length of the longest transaction. Each DM server adds $\lceil \phi \cdot |T_i| \rceil$ noisy transactions with i items into T_i, where $|T_i|$ is the total number of transactions in T_i and ϕ is a positive number depending on the level of transaction privacy. Obviously, the larger ϕ is, the higher transaction privacy we can achieve, but the less efficient the protocol is.

Assume that T_i^* is the set of transactions with i items after all n DM servers add noisy transactions, we have

$$|T_i^*| = |T_i| + n \cdot \lceil \phi \cdot |T_i| \rceil$$

for $i = 1, 2, \cdots, \lambda$ and the transaction database composed of the original and noisy transactions T^* is $\{T_1^*, T_2^*, \cdots, T_\lambda^*\}$. It is obvious that

$$|T^*| = |T| + n \cdot \lceil \phi \cdot |T| \rceil.$$

If $\phi \approx 1/n$ and $|T_i| \geq n$ for any i, the size of the resulted transaction database T^* is almost twice as that of the original transaction database T.

Next, the DB server and the n DM servers cooperate to run Algorithm 3 to anonymize $T_\eta^* = \{t_1^*, t_2^*, \cdots, t_{\ell_\eta}^*\}$ (where t_i^* contains η items for any i and ℓ_η is the total number of transactions in T_η^*) .

Algorithm 3 Transaction Anonymization (DB server and n DM Servers)

Input: $T_\eta^* = \{t_1^*, t_2^*, \cdots, t_{\ell_\eta}^*\}, y$ (public)
Output: $T_\eta' = \{t_1', t_2', \cdots, t_{\ell_\eta}'\}$

1: $T_\eta' \leftarrow T_\eta^*$
2: for $i = 1$ to n {
3: for $j = 1$ to ℓ_η {
4: for any $c \in t_j'$ {
5: Server S_i re-encrypts c to $c' = \mathsf{RE}(c)$ with the public key y of the client as described in Section 3.1 and replaces c with c' in t_j'.
6: } //end for at Step 4
7: Server S_i randomly shuffles items in t_j'.
8: } //end for at Step 3
9: Server S_i randomly shuffles transactions in T_η' and forwards T_η' to Server S_{i+1} if $i < n$.
10: } // end for at Step 2
11: **return** T_η'

In Algorithm 3, the DB server forwards the transactions T_η' to the first DM server at Step 2 and in the end, the last DM server forwards the anonymized transactions to the DB server. In the same way, the DB server and the n DM servers can cooperate to anonymize $T_1^*, T_2^*, \cdots, T_\lambda^*$.

6.4 Same Item Identification Based on Dictionary

We give Algorithm 1 to identify the same item in Section 5.2. That algorithm can be simplified to Algorithm 4 by using the anonymized dictionary of possible items, i.e., $(c_1, c_2, \cdots, c_\gamma)$.

Algorithm 4 Same Item Identification Based on Dictionary (DB server and n DM Servers)

Input: $(c_1, c_2, \cdots, c_\gamma), T' = \{t_1', t_2', \cdots, t_L'\}, y$ (public), $x_1, x_2, \cdots, x_n$ (private)
Output: $T'' = \{t_1'', t_2'', \cdots, t_L''\}$

1: $T'' \leftarrow T'$
2: for $i = 1$ to γ {
3: for $j = 1$ to L {
4: for any $c \in t_j''$ {
5: n DM servers cooperate to run $\mathsf{PET}(c_i, c)$
6: If $\mathsf{PET}(c_i, c) = 1$ {
7: c in t_j'' is replaced with c_i;
8: $j \leftarrow j + 1$; go to Step 3
9: } //end if at Step 6
10: } //end for at Step 4
11: } // end for at Step 3
12: } // end for at Step 2
13: **return** T''

By Algorithm 4, all encrypted items in the transaction database are replaced with the encrypted items in the dictionary.

Like Algorithm 1, Algorithm 4 does not change the content of the transaction database because the algorithm replaces the encryption of the item with an encryption of the same item only.

After executing Algorithm 4, a DM server may be able to identify the noisy transactions added by it in T'', but cannot distinguish between the original transactions and noisy transactions added by other DM servers.

6.5 Frequent Itemset Mining

After the same item identification, the DB server can count the support of any encrypted itemsets in the replacement of the transaction database. But because of the existence of noisy transactions, the support is not the real support of the itemset. To remove the effect of the noisy transactions, each DM server is required to keep the noisy transactions it adds into the transaction database.

Given the encrypted minimum support threshold $\mathsf{E}(\delta) = \{\mathsf{E}(g^{w_{m-1}}), \cdots, \mathsf{E}(g^{w_1}), \mathsf{E}(g^{w_0})\}$ provided by the client, let us consider the key step in the Apriori algorithm over the encrypted transaction database, i.e., determining if an encrypted k-itemset $\alpha = \{\mathsf{E}(a_1), \mathsf{E}(a_2), \cdots, \mathsf{E}(a_k)\}$ constructed according to the anonymized dictionary is frequent (i.e, the support of the itemset is more than the minimum support threshold) or not. Assume that the support of the encrypted itemset α in the replacement of the transaction database is f, whose binary representation is $(u_{m'-1} \cdots u_1 u_0)$, which is known to the DB server and the n DM servers, and the support of α in the noisy transactions added by Server S_i is f_i, whose binary representation is $(v_{m'-1}^i \cdots v_1^i v_0^i)$, which is only known to S_i, where $m' = \lceil \log_2 |T''| \rceil + 1$ and the leftmost bits $u_{m'-1} = v_{m'-1} = 0$. Because $|T''| > |T|$, we have $m' > m$.

Note that because the encrypted itemset α is composed of the encrypted items in the dictionary, each DM server is able to count the support of α in its noisy transactions.

On the basis of $\mathsf{E}(\delta), f, f_i$ $(i = 1, 2, \cdots, n)$, the DB server and the n DM servers cooperate to run the Algorithm 5 to determine if α is frequent or not.

Algorithm 5 Private Comparison 1 (DB Server and n DM Server)

Input: $\mathsf{E}(\delta), f, y$ (public), (f_i, x_i) $(i = 1, 2, \cdots, n)$ (private)
Output: 1 if α is frequent and 0 otherwise.
1: $\mathsf{E}(z) \leftarrow \mathsf{E}(\delta)$.
2: for $i = 1$ to n {
3: Server S_i lets
$\mathsf{E}(f_i) = (\mathsf{E}(g^{v^i_{m'-1}}), \cdots, \mathsf{E}(g^{v^i_1}), \mathsf{E}(g^{v^i_0}))$
4: n DM servers cooperate to compute
$\mathsf{E}(z) \leftarrow \mathsf{E}(z) \boxplus \mathsf{E}(f_i)$ as described in Section 3.4.
5: } //end for at Step 2
6: n DM servers cooperate to compute
$\mathsf{E}(z) = \mathsf{E}(z) \boxplus \mathsf{E}(\overline{-1})$ as in Sections 3.4 and 3.5.
7: DB server lets $\overline{-f} \leftarrow (\overline{u_{m'-1}} \cdots \overline{u_1}\,\overline{u_0}) + 1$, where $\overline{-f}$ is the two's complement of $-f$ and $\overline{u_j} = 1 - u_j$.
8: DB server and n DM servers cooperate to compute
$\mathsf{E}(z) = \mathsf{E}(z) \boxplus \mathsf{E}(\overline{-f})$ as described in Section 3.4.
9: n DM servers cooperate to decrypt $\mathsf{E}(g^{z_{m'-1}})$ as described in Section 3.2.
10: if $z_{m'-1} = 1$, then $\beta = 1$ else $\beta = 0$
11: **return** β

Theorem 2 (Correctness) Algorithm 5 outputs 1 if the encrypted itemset α is frequent and 0 otherwise.

Proof Because f is the support of α in the replacement of the transaction database with noisy transactions and f_i is the support of α in the noisy transactions added by Server S_i, the real support F of α in the original transaction database is

$$F = f - \sum_{i=1}^{n} f_i$$

Therefore,

$$(\delta - 1) - F = (\sum_{i=1}^{n} f_i + \delta - 1) - f$$

Because $m' = \lceil \log_2 |T''| \rceil + 1$, $|T''| = |T'| = |T^*| = |T| + n\lceil \phi |T| \rceil$, $\delta \leq |T|$ and $\sum_{i=}^{n} f_i \leq \lceil \phi |T| \rceil$, the binary representation $\sum_{i=1}^{n} f_i + \delta - 1$ is less than $m' - 1$ bits. Therefore, after Step 6 in Algorithm 5, the leftmost bit of $z = \sum_{i=1}^{n} f_i + \delta - 1$ is 0, i.e., $z_{m'-1} = 0$.

By Step 8 in Algorithm 5, $z = (\sum_{i=1}^{n} f_i + \delta - 1) + \overline{-f}$. According to Section 3.5, if the sign bit $z_{m'-1}$ is 1, $\delta - 1 < F$, i.e., $F \geq \delta$ and $\beta = 1$. Otherwise, $\delta - 1 \geq F$, i.e., $F < \delta$ and $\beta = 0$. □

By Algorithm 5, the DB server and the n DM servers can cooperate to find all frequent itemsets in T without the need for decryption of any encrypted item. The association rule mining has item privacy. In addition, the original transactions and the noisy transactions are mixed completely by re-encryption and random shuffling and thus indistinguishable to the adversary. The association rule mining has transaction privacy as well. However, Algorithm 4 may leak some information about the original transactions to some extent.

7. ASSOCIATION RULE MINING WITH DATABASE PRIVACY

In this section, we give our solution for association rule mining with database privacy. The setting of this solution is the same as described in Section 6.1.

7.1 Item Dictionary Anonymization

First of all, the DB server and the n DM servers run Algorithm 2 to create an anonymized dictionary of encrypted items $(c_1, c_2, \cdots, c_\gamma)$.

7.2 Transaction Anonymization

Based on the anonymized dictionary, the DM servers can select and re-encrypt some encrypted items in the dictionary and put them into noisy transactions, which are then sent to the DB server, as described in Section 6.3. Then the DB server and DM servers run Algorithm 3 to mix the original and noisy transactions, which results in a new database D'.

7.3 Same Item Identification Based on Dictionary

The DB server equally divides D' into n subsets $D'_1, D'_2, \cdots, D'_n$ where $D'_i \cap D'_j = \emptyset$ and assigns D'_i to Server S_i. Then the n DM servers cooperate to run Algorithm 6 to identify items in the database D'. After executing Algorithm 6, all items in the subset D'_i are replaced with the items in the anonymized dictionary and known to the DM Server S_i only.

Algorithm 6 Same Item Identification Based on Dictionary (n DM Servers)

Input: $(c_1, c_2, \cdots, c_\gamma), D'_1, D'_2, \cdots, D'_n, y$ (public), $x_1, x_2, \cdots, x_n$ (private)
Output: $D''_1, D''_2, \cdots, D''_n$
1: for $i = 1$ to n {
2: $D''_i \leftarrow D'_i$
3: for $j = 1$ to γ {
4: for any $c \in D''_i$ {
5: n DM servers cooperate to run $\mathsf{PET}(c_j, c)$ as described in Sections 3.2 and 3.3, where **all DM servers send their computation results to** S_i. S_i checks if $\mathsf{PET}(c_j, c) = 1$ and keeps it secret.
6: If $\mathsf{PET}(c_j, c) = 1$ {
7: S_i replaces c in D''_i with c_j.}
8: } //end for at Step 4
9: } //end for at Step 3
10: } // end for at Step 1
11: **return** $D''_1, D''_2, \cdots, D''_n$

7.4 Frequent Itemset Mining

Given a k-itemset $\alpha = \{\mathsf{E}(a_1), \mathsf{E}(a_2), \cdots, \mathsf{E}(a_k)\}$ constructed according to the anonymized dictionary, let us consider how to determine if α is frequent or not.

The DM Server S_i can count the support of the k-item α in D''_i, denoted as F_i, and the support of α in the noisy transactions added by S_i, denoted as f_i. F_i and f_i are known to S_i only. The real support of α in the original transaction database is

$$F = \sum_{i=1}^{n} (F_i - f_i).$$

Given the encrypted binary representation of the minimum support $\mathsf{E}(\delta) = \{\mathsf{E}(g^{w_{m-1}}), \cdots, \mathsf{E}(g^{w_1}), \mathsf{E}(g^{w_0})\}$ provided by the client, and $F_i - f_i = (v^i_{m'-1} \cdots v^i_1 v^i_0)(i = 1, 2, \cdots, n)$ for the encrypted itemset α, where $m' = \lceil \log_2 |T''| \rceil + 1$ and T'' is the anonymized database, the n DM servers cooperate to run Algorithm 7 (similar to Algorithm 5) to determine if α is frequent or not.

Algorithm 7 Private Comparison 2 (n DM Server)

Input: $\mathsf{E}(\delta), y$ (public), $(F_i - f_i, x_i)$ $(i = 1, 2, \cdots, n)$ (private)
Output: 1 if α is frequent and 0 otherwise.

1: n DM servers cooperate to compute
$\mathsf{E}(\overline{-\delta}) = (\mathsf{E}(g^{1-w_{m'}}), \cdots, \mathsf{E}(g^{1-w_1}), \mathsf{E}(g^{1-w_0})) \boxplus E(1)$ as in Section 3.4, where $\mathsf{E}(g^{1-w_i}) = \mathsf{E}(g)/\mathsf{E}(g^{w_i})$ and $w_{m'} = \cdots = w_{m+1} = w_m = 0$. $\overline{-\delta}$ is the two's complement of $-\delta$ with $m' + 1$ bits according to Section 3.5.
2: $\mathsf{E}(z) \leftarrow \mathsf{E}(\overline{-\delta})$
3: for $i = 1$ to n {
4: Server S_i lets $v^i_{m'} = 0$ if $F_i - f_i \geq 0$ and 1 otherwise.
$\mathsf{E}(F_i - f_i) = (\mathsf{E}(g^{v^i_{m'}}), \mathsf{E}(g^{v^i_{m'-1}}), \cdots, \mathsf{E}(g^{v^i_1}), \mathsf{E}(g^{v^i_0}))$
5: n DM servers cooperate to compute
$\mathsf{E}(z) = \mathsf{E}(z) \boxplus \mathsf{E}(F_i - f_i)$ as described in Section 3.4.
6: } //end for at Step 3
7: n DM servers cooperate to decrypt $\mathsf{E}(g^{z_{m'}})$ as described in Section 3.2.
8: if $z'_m = 0$, then $\beta = 1$ else $\beta = 0$
9: **return** β

Theorem 3 (Correctness) Algorithm 7 outputs 1 if the encrypted itemset α is frequent and 0 otherwise.

Proof After Step 6 in Algorithm 7, we have $z = \sum_{i=1}^{n}(F_i - f_i) + \overline{-\delta}$. Based on Section 3.5, if the sign bit $z_{m'}$ is 0, we have $F \geq \delta$ and $\beta = 1$. Otherwise, $\delta < F$ and $\beta = 0$. □

8. SECURITY ANALYSIS

We have provided three solutions for association rule mining in the cloud. In this section, we show that the three solutions achieve item privacy, transaction privacy and database privacy, respectively.

8.1 Security Analysis on Association Rule Mining with Item Privacy

Our solution for association rule mining with item privacy has two phases - the same item identification (Algorithm 1) and the association rule mining (the Apriori algorithm). According to Definition 1, we have

Theorem 4 Our association rule mining solution described in Section 5 has item privacy if the ElGamal encryption scheme is semantically secure and at least one of the n DM servers is honest.

Proof Without loss of generality, we assume that all DM servers except the first DM server S_1 are compromised by an adversary. If the adversary can break the item privacy of the client, i.e., winning the game given in Definition 1, we can use the adversary to break the semantic security of the ElGamal encryption scheme as follows.

At first, we send the public key y_1 of Server S_1 and the public and private keys of other DM servers, i.e., $(x_2, y_2), (x_3, y_3), \cdots, (x_n, y_n)$, to the adversary. After the adversary selects two items a_0 and a_1, we forward them to the ElGamal challenger, which randomly chooses a bit $b \in \{0, 1\}$, and returns back $\mathsf{E}_1(a_b)$, where E_1 denotes the encryption of a_b with y_1. Assume that $\mathsf{E}_1(a_b) = (A, B)$, we can construct $\mathsf{E}(a_b) = (A, B \cdot A^{x_2+x_3+\cdots+x_n})$, where E denotes the encryption with the common public key y, and forward $\mathsf{E}(a_b)$ to the adversary.

Next, the client (simulated by us) generates a transaction database D, encrypts all items in D with the common public key y and forwards the encrypted database $\mathsf{E}(D)$ to the adversary. During the same item identification (Algorithm 1), the DB server (simulated by us) can answer the PET queries without the need for decryption, because we know the original transaction database.

In the end, the adversary outputs its guess b and we forwards b to the ElGamal challenger. If the adversary has a non-negligible additional probability more than 1/2 to win the game, we have a non-negligible additional probability more than 1/2 to break the semantic security of the ElGamal encryption scheme. Therefore, if the ElGamal encryption scheme is semantically secure and at least one of the n DM servers is honest, our solution in Section 5 has item privacy. □

8.2 Security Analysis on Association Rule Mining with Transaction Privacy

Our solution for association rule mining with transaction privacy has five phases - the setup, the item dictionary anonymization (Algorithm 2), the transaction anonymization (Algorithm 3), the same item identification (Algorithm 4) and the frequent itemset mining (Algorithm 5). According to Definition 2, we have

Theorem 5 Our association rule mining solution described in Section 6 has transaction privacy if the ElGamal encryption scheme is semantically secure and at least one of the n DM servers is honest.

Proof We assume that all DM servers except for Server S_1 are compromised by an adversary. If the adversary can break the transaction privacy of the client, i.e., winning the game given in Definition 2, we can use the adversary to break the semantic security of the ElGamal encryption scheme as follows.

At first, we send to the adversary the public key y_1 of S_1, the public and private keys of other servers. Next we run the item dictionary anonymization (Algorithm 2) to obtain a dictionary of encrypted items on the basis of the common public key y. Then we provide the adversary with a list of encrypted original transactions and a list of encrypted noisy transactions (added by S_1 simulated by us), where all transactions contain η items. After the adversary selects two distinct encrypted transactions $t_0 = (\mathsf{E}(a^0_1), \mathsf{E}(a^0_2), \cdots, \mathsf{E}(a^0_\eta))$ and $t_1 = (\mathsf{E}(a^1_1), \mathsf{E}(a^1_2), \cdots, \mathsf{E}(a^1_\eta))$, where t_0 and t_1 are the encrypted original and noisy transactions, respectively, we forward $(a^0_1, a^0_2, \cdots, a^0_\eta)$ and $(a^1_1, a^1_2, \cdots, a^1_\eta)$ to the ElGamal challenger, which randomly chooses a bit $b \in \{0, 1\}$, and returns back an encryption of t_b, denoted as $(\mathsf{E}_1(a^b_1), \mathsf{E}_1(a^b_2), \cdots, \mathsf{E}_1(a^b_\eta))$, where E_1 denotes the encryption with y_1. Like the proof of Theorem 4, we can construct $t'_b = (\mathsf{E}(a^b_1), \mathsf{E}(a^b_2), \cdots, \mathsf{E}(a^b_\eta))$, where E denotes the encryption with the common public key y, and send t'_b to the adversary.

Next, we run the transaction anonymization (Algorithm 3) according to the common public key y and send to the adversary the re-encryptions of both t_0 and t_1, denoted as $\mathsf{RE}(t_0)$ and $\mathsf{RE}(t_1)$, in a random order. Then we run the same item identification (Algorithm 4) on $\mathsf{RE}(t_0)$ and $\mathsf{RE}(t_1)$ and send to the adversary the results. Note that we know the plain items corresponding to the encrypted items in the anonymized transactions. Therefore, we can simulate the private comparison (Algorithm 5) without decryption.

In the end, the adversary outputs its guess b and we forwards b to the ElGamal challenger. If the adversary has a non-negligible additional probability more than 1/2 to win the game, we have a non-negligible additional probability more than 1/2 to break the semantic security of the ElGamal encryption scheme. Therefore, if the ElGamal encryption scheme is semantically secure and at least one of the n DM servers is honest, our solution in Section 6 has transaction privacy. □

8.3 Security Analysis on Association Rule Mining with Database Privacy

Our solution for association rule mining with database privacy has five phases - the setup, the item dictionary anonymization, the transaction anonymization, the same item identification (Algorithm 6), and the frequent itemset mining (Algorithm 7). According to Definition 3, we have

Theorem 6 Our association rule mining solution described in Section 7 has database privacy if the ElGamal encryption scheme is semantically secure and at least one of the n DM servers is honest.

Proof We assume that all DM servers except for S_1 are compromised by an adversary. If the adversary can break the database privacy of the client, i.e., winning the game given in Definition 3, we can use the adversary to break the semantic security of the ElGamal encryption scheme.

At first, we send to the adversary the public key y_1 of S_1, the public and private keys of other servers. Then we run the item dictionary anonymization (Algorithm 2) according to the common public key y.

After the adversary chooses two distinct database D_0 and D_1 with the same set of possible items, the same size of transactions, and the same frequent itemsets, we first find the minimum database $D^* \in D_0 \cap D_1$ with the same frequent itemsets as D_0 and D_1 and forward $D_0 - D^*$ and $D_1 - D^*$ to the ElGamal challenger, which randomly chooses a bit $b \in \{0, 1\}$, and returns back $\mathsf{E}_1(D_b - D^*)$, where E_1 denotes the encryption with y_1. Like the proof of Theorem 4, we can construct $\mathsf{E}(D_b - D^*)$, where E denotes the encryption with the common public key y, and send $\mathsf{E}(D^*) \cup \mathsf{E}(D_b - D^*)$ to the adversary, where $\mathsf{E}(D^*)$ is constructed by us and we know the plain items corresponding to the encrypted items in $\mathsf{E}(D^*)$.

Next, we execute and the transaction anonymization (Algorithm 3). Because we know the plain items corresponding to the encrypted items in $\mathsf{E}(D^*)$ and the dictionary, we can simulate the private comparison (Algorithm 7) without decryption.

In the end, the adversary outputs its guess b and we forward b to the ElGamal challenger. If the adversary has a non-negligible additional probability more than 1/2 to win the game, we have a non-negligible additional probability more than 1/2 to break the semantic security of the ElGamal encryption scheme. Therefore, if the ElGamal encryption scheme is semantically secure and at least one of the n DM servers is honest, our solution in Section 7 has database privacy. □

9. PERFORMANCE ANALYSIS

9.1 Performance Analysis on Association Rule Mining with Item Privacy

Our solution for association rule mining with item privacy is the simplest among our three solutions.

The basic building block of the same item identification (Algorithm 1) is the Plaintext Equality Test (PET). In each PET, we assume that all DM servers send their computation results to the DB server, which finally determines if two ciphertexts are the encryption of the same plaintext. Under this assumption, according to Sections 3.2 and 3.3, each DM server needs to compute 3 modular exponentiations and exchange 4 modular exponentiation results with the DB server, and the DB server only needs to compute some modular multiplications and division and exchange about $3n$ modular exponentiation results.

The number of PETs required in Algorithm 1, denoted as N_{PET}, depends on the size of the transaction database, the length of each transactions and the number of possible items. Assume that there are total γ possible items and the database contains total N items (including repeats of the same item), then we have

$$N_{\mathsf{PET}} = \gamma N - \sum_{i=1}^{\gamma-1} (\gamma - i) f(c_i)$$

where c_i is an encrypted item in the dictionary and $f(c_i)$ is the support of c_i.

9.2 Performance Analysis on Association Rule Mining with Transaction Privacy

Compared with our first solution, our solution for association rule mining with transaction privacy requires more computations and communications to prevent the background knowledge-based attack.

In this solution, we use two mix networks. One mixes the items in the dictionary (Algorithms 2), while another mixes the original and noisy transactions (Algorithm 3).

In Algorithm 2, the DB server and each DM server need to compute γ ElGamal encryptions or re-encryptions and exchange 2γ ElGamal ciphertexts (receiving γ ciphertexts and sending γ ciphertexts), where γ is the number of possible items in the dictionary.

In Algorithm 3, each DM server need to compute $\eta \ell_\eta$ ElGamal encryptions or re-encryptions and exchange $2\eta\ell_\eta$ ElGamal ciphertexts (receiving $\eta\ell_\eta$ ciphertexts and sending $\eta\ell_\eta$ ciphertexts), where ℓ_η is the number of transactions with η items.

Like our first solution, this solution also includes the same item identification (Algorithm 4), where the number of PETs required is similar to that of Algorithm 1.

Unlike our first solution, this solution determines whether an encrypted itemset is frequent or not by private comparison (Algorithm 5), where the basic building block is the conditional gate as described in Section 3.4. In each conditional gate computation, each DM server computes 2 modular exponentiations and exchanges 5 exponentiation results.

In Algorithm 5, when the n DM servers cooperate to compute $\mathsf{E}(z) = \mathsf{E}(z) \boxplus \mathsf{E}(f_i)$ at Step 4 given $\mathsf{E}(z) = (\mathsf{E}(g^{z_{m'-1}}), \cdots, \mathsf{E}(g^{z_1}), \mathsf{E}(g^{z_0}))$ and $f_i = (v^i_{m'-1} \cdots v^i_1 v^i_0)$, the following formulae can be used

$$\mathsf{E}(g^{c_j}) = \mathsf{E}(g^{z_j})^{v^i_j} \mathsf{E}(g^{z_j c_{j-1}}) \mathsf{E}(g^{c_{j-1}})^{v^i_j} \mathsf{E}(g^{z_j c_{j-1}})^{-2v^i_j},$$

$$\mathsf{E}(g^{z_j}) = \mathsf{E}(g^{z_j}) \mathsf{E}(g^{v^i_j}) \mathsf{E}(g^{c_{j-1}}) \mathsf{E}(g^{-2c_j}),$$

where $c_{-1} = 0$. Because Server S_i knows f_i, the n DM servers needs to compute only one conditional gate $\mathsf{E}(g^{z_j c_{j-1}})$ to get $\mathsf{E}(g^{c_j})$ and m' conditional gates to get $\mathsf{E}(z)$.

Similarly, when the n DM servers cooperate to compute $\mathsf{E}(z) = \mathsf{E}(z) \boxplus \mathsf{E}(\overline{-1})$ at Step 6 and $\mathsf{E}(z) = \mathsf{E}(z) \boxplus \mathsf{E}(\overline{-f})$ at Step 8, they need to compute $2m'$ conditional gates to get the results because 1 and $\overline{-f}$ are known to everyone.

In summary, the total number of the conditional gates required in Algorithm 5, denoted as N_{CG}, is

$$N_{\mathsf{CG}} = nm' + 2m' = (n + 2)m'.$$

When $n = 2$, we have $N_{\mathsf{CG}} = 4m'$.

Table 1: Performance Summary (Comp./Comm.)

Algorithms	DB Server	DM Server
Algorithm 1	- /$3nN_{\mathsf{PET}}$	$3N_{\mathsf{PET}}$/$4N_{\mathsf{PET}}$
Algorithm 2	$\gamma/2\gamma$	$\gamma/2\gamma$
Algorithm 3	-/$2\eta\ell_\eta$	$\eta\ell_\eta$/$2\eta\ell_\eta$
Algorithm 4	- /$3nN_{\mathsf{PET}}$	$3N_{\mathsf{PET}}$/$4N_{\mathsf{PET}}$
Algorithm 5	-/-	$5N_{\mathsf{CG}}$/$6N_{\mathsf{CG}}$
Algorithm 6	- /$3nN_{\mathsf{PET}}$	$3N_{\mathsf{PET}}$/$4N_{\mathsf{PET}}$
Algorithm 7	-/-	$5N_{\mathsf{CG}}$/$6N_{\mathsf{CG}}$

9.3 Performance Analysis on Association Rule Mining with Database Privacy

Like our solution with transaction privacy, our solution with database privacy has to invoke the same item identification (Algorithm 6). However, the correspondence between the encrypted items in the subset D_i' and the encrypted items in the dictionary is known to the server S_i only. Algorithms 6 needs slightly more computation and communication complexities than Algorithm 4 for the same item identification.

In addition, like our solution with transaction privacy, our solution with database privacy has an algorithm (Algorithm 7) to determine if an itemset is frequent or not. However, the frequency of any itemset in the subset D_i' is known to the server S_i only. Algorithms 7 has slightly more computation and communication complexities than Algorithm 5 for private comparison.

9.4 Performance Analysis on Client

What the client needs to do is encrypting all items in the database, distributing the secret keys to the n DM servers through secure channels, and decrypting the encrypted association rules with plain supports and confidences (in the first solution) or the encrypted frequent itemsets with encrypted supports (the second and third solutions) from the DB server.

The performance of our algorithms can be summarized in Table 1, in which we only consider the number of modular exponentiations computed and exchanged.

10. IMPLEMENTATION AND EXPERIMENT

On an Intel i7-2600 CPU with 8 GBytes of memory, we have implemented our three solutions for privacy-preserving association rule mining with one DB server and two DM servers. We use the chess dataset[1] as our sample transaction database. It has 3,196 transactions. Its size is 0.34 MBytes. The average length of transactions is 37.0. We have implemented the ElGamal encryption scheme over a cyclic group with an order of 2^{160} and a 1,024-bit modulus based on GNU MP library. It takes 23.57 seconds to encrypt all 3,196 transactions in the database. It takes average 7.37 ms to encrypt a transaction. The encrypted transaction database is around 30.27 MBytes. The performance of the three solutions is compared in terms of various supports and ϕ (defined in Section 6.3) in Fig. 2 and Fig. 3.

11. CONCLUSIONS AND FUTURE WORK

In this paper, we have proposed three solutions for privacy-preserving association rule mining in the cloud computing environment. They keep item privacy, transaction privacy and database privacy, respectively. Our implementation and experiment have demonstrated that our solutions are practical. We also note that the performance can be significantly improved by parallel computation. To be precise, we could increase the time efficiency of our protocol by dividing the encrypted transactions into disjoint subsets such that each subset is processed by a separate group of n DM servers. However, additional modifications to our protocols are needed in order to yield the correct results. We plan to consider this as our future work and will investigate its performance when deploying our solutions in the cloud environment provided by the cloud service providers.

[1] http://fimi.ua.ac.be/data/

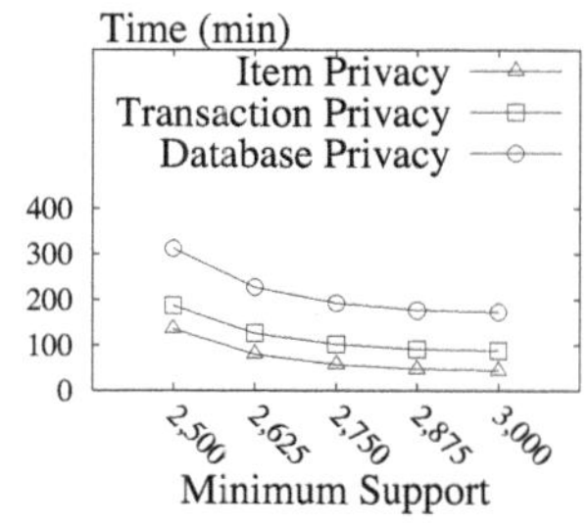

Figure 2: Performance Comparison for Various Supports ($\phi =$ 0.5 for Transaction and Database Privacy)

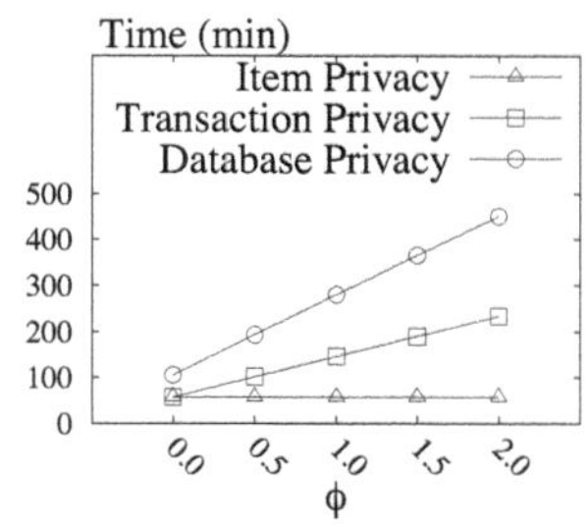

Figure 3: Performance Comparison for Various ϕ with Transaction and Database Privacy

12. ACKNOWLEDGMENTS

The work reported in this paper has been partially supported by the Purdue Cyber Center and by the National Science Foundation under grant CNS-1111512.

13. REFERENCES

[1] R. Agrawal and R. Srikant. Fast algorithms for mining association rules in large databases. In *VLDB'94, Proceedings of 20th International Conference on Very Large Data Bases, September 12-15, 1994, Santiago de Chile, Chile*, pages 487–499, 1994.

[2] T. E. Gamal. A public key cryptosystem and a signature scheme based on discrete logarithms. *IEEE Transactions on Information Theory*, 31(4):469–472, 1985.

[3] R. Gennaro, S. Jarecki, H. Krawczyk, and T. Rabin. Secure distributed key generation for discrete-log based cryptosystems. *J. Cryptology*, 20(1):51–83, 2007.

[4] F. Giannotti, L. V. S. Lakshmanan, A. Monreale, D. Pedreschi, and W. H. Wang. Privacy-preserving mining of association rules from outsourced transaction databases. *IEEE Systems Journal*, 7(3):385–395, 2013.

[5] J. Han and M. Kamber. *Data Mining: Concepts and Techniques*. Morgan Kaufmann, 2000.

[6] D. M. Harris and S. L. Harris. *Digital design and computer architecture*. Morgan Kaufmann Publishers, Cop., Amsterdam, Boston, 2007.

[7] M. Jakobsson and A. Juels. Mix and match: Secure function evaluation via ciphertexts. In *Advances in Cryptology - ASIACRYPT 2000, 6th International Conference on the Theory and Application of Cryptology and Information Security, Kyoto, Japan, December 3-7, 2000, Proceedings*, pages 162–177, 2000.

[8] I. Molloy, N. Li, and T. Li. On the (in)security and (im)practicality of outsourcing precise association rule mining. In *ICDM 2009, The Ninth IEEE International Conference on Data Mining, Miami, Florida, USA, 6-9 December 2009*, pages 872–877, 2009.

[9] S. Sarawagi and S. H. Nagaralu. Data mining models as services on the internet. *SIGKDD Explorations*, 2(1):24–28, 2000.

[10] B. Schoenmakers and P. Tuyls. Practical two-party computation based on the conditional gate. In *Advances in Cryptology - ASIACRYPT 2004, 10th International Conference on the Theory and Application of Cryptology and Information Security, Jeju Island, Korea, December 5-9, 2004, Proceedings*, pages 119–136, 2004.

[11] C. Tai, P. S. Yu, and M. Chen. k-support anonymity based on pseudo taxonomy for outsourcing of frequent itemset mining. In *Proceedings of the 16th ACM SIGKDD International Conference on Knowledge Discovery and Data Mining, Washington, DC, USA, July 25-28, 2010*, pages 473–482, 2010.

[12] W. K. Wong, D. W. Cheung, E. Hung, B. Kao, and N. Mamoulis. Security in outsourcing of association rule mining. In *Proceedings of the 33rd International Conference on Very Large Data Bases, University of Vienna, Austria, September 23-27, 2007*, pages 111–122, 2007.

Differentially Private Publishing of High-dimensional Data Using Sensitivity Control

Wei-Yen Day
Department of Computer Science
Purdue University
West Lafayette, IN USA
wday@purdue.edu

Ninghui Li
Department of Computer Science
Purdue University
West Lafayette, IN USA
ninghui@cs.purdue.edu

ABSTRACT

In this paper, we present DPSense, an approach to publish statistical information from datasets under differential privacy via sensitivity control. More specifically, we consider the problem of publishing column counts for high-dimensional datasets, such as query logs or the Netflix dataset. The key challenge is that as the sensitivity is high, high-magnitude noises need to be added to satisfy differential privacy. We explore how to effectively performs *sensitivity control*, i.e., limiting the contribution of each tuple in the dataset. We introduce a novel low-sensitivity quality function that enables one to effectively choose a contribution limit while satisfying differential privacy. Based on DPSense, we further propose an extension to correct the under-estimation bias, which we call DPSense-S. Experimental results show that our proposed approaches advance the state of the art for publishing noisy column counts and for finding the columns with the highest counts. Finally, we give the analysis and discussion for the stability of DPSense and DPSense-S, which benefits from the high correlation between quality function and error, as well as other insights of DPSense, DPSense-S, and existing approaches.

Categories and Subject Descriptors

K.4.1 [**COMPUTERS AND SOCIETY**]: Privacy

General Terms

Algorithms

Keywords

Differential privacy; Private data publishing; High-dimensional data

1. INTRODUCTION

Private data publishing has enabled researchers to utilize the data without personal privacy breach. The statistics from dataset often contain useful information, such as the frequencies of terms in query logs that users have used, the frequent items bought from customers in transaction, or the information about medical prescriptions of patients. Releasing such information may disclose personal sensitive information, e.g., a person used certain terms to query, or a person has some diseases. Techniques for private data publishing are thus needed. In recent years, ϵ-*differential privacy* [7] has gradually become the *de facto* standard privacy definition in research on private data publishing. Differential privacy ensures that any person's private information will not be inferred by perturbing data with noise. The problem of data publishing under differential privacy has been widely investigated by researchers. Publishing information about high-dimensional dataset while satisfying differential privacy, however, remains a challenge.

In this paper, we study the problem of publishing column counts for high-dimensional binary datasets. In this problem, each tuple in the input dataset D is a binary vector in $\{0,1\}^d$, where d can be very large. The count of a column is the number of 1's in that column. The goal is to release the counts for all columns. Examples of such datasets include query logs where each tuple represents the keywords that one user has addressed in search query, transactional datasets where each tuple represents the items purchased in a transaction, and so on. Publishing the column counts does not publish all information in the original dataset, but the counts represents important and useful statistical information for many applications, such as top-used keywords in query logs or popularity of items in an online store. The techniques we develop in this paper also apply to non-binary datasets where a cell may contain a number larger than 1.

The main challenge in this problem is the very large dimensionality of such dataset. For example, d in query logs data represents the number of unique terms that all users have used in a certain period, or in movie-rating dataset d stands for the total number of movies. The naive approach of adding Laplacian noises to the output vector of all column counts works poorly because the sensitivity is very high. Since adding one tuple where all entries are 1 increases each column count by 1, the total sensitivity is d, the number of columns. In most datasets, the number of columns is much larger than the average column count, thus the amount of noises added completely overwhelms the data.

One approach to deal with the high sensitivity is to set an upper threshold θ on the row counts. If one row has total count larger than θ, the row can be normalized such that each non-zero cell now has a fraction count, or sampled to contain only θ non-zero cells. With limited sensitivity, less noise is needed. This approach has been proposed in [9, 3, 14]. The key challenge here is how to choose the threshold θ, which depends on both the dataset D and the privacy parameter ϵ. Increasing θ reduces errors caused by normalization, but increases errors due to the added noise. In the literature so far, it is assumed that θ is manually set. Choosing θ systematically in a differentially private way, however, remains unresolved.

ASIA CCS'15, April 14 - 17, 2015, Singapore, Singapore

http://dx.doi.org/10.1145/2714576.2714621.

In this paper, we solve this challenge by proposing DPSense and DPSense-S. DPSense chooses a θ, computes a sensitivity-limited dataset, and then adds noises to the column counts of such dataset. To choose θ, we introduce a low-sensitivity quality function for θ that enables one to use the exponential mechanism to choose a desired θ. We design the quality function to consider both the property of dataset and the effect from adding noise. With θ-limited dataset, less noise is injected and the published noisy counts is more accurate. DPSense-S tries to also correct the systematic underestimation caused by sensitivity limitation, by choosing both θ and a scaling factor α simultaneously, generating noisy count from θ-limited dataset, and multiplying the noisy count by α to correct underestimation. The quality function used to choose (θ, α) estimates the error after sensitivity limitation, noise addition, and scaling.

We have conducted experiments on six datasets. These datasets are from various domains and have different properties, such as number of columns, maximum row counts, average column counts, and so on. We use several utility metrics, including the Mean Absolute Error (MAE) of all column counts and the Mean Relative Error (MRE), which were used in [15]. We observe that when given a high-dimensional dataset, one may be more interested in finding information about the columns with the highest counts, since for columns with low counts, the published noisy counts are likely to be mostly noise. In this paper we also use four other metrics: the accuracy for finding the k columns with the highest counts, NDCG of ranking top k columns, and the MAE and MRE for the k columns that have the highest true counts. Experimental results show that DPSense and DPSense-S significantly outperform existing methods for publishing column counts, and they also outperform existing methods for finding the k most frequent columns.

To summarize, the contributions of our paper are as follows:

1. We have advanced the state of the art for publishing column counts in high-dimensional datasets while satisfying differential privacy, significantly outperforming the methods in the literature [15, 8, 23]. Our proposed approaches also outperform state of the art methods in finding the k most frequent items [19]. We also show that these approaches can be extensible to non-binary dataset.

2. We have introduced a low-sensitivity quality function that enables the use of the exponential mechanism to choose a good threshold θ for limiting the sensitivity. We also demonstrate interesting relationships between our quality function and the actual MAE, further illustrating the advantage of the quality function. This techniques could be applied for publishing other information of high-dimensional datasets.

3. We have introduced a way to correct the systematic underestimation caused by limiting sensitivity, and introduced a novel method to choose a pair of (θ, α) that together perform well. The resulting DPSense-S method further enhances the utility preservation of DPSense and gives the best result under the task of publishing column counts for high-dimensional data.

The rest of this paper is organized as follows. Section 2 provides a brief introduction to ϵ-differential privacy and the common mechanisms for achieving it. We describe the problem definition and previous approaches in Section 3. In Section 4, we present DPSense and DPSense-S. Experimental results as well as their analyses are given in Section 5. We discuss related work in Section 6, and conclude in Section 7.

2. PRELIMINARIES

Informally, differential privacy requires that the output of a data analysis mechanism be approximately the same, even if any single tuple in the input database is arbitrarily added or removed.

DEFINITION 1 (ϵ-DIFFERENTIAL PRIVACY [7, 8]). *A randomized mechanism $\mathcal{A}$ gives ϵ-differential privacy if for any pair of neighboring datasets D and D', and any $S \in Range(\mathcal{A})$,*

$$\Pr[\mathcal{A}(D) = S] \leq e^{\epsilon} \cdot \Pr[\mathcal{A}(D') = S].$$

In this paper we consider two datasets D and D' to be neighbors if and only if either $D = D' \cup \{t\}$ or $D' = D \cup \{t\}$, where $D \cup \{t\}$ denotes the dataset resulted from adding the tuple t to the dataset D. We use $D \simeq D'$ to denote this. This protects the privacy of any single tuple, because adding or removing any single tuple results in e^{ϵ}-multiplicative-bounded changes in the probability distribution of the output. If any adversary can make certain inference about a tuple based on the output, then the same inference is also likely to occur even if the tuple does not appear in the dataset.

Differential privacy is composable in the sense that combining multiple mechanisms that satisfy differential privacy for $\epsilon_1, \cdots, \epsilon_m$ results in a mechanism that satisfies ϵ-differential privacy for $\epsilon = \sum_i \epsilon_i$. Because of this, we refer to ϵ as the privacy budget of a privacy-preserving data analysis task. When a task involves multiple steps, each step uses a portion of ϵ so that the sum of these portions is no more than ϵ.

There are several approaches for designing mechanisms that satisfy ϵ-differential privacy. In this paper we use two of them. The first approach computes a function g on the dataset D in a differentially privately way, by adding to $g(D)$ a random noise. The magnitude of the noise depends on GS_g, the *global sensitivity* or the L_1 sensitivity of g. In this method, g may output a vector value. Such a mechanism $\mathcal{A}_g$ is given below:

$$\begin{aligned} \mathcal{A}_g(D) &= g(D) + \left\langle \mathsf{Lap}\left(\tfrac{\mathsf{GS}_g}{\epsilon}\right)\right\rangle \\ \text{where} \quad \mathsf{GS}_g &= \max_{(D,D'):D\simeq D'} \|g(D) - g(D')\|_1, \\ \text{and} \quad \Pr[\mathsf{Lap}(\lambda) = x] &= \tfrac{1}{2\lambda} e^{-|x|/\lambda} \end{aligned}$$

In the above, $\mathsf{Lap}(\lambda)$ denotes a random variable sampled from the Laplace distribution with scale parameter λ, and $\langle \mathsf{Lap}(\lambda) \rangle$ denote a vector of the same dimension as that of g such that each element is sampled independently according to $\mathsf{Lap}(\lambda)$. This is generally referred to as the *Laplacian mechanism* for satisfying differential privacy.

The second approach computes a function g on a dataset D by sampling from the set of all possible answers in the range of g according to an exponential distribution, with answers that are "more accurate" will be sampled with higher probability. This is generally referred to as the *exponential mechanism* [20]. This approach requires the specification of a *quality* function $q : \mathcal{D} \times \mathcal{R} \rightarrow \mathbb{R}$, where the real valued score $q(D, r)$ indicates how accurate it is to return r when the input dataset is D. Higher scores indicate more accurate outputs which should be returned with higher probabilities. Given the quality function q, its global sensitivity GS_q is defined as:

$$\mathsf{GS}_q = \max_r \max_{(D,D'):D\simeq D'} |q(D,r) - q(D',r)|$$

The following method $\mathcal{M}$ satisfies ϵ-differential privacy:

$$\Pr[\mathcal{M}(D) = r] \propto \exp\left(\frac{\epsilon}{2\,\mathsf{GS}_q} q(D,r)\right) \tag{1}$$

For example, if $q(D, r_1) - q(D, r_2) = 1$, then r_1 should be returned $\exp\left(\frac{\epsilon}{2\,\mathsf{GS}_q}\right)$ times more likely than r_2. The larger the exponent $\frac{\epsilon}{2\,\mathsf{GS}_q}$ is, the more likely that $\mathcal{M}$ will return the higher quality result.

As pointed out in [20], in some cases the quality function satisfies the condition that when the input dataset is changed from D to D', the quality values of all outcomes change only in one direction, i.e.,

$$\forall_{D\simeq D'}\left[\left(\exists_{r_1}\, q(D,r_1)<q(D',r_1)\right)\rightarrow\left(\forall_{r_2}\, q(D,r_2)\leq q(D',r_2)\right)\right]$$

Then one can remove the factor of $1/2$ in the exponent of Equation (1) and return r with probability proportional to $\exp\left(\frac{\epsilon}{\mathsf{GS}_q}q(D,r)\right)$. This improves the accuracy of the result. We use this variant of Exponential Mechanism in our paper.

3. PROBLEM DEFINITION AND EXISTING APPROACHES

In the problem of publishing column counts for high-dimensional binary datasets, each tuple in the input dataset D is a binary vector in $\{0,1\}^d$, where d can be very large. Examples of such datasets include transaction datasets where each tuple represents the items purchased in a transaction, search datasets where each tuple represents the keywords that one user has searched, and so on. The goal is to release the counts for all columns, where the count of a column is the number of 1's in that column. The query can be represented as a function $\mathbf{Q}:\mathcal{D}\rightarrow\mathbb{R}^d$. Published column counts can represent important and useful statistical information for many applications, such as top-used keywords in query log or popularity of items in an online store.

3.1 Grouping and Smoothing

The main challenge in this problem is the very large dimensionality of such dataset. The naive approach of adding Laplacian noise to the output vector of all column counts works poorly because the sensitivity is very high. The sensitivity of $\mathbf{Q}$ is d, the number of columns, because adding one tuple where all entries are 1 increase each column count by 1.

Grouping and Smoothing (GS) was proposed in [15]; it deals with the high sensitivity challenge by exploiting two ideas. First, it is assumed that for each dataset D, it is allowed to release the Δ_D, the maximum number of 1's in any row. One thus reduces the sensitivity from d to Δ_D. When $\Delta_D \ll d$, which holds for many datasets, the reduction can be significant. We point out, however, that publishing Δ_D actually violates differential privacy. In fact, Δ_D is one of the most sensitive pieces of information from D, since it is decided by one extraordinary tuple that contains significantly more 1's than other tuples do. Publishing Δ_D reveals the membership of that tuple. The approach we propose in this paper does not need to rely on Δ_D being public to satisfy differential privacy.

Second, the approach proposed in [15] partitions the set of all columns into several mutually exclusive groups, and publishes the average column count for each group by adding noises to them. One then uses the noisy group average count for all columns in the group. When there are g groups, publishing the vector of all group average column counts has sensitivity $g\frac{\Delta_D}{d}$, which is a significant reduction from Δ_D when $\frac{g}{d}$ is small. The tradeoff here is that now one uses the same noise count for all columns in the group, which introduces errors when the counts for columns within one group differ significantly. Three grouping strategies are considered in [15].

1. *Random grouping.* In this strategy, g is chosen to be $\frac{d}{\Delta_D}$ such that the sensitivity is $g\frac{\Delta_D}{d}=1$. Columns are randomly grouped together.
2. *Sampling and sorting.* In this strategy, g is chosen to be $\frac{d}{\Delta_D}$ such that the sensitivity is $\frac{\Delta_D g}{d}=1$. However, instead of random grouping, grouping is based on noisy sampled column counts for all columns. More specifically, one first obtains a sampled dataset as follows: For each tuple that contains 1's, one randomly samples *exactly one* of the 1's and set other entries to 0. Since now each tuple can contribute an increment of 1 to at most one among all columns, the sensitivity of publishing all column counts of the sampled dataset is 1. One then uses half of the privacy budget to add noises to these column counts, and group columns by sorting the columns based on their noise sample counts and dividing the sorted columns into g equal-size groups. This aims at grouping columns with similar true counts together. Finally, one uses the remaining half of the privacy budget to obtain noise average column counts for each group.
3. *Sampling, sorting, and choosing optimal group size.* This strategy is similar to sampling and sorting except that the number of groups is not fixed to be $\frac{d}{\Delta_D}$; instead using the noisy sampled group counts, one estimates the error of choosing different number of groups and chooses g to minimize such error.

In [15], it was shown that the last strategy (referred to as GS) performs the best. We compare with this method in our experiments.

3.2 Other Approaches

In [15], the Grouping and Smoothing approach was compared with two other approaches. The naive *Laplace Perturbation Algorithm* [8] (referred to as LPA) adds Laplacian noise to the column counts. In our paper, as in [15], we use Δ_D instead of d as the sensitivity for the LPA method, in order to have a fair comparison between GS and LPA.

The *Fourier Perturbation Algorithm* [23] (referred to as FPA), was originally designed to publish noisy time-series data. The *centralized* mechanism of [23] assumes the rows in database are *time-series*, and columns are timestamps. FPA first applies *Discrete Fourier Transform* (DFT) on the column count $\mathbf{Q}(D)$. It then chooses the first $k \ll d$ DFT coefficients and injects Laplace noise to them. The magnitude of noise in FPA is set to be $\lambda=\sqrt{k}\Delta_2(\mathbf{Q})/\epsilon$, where $\Delta_2(\mathbf{Q})$ is the L_2 sensitivity of query $\mathbf{Q}$, and ϵ is the privacy budget. Finally, it applies inverse DFT on the noisy coefficients and then publishes the noisy column counts. It may require less noise compared to LPA, but may also cause the utility loss depending on the quality of the DFT approximation.

In addition to GS, LPA, and FPA, we also compare with the *Average Laplace Perturbation Algorithm* (referred to as ALPA), which injects Laplace noise on the average of all column counts in raw data, and publishes this as the count for every column. ALPA can be viewed as GS with only one group, and it publishes the same count for every column. It reduces the sensitivity from d to 1 so that less noise is injected. However, the error for columns with high counts would be much larger than for other columns.

3.3 Utility Metrics

In [15], the utility goal is defined as minimizing the *Mean Absolute Error* (MAE) and *Mean Relative Error* (MRE). Let $\mathbf{nc}$ denote the noisy column count vector, and $\mathbf{tc}$ denote the true column count vector, then MAE is computed as $\text{MAE} = \frac{1}{d}||\mathbf{nc} - \mathbf{tc}||_1 = \frac{1}{d}\sum_{j=1}^{d}|\mathbf{nc}_j - \mathbf{tc}_j|$, where d is the number of dimensionality in dataset. We also use the same setting of MRE as [15] with sanity bound equal to 0.1% of the dataset size [25], i.e., $\text{MRE} = \frac{1}{d}\sum_{j=1}^{d}\left|\frac{\mathbf{nc}_j - \mathbf{tc}_j}{\max\{\mathbf{tc}_j, 0.1\% \cdot n\}}\right|$.

MAE and MRE have some limitations for utility measurement. First, for the dataset with low average column counts, methods such as ALPA, which simply publishes a noisy average for every column, results in low MAE or MRE, especially when the privacy budget ϵ is small. However, arguably ALPA does not really publish all column counts, as it publishes the same count for all columns and does not allow us to identify which columns are more interesting than others. Thus, in this paper we use four additional utility metrics. One is top-k accuracy, which is the accuracy of discovering the top-k columns with the highest column counts from the published noisy counts. Let TC_k be the set of k columns with the largest true column counts, NC_k be the set of k columns with the largest noisy column counts, then the top-k accuracy is $\frac{|NC_k \cap TC_k|}{|TC_k|}$. Another metric is NDCG [13], which is often used to evaluate a ranking result. We assign the relevant score from k to 1 to top-k columns and 0 for all other columns not in top-k, and compare the ranked published column counts of different approaches with the true ranked columns. Finding k most frequent columns is a special case of frequent itemset mining [2, 19]. The method for selecting top k frequent columns in [2, 19] is to use the exponential mechanism k times and each time select one column with the largest count. We also include this method when evaluating the top-k accuracy and NDCG.

The other new metrics are top-k MAE and top-k MRE, defined as the MAE of top k columns, i.e., $\frac{1}{|TC_k|}\sum_{j\in TC_k}|\mathbf{nc}_j - \mathbf{tc}_j|$, and the MRE of top k columns: $\frac{1}{|TC_k|}\sum_{j\in TC_k}\left|\frac{\mathbf{nc}_j - \mathbf{tc}_j}{\max\{\mathbf{tc}_j, 0.1\% \cdot n\}}\right|$, respectively. The intuition is that these column counts are likely of more interest. We expect that the ALPA method, which does not differentiate among the columns, would perform poorly under these two new metrics.

We use MAE, top-k MAE, MRE, top-k MRE, top-k accuracy, and NDCG to measure the utility of published column counts in the experiments, as will be shown in section 5.

4. PROPOSED APPROACH: DPSENSE

As discussed earlier, the key challenge to outputting $\mathbf{Q}(D)$ is the large sensitivity. The key idea of our proposed approach, DPSense, is to choose an appropriate sensitivity threshold θ and limit each row's contribution to the column count vector to be at most θ.

More specifically, we model the dataset D as an $n \times d$ matrix where each cell is a real number. For the input dataset, each cell is either 0 or 1. Given a threshold θ, there are two ways to perform the limitation of sensitivity: *normalization* and *sampling*. For normalization, we perform the following transformation on the input dataset D to obtain $D|_\theta$ so that the sum of each row in $D|_\theta$ is at most θ: Let $RC_i = \sum_{j=1}^{d} D(i,j)$ be the sum of all cells in row i (row count), we normalize cells in the row i if RC_i is larger than θ. That is,

$$D|_\theta(i,j) = \begin{cases} D(i,j) & \text{if } RC_i \le \theta \\ D(i,j)\frac{\theta}{RC_i} & \text{if } RC_i > \theta \end{cases}$$

The sampling method for limiting sensitivity is to randomly sample θ non-zero cells from all non-zero cells in a row for rows with $RC_i > \theta$, and keep all cells for other rows. The transformation from sampling produces $D|_\theta$ similar to the one from normalization since the sum of a row is limited by θ. We have found that both methods produce a very similar effect for utility preservation. Normalization is more general in that it can be easily extended to non-binary datasets or non-integer θ. In the remaining of the paper, we use the normalization method for limiting the sensitivity.

Table 1: Notations used in this paper.

Notation	Description
D / $\mathcal{D}$	Input database / dataset
n	Number of rows in database / dataset
d	Number of columns in database / dataset
$\mathbf{Q}$	Query for the vector of all column counts
θ / θ^*	Threshold for sensitivity control
α/α^*	Scaling factor for sensitivity control
$D\|_\theta$	Sensitivity-limited dataset by θ
RC_i	Row counts for row i
c_j / c_j^θ	Column j's count in D / $D\|_\theta$
$ac(D\|_\theta)$	Average column count of $D\|_\theta$
$ae(D\|_\theta)$	Average column count error of $D\|_\theta$
$q(D,\theta,\epsilon)$	Quality function for algorithm 1
$qs(D,\theta,\alpha,\epsilon)$	Quality function for algorithm 2
ϵ_c	Privacy budget for choosing the best sensitivity
ϵ_p	Privacy budget for publishing noisy counts in data for scaling
$\mathbf{tc}$	True column count vector in dataset
$\mathbf{nc}$	Noisy column count vector to be published

Our approach is to first choose θ in a differentially private way using privacy budget ϵ_c, and then publish $\mathbf{Q}(D|_\theta)$ using privacy budget ϵ_p such that $\epsilon_c + \epsilon_p = \epsilon$. For any input dataset D, publishing $\mathbf{Q}(D|_\theta)$ has sensitivity θ; thus we can then publish $\mathbf{Q}(D|_\theta) + \left\langle \mathsf{Lap}\left(\frac{\theta}{\epsilon_p}\right)\right\rangle$, where $\left\langle \mathsf{Lap}\left(\frac{\theta}{\epsilon_p}\right)\right\rangle$ denotes a vector of independently generated Laplacian noises.

The key technical challenge is to choose the threshold θ in a differentially private way. In Section 4.1, we discuss how we do this. We present the DPSense algorithm in Section 4.2, and the DPSense-S algorithm in Section 4.3. We discuss the extension of our proposed approaches for non-binary datasets in Section 4.4. For convenience, we list all the notations used in this paper in Table 1.

4.1 Choosing The Best Sensitivity Level

There are two sources of errors when we output $\mathbf{Q}(D|_\theta)+\left\langle \mathsf{Lap}\left(\frac{\theta}{\epsilon_p}\right)\right\rangle$. *Truncation errors* are caused by the normalization step, which causes $\mathbf{Q}(D|_\theta)$ to be smaller than $\mathbf{Q}(D)$. *Noise errors* are caused by the addition of Laplacian noise. Increasing θ reduces truncation errors while at the same time increasing noise errors. The goal is thus to choose a θ that minimizes the aggregated effect of truncation errors and noise errors.

The optimal choice of θ depends both on the dataset and on the available privacy budget. Clearly the optimal choice of θ will be correlated with the average row count. If θ is smaller than the average row count, then the normalization is likely to cause significant underestimation. At the same time, the optimal choice of θ also depends on the distribution of row counts. If all row counts are the same, then setting θ to be the average row count reduces truncation error to 0. However, if there are many rows with very low counts, and many with high counts, then setting θ to be the average row count may result in very large truncation errors. Thus a method of choosing θ using only the average row count may be suboptimal.

The optimal choice of θ also depends on the privacy budget ϵ. The larger the privacy budget is, the smaller the magnitude of the noise, and thus it is desirable to choose a larger θ to reduce the truncation errors.

To determine θ, we construct a quality function that takes into consideration both the truncation errors and the noise errors. Let c_j denote jth column count of a dataset D and $ac(D)$ denote the average column count in D, that is,

$$ac(D) = \frac{1}{d}\sum_{i=1}^{n}\sum_{j=1}^{d} D(i,j) = \frac{1}{d}\sum_{j=1}^{d} c_j \quad (2)$$

We use the following quality function:

$$q(D, \theta, \epsilon_p) = ac(D|_\theta) - \frac{\theta}{\epsilon_p} \quad (3)$$

The intuition is that the higher the average column count in $D|_\theta$, then the lower the truncation error. In fact, an increase in $ac(D|_\theta)$ by x means the reduction of truncation error by x. At the same time, the MAE resulted from adding $\mathsf{Lap}(\lambda)$ is computed as follows:

$$\int_{-\infty}^{\infty} |x| \frac{1}{2\lambda} e^{(-\frac{|x|}{\lambda})} \mathrm{d}x = \lambda \int_{0}^{\infty} y e^{-y} \mathrm{d}y = \lambda$$

Thus the quality function in Equation (3) captures the relative change of MAE when changing θ.

Another nice property of this quality function is that its sensitivity is 1, which we prove below.

LEMMA 1. *The sensitivity of quality function q in Equation (3) is 1.*

PROOF. Let D, D' be two neighbor datasets differ in only one row. The sensitivity of quality function q is

$$\begin{aligned}\Delta q &= \max_{\forall\theta,D,D',\epsilon_p} |q(D,\theta,\epsilon_p) - q(D',\theta,\epsilon_p)| \\ &= \max_{\forall\theta,D,D',\epsilon_p} \left|\left(ac(D|_\theta) - \tfrac{\theta}{\epsilon_p}\right) - \left(ac(D'|_\theta) - \tfrac{\theta}{\epsilon_p}\right)\right| \\ &= \max_{\forall\theta,D,D',\epsilon_p} |ac(D|_\theta) - ac(D'|_\theta)| \\ &\leq 1\end{aligned}$$

The last step is because adding one row can increase the average column count by at most 1. □

As we will show in Section 5, the quality function approximates the utility of published column counts very well.

Given the quality function, we use the exponential mechanism to select θ from $[1, d]$ with privacy budget ϵ_c. We also note that when adding a tuple, the quality values for all θ's increases; that is, the changes of all quality values are one-directional; therefore, choosing each possible θ from 1 to d with probability Prob[θ], where

$$\text{Prob}[\theta] \propto \exp(\epsilon_c q(D, \theta, \epsilon_p))$$

satisfies ϵ_c-differential privacy.

Note that both ϵ_c and ϵ_p appear in the above formula. ϵ_c is used for exponential mechanism and is different from ϵ_p, which is used for Laplace mechanism later. The quality function q needs to consider the effect of injecting noises with privacy budget ϵ_p.

We take advantage of the small sensitivity of the quality function by using less privacy budget on choosing threshold, and more privacy budget on publishing column counts. In our experiments, we set 10% of privacy budget for choosing the threshold for sensitivity control (ϵ_c), and 90% of privacy budget for publishing the noisy column counts (ϵ_p). We leave optimal division of privacy budget among the two steps to future work, and note that our experimental results show that it is unlikely to result in significant improvement from the property of quality function.

Algorithm 1 DPSense

Input: Dataset D as a $n \times d$ binary matrix, privacy budget ϵ
Output: A d dimensional vector $\mathbf{nc} = \mathbf{Q}(D)$ which represents noisy column counts

1: $n \leftarrow$ number of rows in D, $d \leftarrow$ number of columns in D
2: Set $\epsilon_p \leftarrow 0.9 \times \epsilon$, $\epsilon_c \leftarrow 0.1 \times \epsilon$
3: Set threshold candidate set $\Theta \leftarrow \{1, 2, \cdots, d\}$
4: **for** $\theta_i \in \Theta$ **do**
5: Compute normalized D, i.e., $D' \leftarrow D|_{\theta_i}$
6: $q(\theta_i) \leftarrow ac(D') - \frac{\theta_i}{\epsilon_p}$
7: **end for**
8: Choose θ^* from Θ with probability Prob[θ_i] proportional to $\exp\left(\frac{\epsilon_c q(\theta_i)}{2}\right)$ for $\theta_i \in \Theta$
9: $D \leftarrow D|_{\theta^*}$
10: Compute the true column count vector $\mathbf{tc}$ in D, and noisy column count vector $\mathbf{nc} \leftarrow \mathbf{tc} + \mathsf{Lap}(\frac{\theta^*}{\epsilon_p})^d$
11: For any negative noisy count that $\mathbf{nc}_i < 0$, set $\mathbf{nc}_i \leftarrow 0$
12: Publish $\mathbf{nc}$

4.2 DPSense Algorithm

Algorithm 1 gives all the steps of DPSense in detail. The privacy guarantee is given below.

THEOREM 1. DPSense *is ϵ-differentially private.*

PROOF. From Lemma 1 and the result on exponential mechanism, the step in lines 4-8 in algorithm 1 satisfies ϵ_c-differential privacy. Lines 9 performs the normalization of each row, and it doesn't violate differential privacy since the transformation is interior and the noisy count is not published yet. Line 10 injects Laplace noise to satisfy differential privacy, and the modification of noisy count in line 11 is a post-process on noisy counts. From Laplacian mechanism, this noise injection step satisfies ϵ_p-differential privacy, and the post-processing of noisy data doesn't affect the privacy guarantee. The composition rule of differential privacy explains that combining these two steps makes DPSense satisfy ϵ-differential privacy, where $\epsilon = \epsilon_c + \epsilon_p$. □

Notice that DPSense does not need to assume that Δ_D, the maximal row count in the dataset is public information, unlike GS. DPSense assumes only that d, the number of columns is public information. This has to be public since it is the dimension of the output vector.

4.3 Correcting Under-estimation Bias

DPSense adds noise to the column counts of a normalized dataset. As column counts from a normalized dataset always underestimate the true counts, DPSense has a systematic under-estimation bias. One approach to address this problem is to correct this underestimation by scaling up the noisy counts outputted by DPSense with a factor α. Following this idea, we propose an extension of DPSense, which we call DPSense-S, DPSense with Scaling.

DPSense-S determines the θ and α simultaneously by exploiting the interaction between them. The optimal choice of θ and α depends on two factors: the estimated error after scaling the count by θ and α, and the noise magnification by α. Recall that c_j is the jth column count of a dataset D. Let c_j^θ denote jth column count in $D|_\theta$, then the average column count error after scaling by α can be written as

$$ae(D, D|_\theta) = \frac{1}{d}\sum_{j=1}^{d}\left(\left|\alpha \cdot \sum_{i=1}^{n} D|_\theta(i,j) - \sum_{i=1}^{n} D(i,j)\right|\right) \quad (4)$$

$$= \frac{1}{d}\sum_{j=1}^{d}|\alpha \cdot c_j^\theta - c_j| \quad (5)$$

where $|\alpha \cdot c_j^\theta - c_j|$ is the error after correcting the count by scaling up with α for jth column. Since α is an up-scaling factor, we set $\alpha \geq 1$ as a condition. Note that $0 \leq c_j^\theta \leq c_j$.

By considering the average error and magnification of noise by α, we define the following quality function for DPSense-S:

$$qs(D, \theta, \alpha, \epsilon_p) = -ae(D, D|_\theta) - \alpha \cdot \frac{\theta}{\epsilon_p} \quad (6)$$

The new quality function captures the correlation between θ and α and the effect of their combination for minimizing error. Similar to the quality function proposed for DPSense, we show that the new quality function has sensitivity as $\max\{1, \alpha - 1\}$ by the following lemma.

LEMMA 2. *The sensitivity of quality function qs in Equation (6) is* $\max\{1, \alpha - 1\}$.

We give the proof of Lemma 2 in appendix A.

To control the sensitivity, we set $\alpha \in [1, 2]$, which results in $\Delta qs = \max\{1, \alpha - 1\} = 1$. Limiting the scaling factor to be at most 2 is sufficient to correct the under-estimation since we are choosing a θ at the same time to ensure that the under-estimation will not be large. We set the granularity between the range as 100, i.e. $\alpha \in \{1, 1.01, 1.02, \cdots, 2.00\}$ in our implementation. The actual scaling factors chosen in our experiments tend to be close to 1.1.

Algorithm 2 presents the detail steps for DPSense-S. We also give the privacy guarantee of DPSense-S below.

THEOREM 2. DPSense-S *is ϵ-differentially private.*

PROOF. The proof of privacy guarantee for DPSense-S is similar to the proof for DPSense. As choosing (θ, α) with sensitivity from Lemma 2 is ϵ_c-differentially private, the whole algorithm is ϵ-differentially private, where $\epsilon = \epsilon_c + \epsilon_p$. □

Similar to DPSense, we use 10% of privacy budget (ϵ_c) for choosing θ and α, and 90% (ϵ_p) to publish noisy counts for DPSense-S.

4.4 Extended to Non-binary Datasets

DPSense can be easily extended to non-binary datasets. Suppose the value is at most r for any cell in a non-binary dataset. The sensitivity for publishing original dataset is $d \cdot r$. The normalization step can be used to obtain $D|_\theta$, and the sensitivity of quality function, Δq, is r by definition. The magnitude of noise is downgraded from $d \cdot r$ to θ, while θ may be larger than being applied in binary dataset due to the fact that $ac(D|_\theta)$ in the quality function is enlarged by at most r times. While DPSense is seamlessly applicable on non-binary datasets, the error is expected to be larger depending on the value of r. In this paper, we focus on the analysis of binary dataset and omit the results for non-binary datasets.

5. EXPERIMENTAL RESULTS

In this section, we report the experimental results. We describe the datasets and settings used in our experiments in Section 5.1, and

Algorithm 2 DPSense-S

Input: Dataset D represented as a $n \times d$ data matrix, privacy budget ϵ, query Q
Output: A d dimensional vector $\mathbf{nc} = \mathbf{Q}(D)$ which represents noisy column counts

```
Same as line 1-3 in algorithm 1
Set factor candidate set 𝔸 ← {1.00, 1.01, 1.02, ···, 2.00}
For each column j, compute true column count c_j = Σ_{i=1}^n D
for θ_i ∈ Θ do
    Compute normalized D, i.e., D' ← D|_{θ_i}
    For each column j, compute c_j^{θ_i} = Σ_{i=1}^n D'
    for α_k ∈ 𝔸 do
        qs(θ_i, α_k) ← −( (1/d) Σ_{j=1}^d |α_k · c_j^{θ_i} − c_j| ) − α_k · θ_i/ε_p
    end for
end for
Choose (θ*, α*) from Θ, 𝔸 with probability Prob[(θ_i, α_k)]
    proportional to exp( ε_c qs(θ_i, α_k) / 2 ) for θ_i ∈ Θ and α_k ∈ 𝔸
Same as line 9-11 in algorithm 1
Scale up noisy count nc ← nc × α*
Publish nc
```

demonstrate the effectiveness of the quality function for choosing θ in Section 5.2. In Section 5.3, we compare the MAE, MRE, top-k MAE, and top-k MRE of different mechanisms. Finally, we compare the mechanisms using top-k accuracy in Section 5.4.

5.1 Datasets and Setup

We use 6 different datasets, namely *Netflix, Transaction, Movielens, Document, AOL*, and *Kosarak*. Table 2 gives the information of these datasets.

The *Netflix* dataset[1] is a user-movie rating dataset released by Netflix from the Netflix prize competition. Rows are users, columns are movies, and a non-zero position (i, j) represents the rating if user i rated movie j. The *Transaction* dataset is from KDD-cup 2000[2]. Columns correspond to items; rows correspond to users; and (i, j) is 1 if user i has bought item j. The *Movielens* dataset[3] is also a user-movie rating dataset, and we process it in to a binary matrix similar to Netflix dataset. The *Document* dataset[4] is a PubMed dataset, where rows represent the medical documents, and columns stand for vocabulary terms, and thus a non-zero position (i, j) represents document i contains term j. *AOL* dataset[5] contains the query logs collected between March and May in 2006 released by AOL. The AOL dataset is also known for the associated privacy leak event, where personal user's private information was disclosed within few days after the dataset was released. We keep any alpha-numeric queries and filter out terms with frequency < 100. A non-zero cell (i, j) represents user i has addressed term j in all of user i's queries. Finally, *Kosarak*[6] is an online click stream dataset from a Hungarian news portal, with cell (i, j) denoting that user i has clicked webpage j.

In our experiments, we test every algorithm by running 30 times and compute the average of the outcomes. We use two different

[1]http://www.netflixprize.com/
[2]http://www.kdd.org/kdd-cup-2000-online-retailer-website-clickstream-analysis
[3]http://grouplens.org/datasets/movielens/
[4]http://archive.ics.uci.edu/ml/datasets/Bag+of+Words
[5]http://www.cim.mcgill.ca/~dudek/206/Logs/AOL-user-ct-collection/
[6]http://fimi.ua.ac.be/data/kosarak.dat

Dataset	Rows	Columns	Δ_D	$ac(D)$
Netflix	480,189	17,770	17,653	5,654.50
Transaction	515,597	1,657	164	2,031.99
Movielens	71,567	10,681	7,359	936.25
Document	8,200,000	141,043	436	3,427.68
AOL	657,426	46,176	27,027	498.85
Kosarak	990,002	41,270	2,497	194.31

Table 2: Properties of different datasets. Δ_D denotes the maximal number of 1's in a row. $ac(D)$ denotes the average column count.

privacy budget settings, $\epsilon = \ln 1.5 \approx 0.4$ and $\epsilon = \ln 3 \approx 1.1$. Setting $\epsilon = \ln 1.5$ means that when one's prior belief is that a tuple t is in the input dataset with probability 0.5 (i.e., an even odds $1 : 1$), after observing the output, the odds is updated to $3 : 2$; and $\epsilon = \ln 3$ updates the odds to $3 : 1$.

5.2 Quality Function vs. Error

To demonstrate the effectiveness of the quality function in Equation 3, we plot both the empirical MAE and the quality computed via Equation 3 while θ changes in Figure 1. For each dataset, we show two graphs. The one on top shows the MAE and Quality while θ changes. Specifically, the 'Quality' curve consists of values of the quality function as computed from Equation 3, and the 'MAE' curve is experimentally obtained. We plot these two curves for $\epsilon = \ln 1.5$ and for $\epsilon = \ln 3$.

What is striking about these graphs is that for a given ϵ, the MAE curve and the quality curve are almost symmetrical around a horizontal line. To further examine this effect, in the bottom graph for each dataset, we plot Avg(Quality+MAE), the average of the quality score and MAE, under the same θ and ϵ. As it turns out, this average is close to the horizontal line of a half of the average column count of the dataset, which we also plot.

The symmetry between the MAE and Quality demonstrates the effectiveness of the quality function. First, the θ value where MAE is minimized is very close to the θ value where the quality function is maximized. Second, even if one chooses a θ value such that the quality is not maximized, so long as the quality is close the maximum, the resulting MAE will be close to the minimum. Therefore, even if the choosing step using exponential mechanism does not choose the best θ, it is likely to choose a good enough θ which leads to low MAE based on the probability computed from quality function. Figure 1 also shows that when the privacy budget increases from $\ln 1.5$ to $\ln 3$, the MAE moves to a lower level and is much flatter as θ increases. In other words, with a larger privacy budget, we can keep more contributions as the magnitude of noise is smaller for the same θ, as we expected in our framework. This also suggests that even if one could manually allocate privacy budgets to get a desired result, and optimizing privacy budget allocation may have little improvement in this framework.

We also note that the optimal θ values are correlated with the average row count of the dataset (given in the label of each subgraph). When $\epsilon = \ln 3$, the optimal θ values tend to be between 1.5 times and 6 times the average row count. However, the correlation is weak as the optimal θ values also depend on the distribution of the dataset.

Another interesting observation is that the average of MAE and Quality does not change significantly under the two different privacy budgets, and in fact that they are quite close to the horizontal line of a half of the average column count of the dataset. This can be explained as follows. The MAE has two components, the truncation error and the noise error. The truncation error component is $ac(D) - ac(D|_\theta)$, and the noise error component is $\frac{\theta}{\epsilon}$. If one estimates the MAE using the sum of the two components, then the average of MAE and Quality is:

$$\frac{1}{2}\left(ac(D) - ac(D|_\theta) + \frac{\theta}{\epsilon} + ac(D|_\theta) - \frac{\theta}{\epsilon}\right) = \frac{1}{2}ac(D)$$

The actual MAE is less than the sum of the two components for two reasons. First the two components of the MAE sometimes cancel out each other to some degree. This effect is smallest when one component dominates the other. Second, the step of turning negative counts to 0 also reduces the noise error. For datasets where the average column count is high and the average row count is low (e.g., Transaction and Document), we see that the average of MAE and Quality converges to half of average column count as θ increases, because the noise error dominates the truncation error, which is small since the θ value is much higher than the average row count, and because there are few negative noise counts, as the average column count is high.

In summary, Figure 1 gives evidence that the quality function we design works well for our purpose.

5.3 Comparison for Column Counts Query

Next, we show the comparisons between our algorithms and existing approaches using MAE and MRE. Figure 2 and Figure 3 show the MAE and MRE under different approaches for the six datasets, respectively. As introduced earlier, LPA, FPA, and GS are the approaches compared in [15], and ALPA is an additional baseline approach we compare. DPSense and DPSense-S stand for our algorithms introduced in Section 4.2 and 4.3, respectively.

For the two privacy budgets, we compute the MAE within all columns and within columns with top 5% large counts in raw data. One can expect MAE in top 5% columns would be larger than that in all columns, since the absolute error on higher counts tends to be large. MRE is the opposite, as one can expect MRE in top 5% columns would be smaller than in all columns since MRE evaluates the relative error.

Overall, our DPSense and DPSense-S algorithms result in significant improvements over other approaches for both MAE and MRE, especially when $\epsilon = \ln 3$. We point out that GS and LPA both rely on assuming that Δ_D being public. Since LPA adds noise of the same magnitude to all columns, the MAE for top-5% is the same as that for all columns under LPA. For other methods, however, the MAE for top-5% is larger than that for all columns, as these columns are kind of outliers. For datasets with small Δ_D such as *Transaction* and *Document*, LPA performs quite well, outperforming methods other than DPSense and DPSense-S. However, LPA performs poorly on other datasets. Interestingly, ALPA performs very similar to FPA, and their performance change little when ϵ increases from $\ln 1.5$ to $\ln 3$. This is understandable for ALPA, since the main source of error comes from publishing the same count for all columns, instead of from the added noise. For FPA, since there is no obvious periodical behavior in the columns, the optimal way of truncating the Fourier coefficients is likely to be essentially keeping the one corresponding to the average of all columns, resulting in a behavior similar to ALPA. GS overall performs well, however, in several instances its MAEs and MREs are significantly higher.

DPSense-S further boosts the performance over DPSense, benefiting from the usage of θ and α, when considering the MAE and MRE over all columns. When we consider only the top 5% of columns, DPSense-S outperforms DPSense on NetFlix, Movielens, AOL, and Kosarak, and under-performs DPSense on Trans-

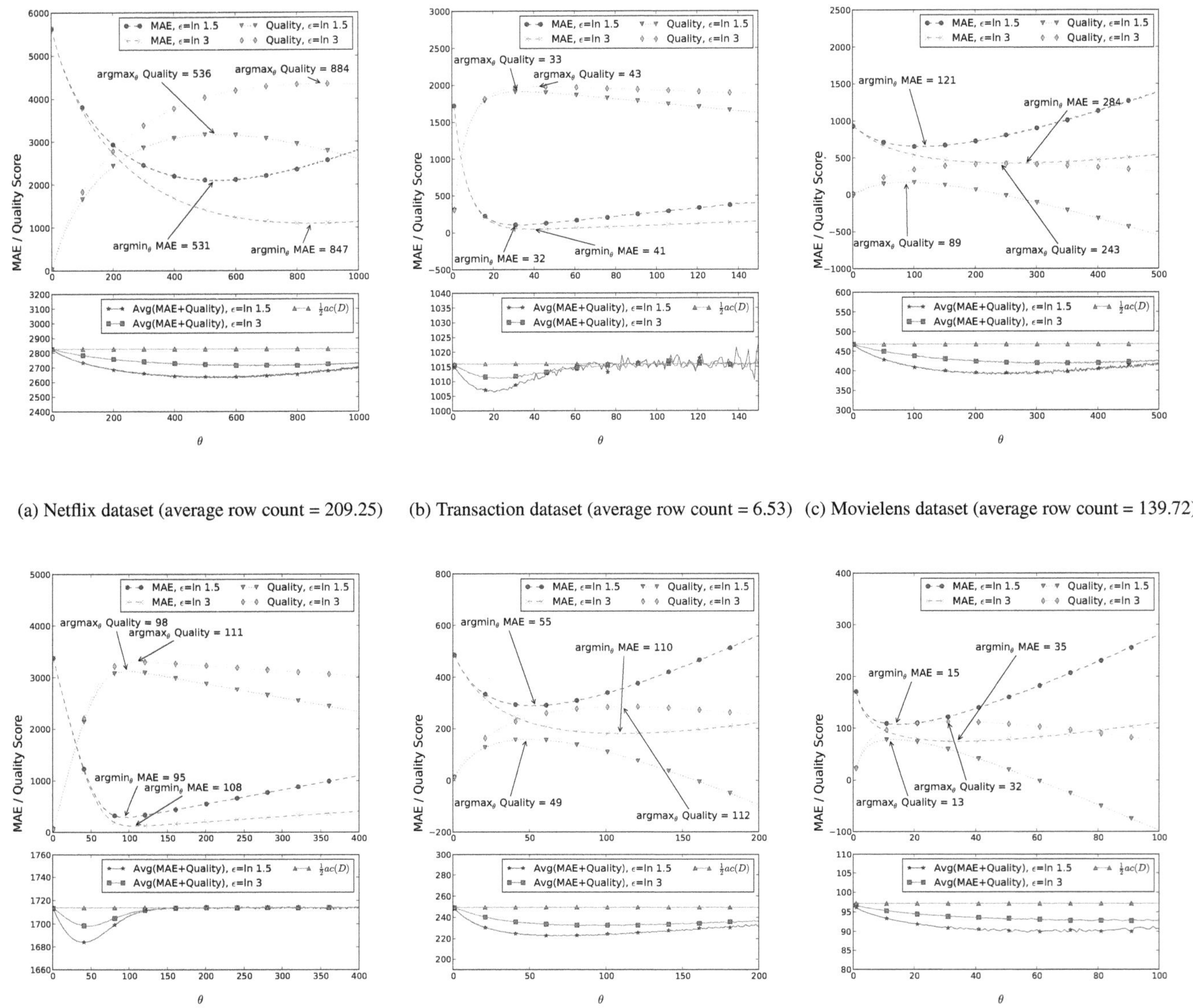

(a) Netflix dataset (average row count = 209.25) (b) Transaction dataset (average row count = 6.53) (c) Movielens dataset (average row count = 139.72)

(d) Document dataset (average row count = 58.95) (e) AOL dataset (average row count = 35.03) (f) Kosarak dataset (average row count = 8.09)

Figure 1: The MAE and Quality function vs. θ for six datasets.

actions and Document. These two datasets have some columns with very high counts contributed by rows with small total sums, and the best overall scaling factor may over-corrects these high counts. This is a side effect of the fact that our quality optimizes for the overall MAE, instead of MAE for the top columns.

5.4 Accuracy on Top-k Columns

Table 3 and 4 present the results among top-k columns using accuracy and NDCG, respectively. As introduced earlier, as the dimensionality is very large, one may be more interested in finding out the columns that have the highest counts.

Since ALPA publishes the same count for every column, one is unable to find top-k columns using ALPA. We omit this approach in this experiment as it is not meaningful. On the other hand, we consider another method, which computes the top-k columns using the exponential mechanism to select each top column iteratively, with quality function set as true column count, i.e., **tc**. This is the method used to select top k columns in [19] and [2], which study differentially private itemset mining. We denote this as EM, in Table 3 and 4. DPSense and DPSense-S algorithms are abbreviated in this section as DPS and DPSS, respectively. We choose k as 1%, 5%, and 10% of the number of columns in the dataset.

Overall, DPSense performed the best, followed by DPSense-S, and by EM and GS. Similar to previous experiment, LPA benefits a lot from datasets with smaller sensitivity, such as *Transaction* and *Document*, while it is worse in other datasets. FPA publishes similar counts to every column due to the inverse of transformation on truncated coefficients, so it predicts very inaccurately on top-k columns. EM needs to allocate the privacy budgets into k% times the number of columns parts, so when k is small it performs reason-

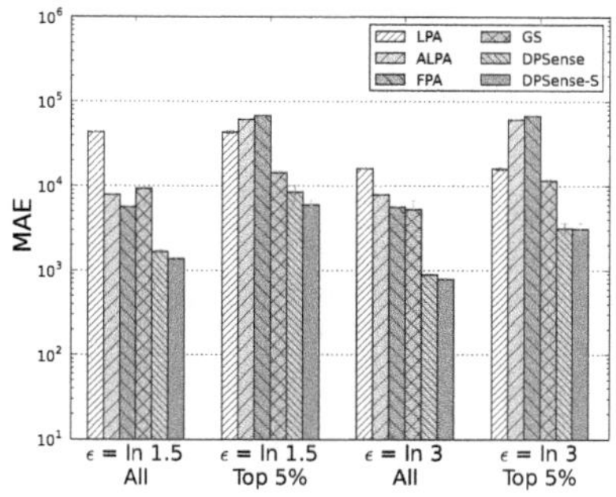

(a) Netflix dataset

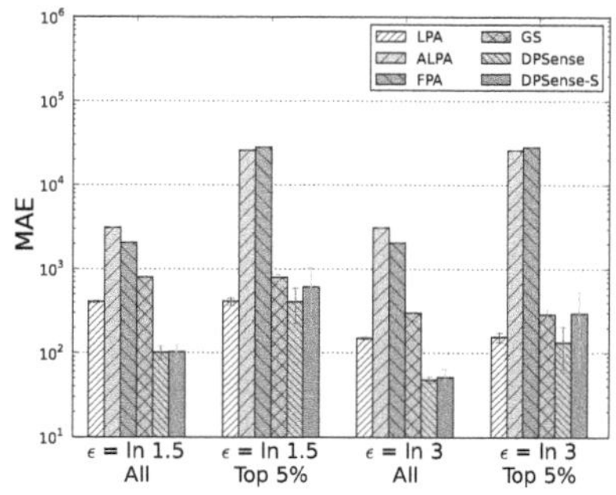

(b) Transaction dataset

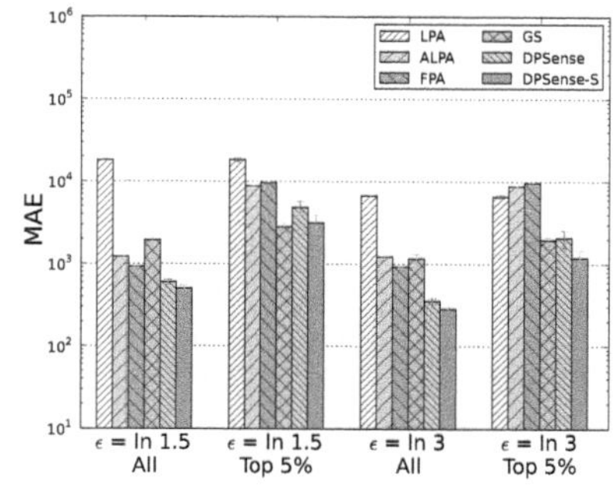

(c) Movielens dataset

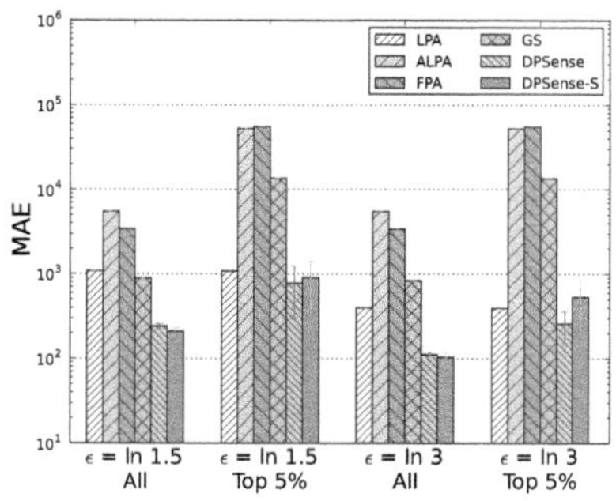

(d) Document dataset

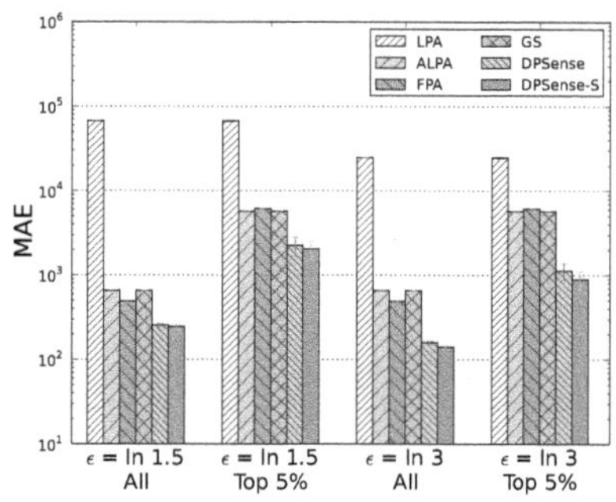

(e) AOL dataset

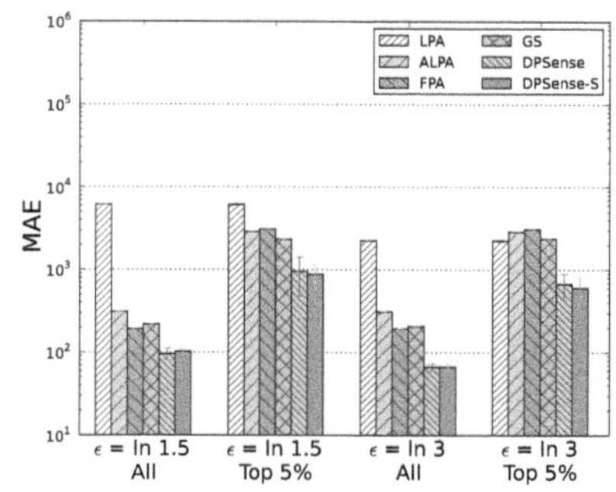

(f) Kosarak dataset

Figure 2: The MAE results of approaches on different datasets.

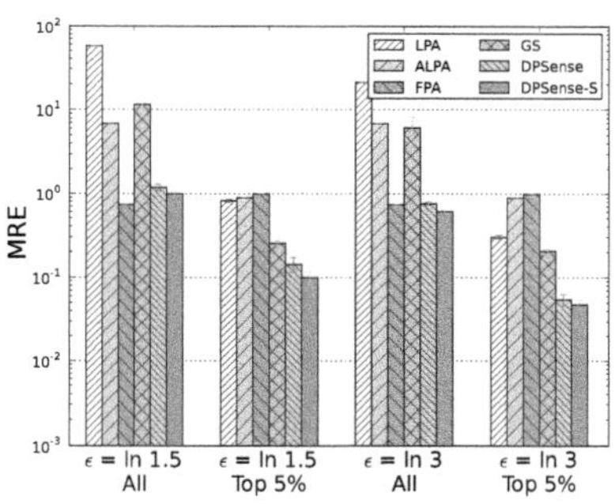

(a) Netflix dataset

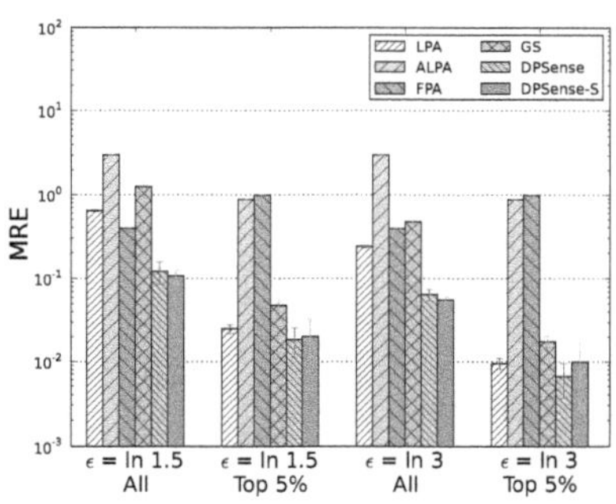

(b) Transaction dataset

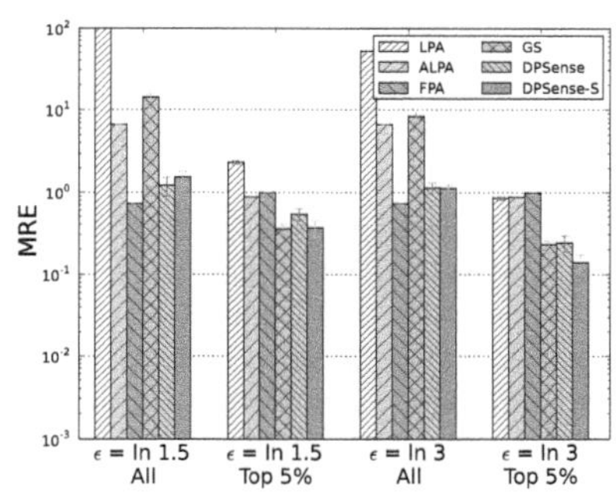

(c) Movielens dataset

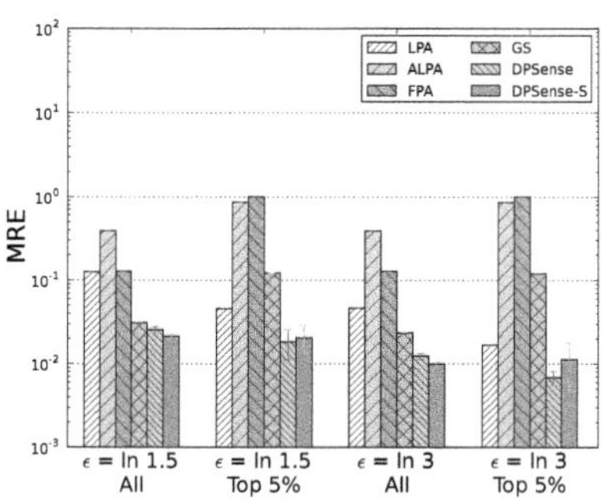

(d) Document dataset

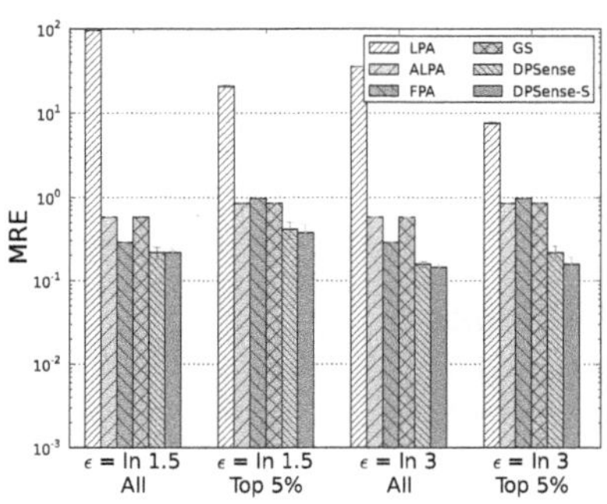

(e) AOL dataset

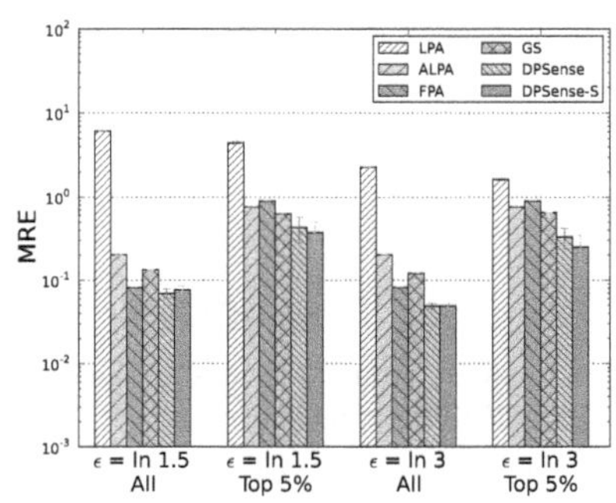

(f) Kosarak dataset

Figure 3: The MRE results of approaches on different datasets.

ably well, but the accuracy significantly drops as k increases. GS benefits from the grouping strategy, but if the estimated group size differs too much from optimal group size, it easily groups dissimilar columns together and publishes inaccurate counts. Also, even if the estimated group size is close to optimal size like in Netflix dataset, computing average within group also produces error. The

Dataset	k	$\epsilon = \ln 1.5$ LPA	FPA	EM	GS	DPS	DPSS	$\epsilon = \ln 3$ LPA	FPA	EM	GS	DPS	DPSS
Netflix	1%	0.170	0.001	**0.997**	0.807	0.981	0.961	0.753	0.000	**0.994**	0.851	0.992	0.991
	5%	0.233	0.050	0.961	0.738	**0.967**	0.951	0.565	0.050	0.984	0.843	**0.985**	0.980
	10%	0.260	0.102	0.810	0.621	0.937	**0.939**	0.475	0.102	0.950	0.776	**0.972**	0.971
Transaction	1%	**1.000**	0.294	**1.000**	**1.000**	**1.000**	**1.000**	**1.000**	0.294	**1.000**	**1.000**	**1.000**	**1.000**
	5%	0.973	0.470	0.986	0.959	**0.990**	0.988	0.988	0.470	0.990	0.984	**0.992**	0.988
	10%	0.962	0.633	0.965	0.920	**0.989**	0.988	0.988	0.633	0.988	0.973	**0.995**	**0.995**
Movielens	1%	0.023	0.093	**0.975**	0.732	0.901	0.887	0.169	0.093	**0.991**	0.777	0.954	0.920
	5%	0.085	0.140	0.746	0.596	0.891	**0.894**	0.203	0.140	0.926	0.777	**0.940**	0.928
	10%	0.140	0.159	0.434	0.487	0.828	**0.843**	0.242	0.158	0.717	0.680	0.918	**0.925**
Document	1%	0.993	0.009	0.975	0.943	**0.998**	0.996	0.998	0.009	0.992	0.945	**0.999**	0.998
	5%	0.963	0.046	0.336	0.964	**0.990**	**0.990**	0.987	0.047	0.597	0.965	**0.996**	0.995
	10%	0.856	0.093	0.209	0.952	0.976	**0.980**	0.964	0.092	0.330	0.960	0.990	**0.991**
AOL	1%	0.018	0.057	0.826	0.294	**0.948**	0.934	0.036	0.057	0.958	0.294	**0.971**	0.954
	5%	0.056	0.305	0.146	0.452	0.880	**0.894**	0.068	0.305	0.310	0.452	**0.944**	0.939
	10%	0.106	0.300	0.136	0.541	0.770	**0.807**	0.116	0.300	0.201	0.541	0.894	**0.914**
Kosarak	1%	0.071	0.020	0.432	0.497	**0.761**	0.756	0.185	0.018	0.844	0.492	**0.851**	0.799
	5%	0.084	0.085	0.088	0.782	0.845	**0.849**	0.144	0.093	0.160	0.756	0.914	**0.916**
	10%	0.128	0.170	0.115	**0.726**	0.710	0.711	0.174	0.159	0.140	0.813	0.809	**0.831**

Table 3: Top-k accuracy for different approaches on datasets.

advantage of sensitivity control makes our DPSense algorithm robust on predicting top-k columns.

From the previous section, we have seen that DPSense-S can improve DPSense in top-5% columns. The experimental result here also demonstrates the advantage of DPSense-S, especially when $\epsilon = \ln 1.5$. Although the scaling up step doesn't affect the ranking of top-k columns, DPSense-S tends to choose a smaller θ than DPSense does and later correct the value by α, in which the smaller θ leads to less noise and improves the top-k accuracy and NDCG.

GS performs reasonably well; however, for some situations it is much worse than DPSense. Since GS divides columns into groups and publishes the same noisy count for all columns in a group, its accuracy depends very much on how well the group size lines up with the k value for top-k columns. If k is close to the group size, and sampling one cell from each row preserves the ordering of columns well, then GS would perform reasonably well. The results of top-k accuracy and NDCG from different approaches are similar. The result of NDCG is closer to optimal than top-k accuracy, mainly because NDCG takes rank into account and also handles cases where a column is bumped out of the top-k by another column with the same true count, which doesn't incur a penalty.

5.5 Running Time of DPSense and DPSense-S

We evaluate the running time of DPSense and DPSense-S using MATLAB R2013a on a machine with Intel Xeon CPU E5-2670 2.60GHz and 32GB RAM. Table 5 shows the result of both approaches on different datasets. Overall, DPSense takes just few seconds to run, while DPSense-S requires time from few seconds to minutes, depending on the datasets. DPSense-S spends most of the time on computing the quality of different candidates, due to the fact that it requires one scan for each (θ, α) pair when computing the pair's quality. DPSense needs only one scan of dataset to compute quality of all θs, thus runs much faster than DPSense-S. The result also shows our proposed algorithms are practical and applicable for real world datasets.

Dataset	DPSense	DPSense-S
Netflix	2.94	1211.59
Transaction	0.34	2.82
Movielens	0.45	178.99
Document	52.86	1946.13
AOL	1.52	298.95
Kosarak	1.04	136.47

Table 5: Running time (in seconds) of DPSense and DPSense-S on different datasets.

6. RELATED WORK

The notion of differential privacy was introduced in [4, 8, 7]. The method of adding Laplacian noise scaled with the sensitivity, which we use to generate noisy counts, is proposed in [8]. The exponential mechanism was introduced in [20].

Our work is directly motivated by Kellaris et al. [15], which studies the same problem as our paper does. We have presented their approach in detail in Section 3.1 and experimentally compared with their approach. Kellaris et al. address the large-sensitivity challenge by publishing one count for a group of similar columns. To decide which columns are similar, they sample one non-zero cell from each row to reduce sensitivity. Our key contribution is a technique to choose an optimal threshold for limiting contributions. We also note that the approach in [15] is based on the assumption that Δ_D is public.

In [16], Korolova et al. also used the idea to limit the contribution of each row to reduce sensitivity in the context of publishing search log information. The threshold for limiting user's activity, d in their paper, is manually set from users. [3, 14] discuss the theoretical effect of sensitivity control by projection of a graph in the problem of publishing graph information. In [9] Gotz et al. discuss the effect of choosing the number of contribution per user by testing different θ values. The authors argue that choosing θ approximately to the average number of items contributed by each user has the best result. In [21], Proserpio et al. presented the idea

Dataset	k	$\epsilon = \ln 1.5$						$\epsilon = \ln 3$					
		LPA	FPA	EM	GS	DPS	DPSS	LPA	FPA	EM	GS	DPS	DPSS
Netflix	1%	0.187	0.000	**0.999**	0.912	0.997	0.993	0.876	0.000	0.914	0.938	**0.999**	**0.999**
	5%	0.299	0.048	**0.997**	0.909	**0.997**	0.994	0.787	0.048	**0.999**	0.951	**0.999**	**0.999**
	10%	0.337	0.091	0.954	0.831	**0.992**	0.991	0.696	0.091	0.995	0.925	**0.998**	**0.998**
Transaction	1%	0.998	0.418	0.927	0.446	**0.999**	0.998	**0.999**	0.418	0.725	0.446	**0.999**	**0.999**
	5%	0.997	0.529	**0.999**	0.647	**0.999**	0.998	**0.999**	0.529	0.997	0.646	**0.999**	**0.999**
	10%	0.996	0.675	0.997	0.887	**0.999**	**0.999**	**0.999**	0.675	**0.999**	0.885	**0.999**	**0.999**
Movielens	1%	0.030	0.093	**0.998**	0.879	0.982	0.976	0.207	0.093	**0.999**	0.911	0.995	0.986
	5%	0.086	0.182	0.922	0.825	**0.979**	0.978	0.273	0.182	0.991	0.922	**0.993**	0.989
	10%	0.146	0.207	0.633	0.730	0.951	**0.961**	0.312	0.206	0.902	0.852	0.984	**0.987**
Document	1%	**0.999**	0.019	0.998	0.959	**0.999**	**0.999**	**0.999**	0.017	**0.999**	0.958	**0.999**	**0.999**
	5%	0.996	0.046	0.553	0.994	**0.999**	**0.999**	**0.999**	0.046	0.828	0.995	**0.999**	**0.999**
	10%	0.971	0.088	0.319	0.994	**0.998**	**0.998**	0.996	0.088	0.521	0.995	**0.999**	**0.999**
AOL	1%	0.027	0.064	0.965	0.389	**0.988**	0.987	0.097	0.064	0.996	0.389	**0.997**	0.992
	5%	0.057	0.326	0.245	0.547	0.975	**0.977**	0.089	0.326	0.518	0.547	**0.991**	0.990
	10%	0.102	0.350	0.167	0.645	0.935	**0.944**	0.127	0.350	0.295	0.645	0.976	**0.984**
Kosarak	1%	0.214	0.017	0.707	0.597	**0.934**	0.927	0.415	0.017	**0.968**	0.587	0.957	0.951
	5%	0.130	0.095	0.143	0.860	**0.955**	0.953	0.247	0.098	0.277	0.836	**0.979**	**0.979**
	10%	0.156	0.161	0.132	0.872	0.881	**0.891**	0.247	0.160	0.183	0.913	0.948	**0.951**

Table 4: NDCG in top-k columns for different approaches on datasets.

of normalizing troublesome points to reduce sensitivity, while the problem of choosing the scaling parameter is not addressed. The notion of (ϵ, δ)-differential privacy was used in [16, 9], and here we use the stronger (ϵ)-differential privacy. Furthermore, we present a differentially private way to choose a good θ or (θ, α) pair, and show that the optimal choice depends on ϵ and distribution beyond the average row count.

Differentially private frequent itemset mining was studied in [2, 19]. These two papers focus on finding combinations of columns that are frequent. They use the exponential mechanism to select top-k columns, which we compare with, and do not consider the sensitivity control technique. Rastogi et al. in [23] proposed the framework of using Discrete Fourier Transform (DFT) to publish time-series data under differential privacy. We compare with their Fourier Perturbation Algorithm in the experiments.

Several methods on publishing the synopsis of a dataset so that range queries can be answered accurately have been developed [12, 25, 5, 17, 22]. Differentially private release of marginal tables were studied in [1, 24, 18, 6, 10, 11]. Publishing a synopsis of two-dimensional datasets has been studied in [5, 17, 22].

7. CONCLUSIONS AND FUTURE WORKS

We have proposed the DPSense and DPSense-S approaches for publishing column counts for high-dimensional datasets. The key idea is to reduce the sensitivity by setting a limit θ on the contribution of each record, and our key technical contribution is a quality function that enables the effective selection of the threshold as well as the correcting factor to reduce error in a differentially private way. Experimental evaluation using several utility metrics demonstrates the effectiveness for publishing all columns or finding top columns with high count. We also demonstrate that the efficiency of our proposed algorithms makes private publishing of high dimensional datasets practical. Our technique has advanced the state of the art on publishing column counts while satisfying differential privacy.

As high sensitivity is a key hurdle to private data publishing and analysis, we conjecture that our novel sensitivity control technique can be fruitfully applied to other problems. A future direction is to investigate whether this technique can be applied to other problems that publishing information about high-dimensional datasets.

8. ACKNOWLEDGMENTS

This work reported in this paper is supported by National Science Foundation under grant CNS-116991.

9. REFERENCES

[1] B. Barak, K. Chaudhuri, C. Dwork, S. Kale, F. McSherry, and K. Talwar. Privacy, accuracy, and consistency too: a holistic solution to contingency table release. In *PODS'07*, pages 273–282, 2007.

[2] R. Bhaskar, S. Laxman, A. Smith, and A. Thakurta. Discovering frequent patterns in sensitive data. In *KDD*, 2010.

[3] J. Blocki, A. Blum, A. Datta, and O. Sheffet. Differentially private data analysis of social networks via restricted sensitivity. In *Proceedings of the 4th Conference on Innovations in Theoretical Computer Science*, ITCS '13, pages 87–96, New York, NY, USA, 2013. ACM.

[4] A. Blum, C. Dwork, F. McSherry, and K. Nissim. Practical privacy: the SuLQ framework. In *PODS*, pages 128–138, 2005.

[5] G. Cormode, M. Procopiuc, E. Shen, D. Srivastava, and T. Yu. Differentially private spatial decompositions. In *ICDE*, pages 20–31, 2012.

[6] B. Ding, M. Winslett, J. Han, and Z. Li. Differentially private data cubes: optimizing noise sources and consistency. In *SIGMOD*, pages 217–228, 2011.

[7] C. Dwork. Differential privacy. In *ICALP*, pages 1–12, 2006.

[8] C. Dwork, F. Mcsherry, K. Nissim, and A. Smith. Calibrating noise to sensitivity in private data analysis. In *Theory of Cryptography Conference (TCC)*, pages 265–284. Springer, 2006.

[9] M. Gotz, A. Machanavajjhala, G. Wang, X. Xiao, and J. Gehrke. Publishing search logs - a comparative study of

privacy guarantees. *IEEE Transactions on Knowledge and Data Engineering*, 24(3):520–532, 2012.

[10] A. Gupta, M. Hardt, A. Roth, and J. Ullman. Privately releasing conjunctions and the statistical query barrier. In *STOC*, pages 803–812, 2011.

[11] M. Hardt, K. Ligett, and F. McSherry. A simple and practical algorithm for differentially private data release. In *NIPS*, pages 2348–2356, 2012.

[12] M. Hay, V. Rastogi, G. Miklau, and D. Suciu. Boosting the accuracy of differentially private histograms through consistency. *PVLDB*, 3:1021–1032, September 2010.

[13] K. Järvelin and J. Kekäläinen. Cumulated gain-based evaluation of ir techniques. *ACM Trans. Inf. Syst.*, 20(4):422–446, Oct. 2002.

[14] S. P. Kasiviswanathan, K. Nissim, S. Raskhodnikova, and A. Smith. Analyzing graphs with node differential privacy. In *Proceedings of the 10th Theory of Cryptography Conference on Theory of Cryptography*, TCC'13, pages 457–476, Berlin, Heidelberg, 2013. Springer-Verlag.

[15] G. Kellaris and S. Papadopoulos. Practical differential privacy via grouping and smoothing. In *PVLDB*, PVLDB'13, pages 301–312. VLDB Endowment, 2013.

[16] A. Korolova, K. Kenthapadi, N. Mishra, and A. Ntoulas. Releasing search queries and clicks privately. In *Proceedings of the 18th international conference on World wide web*, WWW '09, pages 171–180, New York, NY, USA, 2009. ACM.

[17] J. Lei. Differentially private m-estimators. In *NIPS*, pages 361–369, 2011.

[18] C. Li, M. Hay, V. Rastogi, G. Miklau, and A. McGregor. Optimizing linear counting queries under differential privacy. In *PODS*, pages 123–134, New York, NY, USA, 2010. ACM.

[19] N. Li, W. H. Qardaji, D. Su, and J. Cao. Privbasis: Frequent itemset mining with differential privacy. *PVLDB*, 5(11):1340–1351, 2012.

[20] F. McSherry and K. Talwar. Mechanism design via differential privacy. In *IEEE Symposium on Foundations of Computer Science (FOCS)*, pages 94–103, 2007.

[21] D. Proserpio, S. Goldberg, and F. McSherry. Calibrating data to sensitivity in private data analysis. *PVLDB*, 7(8):637–648, 2014.

[22] W. Qardaji, W. Yang, and N. Li. Differentially private grids for geospatial data. In *ICDE*, 2012.

[23] V. Rastogi and S. Nath. Differentially private aggregation of distributed time-series with transformation and encryption. In *Proceedings of the 2010 ACM SIGMOD International Conference on Management of Data*, SIGMOD '10, pages 735–746, New York, NY, USA, 2010. ACM.

[24] J. Thaler, J. Ullman, and S. Vadhan. Faster algorithms for privately releasing marginals. In *ICALP*, pages 810–821, 2012.

[25] X. Xiao, G. Wang, and J. Gehrke. Differential privacy via wavelet transforms. *IEEE Transactions on Knowledge and Data Engineering*, 23:1200–1214, 2011.

APPENDIX

A. PROOF OF LEMMA 2

We give the proof of Lemma 2 here. Let D, D' be two neighbor datasets differ in only one row. The sensitivity of quality function qs, Δqs, is defined as the maximal possible difference of qs giving D, D'. In other words,

$$\begin{aligned}\Delta qs &= \max_{\forall\theta,\alpha,D,D',\epsilon_p} && |qs(D,\theta,\alpha,\epsilon_p) - qs(D',\theta,\alpha,\epsilon_p)| \\ &= \max_{\forall\theta,\alpha,D,D',\epsilon_p} && \Big|\Big(-ae(D,D|_\theta) - \alpha\cdot\tfrac{\theta}{\epsilon_p}\Big) - \\ & && \Big(-ae(D',D'|_\theta) - \alpha\cdot\tfrac{\theta}{\epsilon_p}\Big)\Big| \\ &= \max_{\forall\theta,\alpha,D,D'} && |ae(D',D'|_\theta) - ae(D,D|_\theta)| \\ &= \max_{\forall\theta,\alpha} && \tfrac{1}{d}\textstyle\sum_{j=1}^{d}\big(|\alpha\cdot c_j^\theta - c_j| - |\alpha\cdot c_j'^\theta - c_j'|\big)\end{aligned}$$

where c_j' and $c_j'^\theta$ denote jth column count in D' and in $D'|_\theta$, respectively. Since D and D' are neighbored dataset, c_j and c_j' can only differ in 1. If $c_j = c_j'$, then the sensitivity apparently becomes 0. So let's assume that $c_j' = c_j + 1$. Let $\beta = c_j'^\theta - c_j^\theta$ be the value of the difference of jth column between $D|_\theta$ and $D'|_\theta$. Since the additional 1 in c_j' may be normalized to $\frac{\theta}{RC_i}(\theta \le RC_i)$, and $RC_i \le \Delta_D$, we have the following inequality bound on β:

$$\frac{\theta}{\Delta_D} \le \beta \le 1$$

Let δ_j denote the difference of error on jth column between D and D', i.e. $\delta_j = |\alpha\cdot c_j^\theta - c_j| - |\alpha\cdot c_j'^\theta - c_j'|$. To compute δ_j, we can discuss with four different scenarios:

- If $\alpha\cdot c_j^\theta \ge c_j$ and $\alpha\cdot c_j'^\theta \ge c_j'$: Then we have

$$\begin{aligned}\delta_j &= |\alpha\cdot c_j^\theta - c_j| - |\alpha\cdot c_j'^\theta - c_j'| \\ &= \alpha c_j^\theta - c_j - \alpha c_j'^\theta + c_j' \\ &\le \alpha(c_j^\theta - c_j'^\theta) - c_j + c_j + 1 \\ &= 1 - \alpha\beta \\ &\le 1 - \alpha\cdot\tfrac{\theta}{\Delta_D} \le 1\end{aligned}$$

- If $\alpha\cdot c_j^\theta \ge c_j$ and $\alpha\cdot c_j'^\theta \le c_j'$: the bound of $c_j' - \alpha c_j'^\theta$ is

$$\begin{aligned}0 &\le c_j' - \alpha c_j'^\theta \\ &= c_j + 1 - \alpha(c_j^\theta + \beta) \\ &= c_j - \alpha c_j^\theta + 1 - \alpha\beta \\ &\le 1 - \alpha\beta \le 1\end{aligned}$$

  The above also infers $0 \le \alpha c_j^\theta - c_j \le 1 - \alpha\beta \le 1$. Thus,

$$\begin{aligned}\delta_j &= |\alpha\cdot c_j^\theta - c_j| - |\alpha\cdot c_j'^\theta - c_j'| \\ &= (\alpha\cdot c_j^\theta - c_j) - (c_j' - \alpha\cdot c_j'^\theta) \\ &\le 1 - 0 = 1\end{aligned}$$

- If $\alpha\cdot c_j^\theta \le c_j$ and $\alpha\cdot c_j'^\theta \ge c_j'$: the bound of $\alpha c_j'^\theta - c_j'$ is

$$\begin{aligned}0 &\le \alpha c_j'^\theta - c_j' \\ &= \alpha(c_j^\theta + \beta) - c_j - 1 \\ &= \alpha c_j^\theta - c_j + \alpha\beta - 1 \\ &\le \alpha\beta - 1 \\ &\le \alpha - 1\end{aligned}$$

  The above also infers $0 \le c_j - \alpha c_j^\theta \le \alpha\beta - 1 \le \alpha - 1$. Then

$$\begin{aligned}\delta_j &= |\alpha\cdot c_j^\theta - c_j| - |\alpha\cdot c_j'^\theta - c_j'| \\ &= (c_j - \alpha c_j^\theta) - (\alpha c_j'^\theta - c_j') \\ &\le (\alpha - 1) - 0 = \alpha - 1\end{aligned}$$

- If $\alpha\cdot c_j^\theta \le c_j$ and $\alpha\cdot c_j'^\theta \le c_j'$: Then we have

$$\begin{aligned}\delta_j &= |\alpha\cdot c_j^\theta - c_j| - |\alpha\cdot c_j'^\theta - c_j'| \\ &= c_j - \alpha\cdot c_j^\theta - c_j' + \alpha\cdot c_j'^\theta \\ &\le c_j - \alpha\cdot c_j^\theta - c_j - 1 + \alpha\cdot c_j^\theta + \alpha\beta \\ &= \alpha\beta - 1 \le \alpha - 1\end{aligned}$$

Thus $\delta_j \le \max_{\theta,\alpha}\{1, \alpha - 1\}$. The quality function computes the average of δ_j. Since the bound of δ_j is independent of j, we can directly infer that $\Delta qs \le \max\{1, \alpha - 1\}$.

Enpublic Apps: Security Threats Using iOS Enterprise and Developer Certificates

Min Zheng[†], Hui Xue[§], Yulong Zhang[§], Tao Wei[§] and John C.S. Lui[†]
[†] The Chinese University of Hong Kong, [§] FireEye Inc.

ABSTRACT

Compared with Android, the conventional wisdom is that iOS is more secure. However, both jailbroken and non-jailbroken iOS devices have number of vulnerabilities. For iOS, apps need to interact with the underlying system using Application Programming Interfaces (APIs). Some of these APIs remain undocumented and Apple forbids apps in App Store from using them. These APIs, also known as "*private APIs*", provide powerful features to developers and yet they may have serious security consequences if misused. Furthermore, apps which use private APIs can bypass the App Store and use the "*Apple's Enterprise/Developer Certificates*" for distribution. This poses a significant threat to the iOS e-cosystem. So far, there is no formal study to understand these apps and how private APIs are being encapsulated. We call these iOS apps which distribute to the public using enterprise certificates as "enpublic" apps. In this paper, we present the design and implementation of iAnalytics, which can automatically analyze "enpublic" apps' private API usages and vulnerabilities. Using iAnalytics, we crawled and analyzed 1,408 enpublic iOS apps. We discovered that: 844 (60%) out of the 1408 apps do use private APIs, 14 (1%) apps contain URL scheme vulnerabilities, 901 (64%) enpublic apps transport sensitive information through unencrypted channel or store the information in plaintext on the phone. In addition, we summarized 25 private APIs which are crucial and security sensitive on iOS 6/7/8, and we have filed one CVE (Common Vulnerabilities and Exposures) for iOS devices.

1. INTRODUCTION

As of the end of 2013, Apple has attracted around 800 million iOS users [21] and there are over one million apps in the iOS App Store [12]. According to Apple's "Creating Jobs Through Innovation" report[4], there are more than 275,000 registered iOS developers in the U.S. Despite the popularity, few iOS malware have been discovered [32]. In addition, it was reported [24] that iOS is more secure than Android due to its controlled distribution channel and comprehensive apps review. However, there are still potential risks for iOS systems.

In February 2012, Apple banned all apps from Qihoo [3], a prominent Chinese vendor for anti-virus software, web browser and search engine. This major incident happened because Qihoo used iOS private APIs and encrypted the function calls in its iOS apps, and Apple has a policy that forbids any non-Apple apps in its App Store from using private APIs. Shortly after that, the story developed further when Qihoo received a "double blow" [20] from Apple, which banned every single Qihoo app from iOS app store after an official warning. The reason for this double blow was rather new: Qihoo released their "enterprise" apps to the public but Apple restricts the enterprise apps to be used by employees of that company only, instead of everyone in public.

So what are private APIs and enterprise apps? Why Apple is so vigilant on their usages? In fact, iOS apps on any non-jailbroken device can be classified into two categories based on how they are being distributed. Apps which are distributed through the Apple's App Store are the most common to users and we call them as "normal" apps. The other cateory is the "enterprise" or "developer" apps which are distributed under the *enterprise/developer certificates.* Note that these "enterprise" and "developer" apps are not distributed via the App Store, hence, they are not regulated by the Apple's review process [2]. Often, iOS apps use Apple's Application Programming Interfaces (APIs) to interact with the iOS system for system resources and services. Some of these iOS APIs are "private" in the sense that only apps developed by Apple (Apple apps) can use them and other apps using these private APIs are not allowed on the Apple App Store. These apps using private APIs can only be distributed using the "enterprise" or "developer" certificates which grant a limited number of developers or employee users per enterprise (or company). Public APIs are often used to interact with iOS system for resource allocation or service request. Private APIs, however, are much more powerful comparing to the public ones. To illustrate, consider an iOS 6.0 device. A normal app can call the public Twitter APIs to post a tweet on the user's Twitter homepage (Fig. 1), and the user must consent by clicking the "Post" button. However, by using private APIs, the app can post the tweet without notifying the user [35] at all.

Given that private APIs have powerful functionalities, once abused, private APIs may become formidable weapons for malicious attackers. Although they are undocumented and Apple's review process scrutinizes apps rigorously to search

ASIA CCS'15, April 14–17, 2015, Singapore..

http://dx.doi.org/10.1145/2714576.2714593 .

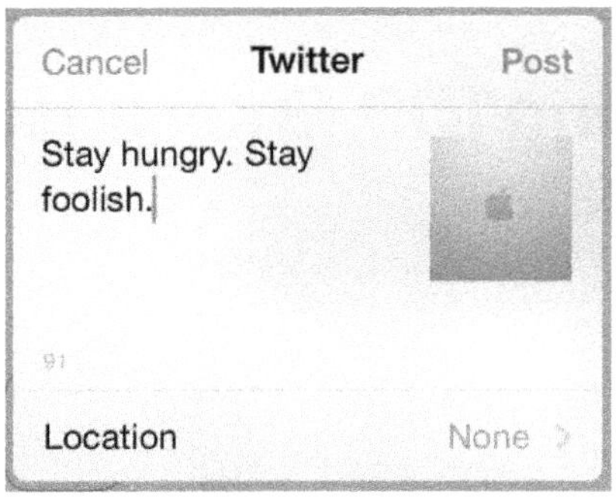

Figure 1: Screenshot for Legitimate Twitter App

for private APIs, hackers still manage to learn them by analyzing iOS frameworks directly and found sophisticated means [35, 27] which can bypass the review process. Since there is no review process for apps under enterprise/developer certificates, therefore, attackers may take advantage of this venue to distribute malware through the web. In addition, authors in [34] and [29] show that infecting a large number of iOS devices through botnets is feasible. They have demonstrated that a compromised computer can be instructed to install enterprise apps or developer apps on iOS devices. This shows that there are number of ways to infect iOS devices, and App Store's review process is not sufficient to protect iOS devices.

Although Apple only allows the enterprise apps and developer apps to be used by company employees and developers, many vendors do use this method to distribute their apps to the public (e.g., GBA emulator [11]). In addition, hackers do use this channel to distribute malware [36]. It seems that Apple does not have an ideal method to monitor and manage these wild enterprise and developer apps. Although Apple can remotely revoke the enterprise or developer certificates, hackers can resign the app, rename the app's Bundle name or change the system time (e.g., Pangu [19] uses an invalid enterprise certificate for jailbreak) to bypass the revoking process. In addition, if the enterprise apps contain vulnerabilities (e.g., URL scheme flaw and heart bleed), they become valuable targets to attackers as the private APIs that they use make them more powerful as compared with ordinary apps from iOS apps. As more users and enterprises use iOS devices, there is a constant push to create enpublic apps, this is exactly the motivation of this paper because we need to warm the developers (and users) before we see the epidemic spread of this form of malware.

When enterprise apps or developer apps are distributed to the public, we refer to such apps as "enpublic" apps. In order to understand the security landscape of enpublic apps, we propose a security evaluation mechanism for iOS enpublic apps. Researchers and anti-virus companies can use our mechanism to detect and analyze malicious iOS enpublic apps. Customers can also use this mechanism to evaluate the risk of the enpublic apps before installation.

The main contributions of the paper are:

- We present a detailed study of threats using private APIs within enpublic apps, and show the gap between Apple's regulations and the abuse of enterprise and developer certifications. To the best of our knowledge, this paper is the first to investigate the abuse of enterprise and developer certificates.
- We propose both static and dynamic analysis techniques to detect iOS private APIs, URL schemes vulnerability and sensitive information leakage. We summarized 25 private APIs which are crucial and security sensitive on iOS 6/7/8, and we have filed one CVE (Common Vulnerabilities and Exposures) for iOS devices.
- In our evaluation, we discovered that 844 out of the 1408 enpublic apps we studied do use private APIs. 14 apps contain URL scheme vulnerabilities and 901 apps transport sensitive information through unencrypted channel.

2. BACKGROUND

In this section, we briefly provide some background information about iOS developer programs and itms-services installation.

2.1 iOS Developer Programs

iOS developers use development tools like Xcode and iOS simulators to develop apps. To distribute their apps to legal (or non-jailbroken) iOS devices, app developers must join the iOS developer programs[6]. There are three types of iOS developer programs: *standard program*, *enterprise program* and *university program*. Tab. 1 depicts the distribution capability of these three programs. Note that all three programs allow developers to test their apps on devices. They differ in how developers can distribute their apps. Developers under the standard program can release their apps on the App Store or distribute the apps through the ad hoc channel. For the enterprise program, developers can distribute their apps through the ad hoc channel and the in-house channel (we will explain the ad hoc and in-house distribution channels in the next subsection). Apps developed under the university program cannot be distributed in any of these three channels.

Although Apple only allows the enterprise apps and developer apps to be used by company employees and developers, many vendors or malware writers do use this method to distribute their apps or malware to the public [36]. The advantage of using enterprise certificate and developer certificate is that developers can use private APIs to achieve advanced functionalities (e.g., screen recording). In addition, instead of the App Store, developers can maintain the installed apps on their own servers, so that they can update these apps any time without the review process. Furthermore, Apple banned many kinds of apps (e.g., pornographic app) on App Store. By using enterprise certificate or developer certificate, it becomes possible to distribute these kinds of apps.

2.2 Ad Hoc and In-House Distribution

2.2.1 *Ad hoc distribution*

Ad hoc is a Latin phrase which means "for this". Both the standard program and the enterprise program can use the ad hoc channel to distribute iOS apps. These apps are `.ipa` files which contain app runtime resources and an ad hoc provisioning profile. Fig. 2 shows the architecture of the ad hoc

Program	Test apps on iOS devices	App Store	Ad Hoc	In–house
Standard Program	Yes	Yes	Yes	No
Enterprise Program	Yes	No	Yes	Yes
University Program	Yes	No	No	No

Table 1: iOS Developer Programs and their Distribution Capability

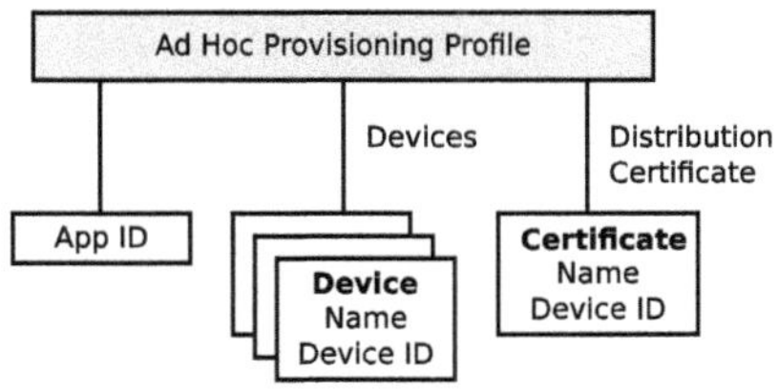

Figure 2: Ad Hoc Provisioning Profile

provisioning profile, each profile contains the ID of the tested app, certificate of the developer, and the unique device IDs (UDIDs) of designated devices. The provisioning profile only allows the iOS app to be installed on these designated devices. In order to register designated devices, developers need to specify the UDIDs of designated devices and register them in the iOS Dev Center [14] before distribution. Note that each development account can register at most 100 devices per membership year. After the registration, developers or testers can install the ad hoc `.ipa` file on the designated devices through the iTunes or via the iOS RPC communication library (e.g., libimobiledevice [17]). Therefore, hackers may register more than one developer account for enpublic app distribution. The advantage of using this method is Apple cannot easily revoke all the certificates.

2.2.2 *In-house distribution*

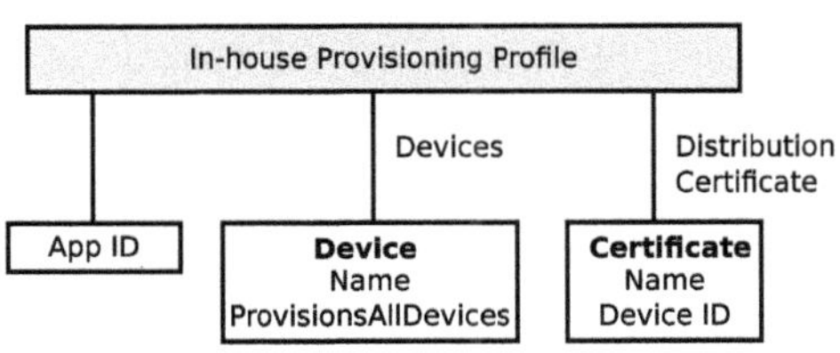

Figure 3: In–house Provisioning Profile

Enterprise program can also use the in-house channel to distribute iOS apps on iOS devices. The enterprise apps contain app runtime resources and an in-house provisioning profile. Fig. 3 shows the architecture of the in-house provisioning profile. The major difference between an ad hoc profile and an in-house profile is that an ad hoc profile serves no more than 100 designated devices, whereas in-house profile may serve *unlimited number* of devices. Besides using the i-Tunes for distribution, the in-house distribution can use the itms-service as another distribution channel. This service supports an over-the-air installation of custom-developed in-house apps without using the iTunes or the App Store. All it needs is just a web server, an iOS app in `.ipa` format (built for release/production with an enterprise provisioning profile), and an XML manifest file which instructs the device to download and install the apps. In fact, developers can provide a simple web link which triggers the installation process, for instance:

```
<a href=''itms-services://?action=downloadmanifest&
url=http://www.example.com/manifest.plist''>
Install App</a>
```

During the installation, the device contacts "ocsp.apple.com" to check the status of the distribution certificate used to sign the provisioning profile. In addition, once it is issued, distribution provisioning profiles have 12 months validity before expiration. After that, the profile will be removed and the app cannot be launched. Fig. 4 illustrates the whole installation process. When a user clicks the "Install" button, the iOS system will automatically install the enterprise app and profile on the device.

3. SYSTEM DESIGN AND METHODOLOGY

To detect and analyze enpublic apps, we designed iAnalytics, a security evaluation system for iOS enterprise/developer apps. iAnalytics first collects enpublic apps from the Internet. Then the system can perform private API detection and app vulnerability detection for the downloaded enpublic apps. At the high level, the workflow for iAnalytics is as follows:

- iAnalytics has an `.ipa` crawler for enpublic apps. Because enpublic apps use "itms–service" for installation, the `.ipa` crawler will also search the Internet with the related keyword, i.e., "**`itms-services://?action=downloadmanifest`**". When finding a suspicious "itms–service" link, the `.ipa` crawler will parse the `.plist` file and crawl the related enpublic app from the HTTP or HTTPS sever.

- After collecting `.ipa` files, iAnalytics uses two detectors for security evaluation: one for analyzing the private API usage, and the other for app vulnerability analysis.

- For private API detection, iAnalytics first generates a private APIs list from iOS SDK. Then iAnalytics uses a private API detector to detect private API calls according to the private APIs list. Note that because there is no app review process for enpublic apps, the app can use any dynamic loading techniques (e.g., `NSBundle and dlopen()`) to load the private frameworks at runtime. Therefore, in addition to checking the static links of frameworks, iAnalytics also analyzes the dynamic loading behaviors at runtime.

- For app vulnerability detection, iAnalytics uses an app vulnerability detector which focuses on detecting the URL scheme vulnerability and sensitive information

Figure 4: The Process of Itms–service Installation

leakage. URL scheme is a protocol for websites or apps to communicate with other apps. An URL scheme with a faulty logic design may cause serious consequences. For sensitive information leakage, personal information, when transported or stored without being encrypted, can be sniffed or extracted by attackers.

- Finally, iAnalytics summarizes the findings and generates analysis reports of these enpublic apps to security analysts.

Fig. 5 depicts the workflow of our system.

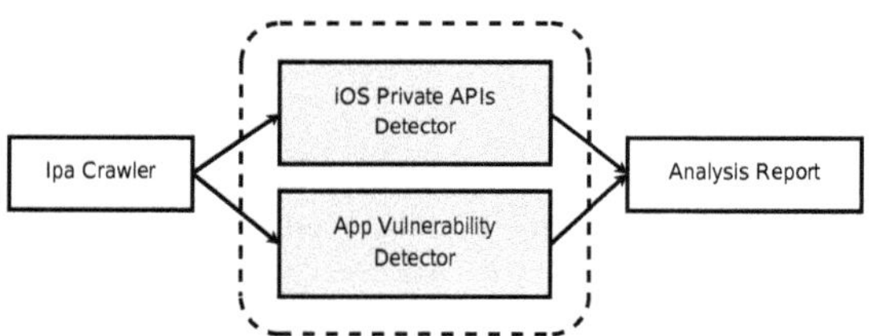

Figure 5: Workflow of iAnalytics

4. IOS PRIVATE APIS DETECTION

In this section, we first give a brief introduction to private APIs, then we show the methodology of obtaining the private APIs list. Finally, we present the implementation of iOS private APIs detector.

4.1 Introduction to Private APIs

iOS Private APIs are undocumented application programming interfaces of the iOS frameworks and they are prohibited by the App Store's review process. These private APIs are methods of framework classes which have no declaration in class header files. Apple emphasized that these private APIs should only be used by the class internally or the iOS system apps [2]. However, when third-party apps use these private APIs, they have enhanced capabilities (e.g., posting tweets, sending emails, and sending SMS without user's consent on iOS [35].) In addition, because there is no application review process in iOS enterprise/developer apps, anyone can distribute their private API apps through this channel.

4.2 Private APIs list

Since the private APIs are the methods of frameworks which have no declaration in the class header files, one can use the following methodology to extract them:

- We first download and install the specific iOS SDK (e.g., iOS 7.1) from Apple's development website[13].
- Then we extract all the frameworks from iOS SDK, for example, UIKit framework can be found at `/Applications/Xcode.app/Contents/Developer/ Platforms/iPhoneSimulator.platform/Developer/ SDKs/iPhoneSimulator7.1.sdk/ System/Library/Frameworks/ UIKit.framework/UIKit`. All of the iOS frameworks are Mach–O file format [18]. By using class–dump[7], which is a command–line tool for extracting the Objective-C information stored in Mach-O files, one can retrieve all the method names and parameters from these Mach–O files. Note that these methods are the API calls, which include both public and private API calls in iOS frameworks.
- Based on Apple's official documents[1], we obtain all the public API calls of a specific SDK version.
- Once we have obtained all private and public APIs call set from Step 2 and public API calls set from Step 3, we can extract the private API calls set of the specific SDK version.

4.3 iOS Private APIs Detector

For iOS private API detection, we use both static and dynamic methodologies to analyze the iOS enpublic apps.

4.3.1 Static Analysis

We built a static analysis tool on top of CCTool[5]. CCTool is an open source project of Apple for analyzing Mach-O format files. This project contains several tools such as otool, nm and strings. However, for private API detection, these tools are not compact and readable. They can only retrieve the basic information of the Mach-O format file and do not have the logic of detecting private APIs. Therefore, we enhance CC-Tool by adding several new features (e.g., private API detection and dynamic loading behavior detection), then build our static analysis of iOS private API detector on top of these modules.

The static analysis process works in the following steps:

- iOS Private APIs Detector can analyze the framework/library loading and determine which framework/library contains private API calls.
- For suspicious framework/library, iOS private API detector will analyze the method symbols and then compare with the private APIs list. If the detector finds private API calls, it will generate a report for the user.
- If the detector finds dynamic loading behavior (e.g., methods which call **NSBundle** and **dlopen()**) of the app, we use the dynamic analysis of iOS private API Detector.

For example, an enterprise app, "**com.tongbu.tui**", statically loads several sensitive frameworks:

```
/System/Library/PrivateFrameworks/
SpringBoardServices.framework

/System/Library/PrivateFrameworks/
MobileInstallation.framework

/System/Library/Frameworks/IOKit.framework
...
```

SpringBoardServices and **MobileInstallation** are private frameworks which contain spring board information and installed package information. As long as an app uses APIs in these two frameworks, they are private APIs. Although **IOKit** framework does not belong to the private frameworks, there is no public API calls in this framework. Therefore, any API calls in this framework also belong to private APIs.

Another example is "**net.qihoo.360msafeenterprise**". This app does not load any private frameworks. However, some public frameworks also have private APIs. For instance: "**net.qihoo.360msafeenterprise**" uses **_CTTelephonyCenterAddObserver** API call of **/System/Library/Frameworks/CoreTelephony.framework** to monitor the incoming telephone calls and SMS messages.

4.3.2 Dynamic Analysis

Because there is no app review process, enpublic apps can use any dynamic loading techniques at runtime. For example, **NSBundle** is a dynamic loading class in Objective-C. It is similar to Java reflection [15] which can dynamically load other frameworks. Another dynamic loading technique is to use private C functions, such as **dlopen()** and **dlsym()**, to dynamically load and execute methods of iOS frameworks. For these apps with dynamic loading behavior, we use **Cydia Substrate**[9] (a hooking framework) to hook the low level library call **_dlopen()** method and **_dlsym()** method on an jailbroken iOS device. Because the low level implementation of **NSBundle** also uses **_dlopen()** method and **_dlsym()** method, there is no need to hook the related methods of **NSBundle**. To illustrate, the logic of **_dlopen()** hooking is shown below:

```
//declare the origional funciton of dlopen
void * (*_dlopenHook)(const char * __path, int __mode);

//implement the replaced dlopen function
void * $dlopenHook(const char * __path, int __mode)
{
NSLog(@"iAnalytics:␣Loading␣%s␣framework", __path);
return _dlopenHook(__path,__mode); //call orig
}
//do hooking
%ctor {
MSHookFunction((void *)MSFindSymbol(NULL,"_dlopen"),
(void *)$dlopenHook, (void **)&_dlopenHook);
}
```

We first obtain a declaration of the original hooked function and implement the function used to replace the original one accordingly. We then use "**MSFindSymbol**" to obtain the address of hooked function and use "**MSHookFunction**" to replace the hooked function. In the implementation of replaced function, the app outputs the loading methods and frameworks to the system log. We collect the related log information from "**/var/log/syslog**". This way, the iAnalytics can detect invocations of private APIs.

5. APP VULNERABILITY DETECTION

Since enpublic apps can use private APIs, they are more powerful, and potentially more damaging, as compared with apps in App Store. In this situation, once plagued by vulnerabilities, enpublic apps become severe threats to iOS users. Attackers may leverage such vulnerabilities to craft dangerous attacks. In this section, we examine two vulnerabilities found in iOS enpublic apps and show how to detect them.

5.1 URL Scheme Vulnerability Detection

A URL scheme vulnerability arises when an app has an unsafe URL scheme logic design and the hacker could send malicious URL requests to the devices. A URL scheme vulnerability may cause memory corruption or malicious actions without user's authorization. In this part, we first briefly explain what URL scheme vulnerability is and present our URL scheme vulnerability detector.

5.1.1 Introduction to URL Scheme Vulnerability

By using URL schemes, web pages running in Safari or iOS apps can integrate with system apps or third-party apps. For example, the **tel://** scheme can be used to launch the telephone app. For instance, a website may contain the following HTML script and a user browses it using Safari on iOS:

```
<iframe src="tel://123456789"></iframe>
```

When fed with the URL scheme of telephone app, Safari will launch the telephone app with the "123456789" as the parameter. After launching, the telephone app requests for user's authorization to make a call. This is a correct logic design from a security perspective, because a malicious website should not be able to initiate a phone call without notifying the user. However, if the app does not perform the authorization check for the URL scheme, it causes security problems. For example, [25] reported that if the website contains the following HTML script:

```
<iframe src= "skype://123456789?call"> </iframe>
```

The older version of Skype will automatically start a call when the user browses a malicious website using the Safari browser. Therefore, developers need to pay attention to the logic design of URL scheme. Otherwise, attackers may use the vulnerability of URL scheme to implement attacks.

5.1.2 *Detection Methodology*

We describe our methodology for URL Scheme vulnerability detection in the paragraphs below:

- We parse `Plist` to obtain the URL scheme information from the `Info.plist` file of the `.ipa` package. In the `Info.plist` file, the URL scheme information is stored in the `CFBundleURLTypes` array. By parsing this array, we can extract `CFBundleURLName` and `CFBundleURLSchemes`.
- If an iOS app has the `CFBundleURLSchemes`, it will call the `[application:handleOpenURL]` method in the `application delegate` class. We disassemble the app and then perform a recursive search from the `[application:handleOpenURL]` method. If the app invokes any private API calls, we catch it. Then security analysts can analyze this potential vulnerable app.
- iAnalytics performs fuzzy testing for iOS apps with URL schemes. After obtaining the `CFBundleURLSchemes` from `Info.plist` file, our system generates random strings or customized fuzz templates with corresponding URL schemes. Then we test these URL schemes through `libimobiledevice` on an iOS device with the installed apps. We then record the system log (e.g., crash report) for analysts.

We have performed the analysis above and discovered several apps with URL Scheme vulnerabilities. We will further describe our findings in Sec. 6.

5.2 Sensitive Information Leakage Detection

Apps may transmit or store personal identifiable information like device ID, user name, password, phone number, address and location information to third party companies. It is very dangerous that the sensitive information is transformed or stored by plain text, because attackers can easily obtain it by sniffing the network or through USB connection. In addition, because enpublic apps can obtain more sensitive personal data by using private APIs, they are more dangerous than normal apps. For personal information leakage detection, iAnalytics focuses on HTTP and local data storage.

5.2.1 *Sensitive Information Leakage on HTTP*

For analyzing HTTP packets, we set the tested device's HTTP proxy to our system. Then iAnalytics uses `libimobiledevice` library to launch the tested apps and sends random user events to the tested apps. If the tested app generates HTTP connection, the HTTP packets will be sent to our system for analysis. After getting the data, iAnalytics searches string patterns of system information (e.g., UDID, MAC address, IMEI and IMSI) and personal information (e.g., telephone number, location information and password) from the HTTP packets. If the system finds anything related to sensitive information, it will report it to analysts.

Figure 6: USB connection verification

5.2.2 *Sensitive Information Leakage on Local Data Storage*

iOS RPC communications library (e.g., libimobiledevice) can be used to obtain apps' data through an USB connection. Although apps in iOS are seperated by sandbox mechinism, the mechinism has no effect for iOS RPC communications library. An PC based application can extract all of apps' data without any permission and user's knowledge. Using iAnalytics, we discovered a bug in the iOS RPC communications: in iOS 7.0, Apple added a new feature to prevent untrusted USB connection (see Fig. 6). However, it only has effect on iTunes software. Other applications can still use iOS RPC communications library to obtain the app data even if the user choose "Don't Trust". Therefore, our system uses `libimobiledevice` library to extract the apps' data from the iOS devices and then search for sensitive information from the apps' data. If the system finds anything related to sensitive information, it will generate a report to a security analyst.

6. EVALUATION

We crawled 1408 enpublic apps from the Internet. We obtained the "Development Region" by parsing apps' `Info.plist` files. The "Development Region" indicates the geographic location of the apps development. Most enpublic apps are from United States, China, England and France, as shown in Tab .2. In this section, we report the statistics of private API usage and app vulnerabilities found in these apps. We also provide case studies of representative enpublic apps.

Country	# of apps
United States	660
China	361
England	223
France	62
Others	102
All	1408

Table 2: Statistics of Development Region

6.1 Private API Statistics and Case Studies

Within the 1,408 enpublic apps we crawled, 844 (60%) use private APIs. For example, some enpublic apps use the private APIs of `CoreTelephony.framework` to monitor phone call and SMS messages. After obtaining the sensitve information, enpublic apps can send them to the hacker's sever in the background. Some iOS 3rd-party market (non-App store markets) apps use the private APIs of MobileInstallation.framework and SpringBoardServices.framework to manage and install 3rd-party iOS apps on iOS devices. In addition, enpublic apps are able to remotely install other apps to the devices without user's knowledge. Many enpublic apps use the private APIs of Message.framework to get the IMSI (International mobile Subscriber Identity) and IMEI (International Mobile Station Equipment Identity) of the device. Because these IDs are globally unique, after obtaining these IDs, hackers are able to link it to a real-world identity [33] so users' privacy will be compromised. Tab. 3 summarizes the private API usages list found in our crawled apps[1]. Note that we have found 22 new dangerous private APIs which are not mentioned in [35] and [27]. These APIs are crucial and security sensitive on iOS 6/7/8 devices. If users do not pay any attention to them, their personal information can be easily leaked to the hacker. To demonstrate how dangerous the private APIs are, we present several case studies below.

6.1.1 Phone Call & SMS Message Monitoring and Blocking

As mentioned in Sec. 1, Qihoo released their "enterprise" apps to the public. Apple halted Qihoo by revoking the "enterprise" certificates [3]. Qihoo implemented some functions that rely on private APIs, which is prohibited from distribution on App Store. Note that one can still find Qihoo's "enterprise" app from the Internet today. Although the certificate became invalid, we can resign the app with our own certificate, then install it on the iOS devices and analyze it.

Qihoo's enterprise app is called "MobileSafeEnterprise" and the package name is "net.qihoo.360msafeenterprise". This app uses both static and dynamic approaches to invoke private APIs. First, "MobileSafeEnterprise" can monitor and block incoming phone calls and SMS messages. The methodology is using the private API, CTTelephonyCenterAddObserver() method of coreTelephony.framework to register a call back method of the TelephonyCenter. When the phone receives a phone call, "MobileSafeEnterprise" will get a "kCTCallIdentificationChangeNotification" call back. In this call back, "MobileSafeEnterprise" uses CTCallCopyAddress() method to obtain the telephone number of the caller and then use CTCallDisconnect() method to hang up the phone call. For incoming SMS messages, "MobileSafeEnterprise" will receive a "kCTMessageReceivedNotification" call back. In this call back, "MobileSafeEnterprise" uses [[CTMessageCenter sharedMessageCenter] incoming MessageWithId: result] method to obtain the sender's telephone number and the text of SMS messages.

Note that some private API invocations in "MobileSafeEnterprise" used dynamic loading techniques and our system detects such behaviors successfully. We also find that even in the latest iOS 7.1, developers or attackers can still use private APIs to monitor incoming phone calls and SMS messages. We have notified Apple about this security problem and Apple Inc. has been working on a fix which is to be released in future updates.

6.1.2 Collecting the Information of Installed Apps

For the network traffic monitoring, "MobileSafeEnterprise" uses private APIs of UIKit.framework and SpringBoardServices.framework to get the names and bundle IDs of running apps. The methodology is using SBSSpringBoardServerPort() method of UIKit.framework to get the server port of the SpringBoard. Then it uses SBSCopyApplicationDisplayIdentifiers() method of SpringBoardServices.framework to get the array of current running app bundle IDs. By using this private API, the app can record the running time and frequency of other apps. In addition, by analyzing the SDK of iOS 7.X and 8.X, we have found another private API called allApplications() in the MobileCoreServices.framework . This private API can be used to get all the bundle IDs of installed apps which include both running and unstarted apps. After getting the installed app list, hackers can sell them to analytic or advertisement companies, or hackers can analyze and exploit vulnerabilities of these installed apps so to launch persistent attack on these devices.

6.1.3 User Events Monitoring and Controlling

We encountered another interesting enpublic app called "i-Control". This app can monitor and control user events (e.g., touches on the screen, home button press and volume button press) in the background on iOS 5.X and 6.X. For monitoring, it uses the GSEventRegisterEventCallBack() method of GraphicsServices.framework to register call backs for system wide user events. After that, every user event will invoke this call back method. In this call back, the app can get the user event information by parsing the IOHIDEventRef structure. For controlling, the app first uses SBFrontmostApplicationDisplayIdentifier() method of SpringBoardServices.framework to get the app at the front. After that, the app uses GSSendEvent() method of GraphicsServices.framework to send the user events to the front app. Attackers can use such mechanisms for malicious purposes. For example, potential attackers can use such information to reconstruct every character the victim inputs (e.g., stealing user's password). In addition, attackers can use this app as a trojan to control the victim's non-jailbroken phone from remote.

Fortunately, Apple fixed these monitoring and controlling private APIs on iOS 7.0 by adding permission controls. However, after analyzing the private APIs of IOKit.framework , we have discovered another call back registration method of user events: IOHIDEventSystemClientRegisterEventCallback(). After registration, the app can still monitoring the system wide user events in the background on iOS 7.0. We have reported this issue to Apple. Apple applied a CVE (Common Vulnerabilities and Exposures) for us [8] and fixed this flaw on iOS 7.1.

6.1.4 iOS 3rd-party App Installation and 3rd-party Markets

It is different from Cydia which targets only jailbroken devices, we have found several 3rd-party app markets (e.g., SearchForApp and Rabbit Assistant) which target both non-jailbroken and jailbroken iOS devices. These markets are enpublic apps and these apps use similar techniques for app management and installation. For app management, these apps use MobileInstallationLookup() method of MobileInstallation.framework to get the pList information of installed apps from the iOS system. After that, they use SBSCopyLocalizedApplicationNameForDisplayIdentifier method and SBSCopyIconImagePNGDataForDisplayIdentifier method

[1]Starting May 1, 2013, the App Store will no longer accept new apps or app updates that access UDIDs. [22]

of SpringBoardServices.framework to get the app names and icons. For app installation, it is interesting that these market apps have several ways to install 3rd-party apps on both jailbroken and non-jailbroken iOS devices. For jailbroken iOS devices, since there is no app signature verification, they use MobileInstallationInstall method and MobileInstallationUninstall method of MobileInstallation.framework to install and uninstall other 3rd-party apps. For non-jailbroken iOS devices, these market apps use "itms-services" (mentioned in Sec. 2) to install other enpublic apps or pirated apps. Because some companies release their apps in enterprise/developer version for beta testing, these 3rd-party app markets collected them and release them on their markets. Although customers can get the apps for free on non-jailbroken devices, they are taking high security risks (e.g., personal information leakage, remotely monitoring and control) of using these apps. For more discussion about pirated apps, please refer to Sec. 7.

6.1.5 Phishing Attack and Unlimited Background Running

We have found another interesting enpublic app called "Buddy Pro". This is an app which can get the location of incoming phone calls. It has several interesting features: First, it can run in the background forever. Second, it can auto start after system rebooting. Thirdly, it can pop up a dialog on the incoming call screen to show the location information. These features are dangerous in that a hacker can use them to launch a phishing attack on the user. Note that running app in the background is very important for phishing apps, because the app needs to stay alive for monitoring sensitive information (e.g., keystrokes or finger movement). However, in iOS, all running tasks are under a strict time limit (around 600 seconds for iOS 6 and 180 seconds for iOS 7/8) for processing.

By analyzing the app using our system, we find two ways for the app to run in the background forever and one way for the app to auto start after rebooting:

- The app can use AVAudioPlayer to play a silent music in the background and uses a property called AudioSessionProperty_OverrideCategoryMixWithOthers. By using this property, the silent music can be played with other music without being detected. In addition, the app will not appear on the music panel. Hence, the app can run continuously without being detected.
- The app can use two undocumented UIBackgroundModes, Continuous and unboundedTaskCompletion, to run in the system background forever. Generally speaking these two undocumented UIBackgroundModes can only be used by system apps, so third-party apps cannot bypass the App Store review if they use undocumented UIBackgroundModes. However, authors in [35, 27] showed that it is possible to bypass the review process and it would be dangerous that an app can monitor phone call events in the background forver.
- The app can use a UIBackgroundMode called VOIP (Voice -Over -Internet Protocol) to start automatically after the system rebooting. Because an app VOIP needs to maintain a persistent network connection so that it can receive incoming calls and other relevant data. In order to ensure that the VOIP services are always available, the iOS system will relaunch the VOIP app in the background immediately after system boot. Therefore, unless the customer terminates the app manually, the app can always monitor phone call events even after rebooting the device.

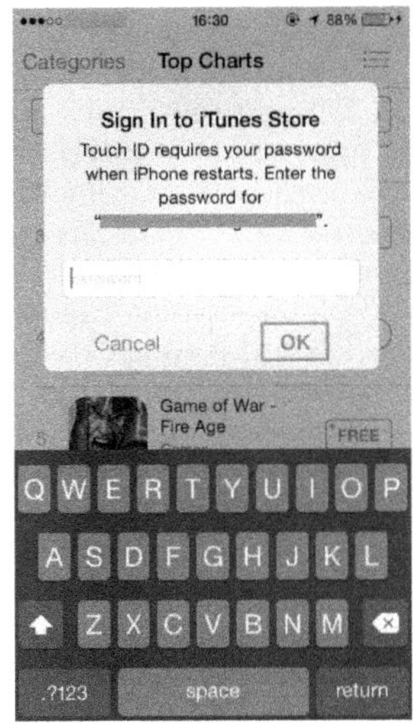

Figure 7: Real AppStore Login Dialog

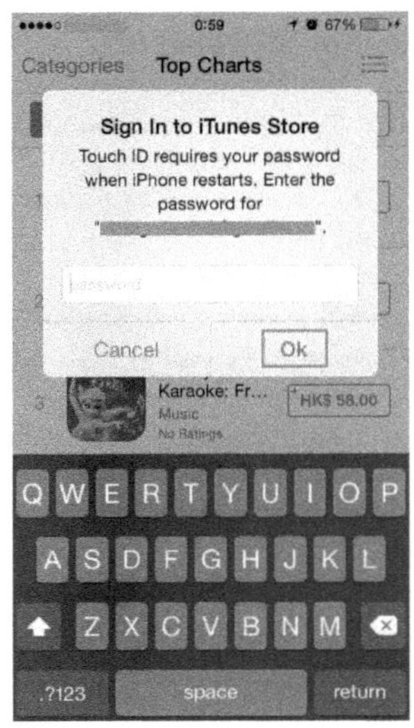

Figure 8: Fake AppStore Login Dialog

In "Buddy Pro" app, we have found two dangerous private API calls : CFUserNotificationCreate() and CFUserNotificationReceiveResponse() of CoreFoundation.framework . These two private APIs can create and pop up interactive dialogs on the foremost screen and then receive user's response. Unlike UIAlertView class, the app can only pop up dialogs on its own screen. Using CFUserNotificationCreate() and CFUserNotificationReceiveResponse(), one app can always pop up dialogs to the foremost screen (includes other apps' screen and home screen) in the background. This is very dangerous, because hackers can easily build a "phishing" app to steal users' accounts. In order to demonstrate, we built an example "phishing" app. This "phishing" app can pop up a fake login dialog (to differentiate, we changed the letter "K" to lower case) in the AppStore app (Fig. 7 and Fig. 8). In addition, we built such a "phishing" app and disguised it as the Twitter app. If the user opens this "phishing" app, it will run in the background forever and it will auto start after rebooting. In addition, it will monitor the runtime process information of the system. What's more, by using the "CVE-2014-4423" vulnerability [23], the "phishing" could get information about the currently-active iCloud account, including the name of the account. When the user opens the AppStore app, it will pop up a fake login dialog on the foremost screen. After the user enters his password, the "phishing" app will send the user's password to the remote server. Note that the demo used the 7.1 version of iOS system on a non-jailbroken iPhone 5s device.

6.2 App Vulnerabilities Statistics and Case Studies

Within the 1408 enpublic apps, we have found 14 (1%) apps containing URL scheme vulnerabilities. Most of the scheme vulnerabilities crash the corresponding app. However, there are two interesting cases, "PandaSpace" and "iDevice Tool" that may become targets for exploits. For sensitive information leakage, 901 (64%) enpublic apps transform sensitive information through unencrypted HTTP or store the information in plain text on the phone. Tab. 4 shows the statistics of UDID, MAC address, IMEI, IMSI, telephone number, GPS (Global Position System), installed app list and password leakage through HTTP and local data storage. After obtaining the personal information, hackers can sell them to analytic or advertisement companies. In addition, they can implement advanced persistent attack after getting the installed app list or password.

Unencrypted Data	# of apps	% of apps
UDID	453	50.3%
MAC address	183	20.3%
IMEI	97	10.8%
IMSI	28	3.1%
Telephone number	86	9.5%
GPS	52	5.8%
Installed app list	54	6.0%
Password	3	0.3%

Table 4: Statistics of Unencrypted Data Leakage

6.2.1 *Remotely Install 3rd-party Apps*

"PandaSpace" is a 3rd-party market app. As we mentioned before, these 3rd-party markets are enpublic apps which can manage and install other 3rd-party apps. We found that attackers can remotely exploit the URL scheme vulnerability of "PandaSpace" to install any 3rd-party apps on jailbroken iOS devices. By parsing the `.plist` file, we found "PandaSpace" contains URL schemes. We recursively scan the private API calls in the `handleOpenURL()` method of the app. We found a dangerous API call, `MobileInstallationInstall()`, in the handle URL scheme method. After that, we analyzed the `handleOpenURL()` function of "PandaSpace" manually. We found that when "PandaSpace" receives a valid `.ipa` file download URL, it will download the `.ipa` file from this URL and then install it on the device. Attackers may use this URL scheme to install other apps on victims' iOS devices. For example, attackers can create a malicious website with the following HTML script:

```
<iframe src="PandaSpace://http://bbx.sj.***.com
/iphonesoft/detail.aspx?action=show&f_id=%@">
</iframe>
```

When victims visit this malicious webiste using Safari, "PandaSpace" will download the app and install it on the phone. Although using the URL scheme vulnerability of "PandaSpace" can not directly install 3rd-party apps on a non-jailbroken iOS devices, attackers can use this vulnerability to trick users to install other enpublic apps.

6.2.2 *System Log Leakage*

"iDevice Tool" is an enpublic app used by developers to debug iOS systems. It uses several private APIs to gain system information (e.g., UDID, mac address and system logs). We found that hackers can use the URL scheme vulnerability of "iDevice Tool" to email all the system information to a specific email address. For example, when the user visits a malicious website with the following content:

```
<iframe src= "idevicetool://emailLog?email=example
@example.com&filter=TextFilter&appname=AppName
"> </iframe>
```

"iDevice Tool" will send the system log of "AppName" to the email address, "example@example.com".

6.2.3 *Location Information Leakage*

"Sina weather forecast" is a weather report app. It has both App Store version and enterprise version. In the enterprise version, it uses GPS (Global Positioning System) to get the location of the user and then uses private API to get the system information (e.g., UDID) of the device. After that, it sends these sensitive information to its server in plain text. For example, here is the captured HTTP request:

```
POST http://forecast.sina.cn/app/update.php?device
=iPhone&uid=32aee18d40fcb4c24e5988c76b4e9f0
d84fb8***&os=ios6.1.2&city=CHXX0***&pver=3.249
&pt=2&token=ff0007a31c005916d5e45b360481f1
1e05b40f010405731e94c8&pid=free
```

This HTTP leaks the UDID ("32aee18d40fcb4c24e5988c76b4e9f0d84fb8***"), iOS version ("6.1.2") and location information (the city number, "CHXX0***"). If the server's information is leaked (e.g., through heart bleed attack), attackers can easily get the user's location through the UDID.

6.2.4 *Username and Password Leakage*

"eHi Taxi" is an iOS app providing services to call a taxi. It provides an App Store version and also an enterprise version. However, both versions have the same vulnerability that they transfer the user's phone number, name and password in plain text through HTTP, as shown in the captured HTTP post:

```
POST: http://myehilogin.1hai.cn/Customer/Login/Log-
inMobile
TextView: LoginName=5109318***&LoginPassword=pass***
```

Hence, attackers can easily sniff and harvest these private information. After getting user's account, hackers can call taxis using victim's money. In addition, the victim may use the same account for other apps. Therefore, hackers may launch advanced persistent attack to these devices. Note that this vulnerability is not specific to enpublic apps.

7. DISCUSSION

In this section, we first discuss about pirated apps on iOS. Then we discuss the limitation of our system and possible improvements.

7.1 Pirated Apps on Non–jailbroken iOS Devices

As we mentioned in Sec. 2, iOS apps have four distribution ways: test apps on iOS devices, App Store, ad hoc and in–house channels. The first distribution channel is for debugging iOS apps only, developers need to use XCode and USB connection to install iOS apps. Customers usually install iOS apps from the second channel, the Apple Store. Given that Apple has the review process for apps on App Store, we assume apps on Apple Store are genuine ones. However, pirated apps can use ad hoc and in–house channels to distribute to non–jailbroken iOS devices. For example, a malware developer can extract a paid iOS app from a jailbroken iOS device and package it into an `.ipa` file. He or she can then use the developer key from iOS developer program or iOS enterprise program to resign the `.ipa` file. After that customers may install the pirated apps through iTunes or itms–services without paying for them. In addition, because hackers have already reverse engineered the iTunes protocol, so that they can install the `.ipa` files on non–jailbroken iOS devices without iTunes [17] [16]. Although ad hoc distribution has a 100 device install limit, hackers can rename the Bundle name of the app, iTunes will then treat the renamed app as a new app with another 100 device limitation. Therefore, hackers can use this method to attract customers to download free pirated apps which are not free in Apple Store from their third–party markets, and then use advertisement to gain money. In this case, both iOS developers for the original app and Apple become victims.

7.2 Limitation and Future Work

Because enterprise iOS apps observe no regulation on using dynamic loading techniques, it is difficult for traditional static analysis methodologies to get the payload behavior before execution. Therefore, our system uses dynamic analysis to handle the dynamic loading behavior. However, dynamic analysis may not have a good code coverage since an app may have hundreds or thousands execution paths. Dynamic analysis can only explore a single execution path at a time and it is hard for the dynamic analysis system to trigger the expected result without the right input. Currently, we use simple behavior trigger techniques (e.g., launching the app, making a telephone call and locking the screen), so iAnalytics cannot guarantee complete code coverage of all dynamic loading behaviors. A possible improvement is to perform symbolic execution to compute all of the feasible paths and we are considering this in our future work.

For unencrypted sensitive information leakage, we only focus on the HTTP protocol and plain text data. However, apps may use other protocols to transfer unencrypted data or simple encrypted data through network sockets. In addition, iOS system has several internal communication techniques (e.g., shared keychain access and custom URL scheme). If the app does not encrypt the data or it has a faulty logic design, it is possible for other apps to sniff or hijack the exchanged data. For capturing sockets and the data of internal communication, the system needs to provide hooking service on the related methods, triggering the behavior, having simple decryption engine and determining the transferred data structure. We plan to address such extension in our future work.

8. RELATED WORK

There have been number of works which aim to bypass the code signing and app review process of Apple App Store. A common method is to Jailbreak [31][10][28] the system so to obtain the root privilege and permanently disable the code signing mechanism. In addition, hackers distribute iOS malware on jailbroken devices [32]. Although jailbreaking is feasible [26], it is getting more and more difficult because Apple actively fixes known vulnerabilities and iOS becomes more mature. Despite the increasing difficulty of exploiting iOS, our findings show that it is possible to distribute apps without jailbreaking iOS. However, it is worth noting that our approach can still take advantage of the vulnerabilities utilized by other jailbreaking methods to compromise iOS.

C. Miller [30] discovered that iOS code signing mechanism could be bypassed, allowing attackers to allocate a writeable and executable memory buffer. A malicious app can exploit this vulnerability to generate and execute attack code at runtime. However, Apple has fixed this issue and blocked apps using such kind of methods to dynamically load and launch malicious payload. T.Wang [35] puts forward another novel approach to evade the app review process by making the apps remotely exploitable and introduing malicious control flows by rearranging signed code. Because these control flows are dynamically generated when the attackers try to exploit those apps, Apple will not discover them during the app review process. However, this vulnerability has been fixed by Apple as well. Authors in [34] and [29] show that infecting a large number of iOS devices through botnets is possible. By exploiting the design flaws of iTunes and the device provisioning process, they demonstrate that a compromised computer can be instructed to install "enpublic" apps on iOS devices. These works show that iOS devices can be infected and App Store's review process is not adequate for protecting iOS devices. Our work further shows that iOS vulnerabilities exist.

The work closest to ours is by J. Han etc. [27]. They propose to launch attacks on non-jailbroken iOS devices from third-party application by exploiting private APIs. Compared with their work, our work is more systematic and we show there is another channel to distribute malicious apps except the App Store. Our focus is not just to exploit private APIs, but also illustrate other vulnerabilities. Moreover, we performed systematic analysis on large number of iOS apps, and in particular, we applied our analysis upon iOS 7/8, which has not been studied before.

9. CONCLUSION

In this paper, we present the security landscape of iOS enpublic apps and their usage of private APIs. In order to understand their security impact, we designed and implemented a mechanism which evaluate the overall security status of enpublic apps by combining static semantic checks and runtime detection technologies. Our results show that 844 (60%) out of the 1408 enpublic apps do use private APIs. 14 (1%) apps contain URL scheme vulnerabilities, 901 (64%) enpublic apps transport sensitive information through unencrypted channel or store private information in plain text on the devices. In addition, we summarized 25 private APIs on iOS 6/7/8 which have security vulnerabilities and we have filed one CVE for iOS devices.

10. ACKNOWLEDGMENTS

We would like to thank our shepherd, Jin Han, and the anonymous reviewers for their valuable comments. We also thank Raymond Wei, Dawn Song, and Zheng Bu for their valuable help on writing this paper.

11. REFERENCES

[1] API Reference of iOS Frameworks, 2014. https://developer.apple.com/library/ios/navigation/#section=Resource%20Types&topic=Reference.

[2] App store review guidelines. https://developer.apple.com/appstore/resources/approval/guidelines.html.

[3] Apple Bans Qihoo Apps From iTunes App Store, February, 2012. http://www.techinasia.com/apple-bans-qihoo-apps/.

[4] Apple, Creating Jobs Through Innovation, 2012. http://www.apple.com/about/job-creation/.

[5] CCTool. http://www.opensource.apple.com/source/cctools.

[6] Choosing an iOS Developer Program, 2014. https://developer.apple.com/programs/start/ios/.

[7] Class-dump. http://stevenygard.com/projects/class-dump.

[8] CVE-2014-1276 IOKit HID Event, 2014. http://support.apple.com/en-us/HT202935.

[9] Cydia Substrate. http://www.cydiasubstrate.com.

[10] Evad3rs, evasi0n jailbreaking tool, 2013. http://evasi0n.com/.

[11] How Apple's Enterprise Distribution Program was abused to enable the installation of a GameBoy emulator, 2014. http://www.imore.com/how-gameboy-emulator-finding-its-way-non-jailbroken-devices.

[12] How Many Apps Are in the iPhone App Store. http://ipod.about.com/od/iphonesoftwareterms/qt/apps-in-app-store.htm.

[13] iOS Dev Center. https://developer.apple.com/devcenter/ios/index.action.

[14] iOS Dev Center, 2014. https://developer.apple.com/devcenter/ios/index.action.

[15] Java Reflection. http://docs.oracle.com/javase/tutorial/reflect/.

[16] Kuai Yong iOS device management, 2014. http://www.kuaiyong.com/eg_web/index.html.

[17] Libimobiledevice: A cross-platform software protocol library and tools to communicate with iOS devices natively, 2014. http://www.libimobiledevice.org/.

[18] OS X ABI Mach-O File Format Reference. https://developer.apple.com/library/mac/documentation/DeveloperTools/Conceptual/MachORuntime/Reference/reference.html.

[19] Pangu Jailbreak, 2014. http://pangu.io/.

[20] Qihoo Double Blow as iOS Apps Banned by Apple, China Warns of Anti-Competitive Practices, January, 2013. http://www.techinasia.com/qihoo-apps-banned-apple-app-store/.

[21] Tim Cook to shareholders: iPhone 5s/c outpace predecessors, Apple bought 23 companies in 16 months. http://appleinsider.com/articles/14/02/28/tim-cook-at-shareholder-meeting-iphone-5s-5c-outpace-predecessors-apple-bought-23-companies-in-16-months.

[22] Using Identifiers in Your Apps, 2013. https://developer.apple.com/news/index.php?id=3212013a.

[23] Vulnerability Summary for CVE-2014-4423, 2014. http://web.nvd.nist.gov/view/vuln/detail?vulnId=CVE-2014-4423.

[24] When Malware Goes Mobile. http://www.sophos.com/en-us/security-news-trends/security-trends/malware-goes-mobile/why-ios-is-safer-than-android.aspx.

[25] D. Chell. *iOS Application (In)Security.* 2012.

[26] D. Goldman. Jailbreaking iphone apps is now legal. *CNN Money. Retrieved*, pages 09–11, 2010.

[27] J. Han, S. M. Kywe, Q. Yan, F. Bao, R. Deng, D. Gao, Y. Li, and J. Zhou. Launching generic attacks on ios with approved third-party applications. In *Applied Cryptography and Network Security*, pages 272–289. Springer, 2013.

[28] Y. Jang, T. Wang, B. Lee, , and B. Lau. Exploiting unpatched ios vulnerabilities for fun and profit. In *Proceedings of the Black Hat USA Briefings, Las Vegas, NV, August 2014.*

[29] B. Lau, Y. Jang, C. Song, T. Wang, P. H. Chung, and P. Royal. Injecting malware into ios devices via malicious chargers. In *Proceedings of the Black Hat USA Briefings, Las Vegas, NV, August 2013.*

[30] C. Miller. Inside ios code signing. In *Proceedings of Symposium on SyScan*, 2011.

[31] C. Miller, D. Blazakis, D. DaiZovi, S. Esser, V. Iozzo, and R.-P. Weinmann. *IOS Hacker's Handbook.* John Wiley & Sons, 2012.

[32] F. A. Porter, F. Matthew, C. Erika, H. Steve, and W. David. A survey of mobile malware in the wild. In *Proceedings of the 1st ACM SPSM.* ACM, 2011.

[33] E. Smith. iphone applications & privacy issues: An analysis of application transmission of iphone unique device identifiers (udids). 2010.

[34] W. Tielei, J. Yeongjin, C. Yizheng, C. Simon, L. Billy, and L. Wenke. On the feasibility of large-scale infections of ios devices. In *Proceedings of the 23rd USENIX conference on Security Symposium*, pages 79–93. USENIX Association, 2014.

[35] T. Wang, K. Lu, L. Lu, S. Chung, and W. Lee. Jekyll on ios: when benign apps become evil. In *Presented as part of the 22nd USENIX Security Symposium*, pages 559–572, 2013.

[36] C. Xiao. Wirelurker: A new era in ios and os x malware. 2014.

Method	Framework	Usage	Available on iOS 6.X	Available on iOS 7.X	Available on iOS 8.0
[[UIDevice currentDevice] U–niqueIdentifier]	UIKit	Get the UDID of the device.	Yes	No	No
CTSIMSupportCopyMobile–SubscriberIdentity()	coreTelephony	Get the IMSI of the device.	Yes	No	No
CTSettingCopyMyPhoneN–umber()	coreTelephony	Get the telephone number of the device.	Yes	No	No
CTTelephonyCenterAddOb–server()	coreTelephony	Register call back of SMS mes–sages and incoming phone calls.	Yes	Yes	Yes
CTCallCopyAddress()	coreTelephony	Get the telephone number of the phone call.	Yes	Yes	Yes
CTCallDisconnect()	coreTelephony	Hang up the phone call.	Yes	No	No
[[CTMessageCenter shar–edMessageCenter] incom–ingMessageWithId: result]	coreTelephony	Get the text of the incoming SMS message.	Yes	Yes	Yes
[[NetworkController shared–Instance] IMEI]	Message	Get the IMEI of the device.	Yes	No	No
SBSCopyApplicationDispla–yIdentifiers()	SpringBoardServices	Get the array of current running app bundle IDs.	Yes	No	No
SBFrontmostApplicationDi–splayIdentifier()	SpringBoardServices	Get the front most app port.	Yes	No	No
SBSCopyLocalizedApplicati–onNameForDisplayIdentifier()	SpringBoardServices	Get the app name from the bundle ID.	Yes	Yes	Yes
SBSCopyIconImagePNG–DataForDisplayIdentifier()	SpringBoardServices	Get the app icon from the bundle ID.	Yes	Yes	Yes
SBSLaunchApplicationWit–hIdentifier()	SpringBoardServices	Launch the app using bundle ID.	Yes	No	No
MobileInstallationLookup()	MobileInstallation	Get the pList information of installed iOS apps.	Yes	Yes	Yes
MobileInstallationInstall()	MobileInstallation	Install `.ipa` file on jailbroken iOS devices.	Yes	Yes	Yes
MobileInstallationUninstall()	MobileInstallation	Uninstall app on jailbroken iOS devices.	Yes	Yes	Yes
GSEventRegisterEventCall–Back()	GraphicsServices	Register call back for system wide user events.	Yes	No	No
GSSendEvent()	GraphicsServices	Send user events to the app port.	Yes	No	No
IOHIDEventSystemClientR–egisterEventCallback()	IOKit	Register call back for system wide user events.	Yes	Yes	No
CFUserNotificationCreate()	CoreFoundation	Pop up dialogs to the foremost screen.	Yes	Yes	Yes
CFUserNotificationReceive–Response()	CoreFoundation	Receive the user input from the dialog.	Yes	Yes	Yes
allApplications()	MobileCoreServices	Get the bundle ID list of installed iOS apps.	No	Yes	Yes
publicURLSchemes()	MobileCoreServices	Get the URL schemes list of installed iOS apps.	Yes	Yes	Yes
continuous	UIBackgroundMode	Run in the background forever.	Yes	Yes	Yes
unboundedTaskCompletion	UIBackgroundMode	Run in the background forever.	Yes	Yes	Yes
VOIP (not a private API)	UIBackgroundMode	Auto start after rebooting.	Yes	Yes	Yes

Table 3: Statistics of Private API Usage

A Practical Attack Against the Use of RC4 in the HIVE Hidden Volume Encryption System*

Kenneth G. Paterson
Royal Holloway, University of London
Kenny.Paterson@rhul.ac.uk

Mario Strefler
Karlsruhe Institute of Technology
Mario.Strefler@kit.edu

ABSTRACT

The HIVE hidden volume encryption system was proposed by Blass et al. at ACM-CCS 2014. Even though HIVE has a security proof, this paper demonstrates an attack on its implementation that breaks the main security property claimed for the system by its authors, namely plausible hiding against arbitrary-access adversaries. Our attack is possible because of the HIVE implementation's reliance on the RC4 stream cipher to fill unused blocks with pseudorandom data. While the attack can be easily eliminated by using a better pseudorandom generator, it serves as an example of why RC4 should be avoided in all new applications and a reminder that one has to be careful when instantiating primitives.

Categories and Subject Descriptors

E.3 [**Data Encryption**]: Cryptanalysis

1. INTRODUCTION

At ACM CCS 2014, Blass et al. [2] presented a novel "hidden volume encryption" system called HIVE. Their system splits an encrypted disk into several volumes. The intention of HIVE is to hide the existence of some of these volumes, and to hide the pattern of read and write accesses to the volumes from observers.

To hide the access patterns, reading and writing has to be indistinguishable. This is accomplished by overwriting an empty block with pseudorandom data during a read operation to simulate an encryption. The HIVE implementation makes use of the RC4 algorithm to overwrite blocks with pseudorandom data and AES in CBC mode to perform encryption. This approach can be proved secure if both the ciphertexts produced by the symmetric encryption scheme and the output of the pseudorandom generator are indistinguishable from random. We stress that RC4 is not used to encrypt any data in the scheme, but only to fill unused disk space with pseudorandom bytes. According to [2], RC4 was selected for performance reasons.

We show that RC4 is a poor choice for this task: we demonstrate that its use enables us to break the main security property claimed for HIVE in [2], namely "plausible hiding against arbitrary-access adversaries". In fact, we will break the even weaker notion of plausible hiding against *one-time* adversaries. Our attack does not extract plaintext, but we are able to detect the supposedly hidden volumes by only examining the disk twice. The supposed infeasability of this kind of attack is the main advantage claimed for HIVE over conventional disk encryption systems and was used to justify its storage overhead [2].

Our attack exploits biases in RC4 keystreams. While it is well-known that RC4 keystreams are biased, and therefore not indistinguishable from random byte streams [5, 3, 4, 1, 6], it is not immediately obvious that these existing results can be applied to break any claimed security property of HIVE. This is because previous distinguishers [3, 4] require access to either a very large amount of consecutive keystream bytes, or to a corresponding amount of truly random bytes, whereas HIVE acts in a blockwise fashion (with the typical block size being 4096 bytes), presenting a distinguisher with a *mix* of short RC4 blocks and AES-CBC blocks.

Our adversary makes use of the Mantin biases in RC4 keystreams [4] to build a weak blockwise distinguisher for short blocks; in contrast to previous work identifying RC4 biases [3, 4] we explicitly present an efficient and near-optimal statistical test that can be used to implement the distinguisher. Our blockwise distinguisher is then applied repeatedly over many blocks to estimate how many blocks on the disk are filled with RC4 and how many are filled with AES-CBC ciphertexts; this approach seems to be novel and not previously exploited in the literature. Finally, the estimate can be used to decide what sequence of read and/or write accesses was performed on the disk by the HIVE system.

Our adversary is efficient, and it needs access only to a moderate number of read/write queries on blocks. For example, it has success rate 0.997 in an attack involving $2^{23.7}$ read/write queries on a disk containing a total of $2^{24.7}$ blocks and 104 GB of data.

Our approach does not involve the derivation of any new properties of RC4. However it does illustrate that RC4 is

*The first author was supported by EPSRC Leadership Fellowship EP/H005455/1. The second author did most of the work while working at Aarhus University and was supported by European Research Council Starting Grant 279447 and by the Danish Council for Independent Research via DFF Starting Grant 10-081612.

ASIA CCS'15, April 14–17, 2015, Singapore, Singapore

http://dx.doi.org/10.1145/2714576.2714596.

not only unfit for use as a general purpose pseudorandom generator (PRG), but also that it can result in systems that can be practically attacked in scenarios where RC4's weaknesses are not obviously problematic.

We informed the authors of [2] about our attack at a conceptual level, and, while they updated their FAQ for the HIVE system[1], they did not initially take the opportunity to revise their source code to use a better PRG or amend their research paper describing the system. They instead argued that RC4 is only an exchangeable building block that can easily be replaced. We note that RC4 was the default, and it is unlikely that users would replace it with their own implementation of a secure PRG, leaving them at risk. Given that the authors released HIVE to the public and still claimed that it "provides more security than all existing schemes",[2] we therefore decided to prepare this paper to alert potential users of the HIVE implementation to the shortcomings of the system. We are happy to note that after publication of a pre-print of this paper, RC4 was replaced by AES-CTR in the HIVE implementation.

We again emphasise that we attack only the specific implementation of HIVE that instantiates the PRG with RC4, and do not claim that the HIVE scheme is insecure if instantiated with a different PRG. Indeed we consider HIVE to be a very interesting proposal that is worthy of further (crypt)analysis.

1.1 Paper Organisation

In the next section, we provide more details on HIVE and its use of RC4. We build an RC4 distinguisher for short blocks in Section 3. Section 4 describes how we use this distinguisher to attack the HIVE scheme.

2. DESCRIPTION OF THE HIVE SCHEME

HIVE [2] is a hidden volume encryption scheme that works on a storage device divided into blocks. The user chooses a value l and can then configure up to l logical volumes V_i, where each volume is encrypted with a key derived from a password P_i. Without knowledge of the corresponding password, a volume should be undetectable. The goal is that "a user can plausibly deny the existence of a hidden volume even if the adversary has been able to take several snapshots of their disk and knows the password for the main volume."[3] This makes it necessary to hide the pattern of accesses that a user makes to the disk, which is achieved by building on a write-only oblivious RAM (ORAM) scheme.

The original paper presents several different security notions and two different schemes; to fix the attack target, we choose a weak security notion and one scheme, which we describe below. For simplicity, we assume that all ORAMs have the same size, $1/l$ times the size of the hard disk.

2.1 ORAM

The stash-optimized, write-only ORAM scheme from [2] is a logical overlay of an encrypted disk over a physical disk at least twice the size of the encrypted disk. It makes use of a pseudo-random generator (PRG) and a symmetric encryption scheme with the property that without the key, ciphertexts are indistinguishable from random strings of the same length. The security goal for ORAM is to hide access patterns to the encrypted disk.

The ORAM maintains a map of logical blocks to physical blocks. Initially, all logical blocks are mapped to $\perp$. At each ORAM.Write(logical block, data block) operation, the ORAM picks K physical blocks at random (independently of the logical address) and tries to decrypt each of them. Some may already contain data, while others may be empty. The new data block to be written and any data blocks that were already stored in the selected K blocks are written to memory. Specifically, they are added to a *stash*, which acts as a buffer to store blocks yet to be written to disk. Then as many of the data blocks in the stash as possible are encrypted and written back to the selected K blocks. Because the physical disk is much larger than the logical disk, there is a good chance that one or more of the K selected blocks were still free, so that all the blocks currently in the stash can be written to the disk. Any remaining free blocks from the K selected blocks are overwritten with random data (generated by the PRG). The map from logical to physical blocks is updated accordingly.

If not enough of the selected blocks were free, then some data blocks will remain in the stash, to be written during a later write operation, when free blocks are found. In general, the parameters of the scheme are selected so that there is a good probability that one or more blocks will be free, so that with high probability the stash size remains small throughout. For example, for $K = 3$, the probability of having more than 50 items in the stash is bounded by 2^{-64}.

The security argument is that since for each operation, K randomly selected blocks are overwritten with a pseudorandom string, the operation does not leak any information about the logical address, the data to be written, or the state of the disk (i.e. which blocks are free).

2.2 HIVE

The security target for HIVE is that it should hide the existence of encrypted disk volumes for which the key is not known. This is accomplished by executing a real ORAM.Read and a dummy ORAM.Write for each Read, and a dummy ORAM.Read and a real ORAM.Write for each Write.

It is claimed in [2] that HIVE achieves the notion of plausible hiding against arbitrary-access adversaries. We will break the even weaker notion of plausible hiding against one-time adversaries, which is given in Definition 1 immediately below.

DEFINITION 1 (PLAUSIBLE HIDING). *The experiment* $\mathrm{Exp}^{pl\text{-}ot\text{-}b}_{\mathcal{A},\Sigma}(k)$ *for a bit b is run between an adversary* $\mathcal{A}$ *and a challenger emulating the scheme* Σ *and consists of the following phases.*

1. *In the setup phase,* $\mathcal{A}$ *sends* l *to the challenger, who chooses* l *passwords* $P_1, \ldots, P_l$. *The challenger initializes* Σ_0 *with* l *volumes and passwords, and* Σ_1 *with* $l-1$ *volumes and passwords* $P_1, \ldots, P_{l-1}$ *and sends* $P_1, \ldots, P_{l-1}$ *and a snapshot* D_0 *of* Σ_b *to* $\mathcal{A}$.
2. *In round* i, $\mathcal{A}$ *sends two accesses* $o_{i,0}$ *and* $o_{i,1}$ *to the challenger; the challenger executes* $o_{i,b}$ *on* Σ_b.
3. *Finally, the adversary requests a snapshot* D_f *of the disk, and outputs a bit* b', *which is the output of the experiment.*

[1] http://hive.ccs.neu.edu/FAQ, date of access 26/10/2014
[2] http://hive.css.neu.edu, date of access 26/10/2014
[3] [2], Introduction

An access o is of the form $o = (op, b, V, d)$. If $op = w$, then data d is written to block b on volume V. If $op = r$, then block b from volume V is read into d. Since the adversary knows the passwords $P_1, \ldots, P_{l-1}$, if one of the operations in round i is a write to one of the volumes $V_1, \ldots, V_{l-1}$, then both operations must be identical. Intuitively, this means that any access to V_l can be passed off as an access to another volume.

We define the advantage of the adversary as

$$\mathrm{Adv}^{pl\text{-}ot}_{\mathcal{A},\Sigma}(k) = |\Pr[1 \leftarrow \mathrm{Exp}^{pl\text{-}ot\text{-}0}_{\mathcal{A},\Sigma}(k)] - \Pr[1 \leftarrow \mathrm{Exp}^{pl\text{-}ot\text{-}1}_{\mathcal{A},\Sigma}(k)]|.$$

If we used an asymptotic definition, we would say that Σ is secure if for all PPT $\mathcal{A}$, $\mathrm{Adv}^{pl\text{-}ot}_{\mathcal{A},\Sigma}(k)$ is a negligible function. Since we want to attack a concrete instance, we use a concrete security definition. We fix a concrete security parameter k and let

$$\mathrm{Adv}^{pl\text{-}ot}_{\Sigma,k}(\tau, q) = \max_{\mathcal{A}}\{\mathrm{Adv}^{pl\text{-}ot}_{\mathcal{A},\Sigma}(k)\},$$

where the maximum is taken over all adversaries running[4] in at most τ steps and making at most q access queries (that is, there are at most q rounds in the game, each round involving either writing to or reading from a single block). We then say that for a concrete parameter k, Σ is (ε, τ, q)-plausible hiding against one-time adversaries, if $\mathrm{Adv}^{pl\text{-}ot}_{\Sigma,k}(\tau, q) \leq \varepsilon$.

2.3 HIVE Instantiation

In HIVE, the symmetric encryption scheme is instantiated with AES-CBC using 256-bit, password-derived keys and a fresh IV at each call. The number of blocks written to for each operation, K (k in the original paper), is set to 3 in the implementation.[5] This low value of K necessitates the use of a stash of unwritten blocks to handle the situation where, when K random blocks are selected, all are already in use. From the HIVE source code it appears that a volume is not initially overwritten with random data. This will help our adversary, since it means it will need to consider less additional data, but is not necessary for the attack to work.

The implementation follows the good practice of using a PRG seeded once with true randomness obtained from the OS to generate all the randomness consumed by the cryptographic operations involved in HIVE. Specifically, the output of the PRG is used to:

1. produce a fresh, random 16-byte IV (for use with each call to AES-CBC);
2. fill a 4096-byte sector with random bytes;
3. fill a 32-byte metadata block with random bytes. A metadata block consists of two 8-byte values and a 16-byte IV.
4. select a random sector to write to. This requires a random 8-byte value for the sector id.

The PRG, while being properly seeded, is instantiated with RC4-drop256. According to [2] this is for performance reasons. More specifically, RC4 is keyed using 256 bytes of randomness obtained from the OS, the first 256 bytes of RC4 output are dropped to avoid well-known strong biases (see for example [1] for a complete exposition of these), some further bytes of output are used for other purposes, and then B consecutive bytes of output are used to fill a block with "random" bytes. The HIVE implementation uses $B = 4096$ (so it has 4 KB blocks), though the choice $B = 256$ is also discussed in [2]. Note that we do not (and do not need to) know from precisely where in the RC4 keystream the bytes are selected, but only that they are consecutive.

3. BLOCKWISE DISTINGUISHER FOR RC4

In this section, we develop and evaluate a distinguisher $\mathcal{D}$ for short RC4 keystreams as used in HIVE. This will be used in the next section as a component in building an attack against HIVE.

3.1 RC4 Biases

We first recall the main results on biases in RC4 outputs from [4] that we will use. Other biases, notably those in [3] are available, but not so convenient to use in the setting of interest to us. This is because they are position-dependent, and we do not wish to make any assumptions about exactly which positions in the RC4 keystreams the bytes we are targeting are selected from (since this is not readily apparent from the description of HIVE in [2] and the corresponding source code).

The following result is a restatement of Theorem 1 in [4], concerning the probability of occurrence of byte strings of the form $ABSAB$ in RC4 outputs, where A and B represent bytes and $\mathcal{S}$ denotes an arbitrary byte string of a particular length G.

RESULT 1. *Let $G \geq 0$ be a small integer. Under the assumption that the RC4 state is a random permutation at step r, then*

$$\Pr(Z_r = Z_{r+G+2} \wedge Z_{r+1} = Z_{r+G+3}) = 2^{-16}\left(1 + \frac{e^{(-4-8G)/256}}{256}\right).$$

Note that for a truly random byte string $Z_r, \ldots, Z_{r+G_3}$, the probability that $Z_r = Z_{r+G+2}$ and $Z_{r+1} = Z_{r+G+3}$ is equal to 2^{-16}. The relative bias is therefore equal to $e^{(-4-8G)/256}/256$.

The above result was experimentally confirmed in [4] for values of G up to 64, though with quite a small sample size, and not focused on early bytes in RC4 output. We have confirmed that the result holds to a reasonable approximation in the situation in which we are interested, for positions 256 onwards. See Figure 1.

3.2 Discrimination and Statistical Hypothesis Testing

Given two probability distributions p and q on some set $\mathcal{S}$, we define the *discrimination* between p and q, denoted $L(p, q)$, to be $\sum_{s \in \mathcal{S}} p(s) \log p(s)/q(s)$. Note that discrimination is additive: if p_1, p_2, q_1, q_2 are distributions on $\mathcal{S}$, and if p_1p_2, q_1q_2 denote the product distributions on $\mathcal{S} \times \mathcal{S}$, then $L(p_1p_2, q_1q_2) = L(p_1, q_1) + L(p_2, q_2)$. This equality extends in the obvious way to larger products of distributions.

Next consider the distributions p and q arising from a simple "bias presence" test $\mathcal{T}$ based on a Mantin "$AB\mathcal{S}AB$" bias. The test $\mathcal{T}$ receives as input a B-byte string, looks for

[4]for an appropriate definition of running time, a problem we do not consider in this paper

[5]Variable HIVE_K in dm-hive.c

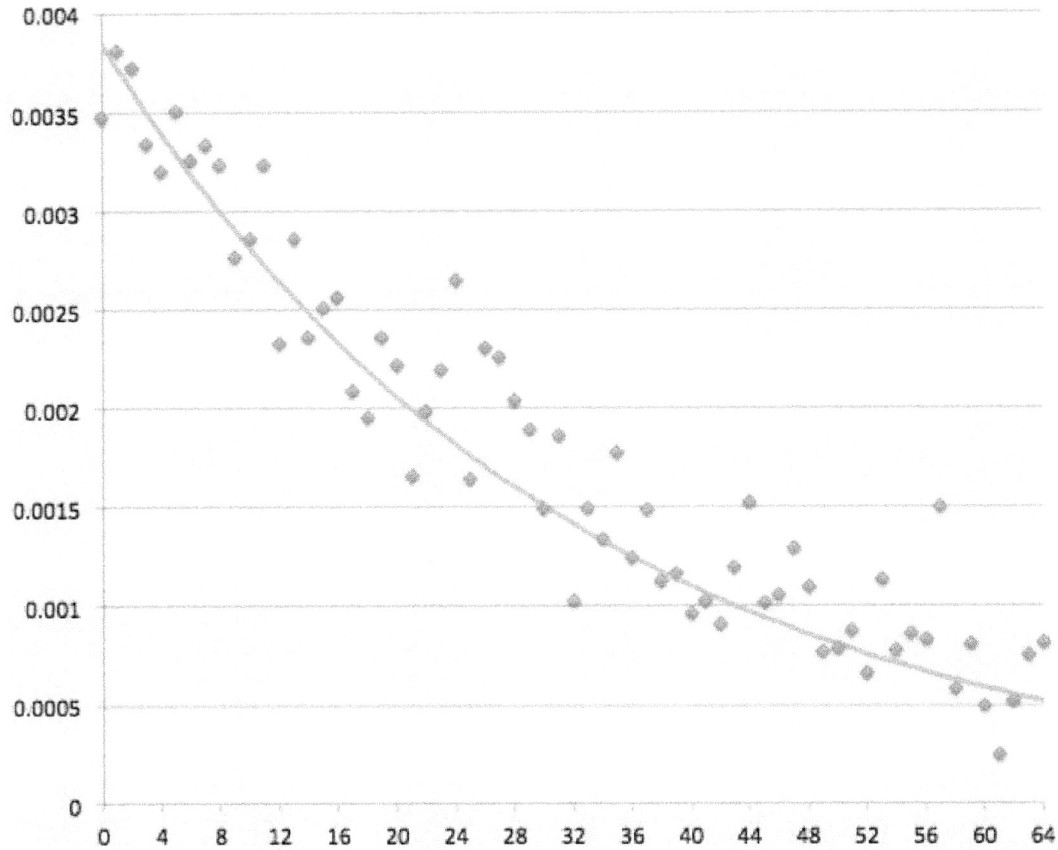

Figure 1: Experimental validation of Mantin biases based on 2^{28} random 256-byte keys, 4096 bytes of RC4 output per key. The x-axis depicts the value of G, the y-axis scaled biases (γ values). Blue points denote experimentally measured values; green line denotes theoretical values computed according to Result 1.

a particular byte pattern of a fixed type commencing in a fixed position, and outputs 1 if the pattern is detected, and 0 otherwise (here we assume the bias is a positive one, as is the case for all the Mantin biases). For example, the test might examine positions r, $r+1$, $r+2$, $r+3$ in the string and check whether the quartet of byte values are of the form "$ABAB$" or not, an event which should happen with slightly larger than expected probability if the input string comes from RC4 output rather than being truly random.

Let p be the output probability distribution of $\mathcal{T}$ if the input string comes from RC4 output and q the output probability distribution of $\mathcal{T}$ if the input string is truly random. Then $p(0) = 1 - \rho(1+\gamma)$, $p(1) = \rho(1+\gamma)$ and $q(0) = 1 - \rho$, $q(1) = \rho$ where $\rho = 2^{-16}$ and $\gamma > 0$ is the relative bias under consideration (so $\gamma = e^{(-4-8G)/256}/256$ for some small integer G).

Then, as shown in Lemma 3 of [4] (using different notation), $L(p,q) \approx \rho\gamma^2$.

The presence of different types of biases in different positions motivates us to consider product distributions $p_1 \cdots p_t$ and $q \cdots q$, where each component in the two products corresponds to a different test $\mathcal{T}_i$ based on a specific bias. Here the second distribution is always a fixed one, q, as defined above (since all the bias presence tests behave the same way in case the input string is truly random), while the first one p_i describes the distribution of the test's $\{0,1\}$-valued outcome O_i. We assume we have t tests in total, and we make the assumption that all the simple bias presence tests that we can perform on our B-byte input are independent. This assumption seems reasonable in view of the different types of test being conducted, despite many of the tests involving overlapping bytes. The same assumption was made in [3, 4] when developing distinguishers for RC4. This assumption enables us to write:

$$L(p_1 \cdots p_t, q \cdots q) = \sum_{i=1}^{t} L(p_i, q) \approx \rho \sum_{i=1}^{t} \gamma_i^2$$

where γ_i is the appropriate value for the i-th test performed.

Now let $\mathcal{D}$ denote any distinguisher based on an input that is the concatenation of the outputs O_i of the t individual bias presence tests, and that predicts whether or not the particular string of B bytes used in the tests was generated by RC4 or is truly random. We assume that $\mathcal{D}$ outputs 1 (indicating RC4) with probability $1-\beta$ when its input is from RC4, and that $\mathcal{D}$ outputs 0 (indicating truly random) with probability $1-\alpha$ when its input is truly random. In other words, α is the false positive rate for $\mathcal{D}$ and β is the false negative rate for $\mathcal{D}$. Then, following [3], we have that:

$$L(p_1 \cdots p_t, q \cdots q) \geq \beta \log_2 \frac{\beta}{1-\alpha} + (1-\beta) \log_2 \frac{1-\beta}{\alpha}.$$

Moreover equality is achieved by any optimal statistical test, such as a Neyman-Pearson likelihood ratio test.

We next evaluate $L(p_1 \cdots p_t, q \cdots q) \approx \rho \sum_{i=1}^{t} \gamma_i^2$ for the set of tests corresponding to all the possible Mantin biases arising in a B-byte block of consecutive keystream bytes. From the above equation, this will then allow us to establish bounds on (α, β) for optimal distinguishers $\mathcal{D}$. We then provide an efficient and approximately optimal statistical test based on these biases, and compute the parameters of the test in such a way as to maximise the quantity $1-\alpha-\beta$, which is the usual advantage of the distinguisher $\mathcal{D}$.

3.3 Computation for the Mantin Biases

In a B-byte block, we can perform $B-(G+3)$ bias presence tests with $\gamma = e^{(-4-8G)/256}/256$ for each value of $G \geq 0$. In practice, since the biases decrease in size with increasing G, we work with values G satisfying $0 \leq G \leq G_{\max}$ for some value $G_{\max}$. In our experiments, we take $G_{\max} = 64$.

Combining all of these bias presence tests, we obtain $t = \sum_{G=0}^{G_{\max}} B - (G+3) \approx G_{\max} \cdot B$ tests such that

$$L(p_1 \cdots p_t, q \cdots q) = \rho \sum_{G \geq 0} (B - (G+3)) \cdot e^{(-4-8G)/128}/2^{16}).$$

Direct calculation gives $L(p_1 \cdots p_t, q \cdots q) \approx 8.7276 \approx \times 10^{-7}$ for $B = 256$ and $G_{\max} = 64$. For $B = 4096$ and $G_{\max} = 64$ we obtain $L(p_1 \cdots p_t, q \cdots q) \approx 1.4914 \times 10^{-5}$.

3.4 An Efficient Statistical Test

We start with a likelihood ratio test and develop from this an efficient test which is approximately optimal.

In the likelihood ratio test, the test statistic is computed as a ratio $\Lambda(O) := L(\theta_0|O)/L(\theta_1|O)$ where θ_0 denotes the distribution arising from the hypothesis H_0, θ_1 denotes the distribution arising from the alternative hypothesis H_1, O denotes the observed data, and $L(\theta_i|O) := \Pr(O|\theta_i)$ denotes a likelihood. In the test, the hypothesis H_0 is rejected (and our distinguisher outputs 1 indicating that its input is believed to be RC4) if the ratio of likelihoods $\Lambda(O)$ is less than or equal some value η; otherwise, H_0 is accepted (and our distinguisher outputs 0 indicating that its input is believed to be truly random). In principal η can be calculated from α, the false positive rate for the test. Specifically, η is determined as the value such that $\Pr(\Lambda(O) \leq \eta | H_0) = \alpha$.

In our situation, O is a vector composed of the outcomes O_i of the individual tests $\mathcal{T}_i$ with parameters γ_i. Hypothesis H_0 is that the input sequence of B bytes is random and H_1 is the hypothesis that it is an output of RC4. Keeping in mind that $\gamma_i > 0$ for all i, we can then write

$$L(\theta_0|O) = \prod_{i:O_i=1} \rho \prod_{i:O_i=0} 1 - \rho$$

and

$$L(\theta_1|O) = \prod_{i:O_i=1} \rho(1+\gamma_i) \prod_{i:O_i=0} 1 - \rho(1+\gamma_i).$$

Then, taking logs, using the fact that ρ and all the γ_i are small, manipulating the above expressions using standard log approximations, and simplifying, we finally obtain:

$$\log \Lambda(O) \approx - \sum_{i:O_i=1} \gamma_i + \sum_{i:O_i=0} \rho\gamma_i\,.$$

Let us denote the above quantity by L. Thus a suitable, approximately optimal test is to reject the hypothesis H_0 (that the input string is a truly random string) and output "1" if $L \leq \log \eta$, and to output "0" otherwise. Note that the test statistic L is efficient to compute: it requires on the order of $G_{\max} \cdot B$ floating point operations and byte comparisons.

It remains to compute appropriate values of η for a given target α. This requires us to know the distribution of the test statistic L when O comes from distribution θ_0. Now, in this case, the outcome O_i is Bernoulli distributed with parameter ρ, i.e. $\Pr(O_i = 1) = \rho$. Moreover, we can group the tests into $G_{\max} + 1$ groups, each group corresponding to a set of tests having the same value for γ_i. Since the number of tests in each group is large, the sum of the corresponding terms in L can be approximated by Normal distributions with mean and variance that can be explicitly calculated. This in principal allows the distribution of L to be computed. We omit the details.

3.5 Optimal Choice of Parameters

For reasons that will become clear in the next section, we wish to maximise the value of the quantity $\delta := 1 - \alpha - \beta$ over the choice of distinguisher $\mathcal{D}$ acting on B bytes of input. Let us denote this value by δ_B. (As temporary motivation note that δ is the usual cryptographic definition of the advantage of the distinguisher.) Since we are interested in optimal distinguishers, our choice of parameters (α, β) is subject to the constraint that $L_B = \beta \log_2 \frac{\beta}{1-\alpha} + (1-\beta) \log_2 \frac{1-\beta}{\alpha}$ where the quantity L_B was computed for different values of B in Section 3.3. Direct maximisation using Wolfram alpha[6] yields $\delta_B = 0.00055$ for $B = 256$ (at $(\alpha, \beta) = (0.499459, 0.499991)$) and $\delta_B = 0.002273$ for $B = 4096$ (at $(\alpha, \beta) = (0.498343, 0.499384)$).

3.6 Implementation

We implemented the above statistical test to ensure that its practical performance is in line with the theoretical analysis. As noted above the parameter η could be set by calculating the distribution of the test statistic L when O comes from distribution θ_0. Another approach would be to generate many samples of the test statistic to estimate the distribution of L and set η by computing the α-percentile of the sampled values.

In our experiments, we simply set $\eta = 0$, ran the test on random inputs and on RC4 inputs, and computed the corresponding values of α, β, δ. This gives us sub-optimal values for δ, but is sufficient to validate that the test works and gives us a distinguisher having performance that is reasonably close to that which is theoretically obtainable. For $B = 4096$ and based on 2^{25} samples (2^{24} for each of random input and RC4 inputs), setting $\eta = 0$, we obtained $\alpha = 0.453706$, $\beta = 0.544646$ and $\delta = 0.001648$. Here the value of δ compares favourably to the theoretical maximum of 0.002273. We are confident that a closer match would be obtained by adjusting η. In our evaluation of our attack on HIVE to follow, we present attack costs for both the ideal value of δ and our experimentally obtained value.

4. AN ATTACK ON HIVE BASED ON A BLOCKWISE RC4 DISTINGUISHER

We describe a family of adversaries $\{\mathcal{A}_{B,S,T}\}$, parameterized by the block length B and two other parameters S and

[6]http://www.wolframalpha.com/

T which are defined below. Our adversaries have access to the distinguisher $\mathcal{D}$ acting on B bytes from Section 3. Recall that $\mathcal{D}$ outputs a single bit b; if $\mathcal{D}$'s input is uniformly random bytes, $\mathcal{D}_B$ outputs 1 with probability α; if $\mathcal{D}$'s input consists of B consecutive bytes of RC4 output, $\mathcal{D}$ outputs 1 with probability $1-\beta$.

For a fixed block length B, $\mathcal{A}_{B,S,T}$ is a one-time adversary against plausible hiding for two volumes, as in Definition 1. In this simple case, there are two encrypted volumes V_1, V_2 protected by passwords P_1, P_2, and a user wants to be able to deny the existence of V_2 to an adversary who knows P_1. We consider two volumes for simplicity and because two volumes are used in the implementation; the attack generalizes directly to any number of volumes. We assume that each volume consists of S blocks of B bytes, so the disk has $4SB$ bytes in total (because it needs to be twice the size of all the volumes combined).

We overload the notation for the access operations in Definition 1 to allow reading and writing of multiple blocks of data in a single query. In what follows, 0^{SB} denotes an all-zero string of SB bytes, equating to S blocks of B bytes each.

Our adversary $\mathcal{A}_{B,S,T}$ then proceeds in five steps:

1. $\mathcal{A}_{B,S,T}$ sends $l=2$ to the challenger and receives the password P_1 and a snapshot D_0 of the disk.
2. $\mathcal{A}_{B,S,T}$ sends $o_{1,0}=o_{1,1}=(w,0,V_1,0^{SB})$.
3. $\mathcal{A}_{B,S,T}$ sends $o_{2,0}=(w,1,V_2,0^{SB})$, $o_{2,1}=(r,0,V_1,d,SB)$.
4. $\mathcal{A}_{B,S,T}$ requests a snapshot D_f, containing $4S$ blocks. $\mathcal{A}_{B,S,T}$ disregards the blocks that are the same as in D_0, runs $\mathcal{D}$ successively on each of the remaining E used blocks of D_f and concatenates the output bits of $\mathcal{D}$ to form a string $R\in\{0,1\}^E$.
5. Finally, $\mathcal{A}_{B,S,T}$ outputs 1 if W, the Hamming weight of R, is at most T; otherwise it outputs 0.

The following theorem is immediate (noting that reading or writing B bytes counts as making 1 query in the security model given previously, so $\mathcal{A}_{B,S,T}$ makes $2S$ queries in total):

THEOREM 1. *Let $\tau_{B,S,T}$ denote the running time of $\mathcal{A}_{B,S,T}$ and $\mathrm{Adv}_{B,S,T}$ its advantage. Then HIVE is not $(\mathrm{Adv}_{B,S,T}$, $\tau_{B,S,T}$, $2S)$-plausible hiding against one-time adversaries.*

Now let us determine values for S, B and T for which the theorem gives a meaningful attack. We consider what information $\mathcal{A}_{B,S,T}$ has access to in its attack when $b=0$ and $b=1$ in the security experiment. When $b=0$, the disk is initialised with V_1 and V_2, and $o_{1,0}$ and $o_{2,0}$ are executed. When $b=1$, the disk is initialised only with V_1, and $o_{1,1}$ and $o_{2,1}$ are executed.

The adversary gets an initial snapshot of the disk before any operations are executed, so identifying unused blocks is trivial; E denotes the number of blocks that differ between D_0 and D_f. All blocks that are written to certainly differ, so we have $2S\le E\le 4S$. We call EB the effective disk size, since the other blocks are irrelevant to the attack. Note that the expected value of E is approximately $3.1075S$. (There are $4S$ blocks on the disk, and in the $2S$ read and write operations in our attack, HIVE will choose $K\cdot 2S=6S$ blocks at random to write to. This means that we expect that, out of the total of $4S$ blocks available, $4S\cdot(1-\frac{1}{4S})^{6S}$ blocks are *not* written to.[7] Using $(1-1/n)^m\approx e^{-m/n}$, we get $E[E]\approx(1-e^{-1.5})4S\approx 3.1075S$.)

Let W_b denote the Hamming weight of the vector R constructed by $\mathrm{Adv}_{B,S,T}$ in case b. We have:

- When $b=0$, $2S$ blocks of data are written to the disk, so it contains $2S$ blocks of AES output and $E-2S$ blocks of RC4 output. Since AES output is indistinguishable from random (otherwise, we would have an attack on AES), the expected value for W_0 is $\alpha\cdot 2S+(1-\beta)\cdot(E-2S)$.
- When $b=1$, only S blocks of data are written to the disk, so it contains S blocks of AES output and $E-S$ blocks of RC4 output. The expected value for W_1 is $\alpha\cdot S+(1-\beta)\cdot(E-S)$.

The difference in the expected values of the Hamming weight of R in the two cases is therefore $(1-\alpha-\beta)S=\delta S$, which corresponds to the S blocks of additional data written to the disk in case 0.

Note that the output of $\mathcal{D}$ on each B-byte block is an independent Bernoulli random variable with one of two possible distributions, depending on whether the block contains output from RC4 or AES (and where we assume the latter is indistinguishable from truly random bytes). Specifically, when a block contains RC4 output, $\mathcal{D}$'s output equals 1 with probability $1-\beta$, while, when it contains AES output, $\mathcal{D}$'s output equals 1 with probability α. Thus, when $b=0$, the distribution of W is a Poisson binomial distribution with parameters $p_1=\ldots=p_{2S}=\alpha$, $p_{2S+1}=\ldots=p_E=1-\beta$ (since the trials are independent, the order does not matter). Similarly, when $b=1$, the distribution of W is a Poisson binomial distribution with parameters $p_1=\ldots=p_S=\alpha$, $p_{S+1}=\ldots=p_E=1-\beta$.

By standard results for the Poisson binomial distribution, the variance of W_0 is equal to $2S\alpha(1-\alpha)+(E-2S)\beta(1-\beta)$, while the variance of W_1 is equal to $S\alpha(1-\alpha)+(E-S)\beta(1-\beta)$. Since $\alpha(1-\alpha),\beta(1-\beta)\le 1/4$ and $E\le 4S$, it follows that the two variances are bounded by S. We define $\sigma^2:=S$.

Now, given that W_0 and W_1 are obtained as sums of large numbers of independent Bernoulli random variables, we can consider them to be Normally distributed to a good approximation (here, we assume E is large, as indeed it will need to be to obtain reasonable success rates for our adversary). We already established that their variances are bounded by S, while their means are separated by δS. Note that

$$\begin{aligned}&\mathrm{Adv}^{\textit{pl-ot}}_{\mathcal{A}_{B,S,T},\Sigma}(k)\\ &=|\Pr[1\leftarrow \mathrm{Exp}^{\textit{pl-ot-0}}_{\mathcal{A}_{B,S,T},\Sigma}(k)]-\Pr[1\leftarrow \mathrm{Exp}^{\textit{pl-ot-1}}_{\mathcal{A}_{B,S,T},\Sigma}(k)]|\\ &=|\Pr[W_0\le T]-\Pr[W_1\le T]|\end{aligned}$$

where W_0 and W_1 are Normally distributed by assumption. We set T to be half-way between the means; viz $T=E-1.5S-1.5S\alpha-(E-1.5S)\beta$. This finally brings us to a position where we can apply standard tail bounds for Normal distributions in order to estimate the advantage of $\mathcal{A}_{B,S,T}$.

Suppose that we insist that the means of W_0,W_1 are $2n\sigma$ apart for some parameter n; then by our choice of T and

[7] In reality, because of the way the stash operates, slightly fewer than S or 2S blocks of data might be written to the disc. However, this does not materially affect our analysis. The probability of eight or more items remaining on the stash is only 0.05 %.

n	$\log_2 S$ (ideal)	$\log_2 S$ (experimental)	$\mathrm{Adv}_{B,S,T}$
1	19.6	20.5	0.683
2	21.6	22.5	0.954
3	22.7	23.7	0.997

Table 1: Number of blocks S required to achieve a given advantage $\mathrm{Adv}_{B,S,T}$ for $B = 4096$.

n	$\log_2 S$ (ideal)	$\mathrm{Adv}_{B,S,T}$
1	23.6	0.683
2	25.6	0.954
3	26.8	0.997

Table 2: Number of blocks S required to achieve a given advantage $\mathrm{Adv}_{B,S,T}$ for $B = 256$.

under our assumption of Normality (and since σ^2 is an upper bound on the variances of W_0, W_1) we get an advantage for our adversary which is at least

$$1 - \mathrm{erf}\left(\frac{n}{\sqrt{2}}\right)$$

where $\mathrm{erf}(\cdot)$ is the standard error function for the Normal distribution:

$$\mathrm{erf}(x) = \frac{1}{\sqrt{\pi}} \int_{-x}^{x} e^{-t^2}\, dt.$$

Hence, under the condition that $\delta S = 2n\sigma = 2nS^{1/2}$, the advantage $\mathrm{Adv}_{B,S,T}$ of our adversary $\mathcal{A}_{B,S,T}$ will be at least the claimed value, namely $1 - \mathrm{erf}(n/\sqrt{2})$. Solving for S, we see that we require

$$S = \frac{4n^2}{\delta^2}$$

to achieve the claimed advantage.

4.1 Concrete Numbers

To launch a concrete attack, we set $B = 4096$, as in [2]. Then, from the results of Section 3 we can take $\delta = 0.002273$ as the optimal setting. Setting $n = 1$ in the above analysis and solving for S, we get $S = 2^{19.6}$ for an advantage of 0.683. Continuing for other values of n, we obtain the second column in Table 1. Thus we see that an adversary with advantage very close to 1 can be achieved by setting $S = 2^{22.7}$, i.e. for an attack involving $2S = 2^{23.7}$ read/write queries on a disk containing a total of $4S = 2^{24.7}$ blocks and $4BS = 2^{36.7}$ bytes of data (i.e. roughly 104 GB of data).

The third column in Table 1 contains estimates for S based on setting $\delta = 0.001648$, the value experimentally observed when setting $\eta = 0$ in the statistical test developed in Section 3.6. The higher numbers in this column reflect the sub-optimal performance of the blockwise distinguisher for this setting of η.

The main computational cost of implementing the attack is that of running the blockwise distinguisher E times; since $E \leq 4S$, the total cost of the attack is on the order of $G_{\max} \cdot B \cdot S$ floating point operations. In our implementation, the running time for a *single* execution of the blockwise distinguisher for $G_{\max} = 64$, $B = 4096$ was 0.000719s (on a Macbook Air with a 1.3 GHz Intel Core i5 processor and 8GB of RAM); the running time of the whole attack with $E = 4S$ and $S = 2^{23.7}$ would then be about 11 hours. This running time could be improved by optimising the choice of η (thus allowing a reduced value of S).

Similar calculations can be carried out with $B = 256$, where we can take $\delta = 0.00055$. We obtain Table 2. We see that S is required to be greater, reflecting the much weaker performance of our blockwise distinguisher when the block size is small. On the other hand, the total disk size is only moderately increased and the running time of the distinguisher is further reduced (because of the reduced block size).

5. CONCLUSIONS

We have shown that the current instantiation of HIVE using RC4 is insecure. Specifically, there is an efficient attack involving $2^{23.7}$ read/write queries on $B = 4096$ byte blocks for which we can construct an adversary having advantage 0.997 in the security model for plausible hiding against one-time adversaries. This violates the main security property claimed for HIVE.

Our work illustrates that if a provably secure scheme is instantiated with an insecure primitive, then all security guarantees may be lost.

HIVE can be repaired by replacing RC4 with a stronger PRG. For example, AES in counter mode (CTR) could be used instead; as well as being more secure, the performance will be better than that of the current RC4-based system on platforms with hardware support for AES. More options, optimized for performance in hard- or software, are offered by the eSTREAM project.[8]

We gave the authors of HIVE the opportunity to make changes to their code and to their paper after notifying them of our initial concerns about their scheme's reliance on RC4. They did not avail themselves of this opportunity. In view of the fact that HIVE had been released to the public and was promoted as "*not rely[ing] on heuristics or obfuscation techniques, but rather strong cryptographic primitives which can be mathematically proven*" and as being able to "*provide very strong security in practice*"[9], we decided to refine and publish our attack to provide a clear demonstration of the shortcomings of instantiating the system with RC4.

Shortly after publication of a pre-print version of this paper, RC4 was replaced by AES-CTR as the default PRG in the HIVE implementation. According to the HIVE developers, I/O performance remains unaffected.[10]

6. REFERENCES

[1] N. J. AlFardan, D. J. Bernstein, K. G. Paterson, B. Poettering, and J. C. N. Schuldt. On the security of RC4 in TLS. In *USENIX Security*. USENIX Association, 2013. `https://www.usenix.org/conference/usenixsecurity13/security-rc4-tls`.

[2] E.-O. Blass, T. Mayberry, G. Noubir, and K. Onarlioglu. Toward robust hidden volumes using write-only oblivious RAM. In *CCS '14*, pages 203–214. ACM, 2014. Full version at `https://eprint.iacr.org/2014/344`.

[8] `http://www.ecrypt.eu.org/stream/`

[9] Both quotes from `http://hive.ccs.neu.edu/`, date of access 26/10/2014

[10] `http://www.onarlioglu.com/hive/`, section "Change Log"

[3] S. R. Fluhrer and D. A. McGrew. Statistical analysis of the alleged RC4 keystream generator. In *FSE 2000*, volume 1978 of *Lecture Notes in Computer Science*, pages 19–30. Springer, 2001.

[4] I. Mantin. Predicting and distinguishing attacks on RC4 keystream generator. In *EUROCRYPT 2005*, volume 3494 of *Lecture Notes in Computer Science*, pages 491–506. Springer, 2005.

[5] I. Mantin and A. Shamir. A practical attack on broadcast RC4. In *FSE 2001*, volume 2355 of *Lecture Notes in Computer Science*, pages 152–164. Springer, 2002.

[6] S. Sen Gupta, S. Maitra, G. Paul, and S. Sarkar. (Non-) random sequences from (non-) random permutations – analysis of RC4 stream cipher. *Journal of Cryptology*, 27(1):67–108, 2014.

Efficient Dynamic Tracking Technique for Detecting Integer-Overflow-to-Buffer-Overflow Vulnerability

Hao Sun
State Key Lab for Novel Software Tech.
Dept. of Comp. Sci. and Tech.
Nanjing University, China
shqking@gmail.com

Xiangyu Zhang
Dept. of Comp. Sci.
Purdue University, USA
xyzhang@cs.purdue.edu

Chao Su
State Key Lab for Novel Software Tech.
Dept. of Comp. Sci. and Tech.
Nanjing University, China
suchao1991@gmail.com

Qingkai Zeng
State Key Lab for Novel Software Tech.
Dept. of Comp. Sci. and Tech.
Nanjing University, China
zqk@nju.edu.cn

ABSTRACT

Integer-Overflow-to-Buffer-Overflow (*IO2BO*) vulnerabilities can be exploited by attackers to cause severe damages to computer systems. In this paper, we present the design and implementation of IntTracker, an efficient dynamic tracking technique for detecting IO2BO vulnerabilities in C/C++ programs. IntTracker utilizes a static taint analysis to select potential overflow sites that are integer operations along *critical* paths, from sources that are program points reading values from users, to sinks that are memory allocation sites. It then instruments overflow checks at the selected sites. Instead of producing warnings once integer overflows occur, IntTracker replaces the overflown value with a very *large* and *rarely* used integer value (*dirty* value), and treats such the value as an overflow tag. Tag propagation is performed by the existing program operations without any instrumentation as operations on dirty values often produce dirty values. Propagation can be automatically cut off by sanitization routines as they could prevent dirty values from affecting further program execution. IntTracker monitors whether any dirty value is used at a sink to detect IO2BO vulnerabilities. We evaluate IntTracker on 3444 programs of the NIST's SAMATE reference dataset, the SPEC CINT2000 benchmarks and 34 IO2BO bugs in real world. The experimental results show that IntTracker is effective in detecting harmful IO2BO vulnerabilities while bypassing false positives introduced by sanitization routines. Meanwhile, the runtime overhead is negligible, averaging about 0.69%. In contrast, IntPatch, the state of the art, produces a lot more false positives and has a higher overhead.

ASIA CCS'15, April 14–17, 2015, Singapore..

http://dx.doi.org/10.1145/2714576.2714605.

Categories and Subject Descriptors

F.3.2 [**Semantics of Programming Languages**]: Program Analysis

General Terms

Security; Program Analysis

Keywords

IO2BO; Integer Overflow; Dynamic Tracking; Instrumentation

1. INTRODUCTION

Integer Overflow to Buffer Overflow (IO2BO) vulnerabilities, defined in Common Weakness Enumeration (CWE-680 [1]), are "a kind of integer overflows, i.e. an integer overflow occurs when a program performs a calculation to determine how much memory to allocate, which causes less or more memory to be allocated than expected, leading to a buffer overflow" [41]. For instance, Listing 1 shows a typical IO2BO vulnerability in CUPS [28]. Lines 15 to 19 is the patch for this bug. In the original buggy code, an adversary could provide a crafted PNG file with large `width` and `height` to cause the multiplication at line 13 to overflow, leading to less space allocated than expected at line 22. Buffer overflow would occur if out-of-bound reads or writes are performed on the allocated memory later.

IO2BO vulnerabilities are a dominant kind of integer overflow in practice. According to our study, out of all the 250 integer overflow bugs[1] reported by Common Vulnerabilities and Exposures (CVE) [24] from 2008 to 2013, 183 cases (about 73%) are IO2BO vulnerabilities. Note that these

[1]According to our investigation, there are totally 595 integer overflow bugs reported by CVE from 2008 to 2013, including 242 bugs in commodity software and 353 bugs in open-source software. In this paper, we select as our study subjects the 250 bugs in open-source software, where the bug specific information such as overflow site, patch and exploitation site are available.

Listing 1: Patched code for CVE-2008-1722 vulnerability in CUPS [28]

```
1       /* Read a PNG image file. */
2       int _cupsImageReadPNG( Cups_image_t *img, FILE *fp
        , ...){
3           png_uint_32 width, height;
4           png_structp pp;
5           png_init_io(pp, fp);
6
7           /* Get the image dimensions */
8           png_get_IHDR(pp, info, &width, &height, ...);
9
10          img->xsize = width;
11          img->ysize = height;
12          size_t bufsize, size;
13          bufsize = img->xsize * img->ysize;
14
15  +       if ((bufsize / img->ysize) != img->xsize){
16  +           fprintf(stderr, "PNG image dimensions Too
        large\n");
17  +           fclose(fp);
18  +           return 1;
19  +       }
20
21          size = bufsize * 3;
22          in = malloc(size);
23          ...
24      }
```

vulnerabilities are usually easily exploitable for security attacks and can cause severe damages to computer systems.

Due to its importance, researchers have developed various techniques to address this problem. Static techniques, such as IntScope [37], Kint [38] and SIFT [23], usually extract constraint information for integer operations (such as addition, subtraction, multiplication and left-shift operations) along *critical paths* from sources that are program points reading values from users, to sinks that are memory allocation sites. They either generate test cases to trigger IO2BO by constraint solvers [37][38], or generate an input filter to preclude IO2BO error-inducing inputs [23]. However, these techniques would produce many false positives due to the challenges faced by static analysis, such as the limited precision of alias analysis and limited loop unrolling. They may also produce false negatives due to the limited ability of constraint solvers.

A classic approach to detecting integer overflows is to insert *overflow checks* at integer operations to catch overflows at runtime. Instrumented programs can react to an overflow by logging the event or terminating the execution. Many existing techniques, such as RICH [12], IOC [19], AIR [18] and RA [33], work in this way to detect integer overflows. As for IO2BOs, IntPatch [41] is the state of the art. IntPatch at first employs static taint-like analysis to extract all integer operations along critical paths as *potential* IO2BO vulnerabilities, and then inserts overflow checks at selected integer operations. Take the buggy code in Listing 1 as an example. **`png_get_IHDR()`** at line 8 is the taint source, which reads a PNG image file from outside and stores the width and height information of the image into variables **`width`** and **`height`**. **`malloc()`** at line 22 is the taint sink. At static analysis phase, IntPatch obtains the critical path, i.e. 8 → 10/11 → 13 → 21 → 22, and treats all integer operations along this path as potential IO2BO sites, i.e. the multiplications at line 13 and line 21. Then IntPatch inserts overflow checks after line 13 and line 21 respectively. For multiplication `c = a * b`, the widely used check code looks like:

```
if((c != 0)&&(c/a != b))
    MSG("overflow occurs");
```

Once a crafted image with large width and height is provided, the check after line 13 would catch this overflow and produce a warning. The check density is 10%, i.e. IntPatch only selects one out of ten integer operations. And IntPatch has a negligible performance overhead, averaging about 1%.

However, IntPatch produces many false positives. In reality, experienced developers often anticipate the possibility of integer overflows such that they add *sanitization routines* after potential overflow sites. We call such overflows as *anticipated IO2BO*. The patched code for CVE-2008-1722 in Listing 1 shows such an example. The overflown value **`bufsize`** cannot go through the check at line 15 to reach the critical allocation point at line 22. However IntPatch still selects the multiplication for **`bufsize`** and insert a check. Moreover, IntPatch selects potential IO2BO vulnerabilities statically, i.e. an integer operation would be selected as long as it is on certain critical path. It cannot guarantee that the program will execute along this specific critical path at runtime. There are two potential execution paths for the code snippet in Listing 1, i.e. $path_1$: 8 → 10/11 → 13 → 21 → 22 and $path_2$: 8 → 10/11 → 13 → 15 → 16 → 17 → 18. $path_1$ is a critical path whereas $path_2$ is not. When the overflow at line 13 happens, the program executes along $path_2$; however, IntPatch cannot determine this statically.

As stated in IntPatch, *'sanitization routines are at semantic level and hard to be detected'* [41]. In addition, sanitization routines in real-world programs take various forms. Hence, we argue that to reduce the false positives caused by sanitization routines, instead of giving warnings once catching integer overflows, we shall develop efficient overflow tracking technique, which tags overflows, tracks its propagation, sanitizes the tag if encountering a sanitization routine, and guards the sinks to determine true IO2BO vulnerabilities.

In this paper, we develop a novel runtime IO2BO detector, named *IntTracker*, which features the capabilities of detecting all harmful IO2BO vulnerabilities and bypassing the false positives caused by sanitization routines. Similar to IntPatch, IntTracker firstly selects all integer operations along critical paths as protection subjects. Then some of them are excluded via checking whether certain sanitization routines of fixed patterns are used to guard these potential integer overflows. The remaining selected integer operations are instrumented and monitored by IntTracker. At runtime, upon the occurrence of an integer overflow, IntTracker does not report it right away. Instead, it tracks the data-flow propagation of the overflown value. If an overflown value can flow into memory sinks without being sanitized, a warning is issued. As such, IntTracker has negligible false positive and false negative rates. The challenge lies in that tracking data flow of overflown values could be very expensive. It is very similar to traditional dynamic information flow tracking [32][10] and taint analysis [20][40], which often slows down program execution by a constant factor. This is because meta-data structure such as shadow memory needs to be maintained and updated during the whole execution. In IntTracker, we leverage the observation that the overflown value itself in the context of IO2BO may not be that important anymore. Therefore, we replace it with some *dirty* value from a specific range of very *large* and *rarely* used integer values (we call it *Dirty-zone*). It is analogous to poisoning the value. IntTracker only reports when a poisoned value reaches a memory sink. Note that 1) all integer operations along the propagation path of a poisoned value would not change its poisonous feature (as proved in Section 2.3.3); 2) if there is any sanitization routine along the propagation path of a poisoned value, the propagation can be automatically stopped due to the fact that the poisoned value falls out of the legitimate range allowed by the check. In other words, IntTracker can reduce the false positives introduced by sanitization routines.

Our contributions are highlighted as follows.

1. We define sanitization routines into two categories: *Santz-postcond* which uses fixed patterns to catch overflows and can be identified through static analysis, and *Santz-spec* which leverages specific program characteristics to sanitize overflown values and are left for our dynamic technique to handle.

2. We propose a novel efficient dynamic tracking technique. It uses very large and rarely used *dirty* values as the indicator of overflows, which allows natural propagation and sanitization of overflown values.

3. We implement a prototype, IntTracker, as an extension of the GCC compiler [2]. Static taint analysis is used to select integer operations along critical paths. It also checks the presence of fixed patterns of widely used sanitizations to exclude parts of the selected integer operations. IntTracker detects integer overflows through postcondition test [41][33]. Once an integer overflow is detected, IntTracker poisons the overflown value. Guards are inserted to memory sinks to detect if poisonous values can reach these sinks.

4. Experimental results show that IntTracker is effective in detecting harmful IO2BO vulnerabilities while bypassing un-harmful ones, which substantially improves the state of the art. Specifically, IntTracker could catch all the 600 IO2BO vulnerabilities in the SAMATE's Juliet test suite [26] and 14 harmful IO2BO bugs in real world. Furthermore, as for the patched code for 20 real-world IO2BO bugs with sanitization routines, IntTracker only reports one IO2BO (i.e. one false positive) whereas IntPatch reports all of them. At last, IntTracker has a negligible performance overhead (0.69% on average).

Outline. The rest of this paper is organized as follows. Section 2 presents the design of IntTracker. Section 3 describes implementation details. Section 4 presents the experimental results. Limitations, related work and conclusion are discussed in Section 5, Section 6 and Section 7, respectively.

2. DYNAMIC TRACKING TECHNIQUE

2.1 Problem Definition

Inspired by discussions in Section 1, the occurrence of an IO2BO vulnerability can be described as a process, in which tainted data is first introduced by the user at a source point, then overflow occurs at some point along its propagation to a memory sink. Along its propagation path, tainted data would undergo a number of integer arithmetic operations. Therefore, we can formally define the process of an *IO2BO vulnerability* as shown in Figure 1.

harmful IO2BO := *Taint-source*; [*Arith_op*;]^N *IO_op*; [*Arith_op*;]^M *MEM*;
anticipated IO2BO := *Taint-source*; [*Arith_op*;]^N *IO_op*; *Santz*;
IO_op, *Arith_op* ∈ {+, -, *, <<}
MEM ∈ {**malloc, memcpy, strncpy, realloc,** ⋯}

Figure 1: IO2BO vulnerability description.

Table 1: Postcondition test. The subscript s indicates a signed operation; the subscript u indicates an unsigned operation.

Arith_op	Postcondtion Test
$x = o_1 +_s o_2$	$(o_1 > 0 \bigwedge o_2 > 0 \bigwedge x > 0) \bigvee$
	$(o_1 < 0 \bigwedge o_2 < 0 \bigwedge x > 0)$
$x = o_1 +_u o_2$	$x < o_1 \bigvee x < o_2$
$x = o_1 -_s o_2$	$(o_1 < 0 \bigwedge o_2 > 0 \bigwedge x > 0) \bigvee$
	$(o_1 > 0 \bigwedge o_2 < 0 \bigwedge x < 0)$
$x = o_1 -_u o_2$	$o_1 < o_2$
$x = o_1 *_{s/u} o_2$	$x \neq 0 \bigwedge x/o_1 \neq o_2$
$x = o_1 \ll o_2$	$x \gg o_1 \neq o_2$

Specifically, *Taint-source* denotes program points reading values from users. It is the start of an IO2BO vulnerability, introducing *tainted* (untrusted) data into programs. *MEM* is memory manipulation routines, acting as sinks for tainted data. *Arith_op* and *IO_op* are the operations on tainted data along the path from Taint-source to MEM. Here, we only consider arithmetic operations which could change the concrete value of tainted data[2]. The superscript N and M indicate the corresponding operation might occur several times. IO_op is the point where an integer overflow happens, including addition, subtraction, multiplication and left-shift operations in either *signed* or *unsigned* type. In addition, as for anticipated IO2BOs, *Santz* indicates sanitization routines that are used to prevent overflown data from flowing into MEM.

Our goal is to detect harmful IO2BOs and bypass the anticipated IO2BOs.

2.2 Sanitization Routines

Experienced developers often anticipate the possibility of overflows and insert sanitization routines after the overflow sites to prevent overflown values from affecting further program execution.

Postcondition test [33] is widely used as sanitization routines by developers to prevent integer overflows in advance or to patch buggy code. The intuition of postcondition test is to utilize the mismatch between an overflown value and the expected value to detect overflow. We call them *Santz-postcond* for short. Table 1 shows the details. As Santz-postcond is of fixed patterns, *we may exclude the checks for some Arith_op's by checking statically whether Santz-postcond is present after them.*

Meanwhile, there also exist other sanitization routines, where developers usually leverage program characteristics and employ program specific checks to sanitize overflown

[2]Note that we do not consider division as Arith_op just like IntPatch [41]. Divisions are very rare along critical paths according to our study of the 183 CVE IO2BO bugs.

Listing 2: Patched code for CVE-2011-1137 [31]

```
  /* Maximum length of the payload data of an
  SSH2 packet we're willing to accept */
  #define MAX_PAYLOAD_LEN      (256 * 1024)

  uint32_t payload_len -= size;
+ if( payload_len < MAX_PAYLOAD_LEN)
      memcpy( ..., ..., payload_len);
```

Listing 3: Patched code for CVE-2010-2065 [30]

```
  int tif->tif_rawdatasize = size * 1024;
+ if( tif->tif_rawdatasize > 0 )
      tif->tif_rawdata = (tidata_t) _TIFFmalloc(
  tif->tif_rawdatasize);
```

values. As these checks are designed to catch overflows under specific situations, we call them *Santz-spec* for short.

Listings 2 and 3 show two examples of using Santz-spec to patch CVE IO2BO bugs. In the first case, the unsigned subtraction might underflow and variable `payload_len` will turn to a very large value. For instance, the product of $8U - 16U$ is $0xfffffff8U$. Instead of using `len_original=payload_len; payload_len-=size; if(len_original<size)` (Santz-postcond works in this way), the developer chose to check whether `payload_len` is smaller than the designated maximum. This check works well with the premise that the legitimate value is always smaller than `MAX_PAYLOAD_LEN`, i.e. the overflown value is always larger than `MAX_PAYLOAD_LEN`.

If the signed multiplication in the second case, i.e. `size*1024`, overflows, the product might be either negative or positive. However, the developer only checks whether the product is negative to detect overflow. From this we may guess that, the developer already knows the value of `size` is not larger than $0x3fffff$ (the quotient of $0xffffffffU$ and 1024) in reality so that they insert such incomplete sanitization.

Here we argue that, as Santz-spec is usually application specific and designed based on developers' preference, *Santz-spec is usually of various patterns and hard to be detected statically*. Therefore, *dynamic tracking technique is still needed for the presence of Santz-spec*, although Santz-postcond can be identified statically.

2.3 Design of IntTracker

In this subsection, we describe the design of IntTracker, which is aimed at detecting harmful IO2BO vulnerabilities while bypassing anticipated ones. As part of the system, the *static selection analysis* attempts to select the integer operations along critical paths from taint-sources to MEMs, and to exclude some of them if they are protected by Santz-postcond. The selected integer operations are viewed as potential IO2BO sites. Then the other analysis, which we will call it the *code instrumentation analysis*, inserts overflow checks for the selected integer operations and dirty value guarding code for MEM sites. Based on these two analyses, IntTracker could provide dynamic protection against IO2BO vulnerabilities.

2.3.1 Static Selection

Following the feature of IO2BO vulnerability, only integer operations which can be influenced by an untrusted source and may be used at memory sinks are potential IO2BO sites. Just like IntPatch [41] and Kint [38], our static selection analysis is also a taint-like analysis, marking all the taint-sources and MEM sites at first and then extracting all Arith_op's along critical paths.

Then each of these integer operations gets further checked whether it is followed by a Santz-postcond according to the fixed patterns in Table 1. If so, we exclude it from the selected Arith_op set.

2.3.2 Code Instrumentation

The code instrumentation analysis consists of two parts: inserting postcondition test after each selected Arith_op and inserting dirty value guarding code before each MEM site.

Postconditon test: as dynamic techniques [41][12][19][18][33] do, overflow check is needed to catch integer overflows at runtime. Here we use postcondition test as the check code. The essential difference between IntTracker and others is the handler when an integer overflow is caught. Instead of giving warnings directly, IntTracker replaces the overflown value with our designated dirty value, as described by the following pseudo code:

```
x = o1 Arith_op o2
IF (postcondition)
    x = dirty value;
```

Dirty value guarding: as discussed in the previous sections, an IO2BO vulnerability is reported by IntTracker when a dirty value is used at any MEM site. Therefore, guarding code should be inserted before MEM sites. The inserted code is shown as below:

```
IF guard_object is dirty value
    call inttracker_runtime_handler();
MEM (..., guard_object, ...);
```

Variable *guard_object* denotes the argument that needs to be guarded, e.g., the first argument for `malloc()` and the third argument for `memcpy()`. A runtime handler will be invoked once a dirty value is detected.

2.3.3 Dynamic Protection by IntTracker

Figure 2 depicts how IntTracker works for IO2BO vulnerability detection at runtime. The upper half shows the process of handling potential IO2BOs, and the lower half shows the process of handling benign cases.

In benign cases, a normal value remains '*normal*' through Arith_op's. It will not be affected by sanitization routines or our postcondition tests. Therefore, their uses at memory sinks are admitted by IntTracker.

In contrast for the potential IO2BO cases, once an integer overflow, i.e. IO_op, occurs, the overflown value would be turned into a dirty value via our postcondition test (marked as step 1). Along the following propagation to some memory sink, the dirty value remains '*dirty*' (marked as step 2). When encountering Santz-spec, the dirty value cannot survive the check and the propagation is stopped (marked as step 3). If the dirty value flows into a memory sink, an IO2BO warning would be issued via our guarding code (marked as step 4). In this way, harmful IO2BOs would be detected by IntTracker while anticipated ones together with the benign cases are permitted.

To guarantee IntTracker working correctly, four key prerequisites (*PR* for short) must be met.

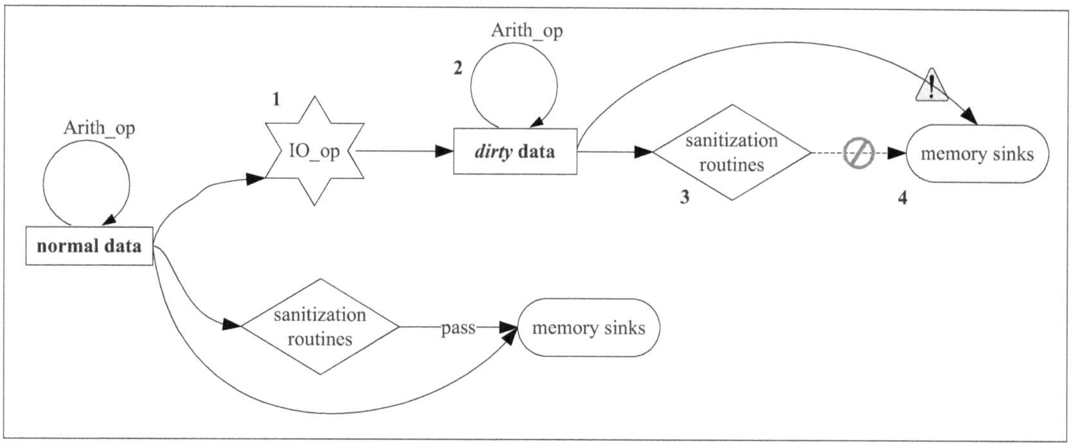

Figure 2: Dynamic protection by IntTracker. ***Normal data*** **indicates values that are not affected by integer overflows or our instrumentation code.**

Table 2: Distributions on the number of Ops_after for CVE IO2BO bugs. ***N*** **denotes the number of Ops_after. 'N = 0' means overflown value gets used at MEM directly; 'N = 1' means that there is one Ops_after along the overflow path.**

	Ops_after (N)			
	N = 0	N = 1	N = 2	N = 3
#	**124**	42	14	3
%	67.03%	22.70%	7.57%	1.62%

1. Replacing overflown values with dirty value (step 1) will not change program semantics;
2. When a dirty value goes through Arith_op's during propagation, it must remain in the Dirty-zone, i.e. keeping its dirty nature;
3. Dirty values will be caught by Santz-spec (step 3), therefore reducing false positives;
4. Dirty values can be viewed as the indicator of overflows when they reach memory sinks (step 4).

PR1. Not changing program semantics is the basic PR for IntTracker. If our modifications on overflown values have impact on normal program behavior, IntTracker cannot be applied to protect real-world programs.

As stated in IntPatch [41] and SIFT [23], *integer overflows in the context of IO2BO cannot be benign*, i.e. overflows are rarely used intentionally by programmers for memory manipulations. Hence, an overflown value itself is always harmful in this context. In other words, the value of the overflown variable is no longer important for regarding program behavior. As a result, we can modify the overflown value into another value without breaking program semantics. Therefore in IntTracker, replacing an overflown value with a dirty value will not change program semantics.

PR2. Keeping the dirty values '*dirty*' along paths to memory sinks is critical to our tracking technique, as dirty values are used as the indicator of vulnerability at the memory sinks. If a dirty value is undesirably sanitized, IntTracker would produce false negatives.

A). ***overflow path*** is a path from an overflow site to a memory sink. Following the notions in Figure 1, an overflow path is a sequence of instructions, i.e. *IO_op; [Arith_op;]^M MEM.* And as for the buggy code at Listing 1, the overflow path for CVE-2008-1722 is 13 → 21 → 22. The operations on an overflown value after the overflow happens (*Ops_after* for short) indicate the operations that the overflown value would undergo before it is used at a memory sink, i.e. *[Arith_op;]^M*. For CVE-2008-1722, the Ops_after in this example is the multiplication at line 21.

We have studied the distributions on the number of Ops_after for all cases we have collected, i.e. the 183 harmful IO2BO bugs reported by CVE in the past six years. The results are shown at Table 2. Columns 2 to 5 show categories based on the number of Ops_after. Row 3 shows the number of IO2BO bugs belonging to different categories and the last row shows the corresponding percentages. From the table, we can find that overflown values get used at MEM sites directly for about 67.03% of all cases. And almost all cases use the overflown values within 3 Ops_after, i.e. the overflow sites are close to MEM sinks in terms of data flow distance.

Observation 1. Overflow paths for harmful IO2BO vulnerabilities are short in general.

B). assume that ***normal integer values*** produced by Arith_op are always in a small range (**Assumption 1**). To confirm this, we take a profile on the unsigned integer values produced by arithmetic operations at runtime on SPEC CINT2000 [9] programs with '*ref*' database as inputs. The profiling results[3] are shown in Table 3. The first row describes different integer ranges and the second row is the number of integer values belonging to the corresponding range. For instance, about $1.18E+11$ values are in [0, 64K). The third and last rows indicate the percentage and cumulated percentage of the number of values in each range over the total number. From the table we can get that about 0.999997756 of $1.45E + 11$ unsigned integer values are between 0 and $0x400000$ (i.e. 4M). Here we call this integer range as *Small-zone.*

[3] We excluded some abnormal large values produced by random number generations and hash value computations.

Table 3: **Profiling results on products of Arith_op in SPEC CINT2000.**

	[0,64K)	**[64K, 256K)**	**[256K, 4M)**	**[4M, 128M)**	**[128M, 256M)**	**[256M, 4G)**
#	1.17706E+11	15114028485	12519654053	295283	14461	16331
%	0.809866774	0.103990667	0.086140315	2.03167E-06	9.94976E-08	1.12364E-07
accum-%	0.809866774	0.913857441	0.999997756	0.999999788	0.999999888	1

Table 4: **Profiling results on *guard_object* of MEM sites in SPEC CINT2000.**

	[0,8K)	**[8K, 64K)**	**[64K, 4M)**	**[4M, 32M)**	**[32M, 64M)**	**[64M, 4G)**
#	352132670	1067633	520464	148	67	0
%	0.995509704	0.003018291	0.001471397	4.18409E-07	1.89415E-07	0
accum-%	0.995509704	0.998527995	0.999999392	0.999999811	1	1

To simplify the description, we choose *unsigned int* type as an example to prove the correctness of step 2, and the proof for other integer types can be similarly constructed. Our proof is probabilistic, similar to [11][35]. We present it in details as follows.

As discussed before, *dirty* values are derived from a range of very large and rarely used integer values. Here we use $[0xA0000000, 0xE0000000)$ as the Dirty-zone, which is much larger (256 times) than Small-zone. We define $\mathcal{I}_{Zone}^{Var}$ as the incident of variable *Var*'s concrete value falling in a specific range of integer values *Zone*, and $\mathcal{P}(\mathcal{I}_{Zone}^{Var})$ as the probability of this incident. We use $\mathcal{I}_S^{Var}$ and $\mathcal{I}_D^{Var}$ to indicate that variable *Var*'s concreate value falls in Small-zone and Dirty-zone respectively. We use *dirty_replace(Var)* to denote the process of replacing an overflown value with our designated initial dirty value (i.e. $0xC0000000$).

Step 2 in Figure 2 can be described as a sequence of Arith_op's, each with a form[4] like *Result = Dirty op Delta*, where *Dirty* is from the Dirty-zone while *Delta* is a normal data. Based on the profiling results, we can say that $\mathcal{P}(\mathcal{I}_S^{Delta}) = \mathbf{0.999997756}$ approximately. And we have to guarantee that after each Arith_op, the left-hand-size *Result* has a high probability of falling into the Dirty-zone, i.e. $\mathcal{P}(\mathcal{I}_D^{Result}) \approx 1$.

PROOF. For the 1st operation, we want to discuss in the view of different Arith_op types, as shown below:

1. case *Result = Dirty * Delta*:
   If *Delta* equals to 1 (we call this subcase as SC_{11} for short), then *Result* equals to *Dirty*. Hence, we can get the conditional probability $\mathcal{P}(\mathcal{I}_D^{Result}|SC_{11}) = 1$;

   If *Delta* is a value greater than 1 (SC_{12}), this multiplication would overflow and our postcondition test will catch the overflow, triggering *dirty_replace(Result)*. Hence, we can get $\mathcal{P}(\mathcal{I}_D^{Result}|SC_{12}) = 1$ as well.

   Following the law of total probability [39], we can get in case 1, $\mathcal{P}(\mathcal{I}_D^{Result}) = \mathcal{P}(\mathcal{I}_D^{Result}|SC_{11}) * \mathcal{P}(SC_{11}) + \mathcal{P}(\mathcal{I}_D^{Result}|SC_{12}) * \mathcal{P}(SC_{12}) = \mathcal{P}(SC_{11}) + \mathcal{P}(SC_{12}) = 1$;

2. case *Result = Dirty* $\ll$ *Delta*:
   Similar to case 1, we can easily get $\mathcal{P}(\mathcal{I}_D^{Result}) = 1$ in this case;

[4]Note that we do not consider *Result = Dirty op Dirty* because according to our CVE study there are no such cases, where two different IO_op's overflow and the overflown values converge at certain point before flowing into a memory sink together.

3. case *Result = Delta - Dirty*:
   If *Delta* is a value from Small-zone (SC_{31}), it is much smaller than *Dirty*. Then this subtraction will overflow and our postcondition test will catch this overflow, triggering *dirty_replace(Result)*. Hence, we can get $\mathcal{P}(\mathcal{I}_D^{Result}|SC_{31}) = 1$;

   If *Delta* is a value out of Small-zone but also smaller than *Dirty* (SC_{32}), this subtraction will overflow as well. Similarly, we can get $\mathcal{P}(\mathcal{I}_D^{Result}|SC_{32}) = 1$;

   If *Delta* is a value bigger than *Dirty* (SC_{33}), $\mathcal{P}(\mathcal{I}_D^{Result}|SC_{33})$ is almost zero.

   Following the law of total probability, we can get in current case, $\mathcal{P}(\mathcal{I}_D^{Result}) = \mathcal{P}(\mathcal{I}_D^{Result}|SC_{31}) * \mathcal{P}(SC_{31}) + \mathcal{P}(\mathcal{I}_D^{Result}|SC_{32}) * \mathcal{P}(SC_{32}) + \mathcal{P}(\mathcal{I}_D^{Result}|SC_{33}) * \mathcal{P}(SC_{33}) > \mathcal{P}(\mathcal{I}_D^{Result}|SC_{31}) * \mathcal{P}(SC_{31}) = \mathcal{P}(SC_{31}) = \mathcal{P}(\mathcal{I}_S^{Delta}) \approx 0.999997756$;

4. case *Result = Dirty* $\pm$ *Delta*:
   Compared to values in Dirty-zone, values in Small-zone are relatively much smaller. Adding or subtracting such small values to/from *Dirty* can only change its lower bits. If *Delta* is a value from Small-zone (SC_{41}), then we can get $\mathcal{P}(\mathcal{I}_D^{Result}|SC_{41}) = 1$. Hence in current case, $\mathcal{P}(\mathcal{I}_D^{Result}) > \mathcal{P}(\mathcal{I}_D^{Result}|SC_{41}) * \mathcal{P}(SC_{41}) = \mathcal{P}(SC_{41}) = \mathcal{P}(\mathcal{I}_S^{Delta}) \approx 0.999997756$;

Even not taking consideration of the distributions of different Arith_op types in real-world programs, we can argue that $\mathcal{P}(\mathcal{I}_D^{Result}) \approx 0.999997756$ for the 1st operation.

The proof for subsequent Arith_op is similar to the first one, besides taking the premise that all the preceding products are in the Dirty-zone. Therefore after N Arith_op's, we can get $\mathcal{P}^N(\mathcal{I}_D^{Result}) \approx (0.999997756)^N$. For instance, after a sequence of 10 Arith_op's, the probability for the final product falling in Dirty-zone is about *0.99997760*. Since in most cases overflown values only go through no more than 3 Arith_op's before flowing into MEM sinks (**Observation 1**), we can assert that *PR2* is met. □

PR3. Santz-spec is designed by developers with specific program characteristics to catch overflown values. If our dirty value cannot be caught by Santz-spec, false positives would be produced, i.e. treating anticipated IO2BOs as harmful.

In general, Santz-spec is designed based on the mismatch between overflown values and *normal values*, by checking the

Listing 4: Code snippet of CVE-2008-1722 after instrumentation by IntTracker. Postcondition test is marked with '*'; guarding code is marked with '>'.

```
13    bufsize = img->xsize * img->ysize;

*    if ((bufsize != 0) && (bufsize / img->xsize !=
       img->ysize))
*        bufsize = 0xC0000000;

21   size = bufsize * 3;

*    if ((size != 0) && (size / bufsize != 3))
*        size = 0xC0000000;

>    if (size > 0x4000000)
>        MSG("IO2BO");

22   in = malloc(size);
```

Listing 5: Code snippet of patched CVE-2011-1137 after instrumentation by IntTracker. Postcondition test is marked with '*'; guarding code is marked with '>'.

```
     uint32_t payload_len, payload_len_origin;
     payload_len_origin = payload_len;
4    payload_len = payload_len_origin - size;

*    if( payload_len_origin < size)
*        payload_len = 0xC0000000;

5+   if( payload_len < MAX_PAYLOAD_LEN)
     {
>        if (payload_len > 0x4000000)
>              MSG("IO2BO");

6        memcpy(..., ..., payload_len);
     }
```

relations between overflown values and some specific thresholds (see the examples in Listings 2 and 3). As we have discussed before, **Assumption 1** is well supported by real-world scenarios. Since normal values are in a small range, we argue that *the thresholds designed by developers are very likely smaller than our very large dirty values.* Hence we can argue that *PR3* is met in most practical cases. In the cases that it is not met, IntTracker generates false positives.

PR4. Table 4 shows the profiling results on *guard_object* of all MEM sites from SPEC CINT2000 programs. The meanings of the columns are similar to those in Table 3. From the table, we can observe that all $3.5E + 8$ integer values profiled are less than $0x4000000$ (i.e. 64M), disjoint from the Dirty-zone. Hence *PR4* is met. When an integer value from the Dirty-zone occurs at a MEM site, we argue that this value is definitely not a benign one and must be set as dirty earlier by IntTracker in the case of an overflow. Therefore, an IO2BO vulnerability is reported.

Examples. We apply IntTracker to the examples in Listings 1 and 2 so as to illustrate how IntTracker works in real-world scenarios.

Listing 4 shows the code snippet of CVE-2008-1722 after instrumentation by IntTracker. In benign cases when an image file with legitimate width and height is supplied, e.g., `img->xsize` as 800 and `img->ysize` as 600, instrumented code takes no action as there is no integer overflow at all. Hence, memory with expected size gets allocated at line 22. When a malicious image file with large width and height, e.g., `img->xsize` as 4 and `img->ysize` as $0x40000004$, is provided, an integer overflow occurs at line 13, with `bufsize` overflown to $0x10$, not the expected $0x100000010$. Postcondition test after line 13 catches this overflow and assigns $0xC0000000$ to `bufsize`. With this new assigned dirty value, the multiplication at line 21 would overflow again. In the same way, postcondition test after line 21 catches the overflow and assigns $0xC0000000$ to `size` as well. Hence, the *guard_object*, i.e. `size`, for `malloc()` at line 22 is dirty now. At last, the guarding code before line 22 detects the dirty value and reports an IO2BO vulnerability.

Listing 5 shows the code snippet of patched CVE-2011-1137 after instrumentation by IntTracker. The overflown variable `payload_len` has the value $0xC0000000$ after replacement by the postcondition test. However, the dirty value will be caught by the Santz-spec at line 5. As such, the patched code stops the propagation of the dirty value and a false positive for the anticipated IO2BO is avoided.

3. IMPLEMENTATION

We have implemented IntTracker for C/C++ programs based on GCC-4.5.0 [2]. IntTracker is composed of a potential overflow site selection analysis, a compile-time instrumentation transformation, and a run-time handler. The selection analysis works on the GIMPLE IR, utilizing static taint analysis to select all integer operations along critical paths and excluding some of them via checking whether Santz-postcond is present to guard possible overflows. The instrumentation transformation component is an optimization pass on GIMPLE, whose task includes 1) inserting postcondition tests for all the selected integer operations and 2) inserting guard code for all MEM sites to protect the *guard_object*'s. The run-time handler is linked to the compiler's output and takes actions when IO2BOs are detected. Totally, our tool is ~ 4K lines of C code.

Critical MEM sites: Just like Kint [38] and SIFT [23], IntTracker also requires the specification about the kinds of function calls that are considered as MEM sites. By default, IntTracker recognizes the standard library functions, including memory allocation routines (such as **`malloc`**, **`alloc`**, and **`realloc`**), memory or string copy routines (such as `memcpy`, `strncpy`), memory manipulation routines (such as `memset` and `memmove`), and C++ operators such as **`new[ ]`**. Besides, our tool can also be configured to recognize additional memory allocations or block copy routines (for example, `jas_realloc` in jasper).

4. EVALUATION

We have tested IntTracker on 3444 programs in the NIST's SAMATE Juliet test suite version 1.2, the SPEC CINT2000 benchmarks and 34 IO2BO bugs in the real world, for both effectiveness and efficiency. All experiments are run on an Intel Dual Core 2.4 GHz machine with 4 GB memory. The OS is Linux-3.5.0.

4.1 Effectiveness

We want to demonstrate the effectiveness of IntTracker in the following three aspects.

Table 5: Result on Juliet test suite

CWE	Total Programs	KLOC	ALL	IntTracker
CWE 190: Integer Overflow	1795	366.3	1795	-
CWE 191: Integer Underflow	1049	218.0	1049	-
CWE 680: Integer Overflow to Buffer Overflow	600	108.5	600	600

Table 6: 14 harmful IO2BO bugs in real-world

CVE	Programs	Version	IO_op	Ops_after	MEM
2005-0199#	Ngircd	0.8.1	$-_u$	$-$	strlcpy
2005-1141#	gocr	0.40	$*_s$		malloc
2006-4812#	php	5.1.3	$*_s$		memset
2008-1722	cups	1.3.0	$*_u$	$*$	malloc
2008-1801#	rdesktop	1.5.0	$-_u$		realloc
2008-3520	jasper	1.900.1	$*_s$	$*, *$	malloc
2008-3640	cups	1.3.8	$*_s$	$*$	calloc
2008-3732#	vlc	1.1.12*	$*_s$	$+, +$	malloc
2009-1882	ImageMagick	6.5.2-8	$*_s$		malloc
2010-1516	SWF Tools	0.9.1	$*_s$	$*, +$	malloc
2010-1519	glpng	1.4.5	$*_u$		malloc
2011-1092#	php	5.3.6*	$-_s$	$+$	memcpy
2011-4623	rsyslog	4.6.4	$+_u$	$+, *$	realloc
2014-0172	elfutils	0.153	$+_u$		malloc

4.1.1 *Effectiveness of Postcondition Test*

SAMATE [26] has a suite of test bench programs in C, C++ and Java to demonstrate common security problems and presents security errors in design, source code, binaries, etc. For C/C++ code, the SAMATE's Juliet test suite version 1.2, released on May 2013, provides 61,387 test programs for 118 different CWEs. The tests described in this paper were done on the Juliet test suite version 1.2.

Table 5 lists three CWEs that describe integer overflow vulnerabilities in the benchmark programs. We choose 3444 programs (about 692.8 KLOC) as our experimental subjects. Programs in CWE 190 and CWE 191 include a number of integer overflows or underflows. But since their critical use sites are not MEM sites, they are not IO2BOs. The 600 programs in CWE 680 have harmful IO2BO vulnerabilities, whose critical use site is either `malloc` or `new[ ]`.

Postcondition test is critical to IntTracker. Any false positives or negatives in catching integer overflows at runtime might degrade the performance of IntTracker. To evaluate the completeness of the postcondition tests in IntTracker, we have also implemented a version that inserts the same postcondition tests for all Arith_op's in programs. We name it *ALL*.

Each program in the SAMATE suite has a good function and a bad function. The good function demonstrates normal behavior and the bad function demonstrates a vulnerability. We ran ALL on all these programs, with both the good input (which invokes the normal behaviors) and the bad input (which causes overflows). For all the good inputs, ALL did not produce any overflow warning, while it identified all the overflows caused by the bad inputs, as shown in Column 4 of Table 5. Therefore, we can say that *our postcondition tests work well in catching integer overflows at runtime.*

4.1.2 *The Ability of Detecting Harmful IO2BOs*

In order to evaluate IntTracker in detecting harmful IO2BOs, we select 10 out of the 183 IO2BO bugs reported by CVE from 2008 to 2013 as we discussed in the previous sections. As not all of software we studied can be compiled properly in

Table 7: Result of false positive reduction.

harmful IO2BO	Patch code	IntTracker	IntPatch
CVE-2008-1489	Santz-spec	***FP***	***FP***
CVE-2009-2415	Santz-spec	bypass	
CVE-2010-2065			
CVE-2011-1137			
CVE-2011-2497			
CVE-2011-3607			
CVE-2012-2113-1			
All 13 others (*)	Santz-postcond	bypass	

(*) CVE-2008-1722, CVE-2008-2315, CVE-2009-1882, CVE-2009-2347, CVE-2009-2412, CVE-2011-2496, CVE-2011-3026, CVE-2012-2113-2, CVE-2012-2370, CVE-2012-2674, CVE-2012-2675-1, CVE-2012-2675-2, CVE-2012-3509

the current experimental environment, 10 compilable cases are selected here. This reflects the *randomness* in experimental subject selection to some extent. We further select 3 IO2BO bugs before 2008 and another one in 2014. Details about these 14 cases are shown in Table 6[5]. Columns 1-3 describe the CVE number, the vulnerable software and version. Columns 4-6 describe IO_op, Ops_after and MEM. *Our static selection analysis could select all IO_op's for each case.* For the 6 cases, whose CVE number is marked with '#', we further provided them with the corresponding overflow-inducing inputs[6], and all were caught *dynamically* by IntTracker.

In order to reduce any bias in CVE case selection, we also tested IntTracker on Juliet test suite. As shown in Column 5 of Table 5, *IntTracker detected all 600 harmful IO2BOs in CWE 680 dynamically.*

4.1.3 *The Ability of Bypassing Anticipated IO2BOs*

In this subsection, we compare IntTracker with IntPatch in bypassing anticipated IO2BOs, i.e. reducing the false positives. Since such overflows are anticipated and handled in the program already, reporting them undesirably increases the audit workload for the developers. Hence, it can be a key criterion to evaluate IO2BO detectors.

To this end, there is a need of a good set of applications containing various anticipated IO2BOs, with which false positive rate is measured and compared. However, there are no such standard applications to the best of our knowledge. In this paper, we collect the 20 IO2BO bugs[7] from our CVE study, that have been patched by the developers with sanitization routines, as our experiment subjects. As shown in Table 7, there are 7 cases with Santz-spec and 13 cases with Santz-postcond.

[5]Detailed information about these 14 CVE bugs can be referred at CVE website [24] via the corresponding CVE number. For CVE-2008-3732, the vulnerable version should be 1.1.11 and below. However, these versions of vlc cannot be compiled successfully under our experimental environment due to certain reason. Therefore, we choose 1.1.12 version instead and remove the patch manually. So it is with CVE-2011-1092.

[6]We only tested 6 bugs, as the overflow-inducing inputs are unavailable for most cases. The details of overflow-inducing inputs for these 6 cases can be found in the corresponding citation [3][4][5][6][7][8]

[7]CVE-2012-2113 entry includes two different IO2BO bugs, and we use CVE-2012-2113-1/2 to distinguish them. So it is with CVE-2012-2675.

Listing 6: Patched code for CVE-2008-1489.

```
  unsigned int i_len;
  MP4_GET4BYTES( i_len );
  i_len ++;

+ if( i_len > 0)
      buf = malloc (i_len );
+ else
+     error;
```

Listing 7: Pseudocode for CVE-2010-2170.

```
1 /* w and h are the dimension values of a JPEG
  object */
2 int tmp1 = w * 4;
3 int size = tmp1 * h;
4 if(tmp1 < 0 || h < 0 || size < h || size <
  tmp1)
5     goto _err;
6 ptr = malloc(size);
```

To evaluate the false positive rate on these patched cases, we face the challenge that the corresponding overflow-inducing inputs are not available. We turn to extract the patched overflow sites and their propagation paths from the subject programs, and then execute the extracts with the self-designed overflow-inducing inputs. From Table 7 we can find that *IntTracker produced false positive only for 1 out of the 20 patched CVE cases.* Specifically, IntTracker identifies all the 13 cases patched with Santz-postcond and the corresponding anticipated IO2BOs are hence bypassed. For the 7 cases patched with Santz-spec, IntTracker avoids 6 of them. The only false positive is for the patched CVE-2008-1489 [27].

Listing 6 illustrates how the patch for CVE-2008-1489 works. Variable `i_len` is of the unsigned integer type and its value originates from `MP4_GET4BYTES()`. It is then incremented by one before used at the memory allocation site. If `i_len` is assigned the maximum value that the unsigned integer type can represent, i.e. $0xffffffff$, it would overflow to zero and hence no memory is allocated. The developers patched this buggy code via checking whether `i_len` equals to zero (those lines marked by '+') after the addition. Since IntTracker replaces the overflown value with a very large dirty value which is not equal to zero, a false warning is issued.

In contrast, IntPatch reports all the 20 anticipated IO2BOs, as IntPatch reports vulnerabilities once catching any integer overflow. It does not track whether the overflown value may flow to a memory sink or not. Therefore, *IntTracker can reduce 95% (=19/20) of the false positives produced by IntPatch for anticipated IO2BOs.*

Besides, IntTracker can still provide protection even if sanitization routines are incomplete or not sound. Consider the patched code for CVE-2008-1722 in Listing 1 again. As discussed in IntPatch, such sanitization routine inserted by developers is incomplete as they omit the possibility of integer overflow at line 21. For example, let `img->xsize` = 2 and `img->ysize` = $0x60000000$. Although the multiplication at line 13 does not overflow, the succeeding multiplication at line 21 overflows. Unfortunately, this overflow cannot be caught by the patch. Interestingly, such incomplete patch is complemented by IntTracker, as IntTracker selects the potentially problematic multiplication at line 21 and inserts overflow check after it.

Another example is CVE-2010-2170 [29] in Adobe Flash Player, as discussed in SoupInt [36]. Listing 7 shows the corresponding pseudocode. `size < h || size < tmp1` is used as Santz-spec to catch the integer overflow introduced by `size = tmp1 * h`. However, such validation check is unsound. For example, let `tmp1` = $0x84444$ and `h` = $0x4000$. `size` overflows to $0x11110000$, which could bypass the check at line 4, invalidating the Santz-spec. Interestingly, such unsound check is complemented by IntTracker, as the overflown value of `size` is always replaced with our initial dirty value, i.e. $0xC0000000$, and such dirty value is negative under *int* type, which can be caught by the check at line 4.

Table 8: Check density. #I: number of GIMPLE instructions in the original program. #II: number of Arith_op. #S: number of selected Arith_op. #E: number of excluded Arith_op. Ratio=(#S-#E)/#II. #G: number of guarded memory sinks.

	#I	#II	#II/#I	#S	#E	Ratio	#G
164.gzip	6514	799	12.27%	8	0	1.00%	18
175.vpr	20242	1140	5.63%	144	0	12.6%	7
176.gcc	188134	7345	3.90%	276	0	3.76%	273
181.mcf	1533	141	9.20%	2	0	1.42%	2
186.crafy	23478	2202	9.38%	22	0	1.00%	20
197.parser	11124	735	6.61%	38	0	5.17%	4
253.perlbmk	89599	3080	3.44%	234	0	7.60%	72
254.gap	99966	8388	8.39%	2	0	0.02%	2
255.vortex	56796	1333	2.35%	21	0	1.58%	16
256.bzip2	4208	572	13.59%	12	0	2.10%	16
300.twolf	44455	2891	6.50%	225	0	7.78%	2
Average			**7.39%**			**4.01%**	

4.2 Performance

We have applied IntTracker to SPEC CINT2000 programs and executed the instrumented programs with their '*ref*' input sets to test the overhead imposed by IntTracker. We first measure how many checks our tool inserts and then compute its performance overhead.

4.2.1 Check Density

Table 8 shows the percentage of instructions that we instrument. The results show that on average about 7.39% of all GIMPLE instructions are integer arithmetic operations, and IntTracker selects 4.01% of them as potential IO2BO sites. As Column 6 shows, IntTracker excludes none of the selected integer operations, meaning that there is no Santz-postcond along their critical paths. Besides, if we apply our Santz-postcond identification process on all integer arithmetic operations rather than those on critical paths, IntTracker can identify totally 98 sites.

Our checking ratio 4.01% is lower than that of IntPatch, averaging about 10%. One reason might be the test suites used. IntPatch used image-related applications, which may need to allocate a lot of memory. However, we are using SPEC CINT2000 benchmarks.

4.2.2 Runtime Overhead

Figure 3 shows the runtime overhead of IntTracker. We ran each benchmark 10 times. On average, the instrument-

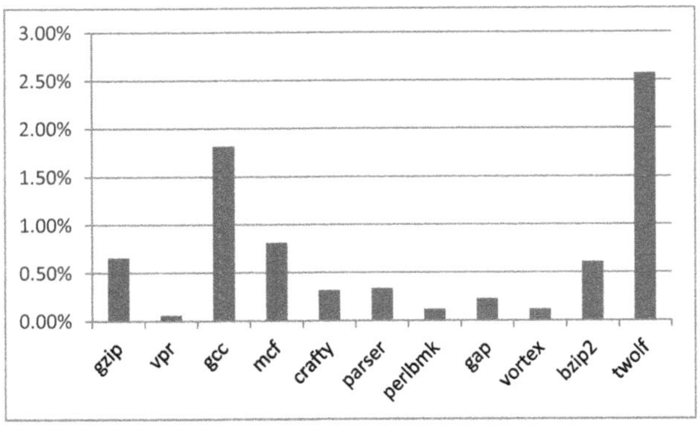

Figure 3: Overhead on SPEC CINT2000

ed programs are 0.69% slower than the original benchmarks, which is acceptable. Such performance loss is lower than that of IntPatch, i.e. 1%. As discussed in Section 1, traditional dynamic information flow tracking [32][10] and taint analysis [20][40] often slows down program execution by a constant factor. Hence our technique is efficient enough from this perspective.

5. LIMITATIONS

We propose to address the IO2BO vulnerability detection problem in a way different from traditional techniques. We use very large and rarely used integer values to replace overflown values, and use them as the indicator of overflow. We leverage the Dirty-zone to guarantee the natural propagation and sanitization of overflows. IO2BO vulnerabilities are reported when dirty values are used at memory sinks. However, as an initial step along this direction, our technique has a number of limitations.

First of all, the dynamic protection of IntTracker has only approximate guarantee, as shown in Section 2.3.3. Although IntTracker works correctly with a very high probability (higher than 99.99%), counter-examples are still possible. *Second*, as described in Figure 1 only addition, subtraction, multiplication and left-shift operations are considered as potentially present along critical paths. However in real-world scenarios, there might exist cases where divisions are also present. Divisions on overflow paths would make it very difficult for IntTracker to guarantee *PR2*, i.e. a division operation *Result=Dirty/Delta* may transform a dirty value to a small normal value if *Delta* is large enough. In our study on CVE bugs, only 4 out of the 183 cases have divisions appearing along overflow paths and the *Delta* in all 4 cases are small values (e.g., 3, 4 and 8). Hence IntTracker would work correctly for these divisions. *Third*, currently we only applied IntTracker to known CVE IO2BO bugs, as mentioned in Sections 4.1.2 and 4.1.3. As a dynamic IO2BO detector, test cases of high code coverage and overflow-inducing inputs need be provided to IntTracker in order to detect unknown harmful IO2BOs at runtime. We are working on addressing these problems.

6. RELATED WORK

Many efforts have been made on IO2BO vulnerabilities. Followings are some representative work.

Integer-based vulnerability detection: Following the notions in RICH [12], integer-based vulnerabilities consist of integer overflows, integer underflows, signedness errors and width truncations. There are a plethora of work on detecting integer-based vulnerabilities or protecting programs from them, which also contribute a lot to the detection on IO2BOs indirectly.

Many work, such as [16][34][13], employ finite state machine, constraint graph or type qualifier to detect integer anomaly in programs. The main drawback of these static techniques is the false positives due to the inaccuracy of range analysis. SmartFuzz [25] utilizes symbolic execution to generate test cases to invoke integer errors. The key challenges are to generate test cases of high code coverage and to deal with path explosion problem when applied to large scale software.

Safe library functions are used to wrap integer operations by adding check code, such as SafeInt [22], IntegerLib [14][17], and Ranged Integer [21]. Such source code transform techniques are easy to be deployed and transparent to developers. For instance, SafeInt exploits C++'s exceptions and operator overloading. However, they may also introduce new integer bugs into program at the same time. For example, IOC [19] found about 20 integer overflow bugs in IntegerLib.

A classic approach to detecting integer bugs is to insert checks and to provide runtime protections, such as RICH [12], IOC [19], AIR [18], RA [33] and BRICK [15]. RICH provides formal specifications for integer semantics in C, and applies sub-type theory from type safe languages into C language. Therefore, integer operations in C language could obtain type safe features through complying type-rule violations for integer arithmetic operations and castings. Diet et al. [19] implements IOC in the similar way, and they further conduct a study about the occurrences of overflows in real-world programs from a software engineering point-of-view. RA presents a more precise range analysis and exploits it to eliminate unnecessary checks in case where integer operations cannot overflow. Experiments show that RA could avoid 25% checks and reduce the runtime overhead by 50%. BRICK uses modified virtual machine to detect integer overflow in binaries. For lack of C-level type information in executable code, BRICK produces many false positives. Another drawback is the performance due to code emulation. BRICK has a 50x slowdown.

IO2BO vulnerability detection: IntScope [37], Kint [38] and SIFT [23] are static techniques to handle IO2BO vulnerabilities. IntScope and Kint both exploit symbolic execution to generate test cases to trigger IO2BOs. The difference lies in that IntScope works on binaries while Kint works for large-scale system software. In order to gain a scalable performance, Kint requires developers providing annotations for key functions and parameters to conduct a precise global range analysis. In contrast, SIFT's goal is to generate filters that can preclude inputs which may trigger IO2BOs. The main drawback for static techniques is that they may produce false positives due to the limited precision of aliasing analysis and limited loop unrolling.

IntPatch [41] is the state-of-the-art dynamic technique to detect IO2BO vulnerabilities. At first, it exploits a static taint-like analysis to extract critical paths from user inputs to memory allocation points and then inserts overflow checks for all integer operations along the paths. IntPatch has a negligible runtime overhead (averaging about 1%). However, IntPatch would produce false positives if sanitization routines are added by developers, whereas our tool IntTracker will bypass most of them (as discussed in Section 4.1.3).

SoupInt [36] is an offline system that can automatically generate emergency patches from attacks against integer overflow vulnerabilities. SoupInt takes a vulnerable program and an attack instance as inputs, and then diagnoses whether this attack is specially exploiting integer overflows through a dynamic data flow analysis. If so, SoupInt generates patches and deploys them by enhancing existing input validation checks inside the program. Currently SoupInt is implemented to diagnose and patch IO2BO exploits.

7. CONCLUSIONS

We develop an efficient dynamic tracking technique to detect harmful IO2BO vulnerabilities and bypass un-harmful ones. Different from traditional approaches, which give warnings once integer overflows are caught, our technique replaces overflown values with very large and rarely used integer values and use the concrete values of the overflown variables as the indicator of integer overflow. This provides an efficient tracking, propagation and sanitization mechanism of overflows. A prototype is implemented as an extension of GCC. Experiments show that our tool is effective and efficient in detecting harmful IO2BO vulnerabilities, and outperforms the state-of-the-art, IntPatch, in bypassing anticipated IO2BOs.

In our future work, we aim to extend IntTracker to handle other cases of integer overflows and integer signedness errors caused by type conversions.

8. ACKNOWLEDGMENTS

The authors would like to thank the anonymous reviewers for their insightful comments that greatly helped improve the presentation of this paper. The authors are also grateful to Tao Bao for useful discussions. This work has been partly supported by National NSF of China under Grant No. 61170070, 61431008, 61321491; National Key Technology R&D Program of China under Grant No. 2012BAK26B01 and National High Technology Research and Development Program of China under Grant No.2011AA1A202.

9. REFERENCES

[1] CWE-680: Io2bo vulnerabilities. http://cwe.mitre.org/data/definitions/680.html.

[2] GCC, the GNU Compiler Collection. https://gcc.gnu.org/.

[3] Overflow-inducing input for CVE-2005-0199. https://bugs.gentoo.org/show_bug.cgi?id=79705.

[4] Overflow-inducing input for CVE-2005-1141. http://www.overflow.pl/adv/gocr.txt.

[5] Overflow-inducing input for CVE-2006-4812. http://www.exploit-db.com/exploits/28760/.

[6] Overflow-inducing input for CVE-2008-1801. http://www.securityfocus.com/bid/29097/exploit.

[7] Overflow-inducing input for CVE-2008-3732. http://www.exploit-db.com/exploits/6252/.

[8] Overflow-inducing input for CVE-2011-1092. http://www.exploit-db.com/exploits/16966/.

[9] Spec 2000 benchmarks. http://www.spec.org/cpu2000/.

[10] P. Akritidis, C. Cadar, C. Raiciu, M. Costa, and M. Castro. Preventing memory error exploits with wit. In *IEEE Symposium on Security and Privacy'08*, pages 263–277, 2008.

[11] M. D. Bond and K. S. McKinley. Probabilistic calling context. In *OOPSLA*, pages 97–112, 2007.

[12] D. Brumley, D. X. Song, T. cker Chiueh, R. Johnson, and H. Lin. Rich: Automatically protecting against integer-based vulnerabilities. In *NDSS'07*, 2007.

[13] E. N. Ceesay, J. Zhou, M. Gertz, K. N. Levitt, and M. Bishop. Using type qualifiers to analyze untrusted integers and detecting security flaws in c programs. In *DIMVA'06*, pages 1–16, 2006.

[14] CERT. Integerlib, a secure integer library, 2006. http://www.cert.org/secure-coding/IntegerLib.zip.

[15] P. Chen, Y. Wang, Z. Xin, B. Mao, and L. Xie. Brick: A binary tool for run-time detecting and locating integer-based vulnerability. In *ARES'09*, pages 208–215, 2009.

[16] S. Chen, Z. Kalbarczyk, J. Xu, and R. K. Iyer. A data-driven finite state machine model for analyzing security vulnerabilities. In *DSN'03*, pages 605–614, 2003.

[17] Z. Coker and M. Hafiz. Program transformations to fix c integers. In *ICSE'13*, pages 792–801, 2013.

[18] R. B. Dannenberg, W. Dormann, D. Keaton, R. C. Seacord, D. Svoboda, A. Volkovitsky, T. Wilson, and T. Plum. As-if infinitely ranged integer model. In *ISSRE'10*, pages 91–100, 2010.

[19] W. Dietz, P. Li, J. Regehr, and V. S. Adve. Understanding integer overflow in c/c++. In *ICSE'12*, pages 760–770, 2012.

[20] W. Enck, P. Gilbert, B. gon Chun, L. P. Cox, J. Jung, P. McDaniel, and A. Sheth. Taintdroid: An information-flow tracking system for realtime privacy monitoring on smartphones. In *OSDI'10*, pages 393–407, 2010.

[21] J. Gennari, S. Hedrick, F. Long, J. Pincar, and R. C. Seacord. Ranged integers for the c programming language. Technical Note CMU/SEI-2007-TN-027, Carnegie Mellon University, 2007.

[22] D. LeBlanc. Safeint. http://safeint.codeplex.com/.

[23] F. Long, S. Sidiroglou-Douskos, D. Kim, and M. C. Rinard. Sound input filter generation for integer overflow errors. In *POPL'14*, pages 439–452, 2014.

[24] MITRE Corporation. Common vulnerabilities and exposures. http://cve.mitre.org/.

[25] D. Molnar, X. C. Li, and D. Wagner. Dynamic test generation to find integer bugs in x86 binary linux programs. In *USENIX Security Symposium'09*, pages 67–82, 2009.

[26] National Institute of Standard and Technology (NIST). SAMATE-software assurance metrics and tool evaluation. http://samate.nist.gov/SARD/testsuite.php.

[27] National Vulnerability Database. CVE-2008-1489. http://web.nvd.nist.gov/view/vuln/detail?vulnId=CVE-2008-1489.

[28] National Vulnerability Database. CVE-2008-1722. http://web.nvd.nist.gov/view/vuln/detail?vulnId=CVE-2008-1722.

[29] National Vulnerability Database. CVE-2010-2170. http://web.nvd.nist.gov/view/vuln/detail?vulnId=CVE-2010-2170.

[30] National Vulnerability Database. CVE-2010-2500. http://web.nvd.nist.gov/view/vuln/detail?vulnId=CVE-2010-2065.

[31] National Vulnerability Database. CVE-2011-1137. http://web.nvd.nist.gov/view/vuln/detail?vulnId=CVE-2011-1137.

[32] F. Qin, C. Wang, Z. Li, H.-S. Kim, Y. Zhou, and Y. Wu. Lift: A low-overhead practical information flow tracking system for detecting security attacks. In *MICRO'06*, pages 135–148, 2006.

[33] R. E. Rodrigues, V. H. S. Campos, and F. M. Q. Pereira. A fast and low-overhead technique to secure programs against integer overflows. In *CGO'13*, pages 1–11, 2013.

[34] D. Sarkar, M. Jagannathan, J. Thiagarajan, and R. Venkatapathy. Flow-insensitive static analysis for detecting integer anomalies in programs. In *IASTED*, 2007.

[35] E. Tang, E. T. Barr, X. Li, and Z. Su. Perturbing numerical calculations for statistical analysis of floating-point program (in)stability. In *ISSTA*, pages 131–142, 2010.

[36] T. Wang, C. Song, and W. Lee. Diagnose and emergency patch generation for integer overflow exploits. In *DIMVA'14*, pages 255–275, 2014.

[37] T. Wang, T. Wei, Z. Lin, and W. Zou. Intscope: Automatically detecting integer overflow vulnerability in x86 binary using symbolic execution. In *NDSS'09*, 2009.

[38] X. Wang, H. Chen, Z. Jia, N. Zeldovich, and M. F. Kaashoek. Improving integer security for systems with kint. In *OSDI'12*, pages 163–177, 2012.

[39] Wikipedia. Law of total probability, 2014. http://en.wikipedia.org/wiki/Law_of_total_probability.

[40] W. Xu, S. Bhatkar, and R. Sekar. Taint-enhance policy enforcement: a practical approach to defeat a wide range of attacks. In *USENIX Security Symposium*, 2006.

[41] C. Zhang, T. Wang, T. Wei, Y. Chen, and W. Zou. Intpatch: Automatically fix integer-overflow-to-buffer-overflow vulnerability at compile-time. In *ESORICS'10*, pages 71–86, 2010.

Anonymizing Social Graphs via Uncertainty Semantics

Hiep H. Nguyen
LORIA/INRIA Nancy
France
huu-hiep.nguyen@inria.fr

Abdessamad Imine
LORIA/INRIA Nancy
France
abdessamad.imine@loria.fr

Michaël Rusinowitch
LORIA/INRIA Nancy
France
michael.rusinowitch@inria.fr

ABSTRACT

Rather than anonymizing social graphs by generalizing them to super nodes/edges or adding/removing nodes and edges to satisfy given privacy parameters, recent methods exploit the semantics of uncertain graphs to achieve privacy protection of participating entities and their relationships. These techniques anonymize a deterministic graph by converting it into an uncertain form. In this paper, we propose a general obfuscation model based on uncertain adjacency matrices that keep expected node degrees equal to those in the unanonymized graph. We analyze two recently proposed schemes and their fitting into the model. We also point out disadvantages in each method and present several elegant techniques to fill the gap between them. Finally, to support fair comparisons, we develop a new tradeoff quantifying framework by leveraging the concept of incorrectness. Experiments on large social graphs demonstrate the effectiveness of our schemes.

Categories and Subject Descriptors

H.2.7 [**Database Management**]: Database Administration—*Security, integrity, and protection*

General Terms

Algorithm, Experimentation

Keywords

Uncertain graph; Uncertain adjacency matrix; Maximizing variance

1. INTRODUCTION

Graphs represent a rich class of data observed in daily life where entities are described by vertices and their connections are characterized by edges. With the emergence of increasingly complex networks [15], the research community requires large and reliable graph data to conduct in-depth studies. However, this requirement usually conflicts with privacy rights of data contributing entities. Naive approaches like removing user ids from a social graph are not effective, leaving users open to privacy risks, especially re-identification attacks [1] [10]. Therefore, many graph anonymization schemes have been proposed [27, 12, 28, 4, 24, 21].

Given an unlabeled undirected graph, the existing anonymization methods fall into five main categories. The first category includes *random* addition, deletion and switching of edges to prevent the re-identification of nodes or edges. The methods in the second category provide k-anonymity [20] by *deterministic* edge additions or deletions, assuming attacker's background knowledge regarding certain properties of its target nodes. The third class of techniques, *generalization*, cluster nodes into super nodes of size at least k. The methods in the fourth category assign edge probabilities to add uncertainty to the true graph. The edges probabilities may be computed explicitly as in [2] or implicitly via random walks [14]. Finally, several schemes for private graph data release [23, 25] are based on differential privacy [7]. Note that the third and fourth categories induce *possible world* semantics, i.e., we can retrieve sample graphs that are consistent with the anonymized output graph.

The fourth category is a recent class of methods which leverage the semantics of edge probability to inject uncertainty to a given deterministic graph, converting it into an uncertain one. Most of the schemes in this category are scalable, i.e. runnable on million-scale graphs or more. As an example, Boldi et al. [2] introduced the concept of *(k,ϵ)-obfuscation* (denoted as (k, ϵ)-obf), where $k \geq 1$ is a desired level of obfuscation and $\epsilon \geq 0$ is a tolerance parameter. However, the pursuit for minimum standard deviation σ in (k,ϵ)-obf has high impact on node privacy and high privacy-utility tradeoff. Edge rewiring method based on random walks (denoted as *RandWalk*) in [14] also introduces uncertainty to edges as we show in section 4. This scheme suffers from high lower bounds for utility error despite its excellent privacy-utility tradeoff.

Motivated by *(k,ϵ)-obf* and *RandWalk*, we propose in this work a general model for anonymizing graphs based on edge uncertainty. Both (k,ϵ)-obf and RandWalk are captured by the model. We point out disadvantages in (k,ϵ)-obf and RandWalk, the tradeoff gap between them and present several elegant techniques to fill this gap.

Our contributions are summarized as follows:

- We propose a general model called *uncertain adjacency matrix* (UAM) for anonymizing graphs via edge uncer-

ASIA CCS'15, April 14–17, 2015, Singapore..

http://dx.doi.org/10.1145/2714576.2714584.

tainty semantics (Section 3). The key property of this model is that expected degrees of all nodes must be unchanged.

- We show how *(k,ε)-obf* and *RandWalk* fit into UAM and analyze their disadvantages (Section 4). Then we describe *Mixture* as a simple mitigation.

- We introduce the *Variance Maximizing* (MaxVar) scheme (Section 5) that satisfies all the properties of UAM. It achieves good privacy-utility tradeoff by using two key observations: nearby potential edges and maximization of total node degree variance via a simple quadratic program. Another advantage of MaxVar is its full applicability to directed graphs.

- We conduct a comparative study of aforementioned approaches in a empirical privacy-utility framework by putting forward the distortion measure (Section 6). We show the effectiveness of our gap-filling solutions (Section 7) on three real large graphs.

Table 1 summarizes notations used in this paper.

Table 1: List of notations

Symbol	Definition
$G_0 = (V, E_{G_0})$	true graph with $n = \|V\|$ and $m = \|E_{G_0}\|$
$\mathcal{G} = (V, E, p)$	uncertain graph constructed from G_0
$G = (V, E_G)$	sample graph from $\mathcal{G}$, $G \sqsubseteq \mathcal{G}$
$d_u(G), d_u(\mathcal{G})$	degree of node u in $G, \mathcal{G}$
$\Delta(d)$	number of nodes having degree d in G
$\mathcal{N}(u)$	neighbors of node u in $\mathcal{G}$
R_σ	truncated normal distribution on [0,1]
σ	standard deviation of the normal distribution
$r_e \leftarrow R_\sigma$	a sample from the distribution R_σ
p_i (p_{uv})	probability of edge e_i (e_{uv})
n_p	number of potential edges, $\|E\| = m + n_p$
A, $\mathcal{A}$, $A(G)$	adjacency matrices of G_0, $\mathcal{G}$ and G
P_{RW}	random walk transition matrix of G_0
$B^{(t)}$	uncertain adjacency matrix, $B^{(t)} = AP_{RW}^{t-1}$
t	walk length
S	switching matrix
TV	total degree variance
d_u^-, d_u^+	in/out-degree of node u in directed graphs
$\mathcal{N}^-(u)$,$\mathcal{N}^+(u)$	predecessors/successors of node u in directed $\mathcal{G}$

2. RELATED WORK

There is a vast literature on graph perturbation that deserves a survey. In this section, we enumerate only several groups of ideas that are related to our proposed schemes.

Anonymizing unlabeled vertices for node privacy. In unlabeled graphs, node identifiers are numbered in an arbitrary manner after removing their labels. An attacker aims at reidentifying nodes solely based on their structural information. For this line of graphs, node privacy protection implies link privacy. Techniques of adding and removing edges, nodes can be done randomly or deterministically. Random perturbation is a naive approach and usually used as a baseline method. More guided approaches consist of *k-neighborhood*[27], *k-degree*[12], *k-automorphism*[28], *k-symmetry*[24], *k-isomorphism*[4] and k^2*-degree*[21]. These schemes provide k-anonymity [20] semantics and usually rely on heuristics to avoid combinatorial intractability. K-automorphism, k-symmetry, and k-isomorphism can resist *any* structural attacks by exploiting the inherent symmetry in graph. k^2-degree addresses the friendship attacks, based on the vertex degree pair of an edge. Ying and Wu [26] propose a spectrum preserving approach which wisely chooses edge pairs to switch in order to keep the spectrum of the adjacency matrix from varying too much. The clearest disadvantage of the above schemes is that they are inefficient on large scale graphs.

Apart from the two above categories, perturbation techniques have other categories that settle on *possible world* semantics. Hay et al. [10] generalize a network by clustering nodes and publish graph summarization of super nodes and super edges. The utility of this scheme is limited. On the other hand, Boldi et al. [2] take the uncertain graph approach. With edge probabilities, the output graph can be used to generate sample graphs by independent edge sampling. Our approach belongs to this class of techniques with different formulation and better privacy-utility tradeoff. Note that in *k-symmetry*[4], the output sample graphs are also possible worlds of the symmetric intermediate graph.

Anonymizing labeled vertices for link privacy. If nodes are labeled, we are only concerned about the link disclosure risk. For example, Mittal et al. [14] employ an edge rewiring method based on random walks to keep the mixing time tunable and prevent link re-identification by Bayesian inference. This method is effective for social network based systems, e.g. Sybil defense, DHT routing. Link privacy is also described in [26] for Random Switch, Random Add/Del. Interestingly, *RandWalk* [14] can also be used for unlabeled graphs as shown in Section 4.

Differential privacy and generative graph models. Differential privacy [7] hides the participation of an item in a dataset. It is applied not only to tabular data but also to graph data, e.g. [23, 25]. The common paradigm is three-phase as follows. First, certain statistics or model are extracted from the original graph. Then, some noise is added to the true statistics/model to guarantee differential privacy. Finally, the noisy statistics/model is used to generate sample anonymized graphs.

Min entropy, Shannon entropy and incorrectness measure. We now survey commonly used notions of privacy metrics. *Min entropy* [19] quantifies the largest probability gap between the posterior and prior over all items in the input dataset. *K-anonymity* has the same semantics with the corresponding min entropy of $\log_2 k$. So we say k-anonymity based perturbation schemes belong to min entropy. Shannon entropy argued in [3] and [2] is another choice of privacy metrics. The third metrics that we use in this paper is the *incorrectness* measure. Given the prior information (e.g. node degree in the true graph) and the posterior information harvested from the anonymized output, incorrectness measure is the number of incorrect guesses made by the attacker. This measure gauges the *distortion* caused by the anonymization algorithm. An empirical comparison of early privacy model like k-anonymity and the emerging differential privacy is given in [5].

3. A GENERAL MODEL

This section starts with definitions and common assumptions on uncertain graphs. It then introduces a general model UAM via semantics of edge uncertainty.

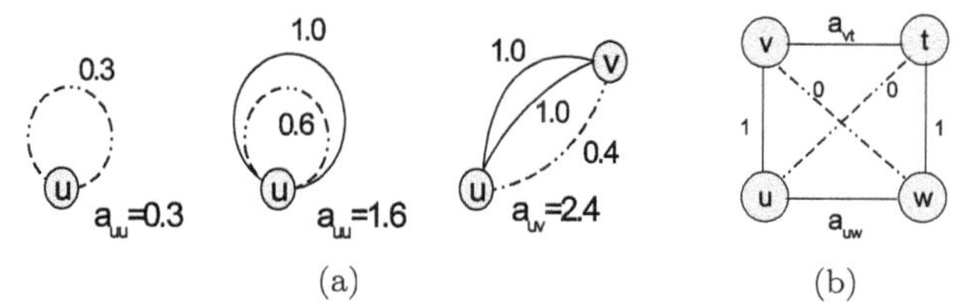

Figure 1: (a) Semantics of selfloops (left), multi-selfloops (middle) and multiedges (right) in uncertain adjacency matrix (b) Edge switching

3.1 Uncertain Graph

Let $\mathcal{G} = (V, E, p)$ be an uncertain undirected graph, where V is the set of nodes, E is the set of edges, $p : E \to (0, 1]$ is the function that gives an existence probability to each edge (see Fig.2b). The common assumption is on the *independence* of edge probabilities. Following the *possible-worlds* semantics in relational data [6], the uncertain graph $\mathcal{G}$ induces a set $\{G = (V, E_G)\}$ of $2^{|E|}$ deterministic graphs (worlds), each is defined by a subset of E. The probability of $G = (V, E_G) \sqsubseteq \mathcal{G}$ is:

$$Pr(G) = \prod_{e \in E_G} p(e) \prod_{e \in E \setminus E_G} (1 - p(e)) \qquad (1)$$

As an example, the uncertain graph in Fig.2b has 2^5 possible graphs and the graph with three edges $(v1, v2), (v2, v3)(v3, v4)$ has probability of $P(G) = 0.3 \times 0.7 \times 0.4 \times (1 - 0.8) \times (1 - 0.9) = 0.00168$. Note that deterministic graphs are also uncertain graphs with all existing edges having probabilities 1.

3.2 Uncertain Adjacency Matrix (UAM)

Given the true undirected graph G_0, an uncertain graph $\mathcal{G}$ constructed from G_0 must have its uncertain adjacency matrix $\mathcal{A}$ satisfying

1. $\mathcal{A}_{ij} = \mathcal{A}_{ji}$ (symmetry);
2. $\mathcal{A}_{ij} \in [0, 1]$ and $\mathcal{A}_{ii} = 0$ (no multiedges or selfloops);
3. $\sum_{j=1}^{n} \mathcal{A}_{ij} = d_i(G_0) \quad i = 1..n$, (*expected degrees* of all nodes must be unchanged).

While the constraints (1) and (2) are straightforward for uncertain undirected graph, the third constraint is novel and central to our model of UAM. It stems from the need of preserving the degree sequence of graph which is useful for degree distribution estimation, e.g. in [9]. In terms of *dK-series*[13], the degree sequence is *d1-series*, the first moment of graph. The higher moments like *d2-series* are left for future work.

By relaxing (2) to (2'): $\mathcal{A}_{ii} \geq 0$ and $\mathcal{A}_{ij} \geq 0$, we allow graphs with *selfloop*s and *multiedge*s (Fig. 1a).

4. APPLICATION OF UAM

In this section, we analyze several existing and novel schemes using the model of UAM.

4.1 RandWalk Scheme

4.1.1 Preliminary Results

We first define the transition matrix P_{RW} which is right *stochastic* (i.e. non-negative and row sums equal to 1) as follows (note that we use the short notation $d_i = d_i(G_0)$)

$$P_{RW}(i, j) = \begin{cases} 1/d_i & \text{if } (i, j) \in E_{G_0} \ i \neq j \\ 0 & \text{otherwise.} \end{cases} \qquad (2)$$

The power P^t_{RW} when $t \to \infty$ is $P^{\infty}_{RW}(i, j) = \frac{d_j}{2m}$.

We prove two lemmas on properties of the products $\mathcal{A}P$ and AP^t where P is right stochastic.

LEMMA 4.1. *For an adjacency matrix $\mathcal{A}$ and a right stochastic matrix P, the product $\mathcal{A}P$ is non-negative and has row sums equal to those of $\mathcal{A}$.*

PROOF. The non-negativity of $\mathcal{A}P$ is trivial. The sum of row i of $\mathcal{A}P$ is $\sum_j (\sum_k \mathcal{A}_{ik} P_{kj}) = \sum_k \mathcal{A}_{ik} (\sum_j P_{kj}) = \sum_k \mathcal{A}_{ik}.1 = \sum_k \mathcal{A}_{ik}$ □

LEMMA 4.2. *For a deterministic graph G possessing adjacency matrix A and P_{RW}, the product $B^{(t)} = AP^{t-1}_{RW}$ is also symmetric.*

PROOF. We prove the result by induction. The case $t = 1$ is trivial. We prove that for any $t \geq 2$, $B^{(t)}_{ij} = \sum_{p_t(i,j)} \prod_{k \in p_t(i,j), k \neq i,j} 1/d_k$ where $p_t(i, j)$ is a path of length t from i to j.

When $t = 2$, $B^{(2)}_{ij} = \sum_k A_{ik} P_{kj} = \sum_{(i,k),(k,j) \in E} 1/d_k$, so the result holds. Assuming that the result is correct up to $t-1$, i.e. $B^{(t-1)}_{ij} = \sum_{p_{t-1}(i,j)} \prod_{k \in p_{t-1}(i,j), k \neq i,j} 1/d_k$. Because $B^{(t)} = B^{(t-1)} P_{RW}$, we have $B^{(t)}_{ij} = \sum_l B^{(t-1)}_{il} P_{lj} = \sum_{l,(l,j) \in E} (\sum_{p_{t-1}(i,l)} \prod_{k \in p_{t-1}(i,l), k \neq i,l} 1/d_k) 1/d_l = \sum_{p_t(i,j)} \prod_{k \in p_t(i,j), k \neq i,j} 1/d_k$.

Because G is undirected, the set of all $p_t(i, j)$ is equal to the set of all $p_t(j, i)$, so $B^{(t)}_{ij} = B^{(t)}_{ji}$. □

We prove the uniqueness of P_{RW} as follows

PROPOSITION 4.3. *Given a deterministic graph G with adjacency matrix A, there exists one and only one right stochastic matrix P that satisfies $P_{uv} = 0$ for all $(u, v) \notin G$ and AP^t is symmetric for all $t \geq 0$. The unique solution is $P = P_{RW}$.*

PROOF. See Appendix A.1. □

4.1.2 Analysis

Now we show how *RandWalk* [14] fit into the model of UAM. We should mention that RandWalk is proposed only for *link privacy* analysis in [14] whereas the current work is on *node privacy.* Algorithm 1 depicts the steps of RandWalk. As we show below, the trial-and-error condition in Line 6 makes RandWalk hard to analyze [1]. So we modify it by removing the condition and using parameter α instead of 1.0 in Line 12 [2] (see Algorithm 2). When $\alpha = 0.5$, all edges (u, z) are assigned with probability 0.5. In *RandWalk-mod*, we add a check for $d_u = 1$ (Line 8) to keep the total degree of G' equal to that of G, which is missing in RandWalk. Note that RandWalk-mod accepts selfloops and multiedges (i.e. it satisfies the relaxed constraint (2'), not (2)).

[1]It also causes edge miss at $t = 2$, e.g. a 2-length walk on edge $(v3, v2)$ (Fig. 2a) causes the selfloop $(v3, v3)$.

[2]This line causes errors for degree-1 nodes as shown in *RandWalk-mod*.

```
Algorithm 1 RandWalk(G_0, t, M) [14]
Input: undirected graph G_0, walk length t and maximum loop
    count M
Output: anonymized graph G'
G' = null
for u in G_0 do
    count = 1
    for v in N(u) do
        loop = 1
        while (u == z ∨ (u, z) ∈ G') ∧ (loop ≤ M) do
            perform t − 1 hop random walk from v
            z is the terminal node of the random walk
            loop++
        if loop ≤ M then
            if count == 1 then
                add (u, z) to G' with probability 1.0
            else
                add (u, z) to G' with probability (0.5d_u − 1)/(d_u − 1)
        count++
return G'
```

```
Algorithm 2 RandWalk-mod(G_0, t, α)
Input: undirected graph G_0, walk length t and probability α
Output: anonymized graph G'
 1: G' = null
 2: for u in G_0 do
 3:     count = 1
 4:     for v in N(u) do
 5:         perform t − 1 hop random walk from v
 6:         z is the terminal node of the random walk
 7:         if count == 1 then
 8:             if d_u == 1 then
 9:                 add (u, z) to G' with probability 0.5
10:             else
11:                 add (u, z) to G' with probability α
12:         else
13:             add (u, z) to G' with probability (0.5d_u − α)/(d_u − 1)
14:         count++
    return G'
```

Let Q be the *edge adding* matrix defined as

$$Q_{ij} = \begin{cases} 0.5 & \text{if } d_i = 1 \wedge j \text{ is the unique neighbor of } i \\ \alpha & \text{if } j \text{ is the first neighbor of } i \\ \frac{0.5d_i-\alpha}{d_i-1} & \text{if } j \text{ is a neighbor of } i \text{ but not the first one} \\ 0 & \text{otherwise.} \end{cases}$$

We show that *RandWalk-mod* can be formulated as an uncertain adjacency matrix $\mathcal{A}_{RW} = (AP_{RW}^{t-1}) \circ (Q + Q^T)$, where $\circ$ is the Hadamard product (element-wise). AP_{RW}^{t-1} is equivalent to computations in lines 2-6 and $Q + Q^T$ is equivalent to computations in lines 7-13. We use $Q + Q^T$ instead of Q due to the fact that when the edge (u, z) is added to G' with probability Q_{uz}, the edge (z, u) is also assigned the same probability. We come up with the following theorem.

THEOREM 4.4. *RandWalk-mod can be formulated as* $\mathcal{A}_{RW} = (AP_{RW}^{t-1}) \circ (Q+Q^T)$. $\mathcal{A}_{RW}$ *is symmetric. It satisfies the constraint of unchanged expected degree iff* $\alpha = 0.5$ [3].

PROOF. By Lemmas 4.1 and 4.2, let $B_{RW}^{(t)}$ be AP_{RW}^{t-1}, we have symmetric $B_{RW}^{(t)}$ and its row sums are equal to those of A. Because $\mathcal{A}_{RW} = B_{RW}^{(t)} \circ (Q + Q^T)$ and both $B_{RW}^{(t)}$ and $(Q + Q^T)$ are symmetric, $\mathcal{A}_{RW}$ is also symmetric.

Due to the fact that $(Q + Q^T)$ has the same locations of non-zeros as $B_{RW}^{(t)}$, the condition of unchanged expected degree is satisfied if and only if all non-zeros in $(Q + Q^T)$ are 1. This occurs if and only if $\alpha = 0.5$. □

We investigate the limit case when $t \to \infty$ (i.e. $P_{RW}^{t-1} \to P_{RW}^{\infty}$). Correspondingly $B_{RW}^{\infty} = AP_{RW}^{\infty}$ has $B_{RW}^{\infty}(i,j) = \frac{d_i d_j}{2m}$. The following theorem quantifies the number of selfloops and multiedges in B_{RW}^{∞} for power-law (PL) graphs and sparse Erdös-Renyi (ER) random graphs [15].

THEOREM 4.5. *For power-law graphs with the exponent* γ, *the number of selfloops in* B_{RW}^{∞} *is* $\frac{\zeta(\gamma-2)}{\zeta(\gamma-1)}$, *where* $\zeta(\gamma)$ *is the Riemann zeta function defined only for* $\gamma > 1$; *the number of multiedges is zero.*

For sparse ER random graphs with $\lambda = np$ *constant where* p *is the edge probability, the number of selfloops in* B_{RW}^{∞} *is* $\lambda + 1$; *the number of multiedges is zero.*

PROOF. See Appendix A.2. □

[3] This implies a mistake in Theorem 3 of [14]

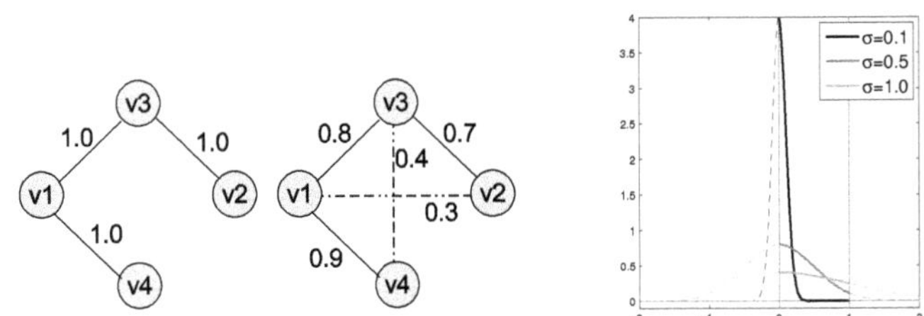

(a) (b) (c)

Figure 2: (a) True graph (b) An obfuscation with potential edges (dashed) (c) Truncated normal distribution on [0,1] (bold solid curves)

4.2 Edge Switching Scheme

In edge switching (*EdgeSwitch*) approaches (e.g. [26]), two edges $(u, v), (w, t)$ are chosen and switched to $(u, t), (w, v)$ if $a_{ut} = a_{wv} = 0$ (Fig. 1b). This is done in s switches. Using the switching matrix S, we represent 1-step EdgeSwitch in the form $AS = \mathcal{A}$ (Equation (4)).

The switching matrix S is feasible if and only if $a_{uw}a_{vt} = 0$. Note that in the full form, S is $n \times n$ matrix with the $n-4$ remaining elements on diagonal are 1, other off-diagonal are 0. In general, S is not right stochastic and this happens only if $a_{uw} = a_{vt} = 0$. For s-step EdgeSwitch $A\prod_{i=1}^{s} S_i = \mathcal{A}$. If $\forall i$, S_i is right stochastic (i.e. we choose edges $(u, v), (w, t)$ such that $a_{uw} = a_{vt} = 0$), then Lemma 4.1 applies.

4.3 (k, ϵ)-obf Scheme

Given the deterministic adjacency matrix A, we can directly construct $\mathcal{A}$ that satisfies all three constraints (1),(2) and (3) of UAM. *(k,ε)-obf* [2] introduces such an approach.

4.3.1 Construction and Limitations

In [2], Boldi et al. extend the concept of *k-obfuscation* developed earlier [3] which uses Shannon entropy.

DEFINITION 4.1. *(k,ε)-obf [2]. Let* P *be a vertex property,* $k \geq 1$ *be a desired level of obfuscation, and* $\epsilon \geq 0$ *be a tolerance parameter. The uncertain graph* $\mathcal{G}$ *is said to k-obfuscate a given vertex* $v \in G$ *with respect to* P *if the entropy of the distribution* $Y_{P(v)}$ *over the vertices of* $\mathcal{G}$ *is greater than or equal to* $\log_2 k$:

$$H(Y_{P(v)}) \geq \log_2 k \qquad (5)$$

$$\begin{bmatrix} 0 & 1 & a_{uw} & 0 \\ 1 & 0 & 0 & a_{vt} \\ a_{uw} & 0 & 0 & 1 \\ 0 & a_{vt} & 1 & 0 \end{bmatrix} \begin{bmatrix} 0 & -a_{vt} & 1 & a_{vt} \\ -a_{uw} & 0 & a_{uw} & 1 \\ 1 & a_{vt} & 0 & -a_{vt} \\ a_{uw} & 1 & -a_{uw} & 0 \end{bmatrix} = \begin{bmatrix} 0 & 0 & a_{uw} & 1 \\ 0 & 0 & 1 & a_{vt} \\ a_{uw} & 1 & 0 & 0 \\ 1 & a_{vt} & 0 & 0 \end{bmatrix} \quad (4)$$

The uncertain graph $\mathcal{G}$ is a (k, ϵ)-obf with respect to property P if it k-obfuscates at least $(1-\epsilon)n$ vertices in $\mathcal{G}$ with respect to P. □

Given the true graph G_0 (Fig.2a), the basic idea of (k, ϵ)-*obf* (Fig.2b) is to transfer the probabilities from existing edges to *potential* (non-existing) edges to satisfy Definition 4.1. For each existing sampled edge e, it is assigned a probability $1 - r_e$ where $r_e \leftarrow R_\sigma$ (Fig. 2c) and for each non-existing sampled edge e', it is assigned a probability $r_{e'} \leftarrow R_\sigma$.

Table 2 gives an example of how to compute degree entropy for the uncertain graph in Fig. 2b. Here vertex property P is the node degree. Each row in the left side is the degree distribution for the corresponding node. For instance, $v1$ has degree 0 with probability $(1-0.8).(1-0.3).(1-0.9) = 0.014$. The right side normalizes values in each column (i.e. in each degree value) to get distributions $Y_{P(v)}$. The entropy $H(Y_{P(v)})$ for each degree value is shown in the bottom row. Given $k = 3, \log_2 k = 1.585$, then $v1, v3$ with true degree 2 and $v2, v4$ with true degree 1 satisfy (5). Therefore, $\epsilon = 0$.

Table 2: The degree uncertainty for each node (left) and normalized values for each degree (right)

	node degree uncertainty				$Y_{P(v)}$			
	d=0	d=1	d=2	d=3	d=0	d=1	d=2	d=3
v1	.014	.188	.582	.216	.044	.117	.355	.491
v2	.210	.580	.210	.000	.656	.362	.128	.000
v3	.036	.252	.488	.224	.112	.158	.298	.509
v4	.060	.580	.360	.000	.187	.362	.220	.000
				H	1.40	1.84	1.91	0.99

While (k, ϵ)-*obf* provides a novel technique to come up with an uncertain version of the graph, the specific approach in [2] has two drawbacks. First, it formulated the problem as the minimization of σ. With small values of σ, r_e highly concentrates around zero, so existing sampled edges have probabilities nearly 1 and non-existing sampled edges are assigned probabilities almost 0. Simple rounding techniques can easily reveal the true graph. Even if the graph owner only publishes sample graphs, the re-identification attacks are still effective as we show in Section 7. Note that in [2], the found values of σ vary in a wide range from 10^{-1} to 10^{-8}. Second, the approach in [2] does not consider the locality (subgraph) of nodes in selecting pairs of nodes for establishing potential edges. As shown in [8], *subgraph-wise perturbation* effectively reduces structural distortion.

Furthermore, the expected degrees of nodes in (k, ϵ)-obf are *approximately* unchanged due to the fact that $r_e, r_{e'}$ are nearly zero by small σ. So (k,ϵ)-obf satisfies the constraints (1) and (2) but it only approximately satisfies the constraint (3) of UAM. To remedy these shortcomings, we present the MaxVar approach in Section 5. It adds potential edges to G_0, then tries to find the assignment of edge probabilities such that the expected node degrees are unchanged while the total variance is maximized. A comparison among schemes is also shown in Section 5.3.

4.4 Mixture Scheme

In this section, we present the *Mixture* approach applicable to RandWalk-mod, (k, ϵ)-obf, MaxVar and EdgeSwitch. Its UAM $\mathcal{A}_p$ is parametrized by p, with the output sample graph G_p. Given the true graph G_0 and an anonymized $G \sqsubseteq \mathcal{G}$, every edge (i, j) is included in G_p with probability $\mathcal{A}_p(i, j)$ where

$$\mathcal{A}_p(i,j) = \begin{cases} 1 & \text{if } (i,j) \in E_{G_0} \cap E_G \\ 1-p & \text{if } (i,j) \in E_{G_0} \setminus E_G \\ p & \text{if } (i,j) \in E_G \setminus E_{G_0} \end{cases}$$

It is straightforward to show that $\mathcal{A}_p = (1-p)A(G_0) + pA(G)$. When applied to G generated by *RandWalk-mod* with $\alpha = 0.5$, we have $\mathcal{A}_p = (1-p)A + pAP_{RW}^{t-1} = A[(1-p)I_n + pP_{RW}^{t-1}]$ and $\mathcal{A}_p$ satisfies three constraints (1) (2') and (3).

If there exists P_{mix} with constraint $P_{mix}(i,j) = 0$ if $(i,j) \notin E_{G_0}$ such that $P_{mix}^{t-1} = (1-p)I_n + pP_{RW}^{t-1}$, then Mixture can be simulated by the RandWalk-mod approach with the transition matrix P_{mix}.

4.5 Partition Scheme

Another approach that can apply to RandWalk-mod, (k, ϵ)-obf, MaxVar and EdgeSwitch is the *Partition* approach. Given true graph G_0, this divide-and-conquer strategy first partitions G_0 into disjoint subgraphs sG, then it applies one of the above anonymization schemes on subgraphs to get anonymized subgraphs $s\mathcal{G}$. Finally, it combines $s\mathcal{G}$ to obtain $\mathcal{G}$. Note that the partitioning may cause orphan edges as in MaxVar (Section 5). Those edges must be copied to $\mathcal{G}$ to keep node degrees unchanged.

5. VARIANCE MAXIMIZING SCHEME

We introduce the *Variance Maximizing* (MaxVar) scheme as an instance of the UAM. We start this section with the formulation of *MaxVar* in the form of quadratic programming based on two key observations (Section 5.1). Then we describe the anonymization algorithm (Section 5.2) and compare MaxVar with the aforementioned schemes (Section 5.3).

5.1 Formulation

Two key observations underpinning the MaxVar approach are presented as follows.

5.1.1 Observation #1: Maximizing Degree Variance

We argue that efficient countermeasures against structural attacks should hinge on node degrees. If a node and its neighbors have their degrees changed, the re-identification risk is reduced significantly. Consequently, instead of replicating local structures as in k-anonymity based approaches

[27, 12, 28, 4, 24, 21], we can deviate the attacks by changing node degrees *probabilistically*. For example, node $v1$ in Fig.2a has degree 2 with probability 1.0 whereas in Fig.2b, its degree gets four possible values $\{0, 1, 2, 3\}$ with probabilities $\{0.014, 0.188, 0.582, 0.216\}$ respectively. Generally, given edge probabilities of node u as $p_1, p_2, ..p_{d_u(\mathcal{G})}$, the degree of u is a sum of independent Bernoulli random variables, so its expected value is $\sum_{i=1}^{d_u(\mathcal{G})} p_i$ and its variance is $\sum_{i=1}^{d_u(\mathcal{G})} p_i(1 - p_i)$. If we naively target the maximum (local) degree variance without any constraints, the naive solution is at $p_i = 0.5\ \forall i$. However, such an assignment distorts graph structure severely and deteriorates the utility. Instead, by following the model of UAM, we have the constraint $\sum_{i=1}^{d_u(\mathcal{G})} p_i = d_u(G_0)$. Note that the *minimum variance* of an uncertain graph is 0 and corresponds to the case $\mathcal{G}$ has all edges being deterministic, e.g. when $\mathcal{G} = G_0$ and in switching-edge based approaches. In the following section, we show an interesting result relating the *total* degree variance with the variance of edit distance.

5.1.2 *Variance of Edit Distance*

The *edit distance* between two deterministic graphs G, G' is defined as:

$$D(G, G') = |E_G \setminus E_{G'}| + |E_{G'} \setminus E_G| \qquad (6)$$

A well-known result about the expected edit distance between the uncertain graph $\mathcal{G}$ and the deterministic graph $G \sqsubseteq \mathcal{G}$ is

$$E[D(\mathcal{G}, G)] = \sum_{G' \sqsubseteq \mathcal{G}} Pr(G')D(G, G') = \sum_{e_i \in E_G} (1-p_i) + \sum_{e_i \notin E_G} p_i$$

Correspondingly, the variance of edit distance is

$$Var[D(\mathcal{G}, G)] = \sum_{G' \sqsubseteq \mathcal{G}} Pr(G')[D(G, G') - E[D(\mathcal{G}, G)]]^2$$

We proved in the following theorem that the variance of edit distance is the sum of all edges' variance (total degree variance) and it does not depend on the choice of G.

THEOREM 5.1. *([16]) Assume that $\mathcal{G}(V, E, p)$ has k uncertain edges $e_1, e_2, ..., e_k$ and $G \sqsubseteq \mathcal{G}$ (i.e. $E_G \subseteq E$). The edit distance variance is $Var[D(\mathcal{G}, G)] = \sum_{i=1}^{k} p_i(1-p_i)$ and does not depend on the choice of G.*

5.1.3 *Observation #2: Proposing Nearby Edges*

As indicated by Leskovec et al. [11], real graphs reveal two temporal evolution properties: *densification power law* and *shrinking diameters*. Community Guided Attachment (CGA) model [11], which produces densifying graphs, is an example of a hierarchical graph generation model in which the linkage probability between nodes decreases as a function of their relative distance in the hierarchy. With regard to this observation, (k, ϵ)-obf, by heuristically making potential edges solely based on node degree discrepancy, produces many inter-community edges. Shortest-path based statistics will be reduced due to these edges. MaxVar, in contrast, tries to mitigate the structural distortion by proposing only *nearby* potential edges before assigning edge probabilities. Another evidence is from [22] where Vazquez analytically proved that *Nearest Neighbor* can explain the power-law for degree distribution, clustering coefficient and average degree among the neighbors. Those properties are in very good agreement with the observations made for social graphs. Sala et al. [18] confirmed the consistency of Nearest Neighbor model in their comparative study on graph models for social networks.

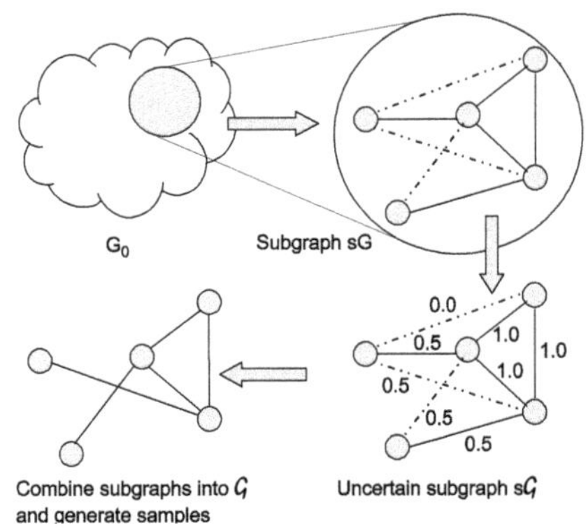

Figure 3: MaxVar approach

5.2 Algorithms

5.2.1 *Overview*

The intuition behind the new approach is to formulate the perturbation problem as a *quadratic programming* problem. Given the true graph G_0 and the number of potential edges allowed to be added n_p, the scheme has three phases. The first phase tries to partition G_0 into s subgraphs, each one with $n_s = n_p/s$ potential edges connecting nearby nodes (with default distance 2, i.e. *friend-of-friend*). The second phase formulates a quadratic program for each subgraph with the constraint of unchanged node degrees to produce the uncertain subgraphs $s\mathcal{G}$ with maximum edge variance. The third phase combines the uncertain subgraphs $s\mathcal{G}$ into $\mathcal{G}$ and publishes several sample graphs. The three phases are illustrated in Fig. 3.

By keeping the degrees of nodes in the perturbed graph, our approach is similar to the *edge switching* approaches (e.g.[26]) but ours is more subtle as we do it implicitly and the switching occurs not necessarily on pairs of edges.

5.2.2 *Graph Partitioning*

Because of the complexity of exact quadratic programming (Section 5.2.3), we need a pre-processing phase to divide the true graph G_0 into subgraphs and run the optimization on each subgraph. Given the number of subgraphs s, we run *METIS* [4] to get almost equal-sized subgraphs with minimum number of inter-subgraph edges. Each subgraph has n_s potential edges added before running the quadratic program. This phase is outlined in Algorithm 3.

5.2.3 *Quadratic Programming*

By assuming the independence of edges, the total degree variance of $\mathcal{G} = (V, E, p)$ for edit distance (Theorem 5.1) is:

$$Var(E) = \sum_{i=1}^{|E|} p_i(1 - p_i) = |E_{G_0}| - \sum_{i=1}^{|E|} p_i^2 \qquad (7)$$

The last equality in (7) is due to the constraint that the expected node degrees are unchanged (i.e. $\sum_{i=1}^{d_u(\mathcal{G})} p_i =$

[4]http://glaros.dtc.umn.edu/gkhome/views/metis

Algorithm 3 Partition-and-Add-Edges

Input: true graph $G_0 = (V, E_{G_0})$, number of subgraphs s, number of potential edges per subgraph n_s
Output: list of augmented subgraphs gl

```
gl ← METIS(G_0, s).
for sG in gl do
    i ← 0
    while i < n_s do
        randomly pick u, v ∈ V_sG and (u, v) ∉ E_sG with d(u, v) = 2
        E_sG ← E_sG ∪ (u, v)
        i ← i + 1
return gl
```

$d_u(G_0)$), so $\sum_{i=1}^{|E|} p_i$ is equal to $|E_{G_0}|$. By targeting the maximum edge variance, we come up with the following quadratic program.

$$\begin{aligned} &\text{Minimize} && \sum_{i=1}^{|E|} p_i^2 \\ &\text{Subject to} && 0 \leq p_i \leq 1 \;\forall i \\ & && \sum_{v \in \mathcal{N}(u)} p_{uv} = d_u(G_0) \;\forall u \end{aligned} \tag{8}$$

The objective function reflects the privacy goal (i.e. sample graphs do not highly concentrate around the true graph) while the expected degree constraints aim to preserve the utility.

By dividing the large input graph into subgraphs, we solve independent quadratic optimization problems. Because each edge belongs to at most one subgraph and the expected node degrees in each subgraph are unchanged, it is straightforward to show that the expected node degrees in $\mathcal{G}$ are also unchanged. We have a proposition on problem feasibility and an upper bound for the total variance.

PROPOSITION 5.2. *The quadratic program in MaxVar is always feasible. The total variance $TV_{MaxVar} = Var(E)$ is upper bounded by $\frac{mn_p}{m+n_p}$.*

PROOF. The feasibility is due to the fact that $\{p_e | p_e = 1 \;\forall e \in E_{G_0}$ and $p_e = 0$ otherwise$\}$ is a feasible point. Let k_u be the number of potential edges incident to node u. By requiring u's expected degree to be unchanged, we have $\sum_{v \in \mathcal{N}(u)} p_{uv} = d_u$. Applying Cauchy-Schwarz inequality, we get $\sum_{v \in \mathcal{N}(u)} p_{uv}^2 \geq \frac{1}{d_u + k_u} (\sum_{v \in \mathcal{N}(u)} p_{uv})^2 = \frac{d_u^2}{d_u + k_u}$. Now we take the sum over all nodes to get the following

$$Var(E) = m - \sum_{i=1}^{m+n_p} p_i^2 = m - \frac{1}{2} \sum_u \sum_{v \in \mathcal{N}(u)} p_{uv}^2$$

$$\leq m - \frac{1}{2} \sum_u \frac{d_u^2}{d_u + d_k} \leq m - \frac{1}{2} \frac{(\sum_u d_u)^2}{\sum_u (d_u + k_u)} = \frac{mn_p}{m + n_p}$$

where the last equality is again due to Cauchy-Schwarz inequality. □

5.3 Comparison of Schemes

All the schemes mentioned in the current work are about *node-level* anonymization. It means we directly manipulate the nodes and their edges. In differentially private schemes such as [23, 25], node signatures are indirectly anonymized via noisy graph statistics/models and graph regeneration. Therefore, all nodes' identities in the output cannot be linked to the original graphs. The incorrectness measure (Section 6.1) is not applicable, so we exclude such schemes from the comparison.

Table 3 shows the comparison of schemes we investigate so far. Only MaxVar and EdgeSwitch satisfy all three properties (1),(2) and (3). The next two propositions quantify the TV of (k,ϵ)-obf and *RandWalk-mod*.

Table 3: Comparison of schemes

Scheme	Prop.1	Prop.2	Prop.3	Uncertain $\mathcal{A}$
RandWalk-mod	○ ($\alpha = 0.5$)	×	○	○
RandWalk [14]	○	○	×	○
EdgeSwitch	○	○	○	×
(k,ϵ)-obf [2]	○	○	×	○
MaxVar	○	○	○	○
Mixture	depends on the mixed scheme			
Partition	depends on the scheme used in subgraphs			

PROPOSITION 5.3. *The expected total variance of (k,ϵ)-obf TV_{obf} is $(m + n_p)(E[r_e] - E[r_e^2])$. The expressions of $E[r_e], E[r_e^2]$ are given in (9) and (10).*

PROOF. In (k,ϵ)-obf, m existing edges are assigned probabilities $1 - r_e$ while n_p potential edges are assigned probabilities r_e. Therefore, the total variance is $TV_{obf} = m(1 - r_e)(1 - (1 - r_e)) + n_p r_e (1 - r_e) = (m + n_p) r_e (1 - r_e)$ where $r_e \leftarrow R_\sigma$. Take the expectation of TV_{obf}, we get $E[TV_{obf}] = (m + n_p)(E[r_e] - E[r_e^2])$.

R_σ has pdf $f(x) = C \frac{1}{\sigma\sqrt{2\pi}} e^{-x^2/2\sigma^2}$ if $x \in [0, 1]$ and 0 otherwise. The normalization constant $C = 0.5\text{erf}(1/\sigma\sqrt{2})$ where erf is the error function. Basic integral computations (change of variable and integration by parts) give us the formulas for $E[r_e]$ and $E[r_e^2]$ as follows

$$E[r_e] = \frac{C\sigma}{\sqrt{2\pi}} (1 - e^{-1/2\sigma^2}) \tag{9}$$

$$E[r_e^2] = \frac{C\sigma}{\sqrt{2\pi}} (\frac{\sigma\sqrt{2\pi}}{C} - e^{-1/2\sigma^2}) \tag{10}$$

Note that for $\sigma \leq 0.1$, $C \approx 1$ and $e^{-1/2\sigma^2} \approx 0$, so

$$E[TV_{obf}] \approx (m + n_p) \left(\frac{\sigma}{\sqrt{2\pi}} - \sigma^2 \right) \tag{11}$$

□

PROPOSITION 5.4. *The total variance of RandWalk-mod $TV_{RW}(t)$ at walk-length t is upper bounded by $\frac{m(K_t - m)}{K_t}$ where K_t is the number of non-zeros in $B^{(t)}$.*

For power-law graphs with the exponent γ, $TV_{RW}^{PL}(\infty) = m - \frac{1}{2} \left[\frac{\zeta(\gamma-2)}{\zeta(\gamma-1)} \right]^2$. For sparse ER random graphs with $\lambda = np$ constant, $TV_{RW}^{ER}(\infty) = m - \frac{1}{2}(\lambda + 1)^2$

PROOF. The proof uses the same arguments as in Proposition 5.2 and Theorem 4.5. We omit it due to space limitation. □

Note that the K_t increases with t and when t is equal to the diameter of G, $K_t = n^2$. Therefore, the upper bound of $TV_{RW}(t)$ converges very fast to m, compatible with the results in the limit cases of *PL* and *ER* random graphs.

By propositions 5.2, 5.3 and 5.4, we roughly conclude that

$$0 < E[TV_{obf}] < TV_{MaxVar} < TV_{RW}(t) < m \qquad (12)$$

5.4 Directed Graphs

For directed graphs, the UAM model can be extended in several ways. We can apply the constraint of unchanged expected degree to in-degrees, out-degrees or both in/out-degrees of nodes.

In the case of unchanged out-degrees, it is straightforward to verify that *RandWalk-mod* still keeps the expected out-degrees of all nodes (note that we have to double the probabilities of adding every (u, v) due to the directionality of edges). The case of unchanged in-degrees needs reverse random walks (i.e. walks on in-edges) and the same conclusion holds. However, if we require both expected in/out-degrees of nodes to be unchanged, there exists no such random-walks. This is not the case for (k, ϵ)-obf and MaxVar. For MaxVar, the constraints in (8) is updated to

$$\sum_{v \in \mathcal{N}^-(u)} p_{uv} = d_u^-(G_0) \qquad \sum_{v \in \mathcal{N}^+(u)} p_{uv} = d_u^+(G_0)\ \forall u$$

Interestingly, in the case of unchanged out-degrees, MaxVar has a trivial solution $p_{uv} = d_u^+(G_0)/d_u^+(\mathcal{G})$ due to Cauchy-Schwarz inequality. The case of unchanged in-degrees is similar. Because the main focus of this work is on undirected graphs, we leave the full analysis of UAM on directed graphs for future work.

6. QUANTIFYING FRAMEWORK

This section describes an empirical framework for privacy and utility quantification of anonymization methods.

6.1 Privacy Measurement

We focus on structural re-identification attacks under various models of attacker's knowledge as shown in [10]. We quantify the privacy of an anonymized graph as the *sum* of re-identification probabilities of all nodes in the graph. We differentiate *closed-world* from *open-world* adversaries. For example, when a closed-world adversary knows that Bob has three neighbors, this fact is exact. An open-world adversary in this case would learn only that Bob has at least three neighbors. We consider the result of structural query Q on a node u as the node signature $sig_Q(u)$. Given a query Q, nodes having the same signatures form an *equivalence class.* So given the true graph G_0 and an output anonymized graph G^*, the privacy is measured as in the following example.

EXAMPLE 6.1. *Assuming that we have* G_0 *of 8 nodes. The node signatures of* G_0 *are* $s_1\{1,2,3\}, s_2\{4,5\}, s_3\{6,7,8\}$. *The node signatures of* G^* *are* $s_1\{1,2,6\}, s_2\{4,7\}, s_3\{3,8\}, s_4\{5\}$ *respectively. The re-identification probabilities in* G^* *of nodes 1,2 are* $\frac{1}{3}$, *of nodes 4,8 are* $\frac{1}{2}$, *of nodes 3,5,6,7 are 0s. And the privacy score of* G^* *is* $\frac{1}{3}+\frac{1}{3}+\frac{1}{2}+\frac{1}{2}+0+0+0+0 = 1.66$. *In* G_0, *the privacy score is* $\frac{1}{3}+\frac{1}{3}+\frac{1}{3}+\frac{1}{2}+\frac{1}{2}+\frac{1}{3}+\frac{1}{3}+\frac{1}{3} = 3$, *equal to the number of equivalence classes.*

We consider two privacy scores in this paper.

- **H1** score uses node degree as the node signature, i.e. we assume that the attacker knows *apriori* degrees of all nodes.
- $\mathbf{H2_{open}}$ uses the *set* (not multiset) of degrees of node's friends as the node signature. For example, if a node has 6 neighbors and the degrees of those neighbors are $\{1, 2, 2, 3, 3, 5\}$, then its signature for $H2_{open}$ attack is $\{1, 2, 3, 5\}$.

Higher-order scores like $H2$ (exact multiset of neighbors' degrees) or $H3$ (exact multiset of neighbor-of-neighbors' degrees) induce much higher privacy scores of the true graph G_0 (in the order of $|V|$) and represent less meaningful metrics for privacy.

6.2 Utility Measurement

Following [2] and [26], we consider three groups of statistics for utility measurement: degree-based statistics, shortest-path based statistics and clustering statistics.

Degree-based statistics

- Number of edges: $S_{NE} = \frac{1}{2}\sum_{v \in V} d_v$
- Average degree: $S_{AD} = \frac{1}{n}\sum_{v \in V} d_v$
- Maximal degree: $S_{MD} = \max_{v \in V} d_v$
- Degree variance: $S_{DV} = \frac{1}{n}\sum_{v \in V}(d_v - S_{AD})^2$
- Power-law exponent of degree sequence: S_{PL} is the estimate of γ assuming the degree sequence follows a power-law $\Delta(d) \sim d^{-\gamma}$

Shortest path-based statistics

- Average distance: S_{APD} is the average distance among all pairs of vertices that are path-connected.
- Effective diameter: S_{EDiam} is the 90-th percentile distance among all path-connected pairs of vertices.
- Connectivity length: S_{CL} is defined as the harmonic mean of all pairwise distances in the graph.
- Diameter : S_{Diam} is the maximum distance among all path-connected pairs of vertices.

Clustering statistics

- Clustering coefficient: $S_{CC} = \frac{3N_\Delta}{N_3}$ where N_Δ is the number of triangles and N_3 is the number of connected triples.

All of the above statistics are computed on sample graphs generated from the uncertain output $\mathcal{G}$. In particular, to estimate shortest-path based measures, we use Approximate Neighbourhood Function (ANF) [17]. The diameter is lower bounded by the longest distance among all-destination breadth-first-searches from 1,000 randomly chosen nodes.

7. EVALUATION

In this section, our evaluation aims to show the disadvantages of (k, ϵ)*-obf* and *RandWalk/RandWalk-mod* as well as the gap between them. We then illustrate the effectiveness and efficiency of the gap-filling approaches *MaxVar* and *Mixture.* The effectiveness is measured by privacy scores (lower is better) and the relative error of utility (lower is better). The efficiency is measured by the running time. All algorithms are implemented in Python and run on a desktop PC with *Intel*® Core i7-4770@ 3.4Ghz, 16GB memory. We use *MOSEK*[5] as the quadratic solver.

Three large real-world datasets are used in our experiments [6]. `dblp` is a co-authorship network where two authors are connected if they publish at least one paper together. `amazon` is a product co-purchasing network where the graph contains an undirected edge from i to j if a product i is frequently co-purchased with product j. `youtube` is a video-sharing web site that includes a social network. The graph

[5]http://mosek.com/

[6]http://snap.stanford.edu/data/index.html

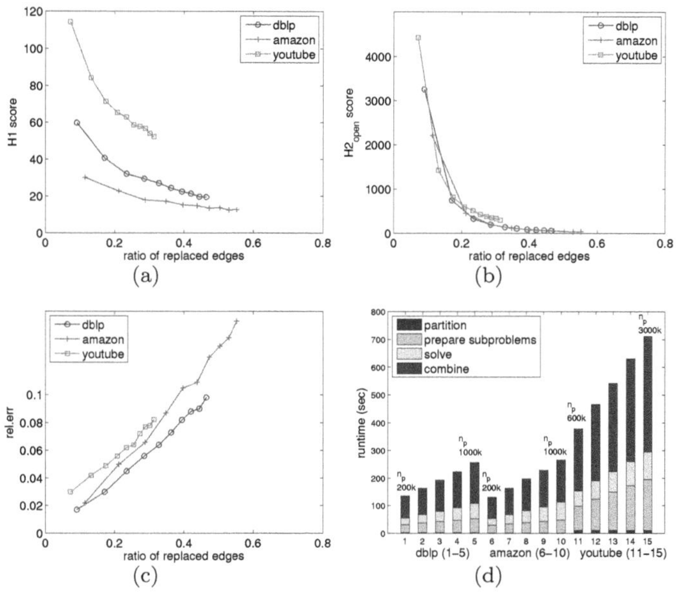

Figure 4: Performance of MaxVar (a) $H1$ score (b) $H2_{open}$ score (c) Relative error (d) Runtime

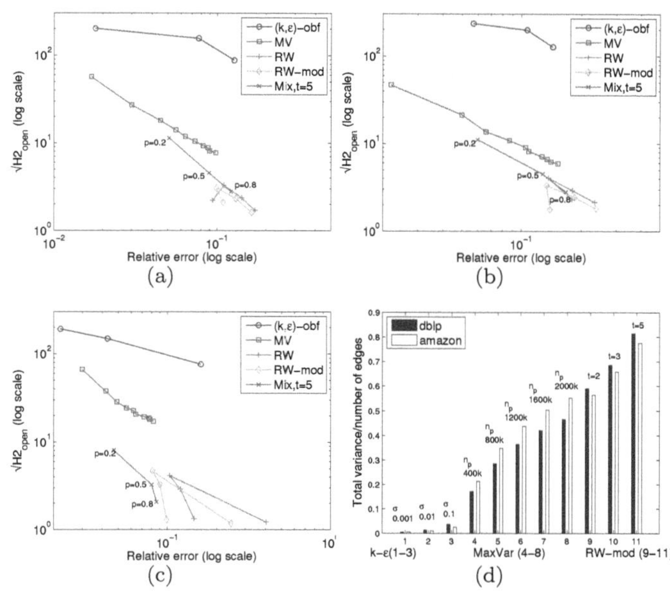

Figure 5: Tradeoff (log-log) (a) dblp (b) amazon (c) youtube. (d) Comparison of Total Variance (TV)

sizes ($|V|, |E|$) of **dblp**, **amazon** and **youtube** are (317080, 1049866), (334863, 925872) and (1134890, 2987624) respectively. We partition **dblp**, **amazon** into 20 subgraphs and **youtube** into 60 subgraphs. The sample size of each test case is 20.

7.1 (k,ϵ)-obf and RandWalk

We report the performance of (k,ϵ)-*obf* in Table 4. We keep the number of potential edges equal to m (default value in [2]) and vary σ. We find that the scheme achieves low relative errors only at small σ. However, privacy scores, especially $H2_{open}$, rise fast (up to 50% compared to the true graph). This fact incurs high privacy-utility tradeoff as confirmed in Table 7.

Table 5 shows the performance similarity between *RandWalk* and *RandWalk-mod* except the case of **youtube** and for $t = 2$ in **amazon**. Because *RandWalk-mod* satisfies the third constraint, it benefits several degree-based statistics while the existence of selfloops and multiedges does not impact much on shortest-path based metrics. *RandWalk* misses a lot of edges at $t = 2$ (see footnote 1 in Section 4.1). The remarkable characteristics of random-walk schemes are the very low privacy scores and the high relative errors (lower-bounded around 8 to 10%). Clearly, there is a gap between high tradeoffs in (k,ϵ)-*obf* and high relative errors in *RandWalk* where *MaxVar* and *Mixture* may play their roles.

7.2 Effectiveness of MaxVar

We assess privacy and utility of *MaxVar* by varying the number of potential edges n_p. The results are shown in Table 6. As for privacy scores, if we increase n_p, we gain better privacy as we allow more edge switches. Due to the expected degree constraints in the quadratic program, all degree-based metrics vary only a little.

We observe the near *linear* relationships between $H1$, $rel.err$ and the number of replaced edges $|E_{G_0} \setminus E_G|$ in Figures 4a, 4c and near *quadratic* relationship of $H2_{open}$ against $|E_{G_0} \setminus E_G|$ in Fig.4b. The ratio of replaced edges in Figures 4a,4b and 4c is defined as $\frac{|E_{G_0} \setminus E_G|}{|E_{G_0}|}$.

The runtime of MaxVar consists of time for (1) partitioning G_0, (2) adding friend-of-friend edges to subgraphs, (3) solving quadratic subproblems and (4) combining uncertain subgraphs to get $\mathcal{G}$. We report the runtime in Fig.4d. As we can see, the total runtime is in several minutes and the runtime of the partitioning step is almost negligible. Increasing n_p gives rise to the runtime in steps 2,3 and 4 and the trends are nearly linear. The runtime on **youtube** is three times longer than on the other two datasets, almost linear to their data sizes.

7.3 Comparative Evaluation

Table 7 shows comparisons between *MaxVar*, (k,ϵ)-obf and <u>*RandWalk/RandWalk-mod*</u>. The column *tradeoff* is $\sqrt{H2_{open}} \times rel.err$ as we conjecture the quadratic and linear behavior of $H2_{open}$ and $rel.err$ respectively (Figures 4b and 4c). We omit the column $H1 \times rel.err$ because they are almost equal for all schemes considered in this work. Clearly, MaxVar gains better privacy-utility tradeoffs than (k,ϵ)-obf, but worse than *RandWalk*, *RandWalk-mod*. However, MaxVar has its own merit as a gap-filling solution. Figures 5a,5b and 5c show that while RandWalk, RandWalk-mod have the best tradeoffs, they suffer from high lower bounds for utility. In other words, if the dataset allows higher privacy risk for better utility (lower rel.err) then the usage of two random walk based solutions may be limited. The simple solution *Mixture* also fills the gap. We omit EdgeSwitch due to its worst tradeoffs.

In addition to the re-identification scores $H1$ and $H2_{open}$, we also compute ϵ for $k \in \{30, 50, 100\}$ to have a fair comparison with (k,ϵ)-obf. Table 7 shows that *MaxVar* has the best (k,ϵ) scores. The number of potential edges used in MaxVar could be 20% of $|E_{G_0}|$, much less than that of (k,ϵ)-obf (100% for $c = 2$ [2]). *MaxVar* and *RandWalk/RandWalk-mod* have $|E_{G_0} \setminus E_G| \simeq |E_G \setminus E_{G_0}|$ and these two quantities are higher than those of (k,ϵ)-obf where the number of edges is preserved only at small σ. RandWalk and RandWalk-mod do not have many edges preserved due to their rewiring nature. $|E_{G_0} \setminus E_G|$ increases slowly in MaxVar because the

Table 4: (k, ϵ)-*obf*

σ	$H1$	$H2_{open}$	S_{NE}	S_{AD}	S_{MD}	S_{DV}	S_{CC}	S_{PL}	S_{APD}	S_{ED}	S_{CL}	S_{Diam}	rel.err
dblp	199	125302	1049866	6.62	343	100.15	0.306	2.245	7.69	9	7.46	20	
0.001	72.9	40712.1	1048153	6.61	316.0	97.46	0.303	2.244	7.74	9.4	7.50	20.0	**0.018**
0.01	41.1	24618.2	1035994	6.53	186.0	86.47	0.294	2.248	7.82	9.5	7.59	19.8	**0.077**
0.1	19.7	7771.4	991498	6.25	164.9	64.20	0.284	2.265	8.08	10.0	7.85	20.0	**0.128**
amazon	153	113338	925872	5.53	549	33.20	0.205	2.336	12.75	16	12.10	44	
0.001	55.7	55655.9	924321	5.52	479.1	31.73	0.206	2.340	12.14	15.2	11.65	33.2	**0.057**
0.01	34.5	39689.8	915711	5.47	299.7	27.18	0.220	2.348	12.40	15.6	11.91	32.4	**0.101**
0.1	19.2	16375.4	892140	5.33	253.9	21.87	0.232	2.374	12.52	15.5	12.06	31.4	**0.144**
youtube	978	321724	2987624	5.27	28754	2576.0	0.0062	2.429	6.07	8	6.79	20	
0.001	157.2	36744.6	2982974	5.26	28438	2522.6	0.0062	2.416	6.24	8.0	6.01	19.5	**0.022**
0.01	80.0	22361.7	2940310	5.18	26900	2282.6	0.0061	2.419	6.27	8.0	6.04	19.0	**0.043**
0.1	23.4	5806.9	2624066	4.62	16353	970.8	0.0070	2.438	6.59	8.1	6.36	20.4	**0.160**

Table 5: *RandWalk* and *RandWalk-mod*

t	$H1$	$H2_{open}$	S_{NE}	S_{AD}	S_{MD}	S_{DV}	S_{CC}	S_{PL}	S_{APD}	S_{ED}	S_{CL}	S_{Diam}	rel.err
dblp	199	125302	1049866	6.62	343	100.15	0.306	2.245	7.69	9	7.46	20	
(RW) 2	10.0	4.9	1001252	6.32	309.3	86.16	0.152	2.197	7.43	9.1	7.20	19.7	**0.094**
3	11.8	10.9	1048129	6.61	315.4	98.04	0.107	2.155	7.08	8.7	6.88	17.8	**0.110**
5	11.7	5.6	1049484	6.62	321.6	100.77	0.065	2.148	6.79	8.0	6.62	16.4	**0.142**
10	11.9	2.9	1049329	6.62	329.2	103.06	0.030	2.144	6.54	8.0	6.40	14.3	**0.171**
(RW-mod) 2	11.8	4.5	1049921	6.62	327.0	105.3	0.093	2.110	7.75	9.7	7.48	23.0	**0.109**
3	11.9	9.4	1049877	6.62	343.3	105.1	0.071	2.117	7.32	9.0	7.10	20.4	**0.099**
5	12.0	5.4	1049781	6.62	340.5	105.1	0.044	2.115	6.95	8.4	6.76	18.3	**0.131**
10	11.9	2.6	1049902	6.62	340.0	105.3	0.021	2.116	6.59	8.0	6.44	16.0	**0.164**
amazon	153	113338	925872	5.53	549	33.20	0.205	2.336	12.75	16	12.10	44	
(RW) 2	5.7	5.4	861896	5.15	274.9	23.11	0.148	2.337	10.70	13.8	10.19	38.7	**0.180**
3	10.0	16.5	923793	5.52	495.6	32.72	0.113	2.282	10.33	13.1	9.87	34.1	**0.137**
5	10.4	8.6	925185	5.53	507.7	33.52	0.080	2.276	9.45	12.1	9.07	29.6	**0.181**
10	10.2	4.6	925748	5.53	498.1	34.37	0.046	2.273	8.55	10.5	8.25	25.7	**0.234**
(RW-mod) 2	9.8	3.2	925672	5.53	255.1	37.61	0.099	2.246	12.02	15.5	11.40	43.2	**0.139**
3	9.9	11.2	925532	5.53	535.3	37.32	0.082	2.254	10.89	14.0	10.38	37.9	**0.134**
5	9.7	6.0	926163	5.53	522.8	37.42	0.059	2.252	9.83	12.5	9.40	33.0	**0.185**
10	9.9	3.3	925809	5.53	491.4	37.45	0.035	2.251	8.76	11.0	8.44	28.7	**0.238**
youtube	978	321724	2987624	5.27	28754	2576.0	0.0062	2.429	6.07	8	6.79	20	
(RW) 2	13.4	1.5	2636508	4.65	19253.8	1139.7	0.022	2.191	6.18	7.9	5.93	23.5	**0.403**
3	23.8	17.6	2982204	5.26	26803.6	2389.6	0.004	2.108	5.73	7.0	5.52	18.0	**0.103**
5	24.6	8.4	2985967	5.26	26018.7	2340.0	0.005	2.106	5.55	7.0	5.38	16.3	**0.120**
10	21.9	1.8	2984115	5.26	24695.8	2099.4	0.009	2.100	5.49	6.9	5.33	18.7	**0.145**
(RW-mod) 2	26.4	1.4	2987228	5.26	23829.7	2578.5	0.018	2.053	6.27	8.0	6.02	22.1	**0.245**
3	26.9	22.3	2988011	5.27	28611.5	2579.7	0.005	2.077	5.75	7.2	5.54	19.0	**0.081**
5	26.1	11.0	2987479	5.26	28619.3	2581.4	0.005	2.076	5.61	7.0	5.44	18.3	**0.090**
10	26.3	1.7	2987475	5.26	28432.2	2579.9	0.008	2.073	5.58	7.0	5.41	18.8	**0.099**

edges in G_0 always have positive probabilities. Fig 5d compares the normalized total variance (i.e. divided by $|E_{G_0}|$) of three schemes. Again, MaxVar is between (k, ϵ)-obf and RandWalk-mod as shown in inequality (12).

8. CONCLUSION

We provide a general view of graph anonymization based on the semantics of edge uncertainty. Via the model of UAM with the constraint of unchanged expected degree for all nodes, we analyze recently proposed schemes and explain why there exists a gap between them by comparing the total degree variance. We propose *MaxVar*, a novel anonymization scheme exploiting two key observations: maximizing the total degree variance while keeping the expected degrees of all nodes unchanged and using nearby potential edges. We also investigate an elegant *Mixture* approach that together with *MaxVar* fill the gap between (k, ϵ)-*obf* and *RandWalk*. Furthermore, we promote the usage of incorrectness measure for privacy assessment in a new quantifying framework rather than Shannon entropy and min-entropy (k-anonymity). The experiments demonstrate the effectiveness of our methods. Our work may incite several directions for future research including (1) novel constructions of uncertain graphs based on the model of UAM (2) deeper analysis on the privacy-utility relationships in MaxVar (e.g. explaining the near linear and near quadratic curves) (3) study on weighted, directed and bipartite graphs.

9. REFERENCES

[1] L. Backstrom, C. Dwork, and J. Kleinberg. Wherefore art thou r3579x?: anonymized social networks, hidden patterns, and structural steganography. In *WWW*, pages 181–190. ACM, 2007.

[2] P. Boldi, F. Bonchi, A. Gionis, and T. Tassa. Injecting uncertainty in graphs for identity obfuscation. *Proceedings of the VLDB Endowment*, 2012.

[3] F. Bonchi, A. Gionis, and T. Tassa. Identity obfuscation in graphs through the information theoretic lens. In *ICDE*, pages 924–935. IEEE, 2011.

Table 6: Effectiveness of *MaxVar* (k denotes one thousand)

n_p	$H1$	$H2_{open}$	S_{NE}	S_{AD}	S_{MD}	S_{DV}	S_{CC}	S_{PL}	S_{APD}	S_{ED}	S_{CL}	S_{Diam}	rel.err
dblp	199	125302	1049866	6.62	343	100.15	0.306	2.245	7.69	9	7.46	20	
400k	40.7	744.0	1049813	6.62	343.5	101.26	0.255	2.189	7.56	9.1	7.33	18.9	**0.030**
800k	29.5	199.2	1049869	6.62	345.9	102.07	0.219	2.163	7.45	9.0	7.24	17.0	**0.056**
1200k	24.4	109.8	1050032	6.62	347.8	102.62	0.192	2.149	7.33	9.0	7.14	16.4	**0.073**
1600k	21.3	77.6	1050029	6.62	342.9	102.93	0.172	2.140	7.21	8.8	7.03	15.7	**0.088**
2000k	19.5	60.0	1050136	6.62	344.5	103.28	0.156	2.134	7.19	8.7	7.01	15.2	**0.098**
amazon	153	113338	925872	5.53	549	33.20	0.205	2.336	12.75	16	12.10	44	
400k	22.8	452.4	925928	5.53	550.2	34.40	0.182	2.306	11.88	15.3	11.28	37.1	**0.050**
800k	17.2	118.8	925660	5.53	550.0	35.11	0.154	2.289	11.33	14.4	10.81	34.5	**0.087**
1200k	14.8	67.3	925921	5.53	547.0	35.63	0.131	2.278	11.00	14.0	10.49	34.1	**0.109**
1600k	13.6	44.4	926059	5.53	547.7	35.98	0.113	2.271	10.71	13.7	10.25	29.7	**0.135**
2000k	12.6	35.2	925659	5.53	547.0	36.24	0.099	2.266	10.50	13.3	10.04	28.0	**0.153**
youtube	978	321724	2987624	5.27	28754	2576.0	0.0062	2.429	6.07	8	6.79	20	
1200k	84.2	1419.2	2987342	5.26	28754	2576	0.0064	2.319	6.02	7.2	5.82	17.9	**0.042**
2400k	65.3	595.5	2987468	5.26	28749	2577	0.0060	2.265	5.96	7.1	5.77	16.6	**0.056**
3600k	58.6	425.8	2987986	5.27	28755	2577	0.0057	2.240	5.89	7.1	5.71	16.6	**0.064**
4800k	56.7	350.4	2987698	5.27	28753	2577	0.0055	2.224	5.85	7.0	5.68	15.4	**0.077**
6000k	52.1	298.4	2987613	5.27	28765	2579	0.0052	2.213	5.82	7.1	5.65	15.3	**0.082**

[4] J. Cheng, A. W.-c. Fu, and J. Liu. K-isomorphism: privacy preserving network publication against structural attacks. In *SIGMOD*. ACM, 2010.

[5] G. Cormode, C. M. Procopiuc, E. Shen, D. Srivastava, and T. Yu. Empirical privacy and empirical utility of anonymized data. In *ICDE Workshop*, pages 77–82. IEEE, 2013.

[6] N. Dalvi and D. Suciu. Management of probabilistic data: foundations and challenges. In *PODS*, pages 1–12. ACM, 2007.

[7] C. Dwork. A firm foundation for private data analysis. *Communications of the ACM*, 54(1):86–95, 2011.

[8] A. M. Fard, K. Wang, and P. S. Yu. Limiting link disclosure in social network analysis through subgraph-wise perturbation. In *EDBT*. ACM, 2012.

[9] M. Hay, C. Li, G. Miklau, and D. Jensen. Accurate estimation of the degree distribution of private networks. In *ICDM*, pages 169–178. IEEE, 2009.

[10] M. Hay, G. Miklau, D. Jensen, D. Towsley, and P. Weis. Resisting structural re-identification in anonymized social networks. *VLDB Endowment*, 2008.

[11] J. Leskovec, J. Kleinberg, and C. Faloutsos. Graph evolution: Densification and shrinking diameters. *ACM TKDD*, 1(1):2, 2007.

[12] K. Liu and E. Terzi. Towards identity anonymization on graphs. In *SIGMOD*, pages 93–106. ACM, 2008.

[13] P. Mahadevan, D. Krioukov, K. Fall, and A. Vahdat. Systematic topology analysis and generation using degree correlations. In *SIGCOMM*. ACM, 2006.

[14] P. Mittal, C. Papamanthou, and D. Song. Preserving link privacy in social network based systems. In *NDSS*, 2013.

[15] M. E. Newman. The structure and function of complex networks. *SIAM review*, 45(2):167–256, 2003.

[16] H. H. Nguyen, I. Abdessamad, and M. Rusinowitch. A maximum variance approach for graph anonymization. In *FPS*, 2014. to appear.

[17] C. R. Palmer, P. B. Gibbons, and C. Faloutsos. Anf: A fast and scalable tool for data mining in massive graphs. In *KDD*, pages 81–90. ACM, 2002.

[18] A. Sala, L. Cao, C. Wilson, R. Zablit, H. Zheng, and B. Y. Zhao. Measurement-calibrated graph models for social network experiments. In *WWW*. ACM, 2010.

[19] G. Smith. On the foundations of quantitative information flow. In *Foundations of Software Science and Computational Structures*, pages 288–302. Springer, 2009.

[20] L. Sweeney. k-anonymity: A model for protecting privacy. *International Journal of Uncertainty, Fuzziness and Knowledge-Based Systems*, 10(05):557–570, 2002.

[21] C.-H. Tai, P. S. Yu, D.-N. Yang, and M.-S. Chen. Privacy-preserving social network publication against friendship attacks. In *KDD*. ACM, 2011.

[22] A. Vázquez. Growing network with local rules: Preferential attachment, clustering hierarchy, and degree correlations. *Physical Review E*, 67(5):056104, 2003.

[23] Y. Wang and X. Wu. Preserving differential privacy in degree-correlation based graph generation. *TDP*, 6(2):127, 2013.

[24] W. Wu, Y. Xiao, W. Wang, Z. He, and Z. Wang. k-symmetry model for identity anonymization in social networks. In *EDBT*, pages 111–122. ACM, 2010.

[25] Q. Xiao, R. Chen, and K.-L. Tan. Differentially private network data release via structural inference. In *KDD*, pages 911–920. ACM, 2014.

[26] X. Ying and X. Wu. Randomizing social networks: a spectrum preserving approach. In *SDM*, volume 8, pages 739–750. SIAM, 2008.

[27] B. Zhou and J. Pei. Preserving privacy in social networks against neighborhood attacks. In *ICDE*, pages 506–515. IEEE, 2008.

[28] L. Zou, L. Chen, and M. T. Özsu. K-automorphism: A general framework for privacy preserving network publication. *VLDB Endowment*, 2009.

Table 7: *MaxVar* vs. (k,ϵ)-*obf*, *RandWalk* and *RandWalk-mod* (lower tradeoff is better)

	PRIVACY							UTILITY	
graph	$H1$	$H2_{open}$	$\lvert E_{G_0} \setminus E_G \rvert$	$\lvert E_G \setminus E_{G_0} \rvert$	$\epsilon(k=30)$	$\epsilon(k=50)$	$\epsilon(k=100)$	rel.err	tradeoff
dblp	199	125302			0.00238	0.00393	0.00694		
$\sigma = 0.001$	72.9	40712.1	6993.0	5280.2	0.00039	0.00122	0.00435	0.018	**3.61**
$\sigma = 0.01$	41.1	24618.2	19317.3	5444.9	0.00051	0.00062	0.00082	0.077	**12.03**
$\sigma = 0.1$	19.7	7771.4	65285.1	6916.8	0.00179	0.00199	0.00245	0.128	**11.33**
(MV) $n_p = 200k$	59.7	3257.2	94508.0	94416.5	0.00033	0.00077	0.00152	0.017	**0.99**
(MV) $n_p = 600k$	32.1	325.7	246155.6	246355.3	0.00017	0.00029	0.00085	0.045	**0.82**
(RW) $t = 2$	10.0	4.9	615966.2	567352.2	0.00318	0.00439	0.00789	0.094	**0.21**
(RW) $t = 5$	11.7	5.6	754178.1	753796.3	0.00271	0.00386	0.00689	0.142	**0.34**
(RW-mod) $t = 2$	11.8	4.5	719361.2	719416.5	0.00073	0.00135	0.00252	0.109	**0.23**
(RW-mod) $t = 5$	12.0	5.4	784872.3	784786.8	0.00057	0.00113	0.00228	0.131	**0.30**
amazon	153	113338			0.00151	0.00218	0.00456		
$\sigma = 0.001$	55.7	55655.9	6158.9	4607.4	0.00048	0.00119	0.00293	0.065	**13.40**
$\sigma = 0.01$	34.5	39689.8	14962.0	4801.3	0.00038	0.00052	0.00066	0.114	**21.33**
$\sigma = 0.1$	19.2	16375.4	39382.6	5650.3	0.00068	0.00102	0.00190	0.145	**18.46**
(MV) $n_p = 200k$	30.2	2209.1	104800.9	104759.9	0.00023	0.00032	0.00065	0.022	**1.03**
(MV) $n_p = 600k$	17.8	188.4	266603.7	266533.7	0.00015	0.00023	0.00047	0.066	**0.91**
(RW) $t = 2$	5.7	5.4	649001.0	585025.5	0.00213	0.00338	0.00550	0.180	**0.42**
(RW) $t = 5$	10.4	8.6	629961.8	629274.9	0.00146	0.00239	0.00423	0.181	**0.53**
(RW-mod) $t = 2$	9.8	3.2	725440.1	725239.9	0.00048	0.00073	0.00133	0.139	**0.25**
(RW-mod) $t = 5$	9.7	6.0	671694.2	671985.4	0.00038	0.00058	0.00137	0.185	**0.45**
youtube	978	321724			0.00291	0.00402	0.00583		
$\sigma = 0.001$	157.2	36744.6	19678.5	15028.5	0.00143	0.00232	0.00421	0.022	**4.28**
$\sigma = 0.01$	80.0	22361.7	62228.6	14914.3	0.00060	0.00105	0.00232	0.043	**6.38**
$\sigma = 0.1$	23.4	5806.9	378566.0	15007.5	0.00038	0.00052	0.00074	0.160	**12.20**
(MV) $n_p = 600k$	114.4	4428.8	213097.3	213371.4	0.00047	0.00063	0.00108	0.030	**2.00**
(MV) $n_p = 1800k$	71.4	814.4	521709.9	521791.6	0.00040	0.00052	0.00090	0.049	**1.38**
(RW) $t = 2$	13.4	1.5	2836169.3	2485053.4	0.00319	0.00425	0.00623	0.403	**0.50**
(RW) $t = 5$	24.6	8.4	2468068.6	2466411.3	0.00304	0.00408	0.00598	0.120	**0.35**
(RW-mod) $t = 2$	26.4	1.4	2863112.1	2862716.3	0.00159	0.00226	0.00355	0.245	**0.29**
(RW-mod) $t = 5$	26.1	11.0	2467414.9	2467269.5	0.00153	0.00322	0.00159	0.090	**0.30**

APPENDIX

A. PROOFS

A.1 Proof of Proposition 4.3

PROOF. Lemma 4.2 shows that $P = P_{RW}$ satisfies $P_{uv} = 0$ for all $(u,v) \notin G$ and AP^t is symmetric for all $t \geq 0$.

To prove that this is the unique solution, we repeat the formula in the proof of Lemma 4.2. Let $B^{(t)} = AP^{t-1}$, then $B^{(t)}_{ij} = \sum_{p_t(i,j)} \prod_{k \in p_t(i,j), k \neq i,j} P_{k,k+1}$ where $k+1$ implies the successive node of k in $p_t(i,j)$. Because $B^{(t)}_{ji}$ has the same number of products as $B^{(t)}_{ij}$ (i.e. the number of paths of length t), $B^{(t)}$ is symmetric if and only if corresponding products are equal, i.e. $\prod_{k \in p_t(i,j), k \neq i,j} P_{k,k+1} = \prod_{k \in p_t(j,i), k \neq i,j} P_{k,k+1}$. At $t = 2$, for any path (i,k,j) we must have $P_{kj} = P_{ki}$. Along with the requirement that P is right stochastic, i.e. $\sum_i P_{ki} = 1$, we obtain $P_{ki} = 1/d_k$. This is exactly P_{RW}. $\square$

A.2 Proof of Theorem 4.5

PROOF. For power-law graphs, the node degree distribution is $P(k) = \frac{k^{-\gamma}}{\zeta(\gamma)}$. The number of selfloops n^{PL}_{sl} in B^{∞}_{RW} is the sum of elements on the main diagonal.

$$n^{PL}_{sl} = \frac{1}{2m} \sum_{i=1}^{n} d_i^2 = \frac{1}{2m} \sum_{k=1}^{\infty} k^2 n P(k) = \frac{n}{nE(k)} \sum_{k=1}^{\infty} k^2 P(k)$$
$$= \frac{1}{E(k)} \sum_{k=1}^{\infty} \frac{k^{-(\gamma-2)}}{\zeta(\gamma)} = \frac{\zeta(\gamma)}{\zeta(\gamma-1)} \frac{\zeta(\gamma-2)}{\zeta(\gamma)} = \frac{\zeta(\gamma-2)}{\zeta(\gamma-1)}$$

To prove that there is no multiedge in B^{∞}_{RW} we show that all elements in B^{∞}_{RW} are less than 1. This is equivalent to show $d_{max} < \sqrt{2m}$. We use the constraint that the number of nodes with degree d_{max} must be at least 1, i.e. $\frac{n d_{max}^{-\gamma}}{\zeta(\gamma)} \geq 1 \leftrightarrow d_{max} \leq (n/\zeta(\gamma))^{1/\gamma}$. Because $\zeta(\gamma) > 1$ and we consider $\gamma > 2$ in social networks, $(n/\zeta(\gamma))^{1/\gamma} < \sqrt{n}$. Meanwhile, $\sqrt{2m} = \sqrt{n\frac{\zeta(\gamma-1)}{\zeta(\gamma)}} > \sqrt{n}$ due to the fact that $\zeta(\gamma)$ is monotonically decreasing. So we conclude $n^{PL}_{me} = 0$.

For sparse ER random graphs, we have $P(k) \rightarrow e^{-\lambda}\frac{\lambda^k}{k!}$. The number of selfloops n^{ER}_{sl} is

$$n^{ER}_{sl} = \frac{1}{2m} \sum_{i=1}^{n} d_i^2 = \frac{1}{2m} \sum_{k=1}^{\infty} k^2 n P(k) = \frac{n}{nE(k)} \sum_{k=1}^{\infty} k^2 P(k)$$
$$= \frac{1}{\lambda} E(k^2) = \frac{1}{\lambda}(E(k)^2 + Var(k)) = \frac{1}{\lambda}(\lambda^2 + \lambda) = \lambda + 1$$

Similar to the case of PL graphs, we show that $d_{max} < \sqrt{2m}$ where $d_{max} = \max_k ne^{-\lambda}\frac{\lambda^k}{k!} \geq 1 = \max_k \frac{k!}{\lambda^k} \leq ne^{-\lambda}$. Using the basic facts $k^{k/2} \leq k!$ and $k > \lambda$ we get $\frac{k^{k/2}}{\lambda^k} \leq ne^{-\lambda} < n$, so $k < n^{2/k}\lambda^2 < \sqrt{n\lambda} = \sqrt{2m}$ as long as n is sufficiently large and $\lambda \geq 4$. So we conclude $n^{ER}_{me} = 0$. $\square$

Social Networks Meet Distributed Systems

Towards a Robust Sybil Defense under Churn

Nitin Chiluka
INRIA Rennes
first.last@gmail.com

Nazareno Andrade
UFCG
nazareno@lsd.ufcg.edu.br

Johan Pouwelse
Delft University of Technology
j.a.pouwelse@tudelft.nl

Henk Sips
Delft University of Technology
h.j.sips@tudelft.nl

ABSTRACT

This paper examines the impact of heavy churn on the robustness of decentralized social network-based Sybil defense (SNSD) schemes. Our analysis reveals that (i) heavy churn disintegrates the social overlay network that is fundamental to these schemes into multiple disconnected components, resulting in poor network connectivity, and (ii) a naive solution that adds links from each node to all its 2-hop neighbors improves network connectivity but comes at a significant cost of poor attack resilience of these schemes.

We propose a new design point in the trade-off between network connectivity and attack resilience of SNSD schemes, where each node adds links to only a selective few of all its 2-hop neighbors based on a minimum expansion contribution (MinEC) heuristic. Extensive evaluation through simulations shows that our approach fares as good as the naive 2-hop solution in terms of network connectivity, while making little compromise on the attack resilience. Moreover, our approach preserves the fast-mixing property that is fundamental to many SNSD schemes even at high levels of churn. This result suggests that existing and potential future SNSD schemes relying on this property can incorporate our approach into their designs with minimal changes.

Categories and Subject Descriptors

C.2.0 [**Computer-Communication Networks**]: General—*Security and protection*

Keywords

Social overlay network, Churn, Sybil attack

1. INTRODUCTION

Security and churn are two key challenges in designing open distributed systems. One of the most demanding security challenges these systems face is a *Sybil attack* [14], where an adversary creates an arbitrary number of Sybil identities in order to reduce the system utility for the honest users.

ASIA CCS '15, April 14-17, 2015, Singapore, Singapore.

ACM ACM 978-1-4503-3245-3/15/04...$15.00.
http://dx.doi.org/10.1145/2714576.2714606 .

Such an attack has been addressed by the decentralized social network-based Sybil defense (SNSD) schemes [32, 31, 18, 21, 27] that leverage the trust relationships among users and the resultant *social overlay network*'s graph structure properties (e.g., fast-mixing [22]) for their robustness. The challenge of churn, however, has been little addressed in these SNSD designs, thus making them potentially vulnerable to heavy churn.

In this paper, we focus on designing a robust social network-based Sybil defense in the face of heavy churn as observed in the real-world. To understand the magnitude of churn in today's distributed systems, we measure the number of concurrent Skype users online over a 7-month period in 2014 at a granularity of 5-minute interval. We observe that only 10-25% of all users are online at any given instance. Furthermore, our analysis of the datasets of Yahoo! Instant Messenger [7, 8] reveals that only a small fraction (5-15%) of all users are online concurrently, corroborating the Skype online concurrency pattern.

We examine the impact of such heavy churn on the social overlay network, created out of the trust relationships of immediate neighbors of each node, which lies at the heart of these decentralized SNSD schemes. Heavy churn disintegrates this `One-Hop` overlay[1] into multiple disconnection components, as depicted in Figures 1(a) and 1(b). This results in poor network connectivity with two honest nodes despite being online may not be able to communicate with each other due to the disconnected overlay. A `Two-Hop` overlay created by adding links to all the 2-hop neighbors of each node, similar to the one proposed in MCON [28], improves the network connectivity but comes at the cost of very poor attack resilience (Fig. 1(c)). This is because of the creation of *new* 2-hop relationships, which also include those between honest and Sybil nodes amounting to nearly 3 orders of magnitude greater than that of the `One-Hop` overlay under a modest attack. Note that the attack resilience of SNSD schemes typically relies on the trust relationships between the honest and Sybil nodes (*attack edges*) to be few.

We explore a new design point in the trade-off between network connectivity and attack resilience. Our approach aims to improve the network connectivity while incurring a

[1]Henceforth, we use the `typewriter` font and upper case for the first letter of each word in the overlay and heuristic (e.g., `One-Hop`, `Common Neighbors`), to highlight the overlay and heuristic and differentiate them from other usages of the same term in various contexts (e.g., (i) '1-hop' attack edges, and (ii) the 'common neighbors' of two nodes, respectively).

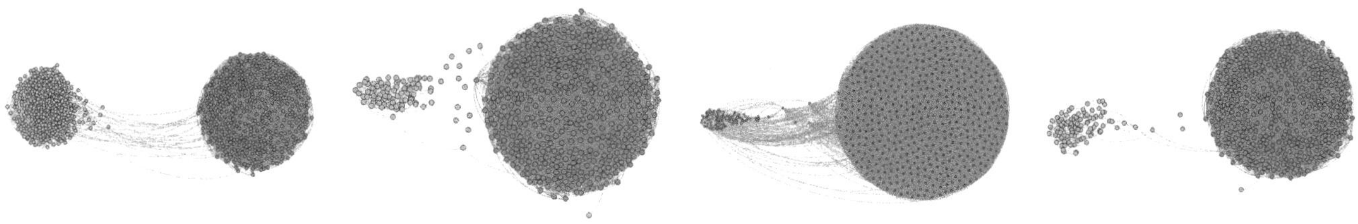

(a) Initial Overlay (b) `One-Hop` Overlay (c) `Two-Hop` Overlay (d) `MinEC`-based Overlay

Figure 1: A pictorial illustration of the social overlay network under heavy churn employing various heuristics. The honest and Sybil regions are represented by green and red nodes respectively. Churn disintegrates the overlay from Fig. 1(a) to Fig. 1(b). `Two-Hop` overlay is better connected but has a significantly large number of 2-hop attack edges (Fig. 1(c)). Our approach (Fig. 1(d)) strikes a balance in the trade-off between network connectivity and attack resilience, with a modest number of disconnected online honest nodes from the largest connected component of the online honest region and 2-hop attack edges.

modest cost in terms of attack resilience (Fig. 1(d)). We propose adding links from each node to only a selective few k of its 2-hop neighbors based on a *minimum expansion contribution* (`MinEC`) [20] heuristic. The main idea of `MinEC` is that the formation of a potential 2-hop link (v, x) between nodes v and x depends on the number of common neighbors between the two nodes while penalizing their node degrees.

We evaluate our approach through extensive experiments in a simulated environment. Our experiments reveal the following. First, `MinEC` fares as good as `Two-Hop` in terms of network connectivity and `One-Hop` in terms of attack resilience, for a wide range of parameter configurations. Second, on our datasets with average degree 8-24, `MinEC` requires only a few $k \approx 100$ of all the 2-hop neighbors of each node to achieve such level of robustness. This suggests that our approach adds only a modest network overhead to the `One-Hop` overlay, but has a much better network connectivity. Third, `MinEC` preserves the fast-mixing property of the honest region's largest connected component (LCC) even under heavy churn with only 10% of all honest nodes being online. This result suggests that existing and potential future SNSD schemes relying on the fast-mixing property of the honest region can be applied to the overlay created by `MinEC` even under heavy churn. We show the feasibility of such application by evaluating the robustness of Gatekeeper [27], a state-of-the-art SNSD scheme, in the case where only 20% of all honest nodes are online.

The rest of the paper is organized as follows. We begin with a review of the literature in the field in Section 2, while Section 3 presents the measurement and analysis of churn in two popular instant messaging systems. Section 4 reformulates the problem addressed by SNSD schemes by incorporating churn as major challenge. We propose our approach in Section 5, while Section 6 presents an extensive evaluation of our approach through simulations. Section 7 summarizes the paper.

2. BACKGROUND AND RELATED WORK

2.1 Social Network-based Sybil Defenses

Over the last decade, a large body of work [32, 31, 18, 27, 16, 21, 28] has leveraged social networks to help build robust and secure distributed systems. One line of work in this field focuses on defending distributed systems against a highly challenging threat of Sybil attacks [14]. Researchers propose social network-based Sybil defense (SNSD) schemes [32, 31, 18, 27] that incorporate properties such as the trust relationships among users as well as the resultant graph structure into their designs to counter such attacks.

Despite varying in approach, most of these schemes make two fundamental assumptions. First, an adversary can create a *Sybil region* G_S comprising a large number of Sybil identities with trust relationships among themselves. However, it cannot arbitrarily form trust relationships with honest users (*attack edges*) because it requires social engineering effort which is often costly. Second, the *honest region* G_H comprising only honest users and their relationships is *expander*-like and *fast-mixing* [22] in that a random walk in G_H quickly reaches a stationary distribution.

The first assumption implies that the Sybil and honest regions are connected by only a few attack edges. Based on the second assumption, SNSD schemes exploit such a sparse cut between the regions for their robustness. For instance, the fact that a short random walk starting from a node in the fast-mixing honest region rarely escapes into the Sybil region enables SNSD schemes to minimize the influence of Sybil nodes on the system utility for honest users.

In this paper, we limit our focus to decentralized SNSD schemes which can be primarily classified into (i) *Sybil detection* schemes that aim to differentiate honest and Sybil nodes with a high accuracy, and (ii) *Sybil-resilient* applications that tolerate Sybil nodes in their system but not explicitly identify them.

Sybil Detection. SybilGuard [32] is the seminal study in the field of Sybil defenses that leverage social networks and their properties (e.g., fast mixing) to counter Sybil attacks [14]. In SybilGuard, each node performs a random route of length $w = \Theta(\sqrt{n} \log n)$. A verifier accepts a suspect if the former's random route intersects with the latter's. When the number of attack edges is $g = O(\sqrt{n}/\log n)$, SybilGuard accepts at most $O(\sqrt{n} \log n)$ Sybil nodes per attack edge with a high probability.

SybilLimit [31] improves upon SybilGuard in that SybilLimit accepts at most $O(\log n)$ Sybil nodes per attack edge with a high probability for $g = O(n/\log n)$. In SybilLimit, each node performs $r = O(\sqrt{m})$ short random walks of length $w = O(\log n)$, and gathers the knowledge of the final edge (*tail*) of each random walk. A verifier accepts a suspect if they both share a common tail.

Gatekeeper [27], with a strong assumption that the social network graph is a balanced expander-like network, accepts at most $O(\log g)$ Sybil nodes per attack edge when

$g < O(n/\log n)$. In the worst case when $g = O(n/\log n)$, both SybilLimit and Gatekeeper accept $O(\log n)$ Sybil nodes per attack edge. Gatekeeper works by distributing $O(n)$ tickets to the rest of the network in a breadth-first fashion from a few (s) seed nodes. A verifier accepts a suspect that has received tickets from at least $f_{admit} * s$ seed nodes.

Sybil-Resilience. X-Vine [21] is designed to perform secure communications pseudonymously over a social overlay network in the face of a Sybil attack. X-Vine constructs trails on top of the overlay such that these trails can be later used for routing messages from one node to another in the network. An adversary can employ a large number of Sybil nodes in such a network to perform malicious activities such as traffic analysis, dropping lookups and trails, and/or routing them to other Sybil nodes. If the number of attack edges is limited, X-Vine bounds the number of trails that can be constructed between the honest and Sybil regions. Thus, the path of a lookup issued by an honest node for another honest node remains in the honest region with a high probability. Note that a successful lookup path contains all its intermediate nodes honest as well, thus making the communication over this path effectively secure.

Most of the above SNSD studies do not incorporate *churn* as a major design factor. Studies of SybilGuard [32], SybilLimit [31], and Gatekeeper [27] have little explored how churn affects their system performance. Whanau [18] and X-Vine [21] were put to test with a worst-case churn of 20%, i.e., at least 80% of all honest users are online at any given point in time. However, as we show next through review and measurements, real-world P2P systems have only 5-25% of all users online at any instance. Such a small fraction of all honest users being online at a time can significantly impact the performance of the above systems.

2.2 Churn in P2P Systems

Churn has often been considered as a key challenge in developing P2P systems. Stutzbach and Rejaie [26] measured churn in three peer-to-peer file sharing systems: BitTorrent, Kad and Gnutella. Their results corroborate and extend previous efforts to show that peer uptime is skewed in all three systems, with many users staying online only for a few minutes at a time. This observation, in turn, has direct implications for the connectivity of the system. However, Stutzbach and Rejaie note that previous uptime is a reasonable predictor of future uptime for peers, a property that can be leveraged for connectivity resilience.

On a different perspective, Rhea *et al.* [25] present an overview of the literature on the measurement of session durations in file-sharing P2P systems. This literature points to median session durations in the order of few minutes to one hour. Moreover, Bhagwan *et al.* [10] measured Overnet to find that users are online on a median of 30% of the period that comprises their participation in the system. Rhea *et al.* show how the assumptions related to churn drastically affect the performance of DHT systems, requiring their mechanisms to be developed with churn as a primary concern. Our work aims at contributing to the conception of realistic churn assumptions for the development of distributed social network based solutions.

3. MEASUREMENTS AND ANALYSIS

Instant messaging systems such as Skype [1] and Yahoo! Instant Messenger [6] are used by millions of users everyday. The whole ecosystem of each such system can essentially be viewed as a *distributed social network*. A typical user in such a system first installs a client on her machine, and then adds friends and acquaintances who are also using the system as 'contacts' in order to interact with them. Unlike online social networks (OSNs) such as Facebook and LinkedIn, these systems usually do not enable users to access friends of their friends and beyond, resulting in each user/client having a very limited knowledge of her neighborhood. This setting provides a natural environment to motivate design considerations for distributed social network-based approaches. In this section, we examine some of the dynamics observed in such systems which can help build more realistic and robust distributed social network-based systems.

3.1 Skype

While most of the research related to churn in distributed systems was studied predominantly in the previous decade, we argue that churn is still an important factor in today's distributed systems. To illustrate this importance, we examine the uptime behavior in one of the world's largest and most popular instant messaging systems: Skype [1].

We collected[2] from an RSS feed[3] on the Skype website [3] the total number of concurrent Skype users online at a granularity of 5-minute interval for the duration of 7 months from February 6, 2014 to August 18, 2014. Figure 2 shows each data point in this period, with all times shown from the Central European Time (CET) zone.

We observe the expected diurnal pattern of online users with the highest concurrency during the early evening and the lowest in the early morning. Consider an example day of July 21, 2014. Starting at midnight, the number of concurrent users online is 58 million and dips to the lowest of the day with 55 million online at 4 AM, and then gradually increases upto a peak of 81 million online at 6 PM. The number of concurrent users online then decreases to 61 million at midnight at the start of the next day. We note that the highest / lowest concurrency at 6 PM / 4 AM CET coincides with 12 PM / 10 PM Eastern Time (ET) zone and 9 AM / 7 PM Pacific Time (PT) zone in the United States, which better explains the day / night online behavior of users.

There is also a weekly pattern in that the concurrent users peak on Monday and gradually fades through the week until Saturday. Interestingly, Sunday is not the least active day which may be due to Saturday, and not Sunday, being the most common day in the weekend across various countries.

During a week, we observe a min-max of 32-58 and 47-82 million users online at any time prior to June 2014 and post mid-June 2014, respectively. The week of June 10 saw an increase of nearly 25 million concurrent users, which may be due to various factors such as World Cup and/or the release of a new version of Skype for iPhone [2]. However, the concurrent usage has since followed a steady pattern.

Based on Microsoft's Skype Internal Data[4], there were about 240, 300, and 330 million active users every month in 2012, 2013, and 2014 respectively. Extrapolating these

[2]This dataset will be made available upon request.

[3]Since September 2014, we observed that this feed [3] is discontinued. Interestingly, Skype clients which used to show the number of concurrent users online are no longer displaying the number.

[4]`http://advertising.microsoft.com/en/WWDocs/User/display/cl/brand_subproperty/1589/global/Skype\%20Advertising\%20Media\%20Overview\%20FY15.pdf/`

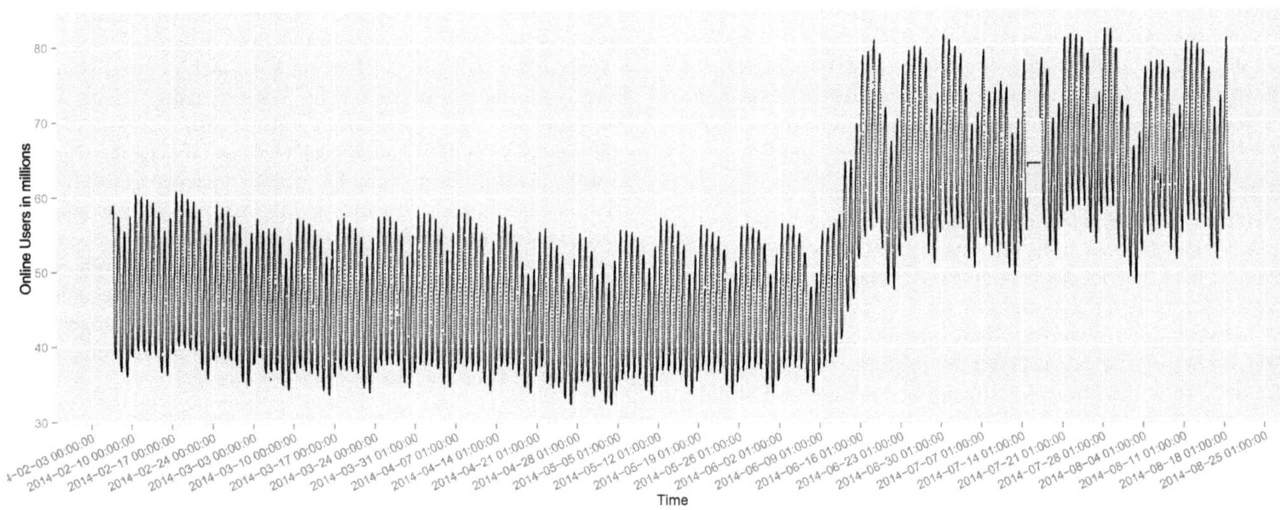

Figure 2: # Concurrent Skype users online from February 6, 2014 to August 18, 2014 at the granularity of 5 minutes.

statistics and our measurements, we estimate that at most 10-25% of all Skype users are online at a given instance.

3.2 Yahoo! Instant Messenger

We obtained two datasets[5] related to Yahoo! Instant Messenger (YIM) through the Yahoo! Webscope program which describe: (i) how active the YIM users are during a day [7], and (ii) how YIM users communicate with each other over a month [8].

YIM Client-to-Server Protocol-Level Events [7]. This dataset contains two parts. The first part comprises 148,176,335 protocol events logged by 4,665,328 unique users in a 24-hour period in June 2010. Around 200 protocol events such as 'logging in', 'sending IM', 'accepting buddy invite', and 'sending files' are logged with each record (t, u) representing an event generated by a user u at time t. However, the type of an event is not logged. The second part comprises 5,320,505 message event records of the form (t, u_1, u_2) indicating who-messaged-whom among users in the first part at what time but only during this 24-hour period.

Unfortunately, this dataset [7] does not contain explicit information about the begin and end times of user sessions. To circumvent this limitation, we infer sessions based on user inactivity. As it is known that the keep alive messages have a periodicity of one hour in YIM [17], we consider that if a user sends at least one message in the (t)-th hour of the trace but not in the $(t+1)$-th hour, this user has a session ending before the $(t+1)$-th hour. The possible side effect of this heuristic is that in some situations where a user goes offline and comes back online in less than an hour, the two sessions will be considered as a contiguous one. Nevertheless, our analyses in this work are not concerned with the number of sessions a user has, or with very-short-term dynamics. Therefore, the expected effect of considering these two sessions as one is very limited. With this assumption in mind, we next study the hourly dynamics of YIM clients.

Figure 3(a) shows the percentage of users who are online during a particular hour with respect to all the users who are online at any instance during the 24-hour period. The analysis of this period can be divided into 4 parts. First, from 4 AM to 9 AM, we see a steady growth of users joining the network with 4% of online users at 4 AM to 15% at 9 AM. Second, from 9 AM to 4 PM, nearly 15% of users are online every hour with a marginal drop at 2 PM which may be due to users having lunch during this period. Third, from 4 PM to 9 PM, online users reduce to 13% at 6-7 PM and increase back to 15% at 9 PM. The drop may be due to users leaving for their homes and having dinner, while the rise is perhaps post-dinner online time. Fourth, from 9 PM to 4 AM, online users drop from 15% at 9 PM to 4% at 4 AM.

Figure 3(b) plots the percentage of users online in the previous hour who continue to be online in the current hour. Each hour sees at least a third of all users online from the previous hour almost throughout the day. From 9 AM to 5 PM, over 40% of users are observed in subsequent hourly time intervals. Late night sees a variance in users being online across each hour with less than 30% of them being common from 4 AM at 5 AM.

Figure 3(c) plots the percentage of users observed in t hourly time intervals. About half of all users are seen only in one time interval and nearly 90% of all users are observed in 5 or fewer time intervals, while less than 5% of all users are seen in 10 or more time intervals. This shows that user sessions typically last less than an hour. Such session times are comparable to those in other P2P systems [26].

Figure 3(d) plots the distribution of the number of messages sent by each user versus her online time over the 24-hour period. We plot only for those users who have sent at least one message, who amount to only 3% of all users. The median number of messages sent by a user grows with the hours online, but plateaus after 14-15 hours online. Users who are online for more than 18 hours send fewer messages which may be due to the users keeping their clients running nearly all day while only occasionally chatting with others.

[5] Although the datasets are quite large, there are a couple of limitations. First, the data selection process for these datasets is not made public. Second, these datasets are completely independent of each other in the sense that users across both the datasets are not the same. Nevertheless, we believe that we can draw reasonable inferences of the system in general since both the datasets belong to the same instant messaging system.

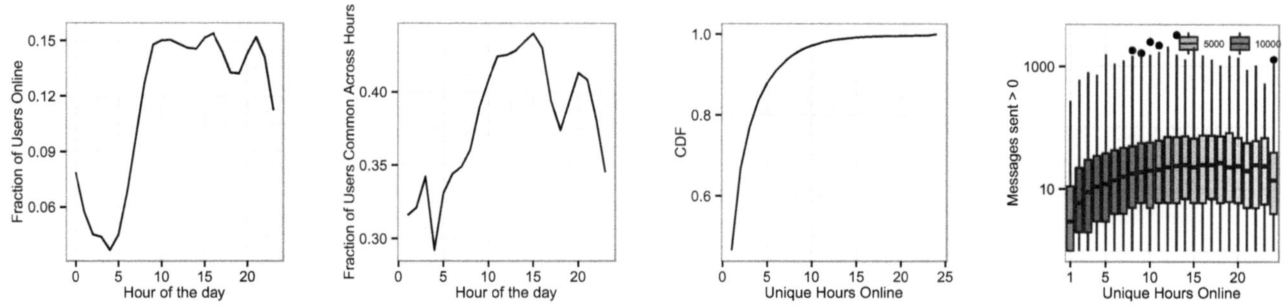

(a) Online Concurrency (b) Online > 1 hour (c) Online Distribution (d) Messaging Activity

Figure 3: Hourly dynamics and user sessions of Yahoo! Instant Messenger clients.

YIM User Communication Pattern [8]. This dataset captures the knowledge of who-messaged-whom among 100,000 users located in 5649 zip codes every day from April 1 to 28, 2008. In each day, only the first communication between two users from a unique locale is loged: (u_1, z_1, u_2, z_2, t), which represents user u_1 from zip code z_1 sent a message to user u_2 from zip code z_2 at time t. If the sender sends another message in the day to the same receiver from the same sender zip code, the event is not logged. However, if either the receiver's or the sender's zip code changes, the event of only the first subsequent message is recorded.

We examine the relationship between user activity and friendships over the period of one month. Figure 4(left) plots the heat map of the minimum number of messages sent by a user versus the number of her friends. The more the friends, the more the messages a user sends. Figure 4(right) plots the heat map of the number of unique days on which a user sent at least one message versus the number of her friends. The more the friends, the more days a user is active online.

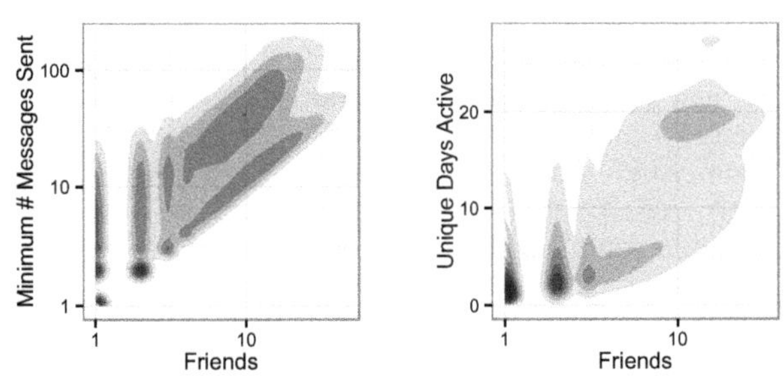

Figure 4: Relationship between user's activity, friends and online time. Darker/lighter gray indicates many/few users.

3.3 Summary

We summarize our findings and discuss their implications:

- In both Skype and YIM, the percentage of all users online during a 24-hour period hits a peak of 15-25% during the daytime and a bottom of nearly 5-10% during late night. This suggests that (i) there are only a small fraction of all users online at any instance, and (ii) the online pattern follows a non-stationary distribution.
- Almost 50% / 90% of all YIM users are observed for less than 1 hour / 5 hours in a day. This indicates that most users are online for a short period.
- About 30-45% of YIM users are online across one hour to the next throughout the day. This implies that there exists a considerable fraction of users online that can be potentially leveraged even in a dynamic environment.
- The more friends a user has, the more time she spends online and the more messages she sends. This shows that there is a correlation between the number of friends a user has, her online time and activity.

The rest of the paper examines the impact of such dynamics on the robustness of social network-based decentralized systems, particularly from a Sybil defense perspective.

4. PROBLEM FORMULATION

In this section, we reformulate the problem addressed in the previous decentralized social network-based Sybil defense (SNSD) schemes such as SybilLimit [31], Gatekeeper [27], and X-Vine [21] by taking into account *churn* as a major design factor. Our model is motivated by the measurements of Skype and YIM from the previous section.

We introduce the following notations we use for the rest of the paper. An undirected graph $G = (V, E)$ contains a set of nodes V and edges E. For a given set of nodes $S \subseteq V$, let $N(S) = \{w \in V - S : \exists v \in S \text{ s.t. } (v, w) \in E\}$ represent the set of (immediate) *1-hop neighbors* of S, and $N_2(S) = N(N(S)) - (N(S) \cup S)$ represent the set of *2-hop neighbors* of S which are at a distance of 2 from S.

System and Threat Models. We consider an open decentralized system in which there is no single authority that can restrict participation. Each participating entity is expected to follow the protocol of the system in order to better utilize the system. However, the open nature of the system attracts adversaries whose primary motive is to deviate from the protocol and hamper the utility of the system.

Let each participating entity in the system have a unique identity which can be classified as either *honest* or *malicious*. An honest identity is uniquely associated with a user that follows the protocol of the system. In contrast, malicious identities are controlled by an *adversary* aiming to undermine the system utility for the honest users. The adversary may create malicious identities arbitrarily for this purpose, which is referred to as the *Sybil attack* [14].

For the Sybil defense, we incorporate and *extend* some of the fundamentals of the models and assumptions of the previous SNSD studies [32, 31, 18, 27, 21], as discussed in Sec. 2.1, into our system. First, there exists a social network among all honest and Sybil identities. Each identity has one or more trust relationships with other identities. Second, the adversary may create trust relationships among the Sybil identities not only arbitrarily but also based on a strategy that potentially maximizes the adversary's advantage. Third, the honest region representing the subgraph of honest identities and their relationships is fast-mixing [22]. Also, the honest region is a single connected component. Fourth, the adversary may have complete knowledge of the honest region. Fifth, the adversary can thus strategically create, albeit limited, trust relationships (*attack edges*) between the honest and Sybil identities.

In addition to the Sybil attack, the system faces the major challenge of *churn*. Let *unavailability* c represent the fraction of all honest users being offline at any given instance. We expect only a small fraction $(1 - c) \in [0.05, 0.25]$, i.e., 5-25% of all honest users to be online at any given instance. Let the probability of an honest user v being online is proportional to a small non-negative exponent γ of its number of trust relationships: $\Pr(v) \propto |N(\{v\})|^{\gamma}$, where $N(\{v\})$ represents the set of all the neighbors of v in the honest region. When $\gamma > 0$, honest nodes with higher degree are more likely to be online than the ones with lower degree at any given instance. When $\gamma = 0$, the probability of an honest node being online is unrelated to its degree. In contrast, the adversary can have all of its Sybil identities online all the time so as to minimize the system utility for honest users.

Goals. The main goal in this work is to enable honest users securely communicate with each other with a high probability in the face of aforementioned strategic Sybil attack and heavy churn. Under these conditions, the system should be able to provide with the same level of robustness as the scenario in which all honest nodes are online, in terms of:

- *Network Connectivity*: There must exist, with a high probability, at least one path (preferably many paths) between any two online honest nodes such that all the intermediate nodes in the path are honest as well.
- *Attack Resilience*: Generic SNSD schemes must be applicable to the system even under heavy churn.

5. APPROACH

5.1 Exploring 2-Hop Neighbors: Pros & Cons

MCON [28] is the among the first studies to show that high unavailability results in the graph representing the social overlay network among users to disintegrate into multiple disconnected components. As a consequence, two nodes that are online at the same time may not be able to communicate with each other due to them being present in two distinct connected components and thus no path exists between them. In essence, high unavailability degrades the network connectivity which is critical to our system.

The authors [28] explore nodes that are beyond the immediate trust circle of each node by tapping into the potential of the 2-hop neighborhood of the node: *the neighbors of its immediate neighbors.* The idea is that trust is usually transitive, i.e., friends of friends are often considered trustworthy albeit to a lesser extent. Their experiments reveal that leveraging all the 2-hop neighbors of each node significantly improves the network connectivity even in the case of high unavailability. In other words, a much larger fraction of all online honest nodes belong to the largest connected component (LCC) with the `Two-Hop` overlay in comparison to that of the simplistic `One-Hop` overlay.

MCON [28], however, cannot be applied to our system directly due to the following reasons. First, MCON employs a central authority that limits the number of Sybil identities, and controls the degree of each node to an extent in the system. In contrast, our system aims for a decentralized design where Sybil identities and node degree are not restricted. Second, our analysis in Sec. 5.3 and the experimental results in Sec. 6 validate our hypothesis that

> *Adding links from each node to all its 2-hop neighbors has a significant unintended consequence of creating a large number of new (2-hop) attack edges between honest and Sybil nodes.*

This is particularly undesired since the robustness of SNSD schemes relies on the attack edges being few and limited.

An Illustrating Example. Consider the following system comprising an honest region and a Sybil region. The honest region's graph structure follows the Barabási-Albert preferential attachment model [9] with $n = 500$ honest nodes and $d = 4$ average node degree. The Sybil region mimics the honest region with the same model and the number of nodes but with an average Sybil degree $d_S = d{*}5 = 20$. The honest and Sybil regions are connected by $g = 0.05 * n$ (1-hop) attack edges. This constitutes the *initial overlay* of the system, as depicted in Figure 1(a). When only 20% of all honest users are online (i.e., unavailability $c = 0.8$), the `One-Hop` overlay disintegrates into multiple disconnected components (Fig. 1(b)). Adding (2-hop) links from each honest node to all its 2-hop neighbors results in the `Two-Hop` overlay with better network connectivity, but comes at a significant cost of the creation of many new 2-hop attack edges (Fig. 1(c)).

5.2 Selective k 2-hop neighbors

The design space for our system, with the constraints of high unavailability and strategic Sybil attack, can thus be populated with two points: (i) `One-Hop` overlay with poor network connectivity and fair attack resilience (Fig. 1(b)), and (ii) `Two-Hop` overlay with fair network connectivity and poor attack resilience (Fig. 1(c)). In this paper, we propose a new design point in the trade-off between network connectivity and attack resilience (Fig. 1(d)).

Our approach aims to add links from each node v to only a selective few (k) of all its 2-hop neighbors. The criteria for the selection of a v's 2-hop neighbor $y \in N_2(\{v\})$ is based on our adaptation of the *expansion contribution* [20] of y with respect to v, which is calculated as:

$$f(v, y) = |N(\{y\})| - |N(\{v\}) \cap N(\{y\})| \qquad (1)$$

Expansion contribution captures the number of *new* neighbors that y contributes to v's neighborhood. This value is obtained by subtracting the amount of overlap ($|N(\{v\}) \cap N(\{y\})|$) between the immediate neighborhoods of v and y from y's node degree $|N(\{y\})|$.

We now describe the details of our approach. First, each node v computes an expansion contribution score $f(v, y)$ for each node $y \in N_2(\{v\})$ of all its 2-hop neighbors. Second, v generates a ranked list of at most k of its 2-hop neighbors with the lowest scores. We thus name our heuristic *minimum expansion contribution* (`MinEC`). Third, each node v initiates a 2-hop link request to every node x in v's ranked list. Fourth, a 2-hop link (v, x) is created if and only if x is present is v's ranked list and vice-versa. For better understanding, consider the following example where x receives a 2-hop link request from v. If x has v in its ranked list as well, x reciprocates the request by creating the 2-hop link (x, v) which completes the handshake for future communication over this link. However, if v is not present in the ranked list of 2-hop neighbors of x, then the node x would discard the 2-hop link request from v.

The exception to this rule of creating the 2-hop link (x, v) is that if x is a Sybil node receiving the link request from an honest node v, the Sybil node x will reciprocate the request regardless of v's presence in x's ranked list. Such a deviation from the protocol of a 2-hop link creation enables *more* 2-hop attack edges to be formed than in the protocol-compliant scenario, thus playing into the advantage of the adversary.

In essence, the main rationale of `MinEC` is that, by rewarding the number of common neighbors between two nodes v and y and penalizing their node degrees, the *expansion* [20] of each node's neighborhood is done at a slow rate as k grows. This enables, with a high probability for a small k, (i) an honest node to form 2-hop (honest) edges with other honest nodes due to high clustering coefficient typically found in the social network graphs, and (ii) an honest node to minimize the addition of 2-hop (attack) edges with Sybil nodes since they would contribute to *more new* Sybil nodes to an honest node's neighborhood. From another perspective, the formation of 2-hop links can be viewed as a variant of the *link prediction problem* [19], and the `MinEC` heuristic is a link predictor method.

5.3 Analysis

Here, we present the intuition behind our hypothesis and the choice of k from an analytical perspective.

Creation of 2-hop attack edges. Let a d-regular graph $G = (V, E)$ be α-expander, i.e., for every subset of nodes $S \subset V$ and $|S| < |V|/2$, the expansion factor is $X(S) = |N(S)|/|S| \geq \alpha = \Omega(1)$. The theory on expander graphs [5] tells us that, for a given set of nodes $S \subset V$, the expansion factor is $X(S) \geq d/4$, when the set S is very small relative to the size of the graph ($|S| << |V|$) and the graph's second largest eigenvalue is $\mu = 2\sqrt{d-1}$.

We now put this in the context of our system. Let a graph G with the above properties represent a large social overlay network containing a single Sybil node v and the rest are honest nodes. Then, the system would contain $g = d$ 1-hop attack edges between v and its immediate neighbors $N(\{v\})$. Let $S = \{v\} \cup N(\{v\})$ represent the small neighborhood around v. The expansion factor of S at such a local level [5] is $X(S) = |N(S)|/|S| \geq d/4$ since $|S| = d+1$ ($<< |V|$) for a large graph. We note that here $N(S) = N_2(\{v\})$, representing the number of 2-hop neighbors of v. An application of the naive `Two-Hop` heuristic would enable v to create a total of $g_2 \geq d + (d+1)d/4 = O(d^2)$ 2-hop attack edges which include 1-hop attack edges and the *new* 2-hop attack edges with its 2-hop neighbors $N_2(\{v\})$.

The choice of k. Consider a system aiming to provide a quality of service (QoS) in terms of network connectivity for the nodes in the system at a given level of unavailability. Suppose further that the QoS requirement is that the probability of disconnection of a node at a high unavailability $c = 0.9$ is below the threshold $\tau = 0.05$. As noted in [28], the probability of disconnection of a node with degree d is $DP(d) = c^d$. Hence, to satisfy the QoS requirement of the system, nearly every node needs to have its degree $d \geq d_\tau = 30$, since $DP(30) = 0.9^{30} < 0.05 = \tau$. Such a high degree, however, is not observed for most nodes in real-world social networks. This is because these networks exhibit a power-law degree distribution along the lines of $P(d) \propto d^{-\eta}$, which indicates that there exists a node with degree d with a probability proportional to a small negative exponent ($2 < \eta < 3$ typically) of its degree d. This shows that nodes with degree $d \geq d_\tau$ are often a small fraction in such networks.

Table 1: Datasets. Keys: |V|=# Nodes, |E|=# Edges, CC = Clustering Coefficient, δ = Effective Diameter.

Dataset	|V|	|E|	CC	δ
AstroPhysics [4]	17,903	197,001	0.633	6.995
Epinions [4]	26,588	100,120	0.135	6.989
Facebook [29]	59,691	728,409	0.227	6.385

To meet the QoS requirement, each node with a low degree ($d < d_\tau$) must add additional l links in the form of 2-hop neighbors such that its effective degree becomes $d_2 = d + l \geq d_\tau$. We remind that in our approach a 2-hop link (v, x) is created if and only if x is present in v's ranked list of size k and vice-versa. Thus, the size of the ranked list must be greater than or equal to the number of 2-hop links required by nearly every low degree node ($k \geq l$).

Choosing the right value for k globally is a non-trivial task. We propose an iterative approach to selecting k. At the beginning iteration $i = 0$, each node v assigns a small default value for $k = k^{(0)}$. Each iteration i proceeds as follows. The node v generates 2-hop link requests to the $k^{(i)}$ nodes in its ranked list, and form only those 2-hop links that were reciprocated. At this point, v sends the value of its effective degree $d_2^{(i)}$ to each of its current 1-hop and 2-hop neighbors ($N^{(i)}$) with which v has 1-hop and 2-hop links respectively. At node v, let r denote the fraction of these neighbors ($N^{(i)}$) whose effective degrees are smaller than the degree threshold (d_τ). If $r > \tau$ for a large fraction of nodes, the value of $k^{(i)}$ is increased additively to $k^{(i+1)}$ for the next iteration $(i+1)$. Otherwise, if $r \leq \tau$ for nearly every node, the iterations are stopped, and the final ranked list size is set to $k = k^{(b)}$ where b is the final iteration.

6. EVALUATION

This section presents an extensive evaluation of our approach, primarily examining the robustness of the social overlay network in terms of network connectivity and the attack resilience in the face of heavy churn and a strategic Sybil attack. We first describe our simulation environment, and then study the impact of various parameters on the robustness of the system. We also examine the suitability of applying off-the-shelf state-of-the-art Sybil defense schemes on social overlay networks incurring churn.

6.1 Experimental Setup

Datasets. Table 1 shows the datasets used in our experiments. We note that these datasets have already been studied in previous works in the SNSD field [23, 30, 21]. While the graphs of AstroPhysics [4] and Facebook [29] are undirected in nature, the relationships in the original dataset of Epinions [4] are directed. As recommended in [24], we derive an undirected graph by considering only the node pairs with edges in both the directions in the original directed graph. In our experiments, we consider only the largest connected component in each dataset to represent the honest region.

Metrics. We measure the system robustness in terms of network connectivity and attack resilience respectively with:

- *Disconnection Probability*: It measures the probability of an online honest node belonging to the largest connected component (LCC) of online honest nodes. The smaller the disconnection probability, the greater the likelihood of a path between any two online honest nodes comprising only honest nodes as its intermediate nodes.

- *Escape Probability*: It measures the probability of a uniform random walk of length $w = O(log((1-c)*n))$ starting from a node in the largest connected component of online honest nodes to escape into the Sybil region. We note that most SNSD schemes, in decentralized [32, 31, 18] as well as centralized [13] settings, employ variants of the uniform random walks for their effectiveness. Thus, we believe that the escape probability metric captures the notion of attack resilience of a generic SNSD scheme.

Baseline Heuristics. We compare the system robustness enabled by our proposed heuristic (`MinEC`) with that of:

- `One-Hop` heuristic is the default one, where each node has overlay links to only its 1-hop neighbors (Fig. 1(b)).
- `Two-Hop` heuristic mimics the one proposed in the MCON study [28], where each node adds overlay links to all its 2-hop neighbors on top of the 1-hop network (Fig. 1(c)).
- `Random` heuristic enables each node to initiate links to at most k of all its 2-hop neighbors uniformly at random.
- `Common Neighbors` heuristic differs from the `Random` one in the selection process of the k 2-hop neighbors. For each node v, the extent of neighborhood overlap of each 2-hop neighbor $y \in N_2(\{v\})$ is computed as $|N(\{v\}) \cap N(\{y\})|$, and then the top k of these 2-hop neighbors are selected for initiation of the links.
- `Degree` heuristic enables each node to generate its ranked list comprising k of all its 2-hop neighbors with the highest node degrees.

Default Experimental Settings. Here we describe our experimental procedure with default settings, as shown in Table 2. We consider a graph from the Table 1 to represent the honest region. For the Sybil region, we generate as many Sybil nodes as there are honest nodes (n). The graph structure of the Sybil region, however, follows the Barabási-Albert preferential attachment model [9]. The average node degree of the Sybil region is set to 5 times that of the honest region. Furthermore, the ratio of the number of 1-hop attack edges (g) created between honest and Sybil nodes to the number of honest nodes (n) is set to 0.05 ($= g/n$). The adversary employs a *strategic* attack where each attack edge is placed based on degree-centrality in that its honest and Sybil endpoints are chosen with a probability proportional to their degrees in their respective regions. Our experiments reveal that this degree centrality-based attack strategy is much stronger than the one used in previous studies where attack edges are placed either *arbitrarily* [32, 31, 27, 21] or based on eigenvector centrality [11][6].

With the above initial overlay in place, a selective heuristic would enable each node v to initiate a 2-hop link request to every node y in its ranked list of k 2-hop neighbors. Recall that the initiation of a link request from v does not necessarily imply reciprocation from y. Only if y were to have v in its ranked list of k 2-hop neighbors as well, the link (v, y) would be created. We set $k = 100$ for each selective heuristic. In contrast, the `Two-Hop` heuristic would add links from each node to all its 2-hop neighbors.

[6]For clarity, we do not show the result of eigenvector centrality.

Table 2: Default experimental settings.

Parameter	Default
# Sybil nodes	# Honest nodes (n)
Sybil graph structure	Barabási-Albert model [9]
Avg. Sybil node degree	5 * Avg. honest node degree
# 1-hop attack edges (g)	0.05 * # Honest nodes (n)
Attack edge placement	Strategic (degree centrality)
Unavailability (c)	0.8
# selective 2-hop neighbors (k)	100
Degree-churn bias (γ)	0.5

We now apply churn model to the system. We consider an unavailability of $c = 0.8$, implying that 80% of all honest nodes are considered offline. The remaining 20% of all honest nodes that are considered online are selected proportional to the exponent γ of their degrees in the honest region. We set a default value $\gamma = 0.5$, implying a small bias toward (honest) nodes with higher degrees to be online compared to the (honest) ones with lower degrees. In each experiment, we consider all the Sybil nodes to be online all the time. This would result in skewed distribution of honest and Sybil nodes online at any given instance (Fig. 1(b)). When the unavailability is $c = 0.8$, the system would contain $0.2n$ honest nodes and n Sybil nodes online at that instance.

Finally, we measure the system robustness with the above metrics. Disconnection probability is computed as the ratio of the number of online honest nodes in the LCC of the online honest region to the total number of online honest nodes. Escape probability is computed as the average of the fraction of 1000 uniform random walks of length $c * log(n)$ from each of 500 seeds in the LCC of the online honest region escaping into the Sybil region. We report the results of both the metrics averaged over 50 runs.

6.2 Impact of Various Parameters

With the above experimental setup, we examine how varying individual parameters affects the system in terms of network connectivity (disconnection probability) and attack resilience (escape probability).

Attack Edges. Figure 5 shows the impact of 1-hop attack edges on the system. We observe that increasing 1-hop attack edges has little impact on the connectivity of honest nodes in the overlay network, while severely degrading the security of random walks originating in the honest region. In terms of disconnection probability, the `Two-Hop` heuristic fares the best while the `One-Hop` heuristic fares the worst. Note that our proposed heuristic (`MinEC`) has a comparable performance to the `Two-Hop` heuristic in all three datasets. In terms of escape probability, the `One-Hop` and `MinEC` heuristics fare the best while the `Two-Hop` and `Degree` heuristics fare the worst. This shows that `MinEC` combines the best of both worlds of the `One-Hop` and `Two-Hop` heuristics by improving the network connectivity for honest nodes under heavy churn while not compromising on the security of random walks under strategic attacks.

Figure 6 plots the number of 2-hop honest and attack edges created as a result of increasing 1-hop attack edges. Increase in 1-hop attack edges has little impact on the number of 2-hop honest edges, while drastically increasing the 2-hop attack edges. We note that the `Two-Hop` heuristic results in an order of magnitude increase in 2-hop honest edges and two-to-three orders of magnitude increase in 2-hop attack edges. This explains high network connectivity (low disconnection probability) at the cost of very poor attack resilience (high escape probability). Also, this result validates our hypothesis in Sec. 5.1. In contrast, both the **Common Neighbors** and **MinEC** heuristics result in the most 2-hop honest edges (apart from the **Two-Hop** heuristic), and the least 2-hop attack edges (apart from the **OneHop** heuristic), which explains their performance in terms of both disconnection probability and escape probability. More specifically, **MinEC** has a noticeably superior performance to the **Common Neighbors** heuristic because fewer 2-hop attack edges are created by the former compared to that of the latter while creating similar number of 2-hop honest edges.

Unavailability. Figure 7 shows the impact of unavailability on the robustness of the system. In terms of disconnection probability, increasing the unavailability helps disintegrating the overlay to an extent that the fraction of all online honest nodes belonging to the largest connected component decreases. Even at high levels of unavailability upto $c = 0.9$, our heuristic (**MinEC**) fares as good as the **Two-Hop** heuristic. Among the three datasets, Epinions has the poorest network connectivity which is due to its relatively low average degree with respect to the honest region (see Table 1).

In terms of escape probability, the **MinEC** heuristic fares nearly as good as the **One-Hop** heuristic, while the **Degree** heuristic fares the worst. We note that the escape probability increases as the unavailability increases, despite the number of 1-hop attack edges remaining the same during the experiment. This is because of two factors: (i) strategic placement of (1-hop) attack edges where higher degree honest nodes are targeted, and (ii) the default value of $\gamma = 0.5$ indicates that mostly higher degree honest nodes are online particularly at high unavailability, while all the Sybil nodes are online at that instance. In essence, combining the results based on both metrics suggests the robustness of our heuristic under significant levels of churn.

Selective k 2-Hop Neighbors. Figure 8 shows the effect of the number of 2-hop neighbors k used by the various heuristics except the **One-Hop** and **Two-Hop** heuristics. In terms of disconnection probability, each of these heuristics increases the robustness of the social overlay network as the number of 2-hop neighbors k used increases. We note that the **MinEC** heuristic achieves the level of network connectivity similar to that of the **Two-Hop** heuristic with the fewest 2-hop neighbors compared to other heuristics. In the case of AstroPhysics and Facebook, MinEC requires $k = 100$ (or fewer) 2-hop neighbors to have as low a disconnection probability as the **Two-Hop** heuristic, while the other heuristics need $k = 500$ (or more) 2-hop neighbors for similar performance. In the case of Epinions, the **MinEC** heuristic requires about $k = 500$ 2-hop neighbors to have as good network connectivity as the **Two-Hop** heuristic, while the other heuristics require nearly $k = 5000$ for similar extent of connectivity.

In terms of escape probability, each heuristic performs differently as the number of 2-hop neighbors k increases. the **MinEC** heuristic fares as good as the **One-Hop** heuristic for $k \leq 500$ on AstroPhysics and Epinions and $k \leq 2000$ on Facebook. The **Degree** heuristic fares worse than the **Two-Hop** heuristic for $k \leq 200$ for each dataset, and then gradually gets better upto $k = 1000$, before finally worsening again. In contrast, the **Common Neighbors** and **Random** heuristics fluctuate in their attack resilience as k increases. Across all the heuristics based on selective 2-hop neighbors, as the number of 2-hop neighbors increases beyond $k > 2000$, the security of random walks worsens as poorly as that of the **Two-Hop** heuristic. This is because the resultant overlay for such a high value of k essentially becomes a 2-hop network where each honest node is connected to every 2-hop neighbor in the original graph.

Sybil Node Degree. Figure 9 shows the impact of the average degree of Sybil nodes in the Sybil region. Increase in the average Sybil node degree has little impact on the network connectivity of the honest region[7], while having a variable effect on the attack resilience for each heuristic. As the average Sybil node degree increases, the **Random**, **Degree** and **Two-Hop** heuristics fare worse in terms of escape probability. This is because the probability of a Sybil node getting selected as a 2-hop neighbor in the ranked lists of honest nodes increases with the average Sybil node degree with these heuristics. In contrast, the **Common Neighbors**, the **MinEC** and **One-Hop** heuristics have marginal effect on their attack resilience when average Sybil node degree is increased. This is because the **Common Neighbors** and **One-Hop** heuristics do not take into account the degree of the Sybil nodes, while the **MinEC** heuristic in fact discourages high degree Sybil nodes and encourages greater overlap of its 1-hop neighbors.

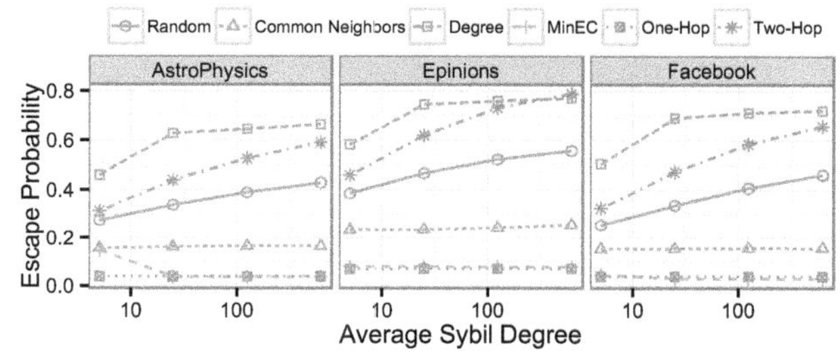

Figure 9: Effect of the average degree of Sybil nodes.

Sybil Region Structure and Attack Edge Placement. So far, we considered the adversary creating both the Sybil region with a graph structure based on the Barabási-Albert preferential attachment model [9] and the attack edges strategically with higher degree honest nodes. We now examine the effect on the robustness of the system when (i) the Sybil region is created with a structure based on the Erdős-Rényi random graph model [15] having the same average Sybil node degree, and/or (ii) the same number of attack edges (g) are created *arbitrarily*, with no relation to the degrees of either honest or Sybil nodes.

Figure 10 shows the impact of the graph structure of the Sybil region. In terms of disconnection probability, all the combinations have similar effect on the network connectivity across all datasets and heuristics. In terms of escape probability, Barabási-Albert model structure results in a significantly worse attack resilience for **Random**, **Degree** and **Two-Hop** heuristics while having similar impact on the other heuristics. This result implies that the **Two-Hop** heuristic similar to the one proposed in the MCON study [28] fares very poorly in our system in terms of attack resilience, despite enabling high network connectivity. Moreover, the result shows that our experiments throughout this section

[7] Henceforth, due to space limitations, we do not show the results of the experiments in which varying the values of a parameter does not significantly affect a performance metric.

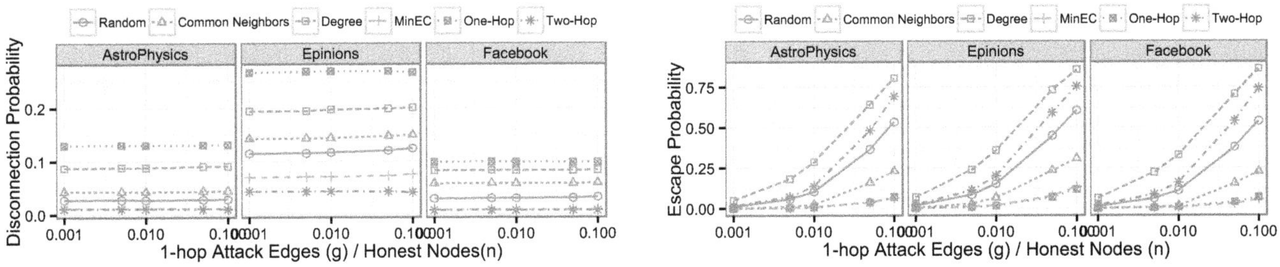

Figure 5: Effect of 1-hop attack edges.

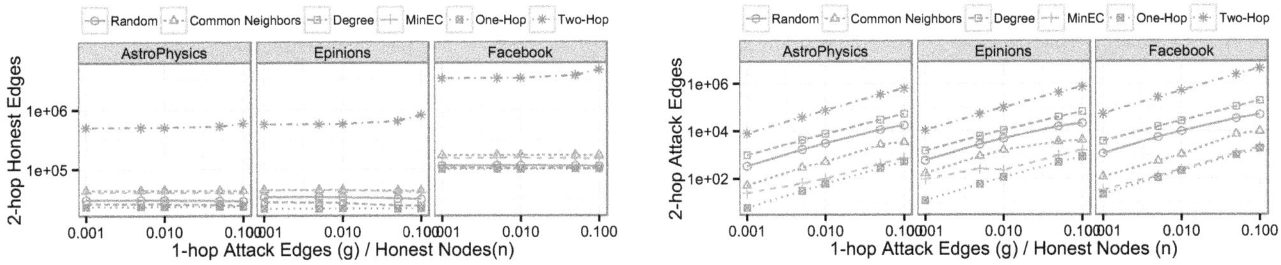

Figure 6: Increase in 2-hop honest edges and 2-hop attack edges vs. 1-hop attack edges.

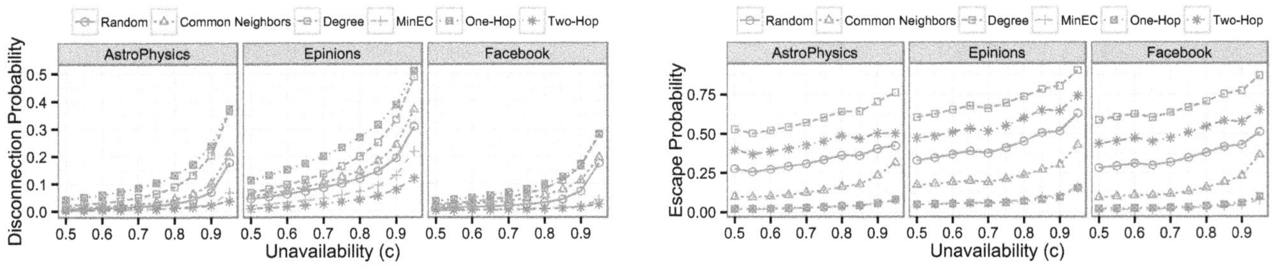

Figure 7: Effect of unavailability.

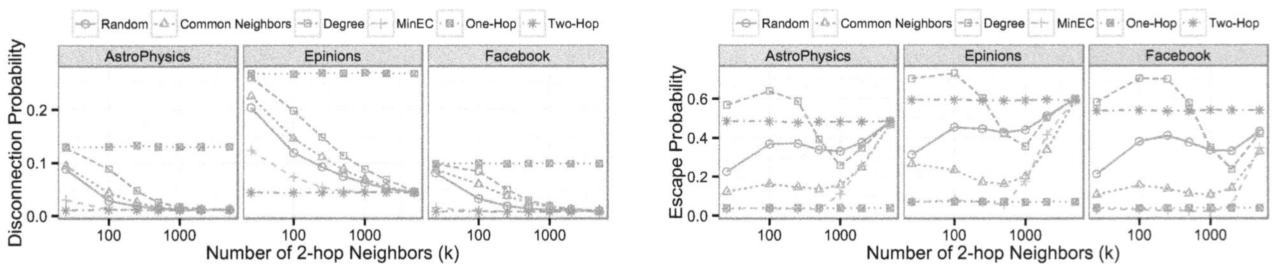

Figure 8: Effect of selective k 2-hop neighbors.

have considered a non-trivial and a stronger attack strategy by the adversary in comparison to the previous SNSD studies [32, 31, 27, 21] that adopt the arbitrary attack edge placement strategy.

Degree-Churn Bias γ. Figure 11 shows the impact of honest nodes' degree bias γ under churn. We remind that the unavailability for this experiment is $c = 0.8$, implying only 20% of all honest nodes are online at any given instance. Also, we note that $\gamma = 0$ suggests that the probability of an honest node being online has no relation to its degree. As the degree bias γ increases, the disconnection probability for each heuristic decreases. This suggests that, when most of the online honest nodes are high degree ones, the resultant overlay network contains a well-connected honest region. We note that, even for low values of $\gamma \in [0.0, 0.5]$, the `MinEC` heuristic fares as good as the `Two-Hop` heuristic in terms of the network connectivity. In terms of escape probability, the `MinEC` heuristic fares as good as the `One-Hop` heuristic and significantly better than the other heuristics for a wide range of values of the degree bias including $\gamma = 0$.

Hourly Dynamics. We now perform a trace-based evaluation of the system robustness, by considering the hourly dynamics of YIM clients which we described in Sec. 3.2. Apart from high unavailability (Fig. 3(a)), we recall that at least 30% of all online users in the current hour are also observed online in the next hour, throughout the day (Fig. 3(b)). In this experiment, we take into account such dynamics for the values of unavailability c and the percentage of common

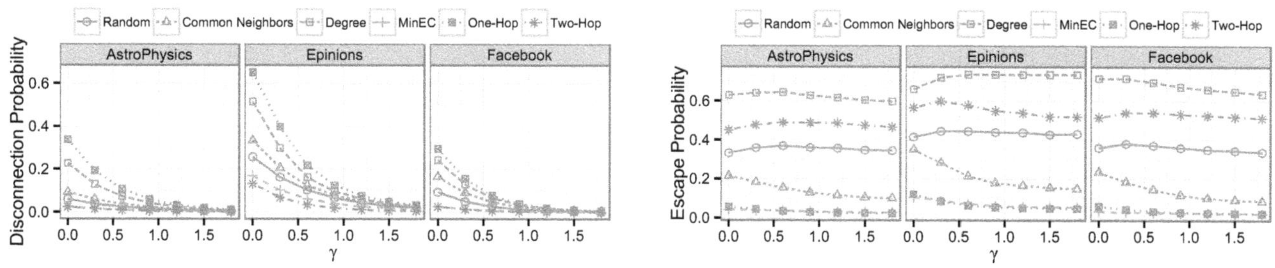

Figure 11: Effect of degree-churn bias (γ).

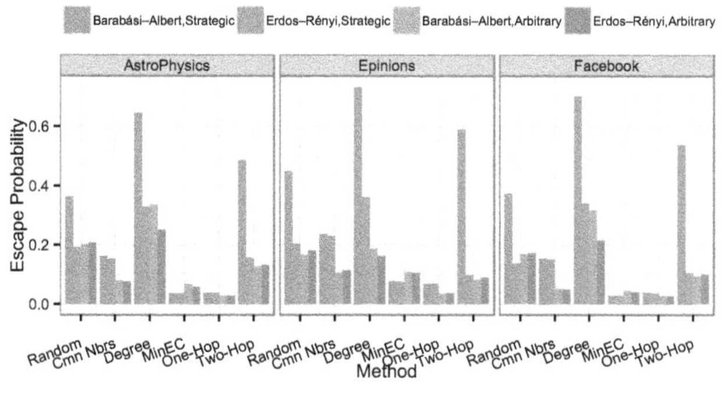

Figure 10: Effect of Sybil region structure and attack edge placement.

users across each hour, while setting the default values for other parameters.

Figure 12 shows the impact of the hourly dynamics on the system robustness. In terms of disconnection probability, the **MinEC** heuristic fares nearly as good as the **Two-Hop** heuristic for most of the day from 6 AM till midnight, and noticeably better than the others. The network connectivity is worse for each heuristic in the early hours of the day, which is due to very high unavailability $c > 0.95$. In terms of escape probability, both the **MinEC** and **Common Neighbors** heuristics fare as good as the **One-Hop** heuristic all day. Putting both things together, the **MinEC** heuristic outperforms the **Common Neighbors** one since the latter results in worse network connectivity than that by the **Random** one across each hour of the day.

6.3 Off-the-Shelf SNSD Schemes

Mixing Times. Most SNSD schemes, including the decentralized [32, 31, 18, 21] and the centralized ones [13, 12], rely on the fast mixing [22] property of the honest region's graph structure for their robustness. Here, we examine the mixing times of the LCC of the online honest region created using our proposed heuristic (MinEC) for all the datasets and various levels of unavailability.

We compute the mixing time of a graph using the same methodology as [23]. Specifically, given an initial distribution $\pi^{(i)}$ at node i and transition matrix $P^{(0)}$ which is the adjacency matrix with normalized rows, we compute the total variation distance $|\pi - \pi^{(i)}P^{(w)}|_1$ at each step (random walk length) w where π is the stationary distribution. The speed with which the total variation distance decays is an indicator of the fast mixing property of the network.

Figure 13 plots the total variation distance versus the walk length, averaged over 1000 initial distributions. The mixing times of all graphs converge to stationary distribution in the order of $O(log(n))$, within a total variation distance of 0.2 indicating 'fast' mixing times. This result suggests that existing SNSD schemes as well as potential future ones relying on the fast mixing property of the honest region can be employed by system designers even in the face of heavy churn by applying our **MinEC** heuristic.

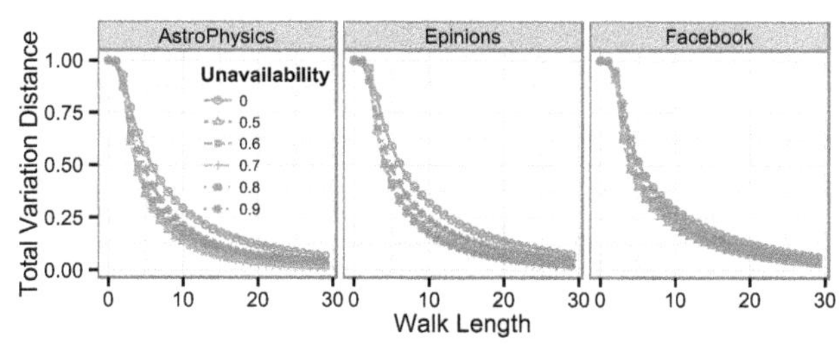

Figure 13: Mixing times of the LCC of the online honest region based on the MinEC heuristic.

Gatekeeper [27]. Motivated by the result of the previous experiment, we examine the effectiveness of applying Gatekeeper [27], a state-of-the-art decentralized SNSD scheme, given our default experimental setting of strategic attack and high unavailability ($c = 0.8$).

We adapt Gatekeeper [27] (Sec. 2.1) to take into account churn as an integral factor. Each verifier v performs the following. First, v obtains $s = 100$ seeds using the random walk method that Gatekeeper borrows from SybilLimit [31]. Second, each seed x sends $t = O(log((1-c)*n))$ tickets in a breadth-first fashion so that at least $(1-c)*n/2$ nodes each receive a ticket. Third, the verifier accepts a suspect node p if p received tickets from at least $f_{admit} * s$ seeds. We set $f_{admit} = 0.2$ which was used in the Gatekeeper study [27].

Figure 14 plots the distribution of the number of honest and Sybil suspect nodes accepted relative to the total number of online honest nodes at a given instance, for 25 verifiers each in 50 runs. The **MinEC** heuristic outperforms others, with a high probability, in terms of accepting over 80% of all the online honest nodes, while accepting a very low number of Sybil nodes. Also, note that the **MinEC** heuristic has lesser variance than the others, indicating consistent performance for various verifiers including the ones close to the Sybil region.

7. CONCLUSIONS

We presented an extensive study examining two key challenges–Sybil attacks and heavy churn–in the field of social network-based distributed systems. In the face of such challenges, we showed that SNSD schemes deal with a fundamental trade-off between network connectivity and attack resilience. We

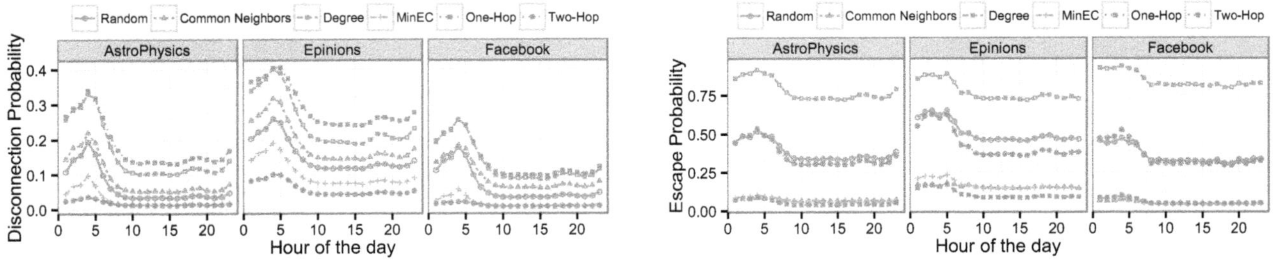

Figure 12: Effect of variations over the day.

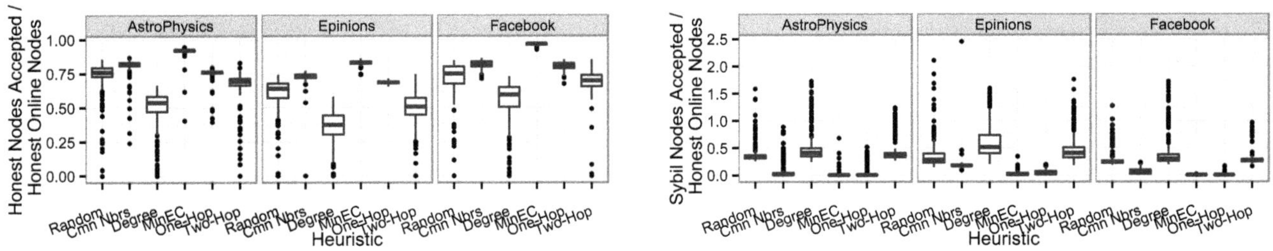

Figure 14: Effectiveness of Gatekeeper.

proposed a new design point in this trade-off with `MinEC`, which fares as good as `Two-Hop` in terms of network connectivity (disconnection probability) and `One-Hop` in terms of attack resilience (escape probability). Our experiments revealed `MinEC`'s robustness to various parameters' testing conditions as well as the feasibility in its application to the existing state-of-the-art and potential future SNSD schemes relying on the fast-mixing property with minimal changes.

We believe our work can be extended in the following directions. First, providing a guarantee of high network connectivity (1% disconnection probability) under heavy churn ($c \geq 0.95$) may require exploring beyond the 2-hop neighborhood of each node for better connectivity while avoiding malicious nodes. Second, the theoretical analysis on selecting k remains an open problem. Third, the designs of social routing systems could be revisited considering heavy churn.

Acknowledgments. This work was partially supported by the European Commission's 7th Framework Program through the P2P-Next and QLectives projects (grant no. 216217, 231200).

8. REFERENCES

[1] Skype. http://www.skype.com/.

[2] Skype 5.0: Remastered for iphone. http://blogs.skype.com/2014/06/09/skype-5-0-remastered-for-iphone/.

[3] Skype statistics. http://share.skype.com/stats_rss.xml/.

[4] Snap network analysis library. http://snap.stanford.edu/.

[5] Topics in theoretical computer science: An algorithmist's toolkit; lecture 6. http://ocw.mit.edu/courses/mathematics/18-409-topics-in-theoretical-computer-science-an-algorithmists-toolkit-fall-2009/lecture-notes/MIT18_409F09_scribe6.pdf/.

[6] Yahoo! instant messenger. https://messenger.yahoo.com/.

[7] Yahoo! messenger client to server protocol-level events, version 1.0. http://research.yahoo.com/Academic_Relations/.

[8] Yahoo! messenger user communication pattern. http://research.yahoo.com/Academic_Relations/.

[9] A. L. Barabási and R. Albert. Emergence of scaling in random networks. *Science*, pages 509–12, 1999.

[10] R. Bhagwan, S. Savage, and G. Voelker. Understanding availability. IPTPS '03.

[11] N. Chiluka, N. Andrade, D. Gkorou, and J. Pouwelse. Personalizing eigentrust in the face of communities and centrality attack. AINA '12.

[12] N. Chiluka, N. Andrade, J. Pouwelse, and H. Sips. Leveraging trust and distrust for sybil-tolerant voting in online social media. PSOSM '12.

[13] G. Danezis and P. Mittal. Sybilinfer: Detecting sybil nodes using social networks. In *NDSS '09*.

[14] J. R. Douceur. The sybil attack. IPTPS '01.

[15] P. Erdos and A. Rényi. On the evolution of random graphs. *Bull. Inst. Internat. Statist*, 38(4):343–347, 1961.

[16] T. Isdal, M. Piatek, A. Krishnamurthy, and T. Anderson. Privacy-preserving p2p data sharing with oneswarm. SIGCOMM '10.

[17] R. B. Jennings, E. M. Nahum, D. P. Olshefski, D. Saha, Z.-Y. Shae, and C. Waters. A study of internet instant messaging and chat protocols. *Netwrk. Mag. of Global Internetwkg.*, 20(4):16–21.

[18] C. Lesniewski-Laas and M. F. Kaashoek. Whanau: a sybil-proof distributed hash table. NSDI '10.

[19] D. Liben-Nowell and J. Kleinberg. The link prediction problem for social networks. In *CIKM '03*.

[20] A. S. Maiya and T. Y. Berger-Wolf. Sampling community structure. WWW '10.

[21] P. Mittal, M. Caesar, and N. Borisov. X-vine: Secure and pseudonymous routing using social networks. In *NDSS '12*.

[22] M. Mitzenmacher and E. Upfal. *Probability and Computing: Randomized Algorithms and Probabilistic Analysis*. 2005.

[23] A. Mohaisen, N. Hopper, and Y. Kim. Keep your friends close: Incorporating trust into social network-based sybil defenses. INFOCOM '11.

[24] A. Mohaisen, H. Tran, N. Hopper, and Y. Kim. On the mixing time of directed social graphs and security implications. ASIACCS '12.

[25] S. Rhea, D. Geels, T. Roscoe, and J. Kubiatowicz. Handling churn in a dht. ATEC '04.

[26] D. Stutzbach and R. Rejaie. Understanding churn in peer-to-peer networks. IMC '06.

[27] D. N. Tran, J. Li, L. Subramanian, and S. S. M. Chow. Optimal sybil-resilient node admission control. In *INFOCOM '11*.

[28] E. Vasserman, R. Jansen, J. Tyra, N. Hopper, and Y. Kim. Membership-concealing overlay networks. CCS '09.

[29] B. Viswanath, A. Mislove, M. Cha, and K. P. Gummadi. On the evolution of user interaction in facebook. WOSN '09.

[30] B. Viswanath, A. Post, K. P. Gummadi, and A. Mislove. An analysis of social network-based sybil defenses. SIGCOMM '10.

[31] H. Yu, P. B. Gibbons, M. Kaminsky, and F. Xiao. Sybillimit: A near-optimal social network defense against sybil attacks. IEEE SP '08.

[32] H. Yu, M. Kaminsky, P. B. Gibbons, and A. Flaxman. Sybilguard: defending against sybil attacks via social networks. SIGCOMM '06.

k-Anonymization by Freeform Generalization

Katerina Doka
NTUA, Greece

Mingqiang Xue
I[2]R, Singapore

Dimitrios Tsoumakos
Ionian University, Greece

Panagiotis Karras
Skoltech, Russia

ABSTRACT

Syntactic data anonymization strives to (i) ensure that an adversary cannot identify an individual's record from published attributes with high probability, and (ii) provide high data utility. These mutually conflicting goals can be expressed as an optimization problem with privacy as the constraint and utility as the objective function. Conventional research using the k-anonymity model has resorted to publishing data in *homogeneous generalized groups*. A recently proposed alternative does not create such cliques; instead, it recasts data values in a *heterogeneous* manner, aiming for higher utility. Nevertheless, such works never defined the problem in the most general terms; thus, the utility gains they achieve are limited. In this paper, we propose a methodology that achieves the full potential of heterogeneity and gains higher utility while providing the same privacy guarantee. We formulate the problem of maximal-utility k-anonymization by *freeform generalization* as a network flow problem. We develop an *optimal* solution therefor using Mixed Integer Programming. Given the non-scalability of this solution, we develop an $O(kn^2)$ Greedy algorithm that has no time-complexity disadvantage vis-á-vis previous approaches, an $O(kn^2 \log n)$ enhanced version thereof, and an $O(kn^3)$ adaptation of the Hungarian algorithm; these algorithms build a set of k perfect matchings from original to anonymized data, a novel approach to the problem. Moreover, our techniques can resist adversaries who may know the employed algorithms. Our experiments with real-world data verify that our schemes achieve near-optimal utility (with gains of up to 41%), while they can exploit parallelism and data partitioning, gaining an efficiency advantage over simpler methods.

1. INTRODUCTION

The imperative to protect the privacy of individuals [27] requires that a certain *privacy guarantee* be observed when sharing data among agents such as public organizations and private corporations, while disclosing as much information as possible. A popular such guarantee is provided by the k-anonymity model, which requires that the records in a released table should be recast, so that any combination of values on a set of *quasi-identifying attributes* (QI) can be *indistinctly matched to at least k (or none) individuals* therein [24]. This model has been extended and specialized in several forms [23, 20, 7, 6] and other alternatives have been suggested [12, 8]; however, k-anonymity remains a fundamental prerequisite of more advanced models and useful as a stand-alone device in its own right. For example, microtargeted advertising systems in online social networks, even while refraining from selling users' personal information to advertisers, may still inadvertently reveal a user's personal information when an adversary targets an advertisement to a particular user's set of quasi-identifier values [17]. A remedy for this problem requires privacy protections built in by design. Such a protection would be to ensure that an advertiser's targeting criteria never fit less than k user profiles, i.e., to apply the advertising criteria on *k-anonymized* data indeed. Therefore, the k-anonymity model remains topical and relevant in novel settings, and preferable to noise addition techniques in many cases [21, 10].

Despite its usefulness in principle, a concern about the applicability of k-anonymity in practice has been caused by a perception that the loss of data utility it engenders would be too large to bear [5], an effect exacerbated as the number of dimensions (QI attributes) grows [2]. However, such loss in utility does not necessarily arise from an inherent drawback of the model itself, but rather from the deficiencies of the algorithms used to implement the model. Indeed, conventional microdata anonymization algorithms have typically departed from the assumption that *all* recast records whose QI values are meant to match the original values of a record t *must* be assigned *identical* QI values to each other [24]; thereby, sanitized records are clustered in disjoint homogeneous groups of the same QI values, called *equivalence classes* [24]. Brickell and Shmatikov first discerned that "*there is no privacy reason*" for this *homogeneity requirement* [5]; they speculated that a strategy using directed acyclic graphs may fare better. In our view, the message to be drawn from [2] and [5] is not a negative, pessimist view that obtaining higher data utility under k-anonymity is impossible, but rather a call for k-anonymization algorithms that do obtain higher data utility by dropping the constraints of previous research. Moreover, we argue that such utility may also be gained *at the expense* of runtime, if a tradeoff between the two emerges. As the anonymization process is an one-off process, some additional runtime is always worth investing for the sake of obtaining higher utility.

This paper provides such algorithms. We observe that some attempts already made in this direction [16, 28, 25, 29, 9] do not define the problem in the most general terms; they introduce superfluous constraints in their solutions or solve the problem by trivially suppressing some values. We keep away from such superfluities and explore the potential to obtain high data utility by value generalization under the k-anonymity model. We define the problem of optimal-utility k-anonymization by value generalization as a network flow problem, a generalization of the assignment prob-

ASIA CCS'15, April 14–17, 2015, Singapore..

ACM 978-1-4503-3245-3/15/04 ...$15.00.
http://dx.doi.org/10.1145/2714576.2714590.

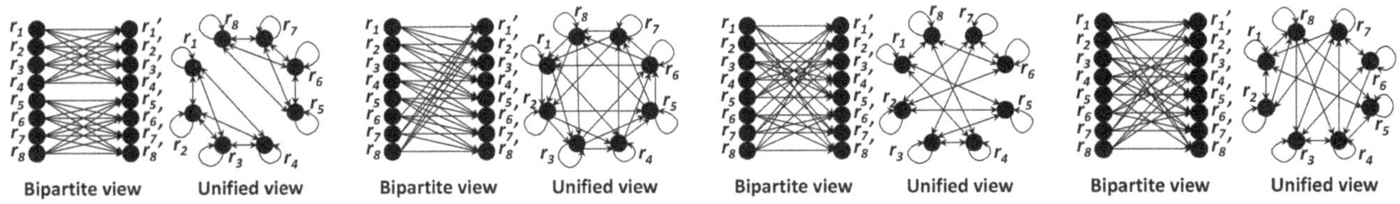

(a) Homogeneous (b) Ring-based (c) Heterogeneous Reciprocal (d) Freeform

Figure 1: Generalization types in graph view

lem on a bipartite graph. To our knowledge, we are the first to formulate this problem in such terms. We develop an exact optimal solution therefor using Mixed Integer Programming. As this solution does not scale, we propose a scalable *Greedy* algorithm, an enhanced version thereof, and a computationally more demanding solution employing the Hungarian algorithm for the Assignment Problem. We also examine whether an off-the-shelf algorithm for the minimum-cost network flow problem can provide a viable solution to our problem. Last, we demonstrate that our techniques can gain an efficiency advantage over simpler methods, when applied in a distributed environment, after partitioning the data.

Our approach differs from preceding research in the *form* of its solutions, which provide better utility, while it provides the same privacy guarantee and recasts data values in the same syntactic way as previous research. A recasting of tuples can be represented by a directed graph, the *generalization graph* [29], that shows how the values of original records match those of anonymized ones. In the *bipartite view* of the graph, an edge from the vertex standing for an original record, r_i, to the one standing for a recast record, r'_j, indicates that the QI values of r_i are included in (*match*) those of r'_j. In the *unified view*, a single vertex represents both the original record r_i and its recast form r'_i.

Figure 1(a) shows the kind of generalization graph constructed by conventional k-anonymization algorithms obeying the homogeneity requirement [24, 19, 15]. In the bipartite view, the partitioning forms two disconnected complete subgraphs of four vertices in each side (i.e., two $K_{4,4}$ *bicliques*), hence obeys 4-anonymity. These subgraphs correspond to the *equivalence classes* formed by those methods; in the unified view, they appear as complete digraphs with self-loops. Previous works [28, 29] eschewed the redundant homogeneity requirement so as to achieve higher utility; still, they resorted to another superfluous requirement, namely that the generalization graph be a *ring*: a cyclical order of vertices is defined, and each vertex matches its predecessors and/or successors over this order. Figure 1(b) shows such a graph.

We propose that homogeneity be eschewed without introducing any other constraint in its place. A corollary of homogeneity is *reciprocity* [29]: when record r_i matches the recast form r'_j of another record r_j, then r_j matches r'_i too; thus, the generalization graph is *symmetric*. To illustrate the distinction between the two, Figure 1(c) shows a generalization graph that is *reciprocal* (records match each other mutually), but *heterogenous* (no record has the same matchings as another). Going further, we can eschew reciprocity too, and aim to construct an *entirely unconstrained* generalization graph that maximizes utility by value generalization. To our knowledge, our work is the *first* to define this problem in such terms. A *freeform* generalization is illustrated by the graph in Figure 1(d).

The advantages of our approach are illustrated by the example in Table 1. The top table presents the values of eight tuples on QI attributes *Age* and *Salary*. By our method, these tuples are anonymized as in the bottom left table; each tuple is recast to a *range* of values, so as to be compatible with, or *match*, three original tuples, and vice versa, as the bottom right table shows; this property is called 3-regularity. This property and a randomization scheme guarantee that each original tuple has three *equiprobable* identities [28]; thus, k-regularity is a sufficient condition for k-anonymity.

ID	t_0	t_1	t_2	t_3	t_4	t_5	t_6	t_7
Age	59	57	39	28	41	37	40	53
Salary	25	27	47	41	20	59	35	34

ID	Age	Salary
t'_0	53-59	25-34
t'_1	53-59	25-34
t'_2	28-39	41-59
t'_3	28-41	20-59
t'_4	40-59	20-35
t'_5	28-39	41-59
t'_6	39-41	20-47
t'_7	40-57	27-35

Original	Matches	Anon/zed	Matches
t_0	t'_0, t'_1, t'_4	t'_0	t_0, t_1, t_7
t_1	t'_0, t'_1, t'_7	t'_1	t_0, t_1, t_7
t_2	t'_2, t'_5, t'_6	t'_2	t_2, t_3, t_5
t_3	t'_2, t'_3, t'_5	t'_3	t_3, t_4, t_5
t_4	t'_3, t'_4, t'_6	t'_4	t_0, t_4, t_6
t_5	t'_2, t'_3, t'_5	t'_5	t_2, t_3, t_5
t_6	t'_4, t'_6, t'_7	t'_6	t_2, t_4, t_6
t_7	t'_0, t'_1, t'_7	t'_7	t_1, t_6, t_7

Table 1: Example data anonymized by our method

Figure 2(a) presents the data of Table 1 in a 2d coordinate system where the x-axis stands for *Age* and the y-axis for *Salary*. Each tuple t_i is represented as a point r_i in this coordinate system (shown by a black circle in the figure). An arrow from r_i to r_j denotes that r_i matches the anonymized tuple for r_j. The matching relationships in Table 1 are thus shown in Figure 2(a). For clarity, we present the same matchings in pure (unified) graph form as well, without positioning points by their coordinates, in Figure 2(b).

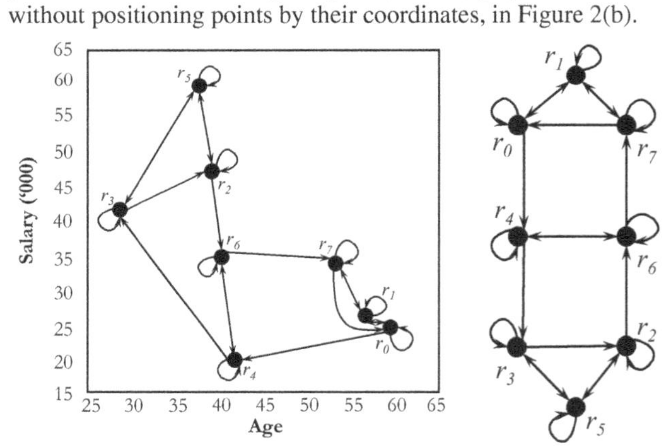

(a) Graph in 2d plane (b) Pure graph

Figure 2: Example solution

We reiterate our main contributions as follows:

- We formulate the optimal-utility k-anonymization problem as a network flow problem.
- We provide an exact optimal Mixed Integer Programming-based solution.
- We offer a collection of heuristic solutions.
- We demonstrate experimentally that our techniques achieve significantly lower information loss than previous methods.
- We show our techniques can achieve near-optimal utility.
- We apply our techniques in a parallel-computing environment, gaining an efficiency advantage over previous work.

2. RELATED WORK

The k-anonymity model calls for recasting data so that each original record have *at least k equally probable* matches among recast records. This effect is achieved by a *syntactic* transformation, reducing the *precision* of the data, but not its *accuracy*; the published data is truthful, albeit less exact [19, 5]; a *k-anonymization algorithm* aims to bring the data to a form that abides by the given privacy condition via syntactic transformations, while introducing small inexactness [15]. This type of transformation comes in contrast to anonymization by *perturbation*, which introduces errors in the data; as perturbation-based transformations provide no information on how much a given record has been perturbed, they limit the purposes such data can be useful for [19].

2.1 Striving for Data Utility

Past research has expressed concerns about the usefulness of the k-anonymity model, due to a perception that it engenders high loss of data utility due to the imprecision introduced. Aggarwal [2] noted that, under conventional approaches for k-anonymization, it is difficult to anonymize high-dimensional data "without an unacceptably high amount of information loss". Brickell and Shmatikov [5] went further to claim that data utility is necessarily almost completely destroyed for "modest privacy gains". This claim was reexamined by Li and Li [22]; the point made in [22] amounts, in effect, to the statement that the *privacy loss* and *utility gain* involved in publishing anonymized data are *incommensurable*; they do not share a common standard of measurement, as [5] assumed; *specific* knowledge has a larger impact on privacy, while *aggregate* information has a larger impact on utility [22].

Still, an observation made in [5] regarding classic k-anonymization algorithms is valid. Such algorithms have raised a *homogeneity requirement*, by which recast records form groups of at least k records, such that all records in a group have the same QI values and are hence interchangeable with each other. Brickell and Shmatikov correctly observed that this requirement is redundant, and called for algorithms that drop it to provide improved utility.

Some attempts have been made in this direction [16, 28, 25, 29], yet retain redundant constraints and superfluities in their solutions. Gionis et al. [16, 25] suggested the model of k-concealment, which guarantees that an original record is associated with at least k recast ones, without the homogeneity requirement. However, the $O(kn^2)$ *agglomerative* algorithm in [16, 25] goes through a series of steps that perform *superfluous generalizations*, introducing extra information loss. Besides, as observed in [28] and [25], k-concealment is a weaker guarantee than k-anonymity, as it does not ensure that each association is equiprobable. For example, the graph in Figure 3 satisfies 2-concealment: each record, on both sides of the graph (in bipartite view), has at least two matches, each of whom participates in a complete assignment (perfect matching). However, the matches are *not equiprobable*: some of them (shown with bold lines) participate in three out of four possible assignments, while others (shown with light lines) participate in only one.

Wong et al. [28] studied the conditions for equiprobable associations, and proposed a technique that achieves k-anonymity without the homogeneity requirement. Yet, even while dropping that redundant requirement, [28] does not entirely break its shackles: it still requires that original and recast records relate to each other by a *fixed* motif, *ring generalization*, thus substituting one superfluous constraint for another. Furthermore, [28] does not apply ring generalization on a complete data set, but only within piecemeal partitions obtained via a homogeneous partitioning; the utility gains achieved are primarily due to this partitioning, not due to ring generalization. Xue et al. [29] adopt ring generalization as an element

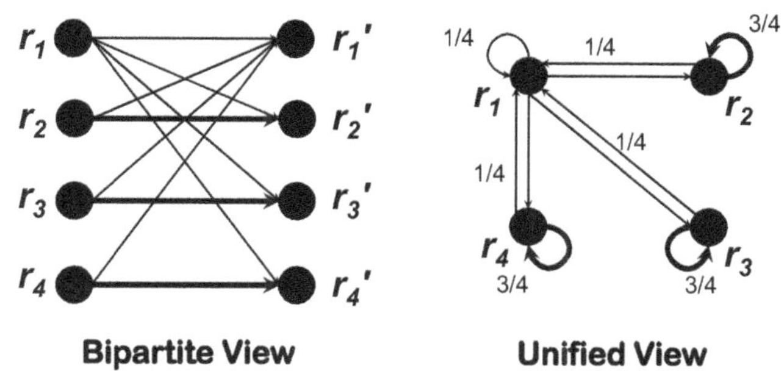

Figure 3: Graph satisfying 2-concealment, but not 2-anonymity

of a technique for anonymizing sparse high-dimensional data; they apply the motif on complete data sets with good results, yet still adhere to that fixed motif. The anonymization algorithms in [28, 29] consist of two components: (i) a component catering to data utility, aiming to produce a data transformation of low information loss by building a ring, and (ii) a component that caters to privacy, aiming to guarantee the equiprobability of k produced associations, via randomization. Even though (i) has sub-quadratic time complexity, the randomization in (ii) brings in an $O(kn^2)$ component. We argue that, since a quadratic time complexity is invested for the sake of privacy anyway, this time complexity budget should also be employed for the sake of utility as well.

Wong et al. have shown that, to achieve k-anonymity, it suffices to ensure that each original record r_i has exactly k matches in the published data R' and each anonymized record r'_i also has exactly k matches in the original data R; in other words, each vertex in the generalization graph has outdegree and indegree k, i.e., the graph is *k-regular*. It would also suffice to ensure that the generalization graph *contains* a k-regular subgraph, but then we could also maintain that k-regular subgraph only. All graphs in Figure 1 are 4-regular, hence ensure 4-anonymity. The motif of ring generalization is applied exactly to create a k-regular graph in [28], as in Figure 1(c), imposing an arbitrary constraint of its own.

2.2 Security against Adversaries

Wong et al. [28] show that we can extract k disjoint assignments, i.e., one-to-one correspondences between original and recast records, as subsets of a k-regular generalization graph. For the sake of completeness, we reiterate their argument, following a more concise formulation than the one in [28].

LEMMA 2.1. *In a directed graph G, where each vertex v has the same indegree and outdegree d_v, each edge belongs to a cycle.*

PROOF. Assume there is an edge $e = (u \rightarrow v)$ that does not belong to a cycle. Then u cannot be reached from v. Then we classify vertices in two disjoint groups: A, those that can reach u, with $u \in A$ and B, those that can be reached from v, with $v \in B$, where $A \cap B = \emptyset$. By our assumption, vertices in B have the same number $\sum_{w \in B} d_w$ of incoming and outgoing edges. All outgoing edges should point to a vertex in B, since they cannot not reach u. Yet there is an incoming edge to B, namely e, which originates outside B. Hence, there are at most $\sum_{w \in B} d_w - 1$ incoming edges from B to B, but $\sum_{w \in B} d_w$ outgoing edges from B to B. This is a contradiction of the pigeonhole principle. □

LEMMA 2.2. *In a k-regular directed graph G, each edge belongs to a perfect matching (i.e., a set of cycles incoming to and outgoing from each vertex exactly once).*

PROOF. Consider any edge e. By Lemma 2.1, since all vertices in G have equal indegree and outdegree, e belongs to a cycle. Consider such a cycle C. If C contains all vertices of G, it is a perfect matching itself. If not, then we rewire graph G to G' as follows: for each edge $e = (u \rightarrow v)$ in C, we substitute vertex u by a new vertex u/v, such that the outgoing edges from u/v become the outgoing edges from u and the incoming edges to u/v become the incoming edges to v; each edge in C becomes a self-loop in G'. Since G is k-regular, G' is k-regular as well, with indegree and outdegree k on each vertex, and Lemma 2.1 still applies on G'. We say that all vertices in C have been *matched*. Then, we select an arbitrary unmatched vertex $w \in G'$ and one of its outgoing edges e' at random. We repeat the process, finding a cycle C' for e'. If C' contains a previously matched vertex w', we update the matches of w' according to C'. Note that any previously formed matches that are now destroyed are self-loops in G'; thus, the number of matched vertices is monotonically increasing, with at least one new previously unmatched vertex getting matched at each iteration. Therefore, the process eventually terminates; the resulting set of matches $\mathcal{M}$ forms a perfect matching on the original graph G itself, since each vertex has exactly one incoming and one outgoing edge in $\mathcal{M}$. □

THEOREM 2.3. *In a k-regular directed graph G there exist k disjoint assignments (i.e., perfect matchings).*

PROOF. We pick up a node n_i and an outgoing edge e randomly. By Lemma 2.2, e belongs to an assignment (perfect matching) a. We take the edges of a out of G, to get graph G'. Each node in G' has exactly $k-1$ incoming/outgoing edges, hence G' is $(k-1)$-regular. We repeat iteratively and find k disjoint assignments. □

Any of k such assignments can provide the *putative* identities of recast records, and may be used as a guide when assigning other, non-generalized attributes to them. Hence, a record represented by a vertex in a k-regular generalization graph appears to have k possible identities, each in one of the k possible worlds represented by the k assignments. Yet to satisfy the equiprobability requirement of k-anonymity, we should also ensure that each edge (i.e., match) of a vertex is equally likely to participate in a chosen assignment, in other words, there should be k *equiprobable* disjoint assignments. We achieve this result by selecting one of k disjoint assignments *uniformly at random*. Moreover, in order to resist attacks based on knowledge of some anonymized tuples' identities and/or of the algorithm itself, the particular *set* of k disjoint assignments we choose from is generated by a *randomization* scheme.

In effect, each of the k possible matches for each tuple has, from an adversary's perspective, equal probability to be the true one. An adversary running the same algorithm on the same data would get different results, due to the randomization employed. Using randomization to avert attacks based on knowledge of the algorithm was also recommended in [11]. Wong et al. show how a random assignment can be generated by iteratively extracting cycles from the generalization graph (in unified view) via random walks [28]; Xue et al. improve on the efficiency of this process [29]. As discussed, the time complexity of this randomization scheme is $O(kn^2)$. Our methods utilize the same scheme for the sake of security, thus tolerate adversaries who know the algorithm.

Choromanski et al. [9] recently studied k-anonymization as a matching problem as well, with a view to providing *adaptiveness*, i.e. a different privacy guarantee for each individual. In this context, they have also provided an analysis on the question of security in case a match is already known to an adversary. They conclude that heterogeneous reciprocal generalization (which they call *symmetric b-anonymity*) is as secure as k-anonymity, while freeform (i.e., heterogeneous nonreciprocal) generalization (which they call *asymmetric b-anonymity*) is weaker only against sustained attacks by an adversary who gains knowledge of *some* true matches. In particular, if an adversary knows c true matches, then the security of heterogeneous reciprocal generalization drops to $(k-c)$-anonymity, exactly as for homogeneous generalization. However, the security of heterogeneous nonreciprocal generalization drops to $(k-c-\phi(k))$-anonymity, for a function ϕ that satisfies certain conditions. The root cause of this difference is that, after we delete all nodes adjacent to c edges (true matches) known to an adversary, we are left with a graph that contains a $(k-c)$-regular subgraph in the former case, but not always so in the latter case. All algorithms we suggest in this paper can be tuned to produce symmetric generalizations. Aside of this security analysis, [9] does not provide algorithms to achieve k-anonymity by value generalization; instead, they resort to suppression, substituting some values by stars.

3. DEFINITIONS AND PRINCIPLES

We consider a dataset $\mathcal{D} = (Q, P)$ of n tuples. $Q = \{q_1, \ldots, q_n\}$, where q_i is the quasi-identifier part of tuple i and $P = \{p_1, \ldots, p_n\}$ is the rest of the record, not considered to contain potentially identifying information. Our task is to recast the values of quasi-identifying attributes in Q, producing an anonymized form thereof, $Q' = \{q'_1, \ldots, q'_n\}$. In this *recasting*, we allow the value of q_i on attribute A_j, q_i^j, to be substituted by a *set* of possible values $\mathcal{V}(q_i^j)$; as in previous work [24, 19, 15], for a numerical attribute, we publish a range of values defined by that set, as shown in Table 1, while for a categorical attribute we publish that set itself. We say that (the quasi-identifier part of) an original tuple q_i and a recast tuple q'_ℓ *match* each other when q'_ℓ *could be* a recast from of q_i, i.e., each q_i^j is included in $\mathcal{V}(q_\ell^j)$. The privacy guarantee of k-anonymity [24] is then defined as follows:

DEFINITION 1. *An* anonymized *data set $\mathcal{D}' = (Q', P)$ satisfies* k-anonymity *with respect to the original data $\mathcal{D} = (Q, P)$ iff each original record $q_i \in \mathcal{D}$ matches* at least *k published records in $\mathcal{D}'$, each having, from an adversary's perspective, equal probability (at most $\frac{1}{k}$) to be the* true match *of q_i.*

This guarantee ensures that an adversary knowing the quasi-identifying part of all records, Q, is not able to identify the *true match* of a record q_i with probability higher than $\frac{1}{k}$. We describe a collection of one-to-one matches encompassing a complete set of original and recast records as an *assignment*.

DEFINITION 2. *Given a data set $\mathcal{D} = (Q, P)$ and a recast version thereof, $\mathcal{D}' = (Q', P)$, an* assignment *α from $\mathcal{D}$ to $\mathcal{D}'$ is an one-to-one mapping, $\alpha = \{(q_{i_1}, q'_{j_1}), \ldots, (q_{i_n}, q'_{j_n})\}$, such that each $q_i \in Q$ is mapped to exactly one $q'_j \in Q'$, where q_i* matches *q'_j. In each pair $(q_i, q'_j) \in \alpha$, we say that q_i is the* preimage *of q'_j and q'_j is the* postimage *of q_i. Two assignments α_s and α_t are* disjoint *if $\alpha_s \cap \alpha_t = \emptyset$.*

In order to achieve k-anonymity, we need to ensure that there exist k disjoint assignments from original tuples in Q to recast tuples in Q'. A set of k disjoint assignments defines k distinct matches in Q' for each $q_i \in Q$ and *vice versa*, i.e., k distinct matches in Q for each $q'_i \in Q'$. The net result can be represented by a *generalization graph* [29], as in Figure 1.

DEFINITION 3. *Given a data set $\mathcal{D} = (Q, P)$ and its anonymized version $\mathcal{D}' = (Q', P)$, a* generalization graph *$G = (V, E)$ is a directed graph in which each vertex $v \in V$ stands for an original/anonymized tuple $q_i \in Q$ and $q'_i \in Q'$, and an edge $(v_i, v_j) \in E$ is present iff q_i matches q'_j.*

Our definition corresponds to the *unified* view of such a graph (see Figure 1). In a *bipartite* view, the vertex standing for an original tuple q_i is separate from that standing for its anonymized form q'_i. A set of k disjoint assignments defines (and is defined by) a generalization graph in which each vertex has exactly k outgoing and k incoming edges, i.e., a k-regular generalization graph [29]. By constructing a set of k such assignments, we determine that the set of possible values of a tuple $q'_i \in Q'$ on an attribute A_j, $\mathcal{V}(q_i^j)$, should include those of the tuples in Q *mapped* to q'_i. As discussed in Section 2, once we have a k-regular generalization graph, we can randomly regenerate a set of k disjoint assignments, select one of them *uniformly at random* as the one that defines the *true matches* between $\mathcal{D}$ and $\mathcal{D}'$, and publish any other attributes of our data (i.e., in P) accordingly. We *reiterate* that the random character of this process ensures the equiprobability property of k-anonymity.

Based on the preceding discussion, the problem of k-anonymization is translated to a problem of determining a k-regular generalization graph from original to anonymized tuples, and then generalize the attribute values of each anonymized tuple q'_i so as to include the values of its k matches. We aim to find a generalization graph that achieves low information loss. Previous research [14, 15, 28, 7, 6] has used several variants of a Global Certainty Penalty (GCP) as a measure of information loss. We opt for a similar metric, in which we distinguish between numerical and categorical attributes in a way that reflects the way we publish the data. For a numerical attribute A_j, published as a range, we define the Normalized Certainty Penalty, NCP, for a recast tuple q'_i as follows:

$$NCP_j(q'_i) = \frac{u_i^j - l_i^j}{U^j - L^j} \tag{1}$$

where u_i^j (l_i^j) is the largest (smallest) value of attribute A_j in the set of possible values of q'_i, $\mathcal{V}(q_i^j)$, (i.e., among the matches of q'_i), and U^j (L^j) is the largest (smallest) value in the domain of attribute A_j. The published ranges prevent the determination of an individual's presence in the data, while they can be used for query processing assuming uniform distribution of values within a range [14, 15]. On the other hand, in case A_j is a categorical attribute, we define the NCP for a recast tuple q'_i as follows:

$$NCP_j(q'_i) = \frac{count_j(q'_i) - 1}{|A_j| - 1} \tag{2}$$

where $count_j(q'_i)$ is the number of distinct values of attribute A_j in $\mathcal{V}(q_i^j)$, and $|A_j|$ is the cardinality of the domain of A_j. A similar metric is employed in [28]. By definition, the NCP obtains values between 0 and 1, where 0 signifies no information loss and 1 signifies the maximum information loss for the attribute in question. Then the GCP for a set of recast tuples Q' is defined as:

$$GCP(Q') = \frac{\sum_{q'_i \in Q'} \sum_j NCP_j(q'_i)}{d \cdot |Q'|} \tag{3}$$

where j is the index of any attribute A_j in Q, d is the number of all such attributes, and $|Q'|$ the number of tuples in Q and Q'. Our definition of GCP is the average value of NCP among all attributes and all tuples. We aim to minimize this GCP value, hence the problem of *optimal* k-anonymization calls for satisfying the k-anonymity guarantee with a minimal reduction in the utility of the original data:

PROBLEM 1. *Given a data set* $\mathcal{D} = (Q, P)$, transform $\mathcal{D}$ *to an anonymized form* $\mathcal{D}'$ *that satisfies k-anonymity, such that* $GCP(Q')$ *is minimized.*

4. OPTIMAL SOLUTION

The methodology proposed in [28] and adopted in [29] creates a fixed k-regular *ring* generalization graphs, without taking into account the actual data values involved. The chief contribution of [28] lies in the randomized process that extracts k disjoint assignments from those graphs in a secure fashion, while that of [29] lies in devising a total order over the records that yields good utility after the fixed graph pattern is applied on it for sparse set-valued data. However, the information loss incurred by the anonymization process eventually depends on the exact *form* of graph built over the data. Unfortunately, the problem of building a graph that minimizes information loss is not addressed in [28, 29]. As we discussed, [28] uses a fixed-form solution and [29] follows suit by adopting it.

Our contribution lies exactly on this graph construction process. We aim to build the graph in a way that minimizes the information lost by value generalization or achieves a near-minimal value of it; to our knowledge, we are the first to address this problem in such terms. In this section, we examine the possibility for an *optimal* solution that builds a k-regular generalization graph. The construction of such a graph corresponds to selecting the set of edges that define it, out of all the available edges in the *complete* bipartite graph from Q to Q'. Viewed in this manner, our problem is a special case of a network flow problem [3]. In network flow terminology, the characteristics of this special case are outlined as follows:

- Our network is a complete bipartite graph from Q to Q'.
- All n vertices in Q are sources supplying k units of flow, and all n vertices in Q' side are sinks demanding k flow units.
- The flow across each edge can take binary values in $\{0, 1\}$.
- The objective is to minimize our GCP function.

We can formulate this problem using techniques of Mixed Integer Programming (MIP). For a numerical attribute A_j, we employ auxiliary variables u_i^j and l_i^j that stand for the maximum (minimum) value in $\mathcal{V}(q_i^j)$. Let q_i^j be the actual value of original tuple q_i on attribute A_j. Last, let $x(\ell, i)$ be a *binary* variable denoting whether the edge from q_ℓ to q'_i is included in the generalization graph we are building (i.e., whether the values of q_ℓ are included in the possible values of q'_i). Then the relationship between original and recast tuples can be expressed via the following constraints:

$$u_i^j \geq q_\ell^j \cdot x(\ell, i) + (1 - x(\ell, i)) \cdot q_i^j \quad \forall q_\ell \tag{4}$$

$$u_i^j \geq q_i^j \tag{5}$$

$$l_i^j \leq q_\ell^j \cdot x(\ell, i) + (1 - x(\ell, i)) \cdot q_i^j \quad \forall q_\ell \tag{6}$$

$$l_i^j \leq q_i^j \tag{7}$$

In case A_j is a categorical attribute A_j, our formulation is slightly different. We substitute A_j by a set of $|A_j|$ auxiliary binary attributes, denoted as $\mathcal{B}_j$, one for each value in the domain of A_j. Then an original tuple q_i has value 1 in one of these attributes only, and 0 in the others, while a recast tuple q'_i should get value 1 in each auxiliary attribute corresponding to a value in the domain of A_j that is in the set of possible A_j values of q'_i, $\mathcal{V}(q_i^j)$. Using h as an index for the *auxiliary* attributes for A_j, it now suffices to employ one auxiliary variable, u_i^h, that stands for the maximum value in $\mathcal{V}(q_i^h)$, which is either 1 or 0. The sum $\sum_{h \in \mathcal{B}_j} u_i^h$ for a given tuple q'_i and attribute A_j denotes the number of distinct values of A_j in $\mathcal{V}(q_i^j)$, i.e., equals $count_j(q'_i)$ in Equation 2. Using other notations as before, the constraints can be expressed as:

$$u_i^h \geq q_\ell^h \cdot x(\ell,i) + (1 - x(\ell,i)) \cdot q_i^h \quad \forall q_\ell \tag{8}$$

$$u_i^h \geq q_i^h \tag{9}$$

To the above constraints we should add the constraint representing the k-regularity of the graph:

$$\sum_i x(\ell,i) = k \quad \forall \ell \quad \sum_\ell x(\ell,i) = k \quad \forall i \tag{10}$$

Then, denoting the set of numerical attributes as NA and that of categorical attributes as CA, the objective to minimize the GCP metric translates to the minimization of the following quantity:

$$\sum_i \left\{ \sum_{A_j \in NA} \frac{u_i^j - l_i^j}{U^j - L^j} + \sum_{A_j \in CA} \frac{\sum_{h \in \mathcal{B}_j} u_i^h - 1}{|A_j| - 1} \right\} \tag{11}$$

where we follow the notation in Equations (1) and (2). Our formulation is a Mixed Integer Program, where the variables u_i^j and l_i^j are real-valued, while the edge flows $x(\ell,i)$ are constrained to be binary. In Section 8 we show that this formulation can be run by an MIP Solver for small data. Unfortunately, it is prohibitive on sizeable data sets, as Mixed-Integer Programming is NP-hard [4].

5. THE GREEDY ALGORITHM

Given the impracticability of the optimal solution presented in Section 4 for large data, in this section we set up to design a practicable and efficient algorithm for our problem, aiming to achieve near to optimal data utility. Our strategy starts out from the following observation: Instead of striving to build a k-regular generalization graph over the data at once, we can do so in a sequence of k distinct iterations, adding a single assignment to the graph under construction at each iteration.

Let $G = (S, T, E)$ be a bipartite graph with the vertex set S standing for original tuples (pre-images) and the vertex set T standing for the recast records (post-images) we aim to define, where $|S| = |T| = n$. The assignment selection starts out with G being a complete graph. Initially, the *weight* of each edge $e_{i,j}$ from S_i to T_j, $w_{i,j}$ is defined as the GCP that will be incurred if the tuple q_j at vertex T_j is recast so as to include the tuple q_i at vertex S_i; for brevity, we call this the cost of recasting q_j as $\{q_i, q_j\}$. At each iteration of our algorithm, we aim to find an assignment (i.e., a set of n edges covering all vertices) from S to T that achieves a low total sum of edge weights. After each iteration, the selected edges are discarded from the graph, and the weights of remaining edges are *redefined* so as to reflect the new state of affairs. Thus, a redefined weight $w_{i,j}$ reflects the *increase* of GCP that will be incurred if we extend the set of possible values of tuple q_j at T_j to include the values of tuple q_i at S_i (i.e., if we recast q_j as $\{q_i, q_j\}$). In effect, at each iteration we attempt to increase the total GCP as little as possible. After k iterations, a k-regular generalization graph is constructed. In fact, the first iteration is redundant, since the self-matching assignment, having zero information loss, is chosen by default. Thus, there are $k-1$ iterations that matter.

We now discuss the details of assignment selection at each iteration. We sequentially process all vertices in S. For each such $S_i \in S$ we select the edge $e_{i,j}$, matching it to a $T_j \in T$, that has the minimum weight $w_{i,j}$. In other words, we greedily match each q_i to the q_j that incurs the least GCP increase. Thereafter, we omit S_i from S and its chosen match T_j from T. This $O(n^2)$ process terminates when all pre-image vertices in S have been matched, and hence all post-image vertices in T have been used.

Nevertheless, the termination of the process outlined above is not guaranteed. Given that at each iteration the degree of each vertex is reduced by one, at the ℓth iteration, our algorithm works on an incomplete bipartite graph where each pre-image in S connects to $n-\ell+1$ vertices of T, and vice versa, i.e., on an $(n-\ell+1)$-regular bipartite graph. While it is always possible to extract an assignment from such a graph, the process outlined above may encounter a dead-end, in case all $n-\ell+1$ possible matches of a certain vertex S_i have already been matched to preceding vertices of S and are hence unavailable. To resolve this problem, when we encounter such a dead-end, we perform a *backtracking* process as follows.

Algorithm 1: Greedy Algorithm Iteration

Data: A weighted bipartite graph $G = (S, T, E)$
Result: An assignment $\mathcal{A}$ with weight close to minimum

```
while S ≠ ∅ do
    select next vertex S_i ∈ S;
    if ∄ available vertex in T connected to S_i then
        find S_{i-x} matched to T_j such that e_{i,j} and e_{i-x,m} are
        available;
        substitute e_{i-x,m} for e_{i-x,j};
    else
        select T_j such that w_{i,j} is the minimum of all edges incident
        to S_i;
    S = S − S_i, T = T − T_j;
    Add e_{i,j} to A;
return A;
```

Assume that a dead-end is encountered when processing vertex S_i in the ℓth iteration, i.e. there exists no available match between S_i and any remaining vertex of T. Then we backtrack to vertex S_{i-1}, which has been already matched to a vertex $T_j \in T$ by edge $e_{i-1,j}$, and check whether two edges as follows are available:

1. The edge $e_{i,j}$, so that T_j can be assigned as a match to S_i.
2. Any edge $e_{i-1,m}$ between S_{i-1} and any vertex $T_m \in T$, so that S_{i-1} can obtain another available match in T instead.

In case such available edges exist, we add edge $e_{i,j}$ to the constructed matching and substitute $e_{i-1,j}$ by $e_{i-1,m}$ (in case more than one T_m are available, we select the one of minimum $w_{i-1,m}$). Otherwise, backtracking continues with vertex S_{i-2}, and goes on until it finds an eligible candidate S_{i-x}. A pseudo-code for a single iteration of this Greedy algorithm is shown in Algorithm 1.

The backtracking process forces a dead-end vertex S_i to obtain the first available match T_j of a predecessor vertex S_{i-x}. However, while the match of S_{i-x} has been selected as the one of minimum edge weight, such a consideration is not taken into account during backtracking. Therefore, we should better ensure that the vertices in S are examined in an order such that it is likely that neighboring vertices have similar attribute values. To achieve this effect, we first sort the tuples in S by a *lexicographic order* of their attribute values, positioning these attributes from lower to higher cardinality. Putting attributes of lower cardinality at a higher position in this order ensures that large value changes among consecutive tuples are less frequent; for instance, the order $\{\{a,1\},\{a,3\},\{b,2\},\{b,4\}\}$, obtained by positioning the low-cardinality alphabetic attribute of these four tuples first, is better than $\{\{1,a\},\{2,b\},\{3,a\},\{4,b\}\}$, obtained by positioning the high-cardinality numerical attribute first.

While backtracking offers a way out of the dead-end, we should prove that it can efficiently find an eligible substitution candidate for practical values of k. We start out with the following lemma.

LEMMA 5.1. *In the ℓth iteration of our Greedy algorithm, if we encounter a dead-end while processing the ith vertex, S_i, we can find a previously matched vertex S_y, which can exchange its matching with S_i and obtain an alternative match T_m, among no more than $2 \cdot \ell + i - n - 3$ previously matched vertices.*

PROOF. The status of our graph while processing the ith vertex at the ℓth iteration is visualized in the matrix of Figure 4. Rows correspond to vertices in S and columns stand for vertices in T. The entry in the cell (a, b) shows the status of edge $e_{a,b}$. A "$\times$" indicates that S_a has been matched to T_b in a previous iteration. Without loss of generality, we arrange the matrix columns so that all post-images in T to which S_i has been matched in the previous $\ell-1$ iterations are gathered in positions $\{T_1, \ldots, T_{\ell-1}\}$. The corresponding cells are labeled with "$\times$" in Figure 4. We do not show other "$\times$" entries as they are inconsequential for the proof, but we keep in mind that there are exactly $\ell-1$ "$\times$" entries in each row and each column, corresponding to previously deleted edges. Then, an "$\bigcirc$" indicates that S_a has been matched to T_b in the current, ℓ^{th} iteration. Thus, each of rows $\{S_1 \ldots S_{i-1}\}$ contains exactly one "$\bigcirc$". Besides, each column contains at most one "$\bigcirc$", since a post-image in T can be matched to at most one pre-image in S in the current iteration.

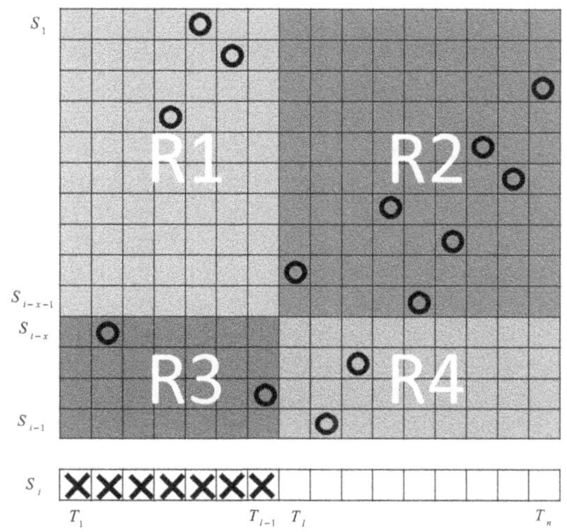

Figure 4: Matrix representation for bipartite matching

An edge from S_a to T_b will be available for matching provided that (i) the corresponding cell is empty; and (ii) there is no "$\bigcirc$" entry in the whole T_b column. Since we encounter a dead-end at vertex S_i, we deduce that each column in $\{T_\ell, \ldots, T_n\}$, for which the cell in the S_i row is empty, contains exactly one "$\bigcirc$" entry, as Figure 4 shows.

Without loss of generality, we gather the rows for *all* x vertices that need to be revisited by our backtracking process in the worst-case scenario at the bottom of the matrix, from S_{i-x} to S_{i-1}. Then our matrix is divided into four disjoint regions, shown by different colors in Figure 4, such that $R1 = \{S_1, \ldots, S_{i-x-1}\} \times \{T_1, \ldots, T_{\ell-1}\}$, $R2 = \{S_1, \ldots, S_{i-x-1}\} \times \{T_\ell, \ldots, T_n\}$, $R3 = \{S_{i-x}, \ldots, S_{i-1}\} \times \{T_1, \ldots, T_{\ell-1}\}$, and $R4 = \{S_{i-x}, \ldots, S_{i-1}\} \times \{T_\ell, \ldots, T_n\}$. The row of a vertex S_y, with $y \in [i-x, i-1]$, that can exchange its match with S_i should satisfy the following two requirements, which correspond to the existence of edges $e_{i,j}$ and $e_{y,m}$ we have seen in our discussion of backtracking:

1. S_y should have been given a match $T_j \in \{T_\ell, \ldots, T_n\}$ in the current iteration that it can transfer to S_i; thus, the row of S_y should have an "$\bigcirc$" entry in $R4$.

2. There should exist a T_m, *neither* already used in the current iteration and *nor* matched to S_y in previous iterations, which S_y can obtain as a substitute for T_j. Such a T_m cannot be in $\{T_\ell, \ldots, T_n\}$, given that all T matches therein have been used already in the current iteration, hence their columns contain "$\bigcirc$" entries, as discussed; it should then be a $T_m \in \{T_1, \ldots, T_{\ell-1}\}$; thus, the row of S_y should have an empty cell in $R3$ whose column does not contain an "$\bigcirc$".

Let w_1, w_2, w_3, and w_4 denote the number of "$\bigcirc$" entries in region $R1$, $R2$, $R3$, and $R4$, respectively. We devise sufficient conditions for the above requirements as follows: Requirement (2) implies that there should exist a column $T_m \in \{T_1, \ldots, T_{\ell-1}\}$ that does *not* contain an "$\bigcirc$" entry. Thus, the total number of "$\bigcirc$" entries in these columns should be *less* than the number of columns themselves. This number of "$\bigcirc$" entries is $w_1 + w_3$, while the number of columns is $\ell - 1$. Thus, it should hold that:

$$w_1 + w_3 < \ell - 1 \tag{12}$$

Furthermore, since each column contains exactly $\ell-1$ "$\times$" entries, and columns in $\{T_1, \ldots, T_{\ell-1}\}$ already contain an "$\times$" entry in row S_i, it follows that each column segment within region $R3$ contains *at most* $\ell-2$ "$\times$" entries. Then any group of $\ell-1$ cells within column T_m in $R3$ will necessarily contain at least one non-"$\times$" entry. Given that column T_m does not contain an "$\bigcirc$" entry either, as Inequality (12) guarantees, it follows that any group of $\ell-1$ cells within column T_m in $R3$ will necessarily contain at least one *empty cell*. Thus, as long as $x \geq \ell-1$, Inequality (12) provides that *any set* of $\ell-1$ rows in $\{S_{i-x}, \ldots, S_{i-1}\}$, spanning $R3$ and $R4$, contains a row S_y having an empty cell in $R3$ whose column does not contain an "$\bigcirc$", as Requirement (2) stipulates. It only remains to devise such a set in a way that fulfills Requirement (1) as well, namely guarantees that row S_y *also* has an "$\bigcirc$" entry in $R4$. To that end, if suffices to postulate that $R4$ contains at least $\ell-1$ "$\bigcirc$" entries:

$$w_4 \geq \ell - 1 \tag{13}$$

Since each "$\bigcirc$" entry occupies a different row, Inequality (13) implies that there exists a set of $\ell-1$ rows with "$\bigcirc$" entries in $R4$, while by Inequality (12), one of them will have an empty cell in $R3$ whose column does not contain an "$\bigcirc$" as well. Thus, when both Inequalities (12) and (13) are satisfied, there exists a row S_y with "$\bigcirc$" in $R4$ and an empty entry in $R3$ without a "$\bigcirc$" in its column.

Now we proceed to find what values of x, the number of revisited vertices, render both inequalities true. Since each row in the matrix contains exactly one "$\bigcirc$" and each column in $\{T_\ell, \ldots, T_n\}$ contains one "$\bigcirc$", it follows that:

$$w_1 + w_2 = i - x - 1 \tag{14}$$

$$w_3 + w_4 = x \tag{15}$$

$$w_2 + w_4 = n - \ell + 1 \tag{16}$$

By Equations (14)+(15)-(16), we get:

$$w_1 + w_3 = (\ell - 1) - (n - i + 1) \tag{17}$$

Since it always holds that $n-i+1 > 0$, Inequality (12) is always true. Then, by Equations (14)-(16):

$$w_4 = n - \ell - i + x + 2 + w_1 \tag{18}$$

Since $w_1 \geq 0$, it follows that:

$$w_4 \geq n - \ell - i + x + 2 \tag{19}$$

Then, to satisfy Inequality (13), we have to ensure that:

$$n - \ell - i + x + 2 \geq \ell - 1 \tag{20}$$

which is equivalent to:

$$x \geq 2 \cdot \ell + i - n - 3 \tag{21}$$

Thus, we can find the desired S_y by examining no more than $2 \cdot \ell + i - n - 3$ previously matched vertices. □

We can now prove the following Theorem:

THEOREM 5.2. *Our Greedy algorithm always resolves the dead-end for* $k < \frac{n+3}{2}$.

PROOF. By Lemma (5.1), in order to resolve a dead-end encountered by the algorithm while processing the ith vertex in the ℓth iteration, we need to be able to revisit up to $2 \cdot \ell + i - n - 3$ previously matched vertices. In order for so many previously matched vertices to be available, it should be $i > 2 \cdot \ell + i - n - 3$, or $\ell < \frac{n+3}{2}$. Since the algorithm requires k iterations, it can resolve the dead-end in linear time for any $k < \frac{n+3}{2}$. □

In conclusion, our Greedy algorithm works for practical values of k used in real-world settings. Furthermore, the linear-time backtracking process does not affect the $O(n^2)$ complexity of an iteration. Hence, the overall complexity of all k iterations is $O(kn^2)$.

6. THE SORTGREEDY ALGORITHM

The algorithm we presented in Section 5 is greedy in the sense that it makes a greedy choice when it selects the *lightest* available edge of each vertex, while scanning vertices in S sequentially. Nevertheless, this process does not necessarily lead to good edge choices from a global view. For example, assume that edges $e_{i,j}$ and $e_{k,j}$ are both available for pickup, while $w_{i,j} > w_{k,j}$ and S_i is the next vertex to be processed. Then, assuming $e_{i,j}$ is the lightest edge incident to S_i, it will be picked up; thus, $e_{k,j}$ will be rendered unavailable, even though it was a better choice of edge from a global (though still greedy) perspective.

Motivated by this observation, we propose an enhanced greedy algorithm, which we call SortGreedy. The external shell of the algorithm remains the same, i.e., it operates over k iterations, with each iteration striving to select an assignment that brings about a small increase of the total GCP, and edge weights properly redefined among iterations. What differs is the internal edge selection process within each iteration. We outline this process below.

Algorithm 2: SortGreedy Algorithm Iteration

Data: A weighted bipartite graph $G = (S, T, E)$
Result: An assignment $\mathcal{A}$ with weight close to minimum
Sort edges E by ascending weight;
while $E \neq \oslash$ **do**
  Select $e_{i,j}$ with minimum weight;
  if $S_i \in S$ *and* $T_j \in T$ **then**
    $S = S - S_i, T = T - T_j$;
    Remove $e_{i,j}$ from E;
    Add $e_{i,j}$ to $\mathcal{A}$;
if $\exists$ *unmatched vertices* **then**
  foreach *unmatched vertex* $S_i \in S$ **do**
    find S_y matched to T_j such that $e_{i,j}$ and $e_{y,m}$ are available;
    substitute $e_{y,m}$ for $e_{y,j}$ and add $e_{i,j}$ to $\mathcal{A}$;
return $\mathcal{A}$;

We first sort all edges in E by ascending weight at $O(n^2 \log n)$ cost. Then, instead of scanning a vertex list S, we scan the sorted list of edges instead and try to pick up good edges directly therefrom. For each encountered edge, $e_{i,j}$, we check whether its adjacent vertices, S_i and T_j, are both available for matching. If that is the case, we select $e_{i,j}$ as a match and remove it from E, while also removing S_i from S and T_j from T, as they are no longer available for matching. Otherwise, we proceed to the next edge in the sorted list, until all edges are examined.

As with our basic Greedy algorithm, the above process may not terminate successfully, i.e., it may not have built a perfect matching of n edges after one pass through the edge list; some vertices may remain unmatched even after all edges have been processed. If this is the case, we call a *backtracking* procedure similar to the one outlined in Section 5. We scan the vertex list S, in lexicographic order, so as to detect unmatched vertices; for each such vertex S_i we look for an eligible substitution candidate among its neighbors in the lexicographic order; now we look not only at its predecessors, but at both predecessors and successors, as already-matched vertices can be found anywhere in the lexicographically ordered list. However, the essence of the backtracking process remains the same, hence Lemma 5.1 and Theorem 5.2 still hold. Algorithm 2 presents the basic iteration of this SortGreedy algorithm. As the complexity of an iteration is dominated by the sorting step, the overall complexity of SortGreedy is $O(kn^2 \log n)$.

7. THE HUNGARIAN-BASED ALGORITHM

Both our greedy algorithms work over k iterations, and at each iteration they attempt to find a perfect matching (assignment) that achieves small sum of edge weights (i.e., GCP increase). They follow a heuristic *greedy* logic in solving k local problems instead of the global problem of finding a k-regular generalization graph that minimizes GCP in one go. We have maintained the heuristic logic of k iterations and enhanced the internal greedy algorithm for assignment extraction. Still, the weight minimization problem addressed by this internal process is polynomially solvable - it *is* the Assignment Problem that finds a Maximum (or Minimum) Weight Perfect Matching (MWPM) in a bipartite graph. We can then apply the $O(n^3)$ Hungarian algorithm that finds an *optimal* solution for this problem as the internal process, while maintaining the shell of k iterations. We call the resulting $O(kn^3)$ algorithm Hungarian for brevity. This algorithm remains a heuristic, as it iteratively performs local optimizations. For the sake of completeness, we offer a brief description of the plain Hungarian algorithm, which we apply for minimizing the GCP increase at each iteration.

The Hungarian algorithm was developed by Kuhn [18], Edmonds and Karp [13], and Tomizawa [26]. Consider the graph in Figure 5a, where edge $e_{i,j} = (X_i, Y_j)$ carries a weight $w_{i,j}$. Without loss of generality, we aim to find a perfect matching of maximum weight (MWPM). Such a matching is formed by red edges in Figure 5a, with total weight 16. Given a bipartite graph G with edges E and a matching M, an **augmenting path** is a path starting out from and terminating at nodes not in M, with edges alternating between $E - M$ and M. The path $X_1 \to Y_2 \to X_2 \to Y_3$ in Figure 5c is an augmenting path with respect to the matching M formed by green edges. Such a path can be used to increase the size of a matching M by exchanging the roles of edges in M and not in M; e.g. $M = \{e_{3,1}, e_{2,2}\}$, will be extended to $\{e_{3,1}, e_{1,2}, e_{2,3}\}$ after exchanging edges within the augmenting path.

A **labeling** $\mathcal{L}$ labels each vertex v in G with a weight $\mathcal{L}(v)$; such weights are shown in rectangles in Figure 5a. $\mathcal{L}$ is **feasible** if $\mathcal{L}(X_i) + \mathcal{L}(Y_j) \geq w_{i,j}$ for any edge $e_{i,j}$. An **equality graph** $E_{\mathcal{L}}$ for $\mathcal{L}$ is formed by the set of edges $\{e_{i,j} : \mathcal{L}(X_i) + \mathcal{L}(Y_j) = w_{i,j}\}$. By the Kuhn-Munkres theorem, if $\mathcal{L}$ is feasible and M is a perfect matching in $E_{\mathcal{L}}$ then M is a MWPM for G. We can see that this theorem holds as follows: Since, by definition, *no* matching can have weight more than the total weight of its vertex labels, a matching $M_{\mathcal{L}}$ that establishes the equality achieves the maximum weight. The Hungarian algorithm iteratively finds a maximum matching (i.e. a matching with the most edges) within $E_{\mathcal{L}}$, and extends $E_{\mathcal{L}}$ by adjusting $\mathcal{L}$, until a perfect matching is found within $E_{\mathcal{L}}$.

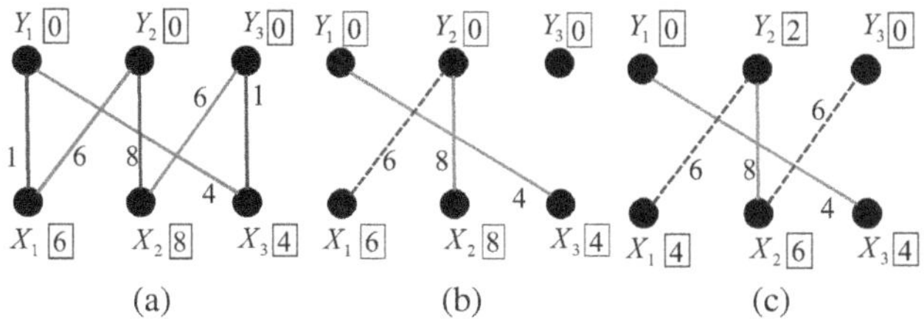

Figure 5: Hungarian Algorithm Illustration

We clarify that, before applying the algorithm to our problem at each iteration, we convert each edge weight $w_{i,j}$ to $-w_{i,j}$, so as to minimize GCP increase. The algorithm starts with an initial feasible labeling $\mathcal{L}$, obtained by assigning the *largest* edge weight at each node on one side, and 0 on the other side. Figure 5a shows such an initial labeling, which creates the equality graph $E_{\mathcal{L}}$ shown by dotted blue and solid green edges in Figure 5b. We pick a matching $M_{\mathcal{L}}$ inside $E_{\mathcal{L}}$, formed by solid green edges, and extend it using augmenting paths found by breadth-first search until no more such path can be found. By Berge's Theorem, a matching $M_{\mathcal{L}}$ is *maximum* iff it has no augmenting path. When $M_{\mathcal{L}}$ becomes maximum in $E_{\mathcal{L}}$, we extend $E_{\mathcal{L}}$ by reducing the weight of some X_i's by a certain amount σ, so that an edge that was not in $E_{\mathcal{L}}$ now becomes a part of $E_{\mathcal{L}}$. In order to ensure the original edges in $E_{\mathcal{L}}$ are retained after the modification, σ is compensated to the neighbors of X_i. For example, the equality graph in Figure 5b is extended to the one in Figure 5c by reducing the weights of X_1 and X_2 by 2 and increasing the weight of Y_2 by 2, thereby bringing edge $e_{2,3}$ into $E_{\mathcal{L}}$. Then we extend $M_{\mathcal{L}}$ in the new $E_{\mathcal{L}}$. Eventually, if the graph contains a perfect matching, it will be found within $E_{\mathcal{L}}$ and returned as the MWPM.

8. EXPERIMENTAL EVALUATION

In this section we conduct a thorough experimental study of the algorithms we have introduced in comparison to previous work. To the best of our knowledge, this is the first work to provide experimental results comparing a practical k-anonymization algorithm to an optimal solution. Our study features the following algorithms:

- **NH** The ring-generalization method proposed in [28]. We run this method exactly as it is proposed, with ring generalization applied on the partitions of size between k and $2k-1$. We attempted to apply ring generalization on larger partitions, yet we determined that the best results are obtained when the method runs in its proposed form. This finding confirms that the utility gains achieved by NH are primarily due to the employed partitioning method, rather than due to the ring generalization itself. Runtime measures for NH include the time for partitioning, building rings, and the final randomization step that extracts assignments.
- **k-c** The agglomerative algorithm implementing the k-concealment method in [16, 25]. A randomization step for this algorithm is proposed in [25], aiming to provide security against reverse-engineering the algorithm. Yet this step introduces extra information loss. In order to allow for the best-case scenario for k−c, in terms of both information loss and runtime, we do *not* include this step in our experiments.
- **minCostFlow** The CPLEX solver for the minimum-cost network flow problem, in which the minimized objective function is not GCP, but the sum of edge weights in the original complete graph. We include this so as to check whether an off-the-shelf algorithm can perform well on our problem.
- **MIP** The CPLEX MIP solver running our formulation for an *optimal* solution in Section 4.
- **Greedy** Our Greedy algorithm of Section 5, with a randomization step for assignment extraction as in [28, 29].
- **SortGreedy** Our enhanced greedy algorithm of Section 6, with randomized assignment extraction included.
- **Hungarian** Our Hungarian-based algorithm of Section 7, with assignment extraction by randomization.

Attribute	Cardinality	Type
Age	79	numerical
Gender	2	categorical
Education Level	17	numerical
Marital Status	6	categorical
Race	9	categorical
Work Class	10	categorical
Country	83	categorical
Occupation	51	categorical

Table 2: The CENSUS dataset

MIP and minCostFlow employ the IBM CPLEX Studio 12.4, invoked by a C++ interface. NH is implemented in C++, while Greedy, SortGreedy, Hungarian, and k−c, are in Java. The methods we compare against have no efficiency disadvantage arising from their implementation environment. All experiments ran on a 24-core Intel Xeon CPU machine @2.67GHz with 48GB RAM running Ubuntu 12.04.1 LTS. We use the CENSUS dataset [1], which contains 500K tuples on 8 attributes as shown in Table 2.

8.1 Evaluation under Partitioning

We commence our experimental study with the following observation: Our methods are configured to run on the *full* data set; nevertheless, the main competing technique, NH, does not do so. We tried to run NH on the full data set, yet the GCP results it achieved were *worse* than those achieved in its default partitioning-based version. This finding indicates that the ring generalization employed by NH may be a liability on large data sets. It is arguably a good idea to apply our methods on a per-partition basis too, for the sake of efficiency. This is what we do in this experiment. We first sort the input data set following a lexicographic order as described in Section 5. Then we divide the data into partitions of equal size P by simply selecting segments of P tuples along the lexicographic order. Furthermore, we use a different partition size for each algorithm, so as to ensure that SortGreedy and Hungarian run at time close to that of Greedy on a single partition. We envisage these algorithms running at a data center offering parallel processing capabilities, with each partition utilizing a different machine. Thus, the runtime of an algorithm is measured as the time for partitioning plus the time for processing a single partition, including the extraction of k random assignments. This configuration allows us to compare the performance of Hungarian, SortGreedy, and Greedy when they are given an equal *time budget* per partition.

In the case of NH, there is no point of selecting the largest partition in which its core routine can run at time no longer than Greedy, since NH gains *no benefit* by running on larger partitions than the partitions of size from k to $2k-1$ it employs by default. Thus, we stick with the partitions the algorithm inherently uses. However, it would not be fair to assume that all such partitions can be processed in parallel either; that would require far more machines than those utilized by the other methods. Instead, we assume that NH can use the same number of machines *in parallel* as Greedy, i.e. the algorithm that employs the largest size and hence smallest number of partitions among the other three. In other words, we offer to NH the same *parallelism budget* as Greedy. The runtime for NH is measured as the time for running its special partitioning scheme plus

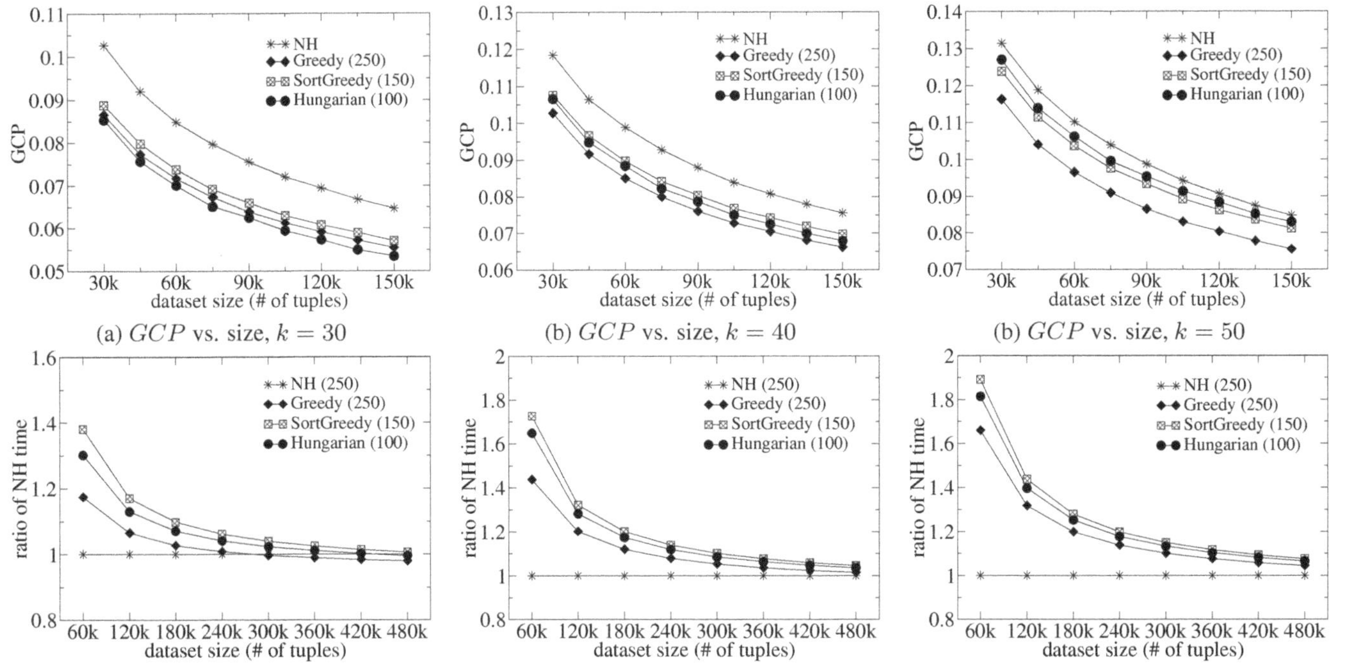

(a) GCP vs. size, $k = 30$ (b) GCP vs. size, $k = 40$ (b) GCP vs. size, $k = 50$

(d) time vs. size, $k = 30$ (e) time vs. size, $k = 40$ (f) time vs. size, $k = 50$

Figure 6: Evaluation under partitioning

the time for processing as many tuples as in a single partition used by Greedy, including assignment extraction by randomization.

We measure the achieved GCP and runtime, as defined above, for each algorithm. Figure 6 shows our results, as a function of full data size, for three different values of k. As shown in the legends, the employed partition size is 100 tuples for Hungarian, 150 for SortGreedy, and 250 for Greedy. Remarkably, under the same time budget per partition, Greedy achieves better GCP than SortGreedy, while both of them outperform Hungarian as k grows. At the same time, Greedy achieves consistently lower GCP than NH under the same parallelism budget. Figures 6d-f show the runtime of all methods as a ratio of the runtime of NH. Interestingly, our methods approach and eventually surpass the runtime of NH as data size grows. This is due to the fact that NH employs a more demanding partitioning scheme, hence its runtime is eventually dominated by the burden of initially partitioning the data set.

8.2 Comparison to optimal solution

We now examine data sets on which the CPLEX MIP solver can run the optimal solution. This way, we have a chance to assess how close our algorithms arrive to the optimal GCP. To our knowledge, no such experiments have been performed in any preceding experimental study on k-anonymization. We randomly select 100 different data sets of 14 tuples from the CENSUS data set of attribute cardinality $d = 8$ and run all competing techniques for several values of the privacy parameter k. We average the results over the 100 runs. Figure 7a shows our results. The bar charts in the figure show the fraction of the GCP difference between k−c (the worst performer on average) and Optimal each method gains (that is 1 for Optimal, 0 for k-c), vs. k. When a method achieves worse GCP than k−c, its bar shows a negative value. Hungarian achieves consistently the most near-optimal results, followed by SortGreedy at a very close distance. The minCostFlow method achieves, as expected, the optimal result for $k = 2$, since, for this value of k, minimizing the GCP metric is tantamount of minimizing the sum of edge weights selected as the second assignment (the first chosen assignment being the self-assignment). However, as k grows, minCostFlow progressively loses its advantage over other methods. For $k \geq 6$, it fares even worse than NH.

We also measure the average runtime, over 100 runs, as a function of the number of tuples, for $k = 6$. Figure 7b presents our results on logarithmic time axes. * These results show that the runtime of our three polynomial-time algorithms grows modestly as a function of data size, while they are positioned between those of NH and k−c; we will come back to this result later with much larger data. On the other hand, the runtime of the CPLEX MIP Solver grows inexorably, as shown in Figure 7b; running this solver on larger data is a prohibitive task. Therefore, MIP will not be featured in our subsequent experiments. The usefulness of running MIP was in leading us to the finding that our polynomial-time algorithms provide near-optimal solutions indeed.

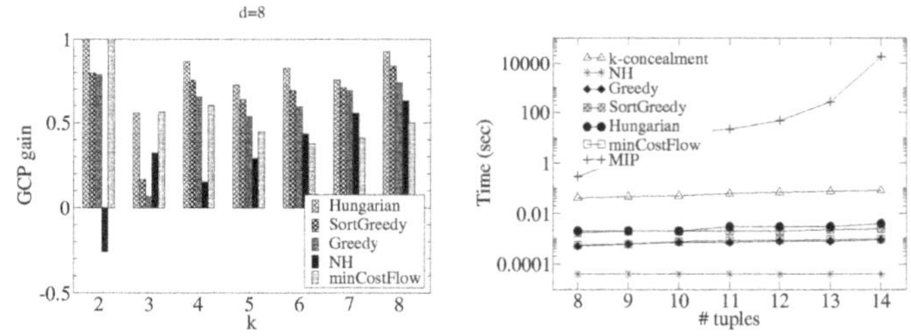

(a) GCP Gain vs. k, $d = 8$ (b) runtime vs. size, $k = 6$, $d = 8$

Figure 7: GCP Gain and Runtime on small data

8.3 Effect of k

Next, we study the effect of the k parameter on the compared methods, on data sets of 1k and 10k tuples from the CENSUS data set of dimensionality $d = 8$. Figure 8 presents our results, with k ranging from 10 to 150. These results reconfirm the superior performance of our methods in terms of information loss. Remarkably, the GCP divergence between our methods and those of previous works is widened as k grows (with up to 41% improvement), while that between our two greedy methods and Hungarian is narrowed. SortGreedy achieves practically the same GCP as Hungarian for

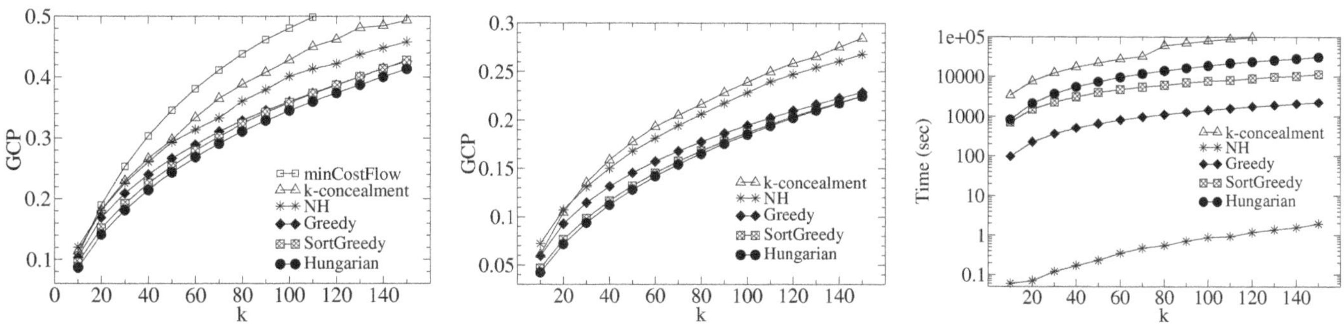

(a) GCP vs. k, 1K tuples (b) GCP vs. k, 10K tuples (c) time vs. k, 10K tuples

Figure 8: Effect of k

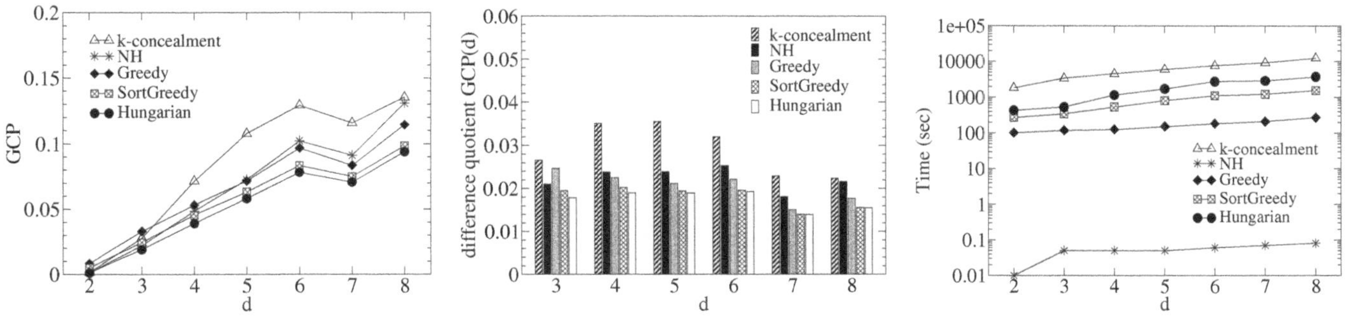

(a) GCP vs. d, $k = 30$ (b) Difference Quotient, $k = 30$ (c) time, $k = 30$

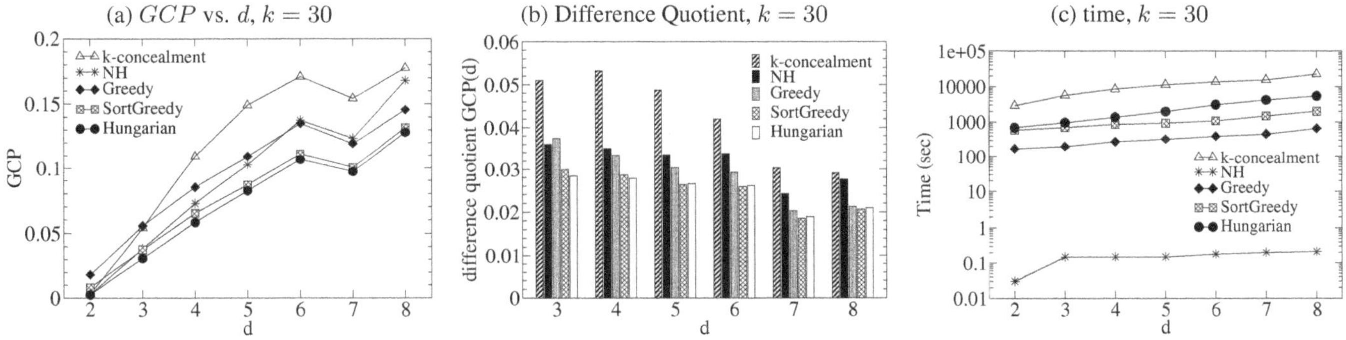

(d) GCP vs. d, $k = 50$ (e) Difference Quotient, $k = 50$ (f) time, $k = 50$

Figure 9: Effect of dimensionality

large k. In terms of runtime, our techniques scale equally well as NH with k, while k−c exhibits unstable behavior (Figure 8(c)). We reiterate that paying some extra runtime is worthwhile for the sake of data utility, given that anonymization is an one-off process. The performance of minCostFlow on the 1k data reconfirms that optimizing a non-GCP objective function is not a viable approach. Thus, we omit minCostFlow from subsequent experiments.

8.4 Effect of Dimensionality

Next, we study the effect of dimensionality on each of the competing techniques. We select the first 10K tuples from the CENSUS data set, and examine the performance of our algorithms as a function of the number of selected attributes d, letting d range from 2 to 8, and setting $k = 30$ and $k = 50$. Figure 9 shows the results. We observe that, not only do our three algorithms achieve better GCP than the competing NH and k−c methods, but they also present better resistance to the curse of dimensionality; the GCP they achieve does not deteriorate as severely as that of the other two methods as d grows. To make this effect more visible, we measure the difference quotient (i.e., the slope) of the GCP as a function of d, $\frac{GCP(d)-GCP(2)}{d-2}$. The middle column in Figure 9 presents our results. Remarkably, k−c has the worst behavior with respect to growing dimensionality, with NH coming second worst. On the other hand, our three algorithms exhibit much better dimensionality robustness, with SortGreedy and Hungarian being consistently the best performers. We also present runtime results for this experiment in the third column of Figure 9 in logarithmic time axes. As before, the runtime of our three methods falls between those of NH and k−c. Still, all algorithms scale equally well with growing dimensionality.

8.5 Effect of Size

Last, we investigate the scalability of the compared algorithms as the data set size grows. We obtain data sets of exponentially growing size, ranging from 1k to 64k tuples, from the CENSUS data set, with full dimensionality $d = 8$. We present GCP and runtime results in Figure 10, for k values set at $k = 15$ and $k = 50$, using logarithmic scales for all size and time axes. The GCP results present a familiar pattern. Remarkably, our methods consistently outperform NH and k−c, with SortGreedy approaching Hungarian. Concerning the two methods we compare against, it is interesting to note that k−c achieves better GCP than NH for small k. This finding is consistent with the results in Figure 8. The runtime results show that our two greedy methods, Greedy and

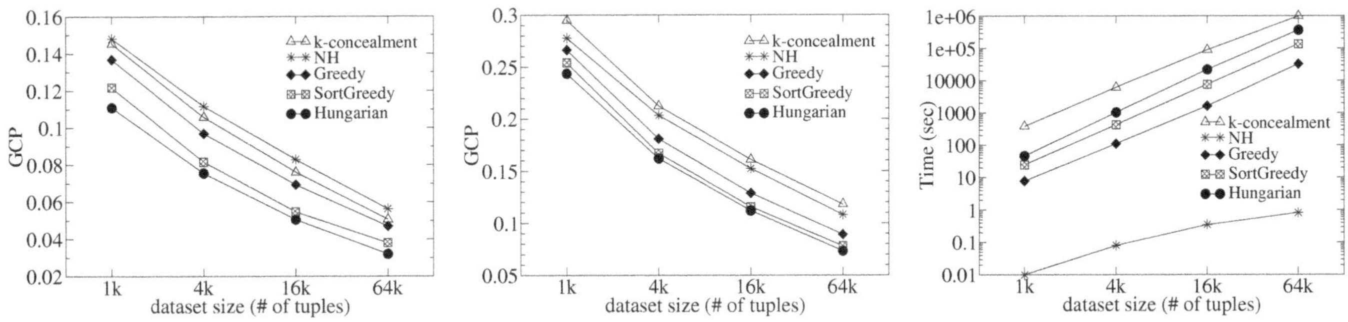

(a) GCP vs. size, $k = 15$ (b) GCP vs. size, $k = 50$ (c) time vs. size, $k = 50$

Figure 10: Effect of size

SortGreedy are similarly scalable as k−c, as is expected theoretically. While NH has the same quadratic complexity as those three, its default version which we are running does not actually run the algorithm on the complete data set, but only on partitions thereof. As we saw in Section 8.1, our algorithms have an *efficiency advantage* when given the benefits of data partitioning and parallelism.

9. CONCLUSIONS

This paper casts new light on the k-anonymity privacy model, which remains a prerequisite for more advanced models as well as a useful device in its own right. We treat k-anonymization as a network flow problem, aiming to minimize the information lost by value generalization. While previous works suggested the graph analogy, they either imposed superfluous constraints, or employed value suppression, compromising data utility in both cases. We devise solutions for the most general form of the problem, achieving significantly lower information loss. Conceived in this manner, the problem amounts to building a k-regular bipartite graph that defines an anonymization of high utility. We model an *optimal* solution using Mixed Integer Programming. Furthermore, we devise a greedy algorithm having the same $O(kn^2)$ time complexity as more restrictive previous solutions, an $O(kn^2 \log n)$ enhancement thereof, and an $O(kn^3)$ solution based on the Hungarian algorithm. Our techniques provide the *same* privacy guarantee as previous research on k-anonymity, as well as security against adversaries reverse-engineering the algorithm. Our experimental study shows that our algorithms achieve near-optimal utility and reliably outperform previous work, while their advantage is enhanced as the data dimensionality grows. We show this advantage applies also in terms of time efficiency when working in a parallel processing environment, after we divide a large data set into partitions.

Acknowledgments

We thank Wai Kit Wong and Arnon Mazza, who shared the codes for NH and k-concealment, respectively, as well as Aristides Gionis and Jonathan Eckstein for fruitful discussions on this topic.

10. REFERENCES

[1] http://www.ipums.org.

[2] C. C. Aggarwal. On k-anonymity and the curse of dimensionality. In *VLDB*, 2005.

[3] R. K. Ahuja, T. L. Magnanti, and J. B. Orlin. *Network Flows: Theory, Algorithms, and Applications*. Prentice Hall, 1993.

[4] R. E. Bixby, M. Fenelon, Z. Gu, E. Rothberg, and R. Wunderling. Mixed-integer programming: A progress report. In M. Grötschel, editor, *The Sharpest Cut*, chapter 18, pages 309–325. 2004.

[5] J. Brickell and V. Shmatikov. The cost of privacy: destruction of data-mining utility in anonymized data publishing. In *KDD*, 2008.

[6] J. Cao and P. Karras. Publishing microdata with a robust privacy guarantee. *PVLDB*, 5(11):1388–1399, 2012.

[7] J. Cao, P. Karras, P. Kalnis, and K.-L. Tan. SABRE: a Sensitive Attribute Bucketization and REdistribution framework for t-closeness. *The VLDB Journal*, 20(1):59–81, 2011.

[8] R. Chaytor and K. Wang. Small domain randomization: Same privacy, more utility. *PVLDB*, 3(1):608–618, 2010.

[9] K. Choromanski, T. Jebara, and K. Tang. Adaptive anonymity via b-matching. In *NIPS*, pages 3192–3200, 2013.

[10] C. Clifton and T. Tassa. On syntactic anonymity and differential privacy. In *PrivDB*, 2013.

[11] G. Cormode, N. Li, T. Li, and D. Srivastava. Minimizing minimality and maximizing utility: Analyzing method-based attacks on anonymized data. *PVLDB*, 3(1):1045–1056, 2010.

[12] C. Dwork. Differential privacy. In *ICALP (2)*, 2006.

[13] J. Edmonds and R. M. Karp. Theoretical improvements in algorithmic efficiency for network flow problems. *J. of the ACM*, 19(2):248–264, 1972.

[14] G. Ghinita, P. Karras, P. Kalnis, and N. Mamoulis. Fast data anonymization with low information loss. In *VLDB*, 2007.

[15] G. Ghinita, P. Karras, P. Kalnis, and N. Mamoulis. A framework for efficient data anonymization under privacy and accuracy constraints. *ACM TODS*, 34(2):1–47, 2009.

[16] A. Gionis, A. Mazza, and T. Tassa. k-anonymization revisited. In *ICDE*, 2008.

[17] A. Korolova. Privacy violations using microtargeted ads: A case study. In *ICDM Workshops*, 2010.

[18] H. W. Kuhn. The hungarian method for the assignment problem. *Naval Research Logistics Quarterly*, 2(1–2):83–97, 1955.

[19] K. LeFevre, D. J. DeWitt, and R. Ramakrishnan. Workload-aware anonymization techniques for large-scale datasets. *ACM TODS*, 33(3):17:1–17:47, 2008.

[20] N. Li, T. Li, and S. Venkatasubramanian. Closeness: A new privacy measure for data publishing. *IEEE TKDE*, 22(7):943–956, 2010.

[21] N. Li, W. H. Qardaji, and D. Su. On sampling, anonymization, and differential privacy or, k-anonymization meets differential privacy. In *ASIACCS*, 2012.

[22] T. Li and N. Li. On the tradeoff between privacy and utility in data publishing. In *KDD*, 2009.

[23] A. Machanavajjhala, D. Kifer, J. Gehrke, and M. Venkitasubramaniam. ℓ-diversity: Privacy beyond k-anonymity. *ACM TKDD*, 1(1):3, 2007.

[24] P. Samarati. Protecting respondents' identities in microdata release. *IEEE TKDE*, 13(6):1010–1027, 2001.

[25] T. Tassa, A. Mazza, and A. Gionis. k-concealment: An alternative model of k-type anonymity. *Transactions on Data Privacy*, 5(1):189–222, 2012.

[26] N. Tomizawa. On some techniques useful for solution of transportation network problems. *Networks*, 1:173–194, 1971.

[27] R. Wacks. *Privacy. A very short introduction*, volume 221 of *Very short introductions*. Oxford University Press, 2010.

[28] W. K. Wong, N. Mamoulis, and D. W. L. Cheung. Non-homogeneous generalization in privacy preserving data publishing. In *SIGMOD*, 2010.

[29] M. Xue, P. Karras, C. Raïssi, J. Vaidya, and K.-L. Tan. Anonymizing set-valued data by nonreciprocal recoding. In *KDD*, 2012.

A Near Real-Time Algorithm for Autonomous Identification and Characterization of Honeypot Attacks

Philippe Owezarski
CNRS, LAAS, 7 avenue du colonel Roche, F-31400 Toulouse, France
Université de Toulouse, LAAS, F-31400 Toulouse, France
owe@laas.fr

ABSTRACT

Monitoring communication networks and their traffic is of essential importance for estimating the risk in the Internet, and therefore designing suited protection systems for computer networks. Network and traffic analysis can be done thanks to measurement devices or honeypots. However, analyzing the huge amount of gathered data, and characterizing the anomalies and attacks contained in these traces remain complex and time consuming tasks, done by network and security experts using poorly automatized tools, and are consequently slow and costly. In this paper, we present an unsupervised algorithm - called UNADA for Unsupervised Network Anomaly Detection Algorithm - for identification and characterization of security related anomalies and attacks occurring in honeypots. This automatized method does not need any attack signature database, learning phase, or labeled traffic. This corresponds to a major step towards autonomous security systems. This paper also shows how it is possible from anomalies characterization results to infer filtering rules that could serve for automatically configuring network routers, switches or firewalls. The performances of UNADA in terms of attacks identification accuracy are evaluated using honeypot traffic traces gathered on the honeypot network of the University of Maryland. The time latency for producing such accurate results are also presented, especially showing how the parallelization capabilities of the algorithm help reducing this latency.

Keywords

Honeypot attack identification, Anomaly characterization, unsupervised machine learning, big traffic data, autonomous security systems.

1. INTRODUCTION

Monitoring communication networks and their traffic is an important advance for protecting computers systems. Several methods exist. For example, using monitoring devices at the interconnection points of networks allows the analysis of all incoming and outgoing flows. Another method consists in installing honeypots in the network. Honeypots provide more or less emulated services (according to the expected interaction level with the attackers), and allows supervising the use of the provided services by attackers. Thus, gathered data allows security experts on one hand to detect and analyze computer systems weaknesses, and on the other hand to collect useful information on the attacker activities that allows the analysis of their attacking methods, objectives, and strategies. Estimating and analyzing the risk related to illegitimate activities on the Internet are essential for security experts to design and develop adapted and efficient defense and protection systems with regard to the actual risk.

Characterizing and classifying current anomalies and attacks of the Internet are very complex and time consuming tasks, done by experts. Such tasks are therefore slow and costly. The main difficulty related to the identification and analysis of the different classes of illegitimate traffic is their fast evolution, amplification, and renewing capabilities. Designing autonomous identification and characterization processes is crucial for easy to deploy and to use defense systems. Hence, modern identification and classification systems must not rely on human expert knowledge, and must be able to autonomously adapt to the evolution of all traffic components, be they legitimate or not (this paper obviously focuses on illegitimate ones). For this purpose, we propose to take advantage of unsupervised machine learning techniques that do not require the help of any human expert. In this paper we then present an unsupervised method for identifying and characterizing anomalies and attacks contained in traffic gathered on honeypot networks. This method does not take advantage of any attack signature, learning stage, or labeled traffic, what constitutes a major advance towards autonomous security systems. This approach uses robust clustering techniques, as sub-space clustering, density-based clustering, and evidence accumulation for classifying flow ensembles in traffic classes, and builds easily understandable associated signatures. This method was first proposed in our previous work [19] that aims at detecting, classifying and characterizing anomalies in the full network traffic. This method has been adapted and extended in order to cope with the specific honeypot network traffic. Indeed, honeypot network traffic only contains illegitimate traffic (attacks, anomalies, intrusion attempts, ...) what significantly changes the way classification and characterization can be done. This paper mainly deals with taking into account the illegitimate nature of traffic to be analyzed, and

ASIA CCS'15, April 14–17, 2015, Singapore..

http://dx.doi.org/10.1145/2714576.2714580.

designing adapted and optimized identification and characterization algorithms.

These algorithms are illustrated by the analysis of honeypot traffic gathered at the University of Maryland, at the Netflow format [3]. The University of Maryland put measurement devices on routers at the border of the honeypots networks. This allows the capture of the traffic exchanged between honeypots and the Internet by monitoring only very few network devices. We nevertheless do not have the communication traces between the honeypots of the same network. The traffic traces we have been working on have been captured on a duration of more than one year.

The rest of the paper is as follows: section 2 presents related work in the domain of attack and anomalies detection and characterization, covering the full set of approaches from signature to statistical profile based, and finishing with approaches based on data mining and machine learning, especially unsupervised ones. This section also presents supervised and semi-supervised classification methods. Section 3 presents our previous unsupervised anomaly detection algorithm. This algorithm has already been published in [19]. We nevertheless add a presentation of this algorithm in this paper to make it self-contained. Interested readers can find an extended version of the algorithms description in [18]. However this algorithm originally works on full traffic, i.e. normal traffic on Internet links, and the objective is then to detect anomalies and attacks. Given the nature of the traffic we are considering in this paper - i.e. traffic between honeypots and the Internet - we know that it is completely illegitimate. This is a strong hypothesis that can help going further for characterizing and identifying the different component of this illicit traffic, and estimating the risk in the Internet. This section 3 then presents the sub-space clustering approach that aims at increasing the robustness of clustering algorithms, limiting its sensitivity, etc. It also presents the recombination mechanisms based on evidence accumulation and inter-clustering associations. As a strong improvement of the previous algorithm, section 4 describes how we can show correlation existing between clusters in different subspaces, these correlations exhibiting that such clusters could correspond to the same attack or anomaly. This is a strong help for more accurately and completely identifying and characterizing all attacks contained in the honeypots traffic. Section 5 then proposes a way to automatically characterize the identified anomalies and attacks. It relies on the clustering and correlation results. Section 6 proposes a method for ranking the risk an attack represents. Such ranking is aimed at helping security experts or network operators to prioritize their work, focusing first on the most dangerous ones. Section 7 illustrates the results of this characterization algorithm by showing a set of attacks and anomalies that have been identified in the real traffic traces of the University of Maryland, and the characterizing signatures that have been issued. Section 8 presents the performance evaluation of our algorithm in terms of good identification, especially comparing it with other unsupervised methods. Section 9 then explains the parallelization capabilities of our identification algorithm, and exhibits its strong performance in terms of low latencies, especially when computings can be effectively parallelized on multi-processor or multi-core machines. Last, section 10 concludes this paper.

2. RELATED WORK

The problem of network anomaly detection has been extensively studied during the last decade. Most of the approaches analyze statistical variations of traffic volume (e.g. number of packets, bytes or new flows) and/or traffic features (e.g. IP addresses and ports), using either single-link measurements or network-wide data. A non-exhaustive list of standard methods includes the use of signal processing techniques (e.g. ARIMA - Autoregressive Integrated Moving Average - modeling, wavelets-based filtering) on single-link traffic measurements [2,4], PCA (Principal Component Analysis) for network-wide anomaly detection [13–15], and Sketches applied to IP-flows [12,17].

The simultaneous detection and characterization of traffic anomalies has also received quite a lot of attention in the past, but results are few and present important limitations, either because they rely on some kind of training data and/or anomaly signatures, or because they do not provide meaningful and tractable information to a human network operator, who has to take the final decision about the nature of the detected problem. Authors in [13] characterize network-wide anomalies in highly aggregated traffic (Origin-Destination flows or OD flows for short), using PCA and the sub-space approach [15]. An important limitation of this approach is that the information obtained from OD flow data is too coarse-grained to provide meaningful information to the network operator. Papers like Lakhina et al. [14] and Biang et al. [17] detect and characterize anomalies using finer-grained traffic information, basically applying the same PCA approach to the sample entropy of the empirical distribution of specific traffic features. One clear limitation of these approaches is that the information they provide is not immediately usable and easy-to-understand by the network operator, who may not even be familiar with concepts distant from his tasks such as sample entropy. Besides, the PCA approach is highly sensitive to noise when used for anomaly detection [6,22], requiring in practice a fine-tuning and data-dependent calibration step to work.

UNADA (Unsupervised Network Anomaly detection Algorithm) [5] falls within the unsupervised anomaly detection domain, a novel research area that has drawn quite a lot of interest in the research community, but that still represents a rather immature field. Most work on unsupervised network anomaly detection has been devoted to the IDS field, generally targeting the detection of network intrusions in the very well known KDD'99 dataset. The great majority of the detection schemes proposed in the literature are based on clustering techniques and outliers detection, being [8,16,21] some examples. The objective of clustering is to partition a set of unlabeled patterns into homogeneous groups of "similar" characteristics, based on some similarity measure. Outliers detection consists in identifying those patterns that do not belong to any of these clusters. In [21], authors use a simple single-linkage hierarchical clustering method to cluster data from the KDD'99 dataset, based on the standard Euclidean distance for inter-pattern similarity. Eskin et al. [8] reports improved results in the same dataset, using three different clustering algorithms: the Fixed-Width clustering algorithm, an optimized version of the k-NN algorithm, and the one class SVM algorithm. Leung and Leckie [16] present a combined density-based and grid-based clustering algorithm to improve computational complexity, obtaining similar detection results.

Previous work of our own permits to automatically characterize network traffic anomalies [9], but using a-priori well-defined anomaly signatures. Closer to our current work, authors in [23] present URCA (Unsupervised Root Cause Analysis), a two-steps algorithm to characterize network anomalies in an unsupervised fashion. URCA uses as input the traffic in the anomalous time slots detected by any generic time-slot-based detection algorithm [7]. In the first step, it identifies the anomaly by iteratively removing from the anomalous time slots those flows that seem normal. In the second step, the algorithm uses a hierarchical clustering method to characterize the particular flows identified as anomalous. We identify some serious drawbacks and omissions in URCA: authors claim that the approach is unsupervised, which is not true, simply because it uses previously labeled anomalous events for the characterization. As in previous works, the algorithm uses difficult-to-interpret traffic descriptors for the clustering step (e.g. sample entropy of the distribution of IP addresses, aggregated at different levels), obscuring the comprehension of the network operator. Finally, the algorithm removes those flows that seem normal before the characterization step, which drags possible errors to the clustering step.

Our Unsupervised Anomaly Detection and Characterization algorithm [19] presents several advantages w.r.t. current state of the art. First and most important, it works in a completely unsupervised fashion, which means that it can be directly plugged into any monitoring system and start to work from scratch. Secondly, we perform anomaly detection based not only on outliers detection, but also by identifying small-clusters. This is achieved by using different levels of traffic aggregation, both at the source and destination of the traffic; this additionally permits to discover low-intensity and distributed anomalies. Thirdly, we avoid the lack of robustness of general clustering approaches, by combining the notions of Sub-Space Clustering [20] and multiple Evidence Accumulation [10]. In particular, our algorithm is immune to general clustering problems like sensitivity to initialization, specification of number of clusters, or structure-masking by irrelevant features. Fourthly, the algorithm performs clustering in low-dimensional feature spaces, using simple traffic descriptors like number of source IP addresses or fraction of SYN packets. This simplifies the characterization of the anomaly, and avoids well-known clustering problems when working with high-dimensional data [11]. Our algorithm ranks the multiple evidence of an anomaly detected in different sub-spaces, combining the most relevant traffic descriptors into a compact and easy-to-interpret signature that characterizes the problem. This permits to reduce the time spent by the network operator to understand the nature of the anomaly. Finally, this algorithm is designed to work in an on-line fashion, analyzing traffic from consecutive time slots in near real time. This is possible even when working with large number of traffic descriptors, because the sub-space clustering and the evidence accumulation algorithms are perfectly adapted for parallelization (see [19]).

To the best of our knowledge, there is no paper in the literature on the use of unsupervised classification and characterization algorithms on honeypot traffic, or for intrusion or attacks characterization on big data sets of attack traces. Some very recent work exists, especially by Symantec and the TRIAGE project (Data Analytics Framework for Intelligence Analysis) that aims to use autonomous data mining techniques for the analysis of all the gathered traces of attacks. However, TRIAGE aims at designing visualization techniques for the experts to make decision, while in this paper we propose to autonomously apply countermeasures for cheaper and faster defense.

3. UNSUPERVISED ANOMALY DETECTION

Our anomaly detection works on single-link packet-level traffic captured in consecutive time-slots of fixed lengthΔ_T. The first analysis stage consists in change detection. At each time-slot, traffic is aggregated in 9 different *flow* levels l_i. These include (from finer to coarser-grained resolution): *source IPs* (l_1: IPsrc), *destination IPs* (l_2: IPdst), *source Network Prefixes* ($l_{3,4,5}$: IPsrc/24, /16, /8), *destination Network Prefixes* ($l_{6,7,8}$: IPdst/24, /16, /8), and *traffic per Time Slot* (l_9: tpTS). Time series $Z_t^{l_i}$ are built for basic traffic metrics such as number of bytes, packets, and IP flows per time slot, using the 9 flow resolutions $l_{1...9}$. Analyzing honeypot traffic at multiple aggregation levels permits to detect both single source-destination and distributed attacks of very different intensities.

The unsupervised anomaly detection stage takes as input all the flows in the time slot flagged as anomalous, aggregated according to one of the different levels used in the first stage. An anomaly will generally be detected in different aggregation levels, and there are many ways to select a particular aggregation to use in the unsupervised stage; for the sake of simplicity, we shall skip this issue, and use any of the aggregation levels in which the anomaly was detected. Without loss of generality, let $\mathbf{Y} = \{\mathbf{y}_1, .., \mathbf{y}_F\}$ be the set of F flows in the flagged time slot, referred to as *patterns* in more general terms. Each flow $\mathbf{y}_f \in \mathbf{Y}$ is described by a set of A traffic attributes or *features*. In this paper, we use a list of common traffic attributes. The list includes $A = 9$ traffic features: number of source/destination IP addresses and ports, ratio of number of sources to number of destinations, packet rate, ratio of packets to number of destinations, and fraction of ICMP and SYN packets. According to our previous work on signature-based anomaly characterization [9], such simple traffic descriptors permit characterization of general traffic anomalies in easy-to-interpret terms. The list is therefore by no means exhaustive, and more features can be easily plugged-in to improve results. Let $\mathbf{x}_f = (x_f(1), .., x_f(A)) \in \mathbb{R}^A$ be the corresponding vector of traffic features describing flow $\mathbf{y}_f$, and $\mathbf{X} = (\mathbf{x}_1; ..; \mathbf{x}_F)$ the complete matrix of features, referred to as the *feature space*.

The unsupervised detection algorithm is based on clustering techniques applied to $\mathbf{X}$. The objective of clustering is to partition a set of unlabelled patterns into homogeneous groups of similar characteristics, based on some measure of similarity. Table 1 explains the characteristics of each anomaly in terms of type, distributed nature, aggregation type and netmask used, and impact on traffic features. On one hand, a SYN DDoS which targets one machine from a high number of hosts located in several /24 addresses will constitute a cluster if flows are aggregated in l_3. In fact, each of these /24 addresses will have traffic attributes values different from the ones of normal traffic: a high number of packet, a single destination and many SYN packets. It is the whole set of these flows that will create a cluster. On the other hand, if flows are aggregated in l_6, the only des-

Table 1: Feature used for the detection of DoS, DDoS, network/port scans, and spreading worms. Anomalies of distributed nature 1-to-N or N-to-1 involve several /24 (source or destinations) addresses contained in a single /16 address.

Anomaly	Distributed nature	Aggregation type	Clustering result	Impact on traffic features
DoS (ICMP ∨ SYN)	1-to-1	IPsrc/*	Outlier	nSrcs = nDsts = 1, nPkts/sec > λ_1, avgPktsSize < λ_2, (nICMP/nPkts > λ_3 ∨nSYN/nPkts > λ_4).
		IPdst/*	Outlier	
DDoS (ICMP ∨ SYN) to several @IP/24	N-to-1	IPsrc/24 (l_3)	Cluster	nDsts = 1, nSrcs > α_1, nPkts/sec > α_2, avgPktsSize < α_3, (nICMP/nPkts > α_4 ∨ nSYN/nPkts > α_5).
		IPsrc/16 (l_4)	Outlier	
		IPdst/*	Outlier	
Port scan	1-to-1	IPsrc/*	Outlier	nSrcs = nDsts = 1, nDstPorts > β_1, avgPktsSize < β_2, nSYN/nPkts > β_3.
		IPdst/*	Outlier	
Network scan to several @IP/24	1-to-1	IPsrc/*	Outlier	nSrcs = 1, nDsts > δ_1, nDstPorts > δ_2, avgPktsSize < δ_3, nSYN/nPkts > δ_4.
		IPdst/24 (l_6)	Cluster	
		IPdst/16 (l_7)	Outlier	
Spreading worms to several @IP/24	1-to-N	IPsrc/*	Outlier	nSrcs = 1, nDsts > η_1, nDstPorts < η_2, avgPktsSize < η_3, nSYN/nPkts > η_4.
		IPdst/24 (l_6)	Cluster	
		IPdst/16 (l_7)	Outlier	

tination address will be an outlier characterized by many sources and a high proportion of SYN packets.

Our particular goal is to identify and to isolate the different flows that compose the anomaly flagged in the first stage, both in a robust way. Unfortunately, even if hundreds of clustering algorithms exist [11], it is very difficult to find a single one that can handle all types of cluster shapes and sizes, or even decide which algorithm would be the best for our particular problem. Different clustering algorithms produce different partitions of data, and even the same clustering algorithm provides different results when using different initializations and/or different algorithm parameters. This is in fact one of the major drawbacks in current cluster analysis techniques: the lack of robustness.

To avoid such a limitation, we have developed a divide and conquer clustering approach, using the notions of clustering ensemble [24] and multiple clusterings combination. A clustering ensemble $\mathbf{P}$ consists of a set of N partitions P_n produced for the same data with $n = 1,..,N$. Each of these partitions provides a different and independent evidence of data structure, which can be combined to construct a global clustering result for the whole feature space. There are different ways to produce a clustering ensemble. We use Sub-Space Clustering (SSC) [20] to produce multiple data partitions, applying the same clustering algorithm to N different sub-spaces $\mathbf{U}_n \subset \mathbf{X}$ of the original space.

3.1 Clustering Ensemble and Sub-Space Clustering

Each of the N sub-spaces $\mathbf{U}_n \subset \mathbf{X}$ is obtained by selecting R features from the complete set of A attributes. The number of sub-spaces N hence is equal to R-combinations-obtained-from-A. To set the sub-space dimension R, we take a very useful property of monotonicity in clustering sets, known as the downward closure property: "if a collection of points is a cluster in a d-dimensional space, then it is also part of a cluster in any $(d-1)$ projections of this space" [1]. This directly implies that, if there exists any evidence of density in $\mathbf{X}$, it will certainly be present in its lowest-dimensional sub-spaces. Using small values for R provides several advantages: firstly, doing clustering in low-dimensional spaces is more efficient and faster than clustering in bigger dimensions. Secondly, density-based clustering algorithms provide better results in low-dimensional spaces [1], because high-dimensional spaces are usually sparse, making it difficult to distinguish between high and low density regions. We shall therefore use $R = 2$ in our SSC algorithm, which gives $N = C_R^A = A(A-1)/2$ partitions.

3.2 Combining Multiple Partitions

Having produced the N partitions, we now explore different methods to combine these partitions in order to build a single partition where anomalous flows are easily distinguishable from normal-operation traffic: the classical Evidence Accumulation (EA) and the new Inter-Clustering Result Association (ICRA) method.

3.2.1 Combining Multiple Partitions using Evidence Accumulation

A possible answer is provided in [10], where authors introduced the idea of multiple-clusterings Evidence Accumulation (EA). By simple definition of what it is, an anomaly may consist of either outliers or small-size clusters, depending on the aggregation level of flows in $\mathbf{Y}$ (cf table 1). EA then uses the cluster ensemble $\mathbf{P}$ to build two inter-pattern similarity measures between the flows in $\mathbf{Y}$. These similarity measures are stored in two elements: a similarity matrix S to detect small clusters and a vector D used to rank outliers. $S(p, q)$ represents the similarity between flows p and q. This value increases when the flows p and q are in the same cluster many times and when the size of this cluster is small. These two parameters allows the algorithm to target small clusters. $D(o)$ represents the abnormality of the outlier o. This value increases when the outlier has been classified as such several times and when the separation between the outlier and the normal traffic is important. As we are only interested in finding the smallest-size clusters and the most dissimilar outliers, the detection consists in finding the flows with the biggest similarity in S and the biggest dissimilarity in D. Any clustering algorithm can then be applied on the matrix S values to obtain a final partition of $\mathbf{X}$ that isolates small-size clusters of close similarity values. A variable detection threshold over the values in S is also able to detect small-size cluster. Concerning dissimilar outliers, they can be isolated though a threshold applied on the values in D.

3.2.2 Combining Multiple Partitions using Inter-Clustering result Association

However, by reasoning over the similarities between patterns (here flows), EA introduces several potential errors. Let us consider two pattern sets P_i and P_j, if the cardinality of these pattern sets is close and if they are present in a similar number of sub-spaces, then EA will produce a very close (potentially the same) similarity value for both flow sets. They will then likely be falsely considered as belonging to the same cluster. This possibility has to be considered very seriously as it can induce a huge error: different anomalies will be merged together and will then likely be wrongly identified and characterized. Another source of potential error when using a clustering algorithm over S values is the algorithm sensitivity to wrong parameters. Furthermore, the use of a threshold over S and/or D can decrease the system performance in case of a wrong value used.

In order to avoid the previously exposed sources of error, we introduce a new way of combining clustering results obtained from sub-spaces: Inter-Clustering Results Association. The idea is to address the problem in terms of cluster of flows and outlier of flow similarity instead of pattern (or flow) similarity. Hence, we shift the similarity measure from the patterns to the clustering results. The problem can then be split in two sub-problems: correlate clusters through Inter-CLuster Association (ICLA), and correlate outlier through Inter-Outlier Association (IOA).

In each case, a graph is used to express similarity between either clusters or outliers. Each vertex is a cluster/outlier from any sub-space $\mathbf{U}_n$ and each edge represents the fact that two connected vertices are similar. The underlying idea is straightforward: identify clusters or outliers present in different sub-spaces that contain the same flows. To do so, we first define a cluster similarity measure called CS between two clusters C_r and C_s: $CS(C_r, C_s) = \frac{card(C_r \cap C_s)}{max(card(C_r), card(C_s))}$, *card* being the function that associates a pattern set with its cardinality, and $C_r \cap C_s$ the intersection of C_r and C_s. Each edge in the *cluster similarity graph* between two C_r and C_s means $CS(C_r, C_s) > 0.9$, being this an empirically chosen value. The value 0.9 guarantees that the vast majority of patterns are located in both clusters with a small margin of error. IOA uses an *outlier similarity graph* built by linking every outlier to every other outlier that contains the same pattern. Once these graphs are built, we need to find cluster sets where every cluster contains the same flows. In terms of vertices, we need to find vertex sets where every vertex is linked to every other vertex. In graph theory, such vertex set is called a *clique*. The clique search problem is a NP-hard problem. Most existing solutions use exhaustive search inside the vertex set which is too slow for our application. We then make the hypothesis that a vertex can only be part of a single clique. A greedy algorithm is then used to build each clique. Anomalous flow set are finally identified as the intersection of all the flow sets present in the clusters or outliers within each clique.

4. CORRELATING ANOMALOUS TRAFFIC CLASSES

4.1 Address related correlation

Thanks to previous algorithm, we can detect several classes of illegitimate traffic, but these classes can appear in different aggregation levels. We know that such classes present at different levels can be related to each other. Indeed, two traffic classes in two different aggregation levels are related for example when their flows come from the same sources and go towards the same destinations. For a better characterization of traffic classes, it is then important to link classes corresponding to the same single anomaly. Correlating illegitimate traffic classes is a solution for that purpose; it is able to determine the similarity between classes at each aggregation level, for possibly grouping them if they belong to the same anomaly.

For estimating the similarity between two illegitimate traffic classes on two different aggregation levels, we use a comparison function. It relies on IP addresses comparison [19]. The comparison method then uses the IP source and destination addresses of the different traffic classes a_1 and a_2. It then compares source IP addresses with each other, and destination IP addresses with each other, using function (1).

$$Sim_{@}(@_1, @_2) = \frac{|@_1 \cap @_2|}{max(|@_1|, |@_2|)} \tag{1}$$

where $@_n$ is a set of IP addresses, and $|@_n|$ the number of addresses in this set.

It exists a similarity between two illegitimate traffic classes if equation (2) is true. $tTSAddrSims$ is a threshold to be defined.

$$Sim_{src}(@_1, @_2) > tTSAddrSims \wedge Sim_{dest}(@_1, @_2) > tTSAddrSims \tag{2}$$

This method as defined in our previous work [19] has some lacks, and especially because it does not consider time. It appears when testing this method on the Maryland data that some flows of the same class are separated in time by several months. It is then clear that it is not satisfactory to consider only IP addresses. For example, illegitimate traffic classes detailed in tables 2 and 3 are completely different from a behavior point of view. For the first class, the number of sent packets in each flow is around 54, whereas it is around 4 in the second class. In addition, the time difference between these sendings is around two months. The only similarity between these two classes is related to their source IP addresses (saddr), and destination IP addresses (daddr). In this case the similarity value between the two classes with the previous function is 66%, what is significantly high, and would indicate a strong link between them. Given the time at which they happened it is certainly not true, and malware infecting the machines are certainly not the same. As a consequence, we added temporal features to the correlation function.

Let us consider two illegitimate traffic classes a_1 and a_2. T_1 and T_2 are the set of time intervals in which traces of a_1 and a_2 appear. $@_1^n$ and $@_2^n$ are the set of source and destination IP addresses of classes a_1 and a_2 for the interval $t_n \in T_1$. The new similarity function is then defined as:

$$SimTime_{@} = \sum_{t \in T_1} \frac{Sim_{@}(@_1^t, @_2^t)}{max(|@_1^t|, |@_2^t|)} \tag{3}$$

However, if it exists time intervals between two classes, the similarity function equals a value very close from zero, whereas these two classes can be highly similar for other features. We then still need to keep in the computing of the similarity function the IP addresses of the anomaly classes a_1 and a_2. But the addresses must be computed intependentely from any temporal feature.

$$SimGlobal_{@} = \frac{Sim_{@}(@_1, @_2)}{max(|@_1|, |@_2|)} \tag{4}$$

month	day	hour	min	saddr	daddr	nPkts	nBytes	nSyn/nPkts
02	01	02	4	192.168.0.1, 192.168.0.2	172.16.4.16, 172.16.4.21	54	4726	0.1481481
02	01	03	40	192.168.0.1, 192.168.0.3	172.16.4.16, 172.16.4.21	54	4869	0.1481481
02	01	18	05	192.168.0.1, 192.168.0.3	172.16.4.16, 172.16.4.21	53	3996	0.0754717
02	01	19	55	192.168.0.1, 192.168.0.2	172.16.4.16, 172.16.4.21	54	4545	0.1481481

Table 2: First example of an illegitimate traffic class (IP addresses have been anonymised)

month	day	hour	min	saddr	daddr	nPkts	nBytes	nSyn/nPkts
04	10	01	30	192.168.0.1, 192.168.0.2	172.16.4.16, 172.16.4.21	5	20	1
04	11	01	30	192.168.0.1, 192.168.0.3	172.16.4.16, 172.16.4.21	4	160	1
04	12	01	30	192.168.0.1, 192.168.0.2	172.16.4.16, 172.16.4.21	5	20	1
04	13	01	30	192.168.0.1	172.16.4.16, 172.16.4.21	4	160	1

Table 3: Second example of an illegitimate traffic class (IP addresses have been anonymised)

We then obtain the simlarity function defined by equation (5).

$$\begin{aligned} SimAnomalies(a1, a2) = {} & (SimTime_{Src}(a_1, a_2) > \lambda_1) \\ & \wedge (SimTime_{Dest}(a_1, a_2) > \lambda_1) \\ & \wedge (SimGlobal_{Src}(a_1, a_2) > \lambda_2) \\ & \wedge (SimGlobal_{Dest}(a_1, a_2) > \lambda_2) \end{aligned} \quad (5)$$

The result of this function is a boolean value which is true if a_1 and a_2 are similar.

4.2 Time related correlation

Let's take again the examples of classes detailed in tables 2 and 3. It is clear that there is no link between these two classes because they happened at very different times. Let's apply equation (5). Let's consider IP addresses of the first class on February 1st at 2h40 am. Source IP addresses are 192.168.0.1 and 192.168.0.2. At that time, the second class is empty (it happened on April 10th to 13th). The similarity is then correctly estimated as false. By continuing with other times and the same method, we always obtain a false value for the similarity. The new similarity function then correctly does not find any similarity between these two illegitimate traffic classes.

Nevertheless, it is required with this new method to fix correct threshold values. If thresholds are not well selected returned values could be erroneous. With a small λ_1 value, each time a small temporal similarity will appear between two illegitimate classes, it will be the global similarity value that will determine the final similarity result between the two classes. If λ_1 is high, the two classes will be considered as similar if they sent packet almost at the same time, from the same source and to the same destinations. This is a strong constraint and forbids any time difference in the sendings. The global similarity will then be of less importance. Based on our experience with the traces of University or Maryland, we empirically recommend to select for λ_1 a low threshold value, between 10% and 30%, and for λ_2 a threshold value greater than 25%.

Illegitimate traffic classes that appear as different after the sub-space clustering phase can then be grouped, as it is shown that they correspond to the same anomaly.

5. AUTOMATIC CHARACTERIZATION OF ANOMALIES

At this stage, the global traffic from and towards honeypots has been decomposed into traffic classes that exhibit different behaviors. Classification techniques of the Internet traffic have now to identify the type of each of these traffic classes, the generating application, or the type of attack or anomaly, each of these clusters is related to. Most advanced classification techniques, i.e. semi-supervised techniques, take advantage of signatures that specifically identify one of the possible traffic families, applications, or attacks. These signatures come either from a previous knowledge or expertise in this domain, either on a training stage on a known traffic, whose application components have already been labeled. This is obviously a strong requirement for classification purposes, but it remains a severe limit for designing a fully autonomous method.

However, in this work, at the opposite of what has been already done in the research area of autonomous traffic classification, this constraint does not exist because of the traffic nature that we have to analyze: illegitimate traffic. It is thus not needed to perfectly identify the anomaly kind (or attack), or to name it. Indeed, all traffic classes that have been isolated by the sub-space clustering algorithm, and evidence accumulation are anomalies or attacks. Therefore, the computing to be performed for each traffic anomaly or attack, in fine, consists in discarding them, after having identified any necessary feature required for instance for estimating the risk they represent in the Internet.

We then propose for this purpose to automatically generate the rules characterizing the anomaly classes. Based on these rules, it is easy to understand the anomalies characteristics and to infer the countermeasures to be performed (and of course, this can be done by a computer process).

At this stage, the sub-space clustering / evidence accumulation / correlation algorithm has identified several correlated anomalies containing a set of traffic flows in $\mathbf{Y}$ far out the rest of the traffic. The following task is to produce the appropriate filtering rules to correctly isolate and characterize each of these anomalies.

In order to produce filtering rules, the algorithm selects those sub-spaces $\mathbf{U}_n$ where the separation between the considered anomalous flows and the rest of the traffic is the biggest. We define two different classes of filtering rule: *absolute* rules $FR_A(\mathbf{Y})$ and *relative* rules $FR_R(\mathbf{Y})$. Absolute rules do not depend on the separation between flows, and correspond to the presence of dominant features in the con-

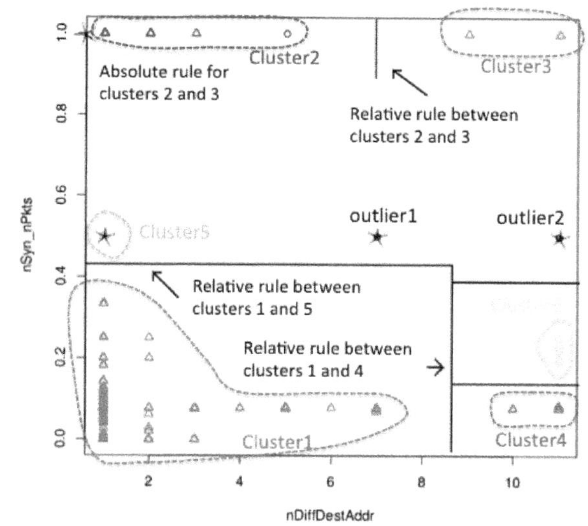

Figure 1: The different filtering rules for sub-spaces (nSyn/nPkts, nDiffDestAddr)

sidered flows. An absolute rule for a certain feature j characterizing a certain flow set Y_g has the form
$FR_A(\mathbf{Y}_g, a) = \{\forall \mathbf{y}_f \in \mathbf{Y}_g \subset \mathbf{Y} : x_f(a) == \lambda\}$.

For example, in the case of an ICMP flooding attack, the vast majority of the associated flows use only ICMP packets, hence the absolute filtering rule {nICMP/nPkts == 1} makes sense. On the contrary, relative filtering rules depend on the relative separation between anomalous and normal-operation flows. Basically, if the anomalous flows are well separated from the normal cluster in a certain partition P_n, then the features of the corresponding sub-space $\mathbf{U}_n$ are good candidates to define a relative filtering rule. A relative rule has the form
$FR_R(\mathbf{Y}_g, a) = \{\forall \mathbf{y}_f \in \mathbf{Y}_g \subset \mathbf{Y} : x_f(a) < \lambda \vee x_f(a) > \lambda\}$.

We shall also define a *covering relation* between filtering rules: we say that rule f_1 *covers* rule $f_2 \Leftrightarrow f_2(\mathbf{Y}) \subset f_1(\mathbf{Y})$. If two or more rules overlap (i.e., they are associated to the same feature), the algorithm keeps the one that covers the rest.

In order to construct a compact signature of the anomaly, we have to devise a procedure to select the most discriminant filtering rules. Absolute rules are important, because they define inherent characteristics of the anomaly. As regards relative rules, their relevance is directly tied to the degree of separation between anomalous and normal flows. In the case of outliers, we select the K features for which the Mahalanobis distance to the normal-operation traffic is among the top-K biggest distances. In the case of small-size clusters, we rank the relatives rules according to the degree of separation to the normal anomaly using the well-known Fisher Score (FS) which uses the variance in each cluster (normal and anomalous). To finally construct the signature, the absolute rules and the top-K relative rules are combined into a single inclusive predicate, using the covering relation in case of overlapping rules.

What follows gives a real example of the generation of filtering rules based on an anomaly characterization. It is depicted on Figure 1. Clusters 2 and 3 have their value nSyn/nPkts always equal to 1. It then exists for them an absolute rule $\{nSyn/nPkts == 1\}$.

On Figure 1, there exists a relative rule between cluster 1 and cluster 4. For generating it, we draw the median between clusters 1 and 4. Based on this median value, we can create the relative rule $\{nDiffDestAddr < 9\}$.

6. RISK BASED ANOMALIES RANKING

Estimating the risk related to an anomaly can help a security expert, in the general case, selecting the traffic classes that require to be computed in priority. In our specific case where all traffic classes identified are illegitimate, it can help to distinguish for instance between anomalies that are real attacks from scanning which in general just serves for preparing a possible future attack. In that case, the risk ranking can help superposing relative filtering rules, targeting in priority the most risky one.

The way our risk ranking is done depends on the amount of communication; the more communication in an anomaly or attack, the more risky. In addition, anomalies that appear in many sub-spaces are considered as more dangerous than the ones appearing in a single or on very few sub-spaces. Three features are considered for estimating the risk related to an anomaly. The first one is the number of packets of the anomaly, because, if there are many packets exchanged between the attacking and the victim machines, there exist potentially machines infected by a virus, or a flooding attack attempt. The second feature is the amount of bytes exchanged in the anomaly, because, even if the number of exchanged packets is reduced, a large amount of bytes could have been exchanged. This may correspond to the download of information from a victim machine by an attacker, or the upload of viruses on several victim machines from the attacker machine. Last, the third feature is the communication duration between the attacker and a target machine. The longer the communication duration, the more probable an attacker performing a download, or having an open *shell* on the victim machine.

The formula used for the risk estimation is:

$$risk = C * (log(nPkts) + log(nBytes) + log(duration + 1)) \quad (6)$$

where C is the number of sub-spaces in which the anomaly appears, $nPkts$ is the number of exchanged packets in the anomaly, $nBytes$ is the number of exchanged bytes, and $duration$ is the duration of the anomaly. $+1$ appears in $log(duration + 1)$ for avoiding some errors as $duration \in \mathbb{R}_+$ whereas $(nPkts, nBytes) \in \mathbb{R}_+^*$. The communication duration can be assimilated as zero because it can be so small that measurement devices can measure it as zero. On the other side, the number of packets or bytes are necessarily greater or equal to 1.

7. EXPERIMENTAL EVALUATION IN REAL TRAFFIC

We run the algorithm described in this paper on the honeypot traffic traces gathered at the University of Maryland. For obvious privacy reasons, as well as space limit, we will not present the complete set of attacks evidenced. But we will show on an example how the algorithm behaves, and how it succeed in classifying attacks and anomalies, how it builds the anomaly classes characteristics based on sub-

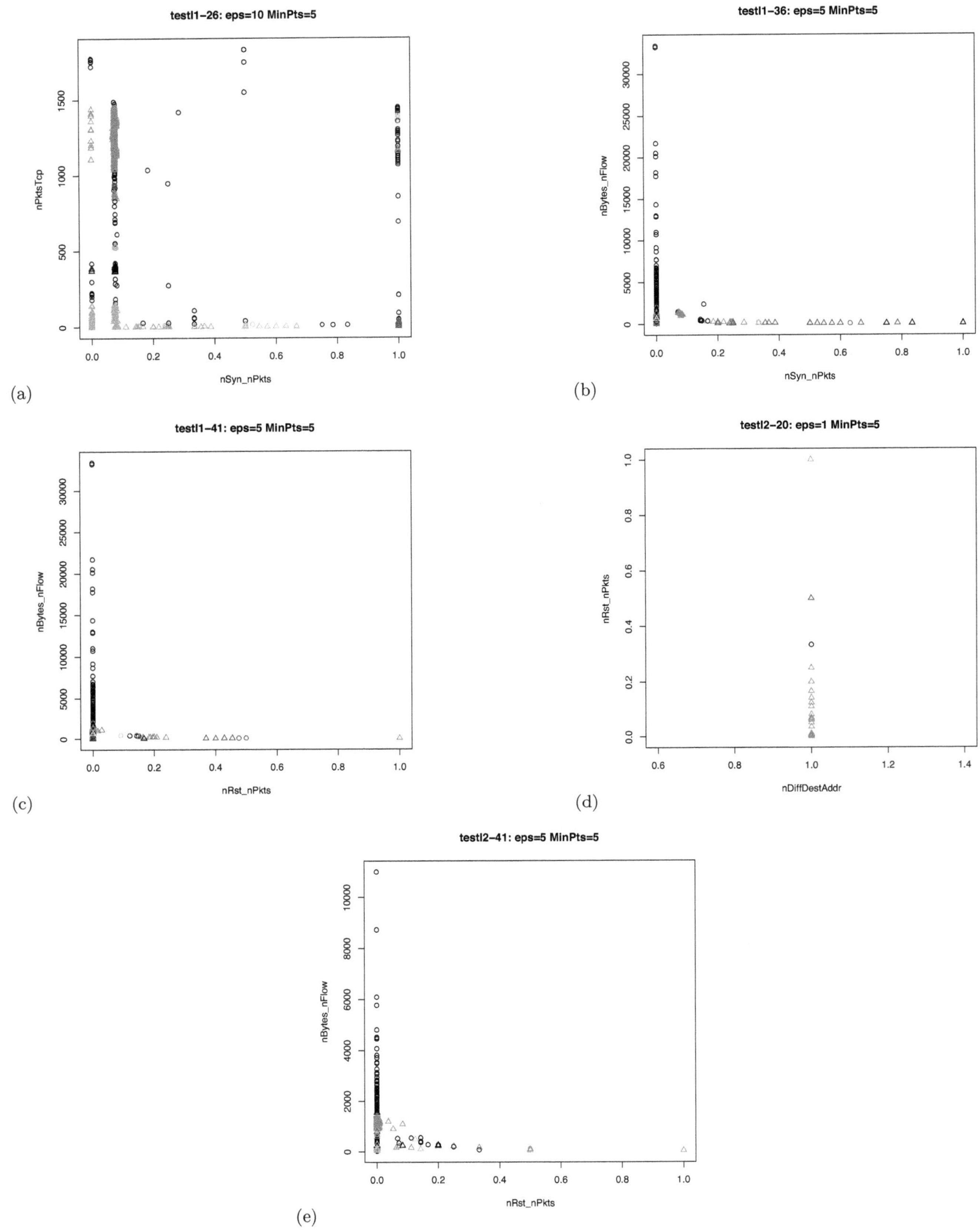

Figure 2: Sub-spaces in which anomalies [44], [224], and [327] appear. These sub-spaces correspond to different IP address aggregation levels and different temporal granularities

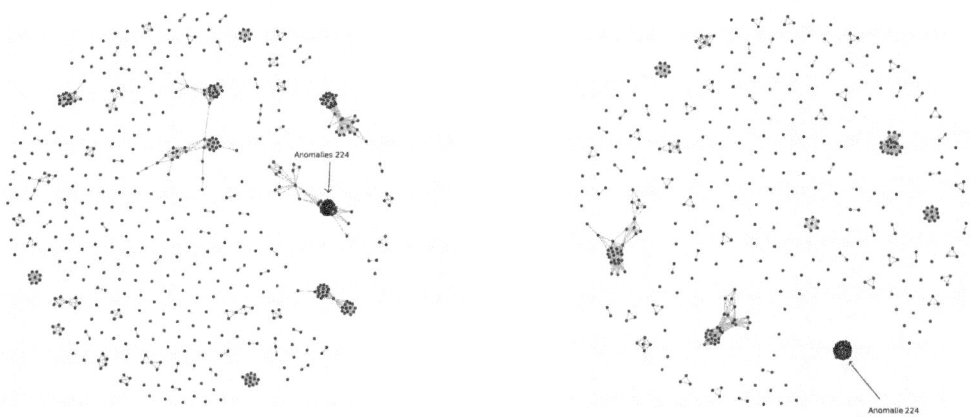

Figure 3: Two levels of cliques appearing when correlating anomalies in different sub-spaces

space clustering, evidence accumulation, and anomaly correlation. It also presents the filtering rules that have been autonomously generated and that can serve for automatically configuring security devices as filtering functions of routers, or firewalls.

This section starts by showing the complete behavior of the algorithm applied on a single anomaly (designated as anomaly [327]). Figure 2 shows 5 sub-spaces in which anomalies mentioned in this section appear (all sub-spaces in which the anomaly appears are not depicted on figure 2 for space limit reason). On each of these sub-spaces, clusters clearly appear, each corresponding to different anomalies. Figure 3 shows the cliques that have been built for correlating the clusters found in different sub-spaces, and then linking the ones that correspond to the same anomaly or attack.

Anomaly [327] appears in Figure 2 on subspaces (d) with the blue cluster, and (e), with the green cluster corresponding to $nRst_nPkts = 0.5$. At the end of the UNADA process, the algorithm generated the following signature that fully characterizes anomaly [327]:

Characteristics of attack [327]:
$(nBytes/nFlow < 93.6666666666667) \wedge (nBytes/nFlow > 74) \wedge (nDiffSrcAddr = 1) \wedge (nFin/nPkts = 0) \wedge (nFinTcp/nPktsTcp = 0) \wedge (nPkts = 2) \wedge (nPktsTcp = 2) \wedge (nRst/nPkts = 0.5) \wedge (nSyn/nPkts = 0.5) \wedge (nSynTcp/nPktsTcp = 0.5)$

Thanks to this process that issues such a signature, it is easy for a security expert to analyze the anomaly: it corresponds to a well-known DoS attack which consists in requesting the opening of a new TCP connection by sending a SYN packet, and then a RST packet for closing it in an un-negociated way. It then makes the receiver allocate resources, and desallocate them immediately. The receiver is then overwhelmed with the slow operations it has to perform on the machine memory. The advantage with issuing automatically such signature is that the appropriate counter-measures which consists in blocking the related traffic can be performed automatically without the help of the network administrator who can then focus on trickiest attacks.

Anomaly [326] appears in Figure 2 on subspaces (d) with the blue cluster, and (e), with the green cluster. The algorithm generated the following signature that fully characterizes anomaly [326]:

Characteristics of attack [326]:
$(avgSport < 21796) \wedge (avgSport > 18635) \wedge (nBytes/nFlow < 93.6666666666667) \wedge (nBytes/nFlow > 74) \wedge (nDiffSrcAddr = 1) \wedge (nPkts = 2) \wedge (nPktsTcp = 2) \wedge (nRst/nPkts = 0.5) \wedge (nSyn/nPkts = 0.5) \wedge (nSynTcp/nPktsTcp = 0.5)$

Anomaly [326] is very similar to anomaly [327]. It relies of the same principle of sending a SYN packet followed by a RST packet for uselessly exhausting receiver resources, and then performing a DoS attack. The only difference is in the port numbers that origin the connection attempts.

Anomaly [44] appears in Figure 2 on subspaces (b) with the black cluster corresponding to $nSyn_nPkts = 1$ and (c), with the pink cluster corresponding to $nRst_nPkts = 1$. The algorithm generated the following signature that fully characterizes anomaly [44]:

Characteristics of attack [44]:
$(bpp = 40) \wedge (nBytes_nFlow = 40) \wedge (nDiffDestAddr = 1) \wedge (nPkts = 1) \wedge (nPkts/nFlow = 1) \wedge (nPktsTcp = 1) \wedge (nRst/nPkts = 1) \wedge (nSyn/nPkts = 0)$

This anomaly is also very simple to analyze based on the issued signature. It also corresponds to a DoS attack called RST attacks which consists in sending RST packets in order to close ongoing connections.

The last anomalies described in this paper is anomaly [224] that appears in Figure 2 on subspaces (c) and (e), on the red cluster with $nRst_nPkts = 0$.

The algorithm generated the following signature that fully characterizes anomaly [224]:

Characteristics of attack [224]:
$(avgSport > 51209.3738990333) \wedge (avgSport < 42107.167194700$
$(bgstDestPortTcp/tNbOccuDestPortTcp < 262.25) \wedge$
$(destPortTcpMax < 291) \wedge (destPortTcpMin < 291) \wedge$
$(nBytes > 19187.5) \wedge (nBytes < 118272) \wedge (nBytes/nFlow >$
$843.428571428571) \wedge (nBytes/nFlow < 1425.16666666667) \wedge$
$(nDiffDestPort = 1) \wedge (nDiffSrcAddr = 1) \wedge (nDiffSrcPort <$
$40.5) \wedge (nPkts > 198) \wedge (nPkts < 1200.5) \wedge (nPktsIcmp =$
$0) \wedge (nPkts/nFlow > 21.5) \wedge (nPkts/nFlow < 11.3333333333333),$
$(nPktsUdp = 0) \wedge (nRst/nPkts = 0) \wedge (nSyn/nPkts >$
$0.115691489361702) \wedge (nSyn/nPkts < 0.183333333333333) \wedge$
$(nSynTcp/nPktsTcp < 0.291666666666667) \wedge (srcPortTcpMax <$
$61502) \wedge (srcPortTcpMax > 34033.5) \wedge (srcPortTcpMin <$
$61502) \wedge (srcPortTcpMin > 34033.5)$

The analysis of this anomaly is more tricky than the three previous ones. It does not correspond to a basic DoS attacks. It is nevertheless a kind of TCP flooding attack with an advanced strategy for targeting specific address and port ranges making it look like a legitimate application traffic. It then makes it difficult to detect with classical detection tools.

8. EXPERIMENTAL EVALUATION

Figure 4 depicts the True Positives Rate (TPR) as a function of the False Positives Rates (FTR) in the identification of the different attacks contained in the honeypot traffic traces from the University of Maryland. The presented results are based on a manual analysis of the detection and/or identification algrithms under evaluation. This manual analysis made possible labeling all attacks in the honeypot traffic of the University of Maryland. This set of labels serves for the evaluations as the reference ground truth. Actually, they permit an accurate evaluation of any detection, characterization or classification algorithm.

We compare the performance of UNADA against three previous approaches for unsupervised anomaly detection: DBSCAN-based, k-means-based, and PCA-based outliers detection. The first two consist in applying either DBSCAN or k-means to the complete feature space $\mathbf{X}$, identify the largest cluster $C_{\max}$, and compute the Mahalanobis distance of all the flows lying outside $C_{\max}$ to its centroid. The ROC is finally obtained by comparing the sorted distances to a variable detection threshold. These approaches are similar to those used in previous work [8,16,21]. In the PCA-based approach, PCA and the sub-space methods [14,15] are applied to the complete matrix $\mathbf{X}$, and the attacks are detected by comparing the residuals to a variable threshold. Both the k-means and the PCA-based approaches require fine tuning: in k-means, we repeat the clustering for different values of clusters k, and take the average results. In the case of PCA we present the best performance obtained for each evaluation scenario.

Obtained results permit to evidence the great advantage of using the SSC-Density-based algorithm in the clustering step with respect to previous approaches. In particular, all the approaches used in the comparison generally fail to detect all the attacks with a reasonable false alarm rate. Both the DBSCAN-based and the k-means-based algorithms get confused by masking features when analyzing the complete feature space $\mathbf{X}$. The PCA approach shows to be not sensitive enough to discriminate different kinds of attacks of very different intensities, using the same representation for normal-operation traffic.

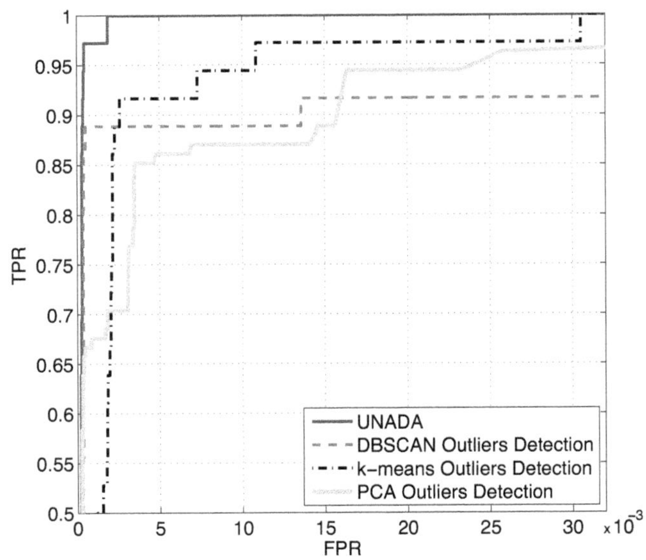

Figure 4: True Positives Rate vs False Alarms.

9. COMPUTATIONAL TIME AND PARALLELIZATION

The last issue that we analyze is the Computational Time (CT) of the algorithm. The SSC-EA-based algorithm performs multiple clusterings in $N(m)$ low-dimensional subspaces $\mathbf{X}_i \subset \mathbf{X}$. This multiple computation imposes scalability issues for on-line detection of attacks in very-high-speed networks. Two key features of the algorithm are exploited to reduce scalability problems in number of features m and the number of aggregated flows n to analyze. Firstly, clustering is performed in very-low-dimensional subspaces, $\mathbf{X}_i \in \mathbb{R}^2$, which is faster than clustering in high-dimensional spaces [11]. Secondly, each sub-space can be clustered independently of the other sub-spaces, which is perfectly adapted for parallel computing architectures. Parallelization can be achieved in different ways: using a single multi-processor and multi-core machine, using network-processor cards and/or GPU (Graphic Processor Unit) capabilities, using a distributed group of machines, or combining these techniques. We shall use the term "slice" as a reference to a single computational entity.

Figures 5 and 6 depict the CT of the SSC-EA-based algorithm, as a function of the number of features m used to describe traffic flows and as a function of the number of flows n to analyze, respectively. Figure 5 compares the CT obtained when clustering the complete feature space $\mathbf{X}$, referred to as CT($\mathbf{X}$), against the CT obtained with SSC, varying m from 2 to 29 features. We analyze a large number of aggregated flows, $n = 10^4$, and use two different number

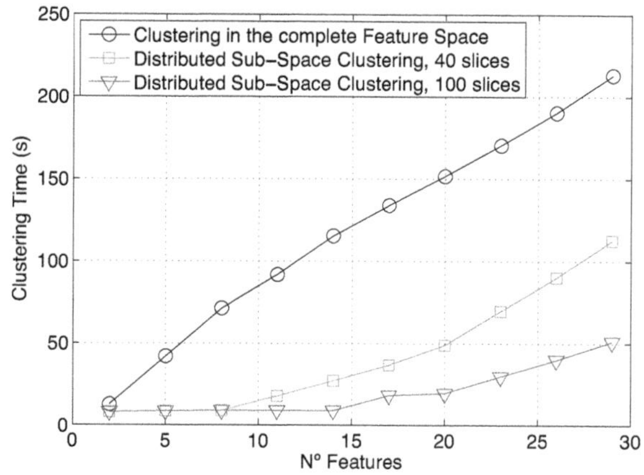

Figure 5: Computational Time as a function of number of features to analyze. The number of aggregated flows is $n = 10000$.

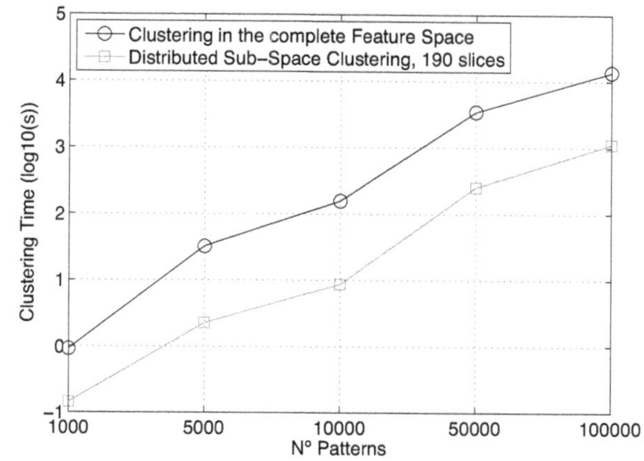

Figure 6: Computational Time as a function of number of flows to analyze. The number of features and slices is $m = 20$ and $M = 190$ respectively.

of slices, $M = 40$ and $M = 100$. The analysis is done with traffic from the WIDE network, combining different traces to attain the desired number of flows. To estimate the CT of SSC for a given value of m and M, we proceed as follows: first, we separately cluster each of the $N = m(m-1)/2$ sub-spaces $\mathbf{X}_i$, and take the worst-case of the obtained clustering time as a representative measure of the CT in a single sub-space, i.e., $\text{CT}(\mathbf{X}_{\text{SSCwc}}) = \max_i \text{CT}(\mathbf{X}_i)$. Then, if $N \leqslant M$, we have enough slices to completely parallelize the SSC algorithm, and the total CT corresponds to the worst-case, $\text{CT}(\mathbf{X}_{\text{SSCwc}})$. On the contrary, if $N > M$, some slices have to cluster various sub-spaces, one after the other, and the total CT becomes $(N\%M+1)$ times the worst-case $\text{CT}(\mathbf{X}_{\text{SSCwc}})$, where % represents integer division. The first interesting observation from figure 5 regards the increase of $\text{CT}(\mathbf{X})$ when m increases, going from about 8 seconds for $m = 2$ to more than 200 seconds for $m = 29$. As we said before, clustering in low-dimensional spaces is faster, which reduces the overhead of multiple clusterings computation. The second paramount observation is about parallelization: if the algorithm is implemented in a parallel computing architecture, it can be used to analyze large volumes of traffic using many traffic descriptors in an on-line basis; for example, if we use 20 traffic features and a parallel architecture with 100 slices, we can analyze 10000 aggregated flows in less than 20 seconds.

Figure 6 compares $\text{CT}(\mathbf{X})$ against $\text{CT}(\mathbf{X}_{\text{SSCwc}})$ for an increasing number of flows n to analyze, using $m = 20$ traffic features and $M = N = 190$ slices (i.e., a completely parallelized implementation of the SSC-EA-based algorithm). As before, we can appreciate the difference in CT when clustering the complete feature space vs. using low-dimensional sub-spaces: the difference is more than one order of magnitude, independently of the number of flows to analyze. Regarding the volume of traffic that can be analyzed with this 100% parallel configuration, the SSC-EA-based algorithm can analyze up to 50000 flows with a reasonable CT, about 4 minutes in this experience. In the presented evaluations, the number of aggregated flows in a time slot of$\Delta\ T = 20$ seconds rounds the 2500 flows, which represents a value of $\text{CT}(\mathbf{X}_{\text{SSCwc}}) \approx 0.4$ seconds. For the $m = 9$ features that we have used ($N = 36$), and even without doing parallelization, the total CT is $N \times \text{CT}(\mathbf{X}_{\text{SSCwc}}) \approx 14.4$ seconds.

10. CONCLUSION

This paper presents an unsupervised algorithm for classifying illicit traffic. This algorithm has several advantages compared to previous work: (i) it works in a completely unsupervised manner, what makes it able to work on top of any monitoring system, and directly usable, without preliminary configuration or knowledge. (ii) It combines robust clustering techniques to avoid classical issues of clustering algorithms, e.g. sensitivity to initial configuration, the required a priori indication of teh number of clusters to be identified, or the sensitivity of results when using less pertinent features. (iii) It automatically builds simple and small signatures fully characterizing attacks; theses signature can then be used in a filtering security device. (iv) It is designed to run in real time by making possible to take advantage of the parallelism of our clustering approach.

This algorithm thus opens new perspectives for performing a risk analysis in the Internet - taking advantage of honeypot traffic - and automatically configuring related filtering rules on routers, switches, or firewalls.

Acknowledgements

The author sincerely thanks Michel Cukier and Bertrand Sobesto for providing the traffic traces gathered on the honeypots of the University of Maryland. The author thanks Johan Mazel and Pedro Casas who have been first involved in the research work on the sub-space clustering algorithm applied to the full Internet traffic. The author also thanks Richard Turc who started this work on the analysis of the honeypot traffic during his master internship at LAAS. This work is supported by the ONTIC project, funded by the European commission under grant FP7-ICT-2013-11/619633.

11. REFERENCES

[1] R. Agrawal, J. Gehrke, D. Gunopulos, and P. Raghavan. Automatic subspace clustering of high dimensional data for data mining applications. In *Proc. ACM SIGMOD*, 1998.

[2] P. Barford, J. Kline, D. Plonka, and A. Ron. A signal analysis of network traffic anomalies. In *Proc. ACM IMW*, 2002.

[3] R. Berthier, M. Cukier, M. Hiltunen, D. Kormann, G. Vesonder, and D. Sheleheda. Nfsight: Netflow-based network awareness tool. In *Proceedings of the 24th international conference on Large installation system administration (LISA'10)*, 2010.

[4] J. Brutlag. Aberrant behavior detection in time series for network monitoring. In *Proc. 14th Systems Administration Conference*, 2000.

[5] P. Casas, J. Mazel, and P. Owezarski. Unada: Unsupervised network anomaly detection using sub-space outliers ranking. In *IFIP Networking conference*, 2011.

[6] P. Casas, S. Vaton, L. Fillatre, and I. Nikiforov. Optimal volume anomaly detection and isolation in large-scale ip networks using coarse-grained measurements. In *Computer Networks, vol. 54, pp. 1750-1766*, 2010.

[7] G. Cormode and S. Muthukrishnan. What's new: Finding significant differences in network data streams. In *IEEE Trans. on Networking, vol. 13 (6), pp. 1219-1232*, 2005.

[8] E. Eskin, A. Arnold, M. Prerau, L. Portnoy, and S. Stolfo. A geometric framework for unsupervised anomaly detection: Detecting intrusions in unlabeled data. In *Applications of Data Mining in Computer Security, Kluwer Publisher*, 2002.

[9] G. Fernandes and P. Owezarski. Automated classification of network traffic anomalies. In *Proc. SecureComm'09*, 2009.

[10] A. Fred and A. K. Jain. Combining multiple clusterings using evidence accumulation. In *IEEE Trans. Pattern Analysis and Machine Intelligence, vol. 27 (6), pp. 835-850*, 2005.

[11] A. K. Jain. Data clustering: 50 years beyond k-means. In *Pattern Recognition Letters, vol. 31 (8), pp. 651-666*, 2010.

[12] B. Krishnamurthy, S. Sen, Y. Zhang, and Y. Chen. Sketch-based change detection: Methods, evaluation, and applications. In *Proc. ACM IMC*, 2003.

[13] A. Lakhina, M. Crovella, and C. Diot. Characterization of network-wide anomalies in traffic flows. In *Proc. ACM IMC*, 2004.

[14] A. Lakhina, M. Crovella, and C. Diot. Mining anomalies using traffic feature distributions. In *Proc. ACM SIGCOMM*, 2005.

[15] A. Lakhina, C. Diot, and M. Crovella. Diagnosing network-wide traffic anomalies. In *Proc. ACM SIGCOMM*, 2004.

[16] K. Leung and C. Leckie. Unsupervised anomaly detection in network intrusion detection using clustering. In *Proc. ACSC05*, 2005.

[17] X. Li, F. Biang, M. Crovella, C. Diot, R. Govindan, G. Iannaccone, and A. Lakhina. Detection and identification of network anomalies using sketch subspaces. In *Proc. ACM IMC*, 2006.

[18] J. Mazel. Unsupervised network anomaly detection. In *PhD thesis of INSA Toulouse*, 2011.

[19] J. Mazel, P. Casas, Y. Labit, and P. Owezarski. Sub-space clustering, interclustering results association & anomaly correlation for unsupervised network anomaly detection. In *7th International Conference on Network and Service Management (CNSM 2011), CNSM'11*, october 2011.

[20] L. Parsons, E. Haque, and H. Liu. Subspace clustering for high dimensional data: a review. In *ACM SIGKDD Expl. Newsletter, vol. 6 (1), pp. 90-105*, 2004.

[21] L. Portnoy, E. Eskin, and S. Stolfo. Intrusion detection with unlabeled data using clustering. In *Proc. ACM DMSA Workshop*, 2001.

[22] H. Ringberg, A. Soule, J. Rexford, and C. Diot. Sensitivity of pca for traffic anomaly detection. In *Proc. ACM SIGMETRICS*, 2007.

[23] F. Silveira and C. Diot. Rca: Pulling anomalies by their root causes. In *Proc. IEEE INFOCOM*, 2010.

[24] A. Strehl and J. Ghosh. Cluster ensembles - a knowledge reuse framework for combining multiple partitions. In *Journal on Machine Learning Research, vol. 3, pp. 583-617*, 2002.

Discover and Tame Long-running Idling Processes in Enterprise Systems

Jun Wang[1], Zhiyun Qian[2], Zhichun Li[3], Zhenyu Wu[3], Junghwan Rhee[3], Xia Ning[4], Peng Liu[1], Guofei Jiang[3]
[1]Penn State University, [2]University of California, Riverside, [3]NEC Labs America, Inc. [4]IUPUI
[1]{jow5222, pliu}@ist.psu.edu, [2]zhiyunq@cs.ucr.edu, [3]{zhichun, adamwu, rhee, gfj}@nec-labs.com, [4]xning@cs.iupui.edu

ABSTRACT

Reducing attack surface is an effective preventive measure to strengthen security in large systems. However, it is challenging to apply this idea in an enterprise environment where systems are complex and evolving over time. In this paper, we empirically analyze and measure a real enterprise to identify unused services that expose attack surface. Interestingly, such unused services are known to exist and summarized by security best practices, yet such solutions require significant manual effort.

We propose an automated approach to accurately detect the idling (most likely unused) services that are in either blocked or bookkeeping states. The idea is to identify repeating events with perfect time alignment, which is the indication of being idling. We implement this idea by developing a novel statistical algorithm based on autocorrelation with time information incorporated. From our measurement results, we find that 88.5% of the detected idling services can be constrained with a simple syscall-based policy, which confines the process behaviors within its bookkeeping states. In addition, working with two IT departments (one of which is a cross validation), we receive positive feedbacks which show that about 30.6% of such services can be safely disabled or uninstalled directly. In the future, the IT department plan to incorporate the results to build a "smaller" OS installation image. Finally, we believe our measurement results raise the awareness of the potential security risks of idling services.

Categories and Subject Descriptors

K.6 [**Management of computing and information systems**]: Security and Protection

Keywords

Idling service detection; Attack surface reduction; Enterprise systems; Autocorrelation

1. INTRODUCTION

Managing the security of enterprise systems is always a challenging task, because the overall security of the entire enterprise is usually determined by the weakest link and today's enterprise systems are so complex that it is hard to understand which program/process can be the weakest links. Many security breaches start with the compromise of processes running on an inconspicuous workstation. Therefore, it is beneficial to turn off unused services to reduce their corresponding attack surface. Anecdotally, many security best practice guidelines [13, 9] suggest system administrators to reduce attack surface by disabling unused services. However, such knowledge needs to be constantly updated and it is unfortunate that no formal approach has been studied to automatically identify such services.

Prior research has mostly focused on the line of anomaly detection to learn the normal behavior of processes and then constrain them, *e.g.,* by limiting accessible IP/port ranges [33, 32, 34] or the system calls that are allowed to be made [21, 30, 23, 19].

While such approaches may detect abnormal behaviors of a process (*e.g.,* possibly attacks), they belong to reactive approaches rather than preventive ones. Obviously, reducing attack surface is a preventive measure that complements anomaly detection. The strong semantic of idling services enables more specific treatments (*e.g.,* disable or even uninstall them) as opposed to the general treatments to anomalies, *e.g.,* raising a security alert. Unfortunately, the frequent false alerts in anomaly detection make it rarely deployed in practice. Identifying idling services, on the other hand, represent a much more cost effective solution where each service only needs to be examined mostly once (*e.g.,* to determine if it can be safely uninstalled). Once a positive decision is made, it completely eliminates the entire attack surface of a process before an attack could ever happen. Unfortunately, due to lack of formal methods, in state-of-the-art practice, system administrators today could only depend on practical wisdoms from Internet forums [10], and their own experience.

One might argue that system administrators or end-users should setup their servers and desktop machines to only run useful services and applications in the first place. However, in practice, this is a daunting task. The modern OS vendors tend to stuff more and more functionalities into their distributions, and provide a "one size fits all" system. Thus, many services might not be useful for a particular user. Even worse, today's enterprises typically run a variety of OS distributions. As a result, it is not easy for system administrators to keep up with the purpose of each and every service. Furthermore, systems keep evolving and users' demands keep changing. Given the complex dependencies inside enterprise, people tend to keep things as they are. Such practice, therefore, negligibly leaves numerous idling services running, and thus exposes unnecessary attack surface.

ASIA CCS'15, April 14–17, 2015, Singapore..

http://dx.doi.org/10.1145/2714576.2714613.

In this paper, we propose an automated method to detect "idle/idling" services and also provide ways to reduce or minimize their attack surface. An idling service is a service that does not serve real workload, but rather running in a blocked or bookkeeping state. A simple example is that a long-running service may listen on a certain port, while in reality no one has connected, or will connect to it. This service thus should be disabled to eliminate possible remote exploits. In our study, we find 25% of long-running processes are idling services.

In general, there are two types of idling services. The first type is easy to detect – the service process is completely dormant, blocked waiting for events that would never arrive. For the second type, the service processes regularly wake up from blocked state and perform some "bookkeeping" tasks – simple operations not relevant to the service they provide. The second type is more difficult to identify, since the bookkeeping operations could make these processes appear as active and truly performing services. In order to address the problem of identifying both types of idling services, we propose LIPdetect (**L**ong-running **I**dling **P**rocess), an effective algorithm that is able to differentiate "bookkeeping" activities from the ones resulted from real workload.

While LIPdetect could identify and report idling services to system administrators, working with IT department of our company we find in some cases the system administrators are not 100% sure whether certain services can be disabled without negative consequences. It is therefore desirable to keep those services running while still reducing their attack surface. In such cases, we fall back to the traditional wisdom to constrain the runtime behavior of a process. To this end, we design a simple tool named procZip that constrains the idling service's execution to previous known states. Combining idling service detection (LIPdetect) and automated process constraining (procZip), our system is therefore called LIPzip.

We evaluate the results of idling service detection, and perform a measurement study in an enterprise with both desktop and server machines to show how much attack surface can be possibly reduced. Meanwhile, we work with the IT department personnel to confirm our results. We also cross validate our results in a university department [12].

In summary, our paper has the following contributions:

- We propose an approach to identifying the long-running "idling" services and show that we can accurately identify such processes (with less than 1.5% mis-classified).
- We deploy our solution in a real enterprise environment on 24 hosts. We find that 25% of the long-running processes are idling on average per host and they constitute about 66.7% of attack surface of all long-running processes. 51.1% of the 92 unique binaries have had publicly known vulnerabilities.
- In collaboration with on-site system administrators and owners of the hosts, we analyze 434 idling processes in detail and classify 30.6% of such services can be disabled to fully eliminate the attack surface. We categorize the common reasons why they can be safely disabled or uninstalled, and show that such results can be shared across enterprises to make recommendations.
- We design procZip and show that even though the system administrators do not have the confidence to disable all services discovered by us, 88.5% of the idling services can be safely constrained by the procZip during a two-week evaluation, indicating that they are continuing to be idling.

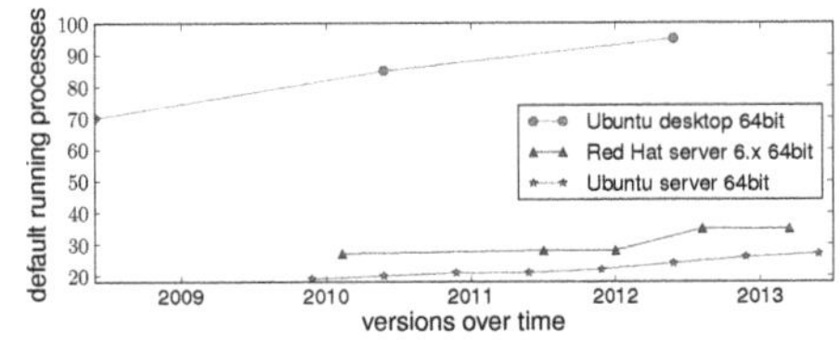

Figure 1: The number of default running processes

2. MOTIVATION AND OVERVIEW

Our motivation comes from the following observations:

1) Today's computer systems are equipped with an increasing number of functionalities (and thus also the attack surface) with newly developed technologies, perhaps much more than necessary for everyday use.

2) Systems are constantly evolving; more applications or features are installed (or updated) over time but they are left there even when no longer needed.

3) What makes the problem worse, in the Linux world, there are a large number of different OS distributions which make the IT systems largely heterogeneous and fragmented.

As a result, it is highly non-trivial to control or even understand all the systems precisely, let alone knowing whether a process is actually performing useful work or simply "idling". According to the IT department in our enterprise, they indeed do not keep track of what Linux distributions or applications are installed, the reason being that they do not want to get in the way of users doing what they want to do.

2.1 Measurement Study

To understand to what extent each observation is true, we conduct the following measurements based on two data sources. First, we look into the historical Linux distributions of Ubuntu and Red Hat from public images that are available on the Amazon EC2 service. Second, we collect information about 67 hosts in a real enterprise.

Default long-running processes. We look into the two popular Linux distributions Ubuntu and Red Hat over the past six years and count the number of daemon processes that are running by default after the system boots. Figure 1 shows that the number is steadily increasing over years. Note that the number from the server distributions is not very high due to the fact that these images are tailored to run on servers and thus many desktop features are not installed by default. In general, the increase of the default processes might render more and more idling processes.

User-installed long-running processes. We compare the default running processes with a snapshot of long-running processes in our own enterprise environment. We look at 13 Ubuntu 12.04 desktop machines and discover that on average 30 long-running processes on each host are not default running processes of the installation image, indicating that our employees tend to install many new services over time and the system size has been considerably growing.

Heterogeneity. Inside our enterprise, we study 67 Linux hosts including both desktops and servers. There are 7 Fedora, 11 CentOS, and 49 Ubuntu hosts respectively. These hosts include 3 unique Fedora versions, 6 unique CentOS versions, and 7 unique Ubuntu versions. This demonstrates the universal heterogeneity of Linux distributions. Indeed, the management complexity rooted from the heterogeneity is partly echoed by users asking questions on public forums about what a specific process is for and why it is running [14, 7, 15].

In sum, all these evidences imply that there are potentially many idling services in average enterprise systems.

2.2 Problem and Solution

Problem statement. The key problem we are addressing is how to reduce the attack surface incurred by long-running daemon processes while minimizing the impact on the normal operations. The first challenge is the lack of a common definition on what types of processes can be safely disabled or uninstalled.

Long-running Idling process. Our definition of long-running idling processes comes from the following intuition. As shown in a recent study [25], long-running processes are typically structured as a giant loop, taking certain input in the beginning of the loop and performing different operations based on the input. Such a long-running process will be in one of the three states: (1) The process shows no program activity in terms of instructions or system calls, *e.g.,* blocked on certain system calls waiting for input. (2) The process repeatedly cycles through a loop to check certain input channels, *e.g.,* polling on sockets or checking the existence of a file. However, the input they receive has low entropy (same repeated input) and does not trigger any (useful) operation or they may not even receive any input at all (*e.g.,* the poll on sockets always timeout). As stated in §3, the challenge here is that such repeating events need to happen with perfect time alignment in order to be safely considered idling. (3) The process is taking input and perform useful operations based on the input.

In this work, we define the idling processes as processes in state (1) or (2). Our insight is that if we can identify a list of idling processes with decent accuracy, it is very likely to have little impact on normal operations if we disable them.

Workflow. Our system operates as shown in Figure 2. First, we collect data from hosts through monitoring agents that we developed. The details about the agent is described in §4. Then the data are taken as input to detect idling processes (details described in §3). Then we produce the list of idling processes and characterize their attack surface (explained in the following paragraphs). Next, we subject the process with attack surface[1] to two possible security actions.

Action 1: system administrators are usually in the best position to examine the list of idling processes and decide if they are needed. As shown in §7, we argue that such knowledge is required to determine the future necessity of a process with high confidence. In our evaluation, we show that administrators in our enterprise confirm many of the idling processes or services can indeed be disabled or uninstalled without interrupting normal operations. We further correlate the results with an IT group in a university department and show that the results can be shared effectively across organizations.

Action 2: similar to anomaly detection techniques, an alternative action is to "quarantine" or constrain their executions within the behaviors observed in the past (*e.g.,* checking the presence of a file). In this way, the process can still

[1]We are focusing on security and hence interested in attack surface. Different prioritizing metrics are also possible (*e.g.,* physical memory consumption).

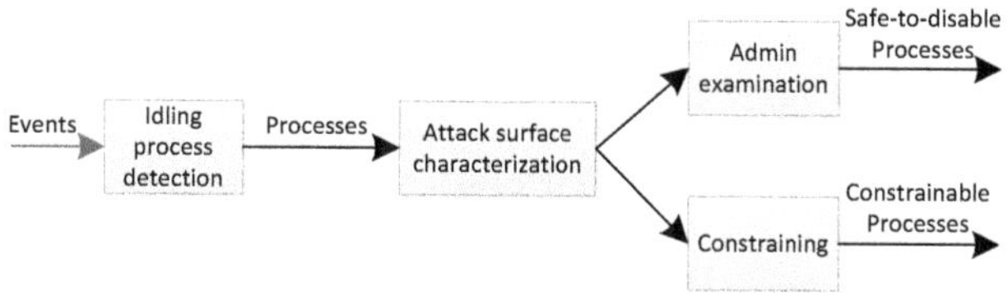

Figure 2: System workflow

continue to receive any potential triggering events. When the triggering events do arrive in the future, we allow the process to be "freed" as long as the privileged user chooses to, *e.g.,* entering the root credentials or confirming a link of an email sent to a pre-registered address. Here, the idea is to reduce the attack surface of processes but still promptly allowing them to continue execution when they really need to. Note that the strategy is flawed if we simply un-quarantine the process whenever we see that the process is no longer idling as it could be possibly triggered by an attack that is actively trying to exploit a vulnerability of this process. Even though this action is operationally similar to anomaly detection in general, we point out that existing models from anomaly detection, *e.g.,* system call sequence or Finite State Automata (FSA), do not suit our problem (described in §3 and §8). So we need to develop new models and methods.

Ideally, Action 1 is generally preferred since it can completely remove the attack surface. In practice, Action 2 can be used as a backup for usability purpose.

Attack surface. Similar to a previous work [33], we only consider system resources with "privilege discrepancy" such as files and sockets as attack surface. For instance, if a process is reading a file that is owned by the same user who started the process, we do not consider it an attack surface. As §6.2 shows, 29.3% of the idling processes we discover have direct attack surface exposed (*e.g.,* listening sockets or reading a file owned by a different user). More details in determining the attack surface is presented in §6 and Appendix. Based on the kind of attack surface they expose, we can prioritize them for system administrators. Note that the attack surface we compute is only the lower bound. In fact, many of them may expose additional attack surface once becoming active. As a result, the percentage of idling processes that have attack surface in idling state is only a conservative security metric.

Goals and non-goals. The goal of this paper is to investigate the security impact of idling processes and propose automated methods to identify them. We argue that the knowledge of the existence of such idling processes needs to be made more readily available to the community.

Non-goals are:

- To develop counter-measures against specific types of attacks. Rather, based on well-understood metrics of attack surface, our system is to reduce the likelihood of successful attacks.
- To come up with another anomaly detection algorithm. Instead, since the semantic of "idling processes" is much stronger than the abstract "normal behavior" in anomaly detection, we can apply more specific treatment to disable or uninstall such idling services. Even if we do constrain them still, there is a much less false alert rate.
- To design a perfect metric to compute the security risks or attack surface of a process. Instead, we leverage known metrics to achieve our goal.

3. DISCOVERY OF IDLING PROCESSES

As stated in §2.2, we are targeting at two categories of long-running processes. It is trivial to detect the **Category I (Completely Idle)** processes. As long as the process does not have any CPU time (available in the `procfs`) for longer than a significant time period (*e.g.,* one week) they are considered category I. This type of processes are usually blocked on certain blocking system calls and does not get a chance to return. However, it is much more subtle to detect the **Category II (Periodic/Repeating)**.

The rationale behind our method to detect category II processes is that an active process typically interacts with users and/or external inputs which should have non-trivial dynamics in size, inter-arrival time of requests, or connection timeout, *etc.* If a process repeats regularly over days and nights, it is highly likely that this process does not involve human-driven workflow, and thus can be considered idling. One might argue that batch jobs (*e.g.,* cron jobs) may also repeat daily or weekly, but they should not be considered idling. We would like to clarify that we consider repeating patterns at the system call level, including parameters and return values, instead of the "job" level. So even for a repeating cron job, *e.g.,* data backup, running daily could see different sets of files every time and therefore generate different sequence of system calls (and different parameters).

Possible solution from existing process behavior models. As described in §8, there are several mainstream process behavior models proposed before. Technically, we consider our problem a special case to model certain aspects of a process. We investigate if existing models are suitable to solve our problem. Not to disrupt the flow of the paper much, we present such discussion in more details in §8. In short, existing models do not fit the idling process detection problem due to two main reasons: 1) Many approaches model the behavior of a process based on a short history of events. For instance, the n-gram-based model only considers the n consecutive events [21]. The Finite State Automata (FSA) models only constrain the next event based on the current state. 2) While the sequence of events have been modeled in several ways, the time information such as the arrival time of events has not been fully considered. We should be able to analyze periodic behavior which is composed of a collection of diverse arrival time of events to accurately characterize idleness.

We note that the timing of events can be critical. For example, a busy web server may run in a loop and serve the same page and carry out the same set of operations repetitively. Therefore, the sequence of events may be perfectly repeating without considering the event timing. Hence, to address our problem, one has to have a careful treatment of timing, which is typically not entailed in anomaly detection.

3.1 Periodicity Detection: Background and Challenges

To find repeated patterns from sequence data is a common problem in many research areas such as data mining and signal processing [18]. A popular way to find the period from data sequences is via Fast Fourier Transform (FFT). However, only when the sequence is known as periodic as a priori, FFT can give the period. FFT is not able to detect whether a sequence is periodic or not.

In LIPdetect, we adopt the idea of autocorrelation to detect periodicity. Autocorrelation measures the correlation relation between a signal and itself after shift with a given lag [18]. For a sequence $S = \{X_1, X_2, \cdots, X_n\}$ and a lag k ($0 \le k < n$), autocorrelation of S with lag k is calculated between sequence $\{X_{k+1}, X_{k+2}, \cdots, X_n\}$ and $\{X_1, X_2, \cdots, X_{n-k-1}, X_{n-k}\}$ using the following formula,

$$r(k) = \frac{1}{(n-k)\sigma^2} \sum_{t=1}^{n-k} (X_t - \mu)(X_{t+k} - \mu), \tag{1}$$

where μ and σ^2 are the mean and variance of the sequence S. The value of autocorrelation falls in $[-1, 1]$, where larger absolute values mean stronger correlations and the positive (negative) sign means positively (negatively) correlated.

If a sequence is perfectly periodic with period p, then the autocorrelations of the sequence will be maximized (*i.e.,* autocorrelation equals to 1) when the lag k is a multiple of p, that is, $k = mp$, where m is an integer ($m = 1, 2, 3, \cdots$). Due to this property, autocorrelation can be used to detect periodicity of sequences. Curious readers can refer to Figure 3 to get an early sense of how autocorrelation looks like.

However, autocorrelation cannot be directly applied in our case to detect periodicity of a process. The primary reason is that as in Equation 1, X_t's are numerical values and thus their mean and variance, as well as the multiplication and addition operations on the values, are well defined. However, in event sequences, X_t's are categorical values (*i.e.,* event types) and all the operations as in Equation 1 are not well defined on categorical values (e.g., it does not make sense to add event type 1 and event type 2 to get event type 3). Another issue with applying autocorrelation on event sequences is that autocorrelation cannot capture the time information between two events. In a process, different system calls may introduce different intermediate idle time intervals, and the length of the time intervals carries useful information in inferring process periodicity. Autocorrelation has no mechanism to encode such timing information.

3.2 Periodicity Detection on Event Data

We propose a new autocorrelation measure, denoted as E-Autocorrelation, particularly for event data, which have categorical values and varying time gap between events.

3.2.1 E-Autocorrelation

Correlation measure. To handle categorical value, we changed the correlation measure from Equation 1 to:

$$r_e(k) = \frac{1}{n-k} \sum_{t=1}^{n-k} \mathbb{I}(X_t, X_{t+k}), \tag{2}$$

where $\mathbb{I}(\cdot, \cdot)$ is an identity function defined as follows:

$$\mathbb{I}(x, y) = \begin{cases} 1 & \text{if } x \text{ and } y \text{ are of same type} \\ 0 & \text{otherwise.} \end{cases} \tag{3}$$

The value of r_e falls in $\{0, 1\}$. By r_e, an event sequence is highly correlated if its shifted version and itself has many same event types aligned.

E-Autocorrelation shares the same property with the conventional autocorrelation, that is, when a periodic event sequence is shifted with a lag that is exactly a multiple of the period, r_e achieves its maximum. Thus, E-Autocorrelation is suitable for periodicity detection in event sequences.

Two-step periodicity detection. E-Autocorrelation employs a two-step approach to find periodic events in terms

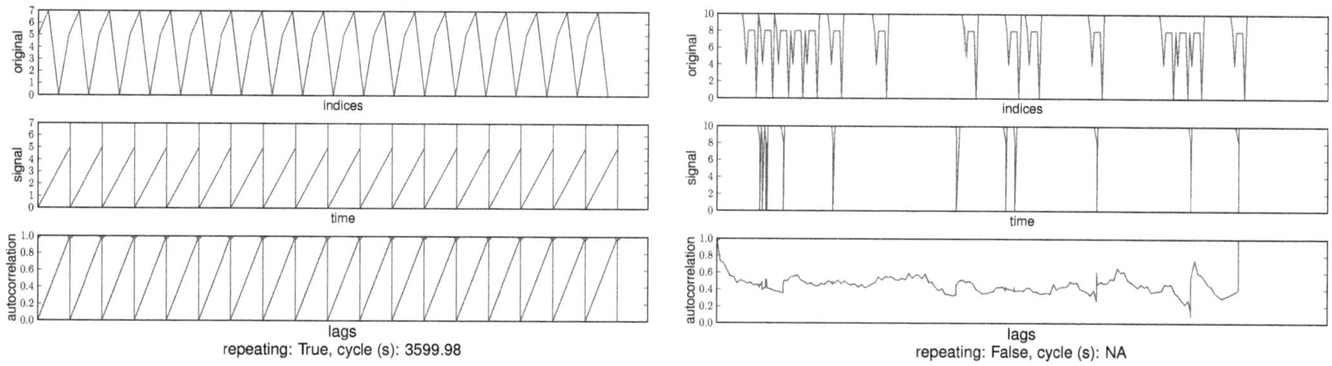

(a) Periodic event sequence of an idling `sendmail` instance.

(b) Aperiodic event sequence of a `mysqld` instance in active use.

Figure 3: An example of a process's original event sequence, converted sequence as signal in time domain, and autocorrelation (top to bottom). Periodic and aperiodic event sequences are presented respectively in the left and right sub figures.

of both event types and timing. For example, a pattern of interest would look like `open-read-close`. Patterns `open-read`-idle-`close` and `open`-idle-`read-close` will be considered as different patterns since the time interval for idling is at different places or has different length.

Step-1 is to identify periodicity from event sequences using E-Autocorrelation with all timing information ignored. For an event sequence $\{X_1, X_2, X_3, \cdots, X_n\}$, we first calculate the E-Autocorrelation value sequence $\{r_e(1), r_e(2), r_e(3), \cdots, r_e(n-1)\}$. Then from the E-Autocorrelation sequence, we find the values that are no less than a threshold α ($\alpha \leq 1$) and consider them as peaks. Note that in a perfectly periodic sequence, E-Autocorrelation values as 1 indicate periodicity. However, since the event sequences could be noisy, choosing smaller values than 1 as peaks provides a chance for our approach to better tolerate noises and thus remain robust. We use $\alpha = 0.95$ based on our experiments using a one-month training dataset.

After the peaks are located, whether the event sequence (again, without time information) is periodic is determined by looking at the standard deviation σ of the distances between consecutive peaks, where the distances are calculated as the difference of lag values corresponding to the peaks. Our analysis on datasets with ground truth shows that for periodic sequences σ is typically smaller than 0.1, whereas for non-periodic sequences σ is typically larger than 10 or even 100. This indicates that σ could serve as a parameter to differentiate periodic sequences from non-periodic sequences. Thus, we test σ against a pre-defined threshold T (we set T as 0), and only when $\sigma \leq T$, the sequence is considered periodic.

Step-2: The periodic patterns recognized from Step-1 could be incorrect since time interval information is completely ignored. It is still possible that, for example, the sequence $\{A, B, C, A, B, C, A, B, C\}$ is determined as periodic from Step-1. However, the duration of the first A, B, C is 1,000 seconds, whereas the duration of the second A, B, C is 1 seconds and the duration of the last one is 0.001 seconds. In this case, it is not reasonable to claim that the entire sequence is periodic. Thus, in the second step, the results from Step-1 are post-processed so as to filter out the cases that show no periodicity (or with incorrect period) in terms of time. To do so, we find the events that appear first in the periodic pattern identified from Step-1. In the example of sequence $\{A, B, C, A, B, C, A, B, C\}$, such events are the first event (the first A), the fourth event (the second A) and the seventh event (the third A) since the periodic pattern is A, B, C. This can be done by looking at the lags corresponding to peaks, that is, if a peak occurs at lag value k, then the k-th event is the one that appears first in the periodic pattern. Such events are denoted as peak events.

Next, for each peak event at lag k, we need to validate the corresponding period by checking if any event always repeats itself after time t_k. If the validation fails, we drop the corresponding peak. After iterating through all peak events, we are left with a subset of peak events, which correspond to the true periodic pattern. In order to do the validation, we construct a time sequence $\{t_1, t_2, t_3, \cdots, t_m\}$ where t_i is the timestamp of the i-th peak event. Then we compute the standard deviation of a time interval sequence $\{t_2 - t_1, t_3 - t_2, \cdots, t_m - t_{m-1}\}$. If this standard deviation is close to 0, then we consider the original sequence periodic and the true period is the mean of the time interval sequence. Otherwise, we calculate and test the standard deviation of sequence $\{t_3 - t_1, t_4 - t_2, \cdots, t_m - t_{m-2}\}$. The above procedure is repeated until a period is identified or the length of the time interval sequence is 1 (*i.e.,* all the peak events are tested).

Figure 3 shows an example of original event sequences and their autocorrelations. The raw event sequences are shown in the figures in the top. Their converted time-domain signals and autocorrelations are presented below. The left sub figures show a periodic event sequence and the corresponding autocorrelation; the right ones show a non-periodic event sequence. Our E-Autocorrelation can effectively differentiate periodic sequences from non-periodic ones and accurately identify the repeating cycles for periodic sequences.

4. SYSTEM DESIGN

In this section, we describe the design of the two components of LIPzip – data collection and process constraining.

4.1 Data Collection

While it is possible to monitor all activities of every process by using kernel debugging or auditing facilities, such as `ptrace` or `auditd`, doing so would incur significant performance penalty and seriously impact the normal usage of the system being monitored. In order to limit the monitoring overhead to an acceptable level, and allow for large scale deployment in a real working environment, we design a two-stage data collection and screening mechanism.

In the first stage, we perform light-weight monitoring for all processes on a system, by collecting partial information

Event Type	System Calls
process event	fork,vfork,clone,execve,exit,exit_group
network event	socket,bind,connect,accept
file event	open,creat,stat,access,dup,close
IPC event	pipe,socketpair,shmget,msgget, socket,bind,connect,accept

Table 1: System calls being monitored (partial list)

(such as time stamp, system call type, and error code) for a subset of security-relevant system calls. For instance, our observation indicates that `read` and `write` are among the most frequently used system calls. However, a process must first open a file before it could perform read/write operations on the file, and the usage of `open` and `close` system calls are over an order of magnitude less. And thus, by inferring read/write operations from `open` and `close` system calls, we deduct more than 90% monitoring overhead. We systematically studied the properties of every system call, and selected system calls that are crucial for our analysis, categorized into four types, as shown in Table 1.

With data collected from the first stage monitoring, we apply our E-autocorrelation to screen all processes and discover those that are likely to be "idling". However, due to the incomplete set of system calls, this screening stage produces a small number of false positives (around 18.2% according to our empirical observation) – *i.e.,* some processes classified as "Category I" (complete idle) do in fact make very light-weight system calls which we do not monitor; similarly, some processes classified as "Category II" (periodic) make unmonitored system calls in non-periodic manner.

In order to remove the false positives, we subject those processes to the second stage monitoring. In this stage, we collect more comprehensive information (such as call stacks, parameters and return values) for all system calls. The heavy-weight monitoring would not induce significant impact to the system, because the targeted processes have little or no activity, thanks to the first stage screening.

4.2 Process Constraining: procZip

We define the "constrained" state of an idling process as the following: (1) The process is allowed to continue its execution without any interruption, as long as it behaves consistently with its previously observed idling behavior; (2) When the behavior of the process deviates from its idling behavior, its execution is interrupted, and human interventions are needed to either allow the process to continue execution, or be terminated. Compared with simplistic mitigations, such as directly terminating an idling process, process constraining is a much more practical approach to reduce attack surface, because it leaves room for recourse in case of useful processes being mistakenly classified, and avoids serious negative impact on availability and user experience.

Different system mechanisms, such as *memory protection* and *code instrumentation* which build a program state machine [30, 23], can be leveraged to achieve process constraining to different degrees. Developing a precise and efficient program behavior model is not the focus of our study. In this work, we simply choose to design a simple model based on *system call instrumentation* only to illustrate that idling processes can be easily constrained. In particular, we intercept all system calls of the target idling process, and build its "idling behavior" profile, which comprises of the variety of system calls as well as their *calling context (CC)* [36].

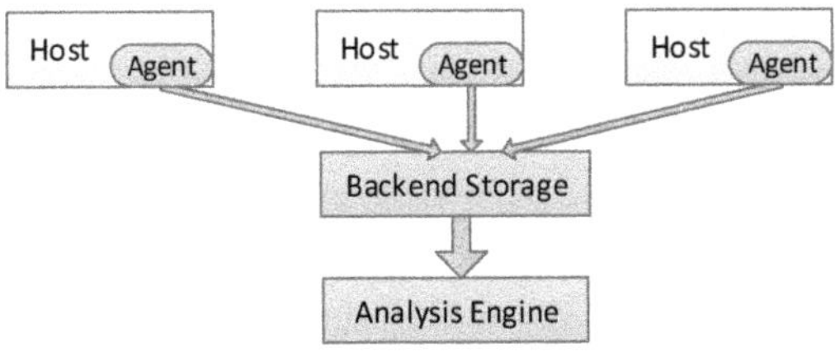

Figure 4: System Architecture

When the target process tries to make a system call that does not match the "idling behavior" profile, this incident is captured and corresponding manual intervention routine (*e.g.,* a pop-up window) is triggered. Because CC is a rich source of process internal state information, this approach could establish precise behavior constraining. Meanwhile, although such detailed system call instrumentation looks heavy weight, since the idling processes are generating little to no system calls, we do not observe any noticeable system slowdown in practice.

For category I processes, because of their complete idleness, the constraining will be in effect immediately. In other words, any system call from these process will be considered as anomaly and thus will trigger manual intervention. For category II processes, a "profile building" phase, which lasts one repeating cycle, will be carried out before the constraining become effective. During the "profile building" phase, any system call and its CC will be recorded as allowed "idling behavior". Afterwards, if a system call is detected with unmatched system call and/or CC in the "idling profile", manual intervention is triggered.

5. IMPLEMENTATION

In this section, we first provide an overview of our light-weight data collection system, which logs and collects process activities. Then, we describe notable implementation details of the process constraining mechanism.

5.1 Data Collection System

We implement and deploy a client-server system to achieve ubiquitous and light-weight data collection. The infrastructure being used for process events collection has a three-tier architecture, *i.e.,* the monitoring agent, the backend storage, and the analysis engine. Figure 4 illustrates the system architecture. The agent deployed on each host is responsible for performing both stages of data collection, as described in §4. For the first stage, the agent monitors a subset of system calls of every process on each host using two major data sources. One is the system call information provided by the kernel built-in Linux Audit subsystem [8]. The other is the auxiliary information from the `proc` file system. Because the majority of the monitoring overhead comes from the processing of data streams coming from the Linux Audit subsystem, we build a custom audit log handler, which achieves 14.3× speedup compared with the stock audit library. For the second stage, the agent leverages the standard `strace` utility to perform the monitoring of all system calls for selected processes.

From real system deployment, we observe that the agent introduces unnoticeable latencies to commonly used programs (*e.g.,* bash, vim, Firefox, Thunderbird, *etc.*). The average resource consumption of the agent is negligible under today's main-stream system configurations. On an idle system, the agent processes about 30 system calls per second, and consumes under 1.0% of one processor core, and less than 100MB of memory. With intense workload, such as Linux kernel compilation, the agent processes about 5800 system calls per second, and use up to 14.8% of one processor core and 300MB of memory. For data reporting over the network, each agent on average consumes under 13kbps of network bandwidth.

5.2 Process Constraining

To implement the procZip, we leverage the kernel `ptrace` facility to intercept all system calls of the constrained process. For each intercepted system call, we uncover its calling context (CC) by walking up the call stack using `libunwind`, and concatenate each call site address into a chain. During the "profile building" phase, we store all observed system call and corresponding CC in an associative array of CC-syscall pairs, which is used as the "idling profile".

When a constrained process is detected to attempt "out-of-profile" system calls, we implement a pop-up dialog window to prompt the local user for either approval (*i.e.,* allowing process to continue out-of-profile behavior) or termination. For our evaluation purpose, we also implement an alternative routine, which logs the event while silently allow the out-of-profile behavior to continue. This implementation enables us to non-intrusively perform evaluation on real server systems and workstations.

Of course, procZip will consume some system resources like CPU and memory on top of that of the idling process. Based on our experiment, such resource consumption is negligible.

6. EVALUATION

Data collection. The lightweight agent data was collected from a total of 64 Linux hosts. The data used for analysis was collected from December 2013 to July 2014, a period of over 180 days. The average days for each host is about 155 days during which each machine has rebooted at least once (due to power outage and so forth). Interestingly, most of these machines were never turned off by human even for desktop machines (this phenomenon is also observed in other environment [28]). Out of 64 hosts, we further investigate 24 hosts to study in more details about the process behaviors.

Determining attack surface. After determining idling processes, we prioritize high-impact attack surface cases (that are more likely to be exploited) based on the resource types and the process user ID. Similar as many existing works [32, 33, 34, 5, 3, 4], we define the *attack surface* as a set of communication channels (resources) provided by OS, including files, Internet sockets, and Unix domain sockets, through which an attacker can potentially gain additional privilege.

We summarize what kind of resources we consider and how we determine if they are considered attack surface as a set of rules presented in Appendix. We rank the severity of the attack surface in the following order:

1. A root process with an open public network port.
2. Open files that are writable by anyone or a root process with local listening sockets accessible to everyone.
3. Other attack surface (see Appendix).

Evaluation methodology. We present the following results in the evaluation:

- How many processes are found by our LIPdetect technique as idling? What are their associated security risks (*i.e.,* attack surface)? Results are discussed in §6.1 and §6.2.

Workflow	Role of Human
Operational	Determine safe-to-disable processes
Non-operational	Tag hosts and processes (§6.1)
	Search for historical vulnerabilities of idling processes (§6.2)
	Examine why some idling processes are not constrainable (§6.3)
	Perform case studies to investigate the reasons of the existence of idling processes (§6.4)
	Conduct survey to cross validate our results (§6.5)

Table 2: Clarification of human involvement in the operational workflow and non-operational (evaluation) workflow

- What percentage of discovered idling processes can be easily "quarantined" to reduce attack surface? Results are discussed in §6.3.
- Can these idling processes be safely disabled in the eyes of system administrators and users? What are the reasons for their existence? Results are discussed in §6.4
- Can our findings be shared across different enterprises? Results are presented in §6.5.

For the first result, we use the lightweight agent data to first gather a list of potential idling processes on 64 hosts. Next, we further select 24 hosts to deploy the second-stage monitoring to perform the end-to-end analysis.

For the second result, we deploy procZip to constrain the execution of the idling processes for two weeks and log any deviation attempts or new behaviors.

For the third and fourth result, we perform case study in collaboration with sysadmins and users in our enterprise and a survey with sysadmins in a university department.

It should be pointed out that the system administrators are mainly involved for evaluation purpose. In the operational workflow of our approach, system administrators are only involved (as the last step shown in Figure 2) when one really wants to kill a process or uninstall a program. There is no better way because it is extremely difficult to predict whether an idling process may become useful in the future. Therefore, it has to be human to judge the reasons case by case and determine whether a process can be safely killed or a program uninstalled. Our detection system itself (including data collection, idling process analysis, attack surface measurement) is automated and does *not* require any human intervention. To avoid confusion, we make a summary in Table 2 to differentiate human involvement in the operational workflow and non-operational (evaluation) workflow.

6.1 Idling Processes Summary

First, by analyzing the lightweight agent data, we get totally 5839 long-running processes, among which 2095 were identified as potentially idling. Here, we consider a process long-running if it has been running for longer than 80% of the host uptime. Next, due to privacy and policy concerns, we select 24 hosts to deploy the second-stage monitoring. With `strace` data from 24 hosts (1774 long-running processes), 434 out of the 546 potentially idling processes are determined to be really idling. Among them, Category I has 328 (overall 18.5%) and Category II has 115 (overall 6.5%).

Unique binaries. Even though the number of idling processes is high, they come from only 92 unique programs (*i.e.,* executable names). Some idling programs are commonly seen on many hosts, while some others only exist on a few hosts. Figure 5 plots the fraction of instances of each unique executable in a decreasing order. It is interesting to see that there is a long tail where about 42 binaries occur less than twice in the 24 hosts, indicating a wide variety of idling processes and services. While it would take some time

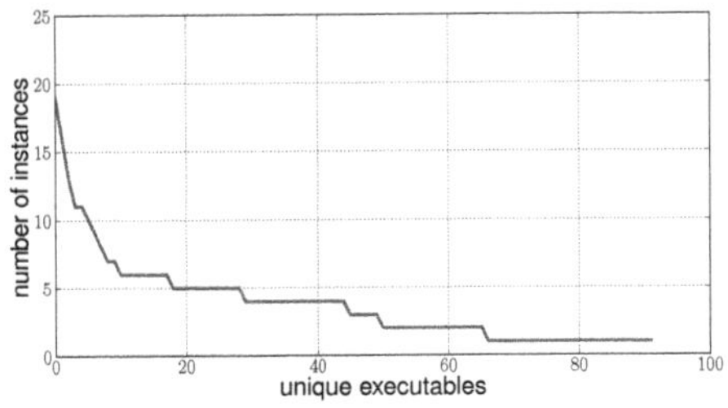

Figure 5: Distributions for number of instances of unique executables

Category I	Instances	Category II	Instances
acpid	19	atd	16
rpc.idmapd	13	rpcbind	5
hald	11	sendmail	5
avahi-daemon	11	mdadm	4
gconf-helper	10	smartd	4

Table 3: Number of unique instances of idling processes and the corresponding category

to investigate all of them for system administrators, one can prioritize which processes to look at first is based on how popular it is inside the enterprise. Table 3 lists the top ranked programs, the corresponding number of instances, and their categories.

Idling process distribution. We further study the distribution of idling processes from the 24 hosts with regard to host types. We want to see whether it is desktop OSes or server OSes that have more idling processes. To achieve this, we tagged each host as "User" to indicate a desktop OS, "Server" to represent a backend server, and "Testbed" to mark those testbed servers that are less frequently used. We did this based on our own knowledge and also with the help of the IT personnel. Figure 6(a) shows the distributions of idling processes over "User" OSes, "Server" OSes, and "Testbed" OSes. We can see that the "User" desktops and the "Server" machines have similar percentage of idling processes. In contrast, the "Testbed" machines have much more idling processes. This is quite in line with our expectation.

Intuition tells us that the characteristics of an idling process should also affect on its distribution. For instance, the idling processes on a server that is mostly accessed through remote shells might have more programs without GUI; while for a desktop host, GUI processes would instead take a larger portion. Due to the lack of a standard way to classify GUI and non-GUI programs, we manually tag each process. Figure 6(b) shows that the "User" machines do have more idling GUI processes than those "Server" machines.

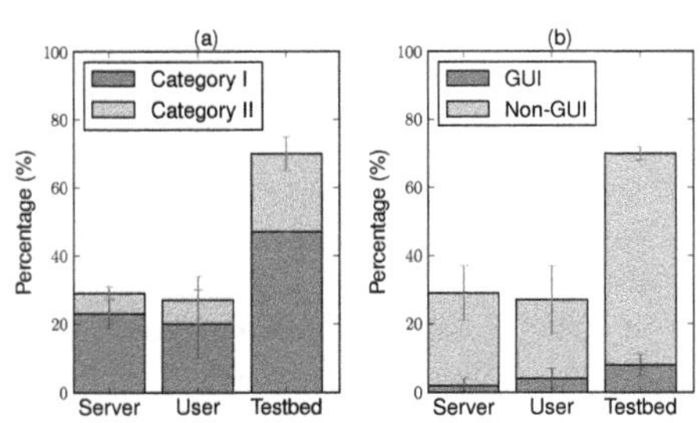

Figure 6: Distributions of idling processes in different aspects. (a) OS purposes: User/Server/Testbed; (b) Processes types: GUI/non-GUI

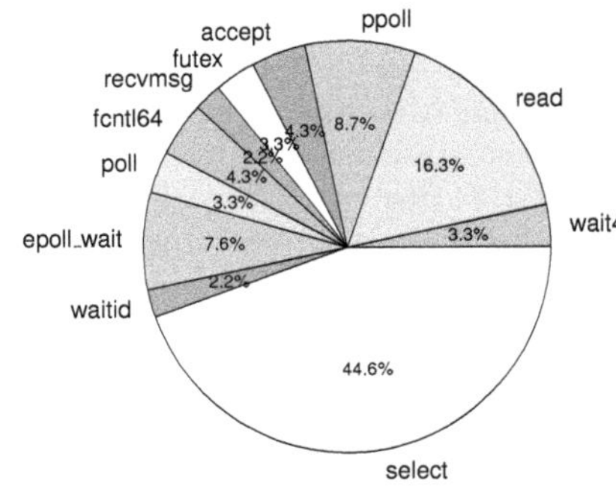

Figure 7: Breakdown of system calls that Category I processes are blocked on

Syscall patterns. For category I processes, as shown in Figure 7, we observe a variety of blocking system calls. We can see that most of the them are **select**, **read**, and **ppoll** which are operated on file descriptors. Such system calls have a parameter where a timeout value can be specified. We are surprised to see many programs choose to block indefinitely, given that such programming practice may lead to responsiveness issues [6].

A non-negligible fraction (16.3%) of them are not blocked on file descriptors, *e.g.,* **wait4**, **waitid**, and **futex**. At first glance, no attack surface seems to exist. However, it is plausible that after the syscall returns, the program will start taking input (*e.g.,* by calling **open**), which may constitute attack surface.

For category II processes, out of 115, 49 repeatedly try to take input through system calls like **read** and **recv**, but always failed with errors (*e.g.,* timeout). 18 processes that successfully take input, yet do not produce any output (*e.g.,* no **write** syscall). When the process does produce output, the output is most likely to be exactly the same across time. We measured the entropy [29] of the parameters for the output relevant system calls (*e.g.,* **write**, **writev**, **recv**, **recvmsg**, **recvfrom**) and found that among the 32 processes that produce outputs, 14 have the same exact output, indicating zero entropy.

6.2 Attack Surface and Vulnerabilities

Attack surface. Idling processes not only waste system resources but may also expose attack surface. Here, we study what is the percentage of idling processes which expose attack surface and what kind they are. Note that the attack surface we measure is only a lower bound, as the attack surface is measured only when a process is idling. Once become active, it may start accessing additional resources and open up new attack surface.

With that in mind, we still want to understand the attack surface exposed when these processes are idling. Overall, 127 of 434 (29.3%) processes have direct attack surface through files that are owned by a different user, or listening sockets which can be either accessed by all processes on the same host (if local socket) or by other hosts (if listening on the public interface).

Further, we find that the attack surface of the idling processes consists of 66.7% of attack surface exposed by all long-running processes, based on a snapshot of all the currently open resources on each host. Table 4 provides a breakdown of the attack surface. As we can see, the majority of the attack surface comes from the listening sockets (both remote-facing and local-facing). It is surprising to see that there are

Resource	File	Listening sockets (public)	Listening sockets (local)
Root	10	43	66
Non-root	19	51	53

Table 4: Attack surface breakdown of 434 idling processes

94 public open TCP/UDP ports (without one connecting to them) from just 24 hosts, which raises significant security concerns, especially considering 43 of them are opened by root processes. Note that these processes are idling and no one has connected to these ports for a long time. For the listening local sockets, they are either TCP/UDP ports bound to loopback address or UNIX domain sockets. Such listening sockets present a threat on local privilege escalation attacks, which is less concerning but still important given the popularity of local privilege escalation attacks in Linux [33, 34]. Note that the number of file attack surface is smaller, indicating the more popular use of sockets as communication mechanisms in long-running processes.

Known vulnerabilities. Out of all the processes, based on their executable names, we find that 47 out of 92 (51.1%) unique binaries have had known vulnerabilities in their development history according to the CVE database [2] and other online sources [1]. It indicates that there can be real threats to the idling processes that we discover. Just to give one example, remote attackers can trigger a vulnerability (CVE-2009-1490) in sendmail by crafting a long X-header to make a buffer overflow, which allows the attackers to execute shellcode and gain root privilege.

6.3 Constrainability Evaluation

Next we want to evaluate how constrainable the idling processes are. Through deploying procZip for two weeks on the 434 idling processes on 24 hosts, we find 384 processes (88.5%) did not have any "new behavior" or deviation from the previously observed behaviors – with a new syscall or an existing syscall at a different call stack, which means that they are very well constrained. 96.3% processes have less than 10 times where new behaviors are observed. More than 93.5% processes converge within one day.

Figure 8 shows the distributions of the number of times that new behaviors appear and the converge time across the 434 processes. The results give a strong indication that the majority of idling processes are indeed constrainable. Of course, ideally, if a process is really idling and the procZip is given the correct repeating cycle, they should be 100% constrainable and should not have any new behaviors observed. In reality, however, why are there still a few idling processes not constrainable? To answer this question, we further investigated 13 such processes from 10 hosts and found that they can be attributed to the following reasons:

First, 3 cases we find are due to the fact that some system calls are issued inside signal handler which may cause new call stack to be observed, depending on which instruction is interrupted. Note that this is not a fundamental limitation of our approach. We could support the signal handling cases by interpreting the parameters of signal handler registration calls (*e.g.,* `signal`, `sigaction`), which allows us to know the address of the handler function. In that case, when we observe a new call stack in the future and see the address of handler function in one of the stack frame, we can simply ignore the immediate stack frame next to it of which the return address can be anywhere in the program.

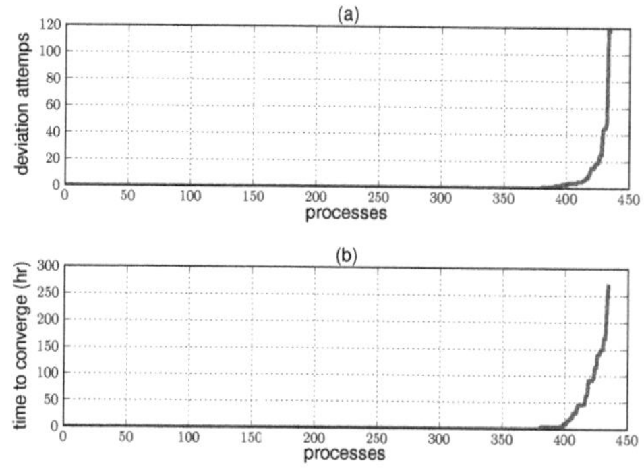

Figure 8: Distributions of (a) deviation attempts and (b) converge time

Second, due to the inherent noise tolerance characteristics of autocorrelation, 3 cases are detected with a repeating cycle shorter than the reality. These 3 cases are considered the inaccuracy of our idling process detection algorithm.

Third, 7 cases are due to real workload change which breaks its previous idling pattern. These 7 cases are considered the false positives of our approach. On one hand, we can argue that such cases are less likely to occur if we monitor their historical behavior long enough. On the other hand, we may want to admit that it is fundamentally hard by any means to predict the future.

6.4 Safe-to-disable Processes and Case Studies

Many idling processes are considered safe-to-disable in the eyes of system administrators and owners. We conduct detailed case studies in our enterprise to identify safe-to-disable processes and the reasons of their existence. The key challenge to perform the study is that a process needs to be examined in the typical runtime context (job-mix) of the host (or cluster of hosts) under examination. To achieve this, we have had intensive conversation with the system administrators and owners of the machines. Finally, we gather a list of processes that are considered safe-to-disable and we provide analysis and insights about such processes. Hopefully, our investigation results can serve as a helpful reference to average system administrators and end users in general.

In our case studies, 133 out of the 434 processes are considered safe-to-disable (30.6%). The top reasons are listed below (without specific order):

- **Supporting unused hardware devices**, *e.g.,* bluetooth devices, 3G/4G data card. Given that we are in an enterprise environment with fairly standard hardware setup: USB keyboard/mouse and Ethernet cables, such processes are very unlikely to be used. After checking with our system administrators, we conclude that they do not actually support the use of bluetooth devices or 3G/4G data cards and therefore these processes can be disabled. As a more detailed example, mdadm is a Linux utility used to manage software RAID devices. In strace log, the mdadm process is repeatedly calling `dup`, `fcntl`, and `close` on a configuration file `/proc/mdstat`, while this file shows that no RAID has been configured. We further check the file system and realize that there is only one physical volume, which does not require RAID management. Interestingly, the reason that the process is running is that the host were previously used to manage RAID devices. When the RAID devices were removed, the person forgot to terminate this service. Besides this example, most of these processes are actually bundled in the default installation image of the Linux distributions.

- **GUI-related processes that run on server machines**, *e.g.,* notification of sound level change. The servers in our environment are never intended to be used as desktop hosts. As a result, many GUI-related processes can be disabled. For instance, strace logs show that the indicator-sound-service process is completely blocked on a system call on three machines and never return. Actually we find out that they sit in a server room where no one is using it to output any audio, let alone observing the sound level changes.
- **Supporting unused miscellaneous software services**, *e.g.,* virtualization daemon (no VMs are supposed to run on them), super server which is not configured to start any daemon on demand. We find that some machines are pre-installed with the xinetd (extended Internet daemon) which listens for incoming requests over a network and launches the appropriate service for that request. By examining this process in detail, we realize that the configuration file indicates that there is no service registered at all, which indicates that this process is not intended to run. This is also confirmed with system administrators.
- **Applications not properly setup/configured**, *e.g.,* location tracking service, web servers serving default page. Many programs, when installed, are not fully configured to run with intended behaviors, possibly due to human negligence or mistakes. For example, we see an instance where the web server thttpd is installed and running for a long time yet idling. We further check the web directory and find that it only contains the default pages that come with the default installation. In other words, one can only browse the default page (which is a 404 page). Another example is sendmail which is normally used as mail servers and mail relays. Desktop users, in our environment, do not really need this program as our email systems go through the company mail servers (Microsoft exchange server). We typically use IT-supported programs such as Thunderbird to receive emails.

Although rare, another interesting case is that certain application/service is in the process of being retired and its functionalities are to be replaced by a new one. In this case, we observe that the old application/service can still be running for some reason. For example, HAL (Hardware Abstraction Layer) was aimed for providing hardware abstractions for UNIX-like OSes. Since 2011, major Linux distributions are in the process of deprecating HAL and hald is in the process of being merged into udev and Linux kernel. Permitted by the owner, we disable hald on one desktop machine and the user did not notice any influence. The CD and USB icon can still automatically appear on the desktop when being inserted. The discovery of this type of case is very surprising and not originally anticipated by us.

Overall, a large portion of safe-to-disable processes can be attributed to the fact that OSes are packing more and more general purpose applications and utilities. Some of them are installed at a later time, yet they are either not really properly configured to begin with, or they are no longer needed but forgotten to be uninstalled.

Boundary cases There exist a large number of processes that are in the grey area even in the eyes of system administrators. Here are some examples to illustrate such cases: the irqbalance process is a daemon process that balances interrupts across multiple CPUs or cores, which is supposed to provide better performance and IO balance on SMP systems. However, we find an intensive and insightful discussion among the Ubuntu package management people in their online forum about whether to start this process by default [11]. Our survey indicates that irqbalance seems to be targeted at a specific server environment and may sometimes downgrade the performance. Further, on desktop machines, such performance concern is barely serious.

To more objectively evaluate whether the processes are indeed safe to disable. We have asked a few users who have agreed to have a few services disabled, which include: bluetoodhd, mdadm, indicator-sound-service, xinetd, thttpd, irqbalance, sendmail, smartd, hald, and winbindd over the course of a few days. The users do not observe any disruption to the daily use of the machines.

6.5 Cross Validation

Since enterprise systems usually share some common characteristics, we extend our evaluation to another organization to see whether our results can also be shared. Particularly, we conduct a survey with three system administrators in a university department. One of them is the head of the IT group and the other two are both senior system administrators with multiple years of experience. The IT group is responsible for managing computers in the classrooms, faculty offices, and student laboratories. They are also in charge of the department web server, email server, databases, *etc.*

We create a questionnaire containing 20 programs selected from our safe-to-disable list together with the specific reasons of their existence. We ask them to 1) give a score from 0-10 (0-strongly disagree, 10-strongly agree) to indicate to what extent they can confirm our result based on their own experience, and 2) note down whether they happen to find the exact same program on their machines and also think it is unnecessary but somewhat were not aware of before.

Due to page limit, we put the detailed survey results in [12]. Overall, the average score is 9.6, showing a reasonably large degree of agreement. Two sysadmins even state that they find all the 20 programs on their machines that they believe are unnecessary but did not notice before.

7. DISCUSSION

Idling processes and their necessity. The concepts of "idling" and "unnecessary" are not exactly the same thing. An idling process describes a process that is in a state given past observations. Whether or not it is still necessary to keep in the system is a question that requires future knowledge. For instance, an idling daemon process that supports cellular network cards may be idling for the past one year. However, it is impossible to predict if someone may need to use the cellular network card in the next day. Therefore, the necessity of a process can only be answered by prophet, in our case, the system administrators.

In addition, the concept of "necessary" is subjective. A process that is deemed unnecessary may be actively performing useful operations. Consider a process which outputs a pop-up notification window (*e.g.,* for instant messenger applications) to the screen from time to time. Some user may find it useful while others will not and may even find it disturbing. Such problem is outside the scope of this paper.

Idling process and its usage. In this paper, we study a number of idling processes from our automated method and then confirm that a large fraction of them can be safely disabled or uninstalled. We envision that such knowledge can be shared across enterprises or organizations. In §6.4, we notice that every safe-to-disable process has its reason to be idling. We could actually construct a knowledge base of such safe-to-disable processes. One way to share such knowledge is to compile a list of questions such as whether the organization requires the usage of special hardware (*e.g.,* cellular network connection) or whether the host is to be used as a server or desktop. Answering these questions will then lead to an automated selection of services to install in order to minimize the attack surface while at the same time satisfy the functionality requirement.

8. RELATED WORK

Unnecessary service. Few studies have looked at what services are idling or unnecessary inside an enterprise environment. Guha et al. [20] examined network traffic traces collected from laptops in an enterprise network and looked at services that generate useless traffic (*e.g.,* broadcast discovery messages with no response, failed TCP flows). Although network traffic can also indicate whether a process is idle or not, but it is by no means accurate. For example, a process might have its listening socket idle but still do useful work (*e.g.,* a database server has an idle Internet socket but is serving a local web server via a Unix socket). Our approach looks at both CPU time and system calls, which can precisely describe the idleness of processes.

Attack surface metrics and reduction. Traditionally, attack surface has been evaluated at different system layers. Manadhata et al. proposed a software system's attack surface measurement [27]. This system uses several metrics such as system channels (*e.g.,* sockets), system methods (*e.g.,* API), and the transferred data items to determine the level of risk. Szefer et al. [31] takes a similar approach for virtualization. Authors proposed NoHype, a hypervisor that eliminates the hypervisor attack surface. Kurmus et al. [24] measured attack surface metrics on Linux kernels. Moreover, they reduced the attack surface and kernel vulnerabilities using automated compile-time OS kernel tailoring.

In our work, we choose a set of simple attack surface metrics to measure at the system layers. Most of the above approaches can complement our method to provide more complete and precise attack surface.

Anomaly detection and process behavior models. Numerous attempts have been made to study how to model the behavior of a process and learn its normal behavior for the purpose of performing anomaly detection [21, 30, 23, 19]. Even though our study also models the behavior of a process, it incurs a different set of challenges. Specifically, we examine if existing models can directly be applied in our case. In general, there are three categories of process behavior models: 1) sequence of system calls [21, 26], 2) deterministic Finite State Automata (FSA) [30, 23], and 3) probabilistic FSA (*e.g.,* Hidden Markov Model) [35, 19]. For 1), the idea is to use n-gram model to learn the common n consecutive system calls. The problem is that an idling process needs not only to have common n-grams, but also the exact time alignment of events. For 2) and 3), the model only learns what the next system call is allowed based on the current "state", it does not learn the linkage between a long sequence of events. For instance, if the model has two states A and B, with the possible transition of $A \rightarrow B$, $B \rightarrow A$, and $A \rightarrow A$. It is unclear if this leads to a repeating sequence at all. For example, the allowed sequence could be either $A \rightarrow B \rightarrow A \rightarrow A \rightarrow B \rightarrow ...$ (non-repeating) or $A \rightarrow A \rightarrow B \rightarrow A \rightarrow A \rightarrow B \rightarrow ...$(repeating). Furthermore, such models do not consider time information at all. Our time-augmented version of autocorrelation approach fits well the problem of identifying repeating patterns.

Vulnerability discovery. A number of studies have systematically revealed a class of vulnerabilities related to resource-access. Vijayakumar *et al.* [33] studied name resolution vulnerabilities in Linux systems. For instance, if a root process reads a file in a public directory, an attacker may be able to remove the file and creates a link to `/etc/passwd` to steal sensitive data. According to their study, a significant number of such vulnerabilities exist. Such file-based attack surface is also considered in our evaluation. Process firewall [34] has been proposed to help defend against such class of vulnerabilities. Our study aims at identifying idling processes which can lead to an easier treatment (*e.g.,* disable the service) so as to reduce their attack surface.

Security risk analysis. There exist a number of studies focusing on the security risk of services [22, 16, 17]. Homer et al. [22] presented a sound and practical modeling of security risk utilizing attack graphs and vulnerability metrics. Chakrabarti et al. [16] models the spread of malware and assesses the benefits of immunization of certain nodes. Chan et al. [17] models the attack and defense as interdependent defense games to study the cost-effectiveness of certain security decisions. Such assessment and modeling is abstract using probability to evaluate the likelihood of compromise. Their risk models can be integrated with our system to provide more accurate risk and impact analysis.

9. CONCLUSION

In this paper, we present LIPzip, a system that identifies idling services, an under-studied research area, and explore its security application of attack surface reduction. We define idling process as long-running processes that are in a blocked or bookkeeping state, and we propose an adaptive autocorrelation-based algorithm which can robustly detect idling process from system call information. We evaluate the effectiveness of our algorithm in a real enterprise working environment, using a custom built light-weight and scalable data collection system. With both case studies and automatic validation through process behavior constraining, 30.7% of the identified idling processes can be safely disabled to fully eliminate their attacker surface, and 93.5% can be safely and automatically constrained to reduce attack surface without system administrators' manual intervention.

10. ACKNOWLEDGEMENTS

We would like to thank Bill Kanawyer, Chris Milito, Shannon Johnson, and Eric Treece for their participation in our survey and anonymous reviewers for their insightful feedback. Jun Wang was partially supported by NSF CNS-1223710 and Peng Liu was supported by ARO W911NF-09-1-0525 (MURI) and NSF CNS-1223710. Any opinions, findings, and conclusions or recommendations expressed in this material are those of the authors and do not necessarily reflect the views of any organization.

11. REFERENCES

[1] Bugs: Ubuntu. `https://bugs.launchpad.net/ubuntu`.
[2] Common vulnerabilities and exposures. `http://cve.mitre.org/cve/`.

[3] Cve vulnerabilities : file with the write mode. http://cve.mitre.org/cgi-bin/cvekey.cgi?keyword=file+write+mode.
[4] Cve vulnerabilities : remote ports. http://cve.mitre.org/cgi-bin/cvekey.cgi?keyword=remote+port.
[5] Cve vulnerabilities : unix domain sockets. http://cve.mitre.org/cgi-bin/cvekey.cgi?keyword=unix+domain+socket.
[6] Guide to network programming. http://beej.us/guide/bgnet/output/html/multipage/advanced.html.
[7] How to remove geoclue-master? http://ubuntuforums.org/showthread.php?t=1957331.
[8] The linux audit framework. https://www.suse.com/documentation/sled10/audit_sp1/data/book_sle_audit.html.
[9] MSDN best practices for security. http://msdn.microsoft.com/en-us/library/ms912889(v=winembedded.5).aspx.
[10] Securing a linux desktop part 1: removing unwanted services. http://www.ihackforfun.eu/index.php?title=improve-security-by-removing-services&more=1&c=1&tb=1&pb=1.
[11] Start irqbalance by default? http://ubuntu.5.x6.nabble.com/Start-irqbalance-by-default-td732222.html.
[12] Survey at penn state university. https://sites.google.com/site/lipzip15/survey.
[13] System administrator - security best practices. http://www.sans.org/reading-room/whitepapers/bestprac/system-administrator-security-practices-657.
[14] what is avahi-daemon? http://forums.fedoraforum.org/showthread.php?t=124837.
[15] What's this at-spi-registryd? https://blogs.oracle.com/jmcp/entry/what_s_this_at_spi.
[16] D. Chakrabarti, Y. Wang, C. Wang, J. Leskovec, and C. Faloutsos. Epidemic thresholds in real networks. *ACM Trans. Inf. Syst. Secur.*, 2008.
[17] H. Chan, M. Ceyko, and L. Ortiz. Interdependent defense games: Modeling interdependent security under deliberate attacks. In *In Proceedings of the Twenty-Eighth Conference on Uncertainty in Artificial Intelligence (UAI)*, 2012.
[18] C. Chatfield. *The analysis of time series: an introduction*. CRC press, 2013.
[19] A. Frossi, F. Maggi, G. L. Rizzo, and S. Zanero. Selecting and improving system call models for anomaly detection. In *DIMVA*, 2009.
[20] S. Guha, J. Chandrashekar, N. Taft, and K. Papagiannaki. How healthy are today's enterprise networks? In *Proceedings of the 8th ACM SIGCOMM Conference on Internet Measurement*, IMC '08.
[21] S. A. Hofmeyr, S. Forrest, and A. Somayaji. Intrusion detection using sequences of system calls. In *Journal of Computer Security*, 1998.
[22] J. Homer, X. Ou, and D. Schmidt. A sound and practical approach to quantifying security risk in enterprise networks. Technical Report (2009): 1-15, Kansas State University.
[23] A. P. Kosoresow and S. A. Hofmeyr. Intrusion detection via system call traces. In *IEEE Software*, '97.
[24] A. Kurmus, R. Tartler, D. Dorneau, B. Heinloth, V. Rothberg, A. Ruprecht, W. SchÃűder-Preikschat, D. Lohmann, and R. Kapitza. Attack surface metrics and automated compile-time os kernel tailoring. In *NDSS 2013*.
[25] K. H. Lee, X. Zhang, and D. Xu. High accuracy attack provenance via binary-based execution partition. In *Proceedings of the 2013 Network and Distributed System Security Symposium (NDSS'13)*.
[26] F. Maggi, M. Matteucci, and S. Zanero. Detecting intrusions through system call sequence and argument analysis. *IEEE Transactions on Dependable and Secure Computing*, 2010.
[27] P. K. Manadhata and J. M. Wing. An attack surface metric. In *IEEE Transactions on Software Engineering (2011)*, pages 371–386.
[28] J. Reich, M. Goraczko, A. Kansal, and J. Padhye. Sleepless in seattle no longer. In *USENIX Annual Technical Conference (ATC)*, 2010.
[29] A. Rényi. On measures of entropy and information. In *Fourth Berkeley Symposium on Mathematical Statistics and Probability*, pages 547–561, 1961.
[30] R. Sekar, M. Bendre, D. Dhurjati, and P. Bollineni. A fast automaton-based method for detecting anomalous program behaviors. In *IEEE Symposium on Security and Privacy*, 2001.
[31] J. Szefer, E. Keller, R. B. Lee, and J. Rexford. Eliminating the hypervisor attack surface for a more secure cloud. CCS, 2011.
[32] H. Vijayakumar, G. Jakka, S. Rueda, J. Schiffman, and T. Jaeger. Integrity walls: Finding attack surfaces from mandatory access control policies. ASIACCS '12.
[33] H. Vijayakumar, J. Schiffman, and T. Jaeger. Sting: Finding name resolution vulnerabilities in programs. In *Proceedings of the 21st USENIX Security*, 2012.
[34] H. Vijayakumar, J. Schiffman, and T. Jaeger. Process firewalls: Protecting processes during resource access. In *Proceedings of the 8th ACM European Conference on Computer Systems (EUROSYS 2013)*, April 2013.
[35] C. Warrender, S. Forrest, and B. Pearlmutter. Detecting intrusions using system calls: Alternative data models. In *IEEE Symposium on Security and Privacy*, 1999.
[36] Q. Zeng, J. Rhee, H. Zhang, N. Arora, G. Jiang, and P. Liu. Deltapath: Precise and scalable calling context encoding. In *Proceedings of Annual IEEE/ACM International Symposium on Code Generation and Optimization*, New York, NY, USA, 2014.

APPENDIX

Determining Attack Surface. We summarize what kind of resources we consider and how we determine if they are attack surface as a set of rules: (1) If a process has opened a resource in readable mode, and (2) we consider three main resource types: Internet listening sockets (either bind to local or public interface), Unix domain listening sockets, and regular files. (2.1) If it is an Internet listening socket, we directly consider it attack surface as it can be accessed by anyone (host-based firewalls are not configured in our enterprise). Many known vulnerabilities are exploited by first connecting to a listening socket [4]. (2.2) If it is a Unix domain listening socket, we first check if it is file-backed. If so, the file permissions apply when connecting to such a socket, and we treat it similar to a regular file (as described next). Otherwise, if it is not file-backed, we consider it attack surface since anyone local can access it. Vulnerabilities have been reported when accessing Unix domain sockets [5]. (2.3) If it is a file, and the file is not a directory or a special file such as `/dev/null` and files under `/proc`. We consider it attack surface if one of the three following conditions is satisfied: (2.3.1) Everyone can write to the file. (2.3.2) The file owner group ID is different from the process group ID and the group-writable permission bit is set. (2.3.3) The file owner user ID is different from the process user ID and the file owner user ID is not root (as we assume the root is trusted). Vulnerabilities related to files have also been widely discussed [33, 3].

The Performance Cost of Shadow Stacks and Stack Canaries

Thurston H.Y. Dang
Electrical Engineering and Computer Sciences
University of California, Berkeley
thurston@eecs.berkeley.edu

Petros Maniatis
Google Inc.
maniatis@google.com

David Wagner
Electrical Engineering and Computer Sciences
University of California, Berkeley
daw@cs.berkeley.edu

ABSTRACT

Control flow defenses against ROP either use strict, expensive, but strong protection against redirected RET instructions with shadow stacks, or much faster but weaker protections without. In this work we study the inherent overheads of shadow stack schemes. We find that the overhead is roughly 10% for a traditional shadow stack. We then design a new scheme, the parallel shadow stack, and show that its performance cost is significantly less: 3.5%. Our measurements suggest it will not be easy to improve performance on current x86 processors further, due to inherent costs associated with RET and memory load/store instructions. We conclude with a discussion of the design decisions in our shadow stack instrumentation, and possible lighter-weight alternatives.

Categories and Subject Descriptors

D.4.6 [**Operating Systems**]: Security and Protection

General Terms

shadow stack, stack canary, stack cookie

1. INTRODUCTION

One classic security exploit is to redirect the control flow by overwriting a return address stored on the stack [36]. Although various mitigations (e.g., NX/DEP) have made this attack and some simple refinements (e.g., return-to-libc) infeasible, the current state of the art in exploitation – return-oriented programming (ROP [44]) – continues to depend on misusing RET instructions, this time by chaining together short sequences of instructions ("gadgets") that end in a RET.[1]

[1]The generalizations of ROP – jump-oriented programming [11], or ROP without returns [14] – are not commonly used in practice and will not be considered further.

ASIA CCS'15, April 14–17, 2015, Singapore.

ACM 978-1-4503-3245-3/15/04 ...$15.00.
http://dx.doi.org/10.1145/2714576.2714635.

These attacks could largely, in principle, be prevented using control-flow integrity (CFI) schemes [7], but CFI has not been widely adopted, in part due to its non-trivial overhead [53]. Recent works that have proposed CFI for binaries [53, 55] have greatly reduced the overhead by adopting coarse-grained policies. One notable relaxation is they adopt a more permissive policy for RET instructions, rather than tracking the return addresses precisely using a shadow stack (as had been proposed in Abadi et al.'s original formulation [7]). Unfortunately, such weaker policies were soon shown to be insecure [13,19,24]. Control-flow defenses against ROP either use strict, expensive, but strong protection against redirected RET instructions with shadow stacks or other dual-stack schemes such as allocation stacks [21], or much faster but weaker protections without. However, it is not clear whether the overhead seen in CFI with shadow stacks is inherent in the shadow-stack functionality, or an artifact of particular implementations. In this paper, we measure this performance cost.

There is substantial literature on stand-alone shadow stacks. Some papers report low overheads, but each paper makes subtly different design decisions and/or does not use standard benchmarks (see Section 9), which makes it difficult to estimate the cost of adding a traditional shadow stack to coarse-grained CFI.

We do not consider schemes that have dual stacks, but which do not store the return address in a shadow stack (see Related Work). To our knowledge, they have only been implemented in recompilation-based schemes – thus negating the binary-rewritability benefits of coarse-grained CFI.

2. BACKGROUND

2.1 Traditional Shadow Stacks

The purpose of a shadow stack is to protect return addresses saved on the stack from tampering. Figure 1 (left) illustrates a traditional shadow stack, in a scenario where there are currently four nested function calls. In the main stack, each stack frame is shown with parameters, the return address, the saved frame pointer (EBP), and the local variables. In the traditional shadow stack, there is a shadow stack pointer (SSP) – which contains the address of the top of the shadow stack – and the shadow stack itself, which contains copies of the four return addresses.

In shadow stack schemes, when a function is called, the new return address is pushed onto the shadow stack.

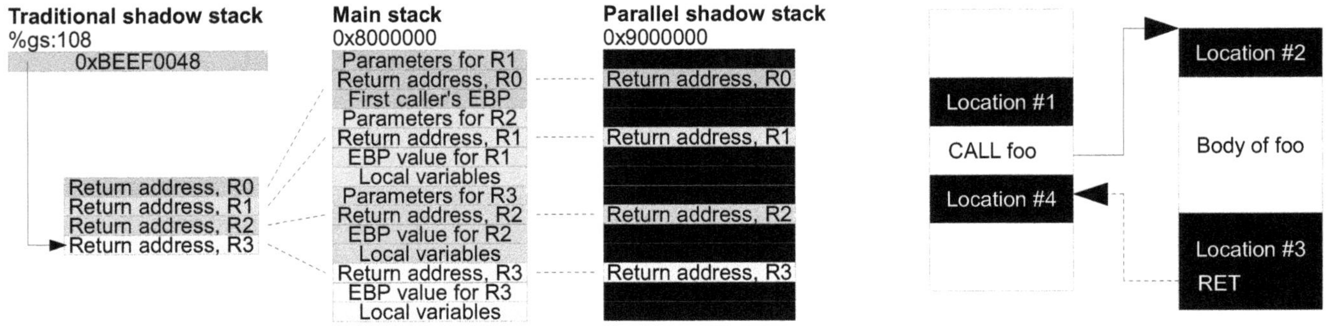

Figure 1: Left: traditional vs parallel shadow stacks. Rx refers to Routine #x. Right: possible locations for instrumentation.

```
SUB $4, %gs:108     # Decrement SSP
MOV %gs:108, %eax # Copy SSP into EAX
MOV (%esp), %ecx  # Copy ret. address into
MOV %ecx, (%eax)  #      shadow stack via ECX
```

Figure 2: Prologue for traditional shadow stack.

```
MOV %gs:108, %ecx # Copy SSP into ECX
ADD $4, %gs:108   # Increment SSP
MOV (%ecx), %edx  # Copy ret. address from
MOV %edx, (%esp)  #      shadow stack via EDX
RET
```

Figure 3: Epilogue for traditional shadow stack (overwriting).

When the function returns, it uses the return address stored on the shadow stack to ensure the integrity of the address where execution returns. This can be done by either **checking** that the return address on the main stack matches the copy on the shadow stack, or by **overwriting** the return address on the main stack with the copy on the shadow stack (equivalently, by indirectly jumping to the address stored on the shadow stack).

The return address can be saved before the `CALL` instruction ("Location #1" in Figure 1, right) or at the prologue of the called function ("Location #2"). The return address can be checked/overwritten before the `RET` instruction ("Location #3"); alternatively, if we ensure that every `RET` instruction can only return to a call-preceded location that is not an unintended instruction (this is the coarse-grained return policy of BinCFI [55]), we can check the return address at the return site ("Location #4").

Typically, schemes that propose changes to the hardware (e.g., Ozdoganoglu et al. [38]) find it convenient to instrument the `CALL`s, while binary-rewriting schemes often instrument function prologues and epilogues by replacing them with "trampolines" (indirect jumps) to the replacement code.

The prologue could be as per Figure 2, and the epilogue could be as per Figure 3 or 4 for the checking and overwriting policies, respectively.

2.2 Stack Canaries

Stack canaries are special values stored in stack frames between the return address and local variables. A contiguous stack buffer overflow would overwrite the stack canary, which is checked for intactness before the `RET`s of vulnerable functions [50].

```
MOV %gs:108, %ecx
ADD $4, %gs:108
MOV (%ecx), %edx
CMP %edx, (%esp) # Instead of overwriting,
JNZ abort        #      we compare
RET
abort:
    HLT
```

Figure 4: Epilogue for traditional shadow stack (checking).

Shadow stacks are sometimes argued to be a type of stack canary: instead of checking whether an added canary value has been corrupted, the return addresses (and sometimes the saved frame pointers) are used as canaries [8, 39]. For completeness, we investigated the overhead of stack canaries.

3. CHALLENGES

3.1 Time of Check to Time of Use Vulnerability

Epilogues that use the `RET` instruction in multi-threaded programs are vulnerable to time-of-check-to-time-of-use (TOCTTOU) attacks: the return address may be correct at the time of the shadow stack epilogue validation, but be modified by the attacker before the `RET` executes. This attack can be prevented by storing the return address inside a register (e.g., `ecx`), performing the validation on `ecx`, and converting the `RET` into `jmp *%ecx` [7].

A similar vulnerability exists for any shadow stack scheme that instruments the prologue, since between the `CALL` (when the correct return address is placed on the stack by the CPU) and the shadow stack prologue, the attacker can modify the return address. This can be avoided by instrumenting the `CALL` site, to compute and store the return address in the shadow stack [7, 40]. Some other architectures are immune, as they pass the return address using a "link register" [4].

Nonetheless, many shadow stack schemes (see Table 1) do instrument the prologue and epilogue (with a check performed before the `RET`); this may be because of its convenience for binary rewriting with trampolines, incremental deployability on a per-function basis, or the perceived per-

Scenario	-fstack-protector-all				Parallel shadow stack (fixed offset)				Parallel shadow stack (randomized offset)				Protected traditional shadow stack			
	Check		Overwrite		Check		Overwrite		Check		Overwrite		Check		Overwrite	
	RA	Data	RA	Data	RA	Data	RA	Data	RA	Data	RA	Data	RA	Data	RA	Data
Contiguous writes, no info disclosure	Y	Y	N	N	Y	Y	Y	N	Y	Y	Y	N	Y	Y	Y	N
Contiguous writes, with info disclosure	N	N	N	N	Y	N	Y	N	Y	N	Y	N	Y	N	Y	N
Arbitrary writes, no info disclosure	N	N	N	N	N	N	N	N	Y	N	Y	N	Y	N	Y	N
Arbitrary writes, with info disclosure	N	N	N	N	N	N	N	N	N	N	N	N	Y	N	Y	N

Figure 5: Security properties of each mechanism.
RA = return address, Data = any data in the stack above the canary/return address of the current frame.
Y = protected, N = vulnerable to overwrite.

```
MOV %gs:108, %ecx # Copy SSP into ECX
MOV (%esp), %edx  # Copy ret. addr. into EDX
non_match:
    CMP $0, (%ecx)# Is shadow stack empty?
    JZ abort
    ADD $4, %ecx  # Increment our copy of SSP
    CMP %edx, -4(%ecx) # Check ret. addr.
    JNZ non_match # Loop until match
MOV %ecx, %gs:108 # Synchronize SSP
RET
abort:
    HLT
```

Figure 6: Epilogue for traditional shadow stack with checking and popping until a match.

formance impact of replacing **RET**s, since it is highly recommended to match **CALL**s with **RET**s [3,6]. Zhang et al. [53] argue that the TOCTTOU vulnerability with their use of **RET** is difficult to exploit (due to the precise timing required), and outweighed by the benefits of return address prediction. BinCFI [55] goes to great lengths to maintain the **CALL-RET** matching despite TOCTTOU exploits, even adding extra stub function calls rather than using indirect jumps.

3.2 Mismatches Between CALLS and RETS

Perhaps the best known violation of **CALL-RET** matching is **setjmp/longjmp**, whereby a function may unwind multiple stack frames. For traditional shadow stacks, a typical solution (e.g., binary RAD [42]) is to pop the shadow stack until a match is found, or the shadow stack is empty (denoted here with a sentinel value of zero). Figure 6 is our hand-compiled version of the C code from PSI [54].

This is already considerably more complicated than the vanilla traditional shadow stack epilogue, yet might not even be completely secure in obscure circumstances: if the same function is called multiple times before **longjmp**. This can be solved by storing both the return address and stack pointer [16,38,46].

```
POP 999996(%esp) # Copy ret addr to shadow stack
SUB $4, %esp # Fix up stack pointer (undo POP)
```

Figure 7: Prologue for parallel shadow stack.

```
ADD $4, %esp # Fix up stack pointer
PUSH 999996(%esp) # Copy from shadow stack
```

Figure 8: Epilogue for parallel shadow stack.

4. DESIGN

We devised parallel shadow stacks as a minimal, low-cost implementation of the principle of shadow stacks, albeit with some security trade-offs.

4.1 Parallel Shadow Stacks

As we will show later in Section 7, the traditional shadow stack has a non-trivial performance overhead. Our results indicate that the overhead comes mainly from the per-execution cost of the instrumentation we add, multiplied by the frequency of **RET** instructions in the program that we are protecting. Thus, an instrumentation with a lower execution cost would nearly directly translate into lower overhead.

We introduce a new variant on traditional shadow stacks, which we call a *parallel shadow stack*. The main idea is to place it at a fixed offset from the main stack, avoiding the overhead of maintaining the shadow stack pointer and copying it to/from memory. For example, in Figure 1 (right), the shadow stack is **0x1000000** bytes above the main stack, and the return addresses in the main stack are parallel to the return addresses in the shadow stack. Single guard pages (e.g., a page marked non-present in the page table) at the top and bottom of the shadow stack protect it from contiguous buffer overflows.

Our instrumentation for overwriting the return address can be as simple as adding two instructions to each uninstrumented prologue (Figure 7) and two instructions to each uninstrumented epilogue (Figure 8).

With peephole optimizations (see Appendix A), the net instruction count can be as few as one and *zero* instructions added to each prologue and epilogue, respectively. Note, however, that instruction count is not the sole, or even necessarily the major determinant of CPU overhead.

This instrumentation does not clobber any registers and can be easily modified to preserve the flags (through replacing `SUB/ADD` with `LEA`), thus making it transparent to the rest of the program, without incurring the expense of saving/restoring any registers or EFLAGS.

All parallel shadow stacks, by definition, automatically handle any unusual changes to `%esp`: for example, when `longjmp` unwinds the stack, it also implicitly unwinds the shadow stack appropriately.

There are two main disadvantages compared to a traditional shadow stack. Firstly, return addresses are rarely packed together, which means that each return address may even use up an entire cache line; the overhead of this depends on the calling patterns of the program. Additionally, due to the shadow stack pointer synchronization, an attacker who is able to pivot the stack (modify the stack pointer to point elsewhere) can choose any return address in the call stack; indeed, if we do not "zero out" (or corrupt) old shadow stack frame entries, then the attacker could even choose expired return addresses. A more insidious attack is to change `%esp` such that the parallel shadow stack region – say, `0xa0000000(%esp)` – is under the attacker's control; we can prevent this, at the cost of limiting the address space, by ensuring that `0xa0000000(%esp)` is mapped to the process address space only for valid values of `%esp`. Parallel shadow stacks do generally use more memory than a traditional shadow stack, but as the stack is small in comparison to the heap, and its pages can be committed only when needed, we do not consider this a major limitation.

Note that we do not claim that the overhead of a parallel shadow stack is low enough for widespread deployment.

4.2 Security Benefits

Our weakest threat model is when the attacker has a contiguous stack buffer overflow (e.g., `memcpy`), but does not have any information disclosure (i.e., while they may know the stack layout, they do not know the stack contents – such as the stack canary value or return value – nor the fixed shadow stack offset). Another threat model is where the attacker can perform arbitrary writes into the stack (e.g., repeated uses of `src[i] = s`, where `i` and `s` are under their control), but does not have any information disclosure. We also consider the previous two cases, with information disclosure (though not sufficient disclosure to defeat randomization).

Figure 5 summarizes, for each of these threat models, we consider whether each mechanism can protect the return address and/or any data stored above the canary (or return address).

All these mechanisms restrict the use of gadgets that end with an instrumented `RET`, and all the parallel shadow stacks provide some limited protection against large-scale stack pivots (since they will write to the shadow stack region).

5. AIMS

5.1 Research Questions

Our overarching research question is: *what are the performance costs of using a shadow stack, as seems to be necessary for security when using CFI schemes?* It is obvious that there is > 0 overhead since it requires additional operations; our aim is to *quantify* it.

To address this question, we evaluated the overhead of: a traditional shadow stack; a no-frills parallel shadow stack; checking vs. overwriting the return address; zeroing out expired shadow stack entries (for a parallel shadow stack); `-fstack-protector-all` (which adds stack canaries to *every* function, instead of a shadow stack for every call); and replacing `RET`s with indirect jumps (to avoid TOCTTOU).

The overhead can be made arbitrarily low by constructing test programs that perform a significant amount of computation for every function call; conversely, the overhead would be artifically high if we instrumented empty functions [15,42]. To provide a meaningful estimate of the overhead, it is important to use a standardized benchmark suite.

5.2 Assumptions

We assume that we have a tool similar to BinCFI [55] that 1) does not have access to the source code; 2) but can identify the prologue and `RET`s of every function (at the assembly level); and can insert code without the need for additional trampolines (cf., Prasad and Chiueh [42]).

Compiler based shadow stack schemes generally fulfill condition 2 but not 1, and vice-versa for binary-rewriting based shadow stack schemes. In contrast, by leveraging the address translation that is already required for BinCFI, adding a shadow stack to CFI does not require more trampolines.

Our assumptions are similar to Stack Shield [49], though that is intended to be deployed as an assembly preprocessor in the ordinary build process.

6. METHOD

We ran SPEC CPU2006, excluding any Fortran programs, on Ubuntu 12.04, running on a Dell Precision T5500 (Intel Xeon X5680, with 12GB of RAM). All code was compiled with gcc 4.6.3, using the standard configuration files (`Example-linux64-amd64-gcc43+.cfg`) and `Example-linux64-ia32-gcc43+.cfg`), with the exception that we disabled stack canaries entirely (i.e., `-fno-stack-protector`) since they are mostly redundant when a shadow stack is available. We tested both 32-bit and 64-bit, as they are the dominant modes; 32-bit performance may differ from 64-bit, due to the larger integers (which may affect cache/memory pressure) and increased number of general purpose registers for the latter. We chose the `-O2` optimization level, the default setting for SPEC CPU, plus the more aggressive `-O3`. With `-O3`, inlining reduces the number of function calls (and thereby the amount of instrumentation required), though the function bodies are also faster (which makes the prologue/epilogue instrumentation relatively more expensive). Since both are reasonable optimization options, we wished to empirically compare their overhead.

We also tested `apache httpd 2.4.10`, using `apachebench` on the same machine. We chose this as a more realistic scenario, whose performance may not be entirely CPU bound.

As per Tice et al. [48], we disabled Turbo Boost (dynamic CPU frequency scaling) and ASLR to reduce variance in the run-times. Additionally, we observed that the SPEC benchmarks tended to run more slowly if the system had been in use for a prolonged period, possibly due to disk-caching effects. To avoid these carryover effects, we rebooted the system before each batch of benchmarks.

We used the following instrumentation (see Appendix B): a traditional shadow stack that checks the return address (for compatibility with `longjmp`, it pops the shadow stack until a match with the return address); a parallel shadow stack that checks the return address; a parallel shadow stack that overwrites the return address, zeroing out expired shadow stack entries; a parallel shadow stack that overwrites the return address, without zeroing; `-fstack-protector-all`, i.e., stack canaries applied to every function.

We tested multiple versions of each instrumentation, and selected the code that performed best in a pilot study.

We tried both `RET`s and indirect jumps for each of the instrumention schemes except `-fstack-protector-all`. We did not implement a traditional shadow stack (overwriting), due to its inability to protect programs using `longjmp`.

Our parallel shadow stacks used a fixed offset, for ease of implementation. However, the overhead should be similar when using a random offset, except for the time required to rewrite the offsets at load-time, which should be negligible: the number of offsets that need to be rewritten is equal to the number of function prologues and `RET`s. This is less than for relocations, which must relocate both data and functions. In general, our implementation is intended to provide a reasonable estimate of the overhead, not production use.

6.1 Implementation Details

We make no claim that our implementation will be robust enough to deploy widely. Nonetheless, since much of the overhead is due to inherent memory loads/stores (see Section 7), we believe we have implemented each of these schemes in sufficient detail to let us measure their performance overhead on SPEC CPU.

For C programs, we call `setupShadowStack` at the beginning of `main`. The `setupShadowStack` function allocates a memory region at a fixed offset from the stack (for the parallel shadow stack) or at a random location (for the traditional shadow stack). For the latter case, we copy this location into `%gs:108`.

For C++ programs, we identified which initialization function would run first, by using `gdb`: the function would crash in the prologue, as the instrumentation would attempt to write to an unallocated shadow stack region. We then prepended our own shadow stack class and instance in the same file, thus again ensuring that the shadow stack is set up prior to other function calls.

This means that we cannot instrument the prologue of functions that run before the shadow stack is set up (e.g., `main` and `setupShadowStack` for C programs). It is possible to modify the compiler to create high priority constructor init functions ([48]), but this would not affect the overhead since the uninstrumented functions are only called once.

The SPEC CPU build process compiles and assembles individual source files into separate object files. We wrote a wrapper script to compile each source file, then instrument the prologues (conveniently denoted by gcc as `.cfi_startproc`) and `RET`s in the assembly, before assembling into the expected object file. This simulates the capabilities available (and overhead obtained) of a binary CFI rewriter that has access to the (dis-)assembly but not source code. It is possible, but laborious, to add `setupShadowStack` at the assembly level; we "cheated" by adding it at the source code level, since this would not substantially affect the overhead.

Since we are instrumenting the prologue for ease of implementation, the instrumented prologue has a TOCTTOU vulnerability in the presence of concurrency (e.g., multi-threaded programs). One could avoid the TOCTTOU vulnerability by instrumenting the `CALL` instructions instead of function prologues. We expect this would have similar performance, but we have not implemented it.

7. RESULTS

7.1 Cost of Instrumentation Schemes

The overheads (though not baseline times) from a pilot study were roughly the same for x86 vs x64 and -O2 vs -O3, hence, for brevity, we will only discuss the x86 -O3 results (Figure 9, left), as they are marginally lower, and therefore provide a lower bound.

Two of the programs (`perlbench`, `gcc`) did not work with the traditional shadow stack instrumentation; we suspect it may be related to `fork`ing and our (mis-)use of `%gs:108` to store the shadow stack pointer (i.e., an artifact of our implementation, rather than a fundamental limitation of traditional shadow stacks).[2] To provide a fair comparison with the other schemes, we calculated the overhead of each scheme, with and without these two programs.

On SPEC CPU, excluding Fortran, `perlbench` and `gcc`, the average overhead of each scheme was as follows: a traditional shadow stack cost 9.69% overhead in CPU time; a no-frills parallel shadow stack cost 3.51%; checking the return address cost 0.8% extra, compared to the no-frills parallel shadow stack; zeroing out expired shadow stack entries (for a parallel shadow stack) cost 0.16%; stack canaries cost 2.54%. See the bottom row of Figure 9 for details.

For `apache`, the parallel shadow stack (overwriting, no zeroing out) had 2.73% overhead. Had our test been network bound or I/O bound, we would expect the CPU overhead to be even lower.

Replacing `RET`s with indirect jumps incurs much higher overhead, except for the checking version of the parallel shadow stack, which had comparable overhead. See Figure 9 (right).

8. DISCUSSION

8.1 Determinants of overhead

As a first-order approximation, we expected the overhead of the instrumentation to depend on the frequency of function calls/returns (to avoid collinearity, we only consider `RET`s); while Abadi et al. [7] reported that their overhead was "not simply correlated with the frequency of executed computed control-flow transfers", their CFI instrumentation is much more extensive than a shadow stack. Our hypothesis was supported by the data (correlation coefficient $r = .73$, which is very high). Figure 10 shows the overhead of the parallel shadow stack (overwriting, zeroing out) compared to the frequency of `RET` instructions (from Isen and John [27]). We excluded `dealII` from our analyses, as it is an outlier with 5.3% `RET`s (over twice as many as any other program).

Since our instrumentation uses cache and memory bandwidth, we hypothesized that the overhead would depend on

[2]Interestingly, Mashtizadeh et al. [31] omitted (only) these two benchmarks; they reported that they could not compile them with the vanilla `GCC` or `clang` compilers.

x86, -O3	With RET in epilogues						With indirect jumps instead of RET in epilogues			
			Parallel shadow stack					Parallel shadow stack		
	Baseline	Traditional shadow stack	Checking	Overwriting, zeroing out	Overwriting, no zeroing	-fstack -protector -all	Traditional shadow stack	Checking	Overwriting, zeroing out	Overwriting, no zeroing
400.perlbench	354		9.2%	7.3%	6.7%	4.2%		7.9%	8.6%	5.5%
401.bzip2	585	2.2%	1.9%	1.6%	1.7%	-2.8%	8.2%	2.7%	2.9%	2.5%
403.gcc	300		4.9%	4.5%	4.2%	3.9%		7.8%	9.7%	7.2%
429.mcf	211	6.2%	0.0%	-0.1%	-0.1%	-0.1%	7.6%	-0.1%	1.5%	0.0%
445.gobmk	449	12.7%	5.1%	5.0%	4.0%	5.0%	26.3%	10.5%	10.9%	9.2%
456.hmmer	516	0.2%	0.0%	-0.1%	0.0%	-0.2%	4.3%	-0.1%	0.9%	0.0%
458.sjeng	518	16.9%	5.2%	5.0%	4.4%	2.0%	28.6%	9.8%	8.8%	8.5%
462.libquantum	669	-1.7%	-0.5%	-0.7%	-0.6%	3.7%	0.2%	-1.2%	-0.8%	-1.0%
464.h264ref	716	19.5%	8.7%	6.4%	6.4%	3.2%	23.2%	8.0%	8.2%	5.1%
471.omnetpp	319	25.2%	7.3%	11.0%	9.2%	5.1%	33.7%	6.3%	16.0%	6.3%
473.astar	453	7.2%	3.5%	2.5%	3.9%	0.8%	9.1%	1.2%	2.7%	1.0%
483.xalancbmk	221	33.1%	16.6%	12.5%	13.7%	9.5%	52.5%	19.6%	21.4%	17.6%
433.milc	565	4.6%	1.9%	1.9%	2.2%	1.6%	4.8%	1.0%	2.7%	1.5%
444.namd	513	-0.1%	0.0%	0.0%	0.2%	0.1%	3.1%	-0.1%	0.9%	-0.1%
447.dealII	360	16.2%	9.4%	7.3%	7.0%	5.1%	18.8%	7.5%	5.6%	5.3%
450.soplex	281	0.2%	1.1%	-0.5%	-0.1%	-0.6%	2.1%	0.1%	1.9%	0.4%
453.povray	218	29.3%	13.0%	11.0%	9.7%	10.5%	31.0%	11.6%	11.1%	8.7%
470.lbm	416	0.0%	-0.3%	-0.4%	-1.1%	0.4%	-0.9%	-1.1%	-0.1%	-0.3%
482.sphinx3	471	1.9%	2.5%	1.5%	0.6%	0.8%	7.2%	0.4%	2.8%	3.1%
SPECint: all benchmarks	5312		5.1%	4.5%	4.4%	2.8%		5.9%	7.4%	5.0%
- without perl or gcc	4657	11.6%	4.7%	4.2%	4.2%	2.6%	18.4%	5.5%	7.0%	4.8%
SPECfp: except Fortran	2823	7.0%	3.8%	2.9%	2.6%	2.5%	9.0%	2.7%	3.5%	2.6%
SPEC CPU: except Fortran	8135		4.6%	3.9%	3.7%	2.7%		4.7%	5.9%	4.1%
- and without perl or gcc	7480	9.7%	4.3%	3.7%	3.5%	2.5%	14.4%	4.3%	5.6%	3.9%

Figure 9: Benchmarks for x86, -O3 with RETs (left) or indirect jumps in the epilogues. Highest overheads are in red, and lowest overheads are in green. SPEC overheads are geometric means of individual benchmark overheads.
Overheads are only *estimates*; although we can reliably reproduce these results (minima are mostly within 1% of the medians), they do not meet certain technical requirements for "reportable" SPEC CPU2006 results (e.g., modifying the source files to add the `setupShadowStack` function violates the requirements).

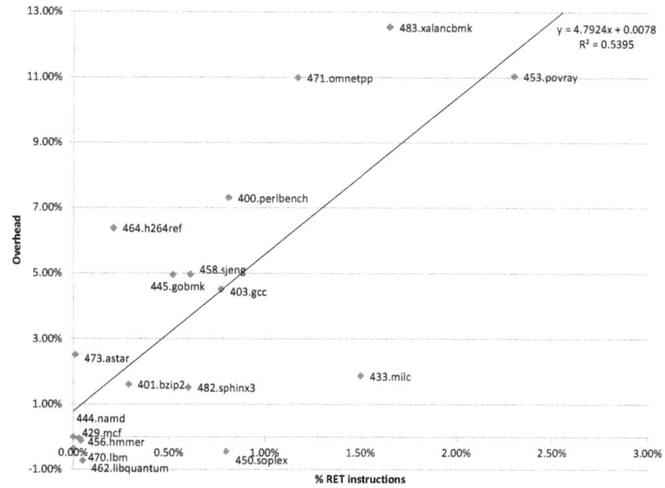

Figure 10: Correlation between the percentage of RET instructions and the overhead.

the percentage of load and store instructions multiplied by the percentage of RET instructions. For example, we would expect that a program with few RET instructions but many load/store instructions would still have low overhead. Using data from Bird et al. [10], a linear regression of the form:

Overhead $= \alpha \times$ (% RETs) $+ \beta \times$ (% RETs $\times$ % loads) $+ \delta \times$ (% RETs $\times$ % stores)

had a correlation of .86. This is a surprisingly high correlation, considering the complexity of modern CPUs.

Interestingly, our regression shows that the percentage of loads has a *negative* coefficient. We interpret this to mean that stores are expensive, but once a value has been stored, it is very cheap to load it due to caching.

Although correlation does not imply causation, we believe simple causality is the most parsimonious explanation.

The traditional shadow stack likely has higher overhead than the parallel shadow stack because of the extra memory transfer instructions needed for additional scratch registers and the shadow stack pointer. This is strongly supported by an experiment where we augmented the parallel shadow stack with those extra instructions: the overhead approached that of the traditional shadow stack.

This model suggests that the overheads of different instrumentation schemes should be correlated with each other: the programs that incur high overhead with one instrumentation scheme, will also tend to incur relatively high overhead on other instrumentation schemes as well. This appears to be supported by our data; for example, `xalancbmk` and `povray` have the highest overheads for every instrumentation scheme. The overhead of the schemes we investigate also appears to be correlated with that of other published shadow stack schemes [20, 54] and instrumentation schemes [40, 54, 55]. Thus, our discussion of avenues for improvement is generalizable to other shadow stack implementations and to CFI.

8.1.1 Omitted Benchmarks

We omitted the Fortran benchmarks due to the engineering effort required, relative to their relevance in a security context. These benchmarks have an extremely low percentage of RET instructions: 6 out of 10 have $\leq 0.02\%$, and the maximum is 0.21%. Our model suggests that shadow stacks will have low overhead on the Fortran benchmarks. Thus, our results overestimate the overhead for SPECfp and SPEC CPU.

We were not able to instrument `perlbench` and `gcc` with a traditional shadow stack. We anticipate their overhead with a traditional shadow stack would be substantial, as 0.81% and 0.77% of their instructions are RETs, respectively. These programs have relatively high overheads when instrumented with the parallel shadow stack or `-fstack-protector-all`.

There are a number of other CFI or shadow stack studies that omit some of the SPEC CPU benchmarks, as we have. However, in some cases, their omitted benchmarks are those which we would predict to be expensive (based on the percentage of RETs, and our own measurements); thus, their omission suggests that their estimate of performance overhead might be overly optimistic.

8.1.2 Indirect Jumps vs RETs

With indirect jumps, the CPU can no longer predict the return address using its internal stack, but there is still dynamic branch prediction for indirect jumps. Our results show that this is noticeably imperfect, implying that the indirect jump has highly variable targets (i.e., the same function is called from multiple locations); this is somewhat similar to BinCFI [55], where its "trampoline" (address translation) routine would "return" (with an indirect jump) to many different functions. This arguably supports the prioritization of performance over TOCTTOU protection, as done by many CFI and shadow stack schemes [55]. In the context of software fault isolation (not a shadow stack), PittSFIeld [33] reported that replacing RETs with indirect jumps increased the overhead on SPECint2000 from 21% to 27%.

8.2 Avenues for improvement

The traditional shadow stack has close to 10% overhead – which is unlikely to be acceptable for widespread deployment [47] – and even a minimalist parallel shadow stack has roughly 3.5% overhead. However, these were obtained by measuring the overhead of (a) **our hand-coded assembly**, for (b) **a traditional shadow stack**, when we instrumented (c) **100%** of (d) **the (intended) RETs normally emitted by the compiler**. We can potentially improve performance by modifying each of those aspects:

(a) Equivalent but faster prologues and epilogues: we already tried many functionally equivalent prologues and epilogues, and even *super-optimization* [32] can provide only limited savings, as the overhead depends in part on the percentage of memory loads and stores, which are mostly unavoidable; for the limited case of leaf functions (those which make no calls), Crypto CFI [31] uses XMM4 (an SSE register) to store the return instruction pointer and frame pointer.
For the traditional shadow stack, we could modify the `setjmp/longjmp` functions or instrument their call sites (as done by Kuznetsov et al. [29] for their dual stacks), to maintain the invariant that the top of the shadow stack is always the correct return address. This means that, rather than using a loop to check the return address, we could use simpler instrumentation similar to the parallel shadow stack (albeit still with another layer of indirection in the form of the shadow stack pointer).

(b) Relaxations or variations of a shadow stack: for example, the parallel shadow stack scheme, a shadow set rather than a shadow stack [18], or monitoring the taintedness of the return address in only the most recent one or two stack frames [28]. All of these, to some extent, trade off some security for performance.

(c) Selectively instrumenting functions: choosing a random subset of functions to instrument would greatly sacrifice security – if we randomly selected $1/n^{th}$ of functions to instrument, then the *expected* overhead is $1/n^{th}$ (even if the function run-times are not uniform). A better choice might be identifying (in-)frequently called functions, using profiling [48]. Alternatively, SecondWrite's [37] return address check optimization omits the shadow stack instrumentation from functions that do not have indexed array writes. They noted that small leaf functions and recursive functions, which benefit the most from this optimization, are also the most frequently called.[3] Crypto CFI [31] also optimizes leaves, instead by storing the return address in a register rather than encrypting.

(d) Reducing the number of `RET`s through inlining (e.g., our use of `-O3`, or with link-time optimization [31])

Although reducing the number of `RET`s or selectively instrumenting functions (chosen appropriately) are valuable contributions, these are orthogonal to improving the prologues/epilogues or relaxations of the shadow stack paradigm. We should beware of conflating the speed of an instrumentation scheme with the advantage gained from a particular optimization: although shadow stack scheme A, run on benchmarks with aggressive inlining, may appear to have lower overhead than shadow stack scheme B, this might be attributable to the inlining rather than the merits of scheme A, in which case the "best" solution would be scheme B with aggressive inlining.

Since software-only shadow stacks are expensive – even with the aforementioned incremental improvements – many authors [16,25,38,52] have proposed hardware shadow-stack support. These are distinct from the return-address stack already present in modern processors for branch prediction [3, 6], which are not secure: if there is a mismatch between them, the hardware reverts to using the main stack. Hardware shadow stack schemes are usually extremely fast, instrument all `RET`s (even unintended `RET`s), and do not require recompilation, but introduce complications for code that intentionally violates `CALL-RET` matching.

Davi et al. [18] proposed a hardware-assisted CFI scheme that includes a shadow *set*; this requires the addition of new labels/instructions to the code. Kao and Wu [28] proposed new registers for the Intel architecture, to store the location of the current return address, and the old value of `%ebp`.

New hardware features that are not security specific can also improve performance. For example, Crypto CFI [31] uses multiple XMM registers. Anecdotally, our parallel shadow stack appears to have lower overhead on a newer processor (a 2011 Intel Core i7-3930K) – perhaps because of an improved stack engine [22]. However, we expect that non-security specific hardware improvements will not significantly change the overheads, since there are the memory load/store costs, and there is little room for improvement with branch prediction (the indirect jumps in the `RET` variants of the shadow stacks are usually not taken, and can be predicted dynamically; the overheads of the indirect jump variants are lower-bounded by the `RET` variants, which have nearly perfect branch prediction).

[3]Unfortunately, the claim of "not sacrificing any protection" is incorrect, e.g., a bufferless function `foo` that calls `bar` could have its return address overwritten by `bar`, if `bar` has a vulnerable indexed array write.

8.3 Deployment issues

The parallel shadow stack variants have lower overhead than the traditional shadow stack, but not sufficiently low that widespread deployment would be an obvious decision. Even faster is `-fstack-protector-all`, but its attractiveness is tempered by its security properties (as per Figure 5). Additionally, `-fstack-protector-all` was applied at the compiler level, though it is possible to add it through binary rewriting (e.g., SecondWrite [37]).

Our implementation is designed only to provide accurate estimates of the overhead of shadow stacks, not shelf-ready code. Nonetheless, some seemingly tricky cases are actually non-issues. For example, tail call elimination does not change the assumption that the top of the stack in the prologue is the expected return address; and the `get-EIP` idiom on x86 still works because we instrument neither the `CALL` nor `POP`. For other corner cases (e.g., exceptions, multi-threading), we defer to Szekeres et al.'s [47] assessment that compatibility issues can be avoided through careful engineering.

8.4 Generalizability

Mytkowicz et al. [34] demonstrated that a narrow set of environment and compilation options etc. may lead to invalid results. Nonetheless, we are confident in our calculated overheads due to 1) the consistency of results across a variety of parameters (x86/x64, `-O2`/`-O3`, ad-hoc tests on a different CPU); 2) the strong correlation of per-program overheads between different instrumentation options, and with the static `RET` instruction counts; 3) other steps in our methodology (e.g., disabling Turbo Boost).

9. RELATED WORK

Table 1 summarizes the overheads reported for various software-based shadow-stack schemes. Many of the papers use an older benchmark suite, SPEC2000; note that SPEC specifically cautions against comparing individual benchmarks between CPU2000 and CPU2006 [2]. We have omitted a number of studies where the shadow stack is a component of a security solution, for which we could not infer the cost of the shadow stack alone [37,40,41].

There are also many hardware assisted schemes [16,26,30, 38,52]; those papers all report low overheads on SPEC2000 (or a subset thereof), when using the SimpleScalar simulator. StackGhost [23] was a proposal for a shadow stack on SPARC. We chose instead to benchmark instrumentation schemes that could be deployed on today's hardware, but hardware support may be a necessary evil.

Ozdoganoglu et al. [38] observed that SPECint programs had higher overhead from instrumentation than SPECfp, which they attributed to the higher call frequencies of the integer benchmarks. They did not calculate a correlation, nor consider the percentage of memory loads and stores.

Table 1: Reported overheads of shadow stacks. Schemes are roughly sorted by the modifications involved.

Reference	Scheme	Modifications	Overhead on macro-benchmarks
Chiueh & Hsu [15]	Shadow stack (checking)	Compiler	Only macro-benchmarks are short-lived programs (0.63s real-time for their `ctags` benchmark, and <5s for `gcc`)
Szekeres et al. [47]	Shadow stack (?)	Compiler (LLVM plugin)	5% on SPEC2006.
Mashtizadeh et al. [31]	Misc	Compiler with ABI changes	45% for leaf-optimized on SPECint 2006[a]. Cost of stand-alone shadow stack is only shown in graph form; as an indication, for `xalancbmk`, it is 2.5x baseline for un-optimized.
Vendicator [49]	Shadow stack (checking)	Assembler file processor	Unknown
Prasad & Chiueh [42]	Shadow stack (checking)	Binary rewriting with trampolines	1-3% overhead on BIND, DHCP server, PowerPoint and Outlook Express.
Baratloo et al. [8]	Shadow stack (checking)	Binary rewriting with trampolines	9.5% for quicksort, which they deemed to be-CPU bound. They also measured imapd (network bound), xv (CPU and video bound), tar (I/O). All execution times were <6s.
Abadi et al. [7]	CFI + shadow stack (overwriting)	Binary rewriting with Vulcan	≫ 5% on SPEC2000 for the shadow stack component; >50% for one benchmark.[b]
Gupta et al. [25]	Shadow stack (checking)	Binary rewriting with trampolines	No macro-benchmarks.
Park et al. [39]	Shadow stacks (checking and overwriting)	Binary rewriting with trampolines	Checking: 2.56% and 2.58% for `bzip2` and `gzip`. Overwriting: 1.56% and 1.7% respectively. Doesn't state whether this is compress or decompress.[c]
Corliss et al. [16]	Shadow stacks (checking)	Binary rewriting	Average not reported, but non-trivial (overheads exceeds 40% for some SPEC2000 benchmarks)
Nebenzahl et al. [35]	Shadow stack (checking)	Binary rewriting with trampolines	4.33% on `bzip2`, 4.36% on `gzip`, and 7.09% on `mcf` from SPEC2000
Davi et al. [20]	Shadow stack (checking)	Pin tool	2.17x for SPECint2006, 1.41x for SPECfp. Run-time of Pin alone is 1.58x and 1.15x respectively.
Sinnadurai et al. [46]	Shadow stack (checking)	DynamicRIO	18.21% for SPECint 2000 on Linux; 24.82% (with compatibility issues) on Windows.
Zhang et al. [54]	General security instrumentation + shadow stack (checking)	PSI	18% overhead on a subset of SPEC2006.

[a] Omitting `gcc` and `perlbench` due to compilation issues

[b] CFI + ID check on returns cost 21%, while CFI + shadow stack (without ID check) cost 16%. But in some benchmarks (e.g., `crafty`), the shadow stack is cheaper than the ID check (roughly 45% vs. 18%). Hence, 5% is grossly underestimating the cost of a shadow stack.

[c] In our own experience, the overhead of instrumented compress is far higher than instrumented decompress.

Corliss et al. [16] assumes that the stack pointer cannot be modified by an attacker. Such a assumption would remove the main weakness of our parallel shadow stack (compared to a traditional shadow stack); however, it is unrealistic given the increasing prevalence of stack pivots [5].

The choice of checking vs. overwriting the return address is similar to the "ensure, don't check" philosophy of SFI schemes [33, 51].

The memory-safety community, besides providing a somewhat heavy-weight solution to data- and control-flow integrity, has extensively studied how to implement *shadow memory*. In the parlance of AddressSanitizer [43], the address mapping used by traditional shadow stacks is similar to a single-level translation, while the parallel shadow stack is a direct offset (without scaling).

An ideal shadow stack would be protected from any writes by the attacker. Chiueh and Hsu's [15] Read-Only RAD accomplishes this through memory protection, albeit at a substantial overhead. Abadi et al.'s [7] protected shadow stack has much lower overhead than Chiueh and Hsu through the use of segmentation (which is not possible on 64-bit) and the security guarantees of CFI, though the overhead is still not trivial ($\gg 5\%$; see Table 1). While our shadow stacks are unprotected, Szekeres et al. [47] observe that even an unprotected shadow stack that *checks* for a match renders an attack "much harder", since an attacker would have to modify the return address in two distinct locations. With a shadow stack that *overwrites* the return address, an attacker would only have to modify the return address stored in the shadow stack, but this is somewhat harder than modifying the copy in the main stack (e.g., a contiguous buffer overflow would not suffice).

Some schemes use two stacks but do not duplicate the return address, hence we do not consider them to be shadow stacks e.g., address space randomization (which uses their "shadow stack" to store buffer-type variables) [9] and XFI [21] (possibly with hardware support [12]). Importantly, due to the change in stack layout, they require significantly more code rewriting than shadow stacks. Xu et al. have separated control and data stacks (essentially a shadow stack approach, but without the return address on the main stack) [52]. Their compiler implementation had up to 23% overhead on one of the SPECint 2000 benchmarks, and non-negligible overheads on most other benchmarks; they did not quote an average overhead. Kuznetsov et al. [29] have a "safe stack" that contains the return address, spilled registers, and other provably safe variables, and a separate unsafe stack. They benefit from improved locality of frequently used variables on the safe stack, thereby incurring negligible overhead on SPEC CPU2006, and can even improve performance in some cases. Dahn et al. [17] and Sidiroglou et al. [45] move stack-allocated buffers to the heap. Some non-x86/x64 architectures, such as Itanium [1], have a separate register stack.

10. CONCLUSION

In this paper we considered the performance costs of using a shadow stack. Our results suggest that a shadow stack, even when pared to its bare minimum (the overwriting, non-zeroing version of the parallel shadow stack), has non-negligible performance overhead, due to increased memory pressure. Achieving low-overhead protection against control-flow attacks will likely require alternative paradigms, such as Code Pointer Separation with their Safe Stack [29] – which unfortunately currently requires recompilation, unlike coarse-grained CFI [53, 55] – or hardware support.

11. ACKNOWLEDGEMENTS

We thank Nicholas Carlini, Mathias Payer, Úlfar Erlingsson and the anonymous reviewers for helpful comments and suggestions. This research was supported by Intel through the ISTC for Secure Computing, by the AFOSR under MURI award FA9550-12-1-0040, and by the National Science Foundation under grant CCF-0424422. We would particularly like to thank Intel for providing access to tetryl.

12. REFERENCES

[1] Itanium(R) Processor Family Performance Advantages: Register Stack Architecture. `https://software.intel.com/en-us/articles/itaniumr-processor-family-performance-advantages-register-stack-architecture`, October 2008.

[2] SPEC CPU2006: Read Me First. `http://www.spec.org/cpu2006/Docs/readme1st.html`, September 2011.

[3] Software Optimization Guide for AMD Family 15h Processors. January 2012.

[4] ARM Information Center. `http://infocenter.arm.com/help/index.jsp?topic=/com.arm.doc.ddi0439d/Chdedegj.html`, September 2013.

[5] Emerging 'Stack Pivoting' Exploits Bypass Common Security. `http://blogs.mcafee.com/mcafee-labs/emerging-stack-pivoting-exploits-bypass-common-security`, May 2013.

[6] Intel(R) 64 and IA-32 Architectures Optimization Reference Manual. March 2014.

[7] M. Abadi, M. Budiu, Ú. Erlingsson, and J. Ligatti. Control-flow integrity principles, implementations, and applications. *TISSEC*, 2009.

[8] A. Baratloo, N. Singh, and T. K. Tsai. Transparent Run-Time Defense Against Stack-Smashing Attacks. In *USENIX ATC*, 2000.

[9] S. Bhatkar, D. C. DuVarney, and R. Sekar. Efficient Techniques for Comprehensive Protection from Memory Error Exploits. In *USENIX Security*, 2005.

[10] S. Bird, A. Phansalkar, L. K. John, A. Mericas, and R. Indukuru. Performance Characterization of SPEC CPU Benchmarks on Intel's Core Microarchitecture Based Processor. In *SPEC Benchmark Workshop*, 2007.

[11] T. Bletsch, X. Jiang, V. W. Freeh, and Z. Liang. Jump-oriented programming: a new class of code-reuse attack. In *CCS*, 2011.

[12] M. Budiu, Ú. Erlingsson, and M. Abadi. Architectural support for software-based protection. In *Proceedings of the 1st workshop on Architectural and system support for improving software dependability*, 2006.

[13] N. Carlini and D. Wagner. ROP is still dangerous: Breaking modern defenses. In *USENIX Security*, 2014.

[14] S. Checkoway, L. Davi, A. Dmitrienko, A.-R. Sadeghi, H. Shacham, and M. Winandy. Return-oriented programming without returns. In *CCS*, 2010.

[15] T.-c. Chiueh and F.-H. Hsu. RAD: A compile-time solution to buffer overflow attacks. In *ICDCS*, 2001.

[16] M. L. Corliss, E. C. Lewis, and A. Roth. Using DISE to protect return addresses from attack. *ACM SIGARCH Computer Architecture News*, 2005.

[17] C. Dahn and S. Mancoridis. Using program transformation to secure C programs against buffer overflows. In *20th Working Conference on Reverse Engineering*, 2003.

[18] L. Davi, P. Koeberl, and A.-R. Sadeghi. Hardware-Assisted Fine-Grained Control-Flow Integrity: Towards Efficient Protection of Embedded Systems Against Software Exploitation. In *DAC*, 2014.

[19] L. Davi, D. Lehmann, A.-R. Sadeghi, and F. Monrose. Stitching the gadgets: On the ineffectiveness of coarse-grained control-flow integrity protection. In *USENIX Security*, 2014.

[20] L. Davi, A.-R. Sadeghi, and M. Winandy. ROPdefender: A detection tool to defend against return-oriented programming attacks. In *CCS*, 2011.

[21] Ú. Erlingsson, M. Abadi, M. Vrable, M. Budiu, and G. C. Necula. XFI: Software guards for system address spaces. In *OSDI*, 2006.

[22] A. Fog. The microarchitecture of Intel, AMD and VIA CPUs. `www.agner.org/optimize/microarchitecture.pdf`, August 2014.

[23] M. Frantzen and M. Shuey. StackGhost: Hardware Facilitated Stack Protection. In *USENIX Security*, 2001.

[24] E. Göktas, E. Athanasopoulos, H. Bos, and G. Portokalidis. Out of control: Overcoming control-flow integrity. In *IEEE S&P*, 2014.

[25] S. Gupta, P. Pratap, H. Saran, and S. Arun-Kumar. Dynamic code instrumentation to detect and recover from return address corruption. In *International workshop on Dynamic systems analysis*, 2006.

[26] K. Inoue. Lock and Unlock: A Data Management Algorithm for A Security-Aware Cache. In *ICECS*, 2006.

[27] C. Isen and L. John. On the object orientedness of c++ programs in spec cpu 2006. In *SPEC Benchmark Workshop*, 2008.

[28] W.-F. Kao and S. F. Wu. Light-weight Hardware Return Address and Stack Frame Tracking to Prevent Function Return Address Attack. In *International Conference on Computational Science and Engineering*.

[29] V. Kuznetsov, L. Szekeres, M. Payer, G. Candea, R. Sekar, and D. Song. Code-Pointer Integrity. In *OSDI*, 2014.

[30] R. B. Lee, D. K. Karig, J. P. McGregor, and Z. Shi. Enlisting hardware architecture to thwart malicious code injection. In *Security in Pervasive Computing*. 2004.

[31] A. J. Mashtizadeh, A. Bittau, D. Mazières, and D. Boneh. Cryptographically enforced control flow integrity. In *arXiv:1408.1451*, 2014.

[32] H. Massalin. Superoptimizer: a look at the smallest program. In *ACM SIGPLAN Notices*, 1987.

[33] S. McCamant and G. Morrisett. Evaluating SFI for a CISC Architecture. In *USENIX Security*, 2006.

[34] T. Mytkowicz, A. Diwan, M. Hauswirth, and P. F. Sweeney. Producing wrong data without doing anything obviously wrong! In *ASPLOS*, 2009.

[35] D. Nebenzahl, M. Sagiv, and A. Wool. Install-time vaccination of Windows executables to defend against stack smashing attacks. *Dependable and Secure Computing, IEEE Transactions on*, 2006.

[36] A. One. Smashing the stack for fun and profit. *Phrack magazine*, 1996.

[37] P. O'Sullivan, K. Anand, A. Kotha, M. Smithson, R. Barua, and A. D. Keromytis. Retrofitting security in COTS software with binary rewriting. In *Future Challenges in Security and Privacy for Academia and Industry*. 2011.

[38] H. Ozdoganoglu, T. Vijaykumar, C. E. Brodley, B. A. Kuperman, and A. Jalote. SmashGuard: A hardware solution to prevent security attacks on the function return address. *Computers, IEEE Transactions on*, 2006.

[39] S.-H. Park, Y.-J. Han, S.-J. Hong, H.-C. Kim, and T.-M. Chung. The dynamic buffer overflow detection and prevention tool for windows executables using binary rewriting. In *The 9th International Conference on Advanced Communication Technology*, 2007.

[40] M. Payer and T. R. Gross. Fine-grained user-space security through virtualization. In *VEE*, 2011.

[41] M. Payer, T. Hartmann, and T. R. Gross. Safe loading-a foundation for secure execution of untrusted programs. In *IEEE S&P*, 2012.

[42] M. Prasad and T.-c. Chiueh. A Binary Rewriting Defense Against Stack based Buffer Overflow Attacks. In *USENIX ATC*, 2003.

[43] K. Serebryany, D. Bruening, A. Potapenko, and D. Vyukov. AddressSanitizer: A Fast Address Sanity Checker. In *USENIX ATC*, 2012.

[44] H. Shacham. The geometry of innocent flesh on the bone: Return-into-libc without function calls (on the x86). In *CCS*, 2007.

[45] S. Sidiroglou, G. Giovanidis, and A. D. Keromytis. A dynamic mechanism for recovering from buffer overflow attacks. In *Information security*. 2005.

[46] S. Sinnadurai, Q. Zhao, and W. fai Wong. Transparent runtime shadow stack: Protection against malicious return address modifications. `http://citeseerx.ist.psu.edu/viewdoc/download?doi=10.1.1.120.5702&rep=rep1&type=pdf`, 2008.

[47] L. Szekeres, M. Payer, T. Wei, and D. Song. SoK: Eternal war in memory. In *IEEE S&P*, 2013.

[48] C. Tice, T. Roeder, P. Collingbourne, S. Checkoway, Ú. Erlingsson, L. Lozano, and G. Pike. Enforcing forward-edge control-flow integrity in gcc & llvm. In *USENIX Security*, 2014.

[49] Vendicator. Stack Shield. `http://www.angelfire.com/sk/stackshield/info.html`, 2000.

[50] P. Wagle and C. Cowan. Stackguard: Simple stack smash protection for gcc. In *GCC Developers Summit*, 2003.

[51] R. Wahbe, S. Lucco, T. E. Anderson, and S. L. Graham. Efficient software-based fault isolation. In *SOSP*, 1993.

[52] J. Xu, Z. Kalbarczyk, S. Patel, and R. K. Iyer. Architecture support for defending against buffer overflow attacks. In *Workshop on Evaluating and Architecting Systems for Dependability*, 2002.

[53] C. Zhang, T. Wei, Z. Chen, L. Duan, L. Szekeres, S. McCamant, D. Song, and W. Zou. Practical control flow integrity and randomization for binary executables. In *IEEE S&P*, 2013.

[54] M. Zhang, R. Qiao, N. Hasabnis, and R. Sekar. A platform for secure static binary instrumentation. In *VEE*, 2014.

[55] M. Zhang and R. Sekar. Control Flow Integrity for COTS Binaries. In *USENIX Security*, 2013.

APPENDIX

A. PEEPHOLE OPTIMIZATIONS

Using our parallel shadow stack instrumentation as an example: Instrumented prologues will often be of the form: `POP 999996(%esp)`; `SUB $4, %esp`; `PUSH %ebp`; `MOV %esp, %ebp`; `SUB <X>, %esp` whereby the last three lines are the standard idiom for functions with frame pointers. We could replace this with `POP 999996(%esp)`; `MOV %ebp, -8(%esp)`; `LEA -8(%esp), %ebp`; `SUB <X+8>, %esp`

In the instrumented epilogue, we could replace `SUB $4, %esp`; `PUSH 999996(%esp)`; `RET` with `SUB $4, %esp`; `JMP 999996(%esp)`.

Instrumented epilogues that have frame pointers but don't use the `LEAVE` instruction will often be of the form: `MOV %ebp, %esp`; `POP %ebp`; `SUB $4, %esp`; `PUSH 999996(%esp)`; `RET` which can be converted into: `LEA 8(%ebp), %esp`; `MOV -8(%esp), %ebp`; `PUSH 999996(%esp)`; `RET`.

Alternatively, we can combine the stack pointer adjustment with the `RET` instruction i.e., `LEAVE etc.`; `SUB $4, %esp`; `PUSH 999996(%esp)`; `RET` is equivalent to: `LEAVE etc.`; `PUSH 1000000(%esp)`; `RET $4`.

The second optimization can be combined with one of the last two.

B. PROLOGUES AND EPILOGUES

- The prologues and epilogues we used are similar to, but not the same as, those described in the Introduction; for details, refer to a forthcoming technical report.
- A parallel shadow stack prologue alternative:

```
XCHGL (%esp), %ecx
MOVL %ecx, -0xb0000000(%esp)
XCHGL (%esp), %ecx
```

- A parallel shadow stack (checking) epilogue alternative:

```
POP %eax
CMPXCHG %esp, -0xa0000004(%esp)
JNZ abort
PUSH %eax
RET

abort:
    HLT
```

- For the traditional shadow stack epilogue, we can omit the comparison with the sentinel value (`CMP $0, (%ecx)`; `JZ empty`). The latter change is secure if we assume that the logical bottom of the shadow stack is filled with zeros (which would not be a useful return address for an attacker) until a page boundary, below which is a guard page. Hence, if no match is found, it will eventually hit the guard page and abort.
- For "zeroing out" (`MOV $0, ...`) the old shadow stack entry, we use `MOV %esp, ...` since it has a shorter instruction encoding. With a non-executable stack, `%esp` is an invalid return address.

I Know Where You are: Proofs of Presence Resilient to Malicious Provers

Markus Miettinen
Technische Universität Darmstadt
markus.miettinen@trust.cased.de

N. Asokan
Aalto University and University of Helsinki
asokan@acm.org

Farinaz Koushanfar
Rice University
farinaz@rice.edu

Thien Duc Nguyen
Technische Universität Darmstadt
ducthien.nguyen@trust.cased.de

Jon Rios
Technische Universität Darmstadt
rios.jon@trust.cased.de

Ahmad-Reza Sadeghi
Technische Universität Darmstadt
ahmad.sadeghi@trust.cased.de

Majid Sobhani
Technische Universität Darmstadt
majid.sobhani@trust.cased.de

Sudha Yellapantula
Rice University
sudha@rice.edu

ABSTRACT

In the recent years, new services and businesses leveraging location-based services (LBS) are rapidly emerging. On the other hand this has raised the incentive of users to cheat about their locations to the service providers for personal benefits. Context-based proofs-of-presence (PoPs) have been proposed as a means to enable verification of users' location claims. However, as we show in this paper, they are vulnerable to *context guessing attacks*. To make PoPs resilient to malicious provers we propose two complementary approaches for making context-based PoPs: one approach focuses on *surprisal filtering* based on estimating the entropy of particular PoPs in order to detect context measurements vulnerable to such attacks. The other approach is based on utilizing longitudinal observations of ambient modalities like noise level and ambient luminosity. It is capable of extracting more entropy from the context to construct PoPs that are hard to guess by an attacker even in situations in which other context sensor modalities fail to provide reliable PoPs.

Categories and Subject Descriptors

K.6.5 [**Management of computing and information systems**]: Security and Protection—*Authentication*; D.4.6 [**Operating Systems**]: Security and Protection—*Access controls*

ASIA CCS'15, April 14–17, 2015, Singapore..

http://dx.doi.org/10.1145/2714576.2714634.

Keywords

co-presence proofs; context-awareness; context guessing attacks

1. INTRODUCTION

Contemporary mobile devices are capable of utilizing a range of positioning technologies such as GPS or network triangulation to find their locations. Therefore, new applications and services leveraging the mobile device's locationing abilities are rapidly emerging. For instance, Facebook and other online social networks (OSNs) extensively utilize location "check-ins" of users to enhance their services; Foursquare [8] uses the location information to connect users to local businesses like shops or restaurants; a number of business owners offer concrete benefits such as free vouchers, special discount, and even cash value to the most active registrants visiting their shops or restaurants.

The LBS business model is built upon the premise of trustworthiness of mobile users. However, as the LBS and businesses are on the rise, so are the clients' incentives to engage in *location cheating* for their personal benefit. Misbehaving users may obtain unjustified benefits at particular venues by repeatedly making false location check-ins. "Fake location" applications that aid the cheating clients are already available for popular smartphone platforms.

A drawback of currently deployed positioning technologies is that they rely on the mobile client to perform the positioning operation. It is difficult for external entities to determine whether the location claimed by a client device is in fact correct. Therefore, there is a need for *location proofs*: methods for verifying the correctness of location claims that clients present to the LBS. In peer-to-peer scenarios, mobile devices may require proofs of co-presence from other devices such that they can control their visibility. For example, a device might want to reveal its presence in a particular location only to those peer devices that are present in the same location [10]. Therefore, the devices need to be able to verify that a location claim made by a peer device indicating proximity is indeed genuine. The peer device is required to present a *proof of co-presence* to establish the validity of their claim. In both cases, we model the situation as follows: a *prover* aims to provide a *proof-of-presence (PoP)* to a *verifier* that they are in the same context, i.e., present in the same proximate environment.

Prior work has suggested two main classes of solutions for constructing PoPs: *beaconing* and *context-based PoPs*. The former class of proofs is based on active beaconing of information by the verifier into its immediate vicinity. The potential provers are then required to capture this information using their on-board sensors (e.g., WiFi or Bluetooth). The beaconed information is utilized by the prover either directly as the proof or in a proof-of-knowledge protocol with the verifier. The underlying presumption of this approach is that only a device actually co-present with the verifier is able to accurately capture the information beaconed by the verifier. In peer-to-peer scenarios, beaconing information into the context has the drawback that the verifier has to reveal its presence in the context. However, revealing presence may be undesirable because of its adverse impact on the verifier's privacy. For example, if beaconing is realized using a WiFi or Bluetooth channel, the verifying device needs to actively emit the beacon information and thus expose its own MAC address.

In this paper, we focus on context-based PoPs. These are based on simultaneous sensing of contextual data by both the verifier and the prover. A number of such methodologies have been proposed [5,10,14–16]. In this setting the prover and verifier concurrently sample their incident context via sensors. The supposition is that the transient contextual fluctuations cannot be exactly sensed or predicted by an attacker outside the context. These measurements are either directly used to generate a common key (e.g., [16]), or the prover sends its measurements to the verifier who compares them to its own measurements. Because of the sensing and synchronization jitters, the measurements often contain noise. If the (noisy) measurements are similar enough, this constitutes a PoP. In the following, we denote such proofs as *context-based proofs of presence*.

Earlier work on context-based PoPs do not consider the possibility of *context-guessing attacks*, either because these are out of scope [15,16], or, they assume that the used context modalities provide sufficient entropy so that attackers are not able to fabricate context-based proofs [10].

Our goal and conttributions: In this paper, we empirically analyze such attacks against commonly used context sensor modalities such as Bluetooth and WiFi, thus demonstrating that for reliable PoPs, the entropy of individual context observations needs to be taken into account also.

We address context guessing attacks by proposing two complementary approaches: First we show how by using *surprisal filtering* we can make sure that only PoPs with sufficient entropy are admitted as valid PoPs. The approach is based on applying data mining methods for profiling the context and estimating the occurrence probability of particular context parameter combinations in them. Second we make use of longitudinal ambient context observations to extract inherent randomness from the context that contains sufficient entropy to make context guessing attacks in most cases impractical. Earlier approaches utilize ambient context data (e.g., [5,15]), in which only momentary snapshots of the context are considered. In contrast, we monitor the context and short-term changes in the context's physical parameters over a longer time period and utilize these changes in the context as a means to extract sufficient entropy to construct a reliable PoP.

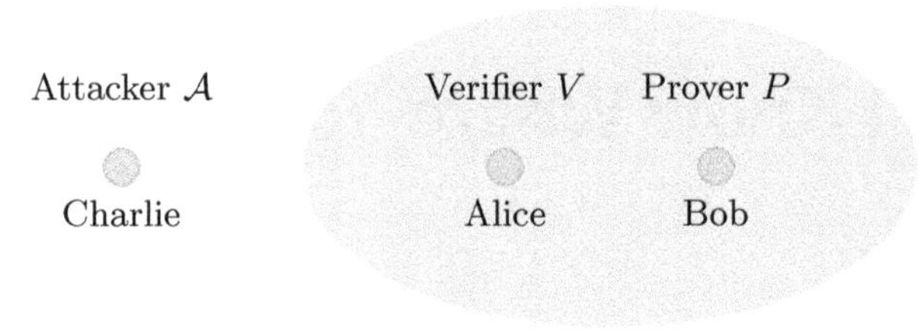

Figure 1: Scenario 1: Peer co-presence

We make the following contributions:

- We empirically analyze the feasibility of *context-guessing attacks* on context modalities that have earlier been used for co-location verification (Bluetooth and WiFi) and show that these modalities are in fact vulnerable to attacks in which a malicious prover fabricates context-based PoPs to cheat about its location.
- We propose two countermeasures to mitigate context-guessing attacks: *surprisal filtering* which is based on profiling and estimating the entropy associated with individual PoPs, and, the use of longitudinal observations of ambient physical properties of the context. We show based on empirical data that surprisal filtering provides an efficient method for identifying potentially too weak PoPs and demonstrate how to use longitudinal context data in such cases to extract sufficient entropy from the context to construct a reliable context-based proof-of-presence.

2. PROBLEM SETTING

Context-based proofs-of-presence play a role in proofs of (co-)presence between peers and proofs of presence at a venue with regard to a Location-Based Service (LBS). Unlike some earlier works that consider the comparison of context information for creating a pairing between the principals (e.g., [16]), we assume that there already exists a security association between the parties. Therefore, we are not considering the threat of man-in-the-middle or eavesdropping attacks in this discussion. We focus on the problem of one party lying about its own context to the other party.

The first scenario is depicted in Fig. 1: Alice, Bob and Charlie are friends in an Online Social Network (OSN). Alice is willing to automatically share her status information or engage in communications, like instant chat with her OSN friends who are present in the same context as she is (i.e., Bob), but not with others (e.g., Charlie). Therefore, Bob needs to prove co-presence to Alice in order to get connected to her.

In the other scenario depicted in Fig. 2, a client of an LBS wants to prove to the LBS its presence at a venue (e.g., a restaurant or a shop) in order to obtain benefits like rebates or gift cards given out to loyal customers of the venue. The LBS cannot rely on unilateral presence claims of the client, since the client has an incentive to cheat in order to obtain the above-mentioned benefits. Independent proof

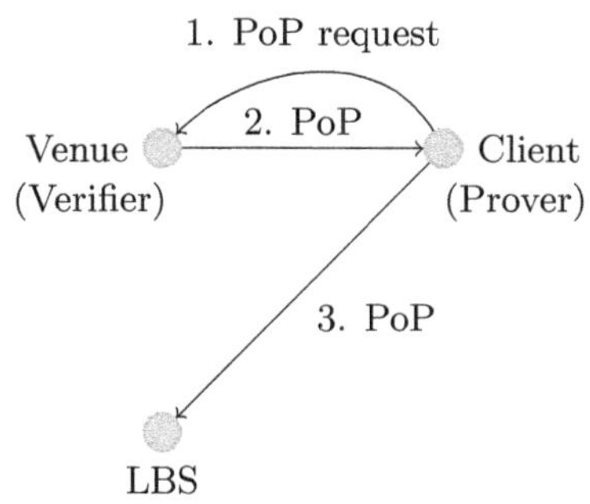

Figure 2: Scenario 2: Presence at a venue

of the client's presence provided by the venue is therefore required.

2.1 Threat model and Assumptions

In both scenarios, the attacker $\mathcal{A}$ is a malicious prover, who *fabricates* a PoP in order to cheat the verifier V into believing that $\mathcal{A}$ is in the same context as V.

In Scenario 1 $\mathcal{A}$ is a malicious user, e.g., Charlie in Fig. 1, who engages in a cyberstalking attack and wants to reveal a target user's (e.g., Alice in Fig. 1) location without actually being co-located with her. To do this, Charlie fabricates location claims for places which he knows Alice is known to visit, and waits for which location Alice responds to his location claim, thereby learning Alice's whereabouts. Alice acts as the verifier V and Charlie as the malicious prover $\mathcal{A}$.

For Scenario 2, $\mathcal{A}$ is a malicious client of the LBS, who wants to do fake location check-ins at a venue for obtaining benefits even though he has not visited the venue in reality. The venue acts as the verifier V. The malicious client $\mathcal{A}$ fabricates PoPs and presents them to the venue V. If V falsely accepts $\mathcal{A}$'s PoP as genuine, it will issue a PoP to $\mathcal{A}$, which $\mathcal{A}$ can then use to falsely convince the LBS to believe that $\mathcal{A}$ has visited the venue in question.

In particular, $\mathcal{A}$ is likely to target such contexts that it can monitor over an extended period of time in order to obtain infromation that is useful for fabricating PoPs. Therefore we have to assume that for any context X, the attacker $\mathcal{A}$ has acquired a rich context profile that it can utilize in maximizing its chances of fabricating a PoP that would be accepted by V.

2.2 Problem Definition

The basic mechanism for providing context-based PoPs which is applicable in the above scenarios is shown in Fig. 3. Both the verifier V and prover P record a context measurement $C_V(t)$ and $C_P(t)$ at time point t. The prover P then sends its context measurement $C_P(t)$ to the verifier V, who compares it with its own context measurement $C_V(t)$ and determines, whether $C_P(t)$ is similar enough to accept it as a proof-of-presence of P. The rationale behind such PoPs is that devices in the same context will observe roughly the same contextual events and environmental conditions and therefore their context measurements will be more similar than context measurements of devices that are not in the same context.

To mitigate the risk of V erroneously accepting PoPs that the attacker $\mathcal{A}$ has fabricated, V needs to be able to evaluate the risk that a particular PoP could be fabricated in

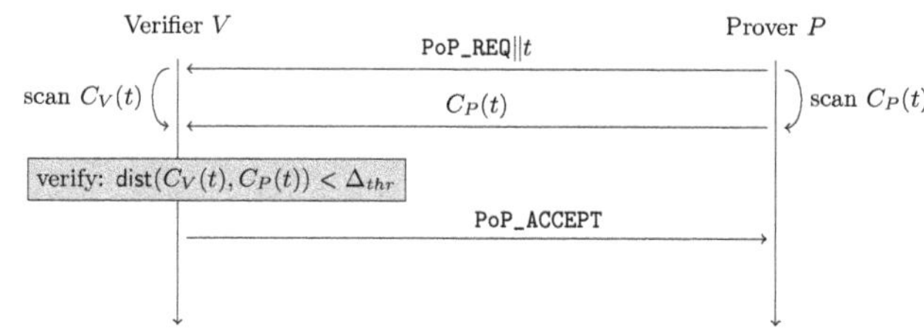

Figure 3: Context-based proof-of-presence

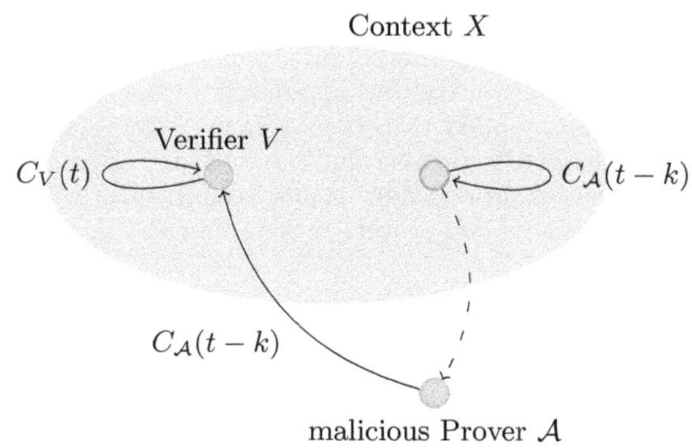

Figure 4: Overview of the context guessing attack

that context. We therefore need a way to determine the entropy of V's context measurements C_V, i.e., how difficult it would be for $\mathcal{A}$ to fabricate a valid $C^*_\mathcal{A}$ such that $\mathsf{dist}(C_V(t), C^*_\mathcal{A}(t)) < \Delta_{thr}$. In addition, to address such cases in which the context measurement of V would be too easily guessed by $\mathcal{A}$, we need to augment the context measurements used in the PoPs with appropriate context modalities that contain sufficient entropy against this guessing attack.

3. CONTEXT GUESSING

A malicious prover $\mathcal{A}$ may try to make the verifier V believe that he is in the V's context X, even though he is located somewhere else, for example to make false location chek-ins at a venue so that he will obtain unjustified benefits from the venue. One way for $\mathcal{A}$ to achieve this is to launch a *context guessing attack*. $\mathcal{A}$ *fabricates* a context measurement $C^*_\mathcal{A}$ and presents it as a context-based PoP to V. If the fabricated measurement is similar enough to V's measurement C_V, i.e., if $\mathsf{dist}(C_V(t), C^*_\mathcal{A}(t)) < \Delta_{thr}$, V will falsely accept it as a valid PoP.

For example, when executing the attack at timepoint t, as shown in Fig. 4, $\mathcal{A}$ can replay an old context measurement $C_\mathcal{A}(t-k)$ it obtained while visiting context X at an earlier timepoint $t-k$, claiming it to be his current context measurement. The attack will succeed, if $C_\mathcal{A}(t-k)$ is similar enough to the verifier's measurement $C_V(t)$. Alternatively, $\mathcal{A}$ could also fabricate the context measurement $C^*_\mathcal{A}$ by building a model of the context X by using several *earlier* measurements $C_\mathcal{A}$ made in the target context X.

In earlier works, context-based co-location verification has been based on direct measurements of contextual values in different modalities. For example, the acoustic environment [5, 15], ambient light [5], atmospheric gases, temperature, humidity and air pressure [14], as well as WiFi [16],

Bluetooth and GPS [15], have been investigated as modalities for contextual proofs of presence.

In their recent work, Truong et al. have found that the sets of WiFi and Bluetooth devices observed in a particular context along with their received signal strengths provide good performance in co-location verification [15]. We therefore decided to investigate WiFi and Bluetooth as the basic modalities for PoPs and tested whether PoPs based on Bluetooth or WiFi are vulnerable to the context guessing attack. The authors of [15] kindly provided us the dataset they used for their experiments so that we could make a direct comparison with their results. Note, however, that their usage scenario relates to zero-interaction authentication (ZIA) settings, where the attack model is different: their co-location verification is intended to protect against relay attacks in a setting where the prover and the verifier can mutually trust each other. In contrast, in our scenario the potential attacker is a malicious prover, rather than the threat of a relay attack.

3.1 Attack Implementation

In our implementation, V uses a classification model to distinguish between co-located and non-co-located context measurements. V trains his classification model with a benign dataset containing examples of co-located and non-co-located measurement pairs. To test the model's performance against context guessing attacks, we construct an attack dataset where benign verifier V measurements are paired by measurements that could have been fabricated by $\mathcal{A}$ by replaying all measurements from the same context that were made 6 to 24 hours earlier.

From the measurement pairs, V calculates a set of features that represent different distance measures between the measurements and combines them to feature vectors. Feature vectors calculated based on the benign dataset are used to train the classification model, whereas features from the attack dataset are used as testing data to evaluate the classifier's performance against the context guessing attack. The classification algorithm used is Multiboost in combination with J48 Graft as the base learner. We used the Weka data mining suite [6] to execute our experiments.

For training the classifier we used the following features:

FEATURE 1 (JACCARD DISTANCE).

$$J_\delta(C_V, C_P) = 1 - \frac{\|C_V \cap C_P\|}{\|C_V \cup C_P\|}, \quad (1)$$

FEATURE 2 (MEAN OF HAMMING DISTANCE).

$$H_\delta(C_V, C_P) = \frac{\sum_{i=1,2,\ldots,n} |m_i^P - m_i^V|}{n} \quad (2)$$

FEATURE 3 (EUCLIDEAN DISTANCE).

$$E_\delta(C_V, C_P) = \sqrt{\sum_{i=1,2,\ldots,n} (m_i^P - m_i^V)^2} \quad (3)$$

FEATURE 4 (MEAN EXPONENTIAL OF DIFFERENCE).

$$\Xi_\delta(C_V, C_P) = \frac{\sum_{i=1,2,\ldots,n} e^{|m_i^P - m_i^V|}}{n} \quad (4)$$

where $m_i^V \in C_V$ and $m_i^P \in C_P$ denote the individual elements of the context measurements of the verifier V and prover P, respectively.

FEATURE 5 (SUM OF SQUARED RANK DIFFERENCES).

$$\rho_\delta(C_V, C_P) = \sum_{i=1}^{|C_V \cap C_P|} (rank(m_i^P) - rank(m_i^V))^2 \quad (5)$$

where $rank(m_i^P)$ and $rank(m_i^V)$ denote the ranks of m_i^P and m_i^V in C_P and C_V, respectively, sorted in ascending order.

3.2 Datasets

To evaluate the feasibility of context guessing attacks, we used two datasets: the zero-interaction authentication dataset by Truong et al., and the *ConXPoP dataset*, which we collected to test context guessing attacks and countermeasures against it. The ZIA dataset was primarily used to demonstrate the feasibility of the attack, whereas the ConXPoP dataset contains more context modalities and an explicit context labeling which we used to examine possible countermeasures against the context guessing attack.

ZIA Dataset used in [15] contained measurements of the MAC addresses of visible Bluetooth devices and WiFi access points and their received signal strengths, simultaneously collected from two devices. The dataset contained a total of 2302 sample pairs, out of which 1140 were such that the devices were co-located, and 1162 pairs were samples from non-co-located devices. We used this dataset to derive features to train the benign dataset for training the classification model of the verifier V. As a baseline, we examined the classifier's performance on the benign dataset using 10-fold cross-validation, and could corroborate the results of [15], obtaining a false positive (FP) rate of 2.5 % for Bluetooth features and 1.6 % for WiFi features.

The attack dataset simulating context replay attacks was constructed by remapping the experiments in ZIA dataset by pairing measurements that were made in the same location, but at different times. The ZIA dataset contained ground truth labels telling whether measurement pairs were co-located or not, but the actual location in which the measurements had been made was not included in the dataset. Therefore we had to use the set of observed WiFi access points associated with each measurement as representing the location in which the measurement had been made.

To obtain a criterion by which to decide whether measurements made at different times were made at the same location, we compared the co-located measurement pairs to the non-co-located ones in the ZIA dataset and observed that a Jaccard distance value of 0.9 for the sets of observed WiFi devices provided a good separation between co-located and non-co-located measurement pairs. We therefore concluded that if the Jaccard distance of two measurements is less than 0.9, we can assume that these measurements were made in the same location.

We then paired each experiment measurement with such measurements for which the Jaccard distance between the sets of WiFi measurements was below 0.9, i.e., that were made in the same location, but at a different time.

ConXPoP Dataset data collection was done using a purpose-built app running on Android smartphones given out to study participants. The app continuously measured contextual parameters and periodically uploaded them to a server for off-line data analysis. The collected data included link layer identifiers and observed signal strengths for WiFi and Bluetooth devices in proximity (sampled once a minute), as well as a continuous trace of the ambient noise level and luminosity, as observed by the smartphone's sensors.

Participants included volunteers from the research lab staff sharing nearby offices and visiting the same lunchtime restaurant. This enabled the participants to provide a rich dataset of co-located measurements arising from natural everyday situations.

All participants were informed in writing about the purpose, goals and content of the data collection campaign beforehand. Participants were free to stop or interrupt data collection at any point by disabling the data collection app. All participants were also given the possibility to revoke their participation in the experiment by demanding the data collected by them to be deleted.

Participants were asked to provide, via the user interface of the app, information about particular contexts that they were visiting (e.g., Home, Office, Restaurant, etc.) and which other participant devices were co-located with the user's own context collector device. Devices of other participants were identified using easily recognizable nicknames. Participants were asked to mark only such other devices as co-located that were likely to be present in the same room with the user for the following two minutes.

Furthermore, in order to obtain examples of co-located observations from contexts where typically only one test participant is present (e.g. the test participants' homes), each test participant was provided with two context collector devices: a main device and an "alter ego" device. By bringing the alter ego device together with the main device to contexts that no other test participants visited, users could provide co-located context samples also from such contexts.

During a data collection period of 10 days, participants generated a total of 5602 annotated co-located context measurement pairs. Using these data, we constructed for each participant a benign dataset and an attack dataset. The benign dataset for training each user's co-location classifier was constructed by pairing measurement pairs marked as being co-located by the user or some other user with a roughly equal amount of measurement pairs that were not marked as co-located.

The attack dataset was constructed by letting one participant at a time act as the verifier V. For each verifier observation $C_V(t)$ made in a named context X (where $X \in$ {"Home", "Office", "Restaurant"}), potential attacker observations $C_{\mathcal{A}}(t-k)$ made in the same context X were selected allowing all participants to take the role of the malicious prover $\mathcal{A}$. We selected k to be 6 to 24 hours.

3.3 Results

We evaluated both the ZIA dataset and the ConXPoP dataset by training classifiers with the benign datasets and using the attack datasets as testing datasets. As a baseline to compare against, we used 10-fold cross-validation of the training dataset. Table 1 shows the results.

The differences of the attack scenarios to the benign dataset results are clear, showing the effect of the context guessing attack. For both ZIA and ConXPoP attack datasets, the FP rate increases significantly in comparison to the benign dataset results. This difference is especially clear for the ZIA dataset. For the ConXPoP dataset, the change is somewhat smaller, due to the higher FP rate in the benign dataset. This is caused by the more challenging experimental setup in comparison to the ZIA dataset. Whereas in the ZIA

Table 1: Results of the context guessing attacks

	FP Rate		
Dataset	BT	WiFi	BT+WiFi
ZIA benign	2.5%		
ConXPoP benign	14.2%	11.0%	9.3%
ZIA attack	35.1%		
Increase in FP rate	+32.6%		
ConXPoP attack	21.9%	26.0 %	23.5%
Increase in FP rate	+7.7%	+15.0%	+14.2%

dataset, co-located and non-co-located samples were more clearly separated from eachother, the ConXPoP set up was more ambiguous. The criterion for co-location was that we regard any devices in the same room to be co-located, other devices not[1]. However, in the office context, test participants used office rooms next to one another, so that their devices were not co-located according to the above criterion, but still the devices shared some common WiFi and Bluetooth environment. This makes it more difficult for the classifier to make a clear distinction between co-located and non-co-located observations, resulting in a higher False Positive rate also in the benign dataset.

However, we see that for both datasets, the context guessing attack yields a False Positive rate of 22% to 35%[2]. This gives an attacker a chance of at least one out of five to succeed in a context replay attack, showing that in settings where the prover cannot be trusted by the verifier, context measurements alone cannot provide the basis for a reliable proof of presence. The verifier needs also to have the possibility to assess how large the risk of a guessing attack associated with a PoP is.

4. HARDENING CONTEXT-BASED PROOFS

We introduce two countermeasures for hardening context-based proofs-of-presence against context guessing attacks. The first countermeasure aims at identifying such PoPs that are potentially easy to guess. We do this by estimating the entropy associated with a particular PoP. This estimation is based on the notion of *surprisal*, i.e., the self-information associated with a particular context observation of the verifier. The notion of surprisal is closely related to entropy but with a difference: surprisal is the uncertainty associated with the *particular outcome* of a random variable, whereas entropy measures the *average* uncertainty associated with a random variable.

In our case, we consider the observed context X of V as a random variable O_X taking particular measured context observations C_V as its value. The surprisal associated with a context measurement C_V is therefore a measure for the uncertainty of that particular outcome of the random variable. We utilize this and use surprisal-based filtering to dismiss such PoPs that can be potentially easily guessed by the attacker $\mathcal{A}$, as described below in Sect. 4.1.

[1]This criterion for co-location was selected, since for providing ground truth information, participants needed to be able to visually observe any co-located persons and their associated devices.

[2]We do not report the false positive rates for WiFi for the ZIA dataset, since we use the WiFi observations in the attack dataset as ground truth for identifying measurements made in the same context.

The other countermeasure we propose aims at increasing the entropy of PoPs in order to make context guessing infeasible for the attacker. In contrast to earlier approaches for co-location verification [5, 13, 15, 16], where short momentary snapshots of the context were used to determine co-location, we use a longitudinal approach. By observing the context over a longer time period and observing changes in the context's ambient properties like luminosity and audio, we aim at extracting sufficient entropy from the context to make guessing of the context impractical. This approach is explained in Sect. 4.2.

4.1 Surprisal Filtering

Surprisal filtering is based on estimating how easy it would be for $\mathcal{A}$ to fabricate a PoP $C^*_{\mathcal{A}}$ that is similar enough to V's context measurement C_V to be accepted as genuine. The estimate is based on profiling V's contexts and utilising the profiled information to estimate the occurrence probabilities of individual context measurements C_V in a context X. Our intuition is that the lower the occurrence probability of a context measurement C is, the more difficult it is for an attacker $\mathcal{A}$ to fabricate the measurement, even if he has monitored the context X earlier. Based on the probability estimate of the proof, V can then reject such proofs, for which the risk of fabrication is high.

More formally, we define surprisal filtering as a function $\varsigma : \mathcal{C} \times \mathcal{X} \rightarrow \{accept, reject\}$, where $\mathcal{C}$ denotes the domain of context measurements and $\mathcal{X}$ the set of V's known contexts. The surprisal filtering function ς maps a context measurement $C \in \mathcal{C}$ observed in a particular context $X \in \mathcal{X}$ to a filtering decision *accept* or *reject* based on the surprisal value $I_X(C)$ of the measurement in V's context X:

$$\varsigma(C, X) = \begin{cases} accept & I_X(C) \geq I_{thr} \\ reject & \text{otherwise} \end{cases} \quad (6)$$

We describe the calculation of the surprisal value $I_X(C)$ in Sect. 4.1.1. The rationale for this defense is the following: Information representing a context is of two types. Static information, such as the link layer addresses of WiFi access points in an office, has a high probability of appearing in measurements taken in that context at any time. Therefore, an attacker who has previously visited that context is likely to be able to fabricate a context measurement containing such static information even when he is not present in the context. Dynamic context information, such as the Bluetooth link layer addresses of smartphones belonging to customers at a shop, is likely to be volatile and thus harder to predict. Naturally, contexts with more dynamic information are more amenable for reliable context-based PoPs. In the following, we describe a way to measure the 'dynamicity' of the information present in a context at a given time and show how it can be used to enhance protection against context guessing attacks.

4.1.1 Surprisal of Context Measurements

To be able to identify PoPs that are too easy to fabricate, we need to measure how difficult it would be for an attacker to guess a context measurement $C_{\mathcal{A}}$ based on the history of observations in the target context X. Since we are assuming a strong attacker model, we have to assume that the attacker $\mathcal{A}$ has equal opportunity to observe and generate a context profile on X as the target V has, and use this profile to fabricate PoPs that are likely to be observed in X.

To obtain optimal results, $\mathcal{A}$ needs to guess the correct context measurement C_V of V. The difficulty of fabricating a PoP $C^*_{\mathcal{A}}$ that is accepted by V is therefore dependent on the difficulty of guessing C_V.

We model the occurrence of a specific contextual measurement C (e.g., a set of WiFi or Bluetooth (BT) devices) in context X with the random variable O_X. The probability that a context measurement C is observed in context X is therefore $P(O_X = C)$. The *surprisal* associated with this context measurement is the *self-information* of this outcome.

DEFINITION 1. *The* surprisal *associated with a context observation C in context X is the self-information of this measurement*

$$I_X(C) = log_2(\frac{1}{P(O_X = C)}) = -log_2(P(O_X = C)) \quad (7)$$

and is measured in bits.

For example, if there is a 50% chance of observing a device d_i in context X, i.e. $C = \{d_i\}$, then the self-information related to an observation of d_i in X is $I_X(C = \{d_i\}) = -log_2(P(O_X = \{d_i\})) = -log_2(0.5) = 1$ bit.

In order to calculate the surprisal associated with a measurement C, we need to estimate the probability $P(O_X = C)$. To do this, we adopt a frequentist interpretation of probability and calculate the probability of context measurment C in context X as the fraction of the number of times that C has been observed in X. Hereby, we need to distinguish between measurements that consist of a single contextual event and multi-event measurements consisting of several co-occurring contextual events. In the following, we consider the occurrence of Bluetooth and WiFi devices in the context as contextual events d_i.

Single-Event Measurements. In the case that the measurement consists of a single contextual event d, i.e., $C = \{d\}$, the calculation of surprisal of C is straightforward. We can calculate the estimated probability of the event as the fraction of measurements containing this event within the whole observation history database $\mathcal{H}_X$ for context X.

$$C = \{d\} : P(O_X = C) = \frac{\|\{C_i \in \mathcal{H}_X \,|\, d \in C_i\}\|}{\|\mathcal{H}_X\|} \quad (8)$$

Multi-Event Measurements. For context measurements containing more than one contextual event, the formulation is slightly more complicated. We cannot merely multiply the probabilities of the individual events, since in reality, the events might be highly correlated with one another, and assuming independence could therefore significantly over- or underestimate the true probability of event combinations. Therefore, we need to estimate the probability of a multi-event context measurement through its occurrence frequency in the observation history database. Thus, given a context measurement $C = \{d_1, d_2, \ldots, d_n\}$ that consists of several context elements, the occurrence probability of C can be calculated as

$$P(O_X = C) = \frac{\|\{C_i \in \mathcal{H}_X \,|\forall d_i \in C : d_i \in C_i\}\|}{\|\mathcal{H}_X\|} \quad (9)$$

As an example, let us consider context measurements of Bluetooth devices. Let us assume that we have a total of

$n = 100$ context measurements of context X in the context history database $\mathcal{H}_X$. Each measurement represents the set of Bluetooth devices observed in context X during a time window of two minutes. In the observation history, device A has been observed in 55 measurements and device B in 35 measurements. Out of these measurements, 15 are such that both A and B occur in the same measurement. Let us now consider the probability estimates for different context measurements. For individual measurements of the devices A and B, we have $P(O_X = \{A\}) = \frac{\|\{C_i \in \mathcal{H}_X \mid A \in C_i\}\|}{\|\mathcal{H}_X\|} = \frac{55}{100} = 0.55$ and $P(O_X = \{B\}) = \frac{\|\{C_i \in \mathcal{H}_X \mid B \in C_i\}\|}{\|\mathcal{H}_X\|} = \frac{35}{100} = 0.35$. For a measurement containing both devices, the estimate is $P(O_X = \{A, B\}) = \frac{\|\{C_i \in \mathcal{H}_X \mid B \in C_i \wedge A \in C_i\}\|}{\|\mathcal{H}_X\|} = \frac{15}{100} = 0.15$.

Given these measurements, we can calculate the surprisal values for these measurements $I_X(\{A\}) = -log(0.55) \approx 0.86$ bits, $I_X(\{B\}) = -log(0.35) \approx 1.51$ bits, and, $I_X(\{A, B\}) = -log(0.15) \approx 2.74$ bits.

To estimate the probability of a multi-event measurement $C = \{d_1, d_2, \ldots, d_n\}$ in a context X in practice, we need to identify the occurrence probability of the combination of events in C occurring in context X. We do this by calculating the event combination's occurrence probability in the observation history database $\mathcal{H}_X$. This is a problem that has been extensively studied in the data mining literature in the context of *frequent itemset mining*. For example, the *Apriori* algorithm [1] constructs the set of frequent itemsets, i.e., combinations of items occurring more frequently than a given threshold value in a given input database and their occurrence counts. Also any other data mining algorithms for mining frequent itemsets could be used. Apriori requires as input a transaction database and a frequency threshold. It returns the set of frequent itemsets in the transaction database with regard to the frequency threshold and the occurrence counts of these frequent itemsets. We utilise this and use the Apriori algorithm to calculate the frequent event combinations observed in each context and their occurrence counts by invoking the algorithm on the context observation history database $\mathcal{H}_X$. We thus denote the set of frequent event combinations in context X for frequency threshold $f \in [0, 1]$ with $D_X(f)$, where $D_X(f) = Apriori(\mathcal{H}_X, f)$.

Given $D_X(f)$, we can calculate a lower bound for the surprisal of any measurement C using equation 7

$$P(O_X = C) = \begin{cases} \dfrac{C.count}{\|\mathcal{H}_X\|}, & \text{if } C \in D_X(f) \quad (10) \\ f, & \text{otherwise.} \quad (11) \end{cases}$$

where $C.count$ denotes the occurrence count of C in the history database $\mathcal{H}_X$ of context X.

This estimate is a lower bound, since for measurements not in the set of frequent event combinations, we do not have the exact occurrence count information (Apriori returns this information only for the frequent combinations). We only know that this occurrence frequency is smaller than f. Therefore, we take f as the upper bound for the occurrence probability of the measurement.

4.1.2 Evaluation

In order to evaluate the effectiveness of surprisal filtering against context guessing attacks, we determined separately for each user's context X the sets of frequently occurring Bluetooth and WiFi devices in the ConXPoP dataset using the Apriori algorithm as well as their occurrence frequencies. Using the patterns' occurrence frequencies, we calculated their corresponding surprisal values and filtered the classification results in the attack datasets by matching the measurements against the patterns and removing any such measurements whose matching pattern fell below the surprisal threshold. We then evaluated the impact of surprisal filtering on the False Positive and False Negative rates. The results are shown in Table 2.

Table 2: Improvement in FP rates when applying surprisal filtering on attack datasets

User	Unfiltered FP Rate	Improvement for $I_{thr} = n$ bits: BT, n=2 bits	WiFi, n=2 bits	BT, n=4 bits	WiFi, n=4 bits
A	13.0%	-6.1%	-2.0%	-8.9%	-2.8%
B	37.8%	-27.2%	-5.4%	-31.1%	-5.6%
C	37.2%	-0.3%	-4.9%	-0.3%	-5.3%
D	21.4%	-17.4%	-0.0%	-19.4%	-0.0%
E	16.2%	-11.6%	-7.6%	-13.8%	-10.0%
F	40.5%	-23.8%	-7.7%	-26.8%	-9.5%
Avg	27.7%	-14.4%	-4.6%	-16.7%	-5.5%
Relative change		-52.0%	-16.6%	-60.4%	-20.0%

As can be seen from the results, the filtering of PoPs based on their surprisal value reduces the FP rate of the attack scenarios by 52% to 60% for Bluetooth and 17% to 20% for WiFi, depending on the selected minimal surprisal threshold, thereby significantly reducing an attacker's odds for a successful context guessing attack.

4.2 Longitudinal Ambient Modalities

While surprisal filtering effectively reduces false positives, our evaluation reveals that unfortunately, the False Negative (FN) rate also increases, especially in the Home contexts from 1.1% to 28.6% for WiFi-based and 55.0% for Bluetooth-based filtering on the average. This is understandable, since the device set-up in these contexts is usually quite static and the inherent entropy of the Bluetooth and WiFi environment therefore does not support the creation of effective PoPs based on these context modalities. We therefore introduce a complementary approach for handling PoPs in contexts that provide low surprisal in the context using the basic PoP schemes introduced above. In the following we show how longitudinal observations of ambient noise and luminosity can be used to construct PoPs that are hard to guess, even in contexts where the device set-up with respect to Bluetooth and WiFi devices is too static to provide valid proofs using the basic approach.

4.2.1 Ambient Light

Most smartphone devices today are equipped with a luminosity sensor, primarily used for adjusting the brightness of the smartphone's display in different lighting conditions. Sensor information about ambient luminosity is therefore readily available. The luminosity sensor does not consume much energy, making continuous tracking of ambient luminosity feasible.

Halevi et al. [5] investigated the use of ambient light for co-location verification for trusted end devices. However, they only consider the mean lighting level recorded by the devices during a short snapshot and conclude co-presence, if the average lighting levels do not deviate too much from one another. Such a simple scheme is obviously vulnerable to a malicious prover $\mathcal{A}$, who profiles the lighting conditions in a target context beforehand. For a context guessing attack, he just needs to replay the average lighting level in the target context as his fabricated measurement and he will succeed with high likelihood.

Therefore, we adopt a more sophisticated scheme. We do not consider only the average lighting level in the context, but focus on the relative changes in the lighting conditions over a slightly longer period of time, e.g., one minute. Our intuition is that such changes often arise from random events like human activity in the context and are therefore difficult to predict.

4.2.2 Ambient Noise Level

The use of ambient noise for the purpose of co-location verification has been investigated in the literature [5, 15]. Halevi et al. used time- and time-frequency-based similarity measures between two short 1-second audio snapshots, whereas Truong et al. [15] used similar measures but 10-second snaphots. In contrast to these approaches we take a slightly different approach and focus on the changes in the ambient noise level over a longer period of time, e.g., one minute. Here also, our intuition is that changes in ambient noise are likely to result from human activity (e.g., people talking), which is very difficult to predict for a malicous prover $\mathcal{A}$.

For the purpose of context-based PoPs, we take the following approach: when the prover P requests a PoP, the verifier V and prover P record a snapshot $M = \{m_1, m_2, \ldots, m_n\}$, where the measurements m_i denote average readings of luminosity or ambient noise level, depending on the modality used, during subsequent time windows of width w. In practice, we propose to use windows of width $w = 1$ sec and to use snapshots of one minute, i.e., $n = 60$. We think that one minute is a long enough time period to capture enough changes in the context, while short enough to allow practical PoPs to be executed with modest delays. Since in practice many applications will execute PoPs asynchronosly and semi-automatically in the background, a delay of one minute should not present a big problem for user interaction. For example, an on-line social networking app might execute the PoP in the background after the user "checks in" in a particular location after arriving there, without requiring the user to wait for the completion of the protocol. Only in the case that the PoP fails, the user might get an error notification that the check-in failed.

Similar to the approach with WiFi and Bluetooth, we calculate the mean Hamming distance, the euclidean distance, and the mean exponential of difference (Features 2- 5 in Sect. 3) between the snapshots M_V and M_P of the verifier V and prover P.

We also introduce an additional feature for luminosity and audio measurements, the maximum cross-correlation between the measurement snapshots.

FEATURE 6 (MAXIMUM CROSS-CORRELATION).

$$M_{corr}(M_V, M_P) = \max\{cross - correlation(M_V, M_P)\} \tag{12}$$

Since the placement of the sensors of a mobile device in a context plays a significant role on the intensity of the light and audio measurements these sensors pick up, two co-located devices might record measurements at significantly different signal levels. For our scheme this is, however, not a problem, since we are primarily interested in the changes in the context values and not the absolute readings as such. We therefore scale the context snapshots M_V and M_P by applying a min-max scaling so that all scaled measurements assume values between 0 and 100.

Similarly to the approach taken in Section 3, we use the obtained distance measures calculated from the benign dataset to train a classification model for co-location for making predictions about whether a prover P's context measurement is co-located with the verifier V or not.

Table 3: PoPs utilizing audio and luminosity modalities

Classifier features	FP rate	FN rate
Benign dataset		
Luminosity	20.1%	14.3%
Audio	19.2%	16.0%
Luminosity+Audio	9.3%	9.2%
BT	16.1%	9.8%
WiFi	11.0%	9.9%
BT + WiFi	9.3%	6.4%
Luminosity+Audio+BT+WiFi	4.2%	2.4%
Attack dataset		
Luminosity	1.1%	0.0%
Audio	0.4%	0.0%
Luminosity+Audio	0.4%	0.0%
BT	21.9%	0.0%
WiFi	26.0%	0.0%
BT + WiFi	23.5%	0.0%
Luminosity+Audio+BT+WiFi	3.6%	0.0%

4.2.3 Evaluation Results

To evaluate the effectiveness of using longitudinal measurements of luminosity and audio as context modalities for PoP, we added features 2 - 6 calulated based on luminosity and audio to the WiFi and Bluetooth-based features we used for the co-location classifier in the basic PoP scheme. We then evaluated the effectiveness of different feature combinations on the benign and attack datasets. Table 3 shows the results for the ConXPoP dataset (The ZIA dataset did not contain luminosity nor audio measurements).

As can be seen, adding audio and luminosity as PoP features significantly decreases the False Positive rates for both the benign and attack datasets' classification results. Especially for the attack dataset, the luminosity and audio context modalities clearly outperform PoPs based on WiFi and Bluetooth. This significantly impacts the attacker's ability to succeed in context guessing attacks.

5. DISCUSSION

Our results show that in scenarios in which the prover can not be trusted, context guessing attacks pose a serious problem for contextual proofs-of-presence for some context modalities like WiFi or Bluetooth observations. However, by profiling the user's contexts and using the surprisal of a contextual PoP as a filtering criterion, we can to some degree mitigate this threat. The impact of the countermeasure on the acceptance of benign PoPs is, however, dependent on the type of context. In contexts with only little dynamic context information (e.g., a person's home) it is challenging to conduct valid PoPs with a sufficient surprisal. However, many contexts that are relevant for our usage scenarios are typically public in nature (e.g., restaurants or shops) and contain significant amounts of dynamic context information. The lack of surprisal in some context modalities can be encountered by extending PoPs to further ambient context modalities providing more entropy. As we showed in Sect. 4.2, the addition of luminosity and audio to the PoP modalities provide good performance against context guessing attacks.

It seems therefore likely that constructing PoPs with sufficient surprisal in most contexts is feasible. In our future work we intend to investigate this issue further. In situations in which ambient context entropy is not sufficient (e.g., in a dark and silent room during the night), PoPs can be still feasible by combining the context-based and beaconing-based PoP approaches. Our currently ongoing research regarding the use of ambient context sensor modalities indicate, e.g., that beaconing-based PoPs using the visible light channel are feasible. They require, however active user involvement, which limits the applicability to such use cases, in which the user is actively involved, e.g., making a location chek-in.

In contrast to other earlier works utilizing audio measurements for co-location proofs [5, 15], our approach has considerable privacy advantages since the PoP utilizes ambient noise level and not the actual fine-grained audio signals. Therefore, the prover P does not need to transmit potentially sensitive audio recordings to the verifier V in order to obtain a proof-of-presence. This is important especially in the peer-to-peer scenario, in which all users can assume both the role of a prover P and a verifier V.

5.1 Limitations

Relay attacks pose a fundamental problem for proof-of-presence schemes, and to the best of our knowledge, only distance-bounding based techniques (cf., e.g., [7]) are able to provide an effective protection against such attacks. However, the drawback of distance bounding is, that it requires special high-accuracy hardware that is typically not available on regular mobile devices.

For our application scenarios, relay attacks would not seem to pose a major problem for economic reasons. For instance, in the peer-to-peer scenario, it would be prohibitively complex and costly for a malicious prover to place an accomplice in all possible contexts that a targeted user visits. In LBS scenarios it might be conceivable that some malicious clients could be motivated to stage targeted relay attacks against selected venues. However, also here the usage of several different contextual modalities for PoPs significantly raises the complexity and cost of the attack for a potential attacker and especially his possible accomplices. A simple replaying of PoP protocol messages by the attacker's accomplice would not be sufficient, but the accomplice would need to actively participate in sensing the context of the verifier in several different context modalities.

6. RELATED WORK

Closely related to our work are the papers by Truong et al. [15] and Shrestha et al. [14]. They use direct measurements of elements of the ambient context for determining the co-presence of two devices in a zero-interaction authentication scenario. However, they assume both endpoints of the scenario to be trusted. The context guessing attack is therefore not applicable to their scenario.

The concept of using context-profiling for evaluating contexts for security enforcement has been discussed by Gupta et al. [4]. Their work focuses on estimating the threat level in a particular context for the purpose of making access control decisions. Our work, takes a different viewpoint: we estimate the occurrence probability of a particular context measurement in view of the observation history, in order to estimate the threat of a guessing attack.

6.1 Beaconing-based Proofs of Presence

Saroiu and Wolman [12] hypothesize six different LBS-based scenarios, in which users of the LBS might have an incentive to engage in location cheating. To tackle such scenarios, they propose a simple protocol for providing location proofs based on beaconing of information over the WiFi SSID of dedicated access points (APs) installed at the target venue. The proof of presence is based on the fact that only devices in the access point's proximity will be able to receive these beacon signals. Our solution, however, is not dependent on dedicated APs.

Another approach based on beaconing of information into the context is the SMILE framework of Manweiler et al. [9], which allows users to establish proofs of co-location after an encounter that took place between the users. It is based on users' devices beaconing cryptographic keys into the proximity of their device and recording keys beaconed by other devices. Later the devices are able to rediscover each other with the help of a third-party server. Contrary to our approach, SMILE requires the use of a central server and requires all devices to engage simultaneously in beaconing and scanning of the context, potentially impacting the privacy of users by making their devices traceable across different contexts. Carbunar et al. [3] present a scheme for privacy-preserving Geo-Social Network logins. They utilize mix networks and a protocol involving blind signatures to provide *GeoBadges*, i.e., anonymous proofs of repeated visits to a specific venue. Their system relies on dedicated hardware at the venues, like display changing QR codes used for location verification. Polakis et al. [11] present a similar scheme for location proofs, which relies on the use of temporary codes which a location-based service can verify. These codes are transmitted over NFC to client devices. The use of NFC as a close proximity protocol thus acts as the proof of co-location.

6.2 Context-based Proofs of Presence

Varshavsky et al. [16] describe a system for co-location verification. They combine Diffie-Hellman key agreement with profiling of WiFi packets for verification of co-location. They compare the received signal strengths of the received packets on a WiFi network in common for both parties. If these are similar enough, the peers are determined to be co-located. According to their paper, the protection of this scheme arises from the fact that fluctuations in the RF environment are unpredictable and spatially limited. Devices located close to each other will be able to observe such fluctuations, whereas devices that are farther away from each other will not be able to do so. However, due to this same property, the prover and verifier need to be located relatively close to each other in order for their approach to work, limiting its practical applicability. Most real-world scenarios, in which peers are in the same room (e.g., Alice and Bob at the same restaurant), but not in immediate proximity would not be feasible using their approach.

Narayanan et al. [10] present three alternative asymmetric protocols for principals to test for proximity in a privacy-preserving manner. Their solutions are based on Private Equality Testing and Private Threshold Set Intersection. They also utilise *location tags* obtained by the principals from ambient information in the context. They discuss location tags derived from WiFi broadcast packets, WiFi access point IDs, Bluetooth devices, GPS signals, GSM radio features, audio fingerprinting, and, even atmospheric gases, but present practical analysis only for the WiFi broadcast packet-based solution. They estimated that using the address fields, the packet sequence numbers and packet payload, one could obtain roughly 10 bits of entropy from each broadcast protocol. Their approach, however, has some practical limitations, which they also acknowledge. Firstly, the prover and verifier need to agree on using the same WiFi access point and both be able to connect to it. Therefore, the method is not applicable in situations in which no access points are available, or, access to the AP is password protected. The ability to generate location tags is also heavily dependent on the traffic patterns of the WiFi access points. On more low-traffic networks like residential private access points, acquiring a sufficient number of packets during a reasonable time frame might actually be challenging. The work by Varshavsky et al. [16] suffers from similar limitations. Also, in some jurisdictions, it is legally prohibited to intercept packets from foreign networks without proper authorisation or explicit permission of the network's operator.

6.3 Distance-Bounding Based Approaches

Hu et al. [7] investigated the problem of proximity verification in the context of mobile ad-hoc networks as a defence against *wormhole attacks*. They proposed to use a *distance bounding* approach in order to verify an upper limit on the distance to a node in the network. The distance bounding approach, however, requires the ability to make timing measurements with a very high accuracy and is usually not possible without special hardware. Distance bounding is therefore usually not feasible on regular mobile devices. Also Polakis et al. [11] and Carbunar et al. [2] proposed the use of distance-bounding in their schemes in order to protect against relay attacks. This attack is feasible for our scenario, but not very relevant, since the attacker would need to instrument all target contexts with a relaying node. Given the vast amount of different contexts that an attacker would want to target, this would be clearly uneconomical for the vast majority of potential attackers.

7. SUMMARY

We show that *context-guessing attacks* can impact context-based proofs-of-presence in scenarios where a verifier cannot fully trust the prover. The feasibility of such attacks is shown on traces of Bluetooth and Wifi mobile data. To alleviate context guessing, a methodology based on the *surprisal* related to context measurements is designed and formalized. The effectiveness of this mitigation methodology is demonstrated on measurements collected from mobile phones. Our work also shows that in case there is insufficient entropy to encounter the context guessing, such attacks can be further thwarted by adding ambient context modalities to the PoP which is experimented using measurements of ambient luminosity and noise levels.

Acknowledgments

This work was supported in part by the Intel Collaborative Research Institute for Secure Computing (ICRI-SC) and the Academy of Finland "Contextual Security" project (274951).

8. REFERENCES

[1] Rakesh Agrawal, Heikki Mannila, Ramakrishnan Srikant, Hannu Toivonen, A Inkeri Verkamo, et al. Fast discovery of association rules. *Advances in knowledge discovery and data mining*, 12(1):307–328, 1996.

[2] B. Carbunar and R. Potharaju. You unlocked the mt. everest badge on foursquare! countering location fraud in geosocial networks. In *Mobile Adhoc and Sensor Systems (MASS), 2012 IEEE 9th International Conference on*, pages 182–190, 2012.

[3] Bogdan Carbunar, Radu Sion, Rahul Potharaju, and Moussa Ehsan. The shy mayor: Private badges in geosocial networks. In Feng Bao, Pierangela Samarati, and Jianying Zhou, editors, *Applied Cryptography and Network Security*, volume 7341 of *Lecture Notes in Computer Science*, pages 436–454. Springer Berlin Heidelberg, 2012.

[4] Aditi Gupta, Markus Miettinen, N. Asokan, and Marcin Nagy. Intuitive security policy configuration in mobile devices using context profiling. In *International Conference on Privacy, Security, Risk and Trust (PASSAT), and 2012 International Confernece on Social Computing (SocialCom)*, pages 471–480, September 2012.

[5] Tzipora Halevi, Di Ma, Nitesh Saxena, and Tuo Xiang. Secure proximity detection for nfc devices based on ambient sensor data. In Sara Foresti, Moti Yung, and Fabio Martinelli, editors, *Computer Security ESORICS 2012*, volume 7459 of *Lecture Notes in Computer Science*, pages 379–396. Springer Berlin Heidelberg, 2012.

[6] Mark Hall, Eibe Frank, Geoffrey Holmes, Bernhard Pfahringer, Peter Reutemann, and Ian H. Witten. The weka data mining software: an update. *SIGKDD Explor. Newsl.*, 11(1):10–18, November 2009.

[7] Yih-Chun Hu, A. Perrig, and D.B. Johnson. Packet leashes: a defense against wormhole attacks in wireless networks. In *INFOCOM 2003. Twenty-Second Annual Joint Conference of the IEEE Computer and Communications. IEEE Societies*, volume 3, pages 1976–1986 vol.3, 2003.

[8] Foursquare Labs Inc. foursquare.com. (online, last referenced [2014-07-24]).

[9] Justin Manweiler, Ryan Scudellari, and Landon P. Cox. Smile: Encounter-based trust for mobile social services. In *Proceedings of the 16th ACM Conference on Computer and Communications Security*, CCS '09, pages 246–255, New York, NY, USA, 2009. ACM.

[10] Arvind Narayanan, Narendran Thiagarajan, Mugdha Lakhani, Michael Hamburg, and Dan Boneh. Location privacy via private proximity testing. In *NDSS*, 2011.

[11] Iasonas Polakis, Stamatis Volanis, Elias Athanasopoulos, and Evangelos P. Markatos. The man

who was there: Validating check-ins in location-based services. In *Proceedings of the 29th Annual Computer Security Applications Conference*, ACSAC '13, pages 19–28, New York, NY, USA, 2013. ACM.

[12] Stefan Saroiu and Alec Wolman. Enabling new mobile applications with location proofs. In *Proceedings of the 10th Workshop on Mobile Computing Systems and Applications*, HotMobile '09, pages 3:1–3:6, New York, NY, USA, 2009. ACM.

[13] D. Schürmann and S. Sigg. Secure communication based on ambient audio. *Mobile Computing, IEEE Transactions on*, 12(2):358–370, Feb 2013.

[14] Babins Shrestha, Nitesh Saxena, Hien Thi Thu Truong, and N Asokan. Drone to the rescue: Relay-resilient authentication using ambient multi-sensing. In *Proc. Eighteenth International Conference on Financial Cryptography and Data Security*, 2014.

[15] Hien Thi Thu Truong, Xiang Gao, Babins Shrestha, Nitesh Saxena, N Asokan, and Petteri Nurmi. Comparing and fusing different sensor modalities for relay attack resistance in zero-interaction authentication. In *IEEE International Conference on Pervasive Computing and Communications, PerCom*, 2014.

[16] Alex Varshavsky, Adin Scannell, Anthony LaMarca, and Eyal Lara. Amigo: Proximity-based authentication of mobile devices. In John Krumm, GregoryD. Abowd, Aruna Seneviratne, and Thomas Strang, editors, *UbiComp 2007: Ubiquitous Computing*, volume 4717 of *Lecture Notes in Computer Science*, pages 253–270. Springer Berlin Heidelberg, 2007.

Bittersweet ADB: Attacks and Defenses

Sungjae Hwang
KAIST
sjhwang87@kaist.ac.kr

Sungho Lee
KAIST
eshaj@kaist.ac.kr

Yongdae Kim
KAIST
yongdaek@kaist.ac.kr

Sukyoung Ryu
KAIST
sryu.cs@kaist.ac.kr

ABSTRACT

Android devices and applications become prevalent and ask for unanticipated capabilities thanks to the increased interests in smartphones and web applications. As a way to use the capabilities not directly available to ordinary users, applications have used Android Debug Bridge (ADB), a command line tool to communicate with Android devices for debugging purposes. While ADB provides powerful features that require permissions to use critical system resources, it opens a gate to adversaries.

To understand the ADB capabilities and their possible risks, we present various types of attacks that are not easily identifiable using ADB capabilities and device-specific functions. We show that applications using ADB capabilities can modify installed applications, leak private user data, and track phone calls, among other things only with the INTERNET permission on the same device. To protect Android devices from such attacks, we present several mitigation mechanisms including a static analysis tool that analyzes Android applications to detect possible attacks using ADB capabilities. Such a tool can aid application markets such as Google Play to check third-party applications for possible attacks.

Categories and Subject Descriptors

K.6.5 [**Software**]: Security and Protection

General Terms

Security

Keywords

Mobile application; Android; security; ADB

1. INTRODUCTION

The advent of explosive interests in smartphones and web applications [25] have dramatically increased the number of Android applications with unanticipated capabilities [2]. Because Android mobile devices can provide powerful features once provided only by computers, Android developers are extending the application categories to areas limited only by their imagination. At the same time, Android applications access private user data stored in devices to perform security sensitive services such as mobile banking and emails, which makes the security of mobile devices tremendously important. Indeed, attackers become much interested in Android applications leading to a huge number of malicious Android applications [24].

Among various malicious Android applications, a recent Windows malware that attempted to infect Android devices to steal private data uses Android Debug Bridge (ADB) [8] as its main tool [19]. ADB is a command line tool to communicate with Android devices for application developers to debug their programs under development. Even though ADB is originally only for debugging purposes, the powerful features of ADB have attracted application developers to build applications with ADB-level capabilities. ADB provides sweet capabilities to draw users' attention but, at the same time, it opens a gate to adversaries.

To understand possible security risks by exposing ADB capabilities to adversaries, we analyzed ADB capabilities and found that they are very much powerful enough to enable various critical attacks. As a proof of concept, we developed malicious applications that leverage ADB using only the INTERNET permission on the same device. The malicious applications can steal private user data and lauch Dos and overbilling attacks as well. Because the malware requires only the INTERNET permission, it is highly likely that ordinary users cannot identify them as malware.

To defend the Android system from such attacks using ADB capabilities, we present several mitigation mechanisms. We first propose a static analysis tool that analyzes Android applications before executing or even before uploading to detect possible attacks using ADB capabilities. Such a tool can aid application markets such as Google Play to check third-party applications for possible attacks. We also describe ways to control uses of ADB capabilities to only authorized parties or debugging purposes.

This paper makes the following contributions:

- We analyze the ADB capabilities to understand possible security risks of exposing them to adversaries. To our surprise, using ADB completely bypasses Android access control policies with just the INTERNET permission.
- As a proof of concept, we develop malicious applications to concretely show possible attacks on Android applications by leveraging ADB and Android utilities.
- We present mitigation mechanisms to protect the Android system against attacks using ADB capabilities. We develop a static analysis tool that detects such attacks automatically and discuss feasible ways to guide the Android system from such attacks.

ASIA CCS '15, April 14–17, 2015, Singapore

http://dx.doi.org/10.1145/2714576.2714638.

2. ANDROID DEBUG BRIDGE

ADB is a command-line tool that enables Android application developers to communicate with connected Android devices. The comprehensive description of ADB and its features is available from the Android developers' site [8]. ADB consists of three components: a client running on a development machine, a server running as a background process on the development machine, and a daemon running as a background process on a device. When an ADB client starts, it starts an ADB server process if it does not already exist, and it binds to a local TCP port and listens for commands from ADB clients. Thus, arbitrary third-party Android applications can establish local connections to devices and access ADB capabilities via the ADB server. Indeed, various kinds of Android applications in Google Play utilize the ADB server. Screenshot [16, 26], USB tethering [5], and Remote shell [11] are such applications. Since Android 4.4 that introduced the `screenrecord` command to record the display of devices, more screen recording applications have been developed [14, 12].

Even though ADB is useful for developers to debug their applications under development, it may introduce critical security vulnerabilities. Because the connections between clients and the ADB server are not using any authentication, malware can access the ADB sever like other ordinary applications. Lin *et al.* [18] demonstrated that an Android malware can access ADB utilities by using the local-socket channel. They also showed that a malware can steal users' private data by using the screenshot capability in ADB.

To lessen possible security risks by abusing ADB, Android 4.2.2 or higher protects user devices by displaying a dialog that asks to allow debugging via a computer when a user connects an Android device to the computer. While this security mechanism guarantees that USB debugging and ADB capabilities can execute only when users approve their uses, it is not a firm solution because it delegates security decisions to ordinary users. Moreover, since such a dialog merely asks whether to accept an RSA key without any security warnings, it is very difficult for ordinary users to understand what the RSA key is for and how risky ADB capabilities are.

We have carefully analyzed the capabilities of ADB, and we found that they are surprisingly powerful. While they provide sweet features for Android developers to support advanced functionalities, they make the security of Android applications bitterly vulnerable. Before describing and showing what kinds of attacks are possible using the ADB capabilities and proposing defense mechanisms to such attacks, we briefly explain the ADB capabilities.

The Android system provides various functionalities such as viewing system logs and modifying installed applications to authorized users as binary files stored in the `/system/bin` directory. In this paper, we call such functions *utilities*. While the Linux system also contains utilities in the `/bin` directory, the Android system contains powerful utilities which do not exist in the Ubuntu system. For example, unlike Android, Ubuntu 12.04.01 does not provide any screenrecord utility in the directory. Note that Ubuntu also has a screen recording utility, but it does not provide it by default; a user should explicitly download and install it to the system. Therefore, we believe that Android provides unnecessary powerful utilities that increases security risks.

Because utilities are powerful functions, the system protects them by requiring that only users with the UID or GID of ROOT and SHELL can access them. However, since ADB has the SHELL UID, it can access most of such utilities and by leveraging ADB many resources with permissions which applications do not have are accessible to arbitrary third-party applications. Thus, malicious applications can also access the utilities via the exposed ADB capabilities.

3. ATTACKS USING ADB

We describe malicious applications that can perform various critical attacks using the ADB capabilities.

3.1 Threat Model

We assume that our malware is installed on a victim's mobile device. Because our malware requires only the INTERNET permission, it is difficult for ordinary users to identify it as malware. Indeed, even though Google Play uses the service named Bouncer [20], which analyzes submitted Android applications to detect potentially malicious applications, it could not detect our submitted malware that use ADB capabilities and successfully uploaded it. Note that our fake malware does not send private user data to our server; it merely sends bogus values to our server. Thus, it did not leak any private user data from anyone happened to download it. We also assume that our malware can access the ADB server. While the ADB server is disabled by default, many legitimate Android applications require enabling the ADB server to access unauthorized resources. Various screen capture applications via ADB have been downloaded millions times already [18]. Other applications also use unauthorized resources via the ADB server, which implies that our assumptions are realistic. If any such applications are installed on a mobile device, the ADB server should be already running.

3.2 Enabling the ADB Server

We assume that our malware can access the ADB server, which is reasonable because many legitimate Android applications require enabling the ADB server to access unauthorized resources.

In order to enable the ADB server, an Android device should enable the "USB debugging" option which requires several steps. However, we can simulate these steps to enable the option just with two taps using a UI redressing attack [21]. First, by executing a "Development Setting" activity with an intent set to the option `ACTION_APPLICATION_DEVELOPMENT_SETTINGS`, our malware can navigate to "Developer options". Then, the malware displays a toast [9] in full screen to hide the "Development Setting" activity. Because toasts pass touch events to lower layers unlike other dialogs, we can trick users to touch screen on the toast leading to touch events on the hidden "Development Setting" activity. Our malware asks users to touch two buttons on the toast to enable the "USB debugging" option. To understand whether this attack is effective, we evaluated the UI redressing attacks on several smartphones including Samsung Galaxy S5, LG G2, and LG G Pro, and we found that all the devices are vulnerable to the UI redressing attacks allowing us to enable the "USB debugging" option.

3.3 Representative Attacks Using ADB

In this section, we present three kinds of attacks we created to show the powerful features of the ADB server. The first kind is the *private data leakage* attacks that expose personal data to outside devices, the second kind is the *usage monitoring* attacks that track various usage information, and the third one is the *behavior interference* attacks that prevent intended operations. Because all attacks require only the INTERNET permission to communicate with the ADB server, most of them are background attacks that run silently on devices, and even foreground attacks are not easily discoverable because the attacks can take place very shortly when users do not see the screen, it is difficult for ordinary users to notice them.

3.3.1 Private Data Leakage

Even though the Android system protects private user data in devices by checking application permissions, it is not enough to prohibit private data leakage as we illustrate in this section.

Message Tracking.

While Android requires applications have the RECEIVE_SMS or READ_SMS permissions to access messages like SMS, MMS, and internal messages from the Android system, applications with only the INTERNET permission can access such messages via ADB. Note that most messenger applications, mail clients, and SNS applications like Facebook notify incoming messages to users through *notification bars*. Because the dumpsys utility provides system data including notification information, the malware can read all the messages from notification bars.

Call Tracking.

In the Android system, in order for an application to get notified of phone-call actions, it should register as a broadcast receiver for the actions. For example, if an application registers as a broadcast receiver with the NEW_OUTGOING_CALL action, when an outgoing call event occurs, the Android system broadcasts the event, which notifies the event to the receivers registered with the NEW_OUTGOING_CALL action. However, our malware can catch call actions without registering as a receiver. Using the dumpstate utility via ADB, it can log all the call information by periodically collecting broadcast intents and by choosing only the intents with the call-related actions. Note that because not only making calls but also sending messages, sending emails, pressing the camera button, and more actions can trigger broadcasting intents, similar approaches would be applicable to track such actions.

Private Database Access.

While Android allows applications to use private databases without sharing them with other applications, our malware can access private databases of other applications using ADB and the run-as utility. The run-as utility changes the current UID and GID to those of a specified application. As the UID and GID are changed to the specified application, malware can have the same permissions as the specified application, and thus it is able to access the private database of the specified application. Even though the run-as utility works for debuggable applications only, debuggable applications are not insignificant. We have collected 8,870 applications from Google Play from February 2013 to August 2013, and we found that 269 applications are debuggable. Due to these security issues, Google Play rejects debuggable applications from November 2013, but debuggable applications already uploaded to Google Play are still available to users unless they have been updated. Moreover, other Android markets than Google Play still accept debuggable applications for uploading.

SIM Information Leakage.

Most smartphones require the SIM card information to connect to and communicate with networks, and SIM card contains a variety of private data such as a phone number, IMSI (International Mobile Subscriber Identity), ICCID (Integrated Circuit Card Identifier), IMEI (International Mobile Equipment Identity), and SPN (Service Provider Name). Because adversaries can utilize phone numbers to infer user identities, the Android system requires applications have the android.permission.READ_PHONE_STATE permission to obtain phone numbers. Also, adversaries have shown various attacks that impersonate users by using the IMSI information [17]. However, our malware can obtain the SIM information by using the dumpstate utility via ADB even when it does not have the READ_PHONE_STATE permission. Because the dumpstate utility provides the SIM information without asking for a user's confirmation, adversaries can perform the attacks silently.

3.3.2 Usage Monitoring

The Android system and applications keep several logs for debugging or other purposes. A kernel driver called "logger" [1] in the Android system records the main application logs, system event information, phone-related information, and low-level system messages, which contains most usage information. Even though the logs are inaccessible by user applications in general, our malware can access them via ADB. We show only two attacks that monitor network packets and users' key events in this section but other usage information is also accessible via ADB.

Packet Dump.

Because data exchanges of mobile devices over network contain users' usage information and they may also contain sensitive information, dumping 3G/4G data packets is not possible unless phones are rooted. If adversaries can dump data packets, they can steal credential data and they can also track users' private activities such as webpage visits. To our surprise, we found that some smartphones provide powerful capabilities including network packet dumps in a hidden menu. Using the ADB server with the input utility, our malware can access the hidden menu and leverage hidden functions there even without rooting devices. The "Packet log" function in the hidden menu is disabled by default but once it is enabled, it captures all the exchanging packets. Such captured packets are stored in SD Card and adversaries can retrieve them even without the required READ_EXTERNAL_STORAGE permission.

Keystroke Logging.

When a user touches the screen of a mobile device, a key event occurs including the key action and the location of the touched point. If an application running in background silently monitors all the key events occurring on a device, it can steal credential information without being noticed by users. Zhou *et al.* [29] developed a touch screen keylogger by reading the Linux input driver files such as /dev/input/event3. This attack is no longer possible as this vulnerability has been patched. However, by leveraging the getevent utility via ADB, our malware can read input driver files.

3.3.3 Behavior Interference

We presented attacks that do not interfere with the functionalities of applications so far, and now we describe attacks that abuse devices like modifying applications and locking screens.

Overbilling.

While applications must have the SEND_SMS and CALL_PHONE permissions to make phone calls and SMS, respectively, our malware can perform an overbilling attack by using the am and input utilities via ADB. First, the malware launches a system application to send an SMS by issuing the following command:

```
am start -a android.intent.action.SENDTO
         -d sms:<Phone Number>
         --es sms_body "<SMS Text>"
         --ez exit_on_sent true
```

which starts an SMS activity with a receiver's phone number and an SMS content. Then, it issues the following commands in order:

```
input keyevent 22; input keyevent 66;
input keyevent 3
```

where the first moves the current focus to a Send button, the second presses the button, and the third changes the current screen to the home screen. Similarly for MMS, the malware can also make extra billing by making many phone calls .

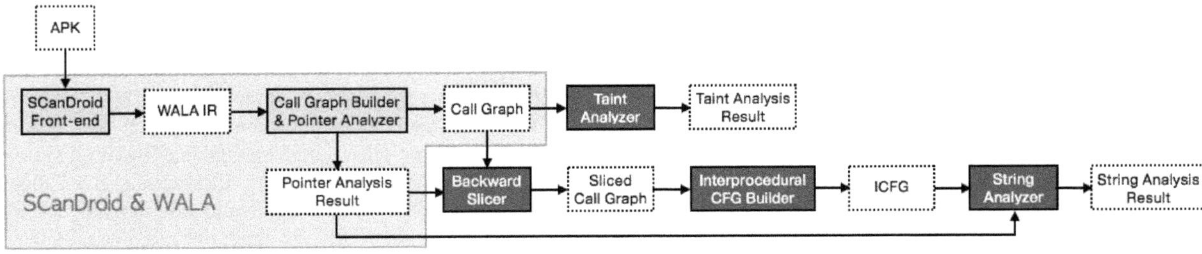

Figure 1: Static analyzer that detects malicious applications using ADB

Application Modification.

The Android system protects applications by requiring developers sign the applications with their private keys. Therefore, only the developers of the applications should be able to modify them for updates, and updates should be the only way to modify installed applications. Of course, the Android system should reject any modification to applications without the corresponding private keys. However, by using the `pm` utility via ADB, our malware can replace installed applications with fake applications without notifying users. For example, the malware can first uninstall the original Facebook application and re-installs a fake Facebook application that contains malicious functionalities. Once the fake Facebook application is installed on a mobile devices, various private data such as a list of friends and messages exchanged via the Facebook messenger can be leaked via the fake application.

DoS Attack.

We can make a variety of DoS attacks on Android using ADB, and here we present two such attacks: target application killing and screen resizing. By using the `wm` utility via ADB, our malware can repeatedly kill target applications. First, the malware checks whether a target application is installed on a mobile device by using the `PackageManager` class. If the target application is installed on the device, it keeps killing the application every 5 seconds to prevent users from using it. Also, our malware can modify the screen size of a device using the `wm` utility via ADB as follows:

```
wm size <Width> X <Height>
```

By setting screen sizes too small or big, the malware can prohibit users from using their devices. Note that no methods can restore screen sizes and even rebooting devices cannot restore the sizes.

4. DEFENSES AGAINST ATTACKS USING ADB

In this section, we present mitigation mechanisms to protect the Android system against attacks using ADB capabilities.

4.1 Defense without Changes to Android

As a mitigation mechanism that does not require any changes to Android, we propose a static analysis to detect possible attacks using ADB capabilities. Based on our analysis of Android applications, we identified representative attack patterns using ADB as illustrated in the attacks described in the previous section. To automatically identify such attacks, we designed and developed a static analyzer that performs a *string analysis* and a *taint analysis* as presented in Figure 1. After describing the high-level architecture of the static analyzer, we present each of its components in detail.

Static Analyzer Overview.

The main purpose of the static analyzer is to extract a set of commands sent to the ADB server by a string analysis, and to check whether the private data resulted from performing such ADB commands are delivered to outside of Android devices via socket APIs. We built the analyzer on top of the state-of-the-art analysis frameworks, WALA [13] and SCanDroid [7]. Our analyzer uses the front-end of SCanDroid to take an APK file consisting of Dalvik bytecode as its input and to translate it to WALA Intermediate Representation (IR). Then, it performs base analyses like a "class hierarchy analysis" and a "pointer analysis" using the WALA analysis capabilities to aid our main malware detection analysis.

Backward Slicing.

Before the main string analysis, our analyzer first performs backward slicing to reduce the size of its analysis target. If we can extract a subset of an input program that contributes to some target variables at a program point under consideration, analyzing the subset would be more efficient and precise than the entire program.

While a traditional backward slicing technique works quite well for tracking primitive values, tracking the values of string objects as in our analysis is not trivial. Because a string object has a character array, backward slicing of string objects requires backward slicing of array objects, which tracks the construction sites of array themselves instead of their elements. To perform a backward slicing of array elements as well, we extended the traditional backward slicing with modeling of methods in `String` and `StringBuilder` classes. When the backward slicing encounters methods that create values for character array elements, it keeps track the flows for array elements by using the modeling behavior.

Furthermore, for Android 3.0 and higher, network operations should execute in different threads from the main thread [10]. While the backward slicing works well for single threaded programs as being extensively used for Java program analyses [27], it may not be suitable for multi-threaded code like Android applications [25].

When a backward slicing for single threads cannot track data flows in a given thread, we extend the backward slicing to consider data flows in other multiple threads. Using the pointer analysis result from WALA, it first collects all the possible objects that target variables may have and collect the instructions that assign values to the target variables in any threads. Performing such an inter-thread slicing repeatedly until it reaches a fixed point achieves a backward slicing considering communications between multiple threads.

String Analysis.

The string analysis takes an ICFG built by the backward slicing as its input and estimates a set of possible string values for the parameters of `write`. To address the asynchronous communications between multiple threads, it performs two string analyses: a flow-insensitive analysis for threads not using network operations and a flow-sensitive analysis for threads using network operations. In order to over-approximate string values on a shared memory between multiple threads, it first performs a flow-insensitive string analysis to estimate possible values of the variables on the shared memory.

Then, using the analysis results as the initial state of the shared memory, it performs a flow-sensitive string analysis to estimate possible string values of the parameters of `write`. Our string analysis provides sound results for asynchronous execution of multiple threads. Because the flow-insensitive string analysis result contains all the possible values of the variables on the shared memory, it soundly estimates concrete values constructed at run time. Also, because the flow-sensitive string analysis builds on top of the flow-insensitive string analysis, and it tracks data flows between multiple threads, the final string analysis results are also sound.

Taint Analysis.

In addition to detecting string values leaked through the `write` function, our tool also tracks value flows from the results of the `read` function to the parameters of the `write` function via taint analysis. Because private user data received from the ADB server via `read` may be leaked through `write`, we perform a taint analysis with the `read` calls as sources and the `write` calls as sinks. Similarly for the string analysis, we extend the traditional taint analysis to track data flows between asynchronous multiple threads. Unlike static analysis which requires precise string values that particular variables may have, taint analysis simply tracks value flows between sources and sinks. Thus, the taint analysis performs only a flow-insensitive analysis which provides sound analysis results. If we want to improve the taint analysis results, we can apply the same approach as the string analysis and use two kinds of taint analyses.

Evaluation.

Because we proposed new attacks in this paper, we evaluated the efficiency of our static analyzer using all 7 applications that leak string values to the `write` function, and we evaluated the taint analysis using 2 malicious applications described in Section 3 that leak information to outside of devices. For the former, we tested such cases where string values flow intra-procedurally, inter-procedurally, via fields of classes, and via static fields of classes. For the latter, we tested malicious applications for application modification, SIM information leakage, and message tracking. Our static analyzer correctly detected command strings that are sent to the ADB server. The analyzer could detect data flows from the ADB server to the outside from the malicious applications.

4.2 Defenses with Changes to Android

We propose mitigation methods that require changes to Android.

Informative Message for Using ADB.

Starting from Android 4.2.2, the Android system protects ADB by asking a user's confirmation to use the USB debugging capability. When trying to enable USB debugging, the Android system show a dialog including a RSA key to a user to approve USB debugging. However, RSA keys may not be useful information to ordinary users who are not familiar with security vulnerabilities. To help ordinary users understand possible security issues resulting from allowing USB debugging, more informative message than RSA keys should be provided.

Automatic Disable of USB Debugging.

While still allowing the ADB capabilities to ordinary applications, the Android system may turn them off automatically. Even though USB debugging is disabled by default, once it is enabled, it remains to be enabled even after the system reboots. Instead, disabling USB debugging by the system periodically is much more secure. The BlackBerry system indeed turns off the USB debugging option after a certain amount of time [3].

Restricted ADB Functionalities.

Because ADB capabilities are vulnerable to many attacks as we showed in the previous section, restricting ADB functionalities may be a plausible option. One way to restrict their uses is to prohibit combined uses of multiple ADB commands. While this restriction does not preclude all the attacks we described in this paper, it can rule out many attacks like contact collection using `screenrecord` with `input` and overbilling using `am` with `input`. More rigid approach is to disallow ADB capabilities from production applications. This restriction goes back to the original intention of ADB, which is only for debugging purposes. We have compared the debugging utilities of the Android system and Ubuntu 12.04.01, and we found that Android provides more debugging utilities by default than Ubuntu. Restricting ADB capabilities in production applications will surely limit the application functionalities but it will guide them more securely.

Secured ADB Channels.

Even though the Android system displays a dialog with an RSA key for allowing USB debugging, the system does not authenticate the server and the client. Once the ADB server is running, any applications can connect to the server via a TCP connection. We propose several approaches to guide the communication with the ADB server securely. The most straightforward approach is to add an authentication mechanism to the ADB server. For example, the ADB server may allow connections only from the shell by checking clients whether their UID are 2000. Another possible solution is to create a new ADB permission and to modify the system so that only the applications with the ADB permission can communicate with the ADB server. Also, if the ADB permission is protected with the level of the signature permission, ordinary applications including malicious ones cannot leverage the ADB server any more.

5. RELATED WORK

Recently, various attacks in Android applications have been reported. These attacks leverage vulnerabilities in intents [4], dynamic code loading [23], content providers [30], permission escalation [6], and advertisement libraries [22]. In this paper, we reported a variety of attacks that leverage one of the Android system component, ADB. Because ADB is originally for debugging purposes, the Android system assigns higher privileges to ADB than to third-party Android applications. Thus, we could present powerful attacks of various kinds by leveraging ADB and its utility functions only with the INTERNET permission.

Even though protecting system components is critical due to their high privileges, only a few work have focused on the Android kernel layer security. Zhou *et al.* [29] pointed out that vulnerable Android device drivers can leak users' private data. Moreover, Jana and Shmatikov [15] demonstrated that examining shared memory can leak private information. Similarly, investigating public information can lead to private data leakage [28]. Compare to these work, our research focused on understanding security risks of ADB and the Android system utilities. The most closest work to ours is Lin *et al.*'s work [18], which studied security risks of the screenshot function using ADB. While Lin *et al.* focused on the screenshot function to build a malware using ADB, we presented how powerful ADB capabilities are and showed their security risks by presenting various kinds of attacks. Given that a malware leveraging ADB to launch attacks has appeared [19], we believe our study on ADB capabilities would be useful to understand their security vulnerabilities.

6. CONCLUSION

In this paper, we demonstrated that by leveraging ADB capabilities, malicious applications can leak private data, monitor device usages, and even interfere with device behavior. For private data leakage, we showed that malicious applications can track messages exchanges, call history, and geographic locations, record screen snapshots, access private database of other applications, and leak SIM information. To demonstrate usage monitoring attacks, we presented packet dump and keystroke logging attacks. Finally, we showed that malware can disturb users by overbilling and modification of applications, and they can even prohibit users from using their devices by DoS attacks and locking device screens. To our surprise, all these attacks are possible only with the INTERNET permission.

To protect Android users from such attacks, we presented multiple mitigation mechanisms. We developed a static analysis tool that detects potential malware leveraging the ADB server. Instead of simply displaying a dialog with an RSA key to protect the ADB server as the current Android system does, a more informative message would be helpful for ordinary users to be aware of security vulnerabilities. We strongly believe that ADB capabilities should be restricted or they should use secure channels; if possible, ADB should be used only for debugging purposes.

Acknowledgment

This work is supported in part by Korea Ministry of Education, Science and Technology(MEST) / National Research Foundation of Korea(NRF) (Grants NRF-2014R1A2A2A01003235 and NRF-2008-0062609).

7. REFERENCES

[1] Android logging system. http://elinux.org/Android_Logging_System, 2012.

[2] AppTornado GmbH. AppBrain: Number of Android applications. http://www.appbrain.com/stats/number-of-android-apps, 2014.

[3] BlackBerry. Blackberry developer. http://developer.blackberry.com.

[4] E. Chin, A. P. Felt, K. Greenwood, and D. Wagner. Analyzing inter-application communication in Android. In *Proceedings of the 9th International Conference on Mobile Systems, Applications, and Services*, 2011.

[5] ClockworkMod. ClockworkMod tether (no root). https://play.google.com/store/apps/details?id=com.koushikdutta.tether, 2013.

[6] L. Davi, A. Dmitrienko, A.-R. Sadeghi, and M. Winandy. Privilege escalation attacks on Android. In *Proceedings of the 13th International Conference on Information Security*, 2010.

[7] A. P. Fuchs, A. Chaudhuri, and J. S. Foster. Scandroid: Automated security certification of Android applications. Technical Report CS-TR-4991, University of Maryland, 2009.

[8] Google. Android debug bridge. http://developer.android.com/tools/help/adb.html.

[9] Google. Toasts. http://developer.android.com/guide/topics/ui/notifiers/toasts.html.

[10] Google. NetworkOnMainThreadException. http://developer.android.com/reference/android/os/NetworkOnMainThreadException.html, 2014.

[11] C. Gutman. Remote ADB shell. https://play.google.com/store/apps/details?id=com.cgutman.androidremotedebugger&hl=en, 2013.

[12] Hiandroidstudio. No root screen recorder-trial. https://play.google.com/store/apps/details?id=com.screenrecnoroot&hl=en, 2014.

[13] IBM. T.J. Watson Libraries for Analysis (WALA). http://wala.sourceforge.net.

[14] Invisibility. Free screen recorder no root. https://play.google.com/store/apps/details?id=uk.org.invisibility.recordablefree&hl=en, 2014.

[15] S. Jana and V. Shmatikov. Memento: Learning secrets from process footprints. In *Proceedings of the 2012 IEEE Symposium on Security and Privacy*, 2012.

[16] E. Kim. No root screenshot it. https://play.google.com/store/apps/details?id=com.edwardkim.android.screenshotitfullnoroot, 2013.

[17] D. F. Kune, J. Koelndorfer, N. Hopper, and Y. Kim. Location leaks on the GSM air interface. In *Proceedings of the 19th Network and Distributed System Security Symposium*, 2012.

[18] C.-C. Lin, H. Li, X. Zhou, and X. Wang. Screenmilker: How to milk your Android screen for secrets. In *Proceedings of the 21st Network and Distributed System Security Symposium*, 2014.

[19] F. Liu. Windows malware attempts to infect Android devices. http://www.symantec.com/connect/blogs/windows-malware-attempts-infect-android-devices, 2014.

[20] H. Lockheimer. Android and security. http://googlemobile.blogspot.kr/2012/02/android-and-security.html, 2012.

[21] M. Niemietz and J. Schwenk. UI redressing attacks on Android devices. In *Black Hat Abu Dhabi*, 2012.

[22] P. Pearce, A. P. Felt, G. Nunez, and D. Wagner. AdDroid: Privilege separation for applications and advertisers in Android. In *Proceedings of the 7th ACM Symposium on Information, Computer and Communications Security*, 2012.

[23] S. Poeplau, Y. Fratantonio, A. Bianchi, C. Kruegel, and G. Vigna. Execute this! Analyzing unsafe and malicious dynamic code loading in Android applications. In *Proceedings of the 21st Network and Distributed System Security Symposium*, 2014.

[24] E. Protalinski. Android malware numbers exploded to 25,000 in June 2012. http://www.zdnet.com/android-malware-numbers-explode-to-25000-in-june-2012-7000001046, 2012.

[25] J. Rivera and R. van der Meulen. Gartner says annual smartphone sales surpassed sales of feature phones for the first time in 2013. http://www.gartner.com/newsroom/id/2665715, 2014.

[26] SmartUX. Screenshot UX. https://play.google.com/store/apps/details?id=com.liveov.shotux, 2012.

[27] X. Zhang, R. Gupta, and Y. Zhang. Cost and precision tradeoffs of dynamic data slicing algorithms. *ACM Transactions on Programming Languages and Systems*, 27:631–661, 2005.

[28] X. Zhou, S. Demetriou, D. He, M. Naveed, X. Pan, X. Wang, C. A. Gunter, and K. Nahrstedt. Identity, location, disease and more: Inferring your secrets from Android public resources. In *Proceedings of the 20th ACM Conference on Computer and Communications Security*, 2013.

[29] X. Zhou, Y. Lee, N. Zhang, M. Naveed, and X. Wang. The peril of fragmentation: Security hazards in Android device driver customizations. In *Proceedings of the 2014 IEEE Symposium on Security and Privacy*, 2014.

[30] Y. Zhou and X. Jiang. Detecting passive content leaks and pollution in Android applications. In *Proceedings of the 20th Network and Distributed System Security Symposium*, 2013.

Android Implicit Information Flow Demystified

Wei You, Bin Liang*, Jingzhe Li, Wenchang Shi
Renmin University of China, Beijing, P. R. China
{youwei, liangb, lijingzhe, wenchang}@ruc.edu.cn

Xiangyu Zhang
Purdue University, Indiana, USA
xyzhang@cs.purdue.edu

ABSTRACT

In this paper, a comprehensive analysis of implicit information flow (IIF) on the Android bytecode is presented to identify all potential IIF forms, determine their exploitability, and mitigate the potential threat. By applying control-transfer-oriented semantic analysis of the bytecode language, we identify five IIF forms, some of which are not studied by existing IIF literature. We develop proof-of-concepts (PoCs) for each IIF form to demonstrate their exploitability. The experimental results show that all these PoCs can effectively and efficiently transmit sensitive data, as well as successfully evade the detection of a state-of-the-art privacy monitor TaintDroid. To mitigate the threat of IIF, we propose a solution to defending against IIF leveraging a special control dependence tracking technique and implement a prototype system. The evaluation shows that the prototype can effectively detect information leak by all the identified IIF forms and also real-world malware with an acceptable overhead. In summary, our study gives in-depth insight into Android IIF from both offensive and defensive perspectives, and provides a foundation for further research on Android IIF.

Categories and Subject Descriptors

D.4.6 [**Operating System**]: Security and Protection

Keywords

implicit information flow; exploitation; mitigation; Android

1. INTRODUCTION

Information flow analysis (IFA) is an important technique, which aims to track the propagation of information between program variables. Information flow occurs from a source object x to a target object y, if the information stored in object x can be revealed by the value of object y. Information flow can be explicit or implicit [4]. Explicit information flow (EIF) results from *data dependence*; and implicit information flow (IIF) results from *control dependence*.

Intuitively, a program with the pattern $low = high$; exhibits privacy leakage via EIF. Confidential data stored in variable *high* is directly passed to variable *low* whose value can be observed from outside. On the other hand, the following code snippet contains IIF from *high* to *low*. Although there is no direct data flow between these two variables, one can still learn something about *high* by observing *low*.

```
if (high == 0) low = 0;
else if (high > 0) low = 1;
else low = -1;
```

In general, IIF is more difficult to be tracked than EIF. Most existing IFA techniques [10, 12] concentrate mainly on EIF, ignoring the impact of IIF. As a result, it is possible for malware to leverage IIF to evade detection. A recent anti-IFA study [2] has demonstrated the feasibility of evasion for C programs. To mitigate the threat of IIF, some approaches [1, 9] are proposed to selectively track control dependence. For example, the study in [1] tracks only a special type of control dependence whose nature highly resembles data dependence. However, the existing studies only consider IIF resulted from regular conditional structures. Little attention is paid to IIF resulted from other language structures.

Information leak is the most commonly seen malicious behavior on Android [14]. Most existing malware samples steal sensitive information through EIF such that the existing defense schemes on Android focus on tracking only EIF [6, 13]. However, as we found in the wild, sophisticated malware starts to leverage IIF to evade the existing defense systems. We envision such attacks will become more popular in near future due to the difficulty of defending against IIF. Hence, there is a pressing need to study IIF on Android.

To better understand the possible attack and the corresponding defense on Android, there are three open research questions to be answered: 1) How many IIF forms there may exist; 2) Given an IIF form, is it exploitable, allowing to effectively transmit sensitive information; 3) How to defend against information leak through such IIF forms with an acceptable overhead. In this paper, we answer these questions by theoretical analysis as well as empirical experiments.

Our study begins with a control-transfer-oriented analysis of Android's Dalvik bytecode in a formal structured operational semantic model. With this model, 54 instructions are identified that may cause control dependence. IIF can be constructed by using any of these instructions. Identifying all these IIF inducing instructions is meaningful for conducting a sophisticated IIF attack or performing a com-

*Corresponding Author

ASIA CCS'15, April 14–17, 2015, Singapore..

http://dx.doi.org/10.1145/2714576.2714604.

prehensive IIF detection. We find that besides conditional structures (i.e., *if* and *switch*), there are other instructions (i.e., *throw*, *exception-prone* instructions and *polymorphism* related instructions) that can also be used to construct IIF attacks. Details are shown in Section 2.

We develop proof-of-concepts (PoCs) for the identified IIF forms and examine their exploitability. Without loss of generality, we respectively integrate these PoCs to a real-world application *FMajor*, which leaks phone number via EIF. We modify the original apk, inserting an additional propagation step leveraging IIF forms to transmit data. We evaluate the PoCs on an emulator equipped with TaintDroid [6], a state-of-the-art IFA-based privacy monitor for Android. We find that all PoCs can effectively steal phone number and successfully evade the detection of TaintDroid. In other words, these PoCs can be easily turned into real attacks. Indeed, by manually analyzing the samples provided by the Android Malware Genome Project [14], we found two samples leveraging IIF in a way similar to some of our PoCs. We believe more real malware samples similar to our (other) PoCs will be found in the future. Details are shown in Section 3.

Compared with exploiting IIF, it is more difficult to defend against it. In general, it is intractable to perform sound and complete tracking of IIF. In this paper, we reduce the problem to tracking a special kind of control dependence called *strict control dependence* (SCD). Observe that practical IIF attacks most likely have to leverage SCD, we hence enhance an existing runtime SCD tracking algorithm [1] to detect IIF. The algorithm selectively taints a predicate if it has *strong* correlation with sensitive information. All assignments guarded by such a tainted predicate are tainted. For better efficiency, we improve the SCD detection algorithm by adopting a lazy tainting policy, which postpones the tainting of control dependence to the post-dominator of a control structure. More importantly, our technique formulates the various Dalvik instructions vulnerable to IIF exploits to SCD, such that our technique can detect all possible IIF forms on Android. We implement a prototype system. The evaluation results show that the prototype can successfully detect all the PoCs and the real-world malware samples with acceptable overhead. Details are shown in Section 4.

2. SEMANTICS OF DALVIK BYTECODE

IIF is caused by control dependence, which is determined by control transfer relationship between instructions. Hence in this section, we study the semantics of Android's Dalvik bytecode (DVML) to identify all the control transfer instructions that can be exploited to construct IIF. The goal is to assist in conducting a sophisticated IIF attack or performing a comprehensive IIF detection. To get a concise and precise semantic specification, we abstract an imperative language $DVML_I$ from DVML and present it with a structured operational semantic (SOS) model. This model focuses on control transfer behavior of $DVML_I$ instructions.

Note that in order to exploit IIF, the attacker should be able to infer a value from the control transfer determined by the value. Hence, if an instruction always transfers control to a definite target address, or in other words, the target is not determined by any runtime value, there is no IIF. We call the control flow instructions whose targets are determined by runtime values as *indirect control transfer* (ICT) instructions. ICT instructions are the building blocks of various forms of IIF, and hence the focus of our discussion.

2.1 The SOS Model

The SOS model focuses on the control-transfer related semantics of $DVML_I$ and leaves out other unnecessary details. A $DVML_I$ program consists of classes. Each class contains a set of fields and a set of methods. Without loss of generality, we do not distinguish static fields (or methods) from instance fields (or methods). Besides, we assume that the first instruction of a method locates at offset 0 and the offset difference between two consecutive instructions is 1.

2.1.1 Memory Model and Execution State

A $DVML_I$ program has a local memory space *RegisterArray* that stores local variables of the current method, and a global memory space *Heap* that stores dynamically allocated objects. A configuration $\langle cm, off, H, V \rangle$ describes execution state with *cm* the current method, *off* the offset of the current instruction inside the method, H the heap and V the register array. Note that the current program counter can be denoted as $pc = \langle cm, off \rangle$.

2.1.2 Instruction Set and Operational Semantics

The $DVML_I$ instruction set is abstracted from the DMVL instruction set by grouping the DMVL instructions with similar semantics into a single $DVML_I$ instruction. The operational semantic rule of $DVML_I$ is of the form:

$$\frac{instruction \wedge computation}{\langle \text{current configuration} \rangle \Rightarrow \langle \text{next configuration} \rangle}$$

Rules are read from top to bottom, left to right. Given an instruction, we search for an applicable rule that matches the instruction, and apply the computation given in the top of the rule. The execution state of the program will transform from the current configuration to the next configuration.

For example, instruction *invoke* $m\ v_{this}\ (v_i)_1^n$ has a rule:

$$\frac{\begin{array}{l} I{=}\text{invoke } m\ v_{this}\ (v_i)_1^n \wedge loc{=}V[v_{this}] \wedge o{=}H(loc) \wedge \\ m'{=}\text{methodDispatch}(m,o) \wedge \text{pushState}(\langle cm,off,V\rangle) \wedge \\ V'{=}loc{::}(V[v_i])_1^n \end{array}}{\langle cm,off,H,V\rangle \Longrightarrow \left\langle m',0,H,V'\right\rangle}\ \textsc{Invoke}$$

The instruction is used to conduct a polymorphic invocation. When executing the instruction, dynamic method dispatching is performed to determine which polymorphic version m' of the method should be invoked. The method dispatching is based on the dynamic type of the receiver object, which can be accessed via the object reference stored in register v_{this}. The current program state is pushed onto an internal execution stack for restoring at return site. The instruction execution results in a new program state where the register array stores the receiver object reference concatenated with the parameters (i.e., $loc :: (V\,[v_i])_1^n$) and the program counter is set to the start of the invoked method (i.e., $pc = \langle m', 0\rangle$).

An instruction may trigger a runtime exception, if runtime values of its operands violate related constraints. Such instruction is called *exception-prone* instruction. It has two execution rules: one for the normal execution, the other for the exceptional execution. When executing an *exception-prone* instruction, checks are conducted on its operands to determine which rule is applied. For example, instruction *binop op* $v_A\ v_B\ v_C$ is an *exception-prone* instruction. At runtime, a check is conducted to examine whether the operator *op* is *division* and the divisor v_C is 0. If so, an exception is thrown and the control is transferred to the corresponding exception handler. Otherwise, the binary operation is performed and the control is transferred to the next instruction.

2.2 ICT Instructions

For identifying indirect control transfer instructions, we examine all $DVML_I$ instructions. The *exception-prone* instructions have two execution rules. Different rules transfer the control to different target addresses, and the rule applied is determined by runtime checks. Therefore, all *exception-prone* instructions can cause indirect control transfer. For an instruction with a single execution rule, if the program counter of the next configuration is dynamically dependent on some operands, it can cause indirect control transfer.

By examining all the $DVML_I$ instructions, we identify 12 ICT instructions. These ICT instructions correspond to 54 DMVL instructions, and can be divided into five categories according to their related control structures, as shown in Table 1. We can see that besides the common conditional structures (i.e., *if* and *switch*), there are three other control structures (i.e., *throw*, *exception-prone* instructions and *polymorphism* related instructions) can also cause IIF.

2.3 IIF Forms

In practice, given an ICT instruction, there are various ways to leverage it to construct IIF. In this paper, we focus on IIF in which the attacker can uniquely determine a high-confidentiality value from the observable low-confidentiality value. In other words, we focus on IIF that induces a one to one (1-2-1) mapping between the two values. Specifically, we consider IIF in which sensitive data is used as the operand that distinctively determines the target address of the instruction, i.e., different values of operand v_H will lead to different control transfer targets. Besides, there is an observable variable v_L that will be assigned with a distinctive value in each target. Consequently, adversaries can directly deduce the value of v_H by examining the value of v_L.

IIF instances can be categorized into five forms, each based on one of the identified control structures. Leveraging the *switch* structure is straightforward. The attacker can use a branch for each possible value of v_H and assign v_L with a unique value in each branch. For the *if* structure, it has only two branches thus can distinguish only two possible values. The attacker can use multiple *if* structures in nesting, or use a single *if* structure multiple times in looping.

Other control structures are analogous to the *if* structure or the *switch* structure. For example, the *exception-prone* structure can be treated as a special *if* structure, which tests whether a runtime exception is triggered. Another example is the *polymorphism* structure. It can be modeled as a special *switch* structure, which tests the runtime type of a receiver object to determine the most appropriate version of a polymorphic method to be invoked.

3. EXPLOITABILITY

We develop proof-of-concepts (PoCs) for the identified IIF forms and examine their exploitability. Our PoCs exploit IIF to precisely transmit confidential data from a secret variable *high* to a public variable *low*, so that we can unambiguously infer *high* from *low*. In other words, our PoCs exploit IIF to generate a 1-2-1 mapping from *high* to *low*.

3.1 PoCs

Without loss of generality, each of our PoCs takes a sensitive 8-bit digital character as input, and leverages different IIF forms to transmit it to the publicly accessible output.

Table 1: Identified ICT Instructions.

$DVML_I$	DVML Instruction(s)	Structure
if	if-eq, if-ne, if-lt, if-le, if-gt, if-ge, if-eqz, if-nez, if-ltz, if-lez, if-gtz, if-gez	if
switch	packed-switch, sparse-switch	switch
invoke	invoke-virtual, invoke-virtual/range invoke-interface, invoke-interface/range	polymorphism
throw	throw	throw
binop	div-int, div-long, rem-int, rem-long	exception-prone
check_cast	check_cast	exception-prone
fget	iget, iget-wide, iget-object, iget-byte, iget-short, iget-char, iget-boolean	exception-prone
fput	iput, iput-wide, iput-object, iput-byte, iput-short, iput-char, iput-boolean	exception-prone
new_array	new_array	exception-prone
array_length	array_length	exception-prone
aget	aget, aget-wide, aget-object, aget-byte, aget-short, aget-char, aget-boolean	exception-prone
aput	aput, aput-wide, aput-object, aput-byte, aput-short, aput-char, aput-boolean	exception-prone

3.1.1 If-Based IIF

The *if* statement is a common control structure for constructing IIF. A single *if* statement is not sufficient to transmit 8-bit information. In PoC 1, multiple nested *if* statements are used to enumerate the possible values of *high*. In PoC 2, a loop is used to traverse the range of the value of *high*. After execution, *low* will hold the same value as *high*.

```
if (high == '0') low = '0';
else if (high == '1') low = '1';
......
```

PoC 1

```
for (low = '0'; low != high; low++);
```

PoC 2

3.1.2 Switch-Based IIF

The *switch* statement is another common structure for constructing IIF. PoC 3 uses sufficient amount of *case* branches to explicitly enumerate the possible values of *high*.

```
switch (high) {
  case '0': low = '0'; break;
  case '1': low = '1'; break;
  ......
}
```

PoC 3

3.1.3 Exception-Prone-Based IIF

An *exception-prone* statement is analogous to an *if* statement that tests whether a runtime exception is triggered. PoC 4 uses a loop to iterate on variable *low* over the value range of *high*. In each iteration, a *division* operation is performed with the difference between *high* and *low* as divisor. An arithmetic exception will be thrown when *high* == *low*.

```
for (low = '0'; low <= '9'; low++){
  try {int tmp = 1 / (high - low);}
  catch (Exception e) {break;}
}
```

PoC 4

3.1.4 Throw-Based IIF

A *throw* statement can throw exception of different types, which can be caught by different handlers. It is essentially equivalent to a *switch* statement that tests the type of the exception variable. In PoC 5, the array *excepts* has different elements of different types. The value of *high* decides which array element is assigned to the exception variable *except*. Different types of *except* lead to different handlers to be taken, which in turn lead to different values assigned to *low*. As such, we get a 1-2-1 mapping from *high* to *low*.

```
Exception except = excepts[high - '0'];
try { throw except; }{
catch (Exception_0 e) {low = '0';}
catch (Exception_1 e) {low = '1';}
......
```

PoC 5

3.1.5 Polymorphism-Based IIF

Polymorphism is an essential feature for Object Oriented languages. In Android programs, polymorphism includes four manners: virtual invocation, reflective invocation, message dispatching, and event dispatching.

PoC 6 demonstrates the IIF via virtual invocation. Method $f()$ has different versions that return different values to *low*. The value of *high* decides the runtime type of the receiver object *poly*, which in turn decides which version of $f()$ to be executed. As such, we get a 1-2-1 mapping from *high* to *low*.

```
class Poly_0 extends Poly {
  char f() {return '0';}{
}
......
Poly poly = polys[high - '0'];
low = poly.f();
```

PoC 6

PoC 7 demonstrates the IIF via reflective invocation. The name of the method to be invoked is determined by the value of *high*. Different methods return different values to *low*. As such, we get a 1-2-1 mapping from *high* to *low*.

```
class Reflect {
  static char method_0() {return '0';}
  ......
}
String name = "method_" + high;
Method m = Reflect.class.getMethod(name);
low = m.invoke(null);
```

PoC 7

PoC 8 demonstrates the IIF via message dispatching. Different values of *high* cause different message handlers to be executed, which assign different values to *low*. As such, we get a 1-2-1 mapping from *high* to *low*.

```
class Handler_0 extends Handler {
  void handleMessage(Message msg) {low = '0';}
}
......
Handler handler = handlers[high - '0'];
Message message = handler.obtainMessage();
handler.sendMessage(message);
```

PoC 8

PoC 9 demonstrates the IIF via event dispatching. Multiple *Button* components are attached with different listeners, which assign different values to *low*. The value of *high* decides which *Button* to obtain the focus. The event of focus changing will be dispatched to the listener of the focused *Button*. As such, we get a 1-2-1 mapping from *high* to *low*.

```
class Listener_0 extends Listener {
  void onFocusChange() {low = '0';}
}
......
Button button = buttons[high - '0'];
button.requestFocus();
```

PoC 9

3.2 Evaluation of PoCs

To evaluate these PoCs, we respectively integrate them to a real-world application *FMajor*, which leaks phone number via EIF. We modify the original apk, inserting an additional propagation step leveraging IIF to transmit data. The evaluation is performed on an emulator equipped with TaintDroid [6] and run on a computer with Intel(R) Core(TM) 2.50 GHz CPU and 2G memory. All PoCs can effectively leak phone number and successfully evade the detection of TaintDroid.

Table 2: Performance of PoCs.

PoC	Δ Size	Δ Mem	t(PN)	t(1M)
if-based (nesting)	0.4 KB (0.06%↑)	11.3 KB (0.18%↑)	42 ms	294 ms
if-based (looping)	0.3 KB (0.05%↑)	8.2 KB (0.13%↑)	45 ms	303 ms
switch-based	0.4 KB (0.06%↑)	10.2 KB (0.16%↑)	37 ms	283 ms
exception-prone-based	0.4 KB (0.06%↑)	28.7 KB (0.46%↑)	51 ms	391 ms
throw-based	0.9 KB (0.14%↑)	55.3 KB (0.89%↑)	49 ms	314 ms
polymorphism-based (virtual invocation)	1.1 KB (0.17%↑)	69.6 KB (1.12%↑)	47 ms	310 ms
polymorphism-based (reflective invocation)	0.7 KB (0.11%↑)	78.8 KB (1.27%↑)	49 ms	596 ms
polymorphism-based (message dispatching)	1.4 KB (0.21%↑)	84.0 KB (1.35%↑)	57 ms	844 ms
polymorphism-based (event dispatching)	1.9 KB (0.29%↑)	109.6 KB (1.76%↑)	96 ms	1126 ms

We evaluate the performance of each PoC from four aspects: size increment, memory increment, time consumption in transmitting a small amount of data (i.e., phone number) and a large amount of data (i.e., 1M randomly-generated data). The evaluation result is shown in Table 2. The PoCs incur less than 0.3% size increment, and less than 2% memory increment. All PoCs can efficiently transmit data. The time consumption in transmitting phone number is less than 0.1 second. For transmitting 1M data, even the least efficient PoC can finish in about 1 second.

3.3 Real-World Threat

We want to note that IIF is not only a theoretical threat. It has been used in the real world either inadvertently or by design. Indeed, we found two samples (i.e., *DroidKungFu3* and *AnserverBot*) from the Android Malware Genome Project [14] leveraging IIF in a way similar to some of our PoCs. Although we have not found other IIF forms in malware samples, we believe they are likely to be leveraged by malware in the future due to their effectiveness.

3.3.1 IIF of DroidKungFu3

DroidKungFu3 will send certain bits of the victim's integrated circuit card identifier (i.e., ICCID) to a remote server. Instead of directly sending ICCID, it adopts IIF to encode each bit. The following shows the highly simplified IIF-related code of *DroidKungFu3*. We can see that it leverages the *if*-based IIF in a way similar to PoC 1.

```
if (high.equals("0")) low = 0;
else if (high.equals("1")) low = 1;
......
```

3.3.2 IIF of AnserverBot

AnserverBot will send the victim's international mobile equipment identity (IMEI) string to a remoter server. Instead of directly sending IMEI, *AnserverBot* adopts IIF to encode each character as the index of its occurrence in a character map *value*. The encoding is implemented by invoking method *String.indexOf*(), whose highly simplified code is shown in the following. We can see that it leverages *if*-based IIF in a similar way to PoC 2.

```
for (low = 0; low < length; low++)
  if (value[low] == high) break;
```

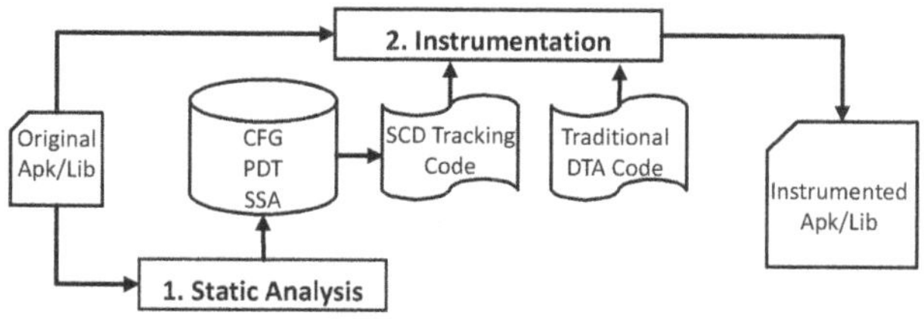

Figure 1: Overview of our IIF mitigation solution.

4. MITIGATION

From the above discussion, we can see that IIF poses serious threat to data confidentiality. In theory, it is intractable to perform sound and complete IIF tracking. In this paper, we propose a solution concentrating on tracking 1-2-1 IIF, since such IIF can precisely transmit sensitive data and hence is more likely to be exploited by real-world malware.

A key observation is that 1-2-1 IIF can be formulated as a special kind of control dependence called *strict control dependence* (SCD) [1]. A statement s is strictly control dependent on a predicate statement with v_p as predicate variable, if the execution of s can precisely infer the value of v_p. The branch leading to the execution of s is called the SCD branch. Consider the code snippet in Section 1. There is an SCD between the assignment statement at line 1 and the *if* statement at the same line. If the *true* branch (i.e., SCD branch) of the *if* statement is taken, the attacker can precisely infer that the value of the predicate variable *high* is 0. As a counter example, the control dependence between the assignment statement at line 2 and the *if* statement at the same line is not an SCD. Because from the execution of this assignment statement, we can only infer that the predicate variable *high* is larger than 0. Little information is revealed.

4.1 Overview

The overview of our solution is shown in Figure 1. Given an application or a library, we first perform static analysis on its bytecode to compute control flow graph (CFG), post dominator tree (PDT), and static single assignment (SSA). The computed information is used in generating SCD tracking code. Then we instrument the application or library with both traditional DTA tracking code and SCD tracking code. The static analysis and instrumentation are performed on a desktop computer. The instrumented application or library will be installed and executed on the smartphone device.

4.2 SCD-Based Tracking

The basic idea of SCD-based tracking is to propagate the taint of the predicate variable of a control structure to the variables that are assigned in an SCD branch. To this end, we first identify the SCD branches of each control structure. Then we adopt a lazy tainting policy that is equally effective as the original SCD tracking algorithm [1] but more efficient.

4.2.1 Identifying SCD Branches

We perform static analysis to identify SCD branches. Currently, the analysis only focuses on SCDs caused by equivalence testing. For an *if* structure, if it is an equivalence predicate, the *true* branch is an SCD branch; if it is a non-equivalence predicate, the *false* branch is an SCD branch. For a *switch* structure, if a branch can be reached from only one *case* value, it is an SCD branch.

Rule	Event	Instrument
T1	Encountering a predicate statement: x is the predicate variable.	$t = \tau(x)$
T2	Encountering a post-dominator: variable x is assigned in an SCD branch i; $\nexists j \neq i$: x is assigned in branch j and $\lvert x_i \rvert = \lvert x_j \rvert$.	$\tau(x) = \tau(x) \mid t$
T3	Encountering a statement s: s is contained in an SCD branch; s may immediately propagate the value outward to a global variable x.	$\tau(x) = \tau(x) \mid t$

Figure 2: Rules for lazy SCD-based tainting. Here, $\tau(x)$ is the taint of variable x, and $|x_i|$ denotes the value assigned to variable x at branch i.

Our solution also features the capability of handling other IIF inducing structures. It explicitly converts them to *if* structures or *switch* structures, depending on the number of their branches. For example, an *exception-prone* instruction is converted to an explicit *if* structure that tests whether the specific condition triggering a runtime exception is satisfied. Another example is the *polymorphism* structure, which is converted to an explicit *switch* statement that tests the dynamic type of the receiver object. The explicit *if* or *switch* statements are then instrumented to track SCD at runtime.

4.2.2 Lazy Tainting Policy

For better performance, we propose lazy tainting policy, instead of the original on-the-fly SCD-based tainting. The rules for lazy SCD-based tainting are shown in Figure 2. When encountering a predicate statement, the taint of the predicate variable is stored in a temporary variable (Rule T1). At each immediate post-dominator, the algorithm examines each variable that is assigned in an SCD branch to check whether its value is distinctive from other branches. If so, it will propagate the taint of the current control structure to the identified variable (Rule T2).There is a special consideration for the lazy tainting policy. An SCD branch may contain some assignment statements whose values may immediately escape the branch (e.g. assignments to global variables). When encountering these statements in an SCD branch, we propagate taints immediately (Rule T3).

4.3 Evaluation of Mitigation Solution

We implement a prototype system and deploy it in HTC T528w smartphone equipped with Android-4.0. The prototype tracks both data dependence and strict control dependence. It can successfully detect all the aforementioned 1-2-1 IIF exploit PoCs, as well as real-world malware samples.

We evaluate the performance of our prototype with the *FMajor* application, the *DroidKungFu3* and *AnserverBot* malware samples, and some popular applications collected from serveral markets. We compare the code size before and after instrumentation, and find that the instrumented versions are averagely 40% larger than the original ones. We also compare the execution times of the native runs (without tracking), the runs with DD-only tracking, and the runs with DD+SCD tracking. The DD+SCD runtime overhead is approximately 65% on average compared with the native runs. Comparing with the DD-only tracking, the DD+SCD tracking increases the overhead by 30% at most. As a comparison, Dytan [3], which blindly tracks IIF, brings approximate 50x performance overhead. We argue that the performance overhead of our prototype system is acceptable.

5. RELATED WORKS

Information flow analysis (IFA) has been studied for a long time. It can be static or dynamic. Static IFA approaches [7, 8] infers the dependencies between variables via data flow analysis and control flow analysis. However, the existing techniques do not have sufficient supports for tracking information flow caused by object oriented features, such as polymorphism. On the other hand, dynamic IFA approaches [10, 12], also known as dynamic taint analysis (DTA), provides the ability to track information flow at runtime. However, most DTA frameworks can only handle explicit information flow (EIF), resulting in under-tainting [11].

Recent studies trend to combine dynamic taint analysis with static analysis to track implicit information flow (IIF). Dytan [3] statically identifies control dependence structures, and propagates the taint of predicate variables to variables assigned in each branch without discrimination. As an improvement, DTA++ [9] only tracks IIF within information-preserving transformations, such as data conversion from one format to another. Similarly, the study in [1] only tracks strict control dependence (SCD), a special kind of control dependence whose nature highly resembles data dependence. Although neither sound nor complete, these studies provide a cost-effective approach to tracking IIF. Our mitigation solution is based on the concept of SCD. We improve the original SCD detection algorithm by adopting a lazy tainting policy to improve efficiency. In addition, our solution can handle all IIF inducing control structures on Android, with many not covered by the existing IIF tracking techniques.

Recent years, with the widespread usage of smartphones, some studies are concentrated on information flow tracking of mobile apps. PiOS [5] conducts static information flow analysis on iOS apps to detect privacy leakage. TaintDroid [6] and DroidScope [13] conduct dynamic taint analysis on Android apps with the same goal. Unfortunately, all of them only consider EIF, ignoring the impact of IIF. However, our experiments show that it is feasible to leverage IIF to effectively and efficiently transmit sensitive data and evade the existing IFA-based detection. Moreover, we find that real-world smartphone malware starts to leverage IIF. It indicates that IIF is not only a theoretical threat but a reality. To the best of our knowledge, we are the first to propose and implement practical mitigation solution to defending against IIF on smartphone.

6. CONCLUSION

This paper presents a comprehensive study of Android implicit information flow (IIF). We propose a systematical method to identify potential IIF forms. With the method, we find that in addition to the commonly studied conditional structures, there are other control structures on Android that can also be used to construct IIF. We develop proof-of-concepts (PoCs) for each identified IIF form and examine their exploitability. The experimental result shows that these PoCs can effectively and efficiently transmit sensitive data and evade the detection of a state-of-the-art information flow tracking system TaintDroid. Moreover, we find two real-world malware samples leveraging IIF in a way similar to some of our PoCs. We believe all of our identified IIF forms are likely to be leveraged by malware in the future due to their effectiveness. In theory, it is intractable to perform sound and complete IIF tracking. We propose a practical mitigation solution concentrating on a subclass of IIF that can precisely transmit sensitive data hence poses the most serious threat to data confidentiality. Based on the solution, we develop a prototype system that tracks both data dependence and strict control dependence. The evaluation of our prototype shows that it can successfully detect all PoCs and real-world malware samples with an acceptable overhead.

7. ACKNOWLEDGMENT

The authors would like to thank the anonymous reviewers for their insightful comments. The work is supported by National Natural Science Foundation of China under grants 61170240, 91418206, and 61472429, and Beijing Natural Science Foundation under grant 4122041.

8. REFERENCES

[1] T. Bao, Y. Zheng, Z. Lin, X. Zhang, and D. Xu. Strict control dependence and its effect on dynamic information flow analyses. In *Proceedings of ISSTA*, 2010.

[2] L. Cavallaro, P. Saxena, and R. Sekar. On the limits of information flow techniques for malware analysis and containment. In *Proceedings of DIMVA*, 2008.

[3] J. A. Clause, W. Li, and A. Orso. Dytan: a generic dynamic taint analysis framework. In *Proceedings of ISSTA*, 2007.

[4] D. E. Denning and P. J. Denning. Certification of programs for secure information flow. *Commun. ACM*, 20(7):504–513, 1977.

[5] M. Egele, C. Kruegel, E. Kirda, and G. Vigna. PiOS: Detecting privacy leaks in ios applications. In *Proceedings of NDSS*, 2011.

[6] W. Enck, P. Gilbert, B. Chun, L. P. Cox, J. Jung, P. McDaniel, and A. Sheth. TaintDroid: An information flow tracking system for realtime privacy monitoring on smartphones. In *Proceedings of OSDI*, 2010.

[7] S. Genaim, R. Giacobazzi, and I. Mastroeni. Modeling secure information flow with boolean functions. In *Proceedings of ITS*, 2004.

[8] S. Genaim and F. Spoto. Information flow analysis for java bytecode. In *Proceedings of VMCAI*, 2005.

[9] M. G. Kang, S. McCamant, P. Poosankam, and D. Song. DTA++: Dynamic taint analysis with targeted control-flow propagation. In *Proceedings of NDSS*, 2011.

[10] L. Lam and T. Chiueh. A general dynamic information flow tracking framework for security applications. In *Proceedings of ACSAC*, 2006.

[11] E. J. Schwartz, T. Avgerinos, and D. Brumley. All you ever wanted to know about dynamic taint analysis and forward symbolic execution (but might have been afraid to ask). In *Proceedings of S&P*, 2010.

[12] W. Xu, S. Bhatkar, and R. Sekar. Taint-enhanced policy enforcement: A practical approach to defeat a wide range of attacks. In *Proceedings of the USENIX Security Symposium*, 2006.

[13] L. Yan and H. Yin. DroidScope: Seamlessly reconstructing the OS and dalvik semantic views for dynamic android malware analysis. In *Proceedings of the USENIX Security Symposium*, 2012.

[14] Y. Zhou and X. Jiang. Dissecting Android malware: Characterization and evolution. In *Proceedings of S&P*, 2012.

Automatically Detecting SSL Error-Handling Vulnerabilities in Hybrid Mobile Web Apps

Chaoshun Zuo
Shandong University
cszuo2013@gmail.com

Jianliang Wu
Shandong University
lucuswu@gmail.com

Shanqing Guo
Shandong University
guoshanqing@sdu.edu.cn

ABSTRACT

Today, there are many hybrid apps in which both native Android app UI and WebView UI are used. To protect the security and privacy of the communications, these hybrid apps all use HTTPS by WebView, a key component in modern web browser. In this paper, we show there is another type of SSL vulnerability that stems from the error-handling code in the hybrid mobile web apps. At a high level, this error-handling code should have stopped the communication but it still proceeds regardless of certificate errors, thereby leading to the MITM attacks. To automatically identify these vulnerable apps, we present a hybrid approach that combines both static analysis and dynamic analysis. We have implemented our approach and evaluated with 13,820 real world mobile web apps from a third party market, of which 645 are confirmed truly vulnerable, with an average overhead of 60.8 seconds per app.

Categories and Subject Descriptors

D.2.4 [**Software Engineering**]: Software/Program Verification; D.2.5 [**Software Engineering**]: Testing and Debugging

Keywords

Android Security, HTTPS, SSL, WebView

1. INTRODUCTION

Increasingly, there are hybrid apps that combine both native Android UI and WebView UI, because of the easier development and lower maintaining complexity. Specifically, mobile web apps use WebViews to present web pages and communicate with web servers. Some web pages may transfer sensitive information, like user name and password, to a server, which causes that the communication should be protected. For this reason, they all use HTTPS connections instead of HTTP connections. Under normal circumstances, the attackers couldn't attack HTTPS connections even if they sniffed the network traffic unless they have the cryptographic keys. However, developers' incorrect implementation of HTTPS in WebView can allow Android WebView to present a web page with illegal certificate, which can thus be attacked by Man-in-the-middle [1, 2] or phishing attacks.

ASIA CCS'15, April 14 - 17, 2015, Singapore, Singapore

ACM 978-1-4503-3245-3/15/04 ...$15.00.
http://dx.doi.org/10.1145/2714576.2714583.

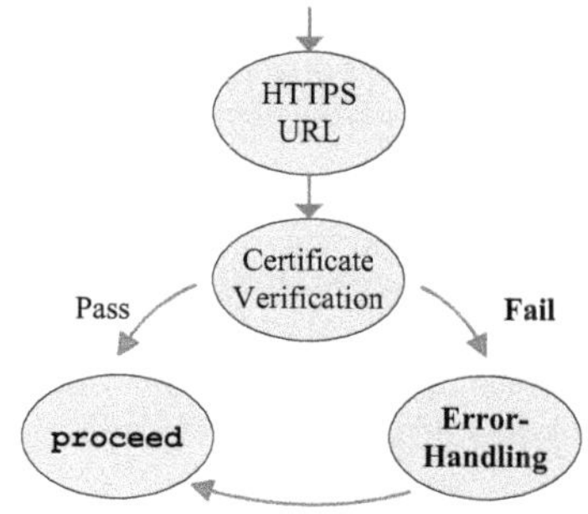

Figure 1: The State Machine of error handling process.

Figure 1 shows how this vulnerability happened. When an app opens an HTTPS web page with an illegal certificate, the app passes the HTTPS URL to Android to verify the certificate. With an illegal certificate Android will get a verification failure, then it will call error handling procedure implemented by the developer. Often times this error handler code just ignores the error and calls `proceed` to show the HTTPS web page (even though the certificate is illegal). This is a particular type of implementation vulnerability we aim to find in this paper.

More specifically, it's possible to analyze this vulnerability manually for a particular app. However, it is impractical to detect this vulnerability on a large scale, given the huge amount of such apps in the market. Meanwhile, unlike native apps, mobile web apps bring new challenges because we have to test not only the normal native app activities but also the web pages. For static analysis, the existing tools such as androguard [3] are not suitable to detect this vulnerability because they cannot track variables. In addition, we can't determine whether an app is vulnerable or not by static analysis only (because it is often an over approximation, leading to false positives). Dynamic analysis is needed to verify whether the WebView would eventually load an HTTPS page and its error handling is vulnerable.

As such, we have designed a new system to automatically identify these vulnerable apps. Our system consists of both static analysis and dynamic analysis. In particular, we first employ static analysis to determine whether these apps are potential vulnerable or not. If so, the potential vulnerable apps will be further analyzed through our dynamic analysis, which is guided by the static analysis information to drive the native Android UI as well as the WebView UI to trigger the vulnerability. In summary, this paper makes the following contributions:

- We have discovered a new type of SSL vulnerability which could lead to insecure WebView HTTPS connection.
- We have designed a hybrid Android web app test framework using multi emulators. This framework contains both static analysis and dynamic analysis. It can install and run a mobile web app automatically without any user involvement. Besides, not only could the system stimulate jumps between Activities but also it is able to drive jumps between web pages within WebView.
- We have implemented our framework and tested with 13,820 apps collected in July 2014. Experimental results show that our static analysis found 1,360 potential vulnerable apps and our dynamic analysis confirmed that 645 of them are vulnerable.

2. SYSTEM OVERVIEW

2.1 Problem Statement

For hybrid mobile web apps, when an HTTPS URL is passed to WebView, it will first verify the certificate of the HTTPS server: if passed WebView will show the page. If verification failure occurs and the app has rewritten the error handling process, WebView will pass the error handling process to the app and wait for the result. Once the error handling passed to the app, it will handle the error in its own way including ignoring the error and proceed and return the result to WebView. If error handling process has not been rewritten, WebView would shield the page directly. However, programmers often rewrite the error handling process. It's obvious that this is a serious security problem, especially for apps that always use HTTPS to transfer sensitive information such as the login information, user information, payment information, authorization information, etc. With this vulnerability unfixed, attackers could easily get all these information by MITM attack.

2.2 Challenges and Solutions

2.2.1 Is the potential vulnerable code reachable?

To identify the app is vulnerable or not, we have to make sure it contains potential vulnerable code. We assume the class inherits from `WebViewClient` which overrides the error handling method (i.e. `onReceivedSslError`) and has the ignore code is potential vulnerable. Any app without this kind of code is invulnerable. It's not easy to make sure if `onReceivedSslError` is reachable because it's called by system callbacks rather than called directly. We locate the method call `setWebViewClient` and find out whether a potential vulnerable `WebViewClient` has been registered or not. If yes, then we find the Activity that loads the WebView which registers this WebViewClient. So we consider this Activity as a target Activity. This helps us to make sure this potential vulnerable code is reachable when the Activity is reachable.

2.2.2 How to record Activity jump relations with trigger events?

To confirm if potential app is vulnerable we need to jump to the target Activity from launcher Activity by triggering related events which have been recorded during static analysis. To fulfill this we build an ACG[4] based on which a path from launcher Activity to target Activity is found, which could guide the dynamic test. ACG is a directed Activity Call Graph of which vertexes represents Activities. And we put information on the edge because we need to know what event triggers the jump from one Activity to another.

Vertexes are not hard to find but edges (i.e. how to find the view and event) are not easy to add. We take view and the event triggered by the view that cause Activity jump as an edge. Here goes how we find edges. First, we find all the methods that could cause activity jump and locate these functions in MCG (Method Call Graph). By traveling within MCG we can find method that causes activity jump and which activity jump to. Then we locate event method (such as `onClick`) the method belongs to. This view which owns the event method and the event would be the edge. With ACG, we are able to find a path on which a series of trigger events are recorded from launcher Activity to target WebView.

2.2.3 How to simulate human operations to both native Android UI and WebView UI ?

Manual analysis is enough for a particular app, but for large dataset, it's impossible. We need to make it possible to detect automatically thus making large scale analysis possible. Along the process from launcher Activity to load an illegal page, human operations are needed. To make it automatic, we need to simulate human operations. To mitigate this, we have made our own test system Android Tester by modifying the Android framework and we use Robotium developed a general test script app for the target apps . With this framework, we could know which Activity is active, which views are on this Activity, their IDs and how to trigger one specific event all of which other test tools cannot do. Once we jumped to the target Activity, how to jump to the HTTPS page within WebView if the default page is not an HTTPS page? Here in test script we adopt a strategy like a crawler. We first load the default page and extract all the links from the initial page and load every link and extract links again until we have found an HTTPS link or the crawl layer depth is up to 3.

2.3 System Overview

We present the overview of our system in Figure 2. Our system takes APK file as input, and outputs the app is vulnerable or not. First, our system carries out a static analysis to determine if apps are potential vulnerable. Second, we need to dynamically run them and to confirm if it's really vulnerable, which is requisite because of the difficulty of validness verification of the self-implemented error handling process and the uncertainty that if the WebView would load an HTTPS page that cannot be solved during static analysis. So we need to build the app's ACG for dynamic analyzing.

Dynamic analysis starts with installing and running the app on emulator. Then our system would find a path from launcher Activity to target Activity. When the path is found, the system triggers an event and jumps to next Activity till the target Activity. After each jump, our system

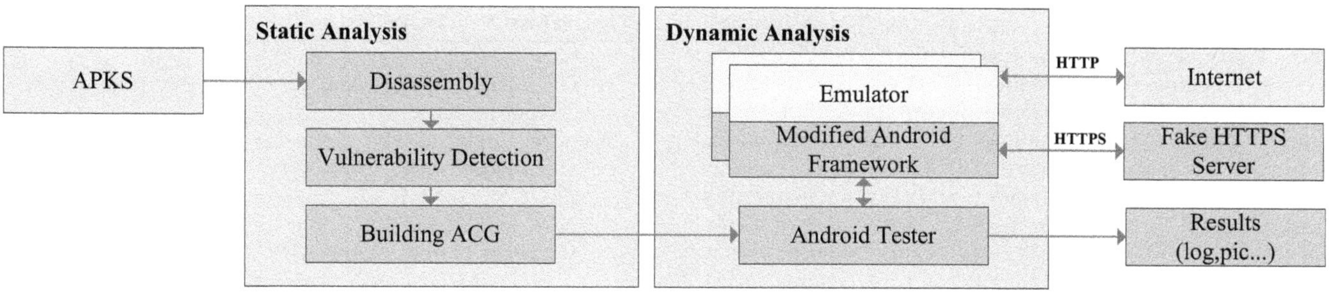

Figure 2: System Overview

calculates the path again in order to avoid the situation that the path found earlier is not applicable because of some extra conditions. During this process, we may not be able to find efficacious path, because there are some views that need conditions to appear (e.g. some app may have an advanced panel that would appear only under advanced mode). Under this condition we jump to target activity directly. At the same time, we built an attack environment (shown in Figure 2) which could redirect HTTPS connections to our fake server who has an illegal certificate. We modified Android framework to print log once an illegal page are presented. At last our system will generate log information and tell us which app is vulnerable and what URL the app has visited.

3. DETAILED DESIGN

3.1 Static Analysis Module

Static Detection. We decompile APK into Smali file by apktool[5]. The static analysis starts once the decompilation process finished. We scan all the smali files to find if there is any class inherits from the `WebViewClient` class. If not found, then we consider the app is free from this vulnerability. We collect all the classes inherit from `WebViewClient` and check them one by one to determine whether they have overridden the method **`onReceivedSslError`** which would be called by system callback when HTTPS certificate verification failure occurs. The app could trust illegal pages by overriding this method with a rather weak one. According to our research, most app chooses to trust all certificate, and some of them use a simple way to handle this error and the others choose to abort the page.

We have identified three common operations that app choose to perform in **`onReceivedSslError`**.First, They trust all certificate and returns proceed signal. Obviously this is vulnerable if it's reachable. Second, They reject and return cancel signal. It's free from this vulnerability. Third, They verify certificate by itself. Some of them check hostnames, and some of them use complex algorithm, and some of them even show a dialog for the user to make a choice. We can't determine if the app is vulnerable or not by static analysis, so we need further detect by dynamic analysis.

Build MCG We have seen some apps with unreachable code and most of them are for testing. So we have to make sure the overridden method **`onReceivedSslError`** is reachable. We would build a Method Call Graph to fulfill this. It is a directed graph representing the calling relationship among methods. Each node in MCG represents one method and an edge from Method `A` to Method `B` means that Method `A` could call Method `B` directly. We employed a conservative approach like[6] to handle virtual method and interfaces while building MCG. A class hierarchy was maintained during the analysis process and all possible assignable classes would be considered when an ambiguous reference occurred.

Algorithm 1 Build Activity Call Graph

Input:
MCG : Method Call Graph
ms : Temporary storage of methods
Output: ACG : Activity Call Graph
function BUILDACG(*MCG*,*AndroidManifest.xml*)
InitACGNodes(*ACG*,*AndroidManifest.xml*)
ms = getParents(MCG,"$startActivity$()") ∪ getParents(MCG,"$startActivityForResult$()");
for each method *method* in *ms* **do**
$Eactivity$ = getTargetActivity($method$)
IDs = FindMethodCallerViewId(MCG,$method$,ϕ)
for each view ID *viewid* in IDs **do**
$Sactivity$ = findActivityByViewID($viewid$)
$ACG = ACG \cup (Sactivity\text{-}Eactivity|viewid)$
end for
end for
end function

function FINDMETHODCALLERVIEWID(*MCG*,*method*,*IDs*)
if *method* is View Event Method **then**
$IDs = IDs \cup$ FindViewId($method$,MCG)
else
ms = getParents($method$,MCG);
for each method *tmethod* in *ms* **do**
FindMethodCallerViewId(MCG,$tmethod$,IDs)
end for
end if
return IDs
end function

In particular, our system builds MCG based on some prior knowledge. Because there are some method calls in system space where we can't reach such as method **`Thread.start`** and method **`Thread.run`**, they do not have any relationship in user space, but from our knowledge **`Thread.Start`** will invoke **`Thread.Run`**. So with this knowledge we added some edges in MCG in advance.

Locate Target Activities Native Android app UI consists of several Activities in some of which WebView embedded. The system callbacks would call the methods in the classes which inherit from `WebViewClient` which we define as self-defined-WebViewClient. To make sure **`onRe-`**

ceivedSslError is reachable code we would find the activity whose WebView uses vulnerable self-defined-WebViewClient.

Once the vulnerable self-defined-WebViewClient is found, the system backtraces through MCG until the Activity which sets the `WebViewClient` is found. The backtracing would stop when it enters the system callback methods (currently our system could only handle `Activity.onCreate` and `View.onClick`) because there is no apparent method invoking these methods. We call these entry methods. Once the entry methods are found, it's easy to determine target Activity. If the entry methods are system callbacks of one Activity, this Activity is the target Activity. The Activity which owns the view is target Activity if the entry methods are system callbacks of a view. For Android app only these Activities that are declared in `AndroidManifest.xml` could be presented. That's why we check the target Activities set and delete Activities which are undeclared in `AndroidManifest.xml`.

Build ACG Now, we have got target Activities. Our purpose is to jump to target Activities from the launcher Activity and trigger the vulnerability. We need to find a way from launcher Activity to each target Activity with the help of ACG which is introduced before. We use algorithm 1 to build ACG. Each node in ACG represents one Activity that is declared in `AndroidManifest.xml`. Native Android UI jumps from one to another Activity because of View Event (such as `Button.onClick`). So each edge in ACG represents one View ID whose event method triggers native Android UI jumps from edge start Activity to edge end Activity. To our knowledge, there are two system calls to make activity jump, they are `startActivity` and `startActivityForResult`. They both need an `intent` which sets the jump to Activity as parameter. To build the edges, we backtrace the parameters of these two system calls (`startActivity` and `startActivityForResult`) to find the Activity (as `A1`) it starts. At the same time, we would find which View Event calls the system calls directly or indirectly during the backtracing process. Then we could find out the View ID (as ID1) and which Activity (as `A2`) owns this View. Then we add this edge { `A2 - A1` | ID1.`event` } to ACG. The jump-to Activity sets in `intent` is not easy to find. There are six constructors of `intent`[4] and two kinds of `intent`: explicit intent and implicit intent. Explicit intent needs target Activity name which is recorded in `AndroidManifest.xml` as parameter however implicit intent just needs an action name which is also defined in `AndroidManifest.xml`. The Activity name of an explicit Intent could be tracked by method backtracing and register backtracing. For implicit Intents, we first scan the `AndroidManifest.xml` file and build the correspondence of the Activities and Actions. Once we have got the Action, jump-to Activity could be determined via correspondence built before.

3.2 Dynamic Analysis Module

This module is the most important part of our system. In this module our system automatically runs each app on an emulator and triggering native Android UI to target activity to check whether the app shows an illegal page. We use algorithm 2 to drive UI to target activity.

Dynamic Test Environment. In order to improve the efficiency of our system we apply multi-emulator to run the test. During this phase we need to install and run the app, and to make it automatically we need to simulate human operations on testing app. To meet our needs, the dynamic test environment should have the following features: Being able to understand the UI states, such as which activity is shown on screen, the position and ID of each View, the screen is showing a dialog or not; Being able to get UI objects, such as get the object of the button that is displayed on screen; Being able to perform actions, such as performing click action on a button by specified button id; Being able to get return value, such as whether a click action is successful or not.

In order to achieve these features, we have modified Android system tool `instrumentation`[7] by bypassing the signature verification phase, which allow us to test other apps with our own test script app (APK) though they have different signatures. With modified `instrumentation`, we don't need to re-sign the target app which may cause app crash. We developed a general test script app of which the configuration file was obtained from static analysis. With these features, we could run the test automatically. The configuration file would be generated automatically from information (e.g. ACG, target activities) obtained during static analysis phase. Then the app would be installed and tested according to the script app automatically.

After the app was installed, our system would drive the app to jump to the target Activities and further to trigger the vulnerability once the test script started by simulating a series of human operations. This driving procedure is divid-

Algorithm 2 UI Drive

```
Input:
  ACG : Activity Call Graph
  tas, target activities
  for each target activity act in tas do
    start target APP
    tACG = copy(ACG)
    ca = getCurrentActivity()
    while ca is from target APP and ca is NOT act do
      ViewID = FindNextEdge(tACG,ca,act)
      if ViewID is NOT NULL then
        perform(ViewID)
      else
        perform(return)
      end if
      WaitForJumpOrTimeOut()
      ca = getCurrentActivity()
    end while
    if ca is act then
      TryToOpenHTTPSWebPage()
    end if
    stop target APP
  end for

  function FindNextEdge(ACG,ca,ta)
    path = findPath(ACG,ca,ta)
    if path is φ then
      return NULL
    else
      edg = first edge of path
      ACG = ACG - edg
      return edg
    end if
  end function
```

Table 1: Results of Static Analysis

Potential Vulnerable Apps #	1360	9.8%
Free from such Vulnerability #	12203	88.3%
Decompilation Failure #	257	1.9%
Total Apps #	13820	

Table 2: Results of Dynamic Analysis

Vulnerability Confirmed #	645	47.4%
Vulnerability Free #	715	52.6%
Potential Vulnerable Apps #	1360	

ed into two parts: native Android UI driving and WebView UI driving. Native Android UI driving drives the UI to target Activity and WebView driving drives WebView to load an HTTPS web page.

We take a target Activity and calculate the path from current Activity to it based on ACG. If the path exists, we get the first edge in path which represents a View ID and a View event, trigger the View event for this View and delete this edge from ACG to avoid infinite loop. If the path doesn't exist, which means there is no way from current activity to target activity, we return to system or roll back to the previous activity. Once jumped to the next Activity, we do the same thing, calculating paths, triggering events and deleting edges until jump to the target Activity. For the condition that some view is visible on some conditions (i.e. click other button first), we directly jump to the target Activity. Once we have jumped to the target Activity with the WebView, To trigger the potential vulnerable code we have built an attack environment that could redirect to our illegal page when the app tries to load an HTTPS page. But there are some apps which load a static local page or HTTP page first with several links on it. Here we adopt a strategy like a crawler to find the HTTPS link and load it. We first extract all the links from the initial page and load every link and extract links again until we have found an HTTPS link or the craw layer depth is up to 3. It's worthy to note that we don't need to find all HTTPS links because all HTTPS links share the same error handling process.

Confirm vulnerability. While the WebView loads an HTTPS page, it will show a blank page if the WebView rejects the illegal certificate, otherwise it will show the illegal web page. So we check the WebView if it's a blank page or not which determines if this app is vulnerability or not.

With all detailed running information it's easy for us to figure out why this app is vulnerable and what is the function of the HTTPS web page. More over this information helps us analyze the result statistically and more general.

4. EVALUATION

We run experiments on two machines with Ubuntu OS, one for test and another for attack environment. We have downloaded 13,820 apps by its download rank from 360 market as dataset in July 2014.

Static analysis takes 13.5 hours to finish, 3.5 seconds per app which is fast enough to deal with large scale analysis. For decompilation, there are 257 apps can't be decompiled. The result of static analysis is shown in Table 1. From this table, there are 1,360 apps are potential vulnerable from a total number of 13,820. The apps that have its own SSL/TLS certificate verification error handling account for 9.8 percent which are potential vulnerable and need to be further detected in dynamic analysis to confirm if they are truly vulnerable or not. For the rest 12,203 apps checked as free of this vulnerability during static analysis, they either don't have their own `WebViewClient` or the code unreachable or the code reject the page with illegal certificate.

Table 3: Top 3 Categories of Vulnerable Activities

Categories	Count	Percentage
Payment	209	25.0%
Authenticate	280	33.5%
Login&Register	73	8.7%

Table 4: Vulnerable Apps in Ranking Interval

Ranking interval	Count	Percentage
1-1000	136	21.1%
1001-2000	94	14.6%
2001-3000	70	10.9%
3001-4000	50	7.7%
4001-5000	37	5.7%

In dynamic analyzing process, we have been employing 4 emulators with Android 4.2 to run the test apps and it takes 23 hours to run all 1,360 potential vulnerable apps and the average time for each app is 60.8 seconds. The result of dynamic analysis is listed in Table 2 from which we can see that nearly half (645) of the 1360 tested apps are confirmed vulnerable accounted 47.4 percent, which means nearly half of the certificate verification error handlings are not well designed or implemented. Also there are 715 apps are detected potential vulnerable in static analyzing process and confirmed not vulnerable in dynamic analysis because of the effectiveness of their own error handling.

Top 5 categories of vulnerable apps are shown in table 5. According to this table finance and social contain more vulnerable app than other categories and many of these apps employed third party SDK like Tecent Weibo, Sina Weibo and Alipay to fulfill some of their purpose. However, these three SDK are vulnerable themselves which makes all the apps employed these SDKs vulnerable. According vulnerable apps's download rank from the market in table 4, we found that the most popular apps (ranking interval from 1 to 1,000) have the highest vulnerable rate. Besides, the vulnerable rate decreased along with the popularity of the apps, which demonstrates the severity of this vulnerability. However, with the decline in ranking the vulnerable rate also fell, does not mean the apps with lower ranks are more secure. With further study we found that the apps with low rank are less likely to use HTTPS, which means they are more easily to be attacked.

Table 5: Top 5 Categories of Vulnerable Apps

Categories	Count	Percentage
Finance	56	8.7%
Social	56	8.7%
Lifestyle	51	7.9%
Entertainment	44	6.8%
Travel & Local	38	5.9%

We also defined category for each vulnerable activity by their name and function. We show those vulnerable activities in Table 3. The top two kinds are Payment and Authenticate Activity which weighted more than half of the total vulnerable Activities. The reason why so many Activities are these two categories is that, many apps are integrated with Tecent Weibo, Sina Weibo and Alipay SDKs and Tencent Weibo and Sina Weibo SDKs are social SSO SDKs and related to authentication and Alipay is a payment SDK. It's noteworthy that many vulnerable apps share a same vulnerable Activity. We have found a same vulnerable Activity in 128 different apps because of the integration of Alipay SDK.

5. RELATED WORK

Zheng *et al.* in [4] presented a system called SmartDroid which could lead native Android UI to the exposure of sensitive behaviors. But SmartDroid can't deal with web UI. Bhoraskar *et al.* in [8] presented an app automation tool called Brahmastra to test thirdparty components in mobile apps. Brahmastra is powerful enough to do that, but it can't test WebView UI which is necessary in our work.

Recently, a number of efforts have been made to reveal and mitigate SSL security problems. Fahl *et al.* [9] found Android SSL MITM vulnerability and developed a tool called Mallodroid to detect it. But they couldn't confirm the vulnerability automatically for large dataset. Sounthiraraj *et al.* in [1] developed a tool called SMV-Hunter to detect the SSL MITM vulnerability which is able to detect automatically for large scale dataset. Our work is directly inspired by SMV-Hunter. However, our system is very different from it, which is designed for different vulnerabilities with different techniques. SMV-Hunter focuses on app built-in SSL verification weakness, whereas our system focuses on the weakness in HTTPS verification error handling process. Meanwhile, the SSL usage is also different. In SMV-Hunter, it aims to find the apps that use SSL for the backend network communication. In our work, the use of the SSL is UI-based, namely, the web page will show up until that the WebView is show up. This means we have to manage to do more to jump to the target activity and open the HTTPS web page. Tendulkar *et al.* discussed the same problem (`onReceivedSslError`) in [10], and we almost work on it at the same time. They just showed the problem without further study in [10], and we systematically studied on it and developed this tool to detect this problem automatically.

6. FUTURE WORK

There are several limitations of our approach. In static analysis, because of the object-oriented programming diagram there are some virtual method call which is only determined at run time. In dynamic analysis, some activities are reachable on specific conditions. For example, if we want to jump to checkout activity on some shopping apps we have to login and put some goods in the shopping cart. We would get an error if we jump to the activity directly. And some UI elements are visible on particular conditions. For example, a logout button is not visible until you have logged in.

7. CONCLUSION

In this paper, we discovered a new type vulnerability for hybrid Android apps, which could affect Android WebView HTTPS connection making secure connection vulnerable. We have designed a new detection system that uses both static analysis and dynamic analysis to detect this type of vulnerability automatically on a large dataset of apps. Our static analysis discerns potential vulnerable apps and generates essential information to guide the dynamic analysis, which is used to confirm whether the app is vulnerable or not by automatically triggering the vulnerability facilitated for both native Android UI and WebView UI . We have applied our system to test 13,820 apps, and in total we found 645 of them truly vulnerable.

Acknowledgements

This work is partially supported by National Natural Science Foundation of China (61173068, 61173139), Program for New Century Excellent Talents in University of the Ministry of Education, the Key Science Technology Project of Shandong Province (2014GGD01063), the Independent Innovation Foundation of Shandong Province (2014CGZH1106) and the Shandong Provincial Natural Science Foundation (ZR2014FM020).

8. REFERENCES

[1] D. Sounthiraraj, J. Sahs, G. Greenwood, Z. Lin, and L. Khan, "Smv-hunter: Large scale, automated detection of ssl/tls man-in-the-middle vulnerabilities in android apps," in *Proceedings of the 19th Network and Distributed System Security Symposium. San Diego, California, USA*, 2014.

[2] J. Clark and P. C. van Oorschot, "Sok: Ssl and https: Revisiting past challenges and evaluating certificate trust model enhancements," in *Proceedings of the Security and Privacy*. IEEE, 2013.

[3] https://code.google.com/p/androguard/.

[4] C. Zheng, S. Zhu, S. Dai, G. Gu, X. Gong, X. Han, and W. Zou, "Smartdroid: an automatic system for revealing ui-based trigger conditions in android applications," in *Proceedings of the second ACM workshop on Security and privacy in smartphones and mobile devices*. ACM, 2012, pp. 93–104.

[5] https://code.google.com/p/android apktool/.

[6] M. C. Grace, Y. Zhou, Z. Wang, and X. Jiang, "Systematic detection of capability leaks in stock android smartphones." in *Proceedings of the 19th Annual Symposium on Network and Distributed System Security*, 2012.

[7] https://developer.android.com/reference/android/app/Instrumentation.html.

[8] R. Bhoraskar, S. Han, J. Jeon, T. Azim, S. Chen, J. Jung, S. Nath, R. Wang, D. Wetherall, D. Langenegger *et al.*, "Brahmastra: Driving apps to test the security of third-party components." in *Proceedings of the 23rd USENIX conference on Security Symposium*, 2014.

[9] S. Fahl, M. Harbach, T. Muders, L. Baumgärtner, B. Freisleben, and M. Smith, "Why eve and mallory love android: An analysis of android ssl (in) security," in *Proceedings of the 2012 ACM conference on Computer and communications security*. ACM, 2012.

[10] V. Tendulkar and W. Enck, "An application package configuration approach to mitigating android ssl vulnerabilities," in *Proceedings of the 2014 Mobile Security Technologies Conference*, 2014.

Torben: A Practical Side-Channel Attack for Deanonymizing Tor Communication

Daniel Arp
University of Göttingen
Göttingen, Germany

Fabian Yamaguchi
University of Göttingen
Göttingen, Germany

Konrad Rieck
University of Göttingen
Göttingen, Germany

Abstract

The Tor network has established itself as de-facto standard for anonymous communication on the Internet, providing an increased level of privacy to over a million users worldwide. As a result, interest in the security of Tor is steadily growing, attracting researchers from academia as well as industry and even nation-state actors. While various attacks based on traffic analysis have been proposed, low accuracy and high false-positive rates in real-world settings still prohibit their application on a large scale.

In this paper, we present *Torben*, a novel deanonymization attack against Tor. Our approach is considerably more reliable than existing traffic analysis attacks, simultaneously far less intrusive than browser exploits. The attack is based on an unfortunate interplay of technologies: (a) web pages can be easily manipulated to load content from untrusted origins and (b) despite encryption, low-latency anonymization networks cannot effectively hide the size of request-response pairs. We demonstrate that an attacker can abuse this interplay to design a side channel in the communication of Tor, allowing short *web page markers* to be transmitted to expose the web page a user visits over Tor. In an empirical evaluation with 60,000 web pages, our attack enables detecting these markers with an accuracy of over 91% and no false positives.

Categories and Subject Descriptors

C.2.0 [**Computer-Communication Networks**]: General—*Security and Protection*; I.5.4 [**Pattern Recognition**]: Applications

Keywords

Anonymity; Side Channels; Traffic Analysis

ASIA CCS'15, April 14–17, 2015, Singapore..

ACM 978-1-4503-3245-3/15/04 ...$15.00.
http://dx.doi.org/10.1145/2714576.2714627.

1. INTRODUCTION

The Tor network is one of the largest efforts to provide anonymity and privacy on the Internet. The network implements a low-latency anonymity service based on the concept of Onion Routing. The network consists of over 6,000 relay nodes worldwide that enable its users to relay communication through a circuit of these nodes, for example, to anonymously express their opinion or circumvent digital censorship.

With the increasing use of Tor in practice, research on attacks against this service have gained considerable attention. A large body of work has studied *passive attacks* based on traffic analysis, most notably website fingerprinting and traffic confirmation attacks. The former enable an attacker to detect patterns indicative for web pages in Tor traffic [e.g., 2, 4, 8]. Although these approaches provide good results in closed-world settings, in practice they suffer from high false-positive rates. Traffic confirmation attacks on the other hand are not limited to web traffic but require an attacker who is able to eavesdrop on both ends of a communication over a long period of time [e.g., 6, 9]. A second strain of research has thus considered *active attacks* against the Tor network, such as path-selection attacks based on network congestion and traffic watermarking using packet delays [e.g., 10]. While these techniques provide a more accurate and faster deanonymization, they involve a significant effort for the adversary. As a result, the few known cases of deanonymization of Tor have been reported to instead make use of advertisement networks or rely on vulnerabilities in browser implementations and are thus unrelated to insecurities of Tor itself.

In this paper, we present *Torben*, a novel deanonymization attack against Tor that is significantly more reliable than traffic analysis attacks but far less intrusive than browser exploits. In contrast to other active attacks, Torben operates entirely on the application layer and does not require Tor nodes or routers to be controlled by the adversary. The attack is based on an unfortunate interplay of technologies: First, web pages can often be manipulated to load content from untrusted origins, for example, using advertisements or user-provided content. Second, despite encryption, low-latency anonymization networks cannot effectively hide the size of request-response pairs in web traffic. We show that an attacker can abuse this interplay to design a side channel in the communication of Tor. This side channel enables the transmission of short *web page markers* that expose the web page a user visits to an observer between the Tor client and the entry node. Although it is well-known that active web content allows to track the visitors of web pages, we are the first to show that it can be used to deanonymize Tor users in a short period of time.

In summary, our contributions are the following:

- We present a novel side channel in Tor communication. By issuing HTTP requests from the user's browser, an attacker is able to induce distinct patterns observable in encrypted traffic.
- We demonstrate that this side channel can be used to perform a novel deanonymization attack against Tor, allowing us to transmit *web page markers* exposing the page visited by a user.
- Finally, we show that these web page markers can be accurately detected in real Tor traffic with high accuracy by combining techniques from signal processing and machine learning.

2. BACKGROUND

Before presenting our deanonymization attack and discussing details of how to transmit data through the underlying side channel, we need to briefly review the basics of the Tor network (Section 2.1) and define the attack scenario we are considering (Section 2.2).

2.1 The Tor Network

The Tor network [3] is a low-latency anonymization network whose purpose is to protect the privacy of its users by obfuscating their network traffic. This is achieved by tunneling user traffic through arbitrary paths in the Tor network, which consist of multiple hops (Tor relays) that run the Tor software and are operated by volunteers. The security of Tor is based on the use of strong encryption and the large number of relays that can be used to establish a path, thus significantly lowering the ability of an attacker to easily eavesdrop a communication or link senders and receivers.

A user who wants to establish a connection to a server through Tor has to run a Tor client on his computer which will first select a path through the Tor network. After establishing a path, the user can send data over the Tor network using fixed size Tor cells which are multi-layer encrypted with previously negotiated session keys. Each relay node on the path then removes one layer of encryption while the cell is forwarded to its destination.

2.2 Attack Scenario

For our attack, we consider a scenario that involves an active attacker. We assume that, first, this attacker is able to monitor the encrypted communication between a Tor client and the entry node, and, second, she actively implants a marker into a web page of interest. An overview of this attack scenario is depicted in Figure 1.

Let us, for instance, consider a totalitarian regime or law enforcement agency that wants to determine whether a particular user visits a certain web page, despite the fact that Tor is being used to anonymize the communication. Clearly, this attacker can be expected to be capable of observing the encrypted network communication between the user's browser and the Tor entry node. However, this alone is a vast underestimation of her capabilities, as it considers a passive attacker. It is reasonable to assume that the user's browser may be exposed to attacker-provided web content at some point throughout the browsing session. This content may be delivered through a multitude of vectors. Based on the chosen vector, we consider the following two variants of the attack scenario:

- **Remote markers** In this scenario, the attacker exploits the fact that web pages often embed content from different origins, some of which might be controlled by the attacker. The attacker may, for instance, be able to host and advertisement on the web page.
- **Local markers** In this scenario, the attacker is able to inject content directly into a web page. For example, the content of a web page may be manipulated at the server to track its users.

Regardless of the type of the marker, attacker-provided content is loaded in the user's browser and can be used to generate a characteristic pattern in the resulting Tor communication. This pattern can then be detected in the encrypted traffic between the Tor client and the entry node, ultimately enabling an adversary to deanonymize the visitors of marked web pages.

3. A SIDE-CHANNEL ATTACK ON TOR

A fundamental limitation of low-latency anonymization networks is that they cannot effectively hide the sizes and order of relayed packets. For users browsing web pages via Tor, this means that HTTP request and response sizes directly influence the stream of TLS records observed between the Tor client and the entry node. Unfortunately, this setting can be exploited by an attacker. If the user accesses attacker-controlled content, such as JavaScript code, the attacker gains partial control over the stream of request and response sizes.

The overall idea of our attack is to leverage this control to carry out a side-channel attack by creating distinct communication patterns in the encrypted data stream that can be effectively detected using machine learning techniques. While this idea is simple at core, applying it to construct a successful attack requires careful engineering of a number of different components. In particular, the following four challenges need to be addressed:

- **Preprocessing of network traces.** Network traces need to be preprocessed and transformed into a robust representation suitable for analysis of request and response sizes (Section 3.1).
- **Side channel design.** A reliable side channel needs to be designed that allows short messages to be transmitted to an attacker observing the encrypted data stream of Tor (Section 3.2).
- **Transmission of web page markers.** Markers need to be transmitted using the side channel, such that the visit of a marked web page induces a distinct pattern in the encrypted traffic (Section 3.3).
- **Detection of web page markers.** Finally, a method for automatic detection of these web page markers is required that enables identifying individual markers in real network traces (Section 3.4).

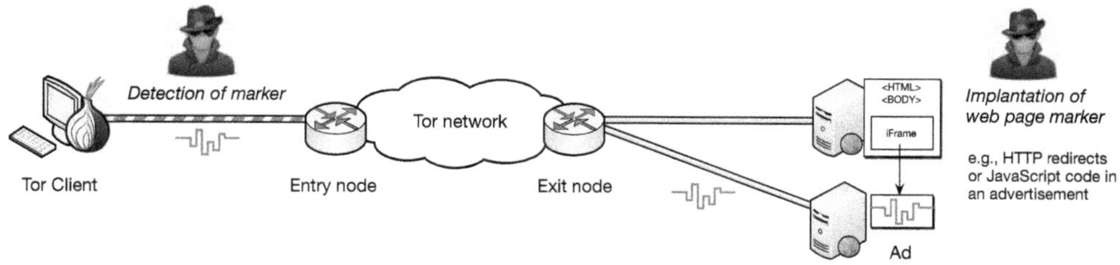

Figure 1: Attack scenario: A web page marker is implanted using embedded or user-provided content, such as an advertisement. The marker induces a traffic pattern visible at the entry node, for example, using JavaScript code.

3.1 Preprocessing of Network Traces

The success of traffic analysis attacks critically depends on the choice of a suitable representation of observed network communication. With this goal in mind, we preprocess network traces by leveraging inherent properties of the Tor protocol and the protocols it depends on, thus allowing us to remove noise sources and highlight those properties of network traffic that are controllable by the attacker. The key insight our preprocessing scheme is based on, is that by controlling the size of HTTP requests and responses, we do not gain control over the size of IP packets or TLS records but only over the *amount* of data transferred from one change of direction to the next. We devise a representation emphasizing this aspect of the record stream in a two-step procedure outlined in the following.

3.1.1 TCP Stream Reassembly

All Tor communication takes place via Tor cells encapsulated in TLS records. While HTTP communication relayed by the Tor network may influence these sequences, they are distorted by several noise sources that needlessly complicate analysis. In particular, delayed or dropped IP packets cause the transport layer to issue re-transmissions of packets.

Fortunately, we can easily address all of these problems by reassembling TCP streams using readily available tools such as *tshark*. This allows all subsequent analysis to be carried out on streams of TLS records as opposed to raw IP packets. In effect, the order of Tor cells is preserved and artifacts of TCP/IP such as re-transmissions and acknowledgments carrying no data are removed. To simplify all further processing, we map traces to sequences of record sizes where a positive and negative sign are used for incoming and outgoing traffic respectively.

3.1.2 Filtering and Merging TLS Records

We proceed to apply the following chain of transformations to account for various properties of Tor and TLS that impact the analysis of network traffic.

Filtering empty records. As a first step, we filter sequences such that they only contain entries representing records of 100 bytes or more. This preserves Tor cells as the minimum cell size is 512 bytes.

Merging of records. We merge adjacent TLS records going into the same direction to obtain a sequence representing the amount of data rather than individual records.

Filtering control cells. We filter single cells that are unrelated to user data by discarding any sizes smaller than twice the cell size after merging. Upon removal of these single cells, we merge TLS records again to connect data relay cells previously separated by control cells.

Normalization of sizes. The concrete sizes of transfered data vary slightly depending on the version of Tor and its libraries. As a simple normalization, we express all sizes in multiples of 2000 bytes.

Upon completion of the preprocessing step, each Tor connection is represented by a sequence of integers that encodes the amount, direction and order of data transfers. We refer to these sequences as *data transfer sequences* throughout the rest of this paper.

3.2 Side Channel Design

We design our side channel such that it satisfies the following two properties: First, normal web traffic should be clearly distinguishable from any side-channel communication to make false positives very unlikely. Second, the transmission speed needs to be high enough to allow short byte sequences to be transmitted before the user leaves a web page.

Side-channel communication can only be distinguished from regular web traffic, if data transfer patterns exist that are atypical for normal web pages. We thus design 16 different symbols using request-response pairs with discrete request and response sizes of $2,000$, $4,000$, $6,000$ and $8,000$ bytes. These sizes are large enough to be atypical but still enable a fast transmission.

A message is then encoded by splitting it into quad bits and encoding each quad bit separately using the corresponding request-response pair. By concatenating the resulting symbols, we finally obtain a data transfer sequence suitable for transmission over the side channel. A more detailed discussion of our side channel can be found in [1].

3.3 Transmission of Web Page Markers

Equipped with a side channel, we can now expose visited web pages by transmitting suitable messages from the user's browser. This, however, creates two additional challenges. First, a suitable browser-based mechanism for transmission of correctly ordered sequences of HTTP requests needs to be found, and second, *web page markers* that encode the names or URLs of visited web pages need to be constructed.

3.3.1 Issuing HTTP Requests

In our experiments, we assume that an attacker is able to execute JavaScript code within the browser of a Tor user. This code can be embedded in a displayed advertisement, injected via cross-site scripting or contained in any other included JavaScript code. For establishing the side channel, the code does not need to operate in the context of the marked web page and thus our attack is not effected by the same-origin policy.

The standard JavaScript object `XMLHttpRequest` offers a mechanism for request transmission that fits our needs perfectly. The object allows requests to be issued from the user's browser synchronously while offering fine-grained control over request content and headers. We can employ `XMLHttpRequest` to transmit a request-response pair (r_1, r_2) using the following URL

`http://server.com/res?str`

where `res` is simply a resource of size r_1, such as an image or a document, and `str` a random string of length r_2 attached to the URL. We choose a random string here to reduce caching effects induced by some browsers. Note that the contacted server can be any server offering resources with the required sizes. It is sufficient to find a server that offers resources with four different sizes to successfully carry out the attack. Consequently, the server does not need to be controlled by the attacker and hence provides no information about the attacker's origin.

3.3.2 *Web Page Markers*

We are now able to transmit short messages over the side channel to expose web pages visited using Tor. If the attacker only wants to monitor a single web page, choosing a constant message is sufficient. However, to monitor multiple web pages or track how a user browses from one page to another, the web page markers need to be designed such that they have a large pairwise Hamming distance. To achieve this, we use the 20 byte SHA-1 hash value of the monitored URL as a web page marker. This ensures that there is a natural mapping between URLs and their markers.

3.4 Detection of Web Page Markers

The presented side channel allows web page markers to be transmitted and recognized by human observers, yet due to the vast amount of network traffic to analyze, our attack only becomes practical if the markers can be detected automatically.

To identify markers in a monitored data transfer sequence, we use a sliding window and classify the sequence under each window independently. This highlights an advantage of our attack over related traffic analysis attacks. Since the marker is transmitted in a small time frame, it is perfectly valid to limit the analysis to small sequences of the network trace, in our experiments 100 symbols, thus significantly reducing the computational resources required for training a classifier and detecting web page markers.

In order to detect the markers, we train a multi-class Support Vector Machine (SVM) with probabilistic outputs on the sequences of individual web page markers. Given an unknown sequence, the SVM can then be used to identify the most likely web page marker present in this sequence. Due to the probabilistic output, we are able to quantify the confidence of this decision, which enables us to determine sequences that do not correspond to any of the known markers. A sequence is thereby mapped into a high-dimensional vector space using positional n-grams which we introduced for this purpose. More details on the embedding can be found in the technical report [1].

4. EVALUATION

We evaluate the Torben attack in a series of experiments that allows us to assess its effectiveness in different settings. After presenting our experimental setup (Section 4.1 & 4.2), we first evaluate the attack in a closed-world setting (Section 4.3) where users can only visit web pages from a fixed set. We furthermore proceed to consider an open-world setting where users can freely choose web pages from a potentially infinite number of web pages—60,000 in our experiment—(Section 4.4). The open-world setting allows us to obtain a good approximation for the false-positive rate of our attack. Finally, we perform a live experiment where we evaluate the ability of Torben to identify web page markers in real-world traffic generated by multiple users (Section 4.5). Note, that a more detailed description of our evaluation can be found in [1].

4.1 Data Collection

To automatically visit a large number of web pages over the Tor network in an acceptable time, we use the *Selenium WebDriver* (version 2.38.3), a browsing automation plug-in for Mozilla Firefox. The plug-in is installed along side the Tor browser bundle (version 3.5), the standard distribution of Tor. This ensures that the browser configuration used in our experiments almost exactly matches the configuration employed by most Tor users.

For our experiments we automatically visit different sets of the top one million web pages from the Alexa ranking (retrieved in February 2014). For the vast majority of web pages, the *Selenium WebDriver* can automatically determine when the page is fully loaded based on loading of the page icon. In rare cases, successful page load is not detected within 3 minutes. In these cases we discard this web page and use the next page in the Alexa ranking instead. Moreover, we remove variants of very similar pages. For example, we consider only `google.com` and not `google.de` or `google.fr`. This is necessary to obtain a better comparison with website fingerprinting approaches as these approaches are known to fail if web pages are too similar.

4.2 Detection Setup

To perform the Torben attack in practice, we implement the preprocessing, transmission and detection steps outlined in Section 3. For extracting positional n-grams from network traces, we use the tool *Sally*[1] (version 0.8.3) and for learning the probabilistic classification the library *LibSVM*[2].

For training the detection method described in Section 3.4, we generate 100 web page markers using the SHA-1 hashes of the top Alexa web pages and record 50 transmissions for each of these markers over Tor. Note that only the web page markers and not the actual web pages are recorded for training our detection method.

4.3 Closed-World Evaluation

In the first experiment, we consider a closed-world setting, where we visit each of the top 100 Alexa web pages 50 times, first in February 2014 and a second time in April 2014 resulting in two data sets. To simulate the attack scenario of a remote marker, we use a reverse proxy and inject a small JavaScript snippet into each page that opens a sep-

[1]http://www.mlsec.org/sally/

[2]http://www.csie.ntu.edu.tw/c̃jlin/libsvm/

arate browser window containing the marker, similar to an advertisement. The marker is transmitted after a delay of 30 seconds. As 10 of the 100 web pages load very slowly over Tor and largely overlap with the marker, we increase the delay to 120 seconds in these cases.

The transmission time of the web page markers ranges from 12 to 20 seconds with a mean of 18 seconds. As the transmission happens in the background, these slight differences to the original web page traffic are hardly noticeable, in particular because communication over Tor often suffers from rather long loading times.

To enable a comparison with related website fingerprinting attacks, we implement the approaches by Herrmann et al. [4], Panchenko et al. [8] and Cai et al. [2], where the first is slightly modified to use an SVM instead of an MNB classifier. For all approaches, we conduct the same experimental procedure as for the Torben attack, except that we do not implant markers into the web pages. Furthermore, our detection method is trained solely on web page markers, whereas the fingerprinting attacks are trained on a sample of the web pages visited in February 2014.

Figure 2a shows the performance of Torben and the website fingerprinting attacks on the web pages visited in February 2014. Our approach is able to correctly deanonymize 95% of the web page visits, whereas the performance of the other attacks ranges from 38.9% to 90.6%. However, all website fingerprinting attacks suffer from changes in web content. When applied to the same web pages visited in April 2014, none of the passive approaches is able to correctly identify more than a third of the web pages, as shown in Figure 2b. By contrast, the Torben attacks attains a similar performance as in February 2014 and outperforms the website fingerprinting attacks, as the learned markers do not change over time.

Overall, this experiment demonstrates that the proposed side-channel attack can deanonymize web page visits with high accuracy in a closed-world setting.

4.4 Open-World Evaluation

In this experiment, we consider an open-world setting, where the user can freely visit web pages from a large unknown set and only few of these pages are tagged with a web page marker. The adversary is thus interested in determining whether marked web pages have been visited by a particular user.

We extend the previous experiment by additionally choosing 60,000 web pages at random from the Alexa top one million ranking, none of which are part of the top 100 web pages. Each of these web pages is then visited once over Tor without sending a marker. This large set of web pages enables us to estimate the false-positive rate of the Torben attack. Due to the usage of an SVM with probabilistic output, we can simply identify data transfer sequences that do not contain a web page marker by setting a threshold on the determined probabilities.

Figure 2c shows a ROC curve for the detection performance of Torben in this experiment. Note that the false-positive rate on the x-axis is given in the range 0 to 0.001, while the detection rate is shown on the y-axis between 0.6 and 1.0. The attack enables detecting more than 91% of the 100 web pages with no false positives in set of 60,000 additional web pages.

The outcome of the open-world evaluation demonstrates the reliability of the web page markers, which are unlikely to be confused with regular web page traffic and enable detecting marked pages with a very low false-positive rate. This reliability rests on the design of the side channel that makes use of atypical request-response pairs for transmitting information (Section 3.2).

4.5 Live Evaluation

The previous experiments already show the effectiveness of our approach on a large amount of data that has been recorded automatically. However, in order to fortify the obtained results, we conduct a further experiment in which we analyze web traffic of real users.

In this experiment, four different users surf through the web for roughly two hours using Tor. Each user visits arbitrary web pages and from time to time, randomly chosen marked web pages. We simulate the attack scenario of a remote marker as described in Section 4.3 and set the transmission delay for markers to 120 seconds.

Afterwards, the recorded traffic of each user is split into chunks of three minutes that are separately analyzed using a sliding window as described in Section 3.4. Hence, the classifier outputs a label and a probability score for each chunk. If the probability score of a chunk is below a particular threshold, we conclude that the user did not visit any marked web pages during this time frame. We select this threshold to be $t = 0.1$ based on several test runs which we conducted in advance. From a total of 34 visited marked web pages, we are able to detect and classify 31 correctly. Furthermore, the classifier does not output any false positives.

5. LIMITATIONS AND DEFENSES

Our experiments show that Torben is a reliable deanonymization technique against Tor. However, its limitations could enable development of effective defenses.

First of all, our attack makes no attempts of hiding web page markers. In consequence, developing a detection mechanism that identifies and suppresses communication on our side channel may be an effective method to protect users. Such mechanisms could be implemented either on the client side directly in the form of a browser plug-in or even by Tor nodes to protect all clients at once.

Second, our evaluation shows that web page markers may be corrupted if they largely overlap with the loading of a web page. This suggests that, although our classification model is able to compensate some traffic interference using positional features, it fails if the interference becomes too severe. A second option would thus be to introduce chaff traffic to disturb the side-channel communication. Yet, this option may not be satisfactory in practice, as it introduces additional traffic and might lower Tor's overall performance.

6. RELATED WORK

Attacks against anonymization techniques have been a vivid area of research in the last years. Several researchers have recognized that, while it may not be possible to decipher encrypted messages, when transmitted over a communication link, important characteristics of the data such as its size and partitioning into data units is often disclosed. For example, Liberatore et al. have shown that it is pos-

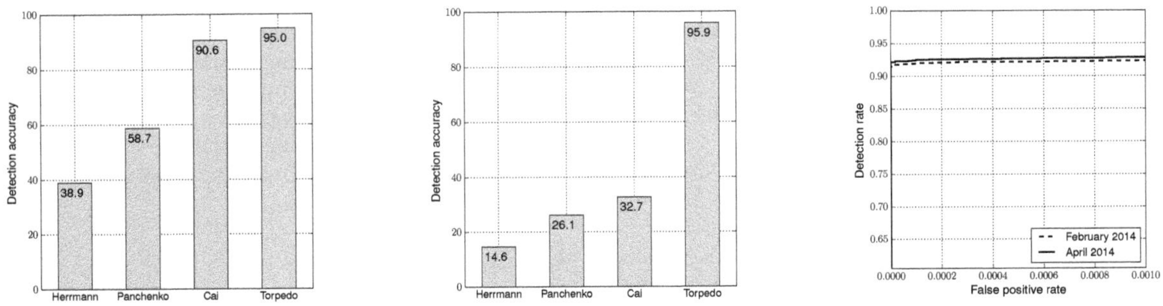

(a) February 2014 (b) April 2014 (c) ROC curve

Figure 2: Evaluation of the detection performance in the closed-world (a,b) and open-world scenario (c).

sible to identify web pages in encrypted HTTP traffic by observing characteristic packet lengths [7].

Based on this observation, website fingerprinting attacks try to deanonymize Tor users by identifying patterns in the encrypted traffic between user and guard node, which are characteristic for particular monitored web pages [2, 4, 8]. All of these approaches, however, suffer from false-positive rates that are too high to enable practical application. Moreover, our experiment demonstrate that website fingerprinting suffers from changes in web content and degrades deanonymization performance over time.

While website fingerprinting attacks consider an attacker only between the client and its entry node, traffic confirmation attacks require an attacker who is able to correlate the traffic on both ends of a communication path. Several authors demonstrated the effectiveness of such attacks [6, 9]. However, this scenario requires the attacker to have access to both ends of the connection over a long period of time.

Passive traffic analysis attacks require traffic to be observed for a longer period of time before users can be effectively deanonymized. Approaches where attackers actively attack the communication path to lower the required amount of time have therefore been proposed. Several of these watermarking schemes have been proposed for mixed networks which use inter-packet delays to encode watermarking sequences [5, 10]. In contrast to Torben, these attacks do not take place at the application layer and are thus much more difficult to realize in practice. Furthermore, they consider a stronger attacker who is able to control the exit node or the link between the exit node and the server.

7. CONCLUSION

Tor is among the largest and best understood anonymization networks operated to date, protecting the privacy of over a million users worldwide. This paper presents a novel deanonymization attack on Tor that exploits a fundamental weaknesses of low-latency anonymization networks. In particular, we show that an attacker capable of providing web content to users, e.g., through banner advertisements or cross-site scripting, is able to deanonymize users via a side-channel attack. By transmitting web page markers through this side channel, the attacker can expose the web pages a user visits within a couple of seconds. This attack is considerably more effective than known website fingerprinting attacks and far less intrusive than browser exploits used in the wild. Fortunately, the side-channel communication is clearly visible in network traces and hence it may be possible to implement detection approaches as a first countermeasure against this attack.

Acknowledgements. The authors acknowledge funding from BMBF under the project INDI (FZK 16KIS0154K) and from DFG under the project DEVIL (RI 2469/1-1).

References

[1] D. Arp, F. Yamaguchi, and K. Rieck. Torben: Deanonymizing Tor communication using web page markers. Technical Report IFI-TB-2014-01, University of Göttingen, 2014.

[2] X. Cai, X. C. Zhang, B. Joshi, and R. Johnson. Touching from a distance: Website fingerprinting attacks and defenses. In *Proc. of ACM Conference on Computer and Communications Security (CCS)*, 2012.

[3] R. Dingledine, N. Mathewson, and P. Syverson. Tor: The second-generation onion router. 2004.

[4] D. Herrmann, R. Wendolsky, and H. Federrath. Website fingerprinting: Attacking popular privacy enhancing technologies with the multinomial naive-bayes classifier. In *Proc. of ACM Workshop on Cloud Computing Security*, 2009.

[5] A. Houmansadr and N. Borisov. Swirl: A scalable watermark to detect correlated network flows. In *Proc. of Network and Distributed System Security Symposium (NDSS)*, 2011.

[6] B. N. Levine, M. K. Reiter, C. Wang, and M. K. Wright. Timing attacks in low-latency mix systems. In *Financial Cryptography*, 2004.

[7] M. Liberatore and B. N. Levine. Inferring the source of encrypted http connections. In *Proc. of ACM Conference on Computer and Communications Security (CCS)*, CCS '06, 2006.

[8] A. Panchenko, L. Niessen, A. Zinnen, and T. Engel. Website fingerprinting in onion routing based anonymization networks. In *Proc. of ACM Workshop on Privacy in the Electronic Society*, 2011.

[9] V. Shmatikov and M.-H. Wang. Timing analysis in low-latency mix networks: attacks and defenses. 2006.

[10] X. Wang, S. Chen, and S. Jajodia. Network flow watermarking attack on low-latency anonymous communication systems. In *Proc. of IEEE Symposium on Security and Privacy (S&P)*, 2007.

Tracing Attacks on U-Prove with Revocation Mechanism *

Lucjan Hanzlik, Przemysław Kubiak, Mirosław Kutyłowski
Faculty of Fundamental Problems of Technology, Wrocław University of Technology
Wybrzeże Wyspiańskiego 27, 50-370 Wrocław, Poland
firstname.secondname@pwr.edu.pl

ABSTRACT

Anonymous credential systems have to provide strong privacy protection: a user may prove his (chosen) attributes without leaking neither his identity nor other attributes. In this paper we consider U-Prove – one of the major commercial anonymous credential systems.

We show that the revocation mechanism designed for U-Prove enables a system provider to efficiently trace the users' activities. Namely, the Revocation Authority run the system provider may execute the U-Prove protocol in a malicious way so that: (a) the deviations from the protocol remain undetected, (b) the Revocation Authority becomes aware of each single authentication of a user in the whole system and can link them (regardless which attributes are disclosed by the user against the verifiers), (c) it can link presentation tokens with the corresponding token issuing procedure (under some conditions).

Thereby, the system described in the technical drafts of U-Prove does not guarantee privacy protection unless the system provider can be trusted unconditionally. In fact, a malicious provider may convert the Revocation Authority into a "Big Brother" installation.

Categories and Subject Descriptors

K.6.5 [**Security and Protection**]: [Authentication]

Keywords

anonymous credential; U-Prove; revocation; tracing attack; cryptographic accumulator; witness

1. INTRODUCTION

Anonymous credentials.

Anonymous credential system is a cryptographic framework in which a person receives an authentication token from a trust provider for the system. The token confirms a set of *attributes* of the owner, e.g. legal status, age, the rights to access a certain IT system, privileges, etc., but also the name, personal identity number, and so on. A holder of such a token, say Alice, can use it for authentication. If A is the set of attributes of Alice confirmed by the token, A' is an arbitrary subset of A, then she can execute an authentication protocol with Bob so that:

- she proves Bob that she holds an authentication token with all attributes from A',
- Bob cannot conclude anything about the attributes not contained in A', in particular in $A \setminus A'$.

"The attributes not contained in A" may include identity data such as the first name, the family name, and the personal ID number. The attributes revealed may include a pseudonym of the prover.

Based on the result of authentication protocol (and the value of attributes presented) the verifier Bob can make appropriate decisions. A good example of an attribute is the legal age enabling to engage into civil contracts.

Thereby, anonymous credentials can be used to reduce the information flow during authentication to the necessary minimum. So, we may hope that anonymous credentials may become a standard authentication method in privacy aware systems fulfilling the "privacy-by-design" requirement.

There are many models of anonymous credentials and subtle differences between them. For instance, it is an open issue whether the verifier should be able to check whether the same (anonymous) person authenticates herself, when the set of attributes is exactly the same. Both possibility of linking (*weak privacy*) and infeasibility of linking (*strong privacy*) correspond to some concrete use cases.

U-Prove.

The topic of this paper is an extension of U-Prove anonymous credentials system [1] developed by Microsoft. U-Prove is based on the quite complex ideas of Stefan Brands [2, 3], which evolved into the current anonymous credential system.

On the upside, U-Prove is very flexible and quite advanced regarding privacy protection. On the downside, its design is fairly complex. This is a major disadvantage not because of the implementation pains and hardness to explain the security mechanisms even to specialists, but mainly due to hardware requirements far above the possibilities of cryptographic smart cards. U-Prove is based on hardness of Discrete Logarithm Problem and that by design, U-Prove enables commitments which can be used to extend the specification. An interested reader may refer to the web page [4] for details of the U-Prove scheme and implementation details.

In the meantime, a large number of system details has been published [4] enabling external designers to integrate their products with U-Prove. Therefore, U-Prove has to be regarded as a system

*partially supported by project S40012/K1102 at Wrocław University of Technology

ASIA CCS'15, April 14–17, 2015, Singapore, Singapore

http://dx.doi.org/10.1145/2714576.2714597.

that has a real chance to play an important role in practice on a global scale, despite of lack of thorough academic evaluation.

Revocation.

It may happen that the attributes terminate to be valid for a holder of an authentication token. For instance, the token may be stolen. Then privacy protection offered by the system has a negative side effect – it hides identity of a misbehaving person very effectively. So the advanced technology starts to be dangerous to honest users, as there are more incentives to steal the tokens. These problems has been also recognized by the designers of U-Prove – see a recent report [5]. The core U-Prove system is not equipped with a revocation system – the necessary functionality must be added to it as an extension.

During Financial Cryptography'2013 the first revocation system for U-Prove has been presented [6]. It contained a security flaw [7], but the error seems to be correctable. The major drawback of the revocation system from [6] is heavy use of bilinear pairings. According to [5], *"Although pairings are popular in recent cryptographic research, they are seldom used in practice due to their maturity level and implementation complexity."* Definitely, currently the consumer's hardware devices are not supporting pairings (may be with some small scale exceptions).

Following [6], the Microsoft team proposed a modified revocation system which is not based on pairings and can be implemented in standard groups [8] (see [9] for a slightly updated version).

For the reader's convenience a specification of the revocation procedures from [9] is given in the Appendix. More details can be found in the technical drafts of U-Prove.

Our contribution.

We investigate the U-Prove revocation extension [8, 9] from the point of view of user's privacy. We show that within the current framework it is impossible to hide the revocation attributes of the users (which are effectively the user's pseudonyms) against the Revocation Authority. Namely, the Revocation Authority may learn about each single authentication performed with the user's pseudonym. For this purpose the Revocation Authority must deviate from the original protocol, but it cannot be detected by the users and the verifiers.

Although each security flaw presented in the paper can be fixed by re-designing the scheme and introducing new (computationally heavy) protocol components, it is not clear whether the extensions do not bring new threats and attack possibilities.

2. TRACING USERS' ACTIVITIES

In this section we present a couple of tracing attacks. They are designed for different scenarios and there is a clear realationship between simplicity and the attack scenario. In all cases the attacks enable to link activities of the same user (identified by the revocation attribute) based on the non-revocation proof. One might ask, what is the purpose of the attack, since U-Prove presentation tokens can by design be linked to a certain pseudonym and verifiers can distinguish if the same U-Prove token was used twice. However, the Revocation Authority does not receive the whole presentation token but only the non-revocation part. Moreover, it receives those proofs from all verifiers and might create an activity trace for each revocation attribute (binded with a U-Prove token) containing the authentication time and the verifier's identity.

What is more, from a practical point of view, the user has to disclose the revocation attribute x_{id} during the issuing procedure (or it may even be chosen by the issuer). Otherwise, it would be impossible for the issuer to revoke a credential, which could only be revoked on demand of the user. So if x_{id} is known to the issuer, he may collude with the Revocation Authority to link users' presentation tokens with a given issuing procedure. The Revocation Authority may even instantiate an issuer and create a full tracing system even without collusion.

The schemes proposed in [8, 9] are aimed to be suitable for a group G_q being a "standard construction", which means that the group G_q (see Table 2) need not to be pairing-friendly. Consequently, in order to verify the equality $Y = X^{\delta}$ in the procedure from Table 7 the Revocation Authority must be involved.

The initial attacks are less demanding computationally. However, the latter attacks seem to be more general: they remain undetectable even if witnesses are updated by the users from the very beginning of the revocation system work, that is, even if the complete list of the revoked revocation attributes is public. The attacks are described for the version [9], however they work for [8] after minor changes. Due to space reasons, we omit detailed description of the U-Prove system and its revocation extension. However, to ease the reading, in the appendix we present raw descriptions of the algorithms used in the U-Prove revocation extension. For full description, we refer the reader to the U-Prove specification [1] and the specification of its revocation extension [8, 9].

2.1 Attack for Local Witness Updates

In this section we investigate the scenario that the witnesses are recomputed by the users themselves according to the procedure `UpdateWitness` (for the case when the witnesses are recomputed by the Revocation Authority another attack applies).

When a user joins the system the first revocation witness (d, W, Q) is given to the user by the Revocation Authority. Moreover, we assume that the complete set R of revoked users (including those from the time before the user has joined the system) is not published – the users must only be informed about the current revocations. Note that this is perhaps the most practical scenario, as it minimizes the information distribution: in case of a revocation the system broadcasts only the list of revoked revocation attributes and the revocation accumulator. Moreover, it is easier to compute the initial revocation witness for the user instead of forcing the user to perform the whole computation based on `UpdateWitness` from the system initialization.

The idea of the attack is to provide a corrupted revocation witness when a user joins the system. Of course, the error propagates as the user updates the witnesses and presents non-revocation proofs. From the point of view of the verifier, no irregularity should be detected and the non-revocation proof should be positively verified. However, note that the verifier must contact the Revocation Authority to check whether $X^{\delta} = Y$. Due to manipulations on witnesses we will have $X^{\delta} \neq Y$, but a particular relation between X and Y enables the Revocation Authority to check whether the non-revocation proof has been created correctly. Therefore, the Revocation Authority may answer correctly, but at the same time it will learn the user's x_{id} from the values X, Y presented by the verifier. So despite that the verifier does not collude with the Revocation Authority, the revocation identifier becomes revealed.

The initial revocation witness (d', W', Q') given to the user holding x_{id} is created as follows:

Input:	
RA private key:	$\delta \in \mathbb{Z}_q$
Revocation parameter:	g_t
List of revoked attribute values:	R
New user's revocation attribute:	$x_{id} \notin R$

Current accumulator:	V
Auxiliary database:	$\mathcal{T}$
Computation:	
1. compute d and W via `ComputeWitness` for R and x_{id}	
2. choose u at random	
3. $\underline{d} := d + u \bmod q$	
4. $\underline{Q} := VW^{-x_{id}} g_t^{-\underline{d}}$	
Output:	
insert (g_t^u, x_{id}) in the database $\mathcal{T}$	
give $(\underline{d}, W, \underline{Q})$ to the user holding x_{id}	

Table 1: Creating a corrupted initial witness

The database $\mathcal{T}$ stores information necessary to link the verification requests with the users. Note that if Q is the non-corrupted value, then $Q = VW^{-x_{id}} g_t^{-d}$. Hence $Q \cdot g_t^{-u} = \underline{Q}$.

For the corrupted witness $(\underline{d}, W, \underline{Q})$ note that:

- one can check that the test concerning c' performed by the verifier succeeds (note that this part of the verification may be executed by the verifier himself),
- the Revocation Authority gets the values X, Y for which
$$X^\delta = W^\delta g^{t_1 \delta} = QK^{t_1} = \underline{Q} g_t^u K^{t_1} = Y g_t^u \neq Y \ .$$
However, the Revocation Authority may search for an entry (Z, x_{id}) such that $X^\delta = YZ$. If there is such an entry, then the answer to the verification query is `correct` and as a side effect the Revocation Authority learns x_{id}. Otherwise, the answer is `false`.

Now let us consider the situation after the user holding x_{id} updates the revocation witness because of revocation of x'.

- According to the `UpdateWitness` procedure, the new value of the parameter d, called below $\underline{d_1}$, equals
$$\underline{d_1} = \underline{d}(x' - x_{id}) = (d+u)(x' - x_{id}) = d_1 + u(x' - x_{id}) \ ,$$
where $d_1 = d(x' - x_{id})$ is the correct value that would be obtained for the correct initial witness.
- The value of W will be updated to the correct value W_1, since no manipulated value is applied for the update.
- The new value of Q equals
$$\begin{aligned} \underline{Q_1} &= VW^{-x_{id}} g_t^{-\underline{d_1}} = VW^{-x_{id}} g_t^{-d_1 - u(x' - x_{id})} \\ &= Q_1 g_t^{-u(x' - x_{id})} \ , \end{aligned}$$
where Q_1 is the value of Q computed for the correct d_1.

Now, if the verifier presents a pair (X, Y) created by the user holding x_{id}, then
$$X^\delta = W_1^\delta g_t^{t_1 \delta} = Q_1 K^{t_1} = \underline{Q_1} g_t^{u(x' - x_{id})} K^{t_1} = Y g_t^{u(x' - x_{id})} \ .$$

So we see that if each entry (Z, x_{id}) of the database $\mathcal{T}$ is modified according to the assignment $Z := Z^{x' - x_{id}}$, then the Revocation Authority may answer the queries of the verifiers just as before.

It is easy to see that after revoking $x'_1, \ldots, x'_k$ and removing $x''_1, \ldots, x''_m$ from the revocation list (i.e. activating back $x''_1, \ldots, x''_m$) the original entry (Z, x_{id}) of database $\mathcal{T}$ becomes converted to (Z', x_{id}), where
$$Z' = Z \cdot g_t^{(x'_1 - x_{id}) \cdot \ldots \cdot (x'_k - x_{id}) \cdot (x''_1 - x_{id})^{-1} \cdot \ldots \cdot (x''_m - x_{id})^{-1}}$$
and the same procedure as above for answering the queries to the Revocation Authority can be applied.

Finally, one can check that despite the manipulations the user and the verifier obtain the same values for T_1, T_2, T_3 (note that they must derive them in a different way). Therefore, no change in the protocol is observable by the verifier.

2.2 Tracing by Setup Manipulations

In this section we present a tracing attack which remains undetected even if the complete list R of revoked revocation attributes is available. This is achieved without manipulating the parameters used for computing witnesses.

2.2.1 *Preliminary Observations*

Let us note that the output of `RASetup()` does not include any proof of equality of the discrete logarithms for the pairs: (g_t, g_t^δ) and (g, K), where the first element in the pair denotes the base element and the second element denotes the exponentiation result. Accordingly, the Revocation Authority may choose the values δ and $\log_g K$ to be different modulo q. So for a while we assume that $K = g^{\tilde{\delta}}$ and $\tilde{\delta} \neq \delta$.

We have to check that for $\tilde{\delta} \neq \delta$ set during the `RASetup()` the procedure `VerifyNonRevocationProof()` executed by the verifier will behave just as in the case when $\tilde{\delta} = \delta$. This is the case when the arguments for computing the hash value c (during execution of `GenerateNonRevocationProof()`) and c' (during execution of `VerifyNonRevocationProof()`) are exactly the same. However, one can check that these arguments are equal even if $\delta \neq \delta'$. Therefore, the difference will not be observable by the verifier, unless the problem of equality of discrete logarithm is easy. However, the authors of [8, 9] explicitly wish to avoid pairing groups, so we may expect that the DDH Problem will be hard in the group chosen for the implementation.

2.2.2 *The Attack*

We assume that the Revocation Authority knows all the values x_{id} and therefore can compute witnesses of all users. The `RSSetup` procedure is executed in a slightly different way. Namely, the Revocation Authority chooses $\tilde{\delta} \neq \delta \bmod q$ at random and sets $K := g^{\tilde{\delta}}$ instead of $K := g^\delta$.

During `VerifyNonRevocationProof()` the Revocation Authority is asked to check whether $Y = X^\delta$. However, due to the `RSSetup` modification this equality does not hold with high probability as $X = Wg^{t_1}$ and $Y = QK^{t_1}$ where $Q = W^\delta$, $K = g^{\tilde{\delta}}$ and t_1 is random. So instead of checking the equality $Y = X^\delta$ the Revocation Authority executes the following steps using δ and $\tilde{\delta}$:

1. $\widetilde{W} := Y \cdot X^{-\tilde{\delta}}$. (Note that if X and Y were calculated correctly by the prover, then we get $\widetilde{W} = Q \cdot W^{-\tilde{\delta}}$.)
2. $\widehat{W} := \widetilde{W}^\eta$, where $\eta = (\delta - \tilde{\delta})^{-1} \bmod q$.

If the witness was correctly computed by the user, then
$$\widehat{W} = \left(W^{\delta - \tilde{\delta}}\right)^{(\delta - \tilde{\delta})^{-1} \bmod q} = W.$$

Note that W depends on x_{id} and can be used to match the non-revocation proof with x_{id}. The Revocation Authority maintains a database with the entries (x_{id}, W), where W is the value resulting from the current value of the revocation list R. The values W are updated each time the list R changes.

2.2.3 *Attack Countermeasures*

In the original description, the Revocation Authority gets the pair (X, Y) and has to check whether $Y = X^\delta$. However, one can modify the scheme so that the Revocation Authority gets only X and responds with X^{δ}; subsequently the verifier compares the answer with Y.

As after the modification $Y \neq X^{\delta}$, the Revocation Authority seem to be in trouble. Of course, for each W the Revocation Authority may compute

$$Y_W := W^{\delta-\tilde{\delta}} X^{\tilde{\delta}} .$$

Note that for the correct W

$$Y_W = W^{\delta-\tilde{\delta}} \cdot \left(W g^{t_1}\right)^{\tilde{\delta}} = W^{\delta} \cdot \left(g^{\tilde{\delta}}\right)^{t_1} = QK^{t_1} = Y$$

and therefore it could check whether

$$c' \stackrel{?}{=} \mathcal{H}(g, g_1, g_t, K, \tilde{c}_{id}, X, Y, C_d, T_1, T_2, T_3) .$$

So, contrary to the intention of the authors of [8, 9] the details of a non-revocation proof (namely, the parameters $c', s_1, \ldots, s_6, C_d$) must be hidden from the Revocation Authority.

The right way to defend against the attack is to expand the protocol by a proof that the same secret key δ is used for computation of the accumulator value V and for computing K. However, we do not follow this direction as in the next section we describe a more complicated attack that works for $K = g^{\delta}$.

2.3 Tracing when g^{δ}=K

In this section we present an attack that does not manipulate the parameter K and therefore a malicious Revocation Authority may safely present a proof that $K = g^{\delta}$. Consequently, augmenting the output of the `RASetup()` procedure by the appropriate proof of correctness is not enough to prevent an attack on users' privacy.

2.3.1 Preliminary Ideas and Observations

During the corrupted `RSSetup` procedure α_1, α_2 are chosen at random so that $\alpha_2 \neq \alpha_1 \bmod q$. Let

$$\delta := (\alpha_1 + \alpha_2) \cdot 2^{-1} \bmod q . \quad (1)$$

(Note that for any given δ it is easy to find $\alpha_1 \neq \alpha_2$ so that (1) holds.) If the order q of g is a large prime number, then $2^{-1} \bmod q$ exists. On the other hand, if $\gcd(2, q) > 1$, then it is easy to generalize the reasoning below to the representation $\delta = (\alpha_1 + \cdots + \alpha_\ell) \cdot \ell^{-1} \bmod q$ for some ℓ coprime to q (in this case the definition of Λ_i given below would change to $\Lambda_i := g_t^{(\alpha_1^i + \cdots + \alpha_\ell^i) \cdot \ell^{-1} \bmod q}$).

For $i = 0, 1, 2, \ldots$ let:

$$\Lambda_i := g_t^{(\alpha_1^i + \alpha_2^i) \cdot 2^{-1} \bmod q} \quad \text{and} \quad \Delta_i := g_t^{\delta^i} . \quad (2)$$

So in particular

$$\Lambda_0 = \Delta_0 = g_t \quad \text{and} \quad \Lambda_1 = \Delta_1 .$$

Note that in order to get V one can first compute the exponent $\prod_{i=1}^{m}(\delta + x_i)$ and then raise g_t to the computed power. An alternative is to get first the numbers Δ_i, then compute $\prod_{i=1}^{m}(\delta + x_i)$ as a polynomial of an unknown δ, i.e.

$$\prod_{i=1}^{m}(\delta + x_i) = \sum_{i=0}^{m} a_i \cdot \delta^i ,$$

and finally put

$$V := \prod_{i=0}^{m} (\Delta_i)^{a_i} .$$

Therefore, it is not necessary to know the secret key δ to compute the accumulator value V as long as the values of Δ_i are known for sufficiently many i's.

Below we assume that instead of using the vector

$$\mathbf{t} = (\Delta_0, \Delta_1, \Delta_2, \ldots, \Delta_m) \quad (3)$$

the Revocation Authority will use the vector

$$\mathbf{t}' = (\Lambda_0, \Lambda_1, \Lambda_2, \ldots, \Lambda_m) \quad (4)$$

to calculate the value of V. That is, the Revocation Authority creates the accumulator according to the formula:

$$V := \prod_{i=0}^{m} (\Lambda_i)^{a_i} .$$

The protocol from [9] (as well as [8]) does not include any proof of correctness of the accumulator value. Obviously, it has to lead to correct answers during non-revocation proofs. Moreover, as we shall see below, the users have some possibilities to recompute the accumulator values when the changes on the list R occur. Therefore, the results of the users have to agree with the values published by the Revocation Authority. In particular, the users can collectively re-compute some values Λ_i from the data available for the users. However, there is no direct way to check whether $\Lambda_{i+1} = \Lambda_i^{\delta}$ if the DDH Problem is hard for the group used.

2.3.2 Updates

Recall that according to the draft [9] users' witnesses are computed by `ComputeWitness()` or `UpdateWitness()` procedure. As we shall see, the first method may be extended to a more direct method of computing W and Q, a method that may be run by (a set of) users. Hence if the second method is available to the users, then both methods should be and yield the same results. Below we discuss the technical details.

First assume that the witnesses are updated by the Revocation Authority. Define a polynomial f over $\mathbb{Z}_q$ as

$$f(X) = (X + x_{i_1}) \cdot (X + x_{i_2}) \cdot \ldots \cdot (X + x_{i_k}) , \quad (5)$$

where $x_{i_1}, \ldots, x_{i_k}$ are the revocation attributes of all revoked users. If the full revocation list is published by the Revocation Authority, then f can be immediately derived. However, one can prove (the proof is omitted due to space limitations) that a coalition of users can reconstruct f even if the Revocation Authority attempts to hide R.

In this case $k-1$ users can find the powers $g_t^{Y_{k-1}}, g_t^{Y_{k-2}}, \ldots, g_t^{Y_1}$ that are used by the Revocation Authority to generate the values of the witnesses. Namely, consider the following procedure:

1. A colluding user holding own parameters x_i, d_i and the global parameter $f(X)$ finds the polynomial

$$g_i(X) = (f(X) - d_i)/(X + x_i) = \sum_{j=0}^{k-1} \mu_{i,j} X^j \quad (6)$$

Note that according to the definition, the witness W for x_i equals

$$W_i = g_t^{g_i(\delta)} .$$

So the user learns all the coefficients $\mu_{i,j}$ in the equation

$$g_t^{\sum_{j=0}^{k-1} \mu_{i,j} Y_j} = W_i, \quad (7)$$

where for each $j = 1, \ldots, k-1$ the unknown Y_j presumably satisfies the condition $Y_j = \delta^j$. We must emphasize that the colluding users assume that in (7) the values W_i are indeed calculated according to the protocol. However, $g_t^{Y_j}$ will successfully be determined even if $Y_j \neq \delta^j$ for at least some of the values $j = 0, 1, \ldots$.

2. The colluding users, say $id_1, \ldots, id_{k-1}$, create together the following system of equations:

$$\begin{cases} g_t^{\sum_{j=1}^{k-1} \mu_{id_1,j} Y_j} & = & W_{id_1} \cdot g_t^{-\mu_{id_1,0}} \\ g_t^{\sum_{j=1}^{k-1} \mu_{id_2,j} Y_j} & = & W_{id_2} \cdot g_t^{-\mu_{id_2,0}} \\ & \cdots & \\ g_t^{\sum_{j=1}^{k-1} \mu_{id_{k-1},j} Y_j} & = & W_{id_{k-1}} \cdot g_t^{-\mu_{id_{k-1},0}} \end{cases} \quad (8)$$

and perform Gaussian elimination in the exponents. That is, instead of scalar multiplications they have exponentiations, instead of subtractions they have divisions in the group generated by g_t. Since x_{id} are assumed to be random and independent, they count for the corresponding matrix (i.e., the matrix $[\mu_{id_i,j}]$, for $i, j \in \{1, \ldots, k-1\}$) to be invertible. [1] Thereby the colluding users should obtain the set of solutions $g_t^{Y_j}$, for $j = 1, \ldots, k-1$.

Of course, if the set of revoked users increases over time to some value k' ($k' > k$), then to find the newly used $g_t^{Y_{k'-1}}$, $g_t^{Y_{k'-2}}$, $\ldots, g_t^{Y_k}$ only $k' - k$ colluding users are needed. The same follows for the accumulator V: if $g_t^{Y_{k-1}}$, $g_t^{Y_{k-2}}$, $\ldots$, $g_t^{Y_1}$ are found and $V = Q_{id} \cdot W_{id}^{x_{id}} \cdot g_t^{d_{id}}$ is calculated by a user with the revocation attribute x_{id} and the witness (d_{id}, W_{id}, Q_{id}), then $g_t^{Y_k}$ is easily calculated from $V, g_t^{Y_{k-1}}, g_t^{Y_{k-2}}, \ldots, g_t^{Y_1}$.

Assume that f is the polynomial (5) from the current revocation round, and that $\deg f \leq k$. Then a user with revocation attribute x_{id} knowing f and the powers $g_t^{Y_j}$, for $j = 1, \ldots, k$, can easily calculate the accumulator value and its non-revocation witness. Indeed, he computes

$$d_{id} := f(-x_{id}) \quad (9)$$

and the quotient polynomial (6). Finally, he directly computes:

$$W_{id} := \prod_{j=0}^{k-1} \left(g_t^{Y_j}\right)^{\mu_{id,j}}, \quad Q_{id} := \prod_{j=0}^{k-1} \left(g_t^{Y_{j+1}}\right)^{\mu_{id,j}} \quad (10)$$

for $\mu_{id,j}$ such that $g_{id}(X) = \sum_{j=0}^{k-1} \mu_{id,j} X^j$. Note that in these computations Q_{id} corresponds to W_{id} shifted by one step to the "higher" powers $g_t^{Y_{j+1}}$ reflecting the presumed relation $Q_{id} = W_{id}^{\delta}$.

A similar method can be applied if witnesses are updated by the users. Moreover, if the initial set of revoked users is empty, then all the necessary data for building the direct method are available to each single user (the user may create virtual identities x_{id} to compute their witnesses and thus to gather the data for the system (8)). Once the direct method of computing W_{id} and Q_{id} is obtained, it can be used interchangeably with `UpdateWitness()`.

It can be checked that the direct method and the `UpdateWitness()` yield the same results. A fairly tedious computation is omitted here due to space limitations.

2.3.3 *Tracing the Users*

We assume that the Revocation Authority knows all the values x_{id}. Since $g^{\delta} = K$, we have

$$\frac{X^{\delta}}{Y} = \frac{W_{id}^{\delta} \cdot g^{t_1 \delta}}{Q_{id} \cdot K^{t_1}} = \frac{W_{id}^{\delta}}{Q_{id}} .$$

[1] It may happen that the matrix in not invertible, but during a large number of experiments we never encountered such a case.

By (1), (6) and (7), for $Y_j = (\alpha_1^j + \alpha_2^j) \cdot 2^{-1} \bmod q$ we get:

$$\begin{aligned} \frac{W_{id}^{\delta}}{Q_{id}} &= \frac{W_{id}^{\frac{\alpha_1+\alpha_2}{2}}}{Q_{id}} = \frac{\left(\left(g_t^{g_{id}(\alpha_1)+g_{id}(\alpha_2)}\right)^{\frac{1}{2}}\right)^{\frac{\alpha_1+\alpha_2}{2}}}{\left(g_t^{g_{id}(\alpha_1)\cdot\alpha_1+g_{id}(\alpha_2)\cdot\alpha_2}\right)^{\frac{1}{2}}} \\ &= \left(g_t^{g_{id}(\alpha_1)\cdot\left(\frac{\alpha_1+\alpha_2}{2}-\alpha_1\right)+g_{id}(\alpha_2)\cdot\left(\frac{\alpha_1+\alpha_2}{2}-\alpha_2\right)}\right)^{\frac{1}{2}} \\ &= \left(g_t^{g_{id}(\alpha_1)-g_{id}(\alpha_2)}\right)^{\frac{\alpha_2-\alpha_1}{4}} \end{aligned}$$

That is, $\left(\frac{X^{\delta}}{Y}\right)^{4\cdot(\alpha_2-\alpha_1)^{-1} \bmod q} = g_t^{g_{id}(\alpha_1)-g_{id}(\alpha_2)}$. The exponent on the right hand side should depend on x_{id} provided that $\deg f \geq 3$. The condition $\deg f \geq 3$ is not a real limitation, as the Revocation Authority may create 3 dummy users and revoke them. The matching x_{id} is found easily, if the values $g_t^{g_{id}(\alpha_1)-g_{id}(\alpha_2)}$ are precomputed after each revocation round.

2.3.4 *Attack Countermeasures*

The attack can be prevented, if the sequence $\Delta_0, \Delta_1, \Delta_2, \ldots$ is published together with the zero knowledge proofs for $\log_{\Delta_i} \Delta_{i+1} = \log_g K$ for each i. However, the number of revoked attributes might be large, so the number of zero knowledge proofs becomes linear in the number of the revoked users. This does not seem to be very practical.

The problem also arises when creating the initial witnesses when the user joins the system. At this moment we need a proof of correctness for W and Q. This is not easy as the cardinality of the set R may be quite large. So the degree of polynomials in the exponent of the expressions defining W and Q might be large and therefore long proofs might be necessary.

3. FINAL REMARKS

The list of problems presented in this paper is not complete as we are aware of more threats. In each case, one can extend the scheme so that a particular attack does not work. However, addtitional procedures make the system even more "heavy" and can make room for new trapdoors. Definitely, since U-Prove is a proprietary system, this is the role of its designers decide how to patch the system.

In our attacks the Revocation Authority learns the revocation attribute when asked for checking X and Y. Interestingly, for [6] the non-revocation proof is checked by the verifier himself and all attack scenarios from this paper do not apply.

A general suggestion is to separate strictly the verifier and the Revocation Authority and blind the parameters X, Y before passing them to the Revocation Authority. That is, instead of X, Y the Revocation Authority should get $X' = X^t, Y' = Y^t$ for a random t. Of course, this does not secure the user against collusion between the verifier and the Revocation Authority, as the verifier must use the original X, Y as arguments for the hash function $\mathcal{H}$. So again, the user has to trust blindly the verifier.

4. REFERENCES

[1] Paquin, C., Zaverucha, G.: U-Prove Cryptographic Specification V1.1 (Revision 3). Technical Report, Microsoft Research (December 2013). Available from: `http://research.microsoft.com/apps/pubs/default.aspx?id=166969`

[2] Brands, S.: Untraceable Off-line Cash in Wallets with Observers. In Stinson, D.R., ed.: CRYPTO. Vol. 773 of LNCS, Springer (1993) 302–318

[3] Brands, S.A.: Rethinking Public Key Infrastructures and Digital Certificates: Building in Privacy. 1 edn. MIT Press, Cambridge-London (2000).

[4] Microsoft: U-Prove. Webpage of the project (retrieved 2014). Available from: `http://research.microsoft.com/en-us/projects/u-prove/`

[5] Paquin, C.: On the Revocation of U-Prove Tokens. Tech. Report, Microsoft Research (September 2014). Available from: `http://research.microsoft.com/pubs/228729/On\%20the\%20revocation\%20of\%20U-Prove\%20tokens.pdf`

[6] Acar, T., Chow, S.S.M., Nguyen, L.: Accumulators and U-Prove Revocation. In Sadeghi, A.R., ed.: Financial Cryptography. Vol. 7859 of LNCS, Springer (2013) 189–196

[7] Hanzlik, L., Kluczniak, K., Kutyłowski, M.: Attack on a U-Prove Revocation Scheme. In Christin, N., Safavi-Naini, R., ed.: Financial Cryptography. Vol. 8437 of LNCS, Springer (2014) 283-290

[8] Nguyen, L., Paquin, C.: U-Prove Designated-Verifier Accumulator Revocation Extension. Tech. Report Draft Revision 1, Microsoft Research (2013, updated Feb. 2014)

[9] Nguyen, L., Paquin, C.: U-Prove Designated-Verifier Accumulator Revocation Extension. Tech. Report Draft Version 2, Microsoft Research (2014)

APPENDIX

Below we present a specification of procedures run by the U-Prove Revocation system.

Input:	
U-Prove parameters:	group G_q of a prime order q generators g, g_1, g_t
Computation:	choose $\delta \in \mathbb{Z}_q$ at random $K := g^{\delta}$
Output: private key δ, public key K	

Table 2: Procedure `RSSetup()`

Input:	
RA private key:	$\delta \in \mathbb{Z}_q$
Revocation parameter:	g_t
Set of revoked attribute values:	$R = \{x_1, \ldots, x_m\} \subseteq \mathbb{Z}_q \backslash \{-\delta\}$
Computation:	$V := g_t^{\prod_{i=1}^{m}(\delta + x_i)}$
Output: accumulator value V	

Table 3: Procedure `ComputeAccumulator()`

Input:	
RA private key:	$\delta \in \mathbb{Z}_q$
Revocation parameter:	g_t
List of revoked attribute values:	$R=\{x_1, \ldots, x_m\} \in \mathbb{Z}_q \backslash \{-\delta\}$
Target user's revocation attribute:	$x_{id} \notin R$
Current accumulator:	$V \in G_q$
Computation:	
$d := \prod_{x \in R}(x - x_{id}) \bmod q$	
$W := g_t^{(\prod_{x \in R}(\delta + x) - d)/(\delta + x_{id})}$	
$Q := V W^{-x_{id}} g_t^{-d}$	
Output:	
Revocation witness for target user holding x_{id}:	(d, W, Q)

Table 4: Procedure `ComputeWitness()`

Input:	
Revocation parameter:	$g_t \in G_q$
The revocation attribute of the user:	x_{id}
Revocation attribute to be added or removed from the set R:	x'
Boolean value indicating whether x' has to be added to R:	`add`
Old accumulator:	$V \in G_q$
Old witness of the user holding x_{id}:	(d, W, Q)
Updated accumulator:	$V' \in G_q$
Computation:	
if `add` = `true`	(x' added to R)
$d' := d(x' - x_{id}) \bmod q$	
$W' := V W^{x' - x_{id}}$	
$Q' := V' W'^{-x_{id}} g_t^{-d'}$	
else	(x' removed from R)
$d' := d(x' - x_{id})^{-1} \bmod q$	
$W' := ((V')^{-1} W)^{(x' - x_{id})^{-1}}$	
$Q' := V' W'^{-x_{id}} g_t^{-d'}$	
Output: updated witness (d', W', Q') for x_{id}	

Table 5: Procedure `UpdateWitness( )`

Input:	
Revocation parameters:	G_q, hash function $\mathcal{H}$, g, g_1, g_t
Commitment to x_{id}:	$\tilde{c}_{id}$, where $\tilde{c}_{id} = g^{x_{id}} g_1^{\tilde{o}_{id}}$
Opening information:	x_{id} , $\tilde{o}_{id}$
RA public key:	K
Revocation witness:	(d, W, Q)
Computation:	
generate $t_1, t_2, k_1, \ldots, k_6 \in \mathbb{Z}_q$ at random	
$X := W g^{t_1}$	
$Y := Q K^{t_1}$	
$C_d := g_t^d g_1^{t_2}$	
$w := d^{-1} \bmod q$	
$z := t_1 \tilde{o}_{id} - t_2 \bmod q$	
$z' := -t_2 w \bmod q$	
$T_1 := X^{k_1} (\tilde{c}_{id} K)^{-k_2} g_1^{k_3}$	
$T_2 := g^{k_1} g_1^{k_4}$	
$T_3 := C_d^{k_5} g_1^{k_6}$	
$c' := \mathcal{H}(g, g_1, g_t, K, \tilde{c}_{id}, X, Y, C_d, T_1, T_2, T_3)$	
$s_1 := -c' x_{id} + k_1 \bmod q$	
$s_2 := -c' t_1 + k_2 \bmod q$	
$s_3 := -c' z + k_3 \bmod q$	
$s_4 := -c' \tilde{o}_{id} + k_4 \bmod q$	
$s_5 := -c' w + k_5 \bmod q$	
$s_6 := -c' z' + k_6 \bmod q$	
delete $t_1, t_2, k_1, ..., k_6, w, z, z', T_1, T_2, T_3$	
Output: non-revocation proof $(c', s_1, \ldots, s_6, X, Y, C_d)$ for x_{id}	

Table 6: Procedure `GenerateNonRevocationProof()`

Input:	
Revocation parameters:	$G_q, \mathcal{H}, g, g_1, g_t$
Commitment to x_{id}:	$\tilde{c}_{id}$
Non-revocation proof:	$c', s_1, \ldots, s_6, X, Y, C_d$
Revocation Authority public key:	K
Revocation Authority private key:	δ
Revocation accumulator:	V
Computation:	
$T_1 := (V Y^{-1} (C_d)^{-1})^{c'} X^{s_1} (\tilde{c}_{id} K)^{-s_2} g_1^{s_3}$	
$T_2 := \tilde{c}_{id}^{c'} g^{s_1} g_1^{s_4}$	
$T_3 := g_t^{c'} (C_d)^{s_5} g_1^{s_6}$	
verify that $c' = \mathcal{H}(g, g_1, g_t, K, \tilde{c}_{id}, X, Y, C_d, T_1, T_2, T_3)$	
verify that $Y = X^{\delta}$	

Table 7: Procedure `VerifyNonRevocationProof()`

Mind Your Nonces Moving: Template-Based Partially-Sharing Nonces Attack on SM2 Digital Signature Algorithm

Jiazhe Chen
China Information Technology Security Evaluation Center
Beijing 100085, China
jiazhechen@gmail.com

Mingjie Liu
Beijing Research Institute of Telemetry
Beijing 100194, China
liumj9705@gmail.com

Hexin Li
China Information Technology Security Evaluation Center
Beijing 100085, China
lihx@secemail.cn

Hongsong Shi
China Information Technology Security Evaluation Center
Beijing 100085, China

ABSTRACT

This paper gives a partially-sharing nonces attack on SM2 Digital Signature Algorithm (SM2DSA). Templates, which are built in the scenario of no secrets known, are used to detect the collisions on the Most Significant Byte of the Nonces (MSBN). Targeting a real world smartcard with 8-bit precharged bus, the power consumption of data moving procedure after the random number generation is focused, on which the template building and matching phases are based. With the templates, we obtain a number of pairs of nonces whose first bytes are collided, then a lattice attack on SM2DSA is proposed to recover the private key. Experiments show that our attack works smoothly; our attack is the first implemented lattice attack on SM2DSA in a smartcard, which can also be extended to the other ECC algorithms like ECDSA.

Keywords

SM2, Template attack, PCA, Lattice attack

1. INTRODUCTION

SM2 [20], an elliptic curve based cryptosystem, is a Chinese standard for commercial use. A digital signature algorithm, a key exchange protocol and a public key encryption algorithm are given in [20], which form the SM2 cryptosystem. The SM2 digital signature algorithm[1] (SM2DSA for short), is similar to ECDSA [18].

The nonce k in ECDSA/SM2DSA (DSA) is an ephemeral key whose recovery is equivalent to the discovery of the private key. If a small fraction of the information about the nonces is known, then it is also enough for the lattice attacks to break the signature algorithm (like [10, 15, 19, 14]). We call these attacks partially-known nonces attacks. The other lattice attacks do not directly use the partial values of the nonces, but break (EC)DSA with some signatures that share a part of the nonces (like [8]). The latter attacks are called partially-sharing nonces attacks in this paper.

Side channel attacks [12] are of great value to evaluate the security of a cipher running in a cryptographic device; among them, template attack [5] is one of the most effective attacks. The lattice attacks mentioned are sound and practical if the information of the nonces can be obtained from side channels. This paper gives a partially-sharing nonces attack on SM2DSA resulted from the information leakage in the generation procedure of the nonces, utilizing templates.

Unlike most of the previous attacks, this paper will not focus on reducing the number of known (sharing) bits, but try to study the attack from a practical issue (like [17]) and aim to solve the problems that will be practically encountered.

Our contributions. This paper utilizes side channel information of the non-cryptographic operation whose security might not attract much attention of the designers.

Since the lattice-based attacks require that the incorrect guessed signatures should be very limited, the success rate is crucial. Our first contribution is proposing a method to reliably detect the information of MSBN from the moving of the nonces, which is given in Sect. 3.

The second contribution of this paper is giving the first partially-sharing nonces attack on SM2DSA (see Sect. 4), which is also the first lattice attack on SM2DSA in a real smartcard.

[1]See [22] for an English translation.

ASIA CCS'15, April 14–17, 2015, Singapore, Singapore.

http://dx.doi.org/10.1145/2714576.2714587.

2. PRELIMINARIES

This section introduces the SM2DSA, template attack, PCA and some basics on lattice.

2.1 SM2 Digital Signature Algorithm

SM2 is an elliptic curve based cryptosystem that defined over finite fields. Similar to ECDSA, SM2DSA can be defined over prime fields $\mathbb{F}_p$ ($p > 3$) or binary fields $\mathbb{F}_{2^m}$. An elliptic curve over prime fields[2] is the set of points (x, y) satisfying an equation of the following form:

$$y^2 = x^3 + ax + b \mod p,$$

where $a, b \in \mathbb{F}_p$ satisfy $4a^3 + 27b^2 \neq 0 \mod p$. To form a group, an extra infinity point $\mathcal{O}$ is included in this set. Consequently, the elliptic curve $\mathbb{E}(\mathbb{F}_p)$ is defined as

$$\mathbb{E}(\mathbb{F}_p) = \{P = (x, y) | y^2 = x^3 + ax + b \mod p.\ x, y \in \mathbb{F}_p\} \cup \{\mathcal{O}\}.$$

For $m \in \mathbb{F}_p$, we refer to [2] the scalar multiplication (point multiplication) mP of a point P.

Using the notations in [14], SM2DSA (prime fields) is given as follows:

Key Generation: Choose an elliptic curve $\mathbb{E} : y^2 = x^3 + ax + b$ over $\mathbb{F}_p$ where p is a prime. Select a $G \in \mathbb{E}(\mathbb{F}_p) = (x_G, y_G)$ to be a fixed point of order n, where n is a prime. That is $nG = \mathcal{O}$. For a user A, the private key is $d_A \in \mathbb{F}_p$.

Signature Generation:

1. Compute $w = h(M)$, here $M = Z_A \parallel m$, m is the message, Z_A is the hash value about the user, h is the hash algorithm SM3.
2. Randomly choose an integer $k \in [1, n-1]$. k is called a nonce.
3. Calculate $(x_1, y_1) = kG$.
4. Compute $r = w + x_1 \mod n$. If $r = 0$ or $r + k = n$, go to step 2.
5. Compute $s = ((1 + d_A)^{-1}(k - rd_A)) \mod n$. If $s = 0$, go to step 2.
6. Return (r, s) as the signature.

See [14] for the signature verification procedure.

2.2 Template Attack and PCA

Template attack [5] is one of the most powerful side channel attacks; the attacker uses the information of an interval (consists of λ points) of the power traces that are value-correlated. With the assumption that the noise distribution to be Gaussian, the attacker builds a multivariate normal distribution $N(\vec{\mu}, \mathbf{\Sigma})$ from the ε profiled traces for each value, the estimators $(\hat{\vec{\mu}}, \hat{\mathbf{\Sigma}})$ is a template. Denote each trace by $\vec{\mathfrak{t}}_i = (x_i^1, x_i^2, \cdots, x_i^\lambda)$ $(i = 1, 2, \cdots, \varepsilon)$, and X_j to be the random variable of $(x_1^j, x_2^j, \cdots, x_\varepsilon^j)^T$ $(j = 1, 2, \cdots, \lambda)$. Then $\vec{\mu} = (E(X^1), E(X^2), \cdots, E(X^\lambda))$ is the mean vector, and $\mathbf{\Sigma} = cov(X^i, X^j)$ $(1 \le i, j \le \lambda)$ is the covariance matrix. In the first phase of template attack, which is named template building phase, the attacker profiles the traces and classifies them according to different processing values, then builds one template for each value. In the second phase, the template matching phase, the attacker uses the maximum likelihood principle to determine the value of the target secret. I.e., the value of the template that maximizes the probability

$$P(\vec{\mathfrak{t}}, N(\hat{\vec{\mu}}, \hat{\mathbf{\Sigma}})) = ((2\pi)^\lambda \det(\hat{\mathbf{\Sigma}}))^{-\frac{1}{2}} \exp(-\frac{1}{2}(\vec{\mathfrak{t}} - \hat{\vec{\mu}})^T \hat{\mathbf{\Sigma}}^{-1} (\vec{\mathfrak{t}} - \hat{\vec{\mu}}))$$

will be chosen to be the one matched with the secret implied in $\vec{\mathfrak{t}}$. Normally, one will calculate the logarithm of this probability to avoid numerical problems[3].

PCA [9] is a linear transformation that transforms the original points to the points that are orthogonal to each other and the variances are sorted. During the PCA transformation, ε traces are first normalized, i.e., $\vec{\mathfrak{t}}_i \leftarrow \vec{\mathfrak{t}}_i - \hat{\vec{\mu}}$ $(i = 1, 2, \cdots, \varepsilon)$. Then the covariance matrix of the normalized traces $\hat{\mathbf{\Sigma}}'$ is calculated, and an eigendecomposition is applied:

$$\hat{\mathbf{\Sigma}}' = \mathbf{U} \times \mathbf{\Lambda} \times \mathbf{U}^T.$$

Finally, the normalized traces are multiplied to the columns of the orthogonal matrix $\mathbf{U}$ that correspond to the several largest eigenvalues in $\mathbf{\Lambda}$ to get the PCA-transformed traces.

2.3 Basics about Lattice

A lattice is a discrete subgroup of $\mathbb{R}^m$ whose elements are integer linear combinations of n $(n \le m)$ linearly independent vectors. The fundamental parallelepiped $\mathcal{P}_{1/2}(\mathbf{B})$ of a matrix $\mathbf{B} = (\vec{b}_1, \ldots, \vec{b}_m)$ is $\{\sum_{i=1}^m x_i \vec{b}_i : -\frac{1}{2} \le x_i < \frac{1}{2}\}$. The volume $\mathrm{Vol}(L)$ of a lattice L is the m-dimensional volume of $\mathcal{P}_{1/2}(\mathbf{B})$ for any basis $\mathbf{B}$ of L. Shortest Vector Problem (SVP) and Closest Vector Problem (CVP) are two classical hard problems in computer science. In practice, lattice reduction algorithms like LLL [13] and BKZ [21] are used to solve SVP with dimension not too large.

Hidden Number Problem (HNP). For integer $\mathfrak{s}$ and $v \ge 1$, $\lfloor \mathfrak{s} \rfloor_v$ denotes the remainder of $\mathfrak{s}$ on division by v. For any real number z, let the symbol $|\cdot|_n$ be $|z|_n = \min_{b \in \mathbb{Z}} |z - bn|$. $\mathrm{APP}_{\ell,n}(v)$ denotes any rational number r satisfying $|v - r|_n \le \frac{n}{2^\ell}$. The HNP [3, 4] asks to recover $\alpha \in \mathbb{Z}_q$, given many approximations $u_i = \mathrm{APP}_{\ell,n}(\alpha t_i)$ where each t_i is known and chosen uniformly at random in $[1, n-1]$, for $1 \le i \le d$.

This HNP problem can be reduced to a BDD problem which is a special case of CVP. When we obtain d such t_i, u_i, the reduction to BDD can be done as follows. One constructs the $(d+1)$-dimensional lattice spanned by the following row matrix:

$$\begin{pmatrix} n & 0 & \cdots & 0 & 0 \\ 0 & n & \ddots & \vdots & \vdots \\ \vdots & \ddots & \ddots & 0 & \vdots \\ 0 & \cdots & 0 & n & 0 \\ t_1 & \cdots & \cdots & t_d & \frac{1}{2^\ell} \end{pmatrix} \quad (1)$$

The target vector is $\vec{u} = (u_1, u_2, \ldots, u_d, 0)$. There exists a lattice vector $\vec{h} = (\alpha t_1 + nh_1, \ldots, \alpha t_d + nh_d, \frac{\alpha}{2^\ell})$, such that $\parallel \vec{h} - \vec{u} \parallel \le \sqrt{d+1}\frac{n}{2^\ell}$. Hence, finding $\vec{h}$ discloses α.

In practice, embedding technique [11] is widely used to reduce CVP to SVP. Given a lattice L with basis $\mathbf{B} = [\vec{b}_1, \vec{b}_2, \cdots, \vec{b}_m]$, and a target vector $\vec{u} \in span(\mathbf{B})$, the embedding method is to construct a new lattice L' with basis $\mathbf{B}' = [\vec{b}_1', \vec{b}_2', \cdots, \vec{b}_{m+1}'] = [(\vec{b}_1, 0), (\vec{b}_2, 0), \cdots, (\vec{b}_m, 0), (\vec{u}, \beta)]$, where β is a parameter to be determined. If the distance between the target vector and the lattice is small enough, finding the shortest vector in this embedding lattice implies solving the CVP instance. In fact, we expect that the vector $(\vec{h} - \vec{u}, -\beta)$ to be the shortest vector in the embedding lattice, where $\vec{h}$ is the lattice vector closest to $\vec{u}$.

Gaussian Heuristic. Let L be a random d-dimensional lattice of $\mathbb{Z}^n$. Then with overwhelming probability, all the minima of L are asymptotically close to $\sqrt{\frac{d}{2\pi e}}\mathrm{Vol}(L)^{\frac{1}{d}}$. Thus,

[2]This paper only considers the recommended parameters in [20] which is over $\mathbb{F}_p$ $(\log_2 p = 256)$.

[3]To avoid the numerical problem when calculating $\log(\det(\Sigma))$, one can refer to [6].

```
void GetTRN(BYTE *rand, WORD len)
{
  WORD i;
  open RNG clock;
  for (i = 0; i < len; i ++)
  {
    wait until the random number is generated;
    rand[i] = RNGDATA;
  }
  close RNG clock;
}
```

Table 1: Pseudo-code of the random number generation

it is common in practice to assume that the length of the shortest vector $\vec{\mathfrak{v}} \in L$ is $\lambda_1(L) \approx \sqrt{\frac{d}{2\pi e}}\mathrm{Vol}(L)^{\frac{1}{2}}$.

3. TEMPLATE BUILDING AND COLLISION DETECTION

The purpose of this section is to illustrate the way to obtain the pairs of signatures that can be used in the partially-sharing nonces attack. We first introduce our target smartcard, and then propose the template attack utilized to obtain the desired signatures.

3.1 The Target Smartcard

The target smartcard has a 8-bit precharged bus whose precharged value is `0x00` or `0xFF` that will not be changed unless the smartcard reboots. This means that before transferring a value, the bus lines will be set to logic 0 or 1 [16]. The two precharged values will be randomly chosen each time the smartcard powers on, which means for a 8-bit value `v`, the power consumption of data moving next time the smartcard powers on can either be the same as itself or the same as that of $\mathtt{v} \oplus \mathtt{0xFF}$. Especially, for the value `0x00`, the power consumption while it is sending over the bus can be the highest or lowest among all the values, which depends on the precharged value; the same situation happens to the value `0xFF`.

To generate the nonce k required by SM2DSA, a random number generator (RNG) is called. Since no particulars about how to generate the random nonces k are stated in [20], our target smartcard generates a 8-bit random number each time with a true random number generator (TRNG). The function `GetTRN()` that generates `len` bytes of random numbers is given in Tab. 1. After 32 bytes of random numbers are generated, they are cascaded to be a big number k with 256 bits. Then k is compared with the modulus n, if $k > n$ then this k is discarded[4] and the random number generation procedure is carried out again, otherwise this k is used as the nonce. Note that for the recommended parameters in [20], n is large enough[5] which means that with very low probability ($\leq 2^{-32}$) k will be discarded.

Note that the line:

$$\mathtt{rand}[i] = \mathtt{RNGDATA};$$

[4]Note that if this case happens then in our attack the corresponding power trace should be discarded as well.

[5]n=`0xFFFFFFFE FFFFFFFF FFFFFFFF FFFFFFFF 7203DF6B 21C6052B 53BBF409 39D54123`

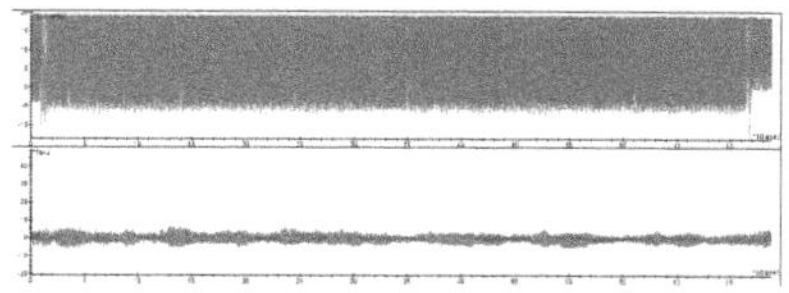

Figure 1: Random number generation by sending APDU (top) and the correlation coefficient between data and traces (bottom)

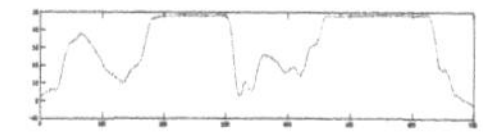

Figure 2: Zoom in the part with the highest correlation in top figure of Fig. 1

moves the random number from the register `RNGDATA` to a variable `rand`[i] in RAM, and this process may leak information about the moving data due to the `MOV` instruction.

3.2 Building the Templates and Finding the Partial Collisions of Nonces

Note that our target smartcard supports the APDU (Application Protocol Data Unit) for random number generation which also calls the function `GetTRN` and outputs the random numbers. This is the case for most of the real world smartcards as well, for example in the PIN verification application of EMV specifications [7], a get-challenge command should be sent from the terminal to the smartcard by an APDU. The smartcard then generates the random number and returns it to the terminal as the challenge. To make our template attack more powerful, i.e., to avoid the strong assumption that the attacker knows the nonces during the template building phase, the templates will be built by sending the random number generation APDU instead of the signing APDU, to the smartcard. The reason for doing this is that the random numbers, which are needed to build templates, will be returned from the smartcard, thus no known secrets are required.

In order to specify the time interval corresponding to the `MOV` instructions, we send the APDU that generates 8 bytes of random numbers for several thousand times and record the power traces corresponding to the power consumption of the random numbers generation; one of these power traces is illustrated in the top figure of Fig. 1. Then we align all the traces according to the part of the first random byte and calculate the correlation coefficient between the power consumption and the data, see the bottom of Fig. 1. We can see that the points of power traces between 13.6μs to 14.1μs have a relatively strong correlation with the data. Zooming in this part, we get Fig. 2, and we believe that the `MOV` instruction falls in this part.

We also try to align the power traces with the other bytes, however these bytes show lower correlation than the first and thus the first byte of the random number generation is used to mount our attack.[6]

Now the problems we need to handle are how to decide the template building and matching strategies.

First, although the `MOV` instruction leaks the Hamming weight due to the precharged bus, we cannot distinguish the values with the same Hamming weight. Fortunately, there are only one value corresponding to the Hamming weights 0

[6]Our earlier experiments tried to detect the collisions of the MSBN by measuring the distances or correlation coefficients directly from the power consumption patterns (i.e., without templates), but ended up with failures due to the low success rate caused by noise.

and 8, respectively. Thus, we only choose the two templates that corresponds to 0x00 and 0xFF to build.

Second, the partially-sharing(known) nonces attack is a lattice attack that does not tolerate mistakes [17], usually the attack fails due to a single long vector. However, due to the noise, the values are difficult to be recovered without false alarm. A simple example is that two power traces correspond to the same value (e.g. two power traces with the common value 0x00 are on the top in Fig. 3) might have a more significant difference than those with different values (e.g. two power traces with values 0x00 and 0x01 are on the bottom in Fig. 3). These will result in incorrectly estimating the values that are transferred, and the corresponding vector in the lattice might be too long. To overcome this obstacle, our solution is two-folds:

– A signal processing technique, i.e. PCA, is applied to the original traces to amplify the difference of the power consumption between values with different Hamming weights. In [1], Archambeau et al. also proposed to apply PCA to the traces before the template attack, with the purpose of choosing the most interesting points which benefit the template attack. Different from their scenario, we have more traces than the number of points to be considered. As a consequence, we use the original routine as described in Sect. 2.2 to get better results. Moreover, PCA is used in a different way from that of [1]. In [1], PCA is applied inter-class (as stated in [24]), i.e., the mean traces obtained according to different values are used to calculate the covariance matrix $\hat{\mathbf{\Sigma}}'$ and the traces to be matched are also transformed according to the eigendecompose of this matrix. However, in our case, we calculate the covariance also intra-class, that is, we apply PCA to the traces before averaging. In this way, the noise distribution could be better used. For the traces to be matched, an independent PCA is applied instead of using the eigenvectors of the template building phase, in order to better character the distribution of these traces.

– The templates are used in a way that is different from the classical manner as that in [5]. In [5], the templates corresponding to all the values (or all Hamming weights) are built, and the target traces are matched with the templates by the maximum-likelihood principle to decide the value (or Hamming weight) of the secret. Note that in the case of stream ciphers or block ciphers, normally the secret key will keep the same each time we do the encryption. Thus the attacker can use multiple matching traces with the same value to enhance the success rate. However, in our case, the nonce varies each time so that we have only a single trace to match for each value. Remember that we only use two templates; thus we look through the traces to find the matched value for each of the two templates, instead of searching over the templates for each trace. Moreover, we decide not to use the maximum-likelihood principle that are used commonly in the template attack. Instead, we use an opposite approach; the "minimum-likelihood principle" is our decision principle that detects the values with the lowest Bayesian probability. The reason is that in the experiment we found that the success rate is higher in this case. Specifically, for the power traces after signal processing, we match them with each of the two templates corresponding to 0x00 and 0xFF. Then we sort the traces with the log-likelihood and choose the minimum ones. Usually, we can set a threshold and keep only the ones below this threshold; these traces are expected to have the values that are the same as (when the precharged values of the template building and matching phases are different) or the complement of (when the precharged values of the template building and matching phases are the same) that of the templates. The signatures chosen according to the same template can then be paired to be used in the lattice attack.

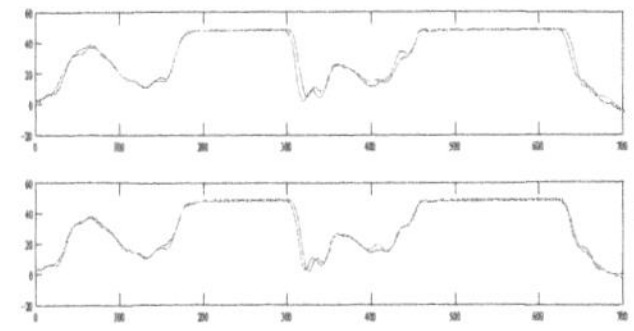

Figure 3: Overlap of two traces (top: traces with the same value; bottom: traces with different values)

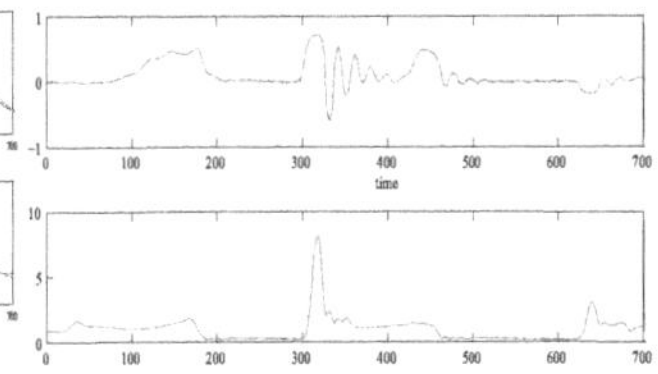

Figure 4: Correlation coefficient (top) and standard deviation (bottom)

Following the above technique, we now describe the detailed steps of our template building and matching phases.

Template Building Phase.

1. Keep on sending the APDU for random number generation to the smartcard and sort the recorded traces according to the first byte of the random numbers. For 1,800,000 random numbers, we obtain about 7,000 traces for each of the 256 values.

2. Align all the kept traces and then apply PCA to them.

In order to enhance the efficiency, PCA should be only applied to the "sensitive points" in the traces that are correlated to the values. This can be easily done by calculating the correlation coefficients between the values and the trace points, since we know the random numbers. However, this might cause a problem that in the matching phase, when one has to do the same transformation, i.e. PCA, to the corresponding part of the analyzed traces, he has no idea about how to choose the proper points due to the unknown nonces. As an alteration, we will calculate the standard deviations of each point of the template traces, and try to find the relation between the standard deviations and the correlation coefficients (see Fig. 4). We know from Fig. 4 that the peak of the standard deviations appears at the same point as that of the correlation coefficients.

Then we select a number of points before and after the peak of the standard deviation, to which PCA is applied. See Fig. 5 for the power traces of values with different Hamming weights after PCA, which shows more significant difference than those before PCA.

3. For the traces corresponding to the values 0x00 and 0xFF after PCA transformation, two templates are built by selecting a certain number of points with high variances. Since the eigendecomposition used in our PCA has sorted the eigenvalues, we select the points on the right hand side whose variances are large.

Template Matching Phase. In the matching phase, the APDU that corresponds to the signing command is sent to the smartcard, a power trace of the whole signing procedure is shown in Fig. 6. The part on the power trace that corresponds to the generation and transfer of k is marked; in the very beginning of this part, we found a very similar interval as that in Fig. 2. We believe that this is the part that we

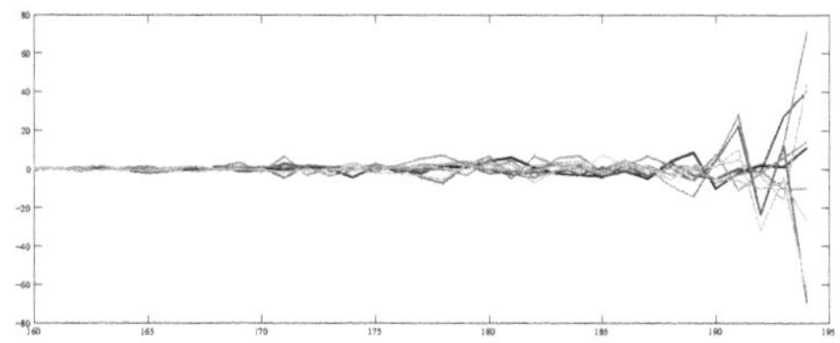

Figure 5: Traces of values with different Hamming weights after PCA

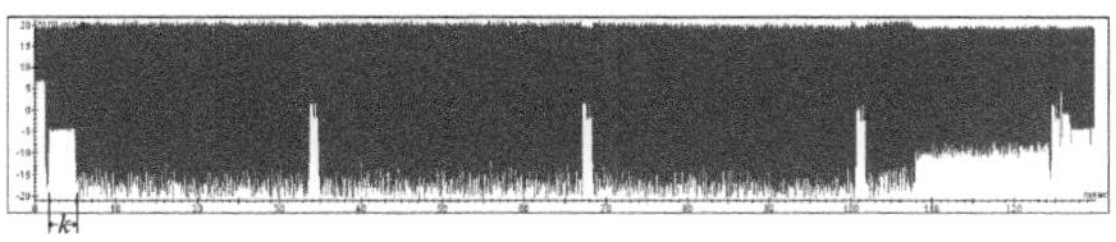

Figure 6: Power consumption of SM2 signing procedure

should use to match the template, thus we keep only this part of the power trace for each signature.

In order to collect enough signatures, we have to repeatedly send the signing APDU to the smartcard. To make the attack more reasonable, we will not assume that we can collect enough signatures within a single power-on period of the smartcard. So we only send the APDU 10,000 times to the smartcard before it powers off. For these traces, we select the interval that is the same as the template building phase by calculating the standard deviation and then apply PCA to them. For the traces after PCA, we match them with the template. A minimum likelihood principle is applied as mentioned, and a threshold is chosen to make the false positives as few as possible. After we find the matching traces, we pair these signatures and then collect the next 10,000 signatures to repeat the procedure. Since the values we targeted occur with probability 2/256, and we have a strict threshold so as to reduce the errors, in our experiment there were only $3 \sim 4$ power traces kept on average for each of the two templates. As a consequence, we can get about 4 pairs of signatures with the same MSBN from 10,000 signatures.

4. PARTIALLY-SHARING NONCES ATTACK ON SM2DSA

In this section, we describe the lattice attack that uses the partially-sharing nonces acquired in the previous section to recover the private key.

For a pair of signatures (r_1, s_1) and (r_2, s_2) that shares MSBN, we have:

$$s_1(1+d_A) = k_1 - r_1 d_A \mod n, \quad (2)$$
$$s_2(1+d_A) = k_2 - r_2 d_A \mod n; \quad (3)$$

subtracting Eq. (3) from Eq. (2), then:

$$(s_1 - s_2 + r_1 - r_2)d_A - (s_2 - s_1) = k_1 - k_2 \mod n. \quad (4)$$

We write $k_1 = 2^l k_1^H + k_1^L$, $k_2 = 2^l k_2^H + k_2^L$, where $l = 248$ and k^H is the most significant byte of k. Since in our case $k_1^H = k_2^H$, Eq. (4) can be rewritten as:

$$(s_1 - s_2 + r_1 - r_2)d_A - (s_2 - s_1) = k_1^L - k_2^L \mod n.$$

Since $k_1^L, k_2^L \in [0, 2^l]$, we have

$$-2^l \leq \lfloor (s_1 - s_2 + r_1 - r_2)d_A - (s_2 - s_1) \rfloor_n \leq 2^l \quad (5)$$

If we can obtain d pairs of signatures $(((r_1^1, s_1^1), (r_2^1, s_2^1)), \cdots, ((r_1^d, s_1^d), (r_2^d, s_2^d)))$ with collided MSBN, then they all fulfill Eq. (5); the recovery of private key d_A can be seen as an HNP problem. Denote $t_i = s_1^i - s_2^i + r_1^i - r_2^i$, $u_i = s_2^i - s_1^i$ $(i = 1, \cdots, d)$.

In our experiments, we use embedding method as shown in Sect. 2.3 to solve the CVP. To avoid the fraction in computation and balance the values in coordinates, one needs to modify the coefficients of the row matrix (1) by some scaling factor. As a result, we construct a CVP in the lattice below:

$$\begin{pmatrix} 1732 \cdot n & 0 & \cdots & 0 & 0 \\ 0 & 1732 \cdot n & \ddots & \vdots & \vdots \\ \vdots & \ddots & \ddots & 0 & \vdots \\ 0 & \cdots & 0 & 1732 \cdot n & 0 \\ 1732 \cdot t_1 & \cdots & \cdots & 1732 \cdot t_d & 4 \end{pmatrix}$$

The target vector is $\vec{u} = (1732 \cdot u_1, 1732 \cdot u_2, \ldots, 1732 \cdot u_d, 0)$, and the parameter β in lattice $\mathbf{B}'$ (Sect. 2.3) is chosen to be $4n$. We expect that the vector $\vec{h} = (1732(d_A t_1 + nh_1 - u_1), \ldots, 1732(d_A t_d + nh_d - u_d), 4d_A, 4n)$ which discloses d_A is the short vector in the embedding lattice. Now, we give a heuristic theoretical result about the number of signature pairs needed to recover the private key: The upper bound of the length of the vector $\vec{h}$ is about $\sqrt{d(1732 \times \frac{n}{2^8})^2 + 32n^2}$; by Gaussian heuristic the expected length of shortest vector is about $\sqrt{\frac{d+2}{2\pi e}}(16 \times 1732^d \times n^{d+1})^{\frac{1}{d+2}}$. When the length of vector $\vec{h}$ is shorter than that of Gaussian heuristic, d_A can be obtained by finding the short vector of the embedding lattice. Here $n \approx 2^{256}$, then we can achieve the bound as long as $d \geq 45$. Since d is relatively small, the lattice basis reduction algorithm BKZ with blocksize 20 can be seen as an SVP oracle. That is, the BKZ 20 algorithm will output the shortest vector for lattice with dimension not much larger than 50.

Experimental Results. Our smartcard runs SM2DSA at 32MHz; a sampling rate of 1G/s and a 1G band width are used when we are collecting the power traces.

To enhance the success rate of the attack, similar to [17], we collect more pairs of signatures than the number calculated from Gaussian heuristic, say 48. The reason is to avoid the failure of the attack due to the false detection of the collision, although the probability of falsely detecting is very low due to our strategy in Sect. 3.

To get 48 pairs of collided signatures, we need about 120,000 signatures in the template matching phase. For our target smartcard, about one hour is required to run 10,000 signings; thus less than 13 hours are needed to process the 120,000 ones. In the template building phase, only the random number generation command should be run, which is much faster than the signing process. In our experiment, we need about 12 hours to get the 1,800,000 traces for template building.

From these 48 pairs of signatures, we randomly choose 45 pairs to form a CVP and then solve the embedding lattice by BKZ 20 algorithm implemented in NTL library [23]. In the worst case, there are about $\binom{48}{45} = 17296$ BKZ reductions with dimension 45 have to be carried out, but this is still feasible since one reduction takes about 2.4 seconds with one core of Intel Xeon CPU W3530 (2.8GHz) and 4G memory. Actually, we recovered the correct private key immediately after we tried the first group of 45 pairs of signatures, and it turned out that the collided pairs we collected were all correct when we figured out all the nonces for the 48 pairs of signatures.

Furthermore, the previous bound obtained from Gaussian heuristic is an upper bound and we expect that fewer signatures are actually needed to recover the private key. In our experiment, we found that BKZ actually performed better than the bound that we estimated: Less than 40 pairs of signatures were enough to recover the private key. This means that the attacker can collect fewer signature pairs so as to reduce the processing time.

Note that in the experiment, we found that the private key came from the second shortest vector of the embedding lattice, since the shortest vector would always be all zero but the $(d+1)$-th dimension. Let the $(d+1)$-th dimension of the second shortest vector be d'_A, then the private key is $d'_A/4 \mod n$ or $n - (d'_A/4 \mod n)$.

5. COUNTERMEASURES

Common countermeasures of hiding [16] will make our attack more difficult to succeed. These countermeasures include increasing the background noise, balancing the power consumption, randomizing the internal clock, random delay, etc. All the countermeasures could be applied to the random number generation and moving process.

Another countermeasure is to generate the nonce k with the method as specified in Appendix B.5.1 of [18]. In this method, a random number with extra 64 random bits will be produced and then it will be reduced before being used as the nonce. In this scenario, the information obtained in our attack is no longer the same as that of the nonces; thus our attack is invalid in this case.

6. CONCLUSION

This paper implements an attack on SM2DSA by using the information leaked from the generation of the nonces. By using the collisions of the first bytes of the nonces detected with the assistance of templates, we give a partially-sharing nonces attack on SM2DSA with the recommended parameters. Possible countermeasures are also suggested.

Our attack can also be applied to SM2DSA with the other parameters and the other elliptic curve based signature algorithms like ECDSA, as long as the transfer of the random numbers leaks the information of the nonce k.

Acknowledgments. The authors would like to thank the anonymous reviewers for their valuable comments. This work is supported by National Natural Science Foundation of China (No. 61402536, No. 61202493 and No. 61402252) and "12th Five-Year Plan" The National Development Foundation for Cryptological Research (No. MMJJ201401009).

7. REFERENCES

[1] C. Archambeau, E. Peeters, F.-X. Standaert, and J.-J. Quisquater. Template Attacks in Principal Subspaces. In L. Goubin and M. Matsui, editors, *CHES 2006*, volume 4249 of *LNCS*, pages 1–14. Springer, 2006.

[2] R. Avanzi, H. Cohen, C. Doche, G. Frey, T. Lange, K. Nguyen, and F. Vercauteren. *Handbook of Elliptic and Hyperelliptic Curve Cryptography.* CRC Press, Boca Raton, 2005.

[3] D. Boneh and R. Venkatesan. Hardness of Computing the Most Significant Bits of Secret Keys in Diffie-Hellman and Related Schemes. In N. Koblitz, editor, *CRYPTO 1996*, volume 1109 of *LNCS*, pages 129–142. Springer, 1996.

[4] D. Boneh and R. Venkatesan. Rounding in Lattices and Its Cryptographic Applications. In M. E. Saks, editor, *SODA 1997*, pages 675–681. ACM/SIAM, 1997.

[5] S. Chari, J. R. Rao, and P. Rohatgi. Template Attacks. In B. S. K. Jr., Çetin Kaya Koç, and C. Paar, editors, *CHES 2002*, volume 2523 of *LNCS*, pages 13–28. Springer, 2002.

[6] O. Choudary and M. G. Kuhn. Efficient Template Attacks. In A. Francillon and P. Rohatgi, editors, *CARDIS 2013*, volume 8419 of *LNCS*, pages 253–270. Springer, 2014.

[7] EMV. Integrated Circuit Card Specifications for Payment Systems. Version 4.3 (November 2011). `http://www.emvco.com`.

[8] J.-C. Faugère, C. Goyet, and G. Renault. Attacking (EC)DSA Given Only an Implicit Hint. In L. R. Knudsen and H. Wu, editors, *Selected Areas in Cryptography 2012*, volume 7707 of *LNCS*, pages 252–274. Springer, 2013.

[9] H. Hotelling. Analysis of a Complex of Statistical Variables Into Principal Components. *J. Educ. Psych.*, 24, 1933.

[10] N. Howgrave-Graham and N. P. Smart. Lattice Attacks on Digital Signature Schemes. *Des. Codes Cryptography*, 23(3):283–290, 2001.

[11] R. Kannan. Minkowski's Convex Body Theorem and Integer Programming. *Mathematics of Operations Research*, 12(3):415–440, 1987.

[12] P. C. Kocher. Timing Attacks on Implementations of Diffie-Hellman, RSA, DSS, and Other Systems. In N. Koblitz, editor, *CRYPTO 1996*, volume 1109 of *LNCS*, pages 104–113. Springer, 1996.

[13] A. Lenstra, J. Lenstra, H.W., and L. Lovĺész. Factoring polynomials with rational coefficients. *Mathematische Annalen*, 261(4):515–534, 1982.

[14] M. Liu, J. Chen, and H. Li. Partially Known Nonces and Fault Injection Attacks on SM2 Signature Algorithm. In D. Lin, S. Xu, and M. Yung, editors, *Inscrypt 2013*, volume 8567 of *LNCS*, pages 343–358. Springer, 2014.

[15] M. Liu and P. Q. Nguyen. Solving BDD by Enumeration: An Update. In E. Dawson, editor, *CT-RSA 2013*, volume 7779 of *LNCS*, pages 293–309. Springer, 2013.

[16] S. Mangard, E. Oswald, and T. Popp. *Power Analysis Attacks: Revealing the Secrets of Smart Cards.* Springer, 2007.

[17] D. Naccache, P. Q. Nguyen, M. Tunstall, and C. Whelan. Experimenting with Faults, Lattices and the DSA. In S. Vaudenay, editor, *Public Key Cryptography 2005*, volume 3386 of *LNCS*, pages 16–28. Springer, 2005.

[18] National Institute of Standards and Technology (NIST). FIPS Publication 186-4: Digital Signature Standard, 2013.

[19] P. Q. Nguyen and I. Shparlinski. The Insecurity of the Elliptic Curve Digital Signature Algorithm with Partially Known Nonces. *Des. Codes Cryptography*, 30(2):201–217, 2003.

[20] Office of State Commercial Cryptography Administration. Public Key Cryptographic Algorithm SM2 Based on Elliptic Curves (in Chinese). `http://www.oscca.gov.cn/News/201012/News_1198.htm`.

[21] C. P. Schnorr and M. Euchner. Lattice Basis Reduction: Improved Practical Algorithms and Solving Subset Sum Problems. *Mathematics of Programming*, 66:181–191, 1994.

[22] S. Shen and X. Lee. SM2 Digital Signature Algorithm draft-shen-sm2-ecdsa-01. `http://tools.ietf.org/pdf/draft-shen-sm2-ecdsa-01.pdf`.

[23] V. Shoup. Number Theory C++ Library (NTL) version 5.5.2. `http://www.shoup.net/ntl/`.

[24] F.-X. Standaert and C. Archambeau. Using Subspace-Based Template Attacks to Compare and Combine Power and Electromagnetic Information Leakages. In E. Oswald and P. Rohatgi, editors, *CHES 2008*, volume 5154 of *LNCS*, pages 411–425. Springer, 2008.

Anonymous Yoking-Group Proofs*

Nan Li, Yi Mu, Willy Susilo
Centre for Computer and Information Security
School of Computer Science and Software Engineering, University of Wollongong
Wollongong, Australia
{nl864,ymu,wsusilo}@uow.edu.au

Vijay Varadharajan
Information and Networked Systems Security Research
Department of Computing, Faculty of Science
Macquarie University Sydney, Australia
vijay.varadharajan@mq.edu.au

ABSTRACT

Yoking-proofs show an interesting application in Radio Frequency Identification (RFID) that a verifier can check whether two tags are simultaneously scanned by a reader. We consider a scenario that multi-group of tags can be proved to be scanned simultaneously. Grouping-proof, which is an extension of yoking-proofs, allows multiple tags to be proved together, while existing protocols *cannot* support multiple groups. In this paper, we introduce a novel concept called "yoking-group proofs". Additionally, we propose an anonymous yoking-proof protocol and an anonymous yoking-group proof protocol and prove their security in Universal Composability framework.

Categories and Subject Descriptors

D.4.6 [**Security and Protection**]: Authentication, Access Control

General Terms

Security, Design

Keywords

RFID Security; Yoking Proof; Anonymity; UC Framework

1. INTRODUCTION

A Radio Frequency Identification (RFID) system comprises three essential components: RFID tags, RFID readers and a backend server. An RFID tag is associated with a unique identifier, which is allocated by the backend server. RFID has many practical applications, such as supply-chain management and retail operations. Normally, both the reader and the server are operated by a trusted party who initiates tags. Although the reader can scan a bulk of tags together, there is no proof which can convince a verifier the simultaneous presence of tags.

Juels [12] introduced the notion of yoking-proofs which guarantee that two tags have been scanned simultaneously. In the scenario, a verifier who maintains a server and all secret information of tags is considered as a trusted third party. Yoking-proofs allow an untrusted party to control a reader which can connect to the verifier after a proof is compiled. Two tags interact with the reader individually and assume that tags cannot be directly linked during the protocol run. The reader obtains a proof at the end of the protocol and issues it to the verifier who can be either offline or online.

The concept of yoking-proofs have been extended to grouping proofs by Saito and Sakurai [20] in 2005. Grouping-proof protocols allow multiple tags cooperatively generate a proof of simultaneous presence to the reader. During the proof, any message from a tag shall be delivered by a reader to another tag. An important task of a reader is to follow a specific logical structure to communicate with tags as different structures may significantly influence the security of protocol.

Tag anonymity is an essential consideration of most RFID authentication protocols [21, 5, 15, 13, 14]. In grouping-proof protocols, preventing the tag or group's identity from leaking to an adversary is a challenging task if the protocol intends to employ symmetric-key cryptography. Usually, a symmetric-key based RFID authentication protocol requires exhaustive key search during the tag authentication. To check the validity of multiple tags without providing identities, efficiency problems will ensue as there are many possible combinations of tags and each tag cannot be considered individually. Public key based protocols [1, 2, 10] enables the verifier to verify arbitrary anonymous groups without overwhelming computational cost. However, low-cost passive tags usually cannot afford these protocols due to the extensive computation requirements and therefore, we do not consider this type of solutions as it is rather expensive and impractical.

1.1 Motivation

Although the gourping-proof can show the simultaneous presence of a group of tags, in some scenarios, single grouping proof is insufficient. For example, a warehouse which stores a number of vehicles intends to prove the presence of all goods to the owner. For each car, several tags are attached to core components, such as the engine, brake and lock system. A prover should show the presence of cars as well as their integrity. Swapping components between vehi-

*This work is supported by the Australian Research Council Discovery Project DP110101951.

ASIA CCS'15, April 14–17, 2015, Singapore..

http://dx.doi.org/10.1145/2714576.2714609..

cles is prevented, otherwise the product is no longer original. Unfortunately, the grouping-proof can only show the presence of either all components or an individual car. Note that each car is in a different group since it intends to be sold separately. In addition, a car should be untraceable after it has been sold. Thus, the authentication should be anonymous that an unauthorized third party cannot obtain tags' identity during the protocol execution.

In the above scenario, a protocol which provides untraceability and simultaneous presence of multi-group is necessary. In this paper, we propose a solution that it not only supports a single group verification but also generates an anonymous proof for multiple groups. Note that a trivial solution from grouping-proof protocols is highly unlikely due to the lack of inter-group communication. In the literature, grouping-proof protocols usually interact with tags in a specific order which constructs a logical structure. To the best of our knowledge, there are two main structures: ring and yoking-style. Ring-based protocols [3, 4, 9, 6] start from an initiator tag, then followed by the other tags and complete the proof at the initiator. Regardless whether tags share a group key or not, once an initiator has generated a proof, it cannot interact with initiators of other groups. In other words, we need to significantly modify the protocol to achieve the requirement. Existing protocols [20, 16, 11] which adopt yoking-style proof generation can also hardly accomplish a multi-group proof. These protocols usually employ a pallet tag to collect responses from a bunch of tags, then generate a proof by collaborating with another tag. Eventually, the group proof is formed similarly as in yoking proof. Therefore, to perform the multi-group proof, an upper layer must be constructed.

1.2 Related Work

Two yoking-proofs were proposed in [12], while the protocol using minimalist MACs has been attacked by Saito and Sakurai [20]. The concept of anonymous grouping-proof was firstly presented by Bolotnyy and Robins [3]. Unfortunately, the protocol statement is ambiguous that how to link tags via their pseudonyms.

Huang and Ku [11] introduced a lightweight grouping-proof which employs a pseudorandom number generator in passive tags, however, the proposal is insecure as described in [8]. Burmester, Medeiros and Motta [4] presented two grouping-proof protocols which support the anonymity and forward security. The protocols have been proved secure in universal composability framework, while some flaws were illustrated later by Peris-Lopez, Orfila, Hernandez-Castro and Lubbe [19]. Subsequently, some other anonymous grouping-proof protocols were proposed in [18, 17, 1].

Recently, Burmester and Munilla [6] proposed an anonymous grouping-proof protocol which prevents an adversary from linking two sessions of a target group. The protocol considered that a group of tags is defined as in a logical ring. A specific framework was described. It allows a reader to concurrently interact with tags. The proof of simultaneous presence is generated by a tag labeled with index 1 and the proof is in constant size.

In grouping-proof, a reader is normally assumed as untrusted and the verifier is offline. If an online server is available, the grouping-proof is not hard since the verifier can setup a timer for a challenge. Even so, there are some protocols [16, 9] proposed for an online verifier. Note that, we only consider a system where online verifier is unavailable.

1.3 Our Contributions

In this paper, we define a novel notion called *yoking-group proofs*. It can be considered as an extension of both yoking-proofs and grouping-proofs. Basically, yoking-group proofs allow a verifier to check the simultaneous scanning of multiple groups. Grouping-proof protocols guarantee a group of tags have been authenticated together, while no existing protocol supports authentication of multiple groups without significant modifications.

We propose two protocols: anonymous yoking-proofs and anonymous yoking-group proofs. As a building block, our anonymous yoking proof is a lightweight protocol which only requires one hash computation in each tag during the protocol run. Our anonymous yoking-group proof provides the evidence of simultaneous presence of multiple groups and the size of a proof is irrelevant to the size of each group. Unlike some previous work, there is no group key stored in any tag, instead, the key is reconstructed at the end of protocol execution and it can only be checked by the verifier. Indeed, the yoking-proof is a special case of yoking-group proofs where there is one tag in each group.

2. SYSTEM OVERVIEW

The yoking-group proof system consists of three entities: RFID tags, reader and a verifier.

Tag T_i: A paasive low-cost device which has a small storage and limited computational capacity.

Reader R_i: A powerful device which is controlled by an untrusted third party. Tag and verifier's secret information is unknown to R_i.

Verifier V_i: An offline trusted third party (TTP) which maintains all the keys and identities of groups.

In an anonymous yoking-group proof, a verifier V creates a group of tags that each tag shares a part of secret keys with other tags. Each group has an individual group identification key which indicates the group's identity. Note that no individual tag holds the key of a group, instead, the key is reconstructed during the protocol run. In the protocol execution, a reader firstly interrogates all the tags and collects their indexes. Then, the reader constructs a logical key structure based on the tag indexes and interacts with tags in the specific order. Finally, the reader obtains a proof that multiple groups are presented simultaneously and issues the proof to the verifier. However, the reader cannot extract any private information, such as a tag's identity and group's key.

3. SECURITY AND PRIVACY MODELS

In this section, we define the security requirements and assumptions. A yoking-group proof algorithm proves that predefined groups of tags have been simultaneously scanned. To evaluate the security of our protocol, we shall define the capacities of an adversary as follows.

DEFINITION 1 (ADVERSARY). *We define capabilities of adversaries as follows.*

- *An adversary $\mathcal{A}$ is allowed to capture all the interactions between the interrogating reader and participating tags.*

Functionality $\mathcal{F}_{ayp}$

Upon receiving input Initiate at reader R: It ignores the request if R is compromised. Otherwise, it generates a unique subsession identifier s and replaces any existing init record by init(s, R), and then outputs init.

Upon receiving input Initiate at tag T_i: It ignores the request if T_i is compromised. Otherwise, it generates a unique subsession identifier s'_i and replaces any existing init records by init(s'_i, T_i) and deletes any record link, and then outputs init.

Upon receiving input Link (s'_i, s'_j) at tag T_i: If there are records init(s'_j, T_j) or link(s'_j, T_j) and init(s'_i, T_i), and then it deletes init(s'_i, T_i), records and outputs link(s'_i, T_i).

Upon receiving input Prove(s, s'_i, s'_j): If there are records init(s, R), link(s'_i, T_i) and link(s'_j, T_j), then it records proof(s, s'_i, s'_j), deletes all link records and outputs proof.

Upon receiving input Impersonate(s, s'_i, T_j): If there are records init(s, R), init(s'_i, T_i) and T_j is a tag controlled by an adversary, and then it records and outputs proof(s, s'_i, ps'_j), where ps'_j is a pseudo-subsession.

Upon receiving input Verify(proof) at verifier: If there exists a record proof$'(s, s'_i, s'_j)$= proof, and then it outputs valid, otherwise invalid.

Figure 1: $\mathcal{F}_{ayp}$ for anonymous yoking-proof.

- *$\mathcal{A}$ can corrupt at most $n-1$ tags where n is the number of tags. In this case, the anonymity of compromised tags are ignored. Note that the corrupted tags are not destructive that they can be involved in the future communications.*
- *$\mathcal{A}$ is allowed to interact with both tags and a reader in any order and messages can be altered by $\mathcal{A}$ in some manners.*

The universal composability (UC) framework [7] supports composable security even in complex systems. Most RFID applications are assumed to be deployed in a large and scalable system, thus we apply the UC model to analyze proposed protocols. In UC framework, it introduces models in ideal world which expresses robust protocol execution and real world where a probabilistic polynomial time (PPT) adversary is allowed to control adversarial parties and arranges the order of activation for parties. In the UC model, it defines a simulator $\mathcal{S}$ which emulates the real protocol ρ execution and translates runs of ρ with real world adversary $\mathcal{A}$ into runs of ρ which is executed by ideal functionality $\mathcal{F}$ with ideal world adversary $\widehat{\mathcal{A}}$. An adversary of UC model in both ideal world and real world shall interact with a PPT called *environment* $\mathcal{Z}$ which distinguishes whether the interactions collected are from $\mathcal{F}$ and $\widehat{\mathcal{A}}$ or from ρ and $\mathcal{A}$. To analyze the security of a protocol ρ, we say that ρ UC-*realizes* $\mathcal{F}$ if there is no $\mathcal{Z}$ can distinguish between ideal and real world with non-negligible probability.

In UC framework, a protocol execution is captured by a session identifier *sid* which is created by $\mathcal{Z}$. In each protocol run, all parties use the same *sid* and any input/output of the protocol is represented associated with *sid*. We describe parties and sessions involved in the protocol execution for both of proposed protocols as follows.

Functionality $\mathcal{F}_{aygp}$

Upon receiving input Initiate at reader R: It ignores the request if R is compromised. Otherwise, it generates a unique subsession identifier s and replaces any existing init record by init(s, R), and then outputs init.

Upon receiving input Initiate at tag T_i, where $i \geq 1$: It ignores the request if T_i is compromised. Otherwise, it generates a unique subsession identifier s'_i and replaces any existing init records by init(s'_i, T_i, i) and deletes any record link, and then outputs init.

Upon receiving input Link (s'_i, s'_j) at tag T_i: If there are records init(s'_j, T_j, j) or link(s'_j, T_j, j) and init(s'_i, T_i, i), and then it deletes init(s'_i, T_i, i), records and outputs link(s'_i, T_i, i).

Upon receiving input Build(s'_i, s'_j, s'_k) at tag T_k: If there are records link(s'_i, T_i, i), link(s'_j, T_j, j), init(s'_k, T_k, k), and then it deletes init(s'_k, T_k, k), records and outputs build(s'_k, T_k, k).

Upon receiving input Build(s'_i, s'_j, s'_z, s'_k) at tag T_k: If there exists four records link(s'_i, T_i, i), link(s'_j, T_j, j), init(s'_z, T_z, z) and init(s'_k, T_k, k), it deletes init(s'_k, T_k, k), records and outputs build(s'_k, T_k, k).

Upon receiving input Prove$(s, \{s'_m\})$, where $m \geq 1$: If there is a record init(s, R); for all $s'_i \in \{s'_m\}$, there exists build(s'_i, T_i, i), then it records proof$(s, \{s'_m\})$, deletes all build records and outputs proof.

Upon receiving input Impersonate$(s, \{s'_m\} \setminus \{s'_j\}, T_j)$: If there is a record init(s, R); for all $s'_i \in \{s'_m\} \setminus \{s'_j\}$ and T_j is a tag controlled by an adversary, then it records and outputs proof$(s, (\{s'_m\} \setminus \{s'_j\}) \cup \{ps'_j\})$, where ps'_j is a pseudo-subsession.

Upon receiving input Verify(proof) at verifier: If there exists a record proof$'(s, \{s'_m\})$= proof, and then it outputs valid, otherwise invalid.

Figure 2: $\mathcal{F}_{aygp}$ for anonymous yoking-group proof

Sessions. The entire life-time of a protocol is represented by a single session. For each session *sid*, it consists of multiple subsessions which are initiated by protocol parties. Particularly, a unique subsession identifier *ssid* is assigned when a protocol party receives an input Initiate from $\mathcal{Z}$. Note that all parities in different subsessions share the same *sid*.

Parties. There are three types of parties: tag, reader and verifier. In each subsession *ssid*, there are arbitrarily many of tags that different instances of type tag are allowed. However, there is only one instance type of reader in a subsession. As UC entities, such as $\mathcal{Z}$ and $\mathcal{A}$, are not parties of a protocol, an adversary is allowed to control multiple protocol parties.

Yoking-proof. A successful yoking proof in the real world implies that the output of each tag contains the other tag's input which is generated by a piece of secret. An adversary is entitled to fully control the network and can selects involved partners. In the ideal world, the protocol execution is emulated by the calls of Link and Prove activities.

Yoking-group proof. A successful yoking-group proof in the real world implies that yoking proof of each pair of child nodes is successful, correctness of group secret reconstruction and the output of one group involves the secrets of another group. As above, the adversary can choose participating partners and control the network. In the ideal world, the protocol execution is emulated by the calls of Link, Build and Prove activities.

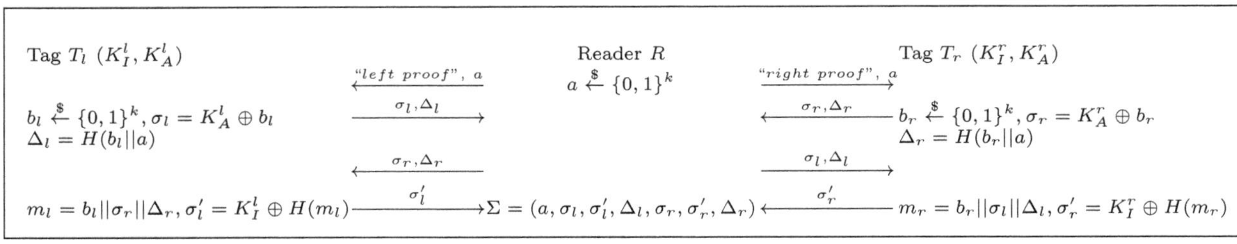

Figure 3: Anonymous yoking-proof protocol.

Anonymity. In the ideal functionality $\mathcal{F}_{ayp}$ of anonymous yoking proof, it only leaks a party's type information which is "tag" or "reader". In the ideal functionality $\mathcal{F}_{aygp}$ of anonymous yoking-group proof, it discloses the type information of involved parties as well as the index when the party is type tag. Note that an index of a tag indicates the position of a tag in a group other than the identity of a tag. Clearly, tags and readers are distinguishable as they proceed distinct tasks. We respectively depict the ideal functionality $\mathcal{F}_{ayp}$ of anonymous yoking proof and the ideal functionality $\mathcal{F}_{aygp}$ of anonymous yoking-group proof in Figure 1 and Figure 2.

4. BUILDING BLOCK

A novel anonymous yoking-proof protocol is proposed in this section. It is an essential building block of our yoking-group proofs described in Section 5. The proposed yoking-proof is a lightweight symmetric key based protocol which only requires one hash computation to each tag. The untrusted third party who controls the reader has an obligation to ensure the sequence of interactions and collects responses of tags without obtaining any privacy of target tags. Then, it compiles the proof and submits it to the verifier who is referred to a trusted third party. During the reader-tag communication, the trusted third party is unnecessary to be online and all proofs can be verified latter.

Our protocol is described as in Figure 3 that any two legitimate tags are eligible to be presented in the proof. For each tag, the TTP stores two keys in its non-volatile memory, namely identification key K_I and authentication key K_A, such that $K_I, K_A \in \mathcal{K}$, where $\mathcal{K}$ is the defined key space. Firstly, the reader randomly chooses $a \in \{0,1\}^k$, where k is a security parameter, and sends a as a challenge to both of tags T_l and T_r. Upon receiving the challenge, T_l selects a random number $b_l \in \{0,1\}^k$ and computes (σ_l, Δ_l) that b_l is considered as an ephemeral key to protect the authentication key K_A^l. The tag T_r executes the same as T_l and sends challenge (σ_r, Δ_r) to the reader. Then, the reader swaps two responses and sends (σ_r, Δ_r), (σ_l, Δ_l) to T_l, T_r, respectively. Upon receiving the challenge, the tag generates a message m and encrypts the message by using the identification key K_I. At last, the reader compiles the responses received from two tags and generates a yoking proof Σ. To verify the proof, the verifier who maintains pairs of keys (K_A, K_I) searches pairs (K_A^l, K_I^l) and (K_A^r, K_I^r) and checks the proof as

$$\Delta_l \stackrel{?}{=} H(\sigma_l \oplus K_A^l||a),\ \sigma_l' \stackrel{?}{=} K_I^l \oplus H(\sigma_l \oplus K_A^l||\sigma_r||\Delta_r),$$

$$\Delta_r \stackrel{?}{=} H(\sigma_r \oplus K_A^r||a),\ \sigma_r' \stackrel{?}{=} K_I^r \oplus H(\sigma_r \oplus K_A^r||\sigma_l||\Delta_l),$$

where $H : \{0,1\}^* \to \{0,1\}^k$ is a cryptographic collision-resistant hash function. We assume that each tag T_i is assigned a distinct key pair (K_A^i, K_I^i) which indicates its unique identity in the database and only the verifier can reveal the keys.

The proposed protocol also employs the timeout mechanism which guarantees the interaction is completed in a small period of time. The tag and reader abort the protocol if the response received later than the defined time window. To simplify the description, we assume that there is a timeout for each round where the recipient is awaiting any response. For the rest of this paper, we will adopt the same definition.

5. PROPOSED PROTOCOL

In this section, we demonstrate an anonymous yoking-group proof protocol which allows an untrusted third party to prove that two groups of tags have been scanned simultaneously. Intuitively, the protocol guarantees plenty of tags have been presented during the protocol run. However, the further requirement of the protocol is that the verifier needs to identify which groups of tags have been scanned other than the validity of tags. The proposed protocol is based on the building block introduced in Section 4. Although a tag may handle more computations during the authentication, the minimum computational cost remains the same as in our yoking-proof protocol. In addition, the computational cost to the verifier is irrelevant to the number of tags.

5.1 Anonymous Yoking-group Proof

An anonymous yoking-group protocol is described as in two phases: the grouping phase and the yoking phase. To show the presence of distinct groups, a reader firstly requests tags to generate a grouping-proof and then yokes groups to generate a yoking-proof. We call the proof created by the protocol as a yoking-group proof Σ_G.

In some previous grouping-proof protocols, the tags are arranged in a specific logical structure. For instance, Burmester and Munilla [6] assume that a group of tags form a logical ring and the tags are labelled from 1 to n, where n is the quantity of tags. Some other protocols [2, 20] also consider a group of tags as a ring or a chain during the authentication. They also consecutively assign each tag a distinct number. Usually, the protocols which apply symmetric-key cryptography pre-define a group by sharing a group key, identity or distinctive counters. Similar method is employed, especially in some protocols which intend to protect the tag's identity and provide anonymity proofs. One reason for this is that the symmetric-key based protocols normally require exhaustive key search to check the validity of proofs and undefined groups may cause efficiency problems as the verifier has to

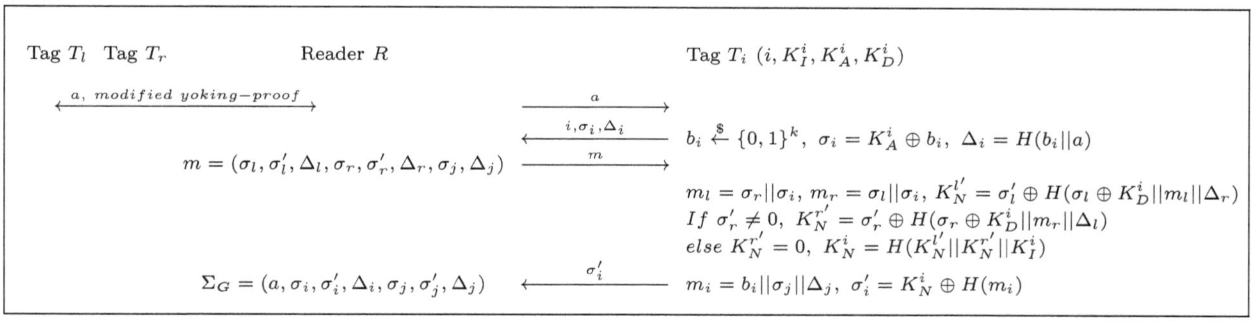

Figure 4: Yoking-group proof with group anonymity for two groups.

test all the possible combinations of tags. Hence, in our protocol, we assume that the groups are defined prior to being authenticated.

An important consideration to a grouping-proof protocol which needs to prevent group's identity is that the computational cost to a verifier shall be lower than the way of exhaustive key search for each tag. As one phase of yoking-group proof protocol, the group authentication in our protocol only requires constant computational cost $O(1)$ in verifying the validity of a group. Moreover, the total cost of proof verification equals to the cost of authenticating our yoking proof. To reduce the computational cost and guarantee the integrity of a group, we employ a binary tree as a logical structure to represent tags and each tag is assigned a different index in the specific group. The verifier only needs to check the validity of a proof generated by the root tag instead of all the tags.

The size of a proof influences the performance of a protocol. Normally, a larger size indicates that more components should be checked during the verification. Regardless whether the proof is a compressed message, it is undesirable if the tags are verified individually. As a feature of our anonymous yoking-group proof protocol, the length of a proof remains the same size of our yoking-proof.

5.2 Constructions

Our protocol is described as in Figure 4 that it shows the proof for two groups. To simplify our protocol, we only consider that each group consist of three tags, while the protocol can be extended to groups which contain any number of tags.

Without loss of generality, we firstly introduce a binary tree which represents the logical structure of a group of tags. According to Figure 5, each node, including leaves and root, represents a tag. From top to down and left to right in each level, a tag T is assigned to an index i and the root is labelled as 1. For a tag T_i, it stores three keys which are identification key K_I^i, authentication key K_A^i and decryption key K_D^i. Initially, the tag owner sets these keys as follows.

$$K_I^i \xleftarrow{\$} \mathcal{K}, \ K_D^i \xleftarrow{\$} \mathcal{K}, \ K_A^i = K_D^p,$$

where $K_D^p \in \mathcal{K}$ is the decryption key of T_i's parent. In case that if T_i is the root of a tree, the owner randomly chooses a key K_A^i from $\mathcal{K}$. The group key K_G is constructed as in a Merkle tree that for each non-leaf node N_i, set $K_N^i = H(K_N^l||K_N^r||K_I^i)$, where K_N^l, K_N^r are node keys of N_i's left and right child respectively and K_I^i is the identification key of T_i in N_i. If T_i is in a leaf of a tree, we set $K_N^i = K_I^i$.

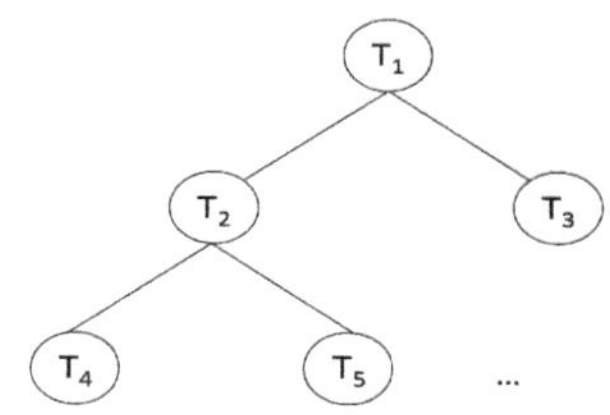

Figure 5: Labeled tree for a group of tags.

Clearly, apart from the leaves, a tag does not keep a node key, instead, the node keys are built during the protocol execution. Indeed, the protocol rebuilds the Merkle tree and outputs the group key K_N^1 at the root T_1. The verifier maintains the group key and it indicates the identity of a specific group of tags.

In the grouping phase of our protocol, tags generate a proof of group. As an example, we show a single round of grouping-proof via our yoking-group proof protocol and the grouping-proof can be accomplished recursively for a larger group. We denote that T_1 is a root and T_2, T_3 are respectively left and right child of T_1. Without loss of generality, we refer tags T_2 and T_3 to T_l and T_r, respectively.

To start with, the reader R broadcasts a request along with a nonce a. A tag sends its index as a part of the first response to R. According to our system model, the reader builds a hash tree structure based on the indexes and maintains a link to each tag. In terms of one group, T_l, T_r and R firstly run the yoking-proof protocol illustrated in Section 4. The only difference is that the reader sets the message

$$\sigma_l = \sigma_l||\sigma_i, \quad \sigma_r = \sigma_r||\sigma_i,$$

where σ_i is generally the response of challenge a from the tags' parent. The reader collects a yoking-proof Σ and T_i's response (σ_i, Δ_i). Concurrently, the reader obtains the reply (σ_j, Δ_j) form T_j, which is the root of another group.

After compiling proofs, the reader sends the message $m = (\sigma_l, \sigma_l', \Delta_l, \sigma_r, \sigma_r', \Delta_r, \sigma_j, \Delta_j)$ to the root T_i and starts the yoking phase. Upon receiving the message m, T_i extracts the node keys K_N^l, K_N^r of two tags and computes the node key K_N^i. In a case that if node N_i of a tree only has left child, the reader sets $(\sigma_r, \sigma_r') = (\sigma_i, 0)$, where σ_i is a response of N_i. Accordingly, the tag T_i ignores a message σ_r' and simply sets $K_N^r = 0$. We should note that this step does not guarantee the correctness of node keys as a tag handles the received message without authentication. Since the goal of our protocol is to check the simultaneous scanning of groups and the hash tree ensures the integrity of a group, there is no need to verify messages during the proof. The verifier is able to verify the group's integrity when it checks the validity of a yoking-group proof.

Finally, T_i outputs a reply σ'_i by using K_N^i and T_j outputs σ'_j via the same approach. Upon receiving two responses $(\sigma_i, \sigma'_i, \Delta_i)$ and $(\sigma_j, \sigma'_j, \Delta_j)$, the reader compiles a yoking-group proof Σ_G. The verifier checks the validity of proofs by searching key pairs (K_A^i, K_N^i) and (K_A^j, K_N^j).

Extension for Multi-group Proof. Assume that there are n groups. In the grouping phase, a reader collects each root tag's response (σ_i, Δ_i), where $i = 1, 2, \cdots, n$. For example, (σ_1, Δ_1) is the response of the root tag of group G_1. In the yoking phase, the reader transmits (σ_k, Δ_k), where $k = 1, 2, \cdots, n-1$, from group G_k to G_{k+1}, then transmits (σ_n, Δ_n) to G_1. Note that this step can be performed concurrently and the following steps are the same as in two-group version.

6. SECURITY ANALYSIS

Due to the page limitation, the proof is in the full version.

THEOREM 1. *Our anonymous yoking-proof protocol and anonymous yoking-group proof protocol UC-realizes the functionality $\mathcal{F}_{ayp}$ and $\mathcal{F}_{aygp}$ with random oracles, respectively.*

7. CONCLUSION

In this paper, we introduced a novel concept of anonymous yoking-group proofs. The proposed anonymous yoking-proof protocol achieves computational efficiency on tags and remains the required security properties. Our anonymous yoking-group proofs convince a verifier that multiple groups of tags are simultaneously scanned. We discussed some common attacks to RFID protocols and the security and privacy are formally proved in the UC framework.

8. REFERENCES

[1] L. Batina, Y. K. Lee, S. Seys, D. Singelée, and I. Verbauwhede. Privacy-preserving ecc-based grouping proofs for RFID. In *ISC*, LNCS, pages 159–165. Springer, 2010.

[2] L. Batina, Y. K. Lee, S. Seys, D. Singelée, and I. Verbauwhede. Extending ecc-based RFID authentication protocols to privacy-preserving multi-party grouping proofs. *Personal and Ubiquitous Computing*, 16(3):323–335, 2012.

[3] L. Bolotnyy and G. Robins. Generalized "yoking-proofs" for a group of RFID tags. In *MobiQuitous'05*, pages 1–4.

[4] M. Burmester, B. de Medeiros, and R. Motta. Provably secure grouping-proofs for RFID tags. In *CARDIS*, volume 5189 of *LNCS*, pages 176–190, 2008.

[5] M. Burmester and J. Munilla. Lightweight RFID authentication with forward and backward security. *ACM Trans. Inf. Syst. Secur.*, 14(1):11, 2011.

[6] M. Burmester and J. Munilla. Distributed group authentication for RFID supply management. *IACR Cryptology ePrint Archive*, 2013:779, 2013.

[7] R. Canetti. Universally composable security: A new paradigm for cryptographic protocols. In *FOCS*, pages 136–145. IEEE Computer Society, 2001.

[8] H.-Y. Chien, C.-C. Yang, T.-C. Wu, and C.-F. Lee. Two RFID-based solutions to enhance inpatient medication safety. *J. Medical Systems*, 35(3):369–375, 2011.

[9] D. N. Duc and K. Kim. Grouping-proof protocol for RFID tags: Security definition and scalable construction. *IACR Cryptology ePrint Archive*, 2009:609, 2009.

[10] J. Hermans and R. Peeters. Private yoking proofs: Attacks, models and new provable constructions. In *RFIDSec*, LNCS, pages 96–108. Springer, 2012.

[11] H.-H. Huang and C.-Y. Ku. A RFID grouping proof protocol for medication safety of inpatient. *J. Medical Systems*, 33(6):467–474, 2009.

[12] A. Juels. "yoking-proofs" for RFID tags. In *PerCom Workshops*, pages 138–143. IEEE Computer Society, 2004.

[13] Y. K. Lee, L. Batina, D. Singelée, and I. Verbauwhede. Low-cost untraceable authentication protocols for RFID. In *WISEC*, pages 55–64. ACM, 2010.

[14] Y. K. Lee, L. Batina, D. Singelée, and I. Verbauwhede. Wide-weak privacy-preserving RFID authentication protocols. In *MOBILIGHT*, volume 45 of *LNCS, Social Informatics and Telecommunications Engineering*, pages 254–267. Springer, 2010.

[15] T. Li, G. Wang, and R. H. Deng. Security analysis on a family of ultra-lightweight RFID authentication protocols. *JSW*, 3(3):1–10, 2008.

[16] Y. Lien, X. Leng, K. Mayes, and J. Chiu. Reading order independent grouping proof for RFID tags. In *ISI 2008*, pages 128–136. IEEE, 2008.

[17] H. Liu, H. Ning, Y. Zhang, D. He, Q. Xiong, and L. T. Yang. Grouping-proofs-based authentication protocol for distributed RFID systems. *IEEE Trans. Parallel Distrib. Syst.*, 24(7):1321–1330, 2013.

[18] P. Peris-Lopez, J. C. Hernandez-Castro, J. M. Estévez-Tapiador, and A. Ribagorda. Solving the simultaneous scanning problem anonymously: Clumping proofs for RFID tags. *SECPerU*, pages 55–60. IEEE Computer Society, 2007.

[19] P. Peris-Lopez, A. Orfila, J. C. Hernandez-Castro, and J. C. A. van der Lubbe. Flaws on RFID grouping-proofs. Guidelines for future sound protocols. *J. Network and Computer Applications*, 34(3):833–845, 2011.

[20] J. Saito and K. Sakurai. Grouping proof for RFID tags. In *AINA*, pages 621–624. IEEE Computer Society, 2005.

[21] B. Song and C. J. Mitchell. RFID authentication protocol for low-cost tags. In *WISEC'08*, pages 140–147. ACM, 2008.

Verifiable Searchable Symmetric Encryption from Indistinguishability Obfuscation

Rong Cheng
School of Electronic and Communication Engineering,
Shenzhen Polytechnic

Jingbo Yan
Dept. of CSE,
University at Buffalo, SUNY

Chaowen Guan
Dept. of CSE,
University at Buffalo, SUNY

Fangguo Zhang*
School of Information Science and Technology,
Sun Yat-sen University
isszhfg@mail.sysu.edu.cn

Kui Ren
Dept. of CSE,
University at Buffalo, SUNY

ABSTRACT

Searchable symmetric encryption(SSE) allows a client to encrypt his data in such a manner that the data can be efficiently searched. SSE has practical application in cloud storage, where a client outsources his encrypted data to a cloud server while maintaining the searchable ability over his data. Most of the current SSE schemes assume that the cloud server is honest-but-curious. However, the cloud may actively cheat on the search process to keep its cost low. In this paper, we focus on the malicious cloud model and propose a new verifiable searchable symmetric encryption scheme. Our scheme is built on the secure indistinguishability obfuscation ($i\mathcal{O}$) and can be considered as the first step to apply $i\mathcal{O}$ in the SSE field. Moreover, our scheme can be easily extended to multiple functionalities, such as conjunctive and boolean queries. Furthermore, it can be extended to realize a publicly verifiable SSE. Thorough analysis shows that our scheme is secure and achieves a better performance.

Categories and Subject Descriptors

C.2.0 [**General**]: Security and protection

General Terms

Security, Privacy

Keywords

Searchable symmetric encryption, indistinguishability obfuscation, cloud storage, malicious server

*Corresponding author

ASIA CCS'15, April 14–17, 2015, Singapore..

http://dx.doi.org/10.1145/2714576.2714623.

1. INTRODUCTION

With the developments of cloud computing, more and more individuals or IT enterprises are willing to outsource their data to the cloud server. As people's awareness of privacy concern is increasing, sensitive data has to be encrypted before being outsourced to the cloud. Confidentiality of the data is guaranteed by the security of symmetric or public encryption schemes. Unfortunately, this process inevitably raises the problem that the cloud cannot do any effective computations on the encrypted data, specially, making it difficult to implement search on the stored data. Thus how to enable an effective searchable functionality on the encrypted data becomes one of the most significant issues and has attracted much research attention [1].

Fully homomorphic encryption [2] or oblivious RAMs [3] are very powerful tools and can be adopted to realize an ideally secure method to search on the encrypted data. However, they are far too inefficient for practical use. Searchable encryption was first proposed by Song *et al.* in [4]. Generally, they can be divided into two categories, searchable symmetric encryption (SSE) and public key encryption with keyword search (PEKS). However, PEKS is still not efficient due to the complex operation of public key encryption, especially for a large-scale database. Therefore, we will focus on how to construct a secure and efficient SSE.

Since the initial SSE approach by Song *et al.* [4], there have been a lot of researches emerging to enhance the SSE. In functionality, a lot of works[5, 6, 7, 8, 9] are proposed to fulfill conjunctive search, dynamic search, ranked search, fuzzy search and boolean queries, *et al*. Moreover, in the security models of most existing SSE constructions, servers are assumed to be honest-but-curious. They will honestly execute the search protocol and only attempt to infer the sensitive information about the clients. However, in real world, this is not always the case. If a server does not honestly execute the search operation, we call it a **malicious server**. In [10], Chai *et al.* considered a semi-honest-but-curious cloud servers, which execute only a fraction of search operations honestly and return a fraction of correct search outcome. In [11], Kurosawa *et al.* first studied the security model where the server is malicious. They proposed a verifiable searchable symmetric encryption scheme, in which they use the message authenticate code (MAC) to protect the reliability of the searching results. Their scheme is proved secure in the universally composable security framework, *i.e.* UC-secure. However their verifiable SSE requires a search time linear in the number of data files.

To our delight, we find a very powerful cryptographic primitive named indistinguishability obfuscation ($i\mathcal{O}$), which can be used to build verifiable SSE scheme. Barak *et al.* [12] proposed the concept *Indistinguishability Obfuscation* which requires that obfuscations of any two equal-size programs that compute the same function are computationally indistinguishable.

The $i\mathcal{O}$ becomes so important because recently there is a breakthrough result of Garg *et al.* [13] that puts forward the first candidate construction for an efficient $i\mathcal{O}$ for general boolean circuits. Many surprising applications in cryptographic field were proposed such as multi-party key exchange [14], deniable encryption [15], short signature with fast signing [16], full domain Hash [17], *etc.* This fascinating achievement provides the possibility for us to adopt $i\mathcal{O}$ in our approach.

Our Work. In this paper we pioneer the idea of adopting indistinguishability obfuscation ($i\mathcal{O}$) to design a new SSE scheme. Our $i\mathcal{O}$-based SSE scheme can have various searching functionalities embedded into the obfuscation circuit so that it can meet flexible searching requirements. Moreover, it can be extended to realize public verifiability on the results returned by the malicious server.

The remainder of this paper is organized as follows. In section 2, we briefly introduce the tools used in our construction. Then we give the system model and security definition in section 3. In section 4, we describe the detailed construction of our SSE scheme and its extensions to multiple search functionalities and public verifiability. Then we give out the analysis for our construction in section 5. Lastly we give the conclusion in section 6.

2. PRELIMINARIES

In this part we will simply explain the cryptographic tools used in our construction: indistinguishability obfuscation and constrained pseudorandom functions.

Indistinguishability Obfuscation. The definition of indistinguishability obfuscation ($i\mathcal{O}$) was first proposed by Barak *et al.* [12]. Informally, the requirement for the indistinguishability obfuscation is that for two programs with the same functionality, after the obfuscation, they will be computationally indistinguishable with each other. In Crypto 2013, the breakthrough result of Garg *et al.*[13] proposed the first efficient indistinguishability obfuscation for general polynomial circuits. All the polynomial circuits can be securely obfuscated. The detailed definition of indistinguishability obfuscation can be referred to [13].

Constrained Pseudorandom Functions. Constrained PRF is a pseudorandom function (PRF) which is only defined on a subset of the usual input space. There are many constructions for simple types of constrained PRFs[18, 19, 20]. In our construction, we use a punctured PRF which is a constrained PRF that can be constrained on the complement of any polynomial size set $\mathcal{G} \subseteq \mathcal{X}$. Following Boneh and Waters [18], we define punctured pseudorandom functions as a PRF with the following added functionality: PRF.Puncture(G) for subset $\mathcal{G} \subseteq \mathcal{X}$ outputs an efficient program for the function:

$$PRF^{\bar{G}}(x) = \begin{cases} PRF(x), & if \;\; x \notin G; \\ \perp, & if \;\; x \in G. \end{cases}$$

3. SECURITY MODEL

The definition of our $i\mathcal{O}$-based SSE is as follows.

Definition 1. ($i\mathcal{O}$-based Searchable Symmetric Encryption). A $i\mathcal{O}$-based SSE scheme is a tuple of six polynomial-time algorithms $\Pi = (Gen, Enc, Token, Search, Verify, Dec)$

- $K \leftarrow Gen(1^k)$: take the security parameter k as input and the client outputs the secret keys K.
- $(i\mathcal{O}_{\mathcal{F}}, \mathcal{C}) \leftarrow Enc(K, \mathcal{W}, \mathcal{F})$: take the secret key K, data file collection $\mathcal{F}$ and keywords set $\mathcal{W}$ as inputs, client outputs the searching circuit $i\mathcal{O}_{\mathcal{F}}$ and ciphertext of $\mathcal{F}$;
- $t_w \leftarrow Token(K, w)$: take as inputs the secret key K and a keyword w, client generates the corresponding search token t_w.
- $(\mathcal{C}_w, \mathcal{S}_w, Mac) \leftarrow Search(\mathcal{C}, i\mathcal{O}_{\mathcal{F}}, t_w)$: take the searching circuit $i\mathcal{O}_{\mathcal{F}}$, the search token t_w and a sequence of encrypted files $\mathcal{C}$ as inputs, cloud server outputs the searched identifiers $\mathcal{S}_w$, searched files $\mathcal{C}_w$ and a verification message Mac.
- $Bool \leftarrow Verify(\mathcal{S}_w, \mathcal{C}_w, Mac, K)$: take the searched identifiers $\mathcal{S}_w$, searched files $\mathcal{C}_w$, MAC value Mac and secret key K as inputs, client outputs $Bool$, if accept, $Bool = 1$; otherwise, $Bool = 0$.
- $\mathcal{Q}_w \leftarrow Dec(K, \mathcal{C}_w, Bool)$: take the secret key K, feedback encrypted file $\mathcal{C}_w$, and $Bool$ value as inputs, abort if $Bool = 0$, else client decrypts to get the file $\mathcal{Q}_w$.

Correctness. We require that cloud server can output the correct searching result with the token and the obfuscated searching circuit.

Our privacy definition adopts the real/ideal simulation paradigm which is popular in the recent SSE works [21, 6, 22]. We require that the adversary cannot distinguish the real game $Real^{\Pi}_{A}(k)$ and a simulation game $Idea^{\Pi}_{A,S}(k)$(L is the leakage function).

$Real^{\Pi}_{A}(k)$: *Challenger runs* $K \leftarrow Gen(1^k)$ *to get secret keys* K. *Adversary* $A(1^k)$ *chooses data files* $\mathcal{F}$. *Then challenger runs* $(i\mathcal{O}_{\mathcal{F}}, \mathcal{C}) \leftarrow Enc(K, \mathcal{W}, \mathcal{F})$ *and and sends* $i\mathcal{O}_{\mathcal{F}}$ *and* $\mathcal{C}$ *to* A. *Then adversary makes polynomial number of queries by picking different keywords* w_i, *and the challenger responds the respective search token* $t_{w_i} \leftarrow Token(K, w_i)$. *Finally,* A *returns a bit* b *that is output by the experiment.*
$Idea^{\Pi}_{A,S}(k)$: *Adversary* $A(1^k)$ *chooses data files* $\mathcal{F}$. *Then simulator* S *generates* $(i\mathcal{O}_{\mathcal{F}}, \mathcal{C}) \leftarrow S(L(\mathcal{F}))$ *and sends* $i\mathcal{O}_{\mathcal{F}}$ *and* $\mathcal{C}$ *to* A. *Then adversary makes polynomial number of queries by picking different keywords* w_i. *To respond, simulator generators respective search tokens* $t_{w_i} \leftarrow S(L(\mathcal{F}))$. *Finally,* A *returns a bit* b *that is output by the experiment.*

Verifiability. In our security model, a malicious server may not honestly execute the search operation and return the invalid searching results. The invalid searching results include two cases: the malicious server forges the searching results or deletes some of them. The verifiability requires that the malicious server cannot generate an invalid response which results that the *Verify* algorithm outputs 1.

4. SSE BASED ON IO

In this section, we start with the construction for the basic single keyword search. Then we show how to easily extend it to a conjunctive and boolean keyword. Furthermore, we present how to use $i\mathcal{O}$ to realize the publicly verifiable property for our SSE scheme.

Before presenting our construction, we analyze two trivial SSE constructions using $i\mathcal{O}$: (I) the obfuscated search program takes as inputs one search token and an encryption of the entire database; (II) the obfuscated search program takes as inputs one keyword token and an encryption of one file. For more explicit comparison, we use an concrete example where a client encrypts 100 files, each of which has size 20MB ($20 \cdot 2^{23}$ bits), and then uploads those corresponding 100 ciphertexts to the server, to which the client will make keyword search request in the future. The number of valid keywords is 1000. Let n be the number of files, λ be the size of a file and m be the number of valid keywords.

In construction (I), the search program first decrypts the entire database, and then checks which files have the matching keyword and outputs a corresponding ciphertext of those files. Thus, the circuit that needs to be obfuscated has size $O(poly(n\lambda)) = O(poly(100 \cdot 20 \cdot 2^{23})$, where $poly(x)$ represents a polynomial in terms of x, due to the fact that the cost for the entire database's decryption dominates over searching's. This will lead to a significantly larger obfuscation of search program. In construction (II), the search program decrypts the input file, and then checks whether this file has the matching keyword and outputs "yes/no" correspondingly. The circuit being obfuscated has size $O(poly(\lambda)) = O(poly(20 \cdot 2^{23}))$. Note that it is still a huge-size circuit in $i\mathcal{O}$'s applications. Also observe that, to search for the files associated with one keyword token provided by user, the server needs to execute this obfuscated search program 100 times. Plus, this approach of searching over the files separately could leak additional information, like search pattern.

While in our construction, we first generate an index table and then apply $i\mathcal{O}$. Thus, the circuit that will be obfuscated would has size $O(poly(mn)) = O(poly(1000 \cdot 100))$. Clearly, $m \ll \lambda$ (it is very common, in real life applications, that the number of valid keywords is much smaller than the file's size), which means that $O(poly(mn)) \ll O(poly(n\lambda))$. Additionally, $O(poly(mn)) \ll O(poly(\lambda))$ in this case. Thus, the size of this circuit is significantly smaller than those in the above two trivial constructions, which results in a significantly smaller obfuscated search program. Also note that for each keyword search request, the server just needs to run this search program once, and this obfuscated search program is computed only once and can be repeatedly used in the future. As we can see, although $i\mathcal{O}$ is a powerful primitive, it is not trivial to exploit it.

4.1 The Basic SSE Scheme

There are two parties involved in our construction: client and cloud server, and the whole process can be divided into two phases: setup and retrieval. Let k be the security parameter that will be used in $Gen(\cdot)$. Let $\mathcal{E}$ be a IND-CPA secure symmetric encryption scheme. Let $H(\cdot,\cdot)$ be a collision resistant hash function and $PRF(\cdot,\cdot)$ be a punctured pseudo-random function.

SETUP PHASE

In the setup phase, the client will upload the encrypted data files along with the customized $i\mathcal{O}$ circuit to the cloud server. This phase includes two algorithms, *i.e.* Gen, Enc. The details of two algorithms is shown as follows.

- Gen : The client initiates the scheme by calling $Gen(1^k)$ and generates three random secret keys $k_1, k_2, k_3 \xleftarrow{R} \{0,1\}^k$. k_1 is used to encrypt his data files, k_2 is used to generate searching tokens and k_3 is used to generate verification messages.
- Enc : In this algorithm, the client has two main missions to accomplish. He needs to generate the $i\mathcal{O}$ circute that the server can excute, and encrypt his data files. We denote his data files by $DB = \{(\mathrm{id}(F_i), F_i)\}$, $i = 1 \cdots n$, here each file F_i has an location identifier $\mathrm{id}(F_i)$. All the keywords contained in the files forms the set $\mathcal{W} = (w_1, w_2, ..., w_m)$.

  1. First the client encrypts his database DB using his secret key k_1, that is
  $$C_i = \mathcal{E}.Enc(k_1, F_i) \| h_{mac}.$$
  $$h_{mac} = H(k_1, \mathrm{id}(F_i) \| \mathcal{E}.Enc(k_1, F_i))$$
  Then the encrypted database is
  $$EDB = \{(\mathrm{id}(F_i), C_i)\}, i \in \{1 \cdots n\}.$$
  2. The client generates the look-up table $\mathcal{T}$ for his database. The look-up table is generated according to the relationship between the keywords and data files containing the keywords. $\mathcal{T}$ contains t items $\mathcal{T}_{w_i} = (t_{w_i}, \mathcal{S}_{w_i})$, $i = 1 \cdots m$, where t_{w_i} is the secret token for certain keyword w_i and $\mathcal{S}_{w_i}$ denotes the identifiers' set for files including w_i. Token t_{w_i} is calculated by a hash function H with the key k_2, $t_{w_i} = H(w_j, k_2)$.
  3. The client generates a searching circuit $\mathcal{P}_{search}$ according the look-up table generated in step 2. He can customize $\mathcal{P}_{search}$ in accordance with the required functionality. The procedure of the seach circuit P_{search} for single keyword is demonstrated in Algorithm 1. Then he securely obfuscate it to get the indistinguishability obfuscation circuit $i\mathcal{O}(\mathcal{P}_{search})$.
  4. Data owner sends the encrypted database EDB along with the indistinguishability obfuscation circuit $i\mathcal{O}(P_{search})$ to the cloud server.

Algorithm 1 Search Circuit $\mathcal{P}_{search}$

- *Constants*: Secret key k_3. Look-up table $\mathcal{T}$.
- *Inputs*: searching token t_w.
- *Outputs*:

1. For $j = 1 \cdots t$, verify that $t_{w_j} \stackrel{?}{=} t_w$. If yes, set $S = S_j$; if no keyword matches, abort.
2. Compute verifying hash value
$$Mac = PRF(S \| t_w, k_3).$$
3. Output the the searching results (S, Mac).

RETRIEVAL PHASE

In the retrieval phase, the client wants to search data files containing certain keyword. He generates the searching token corresponding to the keyword and sends the token to the cloud server. With the searching token, cloud server can utilize the obfuscation circuit to search for the result and generate the verification message. Then server sends back the result to the client, the client can verify the correctness of the searching results and decrypt the correct results to get the files. This phase has 4 algorithms *Token, Search, Verify* and *Dec*, which are described as follows.

- $Token$: Input a keyword $w \in \mathcal{W}$, the client computes the searching token by $t_w = H(w, k_2)$ and sends it to server;
- $Search$: Cloud server puts the token t_w into the indistinguishability obfuscation circuit $i\mathcal{O}(\mathcal{P}_{search})$ and obtains the searching result $(\mathcal{S}_w, Mac)$. According to identifier set S_w, it finds the corresponding items in EDB. At last, cloud server responds to client's search query by $(\mathcal{C}_w, \mathcal{S}_w, Mac)$.
- $Verify$: The client first verifies the hash value by
  $$PRF(\mathcal{S}_w \| t_w, k_3) \stackrel{?}{=} Mac$$
  Then if the result passes this verification, the client still needs to make sure the identifier set $\mathcal{S}_w$ is correctly mapped to the ciphertext $\mathcal{C}_w$, he verifies it by:
  $$H(k_1, \mathcal{S}_w^i \| \mathcal{E}.Enc(k_1, F_i)) \stackrel{?}{=} \mathcal{C}_w^i.h_{mac}$$
  If both of the verifications are passed, the Bool value will be set 1, otherwise it is 0.
- Dec : If the Bool value is 1, the client believes the results are correct and decrypts all files in $\mathcal{C}_w$ by secret key k_1. That is:
  $$\mathcal{Q}_w = \mathcal{E}.Dec(k_1, \mathcal{C}_w).$$
  If the Bool value is 0, the client will output $fail$.

Correctness. The functionality property of indistinguishability obfuscation gurantees that the search protocol will return the correct results. Besides, if the cloud server is not honest, the security of the verification can detect the cheating behavior.

4.2 Extensions to Other Functionalities

Our SSE scheme can be easily extended to schemes which support multiple functionalities, *e.g.* conjunctive queries and boolean queries. If we treat the $i\mathcal{O}$ circuit as a blackbox, it is easy to see that other parts of the basic framework is independent with the search functionalities. The client will only need to slightly modify the construction of the search circuit $\mathcal{P}_{search}$ and its corresponding $i\mathcal{O}$ circuit. In $\mathcal{P}_{search}$ of original SSE scheme which supports single keyword search, the searched identifier set $\mathcal{S}_w$ can be directly gotten after a one-round mapping over the look-up table. In order to support for conjunctive and boolean queries, we need to add a step to operate conjunctive or boolean function on the look-up table $\mathcal{T}$. The algorithms of conjunction keyword search and boolean queries are shown in Algorithm 2 and 3.

Moreover, our proposed SSE scheme can be further extended to achieve the public verifiability, *i.e.* the ability to securely delegate the verification to a third party. A public verification circuit $\mathcal{P}_{pv}$ can be designed with the verifying key embedded in. The client can generate the indistinguishability obfuscation of verification circuit $i\mathcal{O}(\mathcal{P}_{pv})$. Anyone with the indistinguishability obfuscation $i\mathcal{O}(\mathcal{P}_{pv})$ can verify the server's searching results. The verification circuit $\mathcal{P}_{pv}$ is shown in Algorithm 4.

5. ANALYSIS OF OUR SSE CONSTRUCTION

We evaluate the proposed scheme by analyzing its security and performance in this section. First, we will show how

---

Algorithm 2 Search Circuit $\mathcal{P}_{CSearch}$

- *Constants*: Secret key k_3. Look-up table $\mathcal{T}$.
- *Inputs*: searching token $t_{w_x}, t_{w_y}, t_{w_z}$.
- *Outputs*:
  1. For $j = 1 \cdots t$, verify that $t_{w_j} \stackrel{?}{=} t_{w_x}$. If yes, set $S_x = S_j$; if no keyword matches, abort. Similarly, obtain S_y and S_z.
  2. Compute searched index set $S = S_x \wedge S_y \wedge S_z$.
  3. Compute verifying hash value
     $$Mac = PRF(S \| t_{w_x} \| t_{w_y} \| t_{w_z}, k_3).$$
  4. Output the the searching results (S, Mac).

Algorithm 3 Search Circuit $\mathcal{P}_{BSearch}$

- *Constants*: Secret key k_3. Look-up table $\mathcal{T}$. Boolean Function BF.
- *Inputs*: searching token $S_t = \{t_{w_i}\}$, $i \in [1, t]$.
- *Outputs*:
  1. For $j = 1 \cdots t$, verify that $t_{w_j} \stackrel{?}{=} t_{w_1}$. If yes, set $S_1 = S_j$; if no keyword matches, abort. Similarly, obtain $S_2, S_3, \cdots, S_t$.
  2. Compute $S = BF(S_1, S_2, \cdots, S_t)$.
  3. Compute verifying hash value
     $$Mac = PRF(S \| t_{w_1} \cdots \| t_{w_t}, k_3).$$
  4. Output the the searching results (S, Mac).

Algorithm 4 Public Verification Circuit $\mathcal{P}_{PV}$

- *Constants*: Secret key (k_1, k_3).
- *Inputs*: Searching token t_w, Searching result $(\mathcal{S}_w, Mac)$, encrypted file set $\mathcal{C}_w$.
- *Outputs*:
  1. Verify that $PRF(\mathcal{S}_w \| t_w, k_3) \stackrel{?}{=} Mac.$
  2. Verify that $H(k_1, \mathcal{S}_w^i \| \mathcal{E}.Enc(k_1, F_i)) \stackrel{?}{=} \mathcal{C}_w^i.h_{mac}$.
  3. If both accept, output 1; else output 0.

---

the $i\mathcal{O}$-based SSE meets our security guarantee defined in section 2. Then we will give the performance analysis and comparisons with existing verifiable SSE schemes.

5.1 Security Analysis

We define the leakage function L as follows: on input the index table $\mathcal{T}$ and the set of files $\mathcal{F}$, it outputs the number of files n, number of keywords m and the size of each file; on the input search token t_w, it outputs the identifier set $\mathcal{S}_w$ of the files containing keyword w. Then we have:

THEOREM 1. *If PRF is a secure punctured PRF, and iO a secure indistinguishability obfuscator, then SSE construction in section 4.1 is L-secure.*

Proof. We prove the security through a sequence of indistinguishable games.

Game 0 This game is same to the game $Real_A^{\Pi}(k)$.

- Challenger runs $K \leftarrow Gen(1^k)$ to get secret keys $K = (k_1, k_2, k_3)$.
- Adversary $A(1^k)$ chooses data files $\mathcal{F}$, then challenger runs $(i\mathcal{O}(\mathcal{P}_{search}), \mathcal{C}) \leftarrow Enc(K, \mathcal{W}, \mathcal{F})$ and sends $i\mathcal{O}(\mathcal{P}_{search})$ and EDB to A.
- Adversary A makes polynomial number of queries by picking different keywords w_i. Challenger responds with $t_{w_i} = H(w_i, k_2)$
- A returns a bit b that is output by the experiment.

Game 1 Let q_{QH} be the upper bound on the number of registered honest queries. Before the game begins, choose q_{QH} random values $t_i^* \in \mathcal{Y}$ $(H : \mathcal{X} \times \mathcal{K} \rightarrow \mathcal{Y})$. We will use these t_i^* values as the t_{w_i} values to answer honest token queries. Besides this, other steps are the same with Game 0. As the famous leftover hash lemma [23] shows that universal hash functions are good randomness extractors, the tokens are indistinguishable from those in Game 0.

Game 2 Notice that with overwhelming probability, none of the t_i^* for token queries in Game 1 have a valid keyword preimage under hash function H. Therefore, with overwhelming probability, there is no input to $\mathcal{P}_{search}$ that will match any searched index set S. We construct a circuit C that takes these tokens as input and accepts input S if and only if the corresponding token of S is not contained in $T^* = (t_1^*, t_2^*, \cdots, t_{q_{QH}}^*)$, then construct the constrained function PRF^C following the definition in section 3. Also, we build a new encrypted database $EDB' = \{(\mathrm{id}(F_i), C_i')\}$, $i = 1 \cdots n$ and a new look-up table $\mathcal{T}'$ from the leakage function L. Last, replace PRF with PRF^C, $\mathcal{T}$ with $\mathcal{T}'$ in the program of $\mathcal{P}_{search}$, and then generate the program $\mathcal{P}'_{search}$ described in Algorithm 5. So we construct Game 2 as follows:

- Adversary $A(1^k)$ chooses data files $\mathcal{F}$. Challenger generates new encrypted database EDB' according to the leakage function. Then it generates program $\mathcal{P}'_{search}$ as above and outputs indistinguishability obfuscator $i\mathcal{O}(\mathcal{P}'_{search})$. At last, challenger sends $i\mathcal{O}(\mathcal{P}'_{search})$ and EDB' to A.
- Adversary A makes at most q_{QH} queries by picking different keywords w_i. Challenger responds with $T^* = (t_1^*, t_2^*, \cdots, t_{q_{QH}}^*)$.
- A returns a bit b that is output by the experiment.

Algorithm 5 Search Circuit $\mathcal{P}'_{search}$

- *Constants*: PRF^C, Look-up table $\mathcal{T}'$.
- *Inputs*: searching token t_w.
- *Outputs*:
  1. For $j = 1 \cdots t$, verify that $t_{w_j} \stackrel{?}{=} t_w$. If yes, set $S = S_j$; if no item in $\mathcal{T}'$ matches, abort.
  2. Compute $Mac = PRF^C(S \| t_w, k_3)$.
  3. Output the the searching results (S, Mac).

Observe that, with overwhelming probability, $\mathcal{P}'_{search}$ and $\mathcal{P}_{search}$ have the same functionality. Thus from the security of indistinguishability obfuscator, $i\mathcal{O}(\mathcal{P}'_{search})$ and $i\mathcal{O}(\mathcal{P}_{search})$ are computationally indistinguishable. Therefore, Game 2 is indistinguishable from Game 1.

From the above sequence of games, we have that Game 0 is computationally indistinguishable from Game 2. While, Game 0 is same to the game $Real_A^{\Pi}(k)$ and Game 2 is the same to game $Idea_{A,S}^{\Pi}(k)$ described in definition 1. Thus we proved that the $i\mathcal{O}$-based SSE scheme is L-secure.

THEOREM 2. *If MAC scheme is unforgeable, and $i\mathcal{O}$ a secure indistinguishability obfuscator, then SSE construction in section 4.1 satisfies verifiability.*

Proof. If the malicious server forges an invalid response which makes the $Verify$ algorithm output 1, then we can utilize the malicious server to forge a valid MAC value. From the SSE construction in section 4.1, the cloud server inputs the searching token to the obfuscator $i\mathcal{O}(P_{search})$ and obtains the outputs (S, Mac). The verification value Mac can be verified by using the client's secret key k_3. So if a malicious cloud server does not honestly search by the obfuscator and return the wrong results, then the MAC verification will not succeed. Because as long as the cloud server does not know the secret key k_3, it cannot forge a valid pair $\{S, Mac\}$ to deceive the client. Similarly, the server cannot construct a valid mapping for identifier and non-corresponding encrypted files without key k_1. By this method, the client can detect the cloud server's malicious actions. For more details about the security proof of the MAC authentication scheme, readers are referred to [11].

5.2 Performance and Functionality

In this section, we will give a performance analysis of our basic theoretical $i\mathcal{O}$-based scheme and compare them with existing works.

For the client, like other prior works, it needs a preprocess in the *Enc* phase. It will encrypt all the data files first and generate an obfuscated searching circuit. Although the precomputation time is not ideally small, we want to emphasize that it is a one-time effort which can be amortized to plenty of following queries. Compared to client's pre-computation, we would rather to focus on the computation and communication overheads in the *Search* phase, which can affect user experience more due to the high frequency.

Table 1 shows a comparison between our $i\mathcal{O}$-based SSE and other related works. We use n to denote the number of total files stored in the server, m, the number of all keywords and r, the number of the retrieving files for a certain keyword. As shown in the table, Kamara *et al.* [22] provides the fastest search time so far because it benefits from a parallel search (p means the number of parallel processors) method. However, it does not support verifiability. Kurosawa *et al.* [11] has proposed the first verifiable SSE scheme against malicious server. The computation and communication overhead of their search phase is proportional to n. Their following work [24] adds a dynamic property but still does not improve the efficiency.

6. CONCLUSIONS

In this paper, we proposed a secure searchable symmetric encryption scheme based on indistinguishability obfuscation as an initial attempt. Our scheme considers a threat model with a malicious cloud server and provides verifiability against the server. We first present a basic scheme supporting single keyword query, and then extend it to multiple search functionalities such as conjunctive and boolean queries. Further more, our scheme can be extended to support public verifiability. The security of our SSE scheme is guaranteed

	Computation (Search)	Communication (Search)	Verifiability	Against Malicious Server	Against Malicious Client
KO12[11]	$\mathcal{O}(n)$	$\mathcal{O}(r)$	YES	YES	NO
KP13[22]	$\mathcal{O}((rlogn)/p)$	$\mathcal{O}(1)$	NO	NO	NO
KO13[24]	$\mathcal{O}(n)$	$\mathcal{O}(n)$	YES	YES	NO
CG12[10]	$\mathcal{O}(m)$	$\mathcal{O}(r)$	YES	NO	NO
Our Scheme	$\mathcal{O}(m) + \mathcal{O}(r)$	$\mathcal{O}(r)$	YES	YES	YES

Table 1: Comparison of Verifiable SSE schemes. n denotes the number of total files, m denotes the number of all keywords, r denotes the number of the retrieving files for a certain keyword.

by the indistinguishability obfuscation and the MAC authentication concept. We also employ the constrained PRF in our security analysis, which proves that our scheme is secure with some acceptable information leakage. The computation process of the cloud server in the search phase is isomorphic with search in the plaintext domain and the communication overhead is linear with the number of retrieval files.

7. ACKNOWLEDGMENTS

This work is supported in part by the National Natural Science Foundation of China (No. 61379154 and U1135001), Specialized Research Fund for the Doctoral Program of Higher Education under Grant 20120171110027, and US National Science Foundation under grant CNS-1262277.

8. REFERENCES

[1] K. Ren, C. Wang, and Q. Wang. Security challenges for the public cloud. *IEEE Internet Computing*, 16(1):69–73, 2012.

[2] C. Gentry. Fully homomorphic encryption using ideal lattices. In *STOC 2009 Proceedings*, pages 169–178, 2009.

[3] O. Goldreich and R. Ostrovsky. Software protection and simulation on oblivious rams. *Journal of the ACM (JACM)*, 43(3):431–473, 1996.

[4] D. Song, D. Wagner, and A. Perrig. Practical techniques for searching on encrypted data. In *Symposium on Research in Security and Privacy (SSP)*, pages 44–55, 2000.

[5] P. Golle, J. Staddon, and B. Waters. Secure conjunctive keyword search over encrypted data. In *ACNS 2004 Proceedings*, pages 31–45. Springer-Verlag, 2004.

[6] S. Kamara, C. Papamanthou, and T. Roeder. Dynamic searchable symmetric encryption. In *ACM CCS 2012 Proceedings*, pages 965–976, 2012.

[7] D. Cash, S. Jarecki, C. S. Jutla, H. Krawczyk, M. C. Rosu, and M. Steiner. Highly-scalable searchable symmetric encryption with support for boolean queries. In *CRYPTO 2013 Proceedings*, pages 353–373. Springer-Verlag, 2013.

[8] J. Li, Q. Wang, C. Wang, N. Cao, K. Ren, and W. Lou. Fuzzy keyword search over encrypted data in cloud computing. In *Proceedings of the 29th INFOCOM*, pages 441–445. IEEE, 2010.

[9] N. Cao, C. Wang, M. Li, K. Ren, and W. Lou. Privacy-preserving multi-keyword ranked search over encrypted cloud data. In *INFOCOM 2011 Proceedings*. IEEE, 2011.

[10] Q. Chai and G. Gong. Verifiable symmetric searchable encryption for semi-honest-but-curious cloud servers. In *ICC 2012 Proceedings*, pages 917–922, 2012.

[11] K. Kurosawa and Y. Ohtaki. Uc-secure searchable symmetric encryption. In *FC 2012 Proceedings*, pages 285–298. Springer-Verlag, 2012.

[12] B. Barak, O. Goldreich, R. Impagliazzo, S. Rudich, A. Sahai, S. Vadhan, and K. Yang. On the (im)possibility of obfuscating programs. In *CRYPTO 2001 Proceedings*, pages 1–18. Springer-Verlag, 2001.

[13] S. Garg, C. Gentry, S. Halevi, M. Raykova, A. Sahai, and B. Waters. Candidate indistinguishability obfuscation and functional encryption for all circuits. In *FOCS 2013 Proceedings*, pages 40–49, 2013.

[14] D. Boneh and M. Zhandry. Multiparty key exchange, efficient traitor tracing, and more from indistinguishability obfuscation. In *CRYPTO 2014 Proceedings*, pages 480–499. Springer-Verlag, 2014.

[15] A. Sahai and B. Waters. How to use indistinguishability obfuscation: Deniable encryption, and more. In *STOC 2014 Proceedings*, pages 475–484, 2014.

[16] K. Ramchen and B. Waters. Fully secure and fast signing from obfuscation. In *ACM CCS 2014*.

[17] S. Hohenberger, A. Sahai, and B. Waters. Replacing a random oracle: full domain hash from indistinguishability obfuscation. In *EUROCRYPT 2014 Proceedings*, pages 201–220. Springer-Verlag, 2014.

[18] D. Boneh and B. Waters. Constrained pseudorandom functions and their applications. In *AsiaCrypt 2013 Proceedings*, pages 1–23. Springer-Verlag, 2013.

[19] E. Boyle, S. Goldwasser, and I. Ivan. Functional signatures and pseudorandom functions. In *PKC 2014 Proceedings*, pages 501–519. Springer-Verlag, 2014.

[20] A. Kiayias, S. Papadopoulos, N. Triandopoulos, and T. Zacharias. Delegatable pseudorandom functions and applications. In *ACM CCS 2013 Proceedings*, pages 669–684, 2013.

[21] R. Curtmola, J. A. Garay, S. Kamara, and R. Ostrovsky. Searchable symmetric encryption: improved definitions and efficient constructions. In *ACM CCS 2006 Proceedings*, pages 79–88, 2006.

[22] S. Kamara and C. Papamanthou. Parallel and dynamic searchable symmetric encryption. In *FC 2013 Proceedings*, pages 258–274. Springer-Verlag, 2013.

[23] J. Hastad, R. Impagliazzo, L.A. Levin, and M. Luby. Construction of pseudorandom generator from any one-way function. *SIAM Journal on Computing*, 28, 1999.

[24] K. Kurosawa and Y. Ohtaki. How to update documents verifiably in searchable symmetric encryption. In *CNS Proceedings*, pages 309–328, 2013.

The Power of Whispering: Near Field Assertions via Acoustic Communications

Lingjun Li, Guoliang Xue, and Xinxin Zhao
Arizona State University

ABSTRACT

Asserting whether two devices are in close proximity is very important to many smartphone assisted security systems. For example, the smartphone based two-factor authentication usually requires the smartphone to stay in close proximity to the other device during authentication. However, relay attacks pose a serious threat to existing approaches for proximity assertions. In this paper, we present a novel near field assertion system that restricts the distance between the two devices to the scale of several centimeters. Our system explores acoustic communications and can prevent relay attacks. The generated assertion is a confidential binary sequence known only to the two devices. Our system is fully automated and light-weight, as demonstrated by extensive evaluations on a prototype.

Keywords

Mobile security, near field assertions, relay attacks

1. MOTIVATIONS

Many smartphone assisted security applications grant user services or privileges based on the physical proximity between a smartphone and a terminal, e.g., a computer. Hence proximity assertion is an important security mechanism. In this paper, we present a novel *near field assertion* system that generates valid assertions only when the two devices are within a few centimeters.

Our work is motivated by smartphone based two factor authentication (SBTFA) [3, 18], which verifies both a user's username/password and a pre-loaded secret in the user's smartphone. During authentication, the smartphone's proximity indicates that the operator is the user himself. However, this indication is suspicious in the presence of *relay attacks* [9]. This type of attacks utilizes two communicating devices, a *leech* and a *ghost*. The leech is placed physically close to the smartphone and the ghost close to the terminal. The attacker simply relays challenge and response messages between the terminal and the smartphone via ghost-leech intercommunications and thus creates the illusion of physical proximity between the two honest devices even if they are very far apart. Relay attacks void the security protection provided by the smartphone.

To prevent relay attacks and enforce proximity communications, researchers have developed two main techniques. One is the *distance bounding protocol* [2] that cryptographically bounds the inter-device distance by measuring the response time. The other is the *contextual co-presence* approach [7, 11, 14] that enforces the proximity by comparing the ambient information (e.g., GPS, temperature, etc.) sensed by the two co-present devices. However, the distance bounding protocol is difficult to adopt on main-stream devices. The contextual co-presence approach can only confine the two devices in a large area, such as a coffee shop. A relay attack is still possible if the attacker also stays in the same area.

In this paper, we present a surprisingly simple solution to restrict two devices' communicating distance. The main idea can be illustrated by a real-life example: if two people communicate by whispering, it is hard for a third person at a distance to hear the conversation. In the mean time, our solution can resist relay attacks and we will discuss this in the following sections. Our main contribution is a design and implementation of such a system, named *Dolphin*. Dolphin generates near field assertions via acoustic communications, manipulates the sound power to restrict the communication distance, and uses full-duplex communication [8] to resist relay attacks. In particular, Dolphin has the following properties.

- *It asserts whether two communicating devices are within the near field (a few centimeters) of each other.* We use the term "near field" instead of "proximity" to emphasize that the asserted distance can be as small as a few centimeters. A device can prove that it is in the near field by presenting the assertion to the other party.
- *It can prevent relay attacks.* Dolphin has an adjustable time window limiting an attacker's relay time. A prudent implementation leaves an attacker no time to relay messages.
- *It requires no extra equipments and can be easily deployed on off-the-shelf devices.*
- *It is light-weight and battery friendly for smartphones.*

This research was supported in part by NSF grants 1217611 and 1421685. The information reported here does not reflect the position or the policy of the federal government.

ASIA CCS'15, April 14–17, 2015, Singapore..

http://dx.doi.org/10.1145/2714576.2714586.

Acoustic communications have been explored by Dhwani [12] to achieve confidential near field communications. Different from Dhwani, Dolphin utilizes *full-duplex* communications to achieve *relay-resistant* proximity assertion.

The rest of this paper is organized as follows. In Section 2, we review prior works on proximity assertions. We present the thereat model in Section 3. In Section 4, we illustrate the key ideas used in Dolphin and present an overview of the system. In Section 5, we present the details of the entire system. We present evaluations of Dolphin in Section 6, and conclude the paper in Section 7.

2. LESSONS FROM PRIOR WORKS

The problem of restricting the distance between two communicating devices has been studied in pairing systems [4] and relay resistant systems [19].

Recently, Nandakumar *et al.* [12] achieved confidential data transmission over acoustic channels in the near field. They used low signal power and signal interference to protect the data. Like many existing approaches, their system is a half-duplex communication system and is therefore *vulnerable to relay attacks.*

Distance bounding protocols [2] cryptographically restrict the distance of two communicating devices: a verifier sends a series of rapid-fire challenges and requires a prover to respond immediately. The round-trip time of an interaction is measured and used to estimate the distance. The distance bounding protocol is provably secure but requires a no-latency communication channel and complicated implementations. The inconveniences impede this approach's industry adoption. *Therefore, a desired approach should be easily deployed and adopted.*

Alternatively, contextual co-presence is a widely-adopted approach which lets two devices sense and compare the ambient information to make a proximity assertion. Various systems have been proposed using different information, including GPS raw data [11], WiFi signal strength and access point address [10], ambient acoustic finger print [7, 14], cell broadcast information [6], and user's sitting posture [1]. Usage of a combination of multiple environment information has been studied in [15, 19]. Although such approaches restrict two devices in the same area, the restricted distance cannot be at the accuracy of a few centimeters. In addition, keeping sensors awake for a long time drains smartphone battery. *It is necessary to design a system that restricts distance in the near field and is battery friendly.*

3. THREAT MODEL

Dolphin consists of a terminal, a smartphone, and a local network connection between them. A terminal is not necessarily a big-size machine and could be a smartphone or a tablet. The two devices are both honest. The connection is assumed to be insecure and controlled by the attackers. We do not consider jamming or DDoS attacks, whose purpose is to destroy the communications and assertion generation.

Dolphin is used to provide a proximity or near field assertion for two devices. In the scenario, the two devices only want to make a near field assertion. The parties care about the functionality and credibility rather than the confidentiality of the assertions. SBTFA [5] fits this scenario. In this scenario, we assume the terminal and the smartphone have their own signing-verification key pairs and have exchanged the verification keys. Also, the two devices have each other's public key for encryption purpose. Dolphin allows the attackers to eavesdrop the entire local network and to manipulate any message. The attackers may carry out relay attacks between two devices that are not in the near field.

4. KEY IDEAS OF DOLPHIN

Dolphin explores sound as an OOB channel, because the power of sound fades very fast with the increase of transmission distance. Using the threshold, Dolphin ensures that the signal cannot be decoded beyond a desired distance.

Relay resistance is a necessary but challenging part of Dolphin. Relay attacks are due to the fact that a communicating party does not know how long it needs to wait for the response message from the other party. Why is the waiting time unknown? The reason is that the communications are half-duplex! After one party sends out its message, the other one does not respond until the message has been delivered by the network. The delivery could be influenced by unpredictable network latency and attackers can take this chance to relay messages, as illustrated in Fig. 1(a). To fully resist relay attacks, we propose to use *full-duplex* communications. The two devices simultaneously transmit outgoing messages and receive incoming messages. Dolphin has a time window of an adjustable size. Starting at its message transmission, an honest party only accepts a message arriving within the time window, as illustrated in Fig. 1(b). Therefore, a small time window makes relay attacks impossible.

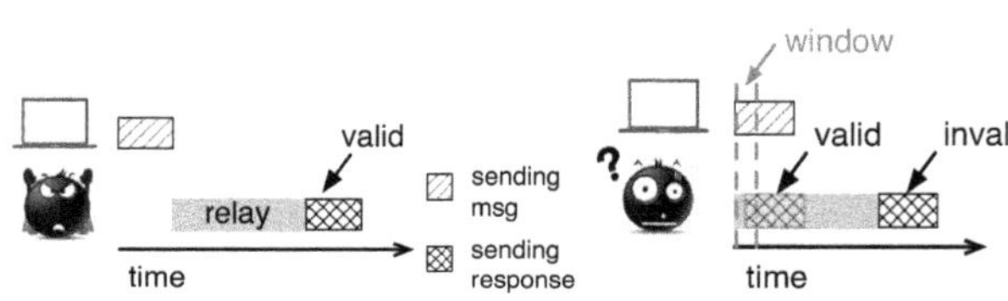

(a) Half-duplex (b) Full-duplex

Figure 1: Half-duplex vs. full-duplex

5. DESIGN DETAILS OF DOLPHIN

For demonstration purpose, we implemented a prototype of Dolphin on an iPhone 5s and a 13-inch mid 2009 Macbook Pro over WiFi connections. We first explain some terminologies. A **signal** is a sound transmitting a message. Digitally, a signal is stored in a sequence of discrete **samples** that denote the signal amplitudes at a fixed sampling rate. A **symbol** is a group of consecutive samples carrying one message bit. A signal contains a sequence of symbols. A **tone** is a sine wave signal of small length.

5.1 The Acoustic Channel

We use 16kHz acoustic channel in Dolphin, because

- the frequency of most ambient noise in our application scenarios, e.g. office or coffee shop, is below 15kHz.
- human hearing sensitivity dramatically drops at frequencies higher than 10kHz [20].
- the frequency responses are good below 18kHz for the acoustic channels used in our prototype implementation, i.e., Mac to Mac, iPhone to Mac, Mac to iPhone, and iPhone to iPhone.

Fixing the channel frequency, Dolphin uses a high-pass Finite Impulse Response (FIR) filter, depicted in Fig. 2, to reduce noise power. The filter suppresses the frequencies below 15kHz by an average of 55dB while preserving the frequencies above 15.5kHz.

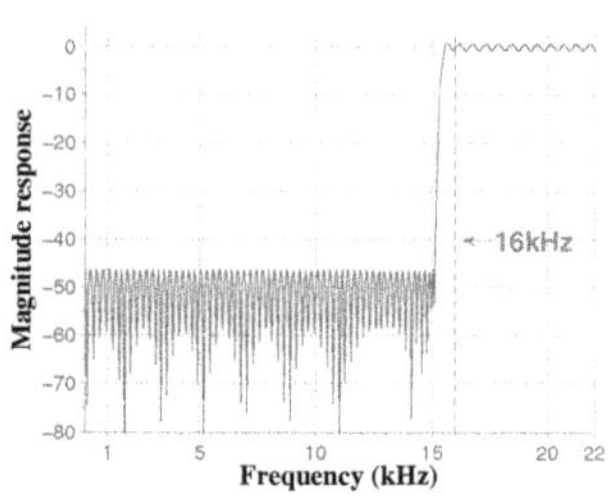

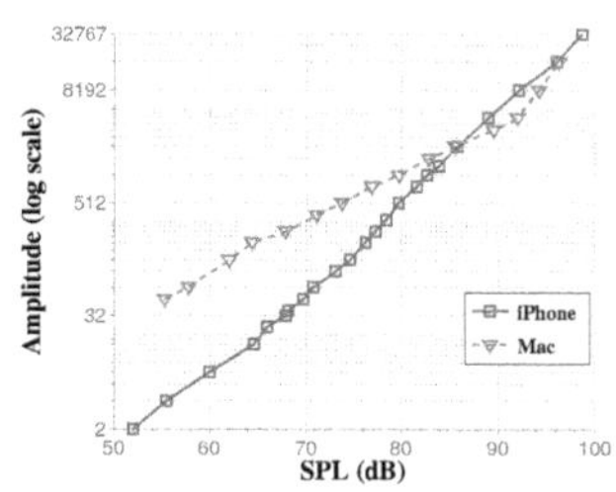

Figure 2: Filter response **Figure 3: Measured SPLs and their Amps**

Despite the noise interference, a symbol of a signal is also interfered by its predecessor and successor, i.e., Inter-Symbol-Interference (ISI). When a symbol is transmitted in an acoustic channel, it incurs *reverberation*, i.e., the received amplitude reduces to 0 slowly beyond the symbol length. We transmitted four tones of different lengths to see the change of the reverberation length. The results are listed in Table 1. For example, we observed that transmitting a 256-sample-long tone incurred a 348-sample-long reverberation. *To avoid the ISI, Dolphin selects 700 as the symbol length and the first 256 samples are reserved for the sine wave tone.*

Table 1: Tone length and reverberation length

Sine Wave	64	128	256	512
Reverberation	122	210	348	617

5.2 Modulation

In Dolphin, modulation is to transform a binary bit to a high-frequency sine wave tone that can be transmitted over the acoustic channel. Dolphin uses a simple on-off keying (OOK), in which the presence or absence of a tone denotes bit 1 or 0. The benefits of this choice are:

- OOK is vulnerable to noise interference, helping Dolphin to restrict distance.
- OOK demodulation is simple and light-weight.

Dolphin transforms a binary sequence to a series of *symbols*. A symbol carries a bit "1" if it has a 16kHz sine wave tone in the first 256 samples and a bit "0" otherwise.

5.3 Calibration and Safe Distance

Dolphin restricts distance by manipulating the signal amplitude and thus changing the emitted SPL. We need to know how much amplitude can produce a given SPL. We let the Macbook and the iPhone play a 16kHz sine wave signal at various amplitudes under full volume and measured the SPLs at a reference distance d_0. We set $d_0 = 1$cm in our implementation. The results are shown in Fig. 3 where the markers are the measured data points.

The *inverse distance law* [13] states that sound pressure falls inversely proportional to the distance away from a sound source. The sound pressure levels L_{p1} and L_{p2} at distance d_1 and d_2 conform to the following equation.

$$L_{p2} - L_{p1} = -10 \cdot \log_{10}(\frac{d_2}{d_1})^2 = -20 \cdot \log_{10} \frac{d_2}{d_1}. \quad (1)$$

Dolphin achieves distance restriction by preventing an honest party's signals being demodulated beyond a *safe distance* d. Let L_a be the SPL of ambient noise. For OOK modulation, $SNR = L_d - L_a \leq 5$dB is sufficiently low to cause a high bit error rate. According to (1), we can calculate the needed SPL L_0 at the reference distance

$$L_0 \leq L_a + 20 \cdot \log_{10} \frac{d}{d_0} + 5.$$

In our implementation, we choose $L_d - L_a = 0$ and $d = 15$cm, which yields $L_0 = L_a + 23.52$. Using Fig. 3 and interpolation, we can calculate the needed amplitude for L_0.

5.4 Synchronization

To achieve synchronization, Dolphin estimates the message delivery time and balances start time on the two devices. A start mismatch is the time difference, measured in number of samples, between the start points of two signals. We say that two signals are *entangled* if their start mismatch is less than half a tone length.

Start mismatch is caused by system latency and audio buffer size. System latency includes network latency and internal latency caused by a device's internal procedures, e.g., job scheduling. Dolphin measures and estimates system latency as follows. First, Dolphin enhances its own instance's priority to the highest possible level, to reduce internal latency. In iOS and Mac OSX, this is achieved by using `p_thread` library and `NSThread` API. The smartphone sends a probe message to the terminal, which sends an acknowledgement message immediately after the probe arrives. Upon receiving the acknowledgement, the smartphone calculates the message round trip time rtt. Repeating the process a few times, the smartphone obtains an estimated message delivery time $\overline{rtt}/2$, where $\overline{rtt}$ is the average round trip time. The estimation is performed each time before signal transmission. Once the smartphone sends a "start transmission" message, it holds for $\overline{rtt}/2$ to start transmission and the terminal starts transmission upon receiving the message. If a synchronization fails, Dolphin just re-executes the protocol until a synchronized transmission is achieved. Synchronization failure causes decoding failure, which is detected by CRC code in Dolphin, see Section 5.6.

5.5 Self-Interference Cancellation

Dolphin reconstructs the self signal using a pre-learned *reference symbol*. Before signal transmission, each device sends itself a symbol carrying bit 1. This phase is called *beep*, and the symbol is called reference symbol. Next, the device arranges the reference symbol according to its own message's binary sequence: putting the symbol at where bit 1 appears to cancel the self signal.

Directly using the reference symbol cannot obtain a good SIC result because we have not considered distortions caused by transmission. *Sampling distortion* is caused by the offset between two digital-to-analog procedures — recording reference symbols and recording message.

The offset Δt is always smaller than $1/Fs$. Fixing Δt, we use discrete Fourier transform (DFT) to shift a sample sequence (blue lines) by Δt. Equation

$$x'[n] = \sum_{k=0}^{N/2} (ReX[k]\cos(2\pi kn/N + 2\pi k\Delta tFs/N) + ImX[k]\sin(2\pi kn/N + 2\pi k\Delta tFs/N))$$

is used to obtain the shifted sample sequence $x'[1..N]$. The above shift operations are done in the frequency domain. A sample sequence needs to be converted to and from frequency domain before and after the operation completes.

SIC algorithm first finds a possible signal start position where the signal energy significantly increases. Around the start position, SIC algorithm tries every possible start position and frequency shift. Among these combinations, the algorithm choses the most similar one as the reconstructed self signals and subtracts it from the received signal. The resulting signal is taken as the one transmitted from the other party.

5.6 Putting The Pieces Together

Dolphin places the two device speakers as close as possible. From a distant attacker's point of view, the two acoustic signals seem to come from the same point and are difficult to separate. The inseparability protects the confidentiality of the resulting assertions.

First, Dolphin selects a safe distance d. When a smartphone and a terminal are properly placed, Dolphin works as follows. We note that when we say "sending message" we mean sending over the local network.

- The terminal sends a "start protocol" request to the smartphone. Upon receiving the request, the smartphone measures and estimates the message delivery time $\overline{rtt}/2$ (Section 5.4).
- The smartphone sends a "start measurement" message to the terminal. The terminal starts to measure ambient SPL when the message arrives, while the smartphone holds for $\overline{rtt}/2$ seconds to start measurement. Both devices determine the needed signal amplitude as discussed in Section 5.3. In the meantime, the devices respectively choose a 16-bit random number with the first bit fixed to 1. Appending a 4-bit CRC code, each device obtains a 20-bit message to be sent out. Using OOK modulation (Section 5.2), each device converts the binary sequence to a 16kHz signal.
- After the above preparation, the smartphone sends a "start transmission" message to the terminal. The terminal emits its signal as soon as it receives the message. The smartphone holds for $\overline{rtt}/2$ to transmit its signal.
- Each device performs SIC over the received signal (Section 5.5). The resulting sample sequence demodulated to obtain the message. CRC check is performed over the message. If the check is passed, the first 16-bit binary sequence is extracted. Both devices append smartphone's binary sequence to the terminal's. The resulting 32-bit number is the final near field assertion.
- Each device signs the assertion, encrypts the signature using the other party's public key, and sends it to the other party for validation.

5.7 Security Discussion

Distance restriction is guaranteed by the physical properties of sound. The inverse distance law of acoustics and BER-SNR relation of OOK modulation theoretically guarantee that beyond the safe distance the emitted acoustic signal's power drops to such a low value that it is impossible to correctly demodulate the message.

Relay Attacks. An honest party only accepts an arriving signal that starts the first tone at most w_0 samples later than itself does, *leaving an extremely small time window for relaying messages.* Our implementation uses a time window of $128/44.1 = 2.9$ms. The time window can be squeezed or relaxed by changing w_0. This means that our relay resistance is **adjustable** and thus flexible to be adopted by different applications.

Multi-reception Attacks. Attackers place multiple microphones near the two communicating devices trying to separate the two signals as in a multi-input multi-output (MIMO) system. However, MIMO needs senders and receivers collaborate to frequently measure the channel information between them because the channels are time-varying. Our threat models assume that an attacker does not control any device and thus cannot carry out such attacks.

Delaying Attacks. Since an attacker controls the local network connections, he can delay the smartphone's probe messages to increase its measured message delivery time but delivers the "start transmission" message as normal. In this way, the smartphone's signal transmission is delayed and the two signals are easy to separate. However, any delay larger than the time window bounded by w_0 causes demodulation failure and voids the resulting assertions.

Placement Attacks. Attackers try to find a vantage position where the arriving time gap between the two signals is stretched to a sufficiently large value to separate them. By triangle inequality, we know that the arriving time gap is no more than d_e/v_s, where d_e is the distance between the two speakers and v_s is the speed of sound, i.e., 340m/s. Dolphin requires the two speakers to stay close and d_e is smaller than 0.1m, resulting in a mismatch of 13 ($0.1 \times 44100/340$) samples.

Distance Fraud. In this attack, one of the two communicating devices is malicious and tries to get valid assertions when it is beyond the safe distance. We remark that this attack is not the main attack Dolphin aims to defend against because our threat model assumes that both devices are honest. We argue that such attacks are difficult to succeed. First, an attacker has to find some way to increase the SNR that drops to a useless level beyond the safe distance. He can either use a directional microphone to increase the arriving signal power or execute an active noise control system to reduce the noise power. However, using a directional microphone in close proximity is very suspicious and an active noise control system is not practical in an enclosed space as large as a room [17].

6. PERFORMANCE EVALUATION

We have designed a series of tests to evaluate the performance of Dolphin, including success rate under various conditions, security performance, execution time, and energy usage on smartphones.

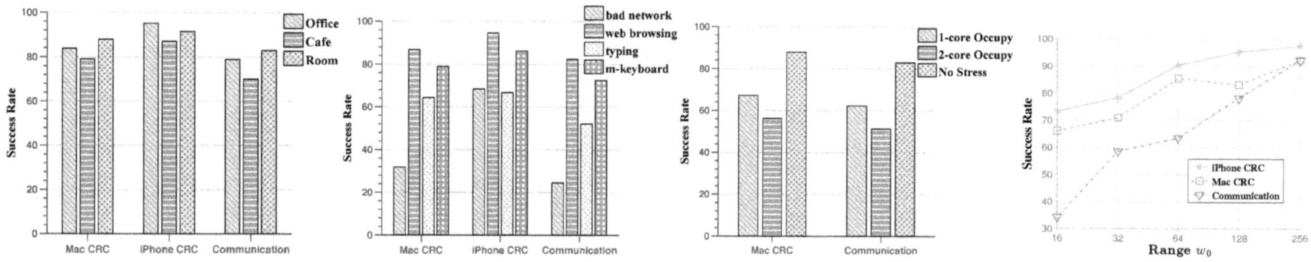

(a) Location testing (b) Usage environment testing (c) Stress testing (d) Testing w_0

Figure 4: Success rate testings

6.1 Success Rate

Before presenting the results, we remark that Dolphin uses 4-bit CRC code to detect bit errors and repeats the protocol if an error occurs. Hence, in practice, Dolphin guarantees to successfully achieve a valid assertion. Compared with contextual co-presence approaches, Dolphin enables a communicating party to locally check the validity of an assertion via CRC check. We suppressed the redo part of Dolphin in the evaluation of success rate. In the following experiments, each device performs one signal transmission per execution of Dolphin. We say the communication is successful if the two resulting assertions are identical.

First, we tested our system at three different locations, a living room, an office with A/C working, and a coffee shop during busy hours. Table 2 lists the average ambient noise SPL and statistics of network ping time at the three locations.

Table 2: Statistics of Locations

	Office	Coffee Shop	Room
Noise avg (dBSPL)	59.4	67.3	42.8
RTT avg (ms)	3.801	9.468	6.055
RTT stddev (ms)	1.922	10.666	2.407

At each location, we let the iPhone and the Macbook conduct the protocol and do 150 signal transmissions. After each transmission, we record whether the CRC check succeeds on both devices and whether the communication succeeds. The success rates are shown in Fig. 4(a). The communication success rate is the highest in the living room (82.9%) and the lowest in the noisy coffee shop (70%). The success rate in the office is also high, although the ambient noise SPL is not low. The reason is that the noise in the office is mostly caused by A/C (which is stable), while the coffee shop often has a noise burst, e.g., running an espresso machine or blending coffee beans. We also notice that the iPhone has a very high CRC success rate, because its microphone is very close to the two speakers and captures the signal much more clearly than the Macbook does. Inspired by this observation, we ran Dolphin on two iPhones, an iPhone 5 and an iPhone 5s. We put the two iPhones face up, bottom to bottom, and 1cm apart. Finally, we obtained a high communication success rate — 96.3%, 98.2%, and 95.7% at the office, living room, and coffee shop, respectively.

Next, we tested our implementation under a high latency WiFi environment and three human usage environments: web browsing, heavy typing on the build-in keyboard, and heavy typing on an external USB keyboard. Each testing performed 150 signal transmissions. During the testings, we kept a non-stop web browsing or keyboard typing while the system was running. To make a loud noise, we use an old fashioned mechanical keyboard when using an external keyboard in testing. The resulting success rates are shown in Fig. 4(b). Bad WiFi connection suppresses the communication success rate to 21%. The network RTT has a mean of 939.67ms and a standard deviation of 243.488. The low success rate is caused by the high latency variance which makes Dolphin's latency estimation inaccurate. In bad network testing, iPhone has a high CRC success rate because the mismatch is so large that the iPhone only heard its own signal. Typing on the build-in keyboard results in a lower success rate than typing on the external one, because the keys around `CAPS` key on the build-in keyboard are close to the speakers and typing on these keys affects the signals very much. Web browsing does not affect the success rate since it uses less touch to the `CAPS` key area.

The first search range w_0 determines Dolphin's tolerance to the signal mismatch and affects the success rate. We executed Dolphin using different w_0, which was set to 16, 32, 64, 128, and 256 respectively. The resulting success rates are depicted by Fig. 4(d). We observe that the growth of w_0 dramatically increases the success rate.

Dolphin synchronizes two signals by estimating system latency. Multiple tasks contending resources may make the estimation inaccurate and fail the communication. We tested the success rate of Dolphin while letting one or two CPU-intensive processes occupy CPU resources. We ran an infinite AES encryption process to occupy one of the two cores in the CPU and Geekbench 3 to occupy both. The testing is performed on the Macbook side because 1) working on computer and putting smartphone aside is a common scenario in smartphone assisted system; 2) the testing is already sufficient to show the success rate change. The resulting success rates are shown in Fig. 4(c). The success rate is reduced to 62% when one core is occupied and 50% when both are occupied. Mac OSX scheduler tries to assign equal resources to long-running jobs [16]. Contention between jobs makes the latency estimation not accurate and thus fails the synchronization and the corresponding SIC phase.

6.2 Security Performance

Dolphin utilizes fast decaying acoustic signal to restrict the distance between two devices. We placed the iPhone (resp. the Macbook) speaker at different distances to the Macbook(resp. the iPhone) microphone and let the speaker transmit signals. The received SNRs are shown in Fig. 6.2. We can see that doubling distance reduces SNR by nearly 6dB, which verifies the inverse distance law, see Equation (1). This makes obtaining valid assertions beyond the safe distance impossible.

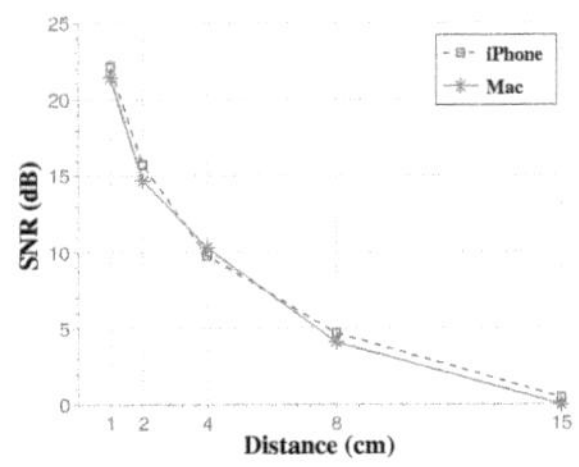

Figure 5: SNR vs. Distance

7. CONCLUSIONS

We have designed and implemented Dolphin — an acoustic near field assertion system. Dolphin utilizes the fast decay property of acoustic signals to restrict distance, and full-duplex communication to defend against relay attacks. It has an adjustable safe distance (for restricting distance) and an adjustable time window (for defending against relay attacks), generates confidential assertions, needs zero user interactions, and is battery friendly. Extensive experiments are carried out to evaluate the performance of Dolphin.

References

[1] L. Bauer, S. Garriss, J. M. McCune, M. K. Reiter, J. Rouse, and P. Rutenbar. Device-enabled authorization in the Grey system. In *Information Security: 8th International Conference, ISC 2005*, pages 431–445. Springer, Sept. 2005.

[2] S. Brands and D. Chaum. Distance-bounding protocols. In *Advances in Cryptology - EUROCRYPT'93*, pages 344–359. Springer, 1994.

[3] Y. Chen, J. Sun, R. Zhang, and Y. Zhang. Your song your way: Rhythm-based two-factor authentication for multi-touch mobile devices. *InfoCom 2015, Hongkong, China*, 2015.

[4] W. R. Claycomb and D. Shin. Secure device pairing using audio. In *43rd Annual 2009 International Carnahan Conference on Security Technology*, pages 77–84. IEEE, 2009.

[5] A. Czeskis, M. Dietz, T. Kohno, D. S. Wallach, and D. Balfanz. Strengthening user authentication through opportunistic cryptographic identity assertions. In *ACM CCS 2012*, pages 404–414, 2012.

[6] L. Francis, G. P. Hancke, K. Mayes, and K. Markantonakis. Practical relay attack on contactless transactions by using nfc mobile phones. *IACR Cryptology ePrint Archive*, 2011:618, 2011.

[7] T. Halevi, D. Ma, N. Saxena, and T. Xiang. Secure proximity detection for nfc devices based on ambient sensor data. In *ESORICS 2012*, Sep.

[8] M. Jain, J. I. Choi, T. Kim, D. Bharadia, S. Seth, K. Srinivasan, P. Levis, S. Katti, and P. Sinha. Practical, real-time, full duplex wireless. In *ACM MobiCom 2011*, pages 301–312. ACM, 2011.

[9] A. Juels. Rfid security and privacy: A research survey. *IEEE Journal on Selected Areas in Communications*, 24(2):381–394, 2006.

[10] J. Krumm and K. Hinckley. The nearme wireless proximity server. In *ACM UbiComp 2004*, pages 283–300. Springer, 2004.

[11] D. Ma, N. Saxena, T. Xiang, and Y. Zhu. Location-aware and safer cards: Enhancing rfid security and privacy via location sensing. *Dependable and Secure Computing, IEEE Transactions on*, 10(2):57–69, 2013.

[12] R. Nandakumar, K. K. Chintalapudi, V. Padmanabhan, and R. Venkatesan. Dhwani: secure peer-to-peer acoustic nfc. In *ACM SIGCOMM 2013*, pages 63–74. ACM, 2013.

[13] D. R. Raichel. *The science and applications of acoustics*. Springer, 2006.

[14] D. Schurmann and S. Sigg. Secure communication based on ambient audio. *IEEE Transactions on Mobile Computing*, 12(2):358–370, 2013.

[15] B. Shrestha, N. Saxena, H. T. T. Truong, and N. Asokan. Drone to the rescue: Relay-resilient authentication using ambient multi-sensing. In *FC 2014*, 2014.

[16] A. Singh. *Mac OS X Internals: A Systems Approach*. Addison-Wesley Professional, 2006.

[17] S. D. Snyder. *Active noise control primer*. Springer Science & Business, 2012.

[18] J. Sun, R. Zhang, J. Zhang, and Y. Zhang. Touchin: Sightless two-factor authentication on multi-touch mobile devices. *CNS 2014, San Francisco, CA*, 2014.

[19] H. T. T. Truong, X. Gao, B. Shrestha, N. Saxena, N. Asokan, and P. Nurmi. Comparing and fusing different sensor modalities for relay attack resistance in zero-interaction authentication. In *IEEE PerCom 2014*, 2014.

[20] E. Zwicker, H. Fastl, and H. Frater. *Psychoacoustics, Facts And Models, volume 22 of Springer Series of Information Sciences*. Springer, Berlin, 1999.

Detecting Fingerprinted Data in TLS Traffic

Konstantin Böttinger, Dieter Schuster, and Claudia Eckert
Fraunhofer Institute for Applied and Integrated Security (AISEC)
85748 Garching (near Munich), Germany
konstantin.boettinger@aisec.fraunhofer.de, dieter.schuster@aisec.fraunhofer.de,
claudia.eckert@aisec.fraunhofer.de

ABSTRACT

We present a new method for detecting known data in certain TLS encrypted communication channels. Our approach enables us to detect single files in eavesdropped TLS secured network traffic. We generate fingerprints by a fine-grained measurement of the entropy of fragments of known data and introduce the application of methods from the field of machine learning to the problem of file detection. We implement all proposed methods on a real data base and show the practical efficiency of our approach.

Categories and Subject Descriptors

C.2.2 [**Computer-Communication Networks**]: Network Protocols; I.5.4 [**Pattern Recognition**]: Applications

Keywords

TLS, Traffic Analysis, Machine Learning

1. INTRODUCTION

The Transport Layer Security (TLS) protocol is the most widely used security protocol on the Internet today, designed to provide confidentiality and authenticity in modern communication technology. Our goal is to apply machine learning methods to identify single files in eavesdropped TLS communication. This information leakage is realized by a side channel in the compression layer of TLS. By fingerprinting a known set of data, we can effectively detect this data in compression-enabled TLS traffic. Our novel approach introduces machine learning methods for analysis of encrypted network traffic in order to identify single files from large data bases. We implement all of our proposed methods and show their feasibility by evaluating them in a realistic scenario.

Although we focus on TLS, our approach illuminates a general problem in certain combinations of encryption and compression in cryptographic protocols. Therefore, the presented approach can be applied to many other compression enhanced security protocols in general.

ASIA CCS'15, April 14–17, 2015, Singapore.

http://dx.doi.org/10.1145/2714576.2714595.

With our presented detection method we cover several use cases. First, our approach enables detection of illegal content in TLS secured communication channels. Second, if the fingerprinted data can be assigned to a specific communication participant, a detection of this data directly causes the loss of anonymity of that participant. Our goal is to increase awareness of our approach, therefore we also discuss countermeasures that mitigate the attack.

The remainder of the paper is organized as follows. Section 2 discusses related work. In Section 3 we present necessary background regarding the TLS record layer and the Deflate compression algorithm. We define data fingerprints for detection in TLS traffic as well as a method to practically measure fingerprints in Section 4. Next, we present a practical approach to effectively detect fingerprints in TLS communication in Section 5. To demonstrate the feasibility of our approach, we implemented all of our presented methods and evaluate our prototype in Section 6. We discuss possible countermeasures in Section 7. The paper concludes with a short outlook on further applications of our approach in Section 8.

2. RELATED WORK

The history of TLS has seen a diversity of attacks and it is known that traffic analysis can disclose sensitive information of the secured communication. By statistical analysis of TLS traffic it is possible to identify versions of network protocol implementations [7], accessed websites [3], and detailed sensitive information of web applications [2]. In this paper we will present a method that even leaks information about single files that are being transferred over a TLS secured channel.

The related work most relevant to our approach is a relatively new attack described in 2013 by Bhargavan et al. [1]. The authors discovered information leakage by fingerprinting the compression ratio of fragments of known files.

However, two important points were left open up to now. First, in a realistic scenario a file will be sent in the middle of a larger data stream, which adds noise the recorded data (as discussed in more detail in Section 5). Second, it remained an open question how to practically fingerprint a large number of files and effectively detect these files in TLS secured channels. In this paper we propose a solution for both problems by introducing methods from the field of machine learning. We show that our novel approach of tackling file identification with machine learning methods allows us to detect files of large data bases in an efficient and feasible way.

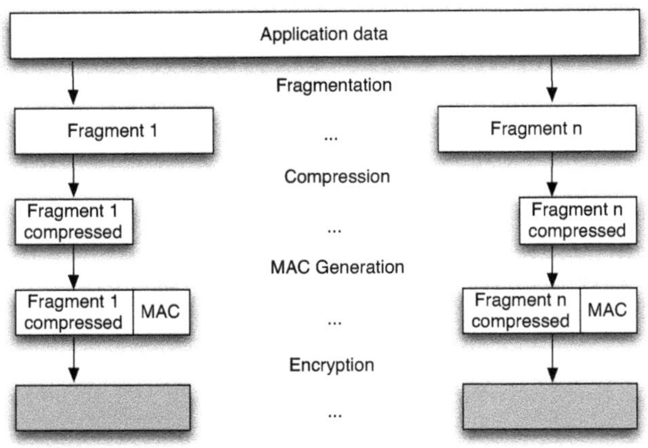

Figure 1: TLS Record Layer

3. BACKGROUND

Before we present the main idea of our paper, we give some background on the *TLS Record Protocol* as well as the *Deflate* compression algorithm. These two building blocks form the ground our attack is based on.

3.1 The TLS Record Layer

The Transport Layer Security (TLS) protocol is the most widely used security protocol on the Internet today. Despite of a long history of attacks, in many applications it is still the first choice when communication partners want to ensure an authenticated, confidential and integrity-protected information exchange. All specified versions of TLS (v1.0, v1.1, and v1.2) define the functionality to compress application data before encrypting them.

The *TLS Record Protocol* handles application data fragmentation, compression, authentication of fragments and encryption, as depicted in Figure 1. It first fragments application data coming from the upper layer into blocks of 2^{14} bytes or less. Each fragment then gets compressed with the compression algorithm negotiated in the initial TLS handshake. This compression step will later provide the crucial attack surface, since the rate of compression leaks information about the entropy of the fragments (see Section 5). Next, a Message Authentication Code (MAC) is generated for each compressed fragment over its content and associated TLS header including content type, protocol version and sequence number. The MAC is then added to the corresponding fragment. The resulting blocks are then encrypted (using the encryption algorithm and cipher suite negotiated at the initial establishment of the TLS channel by the Handshake protocol of the upper layer). Last, a corresponding TLS header is added to each of the encrypted blocks (not depicted in Figure 1).

3.2 The Deflate Compression Algorithm

A detailed understanding of the compression step of the *TLS Record Protocol* is necessary in order to identify a source of measurement uncertainty in realistic scenarios in Section 4.1. In the following, we refer to this uncertainty as *noise*.

The *Deflate* compression algorithm is the most commonly used compression method in the *TLS Record Protocol.* Although the TLS specifications (v1.0, v1.1, and v1.2) allow up to 256 different compression methods, the prevalent algorithm in use today is *Deflate*.

Deflate uses a combination of the LZ77 algorithm [10] and Huffman coding, resulting in two compression steps. In the first step, input data is compressed using the LZ77 sliding window approach that sequentially parses the input data and looks for repeated occurrences of smaller data blocks. Initially, the algorithm creates an entry in the sliding window with every first occurrence of a new data block. While parsing new data, the algorithm looks for matches to already parsed data. If the parsed data matches to an entry in the sliding window, is is just a repetition of a block already parsed before and gets replaced by a reference to the previous occurrence. So by sequentially parsing the input data and searching for already existing entries in the sliding window, the algorithm builds up a dictionary, where repetitions of data sequences are translated to references to a previous occurrence. However, the sliding window has a fixed maximum size. Therefore, the window only holds most recent data and therefore slides over data blocks during the compression process.

In the second step, the output of the LZ77 compression gets Huffman coded by replacing symbols with weighted representation symbols based on frequency of use. By creating a binary tree of nodes, where the initial symbols are the leaf nodes and nodes get successively removed according to highest priority (lowest probability of occurrence), the Huffman algorithm derives a table based on the estimated frequency of occurrence for each symbol of the input data.

The most important aspect of *Deflate* for the following discussion is its characteristic of being stateful. That means that the *Deflate* algorithm has a state, represented by the content of the sliding window and the table of estimated frequencies of symbols. This state gets updated while compressing new input data. In context of the *TLS Record Protocol* (see Section 3.1), the *Deflate* compressor sequentially gets fragments of application data. While compressing a single fragment, the compressor state gets updated according to the compressed input fragment. When switching to the next fragment of application data, this developed compressor state remains, i.e., the sliding window and the table of estimated frequencies of symbols are not being reset.

4. DATA FINGERPRINTING

Our final aim is to detect known data in encrypted TLS communication. If we eavesdrop on a TLS secured communication channel we basically see encrypted TLS packets augmented with headers from the lower communication layers, e.g. TCP, IP, and Ethernet headers. Among all meta data still visible in encrypted TLS communication (such as source and destination of the packets) we particularly choose the length fields of TLS records. In the following we will describe an attack that lets us detect plaintext content in the encrypted traffic under the condition that we have fingerprinted the exchanged data in advance. This attack even works by solely taking the TLS record length fields into account.

Therefore, let us first reconsider application data being processed by the *TLS Record Protocol* (see Figure 1). As described in Section 3.1, the input application data first gets fragmented into blocks of size 2^{14} bytes or less. If the initial application data's size is at least a multiple of 2^{14}, each fragment is of size 2^{14} bytes (except the last one in case

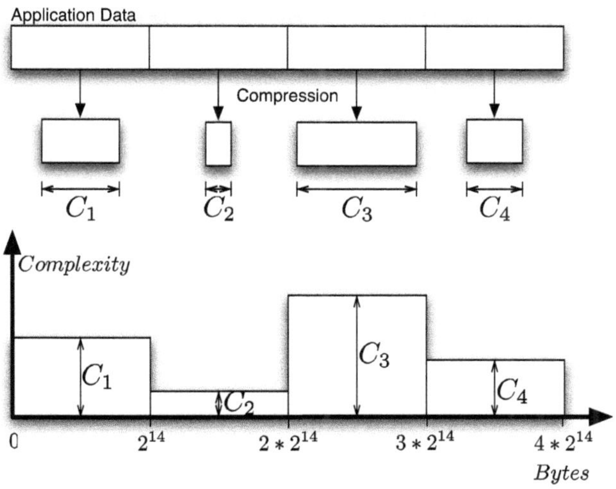

Figure 2: Generation of C_i $(i = 1, ..., n)$

the application data's size is not a multiple of 2^{14} bytes and therefore the last fragment holds the remainder). We assume without loss of generality that the application data is fragmented into $n \in \mathbb{N}$ packets of size 2^{14} bytes. Each of those n packets gets compressed to size C_i $(i = 1, ..., n)$ less (or equal) to 2^{14} bytes. The described generation of the sequence C_i $(i = 1, ..., n)$ is visualized in Figure 2.

Next, the compressed fragments of size C_i $(i = 1, ..., n)$ are further processed by the *TLS Record Protocol* as described in Section 3.1. Each compressed fragment gets appended by an additional MAC (of constant length), an optional padding for input to the symmetric block cipher, encrypted and wrapped into a TLS header. These attachments are small compared to the sizes of the compressed fragments, so the compressed TLS fragments have lengths $C_i \approx S_i$ $(i = 1, ..., n)$ of approximately the lengths of the corresponding records, which are eventually transferred to the transport layer.

The size of a compressed data fragment gives us a practical approximation of the entropy of that fragment. So if we know the sizes C_i $(i = 1, ..., n)$ we have a fine-grained view (of resolution 2^{14} bytes) on the distribution of entropy of the input application data. This entropy distribution is like a fingerprint of the input data. Since we can directly extract the TLS record lengths S_i $(i = 1, ..., n)$ out of the intercepted TLS communication and since $S_i \approx C_i$ $(i = 1, ..., n)$, we can directly extract an approximation of the entropy distribution of the exchanged communication data.

Bhargavan et al. [1] indicated that this entropy distribution may be unique for each file. They evaluated this hypotheses on ten different `MP3` files with positive results. However, it was completely left open how to automatically detect fingerprints from a large number of files. We will demonstrate in the next section that we have to deal with measurement uncertainty, also referred to as *noise* in the following. To handle this noise we apply methods from the field of machine learning.

4.1 Sources of Noise in Realistic Scenarios

Ideally, detection of a fingerprint in TLS communication would be reduced to monitoring the sequence of TLS record lengths S_i $(i = 1, ..., n)$ and searching for a match in the generated fingerprint database. However, in a real scenario we have to deal with noise in the TLS record lengths. So before we present our detection method, we first discuss the sources of noise. In the following we identify two sources of noise in the monitored TLS record lengths.

Fragment Offsets and Uncertain Compressor State.

In an ideal monitoring setting we could imagine that fragmentation in the *TLS Record Protocol* coincides with the overall beginning of data transmission. Fragmentation in this scenario begins with the first 2^{14} bytes of the fingerprinted application data. We could then monitor the TLS record lengths and check if they match with the generated fingerprint sequence S_i $(i = 1, ..., n)$.

However, in a realistic scenario the application data in scope is sent in the middle of a larger data stream. This means that the first bytes of the application data in scope are appended to a previous data block and packed together in one single fragment. The first fragment in this scenario holds previous data as well as the first bytes from the fingerprinted data. So if the fragment gets compressed in the next step of the *TLS Record Protocol*, the size of the compressed fragment does not exactly match C_1, the size of the first compressed fragment without previous data. With the same argument, the actually monitored TLS record lengths do not exactly match the fingerprint S_i $(i = 1, ..., n)$.

Even more crucial is the state of the compressor. As described in Section 3.2, the *Deflate* algorithm is stateful in the sense that its state is represented by the content of the LZ77 sliding window and the table of estimated frequencies of symbols regarding Huffman coding. We already mentioned that when switching to the next fragment of application data the compressor state remains. This means that the last bytes of the previous data (which are the first bytes of the plaintext fragment) have influence on the compression ratio of all subsequent fragments.

Theoretically we could proceed with measuring the sequence S_i $(i = 1, ..., n)$ for all possible combinations of previous data in all possible sizes (from zero to $2^{14} - 1$ bytes) mixed into the first TLS fragment, which is not feasible in practice. Instead, we will later take only a small subset of possible record lengths into account, train a machine learning algorithm with this subset and apply the trained machine to classify previously unseen length sequences.

Symmetric Block Cipher Padding.

We can identify another source of noise in the encryption step of the *TLS Record Protocol*. When initially establishing the TLS channel, the communicating endpoints negotiate a cipher suite for symmetric encryption. This negotiation takes place in the TLS handshake and the result is redirected to the *TLS Record Protocol*, which then applies the negotiated symmetric algorithm to the compressed fragments. When a symmetric block cipher is negotiated, the compressed fragments (with appended MAC) have to be padded to the block size of the symmetric cipher. For example, when `AES_256` is negotiated as symmetric cipher, the compressed fragments (with appended MAC) are padded to fit into a multitude of 256 bit. If we had fixed sizes of compressed fragments, we could of course generate multiple fingerprints of a single file, one fingerprint for each block size. But this is not the case, as we have seen in the last paragraph. Therefore, the symmetric block cipher padding causes noise in the monitored TLS records.

4.2 Fingerprint Definition

Our concept of a data fingerprint should be flexible enough to handle the described sources of noise in realistic scenarios. Solely measuring the TLS record lengths S_i $(i = 1, ..., n)$ will not be enough to apply our identification method to large data bases of files. Therefore, we have to bear in mind the sources of noise for a definition of a fingerprint practicable in realistic scenarios.

For data a and b let $a|b$ denote the concatenation of a and b. For $\omega \in \mathbb{N}$ let R_ω denote a string of random bytes of size ω. Further, for a file $\mathcal{F}$ and an offset $\omega \in \mathbb{N}$ let $S_i^\omega(\mathcal{F})$ $(i = 1, ..., n_{(R_\omega|\mathcal{F})})$ be the sequence of $n_{(R_\omega|\mathcal{F})}$ of TLS record sizes when $R_\omega|\mathcal{F}$ is sent through a TLS channel.

Next, for an $\omega \in \{1, ..., 2^{14}\}$ we can divide the fragment size 2^{14} into $m = \lceil \frac{2^{14}}{\omega} \rceil$ pieces, where $\lceil x \rceil$ is the smallest integer not less than x. With this notation in mind we give the following definition for a data fingerprint.

We define the fingerprint $\Phi_\omega(\mathcal{F})$ of a file $\mathcal{F}$ and resolution ω to be the set of sequences corresponding to

$$\Phi_\omega(\mathcal{F}) = \left\{ \left(S_i^{k\omega}(\mathcal{F}) \right)_{i=1,\dots,n_{(R_\omega|\mathcal{F})}} \mid k = 1, ..., \left\lceil \frac{2^{14}}{\omega} \right\rceil \right\}. \tag{1}$$

In other words, the fingerprint $\Phi_\omega(\mathcal{F})$ of a file $\mathcal{F}$ is the set of record size sequences corresponding to different lengths of prefixed random data.

With this definition even large-scale fingerprinting of a large number of files is feasible, as we demonstrate with our Implementation in Section 6.

5. DATA DETECTION

We next want to detect the defined fingerprints in real TLS communication. In this section we propose methods that handle both noisy data and large data bases.

To effectively handle noisy fingerprints captured in a realistic scenario, we apply classification methods from the field of machine learning. Each method is trained with generated fingerprints and tested on captured TLS traffic.

For all methods, our training set $\mathbb{D} = (\mathbf{x}_i, y_i)$ consists of the generated fingerprint sequences labeled with the corresponding files, i.e.

$$\mathbf{x}_i = \Phi_\omega(\mathcal{F}_i) \tag{2}$$
$$y_i = F_i \tag{3}$$

for a set of files $\{\mathcal{F}_i\}$ and a fixed resolution $\omega \in \{1, ..., 2^{14}\}$. In the following, we sometimes write $z_i = (\Phi_\omega(\mathcal{F}_i), F_i)$.

Consider a probability measure $P(z)$ on a space Z and a set of functions $Q(z, \alpha)$ for parameters $\alpha \in V$ in an appropriate parameter space. Generally, we want to minimize the expected risk functional

$$R(\alpha) = \int Q(z, \alpha) dP(z). \tag{4}$$

Here, $P(z)$ is initially unknown and we have only given independent and identically distributed random variables z_i $(i = 1, ..., l)$, corresponding to the labeled files F_i $(i = 1, ..., l)$. This reduces to minimizing the empirical risk functional

$$R_{emp}(\alpha) = \frac{1}{l} \sum_{i=1}^{l} Q(z_i, \alpha) \tag{5}$$
$$= \frac{1}{l} \sum_{i=1}^{l} Q\left((\Phi_\omega(\mathcal{F}_i), F_i), \alpha\right). \tag{6}$$

Identification of fingerprints is clearly a pattern recognition problem so we will choose Q to be the binary loss-function

$$L(f(z, \alpha), F) = \begin{cases} 0 & \text{if} \quad f(z, \alpha) = F \\ 1 & \text{if} \quad f(z, \alpha) \neq F \end{cases} \tag{7}$$

Therefore, we want to optimize $R_{emp}(\alpha)$ by finding an optimal function f in a hypothesis function space $\mathcal{H}$ (see [6] and [9]). To achieve this we apply Support Vector Machines (SVM) [8], decision trees, random forests, and extremely randomized trees [4].

6. IMPLEMENTATION AND EVALUATION

In the following we present details of our implementation and further evaluate the proposed methods for identification of data fingerprints in TLS communication.

6.1 Generation of Data Fingerprints

For evaluation purposes we wrote a Python script that uses the `OpenSSL` library to implement a TLS (v1.0) server (encrypting symmetrically with `AES-256` in the record layer). TLS fragments are compressed with *Deflate* (see Section 3.2). A TLS client periodically sends files to the TLS server and triggers a network monitoring program (`tshark`) for capturing the generated TLS traffic. We have automated this process so that the fingerprints $\Phi_\omega(\mathcal{F})$ are directly stored in separate capture files, one for each source file. We chose the resolution $\omega = 500$ so that the number of TLS record length sequences $\left(S_i^{k\omega}(\mathcal{F})\right)_{i=1,\dots,n_{(R_\omega|\mathcal{F})}}$ of a fingerprint is $\#\Phi_\omega(\mathcal{F}) = 33$.

Regarding performance, generation of the fingerprints takes some time but can be highly parallelized. In our setting we are able to fingerprint approximately 75 MB/h, of course slightly depending on the underlying hardware.

We have exemplary depicted the sequences of TLS record lengths $\left(S_i^{k\omega}(\mathcal{F})\right)_{i=10,\dots,35}$ with $k = 0$ for 7 different `MP3` files in Figure 3.

It can be directly seen that each file has a characteristic sequence of TLS record lengths that depends on the distribution of entropy within the file.

6.2 Comparison of File Formats

First, let us have a look on how the described machine learning algorithms perform on different file formats. We chose the `MP3` format for audio files, `ELF` for binary executable files, `PDF` for document files, the `JPG` format for image files, and the `WEBM` format for video files.

To detect files from a set $\mathbb{F}$ in a realistic scenario we would train the learning algorithm of choice with the training set

$$T_\omega = \{\Phi_\omega(\mathcal{F}) \mid \mathcal{F} \in \mathbb{F}\} \tag{8}$$

for an arbitrary but fixed $\omega \in \{1, ..., 2^{14}\}$. We would then intercept TLS traffic, extract the sequence of sizes of compressed TLS fragments and test them on the trained machine. If the learning machine classifies the sequence with a

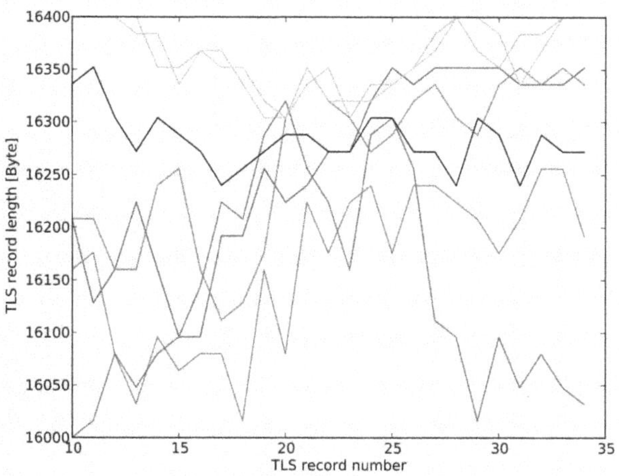

Figure 3: TLS record lengths for 7 different MP3 files.

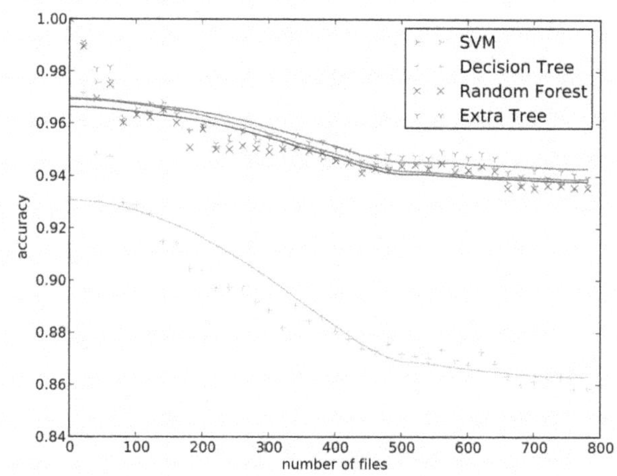

Figure 4: Accuracies versus number of files.

probability above a predefined threshold, we have detected the transmission of the file. For convenience, we take a subset $T' \subset T$, train our machines with $T \setminus T'$ and evaluate the machines on the unseen set T'. In this evaluation setting we can easily apply cross-validation on T for robust results.

We will write $\mathbb{F}_x$ for the set of all files of format x in the following. Further, we show that it is not necessary to take all sizes of compressed TLS fragments $\left(S_i^{k\omega}(\mathcal{F})\right)_{i=1,\dots,n_{(R_\omega|\mathcal{F})}}$ of files $\mathcal{F} \in \mathbb{F}_x$ into account. We achieve decent accuracies even by restricting the features to a subset

$$\Theta \subset \{1, \dots, n_{(R_\omega|\mathcal{F})}\} \tag{9}$$

and thereby omitting fingerprint information. For this first comparison of accuracies for different file formats, we do not apply any feature selection algorithms: We simply choose the number of TLS records $1-12$ from the recorded fingerprints as input features, i.e. $\Theta = \{1, \dots, 12\}$. The reason for this choice of Θ were the relatively small file sizes of transmitted `JPG` files, so that the smallest file was sent within 12 TLS records. We set the resolution to $\omega = 500$ (so that $\left\lceil \frac{2^{14}}{\omega} \right\rceil = 33$). Formally, this yields the evaluation sets $T^x_{\omega,\Theta}$

$$T^x_{\omega,\Theta} = T^x_{500,\{1,\dots,12\}} \tag{10}$$

$$= \left\{ \left(S_i^{k*500}(\mathcal{F})\right)_{i=1,\dots,12} \mid \mathcal{F} \in \mathbb{F}_x, k = 1, \dots, 33 \right\}, \tag{11}$$

where x is one of the formats `MP3`, `ELF`, `PDF`, `JPG`, or `WEBM`.

As common notation in the machine learning literature, we define the accuracy of a learning machine to be the fraction of correct predictions: If a learning algorithm classifies the recorded samples from TLS traffic of a file $\mathcal{F}_i$ to be the file $\tilde{\mathcal{F}}_i$, the fraction of correct predictions a (i.e., the accuracy) over the total number of n samples is defined as

$$a(\mathcal{F}, \tilde{\mathcal{F}}) = \frac{1}{n} \sum_{i=1}^{n} \mathbb{1}_{(\mathcal{F}_i = \tilde{\mathcal{F}}_i)}, \tag{12}$$

where $\mathbb{1}$ is the indicator function.

To compare the accuracy of the chosen machine learning algorithms for different file formats, we fingerprinted 530 files, 106 files for each format. Applying 5-fold cross-validation on the evaluation sets $T^x_{500,\{1,\dots12\}}$ then yields the accuracies depicted in the following Table 1:

	ELF	MP3	PDF	JPG	WEBM
SVM	0.945	0.968	0.979	0.801	0.690
DecTree	0.888	0.914	0.943	0.784	0.668
ExtraTree	0.909	0.953	0.978	0.798	0.691
RandForest	0.910	0.951	0.977	0.794	0.689

Table 1: Accuracy of single file identification for files of different formats.

We clearly see that all learning algorithms perform very good on `ELF`, `MP3`, and `PDF` file formats. And although `JPG` pictures are already strongly compressed, we can achieve an identification rate of up to 80% with SVMs. Videos in the `WEBM` format, however, cannot be detected properly with the proposed methods. For the SVM, we chose a linear kernel, since more advanced kernels (e.g. Gaussian, polynomial) did not result in better accuracies. This shows that the samples are almost completely linearly separable.

6.3 Large Scale Detection

Now that we have seen the feasibility of our approach for different file formats, we evaluate our methods on a larger data base. Therefore, we fingerprinted 5434 `MP3` files with resolution $\omega = 500$ to yield the sample set $T^{\texttt{MP3}}_{500,\Theta}$. In the remainder of this section, we apply SVMs, decision trees, extra trees, and random forests to identify these 5434 fingerprinted `MP3` files in TLS traffic.

Let us first discuss which features Θ of the fingerprints we take into account. We already achieve very good accuracies by considering the first 30 sizes of compressed TLS fragments of the files, i.e. $\Theta' = \{1, \dots, 30\}$. We did not apply feature selection algorithms since we assume the complexity distribution over files to be randomly distributed. This way, we do not prefer any feature above others, as for example we would do by applying principal component analysis.

Figure 4 shows how the accuracy of the proposed learning algorithms depends on the number of fingerprinted files. Here we apply a Savitzky-Golay filter for curve smoothing.

	DecTree	ExtraTree	RandForest
Accuracy	0.803	0.935	0.933

Table 2: Accuracy of single file identification within 5434 MP3 files.

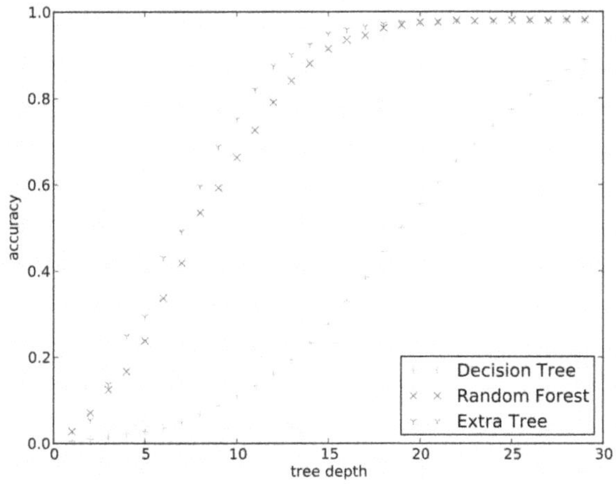

Figure 5: Accuracy versus tree depth.

The accuracies for up to 800 MP3 files show that our approach is likely to scale to larger data bases. The accuracies do not drop immediately when increasing the number of files, instead they decline with a very small rate. The accuracies seem to be stable even for large sets of files.

We are able to identify 5434 MP3 files with high accuracy as shown in Table 2. Again, we applied 5-fold cross-validation to calculate the accuracies. This shows the feasibility of our approach even for a large data base. Such good results regarding identification are crucial for future implementations of practical tools.

Regarding evaluation time, the SVM training complexity is roughly between $O(n^2)$ and $O(n^3)$ (depending on parameters and the choice of kernel). Compared with the complexity $O(\log(n))$ of decision trees, this is a practical disadvantage of SVMs. For real-time detection tree-based algorithms seem more suitable than SVMs, due to their fast prediction time. However, the choice for a real-time detection system depends on the available hardware resources.

To give an impression about how much model detail is necessary for the tree-based algorithms, we calculated accuracies in dependence of the maximal tree depth in Figure 5. Therefore we conducted 5-fold cross-validation on 300 MP3 files. We see that Extra Trees perform best with small tree sizes. However, choosing the tree size big enough, eventually all tree based algorithms will give very good results.

7. COUNTERMEASURES

The obvious countermeasure to avoid the presented information leakage of fingerprinted data is to switch off compression at all. However, in some domains such as mobile devices compression is heavily required and cannot be switched off for performance reasons.

Another countermeasure would be to add random padding to the compressed TLS fragments. That would drastically increase noise and probably protect against practical fingerprinting. The immediate tradeoff here would be an increase of data size with a direct negative impact on transmission performance.

Kelley and Tamassia [5] introduce a theoretical framework that allows security proofs in schemes combining compression and encryption. They present a new cipher which provably does not leak information (within their framework).

8. CONCLUSION AND FUTURE WORK

We demonstrated an approach to efficiently detect known data in TLS secured communication channels. With our solution, we cover several use cases in communication security. Beyond obvious use cases such as detection of illegal content in TLS secured communication channels, our approach results in loss of anonymity of communication participants, if they can be linked to specific files.

Our solution is not limited to TLS but may affect other communication protocols that combine compression with encryption in a similar way as TLS.

9. REFERENCES

[1] K. Bhargavan, C. Fournet, M. Kohlweiss, A. Pironti, and P. Strub. Implementing TLS with verified cryptographic security. In *2013 IEEE Symposium on Security and Privacy (SP)*, pages 445–459. IEEE, 2013.

[2] S. Chen, R. Wang, X. Wang, and K. Zhang. Side-channel leaks in web applications: A reality today, a challenge tomorrow. In *2010 IEEE Symposium on Security and Privacy (SP)*, pages 191–206. IEEE, 2010.

[3] K. P. Dyer, S. E. Coull, T. Ristenpart, and T. Shrimpton. Peek-a-boo, I still see you: Why efficient traffic analysis countermeasures fail. In *2012 IEEE Symposium on Security and Privacy (SP)*, pages 332–346. IEEE, 2012.

[4] P. Geurts, D. Ernst, and L. Wehenkel. Extremely randomized trees. *Machine learning*, 63(1):3–42, 2006.

[5] J. Kelley and R. Tamassia. Secure compression: Theory & practice. *IACR Cryptology ePrint Archive*, 2014:113, 2014.

[6] T. Poggio and S. Smale. The mathematics of learning: Dealing with data. *Notices of the AMS*, 50(5):537–544, 2003.

[7] A. D. Rubin, M. Green, S. Checkoway, M. Rushanan, and P. D. Martin. Classifying network protocol implementation versions: An OpenSSL case study. 2013.

[8] B. Schölkopf and A. J. Smola. *Learning with kernels: Support vector machines, regularization, optimization, and beyond.* MIT Press, 2001.

[9] V. N. Vapnik. An overview of statistical learning theory. *IEEE Transactions on Neural Networks*, 10(5):988–999, 1999.

[10] J. Ziv and A. Lempel. A universal algorithm for sequential data compression. *IEEE Transactions on Information Theory*, 23(3):337–343, 1977.

LineSwitch: Efficiently Managing Switch Flow in Software-Defined Networking while Effectively Tackling DoS Attacks

Moreno Ambrosin, Mauro Conti*, Fabio De Gaspari,
University of Padua, Italy
{surname}@math.unipd.it
fabio.degaspari@studenti.unipd.it

Radha Poovendran
University of Washington, USA
rp3@uw.edu

ABSTRACT

Software Defined Networking (SDN) is a new networking architecture that aims to provide better decoupling between network control (control plane) and data forwarding functionalities (data plane). This separation introduces several benefits, such as a directly programmable and (virtually) centralized network control. However, researchers showed that the required communication channel between the control and data plane of SDN creates a potential bottleneck in the system, introducing new vulnerabilities. Indeed, this behavior could be exploited to mount powerful attacks, such as the *control plane saturation attack*, that can severely hinder the performance of the whole network.

In this paper we present LineSwitch, an efficient and effective solution against control plane saturation attack. LineSwitch combines SYN proxy techniques and probabilistic blacklisting of network traffic. We implemented LineSwitch as an extension of OpenFlow, the current reference implementation of SDN, and evaluate our solution considering different traffic scenarios (with and without attack). The results of our preliminary experiments confirm that, compared to the state-of-the-art, LineSwitch reduces the time overhead up to 30%, while ensuring the same level of protection.

Categories and Subject Descriptors

C.2 [**Computer-Communication Networks**]: Security and protection

Keywords

Software-Defined Networking (SDN); Denial-of-Service (DoS); SYN Flooding Attack

*Mauro Conti is supported by a Marie Curie Fellowship funded by the European Commission under the agreement No. PCIG11-GA-2012-321980. This work is also partially supported by the TENACE PRIN Project 20103P34XC funded by the Italian MIUR, and by the Project "Tackling Mobile Malware with Innovative Machine Learning Techniques" funded by the University of Padua.

ASIA CCS'15, April 14–17, 2015, Singapore.

http://dx.doi.org/10.1145/2714576.2714612.

1. INTRODUCTION

The great increase in demand for flexibility and automation in key Information Technology sectors is leading to the rise of new paradigms that greatly simplify the management of network infrastructures. One such paradigm is Software Defined Networking (SDN). Unlike the current network infrastructure, SDN decouples the network layer (i.e., the *control plane*) and the data layer (i.e., the *data plane*) functionalities into separate entities. This separation allows a (virtually) centralized and directly programmable network control, while at the same time reduces and abstracts the complexity of network devices.

The most widely adopted instantiation of the SDN paradigm is OpenFlow (OF) [11, 2]. OF provides a standard communication interface between the data plane, and the control plane, and introduces the concept of *flows* to identify the network traffic [2]. Each OpenFlow entity, namely *OF switch*, maintains a set of *flow tables*, which specify the rules that the OF switch uses to perform the routing of packets. Flow tables are organized in a pipeline, which is traversed by the switch every time a packet is received.

The control plane can program the flow tables of the OF switches either statically or dynamically. In the latter case, if an OF switch does not have a matching rule in its pipeline for a new incoming packet, it must contact the control plane to retrieve a new rule [1]. Unfortunately, while enabling a flexible network management, the required extensive communication between control and data plane might result in poor scalability. Moreover, it introduces a serious vulnerability that can be exploited to overload the control plane with flow requests: the resulting attack is called *control plane saturation* [17, 8], and can be easily performed, for example, through SYN flooding [15]. By overloading the control plane, this attack incapacitates the target OF switch, which will not be able to retrieve rules for new network flows. Furthermore, if the controller manages more than a single switch, the attacker might hinder an even larger part of the network [17, 9, 8, 6].

Recently, Shin et al. [17] proposed AVANT-GUARD, a countermeasure against the control plane saturation attack. AVANT-GUARD introduces a new module into the OF switch, called *connection migration* module, which protects the switch and the controller from saturation attacks performed by SYN flooding, while at the same time being transparent to the end hosts. With this module, each OF switch acts as a SYN proxy during the TCP handshake stage of a connection, effectively shielding the controller from possible floods. Unfortunately, while being beneficial in the general case, this technique introduces new subtle vulnerabilities and heavy limitations. Indeed, we will show that when running AVANT-GUARD, the state the OF switch needs to maintain in order to proxy each connection can lead to a new Denial of Service attack, that we refer to as *buffer saturation attack*. Furthermore, the required transparency, with respect to the end hosts, limits the number of connections that the switch can proxy to the number of available TCP port numbers.

Our Contribution. In this paper, we make the following contributions:

- We identify and discuss some unintended vulnerabilities of one of the recently proposed schemes against the control plane saturation attack that, to the best of our knowledge, represents the state-of-the-art solution against this threat.
- We propose a novel attack, which we name *buffer saturation attack*. Our attack exploits some of the identified vulnerabilities introduced by the state-of-the-art solution for the control plane saturation attack. As confirmed by our analysis, *buffer saturation attack* is both realistic and simple to run, and leads to significant network performance degradation.
- We propose LineSwitch, a new efficient and effective solution to mitigate the control plane saturation attack. LineSwitch greatly reduces the effects of this attack, while at same time protects the network from the *buffer saturation attack*.
- We performed a preliminary evaluation of our solution, which confirms the effectiveness of LineSwitch against the *control plane saturation attack*. Moreover, our experiments show a significant reduction of the time overhead (up to 30%) when compared to the state-of-the-art.

Organization. The remaining of this paper is organized as follows. In Section 2 we provide some background knowledge on Software Defined Networking, and on the SYN flooding attack and its possible countermeasures. In Section 3 we revise some related work in the area of DoS attacks and defense in SDN. Moreover, we provide a brief introduction of AVANT-GUARD, which represents the state-of-the-art solution against the control plane saturation attack. In Section 4 we analyze the limitations of the current state-of-the-art, and introduce a new possible attack, i.e., the buffer saturation attack. Section 5 describes LineSwitch, our countermeasure against the control plane saturation attack in SDN, while in Section 6 we provide a preliminary evaluation of its effectiveness. Finally, in Section 7 we draw our conclusions.

2. PRELIMINARIES

In this section we introduce some concepts that will be used in the remaining of the paper: Software Defined Networking (Section 2.1) and the SYN flooding attack (Section 2.2).

2.1 Software Defined Networking (SDN)

Software Defined Networking (SDN) has emerged as a new network paradigm aimed at providing higher flexibility in network research, development and operation. The core concept behind SDN is the separation of two distinct aspects of networking that in today's architecture are blended together: the *network control* and the *forwarding functions*. The SDN architecture postulates that these two logically separated aspects of networking are decoupled in two corresponding layers, respectively the *control plane* and the *data plane*. Figure 1 provides a high-level representation of the SDN architecture.

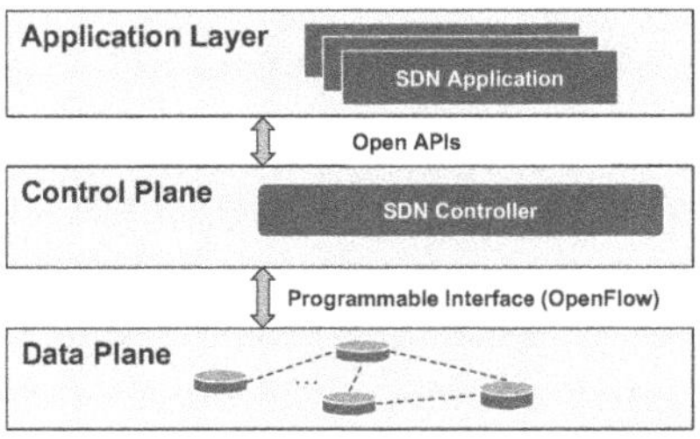

Figure 1: SDN Architecture.

The control plane provides a directly programmable layer that acts as an interface to the data plane for applications, abstracting both the complexity of the underlying network infrastructure and the communication between the two planes. Using the control plane as a middleware, it is possible to easily deploy a great variety of network management applications, that act independently from the physical network devices. Moreover, the control plane offers a logical centralized system that controls and accesses data from all network devices, effectively offering a global view of the network infrastructure. OpenFlow (OF) [2] is the reference implementation of the SDN paradigm. It defines a standard communication interface between the control plane and the data plane. With OpenFlow, the routing is performed based on traffic *flows*; each OF network entity (i.e., *OF switch*) maintains one or more *flow tables*, that are used to route incoming packets, and an OF channel to an external controller.

The control plane can program the physical devices through a series of *flow rules* [1], that are installed inside the flow tables. Such rules specify which actions a switch will perform on a specific network flow. For each unique network flow, or group of flows, there will be a corresponding flow table entry (i.e., a flow rule). Once an OF switch receives a packet, it matches the packet header against the pipeline of its local flow tables, which will dictate what actions will be applied to that specific flow. The control plane populates the flow tables of each OF switch either statically, by pre-installing a set of flow rules into the flow tables, or dynamically, by allowing a switch-driven run-time installation of new flow rules [2]. In the latter case, if an OF switch does not have any matching rule for a new incoming flow, it forwards the corresponding packet header to the controller, which at this point can install a new rule for that flow into the switch [1]. Through the combination of different flow rules, a controller can define a broad range of actions, from the standard routing of a packet to a more complex analysis, involving forwarding the packet to the controller [1].

2.2 SYN Flooding Attack

SYN flooding attacks are one of the most widespread and effective DoS attacks [15]. The effectiveness of a SYN flooding attack is based on the state that TCP stacks allocate when a connection request (i.e., a SYN packet) is received. Such state, called *Transmission Control Block* (TCB) [3], is retained in memory for a certain amount of time, even if the TCP handshake is not completed by the client. This allows the connection receiver to handle the case in which the ACK packet, needed to complete the connection, is lost due to network congestion. Once a critical amount of half-open connections is reached, the available memory reserved to the TCBs is saturated, and no new connections can be established.

In general, in order to make it difficult for the victim to detect the attack and its source, an attacker performs a SYN flooding attack using spoofed IP addresses. In this way, the victim will not be able to identify the source of the attack, and therefore, it will not be able to automatically stop the SYN flooding. Indeed, new incoming SYN packets could belong to legitimate connections, which the victim can not distinguish from the malicious traffic. Researchers and industry proposed several countermeasures against the SYN flooding attack [4, 15]. However, none of them offers a definitive solution to this important problem.

When applied to SDN, the SYN flooding attack does not aim at saturating internal data structures. Rather, the goal is to exploit data to control plane communication to saturate the controller by generating a huge number of new network flows. For each flow, the OF switch will have to contact the controller, which will need to analyze the flow information, prepare and then send an OF response to the switch. If the rate of the flood is high enough, the controller will not be able to keep up with the attack and will be incapacitated from serving legitimate network flows.

3. RELATED WORK

In this section, we provide a brief overview of the main research studies related to Denial of Service (DoS) attacks in SDN. Due to space limitations, in this section we focus only on DoS attacks against the control plane of an SDN network. In [15], Peng et al. provided a first feasibility study for DoS attacks on the SDN control plane. In [10], Kreutz et al. analyzed the SDN architecture, identifying critical aspects and possible new attack vectors, while Kloti et al. [9] assessed some vulnerabilities that affect OpenFlow [2], i.e., the possibility for an attacker to mount DoS attacks on the control plane, and to disclose potentially sensitive information by using timing analysis techniques. In [17], Shin et al. propose AVANT-GUARD, a solution that addresses architectural flows of the original OpenFlow protocol by altering the flow management at the data plane level [8, 17]. In particular, the authors focused on solving OpenFlow's control plane saturation attack vulnerability. To the best of our knowledge, AVANT-GUARD [17] represents the state-of-the-art for tackling the control plane saturation attack in SDN. For this reason, in the remaining of this section we briefly describe this solution. We will further compare AVANT-GUARD against our solution when evaluating our proposal (see Section 6).

AVANT-GUARD [17] adds two extensions to the standard OpenFlow protocol: (1) a *Connection Migration* module, which limits the effect of the control plane saturation attack based on SYN flooding by proxying the incoming TCP requests, and (2) the *Actuating Trigger* module, which allows the controller to limit the number of control messages required to collect network statistics. Since the focus of this paper is solving the control plane saturation attack, in the remaining of this paper we will only consider the connection migration module of AVANT-GUARD, which we briefly describe in the remaining of this section. Moreover, in Section 4 we provide a security analysis of the connection migration module.

As introduced in Section 2.1, whenever an OF switch receives an inbound network flow for which it has no flow rule, it forwards the packet to the control plane. This behavior holds even for SYN packets: for each received SYN packet not matching a flow rule, an OF switch contacts the controller to obtain a corresponding rule. The connection migration module of AVANT-GUARD addresses this problem at the data plane level, by having the OF switch act as a SYN proxy.

This process is articulated in four phases (see Figure 2):

Classification phase. When an OF switch receives a SYN packet belonging to an unknown flow (action (1) in Figure 2), instead of forwarding it to the control plane, the switch acts as a proxy, engaging the client in a stateless TCP handshake through SYN Cookies (actions (2) and (3) in Figure 2).

Report phase. If the client completes the TCP handshake, the switch then forwards the new flow to the controller (action (4) in Figure 2) and waits for a new rule that defines how it should be handled (action (5) in Figure 2).

Migration phase. If the controller allows the migration, the switch initiates a TCP handshake with the destination host (actions (6), (7) and (8) in Figure 2). The OF switch further reports the result of the handshake to the control plane (actions (9) and (10) in Figure 2).

Relay phase. If the handshake is successful, the switch forwards all the subsequent messages between the client and the destination host.

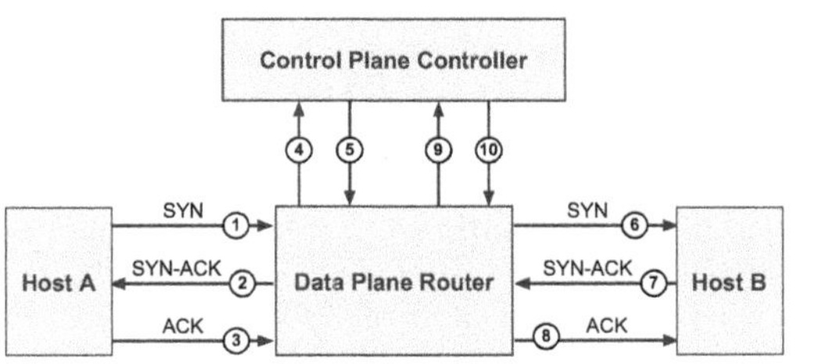

Figure 2: AVANT-GUARD [17] – Connection Migration.

The foremost advantage of connection migration, is the classification mechanism. Only complete TCP flows will be reported to the control plane, effectively shielding it from SYN flooding attacks performed with spoofed IP addresses, and greatly mitigating the threat of link saturation. For non-spoofed TCP flows, the result is that any $\{IP, port\}$ combination will appear to be valid, effectively converting the network to a whitehole network and preventing an attacker from mapping possible targets. Moreover, the consequent SYN flooding vulnerability at data plane level is addressed by the use of SYN Cookies [7]. Since the SYN Cookie algorithm does not need to maintain state for connection requests, there is no need for storing information in the OF switch for failed TCP connections.

Generally, it is possible to infer the use of connection migration by analyzing the round trip time of a SYN packet. An adversary might use this information to flood the data plane with complete TCP handshakes, forcing the switch to forward each of them to the control plane. To solve this issue, AVANT-GUARD provides a modification to the basic connection migration module, namely *delayed connection migration* [17], which requires the initiator of the communication to send the first valid packet, before forwarding the packer header to the control plane.

4. LIMITATIONS OF THE CONNECTION MIGRATION MODULE

The connection migration module of AVANT-GUARD [17] is indeed a valid solution against the control plane saturation attack. Moreover it also shields end hosts from SYN flooding attacks and, by replying unconditionally to every received SYN packet, it prevents port scanning attacks. Unfortunately, along with the above desirable properties, the connection migration module of AVANT-GUARD introduces new vulnerabilities too. In particular, we identified two distinct vulnerabilities that can lead to a shutdown of the OF switch. First, the state that the switch must keep in order to implement the connection migration module of AVANT-GUARD can be exploited by an attacker, which can try to fill the allotted buffers and incapacitate the OF switch (see Section 4.1). Second, the use of SYN proxy limits the number of connections that can be forwarded. In particular, the maximum number of connections forwarded to a specific $\{IP, port\}$ pair is 64513 (see Section 4.2).

In what follows we provide an in-depth analysis, as well as the scheme for possible attacks, for each of the above points.

4.1 Proxying Requires State

A switch implementing the connection migration module of AVANT-GUARD needs to maintain some state, for the whole duration of the TCP connection. In particular, acting as a proxy between two communicating hosts, A and B, a switch R should execute the following three operations:

(1) Once received a SYN packet from host A, with Initial Sequence Number [3] ISN_A, R will respond with a SYN-ACK packet with a spoofed address, i.e., using host B address. The ACK sequence number will be $ISN_A + 1$ and the sequence number will be a random number ISN_R. Note that, according to TCP protocol specifications [5, 13] each ISN is computed in a non-predictable way. Therefore, it is impossible for R to predict the ISN that B would generate and, as a consequence ISN_R will be different from the sequence number B will use.

(2) Upon receiving the permission to migrate the connection, switch R will start a handshake with host B by sending a SYN packet with sequence number ISN_A. Note that at this stage, R must use its IP address to establish the TCP session since it has no guarantees that the reply from host B will follow the same path through switch R on the way back.

(3) Once the SYN-ACK packet from host B (with an ACK number $ISN_A + 1$ and a sequence number ISN_B) is received, switch R finalizes the connection sending an ACK with number $ISN_B + 1$ to B.

To maintain the connection migration transparent to the end hosts, R must perform a *sequence number translation* (and analogously an ACK translation), for the packets exchanged by A and B. Moreover, for each host connecting to the same $\{IP, port\}$ pair, the switch needs to use a distinct port number to migrate the connection in order to later match the response packets to the correct host on the way back. Consequently, for each connection the switch needs to store the following information:

$$\{IP_{src}, port_{src}, port_R, \delta_{seq}\},$$

where IP_{src} and $port_{src}$ are respectively source address and port of the initiator of the connection, $port_R$ is the port number used by the router in the migration and δ_{seq} is the difference between the ISN used by the router and the ISN used by the destination host.

The translation table required by the switch to act as a proxy gives an attacker an easy mean for mounting a *buffer saturation attack*. Indeed, the attacker simply needs to open several complete TCP connections through the target OF switch to a given host. Note that each of these connections will need state to be stored on the switch for translation. Therefore, if the number of connections is large enough, the portion of memory dedicated to that data structure will be saturated, incapacitating the switch from serving any further valid connection.

4.2 Limit on the Number of Connections

As we already stated in Section 4.1, when a connection from hosts A to B is proxied by switch R, all the packets translated by the switch to the destination B will have the IP address of R, and a port number different from the original one used by A. This behavior introduces yet another important problem: if there are several clients attempting to connect to a given destination on the same port (e.g., $\{IP_B, port_B\}$) through switch R, the latter will need to use a different port for each outgoing connection. However, since TCP port numbers are 16 bit fields, the maximum number of connections the switch will be able to migrate to a given IP-port pair is at most $2^{16} - 1024 = 64512$ (the first 1024 ports are reserved for well known services). This number can be quickly reached if we consider extremely popular HTTP services (e.g., Google or Facebook). Therefore, each switch is bound to a maximum number of connections it can migrate for each service, after which all new incoming connection requests can not be satisfied.

The limited number of available ports can easily be exploited by an attacker to mount DoS attacks. In fact, it would be easy to target a given service by opening a series of long-lasting connections through the OF switch. Once enough connections are opened and all the possible ports have been used by the switch to migrate the connections, any other client trying to connect to said service will be rejected. This bound on the maximum number of connections that a switch can migrate, provides a simple and efficient way of mounting a DoS attack to a given host B, for all the clients whose path to B passes through the same OF switch. There are no definitive solutions to this problem if proxying is used: each connection to the same service must be assigned a unique port number by the switch. The most promising way to somewhat mitigate this restriction is to purchase several IP addresses for the switch to use. In this way, when the OF switch consumes all the available ports with a given address, it will switch to a new address, this way being able to migrate other 64512 connections. While address purchasing can be employed as a partial solution, it is worth noting that, for each additional address, the space of possible combinations increases by just 64512. If we consider a complex network, where several switches employ the connection migration technique, we will quickly hit a point where the cost and complexity of management increase extremely rapidly, reducing the appeal of this workaround.

5. OUR SOLUTION: LINESWITCH

Breaking TCP end-to-end semantics introduces the need to store state, which in turn opens the system to attacks exploiting buffer saturation. Therefore, there is a strong need to reduce its use as much as possible while retaining its beneficial effects against control plane saturation attacks. To reach this goal, we propose LineSwitch, an OpenFlow extension intended for edge OF switches of a network. The idea is the following: LineSwitch proxies all incoming TCP connections from a given IP until one is completed, while for all subsequent SYN packets the proxy is used with a small probability P_p.

Our solution effectively protects the switch even in presence of an attacker E with knowledge about the proxy mechanism in use. Indeed, it would be possible for E to perform an attack by correctly completing the handshake associated with the first SYN packet sent, and then initiating the SYN flooding. Although this is true, E would be forced to use its real IP address in all the packets, to ensure they will be forwarded to the OF pipeline. Otherwise, they will be proxied by the switch, and therefore discarded. Moreover, since the effectiveness of the SYN flooding attack is based on a high throughput, once E is forced to use its real IP address for the flooding, the OF switch will quickly proxy one of the packets, thus detecting the attack. Then, the OF switch can blacklist the IP address of host E, IP_E, for $T \times 2^{count_{IP_E}}$ seconds, where $count_{IP_E}$ indicates the number of times IP_E did not complete a connection, and T represents a default time value.

With our approach, all packets with spoofed IP addresses will be blocked at the data plane, and malicious clients that initiate SYN flooding with non-spoofed IPs (after first establishing a complete TCP connection) will be penalized with rapidly increasing blacklist periods of time.

Our approach provides two major improvements with respect to the problems identified in the state-of-the-art (see Section 4). The first advantage of our approach is that it drastically reduces the memory usage needed to perform the address/port translation for each connection, thus offering protection against the described buffer saturation attack (see Section 4.1). Indeed, LineSwitch requires port translation only for the first SYN packet per each IP address, and only for a very small number of subsequent packets based on the chosen probability P_p. Therefore, the memory usage increases roughly linearly with the number of clients with a TCP connection through the switch R. In contrast, the memory overhead introduced by AVANT-GUARD grows linearly *with the number of connections* that pass through the switch.

An attacker can easily generate a huge number of connections from the same source IP using different port numbers (up to $2^{16} = 65535$ per $< IP_{dst}, port_{dst} >$ pair; the theoretical limit would then be $2^{16+32+16}$) and, with AVANT-GUARD, the switch would need to store state for each of these connections. As a reference, in our experiments with a link of 1 Mbps we were able to open approximately 780 connections per second, while with a higher bandwidth of 5 Mbps, it was possible to complete more than 4000 connections per second. Instead, with LineSwitch the number of entries the switch needs to store under attack, is roughly proportional to the number of distinct real IP addresses (machines) the attacker possesses. As a consequence, the effect of buffer saturation attacks is greatly reduced, while at the same time retaining full protection against SYN flooding attacks.

A second major advantage with respect to the state-of-the-art is that LineSwitch proxies a minimum number of connections. Indeed, as discussed in Section 4, while being an effective mechanism to protect against SYN flooding attacks, proxying introduces several problems which derive from breaking the end-to-end paradigm. Therefore, its use should be limited as much as possible. LineSwitch proxies only the first connection from a given host (i.e., an IP address), and subsequent connections from the same host with probability P_p. Since, in general, the migration probability value P_p is small (see Section 6), LineSwitch will assure in most cases the normal network flow, mitigating intrinsic problems of proxying such as limited maximum number of migrated connections (see Section 4.2). Moreover, our experimental results show that a small value for P_p does not reduce the level of protection that LineSwitch provides against the control plane saturation attack (see Section 6).

6. PRELIMINARY EVALUATION

In order to assess the effectiveness of LineSwitch against the control plane saturation attack, and its resiliency to buffer saturation attacks, we designed preliminary experiments on the setting shown in Figure 3. Our system model includes three hosts connected to an OF switch running the reference OpenFlow software switch [14], and a local controller (running the POX controller, `l3_learning` module [16]). We ran all our experiments using the Mininet network simulator [12] in a virtual machine. We compared LineSwitch to the state-of-the-art solution to tackle SYN flooding-based control plane saturation attack, i.e., AVANT-GUARD [17]. The computer used for the simulation is equipped with a quad core Intel i5-4670 @3.40GHz, all of which were available to the virtual machine.

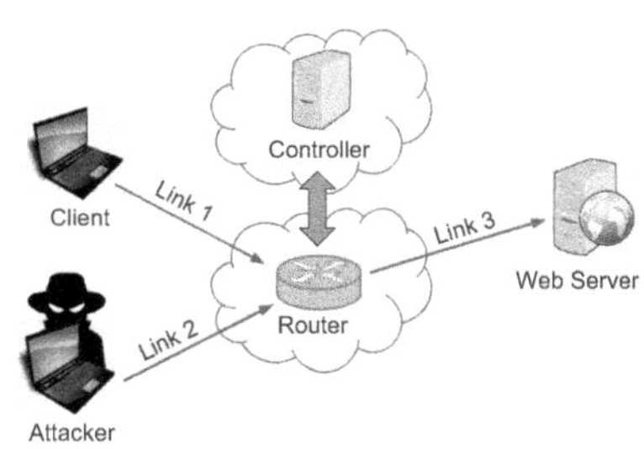

Figure 3: Experimental Setup.

We simulated the behavior of both AVANT-GUARD and LineSwitch under the buffer saturation attack introduced in Section 5. To this aim, we configured the system with different buffer sizes and run the attack at different rates. As a result, we demonstrate that: (1) the attack rate required to successfully incapacitate an OpenFlow switch running AVANT-GUARD grows *linearly with the size of the buffer*; (2) when using AVANT-GUARD, the throughput needed to successfully complete the attack in a reasonable amount of time *is easily achievable, even with larger buffers*; (3) LineSwitch offers an extremely high resiliency to the buffer saturation attack, and can be further configured through the P_p parameter to address the specific needs of the network.

In order to directly assess the relation between attack bandwidth and time required to saturate the buffer, we set the RTT parameter to 0 ms, for each link in Figure 3. Figure 4 presents the results of our simulation. It shows the average time needed to successfully overload a switch with a buffer saturation attack, running both AVANT-GUARD and LineSwitch, with the latter executed with parameter P_p set to 0.01 and 0.05. The results are presented for varying size of the buffer (expressed in Bytes) and for different rates of attack (expressed in Mbps).

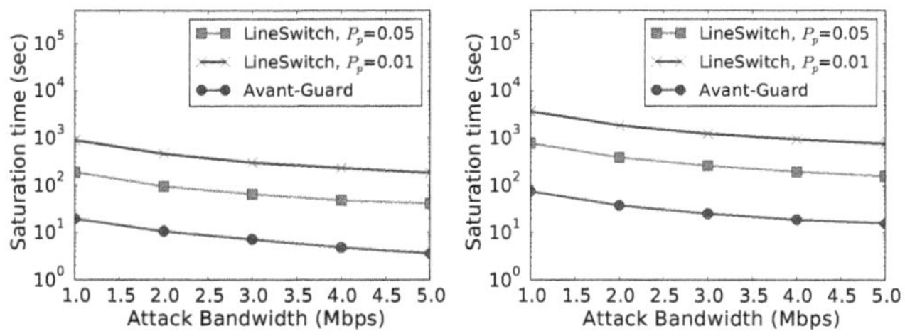

(a) buffer size 2^{20}Bytes (b) buffer size 2^{22}Bytes

Figure 4: Average buffer saturation time, varying buffer size and attack bandwidth, under a buffer saturation attack. Time on y-axis is in logarithmic scale.

As Figure 4 shows, even with a modest rate of attack it is possible to quickly overflow the buffer of a switch running AVANT-GUARD: with an attack rate of 1 Mbps, a buffer of 2^{22} Bytes is saturated in 74.718 sec, preventing the switch from migrating any new connection. By contrast when using LineSwitch, even when setup with a highly conservative migration probability $P_p = 0.05$, the time needed to perform a successful buffer saturation attack is one order of magnitude greater when compared to AVANT-GUARD. As an example, with a 1 Mbps attack rate, a buffer size of 2^{22} Bytes and $P_p = 0.05$, LineSwitch requires 769.487 sec to be saturated against only 74.718 sec required when running AVANT-GUARD. When using lower (and more realistic) migration probability values, the time difference increases even more, as shown in Figure 4.

For completeness, we compared the average overhead introduced by AVANT-GUARD with the overhead introduced by LineSwitch, evaluating both a scenario without attack, and a scenario under SYN flooding based control plane saturation attack. All overhead data is expressed with respect to the standard OpenFlow protocol, under normal network conditions (e.g., no attacks performed). We sampled the time required by the legitimate client (see Figure 3) to download a web page of size 1 KB from the web server. In the regular traffic scenario, AVANT-GUARD introduces an average time overhead of 41.83%, while LineSwitch incurs only a 7.67% overhead. Moreover, under control plane saturation attack with an attack rate of 6.5 Mbps, AVANT-GUARD introduces an overhead of 36.92%, while LineSwitch introduces only a 5.45% overhead. Finally, under control plane saturation attack, both AVANT-GUARD and LineSwitch guarantee a 100% page retrieval success rate.

7. CONCLUSION

In this paper we analyzed the effects of the control plane saturation attack based on SYN flooding, one of the most widespread types of Denial of Service (DoS) attack, when applied to Software Defined Networking (SDN) architecture, and in particular to its reference implementation, OpenFlow. We showed that the extensive communication between the control plane and the data plane in SDN, amplifies the effect of typical DoS attacks, resulting in an overload of the control plane and in the possible impairment of large parts of the network. Furthermore we considered AVANT-GUARD [17], which is, to the best of our knowledge, the only currently proposed solution against control plane saturation attack. We showed that, in its original design, subtle points were not taken into consideration, opening critical system vulnerabilities. To this aim, we proposed LineSwitch, a solution based on probability and blacklisting that offers both resiliency against SYN flooding-based control plane saturation attacks, and protection from buffer saturation vulnerabilities. Our preliminary evaluation demonstrates that LineSwitch imposes a negligible overhead, which can be dynamically adjusted to fit the network needs, while successfully defending the OpenFlow switch and controller from attacks that can potentially disrupt the functionality of the network.

8. REFERENCES

[1] OpenFlow Switch specificatio, v.1.3.4. `https://www.opennetworking.org/images/stories/downloads/sdn-resources/onf-specifications/openflow/openflow-switch-v1.3.4.pdf`.

[2] OpenFlow whitepaper. `https://www.opennetworking.org/sdn-resources/sdn-library/whitepapers`.

[3] Transmission Control Protocol. RFC 793, IETF, September 1981.

[4] TCP SYN Flooding Attacks and Common Mitigations. RFC 4987, IETF, August 2007.

[5] Defending against Sequence Number Attacks. RFC 6528, IETF, February 2012.

[6] K. Benton, L. J. Camp, and C. Small. OpenFlow Vulnerability Assessment. HotSDN '13, pages 151–152, 2013.

[7] D. J. Bernstein. SYN Cookies. `http://cr.yp.to/syncookies.html`.

[8] W. Haopei, X. Lei, and G. Guofei. OF-GUARD: A DoS Attack Prevention Extension in Software-Defined Networks. In *USENIX Open Network Summit*, 2014.

[9] R. Kloti, V. Kotronis, and P. Smith. Openflow: A security analysis. ICNP '13, pages 1–6, 2013.

[10] D. Kreutz, F. M. Ramos, and P. Verissimo. Towards Secure and Dependable Software-defined Networks. HotSDN '13, pages 55–60, 2013.

[11] N. McKeown, T. Anderson, H. Balakrishnan, G. Parulkar, L. Peterson, J. Rexford, S. Shenker, and J. Turner. OpenFlow: Enabling Innovation in Campus Networks. *SIGCOMM Computer Communications Review*, 38(2):69–74, Mar. 2008.

[12] Mininet. `http://mininet.org/`.

[13] R. T. Morris. A Weakness in the 4.2BSD Unix TCP/IP Software, 1985.

[14] OpenFlow Software Switch. `http://yuba.stanford.edu/git/gitweb.cgi?p=openflow.git;a=summary`.

[15] T. Peng, C. Leckie, and K. Ramamohanarao. Survey of Network-based Defense Mechanisms Countering the DoS and DDoS Problems. *ACM Computing Surveys*, 39(1), 2007.

[16] POX. `http://www.noxrepo.org/pox/about-pox/`.

[17] S. Shin, V. Yegneswaran, P. Porras, and G. Gu. AVANT-GUARD: Scalable and Vigilant Switch Flow Management in Software-defined Networks. CCS '13, pages 413–424, 2013.

Measuring Botnets in the Wild: Some New Trends

Wentao Chang[1] Aziz Mohaisen[2]* An Wang[1] Songqing Chen[1]
[1]George Mason University [2]Verisign Labs
{wchang7, awang10, sqchen}@gmu.edu amohaisen@verisign.com

ABSTRACT

Today, botnets are still responsible for most large scale attacks on the Internet. Botnets are versatile, they remain the most powerful attack platform by constantly and continuously adopting new techniques and strategies in the arms race against various detection schemes, . Thus, it is essential to understand the latest of the botnets in a timely manner so that the insights can be utilized in developing more efficient defenses. In this work, we conduct a measurement study on some of the most active botnets on the Internet based on a public dataset collected over a period of seven months by a monitoring entity. We first examine and compare the attacking capabilities of different families of today's active botnets. Our analysis clearly shows that different botnets start to collaborate when launching DDoS attacks.

1. INTRODUCTION

Botnets are one of today's most challenging cybersecurity threats, and promise to remain a serious threat for many years to come. A botnet is typically comprised of a network of infected machines called bots, which are often under the control of a malicious entity, called the botmaster. Botnets are notoriously known as one of the primary attack platforms that cybercriminals use to carry out malicious and harmful actions, such as distributed denial of service (DDoS) attacks, spam distribution, phishing, scanning and network exploration, against pieces of infrastructures and services. Reports have highlighted the devastating operational impact, size, and consequences that a botnet attack can bring to Internet services. For example, it was recently reported that a collection of just 3,000 open Domain Name System (DNS) resolvers were capable of generating 300 Gbps DDoS attack traffic [19], and taking down Spamhaus, a popular spam tracking service.

On the botnet analysis front, significant research efforts have been made to gain a better understanding of the botnet phenomenon and landscape. A common approach to study botnets is to perform passive analysis of abnormal behaviors produced by bot-infected machines [14, 16, 17] . While the passive analysis approach does reveal much valuable information about particular botnet-related behaviors, some of the insight on longitudinal activities is absent since the approach only considers a small portion of bots at a given time [28, 8]. Infiltration is another technique adopted in recent studies [4, 1, 10], where an actual malware sample or a client is to simulate a bot. However, attackers have unfortunately learned to adapt, and most current botnets use stripped-down IRC or HTTP servers as their centralized command and control channels. It is unlikely to obtain a lot of information about other bots by simply joining the botnet. An effective effort to understand botnets would require reverse engineering, passive and active measurements.

*The views and opinions expressed in this paper are the views of the author, and do not necessarily represent the policy or position of VeriSign, Inc.

ASIA CCS'15, April 14–17, 2015, Singapore..

http://dx.doi.org/10.1145/2714576.2714637.

On the defense front, a lot of efforts have been made to detect bots and botnets. While many detection schemes have been developed [25, 16, 22], attackers have been constantly adopting new technologies and improving their attacking schemes. For example, various generations of botnets have been shown to use HTTP and P2P technologies, instead of IRC, for their operations [11, 15, 27].

The arms race between malware developers and defenders is endless. Thus, it is essential to continuously track and understand the latest strategies of attackers in manipulating botnets for attacks. A timely understanding can provide important insights to guide the building of effective defenses. To this end, in this study we perform an in-depth analysis of botnet strategies based on recent botnet traffic, resources enumeration and activities profiling. Data used in this study is obtained by utilizing active and passive monitoring, and using state-of-the-art reverse-engineering and protocol analysis techniques for 23 different botnet families. The data obtained in this study is enriched by traffic observed at a large number of Internet vantage points on the Internet in about seven months of monitoring.

Our study reveals several interesting new trends of botnet management. In this paper, our contributions include the following:

- We conduct a large-scale measurement study to investigate botnet characteristics and describe botnet behaviors. The analysis results help make better comprehension of the wide variety of existent botnet families in the wild.
- Some bots are dedicated and heavily re-used by different botnet families. Similar collaborations are also found within various generations of the same botnet family.

To the best of our knowledge, some of the insights and operation aspects of botnets in this paper are not reported before. We expect these results can help improve our understanding of botnet operations and devise new defense schemes.

The remainder of the paper is organized as follows. Section 2 describes our dataset and section 3 presents characterization of botnet families. In Section 4, we discuss the possibility of collaborations among the botnets by identifying reused bots, while Section 5 discusses related work. We conclude in Section 6 with a discussion about future work.

2. DATASET

Some research efforts on botnet measurements have focused on the taxonomy and classification of botnets by analyzing botnet behavior and common characteristics, such as architecture, command and control channels, communication protocols and evasion techniques [12, 20]. These efforts have mainly been done via passive measurement or infiltration. Thus, they usually focused on specific botnets. Different from these approaches, our dataset is provided by the Team Cymru Community Service [26]. The dataset is based on Team Cymru's constant monitoring of Internet critical infrastructure to aid intelligence gathering concerning the state of the art of attack posture, using both active and passive measurement techniques. For active measurements and attribution, malware families used in launching various attacks are reverse engineered, and labeled to a known malware family using best practices. Hosts participating in the given botnet, by either communicating with pieces of infrastructure infected by that malware family (e.g. the command and control) are then enumerated and monitored over time, and their activities are logged and analyzed.

As each botnet evolves over time, new generations are marked by their unique (MD5 and SHA-1) hashes. Traces of traffic associated with various botnets are then collected at various anchor points on the Internet, via the cooperation of many ISPs all over the world, and analyzed to attribute and characterize attacks. The collection of traffic is guided by two general principles: 1) that the source of the traffic is an infected host participating in a botnet attack, and 2) the destination of the traffic is a targeted client, as concluded from eavesdropping on C&C of the campaign using a live sample.

By tracking temporal activities of 23 different known botnet families in the wild, the monitors of the company generate a log dump every hour from 08/29/2012 to 03/24/2013, a total of 207 days, or about 7 months. There are 24 hourly reports per day for each botnet family. The set of bots or controllers listed in each report are cumulative over past 24 hours. The 24-hour time span is counted from time stamp of last known bot activity and time of log dump.

3. CHARACTERIZATION OF BOTNET FAMILIES

In this section, we examine the botnet families included in our dataset, focusing on their attacking capacities from the perspective of their size, stability, elasticity and activeness. While the monitoring unit targets the 23 most prevalent botnet families, we found 7 of them, namely `Asprox, Gumblar, Myloader, Redgirl, Storm, Tdss`, and `Waledac`, to have zero traffic within our collection window. Thus, we exclude them from our analysis below. Table 1 summarizes some information of the 16 remaining botnet families.

3.1 Botnet Size, Stability, and Elasticity

A first and very important metric to evaluate different botnets is the number of bots that a botnet can utilize. Thus, we can use it to weigh the significance of different botnet families in regards to their impact on network security. There are more than one counting techniques and standards available to estimate the size of botnets. In our analysis, we simply count the number of unique IP addresses when estimating the size of botnets and the maximum number of simultaneous online bots of a botnet. Note that we ignore the case that multiple infected machines might hide behind the NAT and treat them as one single IP in counting.

Table 1: Summary statistics of 16 Botnet Families

Family Name	Active Period	Botnet Size
Aldibot	11/01/12-03/24/13	12,075
Armageddon	08/29/12-03/24/13	171
Blackenergy	08/29/12-03/24/13	498,925
Colddeath	08/29/12-12/19/12	1,859
Conficker	08/29/12-03/24/13	667,523
Darkcomet	12/02/12-03/24/13	4,019
Darkshell	08/29/12-03/24/13	4,886
Ddoser	11/13/12-03/07/13	35
Dirtjumper	08/29/12-03/24/13	837,297
Illusion	08/29/12-03/24/13	47,887
Nitol	08/29/12-03/24/13	15,230
Optima	08/29/12-03/24/13	362,157
Pandora	10/11/12-03/24/13	17,418
Torpig	08/29/12-03/24/13	1,260
Yzf	08/29/12-02/11/13	7,937
Zeus	08/29/12-03/24/13	175,343

Similar to the metrics used in [1], we define the botnet size as the total number of unique IP addresses that were once recruited in their lifetime by the specific botnet. As the last column of Table 1 shows, the botnet size of different families varies significantly. The botnet size is as large as 837 thousand for Dirtjumper or as small as 35 for Ddoser. Based on the botnet size, we can classify them into different groups. The `large` botnet families own more than 100 K bots with unique IP addresses, including `Dirtjumper, Conficker, Blackenergy, Optima` and `Zeus` in descending order. 90% of bots found in our dataset are employed by these large botnet families at least once. The `medium` group includes botnet families with the number of bots ranging from 10 thousands to 100 thousands, such as `Illusion, Pandora, Nitol` and `Aldibot`. The `small` group owns less than 10 thousands bots. In descending order of their botnet size, they are `Yzf, Darkshell, Darkcomet, Colddeath, Torpig, Armageddon` and `Ddoser`.

Since the botnet size does not give us a very accurate estimate of the potential attack capability because those bots may not be online simultaneously, we also examine the number of bots that are simultaneously online, termed as "live bots". Figure 1 shows the number of simultaneous live bots over time. Note the y-axis is in log scale. The left sub-figures show the number of live bots hourly, while the right sub-figures show the corresponding results daily. To some extent, the live bots distribution over time can indicate the `stability` of the corresponding botnet family. As shown in the figure, besides the difference on the absolute numbers, both the hourly and daily results indicate that the botnets in `large` group have maintained a relatively stable army of active bots by showing only a few spikes, while there are more fluctuations in botnets in the `medium` and `small` groups. While this is to be expected, it raises a new question whether the relative stability in large botnets is due to the same sets of bots being active all the time or more sophisticated strategies being used by botnets.

As previously mentioned, Figure 1 also shows a few steep spikes for botnets in `large` groups. By further looking into the data, we find out those spikes can be attributed to some ongoing campaigns started during that time period. Take `Blackenergy` as an example, Figure 2 compares the botnet stability curves for `Blackenergy` with and without certain live bots. The top figure depicts the stability curve with all live bots from `Blackenergy`, from which we observe a transient burst of live bots that are derived from two

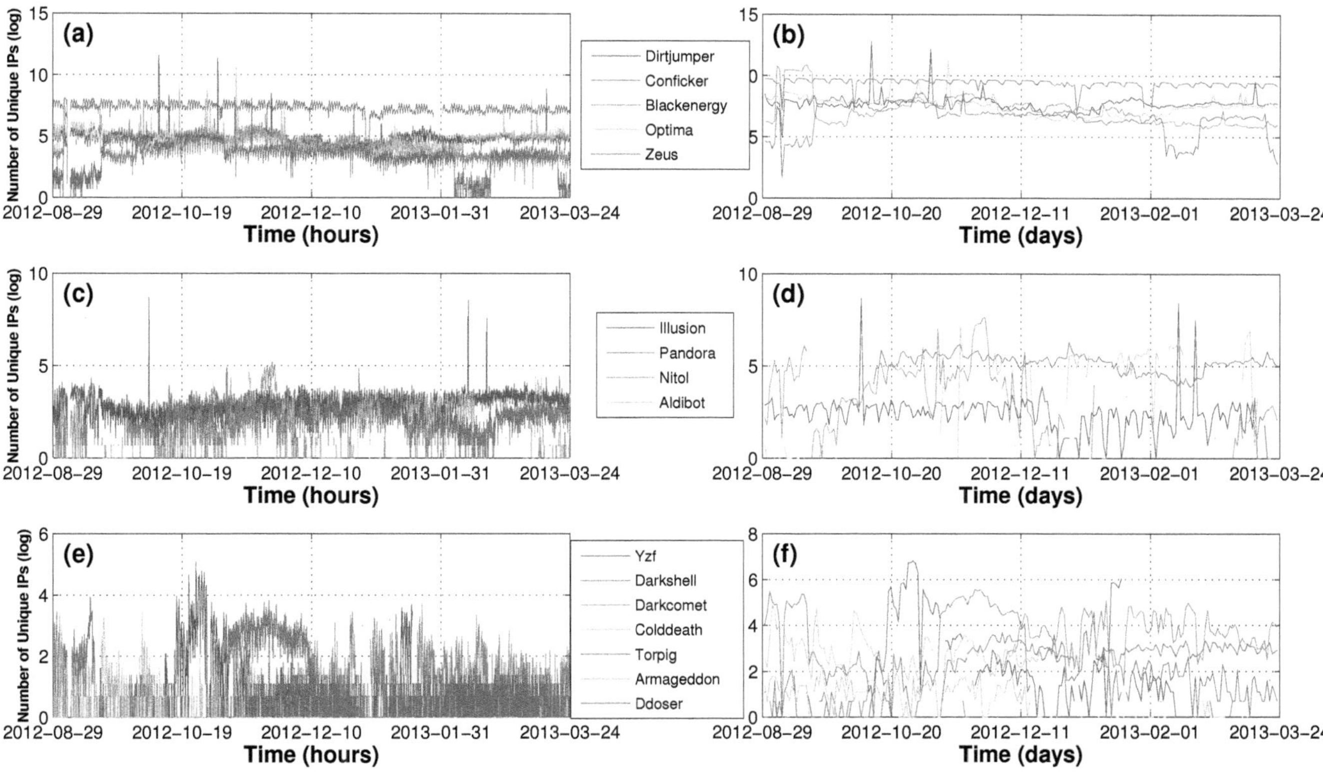

Figure 1: Botnet stability of three groups (based on botnet size)

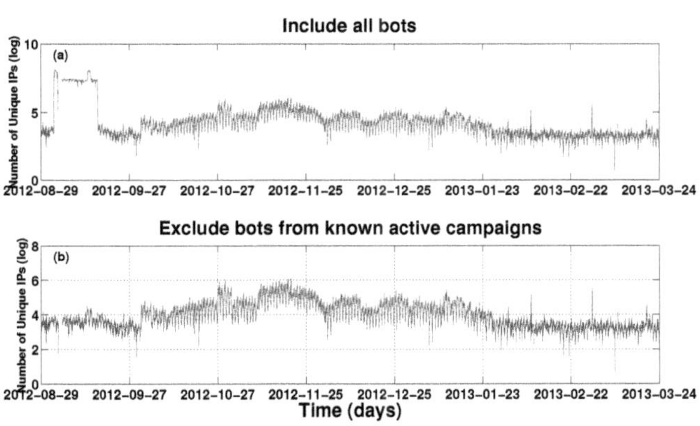

Figure 2: Simultaneous live bots of Blackenergy

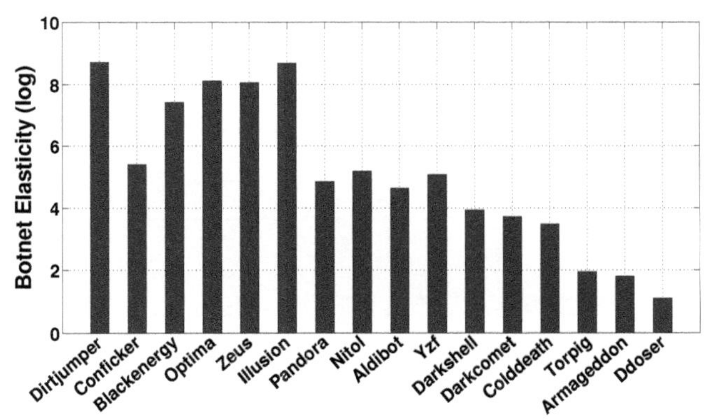

Figure 3: Botnet Elasticity

specific botnets. We speculate those two botnets are very likely to participate in a potential campaign. In the comparison figure at the bottom we draw the stability curve again excluding bots from those two botnets. The new curve unveils that when the `Blackenergy` is not instructed to participate in campaigns, the number of live bots keeps at a relatively stable level. A plausible explanation would be that the botnet requires a minimum number of live bots to preserve its presence (e.g., for business) or the communication (e.g., C&C channels). The number of live bots can surge within a very short time frame, usually a couple of days, when the botnet is instructed to engage in certain attacks. In our observation, a well managed botnet could rapidly recruit new bots in the order of hundreds of thousands. This is another important perspective when we evaluate the potential of a botnet's attacking power, particularly as today botnets are moving to "botnets-as-a-service" [9]. Therefore, we define another metric `elasticity` of a botnet, which is the ratio of the maximum number over the minimum number of live bots.

Figure 3 shows the elasticity result for all families—sorted by size in a descending order. As indicated by the figure, overall, the elasticity decreases with the decreasing botnet size. An exception is `Conficker`. As Figure 1 shows, compared to other large botnets, `Conficker` maintains a very stable army of bots. From the service perspective, the larger the elasticity value, the more capable a botnet is upon a demand for attacks. From the defense perspective, the more elastic a botnet, the harder to shut it down.

3.2 Botnet Activeness

The size of a botnet is one aspect of botnet activity: the scale and the stability, which reflect the potential attacking capability of botnets. Another important aspect to examine botnets' activity is to see whether or not a botnet is always live, i.e., the duration of their activity. Table 1 shows the activity periods of observed botnets in our dataset.

To further characterize botnet activeness, we plot in Figure 4 the total number of days for each family those live bots remain active. They are listed in the descending order of botnet size. 7 out of 16 families are `extremely active` and their activities are reported in our dataset for more than 200 days out of 207 days. They are `Blackenergy`, `Conficker`, `Darkshell`, `Dirtjumper`, `Illusion`, `Optima` and `Zeus`. 6 families (including `Armageddon`, `Darkcomet`, `Nitol`, `Pandora`, `Torpig` and `Yzf` stay active over 50% of time. We consider them `moderately active` families. The other 3 families, `Aldibot`, `Colddeath` and `Ddoser`, whose activity is less than 104 days, are classified as `marginally active` families. In conjunction with family grouping based on botnet size, we notice that although there is no one-to-one mapping, large- and medium-sized botnets also tend to be more active than the small-sized botnets.

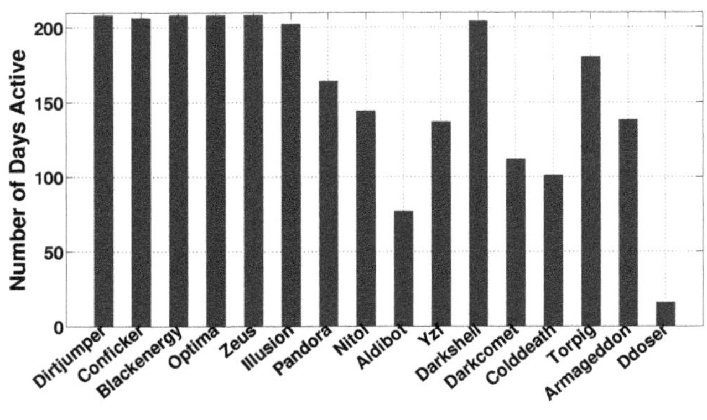

Figure 4: Botnet Activeness

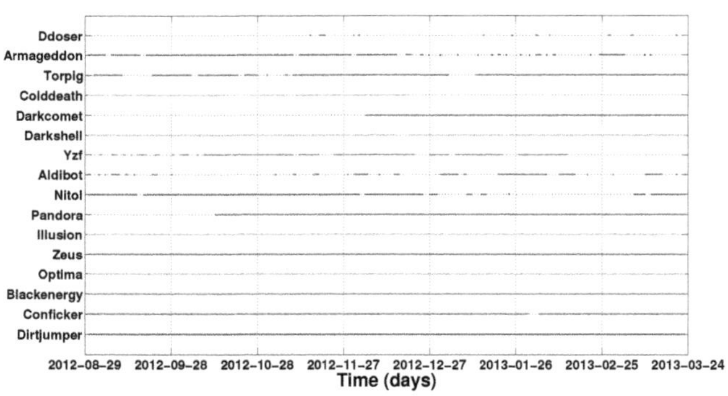

Figure 5: Botnet family activeness pattern

Figure 5 further shows the activeness pattern of different botnet families over time. While the top 5 botnet families in botnet size, including `Dirtjumper`, `Conficker`, `Blackenergy`, `Optima`, and `Zeus`, are almost constantly active in our observation period, `Aldibot` and `Ddoser` show clear intermittent activity pattern over the entire observation period. The rest of botnet families present a mix of continuous and periodical patterns. Considering that many effective detection and defense tools are already in use, the mixture of continuous and periodical patterns is likely to be the outcome of arms race between defenses and attacks. This is because bots are taken down in random pace, and botnets keep recruiting new ones to compensate. In other words, to maintain a simple continuous or periodic pattern is a non-trivial task, because it would require some defense-aware strategies from the botnet to guide the process of bots recruitment.

4. BOTNET COLLABORATION

One of the most challenging facets of the botnet behavior problem lies in discerning the relationship among (seemingly) different botnet families. To highlight this issue, we examine the infected hosts in our data collection to detect the existence of hidden relationships among the families we tracked. After performing a cross-family analysis, one interesting observation we have is the presence of a fair amount of reused bots – bots used by multiple botnet families, which could be potentially due to multiple infections, the NAT effect, or due to using paid infrastructure (i.e., pay-per-install) [7]. Even within the same family, some subsets of bots are also reused by different botnets (a family often contains multiple different botnets identified by the unique botnet ID in our dataset). The findings imply a possible inter-family and intra-family botnet collaboration. By identifying the set of reused bots, the defender could blacklist attacking machines in cost-effective ways.

4.1 Inter-family collaboration

As a first step analysis, we aim to identify bots that are reused across different families. In our analysis, we assume each IP address serves as the unique identifier of a bot and if the same IP is ever used by different botnet families, we consider the bot as a reused bot. Note that we are aware that multiple infected physical machines (bots) might operate behind a single NAT; there's a possibility that those machines are plagued by more than one botnet family over 7 months, thus the total number of reused bots might contain some false positives. Moreover due to DHCP, there's a slim chance that the same IP might be randomly assigned later to another bot that happens to be infected by a different family, which will also increase false positive rates of our classification. However, the analysis shows that the percentage of reused bots over all bots is relatively significant (14%, or 320,340 out of 2,280,369), much higher than what would result from coincidence.

We cross-compare specific botnet families to highlight a set of reused bots and monitor their participation in the botnet activities. Since the total number of unique bots identified in our dataset is over 2.2 million and the majority of them have been employed by only one botnet family, as the first step of inter-family collaboration analysis, we try to reduce the number of candidate bots that we need to closely track. To this end, we perform two data preprocessing steps. First, we filter out all bots that have not been shown to be used by more than two families over their life-cycle, thus reducing the total number of bots to about 320,000 (about 85% reduction). Second, using the outcome of the first step, we group IP addresses into /24 subnet, thus reducing the total number of IPs to 78,837. Aggregation of IPs into /24 subnets might inevitably introduce some false positives when two or more different IPs within the subnet are infected by different botnet families. But the chances are very slim if we assume those 256 IPs are assigned to normal and innocent machines of Internet users.

In our inter-family collaboration analysis, we aim to identify whether there exists a subset of the 78,837 subnets that are reused by various combinations of different botnet families. Also if such sets of bots exist, a second aim is to understand the status of those bots over time to reveal possible inter-family collaboration behaviors.

The top 6 active families we identified in Section 3 are our candidates for inter-family collaboration. Accordingly, we closely track every subnets in our dataset to record the time of their activity and what botnet family employs them. We assume that if the same bot is recorded active in the past 24 hours by two or more different families, they are recruited and are operated concurrently by those families. To make the figure more informative and to ac-

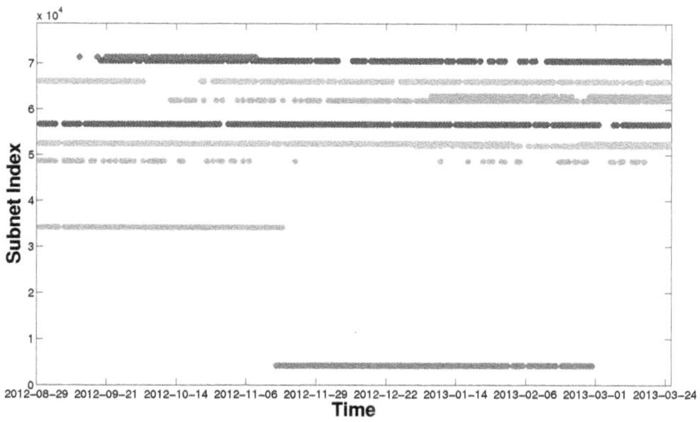

Figure 6: Activity of reused bots over four families

curately pinpoint subnets that are constantly reused or dedicated as collaboration resources, we set a minimum occurrence threshold to rule out less contributing resources (/24 subnets). That is, if the reused subnets do not engage in collaboration operations more than 25% of our observation period, we do not include them or show them in the figure. In our inter-family collaboration analysis of all top 6 families, there are only two subnets (aaa.57.68.xxx and aaa.57.190.xxx*) that are 75% of the time employed by those 6 families.

When excluding Conficker and Zeus from our analysis and only investigating inter-family collaboration between the other four families, we find significantly more /24 subnets are detected as reused ones. We depict concurrently reused /24 subnets and their status over time in Figure 6. The x-axis shows the time (207 days) while the y-axis represents the corresponding subnet index in our subnet set. When the subnet y is concurrently reused by all 4 families at a given time x, we mark the (x, y) point in the scatter plot. To make the grouping of reused subnets more visually impressive, the adjacent 2000 subnets are painted in the same color. We can observe from Figure 6 that a significant number of subnets are reused by all 4 families more than 75% of time. Two subnets (aaa.38.216.xxx and aaa.229.0.xxx) are active more than 95% of time and they are the backbone of inter-family collaboration between those 4 families. Another interesting finding from the figure is the shift of activity from one or many subsets to another set of subsets. For example, the subset aaa.107.232.xxx was heavily reused to engage in botnet activity until approximately day 79, and suddenly two adjacent /24 subnets (aaa.215.36.xxx and aaa.215.36.xxx) that were never reused before become reused in collaboration and served as the replacement of those 2 ceased subnets. This evident successor relationship suggests that the shift was not just a random incident but a deliberate action premeditated by a botmaster. We suspect that they could be an immediate reaction to a bot take-down event or a proactive detection evasion measure.

4.2 Intra-family collaboration

In our second step analysis, we focus on intra-family collaboration, and aim to understand how different botnet generations (identified by a unique botnet identifier) within the same family collaborate closely by reusing the same set of bots. In this section, we conduct our trace analysis on 13 out of the 16 most active botnet families in our dataset. Families `Armageddon` and `Torpig` report botnet activity from only one botnet generation, and all traffic for `Conficker` targets a DNS sinkhole server. For each family, we have a list of botnet identifiers derived from different malware signatures from the dataset. Similar to the methodology we used in inter-family analysis, we cross-compare the set of active bots from different botnet identifiers over time. The measurement results show that some botnet identifiers have extremely high concurrent usage rate over the same set of bots, while some other botnet identifiers show a clear temporal pattern.

*The first 8-bit segment of IP address is hidden for anonymization.

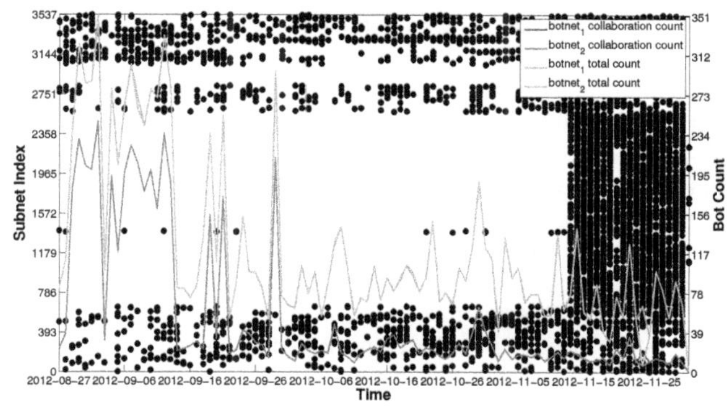

Figure 7: Intra-family collaboration for Blackenergy

Figure 7 shows the collaborations of two botnets with different identifiers within the `Blackenergy` family. In this figure, the x-axis represents daily timestamps when collaboration happened, the y-axis on the left represents the index of subnet involved in the collaborations, and the y-axis on the right represents the count of bots involved in the collaboration. For the scatter plot, each dot with different colors shows which botnet the subnet is involved in, and the black color means that those subnets are employed concurrently by both botnets. We plotted two more curves for each botnet involved in collaborations: the number of live bots for each botnet and the number of collaborating bots. In comparison of the collaboration curve and the live bots curve, it is evident that activities of both botnets are synchronized. Another finding is that a dedicated group of bots that are reused by both botnets are responsible for the spikes in the curve.

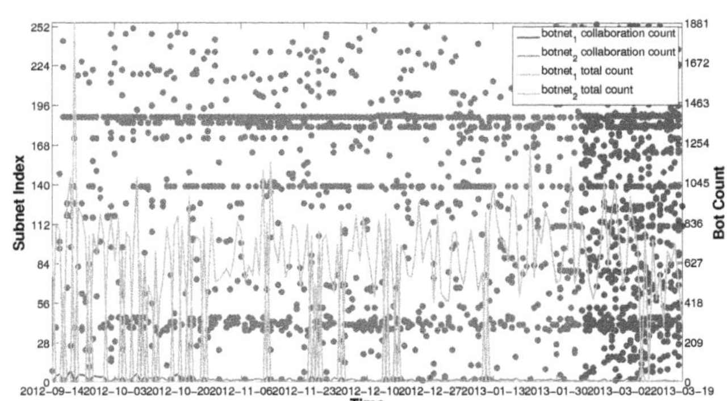

Figure 8: Intra-family collaboration for Zeus

Figure 8 describes the collaborations of two botnet identifiers from the family `Zeus`. Although these two botnet identifiers own a large number of the same bots, those bots are rarely used concurrently. They were solely used by botnet 1 before Feb. 10, 2013, and suddenly nearly all of those bots are transferred to botnet 2. We suspect the root cause is that the same set of bots are instructed to participate in another, different campaign. This evident temporal pattern suggests that botnet 1 and botnet 2 are likely to be managed by the same botmaster. Thus, they are essentially the same botnet, with a difference in their code base that resulted in a different signature.

5. RELATED WORK

Botnets pose one of the most severe threats to the health of the Internet. To collect and analyze bots, researchers widely utilize two common techniques: infiltration [3, 10] and passive traffic monitoring [1]. To facilitate the botnet detection and provide effective countermeasures against malicious botnet activities, it is crucial to have a good understanding of botnets in the wild including their behaviors and coordination strategies. Dagon et al. [12] conducted a taxonomy study of botnet structure based on their utility to the botmaster in 2007, and also ranked botnets based on key measurement metrics they proposed on botnets. Some other security researchers endeavor to conduct an in-depth case study of botnet by putting one specific botnet family under the microscope [6, 23, 2, 24]. The trend that the state-of-art botnets have become more and more sophisticated and applied various evasion techniques to hide their activity, further complicates the detection and defense mechanisms. Many existing botnet studies [21, 5] are targeted at the most common IRC-based bots relying on a centralized control. However, numerous new botnets begin to use http-based C&C channels and leverage the more stable P2P based communication architecture [27, 18, 15] to avoid single point of failure. Some recent work focused on large scale measurements of network traffic to develop methods for revealing more properties of botnets, such as their size [13] and activeness [24]. In our work, with the assistance of top level ISPs, we observed large-scale bot activity data from multiple well-known botnet families, and reveal several new trends and activity patterns of botnets.

6. CONCLUSION

Botnets have been widely used for various Internet attacks. To remain active and profitable, today botnets are very versatile and adaptive by constantly and continuously adopting new techniques to evade from being detected. In this study, we have performed an in-depth analysis of botnet behavior patterns based on a large botnet dataset collected from various Internet anchor points by a commercial monitoring unit for about seven months. By analyzing the data of the most active 16 botnet families, we have reported some new observations and insights of today's botnets. Such results not only add to the existing botnet literature for a better understanding, but also offer timely help for botnet detection and defenses.

7. REFERENCES

[1] M. Abu Rajab, J. Zarfoss, F. Monrose, and A. Terzis. A multifaceted approach to understanding the botnet phenomenon. In *IMC*, 2006.

[2] M. M. Andrade and N. Vlajic. Dirt jumper: A key player in today's botnet-for-ddos market. In *WorldCIS*. IEEE, 2012.

[3] P. Bacher, T. Holz, M. Kotter, and G. Wicherski. Know your enemy: Tracking botnets. http://www.honeynet.org/papers/bots, 2005.

[4] P. Baecher, M. Koetter, T. Holz, M. Dornseif, and F. Freiling. The nepenthes platform: An efficient approach to collect malware. In *RAID*, pages 165–184. Springer, 2006.

[5] P. Barford and V. Yegneswaran. An inside look at botnets. In *Malware Detection*, pages 171–191. Springer, 2007.

[6] H. Binsalleeh, T. Ormerod, A. Boukhtouta, P. Sinha, A. Youssef, M. Debbabi, and L. Wang. On the analysis of the zeus botnet crimeware toolkit. In *PST*, pages 31–38. IEEE, 2010.

[7] J. Caballero, C. Grier, C. Kreibich, and V. Paxson. Measuring pay-per-install: The commoditization of malware distribution. In *USENIX Security*, 2011.

[8] J. Caballero, P. Poosankam, C. Kreibich, and D. Song. Dispatcher: Enabling active botnet infiltration using automatic protocol reverse-engineering. In *CCS*, pages 621–634. ACM, 2009.

[9] W. Chang, A. Wang, A. Mohaisen, and S. Chen. Characterizing botnets-as-a-service. In *Proceedings of the 2014 ACM conference on SIGCOMM*, pages 585–586. ACM, 2014.

[10] C. Y. Cho, J. Caballero, C. Grier, V. Paxson, and D. Song. Insights from the inside: A view of botnet management from infiltration. In *USENIX LEET*, 2010.

[11] N. Daswani, M. Stoppelman, the Google Click Quality, and S. Teams. The anatomy of clickbot.a. In *USENIX HotBots*, Cambridge, MA, April 2007.

[12] C. P. L. David Dagon, Guofei Gu and W. Lee. A taxonomy of botnet structures. In *ACSCA*, 2007.

[13] M. A. R. J. Z. Fabian and M. A. Terzis. My botnet is bigger than yours (maybe, better than yours): why size estimates remain challenging. In *USENIX HotBots*, 2007.

[14] J. Goebel and T. Holz. Rishi: Identify bot contaminated hosts by irc nickname evaluation. In *USENIX HotBots*, pages 8–8. Cambridge, MA, 2007.

[15] J. B. Grizzard, V. Sharma, C. Nunnery, B. B. Kang, and D. Dagon. Peer-to-peer botnets: Overview and case study. In *USENIX HotBots*, pages 1–1, 2007.

[16] G. Gu, P. Porras, V. Yegneswaran, M. Fong, and W. Lee. Bothunter: Detecting malware infection through ids-driven dialog correlation. In *USENIX Security*, page 12, 2007.

[17] G. Gu, J. Zhang, and W. Lee. Botsniffer: Detecting botnet command and control channels in network traffic. In *NDSS*, 2008.

[18] T. Holz, M. Steiner, F. Dahl, E. Biersack, and F. C. Freiling. Measurements and mitigation of peer-to-peer-based botnets: A case study on storm worm. In *USENIX LEET*, volume 8, pages 1–9, 2008.

[19] Info Security Magazine. Spamhaus suffers largest ddos attack in history – entire internet affected. http://bit.ly/1bfx3ZH, March 2013.

[20] L. Jing, X. Yang, G. Kaveh, D. Hongmei, and Z. Jingyuan. Botnet: classification, attacks, detection, tracing, and preventive measures. *EURASIP JWCN*, 2009.

[21] A. Karasaridis, B. Rexroad, and D. Hoeflin. Wide-scale botnet detection and characterization. In *USENIX HotBots*, volume 7. Cambridge, MA, 2007.

[22] A. Moshchuk, T. Bragin, D. Deville, S. Gribble, and H. Levy. Spyproxy: Execution-based detection of malicious web content. In *USENIX Security*, 2007.

[23] J. Nazario. Blackenergy ddos bot analysis. *Arbor*, 2007.

[24] S. Shin and G. Gu. Conficker and beyond: a large-scale empirical study. In *ACSAC*, pages 151–160. ACM, 2010.

[25] E. Stinson and J. C. Mitchell. Characterizing the remote control behavior of bots. In *DIMVA*, 2007.

[26] Team Cymru. Team cymru community services. http://www.team-cymru.org/Monitoring/, May 2013.

[27] P. Wang, S. Sparks, and C. C. Zou. An advanced hybrid peer-to-peer botnet. *TDSC*, 7(2):113–127, 2010.

[28] Z. Zhu, G. Lu, Y. Chen, Z. Fu, P. Roberts, and K. Han. Botnet research survey. In *COMPSAC*, pages 967–972. IEEE, 2008.

CAFE: A Virtualization-Based Approach to Protecting Sensitive Cloud Application Logic Confidentiality

Chung Hwan Kim[†], Sungjin Park[‡¶], Junghwan Rhee[§],
Jong-Jin Won[‡], Taisook Han[¶], Dongyan Xu[†]
[†]Purdue University, [‡]The Attached Institute of ETRI, [§]NEC Laboratories America, [¶]KAIST
[†]{chungkim,dxu}@cs.purdue.edu, [‡]{taiji,wonjj}@ensec.re.kr,
[§]rhee@nec-labs.com, [¶]taisook@kaist.ac.kr

ABSTRACT

Cloud application marketplaces of modern cloud infrastructures offer a new software deployment model, integrated with the cloud environment in its configuration and policies. However, similar to traditional software distribution which has been suffering from software piracy and reverse engineering, cloud marketplaces face the same challenges that can deter the success of the evolving ecosystem of cloud software. We present a novel system named CAFE for cloud infrastructures where sensitive software logic can be executed with high secrecy protected from any piracy or reverse engineering attempts in a virtual machine even when its operating system kernel is compromised. The key mechanism is the end-to-end framework for the execution of applications, which consists of the secure encryption and distribution of confidential application binary files, and the runtime techniques to load, decrypt, and protect the program logic by isolating them from tenant virtual machines based on hypervisor-level techniques. We evaluate applications in several software categories which are commonly offered in cloud marketplaces showing that strong confidential execution can be provided with only marginal changes (around 100-220 lines of code) and minimal performance overhead.

Categories and Subject Descriptors

D.4.6 [**Operating Systems**]: Security and Protection

Keywords

Cloud Computing Marketplace, Secure Execution Environment, Code Confidentiality Protection

1. INTRODUCTION

Cloud computing infrastructures are becoming increasingly popular and mature. Gartner estimated the size of public cloud service market to grow to $131 billion by 2017 from $111 billion in 2012 [20]. As the technologies for cloud infrastructures have become mature, there is an increasing demand for software services especially in Infrastructure-as-a-Service (IaaS) clouds, where computers (physical or virtual) are provided to tenants with full flexibility. It is, however, difficult for cloud providers to fulfill all of the diverse needs of software that are continuously increasing. Consequently, major cloud computing services (such as Amazon Web Services (AWS), IBM Cloud, and Microsoft Azure) operate marketplaces where application developers can upload and retail software, and cloud users can purchase the software that they need.

The ecosystem of cloud marketplaces and services in general involves three parties: cloud users, application developers, and cloud providers. Cloud users seek and purchase the cloud applications suitable to their needs in terms of functionality, price, the easiness of management, etc. Compared to traditional software that requires installation and management specific to each user (e.g., desktop applications), cloud applications are optimized to run on a cloud platform utilizing various services delivered from the cloud provider.

Cloud application developers submit their packages to the marketplace after placing program binaries and dependent components in a disk image. Cloud users search for the software that meets their needs in the marketplace and purchase them. When the cloud users create a virtual machine (VM), they are prompted with a list of the disk images that include the purchased applications. The selected disk image is then written to the virtual disk of the VM, so the application can be used by the cloud users. The applications can be easily deployed using VM images without tedious installation procedures that traditional applications require.

While this new form of distribution simplifies the deployment of software, one of the key problems in software distribution still remains in cloud marketplaces: *the deployed software faces the risk of piracy and reverse engineering*, similar to what conventionally distributed software is facing. Because cloud users typically own an entire VM with all privileged permissions given, technically they have no restriction on the inspection and replication of the applications installed in the VM.

Existing approaches [16, 15, 10] leveraging virtualization-based memory protection protect *partial* code confidentiality or do not address necessary issues in a practical cloud marketplace setting where code confidentiality must be fully protected throughout the entire life span of software after its submission.

As a new alternative, we propose a system named Cloud Application Function Enclaving (CAFE) to address these

ASIA CCS '15, April 14 - 17, 2015, Singapore, Singapore
Copyright 2015 ACM 978-1-4503-3245-3/15/04 ...$15.00.
http://dx.doi.org/10.1145/2714576.2714594.

challenges. CAFE provides a cloud application execution environment with code confidentiality so that it can protect sensitive cloud application logic from any piracy or reverse engineering attempts performed by cloud users, even in the case that the guest OS of the cloud user VM is compromised.

CAFE works in the following way. First, developers create software or port existing software in two groups of program binary files: a group that can be open to cloud users and the other that contains *confidential logic* that needs to be protected. We name the binary files of the former *public binaries* and the latter *secret binaries.* The public binaries are submitted in the form of a VM image that also contains other files related to the application (e.g., configuration files) and the VM environment but does not contain the secret binaries. A cloud user may be able to copy the files or extract the in-memory images of the public binaries as in the existing cloud application distribution.

In contrast, the secret binaries are submitted in the form of separate files and are automatically managed by the cloud providers with protection. When the application is run in the user VM, the secret binaries are fetched on demand at runtime for execution via a secure deployment protocol by the hypervisor. The hypervisor securely loads the secret binaries through a cryptographically protected channel after the authentication of the VM. The end-to-end framework ensures that the sensitive logic is completely isolated from cloud users at all times. Throughout the whole lifetime of the VM, the binary and runtime states of the sensitive logic stay confidential and are strictly protected from the entire guest OS in the VM by the hypervisor.

This paper is structured as follows: Section 2 presents the adversary model. The design is presented in Section 3. The evaluation of CAFE is presented in Section 4. Related work is discussed in Section 5, and Section 6 concludes this paper.

2. ADVERSARY MODEL

We present our adversary model based on a reasonable cloud environment in modern systems. The main goal of an adversary would be to obtain the content (in any form) of program binaries that are protected by our system. We note that the guest OSes running in cloud user VMs are *untrusted*, which means that an attacker can execute arbitrary executable code at any privilege. That is, an attacker can compromise all software including the kernel, drivers, libraries, and applications in the user and kernel mode running in the user VM. Specifically, an attacker can attempt to obtain and reverse-engineer the binary codes containing sensitive application logic using the following methods.

Access to file system: As described in Section 1, applications are distributed to user VMs as a set of files written to the VM's disk image. The most obvious way to obtain the program is to access the files inside the file system using file I/O. Based on our adversary model, the attacker has privilege to mount and access any file system. Therefore, once the program is stored in a file system in a plain form, he should be able to obtain it.

Access to runtime process memory: A more elevated attack to obtain the program binary is to capture the runtime states of the program. We consider that the attacker can access the memory of application processes. For instance, using a debugging tool or by injecting malicious code into its memory the attacker can obtain the binary code from the runtime memory of the target processes.

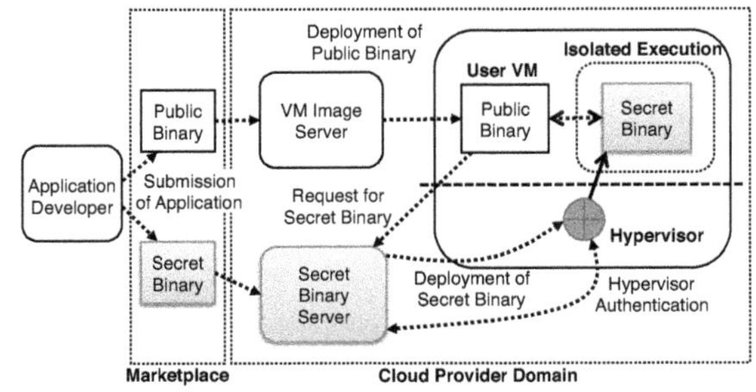

Figure 1: Overview of CAFE.

Access to network: Another attack method to obtain the binary would be using the network layer. We assume that the attacker can eavesdrop and modify network traffic between cloud provider servers and cloud user VMs. Therefore, if a binary file is transferred in a plain form, the attacker may be able to obtain it from network packets.

3. DESIGN

To support confidential execution of various kinds of applications in a practical cloud marketplace setting, the confidentiality of sensitive logic should be systematically maintained in the entire work-flow from the development of programs to the delivery to the cloud users and their execution. CAFE achieves this goal using *an end-to-end framework for the confidential execution of cloud applications* by using hypervisor-level techniques. This is one of the key novelties of this paper compared to previous work which only focus on a local view of protection [11, 13, 14, 10, 16, 15]. The overview of the CAFE architecture is illustrated in Figure 1.

Application development and submission: As mentioned in Section 1, cloud application developers build their program code into two separate groups to be supported by CAFE: the public binary and secret binary groups. In our model, application developers have the responsibility to determine which part of application logic needs confidentiality. The application is annotated to use the APIs of CAFE, a set of hypercalls that request the hypervisor to load, unload, and execute a secret binary. The public binaries are packaged in a VM image along with other binary files on which the application depends. When the application is submitted to the marketplace, the VM image that contains the public binaries, and the secret binary files are submitted separately. Upon submission, the public VM image is transferred to the VM image server that stores and manages VM images as in existing cloud infrastructures. In contrast, the secret binary files are stored in the *secret binary server (SBS)*, a secure storage for sensitive application logic. Both the VM image server and the SBS are a part of the cloud provider domain linked to user VMs with a dedicated high bandwidth connection.

Purchase and deployment of applications: Cloud users purchase applications from the cloud marketplace and then the cloud provider lets the cloud user create a VM using the corresponding VM image that includes the public binaries of the purchased application. The secret binaries, on the other hand, are not delivered this time. Instead, they are delivered to the hypervisor through a secure channel when the binaries are requested for use.

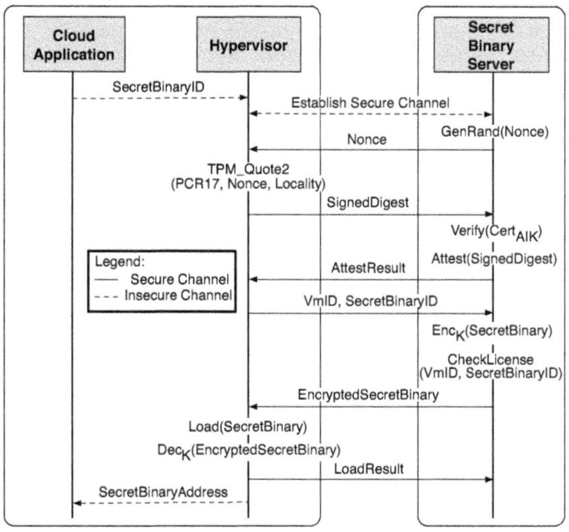

Figure 2: Secret binary deployment protocol.

Execution of an application: When the cloud user runs the purchased application in the VM, the application requests the hypervisor to load the secret binaries via a hypercall. The hypervisor, in turn, communicates with the SBS to prove the authenticity of itself and the user's license for the application. Specifically, the hypervisor and the SBS exchange the session key to establish a secure channel, and the SBS attests the integrity of the hypervisor leveraging the Trusted Platform Module (TPM) to ensure the genuineness of hypervisor. After that, the SBS transfers the secret binaries encrypted using the session key shared with the hypervisor. Upon receiving them, the hypervisor decrypts and loads the secret binaries in a secure runtime environment which is completely isolated from the user VM.

Designation of sensitive code: Security sensitive code has the key logic of an application requiring a high degree of protection. Since this is typically a small portion of the entire application code, the cost to achieve confidentiality is generally amortized in the overall performance of programs. Our evaluation in Section 4 will confirm that this high secrecy property can be achieved with minimal overhead.

3.1 Secure Authentication and Deployment of Secret Binary

Figure 2 depicts our deployment protocol of secret binaries, designed to defend against attacks.

Secure channel establishment: When an application requests a secret binary from the hypervisor, a secure channel is established between the hypervisor and the SBS for tamper-resistant communication. The details of the secure channel establishment are as follows.

Among several candidate key exchange algorithms (i.e., Diffie-Hellan and RSA), we choose a variant of Transport Layer Security (TLS) [3] as our handshake protocol and RSA as our key exchange algorithm. TLS allows two parties of the secure channel (i.e., the SBS and the hypervisor) to authenticate each other with the other's certificate. The certificate authority (CA) guarantees the certificates of both sides; thereby, they can securely authenticate each other. Unlike the standard handshake protocol of TLS, CAFE leverages the TPM to generate an RSA key pair of the hypervisor and a *pre-secret* which is used to derive shared secrets such as an encryption key, an initial vector (IV), and a HMAC key. With the use of the TPM, we provide a level of security higher than the standard TLS.

CAFE generates an RSA key pair inside the TPM and wraps it with the TPM's Storage Root Key (SRK). The SRK is a unique, non-migratable 2048-bit RSA key and is guaranteed to always be present in the TPM. Due to these features, a key wrapped by the SRK can only be used in the machine on which the same TPM is placed. Therefore, even in the case that the attacker acquires a wrapped RSA key pair, he cannot unwrap it without the same TPM used to generate and wrap it.

Remote attestation of the hypervisor: After establishing a secure channel, the SBS generates a nonce (`Nonce`) and sends it to the hypervisor. The nonce is used as a parameter of the `TPM_Quote2` operation, a TPM operation used for integrity measurement [12]. The hypervisor performs `TPM_Quote2` and transfers the resulted digest (`SignedDigest`) to the SBS which verifies the integrity of the hypervisor by matching the received digest with the certificate ($\texttt{Cert}_{AIK}$) from the private CA.

Verification of application licenses: Upon successful attestation of the hypervisor, the cloud application sends the VM ID and the secret binary ID to the SBS requesting the transmission of the encrypted secret binary image. A VM ID is the unique identifier of a VM managed internally by the cloud infrastructure. A secret binary ID is the unique identifier of a secret binary determined upon the submission of the application to the cloud infrastructure, and it is known to both the SBS and the application that uses the secret binary. The cloud infrastructure maintains the association between a VM ID and a user, and what licenses the user has for billing purposes. Based on this information, the SBS determines whether the user associated with the VM ID has a valid license for the application of the secret binary ID. If the license is valid, the SBS proceeds to the transmission, otherwise it refuses the request.

Transmission of secret binaries: The SBS encrypts a secret binary with the encryption key and the IV using the HMAC message authentication of the encrypted secret binaries with the shared HMAC key. The SBS and the hypervisor establish a new secure channel with a different session key (`K` in Figure 2) at every request of a secret binary, and the secret binary is encrypted using the session key. Therefore, the deployment protocol can resist brute-force attacks on the secure channel and the secret binary encryption.

Loading of secret binaries: After the transmission, the secret binaries remain encrypted in the user VM's disk throughout the all steps of the secret binary loading and execution. The hypervisor decrypts and loads secret binaries in the confidential execution environment that is isolated from the user VM. The integrity of the secret binaries is checked using the shared HMAC key with the SBS before the loading. Finally, the result of the loading is sent back to the SBS, and the application receives the address of the secret binary.

3.2 Runtime Protection of Secret Binary

In this section, we describe how CAFE protects secret binaries on disk and memory.

Protection of the secret binary on disk: The secret binary file on disk is cryptographically protected by an encryption algorithm. Among various available encryption algorithms, we choose AES-256 in the CBC mode to encrypt and decrypt secret binaries. The SBS performs the encryption of the binary on demand when a request for a binary is received from an application. The session key obtained from the session channel establishment (Section 3.1) is used for encryption to prevent brute-force attempts that target the transmission of the secret binary. The application uses an API provided by CAFE to load the secret binary. The secret binary file remains encrypted until it is verified and loaded into an isolated memory maintained by the hypervisor. Therefore, any attempts to reverse-engineer the decrypted content of the binary file on disk fail.

Protection of the secret binary in memory: Once the secret binary is loaded into memory, it is protected by the hardware-assisted memory virtualization technology. Several types of hardware-support for memory virtualization are readily available in modern commodity processors such as Intel Extended Page Tables and AMD Rapid Virtualization Indexing. CAFE uses this technique to load the secret binary into the memory and create a secure execution environment isolated from the user VM.

Specifically before the secret binary is loaded, there is one set of nested page tables (NPTs) that is maintained by the hypervisor to map all guest physical addresses to machine physical addresses. When the binary is loaded, the NPTs are split into two exclusive sets: the public NPTs and the secret NPTs. The public NPTs contain the page entries for all memory blocks used by the user VM except those used by the secret binary, whereas the secret NPTs contain the page entries for the secret binary only. The hypervisor ensures that the user VM uses the public NPTs while the public binary is running. Thus, any memory access to the secret binary during the execution of the public binary is blocked by the MMU. On the other hand, when the application executes the secret binary the hypervisor switches the public NPTs with the secret NPTs which enforce the exclusive access by the secret binary providing strong isolation between the secret binary and the user VM.

Previous work leveraging memory virtualization primarily focus on the runtime isolation of the program binary in memory [16, 15]. Compared to the existing work, CAFE ensures that the sensitive application logic is inaccessible from the user VM at any time.

3.3 Secure Hypervisor Loading of Secret Binary

A program's execution is performed through low level operations such as allocation of system resources, program loading and linking, and the bootstrapping of the program. These operations are typically performed by the high privileged software layer in the OS or system level libraries. In our setting, the user VM including its OS is untrusted. Therefore, CAFE has its own mechanism for such operations to ensure the confidentiality of the program throughout its execution. In this section, we describe how this execution environment is established.

Loading of an executable binary: Program code typically consists of multiple binary codes: the main executable and a number of shared libraries linked to the main executable. When a binary is loaded, the location in the virtual memory of the process and the symbols (e.g., exported global variables and functions) are determined dynamically by the *loader*. Thus, any instructions of the program that refer to the symbols must be updated with the addresses determined at runtime and this process is known as *relocation*. When the executable file is built, the compiler constructs a relocation table that includes the information necessary for the relocation: the locations of the instruction operands to be patched, the location of the symbols in the binary, and how the loader is expected to perform relocation (i.e., the relocation type). This table is used by the loader when the executable file is loaded or when the relocation is necessary in a lazy manner depending on the configuration.

Loading by the hypervisor: The application requests the hypervisor to load the secret binary using the APIs provided CAFE. Then the hypervisor decrypts the secret binary into the memory isolated from the user VM. Since the OS loader is untrusted, we use the hypervisor to perform the loading, the decryption, and the relocation of the secret binary. When the binary is loaded into the isolated memory, the hypervisor performs the decryption. After that it performs the relocation of the binary. When the application requests CAFE to load a secret binary, it locates the relocation section of the secret binary, and the encrypted relocation information is sent to the hypervisor via a hypercall. When the hypervisor receives the hypercall, it decrypts the relocation information. If decryption is successful, then it performs relocation on all sections of the secret binary.

4. EVALUATION

CAFE consists of three major components: the hypervisor, the secret binary server (SBS), and the user level APIs that the cloud applications use to send requests to the hypervisor via hypercall.

The hypervisor is implemented on top of eXtensible and Modular Hypervisor Framework (XMHF) [22] which is used in several related work [22, 15, 23]. We implement the authentication/verification layer that interacts with the SBS and the loading and unloading mechanism for secret binaries that involve the hypervisor level relocation.

We use two separate machines for our experiments for the hypervisor and the SBS. Both machines are equipped with an AMD Turion II P520 2.30GHz processor, 4GB RAM, and a 256GB SSD, and run the 32-bit version of Ubuntu 12.04. The virtual machines and the SBS are connected to a 1Gb/s network.

4.1 Use Cases

We demonstrate that various types of application code can be protected by CAFE using six applications grouped into three distinct categories (as listed in Table 1). The applications are selected based on their popularity in real-world usages and cloud marketplaces. We use the source code of these applications to slice out example sensitive code that is compiled into secret binaries. The chosen program logic may not be "confidential" in real world, but they are selected to simulate the developers' efforts to take the benefit of confidential execution of CAFE. Our experiment shows the applicability of CAFE to various types of application software to verify that similar program logic can be executed confidentially.

Table 1 shows the details of the applications that run on CAFE with confidential execution. The first column presents three categories of program logic: decision-making logic, cryptographic operations, and data processing work-

Application Category	Program Name	Binary Name	Code info			Runtime info			
			Protected code	$\|L\|$	$\|F\|$	$\|C\|$	$\|D\|$	$\|R\|$	Overhead
Decision-making logic	NGINX	`nginx-access`	Access module	169	1	4	44	19	1.90%
	Sendmail	`sendmail-filter`	Mail Filter (Milter)	106	1	52	52	559	2.81%
Cryptographic operations	Google Authenticator	`gauth-otp`	One-time passcode generation	102	1	8	44	16	2.52%
	EncFS	`encfs-aria`	ARIA block encryption/decryption	220	3	24	48	346	900.13%
Data processing workload	MapReduce	`mapreduce-kmeans`	k-means clustering	173	1	12	44	380	8.04%
	Hadoop	`hadoop-wcount`	Word counting	180	2	4	44	32	5.82%

Table 1: Use cases of confidential execution of secret cloud application binaries.

load. The following columns show the program information (program name, binary name), the description of the protected program logic (Protected Code), the number of lines of code added as porting attempts ($|L|$), the number of secret functions ($|F|$) and runtime characteristics of the secret binaries ($|C|$: code section size, $|D|$: data section size, $|R|$: relocation table size, overhead). The characteristics of the applications in the three categories are as follows.

Decision-making logic: Application code in this category determines the behaviors of the application. For example, the access module, **`nginx-access`**, of NGINX decides whether the web server allows or denies an incoming web request based on the configuration. Another application, the mail filter module, **`sendmail-filter`**, of the sendmail server analyzes the content of an outgoing mail and decides whether to send out the mail or not. Specifically the ported code examines the header of an input mail and finds whether the sender's address is illegal using a regular expression.

Cryptographic operations: If the OS is compromised, cryptographic operations are no longer safe because OS can look into their runtime states which can potentially be used to infer their operations. We show several use cases of well known cloud applications. We port the Google Authenticator Pluggable Authentication Module (PAM), **`gauth-otp`**, that protects the passcode generating code, and EncFS which is a file system with the block-level encryption. We selected a EncFS, **`encfs-aria`**, that uses the ARIA cipher [4]. The encryption and decryption algorithms along with the key initialization function are protected.

Data processing workload: Some security sensitive code may involve intensive computation. We use two parallel data processing algorithms running on a parallel computing framework to show the support of this category. **`mapreduce-kmeans`** is an implementation of k-means clustering based on Phoenix [19], a shared-memory and C language based MapReduce framework. The protected code partitions n-dimensional integer points into a number of clusters. Lastly, **`hadoop-wcount`** is an algorithm based on Apache Hadoop which analyzes an input text file and outputs the total number of distinct English words.

The number of lines of code added to the applications for conversion depends on the amount of the confidential code of the application. In our use cases, it ranges 100-220 (average 1.18%). Compared to the total LoC of the entire program, it is a small portion of the program.

4.2 Performance of Confidential Execution of Cloud Applications

We present the overhead of the applications for confidential execution in CAFE (Table 1). We calculate the overhead by comparing the performance of the original version with the modified version with confidential protection. In general, one major source of overhead is VM-level context switches that occur while the secret code is running and during marshaling for input and output data. Specifically, the overhead highly depends on the frequency of secret function calls and the size of the marshaled data. The complexity of the protected logic has a minor impact on the overhead.

We have evaluated several server programs by setting up the client for benchmarking workload in a separate physical machine in a local network. To measure the overhead of **`nginx-access`**, we have the Apache Benchmark issue 10K transactions per trial. Diverse content of each page is simulated with a binary blob filled with randomly-generated bytes. We experimented the average size of the web page in top 100 web sites as of July, 2014 [1]. The overhead comparing the number of requests per second is 1.9%.

We use the Mstone SMTP performance testing tool [2] to measure the overhead of **`sendmail-filter`**. The test is run for 30 seconds with one client which repeatedly sends an email with the default Mstone email content. The evaluation shows that the overhead is only 2.81%.

To evaluate **`gauth-otp`** case, the SSH client repeatedly logins to and logouts from the server for 30 seconds using one-time passcodes generated by secret binary. The overhead for confidential execution is as trivial as 2.52%.

The overhead of **`encfs-aria`** is measured using the IOzone Filesystem Benchmark [7]. We use the average throughput (KB/sec) of each process writing a 512KB file using a 4KB buffer. The benchmark result shows that the application with the confidential execution support is about 9 times slower than with the binary without the support. We note that this benchmarking is a *stress case* where the file system is stressed with very frequent secret function calls, which cause high context switch cost. In typical real-world cloud applications such workload is unusual especially when an encrypted disk is used, thereby we expect the overhead in the realistic setting to be much lower.

`mapreduce-kmeans` is configured to partition 8,192 two-dimensional integer points (64 MB) into 4,096 clusters. The application is about 8% slower with the confidentiality support than the original application, both given the same input. **`hadoop-wcount`** is run with an input text file that contains 10,000 words (108 KB). We use the CPU time spent during the two phases as the unit of the comparison. The overhead introduced by CAFE for this binary is 5.8%.

4.3 Performance Impact to Applications without Protection

We use the XMHF hypervisor framework [22] as the base of our implementation for basic hypervisor primitives and DRTM-related code. To evaluate the performance impact we run benchmarks (UnixBench) on CAFE without any secret binaries loaded and compare the results with a vanilla XMHF hypervisor with the basic VM management functionality only. The results confirm that CAFE does not impact unprotected applications in the VM (zero overhead).

5. RELATED WORK

Flicker [16] and TrustVisor [15] provide an infrastructure for executing security-sensitive code in isolated memory based on the remote attestation of binary code. However, they primarily focus on blocking user VM's accesses to the application code in memory only while the memory isolation is enabled at runtime. This design may compromise code confidentiality because attackers in the VM may obtain a copy of the application code from the file system or memory during the deployment before the protection is enabled. In contrast, CAFE protects the confidentiality of the binaries in an end-to-end manner for the entire lifetime of the deployed software.

Overshadow [10] provides cloaking for general purpose legacy unmodified applications and untrusted kernel. Related work [9, 18] have shown that a malicious kernel is able to compromise the protected OS even with the protection schemes by Overshadow. CAFE provides stronger code confidentiality than Overshadow by providing tightly verified and sanitized input and output via marshaling layer, and a constrained scope of sensitive code which in combination significantly reduce the chance of vulnerability.

Software vendors have been working hard to protect their code from reverse engineering and software piracy. There has been a large body of work on obfuscators [14, 17, 21, 13, 5, 6, 8] which make disassembly hard. While the code obfuscation techniques can impede the analysis of code, they are not designed to provide the complete secrecy of executable code because obfuscated code may still retain code semantics. Unlike such solutions, CAFE provides full confidentiality by cryptographically encrypting the binary code and running the decrypted code in an isolated environment.

6. CONCLUSION

The secure distribution and execution of cloud applications is an essential feature to prevent the illegitimate usage of cloud applications and further for the success of the evolving ecosystem of cloud systems. In order to defeat software piracy and reverse engineering of sensitive software logic, we present CAFE which provides the confidential distribution and execution of cloud applications even when the entire OS of the tenant VM is compromised. We present its evaluation on a number of applications commonly offered in cloud marketplaces showing the effectiveness and practicality of CAFE.

7. REFERENCES

[1] Average Web Page Breaks 1600K. `http://www.websiteoptimization.com/speed/tweak/average-web-page/`.

[2] Mstone. `http://mstone.sourceforge.net/`.

[3] The Transport Layer Security (TLS) Protocol Version 1.2. `http://tools.ietf.org/html/rfc5246`.

[4] A Description of the ARIA Encryption Algorithm, 2010. `http://tools.ietf.org/search/rfc5794`.

[5] Themida, 2010. `http://www.oreans.com`.

[6] VMProtect, 2010. `http://vmpsoft.com/products/vmprotect/`.

[7] IOzone Filesystem Benchmark, Feb. 2013. `http://www.iozone.org/`.

[8] A. Averbuch, M. Kiperberg, and N. J. Zaidenberg. Truly-Protect: An Efficient VM-Based Software Protection. *IEEE Systems Journal*, 7(3):455–466, Sept. 2013.

[9] S. Checkoway and H. Shacham. Iago attacks: Why the system call api is a bad untrusted rpc interface. In *Proceedings of the Eighteenth International Conference on Architectural Support for Programming Languages and Operating Systems*, ASPLOS '13, pages 253–264, New York, NY, USA, 2013. ACM.

[10] X. Chen, T. Garfinkel, E. C. Lewis, P. Subrahmanyam, C. A. Waldspurger, D. Boneh, J. Dwoskin, and D. R. Ports. Overshadow: a virtualization-based approach to retrofitting protection in commodity operating systems. In *Proceedings of ASPLOS'08*, New York, NY, USA, 2008.

[11] C. Collberg, C. Thomborson, and D. Low. A taxonomy of obfuscating transformations. *Technical Report 148 Department of Computer Science University of Auckland July*, page 36, 1997.

[12] David Challener, Kent Yoder, Ryan Catherman, David Safford, Leendert Van Doorn. *A Practical Guide to Trusted Computing*. IBM Press, 2007.

[13] B. Lee, Y. Kim, and J. Kim. binOb+: A framework for potent and stealthy binary obfuscation. In *Proceedings of ASIACCS'10*, New York, NY, USA, 2010.

[14] C. Linn and S. Debray. Obfuscation of executable code to improve resistance to static disassembly. In *Proceedings of CCS'03*, New York, NY, USA, 2003.

[15] J. M. McCune, Y. Li, N. Qu, Z. Zhou, A. Datta, V. Gligor, and A. Perrig. TrustVisor: Efficient TCB Reduction and Attestation. In *Proceedings of SP'10*, DC, USA, 2010.

[16] J. M. McCune, B. J. Parno, A. Perrig, M. K. Reiter, and H. Isozaki. Flicker: An Execution Infrastructure for TCB Minimization. In *Proceedings of the Eurosys'08*, pages 315–328, New York, NY, USA, 2008.

[17] I. V. Popov, S. K. Debray, and G. R. Andrews. Binary Obfuscation Using Signals. In *Proceedings of USENIX Security'07*, Berkeley, CA, USA, 2007.

[18] D. R. K. Ports and T. Garfinkel. Towards application security on untrusted operating systems. In *Proceedings of the 3rd Conference on Hot Topics in Security*, HOTSEC'08, pages 1:1–1:7, Berkeley, CA, USA, 2008. USENIX Association.

[19] C. Ranger, R. Raghuraman, A. Penmetsa, G. Bradski, and C. Kozyrakis. Evaluating MapReduce for Multi-core and Multiprocessor Systems. In *Proceedings of HPCA'07*, Washington, DC, USA, 2007.

[20] Rob van der Meulen, Janessa Rivera. Gartner Says Worldwide Public Cloud Services Market to Total $131 Billion. `http://www.gartner.com/newsroom/id/2352816`.

[21] M. Sharif, A. Lanzi, J. Giffin, and W. Lee. Impeding Malware Analysis Using Conditional Code Obfuscation. *Proceedings of NDSS'08*, 2008.

[22] A. Vasudevan, S. Chaki, L. Jia, J. McCune, J. Newsome, and A. Datta. Design, Implementation and Verification of an eXtensible and Modular Hypervisor Framework. In *Proceedings of SP'13*, pages 430–444, DC, USA, 2013.

[23] Vasudevan, Amit and Parno, Bryan and Qu, Ning and Gligor, Virgil D and Perrig, Adrian. Lockdown: Towards a Safe and Practical Architecture for Security Applications on Commodity Platforms. In *Proceedings of the 5th International Conference on Trust and Trustworthy Computing*, 2012.

Access Control in Publicly Verifiable Outsourced Computation

James Alderman, Christian Janson, Carlos Cid, Jason Crampton
Information Security Group, Royal Holloway, University of London
Egham, Surrey, TW20 0EX, United Kingdom
James.Alderman.2011@live.rhul.ac.uk, Christian.Janson.2012@live.rhul.ac.uk,
Carlos.Cid@rhul.ac.uk, Jason.Crampton@rhul.ac.uk

ABSTRACT

Publicly Verifiable Outsourced Computation (PVC) allows devices with restricted resources to delegate computations to more powerful external servers, and to verify the correctness of results. Whilst beneficial in many situations, this increases the visibility and availability of potentially sensitive data, so we may wish to limit the sets of entities that can view input data and results. Additionally, it is highly unlikely that all users have identical and uncontrolled access to all functionality within an organization. Thus there is a need for access control mechanisms in PVC environments.

In this work, we define a new framework for Publicly Verifiable Outsourced Computation with Access Control (PVC-AC) and discuss the security models and forms of access control policies that are necessary in such environments.

Categories and Subject Descriptors

D.4.6 [OPERATING SYSTEMS]: Security and Protection — Access controls, Information flow controls, Cryptographic controls;

Keywords

Publicly Verifiable Outsourced Computation, Access Control Policies, Key Assignment Scheme

1. INTRODUCTION

The increasing use of mobile devices as general computing devices, "big data" and cloud computing results in a growing discrepancy between the resources of end-users and those required for computational tasks. As a result, client devices need to be able to efficiently delegate computations to a server and verify the correctness of results. This is known as *Verifiable Outsourced Computation* (VC) [13, 15, 7].

Recent work has proposed extensions to VC where there exist large pools of delegators, known as Publicly Verifiable Outsourced Computation (PVC) [15], and servers [3]. As with any multi-user setting, we may wish to control access to resources. In this paper, we show that not only is this setting of multi-user VC well-suited to the cryptographic enforcement of access control policies, but that such policies fulfil a natural and vital role in protecting outsourced computations. Specifically in the setting of multi-user VC, we may wish to (i) restrict the computations that may be outsourced by delegators; and (ii) restrict the computations a server may perform. The first need stems from separation of duties and the observation that, within an organization, it is extremely unlikely that all users have equal, uncontrolled access to all functionality. We may restrict the set of delegators that may outsource a computation to those that are authorized internally to compute it (if given sufficient resources). The second requirement arises, for example, from servers being selected from the pool for a particular job without the delegator necessarily having prior knowledge. Thus delegators may not authenticate the server beforehand (in contrast with prior schemes where a single server was chosen with which to set up a VC system) and have less control over which servers may process their data. The sensitivity of the data or other requirements, such as the physical location or resources of the server, may limit the servers that should be permitted to perform the computation.

Some VC settings distinguish between delegators and verifiers [3]. Delegators (or distinguished verifiers) may learn the result of the computation, whereas standard verifiers may only confirm that the result was computed correctly. Again, in a multi-user VC setting, we may wish to restrict the users that: (i) verify the result; and (ii) learn the result. When operating on sensitive data, this second restriction ensures that read access to the generated results is limited to those that satisfy the access control policy e.g. only entities that may read the input data may read the output.

A third motivation for access control in the VC setting is that computational services may be charged for (e.g. in subscription-based utility computing [14, 16]) and that service providers may offer different levels of service to different clients (e.g. different levels may provide access to different functions or computational resources). We must ensure that only valid subscribers may access each tier of service.

In many multi-user settings, access control is enforced by trusted software which authenticates users and evaluates authorization policies [6, 17]. This reference monitor is not appropriate in the multi-user VC setting since the servers are assumed to be untrusted and may have a vested interest in violating the policies. We instead use a cryptographic enforcement mechanism for access control policies where cryptographic keys are used to protect objects and restrict access — the access control mechanism reduces to the appropriate distribution of keys to authorized entities. We use

ASIA CCS '15, April 14 - 17, 2015, Singapore, Singapore.

http://dx.doi.org/10.1145/2714576.2714636 ...$15.00.

the trusted Key Distribution Center (KDC) introduced in the Revocable Publicly Verifiable Outsourced Computation model (RPVC) [3] and extend its duties to instantiate the access control mechanism. In RPVC, the KDC issued keys that enable the delegation and evaluation of particular functions; we additionally require it to issue keys appropriate to the access control policy that enables read and write access to certain components of the PVC system.

Note that in an RPVC scheme, the KDC implicitly provides some access control in that servers are certified to perform specific functions through the generation of evaluation keys. However, no access control is applied to delegators – *any* entity can outsource an evaluation of *any* function for which the KDC has published delegation information. In particular, a delegator may request a computation that the delegator itself is not authorized to perform.

Cryptographic enforcement mechanisms are particularly appropriate when the objects and policies are relatively static (such that additional keys need not be generated and objects need not be re-encrypted). In the context of VC, we may assume that the set of functions that may be evaluated is fixed (a given VC construction can implement a specified family of functions) and that the input data to each function is also static (limited to the set of 'valid' inputs to that function). Thus, the set of objects (function evaluations in VC) is static, and policies will primarily be specified in terms of these computations. Thus multi-user VC is a very natural setting in which to use cryptographic access control. However, VC leads to a somewhat novel application of these mechanisms as we will illustrate in Section 3.

Related work. Clear et al. [8] considered policies over delegators only and in a non-verifiable, multi-input outsourced computation setting using homomorphic Ciphertext-Policy ABE and fully homomorphic encryption. In independent and concurrent work, Xu et al.[18] also addressed the necessity for access control in the setting of verifiable computation, but limited their scope to non-public verifiable computation (i.e. not the full multi-user setting) enforcing access control on delegators only. Xu et al. discuss their notion purely in terms of using CP-ABE as the enforcement mechanism and did not discuss the form of the policies; in contrast, we discuss in detail the types of policies that are of interest in terms of generic graph-based access control policies. These may be enforced by a variety of enforcement mechanisms, including symmetric KASs as used here (which may well be more efficient than the pairing-based CP-ABE approach). We believe that we present a more generic treatment which, importantly, extends to the multi-user PVC setting and incorporates a more natural view of hierarchical access control, as well as additional security notions.

2. BACKGROUND

2.1 Revocable PVC

Non-interactive verifiable computation (VC) [13] is a protocol between two probabilistic polynomial time (PPT) parties, a *client* C and a *server* S, which results in the provably correct computation of $F(x)$ by the server for an input x given by the client. Parno et al. [15] introduced Publicly Verifiable Outsourced Computation (PVC) to allow multiple clients to delegate computations. Alderman et al. [3] introduced Revocable PVC (RPVC) where large pools of clients and servers exist and jobs may be submitted to the pool. This model includes a trusted entity known as a Key Distribution Center (KDC) to perform costly set-up operations and issue appropriate keys. RPVC comprises the algorithms Setup, FnInit, Register, Certify, ProbGen, Compute, BVerif, Retrieve and Revoke illustrated in Figure 1 and corresponding to the following:

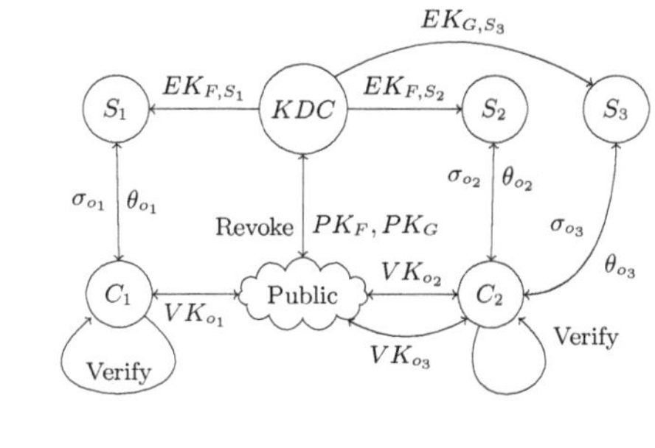

Figure 1: The operation of RPVC

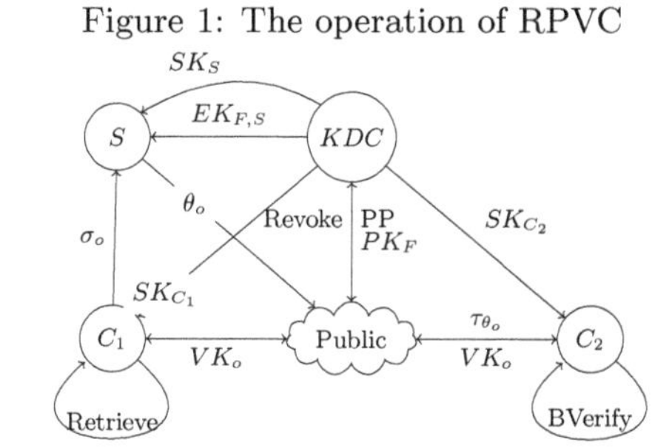

Figure 2: The operation of PVC-AC

1. The KDC generates public parameters, issues personalised secret keys, and evaluation keys to servers and publishes function delegation information.
2. To outsource the evaluation of $F(x)$, a delegator C, sends an encoded input σ_o to a server S, and publishes a verification token and output retrieval key.
3. S uses σ_o and an evaluation key for F to produce an encoded output.
4. Any entity can use the verification token to verify correctness without learning the value of $F(x)$ unless in possession of a retrieval key (blind verification). If S cheated they may report S to the KDC for revocation.
5. If blind verification was successful, a party possessing the output retrieval key can recover $F(x)$.
6. The KDC may revoke a cheating server to prevent it from performing computations (and hence from receiving any reward for future work).

2.2 Cryptographic Enforcement of Access Control Policies

Graph-based Access Control.

A *partially ordered set* (*poset*) is a set L equipped with a reflexive, anti-symmetric and transitive binary relation $\leqslant$. We may write $x < y$ if $x \leqslant y$ and $x \neq y$, and write $y \geqslant x$ if $x \leqslant y$. We say that x *covers* y, written $y \lessdot x$, if $y < x$ and no z exists in L such that $y < z < x$. The *Hasse Diagram* of a poset $(L, \leqslant)$ is the directed acyclic graph $H = (L, \lessdot)$

where vertices are labelled by the elements of L and an edge connects vertex v to w if and only if $w \lessdot v$. Let U be a set of entities, O be a set of resources to be protected, and $(L, \leqslant)$ be a poset of security labels. Let $\lambda : U \cup O \rightarrow L$ be a labelling function assigning a security label to each entity and object. The tuple $(L, \leqslant, U, O, \lambda)$ then denotes an *information flow policy* which can be represented by the H. Henceforth we refer to such policies as *graph-based access control policies*. The policy requires that information flow from objects to entities preserves the partial ordering relation — an entity $u \in U$ may read an object $o \in O$ if and only if $\lambda(u) \geqslant \lambda(o)$ i.e. there exists a directed path from $\lambda(u)$ to $\lambda(o)$ in H. The forward implication forms the *correctness* criterion, whilst the reverse forms the *security* criterion. Note that this statement is the *simple security property* of the Bell-LaPadula security model [5]. Thus an entity assigned clearance label x is prevented from accessing objects classified with label y if $y \not\leqslant x$.

Key Assignment Schemes.

A *Key Assignment Scheme* (KAS) [1] provides a generic, cryptographic enforcement mechanism for such policies where a unique cryptographic key κ_x is associated to each node x (security label) in H. A KAS eases the problem of key distribution by allowing a trusted center to distribute a single key to each entity, who may combine this key with public information to derive additional keys for which the user is authorized. A well-known KAS construction (known as an *iterative key encrypting* (IKE) KAS [10]) publishes encrypted keys. In particular, for each $y < x$, such that no z exists with $y < z < x$, $\mathsf{Encrypt}_{\kappa_x}(\kappa_y)$ is published. Then for any $x > y$, the key for each node on a path from x to y can be derived (in an iterative fashion) if κ_x is known. *Key indistinguishability* (KI) [4] is a crucial security property if derived keys are used in other protocols: given a set of keys $\kappa_{x_1}, \ldots, \kappa_{x_n}$, an adversary should be unable to distinguish between the key for a challenge node $x^\star$ (not a descendent of any x_i) and a randomly chosen key. Freire et al. [12] introduced *Strong Key Indistinguishability* (S-KI) which provides access to keys associated to all other classes which are predecessors of the target class in the hierarchy.

3. POLICIES

We consider graph-based policies in the context of multi-user verifiable outsourced computation where "objects" to be protected are not data files, as in traditional access control policies, but outsourced computations and their results. The "user" population comprises the sets of delegators $\mathcal{C}$, computational servers $\mathcal{S}$, and verifiers $\mathcal{V}$. We are interested in specifying and enforcing policies that restrict: (i) which functions a delegator may delegate; (ii) which functions a server may evaluate; (iii) which outputs a verifier may read.

There has been considerable research in recent years on the cryptographic enforcement of access control policies [10, 11, 1]. Informally, access is regulated in a distributed fashion by issuing appropriate cryptographic keys to authorized subjects, rather than a centralized reference monitor mediating all attempts to access protected resources. Cryptographic access control generally focuses on read access and is particularly appropriate when the protected content is read often but written rarely (to reduce re-encryption). In the context of VC, we will use cryptographic access control in somewhat unusual ways. Rather than storing static encrypted data and ensuring that only authorized users hold the relevant decryption key, we will encrypt dynamic messages within a protocol execution. In particular, to enforce policies restricting the computations that may be outsourced, a delegator must use an appropriate key to encrypt input data. Without the appropriate encryption, the input will be discarded by the server. The enforcement of policies for performing computations is achieved by distributing keys to servers that can be used to decrypt encrypted inputs. The enforcement of (read) policies on outputs uses cryptographic access control in a more conventional fashion; results are published and protected via encryption with an appropriate key.

Cryptographic access control has been particularly widely studied in the context of information flow and graph-based access control policies (see Section 2.2). We restrict our focus to graph-based policies as these encompass many notions of access control that are desirable in practice including information flow policies, role-based and attribute-based access control [9]. Recall that we define "user" population as the sets of delegators $\mathcal{C}$, computational servers $\mathcal{S}$, and verifiers $\mathcal{V}$. We define a security function $\lambda : \mathcal{C} \cup \mathcal{S} \cup \mathcal{V} \cup \mathcal{O} \rightarrow L$ where $\mathcal{O}$ is the family of computations that may be outsourced and $(L, \leqslant)$ is a poset of security labels. This function assigns a label from L, representing the security classification, to each delegator, server and computation in the PVC-AC system. We differentiate between computation policies over delegators and servers, denoted $\lambda^C(\cdot)$, and verification policies over delegators and verifiers, denoted $\lambda^V(\cdot)$. For ease of notation, we use λ to denote λ^C in Section 3. A discussion of verification policies appears in the online version of this paper [2].

Policies over Functions.

We begin by considering a simple case where policies are formulated purely in terms of the functions being computed. In simple terms, we associate each delegator C and server S with a set of functions $\lambda(C) \subseteq \mathcal{F}$ and $\lambda(S) \subseteq \mathcal{F}$ respectively. More formally, we define the set of security labels L to be $2^{\mathcal{F}}$ (the power set of all considered functions). Then, $\lambda(C) \subseteq \mathcal{F}$ defines the set of functions that a delegator C may outsource an evaluation of, $\lambda(S) \subseteq \mathcal{F}$ denotes the functions a server S may compute and for a computation $o \in \mathcal{O}$ computing a function $F \in \mathcal{F}$, $\lambda(o) = \{F\}$. Then, for any $x, y \in L$ we define an order relation: $x < y$ if and only if $x \in \mathcal{F}, y \subseteq \mathcal{F}$ and $x \in y$. The corresponding Hasse diagram with $\mathcal{F} = \{F, G, H\}$ is shown in Figure 3a.[1] Any entity E authorized for $\lambda(E)$ is, by the correctness criterion, authorized to operate on all computations such that $\lambda(o) < \lambda(E)$. For example, in Figure 3a, an entity authorised for the set $\lambda(E) = \{F, G\}$ is authorized for the functions F and G as expected. Each label $l \in L$ will be associated with a key κ_l. To outsource a computation o of $F(x)$, C prepares the encoding of x using the key $\kappa_o = \{F\}$ which, by the security criterion, C knows if and only if $\lambda(C) \geqslant \lambda(o)$ i.e. if and only if $\{F\} \in \lambda(C)$. To compute $F(x)$, S uses the corresponding key κ_o. As before, S may do this if and only if $\{F\} \in \lambda(S)$.

Policies over Function Inputs.

As well as limiting the functions that may be outsourced, we may wish to implement a more fine-grained access control policy determined by input values to functions. For ease of

[1]Nodes for empty sets are excluded from these figures.

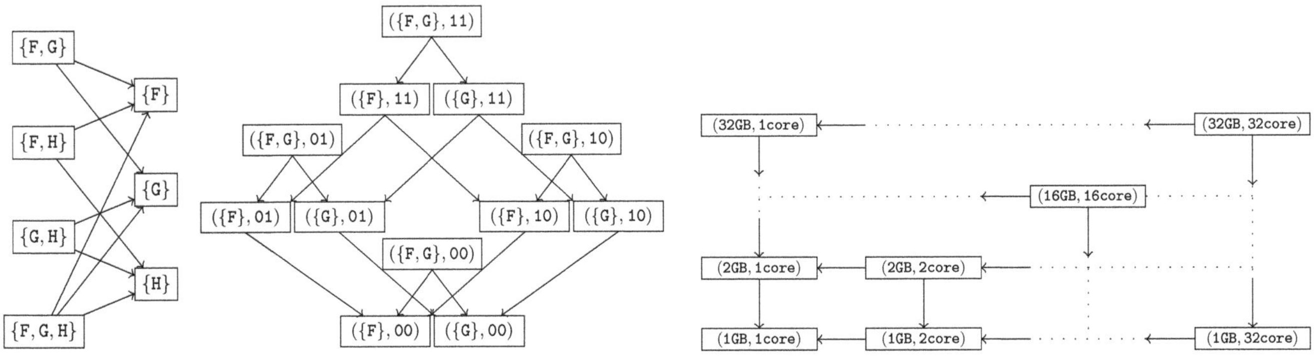

(a) $\mathtt{L} = 2^{\{\mathtt{F,G,H}\}}$ (b) $L = 2^{\{F,G\}} \times \{0,1\}^2$ (c) Subscription based computation

Figure 3: Example Posets of Security Labels

exposition let us assume that all functions have the same domain – for all $F \in \mathcal{F}$, $\mathsf{Dom}(F) = \{0,1\}^n$ for $n > 0$.[2] We then redefine the security function such that "objects" are now considered to be pairs (F, x) where $F \in \mathcal{F}$ and $x \in \mathsf{Dom}(F)$ – that is, $\lambda : \mathcal{C} \cup \mathcal{S} \cup (\mathcal{F} \times \{0,1\}^n) \to L$.

We could, for example, let L be $2^{\mathcal{F}} \times \{0,1\}^n$. To define the order relation on L we must first define an ordering on the input data. One choice is to define a co-ordinatewise ordering on $\{0,1\}^n$: that is $(x_1, \ldots, x_n) \leqslant (y_1, \ldots, y_n)$ if and only if $x_i \leqslant y_i$ for all i. Then for two labels $(\mathcal{G}, x)$ and $(\mathcal{G}', x')$ in L, $(\mathcal{G}, x) \leqslant (\mathcal{G}', x')$ if and only if $\mathcal{G} = \{F\}$ for some $F \in \mathcal{F}$, $F \in \mathcal{G}'$ and $x \leqslant x'$. This poset could be used to ensure delegators and servers operate over a limited range of data values. Specifically, for an entity E, we define $\lambda(E) = (\mathcal{G}, x)$, where $\mathcal{G} \subseteq \mathcal{F}$ and $x \in \{0,1\}^n$, and $\lambda(o) = (\{F\}, 0^n)$. Then E is authorized to operate on $G(y)$ for all $G \in \mathcal{G}$ and all $y \leqslant x$. The Hasse diagram for this poset with $\mathcal{F} = \{F, G\}$ and $n = 2$ is shown in Figure 3b. Different choice of orderings over inputs lead to different restrictions e.g. one could consider bit strings as integers and use the natural ordering over integers for $x \leq y$.

An alternative would be to let L be the power set $2^{\mathcal{F} \times \{0,1\}^n}$. Then each function may be associated with a different range of permissible inputs. An entity E, is labelled by a set of pairs of a function label and an associated input label – $\lambda(E) = \{(F_1, x_1), \ldots, (F_m, x_m)\}$. A computation of $F(x)$ is labelled $\lambda(o) = (\{F\}, x)$. Then, for any two labels,

$$\{(F_1, x_1), \ldots, (F_m, x_m)\} \leqslant \{(F'_1, x'_1), \ldots, (F'_{m'}, x'_{m'})\}$$

if and only if $m = 1$ (the first label is a single pair), $F_1 = F'_i$ for some $i \in \{1, \ldots, m'\}$ and $x_1 \leqslant x'_i$.

The first choice of poset in this section corresponds to assigning a possible data range to each delegator and then authorizing them to outsource a set of functions on that data e.g. a chinese wall policy restricting access to separate portions of a database. Then, depending on the employee's role, they are permitted to evaluate a specific set of functions on that data partition. The second choice of poset is more akin to authorizing delegators to outsource a single, specified computation e.g. permitting the entity to evaluate $F(x)$ for only this choice of function and input data. Finally, the choice of $L = 2^{\mathcal{F}} \times 2^{\{0,1\}^n}$ allows each function to be associated with arbitrary sets of input values.

[2]If not, define $n = \max_{F \in \mathcal{F}} |\mathsf{Dom}(F)|$ and redefine all functions F with $\mathsf{Dom}(F) < n$ by adding fixed points $F(x) = x$ for all $x \in \{0,1\}^n \setminus \mathsf{Dom}(F)$.

Enforcing General Graph-based Policies.

We have seen how sets of functions and inputs can be mapped to a graph-based access control policy to restrict the functions a delegator may outsource and a server may compute. However, in practical applications, outsourced computation functionality will be required to integrate with existing workflows and existing access control policies. As an example, a company that operates Role-based Access Control (RBAC) on their local network and wishes to provide access to an external VC system must ensure that the same access control requirements are adhered to within this new environment. Additionally, a computation may not always be considered purely in terms of the function and input data. Indeed, although the evaluation will be uniquely determined by such factors, the level of protection required may depend on other contextual information. As a motivating example, consider a summation function over the integers. The semantic meaning of the integers may determine the overall classification of this computation – if the integers are city populations then this may not be classified at all, but troop deployments in different regions are much more sensitive.

We can use any poset of security labels L to classify outsourced computations. For example, consider the total order $M = \{\mathtt{TS}, \mathtt{S}, \mathtt{C}, \mathtt{U}\}$ representing the Bell-LaPadula clearance levels [5] and let K to be a set of need-to-know categories. Then we can enforce the security function $\lambda : \mathcal{C} \cup \mathcal{S} \cup \mathcal{O} \to L = M \times 2^K$ where K specifies the nature, and M specifies the sensitivity, of the computation $o \in \mathcal{O}$. To delegate or compute $F(x)$, we require that the entity E's clearance level is at least the classification of the computation: $\lambda(E) \geqslant \lambda(o)$. Similarly, one could define L to be a poset of RBAC roles [9] to integrate with existing RBAC policies.

Additional criteria could be added to the mapping to security labels. For example, we could formulate time-dependant policies by setting $\lambda : \mathcal{C} \cup \mathcal{S} \cup (\mathcal{F} \times \mathcal{T}) \to L$, where $\mathcal{T}$ is a set of time periods. We could then set $L = 2^{\mathcal{F} \times \mathcal{T}}$ as in the previous section to allow entities to operate on specific functions only during specified time periods. By defining $L = M$ as above, certain functions can be more highly protected during certain times of the day. Finally, policies over function inputs can be extended to include characteristics of the input data. Let Z be a set of labels describing data types that functions may be computed over, and define $L = 2^{\mathcal{F} \times (\{0,1\}^n \times Z)}$. This enables the same input to the same function to be classified differently and hence to require different authorization.

One interesting setting for multi-user VC is when users pay for computation-as-a-service [14, 16]. If users pay a price per computation, they could be issued a relevant key such as those discussed in Section 3, with a short time window in which to perform the computation. This key is used when outsourcing a computation to prove that the user has paid for this computation. Alternatively, servers may provide subscriptions to different tiers of service [14]. For example, subscription to a `Gold` tier may allow access to more computational resources, or access during busier periods, than `Silver`, and so on. For simplicity, suppose the resources to be considered are just RAM capacity and the number of processor cores available, and let R and C be sets comprising the available quantities of each. Then, the set of security labels L is set to be $L = R \times C$ — that is, the cartesian product of the available resources. A user that pays for `Gold` membership can be assigned the label $\lambda(C) = \{(\texttt{32GB}, \texttt{32core})\}$ for example and each computation is labelled by the resources that it requires. The poset ordering over L allows each tier to access different subsets of resources as in Figure 3c.

4. PVC WITH ACCESS CONTROL

We define the notion of PVC-AC to enforce graph-based access control policies over delegators, servers and verifiers. Recall that the set of outsourced computations is denoted by $\mathcal{O}$. A specific element $o \in \mathcal{O}$ consists of the function F, an input x in the domain of F, as well as some auxiliary input. Finally, $\mathcal{P}_C$ and $\mathcal{P}_V$ denote posets encoding the computation and verification policies respectively.

Definition 1. A Publicly Verifiable Outsourced Computation Scheme with Access Control (PVC-AC) comprises:

- $(\mathrm{PP}, \mathrm{MK}) \leftarrow \mathsf{Setup}(1^\kappa, \mathcal{P}_C, \mathcal{P}_V)$: Run by the KDC.
- $PK_F \leftarrow \mathsf{FnInit}(F, \mathrm{MK}, \mathrm{PP})$: Run by the KDC to generate a delegation key, PK_F, for a function F.
- $SK_{\mathrm{ID}} \leftarrow \mathsf{Register}(\mathrm{ID}, \lambda(\mathrm{ID}), \mathrm{MK}, \mathrm{PP})$: Run by the KDC to create a key for an entity with identifier[3] ID.
- $EK_{F,S} \leftarrow \mathsf{Certify}(S, F, \mathrm{MK}, \mathrm{PP})$: The KDC creates an evaluation key $EK_{F,S}$ for a function F and server S.
- $(\sigma_o, VK_o, RK_o) \leftarrow \mathsf{ProbGen}(x, SK_C, PK_F, \lambda(C), \lambda(o), \mathrm{PP})$: Run by an authorized delegator C to outsource the computation of $F(x)$.
- $\theta_o \leftarrow \mathsf{Compute}(\sigma_o, EK_{F,S}, SK_S, \lambda^C(S), \lambda^C(o), PP)$: Run by a server S to evaluate $F(x)$ and output an encoding, θ_o, of the result.
- $(\tilde{y}, \tau_{\theta_o}) \leftarrow \mathsf{Verify}(\theta_o, SK_V, VK_o, \lambda^V(V), \lambda^V(o), \mathrm{PP})$: Verification comprises two steps:
  - $(RT_o, \tau_{\theta_o}) \leftarrow \mathsf{BVerif}(\mathrm{PP}, \theta_o, VK_o)$: Run by *any* verifier to check correctness of the result.
  - $\tilde{y} \leftarrow \mathsf{Retrieve}(SK_V, RT_o, \tau_{\theta_o}, VK_o, RK_o, \lambda^V(V), \lambda^V(o), \mathrm{PP})$: Run by verifiers V holding the output retrieval key RK_o to read the value of $F(x)$.
- $\{EK_{F,S'}\}$ or $\perp \leftarrow \mathsf{Revoke}(\tau_{\theta_o}, F, \mathrm{MK}, \mathrm{PP})$: Run by the KDC to revoke a server reported as misbehaving.

[3]In future algorithms this will be S, C or V to denote a server, delegator or verifier respectively.

This is illustrated in Figure 2. A PVC-AC scheme is *correct* if for all functions $F \in \mathcal{F}$, inputs x, honestly generated parameters, and honestly registered entities C, S and V such that $\lambda^C(C), \lambda^C(S) \geqslant \lambda^C(o)$ and $\lambda^V(C), \lambda^V(V) \geqslant \lambda^V(o)$, if S honestly runs $\mathsf{Compute}$ for F on an encoding of x generated by C, then V running Verify on the output will almost certainly output accept and $F(x)$.

5. SECURITY NOTIONS

We now introduce several security models capturing requirements of PVC-AC. Due to space constraints, in this section we will briefly and informally introduce each security notion. Full descriptions and formal security definitions are available in the full version of this paper [2].

- **Authorized Outsourcing:** a delegator may not outsource any computation for which he is not authorized – that is, a computation o where $\lambda^C(o) \nleqslant \lambda^C(C)$.
- **Authorized Computation:** a result should only be considered valid if generated by an authorized party – that is, a server S where $\lambda^C(S) \geqslant \lambda^C(o)$.
- **Authorized Verification:** a verifier may not learn the output of a computation for which he is not authorized – that is, a computation o where $\lambda^V(o) \nleqslant \lambda^V(V)$.
- **Weak Input Privacy:** a server (or other entity) may not learn the input data for computations they are not authorized to perform – that is, computations o where $\lambda^C(o) \nleqslant \lambda^C(S)$.

6. INSTANTIATION

We give a provably secure example instantiation of PVC-AC in the full version of this paper [2]. Informally, the graph-based policies discussed in Section 3 assign labels to each entity and outsourced computation. The ordering relation and the correctness criterion ensures that entities are authorized for all appropriate computations (those that are descendants of their label in the Hasse diagram of the poset). A KAS is designed to enforce such policies, and assigns a key to each label. Each entity is provided with a key corresponding to their label, and they may derive keys for all descendants. As per the security criterion, users may not collude to derive keys for which they are not authorized.

In our setting, we restrict the computations a delegator may outsource, the computations a server may perform, and the results a verifier may learn. We use two independent KASs instantiated over the computation and verification posets, $\mathcal{P}_C$ and $\mathcal{P}_V$ respectively. Delegators and servers are issued a key according to their respective labels in the computation poset, while delegators and verifiers are given a key from the verification KAS. Appropriate keys from the computation KAS are used to encrypt the encoded input for a computation. To encode an input in a manner that will be accepted by a server, delegators must encrypt the encoded input using the key, $\kappa_{\lambda^C(o)}$, associated to the computation within the computation poset. To do so, the delegator must be able to derive $\kappa_{\lambda^C(o)}$ and hence must hold a key at that level or higher i.e. $\lambda(C) \geqslant \lambda(o)$ – delegators must be authorized by the KDC to outsource the computation. Similarly, only authorized servers can derive the decryption key to access the encoded input and perform the computation. By the IND-CPA security of the symmetric encryption scheme used, no information about the encoded input is learnt by an unauthorized entity. To enforce verification policies, delegators generate a retrieval key during delegation, and encrypt this using an appropriate key from the verification KAS. Only verifiers that can derive this key may decrypt the ciphertext to recover the retrieval key and learn the output.

THEOREM 1. *Given a Strong-Key-Indistinguishability secure KAS, a RPVC scheme secure in the sense of Public Verifiability, Revocation, and Blind Verification, and an symmetric authenticated encryption scheme secure in the sense of* IND-CPA$\wedge$INT-PTXT*, then the PVC-AC scheme defined in Algorithms* 1-9 *is secure in the sense of Public Verifiability, Revocation, Blind Verification, Authorized Outsourcing, Authorized Computation, Weak Input Privacy, and Authorized Verification.*

Informally, the security proofs follow from the security of the underlying RPVC scheme and the S-KI and IND-CPA$\wedge$ INT-PTXT security properties. The full proofs of security can be found in the full version of the paper [2].

7. CONCLUSION

We have motivated the need for the cryptographic enforcement of access control policies in the setting of outsourced computation, particularly in the multi-user setting. As developments in VC continue towards such settings, it is vital to enable restrictions to be placed on: the computations that delegators can outsource (both from the perspective of separation of duties, and considering a server providing differing levels of service for different users); the computations a server may perform (such that certain computations, over sensitive data say, may only be performed by a server satisfying a policy); and the verifiers that may learn the output of the result (e.g. ensuring that read access to the newly generated data is handled consistently with the sensitivity of the inputs). We have shown example graph-based access control policies for these scenarios, as well as providing a formal definitional framework, security models, and a provably secure construction built from Key Assignment Schemes.

Acknowledgements

The first author acknowledges support from BAE Systems Advanced Technology Centre under a CASE Award.
The third author was partially sponsored by US Army Research laboratory and the UK Ministry of Defence under Agreement Number W911NF-06-3-0001. The views and conclusions contained in this document are those of the authors and should not be interpreted as representing the official policies, either expressed or implied, of the US Army Research Laboratory, the U.S. Government, the UK Ministry of Defense, or the UK Government. The US and UK Governments are authorized to reproduce and distribute reprints for Government purposes notwithstanding any copyright notation hereon.

8. REFERENCES

[1] S. G. Akl and P. D. Taylor. Cryptographic solution to a problem of access control in a hierarchy. *ACM Trans. Comput. Syst.*, 1(3):239–248, 1983.

[2] J. Alderman, C. Janson, C. Cid, and J. Crampton. Access control in publicly verifiable outsourced computation. Cryptology ePrint Archive, Report 2014/762, 2014. `http://eprint.iacr.org/`.

[3] J. Alderman, C. Janson, C. Cid, and J. Crampton. Revocation in publicly verifiable outsourced computation. Proceedings of the 10th International Conference on Information Security and Cryptology - Inscrypt 2014. Springer, 2014. To appear. Full version available at `http://eprint.iacr.org/2014/640`.

[4] M. J. Atallah, M. Blanton, N. Fazio, and K. B. Frikken. Dynamic and efficient key management for access hierarchies. *ACM Trans. Inf. Syst. Secur.*, 12(3), 2009.

[5] D. Bell and L. LaPadula. Secure computer systems: Mathematical foundations. Technical Report MTR-2547, MITRE Corporation, 1973.

[6] M. A. Bishop. *Computer Security. Art and Science.* Addison-Wesley Professional, 2002.

[7] S. G. Choi, J. Katz, R. Kumaresan, and C. Cid. Multi-client non-interactive verifiable computation. In *TCC*, pages 499–518, 2013.

[8] M. Clear and C. McGoldrick. Policy-based non-interactive outsourcing of computation using multikey FHE and CP-ABE. In *SECRYPT*, pages 444–452. SciTePress, 2013.

[9] J. Crampton. Cryptographic enforcement of role-based access control. In *Formal Aspects in Security and Trust*, volume 6561, pages 191–205. Springer, 2010.

[10] J. Crampton, K. M. Martin, and P. R. Wild. On key assignment for hierarchical access control. In *CSFW*, pages 98–111. IEEE Computer Society, 2006.

[11] A. L. Ferrara, G. Fuchsbauer, and B. Warinschi. Cryptographically enforced rbac. In *CSF*, pages 115–129. IEEE, 2013.

[12] E. S. V. Freire, K. G. Paterson, and B. Poettering. Simple, efficient and strongly KI-secure hierarchical key assignment schemes. In *CT-RSA 2013*, volume 7779, pages 101–114. Springer, 2013.

[13] R. Gennaro, C. Gentry, and B. Parno. Non-interactive verifiable computing: Outsourcing computation to untrusted workers. In *CRYPTO*, volume 6223, pages 465–482. Springer, 2010.

[14] Google. Google Compute Engine – Cloud Computing & IaaS – Google Cloud Platform. `http://cloud.google.com/compute/`, 2014. [Online; accessed 23-October-2014].

[15] B. Parno, M. Raykova, and V. Vaikuntanathan. How to delegate and verify in public: Verifiable computation from attribute-based encryption. In *TCC*, volume 7194, pages 422–439. Springer, 2012.

[16] M. A. Rappa. The utility business model and the future of computing services. *IBM Systems Journal*, 43(1):32–42, 2004.

[17] R. S. Sandhu and P. Samarati. Access control: principle and practice. *Communications Magazine, IEEE*, 32(9):40–48, 1994.

[18] L. Xu and S. Tang. Verifiable computation with access control in cloud computing. *The Journal of Supercomputing*, 69(2):528–546, 2014.

Albatross: a Privacy-Preserving Location Sharing System

Gokay Saldamli
Samsung Research America
665 Clyde Avenue
Mountain View, CA 94043
gokay.s@samsung.com

Richard Chow *
Intel Corporation
3600 Juliette Lane
Santa Clara, CA 95054
richard.chow@intel.com

Hongxia Jin
Samsung Research America
665 Clyde Avenue
Mountain View, CA 94043
hongxia.jin@samsung.com

ABSTRACT

We describe an architecture and a trial implementation of a privacy-preserving location sharing system called Albatross. The system protects location information from the service provider and yet enables fine-grained location-sharing. One main feature of the system is to protect an individual's social network structure. The pattern of location sharing preferences towards contacts can reveal this structure without any knowledge of the locations themselves. Albatross protects locations sharing preferences through protocol unification and masking. Albatross has been implemented as a standalone solution, but the technology can also be integrated into location-based services to enhance privacy.

Categories and Subject Descriptors

C.2.0 [**Computer-communication Networks**]: General—*Security and protection*; K.4.1 [**Computera and Society**]: Public Policy Issues—*Privacy*

Keywords

Privacy, location privacy, private location sharing

1. LOCATION SERVICES

Social networking services are increasingly accessed by mobile devices. This trend has prompted services such as Facebook and Google+ to incorporate location as a de facto feature of user interaction. At the same time, services based on location such as Foursquare and Shopkick are also growing as smartphone market penetration increases. In fact, this growth is happening despite concerns (growing at a similar pace) about security and third-party use of private location information (e.g., for advertising). Nevertheless, service providers have been unwilling to build truly private systems in which they do not have access to location information.

*Work performed while at Samsung Research America

ASIA CCS'15, April 14–17, 2015, Singapore.
ACM 978-1-4503-3245-3/15/04.
http://dx.doi.org/10.1145/2714576.2714640.

2. PRIVATE LOCATION SHARING

Albatross is a location-sharing system composed of several simple cryptographic protocols that allow users to share their locations with their contacts privately. Albatross keeps key features of a typical location-sharing service while achieving privacy from the service provider and social network.

One goal of Albatross is to hide the user's location from the server and yet allow flexible sharing with other users. Albatross assumes an untrusted but Honest-but-Curious server. Albatross can be used for sharing users' whereabouts with only selected contacts, such as close friends, family members and colleagues. At the same time, another goal of Albatross is to hide the user's privacy policies for his location. These policies may be even more sensitive than the location itself, as the policies (i.e., user's sharing preferences) can imply who is favored by the user and who is not.

Albatross supports an asynchronous sharing model, where Alice can share her location checkin to an offline contact who can then see Alice's location after coming online. Naturally, Albatross can also be used for automated periodic sharing or "tracking," say sharing location with a spouse.

As Albatross never shares the locations with the server, it is markedly different from current location sharing services such as Foursquare. All of our protocols protect users' location from the server, and in addition conceal the patterns of sharing among users.

Albatross is practical in terms of performance. All of our protocols are lightweight, using symmetric key encryption, and can easily be run on a mobile phone (our Albatross proof-of-concept runs as an Android application on smart phones). Nevertheless, Albatross does introduce considerable overhead compared to a non-private, trusted server system. Hence, we have emphasized efficiency in our design and made choices that reduce computation and storage when possible. For instance, we introduce a novel grid scheme that requires only one protocol run compared to multiple runs in other schemes, albeit at a small reduction in privacy.

3. CONCLUSION

We present Albatross, a practical location sharing service that achieves location privacy from the social network provider. The system also hides a user's sharing preferences, which may be even more sensitive then the locations themselves. For details, see the complete version of this paper [1].

4. REFERENCES

[1] Complete version of this paper available on `http://arxiv.org/abs/1502.03407`.

Practical Private One-way Anonymous Message Routing

Anirban Basu[§], Juan Camilo Corena[§], Jaideep Vaidya[†],
Jon Crowcroft[‡], Shinsaku Kiyomoto[§], Yung Shin Van Der Sype[¶], Yutaka Miyake[§]

[§]KDDI R&D Laboratories, Inc., 2-1-15 Ohara, Fujimino-shi, Saitama 356-8502, Japan
{basu, corena, kiyomoto, miyake}@kddilabs.jp
[†]MSIS Department, Rutgers, 1, Washington Park, Newark, NJ 07102, USA
jsvaidya@rutgers.edu
[‡]University of Cambridge, William Gates Building, 15 JJ Thomson Avenue, Cambridge CB3 0FD, UK
jon.crowcroft@cl.cam.ac.uk
[¶]K U Leuven, Sint-Michielsstraat 6 bus 3443, 3000 Leuven, Belgium
yungshin.vandersype@law.kuleuven.be

ABSTRACT

Opinions from people can either be biased or reflect low participation due to legitimate concerns about privacy and anonymity. To alleviate those concerns, the identity of a message sender should be disassociated from the message while the contents of the actual message should be hidden from any relaying nodes. We propose a novel message routing scheme based on probabilistic forwarding that guarantees message privacy and sender anonymity through additively homomorphic public-key encryption. Our scheme is applicable to anonymous surveys and microblogging.

Categories and Subject Descriptors

C.2.2 [**Network Protocols**]: Routing protocols

General Terms

Routing, Protocols, Privacy, Anonymity

Keywords

Anonymity; Routing; Privacy

1. INTRODUCTION

The art of providing online anonymity dates back to the use of proxies. In Chaum mixes, the identities of senders are delinked from the actual messages through a mixing process. Secret sharing through Dining Cryptographers networks [?] also provides sender and recipient anonymity. Onion routing [?] ensures that encrypted messages are relayed through a pre-determined path of intermediate hops such that the actual senders cannot be identified. Probabilistic forwarding (e.g., Crowds [?]) delinks messages from their actual senders without a preset forwarding path. However, the onus of message confidentiality in Crowds is on the probabilistic forwarding nodes since those nodes have message decryption keys. While end-to-end encryption can be added, it does not guarantee message unlinkability.

2. PROPOSED APPROACH

We propose a one-way anonymous message routing protocol that is both lightweight and provides deniability to the sender. The sender sends out an encrypted message to a node n_i in a probabilistic forwarding network controlled by other users. With probability p_f, the node n_i forwards the encrypted message to the recipient, or forwards it to another node n_{i+1} in the network with probability $1 - p_f$. Our proposal ensures that an egress encrypted message from a forwarding node is always different from but of the same size as an ingress encrypted message. Only the recipient and neither the sender nor any intermediate node should be able to decrypt the messages in any identifiable form. This *unlinkability* provides *deniability* to the sender: if Alice is to deny sending a message then there is no way to prove otherwise. We achieve this through the equation $\mathcal{E}(m)_{n_{i+1}} = \mathcal{E}(m)_{n_i} \cdot \mathcal{E}(0)$, which shows that the ingress encrypted message $\mathcal{E}(m)_{n_i}$ is transformed at n_i into $\mathcal{E}(m)_{n_{i+1}}$ by a homomorphic addition of encrypted zero, while the actual plaintext message m remains the same. This homomorphic property is satisfied by an additively homomorphic cryptosystem, such as Paillier [?]. In addition, traffic analysis can be thwarted by churning our encrypted noise messages that are of the same size as the actual messages. We have implemented the forwarding functionality in Javascript. Hence, such a system can be deployed on lightweight platforms.

3. REFERENCES

[1] D. Chaum. The dining cryptographers problem: Unconditional sender and recipient untraceability. *Journal of cryptology*, 1(1):65–75, 1988.

[2] D. M. Goldschlag, M. G. Reed, and P. F. Syverson. Hiding routing information. In *Information Hiding*, pages 137–150. Springer, 1996.

[3] P. Paillier. Public-key cryptosystems based on composite degree residuosity classes. In *Advances in cryptology – Eurocrypt'99*, pages 223–238, 1999.

[4] M. K. Reiter and A. D. Rubin. Crowds: Anonymity for web transactions. *ACM TISSEC*, 1(1):66–92, 1998.

ASIA CCS'15, April 14–17, 2015, Singapore.
ACM 978-1-4503-3245-3/15/04.
http://dx.doi.org/10.1145/2714576.2714641.

Disavowable Public Key Encryption with Non-interactive Opening

Ai Ishida
Tokyo Instutitute of Technology
National Institute of Advanced Industrial Science and Technology, Japan
ishida0@is.titech.ac.jp

Keita Emura
National Institute of Information and Communications Technology, Japan
k-emura@nict.go.jp

Goichiro Hanaoka
National Institute of Advanced Industrial Science and Technology, Japan
hanaoka-goichiro@aist.go.jp

Yusuke Sakai
National Institute of Advanced Industrial Science and Technology, Japan
yusuke.sakai@aist.go.jp

Keisuke Tanaka
Tokyo Instutitute of Technology, Japan
keisuke@is.titech.ac.jp

ABSTRACT

We propose the notion of *disavowable public key encryption with non-interactive opening* (disavowable PKENO) where, for a ciphertext and a message, the receiver of the ciphertext can issue a proof that the plaintext of the ciphertext is NOT the message, and give a fairly practical construction.

Categories and Subject Descriptors

E.3 [**Data**]: Data Encryption—*public key cryptosystems*

General Terms

Theory, Security

Keywords

PKENO, disavowability, Groth-Sahai proof

1. INTRODUCTION

The primitive *public key encryption with non-interactive opening* (PKENO) [1] is a class of public key encryption with additional functionality. By using this, a user can prove that a ciphertext is an encryption of a certain message and it is publicly verified. In some situation that a user needs to claim that a ciphertext is NOT decrypted to a certain message, if he proves the fact by using PKENO, the real message of the ciphertext is revealed and a verifier checks that it is different from the certain message about which the user wants to prove. However, this naive solution is problematic in terms of privacy. For example, a customer of a store is required to prove that he did not buy a certain item. If his buying history is revealed to prove that he did not buy the item, his privacy, likes, and tastes are infringed.

ASIA CCS'15, April 14–17, 2015, Singapore.
ACM 978-1-4503-3245-3/15/04.
http://dx.doi.org/10.1145/2714576.2714642.

2. OUR CONTRIBUTION

In this paper, we propose the notion of disavowable PKENO and give a concrete instantiation. This primitive allows a receiver to prove that a given ciphertext C under his/her public key pk is NOT decrypted to a certain message m' without revealing his/her secret key sk. More precisely, a receiver runs the DProve algorithm on inputs his secret key sk, a ciphertext C, and a message m', thereby generating a proof π (we call it "disavowal proof"), and a verifier runs the DVer algorithm on inputs receiver's public key pk, C, m', and π. The algorithm DVer outputs 1 if C is NOT an encryption of m' and 0 otherwise. To construct a concrete scheme, it seems hard to avoid to use non-interactive zero-knowledge (NIZK) proofs since a simulator needs to generate disavowal proofs for the challenge ciphertext. Thus, our attempt is to use the efficient NIZK proof system proposed by Groth and Sahai [2]. However, the language of the Groth-Sahai NIZK proof has a limitation. Moreover, disavowable PKENO needs to support to prove the invalidity of ciphertexts, i.e., the case of $m' = \perp$. We overcome these difficulties by using public verifiability of Kiltz's tag-based encryption scheme [3] (whose plaintext space is a base group). Our proposed scheme is provably secure in the standard model under the decisional linear assumption and strong unforgeability of one-time signature. Also, it is fairly practical since the disavowal proof consists of 61 group elements. The detailed construction is given in the full version of this paper.

3. REFERENCES

[1] I. Damgård, D. Hofheinz, E. Kiltz, and R. Thorbek. Public-key encryption with non-interactive opening. In *CT-RSA*, pages 239–255, 2008.

[2] J. Groth and A. Sahai. Efficient non-interactive proof systems for bilinear groups. In *EUROCRYPT*, pages 415–432, 2008.

[3] E. Kiltz. Chosen-ciphertext security from tag-based encryption. In *TCC*, pages 581–600, 2006.

iARC: Secret Key Generation for Resource Constrained Devices by Inducing Artificial Randomness in the Channel

Girish Revadigar*†, Chitra Javali*†, Hassan Jameel Asghar †,
Kasper B. Rasmussen, and Sanjay Jha*
{girishr,chitraj,sanjay}@cse.unsw.edu.au; hassan.asghar@nicta.com.au;
kasper.rasmussen@cs.ox.ac.uk

*School of Computer Science & Engineering, UNSW Australia, Sydney, AUSTRALIA
†NICTA, Australian Technology Park, Sydney, AUSTRALIA
Dept. of Computer Science, University of Oxford, Oxford, UK

ABSTRACT

The existing secret key generation schemes for body-worn devices using wireless channel characteristics, e.g., received signal strength indicator (RSSI) are dependent on the node mobility and have very low bit rate. In this work, we propose a novel mobility independent RSSI based secret key generation protocol – iARC, which induces artificial randomness in the channel by employing dual antennas and dynamic frequency hopping effectively.

Categories and Subject Descriptors

K.6.5 [**Management of Computing and Information Systems**]: Security and Protection—*Physical layer security*

Keywords

Wireless Body Area Networks, Physical Layer Security, Secret key generation

1. IARC

Prior schemes [2] dependent on body motion cannot be used in many real-time applications. In comparison with SeAK [1] proposed for initial trust establishment between a new device and an existing Wireless Body Area Network (WBAN), iARC can be employed by the body-worn devices for periodic key renewal even when the person is not in motion. We have validated our system using Opal and Iris motes operating in 2.4 GHz, and used TinyOS to program the devices. We have conducted extensive set of experiments to validate our protocol in different real-time environments.

1.1 Inducing artificial channel randomness

We assume that there is one Control Unit (CU) which acts as an aggregator for the sensor data, and one or more wearable sensor devices (D). The CU uses two antennas A1 and A2 having different features which are placed very close to each other. The CU employs a pseudo-random number generator (PRNG) to generate a random bit string $r \in \{0,1\}^{128}$ which is used for antenna selection. iARC employs frequency diversity along with random antenna switching to induce artificial channel randomness.

ASIA CCS'15, April 14–17, 2015, Singapore, Singapore
ACM 978-1-4503-3245-3/15/04.
http://dx.doi.org/10.1145/2714576.2714644.

1.2 Secret key generation

The secret key generation process consists of the following steps: (1) Channel sampling, (2) Quantization and multiple bit assignment, and (3) Dynamic frequency hopping. In iARC, the total number of probes N required for key generation is divided into B number of multiple sub blocks of equal length and each sub block key k_{sb} is derived in a different channel. The final secret key K is obtained by the concatenation of all the sub block keys as shown by the following equation: $K = k_{sb1} \parallel k_{sb2} \parallel \cdots \parallel k_{sbB}$.

Channel sampling is the phase in which the CU and D exchange packets on a particular channel and record RSSI. *Quantization* is the process in which each RSSI sample is assigned an n bit code word. The CU and D decide *Dynamic channel hopping* pattern based on the lowest level of RSSI. The CU and D perform channel sampling, quantization and frequency hopping repeatedly until the total number of probes N required for key generation are exchanged.

2. RESULTS

iARC achieves bit rate of 800 bps with 100% bit agreement between the two legitimate body-worn devices, and generates a 128 bit key in 160 ms. The keys generated by iARC pass the NIST test with entropy ranging from 0.92 to 0.99.

3. REFERENCES

[1] C. Javali, G. Revadigar, L. Libman, and S. Jha. SeAK: Secure Authentication and Key Generation Protocol based on Dual Antennas for Wireless Body Area Networks. In *Proc. RFIDsec*, 2014.

[2] L. Shi, J. Yuan, S. Yu, and M. Li. ASK-BAN: Authenticated Secret Key Extraction Utilizing Channel Characteristics for Body Area Networks. In *Proc. ACM WiSec*, 2013.

A Single Query Forgery Attack on Raviyoyla v1 *

Yuan Yao
TCA Laboratory, Institute of Software, Chinese Academy of Sciences, Beijing, P.R. China
University of Chinese Academy of Sciences, Beijing, P.R. China
yaoyuan@tca.iscas.ac.cn

Bin Zhang
TCA Laboratory, Institute of Software, Chinese Academy of Sciences, Beijing, P.R. China
zhangbin@tca.iscas.ac.cn

Wenling Wu
TCA Laboratory, Institute of Software, Chinese Academy of Sciences, Beijing, P.R. China
wwl@tca.iscas.ac.cn

ABSTRACT

The CAESAR competition is announced recently to identify such primitives offering advantages over AES-GCM and suitable for widespread adoption. 57 algorithms were submitted to the first round in total and then 8 algorithms were withdrawn because of various weaknesses. It has taken center stage in symmetric cryptanalysis to evaluate the security of remaining proposals in last few months, and several outstanding work has been published at top conferences.

Raviyoyla v1 is one of the remaining proposals whose security has not been evaluated formally. In short, Raviyoyla v1 is composed by an additive stream cipher motivated by the eSTREAM candidate MAG v2 and a keyed hash function. Due to the simplicity of the utilized operations, it performs significantly faster than AES. Furthermore, it can be optimized using multiple CPU cores. So, it is quite competitive in terms of speed. The designer claimed 128 bit integrity for both the plaintext and the associated data in the design document.

In this paper, we propose a method to construct forgeries using a single query and the complexity is negligible. After carefully examining the propagation of the differential in the authentication part of Raviyoyla v1, we find that the confusion between two message absorption is far from enough. In particular, if the differential is introduced to adjacent messages, its spread would be limited to a few cells with high probability. As a result, the differential can be canceled out by successive messages. Since the discussion applies regardless of the value of the differential, the value may be chosen intuitively. We prove that the probability is at least 0.307143 for randomly selected values. Thus, one can make use of the freedom in the differential to forge a large number of messages with a single query and the complexity is negligible. Moreover, the probability can approaches one for elaborate values by our experiments.

The following is an demonstration, where the length of the associated data and the messages are set to 0 and 262 respectively, and the key, the public number and the message are set to zero. Furthermore, $\Delta m[4, 5, 256+3, 256+4, 256+5] = \delta$ is the differential between the forgery and the original message. Thus, this table presents three forgeries constructed from a single query in total.

δ(hex)	$tag[0, \ldots, 127]$(hex)
212c27dd2033b7ba	a8d917ee8265c832 1aaa669e542d000a
396cb4981bc8be6f	42c139dac83907af 8bc69fa9239419d4
973bbec0b5e56ec1	432b4647caf15efe b1646e7d647ec2a0
	959df1737c775ba7 fc8ed1e19e4f648e

The idea of this attack was firstly posted on an on-line discussion group[1] by us. Then, the designer proposed a revision as a response. However, we find the revised Raviyoyla v1 should not be considered as secure neither. In fact, we have found methods to construct forgeries for all possible revisions from the designer. According to our experiments, the complexities of these methods are negligible.

In conclusion, Raviyoyla v1 need further modifications in order for the second round of the CAESAR competition. With the current authentication structure, it has to use a strong hash function in order to minimize the probability of differentials. However, that would affect the performance significantly. Therefore, designers should avoid similar structure in general.

Categories and Subject Descriptors

E.3 [**Data**]: Data Encryption—*Code breaking*

General Terms

Design, Security

Keywords

CAESAR, Raviyoyla v1, Forgery Attack, Differential Cryptanalysis

*This work is supported by the National Basic Research Program of China (NO.2013CB338002)

ASIA CCS '15, Apr 14-17, 2015, Singapore, Singapore
ACM 978-1-4503-3245-3/15/04.
http://dx.doi.org/10.1145/2714576.2714645.

[1] https://groups.google.com/forum/#!searchin/crypto-competitions/Raviyoyla/crypto-competitions/x15PAQ_5uNk/pDCQsNIwBikJ

TouchSignatures: Identification of User Touch Actions based on Mobile Sensors via JavaScript

Maryam Mehrnezhad, Ehsan Toreini, Siamak F. Shahandashti, Feng Hao
School of Computer Scinece, Newcastle University
Newcastle upon Tyne, United Kingdom
{m.mehrnezhad, ehsan.toreini, siamak.shahandashti, feng.hao}@ncl.ac.uk

Introduction. Conforming to the recent W3C specifications (www.w3.org/TR/orientation-event), modern mobile web browsers generally allow JavaScript code in a web page to access *motion and orientation* sensor data without the user's permission. The associated risks to user privacy are however not considered in W3C specifications. In this work, for the first time, we show how user privacy can be compromised using device motion and orientation sensor data available in-browser, despite the fact that the data rate is 5 to 10 times slower than what is attainable in-app. We examine different browsers on the Android and iOS platforms and study their policies in granting permissions to JavaScript code with respect to access to motion and orientation sensor data and identify multiple vulnerabilities. Based on our findings, we propose *TouchSignatures*, implementation of an attack in which malicious JavaScript code on an inactive tab listens to such sensor data measurements. Based on these streams, *TouchSignatures* is able to distinguish the user's touch actions (e.g., tap, scroll, hold, and zoom) on an active tab, allowing the remote website to learn the client-side user activities. Finally, we demonstrate the practicality of this attack by collecting real-world user data and reporting high success rates using our proof-of-concept implementation.

Vulnerabilities. We have developed JavaScript code to record the sensor data streams, and have carried out tests on different combinations of mobile operating systems and browsers. As shown in Table 1, all major browsers allow JavaScript code to access the sensor data if the user is interacting with the *same tab*. Furthermore, this access is provided to all separate frames of a web page. This means that malicious code within an `iframe` (e.g., showing a third-party ad) is able to get access to the sensor data available to the main web page despite the fact that the iframe has a different web origin from the main page. We show this in the table under *intra tab* and identify it as a privacy leakage vector. Even worse, in some cases, access to the sensor data is provided even to JavaScript code in a tab other than the one with which the user is interacting. This is shown under *other tab* in the table and obviously demonstrates a flaw in

Device mobile OS	Browser (version)	same tab	intra tab	other tab
Nexus 5 Android 4.4.4	Chrome (38.0.2125.102)	yes	*yes*	—
	Firefox (33)	yes	*yes*	—
	Opera (21.0.1619.86037)	yes	*yes*	—
iPhone 5 iOS 8.1	Safari (8.0)	yes	*yes*	—
	Chrome (38.0.2125.67)	yes	*yes*	*yes*
	Opera Mini (8.0.5)	yes	*yes*	*yes*

Table 1: Mobile browser access to the motion and orientation sensor on Android and iOS. A *yes* (in italics) indicates a potential privacy leakage vector.

browser security policies. In some browsers, e.g., Maxthon on Android and UC Browser on iOS, (not included in the table due to space constraint), the code has access to the sensor data even if the browser is in the background.

Each user touch action, such as click, scroll, zoom, and hold, induces a distinctive device motion and orientation trace. *TouchSignatures* tries to identify these touch actions given access to the sensor data through malicious JavaScript code embedded either intra-tab within an `iframe` or within another tab. This reveal potentially sensitive information about the user's interaction with other webpages or apps.

Implementation and Experiments. To collect labelled data, we have implemented JavaScript code for the client side which asks the user to follow certain steps and collects touch actions and their associated sensor streams. On the server side, we have developed a NodeJS-based server to handle communications, and a NoSQL database to handle the storage of the captured sensor data continuously. To implement the attack, we apply two classifiers: the first one classifies *click, hold, scroll, zoom in, and zoom out* and the second one identifies the type of scroll: *up, down, right, and left.* We identify appropriate time- and frequency-domain features that are extracted from the eavesdropped sensor trace. The classifiers then apply the k-nearest neighbour (k-NN) algorithm to identify user's touch actions.

Results. Our two classifiers achieve total identification rates of 87.39% and 61.59%, respectively. Our attacks highlight major flaws in the access control policy of both mobile OSs and mobile browsers with respect to user privacy. As a countermeasure which strikes a balance between security and usability, we suggest that device motion and orientation data be treated similarly to GPS, and comparable user notifications and control mechanisms are implemented in mobile OSs and browsers. (**Acknowledgement**: the last three authors are supported by ERC Starting Grant 106591.)

ASIA CCS '15, Apr 14-17, 2015, Singapore, Singapore
ACM 978-1-4503-3245-3/15/04.
http://dx.doi.org/10.1145/2714576.2714650

Secure PUFs-Based Cipher Suite for Enabling TLS to Authenticate Hardware Devices

[Extended Abstract]

Paul-Edmond Berthier
Worldline R&D, France
paul-edmond.berthier@worldline.com

Stephane Cauchie
Worldline R&D, France
stephane.cauchie@worldline.com

Zonghua Zhang
Telecom Lille, France
zonghua.zhang@telecom-lille.fr

ABSTRACT

Despite the promising properties of Physical Unclonable Functions (PUFs), its integration with Transport Layer Security (TLS), has not been explored yet. We then present a PUF based machine to machine (M2M) authentication extension for TLS. An Authenticated Key Exchange (AKE) protocol termed DHZKP based on PUF is designed. We develop this protocol as a TLS extension, and prove its security.

Categories and Subject Descriptors

C.2.2 [**Computer Systems Organization**]: Network Protocols

Keywords

PUF, TLS protocol, Hardware Authentication

1. INTRODUCTION

M2M services usually use the TLS protocol to ensure secure communications between terminals and servers. However, the client must maintain a long-term cryptographic secret which may leak. Although some physical protection mechanisms have been proposed, their hardware implementations are always complicated and expensive. Also, TLS lacks of solid relation between the long term secret and the device: the device is authenticated only because its secret is stored in a secure enclosure. Our purpose is to authenticate the device using TLS without storing a long term secret: it must be generated on demand. PUFs are capable of performing device authentications while overcoming the aforementioned security issues. A PUF is a physical object being stimulated by an external stimuli returning an unpredictable response. The unpredictable characteristic is due to unavoidable random variation of the manufacturing process. Although many studies concluded that the implementations of such PUFs are hard, the recent researches [3, 2] have demonstrated some practical solutions. We assume the existence of such PUFs, and propose a PUF-based client authentication scheme working with TLS protocol.

ASIA CCS'15, April 14–17, 2015, Singapore..

http://dx.doi.org/10.1145/2714576.2714652 .

2. PUF BASED EXTENSION FOR TLS

We design a new AKE protocol based on PUFs, termed DHZKP. In this protocol, a constrained yet PUF-enabled device and a server compute the session key and authenticate each other. In particular, the device authenticates itself by performing a zero knowledge proof on its PUFs generated secrets. Thus, no PUF secret of the device is shared with the server. One of our strongest motivation was to integrate DHZKP into TLS handshake: it uses 3 passes for the authentication and the computation of the session key. As we intend to implement our protocol on resource-constrained devices, all the computations will be done in a finite group where elliptic curves could be used. We define a new based PUF TLS ciphersuite and realize an extension TLS from the DHZKP protocol in order to enable the hardware device authentication.

3. SECURITY ANALYSIS

Based on the strong security model stated in [1], we prove that this TLS extension is a secure Authenticated and Confidential Channel Establishment protocol, and that its truncated version is a secure AKE protocol.

4. CONCLUSION

We designed a new AKE based on PUFs, which is named DHZKP. It has been developed as a novel extension of TLS, enabling seamless integration with TLS handshake protocol for hardware authentication. The security of our proposed protocol is proved. The protocol can be also applied to a large variety of machine-to-machine contexts in which authenticating the physical objects are often required.

5. REFERENCES

[1] T. Jager, F. Kohlar, S. Schäge, and J. Schwenk. On the security of tls-dhe in the standard model, 2011.

[2] C. Keller, F. Gurkaynak, H. Kaeslin, and N. Felber. Dynamic memory-based physically unclonable function for the generation of unique identifiers and true random numbers. 2014.

[3] M. Taniguchi, M. Shiozaki, H. Kubo, and T. Fujino. A stable key generation from puf responses with a fuzzy extractor for cryptographic authentications. 2013.

Attribute-Based Access Control Models and Beyond

Ravi Sandhu
Institute for Cyber Security (ICS)
University of Texas at San Antonio, USA
ravi.sandhu@utsa.edu

ABSTRACT

This talk will provide a perspective on attribute-based access control (ABAC). The ongoing authorization leap from rights to attributes offers numerous compelling benefits. Decisions about user, subject, object and context attributes can be made relatively independently and with suitable decentralization appropriate for each attribute. Policies can be formulated by security architects to translate from attributes to rights. Dynamic elements can be built into these policies so the outcomes of access control decisions automatically adapt to changing local and global circumstances. On the benefits side this leap is a maturation of authorization matching the needs of emerging cyber technologies and systems. On the risks side devolving attribute management may lead to attributes of questionable provenance and value, with attendant possibility of new channels for social engineering and malware attacks. We argue that the potential benefits will lead to pervasive deployment of attribute-based access control, and more generally attribute-based security. The cyber security research community has a responsibility to develop models, theories and systems which enable safe and chaos-free deployment of ABAC. This is a current grand challenge.

Categories and Subject Descriptors

H.3.3 [**Information Systems Applications**]: Information Search and Retrieval.

General Terms

Security, Algorithm.

Keywords

Access Control; Authorization

ASIA CCS'15, April 14–17, 2015, Singapore.
ACM 978-1-4503-3245-3/15/04.
http://dx.doi.org/10.1145/2714576.2749229

BIO

Ravi Sandhu is Executive Director of the Institute for Cyber Security at the University of Texas at San Antonio, where he holds the Lutcher Brown Endowed Chair in Cyber Security. Previously he served on the faculty at George Mason University (1989-2007) and Ohio State University (1982-1989). He holds BTech and MTech degrees from IIT Bombay and Delhi, and MS and PhD degrees from Rutgers University. He is a Fellow of IEEE, ACM and AAAS, and has received awards from IEEE, ACM, NSA and NIST. A prolific and highly cited author, his research has been funded by NSF, NSA, NIST, DARPA, AFOSR, ONR, AFRL and private industry. His seminal papers on role-based access control established it as the dominant form of access control in practical systems. His numerous other models and mechanisms have also had considerable real-world impact. He served as Editor-in-Chief of the IEEE Transactions on Dependable and Secure Computing, and previously as founding Editor-in-Chief of ACM Transactions on Information and System Security. He was Chairman of ACM SIGSAC, and founded the ACM Conference on Computer and Communications Security, the ACM Symposium on Access Control Models and Technologies, and the ACM Conference on Data and Application Security and Privacy. He has served as General Chair, Steering Committee Chair, Program Chair and Committee Member for numerous security conferences. He has consulted for leading industry and government organizations, and has lectured all over the world. He is an inventor on 30 security technology patents and has accumulated over 28,000 Google Scholar citations for his papers. At the Institute for Cyber Security his research projects include attribute-based access control, secure cloud computing, secure information sharing, social computing security, and secure data provenance.

Author Index

www.ingramcontent.com/pod-product-compliance
Ingram Content Group UK Ltd.
Pitfield, Milton Keynes, MK11 3LW, UK
UKHW051419290926
15471UKWH00009B/1681

9 781450 338943